REFLECTIONS OF LIGHT

REFLECTIONS OF LIGHT
1995

Caroline Sullivan, Editor
Joy L. Esterby, Associate Editor

THE NATIONAL LIBRARY OF POETRY

Reflections of Light

Library of Congress
Cataloging in Publication Data

ISBN 1-56167-264-5

Proudly manufactured in the United States of America by
Watermark Press
11419 Cronridge Dr., Suite 10
Owings Mills, MD 21117

Editor's Note

There are those who claim that poetry is a dying art. As editor of **Reflections of Light** -- and with a heartfelt thanks to our contributing poets -- I proudly prove those claimants wrong. As evidenced by the size of this book, poetry is not only alive and thriving, but its art spans all ages, races, religions, cultures, and socioeconomic backgrounds. The poets who appear in this anthology display great skill by utilizing traditional and non-traditional poetic forms and presenting unique subjects from which profound insights into the human condition can be gained.

As a reader, you will find experiences in the following pages that are comforting in their fulfilling warmth or shocking in their chilling intensity. As a writer, you will find innovative uses of poetic forms and free-verse, or perhaps even ways in which you would revise another's work. Regardless of how you approach a poem, we at The National Library of Poetry hope you will enjoy the great diversity that follows. It is our goal here to publish new and established writers through our amateur poetry contests, thereby offering the public the freshness of poetry so needed in a world often rent with chaos.

Through the North American Open Poetry Contest, we discovered many exceptional works. While judging the poems is always an artistically and educationally rewarding process, the submission of so many fine works rendered an already difficult task even more formidable. There were some poems, however, which caught the judges' attention and merit special recognition.

Among these are two Italian sonnets: "For Joan of Arc" by Rose Breslin-Blake and "Journey" by Irving York. Both works are exceptional in their subtlety of rhyme and adherence to iambic pentameter.

"The Clearing" by Erika Murphy is a piece with Jungian overtones that portrays a search for life's meaning. Nature brings the persona to a contemplative state in which ideas of being connected to an ancient collective unconscious emerge: "The ancestral wind... voices a ten thousand year-old earth dust / that paints my lungs with cave-etchings / and memories I don't recall." Unfortunately, though the persona is looking beyond the present for meaning, he/she cannot see far enough: "but I see only silent grandparents in rocking chairs."

David Durkee's "Old Bennington Church" is a haunting example of the importance of form in function. The stanza breaks are carefully placed to emphasize the separation the character feels from his/her spouse. "... Its narrow shadow / split the courtyard, the point severed (stanza break) / the two of us, pushing us apart..." The separation of the last stanza, too, functions as meaning when read in the context of its entirety: "... I turned away, the organ surrendered (stanza break) / the last note, its low moan pushed me through the doors." Along with his skillful use of form, Mr. Durkee presents some wonderful images; e.g. "we mingled with the tourists, snapping pictures, / icing each other with glances..."

"Vin Ordinaire" by Donn E. Taylor is a masterpiece of images woven with meaningful allusions. On a literal level, the poem is the story of Gideon in the land of Canaan. Specifically, it recreates Gideon's hiding by a wine press to thresh wheat for his people. This "ordinary" act is juxtaposed with the images of the more purposeful "vintage years." "In vintage years we tasted tang of purpose." This was the time of Moses, of the exodus from Egypt, of miracles and plagues, of "Constant epiphany." On a universal level, the persona is remarking on a lack of faith; i.e. a lack of purpose. Today we need more: "...today we taste / An ordinary wine that wets the lips / But lets the palate thirst." This is truly a remarkable work of art.

Ultimately, Robie Glenn Hall's "Obloquy," a poem about the writer's struggle to create amidst critics' reproach, was chosen as the grand prize winning poem. In the first stanza, the persona describes the writer and the critic: of the writer, "To be a writer is to beg for death"; of the critic, "... Like suckerfish they suck / from my cold lungs the last small warmth of breath: They gag me twice -- not one word must be said / Which might offend the living or the dead."

In the second stanza, the dilemma is whether to compromise one's writing "But one can learn to bend the lung of ink" in order to placate the critics who "... drink / The blood of our labor, then quaff it off / Without so much as one dogmatic cough."

The last stanza offers no resolve. Though the persona does gather the courage to write again, the critics' harsh words still "oscillate and burst/Against the dizzy chamber" of the heart. Writing is done, but with taint of critics' views predicting the creator's fate, thus tarnishing whatever may have been pure.

I do wish I could comment on all the fine poems published here -- there are so many that, like the aforementioned, are unique, fresh, and skillfully crafted works. I congratulate all of you featured here and truly hope you enjoy reading **Reflections of Light**.

Caroline Sullivan, Editor

Acknowledgements

The publication **Reflections of Light** is a culmination of the efforts of many individuals. Judges, editors, assistant editors, customer service representatives, typesetters, graphic artists, layout artists, and office administrators have all brought their respective talents to bear on this project. The editors are grateful for the contributions of these fine people:

Sheree Bernstein, Thomas C. Bussey, Kim Cohn, Amy Dezseran, Chrystal Eldridge, Joy Esterby, Andrea Felder, Jeffrey Franz, Ardie L. Freeman, Hope Goodwin Freeman, Robert Graziul, Paula Jones, John McDonough, Steve Miksek, Diane Mills, Eric Mueck, John J. Purcell III, Lamont A. Robinson, Michelle Shavitz, Jacqueline Spiwak, Jeremy Steinhorn, Cynthia Stevens, Nicole Walstrum, Ira Westreich, and Diana Zeiger.

Howard Ely, Managing Editor

Grand Prize

Robie Glenn Hall / Columbus, OH

Second Prize:

Rose Breslin-Blake / Woburn, MA
David Durkee / Plattsburgh, NY
Joseph Goltz / Silver Spring, MD
Erika Murphy / Denville, NJ
Sara Parker / Hendersonville, NC

Susan Royd-Sykes / Topeka, KS
Marion Shepherd / Columbus, OH
Kate Stewart / Honolulu, HI
Donn Taylor / The Woodlands, TX
Irving York / West Hills, CA

Third Prize:

Lucy Allen / Worcester, MA
Lillian K. Wells Basile / Charlestown, RI
James Batts / Kildeer, IL
Elizabeth Bell / Orlando, FL
Shawn Bentley / Arlington, VA
Francine Boone / Montclair, NJ
Angela Cannon / Annandale, VA
A. E. Carney / Meriden, CT
A. Sherman Christensen / Orem, UT
Merrill Clampet-Lundquist / Philadelphia, PA
C. T. Collins / San Clemente, CA
William Corff / Idabel, OK
Adrianne Costello / Kent, OH
Gloria Damon / Chicago, IL
Adrienne Davis / Seattle, WA
Irene Dell / Carl Junction, MO
Peter DiGennaro / Prospect, CT
Rikk Dunlap / Park Forest, IL
W. Perry Epes / Hendersonville, NC
Lucio Fernandez / Anchorage, AK
Lawrence Flanagan / Excelsior, MN
Ruth Fountain / Austin, TX
John Franklin / Kew Gardens, NY
Joanne Garton / Mansfield Center, CT
Eleanor Gladwin / Decatur, GA
Allison Greene / Santa Cruz, CA
Kristin Hage / Minneapolis, MN
Thrasher Hall / Park Ridge, IL
Grace Hicks / Corsicana, TX

Claire Hicock / Southbury, CT
Gerard Howell / Parma Heights, OH
Elizabeth Humphreys / Akron, OH
David Judice / Los Angeles, CA
Sarah Kallison / San Francisco, CA
W. S. Lane / Hampton Falls, NH
Richard Levering / Hicksville, NY
Patricia Lynch / Simsbury, CT
Paul Marable Jr / Waco, TX
Adeline Martinek / Berwyn, IL
Jerome Mayer / San Marino, CA
Lucinda Moreira / Hillsborough, CA
Shirley Morgan / Gates Mill, OH
Seana Muhart / Sterling, VA
Bob Nevels / Ridgeland, MS
Eric Nimbach / Utica, MI
C. Terry Noe / Brooklet, GA
Oosia / Calabasa Hills, CA
Harriet Poplar / Sequim, WA
David Prosper / Williamsburg, VA
David Rochford / Red Bank, NJ
Nicholas Salvato / Bloomfield, NJ
Gabriel Sciolli / Bethesda, MD
Rebecca Seligman / Boston, MA
Spyros Spyrou / Johnson City, NY
Gertrude Taylor / Hackettstown, NJ
Gregory Thielen / Tempe, AZ
S. Joseph Thomason / Little Rock, AR
Deborah Wheat / Carriere, MS
Rosemary Yasparro / Lynbrook, NY

Obloquy

To be a writer is to beg for death:
To shun the critics' guillotine is luck —
Yes! Watch them gouge! Like suckerfish they suck
From my cold lungs the last small warmth of breath:
They gag me twice — not one word must be said
Which might offend the living or the dead.

But one can learn to bend the lung of ink
Across the paper's windpipe; truncate veins
Yet vacillate to feed true vampires' brains —
Furious fellows insert their fangs, drink
The blood of our labor, then quaff it off
Without so much as one dogmatic cough.

And when the subtle heart gathers to pump
Another rush of blood, the valves are cursed
So that the red words oscillate and burst
Against the dizzy chamber, voices bump
Along vague literary throats like knots
Of Tarot cards or pills, reveal our lots.

—Robie Glenn Hall

Remembrance

One certain song that plucks the strings of memory,
A long-stemmed rose whose scent evokes your name,
The sparkle of champagne in gleaming crystal...
Remembrance flickers round me like a flame.

Yet even as I mourn the wordless ending
Of a rapture that had only just begun,
I bless the fate that brought our lives together
For those days beneath an unexpected sun.

A sun that touched the cold grey world of winter
With a light that held the warmth of Springtime noon,
And yet whose very brilliance seemed an omen,
For a sun that shines too bright may set too soon.

It lies this day beyond some far horizon;
In disbelief I watched it fade and die.
The world is now a place of empty shadows,
The past a distant trace of crimson sky.

Yet life's a pathway strewn with faded memories;
All our summers yield the sad debris of Fall.
Perhaps these too may one day lose their luster,
Grow pale, and dim, and drift beyond recall.

David Rochford

The Sands Of Time

The sands of time so slowly flow, thru the hourglass of life.
A measured portion to expend, filled with happiness and strife.
Allotted time to each is given, no more, no less than fair.
Time to cherish while it lasts, time to love and care.

The sands of time so slowly flow, from the present to the past.
Time that waits for no man, time that will not last.
Look fondly back on yesterday, sweet treasured memory.
But linger not upon it, for the future is the key.

The sands of time so slowly flow, one can barely see.
Measured time appears to be, so plentiful and free.
Advantage must be taken, to do everything one can.
To foster understanding, and to love your fellow man.

The sands of time so slowly flow, ever closer to the end.
Fleeting chances, precious time, for actions to amend.
Ensure the portion given, the slowly moving sands of time.
Are spent per God's intention, in peace with all mankind.

The sands of time no longer flow, opportunities have ended.
Forever gone, the sands of time, measured portion has expended.
Judgment day awaits us all, full accounting one must give.
Justifying actions for, a better world in which to live.

Richard Garrahan

That Something

I see afar from a lofty peak
    A sight that swells my soul with splendor grand
On right and left rugged mountains bare and bleak
    Stand forth God's loftiest land
A wilderness as far as eye can see
    I enjoy in silent reverie

The sun is sinking and the day is waning fast
    Sweet darkness, nature's soothing hand
Has brought the night and stars at last
    To reign supremely o'er the slumbering land
While moonbeams on some river glance
    In their silvery shimmering dance

'Tis far from the haunts of destructive man
    Where the pulse of life throbs with the streams
And takes its course upon nature's plan
    Hurrying not and worrying not, but just lives and dreams
It has charmed me, that something, which brightens life's course
    With an understanding of the universe.

Maynard J. Sears

My Country 'Tis Of Thee

Animation down at the station preoccupation with sidewalk
cracks and aftermaths of homeless lives on Railroad Tracks.
Weatherworn eyes and grey hair pulled pack. Heavy bearded
citizen immigrants make a new landing their Children tightly clinched.

The reservoir of lives and the beating pulse beneath it all from
the day Johnny Shine sang a new Chicago. Ringing high hats
and top hats; the cider and the corn sold inside the kiosk homes.
The ethereal mirth of underground lovers, their sisters and
brothers are all alone.

Screaming reeds screaming needs people eating off what's left in
the street. A rooftop cat's sudden leap over the lives of men with
the skin of dust wrapped tightly around their bodies.

A jubilee of tenderness and violent spells - an aerial view of the
city sold in windows. The brief cased men with patterned nooses
around aging necks walk between the rows of tinted industry
until the lamps are turned off at a dubious hour by urban officials
who work by day and sleep by night and think it's all right -
above the dungeon.

Jamshid Jabbarnezhad

Chroma

Red, the fire thorn blossoms spread
Along paths where weary feet tread;
All blood runs red, runs red.

Black shines the summer night
Shimmering in starry light;
All blackness sparkles bright.

Yellow is autumn's marigold, and
Saffron the seashore's sand;
The golden sun warms all the land.

White falls the winter snow
From clouds close set and low;
All white-robed things in silence glow.

Brown is the good earth in spring
All in furrowed rows for planting;
Brown, love's eyes and sparrow's wing.

Myriad shades are we,
God's children blest and free,
All sharers in one humanity.

Bernard Delos

Vin Ordinaire

(Canaan, in the time of the Judges)

These are no vintage years; today we taste
An ordinary wine that wets the lips
But lets the palate thirst. He comes no more,
Whose spirit through our vintage once infused
His joyous purpose. Habit now prevails:
Raiders come, my neighbor flaunts his Baal, still
His son beats out the wheat in usual ways
In the wine press under an ordinary oak.

In vintage years we tasted tang of purpose:
Exodus! Conquest! Constant epiphany: God,
Master of plagues and pestilence, parted seas —
Of melodies too, and manna's morning miracle;
Stones burst forth into flame and shepherds' staffs
Made flints unfold into fountains. False priests burned,
Justice clear: punishment or forgiveness,
Nothing between —

    But now He comes no more;
Bushes burn in the ordinary way,
And dawn brings only dew. — Thin wine for all:
For me, devout; my neighbor with his Baal—
Even my neighbor's ordinary son, Gideon.

Donn E. Taylor

The Circle

Before there was
and before That...
As if infinity could not be found

Before there was
and before What...
As if virgin was not yet

Before there was
and before Who...
As if creatures were faraway dreams

The sound of the first loud tick of Time
Exploded across the universe
Awakening All to

    tremble awake among the rocks,
    proudly strut on potholed concrete,
    humbly stumble on streets of gold,
      and sleep, exhausted.

To listen ... for another Time.
    James K. Barr

A Spectre Horrible Assails Me

    A spectre horrible assails me, eyes
And fetid wounds dripping pus and black foam-
It strikes with hell-rage, hurling doubt and lies
Against my inner thoughts, in my own home!
From where was hatched this king of monster beasts?
How comes it here, with malice armed, intent?
    Upon my very soul it sucks and feasts-
It cages my mind to soothe the madness pent
Within its own sad, tortured brainhood, fired
With fantasies of violence and hate-

    My waking, seeing mind had sired
Imagination (and fear) to create
An object and returner of the stare
Flung out by questing though- self does self bare.
    Eric Nimbach

Farewell My Rum Cay Island

She longed for sands that once burned
and inky seas that cooled her limbs
while sun rubbed Bahama into her caramel skin.

But when did Bahama say goodbye
when did her island ... rum cay ... say farewell
and when did Harlem first growl at her
with its mouth
held open wide
to swallow every thought of home.

And when she wondered ...
how she came to be on these most frozen shores
on these most concrete plains
lost beyond a will to please

Never again would she taste Bahama filled with silk
but as remembrance
she crooned deeply
from her mother's tongue
of songs known to Africa

singing and singing and singing.
    John William Smith

Dead Issue

Once upon a time I loved my dad
And mom the way a normal child would do.
Naive the boy, until he learned he had
A thousand siblings. How could that be true?

Dad explained my presence here on earth
Which caused a blight upon the family tree:
Mother vanished prior to my birth,
A female-fetus — nameless. Don't you see?

Grandma had a doctor do away
With her unwanted babe, yet save and sell
Mother's store of eggs - blood brothers. Stay
Such steps, for odd relationships will swell.
    Ruth E. Lorenz

The Dream

I dream the tears of children
And prayers a thousand years old.
Eyes of prophets grow dim as lurking light grows.
And frightened, shed their visions - untold.
I am a tree and hear what sleeping eyes won't see.
Listen, listen to the canting song that swings
Through stolen cities and clings like hot ash
Sweeping desert and cloud cresting
Whose sad keens beckon instead resting?
Kilten moon jests loud, "'Tis the willow!"
Silken wind sighs, staying woodlark's billow.
Still stars candle the night
Embracing deaf skies with their cradle of light.
But pinpricks steal their lingering sight
And their voices too, unheard, fade
As an unwary dawn spends her golden coin
On a dream already paid.
Drift on drifting ice flows, the sandcliffs are crumbling.
How blue are my eyes? Black seas rise grumbling.
Tell me more lies and we will live on - in the dream.
    S. K. Lachlan

Dark Song

I flew with Night
And rode her wings
among the stars.
We dipped, and skimmed
the waves — I felt
the beat of spray,
and saw the great
sea caverns yawn.
From dizzy height
we plunged, and rimmed
the world
to spring on Day,
and snatch the first
bright bars of dawn.
    Lora Ann Sigler

Journey

I stood afraid upon the barren peak
And sent a wretched soul to seek the world
Below. Through sullen clouds I saw a creek
That trickled timidly down, snugly curled
Around the mountain etched with nature's braille.
Then sadly it greeted desolation's floor
And crawled ashamedly along a trail
Of heaven's dung, where Noah'd gone ashore.
The sun seared lonely lips until so parched
A drop engulfed desire's shrunken pride.
Macabre pigments dripped upon the prey,
A cadence tolled as eons marched
And at the edge my shadow knelt and cried:
The soul was lost along the troubled way.
    Irving York

Another

This time I write a woman
And she as big as seven hills,
But touching is as touching does
And waiting gets the quills.

Though maybe not unique in me
The skin of love is thin in me
And not too apt to stay,
For I've been known to fall in love
And out within a day.

This waste of talk of loosened love
And I a waste must be,
For this love burst a hold and sank
Upon the sea of me.

S. Joseph Thomason

Life

Life is like the ring, full of victory and defeat,
And the man who wears the crown is the man who won't be beat.

Sometimes you get a pushover and it's not so hard to win,
And you lay him on the canvass till the referee counts ten.
But sometimes your foe has edge in boxing skill,
And the only way to win is to have the greater will.

You start the round a-sluggin' — and you're sluggin' at the bell
And your legs are sort of wobbly and your face begins to swell
And your guts are sorta achin' and your body's yellin' stop,
But you refuse to be a quitter cause you've got to reach the top.
But when the battle's over the ref holds up your hand
And the announcer he announces you're champion of the land,
And you hear the crowd a shoutin' — it really means a lot,
And you know that it is worth it to give everything you've got.

The stars come peeping out as on us steals the night
Saying another round is over in this long and rugged fight.
We pause and nurse our bruises and await the coming dawn,
For we know that with the sunrise our fight continues on.

Life is like the ring, full of victory and defeat,
And the man who wears the crown is the man who won't be beat.

Edwin G. Corr

Michaelangelo

You swirl your colors
and the mixture binds my sadness
I am not blinded
though you intend this to be so
You flash your blacks
in silence
and this paint which sets
your prison
Now flaunts the edge
before me
As I masturbate my heart
to escape
the pending canvas
I'm reminded of the distance
created in your orbit
and the pain
I take for granted
at the hands of human artists.

Barbara Lee Jewell

Showers

Each day you greet me with your one good eye,
And try so hard to open up mine.
Together we fumble through this daily routine,
I approach you as a monster and come out feeling clean.

There have been others like you but some were more bold,
No matter what I wanted, their water shot out cold.
I could hear them chuckle as I fought with all my might,
To readjust the shower head to somehow match my height.

Dirty, happy, relaxed or mad, I have taken many of these,
From a camping ground in Tennessee to a hotel overseas.
But I have never met two that are alike in any way, I'm certain,
And each one tends to baffle me with its different knobs and curtains.

I suppose I should be grateful and I really can't complain,
After all, my other option is a soap bar in the rain.
And I'd be lost without it in my first and waking hours,
So here's to all the hot and cold adventures in the shower.

Kristin E. Hage

The Nursing Home

In wheel chairs they sit and stink
And wait for death and rarely think
Of anything of consequence
Except unyielding circumstance

No pretense of a smile is tried
No shadowing of desperate eyes
That see only emptiness
And unrelenting helplessness

The relatives who come at all
Don't hide revulsion when they call
But act as if they might become
Contaminated by someone

Then with forced gaiety depart
And exult in secret in their hearts
They never stop to think that they
Shall more than visit
The same place one day

John Franklin

Betrayal

The heart has its reasons not to know
And yet I knew, but had hoped to slow
Or even reconcile his leaving,
And I, a bitter thing, and grieving.
For if he had kicked me with his boot
Or if he had made us destitute,
And if he had cursed and called me names
Or had dared to bare his secret shames,
I could have borne all that... but this?
For he was one gone too far to kiss,
Someone I had never truly known
A man of ice and as cold as stone.
Ah, hurry me to a waiting grave,
Remember me for the love that I gave...

Rosemary Muntz Yasparro

A Cask Of Arachnida

The Wasp with single mudded mind
Approaches with bepoised behind
The spider in her stilky lair
And stabandly the lair is bare.

As Edgar Poe did not eschew
Amontilladoish ado,
The spider, mud, and waspapoose
Are all ensconsed for future use.

Howard M. Fitch

The Land Below

From a top a mountain peak, stands a chief with all his pride.
As he stares upon the land below, that was taken from his tribe.
His head he'd nod in anger, as tears fell down his face.
As he stares upon the land below, that was once his family's place.
He stands there in disgust, as he knows his land is gone.
As the land below he stares upon, was once his precious home.
His braves and squaws were forced, to settle somewhere new.
For the land he stares upon below, has roadways running through.
Homes and buildings now decorate, and the trees are cleared away.
He can't believe the land below, has a new look every day.
He fought a long hard battle, but the fighting has had to cease.
All the chief had ever wanted, was a home with love and peace.
But in came others and took his land, like raging hurricanes.
And left his family without a home, and hearts destroyed with pain.
He rarely sees his family, for each can not be found.
For each have had to relocate, upon another ground.
Although his family disappeared, he'll forever always wait.
For the day his family will all unite, and for each will celebrate.
So as you walk across the peak, just always understand.
That what you see below the peak, was another family's land.

Douglas James Hurley

"A Place Of Grace"

How strange, how wonderful, these mysteries of God.
As I continue on this journey into eternity,
The more my knees weaken and faint beneath me.

I long to blossom, to grow and to mature,
Yet my fleshly frailties and weakness often cause an unwanted
  detour.

How very odd that in His presence I feel so small and helpless,
And yet those sweet moments in the light reveal His awesome
  gloriousness...

I look behind me and see years spent striving to do my best,
Now to stumble upon the truth that God's desire was for me to
  learn to rest...

My feeble understanding of a father's heart so full of love,
A God who cares and cherishes his children from above.

All my efforts, works and labor have led me to this place,
A peaceful appointment of rest in His "tender arms of grace".

Judith Hayes

Maternal Sonnet

Flames vanquish in a lifetime's pool of tears
As truth unveils itself to weary eyes.
You gazed the other way for thirteen years.
Now time has lost its meaning with his lies.
A wrenching anger reigns within these walls:
A prison for your heart encased in ice.
Prevailing tension sweeps throughout these halls:
Estranged, you wait in silent sacrifice.
The anguish will outlive us, don't you see?
All love and hope will prove to be in vain.
You're holding on to what can never be;
It's time to turn around and face the rain.
  No words will ever melt the ice away;
  Your heart reserves the power to allay.

Heather Braun

Skin Doll

(dedication for a body of work)
From me, wrapped with elastic,
dripping soft milk of handmaiden's
scent. A place between places,
waiting stretched canvas of girl
fantasy; tearing, wet and scraped
with reminder of darkening itch.
From me. Call me what you
will, but I refuse to be Named.

Allison Laytin Greene

"Though I Walk Through The Valley!"

Four months we had him, only half as long
As while we waited eagerly his birth.
We're not alone, although our grief is strong,
For lo! The bells are tolling o'er the earth.
The tale is old: since Abram laid his son
Upon the altar of his love for God
And David wept in vain for Absalom
Have millions through that shadowed valley trod.
Yet deep at night, when all around is still
I often rise, and clasp pain to my breast
Where once my baby promised dreams to fill-
His tiny fingers to my heart-strings pressed.
Oh, Father God, as I today mourn my small son-
Teach me, dear God, I plead, to pray "Thy Will Be Done."

Marion M. Shepherd

Untitled

In my time, I have felt the pale
Blue August of mourning.
  In this world,
I have seen the stars cry out.
  In truth,
I know not whether
  I am meaningful
As a blade of grass is.
And my test is to find peace
  In the searching.

Aaron J. Torrison

"My Ship And I"

Be still my heart be still for me, I whispered softly to the sea,
Boundless, endless, rising high, waves that leap beyond the eye,
Ever rising, sometimes calm, thrashing, pounding up and down,
Frothy blue and minty green like rainbows bowing on a scene,
The mighty swells so gentle seem, crash against my bow and beam,
A sudden squall and darkening lee, send whitecaps dancing on the sea,
Bolts of lightning, claps of thunder, strike my helm and tear asunder,
The sails so high and filled with fury, pushed my ship the proud and
  worthy,
We pitched and rolled through the night, our only crew, courage
  and fright,
The albatross his head hung low, made sweeping passes off my bow,
On and on she rocked and rolled, twixt sky and sea and ocean blue,
From Africa to Timbuctu, she sailed the Horn, Tahiti too,
Then into the dawn through calmer seas, my ship and I, now
  sails with ease.

Edward Mancini

Inspired By Neitzche's Three Metamorphoses

I am the camel
carrying my own big burden.
Like a carcass on my back
or a tumor in my belly,
it weighs me down.

I am the lioness,
destroyer of useless "values",
ripping apart your fleshy attachments.

I am the child,
the playful artist,
creating,
without ego,
a new world,
by feeling my ancient memories.

Kira Jeanne Cassidy

Cocktail Facial

Been giving myself a
cocktail facial
For That Tired Feeling
cocktail facial
on the rocks
My mother's crazy, I explained
or was a week ago
And my father? kind, hard man
is away

Some things just slip out
when you've been giving yourself a
cocktail facial
Mint Julep refresher
(avocado for a twist)
Splash and rinse this skin away
Cleanse these pores of tell-tale toxins
Rid my glass of this soiled face that
will gawk and leer at me on Monday morning
Wish I'd been giving myself a cocktail facial
on those Monday morning workdays

Janine Martin

Minimum Wage

Plastic must be the material of the gods.
Color changing bowls are plastic and placidly interesting.
Gooey plastic - the taste is neutral, like the air of Switzerland.
The sight of plastic shoes tastes cheap, shoes made by Rolando,
an illegal Mexican immigrant working for two dollars under minimum
wage at a factory outlet in Spring Falls, Idaho.
Not that neutral, maybe it's Yugoslavian.
Flies make too much noise, and so do very small lizards.
Running over lizards always starts *They Might Be Giants* music to
hum from the house speakers.
Now I flip burgers at Micky D's, but it's minimum wage.
At the end of my shift, I think I might dig a hole, end up in
Australia, and cultivate fruit flies in a small, thatch cottage,
then hypothesize on the theory of existence and the relationships
between the insect and man.
"Gutentaug, ich habe eine katze." says I, nature's plutocrat.
The mouse raises his eyebrows as the tree realizes that it must not
be late for its meeting with the rabbit.
And the plastic garbage pail is pushed through atmosphere, slowly
ascending to the most majestic mountain of all.

Joanne Garton

X 47:

"Blasphemous Day!!",
crying night,
how many more hours does a gargoyle
cry?,
Sitting alone perched on the ledge
of a gothic building,
striving to jump?

Months?,
Days?.

no _____,
in fact the truth is seconds,
mere seconds.......,
then revelation of a new kingdom is born,
with the splatter of feathers on flat rocks,
below.

Robert Sheridan

Sonnette

You wouldn't, if you passed her on the street
discern a different look upon her face
from any other (some mundane disgrace
is stamped upon us all; some small defeat
of every day we wear as rusty chains)
you wouldn't know, for instance, that last night
he yawned, turned to the wall, turned off the light,
said "wake me up at eight" and snored (the pains
that in the dark the broken heart repeats
distilled her sleep) you really couldn't tell
by looking at her as she made the bed
this morning, smoothing back the empty sheets,
she didn't try to stop the tears that fell
or try to quicken feelings that were dead

W. S. Lane

Supernova

Dense rain-tree forest of Cupid beckons you,
Do not get allured, Jennifer,
If geranium blooms at the window of your study-den
Tell him to wait: you are not ready as yet.

Multitudes of visions awaiting
On the shore of your blue eyes for embarkment,
Intend soaring high in the sky all over the horizon
From superhighway to supersonic.
Do not break your journey on the path
At any seductive call from behind.
If it infatuates you in your veins,
Invocate the will-power of celibacy
To control its impudent extravagance.
Sunflower as you are, the genesis of Supernova'
With the shining colors of your potentials
Would Michelangelo emerge out on the earth's new canvas.

Beware of the alluring light of Cupid's hyena eyes,
Do not go astray, Jeni;
You would definitely, develop into Supernova, one day
On the infinite path of the Universe.

Gopal H. Banerjee

Spleen

Coltrane's chords washing
Dust and sorrow
From my sunset blues
And filling the room
Like feathers
The empty bag of my tomorrow.

Feeling like a rotten apple
And knowing it
And still peeling it
Is what some mornings are like.
It is cold and gray and wet
And thoughts are falling back
Like tired salmons.

Outside,
Damp leaves on the ground,
No strength left
To climb back on the branches.
It is the season they say.
Why must there be
A season for surrender?

Gabriel Sciolli

Soliloquy In My Cracked Mirror

Me erroneously the sum of my parts?
   Even tangentially not quite
I say, and I do not exclude these warts.
   (What warts, you delusory light?)

(Forget it)…My brain roiling in a maze?
   Maybe, maybe not. But my math
Suffers in such an agonizing daze
   It must have had an acid bath…

Look, view me. I am in third-dimension
   Yet. Some parts are not in perfect
Jugglery? That is utter deception.
   I am you! Whose math is suspect?

Or do we talk of math and delusion?
   My parts—plus warts and all—adhere
Intact: They are you and me in fusion.
   Mind you, their sum is here and there.
      Lucio B. Fernandez

Vagrants And Blind Boys

Blind boy slides
Feeling tired, grey, and poisoned.
An earthworm swallows the world
And merry-go-round in '70's dress-

Swings flying with leaps;
Feet hurt like a scattered Israel
Climbing shower walls

(There is) No hiding from the fat man
Who hammers a vagrant fist
And looks through piss-like eyes

Still, vagrants walk like bamboo
In a cactus tongued creek with teeth
A homeless man's home, biting
His bloody back shelled by stone

Throw sand down metal, blind boy.
We'll go faster-
These are tough skins

While our mothers
Are lamenting over us
I'll tell you what I've seen…
      Merrill Clampet-Lundquist

Untitled

The cry of sea birds - and days now long gone
Flood back - a riptide in my memory,
And like a tautened sail, my senses run
Before the whipping wind sharp in my face.
The sheen of water mirroring the dawn,
Reflects the ebbing and the flowing sea
Of thoughts my mind encompasses, and one
Am I with every moment they embrace.
The salted scent of ocean heavy on
The breeze brings swift remembrance of the free
Wild water - and the fingers of the sun
Put everything in Heaven in its place!

One with the wind, the sun, the sea, the sky -
And one with all the Universe am I.
      Elizabeth Burt Lukather

Mud Season In Vermont

A madness is redeeming winter now.
Flowers bursting up through mud so infiltrate,
I weave as drunk in their excess
And plod along renewed in her tenacious wake.
And my heart rises with every feathered wing
And beast's lightfooted trip across bleak landscape
And catches hold of change and is reclaimed
From humdrum days by nestmakings in the trees
And rustlings along the sweep of new-sprung leaves
From tightly guarded buds and pollen dust
That tints the air from lime to raisin red.
The smell of musk overcomes the must of last year's embers
And my blood surges to renew itself
In harmony with all of life
A-wing again on spring.
      Patricia Henigin Lynch

New Morning

Newness of dreams bends to the not yet man —
for him there is no other hunger.
The cordial is cloudless
   in voluptuous pledge that quenches
in midnight of seductive need.

Sirocco cannot choke the courage
   of recent young
nor apricots lessen its longing.

Charm of the kiss returns the rapture echo.

Days stand numb like brittle cornstalks
when wind cross the ice fields of afternoon.
Nomadic nature reroutes its course
   each calendar.
Vineyards balance baskets of evening grapes,
the mercury glass holds hours
   of fruited laughter.

He goes into a new morning
when he weeps for the pain of others.
      Emma Crobaugh

Bread Crumbs

My soul cries with a strange remorse
For paths we shared, not quite revealed,
That wind through raptures flowered field.
The seed from which these longings grew
Never blossomed, never sown,
Is grieved for fragrance never known.
And yet she was my life, it seems;
Recalling shadows from my dreams.
The tear that flows does not have pain,
Nor mote, nor anguish as its cause;
More like a song whose sweet refrain
Commands this silent soul's applause.
It flows for weathered memory
Within a heart scarred on a tree.
And two names carved at different times
And in a different century.
Another life to come will yield
A chance to share each others days
If we leave moments, like bread crumbs,
To help us find the way.
      Richard Levering

The Peach Of Rage

Awaken to the enlightenment of mistakes,
For the map of life will never be the same it was back then.
I cannot do everything my sweets,
But those drives I do participate in
I will do better than anyone else.
    FEEL THE "VIBE!"
Can we finish the touch with a dry,
Freeloading sound that seeks passion?
Where can I hang my skeletons
If my forever suitors have stepped out of
The closet behind a sheltered kinship?
    INSIDE MYSELF.
Moving, kissing, shaking
As if I have lived a format full of salary.
Contrary to some, a dollar bill will not replace the feedback
Of one smiling child. One beautiful smile! ONE!
Sailing this all is, with the Bo-Bo Baby.
    PONDER THE PEACH OF RAGE
But still I am living!

Brian Norris

Courage To Climb

I see the tree resting in the meadow
full and old, leaning from the touch of time.
A boy, I recall, dreamed in its shadow
on summer days beneath blue skies and climbed
its leafy arms. A playful nudge from fear
gives birth to unknown courage to explore
higher yet, those thin rubbery limbs near
the top. Heartbeat racing, his spirit soars
reaching for that last branch. Holding tight, he
looks out over a world fresh and untamed
as youth itself, and for the first time, sees
his life need never again be the same.
   I learned something about myself that day,
   that with courage, my dreams won't fade away.

Rikk Dunlap

Ally

I love you and spring sun
gleaming in our small garden
on camellias.

I love you and wave-roughed river
sailing feather fans
of whiling swans.

I love you and sky's bright wind
jumbling clouds and bumblebees
against a blinding blue.

I love you and waking dreams
crowding themes endless
in magic, waiting.

L. Russert-Kraemer

Blake Respectfully Emulated

Mock on, James Joyce,
mock on in ebony night.
(Shakespeare shook his spear,
poised, and hurled it home
and stood aside from his art.)
Your scorn is but a cigarette match's flame,
deep at times, tender, brilliant,
drowned
as Rome's sunfonts are drenched with milklight.

Gerard A. Howell

Stork

With voiceless clatterings - silent cries -
He makes his meteoric rise.
"Caveat Emptor" he would say,
But mandibles won't clack that way.

Soon, swooping with abandoned grace,
He settles on the chimney place,
And standing gauntly silent there
He sways and preens with gentle care.
A "de profundis" he would chant
Excepting that he knows he can't.

Now, gently, bill with bundle ducks
(His heart is singing, "Flat Lux"!)
Mid voiceless clattering, silent cries,
Again, his meteoric rise!

A mother smiles, a baby cries!

Elizabeth Bradner Bell

Grammar's Do-Drop-Inn

my name is grammar, but hell, you can call me fessor, pro and con.
here i stand at the pulpit and i don a certain air. master-elastic and
oh-so-rare, i lace up my ole combat boots, then try on another pair.
you see, i have my gunny-sack of privileges, i have my priorities.

oh how i grow fat as i skip over imperative's back and without a trace
i unlock into higher uppercase as i leap-frog over preposition's
tired and lousy phrase, then sit my lazy bum down into a bed
full of verbs multiplying—oh lordy day. and just as divisions walk in
and shut the door in your face (more or less subtracting)

in walks some funny little munchkin adverb, busy thinking of
   some nobler
tense where he forgot his lunchbox under the wild oak near the
   picket-fence.
sure as fire, he has jumped many a hurdle of a million little
harmonizing adjectives all along the way, all dressed to the nines.

still, he wonders if ever the marriage of a million more privileged
sassy nouns could ever bare to walk away from their illicit verbal wives
or raise a dangling participle or 2 so high up in the air, then
powder their hind-ends in a miracle fixative called infinitive
   reciprocal.

you see, here at the local reststop, we mix 'n mingle at the
   do-drop-inn,
we rub noses with guests full of logic and reputation, all non-stop,

so i spray a whipcream algebraic curve upon their naked bellytops.

David Judice

The Sundering

She drove on down the road past granite hills,
His body slumped, leaden, against her side,
Long rows of grass and fenceposts flashing by
With martial tread. And coming to the town
At last, she fled into the street, yielding
His lifeless frame to strangers who moved like
Robots, slowly, and stared at her with wide
Uncertain eyes; not knowing how she came,
How far, how long they traveled side by side,
Distilling love, till back along the road
Somewhere, he silently shed bonds of Earth
And rose to meet a higher claim. And she,
In savage rending sundered, strangely blind,
Was nonetheless lifted as if on wings
And borne safely through warm September air.
Acknowledging God's sovereign right to call
His own, she found His grace sufficient there
And, reconciled, she willingly let go.

Grace Roberson Hicks

Mother-Love

Small satyr
his brilliant white skin
mocks me
rabbit's ear
dove's breast
fawn's tail
lanugo tickles my lip
I kiss his back just below the neck.
Hind-quarters, flank, thigh
flesh like wet clay
glazed with my finger
running round and round
chalky smell
molds to my touch.
I create, consume.
My hands move quickly
to cover my gaping wound.

Sarah Rush Kallison

Wild Lament

On every walk or stroll or some such voyage for inner peace,
I always brush past a hundred people who will outlive me.
They have my blessings,
pressed tightly in a cellophane wrapper with a satin bow,
an ascension wish to unfurl and let fly as ashes over the sea.

What do you see through your private thoughts?
Is there a world on its own, in a secret soaring orbit
that bears no witness to another
and doesn't claim a boundary in space?

Across the sky a million balloons sweep.
Mirrored hearts, flushed birthday greetings, a red one says;
"I love..." then a twist turns longings blank
or simply snags the trailing string.

What can we say that lifts us onto another plain?
Into what future do we unfold our dreams,
caught like a summer gnat to weave a pattern on the hand,
before release after its intricacies back to its sovereign place?

Is it foolish to fear a destiny
in common with souls so rich and swept by a force,
that illuminates such infinite things?

Oosia

Think No Elephants

In Sunday school
I dreaded leprosy.
Fixated, in high school,
on curatorial displays—
pictures of elephantiasis:
Africans trundling their balls
like pumpkins in a wheelbarrow—
I'd try to imagine dancing.

Now they grow between us,
still-born ones: your fibroid tumor
(white lobes big as five months gone
but never kicked, just clung to
your womb, which had to be
delivered itself);
And still not born: my swollen kidneys,
failing, nefrectomable.

Nights, we nestle in a fetal curl,
either inside the other—
a couple expecting
and not even trying not to think about it.

W. Perry Epes

Untitled

Brooding upon the shadows
I envied my neighbour's garden
Roaming its fertile meadows
My soul began to harden.
Forsaken and hungry I knocked on people's doors
A downtrodden alien who felt no remorse
To accept their abundance, to drink from their source
Till one day I was shaken from my disparaging dream
My still heart awakened by your wistful scream
For nurture and guidance from a beggar like me.
And startled by longing I tore open the trunk
To discover the treasures which long had been sunk
To the bottom of my soul.
Emerging from starvation
Your hunger fills my bowl.

Heidemarie Pilc

My Friend

We embrace:
I feel her small, warm back
with cold palms and fingertips.

Perfume
like sunflowers warmed by the sun
caresses my senses
with wings of butterflies

I feel her small, warm palms
light upon my large, cold back
(now like a frail stem in her hands)
and I cry.

And she,
knowing me and my ways—
of turning toward and reaching out to
the brightest thing in my life,
holds me closer
until the world with its cold sunless nights
disappears.

Fiore Mills

Untitled

Hidden from my eyes
I feel the awesome force
of the one beside me
who's always steered the course
of eras and of worlds
so far beyond
the shorelines of my middling pond.

He resurrects forgotten dreams
long buried in the heart.
Into his eternal schemes
will enter and will part
the dusks and dawns of life.

He's seen my lover's eyes
in a thousand new disguises.
His heavens are quiv'ring with the cries
of joyous births and sad demises.

Eternal longing sweeps
through his relentless breeze
its whisper tinged with hope deferred
and love's immortal pleas.

Esther Ilona Baunach

10

In Truth (Villanelle)

In truth you lead me down a path of lies
I followed blind along the way you lead
So shattered hope must now your love despise

You wondrous looked to my bedazzled eyes
As I believed each word of love you said
In truth you lead me down a path of lies

Passion and romance beneath the starry skies
Illusions that were destined to be dead
So shattered hope must now your love despise

Undying and forever were the ties
That bound us one in one when we were wed
In truth you lead me down a path of lies

In truth my broken heart the truth denies
Would once again believe your lies instead
So shattered hope must now your love despise

My broken heart in truth the truth defies
The anger in my heart could wish you dead
In truth you lead me down a path of lies
So shattered hope must now your love despise.

Angela M. Cannon

In Search Of Tranquility

Basking in sunlight golden, while perched on a rocky shore,
I gazed at glistening waters… 'mid the passing speed boats' roar.
In search of calm tranquility, I breathed deep the air so clear
And felt a spray upon my face with water's edge so near.

Lapping waves sent droplets skyward, to land upon my feet,
Cooling me in heat-of-day as I reclined on nature's seat.
A large gull's cry heard overhead! Against the wind, wings firm,
I watched him flutter out of sight, and ne'er did he return.

The rugged rocks invited all to bask in this retreat.
Their surface, smoothed by tides and time, felt warm beneath my feet.
I watched some youth caste fishing lines, way out beyond the shore.
They shared their pleasures joyfully, although their catch was poor.

Nearby a couple with silvery hair blissfully passed the time,
Replaced by still a younger pair…with child…who liked to climb.
Water skiers take to the waves! Jet skis come and go!
Another boater cruises by…with friend-on-tube in-tow.

The water seems to grant such peace to all who came today,
To watch the waves lap o'er the shore and watch the boaters play.
The cares of life pass swiftly by; and problems seem no more.
All hearts at rest with man and God upon this rugged shore.

Elizabeth (Benda) Humphreys

Intrusion

On daily walks by the covert yon,
I hear a pheasant call the alarm -
"There's the woman of seventy-one!"
To all those who may come unto harm.

The robin red-breast prodding, queries
The Canadian geese on the run,
As a small covey of quail scurries
Under the ascending morning sun.

Piercing cries of a raven, anon!
Warning the forest of my approach -
"There's the woman of seventy - one !"
Give heed to those upon whom encroach.

A woodpecker's carpentering stops,
The chickadees' flighting confusion
And killdeer, feigning injury, drops
Perceiving unwelcome intrusion.

Harriet Poplar

The Dance

Through the frost-lined window
I see a memory of my father
By the lean-to-shed
Scraping coal into a bucket.
He leans on the shovel to cough.
I look away.

Back then, with my father's permission,
I used to finger
Through his dresser drawer
Where he kept his valuables,
Essays, poems, in neat little stacks
With change for me scattered about.

I'm glad I danced with him.
My poodle-skirt swayed
As we Tennessee Waltzed
At Friday Night's dance
In Community Hall
When I was twelve or thirteen.

Julia Margaret Strange

And…

And sometimes at night
I see you outside my
window/ beckoning for my
piety/ I struggle against
the glass and scream
and cry/ your body twists
and turns outside/ I won't
break the glass and I
won't lift the pane/ I
will stand and stare/
eating on the bread of
someday/ drinking on the
wine of never/ One day
I will break/ somebody will/
something must/ Probably me/
Then I will drink and
eat of you/ and never
awake.

Joseph Fisher

Stranger Contradiction

Morning coffee and hour spent,
I spied an ant in silence.
The busy little speck roamed wide;
His day's determination.
With omnipresent stare I studied
His sift, and shift and stutter.
He has no drift, no hint of me,
Shuddering dread or joy.
A squeeze of thumb and he'd be gone-
No thought; no memory.

Does cosmic eye, unblinking Stare
Receive my coffee, hour spent;
The busy little speck roam wide;
My day's determination?
With single sweep my friend was eased to safer climes than these.
Reckless, I did secure and hope
The small and great a stranger contradiction:
Myself great and small as this-
And mercy my greatest gift
To give and to receive.

Joseph Goltz

The Woods

As I plunge down into the murky depths of pine,
I stumble over thorny brambles of thicket and of vine.
But still I plunge down deeper, deeper into the woods.

My enemies are close behind, my pursuers closing in,
for I the hunter am now the hunted, a game where but one may win.
But still I plunge down deeper, deeper into the woods.

The thick fog lays heavily, like a sheet of suspended snow,
the moon unseen and shrouded by an eery sea of woe.
But still I plunge down deeper, deeper into the woods.

The deadly air hangs 'round me, electrified with fear and hate,
each breath becomes a task, and each movement becomes my fate.
But still I plunge down deeper, deeper into the woods.

Then like lightning comes a root, takes my legs from under me,
as I fall forth in a heap struggle in vain to be free.
And thus I have plunged as deep as I have plunged,
And thus I lay eternally in the murky depths of the woods.

Alex Colwell

Time

As long as my memory will hold, I will have you.
I will keep you and hide the key to existence
somewhere between my heart and my soul.

You will be my first and last pet;
And I, one of many owners,
Will tame you and name your worth:
I will exercise you in the sun and under the moon;
I will raise you to the level of my dried up dream.

All this I will do for a lark.

You have won every race in this game, so far.
This feeble athlete is no match for a cheetah
Who is as young as the earth is old
And twice as fast as her movement.

Soon I will lose sight of you (by accident).
You will explode with speed and stay out of reach
To teach me a lesson.

By then, I will have forgotten where I placed the key,
And you will have internalized a petrified me.

Natalie Cole

The Hand Of Destruction

Stubborn in my silence,
I will not be
crumpled in the palm
of a blood-stained hand,
wrinkled and twisted,
straining to control me.
Its fingernails will violate each crevice
of my brain,
unthinking my thoughts.
Crimson blood will seep
into the cracks and form ignorance.
My vocal cords
will be left hanging from my mouth,
a mangled vegetable
unless I defy you,
hand of destruction,
and fear you not.
Your limitations make me avoid you.
I allow myself freedom.
And I will speak.

Adrianne Costello

I Quake

I guarantee if melted,
I'd have no spine or innards.
I had once been red
    and now I am diluted, deluded, diluted.
By white walls.
Educating me to be bound by freedom and reason

"When a certain irritation reaches my skull
    I feel as if...
I could kill a man for being dull."
It's been ten years since I've last said that.

A small boy, today, mother rows away, lay this hand on my lap
The bus ride un-smooth, dim eyes past me reading the ceiling,
    his hand on my lap
Bus ride un-smooth; his hand quaking in my lap
Mother, rows away, slaps the innocuous; and left me groping.

Soon the moon will push that cloud away, find me and smile liplessly
Twice! he's done that and twice! he's found me.
I think I'm too easy to decipher with my yellow tee-shirts
But he doesn't even known how easy he is to find with his fat shark
    face.

G. David Prosper

Old Crows

February's a poet
in search of a rhyme.
Lake ice, green mermaids
pines dancing in time.

March, a spoiled child,
tart silence, loud woe -
deer on the hillside
yellow primrose aglow.

April rides past
on a dappled grey mare -
Shadbush, dogwood
white flowers to spare.

May, a fine lady
tends her garden with care,
halo of sunbeams
daffodils in her hair.

I'm just an old crow
watching the seasons rush by -
fluffing my feathers
wishing I could still fly.

George Monagan

Ode To Daedelus

Ah, Daedelus, you who failed
In the grip of grief,
To mold in firm and bold relief
The fate of Icarus upon the
Final panel of Apollo's Temple Gate;

Did you love too much;
Or perhaps too little
To be thus so deaf to the voice of fate?

In that two edged thrust and throb
Beneath your scar, if you had only heard
That second deeper sob that echoes trough
The mind, hard upon the mettle of cold belief,
You might have used that inner voice
To hammer out the truth
In firm and bold relief!

A. E. Carney

A Four-Inch Piece Of Technology

SHE sang to Me, Her voice captured and frozen
  in Time, in Passion; in Emotion; in
  Love, on a 4 inch piece of Technology.

So Clear, so Real; so Close, I could feel
Her warm breath on the surface of My
neck, as Her lustful voice caressed
My ear.

So Moving as to cause My heart to
increase its palpitation; so Dear, as to
cause a smile to steal across My face; so
Touching, that it caused a tear to form in
the corners of My Soul. . .

But alas, to My Disappointment and Pain,
to My Frustration and Heartache, Her
voice, and presence, were only Captured
and Frozen, on a 4-inch piece of
Technology.

  Anthonye E. Perkins

The Clearing

The crystal hum of ancient trees bubbles
into narrow droplets that slide
off the red leaf
onto the bird's back
and into my steamy brain.
My brain's hot creases cool,
and I taste a pure drop of liquid stillness.
A bird's hymn grows in the air like thick grass,
crisping around my chest's hollow and planting seeds in my feet.
Above, a spider waits patiently in its web,
every moment catching a piece of the wind:
The ancestral wind that cuts through black jackets,
brick houses, diamond rings,
and voices a ten thousand year-old earth dust
that paints my lungs with cave-etchings
and memories I don't recall.
I look for the star-pictures that tell my story,
but I see only silent grandparents in rocking chairs.

  Erika Murphy

Resurrection

A grain of wheat once fell upon the earth,
It lay alone and did not wish to die,
There was no one to know its hollow worth;
It was a thing unfruitful 'neath the sky.

Its golden hue—a thing of beauty to behold,
Its gracile lines still in a tender stage,
Behind its shining armor brave and bold
It held its life within its lonely cage.

Another grain of wheat lay in the ground
And felt its flesh torn open by the rain;
The sun shone down upon its earthern mound
And then it died—but surely not in vain.

A newer life was born from out the old,
A living thing had risen from the dead!
Its beauty had been sacrificed for mould,
Its soul had lived because its heart had bled.

  Vera Pickering

The Kind And The Cruel

How kind is the night to the city.
Jewelled buildings are scraping the skies.
And the traffic that trails
Shining ruby-like tails,
Comes t'ward you with diamond eyes.

How kind is the night to the city,
With sensations of riches and class.
Even pavements are sparkling,
Which, out of the darkling,
Are sprinkles and splinters of glass.

How cruel is the dawn to the city!
What a shame, what a terrible waste!
As dawn rises once more,
On a festering sore,
And the jewels are rhinestones and paste.

  Claire Waeber Hicock

Life Without Love

This heart of mine has lost its beat since you
Left me. I wept on end, slept not a night,
Prayed that you would not forget. Birds that flew
Inside my heart, their wings clipped in full flight.
I'm hurt! Your words cut me like a sharp knife.
My loss, a wound, that stabs at my spirit,
Wrenches my bleeding heart. I possess life,
Yet my heart, scared to live, seems to fear it.
But woe! Life changes and is comprised of
More than hurt and pain. The joy of life can
Still be found without the need for one's love.
Live life to the fullest, that is my plan.
  For loss is merciless and hurts deep down,
  In life and nature is true love found.

  Matt Bergeron

"The New House"

The crimson sun groans
like a beast into its dusky lair
below the world
beneath the painted wave,
the haphazard strokes
of color remain,
kissing the sky,
like spots before
the dazèd eye.

Fantastic whirlpools,
reflections of infinite
violets, silvers,
heaven's fires.

Coming is the beauty of Night
and the stars of her breast!

The flapping hills, hushed, retire.
My new Home!
Arches of the world be stilled
and attend this orchestra,

The theatre we call Night!

  Jason Michael Glenn

Autumn Dance

October's slanted light falls
like incense around an altar,
where timeless we celebrate
milk-warmed at earth's bosom.

Blackbirds explode from fields
abandoned by reapers, protesting
a feast interrupted so ancient,
older than the earth is old.

There in heart's clearing,
your golden face close to mine,
sharing your breath we dance
in the impatience of sunlight.

Embracing an abundance of dreams,
I sway with blood's retreat and
become again your holy sentinel
whitened by time and steadfast.

Know, my soul, I will keep my vigil
and await snows' soft slide
to nourish these roots grasping
fiercely love's whispered litany.

Richard J. De Luca

Castle Remembered

Childhood memories jar the aging soul,
Like leaps from a sun-hot rock into the icy creek.

In the glimpses of days long past, a crumbling castle stands,
Nestled on a hilltop, silhouetted against the rich-blue sky,
With wisps of daffodils freckling the grassy plain.

A bright, red ball rolls down the castle slope;
The little child sobs as it dips into the clumps of green.
Casting aside the daily frets, a family strolls along the river's edge.

In these castle grounds, a lamenting history speaks
In strident and in muffled tones.
Here Hotspur conspired to unhorse the English kings,
And in a hut carved out of rock, the lonely hermit lived.

Age conquers sight, and vision fades.
The outside world takes inward turns, cramping the carefree grain.

The castle now blurs in darkening mist,
The daffodils wilt into sickly gray.
Unseen are the ramblers on the bank of the stream.

But in the clouded sight of quickening age,
A treasured memory snaps into view —
A castle, the lost red ball, and the hermitage.

John E. Turner

An Amish Town

It seems like any town, a spill of cars,
McDonald's, thirty-five miles per hour,
slow, school crossing, Discount House,
Furniture Land, Sohio, lined along the road
which stretches East to West, like a passing day.

Traffic slows behind a buggy rattling
on its homemade wheels. Inside, dark figures
sit erect before a metronome which ticks
for them alone. Or is their pace reality,
contrapuntal to our tunes of haste.

We press on, uncertain. Could we linger here, and
could we too be snatched, backward through the years
named progress, to find another beat. No today is
calling, so we leave on roads which point Westward
towards the sunset where tomorrow lurks in today's dying.

Shirley O. Morgan

Lullaby Of The City To Jeff Gaetano

Tell me, Summertime Man, where do you go, what do you do so late,
long after Autumn Woman has lulled her wildish nature
with mystical prayer and the scent of jasmine and sandalwood.

Do you toss darts or shoot pool
in the loud with noise-music-voices,
in the boozy, smoky places
that live on the loneliness in the city.

Or do you dance with changelings in the moonlight
and wonder of the witch whose cool fingers
you could invite to touch the golden hair
on your bare arms and ankles.

And do you soothe the burning questions of your life
with damp breezes while you stand on rooftops,
face the bay, and look toward the open water.

Tell me, Summertime Man, where are you when Autumn Woman
startles awake, sweating with escape from another trap,
the pounding of her heart accompanied
by the howls and scrabbling feet of her dreaming companion
deep in his domesticated sleep.

Adrienne Davis

Scorched Stalk

She was born
long and thin and maize-colored
Speckled with red freckles.

Indian corn.
Growing in a Chicago field
of backroom-made drugs and rock-gut liquor.

She grew straight
Stayed green.
At heart.
And he came along.

A worm done with poisoning
Tomatoes.
Looking for something
to wipe himself on.
So he did
For twenty years.

And now she is the
bitter scorched stalk
which bears no food
—only his Hatred.

Francine Thornton Boone

The Fells

Great grey crags and soft green paths
Mark the curving fells
Folded in unending line
They cradle lake and town,
Sturdy sheep their talisman,
Wisps of cloud their crown.
Pack-horse pass and rocky fence
Sear their patient sides.
Becks and gills gash foaming cuts
Soft heather soothes and hides.
I am one with crag and pass,
Earthbound yet not apart.
For I've a spring of heather,
One perfect white gull feather
To keep tucked within my heart.

Gertrude M. Taylor

14

Skeleton And Shadow

Flexible tissue, your flesh adjusted
molding skin with a potter's skill
around your diminishing frame

forming a new anatomy as you shrank
bonebrittle slight, already sizes
too small for just bought clothes

Rigid and unyielding, you wore posture
and attitude like armor regimentals
over skeleton and shadow

creating a Gordian knot of shrapneled
complexity; those incised fragments
of circumstance and self

Like many abusers, ambiguous to the end,
I knew you'd withered hollow inside,
ravaged years before the cancer

Like many despots, did you die none the
wiser — cruelty in one wasted hand,
courage pinched tight in the other?

Kate Stewart

On Becky's Return From Europe

Love, second self, thou heart whose heart can see
More clearly and deeply than mind or eye,
The sun so long away returns with thee;
The clouds so long a-low'ring quit the sky.
Confusion and uncertainty have gone,
My oldest friends of darker, colder days,
And taken with them all their deadly spawn:
The guilty things have fled before thy rays.
My muse! My life! No more are we apart!
Thy blessed return has made this part a whole;
Thy presence calms the seas that shake my heart;
Thy breath in me awakes a living soul.
Love, nestle curled and safe upon my breast,
And with my heart, now calm at last, find rest.

Shawn M. Bentley

For Joan Of Arc

I said I heard your voices in the field
Near Domremy call out to me - a girl
Just tending sheep in sun. You told me hurl
Stones, wear iron clothes, raise sword and shield,
Shout men to war. Ride swift, you said, don't yield
Smite English armies in the red grey swirl
Of Orleans siege. Then, with King Charles, unfurl
The flag of France, and claim French honor healed.

All this I told their courts. They swear I bring
You shame, my saints. They curse me as a bold
Heretic, scream witchcraft is my game!
Archangel Michael, let my voice take wing
From this vile cell. I, Joan the Maid, do hold
Christ Jesus, King. I claim Him in the flame.

Rose L. Breslin-Blake

Untitled

As enlighting,
Rooms in shadows arise,
Im-pale with subtle contradiction.
An edge sharp as the stone;
Honing yet, another blade of an idea.

The morning is fulfilling expectant eyes,
Hungry at breakfast! And supper yet to come....

Joseph M. Post

House Of Bread

Storage barns lay wasted, gone
No server at the altar stands
How come we go our way estranged
Apart from bread nor any sense
Half empty, lost, on familiar roads
Depressing hard to stretch half caked dreams
No suffering, nor sin, perse only syndrome
Yet, the House of Bread awaits syndromic man
Who would stagger rather than set his heart at rest
How very, very, sad what prized things do not bear
Neither sorrow, nor joy, nor weaken knees
Thus, the one who did not turn his face away
Awaits you as your House of Bread: Beit-Lechem

Orlando E. Pacheco

goldfish

i used to think that the tip of your
nose pointed to the fairy ring. yet all along
oberon has been dancing danubes around my
pupil.

you never understood my love of
bowlers or why they make me
think of lush white clouds. that doesn't
make you bad but it did make me an
alchemist.

you were giving my circles
edges; soon they would have been
squares.

forgetting is impossible. maybe
moving on is hard but after
all i have the bowlers and the
fairies.

when i saw the goldfish this
morning they looked positively
red. i smiled for then i knew that i was
healing.

Nicholas G. Salvato

Mother's Holiday

I rise, prepare for the holiday
Not with kohl-eyes nor jewels in my hair,
Not with manicured nails nor a rouged face:
I do not leave my room in robes of state.
No. I was not born just to celebrate,
To grant easy smiles to the gathered crowd
Around my table, nor to consecrate
This day to leisure, carefree and proud.

Instead I rise to the usual day,
Pull on jeans, whip a comb through hair now gray,
Jog if there is time to spare; if not, say
Silent oaths to reproach a mother's fate:
Jesus praised Mary but ate Martha's food
And set the rest of womankind to brood.

Lucinda Moreira

And Who Stoops Low To Smell The Breath

And who stoops low to smell the breath
  of a fallen fox,
    its faint scent rising from the cold wet grass?
From what fierce foe, toward what small prey
  did the old red fox seek to have his way?
What broke his heart as he lunged at last,
  as he raced like fire through the pale moonlight?
What hound of heaven was on your tail?
What sought to breathe your scented breath?

And who stoops low to smell the breath
  of a fallen soldier in his final fight,
    his faint scent rising from the same wet grass?
From what fierce foe, toward what weak prey
  did the aging sergeant seek his way?
What grand grenade, unpinned and cast,
  flowered flames in the bright sunlight?
What hound of heaven was on your tail?
What sought to breathe your scented breath?

James Clark Batts

Threads Of Dreams

Shapes and shadows
Of unhappiness
Follow me about
Like misty clouds
While cobwebs
Hang their beads
Of recall
So whisper light
On hazy gossamer
Threads of dreams
Imperceptible at first
'til studied by
The flicker light
Of lanterns
Held in hands
Of actuality.

C. T. Collins

History For Me

'Tis fine to see the cities and wander 'round and 'round,
On and off the subways as they criss-cross underground.
We gaze on glass and concrete, our modernistic art,
Sidewalk superintending as they tear the past apart.

At day's end it's home again, that's history for me,
Out into the villages to taste antiquity.
There mankind is real once more, in sunlight, rain or gloom;
People have respect and give each other elbow room.

Now, New York, is a climber's town — people everywhere,
Most so busy moving they never stop to care.
Politics, in Washington that's everybody's game,
Players have a need for more than 15 minutes of fame.

The traders thrive on hustle in hog butchering town,
While marks send money flying as Vegas bets go down.
Yet, when the day is ended, if only in a dream,
I'll seek my peace beside some still unpolluted stream.

Home again, yes home again that's history for me,
Where air is pure, skies are blue and we can still breathe free.
I'll find the homes of rough hewn logs, bricks with mortar stuck,
Places where they mean it when they wish their neighbor luck.

Eve Lewis-Chase

Dancing Irish Gypsy Wings

Gray angel wings — sun pushes to shine through
oppressed shroud of conformity tapping rhythms with
fingertips as Goddess woman, full of FIRE — fumbles under
restrictive stares and Tight-lipped smiles, uncomprehending
the Bold passion shining behind blue-green eyes.
Glancing aside, fearful such soul-wells might Bewitch them
into the Otherworld — not of Faery or the folk lore they live so
Well, but freedom and full-Bodied Life, where
Abandonment is tossed toward dogmatic minds, and
feet trace Spirals in town square without fear of being
Seen — "Gypsy witch!"
whispered behind white-creamed hands,
gray Eyes, shadowed by years of sunless skies, flicker the
Dancer's fire, longing to know such wildness.
Barefoot Gypsy, beaded anklets, twirls and swirls
colorful floral skirt Flaring out like a solar flare
challenging their spirits, fingers begin to Twitch
inner mental Battles force stillness — kept apart —
from the Lush and Lascivious dancer, Wild Spark
threatening the composed sanity of their starving Irish hearts.

Kisma K. Stepanich-Reidling

The Bus Stop

Every day at the bus stop
our prayers unite us
in the seemingly small,
the insignificant.

We boldly demand
  in our prayers
that the bus come
(apparently life is too short to spend waiting for a
bus)

Every day
  in our sacred moments
    we come together
in the majesty of the insignificant.

Every day
at the bus stop
we come to know
  together
in our silences
that life is truly short.

Spyros Spyrou

I Walked

I walked
past blankets limp from oily sunbathers
keeping a vigil on small fry construction crews
building sand castles and digging to China,

Past the Ferris Wheel and other whirligigs
reflected in the neon shades worn by body builders
at Fast Eddy's next door,

Past sea gulls stealing leftover lunches at Joe's Grill
while nearby somersaulting silver fish
are left behind by autonomous waves,

Past summer homes and fewer footprints
and a place where I could share my secrets
with the sea and feel its heartbeat,

Until,
I saw a lone figure in the distance near the rocks
and sadly and angrily remembered
the recent fate of a walker like me

And turned back dreaming of real castles
with towers and sentinels to keep me safe
while walking in the sand.

Jan A. DiBella

The Choice

If I were to listen to famous grey matter,
    Pathway through which man's thoughts travel,
There'd be precious little of knitting I'd do
    For fear that I'd have to unravel!

Such as a letter, which I would not send
    Or some love that I could not bestow,
Because, though my heart kept on telling me "yes"
    My mind was persistent with "no".

There'd be no more climbs to the mountain tops high
    Where bright sunbeams brush away care;
As I hear a voice in chiding command
    "Come down! Don't you know nothing's there?"

Never again would I sail clouds of blue,
    Or ride with my hopes on a Star;
For if I did, earth-bound one surely would ask,
    "Just where do your think that you are?"

Ah, yes! What great raptures life then would deny
    And how much of joy would depart,
If I were to listen — just to my mind
    And forget that I, too, had a heart!

Margaret Baker Foster

Speechless Eyes

I might compare your eyes to that of gold.
Perhaps I'd dare instead the harvest moon.
Still yet I'd feel that to be somewhat cold,
As though the words have come to me to soon.

I'd want to say instead a stormy night,
Complete with thunder and some soothing rain.
But then I'd feel the words were still not right,
That some may not feel strength but rather pain.

Still more I'd feel urge to say a day,
With sun, and sky, and birds, and life sublime.
But now I realize I'd have to say,
Your eyes are not just that but much more kind.

I guess your eyes mean so much more to me,
Than any words could say or anyone could see.

Ali Deale

Seasons

Leaves, new-green, translucent, shimmer
    Playful dance on fresh spun stem
        Blades of same, shoot upward, quiver,
            Robins herald, "Spring Again!"

Locusts' lusty wing's crescendo
    Frogs in chorus bellow near
        Mockingbird's impersonation
            Proclamate that Summer's here

Trees with modest inclination
    Autumn prompts be brazen gowned
        Shameless, draped in crimson foliage
            Drop their garments on the ground

Silence! Whisper! It is Winter!
    Sparkle softly beds of snow
        Quietly hang your crystal pillars
            Earth is just asleep you know.

Deborah Nichols Wheat

What You Sow Makes A Difference

One day I sowed a seed;
    Protecting and nurturing its growth,
Only to find it was a weed.
    It was something to loathe.

There was a pretty daisy near;
    It was so very full of life.
But no one did see its tear;
    Understand its plight and strife.

The tangled roots of the weed—
    took the flower's strength and power;
I, the gardener, did not take heed.
    All I saw was my daisy flower.

A feeling of impending doom came one day;
    My pretty daisy I might lose.
All because I didn't notice the way
    Consummation of the daisy the weed did choose.

Was I so blind, that I did not see?
    Was I so deaf, that I did not hear?
The day I sowed the seed I cast the sin upon thee.
    Our lives forever changed I fear!

Glenda Newman

Time

Spent with yourself
Questioning the past
Contemplating the future
Time escaping. . .

Your heart full of love
Remembering the agony
Dreaming of warmth
Time escaping. . .

Your mind full of fascination
Reviewing choices made
Planning days ahead
Time escaping. . .

Your body at ease
Tired from years
Pure with relaxation
Time escaping. . .

Your soul at peace
Spirits haunting
Searching for meaning
Time to live. . .

Judy Toneri

Dominion Of One

My license to kill has been renewed
Red lemon stung vision is newly imbued
With memories of you
And the bloodlust we knew
And snide-blind good victims
That are waiting unknown

A full scale war in the middle distance
Laughter Glazed Hunger snapping my pistons
Lo and Behold
The sharp blank honest cold
Stark physician's clean prisons
Anesthesia refined

Straining at the bit
Nibbling at the tit
Mother's Milk soured
Wet stained silk strung dour
'Cross the thrillscape of my leer
'Round the still nape of my dear
Let's ride into the fear
Dominion 1 in Sight.

Peter DiGennaro

17

Interim

I remember the March winds like fingers of pesky children
ruffling the hair I wanted neat for meetings,
the distracting shouts at kites,
the vacations impossible, the improbable springs
I thought would never come. I guess they did.
There were flowers and grasses and moonlight
calm as a cudding cow - and as irrelevant
to my impatience in the shadow.
I suppose there were autumns as well as summers
but they seem to have been consumed by preparation
for something I must have forgotten.
Everything was yet to come. And now it has
as much as it will, leaving hardly more
than a little wisdom.
There is no more shouting, rustling;
the golden years and golden leaves are dull and still;
and the moon is low in the south behind the trees -
just the time for an improbable spring to happen
before leaf-lethal winds begin to blow
and I am chilled and killed by an apprehension,
the leading edge of the cutting edge of snow.

A. Sherman Christensen

Cruising Time

Driving down the highway of endless time,
Seeing the truth that is really mine.
Beating with the endless rhythm of life,
Flowing with quantum leaps of endless strife.
I split the sound down the line,
Open the wound and pour the iodine.

To stand naked mainlined to the soul,
Strike the anvil just to rip open the mold.
Soaring free is a gift not so bold,
Energies of life are not to be sold.
For all that glitters in the light is really gold,
The backstreets of reality are ancient but not old.

Cruising-gliding-riding into the sun,
Knocking at the faceless door when that's done.
Back again to suffer the pain of an endless birth,
Rock on, to the rhythms of joyful mirth.
I know now of the gift of choice,
I'm cruising down the highway of no time.

Toni Baird

On Viewing The Ruins Of An Antebellum Home

Now see
shadows run 'round your perimeter
lengthen into days gone by,
skeletal framework
for imagination's fleshing.
There
  the rust-iron grill where
balconies stood
(the wood now rotted-gone)
and lovers kept spring rendezvous.
Shafts of light strike pillars
with soft tumbling down
of porous sand,
stately columnaded marble with
sky shown through.
What work of man
to lift these pillars high
as though to say:
If these stand, we shall not die.

Bob Nevels

Nippon

Mossed pagodas roofed with gold,
  Silhouetted pines
Bent like pilgrims dwarfed and old,
  Wind voiced roadside shrines ...

Cherry blossoms in the fountain,
  Petals seaward streaming,
Fujiyama, sacred mountain,
  In the blue lake gleaming ...

Bamboo sails of little boats
  Drifting calm and slow,
Where the bleeding lotus floats
  On the mirrored snow ...

Thrasher Hall

The Sometimes-Melting Pot

I have heard there is a melting-pot,
Simmering somewhere
In the kitchen of the world.
And I've heard that this pot is golden,
Tempered by years of fury-hope-fear,
Strengthened with some steel-tipped tears,
And that it is into this
Are thrown we, wanting more than rotten
Potatoes, peasants' meals, meatless bones,
More than water-soup and bread-like stones.

But from this mix of human things
They'll extract some blood, some spit, some sweat:
Make a grotesque scabby meal.
And into the tinny cheery molds
We're quietly dashed (dry as dried herbs)—
So then they spit the wet back in us;
Bake us for several years (or so),
In order that we might be
Savored delicious.

Elisa Tovar

The Butterflies

To Gene

I wonder as I watch them fly
Small stained glass windows in the sky
Have they come to comfort me
And cure my pain before they die
Like tongues of flame, the father said,
To make me know that he's not dead
Will they emerge in a new Spring
To float in soft and gentle wind
Or is it simply that I seek
Any sign to ease this grief

I love you all the time

Christine Finn

Spring Storm Coming

The still, the breeze
the smell of new being
blown from the trees
bringing hope with every
breath I breathe
the miracle of life rides in
on the winds of change
to free my soul of death
for that moment I know
to rest or to grow
to be born or to die
that wind shall blow
and what shall it spark in
another man's eyes

Gregory A. Farmer

Earthly Equity

Oh where and whence is equity,
So many people cry in vain;
Nowhere on Earth can it be found,
So many suffer with their pain.

The world is full of fervent prayer,
For mercy do so many cry;
Though heard, it often seems ignored,
So many mutely wonder why.

The master who must know us best,
Betimes will put each soul to test;
To teach us pain and misery,
Behind the veil of mystery.

Each soul must face eternity,
So many lessons must be learned;
Thus back and forth in space we go,
Until all hate within is burned.

The Equity we can not see
Is in our earthly Karma locked;
Enlightenment we will receive,
When once our mem'ry is unblocked.

Sol Finkelman

Openings

I opened my eyes and I noticed the pain,
So the logical choice was to close them again.
When I closed them I couldn't see day turn to night,
But then neither could I see the night turn to light.

With them closed I could not see the world growing old,
But then neither could I see the youngsters, so bold.
I could not see the tears people cry when they're sad,
But then neither could I see the joys people had.

As I sat in my vacuum, all sheltered in black,
I felt someone reach out — and I somehow reached back.
When we touched I was fearless, I grew brave and strong
And I opened those eyes that were closed for so long.

Then I wept for a moment to grieve what I'd missed;
There was no one there threat'ning my face with a fist.
There were people around me with comforting arms
That enfolded me, bringing a feeling so warm.

Then I noticed the flowers, the sun and the stars,
And I noticed their beauty erased all my scars.
Though I sometimes still notice the pain and despair,
I am sure just beyond them the beauty's still there.

Sheila Mandell Gendron

Olympic Gymnast

A diminutive child
Stands poised
Then with a bound, takes flight,
A taut spring released.
Bars are no barriers,
Arc, whip, soar,
Poetry - precise, controlled,
Her slender frame
Bamboo supple, steel strengthened,
Performs with practiced perfection.
Testing the laws of physics
She moves in exact equations
Until end over end she flips,
Descends triumphant.
A breathless world watches
Roars approval
Drops its heart at her feet
Bedecks her with tributes and flowers,
So petite a child,
A giant.

Edith Bockian

We Criminal

Rock ribbed temperance in disadvantageous plight
strength
becomes perverted, seeking unbridled
abandonment...the criminal comes into its own.

His morality contra-distinctionally vagrant vivacious
desires,
dressed in despondent sensibility
finding secret aspirations tempered
with tension...the crime becomes reality.

Instinctive yields of peril, aggravation
and catastrophe hurling towards
disaster, feeling misfortune laced with
danger...crime in a statement of rage.

Civilized tranquil community scorns the
savage and aggressively
adventurous, shaping antisocial degenerates...made
is the criminal.

Impregnable virility intensified
to its utmost apex transforms amongst tranquil society to discover,
the artist, the genius and...the free spirit of the idol.

Scott L. Teague

Fool's Journey

A fool's journey
stumbling homeward
the path is clear
but the eyes gaze down in fear
distraction calls from both sides,
ignorant bliss.... trap the complacent
knowledge...... trap the proud
(a little bit is a dangerous thing,
and that's all the fool can carry)

No respite,
for time snaps at lazy heels
No rush,
for destiny is a fantasy

Stumbling through paradise,
the task is to look up from the trail, and see

Greater the fool who stares at shuffling feet
when the path is clear
and Eden abounds

Steven Fry

Suffering Is Not Enough

What's the matter here?
Sunflower heads bowed to watery cities
Black holes faceless clown all screaming yellow frills
Cornered cowering color, milky lavender sky
Black trees shiver against crisp air
Never been to me
Sorrow is the banquet upon which we feed
When boy was boy, and girl was girl
Found each other in a wicked world
Bone cold fire in bed
Ran out of places to run to, empty faces gone
Some nights spent crying for unborn children who might make me
Complete
Fight with you this morning, mood as black as coffee, sour
Hold me inside deep
Can still see so much of me still living in your millpond mossy eyes
A butterfly, broken wings, I can no longer take flight
My cocoon was safer, dark, warm
Stars, wise eyes watching over us
Weeping willow, green billowing hair, only whispers truth

Rebecca K. Seligman

19

A Dr. Kevorkian Kind Of Day

An overflux of hormones
supplicating whores moan
in rhythm with a drone bee.
Still
a mouth, a mou-OW-th
moves magically
under medicine.
Drugs of love
and luggage.
Pills of passion.
Shun the past
pass the active.
Petting petals, smooth,
moving grace
gives way to fresh sent scents.
Smile a while, while there's time.
It's a good day for cinnamon.
It's a good day for sin-Amen!
Been a Dr. Kevorkian kind of day.

Seana Kay Muhart

Transformation

For Elie Wiesel

The black bird flies as our life,
taunting us beautifully,
ever-present and departing
to become a gray dot,
a small flake of ash
falling into nothing.
Standing on the ground
I hallucinate,
reach my arm into sky,
catch the bird in one hand.
Nothing is fast here.
My father is sick.
This evening I watch
the two men in his bunk beat him
to steal his portion of bread.
I become the filthy bird,
to fly slowly away
while wishing my father would live,
giving him my portion
which I had reserved for the dead.

Gregory Thielen

Triumph At Twilight

Across the Lake the sun is setting, a majestic fiery ball
  That has flamed the sky with splendor, as I await the eerie call
Of the loon, whose quiet passage—swift and silent though it be—
  Moves underneath chill waters of a somber inland sea.

Now the lowering sun is meeting Damariscotta's murky face,
  Its slanting rays transforming to a glowing red-gold place
What once seemed dark and threat'ning filled with snares and
  unknown space.
God is touching it with beauty. He is filling it with grace.

And suddenly, before the glow of this awesome scene can dim,
  The waters stir, pierced by a beak that's long, and sharp, and slim.
A sleek, black head arises; two blood-red eyes appear;
  A triumphant call surprises the solemn atmosphere.

Then, stretching high, and higher, the loon begins its flight
  In an ecstasy of gladness—out of darkness into light!
And I, who've known dark waters coldly flowing over me,
  Have a glimpse of God's own glory—and of what is meant to be.

Ruth Johnson Fountain

The Race

Life is a cycle, akin to a race
that once we've begun, we quicken the pace
to pursue the dream that all advertize
until we achieve what they call the prize.

Within that circle reserved for winners,
I patiently watched the new beginners
and lamented most for those with great speed
completely consumed with all that they need.

They don't understand the reason they run
or how it all ends, or what had been done,
the blessings they'll loose or the wisdom why
they climb the ladder of success, the lie.

From the emptiness of all my winning,
I must return now to the beginning
to quietly wait while I humbly stand
and ask with my heart to follow God's plan.

For those who finish are seldom content,
they look with remorse at all they have spent
To slowly realize the race is won
by only the few who choose not to run.

Robert C. Parbs

"A Poet's Wish"

If I have written but one poem
  That shall in time be known,
I have created that one poem
  For all the world to own.

If volumes of portentous size
  Should never be my lot,
I would not mourn the lengthy loss,
  For length is soon forgot.

But, with one poem, I should stand
  Immortal to the end,
Alone, unsung, but never banned
  From hearts and minds of men.

Ronald Alfred Walker

Port Of Call

As summer's throngs in fall disband
The ancient ones reclaim the strand
With sullen stomachs, capsized chests,
Astringent thighs and frowning breasts.
A woman rakes her knobby hands
Like plowshares through the silky sands,
Recalls the beach of bygone youth -
Hot summer love, cold autumn truth -
Spies flighty shadows on the beach,
Her long-dead sisters, out of reach,
Their chiming laughter high and clear
Till under clouds they disappear.
She scans the line with opal eye
Where pulsing ocean kisses sky;
Her shoulders freeze, a sharp inhale,
Beholds that long-expected sail -
The ship which never makes a call
Except at life's last evenfall -
Obeys the signal from the bridge
And starts her final pilgrimage.

Lucy I. Allen

Passage

The old queen lay dying under the dripping wisteria.
The old queen lay dying.
Joyously garden fragrances intermingled,
A perfect scent for her last breath.

She kissed the crippled cricket good-bye.
"Where is my luck today?" The old queen asked.
"The channel is narrowing.
The waves are still.
Quickly, quickly, the swanboat leaves.
Your luck is on the other side,"
Whispered her sad eyed friend.

With a crisp chirp and a brave leap,
The tiny creature disappeared trailing a
Threnody of joy and despair.
The measured beats of the wind's
Soft dirge swept the garden,
Matching the broken heart beats.

Quickly, quickly, the swanboat leaves.
Helen L. Douglass

Prism

The sky is that smiling shade of blue
The one that makes you suck in the air
With eyelids half closed
head tilted back
all covered in peace and wonder and the idiot joy of being
Funny how the color of the sky
the color of the air
can so shade you
Impress upon contentment
Inhabit existence
True independence a myth
Existentialism rethunk
A chain reaction food chain chain of fools connection
Relation
Connection
We are all part of it
The sky was that drowning shade of gray
the day you left
I don't remember
yet I know
Leslie Senevey

Hedge Shears

Because he stole
the only rosebud,
the garden was gone for her.
She was five
And his great dog named Paris
hated her when she threw stones at the chickens he raised.

Because he stole the only
white rosebud
the garden was gone,
and a great storm descended upon the city of Rio
each day from 5 to 6 p.m.

Because he stole the only white rosebud
the garden was gone for her.
She was five, he was her father
and on that great night
of the theft,
he buried the moon
beneath the mantle of the earth.
Aliete O. Guerrero

Poetry — Music, Art And Literature

Poetry is literature - a story told in verse
The poet is an author, with feelings to disperse
Poetry is history, philosophy and love
And a poem is a chronicle - of all of the above

Poetry is music - a choral incantation
The poet is a maestro of lyrical orchestration
Poetry is a concert of song and sound and love
And a poem is a symphony - of all of the above

Poetry is classic art - a timeless, visual feast
The poet is an artist with his work a masterpiece
Poetry is a portrait of people, life and love
And a poem is a painting of all of the above

Poetry is everything that helps make life so fine
A moonlit night, a child's face, a glass of vintage wine
And a poem is a diary of all the things we love
Music, Art and Literature - and all of the above
Dr. Donald R. Stoltz

His World

A world of sun and cloud, blue sky
The realm that pilots share on high
While boring through the haze that hides
The clefts where only God presides
It's here you sense true life revealed
You're climbing through the mist and feel
At first the warmth, and then dim light
Before you break out in that bright
Sunlit place where calm prevails
With skies of blue and white contrails
While down below the earthlings crawl
Through all the fog and rains that fall
It's here you share a sight serene
The masters work "forever scene"
But only airmen know this place
Where some will say "I've seen his face"
And yet they ask the question why
Don - What makes you want to fly
Don Fairchild

Of Pen And Sword

I've had my choice of "pen or sword"....
The "sword" I have declined,
And, to my "pen" and writing board,
All due efforts I've consigned.

My favored "pen" I will not forsake
Nor surrender to the "sword",
But with abundant zeal I will partake
For deep within me much is stored.

While writing words: to coin a phrase,
Some of which I am so proud,
Repeatedly I will appraise
That term to be endowed.

I feel excitement everywhere
While writing...I'm not bored
Ah Yes! my feelings: I will declare,
"The PEN is mightier than the SWORD".

I let the "sword" just lay and linger
In sanguineous repose,
While in my hand beneath my finger,
My mighty "PEN" will duel with prose!
Lillian K. Wells Basile

"Tongues Of Sword And Fire"

Thrust upon the waves of life, my love as you can see,
The tongues that I have spoken to you have not been filled with glee.
I flowed along not knowing where my future would proceed,
My life was void of poem or song that I could leave my seed.
I fooled all those who did come near, my secret kept me deep in fear.
A kindly soul perceived my strife, arranged a plan to change my life.
New words are now opened to me with tongues of sword and fire,
They pierced my soul and burned my mind and filled me with desire
I felt the chains of bondage fall away onto the earth
Eyes dulled by years of scrambled thoughts were clear for my rebirth.
Oh tongues of sword and fire rejoice I have fulfilled a need
My eyes brim over with tears of joy for I have learned to read.

The sword; a friend who saw through my deceit
The fire; my desire to be much more complete.

Dolores Johnson

From My Fortress

I waited for the moon to fade,
the western clouds to smother.
I steered from thinking toward you
per-chance I'd not recover.

But now the fading shadows form
a unity of darkness;
and hidden well, I'll dare to well
a time outside my fortress.

I see you in your smile softly
lighting up a morning.
I see the chance, thru circumstance
you harmed without a warning.

Hold not too dear to one who flies
or allow at will to yearn;
for some take flight in early light
and some do not return.

We're as the west wind to the east;
though both decide the weather,
they mix and mingle for a time
but never ride together.

Ron L. Johnson

Requiem Of A Loser

Remember yesterday?
The world was new and we were
Filled with our own sexuality,
We ate eagerly at the apple of life.
Today we are older, the world is grayed,
We must nibble at the core.
Where has it gone, when did it happen?
Life has been a trip through hell
And high water.
Some wins some losses,
Does it really matter?
I dwell upon all the things
I've never done, the songs I've never sung.
I'll have some beer and lay me
Down to sleep, either that or
Break down to weep...

Richard M. Caimens

Harvest

Beneath evening sky of red-gold,
Their husks, empty altars to a savage God,
Reaching feebly towards ghost cloud
As they whisper ancient song to restless sod.
Silent cornfields stand alone,
Burning with sweet prayers come too late,
Grasping at sunbeams, but catching only wind,
All too aware of their somber fate.
Oh how they wail whipped to and fro,
Ghosts of what they once were,
As vagabond crow and crude wagon
Carry away their jewels in dusty blur.
Then, as hollow moon glows, how the cornfields whisper,
Strangers to day's rich golden rays —
Mourning lost hope, and beauty gone —
Standing, dust, beneath an ashen haze,
Pleading for sweet compassionate song
Instead of farmers' rustic chant fair,
But it is too late. The harvest is in.
And only echoes are left upon night's air.

Margaret L. Schroeder

Our Welfare Aristocracy

Our welfare aristocracy toil not nor do they spin,
They need not lift a finger for the living that they win.
The children they beget in idleness are raised,
In idleness those kids will spend all future days.
They have no need for learning, education they can shirk,
There is no need to study when you don't have to work.

Their numbers are increasing, their living is assured,
Every want is provided for, no pain to be endured.
The burden of their care increases year to year,
The cost of their support grows everywhere more dear.
There is no obligation which attaches to their station,
They have no duties owed to city, state or nation.

This sorry scheme is not a dream the devil did devise,
Its origin is Washington, that's where the plan did rise.
The authors of our welfare plan should come as no surprise,
The legislation they produced is neither good nor wise.
Our welfare aristocracy - we laud them to the skies,
Their social caste will last and last - their's is the greatest prize.

Donald E. Brown

White Masks

White masks polished and perfumed
  to hide the cadaverine
   of soul rot
dead since the contract was signed
  chasing away ethos and psyche
  as Love lost
   to titillation and manipulation
  the gods of forgetfulness and control
who
  keep at bay the inner raging
   by scraps and straps
  and all life
   is the role
  and how you are
   scene

William Corff

Obloquy

To be a writer is to beg for death:
To shun the critics' guillotine is luck —
Yes! Watch them gouge! Like suckerfish they suck
From my cold lungs the last small warmth of breath:
They gag me twice — not one word must be said
Which might offend the living or the dead.

But one can learn to bend the lung of ink
Across the paper's windpipe; truncate veins
Yet vacillate to feed true vampires' brains —
Furious fellows insert their fangs, drink
The blood of our labor, then quaff it off
Without so much as one dogmatic cough.

And when the subtle heart gathers to pump
Another rush of blood, the valves are cursed
So that the red words oscillate and burst
Against the dizzy chamber, voices bump
Along vague literary throats like knots
Of Tarot cards or pills, reveal our lots.
Robie Glenn Hall

Reverie Revisited

There is a kind of poignant ache upon a visit, long delayed,
to where we spent our youth.

Remembrance calls to mind events now linked to seeing sites
from yesteryear.

Scenes long past and thoughts of might-have-been
still linger unerased, though time does paint with mists
of fantasy and sometimes blurs our hallowed recollection.

With bittersweet nostalgia as its shield our mem'ry
fights pure truth to hold in fond embrace those facts-flawed
scenes which even passing years can't steal—those dimming
vistas, fading echoes, sailing, sounding through the mind
with no coherence but the feel of rightness in reflection.

We stand in dreamlike trance by road and rock, by lake
and woods to see if places once well known remain the same,
and hear familiar songs of birds in trees now tall and full
that then were bush and sapling.

Yearning for we know not what, we blink a tear that
forms then dies as we acknowledge we'd not trade our present
time for all the yesteryears, however sweet.
Thus we say to Time: Get on with it.
Paul D. Marable, Jr.

Old Bennington Church

The ancient pines swayed in the dry heat,
touched the edges of the church and scraped
the loose paint away until the old walls
could not hide grey cracked ribs, dingy
plate glass windows, or the groan and creak
of the steeple. Its narrow shadow
split the courtyard, the point severed

the two of us, pushing us apart until
we mingled with the tourists, snapping pictures,
icing each other with glances. Through the heat
I needed to move farther away from your luke warm
smile, into the church where the cold
benches lined the walls and the pulpit
embraced the brass organ. It played
old dirges, haunting melodies rumbled along
the isles until I remembered the old promises;
forgotten. I turned away, the organ surrendered

the last note, its low moan pushed me through the doors
where you still floundered through the courtyard, shaded your eyes
and snapped pictures to paste in your scrapbook.
David Durkee

Urban Dwelling

Slumlords
Transient tenants
Windows with many jagged eyes
Steps that squeak and doors that sarcastically greet ya
Every other stair has its mouth wide open, ready to swallow your leg
Dust flies from dimly lit lanterns
Creaky boards resound from the trample of tenants' feet
Wind bangs of the window, demanding to come in
Cockroaches creep and flies loaf on plaster-chipped walls and ceilings
Money floats in exchange for drugs and local whores' polygamy
Sounds of gunshots are the only music played
Bloodied bodies are displayed as decorations
Trapped with all the other agoraphobics
No one to trust outside as well as inside
The only thing that makes them safe is bolted doors and blaring
televisions
Aaron Maltz

Reptiles

Day-Stephanie
    Two years-old, she dances clumsily
        in pink diaper-cushioned overalls
    Under her smiling lips sits a red lizard
    Below her sparkling left eye sleeps a purple turtle

Night-Stephanie and Mother
    A sharp scream slices through the apartment
    Slap
    "Don't cry Stephanie!"
    Slap
    "Oh, you look so cute,"
    Slap
    "Now stop your crying damnit!"
    Slap Slap
    Shiny crimson snakes
        slither through teary streams down Stephanie's face

Next Day-Stephanie
    She waddles in circles
    A maroon crocodile
        rests on her right cheek
Ben Rhodes

Feast

I, mid yellow-eyed carrion glutted,
Under the torch of sun, am butted
By predatory beaks scraping
The rolling flesh, stinging,
Bones bare in the fever heat of feast,
Muscles torn by the yellow-eyed beasts.
Nearby apples ooze sweet sugar death;
The birds keep hacking their rotten breath.
My soul's last moments wrenches,
The last nerve twitches,
Cut by the heavy, battered beaks.
The black-winged birds with squealing shrieks
Fly into Paradise.
Jerome David Mayer

Alchemy Of Necessity

You sleazy, rotten-to-the-core bastard,
You lying, loathsome, lizardly lycanthropos,
You worse than amphibian-reptilian excrescence,
Worse than the slimy, schemey, scaly reptiles—
Their coldness, instinct; yours, cold calculation—
You rancid rind of a reprobate,
You puffed up piece of air-filled pastry
You pismire of a pustule,
You—

"Well, hi there, boss!
And how are you this fine morning?"
LaMarr Thomas

23

The Rituals Of The Gods

Chalice of fine silver, chasuble of gold —
Under vaulted arches the priests recite,
With supplicating arms before the fold
The chanting words dispel the fear of night.
The ancient mysteries of wine and bread —
Silent deacons prepare the cup and host
Watchful eyes of uncomprehending dread
In mute prayer partake the Holy Ghost.
Vigils and ember Saturdays in Lent —
In cloistered rooms haggard figures desist
And fast in solitude, their lives unspent,
An obligation they cannot resist.
An act of faith, of unassuming love,
A word well meant, and a smile from above.

David Pardo

Sonnet - Violets

The violets still are growing there,
Upon the slope, the hillside where
We strolled together long ago.
How we have changed; no warming glow
Steals o'er my heart, your listless eyes
Don't speak to me, and so love dies.
Today, I wondered how the violets grew,
They seemed immortal, while we two
Between us dragged a corpse, and so,
What better place to lay it low?
In fancy there I dug a grave
Cast love within it, set free a slave:
The violets are the marker there,
You know the spot, or do you care?

Adeline Martinek

"From Which Comes My Help."

Expansively the mountains reach
Upward to the sky.
Before their majesty I bow—
Insignificant I.

No power of speech have they,
Beyond a breathless sigh;
Yet strength from their silence flows,
Absorbing it — recreant I.

Without mind or reason, within
The mountain shadows lie
A wisdom far transcending man.
Intellectual infant I.

Unhearing though they always are,
To them goes out my anguished call;
And from their depths of solitude
Comes peace to my turbulent soul.

Billie A. Cooper

Measuring Youth

Let us now weigh the worth of shining stars
With sparkling faces, pentacles of glee.
They dance and wing the rims of amber Mars
Indeed, their play is joy to watching sea.
A languished echo, though, the earth does know
When from the delft the steely comets send.
So, too, the agony of growth is woe
To see the life, so dearly near, expend.
But laden spirits claim a riddance naught
For pleasance far out soars the tears of rue.
The wily flights and falls are soon forgot
As Venus' rays emit a golden hue.
If Argo, Crux, and Ursa want in chance
Then evenings know not heavens twinkling trance.

C. Terry Noe

The Conspiracy Of Indifference

I sit about the sickened sea,
vile with black echoes of lovers
calling for that which sickened seas cannot give.

They cry miserably, pleadingly, helplessly;
and the murky liquid slushes tarnished
slops of indifference.

I and the sickened sea, stoic soul, wounded
heart, abandoned spirit, together in
sombrous wet waste.

I, now, unified with despair's deception,
look to the sky and through the
veiled layers of used time.

I wait openly for that divine message lovers
beg to know, only to find tears of rain
darting my mangled face.

And so, I now sit before myself nearing the
epic of my life, bewildered and unfulfilled,
looking for hope—-
but I only see the conspiracy.

Anthony Daleo

Winter Blues

Today, as I lay idle, sick a-bed,
What mighty, labored thoughts went through my head?
Did I, in mind, the ailing earth set right?
Did I, for clouded souls turn on a light?

For me, did nature's mysteries unfold?
Was I of some brave enterprise made bold?
Was inspiration for a play conceived,
Some long forgotten masterpiece retrieved?

Did I invent a plan to help mankind,
Or were my thoughts of lasting peace inclined?
Was the nature of my thinking global?
Can I tell at least my thoughts were noble?

Sorry am I to have to answer, "No".
I was absorbed with one red nose to blow.

Joan W. Krieger

Autumn Is the Purple Time of Year

The autumn is the purple time of year
When all the leaves of summer disappear
Beach Plums and elderberries now are set
For jelly making and for wine and yet
It takes a lot of doing every day
To wash and pick them over in the way
Your mother did...you put them on a broom
In cheese cloth bags to drip outside the room
Where folks can have a cup of tea and talk
About your mussel and your clamshell walk
At sundown on the marshes you can see
Pale sea lavender or marsh rosemary
You gather it and dry it for bouquets
To keep the memory of these autumn days

Helen Fiske Atkins

Attic Trunk

There are some ragged midnights
when shards of moonlight refract shattered
through cold crystal prisms of my memory
and scurrilous compulsion wrests parts of me
to pull and drag broken pieces of you
clattering groaning from a bed of ashes
up the attic-stepped runway
to fly overloaded into a querulous past.

Gathered within an inevitable inexorable
cobweb net of the brain
are amputated limbs rendering holding useless,
recalcitrant pieces of heart, shameless bits of soul,
unsanctified mangled promises...
all bumping scraping against umbrageous landings
delivering both to unrepentant storage...
as vow carries to the end in a cached garret trunk.

Love's mutilated fragments enmesh without delineation
implode fused, collect a secret collaborated dust
whisper the closing of a once lost baby-blanketed lid
making once again a family of the strangers we became.

Sara M. Parker

The Last Wish

I would not have you bury me in sodden plot
   Where my stallion heart can find no release;
No! Better that you place me where earth is not,
   To traverse silent sands as tidal waves cease.

Or scatter me o'er verdant beckoning hills
   That these eyes may trace wheeling futures below;
Let my windswept spirit drift over whispering rills,
   Laugh freely, dance, scatter flowers, then go.

Or place me in night-twinkling, celestial space
   That I might journey azure realms afar;
Where the brilliant course of a meteor I may trace,
   Then pause, remember love and toss you a star.

Oh please! Let shackling earth remain devoid of me
That I might choose my own eternity.

Gloria Damon

Ever My Destiny

To walk the hallowed fields of France
Where once the sounds of battle played
And trod the ancient Scottish moors
Where once the hounds of folklore bayed
To scale the sheer Tibetan cliffs
And kneel where aged monks once prayed
Will ever be my destiny.

To stand upon the mountain peaks
Where once the mighty eagles flew
And sail across the timeless seas
Where once the angry tempests blew
To wander through Yosemite
And watch its awesome geyser spew
Will ever be my destiny.

To ski across the frozen hills
Where once the lonely trappers trod
And chase the great white arctic whale
Through seas which teem with krill and cod
To look upon the face of God
Will ever be my destiny.

Edwin F. Roble, Jr.

Rebirth

Emerging from the womb of silence came darkness—
With it came the smells of damp earth under musty canvas
charred logs smoldering ashes; the muffled groans and sleepy yawns
reluctant zippers, rustling wraps and wooly blankets
stiff denim, wet flannel, dull thuds of clumsy bodies.

The windows of the soul gaze upon the grey mist rising
touched softly by dawn's awakening hand
the sunlight streaming through tall trees
beads of dew, glistening on bright green leaves.

Holding tight in a silky web of life, cradling your soul
rise—break through your warm cocoon, your quilted nylon shell
your downy cast. Unfold: Your limbs, your newborn body
your mind to the freshness of creation.
Forward into the light

Jeffrey Jc. Fabiszewski

Yesteryear

Where futile antiseptics clash
with senile whims and lapses
and reedy voiced remember whens
and fancies echo memory tricks
on how it used to be

The wizened visage, light-bulbed
and mirrored above the sink,
sees shimmering sunbeams dance
with shadows among
the woodlot's whispering leaves

With palsied hands, he lifts
the faucet's chlorinated liquid
and greedily mouths a chill
sweet nectar from the well
beside the gate where Maw's
red rambler draped the arch,
scattering fragrance on the wind

Irene Prater Dell

Beloved Despot

A tiny Queen's arrived on scene;
With ties umbilical,
Expressions quizzical,
Attitude whimsical,
She reigns supreme.

From cushioned throne, with softest moan
She spews commands,
Unspoke demands
All understand
In tongue unknown.

Lying in her bower, she wields her power;
Who would have thought
So much could be wrought
(Indeed, so much taught!)
By so innocent flower?

Regent yet green, your world yet pristine,
May Fortune befriend you,
The Heavens attend you,
All Creation commend you:
God save the Queen!

Manorama Gotur

25

A Sailor's Tale

There sailed one night a merchant ship called the Rosalee.
With twenty men she headed north, astern a gentle breeze.
Her captain and crew asleep below, with one man on the wheel,
they knew not then their course would bend or what the sea would deal.
When evening tolled the darkest hour, the breeze became a gale,
"Force ten and storm!" cried the watch as Rosalee yawned with sail.
Her bow plunged beneath the swells, then rode them to great heights.
All hands were summoned up on deck to save their ship that night.
"Haul in the sheets and bring her windward!" came the captain's shout.
But a wave astern tore her rudder off and she could not come about.
Adrift in storm she rolled and pitched, a frightening sight to see.
Yet the crew held fast beside her masts, so strong their courage be.
With fate certain, they bid farewell and prayed in voices low,
"Lord have mercy on us sinners who are doomed to the depths below."
Then a mountainous wave slammed in her side and split her hull in two.
The sea opened up and swallowed them, the ship, her captain and crew.
Amid the fury of that perilous hour, God heard them and prevailed.
The storm soon passed and calmed the deep, so went the sailor's tale.

Lawrence Flanagan

A Letter, Late, To My Father

One Sunday afternoon
You tightened your hold on my small hand,
Hurrying me past foetid cages
Where huge bears paced, panting.
You said, be careful, darling,
When I reached too far from the pond's bleak edge,
And gathered me up, dripping water
 wetter than new blood.

Now long shadows from your deep closed eyes
Have found small buds of wisdom you once tucked
Into the pockets of my pinafores, and at last
They blossom,
Nurtured, misted, with the afterflow
Of your love.

Eleanor P. Gladwin

My Beloved Chauvinist

Your eyes blazing reflected light from shards of broken reality,
Your forehead a knot of discarded dream cords and goals unmet,
Your hair a cascade of defiance trapped only by a bandanna
 worn like a wreath of thorns around your temples,
Your lips pressed hard over some beliefs that would later thrash
 and burn in the earthquake of your utterance,
Your very countenance askance — are but manifestations
 of an activist unsung, personality enigmatic.

Demonstrator! Setting placards and signs in the picket fenced
 ambiguity of my mind,
Rioter! Breaking loose the stampeding passions in the prison
 of my heart,
Vandal! Trampling on and tearing down the gossamer trappings
 of my morals. Terrorist! Posing as my hero then holding me hostage
 to the truths salvaged from my illusions,
Vigilante! Directing and self-trafficking the nowhere direction of
 my life,
Tyrant, chauvinist, dictator— all I detest—you are! Ahh and yet:
Master, champion, Lord- searing you-ness on my breast, silken guaranty
to quash and quell the rebellion you incited in a soul now me!

Sylvia Sol Avaricio

Hope

ears longing to hear inspiration ...
a smile illuminating a long face ...
eyes drying from the fallen tears ...

This word ...
 gives the child courage to try
 gives the family that extra something to hold on to
 gives the man the strength to move on
 gives the woman insight to look forward to new horizons

These four little letters can bestow on us
 the courage ...
 that something to hold on to ...
 the strength ...
 the insight to look forward to ...

Therefore, with -hope- we live on ....

Jennifer Forcum

One Child's Death

Like a prisoner in a pink cell, I sit in my dollhouse room.
And if I walk outside my realm my parents words
 Spew forth like machine guns,
Once again wounding my spirit and soul.
The smell of liquor tumbles forth;
 Hangs in the air.
I gasp under
 Its smothering
 effect.
Monday
 through
Friday
I'm on
parole—
Sent to school.
I've become one of the walking dead;
Mechanically smiling, talking ... moving.
No one knows that each evening, the bus—
Yellow and cheerful — returns me to death row.

Claudia M. Nelson

The Driver's Psalm

The Lord is my Chauffeur,
I shall not fear.
I see with his steady eyes,
Hold the wheel with his firm grip.
My peace passes understanding
and I drive as a Christian
For his Name's sake.

Even when I drive through the ice and the snow,
 or the rain and the fog,
I fear no evil; for thou are within me;
Thy eyes and thy hands, they comfort me.
Thou preparest the way before me
 in the midst of the traffic,
Thou givest me cool judgment
 and consideration for others,

Surely a safe journey and home shall await me
And I shall dwell in the house of my Lord forever.

Eleanor Louise Church

Rebecca

I wrap myself around your heart and feel the rhythm start to lift
my soul to the stars

to the angels

Who for a moment with you would give me their wings
and forever sing
of the most beautiful creature to reach their eyes
in all of the skies of the universe.

And then just to touch you they would give me their eternity
with no uncertainty that to feel your hand
would heal the wound of
mortality.

But this I say, that not even for wings nor eternity
would I trade my love.

For with you I can already fly
and to live forever without I would rather die.

Eric E. Collander

Memories

The thoughts and memories flow in to my mind,
like a stream flowing back to its creator.
Many blissful years that I thought would never end,
but they did end in a complete silence of despair.
I remember the day when we would run along the beach
with the wind at our heels,
and the song of the sea being whispered in our ears.
The Fall, when we would spend hours watching the leaves,
glide gracefully, to the ground
White crystals fell mystically, to the frosty white blankets,
that draped the hillside, was our Winter.
Spring, a time of gaiety and laughter.
The new little additions to the world of mother nature.
The songs of the robins twittering their love song
in the branches of the birch trees.
The next part is darkness.
A darkness that will last my whole life through.
Even when the sun does shine and melt away the frost,
there will always be some darkness.
Throughout this circle of life I must remember the old saying
"Life goes on"

Alysha Liljeqvist

I The Broom

I am a broom, a very pretty broom.
But as it goes for all brooms my life is delegated to clean up the dirt.
Well as you can imagine I didn't have much to look forward too.
But I got a lucky break.
I got this job in a church.
My job is to help keep the church clean for those coming to pray
   and worship.
But I found that along with the regular dirt, that I was also
   pushing out some special dirt.
This dirt was the sins of those who during their prayers and worship
found JESUS CHRIST and shed their filthy, dirty sins.
If you will look closely you will see a parallel here.
JESUS took their sins to bare on his shoulders and I am helping
   to sweep them away.
We are both helping to free you of your sins.
But please don't give me any of the credit.
JESUS DID THE DIRTY WORK.
I'm just cleaning up.

David H. Gunn

1969

The Jets won the Super Bowl and the Mets won the World Series
Man walked on the moon and contemporary musicians gathered
at Woodstock
While Richard Nixon became president
What a year it was
And it seems like yesterday
A time when we still feared communism
A time when computers were still primitive
A time when athletes were not overpaid
Yes, we still had problems back then
Life is not perfect and it certainly was not perfect in 1969.
Yet as we have moved forward
Let us not forget that 1969 signaled the end of a decade
That was a very interesting decade
And this decade culminated in a very special year
So for better or for worse
Here's to 1969. Oh what a year!!!!!!

Henry T. Sarnataro

The Bear And The Bird: A Poem Of Love And Forgiveness

In the lush green woods of an August morning, a variety of life
awaits a new day. Trees and flowers are nourished by the sun
as footprints find their way to a cool, quiet stream where a
bluebird has come to rest. The bird flies about, landing on a
branch of a tall, shady tree. On the ground, a squirrel scurries
about while a bright, yellow butterfly gently lands on a pink
flower. Nature is the home of another creature- a gentle brown
bear that rests in the shade of a warm summer's day. The bird
flies near the bear as it gathers twigs for its nest while leaving
berries and nuts for its gentle friend.

One day something was different. The sky darkened. A storm
was brewing. The bluebird flew over to visit the brown bear and
saw him bleeding and wounded. The bird began to flutter about
and saw its friend hurting. The bear lashed out and tore the
bird's wing. Falling to the ground, they were both wounded and
could not help one another. Helplessly, they lay quietly in the
darkened woods. Suddenly, a young camper walking saw that
nature's friends were in need. He quietly whispered, "I will help
you." As the dark sky let out the sound of thunder, the boy
returned with a woman. With little more than love and courage,
the young boy and older woman led the bear and the bird to a
safe place. After the storm passed, the woman and boy returned
to see their wounded friends, but found they were gone. The
young boy began to cry, but the woman gently said to him,
"Do not cry. The bear and the bird are alive." She wiped his
eyes as the sun peeked out from a cloud. Walking back, the
young boy saw footprints near a rock under a tree. He found the
bear gathering leaves and twigs and while the bird was chirping,
fluttering gently above his shoulder. He smiled and said,
"They are friends again."

Joanne C. Caprice

Nothing At All

This is an elaboration,
A description of a fabrication.
Read it and you'll probably sigh.
It's not the truth yet not a lie.
It's something I shall make very clear,
It's everything you want to hear,
It's all you ever wanted to know,
About nothing, no one, and where not to go.
Allow me to deliver this information,
To everyone across the nation.
Know yourself and be aware,
Of everything that isn't there.
This is knowledge from me to you,
It's everything I know about nothing new.
Take my advice and you'll never fall:
Never ask about nothing at all!

Jason Kalakaua Woodward

AARDEATH

A dead chicken lay in the street — shot to death by Johnny Triggerman, 13-year old son of Gunnard Triggerman, a successful business magnate.

A retarded mongoose swung on a tree — hung by the neck, because of the sadism of Waldo Swinger, 37, an insane janitor at Public School No. 68.

Death, sadism, hate, and postulation, smeared on the board of nature and mankind.

A lone aardwolf, hidden among the tall, green trees, came upon a young child chewing on a Goodyear tire, wondering why he exists, and then gazing intently into the corotid infinity of the nothingness above him.

Yes, it was an undulatingly beautiful day in this existential house of loneliness, for all living creatures, living or dead, could find themselves progressing steadfastly to the heights of shamnition.

Then, further along the unknown path upon which the aardwolf travelled, he sighted one of his fellow aardwolves purple and dead. He had been grapepalmed.

He and his fellows united — a pack of enraged aardwolves, foaming incessantly at the ears, silently and assuredly creep into the city at night.... The humans shall pay!

Crawling into the sewers of the city — seething, promulgating in the center now. (Little did they realize that they had forgotten to bring the Trident sugarless gum that their forbearers had so wisely handed down to them in case of the eventual hyperbola).

Suddenly — without the legal 30-day notice — flushing, bleeding... slush... slush... slush. The city was not unprepared.

Trapped like aardwolves! Nowhere to turn! Struggle, stench, striation!

The illustrious leader of the pack, eyeballing this auspicious situation, was brought to the edge of tears. He had been raised from childhood, though, to have a stiff upper lip, which the short, dumpy, syphilitic honeydipper procured from a shrapnel wound in 'Nam.

But it was too little, and much too late.

The aardwolves were no longer. The end of life as aardwolves knew it.

Ah, the best laid plans of mice... and aardwolves.

Donn Weinberg (1972)

Christmas Cheer

Away in a manger long ago
A baby was the reason but we think it is toys and mistletoe
What is the reason for Christmas
There are still people who still don't know

Everyone is back home. All families are relieved
Carols that ring in my ears
Chases away those holiday fears

Why don't you just look up in the sky
There is a star twinkling in your eyes
The star twinkles faith and love
Both of which has come from above
A season that is famous for its tender-loving-care
Swapping stories and gifts
Sitting down for dinner with the blessings and love to share

Cold, snowy, days. Wood logs on the fire
Children bubbling with enthusiasm and hope and desire
Everyone is in a joyful jingle
This is not the time to be hateful and single
Why should I fear those lonely tears
When I can wipe them away and enjoy the Christmas cheer

David L. Harold

A Second Chance

As I passed the trash on the curb there lay
a black metal framed chair with four broken
wheels tangled with hair. Its foundation
still has years of wear with a little spray
paint here and there.
The metal framed chair needs only a few
repairs. It didn't ask to be mistreated
and thrown there. If it had life it would
have wheeled away.... Lying in the dewy
grass, covered with spiders and webs.
But it was not without life long.... When
I saw it lying there, I took it home, it
only needed a few minor repairs.
And with that little care, I now have me a
favored chair.

Edna R. Springs

To My Son

Twenty one years ago today, God blessed me with a boy.
A boy to grow up to be, my every pride and joy.

Sometimes I've done right and wrong, but this is part of life.
And I guess someday you'll see it, when you take on a wife.

You'll both do what parents do,
To teach your children right from wrong,
But always remember: Love, respect, and honesty
Is where it all belongs.

I wish for you what you've given me, a purpose to my life.
And as time goes on, the happiness of children and a wife.

But most of all what I wish for you, is to be happy with yourself.
To take life with a grain of salt, never leaving it at a halt.

As time goes by you will see
Whatever happens is always meant to be.

I know my son, sometimes life's hard to understand.
But my son, not only for you, it's hard for every man.

Twenty one years ago today, God blessed me with a boy.
That boys grown up to be a man.
And son, your still my pride and joy.......

JoAnn Colonna

Dream Girls

Once I had a dream of you
A chance for happiness, a life anew
While fate has made that dream come true
My heart yearns for and misses you
But even though you aren't in view
We have the photos to thumb through
Still I'm puzzled and have no clue
What is your size, your favorite hue?
Who's your best friend or have you two?
Do you go to the park or visit the zoo?
Can you tell time and tie your own shoe?
Do you make mud pies and things with glue?
I know you are pretty and that you grew
And so has all my love for you
You have a new family, new names too
But I will never forget about you
I'm on your side - part of your crew
I want all of your dreams to come true
I'm proud you got your life anew
And with it lots of new love too.

Julie Watson

Why is it that a lake with no fish is still a lake,
A dog with no master is still a dog,
A poem that does not rhyme is still a poem,
Yet,
A heart with no love, is no longer a heart.
  Iggy Arana

Family

With a cry, baby enters the world
A face so soft, so sweet, gentle hands, a sight to behold
Warm loving faces reach down to caress this bundle of joy
Mom and Dad bathe in ecstasy, holding hands to greet their newborn.

Years go by, along with tears and happiness
A teenager beset with the pains of growing up
Blossoms into a young woman or man, full of hope
The sky is the limit, one crosses the threshold into another phase.

The Family is there to lend a helping hand
A confidante, a well of wisdom, a true friend.

Faced with many options, it is hard to choose
Eager to excel, be successful and never lose
The many games in the cycle of life
Comes a time for one to seek a husband or wife
Hoping the decision is right
Laying in bed pondering about it during sleepless nights
Or follow the stars, stay single and free
Do what you want to do, let fate decide what the outcome will be.

Remember, the Family is always there, ready to catch you when you fall
The Family, a "Giving Tree", guides us through our journey on
    this earth.
  Elizabeth Sharman

Around The Pole

Students holding hands, praying around
A flag pole at school,
Asking God to teach them to live by the
Golden rule.

Looking up at the stars and stripes on the
Pole above,
And thanking God for this land that
We love.

Asking that God go with them all thru
Their education.
And lead them in the future, to improve our nation.

Since you can't pray in school, as I
Have been told, thank God you can join hands and
Pray around a flag pole.

So let's extend the flag pole circle to every boy and girl,
Who are attending schools anywhere in this world.

Why our children can't pray in school
I don't understand,
While all elected leaders are sworn in
with a bible under their hand.
  Edgar Cox

The Poinsettia

Balancing under the heavy rain -
    a thin lady with a red umbrella.
The wind which blows her green skirt -
    transforms her a poinsettia.
Winds and rains are the Creature's long time fight.
To run after a female shadow isn't my right?
  Can N. Ho

On Knowing You

A time before, you did not exist for me
A flower, whose bloom is turned the other way
A name I heard indifferently
Thoughts that drifted without cause to stay

You were a shop of curios
With treasures stashed behind the glass
But the windows had been darkened so
And I walked by too fast

Even so, I did not see you then
Nor care what sent the laughter to your eyes
I could not feel you in the silence
Nor wish you near to share the sun's slow rise

How gently you dared shape a formless dream
Gave definition to a burst of need
Created with your warmth a closer theme
Translated thoughts that others could not read

I might have passed your half-turned blossom by
Had its freshness not encircled me
Yet loving you took root so easily
I cannot hope that I'll break free
  Donna C. Baer

The Trip

A growing brightness blinded me.
A flowered hand-made teddy bear was my comfort.
The plastic bracelet hung on me like a memory.
An airy gown was my only protection.
Faces in a circle surrounded me.
Mumbling, hurried voices filled the air.
Tears started to run down my face like a waterfall.
My stomach was tied in knots.
A calm feeling came over me as a woman wheeled me to my savior.
My mind was blank until I became conscious.
The touch of someone's hand soothed me.
I felt my eyes fading.
Animals and balloons filled the air.
A group of smiling faces looked down upon me.
Memories flood my mind of this moment that was over in
    a blink of an eye.
  Ashley P. Walsh

Friends, A Friend!

Friends may come and go, but this Friend,
A Friend! Sticks closer than a brother.

Friends may forsake you when things get rough, but this Friend,
A Friend! Will never leave you nor forsake you.

Friends may fool you to elevate your ego, but this Friend,
A Friend! Will tell you the truth and give you a humble spirit.

Friends may give false hope and confidence, but this Friend,
A Friend! Will give blessed hope and assurance.

Friends may pretend to be trustworthy, but this Friend,
A Friend! Will concealth a matter.

Friends may love sometimes when you love them, but this Friend,
A Friend! Loveth at all times.

Friends may know you for a period of time, but this Friend,
A Friend! Knoweth our beginning and end.

Friends may provide limited protection to help a friend, but this
    Friend,
A Friend! Has all power and is our present help in time of trouble.

Friends may unknowingly say, "I will die for you," but this Friend,
A Friend! Has shown and truly given His life for his friends.

Friends, friends and friends are nice to have, but this Friend,
A Friend! That became my life is Jesus, Jesus is a Friend!
  Juane Dunigan

29

Our Moon

I give you a gift, a gift of light
A gift to guide you through the night
If ever our lives should be a part
Have no fear, just take heart
Just look high and focus your eyes
Our moon will shine like a diamond in the sky
So wherever you go if you need my love
Just remember our moon we share above
Just like me it won't go anywhere
Just because you can't see it
Don't mean it ain't there
It will follow you around
Through night and day
Just like my love for you
It will never go away
The moon is a reminder that my love is true
Because there's only one moon and only one you.

John E. Colburn

Untitled

Who starts my day with a smile?
  A giggle and a laugh or two.
A great big kiss and a hug.
  And a caring "I love you".

Who's raring to get started to play?
  A hug and a pat for his dog.
Ready to go! Let's play ball.
  I'll race you all the way.

Who is this happy smiling person?
  Who goes from morn till night
I'm sure you have already guessed.
  He is my grandson, he is a pure delight.

Helen Jarsulic

We'll Dance

It was acid, downers, pot and speed that took your mind.
A good rehab Mom and Dad knew they had to find.

Getting drugs, you thought you needed, explaining "Nobody understands."
It was rehab that took your legs and left you your hands.

Because of all this for you, I didn't show any care.
To you life was not worth living from a wheelchair.

I thought I could handle the day that you would go,
Your passing affected me deeply, this I think you know.

Now it's too late to tell you, "For you, I do feel love."
I know you can see it though from the skies above.

I'm sorry for the way I sometimes acted towards you, I know it was
  wrong
But when I get to Heaven **WE'LL DANCE** to your favorite song.

Angie Brewer

"First Love"

A first love that is lost in the wind
A love that can never be rekindled again
A feeling of hope, a feeling of despair
A lack of love, a lack of care
Feelings so old, emotions so new
Something that's not very easy getting used to
Tears on my pillow, a frown on my face
Finding someone else to take your place
Wishes and dreams coming true once more
Opening up another door
Looking inside and seeing the truth
Searching deeper for even more proof
Proof of which there is not enough
Why is your first love always so tough?

Cherlyn Paul

Friendship

Everyday I go to school, see different faces, different places.
A group sits apart from a single person. That person is me.

I feel lonely, left out. I'm a newcomer at school. No friends.
No one I know is here.

A girl sees me sitting alone and asks me "would you like to join us?"
"Sure" or "Yes" I answer. A huge sigh of relief leaves my chest.
I take a deep breath. I continue to join them from days to come.

Friendship, I miss, because I had a lot of friendship happening
at my old school. Friendship has only found me 6 times at my
new school.

But you'll see, soon. Soon I will have people who know me. I will
have people saying "Hi" and "How are you?" But best of all I will
have friends. Friends who care about me.

Friends should keep in touch always. Because that's what friends,
do in order to have friendship.

Some people learn the hard way. They chose not to make
friends, so now they have no one to trust, care, and like them.

I'm glad friendship has found me at least 6 times. It's a fresh
start. I will soon adjust and learn more about different faces,
and different places.

Jasmine Jenkins

Virgis - A Source Of Strength

I met her first when I was married and fully grown,
A lady tall, blind but oh so mentally strong.
She asked for my wife's hand, a daughter she mourned
For she was growing old and so all alone.
I granted her request and Viola Virginia agreed
Because we both somehow felt her need.

Things went smoothly for a number of years
Then fate took a hand, causing burdens and tears;
Virgis fell, her age and handicap taking its toll,
It was as if God had determined she had reached her goal.
For years she gave her life in service to others
Yet in this hour of her need there were no sisters and brothers.

Years earlier Virgis must have had a vision
She adopted a young married Lady, it was a wise decision.
Viola Virginia was the child she always longed for
Now in her declining years that child is her vigor.

Charles F. Graham

Flame Out

I didn't want to bother you while you lay there murmuring
a little in your sleep. I didn't want to touch you as
you lay there sleeping or are you awake dreaming of your new love.
I didn't want to show you the new moon shining through our
window. The moon we once loved by. My heart is empty now,
but they found that the moon was an empty shell too didn't they.

I didn't want to awaken you where you lay, then like a homing
bird your hand reached out to caress a once loved spot,
touched, then moved away. The touch was not for me. The moon
shone coldly through the window then my love had turned to
ashes, but they said the moon was ashes too didn't they.

I didn't want to touch you while you lay there sighing
a little. Did it hurt you too, giving up our love dreams?
We flew above clouds of silver on our dream trips, with
the moonlight touching the wing tips then the sea far below.
We touched each other too and loved. That flame we had will
burn no more for me, but they said the moon had flamed out
too, didn't they?

Jacqueline Vogelsang

The Humor Of Love

Two worlds collide in one life giving breath,
A man and a boy to be parted by death.
Point of view, attitudes are born to conflict,
The righteous old man and the young derelict.

Good humor to man may be anger to boy,
Boy's mischievous jauntings may chase the man's joy.
On opposite wavelengths are unlikely friends,
Two paths that must cross, must pursue different ends.

Despite their misfortune, their unhappy fate,
Beneath stubborn dogma and heated debate,
Through protest and preaching, defiance, and loathe,
A bitter irreverence tells one ancient troth.

When agony ends and the elder departs,
Then laughter strikes both in the heart of their hearts.
Their laughter sings on through the Heavens above,
The man and the boy share the Humor of Love.
        Douglas E. Heric

Survival Song

What does it take to survive these days?
A man and woman cautious in all their ways

What does it take for a child to see adulthood?
Crime prevention to stop the killings in our neighborhoods

What does it take to get law and order?
A technique that reaches every man no matter what color

What does it take to survive the pressure?
A walk with God it's greater than any treasure

Survival is the tune and drumming melody
That beats in every heart even the small crack baby
        Beverly Hughes

Life Dream

A child is waiting eagerly to meet the new found morning
A man returns unknowingly to a place he once knew well
A woman is crossing so securely to a side she's never seen
A dog is whimpering in the night from his unbroken dreams
The nail is driven in the wood and can be removed at will
The wood will never be the same an ugly scar will still remain
The sun still shines on sand and sea and rain still falls on forests
But we are growing far too fast and we simply can't ignore it
Adjusting life within ourselves is really all we do
This must be part one of it to prepare us for part two
Love is but a gamble you can win or you can lose
Live life and accept it come on now you can see it through
Winding up and sliding down we're taught lessons everyday
Simplify them if you can or be confused in many ways
Idealistic fantasies to cheer you when you're bored
Memories and friendships to heal you when love makes you sore
And swinging on a wooden swing behind an ivory castle
There we sat escaping and avoiding life's big hassles
And jumping off the swing I feel we've wasted too much time
And turning 'round - yup, there it was life was creepin' up behind
Then suddenly out of the light the telephone was ringing
It interrupted everything - I recall we all were singing
        Jody Bodine

Wonderland

There is another land way off above the blue
A sunny wonderland where someday I'll find you
And when I go up there you'll come and take my hand.
We'll walk down golden sands through wonderland
I know that place exists my dreams have told me so
It is a sunny land where golden flowers grow
And when I meet you there you'll come and take my hand
And we will live again in wonderland.
        Evelyn Floria Stevenson

Freedom Of The Press

In the famous land of the free I wanted the freedom to roam
a middle sized helicopter, in the air, over your home.
I built a crate with skill and with ease.
All made of wood, to ship overseas.

With a helicopter I could take it to the front lawn grass;
My yard's gate was small, wouldn't let it pass.
Said a clerk, with posture and poise: "Y'can't make that kind of
    noise!
It is by decree, that the people who live here, from noise
    should be free"

Years went by in the land of the fee - for the press to bring news to
    me.
Freedom for me to drink my beer, while watching TV to see and
to hear.
One day, overhead, something started to roar,
one helicopter, then two, and three and some more,

My screen went blind; helicopters were nine.
They rose and descended and circled in line.
They took the freedom to describe alive
a man, suspected to have murdered his wife.

A city official with posture and poise
didn't say: "You can't make that kind of a noise!
It is a residential zone, and it is by decree,
that the people live here, from noise should be free."
        Emanuel Azmon

To My Wonderful Wife

The night we met was in '43.
A night that will go down in history.
The place was Fort Worth
Which was to give birth
To a love that did grow
Though continents apart.

At first we wrote carefully,
Soon we wrote lovingly,
Later we wrote expectantly,
Our love had blossomed undeniably!

The night we Wed was in '44.
I caught my breath as you came thru the door
What beauty, what grace
So slow seemed the pace
But soon by God's grace
We did vow and embrace.

It's been a wonderful 50 years, dear
Blessed with more laughs than tears, dear
God blessed us with children and grandchildren too.
And I praise Him tonight for such a sweetheart as you!!!
        Everett Elder

Job Pains

By the beige file cabinet, I saw him:
a rhino, staring back at me with dull and muddy eye.
I stared back; I'd seen him before.

He lumbered to his knees, then rose
on stumpy legs and plodded toward me - too familiar.
He pressed in: a mammal steamroller, squashing me
into the loose files on top of my desk, pressing a
stapler into my thigh, mashing my rolodex. His horn
pierced the computer, taking it high on his head,
smoking and sparking as he gathered speed and charged
past the receptionist.

I lay there panting, wishing it were lunch time.
        Alison Huber

An Open Note To My Birthparents

If only I could see you once and store your faces in my mind:
A part of my own self to see, for I gaze in the mirror and yet I'm blind.

If only I could know my past—To learn the truth would help me heal;
Unlock the door of my self-doubts; explain the ways I act and feel.

If only I could talk to you, I'd have so much I'd want to say!
I'd thank you for giving a part of yourself to those who helped form I am today.

If only I could retrace your steps and discover the reasons it could not be:
If, for unknown reasons, you gave me away—or if love for me caused you to set me free.

If only I could explore your hearts and you could see what I've gone through, too—
Not to cause pain or inflict wounds of guilt, but to forge some bond between me and you.

If only I could see you once, the people who gave me being—
I want to abandon the blinders I've worn and finally focus on seeing.

Jennifer E. Bates

"A View Of Life"

In a field called life as I weed through strife, a vision I did see!
A picture clear of my true self in a field of weeds I struggled for my life.
These weeds were large and very green, so thick and tall I could not see.
So worry not, I blindly rushed to romp and stomp and crush and thrash and tear these ugly stalks of life's despair.
But on this day as I did romp, I ran into an awesome stalk!
So thick and green with thistle coverage, with beauty rich and clear.
As I looked up its tall lean shaft to glean the top I could not see, control was lost to unknown fear.
So anxiously I ran amuck to view this awesome gleaming stalk!
I rushed through weeds of tall acclaim and in my haste to view the top, to my dismay did I get lost.
So in this field of weeds that I did use for cover, I was now lost and could not find of that which I did just discover.
So in anger did I attack and placed these weeds into a sack.
And as I weeded this field of pain, my vision began to clear, and to my great pleasure and surprise
my stalk of green with thistle coverage began to re-appear.
So proud I was to re-discover, my field of vision now had no cover.
So on I weed to the edge of this field to view this stalk in all its splendor,
The leaf-like arms did gently beckon to view the "ROSE" that smiled from heaven.

Daniel A. Richardson

Untitled

Below the lofty clouds,
    a placid meadow lies,
    littered with Sycamores
    that graze azure sky.
Via boat through the river,
    that carves the tranquil green,
    blessings many, from graceful nature,
    can easily be seen.

The sacrosanctity of this lowland
    is unmatched, except by the church,
    as Weeping Willows mingle with
    Elms, Oaks, and Birch.
The site of the majestic river,
    in the midst of the foliage growth,
    can remind the poor, discouraged soul
    that the world still has some hope.

Jason Gretencord

Metamorphosis

As darkness intrudes on the crimson sky,
A prayer comes forth from an open mouth.
Stretching outward and upward it goes,
Filling the air with its cries of pain.

The sender varies from day to day, always remaining the same.
The stars are formed and united as one,
As the prayer slowly and diligently becomes.
With an eternal hope the last breath is uttered.

As moonlight falls upon the land,
A teardrop is released, then captured again.
Transformed from pain it's a personal release,
As the prayer is now complete.

Dawn J. Robinette

A Preacher

Oh! for a Preacher for this hour
A Preacher of Redemption, a Preacher of Power,
A flaming desire, a prayful request,
That call for victory in Jesus name.

Oh! for a Preacher to awake the Church
To proclaim the Master's request,
To a dying world, a rebellious race,
To make known the gift of Jesus grace

The call is given, noble Christians arise,
Onward we march united in Christ,
The joyful Preacher now proclaim,
Throughout the earth in Jesus name,
Maranatha, Maranatha, Maranatha.

Dr. Byron C. Robinson

Rebirth

The voice of death calls to me,
    a raspy voice just like the wind.

It awakens my soul then pulls it, entices it
    out of my body, leaving it an empty shell.

I whisper "I love you" to my friends and
    family - my loved ones start to cry.

Death comes - my eyes close and my
    pulse slowly stops.

A tunnel forms - alive with luminescence
    it whirls and twirls

Slowly I move forward - walking, yet
    floating; my fists clenched tight

I get to the end and I bow my head.
    A moan escapes my lips.

The tears flow freely; I raise my
    head ready to face the future.
I know I will make it.

Jessica Brown

What Is Wealth

Eagerly I came to my brand new home,
A young mother, two children, a husband and
financially stripped to the bone.
I stayed at home and took care of the house,
While he went to work like a dutiful spouse
Time passes quickly, God has been good,
I wouldn't change anything—even if I could.
My rewards are around me, my family, my friends,
I want it to go on, but I know it will end.
But for now I am happy and healthy,
And if you add it all up...Yes I feel I am oh, so wealthy.

Florence Enrico

Memories

I look out the window and I see
A reflection of what was
And what has come to be
Memories of childhood deep in my thoughts
Hopes of the future not hard to find
As I look out across the land
My thoughts wander to what
The future holds for me
Will my dreams come true?
Will I always be blue?
My thoughts go back
To the child I knew
And playing with dolls
Was the thing to do
How times have changed
Since these innocent days
In more than one way
Although I will always be
A child at heart
These times can only be memories

Angela Rakoczy

To Kevin Carter

What had you seen Kevin Carter that the world already didn't know?
A reluctant, poignant witness to man's inhumanity to man,
Recording bigotry, fratricidal violence, immortalizing stark
Images of repression, lurid faces of death, ecce signum.

You claimed Pulitzer fame, sadly earned it,
Depicting a poignant metaphor for Africa's despair:
A macabre photo of a vulture watching a Sudanese girl
Emaciated, naked, bloated innards, prone to lifeless, scorched earth;
A photosynthesis of mankind's eternal bondage to Adam curse,
Its futile yearnings for a full life stigmatized by Cain's hand of death.

You chased away the Sudanese vulture but that one
In your mind you cannot. Desperate to sooth your spirit, soul, you
"Sat under a tree for a long time smoking cigarettes and crying,"
still you found no succor, only emptiness, sans solace.

Did you end it all K.C., saying "I won't be a part of it anymore,
No longer a witness to man's darkest facets of madness,
For he has digressed to the lowliest beastly nature,
Masking himself with myriad disguises, that
Now he's faceless, devoid of soul?"

Donald A. Danlag

Beers With Laura

The young brown-haired queen enters the building possessing
a slight smile accented by her diamond-like eyes sparkling.
I follow this daughter of the kilt through the masses
congregating in this smoke-filled watering hole.
She worships not God but perhaps a mutt named Reveille or
the summer sun that she sacrifices herself to.
It is night now and she has been purged of her Baptist
schooling so she must worship bottles of Bud Light.
Like many people she is a native Texan but does not possess a
twang in her vocal repertoire. Though true to her state she
claims to dance the two-step with relative ease. Her only current
boyfriend is an apathetic white cat whom will not accompany her to
College Station. This stumbling Aggie leads me from barkeep to
barkeep making me supply her with desirable amounts of firewater.
She keeps drinking as the lights flash and reflect off her
freckled nose. In the wee hours of this morning of the moon the
stumbless finds herself planted on a naked seat in a dark area of
the club. She grabs handfuls of air as she gropes her way out the
door into the night and climbs into an expensive car. What is not
known won't hurt, what is not remembered will not be discussed.

Brian Bernard Williams

Life's Real Treasure

There is a place within my heart where all my friends can go
A special place for only them that only they can know
And no one knows, not even I, the love that waits in there
For I cannot express in words to them how much I care

Friends of mine, dear friends of mine
You've given me great pleasure
Love divine, sweet love divine
A friend is life's real treasure

There is a love within my heart for all my friends to know
A special love for only them when they are feeling low
Oh, I will always love my friends with love beyond compare
And be someone to lean upon when they are in despair

Heart is thine, my heart is thine
Forever for your pleasure
Love divine, sweet love divine
You are my life's real treasure

Gary D. Tucker

The "All" Of Me

I know not yet the "all" of me.
A statement filled with irony.
Who else but I should know the "me"?
Oh, tell me who would have the key?

    To what's inside but doesn't show.
    Why inner sad, though outward glow?
    Why sometimes glad though tears do flow?
    Oh, tell me why—I want to know.

Are my dreams the "me" I know not yet?
Elusive—Concealing—Coverlet.
These dreams so easy to forget.
Oh, tell me dreams—Will you abet?

    Is the "me" akin to Universe?
    Weaving patterns all diverse.
    Going forward, then reverse.
    Oh, tell me please—I humbly urge.

Will I ever know the "all" of me?
Will it always be a mystery?
Or does death alone hold the key?
Oh, tell me death—What irony!

Glory Strauss

An Unsuspecting Storm

A storm is building in the East
A storm that you would suspect the least
Gentle breezes are the first to show
With a teardrop of rain, a dancing flake of snow
Leaves of memories scatter and tumble
While in the distant there is a definite rumble
Then ominous clouds rake the milestone of life
Howling winds bring heartbreak, sadness, grief and strife
Homes are wrecked and children cry out
Why should all this come about
With a devastating fury it spends itself
So look around and see what's left
Thru parting clouds a light appears
It only proves that someone cares
So claim your treasures and face the sun
For you and me life has just begun.

Benny J. Perry

A Thousand

A thousand times I've dreamed of your touch,
A thousand times I've listened for your voice.

A thousand times I've prayed for so much,
A thousand times I've said your name to myself.

A thousand times I've kissed your sweet lips,
  swam in the depths of your eyes.

A thousand times over you've brought me to happiness,
A thousand times over you've been my only choice.

A thousand times over I've been blessed,
A thousand times over I'd die for you.

A thousand times over I've held you close
  and whispered "I love you" a thousand times.
    David G. Siller

Seasons of Life

I NEED WINTER

A time of peace and quiet,
A time to rest and reflect,
To restore energy...regenerate.
Through solitude comes renewal.

I NEED SPRING

The beginning of all that has been sleeping.
The excitement and celebration of life.
Flowers bursting forth,
Birds singing, love growing.

I NEED SUMMER

To once again feel the warmth of the sun.
To walk in a meadow of wildflowers.
To sip lemonade under an old oak tree.
To be one with nature again.

I NEED AUTUMN

The season of gathering -
A time of harvest,
Of breathtaking foliage and falling leaves.
A reminder that we reap what we plant.
    Donna L. Kosch

"The Wall"

A memorial of granite black as the night.
A timeless looking glass reflecting the sunlight.
Reflecting the heavens if you look just right.
The memorial of granite black as the night.
Columns of names written on the sleek walls.
The timeless looking glass seems so tall.
A hand reaches out to touch a name.
Reflections on the wall the faces never change.
The sadness is there it reflects in their eyes.
Tears fall in silence as they remember those who died.
Sons and daughters, fathers, brothers and mothers.
Friends and lovers, on those sleek walls their names cover.
The memorial of granite black as the night.
Reflecting the heavens, if you look just right.
    Cynthia D. Kanz

Angel

There once was a storm in my sight
And I couldn't look left or right.
Till out of the hate-filled darkness,
An angel came with feelings that I could not name.
And somehow, the angel, with a beauty of mind and soul
Made me feel completely whole.
The closer the angel came, the more I knew
That love and trust was being offered for two.
Once I accepted, the dark cloud was rejected.
And you, with your love shining bright
Have become the angel in my sight.
    Chris Slabic

Ledge

With one step I lose my edge
a twenty story drop off the building ledge
think first of my pain and sorrow
then of life with no tomorrow
Clashing emotions fill my head
pavement emits stench of dread
then life passes before my eyes
I hit the ground and my body dies
next comes sirens taste of blood
as I lay in dirt and mud
great darkness shrouds me
with the zippers close I cannot see
Soon is the coffin closed and sealed
into the earth dropped and wheeled
through tunnels of darkness and funnels of light
with suicide lost heaven's wealth
but first to learn to love myself
    Edward Michael James Perry

Night Dawns On A Drunk

The night falls desperately -
A virus and a revelation.
Like the day, the night has its dawn-
And night dawns on a drunk.
He sleeps. He sleeps with death,
Never knowing which drink belongs to death,
And so he drinks.
He sleeps. He sleeps in his chair,
Cradling in his arms the half-dead bottle;
His lover and his dream.
He sleeps. He sleeps through his days,
Wondering why he never had a break
In all his broken life.
And night dawns on a drunk near twilight,
And for the first time he sees
(In all his sightless life)
That night is dark-
As dark as a dream of death.
    Daniel J. Bristol

Untitled

"Little boy lost" (the classified said)
"Abandoned by father" (Is just how it read);

Needs Daddy to love him, but hasn't a clue
Why Daddy had left him before he was two.

Now living with Mommy and Pop Pop and Nan
Asking the questions a four year old can.

But how can you tell such a sweet little guy
About drugs and addiction and getting so high!

That you run far away, as far as you can
And try to forget that you once were a man.

To "Little boy lost" there will be no reply
He'd be better off if his Daddy would die!
    Carol A. Wright

The Flight

Here I am thinking
about times gone by.
Remember when we wished to fly?
Then one night our wish came true,
we flew so high we touched the moon.
I was unaware that when I landed
you hit the ground and never made a sound.
I often think about that night
when we took our fateful flight.
What were we thinking of,
what was in our sight?
Was it important enough to take your life?
    Heidi E. Barber

Believe

The artist paints a heavy line
  Across the pristine canvas face,
Then lightly brushes up and down
  As though to fill the empty space.
With palette knife he adds paint here and there.
  A masterpiece! We slyly smile.
Those blobs of paint will never be.
  The artist, calmly, all the while
Paints on, and we begin to see
  The picture that was his alone
In the recesses of his mind.
  Why is it we are ever prone
To doubt the greatness of mankind?
  Gladys Loveland

Burning Bridges

Yes, there it was, a step away, just there
Across the street, in fading daytime's light.
They would all be there with glass in hand
Forging fragile friendships of the night.

There'd be laughter, hollow, forced and loud
The shut out broken dreams, lost hopes, old hells -
The game, the bets, the glasses always raised
To drink away sad sounds and sights and smells of burning
bridges.

Oh, he had known real love, a woman's warmth,
A passion not denied, a tender band
Of love - and fear of tightening bonds of faith,
The future threatening things unknown, unplanned.

Another time, another night, another town.
There must be somewhere he could find escape
From broken dreams, lost hopes of warmth and love,
The promises of faith he couldn't keep.

So - on again to face the lonely night
To other lighted dens and other hells
To drown again forsaken dreams and hopes
And drink away the sights and sounds and smells of burning bridges.
  Ellie Roulston

Sunset Energy

The monument became a golden stream
across the water of the tidal pool.
It was as if the obelisk breathed forth
a living tongue to join two circling shores.

This monolith had stood alone, apart,
an alien shape against massed cherry blooms—
a frigid stone, sharp-cornered, permanent,
a thrusting to elicit pride and awe.

All else was curves or movement near the pool:
black trunks and twisting boughs of cherry trees—
the fragile short-lived blossoms, pink and white,
of people mingling, looking, smelling, touching.

And when the tall, imposing obelisk
imposed upon the scene its shaft of rippling gold,
my sense of peace and shared delight became
a taut awareness, trembling and explosive.
  Elizabeth A. Vinson

Make This Poet Rich

My wad o'lettuce, always lean,
Affords so little it's obscene;
Kept down and out, I got no frills,
Expenses keep me payin' bills.

  The bread I win don't stay to see,
  How much I'd love a shoppin' spree;
  I'd like, just once, to get ahead,
  So help me, all I see is red.

  Piranhas, fat and filled with greed,
  Oppress me for my chicken feed;
  Employers seek productive days,
  Then turn around and say, "no raise".

  Reward me. Let me roll in wealth,
  I need more bacon for my health;
  Contentment seems to run and hide,
  How long must riches be denied?
  Bill Graham

In Memory Of My Grandpa, Edward Palmer

Everyday I hesitated to answer the phone,
  Afraid, every time the phone would ring,
  Knowing, sometime it would soon bring news,
That you would be gone; one more time the phone rang,
  In that instant I knew you had passed on,
I know now Grandpa that you are not in pain,
  Grandma will be glad to be with you again,
The two of you are reunited up in the Heavens,
  To live together in the everlasting life;
  Though some of your family could not be here,
  Those of us that were, were always near;
  I pray that you can forgive those,
  Who could not be found, because I know,
  That they will never forgive themselves,
  For not being around;
  We all love you and will miss you,
But someday, we will all be together again,
  Then, we will never be apart,
But for now, Grandma and Grandpa you will,
  ALWAYS BE IN OUR HEARTS.
  Amie Palmer

The Whispering Water

A Mussel shell clamped down tight,
afraid to open and see the sights.

Water flowing over, sweet and light.

The water whispers, "There's no need for fright.
  Let go of thyself and explore Life's delight."

Mussel, feeling the calm waves of the water,
  begins to open knows it will obey.

Mussel slightly opens its shell seeing
  the water and knows it means well.

Prompting the water says,"Come a little farther from out of thy shell.
  I have lots to show you and plenty to tell."

Mussel opening more and more while
  water tells of many other shores.

Water says to Mussel,"Open slightly more and I will take you to
  those other shores, where you and I will explore.

Mussel says to Water,"That would be grand but I am still a bit afraid.
  Tell me of what will happen to us at the end of the day."

Water assuringly replies,"There is no need to be afraid.
  Here I am and here I will stay,
  encircled about you to guide you just one more day.
  Cathy D. Feldman

Loving Him... When

I only loved him, when I first set eyes on him.
After that, it all went down hill.
This same man was once my awakening star.
He was a flower that bloomed in my heart,
And fed on my very blood.
He would turn my rainy days into days of sunshine.
He would take two pennies and with the snap of his finger,
He would turn them into roses of joy.
Yet, ten years later, this very same man...
Made me feel like a trapped mouse.
He reprimanded me like a child
And cursed the ground I walked on.
He kissed the dog and brought the cat roses of yarn to play with.
He fed the fish every day.
Yet, I was left in a corner of misery, crying to be loved.
This, once magical man,
Let my love slip through his talented hands.
I walked into the night and the stars had no answers for me.
But I was convinced,
I only loved Him, when I first set eyes on him.

Andrea Traywick-Jones

Again

Again I am here
Again I am lost
With no one to hear
and no one to touch
I wonder sometimes if maybe I'm wrong
I wonder sometimes if maybe I'm gone
Do they think of me alone in the dark
Do they think of me
When light comes to spark
Remember the smell of a cold winters night
Remember the feel of a dead ringers bite
Do they see the white of the sky
or the blue of the flame
Do they know what they want
And want what the know
Do they know where they are
Are they where they know
Again I am here
Again I am lost
With no one to hear and no one to touch.

Emily Davina Hall

Dancer With Gold Claws

Dipping slender stilts in the gulf, she wades
all absorbed in tiny movements below
the surface of her mirrored, lit, green stage.
Her feathered headdress bobs at fish aglow.
She scoops, then arches the long ivory neck
gracefully, as flashes of silver flit
away. She beams those soft yellow eyes flecked
with brown at her focus point and pirouettes
in her golden slippers. White wing feathers
lift and fall; water droplets spray while she
flutter dances in her pursuit, whether
the passing audience marvels to see
The Snowy Egret Ballerina Show
or views that odd orange beak and gold claws.

Gail Adams

The Truth

My heart sometimes feel that I am all alone in this world of ours
All I do is think all hours
Which do causes me great pain
Knowing that I'll have nothing to gain
Lost in a world which I made and created
Life and Love can never be related
In my book
With just a look
I know that a glance or a mere touch can destroy it all
The idea about love sometimes capture my soul
Thinking that my mind will never give it all
For it played a fool
The truth love hurt and played trick
There is pain which I have grown to be sick
The truth is I'm afraid to give it a chance
Because I don't want to lose my heart
For me it will always dance
For it is not another piece of art
To be thrown away in the darkness
For love can cause me only to be more lonely

Chia Lee

Where Do I Go From Here?

Where did we go wrong? The walks, the talks, the touching.
ALL IS GONE! No more sharing.

Where did we go wrong? The zoos, the circus, the concerts.
ALL IS GONE! No more laughter.

Where did we go wrong? The surprises, the trips, the adventures.
ALL IS GONE! No more secrets.

Where did we go wrong? The dances, the parties, the picnics.
ALL IS GONE! No more caring.

Where did we go wrong? The cards, the letters, the flowers.
ALL IS GONE. No more pictures.

Where did we go wrong? The cocktails, the dinners, the shows.
ALL IS GONE. No more contact.

NO MORE PASSION.
NO MORE KISSES.
NO MORE CARESSES.
NO MORE DREAMS.

WHAT IS LEFT?

Eyes that cry. Empty arms.
A broken heart. Lonely nights.

WHERE DO I GO FROM HERE?

Hunter

Colors

Why do we have Racism?
All it causes is trouble and violence in the world.
Everyone in the world is different.
Different colors, religions, and people in general.
We shouldn't have racism just because people are different.
We should all be one and love people no matter what color they are.
God created us all equal.
No one color is better than another.
We should all care about each other and teach everyone to like
another person even though their color is different.
People are not just their colors, they are real human beings
inside with feelings.
The people in the world today are made up of a rainbow of colors.
A rainbow is supposed to be joined of all colors and it makes
a beautiful sight.
Let's join this rainbow and make this world a better place to live
for our generation and generations to come!

Bridget Fryman

The Seashore

On the sand, there I lay
All my troubles far away
Distant from the city and my problems there
Tests, gangs, drugs, all which I bear
Just able to rest in my own peace
The crowds and noise suddenly cease
And I have a chance to think, if only I were an animal
Would I still have the troubles I now toll?
Alas, nay I would not
Nor the pleasures I forgot
The good times that outweigh the bad
The times when I was happy not sad
True, life is not as terrible as it may seem
Most is wondrous, like a dream
And so pleased am I to have it so
That I think now it is time to go
Back to my home, family, and friends
To face life's twists and bends
But I will never lose this place I adore
My special place on the seashore

Jaime Jordan

Black Father To His Newborn Son

I'm your Father little brown boy
All snuggled to my chest.
I see in you, my little boy—
Makings of the best:
Full, strong body; piercing eyes;
A commanding voice as you kick and cry.
One day you will walk, my little brown boy—
But first, you must learn to crawl.
One day you will stand...little brown boy—
Tall Tall! Tall!!
Doors must be opened, my little brown boy,
For you, where I dared not tread.
Lights must shine brighter...little boy—
Perhaps, more blood to be shed.
But as sure as little blades of grass, my boy—
Pierce God's earth, so quietly—
So shall your strong, black legs, my boy—
Break the shackles! Sounds of thunder...loudly!
My little brown boy.

Gloria C. Anderson

Our Country Church

The neighbors joined together to lift their hearts in prayer,
   all their families joined them as they bowed together there.

The church was built on a firm foundation,
   it was there we received our salvation.

The hymns were sung by the choir gathered there,
   Rock of Ages and Sweet Hour of Prayer.

In this life of failing relationships and memories that pass,
   there was a harbor we could cling to where our love would always last.

The choir sang together with a joyous sound,
   What a Friend in Jesus, we have found.

All the holidays and special occasions, we would say a special prayer,
   and the close ties we felt as we joined together there.

The families shared together through the triumph and the tears,
   all the close memories that we gained throughout our childhood years.

It was a close knit family from the farms near and far,
   they had the common values, that made us what we are.

It was a small congregation, some young and some were old,
   their friendships through the years have been like solid gold.

Betty Williams Rhoden

Death

With the transmigration of the soul
All will balance and fold

The shades of life ascend towards their chosen ne plus ultra

But with continuing apprehension they observe the circling harmattan
Its resolution,
damnation

Yet it can never intercede,
For it can only entice,
And hope,
But not pray,
For that is not its way

With one final wassail it ends,
And then begins.

Bill Aulson

Blind Light

God of love, God of power, blood of faith, wine of flesh,
All will fly into the womb of death. Heart and soul shall
never grow old. Heart and soul shall throughout eternity
always be bold. Body and mind will always be found, the
spirit of joy will always be sound.

In growth and wisdom shalt thou prosper, prosper shall he in
the light of God. Who shall enter into the womb of death?
Who shall die and who shall be reborn? Will it be you or will
it be me, will it be all or will it be none? Who shall live
to eat the flesh of death?

God, my father, my wonderful creator, king of my soul and all
encompassing planets, What will thou do to my soul?
Will I be grateful in the awakening of my sleep, or will I die
amongst the wicked living in their death that they have prepared
for themselves. Come forth my Father and sheweth thee the
path of my soul. I have looked up into the sun where dawns
the mystery of the beginning. With a quick burst of explosion
all heavenly bodies are brought back into the light, God's Wisdom
Masters All.

Japhus E. Buchanan

Precious Time

Too often we're not satisfied with what we have
Always asking for something more
Failing to realize that with each new day
We gain something we hadn't had before
Sure we're one day older
Some may frown at the thought
But one more day of life
Is what we've actually got
One more day to laugh and joke
Spending time with family and friends
Something we've all taken for granted
That precious time we hope will never end
I've taken too many things for granted in my life
I've also done things I wish I hadn't done
There are also many things I'm truly thankful for
And my life is the most important one
Life can end so suddenly
With little or no time to prepare
Don't waste your precious time
Let your family and friends know you care

Brandi Blackard

And You Were There

Amongst the trees
   Amid the skies a single cloud
   Passes by, the green fields our bed we hide.

Oh beating hearts you sound of thunder, all
   sweet that sound young with laughter.

Morning dew sets across our brow, through
   nightless passes that embraced us now, we
   lay here all in wonder with faces of smoke
   and eyes of fire.

Oh how sweet to remember, you spring filled
   nights of wonder.

    Charlton Brown

Persistence

Waves disgorging their spume on the shore
An expulsion of phlegm from the mighty seas
Inhaling it into its bosom once more
To echo and encore this bizarre behavior

A constant motion of surge and retreat
And left in its wake; fine grains of sand
As it powerfully nibbles the rocks with each beat
It is,
   the constant,
     the pulse,
      of our changing land

    Joan Morris

Who Am I?

A graceful, floating spirit - free to roam at will.
An impatient, shackled object - fettered - fretful!
A breeze, swirling crisp leaves.
A leaden, uncomfortable silence.

The fragrance of the sweetest incense - priceless - rare.
The stench of dreary plodding - the dankness of despair.
A dancing sunbeam; a butterfly.
A shuddering guilt of terror-I!

A bouncing ball; a baby's laugh.
A tortured dream that haunts the night.
An angel with the gift of peace.
A bitter, aching urge to fight!
All these, no more am I.

    Echo Harrison

God's Special Recipe

He took the WISDOM of Solomon,
And added the PATIENCE of Job;
He took the LOVE of His disciples,
And borrowed some SOFTNESS from His robe.

While carefully mixing these,
He added His Father's KNOWLEDGE;
This He knew came from life itself,
And not from books or from college.

He then added His FORGIVENESS for one's sins,
And His own LOVE for a child;
He then thought for just a little while,
And under "MOTHER" was His recipe filed.

When we think of our Mother,
A prayer we should say with a bowed head;
For God knew beforehand what He created,
In His own image, it has been said.

Up in Heaven, a light shined brightly,
From the smile of God because He knew;
When a woman achieves Motherhood,
His RECIPE is tried and true.

    Barbara A. Woss

Night Singer

I am the countless voices that whisper in your dreams
And all the shifting shadows which are never what they seem.
I call to you in winds; sighing through endless nights.
And melt back into darkness with touch of morning light.

Are those my steps behind you, or echoes in the icy night air?
You turn with pounding terror, and find I am not there.
See my reflection in the mirror, watching as you sleep.
Do not seek to know the purpose of the vigil that I keep.

Someday you will feel my touch and hear my dark night song.
This is your human destiny, and your wait will not be long.

    Debra M. Richardson

"You Can Go Home Again"

You can go home again - I know, that's where I've been
And an awful lot of things are still the same.

There's the same gold apple tree, and the swing Dad made for me
And the name shows on the mailbox pale and faint

Inside the folks have changed, but to me it looks the same
cause I can picture in my memory

Dad's in his rocking chair, by the woodstove over there
and mama's planting flowers by the lane.

You can go home again - I know, that's where I've been,
And an awful lot things are still the same!

There's rows and rows of lilacs, though the river's not so high
And the trees that Daddy planted reach almost to the sky

The piano doesn't play in the parlor anymore
But I hear a family's footsteps running cross the floor.

There are a couple headstones that never used to be
But when I see the Homestead, it's home again to me!!

    Betty Wheeler

Liberty And Justice...For All?

It's become evident - justice yields only to power and money;
And anyone who wields a badge can tip the justice scale.

In this territory, which was meant to be The Land of the Free,
Only the high, white and mighty have been given the
Opportunity, and have taken it freely to oppress
Women, children and every other minority in our country.

The home of the Brave, I'm sorry to say,
Was born of my ancestors, who built it with the
Blood, sweat and tears of slaves.

The hopes and dreams of my entire generation
Were shot down with the assassinations of King and Kennedy.

The most recent assault on America was seen around the world
As we felt the final blow hurled at Rodney...and democracy.

And the fires now bring to light our common plight;
For when there is no justice, there is Just-Us.

Let us join together peacefully to quelch the flame,
Bring about change, and restore human dignity!

    Denise Butler Presti

The Wish

You came to me a few years ago...
And asked me for my number...

To this day I don't know why...
All I can do is wonder...

You know it may be plain to see we are attracted
  to each other...
When you could have any beautiful woman and why
  with me you bother...

You are my lover and good friend...
I can only hope it will never end...

When we make love and you hold me tight...
I can only wish you stay all night...

You have a career, family and wife...
But still you manage to find time for
  me in your life...

I am good for you and you are for me...
And that is the way it's supposed to be...

I have this hunger, need and thirst...
If I could only have but one wish...
And that is... I could have met you first...

    Barbara Nordin

Prick Driven

My husband told me he didn't love me.
And besides I wasn't bringing in any money.

He took our $40,000 and left for Ventura.
Snarling, "You can't do anything" he slammed the door.

While he was in the mental hospital,
I bore our second child.
Nurtured two children and him.

I can also, besides caring for two children
and an ill husband, knit, sew, crochet, swim,
play tennis, play golf, write shorthand, cook,
compute, calculate, make sweet love,
make sweet babies, hem a dress, flirt
audaciously, wink outrageously,
talk dirty, ride a bicycle, snap my brassiere,
look cross-eyed, act silly, make fun of myself,
Pain, day dream and float images.

My boss gave me two months to find another job.
He snarled, "You can't do anything."
(They were really getting rid of older workers.)

I cooed, "Ooh dada, it's the retirement raga."

    Jane Besen

The Song Of The Brook

The brook opens its lips
And breathes eloquent water over pebbles and stones
That dance in vaudevillian twists
In their autumn beds.

The dogs watch,
Peering into the flirt of sun and wave.
A butterfly flicks her ear
Before it passes and melts into the stream below.

Up on the hill, broken rocks sprawl in ancient forms,
Like helmets and armor from one of Alexander's battlefields,
The song of the brook stretches the air, lingering,
But rain blurts, and winter will come.

    Alice Moolten Silver

My Little Helper

My little helper watches me with such a patient eye,
And bides his time so peacefully, until the time is nigh.

Then, when my hand goes to the door that leads into my shop,
He gleefully sets out after me, and lets all other matters drop.

He follows me into the shop and turns on lights and fan,
And eagerly sets out to do whatever job he can.

I take him with me to my bench and lift him up and set him down.
There he will stay and work with me, never asking to get down.

He plays with things I make for him, and so the time goes by.
He never seems to tire of this; I look at him and sigh.

I think of how much joy he brings, each day we labor so,
Of how I long to keep him here and never let him go.

But grandsons are not ours to keep and summers do pass by.
Soon they will change to other things more appealing to the eye.

But, for now, I am content to sit and teach him what I can,
And try to help this little soul grow up to be a man.

For my little pint sized helper who acts so brave and bold,
Is only just a little guy no more than three years old.

    Frank Arthur

A Day With Mother Nature

The sun is shining so bright in the sky
and clouds begin moving in thunderously quick.
Now the sun's all covered by black massive clouds.
It is starting to get dark,
and it's raining and slick.

    Crash!
      Boom!
        Bam!

The lightning strikes the tree so fast.
You don't know how long the poor tree can last.
A fire starts, but is soon put out.
There is smoke drifting here and about.

Then as fast as they came,
the clouds drift away.
And the moon shows up bright
as it ends a new day.

    David Capriccioso

New Love

I just can't stop thinking of you
And don't want to stop dreaming of you
Every new love is a change
And at first a challenge to get arranged

We all say we'll never do it again
But a relationship more than just friends
By getting use to each others different ways
And missing one another when their away

Sometimes those feelings you hold inside
Can be controlled by your heart an mind
You wonder should you follow them through
Is your new love feeling the same way too

They say an old love, don't fade away
That in the heart it keeps its place
That you don't forget where your loves went
That your memory stores it in

Even tho' it may be so true
I want no other old or new
Now that my hearts in love with you
My memory awaits all that we can do

    Cathy H. Dimeglio

Dreams

Dreams are believed in,
And dreams are forgotten.

Some dreams live on,
And others die down.

Believe in your dreams,
And make them come true,

Or later on in life,
A whisper of what might have been
Could come crying out, "You should have believed,
You should have taken the chance."

Follow or Forget.
Alaina Lackey

Unity

I will arise and go now,
and enter into a new life.
Where I am no longer a solitary creature,
but am a component of unity.

And there I will discover the solidity of faith,
the strength of security,
and the sweetness of companionship.

And I will offer encouragement,
provide understanding,
and share my desires.

And my soul will overflow with thankfulness,
invite hope,
and welcome his love.

And I will treasure my life partner......
For he is the light that illuminates my world.
I will arise and go now,
and enter into a new life.
Denise Bassham

The Moose And Maine

My name is moose, my home is Maine,
And every year I have this fear
That this will be the end.

I don't have to read the papers,
Even if I knew how
To know the season has just begun.

I smell the powder in the air,
And know that death is just around the corner.

I see the hunters in their trucks,
With loaded guns and lots of beer.

I don't want to see my face
Hanging over a fireplace
Looking down on my killers.

I called my family and friends
And we had a meeting.
Then we crossed the river to go to Canada and wait.

When we return there will be peace,
And Maine again will be
Our Pine Tree State.
Edith A. Yeager

The Beach

As I lie here in my lounge chair
and feel the soft sand sifting between my toes,
I observe the bright sun's glare
upon the water and the shore.

I hear the roar of the sea and the crashing of the waves.
It's as if it's singing a song to me,
then the white foam draws away.

Along I drift into a subconscious state
where all my troubles and trials are not mentioned.
Images appear as my mind creates
a world which releases my tension.

Beads of sweat trickle down my back
from the encompassing warmth of the sun,
causing me to feel more and more relaxed
as if the day has just begun.

Every sense is awakened as I continue to float.
Inhaling every breeze, I am my own sail boat.

As the day journeys to an end,
I stop and wonder for a moment or two
where I fit into a place of such magnitude.
Ellen Wean

Retrospection

I sat and watched the clouds slip by
And felt as though I wanted to cry
For how quickly the years have gone that way
From my childhood to this very day
Memories of my mother whom I miss most of all
Happy and sad days so easy to recall
True friends I made along the way
They aren't many I must say
But like the clouds in the sky
Many people I meet and they slip by
And so my life goes on and on
Wondering with each new dawn
What challenges I will meet this day
As I watch the blue sky hide away
Under the clouds of a lonely gray.
Edna F. Jacobson

A Journey To Peace

I climbed love's highest mountain
and felt the pain of its grip
Occasional expressions of tenderness
held me in my imaginary imprisonment...there is peace.

Anguish became my best friend through
endless wanderings in the valley of confusion.
Downpours of despair and discouragement
transformed into tranquil aspirations of rejuvenation...there is
hope.

I see a meadow, but I am afraid
What lurks in the systematic swaying of the grass?
The gentle breeze wrapped in nature's warming rays
Encourage me to come...there is trust.

I want to stay and walk barefoot on the creek's jagged rocks.
I want to drink life's nourishing nectar
and be cradled in its contentment.
And yet I must press onward, I must.
It matters not where fate may take me
But that I am ready for my journey.
Come, walk with me...there is peace.
Judith A. Cromwell

The Builder

A builder fashioned a house with care
And filled it with furnishing rich and rare.
The drapes were woven with threads of gold;
The carpets were marvels to behold.
But alas the mansion failed to stand,
For it was built on the shifting sand.
So it is with a life that's built with care.
No matter how or when or where,
It cannot stand when trials knock,
Unless it's built on the solid Rock.
For the mightiest man in all the land
Is but a pebble in God's hand,
And though he walk a scornful way,
He'll bow his knees somewhere, some day.

Bernice Nethery

Sweet Woman

I believe in women's equality
And for women to see,
Though most men consider them second degree,
A woman is a creator, and man is her pawn,
In the womb of a dear woman I was born.

I am a dreamer
With a gentle soul,
Searching for the woman
Who can light up my dawn,
Could it be you sweet woman
I have just known,
Not long ago and I have sworn
To tell you of my plea,
For a friend to share my aspirations, emotions
My loneliness to bare.

Could it be you sweet woman
Who looks deep in my eyes,
Trying to detect the truth or lies,
I am an open book for you to see
So you may decide to stay or flee.

Albert Rozane

Untitled

There's a special man in my heart,
And from there, he will never part.
Everyday and night when we're together,
We see our love grow, and hope it lasts forever.

Love makes itself known in many ways.
A look, a touch gets us through the darkest days.
Magically, somehow, we know "we" were meant to be.
This is all so real, yet feels like the greatest dream.

He inspires me in a fulfilling way.
We are as one; heart, mind, and soul everyday.
Mere words could never say how much he means to me.
He's full of abundant love, trust, and deep understanding.

When we are alone, and that is quite rare,
We have so much to give each other, so much to share.
This man I speak of is none other than
My devoted husband, passionate lover, and ultimate friend!

Brenda Lynn Russell

the sun shines out

kiss the little girl goodbye
and give salute to the queen of night
embrace cheap sex and animal rights
lift the dress and dim the lights
    this haven of youth and fire
    and the lust proclaimed to save these lives
    the passion of passion's loss still stings
    in the broken empty air of dawn

so heed the loathsome wanderer
and dance on such light airs
(minstrel, wander, sing the songs
that brought us to our knees)

and now the stone of face has turned
every expectation etched
by hope and expectation's loss

now and forever
kiss the little girl goodbye

Jay Morgans

Tuesday, July 26

I dreamt I swam across the river styx
and had a visit with the bolsheviks..
I play the games so well, I always please.
I keep the ace of spades inside my sleeve.
I tried my best to be a scientist.
Some still insist I am a humorist.

Imagine you have every problem solved
and then be careful. Don't get too involved.
I never yielded to my leader's views.
That's why I always sought important news.
I comprehend at times some mysteries
that some ears never hear, eyes never see.

When temptations overwhelm, just say "No."
"Just say, "Woe! Whoa! Go Go! "So so! No!"

David P. Boyd

The Stranger

I heard the knock
And hastened to open the door.
I could not see you face,
And although we had never met,
I knew you and why you had come.
Somewhat reluctantly I admitted you.
Then to the rhythm of an unheard melody
We glided across the floor.
Our bodies moved to and fro
Until finally I collapsed in your embrace
And gave into your insistent demands.
The present left, a retreating light,
As I went slowly towards the unknown.
A vast emptiness where I knew not
What each moment would bring.
And then I realized
Here there would never be
Pain, despair or trouble.
With that thought, I gave in,
And welcomed you as a friend.

Carolyn Markel Giles

Poem In June

I awoke blanketed by sunlight,
And held my birthday brightness in hands
Unwilling, but signs of love surrounding
Cheered, and so I fingered small, soft ways
   To match the Grace
   And thank the Light.

I lingered visited by cloudshade,
And held child-linking letters in hands
Enfolding, then rain and tears down-pouring
Chilled, and awkward anguish probed the pain
   To snatch the Joy
   And blur my Sight.

I rested comforted by nightfall,
And cast my birthday behind with hands
Releasing, then Compline chants remembered
Calmed, and persevered with paean's praise
   To grace the Watch
   And light the Dark.
     Irene Marie Steffens

The Way It Works

Now and again I think of her ways,
And how they bothered us in those days.
How terribly out-dated her rule,
And how she insisted on Sunday School

She maintained her composure all the time,
And with a firm disposition, she kept us in line.
When she gave us chores, it seemed so mean,
But our home was healthy and fresh and clean.

She monitored our T.V. and watched how we ate,
And made it clear how to act on a date.
I'm sure she wondered if it was taking affect.
(Oh, how we hated her with love and respect.)

It's my turn now, and I remember those days—
Her words are mine and so are her ways.
I kept her values and have passed them on
To my two children, who have grown and gone.

My son now awaits a child of his own.
I expect things will be the same in his home.
This will be good, because now I can see,
How right my mother was when she was rearing me.
     Edith Caldwell

To Mother

From the first time I opened my eyes at birth, you loved me...
And I knew. Your loving hands diapered me, fed me,
Held and rocked me,
   And took away my fears.

Through childhood your gentle voice taught me of God and his ways,
Day after day, precept upon precept.
You patted me, hugged me, loved me,
   And wiped away my tears.

With steadfastness and patience you guided me
Through sometimes rebellious teen-age years; you forgave me.
You shared my sorrows and my triumphs, you were my friend...
   And while I grew through the years,

You were a shining example, always, of service to your family,
And to the Lord. The smell of freshly baked bread
In the kitchen, upon returning from school,
   Lingers in my memory still.

I remember your singing and your laughter...the security I felt to be
At home. Knowledge and culture were important to you and so became
Important to me. Thank you for the example of love for family,
For fellowman and for the Saviour that I see still, ...and may follow.
     Diane Bryce Patterson

Untitled

I love you more than love itself
And I know I say "I love you"
   More times than you can count
And that may make you wonder
   About the sincerity of what I say
Well the words "I love you"
   Are the true expression of my feelings for you
And since these feelings
   Are always present in my heart
It only seems natural
   To constantly tell you
"I love you"
     Dave Gibb

Untitled

I am not the greatest,
   And I know this.
Mom treats me like nothing,
   And I accept this.
Treats my brother and sister like royalty,
   And I envy this.
Always putting those two in the spotlight,
   And I don't have this.
Calling me a failure, a nothing, a nobody,
   And I have to take this.
One day I will be at peace,
   And I wait for this.
At peace where no one will
   ignore,
   scare,
   or hurt me,
And I will wait for this,
And I will pray for this.
     Idulia F. Lovato

The Room

I have a room within my heart
And I locked it years ago.
Now when I'm hurt and all alone
There's no place for me to go....

I wander the hallways and listen at doors,
There are other rooms but they're bare.
All my belongings are in the room
That I locked cause I didn't care.

But even if I found the key,
I think I've forgotten the way
To the happiness that's behind that door......
The kind that will stop and stay.

Houses in my sleep at night
I've dreamt them countless times before.......
I wander solitary hallways
Searching for the hidden door.
     Janet A. Vair

In Memory Of—

Oh, soldier boy, the hurricane of war has passed
And in its path your footprints still hold fast;
In Normandy, where once contented cattle trod
The battle raged, and bore you home to God.

Out in a field, where now your mangled limbs remain
Amid the winds that drowned your cries of pain,
The clouds of war, I swear shall pass and be no more;
I promise you, you have not died in vain...
I promise you, you have not died in vain...
Oh, soldier boy, you have not died in vain.
     Frank Ucman

In The Roses

This morning I heard your whisper in the roses
and I saw your smile in the outlined echoing pattern of the petals.
I need no reassurance to know how much you love me,
we go beyond the boundaries of so many years and lifetimes.
The leaves are releasing and as each one dances to its resting place
I am reminded of just how easy it is for me to let go
when we are together.
In your eyes I experience all the scenery.
We are Native Warriors dancing and playing our drums around a fire.
Inside a hut by the ocean, palm trees and hibiscus,
a cooking pot bubbling,
you are soothing me with your touch.
Upon a flat top pyramid, a great ritual for which you are
preparing me and I am completely surrendered.
A falcon flies above. He calls out,
"All is love, all is sacred."
This morning the raindrops fell from the sky caressing the roses
and I felt your hand brush my cheek.
I took petals from the roses
and smoldered them on a charcoal with frankincense, orris and yarrow.
As the essence filled me I felt your hands on my shoulders
and your breath in my ear.
You are always with me but it is in the roses that we are eternal

Amy Ford

The Bane Of Onizuka

"I wanted to fly,
and I was given the chance
to soar far above the earth.
I've had always
a desire to reach beyond the sky.
As I entered the
pallid phoenix
I had no idea that
I was to be cleansed in its ashes.
As I stopped myself
within the Eyes of the Eagle,
I did not know
that I was to soar
higher than any living man could fly.
Upward, forward,
faster and faster...
The earth released its grip on the great bird,
and so did life;
Now I fly
forever."

John C. R. Croft Jr.

Voices

As I sat in solitude a sudden calmness caught my mood
And I was struck with rapturous peace
T'was then my solitude did cease.

For spirits in my room did stalk and spoke the words
I longed to talk, and in the dense cold of the dark
They spoke the words deep in my heart
Words that my lips would not impart. But then my young
Heart did grow older; my joy first shuddered then it
Smouldered. These words unfinished sharply died
And troubled was my soul inside. My head was sick for
Now was lost the treasure that I longed to boast.

I stumbled then from out my room and into midnight's
Darkest gloom; alone I went into the mist
Unto the place I can't resist. And there upon the
Ocean's shore I sat for a day or a week or more.

There was no time in the world whence I dwelt
And the waters seemed to share the abandonment I felt.
Then I dragged my weary body to the shelter of my home
And sat at the table in my room alone.

Helen M. Lombardi

My Little One

I watch you as you sleep. You twitch,
and I wonder what it is that you are
seeing inside your mind. Curled up—
a little ball of fur. Incoherent of
the world around you. I call to you
but you remain in a dreaming state,
free of life's interferences and at peace
with yourself.

You awaken with a yawn as wide as your
heritage. Stretching, the dark slits
of your green eyes widen as you become
more alert. You watch me watching you
and you muster a faint meow. I smile.
We seem to understand each other.

You give me great joy. You, so full of sweetness
and affection. My special friend upon my lap,
sensing when I am troubled. I believe you would laugh
if you could, as I tease you with an old
shoelace. With you, my little one, there is a simple
happiness that is silently understood.

Jacqueline M. Palasek

The Beauty Of Friendship

My friends are a gift that God has sent,
And I'll never forget what they've meant.

All of our lives we'll find new friends,
And the good and the bad will softly blend.

But some friends are so very dear,
And to our hearts they'll always be near.

The ones that stuck by you in need,
The ones that planted that tiny seed.

That tiny seed grew to a graceful tree,
Whose many deep roots are said to be our memories.

What would I do without my friends?
Who in time of trouble their help they lend.

I'll always keep them in my thoughts,
Over smooth ground or rugged rocks.

For we are joined by a special bond,
And we'll remember each other our whole lives long!

Courtney Jones

Swingtime

I have seen the seasons come and go,
and in time I was forgotten.
My paint has slowly faded
and my chains have nearly rusted through.
But, now I wait with pride,
for I have found a heart
that truly does need and cherish me.
She came to me with tears in her eyes
and gently sat upon my worn seat.
She spoke to me as though I was her best friend,
maybe in the past I really used to be.
She told me her thoughts, her fears,
as she slowly began to swing.
She flew as high as my old chains would go,
and I held her safely within my reach.
She would not fall, I would always keep her near.
The time we now spend together
has made us both whole again.
Together we are not alone,
for she will always remember me.

Andrea Buller Hargett

43

I Am A Candle

I am a candle lit by His hand
And it is my duty by it I will stand.

I am a candle made of wax and some thread
I await my Master while He is abed.
Tomorrow He'll use me and my light will shine,
Then gutter and fade until the next time.

I am a candle and I have not long
Before my work is ended and my wax is gone.

I am a candle I do what I can
I play my small part in His Master plan.

I'm just a candle not a Duke or an Earl
But I do my small part for the Light of the World.

Heath Anderson

Night

When harsh realities are covered in an opaque blanket,
and kept hidden from my eyes,
I can sleep.

When will the true night fall to hide the pain of Day,
what some find a choking prison,
I find makes me free.

In warm blackness the daggers are dulled,
and happiness seems real,
as I can dream.

When will the true night fall, my eyes sting from Day's glare
I yearn to hide in Shadow,
to find rest.

When we are young we fear this peace,
monsters crawl through it,
stronger monsters walk through the Day.

When will the true night fall, I won't bring it myself,
so greater forces must control,
when I may finally dream.

Gregory Caudill

If Given A Chance

If given a chance I would enter your eyes and drive to your soul
and leaf through the pages of stories untold
through yesterday's window you've locked in your mind
lie memories of a life that you've left behind

I would lift away the sadness and take you on a rendezvous
Illusions of grandeur can always come true
we could rise and go flying on the wings of a dream
and begin a journey of what's never been seen

Turning wild and free like eagles in the splendor of flight
like a hand in a glove the feeling is right
we could rest on a cloud and float on through the heavens
and reign winners in the battle of Armageddon

We could travel the paths that lead to happy places
where no one's sorrows have left any traces
to find the comfort never given so never lost
reaching for the brass ring would be all it could cost

Like a childhood game of hide and seek open your eyes and look
you can write the final chapters of your book
when you're playing the game and being dealt a bad hand
observe what's beside you because that's where I stand...

Frances Letson

Confused

Life has its ups
And life has its downs,
Always going in circles
Like the merry-go-rounds.

The old want to be young,
While the young want to look older,
The rich want to be richer,
And the poor just keep getting poorer.

Inflation is keeping
Us on our toes,
Why is it so out of control?
Who knows!

People take life for granted
Every minute of the day,
Everybody wishes
They could have their own way.

If things don't get straightened out
In this beautiful country of ours,
There won't be anything left for our children
But a world full of scars.

Ann Marie Jan

An Eternal Struggle (The Battle Within')

At night when I gaze at the moon
And marvel at the creator's magnificence
I go to war with myself
to extinguish my own ignorance
inside me their lies the desire
for Positive Refinement
but the manifestation of that desire
is an eternal struggle
I'm quick to point out another's
faults and imperfections
but it takes the force of Mother Earth
to get me to look at my own stained reflection
Self inspection is a must
An elder told me once - that
if I want to change what's without
I must first change what's within'
So that's where I'll begin
with me.

Carl Wharton (xdous)

The Homecoming of Daffodils

As the day star rises
And morning doors open
The breath on the horizon gathers
Warming the dew that wells on the hillside.
It speaks of the homecoming of Daffodils,
The quiescent spirit of their wave in the distance
And of a moment in April
When to night came the first dawn,
Showing a rare imprint of how love is,
How life, beauty and forever become a fast memory
That time buries in the mind's eye
And the heart refuses to forget.
Adrift in the space between winter and summer,
Nightfall and daylight, mother and child,
Dawn seeks to be that moment
When love lies with forever
And Daffodils return.

Judith Vine

Cupid's Love

Of all the trees that tower high
and of men that rage to die,
I think of all the times we had
beneath the golden sky.

When spring was there and flowers bloomed
We sat beneath a crescent moon.

Through grassy fields of daffodils
down paths that never end,
With words that said I loved you then
like now will never end.

When fields and spring and trees are gone
and all is blown away

To whom will your love belong,
will it end, or just fade away?

Bobby Dean

Untitled

I step out of my window
and on to the sky and walk with the eagles
and watch the scene below...
I see the pawns clinging to their own
and the knights raining hell on them
I see the kings and queens on their mighty thrones
holding the world and crushing it slowly
squeezing out the life juices
then selling them to the highest bidder
I turn in to the looking glass and
the eagles fly away and I walk alone
behind the glass people hide
cowering from the past, the dead
I'm stuck between here and there with so many
but I walk alone; from choice, from necessity
I look up and see the unknown; I look down at the game
the pawns have toppled the thrones
and knights are cutting up the kings
and the world lies in the corner forgotten
set aside for want of money, power, companions...but I walk alone

Ben Gaeth

Storytellers

With battered roof and crumbled sill,
And planes, once parallel, now all askew;
With shingles never having tasted paint
And mortar lying crumbled on the ground,
Behold the storytellers.

They played a central part at some lost time,
These houses, factories, sheds, and barns
Watched the generations come and go.
Neglected now, they let the world speed on,
New England's storytellers.

Listen closely; even in decay
They whisper tales that men are wont to heed.
Thick lie the tracks of human history
Along the thoroughfares they guard.
Listen to the storytellers.

When next you travel down a country road
And come upon some structure tumbled down,
With-hold your haste to journey on;
Reflect instead, upon your heritage, and mine.
Value the storytellers.

David C. Schmoll

When I Awake

I will awake each morning
   And see the sweet sunshine of your face.
I will go through each day
   With the excitement of our meeting at
Day's end.
At night, I will snuggle in your embrace
   And know that when I fall asleep,
My dreams of you will bridge the night
   'til morning.
When, once again, I will awake
   to the warmth of your love.

Florence Gingras

Friendships

   Special Friendships are rare as pearls,
and should be cherished and protected from
all dishonest acts, deeds, or jealousies.
This special friendship can be from early
childhood, or later in life. When the
friendship developed is not important, but
the longevity.
   Friendships are formed without vows, but
last longer than most marriages. One reason
is mutual respect, another is, it is easier
to forgive a friend of almost anything, than
a mate.
   I toast to all friendships, new or old.
May you stay in-touch, whether, you live near
or far. Nourish the relationship with care,
concern, understanding, listening, support,
kindness, trust, love, ... and the
knowledge when to be silent.

Barbara Eugenia Hunter

"Changes"

I arise early to greet the dawn
and sneak a look across my lawn
The rain in the night softly fall
flowers in profusion cast a spell
Soon the humming bird will be out to feed
flying from petal to petal in their greed
The sounds of traffic on a highway below
tell me the work force is now on the go
Some of them face the day with dread
wishing they'd stayed home in bed
Someday they'll be idle with nothing to do
maybe they'll learn to love nature to.

Helen Northcutt

An Overused Cliche

A white moon streak crossed the lake to where we sat,
And the trees formed a romantic sanctuary,
You laughed like a little girl,
Talking of how this spot symbolizes our romance,
And how you can not sleep at night until I tell you I love you.

Yet I thought of the true reason why I had come,
Of the new love started here the night before,
And said the only thing to come to my mind,
"This is no longer exciting."

And as you left, you muttered, "Just yesterday you said you love me"
And there alone I watched the streak of the moon move,
And alone, I realized that we were not so well hidden,
Thinking of how at this symbolic spot,
I turned the word love into a cliche.

Brian Callaghan

45

Fantasy Land

Come, fly with me on wings of the wind
  And soar to an unchartered height,
We'll run up a flight of billowing clouds
  That extend way, way out of sight.

We'll sit upon clouds and dip to and fro,
  Ride upon golden sunbeams,
And warm our hearts in the sun's radiant glow,
  And "cat nap" with happy day dreams.

Let's catch at a breeze and hang on the wind,
  Watch arrows of lightning run,
Play tag with birds as they fly away
  Then - slide down a rainbow for fun!

Let's press the "Off" button on a twinkling star,
  Wear moonbeams all thru our hair,
Wrap ourselves in a velvet night curtain
  And relax to a symphonic air -

Now that we're weary and in need of sleep,
  We'll pull up the blanket of night,
We'll turn down the glow of the stars and the moon
  And know we're in heaven all right.
        Eleanor J. Slusher

A Night In The Streets

  With a stone to lay my head
and some cardboard for my bed....
I lie awake looking up at the coal black
sky, stars seem to wink as their prism-like
brilliance illuminate the sky;
others (who are homeless like me),
acknowledge my existence with a nod
and a friendly smile- for no one else
knows we're here except God.

  The crickets and frogs begin their
nightly serenade and sleep will soon come.
A gentle breeze starts up and the palm fronds
sway back and forth in unison as though in a
choreographed musical. The tumbleweeds and
silhouettes of old house frames provide
comfort as they seem to surround me like
sentries protecting hidden treasures like me...
  A diamond in the rough.
        Alice D. Pierce

Remember Me

Homesick in a land that's strange,
  And sometimes lonely too.
Far from all I cherish most...
  But there's job to do.

That's why I'm here, I know,
  And if the choice were mine to make,
I wouldn't come back... no, not yet,
  For something is at stake.
Something we must fight to keep
  And die for... willingly
That dear, that sweet, that precious thing,
  That man calls "Liberty".

And so... until the battle's won
  In Exile I must be.
But just one little thing I want to ask
  That you remember me.
        Joseph M. Montgomery

Untitled

Everyone has moved
And soon will come my turn
But missing all my friends
Is my number one concern

Never seeing them again
Will get me real upset
For then I will remember
The day that we all met

It was the first day of my fourth grade year
When I met my best friend
We told each other, that
Our friendship would never end

Every night, I went to bed
And more the friends I prayed
And on and on I met more people
And more the friends I made
So when I move, I will never forget
About the friends I said goodbye to
I'll just remember our friendships
And how they were so true
        Jessica Lynn Bruni

Disillusion

When we were young, we thrived on fairy tales,
And sought the "Happy ever after."
We lived the life we'd always known:
Sedate, protected, measured by tradition.

The shy and callow youth I met one day
Bore no resemblance to a king
Or knight in shining armor
Forsworn to rouse a sleeping Cinderella.

And yet I greeted him with starry eyes.
He was my dream come true,
A touch of magic in my quiet world.

I talked with him,
And laughed with him,
And walked with him,
And danced with him,
Secure in my Utopia.

And then one day he kissed me,
But failed to say, "I love you."
For want of those three words,
My romance died.
        Josie Goodrich Smith

Ireen

Deserts attack his heart
and surrender their rusty treasures:
Swords, plundered caravans, tanks bereft of their flags.
The mirage is mirrors in which weavers weave
equivocal prayers, marching songs, and shrouds.
The lofty monasteries forbid the monks to listen.
Ireena came.
Streams open in the sand and flow into
the heart of the monk Ireen;
he has forgotten his limbs and the most important member
and the pharmacy and has listened to chickens for ten years.
His name was never Ireen.
Now he does not believe the letters
which conspired with the sand against him,
but when the enzymes of belief stop working,
he transcends his old name in the night and Ireena;
and he could never pass through the gate
as chickens did
when Ireena the visitor departed.
        Aly Afifi

Female

She is an ocean, almost. But it is her daughter
and that daughter after her,
(what thin opposing currents),
seeking beginnings at the ends
of the cold polar circles;
the warm sea floats on top
breeding silver eels and angels fish.

Rise and fall again, again
waves hold and hold,
tear apart
but do not end.

Inconsolable waves
of Typhoons
join, as Neptune's watery knife spears the land,
scattering scales the color of air,
undoing purple scented gardenias in the jungle,
unfrocking brilliant toucans:
some can be saved.

Words and song spiraling in the wonder
of her upright body.

Joan Blake

Who Am I?

Folding his head downward to his chest,
and the agony carving all over his face,
walks the endless road without any rest,
undignified, less than animal and no grace.

With the heavy rattling chains from his dirty feet,
and under the rhythm of the whip marking his back,
day and night being thirsty and nothing to eat,
walks a destination of uncertainty over his neck!

When the black shadows of the relieving night cast over,
clasping himself in a corner singing the blues,
raising his trembling hands and praying to the Life Doner,
says: "Please God, send me death and have me loose!"

George Katsampes

Crystal Sea

I once asked Grandma, "What is death?"
  and the answer she had for me
    "My dearest child," she softly spoke,
    "death is but a crystal sea."
    For you see, the troubles of earth
    matter not at all.
  Life is short if only a breath
while on this terrestrial ball.
  The sting of death alone is slight,
  Then all is quiet, all is night."

So she asked me, "My child now what is death?"
  And I said, "Sweet Victory!"
    "For death alone is not the end,
    but is life as meant to be
      For you see, the Lord of heaven and earth
      laid down His life for all
  He bore the cross and relinquished His breath
for men on the terrestrial ball."
  A tear ran down as she smiled at me
  "My child I'll see you on crystal sea."

Douglas Stormont McClure

Grey Skies

The grey skies seem like they will always stay
  and the bad feelings...I can't keep them away.

My mind drifts off to a different part of me
  where I watch childhood memories that just shouldn't be.

This was the part of me I thought I could hide
  I thought I could keep the past from the present
  and never let the two collide.

I can't understand why he did me so
  but I have to live with it
  and from it I will grow.

Bissi

Maine

When it is cold and dreary
And the birds are flying south,
I turn around and look to find
A way to touch the coast of Maine.

A state where ocean waves
Embrace the naked rocks,
Where the moon and sun play on the water.

The only State that has a town called China,
A lake Chemquasabamticook,
And miles of fields and forests
That give a home to moose and deer.

My unending love goes out to Maine,
A State that means tranquility, serenity and peace.

James F. Yeager IV

Untitled

As the curtain of darkness arises
And the morning awakens to prizes
The dew on the grass glitters with promises
Lost and found of the night before

It sees through the lies of difference
And of the truths of light
Even in the hardest rain
It can see through the night

It can see all of the people
It can hear all of the birds
It can smell the sweet nectars
And put it all in words

So as the morning comes
With the bright and shining sun
You lift your head from drowsiness
For a new day has begun

Crystal Kozora

Untitled

When the cloudy days have past
And the rains no longer last

Our hearts will shed no pain
And the horizon will be ours to gain

The days when I awake to find you by my side
I will rest assured for us, there's no more pain to hide

Donald M. Good

47

Blind To The Wind

A smile in the darkness
And the whispered dreams inside your heart
The reflections of passion burn in your eyes
And to touch your silken lips
Embrace of fire from the winter sun
A sweet dream come to rescue me from myself
When there are no devils left in hell
And no angels left in heaven
And my heart is left wandering the earth
Would you still hold my broken pride in your trembling hands
Or ask me for a single kiss
Would my dreams drift away quietly
Like rainbows in the winter rain
Or would you leave me with a smile
And the words "forever more" poised on your lips
You say that I will never be the same
But alone, with solitude as my companion
I will find the answers locked away
When I hold you

Joshua Ian Goodman

Dark And Lonely Silhouettes

The sun, as it sets, shines through the rain
And the world becomes cold and dark.
Peril overcomes the being
As it huddles in the corner.
The rain upon the surface,
Drips into pools below.
Outside, the raindrops lay upon
The petals of the flowers,
But the thunder and lighting
Is neverending and soon begins
To beat upon its prey and rip apart life.
So fragile, helpless, and lonely,
Death becomes the being,
And the sun will shine no more.
And the pale moonlight, looking through
The window from the outside,
Silhouettes the darkness in the corner.

Holly Jackson

The Critics

How we used to sniff and snicker at the polyester public
And their unseeing, unfeeling, obviously unknowing words:
"I don't know much about art, but I know what I like!"

What did they know of the inspiration that rent that
dripping slash of vermilion across a cobalt field?
Or the remarkable restraint that left the solitary square
to stare in singular resolve?
What did they know of Pollack's passion? Or Georgia's genius?

Only we, "les artistes," (and those enlightened few who had
the eye but not the hand)
Were privy to the secrets that fed our satisfaction.
And we hoarded them, smiling in smug silence at the uninspired fools
Who sniffed and snickered —
At us.

Jo Wilson

Come With Me

Let me take you by the hand
And lead you to the promised land.
The trip is short; the way is clear
I'll take you there; you need not fear.
Give me a chance to lead you there.
Relax, enjoy, have no care.
The best is yet to come, you'll see,
If you will make this trip with me.

Charles W. Shoop

Sometimes I See My Sons

Sometimes I see my sons
And think of times I failed
To comfort sorrows, to meet their needs,
Because I felt my own were greater,
And therefore more important.

Sometimes I see my sons
And remember we are in life together,
Through good days. And days not so good,
But always they comfort me,
With a word, a look, a touch. They understand.

Sometimes I see my sons
With trust and approval in their eyes
That tell me they forgive the faults,
That we are friends, and they recall
The many times of love and care.

Sometimes I see my sons
And marvel that they're mine.
They give me faith and hope.
They say "Hi, Mom", and everything is fine.
They are my pride and joy - and I love them.

Audrey C. Kainu

A Time To Sleep

The old woman sits on her porch swing
And thinks of yesteryears.
Her face reflects the times of her life;
Times of laughter and of tears.

Her hair is the color of winter snow;
Her eyes are old but clear.
Her mind is sharp and unclouded,
And there's little she doesn't hear.

Her hands have seen much better days,
And at times hurt her so;
But her back is still strong and straight,
And her legs still take her where she wants to go.

She feels a shiver as evening nears,
And the wind begins to blow.
She wonders, "How much longer, Lord?";
But in her heart, she knows.

She knows she'll see the winter snow,
And smell the springtime flowers;
Then in her porch swing, she'll close her eyes
And sleep through summer's showers.

Delila Reynolds

Only You

Last week I dreamed a dream,
and this is true,
That I dreamed of love
and it was you.

Last night as I kneeled
to pray up under the stars,
I prayed for love and here you are.

Today I'll just sit and think of you, because
all of my dreams, all of my thoughts
and all of my prayers are of you .....
My love.

In my world of dreams that come true,
and never ending pleasures.
A day has shown itself, a day when love
will be as one, some way, one day
In love .....

Jonathan W. Pitts

Colors

I walked through the pages of my ancestors
and to my surprise what did I see,
A beautiful rainbow of different colors,
races and creed.

How could have I gone through life
without knowing what my past was
or what my future would bring.
A loving world where we can grow.
All the colors, purple, orange and green.

The orange sun with its bright light
that brings a new day for me.

The green grass starting to bloom,
I can smell, it's almost Spring.

And the color purple is the one I love most,
for it's my heart beating to the knowledge given to me.

How could have I gone another day
without knowing all the colors of the
rainbow, purple, orange and green.

Gladys Serrano-Figueroa

"I'm Sorry"

I know we are young,
and to you a relationship may be just fun.
But I don't care what you do or say,
I love you more and more every day.
Can't we just try to stay together.
Maybe it's hard, and maybe I'll cry,
but I know, that I will still try.
Love me, don't leave me,
I can't say good-bye.
I hoped we'd be together forever,
even though one day, I knew it'd be over.
I'm sorry for whatever I did or said,
I promise I'll never do it again as long as I live.
I never meant to make you upset,
I know this is something I'll never forget.
So please can we put this behind us and move on?
I thought what we had would never be gone.

Cheryl Ann Moss

Untitled

As I sit here
and watch the world
through my blind eyes
I wonder
are we all meant to drown?
should we fall to breathe no more
do we grow from the soil
into large, deadly red roses
that sing the song of danger
for a prick of the finger
brings blood the color of its delicate petals
oh and when the sky becomes gray
and then dark as night
the sky will give in to our ongoing thirst
and we drink till we drown
till there's no longer sound
as our dead petals will fall atop the soil of the ground

Alisha Castro

My Aunt

I'm sitting very quietly
and watching my little boy
The water is flowing freely
I'm crying tears of joy

Another significant person in my life
has moved on from this place
but the memories are vivid and glorious
just like the smile that shaped her face

The tears of joy are flowing
despite the heartfelt pain
The joy comes from the knowledge
that her life, was my gain

I knew and loved her my entire life
since I was a baby boy
Now I'm watching my new born son
and I'm crying tears of joy

James E. Small III

On Our Journey I Lost Sight

On our journey together I lost sight of things
and we couldn't quite storm the weather.

I almost pulled you under
But you awoke by the sound of thunder

Only to leave me behind
hurting and loosing my mind

Even though I've grown
You've chosen to go it alone.

Good luck with the journeys you choose
May they be peaceful prosperous and you never loose

I wish things could be different somehow
But I guess that's impossible right now.

This time I'm not loosing sight
I'm holding on to God's light
He'll see us through I'm sure
As his love for us is pure
Just as mine is for you
I know you feel it too.

If you ever need a real friend
I'll be here for you until the bitter end

Donna M. DeAngelis

Untitled

While falling in love; we kissed and cuddled
and we held on tight and loved each other.
Gifts from above; let us laugh and snuggle,
our hearts grew so light; we saw no others.

The day's were apart seem to be so long
you are miles away, and my day's are gray
but never fear, our love will always be strong
seeing you again will brighten my day's.

So never regret the love that we've found
believe, my love for you, is bright and true
we'll never forget our hearts will be bound
I'll be by your side through all that you do.

Whatever may come in the years of our lives
remember forever, our love will not die.

Corinne Turner

Love Comes Softly

Our meeting was so simple
    and yet so dramatic.
We weren't alone, you and I —
    there were others around us.

But we need this time alone, just you and I —
    for this gentle, sweet beauty of loving.
It seems like I've know you for a very long time —
    although it has only been moments.

I have felt your heartbeat close to mine
    and known your touch so gentle.
Your skin is like the softness of a new petal
    and your scent so sweet and clean.

I have been waiting for you for most of my life
    and could only guess at loving you so much.
There could never be a love quite like this one —
    for there could never be another quite like you.

But you are here with me,
    you are real — not a dream.
You are so special, so unique — not to be duplicated.
    you are my love, you are my child!

Barbara Stokell

Christalization

Hold me up to the light of the Son,
and you will see a dazzling rainbow.

Hold me up to the light of the Son -
the glory of Truth passes through me without refraction.
for the Father and I are one:
everything I do and think is the Creator in action.

Hold me up to the light of the Son:
in every facet you shall clearly see
that all my negative karma is undone.
So now I'm truly free.
... Because in the heat and pressure
of thousands of years of lifetimes -
awake... dozing... asleep -
I cut away at my Satan; I cut hard... I cut deep,
until through the dust and blood and bone
once again my resplendent Lucifer shone.

I am a Christal.

John E. Dallas

Mama Julia

Your smile is always bright
And your clothes, they're not too tight.

You have a graceful walk
And a very smooth talk.

You have a twinkle in your eyes
Like the bright stars in the skies.

Your face is very attractive
Lets us know that you're still active.

Your style is not trendy
But be it ever so friendly.

Your personality is warm as can be
It lets you be you, and me be me.

What's your secret to being so loving and kind?
Please tell me, so I can rest my mind!

Giving hugs with a gentle embrace
Within your heart, we have a special place.

A woman who stands beside her man
Giving him encouragement when she can.

A woman of honor and prayer
Gently taking you in her care.

Duana Davis Stallworth

Carefree

Your carefree life is as free as an eagle,
and your heart blows with the wind...
We were supposed to be together,
What happened to that?
My worries fled when you were near,
Why now I just have this fear...
I love you so much can't you feel it in my touch?
And now all I have are these tears,
as I cry at night waiting for the morning light...
And God only knows I love you with all my heart.
As I wish we would have never part...

Felicia Maes

raped

through a swirling mist of abstract shadows
appears a child born from a melody
clean as rain she stands alone
pure and free from the disease

sudden force, attacked she is, advantage taken, mind molested
no feelings from the foe, he's a friend, who would know
scared for life, scream she tries, but help is in the distance
alone she weeps as haunting memories wake her sleep

help arrives slowly and applies the chains
he has done no wrong and she is all to blame
false religion from those in pretty white coats
terrorizes the victim as she sees no hope

but wait, what outstretched hand
comes from yonder heaven and wipes the tears away
a redeemer with a conceptive plan
a shard of comfort for a wounded child

my sister i ask
take hold of the hand
where pain and fear
could never stand

Andrew Brown

Sincerity

You are welcome my friend to search the beautiful seeds of life
that are embedded into the caravans of time.

These words of invitation expressed to you are expressed with
deep sincerity.

As you travel with the caravans of time, you will see many
pleasant and unpleasant realities.

Many pleasures will be camouflaged as unpleasant realities. You
may even feel bewildered.

    My house is open to you.
    My soul is welcome to you.
    Should you need me for assistance my friend,
    I invite you to my roots of joy,
    My trunk of satisfaction,
    My branches of love and understanding,
    My tree of life and a soul of eternal existence.

To you I give a gift of beauty and understanding.

Akenduca Beasley

A Thousand Deaths

Take me
because even after I die A Thousand Deaths
I'll sit in hell
And when they've put me to rest
I'll watch him
until the end of time
and I'll die A Thousand Deaths
in this broken heart of mine

Evelyn A. Verucci

America

It's cold outside, and the snow clouds
  are gathering in the west.
As I look down the road through the grayness,
  I see another guest.

The threat of the storm and the stillness,
  a heavy hand they lay.
But within it's warm and busy,
  for it's Thanksgiving Day.

The smell of the turkey cooking
  —you can hear it pop and hiss—
and the sizzle when it's basted
  not for anything would I miss.

This day is truly American
  —it's this we have fought for—
this and a hundred other things
  we need cherish more and more.
    Jane Dexter Russell

Sunrise And Moonset

Birth and death
Are like
The rising of the sun
And the setting of the moon.

The world rejoices
In the light and glory of your birth.

The sun is highest at noon,
The middle of the day.
The middle of your life
Is one of the highest and happiest points as well,
Your children now young ladies and gentlemen.

Then you have grandchildren
And you watch them grow too.

Soon though, the moon sets
And the day is over.
There will be a new day,
But somewhere, there is a darkness.
    Elizabeth Marjorie Gott

Is There A Tomorrow

Youth where are you going?
Are you rushing by without knowing
That there is a NOW to live,
And there is a lot of you to give
The world needs your enthusiasm, your determination,
Your undiscovered wisdom and your imagination.
Why must you live so reckless and fast?
Don't you know THIS TIME you will carry as your PAST.
Fill the NOW with treasured memories not regrets and sorrow.
For, yes, there will be a TOMORROW.
    Gene Gordy

"Souls And Heart"

Her mind wanders in the breeze,
As she looks in the sunlit trees.
Red, Orange, Brown, and Green,
The trees are large, round, or lean.
Leafless, but not lifeless.

Wandering spirits in the sun,
Laughing, playing, having fun.
Their souls are forever lost,
But not at great cost.
They seek no help to be free,
I wish I could help for they've helped me.
    Anna Carini

'Him'

Like a mother cradling her baby in her
arms, he gave me love and protected me,
  Like rain on a roof, he showered
me with hope.
  Like time ticking away on the second hand
of a clock, he gave me time to know what
I wanted.
  And like the sun, he greeted me with a
kiss of light and a hug of warmth.
  But now he's gone, and I am alone.
No one to do the things he had done.
  But as much as I miss or love
him, I did what I had to do.
  I'm sure there will be others, but none
quite as great as him.
    Angela Harpster

Ageless Christmas Eve

Timeless and tireless they tread
Around sleeping children's beds,
Guardian Angels sent from above,
From our Creator, the source of love.

Children dream of toys and other things,
That only sacrifice and love bring.
Christmas Eve, all is bliss, quiet
Sky studded with stars, an unseen sight.

Children, young and old alike
Are dreaming dreams that take flight
As the Christmas lights twinkle and gleam
All glad for the Child, sent to redeem!
    Alice Sunday Gist

Constant Reminders

The side of the highway sparkles unnaturally
as a roofless house stands as a reminder
of who owns the desert
Life amongst NonLife
The heat drives out visions of grey, hazy hills
ever in the distance, never near
rock and sand reign and only Time separates each

Bridges forever spanning over dried Earth
because water knows this heat well
and hides itself deep
Scattered cattle bones once alive,
now overthrown like litter
are constant reminders,
reminders of the dark bird circling above,
ever lower,
ever lower
    Gregory H. Stott

Our Dreams

Why is life so uncertain.
As children we dream of things.
Things that will make our lives carefree.
But life does not always work out that way.
As we get older our dreams fade.
But we must face life anyway.
And be thankful for each and every day.
I am eighty years old so I know.
So you take each day at a time,
that tomorrow will be a better day
Also be thankful to God each day,
for letting you like to see another day.
So remember your dreams.
And give thanks to God that we are
able to dream.
    Calvin C. Marcum

Miracle

The rain softly falls in the woods,
As a young heifer lies in silent pain.
Low hanging branches lovingly protect,
The miracle that no one can explain.

She rises and stands as she strains,
With no concept of task at hand.
As I watch, she lies back down,
Playing out the drama nature planned.

A baby calf is born before my eyes,
And lies on the ground, making no cry.
The new mother stands, mooing softly,
And tenderly licks her baby dry.

The calf twitches its ears and comes to life,
It opens its eyes and stands on unsteady four.
Love and warmth it knows at once,
Life is a mystery, a miracle forever more.

Dorothy A. Wallace

A Tribute To Elders

The years have been measured in various ways
As changes have darkened or brightened their days.
These elders of ours, so brave and so true
Have lived through so much, their credit is due.

Their early day battles of sickness and strife
Bear witness to those who've weathered the life.
Diphtheria, Smallpox, Polio too
Today claim the lives of barely a few.

They have seen many changes over the years;
The World Wars, Depression, their losses brought tears.
And yet, survivors regrouped and pressed on
To look for solutions, to deal with each wrong.

They teach us acceptance and patience, give love,
And offer their Faith to the Saviour above
For that which they have; with courage they cope
To preserve their power and prestige and hope.

Those of us seeking the American Dream
Should pause to consider their need for esteem.
So let us pay tribute to that generation
For the example they've set for our present-day nation!

Barbara Herlihy-Chevalier

Tender Thoughts All Made Of Glass

Lines of worry are etched in flesh
As desperate breath heaves from my breast
Cigarette burns to greyish ash
A bitter thought, an angry laugh

Lovers kiss in night's cold embrace
Hope vanishes without a trace
A lonely sigh escapes its tomb
Shades are drawn in a darkened room

Betrayal reared its gruesome head
The end of romance long since dead
Sadly I yearn for evenings past
And tender thoughts all made of glass

For betrayal can ne'er erase
That first look of love on her face
The mystic magic of that spring
When love was born and then took wing

Although abused and badly scarred
I cannot make my heart stone hard
Futures loom larger than the past
With tender thoughts all made of glass

Carl Boiteux

Untitled

I can see her from the corner of my eye
as I make my way towards the kitchen.
She sits there brooding.
Waiting.
Waiting for that one solitary mouse to set her off,
soaring, flying, reeling,
into a blood filled storm of rage and fury.
Killing all set down before her,
breaking all bounds of reality,
she finally crashes down to Earth,
and saunters silently to the refrigerator.
Through half closed eyes a look of love greets me,
and again she waits.
This time for a bowl of milk.

I have heard it said many times
that animals often mimic the behaviors
of their masters.

Carmen Cardenas

To My Daughter

Life is such a funny game I tried to do it all the same
As I was brought up years before afraid to open brand new doors

All safe and snug in my little nest I always tried to do my best
To care for my family through the years
I'd always be there to wipe their tears

Something happened along the way problems grew with each
passing day
What happened to my simple life
The easiest thing now was just being a wife

My mother instincts had a block I didn't even want to talk
About the problems that were there hoping they would disappear

Then a phone call came one day that would take you far away
A whole new world was at your door
Worthlessness you would feel no more

Out of this I would also grow I had to learn how to let go
Independence being one of your traits
Would be the key to open the gate

Faith and knowledge came to you
I could not believe how fast you grew

You opened your shell and out came flowing
Loving words and happiness showing

Dianna Couto

Known Me Forever

Your touch on my skin,
As if you have known me forever.
The bliss of your kiss,
As if your lips were made for mine.

He doesn't treat you,
The way a beautiful princess should be treated.

He doesn't or can't appreciate your touch on his skin, nor you
As a feeling person.

If I could I'd give anything to be him, except in return, I'd
believe in you, more than I believe in myself.

I'd give you the grace of nature, the key for happiness, and
the world's most priceless items,
If they were mine to give.

I'd feel, not against you, as he does,
I'd feel with you, uniting us as one.

For I'd give the stars if they were mine to give just to feel
Your touch on my skin and the bliss of your kiss, as if you
Had known me forever.

Jason Dufrechou

Nothing Stays the Same

Compare your body to that of a car
As it gets older it don't go as far,
Your step is much slower
Your eye sight is dim
They get real teary when you think of him.
Great Grandpa is gone.
I sit here alone and the memories are sweet
We heard the patter of babies small feet.
They are grown now and grand parents too
I'm glad I'm one, how about you?
Three children we had, grand children - nine,
Fourteen great grand children
I think that's just fine.
So much love in my family
No fights and no quarrels.
Boys will be boys and girls will be girls.
You can replace a car,
But what ever you do,
You can't replace me
For I'm eighty two.

Iradell Stiegelmeyer

Contemplations

Serenity shrouded her cherubic face
As she quietly rested in the twilight glow.
Her piercing gaze searched below
The present reality and sought to trace
The long road back from her former existence.
Brightening and dimming, her eyes did measure
The scope of her joys, her pain, her pleasures.
Her mind meandered with gentle persistence
As it moved from an archaic point in time
To her prevailing and ever-receding horizons.
She had dreamed the dream of thousands
Who had futilely struggled and labored to find
The essence of living; the reason for dying.
She had pursued her goals without pause or haste;
Though her effort often seemed a cluttered waste
But she found comfort and strength in trying.
Life is but crossing a river at high tide.
She could only sink or gainfully swim.
The margin of difference is very slim.
But it is by swimming that she would reach the other side.

Joe J. Flowers

My Lord's Mother

My heart becomes heavy as I think of my Lord's mother.
As she was there when they nailed him for his brother.

How she watch as they placed the crown upon head.
Also cursed, spit and beat Him until he bled.

Also feel she cried very loud to leave her son be.
Even though Jesus had instructed He came to set them free.

When they took His body down from the cross that day.
She touched His body with her hands and began to pray.

Whenever you feel down and depressed think of my Lord's mother.
As her son came to die for me and you brother.

Pick up God's word and read about all He did for you and me.
Give your life to Jesus as He gave it all to set us free.

Art McSparen

Angel Over Me

When love was young we stood still in time,
as the seasons passed you were still mine.
We discovered a love set aside from the rest,
we shared special moments that are my memories best.
Thoughts of you fill me now, your smile through autumn rain,
the summer sunsets, the winter nights, with you life was never plain.
I only knew you for awhile but how it seemed like years,
and I'll think of you every day even though you can't be here.
But I know you're happy where you are, your spirit soaring free,
I smile when I envision you watching down, my angel over me.

Courtney R. Herold

Time

Feel the minutes tick on
As the seconds roll by
Giving time, time makes changes
As days and years slip by

Rearrange finally changing
Your age 'til you're on your own
Not considering the fact that you're aging
In an absent world all alone

Time will take its toll on you
Time never gets old
Time…Time to move on
Time goes on even when you're gone…Time

Clay A. Wells

Storm

Lightning sets the distant sky aglow,
As the thunder rumbles low.
Birds fly to safety before the wind.
A storm is brewing once again.

Lightning flashes from earth to sky.
Thunder rolls through clouds up high.
Gentle rain drops begin to spatter,
Against the window panes they clatter.

Lightning splits through time and space.
Thunder roars as the earth it shakes.
Rain and hail now loudly fall,
As the wind the trees do maul.

Then at last the fury calms.
The cooling breeze a soothing balm.
Rain's fresh fragrance lingers in the air.
The storm is gone — the sky is fair.

Elizabeth Stiles Erwin

Why Tell Me

Why tell me you'll just be asleep?
As they put you in the ground so dark and deep.
Why tell me in time I will heal?
When I'm not sure how I really feel.
Why tell me the pain will go away?
Because I know deep in my heart it will always stay.
Why tell me remember the way you were?
For I have already memorized your every word.
Why tell me it was meant to be?
When I don't understand why you have to leave.
Why tell me it will be alright to cry?
Please just tell me why you had to die.

Cindy Heath

Summer Love

The waves role gently upon the sand,
as they walk into the sunset hand in hand.

The sun plays softly upon her hair,
as the footprints that led to them are no longer there.

Sea gulls whisper softly as they glide across the skies,
as he holds her hand gently and gazes into her eyes.

She wonders how their love came to be so strong,
as her heart beats with the surf as it plays its beautiful song.

Their love is like the salt air that embraces the land,
their love is eternal just like the sand.

Christina Kasubick

Ozarks Sundown

Some people view Sundown in a negative way
As though something has ended, the death of a day
The demise of the sunlight, the onset of gloom,
and the fear of the darkness then starts to loom.
But when I view these mountains as they
swallow the sun,
I smile, for I realize the opportunities to come.
The chance to behold heaven through the
beauty of the stars,
See the glory in a full moon, gaze at
Venus and wonder of Mars.
The pleasures of Sundown are countless you see,
But there's one that's especially precious to me.
Yes, the night may hold mystery that frightens a few,
but for me it's time for slumber
and sweet dreams of you.

Dean Boyer

This Feeling

The blistering cold pounded away on our hands
As we stood and watched each other stand.
Slow silvery moonglades danced on her hair
And all I could do was to stand and stare.

It took time to surface this feeling of mine
As I read in her eyes that now was the time.
She looked at me as if to say;
Should I go, or should I stay?

My knees shook gently as the trees looked on
And now my feeling was becoming quite strong.
I approached her lips and noticed her at anchor,
And when we had kissed, I encompassed her nature.

This feeling of mine ended up rather fine.
And now these sentiments emerge from my mind.
I saw a dim smirk come over her face,
And I knew it was then that I conquered this race.

Bill Holden

The Journey

So begone the dawn, when I fall from sleep.
Begone the sun, into another realm of black.
When the circle of truth points at me, with the blade first.
I wound myself so I can heal, learning it's eternal.
And I wept.
Let the world sail thru time, with me as its sail.
The wind turns my skin to dust, and my soul into life.
The colors reflect, the way of the world.
And the world reflects, race, beauty, and harmony.
I will stand tall, singing through eternity.
And I wept.

Jackson M. Jenkins III

Sweet Sixteen

From the miracle of birth
As we watch our children grow
We become so very anxious
Till they reach each new plateau

And though the years ahead seem distant
And tomorrow seems far away
Time marches on - it waits for no one
And tomorrow becomes today

We have witnessed metamorphosis
So it comes as no surprise
That as caterpillars shed their cocoons
So little girls become butterflies

And as they make this great transition
From playing dolls to beauty aids
We realize they've slipped away
Just like their childhood fades

And looking back in retrospect
It all seems like a dream
Our beautiful little daughter
Has grown up - she's sweet sixteen.

Evelyn Schneider

Trio

Our voices poured into the Autumn night sky
as wine into a crystal goblet.
Sweetly. Strongly. Smoothly,
all at once as if it were as natural as the night breeze
that lightly kissed our faces.
Three mouths harmonizing into one distinct voice,
a separate entity,
all its own.
No stage, but in our eyes
Lisa's blue trampoline became an amphitheater
just as Cinderella's pumpkin became a coach.
No spotlights, but in our eyes,
The stars cast a celestial hue that could not be
more dramatic, more perfect.
Overhanging elms
Provided acoustics that were mellowed by the
orchestra of crickets.
We sang of Grace Amazing with such conviction
that even then I knew, as I do now,
That our song, our trio would last forever.

Andrea J. Belt

Death

Swiftly yet silently you crawled,
As you snatched my feeble life away
I pray not now my youth still blooms
Like a flower in all its glory

Reflections of better years
Upon my clouded mind replays
The future yet untrodden
I shall never behold

Like a candle lit
I did shine for a moment
But now I must flicker—
and die
Weep not for me when I'm gone
Plant no weeping willows by my grave
Let it be known that the man called death
As at last snatched its prey!

Jacinth James

54

The Music

You hear a voice across the land
Asking for a helping hand
Until you reach where it began
And knowingly you start again

You work with the skill taught for years
And hope to allay the painful fears
Once again you save a life
And return someone to their wife

Until the day you've come to dread
And come upon someone dead
There was a peaceful expression on the face
And the soul that went to a better place

There are nights you try to sleep
And the morning hours do slowly creep
Your try to remember all you've lost
The lives and friends that it cost

You fight to see another day
In hopes that it would go away
You know from home you are so far
And know there's nothing as tragic as war.

Christopher J. Turner

A Father's Love

Who loves you more than me
asks the father to the child.
She turns and answers in a sigh,
but your love is different than I.

He thinks for a moment, then in despair
turns his head to hide the tears,
that twenty-one years have shared.

My love for her is different now
after all my heart's been through.
My little girl who laughed and cried
no longer seems to care.

I will have to let her go
and find her own new life.
The comforts and the pleasures she has known
have only lasted for a while.

She will build her new world
which is different from mine,
and yet, I have a feeling, all love is not lost
and time will bring me mine.

Helen Kilcooley

Rain

Big drops of water blind you as you drive.
At school or work you stay inside.
In the evening you light a fire to warm you up.
You huddle in a blanket and drink hot chocolate in a cup.
You watch the clouds cry, watching for a ray.
When the sun comes up, it brightens your day.
The weather so hot it burns you dry.
Wishing the clouds again will cry.
When it rains, you hope your school or work will flood.
You wear a coat and a hood.
With a friend, you slip and slide in the mud.
Your friend calls you a great bud.
You want to play all the time.
Finally you get to play in the sunshine.

Jeremy Carson

The Lonely Haunted House

When people look and stare
    at that lonely haunted house
Some people say it reminds them
    of the homeless on the street.
So lonely and with no place to go.

The cracked and peeling paint is like
    Their clothes so tattered and old
Their worn out shoes like missing stairs
The tall dry grass and weeds
    Their hair so long and unkempt
Their eyes are the vacant windows
    Seen from outside the house
The low and hollow wind that blows
    Through this lonely haunted house
Makes it as cold as the homeless are
    Each night upon the ground

If only the homeless had
    This lonely house to love,
They each would be warm and well cared for.
    And have a place to go.

Brian Bennett

A Still, Small Voice

I stood with open arms towards the sky
Attempting to conquer the mystery
Held in all that life 'was' and 'is', and why
I can never discover what 'will be'.
Then, amidst the chattering of the rain,
The thunder replied in its bursting voice,
"You ask me of this time and time again,
And always I answer, 'you have no choice!'"
Soon after the sky sent its flashing wrath
To kill my wonder and collapse my will,
I heard, through the storming, a child laugh
As he swiftly ordered all to be still
    And whispered, "strive to overcome the fire,
    And you will someday have what you desire."

Eli Moore

Meditation

Your mind and your body are lovers.
Attracted first by the mere fact of proximity,
they now want to understand each other, know each other,
    be friends, be one.

If you trust or respect one more than the other now,
let that one lead its partner to a quiet place,
where they may contemplate each other,
    undisturbed and unashamed.

Be not discouraged if learning to love is slow;
    it may take a lifetime,
    but you have a lifetime to accomplish it.
And is there another task of equal consequence?

When at last the radiant day comes
    that the pair are no longer afraid of their nakedness,
    no longer boastful of their own uniqueness -
the world will burst into light and song for their wedding.

You will know a joy that is peace and a peace that is joy.
You will remember this day as the beginning of your life;
and since that which is transient has already passed away,
    that which remains can never die.

Eunice Ratnaike

Attain The Mark

Originally, God's creation of mankind was to bring out our best
    attributes.
But, because of our many infirmities, often the best qualities are
    hidden.
So, keep striving for improvement in your life. No matter what
your situation is, don't give up!

Reject the poor substitutes in life, you can make the right decisions,
thereby, the most distinctive qualities will prevail. So, keep
    striving!

Whatever comes your way, ask God for help, he wants to strengthen you
to perform your best, for he makes us more than conquerors in all
things, because he wants us to excel in our efforts. So, strive for
higher heights.

Audrey Cooper

Reality

Take me away,
away from all the pain, all the shame
Images of everybody trying to be the same
Be different they say
but, don't you realize there's no way?
because your way is everybody else's way
block prints of images passing me in the hallway.
You probably don't like this,
everybody struggling for difference
by alikeness
Everyday I see the same,
People with masks hiding their pain,
trying to be someone they're not,
under fake clothing, fake personality
no one lives in the reality
The reality is pain.
The pain is the same.
Welcome to reality.

Dacia Graham

Underwater People...

Held below in solitude,
Away from feeling, away from truth.
They try to hide the feelings,
But they must depend on,
The solvent of life,
To live this underwater life,
Of concealment and pain.
They must try to communicate,
To speak the language of the heart and of the soul,
Because when the sun rises,
Their life vaporizes,
Into a cycle that will forever trap,
Their thoughts.
So don't be afraid of your mind,
But of what you wish you could have said,
To forever have peace of mind,
And not be stuck below the winter glass,
In the underwaterd world of the underwater people.

Bryan T. Walsh

Forbidden Love

In March of 86, we stumbled into something beautiful
Both timid and naive we approached cautiously
Our minds were searching for the meaning
But the feeling in our hearts was overpowering
Anxiously wrestling with the reality of breaking society norms
Spending many a night holding each other in confusion
Consciously thought of a lasting love overshadowed our fears
Awakened with that sentiment our souls united

Carla Campanella

The Willow And The Rose

"Ah, but alas a rose is a rose is a rose."
Babylon, oh Babylon weep no
more for me for thou hast planted the
Willow along the riverbanks for everyone to see;
In moist fertile soil I, the Willow, spread
roots outward to protect the land from eroding floods of water;
Long slender branches bending low and gently swaying in the wind;
Flexible twigs selected for basketry and
alas, catkins to decorate the home do I, the Willow, give;
And when there is a desire to create an object for use
I, the Willow, do offer lumber; My flowers bear the sweet liquid
of nectar, drank by the gods and gathered by the bees
for honey so I, the Willow, might feed you;
I, the Willow, as a hybrid have been selected to adorn riverbanks
and lakes; to provide shade and tranquility through a quiet grace;
Though I may appear to be a self-indulgent tree, I am true to the
purpose of my cultivation protection, beauty, food and peace;
Know me, the Willow, by my various names
Nigra (black), Babylonica (weeping), or
American (pussy).

Cheryl A. Cantley

The Final Waltz

Her body laying motionless on the bed
barely breathing,
as lifeless as a fine China doll,
but when he came a spark returned.

She rose to meet his eyes,
their black endless pits.
He took her in his arms and like
two young lovers their waltz began.
Around the room they danced as if without a care.
He pulled her ever so close to him, the waltz stopped.

She smiled at him while her china shell
smashed into tiny pieces on the floor.
They rose up together, she and death.
She was free now,
for she had danced the final waltz.

Billie Lash

Psalm 1994

Why, God, have you allowed me to
be afflicted for searching for love?
Then why the face of Christ
on the face of the one I have found?

Why have you burdened me with the desire of Moses
and allowed me the strength of a moth
if Exodus is to be my calling?

If only one step is to be mine,
let me see some victory,
and take me at the moment of my shining
so that eternal life will be mine among my kind
and I can inspire another Moses to demand,
"LET MY PEOPLE GO".

Gene L. Woodruff-Rohrer

Reflections On Adolescence

This path I travel I have chosen
Blind to distant ends.
These hands are bloody from the points of black roses
Touched along the way.

These eyes are pierced by the rays
Of a temporary sun.
Yet, desolate and torn this body forward moves
Searching for the peace lost eternally in the mist.

Janice L. Bernhard

Wellness-The Miracle Of Love

It's nice to be healthy and free
Be cheerful and make the heart glad
A merry spirit drives away
The doubts and fears that make us sad,
And you, my dear, will always be
A miracle of dreams come true
You've weaved within my heart a song,
A song of love and care for you.

You see, I've watched you touch the chords
That bindeth the hearts together
And puts within the heart a song
Regardless of the weather.
Please say a prayer for me tonight
Pray, set this fettered spirit free
To wander o'er this universe,
But always be quiet near to thee.

Charles A. Spurlock

Transplant

The family is bleeding, they know their son will not
be coming home.
"The organs are ripe for harvesting, new life come from senseless
death", the doctor pushes.....
Primitive emotions ignite, fueled by a need to continue
intactness, to protect and preserve what is loved and whole.

"Beyond these walls of private grief your son is linked
to immortality as a donor", the doctor continues...
Too soon to discuss philosophy, charity, altruism they think
this beloved body is still warm, still theirs, miracles
happen — perhaps he will go on to another wold?

"Time is all we have and we are running out", states the
doctor walking away in sympathetic frustration...

"Wait Doctor, take our boy", they scream, "but be gentle"...

Amy Jubelirer

Beautiful Day

I open my window and I look outside, it's such a
beautiful day!
There's so much to see as I look at the scenery.
I look up at the pretty blue sky and I watch as the
birds fly by.
I watch as the leaves on those great big trees sway back
and forth in the gentle breeze.
I can see the pretty flowers, all red, purple, and white,
They sure do make a pretty sight.
I even watch and I listen, as the children laugh and play,
They are so very happy, oh, what a beautiful day!
I am so thankful for all that I see, for my God up above
is the one who created this beautiful scene.

Georgetta von Dolln

Trees

They struggle all winter to survive
Being tortured by the cold
Just surviving is hard
In spring they begin to get more life
Hands grow on their many arms
To catch water as it falls
For it is thirsty
Summer is when they have the most life
Being friends to many children playing in them
And a friend to an occasional dog
Fall is the prettiest point in their life
Even though they're withering away
All of their hands fall off
Leaving it
Barren
They begin struggling all over again

Darron Collings

"Within"

Soft is the silk,
Beautiful the body; I wonder,
Could the soul be as fine as the skin?

Be grateful of beauty,
For the stupid mock it;
Only the wise see
What is truly within.

How often I've wished for a girl so pure
That her heart reaches out
And sees within.

How corrupt we are, to see only the out,
When all that we need,
Lies truly within.

Oh! how I was blind, to see only the top;
How stupid of me, to not see within.

How ignorant I was, to not see the truth
How could I not see people within.

My story is told, that much is true;
But look, look down,
And see within you.

Fred Maidment

Suzanne's Allusion

Mother earth and earthly mother
Beauty acquiesced in spirit, finds mirror in another
Heavenly body and bodily heaven

Rotund mountains ascend to supple peaks
Far below, bisected by a valley deep
Within, wellsprings formed by prescience
Without shall flow the nectar of essence

To the north, a granite promontory
Bold in determination, so soft in exhilaration
Atop, above, lies a fissure deep
Ruptured in rapture, taunt in triumph
Fuming with bated breath of earthly pain

To the south lies, a wily, grassy, fertile plain
A fruited isthmus astride a parturient land
Wherein the moon's cycle of unerring grace
A seed was laid by the light of providence's face

Of a body burdened, of muscles torn
Life burst forth, A child is born!

Christopher Steven Dickey

Watching Destiny

Impressions stark and real
Beckoning
Like ever-spinning memories
With the bridging force of steel,
Whether up touching-close or far,
Distant as the first Beginning
Or the moon or even a star.

From a Source vivid and deep
The moon and sky and flowers,
Impressions that lively leap
With sharing forms of will;
Images shaping images
Urging discoveries to their fill.

Ages old, the moon, yet never again the same;
Once so far, unreachable
Then the curators came
As we watched with electric eyes
Trying to grasp reality's game
And hold its fleeting moments
While seeing an image share its fame.

Carl Joseph Davey

Not So Long Ago

It's true all men when they grow up
Become what they always wanted most
But somehow in the struggle they realized
It's not just a title to wear, not just a respect to share
It's a being not often compared
And then who really knows what's right
It's sad to think that all our live's
We plot and plan for what we've wanted
We believe it's all there really is
Until we think about dying
Death hasn't anything to do with it
Yet still we fear and we stop trying
Whatever happened to what we were not so long ago
In the hearts of all men there is the child
The child who use to run wild
Without a seeming single care
But then we know that's just a lie
Every child is a different soul
And inspiration comes from what we're shown
In the end it's how we live that keeps the child smiling.

Burt K. Arthur

Sound Of An Unsound World

Birds' wings fluttering as they fly,
Bees buzzing,
Dogs panting and showing affection,
A slight breeze...
Leaves rustling,
Winds blowing,
A hum at a distance...
Drizzling rain pitter - pattering on the roof.
A melodious tune,
Soft shoes on the wet grass,
Dogs bark
Words...
Dogs growl
Louder words
Sounds of stuff being thrown around
A scream...
A shriek...
More screams
A rifle shot!
Dead Silence
Police Sirens...
Running feet against the cement ground
Screeching cars
Babies cry, children die

Anjali G. Trasy

Autumn In Vermont

The colors are beautiful, that they are,
Bright reds, oranges and purples you see from afar.
The mountainsides glow when the sun rises for the day
And prettier than a picture that will ever come your way.
The crisp in the air, doesn't seem so bad,
When your eyes set on such a memorizing day,
In which you think you've never had.
The smell is so very fresh and clean
Take it all in, it's very quick it seems.
The wind will soon blow these beautiful trees,
And snow will come for a long time to see.
Fill your heart and feel free of burdens and taunts,
This is what you call the best,
Autumn in Vermont.

Denise Siple-Derouchie

Court Jester

Jingle, jingle, jingle, jingle ....

That is the sound that my footsteps make
Before I walk into my fate.
"Ahh...good evening King, Queen, Lords and Ladies."
"Are you ready to be entertained?"
There is laughter already - but I have yet to start.

What are they laughing at?
Could it be my clothes? I am only wearing bright checkered
Colors from head to toe, with bells on my hat and toes.

As long as the King, Queen, Lords and Ladies are laughing,
My fate shall be great!
I will not be sent to the tower of punishment, nor beheaded!

Jingle, jingle, jingle, jingle....

That's what you hear when I dance around.
My job is to entertain all!

Now 'tis time to bid all good-bye...
With my checkered clothes from head to toe
and bells from hat to toes....

Good-bye...

Jingle, jingle, jingle, jingle....

Jamie Pavlakis

Beyond The Dawn

Beyond the dawn is the brightest light
  Before the dawn is the infamous dark
All the dreamer's dreams are in the night
  Dreams of a dawn born in the heart

Possessed by the dawn are the wishes of life
  Captured by the dawn is the dreamer's soul
All the dreamer's hopes erase the anxiety and strife
  As the radiance of dawn seizes the night's control

Resurrected light embodies all that will repeat
  Overwhelming light illuminates the dreamer's plan
All that once was unfulfilled is complete
  The sacred dawn breathes life into the man

Beyond the night rests what must remain
  Before the night is anticipated what's soon to be gone
Dreams are nurtured for what is to gain
  And so the dreamer's life is lived beyond the dawn

Jay Lutz

Autumn

Autumn is the time of year when the leaves
begin to fall.
The leaves fall like a blanket and seem
to cover all.
After the leaves have fallen, the trees all look
so bare, they seem so sad and mournful
without their summer hair.
When the leaves all change color, they're truly
a sight to see,
Red, gold and brown as pretty as can be,
As the days go on and the weather grows
colder, the Old North Wind blows cover our
shoulder.
Away the leaves blow in the wind and rain.
No more to be seem by us, 'til Autumn
comes again.

Gloria Capobianco

Big Red Mountain

Big red mountain, whoa high
Big red mountain, touch the sky
Soaring spirit, eagles glide, far below the buffalo dies

River strong, torrent wide, Mother earth, heaven high
Laughing spirit, freedom cry, touch the earth, touch the sky

Virgin forest, silver stream, golden meadow all agleam
Big red mountain whoa high, big red mountain do not cry

Crack the ground, crash the spear, start of rage, start of fear
Broken carcass on the valley floor, the buffalo dies, the eagles soar

Of what was then, is not now
Buffalo once was, now the plow
Agony reigned far and wide, Indian blood Indians died

Silence waits on the valley floor, charge of calvary is no more
Tribes and warriors of yesterday
Have disappeared and lost their way

Why this carnage had to be, I must admit perplexes me
Whoa mountain, mountain high
Whoa mountain, tell me why
O big red mountain do not cry
Gene Evers

Pray, What Is It?

Life is the breath,
Birth and death,
And it's gone.

Something stronger (pray, what is it?)
Lays the harrow to the green
I've planted. Most unwanted visit, this!

I'm doubtless seen
By some, by those who near me dwell
And doubt the worth of my convictions most,

As one, a rather thorny, toilsome host
To be at this offended.
Though I'm not!

Indeed, I find my arms extended
To this guest, the ghost,
Who digs the earth I deem the best.
Jeffrey Kemper

Conversation With The Beast

"Daddy, you've poured salt in the wound…" "Why?"

The question is asked tonelessly.
Bland, flat curiosity
tastelessness bred from monotony.

"You just want to give me a hug?" "Promise?"

Hope is felt, fleeting and brilliant.
the illusion magnificent
but the child halts, hesitant.

"Do you really promise this time?" "Really?"

Feet move in patterned drudgery.
propelled towards catastrophe
mind slips to altered reality.

Silence, stillness, as the beast comes. Once More.

Throat swallows thick and sticky.
gasp for breath, fleeing death
gathering shreds of sanity.

"Daddy, you've salt in the wound."
J. Prescott

Land Of The Indians

From the land of the Redman
Blows the wind of change
Where clean and peaceful rivers once ran
Has now become the white man's range

Hostility between tribes
A fight for their land
That ended in bribes
That took freedom out of their hands

All of the children's dreams
Destroyed by writing later to be defied
Resulting with a mother's scream
As their children commit suicide

The Indian Spirit
Is much weaker today
In this world they don't seem to fit
And they wish not to stay

Just think if we'd left them alone
Mother Nature might still be strong
But we've ripped at her flesh until she's almost bone
And now she no longer sings her beautiful song
Douglas Lee Gilliland

'The Naivete Of Fate'

All journeys end here. They gather
Bound stone-weighted puppies in the murk of the cold quarry water.

Like the air we can keep no secrets.
We eavesdrop at the window sills and elbows of the world.
We spy and gossip and slander and lie.
The scapegoats have no faces, we do not care.
We just want their blood, their honor. We don't play fair.

Fate grows frustrated with us.
She tries so hard; compulsively optimistic and naive,
Servant to her screaming, gluttonous children.
Her nerves are tight as hairs, they snap and shred, curl inward,
Electric ends hissing and burning.

Eden has shed its soft white skin,
Revealed itself anew with the scaly face of Purgatory.
The trees, mountains and houses steam, swampy lumps and mounds.

The Garden is stagnant with apathy.
It runs wild with the weeds and roaches.

The sun sets far to the South. It will not rise again.
The day retreats,
As misplaced as the fallen angels of the 'perfect' Garden.
Hillary A. Snodgrass

Daylight

The sun comes up over tiers of hills
Bringing light to life below where
Water calls out its whispering message
To ears that waken to this soft humming voice
The birds sing and take flight
For their daily collection of sweet nectar from
Flowers and berries that hide within the
Colorful array of rolling fields
An infant boy cries out for the arms of his mother
Reminding her of the needs of her child
While a little girl begins to play on her own
Until hunger scratches at her belly
Ready now to request nourishment she calls out
To mother who lays quietly
Trying to catch a few last moments of rest before day.
Beth Vacovec

Owed To A Lady

Cast under a sapphire spell, the night
Bows
To her vulgar neon majesty
While Lady Luck
Primps
In the Desert.

Jacks double down
Sipping
Cool drinks as coins rock 'n roll
Over conversations.

Her perfume draws poker-faced pit bosses
A royal flush as
Hearts
Surrender, straight up
On green felt tables.

Like the caged cash,
She comes and goes
While lovers'
Parlay
Numbered kisses on the pass line.

Deborah Murray Malafronte

The Awakening

The alarm clock goes off. Sounding the charge of the light
brigade as my limbs are summon to the call of revere. My mind,
disoriented between the night and day, challenges my wits to
comprehend the stillness of the dawn. In my wakeful slumber
I reflect for a moment. But soon the ecstasy of walking along
a sandy beach on the shores of nowhere, becomes a distant memory
fleeing from my dreamscape. To follow behind the sun, as they
creep past night's shadowy shroud of darkness.

Slowly my limbs comes together in unison, as they
collectively plot against the one part of me that refuses to
acknowledge the new day. My mind, the head collaborator to
this elaborate scheme, tells my arms and hand to do the
unthinkable. Click! On comes the lights, as my eyes are shocked
to a rude awakening. My life hangs for a split second between
the past and present, as time tares away at my existence.
Disrobing me of my tranquil thoughts and clothing me in the
reality of life's daily struggle to... survive another work day.

Everett R. Hubbard

The Sun, Our Son

The sun, it shines in your eyes
Bright and luminescent
The sun shines in you
Golden light through your veins
The sun shines around you
A golden aura.

Liquid energy in your hands and feet
Lighting up the night
Emanating a myriad patterns of colors and hues
A complex tapestry of Joy
Always bright, always light
Our son.

Jer Zenieris

Passage Of Time

The dimensions of time have yet to be understood.
Between the old and young, bad or good.
Each click of the clock represents another second passed away,
This space of time is the first and only one today.
The clock ticks away minute by minute,
The future is approaching quick who knows what lies in it.
How precious has you time been spent,
While the proud hour hand makes its descent.

Janet Heifner

"Linger"

Did you ever linger, in morning's light, to see the world start
  brightening
Don't move a finger, but just linger, as a new day is lightening
Did you ever view the sunrise, the birds awake and singing
What startles you, with surprise, a distant churchbell ringing

It is the morning dew, so moist, that causes grass to glisten
A thought brand new, to hoist, and echoes as you listen
And quietly awake the morn, with all things back in place
Which flower to take, the swan, gentle ripples one can trace

Did you ever laugh so alone, as the sun came o'er the hill
Day's second half, the tone, it will never be so still
Did you ever think each sound, could be held in harmony
Your eyes would blink, heart pound, oh what life appears to be

If you could gather up soft light, and spread it through the day
Or maybe rather, with delight, near cliffs with ocean's spray
Midday at full race, confusion, mornings light once lost is gone
Start with slow pace, infusion, yes the blessings of each morn

So begin the day, yearning, to hear those soundings anew
Gather each ray, start learning, to become a special you
Remove the strength, the notes, set the table with morning's gift
And then at length, it floats, and you will guide its drift

David A. Walsh

Autumn Fair

It is autumn.
Brightly colored leaves are falling.
Time to go to the fair.
Time to see the huge, round, yellow pumpkins.
Time to look at the big, red, shiny tomatoes.
The tasselled corn is ready to eat.
The long green beans are piled high.
The honey from the bumblebees tastes like wild-flowers.
It is delicious.
People jostle one another as they look.
They gawk and gaze at the prize vegetables around them.
How did the judges ever give that one first prize, one mutters
The children start to cry.
They are hot and tired,
Time to go home.
Soon the cold, bitter winter will be here.
No crops are growing.
No one to share their former abundance with.
Will Spring ever return?
Will frozen hearts ever thaw?

Dorothy Zinan

Words Of Dust

Destiny had time to sell, destiny had cast its spell,
bringing about a reasoning fate not to reason being fair.
No knight in shining armor, no night in safety's harbor, merely
a soul in search of the words, words worthy to share.

In bright daylight reasoning logic apart, in quiet of the night
listening only to the heart.

It's a road seemed lonely yet a road deemed only, by a fate
which holds my only peace of mind.
Times I wondered, wonders I pondered, for the true which heals
ailing for a soul's kind.

With words that wedge to demand their heeding or words with
an edge that leave a heart bleeding.

They shall come one day, they shall come and say, words of
ashes to ashes and dust to dust.
I only hope time shows, the only road fate chose, was to write
the words which were felt a must.

Chris Waggoner

Lion's Whelp

How can we be humble, man, when structures
Built by our hands touch the clouds, when it's our

Crafts we watch trailing lights like stars of night
Within the sky? Yet in my arms a child

Makes me laugh at our accomplishments. We
Men can tamper with nature, yet can we

Create life? No, we can only end it.
We men, so mighty in war, why not quit

Fooling ourselves? Even my act of love
Mocks war in its essence, when I give

My turgid sword its way, impaling my
Wife. She creates life, not death, as do high

And mighty men of war. All man's wisdom
Will not cause a seed to grow. Yet we've come

To where we can alter that seed. Maybe
From this human seed we can breed the team

Of men who will lead us away from war,
Who with craft and guile can guide our leaders'

Thoughts heavenward, so we can then reside
As peaceful men, children of God's own pride.

Gary M. Baugher

The Inevitable

Put in the ground, about six feet deep
Buried under a heavy heap
Someday, you too will be in this sad plight
You cannot stop it, try though you might
Rotting there in that enclosed box
Nothing around but dirt and rocks
The stone above bears the title
Of one deprived of that so vital
They say to exercise,
Don't drink or smoke
For otherwise, you too will croak
But what difference does it make
We all go sometime
And so this is the end of this morbid rhyme

Charles Bruce

The House Of Mirrors

Clear blue eyes that reflect an innocence
But a wounded soldier he is.
No one understands
Alone in the house of mirrors
Running to what seems to be an opening
Only to be cut off
Twisting and turning
Catching a flash of his unattainable
The one he can't reach
The cruel whip that wounds him again and again
Tears run freely down those soft, pale cheeks
Without a single shoulder to cry on
Another mirror.
He sees a young old man
Scarred burned and wounded
Alone in the house of mirrors
With the walls closing in.

Heather Hummel

Untitled

I saw him one day
But all I did was glance and walk away
I thought about him every chance
Seeing him put me in a trance
In the halls he'd say Hi
When he walked by
But now things have changed
Every since she came you've seemed strange
She played with your mind
But you can't seem to find
Any reason she did wrong
I hope you don't think I'm to strong
Because inside I'm falling apart
I wish I could start
feeling better
But every time I start feeling better
All I hear is her name
I wish everything could go back and be the same
Back to when I saw you one day
But all I did was glance and walk away

Christine Anderson

No Scrutiny for Harmony

Winter comes with its icy mane
But all the while it stays the same
If spring could only after hope
I'd gladly stay and force a cope
The agony, the tragedy...no scrutiny for harmony

Nations collide in belligerent wars
While the unborn child looks from the stars
They fight and toil for grains of sand
As the politicians for the voting hand
The rivalry, the brutality...no scrutiny for harmony

One day the world will stop
And all the just will rise atop
While the anguished seek but fall awry
As to their question there's one reply:
The insanity, the demagoguery...it's much too late for harmony.

Darnell Vaughn Michaels

"Love Me For The Last Time"

I know this might sound out of place for a lady.
But every woman likes to be loved,
it will be here today and gone tomorrow.
So that is why I am saying out loud "Love me for the last time"
take me in your arms and set off my love alarm
and hold my body close to yours
and put your hands in mines.
Hold me like you will never let me go.
And just "Love me for the last time."
Talk to me nice and sweet, and
place your lips on mines and don't
forget this is for the "Last time"
run your hands though my hair and don't let
me go if tears start to fall from my
eyes wipe them with a tender kiss, and
keep "Loving me for the last time."
And when all of that is over, we will never say Good-bye.
But hold each other very tight and let the tears fall
from my eyes. Because all that will be said is thanks for
"Loving me for the last time."

I'Yanda Harris Fransaw

Time Is Treasure

Time is short, so is this poem
But God is leading me on
To say what I feel within my heart
So take a look everywhere, do your part.

Help someone while enjoying your treasure
God is the one who really will measure
And add up for the final sum
So enjoy all to the fullest under
God's beautiful sun.

Janie R. Harris

Wishes

I wish I was a bird flying in the air.
But I'm afraid of heights, I wish I was a bear.

I prayed I was a fox playing in the forest.
But I'm the latest fashion, I wish I was a tourist.

I thought I was a fish swimming in the sea.
But I can't swim at all, I wish I was a bee.

I could be a dog in someone's house.
But I'm not housebroke, I'd rather be a mouse.

I'd love to be a horse running down a road.
But I don't want no one on my back, I'd like to be a toad.

I wish I was a monkey hanging by my tail.
But I can't stand bananas, I'd rather be a snail.

I could always be an elephant, but I can't remember why.
There way too fat anyhow I'd like to be a fly.

I wished I was human but, my wishes were no more.
Isn't just like people I'm stuck being a bore.

Daniel Bradley Harris

Cross Of Gold

We ask to carry a cross of gold,
But instead we get one of wood.
Why is it so difficult,
When we do the things that we should.

My children you have come so far,
Your burdens are so heavy.
But really in the scheme of it all
Your burdens can be so petty.

And did you ever stop and think at all,
And pay attention to the fact,
That I will help you carry your cross,
But first you have to ask.

And then when your life is over,
And your life's story has been told,
The many times I've helped you carry it,
Will turn your wood cross into gold.

Carrie L. Langton

At Fifty - An Answer

In my youth some thought me eager, hot and undertaking,
But others slack and small,
While my youth was passing with each waking day,
I scorned at time and reached the sky.

Now I shake my head and all my dreams,
Which fierce youth defended, recede with the setting sun.
And while leaves fade about me like summer friends,
With age comforts grow, but I no longer reach the sky.

The cool winter wind goes its way, and I grow pursy and slow,
I now appreciate each passing cloud which lives and dies,
In that reflection of tears, I ask - tell me why?
Since He who knows the rest, knows more than I.

Arthur J. Gajarsa

Nature's Secrets

I wanted to see the dew fall
But it silently eluded me.
Then I though to catch old Jack Frost,
Still this I couldn't see.

The wind blew strong upon my face
And the air became quite nifty.
But when I reached to take a hold
I found my hands were empty.

The moon came up, and it really seemed—-
to me it was a winking.
Then the heavens filled with thousands of stars
And they all started blinking.

So, I thought I'd rise at dawn
And catch a beam from the sun.
Again I came up empty
For I found it couldn't be done.

Who am I but a foolish one,
That I should even dare,
All of Nature's secrets are here for me
Because my God does care.

Bobbi Brantley

College

Sometimes a friend is just a phone call away,
But it's different than seeing her every day.
I'm used to always seeing that happy smile,
Not her faint voice after I dial.
We may fill each other in on the latest gossip without a fee,
Guys, friends, problems whatever it may be.
But, again and again we remind ourselves of the past,
When we were together night and day till our last.
The last day we never thought would arrive,
When we would say our goodbyes and thanks and start new lives.
It's only been a few weeks since then,
I miss you so much I count the days down by ten.
Don't forget I'm always a phone call, letter or thought away,
I know it's long distance but I'm just across the bay.
A friend for life you have made.
This friendship I feel will never fade.
College may separate two friends apart,
But you will always have a place in my heart.

Jacalyn Tapper

"Taken To Task"

To believe should be quite simple for the Bible has shown me the way.
But my faith sometimes sags as I toil day by day.

Could God have planned my doubts when he laid out my life?
Is it part of his work to save me from this world of guilt and strife?

But God if you are listening as I know you have from the start.
You can help me along life's path by first giving me a clean heart.

I often sit and wonder what God has planned for me.
Just what path he wishes me to take and what sights along it
    I will see.

Does God wish for me to live each day on this earth?
Struggling and scraping to survive from the very day of birth

Can God have planned to instruct me thru trials and sore tribulations?
To give my life a meaning with his spiritual motivation.

Does God know that I love him and want to obey his laws?
That often by Satan I am tempted and in my climb to glory I pause

Will God answer my questions in the spirit that they are asked?
Or in my insolence I'll be punished and God will take me to task

Jack L. Benson

Word Pictures

I have always wanted to draw,
   But my hands won't go the way they're supposed to.
I have always wanted to dance,
   But my wheelchair holds me back.
So I write word-pictures
   On things I only dream about.
I write of fairies
   Dancing through fields of willowherb,
Of icy sheaths bending
   The branches of the alders,
Of what it feels like to run
   Through meadows of golden sunset.
My words are shining flowers
   In the tenebrous confines of my world.
I have always wanted to write a famous book -
   Someday I will
     Erin Lamm

The Most Beautiful Of All

God has created many beautiful things
but none as beautiful as you
You are more beautiful than a moonlit night
You are more beautiful than the sun shining through clouds
You are the most beautiful of all God's creations

When God created earth, it was beautiful
When God created day and night, they were beautiful
When God created man, man was beautiful
When God created women, he created something spectacular
And when you were created, He really out did himself.
   James D. Williams

Good Friday - April 1, 1994

You might say an "April Fool" He was;
But not so, for He is a loving Saviour.
Yes, He and mighty God,
Before the foundation of the world
Began, They figured out this plan;
And He didn't renege, He saw it through,
And He did us a favor.
He bought us back; He purchased our souls.
(But still we must give them to Him.)
He took those stripes that we might be healed,
He took those cruelties that we might savor
Peace — the peace of God, the Father, within.
He was crucified—He died.
Then He was raised up—resurrected.
Then He ascended into heaven,
and there He sat down
At the right hand of God, the Father,
With the promise of the Holy spirit
Forever!!
   Dorothy Chaffee

Untitled

I have many beautiful memories of the life I shared with you
But now you've gone and left me and I don't know what to do
Memories are treasured but they leave me blue
Why can't I meet someone even half as nice as you?

It's been some time since you've been gone
But the void won't go away
No one to laugh with and be happy and gay
Each day is an interminably long, lonesome day

Since you have gone the days are so lonely
I miss you so much my one and only
Girls can't go out like the fellows can and do
But stay at home alone just crying, crying just for you.
   Irene Dodds

Bittersweet

Ah, life thou art sweet
   But sweet's mere pain!
For awhile we are happy—
   Then grieved again!

How dearly we pay tomorrow
   For a smile we bear today,
There's naught we get in all the world
   That doesn't demand its pay.
Each black night has its satisfying day,
   Each day is followed by night -
Just as we grope o'er our sorrows and woes
   Before we can see the light!

Yes, Life's a game of Bittersweet,
   Of compensation dear,
But there's consolation in the thought
   We're paid for every tear!
   Helen Marquez

Blind

I'm different from others
But then I'm the same
Because I'm in darkness
No color or light
Some people retreat or run away in fright
I wear dark sunglasses
Even when the sun's not out
I have a dog named Honey
Who helps me all about
I use a special stick
So that I know what is where
I use my ears to hear
Because I can't see what is there
Just because I'm blind
Doesn't mean I'm a freak
I can still walk, read, laugh and speak
I am different from others
But really I'm not.
   Crystal-Marie Apilado

Untitled

Once upon a time — I could shine
But they took my sun from me
The life of yesterday past has
fared away with the only sunset I know
And in my darkest hour I'll remember what
you've done for me. It's time,
to go alone.
Now in confusion I'll jump into
Tomorrow... not knowing — not knowing
Happy days with depressing sunsets —
Saying good-bye
to a life I've never lived...
   Angelo Emile Gastelum

Misnomer?

I found a tiger lily fragile and fair,
By a sparkling stream growing regal and rare,
She reigned over all flowers in queenly grace,
With waxen leaves and lovely exotic face.

Petals curved delicately dancing away,
In the gentle breeze of a warm summer day,
Her shiny black beauty spots set her aglow,
Should not "leopard lily" be more apropos?
   Dorothy Durkee

Vietnam

No reason for war,
But we fought.
We were only boys,
Thought ourselves heroes,
And it could be said we were.
Why were we fighting,
Men died and we lost,
Reasons unknown.
We went on,
Kept fighting
Until killed.
To be taken home in a box,
Devoid of color.
Mourned over
For losing, but fighting for our country,
Showing our identity,
The boy heroes,
We had been there,
We knew,
But now what could we tell.

Courtney Brannon

Untitled

I could poor my hart unto you.
But what good would that do?
I could show you all my dreams
and wish yours come true.
I could share my thoughts of loving moments
and pray yours are all the same.
Although for some odd reason
I concealed my heart out of shame.
I have hidden many feelings
many moments I'd love to share.
Just to save me from embarrassment.
Heartbreak, my greatest fear.
My hart just would not permit it
So instead I grew weak.
Paralyzed from the heart up!
Just too afraid to speak.
Why couldn't I tell you before?
What was it that made it so tough?
For in your eyes I gaze
And in a moment I'd fall in love.

Jennifer Castro

A Devil's Ride

A long time ago, a poor sinner spared
  by the devil's deals, his thoughts were impaired
Blinded by insanity filled with the rage of hell
  a trade was made—nothing but a soul to sell
He was a crazy mother f**ker shown by the life he led
  with the things he'd done he should have been dead
But he kept on going doing all that he pleased
  with a tissue on hand in case the devil sneezed
He lived his life like a wild ride
  the devil over his shoulder, his ol' lady by this side
He was used and abused and then thrown in jail
  a murder in the night there would be no bail
His time had come, he knew it was true
  took a blade to his wrist and cut it clean through
Now he lives in hell but it ain't what he thought
  a trap had been made and he had been caught
So if you come by a man, calls himself Lucifer
  don't stall around and give your thoughts time to stir
Just get on your feet and run like mad
  cuz when the devil deals, you'll get cut bad.

Amanda Shelton

Hope

Look at the blooming frangipani...
Calm down your heart, just sit and listen...
The drums are talking, fire flies glisten,
Tomorrow will again be sunny...

  Beacons of flame-trees, shy and hazy
  On malachite of endless prairie
  Will talk to you like old, good fairy
  How life is fragile, but amazing...

Flickering skies immerse in glare,
Far away lightenings fade like worries...
Listen to drums and their stories;
We must reach further than we dare...

  Don't hush cicadas stubborn chatter;
  It drains away all pain and sorrow...
  Look at the skies - how they are stunning!

Forget the worries... they don't matter,
You'll see ... Just wait, wait till tomorrow...
And smell your branch of frangipani...

John Gallar

Ellis Island

From the boat...not a ship...
came the mundane clothed blur
of questioning, mind-quivering,
moving, mirroring, mass of peoples.

These processing...not welcoming...
foreign speaking Americans — would they
let them in, or send them back...
Back on the boat, another sea-sickening voyage?

Some couldn't...no, they didn't
pass the tests of health requirements.
Some did...their half-smile was overlaid
with an anxious anticipation of the unknown.

Families all...courageous adventurers
knit together in a common trial's bond,
lined the walls and lined the lines
to be passed through — Destiny's Doors.

These families were ours!
Ones and two's and four's and mores,
now dotting the land...our ancestors...who
made this country — "The home of the brave!"

Harriet Trehus Kvingedal

A Worthy Man

Can you go through life without harmin' another soul
Can you reach that worthy goal
Can you live your life a benefit to man
If you try real hard I know you probably can

Or will you let society beat you down
And end up under the ground
Or behind steel bars in a prison cell
With nothin' but sad tales to tell

Can you go through life without harmin' another soul
Or will you miss that worthy goal
Will you leave your talents buried in the sand
Or will you prove yourself a worthy man

Will you leave your talents buried in the sand
Or will you prove yourself a worthy man
Oh will you prove yourself a worthy man

Jeff Botzko

What Shall They Say

Animals, so quiet and graceful
Cannibals, is the thinking their taste
blood is the gruesome death that
this man has no fear, do the animals have no friend?
What shall they say?
What shall they say?

But, they do have a friend and she is I,
why must we scour it's like taking the petals from
a flower, and if they could confer I will always wonder,
What I shall they say?
What shall they say?

How could man be so cold & kill an animal to extinction
this is beyond my distinction please tell me.
What shall they say?
What shall they say?

Animals have a heart with this I will never part
they have a soul that you should know,
their Gods creation, never divert and all that I say is very devout,
This is what I can say.
This is what I can say.

Jenni Jones

Burgundy

Burgundy is a pleasing wine,
Candlelight, dim, while you dine.
Her color is quiet, gentle and true,
As bright as fire through and through.
Color that reflects love and light.
When caught in roses, a real delight.
To hear her speak is truly amazing.
What she says is like a fire blazing,
Sometimes in autumn you will see
This bold color accent many a tree.
A color so sweet, yet tangy and tart,
Exhibits strength,a giant's heart.
So beautiful in nature, but no less
Can be used to brighten a little girl's dress.
Colors cannot prevent friction and strife
But add color and joy to all your life.
To touch burgundy is unbelievable.
Life without her is inconceivable.

Jessica Rogers

Love

Why does this world have to be all hate,
Can't we get along before it's too late?
Each child killing another,
Children turn against their father and mother.
Children take guns to school each day,
Kids can't even go outside and play.
Gunshots go off and babies die,
Teenagers now steal, run-away, and lie.
There is the smell of American blood in the sky,
What person in this world has the right to make another cry?
Guns can be bought too easy,
That the thought of it makes me queasy.
You can't even walk alone down a street,
You'll get robbed, shot, stabbed or beat.
Some people will do anything to get money for dope,
The list is endless, it seems that there's no hope.
Can we ever get this world back on track,
This is the only world we've got, we could get it back.
Parents worry about their kids day and night,
Does this world have love in it, ha, yea right!

Clarissa Maida

"Tactical Sensations"

"Stimulating, tingling water sprays
Caressing my body in the shower,
The velvety touch of baby skin
Or the petals of a fragrant flower,
The smooth, satiny feel of a nectarine,
The fuzzy texture of a peach,
The glowing sensation of a kiss
Planted tenderly upon my lips
In affection and loving friendship,
Caressing hands in body embrace
In times of tension and stress,
The rough, wrinkled texture of a tree trunk,
The sandpaper palms of labored hands,
These varied textures are of interest,
But give me the smooth, soothing ones!"

Ann R. Rubin

I Will Never Give Up Loving You

I will never give up loving you,
'cause of all the good and bad times
we've been through so sweet heart
you know I must really love you

'Cause I always think about you
sometimes I think about the bad
things we've been through but God
was there and he saw us through

That's Why: I will never give up loving you.

Thinking about the times we've
shared I knew you really cared
'cause of the love we've shared

Thank you baby
for being there

Darius La Mar Greene

Adolescent Or Ancient

Let them be young,
Causing trouble, complaining, having fun times with friends,
But burdened with family problems and peer pressure

Then there are the aged,
Able to drive and go anywhere at anytime,
But stressed-out because of work and taking good care of their aggravating "little ones"

I'd rather be young,
Even though time flies while you're having fun,
At least we still have a little time to be wild and free
Getting sunburnt at beaches, going to sleep overs and parties,
Eating frosted pop-tarts and buttery popcorn until you throw-up,
Are just a few things that I like to do since I'm still young

The grey hairs will be growing in soon,
But at least for now I can still enjoy
Being a teenager!

Erica Wolicki

The Waiting Room

Bodies pass to meet those who mourn, while
Childlike I cling to the far-most corner-space of the room;
Gathering dust and comfort
From the spider,
As we stare silently at the intricate webbed patterns of the wall.
The spider and I, we weep
And wait.

Garrick E. Speer

Cape Cod's Fingerprint

Beach plums and honeysuckle
Cedar and pine,
Bike trails, boat sails
Remind me of summertime.

Days spent at the beach,
Or climbing through the dunes;
So many pleasant sounds,
Singing such peaceful tunes.

The child who discovers a starfish with delight,
Or the artist who's inspired by her sight!

In the distance a ship that is flanked by sea gulls,
Cradled in whitecaps, that lap at her hull.

A fisherman's boat that returns with the tide,
Enjoyed the spray from whales, as they played by her side.

Hot bugs, salt air, sand and sea,
Summertime on cape cod,
Has always been a favorite for me!

Cynthia Gillis

Hairpins

It was the sunlit glint of the coal tumbling down the chute into the
   cellar

Soft as the raveled edges of the silk pongee she used to curtain the
windows of the sun parlor of the only house they ever owned
   Bought so that the girls, who were pre-teens, would have a place to
   bring their friends, a place to be proud of

Absolutely straight except for the few special occasions when the
waving iron
   Heated over the flame of the gas stove in the kitchen and cooled by
   searing newspaper until the "burn" disappeared
created the stylish waves of the day's fashion
   Waves like those in the picture taken just before she left Germany
   the first in her family to begin a life in a country where she knew
   no one, did not speak the language, and committed herself to an
   indenture to pay for her passage

The hair style ever culminating in the bun at the nape of her neck
   The hair style together with the accent that brought taunting from
   the children of the very neighborhood they had chosen so carefully
   so that the girls could be proud to bring their friends home

The bun wrapped in a fine hairnet, fastened with hairpins

Hairpins that could no longer hold the straight, fine, still
coal-black hair as she lay in a coma, in the hospital, in her
eighty-third year

The hairpins of Anna Marguerheta Hoffmann Sorensen - my Mother.

Joan S. Krause

Children The Innocent

Candles are burning on the dark starry night.
Children are praying
hands grasping so tight.
Winds whistle calmly, soothing the fright.
Why must they hunger, thirst and crave?
Why must the children run from the grave?
The children, they pray, for they know far to well
that they are the future of the glistening stars.
They pray, holding hands, candles running low,
wanting escape into the night of happiness.
Being the innocent, the children will know,
that life is the future for them to endure.
With knowledge of the mystery of life,
all is in their hands for them to behold.

Erin Moroney Lorino

If You Listen

If you listen to the world you can hear the laughter of
children having fun, the crying of those in distress.

You can hear the joy in peoples hearts, the pain of those
others.

You can hear the sound of a rose blooming, the crackling
of those dying.

You can hear almost anything, if you put your heart to it

Anthony Ori

Essence Of A Dream

As I ponder in this dark and dreadful room,
Chills approach my body, as if a presence were there.
Fingers trembling with fear; not being able to move,
Staring into the wilderness, perfect silence.

Trees blowing back and forth like milkweed in a breeze,
Clouds of deception moving in slowly.
Lonely as a damson in a forest of pine,
A small cove I see in the lighted brink.

Feelings to ascend were strong but frightful,
The aspect of my pale face was almost timid.
Thoughts of heroism raced through my mind,
A rush of bravery came over me, like a stormy wind.

Hurriedly dashing to the opening, appearing in the mist,
Streams of light passing through me, as if I were not there.
As if a dream had pulled me further and further in,
Frozen as a river of the ice age I stood.

Falling to the musty ground,
My eyes opening slowly: like a newborn.
Feeling that softness of my bed,
A dream so down to reality, one I'll never forget.

Dayna Leigh Bye

Water

Spirit on water - move now our beings
Cleansing and lifting, prayer pure and holy
Guiding our senses, touchings and seeings
Centering always - giving you wholly
Our days and tomorrows, moments and hours-
Failed expectations, talents long hidden
Sorrow and joyfulness, weakness and powers
Carelessness, anger, thought that's unbidden.
Water baptismal, at font and at altar
Sacramental, life-giving, in silence falling
To strengthen in courage, never to falter.
Here in the floodtides, the Lord now is calling,
Waterfall, ocean, pond, stream and river
Prodigious and roaring, fountain and giver.

Adelaide Richter

Untitled

Twisted life of despair
Cold, dark and lonely
In the middle of nowhere
My mind starts to scream
Filled with hostility and anger
How I wish it was all a dream
Everyday is a nightmare from which I would love to awake
My soul is torn and bleeding with wounds
So how could my exterior be so damn fake
I try to run from my life of hate
There is nothing to look forward to.
God I believe has fulfilled my fate
Ignorant and frustrated
Why have I lived so long
Where everything I conceived is hated.

Greg Sommer

Cathedral

Red, green, yellow, blue are the colours he never knew
Colours that inspire the cathedral's spiritual fire. Long hours
short life was this man's in all his strife; for he never knew a
wife - this nameless man a ceaseless wonder
Worked all day, throughout the thunder all through terrible
conditions were his premonitions
of a time he would relive
a countryside with room to grow - and land to hoe, and worship there;
but his dreams were in despair
for now there's only fears and woe -
pearls of sweat through the years cry out from the cathedral piers
-caught between the mortar were his tears
Spiritual dreams left behind
for the rich and unkind
a life thank God he'd never find.

Jaime Ann Haeckel

"Hummmmmmmm"

Hi there neighbor, do you look beat!
 Come and sit a spell

Come watch these youngsters run and jump
 and listen to them yell.

It seems like eons and eons ago
 we did the very same.

Today, for us, impossible; to them
 it's just a game.

Soon they'll sing their Alma Maters,
 and thrill to those mighty cheers,

Our times have come and gone my friend,
 we are in our Golden Years.

Don't frown, relax and smile ol' pal
 blink back those 'gator tears.

It's really so much fun to tell of
 the great things we had done,

Prior to our Golden Years.
 Hummmmmmm.

Jack Pfund

Call Upon The Storm

Thunder and lightning, wind and rain
Come and visit our village again.
And with you bring what we need the most —
Inches of rain of which we may boast.

A cloud of dust lingers in the air
While weary farmers are well aware
Their crops are dying even though they're
Giving their children consistent care.

One long lashing is all it will take
To return the life to what looks fake.
Then our villagers can continue
Selling crops for vital revenue.

Gayle Norris

Trial

Sweaty palms, tunnel vision, blaring lights
Dipping into my soul.
Stomach pains, painful breathing, ticking clock
Counting slowly the seconds of my fate.

Slant eyes, flared nostrils, furrowed brows waiting
To attack.
Music - a trip - food - bedroom - TV set - Las vegas
Anything - just anything to escape this moment of
sentencing.

Janette C. Johns-Gibson

Mother's Day Wishes

My gift to you for Mother's Day
Comes with lots of hugs and kisses.
I love you, Mom, for all you do
So here are three special wishes.

I wish you sunshine every day
To make your whole world bright!
I wish you friendship from everyone
To help make your burdens light!

But most of all I wish you love
Because you are love to me.
God has blessed me with a wonderful mother-
 You
The best there could ever be!

Jean Stires

One Day

Diminish the pain abandon the sorrow
cometh not rain only sunshine tomorrow
A part time embrace we enjoy and share
my eyes behold your face even when you're not there
Come forth the time indeed I do pray
for the peace of mind we'll inherit one day

Those tender smiles we both provide
last for a brief while then they hide
For when you leave I am an empty shell
my lonely heart grieves but you cannot tell
Love is bitter-sweets oh taste don't go away
for in time we'll be complete being together one day

A promise to keep of undisputed love
so hard to sleep it's you I think of
This love sometimes hurts especially when I'm alone
yet I knows what it's worth for my heart is your home
Be patient and endure don't let faith slip away
our love is clean and pure and we'll be together One Day

 Loving you everlastingly
 Fredrick Jones

"Day Of The Living"

Standing here in this big city
Confused with directions of places.

Tall skyscrapers climbing to the sky,
Honk of a horn, people hurrying to work,
Children giggling in the park.

A breeze turns the day into night.

Street lights play stars amongst the black sky.
Sirens wailing down the avenue,
Theatre signs blink dramatically for attention.

Whistle for a taxi, a moon hung to end this day of the living.

Beth Storey

the tear

the tear started from her brown eyes, it was a beautiful girl; who
cried because of a rose that died under the moon light; oh such a tear
that ran down the girl eyes. It smoothly ran down the corner of her
nose, and went down her cheek and like a breeze it softly blew off
her chin. It gently fell onto the rose and the tear rolled
in the rose's center core and with the love of one tear
it magically came to life and all of the petals sprinkled
like a twinkling star at night when the sun gleams on it,
as the girl stopped crying the tear disappears into the
sunlight, as dawn rises from her pouch.

douane moses

Self Portrait

Subjective self ever present, Gwendolyn
Considered waste a mortal sin
  Always ate for two
  Goodies, old and new
Explains the body that was never thin.

Known for poetry, nursing and such
Admitted mother of a household bunch
  Stove, refrigerator and sink
  Collectively, individually think
She makes her very best showing at lunch.

The dinner table brings no slouch
"Spicy Carrot Pie", published - stomach, ouch
  Few dollars line the pockets
  The collar's tight over locket
Her royal highness can not move to the couch.

Heredity, family traditions blamed
It's clear the diet's wild, untamed
  Torts, pudding and cake
  Delicious snacks they make
Gwendolyn's willpower must be reclaimed.

   Gwendolyn Trimbell Pease

Poverty

Poverty seems to exist everywhere.
Contributing to both male and female going astray.
Oh yes! Causing them so often, to lose their way.
It seems that it ought to be a law;
That would systematically chase it away.
Oh yes! Banishing old poverty.

Yes, away - away to stay!
Nevertheless, the old vicious cycle;
Goes on and on everyday.
Again, causing someone to often lose their way.
For it appears, even at this present day!
That the old vicious cycle of poverty, is here to stay.

Wouldn't YOU like to see the day?
When the old vicious cycle;
And all traces of its ill effects.
Have vanished completely away.
Poverty, that is:
When it has totally vanished away - away to stay!

   Delores Watts

Storms

The rain, pounding, on my head.
  coolness, the water washing away...
    THE PAIN.
Like a priest, absolving me.
  The water, purifying, my very... SOUL.
Soon the rain, turns to tears.
  The water was my own, the feelings rush...
    TO MY THROAT.
What was once a rain storm turns.
  The rain, becomes a hurricane...
    IT consumes ME.
The rage grows in me.
  The fear, the sadness, the emotions... take OVER.
These emotions are ruling me.
  They take over thrashing...
    like a storming SEA.
Then, as soon as the storm started.
  It ended, everything became... CALM.
The storm quiets, the sea calms.
  The night ends, with the raising ... of the SUN and a HAND.

   Beth Anne Bradshaw

Cornbread The Rhyming Recipe

First you turn the oven on, my dear sister Joan.
Cornbread, cornbread, cornbread pone.

Next you need some lard, so it won't be hard.
Cornbread, cornbread, Oops! The bowl jarred.

Two cups of meal, ground by a wheel.
Cornbread, cornbread, yelled sister Jill.

One cup of flour. Add some milk, that's sour.
Cornbread, cornbread, it'll take half an hour.

Stir a little water in, careful now, not too thin!
Cornbread, cornbread, it always makes you grin.

Stir it up, stir it up- the spoon goes guh-lup.
Cornbread, cornbread, where's the measuring cup?

Fourth cup of mayonnaise, this to some it will amaze.
Cornbread, cornbread, tweets the blue jays.

Pour it in a hot pan, but don't burn your hand!
Cornbread, cornbread, we'll bake it nice and tan.

To put it in the oven, the pan needs a shoven'
Cornbread, cornbread, cornbread lovin'.

While it's baking nice and brown, you can smell it all aroun'
Cornbread, cornbread, then we'll eat it all down.

   Angela L. (Clawson) Hicks

The Dance

I love how life taps you on your shoulder... excuse me,
Could I have the next dance?

You step into the arms of a tune.
Sometimes it's too fast or too slow.
Sometimes swaying to the rhythm is just right.

The beat might be off, but we keep trying for the right note.

Sometimes we just want to sit this one out... watching everyone else
keeping to their movement of life.

   Joyce Kady

High Fashion

She wears her blackness like a shroud—
  covering and concealing the life within.

She wears her blackness like a mantle—
  outwardly protecting the life within.

She wears her blackness like a costume—
  masking and disguising the life within.

She wears her blackness like a uniform—
  restricting and confining the life within.

She wears her blackness like sackcloth and ashes—
  mourning and deploring the life within.

She wears her blackness like a saintly robe—
  ennobling and glorifying the life within.

Covering and concealing,
  outwardly protecting,
    masking and disguising,
      restricting and confining,
        mourning and deploring,
          ennobling and glorifying—

Black is beautiful if a wise selection
  is made from this wardrobe of basic blacks.

   Frances R. Coble

Creatures Of Night

Dark sinister night creatures,
Crawling, slithering, biting-
Down the dark lonely deserted
Road they are coming for you.
You run, you hide-
No release - you look back.
Bright eyes, red eyes, evil eyes-
They are searching for you,
Fresh - you've never been on
This wicked trip.
They know you - they want you-
Terror-they're getting closer,
Right behind you!
Terror explodes into ecstasy
Once you start to explore.
Never going back-never the same-
Don't fight-they own you now-
Give in-go with it,
Because either way there's no escaping
The fangs of the dark creatures of night!!!

Dana C. Good

The Big Picture

I do believe the Lord above
Created you for me to love.
He picked you out from all the rest
Because He knew I'd love you best.

I had a heart and it was true,
But, now it's gone from me to you.
So care for it as I have done
For you have two and I have none.

When I go to Heaven and you're not there
I'll wait for you by the golden stair.
If you're not there by judgement day
I'll know you've gone the other way.

Then I'll retire my angel wings
My golden harp and everything.
And just to prove my love is true
I'll go to Hell to be with you.

Ella Modic-Coon

Creatures Of The Dark

Somewhere south of hell
Creep the creatures of the dark
their dreams are screams/ their cries are lies
their bite precedes their bark

And someplace where it's hotter than the sweetest siren's song
the creatures melt distinctions to the beating of a gong
for night is a woman devouring all light
blackest of the ladies - scavenger of sight
and the sweetest siren's song/so melodious and strong,
turning lions into sheep, making mighty mountains weep

Can't save the day from night's cruel say
can't sing the sharks to sleep.

Joshua Rauch

Untitled

Do you?
Do you feel the way I do?
Do you quiver with my touch?
Feel at ease with the sound of my voice?
Do your eyes light up when you look into mine?
Do you wonder what I am
Thinking when I look at you?
If all of these are true for you
Then yes!
You do feel the way I do!

Danielle M. Fontannay

Breathless

Ice cold Pierces my lungs
   crisp... burning - almost HOT!

How can beauty like this be
   so ...
      ... *unattainable*

The Trek.
   Long.
      ... Harsh
         ... Steep

The Burden
   ...Heavy

At last! The Top of the WORLD!
   ...what a journey ...

BLINDING LIGHT -
   There are no clouds above me to dim it!
   They are all below me
   ...I can see them ... *Clearly*

So quiet. So peaceful. So much beauty.
So much JOY ... it leaves me -
      ... *Breathless*

Deborah Stambaugh

Carriola

Baby baby
Cry no more
'Cause tomorrow
You will grow
You'll be walking
You'll be laughing
And those lonely days of sorrow will be gone
Great things happen after walking:
Friends, school and lots of playing.
You'll be curious, you'll be wondering
What is this, what is that, always
Wanting to go farther, to know more.

Baby, baby cry no more

'Cause tomorrow you will grow

Cristina Olague-Rosales

Deluded Enticement

Gnarled claws encroaching within passive grounds,
   curling itself around the naive heart
   with choking inescapable spirals.
Captivating to suspecting eyes as the smoke
   dims and deadens the senses.
Dreams turn malevolent as the barbed wire
   glistens its crooked smile around its
   young prey.
Will you find release in the unforgiving
   clutches of this man-made trap
   or drag yourself to rest with the
   gashes from your struggles ensuring
   an even speedier departure?

Amy K. Reichenbach

A Season's Metamorphosis

Softly breezing through wavering boughs,
Dancing in the playful shadows,
The wind breathes cool and deeply,
Letting go only enough for leaves to shiver.

Turning over leaves, unveiling glittery silver,
Whispers of Autumn blow insistently,
Pushing the summer gently aside,
Announcing its approaching arrival.

Soon the fireworks of colors explode,
Displaying their beauty for rich and poor,
Memories of summer ebb away,
Falling into the arms of Morpheus.
  Erin Chaye Doyle

Too Much Pain

Too much pain we do share
death, rape, suicide everywhere
murder, incest, crimes committed
too much, too fast in this world we live in.

Children not healthy like they should be
the homeless, the sick, and the hungry
the rich, the ignorance, who really cares?
We need some Angels to make us aware.

The elderly left all alone
the Aids, the cancer, all the cures unknown
the evil, this trash, all this pollution
please dear God inspire a solution!

Where are the farms, the trees, the flowers?
Now apartment buildings, hot macadam, nuclear power
what to tell our little girls and boys
pornography, drugs, synthetic toys.

Oil spills, chemicals, wildlife destroyed
fires, sirens, major madness around
where is the realization to save ourselves,
our God given ground?
  Cheryl A. Derstine

Fresh Kills

A man-made mountain of broken
debris hovers Staten Island waterways and highways.
Automobiles and trucks piss on by;
the thick diesel air combines
with odors of every kind,
arriving from every angle
pulled in like some great magnetic force.

I walked from the top down to one of its bridges.
Gulls and terns intoxicated,
stumbled as they picked through french fries,
chicken bones, plastic toys and rubber tires.
As I approached one of its forgotten estuaries,
my eyes were glued upon the yellow glazed murky water
rippling in a stunned rate of reverberations;;;
Amidst this spinning gyre, a drowning duck
struggled for life as Beethoven's Pastoral
blared from a passing green Chevy pickup.
While rites of passion ring loud,
ceremonial bulldozers
bury the undying in layers of ascension.
  Brian Yank

Darkness

Darkness holds the key to many evil things,
Demons come out at night,
Personalities take wings,

Darkness brings forth a seemingly protective cover,
One does evil deeds without light,
When darkness fall, against one another,

Light removes the cover of darkness,
Personalities rest,
Peace creeps,
Light puts darkness to a test,

Evil deeds are not usually done,
Until the setting of the sun.
  Gwen Bobo

The Dead End Girls

We live in an apartment complex on a dead end street
Despite neighborhood protests, we're here
Society's "Dead end Girls"
Out of the closet, yet purposedly invisible and forgotten
Binding together like lepers of old
Trying to become a family... short term
Hoping for...a new miracle drug...a "T" miscount...supportive visitors
FALSE HOPES!
Death is the more frequent visitor
We deserve to be punished...
Apartment "1A" girl is gone... "3C" went last week
Now their families cry
It won't be long for "2B"
Desperate phone calls to HELP agencies answered by machines
Long torturous hours at clinics
The pain! The sweats! The abandonment!
Hollywood, community leaders, and churches glorify the need for Research
Reality... too late... no hoopla... death comes once more for an Insignificant "Dead End Girl"
  Esmeralda P. Rodriguez

The 'O' Was Dropped

Where did the 'O' go - that the O'Learys dropped
  Did it go down the street - with a hippedy-hop?

Did it spin in the air - like a table-top top?
  Or did it ring around a pillar - like a horse-shoe plopped?

Did it roll over in the clover - and scare the cows?
  While lovers in a church-side - were exchanging their vows?

Did it roll on thru Congress - and pass as a bill
  And even get to signing - by Bill there still

Oh did it make way for Hollywood - and come out on the screen
  With blessings of Maureen O'Hare - just suddenly turn green

Did it roll through a factory - making Irish tableware
  Leaving prints on tablecloths - that win prizes at the fair?

Did it roll right on to Dublin - O'er the rocky road that's there
  And make the feuding parties-sorta fume and pull their hair
  John D. Young

Don't Fall In Love

Have you ever really loved a boy and think he didn't care
Did you ever feel like crying, but think you'll get no where

Did you ever look in his eyes and say a little prayer
Did you ever look in his heart and wish that you were there

Did you ever see him dancing, when the lights were turned down low
Did you ever say "Gosh I love him", but please don't let him know

If you fall in love my friend, you'll see it doesn't pay
It always cause heartbreak it happens everyday

Did you ever wonder where he was at night and wonder where he's true
One day you'll find he loves you and then you'll find you're through

And when he stops loving you, you really don't know why
You see my friend you're losing him, no matter how hard you try

Love is fine, but it hurts too much the price you pay is high
If I had to choose between love and death, I think I'd rather die

Don't ever fall in love my friend you'll be hurt before you're through
You see my friend I ought to know I fell in love with you.

Crystal Shevon Carpenter

White

Black clouds and Winter's mist
Disperse with Spring's sweet kiss.
Wars are raged and never told,
Battles fought, won or lost alone.
While healing sands may dispel,
One man's Heaven or another's Hell,
Foreboding shadows hidden within liquid pools,
Shades drawn on the windows to my soul.
For if I traverse Northern lands,
Soul be cursed, lest bowed head and folded hands
Nay pristine but evil white,
Far removed from warmth, God's Light.
Defeats that man unbeknown to Life.

Edward J. Brown

Far

Freedom from beyond, as the wind whispers,
Distant cries from distant places.

Caught in a time where life is to heartless

I am lost and I don't know which way to go
Every time I turn around to see behind me,
I am blinded by the past.

What is happening is happening to fast.

Caught in place where I'm not sure
I want to be
Will somebody help me?

I look around not a familiar face in sight,
Almost like day has turned to night

As thoughts enter through my mind,
I feel I'm not wanted here.

No one around here has feelings to share.

Innocent faces, in guilty crowd
Not sure if I should feel proud.

One more day goes by as the wind cries far.

Charles V. Nicholas

"I Have Found You"

Oh, my Beloved,
disturbing are these hours,
these moments
in which my soul rests in You
in which I wait for You without fear,
without anxiety and without torment

Beloved, Beloved of mine,
with the hope of Your promises
my feet stand firm
and the sand has stopped being slippery;
the sands now respect my pace
and the sea gull has finally laughed with me

I myself,
have taken my soul by the hand,
and we have finally returned to walk the same path

This path where the saints
have left their perfumes scattered,
where marked, their footprints remain,
the same that I now follow
and where after so much walking,
as they did,
I too have found You.

Elizabeth Paz-Ligorria (Mariabelem)

I Often.....

I often wonder if what I am feeling for you is right.
Do I really deserve you, do you really deserve me?

I often think that your just playing with my mind,
but I guess that's a chance I have to take.

I often feel like I want to be in your arms and
never have to leave. But that is only a dream.

I often say I love and miss you. Wondering if you
believe it, or feel the same.

I often ask myself how this ever started. Then
realize why question a good thing.

I often find myself closing my eyes and picturing
your face, hoping when they open, you are there.

I often desire for you to make love to me, to be
able to feel you close and wish that it never ended.

I often hope that I never lose you because love is
what I really feel for you.

Chona Santos

A Martyr

In death does the spirit still survive?
  Do they see mistakes made while alive?
Do they float thru space forever and a day
  Pondering the errors of their way?

Or will at last ravaged soul find release
  And the taunting of unseen enemies finally cease?
And their hazy gloom filled skies begin to clear
  For at last this sin-filled world is past. Peace is near.

Locked inside his final crypt, the secrets of life
  Go unanswered, and in need amidst stormy strife
That brought him here prematurely, unsated and forlorn
  Unwanted and dehumanized from the day he was born.

My prayer is that he lives to see that inspiring day
  When wretched souls shall rise and finally have their say
And the universe shall be forced to listen to their beleaguered wrong
  Then commence to progress in truth, forward, united, and strong.

Then who is to say that this lost soul lived for naught.
  Think of what his misery and untimely death has brought.
A new day, a new way for the faithful souls that slaved
  To honor a mirage, until a martyr died, and a road was paved.

Charles Kellogg

71

A Part Of Me From God To You

Trusting you in all things is like caring
for you as Jesus does in his grace and love.

Always being there to grow and pray
with you in seeking God's will.

Uplifting you as a part of the body in Christ
so we could become as one in God's sight.

Pleasing you as he would want me to in spirit
and love not seeking unrighteousness.

To always want you by my side no matter what happens so
long as we both shall lift our lives to God in holiness.

Respect, open ears, understanding, and holding you as we seek the
love of Jesus Christ - the utmost of my wishes, hopes, and dreams.

Caring for me as I do for you helping me in all
things as I will with you according to him.

Work together as one in the body of Christ.

Praying that we will live a fulfilling life
asking God's guidance and love.

Giving all to Jesus so that Satan can't crush us and that we
may be examples for one another as well as for others.

Tarrilynn Jagger

Hostile Breath

I hear it, but I can't touch it.
I feel it, but I can't see it.

Move out of its path or
It will knock you down.

It'll cause destruction all around.
It's angry—can't you see.

Who'd dare to stand against it?
You can't stop it so don't even try.

It'll spit dirt all in your eyes.
Grab your baby and hold her tight
I'd hate to see her go off into the night.

These trees don't know it has no control.
Grip your roots and hold on—it doesn't want to
Destroy you, but it might.

Be strong. It's almost done.
In the morning after this battle is won, will
You stand straight and give glory to the sun?

Patricia A. Reid

Daddy's Girls

We are so lucky to have a father full of love,
A man who's the very likeness of our father up above.
Daddy, you taught us right from wrong with loving guidance and
advice.
You helped us walk our journey through life; no one else could suffice.

You've set an example of how to live right,
Follow God's pathway - the Truth and the Light.
With you as our Father we truly delight,
We love you with all of our might.

It fills our heart with joy and pride,
To let you know your deepest prayers are justified.
Our Lord is your Lord and He lives in our heart,
We want to thank you today for giving us our start.

It's our desire to follow the footsteps you've trod,
For you are our father, chosen by God.

Happy Father's Day!

Leesa A. Wheeler and Patsy Hale

Beautiful Cold Desolate

The night is brighter than the past nights tonight, I can see the
shadows of people and the outline of hollow buildings on the pale ground
loudly reflecting up towards the sky so bright so clear
So cold
So cold
So cold
Vast mountains surround me while the entwined wood stands
   ever faithful
by its side slowly growing old, my hardened face stares at this picture,
I can feel the aging lines on my face sinking deeper while the view is
covered in the purest white blanket, it's a still life all desolate,
all beautiful, I'm the only one drowning in her getting cold
So cold
So cold
So cold
Why can't you save me, I need to share this vehement portrait with you
I want to suck on your bones, your skin will cover me to protect my
aging lines while our souls savor a walk on her, the beautiful cold
desolate promenade, hurry! I'm so cold
So cold
So cold

Rico Garcia

This Transient Life

Sometimes it seems a joke,
a bluff, perhaps a trick of light.
This dizzying whir of days that
pass away to shapeless nights.

Dreams of childhood sparkle like jewels
and nourish a young growing soul.
All too soon they begin to fade
and you are left with a piece of coal.

Forcibly one is made to leave
a womb that is warm and dark.
Thrust into a world of pain and hate
where misery is ever stark.

Let me be an honorable visitor here,
not forgetting my once youthful spark.
God grant me this, and when the time comes
I'll gladly return to the dark.

Russell Gilbert

The Fallen Tree Remembers

I did what a tree does, shelter life,
A boy's hopes, dreams, and his strife.
I remember the boy who built his home in my heart
Nailing my boughs, tearing my limbs apart.

I remember the teen locking the small door
On cowboy boots, toy guns, and comics on the floor.
I remember the soldier standing uniformed and mute
Touching my trunk in farewell salute.

I recall the hero with decorated chest,
Leaning his one leg on my roots to rest.
I remember his words in the evening breeze
"My son's a gardener, his specialty TREES".

I remember the old man with grandson and cane
Neath my shade, tell of agent orange and its pain.
I still hear his last words as he shuffled away
"Ah fallen comrade, from heat and storm depart,
But you will live forever in the meadow of my heart".

Nellie Neary

Mother

A warm smile even if there is pain
A burst of sunshine if ever there is rain
This is my best friend of 17 years
The one who brought me life
Is the same one to wipe my tears
Always going out of your way
Just for your family
Being funny and caring
Never anything for yourself
Forever you'll be sharing
I believe my father is very lucky he has someone so special
As we all do
I know we'd be lost
If for some reason we did not have you
You're there through happiness and sad
Always being honest even if I get mad
I can't tell you what your love means to me
Though sometimes it may be hard to see
Know that I'll love you until the very end
Because as long as I can remember, you have been my best friend

Tina Nicole Jones

Carousel

In the deep night of the winter solstice
a carousel turns and turns.
Twelve carved horses in coats of glossy white,
adorned by crimson bridles bright with sapphires,
   turn and turn
and in their turning move from the shadows
into the light of the silent moon.

In that glow
the bridegroom carries his palette of wedding colors
and paints and repaints
   the satin shoulders
   jeweled bridles
   studded saddles
   and silver shoes
of each unmoving steed
and stitches with care a tiny verse along each inside rein,
then steps into the center to await the wedding party.

And as the carousel turns and turns,
the gold ring glows in the moonlight
waiting to be grasped.

Shirley Frederick

Seasons

There you were that day so long ago,
A child alone, standing, watching,
Silent in your solitude.
You came into my life, unaware of the impact—
And then you were gone.

Years later we met again.
You were still silent.
Only your eyes held a promise—
A promise of worlds yet unexplored,
A promise of joy unimagined—
And then you were gone.

Once again you have entered my life.
This time hopes and dreams that seemed
Destined to remain unrealities
Became immeasurable joys
As our hearts and souls melded.

Question after question arises.
Will you leave again
Only to rejoin me
In the winter of our lives?

Valeria W. Jenkins

Temple Dancer

On a temple wall in an ancient land
A dancer sculpted in eternal pose,
About her an aureole - a radiant band
Showers warmth on all who behold.

The cymbals ring on a distant shore,
A drum beats taps for a thousand years,
In perfect rhythm and grace encircling the floor,
A dancer assumes a pose - that very pose appears!

O! extended moment, 'tis a moment sublime,
Art by art annihilates time.
The dancer's pose focuses in one
The past, the present, the divine light of the sun.

Ron Carman

A Mother's Nature

I celebrate a mother's nature,
a disposition that has no gender or progeny
   restrictions;
an ability to listen and support, without making
   threatening predictions;
a manner that is kind but not blind;
a skill to direct patiently, not as a bully;
a belief that growing happens after
   insight, not after rules have been
   pulled tight;
a hope that individual satisfaction and
   success comes from a combination
   of hard work, pain, and passion
And a humor,
   oh yes,
a humor that helps each of
   us comfort our own hurts,
   disappointments, frustrations and
   bring us to a peace that won't
   cease.

Patricia E. Pavloff

In The Likeness Of You

In the likeness of you
a dream came true,
but it wasn't time.

A man grew angry at the choice she made,
resentment grew stronger
and love went away.

Yet a son was born
in the likeness of you
and although it wasn't time, a dream came true.

Bitter memories will all but fade
if we learn not to ponder on the past
or decisions others made.

Today a young man
stands proud and strong,
Dad's love for his son makes life go on.

Who is to say that there is a right time
for the gift that was given a little too soon?
Who says that the sun rises after
or sets before the glorious moon?

Shirley Johnson

To My Son Gary

There's an empty chair at the table
a face, missing 'round the tree
A cheery voice wishing a "Merry Christmas"
and blue eyes smiling, tenderly -
The traditions are so familiar
I feel your presence every where
I love you and miss you, so very much
Sometimes it's more than I can bare
But I know this year, your christmas tree
Is trimmed in jewels of gold
And the Christmas Carols the angels sing
Are sung with harps and bells that toll
So with all the memories of our Christmas Past
Which you were a special part
I hope you know you'll always live
Deep inside my heart

Sue Jester

Feel The Fear

There's an eerie feeling on halloween night,
A feeling of fear and a feeling of fright.
The sky's always dark, and the moon's always full.
For it's halloween, and the night will be cruel.
The ghosts come out, the Goblins too,
You better watch out, their coming for you.
They'll scare you once, then come back for more,
So run to your house and lock your door.
You better run fast and don't look back.
They'll sense your fear, then they'll attack.
You must be brave and you must be strong.
For if you are weak, you won't last long!

Steven D. Nero

A Heart

A heart is a flower,
A flower with love and care.
A love and care so strong
You cannot pick it from the ground.
A heart is stronger than the devil himself.
The heart cannot break a love
between you and someone else.
The heart is powerful in some ways.
Hate will take it away.

William O. Benson

On Entering Poetry Contests...

Serious poetry...for me, that's out —
A humorous bent is what I'm about —
And the only contests I've ever been in
Are Publisher's Clearing House — (I never win!)
But I saw your contest and thought I'd try —
I said "Why not?" (YOU may say "Why?")
In any event, what can I lose?
What if MY ditty's the one you choose???

Polly Glasser

A Prayer From The Heart

Just a prayer from my heart.
A memory fond and true.
In my heart you'll live forever.
I thought the world of you.
It broke my heart to loose you,
the day God called you home.
I hold my tears when I speak
your name,
But the ache in my heart remains the same.
No one knows the sorrow I feel,
When I think of you.
My love will always be with you Baby.

Kelly Kennedy

"Silent Birth"

Deep inside his mother's womb he kicked and turned.
  A joyous movement he did make with love she yearned.
To gaze upon his precious little face.
  His small soft body she longed to embrace.

The birth date was near excitement mounted.
  His family was waiting, the days they counted.
At his birth there was no cry.
  No sound, no breath to show he was alive.

They laid gently in his mother's hand.
  A small still boy - her little man.
He will never see the light of day
  Or pet the stuffed toys on the bed where they lay

The only hope that gives consolation
  Is the angels taking him to another constellation
A heavenly spot with celestial lambs and teddy bears
  To wait for his earthly family who truly cares.

Life was nine months in his mother's womb
  She will never understand why he was taken so soon.
Stillborn today he will soar tomorrow
  Knowing he's in Heaven lightens the sorrow.

P. B. Cerf

Sojourner Truth

Black and White film flickers to life and
a King is beaten down by his saviors.
Music rattles to militant scratches.
A red haired hustler sought light.
History spiked by a scrawny fighting man's image.

A bold black champion spoke.
Wet tears ran down black skin.
For a man killed.
Children cried.

The once unknown name is now littered in common use,
His message written in the blood of his era.
His name has become a fad of fashion.
Who has knowledge of his message, strength, love?

Shaun Evans

Love Prints

I just thought I'd leave a love print
A little memento of my hand prints
These are special from me to you
Just think of all these little hands do

My hands are dandy they like to play
They come in handy each and every day
I have eight fingers and two little thumbs
And that adds up to lots of fun

I use them to play among other things
I love to clap them when mommy sings
There is one thing I'll say again
I left these love prints to make you grin

Teri Launius

The Worth Of Man

Though man may have a store of wealth
A measure of pride, the look of good health
All things to him that seem worthwhile
And yet somehow has lost his soul
Then he is nothing, he is not whole
And if for others no love he can feel
Then he is nil, he is not real
And if he thinks he can amount to something
Yet knows not God, then this man is nothing

Ruth H. Clark

Ellen's Song

It's almost dawn-
A midwinter, midwestern dawn.
The sky is granite,
The wind furious,
The snow deep-
Deep as the sleep I've just had.
I think I'm awake, I know I'm alive.
I want to be back in my dream,
In your arms,
In heaven just moments ago.
You danced into my slumber and hugged me.
I kissed you, held you,
And heard the most beautiful song-
Our symphony.
As the music gently faded
I awoke.
Now as I stare out the window,
The wind is calm,
Snowflakes are dancing...
I'm awake, alive, and still in love with you.

Timothy J. Price

Hall Of Fame

The work he did, miracles He performed, Jesus has
A name that ought to be put in the Hall of Fame.
I understand He didn't come to make himself
A reputation among man. Since He left
things changed, everything He did lives on in
people born again. Miracles performed, people
healed, this we know of His work. Jesus has a name
that ought to be put in the Hall of Fame. Other men and
women can never compare to Christ. They
share a part in the Hall of Fame: even the best
player who played baseball - the greatest man who ever lived,
the plane of salvation to man He gave. Calvary
was all about His death: 3rd day He rose up
from the grave. These two events were enough to
get him famous. Jesus has a name that ought to
be put in the Hall of Fame. The work He did,
the miracles performed, since He left things have changed.
Everything he did lives on in people born again.
Miracles performed, people healed, this we know of
His work. Jesus' name should be put in the Hall of Fame.

A. L. Anderson

A Childhood Memory

His name brings a memory I'll never forget,
A piece of my childhood I'll never regret...

As children we'd play all day and all night,
And so perfect he was that we never did fight..

He held me and helped me through every test,
And became a symbol of the very best...

He smiled through the pain, the fear and the tears,
And had the bravery to survive those seven hard years...

I admire his courage and the way he held on,
even though in the end he knew he'd be gone...

For as god so strongly willed it to be,
I cried at the end for my loss and for he...

I will always cherish my brother, my friend,
in my heart and soul there will be no end...

I love you my brother, and always will,
And my childhood memory will never stand still...

Melora Romano

We Are The Same

As sea-wet ropes are sorely stretched,
a point of humming comes to each.
Life's essence rises, then revealed, as living waters form and bead;
They form to fall, to glisten and to briefly shine,
to splash, and then disburse through time.
We are the same, for when we yield,
the reach of life goes deep inside,
and stretches us, leads us to points where droplets form:
In blood and sweat, in joy and tears, they separate
stand forth and fall, in struggle and in dream deep born -
arise again, unseen, transformed,
drawn upward by the light above!
In word and act, in gift and song, the essence offers hope to all.
Each walks the path of life to God...
At moments then, through voyaging,
may wind be yours, may seas be warm,
may courage by the Spirit form,
and may you place your life in trust
within the larger Life of GOD.
May His face shine on where you are.

E. A. Vinson

"Quiet Time"

It's three or four in the early morn,
A Quiet time because a new day has been born...

I brew a cup of coffee and get my head on straight,
I know it's awfully early but I really feel great...

This is my favorite time of all,
It's so peaceful, I wrap myself in a soft quiet wall...

Out of all the hours of the day,
I'll enjoy my quiet wall and say...

We all need a quiet time for just us,
To enjoy, to just sit and no fuss...

So I'll take my early morn,
And wait for each new day to be born.

Lee Lashbrook

"Friendship"

Sometimes I think what makes a friend,
A shoulder to cry on, a kind word spoken.
Someone who still cares when you've given in,
The heart grows light in the hands of a friend.

A source of laughter to ease the pain
A shared heart when triumph is gained
And kindle the fire while the coals are hot
That the gift of friendship shall want not

Friends may come with the winter snow,
And go with the summer sun,
But friendship survives as sure as the tide
And time nor distance will push it aside.

Robert B. Bullock

"Lost In My Thoughts"

I'm lost in a jungle of all my thoughts,
a touch of reality I have caught.
My dreams start to vanish in a cloud of smoke,
I can't see through, and I start to choke.
Another lost life on the face of the earth,
a fairly good soul, but what is it worth?!
The sun beams down on the skin of my face,
controlled but forgotten, the human race.
One day we all will be sinfully gone,
it seems that the world is one big con.

Samuel Dewayne Shelton

"Beloved Summer Angel"

You slipped away so quietly, without
a single word, the soft rustle of
Angel's wings was all that could be
heard. Early on that summer morning
for reasons only he can understand,
God reached down his loving hand, and
took our mother to heaven above, to
lavish in His tender care, His never-ending
love. Mother, we miss you, we
didn't get to say goodbye, the nights
are long and lonely, and with sadness,
we still cry. You looked so beautiful in
your final rest, when God called you
home, He took the very best. Happy
Birthday Mother, you gave your
daughter and son the greatest gift of
all-life, and your special love. And
for that, we both thank you.

Teresa S. Petell

The Great Race

Mother caresses her new born,
a smile spreading on her face,
dreams of future glory
she lost in the race.

LOOK INTO THE WINDOW OF YOUR FUTURE
TO SEE WHAT SHALL BE-UNINITIATED AS CAN BE.

Young girl stares into the mirror,
planning her own special day,
dreams of future glory
experienced today.

LOOK INTO THE WINDOW OF YOUR FUTURE
TO SEE YOUR PAST-UNAWARE LIFE GOES BY FAST.

Woman glances through her yearbook,
reminiscing of her youth,
dreams of past glory
realizing her sad truth.

LOOK INTO-THE WINDOW OF YOUR PAST
AND WHAT IS IT YOU SEE?

YOUR PAST LOOKING AT YOU.
YOU WANTING TO BE HER-SHE WANTING TO BE YOU

Steven M. Durben

The Dead Tree

Silent in all its glory…
A solemn reminder of the forgotten years,
Seasons reflected in the riverside,
A calling of life once known…
Secretly whispering,
A remainder of beauty;
And…death…
The river gave life to this omen;
And in turn,
   took it away…
The tree still stands by the river,
Lifeless and cold it is
Joy no longer emanates from within.
The river has dried up, and moved on…
But the tree still stands by a memory-
Of a long forgotten friend…
Silent in all its glory,
The eternal whisper of…
   what might have been…

Leah Reid

Renunciation

Thou, to me, this day hath given
   A song unsung, a plea forbidden.
      Spare thou this symbol of my desire.
      Make it my guide in darkest hour
         Fold it close to my heart in prayer
         And keep me worthy to leave it there.

Priscilla M. Clough

The Lost Wish

I wish upon night after night,
A star that shines in the pale moonlight.
It was once hopeful and bright,
But now it is so depressed and dim,
Because of a wish that include him.
The same wish time after time,
But even today it is still not mine.
The little star tried its best,
But it was too weak to complete its quest.
So gave up is what I did,
And now behind the blinds my little
   star is safely hid.

Michelle Bingham

"Eyes"

Is there a quiet and wise shadow in their rich mahogany abyss?
A streak of hidden anger in their predatory black fissures?
A trace of kind generosity in their gentle hazel pools?
A gleam of treachery in their wicked emerald chasms?
A sparkle of vibrant curiosity in their cinnamon splashes?
A shade of innocence in their misty violet caverns?
A look of cool contempt in their icy blue gulfs?
A hint of monotony in their tired grey puddles?
A merry twinkle in their watery azure depths?
The windows to the soul.

Soniya Keskar

The Long Road

It has been a long road.
A struggle over hills and mountains,
But can you foresee your future with me?
Are we in a tunnel, ready to see the sun,
Or are we still struggling in the dark.
Can't we talk about this or do we have to play games!
Why can't you feel the same?
I miss your tender touch and your gentle kiss
but above all this, I miss
you…

Skip Purich

A Musical World

Oh, how this composition of thoughts inspire me through melody
A synthesis of togetherness brought about by harmony
To imagine a world with flats and sharps non-existent
This yearning for a peaceful blend of sound so destined would persist
Oh, how grateful for feelings in tune
For melody seems to atone my visions and comfort my surroundings
Amazing me in its influence of my perception of reality
What a necessary and wonderful achievement
And so that beat lingers on within my soul

Lisa-Kurtz Woodie

"Thought, Word and Deed"

Dear Lord, forgive us when we think
  a thought not pleasing to your sight.
Cleanse our minds and draw us near
  To dwell on Thee both day and night.

Our words should come from careful thought;
  Not just impatient phrases be -
Nor cruel - hurting other folk.
  But gently helping them to see.

May we be guided in our deeds.
  May kindness come from love within.
Our actions tell whose side we're on,
  And Satan's helpless-
    he can't win!
Yes, he'll be banished-
  no more sin!
    Pearl Ficarella

Not Forgotten Love

If we had never met, you would go your way and live your life without
a thought of me, and I would spend this breathless, fleeting day
dreaming of a love unknown - - joys not to be.

I would have pictured you just as you came, tall and full of grace
and lines of laughter at your face.

God was good, he taught us to love, to be happy, carefree and gay.
But, now I look back and remember how we let it slip away.

Time has gone by, our love is forgotten.   You're a dream, a
love I once knew. How could all that magic and rapture fade
completely out of view?

The dreams and memories you brought me so long ago turned into tears.
Now I can only remember the best part of those years.

It is good once again reminiscing and to look each others eyes.
Though the smoke may curl around us, it's too late — we lead
separate lives.

But, to see you again makes me happy to relive for a moment with you,
my first romance not forgotten and recapture the thrill that was you.
    Pat Gaenzle

Remember

Silence is golden or so it's been said
A time to get in touch with thoughts in our head.
Many times it is used and can be worthwhile,
Other times it's not thought to be in great style.

Today in our world there is such a clatter
No one seems to know what really is the matter,
One thing is certain... you can be sure,
Without any doubt, there's got to be a cure.

There's beauty all around us in the sky and on the earth
God has blessed our land and us from the day of our birth.
Our forefathers believed that in God we should trust
So why don't we, as a nation and people, make this a must?

God has given to each of us His everlasting love
We know... He sent His Son from Heaven above.
Our hearts are often restless... we don't seem to remember
They were made to rest in Him... from January thru December.

Prayer is listening and talking in the silence of our soul
To our Creator where our hearts are centered and is our goal.
If we, as human beings, realize our purpose and do our part
We'll recognize and know the unconditional love flowing from
  His Heart.
    Margaret Jo Rose

Ode To A Little Girl

I trembled with wonder when I first held you....
A tiny bundle, so innocent, so new.
  Clinging as a vine would to a nearby tree.
I carried my baby so tenderly.

It tore my heart to let you go on your own;
unattached at last, the vine's grip broken.
  The years to come will stretch our bond
as you meet new friends and journey farther on.

I pray you'll be safe as each day ends
and each tomorrow brings new experience and friends

I am still filled with wonder as I watch you grow
and a sense of pride just overflows.
  When you sing or dance, or say something bright.
It brings forth a realm of emotion so strong...so wide.
  I have never loved so much and yet been so confused
on what to do to control you.

I am sure I will continue to tremble inside
as you mature and I'll watch with pride
  my little girl, you'll always be
and I thank God for the joy that you've given me.
    Kathleen K. Sasso

Trapped

I feel like a prisoner... locked up in chains,
  A touch of goodness has soured into hate.
Large black clouds have covered my days,
  Instead of waking up happy, I wake up in a
    fearful gaze.....
I go to sleep trembling and dream of nil,
  For someone is plotting, hunt and kill.
My heart's in shatters, my eyes in tears,
  I'm tied at the wrists and once again in a
    painful, sick affair...
Threatened in my home, slapped in my face, I just
  can't handle this sad and scary pace....
I have to say thanks to a killer of man,
  and I must get out... if only I can.
    For I know,
      and feel,
        he's working
          on killing me.
    Mary MacWilliams

Love's Way

You walked upon the stairs of light.
A view I pondered with much delight.
My eyes, first were cool and then were not,
For the passion swelled
As day became, a moist summer's night.

The colors in us, ah from blue to red,
As we felt our loins and fell to bed.
Eros was our God, upon we prayed.
The altar knew, the wine and bread.
Our hearts both knew, fire and dread.

A new season now came, no sweet farewell.
Sullen had entered, the passion broken.
The God was Pluto, who now sat the throne,
And visions of us, no longer staged their play.
The cast and director, the Curtain delayed.

For many years, the garden lay barren.
With snow and ice and hearts unforgiven.
But then, the spirit of eternal life,
Sprung garden's growth of joy and love,
As the raven above, became the dove.

    Roberta Whitehead

77

For Rosie..

There is an empty place where once you stood,
A void in time, as though there was
never a moment of joy or sorrow.
You pass through a life in a lightning flash
of thought, the crystal drop of a tear
Or the rainbow sound of laughter.
Why can there never be forever?
The forever we see is an endless
Lifetime of always changing yet
Still the soul we make stays the same.

You come to me through
a misty veil.
In my blindness I listen for your call —
There is only silence. I picture your face
As I sit very still with these memories.
Your breath is soft on my hair.

I reach out my hand to touch you —
You are gone.
Victoria Edwards

Life To Many; Life To Me

Life to many is like a battle;
A war between rival nations;
An endless cycle of troubles, never peace;
And void of new innovations.

Life to many is like a bird;
A bird with a broken wing.
It cannot fly, and eventually will die.
A joyful song it will never sing.

Life to many is like the land
that is barren from lack of rain.
All life is dry and useless,
With small hopes of replenishment again.

Life to many is like the thorn
Who's soul purpose is to curse the soil.
No beauty, sweet aroma, nor worth does it bring,
But a troublesome bother, and sweat, and toil.

But life to me is like a highway.
Yes, with pothole and detour,
But I possess the roadmap to this venture,
For God is my navigator!
Shelleen S. Derrick

Can't You Believe?

When I'm down on myself, my hopes you retrieve
A whisper from your lips like wind through the trees
Let me know anything, I could conquer, I could seize
It's you , why can't you believe?

My worries, my anxieties, you're the one to relieve
Your comforting words bring an inner peace and harmony
You're the only one who can soothe me, a turbulent sea
It's you, why can't you believe?

It's the sound of your voice I rejoice to receive
Like beautiful music singing lovingly to me
Your words of encouragement make me fly so free
It's you, why can't you believe?

Being close to you I long to achieve
Just to be near you puts my troubled soul at ease
In your place, to me, no one else could please
It's you, why can't you believe?
Keri Katalinic

Coffin

Hidden away in the depths of a closet,
A white shoebox full of mortal love,
Vowed never to be opened again.

Inside, a broken frame displaying two people;
One, a young man in a tux,
The other, a young girl in a velvet evening gown:
The love in their eyes as bright as a spotlight.
The prom glass is gone:
In a flash of jealous pain, shattered into lifeless flecks.
A keychain with their names and poetic words of evergreen love.
Pages of romance (lost now) folded, closed.

An abandoned museum of memories to which the door is locked,
Vowed never to be opened again.
Lori Flint

The Basketweaver

The basketweaver, like
a winding river,
twists and stretches his
life's work - remembering the
quiet valleys and villages
he once passed thru.

His patience neverending,
his goal sure,
he weaves with confidence
unfaltering, knowing what lies ahead
from the pain that's past-
like a sailor returning home from the sea.

The basketweaver, intent
in his pride
knows the restless waters
the turmoil of desires
yet like the calm, drifting river waters
he has chosen to be -
what pleases him.
Kathleen Mayes

"Gone"

A darkened tunnel, I'm lost in the past
A winding road, forever last.
Out of the cold, your face appears
Gone in that moment, my every fear.

For one brief moment, I think I can see
A candlelight flicker, a hope for me.
I offer my heart, I offer my soul.
You take it as yours, encrust it with gold.

The blackness evades, day turns to night
I try to escape, for gone is the light.
I reach for your hand, please help me along
My mistake love, you're already gone.
Kelly Yurick

Homeless Moon Dance

The moon came home last night,
against the blistered ruins of East Harlem,
Riding like a silver blimp
past my blindness window.
Across knotted egos and gnarled fears
That scribble graffiti on wrinkled dreams.

This is not home, pretty queen.
For there are no homes in these houses -
Houseless, but never homeless.
As you glide across this dream
Let me grab a piece of your rugged peace.
Tafa Fiadzigbe

My Mad World

Imagine:
A world where elders are threatened by the children daily
(Mother Parks-beaten).
A place where love, trust and loyalty are non-existent (Anita, why?)
Where pride self-esteem and righteousness seldom abide (Five dollars;
I'm yours.) A world where happiness is attacked if seen by others
(Family, neighbor K.K.K., C.I.A.)
Where the safest place for you is with you. (Double lock the door)
Imagine:
A place where the babies are seldom raised by two.
(Another drive-by reported today).
Where family is dead (He/she beat his/her mother for a hit)
Where environment is strictly controlled
(I'm sorry, the house is already sold)
Your dollars are doled (Good day Sir; we'll be in touch)
Where right is a word just for you (Can't we all get along?)
A place where life is cheap (Got killed for his jacket last week)
Imagine a world where a teacher asks his fourth grade class to
draw trees and little sisters grow from a casket, and teacher
discovers it's for the stillborn child she had last week.
Imagine that world. (I live it)

Kevin Williams

In Law's

Do you know the other day I saw,
A young lady running down her in-laws.

She had not one good thing to say,
And I thought this shouldn't be the way.

For you see, I'm blessed with my in-laws,
I surely don't call them Maw and Paw.

But I can lean on them for guidance and love,
Because they were given to me from up above.

My father-in-law was a replacement to me,
For my father went with Jesus to be.

And my mother-in-law is like my best friend,
Her love is undying, it never ends.

So for this disaster that my eyes did behold,
I told her I'd pray her heart would remold.

In the light of the Lord, and the Golden rule,
Do unto others, as you'd have them do unto you.

Miriam W. Easterling

Behind The Clouds

Beyond the blue-grey mist of dawn, came the sun to light the morn.
Abashed it was to reveal not things to sight,
  of yellow morning's usual first delight.
The other day a city stood, just past that charred and smoldering wood.
People went about their chores-no thought of bitter, ghastly wars.
Suddenly, all was gone from there,
  leaving only embers cloaked in sullen, skyward rising towers.
Blackened, stench filled, air hissed and spread in traveling wind.
A silent din spoke of living things turned dead in sleeping hours.
We walked barefoot along the beach that day with one intent....
  to breath sea air and feel salty waves that came and went.
"Fall flat!" my buddy screamed as from the sky two bombers streamed.
One shell fell fast. It bit the air.
It screeched, and whined, and burst right there!
Thus, passed from life another soul that greed and hate
  kept from its goal.
Oh, why this cruel undying hate?
Should one man shape a nation's fate?
We bought the game. We rolled the dice. We paid the price.
Let not our folly cost us twice!

Marjorie Foster Fleming

Private Matters

Don't ask me about my past,
About the withdrawn and lonely me.
Life is not always fair,
and I have learned to care.
Tell me about my sensuality.
About the fine lines of my Hellenic cheekbones,
and my large brown eyes.
My past is withered, like dried flowers.
My heart and soul are alive, and I can still feel joy.
Don't ask me about my past.
It gives me a headache to recall the times in my life
When ten dollars spent meant no more money for a week.
Hold your head up, hold your head up high.
Imitate the dignity of the peacock
as he shakes his colorful tail feathers in the breeze.
Or the beauty of the white swan
swimming in the park in Montsouris.

Marilynn Green

I'm Only A Teenager

I am only a teenager............
  Accept me as I am. Praise me instead of hurting me,
  Yes, I have feelings too.
I am only a teenager............
  Give me guidance and advice.
  Talk to me in a positive way,
  So that we can always be friends.
I am only a teenager............
  I have my own identity,
  I have my own "style".
  I will grow out of this, but not for awhile.
I am only a teenager............
  Show me direction, show me happiness. Don't try to change me,
  Unless I am hurting myself or my family.
I am only a teenager............
  I will soon outgrow this. I will be responsible, I will
  accept failure. I will accept your words of wisdom I will
  show you respect because you have let me be only a teen-
ager.......

Lorraine Montoya

My Deepest Love

The Northern lights flashed
Across the skies,
I saw their beauty once before in your eyes...

You never let me down.
You turned my whole life around...

You loved me from the start,
I guess I always knew deep
within my heart....

For this and so much more.
My love for you will be forever more...

Like the legends of lore, not heard of before.
Our love will be endless and forever more...

Like the deepest depths of sea.
You reached inside as if to touch me.
And set my soul free..
Throughout time and eternity.
I will hold you in the depths of my heart.

With love and respect and pure certainly...
I love you, Joey

Mary Jo Lance (Wood)

Have You Ever

Have you ever walked down a nine-foot wide road
After a big hard rain, and picked up little
snappin' turtles the size of a fifty-cent piece.

Have you ever rode a pine sapplin?
I'll tell you how it's done.
It takes several youngins to pull the top of a
sapplin down to the ground.
Then one youngin gets on, and the others let go of the tree.
And you better be hangin' on tight cause you don't want to get throwed.
Have you ever had a cow chip fight? It's lots of fun.

Have you ever rode a cows tail?
This is what you do.
Pick a big yearlin and grab his tail quick.
Take off runnin' or you will be draggin', cause
that cow ain't going to wait for you.
You better be watching where he's taking you,
or you might just be kissin' one of those pine
sapplins, and that ain't no fun.
Old milk cows won't do, they can't run fast enough

Norma Jean Griffin

Let Me Be

Let me be the fragrance of flowers you smell
after an early springtime rain
or the giant oak providing you shade
on a hot summers day

Let me be the warm sunlight on a cool autumn day
or the crackling fire on a cold winters night

Let Me Be the song you feel like singing, its melody
filling your ears with memories you hold dear
or the dreams you spin as you sleep
dreams that linger deep within

Let Me Be the rain that kisses your face
or the wind caressing your skin like silken lace

Let Me Be the shelter you seek when ever you feel
your world has gone astray
or the shadow beside you wherever you roam
you'll never be alone

Let Me Be all of these things you
for you'll no longer be in a world of strangers
you'll have someone who loves you and together,
we shall share a love, strong as a flowing tide

Lee D. Stewart

Gone

My father died the other day
   Age fifty-six - too young to leave
Remaining behind were his family
   A wife, four kids to mourn and grieve.

A coma took him away that day
   Like a foe quickly grabbing its prey
So still and quiet he did lay
   Machines and monitors having their way.

His body seemed an empty shell -
   With soul and life's fire all expelled
A decision soon would need to be made
   Life support or nature's way?

Unhooked from artificial life -
   A faithful vigil we kept all night
Until his last breath was released
   Our belief in miracles never ceased.

My father's funeral has come and gone
   His life is over, ours goes on
Time is said to ease one's sorrow
   Perhaps it will, in a distant tomorrow.

Mary Greyerbiehl

The Ship Gallilee

Many leagues out to sea, a vessel sailed, named "Gallilee"
All around her waves dashed high, above her was the sullen sky
In wild fury a storm then came, lightning, thunder, pelting rain
The fated ship swayed and lunged, into the billows it did plunge

The ship trembled with great shock, the bow hit a jagged rock
Thrown against it once again, none could save her, not the men.
Aboard the ship all was confusion, everywhere, black delusion.
"Man the lifeboats!" the Captain cried, hoping death to be denied

As the last boat pulled away, a voice called out "Please stay!"
Where is my child, Caroline? My God! has she been left behind?"
A cry burst from the mother, with speed the Captain's brother
Scaled the sinking vessel's side, in search of Caroline, he hied

She was hidden 'neath sails white, eyes wide open in her fright
He lifted her in arms so strong but the sea did grievous wrong.
Rising waves and tossing spray, carried the lifeboats far away
Left behind youth and child to sleep 'neath grim and wild.

Violet A. Morgan

Pieces Of Broken Sand

Back behind the skies of night
All around the noise of sight
During boring suns with exciting thoughts
While trying to teach without being taught.

Outsmarted crystal in blue white skies
transmitted ideas inside people's minds
Before it began it was doing fine
There was love with feelings and love in mind
Now there is fingers without palms and arms that hide.

Positively sad, unstitch the earth, to pieces of broken sand.

Carved into a scratch of sound
Placed upon a path of ground
Moving in direction not pointed upon
In a way that will be our job.

Unwanted plague in thick red blood
Made us decide if we really could love
What a way to fall down
Standing below the road we ride on
Air that holds us high, now leaves us alone to decide.

Positively sad, unstitch the earth, to pieces of broken sand.

Russ Gascoyne

Desert Rat

While riding out Mohave way, I met a man
All bent and gray,
He moaned through lips dust dry and sore,
"That's all there is, there ain't no more!"

"There ain't no more of what?" I cried,
As I watched him stagger side to side,
He only answered as before, "That's all there is,
There ain't no more!"

Then an angry chorus from the sky,
Thundered, "Leave him be and let him die,
That Desert Rat is old and sore,
He's all there is, there ain't no more!"

He disappeared in a cloud of sand,
That swept across that barren land, and
His moan came faintly oe'r and oe'r,
"That's all there is, there ain't no more!"

"That's all there is, there ain't no more,
None to drink and none to store,
Can't stop to rest my weary bones,
Old desert Rats ain't got no home —— no home."

Oliver E. Fowler

Shadows

Shadows, shadows
All dark in our eyes
Flickering, dancing in the light of the night
How ever you see
You'd notice one thing
How the shadows all speak
To themselves and one thing
That thing always seems to be a mockery of life
For it repeats in a small whisper of the might
Life as it moves and acts upon this limited stage
The stage built by man or nature's design
A blank wall in a dark house

That thing we speak of is the twin of our souls
If indeed our souls are in the shape of ourselves
And if we listen to the shadows upon a wall
That we will hear will be thoughts never voiced
A poem dedicated to the falseness of appearances.

Tien Lin Yuan

Old Warriors

Retire? Advance!
All forces gather 'round!
Retreat to higher ground.

So loss of vigor, hearing, sight
Has placed us in a weakened plight,
Shall we withdraw, give up the field?
It is so easy just to yield,
Say, "Let the young take on the fight
To set the world's wrongs all aright."

No! What we've won we must defend
Or life is done before its end.
To quit would tell the war's too tough
To carry on when going's rough.

It is not so. The opposition
Strengthens when we're in strong position.

Age is no excuse for quitting…
Hold to our course! That's more befitting
Old Warriors, as we end our days
Handing the torch on - still ablaze!

Wilhalmena Williams

Memories Of School

Memories of first grade fun to be cool,
All I know is stay in school.

Make friends, then go to grade second
You get there, I remember friends from second,
Friends that mean a lot to you,
All you do is stay in school.

Having fun on weekends waiting for Monday
Instead of swimming in the pool,
Just stay in school.

Having fun at Christmas, you're waiting for it
To be done, even at halloween waiting for a ghoul,
All you do is stay in school.

All these things you remember from "K"
You look back and say
Those things are far away!
Waiting for a surprise!
Then you just open your eyes
You're in third grade!!!

Mike Garcia

Your Vision

When a day gets out of focus and problems cloud my view
All I need do to bring life back to its colorful hue
Is glance at a picture of beautiful you
For there lies the purpose in some things I do

If night's hardness weighs on my bones, my mood may incline
To recall some memory from the surface of my mind
So I walk in the dark in search of the sign
Losing myself in the splendor of a Denise moonshine

For your vision is encased within my hearts beating
You are the friend that I've longed for in meeting
So gazing at moonlight or photo is well worth repeating
You make possible thoughts once defeating

Thomas Dufficy

Another Love

The sun has decided to never shine,
All is gone and lost.
The smile I once thought was mine,
Till my pain became the cost.
The words that he only said for me,
Are there for someone else to hear.
The things about him I refused to see,
Because I needed for him to care.
He's an image haunting my lonely mind,
The love we shared won't ever be replaced.
It's something that I will never find,
Hidden to deep and misplaced.
The pain is touched by his every move,
Each time I see his darkened face,
Is another memory I try to remove,
Filled with a void of empty space.

Lisa Serafini

Untitled

I open my eyes in the half darkness of morning
All is quiet as I listen to the raindrops fall
I can feel without touching,
her presence beside me
Her aroma invades my nostrils
I smile, stretch, turn over and
look into the face of love
She smiles as my eyes drink in
The loveliness of her body
Stretched out in all its naked glory
My hand moves to softly stroke
her hair away from her face
so that I may see love more clearly
I kiss her lips to share her smile
We come together
with stares, caresses, kisses
all silently communicating our love
Sealing our bond
Finding strength in one another
to face the world

Robyn Joule Elliott

The Poet

He sings the poem the wood thrush does,
all liquid clear and colored brown, sings
to the tree to the air around - alone in
his solitude, his poem speaks out of fierce
love and gentle rain and snippets sounding
in the wind snippets of voices heard long
past carried deep within the well of soul
and poet to poet - I know.

Kay V. Deutscher

All Lost

Fields of Clover, forest of green
All lost!   All lost.
By this virus, by this disease.
It sucks values, morals ... life
into its metal bowels
and slowly forms its excretion,
Society.
It eats away at nature, our families,
the world.
Yes, we excuse Industry as being progress,
to ease the unconscious pain we feel
in the innermost primitive core of man.
There is no medicine for this sickness.
We must all adapt.
And look back at our former healthy terrestrial shell
wondering where we went wrong.

Vincent Fields

Fathers Are Partners Of God

I remember you, Dad. You're often on my mind.
all the fun that we had. In memories I find.

I think of you more often, now that MY kids are grown.
All the love that we had. All the joys we've known.

All the times you took me to the circus and the zoo.
I never could have gone to those places without you.

Movies, museums, and concerts in the park.
And I remember how you soothed me when I feared the dark.
You showed me that a man can be gentle and strong.
You gave me your hand, and let me tag along.

"Fathers are partners of God", they say.
You've been His partner, Dad, in most every way.

Lorraine Standish

Passage

As time goes by I wonder why the heart dies
All the hopes and joys of the young have went by
All of the tomorrows have turned into today
If we could do it all over would we do the same
Or change what we thought was wrong
Life has a way of passing while we mark the time
when we are young we do not take the time to ask why
As age catches up with us we start to think
Why has God granted this time on earth
If we were not put here to make a difference
If you and add up all the plus and minus of your life
What would the total be

Mary A. Weekley

"Honey Bunch"

Cooter, Cooter you've been fun
All the way to the age of one
Born on the very first day of spring
God made you with the "BEST" of everything
Hair and eyes and skin so fair
To "Beauty Queens" we can compare
Sometimes sweet and sometimes wild
Never one to just act mild
Love you, love you "O" so much
Thank you Lord for our
   "Honey Bunch"

Philippe Kassouf

The Narrow Road

Walking down that narrow road alone, sorrow and regret is
all to be shown.

The sun rises and the road stares into the night, the road
is long and endless it seems the darkness is there
overshadowing the light.

A ray of sun to crack the door so rarely is found, walking
through fog with silence all around.

Days are long to wait for the time to lay in peaceful
sleep, when the sun will come and the security I shall keep.

Teresa Moreland Schenck

Alone

She sat beneath the willow tree,
Alone.
Her black silken hair fluttered in the breeze,
Alone.
She had to do it she knew,
Alone.
She stood and went to the water's edge,
Alone.
As the cool water encircled her,
Alone.
Not a sound was heard but the rippling of water,
Alone.

Lara Umberger

Memories

   Look out to the horizon where the sea meets the sky. Clouds
drift along lazily against the blue background. Ripples of water
float by and crash on the shore. An occasional boat sails by.
The scene is serene and calm.
   It brings me back to my childhood days. My memories of
young innocence fade into the sand castles I built numerous
summers on the beach. Rows and rows of red striped umbrellas
lined a bed of sand. The smell of Coppertone permeated the
warm, saltwater air. Men trudged by the bathers carrying huge
white ice chests yelling, "Ice cream and ices!" The peacefulness
of a blimp or advertisement floating by on the back of an
airplane is ever-present on my mind.
   Those days camouflaged the harsh reality of life. I was
consumed in its illusionary world and marvelled at its blessings.
It was like G-D was watching over me himself. I felt protected
under the warm sun and sounds of the roaring ocean.
   My father would yell, "Egg Harbor" when we were nearing our
destination.
   I can recall everyone awakening with a start. "Where, where,"
they would say. My father laughed and had a grin of satisfaction
that his prank worked!

Linda Garber

Orange

It rolled on the hard floor,
and banged upside the brown wooden door.

It spun faster than the rest,
I knew my orange was the best.

Green on the bottom, and orange on the top,
and then a patch of yellow that would not stop.

Its bumpy texture had caught my eyes,
and when I squeezed it, it gave me a surprise.

I loved my orange, orange until one day I dropped it,
and now my orange, orange was brown spotted.

Kate Harlin

A Country Road

I walked down a country road today
  along my childhood trails.
Although now I'm many miles away,
  my thoughts travel through wooded vales.
Along the lovely country side
  past meadows rippling in the breeze,
  a flame with flowers and butterflies,
  my fancies travel there with ease.
Down those beloved childhood scenes
  where life is good and I am free
  to run and play or lie and dream
  and watch the clouds play tricks on me...
Sometimes there're faces or other things
  just floating by, a joy so rare.
With wonder I watch them as they change
  and wish that somehow I were there.
Once more to walk that country road,
  to run and play without a care...
My heart would burst into an ode,
  And I would sing because I'm there.

Lula Shaw Siemon

"Why Do We Fight?"

"Why do we fight?" Some people say,
Although some people fight all day.
"Why do we fight?"
And not talk it out.
We do not know, we just shout.
It doesn't make you big,
It doesn't make you cool.
It doesn't make you tough,
But, just a lonely fool.
When we fight, we hurt, we kill,
But, yet our problem remains here still.
If we could have talked for a minute or five
There could have been a boy still here alive.
Whether overseas, or wherever you are,
Please talk it out.
It's better by far!

Shannon Rutherford

Destiny And You

I never think in the past when I think of you.
Always it is present and always it is true.
A special line was drawn in the path of life we live;
And now we're destined to be near and to each other give.

Think of me wherever in the world that you may be,
And you will feel and sense a warmth within, which warmth will just
BE ME.
You came into my life like a bullet from afar.
Your being then shined through me like a heavenly shooting star.

The years will pass and you will find all you ever sought.
You'll meet your goals and climb the hills and do whatever you ought.
But of all the things life has in store,
What we have now is made no more.

Time will pass and your spirits will rise and fall.
You'll know happiness and sadness and passion, but most of all,
Believe and know that I remain as close within your heart,
As anything you'll ever know, as from the very start.

So seek out love and never fear to share,
For near you is that line to me who does so care.
With you then, for now and for everlasting eternity,
Keep me inside, for that was meant to be.

C. James McCallar, Jr.

Without Love

I miss you and I'll always
always love you too
I am now a woman without a family
without ties, without connection, without love
I know I'll never hold you again
to love you again
but except in my prayers you'd kiss me goodnight
and that you've always love me

You say you'd love me forever
it's not forever yet
and now I am a woman without love
I wish I could have done more
a woman without love
without love
without you now what will I do

It's over, it is truly irreversible over
and I'm trying to comprehend
the fullness of this horrible event
now that I'm a woman without love
without you now what will I do

Sophia Samuels

A Part Of Life

I feel like an island lost in a sea of madness,
Always running from my foes and searching for my friends.
There are times when I question the worthiness of life,
But there are times when I hope to never die.
My only prayer is that I'll make it through,
Through each of life's ups and downs that are given to me.
I'll do my absolute best to stay on top,
But you must promise to be there to catch me if I should
  ever fall.

Nicole King

"Angel Glow"

Oh how I'd like to be an Angel, and have
an Angel's glow.

No need to get to know me or judge my color
or my clothes.

Oh how I'd like to be an Angel and have an Angel's glow.

First sight of an Angel the light of love simply flows

If I could be an Angel the warmth I have
would explode.

And every one would love me because
they would automatically know-

Oh how I'd like to be an Angel and have an Angel's glow

So that all might know God sees
the light within us and we all have an Angel's glow.

Oh how I'd like to be an Angel so my
light would be so bright-

That all could feel my warmth when
they needed it in their darkest night.

If only everyone wanted to be an Angel
the battle would be won

Because the light of love within us is where we all begun -

Patricia Susan Henson

Untitled

Once I sat among your ranks
An open ear ready to listen
And time and again I did
Yet you were not there
When an open ear was what I needed
Never did I let you sit in the depths of sorrow
But here I sit drowning in my own despair
No longer do I sit among your ranks
For what you need is not a friend
But a shadow who will always be there
And never expect a thing
Tamra Spielvogel

Rain Forest

As you walk through the rain forest what can you see?
An orchid, a toucan, or a kapok tree.
Way off in the distance a spider monkey howls.
A comely black jaguar goes out on a prowl.

Green tree frogs sit on the kapok tree's trunk.
Some Amazon river alligators take a dunk.
An albino python slithers along.
A macaw vocalizes his obstreperous song.

For all of its beauty it's hard to accept,
That with the destruction we cannot protect
The plants and animals that inhabit the jungle.
For into the rain forest man continues to bungle.
William K. Young

"Our Little House"

This is the house my husband built of brick, and putty, and beams.
And a piece of his heart went into each part.
Along with many wonderful dreams.

This is the house I came to after he made me his bride.
And this doorstep you see is the same one that he carried
me over with pride.

This is the house we live in together as husband and wife;
Where our little ones will grow sharing the love that we know.
God had blessed every day of our life.
Linda Warner

Remembered Love

The years have swiftly vanished
　　And all our youth is gone,
But in my book of memoirs
　　Love for you still lingers on!
I have not forgotten the first time we met
　　Your kiss and fond caress.
How could I forget the black out that night
　　Your loving arms enfolding me tight?
The endearing words you spoke,
Those ardent letters that you wrote
I remember every date - every sweet embrace your tenderness
You were my only happiness
Since we parted, I've never been the same
Each passing day, I've had but one wish, one dream,
That we would meet again,
And I'd hear you call my name!
Oh, what joy it would be,
To know that you still remembered me!
Liberty Rice Conlin

Today You Gave Me A Rose

Today you gave me a rose
and, as I look at it,
it makes me think of many things
of which I'll never forget.

I think of a rose bush by a chapel
in the mountains so high and vast
and a love we shared that glorious day,
a love that will forever last.

You have given me many experiences,
you spoil me it is true.
Yet all those times would have meant nothing
if I could not have shared them with you.

I spend many hours waiting
for the lonely day to close.
Then once again you are here with me
and together we share the rose..
Verna Jackson

Let Me Give Love

Let me give love, Lord, not just when I receive it-
　　and bask in its glow, or delight in its treasures.
I need, Oh, Lord, to give love when unrequited-
　　and even when it is spurned-or seemingly so-
Help me see the shaming pain of any soul forced to beg for love,
　　and open my ears to hear hearts who silently cry for it-
by deeds and attitudes that repel and provoke and irritate.
　　Help me hear the cry for love that pleads for discipline to,
　　　"stop me"
In the tantrums of a child and in the testing of authority
　　so often displayed by confused teenagers.
May my love respond with commendation to silent pleas for
　　encouragement.
　　Give me the strength to give true love,
when it can only be clothed in the repulsive garb of admonition.
　　Teach me to robe myself in the sackcloth of humility, Lest
I guise pride as love.
　　Oh, Lord the world is sick for love, and lack of it breeds
　　violence everywhere.
Open our ears to hear and interpret those pitiful pleas,
　　and help us all proclaim Your love by responding with our own.
Velva Mattix

Blue Vase

I had forgotten how cleanly formed
And beautiful your hands were upon these keys
As thoughtfully you played a tortured Russian tune
That screamed to God for a soul's ease.

A tall girl dressed in silk,
Pale golden eyes fixed on the wall
Above the music rack, you hovered like an icon
For minutes, moments even - that is all.

I had forgotten how, like a harp,
I quivered at your glance in my direction, such
A turmoil you evoked.....
These keys still remember your heart beat, your touch.

O lovely one, long gone,
My arm trembles as it lifts the blue vase
In memory of pale golden eyes —
As in a painting— in a shimmering ivory face!

O golden bird, you have sung your song
And have flown into the sky,
Leaving me, alone, mute, wondering, why?
Kaya Chernishova

I Play The Flute And She The Cello

I play the flute, and she the cello, we meet, each so attuned to
and content with a soliloquy, is a duet possible?

We admire the others instrument, and wonder, what increment of
pleasure may be exacted from a joint overture.

As I tune her instrument, she repays me the compliment. Our
concerto is about to commence.

We play, I her cello and she my flute. Each finds the duet less
pleasurable than a soliloquy, as time, experience and feelings
are needed to develop an appreciation for the others instrument.

I play the flute, and she the cello, we met, each so attuned to
and content with a soliloquy, a duet wasn't possible.

Dr. Wayne Lener

Neverending Quests

Through the trees,
And cross the field,
Pass the prairie,
But not too far,
You will find a new strange thing,
But I cannot say it so,
For there you'll see a farfetched beast,
Which I sit next to it and there is where I'll be,
Helping, protecting, and never hurting,
Just taking the darkness from her-
And into me.
I am filled with all the darkness,
The darkness of all I have touched,
I take the unfortunate souls of beasts,
And I heal their wounds along with the soul,
For I hold it at all inside of me,
As I start back on my Neverending Quest.

Nicky Strahl

Untitled

I love to watch the sun go down
And darkness fall all over town,
And the streets lights send their small array
Out on beautiful St. Andrews Bay.

And people stirring here and there,
While the girls are home fixing their hair.
And the boys are busy getting a car
and stealing dimes from little sisters jar.

And Mother is tuning the radio
On some old tune that we all know.
Father sits back in his easy chair
And keeps a watchful eye at the clock on the stair.

Then the time comes when lovers meet
Not in town, but on some quiet street.
Far away from everyone's sight,
There to remain 'til late at night.

Then morning breaks both fair and cool,
And the first thought in mind is that of school.
You rush right home and make it just right
But the thoughts of that day, ruin that blessed last night.

Sue Allen

Untitled

The sun has shown its face all day
and it falls behind the mountains as we say,

Good-bye,

Good-bye sun your time is gone

Good-bye sun... until the dawn.

Lindsay M. Clay

The Brat

She was a spoiled brat.
And did not care diddle-squat
She didn't care about anyone.
Until the day he came along.
She opened her heart to care for another.
And experienced life's greatest pleasure.
Now that she has found Mr. Right
She does not let him out of her sight.
Soon a problem did arise.
And caught them both by surprise.
She didn't realize how jealous she was.
Until one day they had a fight and she was the cause.
She was very possessive.
And at times, she over reacted.
She didn't want to lose him.
Because life without him is very dim.
So, she tried to control her jealousy
And as a result, he was very happy!!!

Mala Ramnarine

Misery

Cold sweat soaked through his clothes
And dripped into his hollow eyes
His stomach twisted and clenched with pain
From all the disheartening lies
His body shivered with convulsing nerves
From years of his self doubt
Adored by all the world
Yet the world just shut him out
He searched his heart
And looked desperately for peace
But love was far away
And hope was out of reach
Then a frightening thought came to him
As he stared blankly at the wall
There was but a single way to end the pain
He'd have to end it all
Then be in paradise
Where misery holds no sway
He fired a shot into the air
That took his pain away.

William Sybert

To Be...

To be wrapped in your embrace,
And encompassed in your care.
To be intoxicated by the thought,
That you will always be there.

To be helplessly drowning in your laughter
And reveling in your smile.
To walk, hand in hand with you,
To the end of the longest mile.

To be prisoner to your heart,
And hostage to your soul.
To be the perpetual thought—
That your heart will always hold.

To be the most beautiful thing,
That your eyes have yet seen—
To be your vision of eternity,
And what life is supposed to mean.

To be the missing link,
That you've been searching to find.
To be at one with you—
In body, in soul, and in mind.

Missy Johns

Dreaming The Secret

Exit the day for the night
and entering an additional light
inspiring verve with extraordinary height
and magnificently probing the abyss of life
saturating my nebulous sleep
with pervasive tunes from base to peak
everything I sense to degree
is the covert form of clarity
and the beauty and simplicity
that surrounds myself
is comprehensible all about
I feel as if
I were turned inside out
now every obstacle is not a wall
but a connotation for the integral
yet arising with the light
the very next day
to find nothing has changed
it's still the same way

> *Madelyn D. Lizzio*

If Only...

If only I could reach out,
And find that forgotten place,
Hold your hand, comfort your tears,
Wipe the sorrows from your face.

Tell you that tomorrow came,
And I still had you in my heart,
And though the years had passed,
We were never really so far apart.

When I saw angels fluttering,
I felt you were by my side,
And whenever I saw your portrait,
I laid my head and cried.

And the times I've been lost, with no one who understands,
I new that if you'd been here,
I'd have found safety within your hands.

An unconditional emotion would pour, from your heart to my pain,
And wash away the hurt, that for so long has remained.

But you are here my dear Mother, and we've both been weathered,
And I will always be your daughter,
And for that... I will love you forever.

> *Kathleen Cecil*

Letting Go

The time has come for one to realize
And fully understand and know
That the relationship is over in another's eyes
That's part of letting go

It may be very troubling to say
That one is not the foe
But admitting it in a productive way
Is the process of letting go

There will always be the memories
That produce both joy and woe
Living each new moment one can seize
Must be letting go

Trying to hang on to absent romance
Makes recuperating slow
Realizing reuniting has no chance
Is the art of letting go

It is difficult to put it all behind
And feel happy, not just low
But chains of the future one must unbind
For then one is letting go

> *Tom Russell*

"Tempests To Rainbows"

As tempests roar and oceans roll
And ghastly crimes still take their toll
I sit in quietude and search my soul
For meaning of the awesome whole.

Now the human mind adjusts to these
And yearns for return of the gentle breeze.
Then I think of the power in a tiny seed
Bursting with compassion for another's need.

As glistening dewdrops refresh the rose
And placid pools give sweet repose
Where little froglets often doze—-
A peaceful place to see rainbows.

Rainbows, yes, everywhere—-
Signs of His Love—no great surprise
When we open our eyes to Paradise.

> *Willadene L. Nicholas*

The Root

IT plants itself in least obvious places
    and grows without nurturing invading all spaces,
It wraps its vine around unwilling parts
    slowly stunting their growth while attacking the heart;

WE yank at the weeds it has left in its wake
    though our strength is diluted and our bodies do ache,
We claw at the ground where its seeds have been sown
    but with each field we command, yet another has grown;

ITS presence is rampant... it lives and it breathes,
    feeding on the biased; the ignorant; the weak,
It captures the proud; the noble; the kind;
    consuming all good, leaving shreds behind;

Yet and still, we toil on to fight this disease
    through our heartaches and tears, we do fall to our knees
We pray to the SPIRIT, in his shield he must keep US...
    that is the only true cure to master INJUSTICE.

> *Teri L. Elam*

Not For A Rag

He was a bato from the streets, loved by his carnales
and hated by those in authority.
He walked the streets by day and hung out at night,
wore baggy clothes and always sagged.
But this bato would never die for a rag.

He always respected his hommies and rucas,
and never once turned away his carnales.
He was born to a very poor family,
and had to work hard for what he had.
But this bato would never die for a rag.

He lived his life only to please his old man.
Made his father proud to call him his son.
I have only God to thank for the love he had.
He sent his only son to die for me,
and NOT for a rag!

> *Roy Gonzales Jr.*

Untitled

I am rich today, a baby ran to meet me
And put his tiny hand within my own
And smiled, his rosy lips a flower
One lights within his eyes, from heaven shone
And when I crossed the fields, the birds were singing

A golden blossom in my pathway lay
It wasn't much, but oh, the joy there is in it

To have a baby smile at you, In just that way

> *Louise L. Pace*

Oscar The Oyster

Oscar the oyster lived at the bottom of the sea.
And he was just as happy as an oyster could be.
But one day, Oscar fell,
And a small grain of sand got into his shell.
It was just one little grain,
But oh my, it gave him such a pain!
Oscar tried everything to remove it.
He flapped his shell and swished water through it.
He rocked and rolled and shook and spun,
Until he cried, "This is not fun!"
But the grain of sand was stuck like glue.
And poor Oscar sobbed, "This is worse than the flu.
If I can't remove it,
I'll try to improve it."
As the years flew by, Oscar's grain of sand grew and grew.
Then poor Oscar was caught and made into stew.
But Oscar had done what he said he would do.
For the small grain of sand that had bothered him so,
Was a beautiful pearl as white as snow,
A beautiful pearl with a glistening glow.

Koralee Helen Jaspers

Dusk 'Till Dawn

HUSH
and hear the silence of the light
as it slips into the night.

BREATHE
and feel earth's pulse
as it cools and settles from its flight.

DANCE
and sense the rhythm of the water
as the ocean ballets to the shore.

RISE
and sing a joyful song. A new day's dawn
is bursting open morning's door.

Mary Lenore Quigley

Heart's Request

I only want someone to ease my pain
And help this lonely heart of mine
But every girl I meet turns out the same
Why can't I find some peace of mind

This empty feeling chills my being
I need to quench my desire, someone to take me higher
Look me in the eyes, take off your disguise
Cure this lovesick cold, ease this empty load
From me ...

My mind is full of sorry memories
This burden drives me to the floor
My tongue has tasted many salty seas
Open up your door, hold me forever more

My heart can't see any hope for me
All of my emotions are caught in the oceans
Of loneliness, help me find some rest
Don't let me drown, turn your boat around
Help me...

Lee Bailiff

The Witch's Purple Death

Someday, the witch's darkened mirror will soon reflect,
And her extended ears will soon perceive,
The beautiful and diaphanous cry of the cradle.
And the roaring waves shrouding your sign in secret.
On that day, you will be near the saints in heaven.
Your aching soul will be quenched in healing waters,
In quiet and safe reward.
Nowhere will you see the sword that pierced your side,
Nor the evil-eye that cursed your nights
Webbed in sorrow and confusion.
For the nightingale will answer the sorcerer's cry for mercy,
Her bellowing cries for mercy.
And the purple cauldron bubbling curses,
Will turn against her wicked hand.
And the ravenous raven, although wounded,
will eat her claws and jaws.
He will destroy her thorny heart,
And zeal away her purple death,
and will be plunged in hell.

Migdalia Antonetti

Remembering

And so a flood fills my mind
and I am carried away with images and sounds of you
blown and tossed about
I can but feel you,
touch you

A torrent of past encounters with you wash over me,
a down pour
unknown and all of a sudden
swift and furious
then it's over
and I am left
wondering

Michael W. Spencer

The Crossing

The air is crisp and cold,
And I can see my breath rise from my mouth.
An old coat and a small suitcase is all that I have.
The racket of sea gulls flying overhead makes me frightened.
I am small in my dirty dress and socks with holes.
I feel close to no one and afraid of what lies ahead.
Queasy from the rock of the boat, I cling to the railing.
The sky is cluttered with clouds. It is the perfect day for coming.
Feeling for my rosary which dangles from the chain around my neck,
I feel lonely, but safe.
I wrap myself in a blanket which had been given to me by the man in grey.
On the last few days the meals have been stale.
Sleep is all that we can do.
The cries and whines of the children around me bring back memories of home.
When will the nightmare end.
When will the dream begin.
Now cramped in the corner, I stretch my legs and leaf through the Bible Mother has made me bring.
I look at her picture which lies next to my sewing kit.
With my chapped hands I bring the picture closer to me and tears roll down my cheek.
I know I will make it, and I know I will succeed.

Sarah E. Riolo

The Greatest Prayer

I've said a lot of prayers in all of my days.
And I have thanked the lord in a whole lot of ways.
I thank him for my family, my pets, and my friends.
And for keeping me safe from all the world's sins.

I thank him for the places that he has taken me.
And I thank him for the person he has led me to be.
I thank him for my sensitivity, wisdom, and wealth.
And for watching over my life and keeping me in good health.

I have asked him to lead me on the road to success.
And to give me the strength to just do my best.
And I thought God might have forgotten to grant a prayer or two,
But he answered them all the day I met you.

Now, I can't read the future. And I can't change the past.
And I can't guarantee how long our lives will last.
But I have never lied to you. And I never will. I swear.
For, anytime you need me, I promise I'll be there.

As long as you will let me, I'll stand by your side.
If you need someone to hold you, my arms are open wide.
So I ask you, "Let your guard down." My love for you is strong.
And it will always be there. As it has been here all along.

Michael R. Unruh

My Son

To know him is to love him
    and I hope you all will too.
He has a heart of the purest too.
    and this is the story to be told.
His hand reached out to all in need,
    regardless of race, color or creed.
His hand reached out to God one day
    and said "Please help me on my way."
The good Lord answered "Look dear son
    take one day at a time 'til your battle is won."
He has a wonderful sponsor who helped him on his way,
But for the grace of God he wouldn't be here today.
When he first came to this program I thought he wouldn't last
After many years of drinking, it was no easy task.
So all you people out there do not despair
    because God is right beside you with His loving care.
Just stop and smell the roses
    as you pass along life's way
And thank God He's beside you
    to help you day by day.

Margaret Tuohey

"Spring"

The scent of life crawls into my way
and I inhale the Spring.
Clear skies, such (a good) background,
for feeling so high.
Trees resurrecting from their
solstice slumber,
awakening as a Messiah,
returning from the dead.
Leading us all to the land of the living.
life and love, long lost
to the piercing blast of wintery days,
returns to us, hand in hand, on a pilgrimage
to set us free.

Niles U. Comer

The Valley

The bottom of the valley is the loneliest place I know.
And I know this place well.
The upward journey is long and hard with cold, driving snow.
With each slow, painful step I wonder how I feel.

As I look at the top, I see him looking down.
He looks down at me with a look so weak and mere.
I fight for another precious step on the rocky, frozen mound.
I know one day I'll be there and he'll be here.

The walls of the valley are punishing and steep.
Sometimes I trip and fall back again.
Why do I get up? I won't accept defeat!
My time is running out and my chances are getting thin.

Clawing and fighting up this hill has become a way of life.
Maybe I'm getting a little war torn.
Damn this hill, damn that man, and damn this modern strife.
The valley is very cold but the top is very warm.

I know for a fact the top is warm. I've been there before.
I know that for sure. Because that's where I've been.
That taste has me craving for more.
In the back of my mind, I'll soon be there again!

Troy Smith

Graduation

Thud. I knew it was him,
and I tried not to think,
of what the sound would mean.

I groped for my robe, and stumbled out of bed.
As I felt my way into the illuminated room,
I saw him.

Grandpa lay on the floor, sucking hard for air.
I squinted out the early sun that pierced my eyes,
and knelt down beside him.

I queried why he did not call for help.
His proud eyes shot the answer through a single tear.
But beneath the pride, something else glinted.

We began to talk, and as I reached out and clasped his shaking hand,
for the first time,
I saw the fear in his eyes.

The luminous sun painfully crawled from the east, and dulled overhead;
we fell back into our routine, but I could feel it coming.
The cold, sharp reality bit. My own eyes began to wonder.

Like a machine, the process was well oiled with pistons now
    ready to drive...
my childhood to its end.

Shawn Colberg

Rainbows And Leprechauns

I looked outside one rainy day,
and looked in the sky and it was all gray.
Something caught my eye and it was low,
I looked a little closer and saw a rainbow.
I put on my raincoat, my boots, and hat,
and rushed out the door with my kitty cat.
I went to find the rainbow and what to my surprise,
a cute little leprechaun with tiny little eyes.
He asked me some questions and where I was from,
I said here on this he was not fond of.
I asked where's the rainbow, and with a cute little grin,
He said in your heart and took off with a spin.
I will miss that little leprechaun and we may never part,
because we both have the rainbow
Deep in our heart.

Michelle Dalrymple

The Promise

I smoked that same cigarette nine times over
And I'm not going back, don't want to stay sober
Been through this whole act a thousand times
Ringing the bells and sounding the chimes
Turning the pages
I can't take anymore.

I saw that same vision in my dreams before
And I'm not going to do it, going straight through the door
Traced through the lines of eternity's path
Telling the tales, explaining the math
Wanting the same thing
But all to no avail.

God, I'm only seventeen, do you know what I mean?

I heard that same voice calling my name again
Don't know who it is, could it be a friend?
Traveled the course of my heart's miseries
Reaching for you while searching for me
Holding my hands out
For you to return.

God, I'm only seventeen, do you know what I mean?

Laura Lee Kenderes

He Came From Glory

Jesus came to live in a place on earth
And left behind Him streets of gold.

How could a king leave such riches and glory
To die on a cross, for me, so unworthy?

He left a place of mountains filled with flowers
Mansions, and meadows of green.

He left a place of love and comfort
Just so I could go there, too.

He came from Glory
To save us from Hell.

Won't you consider, today
How much it cost,

For a King to come from Glory
To die on a cross, for me, so unworthy.

Kathy Williams

Sitting By The Creek

Sometimes I sit down by the creek
And listen to the water speak.
It tells of times so long forgot,
Of Summer nights and days so hot,
And children playing near the shore,
Splashing, laughing, running and more.
They'd play all day, these children gay,
And laugh the carefree days away.
But then one time they came no more—
No children visited the shore.
The sandy beach then took to seed,
The meadow's now grown in with weeds.
In this same spot the brook still flows,
Yet why it does, I do not know.
The laughter that once filled the years
Now gives way to reflective tears,
As I sit by this lonely creek,
And listen to the water speak.

Ray Dube

A Smile From The Past

A smile from the past. Memories of anger sorrow
and love once had, but his smile hides a soul other than
his own in his heart of pain. A loved one gone but still
there. I look into my uncle's eyes and I see...my father.
    Oh daddy, mommy said you were going to come
home. I waited for many years but your never came.
One day mommy told me you were dead. But when I
look at Uncle Ronnie I see your sad face behind his smile.
    They though you were dead, because they saw
your casket lowered into the hollow ground. They have
forgotten you but they are blind, because you never left.
The flowers on your grave have long since faded away,
for the world has looked the other way.
    Damn them for looking on, because my love has
never gone. I can see what they cannot, for I truly have
not forgot...because I can see you behind Uncle Ronnie's smile.

Steven Ferrell

Hello, Departure

Every morning, with my make-up
and my clothes, I put on my public self.
My hair is combed and bound and free
of leaves and grass. I stand erect, or sit
(ankles demurely crossed), and cover my teeth.
It is with startled recognition that I
come to see myself, a familiar stranger,
recalling eons past—or yet to come—
and I wonder which direction I am going.
Still, it surprises me to realize
the dark, feral pulse in my veins,
to savor the earth's rich, telling fragrance,
my pace quickening when the moon's round,
silver eye peers through the fingers of the trees:
    bright, silent invitation.
More and more, some part of me slips into the night,
    barefoot, naked,
to roll in the dirt and howl in lunar light.

Polly Hairston

Frog Music

Beyond the lane a blue-grey pond lies gleaming in the sun.
And nearby, Red-winged blackbirds pipe their lyrics just for fun.
But to this music critic's ear more pleasing than the rest
Comes from deep within the pond, frog music at its best!

I tip-toe near the concert hall to see if I can see
A glimpse of one participant before he can see me.
I hear a splash! then all is still.
The surface ripples faster,
But on a floating lily-chair there sits the choir master!

From dawn 'till dusk I hear their songs, notes high and low together
The classics of their water-world, no matter what the weather
The trills of Bob-o-links are sweet.
Blue-birds and all the rest.
In early spring I still adore frog music at its best.

Waustella Laurence

A Smile...

A smile starts at the corner of her mouth
And rolls straight through my heart
Blue eyes sparkle, they shine,
Dimples beam, lips are slightly apart.

Love and joy like wildfire spread,
Consuming all in their path
This gift is priceless, beyond compare;
For a lifetime it will last.

Karen Douglass

Happy Birthday!

Three lovely daughters
     And no son!
Until Melanie brought home
     Number One,
The guy from Nebraska—
     Quiet, studious and fun.
He brought to this family a new dimension.
     At lively dinner discussions he pays attention,
Then wisely escapes the constant chatter,
     To read the news and items that matter,
Or quietly watch TV with Pat and Fat Cat.

Jeff, you are a great addition
     To this family of girls.
As your multi-facetted personality
     And sterling character unfurls,
It is easy to see what Melanie saw—
     And such a pleasure to have you as my son-in-law!

     Wanda McCulloh

The Man On The Middle Cross!

I stood one day and gazed at three crosses on a hill,
And on one cross I saw a man, He was so quiet and still.
I wondered as I stood there just what this could mean.
For many times the things we see aren't always what they seem.
I saw His face, I heard HIM say, "It was for you I died."
The love I saw, it touched my heart, I bowed my head and cried.
I looked around, no one was there, so I knew He spoke to me,
It was as if my blinded eyes had just begun to see.
The man was on the middle cross, a stream flowed from his side,
I stood and watched it as it flowed, a cleansing crimson tide.
I knew I could not leave until I'd stepped into the stream.
Freedom from the load I carried long had been my dream.
I took the step, I felt the load, as it lifted from my heart.
I knew I'd found a way of life from which I'd never part.
I knew I'd never be the same while on this earth I trod.
I'd found the way, the only way, I stood and thought of God.

     Thelma McNichols

The Glory Has Departed

Souls meet in an insignificant setting,
and profound love ensues.
Judeph is not aware,
for his charm tenderly affects every girl
as effortlessly as the sun caresses every fragile flower.
Then dark clouds cover the brilliant sun forever?
The waves will never again reach shore...
Judeph is gone.
Love becomes heartache, and has never been so wanting as this.
The dreams of sweet embrace fill sleep.
Yet with waking hours, dreams are not allowed...lest the warm
rain falls.

     Rachele Samartino

To My Mother

She gave the best years of her life with joy for me,
     And robbed herself with loving heart unstintingly.
For me, with willing hand, she toiled from day to day,
     For me she prayed when headstrong youth would have its way.

Her gentle arms, my cradle once, are weary now,
     For time has set the seal of care upon her brow.
And tho' no other eyes than mine their meaning trace,
     I read my history in the lines of her dear face.

And 'mid His gems, Who showers gifts as shining sands,
     I count her days as pearls that fall from His kind hands

     Caroline E. Keith

Commitment

My mind took me a stroll through time
And sat me down in the middle of nowhere
Trying to explain why the breath of commitment
Was in need of resuscitation

As instinct prevails over last night's morals
Material needs surpass life's original destiny
Fighting to stay above water holding on to a reason to live
While it struggles to multiply commitment
As its seed fall leaching to infertile ground

Generational tradition is put on trial
As till death do us part lives on the border of fiction
Turning its back on commitment
Forgetting who it's really related to
While love, understanding, and longevity
Fight to hold the family together

The ultimate basis of civilized survival
Will continue to collide with decay
Until the showers of commitment are allowed to reign
Over the injustice of adulterous pursuits

     Kevin Briggs

There Is Nothing Like A Mother:

A Mother is some one who cares, and always is near you in need,
And She always fills Her daily deed.
She never says No! and does Her best,
to see that you are well, and have some rest.
When you where a baby, She comforted you and protected you
     from harms.
And still to this day She would do the same, with even wider
     open arms

You can only have one True Mother!
And there isn't another True Friend who could be better.
Love Her now, not later!
Give Her what you can, for nothing could be greater.
She's yours alone, awake or fast asleep.
When your lonesome or blue, who do you turn too? Mother! Why?
Because you know She loves you.
Now She's old and gray, but remember She's never far away,
No matter how She looks today.
You know its not Her heart that changes from day to day,
She's still the same in heart and soul",
That's why I say, let Her know! That you only have one Mother!
And that you love Her so, for if you don't tell Her now,
She may never really know!

     Tony E. Kupiszewski

Caribou Mountain

On Caribou Mountain, the wind does rise
and shifts the snow for its eternal disguise

On Caribou Mountain, it is always white,
stark and austere, under cobalt blue skies

In the winter, on Caribou Mountain,
the wind howls and lashes
and when it stops,
the past intrudes
and the laughter of children is heard.

The laughter of children
who all perished one fall,
when influenza swept the town
and no cure could be found
and the trains stopped coming
and the roofs of the houses fell in
and the stark stone walls still reach up to the sky,
as the wind whistles through them.

From peak to peak the snow shifts once more
on Caribou Mountain
like it has, before.

     Louis C. Oswald

Distorted Perception

Distorted perception coming in, altered thought begins.
And so you've changed your point of view, reality missed you.
And then you grow and learn each day, you think about the
   things you say.
When you see life through deflecting eyes, you just have to
   compromise.

So snort your cocaine, and drink your beer, pass that joint over here.
You say you can, but you cannot see, I don't like the way you
   look at me.
Where's reality baby?

It's kind of hard to comprehend, with bogus information coming in.
It's hard to see life distortion free, when you're hiding from reality.
So many years of substance abuse, will it ever really let you loose?
Your environment shaped you through the years, through
   distorted perception and lots of tears.

Sometimes you look back and see, a distorted reality.
Will you ever find who you really are? Is it too late? Have you
   gone to far?
Where's reality baby?
Where's reality baby?

Samuel J. Scamacca, Jr.

Spring

Spring shakes the earth's greenness
And stirs and wakens my lethargic soul.
It invites me to a grateful new aliveness
Which had laid dormant with the snow.
It arises now and it does grow
With each God given day.
It grows with ever changing landscapes
Of buds, trees, flowers, green grass and leaves.
It snaps and slaps my sleepy eyes and nose awake
So in these wondrous riches it may partake.

Susan Barnick

When I Think Back!

I set alone and think of times gone by. I remember the laughter
and tears in my mother's eyes and times of happiness and times
of pain when nothing I said or done could help times when she
had to be alone and work it out on her own. I remember the
times when I would say or do something to hurt her and then
later realize what I had done. I never could make it up to her,
but finally I would say "I'm sorry" and she would always forgive
me. Forgiving and forgetting are two different things. I know
now that I'm older and think back I was wrong and I wish I
never had done those things. It shows me she loved me a lot.
Someone who can forgive over and over time after time really
must love me a lot. I love her too, and always have, but I never
realized how important a mother really is. I'm sorry now for all
the things I did, and didn't do. I know I can't make them up to
her, but I know this is a time I can say something to help and if
she was here I would tell her
"I love her and how sorry I really am."

Renee Nelms

Why We Give Thanks

The pilgrims landed at Plymouth Rock
   and prayed to God for what they got.
They had a feast, a harvest plenty,
   hoping that it would be the first of many.
They struggled hard through winter's cold,
   but through it they were strong and bold.
They established for us a freedom grand
   in America, the promised land.

Valerie L. Parker

Advertisement

It seemed that when it rained, it poured
And that piece of the rock blocked
My run for the border.
I was proud to be your bud,
But when we doubled the pleasure
We doubled the fun
And it kept going and going and going.....
You were the best a man could get
And I got the fever for the flavor,
So we just did it because we deserved a break today.
I've come a long way baby,
But you'll never hate me because I'm beautiful,
And now your love melts in my mouth and not in my hand.
We brought good things to life
Although I raised my hand because I was sure
This wasn't the choice of a new generation.
Why ask why it just feels right, and
I did try to be all that I could be.
Like a rock that takes a licking and keeps on ticking...
The Heartbeat of America.

Sara Kleynenberg

Childhood

Childhood is over when the dolls are packed away,
and the child would rather stay in,
than go outside and play.
When dreams are no longer reality,
and imagination is controlled by fact,
When the future holds scary thoughts,
and the world appears dark and black.
When naps do not seem like such a drag,
and fairy tales no longer come true,
When Halloween arrives,
and people stop giving candy to you.
When life becomes a great big puzzle,
and the future does not seem so far off.
Then your childhood has come and gone,
You must then find your own path to travel on.

Melinda Robertson

Memories

I remember the snowfalls with the tractor pulling the sled,
And the cold frosty mornings with quilts piled high on the bed.

I remember the smoke and ashes that came from our stove that
   burned wood
And how we'd hurry from our bath behind it as quickly as we could.

I remember the springtime with wild flowers and trees so green
You could smell the honey suckle in bloom and hear the drone of a bee

The spring bubbled and churned as it came out of the ground
You could almost see it rushing to the river just by listening to its
   sound

In the summertime the sun laid heavily upon the land
It was a quiet, lazy time that some might consider bland

I remember the hours I fished and the first time I baited my own hook
And nothing can compare to the first catfish I pulled out of our brook

I remember the trees along the hillside changing to shades of gold
And the bushes and leaves seeming almost to burst with more
   color than they could hold

We would rake the leaves and arrange them in a stack
Then jump in the middle when Mother turned her back

I remember all these things as I look back on the years
I can still hear my childish laughter and feel my childhood fears

As long as people have their memories they're never completely alone
All they need do is sit and remember and instantly they are back home.

Patty Embry

91

The Old Dusty Road

I remember walking barefeet in the heat
And the cold, on that old dusty dirty road
I wasn't very old, the tall pine trees would
Shade me from the rain and the sun
I was seven yrs old, it was a mile
to school each way, I would walk everyday.
On that dusty road I did not see
Many cars traveling the road, at night there was no light,
God watch over me in the day, and
night, in rain when I was in pain
When I was alone on the road he
told me to keep straight ahead not
to be afraid. If I meet a stranger
along the way to greet them the time
of day. If there a sign of danger along
the road he would point the way.
I would see people going to the
lake to fish, the men hauling trash
to the dump to burn, and smell the
foul things in the air, I was seven did not really care

Maxcine Fuller

New Love

When the light of morrow has come
And the darkness of the yester has passed,
We hearken to the new song that is sung
And not to be reminded of the past.

A brand new day awakened from above;
Leads us to brighter futures once again.
Those days left behind us are like a glove
Whose purpose is to cover our mass pain.

Such as nature is to the days ahead,
So is love to the chambers to our heart.
As the winds change, our old love becomes dead.
Then, a new love will show us a new start.

Love is like nature in countable ways-
One being, they can both change with the days.

Michelle Phillips

"Legacy Of The American Indian"

The beautiful clear rivers roared
And the Majestic Eagle soared
The American Indian loved this land
Now they survive by the White Man's hand
Like so many animals whom now are extinct
The Indians way of life will never repeat
The Buffalo once roamed thousands by number
But stilled are their hooves, no longer like Thunder
Hushed is the laughter of the children and Squaws
The hunters no longer by the rivers do pause
Perhaps they were savage and did not understand
With Mother Nature and earth they lived hand and hand
The Indian hunted taking only what was need
White Man hunts mostly from greed
The Indians law was the law of the land
Whittled away like rock into sand
The land is contaminated, dirty and poor
No longer do crystal clear waters roar
But one day, perhaps very soon
The Indians revenge will be the White Man's Doom?

Linda Phillips

You Can Count On Me

No love can surpass that of our father and mother,
And the rest of our family too.
But we grew up an learned together
So we know each other through and through.
Sometimes you want to cease to exist.
This feeling can be very strong indeed.
But this feeling you must resist,
If we are both to succeed.
As you are a part of me
Whether the distance between us is far or wide
You will someday be free,
This can not be denied.
When the day is finally here,
That you are set free.
I will be there,
You can count on me.

Ronnie Payne

I Have No Soul!

She screamed at the empty buildings
and they faintly rumbled back the same.
Those empty hulks
spoke more of the truth than she did.
A groan arises from the foundations
to be echoed by her for,
She recognizes the memory
of belonging,
of family.
Meaning life and bustle to both
yet in quietly different ways.
Which one, do you think, would get the most
out of a slamming door?

Daremo

"Unknown Explorers"

There comes a time when memories fade into dreams,
and things are not what they appear to be.
Aged men sit around camp fires
waiting for the day they too will expire.
And whisper tales of long distance voyagers.
Mariners who had sailed to distant shores
whose names have been forgotten forevermore.
Men who wrestled the angry waves
for which they will be remembered as strong and brave.
Did they search for treasures or fame?
Secrets that die hard are not easily explained.
Is it in vain that man must push beyond his domains
to walk upon the unfamiliar terrains.
To confront the burning questions of his mind,
and to recognizes the answers he hopes to find.
Is this not were he has grown
by venturing out from his family and his home,
and seeking for that which is unknown.
For in knowledge there can be wisdom
to choose the roads that life has given him.

Mark Galassi

Blue

Blue is the stream that goes so slow
Around the blueberry patches in a row

Blue is the Blue Jay that flies so high
In the fresh blue morning sky

Blue is the bluebird that chirps a song
Letting us know he'll be coming along

Blue is the bluebell that blooms in the spring
With daisies and daffodils and other spring things,

Blue is a wonderful color!

Soyoung Oh

The Rain...

When I think about the rain, it's so romantic to me,
and to be with someone special,
that makes it even better to want to see.
When you look at the rain, it symbolizes one thing,
All the love you have for someone and all the joy it brings.
All the big drops symbolizes all the hectic problems you may have,
Along with the small, that symbolizes all the many laughs.
Don't forget about the thunder that holds us close together,
And also the lighting that makes up this beautiful weather.
A cloud over here and a cloud over there,
Makes one big cloud for the two of us to share.
So the next time it rains and you're with the person you love,
Just look and smile at the heaven above.
Rain can mean a lot if you let your mind explore,
And a lot of rainy days you'll probably wish for.

Shycole D. Walker

They Came

They came out of nowhere
And took hold of my heart
There was no warning
Swift as a arrow straight to my heart
They are embedded there till time and
fate say it's time to go
They will then leave on their own to
face life with the knowledge of knowing
that they were love
Loved by a stranger who gave them love
freely with no demands and pushed them to
life, knowing they would survive
Now a year or more has passed
Once they were boys, now they are men
Now they bring wives, babies and girlfriends
To the place where they were loved in friendship
Where they were allowed to be,
As they were, with no one to impress

Yolanda Mendoza

The Watcher

I turn the corner on my morning strolls
And walk past well-kept homes.
But her house is unkempt, the shutters fall,
The grass is high and parched, the hedge untrimmed.

Her front door open, she sits on her porch.
The smell of cats and rot
Oppress the sunlit street and fill the air,
And everything around her, all is old.

She sits out in her chair in rain or sun.
Sometimes I cross the street,
Avoid her eyes, the tapping of her cane,
But under her torn hat, she stares at me.

They say that she is rich, her husband dead,
No one to care or love.
She snatches in the food her neighbors leave.
But one day when I walk she is not there.

Oh, is she ill, or gone away, or worse?
Days pass, her chair unfilled,
Her front door shut against the sun and air,
The untouched dishes sitting on her porch.

Pamela Wolfe Roblyer

Reflections of a Prisoner of War

When cannons cease their deafening roar
And we are free men all once more,
When all our friends about us
Sigh at our brave ventures in the sky,
When wines and foods about us heap
And nights are filled with boundless sleep,
When sweethearts press their lips to ours
In nights of passion laden hours,
When love and joy ascend their peak
And laughter crowds the words we speak,
When sunshine tints our darkened past,
Will we a thankful moment cast
To God who made our shroud lines taut...
And pay the debt for life—rebought?

Robert E. McAdam

Love Knows No Time

We were strangers when we first met
and were introduced to one another.
We looked into each other's eyes
baring our souls to each other.

I stared at you, you stared at me,
feeling an uncanny sense of familiarity.
The love we were to embark upon,
seemed leftover from another century.

We let ourselves go and our love grew,
just as we both expected it to.
Your love is with me eternally,
allowing me the freedom to just be.

You have let me into your body and soul
and your karma is entwined with mine,
yet I sense that we have met before,
for true love knows no time.

And now I realize who you really are,
for I have shared your love before.
You're the twin soul that I've yearned for.
I am your planet, you are my star.

Philip Ingrasciotta

Pure of Heart

In the night, with wind whistling threw the trees,
and with the dog barking at the willow, waving in the wind,
and the moon in its splendor glow,
the stars shining with all their might and strength.

As I sit on the soft grass, engorging nature with the sound of
crickets, with a sweet tune, only those who are pure of heart
can withstand, and all the unpure fade within the darkness.

And with a single thought of the nakedness, the real world can
create, within itself the dream can be destroyed, within all the
rudeness of the world I can't believe that there is still beauty,
as splendid as this.

All the beauty in the world cannot make me leave,
this place of mystery and wonder,
and if you could truly say that you have felt this wonder,
and mysterious force of nature, then you are, greatly true of heart.

And, if you feel the wonder,
and you feel the beauty of all the nature around you,
then I can truly say, that you have a gift beyond the
craziness of the world, and beyond life itself.

And you are Pure.

Tiffany Lei Larsen

Jake The Snake

Jake the snake, he ate a rake,
And woke up with a bellyache.
What could he do: He cried "Boo Hoo",
And then he came down with the flu.
Poor Jake the snake who ate a rake
Then cried Boo Hoo and got the flu
He felt so blue, then said, "Kerchoo!"
So Jake, he tried to find a bed,
To lay his sore and swollen head.
But nowhere could he rest for a spell,
for now the rake was in his tail.
Oh me! Oh my! Oh my! Oh me! Why can't I be just plain ole me?
But with this rake inside of me, I can't even slither up a tree.
Then all of a sudden Hiccup! Hiccup! The rake began to shimmy up,
And then another "Hiccup" came,
And then the rake was out again.
So if some food looks really yummy,
Remember Jake and his sore tummy.
The best thing that you ought to do
Is only eat what's good for you!

Kathleen Spear

Are You Ready?

I sit down and dream of the world this way
And wonder if I'm ready if he came today.

Am I ready to accept Him; am I ready for this?
Am I ready to receive Him, and all that He is?

The prayers that I pray and the songs that I sing
Are just a beginning for the real thing.

Have I been good; have I done my best?
Have I done His will before I lay down to rest?

So that when He comes down on that judgement day,
The good He'll reward, and the bad will pay.

I think I can say that I"m ready to go,
To meet my maker in His heavenly glow.

So Lord, if you hear me, please free me from sin
So that I may be ready for the world to end.

Nancy Dovalina

Dead Of Night Philosophizing

Yes it is, that we all search for inspiration
And yes, as a result we find frustration
    Only the answers can still
    The driving force behind the will
And a deep sigh shall find creation

The rivers within achieve near-boil
Strands of emotion hang in endless toil
    Yet it stands as so
    That only I can go
To cease creative seed's search for thoughtful soil

Here it is, the chance for meaning to stay
The door stands open inviting play
    No move was made
    Figure hid in the shade
Door swings shut, strikes down the day

Mind grows hot from over-use
Closed lights will send a friend to loose
    Foundation must crumble
    To keep wild spirit humble
Battle front borders find sleepful truce

Tony Brennan

What Journey?

What journey we are on I think we know
And yet there are times when we forget.
Our journey is through life; its end is death,
Death which is an end and is not an end.
It is an end to earthly joys and sorrows
But a beginning of eternal life or death.
What journey we are on we remember
When there is special joy or particular grief
To spark our memory of where we are
And that we must move on our way.
We cannot truly stop but we can ponder
And delight to see the sights, to hear the sounds,
To smell the smells, to touch and taste life.

Marsha Flora

Summer Storm

You came into my life like a summer storm,
and you left just as quickly.
But the impact you had on me,
was that of a storm on a desert.
I was fading away, and you brought life back to me, gave me hope.
But even as you gave me hope you put a cloud on my sunshine.
You left me in the cool of the morning,
an I was never to see you again.
But I shall always remember you.
You with your beautiful eyes and wonderful smile.
You, the summer storm, that will be in my memory forever.

Lisa Diann Diamond

The Miracle Of My Baby

The day begins as usual, then a pain strikes out so deep,
And you lose the foresight of your laughter that lay so fast asleep.
The time has come to call and your heart begins to pound,
For the doctor awaits your arrival and your new adventures found.

You know that in a while you'll hold a brand new life,
And you'll be known as mother, as well as sister, daughter, and wife.
Then comes the moment when you know the time is near,
And the agony is worth it — as they say, "your baby's here!"

To hold that bundle in your arms and marvel that she's real
There will be no words that you can use to express the love you feel.
Yes, God has granted another wonder, and created for you, a child.
He formed her very being, with dreams, each time you smiled.

He made her soft and tender and because she needs your care,
He molded her small body—inside—for you to bear.
But, now it is all over, and you find your dreams come true,
For she's a masterpiece from heaven, God created, just for you.

Sandra C. Dotherow

Gone But Not Forgotten

When you are feeling sorta give out
And your body is feeling weak
And your mind is sort of fuzzy
And your joints are beginning to creak
Then you remember all of the good times
And you always had time to spare
And you never thought the time would come
When the looking glass revealed "no hair"
Now time has slowly crept upon you
Just learn to take it with a smile
Your body is trying to tell you
It's not old age, it's those vicious miles

Marvin Bennett

Lunchnotes and Sandwitches

Noonbreak and the muse appears
ankledeep in Mississippi riversand
circled by her crimson, ocher colorguard-
   mighty oaks of indiansummer
   her sandwitches who stand
   the Mother's banks for miles
The muse shimmerslife to the last whisper
of the morning's quietshade and sets
the sandwitches to songs of intangible harmonics
while the Mother azures claps and cries in the ancientongue

I am entranced
I have rootedeep into the sand, fostered leaves
and planted at write angles to the sandwitches
pen to paper I spin mercurial tendrils
from the palms of my hands
words eddied away
by the Muse, the Mother,
the lemon brilliance of the midday sun
Susan Royd-Sykes

Woman - Woo-man

Woman - wooman
Are basically materialistic at heart
Therefore and however they
Will cling to anyone or anything
That will prove to them
A certain amount of
Material security -
But the one that takes a man
For what he is - a man and only
A man,
Is the chosen - none of which her mother is dead
And she is not yet been born.
Len Lorenzo

Old Wooden Barns

The old wooden barns of yesterday
Are beginning to fall and crumble away
As each one goes and leaves the scene,
There goes another person's dream.
One of the past, hard workin' days,
When barn raisin's were the craze.
When folks were neighbors and helped each other
My, the work they could do in a day!

The men and boys would cut and build,
While women and girls would put on the meal.
Life was different in those days.
Folks helped each other in many ways,
And would celebrate the occasion
With a barn dance, after the raisin'.

Just think of the fun and country charm
Of exploring youngsters in Grandpa's barn!
The fun and frolic with new hay,
Sights and smells of yesterday.
Within my memory lies the charm,
Of the huge, old wooden barn.
Rebecca York

Waiting on Haiti

Haiti's fate—inevitable?
Awaiting destination
Intercepting with pleas of peace
Total Surrender or Partial Annihilation?
Inkling of tomorrow. Any?

Written on day of decision prior to announcement of
Haiti's surrender September 18, 1994.
S. M. Caran

Our Indian Brother

The old Indian, furrowed with wrinkles, sat on his dust blown floor.
Around him, his adore hut, caked and crumbling
would rise again, nevermore
The smoke from his pipe, rose thru the rafters, like ghostly
visitors, from the past
And the whispering wind, moaned thru the cracks, that this day
would be his last.
He heard in the distance, an Indians cry, his blood brothers
calling to him
And like the brave Indian, that he was, he went out,
to meet them and die!

The clouds are the smoke of their peace pipes
And the rain, the tears they shed when they die
The wind is the wind of their ponies riding hard
And the earth is their mother where they lie

The night is their blanket to cover them
And the stars to guide them as they ride
Great Indians, Navaho, Apache, the Souix
Forever in our hearts, our minds, for all time!
Moe Feldman

Untitled

Joy
Arrived?
Yellow streams of fluid collide.

Warmth across my face,
Beams of happiness race,
As evil blackness surrenders silently,
Is it here, can it be already?

Evil
Has left?
Darkness recedes like the tide.

Things that twinkled and danced blissfully,
Pressed slowly to their limits,
Eventually to be gone, eternity.
Hopelessly, without courage, they blitz.
Inevitable end as they send
Caskets to the solemn.
Peter Carey

Home

The cotton and corn rise high
As another season slowly slips away.
My place rests surely under foot now,
But where will it lay in the future?
With the long winds of fall stowing
Away on the ship of summer, I see
Plainly the beauty of home.
With every setting of the sun the shadows of
Home begin to set in, and mold
Themselves into thin memories.
Long will I yearn for this place of
Flowing fields and slow rain.
How I would like to stay, but the small snakes of doubt
Would poison me to madness.
The ancient oaks that emanate so much
Green and peace will only be fed by my
Tears of memory at my new home.
This land, this place, with its fields of plenty, and thick dusty
Fog of morning imprints upon my mind a true
Vision of my dearest home.
Peter James Zeller, II

The Potter's Art

The Potter's hands were strong and slim,
As he deftly worked with the clay.
I worked the clay as best I could,
But it would not go the Potter's way.!

As fast as I would build it up,
It crumbled and then fell apart.
I thought I'd never get it right
Or understand the Potter's Art.

The Potter took my hands in his
Slowly pressed my hands in the clay.
I began to feel the clay as it bent,
In response to the Potter's way.

Easy, but firm, were his hands on mine
As he taught "not to break, but bend!"
My hands had learned the Potter's way,
As the lesson came to an end.

Memory alone holds moments that shine,
Prints them deep in the heart.
I'll always remember to "bend not break"
The lesson, I learned, from the Potter's Art!

Ruth S. Ozanich

Ghosts

I can hear his voice - calm and reassuring
As he rubbed my back and stroked my leg
Up and down
Each time a little higher till finally he was touching
Where a much loved uncle shouldn't.

I can hear his voice - loud and insistent
And his footsteps, measured and menacing in my home.
Calling to me
Under the bed, behind the toy box filled with little girl toys
And little girl innocence.

I can hear a voice - shocked and horrified
Telling us the unbelievable. Telling us he's dead
At a race track.
I gasp and hold my breath not daring to believe
The joy that clutches my heart

And haunts my mind
Still today -
Like his voice.

Patricia Markert

Friendship

No one knows friendship
  as I.
For one who cares,
  Is always there.
My dearest friends,
Have helped me through,
  death and divorce
  with support.
Never, never have they faultered,
  Or left me alone,
  When I growned.
For them I am grateful,
For helping me heal through this ordeal,
  They listened, a great deal!
  Now I must move on and count
My blessings, for three wonderful children,
a home, a career,
To love and to cherish throughout the years.

Pat Bertini

Christmas A Story

Christmas time is around the bend,
as I am sure Santa will bring my toys with him.
I want a pretty dolly and a bicycle to and
bubby, wagon to pull me to school.

Mama and Daddy don't want much this year,
they say they are thankful for just having us here.

My grandma is weary of the changing times,
I wish Santa would bring her a peace of mind.

My sister and brother all running about to see,
What a cladder on the outside was about.
They quickly raced toward the window to see,
A jolly old man hanging from a tree.
Santa, Santa little Jimmy cried as he jumped for joy
and ran to hide.

Sharon Fowler

A Bird's Eye

I dreamed that I had wings and could fly
As I flew I saw the world through a bird's eye
I realized then why they are always able to sing
Because unlike men destruction they will not bring
The things I saw as I was flying up above
Was a world filled with violence and not with love
Because of the things that I saw and heard
Only made me wish I could remain a bird
But to my regret I awoke from my dream
Because I'm not a bird but a human being
Who saw something in a dream one night
That helped me see the world in a different light
For one night I was able to fly up above
And I saw what the world needs most is love
I wish everyone could takes wings and fly
So they can see the world through a birds eye

Rodney Armstead

Untitled

My Child, my child, you look so small
As I gaze at you from this dim lit hall

With your tousled hair and your arms spread wide
No cares to worry - No faults to hide
I wonder why God who knows my kind
Would trust in me to mold your mind

You chose not me, my little one
You were given to me by a greater one

You'll stay small for such a little time
Then you'll be big - no longer mine

But if I can teach you wrong from right
So that you can win your hardest fight

Then He'll be glad He gave to me
The one I love so much you see

Thomas M. Everson Sr.

More

How could I ever forget the dance floor;
As I gazed in wonder delight at Himself-more.
So many years past, yet even now so near;
I approached you with fear.
Your eyes, only the heart - can the beauty proclaim;
for More; Complete, is your name.
No longer in fear do I come near,
for now you are More; no longer a dream that does flee;
for you are Complete in me.
More, the dance never ends;
with each step the message of Love, the dance sends.

Marsha Ann Hatfield Meek

The Fountain That I Stand On

The summer's bath drips on the floor
As I return, smiling
The deer don't run away anymore
They've given up their hiding

I briskly hiked five miles of woods
With my extra baggage lost
I've earned back 10 years in just four months
Desire and discipline the only cost

It was smart of me to recruit "Water Mocs"
Ignored for 10 years in the closet
They love to grab the muddy rocks
And take me through the thicket

The meadow gives the same sweet smell
I remembered from my youth
While I may be grown, I'm a kid as well
Watch me play as living proof

It's wondrous to go back in time
Especially by my own hand
Once again it's summer and the days are mine
Ah, to be young, is just grand.

Ronald L. Haines

Teach Me, Lord

Teach me, Lord
As I wait before thee,
O' Spirit, take the word
And plant it deep within me.
    Within my repentance furrowed heart
    Hide this wonderful seed
    To never depart
    And remain until it springs forth in deed,
I'm your child to use as you will.
Dear God, guide me by your word
Until my soul shall thrill
In truly knowing you as Lord.
    Let me, I pray
    Daily seek what you'd have me do.
    I draw from your word each day
    A draft of sweetest water to keep me true.

Raymond C. Bishop

I Am Only A Shepherd

Dear father in heaven I come to you with a simple prayer
as I watch over my flock. I ask you to guide me so I can
guide them in a like manner, for I am only a shepherd.

Father I watch over my flock morning, noon, evening and night.
I know this would be a burden to many men, but it is no burden
when you are near. Make your presence felt when I watch
over my flock, for I am only a shepherd.

Father when one is lost from the flock, I will do my best to
find them. For there is much sadness when one is lost and
there is much rejoicing when the lost is found. Give me strength
to find the lost one, for I am only a shepherd.

Father you give me the endurance I need to tend the flock
through the warmth of spring, the heat of summer, the storms
of fall and coldness of winter. Please continue lending me
your needed helping hands, for I am only a shepherd.

Father as I watch over my flock this day, tears come to my eyes
as I remember your amazing grace which saved a shepherd like
me. As I remember Jesus hanging on the cross, I ask that you be
with me during my daily life, for there is no way I could make it
without you, for I am only a shepherd.

Thomas W. Graham

The Reaper

Come to me, the angel of doom,
as I weave a web to be thy tomb.
Yes, you may run and you may hide,
but the angel of death will be at your side.
No one shall pass me on the street,
which has been trodden on by so many feet.

I am the wizard reaper,
the grim and silent reefer,
A spider of the common ground,
who weaves a web of pure sound.
Dressed in black from head to toe,
And calls to those who must go.

Karin Blank

Attitudes

Isn't it strange how our attitudes change,
    As life goes whirling by?
Some things we once thought
    Were a whole lot of rot
Became the apple of our eye.

Those childhood foes we once despised
    Are now good friends and close allies.
Isn't it strange how our attitudes change
    As life goes whirling by?

And, if others seem jolly while you're melancholy
    There's something you have to do,
To change your perspective and make your objective
    A different point of view.

Dismiss your cares for what they are worth.
    Replace them with a bit of mirth,
Nothing can heal you like a smile,
    And make you feel like life is worthwhile.
It's all in your point of view.

Richard W. Engle

Silent Thoughts

Look carefully and you'll see a bit of sadness,
    as the elderly sit and stare.
Feelings of comfort and fulfillment seem to have
    vanished in thin air.
Men and women no longer young, but not yet old,
Devastated by events that cannot be explained
    or told.
Swept away by the anger, the despair, the emptiness
    as their problems are ignored, and considered
    out of line.
Beneath this atmosphere of gloom and difficulties,
    they smile and peer through unshed tears,
Only wanting to embrace their remaining years
    with the return of peace and happiness, void
    of oppression and fears.

Stella Poe

Inner City Blues

The killings, the rapes, the violence must stop
Before another one of your children drop
Life to so many, they seem to don't care
While this act of violence puts us in despair
What happened to the love we used to show
Only hate and evil most seem to know
The families of those who are left behind
Their grief will be till the end of their time
Mothers, Fathers, Brothers, Sisters too
Are crying stop now before one becomes you
Why can't we all just get along
Before our families will all be gone
Destroy your guns, your knives, your hate
Try to find love before it's too late.

Rosalie C. Johnson

'Unlistened'

Dawn faded and appeared the drunken moon
As the needles stained with bleach were slowly placed in the
monkey's eyes
His tail turned to blue as he began to speak
He spoke of all the bad things going on in the world today
He said we would end up like him, a discrete mute figurine
Lathered with glue and covered with wooden chips, broken spleen
He entered the fire and was burned away to ash and bones
Then came the sirens, soon appeared the cloudy mushroom
The radioactive winds blew across their faces
Tearing away their flesh, devouring, disintegrating their bones
Nothing left but one solid steel tree
Up above, hanging from the branches laughing, was the
plastic monkey

Randy D. Thornhill

Ice

Tinsel-trimming hangs from roof's edge
    as the sun melts snow below
    Ice-falls suspended, spilling in the air
        Grasping, clasping and clinging
Glitter-glass cracks and splits upon the walk below
    hurrying to lock the ice-lolly
    Sticking to my tongue

Whirling, twirling, feeling the scrape of blades
    against ice-water slowing melting
    Ice-blinks mirror near the horizon-haze
        Once glimmer-glaze, now scratched and bumpy
As sun sets the shimmering streaks dim.
    And silence

Once green the grass turned brown from cold, cold
    Faded flowers
    Leaves turned inward
        Ah! Behold! Sun awakens and impearls the earth
Ice-fog mists feel cool-crisp beneath my toes
    Dew-drops illume and freshen morning's idiesse.

Susan Cangurel

Unsung

"Man overboard!" was yelled from above
as water he was already treading.
Thoughts over whelmed him in numbers
for his own death he was dreading.
Preservers thrown were to give him faith
when he felt his heart begin to drown.
Remembering all that had happened
he kept a faint smile to avoid a frown.
His boots heavy, were polling him under
as they attempted to save him with a rope.
Beneath the surface he began to relax
once he realized he had lost all hope.
His mind was flooded with a soothing voice
as it spoke to him in this watery grave.
He knew he was hearing her one last time
sinking deep beneath another wave.
It seems he forgot how to save himself
expelling the last breath from his longs.
His only thoughts were of her smiling eyes
and of songs for here he had not sung.

William J. Nave

A Terrible Fate

What is happening to the human race
As we go through time taking up space?
So much prejudice, greed, power and hate
Condemning us all to a terrible fate.

Our morals are trampled under the feet
Of so many who lie, steal and cheat.
To open our eyes what will it take?
Condemning us all to a terrible fate.

Our ozone layer is depleting too fast
Due to sprays, chemicals and gas.
We're destroying our forests at an astounding rate
Condemning us all to a terrible fate.

The earth is contaminated and being destroyed
Stuffed full of trash, garbage and more.
What can we do, how do we compensate?
Condemning us all to a terrible fate.

Polluting our waters with great haste
With oil spills, toxins and nuclear waste.
We're killing our world so it retaliates
By condemning us all to a terrible fate.

Shirley Taylor Wilburn

The Beginning Of Forever

To have and to hold, the first words we said.
As we held hands tightly and I nodded my head.
From this day forward, our first day together.
The start of our marriage, the beginning of forever.

For better, for worse, our love will grow.
Our feelings much stronger with time it will show.
For richer, for poorer, with nothing to hide.
No one can hurt us or damage our pride.
In sickness and in health, together we will be.
Combined only as one, no longer single and free.
To love and to cherish, as our very own.
With deeper feelings, than ever can be shown.
Till death do us part, together we will stay.
And love one another, till God takes us away.

Pamela M. Frankowiak

Alone

Alone in a world where only the best survive,
At a time when it seems like you can't do anything right,
Where many people look down on you as if you are completely
insignificant, there you are, all alone.

Torn between two families,
Each one trying to show you how much they care about you,
Hurting you more by trying to buy your affections,
and still you feel unloved and alone.

Trapped in a period between childhood and adulthood,
Not knowing any responsibility,
Not knowing what to do next,
Trapped in a world of make-believe and all alone.

Scared of what lies in store,
Anxious to know the future, yet only seeing the past,
Afraid of failure,
You're scared and very alone.

Blessed with the gift of life,
You realize you are not the only one,
Looking anxiously ahead, adulthood is creeping up on everyone,
You're blessed throughout your days and no longer alone.

Shannon Marie Humphrey

Flight

Up in the Big Blue a plane crawls by
At about the same speed as the ant
That crawls toward my feet.
Are they really the same speed?
They are to me.

Catching a glimpse of the soon-to-be phantom plane,
I think to me, "My brother's a Pilot."
"Hi Ron!" I yell as I wave at the plane.
"Bye Ron!" I yell as it disappears into the Big Blue.
Is he really in there?
He is to me.

A tickle on my toe interrupts my Up There stare;
Little ant wants my attention,
So I tickle him back and nudge him off.
Just then he flies away!
"Bye Ron!" I yell as I scratch my toe.
Laughing, I think to me, "Is he really in there?"
He is!

Michelle Claus

Remembering

I think of you so often.
    At least a dozen times a day.
I think of all the talks we had.
    And all the plans we made.

We laugh about the funny things
    That you used to do and say.
And then I wipe the gentle tears
    That never seem to go away.

God's word tells me that you're happy,
    Sometimes I think you tell me that to,
When I hear a certain song or smell a certain flower,
    Or see something that reminds me so very much of you.

So even though your earthly life is over,
    And you're in a wonderful new land,
You're never far away from me,
    Because I keep you close at hand.
I look at your pictures and videos.
    I listen to you sing.
And I anxiously await that day
    When God will make us a family again.

Linda Adams

Love For My Sailor

Could the waves that caress the shore
at my feet this morning
be the same that kissed the bow
of the vessel carrying you
through the long night?
As you bare your body and soul to the mercy
of the inconsistent wind and weather,
know that my heart extends its shelter,
from here,
in the harbor of our home.
My thoughts of you are ever constant
and my heart goes out to you
across the icy blue water.
May the winds bring you swiftly and safely
back to my open, waiting arms.
And within our embrace,
let my hungry lips know again
the warmth and love from your own.

Patricia A. Fauci-Morosky

A Face Of Time

Time passes, like a wave crashing
at the edge of the sea
Never to return
Seasons dance along their way,
touching one another
Then they go, giving way to time
Summers' warm breath turns suddenly cool
Winter holds in her hands those last
few emeralds of summer
Turning them to frozen jewels
Time passing, like a child tossing
pebbles to make ripples on a pond
Time catches me and holds me in my place
Only to toss me forward
Splashing ripples on my face...

Paul G. Ruhl

Untitled

At the vast expanse he stared,
At the emptiness within,
At the lost thought and time,
Wasted in lands of fantasy and dreams;
Disgusted by the thoughtlessness
Of the life he had entered
He again let his thoughts wonder
To the end of his perceived entity;

Jumping through doors in his mind
Leaping through memories of his past
As he wishes they could only be,
Flashes of his future, and he'd begin to see.

So Perturbed by the complexity of it all
He wept, and through his tears he saw
Prisms of light and illusions of warmth
Creating pools of tranquility;
Searching the pools he began to see
Reflections, of the haggard man he'd come to be,
By living in his worlds of fantasy.

William J. Opelka Jr.

The Sea Search

We all have been sunk by the anchor of life.
At times, we have felt out of breath and too weak to go on.
Overwhelmed with life, some cannot swim anymore.
Some have been dragged along the bottom,
Some have learned to swim, or stay afloat of the uncontrolled waters.

One may seem they carry the anchor alone....
Untrue.
Everyone is carrying the same anchor,
And we are all looking for a single place to sink it.

Into the whirlpool of happiness,
Let us draw closer with irresistible power into a never-ending
    spinning vortex.
Into vast pleasures, let us be taken....
With or without our wits.

Rebecca T. Stoppel

Tickles

A tickle all tucked in my warm cozy bed
Awaiting a peek from my mother instead
I waited with patience but no sound was heard
No glimpse of my mother not even a word
Longing for the light to shine under my door
I then would know who my mother came for
After many times lifting my tired weary head
My door never opened and no light was shed
I filled up my night with stories never read
You see they were my tickles tucked under my bed.

Linda Mahakian

Madrigal To Morning

Before you view the next sunrise,
Be sure to put on your poet's eye.
For with your poet's eye you will see
A kaleidoscope of beauty that is free.

Like the roses of a misty garden in summer,
The basic colors of life awaken from slumber.
Orange and yellow are the first to portray
The fading darkness, which yields a new day.

Pink and purple are very close behind,
Then white and blue take their place in line.
For when the sun's red face does shine,
It can warm the souls of all humankind.

While we live on a planet so esoteric,
Many fail to love our world and respect it.
Thus, this lowly scribe warns both learned and lay -
Tomorrow's sunrise may be the last one of your days.

Larry Transou

The Sea

Rise tide, high to oblivion.
Beat out your meter.
Pulsating echoes - soundlessly envelop my soul.
Yesterday fades in grains of sand, rushing back to sea.
Willowy whitecaps whispering, tempting even life.
Wisdom wasted in youthfulness is born upon waves,
resurrected through years of man,
and remains dormant.
Fleeting honor washes seaward,
drowned in whirlpools of antiquated memories.
Once again, it's calm.

Linda D. Hersey

First Born, Joy!

First born, Joy!
Beautiful, precious, baby boy.
Days filled with learning and growing
A time for holding, loving, knowing.

First born, Joy!
School, teen years, man, not boy.
Responsible, capable, bright, kind.
Seeking adventure, experience to find.

First born, Joy!
Now suddenly become a soldier boy.
Uniform, training, gone from our sight.
Prepared for war, ready to fight.

First born, Joy!
Beautiful, precious, baby boy.
Dead! Instantly, violently taken away.
In a sealed coffin to come home one day.

First born, Joy!
With us, remembered, forever our boy.
Pictures, memories, what used to be.
Anguish contained, too deep to see. First born, Joy!

Nancy Haydon

Dusky Country

Comfortably, the spiders reside in various halls,
Behind numerous dusty diplomas on the walls;

Conspicuously, the rats share the shifts at the factories,
Enjoying the frequent idleness of the machineries;

Torpidly, the gaunt farm animals stand and lie,
Among sparse crops as rusty tractors silently die.

For the scholars are lost in the labyrinth of bureaucracy,
Entrenched in the system of autocracy.

Tesfaye Tamrie

Pain And Loving

I use to think pain and loving went hand in hand
Because of the various experiences I have had
I avoided intimacy at any cost
And to be vulnerable, I would have to be mad.

In reviewing my painful situations
I see they span from childhood to my adult life
There is a common thread that weaves through them
"Loving means betrayal, abandonment and strife."

Pain is a very deceiving adversary
For it hides behind many different masks
Pain is a separation from and a longing for something
And defining my "something" was not an arduous task.

I now have the tools to heal my pain
I don't ever have to be its victim again
I can move forward without its shackles
And allow my wounds to mend.

Vulnerability and intimacy are no longer my enemies
I have opened up myself to allow them in
Desiring to be loved was all I ever wanted
But loving myself is where I have to begin.

Karen A. Meyerson

Something Special

My dreams are something special
  Because they are about you
Some are just fantasies
  That I hope someday come true
You're always on my mind
  And I stare at you all day
I wonder if I got the nerve to talk to you
  Just what it would be I would say
I love you so much
  And I often wonder why
You just break my heart
  And make me want to cry
It makes me angry
  That this dream won't ever be true
Because you could never love me
  The way that I love you.

Sharon Manszewski

Our Grand Heavenly Father

Our full and complete trust is in Jehovah God,
  Because we know His words to be true.
Thus, we have learned that in His ways we must trod.

This world's fear we will not dread.
  We will follow what the Bible says.
For it teaches us the right road to tread.

We will not shudder because of venereal disease.
  We will be neither fornicators nor adulterers.
Such like ones will not God's kingdom cease.

We want such glorious blessings to be upon us.
  So, to others we spread this good news.
With sincerest confidence and with no distrust.

God has promised us no more death, sorrow, or pain.
  On that we rest assured.
We work hard, so as that grandiose prize we will attain.

To Jehovah God go all our thanks and praise.
  He cannot lie, as He has shown us.
For His many gifts, we are constantly amazed.

Karen Reed

In Memory Of Jermaine Jackson

Live life to its fullest day after day
because you never know
when it'll be taken away.
Let the people you love know you care
because one day they might not be there.
We do all we can to get his life back
or to see his wonderful smile that we all lack.
We all feel bad and are wondering why,
it's the simple fact we never said good-bye.
We remember all the good times
and all he had to gain
but now there's so much emptiness
and so much more pain.
Our world has changed forever
our lives are not the same.
But close within our hearts
his happy face remains.
This battle we will face head on
many obstacles to overcome,
but in the end together this battle will be won.

Tara Bowermaster

"Emotions"

Thoughts through my mind
become feelings in my heart
Sperm enters an egg -
the beginning of my start

Through love I am created
the oneness of two, now becomes the journey of one
my thoughts are only of hatred

Love surrounds me like no other
My father is not here
so the love comes only from my mother

I hate myself because I am a part of him
I run, hide and try to disguise
No matter how hard I try, I still see them
The hatred of my thoughts begins to harden my heart

Tears fill my eyes
they roll like thunder unto the skies

My heart listens to my brain
I wish it were deaf
because there's no medication for this pain

Michael Martin

I Remember

I remember
    being alone full of desire and spunk
Only to realize my stepdad was drunk
He was fighting with my mother
    and it filled me with fear
Nothing ever imaginable
    could prepare me for what I was about to hear
I turned the corner and to my surprise....
My mom and her husband staring eye to eye
He said he would kill her
I swore I wouldn't let him
    so when I ran out the door
        I guess I sort of beat him
I raced to the neighbor's house
    and banged on the door
He's running after me
    calling me a whore
He almost got me but I slipped away
And then I woke up....
    It's time to go play!

Kristina Fagundes

Save The Rainforest

There is a place where animals live
Beneath the shining sun.
Where water flows, and wildlife grows
Where animals all have fun.
We call this place the rainforest,
A beautiful place to be.
But the animals and trees will soon be gone
Because of people like you and me.
We cut down the trees and turn the wood to paper
Or use it so we can build.
But sit down and think about all the trees we've cut
And how many animals' homes we've killed.
We must stop being careless, put an end to our selfishness
And use only what we need.
And when we cut down a tree, whatever it's for
We should plant two new seeds.
There are so many things we can do for our earth
If we only care.
You can never do too much to help
Our world to be repaired.

Sarah Boelig

My Field

There is a field, my favorite spot,
Beside the school near the parking lot.

I love to run through all its grass,
The sun so gold like the finest brass.

I read my books and write my stories
Of the field and all its glories.

In my field where I once stayed
Were many trees where I once laid.

I played go seek among those trees.
I sat in the branches and felt the breeze.

Then over the years it wasn't looked after.
I remembered my happy times, my childhood laughter.

I thought to myself, "That field should be saved!"
So I shouted, yelled, and raved.

I told of its wonderful life and history,
About its sweetness, love, and mystery.

I cleared away all those ugly weeds,
Gathered and planted many seeds.

Now my field is completely restored,
To be protected by me and the Lord.

Margaret Emanuel

Alone

One day you learn the subtle difference
between holding a hand and chaining a soul,
that love doesn't mean security, kisses aren't contracts,
and presents aren't promises -
so you accept your defeats
with your head up and your eyes open,
with grace of a woman, not grief of a child.
You learn to build your world on today
because tomorrow is too uncertain
and futures fall in midflight.
One day you learn that even sunshine can burn your soul,
so you plant your own garden of life,
instead of waiting for someone to bring you flowers.
One day you realize you can survive alone -
you really are strong inside,
you really do have worth,
so you learn and learn
and with each and every goodbye you learn.

Wendy D. Wooldridge

The Pick Up

As I entered the room, I noticed him, sitting alone.
Big and brawny, he was a delight to my eyes, I wouldn't look.
As I sat there, I was vaguely aware of voices around me,
ebbing and flowing in random conversation.
Becoming conscious of his stare, I saw those wonderful
brown eyes, melting, adoring, calling silently.
Thinking wildly: "No, no, go away. I do not want you, this
can't be happening today."
I picked up a newspaper. He stood up, walking purposefully,
quietly toward me.
Every muscle of his handsome body commanded me, trying to
overcome my resistance, demanding that I succumb.
My heart ached and I dejectedly thought, "Okay, okay you will
have your way."
Placing the unread newspaper on the table, eyes downcast, I
shut off the TV and the voices ceased. Silence engulfed me.
Meeting his stare, I walked slowly toward him, picked up his
leash, and took my dog out for his walk, once again.

Marilyn Beaubien

Fear

Fear, that instinct to flee or fight
Binds down my soul in tethers tight
I've learned with time 'tis a better goal
To face my fear, to free my soul.

If I can see through fear's tangled web
Unravel it each by each tacky thread
I find behind its sinister cloak
A fearless thing, a mocking joke.

If I delve behind fear's dreadful aspect
Trusting spirit, love, and intellect
I find a frightened, starving child
Mostly whose face is meek and mild.

Then I can see this child in true compassion
Is nothing more than unrecognized fashion
Better for me to set my purpose to right
And carry the miserable child into the light.....

G. Warren Taylor

The Many Faces Of Blackness

Black is doom, hate and sorrow,
Black is no wisdom of tomorrow.
Black is a child crying out in pain
Knowing that he'll never see his mother again.
Black is death, lurking in the night,
Longing to take another life.
Black is a person who has lost his sight
And to some it may seem that he has lost his life.
Black is the ability to rise and be free.
Black are the faces of my ancestry.
Black is reality!
Black is you and me.

Valerie Hill

Black

Black is the darkness that sweeps the sky,
Black is the sadness of a lost cry,
Black is the solar system moving around,
Black is the ocean depth yet to be found,
Black could be the jacket on a man that bows,
Black could be the spots on a big white cow,
Black could be the smoke moving up high,
Black could be seen in the wink of an eye.

Michelle Vivona

Help Wanted

Trapped and isolated in my own self constructed black hole,
Blame is only tossed towards those who aren't at fault.
Life alternates shedding a cheap luster.
Pride and ignorance keep my wanting eyes from changing to
reaching limbs.
Though my stubborn lips utter no words,
My weak and dependent mind screams for help.

Yuka Cushing

Healing Hope

Golden glow, replacing dark night,
Blessing the trees with warmth and light.
You bring precious hope with this new day,
Softening the harshness of yesterday.

Noonday sun, witness the frantic hurry
Of a world that feeds on meaningless flurry.
Bring a moment of pause to close the gate
To a world of hurriers who hate to wait.

Gorgeous sunset of purple and pink,
Shadows bring peace as you slowly sink,
Ushering in night with its healing sleep
Presenting new leases on life to keep.

Lela Mae Fenton

"Black Love"

Your face fades out of my mind into a
blood stain on the floor God only knows
What awaits for you behind that door.
The door you pushed me through
an exit out of your life but I will be
back creating pain like stabs with a knife
I shall haunt your heart and tease your soul.
Force you out of existence burying
you deep in a hole now I sit in my room
sorting through my thoughts
grinning morbidly as now I know your body rots.

Kimberly Hoff

The Whistling Wind

The beautiful sound of whistling wind the tumble weeds
blowing scarcely across this ghost town. History was once
here now only to see that people no longer live here.

You can see the old bar taverns were once a man would
be playing a piano. Laughter shared between one another,
a few drinks, gambling, dancing and out the swinging
doors the cowboys would start to leave. You feel the
presence of woman all around walking, talking, and
shopping at the only general store in town.

A breeze drifts by me as I feel that someone actually
could be standing there in this empty town. Just hearing
the whistling of the wind, seeing the tumble weeds blow
scarcely across this land, realizing to myself that
history was once here, and the presence of people is
strong enough, that myself and anyone else will believe
once history was and still is in this abandoned town.

Virginia Pickett

Untitled

The beauty of this day lies far beyond my site,
but one day I'll obtain that beauty
until that day, I'll remain incomplete

Keith Hughes

102

Untitled

The sun shines brightly down on the buds
Blowing winds rock them gently
They sway to and fro awaiting for something new
Silently they awaken

They open their eyes to see a smile
The sun warms their very core
Just as silently their smell fills the air bringing joy to little ones
Laughter fills the air but soon dies out

The sun has disappeared and a cold has settled in
Drooping sadly their lives seem to fade
Petals fall like teardrops
And the feet stomp them down

Finally the tall ones drop
Not a sign is left of their beauty
The ground has once again soaked them up
Spitting them out again only in the spring

Rachelle Rivera

Fallen Heroes

A hail of enemy bullets came shredding through the grounds,
bodies torn to pieces by the enemy's deadly rounds.

No second chance at life just memories of their faces,
their last long journey taken to their final resting places.

No one else to hate, no one else to kill,
for ever they will remain on God's forsaken hill.

The ground shook violently and thudded all around,
soldiers running wildly diving for the ground.

Relentlessly the sniper searched for his prey,
to end a young boy's life to make a full day's pay.

Another crack was heard ripping through the ground,
another body torn to pieces by that sniper's deadly round.

For all of you who read...weep, and cry...remember,
all FALLEN HEROES...for freedom they fought and Died.

Luke Biancaniello

Dance To The Tom Tom Tom

A cloud of dust dawning the air, men's feet dancing the rhythm
of bongo drums.
Riotous, ritual dancing, hot bodies sweating from the beat of tom
tom tom.
Voices tiggering chants, shrieks and shrills in harmony to the
drums throbbing tune.
Tribal people encamped around the fire, mockery melting the moon.
Women shaking tambourines, strings of trinkets with an array of
different charms.
The atmosphere of the night dangerously thick until you can feel
the rage of their harm.
Usually a dance of serenity and peace, now dances the dance of war,
Against men upon wooden vessels who came by way of the sea,
In resolution of their fellowmen taken, blood upon grass of the
Mother Country!
Remember my child as you travel forced by way of the sea,
Our dance of peace for the love of you whenever you think of the
Mother Country.
And when you feel no ground roots of the place you were taken from,
Listen deep within the depths of your hearts for the beat of the drums
Dance to the tom tom tom!

O'keather T. Campbell

The Rising Sun

The rising sun,
bringing light to darkness:
and with all its blazing glory,
the promise of a new day will touch us.
For in that ray of sunshine,
we will find hope.
Hope for a better way,
A new hope for peace,
And the never-ending hope for happiness.
And that sun will rise high into the sky,
Its warmth will comfort,
its brightness will remind;
That with each setting of the sun,
we shall never fear,
for darkness will never conquer,
and light will again emerge:
Bringing hope,
Bringing promise,
Bringing life.

Rochelle Trimble

Antediluvian Recollections

Scattered memories,
Broken dreams,
Lost hopes,
Smoldering flames,
All fell out of the jar as I shook it.

When I searched through them,
I stumbled upon more little pieces,
memories of happiness,
dreams that had become reality,
hopes that matured into goals,
and flames that stretched into eternity.

Scattered dark shadows seem to disguise the light,
but when you look more intently,
you find out,
there are two perspectives for each and every piece.

You then realize
that a positive outlook,
affects what you call life: who you are... how you live,
and what memories you cling to.....

Stefanie Joy Hallman

Transition

Lovely Autumn leaves - red and gold and yellow -
Burning in bonfires all along the street,
Smoke-rings curling, vanishing from sight,
Flaming fronds swirling, dancing in the night,
Enchanted by a wind-tune - soothing, soft and mellow.

Gorgeous Autumn leaves - yellow, gold and red,
Fallen to the ground in unrestrained defeat,
Heaped in a mound - withered, cold and dead.

Then, with the magic of a fairy spark,
Flashing into flame dancers - lightning up the dark!

Saddened Autumn leaves - yellow, red and gold,
Lying on the earth, colors growing thin -
I cannot tell where lovely leaves grow cold,
Nor where the fiery colors of the flames begin!

Pearl Liebman Laskowitz

The Kind Of Love

Oh, how I long for the feel of your touch,
Burning in the dark like a dart.
Could it be needed, and wanted at much?
Together, we could make the most beautiful of art.
We could be until the end of forever.
Say you'll give me the best kind of love.
We will act and live as one together,
And surround each other as if we were a glove.
Let's make a better and brand new start.
Take away from me all of the sadness.
Show me and surrender me forever your heart.
Give me the privilege of an abundance of gladness.
But, why should I be so lonely,
I already have my one and only.

Tanya Schenk

A Theatre Of The Face

Tyranny twisted, ripping my soul,
Burning within, seeing the flames aglow.
Red in my eyes, from fury and fear,
   tormented by my own.
Contorted old thoughts, fresh with the years;
Replays in my eyes, but close when your near.
a theatre of the face,
   a grand performance appears.

William Brinson II

For The Love Of A Child

What is a daughter
But a shadow cast by her mother
Always following
Sometimes, on separate; but, parallel paths
And where is the light
That casts this shadow?
Tis the gleam in her father's eye.

What is a son
But a shadow cast by his father
Always following
Sometimes, on separate; but, parallel paths
And where is the light
That casts this shadow?

Oh Mother...

J. V. Soles

Autumn On Martha's Vineyard

Day after day we've had fog and rain,
But better than "H.H.H." which was such a pain!
With royalty and first family we've been endowed!
"World famous Island" we should be proud!
Bumper - to - bumper (people love their cars!)
Many, however, wish they'd fly to Mars!
But merchants and landlords are happy to win,
And deposit the profits of summer that's been.
Town coffers are not bulging, I'm telling you!
What with over-time lawmen and ambulance crew.
But now we're relaxing and breathing fresh air,
And watching leaves turning red, purple and fair.

Signe O. Stenroth

Sister

I can no longer hug my sister and receive the same,
But from this day forward I will never forget her name.
We had our differences but our hearts were near,
Tearing that bond was something I always feared.
I must now collect the memories we shared in the past,
Knowing that for the rest of my life they will always last.
Suddenly one day she left to be with the Lord.
Now I have no one to pick on. "I'm so bored".
Until that day when we both unite high above,
I'll keep her picture close and treasure her love.

Robert E. Wood

Gilmartins'

There were five other taverns on Avenue N,
but Gilmartins' was favored by most blue collared men.

It was a rough sort of place where men congregated
to settle world problems, to agree or debate it.

Joe Ginty the barkeep, soft spoken and poised,
would keep the lads quiet if they made too much noise.

I've been to pubs in Scotland, England and Wales,
And in El Paso where I landed in jail.

I've had cognac in Paris, beer in Berlin,
There're not many bars I haven't been in.

But the one that always stayed in my thoughts
is Gilmartins' Tavern in Brooklyn, New York.

Norman Rasmussen

God's Love

God created this big old world for us all to live in
But he did not mean for it to get in the shape it is in
So who is to blame for all this shame
That brings so much pain
It is not the Lord up above cause he shows us his love
We may not all be rich that live in this Land
We may work hard for the dollar we hold in our hand
We may not live in a house made of stone
Or drive a car we can call our own
We may not have all the riches in this land
But we can know for sure God is holding our hand
And he will lead us to the promised land
So if your rich and you cannot see
What good did the riches do you, you see
So with all your silver and your gold
It will never buy your soul
So how could we go through this life each and every day
And not think of God in some special way
For all the blessings he brings our way
So with the help from the Lord above we can all share his love

Shirley Jeffers

"The Love He Sends"

The love of God, who can begin to understand?
But He says, "Come here, my child, open your hand."
"Oh, Father, there is nothing there but loneliness and pain,
I cannot possibly open it again."

Then, gently, the Father takes another hand so scarred,
'Tis heavily pierced, and deeply marred,
And places it tenderly over my own,
Suddenly, understanding is quietly sown.

For now I know His love means caring,
It is infinite, so full of sharing.
Outward, now, my hand extends to another,
To you...with the love He sends.

Sharon L. Patterson

Untitled

Elvis Presley came from the sticks
But he wasn't like the rest of the hicks
With his curling lips
And his swiveling hips
He charmed the pants off the sniveling chicks.
  (Captured the hearts of)

Dolly Parton has a very sharp wit
The wigs she wears are a very good fit
Her husband despairs at her extra affairs
And wants her to make a clean breast of it.

President Clinton was heard to say
I'll follow in the footsteps of J.F.K.
I'll help you in your role
Said Robert Dole
I called the undertaker and he's on his way.

Dan Rostenowski was a man of all seasons
If it's there I'll take it was the way he reasons
Now he's down and out
We hope for the count
And in the house there'll be less treasons...

G. E. Royalty

The Tears of Angels

The sky has grown shaded
  but how could I have known
that the laughter would have faded
  with feelings left be shown.

The rain now begins to fall
  first gently on my face
and my heart softly calls
  for the lost embrace.

The water then collects around my feet
  and I stand in reflective pools.
while my heart struggles to beat,
  my hand searches for the missing jewel.

Their tears fall from the sky
  slowly soothing my pain
as the angels cry
  for lost loves all the same.

Laura Tougaw

Someday Sedona

I saw you only once.
But I have seen you before.
There in my soul
You drift, keeping watch, beckoning.

Many souls have walked your streets.
Have scaled your banks.
Searching the awe of your seduction
and finding stillness of self.

My time will come for you
to hold me in your embrace.
I hear your whispers, know the breath of your kiss.
Someday Sedona, I'll come to you.

Regina Arnold

Soul Searching

  I can scream and shout in agony,
But she still can't hear me,
She'll hear me yell,
But she won't hear into it;
She won't know what I'm saying.
  I can talk to her with words,
But she still can't understand,
She never will because she doesn't listen with her soul.

Nicole Holmes

Autumn

Autumn brings to view such colors poets must expound,
But I, no poet, as I gaze around,
Do grope for words in rhythmic sound.

Hills once filled with shades of living green
Now fade, not in dismal show,
Yea, brighter still than was the summer's glow.

The trees stand proud to taunt the artist's brush,
Bathed in reds and golds, a flaming rush,
So filled with life no graying temple shows.

Too soon the crimson crowns will fall to earth
And winter's cap will gird mid Autumn's sad surrender,
Could I but pen a line or two, a picture to remember.

A. E. Hillerich

The Search

I stood at the edge of the mountain and looked for it,
but I only saw the stone, hard and cold.
The hill rumbled with knowledge
and I watched it erode.

I stood at the edge of the forest and looked for it,
but I only saw the trees, tall and bold.
The wind whispered the truth
but I watched the leaves wither and the trunks fold.

I stood at the edge of the ocean and looked for it,
but I only saw the water, blue and clear.
Crashing on the shore, it burst into a cloud of angels,
I watched the mist disappear.

I looked for it from the edge,
as I've searched from the start.
But I was blind until I looked with my heart.
Now, I see it in the mountains
I see it in the seas
I see it in the forest
and I see it in me.

Rick Lange

"No Sorrow There"

I feel the chill of deaths dark door,
but I'll rejoice that you suffer no more.
I'll miss you here, more than words can say,
but I know in my heart, I will see you in heaven some day.
Till then I'll hear your sweet voice as you say,
"come here, I love you"......
I will feel your presence as the wind passes by,
and plants a kiss, just beneath my eye.
I love you mom and hold you so dear,
I'll remember you always, with joy not tears.
Her battle is now over, and her race has been run,
Mom now resides with God's Holy Son.
No more suffering, no more pain,
our loss on earth, is heavens sweet gain.
She left this world, with a smile on her face,
for she had the assurance of God's Holy Grace.
There was no sorrow, nor even a tear,
her face held joy not fear......................

Patsy H. Still

105

Ross

On your face, lines appear tattered as the bark of trees,
    But it's the inside that no one really sees;
Been everywhere from your little mountain home a way up there,
    Seen much in your day and time for all to compare;
And those feelings still linger on past the years,
    Perhaps to hide all those shed tears.

        You're a pioneer in my heart/
        From the days of horse and cart/
        Old Glory called you off to foreign war/
        'Though you could've been so much more...

What has time got to do but leave those who still wait,
    Even when the house is silent and empty without trace of mate;
Whispers from long ago enter the present to recount the past,
    Yet you remain ageless in grey and silvery steadfast;
Come go back a hundred years or so,
    To Virginia in the West where the wild rivers still do flow.

        You're a hero of my soul/
        Whence the hills do often take their toll/
        Raised family and kin/
        To be what they have only once been...

    Michael Everett Squires

Time

Time goes on and we think things change,
But it's the same old thing and it isn't strange.
People the same in each generation:
Styles, and codes, the morals may change, but
the same disintegration...
Each era thinks the past years the best
and the present the worst, but who is to know
until the cloudburst...
Then the horrors of war, descend down upon us,
and we cry, what future before us?
The filth and corruption, the loose moral code,
Welcome into our humble abode!
While we wait for the storm to subside,
there's not much left and men have died.
So we scrape the remains, with a speech and a
flourish, and hope this new world will have
more courage.

    Lynn Wilkins

Beyond Love

I've searched for a word, to express my emotions
But lost it remains, a treasure of the ocean.
Determined to express, my feelings from within
I know not the end, or where to begin.
The touch of our lips, the depth of our eyes
The tender embracing cannot be disguised.
Yet this word which I searched for, remains lost at sea
But my feelings and happiness, are clear as can be.
I've finally realized, why this word is such a task
I never had a reason, to search in the past

    Lawrence M. Tencza

Beauty Aflutter

Agile, capricious butterflies dance aesthetically
Coming and going like the day.
Their majestic beauty silences chatter.
Golden orange, soft yellow, turquoise wanderers
Flutter without a care.
Wings, colors, movements
Capture the heart
Like a rainbow in the sky.
God-like beauty enfolds creative nature,
Enthralling, enhancing, awe-inspiring.

    Kathleen D. Clements

"Anger From Within"

I see an image of who I'd like to be,
but my mirror shows me who I really am.

Why must I go on this way,
Who will know or care for me?

When the grown-ups can't fend for themselves,
I must be the adult and do for the family.

No one cares about my life,
Who can I turn to in a catastrophe?

I have very little in my life,
The only peace I have are the words you see.

My life is so complicated,
There's no way out, no where to flee!

    Kerry L. Miller

The Other Me

I put on a face for the world to see,
but nobody knows the other me.
The other me has hopes and dreams
but they all have passed me by, so it seems.

The wheels of fate must be well oiled.
One turn and all of my dreams were spoiled.
Fate had different plans for me;
the other me was not to be.

My plans fell far short of what I thought they would be
when I still had hopes of being the other me.
I sometimes wonder what my life now would be
if I had just had a chance to be the other me.

    Margaret L. Middleton

"Dawn The Glorious End To The Darken Night"

Many trees and crashing waves make their mighty noise;
But none to the noise of the charging Dawn in all its splendor.
Bursting forth from its Blacken cover, Powerful and striking.
Many listen strain their ears, but SILENCE!
Majestic Beautiful all that's glowing.
Dawn enters forth day by day never stopping never resting
always coming.
Ocean Beauty mountains majesty grassland flair fantastic everywhere.
Glowing light a little slight, ever growing into days ever bright!
Many a thing shows its shadowy shape hard to decipher for
but a moment in time.
Friendly words cheerful birds on the rays of Dawn's morning flight.
Echo's from yesterday play it shows itself everyday!
Playing on the clouds and sky, trees are plenty fields a far,
Ocean wide and rivers small Dawn loves them all.

    Walter L. Kittinger

The Old Brown Shoe

The first day you saw me, I was shiny and new,
but now you only treat me like a little old brown shoe.
You took me home and showed me off,
but now my sole has grown so soft.

You took me everywhere you went. You'd wear me everyday.
But now I sit in the closet. That's where I always stay.
Only when the dog comes will I leave the closet to play,
but then my only purpose is to be chewed on and tossed away.

I'll always remember the memories that we shared,
just you and I,
and if my sole could shed real tears,
it would certainly begin to cry.

So please take me out one day,
and pretend it's like old times,
before I commit "shoe suicide"
that devastating crime.

    Stacie Wines

My Little Son

To my son, I love you so
  But off to work I must go

If money would only grow on trees
  I would pluck more than a dozen leaves

But my career won't wait
  And the bills can't be late

And when the work day is through
  I will race right home to be with you

To hear you laugh, and see you play
  Being with you is the best part of the day

Bath time, snack time, off to bed
  So we can both rest our weary heads

Tomorrow will be a new day
  In which to laugh, smile, learn, and play

I love you all day - whether near or away
  Because my only real job, is being your mom.

Lori Ann Cook

Autumn Leaves

Autumn, a season of morning winds, mild
But oft times blowing as if called by the wild.
Hark, autumn leaves rustle throughout the day
Caught by a whirlwind and blown away.

Ripened by the sun, autumn leaves begin to fall
Strong winds and rain may waste them all
Those left behind, glisten with a gentle mist
Glowing with radiance like the amethyst.

Tomorrow, autumn leaves not burnt with frost
Will cluster, else they too will be lost.
Oh! autumn leaves, as the winds begin to blow
Intrigue me with your splendor in the way you know.

Fallen autumn leaves, are trodden each year
With too much strength and too little fear
Listen! hear them crying beneath their breath.
Coming of fall, surely will bring death.

Yvonne Tackett

Success Is The Key

Tomorrow can bring you happiness
  But only if you believe
You must settle for best and nothing less
  In order to achieve.
Mistakes are made as you will find
  Just do not give up and quit
Because failure's all inside your mind
  And positively conquers it.
There's a lot of work you've got to do
  In order to reach your goal
To be a success it's up to you
  To prove all that you know.
Whatever it is you want to be
  Try it and you'll see
That the knowledge you've gotten is the key
  To living successfully.

LaKesha M. Scott

Married To The Corps

She may not wear the uniform
But she stands proud and tall
Saying goodbye to the one she loves
A lonely teardrop falls
She knows her husbands doing
What life had borne him for
And hers was to be waiting
forever in the shore
Holding onto dreams and photographs
Yellow Ribbons, and her heart
War is not the only cause that keeps two loves apart
In peace time too, she knows the call
Of duty soon will come
And she must say goodbye again
Fore the rising of the sun
Her heart both breaks
And beats with pride
As he walks out the door
And time drags on; 'till he comes hope
When you're married to the corps

C. C. Hockett

Sometimes....

I only asked for time and attention,
But sometimes, asking is not enough.
I expected nothing less than to be shown
  the utmost form of respect,
But sometimes, expectations are set too high.
I believed you when you said that you loved me,
But sometimes, people say things they don't mean.

You promised me honesty and sincerity,
But sometimes, promises are meant to be broken.
You told me you'd hold me when I was lonely at night,
But sometimes, talk is cheap.
You assured me that you'd be there for me when I needed you,
But sometimes assurance is only granted by God.

All I ever wanted was unconditional love from you,
But sometimes, wants go unfulfilled.
All I ever pictured was our marriage and our families coming together.
But sometimes, fantasies are mirrors of untruth.
All I ever had faith in was your strong, everlasting commitment to me,
But sometimes,
  Faith is not enough....

Phyllicia Moten

Dear Daddy

It doesn't seem right not to have you here
But the memories we have, to us, are so dear.
I'll never get used to you being gone
And this feeling of being alone.

So many things remind me of you
Things you used to say and do
The way you dressed, the way you walked
The tone in your voice when you talked

The time we all spent together
We will cherish forever
The day I'll see you again, I look forward to
The day I'll get another smile and hug from you.

Mom has found someone new, I guess you know
To share our lives here below
Instead of us being alone, I think you'd want it this way
I really believe you'd say it was ok.

He takes care of us the way you'd want it done
Problems or complaints, I have none
But to take your place, no one could ever do
For there will never be a greater dad than you.

Ranita Hicks

In Clouds

The dreamer slumbers, drifting deeper in sleep...
but the spirit rises with mysteries to greet.
Once a spirit has flown it can shoot past the stars
seeing holiness and truths in this universe of ours.

The clarity free's in that one step beyond.
for the spirits in tune with all harmonious sound.
While embracing it, with much love from within
the vision expands as we see where we've been.

Telepathy reveals those other spirits sent...
dancers of swirling mist in ethereal firmament.
Populating the stars and building cities of light
wanderers all, they're as jewels in his sight.

The loved one comes forth with silver chalice.
In clouds, spirits wait before a shimmering palace
drinking of the sun and of life's sweet nectar,
as love spills out in rays from his scepter.

The dreamer awakens, for now all is clear.
Those dreams of tomorrow are drawing near.
Return to the spring that drink which was given.
and perhaps...we'll all catch a glimpse of heaven.

Lisbeth Hill

Proposal

"With this ring I thee wed" are words repeated every day,
But these words now have new meaning because they're words
  that I'll soon say.

And this ring is like no other that the world has even known,
For this one represents us and to the world will soon be shown.

You, dear, are the diamond, the most precious jewel I know.
You are pure, clear, and simply sparkling with an eternally
  lasting glow.

We know this to be The Christ within you; it's what makes you
  different from the rest.
It's what makes you most attractive; it's what makes you the very
  best.

I represent the setting upon which you proudly sit.
We go so well together; we are a perfect fit.

My job is to uplift you for all the world to see;
To support and to protect you for all eternity.

Christ represents the band itself, He supports the both of us.
Without Him there we're not complete, His presence is a must.

So with this ring I ask you, "Will you be my Wife?";
With this ring I ask you, "Will you complete my life?"

Stephen W. Bannister

To Love Again

I have loved on many occasions
but this love has been very painful
and it is due to this pain
that I choose not to love again

From this choice I have experienced loneliness
this loneliness has also been very painful
and it is due to this pain
that I long to love again

I long for the love of a wonderful woman
this woman must be true, honest and caring
and it will be due to this woman
that I will love again

You are this wonderful woman
the woman that stole my heart
and it is because of our passion
that I am in love again

Robert E. Fortune

Freedom

We don't know where you are going?
But we are very proud of you.
  You are the men and women in uniform
that stands for red-white and blue.
  You are a symbol of freedom and a honor to me.
So today I fly the flag so high, so all can see.
  Yes, we fly the flag of freedom so
all can see.
  Your name is an old glory and we are proud.
  Today our Soldiers are home. We
want them to feel they are not alone,
  We have hugs, kisses and praises for them.
for they are our heroes Now and Then.
  Hurray for the red, white and blue!
Our soldiers are home and we welcome you.

Nancy Volkart

Untitled

Letting go is not something we would like to do.
But we can't change what has happened to you.
Come what may, we won't let go completely,
You will always live on in our memory.
We'll remember the good times, as well as the bad.
And also think of the times we could've had.
We'll remember the laughter and the tears.
God, how we wish you were still here.
I guess time just wasn't on your side.
I wish we could've at least said good-bye.
But how were we to know this would happen?
How could we know we'd never see you again?
It's hard to accept the fact that you're gone.
It's hard for us to pick up and carry on.
It's so difficult to understand,
Why this had to be part of God's plan.
I do not know if you can hear what I have to say.
Whether or not, I'll say it anyway.-

Maribell Uribe

The Quest

We think we know equality
But what does it really mean?
We think we know liberty
But with what vision can it be seen?

If we are like plants that
Enigmatically choose how we grow,
How can what blooms be equal
If the fruits of liberty are to show?

Well, it's the roles, not the faces, that equal
When it comes to determining worth.
Could one role out weight another
When we are uniformly incarcerated by birth?

Our free will exists within an order
Where balance judges our act.
Perform being aware of individual omnipresence
And you mirror how the pendulum swings back.

Equality and liberty seem contradictory
When viewed from a material nest.
Otherwise, they are symbiotic conundrums—
Illuminating life's most divine quest.

Thomas G. Small

Untitled

I thought my day's work was done at six;
But when I got home I was in fix.
My wife said "Help me with the work;
Set the table and slice the pork."

Then after supper to the divan I headed;
But didn't reach it before she blabbered;
"Clean off the car port, the walks and lawn;
And let me know when you get done."

So after I finished to the divan I sneaked;
But before I made it in she peaked;
And said "The sewing machine is broke again;"
I'm telling you I just can't win.

But the next day after work I'm home again,
So I figure I must like and I grin;
She says "I love you, you big fat jerk;
Now let's get to work and make things perk."

A bachelor doesn't get in a fix;
And can lay on the divan after six;
But then he can only look at the wall;
I have my wife and is she a doll.
        Richard D. Fawkes, Sr.

Crayola

Life is a box of crayons,
But why didn't she realize this
When she received the message on the
White telephone,
Or when she left her new
White house in here new
White outfit,
Or when she pulled up
To her daughter and her new "friend" in her
White car and
Refused to let her daughter's friend ride with her?
Maybe he was a stranger-danger to her,
His arms the size of jack-hammers, those hazel eyes.
Maybe if he sat in the car,
He would have disrupted the color scheme.
        Kurt C. Schuett

Ode To The Least Of My Brothers

We played the flute for you, but you did not dance, we mourned
to you, but you did not weep, I am indifferent to the world of
men, to criticize is to judge, I haven't the authority to judge, to
ignore is to condone, I haven't the notion to condone, but out of
simple kindness and humility I will love my brothers and sisters,
no man or woman or child is expendable, each one is my friend
and brother and sister, even the least of them, especially the least
of them, here to teach me the workings of the world and the
Spirit, all in their own fashion, the Spirit does not descend and
speak to me directly, but through the birds and the clouds and the
sky and the mountain streams, or through the willing hands of
the poet and the craftsman and the painter, and I love them all so
dearly, for speaking their hearts to me, the passion with which
the opera singer sings her lovely song, is the same spirit that
moves my pen across this page, we truly are members of one
body, all of us, individuals members, of one body, One Spirit.
The world of men is wretched, now let us create our own world,
in the image of the Spirit, with the sanction of the Spirit, let us
create a beautiful and bountiful world, a true brotherhood of
man, it is warm and beautiful to possess a dream, to adore and
cherish such a dream of love and peace, of human brotherhood.
        Michael P. Maye

"Different"

You see me in the distance, and you all point and stare.
But you don't even know me, you don't even care.
Is there a reason that you hate me so?
Is it because you think my life is low?
Is it because my clothes aren't the best?
Or is it because I don't look like the rest.
An old saying goes, "Sticks and stones may break my bones,
but words will never hurt me."
But they do.
If you only knew.
So go ahead and laugh at me.
But I'll never change the person I've come to be.
So no matter what you say, no matter what you do,
I'll always know that inside of me there beats a heart so true.
        Tanya Gustin

Months In A Life

Born in January on an icy, winter day;
By next February, 'Daddy' was all he could say;
Two short March's later he was flying his first kite;
Two years later, April, he was riding his first bike;

That same year in May this boy was always at my side;
Three Junes later he and I just watched the ocean tide;
Time slipped by to watch him grow an inch, then two, then three;
He hit his first home run in late July of '83;

I held his hand for safety when the water was too deep;
He held my hand and cried when we had Rover put to sleep;
We camped under the stars on one hot, steamy August night;
He was my son, I was his dad, and nothing felt more right;

A few Septembers later he began his high school fame;
October, senior year, he caught the pass that won the game;
Years later, in November, he met a girl at Kansas U;
They married in December and a grandchild soon is due;

The doctor couldn't tell them the exact due date, they say;
Just sometime in January on an icy, winter day;
        Rick Doolin

School

It's hard to imagine twelve years of your life is spent in a place
    called school
Actually the number is thirteen, unlucky like the three legged stool
There we learn to read and write, socialize and get along
How to cope with the world at large and to know right from wrong
We're taught to be as intelligent as our minds will allow us to be
To take pride in all we do and to show our individuality
We complain about going to this place, we dream of being grown
But it's the place we miss the most when we're finally on our own
Cause our friends go and leave us, we realize childhood doesn't last
Then we wonder why we spent our time worrying about it in the past
But then it finally hits us as we take our last walk down the hall
School was really lots of fun - and not so bad after all
        Karen Farmer

Thief Of Hearts

Radiating warming golden hues,
chases away my lingering shades of blue.
Nothing is so fine or of more value,
as angel's holds no greater virtue.
Thief of hearts no worthier conquest,
in a woman's eye's a welcome guest.
No man could ever be as blessed,
for they can never hold what you possess.
A wondrous thing exploding with beauty and grace,
enthroned stately in its rightful place.
Always there when we touch or embrace,
it's the smile you wear upon your angelic face.
        Shala Payne

Lovers Apart

Not a star in the sky, nor the moon glowing above
Can compare to this passion that I know is love.
Though we're hours away, and we're miles apart,
I think of your smile, and warmth fills my heart.
I thirst for that moment when soon we will touch,
But until that time comes, my voice is a hush;
For while you're away the words are so few,
And until you return, I'll be dreaming of you.
I dream of your voice and your tender caress.
I dream of you holding me, and it's pure happiness.
I love your sweet breath, softly brushing my cheek.
The depth of our love is more than words can speak.
When I think of your love and your friendship so true,
All I can say is that dear, I miss you.
When soon we embrace, and hold one another tight,
I know that together we will forever be alright.

Pam Petruna

Untitled

What on this whole, wide, wonderful earth
Can ever outshine the miracle of birth?

I can think of nothing that comes close to the joy
Of holding a new born girl or boy.

A new little being, created with love
Endowed with a soul from heaven above.

A sweet downy head, that wobbles so -
Perfection in miniature, each finger and toe!

A rosebud mouth, and eyes so bright -
Gurgles and coos that bring such delight.

A tiny body, so wondrously strong -
A mind that will grow through a whole life long.

What an awesome task, to nurture this child
Through the days ahead, whether stormy or mild!

But, love, faith and trust will help on the way
(And a sense of humor could save the day.)

Susan Weddell Lind

To Merrie

In the wake of things we do not know
can not fashion
and can not throw
We find that the world is not really our foe

Though this world is full of twists and bends
and sometimes brings to us terrible ends
it also gives to us a great wonder: friends

I think these are its greatest commodity
for they sing a soft soulful melody
and let us laugh and cry at the strangest oddity

Friends give us a great gift
with such a mass we can not lift

A gift that can not be broken or torn
never to be scattered and leave us to morn

A gift that our souls have always known
but sometimes our hearts just have to be shown
that we are loved and we have grown

Karen Westmoreland

Does Freedom Still Ring?

They call out "Let freedom ring".
Can this be what they truly mean?
Yesterday's gone; tomorrow's too far to see.
What will become of you and me?

What was America founded for,
If we cannot live our own lives anymore?
They say we have the right to life,
Yet killing and fighting are causing strife.

Our lives of freedom soon shall pass,
Because we have gone too far to turn back.
What will become of those unborn babies we've slain?
Will their stories live on or be thrown away
So much like the heroes of yesterday,
Whose lives should live on, even today?
But out of rebellion and out of pride,
We've pushed them away and out of our minds.

Now, that song should be telling us our time is growing short.
America, America, what are we living for?
The issues are plain; just look and see,
Are we really, truly free?

Kristin Buller

"Listen"

Listen as Thy Father speaks to us.
Can you not hear Him saying,
My children, "Why...Why must I always punish you?
I gave Adam and Eve the beautiful "Garden of Eden."
Only to take it back, leaving them naked in My world...Yes!
My world. The world that I have given to you, My children.
So that all may live together in peace.
To love each other, spread happiness and too bear more fruit.
Yet, My children...None of this means anything to you.
This universe is mine! My powers have been shown to you.
And yet, you have become deaf, dumb and blind to "His warnings."
He has placed a plague upon this earth.
A plague that takes Hundreds of Thousands of lives each day.
He has raised his rivers, He has opened His earth.
He has cast down from His heavens raging storms.
His wrath is being placed upon us everyday, in every way.
Yet, He spared our lives. He is crying out to us put down your
guns, join hands and love each other as I have loved you.

Lezlie M. Linder

Alchemist (Modern Day)

Seek, a pure life, elixir of life, in our time.
Change, white snow to gold, keep the future to hold,
   before our children fade away.
Grasp, the Philosophers stone, straighten the wrong,
   of modern times.
Break, the Labyrinth of thought, unleash your mind,
   for mankind.
Alchemist, seeks all the needs, rectify the deeds,
   of the human race.
Cry, cry all you want, the stone will change,
   your poison way.
Blind, blinded by the snow, look to the sun,
   the stone will let you go.
Reach, deep in your heart, the elements of the thought,
   thrive on change.

Robert Louis Pastore

Black Forest

The frosty night air enraptures my presence, making me chill, rubbing my hands for some paltry heat.

The moon shines vaguely through the dark, starless sky, animals howl in the distance.

My feet crunch brittle autumn leaves on my unalterable journey down a much traveled path, through a thick wooded forest of almost total blackness.

A cold wind brushes against me, my teeth chatter.

I taste and feel ice...snow crystals fall onto my face...and ice encases tree branches.

Then clouds break away, moonlight fills my vision, the North Star blinks at me as I notice Venus when I scan my midnight roof above me.

A shooting star inexplicably crosses my sight, than fades into nothing on the horizon.

For that moment, I felt ruler of the universe.

Michael Riceardi

The Atomic Thief

The clouds were hot, the ground in flames, as a cacophony of cries chilled my burning veins. The skeletoned landscape appeared to simmer. The spark of life reduced to a glimmer. Lurching forward with seared arms outstretched, the air raid this morning could not be matched. With raw burning eyes, that could barely see, the death and destruction surrounding me. Buildings and streets once familiar to my eye, have vanished and crumbled in complete awry. Staggering and stumbling through flaming debris, while the hot black clouds dried the tears within me. Groping with no hands, on shattered knees while the fire swept wind muffled my pleas. Family, friends, who were once so dear, like the blackened landscape, from my memory are seared. No pain, no tears, no memory, no grief, all stolen from me by an atomic thief. With a feeble shudder, and a dry hiss, I dedicate my soul to August sixth.

Michael Winston Sherrell

The Encounter

Night shadows swirled through the moonlit streets of the sleeping city.

The corner bus stop was desolate except for a huddled woman with pendulous breasts.

Among the sounds of passing cabs and indifferent cars, the strident gait of hurried feet was heard.

The pungent aroma of a cigar arrived shortly before its owner's paunchy stomach.

The silence was broken by the screams of sirens. The intruder's gold watch harmonized.

From deep within the mountainous man came a gentle whisper, "Is the No. 5 on time?"

The bent figure rearranged her bags and said in a coarse voice, "Should be, sir. Should be."

The heavy cloud surrounding the unlikely pair parted with the approach of luminous beams.

The bus stopped. The man climbed into its warmth. It left behind a foul odor.

Theresa Wilkowski

Untitled

Giving birth to a new life ... full of hopes, dreams, expectations.
Climbing the steps of development with this child of mine.
We approach a door that needs to be opened to get to the next flight.
Never expected the door to be locked.
The world stands still ... shattered future plans.
What is the key to open the door ... to be able to continue the journey up the stairs...
Obstacles blocking the path ... we seem to be losing ground.
Total denial that we need help; yet the forces are too strong.
Sitting isolated on the steps ... believing time will make things better.
Waiting.. Waiting... Waiting.....
Feeling overwhelmed acts like a weight over my entire body, making it difficult to move.
Suddenly heat is rising... everything seems to be spinning around.
A decision to either acknowledge my child has special needs; or remain on the stairs... not moving.
Gathering every ounce of inner strength... we stand up... grasping my child's hand we embrace a light.
Difficulties exist... until we accept the help of another person.
Holding His hand we begin to climb up the stairs again.
Each step towards the door teaches us that the key is knowledge.
Courage enables the hand to use the key to open the door.
Slowly walking through the door... a new journey begins..
A re-birth of life... new hopes, dreams, expectations.

Pamela Rae Morgan

Things I Didn't Know

I didn't know the courage and determination from racing trains and climbing trees
would help me face people reading my poetry.

I didn't know when we hurt each other so terribly
the healing would go slowly and painfully, but I would survive.

I didn't know when I burned my journals at the railroad tracks
what I'd learn about myself from the few I kept.

I didn't know the river I love really runs in myself
and the place where my thoughts come will open whenever I'm ready,
wherever I am.

I didn't know the sounds of Canada geese and football and
friends don't go away,
you can call it up from your heart anytime.

I didn't know humongous losses can be gotten over,
friends care enough to help and you are never the only one.

I didn't know growing up in a small town wasn't so bad
until I met people who hadn't, at least I like to go back.

I didn't know the friends you make and lose
are as important as friends you keep - adding to your whole.

I didn't know it doesn't matter what you miss,
if you can know you miss it, you've never really lost it.

Kelly C. McCarthy

The Light

When times get hard and you are weak
Close your eyes so you may sleep

As you wake still filled with despair
Please know there are those who really care

When everything seems dark as night
There will always be one bright light

Switch on that light inside your soul
You will be able to feel loves warm glow

When your energy weakens the light grows dim
God will take over and make it bright again.

LaJuan Pledger

Each Other

We watch the sun kiss the sky with morning drops of gold.
Closing our eyes,
Holding hands,
Clinging to each other for sympathy and support,
We see the sun allow another day to begin.
And we start our first day.
We left our other world behind,
To find another life.
Tears roll down our cheeks.
We had said there'd be no regrets, no pain.
We were only lying to ourselves.
Dying inside,
Wishing not to have to leave our friends, our family.
Still we must go and make our new life,
Alone.
Wishing for someone to tell us we are doing the right thing,
Leaving everything and everyone else behind,
But we will go on with no help from anyone else.
We have only each other.
And that is enough.

Katy Schappel

Untitled

The sunrise, the sky at sunset
Colors of nature fill my mind with wonder.
I am deep in thought and the world is
    part of me.

I see a leaf dancing in the wind-
    twisting and turning,
Delicate dancers moving in time with the
    music of nature.
 A bird joins in the song and it echoes
    across the mountain,
The world is at peace and the song
    Continues.
It rises to the gates of heaven and
    touches the hearts of the angels.

Nancy Estell Davis

Whispers In The Wind

I have heard the angels
Come a whispering on the wind.
God had sent His angels down,
My broken heart to mend.

I can hear them whispering,
When I lend to them my ears.
They were sent to share with me,
Calming all my doubts and fears.

The breeze blows gently on my face,
I feel the brush of angel wings.
And if I listen closely,
I can hear the angels sing.

Sometimes in the breeze, there's the softest voice,
Like the whispers in the wind.
Again the voice is gusty and strong,
Making clear the message they send.

So let the four winds blow across the fields.
Up the hills and down the dells.
I have heard the whispers in the wind,
And I know, truly, It's God's angels.

Margaret Skyles

"Is He Coming Home?"

He is gone. Why is he gone? He said he would
come back to me all in one piece and full of
pride. But why must he go? He mustn't die;
he must stay mine and never die. There he
stands so tall and brave, with all his
stripes in place. He who is there, he is
mine! But then I saw him leave with maybe a
little tear in his eye. But was it for me or
was it for country, flag, or liberty? But he
promised, he would come back to me all in one
piece and full of pride. And now the flags
are at half mast. Why? He didn't come back
to me. It, killed him they said. It, the
war, the fighting, no peace. That's what did
him in. That's why he didn't come home to me.
Yet, as the flags sway, and the "Taps" play, I
know that he did come home to me. And maybe
not physically, but mentally and emotionally,
his memories will always stay at home with me.

Sarah Jean Schmitt

A Sign Of Our Times

She will not leave my mind, that girl who died.
Coming off the ambulance, full of blood,
Motionless, I stood there, my eyes like floods.
Only twenty-one, we were the same age.
I watched as she died, my heart full of rage
A child at home and a baby inside,
Not one death, but two, for her baby had died.
Eyes still open, they did all they could do.
Where is her killer? He needs to see this!
The child wants her mommy, a good night kiss.
Danielle is no more, but her killer's free,
A rookie at this, her face won't leave me.
"You have to be tough," well, that's what they say,
That's easy for them, they'll see a new day.

Tanya B. Osborne

Under The Bridge Of The World

Oh, how does it feel to wake up in
Complete darkness.
No light in sight because the world you
Constantly whole-heartily fought, you still fight.
Under the bridge of shame
People pass, never knowing your name.
Even to you, your life is not the same.
Under the bridge of hopelessness
you lay on a bed of concrete.
When all your life you had a bed of cotton.
Oh, how we take being on the other side
Of that bridge for granted.

Monica Raymo Ladet

Untitled

Walk softly on the marshes of my soul
    Condemning voices bellowing below
Unearth madness flowing through veins
    Comforts darkness living within

Bones in the desert whisper in awe
    Dripping hidden treasures of memories the same
Feeling life's burdens as my own
    Pain glowing in eyes devour my reverence

Growing tired of this hell
    Wrap divine arms around us
Shaking out blackness
    Longing for rebirth...

Mary Monismith

Precious Moment

As I floated my boat out to sea
content to let the waves take me where they may
I welcomed the soft caress of the wind touching me

I lay upon my back with a smile
pleased with this precious moment I have found
letting the time slowly drift by as I dream awhile

I have not a care in the world today
as I listen to the waves gently splash against the boat
blending with the song of nature at play

Gazing above me I look to the clouds up high
and imagine myself floating on one
so peaceful, relaxed and happy am I

Too soon I must surrender to the land
and open my mind once again to reality
But my heart holds the memory as I walk across the sand.

Karen Petrocy

Block Fingers

Maybe I write to release, I'm dying from this disease.
Could I stand without my feet, I write through my defeat.

Your will could never hold me down,
Because you've turned my world around.
And help me to write again,
From pain even now and then.

Without my pen I'd have no words, to write to myself for you.
And the Paper: piece of clean, refreshes minds eye as new.

In times of feeling good or bad,
I jot the words of sound in mind.
Can I word the feel of love so sad,
As I struggle sobbing for one Last Line.

I laugh to myself and almost gleam;
Thinking you're close, sooner it seems.
Starting from blank and bought,
It's now release and nonsense thoughts.

I owe to the one; that made me feel: Even if it's pain, it's oh so
    real.

And at last I know this love inside,
That's in flowing pen on paper rides.

Marji Cruz

Dad

Dark hair intermingled with specks of grey
Countless worries about bills needed to pay
At night his weary bones on a bed he lay
As thoughts of trouble brought on by day
Oddly at a moment unexpectedly he'd get mad
Then as in regret suddenly he'd be sad
A grease splattered face he'd usually have
Or a boil on his face smeared with salve
Tender and kind in a rough sort of way
And these much used words he'd always say
"Shake down the stove Steve, or bring me a cup of Coffee Shirley"
As the years passed his vision failed, it was hard to see
His fits of anger wasn't his fault
His love for things in his heart was sealed like a vault
All of us would sometimes with him fuss
I guess we didn't know how much he meant to us
And it still makes our hearts pound
As we think of him lying in the cold hard ground

Shirley Bridgett

War

Lying still in their beds
covers protect them; pulled over their heads.
Rain tatters untimingly down. Thunder pushes it to the ground
on which buzzing battles from insects can be found.

The little ones cry when they can see
forms which no one else believes.

Clashing wings of unpredictable flight
slay themselves in the flashing night.
Still the rain chases down, into the shells of crisp bodies on the
    ground
of weeping insects with a frown.

Cries on the bedside pole
little ones, come, for daddy's home.

Praying to their insect Queens
who seem to dictate their dreams.
Rain slowing, tossing down on a laughing Lord on the ground.
Facing the sky, then finally drown.

Little ones fear the booming sound,
and a father's love cannot be found.

Phil Trotter

Where Were You Mommy

I'm always wandering around outside all alone
Crossing streets, going to the store, you not knowing I'm gone
The danger around us is plain to see, some caring person should
be watching me

There are many kinds of people who roam our street
You never know my friends or others I may meet
People often offer me bad things to do or try; someone help me
please hear my innermost cry

Darkness is falling I'm cold and afraid
In my pocket I hold a bravery token my sister made
All kinds of bad thoughts roam through my head; wishing I could
be safe and warm in bed

The sound of gunshots filled the air; screams rang all about
Everything happening so fast there was simply no way out
That one blazing bullet came out of nowhere; pierced me in my
back, I fell right then and there

I closed my eyes and took a deep breath; a bright light came I
knew I was near death
I heard my mother's voice crying, "my baby", it was too late
My last glance was a praying old lady

I heard the sirens; flashing lights were around, I laid there still in
a puddle of blood on the ground
The angels gathered around me; I felt no pain; they took me
away; only my body remain

Mommy is crying, tears flowing down her face
Grieving over her dead son whose murderer they'll never trace
She hadn't a clue how I yearned her love and care; mommy it's
okay I'm in heaven they love me here
Where were you mommy

H. Marie James Dawson

Obsidian

Rhymes with oblivion
close to the edge and wanting what's down there but
at the same time afraid
to jump
smooth in my hand and daring me
inside but
at the same time
impenetrable
warning me away
obsidian
close to oblivion.

Kelley A. Mahar

113

Daddy's An Angel

Four year old Branden asks his mommy why,
Daddy is up in the big blue sky.
And mommy answers with a nod of her head,
Daddy's an angel; that was all she said.

He says that I want to go and be with my dad,
This makes his mommy feel so very, very sad.
But mommy would miss you she said with a smile,
We all will see daddy, but not for a while.

Your daddy's job on earth is done.
Go play with your toys and have some fun.
Daddy's an angel and he'll do all he can,
To see that you grow up into a wonderful man.

Remember that mommy and daddy both love you,
And its love that will comfort you thru and thru.
Daddy's an angel; he's up in the sky,
An angel that loves his sweet little guy.

Sandra L. Siford

Lady First

In November of '60 her smile and character served her well, as she danced to many different tunes. The rights of all citizens was a policy she joyously watched developing, life is good! The whole world adores her without a hard sell, no one has a hint of impending doom. Sweetness of life, thoughts of making the world a better place; she really could!

A plethora of wondrous and tumultuous life events; children laughing on the White House Lawn... memories of a child that never would; swiftly premature death makes a claim. Young in years and shouldering tragedy in life's hardball game, did she feel like a pawn? Accepting the good times in life and not dwelling on the bad was her aim.

She brought her winning smile, grace and charm to Dallas, looking lovely dressed in pink. Motorcade, excited people cheering, outstretched hands, high school bands, madman with a rifle. Tragic bewildering historical events up close and personal changed her life in a wink. The world watched as her plans become sweet memories and the growth of a country is stifled.

Behind her wispy veil she followed the caisson and choreo-graphed the safety of her children. Forging ahead on a newly charted course while paparazzi invades and labels her life, "the fast lane." Good and rewarding years pass but a private soul must find public adoration somewhat bewildering. Fortunately for us her grace and beauty will endure long after premature death made its claim.

Leta Koch

Content with Me

Wandering aimlessly through my own
dark and confused thoughts, I stumble
across a God riding a ray of sunshine.
A God with happiness in his heart and
laughter in his eyes. He speaks to me
in tones of love and kindness and gradually
my lonely thoughts slip away.
He takes me in his arms and we
ride on fearlessly to beautiful and distant
lands where he shows me that my joy
could know no bounds.
We dance in fields of great expectations
and wade in pools of immortality. As
the golden light slowly fades around us,
he leads me to a white stallion waiting
to return us to where our endless
journey began.
We come to a clearing where we
must part, but the God I speak of
is here in my heart.

Melanie Greer

Togetherness

Sweet icy eyes
Dark chocolate thighs tremble with pleasure
from the treasure of intimate soul searching.

The connection 2 produce 1 life to give
soul mate to live grow as one life to give.

Strong feeling to believe in you me us
together forever.
Under worst of time together loving
the serene tranquil motionless
matrimonial togetherness

Larry D. Johnson

A Sense Of Being An Eternal Band

How do you see with prophet's eyes?
    Dark crying willow trees
Grey with age, withered and torn by sharp winds.
    Ashes of the future to come.
Yet you speak with a demonic tongue
    tempting creatures of sweet nature
by addicting them to easy technology.
    You are the hunting dog that smells
the prey of yesterday's savior.
    Smoke and sulfur burn your nose
ever down the path to Hades.
    Your flesh, once soft with youth
now burns with age.
    Silk bites with the friction of
desert winds and all you hear
    turns to the pictures of a silent movie.
Forever moving on and forward
    to the concert of misery,
Where the Band plays on for eternity.

Paul Michael Briggs

A Stain On Stained Glass

The church lies smoldering
Darkened steeple swinging softly on silver threads
Like the bell
Ringed with clashing dust
Where the bomb fell.

Fragments of candles burn in scorched-earth holders
Like stars on heaven's velvet
Burnt iron on velvet altars
In a glass cathedral.

Rings of glimmering glass wedges
Stilettos, leaden handled, cleave flesh
Merge with bullets
Flooded with moonlight singing.
The chords of angel choirs float clear
Where soft, soft rain touches lead and steel.

Robert D. Grappel

A Light In The Darkness

The forest grows sideways in shadow
Darkness descends like a starving vulture.
Picking hungrily at the last threads of light
The sun swallowed whole by an army of clouds
Whose neat, orderly ranks will soon consume the endless sky
And I was plunged into darkness
The path before me obscured,
Cast in shadows of deepest black
My mind weary of all sides
My feet trodding along the hard, stone path
Through the darkness but always unerringly
Towards a light which both guides me
And keeps me from adjusting to the darkness

William W. Graves

"The Darkness"

Close your eyes what do you see
Darkness, look at thee.
Love the dark, love it to the end
Don't be afraid the darkness could be your friend.
Most people they want the light with all its white
Well, I'll take the dark, black as night.
I've had brown, yellow, and cream
But if it must be told, dark is good, good as gold.
Dark so sweet, tasty and fine; light is good sometimes.
People in the light they don't know what to do
Act so silly, a little stupid and a fool.
They don't understand that the darkness is cool.
So to all my brothers who wouldn't give darkness a chance
To all my brothers who wouldn't give darkness a dance.
I'll have darkness with darkness comes darkness romance.

Micheal T. Johnson

Yesterday, Today, And Tomorrow

Yesterday our hearts felt as if they would break when our unwed daughter told us she was with child.
Yesterday we were shocked, numbed, and pained; reality had not yet sunk in.
We were about to become grandparents.
For her abortion was not an option; adoption was out of the question.
The burden would be hers alone as the father faded from the picture.
Yesterday she was a junior at the university determined to have this child and complete her education.
Yesterday at times the burden seemed almost too heavy to bear.
With the love and support of family and friends, she faced up to her responsibility.
When the big day arrived, her dad and mom were by her side.
In awe they watched the birth of their first grandchild.
One look at this beautiful little girl and they knew the choice, the pain, the anticipation had all been worthwhile.
No other joy can compare to the joy they felt as they held her in their arms for the very first time.
With those big blue eyes their granddaughter seemed to say "thanks for being here for my mom and me."
Yesterday our beautiful grandchild was dedicated to the Lord.
Today our hearts are bursting with joy as we watch our daughter walk down the aisle to claim her diploma.
Today she has given her daughter one of the best gifts a single mother can give her child,
an education enabling her to support her child and herself.
Tomorrow the future looks bright, because tomorrow she will take her place in front of the classroom.
Not only will she challenge your children to a good education, but tomorrow she and her daughter will be cheering them on.

Patricia H. Collins

Untitled

Love cling to my heart on that cold winter
day. It sent its warmth through my soul.
Love put the sweet smell of passion in
my heart. It unchained my shackles.
Never will I ever know again pain and sorrow
for your love, is love unconditionally.
Hurt no more I say to you, for you shall
never know loneliness again.
Wonder not, for you will never have doubt
plague your mind again.
You now have found that power that rule
all men of this world.
Your heart shall be happy and free
with no chains to hold it down.
Love cling to your heart to, for you are
the one, who sent it through my soul.
Love put its wonderful smell of passion
in your heart as well.
For you called on it to unchain my shackles.

Tony Anthony Partee, Sr.

Untitled

I went to the forest yesterday in the bomb drop zone
Dead trees blocked my path telling me to go home
I felt like I was in a new world strange as it may seem
I felt like I was walking in a demented dream

I met someone called Autumn there
She said she was a ghost
My logic lost as I entered so I let her be my host
Death warmed over was how she looked strange as it may seem,
Acid rain poured down her face in a demented dream

If you ever go to the forest in the bomb-drop zone
Never eat the berries there and never go alone
For it will become your grave yard
Your final resting place
Your body turns to dust and bones and your
mind's in outerspace.

Lisa Ferrara

Random Neatness, Neatly Random

Random neatness, neatly random...
Deborah would like this paradox. The ocean, wind and water, is such a fascinating, moving work of art. Lines crossing lines, dissolving into bubbles, which slide and burst to nothing. Firm, thunderous curves fall to indistinguishable foam which creeps then goes lacy and recedes...
Which is the ocean? At once powerful and weak — a crashing wave leaves but a grain-wide trail of its glory, and that so soon swept clean by another... Such momentary, fragile, powerful beauty.

Linda Jean Nadzan, RSM

Trigger

Seeming to pull back: RECOIL,
Deeper into paralysis,
Deeper into the shadow of myself.

"What seems to be wrong?" she said.
"I'm very much alone, or so I feel".

Planets motionless all around me.
I appear more stagnant every second:
I wait for my spine to snap and send me orbiting,
Like a rocket, someone could light this fuse and send me shooting.
If only someone would set my spine ablaze,
That white-hot ember catalyst;
Someone to unlock this angst and fury.
And set this freedom in motion,
Like the dream of the carousel setting the horses free.

Seeming to pull back...pull back...
Withdraw.
Almost locked into being alone,
This is as far as we go,
"Click, Click".

Michael Stevinson

A Rose

A rose in rose
arose in rows
of frozen rows:

Those throes o'erthrown,
then throve the rose
on thrones of thorns:

Per aura's glows,
ambrosia's flows,
aroma's blows,

furrows and roads
where rode sorrow's
erosive woes —

o'ergrows those groans,
unrolls her cloaks,
unclothes her robes

the floral rose
enthralls her holds,
enfolds their roles:

morose and wrothsome
loathsome lonesome
loads, although...

enclosing lobes
enclosing lodes
of glozen troves...

Eros-arrows
arouse our awes,
our ohs, our ahs...

A rose!

W. Andreas Wittenstein

115

YOUTH - MY CHOICE

YOUTH - POSITIVELY speaking:
  definitely a mystery,
  a thing of Beauty,
  endless energy, to envy,
  robust health, too often squandered,
  a body of notable proportion,
  physical power, underestimated by SELF,
Toned-muscles in total command, by moral values habituallized.
Sharpened-intellects, hungering for wisdom and knowledge.

  Keen perceptions: visual, auditory, tactical...
  well-balanced emoting, fitting the occasion,
  genuine LOVE - sexual included - BUT in control.
A spiritually-bent curiosity - oft unsatiated;
Too frequently doubted by elders.
To mention but a few.

YOUTH - NEGATIVELY speaking:
  a greater, deeper MYSTERY, perhaps;
  BUT diametrically opposed to each above,
Plus others too well-known to mention.

Mary Joyce Schladweiler

Light Of Jesus

Listen, I know I need Jesus.
Do you know you need Him too?
If you open the door,
He will open your heart,
As you change in the things you do.
It's taken some time to answer His call.
It's taken some patience too.
He's called once before.
But you did it once more,
And you didn't do what He asked you to do.
But now He said, "Hush," and you listened instead.
Your eyes opened wide as you heard what He said.
Your smile is true.
And your eyes sparkle bright.
As you open the door.
You have seen the light.

Barbara Carol Kares Troilo

"Lines Of Misunderstanding"

What happens when the sun won't shine anymore,
do you look for another door?
Do you run further inside yourself,
keep on going through the test?

Caught somewhere in between,
a part of you that's never seen.
Friendliness only part of the disguise,
for the sad truth that underneath lies.

Even if you could explain, they'd never understand,
it's almost too much for me to comprehend.

Laughter in our eyes that was once so loud,
never on a day was there ever a cloud.
Hoping the rain would never come,
then one day it suddenly poured down.

Scared and praying we can win this out,
knowing you never in your heart had a doubt.
Keeping faith this will all pass away,
then the sun will forever stay.

Christine Baker

Two Hearts In One

If I just do my thing and you
do yours.
  We stand in danger of losing
each other and ourselves.

  I am not in this world to live
up to your expectations or you mine
  But I am here to confirm you.

  We are fully ourselves, only in
relation to each other can we be one.

  I did not find you by chance, I
found you by an active way of reaching out.

  Rather than passively letting things
happen to me, I can act and will act,
intentionally, to make things happen.

  I now must begin with myself, but!
I must not end with myself. The truth
begins with two and I shall end with two.....

Joseph C. Demasi

Enjoying Those Glorious Days Of Summer!

Sunning, playing, hiking and biking.
Doing these or something more to your liking...
Enjoying those glorious days of summer!

Picnics, grilling, outings and parties
Perhaps sitting under a shade tree sipping Barcardis...
Enjoying those glorious days of summer!

Vacations, hammocks, slides and swinging on swings.
Closing your eyes and dreaming of beautiful things...
Enjoying those glorious days of summer!

Kids laughing, birds singing, flowers smelling so sweetly,
Just basking in nature all to completely...
Enjoying those glorious days of summer!

Chilling winds, frosty air and the impending dread of December,
Just sit back, relax, a sigh, oh remember...
Enjoying those glorious days of summer!

Carol Nelson

Redneck Dare

Don't you dare cry your alligator tears on my snake skin boots!
Don't you dare accuse me of drinking too much beer after work!
Don't you dare tell your friends I love my dog more than you!
Don't you dare drive my truck 'cause you don't know what to do!

Don't you dare "boo" the flag, it stands for liberty and life!
Don't you dare toss my jeans, they fit my body just fine!
Don't you dare crush my cap, it conforms perfect to my head!
Don't you dare laugh at Ma, she's this Redneck's best friend!

Dare this Redneck, anybody dare?
Don't you dare this Redneck, his friends wait over there!
Dare this Redneck, he knows what to do!
Don't you dare this Redneck, it'll all be through for you!

Judy Voss

Alone To Die

Dark
Evil peering through the shadows of the fullmoon light
The smell of decaying flesh fills the air
A stench of blood in the cold pale night
Black as death a mist blinds the way to good
And leads you to a road of evil
And all the black mirrors of the abyss
And cold murky pools of hell
Leave you there to die alone

Cory Smith

The Ceremony

As the ceremony began,
I sat 'long side a ragged bear
who heaved a sigh and
shed a tear from one glass eye.
While a baby doll,
looking pale and thin,
wondered who would tuck her in
and hear her prayers as the light
grows dim.
But smiling was a dimpled girl,
radiant in the candles' light—
who, yesterday, I held so tight
when frightened by the darkened
room, as things were "bumping
in the night."
Then the song began,
the candles flickered,
and in an instant—
we said goodbye to a
wonderful friend.

Julianne H. Ohlrich

Flag Of Our Country

Flag of our country
   A banner so proud
I stand here beneath thee
   My head bowed
I pray that you will always be
   The symbol of truth and purity
May there be freedom and justice for all
   Regardless of color, the big or small
Those who pay false homage to you.
   Be cast aside as is their due
May each one use heart, head and hand
   To keep the creed for which you stand.
Each one in his heart be true
   To God and the red-white and blue.

Alice M. Hutt

My Rainbow

After a summer rain I looked at the sky,
A beautiful rainbow way up high.
From Lake Superior over fields of green,
A more beautiful sight I had ever seen.
Father walking down the lane
With the help of his cane.
Mother in her chair sat sewing neatly,
And the birds all sang so very sweetly.
All this I thank thee on my knees
Forever in my memories.
Lazy carefree summer day,
Smell of clover fresh cut hay.
On cold and frosty winter nights
We walked to see the Northern lights.
Oh so many things to remember,
Now it's my very own September.
All the trees that were so green all summer
Now have turned to autumn color.
I did not accomplish very much
The rainbow was too high to touch.

Helma Sophia Parmley

Inner Healing

The soft wind in my face
A bird's song in my heart
The laughter of a child
This... is inner healing.

The sunlight in my eyes
The sound of running water
A path so green it shines
This... is inner healing.

The warmth of summer days
The colors in a flower
An eagle soaring high
This... is inner healing.

A mother rocks her child
Soft music in my ears
A rainbow in the sky
This... is inner healing.

The passion of a kiss
To hold your hand in mine
To know that I am loved
This... is inner healing.

Deborah Arocho

Flaming Torment

The sun rose in the distance,
A brilliant scarlet flame.
Scorching all it touched,
As shimmering breath it came.

The lake was turning red,
Seemed to shrink in fear.
Flowers quickly wilt,
As soon as they appear.

A red hot wind just hovered,
As heat from burning torch.
I huddled close to shade,
On a stingy narrow porch.

My eyes, two orbs in pain,
A tormented sort of daze.
The flat horizon sank,
In dancing, distant haze.

I sought one cloud above,
It might bring welcome rain.
Only disappointment rose,
My hope was all in vain.

Betty Grace Northup

Your Life

The baby:
   A bundle of innocence
   A miracle to behold.
The child:
   Seeking, learning, testing
   Growing inches every day.
The youth:
   Curious, and yet unsure
   Disavowing family ties.
The adult:
   The need for a mate
   And a nest of their own.
The parent:
   Proud, strong, authoritative
   I know I am somebody.
The grandparent:
   Time is telling me something
   If I haven't made it, forget it.

This is your life, what it's all about.

Christine Johnson

"Nursing Home Visitor"

A gentle touch,
A caring glance,
A friendly chat.

Each familiar face,
Every bright voice,
Some new friends.

Taking minutes to visit,
Filling days with closeness,
Sharing years of memories.

Gail L. West

"Hope"

Shining down in brilliance
A circle of light so bright
We look and see our futures
We touch and view the night
A feeling so strong we share
A harmony of one we become

Soaring above the clouds; creeping
   along the stars
Twilight has set; we see what is ours
Twinkling above us, an outpouring
   of hope that penetrates.
Freedom of this world
Peace and love created.
Pleasure above pain,
Happiness to reign.
Uncluttered thoughts, no doubts to exist
Unreality in our very midst.

Debra Selesky

Freedom's Wings

A single rose of delicate light
A drift in the vast sea of night
unfolds its secret wonders
with the fresh dew of the morn.
The rising sun in a blue, blue sky,
fields of rolling green,
two eyes watch from up above
a ship setting sail at sea.
Cool winds blow and catch the sails
the waters lay calm and still
cut in two by the wooden hull
the starboard bow clears the trees.
What lay's out beyond the sky,
beyond the cliffs of port?
Upon the waves, foaming white
Upon freedom's wings.

Joe McSweeney

Poems

Not all poems are written to delight
A few fill souls with fright
Many are tragic and sad
Some lead to belief authors were mad
Not to forget the ones that bore
Still there are more
Poems that outnumber all the rest
Universally regarded as the best
They are, of beauty and love.

Joseph J. Rutkowski

117

A Special Moment

A fooling memory
A forgotten place
A picture you remember
An expression on a face
A very small moment
That is captured in time
It stays in your heart
But fades from your mind
An emotion you left
A story recalled
A moment of happiness
A person you saw
They stay with you now
they stayed with you then
You'll never forget
How, where, and when

Janet Wells

Blossom

Here in my hand I hold
A fragrance with petals gold,
A softness, a breath, a touch,
A lightness weighing nothing much.
To you would I this blossom send;
On you these golden petals spend
As tribute to the soul of spring,
A fragile, precious, holy thing,
A love, a gentle living part
You've made to flower in my heart.

Jo Anzalone

The Butterfly

It was a cool and sunny morning;
A gentle breeze upon my face;
I watched a yellow butterfly
Dine on Queen Ann's lace.

The butterfly, undaunted by the breeze,
Held on to the flower
With such a seeming ease,
Rocking back and forth the while,
I wondered at its style.
It enhanced the beauty of
The flower . . .
An example of God's Love.

Eve Moore

The Moon Reminds

The moon reminds me as I sit
   A grate of clouds keeps me from it
I, on my part, thinking back
   To when I slept as he now lies
My son of eight whose quiet cries
   Serve to register his place
As one with me outside of grace.
   Asleep, he longs, as I, awake,
To find the clearing in our dreams
   And walk among remembered scenes.

We come to learn what we've once known
Following paths now overgrown
From seeds we scattered long ago
That teach us what we're born to know.

Brian Haley

Brother Of Mine

So handsome, a genius
A heart and soul so fine!!!
Looking threw your eyes...
At this world we live in,
Life and hardship collide
But you... can always make me see the
Sunny side!!!

When my world dies...
My heart and soul to you I give
Because only you can make it survive.

Brother of mine, my one and only
From children... to now,
You've been my inspiration, my pride,
Always standing with me,
Loving me no matter what I have done!!

Battles of my life, you've fought
Till won.
Your my dear Brother,
You are my only one!!!

Jane Cupit

Seed

I'm a core from an apple
   A life of a leaf
I have four souls that come together
   As unity

The core from the apple
That brings life to the leaf

So that the tree will stand
   Tall and green

Green as the core
Green as the leaf
   And
Green moss that grows on each
Side of the tree

Tree standing tall looking at me
Filling new buds everyday
That I see

Feeling it as I feel it to be me

Collette Johnson

Tennessee

Your soul's a pasty shade of gray,
A little different from the way
   that you portray it publicly.
According to what I've been told
Your soul is lovely to behold.
Its sunny colors shine twofold
As butterscotch and marigold.
   I find it cold contemptibly.
Your advocates have erred, my mate.
They see you glitzy, gold, but wait...
Fool's gold get old, revealing slate.
Your false allure will soon abate,
   and on that date, I'll come to see
Them raise the shades just to behold
A storm-gray day (no marigold).
   Your soul, they'll see, is wintery.

Brekka J. Hervey

Addiction

It starts out fun.
A little here, a little there.
A nice buzz feels real good.
A sweet escape.
Until you discover
a little bit isn't enough anymore.
Your dollar buzz turns into more.
But you can handle it,
or so you say.
"What's a little extra cash
for a good time?
There's no harm in it."
Soon the extra cash isn't available.
Now what?
You can give it up
or find another way.
But now you have no choice,
your body craves it
and you give in.

Bonnie BoWell

The Child So Sweet

Once a woman did marry
A man so wrong,
And she did carry
A child so sweet.
That child so sweet came to be;
And the man so wrong
Was wrong to harm the child so sweet.
He beat upon the child so sweet.
"What is the meaning?" the woman asked.
"Why did you beat the child so sweet?"
The man that did and was so wrong wept.
"I do not know why I beat
The child so sweet."
My dear friends do not beat
The child so sweet.
For the child so sweet is our tomorrow.
Do not beat on our tomorrow.
It brings such sorrow
To the world.

Amy Compton

The Wedding Gift...

A New Beginning

The climbing crocus,
   a new beginning.
Uplifting petals,
   new awakening.
Rebirth, renewal,
   a time of joy!

The lighted candles,
   a new beginning.
Flames a-flickering,
   glowing, enriching.
Eternal, lasting,
   a time of love!

June F. Banfe

Getting Together

A path of love for you and me
A secret code to show my cry
Getting together means a lot to me
My love for you is deep, you'll see
I need you here in my arms
The scenery of my heart is in my palms
I love you now more and more
The love that's near it all assured.

Charles Jones

The Joy Life Has To Offer

Deep inside my healing heart
A pain so great - hurting.
So far it seems to stretch,
Like a great abyss,
Without an end in sight.
Full of loneliness and sorrow
It is there I often lose myself
Tangled in a web of emotions
So tightly bound it's hard to see
All the joy life has to offer.
I search to find a way out
But find I'm trapped inside my sorrow.
So exhausted my strength has left me,
Then I find a beacon of hope,
It is my lord, who shows me the way.
He fills the abyss with love overflowing,
Pulls away the delicate strands that bind me,
And shows me the joy life has to offer.

Joseph Odom

Rest Stop Of Life

What is this place of beauty I seek
A place to renew my energy
To look at life and all it brings
Coming home and feeling peace

I go to the garden now and then
And listen to the sounds of nature
I reflect upon the silence within
A quiet reminder to places I've been

I listen to the trees and flowers
Whispering softly of my presence
The gentle caress of a breeze
Tolls away the hours

In this place I know I belong
For this is where I learned
To whistle my merry little song
And say thanks for all I've earned

Edward D. Perry

The Mind Of A Demented "Man"

So nice and kind is he or she,
a pleasurable person is all that we see.

So kind and so gentle to those
in their path, as long as we're
not the victims of their wrath.

So twisted inside their mind
as we know, it won't be long
before the last trigger will blow.

So be aware of the things
that are spoken, because
we never know who will be
his last token!

Julie A. Robertson

Untitled

Life is strange
A real roller coaster ride
One moment high on the mountain
Then sinking like the falling tide
I don't understand
What it's all for
Happiness would be much easier
If I never needed any more
I guess that I should be thankful
For the time we have shared
And hope that in the future
We both have as much as we can bear

Brian Kettering

My Love

My love is like
a red, red, red.
It flows in petal shapes
scraped and swept
from painting knife and brush.
Into the living stream it spills
upon a canvas river bed.

With a splash of orange-red, red, red,
a blush of violet-blue,
the rushing colors merge.
Amorphic, translucent forms
cling like silk around
the smallest ever bud.

The pool at the eddy waits,
receiving into its deep womb
the petals tightly closed.

The whirlpool at the eddy spins
flings out in fine array
my love, my love, like a red red rose.

Jan Ross Deetjen

Loving....

When from within a quiet comes,
A silence of goodness and faith;
A time that has within its place
The fullness of God's own grace.

A peace that unfolds to a greater peace,
A joy few come to know.
The conscious truth of life unfolding
To a greater good within its molding.

And from this quiet place within
An inner strength is found;
A creative cycle of constant good
So each can hear the sound.

Yes in this quiet place, you see,
Resides the God of eternity; where,
Miracles begin with each new thought
And love is the answer we have sought.

Dennis Martin

Untitled

Deep within there is a gaping hole.
  -A void of sorts.
  Containing nothing,
  Yet everything.
Fear, Anger, Hatred.
  Agony, Love and Tears.
  Become one in the void.
  A tormenting ache.
Beginning at the core of my heart,
  It ends not with my soul.
  No miracle meds will ease my pain.
  -Tho at times it is physical.
The passage of time blurs your faces.
  Yet enhances the anguish therein,
  which consumes my existence.

Irene F. LaBelle

Back To Back

Back to back we lie,
A wall between our hearts,
We're here together,
but we're so far apart.

The tears fall silently,
As I watch our love fade,
But you just want to go on,
With this sad charade.

How much longer,
Are we to pretend?
Please answer me,
Why can't we let it end?

Why won't you admit,
This is just a big mistake?
Why can't you admit,
That this is all fake?

Denise Pendergast

What Dream Is This

What dream is this that lifts my heart
Above all sordid earthly things
And lets me hear soft music drifting
Down from where an angel sings?

What dream is this that lets my eyes
See all the beauty of a star
That yesterday was but a gleam of
Silver shining from afar?

What dream is this that weaves a spell
With all its subtle magic charms?
If only I could dream that lovely
Dream forever in your arms.

Helen De Menna

Of Tortured Souls

Of Tortured souls in wandered wait,
Abreast of life, but naught to know.
With soul afire misguided heart,
For death doth bring eternal light.

To search in lust, embark thy soul,
In deliverance from Godly thrones.
Severed from ye wells of thought,
A never ending battle fought.

Within a dream, lies in between.
Reality illusions seem.
All inherent, lost in a sphere.
The waters edge, earths ending pier.

Drink of the well, reflections known.
To quench thy thirst, of dust and bone.
Of tortured souls in wandered wait
Cast thine love at heaven's gate.

Joseph Andruzzi III

The Prize

Open up your heart,
Accept the love, It's here
to stay.
And as the years that
shall pass by.
And you've traveled many miles,
All you'll see, is joy and smiles.
So close your eyes, and realize,
That this time, it's no disguise.
You've won the prize.
It was the love inside of you,
and you've finally let it through.

Gloria A. Quezada

Suicide

Nobody ever cared when she
achieved a goal;
Nobody ever listened when she
had a problem;

Nobody ever went the extra
mile for her when she was in pain;

Nobody could understand what
went on inside her confused mind;

Nobody could feel what was in
her heart;

Nobody knew when she took
her dark, problem filled life
form our world in search for
some light;

Nobody ever cared.

Holly MacCulloch

When Fall Comes

Leaves are falling to the ground
Acorns are dropping all around
Squirrels are racing from here to there

Feel the wind as it chills the air

Colleen Miller

The Wind And The Leaf

The wind blows
Across a single leaf.
The leaf is lifted
As it feels the wind,
Touches the wind,
Loves the wind.
But the wind moves
Ever onward.
And the leaf,
The leaf is left
Feeling alone,
Completely still
In a world of motion.
The wind has moved on,
To other leaves,
Never to pass again.
I am the leaf,
You, the wind.

John A. Specht

Jennifer

In January you were only two, and you
Almost talked like you were four.
I know when you get to be that age,
You'll be talking a whole lot more.

Your beautiful, wavy, auburn hair
Surrounds your pretty face, and
Brightens your shining blue-green eyes,
Your rosy cheeks, and skin so fair-

And, of course, that happy smile,
Of which there is always a trace
This makes everything worthwhile.

But when you look at me and say-
  Hi! Grandma!
There's nothing else can make my day!

Anne R. Davey

Seabeck Storm

Down from lofty, Olympic heights
Across graylit canal and sound
Visitations of December sights
Flecks of white, touching ground

Now icy winds of winter blow
No longer the playful breeze
Stormy embrace laden with snow
Fall vanquished the stately trees

Wave broken boats high on the shore
Buckled timber of marina and piers
Fractured limbs strew earthen floor
Unwanted are such somber souvenirs

Black curtains fall when power fails
Bedeviled again by fortune's trick
Amenities lost as the dark prevails
Save for the glow of oil lamp wick

Down comforters invade my thought
of shivery winds on paths of plunder
Tomorrow view what nature's wrought
For weary body now bids me slumber.

Don Lund

Drowning In Hate

Hate is a lake
Albeit, a small lake
However, its depth is undefined
Whatever color the sky is,
The lake is always as black as night
When the sun burns hot
The lake is always cold
It lures its victims in different ways
It uses the lure of easy money
Or that of instant fame
Its most subtle lure is that
of innocence,
of trust which is later betrayed
Friends and enemies alike
Tie weights of anger around my feet
and throw me into this watery abyss of
hate
God, please help me
Throw me a line
I can't breathe
I'm drowning in hate

Brian Nielsen

The Book

The book sits there
all alone,
I pick it up,
it's cold and dusty.
No one has touched it
in a while,
I open it up,
it contains a
cold winter day.
I start to shiver,
because of its cold words.
I close the book,
I put it down.
It will lay there
alone, again
until another person
comes along.

Jake Grosek

The Sea

As I look into the open sea,
all I ever see,
is waves,
big waves,
little waves,
all I see is waves.

When I look out onto the sunset,
It's glistening currents set,
off into the sunset.

What's this I see,
it's a dolphin staring at me,
I know I'm safe when,
mother natures critters,
are looking after me.

What's this I see,
it's no longer sea,
I see, it's land
the shore of Newfoundland,
that's the province my family found.

Carol Gharzouzi

Together, Hand in Hand

All lovers have their quarrels,
All lovers have their fights,
But most of all my darling,
All lovers have their rights,

The right to live and love, dear,
The right to be alone,
The right to have their happiness,
And children of their own.

And so to you today, dear,
I make this pledge of love,
I shall be yours forever,
Both here and up above.

I'll always love you, darling,
I'll never leave you, dear,
I'll always be as happy
If you are always near.

And when that certain day comes
And we leave this happy land,
My only prayer is that we go
Together, hand in hand.

Charles E. Cook

The Invisible

Above in the sky, above
all thoughts, "it",
that could not be reached
with my mind, waits
quietly above.
I am trying to fulfill,
but it can not be fulfilled
by me.
Invisible for me and you.
How wonderful would it
not be, if I could reach
out and find?
It is impossible because
it is invisible.
The power of the created
is above.
And then I just see it
happens.
The only thing I can do
is be in it... The life.

Annica Kratz

"Back To Shore"

In this ocean of trouble we are
all trying to find the wave that we
need to guide us through our time.
Then you give me your hand and
I am lifted from a drowning situation.
I let go of the anger that has been
pulling me under. Your love brings
me back to shore.

Joan Doranzo

Heart-Spoken Intimacies

Come into my chamber
Allow my pulsating muscle
move you
Dance the song of life
with my rhythmic beat
Transcend to the branches
of the tree of life
Inhale the sweet
intoxication
of rebirth
Come again,
resuscitate me
with your vital flow
So the dance
can begin
once more...

Brennan McCall

Smiles

Silent language
Alluring, extravagant, mysterious
Communicating without using words
Treasure

Cathy Phouthone

Lost

She sits in an empty room,
Alone in the cold.
Weeping softly as the bleak darkness,
Tightens its icy hold.
Memories of a sunlit past,
Echo in her head.
Covered by the shroud of fear,
Fear for the future ahead.
Eyes of a stranger may be,
Staring into her tattered heart.
But its her own voyeuristic demons,
That are tearing her apart.
Lost in a world of her nightmares,
Locked in her own cell.
Burning in the flames,
Of her own personal hell.
Where does she turn in the darkness?
Will she stay lost in the night?
Only the hidden strength in her heart,
Shall reveal the true path to the light.

Dave Stillwell

Reflections

If into a mirror you can stare-
and find a little girl standing there,
try to remember her but beware,
for if she smiles at you-
you may see,
the little girl that you used to be.

DeAnna Garcia

Untitled

Waiting
always waiting in the wings
Waiting
so patient
(good dog, good dog)
I've died for one thousand
while waiting for Papa Death.
he still hasn't shown
but neither has anyone else
Waiting
....again
she's not coming back
...again
...one thousand one...

Christopher Nagy

Treasure Island

I searched for a treasure
an adventure I could find
and it took me to far off places
and folk fair and kind.
but with are item greater and more
important than treasure
that island I did part:
t'was the knowledge that
the greatest treasure;
is the one within the heart.

Jennifer Kendall

Another Day Without You

Each day begins this lonely life
An empty heart from the strife

Alone and cold the sleepless nights
With peace no where in sight

Tear-stained pillows come with each
dawn... Another day without you.

I've grown so tired I must confess
Of all this bitter loneliness

Sometimes I think my heart will break
How much longer must I wait?

Tear stained pillows come with
each dawn... Another day without you.

Oh Dear heart please break the chain
And let my heart be full again

For only you can me free
So all my sleepless nights can be

Dream filled slumber, approach
the new dawn... Heavenly nights beside you.

Cynthia P. Juarez

Summer Fun

Summer makes me think of camping,
And eating marshmallows
as sweet as candy.
Sleeping under the stars,
Like little night-lights in the sky.
Telling ghost stories,
Getting scared as a bird
when it sees a dog.
Drinking soda and feeling it
tickling your throat like a feather,
And jumping in a pool of water
As blue as the afternoon sky.

Danny Prochaska Jr.

The Dance

Jigging the jig or hopping the hopper,
An exciting dance it is.
With a quick tug and jerk,
A spin and a swirl.
A splash and a splash
She dances upon her tail,
Leaping clear of the blue.

Reel her in,
She sizzles back out again.
Slowly bring her to net
And release her to the depths.

Anticipating a repeat performance,
Cast to another shore.
Jigging a jig, hopping a hopper
A lovely way to spend a day.

Clifford M. Medler

An Ode Of The Underpad

A pink one; a white one
An underpad; we're on the run
A couple here; a couple there
Let's put a stack upon the chair.

Putting on just what we need
To do the job, so we can speed
Along. And upon another bed
To place the pads, just how we said.
The laundry has a big job too
To keep ahead of what we do.

When our day comes to an end
The next shift starts the linen trend.
It made me smile, when the resident said,
"I'm glad to have a nice, dry bed."

Dorothy E. Bayer

Gathering Shells

In our bright sunlight
Ancient crows ahead
Sick and dying, yet
Picking up the dead.
Two crows.
Who turn out to be,
When we get close at hand,
Old women in black clothes,
Stiff legged upon the February beach
Gathering shells.

We cling each to each
And, so not to disturb them
Circle round higher ground
Keeping our warm gift between us;
Yet, wondering the while
What cold pleasure they have found.

Charles F. Greiner

Sea Gull

Symphonies; though he plays
A silver, silent song.
The fledgling, now has really fled,
He lies in the black pool, dead.

Though but a dimple in a crimson sky
Singing free thoughts far and wide,
Woe to them who dive too low
To hit the slick: He could not know,
But they say it was a perfect dive.

Dale A. Vedder

121

On Christmas Day

Dear God, we thank you for this day
And all that went before.
Not for the toys so kids can play,
Or green wreaths on the door.

We thank you for our happiness
As well as for our health,
For it's with those we must confess
We measure all our wealth.

But most of all we thank you for
This birthday of your son,
Who guides us through life's many doors
Until our work is done.

We ask for nothing selfish for
Ourselves except your love,
Until we pass that golden door
At last to heaven above.

Please bless the homeless and the poor,
Give health to those who're ill,
And give us courage to endure
So we can do thy will.

Floyd W. King

"Crucified"

The son is in the mind,
    and also in the heart.
How is it that one,
    could tear his world apart?
Now comes a Rainbow,
    is this to be justified?
When the clouds surroundings
    haven't even been tried.
Upon the mind of innocence,
    the Devil stalks his prey,
and feasts upon it,
    as the spirit is saved away.
Judged in a time zone,
    wrong to be denied.
Knowing, come the rapture,
    one will decide.

   "The Reign"
Claudia M. Scarbrough

A Toast

May your life together, get better
    and better
Be healthy, be happy
    blessed with beautiful children
Good times often
Sad times few
Cherish the day you met
    the day you committed
    and the day you said
        I DO.
Barry Kilduff

Spring

Rejoice with me for death has passed
    and freed me from his grasp.
Rejoice with me for new life's begun
    and songs must now be sung.
The death of Winter is gone and done
    and the life of Spring has sprung.
Sing! Every flower, bird and tree
    sing to heaven 'til eternity.
Sing to the sun and the life it's giving.
    Sing! For now life's worth living.
Awake broken hearts it's time to mend.
    Awake! For spring has come again.

Ann F. York

Carefree

I live by the Brize
and by my poetry
into a Leeway...

  I rejoice
when a flower open
with a smile
for kissing a dream

No matter what I was yesterday
as I will be tomorrow
life is you

  I live by thy image
and roll all pure,
my essence
in the kingdom of stranger...
Calvin Louissaint

Happiness Is My Family!

I am so fortunate;
    And doubly blessed by far,
To have a close-knit fam'ly;
    Trouble or strife can't mar.

We share our joys and woes;
    Who could ask for anymore?
Yet when a problem comes;
    We'll gather to the fore.

A crisis did arise;
    With it came grief and tears.
We all pulled together;
    And we overcame our fears.

A weekly trip we made,
    Through snow, and sleet, and sun.
The object of our worries,
    Knew we were all for one.

The crisis finally ended.—-
    The warmth of love we shared;
Is a lasting blessing,
    Knowing a family cared.
Dorothy Michelli

My Lament

My Darling's now deceased
    And, for Him, I'll always pine -
    But, "they" claim - Death is Death
        And, by now, I should feel fine.

But, I'll be damned if I'll adhere
    To what is being said -
    I will not act; I'll not pretend
        when the one I love is dead.

I want to just be able
    to show grief when I am sad...
I want to just be able
    to show anger when I am mad.
I want to exclaim the way I feel;
    it would ease my turbulent ache.
I want my friends to bear with me -
    just as long as it will take.

And then, perhaps, there'll come a time
    When my woe will abate somewhat -
    And, my loss will be mere memory
        But, ne'er will He be forgot!

Dorothy Schreiber

Lost

Love is like the changing seasons

It comes and goes
and gives no reason

Sometimes you have it
in your grasp

And if it's true
it's sure to last

Love can come
with many faces

Its joy can take you
to many new places

But when it's lost
it just brings you sorrow

But look on the bright side
there's still tomorrow
Harry Dalbow

Why?

Why do I go the distance?
And go that extra mile,
If you don't even trust me,
When I try to make you smile.

Why would I be lying,
I'm just not like the rest,
I know you don't trust me,
When you put me to the test.

You try to forget it,
But nothing seems to last,
All you seem to know,
Are the memories of the past.

Someday you might look back,
On your life since your birth,
Then you'll see the past,
Was a few bad days on Earth.

Now please look to the future,
And you'll see your short lifetime,
You'll notice right from the start,
Your life was yours to design.
Beth Odle

Trapped

I'm trapped
and I can't get out
no one can hear me
Even though I shout

Four walls closing in
The room just gets smaller
My growth has been stunted
I won't get any taller

People don't care
all they do is make fun
This is very hard
You can't grow without sun

I will fight to get out
I will kick my way through
I will knock down the walls
I have too much to do
Donna Bellew

If I Be You Be

Oh, I know it's not so
And I doubt if it could be
That if I be a flower
And you be a bee

Make honey with me
Out on the wild prairie
If you could be the bee
And I could be the flower

Not so sweet would be the honey
But oh so free would it be
Because it's all imaginary
That I be a flower and you be a bee

Eugene St. Clair

"Valentine Of Paper"

This valentine is paper
And in time will fall apart
Reflecting only a little
The love that's in my heart

This valentine of paper
Tells you my love is true
Much stronger then this paper
My love from me to you

However this valentine of paper
Is similar you see
It can crumple up in someone's hand
Just like my heart in me

This valentine of paper
That can easily fall apart
Asks you with a lot of love
Walk softy on my heart

Darlene A. McGuire

Poetry

Poetry need not be petty pretty
   and inconsequential
Though sometimes it's so by nature be
But at times too it's painfully
   powerful and brutally beautiful
Sometimes morning mist at others
   raging rain
Sometimes a stolen kiss at others
   too searing pain
The words I seek
When e'er I speak
Are not just for metered time
Nor yet for propriate rhyme
But at best span space and time
As no other medium could
As no other artisia would
Dare stir the immortal fire
I'm a living bell a lonely crier

Dolores R. Butler

To Toni

She taught me love
   and joy and light laughter,
But mostly love -
A black fluff
   with still blocker eyes;
The fluff - the eyes -
   are gone forever.
Her gentle legacy to me:
   To love an animal.
Had my life been lived without
   that legacy,
I would not have lived at all...

Edythe M. Bluske

visionary moonshine

stilling from waltzes half-forgotten
and kisses blown to the wind

extracting from sunsets shared
and down-turned eyes

   as sweet harmonies past
      trickle
   through
      glass tubing
         which funnels
         lazily
   into a jar
      collecting
         reminiscence

while vapors of our spirit
rush to places skyward

and I taste the essence of daydreams

Julie D. Stevenson

Resurgence

To escape the prison of my mind
And know the simplest thing
The meaning of a soft bird call
The magic of its wing
To lift it from the ugly sights
That greet it when it's chained
And send it soaring in delight
It's significance regained

Ira C. Seelig

Untitled

When the land falls dark
and life is silent, love
burns bright within my heart.
As I wait, the passion builds
until no longer can I control
my feelings. I love him. Sometimes
so desperately that even just
hearing his voice can make my
heart flutter. Like a gallant knight,
he has ridden in and swept me
off my feet. As the rain falls
down through the darkness,
who knows the passion it has
for the land, but I, a simple
blade of grass in a shower of love.

Christie Paul

The Source

I open my eyes
And see the light.
Day has entered
Where once was night.
I embrace the light,
Command it stay.
A new life comes
Like brand new day.
Let it enter
Into my soul.
It fills me up,
It makes me whole.
I find the light
Inside my heart
Where it has been
Right from the start.

Jennifer D. Smuda

The Man Of Many Names

The nights are damp and weary
   and nestled in your head
a dream surpasses lazily
   the expectations that you dread.
Somewhere in the mist
   are eyes you cannot see
waiting for your conscience
   to set the others free.
Who is this man you fear?
   Does he seem to be mad?
Are you sure it's not you
   in the dreams you have had?
What is that you're doing
   when you misplace forgotten time?
Are you sure, unaware
   you're not him committing crimes?
Now you know the truth,
   but you're not the one to blame;
yet you must be aware
   of the man you cannot claim.

Hugh A. Prats III

Talk To Me

When a tear sheds upon your face
and no one else can see
Close your eyes, put me in your thoughts
My darling talk to me

When the nights are lonely
and it's with me you want to be
Imagine me next to you
My love talk to me

Talk to me my love
When your spirits may be low
Talk to me my darling
And feel our love grow

Though we are so far apart
We are together in our souls
And when we talk together
In our hearts we will know

So when you see the rising moon
Or the setting sun
Look to the sky and talk to me
And our love will be as one....

Shadoe

Gratuitous

One cannot buy the ocean sea
   And one cannot buy the sky;
Gratis to watch tides tossing free,
   Look at white clouds floating by.

Gazing at the sunset so bright
   Is a wonder that cannot be sold;
It is free - this colorful sight,
   And it is worth much more than gold.

Twinkling stars are like an ornament;
   There is magic in this view;
Never packaged or ever sent,
   The stars are nature's bargain, too.

Huge rocks of mountains glistening
   As they stand so strong and tall;
With echoes that are listening,
   They are not for sale at all.

This is nature in majestic skill
   Created on an elegant scale,
Given to all without a bill;
   It is free and not for sale.

Edith Dinerstein

All I Need

Together we are perfect
and our love's a work of art
I'd die to be beside you
bound together by our hearts
through longing and devotion
we bridge eternity
a spanse of pure emotion
across a wild sea
for all we can accomplish
in everything we're one
if for this it will take my all
then let it all be done
when apart we're half a person
there's nothing can compare
to the touching of emotion
when alone we both are there
the night is always magic
when in it we are freed
our love loss would be tragic
for you are all I need

Charly Flynn

Visions

I looked at a vision of an orchard
and saw its many trees,
many branches filled with much fruit.
The fruit of some was the apple;
of others, the peach and the plum;
yet a common bed for each root.

I looked at a vision of a nation
and saw its many stocks,
many members filled with many creeds.
The creeds of some were dogmatic;
of others, pure profit and lust;
a commonwealth with many weeds.

I visioned an orchard of nations
yet saw but a single tree,
many branches filled with much fruit.
The fruit of each, the enhancement
of others, was constantly fed
an uncommon food from the root.

Hugh Landrum

Artists

Artists draw with paint and easel,
And sculptors use a chisel.
All they want for us to see
Is how they want this world to be.

Poets use just words and ink,
Forming phrases to make us think;
Evoking thoughts of every kind
For painting pictures in our mind

Everett Volk

Sharing

Sharing is someone dear to us
and sharing every moment of time.
Time is the excess of life. And
precious like a diamond when
given to someone on a special
occasion. Sharing and love
come only once in a lifetime
and set forth in sharing our
times to humanity and sharing
is given only by love and caring
and those who love shall be loved

James Curto

Why

If clouds can float in the sky,
And ships can stay above the sea,
Then why is it to be so hard,
For you to understand me?

If trees can grow so tall,
And ants can carry the weight,
Then why is it to be so hard,
To love me, and not to hate.

So if all these wonders in the world,
Can happen day by day,
Then why is it to be so very hard,
To keep my love away?

Candy Carter

A Time For Friends

When the sands of time have shifted
    And sifted down to the sea;
Come, sit and laugh at what has been
    And dream of what might be.

Time will slow so we may meet
    To smile and ask about the day.
Share stories of our daily walks,
    Our hours along life's way.

Like children, we will experience
    A true community.
We will all invite our neighbors
    To share our shady tree.

Linger and count the bobbing boats
    As the sea-waves roll along.
Winds toss and tangle our hair;
    Tugging a sturdy old song.

The date is made and now we know
    To look forward to that thrill.
When next we meet, the sands of time
    Will pause - and may be still.

Jimmie Nell Bush Sutton

The Puff Puff Tree

I rise early
and sip my coffee
and I watch the sun
work its early magic.
The tiny pollen pods
on our tree grow warm
and suddenly explode
into little puff clouds.
I watch and dream
but soon they are gone -
clouds and dreams vanish
into the reality of another day -
Oh, my love -
Why are you not here
to watch and dream with me?

Betty Sue Sessions

Invitation

Let me take your hand, my dear,
And to the woods away,
My horoscope informs me,
A picnic is the "in" thing, today.
We can rest beneath the trees,
Turn our faces to the sun,
And share delicious goodies—
Don't you think that would be fun?

Grace S. Kane

Eulogy For Freshman Year

Freshman year has come and gone,
and so its time is through
we must make best use then
of what we've learned from you.

You taught us how to socialize,
and how to make new friends,
and how to deal with what's behind
life's many little bends.

Although the work was different,
and difficult it seemed,
you set us on a path of learning
of which we'd only dreamed.

The next three years will build upon
the skills we've learned from you.
We'll ne'er forget you, Freshman Year,
and so I bid adieu.

It truly is a crying shame
our lives we can't rehearse,
'cause time is one thing technology
does not let man reverse.

Anthony Valentino

Look Into My Eyes

Look into my eyes,
And tell me what you see.
Look into my eyes,
And tell me what could be.

See what I'm feeling,
And tell me what it means.

Look into my eyes,
And see nothing but me.
Look into my eyes,
And say if you agree.

I can't tell you why,
But stay close by.

Look into my eyes,
And see if you can fake-
What you take,
When you look into my eyes

I feel it strongly,
But is it wrongly?

Look into my eyes,
And tell me what you see.

Bonnie Blake

Lonely Nights

When the table is set for one
And the candles flame
Is the only light I see
I think of the time we spent
You and me
When we are apart
I have nothing to hold
But the memories of us
But sleeping alone
Rolling over and you're not there
Gives me quite a scare
My arms and legs
Stretched out over the bed
So I know that
When you come home
I will touch you
And know that I am
Not alone anymore
I need you here
And I love you

Jack Fisher

Solitude

When the moon's a soft, pale, cradle
And the cool winds whisper low
The crickets sing a cheerful song
And I have no where to go.

When the bright, clear, twinkling stars
Jewel the velvet sky
I sit in quiet solitude
And wonder who am I.

Just one small humble being
In God's enormous plan
Sheltered by His loving grace
Guided by His hand.

Dorothy West Bitner

Interaction

As the sea absorbs the land
And the land absorbs the sea
So am I part of you
So you are part of me
So each contained in each
And each of each a part
So is my heart your own
And you are in my heart.
But it is wrong to call us
The coalescent "We"
For the sea is not the land,
And the land is not the sea,
And although we are welded fast
We still my dear are two
For I have my identity
And surely you are you.
No we represent no "oneness"
But a reciprocity
As the sea absorbs the land
And the land absorbs the sea.

Florence Young

Falling Down

Feather spinning dizzy
and the sun blinds
'round and back again
to touch the Earth.

Jim Schenks

Untitled

When fall starts coming
And there is a chill in the air,
I don't want to be somewhere else
I want to stay right here.

I don't want to be in
France or Spain or Rome;
I wouldn't want to be
Anywhere but home.

Where I can watch the horses
On their canvas of leaves.
Where I can watch the wind
Blowing through the trees.

Where I can watch the robin
Flying to and fro
Where I can watch the squirrel
Not knowing where to go.

Home is where my heart is,
Contentment can be found;
Happiness is everywhere,
With blessing all around.

Crystal Lansenderfer

Color Me Yellow

Tap into the embryo
  and think hard
like the thing that stole the
  memory
Priceless brain.
  I robbed the museum
    stole all my pictures
    stole all my people
  The flicker in the snow
    smelled like spinach, when I
    used to play in the cow
pastures
  Now I'm homogenized
  You think I'm homogenized
But, I'm just between the
    layer of cream
  and the milk
    Between the skin
  and the blood
    Drink

Elizabeth Bouvier

The Crucifixion

The air was hot and heavy,
And thunder filled the sky,
The whole world seemed to wait,
To see our Savior die.

Dressed only in a loin cloth,
With thorns upon his head.
Nails in his hands and feet,
Through which our Savior bled.

Mary standing down below
With her tear filled eye
Asked the age old question
"God in Heaven, why?"

The earth began to tremble
Clouds rolled across the sun
As God answered, Mary.
"On earth his work is done."

"The world became so filled,
With hate and greed beside,
To save you all from sin,
Our Son is crucified."

Daisy Rittgers

Faithless

Inhumane
And ugly
Compelling, yet repulsive
A roar from the Master
A crack of the whip
We are damned for our laughter
We are enthralled
By it.
Crooning, crying
The faithful are dying
Sucked into their Light
Faith due to fright.
At every funeral
The rain will fall
Attempting to wash away grief
But to the angles' dismay
The sadness remains
And the Master makes the air scream.

Heather Blank

Untitled

I remember when love was new
And uncorrupted by knowing eyes,
When we together knew
That more ahead, than behind lies

We now plod but soberly
Where once we floated by,
We once touched but softly
When gingerly, we now must lay.

Though rapture of spiritful youth
Seldom overcomes the solemn elder
    (In wit, way, or word),
I do submit I crave still;
For that which is no longer.

Pray, speak love,
And cast about us the sacred veil.
Can we not blush again?

Drew Mazujian

Life

I pushed my fledglings from the nest
And urged them so to fly.
And now, I sit in loneliness
And wonder why.

Why did you hurry to grow up?
I did not wish it so.
But once you tried your wings it seemed
You couldn't wait to go.

While you were growing tall and strong
I grew more week and slow.
The future opened wide its doors
And bid you go.

I stood and watched with aching heart
You gaily leave that day.
But really, I'd not ask to have
It any other way.

I can't believe how swift the years;
How short the time has been.
Today they toddle by your side
Tomorrow they are men.

Delsa Michie

The Bathroom Prayer

Please raise the seat,
and watch the toilet -
please be careful and
try not to soil it.

Thank you my child,
Bless you dear one-
For paying attention
to what you've just done.

To the girls that read
this rhyme...
Notice the seat before
you preside.

Thank you my Child,
Bless you dear one -
For paying attention
to what you've just done.

Brenda Carter

Friends

What will happen when they
are all gone,
no one to listen
no one to hear
no one to be there
when you need a friend
all the memories you shared
and all the moments that you
told them you cared
what will happen when they
are all gone?

Jessica Emery

Our U.S.A.

Far away countries across the sea
Are no doubt wonderful places to be,
Such as the leaning tower of Pisa;
The streets of gay Paree.

Any state in the Union
Has scenic places galore.
Now that we have Hawaii and Alaska,
Why first seek a foreign shore?

Start out in any direction,
Take time along the way.
There is scenery and fun a plenty
Right here in the U.S.A.

No fashion trend can surpass
Those seen on 5th Avenue.
The scenes throughout the country side
Will catch and hold your view.

Even if there is a great thrill
In a prolonged foreign holiday,
Why not first take a general view
Of the good old U.S.A.?

Eleanor E. Davey

To Jo in September

One day last week I walked alone
around our little lake.
And I remembered walks we shared
on these same precious days.
I listened hard to hear your voice,
even in a whisper.
I must believe that you survive.
I heard September speak your name.

Jane Parker Smith

Compassion

I watched quietly from my car
as a homeless lady walked down
the wide sidewalk.
She pushed a cart filled with her
only treasures.
Compassion jumped into my car and
sat down beside me.
Her chatter filled my heart and soul
so much,
that before the light turned green
I jumped out, gave the lady
twenty dollars, and
Thanked compassion for being
my friend.

Jessica Zamrzla

Today

I got up to face today
as I do all other days.
I ask my Lord to watch
over and keep us
And guide us so we will be safe.
I look at all the beautiful
Things that he made
and then I wonder why
He even loves us.
Or why he even made us.
We go through life and say
Things and do things
That hurt him so.
After all he only gave
His life and died for us.
That we might be saved.

Debbie Singleton

Fate - My Freedom

Early in the morning
as I start to rise,
The only thought that occurs,
is my future ride.

I've waited all week
and now I can't hide.
All my excitement
that's bursting inside.

I hurriedly dress
and head to the shed,
I can eat no breakfast
with this buzz in my head.

I uncover my 'bike'
and shine up the chrome,
though I know it'll be dirty
by the time I get home.

I fire it up
and push it out in the yard,
Waitin' till it's warmed
is the part I find hard.

I'm finally off
and man it feels Great
This is the essence of freedom
I'm glad it's my fate!

James McCabe

Untitled

A feeling must come and go.
As it comes, it is!
And there is nothing more.
But as it goes...
There is a difference,
A learned part of life;
Whether good or bad,
Affecting future goals to make.

Cindy L. Sagunsky

Necessary Abuse

There's nothing treated quite as rude
As mother's little doormat,
Tramped and scuffed by sodden boots
We should rename it sore-mat.
Although we pity its abuse
our pity turns to hisses,
When some mud-ladened visitor
Out trampled doormat misses.

Billy McCray

Her Wedding Day

A warm smile touched her face
as love shown in her eyes,
wetness from tears
rested on her lips
as she stood in satin and lace.
Watching my daughter,
the little girl faded away
and a woman took her place.
Offering her hand,
and her heart
to the man she loved
and swore to never part.
Standing together
in the blush of love
two souls became one
and the promise tomorrow
began today.

Jo Ann Bunker

Webster

Wit and wisdom can be found
As many autumn leaves abound
For what ever reason
For what ever season
As many waves of the sea
Words for you and me
Turning of the page
The making of the sage
Quest for all devised
Look into the new revised
Anything you've ever heard
Beginning with just one word
Be all you can be
Associated with lexicography
Noah Webster said it all

Bruce Marshall

Yesterday Is Gone

The summer breeze turns harsh and cold
as seasons change and we grow old.
The sparks that kindled young desire
no longer light a glowing fire;
but flicker feebly in the wind
when you recall what might have been.
For Yesterday Is Gone

The wistful memories of the past
assure that only time will last.
When I see carefree youth at play,
my thoughts revert to yesterday.
But I can only frame in time
those smiling faces left behind
For Yesterday Is Gone

In looking down the road ahead,
I thank the Lord for daily bread.
I plan no more illusive schemes
or chartered course of lofty dreams.
Like tearful drama in a play, unfinished
tasks remain that way.
For Yesterday Is Gone

Henry Botts

Littlest Of Thieves

I was defenseless as soon
as she came into my life
with her innocent playful ways,
big brown penetrating eyes
stealing all my thoughts,
fluttering long eyelashes
drawing in my soul.
She clutched at my blouse,
then stole an embrace,
absorbed all my kisses,
taking along with it all my hugs.
I knew my heart was unprotected.
Magnetically she stole it.
My thoughts are with her every day.
Now she's gone and I'm incomplete,
incomplete without her,
never to be whole again,
only left with memories,
memories of what could have been.

Georgiana Schmitz

"Limits"

A limit is defined
   As something which restricts:
Amounts of pain one can endure,
   Amounts of pain one can inflict.
Limits control our lives,
   Limits define me:
How much I can hear,
   How much I can see.
Limits follow us
   Everywhere we go:
Amounts of stress we can handle,
   How much we can know.
Why do we need limits,
   Do we need restrained?
Can limits keep us happy,
   Do limits soothe our pain?
Limits hold me back,
   Even cause depression.
Twenty lines or less,
   You've limited my expression!

Dave Whitlock

The Flag

Stand up and cheer
As the Flag passes by
And don't be ashamed
Of the tears in your eyes
Be proud...and thankful
For the land of the free
The land that belongs
To you and to me
Let your chest swell with pride
And your heart beat anew
As the colors pass by
The Red — White — and Blue
Then say a prayer
For the lives men gave
To make this land...the home
Of the free and the brave

Billie Voorhies

Forever

In the midst of the night
As the moon soared through
The darkest hour there was
Havoc in the air as souls
Were being torn apart

As evil was eating the soul
The night grew dim as
The poison fled through
The veins the evil grew
Stronger

As the evil grew stronger
The soul became weaker
There was a silence in the
Night as the darkness soared
The night air

Forever

Evil has taken once again

Butch Ashcraft

These Are The Soldiers

We said our goodbyes to them
As they volunteered for war.
Years of hardship came thereafter
As they fought to keep us free.
Now is the time for us at home
To glory in their deeds.
Lift up our flag, point it to heaven!
These are the soldiers,
These are the men,
Who fought side by side
While we prayed for them.
Memorial days salutes and cheers...
Yellow ribbons, flowers, tears,
Parades for those remembered comrades
Who fell that we should stand...
Will be a fitting tribute
For what they all would do again,
These, our soldiers; these, our men.

Glenn F. Girdham

Street Jesus

I met Jesus on the street today
As walking slowly he drew near.
His step was weak, his hand held out,
He mumbled things I would not hear.
His clothes were ragged, dirty, old,
And beard and hair were thin and gray;
His eyes were haggard and I knew
Had seen a brighter, better day.
He asked my help to right the wrongs
The world had done to his poor sheep,
And I had nothing I could give;
Not council's word nor tears to weep.
Could silvered wisdom, golden rules
Or pious phrases still the hurt
That threw his sacrifice away
And poured his life into the dirt?
What could I give? I turned away,
His hand was empty, he turned too;
"God bless you, son." I heard him say,
"Father, Forgive them what they do."

Edward Horalek

He Hears, He Cares, He Can

He hears our faintest whisper
as we bow our head and pray,
thanking our Lord for His blessings
that He gives to us each day.
He cares when valleys grow deep
as burdens upon us unfold.
When the mountains we climb
become tall and steep and cold,
with His grace it will prove to us
that we really are so bold.
He can guide us to an ocean
that's deep and blue and wide
so that we may prove to ourself
that we can reach the other side.
But if you can't find a mountain
or an ocean that's deep and blue and wide,
I ask thee then my Father
to guide me to your side.

Allyson Schimmel

Ode To A Princess

Take my hand, my love
As we gaze upward into
The starlit heavens.

My heart is stirred
By the majesty
Of this window to the universe
Reflected in your eyes.

Walk with me
In the calm of the night
The serenity broken only
By a rustling gentle breeze
Softly touching your hair
And making it glisten in the moonlight.

Tell me about our future
As I listen to your voice
Flowing like silk, reassuring me
With shared dreams and secrets

Strengthening me with the promise
Of true friendship
And unending love.

Carlos Rodrigo Maglalang

Life Is Beautiful To Me

Life is beautiful to me
As you can see
So many babies born
So many babies die
So many babies adorn
So many people lie
So much violence
So much hate
We could have stopped it
But it's too late
Because we denied
The facts were put aside
Benefits to the rich
What about the homeless and poor?
That doesn't matter anymore
Life is beautiful to me
As you can see

Lucia Summer

Cetacean (Whales)

Gentle giant, hopefully,
As you glide through crystal sea,
Performing breaches artfully,
And diving so your flutes we see,
Rolling, playing, joyfully,
In the great majestic sea.
May you continue - to be.

Carol E. Southerland

Alone

Apart and alone,
aside from the rest.
Solitude my fortress,
silence my weapon.
Deep thoughts flow as music,
concentration surrounds.
No need for the clamor
or touch of a city,
Pure peace as an island,
amid human madness.
Desire abounds,
but only for freedom
to remain as I am,
Apart and alone.

Chris Acosta

A New Day

The moon fades out of sight
At the dawn of a new day —
And darkness turns to light
Across the Milky Way.

The sun begins to rise
Emitting its golden light
Across the cloudless skies
Bathing the earth so bright.

The birds begin to sing
Their cheerful happy tune
And soon they'll take wing
Across the blue lagoon.

Then springs a gentle breeze
So fresh and cooling
Ruffling the leaves on the trees
While their branches are swaying.

All life begins to explore
Each in their respective way,
For what promises to be in store
For the promise of a new day -

Jacqueline Gross

And The Angels Danced....

As father read,
Auras arose
One by one,
And these guardians
Communed together,
Dancing during the psalm...
And when it was over,
They returned,
One by one,
To those of us there,
As one single light
Climbed the wall,
And looked over us
From above....

Jennifer Tanner

The Waltz Of Autumn

The stately oak no one deceives
    Awaiting Jack to paint its leaves.
Jack's brush is deft — no dalliance
    Till all are dressed up for the dance.
Then the oak sways, knowingly.
    Farewell! Farewell!
    Its leaves go free!

Gloria D. Macauley

Hungry Child

Moma I'm hungry.
Baby go to sleep.
Moma I'm hungry.
Baby ain't nothin to eat,
Moma I'm hungry.
God, please help me.
Moma I'm hungry.
Child give me peace.
Moma I'm hungry.
I can't go to the streets.
Moma I'm hungry.
Oh God, have mercy on me.

Dwayne Mitchell

Untitled

Months in seclusion ....
    battling the illusion;
That life was fair,
    and all was right ....
Justice counts its peace at night.

Elizabeth C. DeBaldo-Thode

Untitled

Time hides in despair.
Beads of tears of all the years
Gather at my feet.

The wind hears despair.
Every tear has a story,
A small tragedy.

Darkness surrounds me.
Lost in a sea of blackness.
Once more I am alone.

Coldness of the winds,
The anger of the thunder.
A cacophony.

What is hope for me?
Golden light from the heavens.
Is there hope for me?

Without hope or joy.
Sadness of the heart and soul,
Prolonged suffering.

Judy Chiang

Secret Love

When you're around I smile
because I know you're there
    My heart pounds so loud that
sometimes I think people will hear
    I'll never tell you who I am
because already I'm a very close friend
    Sometimes I think deep down you
already know how I feel
    And that's what makes my love
for you even more real.
    I'll love you always and forever
you know my love for you will
always grow
    I'll lock my love for you
away deep in my heart
    And hope and pray as
friends we'll never part

Donna M. Clegg

Flowered People

The flowers die
Because of lies
That were forced upon the sun.
I wonder when
If ever...
This war we have begun
Will end
And if it does
Who of this war will win?
The flowers or the rain?
It seems to me the flowers should
Because they are in pain.

Julianne Musser

Every Thought Of You

Every thought of you,
Becomes a whispered prayer.
I pray the Lord watch over you,
And keep you in His care.

I have always wanted,
The very best for you.
I always try to show it,
In everything I do.

But being so imperfect,
I find my very best,
Often falls far too short,
When it stand the test.

I turn to the only one,
Who's love is so wide.
He understands my imperfection,
My weakness to Him I confined.

So today, as I think of you,
My spirit is at rest.
I know the one who control all life,
Will give you what is best.

Irene M. Evans

Immortal Love

The last fire will lite,
behind your lovely eyes.
Immortal Love
We'll meet above.
In these thick walls,
together we fall.
To fast to stop.
Separate we'll not.
Come break these chains.
No love's in vain.
I remove you fear.
"I love you," you'll hear.
Pure as a dove,
immortal love.

Alitroi Brandon Lee

Slaughter House Man

Rolling prison
bellowing down farm road
as wild-eyed holsteins
flail against a frigid alabaster sky
going to meet the slaughter house man
with the wet red hammer
held tightly in his calloused hand
cattle innocent
Do not understand
Pounds are dollars
As the slaughter house man
ferociously hollers
"bring him on in"
nervous creatures
have not a place to hide
as skulls and hammers
angrily collide
baptized in pooling blood
Abandoned bovines collapse in hitler's mud -
collapse in hitler's mud

Doug Nimmo

The Cross We Bear

We are each in our small way carpenters -
Beset by worry and care.
And day by day we constantly build -
The cross that we have to bear.

The true road of life we find dusty -
Sharp rocks protrude from the ground.
We yearn to travel in grassy glades -
That apparently can not be found.

We are so beset by life's burdens -
As we travel along its way -
That we suddenly cry out in anguish
And kneel in the dust to pray.

We ask for His aid and forgiveness -
Tears stream from tightly closed eyes.
We then feel His presence around us -
And suddenly realize

That grassy glades and summer skies
Have always been right there -
And our cross becomes much lighter
If we sand it down with prayer.

Charles Frederick Stock

Setting Sun

The sun setting so pretty
    between the sky and earth
I am beginning to realize his love
    for me and its worth
I am seeing my life at
    its first steps
I'm glad you are there to back me up.

Sun sets pretty colors
    times no light at all
I know that if I should stumble and fall
    you'll be behind me all the way
Taking care of me and being more
    than just a friend.

Crystal Lemoyne

"Choices"

If I should have to choose, my Lord,
    Between the world or you,
The answer would be easy now,
    The world will never do.

Of all the treasures I have owned,
    And loves that I have shared,
The peace and hope you've given me,
    Can never be compared.

The ones on earth who love me best,
    Seem to know me least,
But even with my endless faults,
    Your love has never ceased.

So if the world should ask me, Lord,
    Which one I would love,
The answer would be easy now,
    It came from heaven above.

Jean Hynes

Nursing Home Blues

The world stops at the front desk.
Beyond the curtain of despair
Lies the shadow world
Of those on their way out,
Not living, not yet dead.

Angels of mercy
Scurry from room to room
Serving the elemental needs
Of aged infants,
Reduced to utter dependency
On the loving care of strangers.

Diapered, dressed, groomed,
Tied into wheelchairs.
Half-knowing, past caring,
They are sometimes grateful,
Sometimes cranky.
Sometimes cursing a world
Through with them,
Not willing to let them go.

Helen Griffin

Untitled

The periodic chart of the heart:
birth, death, infinity
(from alpha to zen
and then, back again)
The square root of poetry:
mind, spirit, essence
(cosmic equations
in the equilibrium)
Science circles all mysteries
like music, in the spheres, frozen
Religion, like a scavenging ghost,
is charred beyond
any theoretical recognition

The language of the blood
knows no boundaries,
needs no translation,
but remains as ancient
and pivotal as the natural order
of the Universe

Glenngo Allen King

Life Cycle

The womb of night
Births the day-child,
Whose youth and prime vanish with noon;
Quickly aging with each spent hour,
It dies
In the embrace of dusk,
And is lowered
Into a western grave.

How short-lived!
Only memory can revive it.

Sister Barbara Bruns PHJC

Black Coffee

Black coffee and bulldozed dreams
Black coffee messed up schemes
Black coffee and endless cigarettes
Black coffee with strangers I just met
Black coffee and his mighty caffeine
Black coffee and death's trap
Black coffee here is my map
Black coffee keeps me alive
Black coffee helped me survive
Black coffee scared away my breath
Black coffee with the help of death
Black coffee my suicide
Black coffee in you and I hide

Beth Bourassa

To Son and His Wife

May your new home be
    blessed with happiness,
With no discords to
    spoil its charm,
May the walls be strong
    with lasting love
To keep out sorrow
    and harm
May the window's shine
    with sparkling lights
And God's great love
    give you peaceful nights

Florence L. Fisher

Blossom our Possum

O my goshum!
Blossom our possum
Is up side downsum

Beady eyes, skinny tail,
Very pale, not a quail
Female or male?

Our back yard its home
No highway to roam
It's not alone!

Four tiny tails appear
Bringing up the rear
No ounce of fear

Watch your back
It's on the attack
Even the black cat knows that!

Oh my goshum, our possum!
She's not dead
She's just joshin!

Jami Kerzman

Have-Nots

They live on the streets
Boxes for their home.
Nowhere to go
Always they roam.

Since we call ourselves haves
We call them have-nots.
We have all we need
From adults down to tots.

But have-nots have the freedom
They go where they please.
No one to report to
No special needs.

So maybe they're happy
Though they have not a lot.
Maybe they are the haves.
Maybe we're the have-nots.

Amy Luttner

Eve

One little mistake
branded for life...
Trusted the serpent
followed by strife.
She was forgiven...Adam's wife.
Her name was Eve, the giver of life.

All women suffer
for the sin of one,
If it were you
what would you have done?
The first sin ever
had soon begun
a world of sin for everyone.

The sin, it tempts us
down the path of life.
We're standing on the edge
of a razor sharp knife.
And she started it all... Adam's wife.
Her name was Eve, the giver of life.

Joe Keeler

Time

The key to life is in the center.
Break through the walls,
fire up your emotions and
wander through the passages.
Break out of your daze,
follow your conscience
reach the end of the maze.
Is life worth living,
has it yet been found
shall I continue digging?
A choice that I must make!
If I choose death
will it be a mistake?

Adam Dobbs

Young One

A child of fifteen, who
brought such joy
Oh, the pain in your eyes,
If only you were a little boy,
I could hold you in my
arms.
So afraid my son,
Is it something I've done?
Or is it the worms,
who pray on our young?
Fear not my child,
I'll not let you turn wild.

Clara Spears

Black Girl

Oh, black girl what beautiful
brown skin you do have, and
may your offspring wander in
your path. Oh! Black Girl what
what beautiful skin you do have.

I rise in the morning only to see
your face, skin of a black girl
shall never be erased. For you I
beg to take out the trash, Oh!
Black girl what beautiful skin
you do have.

For a black girl, all my life
earnings I would save to touch
a portion of your skin. I most
certainly do crave. I'll stay
true to these words right down
to the end, especially the beauty
of a black girls skin.

Dwayne Cherry

Thundering Rain

Do you hear me?
Can you hear me?
Through the thundering rain.

Are you listening?
You have to be listening,
Can you stop the pain?

Will you show me?
Can you show me?
Through the thundering rain.

Christina Morrison-Wesley

Untitled

The things that go unsaid
But are still inside your heart,
Can be the very things
That tear your world apart

When the people that you love
Are no longer there to share
The feelings that you've hidden
You can't let them know you cared.

Sometimes things just go unsaid
'Cause you think that they should know
The way you feel about them
But what if that's not so

So tell them while you can
The thoughts you feel inside
Let them know while love is living
So you can still feel it when they have died.

Angel J. Bishop

The Doubter

I really try to be a true believer
But I find it hard,
When misfortune befalls me,
To accept the will of God.

Why must people suffer
More than they can bear?
Is He watching over us?
Does He really care?

When these doubts assail me,
As they often do,
I recall my favorite bible verse
From the Book of Matthew.

It comforts me to know,
There were others just like me,
Who found it hard to accept
Life's trials and misery.

Then I remember His kind words,
When I wonder what life's about,
"Oh ye of little faith,
Wherefore didn't thou doubt?"

Gladys B. Vessa

Untitled

A hand was extended towards me
but I was afraid
of what the hand's intentions may be
so I pushed the hand away

I heard my name called by a voice
The voice was soft and warm
But I felt I had no choice
That voice might do me harm

Then I felt a stabbing pain
And so I looked to see
But I could find no one to blame
No one at all but me

Erin Tiemeyer

Thought Circles

Today I think I grew an inch,
But 'twas not in my height.
It was my thoughts that seemed to grow.
And make my circle bright.

The circle that surrounds my mind,
And makes my thoughts go round.
It widened just an inch today.
And all my wond'rings found.

Dolores Bixler

Thoughts

I lay in bed, pretending to sleep
But in my head the eyes still see
Tears fall on my pillow and I weep
To stop these thoughts I pray to be.

I think of things not concerning myself
Not knowing what caused me to start
Unlike the books I see on the shelf
Keeping real and fantasy apart.

By now my pillow is so wet
But no one came to see me through
To talk and get my feelings set
Though they may seem silly to you.

I lay in my bed, now trying to sleep
This time I hope thoughts won't return
That I may have a moment to keep
Of dreams and not concern.

JoAnna L. Madejczyk

The Coach

I wish someday to be a parent
But my reasons seem quite errant.
Could it be that I have met
No good parents as of yet?
Or is it due to slight displeasure
That I receive at my leisure?

Parents always seem to be
Without time and never free.
But kid's spirit can't be smothered
As I am there to keep them mothered,
It's like babysitting now and then.
But now for my own, I have no yen.

We play and run all the day.
But what we gather isn't pay —
Only dirt and sweaty clothes.
At times a chance to trade some blows—
Why we do it I couldn't say,
But I'll be damned
    If they don't let me play!

John McGreevy Russell

Whisper

There's a Lady, so lovely
But not real to me.
She was there, in my morning
Turned a misty memory.

    Then in the illusion
    Of what we call time.
    Forever to never,
    Now no longer mine.
    As the ships of our lives
    Pass through this glistening Sea,
    When you lay down your oars,
    Look to the shore...

    I will be awaiting there...
        Come to me.
        Come to me...

James Michalski

Daddy

My father's heart has been stilled.
But when it beat it was strong willed.
He taught us love; he loved to smile.
And I would walk a long hard mile,
Just say one last time —
I love you Daddy, you were our sunshine.

Joy C. Watson

True Wealth

True wealth is not measured
    by money, you see,
We could own millions
    yet, live in poverty.
This world's supply
    of silver and gold,
Cannot compare to
    the worth of one soul.

A beggar in rags
    can be richer, indeed,
Than he who thinks money
    can meet every need.
The greatest Treasure
    we will ever possess,
Is the love of Jesus Christ
    and His righteousness.

Grace W. Gregg

"Eternal Peace"

Far away,
    by the sea
My soul,
    is set afree.

Beneath the stars,
    that shine on high,
My inner self,
    heaves a sigh.

Beside the surf,
    that breaks and breaks,
I forget the world,
    and all its aches.

Let me rest,
    here by the sea,
To gather courage,
    to meet Thee.

George J. Rotariu

Memories

Comfort is given
By the sound
Silence is taken
Profound
Life will live
Death departs
Holds you
Keeps you
Never parts
Movements are made
Yet everything's still
Tears are shed
But heart's fulfilled.
Glory was
Glory be
Glory always
Memories.

Julie Hunsicker

Love

Sandwiched
    between the nightmare
And screams that make
    the stones cry blood
Are those brief moments
    of exquisite emptiness
There is the place
    called 'love'

Bryan Mercer

Sweetheart

I watched the waves as they
    came crashing down
I saw the shells upon the
    ground
I watched the sun set on the
    sea
I felt all warm inside because
    you were there with me.
The calmness of the sea, the softness
    of the breeze,
The sound of the birds flying
    in and out of the trees.
Together we watched the moon
    rise, as it grew it got bright
It was just you and me on
    this beautiful night.

Gene L. Reaves

High Summer, California

Hills draw close to the
canyon. Golden slopes whisper
of smouldering hay.

Feasting on the heat,
a lizard waits and watches
the arc of the sun.

A hummingbird sits
motionless among jasmine
and guards its domain.

Slick line of sweat slips
down my neck and falls onto
the white sheet below.

Jackie Taylor

Serene Endurance

Wait on Me.
Cast all your cares on Thee,
For the Lord God Almighty
Wants to give to you abundantly.
Trust in me
And see...
All the fruits you bear on My tree.

Beverly Franey

I'll Never Be The Same

I'll never be the same,
'Cause I lost my man!
I'll carry his name,
But I'll never be the same!
He died and went to Heaven,
On a cold and rainy day!
I'll always love him,
But I'll never be the same!
We had so much fun,
In the bright and beautiful sun!
He always called me "Babe,"
Even as he went away!
I'm sure he went to Heaven,
On that cold and rainy day!
He would say, "Look up Yankee,"
As you go on your way!
As I sit and sip my tea,
And get busy today!
I'll always love him,
But I'll never be the same!

Elisabeth Funderburk

Life's Dream

A dream is born within our heart
    Chasing out doubt and gloom
Each tiny road of life we start
    Moves us into a larger room.

A dream becomes reality
    As on we go in faith
Refusing to be discouraged
    The disappointments of life we take

A dream is always roaming
    All roads the mind seems to know
He travels the earth in his searching
    His heart never ceases to go.

A dream is not lost in sorrow
    Heartaches will brighten the view
Pains shadows will flee tomorrow
    Morning will be bright as the dew.

Life's dreams will keep us going
    Whenever the way is tough
When stones of life others are throwing
    A dream will live on through the rough
Beulah Shortridge

Untitled

tree
climbing
rubdown waterfall

sky
diving
dancing like a tear

touch ground
softly screaming
springing wildly
not resisting

the breath that beckons
oh transparent!
is the music
sung forever
One Heart
is the owner
of all these
Eileen McDonald

Homeless Man

A lonely old man
Collecting spare change in a tin can
Dry wrinkled fingers grasp the handle
Prunes shrivel in the sun

Is home on that bench over there?
An alley? A doorway?
Unanswered questions

A man without a home
A fish out of water
Alex Gray

My Butterfly Child

My beloved child of God,
Conceived in loves passion.
Believed to be my precious angel,
Flying high in the clouds.
You are the butterfly of my dreams,
Drifting in the sweet spring wind.
How brief life is for you,
How meaningful your presence.
My special gift from God,
Loved and let go.
Elizabeth Hurst

"To My Father"

Heavenly Father,
    Come unto me.
Teach me to hear Lord,
    Teach me to see.
Teach me to pray Lord,
    Show me your way.
Dear Lord in heaven,
    Don't let me stray.
Heavenly Father,
    Come unto me.
Please hear my cry Lord,
Please hear my plea.
Fill me with joy Lord,
Fill me with love,
Fill me with wonder,
    From up above.
        Amen
Ginny Ray

Untitled

Distance
Controls
Love
Friendship
Hope
It controls your mind and
Feelings
Love is weakened when apart,
But stronger when
Together
Friendships the same and
Hope will always be there
Even when you're not.
Holly Hilderhoff

These

The start of these
Could mean many things -
    looks, expressions or perhaps words;
Anyone could mean peace
    Compromise or war
Would you be willing to take a chance?
    A word of caution - think it through!
    It could mean no tomorrow.
Eugene Calvin Swigart

The Old Vase

This old vase whose luster's gone
Covered with only summer's dust
Is forgotten of its beauty
Never captivating one's eye
While on my table top.

Once beautiful like the autumn's leaves
Colored faintly with earthy tones
Just with a sight to behold
It's a sight to behold
A wonder to grand to tell.

Beauty in its art form
Sculptured finely like snowflakes
A prize I've always known
For a keep sake this is
A treasure in it's right.

With the passing of time
Colors soon fade like rain
I'm amazed of its statue
For this old vase
Has weathered everything but time.
Debby Kaulili

Untitled

Your soul moves into mine
Creating feelings like pictures
That move from the artist's brush
To canvas
And color is present where only
Black and white existed before

Lovely, how separation fades
Like a mirage
Appearing upon the desert floor
In the heat of the day
And then…misting into air
After violet thunder and a gentle rain

What visions are present
When we allow the fire of passions
To give way to the coolness
of a tender heart

And separation is no more
James Reamy

Autumn

The leaves
    crisp,
        crumbling
with each step.

The forest floor
    a multi colored
        rug that is
            swept away by
        the wind.

Blustery days
    filled in by
        long nights.

Apples picked ripe
    and juicy.

Fall… is any season
    better than this?
Juliet Corcoran

My Cry

A day full of shadows.
Dark fills the night.
I must change directions,
seeking a light.

I must stay calm, hang on,
don't fall.
For someone, anyone, may
not hear my call.
Iris H. Davis

Black

Darkness clouds my vision
Darkness fogs my mind
Death lurks behind the corner
And I wait to die

I pray that someone saves me
I listen for reply
I rest aside an empty grave
I live only to die
God would you please save me
God please bring me back
Save me from this hate filled thing
That casts a shadow of black
David Boncic Walsh

Ways To Bend

"Through the glass doors
    darkly"
A quote my memory does not latch onto
The meaning I cannot recall
Outside rain bends yews in twisted
    directions
Men, women, children slosh through
    puddles
Holding half-bent
    umbrellas
Lines form at ticket-sellers'
    windows
A pleading voice "I want to sit by
    my wife"
Resolute, unchanged, "it's the
    policy"
The voice behind the glass
    windows
Margaret by my side softly saying
"Why can't she bend a little"?

Elizabeth Valicenti

"Someone I Never Knew"

They say that dad's are the people
    daughters look up to.
They are the people that know and care,
They are the people that always
    know what to do.
They are the people that tell you
    not to stare.

For I'll never know the joys of
    having a father,
Or have the thoughts of someone
    special, so kind and true.
I wish I had a father figure,
    so big and strong,
I have a father, somewhere, someone
    I never knew.

Jenniffer Simmons

Hate

People live on hate
Day after day
Like something they ate
But comes out in a different way

Hate is what this world is made of
Cause why else would we fight
And there isn't much love
That's why this place isn't right

No one wants to hate
but it's always there
Just like our fate
People say "I don't want to be here"

Hate is painful
and full of fears
I'd like to be vengeful
Instead of hate all these years

But people live on hate
Day after day
And I hope this isn't fate
Having something to say.

Jennifer L. Meyer

Dreams

Enter the unknown
delve into your mind
create productions
with sleep induced
thoughts occurring
at lightning speed.

Even in sleep
the mind continuously
craves stimulation
inventing a story
totally unique
mystifying the brain.

Brenda Faye O'Neal

Untitled

I watch the rain
Descending into the ocean
Becoming just another
Drop of water...
    Meaningless

I watch the days
Passing ever so slowly
Becoming just another day
In a sea of days...
    Meaningless

I watch the people
Pushing through life
As a member
I mix with them...
    Meaningless

Christy W. Walker

The Leaf

The uncontrollable wind,
Despite the futile attempts at control,
Blew her away.

Though the branch tried to stop it,
Pulling back with all its strength,
The leaf was forced to stray.

There was nothing to be done,
No foreseeing the event.
Things just happen sometimes.

But the branch can't accept
This logical fact.
It lets it possess his mind.

The branch starts to decay,
It can't let her go,
The beautiful leaf.

Why hang on, when there is nothing there,
let your mind wander free.

The branch withers away,
Then it sees, but too late,
All the other leaves on the tree.

Christian V. Labas

Lost

I've lost myself somehow.
Fallen into pieces all a jumble.
Somewhere in this muddled mess
Of "should's" and "musts" and "cant's",
There's someone that I wanted to be
Have I lost me? Was I ever there?

Candace Barnes

How Do You Let Go

Never in my mind
Did I think you'd go.
I thought we would always be
A necessity to one another.
To think we shared time,
One of life's most precious gifts.
We had so much in common,
So much of our love to give.
You and I were good together.
So why did you let it go?
One day I could've learned,
And we would be just fine.
But tell me how to let go.
It worked so well for you.
Tell me how to forget.
I only know one way.

Carla Craft

Neighbors

We all come from here and there
Different as can be
Yet brought together on 1 street
By chance we may meet

On a Summer day washing our cars
Or in Fall raking the leaves
We sometimes say, "Hello"
Let's introduce ourselves before we go

Hi Mike, Hi Keith, Hey Carol and Shae
We're going to the park
Let's make it a group event
It would be fun if we all went

Sometimes we just need to talk
Or borrow this and that
No matter if they're young or old
Good neighbors are worth their weight in gold

Darlene Coleman

Love Is

I have given my love to
    different ones, and I
    realized love is not always
    laughter and fun.
It's also being there when
    someone is in pain.
Helping them realize with
    time they can be happy
    again.
Heartaches and trials may
    come our way, but with
    God in our life we will
    have better days.
When we feel no-one
    understands, God is right
    there to take our hand.

Cheryl Jarman

Aggravation

It seems that when you're
    down and out.
That's the time your enemies shout:
Accusations, plain frustrations
threats and damaging abominations!
Sexy, dirty, ugly things!
Makes you, wonder why,
You were taught to never lie,
though people lie about you!
    That's Aggravation!

Jane M. Stewart

Save For Future Use

When in doubt
Don't throw out
Save it, box it, store it
Someday, someone, somewhere
May want it for future use

It may be too small
Or maybe too tall
It doesn't really matter
Fold and pack it away
Keep it for future use

The colors are faded
The styles are past dated
Tell your kids that's okay
We saved these for you
Our future is your present

Joyce E. Lishinsky

Why

Often when I walk
down the street. People
point and stare,
others whisper and giggle
too, why? It's just not fair!
Why was it me, who has
cerebral palsy day after
day I ask, why is every
sport to me such a big
task? Why won't anyone
talk to me or even
give me a chance
rather what they do
all day is just laugh
and glance! It seems that
when I grow older
to my parents I'll
always hover, I'm signing
off just like this I don't
judge a book like this,
"Don't judge a book by its cover!"

Jackie Goldman

Untitled

My Samarkand!
   Dragons guard the gate.
      Within the walls,
         My soul.

No Mongol hoards
   need storm its heights,
No seasons of Despair.

Minarets reach toward an Azure sky.
   An eagle soars!
      and sighs are carried on
         the wind.

A firefly, caught for a moment,
   Held. As life,
      Then set free.
Flickering, it fades,
And shadows form in the distance.

Into a golden cache
   a tear falls, shimmering,
      glistening there as diamonds.
Gone - lost beneath the desert sands of time.

Yet, still, gold for ever reaching dawns
   and rubies of endless sunsets.

This, then, my
   treasure of Samarkand.

Eileen S. Gaarn

"Jamie"

   Never would have
dreamed that such a delicate
bundle of joy would turn into
this rough neck boy!
   Those innocent eyes' of
blue and cheeks so soft and round,
sometimes I wonder if his feet
will ever touch the ground.
   Always busy with those
little hands, a tear falls as I
watch, knowing someday he'll be a man!
"With him from the beginning
thru thick and thin! With him
I'll stay till the very end!"
   Never felt such a joy!.
till the day I looked into
the eyes of my little boy!.

Elaine Wireman

One Immortal Soul

One immortal soul
drifting through space and time
searching...searching...searching

For a home in the arms
of a woman!

One immortal soul
drifting from shell to shell
it has occupied the shells
of those whose hands are torn
From serving and the shells
of those they have served.
Searching...searching...searching

For a home
   in the arms
      of a
         woman.

for Ann Doyle
Brian J. Murray

The Passing (For Grandma)

Trails of mischief,
Dusty roadsides, fog and dew.

How beautiful America,
Tho' skies aren't blue.

Musty, dusty misty rain,
Shadows cloud remembered pain.

Chimes of morning have broken sadness,
Heartbeats rush to find the gladness

Set in search of things unknown,
American quietly holds her own

No pace, no beat, no drums
Listen as the silence hums

Oh America, I long to give
Sweet America, I long to live

Empty hands held someone dear
Empty hearts long to have them near

America please ease the pain,
Bring bright sunshine to replace the rain

The passing won't be the end,
Fond memories...will keep my friend.

Cheryl Kendrick

"You"

No two snowflakes are the same.
Each sunset is unique.
And God creates us by name.
Our mission we must seek.

God's power does not cease here
Just search and we will find
Proof of His works strong and clear
It stuns the human mind.

God made us different too.
In Scripture we are told,
There can't be another you,
God threw away the mold.

On your pilgrimage Beware,
God wants this to be known
Walk the sands of time with care.
You make your prints alone.

You are free to do God's will
When life's journey is through.
God will speak in voice so still,
"These prints belong to you!"

Joseph J. Blanchfield

Signs Of Fall

Leaves are falling,
Elk are calling.
Bullets blazing,
Deer quit grazing.
Birds start soaring,
Bears start snoring.
Mom starts baking,
I start raking.
Then we eat a very special treat,
It's my very favorite thing to eat.
At last we all have a ball,
At my birthday in the fall.

Beau Allen Amundson

Another Woman's Husband

The sound of your laughter
encompasses my broken heart
and shatters my weary soul
with echoes
of opportunities left unclaimed.

Integrity is my lover.
Through night after sleepless night
I grieve...
Because what might have been
lies dead,
destroyed by my self-respecting honor.

Alone in my bed
I pay the piper's price
of never truly knowing love,
or the wonders of you.

In your bed
you lie with her,
never knowing
the choices I have made,
or how deeply I care.

Dianne M. Graham

Undying Love

I want to be with you
Every moment that I can,
To feel the gentle touch
Of your strong hand.

I want to remember
Your bright smile,
Even though you may be facing
A tough and difficult trial.

I want to never forget those
Special and comforting words
You say, they seem to
Always brighten my day.

I want to always be there
For you, cause that's how love
Is when it's true.

I want to spend my life
Remembering and wanting
Wonderful things like I do,
Because I want to spend my
Life always being with you.

Heather Hymer

Only You

Every bee
Every sea
Every ocean
Every tree
has a message just for thee

Every person is unique
In you alone this gem that seek
to help the weary and the weak

So listen listen
listen now
and every sin and I'll
shall bow
to Him who holds
eternal sway
and bringeth glorious
and perfect day

Bill Guthre

"When Jesus Comes Back"

When the day is just beginning;
every thing just falls in place.
All the trees stand tall in Glory;
as if waiting for His Grace.

The birds sing sweetly;
in the green grass below.
As if they knew the hour;
and were ready to go. Ready!

The clouds are white as cotton;
floating thru the space.
And my hands are reaching upward;
to touch my Saviour's face.

My heart gives a flutter;
pounding hard within my chest.
And my Soul responds buried;
deep within my breast.

My mind is praying;
that it has been blessed.
And it is ready;
to take the final test.

Florence E. Maxwell

Happy Day

Some people might think
everyday's a happy day.
But not me. I think
Happy Day is better than
any other day.
Even better than Taffy
Day!
Even better than sitting
on a bay day.
Even better than pay day!
Even better than K day!
Why do I think it's a
Happy Day?
Daisy's coming to stay
and play!
But, hold on there...
Happy Day's tomorrow.
Oops!

Christina Lea Alford

Tears

Everyone was happy,
except for me.
We were alone,
unbothered by spectators.
You gave me a hug,
and was surprised
by my reaction.
You looked into my eyes,
and I into yours.
You watched me desperately,
not knowing what to do,
as water was falling from my eyes
for loved ones you never knew.

Anne-Marie Hyatt

Existence

i
exist not
for you.
you
exist not
for me.
since
we
both exist,
why not
exist
for each
other, too?

Epifanio C. Coles Jr.

Soul Silence

Silence is a wondrous sound
  Expanding space,
A comfort without touch
  Holding everything in its embrace.

Silence is the soul of the universe
Life in creation enters its realm
All that is, finds expanse,
  Dimension's purview
Pure in a constant advance,

Does silence overwhelm
  Perhaps to hold time at bay
Granting warm sweet breath
Passage to a new freeway.

Adeline Tinkovicz Degan

Why

Save the people, village, country
Explosions, shoot so much
Into the houses
Around to protect
Everyone from wrong
Send people away from their lives
Run, walk with hand-carried memories
One man so slowly
Reverent, with respect and sorrow
Into my life he places his bundle
Silent, no more promise
A baby
Why

Charles S. Bentley

Aged Or Not

I've seen anger and pain in your
eyes of wisdom. You have lived
a full life and now you are
still a care giver of them all
I want so much to share your
stories with the younger generations
I care for you and wish I could
take your pain away to give you
still more happier times now that
you are elderly. I see your family
at the time of their visit. They have
complaints that are reasonable.
The care you get you have
accepted. You complain only
when family comes to visit.
I wish only to have you
and two others to care for you.
Let's blame no one when
I care for over forty or more.
Elderly in one home. I'm only one.

Johnnye Belinda Laison

"The Lonely Heart"

A sunless day...Starless night,
Faceless garden...Fruitless sight.
Haunted heart left in distress,
With mournful waves of loneliness.

A wishing heart...Dying heart,
A heart that yearns for a new start.
But first must cease the steady beat,
Of days gone by and mem'ries sweet.

Ah! Yes, it was a heartless thief
That stole my heart...left only grief.
None but a lonely heart as mine,
Can loneliness so well define.

A patient wait while time stands still,
My heart craves love this void to fill.
Broken dreams best left behind,
Can this heart heal? A new love find?

Sweet gift of love come fill my days,
With joy and laughter ...now...always.
Till my garden to full bloom,
Leave no space for tears or gloom.

Frances Kovacs

Memo To The Wild Flower

Millions of dandelions
   facing the sky,

Millions of violets
   so dainty and shy,

Trailing arbutus
   so close to the ground,

Where but in our fair land
   could this beauty be found.

Sweet smell of clover
   comes over the air,

Wild rose in pink beauty
   and anemone so fair,

Goldenrod and marigold
   as bright as the sun,

America, we're happy
   you grow every one.

Ann Fassbender

The Undying Love

As I sit and watch the snow
Fall outside,

I think of you and how much
your love will abide.

As I sit and listen to your song,
Your voice I want to hear all day long.

I will always care a lot about you,
It's hard to live without the two.

But the hardest part of all
Is when I take a fall,

And your not there.
To show how much you care.

Grandma I love you so much,
I wish I could feel your gentle touch.

But for now until I die,
All I can do is just try.

Bert Rozinski

Traveler Of The Sea

There is a lonely traveler.
Far and away, beckoning to me.
Beyond the sea and off the shore.
Beckons to me my lonely traveler.
Show me the secrets of the sea,
Where the waves pound,
With the steadiness of my heart.
Where the foam gathers,
Like a delicate piece of art.
Where the bubbles are made,
With silk spun thread.
Tell me of the fairies,
That live in the deep, dark, sea.
Here are my questions.
   My lonely traveler.
   There you are.
   Here am I.
Far and away, beckoning,
Beyond the sea and off the shore.

Adelaida Biberos

Reaching For You

Somewhere in the night, restless I lie
Feet on the ground, head in the sky
Consciousness soaring, limitless, vast
Creating the future, reliving the past
Tearing at bonds, the fetters of mind
Ripping them asunder, no longer to bind
Expanding forever, encompassing all
Withdrawing to naught, embraced by all.
Freeing my Soul, I mingle with life
Space my husband, Earth my wife

Joseph T. Paulchell III

Lily Lay

Lily lay in lambent light
   fighting shadows of her night.
      Lily lay midst crouching demons

Lily wrestling with day's dawning,
   pushing back the monster's yawning
   maw.

Strident morning crushes dreaming,
   fractures Lily's misty seeming
   being.

Lily lay in lambent light...
   weeping.

Shrinking shadows gather clout,
   Lily knows there's no way out
   of new day's dawning.

Dressed in robe and bunny slippers
   Lily wakens sleeping nippers
   fixes breakfast, lunches, dinner

Lily knows the only winner
   in this game called Life's
      to keep on dreaming.

Ingrid Krause

Depression

Visions of the future,
Filtered through the past,
Give no insight,
To every question of why.

Pointless actions of cause and effect,
Create a paradox of reason,
Futile efforts to be something more,
Are empty promises of life.

Blind expressions of empty love,
Toss aside all hope,
For rare abandoned hearts,
That hold more love than most.

Constraints of pain and pear,
Weigh heavy on a lonely mind,
Burdens of a false facade,
Exhaust a burning heart.

Fading desire to keep pushing on,
Throws my life out on a limb,
Teetering on the edge of time,
Like a candle in the wind.

Greg Helmerick

The Rose

From where the lovely
flowers grow I don't know
Where the withered
Petals blow
I don't know where they go

But I have seen them
In their glory
Breathed luscious scent
Caressed tender petals
Radiant hue has blossomed
Deep in my soul

And having known beauty
Beyond my imagination
Found harmony
Greater than I was aware

Jerry Soner

Dreams Of Dreamers

Dreams of dreamers
fly away
Dreams of dreamers
come forth today
Dreams of dreamers
have sweet hearts and souls
Dreams of dreamers
see and behold
Dreams of dreamers
Dream of sweet dreams
Dreams of dreamers
Dream of starlight
Dreams of dreamers
Goodnight ...

DeErica Angelita Carr

"Breath"

My thoughts are for those little birds,
Flying on the wind.
So much like little words,
Lying on the lips of mine.
My thoughts are for softly,
Softly, of so-
I touch... and I die.
I reach to bird, away the wind blows,
And I am sad
So much like words on my lips,
A spirit reached my soul.
My ashes have been thrown to the air,
And I am free.

Christine Araby

Sacred Night

I speak to the night
For in its silence
Is an endless quality
Of a mystical serene
Glorious beauty
Hallowed in thy
Makings
I speak to the night
For in this sabbath
Closeness to God
There is a prophetic
Leaking of an eternal breaking
Of light
He speaks
And to Him I give
My utmost, Esteem

Claudia B. Dumas

My Night

Night strength is oft-times all I have,
For many days I'm weak.
There seems to be no end to it,
The peacefulness I seek.

My thoughts do stay preoccupied,
They're led to true and stray.
And only when they sleep at night,
Does calm seem here to stay.

The hope that's heavy in my heart,
By thoughts and things anew,
Lead me to need your strength, My Night,
and lay my trust in you.

It's true I long for restful ease,
Though sleep seems far away,
But think of all and wish for you,
To soothe a rueful day.

So soon I sleep with you in dreams,
Your quiet closed 'round me tight.
The peacefulness my soul seeks out,
Stays with me here, My Night.

Judy McBryde

Stifled Talent

Nay, I win no contest
For my skill has not been honed,
Although the seed's within me
It's like a garden overgrown.
I need to cultivate it
And let it breathe with air and light,
Then watch the blooms burst forth
And grow in such delight;
To brighten someone's parlor
Or to chase away despair,
Or simply say to those who read -
I understand, I care!

Doris Langsdorf

Killing Is My Game!

Killing, killing, killing
for no reason at all
why do people do this
just for power over all.

Why can't there be peace
in this world of ours
why can't there be peace
between the super powers.

People killing people
who they don't even know
just for their leader
because he tells them so.

Let's stop this madness
while we have the time
let's stop this madness right now
before another gun chimes

Jacquilyn M. L. Keating

Tears

Silent teardrops
falling, falling
Down my face.
Marchers, marchers
Of a different race
Running, running to solve the
Case, crying, crying
Tears running down my face.

Emmy Matthews

Compare Thee Not

Compare thee not to roses
For she has no such beauty
Hear not her words of surrender
For she deserves no mercy
Share no feelings of sorrow
For she deserves not pity
Give not your love to borrow
For she deserves not any
Her life be long and lorn
So she will have to suffer
Her heart be only torn
Let no man try to love her
Let pain find a way to greet her
Her cries need not be heard
When scars within grow deeper
The meaning of hurt she'll learn
Grief shall bring no guilt
For her heart is colder than ice
Death can find her still
for she deserves to die

Julia A. Uriegas

The Spectacular Smile

A smile is well-nigh miraculous,
For the internal flame it produces
Dispels the innate loneliness and
Dejection life ultimately yields.

Yet the simple message it embodies
Can be easily understood
By everyone from the tiniest infant
To the most hopeless imbecile.

A smile transforms the appearance,
Converting even the wretched
To artistically tranquil beauty
With one paltry upward stroke.

It also transports the spirit,
For who can retain a somber mood
When the warmth of a smile
Has penetrated his soul?

Though devoid of worldly belongings,
A man still possesses the power
To give one of life's greatest treasures
By simply presenting a smile!

Dorothy Scarbrough

Untitled

Look unto me not with pity or sorrow
for this is what you reap
pluck it out

Have I offended thee
weep not
for what you see is yours

I have done this not to myself
I am yours

Bid me not farewell
for I will haunt you

Nor dare you cast me aside
for I will be your demise

Love me
for I am what you harvest

To rid yourself
be kind
be gentle

So shall I go
I will be no other

David C. Caboon

Trust In Me

I wanted you to believe in me,
For to you, I couldn't lie.
I wanted you to trust in me,
Trust was something I couldn't buy.
All I needed was your love,
But it was him you chose, not me.
So each night I ask the stars above,
That one day, you'll trust in me.
I know the pain I've caused you,
But he was sick and full of hate.
I know you wish it wasn't true,
So it is me that you berate.
I'm not ashamed.
I've done nothing wrong,
And I am not to blame.
Through it all I've been strong,
And I hope to stay that way.
I know someday I'll be on my own and
it'll be just me,
But even then I'll always pray,
That one day, you'll trust in me.

Cyndi Perkins

Sweet Farewell

The time has come
For you to depart.
Please take with you
A piece of my heart.
Have faith and be thankful
And never complain.
Love your self
And remain the same.

Diego Gonzalez

Gentle Lady

Pardon me, gentle lady
forgive my awkwardness
In thy presence I am numb
with my manners less

Walk with me, gentle lady
o'er groves this cool fall
Shall we not approach the day again
this time be all

When age has left us wise and grey
with youthful hearts of memory
go not weeping, fairest love
remember nights we rose above

And if I sweat through the dawn of death
or fever bends my mind
I shall not forget our moments
so ever warm and kind.

James M. Ranard

The Sky

A magical mystical wonder,
Filled with bright stars full of
Endless delight.
Never knowing what to expect.
Rain, shine, all of the time,
Or maybe even snow.
All of the wonders in the sky,
May never be known.
All we know is many stars,
Clouds, planes, the sun and the moon,
Fill the endless blue skies.

Ed Wolk

Death's Rope

Flying through the fathering willows,
free as the fondling wanderers,
hoping once to free its fate
and not to twice believe relate.

To be the seas with me so roamed,
to be so free and then enthroned,
ends not the horrid palace of doom,
but share our morbid chalice of loom.

Of fate, our beliefs,
of hate, our debriefs,
nothing more to rebelate,
nor any score to reinstate.

Sorrow seems the agony of hope
in this mallow meandering of rope;
through the testing of my soul
is the resting in your hole:

A place to hide instead of show,
a place to die eternal woes.

John A. Noss

My Heart Once Was

My heart once was just like the sun,
Full of happiness, not vain.
Now it's like an open wound,
Full of fear and pain,
My heart once was red and loving,
Now it's black and blue.
My heart once was in perfect shape,
Now it's broke in two.
When you're young and haven't found
— What life is all about,
Then your heart is very pure
— and is not full of doubt.

Christina Leigh Wright

"Another Spring"

Spring unfolds like a child,
Full of hope and dreams -
Wanting to be free and wild.

Summer, a fiery youth,
With vigor uncontrolled it seems,
Racing to accumulate
Life's material things.

Fall's golden years,
A season of regret,
Hopes and dreams put off until tomorrow
Knowing now, I will never get.

Oh winter, please don't come,
I am not prepared for your cold winds
And barren trees,
For in my heart there lives the dream
That once again, there will be
Another spring for me.

Joyce H. Schiwart

Not Forgotten

I spy the glossy eye
Gone to higher places
Flat, flat, so low down,
Down down down
Dig deeper to my core
Relentless in his sorrow
Tortured tortured pain
Torment so clear
I feel it, I live it,
He will not be forgotten

Jacob Schimming

Sleigh Ride

A blanket of snow
Gently unfolds
As the glistening runners
of the sled grasp hold.

A horses breast
Serves as our bow,
Driving waves of white ocean
Over our prow.

Bundled down deep,
In a layer of fleece.
The horses driving breath
Breaks the solitude of our winter peace.

Cold noses
Taste the evening chill
Occasionally retreating
Behind a woolly frill.

A yellowish hue
Spills across the snow.
The inviting lights
Of our familiar bungalow.

Allister R. Aaron

Untitled

Pow, Pow, Bang, Bang
Getting taken down by a gang
Shot in the head
Shot in the leg
died in pain, because I bled to death
people think this is just a game
but the world is becoming
untamed...

Carolyne Smith

Untitled

Child walk by
Give me no thought
My youth is wasted
My youth is gone.
Have you no mercy,
Play somewhere else
Go to your mothers,
Stay to yourselves.
Child walk by
Don't look my way
My youth is wasted
My heart, dried away.

Craig McNeill

Courage

Facing life, pursuing dreams,
  Going fourth

Overcoming odds, never relenting,
  just going fourth

Dependent, independent, striving,
  to go fourth

Family, friends, love, marriage,
  Always forward

Dreaming of the future, hoping,
  Going forward

As fast as the wheelchair moves.

Ellen Quinn

Captain Cousteau

Thank you
Grandfather of the water plant
earth.
Conscious of human being
Who care for Mother Earth.
Thank you for all your years
of giving and caring for
Others and specific of Mother Earth.
You give love, spirit to others.
Thank you
for protecting Mother Earth.

James J. Poplawski

Grapefruit

How does
Grapefruit find your eye,
How does grapefruit know to spy.

When it is sectioned and smelling sweet,
And it is grapefruit you want to eat,
then, it spy's your eye and spits,
leaves you feeling like the pits.

How does grapefruit find your face,
find your eye and spits in place.
From now on I'll drink the juice,
It won't squirt me,
when I cut it lose.

Ernette B. Pinkney

Mixed Flowers

Yellow, yellow Daffodils
Growing on the hills.
Among the red tulips
And blue forget-me-nots
Pansies with their
Smiling faces
Wishing I could change
Places and fall into their
Graces
But it isn't meant to be
So I'll just admire
Them from afar
And wish upon a star

Gay Margo

A Space In My Heart

I remember a long time ago,
hands that lifted me into a warm embrace.
My mothers hands.

I remember melodious laughter
at one of my childish antics.
My mother's laughter.

I remember worried concern
when I fell and hurt myself.
My mothers concern.

I remember soft gentleness
when she tucked me into bed.
My mothers gentleness.

I remember love.
I remember happiness.
I remember death.

Coming so quickly and taking away
the hands, the laughter,
the concern and the gentleness.

I remember all these things
and cry inside the space in my heart.

Joan Randall

Magic Mirror

Can this be, a magic mirror
hanging on my bathroom wall
my eyes are bright, and shining
and it's not my face at all
no it's not a magic mirror
as my joyful heart well knows
I've just returned,
from a long, long way
and I'm happy to be home
Ann Miraglia

You Never Do Leave

You are my God. My life is yours.
Hard trials may come. You show the
way.
Your path is straight. It may be narrow.
But you are there. Right by my side.
You never do leave.

Although it may seem that I am alone,
It is because the enemy has come,
To steal my faith, by having me wonder
Where is my God?
Where is his love?
Where has he gone?

And when I look to you again
I now can see
It wasn't you that left at all;
It was myself.

Help me to hold this truth I know
You never do leave.
You have the answer
And you will show me on which path
I am to go.
Frances Carter

Control

Control, control
Have I lost it, have I found it?
Did ever I have it?
Control, control
I always wanted it, doesn't everybody?
Mother, Father, Sister
Napoleon, Hitler, Stalin

Faster, faster
A speeding roller coaster
I've lost control
CAREENING
Lightning fast - a Blitzkreig
Hang on, you haven't lost yet

Up hill,
a slowdown
grasping, grasping
CONTROL!!!
gasping, gasping
CONTROL??
Dawn W. Starks

The Sign

For love, the sign is a rose.
For death, the sign is a rose.
But the sign people don't discover
Is the one you should remember,
Which is the sign in the middle,
The mask of the unknown.
Abbey Daniels

To Nurses

I think I know you.
Have I met you before?
Do we ride the same bus?
Do you work in a store?

Let me just think a minute.
I know I know you.
I know how you act
And I know what you do.

You remind me of someone
I've seen on the street,
Who knows how to smile
At whomever you meet;

Or someone who knows how
To help when you can,
Not waiting to see
How the trouble began.

I know whom you act like!
I know him! He sees us!
You act like a person
Whose first name is Jesus!
Gloria Fowler Bildson

Don't Blame God

How dare you say God doesn't care,
He hung the world in midair.

You crucified His only son,
Who gave us hope when there was none.

His words you wrestle to the test,
to see if what He said was best.

Everyone must choose whom he will serve,
with his own reasons in reserve.

Don't blame God for Satan's curse,
the fallen star of the universe.

If only man could understand,
why God still lends a helping hand.

We often do things our own way,
without regard to what He's paid.

But when the tears begin to fall,
He quickly dries them when we call.
Elena Powdrell

John Thomas Hughes

Now we have another son,
  He is our second one.

He was sent from up-above,
  So we will give him all our love.

Oh, we know it isn't right,
  But we want to hug him oh so tight.

He really looks cute,
  Dressed upon his brother's suit.

He lays around all day,
  Then at night he wants to play.

He is just like all little boys,
  Always looking for new toys.

We will teach him right from wrong,
  And we know he will get along.

We will teach him how to pray,
  And we will help him find God's way.

And when he grows up and looks back,
  He will know he was set on the right track.
James E. Hughes, Sr.

My Caring Son

Although we're many miles apart,
He keeps me always in his heart,
And calls me often on the phone,
If he can ever find me home!

And when I'm ill he calls me more,
Oftener than he did before,
Just to check, when day is done,
This blessed, loving, caring son.

And when he calls it makes my day,
The gloominess just fades away.
We talk about just little things,
The kids and what the weather brings.

And so, Dear Lord, you are the One
Who gave to me this caring son.
I thank you for him, when I pray,
Keep him safe from day to day.

Help him in his walk with you
Always to be kind and true,
Knowing always you're the One,
This blessed, loving, caring son.
Frances L. Thompson

Epitaph (For a Politician)

He lied at morn, he lied at night,
He lied when wrong, he lied when right
He lied at times to save his skin,
He lied at times to hide a sin,
You'd think of lies he's had his fill
But here you find him lying still.
Joseph P. Crescenzo

I Saw A Little Mouse

I saw a little mouse
He sat beside the road,
The birds were in the trees
Over the lawn just mowed.

He wanted to cross over
To the field, on the other side,
He thought, he would be safer
In the tall grass, he could hide.

He waited and he waited
Until he thought, it was safe,
He didn't know, there was a danger
A cat sat, washing its face.

A car went by and he waited
Then a truck was gone, at last,
He thought, that he could make it
If he really ran, real fast.

When he got to the other side
The cat, had been scared away,
He dove into, the tall grass
He sure had "Luck," that day.
Elizabeth Jean Humphrey-Leonard

Anger

These spirited words of mine
hurled and flung against your silence
Hang

then like a boomerang
return.

Wooden words are always curved.
Jane S. Borne

The Wedding

Sky took to him a sunset,
He wed her just at dusk.
He wooed her with blue fingers,
And scent of attar musk.

Caressed her with a molten ray,
Then veiled her blushing face;
His touch had set her soul to blaze,
And caused her heart to race.

The alter shared: horizon,
Upon a lilac sea;
A band of stars her diadem,
And clouds to give them lee.

Her gown: majestic rainbow,
Auroric in its hue;
Diaphanous her veil of mist,
With crest of diamond dew.

The wind choir sang as angels;
Sky led his bride to be,
Across horizon's aisle of Time,
Into Eternity.

Diane Gerber Baugh

Glance

Turmoil, pain, fear.
Her eyes glazed over.
Hands folded neatly on her lap.
A cry moved her upper lip slightly.
Pallid, clammy skin.
Leaves fell from her hair.
The sky had darkened.
The horizon was fading.
No longer did she provide warmth,
Nor food,
Nor comfort,
Nor joy.
I'd like to believe she wanted to.
I can't.
She won't let me.
I want to believe everything will be okay.
The wind tells me it's too late.
But, what if.....

Daniel Sean Kaye

Anchor

Her life is tattered.
Her hands are scared.
Her heart is heavy.
Still, she walks strong and tall.

Her journey has been long and hard.
Her eyes are fading with the time.
Her ears hear the pain.
Through it all she hangs on.

Her hair is silky gray.
Her face with lines of years.
Her smile is weak but strong.
The burden soon will fall.

Her strength grows.
Her faith keeps her.
Her love secures her.
Life ends, but she lives on.

Charlotte Aman

Mother

God sent you, Mother
  here to stay.

To be a blessing
  day after day.

Giving all day long
  teaching right and wrong.

Reading the Good Book
  is what it took.

To keep her strong
  and sing a song.

Though you are gone
  you will live on.

In our nurtured hearts
  we will never part.

God bless you, Mother
  you were like no other.

Janet Clark

Mark The Shark

Mark is a great white,
He's been in a lot of fights.
He has a friend named Keith,
With really sharp teeth!
Mark's in love,
With a shark called "Dove".
Dove is a nurse shark,
And doesn't like Mark!
Because he's a great White Shark,
But Dove like Clark!

Jennifer Karalee Graham

Inspiration

Inspiration breeds with-in,
Hidden by fires of ice,
Smoldering embers dim,
Confronting the essence of life,

Confrontation of the spirit,
Withdrawn from mortal view,
Guides us though we fear it,
Endowed to a chosen few,

Battles fought with-in the soul,
Transformed from mere illusion,
Elusive dreams quietly unfold,
Untangled amidst mass confusion.

Elizabeth Clemann

Agony

The hovering hands of shadows
hide the untemperate diary of dignity
sought and sifted, left cruelly
unexplained - truth -
yet many roadways from truth
the cackle of a stirred up brew
leaves hairs ungroomed
and a lonely boat on earthquake waves
pressure is moving quickly -
no time to talk -
steadily in the whirlpool bed
like a cat after its tail
eventually pounding me down
vertically

Alycia Cardone

Activated

She
hides behind the mask
and loves him.

She
hears music
in his words.

She
sees distant planets
in his eyes.

She
wishes for his breath
upon her ear.

She
longs for his tongue
inside her mouth.

She
waits for his heart
to be touched.

Daphne Barbee-Wooten

Owner

The owner overstands.
His home he makes up.
His voice moves hands to go under.
Why and how and where he knows.
His home is metal clean.
His home lives on.
The sun comes to nothing.
I will the owner.

John Donaldson

Time To Go!

  God looked down from upon
His throne, and said it's time for
my children all to come home.
They've waited so long and the
time is right, for the Son of
God to come tonight.
  Lord, this is my dream and
this is my prayer, to meet
your Son high in the air.
But should I go by way
of the grave, I still can't
wait for that glorious day.

Joanne Robbins

Allah (God)

Allah is mighty powerful of
  his words.
Allah is mighty strong in
  his ways.
Allah is mighty brave in
  Mother's Nature.
Allah is mighty sensitive
  of his senses.
Allah is mighty serious
  on his judgements.
Allah's judgements are:
Honest, equal, great, and fair.
If you are honest, equal,
  great, and near.
"ALLAH"

Angelo Raysor

140

We Must Part For Awhile!

Come to me, dear
  Hold me close to your breast,
And show me your sweet, loving, smile -
  Lay your head on my shoulder,
Let it soak up each tear -
  For you see, we must part for awhile!

Believe me, my dear
  I don't want to leave,
So trust me and show me that smile
  My love has not died,
For that, have not fear -
  It's just, we must part for awhile!

Love me, my dear
  And never lose faith,
For your love I will never beguile -
  In these arms, linger heart,
'Til you've shed your last tear -
  Then remember, it's just for awhile!

Harold W. Beebe

Untitled

I have to say I like it best when you
Hold my hand like the stem of a rose
Being careful not to sting me Because
I sting back Because I sting back
With my thorns that scorn things
Beautiful and simple like the lines
On the smoothly rising flesh of your
Palm Smooth like the face of an ocean
Tossed pebble Curving to the currents
Crashing into its surface I fall into
An embrace Like a child falling down
I fall down with the man who loves me-
"I really want this" I think to myself

Julia Ebert

Time

Time isn't measured by the
hours we spend
For moments are fleeting but
memories don't end
Yesterday is far nearer than
the future will be
The images dearer than the
things we now see
Take each moment and hold it
alive in your heart
If you do there is nothing
From which you must part
Take each precious second
just set it aside
Take it out and remember
that you laughed or you cried
The feelings of living and
loving go on
Time only enriches the loves
that have gone

Antoinette M. Ciotti

I Remember Grandpa

I remember grandpa -
How he held me in his arms,
How we read our books together,
How we shared each others charms.

He wasn't just another Grandpa -
He was a loving man.
Oh, how I miss my Grandpa,
Only he could understand.

Anna Jaco

Soul Mate

My dearest soul mate;
how can I describe thee?
You gave me endless love
and lasting loyalty.

Tell me dearest soulmate;
what troubles you tonight.
Let me guide you through your sorrow
to the answers in the light.

I look back in time,
into your mysterious eyes.
From which you grasped my heart
and said your last good-byes.

Love was something we once shared.
Together we made it last.
And if ever I forget passions' meaning,
I'll just look into the past.

Courtney Adams

Through The Years

Time goes by
How fast it can fly

There can never be enough appreciation
For the gift of your creations

Through all of your doubts
You carried us about

You made us strong
And to you we belong

Be proud and stand tall
We'll catch you if you fall

But only to lift you
Up where you belong

And thank God for the gift of you
As you shine forever all around.

We love you!

Jennifer Bacso

Four A.M.

So real! Surreal?
How shall we dally?
On bedding of silk
or canvas by Dali?

How are we suited?
On earth firmly rooted?
Or off on Chagallian
Fantasy flight?

Viscerally? Vasarely.
You're the fire in my belly.
You are my eyes',
my heart's delight.

So I ask... is it illusion
Or will I embrace you through the night
On bedding of silk
Or canvas by Dali?

Jonah Wittenberg

If I Died

If I died,
how would I feel?

If I died,
where would I go?
Above or below.

If I died,
who will I see?
Everyone whose been
there before me.

If I died,
am I able to fly?
Toward the clouds
in the sky.

If I died,
I know I'm gone
from the world,
but my spirit still
lives on.

Indira Snipe

It's Now Or Never

It's never that I will
  hurt you or treat you bad
It's never that I will make
  you feel so sad.
It's now or never
  Sooner or later
It's only for your toke
  my heart will cater
It's now that I will try
  to make it last
It's now that a spell on me
  your love has cast
It's never that I will say
  never come back
It's now or never because
  it's your love I lack
Say it now
  mean it forever
mean it now
  or say it never

Greg Crank

The Light From Within

When I listen and feel your warmth
I am in complete power with myself
Harmony seizes my inner soul
A yellow light glows around me
I see before me the forth ray
Peace engulfs my whole being

Like magic I fly in the wind
Floating on a soft white cloud
A shooting star flashes by me
Heavens burst throughout the sky
Beneath my feet the ocean sparkles
My body tingles with happiness

My soul speeds through destiny
Away from materialistic things
Towards all earthly creations
Loving thy neighbor as thyself
Forgiving all who have injured
Listening to the sound of my soul

June S. Gatewood

Our Land

Rolling on up I-65
  I admire the countryside
This land of ours so beautiful
  this land of ours so wide.

Not many people see the
  beauty of our land
Take hold of one another
  and walk hand in hand.

In Winter the trees are so
  barren and bare
But the beauty of them
  is still there.

Spring is a time
  for love
This is God's will
  from above.

Summer and Fall have their
  fine points, too
So look a little closer at our
  land through and through.

Appreciate our country and what
  God has given us
Share it more with others
  this is so right and just.

Cynthia L. Eby

Untitled

I am
I am a person
I am unique
I am total
I cannot be
what you need
I am
who I am
Experience me
Enjoy me
Do not change me
For then
I no longer
Am.

Anna F. Coderre

Life

Total alarm
I am silk of this
Disorder unleashed
Starting to lynch
In her fear
Your worst enemy
Choice control
Racist human beings
Shame & Regret
Blood boils inside me
It's all insane
I'm feeling sick
I am feeling numb
Terror raids the land
Were going insane
This is the time, grow up
Realize your messed up
Hid from view, secret plans
Knowledge is the we upon
Face reality

Cheryl Tarulli

"Gods Light"

I ask for light to let me see
I ask for light to let me high
I ask for light to let me breath
I ask for light for your heart to see
I ask for light so everyone can see
I ask for light so all children can see
I ask for light to see in the darkness
I ask for light that I might see my
path along life's thorn road
This is why I ask for God's light

Charles V. Maness

Untitled

In the morning
I awake
to see you lying by my side
And it makes things more.
The sun is brighter
the air is cleaner
My love is new all over again,
because you are there.
In the evening
I drift asleep
knowing you are by my side.
And it makes things less.
The dark is less frightening
the silence less still
and the love for that day has passed,
to be born again
with the coming dawn.

Carol M. Kruck

Just So You Could Be Seen, My Love!

My love, my sweet love!
  I believe that a 1,000
Red roses in all of
  their majestic splendor,
couldn't compare to the majestic
splendor in just a single
  strand of your red hair.
Because when God sculptured
  your face in the
serenity of his dreams.
  He took the radiant
softness of a sunrise, and
  placed it into your eyes.
Then colored them with
  emerald greens.
He made the sun to burn
  golden across the
earth and skies.
  Just so you could be seen.
Just so you could be seen. My Love!

Joseph Spears

Question

"Who?" says the owl.
  "I don't know", say I.
"Who?" says the owl.
  Never when or why.
"Who?" says the owl.
  I say, "I don't know."
It must be kind of sad
To always ask but never know.

Gail Sacharski

Daddy

When I was young
I called him "Daddy."
I still do.

As a child,
I was his "Little Girl."
I still am.

He hugged me,
every chance he got.
He still does.

He believed in me,
so I could believe in myself.
I do.

He holds me while I cry,
and makes it all O.K.
He always will.

His hands, those of a working man.
have compassion, have sternness.

I love him, for who he is,
for who he has made me, and most of all,
because he is, and always will be, my
  Daddy.

Christy A. May

Shadows

I am a shadow
  I disappear into the darkness
    Fade into the background
      You see me when you want to

You beg me to dance
  In the light of your dreams
    If only the nightmares
      Weren't as real as they seem

The sweetly sung melodies
  Turn into screams
    Silently pounding away
      The painful memories

Dark gazing eyes
  Watch emotions decay
    In the light of your terror
      Shadows can't go away

Chris Craigie

Foot Prints

Who follows me through the sand?
I don't know, nor understand.
Who it is I shall never know.
Why does their face never show?
When I place my foot to the sand.
I look back but nobody stands.
What a puzzle this turned out to be.
All it is, is footprints that I see.
Even though I'm old and grey,
I still wonder to this day.
When I walk through the sand,
Who follows me where I stand?

Allisonbeth Olszyk

Fantasy

I longed for you my dearest
I even heard your cry,
It rang with song, the clearest
Babies lullaby.

Oh, how I've cuddled you,
I've touched your tender skin
Its softness like a morning dew,
My dreams, my hopes, begin.

You've snuggled closely to my breast
My heart skipped a beat,
The yearning put quietly to rest,
One precious moment, then defeat.

Oh! How real the love we shared
With beauty, it filled my life,
Then reality, returned to me,
These tender moments-could never be.

We all have fantasies and dreams,
To some they all come true,
Others must rise within themselves,
Discover, dreams anew.

Ann R. Barré

Rags To Riches

Leave the house at day's first dawn
I go and drive that big old truck
I think of you while I'm gone
Work all day to make a buck

Hey honey you're the reason
I work hard for my dollar
Your hugging and your squeezing
Make me glad I'm blue collar

Wealthy men can keep their gold
They can't hug and squeeze it tight
All I want is you to hold
Every day and every night

Gold goes up and down each day
If they knew what they're missing
They would trade their gold away
For some loving and some kissing

All my dreams of me and you
They were my only wishes
Darling when you said I do
I went from rags to riches

Jerry R. Van Cleve

You're Just Like All The Rest

You don't know how you've hurt me,
I guess you never will.
You've torn my heart wide open,
from which my love did spill.
I tried to give it to you,
but instead it went to waste.
It spilled all over from my eyes
onto my pillowcase.
I tried so hard to get you
now I finally know I've lost.
What I didn't know was
I'd be paying such a cost.
At first you spent lots of time with me,
and called me everyday.
Now I'm lucky if I get a call,
or even a simple "hey"!
I thought you would be a different,
I thought you were the best.
But I guess that's what I get for thinking,
cause you're just like all the rest.

Brenda L. Scarborough

Answered Prayer

I have been stolen and sold.
I have been scared,
beaten and mistreated.
I was denied my freedom.
I was born and died
someone's property.
I prayed, but my prayer's
went unanswered,
until one day,
My maker called me home.

Jennifer Harden

My Favorite Sport Is Baseball

My favorite sport is baseball,
I have my own ball mitt,
And I like to be on the field,
Rather than to sit!

I usually hit triples,
Doubles, singles, too,
But when it comes to home runs,
Well, I hit a few!

I don't care for catching,
Pitching is all right,
But when you see me up to bat,
Wow! What a sight!!

Jennifer Elliott

Sound Of Silence

Mid the sound of silence
I hear the north wind blow.
Out on the street,
sounds of the traffic flow.

Mid the sound of silence,
the crackle of pouring rain,
further in the distance,
the whistle of a train.

Mid the sound of silence,
birds of the morning sing,
these are a few joys,
that the sound of silence brings.

Craig Pillsbury

Taps-Again?

Not long ago
I heard
a bugle song
hallow
the ground
of a
muted throng.
Not long ago
I heard
Fuglemen vow:
"No more, dear God!"
But now,
winds blow strong
to cow
the song,
the sod.

David Schachter

Dear National Library of Poetry,

(The best library there will ever be)
Just the other day,
I heard somebody say
That the National Library of Poetry
   has a contest -
To see which poems are the best.

Now I know it's too late to enter,
   because the competition's over
But I was wondering if there was to be
   another one soon -
Maybe in the month of October???

Hopefully by this winter
You can send me information
   on how I can enter.

I have a poem I think will win -
I just need to know when to send it in.

Thank You for reading my rhyme,
I'll write another one some other time.

If you have information for me,
Please send it to the address that you see:

Jennifer Griffis

I'm Hurting Inside

I'm hurting inside,
I just want to break down and cry.
Because the pain the pain I feel,
It feels so real.
I never thought I'd hurt,
From a gorgeous looking flirt.
Why did you do it?

Bridget Gracia

Hold On

It was such an awful day
I knew I'd never make it,
My troubles just kept piling up
and I thought I couldn't take it.
But there were things I had to do
So I figured I could fake it.
I'd wear a smile and work a while
and maybe I could shake it.
Well, sure enough, as time went by
I never could mistake it,
I got to feeling better soon,
Praise God! I'm going to make it!

John S. Lyttle

Pain

Pain's no stranger-
I know his name
He calls - unwelcomed -
Like stain
Seeps between
Cracks and grain -
Leaves behind
A residue
In burning hues
Tattooed.

Pain - uninvited -
Consumes with lust
The last crumb and crust
Leaves behind
A broken plate
Inconsolate -
I know his name -
Pain - it's love.

Betty M. Fitzgerald

143

Sadness

Here I am sitting under a cloud
I know not from whence it came
The day once joyous and bright
Is now my dark wilderness
The fire of life burns from beyond
Oh hand of love guide me to its warmth.

John Dodds

Gina's Promise

I wait for thee above the clouds
I know not where, I know not how
But when it's time, and you're set free
You'll head for home to be with me.

You loved me so and I loved you.
You held my hand and led me through
A life of love and joy and smiles
Cut short by pain and many trials.

It's time to go I'm not sure why.
We mustn't fret or doubt and cry
But trust in he who gave us life
To bring us back into the light.

So when it's time and you're set free
Hold my hand and come with me.
I'll lead you as you led me
Together we shall always be
Forever through eternity.
Mother, Daughter
God's children we.

Bette Masters

Either Or

There comes a time when day is gone
I look back on what I've done
I wonder if I've done my best
Or did in part and left the rest.

Did I serve God with all my might
Did I do wrong or heed the right
If only time would turn again
I'd make amends for what I've been.

It cannot be; I must move on
And do it now ere life is gone
Someday I'll go my Lord to meet
And stand before the judgement seat.

As I stand there on judgement day
I'm wondering what my Lord will say
I know you not, or you're my own
Depart from me, Or welcome home.

Barbara E. Pettyjohn

Sister Dear

Oh sister dear so far away,
I miss you so much everyday,
I know you're safe in your world today,
I know now it was God's way,
Even though I don't come to your grave,
Your love and warmth you always gave,
To every living thing you touched,
You should know you're loved so much,
That special song can make me weep,
Your memories are all I have to keep,
So goodbye for now sister dear of mine,
I'll see you again farther down the line.
(In loving memory of Donna)

Bambie Seifrit

Forever In My Arms

I remember the last time
I looked at the stars
And you were in my arms
Sitting together in silence
Thinking of our future
Thinking of each other
And how things will turn out
Wishing we could always be together
But knowing someday
We will part
My love for you grew
Even more that night
And all I want is what I wanted
On that night to have you forever
For all nights to come
To be the same as that last night
To always have you in my arms
And for those nights
To know that I'll never have
To let you go

Bridget Katherin Richmond

The First Look

When my son was born
I looked in his eyes
Beyond this world
And into the next
Seeing Heaven through his Soul

God sent him here
To be in my care
A Great Gift of Love
Came into my life
A feeling of Blessing all around

At that moment
I promised God
I would Love His child
No matter what
Just as He has Loved me

Joan Sullivan

The Road To Hell

The road to hell
I new quite well
I traveled it for years
And hid the tears

I didn't listen to reason
I did it on my own
I did it through all the seasons
And hid the regretful moans

I can't remember happiness
on that road
I can remember the loneliness
but how was I to know

I learned to be sad
and put up with the pain
I learned to hide that I got mad
I soon woke up and got rid
of the years of stains

Jill H. Adams

Untitled

Outside my dream
I pause.
Tami bends
and serves up a familiar refrain.
Twice the necessary
is half the need.
While passing an introduction
I fall into a seam.
Not thrown
for want of the seam.
Just aired,
for a tangent cause.
A hand extended
to an open,
smiling face.

All the while,
an evening's promise
rises high
in a cascading amber glow.

Jim Prendergast

"Moments To Eternity"

What is this minute
I poignantly reckon,
That is now my life
Winding down in seconds?

So much yet to do,
So much yet to learn,
So much bright newness,
So much joy to earn!

I must surrender
The past's deep caring,
I must, thus, tender!
To those newly faring!

Bless all I've done,
Bless goodness won,
I've scarcely begun
To thank Everyone!

Farewell deeds unsung,
My few seconds grow late,
I climb the last rung,
As St. Peter awaits!

Doris Jacobs

Last Year's Garden

Between the pages of my heart
I pressed a fallen rose,
From the dying edge of summer
Where last year's garden grows.

Watered by my teardrops
Angels hold her there,
Beyond the breath of autumn
And far from fields of care.

Her vase a golden chalice
On the mantle of the day,
Where dawn returns the sunshine
Of memory's sweet bouquet.

Though that flower of my heart
Was lifted from her bough,
In the place of love's embrace
I still hold it now.

And on those lanes that I recall
When memory passes thru,
I brush a teardrop from a rose
Where last year's garden grew. Those
Mothers of my Heart

Eugene E. Lovas Sr.

Young Love

On a country lane,
Driving east, windows down,
Music playing, wind brushing my hair,
I listen to James Brown
Almost crying, "Please, please,
Please, please!"
Aware of double meanings,
I agree.
Spring pops, lush with open sky.
Geese fly north.
This is Alabama.
Fluffy white clouds—boil—
A lady on a broomstick, trojan horses,
Flowing beards, satins, gowns and dragons
Amid libraries, books, paintings,
In cities and poems unimaginable!
In the dreams,
Always, I flew.

Ella Robinson

A Flattened Penny On A Railroad Track

An oblong copper obelisk
dully reflects light off its marred surface
from where it rests
atop its long iron bed.
Once a perfect flat circle,
now the face that it bore
of the Great Emancipator is
stretched and scarred.
Only a few small lines of the finely chiseled,
determined face remain.
The rest has been brushed away by the
tremendous pressure of the freight train
as it lumbered over the coin,
transforming it into the aged chunk of metal
that is left to decay scarred and broken.

John P. Heckathorne

Vengeance Everwanting

Jailed, jailed
Dungeoned in unexpressed malice of life
Help has evanesced everlasting
Trapped running in the same circle that leads nowhere
My own separate heterogeneous genocided by society
Can run to neither the edge is so close
To silence all voices
The fumigation of society and family will never fustigate my soul
Always lost through every nothing all jumbled together
Images and vitiated mirages are the same now
Hope is dead hope is everything no longer exists
Ignored ignored
Psychosomatic splintered eclectic mirages are all to true now
Hope is a lost dream
Truth is pain is a diversion to cope with reality
Learn it
Destroy it everlasting never won
In mind and body
Revenge is the sweet wanting
everwanting, everlasting

Gregory T. Howard

Deep Inside

The girl sits silently, watching the world go by,
Each day wondering when she will die.
Abandoned by all, she is alone,
Deep inside of her beats a heart made of stone.

A dark black soul is nestled within,
Emptiness inside of her, where love should have been.
Her life crumbling to pieces, she doesn't know where to turn,
While deep inside of her angry feelings burn.

She doesn't recognize the hate that she feels,
For, to the girl, hate is all that is real.
Pain and suffering is all that she knows,
So deep inside of her anguish grows.

The girl waits bravely for the day to come,
When she will no longer be alone.
The hurt that she feels grows constantly,
But she buries it deep inside so no one will see.

She tries to deny her feelings but no longer can,
She saw how she felt and immediately ran.
The night before her death she stayed up and cried,
But no one could help, for no one knew how she felt deep inside.

Jeanette Ibex

"The Singing Bluebird"

High above in the Tree,
early in the morning
A flock of birds flying high in
the sky and touch down on the ground
like that of an Airplane,
which, remain silent on the earth.
The little bluebird sings a
beautiful song to his Master,
What a wonderful services being held
like in a chapel of the tree top
high on the hillside, in the mass of worship,
the tone of the singing Bluebird.
Her peers sit and pray,
The King love to listen to her
beautiful voice of music, at dawn,
The singing Bluebird,
Her voice so clear and sweet.
I love to hear her sing the
lovely tone early in the morning,
The magic singing Bluebird,

Earnest N. Davis

Going Home

Glacial Handiwork so carelessly arranged
Earth swept by the winds of time
Sporting cloaks of slender grasses standing close
Heads with sepia manes
Spared by the plowman's till
Fields framed by trees and undergrowth
With fences become one
Rows of anticipated harvest stitched in with seed
An occasional glimpse of parallelism
Banks sprawled with blooms of pink and lavender
Billowed by the artificial breeze
Mounds of treetops visible across flat land
Softly cushioned shades of green
Stands of trees locked arm in arm
Spread their dense foliage
Protecting all that lies within
The land and its offspring suffer superficial scars
The roots lie deep within.

Diane Burkemper

Remembrance

Gradually and in fragments a part of my life
enters my awareness,
which I already had to embrace in my past.
Like a tenacious stream of lava it pours through
my grey tissues.
Shining brightly like a flash of lightning a thought
blazes through my memory and brings me back to
my childhood.
A clear and impressive picture flares through my inner
eyes and yet, I have to let it fade. Time takes it back
again into the world between dream and reality.
I glide away as if on a cloud inexorably deeper into
the valley of life.
Time and space consume me in their power and foreshadow,
where I am bound.
After all, I am the product of the fantasy and
wisdom of nature and the infinite universe.

Heidi Rimanich

She Cries Alone

She cries alone
enveloped in darkness, engulfed in loneliness
and isolated from everyone.
Tomorrow in the sunlight she will stride-
her head held high, her eyes bright
with a forced smile to those she recognizes
her eyes averted
to images of the dark night to come.
A painful greeting to those she knows
to those who think they know her.
A courteous verbal exchange
Automatic answers given again and again to appease her friends.
Then she walks away…
into her own world,
into a deep solitude, a blackened darkness
where a neverending loneliness awaits her
as she briefly looks into unknowing eyes
her head held high.

Christina Schuck

Untitled

On summer's eve, on cusp of night
Ere golden sun is shado'ed moon;
When stream and runnel seem to hush
And fair starlight is promised soon;

There I would sit, in dusk's light bathed
Awaiting night's approaching fall,
And muse on themes of many kinds,
Endear'd to me were one and all;

And still do I recall those hours
So spent when bright warm light shone true
Across the fertile leas of youth
And treasured thoughts which bloomed and grew;

And still a zephyr, mem'ry tinged
Will call me back to sacred leas
With haunting whispers, beckoning
Come back and be forever free

Audrey Droesch

There Is A Future…

There is a future way past our time, and it's
filled with green gooey slime. Do you know
what I'm saying, do you hear the chime?
We've got to clean up our act before we run out of time.

But I see the light not very far off a
place where there's fresh air and you never cough!
So now that you've heard go and spread the word.

Jess Stork

Vince Guaraldi Is Okay

Vince Guaraldi is okay.
Especially Jazz Impressions of Black Orpheus.
It's great when you're with a lady,
Drinking Cappucino by the fire,
Telling her that you usually spend the winter
on the Riviera on your yacht,
But it's in the shop — being fixed.
She's disappointed but impressed. She hugs and kisses you madly.
Jazz Impressions of Black Orpheus is great for that.

Oh Good Grief! Is okay, too.
It's great when you've just lost another baseball
game — and you were pitching.
Your psychiatrist has raised her rates from a nickel to a quarter,
All she ever does is say you're "wishy washy" and
jerk the football away from you when you try to kick it.
Your new kite has been eaten by that evil tree.
And every Halloween your best friend waits in the
the pumpkin patch for some deity to appear.
Your dog is out in the backyard fighting the Red
Baron in his Sopwith Camel. Oh Good Grief! is great for that.

Jeff Boggs

Mother

Mother I love you with all my heart
Even tho we're miles apart
You'll always be with me
No matter how far.
For I can't forget the things we shared.
We have been thru good and bad.
But we have always come out ahead.
So on this your special day I would like to say
I'll love you tomorrow as I do today
Even though your far away.
Your always with me night and day
So just remember I love you always

Elizabeth Gordon

"B"'s Poem

As a child she played with me,
even though I called her "B."

And now she's grown older,
She's going away,

She may be gone physically,
But in my heart she'll stay.

There is proof you see where she's been,
She is my loving sister, Miss Jamie Lynn.

Amanda Burley

The Sword

A man shimmers like a sword in the morning sun.
Everybody wrongs him for what he thinks might be fun.
He wants to fight.
All through the night.

Then the day comes of to battle he is gone.
He does fight all through the night.
He slashes and slices during his fight.
Then the battle is done and the enemy is gone.
At that moment he realizes what has come.

All through the rest of his life.
He sits at home alone with only his wife.
He realized that he has committed a sin.
He murdered for his pleasures within.

Now the man shimmers no more.
He is just like his sword, worn and tattered forever more.

Chris Finch

146

Prayer Of A Broken Vessel

Let me share the love of Jesus
Even when I feel abused
Teach me, spirit, with God's Wisdom
Give me strength when I'm accused.

God almighty by thy Power
Restore the shattered Souls to Thee
Who left alone are broken vessels
Yet can be used to set others free

Free from a self-serving nature
Free from the clutches of despair
Wash each heart, Dear Lord, with Scripture
And place in us a right spirit, there

Let us not be confused by feelings
By those who dearly love us too
Teach us to reach out to the burdened
With love and compassion learned from you.

When the strength of our Bodies Weakens
While inside our being the will to serve you
Teach each of us our loving saviour remains
Like you, when we suffer, to not complain.

Ethel Smith

Our Wedding Day

Every second is filled with anxious delight,
Every minute is shared in a whole new light.
The day will hold a promise new,
Of the undying love that is shared by two.
The night will hold the tenderness,
Of a gentle kiss and sweet caress.
Each month will prove that love does grow,
Each year will bring a better tomorrow.
Two lives, two minds no longer are twain,
But united as one, in joy and in pain.
Two hearts joined to fill an empty space,
Now locked together in an unshakable, unbreakable embrace.
What God has joined together, let no man put asunder.

Iris Ann Vaughn

The Purity Of Love

Like a tangle of thistle was the road to your heart;
Every move, every step so cautious and demure.
There was no light to guide my steps, only bleakness and dark.
The closer I came to feeling its presence, I could hear the
Flow of your blood run through your veins.
I could feel the warmth of your being expel through
Every pore of your skin.
Bleakness and dark, now turned into blithe and blinding white.
Thorns now holding sweet smelling blossoms;
Soft music echoing in the aura;
Your hand held out to meet upon my own.
Our fingertips touched in such a loving way.
Our eyes slowly moved to upward glances revealing
Love through the windows of our emotion.
My heart melted into molten ruby that glowed
So elusively upon my bashful face.
I sensed this was love in its rarest form.
I knew this was the fruit of my journey to
A place that gave me your loving heart.

Anastasia Spiris Moustakas

The Knowledgeable And The Inquisitor

What is the world?
Everything all and more as I've been told.
The world.
What is space?
A place of space in space, that place.
The space.
What is time?
A rhyme, a lie, a spy, working all together to
combine. Time.
What is the mind?
Consciousness, the perception of the world unkind.
All of the senses intertwined in a bind. The mind.
What is a place?
A here, a there, a what, a where, a certain space. The place.
What is the soul?
A hole in the being filled by the light still unseen.
The achiever of goals. The soul.
I believe the knowledge. I can reach to the sky.
But still I do not know the answer to the question, 'Why?'
Nor I! For the question 'Why' is beyond the sky.

Jeremy Jowett

A Walk By The Brook

As I walk by the brook,
Everything in the congested world vanishes.
The chaos of the city
The noise.
The hostility.
   All gone.
I sit on a rock covered with moss.
I hear the faint sound of leaves floating by;
I feel a cool breeze.
The water is crystal clear.
White foam gathers at my feet.
An old stone wall far in the distance, marks the boundary
of men gone before,
And it make me happy, knowing that there was someone
who kept this brook company
when it was young.
I'll be back, I whispered,
   Someday

Jayson Cooper

God Is Good Ah Spring

While standing on my porch one winter's day.
Everything looked so bleak and gray.
Then came spring and what a sight.
Everything looked beautiful and bright.
The beauty of the budding trees.
The singing and buzzing of the bees.
The grass growing green.
The flowers bloom sweet.
The animals come out for food to eat.

The sun was shining bright with a breeze now and then.
You turn your head towards the sky.
You might see a cloud go drifting by.
So now it's spring, I sit on my porch.
Look around and see
What wonderful sights that God has given me.
   God is good. Ah Spring.

Ann Mills Filmore

My Girlfriend

You make my world brighter,
Every time that we converse,
When I talk of you,
It brings a smile to my face,
Instead of kicking me when I'm down,
You encourage me to get up,
I am fully charmed about everything we do,
The last thing I want to do is harm you,
For I don't want to see you blue,
Your an extraordinary person and astute,
When I see you anytime your oh so cute,
There isn't anything I wouldn't do for you,
Even wear a suit,
If your in any trouble,
I would be your knight in shining armor,
'Cause I've never cared about or liked
anyone the way I do you,
Do I hope we can grow together
Who knows maybe it will last forever.

Dwayne Bernier

Welcome

Look not into the abyss
Evil lies over the edge of which you've gone
You've pushed
You've pushed hard
Welcome, welcome to the limit
The decision was yours, whimper not
The search for the crossroads was yours
You took the path of self indulgence
Only you
You who shunned family, soul, and God
Now you belong to that abyss
You'll not be aloud to go quietly into that good night
Scream
Scream
Against the dying of the light
I am death, I am the abyss
I am your drug of choice
Welcome
Welcome
Welcome

John A. Chase

Untitled

When the winter cold has changed its course,
    exhausted all its strength;
When the sun we know that warms the earth
    is now much close in length;
When we see the birds that fill the air
    with all the joy they sing,
When the clouds spread by show the deep
    blue sky,
We know it must be spring.
When we see the sprouts of the many plants,
    and they seem to labour thru;
When we see the trees all in their bud
    in many shades and hue;
When we see the soil being turned in the fields,
    and the hour of toil it brings;
When we see the beauty of all the earth,
    We know it must be spring!
Let's carry on, not be depressed by those
    who do not share
The loving wonder of the land when. Springtime is so fair!

Donald H. Ellison

A Most Ordinary Bliss

I spent a life in darkness
Extolling its horrific glory.
But a priestess of self-denial,
I conjured beasts of distress
For sacrifice to this Phantom.
Wanting at once to be rescued,
Yet basking in the familiar torment of my cell.
This oppressive existence was an apparition
Who fled my haunted soul as I came to bear a new life.
This life was always of me,
Yet I denied its truth.
It was finally bore of me.
The grueling labor stung with sweat.
As I finally saw its face,
I wept with joy.
My limp body surrendered to the gray tones which
Guide my floating path
On this ordinary river.

Dorian Potter

Eyes

Eyes, oh bewitching eyes, know you not the power you possess?
Eyes as deep as a bottomless well, into which a fall forever
would be a gift of boundless joy.
Eyes as dark as a moonless midnight sky. How many secrets
hide within your depths?
Fiery pools of darkness that blaze with mad passion and delicious
wickedness.
Tempting and taunting, challenging and daring, how to resist
these eyes of darkness hue?

Dangerous eyes, capable of sentencing a heart to eternal devotion,
while searing a soul with passion's fire.
Tempestuous eyes, so full of stormy darkness, they sing their
siren song.
With a whim, oh how quickly, these eyes do change; to become
those of a beguiling imp.
Eyes of dark ice become sparkling pools of womanly mischief.
In a breathless instant they become the warm eyes of a doe.
How they comfort and bring warmth to a frozen life.

Powerful and bewitching eyes, once more I ask; know you not
the power you possess?

David Bartholomey

For My Son

My son, my son, Innocent powerful one,
eyes shining with honesty and hope;
your midnight fears and fragile tears
hold me up and give me reason to cope.

I fear for your future and pray for your fate,
that you may know love and never hate.
That you may walk with patience and forgiveness
through a life both fulfilling and blessed.

For you I want a better world,
one worthy of your trust and joy;
as pure as your heart and as free as your spirit,
a safe haven for little boys.

Alex Brand

Tribute To Dr. King

The day did come when no one did gaily sing,
For dead and gone was the Mighty King,
Peace on Earth, this was His goal,
His body is dead and gone, not His work or His soul,
He worked for unity between people, black and white,
To live like brothers and not to fight,
Today, yes we can gaily sing,
For the ideas live on of THE MIGHTY KING

Barry Goldman

Autumn Night

The warm blue day of summer soon
Fades quickly into crisper night
When September hangs her lantern moon
And clouds stroke long calligraphy
  in her golden light.

The air is sweet with the breath of vines
Ripening on the dusty hills
Where a flirting wind lifts fragrant wines
To gypsy maples tittering
  in their gaudy frills.
Across the hayfields neatly stitched
With stacks of harvest shocks
The field mice scatter noisily, bewitched
  by a shadow fox.
I gaze and breathe and listen quite
Enchanted with a wonder deep,
Till soft and full the autumn night
Folds earth and me to mellow sleep.

Claire A. Phipps

Fallen Hearts

FALLEN HEARTS fall from the sky
Fall so gently, like a lullaby
Fall like laughter and happiness
Fall in bunches of greatness
Fall to earth, like a star
Fall in the distance afar
Fall like the rain, gently and cool
Fall like the shimmering of a jewel
Fall like the goodness, from God up above
Fall like two people, falling in love

Diana L. Chiaradio

Untitled

I shall follow the conviction of my heart

All my life's efforts seemed to be in vain
Falling from life like autumn leaves in a brisk wind
When this incredible conviction was felt within

Through all the searching one could never foresee
How beautiful and comfortable you are to me
A discovery so real, that now I truly believe

In your eyes I can see, to my life what you will present
From this very day to all those subsequent
It's an overwhelming discovery of what love meant

This flood of emotions is difficult to chart
Two becoming one, a second chance for a new start
Please understand, much longer we will not be apart

For I've truly discovered, the conviction of my heart

Anthony LaBato

Love

Love is like little tiny rain drops
  falling from the sky.
Love is like the grass that never
  stops growing.
Love is long and lasting like the sea
  that never runs dry.
Love is sweeter than all the seasons
  that go bye.
Love is a commitment that you can't break
  until the day you die.

Carmen Delph

The All American Girls Professional Baseball League

The All American Girls Professional Baseball League is in the Hall of Fame. I'll tell you some about their kind of game.

The League started in 1943. The men were at war, that was the key. There were 15 teams altogether, and they played in almost any weather. They played mostly in the Midwest, and they didn't really get much rest. Two of the teams were Rockford and Racine, at this game, they were quite keen.

The first year they went to Charm school, and if they were out past 11:00, they broke a rule. Some of the team snuck out at night, but they hardly ever got in a fight. Sometimes, they tricked their guardians by putting toothpaste instead of oreo cream, even though it was very mean. Many girls were in their teens. Unfortunately, they couldn't wear jeans. They had to wear short, tight little skirts, so they couldn't run in spurts.

They loved to steal bases. You could tell by looking at their happy faces. When they slid into base they got a raspberry, though they always acted very merry. Outfielders flung themselves against the walls, just to catch high fly balls. Some of the batters were very strong, some of the balls flew soooo long.

They were just as good as men. I hope a League like that happens again.

Julia Gallagher

Dinner Bell

On a hot and sweltering day,
farm hands were making hay.
Draft teams were all in a lather,
because of the sultry weather.

Mother and the hired girl,
both were all in a whirl,
roasting beef, baking bread, pies and cake,
cooking potatoes, putting beans on to bake.

Finally mother gave a shout,
and children gathered about,
the large dinner bell,
that had many tales to tell.

DING DONG - DING DONG - DING DONG.
Farm hands would not take long,
to fill the food laden table,
coming from field and stable.

Helen E. Black

Young Wings

If mine were the soul of an artist, Lord, I'd paint a poem of fear.
Fear like that of a mother bird when young wings fan the air.
Wings well nourished by parents; but yet unknown, untried.
Guide and guard them in their flight; stay always at their side.
For now is placed in crucible a task by love enfused.
Hands I once held; young feet did tend; their own strength now must use.
Gone is the pain of aching back; suspense is now my norm.
Small are the cares that plague my mind, if young wings have good form.
Forgive my lack of faithfulness; neglect to trust your love.
Frail is the heart of a mother bird when young wings flutter above.
Extend your arm of protection, should they falter in their flight.
Guard from each snare and destructive force.
Keep young wings in you sight!

Erma C. Statler

149

Twelve Months

January is a month for New Beginnings
February is the month for valentines and lovers
March is a wild wind blowing.
April is for April fools
May is for bare feet running free
June is for love in bloom
July is a big fire cracker
August is school doors opening for eager young faces.
September is when brown leaves fall
October is full of yellow pumpkins and little goblins.
November is the time to eat turkey and give thanks.
December is the time to celebrate Christmas and the birth of Christ.

Carol L. Wallis

Never Wait For Me

When you're feeling sad and lonely,
Feeling like you can't go on,
Just call my name, and there I am.
Anytime, anywhere, I will always be there.
Just name the task you ask of me,
Turn around, and there I'll be.
So you never have to wait for me.

Whatever it is that you need me for,
You know that my heart is an open door.
No questions about who, what or when?
Just call my name, and there I am.
Think of me, and there I'll be.
So you never have to wait for me.

If love from me will set you free,
My heart is open take all your need.
Just remember when you need a friend
Call on me and there I am.
Think of me, and there I'll be.
So you never have to wait for me.

Ayanna N. Burt

Hell's Angel

Walking during the day
Feeling merry and gay
Upon me I felt eyes
a pair I would soon despise
They follow me round
In the air and on the ground
Whenever I turned around
I saw nothing, in the air nor on the ground
So, I continued on my way
Feeling puzzled of this queer day
I continued to where I work
At the door I felt a sudden jerk
I fell to the ground, while turning around
Nothing on the ground, but hovering above
Like a dove
An angel
No ordinary angel
A devilish smile spread cross it face
Its task, to take me to a different place

Justin Till

Feelings

The feelings I feel inside are feelings that are difficult to explain;
feelings of happiness, sorrow, and solitude, all at once. These
feelings I feel always; a feeling of living and not living, a feeling
I have risked and not risked, a feeling of completeness and
incompleteness. These feeling are feelings of life. Feelings I am
not sure about, yet it is many feelings I have within. So for now
I'll continue to learn and grow and continue to feel.

Jeanne Jarecke

My Little Buddy

He was a friend, for whom I cared a lot about, and though my
mind was filled with a certain doubt of how long he would last, I
knew he would pass but I really didn't care. I still took him in,
and helped him cheat death, postponing the day he'd take his last
breath, and through the many years, I know he lived longer here
than he would have anywhere else

Go out and play, and live another day 'cause you deserve that
much, come in and stay, while death's held at bay 'cause you're
my little buddy

The day did come, albeit too soon for me, but at least now I
know that he's free. I did all I know I could, as much as anyone
else would, but no better did he become. Friends come and go,
but he's forever with me and the reason is because he's in my
backyard you see, he might have been only a cat, but to me he
was much more than that and that cannot be hard to believe

Go out and play, and live another day, 'cause you deserve that
much, come in and stay, while death's held at bay 'cause you're
my little buddy...
...Spuddy...

Jason Schabert

Crystal Eyes

Walking in the dark, the wind is blowing strong,
filling my heart with sorrow because I found myself alone.
Emptiness I felt when I realize that you were gone,
everything that we had disappeared with a sigh...

Sorrow remains within my heart but I have to let you go,
where there's no pain, no darkness, where there's just happiness
and love. There is someone standing in front of me, someone
that is bringing light to my soul, I can feel his peace,
I can feel his love.

There is something different about him, something that I have
never seen before. His eyes are like crystal water, pure in love
making me see through him that you are in paradise waiting for me,
to share that happiness that those crystal eyes are showing to me.
The day will come, that will be together again, and will look at
each other, through the crystal eyes again.

Gisela Movilla Serrano

"Sailor"

Seaward I've been calling
Finding nothing there but time.
The sailor knows his season
The loser knows his crime.
Say love is what we're after
The ocean feels the pain
Of all the lost and lonely shipwrecks
Beached along the main.
There is something in this silence
That screams above the waves.
The answer turns a question
The ocean claims a slave.

Jeanne O'Neill

Volcano Syndrome

To whose embrace shall I flee
From these besieging panics?
They force their flow on up my spine
Into my neck...and further
To the center of my brain and there they stop.
There is no place else for them to go
But through my skull volcano.
They will erupt; they will flow forth.
And in the serenity of the aftermath
Will be one there, arms outstretched.

Jim Hogan

A Leader Of Men

Come follow me the Lord did say,
  Fishers of men I'll make you today.
I'll lead you to heaven and a new way of life,
  God's love I will teach you for this world's strife.
My purpose on earth for all men to see,
  Is to die for men's sins on the cursed tree.
Follow me, he said with concerned look on his face,
  There are many to save and this is a race.
Disciples are few to share their faith,
  So I will be with you all over the place.
A leader of men must first follow me,
  Your commitment for sinners I must see.
Concern in your heart to share God's love
  Will overcome all odds with help from above.
So loud and so clear his voice I can hear:
  Follow-me, follow-me, the end is so near.

Byron A. Reinheimer

Retreat

Running in fear, turmoil and anger.
Fists of rage clinch at air;
Despair entombs every thought.

I confront my demon, my love of past;
I stare the truth with truth untold.
Behold the future my feathered friend.

This is the past, the present and the future;
A cornucopia of emotionally-
A bountiful feast for the deprived.

I lash out at my beast of conflict.
I turn to face my demons of sleep.
Back! Retreat... and rebuttal is my sole comfort the evening.
Tomorrow my friend, you shall fly.
Your cage is unlatched-
and I will dwell in the mist of darkness.

Jayson W. Richardson

"A.I.D.S."

Lightning strikes my world above
flames of fire roar with love.
The night's consumed by an evil face
While his crimson guards dance with grace.
And all around me is falling down.
The demons below me sulk and frown
liken to buzzards as they stare and wait,
for many tonight have found their fate.
As I sit back and watch this place,
I laugh aloud to all within this race.
For no one learns,
and no one can see
Everyone thinks,
"It won't happen to me"

Jason M. Perry

Boo-eka Boo-eka

Bring forth the flowers now, lay down another wreath,
For another "A" student with golden capped teeth.
Light another candle then sing another song
He was a good boy and never done no wrong.
Next year he'd be headin' right for pre-med school
Everybody loved him for he was oh so very cool.
He once helped an old lady to get across the street.
He was gentle and kindly and charming and sweet,
But now he lies waxen ice-cold and dead
In a puddle of his own blood, with a hole in his head
Boo-eka! Boo-eka! Bang! Bang! Bang!
It's alleged he got shot by a rival gang.

John A. Scarlett

'The Future Of The World'

The world is a petal of a black rose
Floating in the air
Landing nowhere
Black, lonely, no others around.
Is it bound to stop?
Only time beholds the answer.
Tick-tock, tick-tock, tick-stopped?
Yes.
Yet why?
People on the world made the petal die of cancer
No one cared to share their answers
I will not shed a tear for all those that died.
Why?
Cause before their own eyes they all waved goodbye.
The world was a petal of a red rose!

Jill Sluka

The Land Of Perfection

The grasses grow wildly across the hills.
Flowers are scattered from desert to plain.
The sun beams down from the sky above
And warms the world's terrain.

A child wanders slowly, dreamily,
As she gazes upon the land.
She stoops to pick a flower or two,
To add to the bouquet in her hand.

A graceful, ebony unicorn
Lopes lazily by,
And rears upon its legs
With its horn grazing the sky.

The small child stops
And looks behind her back.
She's shocked to see the Death
To the land beneath her tracks.

You see, when you enter the Land of Perfection,
Things aren't perfect for long.
For we humans have a habit
Of destroying things until the beauty is gone.

Dianne Hartness

Ann Frank

Who do we have from world war II to thank
For commemorating and remembering the Jew, but Ann Frank?
It was she who was a prodigy and wrote a diary in annex
During the second world war, on life and pain, an excellent
Humanitarian book, the diary of a young girl's secret life
In a building in Amsterdam, nothing but a scrap and knife,
In these years this genius captured love and world war's pain,
Which ended in her people's death as well as hers, never again.
She was the one, almost survived, last minute death in camp,
Just before the allies came, and her father found her book, am
I to say, said this poet, how it was left? On the entrance floor,
Where the book case was, guarding what is now the tour cite door.
A pretty three story Dutch building, right by the old "Amstell",
Torn of the decent Dutch, that muggy European Amsterdam;
A short, fifteen year life, and yet Ann Frank was a great person,
For she was a figure of that century, even when history worsened.

Anatole Kantor

151

Fire—

Call me Fire.
For deep within, flames jump
And grow higher with each passing minute.
You see a quiet little mouse
Always hiding in her hole for fear
That a cat will pounce.
But I am so much more.
I rage.
I am slowly going out of control.
You see a meek little princess,
Always doing Mother and Father's will for fear
That she will not inherit the kingdom.
But I am so much more.
Can't you hear my soul
Crackling, as it finds all and destroys all?
Can't you see in my eyes
The heat so intense that it could easily consume Hell?
What IS it you see?
I am so much more.
Call me Fire.

Gina Rose

Immortality

I've no question in the questioning of immortality
For God created irreplaceable, indestructible me!
And I scorn the fear of perishing from paltry rot and rust
For there is no greater peril than that dust returns to dust.
I may glory in the splendor of my God's forgiving eyes
Or writhe in burning brimstone eons far from paradise,
But in smoke or fume or vapor or in moldering grave I be,
He can't undo His handwork; I am me, eternally!
No force can end the what I am! There'll always be a door!
For the good God thought to make me, and I am, forever more!

Jean Fitzgerald

I Know God Is Real

I know God is real when I think to pray
For He takes all my troubles and cares away
And if it be His will that all my troubles remain
He will give me grace to bear all the pain

Then when I look up to Him, He will send down His love
In the laughter of a child or the song of a bird,
A gentle breeze blowing, a new fallen snow or a much needed rain
Or the sun's rays a-shinin' through my window pane

And this I know for it's how I feel
God is always near and I know that he's real

Betty R. Shropshire

Untitled

Not a poet, you say? You are a poem, then,
for I sense the arrangement and rhythm in you.
Tenderness versed with beguilement, words in a
style all yours, language filled with the fire in your soul.

Imagination, adventure and passion create a rhyme
metered uniquely in the workings of your life.
Verses touching the past and present of me,
startling me, holding me, becoming…
A poem entitled "You", and written especially for me.

Barbara A. Morissette

Troubled Garden

Misery, sadness, my heart shadowed by gloom.
For in my life's garden the rose does not bloom.
The suns rays have been shaded by the growth of the weeds.
Light that is so desperately needed for my rose to succeed.
I must go to the mirror and see the image I reflect.
I must go to my childhood and gather up dreams I chose to neglect.
So much time to be made up and memories to sort through.
There will be pain I'll remember, but some happy times too.
I must plant my feet firmly, back straight, head strong.
My heart will lead this journey and my soul will sing the song.
Patience I've been blessed with. Oh Lord please bless me with the will.
My tools have been provided and sharpened with such skill.
With my mind used as a sickle, my anger as a knife.
Each weed will be discarded as a trouble in my life.
Shine down, shine down sweet sunlight, let me feel the
    warmth of your rays on me.
My petals will soon open, my scent will soon fly free.
Watch me blossom, bring life beauty and be all that a rose must be.

Johnna J. Griffin

"No More To Give"

I have no more to give anyone in this world today;
For I've given to others all my life and they have thrown it all away,
No matter if it was in my family or trying to please a boss at work;
Because all these people did from me never gave but only took.

I trudged along thru all my life but all I got was defeat;
As I reached my Golden Years, I feel my work is incomplete,
Now that I look back there isn't any more energy to flow;
While my tomorrow's are here of these times I do not know.

For my wishes have not been fulfilled only blown away in the wind;
I look to the sky and ask the Lord how much have I sinned,
Tears of pain and silent fears are those I never do reveal;
So many opens wounds I do carry and wonder will they ever heal.

Nothing but rain has fallen like tears in my soul;
As the seasons do change my heart remains dull;
Those are my foot prints seen on the lonely shore;
Today brings nothing but sorrow and there's memories no more.

No more to give or hope is all I do feel;
In my face no breath of my being therefore does yield;
Where there use to be an emotion of share is no more brightness; at
one time there was heart of caring and now is only black of darkness.

Barbara Quatroche

Trains

I used to ride the trains at night
    for many lonely hours
        it did not matter where I went
            as long as I did not stop
                I went everywhere and nowhere
                    it really made no difference
                        to me the night was made to ride
                            to think to shed a tear and always
                                always wonder.

Jaime Mercado

Daybreaks

And I fall to the muddied ground in praise.
Glorious, the sun beams forth her blessings
As I awaken to my morning benediction.
I wipe the dew from my eyes to see the sky
Roll eternally over the hallowed land.
My hands dig deep into the dampened earth
To reach her eminent, fertile core.
From the temple of her womb I seek delivery,
But the dark, moist earth chills my breath,
So, I return my sighs to heaven.
They rise to cherish the holy creator,
And I ascend to capture the blessed day.

Julie Jaarsma

My Dream

I dreamt the world came to a stop.
For once everyone forgot to shop.
They stood still just gazing around
Wondering what is that sound?

It is the sound of the breeze which feels so nice.
I did not have to think twice.
Oh! my it is a miracle,
Everyone's holding hands and making a circle.

Are my eyes deceiving me?
What's that I see?
Oh yea all the colors have come together,
Now the whole world will be better.

In the circle there was a dark spot,
Oh! no I just heard a gun shot,
But alas I started to smile
All the guns where on the ground in a pile

Please, please let this dream be complete,
Get all the drugs and guns off the street.
So everyone can walk without fear.
And show one another how much we care.

Albertine Self

All Alone

Crying in the dark
for someone to care.
Searching by day
for someone to share.
Walking alone
on wave soaked shoals.
Chastising myself
for long-lost goals.
Sitting on a bench
watching the stars in the sky.
Looking at two lovers,
hand in hand, walking by.
Sitting in my room,
by myself, with a drink.
Once again alone with nothing to do but think.
Wishing to myself, it wasn't this way.
Praying it'll all be better some day.
Hoping against hope
I'll someday be shown;
I don't need to cry, I'm not alone.

Anthony V. Amero

For Daddy

Daddy, I'm sorry for the things I said,
For the confusion and anger inside my head,
It's been hard for me to admit
That sometimes I lose and sometimes I quit,
It's not your fault that I've made mistakes,
Taken these gambles without knowing the stakes,
You gave me everything I could dream of,
Yet I know it seems I rejected your love,
I got confused and let myself hate
But please tell me that it's not too late,
Please, let's try to make amends,
I won't break, I'm learning to bend,
I'll try so hard to make you proud of me,
Someone you'll be proud for the whole world to see,
And I'll be just as proud of you, Dad,
We'll never again be angry or sad,
Though the times I've said it are precious and few,
I want you to know, Daddy, I love you.

Janine Rupley

Life Goes On

Civilization is both river and bank;
For this image we have Durant to thank.

There is the river-current of the flow
With wars and violence on the go
Stirring deeper areas of destruction
Surfacing greater levels of frustration
Telling us that all is bad,
And we have full reason to be sad
Devoid of hope without a future.
All is lost!

But on the bank there's a new family exhibiting love
Building a home, repairing the damage,
Instructing the young with a vision from above.
Theirs is a future possessed of a hope,
Rebuilding the wall, reshaping the slope,
Protecting the children, securing the good,
Walking the road as the people of God.

I'll take my stand
With them on the land.

Earl W. Johnston

Homeless Children

I feel terrible
for those children who have no home,
for they have nowhere to go,
They always have to roam.

Some have no parents,
Some have no food,
Some are dying,
Some are getting wounds.

Some wish every night,
Wish they had a home,
for those who have no parents,
are all alone.

The homeless children are still out there,
Waiting for love,
Waiting for a happy life,
Waiting for the God to take them above.

Heather Ray

We Are Not Prisoners

We are not prisoners,
For we are free to roam the earth.

We are not prisoners,
For we are given the means and knowledge
To escape any trap.

We are not prisoners,
If we are cripple or cannot see,

For we can walk or run in are minds,
And we can see with in are hearts.

We are not prisoners,
Because we do not just have to "Accept".

We can be free to express ourselves.
We might be in a world that we feel trap,
And unable to escape its grasps, but if
we look with in,
We will truly see we are not prisoners,
But totally unique,
And that we are,.... "We Are Free".

Angela Minter

Holocaust

Darkness, the reality which is grasped tightly in the hands of time
For what mortal man could understand the full extent of this pain, this darkness
With ignorance bred hate: That source of power
Through power man waved thy bloody standard over scores of conquered sheep
Souls lost to mortality, forbidden to reveal their account
I clench my first and close my eyes tightly, trying to explore that reason which is unknown to me
Yet I fail to understand the complexity of complacency
Vivid, horrific images forever etched into my consciousness, but reasons untold

Bill Meeks

Dimes

Dimes I used to carry, no more do I.
For what will a dime buy?
Many years ago, a coke I could buy,
Just a dime.
Then the nickel candy bar,
Went to a dime.
Oh yes! The pay toilet with so many tots in tow,
Under the door they did go.
The only times, I ever saved a dime.
We come to the phone,
Oh the calls I did make, for a dime.
So now the dimes I use to spend,
Have gone the way many things have.
Down the drain.
No more to be.
Times and dimes,
Have met you see.

Irene J. Burgener

I Must Give Praise!

I must give praise...because you were almost gone;
   for whom without, my heart would have no song.
I must give praise...for sweet hazel eyes;
   that finally started to look into mine, to my surprise.
I must give praise...for a delightful soft laugh;
   that makes my heart jump, like a newly born calf.
I must give praise...for "Mom-Mom", one of three words;
   that is without a doubt, the sweetness my ears have ever heard.
I must give praise...for a tender little hand;
   that reaches out for me, to pick you up on command.
I must give praise...for frail little feet;
   that try so hard to walk, when they would rather take a seat.
I must give praise...precious daughter of mine;
   because you were given to me, my very own little sunshine.

Cheryl W. Church

Child's Prayer To Her Daddy

Dear Daddy, I pray you'll come back to me
   For you see I miss you so
You used to come to my little crib
   And, I saw how you glowed

You left me when I was so small
   That I can't realize it all.
And when I meekly call your name
   You never come to me at all

There is a blank spot in my heart
   For I am still very small
My prayer is Daddy, you'll come back, and see
   How proud I can make you of me.

Dorothy Spicer Cole

Take Time

Take time to smell the roses along life's narrow path.
For you see the smell may not last.

Take time to watch the sun set and rise.
For that's what makes the beautiful skies.

Take time to listen to the birds in the trees.
For they are telling you to feel the breeze.

Take time to listen to the rain falling on the roof.
For this will make you appreciate your youth.

Take time to hug your child today.
So they too, will have a wonderful day.

Take time to tell someone you love them.
For tomorrow you may not have them.

Take time to enjoy life
For God will make our problems all right.

Take time to say thank you for what you've got.
For as it is, you have a lot.

Now you have walked down life's narrow path and you have
Done all that's asked. You will see that taking time
Will conquer the mighty task.

Glenda Weekley

God's Lent Child

He was sent from heaven above
for you to care for and nurture
you were chosen as the lucky one
to provide for him a future.

God knew you were strong
and the qualities you hold
with inner strength you raised his child
how you were told.

He expected nothing less than
all that you have done
the compassion displayed have bonded you and his son.

God would want you to know
the child's choice was you
he was thankful for the parents he was given to.

Your world has been shattered now that he is gone
God is aware of your pain - he will help you move on.

The child was borrowed to you
only for a short while
let him reside in your heart.... God's lent child.

Denise Fackrell

Forget!

Forget the dude that met you in the hall
Forget the dude that prevented your fall
Forget the dude that took you to the movie
Forget the dude that's always acting groovy
Forget the dude that called you honey
Forget the dude that needs your money
Forget the dude that made you sob
Forget the dude that needs a job
Forget the dude that stands so tall
Forget the dude that forgot to call
Forget the dude that's always late
Forget the dude that was your mate
Forget the dude that said we were made for each other
Forget the dude that now has another

Jacqueline West

154

Rainbow And Sunsets

Granddaughter, the look of wonder in your eyes I can't
Forget when for the first time you saw
Your first rainbow and sunset.

After you gained knowledge of the laws of physics,
You now know how nature begets
The glorious rainbows and sunsets.

Even though nature has not revealed all her secrets,
We are blessed to behold the awe
Inspiring rainbows and sunsets.

Granddaughter, we have shared throughout the years
The joys of the golden experience of the rainbows
And shared the rich rewards of sunsets.

When you have a granddaughter of your own,
And I have gone to my permanent home,
Remember me when you see rainbows and sunsets.

Doralee Spurlin

Untitled

Oh, the many questions brought, when frail tears arrive;
Forthwith the many answers sought, of why life doth contrive,

So many trials, as would seek, the words of which Christ spake;
Before the day he turned his cheek and died for our sake.

Yet we know well your kindliness and all the love you carry;
And seek, such like your faithfulness, together while we tarry.

Thus, let us bid a good long life to thee, whom we admire;
For weathering such worldly strife, to seek God's great empire.

For as we hence through these end times, enduring life withal;
Awaiting the eternal chimes of our good masters call.

We shall, as thee, subdue the night, with faith as great as day,
That we, through thee should regain sight,
with Christ to lead the way.

Arthur M. Vale

Yesterday's Regret Of Life

I regret I didn't take the time to call an outstanding
friend that I wasn't some what kinder and left some
notes unpinned as I was so cranky and hasty on my way.
    Oh I wish I could change my thoughtless yesterdays
and I'll count the kind of deeds done today. I'll
listen to a trilling note and lift the one caught in my throat.
    My friend there's no such thing as yesterday
you were born to be winner there's no way that
you can lose you just hang in there and whistle when
you're bothered by the blues. When a best friend
disappoints you and you're crying deep inside you
Just somehow grin and bear it and your heartaches always hide.
    My life was empty meaningless I could not
even pray rejection heightened feeling of my lack
of self esteem I then prayed to my precious lord again
for giving me new life.

Diane Lynn Fredenburg Jones

Weeping Willow

Weeping Willow, why do you weep?
Has a child tugged at your branch to break and succeeded?
Has the soil from the earth been dry?
Do you need rain before you die?
Are you straining to catch the butterfly who is teasing you,
but do you always remain unmoved?
Has the snow froze you...does the wind blow you?
It seems, Weeping Willow, that every season you find a reason
    to cry.

Chanel McDonald

Hope

I play with children who are as tall as I, my parents and
friends laughing and singing, how happy they look. The
dark took over and louder they grew, the men fought and
fell all over, was my dad one of them too? I could smell a
sourness the next day, I remember the night darkness took
over, no one said nothing, so I stored it all away. My
father dies and my mother cries, it is not long before she
finds a new best friend. I am now a man, at such a young
age, for I feel I am the last one to care. I see her pain for I
feel mine grow deeper, I do not know if I am happy or sad,
this day she is gone. Her best friend is now my best friend,
this I have chosen on my own, for I do not need anyone. It
was not easy to let go of my companion, for it was all I
knew, I feared the idea, the loneliness, the need to grow. I
learned it was not healthy, to continue to hurt myself, I
could now see, feel and hear clearly. Things began to build
up, do I just store it away? Do I just let go? I have no
control over this! Can I manage without? Do I have the
answers? I have loosened the chains that harnessed my
pain, I cry, I smile, I laugh, I live, I have HOPE.

Joseph A. Lind

Fear

Fear of the forgotten - never big enough to conquer my fears
from a young age - never able to voice my fears
they were used against me - learned to be tough
you don't scare me - you can beat my body - but I'm not there
for one so small I - learned to separate - you can't reach me
so I stayed out of reach all my life
never learned to be a child - never faced my fears
fear holds me back - never asking for anything
disappointment is a way of life - chances I never took them
for fear of failure - not good enough - for success
confidence that might bring change - change this feels strange
old patterns fall back into place - my fear level grows
will I ever be able to live - without fear of failure
you learn to fear anything different than what you're use to
you feel stuck - but you know what - that feels safe
what's to fear - you have lived with that - that's comfortable
learning to let go of my fears is bringing change - to my life
new doors opening - taking chances - makes me feel - like I'm alive
it gives me the feeling of what - hope - I'm overcoming my fears
dream - goal's a future - nothing to fear but fear itself

Helen L. Golding

A Word To My Caterpillar

Oh pretty caterpillar
From afar you look to be
An ugly green worm
But I see your unique and intricate design
What's more, I understand
Your wonderful potential
From within yourself
You possess the power
To become something quite grand
Something entirely different
It is a metamorphosis
My little pet
Breaking through your cocoon
Will be the toughest challenge
Of your life
But to survive, you will need to allow
Yourself the courage to become vulnerable
When you are scared
And alone,
And different.

Christy McGuire

Life

Life is just what we make it
From dawn 'til setting of sun;
Each thing we do is good or bad
In life as this race we run.

If we choose to do the things that are right
We're tempted to do the wrong;
And as we battle with our soul
The winner is always the strong.

Some take the highroad to travel,
Some are satisfied with the low;
Still others are seeking rich rewards
As they journey to and fro.

We have a challenge each new day,
Without it life would be vain;
But with courage and determination
Our goals can be attained.

There are many that might have won this race
If a little harder they had striven;
If they'd thought more of others and not just self,
Of their time and talents given.

Edith Cox Turner

"Shadows"

Shadows cast into the night,
From days of years gone by.
A presence felt within the dark;
But, one you can't deny!
Familiar figures seem to move—-
For seconds, at a glance;
When every spectre of the night,
Must have a time to dance!
Some are bad, and some are good.
But, each assumes the right...
To haunt the halls, and knock on walls;
And come back every night!
If you should peep while others sleep,
Between oh... twelve, and two;
Don't scream in fear if something's there...
You may just scare it too!!!

Carl Wilkinson

Shadow

My sun has turned
From gold to grey
Through the course of passing days.

It used to shine
But now it's dull
Because my mind's so very full.

The rays don't shine
Like they once had.
It makes me very sad.

Because it was me
Who turned and ran on and on across the land.

Me, who ran from my mind,
From my sun, who was so kind.

My sun has become a shadow.
Into the darkness it disappears
So it won't reflect in my mirror.

It doesn't shine in my face or reflect in my eyes
For the tricks to my heart were just lies.

How did it come to this... I wonder.
I have drawn my sun under.

Becky Book

The Hope Of Tomorrow

A state of mind
From loss we grieve,
But grasp for some hope
Near future may bring.
Though we know ours
A fortunate life,
We shut out the cries
In refusal to hear,
As if they never were
And simply don't exist.
But, in our secret hearts we know
The starving are there.
Filled with the food to nourish the body,
They die from the lonely,
And die from the sorrow.
Yet forever we wait
For the hope of tomorrow.

Coralysa Murphy

"Capture The Flash"

Airports, seaports, distanced with many miles in between.
From one to another the traveler's time is consumed upon the journey,
Pausing, brief R and R within the havens, ready to travel again.
The oases are awaiting, the deserts vast, arid, consuming.
Carpe Diem!
Snapshots transcend the generations which follow,
Capturing the moments, in a flash, preserved for posterity.
The self-serving, inattentive, continue the oblivious wandering,
Seeking, not finding, the haven of the soul's desire,
Unfulfilled within, worse still, unconcerned to be, one to fulfill.
The journey continues, ports of call to savor.
Too soon the destination - the journey is all.
Rest stops are awaiting, forcing nothing but freedom
For the liberty of the living, to partake or pass by.
Give and receive, to give and receive. Capture the flash.

John Adams

The Only Thing Left

The only thing that has not been stripped
From the people of colour,
Is their colour.......

You have been tricked and duped
To believe something is wrong
With even that......

Your brain has been taken
Look how you think violence settles all
Your unity has been taken
look how you act one to another
Your love for self has been taken
Look how you carry yourself and "Gun"

Your language has been taken
Now you have a new one of old "Gangsta"
Your pride has been taken
You go the wrong way to regain it
Your roll models have been taken
You fashion yourself after who????
The only thing left
Is the skin "You" are in!!!

D'aria Fakankun

The Magic in Little Things

There is such magic in little things.
From thumbsize acorn the mighty oak springs.
In small winged fruit lurks a maple to be.
The tiny dark cone is an evergreen tree.
A seed that's as drab as dark cloudy sky
Will blossom so pure in the near bye-and-bye.
All wrapped up as small as the head of a pin
Is its fragrance and color and beauty locked in.
In raindrops and snowflakes so fragile and fair
Abides a grand waterfall roaring thunder in air.

Think of it, and marvel at the wonder of it all,
That the scheme of things is built upon such objects very small.

Eilleen Gardner Galer

'Who Are You?'

You came quite suddenly into my life
Full of love, laughter....
A wonderful image
Everything I need
and want
and hope to be.

Who are You?..Still there
Urging me to "cross the river"
Encouraging me to love again.

Who are You?..Awakening promise, desire
All things I do not fear
Yet, somewhere, somehow forgotten.

Who sent you?..to read my thoughts
View my soul...and trust my heart.

Will you bring me..lifelong happiness or
a passing fling...like a gentle, refreshing breeze.

I miss you already...Yet, you are still here.
I need you already...But, you are not there.
I love you, although we've never touched...
Who are you?...And why do I feel you so much?

Judith D. Ross

Lovebugs

On the Southern Gulf, in warm May winds,
Funny little creatures stick together again.
Pesky black dots just float in the air,
But a lovebug's not one bug, a lovebug's a pair.

They flail as they sail, are these insects obsessed?
The female hangs limply, the male does the rest.
She totters around backwards, she's not in this race.
The boy started his motor and he's set the pace.

He lands when he wants to, he's the contriver.
She's the propeller, a proverbial backseat driver.
You know when you watch them and he moves ahead,
He's not letting go, until one of them's dead!

She's so trusting of this paragon to guide her along.
Doesn't she realize, this boy hasn't a brain, he just has a dong?
He impresses his better half, she's too good for the fields.
So he sought out the best, my Mercedes windshield!

Deborah Willett Gravlee

After The Rain

The earth, mirrored in a lake of glass
gave the appearance for all to see,
Each tiny leaf, each blade of grass
scrubbed, polished immaculately.

The birds fluffed and preened their feathers,
While the nectared flowers tempted the bee.
The clouds, once dark had turned to cotton,
floating on a bright blue sea.

It's nature's way of washing
the dirt, the dust, the grime away.
It's only after the rain, the sun
reflects the rainbows beauty of the day

Gloria Mustill

"Tale Of The Desert Rat"

Desert Rat, oh, Desert Rat,
Getting old and getting fat
Dust in your hair, dust on your tongue,
You've been searching for gold since you were young.
finding no pleasure, seeking no gain,
The hot old sun done fried your brain!
The winds keep blowing the tumbleweeds around,
Rattlers crawl in your blanket while you sleep on the ground
My skin's dried up, my lips, they crack,
I'm heading out and I won't look back.
I'm going back East, I've got a plan,
I'm getting out while I still can.
So, Goodbye desert, goodbye sand,
Goodbye to you old rotten man!
Goodbye Tumbleweed...Joshua trees...
Goodbye old desert Rat...Goodbye

Gerri Jaramillo

My Three Sons

I have three sons, three lovely ones
Given to me by the hand of the Lord
Not to have or hold or own
But to guide and keep, to room and board.

They are not mine, but gifts of God
To be enjoyed, but not for naught
They must be fed and reared and taught
Even if it calls for the use of the rod.

They are not all pleasure and joy
Whoever said they love a boy
I guess I did but wonder why
Especially when they start to cry.

Or fight and quarrel and destroy
The things I've worked so hard on
I cannot treasure or enjoy
Moments like these, but I must prod on.

So I'll face this task the best I can
And do the things I must
And if one day I produce a man
It will be because in God I trust...

August G. Blumline

Puanani (Beautiful Flower)

Puanani flies on the wings of enchantment and hope;
Her smile is a paint brush on an old canvas,
washing it with new color and feeling.
Feeling so deep and color so warm.

The artist can't explain how it happened,
everyone hoping it will preserved.

Christine Rodgers

I Know That God Is Not A Man

I know that God is not a man,
God is supportive, tells me "I can".

God encourages me, lights my way.
God makes me smile, throughout each day.

I am floating high in the presence of God.
I don't have to dodge a 'wink' or a 'nod'.

In the presence of the Al-migh-ty,
I soar….I breathe…..I AM FREE….

I am not loved because of my brother or sister
Nor I am looked down upon because I'm not a mister.

Don't have a hissy, or even a fever,
I know that God is not a woman either!!!

Joyce Ingram

Drink From God's Own Blessing-Cup

I looked for beauty and I found
God's love jumped up and did rebound.
A mother duck and goslings nine
Ran up a hill, oh what a time!

The sweetness of that sunny day
Lives on, and sometimes likes to stay.
For often memories won't retire,
Its joy dwells in that great bonfire!

Precious memories, gathered here and there,
Can fill your cup with golden cheer.
For, like a child's bouquet to you,
Sweet memories never leave you blue!

So drink from God's own blessing-cup,
For when the heart is offered up
He'll pour great blessings there on you.
That's why it's wise, to him be true!

So may you ever with beauty see
The things God has prepared for thee.
So drink wisely from his blessing-cup,
His truth and love can lift you up!

Dorothy Koeller Wildt

Our Grandchildren

Grandchildren are our treasures
God's way of giving us more pleasures
To relive again our children's joys
To once again have fun buying toys
To cuddle and hug, little children once more.

It never seems to be a chore
We listen to them, watch them laugh and dance
And know it's God's way of giving us another chance

We can snuggle and kiss them, play, shop or
go to a show, then at last home they go

God gave us these angels to do our part
And everything we do is good for our heart

Geri Ebli

"Our Mother"

Our mother is like no other.
Her grace and beauty is like that of a dove,
she's always overflowing with kindness and love.
The last thirty years she has worked hard and long,
at raising six children to be responsible and strong.
All six of us children will proudly say,
that we are grateful to our mother today.
If it wasn't for our mother's strict rules,
we probably would have grown to act like fools.
So to our mother we want to say,
we love you Mom, for raising us the right way.

Brenda L. Hughs

"Let The Sun Shine In"

You think you've got me; got me down.
Got my chin strap on the ground.
Well I've got a few things to say.
A few things to do.
A few things to show you.
My Head's up high; eye on the Sky.

I can see and sense the presence of the
position essence of my Soul.

The day will come when I'll no longer have to run
To catch a fraction of the action, you have
left behind.

Just as a bamboo Shoot pops its tender head and
trunk up from the Soil.
And will toil to reach maturity; without
being plucked and devoured.

So…Shall…I!

Becky J. Bolden

Is This Real

Time stands still.
Greens and yellows paint the hill.
Visions seem so clear,
My vision is all I hold so dear.

Roses float in water so thick.
The petals feel so slick.
Lonely silence fills the air.
Come out? Do I dare?

Sun beams warm my face.
Dirt strung across my cheeks in a pattern of lace.
My eyes are red,
Tear stains carved in cheeks of lead.

Greed destroys all.
I will be luck to see the Fall.
Bombs that kill the kids so young,
And again Death's song is sung.

Only people dead
Stored in tombs they wed.
The land has left no touch.
Unfortunate is such.

Carol Ferguson

Silence

Can you hear the silence
growing in my room
shivering in my ears
does not calm my fears
wasted —— all those years

Can you hear the thunder
miles away from here
vibrating the smell
of the wind where I am at
Does it help you see —
— what has become of me?

Little children playing
the grasses are swaying
no time to catch the wind
my heart is melting, baying — I'm still here

If a blind man lives through darkness
an imbecile with age
a little boy with no tenderness
who will turn the page
not I —— I'm not here.

Jeanette Reese

Memories Of A Loved Man

A child is born a boy you see
Grows up to be sweet as can be
When a man he marries
Has children of his own
Tries to teach them right from wrong
As he grows old, his children do too
He has grandchildren and great grandchildren
Who loves him so true
His love and their love are always there
And can't you see how much they care?
When tragic news comes that he is ill
There is nothing they can do, it is GODS' will
When he leaves them the pain is so deep
They think of him with memories they will keep
He lived along life, but too short for me
He was eighty-nine, I am thirty-seven
Don't you agree?

Christine Armstrong

The True Awakening

Rude awakening, rude awakening - there goes another siren
Gun shot sounds, down goes the victim
Sons, brothers, husbands or daughters
The world follows the tragic events
In the court, the trial begins
Unanswered question begs for an answer
Does justice serve the deserver?
To a wife, a husband is lost...to a brother, a sister is lost
Lonely, chilled, weary hearts
Attention grabbers - criminals, dreams smashed
In the judiciary system, the trial begins
Souvenirs of the murder presented
Constant reminder of the life forever altered
Guilty or not guilty verdict
Survivors - the victims always losers
The gun trigger happy criminal always win, life jail
Justice always serves little consolation
The victim is victimized forever
The victim's - survivor's empty, lonely, hollow scared
hearts .... lingers forever ....

Juliana Opara

My Banty Hen

My Banty hen
Had six small chicks
They are so cute,
I wish they were my kin.

They eat the beetles abundant
And their mother feeds by their side
Giving them her share.
Their chirps redundant fill the air
Showing her they also care.

Their mother's loving call
Brings them back
When they're lost in the grass so tall

When day turns to night
Their mother's call brings them to her wings,
And their mother tells them:
Now rest in the dark and come out in the light.

Danny Harder

The Flea And Me

That impudent, irritating, illustrious flea
Had the gall and nerve to bite on me.
I graciously asked this tenacious flea,
"Why must you constantly nibble on me?"
He simply smiled and looked at me—
"I simply have to bite on thee
Because I am an average, active flea."
And that's the story of the Flea and Me.
He could never listen to my earnest plea—
To stop biting on poor little me.
God bless the flea—
But why he exists, I cannot see.
Yet he certainly has an affinity for me.

Donnie Morgan-Wiles

Tennis Anyone??

Chose the course - took all the lessons
Had to - it was a social obsession!
Picked a partner
Played in the doubles
That was the start of serious troubles!
Batted them high
Chased them down low
Always kept me on the go!
Ball is the key - -
Had an idea to watch the sky - .
To keep that ball in my eye!
Out like a comet comes the ball I've been spying
Suddenly I realize to myself I've been lying - -
Totally missed it - swinging hopelessly at air - -
Now to face my partner's glare - - -
Oh boy, his expression!!
Suddenly realized my true vocation - -
Watching serenely from the spectator's station!!

Annette Donofrio

Granny's Rocking Chair

Sitting now in the corner
Handed down and looked over
Left long on wear
Granny's rocking chair

I think back now and then
To the times we would spend
Just sitting rocking without a care
And oh the stories you would share

In that chair I sat on your lap
And we would travel back in time
Even though we just sat
To a little girl whose life was so different than mine

You told how you used to ride an old mule named urser
You told me he would bite anyone he wasn't used to
You told me of the farm and the other animals you had
And I could see on your face it made you a little sad

Now Granny time has taken you away
But I thank God for your memory
And when life gets a little tough for me to bare
I head for the corner to sit again in Granny's rockin chain

Ananda D. Morris

Desert Storm War

As you integrate your spiritual belief, hands in
hands together affixed; your goal was all the way
toward success, penetrates obstacle whatsoever
there be, oneness will ever prevail heretofore.

Braveness and sincerity to our country; defensive
from evil doing against... our beloved country
should ever incur, forcefully on your feet you'd
defended thy country we had behold and loved ever.

No matter what happens should anyone, inflict
our rights, peace and dignity, We rise and
shed our blood regardless if called upon to
instill democracy, to one and all, now and forever.

The challenge you have just encountered, thy children
at the fearful desert storm which you cared not life
nor death to face which brought to your Moloka'ians
role model the dignity and heroism for all of us here.

We thank thee for your safe return.. to our dear
beloved island and friends, mostly your loved
ones...your family, welcome, and may your health in
steadfast be tremendously happy, peacefully and healthy.

Irenio C. Vergara

The Artful Dodger

Politics and the artful dodger,
  happily mated to each other,
    as natural a combination
    and as dedicated a pair,
      as a baby and its mother.

Vote for me and I promise you.....
  whatever it takes to win,
    then he looks you
      right straight in the eye,
        with a wink and a silly grin.

The artful dodger is lovable,
  He's everybody's friend,
    but don't take it
      all that seriously,
        'cause it's only just pretend.

Long live the artful dodger,
  a true-blue sporting lad,
    so no need to explain
      and no need to complain,
        when you find out you've been had!

Fritz Hirschfeld

Dandelion

Dandelion, my first and fondest flowers
Happy friends of childhood hours...
Free and abundant as stars you surrounded me
Like tiny suns come down to sparkle
In the dewy green lawn..

Warm afternoons and going home
With a fist full of gold...
Why is it whispered you are a weed
Why does your value need
Diminish with time: in morning
The talk of the town. By evening
mowed down?

They've turned my golden crowns to hay;
Now dandelions are far away...
One turns to dahlias and marigolds
Eventually...and what is lost
But a little fist of gold

Dianne Noreault

No Longer Pain

Emptiness, loneliness, and feelings unexplained
Hatred, betrayal, and undescribable pain
You left us without warning, a friend lost in the night
A pain so unbearable you've given up the fight

Sorrow like a cancer, and there is no cure
Leaving a pain no human should ever try to endure
A plea was made in silence, you left us unaware
Of the hardships you were facing, things you could no longer bear

"God please let it rain to hide my falling tears
God please let it thunder to mask my sudden fears
God please let me die to stop this terrible pain
Please God, I beg you, let it rain

God please calm my beating heart to stop the hurt inside
God please take the evil tongue of all of those who lied
God please let them know that I won't hurt again
Please God let them know this time I will win"

Your plea has now been answered, your quest for peace was won
No pain could ever hurt you now, you never have to run
No one can be sure if we'll ever meet again
But goodbye is forever, so I say farewell my friend

Jennifer Sherman

Have You

Have you awakened to a new day and taken for granted it was to be?
Have you experienced moments when everyone was too busy to
listen to you when you needed a friend? Have you had life
storms, thought it was too much to bear? Have you gone for a
walk, met someone in need of a listener? Have you acknowl-
edged after leaving, there was a smile, hope on their face. Have
you called a friend and they were having a bad day? Have you
belief in God, to bless you with the words? Have you felt
blessed, saying you always make me feel better? Have you
stopped, acknowledged God is in control? Have you started your
day with prayer? Have you noticed the difference it makes?
Have you said thank you Jesus?

Addy Cox

Dreams Of Me

He comes like a dream
He comes when I am alone just like dreams
He comes like the night still and dark
He comes to comfort and bring sensuality
He comes in like April winds.
But, like dreams he leaves,
To allow another to come in its place.
but, the dream of having him and
him being my dream, only comes once.
For the way he holds me and kisses,
my lips, all I can say is
Make all my but lonely dreams come true.
For the ones of love come when
I am holding you in my arms.
And, If I allow my imagination to
run but for one more time;
I hope his dreams are the same
and equal to mine.
Not of any other but the dream of me.

Fanta Fortune

He

He came to this earth to spread peace and joy.
He entered this world as regular baby boy,
He was born in a stable amongst animals and the stars.
He didn't party and go into bars.
He was kind, loving and forgiving.
He was always trying to help the living.
He healed the sick, restored sight to the blind.
He was never too far behind, when danger was near.
For in him there was no fear.
He was ridiculed, stoned, and hung upon a cross,
until his life was a total loss
This man died for you and I, that's why we should
give thanks when we look toward the sky.
Oh how can people be so mean and live a life yet so clean.
This man was pure and yet untouched
That is why he was loved so much.
You see this is one thing we can never be.
He died for our sins so this world could
be pain free.

Judith Noegel-Hingson

Loving Memories

Somewhere out there is a special Dad.
He gives you a smile, even if he's sad.
His touch is always gentle, his love overwhelmingly strong.
Thru all his strength, you feel nothing can ever go wrong.

Look in his eyes and see a reflection
of love and adoration.... known to others as simply, affection.
Eyes the color of blue skies. Eyes silver glittered,
like sun laden waters, eyes never embittered.

I remember the years gone by
and dream of a fairy land.
Only one thing needed dad.......
Just lead me by your hand.

I always remember this
so you're not very far
you're always in my heart.......

you're my own special star.

The love I gave....
you eagerly took....
Dad...I never told you this,
But....."You're the biggest crook"!

Dottie Macik Race

Olivia

He visits her grave with a tear in his eye
He knows the pain will pass as the days go by
He mourns for the loved one he has lost
He ask himself why it happened to her
He loved her a lot
He wiped a tear from his cheek, not
Knowing what to think
Their love was strong like a white
dove's song
As he sat in front of the grave his
head bowed in a silent prayer
All he could do was ask why
He laid a red rose upon the ground
And the words he spoke were soft but strong.
"I love you Olivia. Forever and ever."
He walked off his head bowed wondering
what the near future will bring
Will he find another love like Olivia?
  "Rest in Peace My Love!"

Christie Laird

Who Is My Neighbor

Who is my neighbor?
He lives close to the rain forests; he lives here-next door to me;
He also lives near the great Pyramids and on the other side of the Sea.
That he's my neighbor is a fact-wherever on the Map I place it-
For it is a Law-not made by man-and no one can erase it.

Who is my neighbor?
He's Gentile; Islamic; Indian; Catholic; Protestant; and Jewish;
He's the stranger; the familiar one; my oldest friend, and my newest.
Jesus said I'm to love my neighbor just as I love myself.
Meaning: do not set him aside, up on some lonely shelf,

Just because he's new and different from you in his ways.
You will be the peculiar one, should you leave him there in a haze.
Be a good Samaritan-help make his future bright;
You'll elevate your own laurels to a greater height.

Who is my neighbor?
He is the aged pauper; he's the celebrated young prince;
He's the doctor, the farmer, the prisoner behind a tall fence.
He's any man; any woman; the little Babes, at birth;
It's incredible! But my neighbor is every Human Being on earth!

Florrie J. Forbes

natureboy

you will never have to cry round natureboy
he loves your laugh
loathes your larceny of life
his timid girl
in sundress and sandals
like wool socks and birkenstocks
free lust
argued with
free love
and imprisoned the two to a field of confusion
i'll admit
i helped them escape
paving their path with granola and gratitude
leaving a trail of ashes
of incense and innocence
happy the boy
happy the girl
natureboy
with his
naturegirl

Georgette Moger

The Wonder Of It All

God in his infinite wisdom made all things, great and small.
He made the tiny humming bird and the pine trees so tall.
Then he took a babbling brook, and made waterfall.
He made the little brown sparrow to sing the whole day through,
and miracle of miracles, he made me and you.

Isn't it a marvel, God made the butterfly?
And took a bit of color to splash across the sky?
He made the lion ferocious, and the gentle baby lamb.
He made the owl precocious, and the battering ram.

My finite mind is burdened with the wonder of it all.
Have you heard a whippoorwill answer its mate's call?
When I stop to think about...How great the Lord must be,
He created all this beauty for all men to see

Florence Lang

A Male Child Was Born

A male child was born to a mother still a child.
He needs love and nurturing and she still needs the same.
In the county hospital where he was born, he was secure, warm
dry and fed. But his stay was short.
His home is a place called a project
A mattress he shares is his bed.
No grass, trees or flowers grow here
Just barren land, peeling paint, smelly hallways, plumbing that leaks
No father figure lives here
His very existence depends on welfare.
There is fear for this male child
He's dragged along on his mother's dates
He's hungary soiled and cold.
Will he grow up where drugs and alcohol are prevalent?
Where gun shots are heard in the night?
Will he be strong and stand up for what is right?
We pray that this male child will have a thirst for knowledge
He will grow and become a man.
When his life is over, he will be sorely missed. We will mourn
In spite of why or where he was born.

Dorothy Paul

Mother Nature

A poet captures the beauty of a love's first, long embrace.
He pens it down on paper, for others' minds to trace.

An artist reaps the beauty from a crimson, golden Autumn,
Splashing it on canvas, as his artist's eyes have caught them.

But how we borrow things from nature, yet we seldom will repay.
They're much more than a souvenir, to use for just a day.

Believing we can tame her strength, and put her to our own use,
Sometimes Mother Nature's halter, can be mankind's hanging noose.

How gently her breezes cradle us, but how quickly the cradle's tossed.
There's fire in her eyes at dawn, from tears at sunset lost.

So don't twist her arms of water, or block her breath of wind.
Don't steal the warmth that's in her heart, against her, we'll
  have sinned.

The soil from her bed of fields, is where we'll end some day.
Don't mess that bed that you have made, for that's where you
  shall lay.

Gary W. Seipel

The Pastor's Sermon

The pastor was balding but a jovial man,
He preached of a God who could heal the land;
His wife had passed on earlier, death claimed her wonderful life,
She has gone to a place where there are no troubles or strife;
In his many years preaching he has seen many of his congregation
pass away,
Some are new faces of those sitting out in the crowd today;
He tells of one person's sacrifice because of His love
and how there is no compare,
Many years ago this young man did this because of His
love for us and His care;
Centuries now have come and gone and yet almost everyone
remembers His precious name,
For the love He has shown His people then, even today remains
the same;
There is one who would have you not to believe this as the
preacher cries aloud,
But his congregation has seen the love of the man he
preaches about in his face and how it makes him so humble
and yet so proud!!!

Garland L. Luther

Was He Ever Really There?

When the tips of the pines touch the stars in July.
He runs through the woods with joy in his eyes.
His long black mane whipping in the wind, he has found freedom again.
His long black tail trailing behind, I see him appear and disappear in
my mind.
I feel the cold of the midnight air and I wonder was he ever
really there?

Geraldine Jessup

He's Hurting Me

I'm not aloud to look around, my boyfriend threw me on the ground.
He said that I'm a worthless dog, and no one will find us in the fog.
He tied me up to a tree, then he started hitting me.
I'm getting dizzy, it's getting black, I see the light but I turn back.
I open my eyes to a very weird place, I see the frown on his awful face.
It's getting cold, I have no clothes, I feel his fists, his painful blows.
The pain gets worse each time he hits, but I am there when he
    throws his fits.
I close my eyes, and turn my head, now his fists feel like lead.
He wants to hit, he wants to fight, and now I pray to see that light.
I want it over, I want it done, and when it is I'll get a gun.
I'll hurt him like he's hurting me, and when I'm done I'll find a tree.
I'll tie some rope from way up high, and in that tree we both will die.

Alexa Mitchell

"What Is Fear"

The son asked his father, "What is Fear?"
He sat there and pondered with a look unclear.
Finally he answered to his young child
With an expression that showed he was clearly beguiled,
"The answer, my son, is not a thing I can name,
For everyone fears, but nothing the same.
Some fear the heights, and some fear the dark,
While others may jump at the sound of a bark."
The child then asked, "Father, what do you fear?"
The man sat uneasy and drew his son near.
"Son, the things that worry me and the things that I doubt,
Are not things a mere child need worry about.
Don't be misled, You're not to be blind,
For you are still young, and fear you shall find.
Your youth may be fleeting, and your innocence may grow dull,
But your happiness and eagerness I don't wish to lull.
You'll have time to grow up, and plenty to fret,
Please hold onto your youth, it's early yet.
Go on to bed now, it's getting late,
I'll read you a story, if you want to wait."

Gideon Steinberg

Longing

The dog and I were out in the backyard last evening
he searching eagerly following the scent
parading round the fence
lusting for whatever moved.

I gaze west toward where you are
through the web of bare branches against a somber sky
reaching towards you not knowing when I can touch you
whispering to the clouds not knowing when I can talk to you
listening to the wind not knowing when I can hear you.

I hunch up against the pitiful cold air
and watch the dog
without longing
make the most of the moment
and wish I could extinguish my memory
follow the scents
chase after the birds
challenge the squirrels
play the dog's game
without thought
of what was or will be.

James Zucchetto

162

Ignorant Surrender

Like a snake he slithers silently into my soul
He slides through the cracks of my mind
Like a boa through a maze of rocks
Swiftly seeping into my heart
Able to retreat in a single second —
He waits for
A sense of movement.
Stealthily, he waits for the ignorant surrender of his prey
Until he swallows me whole —
Mind and soul-too slow-
Finish, FINISH, I cry, but alas,
The process won't flow
As well as the venom which so sharply infected my thoughts.
As he comes to an abrupt hovering,
Which won't land or leave,
The snake is able to engulf me whole —
Oh, so slow

Jaime Marinaccio

What He Did

My mother works all day,
He takes "care" of me while she is away;
He hits me for anything I do,
It really hurts a lot too.

I got this bruise on my arm, because I ran away,
From his curses and threats of a lot of pain;
I got this black eye, because I told a lie,
He told my mom it was an accident,
That made me cry.

What he does she does not see,
If I try to tell her;
She just seems to ignore me.

One day he went too far,
and he gave me a frightful scar.
I screamed and yelled as loud as I could,
A neighbor heard and called for help,
As I hoped someone would.

Now I am alive and well and at my mother's side,
This man, he went to jail and now I stand with pride.
However some times I feel real sad, because that man was my Dad.

Joy Brown

Christopher Columbus Rap

Christopher Columbus was a curious man, a curious man was he.
He wanted to find a new way to the East, and so he set out to sea.

In the Nina, the Pinta, and Santa Maria, given by the Spanish queen.
They had water and food and lots of men. The bravest you've
 ever seen!

They sailed for hours and days and weeks. Out on the open sea.
"We'll never get there." The sailors cried. "It'll take an eternity!"

The water got rough, the winds were strong, and tossed the ships about.
"We're tired and hungry and we wanta turn back!" you could
 hear the sailors shout.

Then finally one day, the sea was calm, and the lookout shouted, "Land!"
"I can see birds and trees and places that're covered with a lot of sand."

Columbus was happy he's found his land, his land of treasure and spice
The people on the island welcomed them, and treated them all
 quite nice.

Columbus named the people Indians, and the land San Salvador.
And he thought he'd found a brand new route, and the land he
 was looking for.

We thank Mr. Columbus for taking that trip back in 1942.
Cause if he hadn't found this brand new world, I wouldn't be here.
 Would you?

Emma Jo Tomlinson

Spanky

Spanky is one dog we'll never forget
He was more to us than just a pet
A loving little friend - loyal and true
Who cheered us up when we were blue!

He was our pal for all these years
He brightened our days - calmed our fears
Always at the door to greet you
More than halfway he'd meet you!

A sweet "Little Guy" who was so dear
Hard to believe he's no longer here.
But we remember the good times we had
And knowing that — we won't be sad
Spanky - our dog - our friend - we loved you so!

Charles R. Murray

"His Song"

I heard the other day, this bird about to sing,
He was very small, somewhat ugly, missing part of his wing,
Still - he possessed the will of singing out, his beautiful and sweet
 song,
Oh, his tone was high, sometimes short, then very very long,
I marveled at the way he sang, perched so high up in the tree,
Not a care in the world, not one bit, reminded me - of me,
His head turned left, then turned right, singing well into the night,
Then, he saw her, high up above, slowly gliding in her flight,
She was a beauty, bright in color, hearing his mating call,
His heart pumped fast, as he sang louder, my-he felt so tall,
Then, together, off they flew, the two of them, till I could not see,
If only I could sing I thought, then lonely - I would not be,

Anthony W. Pierce Jr.

Winker Tinker

When Winker Tinker goes to town,
he wears his hat upside down.

He paints his face all white with red,
puts a pointed ear on each side of his head.

He wears baggy pants and big floppy shoes,
a tie around his neck in red, yellow and blue.

He then gets his dog whose name is Rex,
who can do many tricks and walk on his hind legs.

Now he is ready as we all can see,
to make grown-ups laugh and children jump with glee.
Winker Tinker is a clown you see.

Dora Swalm

The Lonesome Cry Of A Wolf

I heard the lonesome cry of a wolf searching for his mate that day
He would stop and call to her as he crossed the mountains far away
He sensed danger all around him but he did not know
That she lay mortally wounded deep in the forest where the tall
 pines grow
He would stop to sniff the air as he held his head up high
In the early winter sun beneath the pale blue sky
In the forest dark and dense he found a place to rest a while
The wolf knew no hunger though he had traveled many miles
He awoke to a strong wind from the north blowing in winter's first snow
There was a familiar scent in the air, one that he would always know
He ran faster as the scent grew stronger showing him the way
To find his dying mate beneath the pine trees where she lay
Affections passed between the two of them as his gray eyes
 seemed to say
That he would never leave the one he loved as he lay down
 beside her on that day
They had been together for seven winters, this one would be their last
He never left her side in a dying tribute of devotion unsurpassed

Barbara J. Brubaker

The Autumn Leaves Of My Life

The autumn leaves of time begin to fall; My mate of life and I
Hear them faintly call
To us, and softly say "It's almost time to fade away.
The cool winds lightly touch our cheeks, and whisper "Love",
And the fire's last embers fade to a glow, just to remind us
What we both already know, it's his plans!
The angels are waiting to take our hands.
They tell us God's waiting, and they'll show us the way
To the promise land.
We do not fear, we're safe we know, and our eyes turn above
We see God standing there looking below.
We see his smile and the arms open wide, offering us a place
To hide.
Our days of trouble are almost done, and we both feel that
We have won, a place together where we can still be,
Sweethearts in heaven as all through our life.
But let me just say, being there now by his side, is the
Same as in life, for he chose me to be his wife.

Annie Lois Rankin

Untitled

The pages of my mind:
Hear your footsteps softly on the wind
See your smiling face-alive like the sun
Feel your caress as a warm breeze
Sense your soul in the calm blue sky
Remember your laugh-lightly as a bubbling brook.
The pages of my mind:
Fill with your passion of a fury storm-etched in my heart
Accept your gentle concern your startling insight
of my deepest feelings
Welcome your love portraying softly falling raindrops
washing away all my pain
Watch the ocean rise up to the sun, only to return
again as my love for you
Dream of floating on a cloud next to your glowing aura.
The pages of my mind will turn on and on... and so
will be turned back now and then to recapture the
the beauty of love.

Irene E. Briggs

We Waited Patiently On The Lord

Now we waited patiently on the Lord and he
heard our prayers, and He sent His angels to help us
solve our problems, and get the things that we need.
Now we may not see those angles but they will be
there, to help us through this life that God has given
us. And God works in a mysterious way and His
works are wonderfully performed. And God has
earthly angels on this earth, and it may be your neighbor
or some stranger that you have never seen before,
that will come to your aid and be that angel in time of
your need. Now life is like a tale that is being told, and
we can make it a beautiful story, if we keep our faith
in God, and do good things. And nothing can be finer,
than to have God's love and mercy, with you all the
time, so keep your faith in God, and extend your love
and mercy wherever you can, and be an angel for the
Lord, right here on this earth, and God will bless you,
and keep you all the days of your life. And when your
life is over on this earth, then you will be an angel for
the Lord in Heaven forever.

Herbert S. Dandridge

Heavenly Drama

With trembling heart I witnessed
Heavenly drama on earth,
As starving, wigless lioness
Stretched into flying arrow
Chased lovely, nimble-footed gazelle,
Inches shielding life from death,
Awaiting destiny's Solomonic sentence:
Grace or Royalty, to prevail.

Will Heaven consent to piercing claws
Drain gazelle's sparkling juice of life,
To sustain pregnant lioness' gift of love?!

Will Benevolence, for life's sake,
Assent slaying harmless life - Nature's royalty?!

With heavy heart I turned my face away to heaven
To witness not the trials on earth,
Where guided by logic, granted in heaven,
Men slaughter each other wholesale, on earth.

Abe Lev

Untitled

I watch as they carry her away,
Heavy in her casket on this cold winter day.
Silently the tears begin to fall down,
And rain begins to hit the ground.
The thunder crashes and loudly roars,
Like millions of people slamming doors.
Slowly we drive to the grave yard,
Oh God, why does this have to be so hard?
Silently they lower her into the ground,
There are sobs all around.
Ashes to ashes, dust to dust,
The wind blows a long, silent gust.
She never committed a single sin,
Lord, never let me come here again.

Erica Engel

"Mom, I'm Home!"

"Mom, I'm home!"
  He'd call, as a tot, as he returned from play...

"Mom, I'm home!"
  He'd call as he returned from a paper route,
  music lessons or school each day....

"Mom, I'm home!"
  He'd whisper from our bedroom door when he
  returned from a date...

"Mom, I'm home!"
  He'd say, when as a Highway Patrolman, he'd
  stop by on a break...

When God called him home at age twenty-eight,
  I heard those familiar words as he entered
  Heaven's Gate..."Mom, I'm Home!"

Carolyn Waters

"My Father"

Did you know my Father?
He was a kind and gentle man,
Hands that knew hard work and love,
Trials and tribulations he did with stand.
Oh tell me, did you know my father?
To visit him, he would meet me at the door,
Unconditional love for me, I always felt it there,
His table you were welcome, no matter rich or poor.
Tell me now, did you know my father?
For in my father I have perceived the Lord,
Unconditional love, a helping hand, always there,
Strength to carry on, the hope of a blessed reward.

Connie Palmer

Spangler's Spring

The trampled, blood field
Held a grass-encircled water fount,
 Known as Spangler's Spring;
The Blue, the Gray came at dark
 To drink in large amount,
To quench their parched and swollen tongues,
 To wash away the blood.

The cold gray streaks of dawn
Saw each behind his line,
 The Cavalryman, the Infantryman, the Cannoneer;
Forgotten the bubbling spring, the thirst
 That brought them together without design,
Forgotten, and replaced with angry spurts of fire.

Somewhere, there is a common route
Marked with understanding and tolerance,
 With acceptance and similarity,
With basic needs, the longing for love,
 Where man may walk with no defense;
And set forth with commitment and hope
 To meet together at Spangler's Spring.

Jeanette C. Noe

The Need

Everyone needs a little help,
help in understanding others,
Also in really looking at ourselves,
and the way we treat one another.
Everyone needs to be heard,
'cause everyone has a message to deliver,
their own special word.
Everyone needs to keep searching and striving,
for dreams they think are too far.
'Cause each makes his or her own reach;
in finding out who they are,
and radiating their shining star.
Everyone needs to be free and happy,
that surely would be a great thing to see.
And let us not forget,
everyone needs to be loved.
Everyone needs to become love.
People, it seems we're a little slow,
We need to make a move!!!!

Daniel L. Haney

My Guardian Angel

Guardian angel and spiritual guide
Help me to put my fears aside.
Knowing that you are watching high from above
Looking for ways to increase our love.
Working together both day and night
Freeing us from poverty, famine and blight.

Guardian angel and spiritual guide
Descend on me now and turn the tide.
So little money, so much in debt
No relief in sight as yet.
Can't you see I need you so?
It's so very hard to just "let go".

Guardian angel, master and guide
Be my comforter, always abide.
There's a home for you deep within
No need to knock, just move in.
Strength and serenity we will find
With you and me, just doing time.

Eleanor A. Nolan

Wallflower

She was a sunflower in a field of weeds, petals outstretched to the sun.
Her eye embraced the beauty of a dream: The gray sky,
 the dead grass, the fallen trees, and one blossoming flower;
But loneliness seemed to overwhelm her.
So, to the dream, she conjured a young boy almost ten times her
 own height.
Golden hair danced on the boy's forehead as he skipped
 merrily towards her budding beauty.
He stopped a foot from the sunflower and stared down with fascination.
Loving arms reached up from the ground.
The boy lifted the beauty from the soil and gently caressed her hands.
Slowly and delicately, he plucked her right arm from her body.
"She loves me," he said in a childish voice.
Then he ripped away her left arm. "She loves me not."
Her legs. "She loves me." Then, ever so carefully, he removed
 her heart with the nail of his little finger.
"She... she loves me not," sadly.
The boy stared at the remains of the sunflower girl curiously.
"Why do you not love me?" he asked. Receiving no answer, he
stuffed the tiny, limbless body into the breast pocket of his shirt.
"I'll keep you close," he said as he walked on through the field,
His love's blood dripped slowly down his chest from where his
 heart once rested.

David Funderburk

Puppy Love

They're holding hands, they're dreaming dreams,
Her eyes are soft, his has a gleam.
They've locked themselves into a world
 Called Puppy Love.

Each anxious breath, each loving glance,
Stirs their heart beats to a merry dance.
This strange emotion, this passing phase
 Called Puppy Love.

The words they say, the sounds they make,
Would make a poet sound like a fake.
Now happy, then sad, what is this thing
 Called Puppy Love?

And so, the world must watch and wait,
And patiently hope by some twist of fate.
They'll grow, within this beautiful state
 Called Puppy Love.

Cecilia Castelino

Mystic Zither

My mother's hands have a life of their own,
Her fingers flit quickly from string to string.
Deftly, she presses the thin metal wire with one hand
While plucking it with the other, letting steel vibrate.
I listen as her soul is released by enchanted hands.

The zither. It is a Chinese instrument invented long ago,
By my ancestors, but cherished in the present
As I watch her soft hands, long nails
Create unparalleled melodies
With light, deliberate touches.

In our living room, she symbolizes a calm glory;
Breathing with her own rhythm, with her own tempo.
"Teach me to live as you do," I think as I watch silently.
She is lost in what she is doing
But looks up suddenly when she senses my presence.

"How do you do it," I ask,
Wanting the secret of her joy,
But she misunderstands for she beckons me instead to
Sit near her and learn how to play.
Yet, perhaps this is her secret.

Angela Liao

"My Courageous Mother"

"The uncrown Queen",
  Her life spotless clean.
Faith strong as a tree.
  She gave life to two, one less than three.
I was only the start.
  They said there is a second heart.
We met July twenty ninth, nineteen twenty six
  On snow white sheets, we were affected.
God choose Mothers to began.
  She'll clean to you, till life shall end.
And be your dearest friend.
  She prayed and never shirked
Responsibilities or work.
  The uncrowned Queen, is my mother
Now, Lord, I pray "Bless" her.
  A grave beside my Daddy, her body rest
They will Lord, her soul, be an honored guest
  In that Heavenly Home so great
The image of an "Uncrown Queen".

  Earl B. Wheeler

A Mother's Warm And Loving Touch

As she carried me for the first time, I could feel the warmth of
her loving touch.

As she gave me my first bath, I could feel her loving hand
gently drying my skin.

As she laid me down to sleep, I could feel her warm lullaby
singing me to sleep.

As I took my first step, I could feel her behind me and
ready to catch me as I fall.

When I needed help with all the troubles that came, she
comforted me in a way I could feel so much love.

As she gets one year older, I will help her like she helped me
and I know I can still feel the warmth and love she gave me
for the first time.

  Angeli Esguerra

For Annie

God bless a grandma on this birthday night—
Her rolled-up sleeves, her bravely tinted hair—
Who minds the stew, and shines the silver bright,
Transfigured, with a new-born love to share.
God bless a grandma as she sorts the socks
And folds the sheets; then tells her child to rest,
And holds the drowsing baby close, and rocks,
Her mirrored self pressed to her own dry breast.

And did Saint Anne, with weary Mary home,
Tuck her in bed; then, tremulously, trace
In His small form her very flesh, her bone,
Her lover's features in that Infant face?
In Miracle's bright shadow, did she, too,
Rejoice that there were dishes she could do?

  Elizabeth U. Hoobler

"Lil' Pleasures"

Did you ever watch a child as he plants an unborn seed,
His tiny hands so gently give, this plant all that it needs,
He watches and waits as days go by, anticipation in his heart,
For he knows with love and kindness, a bud is sure to start,
And then the day, a green sprout appears, and that's the joy of it all,
To have planted this tiny, little seed, and watch it grow so tall.
Such a proud little farmer is he, to have nurtured this from the start,
With a twinkle in his eye, and a song to sing, it's sure
to go straight to your heart.

  Denise L. Sobola

The Weeping Willow

The weeping willow mourns in silence
Her sadness placed on display for all.
Although her numerous outstretched arms
Seem as if asking for a shoulder
To lean on, cry on, share a laugh with
She wishes no one to relieve her
Of her pain, her sorrow, her losses.
She wallows in her grief allowing
The beauty she was bestowed to be
Seen by none because she does not want
To seem arrogant or conceited
By broadcasting her loveliness to
All who come within the boundaries
Of her magnificent fortitude.
She stands alone watching and waiting
For some unknown being to take her
Away from the hardships she has faced —
From the hurricanes and tornadoes
And the pollution which has clogged her
Every fiber. He does not come.

  Heather Bryant

One Of God's Little Birds!

How can one of God's little birds be so happy all the day long?
He's beautiful, he's yellow, he's healthy and strong.
Has so much energy, speedy in his walk
And I'm trying so hard to teach him to talk.
We have our sessions every morn and night,
But so far no words of wisdom, in sight!
All day long he happily chirps,
Eats his honey-bell with never a burp.
He loves his plastic wife,
She's his very life.
Flits to and fro, from bell to his wife, whom he adores.
Playthings on the floor he ignores.
When he sees me eat his little feet
Speedily go down to his yummy seed.
He loves company when he eats,
So do I - and I praise him to the hilt. He eats that up too...
His name? "Sweety Petey".
To me he's a gem and a sweetie.
He's only a bird in his little ole cage,
But I could write enough 'bout him to fill a page!

  Harriet Ahmels

An Army Buddy

An Army recruit is a civilian going to war
He's the most bewildered person you ever saw.
The training tires him, but he meets a friend
They will be buddies to the very end.

Grime and dirt, musket and sword, he sees
Off he goes with his buddy and gang
To that foreign land somewhere overseas.
And finally came the day of the fatal bang
His closest buddy will also bear the pain
For this chap will never come home again.

Some of that gang made it back to their own shore
The bond of friendship will endure for evermore.
Now only the toll of time will take them away
And yet another buddy expired today.
We will always miss a buddy whenever he dies
For one day we too will journey to the skies.

  Joseph S. Weekes

166

A Man At Peace

Each day He is sitting on the rock
  High above the rushing waves
Looking out and taking stock
  Of the beautiful ocean, a gift to man God gave.

At night when I am resting upon the sand
  And the moon is reflecting off the sea
I gaze up toward the ledge and see that lonely man.
  It seems he's where he ought to be.

He never comes down for days at a time -
  His home is a little cave up there.
Peace and contentment, he once said, are all mine.
  Only the sea and wind with them I will share.

  Gordon A. Estabrook

Jackie Was....

Pink and yellow gingham, black velvet and white satin...
High heels, gowns, and pearls balanced with white leather baby boots,
Toy ponies, and teething rings...the simple beauty of a single white
Rose with the detailed elegance of the Sistene Chapel...
"Grandma" to some, royalty to many...white crisp linen on Sunday
Morning...long country walks hand in hand with grandma...the
Brilliance of Easter morning everyday of the week...
The Princess of Camelot

John was.....
The smile of a newborn with the wit of an old man...
The truest of blues found only in the deepest of oceans...
A forever engraved footprint upon life's shore
The Captain of a nation... trading stories with Grandpa...
Listening to the crickets on the backporch by the lake...
A poet, writing the destiny of a nation...
the Prince of Camelot

They were...
Pink and blue shades on back and white memories...the perfect harmony
Of man and woman....they were the prince, the princess, of the fairest
Time of all-Camelot, whose faint sweet music still does chime for all
The world to listen to

  Jennifer Breen

Long Shadows

The sunset casts long shadows on the sand,
High noon-tide's blaze has softened with the day,
Earth's breath grows cool, fog comes presaging night,
All's past that was, and soon will slip away.
No future now holds worry or concern,
Tomorrow will not be, today grows cold,
My day of life, my loves, will soon be done,
Age lives in yesterday, and I am old.
I cannot hold the sun that sets so soon,
I cannot hold the tide upon the sand,
But as the shadows lengthen and grow dim
All that has been I hold within my hand.
Where once I dreamed tomorrow in the dawn,
Where once I held today in strength and power,
Here in this paler light I find
My yesterday in this soft sunset hour.
So as the tide sets outward to the sea
I wait the welcome waning of the light.
The sunset casts long shadows on the sand
Where calm I greet the coming of the night.

  Cecilia M. Roberts

The Final Battle

Indian braves fight with hearts of fire,
hindering in a nearby briar.
They will fight to keep their sacred land,
with a bow and arrow in their hand,
this could be the Indians' last stand.

The white men have come to take this ground,
there they move without the utmost sound.
The cavalry has joined in the fight,
the battle should rage all through the night,
for both sides will move into plain sight.

Bullets and arrows fly through the air,
in this battle anything is fair.
The battle ground is covered in red,
for every man has been wounded,
there was no reason for this bloodshed,
But it's too late for each man is dead.

  Jason McDermott

Death And Dismay

I once knew a boy who was gentle and kind
His heart held such joy, how brilliant his mind
But war did call him and his mind grew dim
It was clouded with death and dismay

Finally the war ended it's his turn to go home
His troubles ascended, no more to be alone
But home seemed so cold with his story untold
It was clouded with death and dismay

No one wanted to hear how his pain could last
It caused too much fear, leave it in the past
His song was too new though it was an old tune
It was clouded with death and dismay

So pills kill the pain they make everything right
And just like the rain they block out the light
Life he's not tasted yet his life has been wasted
It's been clouded with death and dismay

  Joyce Moretz Dirzuweit

In Memory Of Richard Hall

He was born February thirteenth nineteen twelve
His mother said "That's Richard, a picture of ourselves"
He grew up to be a good man, he was nobody's fool
Decided to make his life work, a career of teaching school

He met and married Lois, his pride and joy for life
And raised a real great family, with care through struggle and strife
He served with love his country, when his country was at war
And always he was ready if his country wanted him once more

He could play golf with the best of them
And his bridge was fantastic too
He worked and raised a garden
And would share it all with you

He was always there with a grin on his face
And with this same grin put one in his place
To really describe Richard would be hard to do
He was always kind, honorable also good and true

Now he fought his last hard battle, and heard His Master's call
That's Richard, a heart of gold, and standing ten feet tall.

  Floyd Teeter

Your Lover, Your Friend

Thinking of you, while we're miles apart
Holding you close, here in my heart
Longing to touch you, to be by your side
Babe, I love you, this I'll never hide.
I give you my love, treat it with care
I give you a friend, with whom you can share
My hand in yours, as we pass through each day
A love which keeps growing, a love that will stay.
To me, love is sacred, a commitment within
To love only one, till the very end
To give all you've got, through thick and thin
To always be there, your lover you friend.

Darla Stangel

The Darkened Heart

A quiet corner of a dimmed past
holds an altar to lost love. A heart knowing
hurt unrequited, a collage of dreams left
tattered, hands unsteady at the lonely helm,
a mind searching, unwilling to see the light,
eyes compelled to look beyond the unwatchable.

All of these lying in homage to an unreachable quest,
placed at the altar. Curses and prayer, vigil and homily
protection sought from relentless emotion
in the long night of failure and despair.

Towering castles of sand to offer solitude against
the ebb and flow of eternal ache. Standing firm for a time
they crumble, swept away by the return of painful tides.
As it always does, it shall always be so.
A breeze, and the flame flickers, yet remains.
The battered wick seems short, yet it burns on.
Shadows dance in quiet choreography in front
of the altar, though no one sees,
save the keeper of the flame,
landlord and prisoner at once of the darkened heart.

Edward J. Gannon

Homecoming

When I entered the house it rang with my steps,
Hollow, lonely, cold.

Empty quite long, it seemed like a tomb,
Smelling musty and old.

The life of the structure travelled away,
To a northern, distant land.

I couldn't revive it, no matter, I tried.
It wouldn't respond to my hand.

It's mood I reflected,
Loneliness grows, the aura of home quickly failing.

Without the spirit your presence commands,
It's merely a modern cave dwelling.

Travel to you, this I must do,
Where we abide is home.

Only you can make my life complete,
No matter where I roam.

You are my life, for good or for strife,
this vow I made on day one.

Now three years hence, I love you sweet wife,
Without you, I am undone.

Jeffrey L. Van Dyke

Wandering Child

Born in the South in the days of old
Horses, wagons, and slaves were sold
She had no knowledge on how to succeed
No way of knowing how to take care her needs
Wandering, wandering child is mine
Beautifully made, sweeter than wine
Little opportunity, it never did knock
They took the slaves one day to the dock
Sold - for the highest bid
Lord, they sold my wondering kid
Since that day, life hasn't been the same
I sold my soul and lived in shame
Wandering, wandering child of mine
Beautifully made, sweeter than wine
Forgive me for the weakness in my ways
But remember, I was also a slave in those days

Johnetta Bryant

Unforgotten Memories

Out on the Ole' road, leading to our
   house,
Playing with my sister wearing my hand-me-down
   blouse
As the flowers began to bloom on a
   sunny spring morning
The fish in the pond began to jump
   without warning
We ran across the pasture to the ole' man down the way
He use to watch us and laugh, he would always say:
Don't ever stop laughing or smiling keep your head up high
For we all only have one life to live please don't ask me why
Sitting under the oak tree, as dew fell upon the ground
Just listening to all the different wonderful sounds
Baby birds chirping for their mother in their nests
Soon she flies over, to comfort them with her breast
As I look back of our unforgotten memories of you and I
Tears slowly roll down from my eyes
Happy tears of the way it used to be
Happy tears of our unforgotten memories

Helen M. Butler

Secret Thoughts/Hidden Feelings

How can I tell you what I should not feel?
How can I reveal thoughts I would not will?
Try as I may to put you out of my mind,
Your image remains indelibly enshrined.

"For anyone," they say, "there's only one."
I scoffed, "'Tis only a tale by an old wife spun."
Yet—somehow—everything about you seems so sane;
Life without you is empty and filled with pain.

Your personality draws me like a magnet;
Your voice, your laugh, your smile I covet.
I know I ought not to feel like this —
Ten thousand other worlds to share our bliss!

Floyd E. Merritt

I Danced

I danced with the river last night.
His lapping lips intrigued me.
Come into the arms of my firm banks,
Calling from the moonbeams underneath.

The beat—steady surging against my pillows of succulence
Tenderly tempting, awakening my senses.
Reveling in the encompassing waves.
Lifted beyond the sphere,

I danced with the river last night.
Swaying in raw wetness,
The marshy grasses entanglement,
Oh cling forever with your vines!

Deborah English

The Answer

God gave His Son, that we might live,
How can we thank Him? What can we give?
It's not God's fault, if we fail to look,
For the answers, which are in His book.
It is impossible to please Him without faith,
Have faith in God and have whatsoever we saith.
To set people free, so they'll never be the same,
God's given us permission to use his Son's name.
Laying hands upon the sick, we'll soon discover,
Right before our eyes, they will recover.
God's given us the Holy Spirit as a gift,
Thank Him, Praise Him, our hands we do lift.
Giving us peace the world does not know,
Out of our belly living water does flow.
God has done all He's going to do, now it's up to me and you.
So as Christians, let us do our part,
Change this world for Jesus,
With love which comes from the heart.
Let's use the authority God has given us,
Going throughout the world, praising the name of Jesus.

Freddy Johnson

A Vision Of You

19 years of age she'd be this day
"How come she's not here"? I ask when I pray
At times I wonder if we'd have been close
If the time spent between us would mean the most
A wondering vision, a sister I never met
My older sibling, who I'll never forget
Are you protecting me in heaven?
From life's sharp sting
If you were here I suppose you'd do the same thing
Mom always told me stories of your lovely red hair
And then the sadness in her heart, the rip of misery's tear
An hour you were here, 19 years you've been away
I have the same wonders about you each and every day
Would you have been pretty with a great personality?
Would you have looked like our mother or something like me?
You're an unfinished story and untold tale,
However, I love you... Doreese Ratel

Holly Charles

Imagine How Jesus Felt

Do you feel any pain inside when you think about
How Jesus must have felt,
When they hammered the nails into his hands and feet?
And when they dropped the cross into the ground,
Could you feel the pain of his flesh ripping?
Think about it! You see Christ Jesus went through
This, and so much more for you and me.
In His body and soul he carried the burdens of every sin ever
committed.
Your sins are those which He bore, as well as my own,
And everyone that ever lived.
Imagine the agony Christ's Soul was in
From the burdens in which He carried.
Oh! How Jesus must have felt at that moment,
When He thought, God, His father, had forsaken Him.
He was crucified, then he rose from the dead Victoriously.
This and so much more Jesus went through for you and me.
Jesus Loved us enough to lay down his life, even unto Death.
During our own hardships let us always remember,
What Jesus endured for all mankind.
Imagine how much Jesus loves each of us.

Barbara J. Stiffler

Brian

Baby, I can't tell you
How much you mean to me
Did you ride up on your big, white horse
Or step out of my dreams?
Did the wish I made upon a star
Finally come true
Or did the angels up above
Really send me you?
It must have been the angels
Cause it's heaven in your arms
The whole world seems to melt away
When you hold me safe and warm.
You're the answer to my prayers
The keeper of my heart
That fills with such a longing
Whenever we're apart
The thrill of your touch on my skin
Sends shivers down my spine
I'm proud to walk and hold your hand
And show the world your mine.

Jacci Mohr

Taking Time For Mother

I've been thinking a lot about you, and I'm taking time to say,
How very much I've loved you in so many untold ways.

And I'm taking the time to thank you for always being there,
No matter what the problem was you've always been there to care.

I think of all the heartaches and all the unseen pain,
And all the hurt you've endured, you were always there just the same.

Every time I needed you the memory that time can't erase
No matter how tired or tremendous the strain, the love I saw on
your face.

Sometimes your eyes were swollen, and your hands would start to shake,
You would always say I love you even when your heart I'd break.

I'm taking this time to apologize for all the heartaches I've put you thru,
but most of all to let you know just how much I really love you.

I always thank God for picking you when my seed he planted,
So I thought I'd let you know you're never taken for granted.

One thing I must do is turn the hands of fate,
And tell you Mom how much you're loved long before it's too late.

Brenda Mae Jones

When I Was Eight

Oh those friendly, jolly elves
Hurry and scurry about themselves.
When last I heard them scamper 'round,
Down came Santa with a bound.
It was late, and I was eight when I saw Santa's fate.
Creeping toward him, I soon found out
That Santa was very short and stout.
Fat and old and out of shape,
There was no possible way to escape.
Done with his job, he couldn't stay,
And he couldn't go—I was in the way.
Determined to leave, he gave me a heave
And got stuck up the chimney half-way.
All of a sudden, he started to yell,
"This pain in my chest is giving me hell!"
My parents awoke, and thought they were dreaming.
They didn't know who was screaming.
They saw Santa, and over to the chimney they ran.
They tried their hardest to pull him out,
But Santa was... a dead man.

Heidi Neu

Nature And The Man

Western river of the early dawn,
Hush your downhill angst;
I am the man who has come to listen,
But first have something to say;

You are the nature and I am the man,
I was put on this earth to find where I stand;
If you were the man and I was the nature,
Naked I'd be in a land of blueberries;
Sadly to say though I don't feel that way,
On my back it is nature I carry;

Western river of the dusky break,
I've said my peace no better than best;
Now it is time to give you your turn,
And then we can both get some rest.

Jeremy D. Acker

Always

As I look of the time we spent together.
I always thought it would be forever.
The joy and comfort of having you near.
The time we did have will always be so dear.
Now that it's over it's still hard
to place, never again to join with
your laughter and see your smile
all over your face.
All I have are the memories we
shared, and to always remember
the love and caring that was once there.
As time goes on and years do pass,
These things will always last.
I thank the Lord for giving me
that time, and for knowing I can
always have them on my mind.

Evelyn Hamilton

Tearing Me Up Inside

I love you and that's true
I always want to be with you

People said to set you free
They said you'd never be true to me
And stupidly, I let you go.
And now you'll probably never know

I've cried every night since we broke up
Thinking of you and making up

You'll never take me back I know
I wish to God that it wasn't so

I love you so much I can't describe
And that's what's tearing me up inside

Amanda Jo McCutcheon

Diamond Girl

She is the goddess of light.
I am lost in her castle so Bright.

I feel pain no more. I feel pain no more.
She is my Diamond Girl.

Locked in time by ourselves.
No one near to hear her yell.
As she cries out
For my love.

Held captive in her castle so bright.
She is the goddess of light.
I want to stay with her forever.

Jim Price

The Dream Is Fading

I am ready for world peace.
I am ready for the thought of others to come before oneself.
I am ready for enemies to turn into friends.
I am ready for arguing to be a thing of the past.
  But as I wait the dream starts fading.

I am ready for crime to be forgotten, like a bad memory.
I am ready for jail to have no use, instead of overcrowding.
I am ready for alcohol to be dropped, and drugs to be forgot.
I am ready for the day I can leave a door unlocked.
  But as I wait the dream starts fading.

I am ready for sickness to be extinct, like dinosaurs of old.
I am ready for a cure for aids, cancer and even the common cold.
I am ready for the sadness of mental illness to no longer exist.
I am ready for all children to live long, happy lives.
  But as I wait the dream starts fading.

I can offer a loving heart to show someone cares.
I can offer a helping hand to someone in need.
I can offer a listening ear to people who need a friend.
I can offer support and confidence to others
  so the dream does not have to fade.

Colleen Renee Mazza

Untitled

I am through with the hurt, I am through with the pain.
I am through with the sorrow, I am through with the strain.
Sometime in one's life you must mature and move on.
But you don't realize what you've had
  until it is finally gone.
You were always by my side whenever I needed you.
Our friendship I'll always cherish,
  for I know that it was true.
Those last few months of your life
  were painful and sad... I know.
But to know the pain had left your body
  was the only reason I was glad to see you go.
The last time I saw you, I will always recall in my heart.
For I can never forget that we'll forever be apart.
I'll never forget that you were my best friend.
Until my life and time on Earth will then come to an end.
I think of you with each and every tear.
For I want you to remember, even in the end,
That... I love you Grandma Dear.

Chris Sanchez

Reckless Love

The moon is like glass. The stars are like lights.
I am waiting for you to fill my heart. Before last
night we did not have the love that we needed to
keep our relationship going. I always thought that my
future was going to be spent with you; but know
that dream can never come true. Because of a type of
reckless love. All the heart breaks of this
life can't compare to the pain I feel when we broke
up. I thought that our love would have lasted
forever. My mind is full of thought of how we
spent our days together. I wish that we were still
together. Because I miss the way we talked, the way
we looked into each other's eyes, and the way I
would hold you. I hold dear every moment that
we spent together. I know that people didn't
accepted us at first. But know once we broke up.
People finally understood the love we shared. No
words can express the love I have for you. But
we both moved on to better things. One thing I
will never forget is that the time we spent together.

Jayson Muronaga

Amen

As the sun sets
I await your beastly call
Lying on my virgin bed
Possessed by your hungry eyes

These feelings inside of me are uncontrollable
Your ancient voice comforts me
Drain me of all life flowing through my veins
I want to experience death

As you bring me back to life
I will walk in darkness by your side
My thirst will be quenched by warm blood
I will be immortal

Sinking your teeth into my anemic body
My blood-contaminated, but my love for you is stronger than ever
My lips, stained from your unholy wine that I drink
We are now stronger than death
No one will tear us apart
Not even the Lord himself
You are my sacred prince
And we shall rule the night—together

Cheryl Clayton

How You Make Me Feel Inside

Staring deep into your glistening eyes
I become mesmerized with every sparkle
In return, I send the twinkles from my own
To show the wondrous feelings I hold for you alone
When you are near or from afar, my face begins to glow
Even in a crowded room, you're all I see
But to be alone with you is what I wish to be
For your smile warms my heart
And every soft touch weakens my soul
So to live my life without you, would cause much sorrow
Even as time goes by, and if we are apart
You'll be the true capture of my heart
Because you're the only one who truly knows me
The only one who seems to care
The only time I feel at ease, is when you are there.

Cynthia Rogers

Family

As I look at the photos of people gone by,
I begin to breath heavy, and start to cry.
As I see faces of family, I'll never know,
It's an empty feeling on my face, that
  begins to show.
Of grandma, grandpa and uncle Joe,
Aunt Mary and Janie, and of other
  people I'd know.
It's funny as pictures, and memories,
  keep them so dear,
That through you don't know them,
  they feel awful near,
So as pictures, we have are the
  people, that are neat,
Take pride in them, and memories,
  are yours to keep.
For these times are yours, to
  relax, and see,
All you heritage come to life,
  like it did for me.

Darlene Anne Gunes

A New Civil War

Though I've never been to Gettysburg,
I can hear their silent, anguished cries.
Two armies met, their blood to merge.
They fought and died 'neath azure skies.
I hear long, silent screams today.
Is this blood also shed for nought?
Wade vs. Roe - the modern Court play
Was once acted out in US vs. Dred Scott.

Is it wrong to give a child a chance
to be born and live and sing and dance?
Let's stop the shedding of innocent blood
by stemming the tide of abortion's red flood.
My choice is made. I know it's right.
I speak for the unborn to help win them rights.

Joseph L. Hamel

The Lake Of Fire

I can hear the trumpet sounding.
I can see him on his throne.
I can see the books are open.
Before him, they stand alone.
What is your name? The Lord is asking.
I cannot find it anywhere, your names
not in this book. I'm searching.
The lake of fire is over there.
On their knees with him they're pleading.
Please don't make me go in there.
The lake of fire is eternal.
This punishment, I can not bear.
You will have to go, I'm sorry.
While on earth, you had your chance.
For your wrongs, you were not sorry.
For your sins no repentance.
You can scream and cry and holler.
Begging now is much too late.
For you have sealed your soul forever.
The lake of fire is your fate.

Barbara J. Dick

You're My Mom

As I stop and take the time to look behind me,
I can see you laughing, your love is growing.
As I stop and take the time to look behind me,
I can see you crying, your love is flowing.

Though I may not take the time to show how much I care
any my emotions I did not share,
but you were always there.

You're my mom, and I love you so.
You're my mom and I will never let you go.
As I grow older, I want you to know that
you're number one in my life.

Now, I'm stopping to take the time to look ahead of me,
I can see us laughing. Our love is growing.
Now, I'm stopping to take the time to look ahead of me.
I can see us crying. Our love is flowing.

Now I'm taking the time to show how much I care
and my emotions I can share cause your are always there.

Angel Meyer

Ode To A Special Friend

This Senior man of eighty four
I cannot find him anymore.
It was not long ago I did not have to search
Up at dawn, to the garden, then perch.
Since he already did so much hard work
And very often brought me surprises - silence broke

His loving gifts were my delight
Made all my days so very bright
His throng of kin and friends were neat
But most of which I never got to meet.

I treasure the pleasant memories of him.
And to my death they will never grow dim.
God knew I needed a special friend
But oh, Alas, it had to end.

Anna Daines

Heart To Remember

With every day that passes
I cannot forget the pain of
Two I loved so much
With every day that passes
I long for what I can never hold
And yearn for what I cannot touch
My pain does not show on my face
But it is there, it hurts, and my broken heart
Will cry out in the night
Life has taken nearly all I've ever wanted
But yet it hasn't left me alone
I still have the love of my life
My true love, my only love
We share happiness
We share each other's pain
We share each other's sorrow
And although we may see many tears again
We shall create a new life
And remember today
Tomorrow

Doug Cross

Falling Off The Edge

Afraid to look below,
I can't help but to think the worst.
Holding on with the little strength I have left,
I feel this overwhelming sensation to fly.

I let go.

I slip into the darkness of the night.
Feeling only the wind seep through me.

I soar.

A feeling of complete and utter tranquility,
fills within me.
I am one.

Elizabeth Visconty

Alfred Prayful Lament

I went to a churchyard and kneeled and prayed,
I ask "God" to help me for I grew afraid.
My stomach is lank for I am getting so thin,
Oh my for a handout, some place to crawl in.
My shoes are all worn and come off my feet,
But that's not as bad as my pants in the seat.
The wind, it blows it through my clothes,
All goodness, all gracious I am about froze.
My coat is all ragged and my shirt is all torn,
Oh why in this wide world was I ever born.
My Maw must have known when she first looked at me,
That I was the Black Sheep on our family's tree.

Elsie Brady

Please Rain

A time when it was all alright,
I can't remember a regretless night.
But what I found to be true,
is the sweet memory of you.
It never leaves me, it's at my beck and call,
and it will always be what helps me to fall.
Nothing comes but pain,
the one thing that helps the rain.
It feeds my greatest fears,
and it replenishes my tears.
When I simply have to smile,
I think of you, and it's no longer worthwhile.
No energy is wasted on a laugh,
and it is all relieved to the past.
So for now I will simply be sad,
it's the only thing I've always had.
And though I may be slightly mad,
for that I shall be glad...
    Because it cannot leave me...
      as you did...

Angela Bumgarner

Waterish Eyes

Every time when I look in the mirror,
I can't see a merry face.
All I can see are two waterish eyes,
With all the disappointment and all the confusion.
A tall shadow with healthy dark hair.
A familiar smile for me to catch.
You are just like a cloud passing by,
and a bird flying away.
All I have left is a long-face
with loneliness and sorrow.
I used to be the happiest girl in the world,
but now, I always shed sad tears.
Because of you, all I have are two waterish eyes.......

Jenny Duan

Untitled

Beauty casts her cloak as though a skillful matador
    I charge forth in blinding fantasy
Knowing that her facets are also pure perfection
    perfectly meshing with all that I be
I languish, not feeling the pain of reality
    For beauties veil mantles all
that is outside of my dream
    I walk a pirates plank
hands tied in beauties bond
    So intent upon the vision
the ocean below is unseen
    Though I can not swim
I boldly walk ahead
    How many steps may I take
before the plunge breaks my spell

Herbert G. Buss

Redemption

I killed eleven people, strangers.
I didn't care anything about them.
They found me guilty, I couldn't lie.
Now I wait to die myself.
Now I care about the smallest leaf if only I could see one,
    but there is no window.
I've been studying my case, looking at the photos;
    two boys, a girl, one woman, seven men.
I wonder often where they went
    and I not far behind them,
Each one, precious, the only family of the murderer,
The only ones who see I have awakened from my darkness,
My beast's skin lifeless on the dungeon floor.

A.B. Curtiss

172

Free to Flow

Born of desire for understanding
I crossed the rivers of sorrow
Climbed the hills of pain
Walked through the valleys of depression
Found no one beside me
Cursed quest for a hidden fate
Traveled on for reasons not to be discovered
Throngs of hate clutched my soul
Endless throbs of confusion swelled from within
The light of my path grows dim
Searching in a forest of broken dreams
Am I to die alone
Or just afraid
No shelter from a personal hell
Yet no one attempts to save me
A hand of innocence
Reaching toward my blind eyes
Taking me from reality
Alas my dreams are free to flow
Free to flow.

Doug Raleigh

Don't Give Them A Start

Cocaine is my name
I don't consider your fame;
My brother's name is Crack,
Give him a chance and he will break your back.
Try my cousin dope
And your neck will be on the rope;
We like to reach your brain
And make your life go down the drain;
You think we make you look cool
But, to us you're the world's biggest fool.
We give you power,
Yet your soul and mind we devour;
So, this is our life long policy,
Make a choice and don't be crazy;
Don't do drugs.

Ghire C. Shivprasad

To Know

If only one could see, who's hidden within me.
I don't take people for granted, of what's said of done.
Take them for who they are, treat them as one.
Some think they know me very well inside and out,
really there fooling there selves, my heart is myself.
If my heart is known,
well maybe I won't complain,
think of others who people hurt,
when you know a heart, than you know a person.
That person has feelings also a heart,
that means a life worth livin',
without a heart we have nothin',
without a life causes are empty.
If there's no joy and laughter,
than there's no me.
Don't judge me unless you know me,
to know me is to know my heart.
When you know all of that,
there's a beautiful person,
than you will know me inside and out.

Florence L. Hemple

Distance

So often, I dream of holding you, of looking in your eyes.
I dream of your smile, all of these things that make my body paralyzed.
Just to be near you and hold your fingers between mine,
and feel your gentle kisses, would make all things fine.
I dream of conversations not spoken through the phone,
of laughter, joy and happiness, all of which now seem unknown.
Distance is a burden that seems to surround the heart,
hoping that our love will keep us going, while we have to be apart.
We've made it through some rough times, many more that lie ahead-
but distance makes the heart grow fonder, or that is what is said.
Miles separate us now, keeping you and I apart,
although these miles are between us, my love for you is always
    in your heart.
Thoughts of you fill my mind and keep me busy through the day,
praying that sometime soon, things will be another way.
Until that day, I'll wait for you, and dream of your embrace
I'll dream of laughing with you, of staring at your face,
of walking hand in hand just the way things used to be.
I know that we can make it, I just need to wait patiently.

Jennifer Senft

To My Dear Grandchild

The day you were born was the very start
I experienced the joy of a Grandparent's heart,
Everything you do, I cherish so much
Your kisses, your voice and your gentle touch.
As you ask about Jesus and the things all around
I thank God for you and the joys I have found.
As you grow and you go on your way
Never, never forget how we would pray.
It's not important your status in life
Or who you choose for a husband or wife
What matters most is that Jesus is your friend
Include him in everything to the very end.
I may not give you worldly treasures
But what I can give cannot be measured.
I'm going to leave this old world someday,
I ask you to "Be There" so we can laugh and play.
Oh, I'll be with Jesus, so don't be sad
We'll look for you and your Mom and Dad.
Just "Be There" that's all I ask of you
Look for me for I will "Be There" too.

Diana Faulconer

In The Middle Of Forever

When I found you my life began
I felt a strength I never knew
I thought we had it all
In this land of me and you

You were everything I ever needed
Maybe I was blind and refused to see
All the lies the hurt and pain
of a love that could never be

Why does one partner have to
    give so much
And the other one just take
Why do hopeful dreams have
to be shattered
And a willing heart just break

Wasn't our love suppose to last forever
Wasn't that the way it was
    supposed to be
But somewhere in the middle
    of forever
You turned around and walked away from me.

Elaine A. Creasey

A Little Touch Of Kindness

A little touch of kindness, is this too much to ask?
  I forget a little now and then, remembering is a task!
So would you lend a helping hand, perhaps an ear to listen?
  Then glance but once into my eyes, your kindness makes them glisten.

Perhaps the same old story! "…it's my treasured memory,"
  When I didn't hide because of pride, and many cared for me.
But now my pace is slower, I can't see or hear as well.
  My feelings haven't changed much, my reddened eyes they tell.
Would you pause to hold the door, and dare you think to call?
  Perhaps I'm bent and feeble, but you'll make me feel so tall!

Would you get a loaf of bread, or pay this bill for me,
  Or will you mail a letter, and shovel off the property?
The outside may look worn to you, my features re-arranged,
  Please understand that deep within, my heart is still the same!

I see my youth so clearly, all those "remember when's,"
  And yearn in desperation, for my in-de-pen-dence.
I can only say "I thank you!" as I share some wise advice,
  My heart swells with much gratefulness, God Bless you who were so nice!

Edmund J. Shanks Jr.

I Lost My Love

I found my love the one I need
I found my love the one who doesn't want me.
I found my love the one my heart longs to see
I found my love the one who hurt me
I found my love the one who doesn't care for me
I found my love the one who doesn't think of me
I found my love the one I thought would be forever
I found my love the one whose heart is with another.
I lost my love the one who's never loved me.

Gina Puma

The Deep Hole

As I walked down the dark alley alone,
I found myself slipping like I was going
into a hole. I looked around me to see
if there was water on the ground.
But there was none. I was falling deeper
and deeper. I tried reaching for
something I could grab hold to but there
was nothing. I was breathing hard and
thinking I was going to die. Thought
were racing through my mind, evil
thoughts I couldn't stop. I felt sweat
roll down my face. Then it was over.
I woke up happy that it was all a dream.

Jessica Jones

Couldn't Say

I thought of you last night.
I know you don't want me to,
But I couldn't help crying.
Knowing that you're not nearby
Leaves me feeling hollow inside.
I realize that you had to leave,
But I still want you here with me.
You'll never know what you meant to me,
Nor how much I loved and cared for you.
I wish I would have been able to tell you,
But, some things are hard to say.
Hopefully, my actions told you how I felt.
But, somehow, I doubt that they did.
I know we'll meet again some day.
Maybe then I can tell you everything
That I couldn't say before.

Jennifer Seitz

My Father

He was never called papa or daddy,
  I guess it was unwritten law
That everyone who knew him and loved him
  Had the privilege of calling him pa.

There never was a more gentle man.
  A trait about which we all knew
And the love that he shared with our mother
  Like a beacon, it came shining through.

He chastised us kids when 'twas called for,
  But never without cause or with temper.
If you were real smart, he'd ease up on the strap
  If, before hand, you let out a whimper.

Every year there's a contest in this town
  And everywhere else, so I hear
To pick out or choose a contender
  As the father of this present year.

Now, I know that it's a wonderful honor
  And for non-winners, some will shed tears
But all of we Fee's will remember
That ours was the father of years

Joseph Patrick Fee

The Flame

The day I saw you sitting here,
I had to look away.
The memories so painful,
The thoughts so brief.
Me, my dreams unfulfilled,
My thoughts in a blur,
My mind in a haze.
The light look in my eyes not pain,
But fear,
My body is here,
But my mind is not near.
The flame is burning deep within.
I blew it out with a great pride,
Finally, memories, thoughts and pain are gone,
Burned and singed by the flame of a candle.

April S. Ridge

Magical Morning Of Music

One cold winter morning, before rushing off to work
I had to scrape my windshield.
With a muttered curse I started and heard:
Splintering echo, echo, echo
through the still morning air.

I stopped. I listened…
No sound came to my ears.

My eyes probed the surroundings
but…no one was there.

I couldn't believe -
was that sound just…me?

I scraped again - just once.
Splintering ice echoed, echoed, echoed
like a million shards of glass
tinkling and clinking throughout space.

Magically, my door yard became Carnegie Hall
as I played…ice…on my windshield.

Doreene S. Seale

174

"Am I Dead?"

She looked at him as she said,
"I hate to ask this, but am I dead?"
Last Saturday night on the bed I laid,
and slashed my wrists with a razor blade.
I couldn't take it, not anymore,
Everyone called me a street walking whore.
I really don't care what people say,
But, the worst part about it was that I felt that way,
I couldn't stand playing the "Sweetie girl" role.
I felt I was sinking into a hole.
But, please sir, don't let me die.
If you give me a chance I'll give it a try.
I can handle the truth. I can handle the pain.
I'll handle anything, my loss or my gain.
So you see kind sir, this much is true
If you let me live I'll be grateful to you.

In a soft mournful voice, the old man then said,
"I can't give you a chance, you're already dead!"

Darin E. Richey

Daughter Of A Slave

I am the daughter of a slave,
I have carried my people's strengths,
And determinations,
to let no man walk,
Upon my forefathers' graves.

They fought and died
to help me to live, to survive,
To achieve and simply to be.

Young men, young women, lift up your heads
Follow your dreams.
Achieve above your own expectations.

Look out America!!!!!!
We are here to stay,
And be recognized for our struggles,
From slavery to our grave.

We bear our strengths, identities, knowledge,
Wisdom, and inspirations for all.
We are not the one that is lost.
We too have our place in history!

Eartha L. Christie

Untitled

If not for the sun
I have no warmth
If not for the night
I have no rest
If not for the dew and rain
my character is dry and growth is stagnant
If not for the wind
my soul is still
If not for change
my spirit is complacent
For I am a part of nature
and nature is a part of me
We are one and inseparable
My being dependent upon natures existence
natures existence is for my being
We are one
I am man .

Ed Devore

America, The Beautiful

I see hate, death, and deceit, and can't believe my eyes.
I have seen the children kill, and watched them be killed.
I have seen the poverty, and watched nobody lift a finger.
I have been forced to see racism, now my eyes hurt.

I see the sellers of drugs, and the people who buy them.
I have seen murder, and the people who laugh at it.
I have seen the raped, and the ones who got away with it.
I have been forced to see the gangs, now my eyes are burning.

I see the beatings, then watched the guilty become the innocent.
I have seen thieves steal, and watched them walk free.
I have seen the back stabbing, and the ones who carry the knife.
I have been forced to see the torture, now my eyes have burned away.
I can no longer see, I am finally free from my sight.
I didn't need to see anymore, I didn't want to see any more.

Now if I couldn't hear the lies, life would finally be peaceful.

Glenn Carle

What's Up With That?

Why did you leave me
I have to know, I hope it's not my fault
I didn't want you to go, I wish you could tell me
I'm dying inside, you stepped on my hope
And swallowed my pride, my half of a heart
Has been crying and crying
Whenever I see you, I feel like dying
There's been knocks at this door way
That leads to my heart
But my feelings for you are still alive,
I won't let them fall apart
I will wait and wait, forever for you
How long will I wait?
I don't have a clue
I won't take off my sunglasses I haven't eaten for days
I miss watching you do things in your silly little ways
I haven't changed, I'm not living in sin
But the man with the key still doesn't want to come in
Am I too ugly? Am I too fat?
I just want to know what's up with that?

Erin Shevlin

Distant Closeness

Because of my feelings and how much I care
I have written a poem for our spirits to share

Although at this moment we may be apart
Let yourself feel the wholeness of my heart

The power and strength of completely real love
Was sent as a gift by our Lord from above

With my love that no actions or words can really show
Is a prayer for you to always feel and know

That the sparkle your presence casts upon my eye
Is a brightness that will never die

And the beauty that shines all over your face
Is a blessing my heart will always embrace

Like springtime rain on a new blooming flower
The warmth of my heart on you I will always shower

Because all of these feelings, so alive and so true
Are from the glory of God's Spirit in me and in you

Gina M. Bayless

The Cry Of My Heart

All alone at night when silence is surrounding me
I hear a deep, deep cry inside my heart.
It is the cry of a pain,
that never goes away.
And you just have to learn,
to put it in a corner.
Where it will not disturb.
Until one day, it is able to come out.
In a silent time.
Another day is gone, and night falls in.
With the night comes a terrible cry.
And I know that it is, The Cry Of My Heart.

Belkis Duran

I.T.Q.

IN THE QUIET…
I HEAR the day greet the night … The morning dew quenching
all that thirst… the heart giving birth to love.

IN THE QUIET…
I HEAR leaves change in color, snowflakes in wingless flight…
The footsteps of an ant headed home…

IN THE QUIET …
I HEAR the growth of trees … climbing the airways
Reaching for life … I HEAR a tear dropping from sparkling eyes
and I can HEAR the smile of a caterpillar changing into a butterfly.

IN THE QUIET…
I HEAR the stars pay homage to the sun and the moon flickering
on a calm lake like ivory climbing the silent wall … Unbending.

IN THE QUIET…
I HEAR wings of angels … the gates of peace ... I HEAR the
Master touching my soul…

IN THE QUIET…

Hugh Goodman Jr.

A Shadow

A shadow crossed my path
I heard a voice say, "what are you thoughts today?"
I had a smile upon my face
I didn't quite know the place.

A baby's face appeared
Someone near and dear.
All smiles - all aglow
Someone in the know!

A mystery swept fore - clearly, I could see.
The future - it's near - it's me!
As a shadow crossed my hand
I heard a voice say, "what are your thoughts today?"

Darhla McComb

The Clown

I thought about the clown after he was gone
I knew that his smile was merrily painted on
I saw it in his eyes his vainly
Hidden pain and after I saw I
knew I'd never be the same
When I looked into his eyes
I was looking straight at me
I'm merely just a clown with
my faces painted on and the
people that I meet will forget
me when I am gone

Dino A. Ponce

tool

i know you can hear me, my voice is bleeding
i know you can see me, my eyes are seething
use all of your senses to penetrate me
see through the garbage that inundates me
if you could just smile
my dreams are fulfilled
the nervous relaxing of my soulful shield
the shelter you give
from harsh winter rain.
But why do i write about practical pain?
Why is my pen the tool of a cynic?
the answer of struggling pain lies within it
break up my words
and pick up my thoughts
from the edge of the cliff i'm about to fall off
after every breathless moment, i feel my heart erase
i cannot find a common thread, a foothold to relate
these walls are my jailcell,
my words hold the key
i just need an angel to crucify me

Joseph Corbo

My Shepherd

When in the midst of the desert,
I lift my eyes to the Lord.
I feel the touch of His presence
And I am fed on His word.
He brings the sweet cooling water;
He leads me on when there's no way to go.
He keeps His eyes on the sparrow,
And praise His name, I love Him so.

When on the top of the mountain,
My heart is soaring so high.
He thrills the soul with His spirit;
Joy, peace and comfort are nigh.
He spreads a table before me;
I'm lifted up to heights unknown before.
So, come what may, I will follow.
Praise be to Him forever more.

Alta Mae Santoro

Peace

I searched high and low, for a sign of serenity,
I looked deep within myself,
but I could not find it in me.
I wanted to find peace,
Some peace in difficult times,
When you don't know which way to turn,
to ease your troubled mind.
I tried to understand where this peace could be found,
In a parent or a friend,
it seems I searched the whole town.
I picked up the world, the BIBLE that is!
I read and I read and understanding became a whiz!
I FOUND IT! I FOUND IT! My heart is filled with joy,
As a child who had lost, but found his favorite toy,
My Lord, My God, can give you all things!
He has the peace that passes all understandings.

Andrea Byard

The Old Clothesline Tree

From my window one day,
    I looked out at my tree,
It was all twisted and bent,
    With deep scars that the lightening had rent
No longer a beautiful sight to behold,
No longer supple, no longer straight,
Notched where the clothesline was fastened,
And burdened down with its weight.

I turned and looked in my mirror,
We have a lot in common I see,
Time has changed both of us,
Me and the old clothesline tree.
But the old tree is still useful,
Shade in the summer, color in the fall,
Seems there is a lesson here,
A lesson for us all.

Cora M. Burris

Endless Dream

I feel a wind I cannot see.
    I love a God who's there for me.
I feel content just being me,
    Because I dream an endless dream.

First you have to walk alone,
    and be content with simple things,
Hold a hand, take time to dream,
    And soar the heights in search of peace.

And wrap your arms around the sun,
    And ride the snow clouds to the wind,
And touch a mind with love and peace,
    And touch a heart with happiness.

If I touch one heart thru life,
    And let one life entwine with mine,
Then I have dreamed the endless dream,
    And I have taught the secret things.

I feel a wind I cannot see,
    And I have dreamed the endless dream,
And I have learned the secret things,
    That finally grow inside of me.

Helen M. Foley

Understanding

I love the thunder of your voice
    I love its rhythm, too.
I love your strength and wild free ways
    You're all that's rough, but true.
I love your cold, wet salty kiss
    I'm thrilled by your embrace.
I love you when you're mad with rage
    And beat hard upon my face.
I love you, too, when you softly sigh
    And glide up on the sand.
Oh, sea, you've the power to move me much
    For, my moods you understand!

Evelyn R. Paris

Forgotten

Why do I have these feelings, the hurt the pain ...
I never thought losing someone could be such a strain ...
It's always me, the one left behind and forgotten, treated as nothing
I have feelings but no one seems to care ...
So I just keep to myself, life is so unfair ...
I just want someone to hold me and care ...
Since the one I love has disappeared ...

Angela Franchino

Endless Reasons

I've got a reason, a reason just to love.
I met a fair woman who's beauty is like a dove.
I've got a reason, reasons just to share.
The woman whom I love is with me everywhere.
Her reason just for loving is the same our hearts both share.
For no reason was necessary, our hearts already there.
She is the reason, I give my heart to be.
It really wasn't reasons, for her heart had set me free.
The reasons why I love her someday I might just tell.
If you look into our eyes you'll see it very well.
I could go on with reasons, but to few is not enough.
The reason I wrote this, was simply because of love.

James Douglas Saint-Gaudens

"A Typical Day"

My hands were so busy, Lord, today
I never once folded them to pray
They polished the tables and the chairs
Dusted and vacuumed down the stairs
Washed the dishes and then the clothes
Ironed some shirts, sat and mended hose
Baked some cookies, made a Beef Stew
Not idle a moment, things to do.
But in my heart, Lord, you were right there
With me every moment in silent prayer
I thank you, dear Lord, for all this wealth
For family, home, food and health, Amen.

Gladys W. Hroch

"Being In Love With You"

Being in love with you really makes me smile,
I only hope it will last a long while.
Not any person can make me feel this way!
And I can surely tell you I'm happy everyday!
The love I feel for you is like a wild flower...
That grows and grows with such power.
If you leave me, like that flower I will die...
You will leave me no choice but to cry.
You always stood out in my mind;
A man like you is hard to find.
Promise me will never part;
And always love me with all your heart
With you I want to spend every minute of my life.
Someday I hope to make a perfect wife
I would never love anyone like I love you
When you're not around I only have thoughts of you.
When feeling your body next to mine.
I'm hoping you'll caress me till the end of time.

Christina Rangatore

The French Fry

I found a french fry on the ground,
I picked it up and looked around.
I want to eat it, but have no salt.
I also want a chocolate malt.

A cheeseburger with onions would be nice,
A frosty root beer, over ice,
Sausage pizza and breadsticks will do,
Chips and dip, and ice cream, too.

Eggs and bacon, biscuits with jelly,
Or bagels and cream cheese, fresh from the deli.
Doughnuts, pastries, apple pie,
Ham and melted swiss on rye;

By now I'm hungry as can be
All this food, it seems to me
That I can only wonder why
All this could come from just one fry!

Emily Woodruff

"A Letter To My Mother"

Dear Mom
I promised to write you a letter the last time we
talked on the phone, which be Mother's Day 1977.
    Mom I didn't get a chance to write that letter,
until now, eight months later, I can't say hope you're
fine, and hope to see you soon, because I was
called to your bed-side a week before Christmas,
you couldn't hear nor say I love you, or that I
be sorry for any grief or pain I had caused you during
our time together, for you already be slipping away.
    And although we miss you, we know God knew
best when he called you from this earth into his
heavenly rest.
    So long mom until I take my last walk with
God and he says come home, I have someone
waiting with outstretched arms to welcome you
with the same love she had the day you were born.
    And I will again look into your smiling face.

Gladys Brown

Taxes

It's the end of the year, after all the fun,
I realize now, there's much to be done.
My income tax, dreaded job of the year,
Enough money to meet it is all that I fear.

I gather the bills and all the invoices.
Oh, how I wish I had other choices.
Add, subtract and work thru the night.
At last it's done and I turn out the light.

I roll up my sleeves and write a big check.
I'd like to ignore it, but what the heck,
Uncle Sam needs every cent he can get.
There's never been a surplus of funds yet.

I live in America, where standards are high.
There's plenty to enjoy till the day that I die.
I can keep what I have and cultivate more,
The many good things sort of even the score.

Edna T. Helberg

A Test!

Hear comes the teacher handing out the test.
I really hope that I can do my best.
It is two long pages.
I feel like I've been put in cages.
I look over to the person next to me,
But I'm a boy and she's a she.
I really want to get this done,
So I can go have some fun.
I am really trying to concentrate,
Because tests are things I really hate.
Now my pencil is starting to fade.
Now I'm finished. I hope I get a good grade!

Cody Koehler

I Saw God This Morning

I saw God this morning, he strengthened my belief.
I saw Him in the glimmering of dew drops in a leaf.
I saw Him in the graceful doe that nibbled on the brush.
I saw Him in the lilac bush and in the beauty of a thrush.
I saw Him in the mallards, swimming in the brook.
I saw Him in the big mouth bass upon my grandson's hook.
I saw Him in the rosebush just starting to unfurl.
I saw Him in the innocence of my son's new baby girl.
I saw Him in my daughter's smile and in my sons' tanned faces.
I saw Him in the comfort of my husband's warm embraces.
I heard Him in the goldfinch song and the cooing of the dove
As I stood there in my kitchen surrounded by His love.

Carol E. Benoit

The Water's Light

Ancient Dreamer, fire of life,
I return once again to this beach of strife.
Here beneath the moon, stars, clouds dancing through the air;
I looked into the water and saw my visage rippling there.
If only I could swim into that face's night,
I'd remove this iron clad, my pain, my fright.
Oh why can't I swim into the night?
Cast fear away, find your eternal twilight.
But death will not die and the fear won't go away;
I am grappled to this beach and oh how I pray.
Pray for my freedom, the warm vision in the sky;
Hear me Ancient Dreamer, Ancient Dreamer reply:

Thence through dawn's golden gateway Thou sent,
An angel, lighting the waters with each blazing movement,
Dances faith into my eyes: a jewel within the sea.
I dove into my reflection, boldly to be free.

Andrew Oresto

Growing Old Together

I had a dream of growing old, my friend beside me still.
I sat and thought, "I love this man, I know I always will."

This wonderful man entered my world and made my life complete.
The time that passed was wonderful, the memories so sweet.

The years had passed, my love had grown, his love had grown for me.
We cherished every moment, our love was plain to see.

The dream was great, I held his hand as I had done for years,
And as I did, I looked at him amid my happy tears.

He looked at me and smiled so sweet, I knew that he still cared.
And looking deep into his eyes, I thought of times we'd shared.

We'd laughed, we'd talked, we'd prayed as one our hearts forever true.
This wonderful man of my sweet dream was no one else but you!

This dream was not a dream at all, but a good life shared with you.
How wonderful when dreams are lived, and not as one, but two.

Growing old has happy times when you know that there is love.
I say a prayer of unending thanks to the matchmaker up above.

Geneva Ybarra

Untitled

Black rain came the day
I sat at the fireplace
And did not understand
That though the boy I called
My son, had grown into
A man
Then I stood and out the
Pane I saw a rainbow
And what more did I see
A little boy had grown
To strength his father looking back at me

Amber Sipes

Insecurity

Emotionally drained,
I sit staring blankly
Afraid of the emptiness I feel.
Terrorizing images rage in my memory

Things have changed
My peace has been devoured by time.
This hatred in my heart won't let me forget.

Awareness came all too soon.
Leaving behind a disaster
Raping my innocence
Security is a luxury I have never known.

Brandy Hestand

Yellow Daffodils

I walked into the forest, why was
I scared?
I've been there before, it's just been —
I guess, many-many-years.

The place of comfort, of endless time
The place where I am hers and she is mine
Where my mind is ripped open, my soul
naked and bare
Where she listens, we listen, no one,
Every one is there.

We open, we close - a private place to rest
Our restless hearts our hopes our dreams-
Each holding the others' to their breast.

Softly, softly, the memory unfolds
Life's dream meaning, to love and be loved
This minute, this moment, this memory is life's
Love to us...pure gold.

Bill Buck

"The Beauty Of Life"

As I walk out into the cool, open air
  I see a beautiful world before my eyes.

A world full of happiness and pleasure.
  The flowers carry a secret scent of sweet perfume,

Evergreen trees growing high into the sky.
The sun is as bright as it is warm,
Shining over my face all day.

When the time comes for the sun to go down,
it is still very serene and beautiful.

The full moon ever so round and pure
as the night owls start hooting,
and the wild coyotes are howling.

This is the place I call home.
As I look out from my bedroom window,
I appreciate the beauty of life.

Anita Patel

My Shadow

I'm sitting in my room watching the fire dance.
I see a shadow before me, again I'm in a trance.

What is this that's coming towards me?
Oh! It's only a dream that will never be.
I'm fighting in my covers, I don't want to awake,
For this shadow is my only means of escape.
She is tall and thin and has long hair.
She lays on my floor, all I can do is stare.
She sits up and she is crawling towards me.
We are together now, I feel so free.
The dreams that I have, I wish would come true.
I have my shadow, thank God for you.
Dreams and fantasies that are in my mind
Seems like the only pleasure that I can find.
If my shadow would visit me tonight
Then I'm not alone again for another night.

Jimmie D. Zehring

Fire And Ice

Through the nylon mesh of the blindfold
I see his form, this man-child who
can rob me of myself forever.
He bends closer, and I feel his
hot hands as he explores my familiar body.

Against my back the floor is cold and soothing
I yearn to escape from the volcanic flesh above me,
But the floor yields nothing, and my
childish body is covered and lost.

I can feel the texture of flesh against flesh,
but my mind is elsewhere;
A cool lake, passionless and calm,
Dr. Seuss, T.V., baseball games distance
me from reality.

Immersed in shame and guilt, my
Anger retreats into the background
Simmering and Smoldering beneath a
facade of innocence and complacency.

Each touch, each possessive grip kills a part of Me.
What did I do to deserve this destruction?

Caryn L. Hebets

I'm Caught Within My Body

At times escaping seems impossible,
I see myself in ways that are destructive
it seem there's no stopping,
to stop means trusting others,
I look in a mirror and I don't see what I should see,
that leads to destructiveness
It seems there's no end,
I slowly fade away without knowing it,
I want it to end, but it seems impossible,
the thoughts and actions become real,
so real I believe them, and when I act on them
I slowly fade away, becoming sick and weak,
only to desire freedom,
freedom from the pain and hurt, freedom from my soul,
some would say you would only find freedom through death,
that wouldn't be freedom to me,
I want freedom through life,
freedom from the being within that holds me down,
I want to rise up and be free once again.

Colleen Collins

My Tennessee Childhood Home

Sitting up on this hill, looking down in the valley
I see where my ancestors used to roam
I look over there on that vacant lot
And think of my Tennessee childhood home

The weeds have grown up, the fences torn down
Not a trace of the old house is there
But yonder stands my old apple tree
And memories of my childhood are everywhere

I can still see my Daddy out there plowing
And Mama cooking over the old wood stove
Sure times were hard but we always made it
'Cause our house was filled with lots of love

Now they're gone and I'm here recalling
All the good things sent from God up above
I thank Him for all these wonderful memories
Of my mountain top Tennessee childhood home

Before I die I'd like to come back up here
And build a cabin where we used to roam
And hope that someday my grandchildren
Will have their own Tennessee childhood home

Buna M. Schaible

By The Fireplace - Again

I have so many lessons to learn.
I sit here watching the glowing fire, listening to it crackle.
Instead of enjoying it I am angry, tense, upset with it.
I have to get up and work with it every 20 or 30 minutes, just
   to keep it going.

I want it to be instant fire - light it - sit back - let it roar!
As I take the time to sit and stroke it, I'm beginning to enjoy
   it in new and different ways.
I am starting to relate it, and it to me - care for it, feed
   it, rearrange it, push it, this way and that, pull it back
   again, add to it, make it my fire!

I don't need a fire that can take care of itself.
I don't need relationship that can just care of themselves.
I don't need a life that is managed for me.
Even though these may be the things that I have been looking for!
I need a fire that I can caress, stroke, play with, and maybe,
   God forbid, someday even share!

   James E. Hall

My Wife

It took 19 years to find a woman like you, so beautiful and true,
I sometimes wonder why you love me like you do.
I thank God everyday, I beg, hope and pray.
That with me you'll forever stay.
For with you is true life,
two wonderful kids and the worlds best wife.
You're the Angel I dreamed of, sent from God above,
full of generosity and great love.
I hope that someday to hear you say,
you forgive me for all the stupid things I do and say.
I'd swear to God above
forever with you I will be in love.

   Carl J. Stenger

A Magical World In My Mind

Behold me sits a blank piece of paper
I stare long and hard at it
I have no idea what to write, yet still I sit
I wish it could open a magical world,
Where kingdoms arise and mermaids float
I'd smile in surprise and sit in a magic boat
The boat takes me far to visit King Gerald and Queen Lynn
And there my magic dreams begin
King Gerald says to me, "Visit the mermaids"
Queen Lynn says to me, "Visit the gardens"
I visit the mermaids in the clear blue sea,
I visit the gardens, so beautiful to me
All of a sudden, I'm back on the boat,
Back to the paper, where no mermaids could float
Suddenly the idea came to me
I lift my pencil and smile with delight
A wonderful, magical world, for everyone to see.

   Cherilyn Anne M. Sajorda

To My Once Love

On this day of mine, alone
I think of thee, at each dawn.
   Alone and thinking.
How it could have been and should have been.
   On this day of mine, alone.
Is it late, so late this cannot be?
   On this day of mine, alone.
As time must go on,
We come to our end, alone and thinking.
On this day of mine, alone.
Will it ever be, just you and me,
On our day alone.

   Joan Wyatt-Mackay

Chocolate

Just one more piece of chocolate,
I swear I'm going to quit.
It's not like if I don't get it,
I'll have a chocolate fit.

Chocolate has been with me,
Through my childhood and my teens.
It's just that when you're forty,
It's a difficult habit to wean.

I live each day for my daily dose,
Of cocoa, milk, sugar and butter.
But, I swear to you for one more bite,
I'll go the rest of my life without another.

Please don't think I'm begging,
Even though I'm on bended knees.
All I want is one more bite,
Of Hershey, Reese's, or M and M's please!

I probably shouldn't quit right now,
But enjoy all of it while I can.
Because once Washington sees its hazards,
I'm sure there will be a ban.

   Delores Ruhl

Is It Them Or Is It Me

At least four nights out of the week
I take this long mind searching ride
Most of the time only to be greeted with a frown
Instead of a smile. I sure hate it when they
Return from these two days - because most of
Them seems to come back in a rage.
They say we are all grown up around here - but
There's always animosity in the atmosphere.
So I ask; Is it me or is it them?
Some of them play religious and some pretend to
Be concern - but if you don't keep an eye out
In back - I think some would hit you with an iron.
That's why I wonder; Is it them or is it me?
Shakin' and fakin' is what it's called - so I
know; It's not me at all!!!
One day you can communicate
The next day you have to hesitate
On whether or not to negotiate
Because all these mix emotions continue to rotate
Again I ask; Is it me or is it them???

   Francine Tyler

Being Dead

Death is so cold, it is so sad for the days of the dead
I think at night, being so old, as I lay in my death bed

And I pray... "Dear Lord
Be with me from day to day
I'm so scared, would I be bored"
He then answered me back
"It's not boring, it's filled with love."
Then I said to him back
"You mean where angels are white as dove?"

He said "yes" to me I said "But...
Where shall I get the keys?"
He then answered with glee

"This is when you shall believe
Believe in what you know
Then your soul shall leave
When it leaves you will go.

So don't be afraid my child of the key
For all you've got to do is what you know
Thank you dear Lord for answering me
For I love you and I know what has to be so."

   Jamie Leet

My Dog Is Gone

The inside of me is filled with tears.
  I think that I shall grieve for years
For I want no one to see
  Just what the matter is with me,
But I do so want to cry out loud
  For a friend so dear who wears a shroud
Though it would not be just the thing
  As people would paint and try to bring
Ridicule upon this head of mine
  At grieving for a friend canine.
But I care not just what they think
  My love for him will never shrink
To less than all that I could give
  If it would only make him live
Again to be a friend to me
  With his loving canine company.
But he is gone, and how I grieve!
  Oh why, oh why did he have to leave
And fill the inside of me with tears
  To make me sad for years and years.

  Dale C. Bowen

The Stranger

Once walking through a shady wood alone,
I thought I'd seen a stranger standing out near the road.
But as I took a closer look,
Lent a better ear,
Spread wide my nostrils for another whiff,
Stuck out my tongue to keenly taste
The flavor of the stranger,
I recognized that it was no stranger,
But it was I in a strange disguise.

While seated on the earth in a clearing in the woods,
I thought I'd seen that stranger
playing deceitful games again.
But as I closed my eyes,
Listened to my breath,
Loosened all my muscles
And moved about myself,
I realized that it was not a stranger,
But it was I who'd been telling lies.

  Deborah T. Salahu-Din

My Party

All my friends were drinking
I thought why not do the same
After all it was my party
And I wanted to be part of the gang
I never thought about what would happen
I guess none of us did
We just wanted to party and have fun
Like every other kid
So after the party was over
We jumped in to the car
We headed down the freeway
Zooming past all the cars
All of a sudden the car got out of control
And I didn't know what to do
Every one started screaming for a second or two
Now in complete silence I lay here wondering why
Why I thought it was cool to drink and drive

  Jessica Paruszkiewicz

"My Wonderful Little Boy"

As soon as I first laid eyes on you,
I thought you were too good to be true;

I brought into this world a bundle of joy,
Everything I ever wanted, a perfect little boy!

Every time I see you smile,
I just can't walk away, not even for a little while;

Whenever I have problems and get depressed,
I just think of you and realize I am so blessed;

God brought you from Heaven above,
And sent you to us to cherish and love;

He gave you to me,
And forever grateful I will be;

You've brought me so much joy,
My wonderful little boy!

And I just want you to know,
How very much I love you so.

  Julie Petrausch

My Flower

As in the Spring, Lord, your flowers I watch grow,
  I, too, a flower to produce, you would come to know.,
Born she was on the first day of Spring
  To all a time of your happiness brings;
Dainty and sweet like your Crocus she is,
  Touch of rain on her face, glow appears like jonquils each year,
As the Summer lingers on and Roses appear.
  She'll remind you of them, so elegant and dear;
Wind blowing fields of beautiful green wheat,
  Flowing as freely like her graceful feats;
I've watched her blossom these thirty-one years,
  Into a beautiful lady, loving, thoughtful, that she is;
Only you, Lord, can really know,
  Joys she has given me, tears of happiness I show;
Grant her happiness and peace of mind,
  To me she will always be just one of a kind;
Thank you, Lord, for the ability and power,
  The Earth to grace another beautiful flower.

Dedicated to our daughter, Janet.

  Genevieve Grant

A Poem For Glenn

Not knowing that someday I would not see you again,
I took for granted your loving smile, your gentle touch,
your handsome face.

We explored the many facets of love together-
Young love, first love, steady love, married love,
the love of our children.

Our hands and lips fit as if made for one another - they were.
And when the passion became gentle,
we became as one.

Pain, loneliness, growing apart;
these came and brought with them bitterness and then apathy.
It was as bad as it had been good.

I left, but my heart stayed; yours broke and then failed.
You took my heart and soul with you
when you left this earth.

And though this pain may someday fade,
I will never forget you.
I loved and love you still.

  Evelyn Henderson

Seasons Gone By

My thoughts race back to yesterday when
I tramp the fields, still wet with dew,
And listen to the sounds made by all
God's creatures as they scamper cross the ground.

I draw on rich memories that recall
Stars twinkling in the blackness of night.
Of knowing past Springs with their dogwood
blossoms, and dewberries,
And the dog days of summer blending into the
Amber of Autumn.
The Winter days when the snowbird sings his
Winter song,
And sings it merrily.
When frost is sparking in the sun there on the
Holly trees.
Much like our lives, the seasons mature
And call attention to nature
And in a blink of an eye
All is gone

Jack C. Nobles

Here I Stand

When the pressures of the world come crashing down on me,
I turn and look at you and heavenly bliss is what I see.
The Good Lord has smiled on me and shown me your hand,
With love filling my heart, beside you forever, here I stand.

This feeling within my heart tells me we will always be one,
Together we can chase the stars or quietly watch the morning sun.
Our love will grow with every day, all the pressures it will
withstand,
With love filling my heart, beside you forever, here I stand.

Our time together goes so fast and I may not always tell you,
No matter what life brings us, my feelings will always hold true.
The winds may come and blow and carry me all over the land,
With love filling my heart, beside you forever, here I stand.

Jean Isham

Untitled

Searching for answers,
I walk into the sunlight
Which brightens the brown, red, yellow, and orange
Spread sparingly through the somber green
That clings in vain to Summer.

As the sun reaches for the west,
Searching endlessly for rest,
An Autumn breeze,
Sometimes gentle often firm,
Carries a chilling taste of Winter.

Still, I search for answers.

Pondering this harbinger of cold,
That wandering wind,
I look for hope in the face of the oncoming Winter.

It seems Spring would be a more likely candidate,
For hope.
Yet Spring is not here,
She has traveled to a more Southerly abode.

And the questions remain,
Searching for answers.

Daron M. Carroll

The Path Through The Garden Of Life

Once long ago, in the forgotten depths of my memory,
I wandered through the path of blooming, sunlit garden.
This garden was a haven for all of my flitting thoughts
And the gate that closed it was my sleep, a silent warden.

Questions and pondering blew through the flowers in this unknown place
And the main thought in my footsteps was the wonder of my
purpose in life.
I hurried further as my memory caught sight of a mysterious
curve in the path that I knew not of ere now.
This I knew, was the answer to my questions and the curing of
all strife.

Long did I yearn, and after long hours of aimless wandering through
memories of curtsying roses and the bleeding heart of lost love,
Realized that the answer would not be found in traversing the
road beyond,
But throughout my struggles with the confused and twisting vines
of life
And at my final home, when the curve would curve be reached
and I could lay down my burden and blessing of life.

I experienced this dream of a ramble along this forgotten path,
As when awake, I struggled with the hardships of life, making a
way through,
Getting nearer yet to my final destination, the bend in the dusty
path surrounded by fleeting floral memories.
I knew the answer was yet to come, as much else would come too.

Eileen Chou

Old Calendar

All through the year,
    I was one of your best friends.
You smiled with me always.
    You even marked very special days
So that you won't forget easily,
    And at other times,
You counted the days so anxiously
    For those happy moments to finally come.
I even reminded you about
    Special holidays like Birthday, Christmas
And many other happy times.
    I was a part of the home
And welcome every visitor with a smiling face.
    Indeed, I was a friend to you.
But, you've been so ungrateful to me.
    At the end of the year,
When the family is re-arranging the home,
    You jump as soon as you remember me,
And my place in your new home is the dump site,
    Only Good for making fire.

Emmanuel Moore

Snowfall

A thick blanket of whiteness covered the earth
    I was up
    I had to go
    I went.

Stepping on the sacrosanct whiteness of God's icy powder
Sinking with e'ry step
    On, on, I went towards my bus.

Powdery spray of cool feathers hit my jacket
Like from birds in flight dropped, burst, vanishing.

When the world slept, the whiteness mixed with serene silence
To welcome the kiss of the moon.
Reflecting its joy in an opulent shine.

A fragile majestic every breath threatened to destroy.

Clement Bonsu

Could It Be?

The other day a strange thing happened
I wasn't asleep, just sort of nappin'
When all at once this tiny creature came
And stood before me and spoke my name.
He said,"You need a friend that's plain to see
And no one can be a friend like me.

"I may be small that's very true
but you'd be amazed at what I can do,
I'll have a listening ear when you need to talk,
I'll keep you company on your lonely walks.

"I'll lie at the foot of your bed every night
You'll know I'm on guard and every thing's all right,
I'll keep you company and cuddle up close
And share with you your morning toast.

"When we've been together awhile you'll see
That no friend could be more faithful than me,
It doesn't matter while we share this house
That you are a woman and I'm just a mouse!"
Helen A. Righthouse

As The Summer Ends

As the summer ends,
I watch the leaves float slowly down.
They all turn pretty colors;
Red, yellow and brown.

As the summer ends,
the colors turn so very bright;
And there's not as many hours left of sun
before the night.

As the summer ends,
the nights will soon be cool.
Then before you know it,
"Goodbye", I'm off to school.

As the autumn ends,
the colors disappear from sight.
And now the snow is falling;
All the colors have turned white.

As the autumn ends,
all the bears will go to bed.
Now the ground is fully covered.
I hope we have a sled.
Brian Wiedenhaefer

The Road To.....

Slip me a hand -
I will surely grab onto.
Let us walk in the grip of love.
Let it guide us through life's long journey.

Show me a river -
I will surely leap into.
Let us bathe in the cool water.
Let it lead us to life's peaceful seas.

Catch me a star -
I will surely wish upon.
Let us ride in the moonlit skies.
Let it take us through life's heavens as one.
David J. Turner

Roses

When I look at my beautiful yellow roses
I think of the man I love.
They stand long and strong,
and give me such pleasure.
I think of the man I love when I see my yellow roses,
for it was he who gave them to me.
JoAnn Arredondo

God

I look toward the sky, see a rainbow
I wonder at its brilliant colors
    And I see GOD

I look at a sunset, the warmth fills my heart
I have hope for a beautiful tomorrow
    And I see GOD

I am in awe of all creation, ponder its beauty
Meditate on when it is born, and when it dies
    And I see GOD

I listen to the rain, it refreshes my soul
I know it quenches thirst in man, animal and plant
    And I hear GOD

The wind blows gently through my hair
It cools me and relaxes my body
    And I feel GOD

I watch one human being, then another
I see them feed, clothe and care for one another
    And I love GOD

I am in complete darkness, total silence all my senses at rest
    And I meet GOD
Anne E. Engo

"You Thru My Eyes"

If you walked a mile in my shoes,
I wonder if you would still be as bold.
I think, if you seen you, thru my eyes,
You would know why I say you're so cold...

You claim you've got all of the answers,
You're famous for "I TOLD YOU SO".
But, believe it or not, you're not perfect,
And there's a lot in this world, you don't know...

I know that my life has had some problems,
But I don't think it's your place to say,
I think what you have to remember,
Is we can't all live life, your way...

So instead of trying to dictate,
And telling me how I should live,
Why don't you try understanding,
And see what help you could give...

I don't need your love or your money,
I don't want you to go out of your way,
But I believe the one thing, you should do,
Is to keep quiet, if you've nothing to say...
James P. Hale

Retrospect

When I grow up to be a woman, I thought,
I would at last be free from tears that played me then;
it would not matter if my favorite doll were crushed into a thousand
    bits,
or some small prize I treasured in my childish heart
were suddenly lost forever from my sight.

What irony lies buried here! - to think that years
could bring escape from the slated edge of life.
The fondest dream is broken in the dust,-
the prized possession eludes the longing soul
and tears, - hot, feverish and anguished, flow unabated.

Perchance it is that in the scheme of life
'tis growth that is the purpose of it all;
and this that breaks the heart today
may lend itself to build tomorrow's soul.
Then - one day we may rise to see
that step by step
we walked into Eternity.
June E. Donna

Love

The greatest news arrived today
I would be a Mother in the month of May
A greater thrill could not be had
I was on cloud nine and oh so glad.

A baby boy would thrill our soul
Or a sweet baby girl could take control
This bundle of joy was coming our way
As we patiently waited for the great big day.

Together we prayed for a healthy child
With curly blonde hair and big blue eyes
A child who would make us ever so proud
Like an angel from heaven on a soft white cloud.

God doubled his promise when the day arrived
With a baby boy who had big blue eyes
A curly haired girl with dimpled cheek
Helped make our family absolutely complete.

It was surely a dream God made come true
Enjoyed only by a hand picked few
I thank God every day I live
For two beautiful babies that only he could give.

Evelyn Scott Gregory

"If I Were In Charge Of A Music Store"

If I were in charge of a Music Store,
I would cancel "RAP".
Tuesday all day and Thursday nights.
Also really really really heavy ROCK MUSIC.

If I were in charge of a Music Store,
There would be rainbow pianos,
Singing instruments and talking, walking guitars.

If I were in charge of a Music Store,
you would not have your best clothes on.
You would not have difficult Music lessons.
You would not have "SCALES", to practice.
You would not EVEN have "Scales".

If I were in charge of a Music Store,
I would decorate with golden shiny Music Notes.
Some instruments would be FREE.
A person who sometime forget to practice and
sometimes forget their "SCALES". But.......
They would still be WELCOME IN MY MUSIC STORE.

Howard Bertin

"A Thousand Dreams"

If I had a thousand dreams, my dreams would be of you.
I would dream that God had sent "his angels back with you".
I would dream of all the love and everything we shared and
And I would dream that God had wiped away all my tears.
I would dream, and dream, and dream, "never to wake up,
Because God sent his angels down, the night you wrecked your truck.
You see, God sent me dreams to dream, because he understands.
He walks with me and talks with me and carries me in his hands.
If I had a thousand dreams, my dreams would be of you.
Yes, God sent his angels down and they carried you above.
And then he sent me dreams to dream, because of all his love.

Geraldine Player

If I Could...

If I could, I would take away the pain,
I would hold you and fill you with peace.
If I could,

If I could I would tell you what a difference you make,
How little it takes to love you.

If I could I would instill in you faith
That happiness will find you again!
If only I could,

If I could I would give you hope;
Why can't you see the brightness tomorrow brings?

If I could I would ask your forgiveness,
For even in loving you, I have hurt you.
If only I could,

But I'm not as strong as I'd like,
More selfish than I should

If I could I would love you till....
I can and I will!

Janie E. Huot

My Son,

If I could speak from the heavens,
I would say,

"Hold on and keep the faith,
Remember our Savior's loving grace."

If I could reach from the heavens,
I would,
Hold your hand and touch your face,
I would let you a sample of God's glory taste."

If I could cheer from the heavens,
I would,
Cheer the voice that sang the story,
Of my Savior and his glory.

If I could applaud from the heavens,
I would,
Applaud the hands that play the guitar,
For you are indeed a superstar.

If I could step from the heavens,
I would hug you tight,
To let you know, "You're precious in God's sight."
Love, Mom

Frances M. Harris

If I Had A Wish

If I had a wish I know what I would wish for
I would wish for a puppy named Patches,
a dog with long eye lashes.
She would look like the poster on my wall
but of course she wouldn't be so tall.
I would love her, and feed her, and take
real good care of her.
I know she would follow me every where I go,
It would be fun to watch her go so slow.
When she would sleep with me, I'd give her a
hug and up beside me she'd curl.
BECAUSE she would be the cutest puppy
in the whole wide world.
So from the very wishful start I'd love this
puppy with all my heart!

Gretchen George

If

If I had no eyes to see, would life tragedies bother me?
If I had no ears to hear, would I comprehend a silent tear?
If I had no mouth to talk, would I just be a balk?
If I didn't have these senses, what would be the consequences?
I'm thankful for all these things, tomorrow's another day and
there's always new springs.
To see the jonquil and daffodil, give me a sense of good will.
To hear the sound of the birds, no it's not so absurd.
To be able to laugh and say ha, for that I thank Jah.

Jeanne M. Butler

Diminishing Marginal Returns

How can a market hope to survive,
If not forecasting the future through children's eyes?
Those vacant stares aren't meant to deceive.
Their prayers and dreams adults can't perceive.

Lie, if it eases the painful truth.
Ideals are lost along with youth.
Buried in vaults. Soul dead.
In God we trust? "In Greed" instead.

Commodities of the heart - Take stock of.
Does gold measure success? A child banks on love;
A non-interest bearing account,
Since nothing equals nothing times any amount.

In green terms consider then,
Diminishing gains, oh, business men,
When figuring in the replacement cost
Of an entire generation the profiteers lost.

Joan Mulloy

"Lost Ourselves To Literature"

I know where the lilies flower
If you follow me
We can venture there
The table is glass
Everything simply the best
There's know one who's to judge us away from now
A place where you and I could share
A world we could create
Heaven is our home
Everybody knows
The house of literature is where the flowery flowers grow
Don't try to hide the final true part of you
We lost ourselves to literature
My helpless pen ran out of ink
like a Gladiola that blooms and wilts in the midst of June
Poetry as we both know has overtaken us so
Yes, you are surely
My true love literate dream
As I awake alone

Christopher Yanez

Last Tear

In Memory of Shawn D. Wagner (1979-1994)

Today's the day I'll shed my last tear.
I'll close my eyes to the past and open them
to the future. Lock the doors to all my fears.
Triumph through the days.

Today's the day I'll shed my last tear.
I pray for another yesterday. I pray for one
last moment. I pray to lead you along your way.
I pray this very moment.

Today's the day I'll shed my last tear.
The light in your eyes is no longer. The love
in my heart has grown stronger. To know what
I have lost brings great sorrow. My tears
know no limits.

Cynthia M. Turpen

World War III

War has been declared on man.
Ignorance and fear,
Are its choice of weapons.
Unprotected sex,
Has kept it alive.
Heartache is its gift, when loved ones die.

Its disguise is smoother than the wind.
Camouflaged,
Among family and friends.
Intravenous drugs,
Strengthened its attack.
Arm yourself with knowledge, and fight back.

My friends, "Aids" has become world war III.
So spread the news.
Draft your friends and family.
Help stop the growth,
Until a cure is found.
For now it's the best way to stand our ground.

Catherine M. K. Poulin

Love Song

I'll write you a love song, to woo, to woo.
I'll write you a love song, to woo.
I'll tell of your kindness, your laughter, your smile
And lips that are sweet as the spring first dew.

I'll play you a love a song, ta dum, ta dum.
I'll play you a love song, ta dum.
I'll tell of your goodness, your patience, your strength
And arms that are warm as the hot summer sun.

I'll sing you a love song, a hum, a hum
I'll sing you a love song, a hum.
I'll tell of your fight for the just and the right
And mind that is crisp as the fall leaves undone.

I'll live you a love song and grow and grow.
I'll live you a love song and grow.
I'll love your pure spirit and want to be near it
And treasure your soul while the winter winds blow.

Carol L. Thompson

"The Hunter"

Over the fence and across the field; into the woods I go.
I'm after the biggest Buck around; and I won't accept a Doe.
The snow is getting deep; the wind is hard and cold.
But my gun is full of bullets; the terrain is "good as gold".
Slipping and sliding, tripping and falling, heading for the top of
   the hill.
There I see a very young boy; he was gutting-out his kill.
I pat his back and shake his hand; then leave him to his chore.
Eight-point Buck was fine for him; but I wanted something more.
Twenty miles later; my legs have turned to mush.
My hands and feet are frozen; but I keep on "bustin' brush".
Walking through a clearing; surrounded by thickets and pines.
I saw the monster Buck at last; sharpening up his tines.
He bolted down the hill; and jumped across the crick.
I didn't even get a shot; I guess he was too quick.
I ran along the side-hill; trying to cut him off.
But I fell to the ground exhausted; and began to puke and cough.
I looked across the valley; he was standing on a cliff.
His head stood tall and proud; his neck was thick and stiff.
I turned around and walked away; proud of what I'd seen.
I thought the only Buck like that; was in my wildest dream.

Dana Carlson

"I Won't Forget You"

Holding this pillow wishing it was you,
I'm just praying this wish will come true.
I know you don't love me, at least that's
    what it seems,
At least I still can make love to
    you in my dreams.
Until you come through,
I guess that will have to do.
I won't forget you,
Or those things that we shared
Hold me,
Can't you see that I am scared.
If you can't conceive,
Or find it hard to believe,
I want to tell you it's true,
I won't forget you.

Heather Aucoin

Nancy Girl

I'm not good at writing poems, not good at choice words
I'm not good at many things, but I'm not really "for the birds"
"Nancy Girl," I love you, I knew you from the start
My love for you, shall never part

We have come a long way, and what I'd like to say
I've waited for a long time, for this special day
When you were a little girl, you said you would "marry me"
My answer to you was, "Let's wait and see"
Now wait and see is over, someone else is on your mind
Let me tell you, you've made a wonderful find
Many times waiting brings happiness so true
And so "My Nancy Girl," this will hold true for you

My poem is almost over, but my love for you goes on
Even though there is someone else named John
And if he loves you just as much as I
Then "My Nancy Girl," you met the right guy
As I said before, we have come quite a long way
Something within me told me, I would see this day
May you both have health and happiness, and all my love too
These are my wishes for John and you

Harry B. Sherr

The War Days

    The bombs are falling, all around me
I'm surely glad that none have found me.
    The bombs are falling, day and night
Throughout the long hard battles we fight.

    Bloodshed, color of crimson red
Lying on the soldiers dead.
    Bloodshed leaking to the ground
From the dead we'll hear no sound.

    Bunkers made of heavy stone
Help us save our flesh and bone.
    Bunkers made of warping wood
Will kill us all, will do no good.

    Bullets flying East and West
Hitting soldiers in the chest.
    Bullets flying through the air
Killing soldiers in despair.

    From this day I shall adore
We do not have to fight no more,
    Because this is the end of the war.

Brad Manial

Memories

On a rusty, old nail, in the basement
In a corner behind the door,
Hangs a dusty, old, beat up cowboy hat
A hat that Daddy once wore.

The brim is all wrinkled and tattered
There's not much shape to it now.
The crown is all stained, and dirty
From the sweat of his wrinkled brow.

Although it is all dusty, and dirty,
It has a special attraction, you see.
For this old, dusty, tattered cowboy hat
Is just bursting with memories.

Some men work for a life time
Just to save up silver and gold.
but I wouldn't trade all their treasures
For the memories that this old hat does hold.

Duane Taylor

A Perfect World

In a perfect world the grass would always be green.
In a perfect world stars would shine all night,
In a perfect world the sun would sparkle in the day.
A perfect world—
No smog, no crime, no guns, no hate, no pain.
In a perfect world
Two souls could find each other, when in love.
In a perfect world
Love and respect would rule the world,
Not greed and power.
A perfect world-
No violence, no regrets, no tears, no mistakes.
In a perfect world white and clear is seen,
While on earth too many colors blind our vision.
We see the wrongs, and know what's right.
But courage lacks where selfishness dominates.
Gain of wealth, not respect—
This is what is important in a not so perfect world.

Elizabeth Mushoyan

The Scuffle

Scuffling in the dirt one sunny morning
    in earnest pursuing a poem,
elusively capering and fluttering away
    on the gusting wind,
which I cast off onto the pavement when I
    imagined I saw another worthier one
which got away just before I could find out
    what intensity and hue it was;
I realized it must have been beautiful,
    more breath-taking than the morning,
and I let it go, for when it would reach
    humanity it would bestow its aura
upon the earth and evermore be born.

Jann Marie Foster

I Know

I know in my heart, God is there,
    In heaven on his throne,
When I bring him, my burdens and cares,
    He assures me, I'm never alone!
On God's strength and love, I depend,
    They flow down like a waterfall each day,
He reaches forth an outstretched hand,
    To lead me, so I don't lose my way!
At days end, when I kneel to pray,
    And thank him for his mercy and goodness,
Words can't express, what my heart wants to say,
    In God's love, I've so richly been blessed!

Connie E. Fisher

The Heroine Inside

A heroine lives inside of you.
  In every woman there lives a heroine brave
  and true.

To the housewives who stand by their husbands
loyal and strong.

  To the mothers who teach their children
  right from wrong.

To the little girls who try to fit their
mommy's shoes.

  To the young ladies with worries of boys
  and schools.

To the women who choose to be doctors and
nurses and fight for our lives.

  To the women who choose to be judges and
  lawyers for our freedom they strive.

To the women who put their lives at risk and to
the ones, if put in their position, they would.

  There lives a heroine in every woman.

Like a hero in every man.
Jennafer Worland

Time

Time is a crippled little man with holes
in his pockets where all his wealth
ran through

Time is a white haired prim and proper woman
whose stern glare lies to her grandchildren
to hide the daring frivolous lassy behind those eyes.

Time is a fat old hound lying belly up in the sun
with dreams of chasing rabbits once more

Time is a cleaning lady on her hands and knees
with a pale green rag which once was a part
of a designer original she wore to the prom.

Time is hills and valleys of endless happiness
and sadness without which life would only be
a long straight gray road to mediocrity.
Jenean Cooper

The Outstretched Arm

This town is small but the people have faith
In ideals large, paternal, and safe-
But I'm the one who'll vanish on
The horizon.

The highways are merely extended arms
Reaching to the villages and to the farms-
Beckoning for the souls mired in
Obscurity.

The city called, and I was more than willing
To see storefronts, but not the blood spilling
Out from the victims crushed in its
Hand.

Skyscrapers are fingers tickling the clouds
The streets, a palm, holding the crowds
In the cracks and they're trapped if the
Fingers decide to converge.

I followed the black path to the countryside
Where my sanity and I hope to reside
Out of the mighty fingers of
The urban grip.
Dan Deitschel

A Boston Sailing Captain's Vow

To sail at sea, is the greatest joy,
In life, to me.
With a sturdy ship, of loyal men,
And myself in command of them.
  We will happily sail the seven seas,
  and challenge any chart of longitude and degrees,
From the coldest arctic waste,
To the hottest tropic place.
  We will bravely fight the angry waves and gales,
  and bring to you many, many, strange, enchanting tales.
Even about, the demons that we have met,
  from the deepest oceans depths!
But only when we have sailed the world around,
  and nothing new is to be found,
We all have vowed, that we will come back,
  to home, on land, and stay, and never go back!
Hendryk Zenon Kenna

In Need

Being tired, I lay down and I slept and dreamed.
In my dream, I heard a voice call
It seemed quite near, but yet not near at all.
As I cautiously looked around, an ill-defined figure
appeared and said,
"I am in need."
"In need of what?", I asked. "Where is your need?"
"From where have you come? Where are you going?"
And he said, "I am in need."
"I truly want to find a time, a way, but there are many
things to consider when I schedule my day. Tell me, when
are you most in need?"
And she said, "I AM in need."
Others came from far and near crying, "There is no exit from
need, you hear? "I am in need, I am in need", they said.
But then I awoke in my comfortable bed.
Somewhat disturbed by my strange, short dream, I got up
wondering about that which I had seen.
I looked in the mirror, and what did I see?
I saw Need looking back at me.
Joy M. Steele

Untitled

Am I dreaming? It's hard to tell.

This dream I've lived over and over
in my heart and in my mind.

A dream in which you and I are one,
bounded by an irrepressible, undeniable love.

A love as strong as the love we shared
one dark night.

One night when everything was surrendered.
All our passion unleashed, all our emotions revealed.

It is the love that turns the fantasy real.
It is the love that brings you ever closer to my heart.
It is the love that comforts me when I wonder...
was it only just a dream.
Andrea Kasper

Mother, Says It All!

There are many special Angels,
In our world, of everyday,
No wings are seen, you can be sure,
But they are Angels, all the same!

Some tall, and thin, the fair, the small,
They come in many forms, you see
And quite a few, in larger size,
Like maybe, you, or me!

They may be found just anywhere,
Their colors vary, in every hue,
The rarest Angel of them all,
could possibly, be, YOU!

They've served in every task on earth!
No task too great, or small,
You ask, who all these Angels are?
Mother, says it all!
No recognition, I could ever give,
Mere words, to sing their praise!
For the worthy cause, they choose to live,
Thank God, for a mothers' grace!

Annie Berry

"In Today's World"

There are so many different people
in our world today;
So many different opinions expressed
in different ways.

Many of our morals we hold too
low, but some are held too high;
But have we ever stopped to listen
and ask ourselves "why?"

Is it today's fast pace of the life we live?
Or is it just "time" we have to give?

There's no reason and there's no rhyme;
For God created the heavens
and earth and He took the "time."

The world would be a better
place without war and violence
to overcome;
But discourage "not" and still
show love to everyone.

So remember if love and peace are always sought;
Our hopes and dreams won't be for naught.

Connie Minich

"Alone"

I close my eyes and see my babies born;
  In pain and joy, the gift of life.
I smile and weep for life is sweet and I am whole.

I close my eyes and toddlers roam my heart;
  New words and deeds and toys and joys.
I smile and whisper a prayer of thanks
  For life is sweet and I am whole.

I close my eyes and home from school they come;
  New adventures to disclose, laughter and light,
A rapid babble of day's events shared.
  I smile and listen for life is full and I am whole.

I close my eyes and shed a tear for the memories of
  The "mommy" years that have swiftly passed me by.
It's hard to smile at times like these for life can be
  Bittersweet and there's a longing in my soul.

For here tonight, I close my eyes and there is silence
  And I feel so alone. The babes have grown
And no longer share their days with me. Where can they be?
  I cry aloud for life can be hard and my heart is breaking
And I no longer feel whole.

Judy Dietrich

Two Men, A Chainsaw, And Some Rope

In the yard, now freshly green with the new season's
delicate touch, two men fell a tree,
Whose maple limbs had screamed, then split
under the weight of winter's wrath.

The men, diligent, draw and quarter the doomed
wood sticks with pulverizing saw strokes, yanking
the remains to the ground with slip-knotted nylon.

Seemingly an odd pairing, rather incongruous,
  the two, tenant and his landlord,
    separated by some years, drawn together by
    one woman, struggle with the task at hand.
Appearances deceive.

They work, putting the tree to rest, and enjoy
a beer together afterwards.
Comfortable together, an uncommon ease
between the two, this is their oddness.

Scott Carpenter

The Earthman Sonnet

You do not understand me.
Desire shaped my destiny,
  I do not regret it;
no, I embrace all passion the universe
  would offer me,
rather than be dry, dead, a living shell.

Your indifference is only surface,
  appearances deceive.

Earthman reaching out, never touching.

No words are needed for our invisible
  feeling that floats,
taut air that hums, glowing with life
  of its own.

I paint a picture with words of a
  being that is child,
sweetness, a glow light affectionate
  with fire;
serene eyes with intelligence not human,
unlimited, infinite thinking that does not
  control, defining what it loves.

Sylvia Keck

Looking Down

Father, why have you left me in this world?
Did not know you long enough, not at all.
You resembled me much but your hair curled,
Sometimes I forget you're not here, and call
To you, for my inspiration you were.
No more games or events do you attend,
My intellect and my soul you did stir,
Your rules at times were reluctant to bend.
If you were here today... the things I'd say
Violent nuances of emotion mix,
I'm angry at God, sometimes day to day.
I cried for you when you crossed River Styx.

But now my heart has healed, and the sad frown
Is gone for I know that you're looking down.

Louis S. Crivelli II

Hawk

Yesterday I spied a hawk
Dipping, turning, floating
In wide circles through the sky.
Wings sometimes horizontal
sometimes vertical.
Plummeting to the earth.
Rising with prey hanging from his talons.

Katie Motter

Do You Make A Difference?

When you awoke to start the day
Did you resolve to yourself and say
Lord, let me as a beacon shine
and make the difference for someone today?
Let me give a kind word or deed
to someone who has been bereaved
and did you through your efforts save,
a life, as you travelled along your way?
Did you give a helping hand
to someone lost and all alone?
Did you reach for one who fell,
and rescue them from the jaws of hell?
If you can say yes to all these things
then you made a difference, for someone today.

Nancy R. Binder

Children Killing Children

We all share a world which is in danger right now. We must
make a difference to live here and now. The parents of today
who do their very best, most likely have children who were laid
to rest. Children killing children not thinking very well, now are
serving their punishment in the nearest jail. Some kids go to
school scared to die that day. It just isn't fair that kids should
feel this way. So I hope the parents and children can cooperate to
cut down the high killing rate. We children make tomorrow
whatever it may be. We all can make this world a better place
for both you and me...For our children and their children, for
the whole entire nation.
Make it a better place for all generations.

Rayanna M. Wilkins

Free Will

A reason to think twice about writing a poem
   Do I have it in me to make it something that would sound nice?
Do I feel I want to expose my hidden thoughts to those who have
   not my desires or my insight?
"Yes" I answer to both those questions, on "Why not take the bite"
   To try is truly "Best"
To simply say this is my free will to do this is the test.
   Often we back off on "Never did this before"
But, so be it—
   This feels like it's just a simple outlet for an inner quest.
Well...Did it come out like a breath of fresh air?
   That was surely my intent!!
That's it, now it ends, my feelings have wings and I feel I have done
   What's best for me...What do you think?

Mildred Anderson

Dreams

   I have a wish, and I have a dream.
Do you have a wish, or do you have
a dream. What you should do with your
wishes and dreams, is always work hard
and try to achieve. If things don't work
out, with your wishes and dreams, then
look on the bright side, if you tried to
achieve. If you worked hard, and I'm sure
you did, then things will get better for
as long as you live.
   Don't forget to try your best.

Toni Mentasti

Poem On the Fly

How now brown cow, holy molly brown cow
   Do you hear
   Do you fear
The buzz in your ear
   Swish swish your tail
   Flip the fly and fail
Buzzing around inside, oh dear
   Cannot fight, cannot win
   What will happen if I sin
Where to go and what to do, all I do is stand here and moo.
Such a story with no care, do not read it in your underwear
   Like the fly who buzzes by
   This story will pass you by
After all why should you cry, if all you did was to try and try
   In the end when you look around the bend
      There will be something to mend
      Here I am your friend.
         Your friend

Sean H. Flynn

Untitled

Do you see the ripples of water
   Do you hear a sweet song sung
Do you smell a heavenly fragrance
   Of what is this that has begun?

This is life my friend, of which
   a part is you and me.
What concepts in this menagerie
   can you foresee?

Is your life doomed to suffer, is
   it doomed to wilt and die?
Or is it fated to bloom and blossom
   to reach out to the pedestals on high?

To each his own as the saying goes
   care not for others, it's your own throne.
Push, trample, ruin, destroy
   are these but earth's only joys?

Come with me and we shall discover
   a new establishment of peace and lovers.
There is a place you soon will see
   where there is nothing but tranquility

Linda Derhammer

At Life's End

Do you seek me now for I am not
Do you seek the same things now, I sought
Do you stop and ask why am I not
Do you now yearn to be with me not
Do you miss the things, I then sought
Do you know that now it will be forever not
Do you seek me now, and find me not
Do you know now, I always loved you an awful lot
But now it will be forever not

Stan C. Burt

Going On Vacation Won't Be Back!

   I'm going on vacation and I won't be back,
driving in the ocean in my catalack.
I'm going on to Hawaii and I'm sure of that,
I'm never coming back and that's a fact.
Rockin and a partying and singing a song,
of dancing to the fun all night long.

I'm going to have some fun till dawn,
I won't have to worry about mowing the lawn.

Rachel Streck

189

Christmas Love

Meaningless christmas if this is all
Do you worship at this lowly stall
Then leave Him there and go your way
Not returning again till next Christmas day

Look beyond this manger scene
All aglow with Holy light
You'll see God's sacrificial Lamb
You'll see a day as black as night

The altar prepared, His altar a cross
Offering Himself for a world that is lost
He was born to die, this we must see
He came to the manger, to go to the tree

Meaningful Christmas, He rose from the dead
He ascended to God above
Longing to dwell in each heart with power
To fill each heart with Christmas love

Rebeccar Todd Sparino

Societies Child

Is full of fear, and full of hate
  Does anyone care, will no one listen
The words are there between the lines
  of every rap and metal song
A new breed of societies child
  is strong and bright, just steered in the
  wrong direction
Even the strong arms of the law that
  they though were to protect them have
  apparently failed
Crime and violence has taken charge
  simple law abiding people hide in
The shadows, praying the violence
  won't find and steal their hearts and souls
While drug pushers and baby molesters
  walk the streets with their heads held high

Will today's societies child survive?

Kathy Lutzi

In Shades Of Gray

I'm a young black Christian man in any given neighborhood.
Doing what I feel is right in God's sight,
and trying not to be misunderstood.
Unfortunately, the ignorance of this world is what I must endure.
Because people do not see an individual so their minds don't mature.
I work hard for every cent I get.
So why can't I go to a shop and not be treated like a known suspect?
No sooner do I get inside, or walk down and aisle or two,
a store owner comes in my face and shouts can I help you?
I look around and notice others just walking freely,
but like a child they put on a smile and bring my stuff to me.
They say we shouldn't find these ways at least not in this day.
I still believe, however, some still show it in shades of gray.
I hold no bitterness to the people who treat me that way.
I just lift up my head and say to myself
maybe they'll learn one day.
I know that store owners are only a small reflection
of other groups in the city. Unfortunately, the treatment is the
same to me.
I guess some go through life as they please.
While others, like me, make store owners feel unease.

Peter M. Lloyd

There's A Stairway To Heaven

There's a Stairway to Heaven God's own to ascend,
Don't forfeit that right for the Devil's Den.
Take the High Road to Heaven your pace don't slack,
There're obstacles in the way but don't turn back.

It's a long tiresome journey and you'll want to sit down,
But just keep going soon the Holy Bugle will sound.
There will always be obstruction but everything's alright.
As long as you look to Heaven and keep the Star in sight.

You will ever be scorned and if you ever feel blue,
Remember that God in Heaven to you remains true.
And when you get to Heaven all the Angels will sing,
While praise be your victory let loud the chorus ring.

So shout Hallelujah! while Angel Bands play,
For you have ascended Heaven forever more to stay.

M. Elizabeth Poole Callahan

The Bridge of Life

Farewell my love it's time I said goodbye.
Don't weep my love, now's no time to cry.
It's true I've done some bad things in my life.
You changed all that, when you became my wife.

Goodnight my love, have a pleasant dream.
Don't shiver, life is but a shorten stream.
The bridge of life, crumbles underneath my feet.
Just smile for me, as I leave this world so sweet.

We had our time, we had great memories.
But the thing I love most, is when you came to me.
You showed me things, I never saw before.
You gave me love, hope, and so much more.

So goodbye! My love, kiss my children dear.
Tell them I'm not far away, I am standing near.
Let them know how I loved them so.
And if they cry, wipe the tears that gently flow.

Sweet dreams, my dear I spend a wonderful life 'tis true.
And if I had to do it over, I wouldn't change for anyone but you.

Raul Maldonado

Grandmothers

Grandmothers keep a smile on your face when you're feeling
down. By saying, "What a nice gown."
Grandmothers may act like a clown.
When the sun gives you a frown.

Grandmothers may ask, "Now are you doing today?"
And you will say, "I'm doing okay."
Grandmothers always say,
"I will protect you from anything that gets in your way."

Grandmothers always say, "I love you."
While you say, "I love you, too."
Grandmothers will give you a kiss and a hug.
While you give them a bug.

Maria Ann Robare

Similarities

Weariness, wine, and welcome drowsiness
  dull my search for self, my hunt for love and comfort.
Forgetfulness, relief, and no more diplomacy
  await me in the spring of life, the arms of Morpheus.
Friends, fiends, and people all around
  are put aside with yearning gone unsated.
Dreams, dragons, and dizzy heights
  come live in the amber glow of sleep.
Or is it Death? They seem alike. Both absorb all care.
Both refresh the spirit. But end we call the one.
They are the same: They are the spring of life
  which brings us back to weariness.

Stephan A. George

190

What Is Sky!

From the horizon and over the blue,
down the pathway and through the hue.
Clouds of wonder, shape and form,
patterns of life rough and scorn.

See the light that rises each day,
brightness that enhances on your way.
Warm are the thoughts with just a hint,
of a light brief and fleeting with tint.

Inside your mind the calm will appear,
of a place everlasting implanted so clear.
Take away death, no fear will there be,
to follow paths of peace and eternity.

Marlene J. Wagner

The Bright Moonlight

I sat alone late one night
Dreaming in the bright moonlight
Seeing things from my past
Remembering love that didn't last
Thinking back from now to then
Wanting things I didn't win
Even now as I sit and stare
At the stars shining way out there
I know of all the dreams I've lost
They're gone as fast as morning's frost
But you're the dream I've had so long
I know you'll never do me wrong
As I sat alone late that night
I felt my heart and soul take flight
Knowing that you'll come someday
That you'll take me far away
From my world of pain and plight
I'm dreaming in the bright moonlight.

Tammi Loughrey

"Revealing The Stone"

Look down beneath my feet
dull black slab marks
this man as one of many who
served, but the edges are not visible,
dead yellowish grass invades
the stone and sun dried dirt cakes around the years.
I kneel and begin to brush away the offending weeds and
dirt, the simple title slowly appears,
"SGT US ARMY"
use my sneaker to kick away
more dirt from his name, but it
serves no purpose; why do I think of this dirty,
sunken plate in the ground,
painted a sun faded black
with a gold border, why does this
picture freeze in my eye?
Grandfathers should bring fuller memories.
The year suddenly becomes
visible as a strong breeze carries
away some mocking grass: "1980"

Leonard J. Roberto

Sweeter Days With Jesus

Everyday with Jesus is sweeter then the day before.
  Everyday with Jesus I love more and more.
He showed how to walk and guide me every day.
  I praise him for my life and showing me the way,
Without him I know there's nothing can't do.
  He gives me strength each day just to make in thru.
That is why everyday is sweeter then the day before.
  And in my heart I realize I love him more and more

Richard Montgomery

Life-An Odyssey

Life is a long, complex game of chess,
during which we must endure considerable stress;
in this wild race, we must all participate,
and boldly go wherever we may be led by fate.

Mountains and valleys may obstruct our way,
and life may appear hopeless and grey,
yet, we must plod relentlessly towards our destination,
with our hearts filled with courage and determination.

When we are on the brink of defeat and despair,
we should think of those who for us do care,
encouraged thus, we must fearlessly advance,
then only of success can there be any chance.

During this long odyssey, we may sometimes stumble and fall,
and often even encounter seemingly unsurmountable walls,
but darkness is always a prelude to the welcome dawn,
and barren deserts invariably precede verdant lawns.

Sharath Kumar

Matriarch's Passing

...And now it's over, the wait is through.

She was Grandma and Mom, widow and wife,
Each at the proper time.

The last months were hardest, as she dwindled away,
And the final day drew nigh.

The sorrow is deep at this time, I know,
But perhaps there's a small ray of hope.

After so many years she's rejoined her Max,
Never more to be apart.

We'll see them again, there is no doubt,
Your faith should tell you so.

So grieve and remember, and send her your prayers,
But know that her soul's still alive.

She waits for us both in a far better place,
Where her love will never die.

Richard J. Vogt

Will You Help?

The earth is a massive land,
Each country built by different hands.
People of every color and size,
People have come to realize.
What makes a person isn't their skin,
It's the joy and wonder that lies within.
It isn't money, shape, or home,
We all must live on this massive dome.
The sky's the limit for you and me,
Our lives are filled with opportunity.
We have our needs, but wants remain,
We have no wall, we have no chain.
But there are those who die each day,
For them there is no other way.
They need our help, they need it now,
Can you help, do you know how?
I see beauty, I see light,
Is it your light that's shining bright?
Will you help, or will you not?
If you do, well thanks a lot!

Leanna Stephens

"For Your Return I Live"

For your return I prevail.
Each day I say tomorrow he'll return, when tomorrow comes
  I can not help to say the same words over again.
Everyday my mind, my devotion, yes, even my soul at times tell me;
  Stop you've done enough!
But, a crazed heart stands in the way of all begging for just
  another day.
The birds in the sky no longer sing for my sake,
The garden has asked me not to return and smell the roses,
The grass leading to your lawn, no longer wants my pace to
  touch her face.
My cry to heavens are no more carried by the wind.
Friends have left me, crazy they call me.
Enemies of main have broken their animosity.
For they say I no longer impose a challenge.
Like a candle I stand mute and tearful.
My heart broken and black yet, it holds its breath.
In a ruinous shape it still wishes to remain.
Remain just one more day in hope.
Saying tomorrow he'll return.

Mariam Al Majid

Love Is To Be Treasured

One's love differs from all,
Each is his own to one's soul.
Feelings come within the heart and mind.

Love is blind to some,
Covers up wrong doing and deceitful games.

When you find love it's rare,
Treasure the feelings as long as time is on your side
Precious pearls, rubies and diamonds of jewels are priceless,
But love is more precious than any stone you can find.
If one does not love, they aren't of the human race.

To truly love, you must work at it
Through the heart, mind and soul,
All bodily functions are involved working together to one.

A rainbow of many colors
describes all emotions that must come together to make it beautiful,
And, like the tale says, a treasure is at the end of every rainbow.

Natalie Harris

Forgiveness

Understanding and forgiveness is held in the heart
Each person has the strength to make a fresh start.

A new day begins bright, like the sun shining above
To share life so precious, life given to us in love.

Like flowers glowing in the field so bright,
Like the breeze blowing in the wind so light.

Life is too short to live in anger and fear
A true caring friend is something one must hold dear.

Arise every day with a prayer in your heart,
Manifest strength to have a new start:

Lord, let me be thoughtful in things that I do,
Bestow in me strength, let me live right and true.

Sherree Faries

California

A land of false values, glossiness and
  fleeting fancies.
Beings as ostriches, heads buried for beneath
  the surface, rising occasionally to verify
  the earth's rotation.
Surely flora abounds throughout the year,
  a panacea - for who could bear winter's
  bleakness in a synthetic realm?
But why do we tarry, when elsewhere lies
  perhaps a Paradise?

Susan T. Carlson

Paper Snow

Paper snow - falling quiet.
Earth below - land gently.
Confetti - no -
stand in the snow and watch it
fly so softly down.
One by one each in its place
making white earth's tired face -
Paper snow - cut-outs by God-
so pure in space -
So quickly gone, with little trace but —
Paper snow, I see you still
between the sky and earth —
my mind remembers you until
you pass this way again!

Marianne Fanelli Irvin

"Stranger"

Teardrops fall from empty eyes and
Echo the sound of rain on a lifeless window.
Puddles are forming, and in their glossy
Reflection is a face dull with sadness.
Droplets slowly drizzle down the contours of my face.
They pause briefly on a mouth that used to smile,
But now seems locked in a solemn slant.
They dance awhile upon my skin,
Then fall to the ground with a subtle noise.
Under my feet, they are in a new world
Where their meaning has changed.
They are no longer signs of sadness, instead
Sparkling water in a pool of rainfall.
No longer formed from the purity of my heart,
Never again to be expelled from my tired eyes.
In this new land they are just water,
Changed and polluted.
I see myself now, in their muddled reflection,
And it is then that I know they are what I've become.
My life, like the drops, has fallen away.

Tracy Feldstein

My Special Friend Like The Red Rose

The rose is known for its
Elegance and scent.
My friend is known for her beauty and charm.
The rose is so big and red
And her hair is so shiny and full.
Her lips are so shiny and soft.
On the pedals, it's early morning dew.
The thorns are long and they do hurt.
And her mind is so very keen and sharp.
While the stem takes in its daily water.
My friend takes in her knowledge and faith.
That's why my special friend
And the Red Rose are so alike.
Because when I see her standing there.
She stands so tall and beautiful
As if she's like a Rose in full bloom.

Ronald Cooper

Baby Girl

Where is the baby girl I held in my arms,
embracing her warmly to protect her from harm?
Where is the toddler who stole my heart,
with her precious little smile, so witty, so smart?
Where is the little girl who used to be nine,
with her searching brown eyes that sparkled and shined?
Where is the teenager, inquisitive and bright,
that I worried over daily and every night?
The years passed so quickly, much to my surprise;
my baby girl is a woman, matured before my eyes.
I remember the years as I gracefully grow old,
and picture my baby girl, in this granddaughter I hold.

Mary Richardson

Thoughts of You

My heart, once broken
Empties its mourning into the wind
Perhaps to be healed in some distant circumstance
of place, and time.

My soul, once separated from one
   who gave it comfort
Casts its longing into the sea
Perhaps to wash upon some distant shore
For another to find, and perhaps to return.

But my memories of you
I must carry always
No matter what paths I may take
Perhaps to fade someday into reminiscence
of what was.
   Perhaps to remain, ever vivid,
as a remembrance
Of what might have been
Kevin Loyd

Leah's Journey

In my hell I stood with death.
Endless black corridors that led to nowhere.
Screams of pain and terror vibrate towards me.
Alone and blind, I stumble along,
Wanting to sleep and forget, but unable to stop.
I claw and tear at the walls, trying to escape.
Hands try to save me, but they can't reach me.
I stagger through a doorway.
Behind me, the door closes.
A white room.
Angels surround me and fill me with their happiness.
They lift me to heaven.
My hell is behind me.
My heaven envelopes me.
Leah A. Lykins

"Listen To The Light"

Lord, you know every thought
Enthroned upon my heart
And with your sword of spirit
I cast away each evil dart

I never treaded the unknown for you
For fear that all would crumble
Lord, splinter this blind womb of selfish woe
Form me to grow bold and humble

Through years of moving experience
You fill my deepest streams
Love alone is the rainbow
By which I measure my dreams

Jesus, shining Son, a carpenter dressed in wisdom
Erase my purple sorrow, Oh Creator who's always been
You planted the unknown tree
On which for me you died for sin

You fill my spirit, crawling with hunger
You break me with love, to give me flight
I listen for your fire in the shadow of doubt
For no shadow can exist without a light
Norbert F. Markiewicz

The Season Of Spring

The day is sunny and breezy, a nice spring day.
Flowers are blooming, birds are singing,
The bears are sleeping with there baby cubs.
Come on lets play outside hurry don't be late.
Nick Torres

I'm Gonna Live

I had heart surgery and I'm mutilated and torn.
Especially my legs and chest; I feel very forlorn.
But that will all heal and will no longer matter:
Tho I must change how I eat ... and not get any fatter!!

No sense moaning and crying in my hankie.
Cause I'm scared and hurt and can't play hanky-panky.
So what? I'm past 70 and have had fun all my life.
It hasn't been easy ... I've had my share of strife.

I've still got my hands, my feet and my brain.
I've never found using them too much of a strain.
I can spend time with my kids whom I love and adore;
And I truly believe ...they don't think I'm a bore!

I can still drive and help others less fortunate than I.
So what if I'm mutilated? I surely didn't die.
So, sit up you people in the same boat I'm in.
If you didn't 'live' before ... now's the time to begin.

Just get out and laugh and continue to do so!!
There's no other way to do it; smile, laugh: HO HO!
Get off your tush and do something for others....
Get rid of the violence ... let's be loving sisters and brothers.
Vera K. Sendroff

Beautiful Dream

The wind that blows through unsettled souls
even there but I know not where
the calming of a turbulent sea
on this journey where you are me.

I know not where I come from
I look ahead to the beating of a distant drum
not being there before I shudder
at the thought of looking forward
and not to the past for the other.

Spinning around
feeling the sounds
crying out to the wind
and never finding another.

The eyes they close
to the past as yet unseen
dream a beautiful dream
for these eyes that cannot see
dream a beautiful dream
alone on this journey where you are me.
Kelley Joan Test

I Knew

I knew that he was near
even though he made not a sound.

The gentle blow of the breeze
and the sun shining bright above told me so.

I knew he would never come back,
because in a way he was gone forever.

I know my eyes will never see him again,
but deep in my heart,
there will always be a place
where he will live in eternity.
Mary Fritz

Feminine Horizons

Be prepared, my grandmother said,
Evenings while mother was going to bed.

Learn to cook and save, sew and behave
But find a good man for a rainy day.

A dancer, however, my mother aspired to be,
And she danced on her toes til they bled, you see.

"That's the price of fame," she explained,
Extolling her talents with modest acclaim.

But she gave it all up to marry my dad,
Which she later regretted when the marriage turned bad.

When I grew up and saw the trend,
Security in marriage not the ultimate blend.

One's own career, an alternate goal,
Offered reward of glory, as well as gold.

Toil wasn't easy, threatening men blocked the way,
With ploys of sex and chauvinistic display.

Be prepared, independent, college degree avowed
Compared to the whims of a wedding vow.

Be true to yourself, I have learned on the way,
With God on my shoulder to guide me each day.
        Margaret K. Sullivan

When The Last Petal Falls

Have you ever seen a dying rosebush,
    ever watched it fade away,
known the time of death was coming,
    forbidding evil of nightshade.
The poisoned soil rots the roots
of stems that hold the precious flowers,
slow at first, almost not sensed
then rapid in the final hours.
        As the stems begin strength-loss,
        as the plant starts losing hold,
        as the petals drift off softly,
        as the heart turns ever-cold.
The leaning stalk clings still awhile
        passion flowers fall as tears.
Empty heart cries out denial:
        as the time of death grows near,
        remembering the warm compassion,
        hearing still the silent call,
        pleading at the final chilling,
        cold as ice when the last petal falls.
        William D. Johnson

Discrimination

It doesn't matter what color or race,
every person is one of a kind,
even when you live in this kind of place,
your wanted here so get it through your mind.
Don't let another person put you down.
For who you are or what you can become,
this is a big thing that goes around town,
don't let anybody tell you your dumb.
It's your body, your soul, so don't throw it away,
you are put on this earth to be somebody,
it doesn't matter what the others say,
when this earth comes to its end you will see,
if you are part of this racism nation,
there should not be discrimination.

        Kristen Dimberg

Demon Of The Soul

In every person there is a place for:
evil,
harm,
hurt,
hunger,
But in every person there is a place for:
love,
hope,
joy,
delight,
Why must the negative place be filled?
Why not bring out the positive?
Because it lurks!
        Tim Potts

Waiting

Sitting in front of the rail station.
Examining this detritus life I live.
Staring at a tree-quarter moon as the
wayward clouds pass.

I wait in a shell. A base of protection
I've built for myself, as the cars and people pass me by.

In front of me lies a single Tree.
Leafless for the coming winter.
It has no protection, it has no warmth.

It stands tall and proud for the world to judge.
I find myself envious of the Tree.
Wishing I did not want or need this
shell, but unable to shed it.

Unlike the Tree. I can not expect the warmth to come.
I watch a long haired beauty read the
state of the world across the street.
She is completely unaware of me and does not care to be aware.

I would invite her warmth, but for
now I am still as naked as the Tree.
        Robert S. Gordon

Eyes Of Ignorance

These are the eyes of ignorance.
Eyes found within all of us; yet you say it's not me.
For these eyes only see the outside; do you really
know what's inside of me?

With these eyes we show our ignorance and don't let
others be.

Why should we let our eyes control us?
It's only because we really don't see.
        Wendy Hendrickson

Morning's Night Sun of A Lover's Kiss

Sallow sight, laden tongue, what irresponsive action has begun
Eyes of sand, sands of doors, so hard to move
Motion of sound, silent, peaceful, why so soon
Starkness of day, invasion of light, easy to shun

Warmish, comfort, blissful dreams
Freshness of air, taste of morning dew
Slowly, consensual, refluent to pursue
Our essence stirs, regretful to our teem

Slow lingering kiss, desired embrace
Our lover's curl, acceptance of kind
Rapturous estivation, regale of mine
Delightful play, auspicious place

Wholeness, bonding, soaring as one
A beautiful rising of a morning's night sun
        Michael L. Wright

Beauty

So it is said, "beauty is in the
eye's of the beholder".
To behold is to watch carefully,
To watch carefully is to watch
with a silent ear. A silent ear is to let the
splendor of the vision captured - that which is
given by God, behold the beauty
that you feel, there's an inner of beholding.
Look inside, see the beauty of inner vision that
beholds us. You are a vision, I am a vision,
Two people, three people, many people.
Beauty isn't outward, it cannot be possessed,
But it comes from within.

Beauty is never seen, but -
is a feeling that should never be denied.
Beauty is a song heard with the beauty
that you feel within, beauty is a breeze that
God has blessed upon his creation.
Beauty is the breath of emotions given
by God, for two, for many people to share.
Beauty is all of the things' that is never seen,
but is always there in your soul...

Leo Carswell

To Anne:

Glacial clear eyes, cornered stares
Fair shown hair, subtle deep voice
I sigh with thoughts of rapture and fond

We spend first moments, brief country rides
Filled with words and gentle laughter
No romance to speak of
But kindle wonderment

A voice I await, anxious to hear
New experiences each day I look to hark
But the question remains, to what purview
Will I be allowed to get near

By form, you are exquisite
By style, you are eccentric
By nature, you are kind
By thoughts, you are unobstructed

If the words go unremarked
I shall repeat
You are beautiful
You are beautiful

Lawrence A. Rea II

"She Fell For Him"

Along with the leaves and stars that
fall from the sky so has his love for her
found once in his eyes.
    As he glides slowly down and further
from sight vision of her pain and remorse
begin on this night.
    Each now in limbo, praying and yearning
for the comforts of yesterday once more, looking
for him through closed shattered doors.
    Day by day she starts to fall she builds up
defenses and starts to withdraw.
    Sounds of silence engulf her time she
pretends to her peers that all is fine.
    His touch is gone warm hands turn cold,
her grip grows weaker no more can she' hold.
    Realizing a part has left her side, she
whispers in pain her last goodbyes!
    The pain slowly eases as ground comes
to sight loneliness and remorse will
end on this night!!

Suzanne Royls

Life's Enchanted Truth

Silence invades her thoughts during the quiet of the light.
Fear engulfs the silence of an eternal sleepless night.
Exterior smiles hide a truth,
Shimmering eyes conceal the tear;
A girl alone through childhood,
A woman lonelier each passing year.

Cold eats his heated breath during the endless winter chill.
Winds scorch an arctic heart bringing life against the will.
Careful not to speak aloud,
Expressions don't mask the tale;
A boy sheltered from lonely life,
A man alone to walk the trail.

Seduced by cold embrace, a night alone she will not sleep.
Nourished by silent thought, warmth growing to make him weep.
Stopped by fear of the silence,
Endangered by bitter chill;
They found each other much too late,
Lost in their isolation still.

Tamara L. Needy

Unprevailing Darkness

Unprevailing darkness surrounds his body with fear -
Fear of the unknown provokes a time-worn tear.

His longing for life is apparent but just too unpredictable,
Does he want to live? or survive in his silence defiantly?

Are his thoughts trapped within the brain waves corridor?
Or are they festering upon his tongue like a sore?

If he wants to speak-he can't. Will he ever?
He's caught between destiny and defeat-he's clever.

Only he holds the remedy to the sleep he grasps,
Can he ever erase the scars that forever seem to last?

Lisa Guelde

Untitled

Endless endeavors, sacred lost treasures,
fears of the unknown battles fought people
Left alone. Echoing cries of pain, innocent
victims being slain. Words of wisdom left
to doom, by the few who insist it never
bloom. Whole societies losing faith, brazenly
exchanging it for hate. Children born without
any hope, as their parents struggle
with their addictions to dope. Plain and
simple say the elite, make money work
hard that's what they think, while their
families are suffering as they blink. Like
a disease left ignored, how can you
fight it if not seeking a cure. Live today
as if no tomorrow and see the beauty
we've led to sorrow.

Peggy Wells Weston

Gentle Soul

    I looked upon the morning sky today, and down to a frail
flower. And as I watch the flower bloom, love grew from
it, it had reminded me of my lover's eyes that there nothing
like the sun nor the sea but the eye's of a gentle soul
who's always there for me. As daylight gently heated my
sleeping face, I woke to see the sky above and I thought to
myself our love never ends so it may seem the love never
dies for my gentle soul. The wind blowing whisper's to me a
silent song that's meant to be, a song shared between you
and me. So when I pick a flower and give it to you just
remember how much I love you.

Kerry Roth

To Martha, With Love And Respect...

Softness cradles her facade—covers drawn closely around
   Features Unwrinkled By Time
Eyes twinkling, she quietly makes her plea...
"Pay the girl— Can't work for nothing..."
But... this girl hasn't worked, she's learned,
Gathered information out -of-print unique
To the age-tempered life cycle of
   An Epic Nonegenarian,
A mentor, who measures present day against
   A Tapestry Of Experience
And presents the tally gently in the Sagevoice of knowledge,
That Tender-Calm voice of highsight...   A priceless Gift.
I clip her nails, her dark eyes dart—
"You'll catch it if you cut me!!" Yes,,,,I know.
   What A Lady!
    Nancy Connor

"My Hungry Heart"

I can only spend my lonely days,
Filled with deepest, fondest yearning,
Knowing that you'll never, ever hold me in your arms,
A faint touch on the hand; a chaste kiss on the cheek,
These tiny crumbs must sustain my hungry heart.

I can only wish for happy days with you beside me,
Holding me, and ever loving me, and never, never go.
Though you'll forget me; though you'll forsake me,
I will always hold you deep within my heart
Until I close my eyes forever.
In my dreams you will thrill me and bring me to ecstasy
In your most intimate, passionate, ultimate loving embrace.
    I. F. Norstrand

Dad's Funeral

Withering faces surround me.
Filling my religion with empty words.
The sands wash out the sound.
Hear my need.
Torn from the chains that bind my feet.
Shattering through the emptiness of the night.
Calling me to another time.
Your melancholy essence fills my mind.
Relishing that brighter place.
Falling on the wet grasses,
Laughter and tears.
My sullen breast unwavering with your demise.
Dejected specter.
Burning aromas penetrate the senses. Enduring silence.
    Tammy Bodrie

The Empty House

For many years you stood empty and forlorn,
Finished, save paint on your clapboard sides,
Your darkened windows reflecting the emptiness,
As you stood apart from the other houses
In the small group surrounding the school.
What sad story brought you to this state?
No matter what situation caused your plight,
Mr. Jim, long left by death with two boys and a girl
To bring up with the help of sisters Miss Pattie and
Miss Sidney, when the youngest had left for college
Met and married a teacher and turned you into a home.
A coat of white and red shutters to match the paint
On your tin roof transformed your sadness to happiness.
Your windows smiled with light; your rooms and hallways
Echoed the laughter of young children romping and playing
Games of make believe on your stairs and in and out
Of your many rooms. At last, you fulfilled the purpose
For which, so many years ago, you were started.
    Margie Dudley Haughton

Infinity

In a window sets a candle
Flame shines against the glass
Never to burn out
But alas burns for a reason

Within our hearts lies a love
That last through all our troubles and strifes
With each obstacle we overcome
We can truly say it has grown stronger

Only we can know the true extent of our love
None can extinguish the flame that burns for us
Our love is forever true
The candle that burns is a reflection of our life

A candle that shall burn for infinity
Burns only for the true in love
When our time on earth is done
The people we leave behind keep our candle burning

This candle indeed burns for infinity
    Susan Rena Foster

Sadako And The Thousand Paper Cranes

The lights sparkle and
flicker behind the young girls eyes,
She believes she can hear her mother softly cry.

She grasps the hand that holds hers,
Hoping to comfort and cheer
But it just brings another tear.

She smiles a little smile,
even though it hurts,
She knows she's been through
A lot and she's over the worst.

She holds her bird in one hand
And her mothers hand in the other
Knowing between the two,
Soon they'll be together

She sighs her last time, softly,
And whispers her final words
Ever so gently she whispers
"Please finish my birds".
    Lee Putty

Is There Time

   Why does one long for
   flitting memories and might have beens
is reality an anchor on our souls
   we can't escape
is longing only the fantasy of desire
   or the desire of fantasy
   that we touch in an unguarded moment
   wishing for a perfect love
   to excite us as the first
   thinking there is no time
   for fulfillment of dreams

   Reach out
reach out for the dreams surrounding us
   knowing they are there
   only our denial
   prevents the truth of our happiness
    D. Dale Stack

What God Hath Promised

God hath not promised, sky's always blue
Flower strewn pathways all our lives thro
God hath not promised, sun without rain
Joy without sorrow, place without pain.
God hath not promised we shall not know
Toil and temptation trouble and woe;
He hath not promised, we shall not bear,
Many a burden, many a care.
God hath promised smooth roads and wide
Swift easy travel needing no guide
Never a mountain rocky and steep
Never a river turbid and deep
But God hath promised strength for the day
Rest for the labor, light for the way
Grace for the trials, help from above
Unfailing sympathy undying love

Mary Cotone

Grief

Soft words, sincerely spoken, kindly meant,
Flowing over my dulled mind;
But, oh God, they are not balm for one bereaved!
They are but grains of salt
Dropped into an open wound,
Bringing searing anguish with each one spoken,
A wound too new and fresh for any soothing.

God, ease the pain so I can hear
For I have need of words.

Mary B. Palmer

Backwards

We begin, a child wondering
footsteps are new to us,
and language confuses us
Our minds are just forming
slowly, slowly building
bones our structure, are strong

We grow, the body of a man
yet things we not fully understand
Life and time go by
you walk through it now,
before you would fly

We end, an old man wondering
footsteps are harder to walk
language we hear, but it's difficult to talk
your minds now gone
bones your structure, crumpled

Still you push forward,
but you end where you begin,
backwards

Valerie L. Grabowski

Things Are Not What They Seem

I used to wonder what it would be like
For it to be dark when it should be light
In a country of things, that live free
Why can't we be nice and live peacefully
Why must we fight and hurt one another
Friends against friends, brothers against brothers
Why must people live, in torture and pain
To make others wealthy, and have fame
Are we too good to give a hand
To an elderly person who can not stand
Why can't we accomplish our hopes and our dreams
I guess it's because things aren't what they seem.

Rachel Harkins

Untitled

To the man I married and love with all my heart,
For better or worse and never grow apart.
Every day we're together the closer we get,
That's why I married you on a day you can't forget!

An original idea the 14th of February,
Much to our surprise, it was quite the contrary.
You are my husband and my best friend,
The only one for me which I can depend!

Each new day brings me closer to you,
New challenges and changes we will get through!
We share our secrets, laughter and tears,
We've learned so much in our first year!

We brought two families together,
Not as easy as you would think.
We are strong and love each other,
Everyday we are more in sync!

I love every part of you down to your wiggling toes,
Your touch, your kiss and how you proposed.
You are the best thing that has come into my life,
Happy Anniversary Darling, I'm so proud to be your wife!

Kerri Jo Svoboda

Not Ashamed Of The Lord

I thank and praise the Lord above
For bringing me thru my illness
'Cause it shows and tells me that it's his will
For me to live and continue to be his witness

I'm not ashamed to praise His Son Jesus Christ
Who died on the cross for our sins
And arose then ascended on up to heaven
To give us a new life that never will end

I know there's a lot in this world today
who's not willing to admit they're wrong
But they'd better be changing their mind pretty soon
Or they'll be standing in fire and see they waited too long

Minnie Jane Lyle

To Senior Golfers

The world is full of miracles and some we can believe
For God grants prayerful golfers some gifts we can't conceive.

They drink too much at parties, chase gals tho' they know better
And practice chips and alibis, learn golf rules to the letter.

We love our golf and gals and grog, we're grateful just to play
We've worked and earned the right we think,
and pleased that we can pay.

The years inexorably pass on, some joys we bid bye-bye
But golf is one we cherish still, and play it till we die.

We hope that years will smile on you, with health and friends who care
And may we all meet now and then, and these happy memories share!

And may God hear our eager prayers, drives fly so straight and far,
And chips roll slowly to the pin and putts all drop for par.

It's great to be with folks we love, see friends whom we hold dear
God bless you all - may fortune smile - let's all come back next year.

Philip B. Phillips

The Enemy

He must have been there the day I was born
For he has plagued me all of my life.
He robbed me of all my peace and joy.
And left me only terror and strife.

He chased away the sweet dreams of youth
Sending nightmares to take their place.
And though he stood sometimes near my bed,
I never once caught a glimpse of his face.

The terror and fear soon faded away
Until anger and hate took their part.
I hunted him all the rest of my years
With black murder burned deep in my heart.

At last through a mist I saw my enemy's face,
The one who in hatred my soul did cloak.
Stone after stone I hurled with all my might
Until at long last — the mirror broke.

    R. L. Scott

The Few The Proud

    Like a brick wall he stands,
for his passion is to protect.
    Like a soldier he marches,
his eyes hard to detect.
    Like the real man he is,
he serves his country.
    For his help is much needed
though his next mission being.
    The sky above, the land below
or the sea across.
    He is always ready to protect and serve.
Though seeming only tough and bold,
    beneath his uniform stands a
Handsome, loyal, hard working,
    marine.

    Misti Buoye

Trees...

Have you ever wondered about trees? In ways trees are like people.
For instance, take the oak tree, her roots run wide and far below
the surface giving her a deeper insight and a solid foundation on
which to build her life. The birds and animals look to her for
shelter and support. They have built a trusting relationship,
knowing that her arms will always be open to them through all of
life's circumstances...

The birch tree, on the other hand, is more like a wondering soul.
Her lust for life keeps her roots near the surface reaching far,
ever searching for the instant gratification she so desires. In her
rush, she never bothers to know the things in life deeper than the
surface. For her only concern is to fulfill her own momentary needs.

The oak, plain and nondescript blends into the forest hardly
noticeable. The birch, bright and flashy with her shiny white
coat is sure to stand out in the crowd. Yet the animals have
learned over time not to trust the flashy birch, for with one gust
of a summers storm, the whole shallow existence of the birch can
be uprooted in an instant. The oak too can be damaged in such a
storm, yet she will always have her solid foundation from which
to rebuild her life...

    Kathleen J. Rothleutner

The Molding Of Truth

Strive for the truth.
For the truth holds life in the palm of its hand.
It is with the hand that one shapes the world,
But it is the truth that gives it form.

    Scott Brian Luftglass

Night Shadow

I fear the night,
For it comes sooner every day.
Each time I face it with the same dread,
And try to hide from myself in the dark.
But wherever I turn my soul follows me,
Like a permanent shadow.
Finding strength in the dark, my shadow grows,
Illuminating the blackness of my mind.
No blanket can suffocate this monster,
For it feeds on the night,
Just waiting until the light is out to torture my heart.
No teddy-bear can protect me from this inhuman creature,
Most clearly defined as myself.
No music can drown out its existence,
For it pounds out the loudest chords of life.
So I unlock my mind in the dark of night,
And let my shadow take control.

    Laura Thomas

The Kiss

It was a kiss unlike the thousands which had preceded it,
For it gently transported its participants into a space not sampled
    by previous experience
A space unexplored by the conscious, as though they had moved
    through a crack in the mirror of physical reality
    into a dimension or fragment of an unknown place.
Like two colors blended to form a third, it encompassed their beings
    as one in a manner unexplainable by Gods or religions as it
    transcended beliefs
And left in its wake a multitude of questions which could be posed,
    never answered.

Had it been a union of their souls, an inseparable intermingling;
A glimpse of infinity;
A total release and submission, each to the other, of all distrust
    built by the past;
An embodiment of their spirits in the pureness of joy, in serenity;
Or a momentary achievement in the perfection of love?
The reason for the journey was to be understood by neither.
The ultimate beauty remained with the realization that whatever had
    taken them to wherever they had been had taken them together.

    Phyllis A. Erskine

The Sea

The sea I can still see in your eyes
For it was the sea that tore us apart
Your face is very much a part of me
As the wind and spray swept across your face
And your sandy hair with it
We two stood gazing into each others eyes
With a deep realization of mortality
That sea, that sea I always discerned in your eyes
Whether storm or breeze, that sea was always in your eyes
We knew of the tempest that threatened us, but cared not of it
We wished only to remain in each others arms for eternity
To stand in endless worship of the other
In that we did succeed
Yet a swell of enormous size swept your immaculate eyes away
For ages I have searched abyss and peak
Only to be disheartened time and time again
Anon, I will again be one with the one that I hold so dear
Into the sea you have evanesced, and only there may I find you
I will leave this world of strife, to join you in the murky depths
And again we will be one

    Timothy J. Meyenburg

Untitled

I thank you Lord for giving this day to me
For it's through your eyes that I'm able to see

Whether it's a bright, sunny or cold, drizzly weary day
It's still beautiful Lord, because you made it your way

This is a beautiful day you gave me to rejoice in and to share
Not only to love each other, but to show that we care

The sun's warmth may be hidden behind the clouds above
I still feel your presence and your very special love

It's you Lord, I feel the warmth of your presence deep within my heart
And I know, from me, you will never part

Vicki S. Wood

Between Life And Land

Life is like an old wise man,
For no one but he can understand.
The trivial little everyday things.
like a baby Robin spreading his wings.
This world was not made for bills and loans,
it was made for you to listen to a cow when he moans.
We were not created just to go to work,
We were put here to maintain God's great work.
To love it, and pamper it, like you would your own,
instead people spit on it, and hate it, and
   for that they are disowned.
These are just a few words from the wise man himself,
Take care of your land, as you would yourself.

Rhonda L. Beal

Alone

Alone again — I cannot sin
For now I know were life begins.

Why am I prone — when not alone
To do those things I know are wrong?

Laughing at others — in their mistakes,
Failing to care whose hearts I may break.

Insensitive to other's oddities...
Eyeing and judging them discriminately.

Gossiping — whispering — backbiting too,
As though I have nothing better to do.

I'll look at myself — examine my image.
There I'll find I need to do plenty.

Alone again — I shall not sin
I'm searching for purpose before my life ends.

I've advanced from where I had once been...
Lost in my ignorance — plagued by my sins.

I've woken to where change and growth starts,
No longer wasting my time with a judgmental heart.

But using every moment to cultivate my mind...
Alone again — I cannot — shall not, ever be unkind.

Leola M. Morgan

The Gathering

The people come together and wait.
Generations stand hand in hand,
strangers shoulder to shoulder and wait.
The elk come down out of the mountains
from behind the trees and into the meadow.
A hundred or so of them are here
twice the number of us have come.
Silence surrounds each of us,
awe draws us together.
The echoes carry me home.

Nancy Lecocq

Goodbye

We've been friends for so long,
   for, oh, so many years.

We've shared some good times,
   and we've shared some tears.

You know we didn't always see eye to eye,
   I guess that makes it even harder for me to say, "Goodbye."

But I know God chose you,
   as a flower for His "Garden of Love",

So He gently took your hand,
   and led you above.

To a beautiful place where there is no rain,
   only sunshine for you to see, where there is no pain.

I will truly miss you.
   we will never laugh together,

But in your children's eyes,
   I will see you . . . forever.

Lisa Moore

"A Vapor"

Life is but a vapor, that appeared,
for, oh such a short time!!
And then, it vanishes away,
too quickly, that life of your's and mine!!

Just like a breath of fresh air,
you find in lofty mountain's high!
Or just maybe, the wispy white cloud,
A way up there in the sky!!

No, life does not last forever,
today it's here, but then it's gone tomorrow!
So I'll enjoy this life while I can,
this vanishing vapor, I can only borrow!!

Yes this vapor will disappear,
but memories will go on, that I know!
So I'll do my best to spread love and cheer,
Maybe to be remembered by some sweet soul!!

This barrowed vapor, will touch someone,
and even though, it seemed a short time,
When I am gone, I'll leave behind,
memories of happiness, someone will fine!!

Patricia Jensen

The Master Plan

I expect a miracle from the Lord above,
for only He can save us, and renew our precious love.

The bond that seals us is much too strong
It's not of our own making,
We were united and chosen by God,
To separate is not ours for taking.

In this life we have been given
We go by the Master Plan,
We think we know what we want,
But God has the Ruling Hand.

Temptation is strong, the pull is great
To turn from all good and true,
God gave free mind - but not free heart;
He left the choice up to you.

To serve Him you must come freely,
He'll never force His way,
Lust and love, doubts and regrets
In the past must stay.

God is not finished, He has more to do;
But the real test remains, it's between Him and you.

Maryanne Carson

Time Adjustment

The times have changed and for the worse
For our children to talk they have to curse
They have no respect for themselves nor others
They don't listen to anyone, not even their Mothers
They have no morals, they have no shame
They're violent and don't mind causing others pain
They need someone to give them a wake-up call
They need to be warned that they are headed for a fall
They need role models, with character and grace
They need to learn constructive use of time and space
Their parent need to be interested in the things they do
They need teachers, they need preachers, they need me and you
They need someone to listen to their problems and ideas
They need to be able to express their confidence and their fears
They need to be embraced and shown true love from heart to heart
But most importantly they need to be introduced to God.

Stella James

Conversation With Myself

Throughout life, one struggles
For Reward, punishment.
nothing is free
    except death.
But does one pay a price for death?
does suicide result in an afterlife which causes more suffering?

Run away from your problems.
    You're only hiding from yourself.
Look for that corner, that shield, that door.
    You can never escape.

Wear the mask.
    You will be exposed
        by ME.

Life has no safety net.
Insecurities always exist.
I have no happiness
    only illusion.

Ning Chao

Heaven In Your Heart

There must be heaven in your heart
    for that is where God's music starts
Sung with the breath of love,
    from soul, let lyrics flow.

Through simple acts of philanthropy
    one by one given without thought....
That is the only way to God-
    Give from the heart.

Thinking of self will not do
    there are too many tough times to go through.
All life is cause and effect
    with debts we must pay.

Now more than ever we must share
    Love without question or pause.
It's not too late, for humanity's sake -
    Give from the heart!

Shernise Alexa Allen

I Didn't Take The Time

Give me one more chance to show I love you;
Give me one more chance to prove I care;
Give me one last time to walk beside you,
To hold your hand and kiss your silky hair.

If only I had looked into the future,
If I had seen back then the things that now I see,
Then maybe I'd have taken time more often
When you asked "Daddy, won't you come and play with me?"

Laura L. Scholz

Untitled

Elisabeth, I'm sorry
for the ill things which you heard (that I said)
were my love charms ringing (all but dead)!

Excuse me, but
from old age have I come back speaking to you
some things only half said but still true!

So,
I shall start over with your wondrous free-flowing hair
and be minded of the contemporary styles that you wear.

From now on,
whenever I make comments about thee,
I only shall say good things—you'll see!

Mark Bell

The Children Cry

I hear the children cry
For the pain they hide inside
For the memory of a world they'll never know

I see the mountains brown
With out their soft green crown
Lost to the greed of selfish men below

The rivers can not flow
And nature can not grow
Where the touch of men has torn this great blue ball

The world can not survive
We can not stay alive
Unless we learn respect and love for all

Can we hope to see tomorrow
If we cause all nature sorrow
And destroy the world with out the slightest thought

Our children's children fear
Their eyes will burn with tears
When they look and what deadly hell was wrought.

Sharon Chezum

Purpose By Choice

    In the eyes of will I go to heaven?
For there are many mistakes I've made.
All were in thought of good reasons.
Should sacrifice serve no purpose but fill one's grave?

    When will thought lose its reason
Or free will find its way?
What if compassion lost its interest?
You paint a wall only once surely the color fades.

    Where does time lose its meaning
Or irrational thinking start?
Why must love be forgotten
To heal the pain of a broken heart?

    When will it work to compromise
Not to live a lie?
Many solutions to the problem
But don't take away the weapons, take away the pride.

    My quest in life is not over yet.
So in hell I will remain.
I sacrifice for the purpose
To justify my pain.....

Keith Owen

The Times

We've had many hard times in our lives without finding time to groan -
For we had to learn early in our life that we must carry on -

In the sixties our hearts were lifted in spirit, our voices did
truly ring - when we sang "We shall overcome", There was Dr. King -

Then our hearts were filled with gloom
He was snatched from our mist so fast - but we still could relish
the thought in knowing, Dr. King was free at last -

Now the eighties brought a brand new Era,
And the door was opened wide -
There were many qualms about the outlook
When a black man stepped inside -

Again our hearts were lifted And again we began to pray - for we
knew here was a man with a vision and again we would have our day -

The song we sung was quite different Far from a Christmas Carol -
We shouted for joy from the bottom of our hearts
For you see, then, there was Harold -

I need not tell you what he did For it was plain for all to see -
He was not a Mayor for just a few, He was a Mayor for Unity -

Though now we mourn his passing, His memory shall ever linger still -
While he was a Great Mayor of our city, He had to do his
  Master's Will
Nethus Bryson

Remembering You

One once said, "A memory lives forever"
For with you, it is true

I'll never forget you, the times we had
I'll always regret, the times we didn't have

I know you can't come back
And now I must face the facts

If you are listening, somewhere out there
I wish you were here

I wish we could be together
Forever nothing holding us apart

If only my wish came true
I'd wish to again be with you

For I know your life is gone
For my life is now all wrong

Remember this
And remember this always

You'll always be in my heart
Even though we're apart
Mandi M. Koury

The Meaning Of Love

The meaning of love, is the meaning of life,
For without love, there can be no life,
And without life, there can be no love,
Life is harmony, balanced so right.

And life goes on, in a twinkle of a star,
A breathless life to see, though seen from afar.
And the sparkle that stays so still in time,
Brings hope and faith to ones own mind,
That there is life, and love to see,
In another world, for you, for me.

And as we live, this life as is,
We come to learn, that we must give,
That little love, that gives one life,
And life gives love, to shine star bright.
Give love, and you'll give life.
Nelson Molina

Untitled

In the blue garden
For you they have yearned,
Ballerina so fragile and small
Won't you dance past their glances and turn.

Amongst blossoms in waiting, softly they call
A hush in their voice, hide no secrets at all,
And whispers softly into your ear
Verses only the angels can hear.

Then pearls burst into luster
From their crowns spinning in clusters.
The pearls then melt into streams
That flow into sleep so it seems.

No one can see
No one allowed,
Just little girls' reveries
Here we are found.
Tonya Gliesmann

Good-bye Student Loan!

I started college after living on my own,
and for four straight years I needed a loan.

With little choice, my debt did rise.
Considering the sum, I wanted to cry.

With my degree in hand, life started to sail.
Then a payment book arrived by mail.

One-hundred-twenty payments hung over my head.
For ten long years, this I would dread.

A dependable payee, on time and true;
Not like some who took the money then flew.

With small payments each month I soon came to see,
The loan agency would get rich on me.

Then one day it hit me, there was something to do.
Through hard work and sacrifice my savings soon grew.

I wrote a big check the most in my life.
No more school debt is what I would like.

Before I close and go on my way,
There's a final note I just have to say...

The loan agency did not earn all they thought.
You see, I'm smarter from the education they bought!
William E. Passalacqua

Hope

Dinghies, rafts, - anything that floats,
From Cuba leave daily, they have no boats,
To come to the land of milk and honey,
To get a job and make some money.

No one to give them a helping hand,
Alone and frightened they reach our land,
What is before them? They do not know,
Their hearts are heavy - their feet are slow.

What do we offer these starving people?
A home! a job! food! - they look so feeble,
When will it end? can anyone tell?
'Twould be really nice to see them all fit and well.

Hopefully soon the 'powers' that be!
Will put an end to this misery,
Unite all the families, and give them a start,
Hooray! For America, How Great Thou Art!!
Mariea VanPraet

Picasso's "Guernica" (Prado Museum, Madrid)

The sun has turned mechanical: an electric bulb
Fretted by disparate rays.

A newborn chick with a fish's tail gulps at the air.
There is a hand with four fingers, the nails pointed.

It is not better to be the hairless skull
At the bottom of the picture?

For through his dead hand, clasping a bloody knife
A cowslip—frail, colorless—ventures upwards in hope?

Not that it makes much difference to the eager young man
Who, hatted by a Napoleonic tricolor, must be a soldier.

And there is an equally earnest young woman who runs
Through the street, her long hair streaming.

Yet agony: On the left a mother—head back, teeth rattling—
In her pain laments the broken dead child she is still holding.

On the right, out of the licking flames, another head—
Drowning in fire, arms stretched in screaming soundless sound.

Surely the horse on the left is neighing. But the bull—
Symbol of man's need to conquer and destroy in order to survive—
Stolidly observes man's torturous undulations.

Whose hand holds the lighted candle?

Patricia Dunkel Johnston

Gifts That Return

We sit silent, heedless of the pain that others suffer in huddled
    fright.
We look afar, casting wide our glances so we do not see their plight.
We ignore, refuse to offer even small tokens of hope or faith or care,
Our lives are taken with our own ease, we will not reach out,
    we do not dare.

For then their pain becomes a part of us, and we do not want to
    share their touch,
The spark of hope that we could offer to them would cost us far
    too much.
Our hearts and lives would grow more complicated, filled with
    other's pain,
And then our conscious minds would push us on, to give of
    ourselves once again.

Because we sit, complacent to the cries that others give,
Our lives are bound, bound to the earth, for we dare not to live.
To open wide our hearts, give love, give strength, for us is right
For then we can rise on eagle wings and join in joyous flight.

Released from self, unbound by selfish keeping of our deepest hope,
We learn anew that through all trials and pain we can help others cope
And with the giving of ourselves, our strength and gifts return
    full speed
We earn rewards a hundred-folded and more, by answering
    another's need.

Margaret Jo Monroe

Confection Confession

He loves chocolate.
Give him chocolate
and let the desire begin.
One nibble longs for more.
"I say dear friend,
might you be passing the chocolate store?"

Taken lightly
or perhaps in the dark.
It's a confectious reaction
to the blissful attraction.

He loves chocolate.

Suzan T. Ganzer

Interstate Odyssey

The long road east in a motor home
From California to Pennsylvania
A fiftieth reunion at Brandywine
A search for long lost cousins
And grandma's place.
No house, only land remains
And memories of summers spent
At grandma's house.
Your cousins called you junior
You were that kid again
Walking two miles to Bluefield
Holding grandma's hand.
The Saturday matinee
A chocolate soda afterwards
An odyssey encapsulated during the seven days
On interstate to your Ithaca.

Louise Cassell

Where Love Comes From

God says Merry Christmas to you and to me
From the greatest story of all history

The story of a dream Joseph had one night
Of God telling him his wife would bright us light

Wise men brought this baby gifts of love
God gave us Jesus from his realms above

To die so that we could have life
To take away our strife

This the greatest gift ever known
This is the greatest sacrifice ever shown

So if we forget the reason for Christmas Day
If we forget the price Jesus had to pay

To save our souls and set us free
Let us stop and thank God so graciously

To humble ourselves to love and the reasons.
Because Jesus is the reason for the season

Teresa Dows

The Fireman's Wife

The smell of smoke
  From the house fire
    Lingered on your clothes
      As I held you near me.
        The family was so grateful
          For you saved their baby.
          All your strengths abound
          Even when I hold you close.
            I held you when you were sad
              For the person who died,
              They were just too sick
              And you can only do so much.
                The strong arms that work so hard
                To save the one's hurt,
                And then you come home to me
                For love, strength, and warmth.
                  When you come home in the morning,
                  Tired from your busy shift,
                  I'll be there to support you
                  For you, my Beloved, are my greatest gift.

Leslie Sawyer

Ink

With this pen I am released
from this staggering pain upon my heart.
Write! Write!
Scribble away all of the hurt that he (you) caused me.

Young love, pure and true
Shattered in an instant-
    time stands still.
Slow-motion in my mind forever
    him leaving me.

My mind won't quit running
My head won't let me let go of the memories of you.

How? Why? What did I do?
Be still my heart, be numb.
Don't think, write!
Write, write away all of the grief that he left inside.

My pen is out
but the faint trace of bleeding ink
    which stained my soul...

Michelle Lynne Duvall

Magic Of The Winter Solstice

Starlit nights, silver beams, snow and ice.
Frozen ponds and lakes
Snow covered hills, valleys and trees.
All is made ready for the first of winter, known as the Solstice.
Children fight with snowballs and build snow families too.

Logs burn in fireplaces, Solstice trees in every house.
Decorations abound in gold, silver, red and green.
There is pinecone and strings of fur with Holly interwoven.
Parents make the Solstice meal after hiding handmade presents.
The children are all asleep and soon Father Solstice will visit.

There is the magic of the Winter Solstice.
This is the time for all to show and display their best.
One glimpse of Father Solstice with his needy bag.
Giving that which you most desire.
That which you cannot get alone.

How does he know just what it is?
That which you would love to get.
Besides the letters that we all write to him and his Nercucks.
Those magical frost people who listen to all we say
and report back to Father who thus knows all we desire.

Robert Thomas Lippman

"A Morning Rap-Rhapsody"

   Pre-dawn awakening to maudlin country melodies; still dozing
toes fumble to the kitchen striking an ill-placed door jamb—a
slight cringe—and on to the coffee pot for that habitual aroma and
eye-opening draught. One sip—two—maybe three——Mmmmm!
   Now! Two special lunches for two special boys. One sand-
wich lathered with P, B, and J; the other with just a "smidgen" of
butter and two extra thick slices of turkey. Add to each a bag of
chips, oatmeal cookie and the (almost forgotten) quarter for milk.
   Breakfast is next, as two sets of small feet rumble down the
stairs. Glasses of OJ now await the arrival of steaming bowls of
oatmeal. Sibling banter, clanking of spoons, and "Are you sure
the homework is done?"
   Breakfast over, up the stairs, teeth brushed, hair combed,
shoes tied. Here comes the bus! Grabbing books bags, lunches,
kisses good-bye, out the door.
   "HOUSE NOW SILENT," echoes the clock. Twenty minutes
left to shower, dress, and make the face! Comb the hair! Brush
the teeth!
Don the shoes! Grab the purse! Five whole minutes to spare!
   With keys in hand, and a last check of the house, the door
opens wide to a brilliant sun-filled sky! NOW TO WORK!!!

Sheila Rohrer

Growing Time

Points run deep,
Furrowed rows repeat,
Fresh earth upturns its face toward the sun.

Gentle breezes blow,
Dry away the cold,
Dried clay we mold.

Harrows level down
Dried, plowed ground,
Furrows fold into fields of quiet ponds.

Spring rains flow,
Reaching earth below,
Once molded, quickly grow.

As seeds to earth are sown
So we to life are thrown.
We plow and plant, we till,
Our Harvest——Life!

E. V. Leasure

Waiting Ashore

Upon the shore, a lady stands
    Gazing at the ocean's touch to the sand,
Images pass and protest in minds—in waves,
    A soulful creature grieves such a crave;
In with the tide, a faint figure nears,
    Abroad a massive ship, faces appear,
To whose possession is not known,
    Yet passed beyond the bountiful zone;
Glares are reflected from water to will
    As written in letters from paper by quill.

A hardened outline in the dimness of eventide
    Shown by the luminous moon that does not hide,
By clouds and smoke, not a thing is polluted
    Nor by past and fight, everything is included;
A hand raised by the blackened known stranger,
    Love rekindled, reborn in a sentimental manger,
Joy races across her unwanting facade—-
    She could no longer let her feelings wade;
Floating inward, the vessel nears the land,
    Upon the shore, a lady stands.

Rachel Olson

A Cloak Of Fine Linen

He wears his dignity like a cloak of fine linen.
Gentleness and kindness are his trademarks.

Why, dear God, why Him? Is there really a God?
Why don't you listen? Don't you care?

People are cruel. He is a branded man.
Somehow, in society's eyes
Suddenly ... less than human ... undeserving.

His family is scorned. His lover, too.

Society. A collective term for individuals
living in proximity to one another.
Individual. One person.

Changing society.
It starts with one person. Let that person be me.
I am human. I can choose humanity. And love.

He is rare. A treasurer indeed.
Not all are like him.
That does not diminish his greatness -
or my responsibility.
Perhaps, it increases it.

Mary R. Goodman

Prayer of Hope

The old man awakened to a day dark and cold.
Gently he rubbed his hands, now so wrinkled and old.
Slowly, he arose and sat upon his bed,
Lifted up his eyes to Heaven, then bowed down his head.
Dear Lord, he prayed. I thank you for another day,
for your merciful, tender loving care.
I beseech the Lord, reach down now, touch this great
nation sinking so deep in despair.
On everyday, homelessness, hopelessness, poverty and hunger abound.
Seeds of hatred, prejudice and distrust now fill our glorious land.
Threats of war, disease and famine now make a treacherous stand.
Send to us now Dear Lord, your love and wisdom,
A new hope to be found,
As together Dear Lord we take these mighty tasks in hand.
Beyond this Dear Lord, I shall ask for no more.

Wanda C. Walters

Why Didn't You Tell Me?

Why didn't you tell me. How dark it
gets when it rains. Flowers only bloom in the spring. And
love comes with a long string.
Why didn't you tell me. How cruel
life can be and at times bitter can be sweet. The only
way out is to be discreet.
If we were all born smart
we would have all the answers to our questions. But we have
to learn the hard way. While our dreams crumble in our hands.
and friends disappear to far away lands.
Why didn't you tell me that love
only comes once in your life and it fades away like a
disappearing sunset never to return. While
we live and learn.
Why didn't you tell me how
hard it would all be.
Why didn't you tell me?

Vicki Sementelli

These Hands Of Mine

These hands of mine can:
Give in love or take in greed.
Help those in need or ignore the needy.
Touch tenderly or tear viciously.
Protect our planet or pollute our resources.
Create works of art or destroy what others have created.
Beckon you close or push you away.
Be lifted in peace or raise a fist in fight.
Write words of love or promote ill-will and hate.
Dry a tear or cause the tears.
Tend the wounded or inflict wounds.
Uphold our laws or take the law in my own hands.
Hug a child or abuse a child.

I have a responsibility for these hands of mine.
To do what is right, or let them do wrong.
Only I can decide how to use these hands of mine.
These wonderful hands of mine.

Susan Edwards

Feelings

As I looked into his eyes, I could see the joy, the
happiness, but most of all the love.

As I put my hand on his chest, I could feel his heart pound
just like thunder rolling by.

When I look at him, a little runs up and down my
spine. When I touch him, that feeling comes back.

I guess it's love but I don't know for sure. Every time we
are together and every time we touch, that feeling comes again.

Kelly Marie Mills

Notes From Mignon

Give me a chance to dream big dreams
Give me a path of true direction
Give me a foundation boldly anchored
And I'll give you a me to be proud of.

Give me an opportunity to freely try
Give me support that will not fail
Give me the openness to be me
And I'll give you a me you can't see.

Give me a smile when I have none
Give me the feeling that you really care
Give me zeal from deep within
And I'll give you a me that knows "I can."

For whatever and whenever you give to me
You give to the world we live in
A world that reflects each and every gift
And thrives on the way it is given

Mignon Sims

When I Was A Lad

When I was a lad,
  glad did I dream
Dream of oceans and kings,
  knights and war machines.
Knights and chivalry,
  and war is a game,
Sailing for far-away lands to claim.

When I was a young man,
  glad did I dream
Dream of a quick end to war,
  no chivalry - just settle the score.

The war lasted only about forty days,
  horrendous bombing rained different ways.
Mass destruction requires little chivalry,
  but a quick end to war is fine with me.

Why give a worthy adversary a chance at all?
Because victory, then peace, matter most of all.

Marvin P. Wilson

"Hope For A Broken Wing"

The Bliss of soaring up in the sky
Glee that brings strength to fly
The wonder of passing by
Eventually said Goodbye.

The confident wings are broken...
I tried to fly but everything was in vain
I closed my eyes, prayed for a moment
But found myself without encouragement.

Time dragged me into suffering...
My life seemed hopeless
For me, there was no use going on
However, they say that life must go on.

Thus, time has helped.
My wings finally got into motion
Once again, I have flown on my own
Then found myself through a new horizon.

The trials of life indeed are endless,
But life has its meaning
There is always hope for everything,
Hope for a broken wing.

Vicky Coey

The Gulf War Part 2

The war is over thank God for that.
God helped them all the way, and that's a fact.
Many came home but some did not.
And many people realize that it won't be forgot.
I looked back and wondered, what were they fighting for?
For freedom? No, for pride? No, for our country? Yes.
But was that the answer, why they truly gave their best?
I salute the men who went over there.
Some were very valorous, and many were very scared.
I don't blame them at all; they fought till the fight was done,
And you know, they wouldn't recommend it for sun loving fun.
Bush helped us through, and we're glad it's now over;
Same goes for him 'cause now his job is over. Bush is out;
   Clinton is in
Maybe the Haiti war will be his end.
The world will have other wars to come.
Too bad we're not perfect or we would be having lots of fun.
The future will try to make a perfect plan
For no more wars and for sure, no one like Saddam.
Well the future will hold whatever is to be,
And thank God again the war is over, and we are still free!!!

Monty King

For The Love Of A Mother

God made a heaven, God made an earth
God sent a woman, to give us birth.
For such a task, he sent no other
But the strongest of souls, we call our Mother.

A heart so big and filled with pride
A haven for all, who wander inside.
For the love of her children, is all that she needs.
And when they are hurting, her heart, it bleeds!

For the love of a mother is hard to explain
Ferocious as a lion, yet gentle as rain.
She guides us in wisdom and wonders each night,
Has she done the best job, will they turn out all right?

For the love of a mother, is a sacred delight
And for those who have known it, see the nights twinkle bright!

Linda Slanicka

"He Loves You More"

Who cares if man condemns you
God will love you,
Because you are part of his bosom.

He always will be at your side,
To give you that love, people cannot give,
Because they are trapped
In human conception and perception,
About God's love.

God is for you, as for me,
For me, as for them,
For Christian, for Jewish, Moslem, Buddhist
or Taoist,
For Black, White, Yellow or Red skin.

If you love,
Just remember he loves you more,
Than people can
Regard God's love.

Roberto B. Rosado Rodriguez

Government Butter And Cheese

It's no disgrace to stand in line to receive
   government cheese and butter.
People come from all walks of life, in all kinds of
   fine circumstances.
I know one lady who went home and changed her coat and cap
To go through the line twice.

Three things a man must possess if his soul should live
And know life's perfect good,
Three things would the all supplying Father give,
Bread, butter, cheese, beauty, and brotherhood.

Don't walk in front of me to get the butter and cheese.
I may not follow. Don't walk behind me, I may not lead.
Just walk beside me, and don't get in my line
To get the butter and cheese. Then you will be my friend.

Before God's footstool to confess
A poor soul knelt and bowed his head.
"I failed," he cried, "to get my cheese."
Thou did thy best - - - that is success.
Some have gone away from the line
A lot of times and left empty-handed.

Vaudaline Thomas

Ole Gray Sky

   You bring tears to my eyes, Ole
Gray Sky.

   My skin craws for the sunlight, Ole
Gray Sky.

   Push your clouds to the east or
the west; so my body can humble rest.

   Looking through a small window I
can see the mighty Gray Sky. I ask
myself the question: Why me Gray Sky?
Are you showing a reflection of my Innerself?

   I have come to the conclusion about
the Gray, there is no reason to ask myself
why. Because feeling blue makes all skies
become gray.

   Ole Gray Sky; I cannot blame
you today. I just made you a escape goat
on how I feel today.

Rodney Varnadore

The Gift Of Love

The gift of love is an advantage of power,
   greater than the sun and moon.
It consists of certain insight which leads
   the to the highest of content.
Love has a sturdy balance to give and
   receive, only from ones heart.
Only can a heart full of love, give off such
   strength and will.
With love you are taught the natural ways
   of feeling...A feeling that can provide
   the values of ones overcoming life.
I write this passage to express only the sum,
   of infinite possessions one has when one
   has learned to except love and to receive it.
Being loved, and shown to love, is only given by
   a mother...A mother held in such honor;
Honor to great to say just Mom...I love you.

Tracey Ronkainen

205

"November At The Circle B"

Shortening days and falling snow,
Greet November with a chill hello.
How hard to rise when alarm clocks ring,
Without the sunshine and birds to sing.
But up you must, and out of doors,
Whistling a tune as you do the chores.
Then into a breakfast piping hot,
With tantalizing smells from the coffee pot,
The bacon and eggs, the toast and jam.
You think "What a lucky guy I really am."
Then along comes the mail with news and bills,
You gulp down more of your ulcer pills.
We've got to get busy and raise more pounds,
You think aloud in muttering sounds.
Then finally you turn to your wife and say,
Let's go see those folks' Charolais
That are advertised by the Circle B
In a place called Little Genesee.
get on your coat, lock things up tight,
We gotta be back for chores tonight.

Ruth Bucher Bottoms

Max And Me

Big "old possum" in a persimmon tree,
Grinning down at Max and me.
I shook that tree, "old possum" hit the ground,
'Bout scared the heck outa my old hound.

I said, 'come on Max, let's have some fun,
See if we can make "old possum" run.
Lazy "old critter" just lay on the ground.
I could see this was no fun for my old hound.

Sure enough "old possum" was playing dead,
Didn't move a muscle, not even his head.
I knew this "critter" was playing it cool,
Cause he sure made 'old Max' look the fool.

We headed home feeling sorta low,
Max kept looking back, didn't want to go.
We got home, had some lunch,
Took some time to watch the Brady Bunch.

Max fell asleep then to dream,
And I knew he was chasing "old possum" down by the stream.
But that sly "old critter" went back up the tree,
And finished his lunch, just like Max and me.

Lois Snelling Conder

Pathway

Walking down the hall so dusty and dark
Groping, wandering aimlessly my journey to embark.
I see a light flickering in the night
I must press on with all my might.
I stumble and fall, my wounds open and bleeding
I'd lost sight of the light, a tangled web I was weaving
I stood to brace myself on a solid rock, the ground shifting
I gazed helpless for security my body slowly sinking.
My dress was rags, all bloody and tattered
I knew what I wanted really didn't matter
The light had dwindled down to a smolder
Then I felt a light touch again on my shoulder
I looked my wounds were healed, my feet on solid ground.
I knew from that moment I was glory bound.
I looked once more at the new found light
It wasn't flickering, but burning ever so bright
The light so bright no shadows cast behind
Then I heard...
In the darkness I've wept for you, in the Son you'll shine!"

Tammy Greenway

Endangered

Encaged, in a glass pyramid,
growing smaller by the minute.
Crushed, into eternity, you know
it isn't worth it, you make it
worth your while. You were high
like a king, but now it's the
opposite. Put in a world where
the putrid stench is part of
your everyday. Running, won't help.
An invisible barrier keeps you
inside your eternal hell. There's
no escape. Close your eyes and
hope to God you die. You can't
stand it anymore, your going insane. Living in a world that is
nothing but padded rooms. Your future is told.
Written in the book of existence.
Life may not be like this forever,
or will it? You seem to be used
to it by now. This life might seem
bad to me, but not to you. Yea, this is your endangered life.

Nick Helling

Growing Up In The Hood

Positive Brothers and Sisters
Growing up in Fear, Violence, and Hatred.
Negativity surrounds the exterior
But the interior holds Family, Unity, and Love.
It is a Dangerous hood we live in
When CRACK is sold freely like CANDY.
The hood holds a lot of Positive residents
Who have passed on the Torch to the next of kin.
Uniting and not Fighting
To make a change soo drastic
That growing up in the hood would never be the same.

Rosemary Ordonez

"Far Beyond"

Sifting rocks into another place,
hailing wrongs in our time,
I can't think in sap, looking for some seed,
catching light in a net I've sewn,
don't know what I'm looking for,
don't have to sight you for my dignity.
Leave me alone, don't want to be known.
Colored vision screens sand in time,
all this stuff is just a phase,
money for a blessing wants me to believe,
have a stone for your feelings beneath,
wash away your sins with bleach,
put some color in my salt so it looks polluted.
Leave me alone, don't want to be known.

Thomas Mixa

Moments

Children at play—how happy they seem
Hearing them laugh—listening to them dream
Wanting to play grown-up—they wish away the years
Always asking questions—seeking answers to their fears

Children wishing time—would hurry up and pass
Grown-ups thinking time—goes flying by too fast
Life is full of moments—that just flicker past
You have to capture the good ones—and try to make them last

We never stop learning—this I know is true
It's never too late—to try something new
Enjoy all the moments—when they come your way
Your heart will remember—and moments will always stay

Sylvia Kaliser

Today

What are we trying to be for this my eyes see,
Handfuls of false prophets appear to deceive,
Who do we run to? Who must we believe,
The increase of the wicked take the love away,
Are you going to leave or will you choose to stay?
Helpless persecutors have the need to crucify,
Slipping so far out of reach and never asking why,
Rumors spread like water over the falls of war,
Bringing on the pain and closing every door,
Nations pushing Nations the mighty die in vain,
We must throw angers hate aside and end its game,
We can toss it aside and take in sweet love,
Let us remember how to hold and forget how to shove,
The light should take us in overrule the sin,
Let it show us how to smile a great way to begin,
We will still hear thunder in cool, quite places,
We will still feel the pains and the dark, empty faces,
We all grow weak, but we must stay strong,
The Magic Kingdom quietly waits to judge us all,
The ways we choose, it won't be long... Today.

Kevin T. Lebel

Frozen Tears

Frozen tears of icicles
Hang for dear life between heaven and earth
Creating a cold beauty.

Each hangs with a quiet desperation
Frozen in rigid patterns fearful of their tear drops.

A wan winter sun strikes their icy crystals creating
a new kind of brilliance.
Forcing the frozen tears to eke out their lives
drop by drop.
Frozen tears dread their spills and splashes
For they don't know what awaits them below and beyond.
If they did, they would weep unabashedly.
For you see, they return to the dust of the earth from
which they came, to water and become
    the purple of the humble violet,
    the fragrance of an Easter lily,
    or the beauty of a lovely rose.

Rita C. McDonald

Knowing Inside

The road I have walked,
Has been hard and full of tears.
And no one could possibly understand,
What I went through in all those years.

I've met a lot of people, both good and bad,
Who have helped me without knowing.
And because of all I've seen,
It made me realize where I was going.

I tried not to complain a lot,
Though I know I sometimes did.
Most never saw how I felt inside,
Because it was behind my own lies, I hid.

But once I finally saw were my life was leading,
And were I was taking myself day by day.
I came to realize that I was the only one
I could count on, So I changed my way.

Now I'm working on a law degree,
To help get me to the top.
And I know deep inside my heart,
I am never going to stop.

Vicky N. Trimble

A Heroes Going Home

A blue star that shone in our window
Has changed to one of pure gold.
My brother that was serving our country
Is now serving in a Mightier fold.
Each night from out of the Heavens
We pick a golden star,
It represents you dear Jimmy
And shines for you afar.
As it shines each night Jimmy
God sheds his beam on you
He's keeping you in his loving care
That's why he changed the star to gold from blue.
But since it's changed to gold Jimmy
You do not seem so far and
Each night we look toward heaven and
Pick a golden star.

Neta Walker Laycock

A Light Of Beauty In The Dark

There is an unknown spirit under my bed. It keeps
haunting me filling my head with beautiful visions but
tragic dreams. Holding me down keeping me from breaking
free. Filling my insides full of fear. I want my soul to be
dragged in an enormous light of love, passion, and
happiness. The oppressive disease is calling me back into
its loins, using its temptations of addiction and
withdrawal symptoms. Very clever this disease! Bold
enough to have forgotten God and the devil existing for
a short period of time. I drink to progress a
conversation with my conscience and vegetate off the
light of the moon. Then at last fall into the eyes of
beautiful Sharon, whom I have to dream about whenever
I long for her. From then on the rest of the night brings
on the dangers of depression, which I have battled
numerously. It never ends the same routine, and finally
then, a few seconds of pain and I'm born again.

Mark F. Blanco

The Mariner's Lady

Beneath a rugged wall so steep, below magistral evergreens,
He and I conversed of much, but reticence did swallow us
    Until the winged song did fuss,
    At swaying trees within the aura.

"This woman," he began, (and I soon found that world ill fit for her)
"Bore beauty like the stars of North and grace like damp of
tempest past, entered my days of youthful bliss, my game full
truant of emptiness, With immortality—my God."

His eyes turned toward the western sky, where ocean rains poured
dark in strings, "She with a stallion wind did chase, and I, with
Donkey, felt misplaced, but when her steed did bow to drink the
song of a melodious brook, her shapely figure cleared to view."

"Do tell, I bid thee, do commence," and with a pause of thought
did he, "The damsel did her horse take leave, and left this
precious green grass stage, and mesmerized by what I'd seen
    I sat the sun across the sky."

The silence welcomed salted eyes; we spoke not more for soon
    the morn
Would pose its noble quests on men, and then new he would
    gaze a glaze, Upon his cosmic Christabel......

Matthew R. Modarelli

"Carolyn's Poem"

Hark!
He beckons Me.
He calls My name,
And I turn to thee.

For beneath My soul lies a beautiful rainbow
waiting to shine.

Hark!
He calleth Me.
And from inside it shines for all to see.

He beckons Me, and I wait;
and forever a rainbow doeth shine upon Me.

Oh, beautiful rainbow,
doeth shine.

As its beckoning call echoes in My heart,
DOETH SHINE !

Kathy Morris

Fido, Bingo, Or Butch

You can set your clock by his routine.
He comes everyday at three to play; until he's sent away.
He makes happy sounds and gestures. He aims to please!
He delights my daughter. She wishes we could keep him.
She plays and romps and laughs with him.
She frequently shares her snacks and even dinner.
He delights in his food; eagerly enjoying every morsel
And he always begs for more.
Then at dark, he must be sent away, to the place he goes to rest.
I think the street is really his home.
The child is nine. His name is Joe;
And he has a natural mother.
She isn't canine; but as far as she's concerned
His name may as well be Fido, Bingo, or Butch.
And as far as I'm concerned
Her's may as well be bitch.

Nancy E. Fuelberg

The Presence Of God

In the home where there is love, God's spirit seems to dwell.
He comes just as the heavenly dove, and tells us all is well.

We feel his presence everywhere; each room, each tiny nook.
We know that he is always there; we never have to look.

We feel His majesty and power in everything that we do.
He strengthens us each day and hour, and fills our hearts anew.
Because we're only human, we sometimes feel depressed,
But with God's almighty power, He lets us know we're blessed.

So, we pray for understanding, and it is then that faith begins to grow.
We strive to obey each commandment, and let all of god's
   goodness show.
Each prayer, each psalm, each holy word; we keep within our hearts.
We commit our souls, unto the lord, from whom we will never depart.

A heart that is full of joy and peace is a heart that trusts in God.
Through faith our blessings will increase when to His will in
   obedience we nod.
A home where the spirit of love is pure; a home that is filled with
   prayer,
Is a home where love will long endure, for God builds His altar there.

Mary Major Fields

The Seasons Of A Father's Life

In the spring of a young man's life,
He finds a young bride to be his wife.
Through shaking lips, and inner strife,
He pledges to her, his true love for life.

In his summer years, he has but one great fear;
How to support those whom he holds so dear.
He works from early morn to late at night,
His only true love, holds their child at night.

In his fall, he is still there,
For his daughter's wedding fare.
With strong, trembling hands,
He wipes away a single tear,
In hopes that never ending love will be there.

When winter comes with grandchild on his knee,
"One more season," to his maker he pleads.
Eyes glowing dim, and hair grown gray,
"Keep my love true," at night he prays.

Omar Edward Hopkins

God

God made the trees that sing with each breeze
   He made little girls
God made the land with the touch of His hands
   He made little boys

He put them all together
   In one big wonderful world
With stars above
   To brighten His love
He gave us all that He had....

So we should say
   Thank you each day
For all these gifts we behold
   And take care of each thing
That His love did bring
   To this great, big, wonderful world.

Leonilla Broker

Our Dad, A Love Story

Where ever our Dad was, my brother and I were always nearby.
He made us laugh and dried our tears when we'd cry.
Sometimes, he had to spank us when we were bad.
Pretty soon, we would reach up and say, "I love you, Dad."

Dad would come home tired from work, at night.
He was never too tired to hold mom and us, real tight.
The love in our family continued to grow.
We were never ashamed to let it show.

Then came math problems, driving lessons and Graduation day.
Once again, Dad stood behind us, all the way.
We were soon off to college and weddings came to both of us.
Dad was a proud father, in spite of all the fuss.

Now that we are married, with children of our own,
Grandpa, to the children, is like a precious stone.
Dad's hair has thinned and turned to gray.
But, the love in his heart will be there to stay.

The family has gathered together, again.
It is Father's day and we sit in the den.
We all want to say, "Thank you, Dad, we love you so much,
You've given our lives that extra, special touch."

Martha Parks

Fifth Grade

In the very back corner,
he sat:
His long legs winging beyond the desk;
his ankles hanging beneath the cuffs
of hitched-up pants of navy blue;
his lean wrists springing from jacket sleeves
that would've fit any other boy in the room.

He didn't come often, but when he came
the teacher called on him to read. He did -
in the same low, slow monotone
usually reserved for the delivery of bad news.
Pale and painfully shy, he avoided the view
of every eye, his own face free of all surprises.
Quietly, peacefully, his dark hair draped down
across his forehead like a curtain closing
on what he'd already seen
at sixteen.

Years later, I think of him with shame,
unable to recall if I ever knew
his name.

Mary Harwell Sayler

My Son

The baby is coming but much too soon
He shouldn't be here it's only June

I've been here a month but it has seemed so long
They keep telling me to try and hold on

I still remember the flight here that day
My water broke so early in May

Ten weeks early and he's going to be here
This baby is coming the time is near

After he's born they show him to me and then he's gone
It's a boy 3 1/2 pounds I have a son

I get to see him and he is so small
He looks like a tiny little doll

Twenty one days he had to stay
But now he's coming home today

The next couple years bring heartache and tears
Medical problems and surgeries and all kinds of fears

Now he's three and a healthy growing boy
He is his mothers pride and joy.....

Sheila L. Minor

The Mountain Man

Always drawn to peaks so high,
He sometimes feels they touch the sky,
So to the woods, he often goes,
So much to see and there repose,

He likes the country roads and streams,
For there he can dwell on his dreams,
Born to the mountains, he will stay,
And learn so much in his own way,

He stands quite tall with courage shown,
Surrounded by loved ones, most grown,
Except for three or four still growing,
Who clamber 'round him, their love showing,

And whether far away or there,
All of his kin and friends do care,
And send a special wish to say,
May God bless you on your birthday.

Sheila P. Ratcliffe

Freedom's Ride

Hatchet in right, scalpel in the other
He stalks his raging soul
As God beats down on him with the heat of the sun
Soldiers stab each other's hearts
While blood trickles down their crippled spines
One by one they fall to the ground
Allowing them to rot in the mud
Only to become part of the grass again
And leaving him to trot with the wind
He runs through their dead spirits
Never noticing that they exist
And all this time he is muttering words
Words that he can only hear
Why am I doing this?
What is this for?
Nobody can tell him:
Freedom's Ride!!

Quan Lam

The Memory

I stood at the garden wall and looked down upon the hill,
   he stood beneath with crimson rays of sunset shining on his face,
   ...and I knew that I had seen him in another time and place.

So strange this feeling overcame me as I saw this other man,
   standing there in your place bidding me Good-Bye,
     My mind so filled with images I felt as though I'd cry.
And just as quick he vanished from sight the man who stood below,
   but not before I knew it hurt him so to go.

After then I always new I'd lived here once before,
   I pondered time and time again if we were once in love,
The man who waived and cried to me as I stood high above.

Time traveled by and I grew older...
   ...my mind somehow told me more,
   of the time and place I once knew...in my past before.

If I had the chance to offer you but one piece of advice,
   It would be to be giving of all your heart...
   ...and never once think twice.
For you may be back on this earth again to make amends for now,
And it may be harder than before to fulfill your chosen vow.

Kim Curtis

America, Our Land

America, America, God blessed this land to man.
He stretched this land from sea to sea, across
   the mountains, and through the riverland.
From the west the Indians came, and from the
   east the European.
As people came from there Mother land seeking
   freedom from another land.

Now America is home, for man, who came in
   search for peace and love.
Where the mind is free and the heart is pure
   and the land belongs to you and me.
I love this land America, where I can live
   and work and think and be a neighbor sent
   from God above.
For this is where the world began, a man named
   God and He was lonely and created man to be.
So bless this land American.
   And thank the Lord you can.

Phelps E. Parsons

Nikki

He moves gracefully, yet slyly
He turns the corner to retrieve his prey
Patting his catch, you can hear his gentle, soft purr of accomplishment
Next to the lifeless rodent, he stops playing and begins to stroke
   himself
Then he lays gazing in the sun waiting for something to happen
As he lays peacefully, he can hear the wind blowing gently
Then he hears a sound coming from the brush
Evolving to a running stance, he moves agilely, yet slyly toward
   the bush
Then pushing his head into the bush, he looks around
He finds nothing but twigs and leaves, then shakes them
He moves slowly toward the house
Finds a comfortable place on the sofa and purrs himself to sleep.

   Nicole Danna

Just A Stick Pony

There was a little pony, his name was Drapple Gray.
He wanted so a master, to care for him each day.
To pet him and to ride him, to keep his mane with care.
Thus one day he galloped off to find a friend so debonair.
In the city, down the vale and on the hillside afar.
He sought from house to house until he found this door ajar.
"Come in," said the lady "Come in," said the man.
"You look tired and weary," (Believe me that I am!)
Then Drabble Gray his story told,
   And of his search in vain —
"Whoa!" said the lady. "Whoa!" said the man.
"Let Mark our grandson hold your rein."
He's a good little lad and Christmas is here.
He will take good care of you, have no fear."
So Drapple Gray awaits his master true.
As he bows low and says, "How-Do-You-Do."

   Truth Arthur

Man

   What is man that thou are mindful of him?
He was placed in a line of Glory,
But got cheated to be seated, in the seat of Greed and Power.

Power to love or Power to hate, which one will man instigate?
Man has put himself to the test,
To see who can destroy each other, the best.

Love has changed since way back when.
It's no more open and everybody getting into the trend.
Men are going through men's back door.
Women or going through women's front door.
Never thinking they can go down with opp;
but if you are not careful you can come up with HIV.

What is the true answer to man most ask question.
What will I do while I am here?
Were will I be when I gone?

   Roosevelt Maddrey Jr.

Living On Faith

Living on faith in need of a prayer.
Held in bondage by my worldly cares.
Digging holes just to fill them up,
as I take my drinks from the poor man's cup.
Work all day just to go to bed,
just to get up and do it again.
At times it seems so useless it seems a sin.
Other times its freedom makes me grin,
as I dig my holes just to fill them up
and take my drinks from the poor man's cup.

   Robert B. Glass

"carpenters"

he had simple needs, simple desires, simple pleasures.
he was unpretentious,
a man of few words, of little formal education.
Robert Walker French was a man.
he was my father.

he was born in World War I,
became a man in the Great Depression,
a father in World War II,
a grandfather in the sixties.
he died in the eighties.
he worked, he ate, he slept, he played, usually in that order.
rarely did he relax - he didn't know how.

he was a hunter, a trapper, a fisherman, a gardener.
he was a carpenter and cabinetmaker with few equals.
he was a good provider.
he loved me, but didn't know how to say it.
I didn't either.
we knew we had a bond, both father and son.
I learned to say I love him after he was gone.

he is in good company, Jesus of Nazareth was a carpenter, too.

   Robert W. French, Jr.

Le Coq Fier, Le Roi De La Ferme

The Proud Rooster, King Of The Farmyard

Le coq fier. Majestic. Commanding. Even in death. Beady
arrogant eyes. Head held erect. Red cox-comb. Red beard. Beak
parted slightly. Orange feathers. Burnished copper feathers.
Black and green tail feathers.
Soft even in death.

Taxidermy. Witch doctors thwarting death's decay. Restoring our
proud bird. Eviscerated. Disemboweled. Gutted. Once deprived of
the essential contents of your departed life force, your skin was
peeled off and glued to a plaster mold of your carcass. Yet you feel
soft as a feather-bed. Deceptive. Like the human beauty-business.
Package deals.
Breast enhancements or reductions? Liposuction? Tummy-tucks?

Face-lifts? Ski-slope noses? Glistening-white ultra-bright smiles?
Varicose-vein removals? Unsightly spider-veins? Nail tips?
Colored contact lenses? Silicon breast-implant-plaintiff
class-action suits.
Outraged Nature rejecting cosmetic disfigurement or perfection.

Le coq fier. Honored or humiliated? Worms will not eat your
rotting carcass. Why do you stare so? How did you die? Crowing
triumphantly? Exultantly welcoming the dawn? Or in a bloody
cock-fight, heeled with metal gaffs. Fighting to the death.
Friendly fire.

My friend, yours will never be the tired crow of an aged, infirm
cock spurned by hens, displaced by younger, handsomer, more
aggressive, cock-sure birds. No. You will be beautiful and
proud forever more. Always King of the Farmyard. Non. Tu
seras beau et fier toujours.
Toujours. Le roi de la ferme.

   Laura Tieger

In The Spiritual Realm (Of India)

Sita girl so fresh
Her spirit sewn with praises
She is so real as the priest reveals
And everyone exclaims her honour.

But mountains and mountains of flesh did burn
Prodded with sticks and forced with shame
Were these souls ready for the eternal light,
Or are they the voices of the newborn's scream?

   Tana Pietrzak

Flying Eagle

Beaded braid of long black hair
headdress made from feathers
moccasins stitched to wear
In spite of the cold weather

War drums you will hear no more
fires all are dim
All we have left is this land
to remember him

Walked this land for many moons
Being free like the eagle
You can still hear the spiritual tunes
See his light footed dance majestically regal

War drums you will hear no more, fires all are dim
All we have left is this land to remember him

His hand in mine a tear in his eye
It's the last time you shall see me
for it was his turn to die
He just wanted to be free

War drums you will hear no more, fires all are dim
All we have left is this land, sadly we forgotten him
Linda Parise

A Man Of Pure Gold

A lifetime of memories are flooding my mind, though the words
of the heart are not easy to find. When you're hunting for ways
to say how you feel, "Just A Man", you may think, but to us,
"Man Of Steel".

"Build Up" and "Make Peace", were his mottos of light,
and "A Job That's Worth Doing Is Worth Doing Right".
"Brush Your Teeth", "Wash Your Ears", "Comb Your Hair",
"That's Enough!" Impatient yet kind, he was gentle - but tough!

Going to town with our dad was a real texas treat,
say "Hello", "Howdy do" to everyone that you meet,
shake their hand, tip your hat, stop to chat for awhile,
and above everything else, wear a bright sunny smile!

Sunday most likely, was Dad's favorite day. He would wake us
with singing in a "Loud" sort of way. Keep a tune on your lips
and "Old Spice" on your face, give your best to the Lord and the
whole human race. He asked quite a lot and expected it too, but
never asked more than he himself wouldn't do! And if ever we
failed, he was there with a hand, Never pointing a finger....
just helping us stand!

A lifetime of memories, a life with a plan, who gave more to his
children that most anyone can, you may think "just a man" as our
story was told, But to the family that loves him, he's a
"Man Of Pure Gold!"
Patricia Fleming

Untitled

Oh moon, fiery spear of burning light,
Held by the branches in the night.
Wrap my heart with your serenity,
And quiet content as I sit with thee.

Touch my cheek with your gentle glow.
Whisper my name as if you know,
Filling my eyes with your looming stare,
Will capture my soul in your magic snare.

Holding me tight with your rays of gold,
My breath, in your shadows, you do hold.
And the midnight charm of your embrace,
Will lightly kiss my upturned face.

And as you glide up in the sky,
From my lips escape a lowly sigh.
For the memory of you will always stay,
As this night soon turns into the day.
Rose A. Lantz

Be Encouraged

it's not as bad as it looks
Lift up your head, O' child of the King,
He'll never leave you alone to cry.
You have a friend, acquainted with grief,
the Son of God, Most high.

You are not crushed,
yet hard pressed on every side.
This burden is too heavy for you,
on the Master's shoulder, let it abide.

Perplexed, but not yet in despair
for you, the Savior's blood did atone.
Persecuted, but you know He'll not forsake you
'cause you've made your heart His home.

Your sighing is not hidden from your Father
though you're bowed down, and troubles endure,
Be Encouraged, God's mercy is everlasting
His grace is amazing and His love is for sure.
Loretta M. Brooks

Listen, Listen...

A screaming little girl.
Help me, help me.
Struggling for support.
Let me hold you, what is wrong?
  Life.

Daddy don't leave me.
Tell me stories when you were a boy.
Give me hugs and kisses and treat me like a spoiled little girl.
Teach me good and wrong.
Surprise me with ice cream on a sunny day.
Hold me tightly and don't ever let me go.
Because I love you daddy and I don't want to be
left alone.

Within my heart I don't want to let you go.
Within my heart I have so much love for you.
Within my heart there can't be anyone but you
because within, that's just something I just can not lose.
Victoria Lulgjuraj

Night Child

There is a girl dancing behind the grocery store.
Her bare feet make little sound as she leaps,
runs, and turns on the hard concrete.

  Why does she dance
  in the dark, under stars
  and moonlight instead of
  under the sun?

Her copper-brown hair glints as she flees silently
along with only her shadow for company.

  Soft feet on hard ground
  she runs as tho' possessed.

She appears like a child of night and I find
myself wondering about her.
  Could it be herself she flees?
Lynda D. Ferrell

Untitled

She lies there sleeping, looking so peaceful
her beautiful little face laying against her pillow
I can't help but stare at her in amazement
Her skin is as soft and delicate as a rose petal
Her voice a tiny whisper
No parent could be prouder

But she's not like the others, she's different
She's a "special child"
Sadness, even pain, an ache deep inside
For her, for you, for what could have been
All your hopes and dreams, every things changed
She changed it
The tiny little person that came into our lives
"Our Special Child"

So many wonderful things, it's all so clear
Everyday is precious and we realize how lucky we truly are
No one can say how far she will go
Or what she will achieve in her lifetime
But one thing is for sure, she will always know love.
She's our little girl, our baby, our special child

Nadine Souza

The Bag Lady

Her dress is old her shoes are worn
Her hair a tangled nest
An old stained shawl draped round her neck
Conceals her sagging breasts

I wonder where she sleeps at night
And how does she keep warm
How does she protect herself
From rain and wind and storm

I wonder if she takes a bath
Does she brush her teeth
Oh precious lady where do you rest
Your tired aching feet

A lifetime of possessions
Tied up in a sack
The road she walks is weary
There is no looking back

Calloused hands and wrinkled brow
Yet daily around dusk
She bows her head and offers thanks
For in her God she trusts

Leona Susan Prohm

A Body Of Fire

Her broad muzzle starts the features of her face,
Her pearly white canines set the spark,
Her red eyes are electrifying and are always shining and
    shall always set the flame,
Her long, dark lashes so thin;
Her thick, ebony brows so simple,
Her full hair is the color of autumn's fallen leaves,
Her auburn body is like a show of atomic orange fireworks;
    Brilliant, illuminous, and always sparkling a black night,
Her blue clothes hug her closely like a sea quenching a flame.

A body of fire, Estellastarr, is what you have.

Nehemia C. Fitzgerald

Night Mother

The night envelops my still form
Her shroud is soft and ebon and warm

She lays my weary mind to rest
And gently rocks me on her breast

It is in her dark womb I lay
Silently awaiting the light of day

She is my mother so gentle yet strong
For her loving touch during the day I long

She is always there yet not too close
One half my life is in her repose

Ever listening to my outcries of pain
Ever listening yet never in vain

Though I may scream and curse her wind
I always come back to her arms again

Night mother as you hold your son this eve
Know that in your love he still believes

Todd C. Ely

Her Happiness

Happy was she who loved to love.
Her unconditional style-
A gift, a blessing from God above.

Happy was she who loved to give.
Forever helping others, blessing each person,
In each day she lived.

Happy was she who's day of judgement never came.
Not a person would she accuse.
Not a soul would she blame.

Happy was she who loved to smile.
Happiness and humor-
Elements further enhancing her style.

Happy was she who loved to sing.
A voice of inspiration.
Consistently praising, bringing glory to her King.

Happy was she who loved to love.
Her unconditional style-
A gift, a blessing from God above.

Lisa A. White

In Heaven I Await For Your Love

Hand in hand and eye to eye
Here we stand to say, "Good-bye."

As memories in my mind of the things we did
Are for you to find and never forbid.

'Cause I just about cry thinking of you.
This was a lie and only God knew.

We were meant to be as later we live.
It's our destiny ... not a sin to forgive.

So hold me forever and never let go.
But if you do I want you to know:

That when I look back on all we've done
I won't laugh 'cause you'll be gone.

Maria Blancas

"Swing Into Spring"

My advice to all is live a fruitful Spring.
Here's how I try for an explanation to do this very thing.

I was 8 Springs old when Dad bought a wooden red, white, and
blue baton;
Its top sparkled like the snow. With it, I trained circus ponies,
small dogs, even jungle beasts — lion and tigers —
we both loved them so.

I see poor folks who love homemade ice-cream at parties
and hear the sound, I love, of Dad's spoon asking for more.
Mom, going into action, scraping beaters, her family chore.

Me - I'm a child of the spirit - wind, morning outside a stucco
house where seven did live.
My thing to fetch chicken eggs under the sitting hens, they don't
like to give.
Hunting for Queen's shepherd pups in a woodpile under fresh snow.
Dad's teaching Johnny the Shetland, a sugar-lump trick - take a
red bandanna out of my back pant's pocket;
for Mary Lou a grand animal show!

Retrace your steps and gently realize just as my sick son (Jonathan)
saying 'Love Is In The Air', under Denver's bright Colorado skies.
How gratefulness to God for our past, Leads us to ask for more
than a road of yesterday!
We need a chance to Swing Into Spring blissfully returning to
our happy youth
Because, thank God in heaven we're nicely made up that way.

Mary Lou Anderson

"The Outsider"

He's never let in, always kept at arm's distance.
He's tried to fit in, but is always met with resistance.
He's awkward, strange, a bit out of touch, they say.
The outsider who never see's the light of day.
In his room of silence he sits alone, always alone.
Rocking to and fro, dreaming of adventures and loves
he will never find or come to know. The outsider
exists between two worlds, not really knowing where
he belongs. One, is where the Insiders speak, yet no
sounds are heard, the other, he can understand their
every gesture and unspoken word. Where does his
piece fit in this vast puzzle we call Humanity?
So many years gone unclassified, is he bordering on
normal or bordering on insanity? Will the outsider
ever find his place in this world, or have peace
of mind? Probably not, as long as the insider's
of the world continue to act Deaf, Dumb, and Blind.

Melodie Ann Aszman

A Man

He wasn't very tall;
  His face was dark and grim.
His body was slight and bent.
  Fate had not been kind to him.

He lifted the pick up high
  And swung it to the ground with force;
He dug it deep inside
  Of the hard but rich dark earth.

Now he pulled his body straight
  And looked up at the red, hot sun.
He wiped the sweat from his brow;
  Then started to dig again.

Not till the sun had set
  And the air all around turned cold
Did the man lay down his pick
  And smile in triumph bold.

Marie A. Melaro

How To Win An Argument

She's lulled by the domesticity
He's upset by the stupidity
She's feeling warm, secure and safe
He's concerned about the future, harsh and cold.
The act committed, the gesture done
She announces the terms, the battle begun.

Why do these have the thrust of death?
The finality of being, the wrenching of soul?

The words echoed are spewed with hate (He)
The tears are shed with bitter remorse (She)

Oh, for the better days
When we were young (She)
Oh, for the finer days
When we did love (She)

Oh, how I blame you
For my being (He)
Oh, how I curse you
For draining me of love (He)

When these thoughts are known, it is easy to see
Who wins the argument, it is (he)

Roberta DeUrso

Avoidance

I see an old man walking down the street.
His back is braced against the wind.
I hear his shoes and the pavement meet,
  and catch a glimpse of blue eyes, dim.
His hat is tattered and his pants are torn.
He whistles a dated tune as he walks.
His face is battered, tan and worn.
His shoes are holey and he wears no socks.

A woman passes in her prime.
But he lacks the pride to raise an ardent eye.
He gruffly whispers please, to spare a dime.
She walks away, shakes her head and sighs.

The smell of urine, liquor and decay,
I wish I didn't act this way.

I'll just cut across that yard
And to my relief he slowly staggers out of range.
It shouldn't be too hard,
  to conceal the reality that he caused the change.

Karen Amber Klassen

What A Friend I Have In Jesus

His wondrous works I cannot seem to fathom
His blessings how can I begin to count them
He's my raft when the tides are high
His spirit so sweet and serene, like a lulla-bye
He reaches out and down in times of consternation
In my hour of weakness he is my only consolation
When wrong wraps me up and I try hard to elude
And still when I pray, with benevolence and love, he does exude
What a marvelous feeling to be enamored by my friend from above
To be made free and pure as a precious dove
Have you ever had a friend love you unconditionally?
I assure you no greater love from my friend, especially
When I know that it is not of my own merit
My fears, tears, and pain with him I can share it
When I go to him with a penitent spirit
He never says, "not this — I simply won't hear of it."
To the end he said he would be with us
What a friend, his name is Jesus.

Sheila Dunham

An Observation Of Love, In Silver: And Blue

I noticed the silver in Grandaddy's soft hair,
His blue eyes full of tears, for the grandbaby there.
She slept like an angel, as he wept grieving tears.
Her life only months, and his life many years.

Though Grandaddy believed in whatever God's will,
Yet today, in his hair there was more silver still.
As it did not seem fair that her life was so short,
But I knew she'd live long in her grandaddy's heart.

I could see him reflecting on that cute little smile,
With small hands patting softly, saying "Hold me awhile!"
Oh yes, she was special to this silver-haired man,
And she's left him a lot in her life's shortened span.

As he lifted the veil for one last kiss of love,
Well knowing, she was now with the father above,
I watched, as Grandaddy let his spirit break.
The pain was so great, even I felt his ache.

Well, now there were others in great need of his care,
So he unclenched those big hands, that were folded in prayer.
Then he rose to his feet like the man we all knew,
the soft hair, still more silver, now his eyes, much more blue.

Sylvia G. Follis-Lehr

Uncertain

Her black hair was dancing in the breeze,
His blue eyes were lost in the clouds.
While the restless autumn leaves were bursting with
color as they swept by each other.
Not listening to the sound of their hearts, closing
their eyes to the sadness of their story, and both
hiding what they felt forever.
They turned to gaze at each other one last time,
waved goodbye and walked away.
Sometimes spoken words should never be heard,
Endless battles should never be fought.
Secret whispers should never be told.
And uncertain moments never be known.
Why must they go through this passage of pain?
When there was nothing to have been gained.
Perhaps they never should have met.

Shelly Della Selva

Life's Folly

Upon the threshold of life he stood,
His hair was black and youth was good.
Riches and fame will come, he said.
I'll make my mark in the years ahead.

The years came and the years went by
He gathered his riches and wondered why
He had no friends to talk awhile
Of things gone by and dreams gone wild.

Upon the threshold of death alone,
His hair was white, his youth was gone,
His life was wasted in decay
Of earthly riches and fame, I say.

Why didn't someone tell me he said
Of things that live when I am dead?
That the good we do from day to day
Are the things that last when we pass away.

Upon his wrinkled cheek - a tear
And I wonder, he said, if God would hear
If I should stop to kneel and pray
Be merciful to me on judgement day.

Thomas A. Johnson

A Winter's Rose

Amidst the snow stands a winter's rose.
His petals are so tender and sheen.
His stem is so desirably proportioned.
His leaves are immensely saturated with vitality.
He possess no thorns to offend me.
His elegance gives me hope.
His presence bestows to me felicity.
His touch creates passion.
Through the storms I hear his comforting voice.
He has changed me eternally.
He makes me feel loved.
I could never enjoy another entity
As much as I enjoy him.
Amidst my heart stands a winter's rose.

Marty Elin

My Grandfather

The sun around him always shines
His smile always welcomes
His eyes sparkle and dance
The love he radiates embraces me
The tenderness of his laugh

The warmth I feel in his presence
The smile he smiles is contagious
The eyes which look at me peer deep into my soul
The love I feel for him is immense
The comfort of his laugh

His child-like qualities that remind me life is short
The amazement of aging I feel when I look at him
I want to embrace him, to take care of him, to protect him
I want him to live forever and never grow older
And he will live forever in my heart and soul

My fear and fright of his death
My sadness and tears at the thought
The way I turn child-like in thinking of my feelings
What about his?

Meegan Tracy

Fearless Flight

The sun glistens over the snowcapped hills as the baby bird
discovers his wings.
The chill of the frosty weather subsides and the spirits of life
begin to sing.

The melody of their songs fill the valley with change and the bird
now becomes afraid.
His open wings begin slowly to close and his dreams of soaring
begin to fade.

He pulls his wings in tightly to his body and down his face drips a
lonely tear.
His dreams now become his enemy, his hopes now become his fear.

Yet his heart beats the future inside his chest, a pounding which he
cannot ignore.
Although his task may seem an impossible dream, he knows his
mission is to soar.

So he stretches his mighty wings in the air. His destiny now lies in
the sky.
His courage overwhelms his body and he looks his fears straight
in the eye.

The wind rushes under his feathers, the sky holding him up like a
cloud.
And only because he faced his fears does the eagle soar and be
proud.

Vanessa Murray

214

Black

Black is beauty also the best
Hold my head high and stick out my chest

Try try try and don't stop. If I fail I might get shot

Help my people when they are down
Bring them up without a sound

Eat the scraps that master gave us
Pray to God that he may save us.

I'm a slave so I ain't s**t if I tell then I will get whipped

But now I'm free but I can't take it
Kill my brother just to make it

I am still a slave living in the ghetto
The man took my brother when he was a young fellow

They are racist because I am black
Even tried to get my mother hooked on smack

Now I am shot in the head
Should have listened to what mama said

She can't help me now I'm dead
Now God going to keep me fed.

I miss home and want to come back but can't cause I am Black
Tory Perry

Two Hands

Two hands pressed together
Holding dear the prayers of the heart
Two hands clasped together
Holding close the fabric of their lives

Two hands holding gently
The child born of their love
Two hands cupped firmly
Holding life in the palm of his hands

Two hands strong and firm kind and gentle
Holding you close, safe from danger
Two hands trusted and sure
Surround your heart and hold it dear

Two hands safe and secure
Bring peace and harmony to the hearts of many
Two hands full of love
For all of those who trust in Him above
Renee Blackwell

"Who Were Those Lovers?"

Who were those lovers—walking in the rain—
holding hands and laughing—singing sweet refrains?
Who were those lovers—dancing silently till dawn—
watching fleeting moments pass—as shadows on the lawn?

Who were those lovers—sipping coffee—drinking each other's words,
speaking softly memories—never to be heard?
Who were those lovers—now walking separate paths—
forever missing hours—as they creep past?

Does time stand still for lovers such as these?
Who were those lovers—were they you and me? Yes, my love.
Sharon K. Lane

Ode To Love From The Heart Of A Willing Prisoner

To many, a shackle, heaviest bonds
Holding life as an anchor holds a
Ship in the sea.
Binding wrists and ankles, making
Prisoners of people, and freedom
A thing to be longed for.

Freedom from what?
From two hearts so very close that
The difference is discernible only to God.
From thoughts and feelings that
Fly together to realms known by them alone.
From having two bodies, two hearts,
Two minds with which to share life's
Sorrows and discover its joys.

Freedom from this?
How can any fail to see that this is freedom!
But, if to you a prison it remains,
You may call me a willing prisoner.
Renee L. F. Green

Night Ride Home

Headlights tunnelling through the darkness
Homeward-bound through piney woodland
Home through somber forest looming
And the drifting mist of swampland.

Hamlets passing, quickly, ghostlike,
Shuttered window, dim-lit doorway,
Dreams of home and fitful slumber
Lullaby of wind and roadway.

Up the winding, rocky hill road
Long-passed cities' glow, now paling
Down to cross the narrow river-
Drone of ancient bridge recalling.

Endless weary miles unrolling-
Talk of home and gentle laughter-
With the swiftly healing darkness
Following after, following after.
Muriel C. Boutwell

I Wish Upon A Tree

I wish upon a little tree.
Hope it grants my wish for you and me.
I watch it grow and grow.
I watch a leaf reach out to me.
After a while, it gets very big.
I hope it will still remember me.
I climb to the top of the tree.
Last night for some strange reason...
My tree fell down.
I watched them take it away...my favorite tree.
I missed my tree and went there every day.
Then one day, I made a wish...
There before my eyes was my favorite tree.
I climbed high into the sky.
I knew my tree had come back to me.
I heard each leaf whisper, "I missed you too,
so I came back to you."
I hope we have the same memories together.
For all of life is within a tree and me...
Into another world, a land of hope.
Paul DiBetta

What Goes On In My Head?

What goes on in my head?
How does it know if I'm live or dead?
What goes on in my head?
How does my hand write with a pencil of lead?
What goes on in my head?
How does it know when it's time for bed?
What goes on in my head?
How does it know what I read?
What goes on in my head?
How does it know what I said?
What goes on in my head?
How does it know when it's time to be fed?
What goes on in my head?
How does it know that I like the color red?
What goes on in my head?
How does it know that I have an Uncle Ed?
What goes on in my head?
How does it know if I will wed?

What goes on in my head?

Tara Young

"A Mother's Ring"

Four precious stones God gave to me,
How fortune could a mother be.
Two boys, two girls, these children mine.
Each one a gem, each one divine.
I held the earth, the stars and moon.
In March, April, January and June.

Then — one day I lost a stone,
My precious March not fully grown.
Where have you gone? Why did you go?
For eighteen years I treasured you so.
Your smile was your sparkle,
Your heart made of gold,
You were my jewel to have and to hold.
When you told me you loved me,
You made my world shine.
I entrust you to God, but you'll always be mine.
Yes, I lost one stone much, much too soon,
But with God's care I have April, January and June.

Mary Lou Casey

Love Creature

Come close and Look at Me.
How I wonder what you see?
"another trophy," that's what you said.
Intrigued by lacy patterns intertwined?
Come closer; you could be mine.

Come close and Listen to Me.
I am more than you see—
Oh, Foolish creature do beware
of love lies and sexy stares;
a silken body used as bait.
Come closer; I cannot wait!

Come close and Lie with Me.
not just tonight, but for eternity.
A hunter's skill so divine
but, you misjudged your prey this time.
You took my body; now I take your soul—
Come closer; consumption's my goal.

Death is Love and Love is Death;
Come closer, for your final breath.

Lisa Frazier Straub

Lord, Give Me Understanding

Dear Lord I don't understand
How life can change with a wave of your hand
At times it feels with no rhyme or reason
Like when and why with each passing season

But to take a family and tear it apart
Changing so many lives and striping a heart
I realize life goes on and we do what we can
Lord it makes me wonder what you're doing to man.

To take the ones I really love
either spreading them apart or sending them above
It doesn't seem fair, it doesn't seem right
To take all that love and put it out of sight

I still wonder the reason, for your master plan
Why all this pain in the heart of each man
Are there any answers to all of my questions
or does it still lie a mystery as a part of creation

But Lord this action has caused so much pain
Lord is it really worth it for all that you gain
Help me to see and to understand
For here on earth it is hard to keep faith in hand.

Tina Baker

"The Sea"

At the edge of a cliff, thoughts are free to wander,
   How life goes by without nature to ponder,
Solely for ourselves are we so driven,
   Without ever enjoying what nature has given.

I admire the ocean, so great and vast,
   With the tales it holds of all that is past,
And often wonder how it came to be,
   This thing of beauty that's called, "the sea."

Below the surface, full of dark mystery,
   Are the corners of life and of its history,
Here for a reason and for us to treasure,
   To respect and care for and enjoy with pleasure.

At the edge of a cliff, I feel deep inside,
   That one can imagine with all fears aside,
How nature's creation became to be,
   This thing of beauty that's called, "the sea."

Raven

Stranger Among Me

How many people can one person be?
How many faces do other people see?
When someone smiles, are the motives all good?
Is your smile, in return, ever truly understood?
Do we all have a front so people won't know?
Can we ever be ourselves and just finally let go?
Let go of the memories that hold up our wall.
Let go of the thoughts that led us all for this fall.
Do I open my eyes and really try to see?
Or do I keep my eyes closed to make things easier for me?
Am I really naive in my belief of the heart?
Am I really going to make it, or just completely fall apart?
Will I ever be able to say good-bye to the pain?
Will inner-peace and self-confidence be something
   I'm ever going to gain?
Can I ever get back all the things that I've lost?
Are our experiences all worth the consequences that they've cost?
Will I ever be at ease with the decisions that I make?
Can I learn to give love as well as I can take?
Will the day ever come when these thoughts go away?
Will the hurt disappear, or is it here to stay.

Nicole Brennan

Strength To Carry On

Somalia, Rwanda, Haiti!
How much longer can you stand?
Satan has robbed you of your food.
Terror has spread over your land.

The world hears your crying.
Your babies are dying each day.
You look to the hills from whence cometh your help.
With tears in your eyes you say,

"Though our hope is almost gone,
God, give us strength to carry on!
God, give us strength to carry on!
God, give us strength to carry on!"

Somalia, Rwanda, Haiti!
And all others who share your plight.
Against corruption, violence, and injustice,
Together we must continue to fight!

Somalia, Rwanda, Haiti!
God will answer your prayers.
Don't think for a moment He has forsaken you.
You serve a God who cares!

Louise E. Whitmore

How Swift

How swift the fox runs through the tall grass.
How swift the fox darts by the pond.
How swift it is when it approaches its prey.
How swift it moves as it attacks.
How swift the hawk hovers through the sky.
How swift it flies with such grace.
How swift it is flying over the river looking for its prey.
How swift it is when it dives through the air and grabs a salmon.
How swift the hawk, how swift the fox for they are swift.

Michael J. Harper

"Drifting Back"

Just a child, and not so long ago it seems.
How time flew, so fast! I never heard the screams
It was like falling from the sky, silent and swift
Crashing to the ground. And my mind set adrift.
My memory floating up, into my past like smoke.
I just lay paralyzed, staring through closed eyes and
Drifting back into my wasted youth.
Only now as I lay here can I see the truth.
See all I took for granted and the lies that I believed.
See the love I threw away, and why my mother weeps.
Now time drags on hours to days.
Life's almost gone with no more games to play.
No flags to wave, and all that waits is empty graves.
No tears to shed just fading memories of the dead.
So what can I say, as I lay here through the day, drifting back.

Rocky Marshall

Joy Unfulfilled

I am living, but some consider me non-existent.
I am beautiful, but you can not see me.
I am a gift, but most take me for granted.
I have a heart, but it is forgotten that it can break.
I want love, but that is ignored.
I have feelings, but no one can hear them.
I want a future, but my fate is not mine.
I am full of life, but unwanted.
I am innocent, but I am condemned by selfishness.
There is only one of me, but some think I can be replaced.
Who am I?
I am the baby who will never be held, or kissed, or hugged,
or loved.
I am the unwanted unborn.

Kandy Stewart

Imagination

I was a boy many years ago
However, I'm a boy again
I've reached an age when boyhood starts
One more time, my friend

I'm glad my senior years, enable me to be
Back in my old childhood days, where I fit so comfortably
Oh, those days were wonderful
And now they reappear
What a lucky kid I am
To relieve, what was so dear

I have never been happier
Since I was a tot
I'm happy to return to those carefree days
I'm loving them a lot

So if you ever have a wish
Just wish upon a star
To go back to those childhood days
It isn't very far

Michael A. Miele

We, Me And Thee!

There are times love, I long to be free, me from thee!
However, life's blueprint says "It's not to be!"
It seems, thee blends with me so thoroughly
We're close as bark that hugs its tree!
At times too close we seem to be,
This you that's thee, and me that's me!
As in a mirror, my image can't escape,
I'm never free of thy loves embrace!
Thee loves me, and me loves thee,
Guess that's how it's meant to be!
We and thee reach out in space,
Always seeking the other's place,
When from your presence me is free,
Lost, I quickly search for thee!
When at last the search is ended,
And I'm in thee's presence splendid!
Me and thee again are we,
And I'm happy as can be!
It takes we two to be complete!
Loves perfect equation, can't be beat!!!

Shirley Musillami

Fabric

The thin thread of my sweater
hung loosely by my side,
slowly I tugged at it,
without resistance the thread began to unravel,
a tug-
and it all begins to unravel,
the shape and the form of my garment
dissolves into a pile of twisted wool
all shape and form gone,
new needles pick at the thread,
delicately, plucking, pulling, weaving
forming a new shape
patterns change
my sweater takes on form
directed by the weaver,
new shape,
new life and my sweater fits.

Leon Beckerman

A Friend

A friend is someone who cares for you when you need cared for
Hurts when you hurt
Needs no reason to ask is something wrong
Gives you their love when you need loved
Tells you you're wrong when you are wrong
Lends a helping hand when you need it.
Without asking for something in return
Someone who is there when you have a need for a listening ear
A friend is someone you can trust with all your secrets
A friend doesn't have to be a person for they may be what you
Choose them to be
A friend can only be a friend if you are a friend in return
I am friends with many things in life, and the one thing we
Must all remember is that you never take that friend for granted
I believe that everyone has what they call their best friend
Well I have a friend like that, and that friend of mine fits
The meaning of a friend to a "T"
And that friend is my "Mother"

Kenneth Ray Menser

"Free For All"

I wish I were dead, my teenager said;
I admit I was taken aback.
What hurt her so bad, to make her so sad,
And what in her life did she lack.

One moment of pain, created a strain
As I searched for the hurt in her eyes,
"What's happened to you, to make you so blue"
I asked: but feared her replies.

I drew her to me, holding on desperately
wondering, what in the world I could give
Then she started to cry, began telling me why
She no longer wanted to live.

It seems she was stressed and so darn depressed,
that her boyfriend had found him another,
Life was ugly and grim, and she hated him
And who could she tell but her mother.

A memory past, but memories last
And life is truly worth living,
My daughter is well, my grand-daughters tell.
That love was the gift well worth giving.

Marjorie L. Lucas

I Am "Lady"

I am one of the virtuous ones
I am far from woman or girl
I am graceful, innocent, compassionate, and meek
I am humble and strong!
"Beauty" and "grace" is my strength
The purity and innocence of my heart allows men to trust me
because they know that I am not evil nor spoiled
Though I suffer pain and labor for the birth of man, I am a
graceful maid and servant for my household
I am the shepherd of my vineyard, I prepare and bringeth food to
my family
I mend the wounds, nurse the sick, and reach out to the poor and needy
I wear fine linen and dainty perfume
I speak with wisdom and kindness to everyone
I am cherished by my children, and my husband feels blessed to
have me as his wife
Though to favor "grace" and "beauty" is vain, I praise the Lord for
creating a clean heart in me so that my inward beauty will send a
graceful glow of beauty outside of me for all to see
I am virtuous, innocent, meek, and charming
Look at me...I'm not like all the rest, "beauty" and "grace" is my
strength!
I'm "special" can't you see.... I am "lady"

Sandy Murphy

The Plan

From the genesis of the age, at the origin of man,
I am had a plan.
During the serpents be siege, and the fatal massacre of sin,
I am had a plan.
From the bosom of Abraham, through the seed of David,
I am had a plan.
In the town of the Bethlehem, out the womb of a virgin,
I am had a plan.
During the slaughter of Jew man child, through revelation of the
Baptist,
I am had a plan.
Through the embrace of the race, till the betrayal of mankind,
I am had a plan.
With three rusty nails, and the sentence of Christ,
I am had a plan.
In the destiny of truth, lay the execution of death,
I am had a plan.
At the tomb of His carcass, to the rapture of christ,
I am had a plan.
In defeating the curse of sin, grace pleaded our case for love,
Behold! The plan of I am...

Sharese Archie

Who Am I?

Who am I? During a regular day
I am like the pollen from a dandelion
tossing about from place to place
collecting tidbits from teachers, friends,
and the world alike.
But I am also like a politician at a debate
by getting my two bits in each day.
and at sporting events
I am the wasted talent and heart of an athlete
screaming and clawing to get out.
While with girls
I am like Gomer Pyle
always marching a step behind.
But I mainly see myself as a man in the background
Who worries about others before himself.

Robert Wininger

Untitled

The day we wed, you gave me life
I am so proud that you are my wife.
With the birth of children, a new found joy
Two wonderful girls, I don't need a boy.
I work real hard to provide a good life
I am so proud that you are my wife.
Through ups and downs, through thick and thin
You were so supportive, again and again.
When I advanced, another change in my life
I am so proud that you are my wife.
The changes kept coming some good some bad
The latest one has made me so sad.
With you leaving, for me there is much strife
I was so proud that you were my wife.
I keep on hoping with each new day
That you will come back....maybe today.
There is one more change I need in my life
That's to hear you say, you are proud to be my wife.

Tracy L. Barton

Reality

I fear every step, that I take,
I am so scared that my heart will break.
That's why it was so hard for me to let you in.
But I did, I let you win.
Boy, was that a sin.
You distracted my body, mind, and heart.
Thoughts of you ran through my head.
I dread the thought that you don't love me
the way that I love you.
I never saw you as black, I saw you as a man.
You never saw me as a woman, you saw me as white.
I am not saying that I was colorblind,
Because that would be a lie.
I just saw your color as another pro to add onto your beauty,
Not as a con the way you see mine.
This is fine though, because one day when I am long gone,
your dawn will come.
The dawn that will open your heart and mind,
So that you will find what I have found.
The color of one's skin has no affect on the love one holds within.

Nicole Weinberg

The Abyss

Help...
    I am trapped within this void I call myself.
Lonely,
    Scared,
        Confused,
Not knowing where to turn.

Can I escape this madness?
    Must I remain a victim of this solitude?

I turn to run...

In desperation,
    I reach out to grasp hold of
        Anything...
            Anyone...

But my attempts have failed.
The eternal abyss
    captures and swallows me.
Now, I only feel that I am
    Falling...

Lori Ann LoGioco

The Me Nobody Knows

Sometimes I think how little I know me,
I am virtually unexplored.
I feel sometimes that I stand
On the edge of a huge sea,
And that sea is me.
I have been judged a million times or more
By my face, my body,
But they were only the shore,
I stretch out beyond where eyes can see.
I see myself as an island,
A hard rocky shelf.
Of being separate yet part of the whole,
But the waves of searching
Break against the reefs of my soul
And I search some more
The waves are in me, and through me
The vibrations softly sweep,
The sea belongs to God,
And because I have been allowed to peek,
I know the sea is of God and God is part of me.

Patricia Schaufler

Black Men, Black Me

My black men, my black brothers don't punish me!
I am your sister, wife, daughter, or mother,
My hair may be kinky or very straight,
And my skin maybe very fair or the darkest of darks!
Our foremother's hands were rough from toiling in the fields all day!
I know you've been oppressed and suppressed,
I know you've been hurt, humiliated and pushed to the point of dehumanization!
But my dear Black men and Brothers, don't take out your anger on me.
Don't you remember in our history I too was a Queen, as you were a King!
The whiteman took away our riches and gold bracelets, and made us ankle chains instead.
But we have a responsibility to our children to let them know, we have a proud and noble heritage!
Our saviors hair was as sheep's wool, with his feet as bronze,
One day we'll all see him as he really is!
So my blackmen so very, very low, and the only person lower than you is me, I know one day that this will not be,
But remember my blackmen, I truly love you, for you are me!

Louise Endiaka Milliner

Repeating

The phone rings everyday when I wake up
I answer knowing who it is
He speaks to me with his hypnotic voice
Repeating the word
Like a broken record player
His profound voice bounces through my head
Banging against each eardrum
Repeating the word
He keeps calling me
Never stopping
I can imagine his face
Red burnt skin
Black eyes
Sinful smile
Animal like body
Shivers go through my spine
Repeating the word
Suicide

Zena Noyes

First Thoughts

I've been gifted of another new morning!
I awoke I see I hear
    and among the green and all the creatures
        afoot aflight
I passed another night afloat on a dream boat!
In my bed with firmness under me, I recall
    thanking him that his firm hand has
        supported me, stays near
    while weary bones and weakened heart
        take their rest
    And lighter the load thru slumber.

Shirley E. Sliter-Donovan

An Image Like Thee

God
I fall on the ground before You and pray
Just as Your son did one day.
May this dreadful hour pass, I also ask.
What's required is such a difficult task.
Father take away this bitter cup from me
For I know all things are possible unto Thee.
Yet, it's not what I will,
It's Your will that must be done.
Keep Your Son's image before me,
So, like Him I may become.

Mildred Floy Pierce

219

Untitled

To the edge of my distant world
I bring myself within a million miles
and I see what is waiting there —
my every prisoner, I have freed.
She stands not among them,
she is so far from this cold sea.
And I see that she is surrounded
with flowers from heaven and a warming sun.
The million miles I have traveled here,
and the same I've yet to go,
she will steal the time it takes, and I will be
there soon. And all the stars that I pass,
serve as a reminder of her, the iridescence of her
sea-green eyes, the tranquility of
her gentile smile. Every muscle I have used.
With every step I thought of her.
My desire to be there with her
keeps me warm on this winter night.
I have loved her forever, knowing that
It would drive me home on a night like this.

Toby Logsdon

Motivation

Time passes by faster. Again I stretch my aims out as far as
I can.   Look around you'll see things you wouldn't believe and
above the heavens puffy white clouds. Near by a friend in need
of some subscribes and a hand reaches out to show the way.
But where are we going? "Far away from here" he said.

The road may end here, but the skies have no limits.

John D'Amelio Jr.

Wondering

Standing in the moonlight watching your face
I cannot get over your warmth and grace
Standing in the sunshine watching your glow
I cannot get over how I love you so.
I sometimes wonder what the world would be
If suddenly you should stop loving me

Wondering what life would be without you
Would the sunshine and the sky still be blue
Would the moonlight and stars still shine
Would there ever be another that I could call mine.

Luba Becker

Children Of The Sea

As I look out over the ocean,
I can't help but wonder,
for so marvelous an entity,
the sands, the birds, and the sea.

Will I ever reach the end of the horizon
or will I stare and wonder away my days,
dreaming of mythical mermaids,
and how much they mean to me.

I fall asleep to the songs of the seabirds,
singing to me as I begin to dream,
of the beach, the trees, and the water.
and the children of the sea.

Walter Mallon

Untitled

As I look at this country as beautiful as life
I can't help to feel pain from the sight

Germany so strong-so beautiful-and proud
But still is a presence some say is quite loud

Of skinheads and racists-you can't pick them out
But their message you'll gather there isn't a doubt

A country so gorgeous but houses the pain
Of all that lost their lives in vain

Museums they've become, concentration camps of the past
Now escaping the minds of the young so fast

Some say it didn't happen-with proof in their sight
While hundreds will die in Bosnia tonight...

Victoria Crick

"Listen To His Call"

I miss you in the morning, I miss you more at night
I can't see you in the darkness, I can't find you in the light
wasn't it only yesterday you danced into my sight?
Wasn't it only yesterday your voice gave me great delight?
How can I see you everywhere? When you're no where to be found
Why do I hear you call my name, yet there isn't any sound?
How can I get to heaven, when I am held Earth bound?
How can I ever find you, you're no where to be found
I know that God's in heaven
He plans for one and all
If I'm to get to Heaven, I must obey his call
If I'm to find my loved one, I've only to recall
The promise of our father, that he'll keep us, one and all
Then I'll know that he will find me
Erase the hurt and pain
Rejoin my one and only
Be back with her again!

To My Love-My Life, My Wife!

Peter J. Esposito

Missing James

Labored tears drizzle over my nose,
I close my waterlogged eyes
And try to remember...
But the darkness reveals only emptiness,
The wasted memories no longer accessible,
Buried in the numb reef, my pureless soul.
Frustration humbly coats my shell,
Minds succumbed to the powerful repetitious hands,
The bond sedated by his dues imposed,
the indolent pressure, the stealth of change.
Whoever was, is not
   Whatever bridged, crumbled.
Unsure of even a blissless good-bye,
Every smile dissipated,
Forgotten ... together,
Worlds to part...
You left my heart just days ago,
   reborn in a weed's root;
Searching for the delicate petal I swear exists,
I have been missing you for years.

Kristi Anderson

My Prayer

In the stillness of the night, O God,
I come to you in prayer.
I seek your Holy Presence and find comfort
In knowing that you care.
When I confess my sins to you,
I yearn to hear you say,
"I have heard your cry, my child;
Peace be yours this day."
When at your feet I lay the names
Of loved ones who are ill,
May your loving arms encircle them
And, if it be your will,
Restore to them a way of life
Free from pain or ache.
I ask your guidance when temptation calls,
The right choices to make.
When dark has given way to light
And again I greet the shining sun,
I pray you'll be ever at my side
And grant success to tasks begun.

Ruth Cox

Untitled

I looked for the stars tonight
  I could not find any
I looked for the moon
  And I found it so distant and aloof
I wondered if God was like that
  And it made me feel so small and helpless

Lona Terumi Ichikawa

The First Time

When you made love to me it was so wonderful
I couldn't believe

Never before has it felt so right you made it so easy
When we turned out the light

The taste of your lips when we kissed
I never knew it could be like this

You were so gentle, yet so strong while our bodies touching
Where they belong

Being in your arms, feeling your touch I hope I made you
Feel as much

Sharon Miller

Ego Tripping

The universe is my home
I created it with the touch of my finger and the breath of my soul
The earth is my ball of life which I created with love
I shed my tears into the sea and I am the warmth of the sun
My eyes sparkle like amethysts over the horizon
The wind is my breath and thunder my voice over the darkening sky
Life is the reflection of my breathtaking figure and beauty
Everyone bows down to me for I am the goddess of love
My face glows brightly like mother of pearl
I cannot be misled
I cannot be betrayed, but above all
I cannot be replaced.

Katerina E. Hajjar

Why I Cry

I cry but no one hears.
I cry out in sarcastic tears.
I've felt this way for many years.
I cry out for help and I cry out from pain
but everyone thinks it's all a game.
No one understands my unlimited pain, I cry out in shame.
I cry out but no one hears,
they pay no attention to my hopes and fears.
They see nothing through my tears.
I cry out of worry and stress.
I only try for the best.
But no one sees or even hears
my cry from all these tears.

Kris Ledford

Untitled

Today I smelt fresh spring lightly soaking in my skin.
I experienced the earliness of morning, loneliness,
Quiet destitute.
The crow of a rooster marked the only second of
recognition.
I am absolutely caught up in wonder,
Mere amusement.
Deep thought, but unable to open my mind to myself.
Noon came and quickly left me to appreciate things that
could not linger long.
I was aware of fresh green grass,
Yellow buttercups.
And farm fresh hope.

Waynette Pecaut

Dreamer

As I wipe my eyes of last night's dream
I face the mirror and contemplate the theme
Reflection of my frown appears before me
Because I know not the story
My mind has told me
Memories slowly unfold
As if my mind won't let go
Total recall once more
My brow at ease
Now, I must interpret the dream

Leqia G. Johnson

A Mother's Memories

As he takes your hand in his
I fade to long ago
To a memory of a rocking chair
Where I rocked you to and fro.

You vow to love forever
I have visions of the past
Of a toddler full of curiosity
The discoveries endless and vast.

On your hand is placed a band of gold
While in my mind's eye I can see
The excitement of your first lost tooth
Which you displayed, proud as could be.

A flame of unity between you
I can't help but reminisce
Of the times you pleaded for the car keys
The epitome of teenage bliss.

With an embrace and the touch of lips
My memories I hold dear
And though I watch you leave our nest
To my heart you'll always be near.

Misty Holey

Untitled

And as I walk through the immortal night
I feel a presence behind me
It is as if someone, or something is following me
I try to keep walking calmly ahead
and not to look over my shoulder
A shiver is sent up my spine
and I tremble with fear
It takes the remaining strength in my body not to run
I have no voice to cry out
For fear has robbed me of this
As I go deeper into the forest surrounding me
I become more afraid
The trees grab at my face and waist
trying to keep me from moving on
The plants hug my feet and try to trip me
My dress embraces my body protectively keeping me from harm
My slippers resist the plants
always keeping me moving calmly onward
I am forever moving through the night
Wondering if I will survive

Kate Semmelrogge

Tomorrow

Sometimes, while everyone is sleeping,
I feel troubled, but I don't know why.
I just can't seem to sleep.
My mind wonders from past to present,
Then plunges far into the future,
Seeing many other people while
Traveling through time.
And then, my dreams wither away, as reality
Becomes life, with the day's dawn.
Dreams, are my hidden life,
But fate, has been pre-set,
And that's the way I'll face tomorrow,
Not knowing, what color my life will be.

Thomas F. Hoddinott

I Understood Not

I saw but understood not.
I felt his pain overwhelm me.
I tried but failed to catch,
I coaxed, he whimpered but cried not.
People all around but help from none.
They stared and walked away, no help they gave.
His head hung lower than his tail,
His coat like his eyes...no sign of life did hold.
This starving, sick, dying dog
No one cared to love or feed.
I went for food but he was gone.
I looked and searched in vain.
He haunts my every thought.
What horrible misery his lot in life be,
Unloved, unwanted, unfed...no one to care.
No hope in life has he.
Why oh why so callous must we humans be.
I saw, I cried, I tried, but I understand not.

Shirley M. Whalen

How Can I Thank You

Lord, how can I thank you for all you give for the mother
I have of this place where I live?
Lord, how can I thank you for all that you are it goes
Past my telling that a good mother is what you are.
Lord, how can I thank you for the mother that I have she
cheers me when I'm sad she makes me happy when I cry she
Always there when I need a friend to talk to so that's
What a good mother is.

Tamia McCluney

A Search For Love

At one point in my life,
I felt that love had abandoned me.
So, I searched for miles to find it.
I traveled across the world,
    and couldn't find love.
I climbed the highest mountains,
    and found vast lands.
I swam the deepest oceans,
    but only found creatures of the sea.
Feeling sad and lonely, I went home to my mother.
She told me how good it was to see me
    and that she missed me so.
Only then did I realize that love was with me all along
    and it was growing as the years went on.

Sara Ella Hooper

The Evil Of The Event·

The darkness of the night filled my soul with blackness.
I felt the evil of the chant fill my heart and take my mind.
I could smell the sinister acts that awaited me in time ahead.
I knew the burliness and harshness of the creature in front of
    me was not real.
My mind created this evil picture, but I knew the devils hand
    was stirring this gigantic pot of hate.
As I breathed in the death "it" took my mind, my soul, and
    my body
I was never again myself.
It had stole all of me and owned me without a second glance
behind.

Serina J. Phillips

Time Released Teacher

I was a drifter.
I floated through the rippling waves
with a message on my mind.
I had a purpose for being.
The note enclosed said it was so.
The contents were locked in and time released
by the pressure of expulsion from within.

Although the cap on my being
was only ignited at interval periods,
credit must be given to those who could relate
to the fire that burned endlessly within me
and for heaping coals upon my soul.

Those young eyes, too, can see the sparks in me,
when I attempt at humor and ask thought provoking questions.
They know I care even when
their response is not always there.

Sometimes I dream in hopes that
I have touched the heart of even just one.
Many thanks to those special individuals who have
shattered parts of the bottle and set me free to teach.

Lisa Futch

Goodbye, Pat!

I knew you so well; yet I didn't know you at all.
I had no feelings for you, yet I would hurt when you would fall.

You fathered me, but you were never a true father in return.
I was your daughter, but the position I never really earned.

I'm sure that if we could turn back the hands of time,
We could change a thing or two.

You'd have been more responsible and mature.
I would have been more loving to you.

But the present is here and the past has gone along with you.
Goodbye, my father, Patrick Bell,
I bid you a sweet adieu.

Terry B. Woods

Utopia Of The Mind

Far away in a climate warm,
I found a shelter from the storm,
The sanctuary so long I sought,
Was always there inside a thought,
The peace of mind from deep within,
Felt like a place I've never been,
The sound of water falls flowing clear and true,
The trees were glistening, kissed by morning dew,
As the new day's sun rose into view,
I thought such beauty has been seen by few,
The air was filled with an unblemished scent,
Untainted by man, yet for man it was meant,
Could this place be how Earth might h ave been?
So long ago but never again,
How far have we come? And how much the cost?
Do the things that we've gained outweigh what we have lost?
I guess we must live with what we have done,
But if we don't change then all will be gone,
They can poison the people, and destroy beauty they find,
I have but one consolation, they can't touch my mind.

Timothy J. Huotari

Like A Rose

I was like a rose, I was beautiful inside
I gave and I tried
I had thorns to protect me from those I hated
But now my petals look some what faded
I bloomed as all flowers do, I was there for you
I gave happiness to those who knew me
Like a rose I seemed to be
My soft gentle petals opened wide
Like my arms that stretched out to you, I tried
Now I'm wilting, my petals turn from red to black
Simplicity was something I didn't lack
Now I'm gone, press me in a book
Remember me in bloom the way I used to look
I really did try, I tried
Like a rose I bloomed before I died.
No need to cry or wonder why
All flowers come and go
For what reason we will never know
Like a rose we all bloom before we die
For us to be once in bloom must be the reason why.

William R. Scheutzow, Jr.

The Ring

On this day of your christening,
I give to you this diamond ring.

It was given to me, by my Mom,
To give to my first-born, daughter or son.

But the years have gone by, with no children for me,
What about the ring? I would just wait and see.

When your Mom was born, tears of joy I did cry,
We grew closer together, as the years passed on by.

On the day of her wedding, as your Mom said "I Do"
I made my final decision, to give the ring to you.

For you are her first-born, sent down from above,
An angel, sweet daughter, to cherish and to love.

And so today, as I give you this ring,
I wish you joy, happiness, all the best life can bring.

It will now be your ring, for many years to come.
To give to your first-born, daughter or son.

Tina M. Stucki

"A Thought Of The Earth"

I am tired she cried in a final gasp.
I have endured rape and indignity from
you for long enough!
Your arrogance is utterly offensive,
for you know nothing of my life.
I am the destroyer of races, the creator of life.
Time is not measured for me, I am ageless,
Yet you persist in the thought that you can hurt me.
Poor and ignorant child.
You are an insignificant itch that feels it cannot
Be scratched by my hand.
You will not survive if you persist
in the actions that are destroying you.
I will! I am the only survivor.
You have been alive for the blinking of an eye,
compared to others that I have created.
Yet, you have the arrogance to think you can destroy me.
She yawns, and ponders the next race she will create.
"I enjoyed the dinosaurs immensely."

Nathan S. Garber

Accomplishments

I know I can do it
I have the will to succeed

I suppose it is ingrained in me
this desire to achieve

Yes, I know failure
Yes, I know defeat
But I know in my heart I won't be complete until either
I achieve or face defeat

My will needs to feel complete
but it won't happen
till I strive forward
by making a difference
challenging the unknown
braving it all
by defying all of the opposition

In order to find thy true self
"The Real Me"

Lorraine R. Harris

Ode To A Neighbor

Big foot is alive and well, upstairs, above me he does dwell.
I hear him nightly as he takes a stroll, in his flat, the big-footed troll.
I know he is deaf, he surely must be, a mile away you can hear his TV.
And often, in the wee hours of the night, I'm jarred from my
 sleep by his yell of delight,
as Big Foot runs down his hall and dribbles a 16 pound bowling ball.
His boom box has only a loud bass beat, for the pagan dances
 done by his feet.
He might think the sound is truly great but it makes my walls and
 ceiling vibrate.
Hey, Big Foot, your neighbor is pleading, your racket has started
 my ulcer bleeding.
I know you're nocturnal and play at night, but I work days so
 please be quiet.
Some nights, awakened, I fester and think of ways to help you
 become extinct.
My life has given me many thrills, but my greatest will be your
 return to the hills.
Then, maybe I can get a good night sleep, and not be awakened
 by your big feet.
To my new neighbors, I'll be quickly revealing, walk softly,
 your floor is my ceiling.
Living so close we must co-exist, so loud noises and such should
 cease and desist.
I'll be considerate of you and you consider me, and we'll live
 happily in close proximity.

Neil M. Shuman

223

Chrysalis

When I consider the feast of life before me,
  I hunger to begin.
I want to have those things of life
Which make it sweeter, like love.
I want love pressed into my soul,
  And to feel the pulse of it resounding within me.
I want to give love back in eager handfuls, boldly, crazily
  And watch my lover overflow with it — brim with it.
I want to know that while I was here, I needed someone who
needed me;
that somebody needed what I had to offer,
  and appreciated that I tried hard to give it.
I want to feel secure enough to need somebody sometimes.
I want to trust and love somebody who
trusts and loves me back … just as much, just as well.
I want to reach out and make good memories
For those I want to remember.
I want to live, more than anything I know
And more than even that which is not known to me.
  Life is a feast —
    I hunger to begin.
    Patricia Dunbar

The End

My heart sinks as I feel the hurt.
I keep thinking, why did he treat me like dirt?

His words hit me, hard and deep.
How could he act like such a creep?

I guess we weren't meant to be.
Was it something I said or was it just me?

I thought everything would turn out alright.
But that was before we had the great fight.

He said it's over.
I said fine.
I had thought I was his,
And that he was mine.

Something went wrong.
What it was I don't know.
I really got hurt,
But I won't let it show.

How could I tell it would turn out this way?
Why can't we go back to yesterday?
  Lindsey Erickson

To Glady's And Her Brothers And Sisters

In Memory Of Lee

He stood handsome in his uniform
I knew this man before he was born
He fought the wars, sailed the sea
This man they called Lee
Always a good child and even a better man
This sailor salutes as he marches to the band
Lee served his country well
There are many stories I could tell.

Now Lee sails again, this time not at sea
After weathering the storm of life you see
He established a beach head with all his might
After so much sailing no more wars to fight
You've reached your destination —
At God's early light.
We received your message —
We know you're all right.
Sail on Dear Brother, you've found the shore
You're now in heaven standing at his door.
  R. Stewart

A Mother's Fight

It came as a shocking blow when I learned you were ill,
I knew you were strong; and would now test your will.

I thought of the things that we have never done,
And of my void; had you not met my first son.

I begged and pleaded to God, that He might spare you,
For there were so many things left for us to do.

I wanted my boy to know his father's mother,
And for you and him to love one another.

At times when you thought you were losing the fight,
You hung in there, for you must have seen the light.

At times you were on God's doorstep and He turned you away,
He must have known how needed you were to shun you that way.

Mother, He gave you back to us in His glorious way,
For you get better and stronger each and every day.

If things go right, which I know they can,
You will see my son grow up to be a strong man.

If he grows up to be as strong as he can be,
He will never possess the strength you have shown to me.
  Nicholas A. DaLonzo

I Know That You Loved Me

My dear son, who I loved so much.
I know how troubled you are, losing me,
And I pray that you will be able to carry on,
Because I know that you loved me.

I knew that you were busy, with work and family,
And you didn't have much time to come visit me.
But trust me, dear son, it didn't matter,
Because I know that you loved me.

For along time now, I have suffered in pain.
Now son, it is time for God to take me.
My dear Alex, please do not feel guilty,
Because I know that you loved me.

There will be times, when you feel so alone.
But all you have to do son, is talk to me,
And you will feel my presence deep in your soul,
Because I know that you loved me.

Even though I'm no longer here on earth,
And I know how much you will miss me,
But I'll still be here, within your heart,
Because I know that you loved me.
  Wendy Rowe

Coma

  As I sit here crying,
I know not what I'm crying about,
  Maybe the music has finally penetrated,
Maybe, if only, it has gotten through to me.

  As I look about me,
I know not what I'm seeing,
  Maybe the flowers have finally penetrated,
Maybe, if only, they have gotten through to me.

  As I lounge here dreaming,
I know not what I am dreaming about,
  Maybe the thought has finally penetrated,
Maybe, if only, but I know it is not true.

  As I rest here,
I know not why I am resting,
  I close my eyes and sleep,
One final time…
  Rebecca A. Kashary

The Blues

Oh how I feel. I feel so low sometimes.
I know not what to do. No one hears a word I say. Or even
cares that I exists. There so busy they have not, the time
to even bother. They never really bother, to even listen.
I feel like screaming at times. What my heart really only
knows. Some day I'll show them all the truth. For when I
speak they say I lie. They will not believe a word I say.
They no not the pain I feel. Nor do they even care.
Their Words cut like a sword. As it cuts my heart into.
With each piercing blow, of their word's. They see not how
I bleed. With each piercing blow. All my tears I cry
in silence. Silence is all I have ever known. I'm always
alone. Alone even with the one I love. The pain never
seem's to end. If they only could learn to really love
me. I some how know that things would be, much better.
But they do not even want to care.

Terry L. Perkins

The Bridge Of Transition

I feel that something is wrong, but I don't know what
I know that I am frightened, but I don't know why.

My eyes search frantically, but see no images
I am listening, but hear no sounds.

I am reaching out, but cannot touch, where am I?
The emptiness of eternity surrounds me, covering me with a
blanket of solitude

All that I have left are my thoughts, I must embrace them closely
For if they vanish and fade away, I will no longer exist.

Has the echo of my being been silenced, will the bridge be
completely crossed?
Or is there still time to turn around, time to look for my past?

To await my sight is futile, the minds eye will envision the way
And guide in the unyielding search for my life as it used to be.

My final thoughts and my soul unite in an alliance of strength
Commencing the struggle to escape this in between place that I'm in.

My pilgrimage is long and exhausting, if only I could rest for awhile
But somehow I know that if I do, my bridge will come to an end.

I hear a sound, it travels through an endless tunnel straining to
     reach my ears.
I hear it distinctly, I recognize it now, I hear my children crying.

My eyes are searching and can see worried faces, I am listening
and hear voices
I am reaching out and touch a hand, I can rest now, I am no
longer afraid.

Linda Fisher

Toy Soldier

My heart beats fast like the paces of a drum.
I know there is no time, there is danger I must run.

The lights in the sky, the sounds I hear.
I am frozen now, frozen with fear.

Your moods they swing, like the pendulum on a clock,
there is only so much I can take from your hard verbal knocks.

You tell me I'm nothing I'm no good,
all my life I've been misunderstood.

The things I see the places I've been there is no wonder
I live in sin.

A child of neglect I was placed here for a season,
as time passes by it's just another season.

Just like a soldier that walks in timely steps,
I walk this world alone with only the time that I've kept.

Kim Meurer

Her Thoughts

Lincoln, dear son, I know thy crime,
I know thy fears, thy dreams, thy mind.
I know of the war between the states,
I know the cause, I know the hate.

Remember Lincoln, remember son,
Remember this, thou is one.
This speech will be alright,
Forget the war, forget thy plight.

In this speech that you will tell,
This speech, this tale, they'll know so well.
Honor the brave, the dead, the hurt
Honor them son, but be alert.

Speak now, in clear, strong words,
Quiet their fears, hear the birds.
But careful my son, hate is here,
People now won't shed a tear.

Peace be granted to dull the knife,
And may the dead find eternal life.
Soon my son, you'll be here,
Then you'll see the Union's tear.

Kelly O'Lone

Life

What's this living all about?
I laugh, I cry, I pray, I pout
To my neighbors I try to give
But my burdens weight heavy each day I live.

All my efforts, they are in vain
Attending the church on willow and main
I plead for help and pay my dues
While all the time searching for clues.

Then one day a still small voice
Silently tells me to make a choice
It keeps repeating you're not alive, you're dead
So keep your life or accept "His" instead.

His life is full of truth and grace
He unconditionally loves every face
His crucifixion forgives my sins
Whoever believes cannot lose, but wins.

Now, not I live, but he lives through me
Trust in Jesus and you will agree
His resurrected life will cause you to shout
This is what living is all about.

Karen Ingle

Silent Talk

My mind is full of crazy thoughts,
I laugh, I sing, I cry in my mind,
for words I mumbled out loud and I get caught,
and that's where my true identity I find.

I search the golden horizon for life,
yes, life that give me faith,
yet is such a wide area, and I strive,
walking in my daily maze.

Silent quarrels that make victories,
thoughts won only by imagination,
but yet life itself made my stories,
when I'm only one of God's creations.

My voice echoes leaving pounding headaches,
I re-live my life through memories,
I walk leaving dark traces, and the ground shakes,
when she silent talk is a mere theater of short stories.

Maria L. Garza

Dream

As the night begins, and the cold sets in,
I lay myself in, for my dream to begin...
I start to dream, of how nice it would be
To have you next to me, to hear you say,
I love you... and I'm glad to be with you.

As my dream really sets in, I dream of
how I wish there was a way, to make you
see, what this love has done to me?
How I wish you could come, and step into my dream;
and send me on a heavenly dream stream...

But as this night comes to an end,
and my dream comes to an end,
I wake up to see, that all this time...
You've been laying next to me...
Reymundo Sanchez

I Asked The Willow Tree

I lay under a willow tree, and gazed up at the clouds,
I let my thoughts turn inward, and asked what life's about;
It passes all too quickly, the same as birds in flight,
Just as the changing seasons, as day passes into night.

There is the elusive butterfly, at first just a cocoon,
Later wings explore the world, but it's life is over soon;
Blossoms like soldiers look to the sky, their heads a cocky tilt,
Suddenly a cold frost hits, their faces fade and wilt.

"So what is life then all about?" I asked the willow tree;
The weeping branches seemed to say, "Enjoy being under me.
Enjoy all things you come upon, don't fret with what's to be,
Learn from the past, enjoy the now, and keep me company."
Ruth Gruenebaum

The Homecoming

I was tryin' to get to sleep last night,
I live under a bridge - called a 'bum';
But the night was so cold, and my blanket so thin,
That sleep - it just wouldn't come.

There're a lot of us vets, under bridges,
And our government doesn't care;
But when we up and enlisted, they promised,
'For you we will always be there'.

Well, I got shipped to Pearl Harbor,
I was there on that infamous day;
And then I got sent to Guadalcanal,
Where a boy-turned-man learned to pray.

So, I guess my bridge ain't all that bad,
It's a shelter, and it's dry;
And when you're seventy-one years old,
No one wants to see you cry.

Sure, I wish I had a home,
A family, or a friend;
The warmth that comes, with candle-glow,
Denied me, to the end.
G. & P. Sanders

I Had A Dream

I had a dream last night
I had to choose a mother, and a father too.

And right before I sprang awake
I knew which ones that I would take.

They were the ones I already had.
Normalea Rabeka Payeur

Why Not Me

I love the rain coming down on my head
I love the flowers in my spring garden's bed
I love the moon on a cool summers night
I love the sky when the stars are bright

I love the sound of crickets when weakness greets my eyes
I love the birds singing when darkness says goodbye
I love the sound of love songs in the air
I love to hear silence when the night draws near

I love the smell of freshly baked bread
I love a new hair-cut, and I love to be fed
I love peace, joy and harmony
I love the thought of holy matrimony

I love to trust
To love, I must
But many times I ask thee
Why is it that nobody loves me?
Moses A. Thompson

Please Save Our Children

Little children of our world, don't be afraid to say,
  I love you Jesus, for he is the only truth along
  your spiritual way.
He will guide you and help you when you fall
  He will be there to pick you up for he is gracious
  when he calls.
So, sing praises with a song, so fill your heart
  with a hungry love, for when you have Jesus,
  you can never go wrong.
So be strong little children, he is here for you
  What he has is a love that's true!
Blessed are you, for you are mine, this my dear children
  Is my promise to you for all time.
So feel at ease, with a peaceful heart, for I have
  loved you from the very start!!
Laurie Kidder

The Passing Of Pretty Poetry

Are the poets all gone?
I mean the ones who weave rhymes. Is the absence of meter
A sign of the times?

Is there an unconscious stricture
Governing those who eschew lines melodic and substitute prose?

Are the poems intended to bury their thrust as though they were
masking an immoral lust?

What can be blamed for this change in an art which for ages has
held a fond place in the heart?

It was a rhyme of the sixties which stigmatized verse and branded
A statesman as something much worse.

For it stirred deep emotion in its self-serving role
And shook the resolve of a sensitive soul.

We can never be sure what this chant had to do
With Lyndon's decision to say he was through.

But the chances are good that uppermost in his mind
Was his image as judged by those coming behind.

And how could he feel
When children would say
How many kids did you kill today?
Max W. Garvey

"Thank You"

I met you when the year was new,
I met you when my troubles were few

Those few were quickly multiplied
but you made me laugh when I would've cried.

You crossed the bridge over burning land
and subconsciously gave me your hand

I grabbed it so instinctively,
too fast for my own eyes to see

If I had let go, I'd have hit the ground
before I could see the friend I have found.
You helped me drown out all my sorrow
and pushed it 'til the last tomorrow.

I saw just negatively,
but you're pushing that away from me.

When I see the rainbow above your head
I'm seeing positive instead

And at the end, your heart of gold
reminds me of what I have been told;

I can't see much with eyes half closed,
but you're the other half exposed.

Lydia Guerrero

Knowledge Reins Supreme

I amaze myself so I say to myself
I must be gifted. Gifted with
enough knowledge to successfully help
others uplift theirs. Uplift theirs in a way
that's safe for everyone - "UNIVERSALLY"
The only fee I try to charge is for
the next person I'm speaking to - is for that
person to take the knowledge I'm giving free "Personally"

It's an even swap - I think you'll
see it that way too. At first it
might look like I'm giving something
for nothing, but I do get something in
return. Our knowledge expands with peace,
and we all receive more room to learn!

Phillip Borden

Untitled

The voice so sweet like sugar cane,
I must come in out of the rain;
Myself again, the dreams pertain
Continued simplicity, is what I ask of thee;
Stick with me, and you will see,
A friendship with no fallacies.

Loyalty is certainly a factor,
For you see I'm not an actor,
I say my lines, I write my rhymes,
This expression a new art,
No games, no lies, and no surprise,
Just fill your eyes and fantasize;
Openly, warmly, you receive me,
Now I wish to know how you perceive me;

How long before the moon
mystically over your pool looms,
Would you have beckoned the call
Or was there no longing at all?
The thought you see could certainly be reality,
It is all due to my own insecurity.

Margo Agrimi-Hayes

Thinking Of You

Reminiscing of all the time we spent
I never realized what it has meant.
You taught me a lot of things,
From that my feeling I bring.

Now that your gone home
I feel so so deeply alone
Sometimes I have self-misery
from all the grief inside of me.

But me day I'll be there
with you in the Lords lair.
I'm trying to live my life right.
So I can to see the light.

You taught me that life goes on
After someone has passed and gone home.
I have accomplished many goals
Thanks to you, the mom, that paved the road.

Lance Tatum

On The Way To School One Day

As I walked to school one autumn day,
I noticed the beautiful flowing brook along the way.

The sky was so blue I could see forever;
The blue sky seemed to bring the things around me together.

My books were tied together and my lunch was in a brown paper bag.
The wind, blowing through the trees, caused the limbs to wag.

We had no fancy buses or cars; instead, we had to walk afar.

The water was rushing over the rocks along the way; the animals
And frogs were making sounds with some degree of life that day.

The rabbits were hopping along with their ears up high to hear
the Noise so near. The movement of the animals was made to
ensure they were safe from fear. What is within us, we cannot
tell; From where comes this longing that sounds like a bell.

As I approached the school and heard the bell ring,
I knew that freedom was a passing thing.

Now was the time to give my thoughts to learning some way.
Before too long, it would be time for me to stroll back home that day.

The rules of nature, the search for things of life for all,
Nurture of friends, and love of freedom will bring to me an open
   path home before night fall.

Robert L. Wiley

Think Of Me

Now that I can no longer stay at my home,
I now must rely on you for my daily care.
Think of me as your Mother, Father, Sister, or Brother.
When I can no longer feed myself, and cannot tell you
how hungry I am, or that I am wet and need to be changed.
Do give me care, and think of me as your Mother, Father,
Sister or Brother.
And when you turn me over at night and notice that I can
not moan or open my eyes, for I am a frozen form, be
gentle with me, lay me on my back, pull my covers up
below my chest, place both my hands one on top of the other,
on my stomach, and let me forever rest.
Please, think of me as your Mother, Father, Sister or Brother.

Patricia Manning

Sunday School Worker's Prayer

As a Sunday School Worker I'd like to be
I pray, dear Lord, to be more like thee.
Help me to be faithful and loyal.
To treat all people like they are royal.

Help me, Lord, to take the time to prepare.
To try my best to always be there.
When I think about making an excuse,
Guide my thoughts to a better use.

Help me to listen to what You say.
So I can help others to know Your Way.
Help me to have an open ear,
So I can listen to things they hold dear.

To brighten someone's day might not take much.
A friendly word, a smile or a simple touch.
Just to let them know that you care.
If there's a problem, you'll always be there.

Help me, Lord, as I go along my way
To make it here early each Sunday.
So I will be ready as the people arrive
By my enthusiasm, they'll know You're Alive!

Shari L. Grimes

In The Name

'The Lord is my shepherd' 'Hallowed be Thy name'
I pray to the Lord, this day goes without shame
Let me be successful, let me be without blame
In the name of Jesus, this I pray —Amen

In the name of Jesus, Lord I do pray
In the name of Jesus, this is what I say
Help me through this time, oh Lord, for the devil he is strong
In the name of Jesus, I pray this all day long

Tonight I kneel before my bed, and I pray unto the Lord
Bless those around me Lord, bless them evermore
And if I should die before I wake, please Lord take me in
In the name of Jesus, this I pray -Amen

Mitchell Leslie

"Time For A Change"

This time it will come from the heart,
"I promise we won't ever part!"
Come with me and rearrange,
"I love you," but please don't ever change.

I'm here, your there,
Never no time for some loving care,
Your life is mine, and "I control,"
Head high, smile big, and begin your starring role.

Your crying, and black and blue,
But remember your mine and I own you.
You do as I say on my stage,
Because as my wife you will change.

No time of my own to do as I please,
My acting debut is finally a cease.
As we part and disengage,
I have my own life now and,
"Time for a Change."

Sharon VanMeter

U.S.A. Blessed

A journey I was blessed to take, into another country,
I saw the suffering that goes on, where children work like men.
Proud, poor, caring people see death come by each day,
Never knowing how to write, or even own a pen.
This Thanksgiving, when we celebrate our blessings,
I cry.

Lois Gregg

Alone

I curl up inside myself all alone in my world
I pull away from the cold, harsh world
that has hurt me so very often.

I'm afraid to love again I fear I might get hurt.
Like a turtle, I crawl inside my shell
away from the world, away from my hell.

Sometimes I get so lonely I decide to try again
Then I poke my head out to look at life once more.

Will I ever find the strength to really re-enter the world
or will I just sample pieces then crawl into my shell again

Can I live in this world, can I survive the pain?
Or have I condemned myself to a lifetime of loneliness
and a life trapped in my shell without someone to love?

Melodie Beavers

Dolls That Are Not

I said no, and she got sad
I really didn't want to, but life hasn't been fair
Always, always I had to deny, I had no money, never knowing why.

She was only five in years
But going to forty considering needs
I worked days, I worked nights
Still the money I got was never enough.

One room that's all we ever had
One chair, one table, and one small bed
The worst, however, was the terrible smell
Coming in constantly from the nearby sewer.
If I could have just one night breathing fresh air
The world would be mine and I would lose despair.

I kept praying, I kept begging; may be God or Jesus would help
I just wanted to buy a small toy for my little girl
Before she was too old to even care.

Here in Santiago's shanty town dreams remain illusions
Regimes come, regimes go
But some little girls never get
Their own unforgettable first dolls.

Kathy Litvak

The Antique Carousel

Today I relived a childhood joy.
I rode a carousel. "Merry-Go-Rounds"
We called them then,
Revolving thrones of enchantment.
I'd hold on tight as I pranced and whirled
Astride a graceful steed
Then I'd release a hand
To wave to loving faces in the crowd
Admiring my feat. So did others
Of all ages, mount to savor the fantasy.
Less magic now, as a lowly pig
Replaced my gallant stallion.
And the riders today
Were "old folks" like me
Taking a stand for the inner child.
But the music was there and the memories
Flooded my circling mind:
Of other days and other rides and
Simply "others". Today I relived
A childhood joy. I rode a carousel.

Margaret A. Paul

Morning

I'm looking out my window now and see the dawning of the day.
I rush to open the window to catch a piece to save.
The red, pink, and yellow hues seem to push forth the sun with
     little effort.
The lace curtains stir in the warm summer breeze as a lone dove
     coos on a telegraph pole.
I can hear the traffic on Turner Street and the irate driver
     who honks his horn for the third time for someone who is late.
I can smell coffee boiling and bacon frying. I realize I am
     very hungry.
I quickly say a little prayer all will go well today and
     close the window quietly so I don't wreck what has just begun.

Stacie Shoemaker

Empty Footsteps

As I was walking along the moonlit beach
I saw a shadow standing in front of the clear blue waves
I approached the stranger with awe
The man was holding a single rose in his left hand
He seemed to be waiting for someone
As the wind blew, my body was pulled towards the rose
I couldn't take my eyes away from his
Our lips met and we kissed
It started to rain and thunder
Ice cold raindrops stung against my hot, steamy skin
Lightning struck and he fell to the ground
I ran for help, but when I returned with the ambulance
It was too late
My hero was dead

Nikola Bodman

Dancing In The Sky

At Moonrise
   I saw night dancing in the sky.
   Effervescently twisting and turning
   She waltzed in rhythmic beauty
   Among the stars and down the Milky Way.

   Each star winked as she passed by
   In a dress of gossamer and filet.
   She cast a glimmer on celestial things
   And danced capriciously in lunar beams.
   Fireflies folded lacy luminescent wings
   And drifted softly into evening dreams.

Come Moonset
   The mystic night danced the last round,
   Slipped behind the ethereal screens,
   Shaking star dust from her silvery gown
   Was ensconced by the estival day.

Kay Tomlinson

In The Midnight Of My Dreams

She walks quietly in the midnight of my dreams
I see her standing before me, skin pure white.
Her hair of gold, beckoning me to caress.
Our eyes meet and all is still.
Our hearts pound with the anticipation of flesh yet tasted.
I move close to her and she tingles.
I take her close and she trembles.
We lay on a bed of roses;
I in her, she in me
She holds me close; yet still forbidden.
We take each other to passion's promise.
Our struggle of bodies becomes as one.
We move with deliberate action.
Slowly, slowly we reach each other.
She screams in pleasure, as I in ecstasy.
We are one, quietly in the midnight of my dreams.

Randall L. Collins

The Gift Of Sight

As I look up at the big blue sky
I see puffy white clouds drifting by

I lower my eyes and I see a big tree
Its new spring leaves waving back at me

Little grey squirrels scurrying all around
Searching for peanuts I tossed on the ground

Blades of grass are blinking with dew
as if to say, "I love you too!"

The buds on the rose bush are waiting for June
While birds in flight are singing their tune.

Bright tulips waking, spread petals supreme
From Heaven Comes Nature's promise of spring

Who wants to give up all of these great pleasures
For the thought of never again seeing such treasures?

As night time comes it's replaced with a big moon
Sleep comes—Sunrise will return it all soon.

Mildred Marsh Ruton

The Sea

In the deepness and the darkness in the dark blue sea,
I see something that no one can ever believe,
I see wiggly lines and perfect shapes,
Which no one can capture the beauty on tapes.

It's hard to describe
It's hard to explain
When I describe this
I try not to be vain.

It's just something I've seen
The truth will bend.

Katherine Kirkpatrick

How Long?

I often sit to watch the world of its beauty or some cruel words.
I see the sun, the birds and the bees.
But half the time it's meaningless when it cannot be shared.
How long must I search 'til my life is fulfilled?
To search and search and yet never to find.
To finally realized I have left it behind in some past relationship,
When I was the only one who cared.
How long must I search 'til my life is fulfilled?
It's hard to achieve what I am looking for, when no one can
Really hear what I say.
I don't want to be alone—I need what that someone has.
How long must I search 'til my life is fulfilled?
I had it before—but never had seen it, but now I am wise,
Mature and still growing: Though one never stops.
Life is to be lived: Not questioned, not feared.
How long must I search 'til my life is fulfilled?
I will live each day to its fullest, though everyone needs
Someone to walk through life's path. I need that someone for
Today, tomorrow and for always.
But how long must I search 'til my life is fulfilled?

Mary Crago

Joyful Life

I shall work as long as Morning comes to this world.
I shall sing as long as there are birds in this world.
I shall endure as long as the wind blows hard.
I shall get wet as long as it is raining.
I shall pray as long as I have friends in this world.
I shall climb as long as there is a mountain.
I shall study as long as there is the moon in this world.
I shall blossom as long as there are flowers.
I shall protect as long as I have love in this world.
I shall smile as long as there is the sun in this world.
I shall go back there as long as there is the sea.

Michiyo Sugawara

229

A Mother's Nighttime Reverie

When I look at you
I see your grandmother's rosebushes in full bloom.
I see a lone star arch across a sky of sapphire blue.
I see my life emblazoned in brilliant hue,
My widest dreams come true.

And when I look at you
I see the eagle's effortless glide
I think, "They have no dark secrets to hide."
The eternal link of the ages
    Manifests in your determined strides
Cherished images of loved ones long gone,
    Flash in your laughing eyes.
I see you and I see "them", side by side,
    And I'm filled with an all encompassing pride
        When I look at you.

    Envoy
In this life I hope to impart
The joy and delight you've brought from the start
You are the children of my heart.
    I see Now, I see Then,
        Happily, I anticipate When.
    Maureen Hogan Zweig

Traveler

With whispering winds of the desert,
I set upon a journey from which I can never return.

My new home is heaven and earth.
My only companion the lonely and quiet wind.
I go wherever my companion takes me.
I travel through ocean and desert.
I rest under the cool shade of trees.
I play on fields that are filled with joy and happiness.
I sleep on soft clouds of sky while shining stars of night watch
    over me!
I am a traveler.
    Taiwon So

The Kingdom

"I shall be king," Amoeba said.
"I shall evolve and grow,
'Til I am Master over all
That I shall make and mold."

It strained and groaned to grow a fin,
And tail to follow after.
Then arms and legs and upright gait,
Absurd to point of laughter.

If this could be, then tell me, do,
Why still appears to me,
This microscopic mite still lives?
"What happened, O Amoeb?"

Amoeba you didn't get to be here
By some "Big Bang" accident.
If you became King, then tell me, please,
Where did your kingdom went?

What happened to your progeny?
They're still the same, I see.
To make a man, to build a world,
Takes One more Supernal than thee.
    Marene Deaton

Morning Prayer

As I slowly joy along
    I sing to thee a praise. A song.

I thank thee for this newborn day.
This lovely world in which we stay.
To grow develop, spiritually,
And serve our fellowman for thee.

I lift my eyes to thy vast sky,
To other spheres that pass us by.
And then my captive eyes behold,
A slice of moon a star enfold.
To frame its beauty for our gaze,
Dear Lord, thou hast such wondrous ways

I thank thee for the greenery, in which thou dressed the trees to be
A sweet refreshing source of shade, along my daily promenade.

My ears are filled with sweet bird calls,
Which lift my heart and so enthralls...
All this forms a kaleidoscope,
That fills our world with so much hope,
Oh, what a lovely place to be
'Til I someday return to thee.
    Libby McSheehy

This Man

I have sat in this same rocking chair for twenty years waiting for him
I stay in a small town with small notions; and people, well people are
just people here. This man, this man came along and changed
everything.

The first time I saw him, his bright light warmed my face. His
eyes were holding mine and his hands were moving in transitory
whisper waves. After one glimpse he made it graciously possible
for me to account for every step I made in life.

I have sat in this same rocking chair for twenty years waiting for
him; twenty years indeed.
I stay in a small town with small imperatives,
small intentions; and living, well it's just plain ole living here.
This man, this man gave me hope,
and he changed my way of thinking forever.
He changed everything.

I still sit in this rocking chair, preparing for my departure, waiting
for some sign; a glaring light down the road or wind tapping my
shoulder, but he never shows.
My journey is just beginning and my path is not clear,
but I know this man will come for me soon.
    Sonja Dunlap

The Tour Bus

The tour bus stopped and I got off to take a look around
I stepped back into decades past, onto sacred, hallowed ground
    I gazed the open landscape green, where a hundred years before
sabers clattered in the sun, the cannon voiced its angry roar

Of a sudden I could see it all, my tears be not denied
for emotions never touched by time, somewhere between shame
and pride
    That Death had claimed so many here, one could not ignore its smell
Lest I cried within my aching heart, God forgive this part of hell

Then a figure gaunt and haggard came slowly into view
Thru the swirling mist beyond his time, in a tattered coat of blue
    He spoke in but a whisper, "We're all condemned here to this day,
so read ye well between the lines of what the history books will say."

And in less time than it takes to die, I stood alone again
and as he faded back to his last day, I was touched by more than wind

That's been twenty years ago, by the sun's continued burn
On that field in Pennsylvania, its lessons too late learned.
    God; Dear God, will we never learn?!?
    E. M. Adkins

Your Tracks

You made footprints that day in the snow
I stretched my legs as far as they would go

I took giant steps and didn't care to look back
I wanted to walk like you, following your every track
When we walked I was right behind you
One time I stepped on the heel of your shoe

As Cold or as lonely as it could be
I always knew you'd take care of me

I remember falling hard onto the ground
You gently picked me up, you'd never let me down

When we finally got up to the top
My little legs were tired as could be
But all I cared about was you being proud of me

I learned a lot about myself that winter day
and although time changes and seasons stray,
The memories of your tracks will always stay

I love you Dad!

Michael Montoya

"Not Really Worryless"

As I walk down the road of life
I think about my past,
I think about how carefree I once was
and wish it could always last.
When I was small I had no worries.
Well, none that really mattered,
but as I look at my life now
it seems so torn and tattered.
This is supposed to be the greatest times
in my life where values and friends will change,
but really I'm just confused.
My worries and problems seem so strange
When really they're just petty problems
about freedom, friends, and boys.
I'm never satisfied with the age I am.
I want to be older and older,
but then I'll want to be younger
and wish to be carefree.
But as I think about it, I
never was carefree.

Minna Dubin

Wind Blown

As I sit here, with the wind blowing by me,
  I think of what a great day this would be,
  for flying kites.

Just as the thought came to mind a child went running by,
  led by a string held tight.

As many times before,
  I am reminded of the wheelchair,
  bound to me.

If I could only be free of it,
  life would then be a pleasure.

As if sensing my despair,
  the child approached me.

I looked upon him,
  with questioning eyes.

Only to be greeted,
  by a fistful of string.

Only then did I experience the freedom of life,
  on that afternoon, while flying a kite.

Now I will never let anything hold me back.

Because now I am one with a wind blown kite.

Teresa Suggs

Untitled

As I sit here listening to the music from the radio,
I think of you so far away but yet so close to me,
It has been several months since I saw you last,
And I can count the weeks and days till I'll be near you once again.
You said that what we had is only purely physical,
God only knows how I tried to believe what you had said,
But since you have been gone I have only realized one thing,
I honestly and truly loved you then without listening to myself.
My heart, mind, soul and body completely tell me,
That it is you and only you that I will ever love.
Heaven only knows if that love will be returned,
I'll take my chances no matter how it may hurt,
Yet it may be heavenly, depending on you, my love.

Sharon J. Shanholtzer

Together Forever

Sometimes when I look at the big blue sky,
I think of you up in the heavens on high.
Way up in that far away place up above,
Looking down on us with so much love.

In that wonderful place, there is nothing bad,
And you remember only the good times we had.
Though we live in a place of fear and hatred,
You live in that place that is holy and sacred.

Closer to God, that is one thing you are,
Though to us it seems, that you are so very far.
You are with each one of us in our heart,
And we will never truly be apart.

So I know now that you are here with me,
Though your body and your face I cannot see.
And the memories of you will live on forever,
Cause I know someday we will again be together...

Karyn C. Nelson

The Woods

  The woods are a special place to me.
I think someday I would like to live there
where it's peaceful and in the morning when I
get up I can listen to the bird chirping and the
animals playing. It will be so sweet there with
the animals. And I won't have electric or
any powered stuff I will just have coal lamps and some
blankets to keep me warm in the winter so they don't
have to cut the trees down and the forest will
always look the way when I moved in there.
I will have a brick house too.

Leslie Verhegghe

Stay

I watch you, as you're packing to go away
I want to, get down on my knees and beg you to stay
but I don't think, it will make a difference any way
oh I just want to say stay, stay
I just want to say stay, stay
please don't go away, and leave me in misery
I know things would change, if you would believe in me
I need one more chance so I could show you how I can be
oh I just want to say stay, stay I just want to say stay, stay
so this is it, you've gave up all hope of loving me
it's time you said, to spread out your wings, you want to be free
any way, you feel you'll be better off without me
I just want to say stay, stay I just want to say stay, stay
I just want to say stay, stay please don't go away

Sid J. Garcia

A Grandson's Prayer

Dear Lord, my Grandma's on the way, it's time for her to go.
I thought that I might tell you some things you'll need to know.....

Grandma loves her children so save a place for me,
Or she will tell you quickly the way it's going to be.

Grandma is a teacher, she'll need a classroom too,
And fill the chairs with children learning something new.

And grandma likes to travel to places far away,
She'll need a phone to call her friends to brighten up their day.

And she'll need lots of hand cream and kleenex by the scores,
Give her lots of books to read and open up the stores.

She'll want a glass of water and don't forget the ice,
And grace her hands with precious stones, diamonds would be nice.

See, Grandma likes things fancy and everything done right,
She needs her hair done weekly and she likes pink and white.

She'll need the best of everything when we walks through that door,
But no matter what you give her she'll always give you more.
And Lord, please ease my sorrow, for she is not so near,
And let her memory live in me as the days turn into years.

Stephen Ingersol

The Long Talk

We had a long talk the other day, the Lord and I.
I told him of a need stronger than human love,
Compelling, searching, hurting.
He looked at me and understood.
We had a long talk the other day, the Lord and I.

He was kind, so kind it made me feel sinful.
How could I have ever hurt the Lord?
Forgive me, I said.
He looked at me and understood.
We had a long talk the other day, the Lord and I.

I took his hand. It was wounded.
Had I done that? He said he loved me.
I want to be with you always, I said.
He looked at me and understood.
We had a long talk the other day, the Lord and I.

I want to tell others about you. Please help me.
I can't do it by myself.
If you help me, I will try.
He looked at me and understood.
We had a long talk the other day, the Lord and I.

Teresa A. Gardner

My First Day

Stepping on new territory on my first day
I took a hot long bath
Letting go all my anger
Emotions
And curiosity
Letting it slowly dissipate deep down
To the synoptic world of nothingness
With a cleansed mind and soul
I reminisced my journey
Questioning and philosophizing my new life
Was there a purpose to it?
Have I accomplished my desires?
Or will I?

Stanley Wong

Exit 13

In all ways possible,
I try to get away,
From you and your tattered libido,
Seemingly forever I have listened and have been taught,
To follow you down your straightedge lifeline.
I slap your hand now as you reach to grab my ear,
You never left the highway,
You have worn this road thin and trite.
Because of this I will not follow you.
I have learned to take a chance,
I dance to tension, and laugh at circumstance,
I will hit your back and touch your life,
Like a fallen breath from a dove.
Yet you will not chase me when I leave,
Or wonder where I have gone,
I got off at Exit 13,
You fear your lives, to follow.

Kristen Hart

Hope

On the periphery of your consciousness
I walk so lightly that my step leaves no mark
in the sands of time
My form as vague as a wisp of fog
drifting over the warm earth
on a cool night....
With an ethereal presence I tread
the perimeter of your mind and
When you wish to draw me
into your circle of thought I come willingly
to light the darkened corners of your life....
Summon me as often as you need a refuge,
a bit of time to dream,
to renew yourself with a fresh new flame...
For in using, I am replenished
my name is Hope.

Louise Sprague

Untitled

I remember the night the war began.
I was among friends,
    staring at images on a tiny screen
Unable to make sense of the reality set before me.
I did not agree with the reason for war then,
    and in many ways I do not now.
But I realize that we are there for the duration,
    and the men and women that now stand
        poised in the middle of the Storm
    may not have agreed with the reason either.
Looking back, I realize how lucky I was
    to be able to find solace amongst my sisters
    and to have the freedom to watch the events unfold.
I think that it is our duty that we support our troops
    in thoughts, in prayer, and in actions.
So that they may return safely
    to find solace in their rooms full of
    friends.

Nancy L. Bartell

Daddy's Girl

I was Daddy's little girl from the moment
I was born.

He never whipped me nor beat me, not even
so much as a scorn

I inherited his looks, his ways, his heart

The only thing that has done for me is
torn me apart

I miss him more and more as the years fly by

Hoping he's happier day by day way up there
high in the sky

I live my life as if to say.

I will carry my hopes and dreams out and
hopefully see him again one day!

Terri Parker Castillo

Precious Baby Boy Full Of Laughter And Joy

My precious baby boy full of laughter and joy. When you were
born I was happy and my heart was full of joy. I felt like a little
kid on Christmas opening his toys. My precious baby boy full of
laughter and joy. From your blondish, blonde hair to your big
blue sparkling eyes and made me the proudest father in the world
and happiest man alive. When you were born I remember
cutting your cord. Then I knew you were very special and going
to be loved and adored my precious baby boy full of laughter and
joy. Do what you believe, and in your heart you will achieve
and in your mind be strong, do what is right and not wrong.
Learn your lessons well and then your grand kids you can tell.
So be a leader and your own man. If someone negative come to
you and say you can't do something look them in the face and
say you can. My precious baby boy full of laughter and joy.

Kevin D. Rusten

The Flame And The Fire

You were the fire
I was the flame
Together we danced
And our names took on fame
We were told that we danced so well
I know for me
I was under your spell
You, the fire
Let me dance and be free
Without a care of who was looking at you and me
I, the flame burned with such desire
As I danced to the power of your fire!

Mary M. Perifimos

The Rose

Such a beautiful sight
Standing there in all your glory
How proudly you display yourself
Like a queen adorned before her king

It was a very humble beginning
The nurturing earth gave you strength
Never did you think to give up
But pondered the reason for existence

Suddenly you felt like you would burst
Something wonderful was happening
The sun fell in love with you
And gently caressed you into bloom

Look at what you have become
So confident - so bold
Maybe one day I could too
Emerge - a rose

Karen P. Brand

Words Of My Mind

I'm torn from love
from life
from death
from wildness
from my destiny

Though you looked me in my eyes
so many times

Did you see my tears of blood fall
into the oceans?
My pain that crumbled
my soul?

You make me laugh and cry at the same
time because it is the love that hides
beneath me

Don't ever leave me behind with wounds in
my heart and sorrows that will last a lifetime

because
I Love You

Amber Stucke

A Passing Thought

A moment's stillness
A word or thought
A passing feeling
A meaningless talk.

A withering flower
Bent in the breeze
Nothing to support it
But other little trees.

Paper and string
And meaningless things
these things mean more to me
than anyone's dream.

Cynthia Koncki Marlowe

Untitled

The sky above is growing dim
All my thoughts direct to him
with his arms he doth embrace
Golden light upon his face
The only deep and yearning love
Come forth with the stars high above
Only when the sun is gone
Do we expect the coming dawn
Cool night air calm and still
Crickets sing sharp and shrill
Content for the moment am
Resting peaceful baby lamb
Darkness falls the moon does rise
Floating gently in the skies
Lone wolf at the heavens bay
Wanting forth to come the day
Me, I wish the night would last
Encompass us upon the grass
The theatre above has shown
That we ourselves are not alone.

Lori Campbell

I Was Born in the Ghetto

I was born in the ghetto
And the need just to eat,
It gave me a hunger
That I can't let go of.
My gut runs
up to my brain.
There it gets in the way of
my mind,
And backs up my best
reasoning
Like a clogged toilet
of white porcelain.
The ghetto sings to me
in the prison.
And I know in my home
I'm uneasy.
Cause and effect are very real.

Tabor Lyn

Mr Pig

Mr. Pig said
it's my pleasure to
make this place
STINK!
This he said
just as
he began to
WINK!

Paul Eckdale

The Wind Shifts

I am the revelator,
of mask and mirror

Walking the mystic stream,
hoping for the fulfillment
of the dream;

A visit; to the sun;
Remembering the wings of Pegasus.

Enchanted as Guenevere;
dancing in Arthur's night market;
Measuring guilt
by the weight of our conscience;

Waiting …
Waiting for the next wind shift;
a spiritual time machine,
That sets my soul adrift.

Zione Walsh

The Nightmares Won't Go Away

A darkness fell upon the room
A cold silence swept across my brow.
I look out the window counting the
stars but it does not help.
I stare at the shadows on the wall.
Their forms represent the dying
figures in the camps.
Oh no!
This can't be happening again.
Why?
I close my eyes, yet the nightmares
won't go away.

Kirk Muckle

My Angel

He came to me when he saw me crying,
  a beautiful angel he was
flying slowly above me
  giving me a beautiful star.

He took my tears away,
he consoled my empty heart.
He told me he came from heaven
  to give me his hand.

He was a beautiful angel
Oh! how beautiful were his wings.
  He looks so soft and charm
but he disappeared in the wind.

He left me his smile
and the steps to follow him.
He just came to ease my pain
  because he never forget me.

That angel was my brother,
  he came to protect my soul.
He is the only one who makes me happy,
  the person which I love the most.

Maria del Sol Jimenez

Forever Mother

Mother is always
A child's biggest fan….
She's there by his side
'Till he's a grown man.

Throughout his childhood
She helps him, you see,
To become the man
She sees him to be.

Mother's not selfish….
She gives of herself.
She doesn't need money;
Her love is her wealth.

Mother will always
Be a child's first friend….
A loving relation
We can't comprehend.

She'll be there for him
Through joy and strife…
Once you're a mother,
It's your job for life!

J. Max Davis

The Soldier

He turned and heard
A chivalrous call
That beckoned deep
From within the walls

Seeking the battle
He turned to go
Facing the giant
Nameless, his foe

Thrusting his sword
He found his mark
Then wept in sorrow
For the frivolous lark

Defeated by victory
He shadowed all light
Whispering his name, then
Removed by the night

Susan Duncan

Fashionably Schizophrenic

While disguising the suffering
A commander sits expressionless,
with fearless eyes
In the quest for supremacy.

Warriors like chess pieces
preparing for battle
strike an elegant pose
On a canvas of bloodshed.

Yet stiff and heavy when captured
In regal awkwardness the king
in deluded formality demonstrates
detached emotion.

As his repressed pawns abandon
their suppression
because of his pulsating speeches
of emerald nothingness.

Yet time only remembers
the commanders' sense of dignity
coverted everything in his quest
for supremacy.

Terrence Temes

The Glass On The Wagon

A glass upon the wagon stood,
  A common piece of art.
A simple frame from which to see,
  The bottom of the cart.

It doesn't give a sharper view,
  Of microbes, fish and worms,
It only shows how much in life,
  In ways there are to learn.

It pulls the sun and shows its color,
  And spreads it on the seat,
In formulas of algebra and calculus,
  Too vast to be complete.

And from its shadow a timing glow
  Across a bed of boards.
Whose cracks in which now act instead,
  Of symmetry and Euclid's chords.

It fills with water and dries with sun,
  And measures each as time moves on,
And casts each one for all to see,
  Amid God's great perplexities.

Milton W. Armiger

Rainbow

I am a rainbow—
a curve of mixed colors
in a changing sky.

Red is anger,
burning like a fire within me.
As I let my anger out,
I become orange—
the bridge to happiness.
Yellow is happiness,
shining bright like the summer sun.
Envy turns my yellow to green,
leading to sadness.
Blue is sadness,
mourning a loss.

I am a rainbow—
created by the rain
of sadness and anger
glowing in the sunshine
of happiness.

Sarah K. Duke

Sane...93

Death upon
a different way.
Kill the sun.
Kill the day.
Drown the night
in my pain.
Kill myself.
It's all the same.
Let the rain
cover me.
Wash the sane
out of me.
Now I feel
insanity.
The only sane
inside of me
is the love
I feel for she.

Michael Cofane

Untitled

A smoker
A drinker
I stare at the man
He gives me the finger
A sign of our times
A voice of youth
We can't fight for ourselves
It's up to you
So sing that song
Pain that canvas
Because alone we
Can't cover our asses
It is not what we say
It is what we do
We should live our own lives
Practice as we preach
Stand up for our own rights
And be thankful for that which we eat

Steven T. Fisher

Maiden Flight

Soaring high thru clouded sky,
A fearless stroke maintains the climb,
When sudden breezes toss awry,
And shift the balance caught in time.

Like cresting wave at ocean's edge,
Carelessly perched upon the air,
The fledgling hangs on shifting ledge,
Awaits the crush with unknown fear.

Then midway thru the crashing roar,
As surf glides in to kiss the sand,
Young glider now careens toward shore,
Yet sets down softly on the land.

Suzanne Brock

A Shelter

Though storms are raging all around,
    a sheltered place I see.
The "Rock of Ages" shield that spot-
    a hiding place for me.

I fear no storm when I am hid
    Beneath its sheltering arm;
For Christ I know, will keep me safe,
    From danger, fear and harm.

I am secure, I have no fear,
    Christ gave His life for me.
I'll glory in His saving power
    Till heaven's gates I see.

Pauline Chism

Not Yet Love

A victory not yet won
A flower not yet seen the sun
A dream not yet conceived
A lie not yet believed
A song not yet sung
A day not yet begun
A hope not yet dreamed
A soul not yet cleaned
A race not yet run
An errand not yet done
A tear still yet to weep
A promise still yet to keep
A story not yet told
A dead man not yet old
Something not yet done
But soon will come

Stacha Simms

What Is A Hug?

Two hearts expressing
A gentle embrace of love
Tenderness and Mercy
Coming down from God above.

A hug expresses Joy
Happiness and Gladness
A hug gives Comfort
To a friend in Sadness.

God invented hugs
Because we need each other
They give Strength and Courage
To a sister or a brother.

Whether you hug another person
Or you hug your precious pet
At that very moment
All your needs will be met.

With unity of the Spirit
In the bond of Love
we find Peace and Contentment
In a hug from Above.

Marjorie S. Siegel

The Rose

A tear in the heart
A gentle touch
The sweet fragrance
The thorns of contradiction
Blood soon trickling down.

A flower of mystery and pain
when seen from a far
it looks beautiful to touch
when picked up
tremors of pain fill the body.

The sweet fragrance
brings people back though.
It's called bittersweet love
To me it's life.

Lindsey Leigh Dinga

Someday

Imagination
A wonderful thing
Maybe tomorrow

Peter Ramponi

A Time Ago

The body stoops
A hand goes out and
picks up from the gravel
A fragment of white sea shell.
For a moment, a roaring
The ancient sea fills the space
That just now was mine.
Moving diamond shapes
grasses flowing.
The sudden cry of a bird
echoes all along the bluesky.
A herd of mule deer crosses the horizon
hooves like scintillating brass
A laugh rings like crystal
in the empty sky.
Bluesky loves Three Trees

Bluesky

Death

Who is this tired grey-haired man
A knocking on my door?
A sweet and comic smiling face.
His wrinkled robe trailed on the floor.

Not a word he says to me,
But beckons with his hand.
My knees, though weak, will follow him.
The glass he holds is out of sand.

I turn around and look back;
Still lying on my bed
I see myself in the mirror
Watch the mourners bow their heads.

Lowell Sullivan

My Gentle Gardener

The seeds were planted
    a long time ago.
But you were the one
    who helped them to grow.
You watered and fed them
    you gave them your care
When others couldn't see them
    you knew they were there.
The seed of self confidence
    was buried so long
You made me feel smarter,
    you made me feel strong
The seed of identity
    you helped it to grow
Into the flower of my personality
    that I needed to know
Thank you my gentle gardener
    for the love that you've shown
Whatever I accomplished
    I couldn't have done it alone!

Martha E. Ebner

Love

Seeking love in solitude
Along the water's edge
Where soft ripples, white and blue
Tenderly wash each rocky ledge.
The twilight of the autumn moon
Beckons to the willow tree.
Fluttering lovers, as butterflies
To light upon its knee.
But, I as a heron stands
Cold water to the knees
Caressing of the moving sand
The only love, left for me!

Vivian Archie Mathews

Miracle Of Love

Today
a miracle
smiled at me
and gazed into my eyes.
A halo of beauty
caressed her face;
there was music
in her sighs.

And when
she touched my hand
with hers
and reached
for the world above,
the miracle of life
became real to me
as I held
our miracle of love.

Laura Winters

Untitled

It is a leap from love to nothing
A pain so deep, an incision.
Nothingness is truth
Remembering is all lost.
Your eyes are exposed
Without obscurity, just reality.
How love once protected
Turned to fear, extreme fright.
Clouds are dim, dark now
And roads crumbled.
The grass is no longer green
And constant thunder awakens the mind.
You lie, cold, undisturbed
And await morning
For someday could be a brighter day.

Shara Krause

I Am Who I Am

I am who I am
a part of God's vast universe
created in His image
encompassed by His hands
contained by His love
enlightened by His Spirit
consuming my time, being who I am.

Pat Hodson

'Just A Dream'

I keep telling myself you are
  a past that used to be.
Then why last night were you
  there again with me?
I've given up on you, and
  started anew.
Then why were you there again
  last night just like you
  used to be?
Go away and let me be, not
  even a dream do I want
  you to be!
Go away and stop haunting me,
  you mean nothing more to me!
Not even just a dream do I want
  you to be.
Please, just go away and leave
  me be.

Patricia A. Robinson

Abduction

You visit upon a dream mist.
A Presence caressing my mind.
Energy surrounds sight and sound.
To your will, my body is bound.

Earth becomes a pebble in motion.
The sky is a vast, dark ocean.
My thoughts are a cresting wave,
Suspended in your time, to save.

White light precedes a fire storm.
Grayness blankets your cosmic form.
Blueness conveys searching souls.
Black depths relay your timely goals.

Upon the cosmos, life's immense stage.
You are the guide, mentor, sage.
I am a twinkling star extolling rage.

Lorna Morris-Cyr

Remembrance

You'll never be forgotten
A quiet leader for us all.
No matter what happened,
You never let us fall.
Nicest person to ever live,
All you wanted to do was give.
So determined, and so clever,
In our hearts you'll
be remembered forever.

Michelle Flynn

Spring Song

A redbird's singing, "Pretty, Pretty!"
A robin's hopping 'round!
A jonquil's shouting, "Sunshine!"
And I shout, "Spring's been found!"

  Springtime after winter,
  Greentime after snow,
  Spirits soaring high again!
  After often sinking low.

Someone's got a fishing pole
Someone's got a plow
Someone's got rake to use,
And a garden to plant right now.

  Soon we'll plant potatoes
  And English peas in a row.
  We'll wash blankets, shampoo rugs,
  And some will spring clothes sew.

Dad will oil the mower;
Mom will bake a cake.
And after an April shower,
The sun a bow will make.

Winnie Saffle

Ocean Breeze

S weetly sings the ocean breeze
A s I walk among the reeds
R ushing water from open seas
A pparently among the leaves
H eart of pleasure, heart of gold
A wesome treasures still untold
R ippling water beneath my feet
L isten to the song so sweet
E very morning, noon, and night
S oftly listen with all your might
S weetly sings the ocean breeze

Sara L. Harless

A Single Rose

There it lies
a single rose
on a bush
of many thorns
waiting for others to appear
so it won't be alone
on that big bush
as day's pass
it get's older
and he feels more alone
thinking will it die by itself
finally a bud appears
but it's too late
fore that single rose
has already fallen

Kathy Mihalek

Ode To Wrigley Field

I was barely alive, maybe five,
  a skinny little squiggly.
But I was in awe at what I saw
  when I first laid eyes on Wrigley.

Dad held my hand in Wrigley land,
  where I lost my baseball virginity.
The sky was blue, the thrill was new,
  it seemed to me divinity.

I had my mitt in which I spit;
  it was the ballplayer's habit.
For there might be a foul near me,
  in which case I could grab it.

I now drink beer and groan and cheer
  as players come and go.
The worst, the best, the middlin' rest.
  It's part of baseball's flow.

When robins sing their April thing
  and springs to summers yield,
I still will cheer, perhaps not here
  for Cubs and Wrigley Field.

Morton H. Kaplan,

(Prof., Columbia College)

The Storm

I saw you through the clouds,
a sudden bolt of lightning
burst from the sky.
My eyes wouldn't close
until I was blind.
The rain fell into the night,
with puddles along the way.
Morning broke.
The sun came out,
shining through your closet window.
The children ran outside,
playing in the park.
The storm was over.
Once more,
we are waiting...and watching
for the same storm
to come again.

Rosanne M. Crimo

A Tree

A tree
  A tree
    A tree
Is what I wish to be

With roots that run deep in the ground
To hold me stead fast all the year round

With long sturdy limbs
That will dance the four winds

With lots of leaves to cover my crown
To offer shade to those on the ground

With a sturdy trunk
For squirrels to run round

With nooks and crannies in my bark
To shelter the creatures from the dark

A tree
  A tree
    A tree
Is what I wish to be
    Sandra L. Berry

Sunrise, Sunset

The sky
A vast canvas
The sun
A brush in the hand of God
Pulling the brush up
Paint flows into place
Designing ribbons of color
Orange, red, yellow
Morning has come
The picture is done

The brush begins its descent
Paint overly wet
Beginning a new masterpiece
Purple, blue, magenta,
Black...
Stars spattered in place
As if scattered by a toothbrush
The artist content with his work
Rests for the night
    Victoria Goldrick

To My Wife

A stunningly brilliant princess
A wise and perfect queen
The delicate form that fills my arms
Is the star that lights my dreams.

So pure and fine and true and right
No flower could be so smart
As this the morning glory
That blooms within my heart.

An exquisite tender loving swan
So firm and full of life
The graceful form that fills my arms
Is my precious precious wife
    J. D. Lincoln

Heidelberg

In Heidelberg,
A woman lovingly arranges flowers
Yellow roses in great profusion
Each carefully cut and displayed.

Smiling in the sunshine
Absorbed in her work
Not even thinking of those
Who will admire her art.

In Heidelberg,
A statue to a king of old
Stands at the end of the ancient bridge
Gawked at by unknowing tourists.

Five times overs the centuries
The River Neckar has risen
To destroy the old bridge
And it will again.

In the great sweep of time
A moment in the sun
And a statue washed away
Mean just as much.
    William Krist

Hope

No definition of hope,
a world of jealousy and hate.
Children governed by starvation,
mourning their own fate.
The killing of the innocent,
pleasure taken from greed.
Opinions never to be voiced,
nobody to hear their plead.
Taken from a mother,
the heart not yet to beat.
Outcome of mistakes,
consequences still to meet.
Helpless are the children,
victims of a sense of pride.
To witness civil war,
holding their fears inside.
The game of life and death,
prejudice of a race.
Nothing to leave the children,
but a world they can't bear to face.
    Regina Kalitz

"My Empire Is Crumbling"

A place I could call my own,
A world that took years to build,
Now my empire is crumbling;
My warriors have been killed.

Failure does not sit well
Within my mind or heart.
And as I watch the bricks fall,
I'm like a fool without a part.

I can only sit and wonder,
What will this defeat yield?
I feel there will be more bloodshed,
More fights on this battlefield.

Will I be able to face the next duel
Despite all of my hidden fears?
Even with a knight in shining armor,
I won't avoid the tears.

How splendid it was to be at the top,
Oblivious to the pain of the poor,
Here's your dose of reality, kid:
Life is a never-ending war.
    Karen Subers

I'm Dreaming Of A World

I'm dreaming of a world,
a world without police,
can you imagine that?
A world with no need for police,
no need for locks on your doors.

A world where everyone plays,
plays fairly, honestly, openly,
a place where even losers,
are considered to be winners,
as long as they try their best,

I'm seeing my vision clearly,
neighbors actually helping neighbors,
members of different races embracing,
members of vastly different religions,
agreeing on the notion of spirituality.

I sit here on my bench patiently,
quietly waiting for my world to arrive,
I see the wind whipping through trees,
they'll be here long after I'm dead,
maybe they'll see the world in my head.
    Stephen D. Manning

Traveler's Prayer

A zipper bag
A zipper bag
I'm stuck between two holes
one that's open
one that's closed
I don't know
which way to go,
the path so unreal
Detail on the other end
Both travels to extreme

Mileage that still adds up
Experience is on its way
There's a fork in the forbidden path-
destiny all alone
Or the fields of harvest every year
that smile give October cheer

Orange and black
Colors that mask
Let me curl and burn in gold of death
Better than to die sealed and breathless
    Sean Hofmans

The Light Of The Moon

As the wind blew
Across his face
It left nothing
Not a trace
Of what had happened
Only hours before
Something so terrible
Something like war

As the sky grew dark
They had crouched in a hole
Nothing moved
Not a soul

Then a rifle fired
And that was it
His friend lay dead
In the tiny pit

He looked up at the dark sky
And he saw a single star
"For we are humans" he said
We will leave a scar.
    Sarah Irving

Old Glory

Neighbor, let's start a wave
  Across our free land.
Let it begin in your
  own right hand.

Wave old glory high
  with her red, white and blue,
While encouraging your neighbor
  to raise his flag too.

Momentum will build as
  the wave grows in length.
Loyalty will bring unity
  and give our country strength.

As the stars and stripes wave
  across this land of ours,
Look heavenward, Old Glory
  is reflecting the stars.

Lets salute Old Glory
  with a hand upon our heart
As we whisper a prayer
  "God give us a new start".
  Viola June Moore

Spring Performance

The curtain rises.
Act. I
  March,
  with lingering snows
  blustery winds
  teasings of spring
  in a bright crocus
  intends to steal the show,
but...

Act. II
  April slips on stage
  with an occasional summery day
  daffodils and hyacinths
  nourishing showers
  Easter joys,
yet...

Act. III
  Lovely May appears
  with soft sun and breezes
  apple blossoms and tulips
  lacy green trees
becoming the glorious "Star of Spring."
  Rose Marie Petranek

The Story Of Creation

The first by God created
Adam was his name
Adam ate an apple
and put the world to shame
but when he had to grapple
with that which he had wrought
and saw what cause it gave to grieve
he slyly cast about and sought
to blame the whole affair on Eve
So then upon all womankind
an Evil spell was laid
Forever hence she was to find
a lowly role to play as maid
and serve as man's caretaker
a troubled trail e'ermore to plod
imposed by Him her maker
to clearly mark her newborn state
a most strange fate to contemplate
Now don't you think that odd
of God?
  Richard Johnston

All That I Ask

I can count all of my yesterdays,
All my tomorrows are yet unborn.
Against the measure of time,
Who will see the path that I've worn?

All that I ask is to be free,
to walk with you side by side.
Will love and destiny be enough
to see us through, and be our guide?

As I know not how far
or how long my journey will be,
all that I ask for is God's grace to
have someone to travel with me!
  Richard S. Misener

Expectations

Could I be, should I be,
  All that I expect to be.
If I were, would it change:
Would it really stop the pain,
Of not being all that I expect to be.
  Sheila F. Vasseur

The End

I feel the end of me is near.
All through my life there has been fear.
Fear for the mere reality.
Fear that there's no morality.

There is no care left for me here.
All now is gone that I held dear.
I've tried to hold on, but couldn't,
I asked you to, but you wouldn't.

I have screamed all that I can
I'll give my soul to him to scan.
Now that I have come to the end.
I'll give my soul to him to mend.
  Valerie Ann Byers

Flowers

To see the flowers
All through the hills,
To see the white,
Like daffodils,
To see the trees,
And flowers bloom,
Like a butterfly,
In its own cocoon,
To feel the sun,
And all its warmth
This is what I think of flowers
And all of nature's storms
and powers.
  Tiffany Evans

Untitled

Follow me into the unknowing
Always wondering where we are going

Ask me I've been there before
I never want to be there anymore

I don't want to see daylight again
then my struggle will finally end

Your always wanting a reason to die
I'm always wanting a reason to fly.
  Thompson Peter Hornett

Victims Of The Wind

One single leaf,
Almost dead and brown.
Clinging pitifully, helplessly,
To its home on the bough.

Behold, the wind!
It howls and rushes,
Knowing no mercy.
With it, sweeps away
Lost souls,
Lost in the wind.

The single leaf,
Torn from its home,
Swirls and twirls in the air,
As it comes closer, closer
To the floor of the earth.

As the leaf lies there,
With others surrounding it,
It gasps for one last breath
And realizes,
They were all victims of the wind.
  Youlim Yai

A Brief Solace

Alone in the world we begin
Alone in the world at the end
The only comfort, our only hope
Is to be together in the middle
As we walk down our pathway of life
Tendrils of shadows rise upon this path
Encompassing the views of all
Follow this path to its end
Even as it grows darker
ones spirit grows stronger
And at the end of this path....Salvation
All darkness is lifted
And there she stands
Love, beauty, and tranquility
Even if it is only fleeting
It is our chance to not be one but two
Darkness vanquished momentarily
Because in birth we are alone
And in death alone once again
  Matt Muhich

My Mom

From birth to youth
and beyond I am the child

Blessed by her love
caressed by her caring
nurtured by her strength

I am the child
bestowed pride in heritage
courage in faith
instilled by the quiet dignity
of example

gathered about are
the children of the child
and the countless many
touched by the beauty of her being

I am the child
of this fair warrior
fiercely proud
though gentle kind and wise

now lies still
the noble heart yet in the child lives
  Michael D. Evans

For Arnold

Death slips quietly in
and bustles away pieces of my heart
the silence of emptiness fills the room
pulsating with her sighs

Death rides crescendos of silence
longings for the laughter
the touch, the smile dreamed of
whispers reach into the past

Death thunders into my heart
reverberating with torments of loss
sopranos away the life-song
with sobs of good-bye

Music holds her breath
buried deep within the soul
a chord unfinished
for the song unsung.

Margaret Carbo

"Betsy Bee's Day Out"

I think I'll go to school today.
And chase the kids while they play.
I think I'll buzz around their heads
And scare the ones that are wearing Keds.
The kids that are playing for square are
wearing red.
And they really dread me landing on
their head.
When I get tired and don't want to play.
I think I might just flyaway.

Whitney Resler, Age 10

Step By Step

Learn how to take it step by step,
   and day by day.
Remember the memories kept,
   in every way.
You are the light of my life,
   the sparkle in my eye.
I will never forget you,
   as the days go by.
You mean so much to me,
   and I know why,
It is because you've touched my heart,
   in so many ways.
I know we will never part,
   as long as we take it,
      day by day.

Kelly Lottermoser

The Martial Way

Work and discipline; day after day,
And each is harder than the last.
Always physically and mentally aware;
And full of moral and stamina.
Preparation for that day;
When your knowledge is needed,
If there is a day!
The biggest fight, is the fight within.
If heart and spirit is pure,
You will master your goals.
Now! The Master will pass his knowledge
Until his very death!

William Lillie

Bed Of Dreams

I see him coming
And feel his presence.
I look into his dark eyes
And feel not afraid
For hidden deep within
Is the secret to love and compassion.
I take his hand and together
We walk through the clouds.
We had been separated too long,
But now we are as one.
He puts his arm around me
And I feel his power and strength.
His lips meet mine
For what seems an eternity.
I know what he wants
And am willing to give it all.
I am to be his mistress
For all eternity
And shall slumber forever
In his bed of dreams.

Yvonne D. Dunson

When I'm Lonely

When I'm lonely
   and feeling blue,
This is what I often do;
Pray for guidance
   and for peace,
Wanting comfort at the least.
Seeking wisdom from above,
Asking somehow to be loved.
Then I thank the
   Lord on High,
For my blessings by and by.
So when you're lonely
   and feeling blue,
This is something you can do ...
   if you want to.

Susanne M. Fowler

Lonely People

When you have a good life
and feeling very secure,

Then encounter someone
Whose life is not in gear.

Their lives are stressed and on the
inside very troubled too,

But spirit holds them up when
they smile at me and you.

I wonder when they leave us
and are out of sight,

Alone again, how they face the
long, long night.

If you and I could recognize
these people in our lives,

Go out of our way to give that
smile, a hug, make closer ties.

It surely would be a better world,
a world that can come true.

Take the time, reach out,
and it will be for you.

Patricia Cantrell

"It's Love"

It's love that lightens every heart
and fills a heart with joy
love that builds a friendship
that time and distance cant destroy.

It's love that makes life wonderful
in a way words can't define.
And love that give such meaning
to this special heart of mine

It's love that poets write
for song to be sweet and fair
love that gives a magic touch
to moments sweethearts share

It's love that holds the secret
of making dreams come true
and love that give devotion
to last a lifetime through.

Marylou V. Hare

Step-Daughter

At the start you won my heart
and gained a fathers love.
Though the years and all the
tears our love grew ever stronger,
Now your gone it seems so long
and I miss you everyday.
Until the time God calls me home
I hope you will remember, that I
love you with all my heart my
darling little step-daughter.

Randy Smith

"I'll Always Love You"

I love you,
And I always will:
Wherever I am,
Whatever I feel.

You are the one
Who has stolen my heart!
And what will I do,
When we are apart?

I know you don't love me,
But what can I do?
NOW and FOREVER
I'll always love you!

Wherever you go, whatever you do,
Please always remember:
I'LL ALWAYS LOVE YOU!

Maria Michelle May

Time

Time goes by
And I wonder why
Life can't be
Simple for me.

Everything's so complicated
And I'm not that sophisticated
Things around me change
As I roam the range.

I'm lost
And I might just toss
All the energy in me
And give into thee.

C. M. Marshall

Change

The time has run out
and I am still the same.
I have not changed,
though I have learned a lot.
Changing shows a desire,
a desire to be liked by others,
and I don't like to mislead
as that causes them to hate.
Their hate causes me no pain.
I have become immune to the feeling
of that emotion,
as they can not just give
their hate and walk away.
Instead, they must stay
and watch for my reaction,
and when I give none,
they say it again
"I hate you".
The words do not change,
and neither do I.

Rebecca Rollins

Firsts

Look beyond the tunnel
and in my eyes you'll see,
the brightness of the sparkle
your warmth has given me.

Look into my soul
searching you will find,
a strength brought out in me
no other like its kind.

Look into my heart
and only gaze awhile,
and you can see the love
shining bright with every smile.

Let our past be memories
of times we once knew,
a future of growing
sharing as two.

No beginnings or endings
could ever take away,
the love I have to give to you
in my own special way.

Renelda Gallagher

"Love"

I have found the way to love my dears:
And, it is not thru possession,
nor any of our fears:
Thru breezes of freedom,
showers of delight:
God brings in the sunshine
that fades away the night.

Laura Knaus

"Another Rainstorm"

I lie in my bed
And listen intently
To the wind outside my window
That is blowing not so gently.
As it blows harder I hear its howl,
A cry against my window.
It screams, "Let me in! Let me in!"
I softly shake my head - "No."
Thunder comes suddenly,
A loud "Boom" to accompany the wind.
Lightning streaks across the sky,
And rain begins to fall again.

Shannon Kirby

Untitled

When good men go to jail,
and justice is a game.
When true love doesn't count for nothin',
Life will never be the same.
There really was a "Once upon a time"
And dreams mattered to us all.
We had the magic and the music then,
but fear of flying made us fall.
When the crimes against humanity,
cause the world to take a look.
And the empty chapters written down,
finally turn into a book.
When the Ivory Towers crumble,
and the Halls of Justice fall.
The people then will come together,
saying "Heaven help us all."

Kurtis Laughead

To My Husband

I heard his voice
And my heart jumped

I asked if I could help
And he took my arm

He asked me my name
Though I did not his

He asked me for my hand
And I gave my heart

He asked me to be his eyes
And I gave him all of me

And I melted into his soul
And we became one

He asked me for immortality
And I gave him sons

And then one day he slipped away
And now in my solitude, I long for him.

Licia L. Allman

Unknown Soldier

Somewhere across the river
And not so far behind
Lies the heart and soul unrestless
of the love he left behind
And somewhere in the distance
her tears forever flow
For the love of a soldier
and the war he had to go
He was just a young man
at age 25
In her heart he'll be remembered
his memories will survive
Proud and brave he fought a war
He fought for what he believed
for some it was just purpose
For others to be free
Etched in stone the year he died
his gravestone still remains
In a field where grass grown high
Unknown became his name

Nicholas Logiacco

Candlesticks

Each year they take me out again
and polish me so bright

And put me on the mantel so
I can spread some light

Oh all around the room - I see
some goodies spread beneath the tree

I hear the children happy cries
Oh how I sparkle when they sigh

But after Christmas said and done
I'm gently laid away

And I must wait until next year
To spread a Christmas cheer

Mary Mazzoni

"Listen Politician"

Keep your television
And prescribed friendship;
Your civil lordship
And disposition.
May they be shouldered by the unwilling.
A coercive brain scrubbing,
To cure the rebel.

But, in touching myself
May I cogito, ergo, zoom.
Come on windy notions
Wave white flagging motions.
Overturn the lecturn, boom.
But money manacles,
Biting social shackles,
And now, just a submissive rebel.

Rod Davis

Lessons Of Life (Father To Son)

We stepped into the wilderness
and snatched the forest's birth.
He said to feel the morning's fog
and clench the winter's earth.

Grasp the scent of the windswept pine
and hold it for all it's worth.
For if you divorce earthly man,
you'll possess a heaven on earth.

I know I am closer to God
as I sense Him from this peak.
His love and joy transcend the clouds
when His majesty I seek.

He placed a bit of heaven in
a stream that is filled with trout
and in the bugle of an elk
inducing a rival's route

You must live life to the fullest.
That will be the greatest test...
that no man may say about you,
He did not give it his best.

Micheal J. Chavis

Life

A bud bursts open
And the bloom is full
Of vivid colors. It grows
Bigger until it can grow
No more. Then it wilts,
Dies, and fades away.

Suzanne Pointer

Time

Will time erase this burning pain
And soothe this restless mind
For I am left to walk alone
A path we walked one time

Will time erase the vows we made
My love to have and hold
Will I not always be the first
To wear your ring of gold

Will time erase the memories
Our laughter, tears and sorrow
Will you recall our yesterday's
And dream of me tomorrow

Time won't erase my gift of love
For sometimes fate is kind
We share a precious baby girl
The part of you is mine

Time won't erase our yesterday's
Forever was my vow
But I will find contentment, dear
To know you're happy now
Marcella Whitt

Untitled

He may look out that window
and stare.
I wonder what we may see?
I wonder what he is thinking?
He may just be day dreaming.
But what could he imagine?
Do you think he may have questions,
or does he wonder at all?
His mind is a mystery,
A Puzzle
and Perplex.
He may just look out that window.
If only he could tell us
what he may see
or think,
imagine
or wonder,
but what can you expect....
He
is only a cat.
Misti Goodknight

Now She's Gone

My mother left
and that was that.
Would I see her again?
Or was now the time to say good-bye?
A single tear rolled down my cheek
To let my mother know
She would not be forgotten.

When mother leaves,
Child feels forgotten.
Do I feel forgotten?
What do I feel?

My mother
Is going off to war.
I don't know
Where I am, what to do, what to feel.

I'll be strong
For me, for Dad
No time to lose, must say good-bye
Another tear
So she'll always be remembered.
Tovah Heller

The Journey

The shadow of the moon
And the mist of midsummer
Converge too soon
For the ambitious mother

The child has driven
The sanity of youth
Beyond comprehension
To the place where one's aloof

Lost in her ambition
The mist did run
Listen to your intuition
Look towards the morning sun

The child's destination
Would someday become
The end of your anxious journey
Just like the risen sun
Richard Robert Poe

Still I Love You

...And the willow, us beholds
...and the pond...our existence shows
We grew up by the banks..
Through life...we drank
Best wine and worst brands..
How could I forget..
The heart begets
What the mind forgets,
Or the heart's drum beats
When the mind recollects..
Visions hit me..
Dreamer.. plain awake..
Sometimes blurred..
Sometimes vague..
And, in the chill of winter's worst
All I feel is your hand's worth..
The smile that hosted me for years...
yet.. I long for in my fears..
I love you.......still.
Mani Hassan

"Angel's Song"

As the winds begin to blow,
    And the seas begin to rise:
In the silence of the day,
    We see the master's eyes.

Suddenly, there is no voice,
    Only angels singing song:
As, we begin to see,
    The spirit going home.

It shines so brilliantly,
    As suns above and below:
It is the truth of his way,
    With shimmering essence aglow.

I turn to you as I wave good-bye,
    Though I know it won't be long:
For in the silence of a day,
    The angels sing their song.
Mary H. Jeffery

Untitled

    Captured by the mechanical eye
are moments to remember,
    Thoughts of yesteryear gone by.
P. K. Hoer

Poetic Thoughts

I read this in the paper,
And thought that maybe I,
Could write just a few lines
To be "remembered by".

I could write about the weather,
Or I could write about my cats,
Or I could write about the styles
Of the ladies' new fall hats.

I could write about politics,
Or the state the world is in,
Hoping that someday it will be
The way it should have been.

I could search the wide world over,
And I would surely find,
The subject that seems to be
Always on my mind.

It's about love and peace and friendship,
And doing unto others,
And thanking God for the little things
That could make all of us brothers.
Ruth Anderson

Life-Ride

You can only ride once
And time is limited

You choose the ride
Ride toward your dreams

To ride with confidence
Without fears...

Live, really live
Enjoy the ride

Fears will fade

Ride to new heights
You call the shots

Take your time, take care of yourself
If the ride bores you, changes it

Life-ride is free
Just get on
William M. Gould

Reflections

I look in the water
And what do I see?
A beautiful girl
Looking back at me!

She seems quite familiar
I don't know where from;
A mermaid she's not
Her name will soon come.

Now I remember
The girl that I see!
Of course she's familiar,
She's no one but me!
Patricia E. Guilmette

241

Child Of Mine

Who do you think you are?
And where do you think you came from?
Your blood, was once my blood.
If you think yourself so great,
I must think myself greater.

You are the apple,
I am the tree.
As the tree is proud of the apple,
Why not, the apple be proud of the tree.

Pauline Safka

Mother's Love

"There is a love that never dies
And you can tell by your Mother's eyes
That love is for you and for me
Whether on land or far out to sea.
When we get big and go to war
As our Father's have done before
And in a year or two come home and see
A vacant place where Mother used to be
Down in the grassy grave she sleeps
Where we may constant vigil keep
But still the love that never dies
Is shining in her lifeless eyes."

V. B. Briant

Heartache

If your heart has ever broken
And your life left cold and bare
There's never been words spoken
And there's nothing that can spare
You the pain and all the sorrow
Of the love you no longer share
Love is something that you borrow
And the heartache is your fare
Here today and gone tomorrow
Till another comes your way
This is something I can tell you
Love is never here to stay
If you're not left for another
Then death, takes it away.

Rosie Sias

Untitled

I know that there shall never be
another one so dear to me
as the one who crossed the great divide
as slowly as the ebbing tide.
One who was always there beside me
on this land or on the sea.
One who was always there to guide me
in the hills or on the lea.
One who shall never more give mirth
in the home or on this earth.
I know that there shall be no other
as dear to me as was my mother

W. A. Cadogan

Is It There

Is it there, up there
Are the stars really stars
Is the moon something great
Are the dreams we wish for,
Are they coming true.
Is what I said, is it really here.
I was only a child
So then I knew.

Rhonda Huddleston

Untitled

Daring and masculine
Ardent and warm
Not meek but gregarious
Intense, like a storm.
Enduring in thought
Larger than life

Radiant eyes, so
Onerous to fight.
Yearning to fly,

Where fortune may call
Invariably free
Inhibited by walls.
Take heed; he is fragile
Although he seems cold;
Love burns in his heart
A story yet to be told.

Theresa Konzel

Trapped
(With The Wonders In Life)

The wonders in life
Are the things I adore.
But sometimes in life
You can't get anymore.

Those are the times in life
Where you usually feel trapped,
Where your wonders in life
Feel so very wrapped.

So remember to think
About what you adore.
Because sometimes in life,
You can't get anymore.

Mishayla Spendlove

"Eternity"

Emblazoned on my conscious mind
Are the words I groped to find.

I truly felt her forceful presence.
My being filled with her essence.

The windows of her soul took hold;
Her searching eyes did thus unfold

Auras of white that blessed my eyes
Her Higher Self was oh, so wise.

The message came through, loud and clear.
This earthly life we hold so dear

Is not your fate, have not dread fear,
Let go your worldly things, held dear.

For where you go 'tis destiny
Your soul is for eternity.

Richard Stannard

Day Has Gone

Day has gone, and so has the mist
    as I lay my head down to rest.
Day has gone, but the tears stream
    on.
Day has gone but the mourn goes
    on.
Day has gone and so has my
    love.

Peyton Walker

Mixed Emotions

When one is just a simple dolt
Around age 23
One doesn't think too much
About the cause of liberty.

When flags wave and bands play
A lump gets in the throat
The marching of soldiers
Can set the tears afloat.

But as we go along in life
We may discover to our horror
That all the glory that we see
Was bought with others' sorrow.

Why did Columbus murder millions
For the church
And was it really necessary
To leave the Indians in the lurch?

Were slavery and the Persian Gulf
Truly righteous actions
Or was it really greed and oil
That caused these infractions?

R. Eugenia Walters

Holocaust Museum

I was broken into pieces
    as I came out of that place.
        Everywhere there had been
        stick figures

Like the first scrawlings of children.
    Only these were real people once,
        ripped from a green summer,
        shoved into viscous dark,

And shipped to landlords
    of a unique killing field.
        Death came into my quiet.
        I will always see the shoes,

All sizes, broken, moldy,
    the eye glasses, knives, forks,
    and at the end —
        the hair, the hair!

Nathalie Ketterer

On Seeing Her For The First Time

Could beauty be her name,
As I look into her eyes,
For they are as brilliant,
As colors from the skies.

The hair atop her head,
So fair and blond and grand,
Sparkles like a ray of sun,
That falls upon the sand.

Her face could light the darkness,
The moon no brighter glows,
No angel's song could capture,
The beauty it bestows.

Her voice is like a gentle song,
That plays a lovely tune,
And if she spoke the whole night long,
The air it would perfume.

As fragile as a newborn doe,
She floats along her way,
And if we were another thing,
She'd be a sunny day.

Michael McLaughlin Jr.

"Ben"

You stand there silently
  As I mumble on
Trying to ignore me
  As if I had done wrong
Times go on
  And I leave you
But, you never realize
  That you are alone
I try to impress you
  Doing my best, indeed
Nothing seems to please you
  How can that be?
Should I give up hope
  But when it comes to Love
'Tis I who loves you most
    Naomi Duncan

Portrait Of The Night

The beauty of the night came to me
as I rode down a long, narrow road.

The sky was dusty blue velvet
with stars twinkling here and there.

A big orange moon played hide and seek
among the floating clouds.

Tall, dark trees reaching toward the sky
made eerie shadows play on the road.

My heart took in the haunting picture
and the lonely feeling it left
brought tears to my eyes.

God spoke to my heart, My child,
keep this picture and never let it go,
for I will never paint it this way again.
    Pauline Buchanan

The Sun Is Forever Healing

  Gentle tides roll in and out
as I think of you.
I walk along a secluded shore
with only the light
shining from the moon.
The echo of the waves,
are as if they are whispering to me
the sound of tranquility.
I remember you by the
sea of blue,
the nights were so cold
but warm were you.
My tears splash in the ocean
like raindrops from the sky.
  Yet, perhaps maybe
if the sun were shining
it would dry these tears I cry.
    Victoria Miller

Life

If you live your life day by day
  as if each day might be the last
put aside all your worries
  and forget about the past
and make the most of everything
  that life is offering you
you'll live a life of happiness
  in which your dreams come true.
    Lois J. Adams

I Picked A Rose

The petals are soft
As if velvet and such;
Yet durable and strong,
And so pretty to touch.
  I picked a rose.

The stem is so strong;
Not bending but straight,
And the stem has its thorns
As does life and its fate.
  I picked a rose.

The leaves are green;
Simple, but pure.
They extend from the stem
And are lovely for sure.
  I picked a rose.

They make up a flower
So beautiful and free.
It's of nature's beauty,
For all the world; to see.
  I picked a rose.
    Kenneth E. Vergith

"One Hundred Fine"

One hundred fine - percentage made,
as palm trees line - viridian shade.
The deepest, truest one sublime,
'tis in the land - one hundred fine.

And century lives - then merely child,
the freshest and the one so mild.
And with each year - one hundred fine,
the gorgeous view of palm trees line.

I've sung this song a thousand times,
the lyrics of one hundred fine.
The true percent - 'tis gold of rhymes,
viridian deep and love divine.

One hundred fine - percentage made,
as palm trees line - viridian shade.
The deepest, truest one sublime,
'tis in the land - one hundred fine.
    Mark W. Haggerty

"Time"

It comes and it goes,
As quick as a wink,
Yet we never again,
Will have a chance to relive.
  Our choice is to use it,
  To it's fullest demand,
  Or be lazy and squander,
  For which will you stand.
For time is an element,
A gift from above,
And just how we use it,
Will be unveiled in life's helm.
  We're accountable human's,
  When life draws to the end,
  Of what did we do with,
  Our life as "Time" spent.
    Pamela Alice Magee

David

Here...
between the moon
and the dark side of the sky,
The heart is always saying
goodbye...
    Muriel Rail Giterman

Two Voices

Two voices I hear calling to me
As the sky is becoming gray
One voice says to let myself free
Yet the other pleads me to stay

If I decide to set myself free
Then I would have to say good-bye
And more on to whatever maybe
Yet part of me I know would die

Away I said I'd never run
But that may be what I need to do
Clouds are starting to cover the sun
It's time to find out what is true
    C. Kritzman

Leaves

Leaves can cascade here no more
As they used to from each roof
Colored like a rusty ore,
In driveways soon to meet rebuff.

The horizon of their shower
Seemed an endless task to rid.
Children used some like a flower,
Or as wreath around their head.

As though Nature's limits burst
They would blanket drives and gravel;
Maple plummeted at first,
Then Elm and Oak to roads to travel.

Leaves, once fallen from old trees
Now bulldozed flat and laid to rest,
No more bother human eyes
But no more warm a bird's nest.
    Margaret Steuermann

Reflections Of A Thought

The leaves are rustling
As winter draws nigh
For sure it is fall
That we are seeing with sigh
And shortly thereafter
Much more can be said
The children will hustle
To stay warm in their bed
The wind will be hissing
As the trees brace for winter
Not knowing for sure
If they're in imminent danger
Yet much can be said
On the beauty of nature
Our children are precious
And our trees stand in stature
It's just the beginning
Of those things that I sought
As I pondered and wondered
This wonderful thought
    Ramon C. Valverde

At Peace

Peaceful are the waters
At that glowing moment of dusk
When dimming rays send tranquil
  unity throughout the sky.
Gone are all the tensions of life
As that one moment of blazing orange
Wisps everything out of your mind
Making life easier to bear
And peace the utmost goal.
    Kerin L. Carmody

The Wage Of War

The famine begins
as winter sets in...
the earth trembles
in its wake.

Mother's are crying
as their children start dying
in a war neither side
will forsake.

And who'll take the blame
when they look upon, with shame,
the devastation their greed has wrought?

Who'll drop to their knees
and pray, "God forgive me please...
the war I waged was for naught?"

Karen E. Roberson

As Is

As darkness is to wondrous light,
As wrongness is to valiant right,
As the moon is to the vibrant sun,
As death is to life not yet begun,
As the desert is to the bountiful sea,
As he who is joyful to him not free,
As the raven is to the graceful dove,
As all of which I despise is to you,
My love.

Shana N. Graves

"Welcome To My Room"

My room is where we meet,
At day's end.
It is where I can gently, firmly,
Hold you to my breast.
These moments at day's end,
I cherish above the rest.

No interruptions, you are mine then.
I kiss your lips and caress your skin.
Until there is the sound,
Of one heartbeat,
Until not only our bodies,
But our souls meet.

I love my room for affording,
A haven for you and me.
For in this whole wide world,
There is no other place we can be.

Morning sun brings your absence, the reality.
You exist in mind only,
You are my fantasy.

Marvis Donovan

Proclamation

Fools cry
At lost memories
Of happiness.
Forever in search
Of time, but
Never finding
A future.
Beyond all my
Dreams of God
Should I claim
To be a fool?
Or am I safer
To remain wise
In the eyes
Of death?

Marie D. Bukowski

To Shannon

As I sit in awe and wonder
At the miracle of birth
And how little ones replenish
The life supply on earth,
My heart's full and o'er flowing
With thanks to God above
For baby Shannon's safe arrival
Through His ever-circling love.

May the granddaughter that I hoped for
On her journey along the way
Experience living to the utmost
And the joy I feel today.
May good health be her real fortune
With happiness four fold,
And let her heritage pass on
To a generation yet untold.

Marjorie A. Schoonover

Mystified

My hours were long ago, as I
awaited at one time, something
that could be caught.

It was enlightening to see,
something I had known once before.

It was like a memory that
   could not be forgotten,
   but only remembered.

It was like a dream which
   destinies could be discovered,
   but only for a moment.

It was in depth,
what many cannot tell is a lie.....

That, cannot make up for the
moments I had lost,
that were withheld in time
but never released.

Rose M. Myers

Fun And Games

Within The Freedom

The birth of a new horizon
Awakening in the dawn
Fresh and full of life

Young and flying high
Always as new as a fawn
Fun and games within the freedom

Age changing youth to a faint line
Falling off in the sunset
Diminished, lifeless

Lost what was once mine
Yet not too old to forget
Fun and games within the freedom

Kristal C. Barnes

Autumn Awe

Fall creation is awaking
Aware of nature's transformation.
Summer days are worn and spent
Failing trees by gusts are bent,
Releasing a myriad of colors
   On
      The
         Earthen
            Floor.

Kathleen M. Lentz

Together

Early morning sunrise.
Awakes to greet the day.
   And many in the world around
Are lost along the way.
   Yet I can climb the mountain high,
Or swim the widest sea
   These things I do, and so much more.
For you are here with me
   Before I knew not where to turn,
I wandered, goals unknown
   There is a certain numbness
That comes with being alone
   Then came along the missing piece
To make my heart complete
   I know no boundaries now, it seems
Refuse to face defeat.
   For together we can reach the stars
And grasp the rising sun
   Yet, without you I would surely fall
Since I am not one, but none.

Michael R. Freeman

Living Life

Live life
Be life
Do life
How could life be short
Yet so wonderful
You're born
You live
You die
Life is like a pansy for some
Life is like a stone for others
Some people are giving during life
Some are selfish and cheap
Don't we all wish there was
Peace on earth while we were
Or are alive
How could such a wonderful world
Be evil
Remember love people of all kinds
When they are alive not dead

Sara Adipietro

"Love"

Wilted in my heart
beautiful transgressions
shadowed upon my face...
A smile is no longer concealed
Melancholy days are over
Dandelions sway in the breeze
A hidden place is revealed
children play...

Many search
but none have found
the sweetness of honey
all hope
few will find
stones turn
leaves fall
and forever you will be
adored in my cellar
buried so deep
in my heart.

Kristen Sauter

Oak Street

Funny, I never noticed the chill
Before - when we were all here
Jumping on the cracks - oops!
"Don't break your mother's back!"

The leaves scattered near around,
our feet, churning with the tacky
bright pink jumping rope.

Yes, all of them have hurried in-
It's six o'clock

The leaves are parting too,
Scratching their way down the street
with the wind that's chilling me.

Now I'm here alone with the
biting pink rope.

I think I must make sure-
I've not broken mother's back

Kathryn Burke

Blue Roses

It began with blue roses
Being in the sun;
The moment was permanent
As wind became identified
With their wisdom;
More than flowers,
Moving in sequence of blues,
They were intellectual.
The sound of their pattern
Was prophetic and sad;
Now they are gone
They will live forever
A pause of blue
In the idea of afternoon.

Lucy Kent

Ball Of Dirt

Ball of dirt is wasting way,
  better find another way.
Ball of dirt is wasting way,
  best for see the coming day.

Man's greed has gone astray,
  the Promised Land has been betrayed.
They took away her display
  and served it up on a tray.
She's been used, she's been abused.
  Now who's the one to lose?
She isn't prey, she's only clay
  Everyone had better pray.
If ball of dirt keeps wasting way
  If wasteful ways are here to stay,
Then wasteful man and wasteful ways
  will never see another day.
Where do all the children play?

Ken Cunnigham

Untitled

"Lost somewhere,
Between sunrise
and sunset,
Two golden hours...
Each set with
sixty diamond
minutes...
No reward is
offered...
For they are
gone forever."

Ray G. Heffner

Childhood's End

Last night I walked alone,
Between the heavens and the seas.
Childhoods end and fantasies.
My thoughts, like the rolling
waves, come crashing in like memories,
of an almost forgotten day.
The sky was open and,
my mind, was floating
down through clouds, memories
come rushing up to meet me now.
Where will I be tomorrow,
when a new day has come to be,
will I still have my sanity?
I can't wait to see.
My joys are slipping away, one
by one, childhoods end and
the day is done.

Owen Hitt

Once I Was A Decimal

Once I was a decimal,
big and black and round,
numbers that surrounded me,
while sitting on the ground.

Once I was a decimal,
and my name was and,
looking to my right,
I saw up to thousands.

Once I was a decimal,
and someone added to me,
some ones, tenths, and hundredths.
and that changed me!

Now I am a whole,
And I am so happy,
looking at myself,
as changed as changed can be!!

Nathan Cardin

Invasion

Hazy,
Blood red sun,
Burning through the exhausted membrane,
of a late day sky.
Leaving his perilous scar,
Across her virgin beauty.
His searing heat
desecrating
the cool balance
of her splendor.

Laura Breen

Old Man

"My Father's dead," I said.
But not one raised a head
or brow in inquiry.
Why can nobody offer sympathy?

He was an old man.
And he was sick.

"My father's died", I cried.
I want to run, to hide
from this raging grief inside.

He was an old man,
and he was mine.

V. A. Gurrera

The Squire's Song

I walked across the battlefields,
bloodstained sword in hand.
I walked, proud though beaten,
across the sullied land.

Underfoot, rasped the red, red
soil, stained with blood and pain.
though my banner flew on high,
my heart lay with the slain.

I saw the eyes of a woman's son,
pleading, but to live.
But the rapier's blade was harsh
this day, and thus, refused to give.

I know in years to come,
when I hear the beating rain,
My mind and heart will wander
far to the innocent and the slain.

The fields will lay as fertile,
for the blood, 'twas shed so pure
Some young maiden's sweetheart,
torn away by valor's lure.

Nilu Dayananda

Winds Of Time

The whispering winds
blow through the trees,
like billowing waves
through the ocean
breeze. The tides roll
in, "Oh! What is it I
see"; a lighthouse
beaming a light so
bright, to help someone
in the night.
The sands of time
wave good- by, to
greet new waves of
Sandy deserts dry.
The winds of time
One cannot see, but
the beauty it whispers
will always be.

Margaret Dailey

The Howling Wind

The howling wind
Blowing in my face
Leaving my eyes
Running with tears

The howling wind
That passes by
Blowing leaves
And crumbling trees

The howling wind
That brings me fear
Leaving my soul
Like a shaking leave.

Walter A. Egeler

September Breeze

As the September breeze,
Blows leaves off trees,
The pollen from the bees,
Causes her to wheeze,
The wind sends a shiver to her knees,
And she looks out at the ocean seas.

Melissa Graesser

"Moving On"

A warm glowing light pierces my eyes,
Breaking through the darkened world
   that lies behind.
The glass shatters and the walls
   crumble.
Into my silent hell I will no
   longer stumble.
My soul is cleansed,
   My mind is pure,
These thoughts filled with pain I
   won't have to endure.
A new sun has risen, the old
   moon destroyed.
I'll keep moving on
   from a past not enjoyed.

Lori Stewart

Winter Wind

Oh, I love November's wind
Brisk, exhilarating Winter wind
Tall pines bowing low with grace
Small ones brushing snow from face

Leaves play racing, run-sheep-run
Or dancing and twirling in Winter sun
Wood smoke casting its pungent pall
Wafting from many valleys small

Winter winds, too, groom the trees
Of splintered limbs and last of leaves
And guarantee the squirrel's nest
Will survive because it stood its test

Even the creatures seem to know
It's play time now before the snow
Binds them to their den or nest
'Tis now their life is at its best

Yes, I love the Winter breeze
Cleansing the air through the trees
Is there anything at all
Like the Winter wind after Fall?

William A. Read

If I Have A Heart...

If I have a heart imbued with love
Buried in the essence of my soul
It's the image given from above
Pointing my way t'ward eternal goal

If I have a heart that reasons not
But prepared to give its love away
Then I live on earth a patriot
Of the heav'nly kingdom ev'ryday

If I have a heart that is benign
Bringing all to joy and soothing calm
Quelling fears and spreading love divine
Then to all I am a healing balm

If I have a heart of love to guide
And my soul is like a healing spa
And the Savior walking by my side
Then to all I am a guiding star

If I have a heart where Jesus reigns
And it steers clear of the path of sin
Then in it the love divine remains
As the Kingdom of God is within

Luke Jayasuriya

Untitled

When I die
bury me in Jamaica
under the golden
coconut tree

Here I'll rest where
winter's gentle
kind people where
hearts are hot
and souls are free

Wash my heart
of needless emotions

Hang
over my eyes sky
full of stars
full of grace

And let my soul roam
through the oceans

Let all the world be
my homeland

My brothers people of every race

Leonard Gogiel

"Invisible"

I tried to get noticed today,
but everyone seemed to brush
me away.
   I tried to get noticed in
basketball, but all I did was
trip and take a good fall.
   I tried to get noticed in
math, but I wasn't paying
attention to the class.
   I tried to get noticed
in the seventh grade hall,
but I'm definitely not a doll.
   I tried to get noticed
today, but I guess I'm
invisible in my own way.

Montana Hodges

Near Dawn

"Go away", he used to say,
But he always said it hesitantly,
Almost apologetically -
As if he knew I wouldn't.

And then he said it more often,
He said it more emphatically...
And angrily,
As if he knew he shouldn't.

So I went away, I ran away
To wait, to wait for what?
For his iced heart to soften?

But now dear God, as it nears dawn,
I see the point I missed.
A change cannot occur,
In what does not exist.

Maxine Dagley

What I Am

I am not made of steel
- But I am not weak

I am not prejudice
- But I sometimes discriminate

I am rarely forgetful
- But I often do forgive

I have felt pain
- But given others relief

I am unique
- But I am not special

I have loved
- But felt hatred

I have criticized
- But I never said I was perfect!

Nicole Marhevko

Love

Well I thought I didn't love you
But I guess I was wrong
That's another life lived and
   another day gone
But tomorrow always comes
   and the sun will always shine
Just as long as our love grows
   and your forever mine
Sometimes I wish you were here
   here to hold me tight
To wipe away my tears
   and love me through the night
Sometimes I'm glad you're gone
   gone so far away
Like a fairy waved her wand
When I wish it all away

Sarah Miller

Silent Screams

In my head I'm screaming
but no-one hears a sound.
I feel my life is spinning
faster and faster around.

I don't face the problem
it just festers and grows.
Why can't I confront it,
it's as plain as my nose.

Why do I fear it so much,
is it as bad as if seems?
It I stop it right now
could I avoid the extremes?

So many trying questions
not nearly enough answers.
The truth as I see it
is veiled like Arab dancers.

Patty Dismukes

The Moon

The moon shines bright,
but only at night.
For when it comes day,
the moon will fade away.
Then the moon will say, don't cry.
I'll be back at the end of the day.

Ryane Reyes

My Job

My job is tiring,
But people don't see,
What they're always doing to me.

Back and forth,
Is where I go,
Saying things I didn't even know.

People pick me up
Any time or day.
I especially hate it
When they have nothing to say.

Once I get relaxed,
There's another ring,
And I hate it
When they decide to sing.

But I have no choice.
This is my home.
Yes, you've guessed it,
I'M A PHONE!

Sesha Seemungal

Enjoy The Moment

You're part of the race
But you can't enjoy the now
You want some peace
But you can't find it somehow
So you crossed the edge
And you start to worry
Your life is frustration
And hurry, hurry, hurry

You had it all it seemed
But you threw it all away
The wife, the kids, the means
All were gone one day
All the joy in life
You filled with agitation
All the good will
Became an irritation

Enjoy the moment while it's here
For pretty soon the moment disappears

Tim Pearson

What Can I Say?

I tried to save you,
But, you did not understand.
I tried to help you,
But, your mind was blind.
I tried to explain,
You acted like you knew everything.
You did not listen,
You did not know anything.
Bang! You kicked my shin,
Then, bumped your own chin
What can I say?
Nothing!
What can I do?
Crying!

C. W. Yang

I Wonder

I often stand and wonder.
Do you wonder too?
Why do stars shine?
Why's the sky blue?
I often wonder,
If you wonder too?

Stephanie M. Lea

Keep Him

The mountain may seem tall,
  but you'll reach its peak-
The valley is too low,
  but only for the weak.

The water may seem rough,
  still your boat will sail-
The ocean is too deep,
  but only for the frail.

Remember to keep the Lord with you,
  so your mountains will seem small.
And when you tumble towards the valley,
  He'll be there to catch your fall.

For He's the waves in life,
  that gently rock your boat.
And His Wisdom is the depths of seas,
  which keeps us all afloat.

Leigh A. Coker

A Tribute To My Doctor

You may be a doctor
But you're lots of fun
Going to you a less scary one.
Doctor's are usually
Cold and primp.
Serious faces that make you cringe,
But your are - a different one
A smile on your face
And a gentle touch,
And a kind word,
That mean's so much,
I came to you, for help and advice
I leave with a much better insight
I as your patient
Give this tribute to you
For being a friend
And my Doctor too.

Margaret Mundo

Free Light

Wherever I may roam,
By land, by sea, by air,
Or even on my cellular,
It's escape from the ordinaire.

Mop and pail, crumby dishes and laundry
Are stashed 'way back and out of sight
To help me free my soul and body
And fill my brain with the light.

Heed my words if you, too, would yearn
To shed your daily rules.
Just venture out in new skin
And join we happy fools.

Mildred L. Culp

A Horse Farm

The grass is green, bright is the sun.
Come with me and we'll have fun.
Let's go riding for the day,
Through the fields of golden hay.
Sunny day and nice cool breeze,
As we go riding through the trees.
Running, jumping through the fields,
Look at what good training yields.
Brown, and Roan, and Blazing White,
Others are as black as night.

Lori Danielle Thompson

"Island Dream"

Sun drenched sands
By oceans shore
Of natures loving gift
Sing of this forever more.

Listen as waves
With caps of white
Roll in and then return
Into the dark of night.

These things of beauty
Which are seldom seen.
Need not to us,
Be just a dream.

Let this tranquil island scene
Become reality for you and me.
For us to share and feel
To love and care—to need.

So dream no more, my love
For it will come to pass
For you and I, someday soon
This dream will last and last.

Ross Wilkey

Fate's Of State's

Man can't govern man
By the laws
Of man, alone

It's gotta be, from his home
More than fate, of state alone

There's gotta be an all mighty
Which ever face, you chose to see

Gotta be an end, to all the fighting
Get on with what we need

Forget all sorrow, pitty
For dreams that never came true

Hold hands, in earnest meaning
With friends whom you help, help you

More than the fate's of state's alone
It's gotta come, from the home

Can't govern
By the law
Of man alone

William Crowley

Night

A dull light of silver is caught
By the stillness of the night.
From the moon it is melted and wrought
To a sword that challenges a fight.

Glittering eyes of the night sky
Stares down in vigil.
The darkness echoing their silent cry
As they watch for their sigil.

Heavy black smothers the night
But allows beams to pass through
Of silvery color, the radiance of light
Until dawn rises and the day starts anew.

Peggy Ahn

Stalling For Fall

I love this quiet month we
    call October

When nature paints the hills
    with red and gold

And the busy growing season
    of the summer

Is winding down and
    finally placed
        on hold.

I like to see the piles
    of yellow pumpkins

When bounty of the year is
    gathered in

And know the inner joy of
    tasks completed

As apples and potatoes fill the bin.
I need this little pause between the seasons
To unbend before I set another goal,

To feel as peaceful as the sleeping garden,
This time of respite for the earth and soul!

Ruth Hunter

White Buffalo Calf

Will there be peace?
Can this white buffalo,
end our woe?
Will the wars cease?

There is a prophecy.
The white buffalo calf is a gift.
Our spirits to lift,
us and them shall be WE!

The calf is female,
it is very sacred.
It is said,
peace will prevail.

Her fleece of white,
as it shines in the moon,
gives us hope that soon,
We can make this world right!

Nancy Craig Scott

The Hunt

The throbbing vessels,
carry two lives,
as interconnected,
as husbands and wives.

The chase, the kill;
do they know what they want?
Or are they both trapped,
in some bestial haunt?

Who is the victor?
Why does he strut?
The magnetic attraction,
of the john and the slut.

The lions give chase,
very regal and proud.
The calves minds bleat,
but their screams are not loud.

They understand something,
these primeval beasts,
without all the bloodshed,
there would be no feast.

Stuart Long

If Only

If only I could run along and
cast out many doubts

If only I could stand the test to
see what life's about

If only I could mend the hearts
of all the ones untold

If only I could reach the souls
that need to be remold

If only during the test of time
I could relate to many matters

The pushers, the drug addicts and
all the baby chatter

If only I could play my role and
whisper a word so sweet
The hungry people would feel much
better and not left on the street
If only I could spread much love
and peace good will toward men
This world would be a better
place and I could be your friend.

Patricia A. Ford

No More Tears Past The Gates

Don't cry now mom
'Cause I now live in heaven
With a halo of gold
and wings of white feathers
I sing with the angels
And walk with the Lord
    Sleep on white cloud
        and fear no more
My body is well now
My mind is so bright
The pain is all gone now
    tears are forgotten

Kimberly Lussier

"Little Holland"

Clickity clackity
Chomp, chomp-chomp,
The shoes of Little Holland
Rattle the doorstep on top.

The windmills a turning
A raw wheated form,
Into a flour of pinwheel breads
For the cool winter storms.

Skating across
The interwinding ice,
The Little Holland of mischief
Enjoys the pinwheel prize.

Ricardo M. Mejia

Snowflakes

I like little snowflakes
    dancing in the air
Little white snowflakes
    in my curly black hair
Shiny white snowflakes
    zooming through the air

Some snowflakes land on my nose
    so cold on my tan little nose
They look so white
    sometimes I let out a fright!

Yikes!

Melody Michel

Untitled

Passages thru my veins
Clogged with cholesterol and care
Block the flow of life thru my heart
Bricks and suction cups are there
I - I have a red rose for you
The petals are as red as my blood
They lie moistened with dew
My sweat waters them for you
The thorns are so large - So sharp
    and pierce thru my sides
I swear that there is poison on them
I'm infected with love - like a virus
Makes me chilled on hot days
and fevers me on cold nights.

Mark F. OBran

Night Encounter - Dream Thing

The little doors I open wide,
Come — do what you will do, I call,
As I creep the long and musty hall.

I bid them out!
In the corridors of my mind,
What ghostly creatures do I find?

In this nothing land of in-between,
Awake - asleep?
What strange appointments I must keep.

Is this unreal, or truly real?
Am I alive or mostly dead?
As I lie drifting - drifting in my bed.

Virginia Alexander

Just Because

Just because I give you
    control
    of my life
    today,
    doesn't mean
    I will tomorrow.

Then sun may be shining
    in my face
    to light
    my way
    and I may not seem
    to need you at all.

But who's to say
    which day
    I love you
    the most.

Pearl M. Russom

Coast Guard Waves

Red glowing night
Cool summer water
Eroding dunes extending down the beach
Waves pounding close to shore
The curl, the motion, the flow
Dropping in, swaying to the movement
Smooth and wet
Shapings of watery thoughts curl
White water destruction
Loss of breath, loss of mind
Air
Black melted night
Sand between the toes
Animal nature collision pause

Mark Filteau

Babe

The only Rock in eternity I
could land on safely -
unconditionally - Babe.
"Point-your-toes", Babe.
My link with reality
with only goodness
My Theo - were I Vincent
Always there believing -
For one fleeting moment -
I have some worth.
Knowing of my death - 22 years
ago and my agony of
existing half alive
The one glimmering star
in a life time of darkness
My only dream
that never became a nightmare.

Mary Mullen

"Nightbreak"

Nightbreak
Darkness rises
Shadows wake
Evil guises

Gather round
In timeless flight
Knowledge found
In depths of fright

The misty glimmer
Of the moon
Black eyes flicker
Sense the doom

And thrice around
The ringless light
Wisdom crowned
Seal the night

Melissa Joy Bernstein

Untitled

Make every
Day a sunny
day, with all your
time in work or
play. Make time
to share with
someone sad, be
kind, be nice, be good and
glad. If you feel
lonely talk to a
friend, they'll listen
to you till the
end. So now you know
3 positive ways,
to make a new
friend everyday!

Tami Brehse

One More Time

Spring has come a million years.
Eyes have cried a million tears.
Breasts have heaved a million sighs.
Hands caressed a million thighs.
Love is still a word sublime,
So I must tell you one more time.
I love you.

William V. Rush

Shadows

Oh! What a dark
day with the stars
gleaming with a
gaze and the shadows
that are formed by
the moon,
The crickets sing
through the death of
the night and wolves
howling at the moon
ready to stalk their
nightly prey. Owooo!

Kenneth L. Davenport

Waltzing Into Eternity

Will you remember the
Desolation in her eyes
When she waltzed into eternity?
Can her voice still embrace
Even the blackest of souls
When she cries as a lover scorned?
Is she just a figment
Of some old forgotten love
Lost in the memories of days passed?
Will the wind whisper her
Name for eternity as
She walks amongst the angels above?
Can her touch bring you back
To those days of old when you
Danced amongst the fields so carelessly?
Feel the lonesome wind, a
Soft and gentle kiss upon
Your cheek, as you lie in fields of gold.
Love is never perfect-
Except for in our dreams.

Trevis R. Badeaux

Forgotten Thoughts

My memory escapes me
did you say that you love me?
My heart didn't hear
did you mean that you care?

You said that you touched me
but I didn't feel you
You might of reached me
but it wasn't real

I'd been watching you closely
but never saw you leaving
I'd been waiting here endlessly
just wanting to believe

You don't seem to remember
you could of forgot
When I said that I needed you
thought that I loved you.

Karen Clancy

"The Way It Used To Be"

On the table I lie,
experiencing a terminal sabbatical.
Holy, sacred and righteous
Full of life
Barely worn,
So forlorn,
The Holy Bible am I.

Karen M. Killen

Untitled

Are her kisses any sweeter
    Do you love her more than me
Have you told her all about us
    or how we used to be

With her, will you be honest
    and truthful from the start
Or will you keep on cheating
    and break another heart

Do you take her to the places
    you used to take me to
Do you find yourself repeating
    the things we used to do.

Questions without answers
    If ignorance is bliss
Then why is it so hard for me
    to cope with all of this.

Sharon Paula Ruiz Rogers

Dreams

Don't mind me,
Don't mind my dreams
Do mind these fights
You know I've fought like this before.
It's not quite what it seems
That's impossible to ignore.
Possible to do
It's understandable to be
Changeable every day,
And impossible to me.
Don't mind my dreams,
It's impossible to ignore,
But possible to do.

Otilia Amarandei

Beautiful Leaf

A beautiful leaf has fallen
Down from our family tree
Leaving her loved ones behind her
With only our memories.

Memories of when she was with us
Giving of self to us all
Always thinking of others
But beautiful leaves must fall.

That beautiful leaf was a treasure
One that we'll always recall
But it was the time and the season
For the beautiful leaf to fall.

It slipped away so quietly
Down from the family tree
To be gathered up at the Judgment
With God for eternity.

Lillian Price

Melodies

You entered my changing life with your
enchanting music.
And when the silver melodies fell from
your caressing fingertips upon the
rippling keys, the unguarded song within
my slumbering heart, stirred and
struggled to be free...
The temptation was too great to resist,
and I surrendered my song to you.

Terry Doty

Marble-ized

Outside of the schoolhouse,
Draw a circle in the clay.
Behind the teacher's back...
A game of marbles we would play.

Mibs: clayies, aggies, clearies
Lined up side by side.
Commies, cat-eyes, swirlies
Occasionally a rare sulfide.

A great American game
That one could really enrapture.
Keeping all the marbles
That one could skillfully capture.

Knuckle down, bony tight,
Shoot targets out of position.
The fun was in the conquest...
The excitement was in the acquisition.

William H. Haithco, Sr.

Terpsichore

Ballet in the warm, watery womb,
Drift in dreamy darkness.
Pirouette and plie, pierce the quiet -
Gasp for breath.

Join the promenade of pain and pleasure,
The arabesque of sorrow and joy.
Forward to the final fandango -
Your cold coffin cocoon.
Dance, butterfly spirit.
Trace the brilliant white light
In cadence with

The choreography of the universe.

Lydia T. Buckwalter

Chinese Spotted Dove

Into my garden
Drops a weary dotted dove
Eating seeds fallen

In quiet preserve
The hunter's son feeds the bird
Harvesting no more

Wild places gone
"Are you my long dead daddy?"
Roll, mobius on

Ron Wong

Memories

I wish that we could have known
each other better and had more time
to share.
Now my search for that special person
will be in Hawaii somewhere
I know that I will miss you, but
will you feel that same or is this a
fantasy or just a game.
Only if you knew that you're the
person I want.
You could take my heart, even
though, my heart has never been touched
Just to give you a picture of me
and one from you is a worthwhile
token. Memories are all that I
will ever have of you softly spoken

Michelle Wright

Hell As Pleasure

With midnights dew upon my lip
Early mornings mist doth drip
That gloaming cup is full of fire
I indulge to take a sip.
With starry nights fain to outshine
Initial dawn's tender vine
Evening sky is filled with marvel
Being teased with all divine.
With splendor upon such gracious hour
Highest peak of lust and power
Vision makes for pleasant time
I emulate sin and not the flower.

Mandy M. Hall

Darkness

The darkness around me
embraces me
restrains me with chains
these golden, dead and eternal chains
connected together in a mysterious code
of desperate cries and fear
Unable to be set free
to fill my lungs with air
a struggle against the angles
and the devils
cheering
and hopeless help
One breath
one candle being blown out
by the tempest
the terrifying tempest
and all turn black as ebony
an everlasting darkness.

Susanne Sondergaard

To Be Free

How like a prisoner is my soul,
Enclosed by bars made not of steel,
But of fears and doubts I conceal;
Their strength too great for my control,
How like a prisoner is my soul.

Oh, how I have longed to be free,
Like a bird who soars in the sky,
My soul with wings; could I then fly
From this cage? - At last, Liberty!
Oh, how I have longed to be free.

Lori Ann Nyce

Tears From Heaven

Every angel has to fly.
Every angel sits and cries.
Every tear that forms a
rain brings a clear day near.

Every loud thunder brings a
softer sound to your fear.
Every puddle that soaks the
ground brings a flower big and proud.
Even the lighting that strikes the
sky has a light in every eye.
The wind is strong and cold, but
warm and weak on different weeks.
The clouds so dark and gray
please tell us when the rain will
fade.
Every angel has a cry.

Tisa Shade

Unwanted

We don't want you
Everlasting nuisance
Go run far away
Go far from our eyes

We don't want you
Stupid little misfit
Go back where you came from
Go far from our eyes

We don't want you
Untalented freak
Go hide in the darkness
Away from our eyes

My heart is not extravagant
I do not wish for much
But I would gladly sell my soul
For an accepting touch
All I want is to belong
I want someone to say
Please don't turn and disappear
I want you here today.

Laura Gruber

Shadow Of The Eagle

Only yesterday,
Everything was
Bright.
But now the
Shadow of the
Eagle
Has brushed the face of
Night.
Strong wings
Gently glide,
To find and touch the
Places
Where we all must
Wait and hide.
Here, apart
And lonely,
Cowering inside.

Patria E. Danielson

Untitled

Fighting in my mind
Excuses right and left
All my doubts appear
Ruining chances—yet—

Coming from my soul
Often I will hear
Unexpected and sure
Reaching my heart's ear
Acceptance—as I am
God cares for me—
Even when I fail.

Karen R. McClellan

Untitled

Shattered dreams
Faded from the past
Come to me like whispers
That cast shadows from the mast
To few a sailor
On this torrent night
My skin has turned pallor
Now my soul can take flight.

Sharon Wavrunek

Illumination

A sparkle of light emerges.
Fascinated by the glow,
it grows and grows.

Touched by the brilliance of what
life holds; reaching for heights
no one knows............

A flame ignited.
Engulfing the masses beyond reproach.
So alive! Burning with great
momentum toward the realms
of enhancement.

Virginia Knowdell

(Gone)

For you nemesis
feelings fierce,
weathered, standing anchored
never growing their promise.

A lover's hope continued strong
while watching the shrinking
to a lesser,
a whisper.

There was a day to shout of joy,
sense timelessness
and magic
for those seedling desires.

The love yearned to soar
to find its boundaries.
Instead, it burrowed along the ground
a thin line, without words or sound.

Lily Sinclair

True Love

A shadow of fear
Fell across the land
As you are griped on the shoulder
By deaths bony hand.

The price of your love
Is a broken heart
For in the end
We learn that all must part.

But your love
Will never die
Though in a coffin
She does lie.

As lovers you were one
But now you are two
You tasted true love
But she wasn't meant for you.

She now lives in a
Much higher and grandeur space
But for you she will always have
In your heart a special place.

Sarah Lynn McGregor

Love

Love is like a flower,
First we plant the seed, it grows,
and we nurture it until it blossoms
into something that we'll cherish,
but once we neglect that flower,
it withers away, and dies.
Love is like a flower.

Wava T. Johnson

"A Poem For Aaron"

A great grandson, my very first
  Fills all my heart each hour.
We waited for him, as the spring,
  awaits the April Showers.

The softest cheeks, the darkest eyes,
  are beautiful to see.
And as I hold him close,
  I think, "How lucky can I be?"

This little one has brought to us
  a whole new world of joy.
We love each moment spent with him,
  our Special Baby Boy.

God granted me some extra time,
  and let me live to know.
A love as big as life itself
  on me He did bestow.

I don't mind growing old at all,
  I'd walk a lot of miles.
to see just one (or maybe two)
  of Aaron's big sweet smiles.

Virginia Carr

My Prayer For Peace Of Mind

Incredible sadness
floods my soul.
The lack of gladness
digging a hole
and dragging me in.

Unexplained tears
well up in my eyes.
Unfounded fears
darken my skies
weighing me down.

Heartache and pain
overwhelm my being.
I just can't explain
this sense of feeling
so all alone.

God, give me strength;
a measure of hope,
and shorten the length
of times I can't cope.
Lord, lift me up.

Maria Scholz

"My Kaleidoscope And Me"

Seas of emerald green.
Flowers of ruby red.
The sun glistening like a diamond,
Angels wings of silk
Silver stars that shine at night
White sand falling through an hour glass.
It's all the colors of my kaleidoscope.
Circling like the planets above
It all fills my heart with love.
To wish upon that shooting star
Winds that blow my kite so far
The moon so full it brightens the night
To watch the sunset into the sea.
All the colors of my kaleidoscope and me.

Samantha Racko

Cherry Blossom

The last spring blossom
fluttering in the breeze
lands in the river
and slides beneath the waves

Victor J. Haag

If I Were A Cloud

If I were a cloud,
Flying high in the sky,
I'd take you on,
The most wondrous
Of rides.
Just think of the places,
We could visit and see,
Oh! What a joy, it would be!

If I were a cloud,
Flying high in the sky,
We'd go to all the exotic places,
We've never seen.
We'd float high above,
The seven seas,
Oh! The fun, it could be!
If you'd like to be a cloud,
Flying high in the sky,
You need only to unite,
Your imagination with mine!

Lynne Louise Skinner

Life's Expectations

Would you forfeit your eyes
For a glimpse of a light
So pure it promises pain.
Should you feel cheated
If you got only night.
And as your keeper laughs
Would you cry
Or would you beg him to see it again.

Pete Necak

Visage

Shadows silently competing
For far too little
sacred space.
That long, slow curve
that begins just beyond the ear
working its way
to a refined, determined chin.
And eyes
beyond color
hiding
revealing
begging -
near laughter
near tears
pleading for hope.
A stray freckle
A hint of a grin
I'm almost afraid to blink.

S. Duncan Green

To God

God, the Creator of heaven and earth,
God, my Father, before my birth,
God, the Supreme, that dwells up above,
God, to you, I give my love.

Yvonne Clarke

Comparisons

Don't dwell upon your troubles,
For Father Time will heal
The heartache and unhappiness
That right now you may feel.

All life is full of ups and downs,
The best comes with the worst,
You cannot know true happiness
'Til you've known sadness first.

To know what's good there must be bad,
Take time to ponder that:
If everybody all were thin
Then no one would be fat.

There'd be nothing as "beauty"
If everything were plain;
We wouldn't see the sunshine
Unless we'd felt the rain.

So when you're on the bottom
And your teardrops fill a cup,
Remember that the only way
To go from there is UP!

Maxine Werber

War

They gave their lives
for glory,
or so goes
the story.

Those soldiers
fallen and lost,
a beach taken
how many lives the cost.

One ville
marked down,
how many dead
laying on the ground.

One more battle won,
another mother at home with one less son.

The battles through history
they are all the same,
the leaders(?) of our countries
must think war a game.

Kevin Price

Mother Earth

I stand here in Sadness
for I am ashamed
For the pain and destruction
We are to blame
We've used her, abused her
We've drained her dry
We've cut her and burned her
We've made her cry
She gave us all she had
every ounce of her soul
She fed us protected us
Sheltered us from the cold
Her beauty is timeless
We've used her in greed
She's old and she's tired
She need's comfort and peace
Our mother Earth
I love you so much
I wish I could give back
all that we've took

LaDena Davidson

My Sad Heart

Let me go my way,
for I have toil hard
and long.
My heart within,
its heavy load, I
bear it all.
Who dare to push me
farther hack.
Each step I have taken
it's not my own,
The master carries me,
He knows the sadness
in my heart,
and whole me always,
close in His arms.

Willie V. Rhodes

Thank You, Mom

Thank you mom
    For listening when others
    thought I had nothing to say.

Thank you
    For being there - helping me
    along the way.
You made me feel important
whenever I was down, I knew I
could depend on you to bring me
back around.
    For many reasons I love you mom
much more than I can say
I'm wishing you a special love,
On this, your special day.

Vicky L. Orr

Same Old Story

Looking, always looking,
For the dream that was once there,
Looking, always looking,
But finding it nowhere.

Searching, always searching,
In the darkness black as coal,
Searching, always searching,
In the shadows of ones soul.

Hoping, always hoping,
That it one day will be found,
Hoping, always hoping,
Yet speaking not a sound.

Living, always living,
Without thinking of remorse,
Living, always living,
Letting life run its course.

Accepting, finally accepting
Life, in all its glory,
Accepting, finally accepting,
It's all the same old story.

Tammy A. Gregg-Rabbitt

The Dive

Into the sea I am born
from a rocky perch
I commit myself
to her majestic splendor,
unimaginable depth and swift anger
into this I go,
more graceful than any bird in flight
transformed into a greater being,
held not by the bounds of gravity
but by the span of a single breath.

Richard Stein

The American Eagle

The mighty eagle flies
forever high.
With the wind beneath
his wings - he soars in the sky.
Looking down from above
he see's field of poppies,
glittering in the sun -
And he bends his wings,
and flying real low
He caresses each bloom
in the sun's afterglow.

Lidi Mary Kyle

Untitled

Forever in waiting
Forever in fear of feeling darkness
Your eyes dance unto me
(a light)
Love-Adoration-Kindness
Your words caress my mind
Feelings and emotions flow
Through my soul and inner being
You possess my every thought
My every word
Every spiritual being
Within me
Razes its guard
Allows you to come
Enter my soul.

Karen S. Capria

The Tree

Bare in Winter,
Forlorn and cold,
Decked with ice and snow.
Comes the Spring,
The warming sun,
Its buds begin to show.
Then in Summer,
All dressed up,
In leaves so proud and green.
Enters Fall,
With brilliant colors,
Prettiest hues ever seen.
The tree it speaks,
Without a word,
Its splendor can't be told.
As seasons change,
And years pass by,
Its story doth unfold.

Linda Weaver

Untitled

Just my friend
From the beginning to the end
More than friends
Never again

Your eyes were kind
But mine were blind
With love for you in my mind

I may never see your face again
But true love is from beginning to end
But only as a friend

Shannon Regan

Making The Garden

A battered straw hat
freckles your face in speckled shade
and you stoop,
slope-shouldered,
in the garden plot.

You embrace the rake
with loving, work-soiled hands
scoring grooves of passion
in the fertile earth.
The rounded rows lying
between your feet
are straight as an aisle in a cathedral.

You sweet-talk to your wedded tool,
enemy of the weeds,
engaging your lips and arms
in perpetual motion
in the dance of garden conception.

You goad the ground
and hack at wayward grass with a reli-
gious fury.
This surely is a prelude to your own
created Eden.

Marie Calame

My Dream

I dream often of a future
     free of drugs, violence, and war
A time when the rich
     share their wealth with the poor.
I dream often of a future
     that I can hold dear
Have a home and raise children
     and do this without fear.
I dream often of a future
     in which cures could be found
For the fatal diseases
     that plague the world round.
I dream often of a future
     in which all people join hands
To make a difference in the world
     and take a strong stand.
I dream often of a future
     where our efforts can be seen
That these things can be reality
     not only MY DREAM.

Wendi Hiller-Siemiatkoski

"Morning Freshness"

AWAKEN, taste morning
freshness, feel body
energy stretching;
see sunlight piercing
sight, bringing
daylight out of night.

HEAR noises stir
imagination, smell
fragrant blossom
scent; know beyond
mind thinking, God's
presence, freedom,
spontaneity, intuition.

ARISE, know faith
calls, gives today,
hope, love enough
for all; deeply
breathe morning
Freshness, God's
miracle, new life.

Lawrence London

Changes

Breaking away is so tough
From family, friends, and you
I will have to find the strength
It won't be easy that I knew

From laughter to friendship
I had it all in my hand
But I turned my hand over
Why I do not understand

Now all I hold
Is a memory of the past
But that is also leaving
From my mind very fast

I am starting all over
A brand new start
New people in my life
They play an important part

My new life I dream of
So wonderful and full of joy
Someone's given me another chance
And I feel like a newborn baby boy.

Kaustab Banerjee

Nightmare

She came to me in solitude
From out the night an angel fair
and smote me with a golden rood
And sweetly smiled at my despair
She stood above my narrow bed
As calm and bright as sunlit snow
Until I knew with sudden dread
That she was my immortal foe
I looked into a lovely face
That mocked me in my hour at need
And there no mercy could I trace
Nor in those eyes wise kindness read
I shuddered for the chill of death
Flowed from those smiling lips to me
And gasping wildly out of breath
I looked beyond the phantasy
Then one by one at last I broke
Those long confining prison bars
And from a troubled dream awoke
Beyond the threshold at the stars.

Pauline LeMarie

Winds Across Time

Through nights passing
from reality to death
Somber winds blow
Skipping from me to myself
Which am I? I do not know!

From the scraper-clad city
to the majestic desert
of my people
Somber winds blow
Am I woman? Am I love?
Which am I? I do not know!

Skipping from life to life
only my moccasins remain whole
And as somber winds blow
I ask: Cherokee, Comanche or Crow?
Which am I? I do not know!

Miranda Running Bear

The Escape

The blue blood crawls out
from the darkness.
The cruciating sensation oozes
from the depth of the inside.
The urge to remain heedless
confuses the mind.
The yearning to have the fortitude
of another
lies beyond the crooked smile.
The air so cold leaving the soul
to quiver,
The emptiness in the body
so overwhelming that,
As I fly from the reality you
can hear my heart
Lingering in the hollow
shadow
of what I'm leaving
behind.

Kerri McCloskey

Untitled

Oh heed me not
     from ye to beyond
I hate the threshold plex
     love/hate
     I can't go on with
     someone I ain't, how
     can you feed me? Not
     with that.
Humble pie I'm into love
The spiritual food awakening yes.
     Step inside my
     romantic
     barrier
fwe fwe fwe
          my
          mind.

Paul V. Stringer

Remembering

Standing here looking out my
     front door,
I can feel you walk up
     behind me.
I can feel you touch me, so
     soft and gentle.
I miss the nights spent in your
     arms.
The long talks, feeling safe
     and warm.
Remembering you is easy
Forgetting you is much harder.

Nancy Ihlenfeldt

Humarock

My skin tingles. The
     Frothy white sizzles and
     Fizzles clinging to arms,
     Legs, flattened hair in eyes.
Tilt my head,
     Shake away the water
     A bit of the confusion too,
     Look to see who's watching.
"Quick paddle."
     "Here comes another!"
I'm off.

William C. Cosgrove

Danmark

Barren trees for empty fools
Frozen ground under you feet—
Icicle tears in your eyes
Passing time telling lies.

Howling wind for noisy minds
The nebulae fill your head—
You wait until you can sleep
Counting secrets that you keep.

Passing trains for lost hearts
All the voices a foreign tongue—
Falling short of the ground
Your own terms keep you bound.

With all its life, there's death
No God does live here—
Nothing melts the living cold
Possessing power you can't hold.

Dark skies for blackened souls
Hovering over the kiosk—
Everything seems to pass you by
All alone, you wait to die.

Laura Kostka

The Living Dead

Those bright shining faces
full of smiles and cheer.
Are they real, or just a ploy?
Are people truly that happy,
or are they dead inside?
Acting out the roles,
feeling nothing deep down.
Are we mere machines,
our brains computer command?
Our feelings the push of a button?
Or maybe we are animals,
doing the tricks we are
trained to do.
Our reward being,
a little touch of life,
instead of just a bone.

Rae Ann Joy Jakubowski

Untitled

Beware Generation X
Get yourself a label
A pigeon hole
Define yourself
Quick
An image to conform to
An ideal to rebel against
Hurry
Politicians are discussing family values
This should scare you

Kathleen Lowe

Beyond

Because I was raised in a compound
guarded by memory, and
fenced in by intellect
Allow me the time to consider
my own reflection
So that when I turn my eyes toward you
I may ascend from this mesh of "isms"
to a place of transparent bonds
and one which is not fenced in.

Laura E. Winne

"You Are The One"

You are the one, I want to...

Devote myself to,
  Give myself,
    Care for you,
      Love you.

You are the one, who...

Holds my heart,
  Makes me happy,
    Fills me with desire,
      Leaves me weak,
        Makes me strong.

You are the one, I...

Dream about,
  Want to hold,
    To kiss,
      Spend my life with.

You are the one, who...

Holds the key,
  Keep my heart with you,
    Or set it free.

Susan Morgan

Definition Of Love

Love is a baby's smile
  Giving you their trust
Giving pleasure beyond measure
  Love is a baby's smile

Love is a lovers embrace
  Their eyes showing they know
No one will ever take their place
  Love is a lovers embrace

Love is giving, not always taking
  Giving support when needed
Showing you care, will always be there
  Love is giving

Love is sharing good and bad
  Helping with words or a touch
Ready to listen when eyes glisten
  Love is sharing

Love is when you give of yourself
  Giving confidence when needed
Lending a helping hand, helping others stand
  LOVE IS LOTS OF THINGS

Laura A. Jackson

To Meriam

Here in Peaceful Silence
God's wonders all around,
filling our heart with happiness,
with the blessings that here abound.

A tender breeze among the trees
our camp fire all aglow.
Hours of tender music
from our little radio.

The memories of the water
where we paddled our canoe,
our visit to the Island,
cool water, blue sky, me, and you.

A weekend to remember,
with hundreds more to share.
You've made my life so wonderful
none other can compare

Ralph

"Letting Go"

Seemingly endless
goes year after year,
growing are the little ones
you hold so dear.

It's terribly hard
you already know,
saying, "Good-bye"
and letting them go.

With a very big heart
and a smile on your face.
You know God is with them,
as they find their own place.

Reminiscing the past
with a contented deep sigh,
the flickering images
of days gone by.

Linda M. Barr

Wild River

Wild river running free
going on into the sea
rushing wildly on and on
never creeping, never sleeping
giving no moment to reflect
in waters that never collect,
but travelling forward through valleys,
hills and canyons, here and there
run free wild river
let not you die out, or slow down,
let nothing of man or nature
block you or deter you,
hear yourself roar like a
charging lion, see yourself
glitter like a flood of wet light,
feel yourself rushing on into the night.

M. L. Baker

Stepping Out

Stepping out this morning
Going places
Been out - Going home.
Stepping out this evening
Going places
Been out - Going home.
Out and Home
Home and Out
What's out is home.
What's home is out.
It's crazy, but it happened.
Don't know why
That's just the way it is.

Lynne E. Adams

Sally Sells Sea Shells

She's standing there
Gold luminescence off her hair
Small toes in the sand
Bare fingers in the sea

Radiant with an archaic smile
She's engrossed by the wonder
Free from evil and bile
Balanced without being under

Gravely she will lose her spirit
Become part of the compact majority
Into which she will solicit to fit
Absent of concrete authority

Patricia Lordi

The Splendid End

A spark ignites orange.
Gold flames leap to red.
Purple fingers flicker dark
Then bright.
Shadows pulse
Tumble
Scream pink.
Buildings kindle
Air crackles
People stare.
At last
Gray haze wastes away.
Blaze dwindles.
Embers grow ruby
Then sooty.
The world
Dies.

V. R. Roadifer

Tomorrow

Where have all my tomorrows gone?
Gone away with the dreams of youth.
Yesterday there were many,
Today there are so few.
If dreams were rekindled,
would tomorrows renew?

Robert C. Newsom

The Butterfly

The butterfly and its beauty
grace the land of earth -
Let not its heart be burdened -
It's gentle from its birth.
He flies with grace and
courage and leaves no fold
unturned. He circles
his inner beauty for us -
so we must learn - that
just as the butterfly
graces the earth -
God in heaven gave us
   birth.

Kriscinda Bailey

Burial

The open grave,
Gray casket
Carried solemnly
in place.
It is so final.
Alone, desolate,
grief choked
I watched,
listened with
deaf ears
As I heard,
"dust to dust"
committed.
To the cold earth.
Numbly I moved
to go, tell me it
Isn't so; No! No!

Mildred Jacobsen

Beautiful Night

Beautiful stars bright and bountiful
Grey, glowing, gloomy, beautiful moon
Shining, shimmering, slippery, sand
Streaming through my fingered hand
Crickets creeping, crawling, cheeping
Woof whinnying, wielding, wailing
Word whispers, wanders, and winds
All along the long hillside
Hoot owl hoot, hoo, hoot, hoo
Birdie hiding, confiding
In her nest, the best, the rest
All around are unseen guests
Beautiful night, bright and bountiful

Quientana L. Avery

Our Love

Our love is like a flower.
Growing more beautiful with each day.
May the good Lord shine upon us.
And show us the way.
May he let us grow old together.
To live and love each day.
For our love is like a flower.
Growing more and more each day.

Nora D. Oller

The Lonely Isle

Farewell, lonely isle at twilight.
Guard well my little love.
May the Good Lord watch o'er him
With his Angels from above.

We'll be together again some day
And you'll perch on your little shelf.
There'll never be one to take your place,
I'll wait for your own dear self.

So dream sweet dreams, my little love
And we'll meet again, I pray
And goodbye to the lonely island
Where you'll sleep till that happy day.

Rose Loewinger

Rekindled

How could it be that I, secure
Had let it happen? Smashing all
Those promises self-made, so sure
My battered heart would not recall
Memories now bittersweet. Dare
I even say aloud his name.
All letters charred. No more to share
That private joy I now disclaim.

Yet still his teasing voice I hear
Inside me, saying secret things
That wipe away my cobweb fear
And keep my mind remembering.
With doubts consumed, this fire in me
Declares the flame, rekindled, free

Milly Steele

"Solitaire"

The loneliest game for the crying man...
He hides within the hearts
But is covered by the spade.
The King overpowers him
And he is forced back into darkness.
Solitaire draws him back to the game
And he is lost within the shuffle.

Vicky Keeran

Rain

Rain is the drip-drop you
hear during a thunder-storm
Rain can make mud today
That is where the children play
Rain is not quite understood
Rain is bad and good
God wiped out the world with Rain
You can grow food with Rain

Nicole Eichenberg

Safe In God's Arms

If I'm, sick, or hurting at all,
He'll be there with open arms.
I'd fall down to the ground,
He'll pick me up out of harm.
I could never hurt anymore,
Because His spirit lives in me
for-ever-more.

Just like in the past, God takes
All the hurt and sorrow away.
If you need a friend, Jesus is there.
Don't worry, do not despair.
Just call on Jesus' name,
And nothing will be the same.

Look toward the Eastern sky
where the white doves fly. That's
where you'll find Him just lift your
hands high. And praise God Almighty
Cause He's the one who makes me see
The crippled walk again, and took away sin.

Cause with Jesus, you're safe in His arms.

Thomas N. Hamby

A Teddy Bear

A teddy bear is fun to squeeze.
He'll never cough,
he'll never sneeze.

He'll sit on a table.
He'll sit on a chair.
Don't give him a haircut,
he never grows more hair.

He has button eyes
and short snout nose.
He has no shoes
and no sets of clothes.

Mine went with me into surgery.
That showed he cared.
They even bandaged his ear.
He said he wasn't scared.

He never asks for gum
and not once for candy.
Just keep yours by your side.
He might come in handy.

Raymond L. Wells

Untitled

Zhengzhou, Chaos, Flattery
How happily the bird sings
For ignorance is its bliss
It worries not the human worries
And concerns itself in feeding

Cities, Patterns, Impressions
The human spirit cannot be defined
But when in doubt, look at bird
And know that life is simple
Though not always kind.

Tom Lenius

The Beginning

I'm lost in a dark cave
help me
I see a growing light
help me
walls suffocate and surround my body
help me
everything stops, everything is done
thank you for helping me.
I hear the sound of a beautiful voice
singing
a soft whisper
shhhh
it's okay now
I'm safe
a crystal waterfall beholds nude dancers
I enter the sea of love
sudden rush
laughing
happiness
true bliss is mine
Liz McGoun

She Drinks Midnight

Like ivy
her supple vines wind and climb,
my back and limbs
a trellis.
Her foliage spreads,
gentle leaves upon my cheek and chest,
inviting the moon.
She drinks midnight
slowly,
as if no one watches.
Stacy Handelman

Untitled

The man is in his 40's
he's been around for a while
we all know his face
we all know his smile
we all know OJ

Now he is in trouble
fighting for his life
did he commit the crime
did he use the knife?

His children have no mother
and he is in jail
the public is confused
while OJ sits — no bail

He probably dreams of running
the length of the football field
now only his mind can travel
because his nightmare is real

What will happen to OJ?
Marilyn Anita Harris

Over The - Shoulder - Spy

Gossip flows through my veins,
I listen intently for interesting bits
of information. Pretending to be
fascinated with my novel my shoulders
are privately hunched over: My ears
are open, my eyes alert, and my
mouth is savoring the replies of
malicious retorts. For I am the
Over-the-shoulder spy.
Marie Shin

World Without Walls

Look for the Forest
Hidden behind trees

Love sometimes bound
in ropes of humility

Reality can grow
in a field of dreams

Where cries are heard
beneath faint screams?

Is this freedom
chained to irony?

Not a house is built
on foundations of fear

Not a city of salt
melting at the touch of a tear

Nor a nation of hearts
turning blacker each year

In unity we'll rise
"There is hope for us all"

To Truth, To Life
To a world without walls.
Tom Fitzgerald

Chance Meeting

What is it that
hides from us
the things we
ought most
to know?
We live amongst
miracles.
Where past and
future meet.
And where a chance
meeting has the
power to change
the world.
DJ Lee

Rational Time

The white brick wall I sit upon
High up on the hill
The Hill of peace
Where the whirling
Craziness of my thoughts
Is calmed by a rational voice
That relaxes my fears
Soothes my pain
Makes me an angel
At peace with the sky and Earth
So I can once again
Rise up
And go to conquer the world
With its limits
Beyond rationality
Kory Bergman

An Inscription To Stephen

Whilst among the quiet flays
I saw a very crow
flight above the fallen trees
upon a breast of snow.
"Tis hardly black," an old man sees
"to go against the flow."
Laura Renee Hogan

Out Of Tune

"Hit just ain't no use," he sighed,
  His face was one huge frown.
"I just ain't in tune myself,"
  And he laid the fiddle down.

Fiddles may be in perfect pitch.
  And sound well to the ear...
But if the player's not in tune.
  He just don't want to hear.

When life seems so discordant,
  And troubles pile up to soon.
Maybe life's not sharp or flat...
  It's the soul that's out of tune.
William D. Gilmer

Monty

I have a dog
His name is Monty
He sleeps just like a log

He wags his tail when he is happy
He barks when he is sad
and he never appears to get mad

He eats his little doggy food
and then he begs for mine
He gets in a bad mood
If I don't give it to him in time

I pick him up
and hug him a lot
I love my little tea cup pup!
Teila L. Millner

The Eternal Sea

Foam crested waves dash on the shore,
Hostage to moon, a ceaseless roar
Restless, the endless billows came
Constant, they always look the same.
High tides crash o'er a sandy dune,
The beach lit by a waning moon.
Wind and storm raged, their frenzy spent
Upon dead trees whose limbs are bent,
Victim of storm and ruthless tides
As a hurricane o'er them rides.
Laura T. Lejeune

Prison Song

I sit here alone,
  Hour upon Hour;
In this cold, lonely Prison
  with vine covered towers.
I see so many problems,
  I see so many tears;
Your loved ones forget you
  You're alone with your fears.
All you have left
  are your hopes and your dreams,
The rest of your world
  falls apart at the seams.
You have one thing to look forward to,
  one certain Day;
You forget how to laugh
  you forget how to play.
I sit here alone,
  Hour upon Hour;
In this cold, lonely Prison
  with vine covered towers.
F. Joann Durio

Untitled

How can I let this happen?
How can I unclasp my hand from yours
    and let you just walk away?
Must the strength come
    from my love for you?
Must that feeling I so cherish
    be drained in such a way?
That which was so good to me
    has turned on me,
And now, as it once brought me such joy,
    it brings me much despair.
My eyes close so as not to see you go.
My tears wash away my smile,
But the strength was there
    and my hand did let you go.
It is not to you I whisper goodbye.
My goodbye is to that
    we could not attain.

Shada Johnson

Nelda and Howard

He misses her.
    How could he not,
    When even birds have stilled
        their song,
    Who wait outside at dawn
    And listen for her bid to
    Come and feed
    And share the sunshine of her day.
And yet, he doesn't miss her.
    How could he,
    When every dawn brings on its
        breath
    A presence so like hers,
    A waiting on some deed of love.
    or music to be sung —
    He breathes that breath
        and lifts on wings,
    To share the suns of all her days.

Virginia L. Edwards

The Plan

The surest way that we can know
how God meant us to live
Is if we fall along the way
Or have cause to forgive.

We've had to know of aching hearts
And spent sometime alone
And carried someone else's load
Had hope when hope was gone.

You have to know some pain, some joy
And keep your spirits high
Trust in the Lord with all your heart
And be prepared to die.

The golden rule was meant for all
To thine own self be true.
The one who watches over all
Is watching over you.

Willie Jean Hull

Something Fell

I see raindrops on the ground
I see them fall and make a sound
They fall like maidens on a wing
Whisping past the soul of me
They cut through trees and flowers too
To watch them fall will make you see
Just what tears were meant to be.

Natalie Buss

My Old House

Old house of my memories
How I remember thee
With holes around the floor
And raindrops through the zinc.

Many times I looked at the mirror
Many times I always dreamed
That I was queen of the fairies
And my husband was a king.

Pictures all over the wall
Pictures of mountains and hills
Pictures telling me the stories
Of the things that I could reach.

Today many days later
And far away from my ground
I can't forget all those years
In my beautiful old house.

Maria T. Santiago

Always In Pain

I can't get my life on track.
How I wish he would come back.
I loved him so much,
Why did he go?!
How much he hurt me,
He'll never know.
I can't forget him,
I can't let him go.
His memory haunts me,
Wherever I go,
He's always on my mind,
He's always in my heart
I wish I could take back the day,
That he broke my heart.
I feel empty and all alone,
I want him back as my own.
But he had it all planned
He thought he was so clever
The only thing he wanted,
Was to hurt me forever.

Shelly Hollabaugh

Be

Chill little birds sit
How that tree breathes its last breath
Oh - sun smile on dark

Say it till the end
The snake crashed on my sofa
Knew my minds thinking

Cute little words said.
Makes my stomach twitch - eyes ache.
Turns it all around.

What's it all about
Oh - bite the dust, my dumb phrase
Chuckle your head off

One day I found it
For your head to be placed in
Nope! - did not fit - crash!

Say good-bye my friend
I'm lost again for now - once
Sit on your toenail

Viviana Caratachea

Fall

Already the leaves are homeless again,
huddling in piles under bridges,
stumbling from doorway to doorway.
They scatter through the streets
sounding like the chattering of teeth
or the clatter
of this old typewriter.
Deep in the yard now, deep as
discarded poems littering my floor,
they blow like vagrant children,
trunk to trunk, wondering
where they belong.
They are waiting,
waiting in parks and under benches,
waiting for the snows
to push them into the earth
where by spring they will have found
their homes
in the roots of budding trees.

Rebecca Balcarcel

Untitled

I'm fake-
hypocritical-
I do things I say not to-
I lie about everything
to my mom and family-
and I pretend
and they believe
no one knows how I am-
I'm confused about life
and how I act-
I don't understand
why I'm so afraid
to just be me
and why do I care if
they get mad
and just go along with their
petty games?-
I don't know,
I guess I'm
just human-

Rebecca J. Cass

The Guardian

Do you feel me near you
    I am always here...
To wipe your tears of sorrow
    and let you know I care...
Do you sense my love
    surround you...
Do you know I'm always
    near...
To hold your hand and help
    you through the hurt of
    many years...
Do you feel my arms enfold
    you...
As they did when I was
    there...

Kathryn J. Mezo

Father God

Father God in Jesus name,
I need a Miracle today.
Hear me Father as I pray,
If not only for this day.
Father God in Jesus name,
Only for my Miracle I shall pray.
Father God in Jesus name
I got my Miracle it is this day.

Marion Hitsman

Venus And Earth

Everyday, everyday, everyday
I awake and return to sleep
and dream of a yak
yellow and brown in the
celestial sun heavenly
warm and furry
empty eyes glistening
Running, running, running
through great fields of
lush grass where the tiny inhabitants
stare up at the saint-like body
approaching
and they watch in wonder
as it seemingly floats over their world,
ever so closer to the sun than they are.

Michael Butler

Best Friend

Kneeling at the altar
  I bare it all.
My pain and sorrow
  I lived the fall.

But it's time to rise above
  and start a new.
I'll walk in the right direction
  with the skies so blue.

I will see more bad times
  but I can work them through.
I'm going to hold onto my dreams
  and think of you.

One day I will be back
  kneeling at the altar once again.
I will pray to my only God
  my only Best Friend.

Samantha A. Greer

Last Night...

Last night,
I came close to death
At least I thought I did.
I hurt so bad
Life became irrelevant
Movements became mechanical
Feelings were demolished.
Last night,
I thought I would die.
You laughed at me
When the pain was unreal.
You abandoned me
In the midst of a raging sea
You pushed me off
An endless cliff
Last night,
I thought it was over
But today,
I live to tell you
I survived.

Sandra R. Johnson

A Real Sweet Friend

Although I had never met you,
  I feel like I've known you
  for a long time.
All I've heard were sweet things
  about you.
You make your friends feel so good.
You seem to understand us, when
  no one else does.
You're someone who is truly glad
  for us, when things are
  going well.
You're always there to listen.
You're a very special friend.

Peggy Jannick

When I Think Of You

When I think of you,
I feel the rainbow against the
grey and purple sky,
I feel the bright and shiny
twinkling stars up so high,
I feel the soft clouds
wondering above the sea,
I feel the sweet coolness
of the mid-winter breeze,
I feel the morning mist
in the early autumn days,
I feel the sweet laughter
on a pretty little girl's face,
I feel the fragrance of the
fresh flowers,
the precious gift of God,
the spring season,
I feel the sweet love within my
heart to carry on.

Shireen Dianne

Womanhood

Today I felt a breeze
I fell down on my knees
I got so confused
I came up with a bruise

Could it have been an Earthquake?
Or have I made a mistake
I need to know the truth
Is my name really Ruth?

They say I'm not really sick
Was that me who threw that brick?
Thank God I'm not a boozer
Then I'd be a real looser.

Today I really feel strange
Why do things have to change
I try to do the things I should
And now I'm coming into womanhood.

Patricia Butler

Within

Amidst a maelstrom of love and hate;
I stand
Whipped about endlessly, by insult
and soothing word.
Drowning in a dark sea;
no sight of land.
Above the idle chatter, my council
not heard.

Shane Strait

"Twice Upon A Time"

Once upon a time
I fell in love
But it was always me
That I was thinking of

I hurt you—I know
There's nothing I can say
Except I'm sorry
Today and everyday

I've learned just how much
You do mean to me
Because I love you
I'll set you free

Your happiness is what
I really care about
Will you ever trust me?
Will there always be doubt?

Twice upon a time-I fell in love
Twice I blew it
Maybe it's your world
And I'm just passing through it...

Paula Kay Cholewa

I Remember This Day

I remember this day.
I felt it eons ago.
As life is forever the same
It is forever changing.
I am not still.
Silently I am moving
With the vibrations of life.

The buds and blossoms remember this day.
They felt it eons ago.
Baring fruit upon branches,
A part of the tree and bush,
Glimmering in sunlight and dew.
Eventually falling to caress the earth
Only to bloom anew.

We remember this day.
For I have nourished the everlasting blossom,
And it has nourished me.
We are all part of each other in all life,
And we remember this day, eons ago.

Renne Rhae

Mesa

I am a mountain.
I have emerged
From the earth's recesses.
Thrusting upward, skyward,
I stand lofty, serene, eternal
Through the eons.
Stark monolith, I am;
Weathered and seared
By the elements - sun, wind, rain;
And tempered by time.
Restless? Not I.
In stark magnificence,
I stand; a lonely sentinel
In the barren wasteland.
I am a guardian of earth's mysteries.
I am a repository of eternal truths.
The world will come, therefore,
And look upon my curious brow;
And be uplifted
By my towering spirit.

Winifred Evans

Different Eyes

Through the golden fleece of time
I have seen and wished they were mine.
All the chests with rusted keys
Which now hold only memories.

Shadows now the presence casts
Nothing ever really lasts.
Today's tomorrows will soon arise
I'll see today through different eyes.

Now, today in all I do
My eyes still will watch for you.
Though different eyes see you from afar
My eyes behold thee, morning star.

Different eyes will thy glory see
Till the dawn keeps you company.
Some may turn away from you
Different eyes with shades of blue.

When at last I find my sleep
Nothing earthly shall I keep.
Dreams will end and memories fade
Yet I shall reap the light of day.

Melanie Lynn Hounshell

A Dream Come True

How it all happened,
I haven't a clue.
I turned and there you were,
Dropped from out of the blue.
It was just like a dream to me
That somehow came true.

Someone I can love — finally!
I'm living out my fantasy!

When life throws a fast ball
You never turn your back or flee.
You help me up when I fall,
You take good care of me.

You're always right by my side
Even when things go wrong.
You're always there to hold my hand,
Your love makes me strong.

I know that you love me
And I don't even know why.
But I know I will be here for you
'Til the day that I die!

Nedra La Shawn Jennings

Dandelion Tears

Lying awake
I hear the rooster crow
I dress quickly
Before the mist returns to vapor
Dandelions
Weighted with tears
Why are they sad
Weeping in the morning
They know death follows rain
Dandelions
Fear it most
The Plague of Hands
Dandelions
Knowing death will soon follow
Watering weeds is foolish
They perish
And are not

Missed.

Maria L. Jonas

I Need You

"Who needs you?"
I heard myself say.
I didn't want God and
I didn't want to pray.
I thought I was old enough
to be on my own,
so much I thought I had known.
Too young to be alone,
but old enough to hold my own,
I opened my eyes in the middle
of despair
and saw you standing there.
With open arms
so full of love
you cradled me just like a dove.
Forgiving me from the bad
I had done,
Forgetting all the pain I caused,
your love for me has never paused.

Rene Sherrod

Missing You

Missing you
I hold myself
'til the early morn.

Time goes by,
Autumn leaves they fall
Upon my crying eyes.

Into the whispering wind
My mind follows
Searching for you.

I walk alone
Along our favorite path
Wishing you were here.

Now I see
As I look down
You are in peace.

Your spirit flies away
To another place
Now I dance alone.

Raman Jayapathy

Honest Feelings

on the day I saw you,
I hoped that you'd be mine;
And with each passing day
I hope it's only matter of time.
Til that day I guess that
I'll just wait around and see;
If by any chance
You might feel the same of me.
Other guys may come and go,
Young loves usually don't last long:
But for guys like you
The feelings' always burning strong.
Other girls may tempt you
With their fast and phony plays:
But me, I guess I'm just to real
To try those put-on ways.
So if the day should ever come
That you would turn to me;
I hope it would be for just myself,
Not for something I couldn't be.

Marla Mounts

I Love You ...

I love you, you know it
I hurt you, I'm paying for it
So many times I've fallen in love
So many times I've been hurt
You warned me once, but I didn't listen
You warned me twice, but I didn't care
The Gods unleash their rain
Or thousands of peoples pain.
It rains down upon my soul
Maybe you don't believe me,
Maybe you don't believe my sincerity
Because I don't cry outwardly
But I can cry no more
No more tears are left in me
I'd do anything and give everything
to have your love returned to me
I love you, I want you, I need you,
Please forgive me and please come back
I need you more then every breath,
I'd give anything, even death.

Randi Burton

He Cares

When morning comes and I'm awakened
I know He really cares for me
When shadows flee behind the dawning
It's then His Beauty I can see
He kisses flowers with His sunshine
Waters trees with morning dew
He tends the Robins and the Sparrows
Listening till their songs are through
Ever watching o're His children
Carefully planning out their day
Waiting gently for their asking
So He can lead them on their way
Caring if they are in trouble
Or if they have some heavy load
It's He who has the strength to carry
Anything down life's long road
Knowing that He cares so deeply
With tender love He understands
Lets me know that my tomorrows
Are secure in His great hands

Pepper Beard

Nature's Walk

While walking through the forest near,
I lay aside my thoughts and fears
And know that my God is near.
I listen to the sounds of songs,
The creeping things that crawl and roam.
I smell the moose so fresh and sweet
And pick the flowers near my feet.
While looking to the bright blue sky,
I see the birds that fly near by.
As the wind comes breezing through,
I blink my eyes for another view.
Pulling my hair from my face,
I felt a strength of loving grace.

Nanette Black

Sounds Of The Morning

When I awake each morning,
I lie there for a spell
And listen to the sounds of the morning
And each has a story to tell.

The clickety-clack of the freight train
As it lumbers down the track,
Loaded with cars for New Orleans
To unload and hurry back.

The ole hoot owl screams in the dawning
From his hollow in the tree.
He's so happy the night is over
And is getting so sl-e-e-py.

The plant whistle is blowing,
Calling its employees to work.
Better hurry and punch the timeclock.
No payday if the work you shirk!

Thank you, Lord, for your watch-care,
You've given me another day.
Help me to be worthy of your blessings,
As I quietly kneel to pray.

Lorene Duncan

To All The Ones I Will Leave Behind

Don't cry for me
I must leave you now
For I have chosen a different path

Don't think of me
As what I have done
But who I am and what I will do

Don't talk of me
As if I am gone
I will always be part of your life

Don't forget me
When I'm out of sight
I shall always be inside your mind

Don't count me out
When you need me most
I will never be out of your reach

With love from me
This is what I give
To all the ones I will leave behind

Ryan Kihn

When I Was Young

When I was young
I owned the world
It all belonged to me
The corner of the dark - red house
A yellow tree
The street in quiet dusk
With lights to see
The world was mine
It all belonged to me

Now in later years
I know, and knowing, grieve
The world is theirs
These younger, greener people
Climb the stairs
Into the dark-red house
For food and prayers
They own the house, the tree, the dusk
The world is theirs

Naomi Greifer Rubin

The Monster Under My Bed

There's a monster under my bed.
I pulled the covers over my head.
I tried to reach the light.
But it was not in sight.
His eyes were big and round.
His hair was bright and red.
I couldn't even move.
I sat there in my bed.
I looked under my bed
and my red teddy bear
was sitting on my sled.

Nicole Barr

I Love

I love her beautiful hair,
I really do care.

I love her blue eyes,
I won't tell any lies.

I love her luscious lips,
And the way she move her hips.

I love her bodacious body,
No she's not naughty.

I really love her,
And I would die for her.

Richard Parks III

Untitled

When I think of you
I see a special person
the Lord gave me.

No matter what we do
or what we say
you love us anyway.

You smiled with us
you laughed with us
and when we cried,
I could see the tears in your eyes

You always made a big fuss
because you were so proud of us.

I am glad the Lord
picked you for us
Because Grandparents
are a must.

With our love we give to you
and we know you love us too.

Kim Lovett

Looking Through

Looking through the trees
  I see the clouds.
Looking through the clouds
  I see the space.
Looking through space
  I see the sky.

Looking in the clouds
  and in the sky
I see angels faces
  looking up.

Maria del Pilar

I Miss You

I miss you when,
I see something funny.
I miss you when,
I am sad.
I miss you more and more when,
I realize I miss you less and less.
You could always make me
smile.
You could even make me
mad.
But you were always there.
When you died, I felt empty.
But I knew you were still there,
somewhere.
At times I think,
"She would of liked that."
But you are gone,
and with you a piece of my heart.

Mary Margaret Derryberry

I Will Not Trespass

While there are some years
I shall try another road
but I will not trespass.
Outside
looking in
I never did belong.
I was a rare bloom.
Perhaps
a weed.
Before I wither
I shall say,
"Goodbye."
Cautiously
I will walk
the other road.

Mary Spurrier

Still Dancing

You swirl with grace as the music plays.
I sit and watch.
Even when the record stops,
your melody stays.
And you are still dancing.

I can see you like yesterday.
I feel your life and love.
The echoes of your laughter
have never died away.
For you were still dancing...

On that day I said goodbye,
I felt myself go numb.
For I could still see you,
and I knew you'd never die.
For you were still dancing...

Even now I'd feel the tears.
But I'd sit there and listen,
For deep within myself I know,
That it's your song I hear.
For you are still dancing...

Leah Rushefsky

A Mother's Fantasy

I come home from work
I sit in my chair.
My body is here
My mind is elsewhere.
High on a cliff top
I quicken my pace.
His lips on my hair.
His breath on my face.
Excitement is soaring
As I fly through the air.
The feel of his being
It's everywhere.
The sense of my wonder
so light and so free.
My past is so vivid
My present, far from me.
A shake on the shoulder
"Hi Mom, it's me."
Back to the present
And into reality.

Valerie J. Huff

The Mirror

Yesterday
I smiled
A boy grinned back at me
Familiar face
But as I turned to go
I glimpsed something new
A deepness
A definition
It was hard for me
To notice the man
In the face
That used to be a boy.

Konrad Peters

"Scared Of Love"

Once I felt a deep love
I thought nothing would
ever make us part.
But time and distance
took their toll.
That love left.
I find that love
now slowly returning
to me.
But now I find
that I'm scared,
scared of love.
The leaving of that love
hurt me deeply
That hurt is what
makes me
scared of love.
Scared of the hurt,
Scared of the pain,
Scared of the love.

Mirjam Troesch

Incarnation

I witnessed
your mother's petals opening around you
the day you dawned
dusky blue, cloud pink, sunlit by the second
through your indignant squalls

Your rosy brilliance
filled up the room
overtook my breath
while God's handservants,
absurd in their attempts
to be equal to you,
bustled and scurried,
attending as you made your choice
to grace us with your day   .
or return to your realm of unbloomed dark.

Standing in streams of blood and water,
shaking like a virgin
I dared to touch your mother's hand,
felt my knees fail and bowed my head
bathed in light commanding genuflection.

Bronwyn Anne Best Jardin

"Homecoming"

Every time I count my blessings,
I recall my country home,
My Mama and my Daddy
Who still live there all alone.
They've been so happy there
As the years have come and gone
And I thank The Lord
For the lives they've touched
And the love that they have shown.

Daddy's sitting on the front porch
Watching for the children to come home
Mama's in the kitchen
Cooking something special for everyone
They're both praying
That it won't be very long
Till we're a hugging and a kissing
And a reminiscing
And the kids are all back home.

Doris Evans

The Farm

I walk outside to let the horses graze,
I remember riding on warm, summer days.

As I walk to the shed,
I hear geese overhead.

Dogs bark across the road,
Trucks drive in for pigs to load.

I enjoy the farm whenever I can,
Because I am back in school again.

We play in the corn,
And come home with clothes torn.

I remember we used to run and play,
Sometimes we would run all day.

The farm is the best place to be,
Come on over and you'll see!

Danielle Brandts

Me

Across the field
I see him running
With his dog
Hard at his heels
An old straw hat
And bare feet showing
A string of fish
Caught at the mill
As he approaches
To my surprise
I can't believe
Just what I see
For underneath
That old straw hat
The boy I see
Is really me

Billy E. Denman

Sad Songs

In passing
I slowed my pace
To hear someone singing
Then I saw your face.

You smiled
Then sang your sad songs
I stopped for a while
Your influence was strong.

Your voice rang out
Your feelings within
Your face showed your doubts
The battle you were trying to win.

If I were never to see your face
Or hear your voice again
I would remember when I slowed my face
To hear the songs of a friend.

Carol A. Cottle

Untitled

While walking down the beach,
I stopped to watch the sea,
It whispered and it giggled,
And said many things to me,
It finally said with all its might,
You're wasting all your time,
You have so little left to use,
And you must begin to climb,
I finally realized it was right,
And then began to walk,
Down the beach toward who knows what,
And the sea no longer talked.

Jay Berkowitz

To Sight Judge

Do you know me
I think not
So why do you judge
You look, you see
Are you sure you're right
If you're wrong then you lose
because you'll never know

Brian Fargnoli

Missing You

It's been a while since I've seen you last.
Although many, many months have already past.
I'll do my best to write and send you money.
No matter what you'll always be my heart, my honey.
Still today I wish you where here.
Better still I'd rather be there.
And I do know now, I'll never drink another beer.
I tried to write you a long, long letter.
Then I thought a poem be better.
I'll try to write about how I feel.
Never again will I steal.
I'll always have you on my mind.
Because a daughter like you is one of a kind.
Even though I see you only once in a while,
It makes my day to think and see your smile.
I'll end this poem with a kiss
To let you know, it's you I miss.

Lawrence Long

Silent Grief

Silent grief swells inward more
As happiness dances upon a distant shore.

A shore oddly within one's grasp -
Love escaped from a desperate clasp.

Come, let's skip across a friendship's grave;
No dual effort for it to save.

And as we dance, oh, do pretend
That this superficial imposter is a beloved friend.

Callous knife dripping with blood from the heart,
As paths hasten to permanently part.

Treasure fond memories - no more in store -
As silent grief swells inward more.

Kari R. Mack

Drop

My tears fell to the ground;
As I thought to myself, "He's gone!"
How I loved him and then I lost him;
What was I to do without him to protect me a night?
He was always there when I needed him;
But where is he now?
They warned me I would lose him;
If I didn't watch him closely;
Could it be that he was in the arms of another;
Could it be that he's being held close?
I couldn't handle it; I wanted him back;
Waking up alone without him;
My life was so empty;
Where did I go wrong?
How could I let him slip away?
I asked myself many, many times;
"Where is my Teddy Bear?"

Mandi Gallegos

A Prayer for Mom

If I should die tomorrow
My only wish would be
That God would send an angel
To keep Mom company.

She'd need an angels patient grace
To soothe away her tears,
And need an angel's gentle hand
To wipe away her tears.

Lillian V. Echols

Tragedy

My heart is clothed in shades of black
As if to mourn, at last,
The death of a strong and silent love
Now buried in my past.

I, in my soul's chambers, dwell.
There, with my lost love.
This love has been condemned to hell
Instead of the heavens above.

A love of which no poets tell
Nor authors ever speak.
This love which trapped, as in a cell,
Now grows with each day weak.

A love once rich with nature's fire
Now gasps amid hell's flame,
And dies an inch for every beat
In a heart which bears my name.

I go now to find my love
And, if death should be the way....
Quick my heart shall cease to beat
And peace be mine this day!

Kathryn R. Visser

I Don't Do It For The Money

I don't do it for the money, if I did I'd be gone.
But I enjoy walking up free, and the misty morning dawn.
I stand out on the prairie, nearly takes my breath away.
You never cease to amaze me. Lord, it's another brand new day.

I don't do it for the luxury, if I did I'd be gone.
But I endure the midday drudgery, in the baking burning sun.
I curse as each little misery, makes its way around the bend.
You never to cease to amaze me. Lord, Your patience never ends.

I don't do it because it's easy, if I did I'd be gone.
But I look forward to the evening, when my working day is done.
When I hold my little baby, I think about Your Son.
You never to cease to amaze me; Lord, for giving us that One.

He didn't do it for the money, if He did we'd be gone.
He didn't do it for the luxury, His road was hard and long.
He died to set us free, because You are Lord of all.
Oh Lord send me. You are Lord of all.

Paul Behle

I'm Human

Look into the inner depths of my soul
   Can't you see the love?
Look past the shallow attitude
   Can't you see the care?
Look beyond the tired expression on my face
   Can't you see the interest?
Read between the lines of all my work
   Can't you see the concern?
Look beneath the outer shell
   Can't you see I'm vulnerable
Be above all the harsh words
   Can't you see I hurt
Understand the stupidity of my actions
   Can't you see I'm confused
Take the time to listen to me
   Can't you see I'm human

Rebekah Clapp

Who I Can I Lean On

Though you feel you have friends around you
don't believe in all the love they give you
because there is only one you can lean on
and believe him to be true

It's not someone you see everyday
but it's someone you can talk to anytime
guess who it is? It's Jesus
the best-friend of any kind

That's who I can lean on
who will protect me at any rate
help me go through good times and bad
Jesus is never late

He always cares no matter what you did
with his help there's no need to be afraid
just ask to be forgiven for
the ways that you have behaved

If I had a choice on who to stand by
a friend or Jesus
I'd pick my savior for no matter
what he always believes us

Tamika Johnson

Night Fall

Stop your crying little one.
Don't you know the day is done?
Peace descendeth in the air.
Can't you feel it everywhere?

Toys laid by and books aside,
Little horse you love to ride,
All are grateful for the rest.
They sleep now, can you do less?

Let your tiny fists give way;
Do not try to hold the day.
Surrender's to the Master's will.
Know that He is with you still.

Carolyn Lazarus

Sexuality

I feel most sexual when I get,
dressed up and step out of my house

Heads turn words float out I'm on,
cloud nine and that's no doubt

When I step into the club, I feel
like Cinderella, the music stops there

I'm at the top of the stair and all
eyes go from toes to my hair

That was before my man brought home the coke
No not Pepsi not Coke a Cola I'm talking Dope

There went my job, my life, my career
And my sexuality? Ha

It stopped right there!

Blanche Reifer

Chocolate

The pictures I paint of you
I see so clearly now.
The disappearing paint that
flows beneath my skin
that loving sweet face I
once knew fades off the
canvas of my mind and yet
my paint brush keeps going...

Rainy Heath

Blue Moon

There is one blue moon for each soul.
Each one has their fantasy.
Some more far out than others.
But each one with its own uniqueness.
Perhaps a dream to be king,
Or to fly on a magic carpet.
Some have dreams of great affluence,
Others just longing to be alone.
No one is without hope.
No one without an aspiration.
Each one wanting something different,
Yet all wanting the same—
To be able to achieve their goal,
And stumble upon their own blue moon.

Joseph Levine

Transcendence

That look is crouched in the air again:
Frightened, unsure, threatening.
I send messages with no mouth -
Pleading for peace.

Your hand curls in upon itself.
So eager to release a mote of your pain.
I send tears with no eyes -
Pleading for understanding.
The beam of your arm arcs to join my face,
Flying to connect and appulse.
I send warning with no words -
Pleading for remission.

I reach to stop the rush of your arm,
Unsure my strength will stop the hurt.
You send fear without understanding -
Pleading for rest.

I stretch to touch your face
Afraid I'm not that brave.
You beg forgiveness without knowing -
Pleading for my return.

Brenda D. Ballard

My Mother Ellen

You were taken away
From us to soon...

My Mother Ellen
I hope you realized how much we loved you
Because, you meant the world to us,

Now, we look at the
Heaven above
Knowing your a Angel now...

Now, we understand
When you said I love you,

Oh, yeah...
My Mother Ellen
You were taken away from us to soon...

How, I wish to God, Mom you were with us today

But, we know someday in our heart's
We will meet again in the heaven above

Until then
My Mother Ellen
Were left to remember
Your love meant the world to us...

Pamela Morris

My Life.......

Turning, Spinning. Faster and faster.
Full of one way streets
Most that seem to be dead ends.
Full of closed doors
That when opened-lead no where.
Not fitting anywhere.
Not on the outskirts
But not inside.
Not knowing what to do
Which way to go
Waiting for others to tell me
What to do, where to go
And when they don't I'm lost.
A brick wall. That's what I try to be.
Trying to ignore the names they call me
But really hearing every word that's said.
Inside another wall crumbles as each word picks at my heart.
Wishing to be brave enough to end it all.
For good. Why not? What's left here?
Help me. Please.

Regina M. Reilly

Happiness

What is happiness?
Happiness is the sun on my face,
The laughter of the children,
My two sleeping cats.

Happiness is the first sign of spring,
The early spring flowers,
The budding trees, robins and April Showers.

Happiness is retirement, relaxing
with no more stress.

Happiness is spending time
with those you love
Saying thanks to God above
No more stress just sunny days!

Juanita R. Myers

Lies

Tell me you love me, and that I
have nothing to fear, but fear itself.
   Tell me you could never intentionally
hurt me, even if you wanted to.
   Tell me that I am important to you,
even though your friends try and
tell me different.
   Tell me that she means nothing
to you, and you have no idea why
she would say otherwise.
   Tell me the rumors going around
are just lies, even if your best friend
said they were true.
   Tell me that when I talk to you,
the sound in your voice isn't saying
goodbye...
   Tell me all these things for all
different reasons, but mainly because
you know I'd die if you told me the truth.

Marina Ramos

My Job

My job has several titles,
I do it every day;
from cashier down to phone man,
learning many different ways.
I push buttons, bag some clothes,
answer phones with big "Hello's"
I work in mens pushing stock;
Troy's pants, underwear, and socks.
I work in Christmas doing displays;
Sue's bulbs, ornaments, and sleighs.
I work in toys, stocking shelves,
with Michelle like Santa;
and us like elves.
You see my job requires a lot;
I work very hard and give all I got.

Annie Jones

"A Child's Vision"

   I lay upon my bed to sleep,
in a tent grown old and worn.
   I could not help but sigh and weep;
my heart was so forlorn.

   Tomorrow I must go away,
from the parents I held so dear;
   for they upon their sick bed lay,
and could not calm my fear.

   With brothers, I must go and stay,
with people strange and new.
   I knew not then, how long 'twould be;
but the days would not be few.

   As I lay upon my bed,
fearing the unknown,
   to my breaking heart and fear filled head;
a vision then was shown.

   A moonbeam streamed down through a hole,
and aching heart restored.
   It eased the pain of my lonely soul;
for there, was Christ our Lord!

Barbara J. Benson

In Memoriam

The house is strangely quiet, though the sun
In lemon colored gay exuberance
Has entered and transformed the darkness there
To bubbling light. Outside the kitchen door
The roses grow in dense profusion still,
And long-haired grass in dewy fragrance plies
An emerald rug.

Thick dust has gathered on the floors and sills,
And smoke no longer makes its path skyward
Up from the tilted roof. The corn he sowed
Still waves and softly welcomes visitors—
But as in silent, lonely sympathy,
The well's run dry...

Lorella Green

Die?

Why? You have everything to live for, nothing to gain. Quit ingesting drugs, alcohol, pain, and guilt. I'm being selfish.

Ok, I don't want to lose my bestfriend. Let the anger out and do what's right! "Walk Your Talk"

If you need me I'll always be there. I promise not to push but, to support you. You need love, compassion, understanding. That can be given. Don't leave me now! This has been the first day of the rest of our lives!

Stop! look! listen!- This could be the changing of the Tides. It breaks my heart too see you in such pain. I want to take it all away but, you have to want that to.

So do what's best for Michael, not me or anyone else. You my dear are like a Diamond in the rough. Just keep your head up.

Be that strong, compassionate man I know you are. You'll never know if you don't try! What have you got to lose? Cause always and forever we'll have that special something. That no one else can ever take away. Remember that our friendship will last forever!

P.S. you can always have your hug and smile, remember It's ours too, you know

Barbara Hansbury

What Happened To The World Today?

What happened to the world today?
Look around,
Where are the dreams of yesterday?

An innocent child holds a gun,
instead of learning to walk,
he learns to run.

People dying everywhere,
reaching out,
for a friend to care.

It's time to stop and take a look,
the world is like an open book.

Hold the child who is crying,
feed the people who are dying.

Take your brother by the hand,
it's time to make this a better land.

What happened to the world today?
It's time to stop,
not look away!

Catherine Bashiruddin

Concerto

Over and over a concerto played, somewhere upon the ivory of
the mind, where upon fingers, sensitive with sentiment, roamed
about, as if seeking a door, a poetic portal,
to be birthed upon the unmarked pages of time...

But its existence was trapped, like a moth in a jar,
and its distance was incomprehensible, like a child reaching for
a star, but as the third day began to lapse,
the lid was quickly loosened, and like a moth eluded my grasp...

'Twas upon that day of extracting, nearing completion,
of adding ink to a creation dipped in heaven's honey,
that suddenly the stream of inspiration dried,
and I sat stunned near the unfinished page, and cried...

It was not anger I possessed, nor pity recessed,
nor bitterness that bore a hole through the heart,
but sorrow, that dark swirl of love and loss combined,
of life and death intertwined...

I shall not cease to mourn for that unfinished concerto
until I sink in earthen dust, to rise before the One I trust,
where I shall capture those wings from a jar, and touch that
unreachable star, when I shall behold my little baby girl.

Gary D. Gresham

Do Not Be Afraid

So many nights I have
sat up crying,
talking to myself,
wondering why things
aren't working out right.
I blame myself — criticize myself —
and just down right degrade myself.
And — when the morning comes — I feel so afraid —
afraid to get up and go on with my day.
But then I say to myself, you have to live for
God has let you rise up — So get up and go on!
And then I mope around trying to get dressed,
getting more and more confused.
While driving I realize - today is a new day - a new dawning.
Do not be afraid, for God will help you to see the light —
 And then, I am not afraid.

Gloria J. Richardson

I Think We Know

I think I see unclear to me
slumber standing.

I think I hear some soft sounds
they know I'm around.

I think I smell lured sweet ways -
how if ever shall I start the day.

I think I touch now the rough, and avoid as many cuts,
before the loud pain becomes too much.

I think I taste and what a waste, the kisses are late.
But we must stand strong and wait — with the tears of faith,
as we wave.

And through us, we must let them be,
See, hear, smell, touch, and taste — everything.

Included is human race.

Roberto Millar

My Gift To You

Happy birthday Jesus, I am my gift to you
So unwrap, open and use me so that I always please you

I give myself to you this day, a gift which is tarnished and used
Asking you to make of me something that's finer than jewels

I want to be your blessing, your love to those I see
For then I'll know that I am the most precious gift I can be

You've given me many talents and many special gifts
But nothing means more to me than your transformation process

You're making me a seed which grows into a tree
You're making me a helper to all who eat from me

You're making me a flower, which blossoms from water and light
The water of your word, and your light that gives me life

You're making me a gift in the true sense of the word
Something that's given freely like the song of a hummingbird

You're making me a gift, one that's chosen and prepared
You're wrapping me in your spirit and keeping me from evil snares

I thank you for this gift I'll be when once the fire is through with
 me
No gold or gems could ever be as pure a gift as I will be

For I have chosen to be given, broken, molded and made
Here I am-your worthy vessel, a surrendered lump of clay.

Lisa Marie Byrd

The Older Runner

Worn, tired muscles;
Stiff joints, aching bones.
You sit on the hard ground, trying to stretch them out,
Wondering why on earth you're doing this again.

Younger runners pass;
Hardly warming up.
But these longer road races are always murder,
And you need every edge you can give to yourself.

The call to the start;
And still butterflies?
Once more the thought goes through you, "I must be insane.
One of these days I will quit coming to these things."

The gun is fired;
The runners all start.
"Pace yourself," you tell yourself. "Don't burn out too fast."
But each mile is easier than the one before.

At last the finish;
Cheers for your success.
You've beaten younger runners, bettered last year's time.
And now you remember why you did it again.

Kate Guesman

Racism

Evil is here on this planet of life
Storms of anger leave us homeless and in pain
A sheltering body of darkness to protect me in vain

The horrifying screams of wretched people
blinded by labels that fool their naive minds
with a crooked smile you try and hide the fears within
The soul manipulated with hypocritical countless lies
choosing racism to cower behind the truth.

Hope is not at all lost as we think
if truth really mattered we'd all be in peace
low and behold I shall defecate my madness on them
only them, the few who lie with dignity,
spoiling the mind of an innocent child

Damn them all to hell, and pray for our daily sins
life begins with a living cell, and the strong will always win
blaming each other, not knowing we are all in this world together.
Ignorant tribes of people who hate, in ten years we'll be dead if
we keep going at this rate.

The signs are here, I know we listen....but, do we hear.

Whisper Thompson

In a Family of Winners

In a family of winners it's quite conclusive
  That everyone's happy and not abusive

With parents that listen and smile a lot
Health and happiness is what you've got

Brothers and sisters that fuss and fight
  All that's normal and perfectly right

The sharing and caring of happiness and pain
  The storms the weather sunshine or rain

It all makes a family a treasure to hold
One is much richer without silver and gold

In a family of winners it's quite conclusive
  That everyone's happy and not abusive.

Jeremy Frank

"My Angel Betty"

You see there is this angel
That looks on me each day,
I hear that sweet soft voice that says,
"I'm always with you, Marty Rae!"
The voice I hear can be no other
Than my sweet, affectionate, loving mother.
She has been gone now for thirty two years,
And I miss her so I still cry for tears.
She was and is the strength in me,
Along with God give me peace and tranquility.
I've carried on the best I could
Have I tried the way she knew I would.
So many times, I've gone astray
I know she'd just say "Kneel and Pray."
"First trust God and then talk to me.
Can't do much more - just be the best you can be."
As time goes on I must confess
Sometimes I get weary and don't do my best.
Same as always, I hear her say,
"God and I love you, my sweet Marty Rae!"

Marty Rae Royer

Living

I'm a lady of age
  Who loves life
And I'm wiling
  to battle the strife.

  There's living
  And loving
  And losing, too.
But it can be good for you.

So go to all ends
To make friends
And winning will happen
  to you and those around you.

Your life is precious to God
  His world is precious to you
So be careful as you move
  through it, in all you do.

Leona E. Hacker

Just Weren't Meant To Be

The sky fades grey and so do we,
You say you love me but that can't be,
Words can't express the way I feel,
But hopefully my heart will heal.

When you look at me I want to die,
Your eyes just make me want to cry,
Your smile is just so sweet
It makes my heart skip a beat.

I loved you and you loved me,
But I guess we just weren't meant to me.

Allison Reynolds

"Silent Love"

I'll never forget that day we met,
you were shooting hoops into the net.
I walked up to you with a little fear,
not knowing that you couldn't even hear.
When I walked up to you I asked you your name,
you didn't answer so I felt ashamed.
But then you noticed me and gave me a smile,
you gave me your phone number for me to dial.
We started dating and we fell in love,
I know God sent you from heaven above.

Kristine Hogle

New Beginnings

Have you ever gone strolling, over the meadows and down by a brook?
In search of something, you know not what.
The cold winter wind, with all its fury you have left behind,
To look for this "something" in which you hope to find.
Possibly an escape from your problems of endless strife.
Or even a firm foundation, on which you hope to build a new life.

Perhaps you ask yourself this question, "Could this be a dream?"
Then you face reality, as you look into a stream.
It's like seeing yourself in a mirror, distorted it's true;
Though vague the resemblance, you know that it's you.

You gaze into the stream, its cool water rushes past,
Your life you compare with the water, so swift, so fast.
Suddenly you have the answer, to that "something" you hoped to find.
It's buried deep within you; the past you left behind.

"Be brave, look onward," cries a voice from the deep;
"Have faith, the past you were forced to trod,
but the future will bring happiness, now that,
You have found yourself, and your God."

James M. Barbee

Autumn

Yellow golden rods nodding,
  In the autumn breeze;
The stately elms and maples.
  are beginning to lose their leaves,

The colorful swirling and dancing,
  As they move along the ground;
From early morn til sunset;
  They make a rustling sound...

The sounds of winter approaching,
  Squirrels scampering from place to place;
Digging holds to store their nuts,
  That are distorting their tiny face.

The call of the large wild geese,
  as they circle the pond to land;
On one of their many winter flights,
  The large gander is in command.

  He honks in flight his orders,
The flock all gracefully descend;
To rest awhile and also to feed,
  many miles to go before journey end.

Esther N. McNeely

By My Side

Man comes and goes
In the blink of eye.
Not him although,
He remains at my side.
My knowledge of him goes beyond the text,
But his wisdom of me is more than I know.
"Don't judge a book by its cover?"
His practice of this is matched by one other.
He holds my deepest secrets in his soul,
Secrets forever to go untold.
He's constantly on my side whatever my action may be,
Even when I'm so unworthy.
I dream with him.
I laugh with him.
I live for him.
I love him.
One life can touch in so many ways.
He knows this, and so do I.
In every way has his touched mine.
Not in the flesh, in the Spirit Divine.

Jessica Benson

Oasis Of My Life

In the darkness of my life, you are my candle.
In the confusion of my days, you are my answer.
In the mist of my fears, you are my security.
In the sadness of my tears, you are my comfort.

In the brightness of my life, you are my smile.
In the happiness of my days, you are my laughter.
In the acknowledgment of my success, you are my strength.
In the warmth of my touch, you are my source.

You are to me a waterfall in a dusty forest,
A star in a dark night,
A rainbow in a cloudy sky.
You are to me an oasis in the darkness of my life.

Fran DeAngelis-Parent

Window

Have you ever sat by your window and seen:
In the daylight, traffic rushing by
In the evening, someone baking pie?
In the daylight, flowers blooming
In the evening, danger looming?
In the daylight, workers rushing
In the evening, water gushing?
In the daylight, destructive wars
In the evening, people crying "no more"?
If you have seen these things through your window
You have experienced many highs and lows

Erna B. Caskie

The Ever Changing Mountains

Sometimes I gaze at the mountain's grandeur
In the early morning mist,
And feel the coolness of the dew
As fresh as an angel's kiss.

Later on I see the rain
Cascading over valley and hill.
It seems as if the mountain understands
The sadness I sometimes feel.

A more glorious sight one could never behold
Than snow on the mountain peak.
How could I see such a marvelous wonder
And not and God's presence seek?

I see the sun rise with the mountain as its curtain
And the world as its stage;
And, yet, the scene is never the same,
But as changing as the playwright's page.

Whether mist or snow, sunshine of shadow,
The mountain's beauty will never cease,
And I will continue to lift up my eyes
And in this beauty find God's perfect peace.

Carol Reel

If You'll Only Look Around

If you'll only look around, heaven's beauty can be found
In the grass, in the trees, in the flowers and the bees
Won't you stop and take a look at the things in the great book
And see all God's wonders, if you'll only look around.

Sometimes aches, sometimes pain over ride and temptation gains
All good thoughts and deeds are pushed aside
From this life you would like to hide
But if you'll only look around, heaven's beauty can be found.

There is trouble on every hand, a lot of things you don't understand
But there is one thing that you are sure is certain
A christian's house is not built on the sand
If you'll only look around, heaven's beauty can be found.

Christine K. Hopper

In The Middle Of The Book

In the middle of the Book
In the middle of the night
A child's mouth moves,
Sincerely mimicking those mouth's crying
Hymns
Hymns that hate, hymns that hurt...
Against those that curse the song.
Harmony of voice heals the soul
It cools the heated madness of the heart.
Night turns to morn
The songs are theory, illiterate
Black and white dots dancing
Out of measure on pages,
Lost to most souls...
    In the middle of the Book
        Cynthia L. Warren

Communing With Nature In The Garden

I commune with nature almost every day.
In the morning, I hear the Steller's Jay
Announcing feeding time for the bird population.
The mourning dove arrives with a noisy flutter
To dine, and his departure sounds like a helicopter.
Then later the garden fountain is their destination,
And I watch them splash and bathe in the water,
But when interrupted they really do scatter.
The squirrel scampers down the tree in play,
With quick movements and acrobatics to display.
The humming birds enjoy their sweet nectar concoction,
And I notice the bees also find it an attraction.
Sometimes some deer wander into the garden to eat.
They nibble on the plants that they find a treat.
In the evening the crickets begin to chirp away.
Then the hoot of an owl brings an end to the day.
I find that nature is a very wondrous thing,
Because of all the enjoyment it does bring.
        Elna S. Halme

Life in a Day

Trees are green, fields are dark
In the night you can hear the dogs bark
Crickets creep, and people weep
Sorrow and death is all around
As people watch with faceless frowns

Joy and laughter, loud and clear
Takes away the peoples fear
Just for awhile they will be fine
Till death sneaks upon them one more time

In the still of the night, the reaper appears
The people hope and pray he doesn't come near
If he should just pass on by
Give thanks to the miracle in the big blue sky

And this is the way,
Of life in a day
        Ellamarie Pabon

The Small Child

Those little one's are very active as they run and play,
In the park, in their yards and also far away.

They are tuckered out from the very long day,
Now welcome the chance to kneel and pray.

"Now I lay me down to sleep" was said by many a child,
When they were young and ready for bed their feelings not to hide.

"God Bless Mom, God Bless Dad" was also said aloud.
Heard by little voices as they spoke very proud.

Sleep has overcome them now, as they lie in their beds.
Pleasant dreams will come to them inside their little heads.
        Helen Adinolfi

Funeral March

Over the prow of my boat I could see her face reflected
in the water that rippled over her lips.
I heard them humming a tune, telling me to come home.

I stretched into the water to touch her lips
and the shiny surface shot toward me. I came up grasping for my
boat, which was gone among the songs of my water-filled ears.

At her funeral I wear white
socks and underwear. I sing along while they play "Taps",
and hold her as we walk her into a hole in the ground.

On the way home I rub my wrists
together
and whistle to myself. She'd been on the boat that day.
She asked me to follow her. My wrists tell me I want to.

A small grin rises on the face that looks back
at me from the medicine cabinet. The eyes watch her row
the boat away. I sit on the bathroom floor, looking at my hands,
humming,
thinking how much I don't like the razor blades,
but like the song.
        David Goldthwait

Last Thought

Happiness, strange feeling and...so far.
In this emptiness.
In this slavery of my own thought.
One thought...death...death.

Not one, around me, is guilty.
The poor side of nature.
Virus of our times...no cure.

Never did I proceed with evil,
then why the anguish...the guilt.
Yesterday is far...so far.

Dark moments in my life... did I have any?
Death...I never was in pain or suffered,
because of your existence,
fear...why so much fear.

Loneliness, friend of mine.
Trying to search for truth...meaning.
Age, my age...naked I cry.

Calm...I need calm.
Must be sincere in judgement...and wait.
Raw reality, but my soul will never be...so far.
        George Guevara

Untitled

Running from day to day she labored
in vain
Time a relentless pursuer
pushing forward
never giving up.

Her thoughts ravaged in years past
The reasons were too many
Now floating to the surface
A long ago forgotten feeling
Hope

The burdens of a tomorrow no longer existing
Time was reshaping itself
Storm clouds changing now disappearing
A song

Listen.....
Can you hear it?
Time is singing a new song.
        Anita Swanson

The Poet

The Poet shares a heartfelt song,
In words that often rhyme,
His pains, his joys, and his deepest fears,
On paper with pen he writes.
It's not the fortune or the fame he seeks,
For these they solace him not,
What he seeks is understanding,
Of himself and of his lot.
For it's in this understanding,
And in the comfort his song brings,
To the hearts of those who hear his rhyme,
This means everything.
For it's here the Poet can consider,
And he understands,
The reward he's reaped, is his gift to share,
The words he writes, with the pen he holds in hand.

Dolores De Cola

The Thought Of Movement

You held my hand long and hard
Incapable of knowing the injustice to the Bard.
Turned and pulled, the fight never ceased,
I never realized the love of a powerless beast.
The years have drove and the lessons carved well
Only now I can't hear the sound of the bell.
When the night permits and the moon allowed to beat,
It is then I can see all of my shimmering fleets.
Unable to prove, they too, wait for the sound
But that impeccable God can never be found.
Wait, wait, wait and wait.
All of this causes me such glorious hate.
Can it be I choose not to hear?
Overcome am I with such degrading fear.

Cheryl L. King

Bootscooting

The sign says country nightclub, but it looks like an old store,
Inside there's a country band, and sawdust on the floor.
Pick your partner and whirl her, whirl her, round the floor.
She came here to have fun, and that's what you are here for.

Bootscooting, Bootscooting. I hope it's what I think it's
going to be, boy finds girl, girl finds boy.
A super night of joy. And Bootscootings where we'll be!!

They use to call it honky tonk, but now the tonks all gone.
And you can't find a honk in any country song.
And if you want to drink, you better just stay home!
So how is a young rowdy going to get along?

Give me an old Buck Rodgers and a Shirley Temple too,
We can have fun Babe, I'll sing and dance with you,
I'll love you all the evening till the morning sun comes through,
And when the sun is rising I'll sing this song to you.

Janelle Skierski

Spring

In the spring of a modern age
In the black and white of a newspaper page
Scrawled headline flash and streak
Proclaiming violence and peace at a peak

Dreams swell, of a young revolution
One to clean old corruption and pollution
All peoples joined hand in hand
All colors meld fresh to stand.

Douglas Thomas Babcock

Distant Anger

Looking back now, I try to capture what was
Instead I find what might have been.
I think of the short time we had or had not
And ask, "was it all a dream?".

It seems the more I try, the harder it gets
To watch you slip through my memory.
Reliving the past each day after day
Never able to fulfill my need.

The deeper I look into the wounds of the past
The more I find, the less I see.
How could I have thought that we were two of a kind
For I know not why you left me.

Posing questions, asking no one
Fearing they will see through tears.
Distant anger I have lived with
Pain and sorrow all these years.

Cheryl Prashker

To Lenny

We were an arranged marriage between two love feast couples.
Introduced as children.
In your Resident's whites, you lay on my bed with our first
   born.
Your daughters now in their servant's starched aprons help me
   prepare your potpie from my garden vegetables.
Your son draws Daddy a picture from an adjoining table.
Last night you told me of the hint of violation.
We lay flannel to flannel with all windows open to the cool
   autumn wind and rain.
A coy woman who disrespected your golden band and you....
The suffering, I feel sorry for her.
You, Lenny the child of my lovers, you the father of my
   children, you who uttered "I'm married!"
We who will walk beside a diamond lake in heaven and have ten
   children adored as progeny by grandparents, will
   entertain God with our potpie.

Ellen Stone Dunlap

The Heavenly Show

There is, the Irish tell us, a "golden elixir" that
introduces us to sleep - "innocent sleep that knits up the
raveled sleeve of care."

This Sunday last, when conditions of the heart would
come to call and hold that innocent sleep hostage - one more
time - sleep was a fleeting partner.

I went out and gazed onto an onyx canvas decorated with
diamond chips that seemed to wink a welcome to their newly
arrived sleepless companion.

The cool morning air rushed toward me, spun around my
body several times, brushed my cheeks gently, ran its
fingers through my hair and said, "be awake dear friend -
the heavenly show is about to begin."

And, as if on cue - a gentle pink blush pushed the onyx
canvas upward and revealed a violet curtain decorated with
puffs of tangerine. Suddenly, gold and silver streamers
arched upward turning the violet curtain to turquoise, spun
around the tangerine clouds - kissing them softly, and all
of a sudden to the eye - we said, "Good Morning to a
Marmalade sky."

Anthony Mann

America Yesterday

America today, from your America a long time ago,
Is a beautiful place,
And a pleasure to know,
Christopher Columbus, who sailed the great seas,
From, the Isle of Genoa, his belief true to make,
Who discovered our America which really was a mistake.
Years went by, and our country grew strong,
Some very special people came to write our nation's song,
From our forefathers and the wars that were led,
With Betsy Ross on her rocker with her needle and thread,
Stitched a flag for our people which was blue, white and red,
From the Civil War to the Great Depression for people who said
   with a tear,
Remember your memories and the days of yesteryear,
We'll fight for our freedom which countries will understand
We'll help one another and preserve this special land.

John Scenti

Before And After

I look in the mirror and all I see
Is a face that belonged to me.

Once there was a love.
So beautiful and gentle - like a dove.
I was foolish and said "Good-bye".
That one word hurt so much I wanted to die.
I thought that after what we had
Had gone away that I'd be forever sad.

But then I met him
And everything in me that was dim
Lit up in me - like magic
Now everything that happens to me doesn't seem tragic.

He made me feel what I thought I lost
And now I know what I went through was worth the cost
Now because I have him.

Jackie Sanchez

The Rhythm Of Life

The rhythmic flow of life
Is a natural dance of grace;
Its beauty is simplicity
A simple, freckled face.

A baby's laugh, a loving touch
Can set your heart aglow;
A mother's prayer is answered
With her voice so soft and low.

A swaying tree, sweet melody,
The wind brushing your face;
The smell of sweet perfume,
The feel of satin, silky lace.

Live your day as if your last,
Breathe deep the jasmine air;
Reflect on clouds, these fleeting ghosts,
White phantoms, spirits bare.

Celestial world, this rhythmic dance,
Holds secrets like a lover;
It waits to spill its sparkling jewels...
A treasure to discover!

Donna Puglisi

Untitled

My eldest son whose seven today,
Is a remarkable child in every way.
He's full of life, of love and joy,
In short, God gave me a wonderful boy.

He's my right hand man, my helper, my friend.
And when his Mother's busy, a hand he'll lend.
He'll help with the dishes, vacuum the rug,
Clean up the yard, give his brother a hug.

I can remember the times he wasn't so well.
When he had two hernias, the times that he fell.
When doctors said he meningitis and wouldn't survive,
God has watched over and kept him alive.

He'll never be perfect, and has much to learn.
He'll raise a fine family and a living he'll earn.
He'll love with his body, his heart and his soul,
And with God's guidance, he'll soon reach his goal.

But today he is seven, and this is his day,
And I'll try to please him, every conceivable way.
I'll suspend the discipline, react like a dove,
If my seven year old man continues to love.

Charles J. Hardman Jr.

For The Sky-Diver

Tonight I see that great Orion
  Is a star-chute harness, gleaming
    Serenely in the sky, and staunchly
      Competent to hold a jumper
        Drifting downward so expertly
          To a pre-planned destination.

Be his star-guide, great Orion!
Hold him steady; give him sureness;
Keep him swaying lightly, easily
Drop him gently; roll him smoothly.

Note his chute's a nodding moon-flower,
  A celestial morning-glory,
    A ballooning open blossom,
      Tugged taut by an eager zephyr
        Plucking at the vine of nylon.

Waft him softly, rocking safely,
Perfect jump to perfect landing.

Emily B. McCain

Like A Summer's Sun

Like a summer sun in a day that turned night,
Is a tender love that once held you tight.
And the day came to an end and you're feeling alone.

With the breezes blown and the wind feeling fine
Is the one you knew, who was one-of-a-kind,
And your mind becomes so still, cause you're missing what's gone.

When, oh when is my one coming back, for I've wandered alone
  just knowing this fact.
That the day is long past gone and her light feels so black.

I've lived two-thirds of my life without feeling her touch.
To have it right now would mean oh so much.
But the gap is much too strong, and I can't go along.

When, oh when will I come to the chart, that her life is not done,
  for she gave me my start.
And a mother's touch lives on in her child's life below.
And the day comes to an end and I'm taking it slow.

With the rushing sea and the ripple from the storm
Makes me think how certain I was formed.
For the seas calm down to say - remember her, can't you see?
And my day has just begun. No one can take her from me.

Jean Halvorson

Enlightenment

The twilight of my life
Is filled with shooting stars
Random sparks
Light my days with new excitements
... As life goes on
New worlds emerge
New life is formed
Discoveries are made
Futures are planned
... And until twilight descends to total darkness
My life will sparkle
Until it finally flickers and fades

Adele Feingersh

What Is Love

First think! What is the meaning of love?
Is it in the mind? Or is it something from above?
Is it the mighty heart controlling from within?
Or is it the feeling of the heart and soul of men?

There is no definite meaning for love,
No matter how true it seem, or pure as a dove,
A place, thing or someone might be,
It is something, the naked eye cannot see.

There are many reasons, why love can't be explained,
It cannot be measured, or just to be gained,
Love is like a theory, until proven a fact,
And it's a long time, before we can see that.

But this feeling is what everyone needs to share,
Until the moon rules the day, love should mean you care,
The feeling or likeness is there, then it grows,
I would think of love, as a fountain that overflows.

Aneise Brown Mayo

A Stolen Childhood

The child that cries day to day.
Is kept from having a normal play.
Living in fear each time she awakens
For she knows her innocents will be taken.
She hides the big secret from those who care.
For much more violence and hurting is feared.
In her mine, she is to blame
She is cheated through life and is
never the same.
Her childhood was stolen over and over again
She grows up in hatred and feeling drained.
For unless she tells and seeks out help
She will never know how to love and what
is supposed to be felt.

Deborah J. Riccio

A Person's Worth

The carefree timeless optimism of our youth
Is now but a faded memory.
Replaced by the stark realism
Of time. needs, and responsibility.

But all is not lost
There's no need to worry or stew.
For age brings forth the maturity
And wisdom to see you through.

While some may feel they have failed
To leave this world a better place,
Perhaps if they would only pause to ponder this
They will be able to save face.
The measure of A PERSON'S WORTH
Changes drastically as we grow older.
But this value, much like beauty
Is truly in the eyes of the beholder.

Gene Hughes

The Heart That Burns The Burden Tear

The heart that burns the burden tear
Is the heart that dies from undying fear
Always weary, it's hard to see clearly
Is the heart that burns the burdens tear
Contemplating, aggravating yes it is
When the days are dark and dreary
And the wind is never weary
You will be alone with the heart that burns
The burden tear
No solutions, just consequences
The rain is falling, tapping, tapping
Against the window with a psychedelic beat
Which displays a rhythm
The rhythm, of the heart that beats
That burns the burden tear

Charlene Williams

Losing To Him

Sweet smelling sweat,
Is the only thing passion has left
Careless whispers fill my empty heart
I pretend I am sleeping
Knowing only his name,
I ask myself
Who is this lying next to me?
My broken heart grasps onto
hauntful happiness.

Seeking security
Finding myself in the arms of loneliness,
Passion has found me; but love is lost.
For who knows the difference
security or loneliness
As I approach the end I can only look for answers
rustled under the thick walls that have embraced
my heart.
My looking glass is misty,
causing frightful uncertainty.
Am I to blame or Him.

Ann Marie Sousa

Growing Into Himself

The tears of the child roll down his face
Is this because of me?

His muscles tighten, his body shakes
Is this because of me?

His eyes show sadness, his head hangs low
Is this because of me?
His mind is wondering, himself unsure
Is this because of me?

Wondering, can I make it, should I try?
Is this because of me?

I sit and watch, can't help but wonder
Is this all caused by me?

I take this time to remember
This is not because of me

It's part of growing,
Part of becoming,
Another, apart from me.

C. M. Ross

271

Baby

A baby to have, a baby to hold,
Is worth more than the world and all of its gold.
A baby's laugh, a baby's cry,
So strong it can bring a tear to your eye.
So soft, so calm, yet ever so small,
Who seems to have no worries at all.
A frown, a smile, then as still as can be,
Which makes you wonder if they can see.
They learn to talk, soon after to walk,
Growing and learning, day by day,
Till soon you find his baby days are slipping away.
No bottles, no diapers; no strained foods,
Only gallantry, tantrums, and changing of moods.
A baby, a child, a teenager, an adult,
Sometimes a devil, an angel, or even a cult.
The years slip by so very fast,
The joys seem to diminish and troubles seem to last.
Growing older until the time will come,
They will have to raise their own little one.

Barbara Soucy Isaman

Mirrored Windows Of Flesh And Bone

There is a window in my soul.
It allows me time to draw from the well.
Time is passing hear the clock tick.
Hurry, I hear the ticking, the ticking of time.
The clock is my heartbeat, pumping ever so fast
Grab helpers to salvage all that you find.
The well is so deep dear heart I think I shall faint.
Life is a gift wrapped up in a dream . . .
When the dreamer arrives he sees the fresh bow.
Asking were did it come from for I do not know.
Why, it came when you were fast asleep all safe in your womb.
It's taken quite a beating, but it still looks shiny new.
Unwrap the fine paper made from flesh and bone.
Look, it is a mirror and the image is you!

Cheryl Chernick

My Special Day - My Friends

We love to go to the senior center, my husband and I.
It always has a down home feeling and is also close by.

Edith Bates comes in with curlers in her hair some days,
But you hardly notice and give a slight gaze.

Augie Amman greets all the girls and boys,
And when we were king and queen in 92,
He still says to me, Hi Queen and I, Hi King, for nothing else will do.

To this years royalty, Queen Rose Shooltz and King Norman Arnst,
I wish them a year of success,
And may they have lots of fun as those before them were so blessed.

Florence Bitterman, a bouncy 90 plus year old,
Enjoys each day, loves strawberries and is still up to her tricks at cards I am told.

Louette, our dear director, runs the center to perfection,
We could find no one better and her phone is always a connection.

To all who made "my special day" such a pleasure,
Bless you all, for friends like you, are to me a great treasure.

Bess Danek

God's Miracle In A Seed

Gardening is a form of worship to me;
  It answers in me some need.
For as my hands place it in the ground,
  I see a family meal,
    Lurking in each seed.
As I place it gently in its row,
  I offer up a prayer!
I feel God's blessings upon me fall
  As if thanking me for putting it there.
When the rains fall from the skies,
  God's watering it I know;
When the seedling, on a bright day
  Does at last appear
I see another of God's miracles.
  An know that He is near!

Betty D. Mason

Smiles

A smile can warm the cold nights and brighten any day,
It can strengthen any weakness and pass all your cares away.

People who are wealthy and considered up in style,
Are so penniless and have nothing if they don't know how to smile.

And, no matter where we roam,
A joyful smile always makes you feel welcomed and not so far from home.

There are false smiles, and there are true smiles, and smiles that are so cold.
But, the ones that are sincere, are the ones that will hold.

It opens the "Gateway to the Heavens", and on earth makes living worthwhile.
So, as we pass someone today, don't just stop and say "hello".

Let's take that extra step and walk that extra mile.
And, without hesitation, and a very warm and friendly smile.

Judith Ann Mckay

The Power Of Love

Love: It's the most powerful force in the universe.
It connects us to God, to our higher self and to one another.
There aren't enough words to tell you I love you, not enough ways,
To show I care, not enough laughter and good times to wish you, not enough wonderful moment to share.
I am very thankful for this year. What a blessings come to mind
You are my dear friend and a wonderful man, so loving and so kind.
Each time I see the sunrise, and the beauties of the day, you are
The unexpected little joys, I find along the way. Yes I am thankful
For this year, and for the small and furry thing. You and your loving
Is what keeps me going, the peace believing brings. I have so much
To thank God for, I don't know where to start, I only know he walks
With me, and lives within my heart, with a whole new beginning
Starting today and every year. I thank God for placing your love
Deep with in my heart.

Dora Robinson

Christmas

We can hear the bells ringing with a happy jolly sound,
It has come that time of the year when Santa comes around
We'll all get our christmas tree ready for Santa to see
We'll all be waiting and hoping very impatiently
We'll leave him a glass of milk and cookies for him to eat
We'll have our stockings ready but there not for Santa's feet
We'll go to bed early so we'll be the first one's up
So we'll be ready to get our gifts and all the neat stuff.
We'll go outside and build a snowman with a sign just for Santa
We'll even go on top of the house and stick a reindeer on the antenna.

Judy Merriman Voltz

My Child, Wherever You Are

For all those nights I didn't get to hug you,
It did not mean that I didn't love you.

Please forgive me if I'm not there for you,
It does not mean I don't care for you.

There are days I'm out walking and pass through the park,
I see children playing and wonder where you are.

I know there will be times in your life, when you're older,
You will think of me; I pray your heart won't grow colder.

I've spent so many hours thinking back to that day,
When the love I carried inside me was taken away.

Just as sure as there's an ocean and a sky above you,
My child, wherever you are...I'll always love you.

It hurts me more than words can say,
Not to be holding you on Mother's Day.
DeNeese Carrigan

The First Time I Walked

Remember the time when a little girl walked,
It give you a special feeling to see her walk.

Your twenty-three month old daughter took her first steps,
twenty-three steps across the front room floor.

In wooden shoes big enough to be roller skates,
but without the wheels instead she slid her shoes.

With sister Nancy and mom to help, you watched
your daughter take her very first steps.

You remember the wooden shoes she walked in,
for six months but you especially loved that little girl,
when she made you very happy because she walked.

That little girl doesn't have wooden shoes now,
but she thanks you from the bottom of her heart,
for what you have done for her.
Janet M. Thill

Windows Of Time

Life is like a window
It gives us a view
Of all that we can see and things we must do.

Life is the growing of two hearts to one,
It carries great freedom to those who do come.

Life is knowing you are not alone,
Of sharing and caring for all who we love,
Making a family and a good home.

Life is like panes of a window in time,
Showing us all it has to offer with no reason or rhyme.
Gloria A. McDonald

Vows Of Love

My love, you have made my life complete.
It is amazing how we ever did meet.
I will cherish you all the days of my life.
I am honored to be known as your wife.

Together we must face our hopes and dreams.
I know it will be harder than it seems.
Trust, not jealousy will be our guide.
We must treasure each day and stand side by side.

You are my lover and my very best friend.
I know our fights we can easily mend.
Know most of all, my love for you is true.
I look forward to so many years with you.
Deborah Triggs

The Choice

"Who am I? I must find myself," the young heart cries.
It hears, "Just do your thing. You're number one."
And still it hungers, starved for meaning to exist.
God made you as you did appear at birth,
Shaped by heredity, environment and choice.

Your genes determine much about you, child:
Your color, features, height and weight and more.
And even your behavior, left unaltered,
Finds its source in chromosomes and genes you did not choose.

And the place where you are put, environment,
Decides somewhat how you will see the world,
And how relate to others like yourself.
Until your later teens you could not choose.

Look up and hope, young heart, at this:
God gave you choice to use to shape the rest.
By choice you break behaviors lying dormant in the genes.
By choice you change environments of hate and ugliness.
By choice you look to Him who gave you power to be His child.
And praise Him, praise Him for the relevance of being.
Judy Mecham

Time

What is time? Is it a place? Is it a thing?
It is a place of infinite possibilities?
It is a place, waiting to be explored.
O, time, how great is thy magnificence.
O, time, how great is thy powers, indeed.
Time, in all thy magnificent splendor,
Where dost thou travel?
Is it across the vast reaches of space?
Tell me, O magnificent time, where dost thou travel?
O, time, your powers are truly wonderful!
Time has the ability of change people.
Time has the ability to change things.
Though we cannot see you, you are ever present.
Only time, and the Lord, can make a difference
In the way man sees things.
O, Lord, Father of time, turn us away from the
Infinite hatred of the world.
Only God and time can see the way things will be.
And only God and time can change them.
Andrew Shelton

Untitled

It's hard not to know...
It kills me so deep within, I don't even know why
Not even in one life do I know
More than one, I have, which one do I belong?
Which one makes me the happiest? I don't even know
In which could I survive? I don't even know
You see, I don't even know myself
In the mirror, a different reflection every time
Like someone behind a mask
Never themselves, never true, is that a smile?
No, just a tear in disguise, is that laughter I hear?
No, just a cry for unwanted help, all alone, I'm strong
At the same time, wounded and helpless
Unheard and misunderstood
Living the life of a strong but weak warrior
Am I capable of taking the pain?
Will I ever rise and fall?
Express, to just get shot down once again? Ashamed
I walk with my head down, without a single heartbeat
Is this really me? I guess I'll never know...
Denise Michele Santos

Untitled

Love is like a burning flame in the fireplace.
It is as heavy as the coals are hot.
It sizzles with the hidden passions and desires of fantasy.
But is quickly diminished with damp harsh words of anger.

Love is the gentle breeze blowing through the evergreens in winter.
The bird that perches itself upon the snow-covered branches
is as light at as the euphoric feeling created by a man and a
    woman conceiving a child.

Love is the tear of a long forgotten memory. Thoughts of a life lived
years ago fill the heart with warmth on a cold December night.
An old journal entry can renew a childhood that was lost in time.

Love is the shape of a rainbow and the color of a square. It is
opposite of hate on the emotional spectrum, yet close enough
to lust to begin with the same letter.
Love is the line between life and death.

Love is who you are and what you feel. It is why you've here
and not there. A carnation may last longer, but a rose means so
much more.
Love is money, and money is power. Power to change this
disease-infected world. But the love of money is self-destructing,
therefore the homeless will continue to be ignored.

Love is not sex without a condom, nor a hug without feeling. It isn't
a newborn baby addicted to cocaine or black eye from you father.

Love is a joke.

Erica L. Behling

"Histormanity"

My history, your history, are forever intertwined.
    It is difficult to separate your history from mine.
Our wars, our scars, our hopes, our dreams,
    From without and from within
Make us more alike than different when
    We look beneath the skin.
Asian, Indian, Black or White, we are less different,
    More alike.
So let's untie the know of fear and realize
    That we are all here.
For the rope of humanity ties us together forever.
Praise God

Gwen Morris Vaughan

"Lost And Alone"

Sometimes in a world that is so insane,
It is hard for you to find a little faith.
When you're crying out, deep inside,
You don't feel as if you have the will to survive.
No one will listen, no one will help
And you're forced to deal with the cards you've been dealt.
So you struggle in the dark to find your way,
But the light guiding you continues to fade.
So I ask you: "What do you do when you are lost and alone?
Do you wait for someone to give you the courage to go home?"

Jessica Morales

Emily

A light comes to my eye,
It is present when thinking of Emily,
a ray of sunshine,
brightening many horizons.
A very precious gift,
such a miraculous fulfillment.
So much determination and fire in her soul.
How proud and grateful I am to be so blessed.
Emily-a special child-so loved.
If only I were born in her skin.

Carol Uden

Anger

The cold blooded anger in me is like a rock.
It is like hard coal burning inside me.
It is a door that's always locked,
That no one can open without a key.

It lies on my chest like bricks.
And is hard to just ignore.
It stabs my heart like a cactus pricks,
And is too much pain to endure.

As I lie there in bed,
I wonder if the pain is ever going to end.
It is all quiet around me, as if everything was dead.
How long will it take to mend?

The new morning is here, and the sun is brightened,
As my pain has lightened.

Carolyn Kregar

Nature's Caress

A warm breeze gently blows over my body,
It is nature's caress.
It speaks of love and understanding.
It says we belong together.
The breeze smells sweet,
Sent from a powerful, but gentle, soft being.
Stay breeze, stay.
Oh, I know you must go and continue on,
But you will come again.
You must stay in motion and touch the universe.
Where do you come from?
I wonder.
Do you have no beginning and no end?
You who are the warm, the good,
The pillow of one's soul.
Pass on, I understand.

John Kelly

The Kingdom Of Heaven

I realized this day that the Kingdom of Heaven is right here now today
It is not a place that we go to   after
That it is just as Jesus said it was
I looked around the table at the rough scarred faces of real men
and women
And knew that God is here in this place   Now
And I realized that wherever God is present   is the Kingdom
And I realized that God is present any and every time we look for God
The Kingdom is an attitude, an awareness, a gentle reality
And we can touch it or be in it or live it   as we choose
What an incredible gift for such common everyday folk as us
From an unconditionally loving God

Joseph B. Kelly

White

A color so plain, a color so white.
It is so beautiful, it can be light.

A flower is white, so delicately frail
So fragile and light, so very pail

White is a cloud, like a cotton ball,
It flows with the wind so high and so tall.

Lace can be white, white is romantic
White is like snow in the Antarctic

Snow fall so gently, so slowly, and carefully
Sometimes it blizzards fast white dots so closely

White is so beautiful, flowers, clouds, lace and snow
So gentle and delicate, many other things to know.

Angelee Lockhart

It Is Here...

It is here
　it is now
　　it is ours:
　　　Our chance
　　　　our choice
　　　　　our time

....A time to heal
and a time to rejoice
....a time to reach out
and a time to touch
....a time to hold hands
and a time to love
....a time to shape together in faith and harmony
the undiscovered country of all of our tomorrows.

It is here
　it is now
　　it is ours:
　　　our chance
　　　　our choice
　　　　　our time...
Cleo Laszlo

Country Life

A simple life, but yet hard,
　It is on a farm
Feeding animals at dawn and dusk
　Smell the air, it is a must
A horse's winnie, a doggy's bark,
　This is home for us, from dawn to dusk
Up early, out late, this is the life
　You must take.
It's not bad don't be sad
If you like it I'll be glad
Crystal Koch

The Flower Gatherers

Gratefully I descend into the valley of deepest sleep;
It is redolent of death.
I reach out to pluck for my own that fatal flower,
when suddenly a sword of sunlight pierces my eyelid,
as the new day plucks me for its own.
Judith Williams

March Thaw

The earth is frozen, the sky is a barren gray;
It is still winter over the land, you say.
Pristine white is the snow that covers,
But underneath, it's the brown of death we discover.

Cold, cruel blasts come from winter's womb,
Like a heart of bitterness, like a tomb,
Eating away life from those that are unprotected,
Frozen sap of the living, left bereft and dejected.

Somberly the world turns locked in winter's grip,
The hours and minutes slowly passing on this trip.
The end seems in sight! There's a warmth on the air,
But time proves it a deception, so you better beware.

Suddenly, how mercilessly the frigid wind returns,
Stinging like the darts of hell it spitefully burns.
Roaring gleefully as it ravages the frail and the weak,
Wresting the insecure from the poor hiding places they seek.

Yet every living thing sighs, anticipating a coming day,
When hearts embracing springtime are free of winter's tyranny.
All, like undaunted daffodils, will break forth from the ground,
Bejewelled, lovely ones march rejoicing in new life found.
Carol Favreau

Rain

I sit by the window and look at the rain,
It looks like teardrops falling.
It's as if the rain has a voice,
And the voice, to me, is calling.

I stare at the rain, the shattered dreams,
Dropping and falling apart,
I wish I could be a beautiful as the rain,
I wish with all my heart.

Sometimes it brings back memories,
Memories of days that have gone by.
I quietly sort out my feelings,
The feelings I have, and I don't know why.

The rain always listens to you,
It's as if it's a quiet friend.
It will always listen to your sorrows,
And to your troubles that have no end.
Jessica Leigh Pittman

Of Death

Death is like a snow flake, that falls gently to the ground.
It melts away and leaves no trace, there's silence all around.
In sorrow, friends and family gather round once more,
To show their love and share a closeness never felt before.
Time passes, memories fade, and things get cloudy in our mind.
Hazy visions haunt us when we are left behind.
But we know in time, we too must go at last,
And hopefully join the one's we loved, who left us in the past.
In fantasy, we meet again and all is well.
We greet each other across the space where God and Angels dwell.
Evelyn C. Nevis

Anarchy In The U.S.A

Something's wrong with our economy
It might as well be Anarchy

There's a black market for guns and drugs
Raping girls for teenage thugs

Psycho killers who walk free
Governments stealing our hard earned money

Races all around come in
Polluting our once beautiful nation

Each new day points towards the way
The way that is, of Anarchy.
Brianne Stanley

Someone Special

Love before he came along was just another word,
It would come fast and go slow leaving you in tears
　I'd heard,
As for now I believe in it,
I wish it would flow easy like sand every grain
　and grit,
My emotions are not easily released when he's near,
For I am scared he will laugh as he listens to hear,
The thought of him brings me up when I'm down,
My sense are so confused I feel like a circus clown,
Yet it is beautiful the way I feel inside,
If I try I can make it all I have to do is be like a
　free bird and glide,
In instances of thoughts in haste,
I think all my love for him is a waste,
My feelings for him are so very strong,
For you are whom I am in love with and be for
　quite long.
Donna S. Brown

Black

Black - My Favorite colour.
It represents a state of nothingness.
No joy, no sorrow. No love, no hate.
Just a peaceful, quiet Nothing.

Night. My favorite time.
It represents the same nothingness.
The same peace.

But not tonight.
Not last night and not tomorrow night.
Now, a new Blackness controls the sky.
A Blackness with the look and feel of Death.
It shadows the city. Warning; teasing.
Does it reveal its power? Yes; everyday.

But the people don't see.
The Blackness has covered their minds. Their hearts. Their souls.
They are no longer horrified by the atrocities of the world they
    live in.
Of the world they die in.
They have become placid. They have become void.
They have become Black.

Black. My favorite colour.

Angela Wheeless

An Old Man's Lament

She gave me all my tomorrows, in her gentle, loving way.
It seems like forever since she lived here; the girl from yesterday.

She loved me when she lived here and when she went on her way.
I know, today, she still loves me; the girl from yesterday.

I gave all the love inside me 'cause no one had loved her that way.
But still she had to leave me; the girl from yesterday.

My house, left vacant and empty, could only have stayed that way
In deference to the way I lost the girl from yesterday.

I knew when I was looking at the stars, so far away,
The same one's were being looked at by the girl from yesterday.

It was not about promises broken or love that went astray.
I can't explain what made me lose the girl from yesterday

I never replaced her presence because no one was quite that way.
She always stayed my Princess; the girl from yesterday

I had no more tomorrows; just a life of sad todays
complete with all my memories of the girl from yesterday.

Anthony E. Cunningham

Untitled

Our weapon is EDUCATION
It shields us from the AIDS invasion
Which can decide your life's duration
It attacks the bodies Immunity
Tearing it down like crime in our community
Knowledge is the way
To save our life today
The declaration has been drafted
The lines have been Drawn
The battle is here
No cure now or near
We ו.eed to arm ourselves
With knowledge not ignorance and fear
Because EDUCATION IS THE FINALIZATION
FOR AIDS EXTERMINATION...

Charlayne Wright

The Snowfall

The snowfall came late last night,
    it snowed and snowed 'till broad daylight
The snow had covered hill and dale,
    even covered the bunny's trail.
Sent the birds close under the eaves
    or searching for the thickest trees.
It has not stopped all day long,
    kept whirling and twirling its silent song.
Everywhere is a veil of white
    for it has snowed from dawn 'till night.

Edith L. Burton

"50th Anniversary"

Today must mean so very much to you...
It stands for fifty years of devotion and
Love between you two...

It's your golden anniversary
Fifty years ago today, you vowed to love
Each other and made it all the way...

You made it through the good and bad
Though times it did get rough..
You had the courage to stand and fight,
For your love was always enough..

It's nice to see a marriage of fifty years
Survive, your rarely see a love that stays
So very much alive...

As your children, we're so very proud to
Be with you today,
We're here to say "we love you"
On your "very special day"...

Janet Diane Leiser

Poetry, A Pathway

Poetry is a pathway to soft colored silence.
It stirs the heart and soul to expel doubts and terror of the night.
Can incite one to burst with cheer,
Throws off the core of density for the fool,
Stretches its arms, a giant tree shading the weary,
Warms the cold whiteness of a frame,
Fills curious minds with the knowledge of self,
While it plays a melody heard by once deaf ears,
Speaks a universal language bringing lonely ones from their
secret places, to share common ground,
Poetry is a pathway to Peace.

Betty Jean Stribling

My Day

I bought a colorful kite,
It was a unicorn and such a sight,
I flew it over the world today
It was wonderful, I had nothing to say.
I saw the seven wonders, all sitting pretty,
And then I saw two people, acting all pretty.
I flew to the Pacific Ocean,
It looked like magic potion.
The unicorn talks to me,
And tells me what to see.
The unicorn is yellow, pink, and blue,
Its love is truly true,
As I sail back home tonight,
I remember all the sights.
I put the unicorn in a safe place,
And went to bed with a smile upon my face.

Donna Castillo

Angela

On a bright sunny morning, I found myself dreaming.
It was a waking dream of a girl with no face.
She came to me like an angel with no meaning.
She was truly of a God send race.

We met facing each other like pawns in a game of chess.
With smiles on both our faces we never knew of the debauchery
underneath.
Love came in quickly and left no mess.
All those care free words uttered under our breath.

Soon happiness turned to a seething sore.
The forest of love soon caught flame.
The strength of sanity was tested more and more.
Now we began to point to each other in blame.

The pawns changed into a king and queen full of rage.
I started to run through the flames to the one I loved.
Would our fates be left up to the mage?
And found that she was gone out into the night never to be seen again.

John Overpeck

My Dream Come True

I once had a dream of a new country
It was clean and beautiful
I had a very good view of this country
The cities were clean and the buildings were very tall
The houses were big and neat
This country was full of cars, vans,
    trains, and trucks
The malls were huge and fantastic
I could tell it was green in nature because of the
    tall beautiful green trees, flourishing
    flowers, and green plants
It smelled as fresh as daisies
The sky was as blue as a running stream of water
The sun would rise and set with a smiling face
It had pleasant sounds
No one thought of my dream
Only one great man thought of letting
    my dream come true
He sent a spirit to tell me
    "good luck in your new country"

Benedette Mutisya

Wings

I never knew why whenever I saw a butterfly
    it would cause me to pause...take notice...so fascinated...

If possible, I would cup my hands and gingerly catch it,
    examining it closely so as not to harm its wings

I'd soon let it go, watching it fly away, feeling,
    for that instant as free is it must have

Now...as I grow, I realize that I too, have wings...that I am
    made just as special
...That the sky is not my limit...that I am infinite in my abilities

...That I should guard my wings...being careful not to allow
    anyone to hold or clip them..
surrounding myself with only those who truly want to see me soar

...That I should live my life with the quiet gentleness in which a
    butterfly lands,
moving forward with the determined vigor in which is takes flight

Now I know that nature is meant to symbolize our lives...to
intimately embrace and swirl into our spirits, making us feel as
    boundless as we are...

...As free as we CAN be
...As uninhibited as we WANT to be

Donna J. Smith

The Calling

I first hear it in February. Strange. February is cold, snowy.
It's a calling that I hear. Far off. But insistent.
And then, I smell it. No, wait - I hear it! The salty ocean.
My mind and body seem to stop - as if lost.

Funny, how it calls. Like a fog horn. It just comes and awakens
the senses, the feelings of something wonderful that will come
further on down the road.
I hear it - this fog horn. Telling me it is time to come back to
the Island. To walk the streets and mingle with the crowds. To
fish from the jetty in solitude. To listen and hear the world go
by in the heat, in the breeze, in the water as it softly touches the
pebble lined shore. This is summer on the Island.

Later, when it is finally time to go there, I hear the colors of
summer, the laughing of people. I hear the excitement of getting
ready to go once again to the Island of Martha's Vineyard.

Joyce J. Lloyd

Untitled

There's a word that should mean, a lot to you and me;
It's a simple one, it's easy; it's called family
Mom, Dad, Uncle Frank & Aunt Dru;
Grandma and Grandpa; and a cousin or two.
There are nieces and nephews; from way back when;
Uncle Joe and Aunt Cindy; and your second cousin Gwen
Remember the get-together; with mom running all over the house
If dad's taking a nap; kids must be quiet as a mouse!!!
Don't run around Grandpa; it makes him dizzy "U" see
And be careful not to knock over Grandma's cup of tea.
Where she's sitting patiently; while Granddaughter Brook
    brushes her hair
Out sheathing baskets are mom's pride and joys,
All grown up men now; but to mom; still boys
Soon;... the get-together is over and done;
So... Mom and Dad sit, remembering the fun.
The caring; the laughter; the love that was shown,
No-one there; felt unloved; or alone.
"Ahhh!!! said Dad "How happy are we"
"Yes" finished mom, for our wonderful family!!!"

Jo Franklin

Reality

I don't know what I want.
It's all there yet I can't reach any of it.
It is just a huge blur,
A dot in the distance,
The idea of it is great and fun,
But the reality is the truth
I don't want the truth
I want the reality to be ideal,
and the ideal to be reality.

Donna M. Ogburn

Family

Family - More than just a name you share
It's also in the way you care
With children of your own spreading time so thin
We still find time for each other
With the force pulling from within.
When parents pass on much too soon
You can still feel their hands
Guide you through your gloom
But through it all, the best you have
Is the family that you call yours.

Joseph T. DeMars

"Leaving"

I don't need anyone to show me where I lost my way
It's all too clear to me
I don't need anyone to help me through the day
I've got my faith to save me.
It seems the distance between me and my dreams is growing
everything is uncertain, nothing soothes my pain but freedom,
that's all I'm asking for.
Free me from this place I've come to call my home,
no longer my home, now what the f**k do I do.
Other things are calling me now,
my chosen road looks like a bad choice...
I can't believe I've allowed myself to be lead this long.
I don't have it in me, need to be on my own,
not responsible for everyone's mistakes,
I can barely account for my own.
and it's all because of the end I was shown
Doing things for other people can't bring satisfaction
if it's not something you would do of your own mind.

Jeff Urban

Where Are You

We hear the sounds of nature, only God could make.
   It's beauty beyond words. His creation,
as are we. You were His to take.

Do you know we are here? What we are doing?
   If you were here, what would it be like?
We miss you. The loss we can bare.

You don't have to worry, your pain is not.
   Your soul is free as a bird in flight.
The problems that were; you need not care.

Can you see, we want to please.
   To keep your memory alive. Take care of
the things you loved: We do with great ease.

   You are there:
With the Master, the Creator, never to part.
   Do you know we love you.
You are in our hearts.
   That's where you are.

Janis Hunt Arms

I Found You

My life is not the same
It's been another game
Now you've come along to make me glad.
Now you're in my heart
We'll never be apart
My darling, you are all I've ever had.
I found you
When I needed someone to love
When I needed someone to share my life
I found you.
My life needed someone like you, my dear
someone who could be near, I found you.
Now I desire,
My heart is afire
Now that I live, all the world that is mine
Lays at thy shrine.
Now I know I'll never complain
You'll always be the same
I'm in heaven—because I found you.

Grandin K. Hammell

"Moon Rise"

The sun begins to set
Its brilliant shine lost - softly,
To make way for an anxious moon.
The birds, who have circled the vast blue sky,
Have landed, in the wake of the orange dusk
And waiting white celestial sphere.
Even the wind,
Having blown its breath all day,
Has begun to whisper - quietly.
The squirrels, having scurried through the day,
Resort to a tranquil and calm place.
The waves in the sea, as powerful as they can be,
Have somehow slowed their path.
Now, no longer angry,
It seems every watchful eye
Has now a secluded passion.
This is the time -
When the day has lost its rumble
When you finally can hear...
I Love You.

Jude Torchenaud

No One Knows

A bullwhip saga, the story goes,
Its dreadful ending no one knows.
Little ones being beat to death,
Earth's pieces looking for breath.

She said, "Hug me, with tender care,
And you will be blessed with drink and air."
We go on in greedy want and no bending,
With wealth amassed and no relenting.

King of the living, we see no wrong,
Breaking cycles 'til the final gong.
Tell me, how do I give this tender care?
By wanting less and being fair.

A bullwhip saga, the story goes.
When it will end no one knows.
Life will stop when time runs out
And there's no more wealth for us to tout.

Jack Cupper

It's Gone

My world has gone black,
Its emptiness means there's no going back.
Everyone's gone and there's only me,
All living things ceased to be.
I'm left floating around,
With my heartbeat as the only sound.
Boom boom, boom boom, over and over everyday,
I'm going insane, there's nothing else to say.
Without love, without care,
Without someone to have my thoughts to share.
Fading away like a memory far back in my mind,
Wondering what happened to that time.
What happened to the happy days,
Where laughter and love couldn't be held no matter what the ways.
It burst forth so no one was left without love,
Even the skies and the birds sang from above.
But now it's gone, burnt in a flash,
Everything fell with a sounding crash.
No more love, laughter or fun,
But most importantly there's left not one.

Angel Gregg

Untitled

There is a place I long to be,
It's far away and near the sea.

I go there when all alone,
I return with a heart of stone.

For I have found the strength to resist,
that which I long for of length to exist.

I find the more I am alone,
it is much harder to turn to stone.

I long for feelings which I could express,
to someone who would know much happiness.

This place by the sea where I long to be,
has led me to want more than I could see.

I will not turn my heart to stone,
For when I'm old, I do not wish to be alone.

Adeline E. Anneski

To Africa

The sun went down in splendor, glowing, bright -
It's far-flung crimson banners lingered still,
The smoke from Pagan wood fires on the hill
Rose to the evening star - swift came the night.

Then silent, purposeful, in lordly might
The lion hunted ceaselessly for prey,
The leopard and the jackal went their way,
And darting screech owls glimmered, palely white.

O rich and lovely country wrapped in sleep,
O tribes untouched by civilizing hands,
Safe in the fastness of those granite rocks
You know not of those things that make us weep.

Continue in your ways, for no man mocks
Tranquillity - that peace on earth demands.

Gillian M. Stone

A Hug

I like to hug and be hugged.
It's great what a hug can do.
A hug can cheer you when you are blue.
A hug is welcome back again and great to
see you, where have you been.
A hug can say I love to see you, I hate to see you go.
A hug can sooth a small child's pain and bring a
rainbow after rain.
A hug there's no doubt about it
We can't live without it.
So, stretch those arms without delay and give
someone a hug today.

John Frank Wells

Deep Inside

Deep inside is your smile
It's hard to reach, but it's on your eyes
Inside my heart and mind
are the things which are hard to define
And problems whose solutions
are yet to be found

Deep inside is my aching heart
The only proof are the tears on the bedside
Who longed for you day and night
Because you are my star that shine

Deep inside are sadness and happiness
That no one can fathom its depth
To fulfill every thing, show your best
Keep the best and strive for the rest

Jose Patricio Banez

What Stays Constant?

Of all the things in this world, what stays constant?
It's not the idea of believing in ourselves,
that changes from day to day.
It's not the trust we have in ourselves to take the right road.
It's not the people who only stick by us when things are good.
So, is it our will to hang on while the hurt of the world is
pulling us down?
Is it the on-going battle against our fear where we will
end up in life?
Is it the friend that wants to see us through the good and bad?
Is it the one person who really believes in us?
Of all the things in this world, what stays constant?
The constant of life is knowing that the sun will come tomorrow
and that our road is waiting in front of us.

Julie Carruth

Not The Same

It's not the same, I want you to know,
It's not the same, when I am alone,
It's not the same, when I don't hear you speak,
It's not the same, when I don't see your face,
It's not the same when I love you so,
It's not the same because I am alone,
But it's not fair, to burden you so,
And it's not fair, but I love you so,
And it's not fair to ask this of you,
And it's not fair for a smile from you,
And it's not fair to call me a poet,
Just a man in love, with just one woman.

Dwight Vincent Collins

Calendar

Be gentle with that calendar on the wall
It's printed neatly for one and all
It tells you the year, the month and the day
Even tells you how long you can stay.

You see a picture of a curly headed baby
Thinking back, memories become hazy
That picture could it possibly be
Years ago - a picture of me?

My how the time flies
And those numbers never lie
They say you were born in December
A long time ago - do you remember?

If we knew all of its past history
It would certainly clear up a lot of forgotten mystery
But lets just think deeply and pray
For no matter what - it carries us away

The pictures you see are truthful
Treat life right and its beautiful
Those big black numbers never lie
On one of those days you will die!

John List

I Am The Ear

I am the ear.
It is my job to listen.
I will listen to all the good things that come your way.
I will listen to all the bad things that you have to bear.
I will listen to all of your problems whatever they are.
Since I am not the mouth my advice may not be sound.
But it is my job to listen,
For I am the ear.

James Godfrey

Ode To Granny Gowns

This flannel granny gown won't let me go,
Its soothing softness lures me so!

Its comfort is too hard to fight.
The cozy night
Pretends a right to stay,
Trespassing on this shining day.

But far too fat my body's grown,
Too many seeds of sloth I've sown,
By lounging long in gowns that pamper
And all my good intentions hamper.

My feet they should be Reebok taken,
This granny gown should be forsaken
For stringent underwear and clothes
My comfort craving body loathes.

So, off you go, huge gown I love,
Into these walking clothes I'll shove
My bulging body — hit the trail,
Against this fat I shall prevail!

'Course, then I'll hike right to the mall
And purchase granny gowns - *size small*!

Alberta Evans Stokes

Wither And Die

As surely as the sun's aries,
it's suddenly taken away by surprise...
A frightening sight for your very eyes,
when everything withers and dies...

Life's expectancy is suddenly short,
people are dying all kind of sorts.
Everywhere we're starting to find,
we're killing off are human kind.

Flowers start to wither and die,
when do we stop and wonder why.
Things of beauty never stay,
they always seem to go away.

Clouds come and darken our dreams,
when ever we are happy there always seems,
a force of evil at every step we take
taking away this life we make.

Death comes one day or another
this life we lead why even bother,
the suffering is quick and many are in vain
I don't think I can take all the pain.

Charles L. Casey II

The Long And Winding Road

The long and winding road seems to never end,
It's the road that leads to the end of your life, my friend.

Each step you take to getting older,
the road seems to get longer and colder.

It seems like every step you take in life gets harder,
but somehow through it all you do it without being a martyr.

The road is like a journey through time,
all through your life and in your mind.

It's like a medieval battle,
a tough journey on the saddle.

Just when you thought you made it to the long and
winding road and life itself, it's only the beginning of hell.

Christina Kunes

Memories Of A Lost Child

Who I am? Where do I belong?
It's the same old melody just a different song.
Does anyone know why I'm so alone?
A million people around me, yet I'm so alone.

I cry for help, but there's no one to hear me
Two million eyes, yet no one sees me
Is it true what they say, that I'm a lost generation?
In a few more years there will be no nations.

I look in the mirror and the reflection cries out
You are but a mere image of yourself, no doubt.
If I could just be given the chance to prove how wrong you are
To show all the world how I refuse to wear these scars

Don't blame me for the color of my skin
Has anyone stopped to learn the person within?
I have no future if I'm compared to all the rest
Just give me a chance, I know I'll pass the test.

I've never been one to follow the crowd and act wild
This is only my experts from the memories of a lost child.

Bernadette L. Austin

The Wondering Years

The wonder years of life are here.
It's time for joy and cheer, fear and yes maybe even
some tears.
It's the time when friends start on a different road
together, apart who knows.
Jealousy, hatred, and even revenge when one hurts
one, but their hearts never mend.
A fear of growing into something new, changing and
becoming on the outside and inside too.
Feelings you thought you'd never have, to get one day
and wonder will it last?
Scared of your thoughts, your new acting emotions.
Wondering if your mind is drunken with a potion.
A potion slowly trickling down to your heart.
A heart so beatened and bruised of emotions hurt,
anger and rage.
A heart filled with joy and laughter, but a heart torn
with a fear.
But a fear of what?
A fear of the becoming wonder years.

Janelle Hailey

Bears Are Forever

What I'm about to tell you, is not in a book.
It's written from the heart, from a bear that was shook

Someone's gentle hands made me, and colored me brown like a bear
Made me boots and a combat suit, then gave me a mission to share

I was shipped in a box to Alaska, then hung on a hook in a store
One day a soldier bought me, I hugged him, 'cause I wasn't
  hanging anymore

The soldier smiled we got in his truck, traveled across town to his den
He stood me up, upon my feet, then called a lady named Lyn

I was listening and heard him say
I got a little soldier for your sister today
Goin home on that plane, keep him very near
Suddenly, I knew my special mission was not here

After all the traveling for this special day
I'm just a little bear with some big words to say
You can hug me, hold me, and I'll pray with you
My mission's forever, each day to get you thru

Bobby W. Bolls

280

Your Life

Your life is a feather, slowly working
  itself to the bottom.

Your life is being buried alive, trying to
  escape for that breath of air.

Your life is trying to reach for publicity,
  but you know that you failed.

Your life is an ocean floor that never
  reaches the top.

Your life is so high, you'll never
  want to come down.

Your life is so confusing, that you can't find
  the right road out.

Your life is a treasure chest, waiting
  to be found.

Your life is something you're still
  looking for.

Why seek that life?

  Joseph Frazzetta

Symbol Of The World

I open my dreaming eyes and take a look around
I've got both my feet planted on the ground
But my heart is reaching way up towards the skies
Playing with the wind where the great eagle flies.

My dreams are being carried by this beautiful bird
When it speaks, it watches me, wondering if I've heard
I continue to see it and he thinks I understand
He lets go of a feather and it falls into my hand.

He speaks once more and then flies away
I am slightly saddened, I wished he would stay
But I glance at my hand holding the colored feather
And I know he will return to bring times even better.

I know it is too colorful to be the eagle's own
I wondered what to do with it, well, I guess I'll take it home
While I wondered the eagle's reasoning, I jumped with a start
Because although there was no wind, the feather split apart.

I was curious to know what was happening to the feather
But with the touch of my helping hands it all went back together
My heart, it speaks, and as I listen I am told
That the fate of the world is this colorful feather I hold...

  Allison Boling

Shane's Song

I have seen the dawn breaking
I've seen flowers seed to awakening
I've seen a myriad droplets linger
Enchanted by light to framed splendour.
I have seen a trillion stars twinkle
I've seen a thousand streams burst to mingle
I've seen fall's forest foliage peak
in their haunted dying beauty
but I am to blame when I see nothing to compare to Shane.
I have heard the cuckoo's dual oath
of rebirth bursting growth
I've heard the rolling waves crash eloquence
against their sculptured end.
I have heard nightingales sing,
the songsters royal king
I've heard symphonies cradle the world
inside their tunes.
But I am to blame when nothing, no nothing
compares to Shane.

  Joseph Ruane

God, Champagne And Roses

Hold out your hand, my dear;
I've held it so many times before.
Surely, you must know...
No one could love you more.

You're the window I gaze through
To see the beauty of my past.
You're the author of the poem—-
That made "Eight Wonders" Last.

You're the sparkle in my champagne.
You're the wonder in my eyes.
And this union in Christ's Grace
Made us a paradise.

And I, I am yours, my love. I thank God, you see.
For in His divine wisdom — He let you marry me.

You're the flight I took — when love's wings were so new.
And now, you're the golden journey that love has seen me through.

You're the window I gaze through to see the beauty of my past.
You're the author of the poem that made "Eight Wonders" last.

These 40 years... this anniversary - Ruby...
Could never shine as brightly... as you do...for me.

  James Heffernan

What Makes Christmas Merry

Outside it's cold and nippy,
Jack Frost is in the air,
Blankets of white covers tree and shrub,
To witness he's been there.

Inside it's warm and cozy,
The fire is burning bright,
Perfume of pine from the Christmas Tree,
Fills the room this special night.

It isn't the snow or the cold outside,
Or the warmth of the fire within,
That brings the Christmas Spirit,
To those who dwell therein.

It isn't the holly or mistletoe,
Nor the presents under the tree,
That fills young hearts and old alike,
With feelings of ecstasy.

But it's the love that is shared,
And the giving and the caring,
Coming straight from the heart,
That makes Christmas merry.

  Alice S. Davis

"For My Wife"

Honey, I want you to know how I love you so
Just like the birds in the tree's
That you see
I want you to believe it's coming from me
My love for you is strong
Hope I'm not wrong
For loving you so long
May I sing you a song?
Honey my love for you is like the wind
It may stop but I don't know when
Loving you just like a flower
I'll love you every hour
My love for you is neat
Without you, life would be incomplete
Now, I hope I don't have to repeat
I love you my sweet

  Aaron Toliver, Jr.

Ode To A Little Boy

Little boy with curly hair
Jet black eyes and face so fair,
Your silent laugh that tugged my heart
And yet too soon we have to part.

You'll never know what it is to run,
Or build sand castles in the sun,
Your carefree years were spent in bed
And for your youth what can be said.

You have two legs and cannot walk,
You have a mouth but cannot talk.
You look at me and I at you
As if to say "What shall I do"?

You lie and wait for someone to come,
You see fleeting shadows on the run.
You do not ask for so very much
Just a smile, A whisper, A gentle touch.

Your arms are rigid, your body small,
Care must be given for fear you would fall,
But the light in your eyes and strong determination,
Show me that I have chosen the right vocation.

Beverly Eskra

The Quest

As the years have passed with untamed speed,
Just a young lad with an iron creed.

As the wheels leave the ground, tears start rollin'.
The parents have found their baby was stolen.

As he embarks this frontier, that marks his life's purpose,
His family is near, but his loneliness surplus.

As the time speeds past, living a life of change;
His pride at full mast, self-discipline at full range.

As the wheels touch the ground of his precious home state,
A young man is found after his parents arduous wait.

As the family comes together once more with loving care;
The time is a tether, so much for them to share.

As he again boards the plane to continue his quest,
his goal still remains to be the nation's best.

As this story unfolds so does his life;
An unpaved road of internal strife.

Chris R. Stricklin

Untitled

Great forces are at work inside the Earth
Just as great forces are inside of us.
A huge mountain rises up magnificently.
It is not built in one day
for something so impressive takes time to rise.
The mountain is built to last,
it does not succumb to its enemies easily.
For powerful forces work against the mountain unendingly.
Rain, snow, wind, and water attack the mountain from all sides,
But the mountain stands proud.
Its foundation far too proud and too deep,
built far too strong.
Not only does the mountain survive, but it grows:
trees grow in vast forests as do flowers in brilliant fields.
Animals populate and reproduce on the mountain,
adding to its beauty. People stop to gaze at the mountain
For its magnitude and resplendence are great.
Just as a mountain of rock is formed in the earth,
A mountain of love has been formed between us.

John Thomas Ehlers

Wise Old Owl

Wise Old Owl Great-Grandma calls you
Knowing eyes opened wide unblinking
Determined brows wrinkling to a V
as you search the world around you for things familiar
Ancient bird-eyes hold secrets of time before memory

Your weeks in our arms can be counted on two hands and two feet
Your feather-soft body untouched by days of use
Your winged-spirit unpricked by human fears
And yet, it seems we are not the first to cradle you
The breath of God still fresh on your skin
sends crisp sweetness into our souls

Did you watch, Oh Owl, as we waited for you?
Know our eyes our laugh our voices before you wiggled into view
Did you eagerly wait with God longing for our kisses and songs of love
Small perfect hands gripping the edge of your gilded perch?

As human language fills your mind
And God's perfect whisperings forgotten
I'll watch you Wise Old Owl, Smile at the paths you choose to fly
and remind you of your curious beginning in this world
Unknown and yet familiar?

Julia S. Field

The Path Of The Heart

We may search for the perfect love
Knowing it only comes from the LORD above
Still the heart desires to find a love of perfection
Wisdom speaks, "Be wise and cautious in your selection."
Perfect love is only perfect in human theory
Loving one's perfection and imperfection is love in reality
The heart becomes strong when making this journey of search
Qualities are gained no matter how circumstances make their approach
The tears of the heart gain understanding, forgiveness, and wisdom
which are not blind
For when it begins to rebuild
It produces the priceless gift
Known as a peace of mind.

Haynesly R. Blake

Passed Away

Traveling the road by the quarter moon,
Landscape lit by the dimmest light,
Our destination arriving all too soon,
By passage of this murky night,

Further along, upon another rise,
Horizon of the way is brought to sight,
Brightness crests the hill, into your eyes,
New images bathed by another's light,

Quickly your companion goes by the way,
Absence of illumination darkens your plight,
To go back to that time and stay,
For one moment everything was alight,

For some you look again in the mirror,
As though in a way your being polite,
Is it the thought of forgetfulness you fear,
Acceptance of the end creates despite,

On all this absolution does not depend,
Between life and death all things meld,
All travels at one time must end,
Always should the celebration of life be held

Eric Harman

God Daughter

Wasn't it just yesterday, I saw you for the first time? An infant, large black liquid eyes, lost in the face of innocence. Your arms stretched out to me, held you close, hearts melting together, creating a bond. Wasn't that just yesterday?

Wasn't it just yesterday, I took pictures of you in your first communion dress. Walking up the church isle, the afternoon light shining through the stained glass windows, illuminating your still so innocent face. An aura of love flowing from you.

Wasn't it just yesterday I watched you at a swim meet? You're oh so small body vying against the older children. Little did they know they were competing against the heart and soul of a champion.

Wasn't it just yesterday, I watched you on stage at one of your many fiddle contests. How shocked the audience was to hear the experience of a lifetime streaming out of a small child. I wonder if they knew how privileged they were?

Wasn't it just yesterday, you donned your first prom dress? Dark blue velvet, trimmed with rhinestones, accenting the sparkle in your dark eyes, the deep spirit of your soul. Was that last Christmas?

Today I received an invitation to your graduation. I can hardly wait to see what tomorrow will bring.

Angelica Morrow

Patrick

Through the mist, I saw a child at play.
Laughing and happy, he called to me,
"I love you, Mom!"

Through the mist, I saw a man—tall and strong—
playing with a child — his own.
And he called to me and said,
"I love you, Mom!"

Through the mist, my veil of tears,
I saw the child-like man.
Dressed in white, he plays with angels now!
And, softly, he calls to me and says,
"I love you, Mom!"

Donna Pittman

Why

As I sat starring into your eyes
Laying beside you holding your
Hand as each minute your heart beat less
And as I think back
My heart beats less too
Now that you are gone
Sometimes I start to think
Of how I will carry on
I never told you how much I cared
Or how much you meant to me
Please don't go and leave me here
Living a life without you
This first year as life goes on
Your memory never faded
Sometimes there are times when
I can't deal with it
And I break down and cry
As I stare in the mirror
And wonder why?

Erin Bryant

The Sea

Foam comes in with a hiss and ebbs with a sigh,
Leaving tiny bubbles like a lace collar along the shore.
Only the cry of a lone sea gull disturbs the semi-quiet,
Heard against the low hum of the ever restless sea.
I sit on night cooled sand, my thoughts ebbing and flowing
    with the waves
As blackened sky becomes paler and ever so slowly the sun rises,
Barely peeking over the edge of my world.
It sends a sparkling crystal path across rising and falling waters
Beckoning me to follow its climb into the sky.
But I must go back to my noisy bustling world
Leaving the Sandpipers to run and play along the shore,
No longer a part of this eternal wild nature of sea, wind and sand.

Diana Forrester Newhall

My Sister, My Friend

A job in the valley, took you away,
leaving your house behind, close by the bay.

Me, I stayed behind to take care of the home,
where love and compassion, were always shown.

You made it so special, I remember oh so well,
when I think of my growing years,
my thoughts on you dwell.

Such inspiration and strength you did show,
Over coming obstacles, some will never know.

Times were tough, for you in many ways,
but I am so proud of the person you are today.

I'm glad your in my life, for there will never be,
another sister that I call, Rose Marie.

Debra Torquemada

Cry

Cry they say,
let all your feelings come out.
Talk they say,
sharing the pain will help.

They think that they can help me,
I used to think that too.
But I have found out there's nothing they can do.

I have cried and cried, 'till I could cry no more.
I have talked and talked, 'till there was nothing left to say.
I have stared blankly at the walls trying to forget the things
I've said or done.

At times I've wished I were crazy,
not knowing things around me
Or a child so full of innocence,
but never growing up.

Jessica Melton

The Hartford Courant

Turn back in your flight, Time.
Let me not stand alone-
Alone to shift for myself and groan
Of better days when love was mine.
When lover's footfalls would arrive
And when wild flowers were in my heart.
A time when we lovers could never part
And the world for us was so alive.
Alas - I had to suffer all the sorrow
Of parting with my love's sweetness forever,
Of having no more our shared pleasures ever.
For our love, there is no morrow.

I have loved once and have grieved,
But have loved again and again believed.

Elizabeth Pettit Varner

283

Part-Time Dad

You may think a trucker's life is really hard and bad,
Let me tell a trucker's tale about my Dad.
Even though he's mostly gone, we love him so.
That's why I sat and wrote this poem, to let him know.

He is a part-time Dad, and a full-time trucker.
He's been across this land, from one coast to the other.
You may think that he didn't care about his kids,
That's where you're wrong, I've written this poem 'cause he did.

He's got so many names, you wouldn't believe the things he's called.
He's 'Slo-poke' on the C.B., and in business his name is Claude.
He's 'Popaw' to two little boys, He's 'Honey' to his wife,
But I've just called him 'Daddy' for my whole life.

He's really a full-time Dad, and a part-time trucker,
Taking good care of his kids and loving their mother.
If you ever met a trucker who was really all that bad,
I pity you so, 'cause you never met my Dad!

Brenda Lee Edmonson

"Touch Me One More Time"

Lay down beside my body
Let your flesh touch mine
Roaming mouth upon my skin
Warm fingers move in time

Kiss me with your body
Beside me where it's warm
Linger with your fantasies
Arouse my moving form

If you could stay with me we'd make love again
I know you have to go, before you do
"Touch me one more time"

My love will fill your body
As yours get lost in mine
Like two shadows on the wall
That move in graceful time

I miss you when you leave
I long to hold you near
To give you all my love
To kiss away each fear

If you could stay with me we'd make love again
I know you have to go, before you do
"Touch me one more time"

Carol Kimzey

Little Sister, Little Brother

Little sister and brother
Let's get involved, there is so many problems
That need to be solved, the problems we see and
Hear each day, is pulling this generation further away
Little sister and brother let's map out a plan, one that
We all can understand. Let's turn in the gun's the real and
The fake lets stop this violence for goodness sake.
Little sister and brother how long do we live in fear?
Can't you see it's getting us nowhere.
Lets stop this violence killing one another I'm talking
To you, little sister and brother. Before you think about
Getting a gun, stop and think do you really want to shoot
Someone? Before you think about pulling that trigger, whatever
The problem, it'll just get bigger. Before you act, take time to
Think, is it worth the level, to which you'll sink?
Let's stop the violence, killing one another,
I'm talking to you
My little sister and brother.

Florence Lorraine Thomas

"Beyond The Distant Mountains"

Beyond the distant mountains
lies a treasure of fortune fame
It isn't a treasure of what you think
but a beauty that can't be claimed
Few people take it seriously but it is as
strong as any power that can overtake
And its power is natural, much more
Natural than any man could ever make
A stream ripples over ridged rocks, and
makes the land of the mountains even truer
As I stop to stare the wind whispers to the
mountain its regal beauty is being noticed.

Jayme Hansen

Life

Life; a deep breath on a foggy morn
Life; a heavy sigh from the chest was torn
Today a great gold star with paste
Tomorrow you choke on the bittersweet taste

Sail away, sail away, on the mind's breeze
Thoughts can control anything you please
Then damp and soggy everything you wear
Shivering and shaking and hiding from stares

Making love to the sun and dance for the moon
Into the arms of desire we will fully swoon
Promise, a sacred word captive in a heart
Tomorrow is here, yet there is not a start

Death in the eyes of a vacant stare
Someone with whom there was a care
Laughter bouncing round every place
then leaves the earth into distant space

Power and wonder surged through a vein
only to bleed and drip on flesh again
Musty books smiled from dank shelves
and in their words, you saw yourself

Alanna Swenson

Miss America 1995 — Heather Whitestone

She was normal when brought into this world,
Life became questionable when she was a little girl,
Cause the reactions from medication left her deaf,
And left parents wondering if she could survive by herself.

Her life started by taking ballet when she was five years old,
And going off to schools and to college as she was told,
Trying to prove her doctor's predictions were wrong,
And to others within her heart that she was strong.

Then she set her goals using the five points of a star,
So anyone can overcome their handicapped no matter who you are,
Your goals in life can be accomplished no matter how hard you strive,
She did it by becoming Miss Alabama and Miss America 1995.

Being deaf does not leave us out of the normal crowd,
She proved to us all and we should be proud,
So be positive, work hard, believe in your dreams,
face your obstacles and build a support team.

Christopher G. Abbett

A Time for Us

Love, an emotion we can't hide.
Laughter, something that comes from inside.
Life, a combination of the two.
This time was meant, for me and you.

Anna Marie Zoland

Untitled

Mere thoughts of him
Lift her spirits and
Tug at the corners of her mouth
Resting upward in the form of a smile
Wandering fragments of unintentional laughter
Blur
Silently, he looks towards her
The vanishing surroundings seem lifeless
While their chocolate eyes meet
Joining, as he crumples his face
Molding his features into "their look"
She returns the knowing expression
Silently
Glancing slowly away they feel at ease
As one

Jessica Montour

Sun—Water

Warm sunlight on my feet
Light green, fresh green leaves catching the sun
against the grey purple hills of Winter past.
Spring flood water rushing, sparkling in the sunshine.
Birds flying, swooping, chirping, swirring, making love
—Spring—new life—Resurrection

Georgia L. Newsom

A Painting Dripping

As I looked upon a person dying slowly and sadly,
  like a drip falling from a painting.
As I saw the beauty that is now passing away,
  as I looked at the death I saw paint dripping away.
She is dead, but the beauty in her is still alive.
As I saw the death of my relative, I said to myself in my mind,
  "She is dead in life, but alive in my heart."

Dripping away our happiness on that day,
  when the painting dripped that's when our happiness was black,
But when I looked at her my soul was bright.
She was as smart as a painter, and as beautiful as a painting,
  and still is inside the heart of a painter.

Johnny Sadoff

Treasured Friend

The time we shared was beautiful.
Like a sunset on the ocean.
This beauty will last forever in my heart.

Our laughter will be remembered in my soul.
Like the memories a child holds.
I will hear our laughter in every smile I see.

Your kiss will linger on my lips.
Like the sweetness of a rose petal.
I will feel them there every passing day.

Your touch was so gentle and inspiring.
Like a warm summer breeze.
I will cherish those moments for all my life.

Talking to you was easy and peaceful.
Like the warmth a fire brings on a winter's night.
There will never be another so comforting.

Our friendship will last forever.
Like a picture you've painted and hung on the wall.
I will treasure it as I treasured you.

Beth Christianson

The Poet

Deep from the heart come the poet's words
  like a well Spring running free
His thoughts flowing like a rippling brook
  to a graceful willow tree.
He may speak of a mother's tender love
  as she cradles her babe so dear
Or the ravage of a violent storm
  that all the world may fear
He may tell of the things that may have been
  and things that are soon to be
But it's deep from his heart he pens the words
  for the joy of you and me.

Dorothy Mae Evans

Big Dreams

Big dreams
like castles in the sand
aren't known for their durability
and they are never quite like you planned.
I've had plenty of big dreams
but each and every one fell through
without affirmative action
big dreams can't come true.
The bigger the dreams
the higher the hopes
the bigger the fantasy
the farther you fall.
Big dreams
like castles in the sand
they're not around for long
you turn around and they're gone - again!

Janet M. LaCross

"Icicles"

Icicles forming on the bottom of the car
  Like dirty daggers hanging from a killer's room
Slush and mud all about
  As if blood had stained them
Cold and smooth icicles
  Like an assassin's attitude
Frigid at the car's underbelly
  And on the bottom of life's sanity

Water, the aftermath of the hot sun
  And finger prints identify
Nothing left but shattered cubes
  Nothing left but a shattered life
Still cold and desolate, melting away
  Hiding in a deserted prison cell
Just waiting for another freezing day
  Just waiting for another freezing day

Jason Kenneth Serafin

Little Daffodils

Little Daffodils go to sleep you've had a big Day
Little Daffodils tomorrow's rain will wash away Dust
Little Daffodils it's time to reach for a Star
Little Daffodils your seedlings are deeply Rooted
Little Daffodils while you sleep, Angels watch over You
Little Daffodils you welcome the Sunlight, you're Flourished
Little Daffodils there's wordings to describe your Beauty
Little Daffodils they're those who admire your Beauty
Little Daffodils new seedlings await your new Comings
Little Daffodils you've captivated all of America
Little Daffodils go to sleep, the Stars and angels watch over You
Little Daffodils rain will wash away the dust, guarded by Angels

Dicky Overstreet

Age

The relic lay agonizingly still,
like the calm after the storm of the sea.
The prison was the physique,
and locked inside was he.

His hinges, frozen with years of rust,
couldn't be coaxed to bend.
But what good is an open cell,
when the captive is chained from within?

For all of his friends took part in the crime,
and all of his friends were caught.
No one could escape the night-watchman,
who weakened senses and muscle and thought.

He was only one of many to pay the price,
of inhaling the sky and of walking the earth.
But inside the solitary candle still glowed,
from the wick lit brilliantly at his birth.

And so he whispered "goodbye" to her and all,
and retreated inside his cocoon.
Sometime near he'll fly like the monarch,
with wing beating softly against the moon.

Bernadette McDougall

Moods

Moods, so complex-
Like the wind, North, South, East or West.

Moods, so unpredictable-
Like the sun - filled with shiny rays,
    but sometimes coal black on the more miserable days.

Moods, so diverse-
Like a breeze - whisking 'cross a silent glittering beach,

Moods, undependable-
Like the chilliest of a cold winter's day,
Sometimes frostbite thawed in such a cunning way.

Moods, uncontrollable-
Like a part of every day living,
Sometimes not a part of every day giving.
Moods.

Cindy Grantham

Rejection

And they all look at you
Like they all know a secret
But you believe there's nothing wrong.

Whether it's just a belief, or what you really know
Doesn't matter anymore
Because you should know by now
That you are so powerless
And your opinion doesn't count.

You watch constantly from the outside
Seeing everyone's little novel in color
Waiting for your number
To be called
So people can see your story
With you on the inside.

Things come too naturally to you
like
Dripping out of a faucet
And you keep laughing
'Cause it's just so hard for all the oblivious others...

And you always know why.

Ashlee Rudert

Listen, My Children, Listen

Listen and think, my children, of the days of yestertime.
Listen, and think of every little rhyme.
For these are the days of tomorrow and yesterday.
These are the times when our minds go out to play.
We do not think of answers, to questions we do not know.
Time has stopped and our minds will only grow.
Reasoning is not by your side to help with any fight.
For you will not know the reason why you are right.
Nothing can harm you, for what is harm?
Every where you go someone is leading you by the arm.
If only it were easier, and time went on this way,
But now our minds have stopped to play.
Growing has begun now, and our minds seem to be laden,
But there is still lots of room for little ideas to be made in.
Time is speeding for us, but the journey's just begun.
Days are getting longer, but are decreasing in fun.
We grow throughout this time of mystery.
Sometimes making a mark in our minds history.
Listen and think, my children, of the days of yestertime.
Listen, and think of every little rhyme.

Christen Majba

My Corner Of Midnight

I sit alone in the darkness, my corner of midnight
Listening to silence, the sounds of my life
With tears flowing down and sadness in my heart
I sit alone and wonder why we had to part
You've been gone so long, it's left me empty inside
I wish this on no one, I wish no one this time
I wait for the day, we'll be united again
It seems like forever, but I'll wait till then
When our time comes, will you know my face
Will your heart reach out to me, is there a smile on your face
Is it what I've wanted, has time stood still
Until we are together, I can wait till then

Judy Stewart

The Other

I lay quietly next to his warm body, pleading for sleep to come,
Listening to the sound of winter sleet, tapping against the pane.

His hands are soft and gentle...
Seeking a response that doesn't come.
My body presses deeper into the darkness,
Hoping to find comfort there.

I close my eyes, as a shiver runs through my body,
Wanting release from the tension building inside.
I can feel the warmth of his hand where it rests flooding into me.
Not the searing, burning touch that penetrates
my very soul at its nearness.

I can smell the heat start to thicken in the room
Breathing quicker, heart beating faster;
Not mine, pounding wildly in my chest
Until the noise thunders in my ears, and I think the world can hear

Silently my heart protests, and then somewhere,
Against the strain and aching,
Somewhere between rest and slumber, as the probing continues...
I lose, and then the dull, swollen, emptiness, begins
Creeping before the anger.

Charlotte A. Haven

Fire Fire!

That summers night while I was sleeping,
little did I know about the fire that was creeping.
That night when I woken while I was sleeping,
to the sounds of the fire alarm shrieking.
I got up and went into the hall,
just in time to see the kitchen ceiling fall.
I ran into my room and picked up the phone,
the phone was dead there was no tone,
but I wasn't about to lose my head.
But to much of my mistake,
my family I almost did forget to awake.
We all ran from the house,
and as we did we all saw a mouse.
As we all four gathered in the yard,
We stood, we watched, but it was really hard.
There I was watching my home get eaten by the
animal called fire,
and all I could do was watch it climb higher and higher.

Clayton Noon

Forever

As she walks through the vast empty field;
little does she know her loved one will soon be killed.
She calls out his name as it echoes back through the
house, she can hear nothing, not even a mouse.
As she walks through the house room to room, she sees a man
lying there, her very first groom. As she looks at the blood
covered floor, she sees the knife in his shirt all tore.
She has so many questions, the first one why?
Why was it him, why did he have to die? As she strains to reach
for the phone, she hears a soft, mumbled groan, she feels a
tear drop fall down her cheek, as her hands feel cold,
shaky, and week. As the last numbers dialed on 911, she knows
the police are soon to come.
As she holds him in her arms just one last time, she wonders,
did he kill himself or who committed this crime.
She remembers all the memories they had together
she knows she'll always love him forever and ever.

Bridgette N. Hood and Kim Herron

Dedication To An Album

A glimpse of the past is enclosed herein,
  Little pictures make us smile or grin,
And preserve a scene which brings joy from within.

Remember the day when we all went
  So happily on our way
To the lake in the mountains, just pleasure bent
  What fun, what a beautiful day.

Time is a thing which never stops
  And memory fades so fast
The bloom from our countenance quickly drops
  Soon youth takes its place in the past.

But a picture preserves in exact detail
  That which we wish to remember
Then over smooth water we can again sail,
  As, long ago, that beautiful day in September.

Alma Shipp

Untitled

Once upon a time,
Love was a splendid thing.
But I can no longer bear the pain
  of watching it crumble before my eyes.
I must leave—
  and pray I have the strength to survive.

Diane Briski

A Visit To Emily's House

During the drive to Massachusetts
little shacks, big shacks packed up against the earth
I wondered how you traveled from Amherst to Holyoke
and back to church.
I came to find inspiration
paid three dollars to walk inside the door
sitting on a brocade piano bench
I purchased a brochure.
Listening to the clock tick away a chime
I saw Vinnie's eyes
watching mine.
I know you, quite often I see you
only to be reminded that nothing really changed
Jacob still wrestles with the angel
for all that you arranged.

And summoned, by white dusted lace
airlessly mantled in glass
your square hemmed pocket
sails without a mast
on yellow sheets and string.

Diane Fesko

The Dancing Fish And The Blue Coral

Deep in the ocean blue, on a sunken ship,
live a silverfish, and a blue coral.
The coral liked to sing, and the fish liked to dance.

When the tide is full, coral sings my life,
below the ocean blue, is full of wonders,
colors, and adventures too, Tee'rah, Tee'rah, dee,
do: May I sing a song for you.

When the sun goes down behind the clouds,
and the ocean look all misty and warm, the
drums aboard the sunken ship, begins to,
beat a mystic tune. The silverfish begins,
to sway, flap his fins, winks his eyes and
away he goes dancing by.

The silvery light of the midnight sky,
and the mystic beat of the mysterious,
Drums, Oh what a wondrous sight.

They sing and dance till morning light.

Eulanhie Anderson

Lilacs

I haven't known her since those warm,
Lolling days of youth.
Still I find her
In overgrown paths of a memory long forgotten.
Purple skin seen through misty eyes
That stretched long before this day.

How can I admit such a meeting
Knowing that as sure as I was once lulled by her breath,
I shall never be in her arms again?

Still I cradle the blossom in my heart.
For I cannot forget
The heaven of her sweet touch
On my lost halo of gold,
And the gaze that met mine
In endless horizons of lavender.

Emily Klare Ladwig

Untitled

There's this girl I know; she is tall and slim, her hair dark and long, her almond shaped eyes are like hazelnut and glow with a bright-light, she makes my heart feel, whole, like I've never felt before. A hunger for life exudes from her being. She wears a smile that's as innocent as a larks.
There's this girl that I know, she is a woman now, masked by ages' gentility, her soul has weathered hard times, but she, she is not hard. Though, she seems numbed by life's bestowments.
There's this woman I know, I love thee, how my heart aches with a pang - but she is numb - numb to me. Her eyes still have a glow but they hide their smile. Her hunger for life seems quenched, her being - is just being, her smile remains innocent, but too rare to remember.
There's this woman that I know, she made me feel good - like I never felt before. I loved thee - how my heart ached with my love for thee. But, but she is numb, numb to me.

Gary S. Alan

Freedom Finally

I broke the chains with my own two hands and cried with joy. No longer bound was I. Finally able to follow my heart and not the harsh unforgiving words that I am so accustomed to. No more shouts or yells or degrading comments to bind my mind and soul. No more cold, hard and hurting irons to bind my hands and feet. I can sing with all the joy in the world, or with all the sorrow. I can now dance in broad daylight with no fear. My eyes can see more than everything, my ears can hear more than all, and now they do it freely. No whip will reprimand me, my stomach will no longer hurt with punishment. I rejoice in words and actions on this happy day. I eat the feast set before me with a happy heart and soul. I listen to the music and am joyful that I am here with my family at last, finally free.

Jamie Blauvelt

Birds In The Trees!

I sat by my window,
looked up through the trees.
A flock of birds were singing in the breeze.
Playing and chirping and flying around
How happy they were.
They didn't want to come down.

Then all of a sudden the Chirping stopped
And all I could see
were the lonely tree tops.
Away through the branches the birds all flew.
To a part of the sky I never knew.

Oh how free it seems to be
To watch the birds fly away from the tree.
Without a care or worry in mind.
The birds flew north in just a matter of time.

I sat by my window feeling lonely and sad.
Wishing that I could have the fun the birds had.
Flying around all happy and free
Without a care in the world
In the top of the tree.

Bernice Frost

Celestial Harmony

A glow is shed by a milky orb
Luminating shadowed and leafy boughs.
Smoothly meandering, a brook flows through,
Strewn with leaves and flower petals.
It glistens as plenilune drops her tears,
Washing over infinite grains of pebbles.
Her silvery stare is cast upon the hills
And down, down, down in the valleys.
The silver crescent speaks of yesteryear,
Of harmony within the heavens.

Joanne Hammer

Untitled

My body aches - lack of satisfaction
Looking for a reaction
My heart is bleeding—-
Old wounds are slow to heal

Time to leave this dungeon I've made
The prison walls are getting small
I've become quite anemic — loss of blood
Trying to escape —-
My senses are blocked — unable to feel

My heart is open
Lying in a puddle of blood —-
drowning in regression

I have lost consciousness,
Can this be for real—-
A state of shock

Trying to be as young and free
And in love
As the child I once was

Before the pain
Long before this waiting game.

Jal Clinkscales

The Prayer

Lord God, touch each and everyone here today,
    Lord in a special way.
Show them that you have wonderful powers,
    And that you someday might be their tower.
Lord bring them on mountains and out of valleys,
    And Lord, please show them the right road and not the
    wrong alley.
Please touch them with your divine healing and your wondrous love,
    For one day you will be descending down just like a dove.
Lord we shall call on the angels from up on high,
    And when we see them we shall never say good-bye.
You see we are not judged by our stature below,
    Our faith will be the only one to show.
Now I will end this little prayer,
    Letting you know that I love and care.
        Amen...

Autumn Miller

The Journey

Shyly, quietly, hesitantly,
    Love begins its life-long voyage.
Hard to determine its beginning,
    Wondering if, where, when, it will end.
We begin as friends, meet as lovers,
    Travel as companions, together.
Through frequent stops, long waits, detours,
    Love grows, trust blooms, faith flourishes.

Together, two become three; then more.
    We meet over questioning, childlike eyes.
With hands reaching, hearts bound together,
    We have traveled years, decades in a moment.
Guiding each other, our children, our family,
    We have become a tradition.
Sharing joys, sorrows, fears, pain,
    Together, we have become one.

Darlayne L. Yliniemi

288

My Love

My love for you is like no other
love I have known.

Feelings of ecstasy overpower my mind
and body.

These feelings carry me through until we
once again passionately fulfill the
cravings of our very souls.

To surrender to your touch is like the
opening sunburst — beckoning you to
conquer what is yours.

Ella Washington

The Special Gift

It can only come from above, spreading wings like Mother Hens
give love. If your heart is right you will see a beautiful light.
The poor, the rich, they both have it, but only a few will ever
understand it. Some take it for granted, some cherish it, only a
few ever find it. For those who rush through it, Pity themselves
in the end for not realizing it. For those who abuse others with
it, will only find out in the end the price they will have to pay
long began. For some it's so powerful that confusion comes from
it, without understanding they seek various ways to destroy it.

Those who really understand it can only love it. They pray for
those who abuse it and cry for those who never got a chance to
use it. For those who waited too late to enjoy the beauty of it
will one day weep for never stopping to realize it. Bless those
who take medication to prolong it, for they too understand it.
For those who cannot see, seasons of the year is when they really
hear. It's so simple to understand that Birds sings about it, even
Bees nourish from it. Say what you want, do as you like, if your
heart isn't right you will never see the light. If your Soul is pure
and you are very sure, enduring pain is only part of the cure.
The path of Life is narrow, how we appreciate this gift
determines our SOUL Value.

Bill Logan, Jr.

Someday . . .

Someday, the world will be a perfect place to live,
Love shall be the only emotion we will give.
Someday, there will be no existence of cruelty and abuse,
Our educated minds shall be put to sensible use.
Someday, we will be united and live as equals,
We'll set aside this old book and begin a sequel.
Someday, hidden differences in customs and beliefs,
Shall be acknowledged and accepted to everyone's relief.

Someday, we will not live in fear,
Greetings shall be shared with strangers and those most dear.
Someday, there will be no guns to protect and kill,
Weapons causing insanity shall be eliminated at will.
Someday, there will be no experience of suffering and pain,
Person to person each will learn and shall gain.

Someday, the environment shall flourish in abundant beauty,
Pleasing Mother-Nature for respecting and doing our duty.
Someday, the sun shall shine radiantly bright,
We will find the power to change and to do what's right.
Someday, we will all be able to say,
It's been a wonderful life from the very first day.

Claudia Angela Morelli

Forever Young

Be brave my love it's time once more to hear the voice of that
one love who bleeds your soul.

Do you not understand this love is not to be? Yet, knowing that
it is, dare not release it to be free...confined it must remain.

A love so old it feels the desolation of the aged and an intensity
so great it cries out in the night and in the private places of the
heart and mind.

Were it not for the memories of things which might have been
you would be free of this cursed love affair with time.

A time when love was young and free...young and
innocent...young and daring...young and everlasting.

And, everlasting it has been, no longer young...no longer
free...no longer innocent...no longer daring...just, everlasting.

So once again, be brave...be strong...be glad that you have that
which should not be...there's no control in love and time...they
come and go but never leave my soul.

Elvia Saldivar Cecil

America's Flag

A merica has a flag, you know,
M any years I hope it waves.
E veryone sings its song, standing in a row,
R ed white and blue, colors that gave freedom to its slaves
"I n God we trust" is our motto, and
C ourage it gives our men at war
A nd forever it should fly, the
'S tars and Stripes we have come to adore
   because it is our flag.
F reedom is the thing it stands for, as is
L iberty, justice and a whole lot more.
A merica has a flag, you know, and it is
G oing to fly forever!

Joy Nichols

Searching The Past

The beam of the flashlight
made a narrow tunnel of brightness
through the dark attic.
Its rays picking out three old, wooden chairs;
lying on the floor, entangled like the forms
from some long-ago lover's triangle
where none had released the other-
legs enlaced; backs unbending.
Two boxes, the bases for cobwebs
and covered with dust and dead flies
held nothing; like empty coffins
in a silent grave.
Leftovers of another time were gone-
leaving behind yesterday's odors and memories;
haunting one who once lived there.
Ancient echoes and dim shadows
had ground into the old floor
or sifted through tiny ceiling cracks-
free at last from the past
like the one holding the flashlight.

Joan Stephen

And You Say.....”Come On Baby”

Each place we go, each sight we see,
Makes me love you more, when you're next to me.
If I have my way, I'll be by your side.
Close to you, stuck like glue - when we swim, walk or ride.
And you say…”Come on, Baby.”

See us ride, side by side — destination unknown.
From the start, heart to heart — close to you, I have grown.
Face to face, every place — we just groove right along.
You're the top, never stop — we sing “LOVE” in our song.
And you say…”Come on, Baby.”

Everywhere, sea or air — we go hand in hand.
Precious joy, we employ — love, we understand.
Arm in arm, soft and warm — stretched out on the beach.
This is clear, we stay near — at least in arm's reach.
And you say…”Come on, Baby.”

Love's the way, everyday — happiness is our goal.
Here we go, toe to toe — mind, heart, body and soul.
There's no doubt, you won out — I dig hanging around.
Ready to leave? Pull my sleeve — we'll check out the town.
And I just love to hear you say…”Come on, Baby!”

Carolyn Ann Shephard

Man

Man is born of many things; of soul, of flesh and blood
Man is born of many things; of evil, of lust and good.

His first years are spent in quiet at his mother's breast
These are the peaceful years, when things are at their best.

Then, comes the toddling years at his father's knee
With the seed of growth instilled, he blossoms like a tree.

All the pleasant years of childhood, the secrets yet untold
Then, with the fleeting years, nature's secrets now unfold.

The youthful mind inquisitive, seeks the learning of the ages
The adventure and knowledge pour from still, white pages.

Thus, filled with knowledge, he seeks things on his own
The mind instilled with other ideas, once more becomes his own.

Early years of manhood, he's now aware of passing years
He makes his way into the world with many unshed tears.

His first romance, then many more, till at last his bride to be
Then more fleeting years go by, and his own son at his knee.

Thus, a cycle, on and on, like an endless chain.
As an old one passes on, a young one takes his place again.

Is this then not eternal life, the continuation of the kin?
With this process oft repeated, since all time began.

Jack W. Dempsey

Despair Or Loving Care

Many people in this world are sad.
  More people than not seem to be mad.
It seems only a few people are really glad,
  With the best reason that can be had.

The Devil has treated them all unfair;
  And when they came to the slough of despair,
He offered no help and left them there.
  Glad ones sought the one who really does care.

God cares so much He gave His Son,
  Who on the Cross their victory won.
When they called on Him new life was begun,
  Forgiveness, freedom, and love in life to run.

Helen Ruth Ewing

Ten Thousand Times Ten Thousand Times

Today my heart beats ten thousand times ten thousands times

He who would slay the Prince of Peace
Man of compassion, dignity, love for all mankind

What manner of man to see him fall unmoved

My heartache throbs ten thousand times his life, my soul to free
To stride, and not to strive toward peace, love, and unity

How shall I now continue - sing, preach or pray
What measure use to direct and chart my rugged way

With pride of self, a determined will and faith in God
He'll guide me still

And if it means my life to give
I'll yield it all The Dream to live

But Jesus please forgive the sin
Purge hatred out - let love flow in

For only when Thy work I've done
I'll take my place beyond the sun

My heart beat thunders ten thousand times ten
For life support - and love support

For Martin Luther King

Eleanor F. Hart

Silent Messenger

Now silently I gaze upon this flower of pastel hue,
Marveling at the tender stalk from which it gracefully grew.
I'm simply captivated by this lovely, flourishing bloom.
Moist with dew and sunlight's rays, its fragrance like perfume.

What peace, what inspiration, I gather from it here,
Transported from my daily toils, it melts my stress and fears.
It surrounds me with serenity, it moves my heart to sing,
As silently to one and all its message sweet it brings.

Its power undeniable while its beauty permeates,
I am truly captive to the bliss that it creates.
Feeling calm and grateful, too, my spirit to enhance
By gathering in its message full of life and radiance.

May each and every onlooker possess the eye to see
As he wanders seeking refuge from this world's calamity.
May each who strolls this garden path, see just what he must see,
To clear his mind or cleanse his heart or set his spirit free.

Day grows short as I tarry her within this garden view,
But I shall hold this moment fresh of a flower that I knew.
As silently I gaze upon this bloom of pastel hue,
Marveling at the tender stalk from which it gracefully grew.

Ellen Russell

Happy Nineteenth Birthday

Happy Birthday to the young man Steve!
May he have many more and continue to weave
That beautiful tapestry of his life,
So firmly woven with no hint of strife -
A carefully - fashioned lifetime of all things good.
He's becoming the man we knew he would
Bringing to all of us pride and joy
Just as we found in the growing boy.

Evelyn Z. Maguire

Worth It?

There's a boy in the park, harassing an old lady.
Maybe somebody should call the police. Maybe
someone should do something, before it gets worse,
But there goes that little punk off running with her purse.
He jumped a park bench, and ran into a cop,
Who tried to slow the kid, but the boy couldn't stop.
You see his parents are out of money, and his mother lost her job,
And his father owes a lot of greenbacks to the local mob.
Heart-pounding, mind-racing the boy ran through the night.
But soon was stopped instantly by a passing black-and-white.
Out of breath, the boy quit, he'd had enough,
And was led into the black-and-white, with his hands in cuffs.
Eighteen months in the state pen.. that ain't too nifty.
And all the lady had was a lousy two-fifty.

Joe Pinciaro

Twilight Psalm

God I am still counting the sandy shore birds,
Measuring the distance of the galaxies
Nothing changes with Him.

The zinnas bloom, rivers flow
  Butterflies fly.

All hope and courage begin and end with Him.
  Love is him mantle
  Straight his path
  Comforts his bosom.

Tho' we falter our steps weary, endless is His mercy.

  He knows our clay fragments
  The cries of our hearts
  Before they are spoken

Come lean upon your Father, for I have known thee,
Before worlds yet unspoken.

Gather your flowers, catch the distilled of the rain.
In the garner of harvest; planted for your hearts token

Shalom, peace dear son and daughter,
For I am your Shepherd.

Augusta Nelson

Inseparable

  My love for you is like a rose in full bloom in the
middle of winter. A thing that any one would appreciate and
admire because of its undying endurance and beauty. Love that
is as strong as my love for you is as the very earth that rose
grows from. I will hold you, my love, until you are picked from
me and put somewhere else and admired. If your maker decides
to have you plucked from me, I will have supported you in what
ever did. I will always consider you mine and I yours because of
the time we have spent together and the way we have made each
other. I have molded you, as you have me, as we've weathered
every storm.
Our love is inseparable.

Donna R. Hayes

Untitled

Man thinks he has evolved to the point where he should
migrate into space,
Yet mankind's inhumanity to mankind here on Earth is
an indescribable disgrace.
God in His perfect wisdom has placed us light years away,
From any other beings we may meet someday.
If and when we become civilized to live in peace and love,
We may be allowed to migrate beyond and above.

James P. Federnok

"When I Think Of You"

When I think of you, I see all I believe in...
Miracles happen, from thoughts I once dreamed in...

When I think of you, I see sunshine and laughter —
a warm resting place; a kiss to come after, a softened embrace.

When I think of you, there are fireworks flying,
a candlelight glowing; a proud father smiling...

When I think of you, I see all I believe in...
The peace in a sunset —
The joy of marriage —
The fun of our loving,
A new baby carriage...
A romantic walk,
A life all brand new —
And forever beginning...
A life filled with you.

There'll be clouds up above, but with big silver linings...
Our faith will endure, and the sun will keep shining...

When I think of you....
Fidelity lives there, and trust is made new...
To have and to hold...my love, I love you.

Darlene DeIorio Benson

African Woman

African woman you are the backbone of earth
more than silver, gold, and diamonds for all its worth
the brilliance in your mind
definitely makes you one of a kind
your features bold and beautiful
to any black man your are plentiful
fullness in those tasteful lips
strut in those hips
power in that strong nose
so hold your head up and pose
towards the heavenly sky
for you are the black man's natural high
therefore keep a bright smile
because you are grace and style
Queen of all
without you a king could not stand tall
remember no strong African woman
no strong African man
African woman

Antanus Pullum

What Is Truth?

Out in the woods in the crisp morning air — you see a flower, a
morning glory in all its beauty...the dabbled sunlight glistening
across the dew, rests nature's tears its petals—and the fragrance
of a thousand flowers, and so many things you feel but cannot see,
waft over you—you sense and feel truth, intangible and fleeting,
but none-the-less—Truth.

A stranger arrives—too late, the flower closes sealing its truth
within; you try to describe the beauty, its form, substance as you
saw it—it can't be done...the late arrival understands...bending
down, he cups the closed morning glory in his hand; yet realizing
he will never know the beauty of its truth as it was the moment it
opened in the morning dew.

So forget things you've read; the sentences and words...think
only of the images that truth creates in your own mind and the
feelings that stir and warm your spirit—these then are the truth—
truth is not in your voice, eyes, ears, nose, or touch; truth isn't
what dreams and visions are about.

Truth is all the things it can be—truth is complete—truth is the
total image engraved fully and indelibly in your mind—truth is
something we all have within us—only we know when it
happens..only we feel its full strength.

The image we perceive and hold within us...becomes our own TRUTH!

Douglas Reagan Whatley

Angel In White

i see an angel in white
morphine the disciple of the sleep god
has temporarily returned me from his realm

i see an angel in white
she is encouraging the medical umbilical
running life and death into and out of my body

i see an angel in white
how she can stand to care for
the valiantly dead the violently dying the viciously mangled

i see an angel in white
a tear flows down her cheek
her only answer is because

i see an angel in white
she will receive none of my medals for valor
though her valor be greater than mine

George William Newport

"My Mother The Angel"

In my mind I can see a picture of one of the world's
most notable angels... my mother.
She is positioned on a rock that symbolizes all the
obstacles she has conquered, and behind her the sun is
setting behind a huge mountain - portraying the obstacles
yet to come.
She is standing with her head slightly bowed in
innocence while a halo dances above her, shining
almost as brightly as her stunning smile.
Around her tattered and torn clothing I can see the ghostly
shadow of a protective, golden armor which God himself
put there to protect her from all the dangers in life.
While she stands there in all her warmth and beauty, I
can see her shed a tear, and I watch this tear trickle
down her cheek and fall upon the red rose she is holding
in her loving, prayer-like formed hands.
Having this picture in my mind and in my heart gives me
a reason to do the best I can to make this angel, my
Mother, proud of me.

Annie Lamplen

The Urban Killing Fields

Senseless violence at a random stage,
Most of which is under age.
Lift the hammer, pull the switch.
Now you've killed the son of a bitch!
You shriek with laughter, and shoot some more.
You shoot another, he hits the floor.
Find some cops and shoot them dead.
Is this the life you really lead?
Went trigger-happy with a gun.
Kill seven people, now that was fun!

Joseph Ciaglia

Janu-Weary Blues

I'm fighting fever, stifling sneezes,
Must have stood in chilly breezes.
Tried to ignore it, found I couldn't,
Thought I'd die! (was afraid I wouldn't!)
Feel some better, tho spine lacks starch.
I think I'll stay in bed 'til March!

Coral L. Stone

The Child-Voice Of Love

Sickle moon hangs in the twilight,
Muted and ethereal in the starless sky,
Wreathed like my heart on this autumn night
By the clouds and mist that around her fly.

Lovely are eyes first stirring with love:
A quickening tempest igniting the soul,
Heady winds that move us and lift us
Higher than where we would normally go.

Chaining me once again to time
Is the touch and the feel of that love,
Like a child-voice innocent and undefined:
A promise of what it may become.

The night sky is barren once again,
Autumn winds now unsuitable company;
Emotion (like the moon) having fled,
Though she inspired my brief reverie.

For I am lost once again and left behind
While the touch and the feel of that love,
Like a child-voice innocent and undefined
Passes through me like a ghost.

John Stephenson Jr.

Lamia

My glittering eyes you cannot resist
My bone-white skin you cannot miss
You're scent is overwhelming, I want your blood, my dear
I see the brightness darkening in your lovely my eyes,
I sense your fear

I am a child of darkness, my lover, perhaps even a tortured mind
A child of the eons, with experience spanning time
I'm immortal and damned, damned to feed on your life
The life I can never have again.
and that painful knowledge cuts sharper then..... a knife

But come, my love, I lust for your blood, that sweetest wine
I enjoy toying with your mind, your fragile will, I will bind
I am the wolf, you are the cunning fox-so maybe I'll bring you
into this sweet, dark secret; this lovely paradox

I'll teach you how to master the night, though you'll
never again see the light of day
Don't be afraid, my dear, I'm not the devil..... my heart is gray
I might make you one of us, pretty one, but first I must drink;
this blood lust burns like fire
I have you now, lover, for I am Lamia.... Vampire

Jason C. Walsh

Now And Then

Then
My dear Luther.
   Now that we are growing older,
you might think our love doesn't
mean much all I need is your electrifying
touch and darling I love you still.

   Now
Now that you are gone
I have to walk alone
each step I make,
each breath I take
I'll still be loving you.

Hattie B. Williams

Untitled

Difficult to accept-
My fate was already assigned.
When will I eliminate the fog?
And think with a clear mind.
My impulsive behaviors.
These unrealistic dreams.
Make insanity the reality,
So sickening it seems.
My inspiration for life -
Now wants to take my hand.
Its wishes will be granted -
If I soon don't take my stand.
Living true to reality,
Even playing the family role.
This could be one fantasy - turned reality,
A dream he never stole.
The lights are flashing, the bells are ringing,
Euphoria … I'm ridding that wave.
Will this remedy - that made me its slave;
Take me to the end - another plot - another grave…?

Andrew M. Lombardo

Untitled

A slender piece of grass drifting in the wind.
My hair drifts too.
Grass, as I hold up a peace
   is nothing
But this is where my mind clicks
   and all the tiny tumblers fall into place.
And the grass becomes something.

The frolic and the play of grass
The grass does not move
   but it still plays.
It plays with our minds.

Andrew B. Kasprzak

A Vision Of Love

When first I saw you standing there
My heart knew that it had to care.
Your splendid image my mind rushed to capture
Not ever have I known such rapture.
That we could share a grand romance
Oh, how my spirit would sing and dance.
Alas, may the prayers of my soul come true
That you love me as I love you.

Janet McNally Brown

Ghosts

My love is a shadow cloaked in my dreams,
My hopes of the past shattered by schemes.
In a crowd passing by, out of reach, out of time.
My love is a shadow but mine, all mine.

My love is an echo, a lost chord of love.
A promise of wealth, a high-soaring dove.
In the shadows of hope, in the lilt of a song,
My love is an echo but gone, now gone.

After nightfall I search through the cares of the day
but it's out of my reach, it's just too far away.

My love is a shadow that follows me ever,
But I can't draw it in, it's too free far too clever.
It's a past joy of youth, it's my own memory.
My love is a shadow that ever taunts me.

Barbara H. Tedd

A Dream Fades

My world was full of laughter. Now its full of tears
My life was full of dreams but now I'm full of fears.

I remember the happy times when wedding bells were heard,
But now I know it was all an act and love is just a word.

Now I know, she never loved him, not the way that he loved her
I only wish she would have told us what her true feelings were.

I always believed in wishes and I believed in hope,
even when the world around me thought it one big Joke.

I believed in happy endings, romance, magic and love
But I realized life isn't fairies and Angels up above.

With only two people my dreams were shared
but they broke my heart I thought that she cared.

I had the vision of their wedding. It was only in my heart.
And in my dreams I always thought that they would never part.

Now I'm left to pick up the pieces of all my shattered dreams.
No one cares and they don't know just what this truly means.

I learned I can't believe in dreams and so I have to say,
You can't live for the future you must live for today.

I don't want it to be like this, I don't want the dream to die,
But I guess they taught me something, it's time to say good-bye.

Anna Street

Useless

I feel so useless inferior
My little daughter
Only six lies there dozing
So very sick I can't get near her
Her small young body
So parched by fever
Her tender lips…
So chapped and dry
She stirs restlessly
She cries… I catch my breath
Hoping… Praying… Let her sleep
So sound, so deep
So as not to feel the fever
Or the pain I'm her Mother
I should be able to help To calm her fears…
Quiet her yelps but I can't
I'm not God… I'm just her Mother
But God He knows
Just how very, very much
I really, really love her!

Hope M. Schmidt

My Blue Princess Sixteen

My wonderful princess in your sweet sixteen
My love and my life in the only thing
That my heart can offer to you in this day
When you got the world in your eyes my love.

You are now my blue princess,
soon you'll be my girl;
later you'll be my honey,
wife, mother, and then,
while this time is coming
for our happiness,
I pray to the heavens
keep joined our hearts.

I'll be always yours,
My pretty sweet sixteen,
and God will be blessing
Our wonderful dreams.

Jose Domingo Rico

293

Granddaughters

My granddaughters are my glowing treasures,
My love for them is without measure,
Old age brings wisdom and love unending
with ability to see things needing mending,
And since I have plenty of time for caring
My girls get "unasked" for advice for sharing,

My granddaughters are beautiful and oh so bright,
I love them greatly, as is my right,
I thank the Lord for their gifts of love,
Each day of my life I send prayers above,
"God keep them, protect them, and most of all
Pick them up, brush them off whenever they fall.
I'm living so very far away I fear
They'll forget how I hold them so dear
I sincerely hope, when I'm no longer here
Funny memories of Grandma crop up year after year.

Barbara L. Sandholt

Yes

Loneliness surrounds me in a window's shroud
my lover has escaped me,
gone from me right now.

Of all the ones I'd rather hold me,
the coldness of the night is last.

Of all the ones that should have loved me,
few have stayed and kept their vows.

So what does the night say when I beg for
sin and death?

An evil cackle fills the silence,
and she answers, "Yes."

Erika E. Frisby

Untitled

As I wake from a peaceful slumber
My mind and eyes begin to wonder
How do I begin to really live?
When all I do is give and give

Empty from the constant demands
Of people always holding out their hands
Waiting with nervous anticipation
Doesn't seem to help the situation

To see myself as just as good
Knowing I'm also a part of the neighborhood
Fills me up with some sense of joy
Instead of being played like some kind of toy

Now I stand just as tall
Knowing I just might as well fall
But now I know that's alright
As I lie down now for the night

Gwendolyn Scott

Daddy

Never there when I needed a friend.
Never there when my broken heart was
in need of a mend.
He carried on with his life, forgetting
about me. Now the time has come to see,
that really, he was never there for me.
Where were you? Where were you dad?
Do you still love me? Do you still care?
Never did I dare, to try and understand
you , to try and talk to you and let
everything out, for there was no
doubt, that you didn't care.

Carrie Ann McGurk

Instant Love

You finally made it into this new world,
My sweet little bundle, my dear little girl,
I waited and waited for nine months to meet you,
It seemed like forever, and boom! there was sweet you.

I thought I was dreaming when you first arrived,
Your fingers, your toes, on each limb there were five.
So tiny your features, so silky your skin,
This wonderful feeling comes from deep within.

I've never experienced such an emotion,
For one little baby, oh! so much devotion!
The two-hour feedings, the changing of diapers,
The baths and the laundry, the baby-fresh wipers!

The hugs and the kisses, the squeezes and all,
What was life before you? I cannot recall!
I still can't believe that you're here next to me,
I saw you and you stole my heart instantly.

I know you were sent here from heaven above,
Just two little words tell it all,
"Instant Love!"

Janet L. Benedetto

A Love Promise

As I sit by my dining room table,
  My thoughts turn to you.
You were the love of my life,
  When you died, I wanted to die too.

You were so loving and good,
  I just know that you are with God.
As I want to be with him and you,
  I'm endeavoring to do my best, before I hit the sod.

Somehow, time has a way of healing us,
  As the days, months and years go by.
The skies that looked so gray,
  Have now become a heavenly sky.

Now I do not want to die,
  As I have found a use for my life.
By helping and encouraging others
  To end this worldly strife.

Through your unselfish life and death,
  I have turned to the Lord.
You taught me well, my Darling
  And I hope to see you again, I give you my word.

Adeline M. Kramer

Well! We All Age

I see a box there from afar
near where the dwellings are
Curious to it's state I rise
moving closer to apprise
this antique structure if I could

Must be a century ago
an architect did construct
this lasting enclosure made of wood

Nature's elements still visit
its slats gnarled and twisted
brown and grey from decay
metal lid that rusts away

From center beam steadfast, a pulley of iron cast
molded beauty past, nonfunctional at last

Rotted hemp draped through rusted groove I dare
once hung a shining pail there

Peering into the abyss, a cylinder of blackened stone
set one by one, by hand alone
a vessel to crystal liquid from below
the vessel's barren, now I know

James H. Coscarella

The Glory Of The Ozarks

The glory of the Ozarks, with her mighty, giant oaks;
Nestled on the glistening lake, live her plain and friendly folks,
The glimmer of the sunrise, on the water crystal clear,
No rushing, pushing, crowding, in the lives of folks down here.

The patter of the raindrops, as they fall upon the leaves,
And the music of the wind, as it dances through the trees,
The fragrance of the dogwoods blooming on the hills,
Combined with grace and beauty of mimosa in the dells.

Overlooking rippling waters, mallards riding on the waves,
The wonder of the work of God, in carving out the caves,
The promise that awaits when the day is done —
Is the splendor and the beauty, in the setting of the sun!

Donna Abell, Jayne Cottrell

My Unreal Home

My home is in a place where you've
never been,

It's a place where people don't know
how to sin,

You're never made fun of and you'd
never be laughed at,

Everyone is friends no matter skinny
or fat,

Horror and evil has never been heard of,

We think peaceful thoughts that are
made out of love,

All the people around you are quiet
and sane,

Together we live one life without pain,

If you could come and visit you'd never
want to go back,

Since unending happiness is one thing
we'll never lack,

I'd stay there forever but this place is not real,

It's my imaginary home that no one can steal,

Amanda Wallover

A Morning By The Water

The water; always turning,
  never ceasing.
The silt; always churning,
  never breathing.
The gilled; always yearning,
  ever leaping.

Oh all ye listen, tis a thing to hear!
so whenever visiting this wet frontier,
there will always be something, yes something to hear...

Ian Cipperly

Yesterday Has Come And Gone

Yesterday has come and gone, forever lost in time
Never to be seen again, just a day in passing time
Tomorrow will be another day, in the never ending cycle
Just hold on to the path it takes and cast your fears away
For every passing day comes another, in its way
So be happy for what you have and not for the impossible
Who knows if tomorrow will end the ever enduring cycle
So forget the worldly matters and look inside your heart
To cast away your troubles.

Angela Bidwell

An Ecological Poem

The trees were leafless...the grass
never grew...the sun was too close for
comfort...the sky lost its hue.

The fields became barren...the
hills, non-existent...the flowers wore
no fragrance...the river was spent.

The stars were without sparkle
the moon, without brilliance...the forest
was exhausted...the beasts stood no chance.

A piece of sky was stolen...the
rain never came...the wind knew
no direction...Life was never the same.

The future is never more bleak if we
ignore the signs of time...that mother earth
is dying and indifference is today's crime...

The land, the air, the sea are
no longer what they used to be....
  If only we all try to change
our ways...then this world
will surely be a better place.

Jennifer O. Manuel

The Roads Before Me

I've traveled this road for so very long
Never thinking of swerving from its path for I saw no other.
How could I?
The path I've chosen has brought me many days of glory and happiness
And memories which I'll never forget.

But those days have since past and now there is only
So much pain
So much sorrow.

Now, during this troubled time,
I question myself if that road was the right one.

But in this time of doubt,
You're there to open my eyes
And tell me to take a chance.

You take my hand and I boldly take a step on a path unseen by me.
With each step I realize how blind I've been.

Beyond this path is no single path, but many.
Perhaps I'll follow this road or journey down another.
Yet, whatever road I choose,
Now I know that there are many roads before me.

Jackson C. Hui

Mother

As a child I learned quickly that you would never be there.
Never to notice the not-so-subtle hints of mental or physical wear
Not to see what's obvious at a young tender age
Not to hear the cries hiding the then unrecognizable signs of rage

As an adolescent I learned quickly the best way: to be silent.
It was much easier than anything for the fear was there of being violent
Withdrawing to be alone with me was taken as a hint by you
I knew you wouldn't ASK for fear I'd MAKE you see.

As an adult I have learned that it's not really just "me" but "we".
So, now we are together all and should have no need of you, you see
"We" should now be able to stand alone and never have any more need
Of you and yours in our lives for "our" recovery you would only impede.

But it isn't so, it's not as it should be. Why do we strive to make
  YOU feel
It's not such a raw deal...for you...you got "multiple" talents in
  this deal
Why do "we" still set ourselves up so you can easily knock us down?
Why do "we" still try to prove to ourselves that you love us and
  you'll be around?

Judy Reeves

295

Jump!

His limbs trembling like
New leaves in the springtime breeze
For lofty heights has called his name.
Despair, distraught, distrust, dislike,
Disapprove, disarray;
His mind consumed.
Wondering, waiting for the green light to say "go"!
SCAREDY CAT, SCAREDY CAT, SCAREDY CAT!
Reverberating in his ears.
Friends encircled at play around his mount
Chanting and scolding his paralysis.
JUMP, JUMP, JUMP
1....., 2......, 3......JUMP!
He stands a statue cast in stone.
He is the only one who says "no".
The whole world in one accord
Agrees on that one solution.
Urging, impressing, coaching, evangelizing.
Finally embracing the world's religion,
He leaps to his honored, glorious death.

Jennifer Hootman

Ms. D.

With one breath she could create a whole new world
New thoughts and ideas in my small head danced
    and twirled.

For now, it was no longer a classroom, but an ocean
    or sea
Within it were interesting, exotic creatures and fish,
    all new to me.

When one special individual has the ability to
    take you to another time and place -
Being uninterested, or tired is never the case.

Eager to learn; for knowledge one can always depend,
    more than a teacher she is also a "great friend".

Not too often do teachers like Miss del Vecchio
    come by -
That it is understandable why her leaving would
    make one cry.

Pages and pages of compliments, I could just go
    on and list -
But not a million pages of written text could
    ever display how much you will be missed.

Brian Wright

The Little Nut That Never Gave Up

He was hanging on. He was at the top.
    No higher could he be.
Though he hung out with some nutty friends,
    His faith was strong as it could be.
But the power of time came with the wind
    That blew him round and round.
He soon fell down upon the earth,
    Where there, he held his ground.
He never gave up from just being a nut.
    He just grew and grew and grew.
Now he's sturdy and strong as one can be.
    As he grew to be a magnificent tree.

Donald Robert Foisie

Mother

Mother, you were always there for me
No matter what I wanted to do or be
Mother, you always gave me the best things in life,
Love, honesty and respect
And if anything was wrong with me, you could soon detect
Mother told me once when I was a child,
Life is not a garden of roses in which you wish it could be
For you would love to smile and smile
And that Mother would love to see
If you stumble in life and fall get up!, brush yourself off,
And stand up, and walk with stride,
And say to yourself, mother gave me the greatest gifts,
Life, love, respect, and pride
Just remember when you go through life
And all the obstacle get in your way.
I will respect what mother use to say.
Thank you Dear God from above
For a sweet mother who gave so much love.

Beulah Hill

In Everyone's Eyes

In everyone's eyes their is a light.
No matter what level, it shines so bright.
As days go by we'll surely see
That everyone's light is meant to be.
Whatever direction we decide to go,
We'll be the master and go with the flow.
As the earth twists and turns, so do we
We can use our light to set us free.
In everyone's eyes there's a light.

Frances Searles

For Joan - God's Miracle Baby

The tear has dried upon her cheek;
No more for answers does she seek.
    Her babe sleeps peacefully in her arms,
Nestled down deep so safe and warm.

    With tenderness she softly hums
The lullaby of Johannes Brahms.
    This child is His gift she knows,
For in her heart He has placed a rose.

Bernice Geigel

No More

After Appomattox an eerie silence fell,
    no more to ever hear, that famous "Rebel Yell".
Soon to stack their deadly arms,
    going home to burnt out farms.

Blue and grey, to stand as one,
    no more to face, each other's gun.
They left so many, but now so few,
    with many endless, chores to do.

The caissons cupboard's are finally bare,
    no more death, hidden there.
Famine and hunger, the enemy now,
    not even a mule to hitch a plow.

Finally fading, the cannon's "bloom",
    no more gore, no more doom.
Heading home, to friends and wives,
    unlike so many, they had their lives.

In the fields, of countless mounds,
    no more parting, of the ground.
No more blue, no more grey,
    each was right in his own way.

John R. Landon

Christ

What is the manner of this man named Christ?
no one can say He did not pay the price
pain was His work and money His blood
He resurrected man from the slime and the mud

He stood on a lonely tower looking down
at men to their greed earthly bound
upon His nakedness He clothed Himself in light
once again, the force of evil was in for a fight

cry out Christ! Your first name Jesus
do not let our conscience in evil tease us
our souls thirst for the purity of love
and once again our eyes turn to above

the star of David is marked with blood
six million Christ died in evil's flood
children of Israel do daily weep
their tears fall in a well so deep

each tear God does weigh in His heart
and pierces Him like a stinging dart
God shall soon send their Messiah
to elevate the spirit much higher

Allan H. Lambert

Real Soon

When I closed my eyes, you were there.
No one could see you, but me.
I've been thinking lately, missing you.
But, you said, I'd see you again...Real Soon.

Now, I'm not one to doubt your word,
but, I must say, I'm a bit concerned.
It's not as easy as one, two, three.
We're parted by more than land, you see.

I look to the left and glance to the right.
Occasionally when I sense a bit of strife,
I think of you, and believe life is worth
so much more than worry can bring.

You really have got me thinking.
I appreciate each day so much more,
since death has parted you and me.
And you said, I'd see you again...Real Soon.

Christine A. Dickinson

"I Don't Know Why We Have To Die"

I don't know why we have to die
No one escapes death, no matter how hard they try
But it somehow seems natural to shed our shell
I don't know if there's heaven or a hell
It would be great if we lived on somewhere
In a place where it doesn't matter how much money you have
    or what you wear
Death is painful for the ones who remain
It breaks our hearts and can drive us insane
But if we believe in the special place where someday we all will go
Our appreciation of life will flourish and grow
All we have is now because we don't know what tomorrow will bring
Death is a sad but natural thing
So hold on to the memory of your beloved family and friends
Your thoughts will be with you until the end
Maybe someday our souls will all meet again
Who knows exactly where or when
So enjoy each moment as though it were your last
And maybe we'll meet once again when the great play of life is recast.

Christine McGuigan

One Woke Up

I sat in a stare,
No one noticed, no one cared.

All at once I heard someone yell,
All at once their voice rang like a bell.

Like a great horned owl,
I saw the wisdom of their howl.

It cried and to make us see it tried,
Haven't you seen enough people already died.

It opened my eyes to the horror we've
been bound,
If we open our hearts we all can be found.

Amanda Bartkoski

Broken Promise

The calendar promises tomorrow is May.. yet
No robin sings spring, no wild flowers delight.... and
Dawn's hour discloses a past frosty night.

The calendar promises tomorrow is May...yet
March winds wildly gust, cold April showers chill... and
Droppings of winter still scar barren hills .

The calendar promises tomorrow is May...and
My heart is singing tho long spring delays... for
I imagine the willow leafed out in green,
Look to the hillside and, it magically seems,
There bloom daffodils yellow, hepatica pink...
The white blight of winter transformed in a wink as
I wish gray clouds swirl away to skies blue,
Vision dandelion splashes of warm golden hue.
I rejoice and am happy and see what is not,
Painting with "pretense" the May spring forgot.

Betty J. Malcomson

I Hope So

People are so angry, so full of stress,
No wonder the world is in such a terrible mess.
Mayors that lie, preachers that steal,
Children that are praying for one square meal.

Soldiers are marching for something to conquer,
We can't keep this up for too much longer.
Machines rip through mountains and tear trees
from the ground.
A women is raped, but no one hears a sound.

the fighting, the killing, mass amounts of blood,
Our world is crumbling with earthquakes and floods.
A man is evicted, he can't pay his dues,
Some jock makes millions endorsing tennis shoes.

So when you walk by and say have a nice day,
"I hope so", is all I have to say.

Aaron P. Johnson

Ship Of Fools

The Captain of the ship of fools does
not know where he is heading to.

He will search and search and travel and travel.
Yet his destination will never be reached

For the ship itself is full of fools
and no help will he get

The Captain of the ship of fools
will travel lost his entire life

For the Captain of the ship of fools
is a fool himself

Ari Bykofsky

Nighttime Healing

There is no sorrow or broken heart God cannot heal.
Nor excruciating pain He cannot feel.
So during your grief
Hold onto your belief.
Our Heavenly Father knows what's best.
When our wounded suffering bodies need rest.

Love and cherish the times you and your loved one once shared.
And always remember how much God cares.
I know it is difficult to thank God now for their temporary stay.
'Cause this moment is nighttime, and not day.

As you release your tears and reflect on the past years,
Remember God is willing and able to carry you through.
His spirit is abiding in your heart to love and comfort you.
'Cause there's nothing on this earth God cannot do.

But at such a time as this,
He's there to take away your pain.
To restore your hope and faith to help you receive
His almighty power and strength again!

Deborah M. Chewning

Blindness!

I'm blind as a bat and I cannot see,
Normal and natural things in front of me.

I worry and fret over the future and bills,
Forgetting happiness, laughter and life's little thrills,

For my vision is really crystal clear,
Yet my perspective so warped I can not see what is near.

With such problems that hinder me and make me blind,
Solutions with answers I'll never find.

Like a fly caught and waiting in a spider's web,
I'm here and alive yet symbolically dead.

Being unable to enjoy what you have given me through time and space,
I've really lost contact with the human race.

If only I could start over and see again,
As through a child's eyes on life's brink to begin.

For the sights, sounds and colors that nature displays,
Cannot come close to man's attempts or ways.

Thank you Lord for your patience and lessons,
Giving me time to comprehend each session.

I may be slow at learning and hard headed as rocks,
But you answer each question and all of my knocks.

Cheryl S. Coté

It Not What It Is

It that wants
not
what it is should not want if
it is true?
is the fire burning?

It is but
not with
what kindling is here.

it needs more to burn. If what is wanted
is true to burn then
It should
not burn
what is not needed. So
it
is true to burn?

It is not.

Eric Byron Nelson

Tuesday

Did you ever get engaged on a Tuesday?
Not a Sunday or a Friday but a Tuesday?
Don't ever ask a louse to be your spouse,
But get your date to be your mate, on a Tuesday.

On the steps she's looking pretty,
He's talking cars and getting giddy.
Out pops a question and a ring,
The most extraordinary thing,
Tuesday will never be ordinary again.

Did you ever get engaged on a Tuesday?
Take a day off from labor,
Spend the time with one you savor.
It's so wild and so mad (you cad),
To call it the best day of work you never had!
You got engaged on a Tuesday.
Today you found your true way.
Good luck! Stay together.
From a Tuesday till forever,
Engaged on a Tuesday: TODAY!

Dana Sheets

What Makes Us Different?

A man walks into a train
Not knowing where he's going or what's his name
A woman lives in darkness
Not able to see the light day
Yet most of us take life for a joke and it shouldn't be that way
A little boy in a wheel chair
Because he can't walk
A little girl lives in silence
Because she can't hear or talk
Yet we're never satisfied always wanting more
Taking for granted what life is really for
A baby is born with a deadly disease
Children are hunger PLEASE, PLEASE, PLEASE
Families are homeless with no place to go
Yet we past them by because we don't care to know
What make us different from any of them
I COULD HAVE BEEN HER
    YOU COULD HAVE BEEN HIM.

Iris Highsmith

"From Cleveland"

I don't recall
Not once, not at all
A sonnet about my beloved town
Between pen and paper
Before my thoughts are a vapor
Let me write these sweet rushes down.

    O Pittsburgh how sad how strange
That no one has sung praise abroad
About morning mist in your valleys,
Red brick paved alleys,
The steep, deep, stubby, but narrow
Cobblestone streets I've trod,
Each visit I take in with hearty wide grin
Pitt air, Pitt sky, Pitt dew
When gone at last
Ancient hills in my past
Impatiently I await another view
Of you, love you—From Cleveland.

Donald J. Williams

Forget-Me-Not

Forget-me-nots are, as they say,
Not to forget them any day.
Just as the flower of a memorable name,
I like it, want to play its game.
Even if we are never one,
I want you to remember what's been done.
Or, if I never see you again,
I want you to remember me until the end.
Just as a friend, if it has to be,
But like the forget-me- nots, don't forget me!

Andrea Link

Life

You are a pea inside a pod,
Not yet given life from God.
Soon you'll be chosen to go to earth below,
To a man and a woman with a parental glow.
They'll raise you and teach you,
   love and protect you.
So when you have grown,
   you'll know just what to do.
For your own child, whether daughter or son,
To help them prepare for their own little one.
Who is but a pea inside a pod,
Not yet given life from God.

Anthony V. Tafua

Home Life

Surrounded by darkness
Nothing but mean faces looking down upon me
With my mind I try to change them but fail
Following with my eyes they slowly leave my sight
Wishing I too could be a cloud far, far away

Trying to picture happy things from what I see
I sit on the porch looking all around
In the background my parents scream
I wonder, why me?

Now laying on my back
I look up at the stars
Thinking of them as angels
I focus on the brightest star
Feeling the star reach out to me
with every sparkle
As if to say
"Don't worry, everything will be okay"

Carrie Sherman

Last Night

I am in the womb all is warm and black;
Nothing I fear, nothing I lack;
I am a child under the covers;
Snug as a bug, all safe and oh so warm;
Overhead my guardian angel hovers.

when...

The door opens and I cower in fright;
In terror I scream into the night;
I know my fear, she enters the room,
"You little bastard, you can't do a thing right!"
She raises her hand to strike again;

when...

She gently shakes me and brings me to the now;
And into her arms I bury and cow;
She has saved me from a time way back there;
Thanks Hon' it was just another nightmare.

H. E. Fry

Snow

The first thing you notice is that it's still
Nothing is moving at all
So take a moment if you will
And watch the snowflakes fall
Just close your eyes and let it in
The beauty of the sound
While nothing is stirring, not even the wind
Only soft white droplets falling down
This is a creation that's full of peace
It puts your mind at ease
Take a deep breath, all tension release
And watch this blanket cover the trees
Let your heart with joy abound
And set your spirit aglow
There's nothing so beautiful as the sound
Of gentle, falling snow.

Jean Davis

To A Fallen Teacher

Halls so quiet and faces so drawn
Nothing is the same since he has been gone.
No more merriment, no more cheers
Only sadness and salty tears.
With his smile gone and his laughter stilled,
There remains a void that can never be filled.
Without him the classroom seems so bare
As we gaze at his desk and empty chair.
He had a brilliant mind and a heart of gold
And a gallant spirit that was true and bold
Then came the dark and rainy day
When the good Lord decided to take him away
Though his visit was a joyful one - only much too brief,
The memories that he left behind will sustain us in our grief.
We asked ourselves why God chose him, for he was so young and gay
Why not a man who hated life or one that was old and gray.
But the Lord has reasons which are sometimes hard to understand,
Which is why He picked him on that day and said, "Come, take
   my hand."
No, things are not the way they were since the day he went away;
But heaven must be a brighter place since he went up there to stay.

Eugenia Battistuzzi

Leading The Way

We started out running and holding each other's hand
Nothing would stop us from completing our plan.
Obstacles were confronted both night and day
But even in them He led the way.

Years slipped away and the run became a walk
Even then we remembered to pray and to talk.
Each of us has faltered and still we can say
But even in them He led the way.

The steps are now slow and at times we must stop
We still have each other we're grandma & pop.
Children all grown and with grand kids we play
But even in them He led the way.

We're learning to adjust and are glad for this life
Still walking hand in hand as husband and wife
The years have gone past and we're turning gray
But even in them He led the way.

Our years together are a treasure of joy and of love
They have been blessed with the presence from God above.
The road ahead may have rough spots of dismay
But even in them He'll lead the way.

Ivan E. Cousins

Blow Out The Flame If My Life Is A Candle

Hand me that blade. Don't ask why.
Now is the time that I must die.

This life's not worth living, it seems more like hell.
I feel like I'm trapped in a cold prison cell.

The days are so long and veiled with pain.
The wind is so cold and the skies only rain.

My soul has turned black. My face has grown deep.
Start digging my hole, in the ground I shall sleep.

I'll have no more troubles. I'll have no more fears.
And never again see the sight of my tears.

So free me, oh blade, from this life I can't handle.
Blow out the flame if my life is a candle.

Joanne M. Yaros

"The Buck Stops Here"

Dear old Harry said it first,
Now repeated by Bill at his supposed best.
Bill is pro-business and Ron carries his banners
As soft money from big business goes to the party coffers.
Robert R. says bigger and better unions are great
Thus making big businessmen squirm un-comfortably at the gate.

Somalia required quick and decisive handling
Yet Bill vacillated and we now "leave" a society crumbling.
Haiti needed Bill's realistic assessment and action
Yet he vacillated again and Cedras laughs at his in-action.
Count the Cuban and Haitan refugees at Guantanamo Bay,
The daily cost to us all should create an animal like bray.

European powers have failed in the ethnic Bosnian battle
By indecision and vacillation and apparent squabble.
Rwanda was not handled as a serious bill of fare
As additional indecision may now also include Zaire.
What has happened to leadership and personal responsibility
In being able to say with conviction:-"THE BUCK STOPS HERE"

Anthony Torres

Untitled

Hello there human one
Now that your daily work is done
I would like to converse with you
To speak of things hidden but true
Point out a path that's rewarding in ways
Show you real beauty as you mold the days

Picture your greatest desire
That one that sets you on fire
Gently open your mind to it all
I'm here waiting for you to call
What is the first thing you want to do
Wanted for years, it's really not new

Your life you would like to change
Perhaps a few things to re-arrange
Let's start by getting to know what's inside
Then quickly your dreams will be satisfied
Think with your mind to clearly see
The absolute truth now hidden in me

When you look within, you're already new
Cause I'm not really me but actually you

Juynne Malone

"A Tree's Whisper"

I stand here planted firm in the ground;
 Nurtured through eternity, w/
  branches that reach towards the sky;

Within my bosom;
 I house security for the weak;
  food for the hungry;
   and shelter from the cold;

Each of my branches slightly sway;
 at your command;
  but I never falter
   I never move;

I remain firm as you planted me
 from my beginning;
  as I will remain throughout time....

Cassandra Jackson

Untitled

O child if I could give you
O child if I could give you
All the things that I have learned
Things that were not given but things that I have earned
I would give you times of sorrow that would last throughout the years
Then I would give you friends who love you to wipe away your tears
I would give you times of joy to set your heart a glee
For these are times my child that sets the spirit free
I would give you times of danger
That fills your heart with fear for these are times my child
That teach us that life is dear I would give you times of toiling
'Till no future you could see for this my child would show you
That life is never free then I would give you time with Jesus
When the flame of life grows cold
For these are times my child that gives you peace when growing old

George F. Neal

After Math

The fission products settled slowly
 o'er the land, the sea, and the concrete
And the fused and twisted Geniac
 was dying where it lay.

The accumulated knowledge of a genus
 passed in review
As failing electrons ebbed their flow.

From concept of cypher
 in pre-logarithmic bliss
To trigonometric function -
 and higher still.

"In the beginning man created abacus,
 slid-rule, and computer - - -"
The core - memory recapitulated,
 and dying intoned -
"My God! What hath Math wrought!

But it was spared part the pain
 if it but knew
For circuits it did not contain
 to calculate what might have been!

Frank L. Ireland

November 21st

I keep having this vision
Of a baby in a crib

Black, fuzzy and moldy
With its swollen eyes

Blinking

Like a rotten orange with eyes.

I keep thinking this baby should be dead,
No one can live in a body so decayed.

But it lays there blinking

And living.

Erin A. Kleider

Grandpa And Me

It was so long ago, just a memory in my mind
of a dance recital I was in that my past has left behind.
Not much I remember of that day except for the car ride
when Grandpa held my unsure hand and looked at me with pride.
It was then I learned about the bond that only we would share,
than ran far deeper than our genes or the color of our hair.
As time went on, Grandpa became old.
He grew fatally ill, now his hand was mine to hold.
He entered the hospital one stormy night
and his frail weakened body fought its last fight.
I know I never told him, my dearest Papa Joe,
about my truest feelings and how I loved him so.
For if I saw him one more time I'd run to him and say
I've missed him and my love for him
grows stronger every day...

Jennifer Rose Sadaka

Goodbye September

I awoke with a memory fresh in my mind,
Of a time long ago,
Like a dream of some kind.
Walking with someone on a woodland trail,
Laughing and talking as birds set sail.
Warmed by the sunlight drifting through trees,
Smelling the scents, of the ferns on the breeze.
Sharing a moment on a September afternoon,
Listening to the crickets and the cady-dids' tune.
A time to be treasured as the days grow short,
Soon on her tail, old man winter comes to port.
So, I'll drink in the beauty as fall descends,
And watch as the Master paints His autumn blends.
And taking the memory of this glorious display,
I'll add it to others that my hearts tucked away.
So I can walk through them now and again,
Especially when winter's drear sets in.
I sleep with a memory fresh in my mind,
Of September retreating as the seasons unwind.

Ivy Pesock

A Thought For Our Minds

We're living in a world where things are very tight,
On news you hear all about the wrong but very little right.

Why spend so much of our money on planets where men
aren't known.

Let's take that same wasted money and straighten here at home.

Let's clear up all the killing, the drugs, the AIDS, and such,

Let's do it for our future, our children and for us.

Geraldine DeVine

My Hair Is Flat

If my hair was any flatter my head would look like a platter
Of pasta, as wispy as thread,
And the snarls that enslave me would be lumpy gravy
You must think my shampoo's made of lead.

But really, it's not - my hair's just this thin,
It catches fleeting thoughts but holds them not in,
So my mouth has these comments that come from my brain
Which have no connection to other thoughts in the train.
But it isn't my fault; I just have no hair
To keep my brain juices from diffusing to air.
I ate all my egg yolks and did what Mom said
Would give me thick curls on top of my head.
Though at the time, as a kid, I gave not a care
To what color or shape or size was my hair;
All I pleaded for was a zig-zag cut,
But this served all the more to make Mom wonder what
Was going on in the mind of this child she had claimed,
Too late to return, and the mind clearly drained.
I botch up names and fudge on grammar,
But am less likely to hold my tongue than clamber.
Eye brows are raised and folks humored, I'm told,
As I spew out new words and misuse the old.
And to say things like "funnest" isn't always the brightest
'Cause we all know "most fun" is always most rightest.
That I'm thought-processingly challenged, friends seem not to care,
I'm sure they've figured out it's all because of my hair.

Emily D. Solie

The Loss Of A Loved One

No words can say the way I feel, nothing can heal the pain,
Of realizing I must go on without seeing your face again.
Our years together were very short, but our friendship was very true.
No one or nothing can ever amount to the love I have for you.
I know that I'm not perfect, but you always had this way,
Of making me feel on top of the world and making everything okay.
Every moment we had together is treasured in my heart,
Because even though you've moved on, our friendship will never part.
We lived life to its fullest, what part of life we shared.
Through all the fun and all the fights, I always knew you cared.
I would give the world and everything to have you back once more,
To hear your voice, and see your face, and greet you at my door.
A part of you is always with me, no matter where you are.
It tears me apart knowing life goes on, and you must be so far.
That gorgeous smile and those baby blues are forever stuck in my mind.
Your gentle ways and loving thoughts are definitely one of a kind.
I miss you and love you terribly, wherever you may be,
But the friendship we have and the love we share will always be
    with me.

Darlene Suduba

"Again"

Has our generation seen too much
    of skirmishes, battles, wars and such?
Our father's blood drenched the sands
    of Bataan, Normandy and other lands.
There were tears, heartbreak, loss and pain.
    Must we really do this again?

We went to Vietnam on our senior trip,
    to fight the communists' ugly grip;
Now our sons have gone to free Kuwait.
    It was easier for us to go than it was to wait.
Wives and mothers have asked since time began
    Must we really do this again?

As long as America continues to stand.
As long as there is evil in any land.
As long as there are mad men
    like Hitler, Mussolini and Hussein;
As long as there is fear, agony and pain
    I think we really must do this again.

John P. Sampson

An Appeal For Peace

O! Mighty Nations of the world! Lay down your weapons
of terror, fury, and hate!
Your suffering, bleeding, dying people cry out in anguish —
Peace! Peace! Let us have Peace!
Is this too much to ask for?
Not Oil, not Diamonds, Silver or Gold-
Just merciful- blessed Peace!
The people are weary of war and the wanton destruction it
brings and leaves behind!
Your women, children and elders are bewildered and frightened!
They cannot understand why these evils are plaguing them!
Their men are taken—their homes burned, their land
destroyed and they know not where to go—what to do!
O! Leaders of Nations—Hear your people's cries!
Lay down your weapons of violence!
Let your people have Peace!

Irma L. Askew

His Home Is The Sea

Alone is the sailor waiting for the dream
Of the biting wind and the gentle breeze
    And the star-glo upon the beam.

Alone is the sailor on a boundless sea
With the darkening clouds to command
    Windswept waves - their majesty.

Alone is the sailor, voiceless is his realm,
His hand tacks hard the spanker aft
    And his heart lies on the helm.

Alone is the sailor searching wild mounds
of liquid coal,
That once again he'll see the horizon,
Long silent line that stretches across his soul.

Alone is the sailor at the threshold of the deep,
While sea gulls cry against the sky
    He's going down to sleep.

Gloria E. Dudra

"My World With You Gone"

Some time has passed, since I let go.
Of the most wonderful feeling, I'll ever know.

I still wonder. Why it was to be.
This wonderful feeling, was left only with me.

A love was felt. So it could only die.
Love dies so hard, it's hard not to cry.

Some time has passed, and all things fade.
Part of me is gone. What price have I paid?

To go on with my life, and find my place out there.
It's hard to go on, with a life you can't share.

The days come and go. The nights are so long.
It's such a lonely place. My world with you gone.

Danny W. Gunter

For Love Of You

My heart is quiet, with thoughts of you, my soul at peace,
for love of you. Yet fear that I might again let love slip away
pulls at my heart, tearing my soul.

My love is yours, in fullness, the gentle vision of your beauty
warms and heals my soul. Turn me not away, but bring me ever
closer to your heart.

Touch me, heal me, let me know love.
My dreams, my life, they're all the same with you.
Return laughter to me...

Jerome Langworthy

Will Be

Do you ever in the darkness and aloneness
of the night, take a moment to just think of
where you are, where you've been and most of
all where you are going?

Before you know it the years are passing,
suddenly, you turn...look back... and the future
is now.

All those choices were vastly more important
than you had anticipated...

and the effect, in some cases has already
ran its course.

Oh, if only...
But what would be different?... Better?
Or possibly...Worse?

Heaven forbid that you should turn back now.
Stay on course. Complete the race.

You still may win...or..lose.

Brenda Smith

Adieu To Summer

Good-byes of summer's dreams dissolve in the mist
Of water color prints among the trees
As I slipped away to escape the misty memories
Of his tear stained day aged face
While hopes of rainbow colors invade my mind
to erase the memory
And fill it with the sparkling sun struck leaves
painted over by fairies
Time is like the leaves falling quickly
With only the blur of brilliant colors left behind
As visions of hours ago become the reality
Of my mind's eye through the rays of yesterday's sun
Only now in the sanctuary of fall's new dawn
May the pain be allowed to seep through
to be expanded
The painted leaves of yesterday,
Fall silently in rhythm to my blood colored tears
As the ray's of yesterday's sun absorbed the pain
And remained only misty water colors

Joyce Mentzer

"Reminiscing"

As I sit here reminiscing I think back and get to wishing,
Of when I was in school in days of yore doing the things I did before.
The games I went to, the fun I had, the grades I got, good and bad.
The teacher scolding for work not done, getting a detention for
chewing gum.

Before you know it, the Senior Prom, wondering who will take you,
Bill or Tom.
What a relief, Graduation Day!
School's finally over and you're on your way.

Now you're grown up, a new life begins, adulthood has started,
your childhood ends.
Life moves on and one day sure as fate you've come to the time
when you have met your mate.

Wedding bells chime and a new phase starts, you promise to give
your love and your heart.
Then come the children — ooh that reminds me to stop my dreaming,
It's time to feed them and start the cleaning.

Annabelle Crum

302

Rival Of The Sky

The mind embraces the torment
    of winters barren trance,
escaping the elusive spirit of the heart...

Winters crying purge,
Bestowed upon roadside trees,
    Depicting fossilized character,
their branches spurned like
torturous twisting hands.
Searching desperately into the
    aloof winter sky...

As flaming colors passionately sketched
Be dazzle the very sky they intimately
    rule,
Defiant clouds attempt to etch
    the horizon deep as a wound...

Lustfully they mimic the solar angel,
    enticing her healing rays.

Donna Marie Vermont

Footprints At My Window

Last night I had a dream
Of your footprints at my window.
A path of which I feel,
Is where the broken hearts go.
Although we are together
Only in mind and soul,
It's funny how our bodies
Never come together whole.
And although these footprints
    seem so light,
I believe you were at my window tonight.
For if I believe it is truly so,
That you were not at my window,
Then all my faith is gone and spent,
And all that we have shared has went,
To vulture's food; death and sorrow
But I hope to see your footprints tomorrow.

Joseph Salemi

Untitled

When I wake up in the morning and think about my day,
Often with no warning brass rings pass my way.
They fill the sky above me, which way do I turn?
Is it selfish of me to grab them all and learn.
If I let the rings go by and do not take a chance,
Will life just pass me by and leave me in a trance.

I see people around me, unhappy with their days.
They let the rings pass by, just stand there in a daze.
I know there is a ring of gold, waiting in the sky.
Even when I am very old, brass rings won't pass me by.
If you do not take a chance and let them swing right by,
You may miss your ring of gold, if you never even try.
I do not need the ring of gold, but if it passes by,
I will be ready, young or old, still reaching for the sky.

George Elliott

Creation Of Monet

I like the life in the picture, will you sell it to me?
Paint me a watercolored dream of the way it should be.
    Make it smooth like water in a country brook,
I want a happy ending, riding into the sunset story of a book.
    Give me the memories burnt into my mind,
I can forget and leave the bad behind.
    Sell me the soft meadow, and there I will stay.
Sell me the life in the picture, the creation of Monet.

Jamie Klasinski

The Gypsy

I fell in love with a gypsy.
Oh, how could that possibly be?

A tall, dark man slipped into my life
At a time when I overflowed with sadness and strife.

The clouds of heaviness hovered above.
I felt worn and weary, and too old to love.

But his flashing black eyes held me as in a trance,
And his kiss made my heart sing, as it started to dance.

The hidden inside of me suddenly grew bright,
As I dreamed of his touch in the darkness of night.

A miracle happened, I no longer felt dead.
Visions of hope flooded my head.

Dreams have a way of disappearing in air.
Life it turns out, is not always fair.

For he left just as quickly as when he came.
My shattered soul will never again be the same.

The ache that I feel has blossomed and grown,
While the seeds of love far away have blown.

To distant lands that I'll never see...
God, why did you let me fall in love with a gypsy?

Jan Clements

Empty Soldiers

Please don't empty another soldier I will lose my mind
old purses reek of a scent left behind

Half empty leaking on shoes worn for school
passed out at the kitchen table plate full of drool

Hidden in my winter coat pocket
soldiers drained burst verbally like a rocket

Afraid to stir in the night ahead
walk softly or you will wake the living dead

Who to confide in when their hearts are full of sauce
you will hear my slurred words I am the boss

So young and confused will I be the same
some siblings still play the game

Years have come and gone some good some bad
wish you were here now my soul feels so sad

I have come through it all emotionally distraught
recovery is the answer where life is taught

True love is here hopefully to stay
for some reason it ends I will be OKAY

Dottie Dunbar

Flight

The stairs are old and gray with age.
On these steps I like to sit, the parched
wood licking the soles of my bare feet.

Brilliant rays from the sun warm me
as a gentle breeze strokes my hair.

From this spot I can see the lake,
a vast ocean of zircons sparkling blue to the horizon.

Tall, graceful dune grass dances to the
soft melody of the waves hitting the shore.

No longer am I just sitting on the steps.
I'm soaring with the sea gulls through the air.

Dolsa Sciaky

To Zoro

No hero was feared as he rode into the night
On a black stallion he sat, his reigns held tight.
His sword he pulled briskly as he waved it overhead
I will not rest until all the thieves are dead.
For it's justice I seek for the needy and the poor
And as I ride tonight I shall leave my mark upon their door
To let them know there's someone and when they speak my name
That Zoro once was here and shall come again,
So fear the mask I wear and always look behind
But, look into my eyes and know that I am kind.
To those who trust me and share my feelings
I ask forgiveness to the evil ones I've been killing.
For it's not a coldness for death I wear beneath my cape
It's justice for all and all namesake.
So when you see my shadow slip into the night
Pray it's goodness you are doing for I will make it right.
I will return in anger and my sword you will feel
And as you die from the blade and your body is still.
I will not pity you as the man so cruelly dead
I will ride away in silence, and leave my mark upon your head.

Don Fuller

November

November blusters down from the mountains
On scudding gray clouds. It flings geese
Across the sky, their honks unravelling
The chilly air. On high desert mesas
Quail fly low, bronzed by the luminous
New Mexico sun. We gaze at yellow
Chamisa, and hills dotted with cedar
Flying past our windows. Someday we
Should stop to smell the sage and gather
Purple Astors. We should bottle the translucent
Mountains air. Our minds grow heady from wishing:
All the pine nuts we would eat from
Roadside stands. All the green chile
and thick round bread fresh from adobe
Ovens. Soon December will rob us of our
Opportunities. Snow, like indecision,
Will lacquer our desires. November, our
Eleventh hour, will have migrated with the geese,
Leaving us with only dreams of next year's
Autumnal promise.

Eve Cobos

Cross My Heart

Every day, I pass your twisted face hanging
on the walls that decorate my day
Imprisoned by Michelangelo, contorted face
mangled body greet me by the water cooler
This murdered man
Homicide shares its space
with Monet's Waterlilies and a crooked
basket holding crushed potpourri
Fearing damnation, my stare finds the floor
littered by multi colored candy wrappers, discarded
one, loving me, he can still obliterate me
Cool water, fills my cup
He lived in them.
Yet, they killed him. Severed veins, sliced arms
ruptured lungs immortalized
The shock of swallowing ice, the big blue
clock says fifteen minutes past.

Christine Liverani

No Place To Go (Homeless Children)

Swings are swaying, children are playing
  On this a cold winter's day.
Some are laughing, some are smiling
  The hours quickly pass away.

One more minute, one more hour
  They hope the day will never end
The sounds of laughter reach skyward
  As the sun goes down around the bend.

Can't they stay a little longer?
  Can't they swing just one more time?
Can't they laugh a little louder?
  No they can't - there is no rhyme.

The swings are still, there is no laughter.
  The only sounds are children's cries.
That was their playground, their only home.
  And everyday, the sad good-byes.

Barbara S. Powell

Ode To New Life

At last without the Bonds of Mortal Body
once again to dance and sing
she plays within the fields with angels
and laughs because she has no wings

The colors glow just as she remembers
so bright and luminous they shine
she reaches out to touch a flower
it reaches back their love entwines

She's gone beyond the mere illusion
that it's bodies that give life to man
into the realm of loving fusion
where all in one and no one stand's alone
once again she's home

From this place she calls us to be with her
to see the walls dissolve before our eyes
to know with love there is no separation
oh yes she lives for always love survives

Ellen Barr

"Himself"

Once it was the blessing, now it is the Lord
  Once it was the feeling, now it is His word
Once His gift I wanted, now the Giver own
  Once I sought for healing, now Himself along

Once 'twas painful trying, now 'tis perfect trust
  Once a half salvation, now it's believing
Once 'twas ceaseless holding, now He holds me fast
  Once 'twas constant drifting, now my anchor's cast

Once 'twas busy planning, now 'tis trustful prayer
  Once 'twas anxious caring, now He has the care
Once 'twas what I wanted, now what Jesus says
  Once 'twas constant asking, now 'tis ceaseless praise

Once it was my working, now His it shall be
  Once I try to use Him, now He uses me
Once the power I wanted, now it's the Almighty One
  Once for self I labored, now for Him along

Once I hoped for Jesus, now I know He's mine
  Once my lamps were dying, now they brightly shine
Once for death I waited, now His coming I hail
  And my prayers are anchored, safely within the vail.

Joseph Mengersen Sr.

Painful Feelings

Hurting, Grieving, Crying, and Wondering. When will this stop,
One day things are bright, then all of sudden pop.

Why is this pain come and go,
My past too quick but my present too slow.

Cease this gap and bring me joys,
Because in my mind there is much noise.

Why is this pain so great,
Of all the things I really hate; loneliness, depression, sadness,
disharmony is what I tell, all these things please go to Hell!

When will my sorrow rest,
In that day my soul is blessed.

Thinking of my painful past and always trying to mend my ways,
All too much in these days.

Faith and hope is what I need,
Lord, all I ask is you plant that seed.

In my heart, my mind and soul,
This is my faithful goal.

When will peace come to land,
In that day my joy at hand; waiting and waiting for that day,
Please turn off my dismay.

Austin Dale Kim

Too Soon The Dawn

Those Texas girls were quite a pair;
One gorgeous, and one - just fair!
And when they heard the music's beat
They couldn't still their dancing feet!

They'd dance from dark until the dawn
And then the magic spell was gone;
For daylight comes all too soon
When you're dancing 'neath the moon.

The Ol' Folks' Home has claimed them now,
And to its rules all must bow.
Some would say they're o'er the hill;
The music's gone, their feet are still.

Yet, some nights when the moon is high
They hear the music in the sky.
And to the beat their hearts dance on,
For all too soon will come the dawn.

Past eighty the years do pile on,
Body sag, hair gray, strength all gone;
But the heart, like music, will still beat
And memories add the dancing feet.

Beatrice Kelley Nichols

The Continuing Cycle

ACT I, The process begins with birth, and then it continues on.
One reaches ACT II, Childhood ... and soon those years are gone.
ACT III, is called Puberty; a natural process, experienced by all,
A state of physical development ... a feeling of standing tall.
ACT IV, and one reaches Adulthood, the time in life to be...
Twenty-one, healthy, and independently free!
It's the time of life when dreams come true, and ambition is at its
  peak;
A time to make one's niche in life, and leave a legacy for heirs
  to reap.
And then the years continue, and one realizes that on life's stage,
The curtains have begun to close, on ACT V, the process of Old Age.
And now the years move swiftly on, and with life's passing cleft,
One moves as did the slaves of old,
toward the mysterious realm called death.
But death is only a gateway, where the process begins again,
For crossing from time to eternity begins a process that will never end.

Doris L. Cooper

In The Wind

Blown like paper in the wind,
One step forward may mean two steps back.
The harder one tries,
May be the harder one fails.
To achieve the length of the journey,
To finish ones destination,
It must be extraordinary.
A cup trying to be filled,
Losing the filling quicker than it gains.
There more the dreams,
The more the disappointments.
To fill ones cup,
To fulfill ones dreams,
It must be grand.

Angela Lothridge

Healed Wounds

Healed wounds will leave a scar;
One that always remains:
For tho it may seem to disappear
The scar remains in the brain.

We may pretend, and then again;
What we say may be true;
But the idle tongue carelessly swung,
Little realize the damage it do.

Now the wound you cast, will last and last;
No matter how I pretend -
But I'll love you dearer, and Dearer, and Dearer;
As this life draws nearer its end.

But a word of advice, should surface:
If you love again as life goes on-
That the things you say, may one day,
Cause a wound that will be your own.

And so I'll part, wounded at heart;
But my love will never fade soon,
It's as true as life, as you struggle and strife,
Scars are left by healed wounds.

James H. Augusta, Sr.

Serenity

A figure walking through a path surrounded by trees.
One who escapes the haunting of the living which she sees.
A figure of beauty amidst the dark colored sky,
A ray of light glimmers upon her thigh.

Her long black hair covers her breasts,
which the bright stars above her attempt to caress.
She walks in harmony with the lilies of the grass.
She has become part of this underworld at last.

A sudden breeze calls out her name.
A vision of nudity, who has no shame.

She yields before a sparkling pond,
which her bright blue eyes gaze upon.
She lays her body upon the grass.
A tired body who has deserted the past.

Barbara Ruiz

Alas, Our Winter's Here

Darkness creeps across the land as tourists disappear.
Our winged friends have all gone too. Alas, our winter's here.
The waves no longer break the shore. Icebergs now fill their space.
Hoarfrost, wind, and drifts of snow, now signify this place.
The Northern Lights dance in the sky to brighten up our day.
We grin and bear the bitter cold, the good old Alaskan way.
And then there comes a time of year that's long awaited for.
Our break-up season will arrive to open summer's door.
And once again the sun returns to nourish all that's here.
The season ends all too soon. Then comes another year.

Barbara Shine

One Precious Life

One precious life has now expired, just by living life
one will get tired.
But to cast your worries in the sand, and your last
breathe snatched away by one careless man.
We both had our on endeavors we're only six-teen and was
to achieve them together!
Even though winds will always change, one pull of a
trigger bought so much pain.
The person(s) who made her life expire, broke so many
hearts with one shot fired.
It seems the rain will never let up I miss you Nicole,
and love you so very much.

Joy Murphy

The Divorce

The Oasis was there...
    Only as long as I stayed, and then it burned.
Blowing sand
    Whipping my spine...
        Covering warm sand with hot...blistering hot.
Hurting my feet
    as my past Oasis layered my path with contempt.
I glanced back, and my eyes were scratched.
Seeing the world now through scarlet rainbows
    That formed crescent tracts on my cheeks
        and more clouded rainbows boiled in my paining eyes.
I ran fast...and faster.
I ran until blisters stung my feet.
The Oasis had been safe...But so small.
    The berries had no more flavor.
I must remember...The berries had no more flavor.
I tore away my clothes and tied them around my feet.
    More than anything I needed my feet...For they were taking me
        to what or where...I did not know or care.
Naked head to ankle, scared I raced toward the horizon.

Eve Sellars

My Angel

My angel was sent from above
Only to fill my life with love
I look at her and what I see
Is innocence, love and curiosity
She is my sun in the morning, and moon at night
She is my everlasting light
When I am feeling down and blue
She perks me up and I am like new
My angel is my daughter, Amanda is her name
Without her in my life I would never be the same
Her smile is very wide, expressions you cannot compare
What would my world be like if she was not there?
So when I am gone and passed away
All I can do is hope and pray
That wherever my angel starts anew
That I will be her "Angel" too

Helen Farinella

"Mother"

How do I tell you how much I care
Or how do I tell you how much I
appreciate everything that we share.

How do I describe what's in my heart
When at times we seem to be worlds apart,
Even though we may fight and scream
You're always there at the end of my dream.

I'll always love you and I want you to know
That the love you want I'll try to show,
But let me make one thing perfectly clear
I really do love you, "Mother dear."

Diana M. Thrasher

Sarajevo Monday

Just another day in the shadow of rubble,
Or digging in the ground for shelter from the
Net of steely shrapnel drawn across the earth,
Across the fleshy tokens of an ancient hate
That the murderers learned from their twisted grandpa,
Holding hatred in their palms like some treasured thing,
An heirloom sodden by blood, soiled by usage;
Next to their assault rifles, dearest to their hearts.
Every one of them knows that his rapes make clearer
Lines of blood and worship, scourging impure decades
Left behind by conquerors remembered in mosques,
In the muezzin's cry; surely it is Christian,
Only God's will, to strip the land of infidels,
To whip the mountains with the keen howitzer's lash,
To tear the flesh from cities, leaving concrete bones.

Jonathan C. Elliott

What Friends Are For

I don't want just one nor two, or even three
    or four.
The selfish part within my soul wants
    many many more.
It can be this. It can be that. It can be
    anything.
It can be all that's lean or fat, but not
    a wedding ring.
Cause you will find the greed in me does not
    want suffering.
It wants not that which slobbers, nor
    that which wets its pants.
Or friends who becomes robbers, nor those
    who say, "I can't."
"So what is it you really want?" my friends
    will ask of me.
And I shall then become quite blunt, and say,
    "Just be a friend and have a cup of
    tea."

Duane F. Hougham

Can I Really Call You Mom?

Can I really call you mom...?
Or is that only what I'm supposed to do...?
Can I really call you mom
even though I don't know you...?
Can I really call you mon...
when you weren't there for me...?
Can I really call you mom...
even though you call me bad things...?
Can I really call you mom...
even though you never understood...?
It seemed like I would always do bad...
and never do good...
You said I could never do right...
and always do wrong...
And still wonder how I could
love you along...

Helena Liberona

Streams

Streams are great for fly fishing
Or just plain out throwing a penny in and wishing,
Streams can be used for floating around on a tube
Or picnicking nearby eating some good food,
Streams are wonderful for taking swims
Or hunting around for stones and gems,
Streams are good to wander with while on your bike
Or something to follow while taking a hike,
Streams are fantastic to paddle around on a canoe
Or just to paddle to a grove of bamboo,
Streams often have pretty things like a waterfall
Or nice big rocks where you'll sit till nightfall,
Streams and poems continue to flow
Why this one has to end we'll never know.

Courtney Sergeant

Untitled

Floating like smoke on a lazy day.
Or like a lie that won't go away.
Wafting there too gray not to see.
What is this hanging between you and me?

Like a dream seen through another's eyes.
A hazy vision through a heavy sigh.
Smoke will gently drift away,
and so will end another day.

Another day and I walk alone
in a world where I don't belong.
A stranger in a stranger land,
there's no way back, so here I stand.

Barbara Grant

Untitled

Did you ever stop to see the sunset?
Or the moon silhouette
Against the midnight sky?
Or have you observed the birds fly?
The pillow white clouds mount above
The beautiful descent of a white dove
Behold the fields where wild flowers grow
The Atlantic Ocean where the blue waters flow.
Or watched the red rose bud,
The laughter of children playing in mud.
Have you watch the trees lowly bend
As the earth send forth her gentle wind.
Did you hear the April showers or Autumn rains
Falling against the window pane.

The squirrels leaping from tree to tree
The butterfly fluttering in the air so free
The morning filled with songs of birds
The silence, not a word.
The earth is the Lord's and all that's within
Take time to listen every now and then.

Brenda Claiborne

Sheer Contentment

Sheer contentment possesses my inner sole as we lie side by side
Our hearts pulsating like a precisioned instrument.
Tranquility slowly flows through every pore in my body
My mind rushes-trying to stop this feeling from being released
   forever, never to return.
Your gently touch and warm sensual kisses stay on my lips as I
   quiver and silently fall asleep
Subconsciously the need and want for you engulfs my entire
   being as I awaken with a glow as if surrounded by the sun.
I feel your tender presence and gently reach for you
You slowly turn towards me while my thoughts are strengthened
Yes... my dreams have become reality.

April Simon O'Malley

Individual Mystique

The planet we are now calling
our home is existing on borrowed time,
and it's soon to be with drawn.
Through hard times chaos, and despair.
A desperate cry crackles in the air.
Individuality, unique no two are
ever exactly the same.
Experiences differently. For each
living soul. No matter how close certain
events.
Seem to be the same.
The outcome bears its individual name.
Just as sure as the mysteries of the
mighty oceans wide, is the mystery
of what happens when two heart's collide!

Bradley Anderson

Victorious King

I dreamed that I awoke on Easter Morning
Our precious Savior did I behold
Descending from Heaven, surrounded by Angels
Swathed in white, with a crown of gold

I looked around in utter amazement
At the crowd coming from near and far
And suddenly my gaze was drawn toward heaven
To a gigantic twinkling silver star

"Behold my son the risen Savior
Who from the cross has set you free
He has broken the chains of sin that bound you
And conquered death eternally"

The Angels blew their golden trumpets
They spread their wings and began to sing
"Hallelujah, Hallelujah he has come for the faithful
Praise the Lord, our Victorious King"

I awoke reluctantly from my dream
Peace and joy now filled my heart
And I looked toward heaven and cried aloud
"Oh my God, how great thou art"

Jean G. Chinchillo

Seven Who Dared

Eager throngs watched the CHALLENGER liftoff,
outbound for vast uncharted space,
unknowing one earth-second later,
they would all meet their Lord, face-to-face...

For one minute twelve seconds of tension,
they soared high above earth's green sod,
and then - with no warning, the shuttle
exploded — and they were with God...

Seven lives: Five men and two women,
snuffed out, o'er the ocean's blue floor-
Gone were the Astronauts seven,
in the blast from that earth-shaking roar...

Eleven children had lost a loved parent-
Whole families were torn apart-
Shocked tears filled the eyes that had watched them—
Unbelieving and stunned, was each heart...

Yet their spirits still live on, eternal;
proof of Mankind's immortality—
They soared on the wings of the morning
- then plummeted down to the sea...

Dorothy R. Cameron

Life's Storms

There are many storms in our lives; trials, tribulations, heartaches,
pain and despair; all we have to do is pray to God, He
will answer prayer.

When the storms are raging, many times I just can't seem to
go on; then I go to my secret place and pray to God, He
gives me strength and makes me strong.

Our faith can look beyond the storms, God can bid my restless
soul to cease; He alone can give my longing heart restful peace.

The many storms in our lives, we just can't fully understand; but we
must pray without ceasing and ask our precious Lord to take our hand.

On this earth we are searching, and many times we began to roam;
But with King Jesus at the helm, He will give us safe passage home.

No one said that life would be easy, there are no guarantees;
so trust in the Lord continually on calm or stormy seas.

We must remember, without faith we are like a ship tossed in
a stormy sea, not knowing our life's course we become lost most
hopelessly.

The Master can calm our life's storms, for the wind and the
waves obey his will; all the Master had to say "peace be still."

Hannah M. Jackson

Paint A Picture

Paint a picture/as vivid as can be
Paint a picture/for everyone to see
  Let your life - be your hands
  Create a masterpiece - for all to understand
  Use all the bright colors - you may need
  Blend them beautifully - for they reflect - all your good deeds

Build a frame
As strong as can be
Made out of your name
For all others to envy and see
  The price it really takes
  To create a work of art
  And the difference just one life makes
  When giving love straight from the heart

Paint a picture/for inspection
Paint a picture/for direction
  Be a role model - everyone would treasure
  Be a role model - who could paint a picture

Francis A. Targowski

Winter Kill

A thick, foreboding curtain of marshmallow fog,
  parting, revealing a splendid form.
    No warning sound,
    No fleeting glance,
Only a free spirit, leaping in silhouette
  against the frosty sky.
The ominous noise of screeching brakes,
  metal meshing with glistening hair and delicate bones.
    No gushing blood,
    No piercing scream,
Only a motionless beauty with outstretched limbs
  and frozen pleading eyes...
    Winter kill
    Winter deer kill

Jane E. Allen

'My' Brother

The path to his house was narrow and small;
Passing through the door he appeared in the hall.
Once so strong, so tall, so sure, so deep —
His diminished presence a view I'd oft repeat.

His eyes showed the pain, the anger, the fear,
As he was instantly comforted by having me near.
For the many unfulfilled years that were to be,
A fact only too obvious to both him and me.

The day at sea was soon at hand,
As I tried to make sense of this demand.
Though, the bright sunshine contradicted the event,
Fate, as ever, is something one cannot prevent.

The passage of time, the softening cries,
And his absence still apparent in my eyes.
But the spot that I hold for him in my heart
Is aglow with memories that will always be a part,
Of memories that will always be a part...

Joann Ligotti

The Song

beautiful and pristine, trees vibrant and aflame:
passions of Fall.
air: cool, moist, running through flowers and trees.
the bouquet: colors when all of nature stands at
Attention.
trees saluting the changing of the guard: amber, chestnut,
crimson.
the order for Man, "explore, investigate, not stagnate."
uncover the treasures that a rock protects,
digest nature: drown your senses in its presence.
relieve the fruits and vegetables:
by first smelling the grass and feeling the rain.
use a rock as a pillow, meadow floors as a mattress, trees as a fan;
the stage is set.
crickets, the violins
birds, the tenors and baritones
creeks and streams, the rhythm.
Allow them to speak to you, because they have a story to tell.

Erik C. Sarvary

Wind

Furtively brushing by my window, eerily whistling
  past the door.
Climbing high in the sky, lifting eagles as they
  circle and soar.
Bowing the faces of wild flowers in silent, reverent
  prayer,
Lifting them up gently, with tender loving care.
Teasingly ruffling the feathers of a proud and
  preening bird,
Running by quickly, unseen, unheard.
Scattering hither and yon nature's seeds
  everywhere,
So all of her golden promises, will take root
  and bear.
What are you mysterious, untouchable, inexplicable
  force?
I am the wind, invisible wind, following my natural
  course.

Gloria S. Fuentes

Silver Anniversary

What happened twenty-five years ago,
Pay attention, I want you to know.

Neal Armstrong stepped on the moon,
We became bride and groom.
While the rest of the world looked into space,
All I could see was your adoring face.

We walked hand-in-hand with friendship and love,
And our marriage was blessed by God above,
With a beautiful daughter and a strong handsome son,
People of four, family of one.

Time has a way of fleeting fast,
But our love will forever last.

Cheryl A. Muscarello

Monet In His Floating Studio

This picture looks to be like a Spring day in Paris to me
People in the boat are having fun to see
Painting, relaxing and rowing
Smoke stacks, clouds, trees
The surrounding waves, the gentle breeze
Comfortable, calm, relax
I would probably never come back
Swimming, playing, hanging out
Looking at this picture, that's all I can dream about
Vacationing seems to be the thing to do
That is the impression this picture brings to me
How about you?
Scenes like this can not express
The imprint of this picture
Cannot be suppressed
I don't think that if you can see
What an impact this has brought on me
Rowing and canoeing seems to be the way
these people have fun
Oh, take me away!

Joey Floccari

Why?

So confused, I wonder why,
People need to cheat and lie
Where is the "Love?" Why so much hate?
Between our neighbor, between our mate.

With life already such a daily grind,
Where is that "Peace" we crave to find?
When "Trust" is dead and the May day call
Is clearly answered "To Hell with All"

When our only way to make things right
Is to hurt and maim, kill and fight.
Then we strangle our dreams with an invisible rope.
And turn our backs to the cry of "Hope"

When will we take the time to see
All the hurt, the pain and the misery?
And, if we see will we lend a hand
to nourish and replenish our diminishing land?

What kind of future is in the make?
And shouldn't we worry for our children's sake?
Will "Love" return and this world survive
Or shall we all perish? I wonder why.

Diane Van Middlesworth

Untitled

Have you ever heard the screaming of two
    people who are supposed to love each other,
Or gone through the pain of slowly losing
    the people who are supposed to be there
    guiding you through the tough challenges of
    life?
Have you ever asked yourself where your
    true home was,
Or had to choose between two people
    you care so much about?
Have you ever had to teach yourself how
    to pick up the shattered pieces of
    your life and move on,
Or ever felt the pain. The pain of loneliness?
Have you ever felt like dying?
Have you ever lain in your bed at night
    and cried yourself to sleep?
Have you ever felt like no one in the world
    understands?

Christina Poling

Leilani

Leilani strolls along the black sand beach
picking up sea shells rolling in by the waves' command.
The water encapsulates her toes as the sand
massages every toe.
Her windswept hair reflects the sun's rays.
As the evening approaches,
she makes her way into the opening of a cave
carved by the thrashing ocean surf.
A grotto waits for her.
Inviting, enticing, intriguing.
Leilani dips her feet into the glass like reflection.
In a pool of heaven sent tears,
she swims and licks her lips
draped with the salt of heaven's teardrops.
Blue reflection ripples away
as the moon takes over.

Janice M. Chang

Him

A mirror shatters, reflecting life;
Pieces of a puzzle, full of strife.
Wanting and needing his love and protection;
Yet always retreating, hurt by rejection.
A child's tears, a mother's woe;
Waiting, in vain, for him to let go.
Let go of the violence, let go of the pain;
Give them a safe-house, and the right to be sane.
Dark days and stormy nights;
A child afraid, through fight after fight.
Mournful cries, of sadness and despair;
Wondering in secret, does anyone care?
Cowering and trembling, waiting for an end;
Hoping and praying, time would soon mend-
    the damage that has been done...by him.

Heather E. Parks

"The Healing Process"

I was showered upon by spears of hate, and my human armor was pierced. I was wounded on the battlefield of life, by the consciousness of man's ignorance. I was attacked, because I was accepted amongst man for representing truth and wisdom. Rocks of prejudice were thrown, striking me from head to toe, because I had a different idea. I was bound, lashed about my back, and the crackling of the whip, still rings in my ears. I was shot in my heart, by a bullet of injustice. I was imprisoned, chained like a wild animal, for this was the rule of my captors, in the darkness of their bitterness. Freedom's storm of time, caused my release from bondage, pain, and suffering, as this was the power of the new world order. Henceforth, I would be accepted for my deeds, praised for my courage, and respected for my philosophy and understanding of all mankind. Thus, was the judgement, and medicine administered to "the healing process", and my wholeness shall be once more.

Anthony J. King, Sr.

Once

Once the dawn's black palm trees stood still in the
pink immaculate sky
Once I was a visionary, penetrating all life's
experiences and freedom
Now I am but just a lifeless soul given into
memories, pain, and fear.
I've learned now of fellow humans way too much to bear
I dare to think within my mind, these are
hungry devils before me
Ones to drool at your flesh, rob you of your joy,
and cripple your soul
My joy has died where once stood gullibility that
my own mom loved me
Dear God, I've blinded myself with fear, pain, and tears
my eyes once penetrated rainbows
Shall my soul, faith, trust, freedom, and happiness return
from the abyss
Shall I sing freely again in my cloths of joy, feeling
the dawn and tasting the stars infinitely.
I miss the soul of the sun.

Crystal Parrish

The Objective

To have an objective in mind,
    places you ahead of the crowd.
Knowing that the pathway is clear,
    you don't worry what is allowed.

Forge ahead - needs not to be said,
    of a person that tries - like you.
If an obstacle's in your way,
    you always know just want to do.

Patience you have without question,
    and you will go the extra mile.
In this day and age of all's fair,
    a child's actions can bring a smile.

Children are what life is all about,
    and what a role model you are.
If children will merely listen,
    with your helping they can go far.

Your objective is try to help,
    make that difference when you're to lead.
Remember throughout your life now,
    it's their little souls you will feed.

Genevieve Lyon Pearl

So This Is Life?

I was a seed,
    Planted by fate -
    Created by love to be able to hate.
I was a child,
    The epitome of innocence -
    Lost in a realm of felonious conduct.
I am a man,
    Proud without conceit.
    Inseparable from my faults.
I must age,
    Gaining patience and knowledge -
    Restoring my inherent innocence.
I will die,
    Absolved from what I once was -
    Separated from my body I vanish virtuously.
I will rise,
    A new extension of my essence.
    I will try again, the soul is infinite.

Craig Tantillo

"Daddy's Little Girl"

Daddy I miss you
please daddy won't you comeback;
you said everything was okay.

Daddy, when I look up at the stars
I'm looking into your eyes,
to say I love you and miss you.
My eyes begin to fill with tears.
It still doesn't feel right without you
    my Daddy.
I miss watching you cook and hearing
    your voice;
Seeing your precious face.

Oh Daddy why did you have to leave so soon.
    I love you Daddy
You're safe now and out of pain
You're in God's arms now,
He will take good care of my daddy.

It's never late to say I love you.
Father, I love you.
I will always be your little girl.

Cindy Rose Bergeron

Stay Away Daybreak

Stay away daybreak remain where you are
Please don't come here stay away far
Because when on the horizon you shall lie
Surely in some way I will certainly die
Four out of fourteen is not much time
So stay away daybreak and let her be mine
I love my dear sweetheart with all of my being
And to my Hilary I will always be giving
She comes from God from my heart and soul
And her happiness will always be my goal
As together we grow throughout the ages
Our book of love will turn the pages
Of how lucky I was to be given that gift
Such in the time of my life it gave me that lift
To live for my sweet Hilary and for that reason
I will try to my death to be here one more season
So stay away daybreak and remain in God's time
Stay away daybreak and let her be mine.

Cam Martindale

Nature

When I think of nature
I think of butterflies flying
and rivers flowing.

When I see nature
I see raccoon prints in the
mud and trees swaying in
the wind.

When I hear nature I hear
birds chirping and bees buzzing.
Nature is special to me.

Jennifer Reams

In Summer I Turn Pagan

In Summer
I turn pagan
Fashioning
My own Garden of Eden

In Summer
The mind slumbers
Leaving the body
To make love
Under palm trees
On the beach

In Summer
I take no heed
Of Winter's coming... there is
No yesterday... no tomorrow
Only today
For which I live
Blessed by the sun
That I take for my own

Barbara Legerwood

A Set Of Tracks

For a short period of time,
I walk destiny's tracks....
hoping that in my heart I
chose not to look back.

They lead me to a loving
road, unknown.....
Have I found a place I own?

Along this path, I find peace
and a special happiness; a
place I never want to leave....
But trying to understand myself
is so hard to perceive.

So, I choose a different path
and go back to the life I had before....
I feel like I'm falling through my
tear's open door....
I don't know what's real
and what's whole....
can you help me find the way
back to my soul?

Dana Abbruscato

"If Every Child..."

If every child was born without guilt,
If every parent would treat their
    child as they are suppose to,
If every child knew only good and no bad,
The world would be a better place
    for all of us.

Carolina Inostroza

Joy!

Here's to the daughter I got when
    I wanted another boy,
at first all she brought me was joy,
Until she grew up we shared all,
    then she met this boy,
To him in secret was she wed,
    with a broken heart no tears
    could I shed
Now that I am old I think of
    all the love to her I haven't told,
Before it's too late to her I will tell
    of all the joy that only mother and
    daughter can hold,
Love, love, love, love

Hilda Gelhaus

Euphoria

When I looked into it,
I was not sure. But I kept
on going, seeking for completion.
It had something to do
with the geese that played
in the softball field, near
the pond, and the leaves
rustling under my feet.
I started to run faster,
my small emotion, growing
each day, somehow trying
to reach euphoria! But,
I knew when I reached it,
it would not be enough but I
kept striving until I thought
I might explode, and then
it would not matter, because
non-existence would be upon me.

Delesia Robinson

Stacy

Thirteen years ago today,
I was overcome by the sweet love song
A tiny baby played
To my heart.

Soft and warm ... so sweet,
As I held you close
And felt your spirit
Join hands with mine.

A gift from God
That grew strong and tall
And beautiful —
And called me Dad.

As the days go by,
My eyes fill with tears of joy and pride,
When I think of you
And the fine young lady you've become.

Happy birthday, Stacy,
My darling little girl.
You warm me like sweet sunshine.
I love you.

John Henry Clark

Predator And Prey

You were the predator
I was the prey
My love you found
My heart you took
The pain you caused
The tears I cried
You were the predator
I was the prey
You found my trust
You took advantage
The pain you caused
The tears I cried
You were the predator
I was the prey
But things will change
As they often do
I will find your love and trust
I will take your heart and advantage.
I will cause the pain you will cry the tears
When I'm the predator and you are the prey

April West

"If I Pass The Way Today"

If I pass the way today.
I will say.
Are you sure this is my day?
I want to see the world again.
Aren't I in luck to have such a
Beautiful life.
Please, be on my side.
"Just give me a bit more time."
My words fell into a sudden
Cold silence.
Well how much longer are you
Going to keep me in suspense?
I don't understand why.
We did not know.
The time passed by,
And nobody told us
When we had to go!
If I pass that way today I will say
I want to see the world again.

Iva Anjos Lobo

If I Were In Charge Of The World

If I were in charge of the world
I'd cancel MTV, broccoli, tater tots
And football.

If I were in charge of the world
There'd be ten ice cream stands
On just one street and baby brothers
Galore for sale.

If I were in charge of the world
You wouldn't have to clean on
Saturday or go to your grandma's
On Friday or wash the car every
Other month.

If I were in charge of the world
A candy bar would be great for you.
Cotton candy, pizza, and
Chocolate wouldn't be fattening.

Jacqueline S. Rood

My Love

If I had never seen eyes
I'd never known where beauty lies,

If I had never held your hand,
I'd never known this thrill so grand.

It took you oh, so long to learn
that it's you that my love yearns.

I've loved you lots since years ago
but you were never free to know.

So now I'll tell you, smiles with tears,
I've loved you darling, all these years;

And now I know your thrilling touch,
your kiss, your warmth...I love you,

Oh, so much.

Gregoria Galarza

By Way Of Introduction

Who are you, I am asked
If I give a name
It only tells what I am called.
Having had many names
it still does not say
who nor what I am.

So who I am depends on who you are
Perhaps
we come from
two different worlds,
yet headed
in the same direction.

Adam R. Karr

"Momma's Little Girl"

She is invincible.
If only her life would always be
a reflection of her childhood.
She laughs when things are funny,
and she cries when things are sad.
Although she is a loving child,
she pouts when she is mad.
On the outside she's so pretty,
and on the inside, so complete,
that her mother wants to keep her
a child for eternity.
She knows she cannot have that,
so she gives her a hug for now,
and smiles and goes on with life,
watching her little child.

Jennifer Wall

Peace

Is it right,
if you are in a war,
to kill a human being
for the sake of freedom
or truth?
What is truth?
Is it right,
to kill a human being
for God?
The crusades are a battle
within ourselves,
we are not truth.

Emily Lammert

Imagination

Clouds can be a transformation
If you use a little imagination
They are a bellowing marshmallow sea
or anything you want them to be
a defiant stallion standing on a hill
or a pelican with a fish in its bill
a fleet of ships with full blown sails
or two children with shovels and pails
a preacher and bride and groom
Fairies, elves, a witch on a broom
a girl and her doll - a boy with a ball
or a huge giant - a bean stalk, so tall
all kinds of animals, you find in a zoo
Look! - There's even a picture of you

Cordelia McElroy

Never Give Up

It times of darkness
I'll be your light.
In times of weakness
I'll help you fight.

When your spirit is low
And continues to fall,
I'll be there to tell you
To give it your all.

You must never give up
When the stakes are high
When you seem to be losing
You still have to try.

And if you grow weary
As the road gets too long
I'll be there to guide you
And help you stay strong.

These words are my promise
In times when you're blue
For they always worked for me
When I heard them from you.

Christina Buffington

All I Want Is You

I'll tell it rather simply;
  I'll say it plain and true
A single thing is all I want,
  And all I want is you.

There are no other riches,
  No treasures or possessions
That ever could compare with you,
  My fondest of obsessions.

You are the very air I breathe,
  The ration that sustains me,
You're all my thoughts tied up as one,
  The laugh that entertains me.

You're all that life need ever give,
  The maximum that's due,
If I could ask for anything,
  I'd only ask for you.

Domestric Williams

Shoots And Scores?

Flying right to the net
In a blind fury,
The goalie must stop it,
And he must hurry.

It bounces off him
And into the boards.
His enemy gets it,
Shoots, and scores.

The goalie feels bad,
The team, defeated.
They seem to think
The other team cheated.

Did the center kick it in
With the tip of his skate?
Will he soon have to meet
His awaited fate?

The ref tries to decide - give or take?
He DID kick it in with the tip of his skate!
To the team the goal is not given,
And the other team is still winnin'!

Christine Kratz

Observing Mom's Struggle

Odd bits of paper, piled
In a meager stack
Along with an old envelope or two.
Words written there, illegible.
A bit on one
A bit on another
List her needs. Fragments.
Fragments of that long
  lonely weary journey
Into death, which does not come.
Dwindling slowly, ever slowly.
These bits, now, her tie
To show she still can BE.
Say I AM. I NEED. I WANT.
  I HURT. I LOVE.
Death tarries. Busy elsewhere.
And so she waits.
Why must death come
  one fragment at a time?

Grace C. Glaude

My Winter Monday...

My house so still
In a world of silence
I feel so alive.

In a world so uncaring, I care.

In a body so quiet.

I

Feel

Loud.

Dorothy J. Van Camp

Before the Storm

Birds in flight
in the dark of night.

Red skies
Black clouds.

Eyes follow....

Fear ascends.

Barbara A. Coscarello

Untitled

I see you everywhere
In cars
In crowds
In treebark
No hiding from your stare
You show yourself to me secretly
Hiding in my mind
I only know your hiding places.
Your dwellings of hell
They are in my mind
To deal with everyday
You're comfortable there
So easy to live with
You are my only friend
With me at all times
To talk to or yell at
You take the crap, then spit it back
You are my conscious

Dawn Secor

Dorks In Cool Clothing

We are all just DORKS
in cool clothing
we dress to impress
and when we speak we regress
we dare to watch
ourselves express
then criticize
and further digress
we pollute the world
and make a mess
we act apathetic
and then protest
we judge a man
by the hair on his chest
and judge a girl
by the size of her breast
we judged education
by the score on a test
and the most alive keep loathing
we're all just DORKS in cool clothing.

Joseph A. Cohen

Raped Of Body And Mind

I stand, naked,
in front of the full length mirror.
My body ashamed.
My mind too bruised
to believe I could be beautiful.

The dirtiness never washes away.
I am always wiping it off
my neck, my arms, everywhere.
I hold myself in my arms protection,
to push the ugliness out my mind.

But I will never forget.
My mind will not allow it.
My body will never stop feeling
the dirty violence
of the dark figure in the night.

Christine DeRosa

Untitled

Where do I fit in,
in God's grand scheme of things?
Just where do I fit-
with paupers or with kings?

Or do I stand alone
at none of these extremes,
With my head held high
and power in my dreams.

Am I just a pawn,
or could I be a knight?
A Bishop?...Much too strict.
A Queen would be alright.

A Queen can move in any way
as far as she wants to go.
Where there is a will,
there is a way, you know.

With faith in all my dreams
and with my head held high,
I will survive this world;
My dreams, my God and I.

Jill Coffee

Daddy

The memories are still fresh
in my mind,
Playing ball in the yard
Your voice behind the plate
As I grow,
I see your lessons,
Your examples,
You taught me how to work,
The early morning trips
to the print shop.
Mowing the yard,
You taught me to play
Together by the river,
and the quiet moments by the bank
just waiting for a bite
Your love lies not in words,
but in strength
I wish someday...
That this strength may be mine,
to give to my own.

Alan Major

I See His Face

I see his face
In odd shaped clouds
In day dreams many
And in summer heat.

I see his face
In winter snow
In domestic chore
In tomorrow's dreams
And in days ago.

I see his face
In angry recalls
in make ups and in
fall leaves

I see his face
in children, in games
and in reflections
I see his face

E. Black

My Special Daughter

One beautiful day
In Sault Ste. Marie
Pamela Jayne was born
Early in the morn

You had a head of hair
That was the color of brown
But a month later
It turned blond all around

Like a little girl in a song
Your eye lashes were unique and long
And then the terrible braces
Brought about the prettiest of faces

Graduation came and went
And soon the marriage word
Which after four happy years
Brought about little David III

Now a second one is on the way
We're all so happy on this day
I love you, Pamela and Davids too
And all because of June 9th in the Soo.

Ione Krueger

Tumbleweeds

The tumbleweeds blow by quickly
In the arms of a restless wind
Whose destination is Tomorrow;
Whose beginning is the end.

The tumbleweeds fly by singing
Tumbling throughout the day,
Whispering, rolling, clinging,
To Hope along the way.

The tumbleweeds drag by moaning.
Tumbling throughout the day,
Screaming, crying, groaning,
Their appeal along the way.

The tumbleweeds bounce by roughly
Etching all they'll ever say
In the dust which is Forever;
In the ashes of their grave.

The tumbleweeds all lie calmly
At the fence as if to say,
"Life is just a journey,
And Time is but a day."

A. Alan Draper

"God's Paintbrush"

The sweep of God's hand
In the fall of the year
Brings about such a change
That we know He is near

As green colors of summer
Become red, yellow and brown
From out in the countryside
Clear into town

And He puts in the sky
That is beautifully blue
Soft cushiony white clouds
Filled with glistening dew

I guess that He paints this
For all people to see
But I feel His painting
Is especially for me

George W. Collins

Empathy

To react, to feel, to share
in the love
we miss the reality
of bleeding for our brother
your pain, my pain
it's all in one
empathy we lack
so the guns are our lover

You see, I feel
mother's crying for their babies
he's young, so young
never taught to feel another
we can stop the terror
remember Home in the past
reach out...change one
and he'll change another
Jaye Lindo

Rosie

A cold, rainy Saturday
in the middle of October

Inside,
my feet are being warmed
by Rosie,
my golden retriever.

Warm feet
under a dog
make a cold rainy day
not so bad.
Ailene Bay

This Time Will Be No More

One's life is centered
In the midst of someone's time
Hours, minutes, and seconds
Tick away in the mind
This time will be no more

From the beginning, life took form
To count the minute we were born
God chose that time for us.
This time will be no more.

Our time started and made
Our hearts grow stronger
We lived that strength to the fullest
This time will be no more

Now time has slowed down
The pendulum oh so weak
The ticking can't be found
Back to dust
No more sound
This time will be no more
Bonnie Hanks

Untitled

Reminiscing, dear, of you,
In the twilights' lazy gloom,
Dreamin' dreams that can't come true,
All alone up in my room.
Don't forget me in your rambles,
As your ship sails on and on
Life's span is just a gamble,
And there's nothing when it's gone.
Oft times I sit and wonder
As I gaze out toward the sea,
If your ship should go asunder,
Would you drift right back to me.
Beulah Manis

Untitled

I came to a place
In the river
Where two bodies of water meet
And become as one.
There within the depth and darkness
The current surged and swelled
Like a pregnant belly
Giving birth to fish,
Birds, raccoons, and reeds.

Soon after,
The birth cry of a fawn
Skipped above and through the waters
And then echoed within the
Surrounding forest
Of ancient oaks
Standing witness
To the Genesis of it all.
John A. Fowler III

Daydream

A Portrait of you
in watercolor dyes
with your eyes full of love
and your arms open wide

The sun filters down
and shadows your face
as your lips reach for mine
and my heart starts to race

With barely a tear
I wash them away
those rose tinted dreams
that lead me astray

My prayers are for you
though where you might be
in only my thoughts
but never with me
Janet S. Eccles

Freedom Sweet Days

Old Daddy sweet day
Indians dance sweet peace
for Daddy sweet rain
white dance for sweet rain
for sweet peace
Brown peace sweet dance
of sweet brown black people
for sweet peace of freedom
Holy Spirit Daddy sweet peace
the bread man said
wine is nice
so lets keep it Holy
   sweet people
cool, cool days hold on
   they said but sweet
Holy Spirit children
yellow people sweet days
   for people for sweet people
   for peace
      and freedom
Jay Slover

The Eagle

He shot an arrow
Into the sparrow.

Along came an eagle,
   and saved her life,
And transformed her
   into a most loving wife.

The sparrow has grown,
And has reached heights once unknown.

The eagle had to be sent from above
And has filled my heart with much love.

I know that my life
   is such a precious gift,
And loving my eagle,
   gives me such a lift.

Through this ordeal
   I did survive.
And I "Thank God,"
   that I am alive.
Barbara Lewallen

Baby Blue

Surrounded by the infant's cries
Is a message of life
And all you need to know
In order to survive.

The use of a looking glass
Is needed, to look into his soul
To discover the secrets
He refuses to disclose.

Through his eyes you need to look
In these waves of ocean blue
The ability to speak lies
So that all may come true.

These words you wish to keep
Are a gift from him to you
Never lose them, and never lose sight
Of the eyes of baby blue.
Benjamin R. Burnett

A Painted Rainbow

In a land that lies at the rainbows end
Is a painted path
For dreams to enter the hills.
A painted butterfly
Softly dressed in white
Flies past a painted meadow.
This is a man's painted world,
But why does he create this painting?
Could it be a dream?
Or possibly memories
Of a world where he was a hero.
Perhaps it's a promise
Forgotten.
For him, it's an unrealized dream,
Becoming a reality.
It's a hope
For tomorrow.
A hope;
Painted into a rainbow.
Esther Friedrichs

Me

In this world I live there
  is an emptiness that
  surrounds me.
At times I'm not alone for there
  are many more that share
  the same feelings.
Just like a roller coaster going
  round and round - up and down.
It will come to an - end then
  a choice we all will make.
Hands in the air we will
  succeed to eventually be free.
The world I live I live
  for me.

Jennifer Strom

The Game

Tennis is life?
Is it?
If tennis were to die
Would my chest no longer
Heave with life?
Would my limbs fall numbly
To my sides?
Would I collapse into a pile
Of nothingness?
Would my soul no longer
Exist?
Would my heart crumble
In your hands?
If tennis were to die
Would I too, die?
I think
Not.

Courtney Parker

Peace

  Peace... peace. What is peace?
Is it the cold rushing water
below your feet? Is it the
luscious green meadows over the hill?
What is peace? Is it the end of war?
Is it mutual agreement of persons?
Peace... where does it begin?
Does, it begin with friendship,
loyalty, or defense? Peace to me
is freedom. How else can I put it?
It is friendship. It is loyalty.
It is all that. But really,
peace is every one of us loving
our neighbors as ourselves.
That is what peace means.

Joseph L. Ortega

grandpa's deelite

my ears have failed me
is my sight to follow?
just what has ailed me?
will i see tomorrow?

i can ponder for ages
of naught will i specify
i cannot hear the sages
only gaze into bright eyes

and now farewell will i bid you
your patience will i cherish
there is no time for who?
it is me - and now i shall perish

James Lynch

The Sound

The sound across from the ocean
Is loud yet cannot be heard
Much like looking at a picture
That does not convey a word

Although larger than a lake
All so calmer than a river
Silent treasures to partake in
Time-consumers rarely give her

And the bridges built to cross her
Each set foot in grand locations
She is merely the proposal
Near to reach our destination

But the soft smell of her thoughts
Are too daring to escape
If you're looking to get lost
Lay in pools without the wakes

And late at night when shores are barren
Her mentor faintly voices
To the sound across from the ocean
"Our distinctions yield no choices"

H. L. Davenport

To Do Or Not To Do

A paramecium
Is not so dumb.
With just one cell,
It does quite well.

A brilliant man,
On the other hand,
Knows some things
That he can't understand.

He gets confused
About what to do —
Should he put on his hat,
Or take off his shoe?

Stuck in the muck
Of indecision,
The genius dwells
With the lowest of cells.

Gordon McLamb

The Answer

Life in its greatest complexity
Is so simple, yet so deranged
No one can understand it.
If one person looks into the center of
His mind and the center of
Life
At the same time, he would
Probably find the answers to all
Of our questions about religion,
Death, and life in general.
The results would be so amazing,
It's just too bad that no one
Has enough courage to look
Into the center of his mind
And the center of life.
I think I will one day,
But first, I have to get away
From hell.

Brandi Ralain Newman

The Key

A new horizon, a new thought -
Is there a perfect way?
Once thought of
The design is the key -
Involvement, commitment I see,
Is part of this key,
The door is wedged tight,
But the Light still gleams bright.

I say, hey, I'm not quite ready,
But that's okay -
A time, a place -
Space to wait,
It's worthwhile;
This query is a quietness -
A willing trek.

C.L. Vernon

Infinity

A place in my heart
Is what you hold
No matter what you do
It still holds true
Love is forever
It never ever ends
But this place in my heart
It aches right now
It is time to mend
Otherwise it will end
And that is the last thing
For I could not bear
Losing you as my lover.

John Tartamella

The Puzzle

The "Land of Shoulda"
  Is where I dwell
it is my own
  Special Hell.

Shoulda done this
  And shoulda said
Haunts me
  As I lay in bed.

It still amazes me
  Shoulda this
Shoulda that
  Drives me crazy.

She shoulda
  shoulda this
Shoulda that
  Will probably be
My epitaph.

Why can't I accept I did my best
Resolve not to should on myself
Find peace and rest?

Elaine H. Colacino

Love

Love... what is Love?
Is love like the butterflies
flew by?
Or love's like the crystal glittering
in the heart.
The question that have so many answers.
  But for me, Love is truth
  and honesty.

Batong Nguyen

315

Love

Love is cruel and untamed.
It brings a smile to your face
and tears to your eyes.
It breaks your heart and leaves
you with pain, that is only
forgotten when the birds
sing again.
Love is naive and innocent,
making even the boldest shy.
It makes your heart and allows it to fly.
Love is that spark that makes us
feel young, giving us feelings
one cannot deny.
Love is prosperous, love is true.
Love is best when shared by two.

Eunice Anne Jaquez

Untitled

It lit too quick,
it burnt out too fast,
just smoke,
a mournful reminder,
cloaks us.
Now is the time,
the ever sweet story's over,
the fire is out,
there is nothing left to stay for,
but I still linger,
the last to leave,
trying desperately to hold on.
I turn to go,
with memories in my heart
and tears in my eyes.

Heather Lee Smith

A Watched Pot Never Boils

I watched a flower,
It did not rise.
It must be afraid of my watchful eyes.

I watched a cat,
It did not blink.
It is that I watch he will think.

I watched a tree,
It did not sway.
It must be that I don't go away.

I watched an egg,
It did not hatch.
Perhaps my staring was like a latch.

I watched a shoe lace,
It did not untie.
"This is hopeless," I said with a sigh.

I walked on in the blinding sun.
When I looked down my shoe lace was
   undone.

Courtney A. MacKilligan

In The Darkness

In the darkness I sit alone
   in my warm and dreary home.
In a town that gives no love,
   I'm asking the moon above
What will become of me?
Will you answer me please?
I have no love of my own, so now,
I'll dream of love unknown
   in my warm and dreary home.

Brittany Wiemer

Who Cares

It is so deep inside of me
It hurts to much to explain
No matter how deep it goes
Or how much it hurts down in
It is always seems to be there within

It is there when I feel down
It is there when nothing else could be
So how can it be there, I can't see

It is sad when I am sad
It cries when I cry
Oh but how happy it could be
Only if I could find the happy in me

I do wish that you could help it
Who are you to care about it
Who can help. Has anyone a clue
Please don't hide it if you do.

Oh how I do love you
But it, that's in me, weighs too heavy
for it hurts to deep within me
I need to know, do you care.

Dianne Fletcher

Fear Lives Here

Fear is black
It is as lonely as the night

Fear is a hole in your soul
That you never fill, never will

Fear is the mind
When it screams and no one hears

Fear is living with
What you can't live without

Fear is the inability to seek
When you already know what is found

Fear is the tunnel
With no rainbow after the storm

Fear is the chill
That robs the body of warmth

Fear is your conscience
To whom you deceive and you lie

Fear is the thief of life
When it steals you blind so you can not see

Fear lives here
Fear lives in your and me

Anne Pipenhagen

Mary 1942-1990

She died.
It was a dark cold day,
And snow lay on the ground.

She died.
Her friends and family came.
They cried.
She did not cry.

If you remember,
Mary was a quiet person,
quiet in the fires of her mind.

Jane Nicodemus Garvan

Love: Highly Over Rated

It wasn't a meeting
It was a collision,
And you and I got on
Like hot gum on the soles
Of new shoes.
You spoke conveniently of Love,
Let the words roll off your tongue
Like an avalanche on my soul,
Then ripped them away
With the alacrity of a thief.
Imagine my surprise
When the rift in my heart scarred over
To find relief in your absence,
Life beyond the wreck.
All told you made off with more
Than my faith,
But I salvaged my shoes
And that's more than you can say
For your soul.

Amie Claire Doggett

The Museum

I went to the museum
It was filled with things to see,
It was so good
It was better than I thought it would be.

The bus ride was long
but I held strong
We broke apart
and we saw nice art.

We went to the school house
and wrote with a quill
we had to sit
and stay very still.

The bus ride back
was not so bad
when we got back
I was very sad.

David Koeppel

The Treasure In Me

The sun came out today,
   it was the first time.
The sky was blue,
   the clouds were long gone.
I stood there amazed.
   I just wanted to share it with you.
I took the key I was wearing,
   it was old and rusted.
I opened up my heart
   and then I threw the key away.
I cleared out the cobwebs
   and I tore down all the doors.
I put in windows instead,
   that allowed the sun to come in.
Finally open and free,
   my first thoughts were of you.
I knew you would be happy to know,
   that behind the locked door
I found a treasure.
   It was me.

Cheryl L. Swartz

"My Little Blue Car"

I'm so proud of my little blue car.
It won't go fast, but it will go far.
I got up this morning and got dressed
Going to see my loved ones way out west.
I try not to worry as I drive along.
I say a prayer and sing a song.
You think I should be locked up!
May I remind you?
All of the monkeys are not in the zoo.

Juanita Myers Murray

Drifting

So cold I watched the wind blow
its breath against my face.

The snow I watched kept falling,
a satin blanket of white lace.

I watched a single snowflake fall,
a tear fell from my eye.

The snowflake slowly melted,
the tear I slowly cried.

Another bit of snow fell
to the ground where it would lay.

It settled there a moment
then drifted far away.

Jolene J. Schrader

Peeled Tears

Beneath the ground a potato cries
  Its eyes reaching all about
Above, something is a stirring
  This spud can't see or shout
Why is this veggie crying
  From within the darkened view
He's planted next to an onion
  That the spade had chopped in two
Nothing is as it seems
  When at first it be glanced
The potato was soon uplifted
  And the stew became enhanced

Carl A. Smith

Vacation Has Ended

Vacation has ended.
It's school time again.
What can I do but try to make friends.
Back to the classrooms
Into the schools,
What can we make of these young fools?
School work is hard
But children will pass.
At the end of spring
We will be gone at last.
Books, pencils and paper
Is all we have to bring.
In my third period Chorus class
All we do is sing.

Donna Matuska

Untitled

A bird sits on a branch's tip;
Its song is joyful and sweet.
So is the song of friendship,
When friendly eyes do meet.

Eva Quezada

Loving Again

When it comes to pain
I've felt it
When it comes to tears
I've cried them
When it comes to doing without
I'm doing that
When it comes to being alone
I'm living that
When it comes to love
I hid.
When it comes to you
I want to love
I want to commit
When it comes to you
the pain stops
the pain heals
the tears dry
And now
I'm waiting to love again.

Denece Washington

"My Parents' Home"

There is a place inside my soul I go
  I've gone there many times,
A place complete, that makes me whole,
  when trouble fills my mind.

By foot or phone I'll always trace
  the places where I've grown,
But no sanctuary could replace
  the one that I call home.

The home where Mom and Dad reside
  that's where my heart will stay,
And though we live apart, inside
  they are never far away.

For when my troubles weigh me down
  and the pressures hard to bear,
I know that if I look around
  Mom and Dad are always there.

It makes no difference where I roam
  the distance cannot sever,
The bond that always brings me home
  In my heart they live forever...

Jennifer Lisa

Secret Love

I have a secret love,
I've hidden away in my heart;
For I can tell no-other,
but, in there, we'll never
be apart.
I have a secret love,
and though he'll never know;
he'll always be a part of
me, wherever he may go.
I have a secret love,
he's perfect in every way,
In my eyes, he can do no
wrong, but a secret he
must stay.
I have a secret love,
It hurt's to keep inside,
how I long to be with
him, but, by the rules I
must abide,

Jonna B. Wightman

Who Knows

I've never seen an angel, although
I've seen a UFO
Trying to convince
My friends of it since
That time in the late sky
I saw it spinning by
If only others knew
The feelings that it drew
To see such brilliant light
An extraordinary sight
Some knowledge they could gain
Of things we can't explain —-

Amy Robideaux

Requiem For Life

My wings reaching for the sky
Know I can't
But have to try
To shed this form and fly
Power, majesty, ease and grace
Floating easily into space
Touch the moon meet the stars
While I'm chained behind these bars
If I could just escape, break free
No happier person would there be.

Jeanne Morin

Blue Iris

Blue iris, freshly gathered,
Laid in fabric pattern pressed;
This was to be your springtime dress
To win friends who mattered.

It awaits your returning after,
A shroud you claimed in spirit's sign,
To make a young girl's statement bind
With nature's gift of laughter.

See how their petals seem to beckon,
Hung delicately in the light.
My fingers trace through misty sight
The lines of life we have to reckon.

Greg Lough

Sophia's Lullaby

Close your eyes, my child and rest
Lay your head on Mommy's breast
Daddy's near to comfort you
Til you sleep the darkness thru.

Angels guard you while you sleep
Sent by God your safety keep
Moonbeams serve as nature's light
To protect you thru the night.

Close your eyes, my child and rest
Lay your head on Mommy's breast
Daddy's near to comfort you
Til you sleep the darkness thru.

As you dream of Teddy Bears
God will wash away your cares
And when again the morning breaks
He'll nudge you lovingly awake.

Close your eyes, my child and rest
Lay your head on Mommy's breast
Daddy's near to comfort you
Til you sleep the darkness thru.

John E. Riegel

Abstracts

Thinking in the abstracts,
  Learning how to cope,
Ways to handle everyday,
  Where's the antelope,
Going down the river,
  In a smelly old canoe,
Sixty seven little men,
  Stop to watch the view,
Wonder why I'm writing,
  Wonder where I've been,
Thinking in the abstracts,
  Ought to be a sin.

Josephine C. Hill

Sanity

Let the night surround you
Let the darkness be your fate
Close your eyes at night
And open your mind's gate.
A quest for an inner peace
And the sandman's touch of rest
Will send you speeding on your way
To a land where you know best
The boundaries of your mind extend
Into a world without a fear
You can't escape this place tonight
Until morning starts to appear
Your fantasies begin to unfold
But the darkness turns to grey
Falling back to Earth so fast
Then in your body you lay
A warmth touches your skin
It's the sun in all its might
You're up pushing it through the day
While waiting for the night.

Christopher Greeley

And There Was Life

And God said,
let there be life.
And there was life.
And he saw that it was good.

There was man of his youth,
bewildered, alone
There was man of his growth,
his breadth, and needs.
Then man became man.

He knew happiness of
life well-lived,
And agony of life well-died.
He knew comfort of brothers
still well and alive.
He relived every life—
a part of the whole.

And all this he found
and accepted as true.

Where has man gone?

Deborah Bass Rubenstein

Spring

"With the coming of Spring
let us not take for granted
what is happening, rather,
let us be aware of every
living being and that
Life itself is a rebirth!"

Ann Bilanych

My Happiness

It hurts me so much to
let you go,
but no matter what
I do you'll never know.
I fell for you harder
than anyone before
and for that my
heart is sore.
Nothing ever made
me as happy
as you always
made me,
but my happiness is
coming to an end.
Time heals all and my
heart will mend,
but there will always be
a place for you deep within.
You were My Happiness.

Angela Culver

Emeritus

Emeritus
Life
Between nowhere and nothing
Sound
Fury
Signifying detritus
Here
Now
Four score
Maybe more
From nowhere to nothing
Gathering detritus
Emeritus

Joseph H. Wellbank

Life

Life is God's gift to live for
life is something special
so your life can't be a bore.

To die is one thing
but to live is another
don't put your life in a sling.

To die without Christ is really bad
but with Him is really and truly good
don't make your peers and elders sad.

Live a life that fits
just as long as it's o.k. with God
so don't let your life go into bits.

Since God gave us a life to live
take it with gratitude
and just give.

Ian Loose

End Of Time

Forever is to long for good bye.
Life is to short for love and
tomorrow never comes. Today
has already been and gone.
What exist cease to exist,
At the end of time

Jennifer Ramirez

Life's Easy

Just when you think
life's easy,
A stone is tossed in your
way,
your battleship is turned,
And there's a problem to
make your day.

Just when you think
life's easy,
A sacrifice is made,
All your dreams tremble,
And your light begins
to fade.

Just when you think
life's easy,
Your problems just
gather within,
Then you feel the deepest urge,
To start all over again.

Daphne C. Watkins

Christmas Is A-Coming

Christmas is a-coming,
  light snowflakes touch the ground;
Christmas is a-coming,
  just feel it all around:
Christmas is a-coming,
  hear carols in the air;
Christmas is a-coming,
  to bring us love to share:
Jesus was born Christmas,
  God's love came down to earth;
Christmas is a-coming,
  let's celebrate His birth.

Grace E. Wiltberger

Rain

Rain is falling on the roof
Lightning flashes and thunder cries!
Splatter, patter sound the drops
Fog rolls in the black clouded skies.

The creek has flooded,
It continues to rain,
The drops slam on the glass
Of the window pane.

I am scared
All alone.
The forest surrounds me,
Surrounds my home.

Winds pick up
The sky turns dark.
Lightning flies,
Sending out sparks!

The rain lets up
It still sprinkles slightly,
Clouds drift apart,
The sun shines lightly.

Jennifer Culbertson

Untitled

In a moment, I shall die;
Like a bind about to fly.
May a student start to learn;
as our world shall slowly turn.
A heart that slowly starts to break;
"I pray the Lord my soul to take."
Soon, that soul will be gone;
But in you're heart, I'll live on.
For hearts can break, but they can heal;
And now you know that love is real.
That peaceful bird has begun to fly,
My time has come. My time to die.

Jerry Vandiver

Alone

Alone
Like a Coke can floating on the
ocean of life—
Used up and thrown away.
Looking for a new owner.
But finding none.
Forever floating.

Charlotte M. Barnes

When Can I Go On?

I get a strange feeling sometimes
like I'm standing alone
beside a river-bed.
And I can see across the river
The world, my life, my dreams, me
Everything, everyone passing by.

I have no control over it,
Over anything that's happening.
I can't scream for it to stop,
I can't run away. There's no where,
No where I can go. I must stay,
alone beside a river-bed.

Jennifer Bucco

I Know

I know......
   Like the moth to the flame,
   I am drawn to your fire.
   Seductively lured...
   By forbidden desire.
Though......
   Your heat will ignite me
   With the lust you inspire,
   And burn me to ashes
   If I dare to aspire.

   ....I know.

Florence L. Bartlett

My Children

Tiny footprints on my floors,
   Little smudges on my doors.
Windows messed by baby faces,
   Bits of food in funny places.
So many tears I wiped away,
   Kissed lots of boo boos everyday.
Words cannot express how much
   you've meant
But this I know, you were heaven
   sent.

Dora McClure Deardorff

Pot Of Gold

I have never seen a rainbow,
Like those in the midwest.
Their generous hue of colors,
Just have to be the best.

At the end of every rainbow,
Is a great big pot of gold.
At least that's what they told me,
Since I was five years old.

So I looked,
   and I searched,
      and I traveled,

Until I finally found,
The one true pot of gold you see,
Is when YOU are around!

Joseph LaRocque

When Springs Arrives

Reaching,
Limbs hopelessly scratch the frozen sky.
Chilled wind — forceful sway.
A solitary tree.
Stale air mumbles of desolation.

Trodding through fallen branches,
Crackling under pressure.
Burnt embers, (spiraling smoke).
Ashes snow to the stone cold earth.

An icicle clings to the arthritic branch,
Its dagger pierces the air.
A cry of defeat as rays of yellow
Thaw...thaw...thaw...

A trickle of life that replenishes
a redbreast's thirsty return.
Drifting with the sun
a dream transforms...
The green beneath bare feet.

Jennifer Munson

Bodies Of Desire

As I imagine our bodies embracing our
lips gracefully touch with sweat beading
off our bodies.
With full desire inside my soul I
can no longer control.

As we make passionate love I
get this feeling inside that I can't
explain sometimes I wonder am I
insane.

All that I am all that I feel
and see I am a women of fire
so I have no shame for my desire.

When he rubs his hands on my body
and slowly takes his fingers and
caresses me down my spine.
I sometimes feel that I might
lose all of my self control and
then he softly whispers in my ear
"Bodies of Desire" then at that moment
I lost my mind.

Dawn Jackson

Passion In Progress

As I cry myself to sleep.
Listening to the wind call my name
I want my ache; my ache to come true
Hear my cry
I want my dream
I need my dream
To come true
My dream has turn to hate
Is it time to give it up?
My dream has turn to anger
Is it time to give it up?
At first my dream seem possible
I will not give up until my dying day

Julie Eyrich

Fairy Tale

Tina Sabrina
Lived on my shoulders
Shinnying up
Through tangled hair
Sliding down ribbons
Whispering stories
Of knights
Who rescued maidens fair

She swam in my tears
And giggled at fears
Then flew away
On wee wispy wings
When my shoulders
Grew older
To bear the burden
Of heavier things.

Frankie Gilliam

Broken Heart

He sits on a chair,
Lonesome and scared.
Tears stream from his face,
Like a stallion in a race.
His heart pounds low,
"Thump, thump," in a row.
He quivers with fright,
Is there no longer a light?
He thinks of the past,
How, in his mind, will last.
The memories they had,
Most good, yet, some bad.
Will he ever cope?
Is there no hope?
He prays "God, give me strength,"
But his words seem to sink.
"Why did she leave me?" "Why did she go?"
He wipes the tears form his face, and
turns to walk away.
Is there something he missed? Yes, he
gives her a final kiss.
He places flowers by her side in the casket
where she lies.

Joe Don Wallace II

Fervent Hope

For those of you who've done this
Longer than I have
I wish I knew your secrets
Wish I knew your paths
Some days they go like clockwork
Others like a year
The love, the fear and anger
Unsurmountable tears
Courage - Faith - New Wisdom
At least they'll be home soon
But days that seems like never
Days that seems like noon

Jane Howe

Landon's Laughter

Lifeguard Landon lays lazily
Longing learning limericks like
Little leaping lizards licking lollipops

Laughing loud Landon's lipsticks
"Luscious lime" leaks lightly
Lingering like Lava leftovers

Latter leaping Landon lands lassoing
Lanky leopard lions lunging
Like large lobsters

Logically lovable lumberjack landon
Learns less lounging like
Lathering leotard laced legend lamas.

Letting Landon laugh loudest longest
Lastest lets love life
Last longer

Cherie Frank

Woodland Sprite

Come hither, young sprite;
Look around you
  at the peace you
  live in.
These woods are untouched
  by human hand,
See the trees unseen
  by human eyes,
Hear the sounds unheard
  by human ears,
And feel your body flood
  with emotion that will
  never touch the human heart.
This is to be your land,
  your realm, your kingdom
  no longer mine.
Allow me to leave in peace
  as that I came in.
Adieu, my prince of spirits.

Jennifer Knighton

We're Special Also

It's true a rose is the
most beautiful flower of
Them all.
Although when you put all
The flowers together
No matter which way you
Look at them, they are
All beautiful in their own
way.
On Interracial children.

Joseph W. Crothers

In The Lonely

Fell unto shame
lost in my innocence

Feel the pressures
underriding my soul

seeking integrity
too far down inside

Loneliness shines out
my mind can't control

How my body cries
he tries to appear

My hidden obsessions
mistaken by fear

The pain will drift me from this place
no explanation to the calm assertiveness

Searching for truth
I am lost, no way out

Drowning in sincerity
I jump to escape

Frustrating anxiety
took it astray.

Corrie Abruzzese

Lost In Space

Little tiny planets
lost in space.

Little toy rockets
shooting for the stars.
Colliding
making one breath filled with life.
Suddenly deflated.
Abortion.

Efrem Crews

Love: A Definition

Love is free, yet there is cost
Love is found but may be lost;
Love releases yet it binds
Love may seek and often finds.

Love must give but also takes
Love destroys...sometimes creates.
Love can see and yet be blind
Love may know but still is kind.

Love disturbs but gives a calm
Love may burn but is a balm.
Love is sudden or may be slow
Love may learn but then must grow.

Love is Youth yet love is Old
Love is Silver but purest Gold.

Doris Lloyd

Love

Love is a lot of things
Love is what I get a lot
Love is a cold glass of water
Love is a loving puppy kiss
Love is a hug from a friend
Love is everything good
'Love is the answer'

Ernest L. Pennell Sr.

Shadows

Shadows of your loveliness
Lurk deep within my mind
Shadows of the one true love
Whom once I left behind

Shadows of the gracefulness
In every step you take
Shadows of the rendezvous
We often tried to make

Shadows of the happiness
Which we will never share
Shadows of the soft words spoken
With tender loving care

Shadows of the love we knew
In our first and last endeavor
Shadows of your smile so sweet
That now is lost forever

Calvin Daniel

"The Little Voice"

Material things can give you comfort
make your heart as cold as ice,
Forget your fellow beings discomfort
And lull you in the hands of vice.

How low and muffled does it sound.
Always listen to that voice.....
You may wander all around,
You have no choice, you have no choice.

Come out of self created dungeon
Where darkness and despair prevail,
The ray of light that is forbidden
Thousands of secrets may unveil.

Sometimes I wonder about this age
And think of those by gone days.
I find myself in a fit of rage
Whenever, I tend to change my ways.

Jawaid Tabassum

Kindness

The quality of mind making
Man like unto a God;
Kindness pure as gold
Reshaping narrow patterns to broad.

A kind voice speaking to someone
Who weary on life's way,
Now can walk a path in the sun,
Transformed in a new day.

The warmth of eternal goodness
In a kind noble heart;
Giving the light of happiness
No more to depart.

Annebi Doombadffe

Another Day

Morning is new
Many surprises ahead;
A conquering feeling
As you arise from bed.

The day is inviting
Abounding with chores;
Testing your knowledge
Tallying the scores.

And as the night approaches
The conclusion is the same;
Has it all been worth the trouble
Of playing this futile game.

Charlotte Murphy

320

Death Of A Season

Leaves wither and fall
mere husks of the life
that they once held.
And the grass that was green
(once upon a time)
is as gray as the steel sky
that looms above
threatening.
The last bird left yesterday
and the absence of his song
leaves my heart as
chilled as the air
that raises the
hair on my skin.
There are faint sounds of sobbing
as the cries
of a mourning stream
are carried to me
on the breeze
that is the breath of winter.

Amy Pennington

The End Of The World

One day the world will end,
Millions will die,
Thousands will cry.

The beast will come and take power.
weeds will take the place of flowers.
He will feed on our pain,
and he will take the Lords name in vain.

The Lord Jesus Christ will come again.
He will rid the world of pain
He will clothe us in this gentle reign.

The time is near so have no fear,
for those who have the mark,
will be cast into the lake of fire,
And followers of the Lamb,
will go higher and higher.

Joey Cruz

Tiny Fingers

Tiny fingers…
Miniature miracles new born,
O' the wonder of the moment
when you first touched me…
So soft… so pink… so warm.

Tiny fingers…
Playing on my heart strings…
Sweet the music that I hear
Inspired by my own miracle,
  'Motherhood'
'Tis called 'A Lullaby',
My dear.

Elisabethe Hughes

Upon Leaving

I will put my eyes in your eyes
My heart in your heart
And fill my soul with yours.
Breathe your breath
Feel your pain
Cry your tears
Until I walk with you again.

Donna Halfpenny

Untitled

The sweat of commotion
Molten movement of mind
Shifting to see
Where I've gotta be

Seeing me hate
Seeing me cry
Colors of the moon
Never enough to satisfy

Seeing me slip
Seeing me slide
Just got a little too close
To where I need to be

The color of emotion
Ever changing shades
Of where I should be
Feelings of colors of places I'm to be

Jennifer Harris

Heidi's Secret

I live in a daydream
Morning and night
I wake up with the sun
And close my eyes tight
I walk around blind
Afraid of my plight
Oblivious in my dream world
Where everything is right
The darkness is comfortable
For all I see is light
Shining like a star
You are in my sight
My love for you - should I tell you?
I don't know I might
But until then I will live in my mind
Where I am safe from all pain -
Well not quite.

Heidi Ristau

"Frances"

The child looks into the loving faces
Mother holds her close and cries
Father looks on from heaven above
And then the child is smiling
knowing she is loved indifferently
and forever.

Jamie Cooper

Little Bundle Of Joy

Tears are cried, babies died,
  Mothers drugged, babies hugged.
They are punished, why?
  They are dying, try?
  The justice, when?
I walked through the hospital,
  my heart breaks,
  The babies ache.
Babies shake with drugs,
  I cover them with hugs.
I try to comfort him with a toy,
  This poor little bundle of joy.

Jennifer K. Davis

Leo Dancing

Song
move placenta
thrust with intent from open womb
color was always her style
leaping from tongue to belly
dissolve the negative
touch sun and spin
she is figure, she is stage
red orange yellow
twisting she is rhythm
sun-

the happy eye is her flair
child prodigy of laughter
I've never learned more about smile
than from hers
the sister mouth, eye of demand
turn the spirit inside-out
throw into air and catch, run and grace
flush with harmony
MOVE WITH DANCE-

Angela Carter

Flotsam

  Ocean waves are pounding.
  Moving beach sand — Where?
  From this land enchanting
  To some other — There?

What of this odious thing — Death?
That forces man, through hidden fears,
To loudly damn, with every breath,
While calling on God's burdened ears
To hold that Clarion's last knell.
Although — 'Tis His call they battle.

  Oh eternal sea — Floating.
  Enticed by that refrain;
  "'Neath celestial lights glowing.
  Be born again — Again!"

Emerson M. Wilson

Interwoven Sunlight

Huddled in a deep fog
my arms
tightly
wrapped around me
I cough, and think
of the days
of sun.
When light
would bounce
off shadowy cliffs,
and the sweet, sweet scent of daises
reigned.
I remember warm sand,
slipping
through small fingers…
and laughter…

But then the grey came
Engulfing my tired soul
now bitter cold, remembering the inno-
cence
of youth.

April Brasel

Desire

If you should so desire
my body to embrace
look deep into my eyes
touch your fingers to my face

No truer passion heightened
by your touch or by your kiss
when you my golden locks of hair
run through your fingertips

Rising up emotion
a deeper passion wakes
your body melting into mine
that brings me to the place

That I will now call paradise
in silent heart and mind
knowing that no other love
compares to yours and mine

If you·should so desire
my body to embrace
look deep into my eyes
touch your fingers to my face

Judith L. Johnson

You Are The One To Blame...

Every time you touched me all
my feelings left me.
I would yell, scream and cry, all
I wanted was to die.
My whole body would go numb,
the whole situation was so dumb.
I did not want a single kiss.
What did I do to deserve this.
I thought you were my "Dad"
but what you did was
really sad.
All my feelings for you are hate,
you said this was normal,
it was fate.
You told me never to tell, but
you can go to hell.
What you did was wrong.
In prison is where you belong.
You must be insane, for you
are the one to blame...

Eric Orta (Daddy)

You Are My Everything

You are my everything
My happiness and my pain
You complete my world
And keep me sane
You fill my heart
With your tender ways
I anticipate loving you
for the rest of my days
You are of my words
The love of my life
I look forward to the day
When I will be your wife
You have made me
Whole in every way
And turned my skies blue
From an eerie shade of gray
You've softened my heart
And made it sing
My one and only, forever
You are my everything.

Joanne Pennell

Falling Petals

Fallen petals beneath my feet
My heart feeling so incomplete
Shattered thoughts
Shattered mind
Falling petals so hard to find
Crystal tears upon my cheek
Falling heavily upon my feet
Moving swiftly like the wind
Feeling the torture time and time again
My heart was burning with desire
Now it sits alone with no fire
Then he came and held me in his arms
And made me feel his loving charms
Now he has come and rescued me
And these falling petals will never be

Chastity M. Baucom

Morning

Day breaks
my lover sleeps
a bird chirps
a dog barks
a truck rolls by,
the sun rises somewhere
behind buildings -
I close my eyes
lay down my head
and dream it all away.

Elizabeth Luick

Lost

Here I stand lonely and lost
My memories will never be
forgotten in my thoughts
I sit here wondering how
things will be,
but for now I'll have to
wait and see
My life has been full of hate
and mistrust
being with guys who's hearts
are full of only lust
me hurting you, you
hurting me
I can't wait for the day
That I'll be set free
because then you'll get to
see the real me.

Jenny Nelson

Farewell

I walk along the board walk it puts
my mind at ease
It's there I think about you
and what you meant to me
It takes me now to a place
that's comfortable and warm
A memory of our yesterdays
when we were one
My memories I bring them
here to sort out the pain
there's something about the ocean
that washes it away
And as I walk along the beach
and admire shoreline shells
I find an inner happiness and
I'm able to bid you farewell...

Darlene Brandafino

Lament

Ye'll not go through th' breaks today,
My son, my poor heart's own.
Ye went in midst but yesterday,
An' nu I be alone.

Carla Jo Underside

Untitled

Dark, rainy nights
never a full moon
cold rains drowning
the snow away.
No stars' shiny lights
no bird's precious tune
just the monotonous sounding
and the fog color grey.

Ivy Mathews

Butterfly (For Joby)

Built to rise above all nets
never cornered
always ready to escape
riding away on a passing current
you have weathered many winds
which plucked you off the wall
and drowned you in a bottle

Your discerning eyes
keep you alive
two looking out and one within
pinpoint spaces safe enough
to rest your wings

You
saw me inside my brown deerskin
you flew through my heart
I am honored that such a gorgeous butterfly
wished to pause and stay
in that same patch of cloudless skies
taken in by my blue eyes

Alexander D. Bingham

Kittens

Kittens like to play
never in the rain.
Kittens like to purr
they also have soft fur.
Kittens can run
they also have fun.
Kittens can get in pots
not when they are hot.
Kittens get on pillows
they watch pussy willows.
Kittens can get fleas
they hate bees.
Kittens play with blocks
they hate dirty socks.
Kittens like to sleep
they wake up when the alarm clock goes beep.
Kittens play with balls
they play with them down the halls.
Kittens are like this,
I don't know why! Goodbye!.........

Jennifer L. Lee

Rush

Rush, rush, rush,
Never time to play.
Rush, rush, rush
Busy every day.

As quickly as a lightning bolt
Your life will pass you by,
As fast as a running colt,
As quick as a sigh.

Your life is like a ticking clock
That will always have the time
But never has the time to stop
Or life will pass you by.

Rush, rush, rush
Never time to play.
Rush, rush, rush
Busy every day.

Carie Stutzman

Isolation

My heart beats to each
new beginning day and beats
while I sleep. Why? No matter
where I go whom I'm with I
feel alone, even if with loved
ones or friends, I ponder.
With every holiday I feel
approaching my stomach aches
for I know I will hide, for
the sounds I hear of everyone
festively enjoying the warmth of
togetherness due to blood lines,
I stay away, why? I sometimes
stare into the heavens and ponder.
With every new birthday I know
as I grow into those
struggling years of achievement, and
age I in my heart seem
to only fade as even those closest
marry and sway away I'll go hide.

Andy R. Hernandez

Untitled

Like shadows in the
night, my mind
becomes one with
the darkness only
to realize that
what it possesses
others criticize and
leave for the dead
to rein over.
Never to be
understood.

David Codding

Jr

Five minutes of pleasure
Nine months of pain
Ten days in the hospital
That's now Jr. came
Your boyfriend says he loves you
And you believe it's true
One minute you are happy
The next you are so blue
Now Jr. is a bastard
His mother is a whore
And Jr. would have never been here
If the rubber hadn't tore

Jennifer Navarra

One

Alone I walk the fields of God.
No earthly love have I.
For those around me
Walk on by.
Alone I laugh; alone I cry.

Why I was put upon this earth
I often ask.
I wonder why?
Alone I came when I was born.
Alone I live; alone I'll die.

Hortencia Acevedo

Magnet

When she calls me I must answer
no matter where I may be
for the simple fact that she beckons
is a stimulus for me

When she wants me she can have me
no matter how hard I resist
for the truth is I adore her
it's for her love that I exist

When she shuns me I go hurting
and the pain is deja vu
for the cycle is ever turning
but there is not much I can do

'Cause when I want love
it must be her love
she is the only I know

So when she calls me
there is no opting
my heart and I must go

Donald Carroll Moragne

Untitled

Land of desolation... Seas of blood....
No moon... no sun... no sky to behold...
Worms eating your flesh...
Demons at your soul...
Your time of living...
Nothing but dying...
Seeking your pleasure...
From a world of pain...
Fires burning...
Raging out of control...
Earthquakes are summoned...
All the ground lies low...
Floods across the plains...
Locusts eating all you know...
Devastation...
Complete and so unknown...
All that is left...
Decimated before your eyes...
No way out... No way out...
Then you'll meet your demise

Jon Beckmon

The Old Velocipede

I used to be rode a lot
    now my rims are bent and covered
with many years of grief.
    My seat is torn and chain is rusty
laying in the weeds next to
    the age stricken barn.

Henley C. Thomas Jr.

Revived

Sad, lonely, broken hearted
No one to turn to
No one seemed to care
I felt my end had started
Just at that moment
In my despair
I called on Jesus name
To my surprise
God brought about a change
Love, joy and peace came
Just at my wits end
He made me alive again
Now I'm happy in Jesus
Thanking and praising Him everyday
After all that He's done for me
I wouldn't have it any other way

Annie L. Williams

"Wild Horses"

They run across the grassy land,
    No place to go - just run.
Where the breeze rubs against their face,
    Where they feel the heat of the sun.
Their feet stomp upon the ground,
    Their manes blow in the air,
They look so beautiful and elegant,
    They have a special flare.
They chase each other all around,
    They love to be together.
It doesn't matter about wind or rain,
    It's their favorite kind of weather.
Their eyes sparkle with sunlight,
    They get a little gleam.
If you look at them close enough,
    You'll feel like you're in a dream.
Horses have their own little world,
    As dull as it may look.
But it's a lot better watching it.
    Than to ever read about it in a book.

Amanda Walling

My Prayer

Some day I'll not be afraid
    No threats of leaving
        will make me cry
I'll watch you with open eyes
    you'll see me at a glance
        but, turn your head
            You've missed the chance

I had to be sure
    you loved me once
If not no more
    this time I'm the winner
        that's for sure

I can't lose, I've made my choice
    No more pain, no sorrow
JUST MY TOMORROWS

Darlene McFarlane

Alone

There's not a star in the sky,
Nor a face passing by,
Not even a ring of the phone,
Nor an animal in my home.
For I am all alone.

Angela Paul

Weird

Weird does not exist.
Normal is forever.
Just as a bright pink sun
Shines in the dead of night.

Just as the sky is a pure green,
The clouds are purple,
The land is blue,
And the ocean is yellow.

The flashing green of space
Compliments
The brilliant red
Of the moon.

The violet stars
Lay,
Deep within the fuchsia core
Of the black, dying earth.

So, in a world where
Weird does not exist,
And normal is forever,
Nothing is "normal."

Dawn J. Reres

My Poor Father

Not even a whisper,
Not even a breeze.
I lost my poor father,
Not even conceived.

War is not fun,
War is not kind.
Many are killed,
Even those who survived.

The flashbacks he has,
Of the horror he lived.
My poor father,
Imagine his kids.

Jeremy Jessup

Amen

Our world is changing day to day
Not for the good, I'm wont to say
The news I hear is always bad
It makes me feel so very sad.

The air we breathe is filled with grime
And all the oceans filled with slime
The sun no longer is our friend
I feel this world is near the end.

Tornadoes, earthquakes, floods, typhoons
Sure seems to me a sign of doom
All in the bible - the final book
In revelations - have a look.

That we could stop what is to be
Does not make any sense to me,
There is no place to run or hide
All we can do is search inside.

To cleanse our hearts, to make amends
To join together family - friends
To pray for guidance from above
And purify our souls with love.

Irene Sandy Fierro

Acquaintances

You know me well, you say.
Not to disillusion
but I'm afraid
not even an inkling.
Do you know me?
What I have done
And what I am
is the difference
you know not of or why.
So please.

Joseph Fincher

And God's Speed

Sitting here with,
Nothing to do.
Except that I am,
Thinking of you.

And wishing so,
That you were here.
Please don't leave me.
This I fear.

I want your love,
It hurts so bad.
Oh please don't,
Make me sad.

Say you'll be mine,
To have and to hold.
I'll be your shelter,
And warmth in the cold.

I am the one,
That you need.
I send my love,
And God's speed.

Augustus W. Johnson III

Park Bench Romance

Every day a new romance
novel graces
her fingertips
   the lady on the bench
with one hand tugging
   at a lock
of dirty blond hair
She waits
for a different cover
picture:
   One with her face and
   someone else's body
   like they do.

She knew they did.

Heidi Fellner

The Rose

The blush on the rose\ a shade
of beauty\ and velvet soft its
Petals\ but its thorns, a warning
To careless hands\ these red
notes of silent music\ rising
from the land. So easy on the
Eye\ These fragrant blossoms of
Regret, or new born passion,\
and neither in hope,\ nor in
thoughtless pleasure,\ pick one\
as if to steal a kiss\ from the
Lips of mother earth.

Joris Alexander

John F. Kennedy

In the streets of Dallas, Texas
November, nineteen sixty three
In a motorcade rode our president
John F. Kennedy.

A snipers bullet pierced his head
But nobody did see.
The man who fired the fatal shot
That killed, John F. Kennedy.

A man of courage, a new frontier
A victorious man was he.
He strove to keep us all from harm
Through his Presidency.

Now silently, he still walks on
Such a precious memory.
The eternal flame will always remain
For John F. Kennedy.

Anne S. Cvar

My Name Is Life

I've given you a start.
   Now it's up to you.
I've made you original.
   You are one of a kind.
I've given you problems.
   Find the answers and deal
   with them.
I've given you emotions.
   Use them wisely.
I've given you intelligence.
   Make good use of it.
I've given you health.
   Take care of it.
I've given you humor.
   "Smile"
I'm worth it.

Carolyn A. Brown

Ode To My Soul

   Rise high, rise high,
O Soul of mine,
   When once you leave
This frail old shell.
   Rise high beyond the
Stars' bright shine,
   For there O soul
I wish to dwell,
   Rise high on shimmering
Wings of light,
   Rise high above the
Birds in flight.
   Rise high into the
   Blue skies calm,
Rise high, O soul,
   Into God's realm.

Elfreda M. Almgren

Untitled

With in my heart there lies a thought
of love for all good things to be

With in my mind three lies a view
That all the world should see

But to bring them out and
Share it all
A way I can not find

Charles H. Freeman

Philosopher's Point

Sunlight shines
O'er dormant water
Refracted myriad
O'er gossamer and pearl
Ripples disturb
The mirror of the surface
Warm waters call
The soul is soothed
When starlight and moonbeams
Gleam o'er silvery shores
A curved seat atop a cliff
Above the dancing, laughing waves
That is Philosopher's Point
There hear the lake whisper
Of peace and tranquility
There many answers are sought
Soft replies from the waves
Of dancing, knowing waters
What one learns....
I cannot say.

Erin Magee

Imagination

The lovely sorrow
of a dragon's heart
is the boom
of a laughing storm.

The edge
of an angry mountain
when it rains
plays games of feelings
and memories.

When animals look
in mirrors of shadows,
a kind moment
of truthful music from the sun
can be heard.

Imagination is never dull
and frantic thoughts
can be so exciting
they'll make you
burst with shiver.

James Henry

Flight of the Spirit

Watching clouds form into works
of art as if directed by the
hand of an artist...
Sunset desert paintings across the
sky that turn into clay colored
walk-ways...
The beauty of a forest clearing with
its carpet of pine needles...
A ray of sunlight that exposes a
new corridor for exploration...
The sound of the wind as it
rearranges fallen leaves...
Tree branches that reach for the sun
and bow to the rains...
The warmth of a handful of earth
containing the power for the renewal
process...
The feeling of being a part of it all,
without the search for answers...

Jeannette Williams

"Life's Colors"

Life's colors tell the story
Of birth to final day
Creating rainbow mem'ries
Within the mind to stay

So kiss the newborn soft and pink
Touch golden locks you may
Witness cries of temper red
For I was born this day

Paint the sky a misty blue
Chase clouds of gray away
Shout from rooftops white with snow
For 'tis my wedding day

Stroke gently hair now silver
Mid purple violets pray
Mourn in black and yet weep not
For I've gone home today

Rejoice mid rainbow mem'ries
Of pastel yesterdays
For in life's colors there I'll be
Forever and always

Gayle Elaine Snyder

Heather

Softly, falls one wispy lock
Of burnished, golden hair
Softly, kissing youthful brow
And briefly resting there.

Wispy lock of gold refined,
Of silken, copper strands
Softly, now upon the cheek
Of Heather gently lands.

As if borne on fairy wings
'tween cheek and brow it flies
Momentarily becomes
A veil o'er Heather's eyes.

Softly, falls her laughter
As she brushes it away
More like a companion
Than a hindrance to her play.

Ddoris Kennard

Untitled

The daisies and Cattails
of early mornings away...
Pale yellow stray kittens and
Kellie from Merriatta
came to play.
Skates, swings, vacant lots
gave way to silly
fantasies
of how it would be when we grew up.
Carefree hours of
joyful play in
the sun and rain,
Forever sweet memories again.

Angela C. Horton

The Freedom Of The Meadow

Softly does the meadow breeze,
over fields and through the trees.
You can't see it but I can,
Imagination takes a hand.
A whisper of the cool white snow
Makes a sound both to and fro.

Gage Simmons

Red Lakes

Shimmering leaves the colors
of life boldly flowing in the breeze
as the sounds of the cotton wood
tree set my spirit free. Peace
and calm comes to my heart
through the vision of these.

The smell of the air brings life to
my blood. The life I'd forgotten living
down in the smog. My heart longs
to see its new blanket of snow. The
clean white only nature can bestow.
In my minds eye I am there.

Jeannie Averill

My Garden

I planted a garden,
Of love hope, and peace.
And offered its bounty,
To all, and for free.

I planted love,
Out in full sun,
To warm up the earth,
Till day was done.

I planted hope,
Under a tree,
Where its roots could run deep,
And yet rest peacefully.

I planted peace,
Where the rain could fall free,
And encourage the spread,
Of tranquility.

With help from mankind,
My garden will flourish,
As fruits from my harvest,
Heal and nourish.

Joyce Lawrence

Tangled Tremors

Caught in the mainstream
of seclusion
Scripted to prophetic
inroads
Challenging indefatigable
piracies
Sanctioned in the
knell of suspicion.

Hear me in words unspoken
In yearnings call
To be with
In the togetherness of life
Quench the thirst of separation
Secure the bond of forgiveness
Erode nightmares tales
Prompting deference for life.

Jo Wollschlager

Untitled

I had sweet dreams
of you and me.
In each other's arms
so tightly embraced
I felt so wonderful
that I was dazed,
so warm with beams and rays
you were so gentle, with
your enchanting grace.

Alice Haynes

Halloween

I'll tell you a tale
Of strange things afoot
They are not what they seem
And they are not as they look

The mist was dark
And filled with gloom
As a ghost caught his tail
On fire by the moon

They lighted the way
For the others to come
Rattling and singing
A chilly tune

Dark are the shadows
That hang on the well
Deep inside where
The witches dwell

Frances E. Long

November

November - is the eleventh month -
    Of the year.
As thanks giving is the fourth
    Thursday in November -
When we give thanks to our savior
    For all we have
As he gave his life for our sins
    So we can be saved
So let's us all celebrate with a
    Big thanksgiving feast of turkey
And dressing with family and friends
    The thanksgiving tradition

Irene Mary Larson

The Thinker

Thinking, as I sit.
Of things past,
Of things to come.
In disgust,
Everything so unjust.

The perspective you have,
Determines the outcome.
Of whether that instant
Stays a thought, or
Becomes a must.

Whoever am I to say,
It should be this,
It shouldn't be that.
A man, that's who;
Living and thinking in this abyss.

Andrew James Long

Flight

Reach high in thy vision,
    Oh soul,
Piercing the clouds
    As they roll.
Though planets appear
And stars interfere,
Wing on through the vast stratosphere.
This trip to the heights
    May reveal
The source of the joy
    That I feel.

Donna S. Van Arsdale

Wondering Silence

I gazed upon leaflets
Of towering green trees,
Wondering — their silent
Whispered rustling of leaves.

I scanned tall gray pillars
Transformed cement and stone,
Wondering — their silent
Stature and colorless tone.

I glimpsed the moon, the stars,
The sun and source of life,
Wondering — their silent
Beauty — enlightenment of night.

The universal silence
With magnitude portrayed,
Unfolds Nature's beauty
Through Mankind's words conveyed.

People transmit movement,
Nature calms their strife.
Why do people pierce silence?
Why does silence pierce night?

Carolyn Spencer

Seeing Eye Dog

Seeing eye dog? Leading my friend?
Oh, my Lord,
When did blindness begin!

I haven't seen her
In many a year.
Will the light change in time?
Does she have any fear?

Approaching now, close enough to see
Those staring eyes, that don't see me.
My tears welling up, deep down inside.
For I remember the light that was
    once in those eyes.

But wait just a minute.
Look at the rest of her face.
Serene, as she walks with her dog,
    pace for pace.
The light that once was there
    in her eyes
Now illumines her whole face
As though God were now her eyes.

June C. Taliaferro

I Could Make A Million

If I could bottle the sunshine,
On a cold and rainy day;
I could make a million,
If I could chase the clouds away.

If I could bottle up happiness,
To give a person that was sad;
I could make a million,
And that would make me glad.

If I could bottle up kindness,
For a person who had hate;
I could make a million,
And wouldn't that be great.

But this is all left up to God,
Who knows our trials and stress;
So as we live in this world,
I'll have to settle for less.

Ellsworth C. Buck

How You Creep Into My Cell

How you creep into my cell
On feathered feet,
    As quietly as the sun steals in
Where drapes don't meet.
    A white silence and there you are,
Standing with soft assurance.
    You know you are welcome now,
Not bold nor yet askance,
    No question where once there was.

    Though we neither speak nor touch
The sharing dilutes the loneliness;
    The darkness melts
As dawning dissolves the night,
    Or moonrise diminishes the clouds,
And my cell is warmer than it was.

James Kerrick

ever green

as the days
once again grow shorter,
evidences of the
beauty to come
are beginning to emerge.
hints of crimson,
yellow,
and orange
are creeping into our visions.
as each day passes
more will appear;
'til at last, only
the fir,
the spruce,
the pine
will prove to be
ever green.

Barbara R. Gay

Sister

A sister is not
Only a sibling,
But, a friend, a
partner, a competitor.
Some sisters are close,
Some are apart.
Some are buddies.
Some are enemy's.
But, my sister and I,
Are just right.

Caitlyn Meacham

-Will To Grow-

Does it come from wishing on a star
or from scenes of afar...
How does the seed of desire turn
into a dream.
When does the seed of a dream, turn
into will of a need.
How does it change from a seedling
to rooted hunger.
When the soil is hard and drought
is nearing?
What makes the need of it grow to
the point of blindness and how
do you let go?
When it is suffocating the breath
from your soul without losing
your heart?

Cassandra Shaw

Whether

If I hurt a little
Or hurt a lot,
And no one cares but me.

If I cry a little
Or cry a lot,
And no one care but me.

If I love a little
Or love a lot,
And no one cares but me.

If I live a little
Or live a lot,
And no one cares but me.

If I hurt, cry, love, live, or die
Then whether I am
Or whether I'm not,
If no one cares-but me.

Florence B. Stewart

Emotional Suicide

It begins with a far away glance,
Or maybe hello and how do you do,
That's when the vision's implanted,
And the process is started anew.

All my hopes are left unarrested,
And my flesh works overtime too,
Creating this vision of beauty,
That I hopelessly get drawn into.

Each memory loads up the bullets,
While my dreams pull the hammer on back.
I've made myself a half-cocked weapon,
Completely armed and ready to attack.

I've thoughtfully planned and pondered,
Every detail and each little part,
But when I finally see her,
I shoot myself straight through the heart.

Each rejection seems monumental,
As my emotions are torn asunder,
I've got to stop doing this to me,
Before I'm buried six feet under.

David L. Henkel

The Wind Howls At Everyone

The wind howls at everyone
or sometimes just a gentle breeze
sometimes you know it's coming
you can feel it in your knees

On a hot day a breeze feels good
your glad it came around
because it's swept you up
when you were feeling down

But sometimes the wind chill factor
makes things very cold
you just have to put your foot down
and take things in control

You have to take things you don't like
and cheer at the ones you do
because the wind howls at everyone
it's not just picking on you

Heidi Helmbrecht

Dream Girl

Last night I dreamed in colors bright,
Orchid, pink and blue.
You were there within my dreams,
I swear to you it's true.

You rushed into my waiting arms,
I held your body close,
And when you laid beside me
Was the part I liked the most.

A soft breeze moved the pink curtains
Blue moon lit up your face.
And then you left this bed of mine
And floated into space.

You went right through the wall somehow
Upon the moonlight's beam.
It broke my heart to watch you
Enter someone else's dream.

Within who's dreams do you belong?
Tho many dreams you see.
I only know I want to sleep
And dream you back to me.

DeLila Mize McCabe

Touch Me Softly

Two feet in the grave with my hand
Outstretched across the barrier of
Time and space between two
Worlds embraced with fear.
Never have I felt so wholly
Your love, nor so patiently
Offered of myself or mine.
You inherited my life in one
Night; you are cursed with the
Gift to walk on amongst the
Pain and growing grief.
I reach for you in what is
Momentless, but touch me
Softly, my love, save your
Clenching grasp for the Earth,
For this is your power that
I can no longer share.

Jason Shanley

Interlude

Recycle, reprocess, redo...
Paper, love, life, recycled!
For all of mine was all of yours
And all of yours was mine
Now it becomes ours to give to her,
Our daughter,
To carry on 'till all of hers becomes...
Recycled!
All of hers will then be his,
And thus again,
The process begins...
Recycling!

Cris Reyes

Heart/Soul

The love I have for you makes my
passion glitter. I speak to you from
the realm of my soul, and the tenderness
of my heart yearns to be with you. You
have set the passion in my soul free.
I long for the day, time our eyes
met, we hold hand and we just kiss.

Johnny Brookins

Progress, Mighty Progress

A lost and lonely lady
passed away the other day.
Her hopes and dreams just vanished
as her spirit slipped away.

Her eyes beseeched a stranger
who ignored her in defeat
while thousands more lay crying
in the gutters and the streets.

Progress, Mighty Progress
Is this all that we've to show
cities that never sleep
and children who'll never grow old.

Cynthia Martin

The Deer Hunt

In the snowy woods
perched in my stand
movements arrive in hesitation
black and white attire

The cry was of a baby
torn lip and whiskerless

She rubbed against my legs, so gently
her body so frail and thin

I fed her soup and crackers,
with coffee on the side

After her meal she nestled
into my coat pocket
like a bird in nest

She is now the queen of a
home where I stay.

George Gessitz

Morning Glory

Rainbow spawned water nymphs
Perform their mesmerizing antics
In the liquid laughter
Of transparent morning mist.

Fat fuzzy bumble bees
Wait patiently,
For nectar laden blossoms
To open their doors for breakfast.

Fashionable petal gowned daisies
Raise proud sleepy heads
For the innocent kiss
Of the morning sun.

Dew drops square dance
In spontaneous rapture
On tiny spider web trampolines
Of filmy gossamer spun silk.

Descending gleefully on slides
Of variegated blades of green
Into the warm nurturing
Arms of Mother Earth!

Judy Hayes

Flowers

Flowers smell scrumptious.
Petals fall softly downward,
When calm breezes blow.

Casey Stork

Chesapeake Bay

The estuary that flows from
Philadelphia to the Atlantic
Providing a home for
Devil fish and fairy fish.
    Where minnows eat sharks
    and sharks flee to desert isles.

Where dolphins dance with flying fish,
crabs and lobsters make love
in muddy caves.

    Where flounders and blowfish
    attach Chinese Men-of-war
    to feel the sting of poison
    liquid fired by jellyfish.

Where the skeletons of sunken ships
give up their wealth to sea urchins
and sea eels.

    Where bones of ancient
    Pirates guard treasures
    sought by pirates
    of a different age.
        Arthur Gallant

Raul's Dream

Alli esta the American Dream
Piece of the pie
Democracy claims "todos iguales,
Levantate by the boot straps
Determination, 'Ganas'"

It is all there
very neatly placed
by color, size, consistency
al alcance
Dark eyes fill with delight

Suena, inside the candy store
soft, chewy chocolates
Red, white and blue jelly beans
cellophane lollipops

Estira la mano
Grasp a fistful
Despierta a la realidad
"The Dream" is encased in glass
Shatter
        Alejandra M. Galarza

Blood Test

Draw the blood
Pierce the skin
    What's wrong with you?
Take it from my head
That's where I am messed up
Take it from my heart
That's where it hurts

Friends come
Friends go — go
    What's wrong with you?
Easy to smile
Pain remains
I feel alone
I am alone?
        Dan Serkland

"True Love"

True Love is bright and shining
Piercing through the darkest night
Finding joy in the knowledge
The beloved walks in light.

True love is not demanding
Neither seeks itself to please
Rather gains the please in the giving
Asking nothing to receive.
        Esther Skinner Wolfe

"Whisper"

    I'll whisper your name; you'll
play my game.
    We'll share our love; alright -
tonight.
    The both of us holding on tight, not
wanting our moments to end. To last
within us at least through the night,
but to hold on to for life.
    I want you to hold me, caress
me - bare - with me; even if it's just
for tonight.
        Love me -
        Once -
    Like you never loved before
and never again!
    Whisper to me; I'll play your
    game.
        Andrea Moore

The Red Tapestry

The faceless cellist
Playing a distorted tune.

The soulless Beetovan
Striking the barren keys.
He is creating a river,
A river of empty tears.

Together they play,
Weaving a tapestry
For the lost love
Misplaced
In the vast desert
Of their hearts.
        Danielle Isasi

Secret Life

I hide in the shadows of the night
Pleading to be noticed
Hungry for the light
My life is a secret
Wearing its disguise
No ones sees my sadness
No one hears my cries
I feel like the forsaken one
Living all alone
Crawling to desolate corners
Fearing the unknown
But there must be others like me
Afraid to show themselves
Hiding their true feelings
Stashing them on shelves
We are the chosen ones
Running in life race
Wanting to be winners
But settling for second place.
        Amanda Brazzeal

Emancipation

If I should die,
Please do not come to see me
In some dark and scented funeral place,
Murmur solemn words
To my cold and lifeless face,
And bury dreams and mortal treasures
With my bier,
For I shall not be there!

But go outdoors
To a field or, to the sea,
And, when you hear the whispers
Of breezes through the trees,
Or the sigh of deep-moving tides,
Or hear the happy whistle of a far-off,
Unseen bird,
Know these sounds are mine,
My joyful triumph song,
For I shall be mingling, at last,
With the universe I love,
And shall be free, free, free!
        Dorothy Keezer

Desert Ballet

Exhale of hot breath;
Prelude to a storm.
The desert winds
Lift and carry
Sand and sage
Across the stage in a
Whirling, twisting column
Of free movement.
A dancing devil of dust
Tempts earth with clouds.
The first theater
Of a desert storm.
A crescendo chorus
Of light and sound
Brings the house down
As the curtain falls
In an applause of rain.
Sorry Sir,
There will be no
Intermission today.
        Julie Jones

God's Flowers

As God walked the Earth.
Proud of its new birth.
He said to himself
Everything looks the same.
So he created colors.
And flowers will be their name.
From the purple of the violets.
To the baby breath's of white.
God made the beauty of each.
Shine so lovely and bright.
Then on a bush that was
graced with nothing but thorns.
He placed the most beautiful
flower of all.
A rosebud so tiny and small.
Kissed it with dew.
Just to show the world.
How much he loves you.
        Betty Edwards

Pure Love

It's not so much traditional,
Pure love is unconditional.
When it's given away,
It doubles back your way.
So try real hard today,
To love someone a special way.
Pure love is clean and free,
And it grows stronger than a tree.
So when you're feeling down and cold,
Remember God's love is strong and bold.
So if you want that pure love.
Take the time to look above,
You'll surely find that pure love.

Glen E. Phillips

Cloudbreak

There is an answer to every
question that rings.

And love deep down somewhere
in all living things.

But once in a while this
is so hard to believe.

When cruelty and unfairness
give no reprieve.

With more patience, forgiveness
and coming from love.

I'll handle this void
As they watch from above.

David Lee Specht

Daydream

clouds burst
rain falls
purple haze hangs over all
clouds shrink
rain stops
innocence around me hops
i dream
surroundings fade
a cat-like boy with eyes of jade
speaks aloud
he is quite near
meaning never reaches ears
nonsense rules
kings are fools
i wonder will it ever end
i awake
my hands they quake
things were so much clearer then

Amy Marie Doud

Eternity

Can words tell the pain and
pleasure's of old,
That blossoms and ripen's in
one's soul,
As they gather one for the longest
flight,
On wings, into the deep and
darkest night,
Light as the clouds that caress,
and give eternal life.

Audrey Schmidt

The Last Moment

As I pick up that cold knife
ready to cut.
I wonder at the same time,
if I leave the world
will I be better off or
will I be worse.
If I'm gone how will the world
of people who love me be
without me.
I think it over and wonder
should I leave and never
come back.
Or should I stay and let the
people who love me with more
wonderful memories of my
laughter and smiles.
I touch the cold blade of the
knife and soon set it down.

Alisa Morris

Reality Is

Reality is hurt inside
Reality is the pain
Reality is mass murders
Reality is insane

Reality is satan
Reality is God's love
Reality is mean
Reality is a dove

Reality is here
Reality is some day
Reality is coming
Reality is now

Charity Doss

Great River

This great river is like a mirror,
reflecting the rays of the sun.
People try to conquer it,
but it knocks down everyone.
The wildlife inside of it,
jump out as if they're scared,
for what's inside it, no one knows,
it never has been shared.
I've smelled this mighty river,
and sometimes, boy, it reeks,
the smell quite often stays around,
it doesn't leave for weeks.
Yes, I've seen this mighty river,
It's very big you know;
Nobody will ever control it,
through anything it will flow.
So if you ever see this river,
you'll know just what I mean;
For the mighty Mississippi will flow
shimmering and sheen.

Cory Speth

Midnight House

Tides of forgotten love
Shards of bitter hate
Shatters of the past
Monotonous
Impeccable
Flowing waves of bitter memories
and the midnight dreams of a young boy.

Joshua Gronsbell

Popcorn

Fluffy and buttery,
Relaxing and warm.
I love the salty taste,
Of newly popped corn.

Light and tasty,
Small and delicious.
It will help conquer,
All of your wishes.

Handfuls and handfuls,
Of this wonderful treat.
It's perfect for snacking,
And great to eat.

Jeremy Martin

A Self-Guide For Third Eyes

Along a road of thorns I crept.
Road signs recognized when I slept.
To see the sun, I faced the east.
So I could rise above the least.
An ego trips those with short sight.
Across the hedge-rows, dark to light.
The birds will sing a song when safe
With wind to carry iron faith.
Across the river to know much more
And never follow foolish lore.
The stories built with idle mind
Will cloud the sky with cup of wine.
A spirit pours with tears of pain.
A sky alit with storms of rain
To wash his ire of John's good-bye!
Just eyes, held on a vacuum spy.
Closed books were read from when I
slept.
Again you read to open text.
A mind of one, the mystic next.

Greg L. Weatherman

Tears Of Sorrow

Tears of sorrow,
roll down your cheek.
I know how you're feeling,
sad and weak.

I can't change what happened,
I can't end your sorrow.
But just hope and pray,
that things will be better tomorrow.

I feel your pain,
I know your grief.
Now I understand why,
you're wishing for relief.

Tears of sorrow,
fill your weepy eyes.
Oh, how I know,
You wish you could of said your good-byes.

Cassidy Williamson

Sunset

If I have one day of being alone,
sitting and wonder and thinking
will the sun ever has its last glow.
Different colours of shady so
beautiful of its on way,
'till that moment on the very next day.
So long sun I'll meet you again,
I wave to you when you're
hiding without a trend.

Francine Jaquinto

Fog

Creeping, crawling, cat-like movements
Rolling across that old cape town
Can you hear that horn a' blowin'?
Echoing down alleys all about

Come, come sweet calm whiteness
Casting shadows on the ground
Peacefully pouncing on every hillside
Engulfing everything in its path

Wonder what's hiding behind its curtain
Waiting, whispering, ready to pounce
Emerging through a cloud of white
All is quiet, all is tranquil

Disappearing without warning
Pulling the stars back into place
Time stands still within its walls
Leaving behind the same but changed town

Gerald Arnold

Wild Stallion

In the mirror I am a wild stallion
running free as the wind.
The lush grass and rapid streams
belong to me.

I am beautiful and graceful,
Yet the closer you get the more
Intelligent and fierce I seem.

I am patient enough to rule over
a herd of calm mares and their
curious colts and foals.
I am as strong as the mighty rapids
I lead my herd along.

Yet when I turn away I am a
young girl with the unique
characteristics of the wild stallion

Amy Evans

Night Show

I saw the ship's
Sail across the sky
What will they think at home
My, oh, my
Fire ember balls of light
Listen closely, it's quiet tonight
A skeptic's crow
A believer's delight
A sci-fi theatre
In this sky tonight
Orgin unknown
It could be our own
But, I haven't seen it
On any late show
Points to ponder
A back shelf book
Sometimes the strange
Needs a second look

John D. Winn

Butterflies

Butterflies flying,
So gracefully in the air,
Soaring high and low,
Wings flapping very swiftly,
Going to the world unknown!

Allison Decker

Sanguinary

Oh, so very
Sanguinary
What's happening
To the children in the city.
Self-inflicted genocide
And everyone says
'It's a pity'

Six children shot
At a neighborhood pool.
The gun fired indiscreetly
While chaos and panic
Burst onto the scene
The gun got away so neatly

What's happened to humanity
Is it sleeping
While insanity
Has its finger on the trigger
And if you don't live there
What should you care
When a 'n***er kills a n***er'

Christian K. Sams

"A Real Christmas"

Tonight, in our modest parlor,
Sat my wife, there with me,
Angelic voices filled the air,
In a corner stood the tree.

How its lights did glitter,
Garbed in tinsel was its hair,
Such a glorious apparition for,
Jesus Christ was with us there.

Before the tree, in a manger,
There the God-child lay,
In peace, gently sleeping,
On a new-made bed of hay.

Up above, a guardian angel,
Lit the room for us to see,
God's greatest gift, a saviour,
A new beginning, the nativity.

Let not this blest occasion ever,
Fade, nor quietly steal away,
There before the tree gifts and wrappings,
For Christ was born on Christmas day.

John Albert

When I Dream Of You

The thought of your voice
saying good night,
Lets me know that
everything's alright.

I fall asleep in you arms again,
The time of our passion
to begin.

When I dream of you,
I want your love.
When I dream of you.
When I dream of you.

The way that you touch me
shouldn't mean,
That this is only a
passing dream.

Dawn brings about a time
I hate.
Because till tonight our love
shall have to wait.

Joyce Harvey

Homeless

As I walk along the street. I
see many people with bare feet.
They are hungry and cold, and
they have no one to hold.
They eat what they find, and
aren't treated kind.
They are treated like trash,
and have no cash.
They eat at food shelves,
because they don't believe in
themselves.
Maybe someday homelessness
will come to an end, and everyone
can be each others friend.

Jennifer Messick

Reflections

I look into your face and
see the lines that pain leaves
I stare into your eyes
and know the trouble you have seen

I see into your mind
knowing what your mind knows
I watch your broken spirit
and see from where you tears flow

Then I come to see your heart
through veins it pumps out fear
So not wanting to know any more about
you I will stop looking into the mirror

Holly Myers

The Rose

A gardener mixing a concoction
seed, earth, water.
The seed starts to break open,
something greenish and brown starts
to grow out from the seed.

The gardener waters it.
It grows green and tall,
red petals on top...... ouch!
Thorns, don't touch the stem
it grows big, the petals are soft.

The flowers weakens,
The petals fall off.
It bends over, turns brown,
it falls apart. It turns to earth,
food for other flowers.

The gardener stands
feet in the earth,
legs are stem,
his body is covered with thorns,
head and arms are the blossom.

Ian Wynn

A Secret

A secret's a secret
  so long as it's kept,
When known by but one
  and no one except,
But once it's told twice
  it's twice as well known—
In a trice it's told thrice
  and the secret is blown.

John D. Bridgers

Belief/Beingness

The answers, my friend?
Seek them from within
　　And
You shall come to know

That you can really grow
Continually progressing and becoming...

Listen with care your beliefs
They are your own drum strumming

Leading ever onward and up
To your own highest, your own best,

Filling to the bring your personal
Happiness cup.....
Centavo

Then You'll Know Me

You say that you're a Christian
Seeking to serve the King,
But all along the pathway
You keep doing your own thing.
You don't know Me!

The Book lies on the table
Its pages nice and clean,
I haven't heard your footsteps
Nor the Bells of Heaven ring.
You don't know Me.

I don't need your money
The riches are all mine,
It's a life of sweet surrender
Open to all mankind.
You don't know Me!

My arms are ready, waiting
To share My riches with you,
But you must open the door
For My Glory to shine through.
Then you'll know Me.
Joyce E. Shafer

Time Flies

In my youth - the Summer time
Seemed to stretch out forever
But now - I barely but an eye
And it's time for Winter weather

Weeks spin by at amazing speed
The days seem to mass together
The months pass by in double time
And we're rushing toward forever

Then you chose what must be done
And calmly set all else aside
There is only so much you accomplish
When time's no longer on your side

You learn to enjoy each moment
Clasping joy and laughter near
Not wasting time with anger
Delighting in those you hold dear

For time has now become relative
It can bless or hurt - as you chose
So make the most of each moment
It goes by too quickly to lose
Christine E. Bogart

An Even Start

I've driven the wicked road
　　Seen old faces worn
Seen young children cold
　　Their clothes tattered and torn

I've been by the wealthy
　　Their angels in white at play
Young and healthy
　　Laughing each day away

The first suffers so
　　In deep desperation
The second will never know
　　such a frustration

Each born naked
　　But with uneven chance
Some lives incarcerated
　　while others enhanced

Let all have an even start
　　Let the gun shot ring in each Man's ears
Make pure every heart
　　for everything conquered and nothing feared
Donald Crombie

Solitude

Unrequited illusion
Self inflicted delusion
Hard reality
Life's seclusion

Unrequited delusion
Self imposed exclusion
Wake up fast
Hell's own fusion

Death before surprise
Never let me close my eyes
Flowers on the garden wall
Truth no disguise

In and out light cracks through
Much to quick to get a view
Eating all the fresh sinew
Edward M. Esposito

Little Cherubs

Little cherubs
sent to earth
Rejected and denied
their birth
Return to God
in their despair
He recommends them
to Mary's care
Who comforts them
and wiping tears
weeps herself
to see...
Thousands thus
'UNWANTED'
How many more
will be?

Cindy VanArsdale

Love

Love is a feeling that two people
　　share, Love is a bonding that cannot
　　compare, Love is amazing it's true
　　and it's fair and one thing is certain
　　it'll always be there.
Love causes heartache, pain, and despair.
Love can be empty if no-one is there.
　　But it is wonderful when you get to share.
And though feeling change and people
　　tend to leave, it's like comparing
　　it to a warm summer breeze.
　　It's warm for a while and brings you
　　a smile and one thing is certain
　　it has it's own style.
Love is terrific it's simple and true
　　and it's really amazing how much
　　　I love you.
Fred Dos Santos

She Goes On Faith

I have a sister who is an Elder
She goes to Church frequently.
It cannot get any better
Because of GOD'S honesty.

She help's everyone
When she is called upon.
But she knows GOD
Whom she depends on.

When I am with her
I see her Faith
I see her smile
I know GOD keeps her safe.

I see her light to shine
As she goes about her way.
She Blesses people and says
"Praise the LORD, each and everyday".

So here's to my sister
May she always be strong.
May she always know love
May she never go wrong.
Helen Smith

Untitled

She walks to a different beat.
She marches to a different drum.
She's always seen defeat,
and hardly has any fun.
They all ignore her.
They try not to look her way.
They hate her because of what
happened one warm fall day.
She tries to forget it.
She wants to get on with her life.
She just can't get over, that she'll
never be a Mom or even a wife.
They don't understand how it feels.
They don't believe this would occur.
They used to whisper and talk but
now they just deny her.
She wants to be accepted,
but now her memory fades.
She has it, that horrible thing called aids.
Amy Hook

Robert's Angel

"Grandma, I saw my Mommy today.
She smiled through the window at me.
Do you believe me Grandma, huh?
You've got to believe me you see.

She came from the woods behind the house
She wanted to check on her boy.
She loved me for such a short while,
and said I was her pride and joy.

Papa, I saw my Mommy tonight.
She wore such a beautiful smile.
She looked at me with so much love,
but could only stay for awhile.

Do you believe me Papa, huh?
You've got to believe me, please do.
I really saw her, I really did.
You know I would not lie to you.

I have to know she's there for me,
her spirit guiding me with care.
I don't remember the time we had,
but I know her love is still there."

Barbara Sherrill

I Was There

I was young and didn't know much
    She was there.

I was cold, needed a touch
    She was there.

I was sad, mad and scared
    She was there.

I felt as if no one cared
    She was there.

She became sick, lost much weight
    I was there.

She prayed to God to give her strength
    I was there.

She held on with all her might.
    I was there.

She slipped away into the night
    I was there.

Jennifer Spaeth

My Sister

I have a sister named Faye,
She's a special lady by name.
I have a sister name Faye,
She's bright, funny, and gay,
When you laugh, she'll laugh with you,
When you cry, she'll cry with you.
I have a sister name Faye,
She's kind witty and brave.
When you need her she's near,
When you want her she's there.
All she wants is for you to be happy,
She never ask for pay.
I have a sister name Faye,
Who has the world at bay.
She brings out the sun on a cloudy day,
She never thinks of herself in dismay.
This lady name Faye,
Makes me proud to say,
That I have a sister name Faye.

Debbra L. Watts

The Animal Thou Fair Moon

Shine down thick
Shine on me
Shine with kick,
Nights are frail
Nights are pail
Shine on me
God's thumbnail.
Change your mind
Heavens no
God's flash light
Full of glow
My girl's cold
Heat things up
Let her be.

Wolf for me
When in full
My clothes down
She then pulls

Bobby McNair

How

How could I wake tomorrow
    should I lose you today
How could I travel down life's path
    without you to guide my way
How could I tell our angels
    He had called you home to rest
How could I make them understand
    His way is sometimes best
How could I see the flowers or
    smell sweet roses wet with dew
How could i do most anything
    without fond memories of you
How could I oh my darling
    ever be the same
'Till the day we'd meet in heaven
    and together be again.

Dorothy Ballinger

Role Model

Model citizen I must be
Showing others right from wrong
wrong from right, to make you
proud as so it may be your
presence overwhelms me to such
a degree. Happy not said
you usually make me.
I perform my hardest each
and every day to be a
Role model so proud for
you as you for me.

Harlan Hartman

Uncle Lee

My Uncle Lee is like the eagle.
Soaring high above the trees.
His soul is free.
Free to roam.
To see the ocean's foam.
He's now the wind in all our sails.
There's one thing I want him to know.
Is that I loved him so!
    Love 4-ever,

Dawn Sutliff

Misty Eyes

My eyes have been misty,
since we've been apart,
the pain of missing you,
is in my heart.

Each day I pray,
to the Lord above,
for some time together,
to share our love.

I miss you dear,
and yet I know,
no need to fear,
our love will grow.

Time will come,
and time will pass,
but a love like ours,
will always last.

Our love is so beautiful,
that I realize,
there is no reason,
for misty eyes.

David A. Krause

Untitled

Four years it has been
Since you have been;
And I still can't go on.
The hours-long chats,
The encouraging pats,
They all are suddenly gone.
I can't erase
Your words or face
Imprinted in my mind;
Your big, strong hands,
Your firm commands,
So frighteningly far behind.
I won't forget,
But will regret
The time forever lost.
I'll apologize
To forever-closed eyes
Covered by Winter's frost.

Jennifer Tumey

Dandelion

He loves me.
    Skip
        Hop
    Bounce
        Spin
He loves me not.
    Stomp
        Hurl
            Scream
        Pout
He loves me.
    Whirl
        Bubble
    Beam
        Giggle
He loves me not.
    Damn weed!

Christen Masaniello

Melting

Ice cream
 Snow balls
  Milk chocolate...
   melt.

Creamery butter
 Meringue pie
  Winter's sleet...
   melt.

Frozen ponds
 Orange popsicles
  Frost bitten noses...
   melt.

Fingers of ice
 Peppermint spice
  Souls on fire...
   melt.

Kissing my skin
 Lips sans a smile
  Your icy gaze
   And, I... melt.
    Ilona Gioia

holy humid holiday

air is not crisp
snowflakes can't fall
this is tropics
sunshine, that's all

plastic pine tree
smells like mildew
iron rod rusting
needles are blue

wreaths untangled
holly's replaced
broken garland
can you find tape

babe in manger
lamb chipped her nose
where's that shepherd
buried in bows

poinsettias grow wild
their bushes climb tall
in december bloom
red rushes the wall
   alida-ruth nitta

Memorial

They sleep;
So many loved ones!
In graves across the land
On gentle hills
And grassy plains
Beneath the sod and sand.

With flowers and flags
We honor them.
Most times without a sign.
But they live close
Within our hearts -
In Memory - in our minds.

They shared our lives
While passing
Enriched us on our way.
Rejoice! And know we'll meet them
In Heaven some glad day.
   Hazel McNeal Graves

Behind A Mask

I wear a mask
So no one sees
The pain inside
My heart it bleeds.

Behind my mask
Is a heart that broke
From things that were
Said as "just a joke."

Behind this mask
Is a pain deep
There are nights
I cry myself to sleep.

Behind my mask
Is a sorrow no one knows
From the pain you feel
When a loved one goes.

Behind this mask
I live alone.
All I want
Is to be left alone.
   Allison Hunt

Untitled

Bubbles....
So perfect
and round slowly,
gracefully they fall to
the ground.
One by one, their
colors do shine.
Brilliance and beauty
brought out by the sun.
Some go here,
some go there,
then there are those -
that go absolutely nowhere.
With a change in the wind,
they start to descend.
Hitting and
popping, not even stopping.
Until all the
bubbles had come to rest.
Looking like fourth of July at it best.
   Betty Jean

For Her My Tear

A tear drop falls
So soft, it falls
Catching feelings
It drips down my cheek
Across my face
For her I cry
For her my tear
Reaches forth
For her it dies
And falls.

She pulls away
So soft, her hand
A tear remains
Beside her I stand
For her I cry
For her my tear
Reaches forth
For her it dies
And falls.
   David R. Navarro

Unborn Child

We wonder about the unborn child.
So still and silent in the womb.
Yet he lives and wants to smile.

Give him the chance to walk his mile.
Don't sentence him into the tomb.
We wonder about the unborn child.

He grows strong and so mild.
Not for the Gods a hecatomb.
Yet he lives and wants to smile.

He wants to grow, into a juvenile.
Without the fate of sudden doom.
We wonder about the unborn child.

Don't seal his fate in exile.
Not to see a sun-lit room.
Yet he lives and wants to smile.

Don't take away his chance, meanwhile
he can live within the womb.
We wonder about the unborn child.
Yet he lives and wants to smile.
   Jannie B. Clark

Untitled

You shared with me your heart
So that mine may beat again
You shared with me your air
So that I may breathe again
You shared with me your soul
So that I may feel again
You shared with me yourself
So that I can love again
I'll share with you my strength
So that you can grow again
I'll share with you my home
So that you can belong again
I'll share with you my son
So that you'll be young again
I'll share with you myself
So that you can love again
   MSJ

Beauty Flows

Beauty flows from you,
Soft and warm in hue,
Fair and wide it goes,
Gentle, fond, fair rose.

Beauty flows forth, dear,
Heart-warming and near,
With you at my side,
Gentle, sweet, love-eyed.

Beauty flows at hand,
Touching heart and land,
Rippling ever-outward,
Gentle, dear, regard.

Beauty flows from you,
Making my heart true.
   James R. Poyner

Untitled

The leaves changing colors.
Soft breezes turn colder,
Blow summer away.

Days shorter so it seems.
Not as sunny as they used to be.
See the leaves fall, winter is near.

See the snow softly fall.
A new season, a new beginning.

A young child awaits now,
For a man said to bring gifts.
Wise in his own way, yet so naive.

So much more to experience, to be
to see, to live, to give.
Sheltered for awhile, but free to grow,
to learn, to love, to remember.

Then one day, be remembered.

Briget Buchanan

Rain

Gently falling from the sky above
Soft, cool, and swift as a dove.
Cleansing the air with a gentle stream.
But is rain really as it seems?
Full of life for each flower pod,
or is rain really tears from God.
I often wondered as a child if I
did something bad;
Is rain Gods way of showing He's sad?

Betty Marcum

The Rain

The wind sang
Soft, Sweet, Slow
Melodies of you
On a stormy night

The lighting bruised me
The thunder cursed me
And the rain drenched me with sorrow

Jason Roppolo

My Dream Of Summer

The sun sets
    softly as
    we walk hand
        in hand
The waves roll
    gently up on
    to the sand
        With the cool
            breeze the trees
                begin to sway
                    foot prints once
                        left are now
                            washed away
As my memories
    of the past wonder
        through my head
            I wake up
                from my dream
                    and rise out
                        of bed

Aimee Fukuyama

The Unheard Sound Of War

A
soldier
hears;
bombs
thunder,
guns
boom,
planes,
roar,
rifles
crack,
but
never
hears
the
bullet
that
kills
him.

gordon e. marsh II

Apels Are Nise

Apels are nise som hav spice
som are yello som are green
som are red with a werm between.

Gabe Buttler

Poetry

Poetry takes a long time to write.
Some bright as the day,
others dark as the night.

Not just used in every day life.
Some dull as a spoon,
others sharp as a knife.

Verses and rhyming,
Don't forget timing.

Expressing your feelings,
understanding the meanings.

It can make you gloomy or sad,
and even altogether glad.

All is fun, there is no doubt,
That's what poetry is all about.

Jessica Christiana Smith

The Promise of Love

There comes a time when you will spend
some special time with a friend.
To touch and share in all you do
and say the words like, "I love you".
To see the stars and birds in wing,
to touch the grass and smell the spring.
Life is short as you may know.
That's why we must take time to show
the little things we feel and mean
to someone else who share our dreams.

Jamie E. Bone

Love For The World

Valleys lush green
Stars bright as day
The sky baby blue
All not as beautiful as
When I look at you

Jonathan Wye

A Picture From Rwanda

Clear, glistening tears
    somehow emerge from
    a leather dry face,
Attached to the starving
    sick-thin body of
    a mother.
She'll be a mother forever,
    if she lives-
    though her children die
One by one in cries
    and screams of agony
    and thirst.
Leaving her a
    widow, childless;
    and hopeless,
    worst of all.

Connie S. Ganger

Strong Black Woman

I stand alone
Sometimes afraid but always aware.
People stare at me,
    but it doesn't matter
Because I am a strong black woman.

I am proud
Not only of who I am,
    but of who I will become.
I let nothing hold me back
Because I am a strong black woman.

I feel pain
Pain only I can feel, inside my heart.
I seek understanding, not sympathy
Because I am a strong black woman.

I am confident,
Therefore, I believe in myself and what I
    can do,
I will succeed
    no matter how hard they try
To hold me back
Because I am a strong black woman.

Alexandra Renee' Taylor

Untitled

Things happen so sudden
Sometimes they happen too fast
Before you're ready
Or before you want it to
But whatever, or whenever
There's no way to stop them
We have to realize
We have to acknowledge.
Maybe it happens for the better
We may not think so
Or may not want to believe it
But we have to live with it
A death is just a new beginning
A new beginning for the dead
And also a new beginning for the living
The dead get to be, finally, at peace
At peace with themselves and all below
We, the living have to begin
Begin to live without someone you love
And will always love for eternity.

Brian Jenkins

Special True Love

You can fall in love
sometimes to fast
you can remember
all your loves from
in the past
But the one love you want
and the one you hopefully
find
is the one that is so special
you leave all those memories
behind
The one that has no comparison
to all the other ones
the one that makes you
realize something different
something else is there
and this one that is so special
is one sent from above
it is what you call
a special true love.

Angie Westfall

Sometimes We Cry

Sometimes we cry
Sometimes we can't help but fly;
We all search for the perfect life
And the answer alludes many of us
  As still others give up.

I find my peace with you in the night
  Beside the soft glow of candle light.

Chris Pankonin

"Tears"

Drip drop, drip drop,
soon becoming a stream,
ever flowing, ever salty,
all from the eye of thee.

A sign of sadness from the heart,
a river of pain let free,
fresh and wet like a spring morning,
all from the eye of thee.

Expression of happiness, a relief,
an innocent child's plea,
the loneliness of a howling wolf,
all from the eye of thee.

Jennifer M. Lembeck

Forgotten Heroes

Here I am
Standing here
Nothing do I have to fear

In the park
Oh, so dark
Misty clouds surround my feet

Click! A sound is heard
A light goes on
And then another far beyond

Till all the lights that were so dark
Have lighted up a field, a park

And now the darkness has become
The light that's found in everyone

Here I am
Standing here
In my field o' dreams

Jeanmarie Brennan

"The Little Mouse"

I saw a little mouse
Standing on its toes
It made a squeak
Took a peek and
Dashed through the door
"Oh Ha, it said
I see a treat
Dropped on the floor
Oh me, oh my
That's a good pie
I'll take it to my nest
For my little quests
Sitting by my door"
That the little mouse did
And all shared
That "Good Piece of Pie"

Eleanoir Massey

The Executioner

The executioner
Stands before me.
Delighting in his grisly purpose.
As my horrified reflection
Stares from his sharpened blade.
The stench of hate
Reeks from his dirty palms.
And his cloak is woven
From the lost souls of youth.

Gretchen Stout

Sanderlings

A little flock of sanderlings
Stands upon the beach
Warming in the winter sun
On one leg each.

As we walk beside them
They turn and hop away
They see us every afternoon
But still they will not stay.

Down along the water's edge
The waves roll in and out.
On two legs now the sanderlings
Flicker round about.

Their feet twinkle so smoothly
They look like toys on wheels
Their beaklets prick the soggy sand
And find their minute meals.

Barbara S. Buitron

Untitled

The night was magical
Stars of the universe
Like a blanket covering earths mystical
Rolling surf
Sweeping the waters
To its shore
Like lovers
Gasping for more
Infinite movement
Through the night
With mornings complement
Earth is now full of life

Danette A. Nakata

Loss

I kept - my sanity on paper -
Still drew a disrupt picture
I know - that time - I myself
Lived the razors edge

Never drew - blood - my sanity
I read aloud - and kept
Under breath - my pain
For my friend - our loss - her brother

Young man - our age - wrecked family
Similar- my own - my friend and
Lover - lost her ties - for him -
When drawn - the gun -

In time - she knew well- the feeling
Of loss - when the great sons birthday
Held a lonely visit

Her feelings - only imagined
By me - for a loss- as close -
I yet - to experience.

Blaise James

The Consequences Of Endurance

I've yet to find a common soul;
Still though I hold for what is true,
To share with me a common goal
And utter harmony pursue.

I scan the world for subtle hints
While reservations cage my mind.
I wonder if my standards make much sense.
Is it them or me that's left behind?

Charles D. Fairchild

Touch Of Snow

Snow touches lightly,
Stirs no wrinkled leaf,
Wakens nothing slumbering —
  Save old grief.

Grace Wenger

Stop And Smell The Roses

He said, "Don't let it get to you
Stop and smell the roses."
But for him, when it came
He couldn't find the door
And could only escape
The other way.

I know there are no fears, now
Where he is
And roses a-plenty
For him to smell
I couldn't know, when my son
Asked me to pray with him
How desperate he was.

So when your son says,
"Mom, will you pray with me?"
Take him by the hand and say,
"Come with me,
And while we pray
God will let us smell the roses."

Frances Swinderman

The Strength In Me

I have to find the
   strength in me
It's buried under
   years of burden.
I need to bring it
   up to see
If I can be the
   person
that I remember
   myself to be.

Faith Rasmussen

Golden Gown

   Mine eyes have ne'er seen
Such a lovely creature as she
Laid out in burnished frock
   'pon pillows of stone

One spare hand to her throat
The other 'pon hardened breast
Lightsome locks of russet red
Made a cradle for her head

The pyre blazed like tinder
When graced by the first flame
People made of her name a mantra
As her golden gown melted away

Gail A. DePiero

Sunset

Every day I go outside to see the
   sunset go down;
With beautiful colors that fill my
   heart with love and joy,
I wonder if I will ever see it again.

I have to go inside right now,
   because,
Darkness is falling upon this
   beautiful sight.

Cary Zerbian

Untitled

Here I stumble in a world of confusion.
Surrounding me. Reality, illusion.
Passing me by, yet so far behind.
Where am I going? Where have I been?
Here I cower in a world of fear.
No matter how I run, terror is near.
Shadows lurking in all dark alleys.
Planning, scheming, death of a foe.
A tortuous end. A horror gallery.
Running, hiding, nowhere to go.
Here I cry in a world of sorrow.
So much sadness. So much pain.
Hoping, praying for joy tomorrow.
Praying for the grief to end.
Too many weeping. Crippled. Dying.
Too many sick. It's hopeless crying.
Sorrow's beginning is lost in time.
Must it last 'til all have died?

Diana Crowley

Untitled

A moment passes with a heartbeat,
Take a deep breath and enjoy that beat,
It may be the last,
Or the first of many.
The breath of life may not be long.
Enjoy the moment,
Savor it, and store it.
Close your eyes,
But open them again hurriedly,
Or they may stay closed forever.
Look around the world,
Forget the future,
Who knows if there is one?
Life may end at any moment -
A moment not too soon,
Yet too far away.

Farida Khan

Big Sister Hand Me Down

She likes to give,
tarot card readings
crystals with pastel glow
Reiki mind-warps and
Funky green disco pants.
"Do what you want,"
I tell her
and she accords:
with 65% Polyester blend
flowered carrots and lime peels
swimming in grape thickness and
Grandma's moldy wall-paper brown
pouring down my legs
like my hangover's answer
to last light's buffet.

Tight crotch with cheek-splitting features
they relax at the floor like drapes.
I pulled on the pair
of spicy trumpets and faked her a smile.

Bob Williard

Final Poem

If I could dare to write you
tell you all the things I left unsaid
it would be good.
But I cannot.
My heart cries in anguish
at its crushed emotions
made meaningless by fate.
My heart roars in anger
at its love left unfulfilled
strangled by the constraints of time.

You left me behind.
moved on
to join life's ebb and flow.
your current pulls me not.
I must content myself with
this timid stream
until some untempered squall
again comes to rain upon me.

Carl Fossum

The Rule Of Life

It's always been the rule of life
That a man has to pay a price,
For whatever he wants to gain
He must be willing to feel the pain.

But it is also part of the rule
That there must be an exemption,
Sometimes a man achieves his goals
Without paying the price at all.

Life could be happy or sad,
It all depend on what man does.
But if success eclipses the price,
Who isn't willing to sacrifice?

And life sometimes can't be so bad,
Sometimes it can be a real surprise,
And as long a man has dreams and hopes,
He's bound to win and not to lose.

Fred P. Alarva

A Song For The World

Oh that I might write a poem or song
That all the world would sing,
A song to rouse the minds of men
And change the hearts of kings.

A song to lift a sin cursed world
And from it strike the fetter,
A song of joy and peace and love
That would make mankind all better.

A song to stop the orphans' cry
And drive away their fears,
One that might lift a drooping soul
And dry the widows' tears.

If I could write some word or line
By which the world would gain,
I should not feel my weakness so
Or fear I'd lived in vain.

James C. Bayles

Have A Nice Day

High school graduates
   That can't even read
A world going hungry
   We refused to feed.

Too many fish
   Are still being caught.
Third world wars
   Are still being fought.

Too many people
   With nowhere to live.
Too many people
   With something to give. (That don't)

Wildlife succumbing
   To polluted seas.
People succumbing
   To incurable disease.

What will be the final nail into mankind's
   coffin?
   A nuclear war?
   An unhealing sore?
   Or just too much, too little, too often....

Frank C. Eddy

What Of The Night

What of the night
That darkened theater
Spotlighted by the moon
Floodlighted by the stars.

Wherein the world
Is but a revolving stage
For a never ending celestial drama
Produced by Jove.

And earthly cataclysm, age and epoch
Are but scenes
Played by mortal mummers
In Eternal divertissement.

George W. Gibson

Deep Dark Despair

It hit me all at once
That day
My daughter sought another way
To live her life apart
From her spouse of many years
Oh Lord the giver of tears
Please make them stop
I must go on
I must see beyond
This deep dark despair
Lying on my back
Waiting for the Comforter to bear
My grief
I realize there
Is only one truth
I wish I had converted in my youth
A mature faith may have lessened my
Deep dark despair
But I must go on
I must trust in my Father's care

Dianne Tharaldson Huseth

Antiquity

They say the earth is warming up,
That glaciers will all melt,
That continents will be submerged.
All creatures and the human blend
Will slip beneath the rainbow's end.

And when, 10,000 years from now,
While searching for antiquity,
They'll find us in our redwood traces
With smiles upon our faces,
Boiled in our own jacuzzis!

Janet Hartley Humphreys

Friendship

Friendship is a special bond
that lasts when all else fails.

Friendship holds a neutral ground
when things are not so swell.

Two lovers can pass in the night
like ships in the sea,

But when the love is gone,
the Friendship will always be.

Christian D. Brazwell

Is My Football Team Ploughing

Is my team ploughing
    that I was used to drive.
and near the harness jingle.
    When I was man a long;
aye the horse trample
    The harness jingle now.
no change though you lie plough.
Is football playing time.
    Along the river shore
with lads to chase the leather.
    Now I stand up no more.
aye. The ball is flying.
    The lads play heart and soul.
The goal stands up the keeper.
    Stand up to keep the goal
Is my friend hearty.
    Now I am thin and pine;
and has he found something
to lie on. A better than mine.

Isebella Carter

Solemn Solace

Do you remember
That in March
The earth awakened,
Its soft soil quick again,
Winter's harshness
Having been lifted
By the mellow winds
Of the coming spring?

Although we barely
Ever see the snow
Where we have come,
Here, too, this is the time
Persephone returns.

The Ides of March
Have taught me that
True love demands
Complete enjoyment
Of all pleasures
Our lovers seek.

Conrad Borovski

Lilies And Lilac

I walk around in a valley of mirrors,
That only reflect your face.
I project my love for you
By walking at a faster pace.
I'd sail my love to you and back.
Lilies and Lilac
It's your love for me I lack
My Lilies and Lilac.

Cathy Leach

Aunt Kate

There is a very sweet Spirit
That rests upon your face
Just like the calm assurance
Left from God's precious grace

You walk with dignity
Knowing what God has done
Telling the love of Jesus
For God's blessing have only begun

There is a gentle way about you
And you are as proud as you can be
For your know the love of Jesus
Is what has made you free

Many have called you blessed
For you've walked throughout this land
Spreading the message of love
To every woman and every man

When you speak a word
There's wisdom that flows through
For in the Word of God
It said, this you must do

Cheryl White

Daniel Eric

You're gone from me, I'll never know
That special joy of watching you grow
From boy child into a man.
The master had another plan.

I nurtured you close to my heart.
I took such care, right from the start.
I loved you from the moment I knew.
I waited impatiently for you.

I ask myself, "how can it be?"
You gave this lovely gift to me.
Somehow I thought, it's just not right.
You gave it; almost; but not quite.

You've got to help me, now I pray.
Show me how to find the way
To accept my loss with grace.
Nothing else can take his place.

Jane Reeder

A Country Day

I believe in early mornings
    That wake up slowly;
No hurry, just gradually rise
    Like the sun.

The world at its best,
    In the sunrise hour;
An entire day - waiting like
    A song yet to be sung.

And then, as quietly as it comes,
    The day shifts into full gear;
With the noise and bustle
    Of all the activities that occur.

Until the twilight time arrives and
    Things slow down again;
Sit on the porch, listen to the crickets
    And thank God for the quiet.

Beth L. Miller

Untitled

Write! Write! Write!
That's all I hear
A little voice inside, that says write
Write about what? I ask
There's no answer, just write!
I'm too tired right now!
I'll do it later!
Okay, I'll write now!
Then distractions come, I don't write
A day or two goes by
I still have not written
Then come the voice again
Write! Write! Says the voice
Yes, I'll write I'll say
Then the process starts all over again
Days and days go by, the voice comes back
Write! Write! I said write!
Realizing it's not my imagination, I reply
Lord I hear your voice, I have the desire,
But I need your discipline!!!

Cametra Puryear

Racism

"Too sensitive"
That's what they say
And you stand waiting
Waiting to be served

"Easily offended"
Seems to be your way
And you start hating
Hating that's been reserved

"Always misreading"
You do it each day
That they've been baiting
Baiting 'til you're unnerved

"Can't understand"
They make you pre-pay
It's kin to berating
Berating what's not deserved

"They're all alike"
If you'd just obey
Racism is abating
Abating to be conserved

Elizabeth Stone

"On Christmas Eve"

The night was dark and still,
The animals all quiet as they wait,
Something was going to happen,
Something wonderful, for man's fate,

A tiny stirring, a movement then,
A small crying sound,
And all the animals came,
A babe to see, they gathered around.

They all knew, this very night,
A great Master, now was born,
Wrapped in a mothers arms
Her face happy no longer forlorn.

And Joseph stood, so proud and tall,
The father of a beautiful boy,
While Mary caressed their son
The animals were filled with joy.

Even the Heaven's were glad,
For the brightest star pierced the sky,
And all mankind would remember,
The night Jesus Christ did first cry.

Evelyn L. Mokracek

Empty Nest

The seasons change
The buds open up
The birds chirp and nest

The wind brings warmth
The flowers flourish
The birds feed their young

The leaves change color
The seeds fall to the ground
The young birds fly away

The wind blows cold
The trees are bare
The empty nests remain

The seasons change
The buds open up
The birds chirp and nest — again

Janet S. Sola

Time In A Bottle

If I could put time in a bottle;
    I would pour in lost days of old.
Beginning with those warm memories;
    from childhood, treasured like gold.
In my bottle, I would store all;
    the precious memories it could hold!

Yes, if I could bottle up time;
    I'd encapsule memories of yester-day.
Joys and laughter of the grandchildren;
    held in time, then, later replay.
Held for some dark and lonely mood;
    then used to brighten up my day!

As I move along earth's rocky path;
    I can see my treasures, o'er and o'er.
But, wait - time- no bottle can hold;
    so, once more, I'll open my bottle.
And as my life's journey nears its end;
    my thoughts and memories I'll outpour!

Then wander thru my garden of memories;
    to relive them all, once more!

Richard M. "Rik" Teed

Untitled

Of all the dads in the state
I wouldn't hesitate
To pick a dad like you
And when we're fishing
Or going to the zoo
I'm always wishing
That there were three of you
And whether I'm going to
Michigan or possibility Timbucktoo
You'll know who I'll miss
And now I'm done with this
So I'll say goodbye to you

Molly Margaret Kubiak

Onondio

I close my eyes to the God of light.
I wrap myself in a blanket of darkness.
    All of nature sings to beauty.
    All of nature sings to sleep.
I call to you, God of Thunder!
I call to you,
    but peacefully you sleep...

Lisa A. Cilibraise

"Reverie Of Love"

I walked into the Garden, and
I thought of you,
And said a little Prayer
I saw a rose
And suddenly you were there!
I looked above
And saw the sky of blue
A bird on wing,
And listened to Him sing
He sang of you!
I walked along
The Garden Path with you
And felt the Grass,
Still wet with morning dew.
I realized as I walked
there with you,
My life, my love, my all
depends on you,
Oh, say you need me too,
I'm so in Love with you!

Ruth Barnsdale Fultz

You And I

I am, you are, we can
I tried, I failed, I cried
This day, this now, that's how
We will, we must, again
We try, we try, we try
The storms, the clouds, the rain
We try again, again and again

It's hard, we tire, we rest and then
We try again, again and again
We look, we see you there
A life ours lived with beauty sure
Our trials and fears obscure
So smile and wipe away
Enjoy each hour and everyday
We pray we pray we pray

Mary E. Kinchner

"Waiting"

When I am down;
I turn my face in a frown.
The days seems long;
When I don't sing a song.

The times I look
At my life; I shook.
Because, I didn't listen;
When I should of been sittin'.

Please, help me to take;
My life not to shake.
To go back into my shell;
So, Lord, "I don't want to go to hell."

When this day I woke up;
To write my life; "not in a cup."
But, to fill that "Love of Waiting;"
When I just sit and hear "Him" saying.

Some day very soon;
Not far away from my gloom.
I will be safe in "Saying"
That I will be in "Waiting."

R. D. D. Gonsalves

I Am What I Am (Through My Daughter's Eyes)

Please accept me for what I am,
I wasn't born "perfect", you see.
And when I go to school,
Kids pick on my deformity.

They laugh, they smirk, they turn away,
They say that they can't play today -
Or any day...
It's such a hurtful thing to say.

My greatest wish if it could be,
Is that they accept me unconditionally - like my cat Mystery,
Who doesn't notice my flaw -
She just cuddles up and taps me with her paw.

I am what I am - please look beyond my face.
And try to understand,
That what nature gave to me,
I cannot replace.

Rachel Stewart Spector

A Soul's Merry-Go-Round

Filled with a Spirit that is not my own,
I watch the world go by
So quickly, it seems I'm watching a merry-go-round.
Only the painted horses have become painted people,
And the mirrors once filled
with the carnival lights and laughing children
Now reflect people,
who seem to have forgotten how to laugh,
and the faces of a clock.
Alone I glance around me and search
for the lever to slow
the spinning wheel down and to find the music box,
Yet on the platform turns...
Until I sit down on the old, wooden horse with its chipping paint
And once again gain the precious, insightful perspective of a child.
The joyful music of the Spirit
once more plays its melody in my
soul.

Lucinda Wilhoite

To My Best Friend

  I am your best friend,
I will stand before you,
  talk to you, give you advice.
I will stand beside you,
  listen to you, let you make whatever decisions
  you feel right.
I will stand behind you,
  support you, catch you if you should fall.

  I am your best friend,
I'll never be far - no matter what.
I am your best friend
and I am here - just look around;
  As I often have.

Lori Ann Zahora

The Ocean

The season is upon us when I must stretch out my long arms.
I will take a deep breath, and hurtle my muscle against my neighbors.
It is time once again to cleanse my body of the wastes left behind.
Do these summer invaders realize the rigorous exercise they put
  me through?
I am growing old and my spirit is forever weakening.
I will call upon the heavens to open up and saturate me with fluid.
I will call upon the winds to plunge me forward,
And I will call upon my friends surrounding me to remain strong.
For after the poisons and the nausea sicken me,
I will vomit my contents upon them, soiling and littering
Thus bruising the sand and rock, and forever scarring.

Teresa Donoher Ryan

Thoughts While Sitting

By My Best Friend's Father's Grave

I wish I would know
I wish I could see
Why life's what it's been
For you and for me.

We all have a purpose
Of this I am sure
We all have a meaning
A reason endured.

But why were we chosen
To live when another
Has died without reason
Their purpose unfinished?

And suppose that their purpose
Was a child or two or three
And when they had died
That child was too young to see

Why life goes on this way
Why we face each unknown day
And why things are
The way they are for you and me.

Louise I. Scheirer

I Am

I am a special person who likes sports,
I wonder if Bo Jackson will ever play
    football again,
I hear birds singing outside,
I see snow on a farms field,
I want world peace,
I am a special person who likes sports.

I pretend that I hit a home run every time
  I pick up a bat,
I feel happy to be alive,
I touch the wet snow,
I worry that the world will end,
I cry when a family member dies,
I am a special person who likes sports.

I understand that life is not fair,
I say do what you want to do,
I dream about what ever I want,
I try to help out any way I can,
I hope that when I die, I die in my sleep,
I am a special person who likes sports.

Matthew Chaple

As I Wonder

As I look up to the clouded sky,
I wonder if my Daddy can now fly.

As I smell the salt in the ocean's air,
I wonder if my Daddy is still at peace there.

As I touch his picture with my tiny hands,
I wonder if my Daddy knows I'm now a little man.

As I cry myself to sleep at night,
I wonder if my Daddy knows I can ride a bike.

As I remember our memories of laughter and play,
I wonder if my Daddy will come back one day.

As my heart has an emptiness deep inside.
I wonder why my Daddy had to Die.

As I counted the days, the months now years,
I wonder if my Daddy's soul will continue to stay near.

As I look up to the sky so blue,
I wonder if my Daddy misses me too.

Melissa T. Maksin

The Eye Of The Beholder

Were I a sculptress
I would cast your body in clay.
My fingers would take pleasure
in remembering every detail
of your perfect form.

Were I an artist
I would portray you in color.
My use of highlights and shadows
would echo the glow
which exudes from your smooth, brown skin.

Were I a photographer
I would focus solely
on your eyes
for within their depth
is the mirror of your heart.

And yet, with all of their beauty
none of these mediums
could possibly capture
the true essence of
YOU.

   Toi Lynn Mooty

Medieval January

   The castle smelled of dampness as the
icy breeze flowed through the open windows,
unsettling the tapestries and applying an air
of exotic mystery to the fortress.
   Fireplaces sparked as the blades of magnificent
broadswords gleamed above the coat of arms on the
wall, while majestic spirits of former kings and queens
sat in antique thrones, comfortably poised.
   Monstrous gargoyles perched silently atop the
stone columns in the corridor, and assembled suits of
armor stood rigid against the wall. The arctic night
wind whistled throughout the castle, yet it was only
strong enough to quiver my bedside candle's flame,
as I drifted off to sleep.

   Kelly Byrd

My Prayer

Dear Heavenly Father, please forgive me
if at times I seem ungrateful for all that
you have given me.
Or if at times I grumble at the duties
I must perform.
If, in my foolish heart I seek treasure,
or long for earthly pleasure I have no
right to seek, give me the strength
to bear the pain of realism,
Dear God, you know that I am weak.
Keep me above pettiness or petulance
when things just don't go my way,
I ask for wisdom and courage
as I face another day.

   Ruth Schwarzbach

Yes, I'm Thankful

I'm thankful for the food and air - that helps sustain my life
I'm thankful for the daily chores - the task, the grief, the strife
I'm thankful for the birds that sing - the soil, the grass, the trees
I'm thankful for the strength and will - to get down on my knees
I'm thankful for my Mom and Dad - who gave me home and love
I'm thankful for the gracious God - who dwells in skies above
I'm thankful for the health He gives - to body, soul, and mind
I'm thankful for the folks I meet - whose thoughts are good and kind
I'm thankful for the things I do - each moment of the day
I'm thankful for the skies I see - blue and clear, or gray
I'm thankful for the skills I have - in work, in play, and such
I'm thankful for my relatives - and love them very much

   Vince Ruffin

Stephen King

Master of the Macabre, His Greatest Claim to Fame,
If it's Terror that You're Looking for, You'll Find it by His Name.
Derry or in Castle Rock, Each a Small Town That's in Maine,
Sheriff Pangborn Seeking Old George Stark, Who's Terribly Insane.
Or Trying to Stop Leland Gaunt, the Devil in Disguise,
So Readers All, You Must Beware, Heed This Warning to the Wise.
You'll be Ensnared with Each New Book, Though You'll Try
   and Put Them Down,
They'll Keep You Reading Through the Night, You'll Jump at
   Every Sound.
I Anxiously Await His New Books to Come Out, For He's the
   King of Terror, Of That There is No Doubt.
I say that I'm His Number One Fan but Annie Wilkes I know I'm Not.
But Every Book that He Has Written is Every Book that I Have Got,
I Feared Along With Woman and Son Trapped by Cujo in Their Car,
Or the Overlook Hotel and Those Strange Ghosts There at the Bar,
The Monster Thing in Derry, the Monster Thing They Just Called It,
The Monster Thing That Took the Children of Anyone It Could Get.
Carrie, the Child, Being Teased and Hurt So Much,
But in the End They Saw Her Way, She Had That Special Touch.
Christine, the Car, Don't Tell It What to do, Don't Get by It or
Its way Cause It's Sure to Get You.
There's Many More I have to Say, I've Read Them, Every One,
The Three New Books I've Just Received, I'll Read From Dusk
   to Dawn.
So, Keep Them Coming, Stephen King, I'll Read Them All, I Know,
And as They Come I'll Buy Each One, My Collection it Will Grow.

   Yvonne Madison

My Philippine Friend

This little lady is a very good friend.
If you need a helping hand she would lend.
She is very smart
And sometimes she works with art.

She has a daughter and two sons
And they keep her on the run
She is an Oriental
And her husband is gentle.

My friend has a cabin in the pines
And it is a cozy place to dine.
She likes to plant seeds
And she keeps her garden free of weeds.

This friend gets involved with many things
And she also likes diamond rings.
She hails from the Philippines
And she came to America to fulfill her dreams.

   F. Marion Daniel

Untitled

If you take the tears from crying eyes will the hurt just disappear?
If you put a weapon in the hand of a frightened man
will he show no fear?
Take the motion from a spinning wheel and watch it stop.
Take the danger out of a naked flame and what have you got.
Could you swear if you had that second chance you wouldn't do
it again?
Why is there blue sky?
Why is there red sky?
Should the blue sky meet the red sky?
There's a right and wrong
There's weak and strong
These are just a few questions I've wondered for so long.
If you know the answers, what would they be?
It's just the ways of the world and that's how it's meant to be.

   Michael Joseph Sutmaier III

Nature's Tiny Gypsys

I saw the glow of a little firefly
Ignite within the field of night
Following the tiny explosion of light
I beheld the secret of a mid-summer's night
The melodious gyrations of a wee maddened cricket,
Strumming his tune upon his tiny brisket
The Honking of a lazy bull frog
  —All seem to try the evening's sky!
A whippoorwill's song sketches and
  Endeavors to catch a soft symphonic
    Call of nature's merry makers' ball !!
A falling star, a murmur in the trees
  Enfolds me with deep harmonies.
The resounding crash of a new-fallen tree
  Embraces to me
Knowledge of a beaver's spree!
All this——nothing more——
Awakens me within my core!

Louis J. Nuzzo

An Untold Story

A rickety shanty beyond the ochre light
illuminates
a southern town and awakens
a ghost
haunted by the torches of slavery,
the humiliation of rape and poverty.

An ashen, young girl rises forward.
With cracked, quivering lips
she decides to break the mold.

She carries the history of her family
through her
skin of desire and
the thoughts of a community's shame.

With no one daring to challenge her whisper.

A rickety shanty beyond the ochre light
shines
a southern town and strengthens
a woman
haunted by the torches of slavery,
the humiliation of rape and poverty.

Mark Rosario

The Way To Mend

  I say to my friends,
I'm able to mend whatever they bend
  So this to you I do send:
One day in a diner I was confronted by a whiner.
  She said, "When I look into the mirror
I see it coming clearer, it's my end that seems nearer.
  I can't defend, it's what I fear
somebody smear it please
  cause it to change or cease.
I yell to HE who compels, NOW!
  But there is no one around — wow!
I must be a mental case;
  how did I become such a sentimental waste,
overwhelmed with haste?
  For who I am — having no grace I'm damned!"
So I said, "Yourself you have crammed
  into your own corner, ma'am.
To me there's no doubt, this feeling's unpleasing.
  PLAN YOUR THOUGHTS PROPERLY
AND DEPRESSION WILL BE CEASING."

Kevin Styer

A Captivating Fantasy

I look at clouds with wonderment.
  I'm intrigued by what I see:
Snow-capped trees and frosted cakes,
  White sand surrounding sky-blue lakes.

Imagination comes alive in me.
  I see life in the guise of a fantasy.

Just as I recognize a form
  Its shape begins to change
And turns into a bit of fluff
  Or something whimsical or strange.

Then dark, foreboding clouds appear
  And rain begins to fall
And the lovely scene that had emerged
  Is lost beyond recall.

But the rain won't last forever
  And fleecy clouds will again float free
And I'll see life through other images
  In another captivating fantasy.

Lois Bloomer

Watchful Eyes

I'm a sensitive black woman
I'm not ashamed to say, I care.
I'm not afraid to bare the fruits of this world
Or to swallow the marrow of the bones of life.

I feel the crust of the burdens
our children of tomorrow must bare.
I see their despair through the marbles
of the looking glass they peer through.

Do I close the shutter of the lens from which I see?
NO.

Keeping peeping until I see the glare of the stare that we can share.

Maria E. Lamar

I'm Thankful

I'm thankful for so many things. I'll only name a few.
I'm thankful for the friends and family that hold me when I'm blue.
I'm thankful for the stars above that light each precious night.
I'm thankful every day I wake for the morning light.
I'm thankful for my loving God who made the golden rule.
And believe it or not, I'm thankful for that dreadful thing called school.
I'm thankful for that book called The Bible that helps us understand
The things that aren't so understandable to the brightest man.
I'm thankful for the green trees, blue oceans, and wide skies.
I'm thankful for an imagination I can let fly high.
I'm thankful for my freedom of both religion and of speech.
I'm thankful to be in a country where I may live in peace.
I'm thankful that my clothes aren't ripped, old, and torn.
I'm thankful for my parents who decided I'd be born.
I'm thankful for my country which isn't constantly in war.
I'm thankful for my splendid life. I couldn't ask for more!

Robin Edmonds

Untitled

Life is full of mazes, not knowing what lies ahead
in each maze you go thru, each journey lies
challenges in which everyone has a destination.
It takes determination in order to go thru the
challenges and obstacles that comes forth to you,
even though our past may challenge our weak areas.
We must uphold our grounds, to seek
thru a passage to complete the maze.

Margaret Johnson Prentice

Thankful

Dear God, I'm thankful for the bed in which I sleep,
I'm thankful for the nice clean pillow slips and sheets,
I'm thankful for the mother, who fixed these nice
   Clean things with care.
Especially thankful for the loved ones who came
to care for me. Because I know dear God, that
it's done through love of thee.
I'm thankful for my babies, with their red curly locks,
And for my dear mother, who makes their little frocks.
Dear God, I'm so thankful for a sweet husband,
who works so hard each day, and spends it all for
medicine, without a grumble that his money goes that way.
   Now dear God, thank you for all you've done
for me, because all good gifts come from you,
As everyone can see.
Thank You Dear Lord.

   Sylvia Lloyd

The Giver, The Seeker, The Loner

The purity in my soul.
I'm waiting to see the angels.
My mind is so deranged, so pure.
So infinitely conscious of the surroundings.
I'm waiting to see the floating islands,
the clouds come down and talk to me.
I'm waiting for the trees to uproot and walk with me.
Talking to me, unseen by impurity.
Making sense to me in my deranged mind.
Floating my feet on the wind and relax to the soothing of the calm
rain. Drifting back to earth and falling into the thickets.
Snakes wrap around me and hiss secrets into my ear.
The mosquitos fly about noticing my will and wanting a sample
of my blood for their children.
   Take What You Want.

   Steve Markley

Eastern Boulevard

Cheap, battered, domestic cars like to cram one another
In a barren and unholy decadence.
Maria had a tattoo of a rose and a sword
Along with trouble counting money.
She stuffed a Copenhagen in her black, vinyl purse
In another tattered Exxon.
You remember Exxon,
They killed the Earth.
Those cheap, fluorescent beer signs
illuminate the cracked, broken glass
Meticulously scattered in a decaying street.
I lose all hope until beauty stares at me
Behind a dirty windshield now getting pelted with tear-like rain.
She laughs at me and leaves forever.
I hope the water from the Heaven's won't melt my bones.
The shadow in front of me is a cheap, plastic Nietzsche figure
Wandering around in a hopeless world always suffering
From a loss of God and desolation.
Where are we supposed to go
Now that the Fischer King has deserted us?

   Todd Karpovich

Under The Sea

   You are like heaven under the sea.
In a big bubble waiting for me. As I swim down under
The sea, all I can think about is you and me. As I swim,
My heart begins to beat, because I am so close to you
I get lots of heat in me. Nobody can make me come to
a halt because my love for you is all in my heart. If I
intend to succeed, all you will love. I will love you
until I die. I promise you this is no lie!

   Mandi Gadell

Essence Of A Man

I looked — and it was made of good stuff.
In a few locations, the fiber had frayed,
But the overall effect was good.
The colors were arousing —
Not too bold, not too dull.
In fact — there existed
A combination of earthly tones —
The ones of brown and tan ——
That so resemble
Rich loam and parched desert.
The texture intrigued —
There was the roughness of suede
And the smoothness of leathers.
Ribbed corduroy dominated,
But was softened by repeated washings.
The scent was fresh and crisp,
With the aroma, as if a halo,
Demanding closer scrutiny.
It drew me close —
This essence of a man.

   Nancy Hockensmith

The Photograph

Father sits upon the piano
in a miniature silver frame.
His was a potent life
held captive by memory
in a three inch square.
Father - the genie in a lamp.
Out, genie! Out!
Appear.
He is twirling me around the dance floor
Crinolines and shiny little girl shoes
the sound, touch and smell of him.

A grandchild He never knew
bangs a sour melody on the piano.
All I notice is the frame's fine silver filigree.

   Laurie A. Stieber

The Healing

The smile on the face will now reach to the eyes
In a relaxing…assuring way
All those sleepless nights will somehow disappear
As the stars in the night dance away

The energy lost will return to the "BOD"
As the jobs left undone are complete
And there will be wondering what took so long
As the healing removes self-defeat

Hurts once experienced will be put aside
As somehow it is learned to forgive
Yet remember there's always a lesson that's learned
Keep on going…yet be positive

For the process of healing can take quite some time
But in ending…we gain inner peace
And we know when the healing has taken effect
Because all of the hurting has ceased!

   Phyllis Y. Smith Thompson

Riverside

Yesterday my love, I called you to my riverside
in a second, you were there.
The brilliance of your smile was matched by the fire in my heart-
my love for you.
Yesterday my love, when I called you to my riverside, you
answered me with your eyes what took my words volumes to ask
There really was no need, it was written all over your face.
I was amazed by your intensity and overwhelmed by your sincerity.
They allowed me to express the freedom that you make me feel inside.
Yesterday my love, when I called you to my riverside, I had hoped
for little but instead was given much. Today I know that I have
been rewarded because when I called you to my riverside, you
not only came, but you took a drink.

Tracye Leeks

Blue Leaves

Blue leaves cascading to the ground
   In amber twilight,
Memories of carefree days when trust was all,
   Except for grand imagination;

And we slew fiery dragons,
   Without shedding a drop of blood;
A place where impenetrable forts were built
   Of leaves or snow;

And little girls became mothers overnight,
   As the new doll arrived;
Where wars ended with the adversaries walking home together,
   And parting promises of, "I'll see you tomorrow;

It was in this place,
   That all our dreams took root,
And stayed with us long after we had dared
   To dream anew.

Tienne

Grandpa

A gentle heart that beat so strong
in children's eyes he did no wrong.

A love that grew be leaps and bounds
we could feel his love though he made no sound.

In mournful days and silent nights
our family love held so tight.

And when the heartbeat slipped away
we prayed his pain be washed away.

As we raise our eyes above
we thank the Lord we had his love.

Kathleen Mannion-Sass

You're Not Alone

Oh Lord, sometimes I feel so alone;
In this harsh reality.
This world of murder and drugs,
And no morality.
But I know in my heart,
That it won't be long till I'll depart.
To a land where no one is alone.
And a place where I'll call "Home, Sweet, Home".
There are days I'd like to hurry the pace,
For that glorious day when I'll see your face.
With your arms outstretched,
For my name has been etched;
On that Lamb's Book of Life!
In this "Home, Sweet, Home",
There will be no more strife;
A land where no one is alone.
I'll be waiting to see you,
On that glorious throne!

Vickie L. Willey

A Writer's Pen

When a writer's pen gathers thought
in expression of the heart:
Words embrace the depth of meaning
desired to impart.

Language is like a painters brush
delicately painting the passion deep within.
Colours of the heart so brilliantly alive:
Like a masters bow means life, to the strings of a violin.

And because the heart becomes so vibrant,
the greatest desire is to share.
To touch the heart of another through expression:
Look at me... Can you see what is there?

Can you see into the heart, touched with beauty?
Do gathered words stir at all within?
Can a writer's pen bring to light:
How precious to life? your heart to win.

A writer trusts the pen
to convey expressions of the heart.
Yet, words become empty visions
when the light leads into dark.

Mel Weed

Autumn Leaves

It was like this last October as we strolled, your hand in mine,
The hillsides were all-glowing with the fresh autumn sunshine.

Do you remember how we danced our way 'cross the carpet of
   leaves?
Ahhh....such a short time ago...now, how my heart grieves!

You were like that autumn sunshine—bright and beautiful and cheery,
Yet when I think about last autumn, my eyes become so teary.

For last October, it seemed to me, the world was a beautiful place;
Each day brought a new discovery, each time I saw your face.

Now as I watch the clouds begin to form and I feel the drops of rain,
I am drawn back to the present, though the memories remain......

Of how you left me, oh so quickly, so unexpectedly, you were gone——
But I must stop this sad remembrance, for as they say, "Life
   must go on."

Now I feel the tears rush to my eyes and I know I must be brave....
As I watch the autumn leaves fall softly upon your silent grave.

Stacey DuVaul

Because Of Her

I am alone...
In pain...
Senseless...
Unable to reach normalcy.

Will time
Alter me,
Or, will it stand... awaiting...
My salvation.

In this instant;
In my Totem state
I feel distance from this Planet.
In this psycho-coma
Something inside of me is shattered.

Shadowed by life's despair,
I tumble in para-normal scenes.
Or, is it all (perhaps?!) because of... Her.

Spiro I. Galic

Come Along With Me

It's off to church on Sunday morning, no matter what the weather,
In snow, sunshine, or in the rain, my spirits floating like a feather.
I'm glad to be on my way, and it doesn't take me long,
To take my scenic route to church, with me singing my favorite song.

But on the way I notice, all these children out at play,
They just don't seem to know, about this very special day.
The fathers are outside mowing, the mothers are hanging up clothes,
The kids are riding their bikes, what's wrong here, they don't
   seem to know.

When just around the corner, there is a church of God,
And it really doesn't matter, whether it's rustic or very mod.
Come along with me, all you people, let's go and learn to pray,
To the one who's so loving and caring, even tho we tend to stray.

Let's learn about that cross on high, and the one who paid the price,
To cleanse our souls of every sin, every heartache, and every vice.
So come along with me and join the crowd, we are just ordinary folks,
Let's change our daily lives and deeds, and then we're free,
   without any yokes!

Laura Buske

Coming Home

Far beneath the surface,
in the darkness, a feeling stirs

Moving through a compulsory
life - an ordinary life

An awareness slipping through religion and society
Going through a young woman's
phobia - no time to calm her

It marches through words like queer and odd-ball
Then suddenly lies dormant as marriage and births take care of years
The feeling is remembered, in a daughter's journey, but put on hold

The sensation growing no longer able to be contained
Continuing untold to counselor, friend or family

Time stops - the container fills
and is pondered - both past and future

Loneliness nudges the sensation
and it begins its ascendance

The heart beats less rapidly as self becomes aware

A deep breath taken as the sensation moves to sunlight
The words slip out,
"Finally I am home"

M. M. J.

"Letting Go"

Love brought two hearts together.
In union, a new being was made.
A tiny hand to hold, only to let go in time.

his first words spoken, first steps taken.
A tiny fall, a bruised knee.
A little hand to hold.
Made it all better.

First day of school. New faces. New friends.
Someone to take my place now.
A smile on his little face, tears streaming down mine.
A bigger hand to let go.

First big game. First dance. First date.
Graduation day. Leaving home for college.
Saying goodbye. Letting a big hand go.

A new friend. A new love. A new wife.
A kiss. A hug. Letting go forever.

Love bringing two new hearts together.

Patty A. Winiarski

"I Can Do Nothing For Them All"

As I walked through the darkness, I came upon a light....
In the light were voices crying for help, but I could Do
Nothing For Them All....
I sought ways to beat the monster that trapped them like a spider
   web ....
But the lining was too strong to cut or break ....
So I sat helplessly for I Could Do Nothing For Them All .....
   One monster of smoke, inhaled another victim with every puff..
While another of bullets, bloodied one whose light slowly
flickered out as it drew closer to its grave.......
The third had the lights running frantically from its
   educational ways.....
Yet all I could do is sit helplessly, for I Could Do Nothing
   For Them All ......
   Once they were thought of as the future.....
Now the future may be no more, for the monster devours the
   lights every hour more and more ....
As I run screaming, "Hurry there's still time," ......
It's as though they don't hear, smiling as I can see the
   crying inside ......
Will this ever end, not while the monster is allowed to live .....
Sorrow and many tears for the victims it claims and has killed..
Yet day to day I can only sit while others careless.....
For the Power Of One Is Not So Great, if I CAN DO NOTHING
   FOR THEM ALL.....

Shatonie L. Reaves

A Cry For Universal Humans

One of the past nights
In the middle of the darkness
I decided to cry, to rebel, to roar
With a primordial voice of the God in a human being

To collect
All the unspoken curses
And the unheard voices
Of the weak and helpless

Sum all the first cries of the newly born
And initiated
And the last breaths of the killed
And terminated

Weep aloud with a temporal and universal cry

Cry as far as the farthest corners of the galaxy
And the Kingdom of God

Rebel against the ideal order of the universe
And the human truth, weakness, and misery

Rebel against the act of creation of life
In the name of its future destruction

Migdat I. Hodzic

Meadow Tree

In a field of clover and timothy,
Is a very wise old oak, called Meadow Tree.

It's a tree that seems to say,
I my dear, will live to eternity.

For here I've stood a many a year,
Watching the seasons change from fall to spring.

Budding in spring,
Full leaves in summer,
Colored in fall,
Bare again in winter.

I've lived in fresh air,
I've lived in polluted smog,
And here I'll stand to go living on.

Laurie B. Gonder

November 8th

The mood of the sky determined her rest
in the open-roofed shanty, her home
the kindness of strangers, a bagel at best
she counted among her unknown.

She'd reared six children, all grown now,
alone with the backbone now marred
and counted a blessing in the dead of winter
the sight of an unlocked car.

Her estate was portable, her wardrobe condensed
to the garments threadbare on her back
a hairstyle was useless, a toothbrush but plenty
of days she'd often lose track.

To learn to share, to get to give
to run out to borrow to give more
thus, thousands she spent, and hours she gave
from a heart which never kept score.

In the long line they found her on November 8th
lying stiff and smiling and cold
with one hand gripped tightly to her old address
and the other a ballot to vote.

Trudy Ann Mitchell-Gilkey

Within Winter's Storm

It moved her-
in the silence of darkness it was approaching,
very rapidly - as if to intimidate,
with sounds of a distant drum beating.
She trembled, yet, she wasn't afraid.
It reached inside her
taking hold of her inner being without consent.
Tightly, she held on,
as its mighty force raged,
with fierceness covering her body
as flicker's of light burned,
captured, taken -
in an embrace of pleasure.
Suddenly, it eased, subsided, moved on.
Calmness set in,
releasing anger,
once again bringing stillness
to the quiet night.
The storm rolled on
to other unexplored skies.

Kathy L. Farmer

"Tree"

You were just meant as cool shade,
In the summertime,
As defense,
Against the scorching sunlight.

Your branches spread outward,
Offering your sincere welcome.

Me, sitting by your side,
Feeling peace within,
Knowing your truth.
For you were a real friend.

Oh, how you've grown and extended shape,
Changing the appearance of your leaves,
    as the seasons lag and falter behind.
Stretched out you stand, inspiring me with your companionship.
Entangled with loving memories,
    your cool spirit lives on for all eternity.

Laurie Garza

"Old Neighbor's New Home"

They have tossed me and tossed me around
in this unfamiliar new home they have found.
I came to this place quite uneased at mind,
thoughts of my old home I have left behind.
The room looks bleak without any love,
I pray to my God in Heaven above.
oh why, oh why do I have to live here,
thinking of memories I hold on so dear.
I once had a castle, my little old home
but now dear Lord, I feel so alone.
Faces are strange, not the loved ones I know,
can I go on hating it so?

I sit by the window when I'm not in bed
and wish and wish that I were dead.
When I was young and a nice fine chap,
I never thought I'd be in this trap.
But now I'm old and pretty feeble,
to me it's quite unbelievable.
So here I am, I guess to stay
until the Lord takes me away.

Madeleine Reinhard

Me

I am but a small entity,
in this vast world we live in.

There is much to be gleaned from it,
my head swirls in a constant motion.

For the times are very chaotic.
The time for peace and tranquility lessens each day.

I desperately cling to this merry-go round
Called life
searching for an end to the poverty, pain,
and suffering we all share.

I can not fully understand, nor
control my destiny.

There is no end in sight, but I
must go on.

Therefore I am.

Kathryn Bowden

"In Time"

In time - you'll experience it, a first love.
In time - love is found, unpredicted, unexpected.
In time - you made me feel safe, protected.
In time - you made me feel love, desire.
In time - we grew separate but together.
In time - I learned about me, you.
In time - what I felt was real, true.
In time - a part of me was a part of you.
In time - things changed dramatically, uncontrollably.
In time - you and I drifted, separated.
In time - I can look back with tenderness, fondness.
In time - I'll treasure the memories we made.
In time - I'll know that you'll always be a part of me.
In time - I hope you find the way.
In time - I wish you security, success.
In time - my aching heart will heal.
In time - I'll learn to love again.

Stephanie N. Vidanoff

Jungle Square

Across the square nobody sees
in your eyes the truth.
I, for ONE, only want to hear
not noise or silence in fact
Just the voice of the deaf passing me
as only the blind see colors.
Long rivers, rocking streams, green grass;
Yet across 125th street reality sets in.
Young men and boys crying in the night,
As the old ones laugh at the bottles...
As the women carry the load all day long
And the babies and children die alone...
Who wonders why and sees the pain?
Who really cares why we walk away?
Do you hear the hurt I see?
Must I remain a silent voice...?

D. L. Williamson

True Freedom

Kite of red sails the vast sea of breath and sighs,
Inching his way further and further from his jailors
Looking over the insignificant mortals, and
Leering at those who once ruled his life.

Yanking at his oppressive leash, seeking
One million different worlds to explore
Urging for the potential omnipotence of
Real freedom. True freedom.

Winds tear and tug, praying to free their new friend.
In a sudden jolt, the string snaps.
Freedom's spirit possesses his soul,
Even as the kite plummets to his death.

Peter A. Ceresa

The Artist

Mid-morning. The crowds edge by,
Innocuous to the artist's fate;
But one steps out, her bearing proud:
"My portrait! Disregard the rate."

His palate stiff, his fingers taut,
He plies the colors, blends each tone.
"Will I paint with a beauty fraught
Where none exists but in mind alone?"

As if in answer to his thought,
She rises. He notes her trembling hand.
No bartered price. But wealth has failed.
The crowds edge by the artist's stand.

Mary Jane Garry, CSJ

"Death"

We never do anything to prepare for our death
... Instead .. We force our family
to choose our space to rest
of course we have insurance - cause we think
It's best — But
Even though we die for sure
we just never so anything about death.

We say we love our family But
our obligations we neglect - So
we leave our loved ones
emotionally empty and or in Financial
debt.

We say we love our family But
we leave them in a mess — cause
we ignore that which comes in naturally
the certainty - called "Death"

Karen Dunn

Little Girl

In my mirror I see, a slender brown haired child, glaring back at me.
Instinctively I step back - so does she - I move forward, again, she
copies me. This little girl seems familiar, have I seen her before?
I reach out in an attempt to touch her - my hand feels only the cold,
hard mirror. She never moves, as though she already knew there was
safety behind the gilded glass. I go down on bended knee, trying
harder to see- this small child standing before me. As I watch
her unmoving face, a solitary tear rolls down her cheek and in the
deafening silence, splatters on the floor at my feet. When again I
face the mirror, the only thing I see, is my own reflection
looking back at me.

Lois Archer

"Love Is All We Are After"

Love and devotion,
Intense feelings of emotion,
Believe in destiny for you must not be kept apart,
Separation of the minds,
Love can be so blind,
The moon that lights the sky
Brings a tear to your eye,
Far away from the city
The days turn into nights
Release and let go of those chaotic fights.
Don't hesitate!
It hurts more when your soul has to wait.
Don't keep your love a mystery
It will only slip away,
Life is just a game
You must reject all shame.
Reach out with open arms, catch the dreams around you.
Unselfish love which reflects the truth,
Love is all we are after...

Nicola Stockberger

Sky And Earth

Caressing sky, a canvas for landscape artists,
    interacting with the sun and atmosphere below

Painting the new dawn with brilliant freshness,
    designing a sunset mural from your palette of colors

Illuminating the warm spring days, green grass
    and wild flowers with the glistening of dew

Enhancing the glow of yellow, oranges, and browns
    of a bountiful summer day

Illustrating the subtle and cold spectrum of a
    glorious fall fantasy

Radiating a winter setting of stark trees and the
    white snow with tinges of your blueness

Stroking the pond and sea, and silhouetting
    forests, mountains, and desert against your vastness

Shyly drawing a curtain of clouds over your face,
    letting rain fall, and rainbows arch close to you
Ultimately shadowing the celestial sky from grey to black,
    where twinkling stars light your way to reawakening.

Marjorie H. Jensen

Nature's Ways And Love's Ways

As the wind whistles its way through the weakened limbs
in the highest tree,
the love in between the wind and the weak limbs
when they met was so strong,
for together they helped the tree by reshaping a home
for the birds,
all made out of strong new limbs of love,
with the love of each other.

Sarah Lynn McElroy

346

The Stallion Of Zeus!

The stallion of darkness flies, across the desert sands and
into the mystic skies
To the ancient Greek lands, where once he did dwell
in a time of many Gods, where once all was well and
olympians there did trod.
But their faith was dying thing, for new Gods the people themselves
did make explaining only that all people are vain, so the old
Gods they did forsake and what is a ruler without a people and
what is a God without commitment much like a church without a
steeple or a mind without contentment
So now the land is a dreadful place
lost to all those that were caring and nowhere can be seen a face
and no music any longer blaring
This land it once was so grand
This land of olympus!

Kathy K. Reckner

"Self-Regeneration"

I can't face my
invention.
I lose sleep over my
invention.
It controls the fear in my hands.
I shake thinking about the
invention.
It forces me to avoid it.
It forces me to bite my nails.
It forces me to procrastinate.
I am scared to change my
invention in fear it will change me first.

How do I confront a future I will never know.
How do I confront a past
I wish I never lived.
How do I confront this
invention that controls my actions
My fear and my well-being.
How did I give it the power to hate me.
How do I how do I? How do you do?

Linda Liu

"Growing Old"

Way down deep in the pit of my soul,
Is a world that only I can control.
Where the sun shines bright at the wave of my hand,
And the stars above twinkle at my command.
In my mind I'm still young, and pretty, and strong,
But my body, so unhealthy, proves my mind wrong.
So whenever the aches and pains get me down,
I climb deep inside to the pit of my soul,
Where my mind and my body will never, ever grow old.

Marilyn Gartner

A Light...

The seeking of God
is breaking my own box
For the sake of the nature of God

The loving of God
is moving my boundaries
For embracing more and more people of God

The following of God
is being with people
whom nobody want to be with but God

Sunju Choi-Chong

Mother Poetry

I need poetry as I take in the mail and remember that my mother
   is dead and can't put a dollar in a letter ever again.

I need poetry. As I plait my child's braids and tell her not to chew
the bows, a poem rocks my body, hushing my pain, whispering,
   "you are your mother."

Poetry hurts. It is the paper cut, unexpected, deep incision in the
mind, unseen, untended wound.

Poetry exhausts. It is the tantrum I need and am forbidden, the race
run against myself and mercifully lost.

Poetry distracts. It is the curiosity with which I count the tiny
pills, the death-wish postponed the time to read one more page.

Poetry satisfies. It is Tom Jones' pear that makes me laugh, the
oil in Aaron's beard, my superfluous self feasting.

Poetry revives. It is the womb where I float safe, and smiling listen
'til moved to speak.
Poetry is my mother alive
and singing
in me.

Kate F. Bilis-Bastos

Well Of Emotion

I ask myself every day
"Is it worth the price I pay?"
And most o' the time I will say
"The answer to it must be `nay'."

Through all the days of my life,
And all the times I feel strife;
When I want to take the knife
And end this thing that we call life-

Sometimes I will truly try,
And sometimes I will just plain cry.
What if the peace is just a lie?
I do, and don't want to die.

I want to reach the very end,
Not to worry who is my friend.
To travel 'round the final bend, never a way back to wend.

'But then again' I start to think,
'There's so much from the cup to drink.
And I have lived only a blink too soon at eternity's brink.

And so I sit here all confused while the cruel Fates are amused.
My opposing thoughts are fused. The well of emotion's all used.

Melissa Hines

More Precious Than Gold

For many to seek true happiness
Is like following a beautiful rainbow.
They see the magnificent colors
So after the pot of gold they go.

I, myself, have chased many rainbows
Only to see them fade away.
Is there a pot of gold? No one knows.
But I kept on searching anyway.

Then that day our eyes did meet.
My heart and soul did honestly know
That you were the one I've longed to greet
And from that point my affection and love did grow.

I knew that no longer would I chase
That elusive rainbow with its pot of gold.
For I know that you are much more precious.
Than any worldly treasure anyone could hold.

Steven W. Hawkins

The Young Ones

The things they say nowadays
Is more than I can bear
Greeting each other as "Hey Dudes"
Today is anything but rare.

The phrases "Chill Out," "Cool"
And "That's really Rad"
Are a few of the kids sayings
That really aren't so bad.

I suppose my elders thought
For more than a thousand years
That the "Young Ones" have a problem
Using what's between their ears.

Now that we have gotten older
And our hair is streaked with grey
We tell the "Young Ones" to use proper English
So they can get a good job with good pay.

Just when we think the "Young Ones"
Totally speak in a foreign tongue
They grow up over night and
Start correcting the language of their young.

Lois Bennett

Virginity

The physical force that acts upon me
is never as strong as the lock that guards me.
The wish to break loose is ever fulfillment
the physical act could never bring me.

The power that keeps me was never more persistently fought,
I bring out temptations that violet these thoughts.
His arms would whip me if I struggle the scold
disguise me, brutalize him, bring the flame to explode!

Escape is vain, though gentleness may reign.
No help. Still far. The angel keeps them apart.
Prisoner for life, in chains you ought to die!
Fugitive I am, help me come alive.

Valeria Olivos

Open House

Your house has many mansions
  is that correct my Lord?
Which one will I find You in
  is it so You won't get bored?

You say You made them all for us
  as we evolved and grow
With each one very different
  to explore and come to know

Which one is Your favorite
  is there one that I should choose?
It doesn't really matter ...
  when I visit I can't lose.

My God, You are mighty rich
  Your property goes sky high
Now ... to reach the estate with the pearly gate
  does that mean I have to ... DIE?

Randi Brownell

Prejudice

Sneaking into your heart like a cancer,
it consumes your soul.
An overwhelming darkness pervades your mind-
reaching,
    extending,
      expanding,
to the very core of your being.
The taint withers your life force until all
that is left is a cold, dark cavern of hatred.

Stephanie R. Bonnick

Save The Children

The only way to stop our children's fatalities
is to return to the old school of values and morality.

Whatever happened to the golden rule and stop sending
and start taking our children to Sunday school.

We must restore the feelings of Black Pride.

Set realistic goal and purposeful strides as we walk
and avoid profanity as we talk.

There is no shame in being black.
Our only shame is in the way we act toward each other.
We must teach our children to love one another.

Restore in our babies a sense of pride
before we can stop this senseless genocide.

Our parents taught us in whom to believe
We got too busy to get down on our knees
and pray to our heavenly Father
or are we just too cultured now to bother.

We must learn to talk instead of shoot it out
believe in each other when there is room for doubt.

Let's start again to share our bread
or pretty soon all our children will be dead.

J. Harris Jefferson

The Christmas Wish:

My wish for Christmas, I believe
Isn't something found under a tree
Not a pretty package with ribbons and bows
But love for one another that continues to grow.

Material things can be bought everyday
But miracles never seem to happen that way,
And God if miracles really do exist.
Please make mine, first on your list

Let us on this night, be all the same
Forgive one another and place no blame
Give everyone on earth a place to live
For Christmas is the time to give

Give the gift of yourself to all you know
And let your feelings begin to show
For if we spread our love around
A truer gift cannot be found.

Robin Rimar

That Look

That look is still in your eyes,
it appears now and then.
I see it more than you realize,
the look that says, we're more than friends.

Friends, we decided we would be,
as lovers we'd never last.
We chose to stop our loving then,
and put it in the past.

For a while, it's been that way,
we seldom ever meet.
When we do, there's not much to say,
but it's, oh so bittersweet.

For the eyes, are the windows of the soul,
I can see in yours as you do in mine.
The feeling, the longing is still there,
But we go on as if we are blind.

We smile at each other and look away,
as if there's something else to see,
When in our hearts we know how we feel,
and that look in our eyes, will always be...

Mary R. Lohr

Captivation

The evil in the world has made a fort around me
It does not let true happiness in
Just a flicker now and then
The hands of sorrow are clasping me
The seed of sadness has been growing
and now has become my roots
It causes me to weep for help
but the fort shields my pleas
I cry in solitude
No one knowing my cause
I am yet a slave of hatred performing my tasks unreluctantly
Days and nights go by like nothingness
Only the tears have movement
"Let me out of this dark chamber!"
But I have become part of its hard, stony floor
Now the seed has taken root
I am forever growing in the soil
of the garden of shattered and imprisoned souls.

Michelle Burgess

River Of Life

It floats and dances on a gentle breeze,
it glides like a ballerina among the trees.
To land so gently on a bubbling stream,
and swept away like an elusive dream.
To be caught in a whirlpool and tossed about,
the current comes by and pulls it out.
Lodged on the rocks its journey seems to end,
'till the swift moving current sets it free again.
Tossed in the rapids, dashed on the rocks,
pulled under by the current, and like that all elusive dream
It surfaces tattered and torn further down stream.
And in a calm pool it finally comes to rest.
How like our life is the journey of the leaf?
Caught in a whirlpool of indecision of life.
Dashed on the rocks of stress and strife.
Thrown into the rapids of shattered dreams.
Then to rest in the calm of the stream.
To regain our hopes, renew our faith, rebuild our strength
and to reform our dreams.
For unlike the leaf, our journey has just begun.

Pamela Ketcham

My First Christmas

My first Christmas was a long time ago,
It happened when I was six years old.
My first grade teacher said;
Santa Claus will come and visit your home
On Christmas eve when everyone is asleep
And fill your stocking with surprises.
I quietly slipped down the stairs
Hung my long black stocking by the fire.
Early Christmas morning when I got up
And took my long black stocking from the nail
What a surprise to find a lump of coal!
When mother came in the room she said,
Jewish people don't believe in Christmas.
My schoolmate asked if I could come and see
Their Christmas tree and all the things she got.
The flickering candles put me in a trance.
And to this day I still like to be with
My gentile friends on Christmas Day.

Nettie Yanoff Schwartz

Adult Language

Maturity is without a hidden meaning
It has more to do with weaning
Self of an absorption with me-ism
Replacing it with a healthy dose of be-ism
Having had a growth that blossoms full
The ability to be free of push and pull
No uncertainty with decisions or otherwise
Even if painful no hesitancy to improvise
An action freeing oneself of a bind
A working out thoroughly in the mind
The most responsible course of action
Regardless of pleasure or abstraction
A definition that is challenging and pure
Derived in its total scope by being secure

Larry L. Whirl

My Visiting Son

He said: "Get on with your life, or don't you have one?"
It hurt to hear him say this, my youngest son, now thirty.

I could have answered: "No, I don't," but I just simply sighed.
How could he know what I feel, a widow of many years?

My life's long been changed, by time I no longer keep,
For only memories hold, the soft-spoken, loving words.

Yet I keep striving to greet God's day, accepting what comes my way.
I care and till my garden for hours, creating is an epiphany.

That is my life, I want to tell him, and little else to add.
The passing years have silenced sounds of friendships and loving
  children.

My ship is grounded in time, but my soul sails on,
In love with nature and the garden's hour.

"He who plants a garden, creates happiness.",
A Chinese philosopher of long ago wisely said.

Walking from the garden path, I glow with pride,
My arms embracing colorful sprays of my garden's flowers.

Rose M. Guatelli

Faithfulness

It is one of the most beloved and enduring attributes of love
It is benevolent in its gracious gifts and demands nothing, but is
  freely given
It is as pure and heavenly as the peaceful symbol of the dove
It is unconditional sacrifice and is as prominent to the heart as
the majestic mountains that grace our planet
Faithfulness is the one who used the universe as his canvas and
created all the beauty that we see around us, it says I am present
when the sky swells in darkness and the clouds began to weep
just before life's unbearable storms but it always manages to peak
through like the first ray of sunshine that slips through after the
storm and the glorious shades of color that burst forth from a newly
formed rainbow that fill our hearts with hope and restoration for a
faint spirit like a revelation or answer from God but it is also
there in our times of rapturous joy to share in our happiness and
augment to it any way possible it will never be judgmental and
wherever it abides and whom ever heart it pervades is blessed among
many because of it's wonderful healing effects on a hurting world
It is the perfect gift receive from a most holy being
Bless our God who is faithfulness

Kendra Hausan "Inspired by God"

To Care

Love is warm and gentle, never cold
It is with you even when old
If sad then look for it
And fire in your heart will be lit
Life is short and goes fast
But love can survive and forever last
Open your heart and give it a try
You may find that it is the ultimate high
If it turns on you do not be sad
Try again 'cause true love never goes bad!

Steve M. Lucas

Our World

Because of greed, this world is full of sin
It just didn't all of a sudden begin
It's been like this since long ago, as far back as Abednigo
Our young girls are having babies
Teens selling dope to drive mercedes
I don't understand what makes it so cool,
When they never finish school
I know it seems these are all complaints
But we are living in a world full of shame
The young boys disrespect the young girls
All they want is someone to rock their world
Look at the diseases with out a cure
Will someone please tell me what about the poor?
They walk around with rags on their heads
Hoping for one decent meal before bed
Time after time we try to hide it
When America the free should try to fight it
It takes more than one to bring changes about
It's sad that because of greed,
Our children of America do without!

Terri Lynn Hurd

The Arms Of Love

The storm rages fiercely outside.
It seems there is nowhere to hide.

The thunder and lightening are so strong.
Loud and rumbling is their song.

Then Mother's arms safe and warm,
Encircle you, and keep you from harm.

Snuggling into her soft smooth neck,
She leans over to give your cheek a peck.

The strength of her love will never allow,
anything to hurt you now.

So when the storms of life prevail,
when all is lost, and your destined to fail.
God reaches down to hold you dear,
his love and kindness is always near.

He will never allow anything to hurt you now.
Evil and darkness to him will bow.

So snuggle into his soft warm face,
where he will be your hiding place.

Korrie Sudwecks

Believers Become Achievers

Life is made of many a goal.
It tests our endeavors so I am told.
Creative planning accomplishes one's best
Although controversy from others challenges the test.
Having the faith to accomplish our deeds devours the weeds
So I say to all believers-become achievers.

Ronnie Cowan

Life?

I finally realized what life is...
It took me a while to think about this.
That everyone and everything will change
No matter how much you try to rearrange.

Sometimes I do things just for spite,
To see if they would possibly turn out right.
If they would fail, which they always do,
I'd just turn away and feel real blue.

Well another day is at an end,
Sometimes I wish it would never begin.
The day can be so boring and long,
Even though I do things which are wrong.

The hurt and pain which I feel inside
Is from feelings in which I hide.
It is nice to have someone to tell,
All your feelings, and they like you just as well.

But one thing I'll never forget,
Is that the Lord has never failed me yet.
So I will keep on searching for my goals,
Because that is the way life goes.

Linda J. Hall

The Cry

One night I heard a sad cry.
It was a cry that was longing for happiness.
As I walked through the cold dark night,
The cry I heard became louder.
It seemed to go with me every step I took,
But when I tried to forget about the cry
The more I would hear it.
But the more I would go to find the cry,
The more I realized the cry was mine.

Wendy S. Merriman

A Cry

A cry was heard last night,
it was a cry with no meaning,
it was not of distress, sorrow or shame,
for the one who cried out was fortunate,
for at that moment their soul was at ease,
If only the world would cry out.

Meghan Moore

Birthday Party

My parents had to plan a party on the day I became eighteen.
It was quite lively, and no one dared to cause a scene.
My whole family came and to my surprise,
Even the ones I disliked most arrived with presents disguised.

All of my closest friends were there to pay their respects
And wore my favorite colors; head to toe in white and black.
My acquaintances arrived late; no homage due.
I knew them very briefly from classes, work, a day, or two.

The white candles illuminated the wan icing on my cake.
Everyone feasted upon every slice they did partake.
Flowers decked the room and ornaments galore,
But yet something was missing, still something more.

The only thing lacking was me, the birthday boy.
For I could not move nor think, nor cry for joy.
I was there in spirit, but in an oak coffin I did lay.
As they lowered the casket, no tears fell on my Happy Birthday!

Raymond O. Squires

Hero

It wasn't his money or his possessions that made him special to me
It was his view on life, the joy and the peace I could see

It wasn't because he was handsome or debonair
Because he had no teeth and very little hair

He didn't have wealth but he did have charm
And he owned this little sixty acre farm

I never saw him dress fancy as I recall
He just wore an old straw hat and bib overalls

His home most people would consider a shack,
They still used the two-hole outhouse sittin' out back

People seemed to be most of his life
His friends, his family and his dear wife

He didn't worry about gettin' things like a lot of people do
He said this world wasn't his home, he was just passin' through

He worked from sun up to sun down givin' it his best
But Sunday he gave to God and that day he would rest

Wherever he would go I would like to tag along
He would always be a whistlin' an old gospel song

When I look back and think of his life it kind of makes me sad
Too bad every kid doesn't have a hero just like my old granddad

Sam Wilbanks

My Love

My love for you is eternal and of no limit to me.
It will last beyond the mountains' fall.
And when they all dry up, each and every sea.
My love will still be there, standing tall.
Past when the sun burns itself out of fuel.
And the Earth may be but a small, lifeless rock.
My love's still there, like a stubborn mule.
As each new day passes, it grows stronger without block.
On a seemingly infinite ocean, it's a single wave.
Gathering itself like it knows the end is near.
But never will it reach the shore, its grave.
Even when knowing this, it yet grows, its destiny clear.

Regardless of what form it may have to take.
My love for you will still remain, always awake.

Sam L. Watson

The Poet

A poet's mind has boundless freedom
It will sway and swing and soar
A poet's taste is hard to fathom
For many loves I will implore

A poet's hand are sure and steady
I have no fear my pen is ready
A poet's light shows life beauty which will never fade
In the light of day or dark of night I will ply my trade

A poet's nerves are like a woven thread
For all doors and ways I must tread
A poet's eyes look with an artistic view
On things that may pass right by you

A poet's ears can hear a symphony in the tide
Open minded in me you can confide
A poet's nose will tell of scents which you cannot disclose
With vivid recollection I can smell a phantom rose

A poet's heart can reach to heights and overwhelm your breath
Or plunge your feelings deep as natures lowest depths
A poet's word can live forever or be divine
I am a poet freely passing through the doors of mine

Melvin P. Hunter

Stillness

The stillness says so many things,
It writes a message upon the land,
Speaking words of wisdom and peace,
And touching the hearts of you and me.

The stillness speaks with words so kind,
With messages sailing through our minds,
It reaches out for you and me,
And tells us quickly what to do.

The stillness comes at anytime,
When the sun rises or set on time,
Early morning or the middle of night
It brings a message without a fight.

It whispers loud upon our ears,
Just listen to me and have no fear,
Because what I'm saying, to you is true,
Have no fear, I'll speak to you.

Words of wisdom rushes through your head
Remember, what I told you, believe what you read,
Joy, peace, love it said,
This message is for you, it's all I had.

Lena G. Hall

The Piggy Poet

There's Irishmen, Englishmen, Germans and Jews,
Italian, Spaniards, Frenchmen and Portuguese too.
There are Norsemen, Swedes, Swiss and Finn,
Aussies, Filipinos and many more true.
But cerebral palsy has no rules,
So lets all help the purple pig,
By paying his dues.

Lloyd E. Wackerle

Motherhood - A Blessing

Motherhood is a great and powerful journey
 It's a long winding road that's filled with learning
Motherhood is seldom easy and carefree
 Often it's difficult to unlock if you can't find the key
Motherhood is tough yet so rewarding
 Looking into little eyes that are so adoring
A child's mother is his most prized possession
 She is his keeper, he is her blessing
When a mother feels she can go on no longer
 A kiss from tiny soft lips makes her feel stronger
He makes her feel that she's wanted and needed
 With small arms wrapped around her she never feels cheated
A woman needs her child, and he his mother
 God planned it that way for He gave them each other.

Kimberley A. Moore

"Untitled"

We look around, dance a bit, and enjoy what's left of it
It's all around,
 the beauty and space,
So fill it up,
 do not wait.
Don't step aside
Take a chance
Twirl a nickel
 or fight a bull.
It all creeps up,
 that thing in us,
But push it back, and watch it live!

Rose Titcomb

351

It's Christmas Everywhere

It's Christmas everywhere
It's Christmas in the country of Iran
It's Christmas on the Isle-of-Mann
It's Christmas everywhere

It's Christmas everywhere
It's Christmas in foreign lands
It's Christmas out on the Saudi sands
It's Christmas everywhere

It's Christmas everywhere
It's Christmas where the sun is bright
It's Christmas in the deep dark night
It's Christmas everywhere

It's Christmas everywhere
It's Christmas in the African Wild
It's Christmas since the birth of the Christ Child

It's Christmas everywhere
Robert F. Gosnell

Rebirth

It appeared dark, desperate, without hope.
Its desolate spirit enveloped my soul,
While despondent complacency extracted its toll.

Mired in a non-lifestyle with no reward,
I ate, slept and existed all alone.
Fear's intoxicating presence was all that shone.

A warm waft of air and a speck of light signal a change.
I feel and see it now, I want to grasp more
Of this comforting call that has touched my core.

Drawn forward to remembrances of inner passion,
I venture toward a life imbued with joy.
Reality is a positive perspective none can destroy.

The splash of a wave, the wisp of a breeze,
And the awe of a sunset are reassurances from above,
That all is complete with my new gift called love.
Michelle Taylor

From A Baby's Eyes

All those faces looking down,
It's enough to make a baby frown;
Each time I try to catch a wink
I hear, "Oh, let me take a peek";
Nodding their heads to make me smile,
And the funny noises, when all the while -
I'd like sometime to look around,
And see this brand new world I've found;
But they all disappear, which seems very strange,
When I'm ready for a diaper change;
Now, when I'm hungry and start to cry -
It's - "Let me feed that sweetie-pie";
If I could only understand-
Being a baby would be just grand!
W. Louise Tanner

"Champs"

Just a quick note to let you know
It's off to Miami you must go
Nebraska is good, but they are not great
They can't compete with Florida State
I asked your wife what would come in handy
And she replied spending time with Ed and Andy
This year instead of coal
I'm sending you to the Orange Bowl
So off you go on your merry way
Because the action starts on New Years Day

Santa
Linda S. Howard

The Golden rule

So your out with someone new, I wonder what's on your mind.
It's funny cause I thought you were special, a one of a kind.
How could I of been so blind to think of you that way,
How was I to know the price I'd have to pay.

My mind is constantly turning away from me ... to you.
Maybe I can face it, it's over, really through.
Maybe this is a lesson learned, one I should have known.
Some feelings you hide so well and others you've never shown.

But the day by day confusion will always be around.
Love is strange to many people, and thoughts don't make a sound.
Although my hurt will make me sad, and I will play me the fool,
Never will forget, Kelli's Golden Rule:

Don't mess around with fire, with fire you'll always get burned.
Although you maybe smart, lessons are never learned.
So back on your feet and think, put on that happy smile,
And don't find another love, it isn't worth your while.
Kelli B. Boyd

Desert Spring

The winter desert waits in cold somnolence,
its grey-brown starkness spiked by faded scrub.
It is an austere demanding land marked and surrounded by sharp
mauve-brown mountains that thrust against the lower reaches of a
cobalt firmament which only hints at shreds of wispy images of
clouds.

On currents filled with sunshine's promise she drifts across the sage
and Joshua trees blessing hidden crannies with her breath which leaves
a tattered trail of beauty seen only by the diurnal lizard's eyes.
Before the eye she drops her treasures, leaving brighter, darker
greens and splashes of bright yellow floating on the desert floor,
dotted by the fuschia bloom or brightened by white desert flowers.
She drops clumps of lighter sage among refreshed smoke trees
and paints spiked orange up and down the valleys. And where is
least expected there is the bright palest lavender blue, her eyes.

As she advances up the slopes of burgundy and burnt sienna
she paints with mossy green on rocks which before stood bare.
She warms the desert air with the sunshine of her smile
and the joy of her laughter, the cactus bloom. And as
she trails yet further, higher, the desert smiles and starts to fade
for summer comes and the desert dreams until spring comes again.
Virginia K. Smith

Youth And Age—(A definition)

Youth is not a time in life,
It's just a state of mind!
In a burning zeal for living,
We can "juvenescence" find.

If we lose enthusiasm
And the world looks bleak and cold,
'Though we've had just thirty birthdays,
We will know that we are old!

When we're planning for the future
And not living in the past,
We're as young as April sunshine,
'Though our next breath is our last.

So, let's count our birthdays differently,
More accurately, it seems;
We're as old as our uncertainties
And as youthful as our dreams!
Olive B. Kirke

September

There's something in the leaning of this sun
Its tarnished rays diluted as with dust
That breathes a sense of golden summer gone.

A few dead leaves, like ghosts of sunburnt days,
Loiter and eddy slow across the path
And herald the bright pall that autumn lays.

There's something in the chilling of my thought
That speaks of summits passed and tasks untried
That joys not now to be attempted. Nought

Dissolves the creeping pain of time's slow turning.
July returns not, nor the blaze of light
In which ripe hopes and full-blown loves were burning.

Nancy Madeira

Ruby

She was orphaned when she was fourteen.
It's unbelievable the things she's seen.

She was beaten, whipped, her mouth washed out.
But she wouldn't dare let out a shout.

"What broke the cycle of abuse?", I asked.
She said it was simple, an easy task.

She thought no one should be treated that way.
And she worked hard at it day after day.

"Treat everyone with love, dignity and respect,
and the rest of your life you'll have no regrets."

She's been my inspiration all of my life.
I'm glad she was my father's wife.

I gave her problems but I wouldn't have another.
I'm more than proud that she's my mother.

To break the cycle can be done.
As you can see it takes just one.

Leah Owens

Once Again

Here we are again, reunited
It's what we said, we always wanted
On each other's faces, there are a few more lines
Never mind, for we can still recall, all the good times

Once again, a year has past
Once again, I hope it'll last
Once again, a step in life
Once again, your friend for life

Here we are again, so much to share
Time after time, and yet we still care
Times have changed, yet closely listen
Revealed is a return, to innocence

Day after day, we laughed and partied together
Serious sometimes, greatly immature at others
We were always together, until the sun shined
And boy wasn't it all, such a grand time

So never forget, because we know we can't stay
For again we must part, on our own separate ways
Keep on smiling, 'til we meet again someday
Perhaps, even before, we are all old and gray

Paul M. Lee

Eternity

I don't feel lonely any more.
I've ceased to end each day
Hoping that with the new one
You'll return.
For there is no time where I am now.
There is no yearning.
The space is vast, endless.
Yet there is no search.
The ethereal lights shine on and on,
And yet they light no path.
Here among them I find they hold no charm,
No promise as I thought they did
When I beheld them from the earth.
There is no joy, no gladness here
No expectation.
Yet neither is there despair.
There is only nothingness,
Eternal nothingness.
At last I've ceased to care.

Meredith Neill

Untitled

The picture, unforgettable -
I've entered the door many a time, but did I really notice,
    the walls, the scent, the love throughout the hallways.
Hush, the sparrow is sleeping.
I've climbed many a step into the glory of her room.
I remember each glass figurine,
    every picture placed gently upon her dresser -
    her bed, a four poster with fresh white sheets.
Hush, I said, she'll awake -
What? Her eyes are closed you say -
Hush, I know she's gone away,
    but I'm still here waiting for her return.
Hush now, the sparrow is sleeping.

Leslie F. Horack

Endless Love

My love for you is endless
I've even forgot about the rest
I've never felt so much love for someone before
What more can you ask for
I'm willing to give you heart
Just as long as you won't break it apart
For if you hurt me, I'll fell so very blue
And I'll just find myself crying over you
But deep down inside I know you're not that king of guy
Who will just walk-out without a good reason why
I have faith in you
I honestly and truly do
So please open up your heart
And let me become a part
A part of your life, for I really believe we belong together
And believe me, my love for you will last forever
For my love for you is so very endless it will never end
And I know I'll never love another as much again
And so I hope you'll give this love a try
For I honestly believe you are meant to be my guy

Kimberly Bolt

"The Hour Glass Of Time"

On laughter's wings
  I've floated away in the memory of what once was
My senses are filled with your dancing eyes
  Piercing straight into my soul
I cannot hide from your existence
  I run, I stumble, I fall
Your being has lifted me higher than I've ever been
  On Angel's wings I've soared
My dreams are not void of you
  You invade my sanity
My steps are above the universe
  I look down and embrace your soul into my heart
Through the hour glass of time
  We will grow old together
I have not touched you yet we've done a million things
  And perhaps in dreams of tomorrow
I will chase your elusive being
  Running, stumbling, falling
Straight into your existence
  Capturing your love - I will surrender.
  Rita Palumbo Graves

Big Wheel

Of all the lovers', of all the men...
I've never wrote to you
With an authors' pen.
Even though, you were all I ever wrote of -
In every single verse...
Because of a love, twenty-two years ago.
So innocent, yet pulled away a long held curse.

No one could ever replace you,
My dearest Big wheel - No pain could match
God's loving seal.

Alone remembering; for-get-me-not's, football,
A silent running stream and a perfectly etched face
In my mind...
Remembering a boy, a hero, a friend of mine.

And yes wheel, I love you still -
where ever you may be....
My first love, from then until eternity.

A wheel of life that began with you and me...
A memory that only we can see.
Is full circle never to be broken.....silently spoken.
  Terri King

Rule of the Sun

In days of strength, veins are fluent with life
Joints surge forward in motion, wheels clear the void without
  hesitation

The rule of the sun, words that will live on

Subtle hues of sand sifting slowly through hand
The sun fills the sky as we drift through the waves
The shore pulls water from the depths and beckons us to sail,
  to run, to work then rest...and dream

But wait... is it strictly possible to dream through
  the night without some sort of unconscious life?
To keep our head above water and live to see
  the next golden flax symphony of basement tile
  floors all of plaid greens and tans holding out their
  putrid hands, begging come walk with me

In days of weakness the heart lies still
the mind lies restless

As we hibernate the sun continues to shine as the
  sun tends to do
But we lie and waste away in the cold light
  of day to sit and do nothing but pray
  C. L. Yaros

"Hummingbirds And Morning Glories"

Two earth's rarest treasures, give me
joy beyond measure.
Hummingbirds and morning glories -
Each a jewel, tells its own unique story.
They both appear for a very
short while -
Whenever I see them, my heart smiles!
The hummingbird, a mystery,
of flitting grace -
The morning glory - a
rhapsody in blue shows her face-
This modern world with
its hectic pace
Scurrying, hurrying,
running human race
Stop and consider, pause and reflect-
Give our creator his due respect!
Take your time, pause and see -
The beauty of the hummingbird
and the morning glory.
  Shirley M. Koenty

Pink Whales

The grass had a trampled path worn,
just a league away from the graves of the iron whales,
you can hear the cries from their sisters far away,
you can hear the singing from their hearts,
the structures of steel, and engine,
rusted in place at New London,

The grass grew bright and green,
just a league away from the graves of the iron whales,
you can hear the crying,
you can hear the singing,
you can see them from the ocean...
  Winston H. Reed III

Little One

A clear November night the moon and stars were bright a child
was just conceived from you and from me a
blessing that we shared someone for us to care and nourish from
within until the day came when she was so
beautiful a child of yours and mind from heaven blessing fell we
named our child CHERELLE

Talking about my LITTLE ONE little person as can be LITTLE
ONE little person LITTLE ONE for me

Before I start my day I have to stop and prey to thank the Lord
each day for sending her my way pretty twinkling
eyes full of laughter and surprise she's always on my mind
thinking of her all the time she is my

LITTLE ONE little person as can be LITTLE ONE little person
LITTLE ONE for me

As I look into her eyes her smiling face I love her gentle touch and
I love her warm embrace she is my everything and everything I say
I'll take her by the hand through my eyes I'll show the way she is my

LITTLE ONE little person little as can be LITTLE ONE little person
LITTLE ONE for me she is my LITTLE ONE little person little
as can be LITTLE ONE little one for me.
  Omar K. Simmons

Adventures Of The Day

My adventures of the day are getting worse,
just patiently waiting for the day I'll burst.

I feel like I'm the only one, looking through a scope,
examining the world not able to cope.

I pay close attention to people;
and I'm puzzled in mind; is there anyone left
whose loving and kind?

I wonder why I'm so fragile in mind. There
are woman more fragile than I, hanging with
the everyday grind.

Do I still have my sanity? Are you still in touch?
When I hear the word sanity, sane and such; I picture people
behind soft walls, whaling those echoing calls, as they
find that their mind is a burdensome crutch; some not even
knowing as much.

Tracy Long-Heaton

"Parents In A Secondary Home"

Parents do not go to the home on their own free will
Just to sit and watch birds on the window sill
They are put there, but have to pay the bill
Parents in a secondary home, from day to day
It is so boring that they just sleep until the day fades away
Parents miss their loved ones so dear
Such a strange place and very lonely there
It is like a prison to them, with much pain and fear
They can't be in a single room, by themselves, but for two, or a pair
Their children can't afford to keep them home
So they are put in a care center for them to roam
Parents are so glad when you come to say hi
But very sad and heart broken, when you say goodby
Children can't stand the hurt, sadness and loneliness, that they bare
Just pray to God, that they are treated with respect, and good care
Parents just sit and dream to pass the time away
Hoping someone will come to see them that day
Same old walls, halls and rooms, they say
So home sick and heart sick, that they want to pass away

Larry Dee Mulford

Dream

In the middle of the night, I lie awake
Just to watch her sleeping.
Run my fingers through her hair
And wonder what she is dreaming.

One soft kiss on her cheek hold her close and tight
As I drift away to dream with her one more night.

Oh' when I'm fast asleep no darkness can be found
Just being next to her there's sun shine all around.

Don't let me wake in the morning
To find that she is gone
I'd cry myself to sleep
And dream from this day on.

Every day I thank the heaven's
For one dream that came true
Heaven sent me an angel
That angel was you.

So if you ever start to wonder
Just how much I care for you
Take a look in the mirror
you'll see my dream that came true.

Stephen D. Kelley

A Parent's Pride

On that cold and raining morn
Just when the sun was about to dawn
A perfect little boy was born
With a smiling face and a great big yawn

Mom and Dad as proud as can be
Knew someday what they would see
A young adult so tall and handsome
Who'd make this day worth a king's ransom

As we watch him walk down that aisle
With his cap and gown and our favorite smile
It's hard to believe the years have flown
And yes, our little boy has grown

To our son we wish you love and success
And of course we always wish you the best
Keep that smile on your face and love in your heart
For your future is off to a wonderful start

Your love of music will always see you through
Even when the sky is not blue
Study hard - learn well - have fun
And with this we guarantee - you'll number one

Mary Ann Ragona

Peace

Sit down, stay awhile I got a few words to spit out-
Just words of knowledge nothin about pull or clout-
People keep playing games with other people's heads-
Whether their topping consist of perms, weaves or dreds-
You see it's not a color thing it's all about the mind-
But wait, for colors not to interfere we would need to be blind-
These games stupid games all need to stop-
Enough with the masks wanna be's and stupid props-
We need people that are true to self true to the game-
Not people out for cheap wealth or fake fame-
You se I'll take the poor genius over the rich dummy anyday-
But while that rich dummy is lost the poor genius will find a way-

Matthew B. Smith

The White House U.S.A.

Take pride in this beautiful structure
Keep out poisonous rot and decay
Cement a foundation of good deeds
The constitution has meant it that way
Here's a call to all future statesmen
To bring back the spirit we knew
And a challenge that every american
Hold a reign on the land where he grew
But as each man is only a human
Not a heavenly myth too sublime
Mistakes are a part of his heritage
And can be rectified with courage and time
Let the walls echo sounds of his valor
And the halls feel the weight of his stand
Let his knowledge be mixed with great honor
Make it awesome to each foreign land
Don't take on a task far beyond you
Or sacrifice duty for play
Keep this symbol of justice and fairness
A white house unsoiled. U.S.A.

Terry Gilmour

The Spirit Within

When you open your heart and mind, there's certain
kind of peace you'll find
The spirit within is a powerful thing, it gives us the power
to laugh and sing
Never let a troubled spirit bring you down, show them happiness
and they'll come around
Don't claim your adulthood until you can see, there's a
little child inside both you and me
Always show children respect and love, and remember we all
have one God up above

Thomas Reuss

"Christmas Time"

Warm fire, cold snow,
kissing under the mistletoe,
Christmas trees with fresh pine scents,
all covered up with ornaments,
decorations a joy at sight,
beautiful lights that shine so bright,
children tearing paper to reveal a toy,
just to sit and watch, is such a joy,
Christmas songs with a cheerful rhyme,
this is what I think of at Christmas time.

Laura M. Hollar

"In Memory Of Dad"

When I was a little girl, I would climb upon my daddy's
knee, look into his bright blue eyes, he was the
dearest one to me. A smile would trickle across his
dear ole face, I knew no one could take his place.
My love for him, no one could know, he would put
me down and say, let's go. There's lots of work
to be done, then we would work from sun 'til sun. I enjoyed my
days back then even tho they look dim. I'd work myself to
death just to be with him. With him getting old, his hair
turning grey, I knew he would not be here for many more days.
To think of that would break my heart, I knew I couldn't stand
for us to part. When doctors said, he was gone, I knew
I was left to face this world alone. Up in heaven, he's there I
know, looking down at me on this earth below.
When I am called from this ole world I
want to go to heaven and be daddy's little
girl, I want to climb upon his knee
and say to him remember me! I know he
will be happy for me to be there. We can
hold hands and walk up those golden stairs.

Martha Louise Day

"The Dreadful Truth"

An aching, burning sensation all night long... I
knew... I just had this feeling, there was something very wrong.

It hurt so bad, a pain that wouldn't go away! It seemed
to stay longer and stay... and stay.

But I didn't know what was wrong with me. Nothing was
wrong as far as I could see.

So, I went to the Doctors, Nurses, everybody, to find out
what was wrong with my body.
Oh No!
Some Terrible Disease, much worse than I thought it would be.
Gigantic hospital, dreary room, and a big scary bed. I
really didn't want to be there. I'd rather have been dead.

As I laid there, very weak and fragile in my bed, I heard
voices... "You can fight through this, you can make it!" they said.

Well, I know I can make it right, I won't give up without
a fight. Things are going "ok" as far as I can see, but I just
have a couple of questions........

Why Leukemia? Why Me?

Liane Wilson

Heroes Of Our Country

Heroes of our country, you have my lending hand
knowing you're the one's, whom saved our precious land
You lived many months, preparing in the hot desert sand
Now tall and proud, is how you should stand

The deaths of many brave soldiers, left my heart in sorrow
I give you my unknown thanks for giving me tomorrow
Everyday I live, you will always have a part
And forever shall you be, deep inside my heart

Your loyalty and bravery will always be known
To every single soldier, you deserve a metal to be shown
The land decided to give you a single day parade
But more than that, I will honor you everyday

I am proud to know, my country stopped the war
Your bravery, honesty and loyalty, I shall always adore
With my right hand over my heart, I will like to say
Thank you soldiers, for another beautiful day!

Tonya M. Hudler

Fairy Artists

Last night fairies visited my garden,
Laden with palettes they flew on silver-tipped wings
Painting springtime bouquets on earth's canvas
With infinitesimal gossamer brushes.

Yellow daffodils circle the bird bath,
Red tulips stand in dress parade beside the walk,
Pink hyacinths cluster at the white fence,
While shy blue violets bloom beneath apple trees.

One artist imbued with pixy intent
Did not paint the white lily-of-the-valleys,
Their stilled bells stirred as the chuckling fairy
Hurried from its playfulness to the garden gate.

Tonight when other blossoms nod in sleep
Satisfied to rest after daylight's sunfilled glory,
A star-tipped baton will awaken the bells
To sway them in rhythm with gentle airy chimes.

If you listen in the stillness and hear
This ethereal lullaby filling the air,
Know that one day the soft touch on your cheek
Is from a fairy creature that believes in you.

Louise L. Mackenzie

The Color Green

Green is a color that I always see,
Lately, though it looks different to me.

All the plain old meadows that I have seen,
Now, suddenly explode with the magical color of green.

Most would think how strange for a man to get so excited,
Over a mere color, no matter how delighted.

However, they do not know or understand,
How this color made its brand.

Me, being a simple man,
I'll explain it as best I can.

Green is so special of a color to me,
Because it is the color of the eyes of beautiful Julie!

Robert Louis Krieg

When You Lose That Person

I remember when, you and I talking, about our past together,
  Laughing about it, crying about it.
We don't do that anymore.

I remember you and I doing things together,
  Making you laugh when you were sad,
  Making me laugh when I was troubled.
We don't do that anymore.

I remember telling you what was happening in my life,
  When we were together.
  You, encouraging and helping me when I needed it,
  Me, giving you advice when you needed it.
We don't do that anymore.

I still talk to you as if you were here with me.
  Still write to you,
  Hoping you can hear me,
Even if you are gone.

  Kristina D. Anderson

Now

Avenues forsaken, winding through my past
Lead me to a crossroads where the view is clear at last
Years of desperation have surely left their scar
But as long as I'm alive, a new horizon can't be far

And I'm here today
Somehow, someway
This chance I'm taking

Fortune's faces trading places
No apology, no one to blame
Visions changing, rearranging
And opening my eyes, I finally see
Now is the place to be

I've said goodbye to the old that was
So let the new begin

Fortune's faces trading places
And gazing at the world, it's clear to me
Now is the place to be
Now is the place to be

  Stefan Shane

Untitled

The gray one scratches
leans back, smiles
tilts forward, watches
blank walls
leans back, scratches
cuts a sense, another sense, another, another, another
looks, searches, perceives
the white one smiles
as a drop of water appears
to reflect off of no one's eye
the white one still smiles
the drop falls
the drop fades
the unfelt black one smiles
in dryness
stillness
a sense, another sense, another, another, another
the gray one returns
the gray one forgets to watch
the gray one fades

  Pat Cannon

Reflection

You deny your fish's death
leave him afloat in his tiny, aquatic world
of blue and green marbles.
Daily at 3:00 you sprinkle
flakes of red and beige onto the surface
of his rippleless coffin,
humming softly to yourself or to him.
Lying on your bed, your head raised slightly
you stare at the flames
that project his still existence onto the wall.
His image swims 'round and 'round,
making you dizzy.
He reaches the surface and bids you
farewell with a flick of his tail-
leaving a drop of water
to trickle down your cheek
as he burrows down into the cool depths
and vanishes into his plastic castle-
never to return.

  Stephanie Kilham

To Sea

Fishermen go to sea to chug of engines and white gull's call,
leaving the docks, the town, the homes short their manly number,
quiet but for the timid tidal lapping about the piers and piles,
and groaning pull 'gainst taut lines by boats in harbor still.
Children, mocking queues, board a honking yellow monster of abduction
leaving the house, the yard, the street without the haunting
  echoes of their play.
With what joy the town, the homes reclaim their fishing fleet
when through the harbor gate they sail to long-awaited haven!
For growing babes it is not so —— their trip is but one way,
each day, each year they swing from us in greater orbit still,
'til such the time and distance that they are like sailors drowned,
no less the loss for those hollow ones who wait on harbor's hill.

  Phil Dehnick

An Asp And Hope

She stands with straight of back,
legs unbowed to face the winds of change.
Knowing that panderings will make
her way a gauntlet of weary bones
and sighs and smells.

Who can hear the cry of pain,
when arcs of flame spark
with pink and yellow lines of smoke?
Those who see with eyes of clear regard
to take the course that weary steps
and faint of heart will shun.

Her feet are slow, the gait unsteady,
but still she tries to find her way
through wisps of smoky lines
where colors merge to form a flame of coursing strength.

The asp with eyes of red and green
stares in feint repose.
She in grandeur looks straight ahead,
thinking of days and ways to skirt the paths that lie afar.

  Susan Perez

357

Human Condition

From positive to neutral to negative,
Lie spectra of attitudes,
Towards reasoning and feelings
Embracing humans.

Reflective of the passion of a kiss,
The coldness of indifference,
And the anger of hate and violence
Endures humanity.

For the individual and society
Here, bound to the reality of nature
From birth to death, endpoints of moans,
In-between laughter, boredom and tears.

Culture molds traditions, beliefs, and behaviour,
Consciously and unconsciously,
Achieving diversity
For the development of individuals.

Life sparkles whatever occurs,
Cope with victory, stand-off or loss,
Head and heart in harmony
Optimize the human condition.

Sam Silbergeld

Clear Water Beach

As far as the deep blues and greens reach
lies God's haven, Clearwater Beach.

Ole faithful pirate ship sails in view
while playful dolphins are long overdue.
Sandcastles formed while music fills the air
and fun seeking tourists let down their hair.

Innocent as children, joined hand in hand,
lovers float on love high above the sand.
With each passing wave, worries roll away.
Upon the young lovers, God's gentle hands lay.

The warm tropical breezes they do feel,
gliding thru the water as tho' they're seals.
Yielding to the warmth of the midday sun,
they and the ocean become as one.

Never enough of this heaven can there be;
unlocked here are the treasures of the sea.
As far as the deep blues and greens reach
lies God's haven, Clearwater Beach.

Linda Renz

Love's Child

A woman dreaming she is pregnant
Lies in silk and pillows and her love's arms.
Sleeping. Knowing her silent power
She is warm, eternal and young.

Beautifully young. Buoyant in love.
Her body a lush island for another.
Her hand falls like a feather to her middle
Searching for the new swelling.
The cloud of sleep holds her thoughts
And delivers a renaissance angel to the bed.
Laughter rains down on the woman's belly
Waiting sweetly to receive a child.
Her mind and body floating in desire,
She wakes and turns to better see her love's face.

Nestled close, she smiles as sleep prevails
And returns her to drifting and dreaming.
Dreaming of the coming of the little one.
To suckle. To love. To teach.

Kiri Bazos

Death-Awakening

The earth-born form to which I seemed so seemlessly linked
Lies lifeless, leaden,
Still, held by the planet which lent to it its substance.
It now returns used and worn to its original home,
As I return to mine.
I float free above that which I had thought was me,
Divesting myself of friend and foe,
Of longing and fear, of event and world.

The vastness opens, welcomes,
Undefined by earth's confines.
The purity seeps into my being gifting me its astonishing freedom,
Freedom to be without becoming, to live beyond cessation,
Beyond pulsation of heart and lungs,
Beyond day and night.
Radiance invites me to itself as I melt into the primacy,
Into the undefiled light.

The light pervades the spaceless vast,
Penetrates the depths of the timeless when.
It is the oneness of the many, the clarity within each seeming,
The being within each becoming my source, my home, truth.

Steve Sklar

Don't Fear Your Feelings

My child, my child, my precious one.
Life is wonderful, life is fun.
But, life will bring onto you challenges true
This is why I'm sharing with you.
Youth is hurried, wild and carefree.
And you will cross bridges that I have seen.
Dating and feelings have not really changed
You will enjoy friendships that you have made.
But, emotions run ramped under a lover's moon.
Your body and mind will begin to argue.
Fear not these feelings, you're normal inside
Just be prepared so no shame you will hide.
Diseases and pregnancies once were hushed.
We know of them now, they've been much discussed.
So learn from others and protect yourself.
When you don't understand, simply ask for help.
I will not condemn nor will I condone.
For I know the feelings of being alone.
No one to ask and too afraid to share.
Fear not these feelings, we've all been there.

Sheila Diehl

Art

Art is expressed in many ways
Like a gloomy day painted in greys
When a potter raises then shapes
A perfect half sphere bowl just for grapes

It's mobile and flows with the times
And helps me create a page full of rhymes
Art will flow through a musician
Unlike the boastful politician

When hammer and chisel conform
The ever flexible takes new form
Art too can express emotions
Stopping time and capturing motions

Art in a sense is infinite
I feel its presence is permanite
Yet still art takes another shape
Tie dye, Timothy, can you relate

Thomas Kihle

Thoughts For Friends

I sit truly realizing for the first time,
Like a light going off in my head,
That we must say good-bye
Sooner than I want to say it.

I want to thank you for all the good times.
I am glad to see how far we've come from the bad times,
But there is so much more—
I want you to know how much you mean to me.

You allow me to be myself when I am not so nice.
You teach me to empathize with others.
You show me the other side of any issue.
You care enough to take the time to be my friend.

So I try to figure out how I can bear to say good-bye,
When I realize I can rest knowing
That no matter how far apart we are,
The bond we share will keep us close always.

I thank God for you always.

Laureen Penn

God's Holy Cross In Hell's Kitchen On 43rd And 9th

Walking down 43rd and 9th
Like all children, I questioned
What I didn't understand.
"Hell's Kitchen, what's that?"
I remember mom's voice saying,
"Bad things have always happened here".
As I walk down the block, I'm slapped.
They stand side by side,
The church and the porno palace.
When I am alone this picture haunts me.
In the burgundy one, a Catholic Mass is held.
The bell rings loudly
Above the maddening traffic noise.
In the other a cattle herder sits.
As he gulps his whiskey from a grimy shot glass,
He watches his meat dance nude in high heels,
On a black shellacked stage.
The bell's toll sounds in her head,
As the snake flashes his bill.
She hears nothing.

Marina Henderson

The Impossible Task

The years have passed,
Like billowy clouds on a windy day.
Some beautiful, some dark lined,
Some stormy and some a sunshine ray.
So fast- where have they gone?
Like clouds- do they disappear?
Only to come back the next time around?
In youth, the years ahead seemed so eternal-
In age, the years behind me seem-
So fast- where have they gone?
A fleeting moment, in the passage of time.
So much to me—so little to eternity.
I stand and I ponder and I turn-
To face all the glories of the earth,
Our time here is so very short—
And now it's my turn,
To master and live the art,
Of putting twenty-four hours into one.
So fast- where have they gone?

Sally J. Nelson

Grow Where You Are Planted

All things that God has made grow where they are planted.
Like Dandelions in the lawn.
Growing, showing bright yellow above the green
Solitary, yet, bold, and delicate.
Such simple beauty, magical as it turns into a white star.
With a puff of air its seeds float skyward.
Cherished by those who can see through a child's eyes.
Settling in many lawns of green to find a home, and grow.
A tiny reminder that all things God has made
grow where they are planted.
His wisdom, held there in the leaves of grass, a message.
Grow where you are planted.
As it is with Gods Love, we grow where we are planted.
As it is with the Dandelion, we spread His Love with a breath.

Laura E. Stepanek

Empty Promises

Washed away feelings,
    like footprints in the sand.
Faded promises,
    become the yellowed photos of yesterday.
Broken hearts splinter,
    like a shattered mirror.
Icy looks,
    are bitter winter winds.
Relationships end,
    feelings,
    promises,
    hearts,
    loving looks,
Die,
    like a loved one passes.

Melanie Reese

Holy Father's Eulogy

He from a far country bravely comes
Like one who Alp's top forepart ramps,
For Polish Tatry are you not sad
Or for high Wawel do you regret?

In front of you marsh the Angels-knights
They give you vigour in many fights,
You'll be the winner with their support
You beat the evil of a strong sort...

Be a defender of the small child
Full of charity, tender and mild,
Through your fervent prayers, day and night
The devil's power shall lose its might.

To change the world of peacy still mute
Can your tall figure in the white suite,
When our globe becomes deep dark
You remain man's confidence's bright spark.

We bow all heads before your throne
Because earthly pride so fast is gone:
Vicar of Christ, John Paul the Pope
Joy of the Christians, their trust and hope!

Mike Svey

Love

Love is only simple thing.
Love can be thrown away,
Or you can be born with it.
But only simple things can be touched or heard.
But why can love be so cruel or turn into Sorrow?
Once you are unloving, you cannot take it back.
Love can turn into hate if you do not treat it with respect.
That is what love is-not a simple thing after all

Marshall Jacobini

True Love

Love feigned——
Like the fleeting butterfly,
Lands here, there, everywhere;
And like the butterfly,
Lives but briefly.

Love feigned—-
Like the firefly at night,
Flashes brightly in the dark;
And like the firefly,
Is lost in the light of day.

But true love——
Like the castles of old,
Is built on a solid foundation of friendship;
And like the castle,
Will withstand the ravages of time.

And true love—-
Like the ships of the sea,
Can weather the storms of life;
And like the ship,
Bring you home safely.

Rick Fleming

The Ebb Of Days

Our days flow past repetitiously,
   like the waters of a great river
   ever moving toward an unseen destination.

We drift with the tide, unthinkingly we follow.
The poet looks at a leaf, riding the crest
   and wonders.
Storms come, waters overflow their boundaries
   angry, muddy, restless, covering defenseless land.
The planter looks at the waste
   and wonders.
Calm days and turbulent life, birth and death——
   growing, changing, slowly we alter.
Like the leaf torn by the waves we
   are no longer the same.
Seeing ourselves reflected
   in the currents of our past
   we approach the last ebb
   in wonder.

Rosemary Bishop

My Mother

My mother, my friend, my mother,
like you, there will never be another.

The love we've shared is so deep,
always in my heart, I will keep.

Trials and tribulations, we've had our share,
but always knowing that God was there.

The time we've shared seems too brief,
which only adds to my grief.

My heart feels like it's been pierced by an arrow,
but I know that His eye is on the sparrow.

And if for the sparrow, He will care,
I know for me, His grace will be there.

I love you, I love you, I know that you know,
and your seeds of love, I promise to sow.

Over now, are your burdens and pains,
and that, my friend, is Heaven's gain.

Rest now, Mother, and you will see,
one day, again, together we'll be.

Kathy Metze Stewart

Good Friends

Do not hasten as we say good-bye
Linger in our warm embrace.
Revel in these special moments
Capture time and hold its place.

Caring friends who help each other
Remain a constant in our lives.
Reflecting on the lives they shared
Impoverished humanity; if no one cared.

Empty spaces left behind
The status quo no longer defined.
The perfume of life grows somewhat fainter
The scent of loss within our mind.

Should we meet again tomorrow
To celebrate another dawn.
Rejoice and savor every moment
The hands of time keep moving on.

Mildred Shavelson Brettschneider

Beauty

Beauty is everywhere. We need only look to see it,
listen to hear it, touch to feel it, smell to enjoy its aroma.
Beauty is waves rolling to the shore, the wind rustling
the leaves, a sun shower, the fresh smell of spring.
Beauty is everywhere we need only be aware.

Norma Rait

Alone

There is no one here only I,
Listening to the soft silence of the night.
Suddenly I hear a cry,
It sounds so distant but then I realize.
It was only I,
crying in the soft silence of the night.
Afraid of the loneliness I was feeling within my heart.
Afraid of the emptiness which was tearing my soul apart.

Veronika Jozsa

Christmas Dove

Christmas bells are ringing,
Little children are singing.

The joy of Christmas is covering the land,
for everyone as it's been planned.

Time is here to spread our love.

Unfold our wings like a thousand
fleeting doves.

To caress the hearts of those we love.

In hope that the Christmas Dove,
can open the door, to bring the
gift of love evermore.

So sing my children across the land,
and give the world a helping hand.

Then fly so high my Christmas Dove,
and spread the word of Christmas love.

Roxanne Mosher

Oklahoma Cowboy's Advice

I went to the Town Pump one evening at seven.
Little did I know I was at risk of losing my heaven.
My beautiful model, my enamorata, my saint,
became a real virago—an angel she ain't!
She picked up my whiskey and icewater and gin
and instead of taking a poke at my chin,
she wasted that last jigger, that cost me my last penny—
and poured it—icewater and all—down my collar! oh, many
are regrets I have offered, but all bore no fruit.
   She walked out with her two escorts and waved goodbye
to boot! I tried to adjust collar, tie, shirt,
or was it bolo and knot! I forget why I bothered
but I am really quite shy and this beautiful newcomer
had given me the eye. I had to sit there soaking and wet.
The bartender tried to help me. He said:
"Drinks are on the house," and they explored in laughter.
Maybe it is superfluous to recall I now look more deeply
for beauty—models don't interest me at all
but my cowgirl girlfriend has answered my call
and we're fishing for rainbows in Snowy Range stream this fall.

Veda Nylene Steadman

The American Dream

In far off lands they wait, papers filed
Lives on hold, plans made, and so they dream
Wonderful dreams, blurred and hazy
Like the movies, slow moving, lazy
They are coming to America.

And now, the big day dawns,
Anxiety, excitement, sleepless nights, the norm
Luggage packed high, spirits packed high
Well wishers wave goodbye, envy in their eye
They are leaving for America.

On a brand new land, they gaze
Impatient, embracing, daring, a little fear
Too late to turn back now, relatives galore
Hugging and crying, laughing, excitement restored
They have landed in America.

In this new home, they remember, the beginning
The gamut of emotions, euphoria to despair
But they hung in there, dug in there
This home of the brave, land of the free
They are living in America.

Kris Singh

Tramps Lament

Spent ten years on the road and rail,
Living life like a fairy tale.
Getting up and falling down,
Never stopped to look around.
Check the weather, look for rain,
Rain's a coming, jump a train,
But I was here a year ago,
Find me somewhere else to go.
Broken bones and memories,
Life's been pretty good to me.
Losing teeth, losing hair,
Tell you boys the world ain't fair,
Although I done and seen a lot, you could put all I got
In a tote sack and a bed roll
Settled down a time or two
One time I spent a year in the same old town.
And let me tell you what I found
Two types of people in this world.
Besides of course boys and girls.
There's tramps and people who wish they were free

Tom Bradley

Longing To Belong

Lonely with people
Lonely by myself
Feeling stored away on a dark closet shelf
When will they take me down
Am I going to drown
In my own tears
How many years
Will this go on
Lonely

Sharon A. Bosch

Cry

Cry, cry, cry in the night
Lonely tears filled her face
Only the good Lord knows
Why she sticks around to get hurt

   It cannot be because of love
   Love's been long gone from the picture

The helplessness of a woman
Trapped by what she thought was love
Beaten down, thrown around
Shattered love

Cry, cry, cry in the night
Cry for a woman who has no rights
Cry for the woman who can't sleep at night
Cry for her broken body and spirit
Cry because she is your mother, sister and grandmother
Cry for her freedom

   Broken promises, dreams
   Broken body, spirit
   Broken love, everything

Cry for the woman who has nothing

C. Merla Jobe

Look

Look at the baby see as he is born!
Look as he steps into his home and sees his new surroundings!
Look as he learns who Mommy and Daddy are!
Look as he takes his first step and glows with happiness!
Look as he takes his first steps into kindergarten and discovers
   his new world!
Look as he makes new friends!
Look as he enters the real world!

Lisa Maria Schefler

Make Sure It's Frigged...

Turned on the T.V. saw about the quake today.
Look at all the death and destruction; what can you say?
Everybody's an expert or so it seems
Journalists, analysts,, seismologists,
Even the stock boy at the A and P.
Shoot out here amongst us cool west coast, state of the art,
Teflon toe-jams, we sure gotta have some relief.
First the riot and old Reginald boy
The fires that burned all those rich folk's toys.
Enough tragedy to shake even the staunchest belief.
Now floods so bad you could surf through your hillside home.
People in despair, walking their days in fear
Families torn apart, their way of life as they have known it gone.
Parents comforting their children and drying both their tears.
The big question is, when will it end?
Everyone knows the earth will mend... itself
Will we be around to see it?

Tommy Rushing

"The Bonds Of Love"

A certain time, a certain place and the
look of love was on your face

You moved your hands, your eyes met mine,
I know I'd love you for all time

We were young, people said "they'll not last,
but the bonds of love had been cast.

Now we're older, your eyes meet mine
and I know we're together for all time.

The things you do, the things you say,
make me love you, much more each day.

We've opened up our hearts like two books
and liked what we saw when we looked.

My time here love will soon be past
We'll marry, have children, the bonds
   of love have been cast.

   Paul E. Preskenis

A Death Crone At Seventeen

Who is the crone
Looking at me with the scared eyes of a child
Whose heart is this that has grown so hard
This woman whose soul has known a thousand tears
Was there ever a child who felt the love of God
The freedom of the earth
Was there ever a heart that was not so heavy
With guilt
Was there ever a time without the pain
Did she know a love sweet and pure
Or was she alone to fight her fiends from within
Who is this spirit unbalanced by hate
Whose smile is embittered by her fate
All hope she lost when they left
All the people she trusted but could not accept
Who is this crone
Standing before me
Who is this woman I have become
How I hate who destiny has made me
Who I have made myself

   Sarah E. Jewel

A Wintery Walk

The winter wind is blowing through my hair,
Looking at the sky I smell the frosty air.
The houses so warm, cozy, and complete
As I stare at them while I walk down an ice-covered street.
I can't help but notice children playing in the snow,
Or relatives or friends kissing under a mistletoe.
Seeing Christmas trees glowing shiny and bright,
They seem to light up the sky on this cold, moonless night.
Jackfrost seems to be nibbling on my terribly cold nose,
While at the same time he's numbing the tips of my toes.
The world seems so content, and perfectly at peace.
And the snow is as white as a young lambs fleece.
Snowflakes are falling and swirling around,
Making an illusion of diamonds on the icy cold ground.
As I look around one last time, being so happy and gay,
I realize what a wonderful way it was to spend this cold,
Winters day.

   Stephanie L. Diehl

Ode For A Golfer

As I stand upon the 18th tee, driver thus in hand;
Looking at yawning fairways, bunkers, lakes and sand.
One thought now crosses my mind, as I set up to swing,
Which of these three places will my tee shot bring?
The fairway, a beautiful place, straight and to the right.
But "O" if I should hook it, it's in the lake and out of sight.
The bunkers to the left, and all that gruesome sand;
That would be an awful place for my ball to land.
So with one quick look, to the left and to the right;
Now I'm almost ready to put this ball in flight.
Waggle the hips, straighten the arms,
Take the club back slow and away!
Who care if I hit it straight or not... for
It's such a Beautiful Day!

   Kenneth Eskridge

"sunset"

sitting on the boardwalk
  looking into the horizon
    the magical hour is upon us

the hot summer breeze
  has become cool and caressing
    as the sun says farewell to this day

all faces are glowing from the lovely hues
  which continue to emanate
    as it descends

how beautiful to behold
  this precious gift from nature
    we watch with anticipation and sadness

    we can never this moment again
      still we rejoice
        awaiting its return

   Yvette Sang'iewa

Less Than Zero

Seeing all the pain, can't make it go away
Lost for all that's real, wonder what I feel
Have I reached the end, for time will never mend
All that feels so low, not knowing where to go
I guess I gotta find, this feeling left behind
Cause I've come to know, feeling less that zero

Uninspired by the truth, looking for the proof
That this will turn around, an emotion not yet found
Keeping this inside, I no longer hide
The pain that left me scarred, has me looking kind of hard
I no longer mask, the time has come and passed
So I will have to go, cause of a feeling less than zero

   Todd Yuengst

Chocolate Chip Bliss.

One night, while riding in a van, someone gave me a cookie.
(Man oh Man)!
It was chocolate chip and it was great!

First I thought of wheat blowing in the wind.
Sugar cane sweet, chocolate chips neat. I thought of the
butter, I thought of a cow. I thought of a chicken, an egg
OH WOW!
I wondered and wondered as I ate that chocolate chip cookie
that was so great!

I thought of the mill, I thought of the man, the flour and how
it began. (How long would that chocolate chip last?)

Then I thought of a little woman in some little town, baking
cookies from a recipe that had been handed down.

   Thomas H. Mickle

Vast Horizons

Time gone by
lost in the vast horizons
Stars scattered like little children
marbles thrown from the hands of gods
Children of the night
Shadows that disappear in the sun
Hearts broken and shattered,
  like mirrors tossed about the floors
To try to repair them would be hopeless
  to sweep them up and pitch them out,
We would risk possibly disposing of a treasure,
  a human heart gone to waste.
Trampled upon like a dirty old worn out doormat
Love is only a word that must be proven
  through the trials in our lives
With love, we hold the world in the palms of our hands,
  without love, we have nothing
We are nothing but useless sex starved emotional creatures
  lost in the vast horizons.

Leann M. Zeglin

From Son To Dad

I had no cares when I was a child, there was
lot's of love, my worries were mild, my Mom and Dad carried
the burden, of raising a family, and stopping the hurting,

My dad was a careful to raise us right, to fear the
Lord, and fight a good fight, his love and kindness
Were one of a kind, a giant of a man, with a humble
Mind, his heart was on Jesus, and he studied so hard, to
get us to heaven, and to strengthen our guard.

My mom is an angel, from the father above,
who has unmatched mercy, and bundles of love, when I
Was sick, she doctored my needs, she sat up at night
For the bible to read, she made sure I was raised.
to the best of her ability, Her standard was high, but
it gave me stability.

Years have gone by, my life has been changed, I
have a wife and two children, my goals rearranged, now I am
the provider, my children have no cares, but I never
would have made it, without Mom and Dad prayers.

For all their raisings, I am very glad,
But I finally had to change from son to dad.

Stan Flowers

"Loneliness"

As I lie here in my bed
Lots of thoughts go through my head
Wondering why, I'm all alone
All my strength, seems to be gone
I'm never happy, always sad
Nothing good happens, only bad
I look back on things, I've done
I don't think, I've ever hurt anyone
It seems I've hurt myself the most
Cause all I can see are lots of ghost
There's an empty feeling, deep inside
It's not like I'm living, but like I've died
Even if I'm in a crowd
And the people are getting loud
It seems that I'm not really there
But at a distance, off somewhere
Loneliness is like, a dread disease
And on your mind, your heart it feeds
Maybe someday, these feelings will be gone
Then I won't feel so all alone.

Lulabelle T. Robinson

Untitled

Feel the heart, sense the thoughts, touch the mind,
Love is a wonder that can be vanished by wrong eyes.
To deliver is to whisper through the sky,
Wondering what is to be behind your eyes.

The thought that enters is the voice that leaves.
Look through the eyes, not the mind, and let love live as one kind.
Words can slash the heart and fall free to the open well.
Senseless thoughts stir the brain, to drive one crazy, the thoughts
  of insane.

Sip of the cup, taste of the heart, the mind is swirling with thoughts
  of "nothing".
The eyes are closed and the hands are clutching.
What are words that are spoke of true,
The realm of wonder bringing times of new.

Lights to the sky, soil to the ground,
The laugh and whisper that make no sound.
The skull is a shelter not a bound.
The open door can be closed with a gentle touch,
The hair can be tattered with the stroke of a brush.

1000 miles of moonlight embrace the sky.
The countless wonders can't be answered with the question "why".

Steve Kersmarki

This Love I Have For You

Love is patient, love is kind,
Love is alive, it grows with time.

Love is honesty, love is trust,
Love is commitment, it is a must.

Do you love me? No more you need ask.
These words you may view each time as you pass.

Yes I love you, yes indeed!
My love it started as a seed.

Blown upon my heart it fell,
quickly it took root so well.

Confirming light it sought to find,
a chance it took, you were so kind.

Growing toward the light each day,
expressing blooms of love array.

A fragrance of a love so sweet,
God planned Himself our hearts to meet.

Formed in His hand the seed He blew,
from heaven this love I have for you.

Todd Edwards

Little Wanda

Little Wanda, oh so sweet
Loved it when she got a treat
Loved the gas fumes, so she would
Suck the pump when 'ere she could

Then one day, so I'm told
Little Wanda passed out cold
And almost left this earthly fold

Since that fateful autumn day
Little Wanda stays away
From that almost lethal pump
That knocked her on her little rump

Now with her Daddy by her side
You can hear her say, with a hint of pride
"I sucked gas and I damned near died!"

M. Calmes

I Sing For My Sister

Low, deep-down, strumming and moaning
Lower still.... weeping and wailing
Holding my belly, tears flowing down
Body's like a rock, belly's taut and firm

Thoughts of all my yesterdays and my babies
Look sound in every measure of what's outside of me
But my soul, oh God, my soul's full of open wounds
Can't ease this pain even with the balm

Evenings pass on to golden ambers just before blackness
Falls, and I weep and mourn flinging curses into its hollow

Thoughts of all my yesterdays and my babies
My burden is my "man-child" alias "boy-child" by his years
Lean, lank and troubled in his heart and in his mind
Sat side-by-side with satan one night 'cause he
Didn't have strength to pull with a mighty force and free himself

Sweet, sweet Jesus, swing down low 'cause I'm
Bent and bowed down on my knees
Keep me within Your loving reach
While my sister sings for me as I penetrate this blackness of
Thoughts of all my yesterdays and my babies.

Muriel Wharton

Man's Ledgers

A balance sheet must compute to the penny
maintaining no margin for error.
Equally weighed from beginning to end
is the ledger of life.

Is there a balance for our lives?
Are they stacked like a row of infinitesimal figures
leading into eternity?
Can lives be more than one or another?

Errors in figures and life
provide challenges and frustrations.
Sums and differences are re-calculated
until two sets match.

At origination,
there are no pluses or minuses.
We are equally calculated in God's design.
Everything has been planned for our measured duration.

Linda Darkes

Untitled

Dream me up a song my love.
Make it as unique as it can be.

Sing it to me softly,
The nights that we lay in each other's arms.
Whisper it to me in the morning.

Wake me with it in the middle of the night,
When I scream in my sleep, as I often do,
Being chased by demons, which are ever so close.
Write it to me.

Read it to me
In all the languages which neither of us know.
Greet me with it when we pass on the streets someday.

Scream it to me when it rains,
Drown out the thunder with it.
Take away my thoughts.

When you act it out in front of me,
Let me be your captive audience.

Rebecca J. Sweigart

Coming And Going

I rambled down a railroad track and met a
man dressed all in black with kerchief tied
into a sack that dangled from a pole in back.

His frayed fedora looked forlorn atop a face
with beard unshorn, and 'neath his trousers
badly torn were shoes that had been weather-worn.

And then he smiled a warm hello as if he wanted
me to know that he was neither friend nor foe but
just a fella on the go.

Skipp Kropp

Untitled

My mother transformed the other day; transcended to another plane
Many experienced her wonderful way; Marina was her name

She chose the leaving of the flesh, as such a simple task
On the morning of that special day, she made one breath her last

Marina spent each day she lived sharing wisdom, words and prayers
The answers to unpleasant situations, flowed from her like a lair

On Monday she wore pretty pink; on Tuesday ate Tai food
Wednesday was our special day; the air heavy with a mood

I woke her up at 10:00 pm; something I'd never done
"Are you breathing ok, I love you"; she smiled like the sun

A great big hug I gave her; one that I loved so much
Wednesday was our special day; the last day of our touch

Remember that you're special; she told me that each day
I urge you all to always know; that you are special too, she'd say

She didn't ask for help that morn; I offered none to her
We knew that magical time we shared; was fully and completely done

No one can take her words away; the words are always mine
I use them, feel them, breathe them, and they always make me shine.

Kim Kromas

Untitled

The rumour of the dragon came
Many hours ere it was seen.
But a hero there was of worldly fame
That happened upon the scene.
This courageous knight upon his steed
Had prepared throughout his life
To kill this dragon and its greed
And rid this town of strife.
Many hours on the practice field
With a slat of wood for blade.
Now with steel and a hardy shield
This dragon would be flayed.
The dragon came unto this fight
On winds only he could ride
and when the smoke had cleared that night
'Twas brave hero who had died.
The villagers knew not what to have said
They knew not how to cope
For hero was not the only thing dead
It was also the death of hope.

Travis Southern

Untitled

I don't understand and I'm eighteen
Love can make you feel happy.
Love can make you feel mean.
Love can make you feel glad.
Love can make you feel sad
And all other emotions in between, I know,
Maybe I'll understand when I'm nineteen!

Wendy Ethridge

After Visiting A Deaf Friend

Thank you Lord that I can hear
Many sounds that I hold dear,
Church bells ringing when I was wed,
Our babies cooing in their bed.
Many birds singing as they greet the dawn,
Splashing in puddles on the cool green lawn.
A "Good morning" greeting at the start of each day,
Children's voices, puppy's bark, all happy at play.
Mother at the piano playing to her hearts desire,
The sound of popcorn popping and bursting on open fire,
Sheep graze in the meadow, the wind rustles the grass,
And the breaking of water by a leaping bass.
A heard of cattle lowing
And a winding brook flowing.
Friends, family knocking at my door,
These are the sounds that I adore.
Be quiet take time to be still.
All you hear will give you a thrill.
Thank you dear Lord for giving to me
The power to hear, the sight to see.

Margaret Story Myers

The Daily Planet

Exclamation points dribble across the page.
Marks of ingenuity, they shine bringing light to our existence.

We live to die.
Guns are our means of expression.
They play painting the world red,
adult actions mastered by juvenile minds.

A man walks as a skeleton, skin clinging to his sweaty body.
I am hungry.

No assistance offered.

I am dying, don't you care?
Tears filled with anger fall heavily upon the earth.

No justice.

A portly man walks in the empty street pointing his gun at the world.
He knows no limit.

He walks past that shadow of a man and fires toward the sky.
A blast so loud it overrides one voice, one person crying
No more.

Rivers of life-giving blood flow together without purpose.
The end of infinity.
Period.

Patrizia Pensa

A Warning

Warning! Warning! Stay off the road.
Miss. Virgin Surprise resides
in our ephemeral abode.
Best take cover. She may explode
bringing death to every zip code.
What's solid turns to gas
encompassing the genial ignoramus
blinded by the fudge of the bombast.
The forecast is ground zero.
You'll see no tomorrow. No sorrow.
No one left to grieve beside the grave.
Many fools think this a tirade.
The message isn't to invade but to evade.
Let war be no more.
Fell the ohm of an orchestral orator.
May its infusion ignite the impassive
to affirmative action toward peace
so all may live. Let's sign life's lease.

Yvonne Van Damme

Rose

Can a woman be compared to a beautiful rose blooming on a bright
   May day
Painted in scarlet
Standing with grace
Waiting to be picked by some worthy face?

Once a bud
Now a flower
Unfolding before our eyes
Its beauty increases day after day
Until it slowly dies.

As the day breaks the rose is preparing
To conquer all troubles coming its way
Though wind is trying to break the stem
And rains are trying to drown the rose,
It firmly stands tall holding onto its petals
For they bring life to the beautiful rose.

It is sad to watch the rose as it grows older
Once so vibrant now so pale are the petals that remain...
Eventually the last petal will fall,

But Rose, you have lived a beautiful life after all.

Lorie-Ann Lee

White Cat

In this sylvan glen we both recline,
Me and this marvelous feline.
Who are you, you mysterious cat
Appearing from thin air like that?
With motion smooth and swift
Effortless as a log adrift.

Behold two hummingbirds flit in
Need I witness nature's sin?
I with beaded brow
Watch two hummingbirds avow,
Their quest for nectar near that twitch
Of tail which now does not switch.

That white creature is transfixed!
It is a duel between, betwixt.
The birds draw ever near until;
There is sound both sharp and shrill.

Then, with a start, those slanted eyes do pierce me through
And make me glad that I am bigger than you!
Alas, would time allow
More contemplation of au naturale.

Margaret Mortland

The Love For One Man

Dear God who watches over me, please help
me solve this mystery. I loved him once, I
love him still, it seems like I always will.
He never calls, he never writes there must
be someone else in his life. I miss him so
it hurts so bad. I miss his kiss, his warm
embrace, but most of all the smile on his
face. I guess he's happy with his new life.
I hope he's loved, happy and glad. Because he
don't need to be sad. I wish him the
best in whatever he does. But most of
all I wish him love and happiness to.
I just wish I had the guts to tell him I
was falling in love with him. But it's
in the past and I have a new friend.
I guess that's all I've ever been. Dear God
please watch over him, because I don't
want to lose a friend.

Sandra Star Nielsen Schif

Gone For Two Months

You've been gone for two months now. It has been hard for me to adjust without you around. I just keep telling myself that you have been busy and have not had time to come out. I try to make myself believe it but I know it is not true.

I walk through the hallway where we always stood thinking I might see you but I know I won't. It is different not seeing you standing there.

I try to make myself believe that life is just a long weekend because I would never see you. I guess life will be a long weekend all my life.

People are always asking me why I miss you so much when they never did see us with each other. I just tell them that they would not understand and they never will because they did not know how I felt about you.

You've been gone for two months and they will never know how I felt.

Nicole Sosbe

Wood Seasons

The fragrance of a thousand blossoms,
meandering in the breeze.
Life abounds in the trees.
Beams of light, dancing through the
canopy. Cool, shaded, how fresh the air;
fruits and berries everywhere.
To see the trees, with their multi-colored
leaves. Making the sunsets golden so bright,
as if trying to hold fast the night.
Lightly dusted in white, covered with
glistening diamonds in the moonlight.
Old trees leaning on young. Waiting
for the warmth of another springs sun.
In their last effort to stand tall. Before they
finally fall.

D. G. Miller

The Death Of A Poet

The words no longer flow...
Melodic moods that once could caress, could whisper
and in a line tell of all love...

Words like the steeping southern dew ... are gone -
Now tense tiny knots are tossed back and forth a dark wall
as I strain to see the forest for the trees...

The soaring flight of philharmonic phrases no longer take me
with them and the effervescent beauty of memorable madness'
have withered to be faded sagas of joy.

The death of a poet is a sad affair - when each line written
doesn't have a next or another -
The paradox to this agony is life ... ingested by cause rather than
reason and then he must start anew
forlorn with the tragic metaphor that life is death and so it is
with the life of a poet

Living each scene created by thought, the prose are conned into
silence by a faulty impasse which he didn't intend ... each page
appears now as the next and the next—all empty. Not of words...of
feeling - of joy - of sight.

At night I am no more alone than the day, and songs I have never
sung but tried to say are now riddles to which the answers
I can't explain...

The pain of a dying poet is everlasting, overcoming, yet rarely noticed -
The irony of it all is that only in death does he live, for those who
see his message his vision - his prayer - and his life.

Rick L. Weldon

B.C. And A.D.

Before the death of Christ,
Men offered animals as a sacrifice,
But after Christ died and rose from the grave,
He prepared the way of all men to be saved,
Before Christ men did not have a future,
But now God is looking for a new creature.
God gave his only begotten son so we can be saved.
He gave him to the grave but it could only hold him three days
He rose from the grave with love in his heart
Giving all man kind a chance for a brand new start.

Raymond Paschal

Halloween Dream

Hoot...You hear an owl screech!!!
Meow...You hear a black cat scratch!!!
Creek. Creek...You hear someone coming!!!
Bang Bang...You hear a gun shot!!!
Help...You hear someone scream!!!
Slam...Your door swings open
YOU SEE... YOU SEE...
Then you wake up, It's your HALLOWEEN DREAM!!!

Nicole Cardwell

The Me In Mercy

There's another word in Mercy; take the letters one and two.
Mercy is what I want for me but what do I want for you?

It's easy to feel merciful long as the problem's not too close.
Can't I pray and say "I'm sorry" then to my friends and self justly boast?

Yet wouldn't I go do something if I truly wanted to feel
Another's pain, and cared to help? Only with action is mercy real.

Daily I must remember God didn't just talk about sinning.
He felt my pain and loved me so, He gave His Son — my new beginning.

There's another part of Mercy, an even harder thing to do,
For if I'm to be merciful, I must include forgiveness, too.

"For me, mercy; for others, justice"
We humans want it each minute.....
This one last thought I leave with you
Justice has the word "us" already in it.

Susan L. Persons

Untitled

Lightning!
Mesmeric, magic;
Dancing, darting, licking,
Threatening, thirsty, cavorting enchantress?
Awesome!

Sunrise!
Solemn, tranquil;
Unfurling, diffusing, exploding,
Morning's promise of evening?
Enigma!

Pauline Mills

Dream Love

Six feet five, blond, eyes of blue
Muscles glowing a tanned bronze hue
Somewhat rugged, yet gentle and kind
A heart so warm, I'm glad he's mine
I dreamed of this man and hoped one day
To feel the strength of his arms embracing me in his soft way
To know his love so tender and deep
And the comfort of his nearness while I sleep
Oh, this man is no longer my dream
He is my true love, my husband, my esteem.

Pamela Markman

366

Two Timeless Hearts

As a new day dawns with the promise of love,
  Morning dew glistening on fairy trees;
A day when two hearts entwine as a fitted silk glove,
  With love radiating like waves on the sea -

A dress of lace and bands of gold;
  And God's promising loving kiss;
A promising heart to have and to hold;
  A forever feeling of wedded bliss -

A tiny hand reaches for a parents love;
  Content feelings are nurtured and grow;
Till spirited soul take flight like winged spread doves;
  The knowing of teaching and life's guidance now show -
Glistening strands of silvering years;
  A touch from an aged hand;
With walls embraced in life's memories held so dear;
  A strong forever love still stands.

Now remembering a tired soul that has moved along;
  But only momentarily apart;
Awaiting till the two souls join in a forever song-
  Of a love from... Two Timeless Hearts
    Tracey Boone

Erlking

The night is quiet, cool, and still.
Most mortals have gone,
for they've felt the chill.
The darkness has now blinded the day,
And now it's time for the Erlking to play.
Eyes of sapphires, hair as icy as frost,
many will gamble...at any cost.
Horrors unseen, and stories untold,
Will pass by as the world grows old.
But now it's dawn, quiet and still,
And the Erlking must go home of his own free will.
    Lindsey James

Funny This Thing Called...

The bright, powerful sun shines gallantly down the round,
multicolored earth.
A single old, wise, and majestic tree sits and
waits for the coming of the year.
A tiny, frivolous acorn floats lavishly, and gracefully down to the
black, rich, and nutrient possessing soil.
Defying gravity in the process.

Funny, this thing called time.

A minute ant searches endlessly for a morsel of food.
Among billions, is this ant any different?
Is it special?
Or does it fall in line with every other ant?

Funny, this thing called difference.

A mother waits excitedly and expectantly for the arrival of a child.
While an old man sits and waits to die.
A father asks his father for reassurance,
Which he can no longer give.
For he is to old and must finish what he has started.

Funny, this thing called life.
    Mark Walker

Milestones to Miracles

I thought my heart would leap out of
my chest just the other day, she took her
first 3 steps, what would have been a
milestone for some, became a miracle
for us, with each day that comes, I am
forever grateful. What is behind each
corner I do not know but, this I do know,
Just a year ago on a dark and starry
night, there came to me, the littlest angel
I have ever seen.
    At first, I did not know, nor could I foresee,
the happiness and inspiration this little girl angel
would bring to me. I did not know because I did not
see, the wings that carried this child to me. In
time, she came to have a rare cancer, and it all
seemed unbelievable but true. Fret not, this child's
will to live is so strong. Our life is so different
now, the journey so long but, if you stop to listen,
I think you will hear, the fluttering of those wings,
because I know, I know those wings are there.
    Shelly Lee West

Memories

My memories come rushing back,
My eyes are filled with tears.
Nothing can replace the loss of the one
you hold dear.
But when it comes time to say "Good-bye"
you are really not prepared,
So many things left unsaid,
So many things unshared.

My memories are all I have,
now that you are gone.
Your pain and suffering is over,
Now you must move on.

You are going to a place that we may one day see,
I'll have to say "Good-bye" now Grandma,
and in my heart you will always be.
I can't tell you how much I'll miss you,
but I'll always carry your memories with me.
    Lorrie A. Thomas

Parting Grace

Lord let me leave this world with grace
My eyes fixed firm upon your face
leaning on thy everlasting arms
that have kept me safe, secure, and warm.

I'd have no doubts or sorrow seen, by those who hold me in high esteem
Nor have the rock of faith I've long since taken
In death's hold, weaken, lost and shaken.

Yea, Lord, you've answered every prayer through life's joy and sorrow
I've felt you there; and when my last breath of life is drawn,
I won't be afraid, for I won't be alone.

So let me leave this world with grace
Eyes bright and a smile upon my face;
So those standing by, somehow will see,
The miracle of eternal life, begin in me.
    Marica Gahan

The Wall

The time has come to go to the wall.
My family and I stand proud and tall.
For those who came when our country did call;
With those in remembrance we stood at the wall.

Daddy ran his fingers along the wall,
and read the names of those brave and tall.
He stopped at a name, with a tear in his eye,
and put down a rose to remember it by.

He said, "This is the place where a great man died,
he fought for our freedom; died for our pride.
And when the time comes, in the midst of the year,
for our country, its people, for them shed a tear!

For someday in time
your country will call,
and you'll onward and fight
and remember the wall."

Molly Stanley

Middle School Woe

My stomach was rumbling,
My fears were great,
My old world was tumbling,
What would be my fate?

I walked in the school office,
Everything around I notice.
I drew my conclusion,
My whole life was a confusion.

I nervously watched the exchange of forms,
And realized, hey! This is the norm.
My Elementary School days are over.
Gosh! I miss them, but I am no quitter.

I am now a Middle school student,
And things are surely different.
Easy or hard, I intend to do my best,
And hopefully I can take care of the rest.

Sapna Beeram

Lucky, Lucky, Lucky Me

Some people always complain about how they feel.
"My finger hurts." Are they for real?
They should look around and try to see
How much worse off they really could be.

Many ever complain, though they can't hear or see.
By some twist of fate, it could have been you or me.
You say you can't run, but can walk anywhere.
What about those you are bedridden or need a wheelchair?

Some suffer so that it nearly drives then insane.
So, please try to bear it, your little finger pain.
Don't wait until you are ill before you pray
For good health to come back to you someday.

Look around. Look around. I beg you, please do.
There are millions who would love to trade places with you.
Compare your problems to others, and you will see
That you should be saying, "Lucky, lucky, lucky me!"

Max A. Hankin

"The Gift Of Life Is Love"

Love cannot be held in the palm of a hand.
Nor is love something that is carefully planned.
Love is a seed which springs into a flower.
Only God can explain love's real true power.
Yet love can be seen in the warm gentle rain
And in the birth of a child, when its mother is in pain.
Love is a smile; or a tender embrace.
Yes love has a home, yes love has a place.
Love fills our lives to make all a new,
with three simple words "I love you."

Russell Diener

"The Swing"

We sat on the swing,
My girl and I
The big, old, green one on the porch
One June day…
And as we sat…
Swinging… arms tightly around each other…
Sipping iced tea in the heat…
Watching cars go by in the street…
We sat there…absorbed in the day…
Very much in love…
Contented… for we knew
That Autumn's coming soon.

Matt Stefon

Our First Meeting

Shocked! I stand trembling inside,
my hands are wet it is too late to hide.
I spot you and you see me,
I am caught in a trap no time to flee.
I grin at you and you return one to me,
Surprise! It's a disguise don't your eyes see?
No I guess not for yours is too,
we both act happy yet we are both so blue.
So-long, farewell, I am leaving my stand,
no wave good-bye nor a shake of my hand.
This is our first meeting since we parted,
it left me uneasy and sad hearted.
I am glad in some ways that I ran across you,
although it hurt I needed it to.
It reminded me of a poem I know,
it says "If you love someone let them go."
And if by chance you shall knock on my door,
I won't mention the past for there is a future in store.
Or if by fate you are seen no more,
I will always remember our times before.

Yvonne Keys

Confused

I've come a long, long distance from the place I used to be
My heart, it is more open, my soul, it is more free
My mind it is much clearer, my will is getting strong
And yet I wonder deep inside, where do I belong?

I've kept a distance from the past
The future I control
And still I'm lost inside myself,
I have no where to go

Some people look straight at me and think I am so strong
"You help some with their problems, you help them carry on.
You show some how to look inside, you pick up on what's wrong."
To help it comes quite easy, for them my strength is there
For me I walk in circles, I cannot let them near

People only hurt you as they find your weakest spot
They tell you what you need to hear, then take all that you've got
I know this story all too well, too well to let them care
I think I belong inside myself
I think I'll just stay here

Kevin W. Kramer

Thoughts At Midnight

And I never really dream anymore,
My world's consumed by black or white.
And I never really dream anymore,
Someone tell me is this wrong or right.

And all the colored leaves have died and fallen,
I no longer hear the blue bird calling,
I find myself accepting our sin,
So I'm trying to sail but there's just no wind,

I'm trying to sail but there's just no wind.

Shana Moscatello

368

Denial

Who am I, I don't know
my life is hidden within your soul,
afraid to ask "I do not dare"
So I say, that I don't care.

You bore my life but truth you hide,
deprived of love with senseless lies
and sleepless nights with satan I share
with trembled fear, cry I don't care.

Who was he that gave me life
in your moment of bliss
then abandoned my love that I so desperately miss
I tell myself that I don't care.

From your womb I was rejected
In your arms felt so neglected
I sense your pain, but you won't share
but it's alright, cause I don't care.

Reflections in your eyes of me,
of who I am, who you think I ought to be
never reaching expectations but forever trying
with tears of despair I cry...."I don't care."

Patricia Earl-Dudley

My Only Love

As the days go by and the length we're apart gets longer
My love for you gets stronger and stronger
In more than words could ever say
My love for you will never die away
You hold a special key to my heart
That no one could ever tear apart
With your warm smile and tender kiss
It's no wonder that's what I miss
I hope to bring you many happy memories that will last for years
but I hope will never bring tears
Just seeing your gorgeous face
Makes my heart race
The best is yet to come and as the nights go by
I will be thinking of you my only love

Michelle Kulkey

The Man With A Mask

I am the man with a mask.
My mask protects me from the reality I fear,
it shields my eyes from that which I have seen.

My mask is a coat of armor;
my words are my weapons
securing this tender being.

My mask shows happiness and sadness,
but still, lost am I.

It was put in place during childhood,
to shield me from screams in the darkness
as I awoke from a deep sleep.
This mask I wore to battle as I opened that door,
and hid the fear
and the tears that fell inside.

Why did the ones I loved create this mask?
My eyes still close with fear as the child tries to sleep.
I'm still that child hiding, wishing to grow without a mask.

Terry P. Foreman

Escape

I am surrounded by people yet I am alone.
My mind is on yesterday and on days to come.
I battle to win but sometimes life makes no sense.
I want to give up, but that also makes no sense.
I'm drifting; the tide is high as well as low, I
dodge and I duck but I still get wet. My tears
are overflowing like the ocean. My stomach is upset.

I meditate for awhile, the ocean is calming, a bird
lands on my shoulder with sweet songs and happy tunes.
Everything is still. There's a rainbow in the distance
and butterflies are on the flowers, at this time, nothing
matters, I would like to stay here always but I know
that's impossible.
The sharp knife of reality will never go away but once
in a while I will escape.

Valencia Rhymer

Lonely

While sitting here with my pen in hand
My mind wanders to a mystical land
Where instead of plotting and scheming
I'm lying back and silently dreaming

I've traveled this land from near to far
Going by plane, train, truck and car
Meeting different people and thinking if only
I'd settled down I wouldn't feel so lonely

She who would accept what I offer of myself
And not to tuck me away like a book on a shelf
To meet someone special to share my life
Someone to call my friend, my lover, my wife

So on I go chasing those mystical dreams
Never to return to reality it seems
But again I awake and think how phony
A dream is a dream and I'm still lonely

Regan Jurkowski

Thanks

I was his wife
My name, half his, still labels me so.
Why am I here? Why do I stay?
I am cast out from the elite-
friends by marriage, not blood.
I do not belong.
But I stayed for my son
so he would know everyday parents, not weekend playmates
and have found my own place.
Those who survive hardships gain respect,
both of self and of others,
a new breed of homesteaders.
Wide windswept plains to the edge of the sky.
Land of few, but strong and proud.
Where rains are scarce, roots search deep.
Where winds whip fiercely, resiliency thrives.
Where grasses grow wildly, primroses emerge.
Maybe thanks are due him, this man who was mine
for freeing me to be of this land
for freeing me to be who I am.

Peggy Jo Mann

Just Think About It

Grow with changes.
Never stop living.
Take what you can, but keep on giving.
Don't stop at love, emotions shall go on.
Don't give up, give yourself a shove.
Reach for the top and remember never give up.

Trisha Lee Honto

Who Am I?

Who am I to you?
My name just words,
My thoughts come and go
Like friends who are only passers - by.

My life just part of history.
My death another pain.
My character and my traits, they are not mine.
My soul; my last free will to voice who I am and what only I can feel.

'Tis my jealousy, my fear, and my hate
That separate me from the monotonous
And indefatigable masses which
Surround us both who are quick to surmise.

Who am I to you?
That is something only you can answer.
For you alone see what you see,
Think what you think, hear what you hear.

Though you see me,
I see you.
In both our eyes
The sun shines through.

Tammy Baker

Treat Him Life A Friend:

The other day you had said gently,
"My nephew is staying with me!"
Mentioning it so very proudly.

I cannot remember exactly his name,
Except believing in his Uncle is the same.
An reflection of family and all that it brings,
Perhaps men discuss their untidy luck.
Or playing poker and going bust,
Knowing you Rick the way that I do,
None of these things have you decided to choose.
Instead giving him as artist pen,
And treat him like your best friend.

He might be so tenderly young,
And wanting to go out and have some fun.
But I think you're an influence by far,
A special way of showing that you care.

And to anyone, you attempt to always be there,
To share a friendly story from within your heart,
I say Rick, you seem to treat him as your friend.

Valda M. Vondall

Peri Nekrou Adelphou.... About A Dead Brother

There you are .....hovering....waiting to consume him...
my only brother of blood and bone.
And I can do nothing but watch ...and pray
as he slips compliantly into your somniatic clutches.

What? A twitch of the eyelid...perhaps an effort to elude you?
I think not...just a twitch...nothing more.

He slows...and slows...the gauges drop,
seventy five....
fifty-five.....
forty........
30/10 and......
he's yours.

Suddenly, the blood pounds in my veins...
and I see as through kaleidoscopes planted firmly in my eyes.

The eons of passings stored in my soul's memory all come into this
one moment....like the rush of a tornadic vortex, blasting and
screaming pain in my gut like no other....then all is quiet

Except for the damned respirator like an old clock:
Click...whee...click....wheeze.... (good-bye Kevin, I love you).

Mark E. Radeke

Through Out It All

God grace and mercy pick me up, when I would fall
My soul was dead, and never use my head, looking
for different resource instead

Neglect myself and had know respect, and at the time
had know regret, and never rest, in my mind I didn't
realize with my children how much I were bless, through
his grace he has given me another chance.

I am a save person today, His spirit is in me always
Morning noon or day I pray God! Please watch over
me through out the day, You will always be in my heart
to stay, His Holy Spirit feel so great.

Today I let go and let God, work it out and today
he has forgiven me for my sin, I can clap my hand,
Stump my feet, and sing and shout, cause he has
given me a clean heart, and all the love he will bring

I know his eye is on the sparrow and he watches
over you and me, you see his grace is amazing
remember when he open up the sea, and his people
were free, just come on and join us and believe
he will give you joy and peace like he did me.

Patricia Bush

Come Forth the Child in Me

Come forth the child in me,
my spirit wants to be free.

Life with its many chains tugs your very soul
until you grow old.

Trials and tribulations beckon me
to surrender to thee,

But the child in me
wants my spirit to be free.

Come without haste,
don't pause nor pace.

Let the child in me be free,
so that the spirit will teach thee.

Oh, what zest, Oh, what truth,
bathe me in thou glorious youth.

Don't crown me with your
sacred honors or dignity,

Help me refrain from the pitfalls
of time and my anatomy.

Come forth the child in me,
my spirit wants to be free.

Monette M. Graham

Battered Women's Nightmare

In the darkness he slips into my mind.
My heart trembles with fear, which was once love.
I feel his presence, though I can not envision him.
My breath becomes faint, as his hands grasp my neck.
He has found me weak and alone, but I am too
Strong to give in so easily.
I beg him to let me live my life.
Sunshine peers threw my window.
I awake.
Even in my dreams, he shall never
be the death of me.

Tessa Lenart

370

"I Am"

My heart is weightless..like the wind winging in flight
My step is nimble..like the flow of time

Sometimes warm embraces my being..clasps my hand
Encourages me to linger then hasten on

I am two people not one..daughter of Gemini
Poignant one moment..utterly ridiculous the next

Somber, desperately drawn and gray
Yet in an instant..exhilarated...gay

Changing...woman..girl or child
Sophisticate...inge'nue..infant

Mind consumed with many thoughts
Personality dwelling in the shell of facade...

Suppressing compulsion, cursing the grotesque
Tender..yielding..soaring away

Blessed that I be..to welcome each day
Ah..but could I change this tumultuous being...
Would be like eyes blind...without seeing.

Minna L. Kapinos

Dream Snatcher

Mother warned me about you, she said you'd do me in.
My teachers said embracing you was not the way to win.

I tried to keep away from you, I kept my nose so clean.
I grew up and I married, I held on to my dream.

We had two kids, a mortgage - our jobs from day to day;
The years went by, routine was set, I didn't see it go astray.

I blamed him for my anger, I felt lonely and neglected
If only I had been more wise; not left you undetected.

I never used you, even once, instead you took my friend
And now our life as man and wife has all come to an end.

Our world was just so perfect, I'd weaved the best dream catcher
You didn't care who's lives you wrecked
COCAINE, you're my dream snatcher.

Sandra Lea McDowell

The Search

I see God through my eyes, no others.
My view is not cluttered with visions of his great sacrifice.
No need to share his pain and death.
I need no other's definition or directions.
I don't need to be pushed, prodded or sent.
It doesn't matter how others have seen Him—I am not compelled
   to force my conclusions or the conclusions of others onto all—
   no need to bare my soul.
My vision goes deeper, my destination more serene, to a place
   that is peaceful, where constant praise and abstinence is
   not required; empty words leading only back to themselves.
I shun the hypocrisy of man's theology, eager to appear reluctant
   to stay—ever changing.
I should not have to prove my worthiness to others—I won't!
My story need not be told.
God does not require one certain mode of worship. In the end
In the end we all worship the same God and the differences are
   immaterial.
When we (God and I) meet—these petty human concerns will be
   redundant.
The years of searching for the "Truth"—the one answer, will be ever-
   gone without a clue left behind.
Replaced by the lasting knowledge that God is God; that I am
   what I was meant to be—a part of Him.
Together we are the Life, the Soul, and the Beauty of each other.

Kelly McArdle

From My Star

From under the stars as a formed human being, I wonder if
my visions are real. Contemplating nightly which star is mine
to ride, I concentrate until my soul jumps forward, sending a
tingling shock that kisses my emotions. Then there I sit, upon
my star. I observe my human form not knowing what to do without
me. Just laying there not knowing to even breath. From my star
I can see operating humans defying the use of their vehicle, not
even realizing they're out of control. From my star I can hear
little sound. Only the echo's of silence. From the earth I hear
mottled screams and lost plea's for help and the human beings
pay no attention. Hovering over the star next to mine I can
sense an angry soul wanting to not be angry. It spits on the
world then drops down to catch its madness sending a bomb
instead, of optimism and hope to the chosen potential hearts,
feeding them words to speak. Now it sleeps in peace on its
star, obviously confident it's chosen the right messengers. The
kiss comes to me again, as firm and as gentle as the first and
leaves me standing in human being form. Are my visions real?
I think so. And now I know, I am guided by eye's I will never
actually see.

Karen B. Thompson

Someday

Not so long ago or so it seems, I'd conjure up the wildest dreams
my wealth was grand and fame was mine but I hadn't reckoned
as yet with time.

The years slipped by quite slowly then and someday, I knew not when
I'd blaze a trail or conquer space I'd set the world a merry pace.

But soon the years more quickly passed and still I had my die to cast
procrastinate no more I vowed with deep concern and wrinkled brow.

And now the years were in a race and I no longer could give chase
my husbands needs I must fulfill and children's voices sometimes shrill
called Mommy that and Mommy this but always paid me with a kiss.

My legacy is not in coin nor history's greats will I join
my fortune now is number seven four girls three boys direct from
   heaven
a good man's faith and lasting love God's guidance sent from up above.

It's true I've never ventured on nor silks and satins do I don
but if sometimes I feel remorse for never charting my dreamers course
my abundant blessings I do list and I know for certain...
I've been blessed.

Helen Sue Sleight

"Alone"

Farther into the darkness of my mind I go, blackness swallowing me.
Narrow angry paths filled with treachery, deadfalls and imperilments.
The denseness confines my thoughts, a prisoner of the dammed.
There is no escape, vicious condemnations snare me, hold me down.
Cursed brambles rip at my tender being, wounded, lost.
Deeper into the pits of hell I fall, fear weeps from each pore.
A cold evilness confines me, I struggle to be free, no escape.
My screams are strangled by the hand of suffering and pain.
Silent tears cannot wash away the loneliness in my soul.
Alone in despair the cruel reality of life crushes and destroys me.
The brutal blackness of my existence smothers the spark of hope.
Lost, deserted and helpless in the forest of life's iniquities.
Besieged by hate, defenseless of the wicked, murdered by fate,
lost forever.

Michele Saddlemire

371

You're An Angel

Every female born becomes a woman -
naturally but not every woman is an
Angel. But you have mastered the art
of beauty that radiates forever in my
heart. Even if Heaven does have scholars
you'd have to be at the head of the
class. You're God's gift to the world!
But gifts to me are not like gifts are
to the world, here today gone tomorrow.
Diamonds and jewels are not gifts but
excuses for gifts. A true gift is a
portion of love. But it's not what you
give me that determines the relationship,
but what you are willing to give me
that determines the relationship and the
quality of love. Love does not consist
of gazing at each other but looking
outward towards the same direction.

Kevin Rainey

Thought For The 90's

How did we get here?
  Neighbor against neighbor
  Son against daughter
  Child against child
  With no love to speak of and no love to give
  Why do we wander from country to country
  Solving all problems except where we live.
Time was we could count on our neighbors
Our leaders our children to be our allies.
God grant us the power
To swing back the pendulum
To sweep away meanness and hate
From our lives.

Sara Eaves

Killer In The Mist

Traveling roads under misty sky,
Never asking the reasons why.
Autumn winds carry wolves' cries.
Killer in the mist who lives with lies.
In shadow night, a candle the only light.
A knife blade gleaming in his hand.
Messages of fear transcends the land.
The burdened child beneath clothes and knife
battles rage within for love and life.
Knowing no fear except his own;
A killer with scars and hate full grown.
Systematic pain molding insanity and despair.
Animosity striking out with knife to bear.

Love the child so damaged inside, without care.
Never to step from darkness; wandering endless fate.
Another victim to hate.
When victims fall, all is too late...
For life disintegrates and time can't wait.
Blood staining earth in mist and rain...
The man-child has discarded reality and pain.

Richard S. Bossone

Jesus Christ The Inspiration Of My Life

I love you,
Not just for the things you do.
I love you with all may heart.
I pray that I will never part.
You died for me
To set me free,
That I will be with you to
eternity.
I thank you for your special grace,
That I will be with you in that special place.

Rita Jean Krupa Falco

The Sea That Courses Everywhere

The sea that courses everywhere, nowhere,
never flows the same way again.
Always going a different way
Upon the planet it commands.

The beauty appears anywhere.
Although not always seen,
It is always there.

The dimness of forever travels the tides
of the universe.
Some, dry as dust; others flood the stars.

Trying to enter: step
barefoot, naked into the shards of its reality.
And a new knowledge of Truth is born.

Morgan Herman Steckler

Soul Murder

There were no clues left behind
No fingertips, bloodstains, or weapons to be found.
No body to be found without a heartbeat
Just without a heart.
No unconscious, lifeless body
Just a self injurious one.
No one noticed the ghastly, ghostly, Emptiness.
No one imagined a murderer about.
No corpse, no murder.

He died a thousand slowed deaths
at the hands of loved ones.
He silently slipped away
early on before a solid body being could be killed.
A sort of life long hibernation
traveling incognito to himself and others.

As his disguise wore thin from effort and age
He sought refuge and the fantasy of recovery.
The illness swept through him
like a maid sweeping dust from under the bed.
Healing is such dirty work.

Kit Erskine

The Bridge

He came home to America from a war they did not win,
No marching bands with flags unfurled did greet this tired Marine;
Just taunting words or looks of hate...there was no welcome to be seen.
Neither pity nor help did he seek or want
Simply to forget - to start again - could this be so wrong?
Surely somewhere inside his hard, cold soul
Remained a spark, an ember just waiting to be burned.
Oh what would it take to help him begin, his dead soul did cry
and yearn?

She offered her hand and took the time to listen
As he spoke of lost men and hopeless missions.
Together they sought not answers or reasons
But searched for hope...a start of a new season.
Only love and understanding can build a bridge
That takes us across dark valleys or over a steep ridge;
Hand in hand they walk each day and face the future unafraid,
Having worked through all the pain, forever together they will remain.

Marcia J. Sturgis

All Alone

In this world we are all alone.
No one to talk to. No one to love.
You had a love you thought was true.
But now you wait for that love to leave you.
You feel all alone.

You go home hoping to find a friend you can call your own.
But when you get there; you find no one who cares.
You are all alone.

You never knew what love was until you met him.
And now your life is full of hope.
But your one true love turns and abuses you.
You wish you were all alone.

You try to be strong but you have to come to realize.
That the only thing keeping you alive.
Is the hope that someday you can have peace of mind.
Then the thought occurs to you.
The place to find love and peace is right in front of you.
You say hello my one true friend.
Now I will never be alone again.
Thank you for allowing me to come home again.

Monica Crosby

The Mourning Dress

Today there is no faltering in choosing what to wear.
No questioning of what will go with what.
It has to be the navy dress, black slip, dark hose, black shoes:
These are my clothes for saying last goodbyes.

It hangs between the business suits and dresses for the night
Among the formal clothes my life requires.
It wasn't there a year ago - it's pushed some others out,
Replacing shirts with stains from baby years.

It's ready to be worn. It's hanging clean and neatly pressed
Just as it was when put away before.
It fits me still, no tighter nor more loose than the last time.
It slips right on and with it comes old griefs:

A frigid day in winter, with the snow piled high around,
The loss again today makes me recall -
The emptiness of absence and the ache of silent need:
We mourn for living as we do for death.

It's over now and I must put it back for the next time:
The buttonhole is torn and needs repair.
The fragile, silky fabric has been frayed but it will mend
Much sooner than the fabric of my heart.

Tamara Gilman

The Coming Of The Night

Black, black was the night
No stars, no moon, to shed their light
Hope, man's everlasting panacea, no more
Gone, gone with the coming of the night
How dare hope linger here
When nothing left, but unquestionable fear
Still wait, is that a light
Or is it just my unearthly fright
No, that cannot be, though I can barely see
It's dark, but surely that is a speck of light
Fighting, fighting, to show its might
Through all the darkness of the night
Man's strength and God's might
Will surely shed this world from all its fright
To displace darkness with radiant light
So we can live in peace, where there will be no night.

Lloyd E. Klatt

Barren Garden

Her garden is barren
No sweet love grows there
No love grows... at all.
There are only memories buried under the starving soil
But no love grows
She has planted so many beautiful seeds
Seeds of silver-eyed exotics, warm mediterranean browns,
and seeds of green-eyed passion-flowers
She planted each and every seed with care and tenderness
She nurtured every seed with adoration and kindness and warmth
She protected every seed from bad weather and bad temper
From selfishness and cruelty
And yet—every single seed that produced a magnificent sparkling bud
DIED...just moments later
Leaving her with only memories buried under starving soil
And a garden where no love grows
And though she waters it constantly with her very own loving tears
Still, no love grows
And the soil writhes in never-ending pain

Tina Fogel

Everlasting Love

A love so strong it could not be forsaken,
None could count the weight of it but the
    two whom it overpowered,
Separation only pulling them closer,
Causing the bonds to become even
    stronger through the distance.
Braving the severest of conditions to be together,
Leaving hearth and home for the sake of love's magnitude.
Forty seven years, a lifetime together,
Hoping, planning, dreaming, working,
    supporting and always loving.
This love cannot be lessened by temporary separation.
It's something that transcends both time and eternity,
With its strength, power, and bond.
And when, at last, it is reunited in the
    presence of the One who authored it.
It shall be even more glorious than all of
    earths greatest imaginings.
Until that time, the Love that first knit those
bonds shall strengthen and sustain.

Patricia E. Haney

We Will Never Forget

We will never forget your laughter,
    nor the Merriment within your eyes.
We will never forget your open arms,
    patting our backs, as we all cried.

We all knew someday you would leave us,
    there was nothing anyone could do.
"But Lord", we were never ready,
    the day she went home to be with you.

How do we say how much we Miss her?
    How do we say, how much we Care?
She taught us the true value of living,
    Love is Precious, so always share.

Our Hearts, have never mended,
    Our Tears, have never dried.
Her Love will always be with us,
    Her Cherished Memory is deep inside.

Thank you God, for the time we had,
    Someday Cancer might have a cure.
Throughout her illness she taught us Love,
    it's just not the same without her.

Melanie J. Hatz

Thinking Of You

It is so sad that we are apart,
not a moment has passed by
without thinking of you.
Now I have someone new.
But when I am kissing her,
I am thinking of you, and
when I am holding her,
I am thinking of you.
Even when I am making love to her
I am thinking of you.
Why should I lie to myself,
I am still in love with you!
It is so crazy, I can't get you out of my mind,
from the moment I open my eyes
until the moment I go to sleep.
Funny how, when we were together I couldn't wait
for the minute to get you out of my life,
and now I am paying the price.
I will love you all of my life,
because I am always thinking of you.

    Mahdi A. Shaheen

"Silence"

There's a silence, oh so silent
not even the keenest ear can hear
yet there's no reason to fear
to me the silence is completely clear
it concerns you and me my dear

It's like sailing on a calm sea
it's like retrieving a lost kite from a tree
It's like a slave being set free
it's peace, it's harmony

It's sunshine, with some rain
It's joy, with less pain
it's ice, melting from the heat
it's me, loving you and feeling
so complete...

    Phyllis L. Mason

Can You Remember WHY I'm Saying This?

I know you love me for who I am,
Not for what I try to be,
I want to return your love,
But I'm trapped in a whirlpool of confusion.
Will I ever return your love?
I only wish I could.
You try to make me understand,
I just tell you I don't want to hear it,
You always seem to continue to talk,
But never listen to me.
You say you love me,
I somehow always run away with my tail between my legs.
Is it because I'm afraid of what will happen next?
I know I'm not afraid of you it can't be,
Because it's like you say,
I love you.

    Robin Domanski

In Appreciation

Outside my kitchen window I often gaze
Not only at the foliage all ablaze,
But also the squirrels running along the stone wall,
While gathering food for storage in the fall.

Pitying them scurrying in the woods and fields,
I help by supplying them food for their winter meals.
Supplying food for the squirrels and their mates
Helps to sustain them in winter as they hibernate.

One morning on a bright day in spring,
I saw a pair of red squirrels proudly bring
Their three baby squirrels to my attention,
Marching proudly, but void of arrogance and pretension.

Oh! how great it would be if we could learn
From these little animals a like concern
For those who lend us a helping hand
By showing appreciation whenever we can!

    Modine G. Schramm

Silent Tears

What do I do with this tear in the palm of my hand
Not shared by my parents who perhaps could understand
Not spoken to friends for a burden to bare
Not given to teachers, neighbors who really could care
What to do with this tear in the palm of my hand.

What to do with this hurt in the core of my heart
Not wanted by me from the very start
Not given a chance by those concerned
Not understood, by any, the causes of the unshown burn
What to do with this hurt in the core of my heart.

What to do with this anger that now seems to surge
Not controlled by need of acceptance to merge
Not noticed by those as I quietly hide
Not touched by any as I silently cry
What to do with this anger that now seems to surge.

Help me someone to wipe this tear from the palm of my hand
Help me someone... parent, friend or teacher to understand
Hug my heart with a smile that you promise to always land
Diminish this anger so that I can survive
Just long enough to wipe this tear from the palm of my hand.

    Vera M. Dodelin

Chasm

I have left you, my darling. You hold a shell
Not the heart and soul of me that dreams and feels
And yearns to share. The me you cannot see
   And could not understand.

I have left you, my darling. The inner me
That laid my hidden bits and pieces at your feet
Like precious jewels. Whose lustre you did not see
   And did not understand.

I have left you, my darling. I tried not to;
I reached out so often, my soul crying for a mate,
My heart bared and wounded. Trying to make you see,
   Trying to make you understand.

I have left you, my darling. Gathered my jewels
Now so dull and worthless. Stifled my plaintive cry,
Bound my broken heart. Sadly, you still do not see;
   Perplexed you cry, "I don't understand!"

    Lucille Ann Green

Wailing

I use the same trusty tie, time after time,
not too long or short.
The weapon round and straight,
the point sharp and short.
I see the raised round form pulsing
just below the surface.
The hollow tip strikes true.
Blood wells up in a swirling stream,
mingling with fluids external
only to be plunged back into the wound once again.

The sound of waves beat upon my eardrums
from the inside.
My mouth is sucked dry,
breath shallow, heart surges.
The concussion past,
I sit and wait
to do it all over, again.

Phil O'Donnell

The Golden Years

Here I sit in my old rocking chair.
Nothing to do but sit and stare,
The golden years are for the birds,
Cause I even have trouble making turds,
They tell me chin up, head high,
You can do it if you only try,
Only do what? Sit in a chair,
Look at the walls and wish I wasn't there,
The years went by way too fast
I'm tired of sitting on my ass,
With all kinds of aches and pains and gas,
My only hope is that it soon will pass,
And I'll be free,
Yes free at last,
With time left yet to enjoy the years,
Yes the golden years with all my tears,
And through it all I'll have to say,
I must only live from day to day.

Theodore A. Blumenberg

The Cross

Take a look at the cross -
Now this is the way, not to be lost.
The cross has a special meaning to us;
GOD'S word was there for us to trust!
Jesus was there on that cross you see?
GOD'S answer for sinners like you and me.

Looking at the cross I see there,
Jesus showing His promise He really did care.
The cross also shows a lot of love to see -
His promise to man that eternal life can be free.
GOD will not let our souls be lost;
That's why Jesus died on that cross.

So when temptation tries to prevail,
You can look at the cross and your faith will not fail.
You can live free from fear and doubt.
Because you truly know, what the cross is all about.

When you look at the cross you must confess;
Jesus gave so much love that He is the best!
Be glad you have that cross in mind,
It will keep you rich in GOD'S love all the time.

Vernon Traverse

JKO

These words hope to speak reams in reverence.
Of a life often secret, passed today.
This private, not public, Today's Mother
with vigilance, stoic love
Shades of Grey.

Candle galas, stately dinners, White House days.
Kremlin visits, Cuban crisis, Cape Cod waves.
Quiet scandal, whispered rumors, starlets pay.
Always beaming, dry eyes streaming
Shades of Grey.

Early Sixties, TV trauma, horrid way.
Backward boots, idled motors, horse's neigh.
Black laced faces, lives in tow, curbside pain.
The wife, Today's Mother
Shades of Grey.

The last days of an icon, So special.
The last act of a king's classic play.
If Camelot be her canvas of living
then the pallet's surely swirled
Shades of Grey.

Thomas Botelho

Shadow Dancers

Shadows rendezvous by glowing flames
Of a white hot fire: A secret tete-A-tete.
Two silhouettes against the starlit night
Bow and curtsy in mutual respect.
Whispered words, low and sweet, echo,
 "Shall we dance?"
Two bodies come together, swaying in time
With ancient music, full of mystic rhyme.
Slow and sensual, tenderness in every line.
Joining in eternal love, becoming one.
Lost souls, found in the beauty of velvet darkness.
Locked in a lovers' embrace for all time.

Suphrina L. Bowers

Matthew

Yahweh is the source behind the glamour
of a young, black male born in Alabama,
He stimulates, renovates, and generates
Power to my soul that man cannot duplicate.

Fanatical, Magical, A Creative Radical
I love the West, I enjoy the Nation's Capital,
That's where the laws are made to govern all people,
But my mind is a weapon, I consider it lethal.

Thank Jehovah for the gifts he's given me, my friend,
Thank Jehovah-Jireh for the trouble I haven't been in,
Thank God for making Matthew a living soul,
Thank Him for what he's done for me to make me whole.

Ambitious, Aggressive, Bold, and Fearless
My love for life makes me an absolute realist,
Perfectionist, Militant, Protagonist, Activist,
There are so many words to categorize this.

My goal in life is to be a great geneticist
It's really awesome to study how the human body ticks!
Oh yes, I have faith, hope, love, these three,
For it's Jehovah-Shalom who EMPOWERS ME.

Matthew Bonner

Somewhere In Time

Entombed by winter's cold revenge
of charcoal skies and endless snowflakes,
I long for springtime, flowers, birds,
and you to warm my shivering heart.

Speak to me of forest-green brooks, pasqueflowers,
and the quickening of heartbeat and pulse
we once shared kissing on busy streets,
behind store-front pillars of passion.

Firelog embers cool and winter darkness descends.
I retreat to the rippling pond of fantasies,
where the joy of springtime and the memory of you
eases the chill of windowpane frost.

I wait; trapped between space belonging to death
and rebirth, heartbreak and happiness, hoping
somewhere in time, I will again know
the fragrance of lilac, the touch of your hand.

Kay Price

Lines From Africa.....

You talk of the new-born crocus
Of daffodils grown fat in their shifts,
Of a world invaded by spring and
Heady with its beauty
You speak an alien tongue.

For a moment - like so much light from a falling star -
You warmed me with memories of the sun
Waking a frozen world from winter's hibernation,
And the smell of the wet, cold earth
Beginning to grow once more.

I yearn for another season:
The sudden, breath-stopping fury of the wind -
In a vigilante search for the first rain -
Angry thunder cries echoing
Against closed windows of the sky.

A flaming torch of lightening flung toward cloud-mountains,
Streaking back to earth again.
Below, the sea runs black and trembling
With fear a froth of white at its mouth.

Shirley R. Shirley

Untitled

The brittle lifelessness
of leaves fallen from the tree.
Their brilliant colors sucked out of them,
leaving the bleak, dull brown,
as cold as the dead, stiff dirt on which they lay.
With no breath of their own,
The cruel wind shaves them to yet another destiny.
A rumble in the distance
Approaching
Louder
The wheels of the truck snap the frail bones
with hollow cracks.
Yet they can not cry out
and the shattered fragments
of the once festive garment of the tree
drift on the pavement.

Sarah Mackey

Last Respects

If we are to go on dying, then why not these men
Of painted honor grant, us merely the ways of human decency

In their streams of laughter, and steady waves of bloodshed
I, nor no man has heard, the murmurings of compassion

Before we are blown through their hell
or burnt in their indifference
May each of our frightened souls
Find empty solace in their certain demise
At the hands of their own wicked lies

So if our humane tears do nothing more
Than to confuse our blood-soaked faces
May they one noble day see,
In our countless names, weeping traces
Of their own fading mortality, and the plight of privileged power
And cast to sorrow no more the fragile youth to die
in the midst of their feuding hour.

Ronan C. O'Malley

The Door Was Always Open

If I could speak I would tell you now
Of tales from menacing streets as I roamed,
Mysteries cloaked in still shades of darkness,

Of lazy playful days in the sun
Butterflies in the breeze, raindrops
Honeysuckle in the morning, and love

And though I returned to you often,
My heart and body broken by adventures taken
Or lessons not so easily earned,

The door was always open

Arms were there to help me
When my willful ways threw fate to chance,
And my spirit filled with folly took to wondering
Of mysteries, yet untold

The door was always open

Neither man nor beast could ask more
Than to live and die in the arms of souls,
Who love enough, to set them free

And the door was always open for me

Priscilla Sands

Empty Hourglass

I find myself counting the days slowly gone by
Of that my soul is so alone and how many the reasons why
An attempt to make things right
When they were wrong from the beginning
Forever I beg it not be long
But time keeps on spending — I look at love
Through other eyes it's never seen by my own
I feel love with each beat of my heart
Still lonelier is all I've grown — I dread the dark sky
That surround the bright moons
During each night that lasts forever
To remind me instead of to find me
A love to be together I search my soul
To find a reason or justification for my plight
While I swing my arms at the voice in my head
Still alone I lose the fight — Where is my other
To be with me to remove my hurt inside, by the time my love
Comes for me I pray I'm still alive — for someone new to
Come into this world of peace within me and share our lives
Rich in love through the sands of eternity

MacArthur Nelson, Jr.

Untitled

To write a poem is to tell a tale
of when I win or when I fail.
Sometimes it's full of heart and passion
I write it down for some satisfaction
because when he read it, it looks more true
It's like learning something I already knew
a feeling I had but could never admit.
At first it was shameful but now feels legit.
I write a poem to define my feeling
and it helps to give me a sense of healing.
So poetry is not only riddles or rhymes
but a palate of feelings and one of
  my favorite pastimes.

Stacey Oliger

Fatigue

He just got tired of being black,
of white folks whispering 'hind his back,
of watching faces dressed with glee,
dismissing all the black in...
He just got tired of smiling smiles,
of grinning grins and hiding tears
that damped his soul in childhood years
and turned his spirit all to mush.
He just got tired, poor fool, got whipped,
so beaten,
he was bound to slip;
and slip, he did—
he came down hard,
Pow! Pow!
Right in his neighbor's yard.
He fell, and falling smiled his last
and closed his eyes upon his past.

Warren Brown

A Momma Who Hurts For Love

I know someone who is quiet and very shy-
off in another world in Dreamland, up so high.
She doesn't have a lot of money, jewelry or clothes-
but she's the richest person, that I'll ever know.

She worries, wonders and frets a lot-
and forgets about all the things she's got.
She gets depressed and cuts herself down-
especially, when there's nobody around.

She is a momma, so she has the right-
to question her future, by day and by night
She has 5 good reasons, that will tell her one day-
how much she means to them, but didn't know how to say:

"We love you Momma, and we care-
Because day and night you're always there."

Roberta Graham

Silence

The day we separated and said good-bye
Numerous tears fell from colored eyes
The soft colors soon turned to a seemingly gray
With the endless flow of tears, I looked away
Knowing this was my last chance to look at you
The best qualities came out, through and through
It's hard to even imagine us apart
With these deep emotions of pain we hold in our heart
But just knowing we'll be united soon one day
All the pain and anger will slowly drift away
And with that last silent glance,
You said good-bye to me.

Stefanie Bennett

Bovine Reaction

Many of times the tracks they have failed,
Often the trains they have been derailed,
But none shall forget the night of the Chessie,
When the engine of the cat made a crash that was messy,
A dark form ahead - breaks thrown - jumped the track,
Screeching to say that the train won't be back,
It fell off the bridge onto a barge,
The hot twisted metal profoundly took charge,
On impact the captain had been thrown to the shore,
His ship floated away with him watching in horror,
It hit the dam at a speed so fast,
It burst the wall with a crash and a blast,
The water came down and rushed through the dirt,
Mixing up mud in a torrent sent down to hurt,
It shorted the wires of an electrical plant,
The generator exploded I'd describe but I can't,
The ball of fire went up - fell on the mud and it glowed,
Electricity ran through a farm a humble abode,
It killed among others a heifer not in its stall,
The cow the Chessie almost hit which had started it all.

Richard O'Donnell

Untitled

I cannot believe we will meet once again
Oh, ancient well of knowledge.
The memories we've shared run through my
blood-full veins every time the clock ticks
in the garden across the Parthenon.
You could never be erased, nor remain a cloudy shadow
in the dusk for your heavens are too enormous;
they cross the sun-drenched horizon calling
my name in nostalgia, and awaiting my presence.

Without me, I was told the flowers do not blossom in the
courtyards, and the fruit does not ripen. I was meant to
step on your land a million times. My beauty reflects upon
the beauty of your faces; it takes on a worldly shape of
personalities. My fierceness comes from you my Spartan
brothers and my wisdom comes from you - Oh, Goddess Athena.
Aphrodite is yet unreached, for her beauty blinds the soul
too deep. So, I await the time of our osmosis, yet it may
seem so far away - As long as you remain my deeply embedded
roots, the days will flash and I'll appear to give
never-ending life to all of nature throughout the year.

Olga Stefaneas

A Young Boys Outing

Spring rains come down and fill the river with rotted clay brown.
Oh majestic river, splashing and waving back...
  Trying so hard to hold onto its sandy bottom that it lacks.

Blue river, sometimes green or brown...
  Depending on what ground you stand.

My river, that trees stand so damned grand...
  Where stone and rock, yes even boulders have failed...
  Then its banks become impaled.

It now can cross...lands green and so supreme...
Full of sun, as so many children's dreams go and come.

River gold and blue, ice your armor will soon form,
  inching down to depths where fishes swarm.

Soon river your waters will swell, and rid us this day's outing...
  that we've yearned for so long, over each winter's storm.

Rains do come down and make little boys frown, now it's time to go
  back into town, so we all do not drown.

Yes river, we will come again to spend time by your bank.
  So until we all see you that coming day...may I just say,
    thank you anyway.

Paul G. Damien

God's Great Love

God in heaven, all around,
oh, what miracles abound.
In thy peaceful place above,
hear our prayers, receive much love.
Jesus evermore our shepherd
lead us where we ought to go,
fills us with thy awe of wonder
nurtures us with lasting love.
Oh, we of little faith
Oft get caught up in self
forgetting the teachings of thy Holy words,
"LOVE THY NEIGHBOR AS THYSELF."
How ungrateful we are at times
when all seems lost,
forgetting, we need but put
our problems in the hands of God,
whose love is blinding.

Marolyn E. Baker

"Coal Miner"

Yesterday is not like today. Yesterday I saw an
old diner by the bus stop, where there were coal
miners dining, up the road I saw a fire burning.
To watch the slate dump burning, would get
your heart and mind to think. Down the row's of
Company houses and the Company store all lived
up on the hill together, also one little church
out there alone waiting to hear good new's
about Jesus. Most miner's pay day to pay
day at the Company store, using the script
coins for food and misc. items, the Company doctor
up there doing all he could for the coal miner's
and their families. No refrigerator. Maybe one
where someone cared to share the ice with the other families.

Ramona E. Hamric

La Espanola

She goes to the street
on a Saturday night....

Golden cross displayed ever so nicely
between her firm and half exposed breasts.

And the black leather and Spandex
announce her piety....

After ten beers and vino fino
she sits hidden in a dark corner
and pleads her love to a companion

And at one o'clock in the morning
she cries into her pillow......

While her father snores peacefully in the next room.

Will Cordero

Silence

The day we separated and said good-bye
Numerous tears fell from colored eyes
The soft colors soon turned to a seemingly gray
With the endless flow of tears, I looked away
Knowing this was my last chance to look at you
The best qualities came out, through and through
It's hard to even imagine us apart
With these deep emotions of pain we hold in our heart
But just knowing we'll be united soon one day
All the pain and anger will slowly drift away
And with that last silent glance,
You said good-bye to me.

Stefanie Bennett

God Sent Bluebirds That Spring

The Bluebirds came out of the west;
On a Westwind, He sent them, His best.
He sent them that spring.

Pa put up Bluebird houses and waited;
He said they would come as time was dated.
He said they would come that spring.

You see, Bluebirds were nearly extinct;
But, sure enough, they came in blue, distinct.
Azure, feeding and mating that spring.

God sent the Bluebirds for Pa's delight,
You see, he was ill, a dying light.
His faith said they would come that spring.

God sent them, Pa's last spring, that spring;
You see, Pa had an omen that spring.
God sent heralds, His sweet Bluebirds, that spring.

Preston L. Jackson, Sr.

Renewal

My troubled spirit sought for rest.
On city streets I found it not -
And so, I walked alone amid
    the stars and desert flowers.
The sky dipped down and stars
    and flowers and sky were mixed
    together. As I became accustomed
    to the night, and moonlight increased,
Horizons slowly lengthened and the
    silhouette of distant mountain peaks
    brought rest and soothing comfort
    to my heart.

"I will lift up mine eyes into the hills..."
How meaningful tonight the Psalmist's words.
I slowly shed the day's frenetic cares —
My Being merged with night and stars and sky
    and space and all infinity.
As I reached out, deep peace embraced
    my soul, and my Spirit, now unfettered,
Found true rest.

Laverne Rupert

"Smile"

If you really want revenge,
On someone you dislike,
Stand up straight and smile wide,
Don't ever look uptight.
Those around will fret and scowl,
And constantly complain,
All because you stood up straight,
And smiled all the same.
A smile can be sad, or it can be inviting.
It can represent sarcasm,
Or make something exciting.
It can tell someone "I love you,"
Or can show someone you care.
It may bring a tear of joy,
Or wipe away a fear.
A smile is always powerful,
And its meaning is rarely the same
Meanwhile, if seeking revenge,
It can drive somebody insane!

Shari Bierce

A Little Child Shall Lead Them

The large beautiful church, was crowded with well dressed people.
On that sunday morning, when the man with ragged clothes walked in.
He looked around with sad apologetic eyes, as some moved away
   from him.
His worn out shoes were hanging, by strings tied around his feet.
Then suddenly a small hand was placed in his, and he heard a
   voice so sweet

He turned and looked at the small girl standing there, a sweet
   smile upon her face.
Welcome to our church sir, you know this is Gods very own place.
Most of the congregation looked ashamed and sorry, as they
   began to sing.
When suddenly a beautiful, clear voice rang out, that made the
   rafters ring.

They looked around in amazement, but the old ragged man was
   no longer there.
In his place stood an angel, in shining white robes, a halo around
   his hair
The little girl with a smile of joy and love, was still holding the
   strangers hand.
Suddenly such joy and peace filled the church, at last they could
   all understand.
   ,,Our Lords words,, and a little child shall lead them...
     Linda Maxwell

Daydream

I thought of you again today
   On the city's crowded street,
And how it would be
   If by chance we should meet.
You would suggest we have coffee
   Just for old times sake,
I would ask about your family
   You would inquire about my mate.
While we quietly sipped our coffee,
   You placed your hand on mine
And I knew without a doubt
   Our love had endured the passage of time.
"I must go!", I say and jump quickly to my feet.
   Then looking back, I wave farewell
To you, my love, on the city's crowded street.
     Margaret Hardy

Reunion

They stand, the long-necked birds,
on upthrust rocks of the sea,
their legs reed-like and strong.
They face into the wind.

We too, although we are splintered
and worn-away like the stones,
face windward and look out to sea.

Oh to shed the years like water off the dark birds' wings-
I would touch your dear scarred face and
together we would bring to life what used to be.

There is a tide pool there,
deep and rich with plankton,
the sea grass waving at its edge.

See how the cormorants rise, soar, and dive
from a height beyond our reach.
     Lydia Priest

A Solstice Prayer

Turning thrice and thrice around
once left, once right, once up, once down,
bent knee to embrace the earth,
for she is the mother of your birth.
The oceans her water spent,
your life from her is lent,
from her soils flesh and blood,
though to her it is only mud.
In her eyes 'tis all the same,
at death, you return from whence you came.
Yesterdays hopes and dreams of power,
find revelation in tomorrow's flower,
and even heroes fame is lost,
in a new generations coming frost.
If you would strive to understand this verse,
and ignorance and pain you have cause to curse,
then journey to the fairy mound,
and circle thrice and thrice around,
and gain the key to immortality.
     Roxanne Horton

The Grand Exit Ball

"Oh, what will you wear to the Grand Exit Ball?"
One bright green leaf asked of another this fall,
"I'm weary of wearing this same emerald hue.
Don't you think that a more daring color would do?"

I guess I will wear my dazzling new gold,
It seems more the style now the weather's grown cold.
What you wonder, I'll bet, is "What will it cost?"
Well, the answer will be, "Just a kiss from Jack Frost!"

"You would look gorgeous in red tinged with wine,
The attention you'd get from the grapes on the vine!
While your sister I think would in orange be stunning,
Or wouldn't a crisp shade of bronze be just cunning?"

"Let us dress in our best for the Grand Exit Ball
And make now a lasting impression on all.
For this, the most colorful dance of the year
I wish all the leaves in the world could be here!"

She came whirling and twirling around in the breeze,
Then glided on tiptoe down under the trees.
And to her delight when she looked all around
Every sister in sight took the same way down.
     Thora Snow Hankins

My Side

My side is full of violence and cruelty
One side is full of love and compassion

My side is full of guns and hate
One side is with people who share and shake

My side never used their mind or heart
One side is like the love on Noah's ark

That side has a right to have a chance
This side had the right to remain silent

Some sides can't see each other at all
It's flooded with these big big walls

So if you come down to my side one day
You might think it's happy and gay

My side won't join with that side at all
Because it's flooded with those big big walls
My side
     Vanessa Sharie Jefferson

Sunshine

A gloomy period, had entered my life,
one that filled every day, with constant, bitter, strife,
stainless steel tinmen, know them very well,
looking at each day, as a walk through hell!!

The blood, the sweat, the tears I have shed,
my body in hard pain, wishing at times to be dead,
I looked up from the wall and into your eyes,
God at that moment, sent me, a sunshine surprise!

There is an aura, that I sense around you,
Like a heavenly shade, of lite turquoise blue
The soft, tender smile, when looking at me
the jokes, the hugs, when you hold me so gently.

Your dainty, soft hands, when touching mine,
sends a deep buried glow, right down my spine.
I start stammering acting just like a kid,
To keep my true feelings for you, well hid.

Yes Daria, God smiled down on me that day,
Said, "Nick; stop! Today won't be all gray
God brings me work to help tow that line,
But six days a week, honey, brings you, sunshine!

Nick Bogdanovs

A Wonderful Friend

God made very few people like you
One who would do whatever they could to
Make a visit mean so much
And warm a person with just a touch.
I don't know what I would have done
If you had not been the one
To help me out with all I had to do
God made one wonderful friend when God made you.

B. M. Mazzarella

The Land Beneath The Mountain

The sun was shining, yet none were awake.
Only me and the mountain, I was scared,
and I started to shake.
As I touched the icy surface,
Shivering nervously as I did,
I wondered if I could do it,
After all, I was just a kid.
With all the might and courage,
that was left in me.
I started to climb and be all I could be.
I looked up, and I saw a new world,
I was no longer just a scared little girl.
Now, there I was at the top,
looking at the land beneath me.
The world seemed so special,
there wasn't anything I couldn't see.
There was love, joy, and happiness,
Every night and everyday.
I want the world to be, like this.
This is how to world should stay.

Sarah Sanghavi

Cubist Art

I sit on a chair in a box. A cube. Six walls.
One is distinguished by its in-out waving wood.
Another lies buried beneath a shroud of tortured nap.
A third is crossed by a welded weave of windows to ceiling space.
The rest cry for individuality.
They beg for the burden of picture frames,
that they too may imprison art
so as to please me in my captivity.

Lynne Haynes

Guardian Angel

He stands alone, trying hard not to be seen.
Only when others threaten her does he turn mean.
You can see in her eyes the love for him she feels.
No one knows just what in her mind reels.
The special way they speak with their eyes,
Tells people they can distinguish the lies.
He follows her every place, afraid to leave her side.
There is a feeling he cannot leave a gap very wide.
If anyone approaches her, his body will tense.
He knows that she fears to be in crowd that is dense.
When she is deep in thought, he presses closer to her.
Protection is etched into his mind, he won't let anyone nearer.
The thing no one comprehends, he's not of her blood nor is he
Romantically in love.
He is her guardian, for time to see her through.
Ridding herself of him is something she would never do.
They share something beyond anyone's understanding.
She never asks for material things or is at all of him demanding
The way he looks at her lets anyone know, that he would do
Anything to take all her pain.

Sherida Wagstaff

Why Do I Still Remain?

I continue to hold,
onto something that is unsuitable and cold;
so why—do I, still remain?

I'm enclosed by four walls,
I find restrictive and small;
so why—do I, still—remain?

At times I can't breath,
my soul cries out to leave;
so why—do I, still—remain?

I question my self-worth,
in a place that's disrespected me since birth;
so why—do I, still—remain?

Many see me and smile,
still hating me all the while;
so why—do I, still—remain?

I've tried unsuccessfully to maintain in an environment that
slowly deteriorates my brain; so why—please—tell me why,
do I—still—remain?

Shall I continue to ask why, be miserably stagnant here—until
I die? No—for I—no longer can remain!

Rita Joy Derrico-White

Rain

Soothing is the rain that falls
Onto the earth it flows,
The trees that echo, storms that call,
The wind it howls and blows,
The darkness comes upon us, as the clouds fill up the sky,
No longer do you see the birds or anything that flies,
But nature has its way you bet,
And it is plain to see,
That all the beauty even yet,
Amazes even me.

Lorraine L. Brown

Love Is Special

Lilies,
Open hearted-ness,
Vases full of flowers,
Especially for the one you love.

In love you have,
Special friends.

Streams of love flow through your body every minute,
People always love something,
Especially for the one you love.
Create new friendships,
In school or in home,
And there is
Living proof everyday that love is special.

Kristina Rose Lollman

Ocean's Majesty

It slowly moved through uncharted,
   open waters.
Surfacing to make a short, explosive-like
   exhalation only then to submerge itself again.
An occasional flip here and there breaks
   its monotonous pattern.
The creatures swiftness is triggered by
   its stream lined, sleek appearance and
   powerful movement.
A whistle and a single - toned squeal is its
   way of navigation throughout the salty,
   inhabited ocean.
The intelligence of this beautiful mammal
   is astounding and brings out much
   curiosity in us.
Not understood by the world outside the sea,
   the dolphin was free.

Melissa L. Papineau

Philosophical Musings

Are we the creation of a superior mind?
Or a random combination of the glutinous kind?....... Whatever

Are we really God's crowning achievement?
Or a speck of dust in the firmament?................. Whatever

Does God watch over us all of our days?
Or stand in the wings and laugh at our ways?......... Whatever

Are we the masters of our fate?
Or have no say if we're early or late?............... Whatever

Is this my one and only life?
Or will I come back with another wife?.............. Whatever

What have we learned in all our schools?
Except that we're nothing but simple fools?.......... Whatever

Is there such a thing as evil and good?
Or are morals a relative attitude?................... Whatever

Which is superior? Mind or matter?
Some say the former, some the latter................. Whatever

Now of all the answers philosophers find,
Do they come from the rational or empirical mind?
Ideas and thinking are our mainstay,
Excuse me, I really meant to say.................... Whatever

Norman E. Smilnyak

Sarajevo

Who'll save the dying father's life
   or bless his poor surviving wife
   or quell their starving infant's wail
Who'll see enough to tell their tale:

How on a bright and clear spring day
   hate scarred the sun laved month of May.
As shells and rockets razed their city
   the just and pure foresaw no pity.

"Not I," said the German, so close yet far,
"Nor I," said the Brit, abhorred by war,
"Nor I," said the Russian, still cold yet free,
"Nor I," said the Yank, from across the sea.

Cry prayers through the clouds and beyond the sky,
   yet how can you say a God exists to justify.

Nickolas A. Vlasic Jr.

By The Heat - Colder

There's a place for me/ us/ we. Some place that's not so cold or far away. A place that green is green and red is red and the only thing that has changed is "This old Heart of Mine" — which seems to have gotten just a little bit more mature. Away from sinners and spoilers that stand in dark places not wanting to be seen, less they be called to work/ change towards the value of self denial and self restraint for the inevitable projection of self "into a new life".

The months have been long and this one longer still. It seems almost as if this is the point to stop trying and program oneself for surrender and accept defeat and think that, the war is over. Surrender might be a virtue, but surrender to what? To whom?

I believe that this is the survival and I am here! I have made it to this point and I cannot divorce my self from struggle, we are one. I cannot cancel my contract with Change and give up this ground on which I stand to the inventors of quicksand and potholes. I will not be victimized. "A man who does not know the grounds on which he stands, will be at the mercy of anyone who does".

Yillie Bey

Love

What is it all about. Is it happy, or is it sad? Is it good or is it bad? Is it meant to happen to all of us or just some of us? When will it be done? Do we like it or do we hate it? Why is it confusing? Why is it good? Why does it hurt when it is over? Love is a mysterious thing, it comes and it goes like a storm. Sometimes you have thunder and lightning and sometimes you have a rainbow. It comes in all different forms. You learn from it and you make mistakes. Sometimes you even crash and burn. Just keep your head up and try to remember one day you will know what it is all about.

Lacey A. Trezek

"Just You And Me"

I'll never forget the day you softly caressed my face,
Or when you gently pulled me to you for that passionate embrace.
"You have become my life," is what your lips were saying,
As you slipped the ring on my finger and in the background our favorite song was playing.

This was the day that everything began to start;
That forever would you own a sacred piece of my heart.
Our parents said our love would not last;
That very soon it would be a forgotten fling of the past.
But, oh how wrong did we prove them to be;
Because through all the mountains we've climbed, and all the storms we've weathered, it's always gonna be "JUST YOU and ME."

Sheila M. Harris

Untitled

Does the past truly fade away?
Or is it just a reminder of a small lingering ache?

When your heart feels so heavy it hurts to see and
the clouds in your head seem to never leave, what
is it you think of - Right now? Today?

No, it's the icons with something to say.

As if you were made of shiny thin glass, they think
they see through you and begin to laugh.

They tell you your way is totally wrong, and you're
not able to sing their song.

So you silently sit where they say you belong.

You try to listen and grow stronger, the day finally
comes when you can stay silent no longer.

As soon as you speak they shatter the glass you thought
was yourself, then pick up the pieces of the empty shell.

So remember, next time when your head fills with clouds,
yesterday can be as close as now.

Kelly A. Craig

Time & Fate

Is time my alliance, my vigor to succeed;
Or is time my enemy, my barrier to exceed.
For time is a gamble, one of which we win or lose.
For fate is a privilege, one of which we can not choose.
And there may be times we choose wrong from right;
Dark times that prove harder than those with light.
But I can't be convinced that there's ALWAYS a turn -
pointing in the direction in which to learn.
From good or bad;
honesty or treason,
Everything we do is done for a reason.
Time and Fate, they travel as two;
Withholding the wisdom in all we do.
If ever I doubt that either is a friend,
my only prayer is for time not to end.
For when I stop believing and begin asking why,
I'll never live my chosen life because I allowed time to die.

Lisa Ambrose

Ocean Grove...The Fishing Pier

It was magnificent reaching out over the surf to greet the sunrise
or the darkness.
It offered space...a chance to get away. It was something
special... something to share.
The fence let you go just so far..it was after all a private place
reserved for a certain few.

On the good days, it was full of activity...invigorating...like a
dream but very real.
And there were some dreary days...drab is the word...when
things weren't so nice...
the world seemed cold and awash.

It withstood many storms perched as it was above the devastating
waves.
But alas it was fragile and in a flash it was wiped away;
all but its memory.
But somehow still you knew it was there for you.

A. Bernard Herrmann

A Moment In Time

Give me the sunset of life...
Or the rainbow after the storm passes...

Bring for my eyes to behold...
The colors of fall
As the trees cast off its leaves

Look above at the celestial sky and gather together
The glitter of all the stars that descend from its birthplace
To sprinkle over me

Or the sea breeze that blows across my face
To caress my spirit and comfort my soul

Bring these treasures to me...
To call my own and

It will never compare to
A moment in time
You have given to me

Mona A. Vidales

Myself

There is nothing so peaceful as a walk in the park,
Or the song of the crickets just before dark.
I love the radiance of morning's first light,
And the beauty and grace of a bird in flight.
I love the sensitivity of a passionate kiss,
In the arms of my wife, this is total bliss.
I love the winter, and the first day of spring,
When nature breathes new life into everything.
I am so thankful for the warmth of the sun,
That makes my summers exciting and fun.
When my summer is over, I enjoy the fall,
For this is the most beautiful season of all.
From the simple beauty of leaves on the trees,
To the chills of the evening, mid-summer night breeze.
Someday my body will go back to the earth,
And the ones left behind will determine my worth.
I hope that someone will be able to see,
That down deep inside, there was some good in me.
That's how life is, and it was meant to be,
When our children are raised, God will set us free.

Rick Howard

Take Control

The lives that we are given are very precious, indeed.
Our Fathers and our Mothers choose the paths we will lead.
Our youth precedes us kindly; so we are told.
Confusing adolescence? Ironic adage always seem to fit.
Never seeing our troubles as only mild intrusions.
Much time listening? To what? We still do not know.
Voices trying to make you. Who? You don't know. There's
no time to ponder! Proceed with your path! Although,
the path has changed now, and; is yours to choose. Always
remember where your path began. Youth is Oh! so
precious until our time goes by, it always seems to die.
Our path is right on schedule, youth dead and gone. Much
to our amazement we grasp our hidden feelings, beginning
to understand. Live your life as you choose and
listen not to they. You have the control now. Youth
can live forever, even when it's lost, all it took was
seeing that life was precious, Indeed. So take control
and have a voice, and let your voice be heard! Live
your life as you choose, Live you life for YOU !!!!!!

Lisa Louise Cherrier

Untitled

Our hearts has been shattered so. Anymore we can't think straight.
Our mines is just a complete blank.
Our hearts have been broken, shattered beyond repair.
We loved you once showed you how much we cared. You were too young,
foolish, full of pride, tried to be tough and strong.
When there's lots of warmth and tenderness hidden inside.
Not yet ready for the responsibilities you took part.
You fought and struggled until you shook.
Soon you became violent with and outrage.
Never once did you stop and realize the ones you
hurt, and destroyed; was "I" your wife and your adorable baby boy.
Our hearts and dreams, as a family are shattered so;
beyond any self control.
We loved you once with a love strong and true.
We hoped it to last forever to never end.
But our lives together as one never really had a chance to begin.
It ended, in tragedy, before it even started, because of shatter,
and to be broken hearted.
You destroyed your life as well, as of our.
We can never mend, it has too many scars and now it must end.
Peggy Burrell

Forbidden

Why must everything be Forbidden?
Our thoughts-
    locked away for no one to know,

Our friendship-
    reduced to mere strangers,

Our feelings-
    denied from admitting the truth

Our love-
    refused too scared to loose what
    we already have,

Everything we feel and want is Forbidden.

Reality won't let us be friends or lovers,
But our hearts won't let us remain strangers.

Why must everything be Forbidden?
Paula Wood

The Beauty Outside

The trees are leaved of, deep, dark green,
Outside, only beauty and should be life are seen.
The birds are chirping a lovely song,
From here, it seems there's nothing wrong.

Inside ones soul is where ugliness hides,
To escape this fear, one runs outside.
Deep, dark secrets buried beneath ones mind,
Seeping outward, at periods in time.

The squirrels run freely, through the just cut grass,
Outside, it's peaceful, the fear is gone at last.
Shadows of pain and faces unknown,
Outside, the beauty has all been grown.

We'll stay out here among the peace,
and leave inside the shadowed beast.
Tranquility must form to hide the fears,
So others won't see the trailing tears.

Peace be there for all outside,
and keep the shadows locked up inside.
and like the animals, set us free,
To run beneath the dark green tree.
Sandy M. Ward

A Private Memoir

Treasured moments,
pack my mind with contemplation.
It is undescribable to anyone but him,
for it will puzzle the rest,
to analyze my sentiment.
Sitting near the ocean, looking to the sky,
his is image so clear in my mind,
creates a reflection
through the rays of the luminescent summer sun.

So far away,
at an instant so close,
captivating its ability,
to form such a vision before me.

He only can create this. . .
he only can make this moment possible. . .
for both us to share.
Sianis Eleni

Chloe

Chloe's so sweet, with pancake hands and
Pancake feet. When she awakes, it's real neat
With her thin legs she's so petite. Watching her play
in her little seat she really seems so elite. No
other could compete, not even our country seat. So it's
not freak to take a peak at Chloe, and be complete.
Rose Marie Jenkins

Together

As a beautiful clear mountain stream runs down so free and gay;
Passing though shadows and sunlight,
Glittering soft golds, greens and blues as it moves on its way.

That is the way you run through my mind, with streaks of
sunlight that turns into golds, greens, and deep dark shadows
of gray.

As the stream finds its way down the mountains deep valley
Let me find may way into your heart and let me stay;

Let us move though this mysterious life together, with its deep
dark shadows, sunlit golds, greens and blues.
Let us grow old together day by day.
Willie H. Walker

A Black Woman

When I walk
    people stop and stare
When I talk
    people stop and listen

Maybe they see
    something different in me
Not seen in every
    female-human-being
A black-proud-African-American-woman
    walking with stride.
Not afraid of her culture
Not hiding her pride
Standing tall knowing where she has came from
Not forgetting her roots
Or where they had begun
    A Black Woman
Tekeah C. Scott

I Was a Fool...

I was a fool to think you needed me.
I was a fool to think you cared.
I was a fool to think you wanted me.
I was the only one who dared.

I was a fool to think you loved me.
I was a fool for trying so hard.
I was a fool to think you trusted me.
You had long ago been scarred.

I was a fool to think you listened to me.
I was a fool to let you lie.
I was a fool to think you loved me.
Some say you are the fool...not I.

Michelle Monday

Before I Met You

Before I met you
I was a lost lonely soul
With nowhere to go
And no potential goal
But like a falling star
That gets everyone's attention
You came in and took all my interest
After I met you
My life turned into a joy
Like a little child with a favorite toy
Now that I know what love is about
I never want to be without
Love you
Love you so very much

Maurice Earl

Summer Nights

Alone -
   I watch the evening come.
The sky turns navy blue.

The moon comes out.
   I watch
And hope you're watching, too.

Wind blows softly through the trees.
   Summer scents come with it.
I hear a symphony of crickets.

I lie awake,
   Hating to waste
A night as beautiful as this.

Summer nights are much
   Too long
Unless they're shared with you.

Laurie C. Smothers

Fusion

To ride upon a cherubim,
If I could only ride with him,
Our hearts would rise above the fray,
And lie in ecstasy all the day.

To soar above the seraphim,
If I could only soar with him,
Our souls would spin beyond this clime,
And fuse together past all time.

Marjorie Perry Russin

Voluntary Slavery

I will love you
I will honor you
I will cherish you
In richer or poorer
Sick or in health
For better or worse
Till death do us part
I will be your slave
Your slave with a smile
But only if I can
Pretend
That I have a choice
A free will
All of my own
Only then
Will I volunteer
For slavery

Tish Bastian

The Robin

I spied you hiding in the green
I will pretend you've not been seen
Cautious head and anxious eye
Determine if you hide or fly.

This garden has become your home
I'll not intrude, it's safe to roam
I like your song, your busy flight
One danger, the cat at night.

Merlyn Churchill Hendren

Untitled

Peace and Justice
I wish it could be

No war
No fighting
or just plain being mean!

Why do people have to
steal to be rich
when they know they
can be punished for it?

I wish I could teach them
a lesson or two
so they would know how
they're making others feel.

Tiffany Lapworth

Wish I Were You

Often at the hour of midnight
I wish upon the sparkling stars.
How come I can't be so bright
instead of locked up behind these bars?

For you were the sports star
and I was the outdoors type.
You worked hard for your first car
while I became the lousy hype.

Now you are a married man
and I'm still single.
You have always had the perfect plan
while I'm out partying just to mingle.

For I still love you the same
even when the cows go moo.
I guess it's all part of the game,
how I wish I were you

Randy Payne

Unrequited Love

Something happened to me that day
I wonder if you felt the same way
It was a feeling so strange, so new
So fresh, just like the morning dew.

It's with me now in all I do
I wonder how it is with you
Will the words ever be said
Or will they buzz around my head

Things can change so easily
But doubt lingers on wearily
Time will pass and we'll move on
The feeling, though, will not be gone

If things could be different
If I could be true
To move all mountains
To be with you.

But pride, you see, is my middle name
And I can't bear to lose the game
Exposure may not go my way
So unrequited I will stay.

Tara Matthews

The Gift Of My Life

If I could give the world a gift
I would first wish to be dead.

This gift would be
The epitome
   of my life
Lived and loved by me.

It could not possibly
Be understood
   by the majority.

These common, everyday people
Caught up in the act
   of being selfless and unoriginal

I want to give
The gift of my
   independent mind.

Creating never before imagined ideas,
Which in their turn
   form a perfect piece of art,
Fragile yet strong and unafraid
To stand alone.

Tirzah Rossi

Untitled

If only I was around you
I would never feel any pain.
You would be able to shelter me
from the hot sun, the snow, and the rain
I want to be with you always
but I know that can never be,
For I may be in love with you,
You're not in love with me.
I've tried everything I can think of
to make you feel the same
But now I guess I realize
you don't want to play my game
Day after day I keep praying
that you'll soon feel this way
But until then I'll sit alone,
While I watch you play.

Rosemary DeSantis

If Just Once

If just once I could have told you.
    If I could have looked into your
eyes to let you know.
Yet, every time I felt it coming,
I stopped it again.
The words just couldn't be found.
If just once I could have felt your
    heart and knew.
If I could have been your feelings,
I would have known.
We could have said so much in
    such a small amount of time.
And yet, the words just couldn't
    be found.
If just once we could have been sure.
If just once you would have let me in.
If just once could have let
our guards down,
Maybe then,
    we could have found the words.

Patricia E. Hughes

Trust In Thee

Lord I put my trust in thee
If I don't where would I be
Out in the wretch world alone
With a mind confessed and almost gone

Lord I know you're always here
To give the love and show you care
Satan is always on your track
Lord just help me not turn back

When Satan knows you love the Lord
That is when he works real hard
It is good to pray all the time
And keep Jesus on your mind

You shall never let a day go by
And thanking God for being alive
Without His spirit your bones are dry
Remember one day you will have to die

Patricia Russell

Search

There is love,
If only you will search it out
Within your heart, not very far.
The love deep inside yourself,
And you'll find that's not very hard.

It's important that you no who you are,
because we all have a purpose,
In the world to go far.
Just search it out, and find yourself.

The mistakes that you make
Can be corrected along the way,
No matter, what others might say.
They make mistakes too, if not the same.

Because we all share the world
In many different ways,
God, has gift us with His love,
To see each new day,
The love we share each day,
Goes far, far, away.
All over the world, there is love.

Linda J. Anthony

Only For Today

You are my precious love my dream
I'll always hope for and I pray
for you the best.

I'll hope life brings you happiness
And that you go beyond my wish
cause I wish you the best.

You so dear to my heart so bright!
No shame you are but about all
That; you are my brightest star and
I'll speak of you.

I'll dream that what you dream
of comes true but in spite of all
that, I'll hope you'll shine through.

There's my star that looks like you
I want to make my wish and hope
you'll come true. Stay strong live
for the day when I come and hear
your voice say "always will be
ours today."

Robert L. Bell

You Can Whisper

You can whisper, if you like.
I'll be listening.
No need to be the troubled one,
sullen and withdrawn;
or fists pounding in the air, yelling,
"I am not my father's son."
No jokes, no stories necessary
here to entertain.
No suit of armor or planned attack
needed to keep the hurt at bay.
There is no judge or jury;
no reason to stand trial.
Just me listening;
you can whisper, if you try.

Maria Limarenko

The Way We Were....

I'll kiss you once, before I go,
I'll love you once, then close the door.

We'll reminisce for the
time we spent,
The way it came
the way it went.

We'll think of our children
that God has sent,
We'll want to go back
We'll want to relent.

But hard as it is
we can't hide the fear,
it's forever deep
and forever here.

Tho, I love you and couldn't steer.
I must confess the fact is clear.

Just another day
a few more tears,
a different year
So very dear...

Melissa Homer

"Old As Time"

Whoever choose to worship me,
I'll shelter and worm eternally,
Welcome souls of young and old.
When I strip them of grace,
I only leave an empty place.
Restless, un good and vice,
Good converts for my advice.
I lead the unholy love pain.
Thrive on meek and hopeless remains.
Evil at the worst,
Always quench my thirst.
I hate the good and the kind.
That team can blow my mind.
Killers and thieves are from my domain,
Where they serve I reign.
I rob the mind, hate the fine.
Red as wine, "Old as Time".

Vicki Johnson

Elegy To The Man

I can not do the show
I'm on the mountain's edge.
The dark ravine below
Beckons me to the ledge.

I'll never understand
Why people have to go.
Someone, give me a hand
To continue the show.

The show can not go on;
It needs the other man;
The plot is all but gone
It's just a broken plan.

My mind is all adrift
I don't know what to do.
My feelings need a lift
Oh, man, do I need you.

Theresa Schanbeck

I'm So Sad

I'm so sad
I'm so sad
I don't know how to be happy or Glad
I'm so sad
I'm so sad
The world seems to me oh so Bad
I'm so sad
I'm so sad
Sometimes I really think
I'm going mad
It's a shame that
I'm so sad

Stephanie Newton

Encircled

Oh frightened child at my breast
I'm swirling in your warmth
a trembling heart seeking rest
such labored, whimpering breath

A velvet hand grasping love
as silken coils circle a face
and tepid tears smear the dove
captive in my embrace

Maureen O'Connor

You And Me

If I had known you better,
I'm sure that friends we'd be.
Because I've learned to like you,
And I feel that you like me.

There's been so many different things,
That we have had to do.
You didn't have time for me,
And I didn't have time for you.

There wasn't time to go around,
We had to pick and choose.
The jobs, the houses, the cars and such,
The kids, their clothes and shoes.

Now old man time has lost his prime,
He's fading fast away.
I certainly hope before he goes,
We'll have another day.

A day to sit and reminisce,
About things of the past.
And even then we may make,
A friendship that will last

Robert L. Washington

Solitude

I'm tired of starting over,
I'm tired of being the one,
Who always has to make the move
when it's all been said and done.

A mental note inside my mind
rewinds back through the years,
of times I tried to make it work
And all the wasted tears.

Love is like a game to me
That I never seem to win.
I don't understand the logic.
Why do I always try again?

Always thought love was something
That I would have once I was grown.
Now I am ready to face the fact
That I might live my life alone.

I don't know if I will be happy,
But I think it is for the best
That I live my life by myself
And give my heart a rest.

Sandi Helms-Merced

"The Living Stone"

Like stone
in a flowing river
like stone
on the grass
I follow the stars
    stone and water
    in emptiness
    what is flowing
My life please wake up
be in time
to admit the empty sky
    go
    go like a living stone

Marek Prejzner

Again

I feel so small, like a child
  In her mother's clothing—
  A hopeless romantic lost
  in a sea of dreams, wishes
Everyone around me is someone
With a place in this world
...where is my place...

I am lost, yes, lost.
  Someone find me, take my hand,
  Pull me out of myself,
  Set my feet on solid ground,
  Open the window to my world
  ...I cannot breathe...

Interpret? Take it for what
  It's worth—how I feel...
  Don't read between the lines
  ...look at me...

Reassurance... That's what
  I need, tell me again
  ...tell me again...

Kristy Buffington

"A Mother's Love"

It's true, God keeps His promises
In many little ways,
From the rainbow at the shower's end
To the sun that lights our day.
But there's no sign, that is clearer,
That shows His love for me
Than the mother that has always cared
As I sat upon her knee.
For, in her eyes, I see His love.
In her hugs, I feel His care,
And her understanding wisdom
Shows His judgement's always fair.
For, in her eyes, I'll always be
"The prayer that once came true"
As God has promised, so has she;
Her love came shining through.
So, when heaven's gates do open up
To my mansion, high above,
I'll thank God for the Mom he sent
Who showed to me, His love.

Robert Louis Senn

Immigrants

Sudden, new faces appear
In my neighborhood-
Swept here by alien forces
That I know of only because
I - along with my neighbors -
Read papers, watch television,
Or listen to the radio. We all
Welcome them for their newness;
Their guts for coming here;
For their perspicacity in
Choosing our neighbors over
Any other! Welcome, Mr. Chan,
To our neighborhood!

Lawrence F. A. Johnson

Friends Are Like Flowers

Friends are like flowers.
In new surroundings
a few wilt and wither;
more pick themselves up,
standing proud mid tears of laughter
or soft conversation.

In warm sunlight
—from seedling to maturity—
they flower
becoming part of us
to console; to give pleasure
to nourish; to treasure.

Valencia Cacciotti

Unrelenting Promise

A tiny seed,
In promising innocence,
Sheds its pod,
Cascading,
Wedging its way into an earthy fold.

In silence,
It keeps vigil with sun and rain,
Until its moment comes...
Bursting forth,
Decked in purpose and profusion.

Whether in fragrance or hue,
Essence or taste,
Its promise is at last fulfilled,
Delighting souls, sustaining life,
Awakening senses that were stilled.

This hardy, yet fragile bloom goes on,
With rhythm, purpose, beauty and grace,
Until at last, it begets its own...

A tiny seed,
In promising innocence.

Margaret J. Geckos

Memories

As I have grown, you have shown,
in so many ways, with those special days.
Remember one, for I can see,
Roaming on the beach, you and me.
We discovered a weathered pile,
upon our faces, perched a smile.
We looked upon the sunlit ocean,
You and me... Father and Son.

Peter J. Hoeltje

The Touch

Someone touched me today
In such a special way
I glowed all over from
    head to feet
I knew right then it was
    God's treat
That I was saved from harm's way
I knew right then I could
    start my day

Lucretia Screen Williams

Earth Day

The environment is losing
in the battle of pollution.
Help the earth, and make a change,
find the best solution

There's a big hole in the
O-zone layer,
but there are lots of people,
who don't take time to care.

Land fills are filling.
filling up fast.
at the rate that they're going,
They surely won't last.

Our natural resources
need less abuse.
Help make a difference.
Recycle, reuse.

The environment is falling
down a long, unhappy slope,
but there's still time to make a change,
remember, there's always hope.

Sarah Vonnegut

Choices

Choices, like voices
    in the dark.
The Sorrowful Call of a distant lark,
    of memories so sweet and yet
full of pain.
The Choices one makes
    where visions remain.

Remind us all of the Simple Truth.
The Choices we make we must endure.
Like the waves on the ocean rise
    and fall.
The Choices we make affect
    us all.

Morgan Metzger DesMeules

Loneliness

I felt cold, I felt alone
In the misty air
I knew
As one tear turned into a million
I knew

I see my fears, as years went by
Though I never knew why it had to be
To see my fears, that it had to be
loneliness
But why did it have to be?

Maggie Urban

Animals

Animals, animals everywhere
in the zoo, in your hair.
Animals, animals see them here.
Animals, animals see them there.
Animals, animals love them all
large or big, even small!

Lauren Rardin

Love, Dad

How can I let you go
In this brief time I've come to know
The greatest joy this life can give
And it is AIDS, I can't forgive
For all the lives it will destroy
As it has come to take my boy

I must be strong and not let it show
That soon his time has come to go
For all his needs I will comply
And never stop and question why
Just make this time with him the best
And worry later when to rest

When he is gone and I'm alone
I'll miss his heart inside our home
He tried to help others, it is true
And did more for the world than most folks do
I know he'll find peace in heaven above
As he's remembered here on Earth, with love

Valerie Ramsey

One Man's Game

Alone
In this dark, cold, cruel, world
No one to love
And no one to hold
Too many broken hearts to mend
Not enough time
For all to heal
Too much power
One thinks he holds
Leading them on
Then laughing
Directly in their troubled faces
Confusion in their sad eyes
As he walks off in pride
Thinking love was meant to be
But he was just a user
And at the end
Made them all feel like losers

Kristin Beckman

The Golden Years

Hold back the tears
In your Golden years.
You know you're old
When the Stones grow cold.
You try to diddle
And it Bends in the Middle.
No use to Sob,...
Just, pat the knob-
Put it away, and say;
"Too bad Old Man,
You've had your day."

Thomas L. Lynch

Riverflow

The river flows backwards
Into our minds and hearts,
As we dream forward
Into the unknowable unknown.
Floating on Mother of Time
We drift/dream her depths,
Sense/see her secrets
Elusively,
As the river flows backwards
Into our bones
To shape/shift the future.

Millicent Rucker

The Why

Consider what you contain
In your imagination
The divine and the forbidden
The heritage you retain.

A creature was humanized
Out of a distant somewhere
Self awareness acquired
It thought and ritualized.

Who, what and why am I
The very first to ask
Peering all around, looking,
At the earth and the sky.

For Nature's endless infinity
The mind went to explain
With spirits, Gods and demons,
A measure of vain futility.

For the who and the why
Rest with us today
The barrier impenetrable
Between you and I-

Kenneth J. Munden

"Faithful One"

Children of the world,
Innocent and small.
Flowers, trees and animals,
All of you stand tall!

The earth is falling under you,
The evils getting deep.
Keep reaching up to heaven
And God will hold your feet.

Hold tight to your dreams,
Follow through with heart.
If part of you is dying,
Search to make a new start.

Don't hold on to what is gone,
Let it go and just move on.

Twenty lines touching ground,
Though it may seem short, I've found;
Twenty lines in this case,
Could make this world a better place.

Lindsey Bixler

Look - Out

Clean, pure,
innocent the air.
Though my stare seemed dishonest
or greedy, it was free -
and I read "No Charge"
on the label for me.
Steady, strong, the mountain said
I belonged to it and it to me,
timeless moment of beauty and truth -
and the label said "For Free."
Heal, restore,
pour in your beauty like oil,
finding cracks and crevices
where the pain of unknowing hides
and then, mountain,
stone me into your hill
that I might forever gaze
with some grace
on the autumn loveliness
of your granite face.

Nanette Herman

Lela

Head deep
into your lavender loveliness
I marvel still
at life laced up tight around

your green trunk. No act of God
has brought you
down.
As I stoop to trace
two
bursting buds,
plum purple with a naked chill,
you shiver… quiver
under winter's last thrill.
A tear struggles
down your slender frame.
I can only sing of life,
when nature saves the best
for last.

Marjorie Josephine Kemp

Aglow With Smiles

A smiling face
is a beautiful thing.
It feels to others
as a breath of spring.

A smiling face
gives much delight
It begins a day
that seems so right.

A smiling face
sets eyes aglow,
and others
feel good, you know.

L. B. Everett

Being Yourself

Being yourself and no other
Is a goal which we need to attain.
When we walk and talk
And think and feel as us,
We walk our own walk,
We talk our own talk,
We think our own thoughts,
We feel our own way.
No carbon copy are we,
Just the individual
Which GOD hath made.
We have a service
To do for Him
That nobody else can do.
Let us be true and faithful
To that which is our call.
Let us march to that
Drum beat within us.
Let us march brave and tall.
Let the world see our colors!

Margaret Rahn

Enigma

My face to the world is joyous
Is my face to the world who I am?

Do I offer you honest emotion
or a mask of some plastic Saran?

Do I proffer advice like a Portia?
Is my judgment astute and benign?

Well I trust you will never discover
Mona Lisa's mysterious sign.

Rhoda Torn

The Forbidden Love

The taste of the forbidden fruit
Is always so sweet
From sneaking a glance
To planning a place to meet.

The thrill of the unknown
Leaves room for heated desires
The longer it builds
The harder to contain the fire.

Knowing you'll never be together
The challenge grows
The passion you feel
Is something he'll never know.

Terri S. Carter

Behind

Underneath the wise
is always the dumb,
Underneath the pain
you still feel the numb.

Behind the strong
lies the weak,
And behind the river
lies the creek.

The strong survive
the weak decay and die

Sometimes your problems
are what they seem
do not be deceived
but always believe.

One day the dumb will be wise
And the weak will survive.

Patrice L. Patrick

Along My Way

The sunshine warm upon my cheek
Is but the touch of God;
I feel His nearness, hear Him speak
Along the way I trod.

The winding creek, the gentle rain,
The sky so blue above;
The verdant green of field and plain
Are touches of His love.

The mountain peak, the chasm deep,
His power bespeaking of;
The fleecy cloud, the wind's soft breath,
The touch of God's own love.

Oh Lord, I feel your Presence near,
For everything I see
Is but the touch of grace and power,
And shows your love for me.

And so, I place my hand in thine
To guide me through this day;
Your Holy Will, not mine, O Lord,
Shall be my only way.

Pauline M. Rodolph

Willow Tree

Oh willow tree, why do you weep?
Is it because you fear change?
Because if you fear change
Then you will fear the world.

Lisa Galvin

The Lie

Suddenly, this train I'm on
is gaining speed
and losing control
it's weaving and wobbling
it's starting to roll!

Those who love me
said, "don't go"
but, I was smart enough
I should know!
I'll be o.k.!
After all, I'm young
and indestructible
Aren't I?

What do you mean,
I'm not?
Who's responsible
for this lie?
No! It can't be me,
I'm too cool!
It's a lie!

Patti Fairchild Bartee

Untitled

Someone who is dear to me
is looking in my eyes.
I am the one who comforts him
and wipes the tears he cries.
Every time I look at him,
this little man of mine.
He holds a certain wisdom
that in me I cannot find.
He knows not of the violence
that engulfs the world today.
He knows not of the frightening games
that shallow people play.
All he knows is in his heart
and carried in his soul
All he does is smile at me
with eyes as rich as gold.
If only all the little children born onto this earth
could hold onto their soul inside
and understand how much they're worth.

Susan Dowling

Fantasy

You look at me, but what you see
Is merely just a fantasy
You just don't understand
You think you know me
Like the back of your hand
But if you really could see through
I am normal just like you

Life is what you make of it
So try to make it last
Like me, try to change your ways
And don't dwell on the past
Mistakes are just a part of life
For we all have made a few
So when you learn to accept reality
Then your fantasy can come true

Stephanie Frank

Untitled

The wind of change
    is on its way
Will it pass me by and say
    "Wait until I blow again."
The wind of change
    is on its way
Will it change direction
    when it's my turn to feel
    its cool breeze upon my face?

The wind of change
    is on its way
But I will not let it
    pass me by!
I'm gonna spread my wings
and fly as high as the wind
will take me.

Victoria Johnson

Whisper Thy Name

Some say love
Is soft as a whisper,
As calm as the sea.

An early morning sun shines,
And birds fly so free.

Cause nobody knows you
Nobody even knows your name;
It's soft as a whisper,
As gentle as the rain.

When lightning strikes
In the distance,
And thunder still remains;

Listen for the whisper
It's calling out your name

Todd Miller

Couples

The love we have together
is tested every day,
the trials and tribulations
will guide us on our way.

To make it in this world of ours
takes love and happiness.
We have to give each other strength
or our lives could be a mess.

Our faults will always be there
no ones life is great.
To always judge each other
could quickly turn to hate.

So to be understanding of people
accepting them as they are,
takes a lot of faith
but will bring us peace by far.

So the love we have together
will never find happiness,
until we trust in each other
and let God take care of the rest.

Sharon Theuerkauf

Full Circle

Full circle
Is the course we've run:
rivers a flame;
acid rain;
Air polluted beyond claim;
soil infused
with lethal gas
There is no hiding place.
Alas!
Is this the end
or can there be
solutions to the circuitry?
Can we guard from devastation
God's supreme, unique creation?

Is it possible ... can it be
There is in our mentality
unused capability
to harness
what we have unleashed
to fashion bold a world at peace?

Margaret A. Golton

Untitled

The dream I dream
is the dream I feel-
I know exactly how it
should be-
But it seems to me
this dream I want-
Exists only to me-
I find a place
I grab onto-
hoping with all my will-
That I finally found-
my dream of dreams-
But I am looking still-
My wish to be happy and
content-
Is a feeling that I love-
But it seems to be-
to reach that Place-
-alone-
Is all I have-

D

My Friends

How you feel about yourself
Is the key
We are all people
And that's the way
It should be
Dark skin
Light skin
It should be the beauty within
Heavy set or thin
You are still my friend
My friend short
My friend tall
God and you
Should love us all

Kylus Harris

Can't Let Go

When the pain
Is too strong, and
I just can not
Fight, I know to
Hold on that I'll
Soon see the light.

When the night
Is so long, it
Collides with the
Day, and the one
That I love is
Still too far away.

I just close my
Eyes and think
Everything is all
Right, because I
Can't let go, I
Just have to fight.

Tara M. Giardino

"Why?"

Peace on Earth; good will to men -
Is what the people sang.
But no one cared to listen as
the bombs exploded and rang.
Death and destruction -
People in pain -
Children crying in the rain.
Political amnesty given to those
inflicting terror on all;
Not much you can do with
your back to the wall.
Where is the love for the world to see?
Where is the peace the Lord
intended to be?
How many people have to die -
How many have to cry?
What is the sense of war and
Death -
Can anyone tell us; why?

Kathy Acton

Beauty Is The Color Red

In abundance from our trees is shed
It also blazes from the bush
From the hills and fields as West we push
To smell the nectar of a rose
To taste an apples sweet repose.
In all the land of gallant color
There surely could not be another
So flaming from our hearts we share
A touch of love that's in the air
I dread to think the void would be
If never the chance I had to see.

Wesley William Heerssen Sr.

My Tree

I sit in my tree and stare at the sky
Its branches envelope me tenderly
I am cradled in its graceful flow
This tree stands like a king at a ball
Seeing my tree makes me feel proud
It's my quiet place where I love to be
Everyone everyone will love my tree

Michelle Lasky

Beauty Of Love

Why does love shun me away? Is
  it because I do not have the
beauty on the outside or is it
  the fact I am not me?
Love shuns me away because I
  have no real reason to love
Another. Because love itself is
  more than a word. The time
that is taken by love is not wasted.
  If by chance it is wasted then
who is to blame? I say it is
  the one who thinks love is
a four letter word. The one
  who can not see beyond
the outside of the small word can
  never understand one self. When
that person can see beyond the
  glass case, then he and he alone
will understand the beauty held
  within love itself.

Mary Carolyn Marshall

The Tulip

A Tulip is a beautiful being.
It buds in the spring when
the rains are still coming down,

Unfortunately the Tulip does not
live long.
It will sit in a vase and fill
the air with color and beauty.

Then one morning you will come
down to your kitchen and look at
the vase on the table and there will
no longer be a beautiful tulip.
It will have wilted and died in
the blink of an eye.

I believe that the Tulip symbolizes the
youth of a child through their
parents eyes.

Monique C. Michaud

A Precious Child

A child is full of love and warmth,
It comes from deep inside.
Their little lives are so special,
They're wonderful to be by,
As days go by and weeks go on
Their faces change so much,
Their actions and their movements,
Seem to be a quick little flash in time,
So as they grow and begin to learn,
The wonders of the world,
From the green grass of home,
To the different buds of the earth,
Just remember their little faces
And love their little smiles,
For after all they're God's little gift,
To you a precious child.

Tammy Renee Bursell

Cry Of The Dark

The darkness tells its own story
It cries out tales of pain and glory
Those distant sounds you hear at night
That wake you in a state of fright
They are the lonesome cries of the dark
They cause the dogs and wolves to bark

The cry of the dark is silent but heard
To those the darkness is preferred
Have you heard the darkness cry?
Have you ever wondered why?
Why it cries such a lonely song
Could such sorrow be so wrong?

The darkness cries so beautifully
It blocks out all reality
It will lift your spirit off the ground
Soon you will be gazing all around
Let the cry of the dark take your mind away
Let it ease all your thoughts of gloom and
  dismay
The cry of the dark is a sacred song
To those whom in darkness truly belong.

Sandra Capestany

The Leaves Will Fall

Life is so much like a tree,
It digs its roots,
Builds its trunk,
Spreads its branches,
And forms its leaves.

There's work to be done,
Plans to be made.
Dreams to be dreamed,
Tomorrow to look forward to.

Then it happens
All too soon,
The leaves begin to fall.

Maureen Reed

Love Is Gone

I can't believe our love is gone.
It doesn't seem it lasted too long.

It was fate, him and I,
days went by and we drifted apart.
I am saddened, I can't lie,
but it was him who broke my heart.

My dreams came true, us together;
He was my friend and the one I loved-
I thought we'd be always forever
but I wasn't the only one he loved.

We finally went our separate ways,
I hope my pain doesn't last very long.
I think of him every passing day-
not forgotten, but our love is gone.

Stacy L. Hickerson

A Flower

A flower is like a breath of spring
It's such a lovely and lively thing
Awaiting the season for it to thrust
It shares its beauty with each of us
The time will come for it to fade
But God will send it back someday

Martha Kendall

PaPa

  Papa today is your birthday and
it feels like you should be here
with me!
  But I know there's a God in
Heaven that will watch over
you for me,
  I will love you always and
forever, and never a day will go by,
  That I don't think of you,
and the love you gave me all
of my life.
  One day we will meet again
in Heaven,
  I know not the time nor the day,
  But I will love you always
my dear Papa forever and ever
always!

N. Soape

Aura

It dwells within the rocks and trees
it gives its essence to the breeze
the sun that shines upon my head
the moon and stars, the grass my bed

And as I look upon the earth
the dark of night, the child in birth
or look upon a cloud on high
the light I see I wonder why

No one else I've heard not tell
of altered sight, of witches spell
deceived by eyes or so I thought
I gave it up lest I be caught

And then one day it came to me
that others saw what I could see
how free it felt to know for sure
that God's true light is all that's pure

William Wayne Cook

Longings

Your beauty is such that
It makes my heart ache
Yearning for a chance
I would give all to take.
Just a few moments to
Find out if they're true,
These feelings I find
Ever hard to subdue.
And if they were.
What of it then?
Would my heart have
to suffer for them again?
Or would it find
One much the same,
Longing for love and
An end to its pain?

William Connally

The Plea

There is nothing I can do
It's not my choice
I pray to God
Hope he hears my voice
Life unlived,
Won't you give it a chance
I'm not
an unfortunate circumstance.

Santos M. Garcia

Just Wondering

Golf is such a wonderful sport
It provides a lot of challenging fun.
It takes a great deal of skillful play.
To be able to shoot a hole in one.

It is amazing though how many miles
A golfer walks throughout the day.
He will push a cart or carry the clubs
And consider it relaxing either way.

But on the days when it is pouring.
You can almost scream and shout
For some of the big time golfers
Are too tired to take the garbage out.

Mary H. Moody

Music

Notes! Notes! - one escapes -
     It travels to your soul -
As it mingles with others
     The journey begins - where?
To the surge of the ocean
     Where the waves crash
In the depth of your being
     Then recedes to memories
Of your childhood - in calm waters
     Then crescendos again and again
Through the veins of your life
     Yearning for more - knowing
The peace and ultimate release
     At the final chord.

Marjory L. Chaloff

When I Was Small

When I was small I learned to crawl,
it was a major feat.
And later on a learned to walk
and toddled down the street.

It was such fun to learn to run
and play with all my friends.
I climbed and fell, it all was swell.
Yet, one day childhood ends.

So, off to war I learned to march
to a drummer's beat so loud.
I couldn't hear the sounds of fear
amid the cadence crowd.

I learned to fight for freedom
my mother understood.
Her loss was but a gesture
to serve the common good.

Now as she mourns beside my name
carved neatly on a wall.
The one thing she cannot forget
is me when I was small.

Lorraine Billings

The Rain Storm!

There once was a rain storm
It was loud and wet
You could see lightning
and hear thunder,
How could you forget?
It makes you jump.
It makes you look.
Your heart goes "thump,"
It's so loud you can't finish
reading your book.

Nicole L. Harris

To Viola On Our Mutual Birthday

When God was making mankind
It was very plain to see
He made two special babies
And they were you and me
'Twas on a cold day in January
That we were placed on earth
It was indeed the 11th
That we were given birth
I am so very happy
That it turned out this way
To have a lovely person
Like you to share my day
I offer you congratulations
And I hope you say the same
Aren't we lucky we have each other
And we have but Him to blame

Lillian LaPrell

Without You

     Without you in my life,
It would seem as though
I'd have nothing.
     So that there should tell
you I believe our relationship
holds something.
     Sometimes I think what
would I do if I lost you,
but I come up with nothing
except the fact that my feelings
are just left feeling sad and blue.
     Without you I wouldn't want
to carry on.
     Because I doubt I could
face the up-coming dawn.
     So now I pray that you
being with me is where
you'll always stay.

Railyn Timmons

"Life's Storms"

A cloud is hanging over me.
It's hard to look beyond.
It's a habit I have hated…
Yet, still I'm very fond.

As I look ahead to blue skies,
there seems to be a wall.
Each time I try to climb it…
I slip-and back I fall.

When the challenge is so far away…
I know I'll make it past.
Yet as the task comes nearer…
My confidence won't last.

This Isn't just a harmless cloud.
It's a dark and dangerous storm.
It will get worse, not better-
As my fate begins to form.

In my dreams I find a ladder,
I climb, and never stop.
As the sunlight hits my face…
I make it to the top.

C. Jeanene Zielinski

Desperate

Entrance into hell,
it's harder to escape.
The mountains are only trivial
to the problems of the day.
Pleasures of joy used sparingly,
no time for you to play,
The lust of hearts in tragedy
make the victim look away.
Silence prevails the setting,
Darkness covers the land,
Even now please let me die
With rare flowers in my hand.

Maren Lindow

Description Of Love

Love is such incredible stuff
     It's rare and it's risky
     It's calm and it's frisky
And sometimes it's terribly tough.
     Painful and perilous
     Joyous and garrulous
It is sometimes erratic and rough.

Tender as a flowering bud
Stronger than sharpened steel
Deeper than bone, deeper than blood
Capricious and fickle - yet very real.

     Quiet as comfort
     Shrill as a scream
     Rough as reality
     Smooth as a dream
     Joy and elation
     Torment and strife

Love is the stuff that gives meaning to life.

Sylvia Vicker Savage

Parting

When night comes around
It's time to say good-bye.
Minutes begin to feel like seconds.
Although they both are holding back
their minds are dreaming alike,
waiting for that glimpse of passion.
For every junction an end must come;
but that moment is worth it all:
the lips lock, slow and lustfully
every motion creates more want
until the surroundings cease to exist
time stands still, running on empty
with hesitation the lips depart,
but the craving remains.

Linda Mielcarek

Who I Am

Black is me.
It's what I'll be.
I don't know why,
But I am glad that I am,
     Black as I come,
     Black as I go,
     Black as I please.
Under uncertain skies I am as free as
A bird unafraid to stretch its wings.
So don't tell me what I ought to be,
For I am my own person you see and
Nothing and no one could ever make
Me change my ways, because who I am
Is myself and myself I will always be.

Stephanie D. Winfree

Dumped

Well it's official
I've heard my dismissal
But I'm still confused
Far from being amused
She'll never be mine
I guess I was never in line.
Is she worth all this time
Does she think I'm slime.
Was I in love
Or was I above
Was it even capable
Or in able
Why did I try so much
Then worry as such

Rob Lenkey

Hard Metal And Roses

Juanita with roses
  Juanita on the corner
eyes shouting sadness
  Juanita where's your mother
flower girl Juanita
  selling by the stoplight
    on the avenida
      Juanita with roses
how old are you
  how many years
    cold cars passing
      hard metal and roses

Juanita, Juanita
  Juanita where's your mother
    Juanita on the corner
      hard metal and roses

Karl Bryan

Daddy's Little Girl

When I was three my daddy said,
just as he gave me a twirl,
that he hoped that I've forever be,
Daddy's little girl.

The age of seven was a wonder,
because I turned into such a pain.
But Daddy said his little girl,
is what I would remain.

By the time I was ten,
I was looking at boys.
My daddy seemed to wonder why,
I no longer liked my toys.

Daddy didn't like the day,
that I turned thirteen.
His little girl was growing up,
what did all this mean?

Now that I'm older,
and I've tried to see the world,
I think we've both finally realized,
that I'm no longer Daddy's little girl.

Kristy M. Besaw

Untitled

Wake up and die right
keep your ways on the
straight and narrow gate
The way of the righteous are
blessed white the ways of the
wicked are cursed in the Lord's sight.

Marrgot Peirce

Only One Way

There is a way to pleasantries-
  Just be nice.
There is a way to happiness-
  Self-sacrifice.
And the way to satisfaction-
  Do it right.
Or the way to one's pride within-
  Out of sight.

But no matter what the case may be,
There's but one way for eternity,
And that is Jesus, our Lord and Christ,
Who gave himself a sacrifice.

Roberta C. Dishman

Poetry is...

Poetry is, in essence,
Just how we feel and act.
Our thoughts are written down,
Though not always exact.

They have a deeper meaning
Than just what is said.
The words come from your heart
And not your head.

For poetry is a subtle
Revealing of the soul,
All of the innermost feelings
That make a person whole.

So as you read poetry
You've got to take your time,
And catch the meaning hidden
Between the written lines.

Rose M. Meis

God Is the World's Best Artist

God is the world's best artist.
Just look around and you'll see
The wonders and beauties of nature
He put here for you and me.

He is not afraid to use his brush
As he paints all the trees and flowers.
Yet, loveliness is best expressed
When he touches nature up with showers.

God's Master-piece is the beautiful sky.
It laughs, then cries, at times.
Yes, God is the world's best artist
Because - "His light so shines."

Margaret A. Rosenberger

"Seventeen"

Seventeen is a funny age;
Just right to make your parents rage;
Help your ma to keep things clean;
Then sometimes - feel pretty mean.

Life gets lonesome sometimes sad
Days will come both good and bad;
So as we go from day to day,
We must take what comes our way.

So don't do anything you'd regret
Life is still worth living - you bet
Be good always - keep your life clean
It sure is great to be seventeen

Nina F. Lonas

I Saw A Man

I saw a man just sitting there,
Just sitting there, just sitting there.
In hospital he sits and stares.
A man lost — without a memory.
Father Frank best with many a duty.
He knows not me nor anyone.
A disease that blunts the brain.
And weakens every muscle, strain.
Is this the coronation of advancing age?
Is this all we can expect of time?

Walter Murray

"Departed Pet"

My precious pet, you'll never know
Just what you meant to me.
The years we spent together,
brought lasting memories.

I, can't escape from thoughts of you,
no matter how I try.
Since you were snatched away in death,
and I was left to cry.

The tears I've shed has "yet" to take
the pain, out of my heart,
And if I cried an ocean,
it would only be a start!

This house, we shared together
is lonely as can be.
It seems no matter where I look,
you're all that I can see.

I hope, someday "my little pet"
this grief I feel will cease,
So my aching, breaking heart,
can once more find some peace!

Thelma L. Meadows

They Didn't Let Me Know

When the death angel came
  Knocking at your door
You were ready to go.
  But, no one let me know.

Even though our age difference
  was far apart
You always had a place in my heart.
  Yet, they didn't let me know.

My thoughts were often of your children
  and how they were getting along.
Fond memories still remain.
  But, they didn't let me know.

One day we'll meet face to face
  the sad memories will all be erased.
No more sorrow or pain.
  Even though they didn't let me know.

Mable Glover Johnston

The Ice Age, Come

Freeze over my heart
Let it be still,
Buried way deep below,
Enclosed forever.

After all, since he
Doesn't love me anymore,
What do I have
To live for?

L. M. Ward

The Sea

Why are you so angry this morning
   Lashing out at the cottages
     That line your shore

What are you saying
   With your thunderous voice
     That you are in command

I hear you
   And I do not doubt you

I'm alone on the beach
   They all left yesterday
     The sunglasses and bikinis

No more little old ladies wading
   With skirts held high

Will you miss them all
   For another year

"I'm happy"
   Now I have you all to myself
     Ramona Smart

Reflections Upon A Dream

I tossed and turned,
Last night's repose
Gave troubled dreams
And tangled bedclothes.
I suffered in slumber
For considered acts,
That as of yet,
Are not even facts.
Yet dreaming gave me
A most rare look,
At how I will feel,
For actions I took.
How strange to suffer
In darkest night,
For things not done
But only that might.
Yet insight is the greatest tool
And last night's pain
Saved tomorrow's fool.
    Wayne J. Summers

You

In my dreams
   Late at night
A vision comes
   Into my sight
Of palm trees blowing
   In a cool spring breeze
Of light rain falling
   And you and me

I only wish
   That I could make
Myself to dream
   And not awake
And even though
   I see you here,
In my dreams
   You are so near

It's oh so hard to face the days
Since you have left and gone away.
    Sheri Hedrick

Untitled

I see you sitting there
Laughing at some joke unheard
Or commenting on someone you know

Saying things neither polite nor rude
And yet, perfect for you.

You turn to me so silently
As I quietly walk by
You ask me to sit with you
To talk and have fun with you.

Yes, I agree to sit with you
'Cause I can see the other side of you
Which many people do not know.

Do not shy away from me
For I only wish to be a friend

And sit here with you
Laugh at some joke
Unheard by anyone else
Or comment on someone we know

Saying things neither polite nor rude
And yet, perfect for this group.
    Miriam Hawn

Dead Air

After the wake is gone
left standing in awe
after the wave is gone
dumb founded is all they saw
after the ripple is soft
we set in silence
after the quiver lays
we anchor in bliss
after the wake is gone
gone, never to return
after the wave crashes
Is always, when we burn?
    Lee Tanner

"Moonlight"

   Turn off the lights and
let the moon, shine down.
   It is wide open in a clear
bright sky, noticing its light on
the ground.
   Shining its peace throughout
the world to know.
   The hatred that is non existent
in my world is more than I
can hold.
   Do not be so bold, the
world is ready to end.
   The memories are shattered,
there is nothing left of my friends.
   So please take me far away,
away from these city lights.
   And bring me here, to
a calm moonlit night.
    Sarah Beebe

The Artisans

Loving-kindness is the hand of Jehovah;
life, His sculpture.
Selfishness, the hammer of Beelzebub;
murder is his art.
    Paul L. Burrell

The End?

Tell us stranger what you look like,
Let us look upon your visage.
We wish to venture to your darkness,
We want to seek and find your message.

Don't come to us too fast or gruesome,
Or pounce on us like raging weather,
Softly blow like summer breezes,
Or like a weightless, drifting feather.

Our minds know not until your coming,
Just how great and bold you are.
The time and place is still a secret,
Is our final near, or far?

It's a wonder to every person,
That mystic thing that we call death.
And what will our consolation be,
After we have finally left..., forever?
    Larry Lorenz

Wish, Hope, Pray And Dream

I wish there was a way I could
let you know how much
I Love You
I hope someday you'll see and feel
How much I am in love with you
I pray that one day you can
trust in me, as I
Trust in you
I dream about the day you
Love me as much as
I Love You
Then I won't have to wish
Hope, pray anymore because my
   Dream came true
Now you know how much
I Love
    Sherry L. Henderson

Necessity

Take my hand
Let's take a walk
Crunch some leaves
Have a talk
How are you doing
How have you been
So much to tell you
Where to begin
Say I love you
A whisper, a hug
Four year old child
Heart feels a tug
Growing and learning
Pulling away
Each moment's precious
Live for today.
    Karmen Hershey

Dogwood

Petals five of palest pink,
Nail notched by sacrificial blood,
Trunk too weak to bear the
   burden of a human cross
Sun shines brightly on it,
Winds blow softly over it,
A token of Heaven's love for man
   is growing here.
    Thelma Guttormson

The Frigid Rest

numb in a brain freeze
licorice mixed
    with the liquor inside me
he wants my recognition
I cease to feel him
    against falling skin
heat rising above me
while I am stillborn
    to the touch
the twisted flow of diversity
climbing to the summit
    of internal paranoia
climatic dreams fogging
the windows in the spotlight
    finding the way
back to the familiar
as I have a hunger
    for my rest in peace

Sarah James

Life

Life is so mysterious,
    Life is amazing and great.
Greet each day with a smile,
    Problems can always wait.

Life is what we make it:
    Happy, content and sweet,
Mixed with occasional sadness,
    Family makes life complete.

Let's sow seeds of kindness,
    Love will make them grow.
Joy and happiness will return,
    We reap just what we sow.

We were each given a talent
    To develop here on earth.
Let's multiply our talents,
    Show others our true worth.

Life is what we make it,
    We've been greatly blessed.
So let's help each other,
    Until our day of rest.

Lillian A. Mink

When A Child Runs

When a child runs
Life shines dull
Spirits crawl beneath the earth.

Memories—reveal themselves—
    through the haze of regret

Life — wilts ——
    and struggle loses meaning

Laughter merges with tears
    as shoulders droop
        and muscles give up their will

    Reasons - must be found
        to get up
            to eat
                and to live

Phil H. Becker

The Answer

Are you tossing in confusion
Like a ship at worst sea;
Are you scared of life's giving,
Need you be troubled.....take heed.

There comes a mighty tempest,
It's told, It will be soon,
Be mighty against your transgressions,
Listen for this tune...

Played on that last day trumpet,
In a twinkling of an eye;
Your ship can come to harbor
And rest itself on high.

Thank You Jesus
For the answer.

J. J. Wills

The Ultimate Love

Love is something beautiful
Like a sun-splashed sky
Or the wide, open country
where the meadows lie.

Love is something precious
Like the cry of a newborn
Or the crisp smell of dew
On a bright, Sunday morn.

Love is something gentle
Like the leap of a fawn
Or the slow, gracious break
Of a breathtaking dawn.

Love is something eternal
Like a gold wedding ring
Or the heartwarming sounds
When Heaven's angels sing.

But above all love is God's
Which is forever and fair
And is by far greater
Then any human care.

Sheri Pfautz

Sunflowers

A tender dream
    like flowers
        grows
            with petals
                soft
            and wet
        with dew
            and quiver
                in the morning light
When waking from within the womb
    of slumber
        sweet
            and yet intense
She hastens to repeat the dance
    of dreamers
        and experience
Planting thoughts of universe
    The seed of life
        Love

Karin Cathryn Whitney

Garden of Dreams

Such a vivid memory
Like I knew all of the characters
Time to tell the story
Like pictures in a book

Another strange day it seems
In the back of my mind a memory
The light breaks through the darkness
The morning soon arrives

I'm going to write you a letter
As if I knew all of the words to say
Searching for an answer
Our secrets are revealed

And now I'll sing you this song
In the garden of our dreams
The truth is love unveiled
Here for all to see

Markus Crash

Sweet Solitude

Changes are like seasons,
like the moods of the sea.
Winds of emotions
bring changes in me.

Waves in these waters
reflect dark mysteries.
Mirrors span across time
and create memories.

I relive days gone by
with a turn of my head.
My mind's eye sees old faces
my ears echo words said.

While entrapped in my daydream
I soar high, lost in space.
Then reality awakes me
Dreams dissolve, with no trace.

Wanda Howard

"Close To Me"

Close to me, so close to me,
Like the stars are to the sky,
You're close to me.
You're as close as day and night,
As time is to eternity,
You're close to me.
What if raindrops,
In a cloud may separate,
They will rise again and
In heaven mate,
It's destiny.
Close to me, so close to me,
Like the rays are to the sun
you're part of me,
And in my heart
You'll always be,
close to me.

Margaret R. Loyko

A Wanderer

A Wanderer passed through a village.
No one saw him when he came,
No one saw him in the village,
No one saw him when he left.
Everybody was guilty.

Michael Shaskevich

Susan

She would come and go
Like the sun,
Radiant in
Beauty and elegance,
In kind happiness
And admirable
Independence.
Her very clothes
Spoke power...
Her name was Susan.

A smile dresses
Her face, masking all
Other emotions
As she mechanically
Does for others-
Feeding first,
Cleaning next,
Entertaining and
Serving all of the time....
Her name is Mommy.

Karen Elizabeth Burkart

Impenetrable Fortress

Waves of pain crash against my heart,
like the surf pounding the tender shore.
The love we felt has become a dark
chasm separating our souls.
My heart has turned to stone and is an
impenetrable fortress protecting its
precious treasure.
Enveloping darkness swirls and dances
around my weary, wounded soul.
Reach out, touch me, let us be as
we were before!
Make me feel the heart-throbbing
passion that was there once before.
The memory of your face slices through
my body like a searing blade of fire.
Alas, the dream will not be and I am
standing alone once more.

Robyn M. Wood

A Tribute

A mem'ry, lovelier than the rose,
Lingers with me, fresh as dew
Nestled in my heart it glows
A shrine, so special, just for you.

The elfin smile that rode your face
And shimmered like some priceless jade
Caressed us all with heart-felt grace
A mem'ry, Dot, that will not fade.

You gave so much down through the years
You helped out in so many ways
'MIdst the laughter and the tears
You set the stage for better days.

Ruth K. Meltzer

Ocean Character

The madness claims the subtle
   lives, from sour grains of sand,
The weaning foam, sucking life
   from slowly dying land,
The anger of the currents
   strength, makes nature beg and bow
Devoured by the icy dark,
   the grains swim circles now.

Kimberly Loar

Who/Why

Sometimes I wonder just who am I
Living today and tomorrow die
What's going on, I'd like to know
Why am I here and where do I go

A mouth, a nose and two small eyes
Why is that such a big surprise
A mind that thinks and eyes that see
Can this all be really me

Sometimes I feel I'm not even here
Sometimes I feel I'm close and near
Sometimes I feel so distant and far
Sometimes I wonder just what is par

Sometimes I'm quiet with nothing to say
Sometimes I'll sing all thru the day
Sometimes I laugh and sometimes I cry
Sometimes I wish I could say goodbye

Time goes by and I'm still here
Just another day, a week or a year
How do I know what I'm supposed to do
Can someone help — can you????

Kay DeBar

"Prisoner Of Addiction"

A Prisoner of addiction—
Locked in its Manacles—
sticking the needle through flesh—
Hoping for the keys to success
Fame as his warden—
for he has the key.
Serving a four-year term—
Bound for wealth, Bound by Wealth.
tripping on Chains—
that he himself has Forged.
Going nowhere—
just a short, fast way to death.

Mark Mitchell Jr.

Phoenix

Rising above oneself
Looking at the world threw
different eyes. It scares
me to know that I will
never be the same. New
body, New eyes, New mind
rising to a new level. As
I ascend I say goodbye
to the old and welcome
what future beholds.

   Watch me fly to the
heavens.

Patrick Roche

Man Behold Autumn

Beloved, gorgeous Autumn
Lord God, you deserve a standing ovation
With a never ending applause.
What a wonderful spectacle
For man to feast his eyes
And, nourish his soul.
Nothing on the printed page,
Canvas, or cloth has ever to compare.
Nature ever changing
Gods own kaleidoscope

Marie E. Welch

Almost Thirteen

Almost thirteen...
Lost in the crowd.
Feeling bad one day.
The next day proud.

   Wondering all the time...
   Why me?
   Is it possible that
   Life can be more scary.

   At my age people say
   Children are to be seen
   And not heard...
   But adolescence is a time to speak
   And express our words.

   You're almost thirteen,
   Life is unreal,
   Adults may not know
   What me feel.

R. Mercer

King Lion's Roar

Angels sing
   love and honor
World wake up
   join the choir
Time fleeting
   death arriving
Prepare your house
   light or fire
The lion comes
   sun or moon
World wake up
   King Lion roars.

Theresa D. Murray

Synopsis Of Love

Love is sweet, love is kind
Love can be very hard to find.
Love is nice, love is lasting
Love can seem like dynamite blasting.

Love you cherish, love you save
Love you get more of when you gave.
Love is a song, love is a poem
Love is found in every good home.

Love is gentle, love is tough
Love we don't seem to have enough of.
Love is food, love is clothes
Love is only where it grows.

Love is Mom, love is Dad
Love is that sweet little babe you had.
Love can live, love can't die
Love can't end with one good-bye.

Love is bright, love is sun
Love isn't always having fun.
Love is below, love is above
But love most important of all, is love.

Mary Hale

A Brick Wall

A wall made of may red squares
Of concrete plastered together
To form a shield from the
Bad like my mother used to do
When she loved me.

Peggy Vint

Memories

Steadfast rocks and gentle streams,
Love felt blankets broken seams,
Teddy bears with one eye blue,
Scents of times in morning dew.
All these hold within their sight,
Their furry paws and watery flight,
The nature of our heart's delight:
Our past, its golden worth, our sight.
For though they stand in plain design,
Seen or felt at our own time,
Their image lives beyond our minds,
Fading soft, so we might find,
Lasting love of self through time.

Morgan Land

Untitled

I will search for enchanted grass,
Make a potion of love in a glass,
After supper this drink he will have,
That would make him drunk with love.

Then, I will look for a wonderful witch
Her witchcraft, to me she will teach.
I would put on his soul a magical spell,
So he would send his lover to hell.

Also, the star I will find in the sky,
To answer my question it won't deny.
Is there hope? Am I waiting in vain?
Uncertainty drives me insane.

Margaret Rainstein

Winter Wishes

Winter wishes
make the sky so white,
it makes the snowflakes
fall in flight.
Winter is the time for
Hanukkah candles,
and makes us wear boots instead
of sandals.
Winter is the time of year
when we cry for joy tear by tear.
Winter wishes is the thing
we can't do in summer, fall, or spring.

Kelly Marie Shinko

Along Life's Road

Early morning sunrise,
Makes dewy grass glisten.
Birds sing cheerfully for us,
When we pause to listen!

When roses are in bloom,
with aromas so sweet.
It's such a pleasure to pick one,
For our neighbor down the street!

There's a beautiful rainbow,
Behind every dark cloud.
We need to be thankful,
and sing praises out loud!

God provides so much
along life's road.
To brighter our day,
and lighten our load!

P. J. Blankenship

Lies...

Broken Hearts and many lies,
Many of my unheard cries,

You said you loved me,
You said you cared,
But now all I feel is lonely and scared.

I need you now, I needed you then,
I need you now as more than a friend,

Sleepless nights and untold dreams,
Little lies and bigger schemes.

I told you then,
I'll tell you now,
We'll be together somewhere...somehow.

Tricia Jayson

The Immigrant

I saw a flag with stars and stripes
Many years ago
It caught my eye and fancy
Waving to and fro.

I asked them what the flag meant
And someone then told me
It's for a land of plenty
Where everyone lives free.

Every time I saw that flag
It stood for some place good
I hoped that I could see that land
But never thought I would.

I saw a lot of turmoil
In the place where my home stood
I wished that I could leave it
But never thought I could.

Many years have since gone by
And when that flag I see
It has a special meaning —
It's waving now for me.

Mildred J. Katemopoulos

Untitled

   The pain in my heart
matches the tears in my soul
   there will never be another like you.

   As a couple, we were unbeatable,
as single I feel weak.

   Your companionship and caring filled
my eyes with love.
   But on that fateful night
of drinking and driving,
   you forgot your destiny.

   As they cover your body in the earth
and our dreams in dirt,
I will always love you, and the
child you will never know.

Tammi Ross

Endless

The silence he brings, into the depth
   of the night
As he peels away my flesh, only to come
   in to my soul and leave me
Helpless and empty once again.

Sandy Wojnowich

Possibilities

Since I wished for you,
"Maybe" became possible.

Since I got you,
"Nothing" is impossible.

Since I held you,
"Impossible" became possible.

Would I be without you,
That thought is not possible,

You are my life,
Making whole of me -
                    Possible.

Kishan Chand

A Glimpse of Time

We knew each other for two days.
Maybe it was just a phase
Or maybe it was love at last
Why did it go by so fast!

The Gallery of My Heart

The memory of the night we had;
is truly a peace of art!
A peace that may only be stored
in the gallery of my heart.

A River of Love

Our love is like the ocean breeze
that floats around calm and free.
Never know were to go or what to do.
But always end up saying I Love You!
And the true love between me and you
Will run till the oceans dry up, and the
breeze
don't blow, so that it can't roam wild,
and free inside our soul.

Karen Cobb

Remembrance

   What memory would be of me, without
me.
   People called friend forget my face,
   The words of my heart linger in
their mind.
   Me being dead, my soul in heaven
   People remembering me not without
a picture.
   Day after day I slip away,
   My mark was made, my love
was shared.
   If I die before I wake,
   Would my love be lost,
   My laugh be forgotten,
   Or would a memory of me
be forever.

Melinda M. Haigler

Loves' Afar

When I see her
   My heart is all a flutter
I can't believe it
   my legs are turned to butter
I need to tell her
   but my mouth begins to stutter
A deep breath I take
   She is gone before I utter
   loves' afar

Mark Lastowicka

Baby Makes Three

Coiled potential gushes
Mighty love rushes
Forth! God's hand
Stretches across chasm
Finding two lovers
...And baby makes three...
Wanting turns inward
Welcoming other and self
Joining in a chance
Dance of romance
...And Baby makes three...
Planted and grounded
Loved and sprouted
From Father's fire; Mother's love
...And baby makes three...
Born of love from above
Apart yet a part
Of parents love
...And Baby makes three.

Martin Schatzman

Condensation

Gray, dim morning
Minds reach out
Like tendrils of the fog itself
Snatching misty threads of dreams.

Half-dawn, half-awakening
A fading of the boundaries
Between night and day
Life and not-life
Constructed and imagined realities
Until with fog conducting dreams
A great subconscious mind emerges.

Countless cells float in gray fluid
Each is an isolated memory
And each is a premonition,
A possible reality that may
Stand solid in the light of day
Or evaporate like the mists of morning
The condensation of cast-off dreams.

Lydia Heard

Move

On the move again...
Move again...
Move again!!
We are on the move again.
Staying here today, on
the asphalt by night fall.
We are on the move again.
We are not professionals;
but, we are well experienced!
We hang our hat on the
trailer wall.
Now it is in the apartment hall.
Check to make sure we
did not leave the dog behind.
Like we accidentally left Mr. Boots
at the edge of no roots.
We are on the move again.
We should be going through
the next town by ten often.

Marjorie Myrick

The Little Boy And The Shadow

Play around your shadow little boy,
move around again and again,
follow your own little world.
Play around
until noon time,
when the shadow
your shadow,
will shrink to your feet,
at your mercy,
to stomp on it,
making you,
for a short while,
the center,
of your own self.

Wilfrid Mirville

Lotus

Floating, Growing, Within Mud, Spotless

Glide
Moving, with others, influence, follow;
Expand
Ideas, not sure, try, change;
Impure
Differences, hatred, evil, not I;
Clear
Exotic, rich, within bad, good.

Kristopher M. R. Hager

Habit

Habit habit habit
Mr. Habit has a habit
of getting into habits
Habit habit habit
Mr. Habit has a habit
of getting hit in the
head with a ball
it is a habit for
Mr. Habit
Habit habit habit

Lacey D. Bonini

Christmas Eve

Once upon a time
My brother Mike and I
Climbed upon our window seat
To watch the yellow moon so high

When suddenly out of the darkness
Dressed in red with a beard so white
Appeared a funny looking chap
Who disappeared into the night

Seeing we were not asleep
He kept on towards duty bound
And waited for our little heads
To rest upon our pillows sound

When I awoke the morning after
Underneath my Christmas Tree
I found some presents from that stranger
Who left them out of love for me

Susan Boyle Vaughan

Christmas Eve

The party's over.
    My guests have gone.
    Silence fills the room.

The sound of laughter disappears.
    Voices ... I no longer hear.

Dirty dishes everywhere,
    Soft drink bottles sitting there.
Coffee maker ... totally drained,
    Empty cups ... with lipstick stains.

Christmas wrappings on the floor,
    Jingle bells hang on my door.
Christmas lights are shining bright,
    They light my windows in the night.

Now Christmas Eve is over
    For another year
    Leaving me with memories
    I hold so very dear.

Phyllis Christina Dunn

"Love Lives On"

My life has just begun,
My heart is not the same
I have to go on living,
In my father's name
When I'm feeling low,
As I now often do
I picture his warm face,
And remember love so true
I miss his loving hands,
The things that he would say
His memory will live on
Inside me,
Each and everyday...

Lisa A. Sacco

Untitled

Can't you see me, while you're away?
My heart is with you, everyday.

Don't cry for no reason,
    or make an excuse.

Look for the answers,
    tell the truth

Love you forever,
    repeat everyday

Don't let your heart
    wander away!

Lisa P. Haun

Heart's Captivity

    With each passing hour of the day
my heart long's for her.

    With each passing moment of the
day my heart belongs to her.

    She alone holds the key that
will release me.

Set me free, I say to thee.
    No this cannot be.
    For I am truly happy,
    in her captivity

Mathes J. McMillan

My Christ Of The Cross

My Master came; He bled and died;
My Lord, for me, was crucified;
On Calvary's cross He bore my shame,
Oh, how I love His blessed name.
For Him, ill will could have no part;
He bore no anger in His heart.
And so He died as He did live,
Whispering, "Father, them forgive."
But then they rolled the stone away.
'Twas a glorious resurrection day.
He reigns on high in heaven above
To share with all His glorious love.
He gave His life, His blood for me,
I'll always humbly thankful be.
He died cast out, alone, apart;
He'll always live within my heart.
So, let your voice in praises sing;
Let the bells of heaven ring;
May He by each one be adored,
Alleluia to our risen Lord!

Marilyn McGowan Godfrey

My Love For Him

Like an eagle in the sky,
My love for him will always fly;
Like a river running fast,
My love for him will always last;
Believe what I tell you,
I will always be true;
No matter what you think,
Our boat will never sink;
Because, our love,
Is a gift from above;
And the stars shine bright,
On our love tonight!

Shelley M. Bass

Dimensions Of Soul

Oh, my darling
My love for you is so
It exceeds being contained
In the dimensions of my soul
For I explode all boundaries
Into heights of tenderness
Then sink to depths of emotion
With your every kiss
Oh, my darling
My love for you is such
Expands the breadth of expression
Mere words are not enough
For these feelings consume
All corners of my being
Beyond what I can comprehend
In the abyss of soul unseen
For you inspire me endlessly
To emotions I never knew
Into dimensions beyond myself
In the name of loving you.

Kimberley A. Segraves

"Real True"

In the fear of the eye
Of the real and true.
Seen by the nieve
In another view.
Straight from the real.
Right from the true.
Life's lesson is heard.
Thank you and I love you.

Zolene Wolf

The End Of My Beginning

Here I lie in the comfort of
my mother's womb,
My mother does not want me,
Now I must face a most terrible doom.

For see I will never be born,
From my mother I will be torn,
I had but only one wish,
I wished she wasn't so selfish,
My wish didn't come true,
She did what she wanted to do.

Now I enter through Golden Gates,
I'm away from all of the
Worlds bitterness and hates,
Now I'm with the Lord,
He is full of love and grace,
I feel privileged for I
have touched his face.

Michelle Vail

Amy

Skipping down the paths of life,
My precious granddaughter goes,
Not thinking of the pitfalls,
Not knowing of life's woes.

The troubles of the life ahead,
The many ups and downs,
Nothing seems to concern her,
Thru life she leaps and bounds.

Hopping, skipping, dancing, playing,
Happily on her way.
This is the day that she turns eight,
And nothing can dismay.

I cannot tell her of tomorrow,
And all that lies in wait.
Just watch her and enjoy it now,
As she goes out to skate.

Someday when she's all grown,
And watching her child play,
Maybe then she'll think of me,
And this real special day.

Marna J. Marshall

Untitled

When you walk through my door
my soul sings
of a longing,
and I, too
raise my voice
to the wind.

The thundering
of my heart
fills my eyes
and I dance
to the rain
that showers me;
cleanses me.

I spill over
with joy.
I am captive
once more.

Lisa Salvata Linton

Here We Are My Sweet Dee

Here we are in this lonely world
My sweet little Dee and I,
She's the one that makes me feel
The way I do inside.
She's always here when I need her,
She's right here by my side,
And I would do most anything
To keep her satisfied.
When times got hard and friends,
Were few I could always count on you.
Thank you for forgiven me for all
The things I brought you through.
Once in life is this lonely world,
You find someone you need,
And for me my sweet and special Dee,
You are that one indeed.

Robert Robinson, Jr.

Chaos

Confusion raging in my mind,
My thoughts so often stray.
I reach out to the one I love,
But she just turns away.
There is a longing in my soul,
A need I can't express.
I try to dream of days to come,
Yet still my thoughts regress.
Standing in a crowded room,
I'm lost and so alone.
The emptiness blows through my soul,
And turns my heart to stone.
I feel the demons in my head,
Trying to break free.
I stand here looking in the mirror,
And wonder who I see.
How long can I walk upon,
This tightrope called my life?
Before I drop into the darkness,
And insanity ends my strife.

Todd Bugg

"Never Been A Mother"

You say you've never been a mother
  Never a child of your own to care
But to me you've been a mother
  On this earth none can compare.

You say you've never been a mother
  Never made a kid's heart glad
But to me you've been a mother
  The best a kid has ever had

You say you've never been a mother
  Never one of your very own
But, to us, these kids you've loved
  Gave the only home we've known.

So don't say "I've never been a mother"
  With all your tenderness and love
Lady, you have really been a mother
  Just like one sent from above.

Nadine Puckett

Death Of A Butterfly

You walked a long time, your hand in hers,
  Never knowing at the time
    Of all the love, of all the joy,
    Of all the everything
      That she would be.

And then one day,
  Through fate, or circumstance,
    Or less,
      The hand is loosened
And the pathway complained, lost.

And now she is seen as pure sunlight
  Or sparkling clear waters
    And the onliness
Of your possible happiness,

As the fingers of your heart
Reach out and curl
And try to grasp
The gentle butterfly
That has taken wing
  And left you alone.

Robert Walter Purser

Reality

Silence comes to those who hear.
  New is old with passing years.
Round is the line without a break.
  Peace is war, love is hate.
Watches that no longer wind.
  Darkness falls upon mankind.

The earth is scorched, solid black.
  Souls trod a beaten track.
Evil quivers, taking flight.
  Blind begins to see a light.
Quiet descends, clouds drift by.
  Gold is sun, blue is sky.

Green appears where none before.
  Demand begins anew for more.
Memories faded, time is passed.
  End is beginning, first is last.
Good, evil, peace and strife.
  Continuous is the circle of life.

Patricia D. Sollock

Cheers Or Tears?

Just the two of us
Nibbling at supper;
Quiet prevails, but sounds
Echo through my mind...
  Squeals, screams,
  Laughter, tears,
  Bouncing balls,
  Clatter on the stairs...
My wife reaches out
To touch my hand,
The last of our kids
Is grown and gone.

William Trutner

Shadows

The hand between the candle and the wall,
produces shadows dark and tall,
the light and flame it separates,
a hidden mind illuminates,
reflecting deep into the night,
secrets made by candle light.

Michael London

Death Of An Angel

You had seen a light
No one else could see.
It was dark for them.
You wished to bring a calm and peace
To your world.
A world that had none.
A world of death and crime.
Then, with a fight for the longing
Of life rather than death,
You, an innocent child,
Had darkness impressed upon you, too.
The darkening, blackness of death.
Then, only after you were gone,
Did they realize,
The beauty of the light
That you stood for.

Sara White

Unanswered Questions

Ask for things we think are right
No one knows for sure
Who's to say if it's wrong or right
Or if there is a cure

Life just happens who knows why
I guess god keeps secrets well
Doing things that trip us out
Maybe life is the living hell

People say Someday at the end of time
There will be a judgment day
How do they know, who told them
Who or what gave anyone the right to say

Some of us follow our instincts
Letting our conscious be the judge
Not wasting time on bad memories
Karma will settle the grudge

Never knowing which day is our last one
Afraid of being hurt we don't plan ahead
Not taking a chance on shattered dreams
Keeping a lock on our heart instead

Susan D. Campbell

Amazon River

Amazon river, you are a mighty river;
No other river comes nearer.
Put your power in my intellect,
So that I will sing your glory.

I love you, mighty river;
I love you, powerful river.
I was born at your banks —
I belong to you.

Amazon river, I live far from you;
But I see you almost every day,
When I fly to see you
In my mind, in my imagination.

All human beings admire you,
Admire your dense, thick rain forest;
Admire your great volume of water;
Admire your gray and crystalline water.

Amazon river, you were born being great
And so was I.
You were born with greatness—
I was born to be great.

S. P. Cordeiro

Eternal Love

What is this feeling?
No words can describe.
Such deep emotion fills my being.
Some call it love, but is that it?
I felt love before, though never this.

Something beckons me from long ago,
As though I've known your soul before.
It stirs me so deep inside,
To look into your familiar eyes.

So many nights I laid awake,
Wondering where you were.
But many lessons we had to learn,
Before our love could be.
Heartache and tears
were the paths we took,
That led us to each other.

Now here we are soul touching soul.
How wonderful, how sweet,
To look into each others eyes
And see eternity.

Rhonda A. Smith

If

If I was invisible,
nobody would bother me.

If I was a bird,
I would soar above the whole world.

If I was not human,
I could be anything
and everything there is to imagine about.

But since I am human,
then the If is only a dream.

Melissa Kindilien

A Very Lonely Death

No one really paid attention,
Nor did anyone care
She sat alone and only hoped,
But love someone, she didn't dare.

She longed for someone to hold her
She longed for a good friend
But that single deep dark secret
She knew, would bring the end.

She wished there was someone to stop her
She didn't want to die
She knew it was the only thing left
Her life was all a lie.

Quietly leaving that lonely room
And entering into another
She took her father's prize possession
And grabbed a small cover.

She sat in the corner and cried
As she took her last breath
For tonight she was to experience
A Very Lonely Death.

Stacy Hanson

Doing Time

On the inside looking out.
Not afraid just very bored
    Six long, slow months - no doubt
Feeling bad as they slam the door.

I am certainly not alone.
Thirty one others to be exact,
    All of us in here to atone
For some stupid illegal act.

The lost of my freedom
Is punishment in itself.
    For in here there is no fun,
And all their smoking destroys my health.

The courts are a joke in this nation.
If your wealthy or a politician,
    You'll probably just get probation
And never see the inside of a prison.

Mike Malinowski

The Seeker

The seeker of things
Not yet quite seen

The seeker of things
Not yet quite been

The seeker with eyes
That pierce the night

The seeker has friends
That protect from freight

The seeker in you
At times will be

The seeker who's blind
And cannot see

The seeker is someone
We all keep inside

The seeker feels
A need to hide

The seeker struggles
To be set free

The seeker in you
The seeker in me

Michele Slauson

Beyond The Mind's Eye

Forgivable, is the child who knows
nothing.
Tolerance, for the fool who knows
too little.
Beware, the narrow intellect of the
aged zealot, who knows all.
Vision is his, who finds knowledge
through discovery, for he shall
also find
wisdom.

Meredith E. Smith

Untitled

I have seen the Evil in reality
or so it seems.
I have seen happiness only in dreams.

Robert Sherman

Untitled

Stare into my deep blue eyes
Now tell me what you see
Listen to my beating heart
And know it's yours for free
Open up your warm, strong arms
Let me feel you near
Hold me nice and close
Shield me from my fear
Kiss me tenderly
Then watch a smile arise
Linger on my lips forever
Silence all my cries
Make me feel a passion
I've never felt before
Promise that you need me
And love me even more
Look into my eyes
You'll see how much I care
Look into my heart
You'll see my love for you is there.

Mara Herskowitz

The Window

I stand still
observing the world
through the window.
Looking forth I see
the moving lights of a city
Flashing with its
screams of enticing joy;
enveloped with cries of thunder
that drive an emotion of passion,
while illuminations of lighting
bring with it unseen visions,
and the many tears of rain
surround and remove—
all its inhibitions.
I stand still
observing the world
through the window.
However, I cannot see myself - past
the reflection of the wall on the glass,
from my own enclosure.

Micheal R. Cox

The Sky

The sky is as blue as the
    ocean,
The stars are as bright as a
    lantern,
The dew on the grass is as shiny
    as brass,
And the trees seem as tall as
    a mountain,
The moon is as yellow as a
    banana,
The sun is as scintillate as
    varnish,
The clouds are as white as
    snow,
And the fog is as damp as
    a tea leaf.

Shannon M. Johnson

Black Rose

She's everything to me,
Ocean pearls, and queen of land and sea.
If I had one wish
That would come true
I'd wish I truly do,
Oh! That I could have you!

But she's a Black Rose
Growing in the desert!
And she never stops to think
About me!
She's a Black Rose,
Growing in the desert!
And if that girl were mine,
I'd be right by her side,
And I'd never let her go!

Matthew A. Gardner

"A Reader's Creed"

I always think the cover
of a book is like a door that
    opens into someone's house
where I have never been before.
    A pirate or a fairy queen
may lift the latch for me,
    but I always wonder when
I knock, what welcome there
    will be.
When I find a house that's
    dull I do not often stay, but
when I find one full of
    friends I am apt to spend the day.
You never know what sort
    of folk will be within
you see, that's why reading
    is so interesting to me.

Rayfus Martin

Take A Stand

Abortion is the killing
Of a life he has created.
Stand up for Jesus
Until this death is abated.

Drugs on every corner
Altering people's mind.
Take a stand for Jesus
Bring sight to those who are blind.

Gang violence is escalating
Innocent people die.
Take a stand for Jesus
Let his name be our battle cry.

Child abuse is rampant
People out of control.
Take a stand for Jesus
Until Satan loosens his hold.

Oh, people of America
Wake up and see.
If we don't take a stand for Jesus
To Satan we lose our country.

Nita Gorman

Untitled

Feelings
of depth and vagueness
in and out of focus
like an oriental landscape
moving with dual nature
as a Hokusai wave
retreats to the ocean
its heart and soul
advances to the shore
its body and mind

Rachel L. Linden-Marshall

Random Thoughts of Plato

Random thoughts
Of Plato
Seized me
Of Socrates
Of Kant of Aquinas
Of Spinoza of Descartes
Of Mendelssohn of Marx
Of the Bal Shem Tov
Of Heschel's grandeur,
And of Buber's Thoo
Books of
Wisdom
Truth
And
Stimulating
Thought questions
For all who would listen.
And respond to the subtle silence
Betwixt the questions and the responses

Ralph J. Silverman

Our Cry

As I watched the movie
of the battered wife
A flood of memories
came back of
that period in my life
At first my feelings
were of anger and pain
By the end of the movie
tears were falling like rain
The price is too high
that women have to pay
Death or life in prison
There has got to be
a better way
Parents teach your children
Educate them well
That somebody this
nightmare for women
will in homes
no longer dwell.

Penelope Jacobsen Hunter

Reflections

As I close my mind
of the sights and the sounds
My own little world
reflects nothing around.
A vast block of infinity
a timeless lapse of shadows
My own little world
reflects only hollows.
Trying to reach away
from the visions and noise
My own little world
will never reflect joy.

Marci Girard

A Picture

Pictures in the past,
of you and me.
Remind me of the ways,
we used to be.

If I would lose
this picture,
I think of how lonely
this world would be.

To lose this beautiful picture,
would be painful for me.
The emptiness I feel inside,
would never be free.

So now I hold this picture,
Ever so close to my heart.
In hopes that me and this picture,
will never be apart.

Nikole Gustkey

A Little Brother

A little brother
Oh what a bother
why is he here with me?
I don't really hate him
but don't know who would
ever date him
And dread him for every
word he says.
He is a little pest and ruins
every dress that mom
ever buys for me. He doesn't
care and is always seen
wearing his underwear.
Geez, why is he here?

Kristen L. Lewis

Hello

Hello
old friend,
it is nice
to see you
again.
To be surrounded
by the warmth
of your hug
and the gentleness
of your touch
as you hold me
while we say hello
after being apart
for a while.

Mary Tripp

Life

Life soars through the clouds
    on its highest
And through valleys
    on its lows
You never know which way
    your life will choose
       until you arrive
Just take your life's highest
    as being proud
And your lowest with understanding
    as just another lesson
       learned in life.

Poncheena Kay Schwarck

God And Heaven

We praise his name
On Sunday night
Give him thanks
And true delight
He helps are prayers
And is always there
He touches our heart
And brightens our sight
So we can be led into the light
And there we will find eternal life
Paradise and true delight
Love and sharing
Family and friends
Niceness and happiness
Are all that is in
There is no fear in heaven
So don't be alarmed
No darkness no hate
That awful stuff
Can't get through the gate

Poppy Quinn

An Ark

Says,
On the breathless lake
An ark awaits for the wind
Tells it the destination.

Fragments of the moon
Dispersed on the water
Sing the silence
Without a sound,
And story the meaning of
Eternity
To its own shadow in the sky.

"…think of you."

At time the lake breathes.
The wind dimly
Starts to rustle.

Breaking the moon in two
The ark steers to someone.

Says,
Tearing the eternity
The ark rows to a moment love.

Takabe Hisamitsu

Waterland

— To A Woman

We lay together
On the river bottom
The salmon's eggs washing over us
The long green reeds
Floating next to us like dancers.

I asked you not to hurt me
To be gentle
So you brought me here
To this waterland
Beyond conquest
Beyond question
Where we sink
And rise together
With a softness like clouds.

You are strong
Powerful
Yet unafraid to expose
Your own soft underbelly.

Peter Damm

The Beach

The soft, smooth sand,
On the soles of your feet,
The bright shining rays,
Of the sun's heat.

The depth of the ocean,
So deep and so wide,
The schools of gliding fish,
Side by side.

The misty, white ruffles,
That crash to the ground,
And send out sprays of water,
Everywhere around.

Stars twinkle,
With every bit of light,
The moon's reflection,
What a beautiful sight.

Wading your feet in the water,
Getting them wet,
This is a joy,
You shall never forget.

Kerrie Boerem

"My Old Sixty Three

I am writing myself a poem
On this my special day
To share the love of God with you
In a very wonderful way
I want you all to know
That I am happy as I can be
Whenever you see me driving
That old nineteen and sixty three
The only car I have ever had
That is very true
God has been a blessing to me
Throughout these many years too
My car is getting old now
As you all can very well see
It also has many problems
But "Buddy" gets it fixed for me
I am so thankful to know
That God is always by my side
For which I give Him the praise
knowing that He is always my guide

Nannie Sue Crumpton

"The Old Lonely Road"

As I was out driving for pleasure
one-day I saw this old man
Walking down this old lonely road and
I thought to myself He hasn't a
soul to care what lonely road he
goes. So I drove up beside
him I said Sir can I give you
a ride. As he turned around to
my surprise I saw the kindest
face in my whole life. He said
Son I want to thank you for
your helping hand but this old
lonely road looks like a street of
gold to me an the end of
it my heavenly father is
waiting patiently. An as I drove
away with one thought in
mind that one day I would
walk that lonely road

Mary L. Howell

Tender Memories

Starlit bliss,
One tender kiss,
A reverie
Of what love was meant to be,
That first rendezvous
When I met you.
Then you departed,
And sadness started.
I will always recall
The joy of it all
When I loved you,
And you loved me,
    So tenderly!

Phyllis Capen

On The Maine Coast

No sound, no sound
    Only silence everywhere
The sky falls back on itself
Clear blue spaces push to gain a peek
Islands dark in shadow
    caressed in lingering pink
    from early sun
Hiding now behind the heavy clouds
Lobster boats cruising as shadows
Rocks rise in the water
Tide whispers away

The day has begun
    and song bursts forth from me
    in praise of God.

Mary Frances Elliott

Dove

O, Dove from high above
open up your wings of love

Spread your love all over the land
as hand in hand we all shall stand

Bring to us all joy and peace
and don't let it ever cease

Come around all the day long
and sing your joyous ole song

For nobody knows what's more true
until you come out of the sky of blue

Kenneth Roberts

My World

Some may say, some will do
Opened my mind to a new point of you

Can you feel, know the strain
In my world can you feel my pain

All you are, all you'll be
Circles of fear is all you will see

As you drift, push through the haze
Brush life aside to survive the daze

WELCOME TO MY WORLD
I am there, you let me be
That distant blur that shape is me

Far behind, Burned in your minds
There I stand realities kind
WELCOME TO MY WORLD

WELCOME TO MY WORLD

Richard Ghazarian

A Mother's Question

A son can either break your heart
or fill it full of love,
He can act like he's sent by the devil
or flew in on the wings of a dove.

A son can make you hurt inside
like you've never hurt before
but because a mother's love is strong
there's not much she can't endure.

A son can make you fill with pride
As he shyly gives you a hug
Or whispers "I'm glad you're my mother!"
Truly gives your heart strings a tug.

What makes a son so capable
of such pain or affectionate love?
The answer lies in her forgiving eyes
and a mother's unconditional love.

Lonnie Carr

Are You A Hugger

Did you hug someone today?
Or show affection in any way?
Just to show someone you care
Or did you feel you wouldn't dare?

Maybe they're waiting for just that,
It's as easy as a little chat,
Just let them know how you feel,
Just a gentle hug, no big deal.

It can sure chase the blues away,
And may brighten someone's day.
It can make you feel better too,
And it's such a nice thing to do.

A senior citizen, so lonely and drear
Needs a hug and a word of cheer.
Friends oft have burdens hard to bear,
Give them a hug and offer to share.

Love and caring make the world go 'round,
A little hug costs nothing I've found,
So let the Lord lead and you will see
What a great hugger you can be.

Velma McBride

Country Boy

My city bride is quite a cook!
Our friends delight to come,
When we invite to dinner,
........and they never leave a crumb.

I dearly love her entrees
And tiny petit fours
And crepe suzettes she does so well.
........I always ask for more.

But I want some country cooking!
Cornbread and pinto beans,
Chicken, fried with gravy,
And 'taters and turnip greens!

If I can't have some country food,
I think I'll simply die!
But I don't know how to tell my wife,
........For it might make her cry.

Ruby Chilson

Donna

Ages long ago and unknown
our souls drank in the light of the sun,
two spirits joined in universal joy
together we became one,
the laughter in your eyes as we stare
gently touches my longing heart,
smiles in radiant starshine
glowed from the start,
hand in hand we hold our union
and wade through the mist of the past,
ascending the precipice of symbiosis
clouds part before our eyes,
we wonder about the past,
did we know our previous selves?
were we joined in the expanse?
our hearts reborn
we inscribe a new chapter to our long story
upon the ancient tablets of the mind,
we have found us once again.

Steven D. Kulp

Future Sight

I look out afar
Out beyond the trees
And search the horizon
That is far from me

I scan the left
And I scan to the right
But what I seek
Is way out of sight

I spy a little nearer
To see something new
But all that I see
Are thoughts that are blue

So here I sit
Feeling lonely and numb
For the sight I seek
Is the sight of freedom

Peter Fox

Love

Privately,
Out of sight;
None to hear
Nor eye to see;

Some new thing
Barely felt,
Yet discerned
By fluttering

Wings of air
Across cheeks,
Touching lips,
Soft and fair.

A gentle shove
By your voice,
Tender, sweet,
I found love.

Kathryn L. Harrison

Madness In A Doomsday Ring

The race to madness
over a myriad years
First gold then steel
Now Space and all its fears
Still nothing to say on meeting
But war and torture is real
No greatness endears one to the other
Even though paintings and words
Sing the virtues of another

Polluting their very air
With not the smallest grain
Of purposeful change
Who can seriously love
The creatures so entrenched
Forever in mud
Calling for new masses
Coming in the new Spring
To believe and race
To what seems a never ending
Madness in a doomsday ring

Samuel Rich

On Stage, October!

October entered a frolicking clown,
Painting foliage to golden, red, brown.

Her ally wind scattered leaves around,
And rustled them along cold ground.

Not a bad way to exit from the blue,
Gaily garbed in breathtaking hues!

As I rake, gathering leaves in heaps,
A comparison to life my mind reaps:

Everything that lives must die, true,
And OLD must make way for the NEW.

For crumbled leaves, life is final,
While Humans believe in Life — Eternal.

Now, I've no more time to daydream,
For October's rascal Wind returns.

And, I must race with frantic pace,
Before it blows piled leaves in space!

Pauline L. Allen

Peace

Peace is great!
Peace is grand
It does not come out of
The palm of your hand.

War is not great,
Peace is more grand.
You have to work hard
For peace on this land.

We can help the poor; give
Them some food.
Not let the rich hoard it all
And be rude.

We have to love one another
If we want peace.
Because if we don't
Violence will increase.

Children are dying
Don't let this happen.
Babies are crying
Let's take some action.

Laurie Finnigan

Forget Me Not

A cluster of flowers,
Peeping at me
From a distance,
Beneath the shadows
    of thick foliage.
A beauty, in the forest,
Hidden from the sight
    of mankind;
Except, for one, treading
    a lonely path,
But blessed for that one
    moment,
To see a jewel
In the wilderness!

Ramon G. Palanca

One Thousand Pieces

It is in one thousand pieces.
People lie, cheat, and walk
all over me.
look what happened, now it is broken.
Does anyone know?
Does anyone care?
Does anyone see the pain it cause me?
No, no-one knows.
No, no-one cares
No, no-one sees my pain.
Or do they, and just not care?
Or maybe they just can't help?
Maybe, people just want to stomp
me into nothing but dust.
No-one should have to live through
the pain of a broken heart.

Machelle L. Lucas

"Ode To Joy"

What heaven -scent
    Perfume doth
Drop to the earth below
    As dew this day

And giving sway
    Doth proclaim like
A gong your name
    Juliet, Juliet, Juliet!!!

William Curram

Untitled

Stumbling as I go.
Picking myself up,
And heading off again.
Mistakes I make,
May hurt you,
I never intend that.
They can hurt me too.
My humanity shows through,
Frailties and misconceptions,
Cloud my thinking.
I can only steer my way,
During moments of lucidity.

William Honeycutt

My Inner Thought

Yellow walls surround me
Piped ceiling above
Colors combined in here
Bare the strange sense of love
Lights above my head
They flick on and off
Strange feeling I'm dead
My mind's completely lost.

Out in the distance
An image appears to me
Looks like someone I knew
But it really couldn't be
A cloud of smoke I see
Colors red and green
The image has gone away
This must be a dream.

Richard Dana Jackson

Clouds

Pathetic Mortals - occupying Earth
Playing Man-made charades
Their daily actions are a death
Acting our ritualistic parades

Mortals, too busy to listen
To look, to extend beyond
The magic of life that glistens
The ache that begins with dawn

Love surrounds each mortal
In ways never understood
Each day is a special portal
Hear the spirit, the values, the good

It is as special as look at the sky
The ever changing clouds of cover
Clouds they say - just clouds up high
No-Mortals, clouds are angels that hover

Watching us in constant motion
The clouds-ever changing perception
Angels showing divine devotion
Patiently awaiting our reception

Robert J. Maloney

My Boy

As he sits there
playing with his toys

I watch in wonder
The magic of this little boy

He has taught me much
at his tender age of seven

The tenderness he touches
deep down in my heart

Now as he sleeps
I kiss his cheek

As I watch in wonder
The love he has to give

Rita K. Rednour

"Look On Me With Eyes Of Love"

My darling, when you look at me
Please see beyond silvered hair
The furrowed brow, the dimming eye
Which time has made, no longer fair.

Through memory's eye see raven locks
That frame a face, both young, and fair
With eyes that glow, with deepening love
And lips that smile with beauty rare.

Oh, look on me with eyes of love.
I pray, my darling you will see
A gentle being, worthy of
The love you have given me.

See this love, within my heart,
My hopes that together, we'll always be
These are the things, I hope you'll see
My darling, when you look at me.

Myrtle A. Treadway

Paronamasia

HEAVEN ON EARTH
POWERS THAT BE
A PLAY ON WORDS
ONLY YOU AND I CAN SEE

Forgive me, I am fading
You are above me
Sitting where I placed you
Before I fell to the sea

Drown in my own sense
In a futile attempt
At your world
In loving contempt

You will remain
I will not fade
In our ways
We are the same

G. A. Powers

"A Baby Is Born"

A baby is born
Precious as can be,
Fresh out of the womb.
Love is the key.

A labor of love
A mother bearing all the pain,
A baby is born
With so much to gain.

Blessed with a healthy heart
A complexion so smooth and fine,
God fashioned and made her
In nine month's time.

For life is precious
And so very dear,
A baby is born out of love
And not out of fear.

A baby is born
Our heavenly father's work is never done,
A miracle from God
A special gift to everyone.

Robert Peterson

Fireman

Mr. Fireman we all adore your
pretty red truck!
   But if we are very careful with
matches and fire and have lots of
luck, we will have no fires!
   And you will be stuck in your
fire station in your pretty red truck!
   We shall keep our ears open
for the sound of your big bell!! It's
there to tell us fire! Fire!! Fire!!
and to say that you and your truck are
on the way to help help!!
   Thank you Mr. Fireman who rides
on your pretty red truck. Pretty red
truck!!!

Rena Glenn Kerr

Fate

Like the moon
Pulls on ocean
Tides and the ocean rushes in
to the waiting shore-
Like eager plants
turn to the solar
warmth of the sun-
Like the trees
pray to Heaven
with upright
leafy arms-
Like lustrous
feathered friends
turn southward-
Like salmon bravely
forage the waters severity-
Like the lush persistency
of the Rain forest-
The truth of friendship prevails-
Ours has become a crescendo
That refuses to be ignored.

Wilbur P. Jones

Summer Bids Adieu!

Goldenrods are waving their farewells
   Pumpkins hugging the vines
Crimson leaves, amber, and brown
   Mournfully floating to the ground.

Bumble bees kissing feverishly
   The marigolds goodbye
Wild geese honking excitedly
   Forming an angle in the sky.

Corn, wheat, all are reaped
   The harvest labor is done
Sparrows chattering
   Calling everyone.

Summer closes her whistling doors
   At Winter's gentle urge
An owl sits alone, inscrutable
   Owning the world.

There's a tinge of spice
   In the air
While all Nature
   Whispers a silent prayer!

Marie Scaletty

Moon Intoxication

Sliver of a moon,
Quiver of a hand;
My lips sense dew
And my eyes breed dark —
Light sheds lies
While fright nails my thighs;
Hospitality running cold,
For I am left alone.
Enlist your lusty love,
Heightened by the hills above;
Fanned upon lush green I lie,
Hidden from the voyeuristic sky.
For your skin I thirst,
So readily I pine - at last, at first.
I beg for naught,
Patience forgot.
All perfection is nil—
The chill escapes,
My life is unfulfilled
As the mist awaits.

Theresa Braun

Untitled

Hell and Damnation
rages at my door
Satan in knocking
I wont let him in
a smile
sharpened teeth
sip some tea
come on in
The bargain bin
of my soul
50 percent off
come on in
look around
paper or plastic
to hell in a handbasket

Mike Dunbar

Call Waiting

The telephone company has
  really gone wild

So many things added, I can't
  keep up, my child.

The latest thing now is
  the "I.D."

So I can know who's
  calling me.

There's the conference call,
  come on folks, hook up, you all.

The one that really makes me spurn
is the one that says, "call return".

The best one yet, you must
  agree

Is the "call waiting" just
  for me.

'Cause you know it may be
  very important. Heaven's
  calling me.

Nannie E. Beall

Autumn

Trees of fiery orange,
  Red, yellow, gold, and tan.
Deep violet and maroon,
  I view from where I stand.
Looking up into the sky,
  A golden sun, birds flying by.
Going south till summer's warmth,
  Making way for snow galore.
Fun-filled days raking leaves,
  Making way for winter dreams,
As I gaze out the window,
  I can't help but ponder,
How God could create such a
\marvelous wonder.
Of all the seasons,
  Winter, spring, summer, fall,
I know which I love most of all.
  AUTUMN

Rachel E. Kester

Observations At 3 A.M.

the coolness comes
refreshing, rushing, stillness
late by dark time
bright white eyes
seek their paths

the moisture forms
on blades of grass
on panes of glass
a quiet moment
as creatures move
prey stalk prey
the sightless sounds
as coolness comes

T. G. Weber

A Wedding Day

Two lovers' hearts instilled embraced
Relationships formed not in haste
It's time to change our universe
Each one of us our hearts in thirst
We take these vows most caringly
Embracing our future most daringly
We hope our friends and family
Join us in our dignity
Our love is ours it's our reward
Sharing our space with our Lord
Take the time and join us now
With your love we'll take our vows

Robert A. McCorkell

Nature's Beauty

Looking at the beauty of a rose ...
Reminds one of how a child grows ...
The innocence of a tiny bud, nurtured
In a garden of love...
Petals blossoming from the sun above...
Through the clouds, bathed by the
Sprinkling rain...
Thorns protecting our flowers from the
ravages of pain...
Take heed to mother nature there is
So much to be learned
Only then, will the flowers grow back,
this we will have earned..

Wanda Peluso

Today

Yesterday resides in the past,
remember it.
Tomorrow has not risen,
anticipate it.
Today is the moment,
embrace it.

Yesterday is history,
chronicled for posterity.
Tomorrow lies on the horizon,
a new dawning still.
Today is rife with opportunity,
grasp it.

Yesterday abounds with all our todays —
untapped, unclaimed, unfinished.
Tomorrow is but a promise,
beckoning.
Today only, do we possess, a fresh
beginning—
unfolding, unchartered, unlimited.

Marie P. Casey

After The Storm

The sea is an old man
Repentant and grieved,
He has smashed, pounded,
Shouted, and raved.
He has struck the wind,
Sassed the sky,
Turned on the very shore
That was his friend.
Now where will
The old man
Rest his weary arms
But upon the bruised
And weeping sand?

Sara E. Sweeney

Run

My dear young friend
Run as fast as you can
Here comes that old man
With that axe in his hand
Race across that field
That keeps you up at night
That field with holes

With snakes ready to strike
Please don't stumble
'Cause you'll be as good as dead
If you fall into his arms
A body found but no head
His voice full of anger and hunger
I know you hear him screaming
As that axe brushes your neck
I know you feel him swinging
Why are you wearing shoes?

Wake up my dear young friend
Shoes with fresh grass stains
Weren't you only dreaming again?

M. Antonio Catarino

"One More Tear"

One more tear
Runaway boy who doesn't care
Little girl full of bruises
One more tear
Moms who cannot sleep
Dads job he cannot keep
One more tear
Drugs are everywhere
Junkies take a dare
One more tear
War and hunger world despair
Greedy people cause it there
One more tear
For you and me
Misty eyes is all I see
One more tear

M. Skleros

Lies

There is such a thing as a good lie,
Sad are lies that make you want to die,
You think you intimately know someone
you then find out it was just for fun.

I now know the truth about you,
Although the thought makes me blue,
I'm really glad you told me so—
Now I'm ready to let you go.

I shan't forget the look in your eyes,
When you told me that final good-bye.
Now that I know I want to cry,
all because of that one little lie.

Karen Holtschlag

In Praise

In God's arm I'll lay once more
Safely placed by heaven's door

Where misery is a thing of past
And happiness is found at last

The world goes on while buglers play
Man's faith in God will always stay

While angels sing and praise the Lord
Life on earth lives by the sword

Salvation is so close at hand
believing that we'll see the "Man"

This "Man" who died for all our sins
Gave us His so our's begins

This "Man" is God, His love so great
Help me Lord pass thru the gate

And when I die I hope He'll say
I've blessed you on this special day.

Kathleen Bruce Calvanese

"Reality"

Imagination intercedes
Reality vanishes
The improbable possible
Energy abounds
The spirit ascends
Success within reach
The awakening
A physical awareness
Acceptance of one's fate

Wilfred G. Sardelli

Today

"Today is the time of my life"
Said Thoreau long ago.
Not yesterday, not tomorrow.
That's something one must know.

Yesterday is gone forever.
And never will return.
Throw all your plans into a fire,
And simply let them burn.

Tomorrow may never come,
Although we'd love it to.
For accidents can happen,
To me and even you.

Let me feel the warmth of sun.
Let me hear the robins sing.
Let me see the moon come up.
Let me watch the birds on wing.

Today, oh Lord, could be my last.
I hope that it's not true.
I love the world that you have made.
I also do love you.

L. V. La Chapelle

Third Planet From The Sun

Dinosaurs walked this
     same ground…
But…they are no longer
     around…
It's a beautiful place
     this Enchanted Land
Full of dreams…yet
     built on sand…
Trees so tall grass
     so green…
Loveliest sight I've
     ever seen…
But things do come and
     things do go…
I don't want to say
     I told you so…
The place I once knew
     and loved so well…
Is very quickly going
     to hell…

Paula J. Gibbs

Say "I Love You"

It's a cure-all for the blues
Say it anytime you choose
It will mean the world to someone
Say "I love You"

When the day seems long and dreary
And you're feeling mighty weary
And the bottom looks like up
Just say "I love you"

If the hill you climb is steep
And the water seems too deep
Don't hang your head in sorrow
Say "I love you"

The world will still go 'round
Chin up! And hold your ground
Just keep on smiling
And tell someone "I love you"

Martina G. Farrah

Memory

Sitting in my mother's room
Scented with perfume.
Rose?
No, Hartnell for Stars. A Star…
Wanting to be a legend.

The shows we gave behind
A tattered sheet.
Friends grown and gone -
Though not really gone.

We cooked pears on the stove
Added sugar to make the climb worthwhile.
The pear tree, the garage roof
I was stuck there, once…
All day.

Stuck in many ways.
But not with tabs from paper dolls,
Not glue, paste or papier-mache -
Things that should stick.
But held by warring against past…
My adult face in a child's crowd.

Lee E. Ruffin

Teardrop

A single priceless diamond
Scrapes Flesh
Plummets Gracefully
Before it collides with concrete
and
Shatters

Nikki Telowitz

Remembering

Meeting you,
     sensing your response;
Liking you,
     becoming your friend;
Knowing you,
     growing closer each day;
Loving you,
     sharing your desires.

Marrying you,
     fulfilling our dreams;
Admiring you,
     doting father of two;
Honoring you,
     praising your success.
Toasting you,
     reaching our golden year;

Losing you,
     shattering my life;
Remembering you,
     cherishing our love - forever.

Lois B. Turner

Children

Children are like precious jewels
Sent from above
Like angels from a far
A gift God sends to all

The love He has to give
The patience He has to keep
The sorrow He has to share
To the bondage between us keep

May His blessing be with us
And His love forever be
May He guide us all the way
From here to eternity

Luly Newton

William

William, William, William
Shakespeare, Shakespeare, Shakespeare
Tell me if you may
Why can't I have my own way.

Looking for Romeo I set
Forth to Venice
Beaming and scheming
My mid-summer's nights dream.

Each character began anew
Nothing is too good for you
As you like it.

Once captured and beginning to trust
It would all deteriorate back to dust.
Temptation, temptation
They all began to stray
Measure for measure
I paid for each glorious bouquet.

My winter's tale of taming the shrew
Always ended with you
Ever wondering how you knew. William?

Margaret Soborowski

Death Call

When the time of my last breath
Shall come upon me as I lay
I shall walk through the valley of death
Fearlessly, as the Lord shows me the way.

He the most Holy, blessed be His name
has always been my guide
In my time of need, He came
And stood right by my side

So, when he does call
To Him, I will gladly go
Unto the Great Death Hall
Of which I do not know

Norma Neiman

Untitled

Reckless abandon
Shameless attraction
Retreating in the mind

Yesterday's gleaming
Slowly receding
A remnant in the eye

Soulful illusion
Thoughtful intrusion
Provoking restless vibes

Feelings of grandeur
Lustrous glamour
Leading to one's demise

Mary Jo Kulhanek

Show

Show your feelings,
Show them now,
Show the people tall and proud.
Show the people how you feel,
Show them that you are for real.
Show them that you need them now
Show them that you hope they're proud.

Tania Barron

Shattered Dreams

Oh dreams, once held so high
Shattered down you lie
Mixed with the sweat of my brow
Crushing my hearts desires.

Once I had built you
A piece by piece
On the strength of my youth
On the faith of my God.

Ah, but it is all spent now
There wasted you lie
With my hopes and desires
Broken by cruel time and destiny.

Dead I lie to the world
Living but dead
A broken heart with broken dreams.

Khatija Khwaja

Alone

She's lost in a world unknown.
She can't get out
For the ends are sewn.

She thought to herself,
"How did I get here?
I'm all alone and by myself!
Did I deserve this?
No!! then why?"
"Why?"

She's not afraid of the dark.
Cause she's there everyday.
But all she needs now,
is just one little spark
To lead her all the way.

She will find herself
on her long journey home.
And even though
She'll still be by herself,
She will no longer be alone.

Linda Karpovage

My Mother

My Mother taught me to be fair,
She gave me much love and care.
When I was only a little, child
She tucked me in always with a smile.
She always said this little prayer,
Because my mother always cared.
Now I lay me down to sleep,
I pray the Lord my soul to keep.
If I should die before I wake,
I pray the Lord my soul to take.
If I should live another day,
I pray the Lord to guide my way.
This was so many many years ago,
Mother is in heaven, this I know.
Her memories are still so very plain
Wish I could hear my mother pray again.

Ruby Hayes

Nothing

Her life was empty
She had nothing
Everything gone
She had no one
Everything was nothing
To her everyone was lost
And she couldn't find a thing
Her heart torn up
People had stomped on her
So she ran
As fast and far as she could
She never stop running
Till one day when she could run no more
And still there was nothing
When she started running
She thought she would find something;
  someone
Maybe someone to care or to love her
She died running
I never told her I loved her or how much I
  cared,
I wish I had.

Paula Kellogg

Brid

She hears the wind Slieve N'Eamon
She squints into the sun.
Transfixed she stands and then is gone,
As back through time she comes.

She feels the wind on Slieve N'Eamon
She stares back at the sun.
The Daughter gone, the Mother born
As backward now she runs.

She is the wind on Slieve N'Eamon
She's wedded to the sun.
She is the Earth, hers is the spawn;
The Primal,
Endless,
One.

Marjorie Perron

"Ode To The Oxymoron"

Men and women
Shut your ears and hearken
To those who fabricate
Peace and destruction
Moronic people with educations
Wasting away what they want
Greenpeacers who pollute
Pro-lifers who slay
Peace corpers plundering the earth
Gaining knowledge and knowing less
Shattering the past with the present
Is this what we don't want?
Earth the unearthed
Supplant the fresh with the seasoned
Propel forth back to finer avenues
Grow younger with age
Don't listen
Unlock your ears
They're just oxymorons

Kevin Weber

407

Silence

crash
silence

Crash
Silence

CRASH
SILENCE

Unbroken silence
the oasis destroyed
by a faultline
in the dreamscape
shattered fragments of a world
mistaken for garbage
no escape
no retreat
nothing but a fading memory
in someone else's mine

Destruction complete
pain overwhelming
desperation overpowering
crash   silence

Lori Hobart

Trees

Trees are tall and proud,
Silent like, never loud.

Trees are green and brown,
With roots underground.

Trees are like us,
Without all the fuss.

What would the world be,
Without the tree?

Michelle McCandless

Start The Love

We've heard and heard
since we were born.
It's hard to imagine.
It's hard to believe.
That the Father was here
and will return.

Does He love you?
Does He love me?
Is it true? Is it true?
He wore thorns around His head,
Carried a cross 'til He was dead.
Is it true? Is it true?

Can we stop and think
about the pain He went through?
Can we stop and think
what can we do?
Listen to what I say.
Start the love. Stop the hate.

Kristin L. Davis

Butterfly

Butterfly butterfly in the
sky, why is it you can fly
so high? When I try to
just say hi you fly away
into the deep blue sky, I want
to be your friend poor butterfly
so please come down from the pretty
blue sky.

Nicole Friedenberg

Ocean Mother

Ocean Mother
  sings to me, her child,
    a song pulsating over time.
Rhythmically she whispers
  the mysterious harmony
    springing from the depths
      of her inner being.
The melody of her passionate heart
  entices my spirit to
    dance with her along
      the sandy shore.
She enwraps me in her
  tidal embrace
    revealing to me the
      treasures of life
        deep within.
She releases me to
  journey home—-
every fiber of my being
  singing her soul-spirited song.

Mary Kemen

Child's Poem

  A black ball
sits upon my bed.

  I hope she doesn't fall,
that little black ball.

  I have a little Kitty.

  She's black and white
all over.

And when I lay her upon
  my bed,

She hides her little head.

Sarah Van Fossen

Women Through Men

She's calm and free,
Sitting here, talking to me!

Beauty; that — she is,
A constant reminder to me,
Of all I want to be.

Unique, above the norm,
Sailing on course; dead ahead,
And through the storm!

Death we have both seen,
Their cries, their screams,
By a diabolic director, it seems.

Like a shining song although,
Abruptly, with casualness,
She glides with womenness!

No mourning, no regrets,
Just cares, concerns,
And sure-bets.

She knows, she is
Woman, woman, woman!

R. Patrick Simes

Untitled

Sanctuary
Sitting 'round
Hiding faces
Underground

Full moon hazes
Starlight blazes
Under the City
By the sea

Saffron flowers
Yielding powers
Against a foe
Concealed in white

Teflon soldiers
Come to battle
In a field
Of midnight light

Leading charges
Through the dark
On a quest
For the heresiarch

Pamela S. Hanko

The Pecans

      questions unanswered

Scattered among the debris, pecans:
small and round,
plump to perfection.
Silence screams within.
Quiet possesses
the countryside remembers:
the slightest touch—
the tiniest gasp—
doomed disbeliEFGHIJKLMNOPQRSTUVWXwhy?
around and around and a
              round
              pecan
              bursts.

Samantha Stavely

Patterns Of Life

I gaze out my window,
snow falling through the air,
I watch with awe each landing flake
knowing God has placed it there.

Each flake is shining crystal
only He alone can make.
This is His way of freshening up
the air for mankind's sake.

Each snowfall is a chance we get
to start our life anew,
each flake a different pattern
representing me and you.

And as the snow is melting
each flake becomes as one,
like we should melt as Christians
to the mold formed by His son.

Pray as we flow among His trees
spreading nourishment to each,
that His word like melting snowflakes
will touch the roots of all we reach.

Thomas B. Kellam Sr.

The Gift

We were
So close to death!
He sat there
Facing us,
With nothing between
But our prayers!
And
He
Turned
And
Walked
Away!

Katherine Stuckey

Life

I love to laugh at life;
So full of stress and strife

My heart is aloft and flying;
Its wings are spread,

Heading towards the Light,
But, I'm not dead!

No, alive and well am I,
Looking life in the eye
and laughing!

Norma Moore

My Baby Brother

My baby brother is beautiful,
So perfect and so right.
His skin is soft colored light;
His eyes, dark and shiny.

His hair is black, braided up tight:
His new teeth are sharp and white.
I like it when he nibbles his toe.
When he laughs his dimples show.

Nichole Thompson

Guilty Feelings

Why am I like I am my Lord
    so quick to blow a fuse
The lady I love I always hurt
    but that's not what I choose

Teach me to treat her with respect
    for I chose her for my wife
Why must I treat her as I do
    I'll love her for all my life

My heart dear Lord, is remorseful
    put a hand upon my head
And bless my mouth with kindness
    and good things to be said, Amen.

Roger D. Cordova

Coupling

Life is given to each unmatched
    So we can share differences.
Time was created for us to enjoy
    Joining memories of life's pleasures.
Love grows in the hearts of many
    Changing live's in time.
        May we always
            Learn from each other...
                Spend time together...
                    Love forever.

Linda T. Wroblewski

"A Feeling"

Casting a glance
    So strong as to lance...
        the heart.

Saying a word
    and to say it...
        as no other has heard.

Listening to thought
    as though it were spoken...
        whether it is or not.

Thinking as one
    as to think union;...
        togetherness.

Rex V. McCoy

This Thing They All Call Love

It all seems so fruitless
So very very useless
This thing they all call love...

A wonderful sting
A joyous thing
This thing they all call love...

So what's the deal
We're all afraid to feel
This thing they all call love...

It's really well worth it
To learn how to birth it
This thing they all call love...

Wira Gernaga

Don't Play In The Rain

It's raining today,
so we are not
going out to play. May
be another day. Because
it is not a good
day to play, so
we'll stay inside
to play today:

Nicole Marie Kotyk

Life

Life is so precious;
    so why can't I enjoy it.
Life is so meaningful;
    so why can't I see that.
Life is full of dreams;
    so why can't I dream them.
Life is full of hope;
    so why can't I believe that.
Life is full of fun;
    so why can't I experience that.
Life is full of surprises;
    so why can't I enhance in them.
Life is full of joy;
    so why can't I feel that.
Life is so short;
    it is going to pass me by.
    so why can't I wake up and see that.

Marie Briles

Playing A Word Game

You can't spell
So you can't play
She runs to her room
Crying all the way

What damage have I done
To my daughter
My only one

If only I new
The damage I had done
She thinks she's stupid
But I'm the stupid one.

Samara L. Bowhay

Day Dreams

'Tis not night but yet I dream,
Soft and tender,
Sweet and true,
So long I dream, it almost seems
Forget the world there's only you;
You sit beside me,
    Hold my hand;
    The swing moves gently
    To and fro;
    Deeper, deeper, though not planned
My stream of thought does flow,
    To a long ago time,
    To a happier time
When you and I were one...
But duty calls, I must move on,
But in my heart you'll stay
    Till next I dream
    And free my mind,
    Again you'll come,
I pray.

Ollis L. Beach

Honor

Soft the winds, like springtime's fingers,
Soft the rains, like Heavens tears,
Soft the years roll by in gladness,
Never hinting storms to come,
Never hinting whirlwind's ravage,
Rain of steel and battle thunder,
War to tear the heart asunder.

Back across the blood-red water,
Marching back with heads held high.
No surrender, mind or body,
No surrender, heart or soul,
Honor be theirs, ever after,
Honor be ours and all shall know.

Patrick Rudy

My Lifesavers

M and M candies ...
stars in the sky ...
teddy bears ...
one small puffy cloud ...
a rain storm ...
a small child's laugh ...
the first snow fall ...
a new born puppy ...
first rose bud ...
last cup of coffee ...
a sunset ...
last bill paid ...
my last breath before my sleep -

Sharron Wakefield

Meditation On A Rose

The red flowers bloom mightily
    solitary sulking at the edge
    of a container too large
The red flowers bloom mightily

A symbol of your love but
    lasting longer

Your gift to me so fragile
I crush them easily pluck
    the pedals blow them to the wind
    they may reach others
    like pieces of your lust
A pedal here or there but never
    the whole flower

The red flower bleed mightily
    the pedals
        drip
            drip
                drip
                    blood red
Karen C. Fox

The Balloon Salesman

Some go high, some go low.
Some go fast, some go slow.
Some drift up, some drift down.
Some are purple, some are brown.
One is fat, one shaped like a hat.
Some are small, some are thin.
Some balloons can even spin.
You can make a house, people too.
You can make a giant shoe.
Some are green, some look mean.
The balloon salesman comes,
Then he goes.
He left a balloon with feet and toes.
With balloons he played a game.
With balloons he wrote my name.
Katie Krupinski

Untitled

She has passed away
Some of the hardest words to say
I must say them today
For she is gone from us now
No more worry to cross her brow
I must contemplate how
I can live without her
I hope they find a cure
And extinguish this disease for sure
But those days are far from here
We all must continue to live in fear
And watch each dropping tear
As the memory of her and others fades
Into the years and decades
Till one day we conquer AIDS
Scot Thomas Hoffman

Worms

Worms, worms, can be found in the urn.
Some wiggle their way into a ball.
Mounds of worms can be found in the fall.
Some are seen crawling down the hill.
Some people search them out for a thrill.
Others look for them to kill.
Some can be found on a hook,
now being used as a lure.
Some look to the earth for a cure.
Wanting to be pure.
Never needing a fur.
Patricia Ann Perkins

Hell On Earth

Every time I turned around
somebody was getting shot!

Every time somebody walks up
to me and say someone is
planning on killing you. But
in this world today kids are
getting killed by kids over
colors, gang violence, and all
types other things too.

Everything that's happening
in our nation it's hell on earth for us!

I pray to God every night
that it doesn't happen to
me or my future kids.

But all I can say it's hell
on earth for us!

Hell on earth is true! I lived
in projects so I know how
the hell on earth is like!
Nicole Super

In Memory Of Bobby Hankins

Today we pause and remember
Someone who touched our life;
A man who loved so many
His friends, his family, his wife.

We will always remember Bobby
And the smile upon his face;
As we all grew to love him
And no one can take his place.

By just the sound of his voice
Or the touch of his hand;
We knew that he cared
And would always understand.

He loved to support the children
When their fair animals were sold;
And a lend a helping hand
To those who were growing old.

Yes, Bobby will be remembered
By his music and his love;
As he gently watches over us
From his heavenly home above.
Lola Moore

What is our love?

Something pure and true,
Something honest and sacred,
Something informal but formal,
Something mysterious and hidden,
Something unpenetrable and essential,
Something uncorrupted and innocent,
Something genuine and content,
Something extraordinary and awesome,
Something unique and worthwhile,
Something spicy and untamed,
Something passionate and sexy,
Something healthy and fortunate,
Something vigorous and powerful,
Something valuable and brave,
Something majestic and elegant,
Something honorable and faithful,
Something adorable and respectful,
Something warm and strong, something I
feel deep in my heart,
When I think of the love between us.
Tanya Diane Clark

From Dusk To Dawn

Something groans in the darkness,
Something reels from the light.
As between twilight and the day,
The night acts out another play.

A beacon beckons us to remit,
Those thoughts which we wish to be rid.
The muck of the night
Draws our minds to bend,
To an unseen force that lies
Somewhere just beyond our hands.

Devils devise destructive deeds;
Demons deceive, deeming demise;
As angels appear above and about;
And a secret silence seems to cease.
Michael Mullen

The River

Life is like a river
Sometimes smooth, sometimes rough
But we always seem to make it
Even when times are tough

When the river is smooth
Things go okay
But when the river gets rough
Things don't go your way

You must learn to fight it
And keep swimming on
Then the river will grow smooth
Even though it took so long

When you learn to fight it
And with the help of friends
The rough parts of the river
Will never be rough again.
Megan Downey

Contrast Sports

Somewhere ends are catching spirals,
Somewhere blocks are thrown,
Fans are cheering by the thousands,
While other thousands groan.

But far along some distant path
Away from cheering masses,
Two runners battle for the lead
In alternating passes.

They run cross field and over hills
Alongside chilly streams.
Photomen and interviews
Are only in their dreams.

There is no break at half-time
No pause between each play
No substitute to bear the load
A portion of the way

Cross-Country is a puzzling sport
Observe when all is through,
Winners get few headlines -
Losers not a boo.
Kevin Lawler

Love Is Like A Butterfly

Love is like a butterfly it makes my
  soul to tell no lie
Of the way I feel for you
  to make me see the way you do

I fly so freely through the world the
  thought of you makes me whirl
I have no feelings of regret because
  a love like ours I'll never forget

My love for you is like a rose yes
  it blooms but still it grows
To never wilt and never to die
  my feelings for you is not a lie

I talk to you with my pen and write
  my feelings that will never end

Love is something you'll always keep
  even while you are a sleep
and when our love is ever shown,
It will have been the best that
  you'll have ever known.

Nancy L. Carpenter

Broken Hearts

Broken dreams and broken hearts
Spiteful schemes true love departs
Memories of past, future gone
Promised with the break of dawn
Looking up to count the stars above
Wishing for someone to love
No one there to hold your hand
No one there who understands
Dying inside day by day
Wishing your life and pain away
But still you go on because you must
Knowing you'll never be able to trust
Walking on all alone
Hearing those familiar moans
Marking off life's long list
Fearing shadows in the mist
Don't look back it's too late now
Nature gives its final bow
What lies ahead you'll never know
Fact, fiction, friend or foe?

Sherri Racki

Sports

There are all kinds of
sports around the world,
  All people play them,
men, women, boys, and girls.
  Some are boring, some are
fun,
  In some you dribble, in
some you run.
  Football, basketball,
volleyball, softball,
  Even in fox hunts there
is a call.
  Swimming, soccer, tennis,
track,
  All you gotta do is get
the knack.
  I like sports, they are all
really great!
  Best of all, they keep
you in shape.

Lisa Luzier

Star Struck

Velvet night with diamond eyes,
Spread so far above my head,
Vast misty black from star to star,
Sprinkled there by unseen hand,
Oh, so close, yet years away,
Patterns seem a signature
Standing there on earthly sphere,
I so small in masterpiece,
Yet a part, because I know,
Amazingly, you know me.

Martha Bell

Button Hole

Just about
St. Patrick Day,
the bulbs I planted
Burst forth in yellow color.
The biggest daffodils
I'd ever seen.

They leaned towards
the evening sun.
They swayed in the breeze,
And stood tall and straight.

They matched my mood.
They played with my mood.
In the buttonhole of
my green blouse.

Sandra Lee Bosworth

Sky

The moon above so full this night,
stands so still, but, oh so bright.
The stars surround, twinkling with glee
The sky performs a show to see.
The world seems calm on this night
as the moon and stars shine so bright.
The moon radiates a calmness below
The sky so lovely from its glow.
Oh, how nice this world would be
if only as tranquil as this sky we see.

Roberta Marie Pankratz

Our Forgotten Veterans

Our lady with the torch
  Stands with tears in her eyes
For our Veterans forgotten
  in wars long gone by.

World Wars I, II, Korea
  and Vietnam too
Veterans who were told
  we'll take care of you.

They didn't enlist
  but were drafted you see
Still they answered the call
  To save you and me.

Some were wounded
  and some did die
Now those who are left
  are forgotten, but why?

Our forgotten Veterans
  they should come first
They went through hell
  they suffered the worst.

Theresa Teague

Sounds Of The Inner City

The slam of a garbage can,
the clink of a basketball
rim after a jam, the
sizzle of bacon and
freshly cooked ham.

The shuffle of feet along
the city's concrete, as
fans roar through the
summer heat.

The beep of a horn as a
tire in torn, and the
screams of a mother who
loses her first born.
The rings of a businessman's
telephone, the snarl as dogs
fight for a bone, the curses
of a detective for his cover
is blown.

The buzzing of hopelessness,
as we are in distress.

Barry Jackson

Dream Hideaway

The new moon brightly shines tonight.
  The clouds have flown away.
Together with stars' sparkling light,
  it's almost bright as day.
A soft breeze gently sways the trees.
  Boughs make a rustling sound.
The dew glistens on grassy leaves,
  cropped closely to the ground.
Night jasmine sends its fragrance here,
  to mix with tall pines scent.
Oh, glorious night, in mountain lair,
  beneath all heavens tent.

John W. Bell, Jr.

Season's

Fall, red, brown, orange, yellow
the colors what do the
mean?

Give and take, live and dies
why, the sign of the season
of pententvood and hope.

Snow covered highways that
for awhile look like driveways,
but suddenly you slide into
spring, and this is what
I really mean.
Summer has come and the flowers
will soon dry, die.

Alli Markow

The Search

I've been swallowed by a giant whale,
the overwhelming life.
I've lived and died and lived again,
been lonely in the night.
I looked for something strong and sure,
something I could see.
And when my search was ended,
I found the strength in me.

Carolyn B. Griffith

A Soldier's Prayer

Dear God in Heaven
Please hear me here tonight
I am only a soldier asking
for you to make me do what's right

Show to me I beg you
Make me understand
Why am I trying to kill tonight
In this far off distant land

Why are my hands so thirsty
Blood fill me with delight
Why do I stop to ask you
For you to make me do what's right

I do not wish to take a life
Or do I wish to have mine taken
What has happened to this World Dear God,
Are we all forsaken

Have we gone beyond your power are we all to blame
Please put an end to this mad war I bow my head in shame

So dear God in Heaven hear me here tonight
I am only a soldier asking for you to make me do what's right

Aridith G. Curbeaux

Sweetheart

Sweet doll of my wildest dreams.
Please let me sleep in your soft lap.
Let me take a nap in your tender arms.
So I will recognize what ecstasy means.

In those hot nights I caressed your body.
I became inebriated with passion.
Nothing else was important, just you.
And the immense happiness of being loved.

I adore your green vivacious eyes.
Your red urgent breasts with nipples of honey.
Your waist of greek marble statue.
Your legs of Diana, The Hunter.

I know that in all the known universe,
only one woman has been so gifted.
Your soul is so limpid, your body is so agile.
Please let me mortgage you with my life.

Juan E. Bahamón

Poems Upon My Beard

Poems upon my beard! Did you hear me my dear?
Poems upon my beard! Of late events have grown quite queer.

The cat flew off the outer space - no sanity is left in place.
Spring flowers bloom from the clouds!
Old men moan and groan aloud.

Chaos reigns amuck in mire. Assigned assassins go for hire.
I say, things are out of sync...
At long last I've found the missing link!

**How dare you even think
You've found the crucial missing link!**

Give him no mind! Let the man think.
Proceed Sir, tell more of the missing link.

The DNA man, the DNA, the brain is made of matter gray.
Between tissue, soul and spirit is only but a lyric
And now I've ascertained the cryptic! ...

Acrimonious lamentation! I am kept from emanation.
'Tis far worse than I had feared ...
Poems upon my beard!
Poems upon my beard!

Gary Goldman

The Mind Of A Cat

Along creeps a spider on its way
Poor insect, unsuspecting prey
A shadow sprawled along the terrain
The whispery tendrils of sand-colored mane
Tightened muscles, waiting, aching
Wheezing breath, the silence breaking
Finally, impatient one
The pounce is short, the job is done
The graceful curves, so delicate and fine
Stand out in the silhouette of the departing feline
Off to the shelter of a maple tree
To dine in peace and secrecy
After this delicious feast
This silky purebred genuine beast
Sets off for the house of the owners, dear
In the living room, there is nothing to fear
Curled up by the fire, comfy and warm
Sheltered from the approaching storm
Asleep and content, feeling well-fed and fat
No one knows what goes on in the mind of a cat

Danielle Beres

My Beautiful Clouds

Oh, how I marvel at the beauty of the clouds
Positioned up high in the sky,
silently passing by
Majestic presents, but untouchable,
and yet not so far in distance
Transforming into any imaginable existence,
fluffy as a feather pillow, and soft as cotton
Tasting of roasted marshmallows,
with a sweet aroma swirling in the air
God's creations are so beautiful to me,
and they exist for everyone to see
Oh, how I marvel at the beauty of the clouds

Catherine Lucas

The Knife

The shadow is once again surrounding my heart, freezing every
pump of joy. Emptiness fills my body, leaving it shriveled
and useless. Childlike, I curl into a ball in the silent
darkness and clutch my hair, fighting my frustrations in
vain. I have lost the battle of love, and my wounds are
beyond painful. My soul and body are consumed in awful
wretches. Stinging tears travel down my face, leaving me
blinded. This torment us utterly destroying the person I am
inside, the person that once stood tall and happy. Now I
sit, crying like a child in a corner of my inflicted mind,
Will my misery stop?
There must be a way, a way to end my torture!
Knowing the life in me shall never return, I reach for the
knife. The lustrous knife of death that will bring me life!
Its radiant steel enters my flesh and my blood escapes cold
with sorrow. Oh, praise the tool of death that cuts life
back into me! Praise the instrument that delivers me from
this insane hell! My distress was my death, but the knife
will give me a life without anguish.

Emily Douglass

Rain, Rain

Rain, rain fall down and touch the pretty people,
Rain, rain fall down and make a puddle,
Rain, rain fall down and make the flowers grow?
　Is that so?

Allison Riker

What Is Faith?

Faith is a blade of grass
Puncturing a concrete path.
Faith is a ray of light
Probing a dark sky's wrath.

Faith is a little bird
Searching seed in a barren land;
Or a blossom
Surviving in a sea of sand.

Faith will walk where it cannot see
And open all doors without a key.
Faith is courage, hope, patience and cheer;
For it walks with God in the absence of fear.

Harold B. Ward

Twilight

Twilight has arrived at last!
Putting the activities of my day in the past.
A quiet time now,
Time to rest before bed,
To gather the thoughts that run through my head.
I gaze out the window as I sit in my chair,
And hear the birds chirp as they glide
Through the air.
And if I look closely through the suns last light,
I can faintly see stars coming out for the night.
A peaceful feeling has come into play,
As I'm settled in my house at that time
Just after day,
That time before night,
Twilight.

Jan Randazzo

Shade Of Blue

I have seen colors pale and bright
Ranging from dark hues to the shade of moonlight.
But nothing can compare to what I saw
When I looked into your eyes and felt a sense of awe.

A blue which I have never seen
Eyes of kindness, never mean.
Eyes like water, pure and clear
A river of salt when you shed a tear.

Blue like the Caribbean Sea.
I see a fantastic image of thee
Looking, gazing through crystal blue,
Searching for love, hoping it is true.

I can see your soul through your eyes
A lovely picture; I'm full of romantic sighs
All because of this shade of blue
I sense feelings which come directly from you.

Jennifer C. Lynch

Finding Peace From Within

Searching for answers,
Reaching for goals,
Struggling for happiness,
Praying for strength,
Opening new doors,
Trying so hard to close old ones,
Digging deeply within,
Touching those feelings you've hidden,
Hoping for comfort with each truth you face,
Finally coming to terms with the reality,
Life is tough,
Life is good,
Life is a gift from above,
And so are you.

Donna Pritzlaff

The Gift Of Life

The gift of life is within us all
  Readily at our beck and call
Flowing through our veins each and everyday
  Keeping us going on our merry way
Our earthly existence it does retain
  The accident victim it will sustain
Its vital nectar so complete
  Preserving the human existence so sweet

Blood donors work a special magic
  Preventing death from causes so tragic
Giving salvation in highest measure
  Greater than all earthly treasure
Unsung heroes who don't complain
  When giving blood of a little pain
To lift the bane of suffering's yoke
  While giving the dying a strong ray of hope
Through scourge and disaster, earthquake and flood
  They selflessly come to donate their blood
In heaven they'll know neither fear nor strife
  Cause God will say "your will gave us a life"

Alexander M. Selkirk Jr.

"Is He Right"

The time has begun, for everyone, to
recognize the Son. Is he right?

For the wicked and insane, they must rebound
from this game, to stop all their pain. Is he right?

We must try to rise above, this world and seek
love, a spiritual gift we deserve. Is he right?

We must seek within were told, to find the light
and our soul, the center to unfold. Is he right?

Order is the ray, we must use, use everyday, to
keep from going astray. Is he right?

The magic that is ours, to use among the stars,
to seek sight at night. Is he right?

The freedom of this goal, to liberise the soul,
the gifts to behold. Is he right?

We are one-not three, when our lower selves are free,
to be what were meant to be. Is he right?

He is the spirit that is us, the reflection of our
selves, our true being in flight. He is right.

John R. Salera

Colors

Black is the night with the soft moon light
Red is the love meaning me and you, but
Red can be sin and we both know that's true
Yellow is the friendship we both red (love)
White is the vows that we both said
Blue is the heaven we both want
Gray is the time when we both fought
Pink is the birth of our new daughter
Purple is the time when I first saw her
Rose is the happiness on my face
Orange is the worry as I pace
Silver is the strength as she grows
Gold is the knowledge that she knows
Violet is the dream that she does want
Green is the laughter she has taught
Lavender is the true memories she had
Maroon is the time when she is sad
Colors are life that we all share
When colors are mixed we all stare all the emotions that come
and go the colors are here to stay which we all know

Carina Quinn

Catalogue

Amber eyes glint at night,
Reflecting back the porch light.
Knowledge of an earlier time,
When we lived by our wits, learning to mine.
The trees, swaying grass and rough rocks too.
Pouncing out to devour our due.
Then, we ruled the earth with cunning and grace.
Long before the human race.
We hid and tracked and hunted immune,
To the tinkling of a collar bell, out of tune.

Bruce Rapsher

Remembering Crystal Beach Park

Remember the Thriller at Crystal Beach Park?
Remember the Bug and Laff-in-the-Dark?
You and your friends, oh how you screamed!
And the laughter forever, that all of you dreamed.

You'd go to the Penny Arcade for some fun,
Then on the Rink to watch skaters till down went the sun.
Night time brought dancers to the Ballroom's smooth floor
To dance to the great bands, who now are no more.

The taffy, popcorn, hot dogs and more,
The picnics and swimming off Lake Erie Shore,
Oh, how you loved to catch Merry-go-round rings,
Or see just how high you could go in the swings.

For good clean Fun and to watch fireworks soar,
Oh, to return to that Park, just once more!

Eleanor Blanchat Ryan

Living In The Mind's Eye

Just where does the time go? The years pass so fast.
Remembering adventures and stories that last.

What are their meanings, and look how things change,
They soak in your memory like droplets of rain.

They splash and make impact at the time they occurred,
Seeping through generations that young hearts are stirred.

Relentlessly endless, each day of our lives,
As we keep looking backward, holding strong to our ties.

Why is the future a scary, cold thought?
Might we be tested on what we've been taught?

When you think of a person you once were close to,
That has passed to the next phase, where skies are so blue,

Do you wonder where they are and what they might see?
Or if they were still here, just how could it be?

But, life is so funny, just where does it end,
When you think of that person, their life starts again.

So I guess they are never really gone from our side,
And, the end of the world, is when memories have died.

Carina L. Florsek

Untitled

One night I took a walk down a long and winding
road. As I came upon each bend in the road I felt a little
fear and as I walked around each turn I realized there was
nothing to be afraid of. Each bend was different and brought
a new experience and I soon began to see that each twist and
turn was only another part of life. But as I came nearer to
the end of the road, the sky grew darker and yet it was the
most enlightened time of my life. I grew more afraid with
each step that I took, for I could not see my destination at
the end of the road. I then turned around to go back the way
I came and found I could not return, there was no way but
forward to go.

Juanita Sisk

"Loveswept"

There is such a thing as being Loveswept
Remembering that first night we met
That wonderful man, so witty, so charming
It was hard to hide the feelings that were alarming

That night we danced all night long
The magnetism was so strong
He swept me right off my feet
Burning me with the intensity of his heat

But we still had much respect
For we didn't know what to really expect
Such anticipation and curiosity was aroused
Yet the heat of romance had to be doused

We have all the time in the world to spend
Learning about each other and to someday apprehend
The feelings inside that we have kept
For this was sure an obsession loveswept

Gertrude Maldonado

Listening For The Ancient Ones

The mesas speak in silence
Repeating, repeating, nothing on the wind.
They cough up rocks and spiky yuccas,
Blue lizards skittering under stones,
Prairie dogs darting across roads,
Ravens picking carcasses left by cars.
Braided sand in dry arroyos, burning in the sun,
Speaks of water's force, now gone.
We are trespassers here,
Unattached to land and sky.

Ghosts of a thousand years,
Voices we cannot hear,
Sing in the empty ruin towers.
Questions vibrate in the stillness.
Who are the ancient ones?
What are the pictures pecked in the cliffs?
Where is the water and the forest?
And who are the gods that stole them?

Jhane E. Marello

Caught

It's time for me to head home
Rest this aching heart of stone,
Sometimes better to be alone,
A king upon an empty throne.

Lord knows when this pain will cease
And bring to this tortured soul...Peace.
Waiting for laughter at a lonely feast
A broken heart, a brand new lease.

This battle always seems to be fought
Between which I'm always caught.
The truth to me is always sought
'Cause love can be sold but, it can't be bought.

All things seem to come and go
while we're caught somewhere between high and low.
Love comes ever so slow,
You and I ... how the cold wind blows.

My soul feels like it wants to fly
But, my heart just can't say good-bye.
All I want is to be by your side...
Even though I need the wide open sky.

Charles J. Wente

Untitled

She's always there for me when things don't go just right,
and when I need a loving hug she's the one who holds me tight.

It's not often that I open up and let my feelings show,
but if I ever need to talk it out I know just where to go.

She's there for me no matter what the price she'll have to pay,
and I'll love her with my heart and soul until my dying day.

Her eye's are full of love and her heart is just the same,
and I'm so close to her that I don't call her by her name.

This may not make much sense but I know that I'm not wrong,
'cause the person I'm describing is the person I call mom.

Elizabeth Snelgrove

My Friend

Here comes that little doggie
Right through my door
I hear the pitter patter on my floor.

She sits down there and looks up at me
Just as cute as she can be
She thinks I am going to feed her, you see!

I tell her there's nothing for her, I can find
She just sits there —-
Hoping I'll change my mind.

When I tell her "all gone, all gone"
She sadly turns and walks away
Only to come another day.

I think she is human
And knows what I say.
Else why would she act that way?

Gladys L. Hill

Ghetto Man

What'cha gone do ghetto man,
  rise early in the morning if you can;

Body all achy with pain and strain,
  from the day before without much gain;

Now comes another day with mouths to feed,
  a good steady job is what you need;

Reach for socks with darned up holes,
  runover shoes with worn out soles;

Pull on pants that's seen too many days;
  been patched and mended in a dozen ways;

Trying to do right, earn an honest wage,
  but sometimes life just won't turn the page;

But you're trying to stay strong for wife and kids,
  even if it means staying on the skids;

'Cause you believe one day your time will come,
  maybe today will be the one;

And if it's not and the day goes by,
  no one can say you didn't try;

So what'cha gone do ghetto man,
  rise early in the morning if you can;

Jeannetta Louise Brown Darby

A Time Remembered

There was a time remembered now, of days beginning in cold,
crowded rooms for sleeping, and dressing under heavy quilts,
then quickly down a narrow stairs to friendly warmth by the
kitchen fire—of smells of coffee, toast and buns.

The kettle hisses and steams until, the basin full, the morning
dabbing of nose and ears and chin and neck, too hot for more.
Then time runs out with breakfast down, the bundling starts until
I think I'll not get out of scarves and gloves, sheep-lined leather
and boots and cap with ear-warming flaps.

The cold strikes sharp as down the wood stairs I half jump and on
my way until once more as daylight fades, I come again to live
inside the house where love makes roaring fires seem cool in days
remembered now.

Harry J. Wade

Piano

I am wooden and melodic; a sweet seducer of sound.
Run your fingers up and down my scales and feel the
reverberations.
Sleek and polished, I sit stately adored with a stripe of black
and white.

Don't blame me for a flat or if your pitch is sharp;
You are at the pedals of my destruction.
If you don't measure up to my staff,
I suggest you change your tone.

Heed the ticking of the metronome,
Perched high upon my shoulder.
The tyrannical tempo endures
As your digits fumble over my octaves,
Like a lame spider.

Julie Michalski

The Raging Storm

The thunderous tunnel
rushes along the clouds
stripping the life from the wind
mortifying the content community.
Marking its territory
like a raging tiger marks his prey.
Randomly searching...hunting
and ultimately destroying anything around its way.
Staging the crime,
selecting the jury,
it goes on to destroy.
Annihilating and maiming anything
within its path.
Cycling to happen another time,
another way.
Centuries parting,
people dying
and
it happens again.

Alana Haro

Woman (Rib)

A woman is to be loved not pushed or shoved,
She was given to man by God above.

Be loving to the woman in your life!
Be it your mother, sister or wife.

A woman bore your children, she cooks and cleans
On a woman you can always lean.

With loving kindness her trust you'll earn.
For just a touch, her love she'll return.

Mothers, sisters, wives and such they all are women.
  God's given special touch.

Diana A. Young

Baltimore Harbor

Smoke stacks and ship masts look down upon factory roofs.
Sailcloth draped like curtains from tenement windows.
Brick warehouses of mill construction enclose wooden piers.
Water towers on factory roofs punctuate the city skyline.
Old clippers moored in yards far from channels.
Faded advertisements painted on brick of windowless walls.
Railroad tracks embedded in the pavement of uneven streets.
Wooden barrels on loading dock edges.
Seafood for sale in the hot sun.
Longshoreman unloading commerce.
Horse-drawn trucks jostled by streetcars.
Clothes lines hang from one apartment to another.
Fire escapes decorate building faces.
Poverty is seen in those faces.
Departing ships offer a way out.
But rust discolors the white hulls.
Industry gives us the gilded age.
Everything is tied to the docks.
Hardship was the picture.
Such was Baltimore life in 1912.

Eric P. Jacobs

Now

"If there's something you need to
say, to someone that you love today. Say it now!
If there's fences that needs mending, unfair
laws that need bending, unsolved mysteries
that needs ending. Do it now!"

"If there's love you need to share, or
perhaps a word of prayer. Share it now!
Time is precious, waste it not, life goes on,
until it stops. Whisper words of love so true,
especially if, it's overdue. Do it now!"

"Don't wait until they're gone, to say
how you feel. They won't be around to hear
it, or know if you're for real.
Time goes by," oh so fast, you won't be
able to hold on, or even make it last.
Lost moments can't be recalled, days gone
by, will not return. But if by chance, somehow
you learn, to cherish each moment and bless them
all. Love God! bless man, be happy if you can. Bring joy,
live peace, dream dreams within your reach. Do it now!

Cleve Esther McSwain

Plastering Holes

I'm plastering holes in the wall,
Scraping the paint off, watching it fall
To the floor in white flakes.
There is dust in my hair and it makes
Me look older. I'm mixing the mortar in a shallow quart tin.
It can't be too thick, it can't be too thin.
If it runs it won't dry
And then I can try
Again. I'm smoothing the cracks, filling the breaks
Surprising how much plaster it takes
To hide all the holes.

I'm plastering holes in my soul,
Covering the doubts up, playing a role
To hide all the cracks, to fill all the breaks
In my crumbling dreams. I have made my mistakes;
There is grey in my hair and it makes
Me look older.

Benjamin D. Santer

House For Sale

In Oxford County the old house stood, among the hill and pine
scented woods.

At the edge of South Paris it could be found, not far from old
Norway town.

A rambling house with a barn, now a boarding house, once a
farm for more than a century.

Its head on high, it bore the wrath of time, wind, angry sky.

To the West is Paris Hill and Norway Lake, formed by ice and
violent quake.

Off to the North courses stony brook, who's waters have tasted
its share of bait and hook.

The fiddlehead and Minnie's place, grace the old town like
country lace, each locked in my memories place.

Oh, how I miss the waterfall by the bridge, the tall church
spire, birch logs burning on the living room fire...

Echoes of the school yard across the way, the sound of laughter
from children at play.

This old heart of mine can hardly bear: To never see market
square, North to Maine, no more will I roam.
I'm a lost poet without his poem.

Edward T. Sullivan

The Senior Class Of 1952

We have come to the place where our high
school days are few. We have struggled
and toiled. We have covered much ground and
soil. We have worked, studied, and played.
We have seen the time when for our test
we would have paid.
Realizing that we are small, yet we believe
there is great work ahead for us, one and all.
We have seen the time when things looked
bad. There have been times when we all were
sad. Yet, with victory we have pulled through
the times of deepest dark blue.
We have seen the time when we wanted to
quiet but we fought like mad to keep our class
from being split.
So here we stand in line leaving our
high school days behind. We represent the
golden treasure of which we have long desired.
And now with our twelve long years of hard
work, we're all mighty glad we did not shirk!

Irene Glass Crowe

Pest

Hurry up; I see you there.
Scramble, run;
Tell the troops to head for cover.
Because I see you having fun.

Who dropped the cookie?
I do not know.
But your little radar
Told the whole world, where to go.

Your straight little line,
Weaving back and forth.
Taking what you think,
Is a heavy load; along its course.

Well you have had your fill,
And you must now go.
Because I said "You are not welcome here;"
So now my bug spray will blow.

Bonnie Biesterfeld

I Realized

I, but a lonely man,
Searched the land above the sea
For the one who could bring change within.
But I found no one but me.

I, but a lonely man,
Searched the hills and dales
For the one who would bring solace to my soul.
But I found no one but me.

I, but a lonely man, then lifted my head toward the sun.
"Lord, where is the one I seek?"
The Lord replied "you are in the place where he is."
I looked and I found no one but me.

John G. Bailey

That Old House

Wandering down the roads and through the woods
Searching for that old childhood home
It's overgrown with trees and weeds now
My heart cries out in pain, as I remember the years gone

The porch is falling in and the roof is almost gone
I walk up the steps and into the doorway
The old wood stove still sits in the hallway
Why did I ever have to grow up and move away

I found a broken picture of Grandma on the mantle
The picture looked the same as it did years ago
Though the house is not the same it used to be
I can still feel the love in this old, old house

The love is strong as ever in this old run down house
I remember all the special times growing up as a child
Only memories are still alive, as I walk away from the house
But the love will be with me forever, as I make my own home today.

Joey Sutton

"I'm Starved, Whatcha' Got?"

The order of the day is life,
Seasoned slightly with victories and strife.
cooked only rare, it's virtually raw.
The future unseen, the past we hardly saw.
We have no choice in the way it's made
You must take and eat or slowly fade.

"I'll have a side order of reality to go."
Is reality life? Or do we really know?
The two together, go side-by-side.
One without the other is an "out-of -order" ride.
One is a gift, the other an event.
One is experienced the other was sent.

"A pitcher of pleasure to quench my thirst."
Your time must be enjoyed or you'll be cursed.
Too much to drink could certainly spell doom.
Too little?..... and your life's an empty room.
Needed is this drink that tops-off the meal.
All three together is usually a good deal.

"How much is it?"

"Forget it kid, It's on the house."

Anthony Angelias

I Am The Wretched Youth

I am the wretched youth.
See my boots, they are black.
See my chains, they clank and clatter.
I am the wretched youth.
No mother or father to speak of,
No one to believe in.
I am the wretched youth
See me in the mall you turn away,
See me with your daughter you pray and pray.
I am the wretched youth.
My facade is my disguise,
Anger in my eyes,
I am the wretched youth
My acts of violence are my cry for help.
Someone touch me,
Someone help me,
No one comes,
They never do.
I am the wretched youth.

John J. Hirst III

Untitled

I hold me up at arm's length,
seeing myself as a glass of water.
Clearer at the top, as I look deeper down into the glass,
the water begins to haze and cloud,
the farther down, the darker the water.
Till looking at the bottom, I see mucky sediment
that's no longer mud, but turning back to stone.

One twirl, two twirls, a tiny whirlpool begins to form,
funneling, down, into my water.
I see more clearly thru the shadowed, cloudy water,
gaining understanding(s) of the
contents of my glass.

Another twirl, the whirlpool gains strength,
I'm beginning to see the bottom layers flake, slightly,
the crust beginning to break.
Looking up I see what once was clear is now cloudy,
the temptation to set the glass down is great.

I gather my courage and wisdom.
I twirl the glass again for I know I must see thru
until my glass is entirely clear, able to be drank.

Jeff Murphy

The Passage Of Innocence

So many of the joys you find in childhood
Seem to fade away as time goes by
No more time to look upon the clouds
Searching for pictures among the skies.

You forget to stop and look upon the world
That's filled with wonder at the magic of life
Instead you dwell upon just those things
That can only cause you much grief and strife.

If only we could retain our child-like views
That fill each day with the wonder of it all
We would gladly trade all the riches of the world
If only for a day we were able to recall.

The sweet smell of the grass after a light spring rain
Watching a kite start to soar up into the open air
Sweet ignorance of how swiftly is the passage of time
Embracing only the moment for it is all we are aware.

Each day as we grow older more of our innocence is lost
Too soon it will be gone forever so dear a price to pay
We yearn to recapture the blind faith we all once had
But you cannot go home without innocence to guide the way.

Cindi Paladini

Never Had Roses

Been everywhere but where I want to be.
Seen everything and things in between.
Still living alone, my spirit and me.
So many questions, so many possibilities.
   Oh, she never had roses.
   She never had flowers from me.
Always busy, no time to spare.
Forget above love, she's working on a career.
These are the eighties, you lookout for number one.
Desperation makes you crazy, loneliness makes you numb.
   Oh, she never had roses.
   And she never had flowers from me.
You read between the lines,
And listen to what they say.
There's always reasons in what you find.
Oooh, tomorrow's just another day.
   Oh, and she never had roses.
   She never had flowers from me.

   Brian K. Wedding

Pink

I've walked you a thousand times
Seen you painted pink in dawn's early light
I've seen you rage, I've seen your glass
You hold deep secrets to the future and past.
I've watched you role up to greet me cold
You've sheltered me from pain
You completely understand, how I think
As I watch the sky's pink stain.

There's long dark days I wander
My mind drifts and wonders
You are the key, unlock my door
I'll see you painted pink once more.

Slowly the days drift on
We strongly walk time along
watch as the blue, fades to grey
Pink paints the end of the day.

Purple roles into midnight blue
Each night that I stand here and watch you
I'll see you tomorrow, as the sun falls from the sky
Watch as the pink sinks and dies.

   Bret Matthew Bradford

Two Souls And The Journey

Two souls now find rhythm together
separate notes, yet forming one chord,
when played their song echoes sweetly...
with melody unheard of before

Two souls now stitched tight to each other
paired fabrics now blend into one,
no longer fine silk nor a cotton...
but a pattern so beautifully spun

Two souls now determined to set out
trusting wind to power their boat,
old sailors have called this "commitment"...
and swear it has kept them afloat

Two souls now assemble one puzzle
each has brought, distinct, its own part,
by sharing their piece with each other...
hence from two...they've now formed one heart

Two souls now beginning a journey
with mountains and valleys to ford,
on mountains you'll find us rejoicing...
in valleys we'll kneel to You Lord.

   David G. McFalls

Thank God, For Moms Like You

Your tender touch, the gleam in your eyes,
Sets off a glow, brighter than sunny skies;
The advice you give, with the good deeds you do,
Thank God, for Moms like you.
Your gleaming smile, the love in your heart,
You convey to us, that's where it all starts;
The touch of your hand, paints a picture so true,
Why we all thank God, for Moms like you.
Your caring thoughts, and the little things you say,
Your presence we hold so dear, day after day;
Your love to us, and our love to do,
Thank God, for Moms like you.
The love we feel are so strong,
Mom, you're very seldom wrong;
And if I die, before this world is through,
I at least, thanked God, for Moms like you.

   Dennis A. Massei

Act III Improvised

September's lessening light
Shadows the approach of dark descending
On a festive day of mirth and song.

What ominous intrusion this momentary pain?
A seething, rushing current
Obliterating sight.

This cannot be; it is not time.
Surely, it will pass.

Celebratory hours with illusions of escape
Cloak night's descending curtain
On an impromptu play of fate.

Vague configurations vertiginously spin
Myriad perceptions too fleeting to be named.
What intercepts this lightspeed folly?
Why does it not register in the brain?

Faceless voices hurry by.
Yet no strangers pass.
For the human heart was sought and found,
Then its visage disappeared.

   Adele R. Minissale

The Playwright Sits Up At Night

Once I knew a woman;
   She changed her name.
   She wouldn't feel her own face;
   She had no smile to blame.
She walked away slowly;
   She ate so fast.
   I had to watch her just because—
I'll never know what the hell she hoped to be.
I'll never know what the hell she thought of me.
What possible reason did I have to be honest to her?

Once I knew a dark place;
   I felt so scared.
   But now the dark place knows me;
   The cold light never cared.
The darkness moves so slowly;
   It holds me fast.
   I have to listen just because—
I'll never know what the darkness hopes to see.
I'll never know why it feels so safe to grieve.
What possible reason could I have to be honest to myself?

   Eric A. Mein

My Loves

Juliet smiles with her eyes.
She is not yet ten months, but is already a social butterfly.
She is playful and has an impish look to her eye.
Juliet is my free spirit.

Jeffrey is the most savvy and dutiful two year old around.
He loves to go outdoors and to read books.
At bedtime he's elfish, but otherwise he's full of tranquility and
serene looks.
Jeffrey is my old spirit.

Joe is intelligent, confident, and a jack of all trades.
Joe is a very loving, considerate and handsome hubby.
He is gentle, always ready to forgive and to laugh with me.
Joe is my soul mate.

Soul mate, old spirit, free spirit - I love you with all my heart
and soul.
I am so lucky to have you three.
You are my life.

Jessica O. Ellison

The Forgotten Woman

Faithful is her middle name as she nurtures her family.
She is the perfect mother, always there to care for her children.
From giving them hugs and kisses to making cookies and lunch,
She works tirelessly for her family.
She's full of grace and duty for her husband;
Encouraging him and fixing his favorite dishes, she's the perfect wife.
Caring for her family has always been her main priority,
Not being selfish to put herself first, she's the forgotten woman.
All of a sudden, on a bright summer day, while she was going
about her usual duties,
She saw her reflection in the mirror; staring back at her was the
shadow of her past.
The children have left the nest, and her husband has left her for
another woman.
Her aging eyes and grey hair hits her for the first time.
She has forgotten to live for herself; she looked back at her
childhood dream.
She wanted to be a dancer: She picks up the phone to call a
dance school,
But drops it back again for lack of courage:
Is it too late now to pursue her dreams?
The forgotten woman is yet to make up her mind.

Jennifer Wall

She Knows

She knows the downfalls of life and its woes.
She knows the loss of a beautiful child with a sweet, soft smile.
She knows his confusion, bitterness, and perhaps hate.
What awaits this child's fate.
She reaches out a hand to grab hold, but only
gets something cold, a feeling of dread of something dead.
She knows life's cruel game and how it will take aim.
She knows life's cruel fate.
She knows how it can turn love to hate.
She knows she must keep her faith or all will be lost.
She knows to pray each day for God to give her strength to stay.
She knows that one day,
She will prevail, and the ones who persecuted her, will go to hell.
She knows to stand tall, not to look down or she too will fall.
She knows one day, she will have all,
and unto her child she will call,
come to me dear child, and I will protect you.
For she has seen all, and I will walk with
you and protect you from life's hate,
because she has seen, and felt all.

Helena Puryear

Tomorrow

She walked in the rain, in a dirty coat and stocking cap.
She looked scared and cold.
The only shelter she could find was in a cardboard box.
Yesterday, she was robbed by two young men in leather.
For only a few dollars and a cheap bottle of booze.
The only other items she had left were in her cart of "goodies"
she found in the garbage can.
When people walked down the street, they stared at her and
laughed at her.
Why was she there? Why didn't they care?
Why don't they help? Who are "they" anyway?
We are they.
Why don't we care about her,
and the people like her?
Where will they be tomorrow?
Will they have a "tomorrow"?

Candy Roberts

Untitled

A girl once felt his great love for this man
She went to him with her problems, so sure he would understand
He lifted her spirits when she was down
He made her smile when she held a frown
When she cried inside and let nothing out
He would take her hand and show her what life was all about
As years went by and she continued to grow
She began to doubt he could teach her everything she would need
to know
The touch of his hand, she didn't want anymore
So sure a better life was on the other side of the door
When she went thru that door, she put him in her past
She was a fool to think this relationship could last
They say a daughter and a father have a special tie
She feels no remorse for never saying good-bye

Courtney Lee

Mother's Love

Mother's love is always true.
She will be there for us, no matter what we do.

When we are sick or well,
Happy or sad.
Mother's there to make us glad.

When times are good
Or times are bad ...
Mother's love is never sad.

Happy am I for Mother being so near!
Where would I be without Mother dear?

She's caring, thoughtful, gentle and still.
I love her so, and I always will.

Bill Barnett

"Flowers"

Flowers can say the most beautiful things
    silently of course.
Only people with imagination can hear them.
Wild flowers are the easiest to hear.
They express themselves the loudest of all.
Everyone has an imagination, IF you can find it
In yourself the flowers will speak to you also.
Flowers are expressed through beauty
    And peoples imagination.
Listen closely and you might hear them.
Sometimes careless children who haven't yet
Found their imagination, or who just aren't
Listening come along and pick them.
That is when and only they fall silent,
    Forever!

Jessica Cook

Renaissance Man

Respite from my sorrows,
Shelter from my anger.
You were my strength and life.
But you are gone, now.
And I am here - with no place to run,
No place to hide.
I stand vulnerable
Unable to resist or understand. Where are you?
My Soul screams in torment.
My Heart writhes in torture.
I need you! You used to protect me.
My trust is gone and my hope is fading fast.

Damn it. I don't need you, or anyone.
I've made it this far on my own.
You claimed you cared
But that was a deceiving lie.
No more! Never again!
I have only myself to trust.
I'm done playing your game.
My game has yet to begin.

Andrew Lindsay

Song Of The Wind

I walked today in moccasin tracks, along the banks on the
    beautiful shore
Though many years have passed since then, its beauty is as before.

From the edge of the Nansemond River, with the naked eye I could see
"Dumpling Island" in its primitive state, which housed the Tribal granary.

Father sky was a beautiful blue and the billowing white clouds rolled by
As I quietly listened, seems I could hear, the gentle breezes sigh.

As I gazed on mother earth around me, in my mind's eye I could see.
My ancient people planting, hunting, fishing, as happy as could be.

I let my thoughts go wandering as I sat on a green carpet of grass
The song of the wind reminded me, you are an Indian lass.

A "Nansemond Indian" you are, with a heritage long and proud
What once was said in whispers, can now be shouted out loud.

The trees being bent by the wind as if remembering the past
Seemed to be nodding their approval, of the return to our
    homeland at last.

I knew "Chuckatuck" was a special place and no words that I could say
Could describe just how close I felt to my ancestors on this day.

As the song of the wind plays on, my spirit is heavenward raised
As I thank the God of creation and offer to Him grateful praise.

And the song of the wind plays on.......

Frances P. Woodard

A Moonlit Life

The evening came spreading its black peace.
Silence spoke her endless rambling, carrying me on a stream
Of unraveling thoughts letting me fall through the mist,
Carried on by the currents, flowing evermore.

Flowing evermore, black peace lulled me.
Flowing evermore, black peace held me.
Held me in the midst, rising from the water.
Held me enshrouding my strength of spirit born.

In vision lost, black peace showed me.
In vision lost, black peace told me.
Told me of my life, in moonlit silence.
Told me of my silence, in moonlit life.

Flowing evermore, onward coursing.

The morning came spreading its pallid light.
Voices starred in blind fury as the mist fell, gathering to
Water the spirit born of strength, carried on by the
Currents, flowing evermore.

Debbie Visnaw

"Escape"

Lost, alone,
Silent as stone,
No family, no food,
She's scared to go home,
Her hand on her stomach,
A child she conceives,
Away from abuse but
She'll starve she believes,
No money, no hope,
How will she cope,
With one black eye and a bloody nose,
She runs away to a place no one knows,
With a gun in her hand,
She closes her eyes,
Trying to be free of the hurt and the lies,
Like a desperate plea for mercy,
She pulls the trigger,
Violence,
Silence,
Can nobody hear her?

Gayathri E. Marasinghe

Smoldering Embers

Willowy shadows from the candles dance across the walls. The
room is silent except for the sound of your contented breathing.
As I lay awake in bed I can feel your body next to me, and the
smell of sweet spice lingers on my skin from our contact. I am
unable to sleep, the evenings events continually play through my
mind. I can still feel your lips on mine, your hot breathy kisses
on my face. Your caressing hands on my body awakening my
flesh and starting a thirst that only you can quench. When we
finally come together, I slowly lower myself to you so you can
enter and fill me with feelings only you can evoke within me.
Slowly, rhythmically we climb together riding a wave of
passion to its climax. To feel the electricity pulsing through us
leaving us in a state of exhilarating exhaustion. To bask in the
afterglow of the love we've just shared will forever be burned
into my memory. Thus I am unable to sleep and I lay awake
content with just listening to the peaceful sound of you sleeping.
I turn to you and lay my head on your chest, your arms encircle
me and in your warm safe embrace I soon succumb to slumber.
Safe in knowing your arms will hold and protect me through the
night as I dream of you.

Donna Paradowski

Hope

Crying.
Silent tears slowly piercing the air.
No one is supposed to know, what would they care?

Life's dreams and expectations slowly dying
and all hope is forgotten.

When reality hits you
you're down - rock bottom.

In spite of the struggle,
Keep your head raised high and remember
you are strong, not weak, don't be shy.

Your hopes, dreams and expectations
won't be fulfilled
with your head bowed low
- beyond the farthest hill.

Look up, look up, there's hope in the air
Reaching out, grasping,
Trying to pull you near.

Whispering, "Don't give up, help is on the way.
Continue to pray, strive and live just for today."

Dawn Hare

Fame and Fortune

I have always dreamed of fame and fortune
Since I was seven or eight.
Maybe I would be a movie star,
Or invent something great.

But who will remember me?
My life has been so ordinary.
Just another forgotten stone
In my family cemetery.

I hoped to someday be rich,
But could never save a dine.
My days are flying by,
And I am running out of time.

I wrote Marilyn Vos savant,
The lady with the highest I.Q.
"I want my life to have been worthwhile,
So Marilyn, what should I do?"

"Produce more than you consume,"
She said, laying my anxiety to rest:
"Whether it is handbooks,
Harmonicas, or happiness."

Carrie Belle Rowe

Four Sisters

On the occasion of a fiftieth wedding anniversary.

Four sisters we've been
    Since - Oh! So young!
It seems as though we
    are now as one!

Sometimes we've fought
    and hurt each other,
But then our love
    we'd re-discover!

We've shared together
    through out the years,
Each other's joys
    each other's tears!

Now, once again
    we gather here,
To celebrate
    Your Golden Years.

Dear sister of ours
    please know for sure -
Our love for you
    will forever endure!

Francis W. Miller

Old Folks

You seldom hear a group our age
Singing God's praises in public on stage.

By our looks, you would think we are old,
But we are still young at heart and good as gold.

Now don't view us with a critical eye,
But pass our imperfections by.

Now you all just listen while we old folks sing,
Because we are going to make Heaven's jubilee ring!

Daniel Neal Allen

Winter Heart

The savage beast of winter has raped me and left his
sinister seed of ice planted in my womb.
With his icy palms of death above, I cried beneath the
frigid fingers so eager to fondle my trees of green splendor.
He had no mercy for my mending heart, 't'was only a
fortnight since my lover held me in his arms.
Yet still he crept into my fertile valley of dreams and
stole my summer moon once high in my sky of tears and smiles.
He moaned with pleasure as my green leaves of hope and
lust faded then fell to the rotten soil of his domain.
Did he know my lover has left yet once again from my
loving touch and warm heart?
Take your season of shame I cried and bury it in my
bosom so filled with pain.
Mother Nature has teased my heart with summers glow,
just as my lover has pierced my soul with his absence.
Now their fickle ways have brought the snow frocked
demon of change into my warm breast.
Take me now, take me wholly from natures torment, from
now to eternity, it will be winter in my heart forever.

Carrie Emily Beck

Come

Come...
    Sit with me.
        Do not talk...
            Read... Or do...
                Anything.

Just sit with me.
    Share my silence.
        And learn to know me.

Come...
    Walk silently with me.
        Through ripe harvest fields...
            Shuffle listlessly with me,
                Through the blanket of leaves in the woods.

Plod with me thru the snows of winter.
    And burst into song with me in the springtime.
        When my heart again is light and gay.

Come...
    Be my friend...
        I need you...
            As you need me.

Donald E. Bobb

The Mind's Own Maze

Grace the mountain tops of avengence
sleeping killers awake, the sun dawns upon a new day
revenge is the word that lingers in your seemingly endless
mind, do you wish to be an angel
an angel of death, which creeps up the gates of the rise, or
do you wish to be saved by the killer of
the mind, and drink from the goblet, ringed with secrecy and
surprise, so, look now, look into my eyes
filled with sorrow, and glance to have the long lived
chance, to kill you would be amorous, but fate is
inauspicious, and the cold wind whispers the sounds from the
Light, so bow down now and prepare your sole, for the roller coaster
into the night.

Brad Anderegg

Earthly Sacrifice

Condemned consciousness. What manner of trickery is this?
Was I not sleeping within the confines of bed solace moments ago?

Trapped. Why can I not move? Squeezed inside a crypt of
wooden terror, I reach out to escape, and find only silver-ridden
wood to to confront me.

Screaming. Should I not cry out? Or is my voice being swallowed
as my body inside this hollow stomach of earth mother?

Darkness. Black as moonless tide pool. I stare at emptiness as I
attempt in vain to plan escape from this horrific, inevitable digestion.

Silence. Deafened by the sound of my own heartbeat. I imagine
the worms and subterranean insects gently pecking at this
wooden womb to feast.

Stagnant. Air heavy with the stench of my blood as my flesh
torn fingers desperately claw at the wood to clutch freedom.

delirious. I laugh at the absurdity of my measly problems still
waiting for me above the ground. All so oblivious to my slow,
calculated demise.

Strained. The fading reality of my heart beat as it weakens with
slow deliverance. I close my eyes trying to cling to the last
shreds of my sanity.

Release. I pray for death to achieve my escape, and offer my
body as a sacrifice to the earth. My fixated eyes forever staring
at the imprisonment of my mortality.

Gabrielle McCloud

Mind Journeying

Running wild, the waves of the sea
Slide and splash a long journey
To the beaching surf
Wetting the work of the sun's warmth
Reflecting the glimmering rays
Making the dancing distance
Look like a forbidden ecstasy
Upon the horizon of never ending
Heavenly clouds and deep blue sea
Sending a dreamy scene
Into the creative imagination
Giving fantasies beyond reality
Warm sensual winds pass
Returning thou to the forever lasting now.

Heather Corman

Memories Of A Lifetime

There he lay, motionless, his mind wandering
Slowly he closes his eyes, going to another place and time.

The crackling of the fire shatters the midnight silence,
Freshly fallin' snow covers the mountains, untarnished and pure,
Like her soul.

Radiant is she, her skin smooth and soft,
He places the ring on her finger, glistening as a distant star.

The ring, a seal,
Dull in comparison to what they share,
Love and passion, untamed.

Love materialized, creation of new life,
No gift could be greater, one woman to one man.

His life, filled with happiness and memories of a great love
All he had to give, he gave
Change, nothing would he for his life was complete.

He wakes, his hand in hers, "Thank You" he whispers.
A tear rolls down his cheek, his eyes shut not to open again.

Where there was once light, there is darkness
A glimmer stands alone, strong and distinct
The love that they share eternal, timeless.

Harry R. F. King

She Identifies With Butterflies

Born again in unconscious beauty,
Slowly she emerges from sleep in a crystalline prison —
Her sentence for having been less than lucky
In another life she led but didn't lead.

Scared, and sure only of what her senses tell her,
She hears echoes of her past, feels footsteps in her future
And sees clearly that her hope for the present
Lies not in where she flies, but in who she touches.

And so she goes, off into a season's eternity,
Propelled by a purpose no more complex that the need of her nature
To drink from the blossoms of being,
Enroute to a rendezvous somewhere on the outskirts of summer.

But for now, having perched indecisively long on my lips,
She chooses to drink from me.
And I, helpless and awed, her pleasure all I feel,
Give up the struggle with myself because, for now at least,
She's real.

Chuck Vail

Footsteps Of Time

Walking on the beech, feeling the grains of sand
Slowly slipping through my toes.
Feelings that my mind is drifting away with the tide.
Each grain of sand goes from one bench to another;
Carrying the thoughts and feelings from each
Person who has walked upon them.
Passing on a bit of knowledge to all.
The picture of her is implanted in my mind,
Like the footsteps of time in the sand.
Her brown eyes sparkle in the moon light.
Wanting to stay forever in her arms,
But only feeling the grain of sand slowly
Sliding through my toes.

Curtis King

Amity

With you all reality escapes me.
Slowly we slip into a secret journey.
But, looking through the glass
I wonder what awaits me.
I can imagine life out there.
The unknown taunting me
whispering the unseen
enticing.

You have taken me on a journey.
If there were a chance we could kiss
just once.
Yesterday you were so beautiful
my body drew near.

I know there was a stream after hours of dryness.
I bent over
nothing to drink.
But I am still this way
looking at the butterflies.
It is common they play in the air.
I sense a rumor.

Anna Innis

Soldiers

Snapping out, back to what we were before
Snapping out, of the madness that kept us going back for more
Clinging to your allegiance like a child to its mother, as you
snapped the spines of our own brothers.

You showed us your dreamed filled sea and your dreamed filled sky
and we paid that wage when you put time as the lock on our cage.
You snapped the spines of our fathers sons as they carried your
rules and beliefs of a thousand tons.

Danielle Avedon

Gremlin

I am the shadowy little gremlin
Sneaking into your night,
Twisting and turning, torturing your sight.
In and out of hallways I follow 'till your wild,
Changing you into a lonesome, helpless child.

A dark shadowy figure,
I steal into unconscious plight-
Always in the background,
Hidden by the light.

I surround you
And confound you
Fill your spirit with eerie dread-
I am the black gremlin
Pounding in your head.

Embrace me
Face me
Ignore me if you dare,
I'll come right back to haunt you-
You know how much I care.

Jill Randolph McAfee

Rare Beauty Should Not Die

Rare beauty should not die. This loveliness
So carefully conceived, the mastery of these movements,
The intricacies of these patterns woven in the fabric
Of the dance should live, caught in time and guarded
In the hearts of those who dance or see this dancing.

The beauty of the storied settings, the grace
And splendor lyrically unfolding from loveliness
To further loveliness, hands and feet
Responding to music's inspiration
Are fleeting eloquence. Hold fast in memory
This vivid present, that what exists so perfectly
May have its being in the minds of many,
Refuting time and denying oblivion.

Florence Breckenridge Palmer

"Best Friends"

Since kids, we were destined friends for life,
So different in many ways, yet many alike.

You stood by my side with such a heartfelt smile,
That glorious day I walked down the aisle.

Both strong-minded and always there for one another,
No matter the day nor the hour.

I wonder if we were friends in another life past,
Maybe that would explain our souls crossing this path.

Through it all,
Big and small.

You are there my friend,
Always until eternity's end,
Best friends.

Carlene M. Pfeister

A Poet's Mint

The fruit of my pen is the song of my soul;
Speaking in rhyme hidden truths unfold.
Phrasings of beauty that trace a scene;
Or slices of wisdom from an untold scene.

I paint a setting with words that care;
My heart is my palate for all to share.
Delicate verses delivered in print;
A verbal landscape from a poet's mint.

Doris V. Frye

Untitled

I pretend not to care
so failure and rejection won't hurt as much.
Attempting to convince everyone including myself
that I am indifferent when deep down
I'm scared to death that people are looking at me,
pitying me, wondering what's wrong with me,
or even worse, not looking at me at all.
If I let my self believe I wasn't indifferent,
I'd be faced to look at myself and see someone
who wanted desperately to do better.
Torn between not caring and wanting to be the best,
I try my hardest to pull off an appearance
of indifference people will admire.
    So caught up in making sure
other people see me the right way,
I forget about living life
I forget about myself

Diana Wogan

My Wish

I'd like to be an artist or a poet, maybe, too
So I could paint on canvas or write some words for you
To see the pictures I can see looking out my window here
While I wait patiently for nature of appear.

Now there's the deer down by the stream and over here hid doe
The little fawn just gambols on and the pheasants strut so slow
The squirrels play up in the trees, the blue jay scolds in flight
The cardinal whistles to his mate, the quail calls out, "Bob White".
Now winter's come, the flowers are gone, the snow spreads a
    blanket fine
And nearly all my feathered friends have flown to warmer clime
But out around the big oak tree, where acorns can be found
The quail and pheasants come to feed if I never make a sound
So I just sit and watch and pray that the faith and trust I see
In God's wonderful creatures may all ways abide in me.

Constance H. King

What Is Worthwhile?

One life to live-what a challenge now!
So let us seek God's favor so we'll know how
To get the most out of life as he guides the way,
Helping us get rid of things that burden our day.

Try dropping all pretense, no shams allowed.
Worry just takes up time we could use head-bowed.
Forgetting self as we seek to make others smile,
Bringing them and ourselves happiness by the mile.

It's not the length of years, but how we use our days,
That fills life with hard work, getting man's and God's praise.
Singing hymns as here we contentedly live,
Enjoying true friends and kin in a life love-filled.

Though sorrow and disappointment also come to us,
We strive through faith and love of God without fuss
To shed the world's evil ways, seeking life's true meaning
As we cast sunshine here smile an eternal place gleaning.

Cornelia Kay Grant

To My Cousin

Dear Cousin Blanche: I just now read
Some mighty fine verse written by you.
"Very good!" I cried, scratching my head.
Then smugly thought, "I'll do that, too."
So, then I recalled my fifth grade class
Where we studied some rhythm and rhyme.
But 'twas years ago, alack and alass!
Iambic pentameter has vanished with time.
Boo hoo! Boo hoo! I'm on the wrong track!
Must leave it to you, possessing the knack.

Holly Wood

"A Smile"

I don't know how many languages exist.
So many people together that don't understand each other.
But, with a smile, understand you can,
smile at the foreigner whose language you don't understand.
That way make sure he'll sit next you.
Smile at the child and dry his tears.
Smile at the senior citizen and offer him respect.
Always smile and your face will be more beautiful
A smile is worth much more than money!
What beautiful faces we would all have!
If we would all smile and not be proud
Smile at your subordinates, to the people that pass by your side.
Look in the mirror; how well you feel!
   Smile dear friend!
If a dollar you put in the beggar's hand
don't look at him with pity or disgust,
  Tell him "Good Day"
Give him your best smile.
I'm sure your heart will smile too!

Carmen M. Ramirez

I Want To Make A Difference

I see so much hate and anger in the world,
so many people working so hard
at being sarcastic.
I know I can make a difference.
I hear so many shrill voices with
an edge cutting like a knife,
to the bone of the soul.
I hope I can make a difference.
I feel the pain of the homeless
doing without, the children with
no clothes or bread—
I pray I can make a difference.
The love that flows between
you and me is something I can give—
Oh Lord, I want to make a difference!

Darlene Neal

To My Children

Oh child of mine, see how you've grown
So many times I wish I'd know
to hold you close and keep you near
and say the things a child should hear.

I'd say. "You make me very proud.'
I'd say, "I love you!", right out loud.
Who would have thought there'd come a day
when you'd be grown and far away?

And now it seems I've missed my chance
to tell you how my heart would dance
the many times you ran to me
with happy face or skinned up knee.

At times, it seemed, all I could do
Was point out what was wrong with you.
Instead of listening with my heart,
I lectured on, wedge us apart.

If I could go back in time,
I'd say how glad I am you're mine.
So you would know you'll always be
a very special part of me.

Christine Furstenberg

Daddy

"Dear Daddy can I talk with you"
So much to say so much to do
So limited is passing time
"Daddy I'm so glad you're mine"

"Daddy say a prayer for me" as you go to surgery
"Ask Jesus not to take you home"
"I still can't make it on my own"

"Daddy what would mama do"
"You know how she would grieve for you"
You've strengthened us along the way
"Daddy don't go home today"

"If not for you I would give up"
"But you have made me strong, and tough"
"So many things I've yet to do"
"Dear Dad; I've learned the most from you"

"When I sing, and play my songs"
"Daddy you will sing along"
As I write I shed a tear, "and praise God daddy you can hear"

"I know you'll teach me how to play"
"Cause daddy's not," going home today!

Barbara J. Cochran Stanley

It's Almost Too Late

Standing in the rain...............
So nobody can see the tears from all of the pain.
The earth is so abused and falling apart..............
It's really enough to break ones heart.
The rain forests and all Gods animals..............
are being torn apart.
If only we could stop all the hate.................
and destruction and make a new start.
There are some who really try with all their might.....
But the horrors and wastefulness continues........
if only by night.
If things continue as today.......................
For the next generation to enjoy Gods wonders...........
there will be no way.

Jean Davis

He

The moon is full and high above
  So now, I lay my head to sleep
To dream of He, my future love
  The one whom my heart dares to keep

Too far away, I know not his face
  Nor fathom his beautiful name
Yet near, I feel his warm embrace
  And his love, so passionate, yet tame

I reach out to touch his milky skin
  And seek out his fiery eyes
And his lips—so full!—for mine to win
  To conquer and meet surprise

I close my reality and await his kiss
  And his words of secret revelation
Anticipation, my heart pounds, no beat amiss
  For soon, I shall drink in celebration

Alas! A light! So bright in my eyes!
  Truth triumphs over my heart
Oh my love, he fades with the sun rise
  Once again—and for now—we must part

Joyce Yray

I'm Now Leading The Way

I know you miss me dearly
So take heart to what I have to say,
The time we spent together
You had always led the way.

We've built many things
The most important, a master piece you see,
It wasn't anything earthly
What we were working on was me.

I've made a difference in the lives of many
That is what my purpose was,
Now I have a higher calling
That's just what God does.

You're not meant to understand that
Until you get to where I am now,
It's really all so very simple
God's chosen me to show you how.

Remember Dad I haven't left you
My spirit is here to stay,
Because of what you've taught me
I'm now leading the way.

Cindy Jackels Martinson

A Tribute

For freedoms cause you answered, with much required you gave,
So when we raised 'Old Glory', proudly it would wave.
You fought to live and dared to die, and bravely took a stand,
And left behind the ones you loved, to fight in a foreign land.
So here's to all the lonely nights when you couldn't stop the tears,
When the enemy was bearing down, and you swallowed all your fears.
To the memory of a foxhole, of sand, and fleas, and rain,
Of standing guard on Christmas Eve, recalling all the pain.
To all the days and weeks and years, the loss of life and limb,
And God bless the ones who can't forget, so the pain they suffer still.
From World Wars to Crisis, from skirmish and to 'Nam,
From Desert Storm to Desert Shield, you served old Uncle Sam.
To all Vets who served, in air, on land, and sea,
We salute your fighting spirit, you're all we want to be!

Jean Smith

Gangs Of Pigeons

Homeric gangs of pigeons
Soar overhead and blot the sun
Not with malice, I am quick to say
But sort of happily and gay
"Follow the leader" is the game they play.
They swoop and dive down one street
Then circle at the corner
And plunge headlong down my avenue.

"Why are they there?" I wonder every day
Such joyous evidence of life.
In a city without much heart.
But that is just the point:
They are an evidence from God
Of just what life is all about.
To people in whom life is dead.
And all is cynicism and mirthless thought.

For who could look skyward
And not celebrate - not we ourselves
But something more primary up there.
In the affairs of man.

Doris M. Seltz

"Strings"

Strings surround me...they beckon to flee.
Soaring out high...the shaking you see.
Attempts at your heart...are heavy in the wind.
My strings caress and delight...you are my love and my friend.
Strings that entrap...will only knot up.
Like teasing with a bone...pulled away from a pup.
My strings fly open...in a gentle breeze.
Yours for the taking...no, they do not tease.
Feels like a perfect situation, a lingering touch just in time.
You're strings are so caressing...they're getting tangled up in mine.
As a ball of string unwinds...trust will come our way.
Strengthening our love...so it won't fly away.
No, there's no spiders web...to be tangled in.
Your strings touch mine, tenderly and, we begin.

Jayne Lynn Brannon

"Facade"

Silence and obscurity-the dwelling for your pain,
     Sobs are lowly in sound, you hide a mighty shame,
Pride and self worth exiled into non-existence,
     The pain cripples the body, but cannot consume the spirit,
Mama, the pain ain't yours to bear alone, I'll fight,
     We'll cry, together we're strong.

A spirit seemingly born to roam,
     No external forces cause your pain,
Its perpetrator lies within our once happy home,
     To others unknowing you hide the hurt well,
But your eyes are soft and glossy;
     They hold your private hell.

Only a silhouette in a dimly lit room seeking solace
     and peace,
Your tears leave it gloom.

Suffering so long, concealing is no use,
     I have come to realize my mother, my friend and
Foundation is a woman abused.

Danny Williams

Nocturne

The sun sinks slowly behind the hill leaving the earth bathed in a soft rosy light. The sleepy birds sing lullabies to the fading streaks of day. One by one the tiny stars add diamonds to the blue velvet sky.

The moon takes up her vigil like am other who watches over her sleeping child. As the liquid moonlight spills lightly over the forest figures, it clothes them in shimmering gowns of iridescent glow.

All through the silence of the night come the sounds of the sleepy forest. Whispering breezes play sweet melodies in the tree tops and the giant trees sway with graceful rhythms as though dancing to their favorite waltzes.

Crickets, frogs, and night birds form a symphony orchestra and serenade all the little forest creatures who find night time the right time for all kinds of ceaseless activity. Such motives and goals are known only to the mysterious animal kingdom.

Winding its way among the secluded glens is a tiny brook familiar to the inhabitants of the wood. Like a narrow band of silver ribbon, it glides swiftly on its way, its foamy ripples jumping over each other as they race one after another, only to rise and fall again in an endless pattern. Slowly, but with continuous activity, silently, but with lulling sounds, and gently, ever so gently, the busy word is hushed and wraps itself in the peacefulness of night.

Chris C. Shoemaker

425

Snowflakes

As the sun settles over the horizon,
softly a shade of darkness comes creeping.
Streams of moonlight cast shadows in the night.
Stillness falls over the land while the crisp
cold air fills our soul.
Glittering small objects fall from above
twinkling the tree tops and flowers below.
Up above the moonlit skies,
soft and warm flakes mount below.
All through the night these crystals have fallen,
caressing the ground with a soft white blanket.
As the daylight approaches shimmering objects
dance in the wind, portraying their sparkling radiance within.
The shade of darkness is raised above so the
snowflakes can now dance in the sun.

Coleen Garneau

Time

Upon a withered branch, the dew glistened
   softly in the moonlight.
The breeze, such as it was, could barely
   carry the little drops onto the
   smooth rock below the tree.
It was here that Nature found a weakness.
The crack, about as large as a hair,
   could be seen crumbling along
   its edges.
No more would I sit upon the polished
   surface of that rock, the rock that
   had served me for many hours of
   peace and contemplation.
The crack, small as it was, killed the
   rock that saved my life.

Bryan Green

Arlington National Cemetery, Washington, D.C.

I've never been in a war, yet I've been told soldiers fell,
with one long look at this cemetery, I truly believe war is hell.
From great walls with names to unknown remains, the only things left
are loved ones and veterans' unrest.
Some deaths gained independence, and some helped out others,
but that made it no easier on the distraught victims' mothers.
Death and despair for the youths of our nation,
right out of high school or college graduation.
With a government that's for the people, it's not run by us.
With a protest on every corner, what's the big fuss?
The number of demonstrations is rising like yeast,
the demands of the protesters is for all wars to cease!
I've been told our fighting force is the best, truly elite
but when it comes to the destruction of human life, there's only
   room for defeat.

Donald Praeger

Untitled

People search forever, and they may never find,
Someone oh, so special, so gentle and so kind.

People search for happiness, but joy may not be there,
To fill your heart with peace, and know you really care.

People search for love for years, and no one is appealing,
Sometimes they shed a lot of tears and never know that feeling.

Well I have found that special one, so considerate and so kind,
I have found that someone, some people never find.

The security and contentment, that fill my life with bliss,
The joy and love that fill my heart, each and every time we kiss.

They say that love is for the young, I know that can't be true.
For now, at this point in time, I am in love with you.

Angela Reiss

"In Unity"

We are happy to greet you here today.
Some of you came a mighty long way.
This is our family reunion, and unity means
We are together.
We will enjoy each other, in any
Kind of weather.
Feel free to join in and let's have fun.
There's delicious food to eat—and everything's done.

Preparing for you was really no bother,
Because all our help comes from God, our Father.
There is nothing like being
With family and friends -
At our next reunion,
We hope to see you again.

Let's be sure to keep in touch with each other.
After all, we're sisters and brothers.
So spread the word in your community.
This FAMILY dwells together
"IN UNITY."

Flora Waymon

Conversations

"Look at him circle there, turning against himself that way.
Some primal urge to clear the nest, before he settles down to rest.
A going back... a retracement to his source,
back to his beginning in answer to some compelling force."

"OO oo OO oo OOOO woo woo, like any Otter Hound would do."

"Rather like the winding of his mainspring to energize him
for the coming day.
As with those tops with which we used to play
each click would make the spring stay tight
and with the rising sun a special ray of light
would release the spring, and send him spinning on with life."

Now, he places each foot with care
driven to make one more faltering round.
The only evidence that pain is there
is how he slowly, gently eases down.
No clicks to make the spring stay tight
or with the morn no special ray of light.
And as the top wobbles on its final round
the silence bids the dawn goodnight.

No OO oo OO oo OOOO woo woo, like other Otter Hounds will do

Burr Manby

Miracle Defined

Some say a miracle is an extraordinary phenomenon
Some say a miracle is beyond all human understanding
And to fathom its origin is too demanding.
To describe a miracle we simply begin by recognizing its Creator;
whose nature is love, and who lives within.
Within our hearts, within our minds;
Who reveals Himself to whom ever He finds.
All His works of beauty are majestic and grand,
Created and nurtured by His loving hand.
But the greatest miracle,
is the love shared one to another;
That creates the miracle of life,
And a Father and Mother.

Carol A. Sturm

426

Untitled

Thank God for what I see
Some see the rain as an interruption to
the day I see it as the nourishment, for
the birth of a rose. The life of the
trees and the lush green pastures. The
path for the rainbow to shine. A gentle
reminder of God's promise. An
appreciation for the sunshine and the
warmth it brings. The light that guides
our way. Fills our hearts with joy. A
time to embrace the song of the birds
and the laughter of the children. The
inspiration for thought. There is so
much to see if you could only find the
hidden picture. There's beauty in
people, places, and things that people
never see after the storm the sun may
not shine right away. That's the time
to find the hidden picture. The beauty
that takes thought to see.

Donna Golden

Untitled

How can you miss something, someone
    some thought
    you never should have had?
It's easy to think - what could have been
    pretend days should have been different.
Nobody wakes up everyday to perfection-
    but I fool myself into thinking it
would have been with you.
    I miss something.
All my perspective is gone. Suddenly I have
needs that weren't here yesterday. Empty stuff-
unfulfilled and all that. Your hands-
    I miss someone.
Logically nothings different - but you've been here
    and gone - so now something is lost -
    a moment that's gone for good.
Dreams of touching for days on end -
    I miss that thought.
        But I never really had it.

Dana Leet

Beyond Beyond

Out there, there must truly be
Something beyond just you and me.
How can things be organized so well
Held together with laws and properties, can't you tell?
Good effort rewards both you and me
Hurt brings suffering and will always be.
From cold there is fire and then it is cold
Things align in the universe and they never release their hold.
There is life and death and family
Hurt and happiness but there is harmony.
Anxiety in learning things without measure
Our motivations were given - both pain and pleasure.
Our universe is growing everyday they say
Problems are ever present so we kneel and pray.

Beyond there is hidden in the light
The creator who feels our love and understands our plight.
I'm wondering if this is all going to an end
It's really a beginning a passing given by a friend.

Gary Laprocino

The Wall

As I look out into the morning air
Something catches my eye, I set and stare.
I detect movement at its strongest point.
Something is missing, and I start to understand.
That massive wall that once stood tall,
Is trembling and shaking and starting to fall.
For there is a hole that is devastating
And it seems that the wall is slowly fading.
Turning away from the stone cold stare
I feel tired, as if I can't go on.
One last glance and what is it I see,
But the hole that once was no longer stares at me.
The wall is strong and complete once again
The part that had been missing is back, like it had been.

David Wayne Crouch

Eyes Beyond Steel

The stranger within me stares out of porcelain eyes.
Something deep inside the caverns of my mind stirs. A rushing
of wings. A flourishing hope.

I despair not the dawning day, nor the ensuing darkness.
Their grip permeates a land that I have long since forgotten.
Shadows, much like dreams, rule me from afar. Vague memories
of stealth and isolation pulsate within my benign consciousness.

For a fleeting moment, the stranger within me awakens. I watch
his hot breath escape my mouth in tiny white clouds. It is a cold day
and he is stalking something that I have never dared to look upon.

A stag wanders in the distance. An eagle soars undaunted into
an approaching storm. A wolf cries and is silent as her wails
echo off towering walls of granite.

Such visions are the essence of life, yet they are lost to me.
Much like tears in rain.

Deep within the bowels of my being the stranger senses these
things and stirs. An intangible fire of recognition has been lit
within me, but I fail to feel its warmth. Deprived of all,
my heart throbs and I long to be free.

But the predator within me is gone.

John D. Shors II

United Nations Inspired

"The United Nations may seem a bit evil,
Something in the nature of a boll weevil,
But one must remember it has some style,
And definitely should stay around awhile.

"Many resolutions the UN does often pass,
Presumably just to help the needy mass,
Yet each day it seems to become weaker,
Ever so much more frigid, mild and meeker.

"Yet out of the United Nations can come,
An especially good little positive plum,
Of assistance to the real world's needy,
Often at the mercy of the terrible greedy.

"If UN Secretary Generals lose humility,
It can often lead to disaster, senility,
And perhaps even the end of the UN for good,
Something that might never be fully understood?

"The United Nations may seem a peace palace,
To Don, Jack, Bill, Jim, May, Joe and Alice,
But for many of us it can mean so much more,
It would be miserable just to shut the door."

Blythe Foote Finke

I'm Looking Into You

I'm looking into you from the other side. Somewhere in the
darkness a song has arrived. But you don't know why it feels so
strange to be in this world with its endless pain. It can't be real!

You watch the video on MTV and you wonder what it's like to
be a central part of that insanity: A star adrift upon melodic sea!

Yes, you wonder still what is going on in your spinning mind,
what it is that you're gonna find in your visions: the key?

Keep on playing although you're all alone. Voice in stereo from
the twilight zone. Expanse of space is your only home.

Yes, you wonder still what is going on in your spinning mind.
Can you ever find in your visions: the key?

You watch the video on MTV and wonder what it's like to
REALLY be a central part of that insanity. A star adrift upon
melodic sea!

I'm looking into you from the other side. I'm very pleased with
what I find. Stay alive and keep an open mind.

Jay Chris Sullivan

The Lonely Sparrows

Dodging the cars in the shopping center, I look for the
Source of the singing birds: It is little sparrows flitting
Among the carts and in the eaves of the overhang.
I watched their happy darting about
I listened to their clear sweet notes.
Of the rushing shoppers, not one noticed, one tripped—
How oblivious to beauty, how remote .
Tell me, little sparrows, sing your song again,
What are you saying?

You have another great gift—with such mobility
You choose this! Why not verdant trees
And fields of grass across the way?
Tell me, little sparrows, sing your song again,
What are you saying?

Brave little birds, unencumbered with rent or mortgage,
Why not leave this perilous place and spend
Your uplifting exuberance elsewhere?
Tell me, little sparrows, sing your song again,
What are you saying?

Harry W. Gordon

Honey Pine

I am the surface where you eat,
spaghetti, salad, butter, rolls —
Crumbs scratch my lacquered shine,
you hold hands over me.
The Friday night hum of a calculator
vibrates through me.
Your head, bills and figures weigh me down.
Years ago, you changed your baby's bottom here.
I winced, but stood on claw feet.
Baby drool, cat scratches and candle wax
burns have shaped my face.
I've been pledged, murphy oil soaped, endusted.
Tomorrow I'll be dipped, sanded, restained.
"Honey pine", she says.

Ebee Conry

Autumn Memories

Autumn is an enchanted time.
Spectacular foliage; scarlet, yellow, brown, orange, and gold.
The beauty is untold, and the memories that it will soon be cold.
Raking leaves as they drop.
Sounds and texture do not stop.
Blue jays, woodpeckers, and chickadees are also part of Autumn leaves;
They can be heard in the bushes and trees.

The charm of Autumn memories.
The blooms of the summer gardens have to fade
to make way for the Autumn days.
Cool and crisp turn the days while all the harvesting is well underway.
Dwindling sunlight is so near.
The Autumn will soon be gone, I fear.
Then the spectacular foliage of scarlet, yellow, brown orange and gold
will just a memories that I have told!

Jennifer Crow

Life Would Be Easier

Life would be easier if children never
        spilled milk, never forgot to be
        polite, never got sick,
and never forgot to do their homework; But, they do!
Life would be easier if children always
        said please, always ate the right things,
and always got along with others; But, they don't!
Life would be easier if children came
        with blueprints, or instruction manuals; But, they didn't!
Instead, children come to us with a lot of needs, desires,
        emotions, talents and gifts...all put together in a package!
The packages are all very different. Some have new wrappings,
        pretty ribbons and are desirable to hold.
Others are tattered and torn and look less desirable.
How we open each package and handle what's inside will determine
        the lasting value and beauty of the gift we find!
Every child is a gift! A package to open!
Life would be easier if each package were pretty and easy to handle,
        But, they aren't!
We are the package handlers, Let's handle with care!

Deborah A. Barrett

Seal

Feet firmly planted on life's highway of cement,
Spirit feeling stifled, beginning to ferment.
Carelessly forgetting the eternal lasting cause,
Lost and absorbed within this world's flaws.

Painfully, slowly, intellectual icicles do drip,
As I remember, words flowing from my lip.
Ahh. I remember, the freedom of a soul,
Momentarily diverted from life's true goal.

To fly, to soar, no limits in sight,
Life, the school, why must we fight?
Silently breathing, in wonder, in awe,
Our countries false riches, becoming the law.

Yes, I remember you, those now gone,
You gave me my truths, showed never wrong.
Now I reminisce, you who were brought to me,
I too, do fly, when I choose to live free.

Jannine Salo

My Sisters And I

My sisters and I when we were grown
spoke of Our Father and Mother
and of the love and caring they had shown
Always to each other,
to us and everyone they had known

They taught us honesty, to love, honor and obey
and as most humans we often did go astray
but My Sisters and I would recall
the most important lesson of all...
God loves you and will hear your prayer
if you ask forgiveness and he knows you really care

Jacqueline Smith

Untitled

They just appear. The weeds in the garden.
Sprouting unexpectedly. Anywhere.

They just appear. No prevention. No prediction.
No cure. The weeds just appear.

Chemicals and powders offer temporary
relief. But again, they just appear. Anywhere.

They overcome the presence of the flowers.
Draining their beauty. But there is one that
survives.

One perfect bud. Oozing with color
and fragrance. Standing tall amongst
the weeds. Reaching out to the sunlight.
Enticing honey bees. Determined to blossom.

Jeanne Masecar

The Promise

I find myself at dawn,
Standing at the water's edge,
Barefoot in the gentle surf, the wind in my face,
My arms outstretched in offering to the heavens.
Holding my heart in my left palm, facing east
Allowing the first rays of the sun to fall upon it.
My soul in my right palm, facing west, still in darkness,
Awaiting the promise of a new day.

As the sun commences its journey across the sky,
I remain immobile, oblivious of the rising tide.
With each breath I take, my lungs are filled with
The moist sea spray.
My feet sink deeper and deeper into the sand,
As the relentless waters, silently engulf me.

A white light appears in the horizon, getting closer and closer,
Casting a silver beam on each palm,
Transforming into doves, my heart and soul.
In unison the gentle creatures take flight in a flutter,
Soaring free to the heavens, leaving behind
A white feather and footprints in the sand.

Fauvette Nudleman

Impassioned Soul

Hidden behind the disguise of a smile is a lonely child
starving for love and acceptance but, only being nourished
by his own starving soul.

Trying to fight back the tears of his bleeding heart only
to drown himself in a watery grave.

His smile is lying to the world and his eyes are curtains
for his soul always remaining closed so others don't see
him hurting. He can still feel the pain and hear the screams
of the haunting soul inside him as if it were a separate entity.

The soul is searching for the light of another or is the light
a way for the soul to escape the flesh of hell.

James D. Bunger

Indian Ghost

Indian Ghost in the pale moon rising,
standing proud and alone on the horizon;
Forgotten chants and Tribal dance,
Indian maids and horses the prance;
A wisp of wood smoke and a river of mirrors,
Taking us back through the years.

Indian Ghost in the pale moon rising,
Standing proud and alone on the horizon;
An eagle feather in his hair, showing to all
that he was there.
Never forgotten with an open mind and soul;
forever traveling to the days of old.
Waiting there to teach us anew on living with
the animals and in the woods too.

Indian Ghost in the pale moon rising watching
his people in the horizon;
Tears in his eyes for that, that is forever lost;
No one knows forever what it had cost.

Hazel Summerkamp

Truth Or Lies, Lays Within

Day is just the start
Start or finish, which do you prefer to see
Seabreeze from the ocean, ocean sprays colors forming blue
Blue skies with cloudy thoughts, thought you really cared.
Careful of surprises, surprise gifts from above
Above the clouds in the air, airplanes drifting East.

Would you give me a chance or stay in a song
And live in a dance though you know that it's wrong.

Fever in my head, headaches me to melt
Meltdown to a different feeling I've never felt.
Material runs deep like water, watering down the soul of man
Man and woman who unite as one
One is a lonely number to plan a life which includes two.
Too many circumstances arise, arise and take a stand
Stand up as we try, try harder to keep it going
Going down in the end, ending up again as one.

Brian G. Tuma

Ethnic Cleansing

Ethnic cleansing is the only cleansing which leaves the filth and
stench of death behind.
It is the only cleansing which devours innocence in multiple gulps.
Ethnic Cleansing is the din of a thousand hoarse throats growling
for equality.
It is the sight of a withered body with an outstretched fist
clinging to a loved one until the final moment of life has ceased.
Ethnic cleansing is a plain man or woman with an exceptionally
tortured heart screeching with utter despair.
It is quivering soul mesmerized with the thought of sanity.
Ethnic cleansing is the look of complete knowledge, knowledge
of pain, on a youthfully ignorant child's face.
Ethnic cleansing's cause is a single thought of prejudice hatching
from a egg in the nest of insanity and ignorance.
This nest is where all humanity is conceived, and lives by
thriving upon it until it takes their soul back into its bowels to be
recycled into another pitiful thought of hopelessness.

Jennifer Tower

Night Train

A long whistle was blowing when the train was leaving. People were sticking out thru' the windows to see those waving still, a dark night seemed yet glowing even though the farewell was no more somewhere heard sobbing, O God, someone crying in deep sorrow of parting.

Over the Pacific the flying was easy, nonetheless, the night was sleepless afloat in the moonlit sky with loving Ma's wrinkled wearing too big a smile, on the table was ready the dinner but no Mom's heart on it, tasteless somewhere heard sighing, O God, someone crouching in longing for home-bound sail.

Busy world was there as dreamed, when the long night was gone nowhere. Leaving behind those many lost; parent and children, male and female alike, bustled cities were the same as been for million years long, still no room for a stranger somewhere heard puffing, O God, someone in every corner of the smoking

Steepled Churches are many, really, many, many, and many to be found everywhere. But found are people weeping outside, not inside beautifully decorated but emptied, souls are sold and lost in this hellish heaven, indeed, more are seen like marching at war somewhere heard preaching, O God, someone sniffing without ceasing, void.

Come, O come, my friends, do not stay there standing still, run around here and there shouting as being felt like, do something for those left behind wheresoever. Can't you hear the whistle blowing again in the night when the night train starts roaring. Forgetting not those on their knees remembering on the wrinkled face tears rolling.

Bo-Joong Kim

Hostage

Poisoned bars rusted brown by time's indifferent passage.
Still the stagnant stench of captivity cannot escape its defenses.
A footstep echoes off into infinity.

And I wonder when I'll be home again and the moon-rise answers never.

Awakened by morning's din, to words foreign and strange.
And I've asked and asked again, for what purpose can this serve.
They feed me but nothing more.

And I ache to breathe you in.

Desperation fills their faces. Perhaps the time is near. One way or another I'll be free.

And I, as tired as can be, feel nothing.

Brad Center

"The Horseman Of Combat"

The fires of darkness have subsided now leaving an eerie stillness about it that suggests to one that death was here.

As the light of dawn begins to illuminate the bloodied soil, traces of the pale horseman's work become the dominant features of the arena of death.

Sounds, strangely unfamiliar to the jungle, start breaking the air now at more regular intervals. Crying and moaning dominate a normally placid setting.

The dust off birds are leaving now, filled with the carnage of his night's work.

For those he has chosen to remain, he will have given the gift of "survival's guilt."

Raindrops are falling now, clearing the stage of sanguid colors so that whoever are the next will be able to start afresh.

And there will be a next, as the horseman on the pale horse is never satisfied.

Jon Bales

We Can Make A Difference

We can make a difference, we can make a difference.
Stop the litter, don't kill a critter.
Make a solution, stop the pollution.
Don't tear off leaves or cut down trees.
If you don't need'em, leave'em.
We can make a difference.
Yes, we can make a difference.
Help the planet, don't just can it.
Help the ozone layer.
All it needs is a prayer.
Make a difference.

Andrea Long

Studying

Trying to think of something to write,
Storming my brain since it hit daylight.
Things slip my mind as time passes on,
The clock ticks and ticks but the
   hands don't move at all.
My head is empty for I have nothing to say,
If it were for me, I'd have someone
   else write my essay.
I have to study the whole day through.
If I want to go to college and to medical school.
To make my teacher proud and show her my best
I guess I'll have to stay up all night
cramming for that algebra test.
Then there's science and foreign languages too,
How am I ever going to last the whole day through?
If I don't work hard and study for school,
I'll probably end up a nobody with nothing to do.
So that's why I try and strive for the best,
So I won't ever end up like the rest.

Angie Valenzuela

Living With Hope

Early morning the sun came shining through the window
Straight down on my pillow
It has been such beautiful days
For which I give thanks and praise

The flowers are blooming
Everyone seems to be smiling
It's as if something or someone
Has turned us into real humans

For lately everyone seems to lose respect for the other
No love between sisters and brothers
All but hatred that surrounds
No love to be found

Today there is hope in the air
Thanks to the bright and shining sun
For taking away our fears
And drying our tears

Give thanks and praise
to God above
For now we live with hope
Peace and love.

Gregory A. Lewin

The Doctor

My little boy knows, I'm not feeling well.
Strange to say, but he can tell.
He tries to tell me how bad he feels,
By rubbing and purring so close to my heels.

He cuddles up close, from head to foot.
As if to say softly, now you just stay put!
I'm here if you need me, just give me a call.
And we'll get rid of that flu, FOR ONCE AND FOR ALL!

Joseph Bommarito

"Treading Water"

Looking into your baby blues
strength in my knees is what I lose.
A cross roads has suddenly appeared
an inevitable separation is what we fear.

Are you the one? Am I the one?
If we are destined then why the stagnation?

Can we be wrong, I don't think so
if we don't do this we will never know.
I understand the problem but maybe I don't want to,
we don't really know the right thing to do.

Say you love me at least for now
so we can move on with our lives.

Accomplishing greatness is overshadowed by doubt
what are your words really all about?
I want a life and a home to share
our moments are getting us close to nowhere.

We have all these break-through talks
but continue treading water.

Allisandra Fairclough

Hands

The newborn's fingers
Stretch out — reaching.
Eager to draw in life giving energy.
Grasping, gripping strong little fingers.
Insecure thumbs tucked inside fists.

Comes a day of discovery!
Hands become play things.
Probing, exploring, sensitive to touch
Thumbs pull out — separating,
getting much stronger, standing alone.

All our life time long,
hands are faithful servants.
Caressing, soothing, patting, holding,
hands lending comfort, doing our work.
Giving us joy and service.

Hands keep busy
Are calloused and scarred.
With life's breath labored,
they claw at the winding sheets.
Finally stilled they lie in repose.

Judy Aldrich

After Christmas, It's Spring

The short gray days of winter
stretch shadows o'er my mind
And even though there's holidays
I'd leave it all behind.

For I hate the cold, the sleet and snow,
the grisly temps of twenty below.
I long for the warmth of May.
Then I remember, that after Christmas,
it's spring!

Never mind the snow, it will all go
The flowers will bloom in spite of
the gloom.
The trees are bare, but I don't care
because, after Christmas it's Spring.

So forget the ache of the cold;
the bite of the winter's wing,
And say farewell to all that and sing,
After Christmas, it's Spring!!

Jeanne W. Carey

The Withdrawing

You were a mighty father
Striding through our childhood with the force of wind.
How could we know your soul was many splinted
Or guess when mother died so young, so unexpectedly
That she would leave a wounded child with us?

Painfully you eased behind your wall, that so familiar wall,
The wall of waiting, where we sentineled our childhood
Watching for a sign of you, looking over,
Waving and smiling benediction on us.

The anguish of your loss hurled brick on frantic brick.
A fortress loomed impenetrable,
A hiding place to spare us from your disability.

Outside your grief blew us a hurricane.
You could not see us bent against the wind,
One brick or two removed we could have touched your hands,
Cupped a chalice for your tears and mixed them with our
own, water for your wine.

It would have been a great communion then,
Not us outside in all that weather,
Searching for entry, bleeding from an unattended wound.

Charleen Jenkins

Anne Frank: Child Of The Holocaust

Whoever, wherever you are
Strike a match in the conscience-stricken heart of abandonment
   darkness,
Light an illuminating candle for Anne Frank
Refugee prisoner of Prinsengrachet 263...Bergen-Belsen victim,
Fertilize her memory with eulogizing tears in perpetuity.

Ghosts...I seem to see her furtive face at the Annex window,
Cinema darling Deanna Durbin enlightens her abstract bedroom wall,
An innocent child housebound to escape the Aryan plague
Looking down in the occupation austerity of the tree-lined
   Prinsengrachet,
A herd of yellow-ill-starred Jews being prodded toward transports,
Tethered houseboats with their diverse roof-gardens defiant in the canal,
Then sentinel Westerkerk clock tolling at quarter-hour intervals,
Timeless, tocsin, uncorrupted by the Nazis,
All of it eventually recorded with fidelity in her posthumous Diary,
A victim's legacy of innocence, faith, hope,
Morality, mortality, Christian nobility in the Godless age of Genocide,
To be read henceforth till the end of time,
A Biblical testament of the Holocaust, immune to neo-Nazi-revisionism.

How can we ever forget, hidden from the world
Anne Frank once lived...here...in this warren...

Gershon Spivack

When Twilight Draws The Curtain

I get up early every morn, about five o'clock or so,
stumble into the bathroom, dress myself from head to toe.
   Gobble down my breakfast grab my flopped hat and coat,
wake the sleeping children, "Don't oversleep," is my daily quote.

   I hasten to the bus stop, drop a letter in the box,
Someone's running past me, like a hound chasing a fox.
   Board a crowded bus, have to stand most of the way,
After working hard eight hours, I've earned more than my pay.
   Once more I step - up on the bus, filled with tired - looking souls,
I pay my fare, struggle between them and hold onto a pole.
   I'm bounced on a fellow passenger, step on a few toes,
I try to be polite, frowns creep into their faces, but that's
the way it goes.

   I ring for my stop, and squeeze myself free from the bus,
I'm glad I took my vitamins, because they add to my just.
   The streets are almost dark now, and I try not to be afraid
When twilight draws the curtain, and night pulls down the shade.

Gloria M. Little

Heartbreak In Purple August

The bright, blue hope of spring has long been
summer-scorched; the jade of June diminished;
July's gold-dust sun overripe, a Halloween pumpkin
lolling in a fading sky.

The pale face turned skyward on purple August
nights is moon-streaked, loneliness dipped in silver,
Romances of summer, with summer, about summer,
their cotton candy glimmer and ferris wheel kisses,
slide down pale cheeks, useless tears falling
into the palm of God's hand.

August pauses, and lingers, a long coppery sigh,
Purple heartbreak lingers also, clenching
sober fist as August unfurls its ungainly tail.

Amy J. Delaney

The Glass World Of Peter Jude

Between us a glass wall, tiny fingers
summoning air into a smaller glass world.
Your new born eyes blinking blue,
seeing but one dawn, one dusk.

Time enough for a single ride,
not for ice cream, but x-rays.
Enough for consultations, baptism, tears,
enough for one kiss of welcome and farewell.

Hushed voices slide away leaving us alone.
Silently I scream through the glass,
watching the last rise and fall of your only blanket.

The tiny white box of your home has no glass.
Each year a single white flower commemorates
a gray day long ago, each flower laid on a brown grass table,
cold stone doing for candles.

No other gift but your picture packaged in glass,
tied in my mind, changing year after year as you grow there.
Images of what you might have been had you but forsaken
tiny wings, my son.

Joseph R. Mascaro

Untitled

With first glimpse, the vastness of her radiance is awe inspiring;
  sunlit rays glisten upon her brow and dance in pirouettes.
Outstretched arms reach up to embrace,
  and yet, withdraw again in the very next breath.
She is undaunted, a seductress, known by many lovers,
  however, each soul that she entices,
    learns quickly of the fury with which she can burn.
Within her arms there is safeness and security, warmth of the womb,
  nevertheless, it is in those same arms that you may break.
Your destiny lies in her hands, wavering unsteadily,
  controlled by the ebb and flow of her passion, by her love and
    rage.
The depth of her charms is so beguiling, danger becomes unfathomable.
Do not so readily let down your guard, take heed;
  discovery is yours, yet only skillfulness and love can guide you.
She is beauty given many names, though she answers unto none of them
  for no spoken word can capture the glory of her spirit.
Tempestuous at times, yet tranquil.
She is boundless and all encompassing.
She is ocean, she is sea and gulf. . .
  and I have loved her unconditionally, now and for all time.

Jean Morgan

Veteran's Park 1979

They played in the ocean as the
sunset over my shoulder
In the distance the ferry returned
the round trip weary from Nantucket
The tide had made private pools
in the folds of the beach
and they jumped and skipped in them
Watch this Mommy
See my shell does seaweed bite
Let us walk and hold hands
(and let time stand still for this twilight)
I was soothed by the tide
my cares set free with its ebb
I wanted to stay forever
but too soon it was time to go

Cheryl Sharp-D'Escopo

The Ladder

Ladders of silvered rope descend,
Swaying down into the satin depths
Of the dark and dimpled lake.

Oh how I long to climb down,
Deep down to the soft and cool receiving ooze.
My tired, fevered feet would curl round the rungs
Woven of light beams, reflected from the shore.

But then how sadly I recall,
I'm made of molecules, corporeal and heavy,
But the ladder, a construct of immaterial
  luminous waves,
Cannot support the embodied weight of human sorrow.

Irene Rudoy

Sugar Sweet Dreams

  Shush precious one, sleep your innocent
sweet dreams of ice cream mountains topped
deliciously with cream.
  Cookie animals to hold our little hand and
coax you to play in the brown sugar sand.
  Chocolate kisses to freckle your rosy
cheeks as colorful jellie beans roll in a game
of hide and seek.
  Hush my baby, sleep your dreams of happy
play and run beside streams of rainbow koolaid.
  Clear blue skies pillow with cotton candy
over dancing lollipops that harmonize so dandy.
  Comfort your fragile body in the puddles of
cherry jello and wave out your laughter in the
sweet flower meadows.
  Rest my beautiful child, lay your mind from
worries and enter your dreams in the
world of sugar sweet stories.

Della Rae Drennan

"Faith"

Sometimes I stroll through flowers
Tall that grow beside my garden wall
Sometimes when faith is very
Low and I cannot see why things are so
I stand among the flowers I
Grow and learn the "answers" I would know!
For among my flowers I have come to see
Life's miracles and mystery
And as I stand in reverie
My faith comes slowly back to me!
And I kneel and thank my
"God for all his blessings
And his love

Alice J. Bramlet

For Little Rhododendron

Pink satin rhododendron, sweet,
Swift water swirling 'round your feet,
Alone and small, yet true and strong,
How do you cling there all day long?
Sunshine glinting on your petals,
Glistening leaves where cool mist settles,
Bright, shining star 'mid rocks of gray,
Welcome butterflies at play.

In this poets' haunt with trilling bird calls,
Do spirits come to hear as night falls?
To listen to the rippling run
Until the rising of the sun?

Do poets of old who joined with friends here
Commune with them as yesteryear?
I think they come on Angel wing,
And leave the notes the songbirds sing,
And scatter beauty in your tresses
Like the beauty love possesses.
More lovely than earthly poets impart,
And can only from an Angel heart.

Delia G. Hall

Seasons

In the summer the swans
swim gracefully on the
sparkling lake, while lovely, fragrant
flowers bloom.

In the autumn the leaves
change colors to red,
orange, yellow, and brown and
then fall.

In the winter the wonderfully,
white snow falls softly
on the green grass.
In the spring the
chipmunks, squirrels, raccoons, and bunnies
come out from hibernating
and wait for the next
year to come around.

Jeni Stockle

Single Vs Married Life

A single life is a lonely life,
    take it from a newly wed wife
I had my freedom, I had my fun,
    I thought I had everything under the sun.
But then came the day at sunny
    Rockaway that changed the entire
    course of my way.
Never did I dream the stranger
    I would meet would soon prove
    to be my reason for living,
    for planning, for giving
And now our own baby boy
    has brought us such joy
Has come to bless our home
    with happiness never known
May God up above always
    keep us in his love.
May we ever be grateful and
never forget how blessed we
were on that day we first met.

Gloria Kovelman

Failed Relationships

A dog is given a bone and is left to enjoy it, but soon it's taken away and the dog is kicked in the face without reason.

Later, he is given a bigger, better bone, and is left to enjoy it, but soon it is taken away and he's kicked in the face even harder.

Finally, he's given the biggest, best, juiciest bone around, the only one he'd be happy with for the rest of his time on earth, the only one that gives him so much joy and satisfaction, the only one he'd protect with his life, and he's left to enjoy it.

But this time he's kicked, beaten, and nearly strangled.
Soon he sobs at just the sight of a bone.
He knows he can't have it, no matter how hard he tries,
    no matter how good it looks,
    no matter how long it's in front
    of him.
So the dog is left to waste away beside a pile of bones, because he can no longer stand the abuse.
...and so he dies;... withered... broken... and lonely.

Alan Stemper

All Things That He did

Taken for granted, a tough healthy man
    Taken for granted, building tools in hand,
Taken for granted, not scared to get dirty,
    Taken for granted, his homes are still sturdy.

Taken for granted, a sociable man,
    Taken for granted, his cigar in hand,
Taken for granted, he enjoyed to dine,
    Taken for granted, he adored his wine.

Taken for granted, a kind, cordial man,
    Taken for granted, a peace pipe in hand,
Taken for granted, he loved all his friends;
    Taken for granted, they never did end.

Taken for granted, a family man,
    Taken for granted, his plate to their hands,
Taken for granted, he loved her, his wife,
    Taken for granted, all days of his life.

Taken for granted, all things that he did,
    Taken for granted, that he'd' always live,
Taken for granted, he'd be there smiling.
    Taken for granted, the bell tolls; he's dying.

Christopher C. Giancola

His Father's Watch

Late at night an old man sits
    takes out his watch to watch it tick,
    stares at its face that shows no age,
    unlike his own where years play and rage.

He turns back its hands to turn back time,
    time remains just the hands unwind,
    looks to the darkness with yesterday eyes,
    remembering when's, wondering why's.

He dreams of lover's goodbye smiles,
    chances lost among the miles,
    longs to see his father once more,
    turns the key in a long-locked door.

Again a boy on sun-washed sand,
    holds tomorrow in his hand,
    laughs as skimmers chase the sea,
    and umbrellas ballet wondrously.

He soars in joy as a bright red kite
    held by a thread to earthly flight,
    while on the shore his father sits
        and takes out his watch to watch it ticks.

Bonnie Harvath

On The Diamond

As we play the game of life-
Taking our turn with its toil and strife-
There are many chances to win or lose-
And it depends upon us, the pitches we choose-

We can make the right pitch, and honor the Name-
Of the one who died that life we might gain
Or, we can swing away at the wild pitches of life
And wind up in trouble, torment, and strife

Moses played the game according to the rule
And learned in his life for life is our school
And honored Him in his Hall of Fame
And gave glory to His Holy Name.

So on that day when the Great Game Begins
And we play before Him, who taught us to win
And on that opening day my heart tells me so
That out on the mound, COULD WELL BE 'OLE MOSES.

Clifford (Jack) Lawson

Loner

No friends, lonely and detached. Scared to try and
talk. Chicken, runs whenever someone comes near.
Cemetery, favorite place to be. Talks for hours to
nothing. Quiet, can't think of anything to say.

Crying, sad and full of woe. Sees a person that looks
like a friend. They come closer. Want to talk, make a
friend, chicken out. Recede to a dark place and quietly
watch them go by. Didn't want to be their friend anyway.

Darkness, time for a walk. Stay away from cars, lights,
and people. Where? Where? The cemetery, go there.
Cracked tombstones, grey and loathing. Hard cold
granite. All dead, all gone, all peaceful. The hoot of
an owl, the heartbreaking wail of a dog. All welcome
sounds to these ears.

Twisted trees with roots reaching toward decaying
coffins. Suddenly tears to eyes that have seen no
happiness. One thought, this is my world. A world with
no friends. The sun is coming, must go. See you later
when the moon is full.

Dawn Edwards

What Is A Best Friend?

A best friend is someone who we can
Talk to, laugh with, share our problems with,
Or just be there for you when you
Think that you have gone around "the bend".

Sometimes we might meet our best friend
In Elementary School or High School, but
It doesn't matter where or when.
Just that they are your best friend.

We all grow older, and we always remember
Our best friends, although they may move
Far away, they are in our hearts to stay.

They're always there if you need a shoulder,
They're always there if you need a listening ear.
Please remember that they're always there
If you need to hear "I love you
And I really do care".

Deborah J. Rutherford

Summer

Snow melts and runs down his face.
Tears going forever never finding a place.
Boarder feels as if he has no home,
The snow left him so all alone.
Nowhere to go nowhere to ride,
The sun left him no more than a mud slide.

Casey Waltman

The Hat He Wore

Straw-woven,
    tattered and sweat-stained,
shaped and stretched and pulled
    this way and that
to conform to ever-shifting weathers and moods,
    the hat he wore
    now restfully hangs on a rusty nail
by the back door.

He wore it when he strolled
through sea-like fields of oats and wheat
that rippled and swayed in the mild evening winds
    of early summer.

Under the blasting heart of a July sun
    it shaded his rugged face
harshly furrowed from long hours
    of squinting dust and hay chaff away.

Constant companion and protector,
it waits in the early morning shadows
    unfeeling, severed of life,
left now only as a memory of someone close to me.

Frank A. Schmainda

Only My Head Could Be Seen

"Before you bury me
Tell me one thing,
Why'd you leave me shaking?"
She laughed through her tears and said,
"I was a fool in a pool with no water.
You poured gin on me when I was on fire!!!!
You left me alone to feel out the dark.
I can't feel an inferno, all I have are tepid sparks!!!"
"So one scoop of dirt will suffice," I hoped,
"to be brushed off between the kneeling and the rice?"
"Don't be stupid," she screamed
"You're doomed to be covered,
undiscovered, my lover,
until only your head can be seen."
With that she proceeded to chill me.
In mud she proceeded to thrill me.
Undeniably real.
my breath to steal.
Until only my head could be seen.

Eric P. Schwartz

The Verdict

Not the first to travel down the long hallway, certainly not the last;
Terrified and Anxious and Nervous (Though others told me all would be well),
I arrived at the cold, antiseptic-smelling room and waited.
I sat on a hard, unyielding chair, as I awaited judgment on the witness stand,
Preparing my defense for the prosecution.
The questions in my mind pinched like needles,
Vaccinating me against my cancerous fears:
Would I be accepted? Would I be understood?
Would I be forgiven? Would I...

Heavy footsteps jerked me out of my medicated stupor.
Sweaty palms and a parched mouth were cellmates with my racing heart.
Accompanied by his escort, he emerged from his chambers,
ready to make his Decision.
His deep, saucer-like eyes surveyed the room,
Searching for something, for someone. Searching for me, discovering me, he acknowledged my presence with a penetrating gaze
Which revealed to him everything he needed to Know.
He reached out to me (As in The Fresco on the ceiling of the Sistine Chapel);
The Child reached up towards the trembling hand,
And smiled up at his Father.

The Verdict had been passed: My newborn son had decided to love me.

Adam Holzman

Count It All Joy

James happens to be none other
  Than our Savior's younger brother
His powerful message for each one,
  Count it all joy when trials come
The testing will make your faith grow strong
  Ask the Father for wisdom, you'll never go wrong
But ask in faith, not a doubt in your mind
  He'll answer your prayer, He'll give you a sign
Both rich and poor will all pass away
  Like the flowers, the grass, of by gone days
A crown of life in return for our love
  He's promised this blessing from heaven above.
So be strong in the Lord when tempted with sin
  Bring forth fruit each day as you labor for Him
Be a good listener, be slow to speak
  Put away anger, be gentle, be meek
Yes, be a blessing to someone today
  Be pure, unstained, His child always

    Janet Lee

Blessed Relief

Oh Dear Lord up above
Thank you for taking the one I love
He was suffering so much pain and grief
I know he welcomed the much needed relief
Take him into your loving arms
Keep him from any further harm
Knowing that he is safe and secure
Makes my loss easier to endure.

    Jerldine Kite

The Storm Sonnet

The trees bow down upon this wind so grand,
that blows across the land to flatten weed.
It cares not for the damage done to land,
and carries on without a single need.

The clouds so deep and dark are 'cross the sky.
They rumble horrid sounds that shake the land.
The movement..swirling..looks to never die.
The lightning reaches out an angry hand.

The rain now comes and pounds upon the land,
This anger brings with him another friend,
The hail sticks by the rain and thinks he's grand,
But soon it stops; their reign comes to an end.

And though so hateful..in the end it shows,
Array of colors from a rainbow glows.

    Jennifer J. Murphy

The Sparrow

The sparrow with song-like chirps (in bursts of song,)
that followed him right along.
With notes so clear, in tone, of this bird -
That is like a song often heard

An a melody that had words.
Another sparrow, on the roof top, heard
these song-like chirps an to him were as a spoken word.

Message heard, decoded and a song went forth in answered song.
For each sparrow had a song;
that followed him right along.

What a chirp! What a tone! What a song!
Message heard; ever so sweet and yet so strong,
In song-like chirps, that followed him
All day long.

    Evelyn Jeanette Beard

Raindrops

There came the late November rains
That drenched my yard
And splashed my window pane
And some got on my pillow.

And there was painful loss
But just the same
I knew that there was much of gain
To follow.

Like morning sunbeams
Through the tear soaked leaves
And blue jays jostling limbs up in the trees
And lingering raindrops fall,

And I recall
As in a dream
A face that smiles
And eyes that beam
And laughter mixed with tears and things
And all the joys that memory brings,

Like lingering raindrops.

    Floyd Emmerling

Untitled

Carrying with the treaded white, milky stars
that fell from within your hand
I found more in these magnanimous trinkets
than in myself or any foreign lands
Sequacious in your distinctive need to mend
a mendious man
Are you likewise troubled of my entangled limbs
Are you likewise troubled that we rest in so similar
fragrances of pain
Are you troubled by the crazy whims of their subconscious
Give us each other's hand as a brittle commandment
softened and made tender by the beat of my heart

    Jacob Kramer

In Loving Memory

To Grandpa
We prayed for you night and day
That God would take care of you.
We wanted you to come back to us,
But God wanted you to come home to him.
  So, we let you go.

You're in God's hands now, as you always have been.
We all love you so very much,
But God loves you so much more.
And you can rejoice eternally at his right hand.

We'll always treasure our times together as a family.
You've been generous and willing to help when
  someone had a need.
Thank you for your caring heart.
You'll always be appreciated, and you'll remain in
  our hearts forever.

It isn't easy losing a loved one.
But we can rejoice because we'll all be
  reunited again.
"When we all get to heaven, what a day of rejoicing
  that will be!"

    Jenni Tucker

Marissa Jayne

There's those dimples with their depths
That hide her secret's in the cleft
And those eyes that speak of mischief everyday
A whirlwind dancing here and there
Not a moment yet to spare
Then in sleep an angels face she does portray
My prayers express the blessing
Of Gods wisdom in his sending
This exhaustive yet delightful bit of him
First A devil then such joy
Playing me just like a toy
A blond haired satan in a blue eyed cherubim
Could I but hold her here for now
Stop all time if I knew how
Drinking up shared innocence from her heart
Then I myself could stay as young
As Marissa Jayne, my special one
And isn't she what life is all about?

Dani McNeil Baldwin

What Happened To Now

What happened to the baby
    that I carried deep inside
What happened to the little boy
    who loved to seek and hide
What happened to the little tike
    who loved to ride upon his bike
    and squeal and scream with pure delight
What happened to the little lad
    who on the first day of school had
    a confrontation between good and bad
What happened to the little boy
    whose love was all mine
What happened to the handsome teen
    who made music all the time
What happened to the young man
    who took young ladies out to dine
What happened is ...
    that little boy became a man
What happened is that time marched on
    like nothing else can.

Carol Williams Glasco

Why

Why is it that I have to write what I can't say
That I want to be with you for the rest of our day,
And to tell you that I love you - that I really care
The dreams and goals of your life I'd like to share.
But when I'm near to you my tongue becomes tied
By the fear that emerges from deep inside.
A fear that says what if she doesn't care
And throws me aside after my soul I've bared.
And so it is my words will remain unsaid
And our life together will be only in my head.
For while I'll never your feelings truly know
I can always dream that it might have been so.

Barrington W. Keist

Untitled

The feeling left me, but the memory was
still there, I knew that I would remember it for
eternity, forever yet to seek me again and
haunt me. The elevation of the thought was
enterprising. It was I who was the envoy of my
forlorn life. I hanker for a new life. I felt so
alone so insolvent, immersed into reality, the
muffled silence was over.

Jennifer C. Smith

My World

That you were my chief endeavor,
That I was your whisper be.
Grasp not so tightly
Breathe the fresh, fresh air.
I feel you shall know
Praise that you felt should come,
That I am there to hold your hand,
The day it should come.
You asked if the warmth was felt,
But, hours you did not know
Simply that I could hold you,
Once again was mine the answer told.
Wasted hours upon the day.
The anguishes that we know.
Days passed and came,
However, the passions all anew
Nights bathed away,
If once to stop and tell you every, every day
I am your devoted lover,
My world - it is you it seems.

Colleen Tuthill Smith

"Grandpa"

Grandpa you were a great man,
that I will never forget.

And even though we have so little
precious memories...

I still hold them dear to my heart;
for they are what keeps us from growing
apart.

And even though you're gone,
just remember my heart is where you will
always belong.

And in my mind, I know you're still watching
over me...
Our precious memories will always be.

Jennifer Marie Hunt

My Goal

At the end of life's road, is the ultimate goal
That I've struggle and strived to attain.
Though difficult the way, I'm determined to stay,
Until I accomplish each goal.

The road may be long, rugged and steep,
But onward and forward, I must go.
For what I'll achieve will help me indeed
To reach and acquire my dreams.

The goals I select are mine alone;
Public goals are foreign to me.
For deep in my heart, I know what I need;
And what I must do to succeed.

Irisdeane H. Charles

Autumn

It is that time of year when the days start getting shorter.
That time of year when a man realizes that his time too is
getting shorter.
It is that time of year when man reflects on his past gone by,
Lost Love, Lost Friends and Past Adventures.
My, how he would like to turn back the Clock.
If only he'd done this, if only he'd done that,
If only he knew then, what he knows now.
But turn back the clock, He never can.
So he longs for Spring and longer Days.
'Cause with new beginnings Old Memories Fade.

Joe A. Smalley Sr.

Lasting Love

It's deepest thunder over lasting love,
That keeps a lonesome heart in deepest pain,
And raindrops of emotion from above,
A strange new lighting just to breathe a name.

Its thunder only brings a storm of doubt,
The lightning kills a joy that has been found,
And leaves a lull of sadness from without,
A sadness that the raindrops try to down.

The lightning could be joy of love not bought,
The raindrops, the balm of mutual trust,
But thunder is the doubt not seen but sought,
From lack of raindrops love will turn to dust.

Let's make thunder something not in vain,
Such as trusting friendship sweet and new,
And follow it with lightning and the rain
And start a love that always will be true.

Joseph Brook Gibson

Questings

What is the purpose of this dance of life, the roles we act
    that make our destiny, this mystic blend of dream with fact?
What are the rules? What goals are there worth striving for and why?
    Carefree pleasure? Happiness? Is the aim to satisfy
our wants, to seek avoidance of all sadness, grief and pain?
    For most of mankind that's the all of life! Alas - in vain!

When young, realities - though cruel - are overcome by dreams,
    till hope is dashed by fortune-ill, or principle-less schemes.
Relief - from pain, or fear, or threat - gives happiness a lift;
    and gratified desires, hopes, lusts; with these it too comes swift.
But not for long! Such means-to-end make only brief resource.
    The aftermath comes quickly - either boredom or remorse!

To crave and then acquire: wealth, power, fame beyond compare,
    provides for happy ego - adulation, envy. Rare,
but emptiness lies therein; no hope higher to ascend
    bears fruit of pure despair - the certainty of glory's end!

And so one asks, "What is it all about? How does one win?"
    And answers, "Hurt no one! Love all! Find happiness within!"

Aaron Kolom

Rectangular Sunlight

Rectangular sunlight
that my window shapes,
out of you I gaze
endlessly
wondering what I am missing,
for I am trapped inside
unloved, uncared for
drowning, drowning
in a bottomless sea of deep darkness

I pace back and forth in my little room,
my own little space that is hollow with sin,
I am inside it... for I let it in.
As my window is painfully locked,
and I turn from it:
I sing

"I stand as I rotate
my presence is unknown,
I walk as I turn
I realize I stand alone."

Allison Hegge

Look Toward Tomorrow

You have many tomorrows
that promise you warmth and love.
With strength and courage
you can turn them into a future of todays.
Don't look back.
Tomorrow is in front of the day that just past.
When darkness is too much to bear
hold on to tomorrow.
It will take you there.

Janet King

When You Are Young

When you are young it's hard to know
That someday soon so old you'll grow
You feel there's so much time ahead
You don't worry about the life you've led
You waste the years while having fun
But you see time has swiftly run
The days and years go flying by
And you'll think back with just a sigh
If I could live my life again
And start all over when I was ten
I know that I can surely see
How much different I would be
Now old age has extended her claws
Drawing me close within her jaws
She'll never turn me loose again
To take a place among young men
She's got me where I'm feeble and tired
To accomplish things I am not inspired
My only thought is to sit and rest
Cause that's the thing that I do best

James W. Norris

Anniversary Poem

It seems like only yesterday
that to Mississippi we ran away!
When we were just in our teens
and had very meager means!
With our hearts full of love and stars in our eyes
we said our vows and made our lifelong ties!
And as the years passed one by one
we had a daughter and then a son!
We've seen them married to their own true love
with blessings from the heavens above!
As time flew by and the grandchildren came
totaling three precious lads and one darling dame!
With each being special in their own way
for which I am so grateful on this day!
To you my darling husband of thirty years
who have held my hand through troubles, sickness and tears!
Given me self confidence, loving care and strength
have made these many years seem so short in length!
So on this very special day of thirty years together
I give unto thee my vow of true love forever!

Glenda Sample

Veins Of Ice

When the wind blows through my hair, I forget the pain.
The agony is truly in my head, though it feels like my heart is
gone now.
Those feelings may never be seen again, for they've been twice
tossed.
My hand may be reaching for yours, but just because they touch,
don't mean I'll grab hold.

Christopher J. Gomez

Grandma

There was once rolling laughter from her soft, young face
That was silenced by the roar of the tyrant's booming voice.
There was the desire to relax on a Saturday morning
That was forced to take part in the folly of his choice.

She wanted a small family of only three or four,
But found herself cooking and cleaning for eight.
She watched as he broke their wills, destroyed their dreams,
Would fight to protect them which only caused more.

Finally now, after 52 long seasons of pain,
The roar was buried by the bitterness that destroys.
Now she smiles though her gums are bare,
Her heart pours out secrets, jewels like fresh rain.

The days go by without fights or tears,
Choices are made with joy, not fear.
Yet still, at times when bearing her heart,
With sudden flash of fright in her eyes,
She turns her head as if to hear
That familiar rage that still echoes in her memory
She sighs, as if to say, "Will I ever really be free?"

Joanne E. Trinkle

Feelings

Have you ever had the feeling,
That you're staring out a window?
Fighting with a loved one,
Then end up feeling real low.
You say it's just a lover's quarrel,
To try and fool yourself.
So what's another argument,
Just put it on a shelf.
You try and say you're sorry,
But can't look her in the eye.
She's sure you know just what you've done,
You told another lie.
This seems to happen all the time,
When ever you go out.
If you would stay at home sometime,
You'd know what love's about.
In time you both can work this out, if you really try.
It always tears your heart in half, when she starts to cry.
Try not to think of just yourself, and set aside your creed.
After all this she still cares for you, she's all you'll ever need.

David I. Doan

Never Look Back......

Never look back,
that's all I said,
these three words,
still ring in my head.

I fear if I look back,
I'll wish I were dead,
It fills me with fear,
these three words,
that deafen my ears.

Mostly happiness today,
but the small piece of sadness of yesterday,
I will never look back...
I fear if I do,
It will cause me to crack!

Chantae Valdez

Where I Belong

There's a place that I know,
That's not far away,
Whatever I do, I'm welcome to stay.

The people I know there must be heavenly sent,
Even with my wrong,
Their love has never bent.

They comfort me,
Like no one could,
Just the way an angel would.

Blessed be those people
For when their love is near
My mountains of troubles would disappear.

Through my mistakes and answers that were wrong,
I learn that
Being home with my family is where I belong.

Josette Corinne H. Dziuk

One with the Night

I have been one acquainted with the night,
That's when my powers are at their height.
I take advantage of those who are alone.
Like the one there on the telephone.
This is a man who carries a gun,
He will make my chase much more interesting and fun.
I'll chase him down until he is tired,
He'll quiver in fear for I am unharmed by the shots he has fired.
I'll rip him to pieces like an old shaggy doll.
He'll scream for his life, but know one cares of his call.
When morning breaks I'll be gone,
I'll return to a statue on the church lawn.

Buck Fischer

A Birthday Wish For Adam

My dearest Adam, today is you special day.
The Anniversary of your birth.
A day I'll forever treasure, even though your away.

I'm certain an "Awesome" party to celebrate you, will be held in Heaven,
As you my precious child should finally be seven.

A party so spectacular, that on earth it could only be a fantasy,
So live it up! Celebrate! In Heaven you need only imagine and it will be reality.
Such a gift you were to me, changing my life so much in your six short years,
You've been gone now almost one year, still never ending are my tears,

Wonderful memories fill this void today, as I recall all the special times we did share,
Oh Adam! As time and memories pass on by I miss you so. Your death was so unfair.

My dear Adam, today I'll sing Happy Birthday to you,
While I wait and dream of the day, we'll celebrate together again, like we used to do,

And I'll seal this birthday wish with countless hugs and a great big kiss.
Then I'll send it to Heaven, for this your seventh birthday, the first I'll miss.

Deborah Marie Hoffman

My Army Friend

You have given us so much.
The army has ended your career.
To give us peace and rest.
God lent you to us as a gift.

We would like you to return.
For what it meant to lose you.
No one will ever know.
Your smile, your loving face, isn't any more.
I think of you in silence.
And secret tears will drop.
Your spirit will be with us.

When my life is through.
And the angels ask me to recall.
The thrill of them all.
I will tell them, I remember you.

You added so much to our lives.
Love to you always, our dearest son.
Forever in our hearts, souls and in our life.
You will always be a part of my life.

Evelyn T. Tallman

Tribute To The Arts

The Arts can diminish prejudice.
The Arts can show the differences and show the connections
   between all of us.
The Arts praise the essence of a person
and makes us more aware of ourselves privately, therefore in a
   none intimidating way.
The Arts can redefine human value. The Arts can teach us and
   enlighten us.
The Arts can speak to us in a most unique way.
If you really listen; You can "feel" the words or music.
You can "feel" what the character feels.
If you can "see" the art form, you can see beyond sight.
You can "see" what the colors conceal.
When you "understand" the message or understand the "mood"
the Arts can "touch you.
When the inspiration for the art form is revealed
the arts have so much more to offer than what is on the surface.
It inspires us to ask questions. Broadens our experience. Creates
   a desire to understand.
The Arts allow for human error, and makes us aware of <u>all</u> the
   possibilities.
The Arts can keep us in touch with ourselves.
The Arts can keep us Human.

Dedicated to Jane Alexander, '94.

catherine rose

The Feeling of True Love

I try to defeat,
The beat of my heart;
I try to control my emotions,
When I see the silhouette of your youth;
But,........but my heart made trick to my feelings,
And I get nervous and confuse.
I tremble from my heart to my feet,
My face shows the redness of my heat,
And I sweat blood thru my pours,
And that what I call love;
Maybe in another occasion,
Or another dimension perhaps;
They call that by another pronunciation,
But I call that love.
.....the feeling of love.....

Demetrio Rivera

Earth

Far away in the depths of the space
The astronauts reached the moon
They thought it will be the perfect place
Where we can be living soon
That was their case
They so easy to forget the Earth is the best
For every human race
Our goal is to keep our environment clean
Earth is the only place of birth
For you, him, and me
The need is the mother of the invention
You know what I mean
We should clean the Earth
The sky and the sea
And live healthy and free
No traces of life on the moon
No creatures, no grass, no trees
That is my idea, I wanted it to be told
To every one of us, young or old
The Earth remains while life continues....

Basem E. Hilal

Peace On Earth

In lowly stable on some straw
   the Babe was born in humbleness
      to teach us peace -
   the Star above, a guide for all to see
      the majesty of His humility.

The Star still shines
   through clouds of greed and lust for power
   to show the dignity of
   washing others feet
   riding an ass
   wearing a crown of thorns
   and dying on a cross
   between two thieves.

Gertrued Hickin Sigmon

Into The Fire

Into the fire calls the flames
The blackness set a bright ablaze
With sanguine dancing bloody silk
And golden flick'ring flowing "milk"

Into the fire calls the heat
A tempest of foul crimson meat
Grim red sinews of a beast
Hungry for souls ready to eat

Into the fire calls the eyes
Lurid red "moons" that seem to cry
That needs, that wants, that human flesh
That calls, that screams, one's soul to mesh

Into the fire calls the beast
Animals run, he starts to feast
On pure good souls to slake his thirst
The purest lives are damned the first

Into the fires, calls again
His dinner of souls never ends
Mortals blood he does desire human sins he does admire

Dying and Burning, Into the Fire

Johnny Kim

439

Darkness

Suddenly I felt a chill starting at my toes,
  the blackness swept over me ending at my nose.

The darkness engulfed me swallowing me whole,
  as I saw my family weeping over my dreary soul.

I did not know where I was or where I had come from,
  or why I could not talk to them or why they heard me none.

Black sides all around me, silk pillow at my head,
  until then I did not know that I was truly dead.

My family weak and sullen regretfully left my side,
  then they closed the coffin leaving me still inside.

My box now six feet under, soil above my head,
  please someone stop them, I'm really not quite dead.

But, yet they could not hear my pleading cries,
  all they heard was thunder from the roaring skies.

Claustrophobia, all around me, I lay there trapped in,
  now I remember why I'm here, for drunk driving was my sin.

I had to party to have fun in every way,
  suddenly, quietly I began to pray.

The angel of death came over me, taking me from my hell,
  to be with God in peace for now and eternity as well.

  Bonnie Bueter

Remission

The weather and I are as one,
The Cancer is the rain and Remission is the sun
Just as the rain slowly starts to flow,
The Disease in me starts to grow.
Harder and harder seems to flow the rain;
that is when I feel so much pain.
And when there seems no end in sight,
that's the time to be tough -
It is the time to fight.
I say when it rains it pours;
Somebody tell me why I was the one
to knock on St. Peter's doors.
So if you have thought of giving up
like I could have done:
Remember it may be raining now,
but one day there will be sun.

  James Wilson

Looking Out My Window

My window gives me beautiful sights
The cerulean blue sky is such a delight
My eyes open wide when large white fluffy clouds appear
I'm impressed by the billowy softness when they are near
Sometimes the sunlight's beauty appears on the cloud
  like a light yellow meadow
My eyes are fascinated by the dark payne's gray shadows
I look at the clouds swiftly rolling by
Where are they going as they fly?
My body relaxes as I travel up there high in the heavens above
My dreams are planned for future and love
When I look out my window it's really a pleasure
This is God's special gift a beautiful treasure
I thank him for this exquisite beauty
All this gives me a feeling of security
When my life on this special earth is over I will shout loud
I miss the cerulean blue sky with the billowy white clouds

  Ethel M. Shannon

Spring

Hear the birds finally coming home,
The cheeping babies facing the unknown,
The new saplings pushing up to stand alone,
This is Spring.

Feel the light morning showers,
The splendor and grace of sweet flowers,
The light sprinkling of pollen powder,
This is Spring.

Drink from a brook bubbling and clear,
Or eat of herbs that just happen to be near,
Taste Granny's pie, delicious and dear,
This is Spring.

Take a whiff of the scent on the breeze.
The pure freedom of the trees,
The fresh saltiness of the seas,
This is Spring.

Gaze at the mysterious moonlit sky,
The silhouette of the dark hills near by,
The stars that twinkle up on high,
This is Spring.

  Cheryl Tian Li Chin

America's Children

America, America, the children with their thrill for the kill.
The children hooked on crack who have no will.
Sex here, aids there, a gun just for respect.
With violence on T.V. shown as fun just what do we expect.
Grown-up's worried about a career.
Never thinking about a child's fears.
Taught to succeed at all cost.
There is no wonder so many are lost.
Seeing their heroes fall from grace.
Knowing that at any time our leaders could destroy the human race.
Joining gangs so they'll get some love and caring.
Killing each other and ruining their life so it's beyond repairing.
Black, white, yellow, brown, or red.
It doesn't matter when you're dead.
So people at least lets try.
Because if we don't more children are going to die.

  Jacob D. Smith

Run Demon Run

  All throughout the house, it was as quiet a mouse.
The children's parents, humbly praying unto the Lord.
  Suddenly two hideous demons, popped up through the floor,
casting gruesome shadows upon the walls.
  They were quietly stealing towards the children's room,
with thoughts of processing the children's souls!
  But oh, did they get fooled! For there upon the bedposts
sat Christ with a flaming two edged sword.
  Oh, how them Demons screeched for mercy and begged for pardon.
  Jesus, stood and threw that sword, the sword landed into the
floor with such force, it split wide the floor, the earth beneath
it, and Hell's damned could be heard with their terrible moans
and groans.
  The Demons quickly dive into Hell's doorway descending back
into their domain. Gladly escaping Christ's wrath.
  Christ stood so tall, so true, heart of gold, eyes of love.
He smile sweetly at the precious sleeping children.
  Christ listened quietly as the parents prayed and yes,
He would remain this day and thereafter.

  Dixie Ann Salmons

"A Country Christmas"

Sycamore balls and popcorn,,, have trimmed a lot of Christmas trees.
The chimneys were even bigger,,, for sliding down with ease.
It seems that Santa Klaus would know,, when I was asleep.
I never got to see him,, even though I tried to peek.

I guess he knew when I dozed off,, he was a smart old man.
Cause, just as sure as shootin',, I'd miss him once again.
But, that didn't bother me none,, cause, next year he'd be back.
My momma said he would,, and, I could count on that.

But, I often wondered,, why he didn't bring me toys.
Mom said! He had saved them,, for the needy girls and boys.
I guess that I was lucky though,, I could make my sled and kite.
Then, I'd wait for summer,, for the fish to bite.

There was lots of love in our home,, from one Christmas to the other.
That's what Christmas is all about,, according to my mother.
I never did see Santa,, looking back it was the best.
I'm glad for those that didn't,, and, feel sorry for the rest.

Del Davidson

Prejudice

To those who dislike a man who's not given
The choice to be born in the country they live in,
They're prejudice

Anyone thinking that it is not right
To bother with those of us who are not white,
They're prejudice

Those men who refuse to mix with a crowd
Where all are not with his religion endowed,
They're prejudice!

The world has numerous problems to solve
Yet I think there is one word which we must dissolve.
That's prejudice!

Carol Kaszubski

Autistic Self

The autistic self
The closed shell
The personality enclosed
By hands unbroken.

Sometimes the shell cracks
And the self peers out
And allows itself to be seen for a moment.
Then the shell closes tightly once more,
Perhaps to crack again at some time.
Perhaps, never again.

Barbara Harrison

Untitled

The garden is alive again for it is Spring!
The crocus and the tulips stir awakened by the birds that sing.
I hear it! My ears can hear!
I see it! I am not blind!
I feel the warmth of it where cold leaves have lain.
I feel the strength of it from the sun, the wind, the rain.
Nothing held immobile by frozen coldness,
Nothing but my heart!
The plowed fields are black and wet and rich with life.
"Freedom is ours" they cry,
"There is no strife."
I breathe too, I live with no awakening no rebirth within me.
Oh Spring, you should bring new hope,
Pray, help me—thaw my heart!

Dorothy A. Teaters

"City Of Darkness"

City of Darkness, a dismal place to dwell.
The closest thing there is to hell.

Where robbers and thieves are the crowd.
Where streets are dirty, dangerous, and loud.

A place opposite of our own.
Where the sound of the wind is a moan or groan.

In the city of Darkness, night doesn't end,
And goodness is just a whisper on the wind.

In this place, raindrops are black,
And the common home is a shack.

If you live there life is an endless doom.
This is the place where the world's scum is swept by life's big broom.

Avoid this place by all means.
Don't be bad or cause bad scenes.

The world is bad, but this is worse.
Stay away from evil's curse.

Love your enemies, be kind,
To the helpless, don't be blind.

The City of Darkness is an awful life.
Stay away from its strife.

Daniel Froggett

Desert Rain

The sun went down today at noon
The clouds even hid the moon
And the sky was a barren wasteland
And the final stake was driven in my heart.

While I am on the East Coast
You are on the West
And a desert full of several hundred species
could care less.

But alas, there in the distance,
I hear something sings my pain
A lone coyote driven by
The lack of peaceful rain.

He stares me down from farther
Than the empty sky I see
The other winds just pass him by
His pain belongs to me.

And as nighttime falls faster
Than a blazing waterfall
I look back as I walk away
Just waiting for his call.

David Bryan

Tuesday Night Darkness

As I step outside in the Tuesday night darkness.
The cold biting wind nips at my bare skin.
The billowing snow is biting cold,
Through all the warmth of cover.

As I step outside in the Tuesday night darkness,
The blackness haunts my soul with unspoken images.
The smell of ice surrounds my frightful thoughts.

As I step outside in the Tuesday night darkness,
The thick, fluffy mass of whiteness
blankets the frozen earth beneath me.
The blue tinted crystals glimmer in the moonlight.

Erin Halferty

Song For Voice And Empty Pockets

Beneath the bright umbrella of my sins
The clouds seem tarnished trumpets of a silver afternoon
Gay as Scott and Zelda at the shore of Juan-les-Pins
Their shadows calling mine from that rich arabesque of dunes.

But I am no fit subject for dufy
No bright translation into art and changeless light
No emblem of sweet youth and liberty
My weighted footfall leans distinctly towards the night.

The little myth of all my witty afternoons
The brittle beauty of my final maquillage
Shall scatter like a thousand coffee spoons
Beneath the burning castles of the plage.

Forsake my heart of all its vanity
That still adheres to this bright blood and bone
(And to this tongue's deceptive euphony
That wags me everywhere beyond the Gates of Rome.)

The Eden I would have is innocence
A swim with all you angels in the bright eternal sea
I thank you for your patience, fortitude and tolerance
And bid you all to pray for me.

Alfred E. Robinson

Heaven Is The Place

Heaven is the place above
    The clouds so very high;
Where people laugh and angels sing,
    And God lets you say good-bye.
He takes you up under His wing,
    Because a child of His you are;
The people below listen and learn,
    That Heaven is not so far.
There is a time in everyone's life,
    When it's time for them to go;
Let go of your mind, hold onto your heart,
    And only love will flow.
Heaven may be the only place,
    Where hearts can join together.
If this can happen in my life,
    That's where I'll live forever.

Ashley Adams

Unrequited

"Practice makes perfect," a wise man once said.
The coldness of sweet trickling down your head,
And of course of the anguish and pain of your work,
Unrecognized, unnoticed, unwanted. You're a jerk
For trying to advance and to succeed
In a world of competition, and conceit.

Dry you tears now; pick up what dignity is left.
Don't walk out that door. Don't go near those steps.
Take stand, don't let them win.
What they have done to you is a sin.
Keep working hard, make them see.
What a mistake they've made; take it from me.

The rejection that you've had to bear is absurd, unjustified, and unfair.
That's life, the way the cookie crumbles;
Youth is spoiled, your childhood tumbles.

The scar that you bear goes down deep.
Pick up your head, you have one more promise to keep
To your father who has supported your quest
To be accepted, to be your very best
NEVER, EVER, GIVE IN TO THEIR PREJUDICE!

Jessica Battaglia

The Other Side

Nights are filled with sadness the guns,
the crimes of pain are a shock to some.
The children are filled with anger and rage
all these things are a shock to those
whom live on the other side.
Nights is filled with gladness
the pop pop games of peace are a shock to some
the children are filled with laughter and playfulness
All these things are a shock to those
whom lived on the other side.

Bryant T. Smith

The Chenille Bedspread

The old house stood empty.
The curtains were down and washed with care.
The dresser drawers were sorted.
The closet stood bare.

In the corner stood a basket of clothes.
Or so I thought until I looked closely.
In it were rags; T-shirts and long johns;
A flannel shirt saved for patching or polishing mostly.

But down in the middle, folded so neatly,
there was a blue bedspread all tattered and worn.
The chenille kind...and obviously of no use.
It was rehemmed and sewn together where torn.

Then I ran my hands over the soft worn blanket
and thought how it should have life anew.
So from the fabric so tattered and worn,
six bears were sewn...teddy bears of blue.

My brothers and sisters, each one seems to say,
"Remember us when we were whole. Rejoice! For there is life
anew!" The blanket may not be there anymore,
But the thread is still strong, and remains in you too.

Elaine Radunz

Nature Sights Spring

Thus the trees are blowing.
The Daffodils are showing.
Watching the sunset beyond the trees.
Listening to the whispering of leaves.

New life around thee.

Red Finches are courting.
Laughter of children absorbing
Orange poppies dancing to thy gentle tune.

New life surrounds thee.

Rain drops falling from heaven.
Bleeding hearts distended.
A gentle choir singing.
Church bells ringing.

New life envelops me.

Heidi L. Yeager

Ode To A Grand! Granddaughter:

Emma Marie Coleman

Emma Marie, you've got what it takes to be
the love of my life, through eternity
you came down from the stars, with love for me
And can't you see? I love you too!

Playtime with you, made everything seem true
years have gone by, and twilight time is neigh
I know you'll always remember and love me too
Even though I'm far away, I love you too!

John Concello

My Operation

From the hustle and bustle of restaurant life
The day of reckoning had entered my life
My deepest fears had been confirmed
It was on to St. Elizabeth's to be interned.

My months before were feared enough
But the four days before were even more tough
I worked in a kind of twilight zone
To ready myself for the great unknown.

Wednesday morning finally came
Eight-thirty arrived all too early just the same
A hazy-ride; an uneasy mind
A thought I couldn't bear it — no peace to find.

I can't tell you my feelings exactly at the time
Because my limbs were being fastened one by one
My claustrophobia was taking on a tremendous climb
My doctor was late — would I survive the time?

The next thing I knew I was being set free
The beloved face I was waiting for was smiling at me
What do you know - I'm alive, well and free
I cheated St. Peter at a quarter to three.

Edna Kallasy

Untitled

it's April again and the acacias are in bloom
the deep yellows are visible for miles

I remember other April's past...the two of us running hand in hand
through the streets of Paris at 1:00 in the morning rushing to see the
Eiffel Tower as if it would fade into the darkness. The tower was
there and we shared the excitement as if we were explorers
discovering a new land.

April also brings us the gathering of friends and family for
Easter. You began a tradition years ago by holding a now famous
Easter egg hunt much anticipated by more adults than children
due to a promise of, "A lotto ticket in every plastic egg"

it's April again...we walk hand in hand into the future
each footstep engraved in memory
our lives have once again evolved
you've held my heart and whispered hope
I've heard your gentle voice
I respond my dear with eternal love
and when this journey brings us to an end
our love will echo forever across the mountains and valleys

it's April again... and the acacias are in bloom

James Perry Rose

"A Poet's Heart"

The exaltation breeds with the fear
The joy cannot be bound even by compromises
my soul sings, my heart flies
and in this I know I am free
When the blinders fall from your eyes
and you see what can be
in a white page,
or a blank canvas
your spirit will soar
your mind will ache
your hands will scream trying to keep up
with the words and imagings that fight to come out...
This is love, this is destiny...

Cheryl Diane Wilson

Boundless Wonders Of Our Creator

Did you ever wonder who created
  The earth and the sky,
  Rivers and valleys and mountains high.

Did you ever wonder who created
  The flowers, the trees and all that grows,
  Warm bright sunshine or winter's white snows.

Did you ever wonder who created
  The sandy white beaches, the oceans so wide,
  Colors in the rainbow arched against the sky.

Did you ever wonder who created
  The many songbirds with their melodious trills,
  Sounds of the hoot owl and the whippoorwill.

Did you ever wonder who created
  The soft gentle rain or the violence of a storm,
  Fresh clean air at the brightness of morn.

Did you ever wonder who created
  The love of a mother, a baby's first cry at birth,
  People of all nations who roam the earth.

Did you ever wonder or merely take for granted the beauties we see,
  Yes, surely it was someone greater than you and me.

Helen Pope Bell

After One Year

There are no painful memories. No more.
The engram of her death upon our minds
Has softened to her legacy of peace.
She passed in grace and beauty, and it seemed
To us, a life cut short - but not to God,
Who shaped her being into a perfect round
And called her to Himself. We feel her love
Around us, like sunlight on wintry grief.
We think she watches from that happy sphere,
And finds her triumph in our own belief.
We wish her well, and trust to meet her there.
Only an act of faith? Then, Thomas, lo!
Her children and her children's children bear
The hallmark of her incomparable soul!

LOUISE (1932-1987)
I have fought the good fight;
I have finished the course;
I have kept the Faith (2 Tim iv, 7)

John B. Dunaway

Special Child

The Lord had a idea from Heaven
The idea was perfectly fine
To send a child down to earth one day
This child would be crippled and blind

This child had a wonderful family
Who helped her though thick and through thin
They gave her all that they had each day
Right on up to the end
They went to see relatives one day
Leaving the special child behind

They had a terrible welcome one day
To find that the child had died

They cried and cried till they could cry no more

Missing her in their hearts
But now we know she can run and play
And her memory will never part

Carrie P. Beohm

A Widow Remembers

How well do I remember
The garden he made for me
Just so that I could see
A plant grow from a seed.

There were roses everywhere,
Bushes, trees and climbing vines;
Some were yellow, some were pink
Some were red and some were white,
All just for me!

Tulips of all colors and impish daffodils;
Profusely graced our hill;
And out from under the lilac tree
Dancing in the gentle breeze,
Elfish daisies peeked and winked
As I sauntered through the garden
That Ted had made just for me.

How well do I remember,
Chattering birds and whispering trees
On a lazy summer afternoon
As I strolled through the garden
Ted had made just for me!

Eugenia L. Parker

Heart Song

I love the day when it is warm, the cool clean air filling my lungs
The green green grass nodding in the breeze. The birds in flight,
the squirrels in the trees. I love to walk down the sidewalk and
listen to the birds singing, and the songs of nature ringing in my
ears. I love to reach the park by my house, to gaze at the green
slopes and lie there and wonder, will this ever disappear? The
sounds of children playing and laughing drift by. The cottony
clouds smile down upon the earth making patterns against the
gorgeous blue sky. Slowly I walk across the field, gingerly
feeling the earth beneath my feet. The smells of the flowers
scenting the air, the wind blowing through my hair. The radiant
sun beaming down, covering everything without a sound, shining
on my skin making me glow. I climb up the hill and stand
by a tree, the tall tree towers over me. It shades the park with
branches of grace. The swings gently move in the breeze, they
seem to be calling- please, please! So I sit on the swing and
move through the air, alone with nature, free, without care. The
beauty of the earth captivates me. My heart feels light as I soar
to the trees. I'm by myself, but I don't care, this beauty is one I
don't care to share! I love the day when it is warm, the smells,
the sounds, the glorious sights it keeps my spirits in the light!!

Andrea Marie Pettee

To The Baby I Lost

You'll never know the way I feel -
the grief I knew, or the pain I felt inside;
the way my heart broke in two
on the day I learned you died.

You were unborn then that is true
but oh how dearly I loved you.

Your tiny body so small and still
on the day I gave birth, but not life to you;
your little nose and hands, I never will forget
or the way the cord was tightly pulled around your neck.

Baby, how I wish you would have lived
I'll never know how sweet you would have been.

However, even though you are now gone;
In my heart forever you'll live on.

Gayle Bilstad

Union In Separation

You, my love, I've been contemplating
The hours seem like endless waiting
Our meeting in my mind I've been creating
Just one moment with you is worth all this anticipating.

Is there anyone who would believe me
If I told them you never leave me?
Would they think that I let you deceive me?
But I call out your name and you're there to receive me.

Because you're in my heart
Who can say that we're truly apart
What time did this love start
It's as timeless as music and art.

Ann Gabriel

"Old Oaken Thoughts"

Oh the rape of the land is easy to see —
    The leveling of hills, and the cry of the tree.
Where once was a high and rolling terrain —
    Now is a flat and boring plain.
Each tree seems to say — "Oh why do we die?"
    "Instead of reaching up to the sky?"
Where once we were able to shelter when needed —
    Now all that happens are thoughts, if we're heeded.
Does anyone listen to what we could say —
    If given a chance on a windy day?
What man seems to plunder for progress is seen,
    As a rape of the land — nature's bad dream.
Even the wildlife questions the change —
    They wander and wonder as homeless they range.
Looking for peace and the quiet of old —
    Never realizing that men are so bold.
Oh, let us step in before they're all lost,
    Before they're all gone regardless of cost.
"Save the open land," cries the twisted oak trees —
    "Let our future remain" — let our vistas be free.

Eileen R. Volpe

In The Corner

Alone in a corner lies the silhouette of a boy.
The life from his smile, his only decoy.
At attention he stands with his hands at his side.
Feeling unworthy with his presence, he retreats back
To hide.

Much from within
Can this boy give.
Few are they who can find
Where the spirit within may live.

Who ever can combine the boy and spirit as one
Has the power to dance among the stars and preside
Over the sun.

The group he belongs to
Is none but his mirror's twin.
Not even, at times, to his own image
Does his vision appear to win.

The boy's place, to him, is very well-known.
So, he sits back, in his shadowed corner,
Bearing a heart that needs to be sown
In the darkened shadow which has only but grown.

Jonathan Streit

It's Only A Shadow You See

Are we like shadows on a wall, keeping ourselves hidden from the light and from the eyes of others? But in doing so, do we become strangers to ourselves?

We can blame the time in which we live and say the world moves at such a fast pace that we must fill our time with places to go and people to see just to keep up.

But is it not really our own fears that keep us from taking the time to look deep into our own shadows and seeing those corners that have been hidden in darkness for so long. Do we look quickly and see only our fears and insecurities? But look past these. Look deeper. Search harder into those shadows. For also hidden behind the light are our hopes and dreams. Do not let your dreams become over shadowed by fear. Walk forward out of the shadows that the light may open your eyes to the hopes and dreams you have kept hidden for so long.

Maybe, when you have taken the time to search your own shadow and have come out of hiding. When you have learned to listen with your heart instead of your ears. When you have learned to see with your heart instead of your eyes. Perhaps then, you can see beyond my shadow, and see who I really am.....

Darlene M. Griffor

Shy

You'll never know what you mean to me.
The love in my eyes you'll never see.

A secret admirer I'll always be
'cause my feelings are trapped deep inside of me.

You'll never know how I'd love your touch.
Never know that your smile means so much.

I hold my emotions like a child at lunch,
how I'd love to talk to you over brunch.

You'll never know how I like your smile,
and how you walk with athletic style.

I wish you'd talk to me for a while,
or my number your fingers would slowly dial.

You'll never know what you mean to me.
The love in my eyes you'll never see.

A secret admirer I'll always be,
'cause my feelings are trapped inside of me.

Chandra Brown

The Cat

The cat.
The magnificent cat.
She carefully stalks her prey as it sits blind to its near fate.
When, at long last, she has polled her options and determined the best
    plan for her attack, she approaches her victim with discretion.
Crouching, as if to camouflage her attack, she pauses and waits
    attentively for the ideal moment to pounce.
Then it happens.
She leaps, with all four limbs aloft, into the air and lands, claws
    outstretched, on the back of the innocent creature.
Ever so delicately she feasts on the still twitching body.
Soon the entire carcass is devoured and she stretches herself in front
    of the window and begins to daintily cleanse her paws and coat,
    holding no regret, no sorrow, no grief for this crime.
The cat.
The extraordinary cat.

Carolyn W. Gesell

Volleyball

This game is now over.

The match is done.

I'm not sure who won or who lost.

It was uneven from the start.

As you have

Much more experience

In the art.

Players on both sides
have rotated
in
and
out

But it always came back to

me   and   you.

I'm exhausted from playing.

I only wish I realized sooner

that we were on

opposite   sides.

Maybe the injuries would be less.

Crystal A. Scott

Isn't Life Strange

Isn't life strange.
The moment that you feel all alone, you're not.
Isn't life strange.
Being in a relationship and feeling like you are the only one in the relationship.
Isn't life strange.
It's good not to cut all ties with old relationship because someday they are there when you need them.
Isn't life strange.
Falling in love with the wrong person is detrimental.
Isn't life strange.
Often wondering if the old relationship was totally over.
Isn't life strange.
Feeling that you're never alone.
Isn't life strange?

Amy Michalek

Moon Man

As they sat by the winding waters,
the moon man danced, he danced to the sound
of rejoice.
As he danced the man grew hotter,
he then heard noises like a distant voice.
From a window comes a lively song,
which makes even the animals lose control.
The moon man is like a zombie set within
his own little throng.
While he danced, he heard the pounding
of his heart, like the deep drum roll of distant
thunder.
So, the moon man finishes his tribal
dance and the people hope for him the best
by luck and chance.
They said fare well to him that night,
and left for home with help from his
guiding light.

Jason Fitzherbert

A Tropical Moonlight

Far away on a tropical island
The moon shone like someone had
A flashlight in the sky.
The plants were as bright as the sun,
The leaves shivered.
The sky was as black as a cat in the night.
The moon shone on the water,
And made a stripe of light.
Vines grew on the trees.....
But wait it's gone,
The island disappeared.
I woke up it was all a dream.

Heather Ineich

Morning's Beauty

The darkened sky is turning gray,
The morning mist has yet to stray.
From the tops of mountains and evergreens,
Floats the songs of birds their only means,
Of greeting the new day, the rising sun,
With cheerful dreams of what's to come.
I stand here in exhilaration,
And listen to this declaration,
Of beauty and of nature's grace,
And hope one day the human race,
Will pause a minute and look around,
So that nature's charm can be found.

Jennifer Germano

The Frenchman

He smiled at me, my heart begin to race.
The nectar of his lips I could almost taste-
My heart I can no longer trust.
This can't be love, it must be lust.

I must listen to my head,
'er down the wrong path I am led.
Oh! What ever would my children say?
I must stop taking that RNA/DNA!

Dixie Darcy

The Beginning

What is one life?
The number of hours
The age, height, weight, sex, or color?
What is one life?

Not to have reached the top of Mt. Everest
But to dearly touch each person you reach for
And to reach for each person you pass
That is one life.

Not to have been an olympic swimmer
But to know more pain than any olympian
And to treat it like part of a gold medal
That is one life.

Not to have entertained thousands in battlefields
But to make each person laugh
Maybe even laugh at themselves
That is one life.

To take life as we find it
Embrace it and love it
Because it's the beginning of life eternal
That is one life!

Judy G. Silvia

"'Twas A Day On 2A"

'Twas early a.m. and up on 2A,
the nurses were having their usual day.
The patients were nestled all snug in their beds,
while Susie did room checks, counting, their heads.
Pat's feet were tappin' cause we were all late,
and she knew once again her ride had to wait.
With Sandy in charge and Lori on meds...
Phoebe was busily making up beds.
In came o.t. and the programs began,
Sally made trivets from tri-colored sand...
at last it was lunch time, we could all leave the floor,
so we beat a hasty retreat out the door.
Well... we gained second wind as the p.m. progressed,
it won't be long now 'til we go home and rest...
C'mon Cindy, Candy, Colleen and Jan,
we've waited about as long as we can!
C'mon Katie and Phil, Joe, Sharon and Kevin,
oh how we love to see 3-11!!!

Janice O'Connor

The Bringing Up

It's hard, it's difficult, almost impossible at times to do,
The nurture, the loving, the guiding of children from me and you.
The raising up from tiny babe, through perils that life displays,
The parental example, the caring and sharing of right/proper ways.

We all! We all must surely do our best to solve this arduous chore,
We must fulfill the responsibility that was cast upon our shore.
There are multitude of choices, but our baby came without even one.
Why shirk the task? Why sometimes choose "It cannot be done?"

Moms and Dads love their children, even when beset by frustration.
The misbehaving, the dirty hands can be solved by parent attention.
We both work, there is not the time; Is this our lame excuse?
Why must we as parents be shackled with this "bringing up" abuse?

The journey of life has promise, however, not with eternal calm.
There are always stormy sojourns that come to cause us mental harm.
It is with cloud of contrition that we may spend the senior years,
if we do not as parents provide the sustenance for all the dears.

The saying is "Hope springs eternal" don't quit along the way.
Remember that it can be done and pleasure will surely come one day.
When we reflect upon results wrought with sacrifice and some tears.
The wholesome life that was provided as grandchildren now appear.

Charles R. Sommers

What If?

What if there is never another you?
The one to make my grey skies blue.
Someone to laugh with when hope is gone,
To pick me up and carry me home.

What if I forget your smile,
The one with the twinkle in your eyes?
What if I forget your love,
And the feeling I got from your warm hug?

What if I forget you, my friend?
Will you still love me until the end?
What if these grey skies never turn blue,
Because there will never be another you?

Jennifer Staten

Summer Vacation

Summer is gone, gathering into memory its realities:
the opaque glint of the sea across the throng of beach
umbrellas, orange, green, purple;
the grittiness of sand, driven by the rising wind into
eyes, hair, sandwiches;
sand in the shower stall, sand in the sheets;
the hot breath of the sun lingering into the warm evening,
laden with the heavy smell of fire igniter in the hibachi;
the young teenagers, nervous on their first visit to the
boardwalk after dark, without parents,
excited, frightened by the stares, the speculative eyes;
the half-hearted struggle to pack the tumbled clothes,
the toys, the beach gear, into the trunk of the car,
the nudge of the long trip ahead,
one car in the endless queue clogging the highway,
the sullen children, mourning the interrupted lessons
in courtship, discovery.

But the thought of autumn rises, with its own realities
the half-forgotten duties, ambitions postponed.
The thought of summer fades.

Anyda Marchant

Cindy's Telluride

Unlike home, I can breath here.
The ozoned oxygen heals heaviness;
aspen leaves flutter my senses to peace.

Christmas scents invade June.
Tired snow tricks me and plays
funny winter games with thick shoe soles.

Under Bear Creek's falls I gasp for air.
Melted snow spray, sunlit crystal
and mountain majesty swallow my breath.

My tears soften Jud Webe's trail.
Somewhere in a field between aspen and spruce
the earth touches me in ways no man ever has.

The peaks beckon bliss, the mountain air new life.
Unbearably beautiful through these
stinging, salted eyes.

Pristine is this place.
It's great jagged horns protect it
from careless intrusions, and invite my awe.

Beth Waitkus

Life's Summers Days

Oh! How long the days of summer
The pictures that young minds remembers
Summer is but a fleeting moment of time
When comparing the memories of days of old
Life begins as a summers day
Traveling through our many emotions
Ending up as a fleeting moment
In our memory of time passing
Love each moment as your last
Keeping your summers images in the past.

Gilbert P. Chouinard

Untitled

The more I gain, the easier it is to see.
The visions of my world's bleakness are only
A detriment...I am forever trapped in a
Slippery abyss of knowledge that works for and
Against. The curse is self - knowledge,
Unavoidable to those willing to live and
Experience. I am lost in an hour glass of sorrow!

Jeremy H. Walser

Musing Or Amusing

Musing, musing, the utilization of man's capacity to think;
  The preoccupation, past and present, of the sage.
Wisdom, oh blessed wisdom, the golden fruit
  Produced by the musings, ah, thinking, of the sage.

Amusing, amusing of self, the absence of using man's capacity to think
  The preoccupation, past and present, of the loaf and the fool.
Foolishness and sorrow, oh how sad, the sour fruit
  Produced by time spent in amusing of self by the loaf, the fool.

Musing, thinking, oh what hard work required to do it productively,
  The loaf and the fool, scared to engage in this hard work,
    run away into idleness, submerged in amusing of self only.
The sage, loving the hard work of musing, devotes time
  And energy, multiplying wisdom to benefit others instead of
self only.

The musing sage, the whole situation evaluates,
  Steps taken only after applying the principle of a look before
a leap.
The loaf, the fool, full of amusing of self, nothing evaluates,
  So where angles fear to tread, there the loaf, the fool rushes
deep.

Joseph O. Olubadewo

Haunted Memories

Memories awake passing dreams, and linger for a moment past.
The scent of burning leaves in fall recapture youth of days gone by.
The eerie darkness of the sky, when the earth stood still and
dreams were mine.
Time passes.
A blanket of snow will soon arrive, holding time in silent skies.
Time passes.
Awaken now to a serenade of spring with birds on wing.
To now prepare for many things.
The future awaits with outstretched arms.
Once more to capture life's enticing charms.
Time passes.
Again the haunting memories are cast.
Time passes.

Carol Sturgis

The Snow

The Snow, it falls so peacefully,
The Snow, it lays so gently upon the earth.
To my delight, I could not count,
the many different flakes in flight.
I stood there cold and silent,
afraid to disturb the blanket of white.

If I should make my position stay,
Undisturbed the snow will be;
But I must make my way towards home,
the Snow has finally reached my knee.

One step at a time, how high I must go,
I look back once, and my foot steps are gone.
The Snow, it falls so peacefully,
The Snow, it lays so gently upon the earth.

John Daka

Nothing Changes

Dew drops trickle upon the soldiered blades;
they alone, stand barren;
brisked by the wind, and shone by the sun.

We break the solitude, and shatter the moment;
yet, after our passing;
the soldiers do not speak, and wind whispers-
still.

Erin M. LaValley

447

Of What's To Come

A chapter of my life is done
The songs I've learned have all been sung
And yet there's still so much to do
As I walk this road along side of you.

The times to come I can't imagine
For what I can accomplish I simply can't fathom
But I know whatever my dreams will be
I'll be able to see them that much more clearly
With you by my side
Helping to guide-me.

We've journeyed together to discover the way
We should live and love from day to day
Through laughter and tears
Through triumph and fears
We've learned that there's one thing that remains the same-
Your love for us all is the reason you came.

And we eagerly step closer on this path we begin
For only along it can all of us win.

Ellen Macieiski

God Hear My Plea!

Everyday, I think of what you've given me.
The sparing of your soul for my happiness.
Then you set forth and gave me life, and wings to fly freely.
Innocents were all I had, then you gave me maturity.
And I grew out of being a child and into a woman.
Now that I've become of you, you've given me a whole new life
    to think about,
The dreams are gone, the innocents are faded, and all I feel is misery.
I ask you for your hand so you can guide me to a place I'd like to be.

I work so hard everyday and all I receive is pain and grief.
Worries from one day to the next.
I try so hard for you to hear my cry,
The days end and I don't hear of you,
Why do you shun me away? I can't explain,
Shall I feel helpless and loose my faith?
Or should I regain my strength and keep waiting for you to hear
    my plea?
My days are but too far away for me to ask you why,
Please Lord hear my prayer, show me a place that you will be,
So then I will have known that you have heard my plea?

Dede Garcia

Together

The day we met we walked on the beach.
The stars where shining so bright.
The day was just right.
It was so great, I think it was fate.
You are the right one,
We had lots of fun,
I want us to be together
and if we were it would be forever.
In your arms I want to be,
I loved the way you hugged and kissed me,
you are my destiny.
You will always be in my heart,
We will never part.
I think of you night and day,
I even pray that we will be together
now and forever.
Now you are mine, it's so fine.
I love you so and I will never let you go.

Jennifer DeMicco

Missing Children

Where are the missing children?
The stolen and not found
Courageous little ones escape
Others...lost and bound

Posters say they've not been seen
Youthful faces drape magazines
We send them to school, but they're not safe
For the scourge of the nation lies in wait

Some carry guns...We wonder why
Adults aren't the only ones
Afraid to die

Our children can no longer play
From their very homes
They are taken today

Where are the missing children?
Whose absence reveals our fate
We must protect them or we'll lose them
The hour is getting late

Alicia F. Dhanifu

Untitled

Reacting to insight,
the stone faces of the masses do not care.
There is not a sensation of hate
that does not stem from affection,
except that belonging to fantasy.
Go ahead and burn,
forever, in the feminine pits of your rage.
Love is the only emotion, love begat shame.
In the eternal utopia of your dwelling,
men do not cry. There is no stronger word
than that which lives on inside,
meaning nothing can compare.
Loyalty forgotten in the long run,
A race for acceptance continues, while hiding
behind the truth that is only a mirror for desire.
This can't go on, while those who do not know
shame are pressured into uniformity of motion.
The rat race continues to search for euphoria,
while the most common reaction is still fear,
ingrained so deeply, you cannot run away.

April Bainter

The Modern Day Lawman And Señorita

Sometimes I surprise myself, that I acquired the dream
The stories from a Midwest cinema, the Saturday screen

The Lawman would woo the Señorita of old
With exploits so brave, so bold

He was always tall and strong, blonde and cool
I saw her dark and mysterious, feminine and new

The Señorita was every man's desire
But only the Lawman could fan that fire

He would touch her hand, but never kiss
This love was too pure, G rated cinema, matinee bliss

No matter how the tale would turn and twist
In the end, he would win, she was always his

Many years, and a thousand Saturday afternoons pass
I find myself holding that dream at last

It is the same, yet different, we touch, and we kiss
The modern day Lawman and Señorita, in wedded bliss...

Gregory Richter

Yibba-dee, bibba-dee, dittle tee doooo!

Yibba-dee, bibba-dee, dittle tee doooo!
The sun and the moon were made for you!
Yibba dee, bibba dee, bibba ba do,
and so is the sky that's so bibadie blue!
We love them so much cause they're there everyday.
Bib bit-ty dee, we dittle tee do. Bibbitty be wa-wa down Echo
Lake way!
Come, sit on Perch Rock with me and feel all the breezes
sailing our way!
Look! See how the water shines, bibbity dooo, making a
rainbow, yibbitty do.
Green and yellow and blue, oh! Yibba be-de-be-t, diddle dee do!
Ring all the bells! Ting ding, cling clang, bong dong, ding dang,
ring ding, ding ding!
They will echo and say, ring ding a ling, come sing sing,
sing with us today!

Barbara von Tobel

Outside My Window

As I look outside my window
The sun bathed fields are all aglow with dawn's first light.
The furrows of the new-ploughed fields are such a lovely sight.
Here and there a pool from yesterday's drenching rain
Is glinting and reflecting light in a never-ending chain.
Here and there a majestic gull is searching for a worm,
Other's hovering above the ground, seeming to wait their turn.
They seem to know just when the farmer thinks it's time to plow.
They're gathering in numbers, I can hear them calling now.
Yes, I can count a hundred, strutting proudly all around.
Such milling and confusion, such a wondrous, lovely view
I feel very close to nature - closer to my father too.
Oh what beauty does surround us - if we only take the time
To look outside our window - to find beauty so sublime
We could search the whole world over, travel many miles away,
But never see such beauty, as I'm seeing here today.
Just a simple little lesson; yet it's plain as it can be
Beauty evermore surrounds us if we take the time to see

Jean M. Owens

Rebirth

As I observe this ethereal morning
The sun comes up with day's dawning
Trees in silhouette against the skyline
Dark green shades of snow covered pine.

From nature's chorus of birds and trees
Is the music I hear upon the breeze
Snow dust sparkles upon a leaf
As the sun creeps up to cast sharp relief.

Each one of us unique in the way we see
I know this day is just for me
Quiet and solitude is my yearning
This is the time of utmost learning.

Heather M. Mathieson

Hopes

Lost in time is where are hopes seem to be,
The world is still yearning to be safe and free.
You can see the terror that interrupts their day,
And feel the strength of an army when it moves in to stay.
Everybody has a dream come true,
to live where they're free under a sky that's blue.
To run and play with all their friends,
To go to bed safe when the daylight ends.
To wake up in the morning and still be there,
To go outside and be able to smell the clean air.
We can all be thankful to live where we do,
In a place where all your dreams come true.

Danielle Schneider

Just Serious Fishing

Today is the perfect day to end all wishing
The sun is smiling in a naughty sort of way
The creek is gently urging me to spend the day
I see no harm in a little serious fishing

Leaves rustling in the wind even birds are singing
My lunch pail is packed with bait, line and hook
To avoid any questions, I proudly tote a book
Now why must that old school bell keep ringing?

Everyday a school day, is just too much education.
I think it's great for girls and all the sissies
Who have nothing to do but primp and act prissy
But it's not for me. A fellow has a reputation!

I know come evening, I'll have busted britches.
But it's all worth a little serious fishing!

James Lanham

The Kiss

Today I woke to
the sun kissing my face

Bringing with it a sort of
peacefulness, unattainable in any other way

Like the feeling of two people
knowing, but neither one admitting it's there

To wake with the sun
Is beautiful, spiritual
with a feeling of belonging

Like keeping your Lovers scent
with you always, when they can't be

Like trusting yourself
in knowing you always
feel the warmth in you

Like waking up in your
Lovers arms, knowing and
Never having to say the words

To me, Waking with the sun
Kissing down on me
Is like waking with you

Adela Matute

Faded Picture

The marshmallow clouds were scattered and few
The sun shone brightly against a background of blue
The birds chirped sweet melodies like those of hymns
The grass glistened supremely, like flawless emerald gems
The luscious fragrance of flowers danced in the air
The trees swayed peacefully and unaware

A harmonious picture to many this may be
But for them pain and hunger is all they see
No joyous todays or tomorrows
For them only despair, hopelessness and sorrow
Desperately searching for a place called home
Day and night in the streets they roam

Does the world really care
Will we sincerely share
Do we hear the homeless children's cry
Or will we simply close our eyes
No fault of yours, what should it mean you
Remember, misfortune could introduce itself to you too

Dana L. Andrews

The Fruited Summertime

The trees that swing and sway,
    The sun that shines by day,
That call of faraway, in The Fruited Summertime.

The waters sweet caress,
    That homey little nest,
Yet that feeling of unrest, in the Fruited Summertime.

Sorrows unwanted kiss, is not always in vain.
    For it is followed by bliss
That a searching eye won't miss.

When you hear that call of faraway,
    You must never answer nay,
Nor when that feeling of unrest,
    Reaches you at your breast,
In The Fruited Summertime...

> *De Kienzle*

I Saw The Bird Dance

Dick and I sat on the patio that morning
The sun was just rising, a new day a-borning.
The wisteria were past — the rosemary, too,
The desert glistened — but it wasn't with dew.
Birds sang their welcome to the peaceful new day —
Sprinklers whispered a promise of life in their own way.
Hummers and orioles drank from nectar-filled feeders,
Finches, wrens, even phoebes, ate from their seeders.
"Old Ugly", the lizard, lay splayed in the sun
As he came from his nest, his night's sleep done.
The bunnies, Scarlet of the South and Nanook of the North
Joined "Big Daddy", the pheasant, as his call echoed forth.
All was as usual — each one in his place
When along came a strange bird, svelte, long-tailed, and with grace.
I, watching, noted that he uttered no sound
But with joy flapped his wings and danced round and round.
He too felt contentment, the love in this place.
Each one "belongs" here in Nature's embrace.

> *Jeanne Snell*

Why

It's hard to explain, what I'm feeling inside
The tears and the pain, I'm trying to hide
The pain is deep inside my heart, like a shivering chill
It attacks my weary body, and holds me at will

For a moment I'm captured, by this wicked spell
I long for the day, to escape from this hell
It's really worse inside, than on the surface it seems
Nothing has ever compared, in the worst of my dreams

The love's since grown cold, and with me it takes
My life's major dreams, and all of my mistakes
I've trusted so much, only to be deceived
It destroys all my notions, and what I believed

One would be foolish, to try love again
You can only give so much, before you begin
To lose the devotion, in heart and in soul
I struggle to hang on, and not lose control

To go on with my life, so empty inside
What I am feeling, I must decide
It's hard to move on, I've been through so much
Forever in a daze, with reality I've lost touch.

> *Amy C. Zickau*

A No Win Situation

A sad, sad story; a mother in grief
the tombstone on the drift, her son beneath.
The frustrating pain still torments her heart
of the terrible day that her loved one depart.

Incarcerated, he was, not a pleasant place to be
Not one moments justice, and parole, he couldn't see.
To deal with it..he had to..it was all he could do.
For he had to stay strong until his sentence was through.

But one of his enemies, obviously full of dismay,
wanted to end his life in a different way.
And while he slept someone ended his life;
they stabbed him several times in the head with a knife.

This has to be the cruelest murder of them all
Having experienced death behind prison walls.
And her son was her only...now nothing she has left.
And each day she relives the nightmare of her son's horrible death.

> *Jenny Craig*

My Wonderful State Of Michigan

When we moved to Michigan in 1919 I was only seven
The vast trees, hills, rivers and lakes seemed almost like Heaven.
We entered the State following along Lake Michigan's shore
The sand dunes overwhelmed us as we'd never seen them before.
Our friendly neighbors showed us new things by the score.
Sliding down hills, ice skating, and seeing deer and native
    animals galore.
Then the beautiful forest with many trees of many kinds
Some furnishing maple syrup and so many kinds of nuts to find
Then spring brought many wild flowers and leeks dug in the woods
Then finding morels in abundances which were especially good.
The fall brought puff balls and mushrooms to gather
Hunting these bounteous treasures in Michigan's beautiful weather.
In summer we were swimming in these beautiful lakes
Then going fishing and hoping big fist would relish our bat.
In these later years we've gone to the U.P. crossing our famous bridge.
Seeing the old copper mines and beautiful tress on each ridge.
I have certainly been blessed in this adopted State of mine
There's no other one like it and just truly sublime.

> *Audrey Baie Henry*

Untitled

Staring out at desert's scene, I sit here all alone.
The view, my friend, astounding... sends chills down to my bone.
Yet all I love is far away, and far are all I've known.
A puzzle piece is missing. For I'm a man away from home.

It's a dream that sent me searching, for thing's I've yet been shown.
I stand before a world of knowledge, fresh seeds wait to be sown.
But I must pass before their time, must leave before they're grown.
That puzzle piece still missing, for I'm a man away from home.

It's new songs that I came looking for, my ears await their tone.
There's trails set for my passing, in lands I've longed to roam.
Yet my heart is feeling empty and at night I hear it moan.
That puzzle piece sits waiting for this man to come back home.

Home...

Now my face has felt the power of the winds the desert's blown.
And the hair I'd thought been tangled seems like it's just been combed.
So, I sit here now and weigh things out for life's not carved in stone.
That puzzle piece just may not fit when I arrive back home.

> *Eric T. Smith*

"Remembering"

You're gone now, but I remember.
The warmth of that sun lives in my heart
when I remember.
Wanna play a game of catch out back?
Do you think the Reds will win it all this year?
I'd love to watch a ball game with you... today!
I'd even watch Lawrence Welk, if I could watch it with you!
Remember the sunday afternoon sing a longs?
How'd that one go about "Mares eat oats and does
eat oats and little lambs eat ivy?"
Are you sure you remember all the words?
Tell me another story Dad, just the way you used to,
When you could still remember.
Nevermind, it's O.K. ... I remember!
You taught me about courage.
Your courage in the not remembering.
I'll always remember the courage!
Day after day, I keep remembering and meeting you
in the memory of the ways in which we were together.
Our love remains ever present, as long as I remember.

Dennis P. Lindsay

"The Warrior's Adrenaline"

Heads roll and people cry,
the warrior feels satisfied watching his enemy die.
Blood stains on his axe he just made,
his eyes are wide for he's far from afraid.

Headless bodies lay on the ground,
the warrior shakes for a kill but there is no one around.
To murder he loves and to slaughter he enjoys,
he is getting revenge for his long lost boys.

The boys were his brothers, now they are dead,
all he can see is the color of red.
Now his adventure is over, what will he do,
the enemy is dead and the warrior is still blue!

The revenge was out of anger so people say,
now the lonely warrior will put his axe away.
Justice was accomplished his job is done,
without his brothers his soul shan't be one.

Joshua F. Swartz

The Shore

When I look out across the surf,
The waves beat the shore with mocking mirth.
but what can I do but watch and stare,
To stop the waves I do not dare.

What treasures do the waves obscure,
From the eyes of men upon the shore.
Their sovereign secrets the waves will keep,
Safely hidden beneath the deep.

What knowledge will go on unlearned,
Through the minds of men so undiscerned.
In answer to my nescient way,
I'm in awe at what the waves might say.

The ocean moves before my sight,
And stars herald the approaching night.
And still the waves continue to beat,
Upon this stone beneath my feet.

Above me now a tapestry,
Of dazzling stars in full array.
Hung above this churning sea,
Until the end of time to be.

June R. Heiss-Moses

The Sunrise

The sunrise may turn into a wind, breezy and light;
The wind in turn, a whirlwind, whirling and fast;
The whirlwind, a tornado, dark and gray;
The tornado may turn into a hurricane, strong and bold,
The hurricane may turn into a tsunami, that causes a flood,
A flood that wet the ground so dry,
A flood that evaporated and turned into rain,
The rain that fell and became drinking water,
Drinking water so sweet and refreshing
That after we drank it,
It turned up in the clouds.
The clouds that cleared,
And showed the moon,
The moon that rose when the tsunami was dead.

Ishan Chakrabarti

Forbidden Dreaming

The dawn breaks; the sun stretches forth its rays in daydreaming.
The wind whispers in the rustling leaves; I hear you calling.
My heart says, "Foolish, foolish, o foolish one!
He neither calls nor hears you cry. Hush, now hush!"

The sun sets and in the sunset, He is everywhere:
His laughter and low chuckles ride and wind.
I see his lips, a smile dawns. I fancy his tongues catching
The raindrop as it falls on paradise. I feel his strong arms.
Then dark falls curtaining the warmth from the land.

In the fading light reality invades:
  I cannot hear his voice-I mustn't even try,
  The mountains cannot be penetrated.
  My heart aches and cries out, "Foolish, O foolish one!
  He cannot call nor wants to hear. Hush now hush!"

Dark has come, night dreams prevail:
  Surely no mountain can keep my love from him,
  For if my love the mountains bar, then, on wings
  It shall be lifted to carry my heart to him.
  Softly, sleep now, o foolish one-hush!
  A new day will dawn.

Ellen Bourgeau

One Life

When I was born
The world was warm
A happy child was I
But, then fire came from the ski
My happy world went by

There was misery and death
As we all held our breath
And prayed, "dear God
Just one more day"
To love you and others, show me the way

I was spared, grew up and fell in love
With a man I could not resist
We vowed our love, which came from above
A love we thought could not exist

Now my life is getting shorter
And I look back in time
A life I'd repeat in the same order
The good, the love, the children are mine
To relish, to thank and to say
"Thank you, God" for making it this way

Gerda M. Hollinger

Life

Life is just a game that bids you to win or lose.
There are many decisions you are destined to choose.

Accomplishing what you want is tough,
Because living can sometimes be rough.

Now you are faced with many trials and tribulations;
But now it is time to devour your innermost temptations.

Beginning a new step can multiply several tasks;
But if you fail don't unveil the pity mask.

Sometimes there are many good things in life,
But you are pressed to make a determining sacrifice.

It's good we all have a chance to live,
Because in the end we all have KNOWLEDGE, POWER, and
LOVE to give.

Jacqueline L. Brown

A Chance To Love

Whether you believe it or not
There are many people out there and I mean a lot.
To find the right person is the name of the game
Just keep in mind, no two people are the same
As like the seasons people change
And in this relationship feelings exchanged.
No one knows how or even why
One person can be a twinkle in your eye.
Unlike the seasons that come and go
There is a love that will never go.
A love that makes your heart beat fast
A love you know will always last.

Brian Murphy

"As Was His Custom"

"As was his custom" a Christian man,
There are things we see and hear, we don't understand.
I was left an orphan, God holds my right hand,
God's granting me the courage to change the things I can.
I want something more, Saul's helping "My Best Friend;"
Saul, my neighbor, an orphan, we'll be friends till the end.
A-m-e-n! A-m-e-n!

"As was his custom" reared in a good home;
A good father and mother, safety he's known.
This man too, has grown. "My Best Friend" my sins atoned.
We're not free from sin; but christian if "you" are
cast thy stones. A-m-en! A-m-en!

"As was his custom" His father, has been there, all along;
In support of his son, where he belongs.
Saul and I, are friends, securing our safety,
before he's gone. What does this say for these wrongs?
Saul more mature in faith, no church, he roams.
Saul loves "My best friend" his light has shown.
They're working together, Saul's the head;
of this throne. A-m-e-n! A-m-e-n!

Bonnie L. Hurt

Destiny

Waves are the footprints of the wind.
They wander out and they wander in.
Do you know where you'd begin?
If you were a wave being pushed by the wind?

Is it our choice to make or is it to be,
Being a wave being pushed on the sea.
I no not know where I'm going.
But I do know where I have been,
Being a wave being pushed by the wind.

Gary J. Caulfield

The Difference

Relatives are many, but family is few
There are those who say they love you
and those who really do
They say "blood is thicker than water"
and while this may be true,
without the love to add its strength
mere blood will never glue
the pieces all together
that form the kind of bond
that lasts until forever
that makes a family strong
so while they say they love you
only actions are the clue
for relatives are many, but family is few

B. Carter Pittman

Hyacinth Time

In hyacinth time while March winds wildly blew
There came the call, our dearest one, for you;
A call that meant relief from this world's pain,
From this world's heartache, warring strife to gain
Admittance to the home above
Where God is Light and Light is love.

Now you are gone. God's holy will be done.
No more you'll walk with us beneath the sun
That shines on scenes that were so dear to you;
The verdant hills, bedecked with violets blue,
The fragrant gardens wet with morning dew.

Spring will mature with splendors unexcelled -
Sweet summer will precede fall's golden days -
Then winter's hoary grip held until dispelled
By boisterous winds directing dark clouds ways
To poignant memories that we all once knew,
In hyacinth time while March minds wildly blew.

Clyde Smithson

Syndrome

The streets were his home
   there he could roam - in peace of day
      and terror of night
People could not understand
   What brought him here?
A war not long ago -
   took a boy and took his soul.
Taught him hate and death
   But the drugs were a refuge from reality
      the booze a sure friend to wile away time.

And as time passes
   the pain lingers on
A boy is forever - he cannot grow
   He's still in a field - twenty years ago.....

James Rooney

Tribute To Bess Truman

There must be many legal matters for her to consider,
There must be weeds in her flower garden to pull,
There must be some formal notes she should write,
But she chose to gather comfort from the written
Words of others.
The fragrance from the flowers on the table scented
the room and filled her nostrils.
Necessary hunger drove her to eat and necessary
tiredness drove her to bed; but
seeking life drove her nightly
to gentle books.

Jason Stoetzer

452

"God"

God is to me my all and all,
There to catch me before I fall,
My peace in the middle of a storm,
Rocking my soul until I'm safe and warm
Loving me although I'm nothing,
Helping me to feel like I'm really something,
Giving me life so full of hope,
And joys through the years that taught me to cope,
With pains and sorrows the help that he gives,
I'll love him with all my heart as long as I live,
Thank you God, my father, mother, sister and brother,
Because to me you're all of these and there is no other.

Essie B. Burt

What Time Is It?

I awoke this morning at some unknown hour, my room was yet dark.
There was no moonlight or sunlight shining through, I turned to
look at the clock, but the clock was without a face. Then I
thought to myself, what time is it?

As I prepare for another day, my spirit is restless, my head is
in a daze. I wonder to myself, just what this strange feeling
could be. I think to myself is this happening to anyone else,
or is it just me. And once more I wonder, what time is it?

As I walk down the street, I notice all the sorrow on the faces of
the people I meet. I see a man asleep on the sidewalk, I notice a
mother walking the street. Then I hear a baby in the distance
crying, and in my heart I feel like dying. Then I look to the
sky, and in a silent voice I ask, Lord what time is it?

When I turn to the news such stories are told. I hear of a father
who has killed his son. A mother is being charged with the death
of her child. We have children killing children, mere babies are
dying in the streets. Fighting and destruction is all over this land,
and it seems that no one is willing to extend a friendly hand.

I see famine and drought widespread. I hear of hurricanes,
tornados and storms of all nature. There are wars and rumors of
wars. I see city against country, country against nation,
and with sorrow in my heart and tears in my eyes, I ask you
world, WHAT TIME IS IT?

Glorious McClendon

Our Mother, The Light Of Love

As she gave us life, we became her life
There were so many lessons to teach
Who knew life could bring so much strife
Goodness and love always prevailed whenever we would beseech

How could any one person give so much
When her own share of life's struggles seemed so great
She was always there, remaining strong with her special touch
Can we tell her how much she gave, please don't let it be too late

We will continue to learn her lessons throughout our remaining years
Without even knowing
We reach for her now through our tears
But she's above us with kisses from her lips blowing

Thank you dear, sweet, kind, loving lady
For your guiding light above
As you leave this earth, each of us gains your strength
And will ride on your wings like a dove

As you grew older, our roles reversed
And we become your mother before it all ends
Now we tuck you in, tell you how much we love you
As your new life begins

Barbara Baker

How

Used to be
These roles were clear for all parties
Men like acting, aggressively conquering
Women flirt around the edge of productivity, chatting
Strong, silent, Marlboro man
Helpless, chatterbox, woman
Mother nature, household ruler, birth, love, giver
Father producer, solely, soulless, financial provider

They marry
So little in common

And now, all of the rules have changed, this decade
They have, into our domain, tried to invade

Purposefully vague
Each are taking over the other's chores
Working women, house husbands
It is easier to get by if nothing is clear
Big surprise that families are confused, society in uproar

Bob Connors

The Children Cry

Many children are crying, and oh how sad
They are being abused by their very own dads
What has happened to the dad's of days gone by,
when they cared for their children and didn't
want to see them cry.

Not only by their dad are they being abused,
but by their mother's and brother's and people
they never knew. Lord, what is happening to
our land? How can we help these children in
pain, who can never trust anyone again.

God help these little children, that sit and
cry, they are so lonely, they wish they could
die. Lord, listen to these little one's prayer,
help them to know that some one care's.
God bless the little children.

Bernice Richardson

"Through These That Cannot See"

I have these eyes, that cannot see,
they are blue and bright as can be.
But, through these eyes that cannot see,
I sometimes wonder, what God has done to me.

I hear the sounds of life go by,
so much violence, that the young must die!
I see through my heart, what's good and bad,
mostly what I see is truly sad.

This world is ours, to live in peace,
even though we're here, on a borrow lease!
I feel God has a special place for me,
but through these eyes, I cannot see.

I smell the scents of time and life,
trying to figure out what is right.
I'm thankful for each passing day,
as I proudly struggle to find my way.

God has given me the peace of mind,
to accept myself, although I'm blind.

Jake O. Roussel

My Family Of Living Oaks

When they cut the timber in the years of long ago
They didn't cut the trees along this old fence row,
So now, like wooden soldiers, where they stand,
Guarding my house my home my land.

Sometimes, in fancy, I stand with them out there
Pretending they are my family, feeling that they care.
Through generations I name them one by one
The dead, the living, from the oldest to the young.

When others view them they only see the trees
But, to me, they are my family waving with the breeze.
Each one becomes a loved one that dwelt here in the past
While I alone am left and my day's are going fast.

I know there's a happier place where their souls have gone
A place in heaven which someday I too shall own
Also I know I'll see them like the big oaks standing
Watching, waiting, waving for my own eternal landing

But in the meantime I'll keep pretending my
    family of living oaks
Are the loved ones I am missing who were
    my former folks.
        Grace Odom Britton

The Stars

The stars are looking down at me,
They look like a sparkling baby bumble bee.
You know what it is that I like?
They are beautiful, sparkling, clean and bright.
The happiest thing about them to me,
Is that you can see them all night.
Isn't that a sight?
The sad thing about it is,
That you can't see them in the morning.
But that's okay,
Because you're in bed snoring.
        Chelsy Z. Briggs

The Lights In The Tunnel

The lights in the tunnel are fading to black.
They lure me down this rocky path.
They shimmer and cry.
Calling my name in a whisper, they draw me closer.
Clear; then vague.
Happy; then forlorn.

The lights in the tunnel are fading to black.
Soft mist envelopes my feet.
There's no turning back.
Reaching out to grab them, I can feel nothing.
Cold; lost.
Empty; lifeless.

The lights in the tunnel have all gone out.
        Elaine S. Hannig

Childhood Revisited

As I recall those days of my childhood,
those so innocent and good,
blurred images slide through my mind
possessed of feelings, so hard to find.
Like a broken projector
this film has no director.
Emotions of freedom and joy, I hear the strongest.
Innocence hid the shortcomings, and my most
gleeful remembrances, sparkling like crystal
droplets, last the longest.
        Jonathan Konkol

Whispers Of Nature

The lilies and the tulips,
they speak to me each day.
I know that I can hear them,
for they talk their own sweet way.
They whisper in the morning,
they speak of love so true.
They murmur in the noontime,
about the skies so blue.
The leaves, they are their hands,
they use to emphasize.
Their petals are the lips,
which speak no made up lies.
At nighttime when the moon kisses them good night,
they close their lips, and drowsiness drifts,
over their hazy eyes.
        Deanna Caudill

Black Clouds

Black clouds are everywhere
They're hiding my heart
I look to the sky, I look to the moon
I look to the sun, to melt my gloom
I look for love, to clear my soul
I look to the heaven for love.

Black clouds are everywhere
They're hiding my heart
I look to the stars, I look to the wind
I look for the rain, to cleanse our sins
I look for love, again and again
I look to the heaven for love.

I'll wait for the maestro, to play my song.
I'll wait for the dancer, to dance again.
I'll wait for the preacher, to say Amen.
I'll wait for the black clouds, drifting away.
I'll wait for the birth, of a new born day.
        Joyce E. White

Looking Out The Window

Looking out the window, daydreaming as the wind blows
thinking 'bout how it used to be
....
When we used to cuddle up to each other
as we watched t.v.
I used to call you "kid" just to upset you
and we used to wrestle; of course you always
let me win.

We were young and so much in love,
I only had eyes for you and you only had
eyes for me.
As time went by, things seemed to change,
now for you it's only a joke,
what I see, what I feel doesn't matter...
and that's where the hurt comes in.

So I'm sitting here looking out the window,
daydreaming as the wind blows, thinking 'bout
how it used to be...
You see nothing has changed for me.
        Claudia Arteaga

colette

just sitting here with thoughts so clear
thinking of her, wishing she was near.
i'm holding this vision,
she's behind my eyes;
inside she leaves a smile
and a feeling i've come to realize.
i've seen sunsets that moved me
and clouds play with the wind.
i've left foot prints near the sea
to be washed away from behind me.
i've chased raindrops in numbers
on a hot summer day and ran through the puddles
like a child gone astray.
but i can't remember
looking back in my past someone as colorful
as colette.
she's a colorful sunset,
a feeling that lasts
the warmth before an evening
turned into the dream sleep caress.

james t. rowe

Daydreaming

I am fed up. Nothing else to do.
Thinking, reasoning, conscious, of deep,
profound introspection feeling empty within.
Imagining, dreaming, visualizing, I'm somewhere else.
Distant, far away, remotely aware
with all the stress, the pressure, and the exhaustion.
Free from harm, impairment, and bondage.
Disremember all the caustic amoral conclusion,
In which the world has to offer.
In a place sheltered with joy,
And never ending peacefulness.
Unbound to be what demand for.
Fantasy is what I called this,
But then again not,
Because illusion can just be cunning.
In such a way to discover,
The impure thoughts,
Of a cynical mortals have beseech.
Release me through all these fears, which conceal my mind.
And let my soul return to reality.

Gary Gutierrez

Living Water

I was the woman standing at the well,
Thirsty and weary with an empty pail.
Thinking of a life spent in vain,
Wondering if it would always be the same.

Why was I there? Knowing very well
Of the long journey home;
The burden of the heavy pail.

As a tear trickled down my cheek
I heard footsteps; a stranger speak.
He had come from Galilee,
Hung on a cross and died for me.
He spoke of raiment whiter than snow,
A mansion he has prepared for me
And the greatest love I would ever know.

"I came to the well to ransom thee,
From unfulfilling water to set you free"
He continued as he took the pail
Sharing living water as we walked from the well.

Hazel Reynolds

My Son

You entered my life not long ago
This blanketed stranger, whom I didn't know
So helpless, sweet, tired, and small
As fragile and slight, as a porcelain doll.

You'll see the world through different eyes
Someone always there to answer your cries
My only hope is you'll live out your dreams
Things in this life aren't as they seem.

Lessons are learned when you try something new
Remember to follow your heart in all that you do
I'll try to help you along the way
Things will get tougher each passing day.

A time will come when you'll go on alone
Leaving me here to watch on my own
I want you to know that you'll need not fear
If you need me I'll always be near.

But, for now, you are mine to kiss and hold tight
To tuck away and whisper good night
So, sleep in peace my darling one
You are my hopes, my dreams, my son.

Anita L. Sams

"A Day Of Thanks"

Today we come together to be with family and friends.
This day is filled with love and laughter from beginning to end.
Aunts, Uncles, and cousins all seem to be in sync
Grandma and Grandpa just make our day complete.
Mom's and Dad's hearts are all afloat
So thankful for such kind folks.
Thanksgiving is a simple affair with turkey and dressing
and nice atmosphere.
The kitchen is full with all those women in there
saying "Thanks Dear Lord for all my family that's here."
It's nice to come celebrate this day once a year
To share love and laughter, be thankful and care.

Ann Fagliano

This Land Of Ours

Brothers and Sisters as you travel
  this life,
Rebels — both black and white
  are always planning strife.

And if they are not agreed with,
  from every point of view,
They will sow a Seed of Discontent
  between your neighbors and you.

But woe be to the sower, for
  his day will surely end
And the Blacks will have their
equal rights, as men among other men.

For in this land of ours, each of us has a place
And no one should suffer hardships
because of Color, Creed, or Race.

Black and White must work together,
then freedom bells will ring.
And we will live together in
  Brotherly love —
Each of us doing our thing.

Josie B. Harrell

Without Care

It is without care that I am to walk through
this life with Christ Jesus as my savior. It is without
care that I am to turn the hands of time from a negative
deem view to that of a positive. It is without care that
I am to walk in faith, diminishing all doubt that is cast
my way. It is without cares of the world that I am to worship
my Lord. It is without care and with love that I am to
biblically learn what I must. It is without care of
vengeance that I must love my enemies. It is without care
that I must refrain from the use of learned idiosyncrasies.

It is without care of the world that I must not
allow my flesh to be tempted but to be controlled by the
God given inspiration of my soul. It is without care that
I turn my attentions and dedications to the God within me.

It is without care that I love the God within side
of you, not noticing the ways of your outer flesh. It is
without care that I not burden myself with the hurts
placed upon me by the people of this world. I give my cares to
the Lord, I am truly without care.

Cynthia A. Barnes

How I Killed My Grandfather

Who is this man
this little man, this old man.
He lies cold there, like a cat
I found someone, frozen stiff in a parking lot.
His swollen hands, his closed eyes,
his pale yellow skin - he does not look real.
His fine suit makes him look good awfully.
I try to remember as I try to cry;
Did he make me laugh?
Did he Norman Rockwell me?
Did he carve a niche in my head where
he can live legendary?
No; I did not even speak his language.
Now I cannot see him, so I cannot cry.
I forgot my tears anyway, like I forgot him.
So I walk away, under sky azure,
asking myself "Who was that man?"

David Oh

Things Made

This clod of dirt, how common
This moment of time, how insignificant
almost, these things went unnoticed by me
until I thought.
Oh how perfect, how sublime
That infinite God made finite things
like earth and men and time

Janette E. Hernandez

"Tidal Waters"

This day,
this time,
pulsates with the forceful energy of a surging ocean:
restless, overwhelming, inspiring, terrifying,
pounding against the rocky shores of my heart.
The cold blueness crashes around
in a loud disruption of its rhythmic beating,
sending a salty spray onto my face.
As I struggle,
blinded,
the tide rolls out quietly,
leaving faded footprints in the sand
of my mind,
forming a new path to be tip-toed upon when the burning
droplets are
cleansed from my eyes.

Christie Ricapito

Three Rounds

This foolish I,
this tissued robot, driven by the sun,
eluding definition or foretelling,
houses wind and fire
and strange perceptions of the uncanny mind,
the sobbing soul.

Floating upon the flood of life, I muse
how through the winding streams of chance
all things relate.
Feeling my lungs inflate,
alive to the beating heart,
quietly I wait.

Knowing that love will come, unsought,
knowing that peace with pain is bought,
I also know that what I know today
gives way tomorrow
to a further thought.

Diana Fabiani Suplee

Reservations

I've got my reservations on this train I ride with you:
This train that takes us swiftly through the night.
Can we buy each other's tickets yet protect each other's pride:
Share our shadows as we still stand side by side?

I've got my reservations on this plane I fly with you:
This plane that flies us higher than the stars.
Will you put your arm around me as we take off and we land?
When we come to earth, will you still hold my hand?

I've got my reservations on this ship I sail with you:
This ship that travels rainbows, lakes, and seas.
Dare you take my love completely - without questioning or doubt,
Knowing fully love is what life is about?

I've got my reservations on this trip I take with you:
This journey to the sunset and beyond.
Please confirm your reservation; for the trip is all that counts:
.....The final destination's out of bounds.

Gadge Bobo

Untitled

There is a special someone who I'd like to dedicate
This very sentimental message from my heart if it's not too late
Many years have passed us by and occasionally we'd speak
But in my heart I'd feel the warmth that often I would seek
The past is over and tomorrow is here
I treasure each moment you are so dear
A friendship begins as friends we did part
But I felt in my heart it was special right from the start
We shared many of our ups and downs as many and as few
And I thought I could not have made it without a friend like you
The past is over and tomorrow is here
I treasure each moment you are so dear
There is nothing as quite as special as my dear friend
Pega, you are my Guardian Angel until the very end.

Deborah L. Betsch

456

"The Beautiful Monarch"

If I could tell you and make you see
This wonderful thing that happened to me.

When I was a child, around eight, I would say
A beautiful butterfly I saw that day.

My teacher told me from a caterpillar it came
And fed on a milkweed but didn't know the name.

I covered a box with a wire screen top
And out into a filed I ran like a shot.

After looking and looking to my dismay,
There on a milkweed this funny creature lay.

Very carefully I placed it, milkweed and all
In the screen covered box as I recall.

Then I waited and waited for this amazing thing
As it crawled up and made a cocoon on the screen.

Then time passed again and lo and behold
This beautiful butterfly began to unfold.

Then with tenderness and love I now can say
I helped nature's miracle fly on its way.

Josephine Rose

"Dare"

Oh how I yearned to see what lay behind
   those dancing, dark brown eyes.

Smooth and sleek, he was sly and the epitome
   of a player.

Camouflaged in the night, he was a canine in heat
   and I was his prey.

Glorified in the day, he was the king of all games
   in search of a queen.

But, I was the bitch,
Who played the player,
And won all his games.

And now as I sit upon my throne
   I suffer.

Erica H. Collins

The Falling Rose

You were our rose in full bloom, so easy to love
Those who knew you, felt your full bouquet

You knew the secret to life, as you gently allowed
Our petals to unfold—slowly, sweetly, softly
Enjoying the fullness and warmth of your love
Enjoying your special gift of classic pride.

Alas, nature's forces intervene too early
And we must sadly observe you

Pushing against the gale
Rising sometimes above the wind
Appearing stronger, but getting weaker
Creating a proud lasting impression.

Alas, the aura is more fragile
the beauty is fading
the strength is leaving
the petals are falling
And we are crying.

Constance Miceli

Morning Water

White gentleness rested in the morning glory blue of sky. A quiet perfect Sunday morning.

We met at Kevin's favorite spot on the lake; a rocky quay at the harbor's mouth with the skyline's backbone stretching in the south. Sunlight sparkled on the surface of the water. Sailboats fluttered their canvas fans. The lake was wearing her best blue dress.

Sweet John, Kevin's care-giver, was our leader. He brought music and began playing a beautiful song I did not know. He touched fire to holy incense - the smoke drifted upward to join the clouds; the scent carried her basket of redolent herbs all around us.

Kevin's mother began, holding the earthenware urn with the last of her son, pouring a portion of his ashes into the lake. A daisy dropped from her fingers into the morning water.

Each of us in turn held our friend one last time and poured his ashes into the hungry lake. A rain of flowers fell from our hands; a bouquet of sweet memories floated on the gentle waves.

Sweet John was last. He gave to the lake what remained in the urn. Kneeling on the quay, he held the urn high above his head for all to see - our eyes and hands yearned to touch again - and smashed it on the rocks before him. The breaking of all our hearts. Then, like a priest kneeling in the earth sowing seeds, he dropped the broken shards of the urn into the lake until the quay was empty.

Michael A. Garcia

Untitled

I feel a void deep inside my skull,
   pining with inmost desires,
      craving my greatest gift.

I am fearful of these things,
   my passion is running away,
      my grip on my insanity grows weak.

What escape is there,
   what relief from these urges,
      what remedy for my pain?

Yes, one lowly thing that awaits me,
   the one thing that all men inherently fear,
      my one escape.

But why does eternal bless escape me?
   Did I do something to deserve this?
      Did I anger my creator in some way?

I search and do not find,
   I pray and do not receive,
      I covet and am not blessed.

Todd Alan Gorman

To My Children

I will share a piece of my heart with you today —
Please keep these words in your hearts,
   your lives through.
Though living at home, or grown, out on you own,
   I've know no "greater joy", than to be titled, Mom.
The pay is low, and hours are quite long —
Other paths I've put on hold, as to care and share
   with you my own.
"Dear children," you are my pay, each day in many ways —
My investment in you will keep, and carry us
   though miles apart.
"Love," will always unite our hearts.

Linda Dinkel

Near The Water's Edge

As I stroll along the beach
The cool white sands caress
    my feet
My racing thoughts and turbulent
    emotions cease
As I look out to sea beyond the
    horizons I see
The deep blue crystal waters
Sparkling like a precious gem
The sun peeping through the
    whitest clouds
Leaving a tingle to my flesh
    and I let go
Of any sense of anxiety.

Fay M. Sherwood

Mama's Red-Headed Embryo

The unborn child sneaks around
the corner scaring death,
as she quietly awaits the
Justice of Peace.

Hands smothered with dirt from
burying the past.
How was she to know that Budweiser
and Chevy's made babies?
Her golden hair and birth hips
lured Mother Nature.

Mama always told me that I was
the product of her lost virginity.

Charlotte Reeves

A World Of Life

Peek-a-boo
    the evening sun
Shining on
    our day of fun.

Cloud tag
    all around
Lots of love
    it does abound

You don't see
    but your smile
    tells it all.
Swing your legs,
    we'll have a ball.

Ring around
    the roses
Blooming thru the earth.
    Thank you for
        the gift of life.
It's my first
    since birth!

Eileen A. Seaman

Nature's Reprise

Our land lies fallow,
the field mouse groused,
with spent shell, misery and gloom;
as the toll stills to rest,
and birds gone to nest,
where best shall the wildflowers bloom?

Jerry F. Ray

Remember The Pond

Remember the pond the grasses
the gentleness of the reeds weaving
sharing their space
with an infinite number of species.

Not to forget the Redwinged Blackbirds
Flitting about
not fearing anything nor anybody
as they display their wings playfully
For the sheer joy of being.

So peacefully beautiful
that seeing them there
and being alive just so
Tells you that life
is a moment from eternity.

And that their calling
is a storage house of memory
that reminds us that we
have all come from that space -
Have lived through that sound
And shall share their dance.

Barbara L. Ginsburg

Memories Of War

It's been years, since the war's end.
The incidents and the scars remain,
Although they seem to be faded by time.
America has seemed to have forgotten
    its best.
The deeds of its brave men linger in
    the past.
And still seem to surface when war is
    threatened in the present.
By those who have the mental scars of
    the past.
Hoping there will never be another,
Let us learn to live and pray together,
    for your neighbor is your friend
    and brother.

James Charles Litz

Seascape

The sea
The lamp lit and stove,
Creaked in the rise of the water,
Clock, tock over the shade.

The time was a picture,
So time was in the dark,
Untold in the arms of her woe.

The light touched with allure,
Against her temples,
And shadow and shoulder reflected.

The beginning moved
With hands even,
Across the light to feel her love.

Warmth allowed with
Painfulness fruited a flower
Against nest.

Jo-Ann Sanchez Lin

Headin' Home

How does it feel to be eighty?
The last station soon may be called
As the sun breaks the haze in
    the westering sky,
There's a dawn that for me will enfold.
I've cornered the memories,
    the good and the bad
Through mountains of joy, dark
    rivers and foam;
Harbored in Peace, yes, I'll
    call it good
As in His silent Grace I'm
    headin' home.

Borghild Wilson

When Sunlight Smiles

When sunlight smiles and rivers croon,
The leaves become the sparrow's home.
When I do sit on rocks of grey,
The clouds dance by to entertain.
When air of sweetness drifts on by.
I hear my love sing lullabies.

When sunlight smiles and warmth ignites,
The grass takes in a breath of life.
When fish swim faster than the breeze,
Their liquid world becomes my dream.
When fragrant shadows lurk behind,
I feel approaching that love of mine.

When sunlight smiles to a closing view,
I know the moon must play here too.
When beams appear on cooling lands,
Starlight enters the stage as planned.
When pleasant laughter fills the night,
I know my love sits by my side.

Genaro Martinez

Reality

Is this reality?
The love in my heart
screaming for you
is this reality?

Is this reality?
the stress in my mind
hammering me away
is this reality?

Is this reality?
the problems in my life
pulling me in million directions
is this reality?

Is this reality?
the originality in my soul
helps me to escape the pressure
is this reality?

What is reality?

Amber Dawn Barlow

Vet

I've done some heart time in
the Love-is-Blind jail,
Got a tattoo of a feline-
Ladies pay my bail
Got a suit that smells like
Toilet water, worsted for the wear
Got a bag o' Dear John letters,
Torn between "I care".

Andrew Sardi

458

Summer Evening

Flash of a firefly,
the lurking cat looks and leaps
and catches darkness.

Edda H. Hackl

The Moon Is My Friend

Sleeping in my tent,
The moonlight shining through
Makes my tent of green
Look like it is blue.
Lying on my pillow,
Listening to the frightful wind,
But I am not afraid
Because the moon is my friend.

Grant Ellington

Family

The days are bright
The nights are dark
Either way were still apart.
Every moment that you're gone,
I miss you even more
And in my heart there is a place
Where you will always be.
I think about you often
And wish you were with me.
I will always think of you as family
And hope you'll think of me.

Andrea Kesler

Pas De Deux

(A Dance For Two Performers)

When the winds blow
the old oak tree
dances
the measured tread
of the minuet,
while the young
green willow
whirls
in a wild pirouette.

Ginevra Ginn Tidman

Untitled

I was on
the outside
looking in
When I saw
you standing
there I
thought my
dreams were
answered
but when
I tried to
get in
the door was
locked and
someone
else had
lost the key

Eric J. Smith

Lonely

The feelings never end,
The pain never goes away,
The tears don't stop,
Will the hurt go away someday?

Wanting to feel important,
Wondering if anyone cares,
Curious if my friends know how I feel,
Is there someone out there?

Wanting to be held,
Wanting to know,
Whatever happens,
You'll never go.

My heart aches for someone,
Each night I go to bed,
Wanting to be loved,
Is all there is to be said.

April Jerset

Break Of Dawn

His head lay softly against
the pillow the sun's first
rays played on every
highlight.
    As he slept I looked
down on his flawless cocoa
Complexion, my eyes followed
every silhouette of his face...
body
    Slowly as if feeling my
love's penetration he turned
toward me.
His ebony eyes sent a rush
of warmth to my heart,
my soul
    I can only pray that
every break of dawn be as enlightening
then there would be no more
needless waves crashing against
the windows of my soul.

Joan D. Ingino

"Strangers"

Allow me if you will,
The pleasure of your company
There are perhaps, too many Winters
Which need forgetting
And two places by the fire,
Will disperse the haunting shadows
You evoke in my memory
the fondness of a yesterday
Of a bright and laughing Spring
Of April rains, and sweet young
flowers
Fireflies and Crickets
On a Summer's evening in June
There's a certain pain, half
hidden in your eyes
Like broken wings, and fading things
Perhaps if you are willing, to share
a secret or two
We may in some quiet place...
Pass the long dark night.

Ashley Bertrand

"Mother To Son"

We're from the same shoot
    The same family tree
Into this world we sprouted
    Call it destiny.

It's Mother to Son
    A 'Special' thing
A closeness on which we're tied
    And you've always been there to
Laugh with me, or even if I cried.

Anyway, I think it's fantastic
    That you were meant to be
A part of my life, my Son
    You'll always be 'Special to Me'!

Clara May Shaw

Does It Really Matter?

The days drag on now-in a haze.
The seasons metamorphose before my eyes.
Am I in a trance-in a state of quandary?
Or am I in limbo-in purgatory?

Is this all there is to existence-
One strike and you've met your zenith?
Not another hope, another chance,
To make amends-find armistice?

My vision of fair play,
Shows a happy beginning in some borough,
a pride and joy to the lineage,
and a hope for the morrow.

A fulfilling passage with travails
that are mere winds in the sails;
To a rewarding downside; to live,
The promise: Paradise-but here on earth.

So that in retrospect upon expiration,
The consensus of all faithful departed
Would be: A wonderful world-
A wonderful life. And it mattered.

Deji Oyewole

"Crystal Death"

My heart's beating fast,
The smoke's burning my eyes,
People ask how I'm doing,
What they hear are a bunch of lies.
If they could only know,
That I haven't slept in days,
All because of a drug,
That turns my mind into a maze.
I try to close my eyes,
But the struggle is just too much,
And my body is so sensitive,
Even to a gentle touch.
Somebody, please help me,
To rest my weary soul,
For the longer I stay awake,
The more I lose control.

Christina M. Avery

The Grand Hello

The leaves are turning on the trees
Their beautiful hues of red and gold
Another season has past
Oh, winter of ice and snow and winds
that blow their gusts of drifting snow
Remember Autumn's glow and bring
An early thaw for Spring time's
Grand Hello

Elaine Martin

The Agency

Amid the nervous giggles
the staff meets
to discuss the problems
of getting together
to discuss problems

Winter Visitor

Branches heavy with ice
reach for the ground
we stay in and drink champagne
the war memorial will wait

Dorothy Sheehan

Winter Evening

It's a cold clear winter evening.
The stars are shining bright,
And Orion on the skyline
Watches o'er the moonless night.

The snow has covered everything,
Even fence and house and trees,
And o'er the fields comes blowing
A chilly winter breeze.

The bear that treads the icy snow
Looks up to his immortal friend
That has always shone up in the sky
And will until the end.

There's a cabin in the forest;
The roof is covered white,
And a candle lights the window
As it shines out in the night.

Nothing is more beautiful,
As far as I may know,
Than a clear cold winter evening
With all things clothed in snow.

Harold M. Magnusen Jr.

How Still!

From my canoe
The stillness is profound...

No ripple mars
The mirror of my pond...

The loons are silent motion
And the fish swim - far below...

My paddle dips are effortless
As I glide to - and fro...

The woods are still...
There is no breeze...

One blue jay screeches
In the trees...

One squirrel scolds him -
That is all...

And one acorn -
I hear it fall...

Helen P. DesChene

The Lavender Hour

"'Tis the hour of Lavender,"
The story lady told me,
"When the air smells of violet
And the wind is in the tree.
When it is not day and
It is not night.
For there is no darkness and
There is no light.
You may see the unicorn play,
For they are not native to the day.
'Tis the time that the birds
Are no longer in song.
Hold tight to the hour,
For it is not long."
And then the story lady took my hand,
And we waited for Lavender to cross the land.

Jamie Carter

Darkness Steals Light

Days and nights divide
The sun is alive
All alone at night
Darkness steals the light.

In a minute of time
Something's on my mind
Don't leave me alone
Heart turns to stone

Sometimes I think
I don't want to think
Sometimes I feel
This life isn't real.

The sun will shine
Reflective tears of mine
In the moonlit night
Things aren't always right.

Cloudy, windy, rain
It's driving me insane
Need to get away
Escape to a sunny day.

Dawn Emery

Reality

After Reading Emerson's "Self Reliance"
I am merely what I think.
The thought I think is me.
Though upon thought makes the link
Which forms my mind's reality.

Mind reflects thinking soul.
Soul and mind complete the whole.

The sole reality's the mind.
Soul is flowing thought.
Soul-mind turns blank, ere blind,
To thought one tries to wrought.

My mind at times transcends the me,
I, the thought that's I, reality.

Thought's more often transcendental
Which reality oft requires,
Yet, reality's coincidental
With thought that thinking inspires.

What I am or think I be
Is, for me, reality.

James T. Guyer

Ticking

It is becoming too much
the walls are closing in
roads I'm driving on are to slow
what's the purpose of my unknown sin
sitting lost in thought
seeing in a complete three dimension
grabbing but not reaching out
feel my untold growing tension
time is in a warped standstill
there are no numbers on this clock
tearing at my insides
is there any real stop
fear rises around my corners
for it is my sun
come to me and bring it bright
this is when we start to have fun

Johnny Bowman

The Programmer

The days pass by,
The world turns round;
The compcenter bustles,
The console lights flash.

The days soon darken,
The world shakes and shakes;
The programmers write code,
The console lights blink.

The days become nights,
The world trembles in fear;
The programmer traces the flow,
The console's light flickers.

The days are now gone,
The world crumbles to dust;
The programmer reboots,
The console's screen grays.

The night's pass too,
Only a mist remains;
The lone programmer works on,
The console reads ERROR.

Joseph S. Fulda

The Parent

The sleepy days, the wakeful nights,
The worries, the delights.

The diapers, the toys,
The messes, the joys.

The laughter, the tears,
The hopes, the fears.

The sounds, the talking,
The steps, the walking.

The running, the puddles,
The tumbles, the cuddles.

The pat-a-cakes, the peek-a-boos,
The tantrums, the "I love you's.

The songs, the rhymes,
The stories, the precious time.

The whispers, the shouts,
The dreams, the doubts.

The listening, the learning,
The wonder, the yearning.

The growing, the providing,
The letting go, the guiding.

Cindy Duley

460

Life

First he created matter,
Then he formed a mind.
You that are His creation,
go forth produce in kind.

Set yourself upon His earth,
Search out and find your spot.
Remember man you have chosen,
thus forever bemoan your lot.

Each must endure life's hardening trail,
Not knowing when your time will end.
For lucifer you did take, his
promises crumbling with the wind.

Now before your life should cease,
Let your voice be heard in heaven high.
Thanking God for Jesus sent,
that soul might never die.

Allen E. Welding

Chills

A lovely life,
Then it was gone,
Taken out of sight.

Once was there,
Then it was not,
No one seemed to care.

In the dark,
I was scared,
Shut out from life.

I seemed to rise,
Soaring above the clouds,
Up up to that lovely dark place.

Deathly chills ran down my spine,
Then I awoke,
I was fine just fine.

Amanda Graffam

Of My Proper Inspiration

The misfortune of the challenger
There above in the space want to
Explore my career to come to the
School and count the what I want.
What misfortune at least terrible
How can occur could be for to miss
Of some error what can not not be to
Know what sorry misfortune what
Surprise of the nature one threshold
That cry in the drift the
Pity that today embarrass in the
Space the challenger all was to
Cloud glory to verb and
To all is finished,

Elena Iris Charneco Perez

Untitled

In a perfect world
there would be no pain
there would be no tears
there would be no sorrow
But we are
far from a perfect world
and I hurt
and I weep
and I grieve.

Gordon R. Landis

Time That No More

For ever yesterday,
There is a tomorrow.
For time spent
Time has to past
Looking in the window of time,
The future looks dim,
One man creates,
Another destroys.
One climbs to the top,
Another falls down.
For everyone that love's
Someone has to hate.
Soon the fire's will come
And time will be no more!!!

Clara Faye Waldon

Me

When I think of you...
    There is an out standing love.
I have a desire to reach a part of
    of you that only you can allow
        me to touch,
            And that's your heart.
During the moment when I have your
heart a haze flow's over me.
It allows me only to see you, feel you
and to be part of you,
    For you my love
        Are myself. At times I
need that inner peace and the right
to love myself allows me to love
other's such as you.

Barbara Jenkins

"Sonny's Wall"

Look yonder on that green hill;
There stands a man so very still
Behind the one so proud and tall,
Stands a mult. — stoned wall.
The wall grew taller day by day.
    So many say!
No stone will crumble, and never fall,
From Sonny's great wall.
The stones - you see;
Represents you and me.
Never a harsh word;
Have we ever heard.
'Bout the one so proud and tall;
Who stands guard his stone wall.
    So many say!
Yes, look yonder on that green hill.
And you'll see a man so very grand,
For there he'll for ever stand;
    So many say!

Judy K. Wicker

Friends

Friends are like years,
    they come and they go.
Some years are fast,
    some years are slow.

Sometimes I wonder,
    what a friend really means.
Maybe a part of life,
    of unbroken dreams.

Cindy Lamb

The Cook-Book-Crook

Did you know,
there was a book,
about a cook and a crook?
Well, it started out,
when the cook took a look,
he shook,
because he saw a crook,
steal his cook-book!
"Stop you crook!"
shouted the cook.
Well that crook,
he was a true snook,
he ran off with that cook-book!
So the cook,
he called the police to come and
take a look!
They looked,
and they looked,
but they couldn't find that
cook-book-crook!

Jessica Beynon

Listen With Your Heart

Listen with your heart—
There's melody in the music
Of a heart beating with love!

Listen with your heart—
There's hope for a better
Life in its rhythm!

Listen to your heart—
There are lyrics that speak
Of peace and compassion!

Listen to my heart—
There's caring and longing
For a fulfilled life in each beat!

Listen to our hearts—
When two hearts listen to each other,
There's syncopation—
A lovely melody is born!

Elizabeth H. Grigg

Diaspora

My tribal heroes are coming home
these days of the gasping summer wind:

    The centipede writhing
    on top of an anthill

    The menacing look
    of the stonefish

    The peal of the centuries-old bell

    The silhouettes of dancing
    butterflies lost in the deep

    The lush bamboo grove
    taunting its virgin breasts
    in reckless abandon
        all day long
            all night long

    The rugged hills and green
    (ancient pastures of my childhood)

    The burst of sunlight
    nursing the still-born dream!

I hear voices and
a loud knock on my door...

Ismael F. Fabicon

Coming Out

I let them out to share with you,
These feelings from my heart.
But now I have to wonder,
Did they push us far apart.

You've had some time to think about,
The things I had to say.
So can you ease my mind.
And tell me everything's okay.

Can there be an end to this?
No-one wants it more than I.
These feelings hurt inside me so,
All I want to know is why.

Bonnie S. Smith

Being A Mother

Being a mother is not just a name,

It's a thousand and one jobs,
They all mean the same.

You can hold the highest office
Or a degree,

Be a Doctor, a Lawyer; or have a
Specialty,

A mother's job starts with the time
She conceives - with the labor,
And struggle of raising they need,

Oh! The hard years, of problems,
Sickness and smiles, of joyous
Occasions of sadness and fear.

A nurse, a teacher, a friend,
And a listening ear.

A shoulder to lean on,
and a vision to see.

That's being a mother!

And I'm glad that's me!!

Dorothy Komperda

Them

They are great
They are grand
Beautiful little creatures
Born to stand
Awaiting eyes
No concept of lies
Innocent mind
So kind
Loving laughter
Smiling everafter
Learning all
Not to fall
Sometimes sad
Sometimes bad
Always good
Sometimes afraid
They question,
Only curious
Wanting answers, waiting patience
They grow, they live, they learn, they die

Deborah Cromer

Untitled

If you had three wishes, what would
they be,
Would you help save the rain
forest, plant a new tree,
Would you help the sick,
take care of the poor,
Because every day,
opens up a new door.
Would you get rid of guns,
drugs, and alcohol,
Would you like to spend more
time at the shopping mall.
We can make this world a better
place step by step each day.
Besides, don't you think God would have
wanted it that way?

Jennifer Curcuru

My Lover's Eyes

They watch, they feel,
They read my every thoughts.
They plead, they sing,
They see my every move.
They know, they care,
They love my every being.
They are my lover's eyes.

Jennie Hallett

Untitled

Love
They say forever
I wonder
There are scared emotions
it's a mystery
They say love is all you need,
    that Love is beautiful
Why is it then the perfect love
I have found is drowning me in tears?
Is this how love feels?
The suffering and the pain?
If this is love then let it die
It hurts so much
Let this love die before my eyes
I want to live
Let this love vanish
it's caused me nothing but torture
I'm slowly dying
Please take this thing that you
call love and destroy it.

Elaine Duonola

Pandering

They linger longest, on losers.
They'd rather broadcast the pain.
A tasteless sop to accusers
and pity mavens the same.

I look away from the view:
the saddened faces exposed;
a bitter expletive, or two.
A door was opened and closed.

No abiding interest in class.
Wretched moments for sale.
Their human interest, so crass;
their color comments, impale.

Clarence O. Foster

Two By Two

Two by two they go by you.
They watch you glide inside.

They look at you and check you out.
You feel them, you see them
but you can't believe yourself.

They welcome your arrival.
They make sure you know you're here.

"Don't be scared," they think to you
but you don't want to know.

You're back at home. You're all alone.
How did it go? They want to know.

You've known about this all along
but you just didn't know.
This is where you're really from,
now you're back at home.

You're life went by
in the blink of an eye.
Oh God what did you do?
You knew you were going to die.

Alan H. Dion

Memories

When you think there's no tomorrow,
think of today.
The fun we've had,
the dreams we shared.
Think of the times together,
as friends we cared.
So even if tomorrow never comes,
think of the memories of today,
keep them and never let them stray.
For they will keep you company on
your darkest day.
And never will you wonder if
tomorrow will ever come,
because today is here to stay.
Forever.
Locked inside your heart.
Memories.

Julie L. Meares

The Healing Touch

how does it work
this osmosis of gentle touch
caressing hands on feverish brow
anguished twitching

nothing seen passes
yet distress abates
arms relax
sobs fade to sighs

stroking and soft murmurs
transcend pills and IVs...
the healing touch of love.

Josephine L. Collitt

Aspects

I look right through my walls,
Through the ceiling to the stars above.
I slip through crowds unseen, unfelt,
Like the aftermath of making love.
My existence is an insecure thing,
Slipping from moment to moment....
"Hurry up! Get it over with!" I sing,
My annihilation hoping to foment.

Craig Rogers

"Darlin' Memories"

Without form, shape or definition
This relationship is growing
Moving in a direction
    yet unknown.

Surpassing any reason
We continue building memories
    of country woods and
    froggy nights.
Skies splashed the color
    of orange - cranberry juice
The score is 6-0 the bottom
    of the first inning.

I ponder the question
"What would I do
    if I had your heart?"
And three little words
    make all the difference.

C. Farrar

Untitled

It has paid me little thought
This time of mine, none
That I can understand at all.
When here, it gives moments of
Peace so rare and jubilant that
I'm sure it plays at games,
Laughing and giving hearts a
Crying time.
It stays still to
Then awake and move; but stay awhile.
I am not sure why my bones ache so.

Harold Shapiro

My Gift

She was the baby girl born to me,
This tiny creature placed nearby
For me to see.

I was told her beauty would grow;
How could this be, I thought
She already glows.

One day when she was eight,
A bike arrived to uncrate.
Determined to ride it, though
Bruised from ankles to knees,
She finally rode off into the breeze.

And like I was told, her beauty did
Grow; but I hadn't noticed because
To me, she was already a rose.

Fannie S. Schanfield

Decoration

sad-eyed window sill
thorny roses posing still

remnant decorations
punctuate love's vacant station

lingering visions ply the will
emptiness of strength to kill

tender soul mis-understood
face of weathered wood

the heart not feeling good
bares a spirit...
    ...ripe for renovation

Jim Otterstrom

Loving You

Thank you for letting me love you,
    Though untimely it may seem,
And any hope of love returned
    Is but a passing dream.

Thank you for letting me love you
    And turning me not away,
For just to be there near you
    Is the highlight of my day.

You are all things beautiful,
    A gracious work of art —
Big, black and beautiful,
    With young and tender heart.

I only ask you let me share
    The many hurts you've known,
For though you're in the hands of God,
    You need not be there alone.

Thank you for letting me into your life
    Where love overshadows pain.
Surely this is sent of God,
    And need not be sent in vain.

Grace M. Ketcham

Through My Eyes

If you could see
    through my eyes
You would know then
    why I smile
I can see the mistakes you've made
    and I can see the pain on your face.
Ah my love,
    your faults
    they are many
But then,
    so are mine
If you could see you
    through my eyes,
You would see that
    your faults and mistakes
Only make me love you more.
If you could see me
Loving you
    Through my eyes

Anita Gayle Click

"One Drop Of Strength"

It starts out alone,
through perilous obstacles it falls,
Seeking the sinew of its unity.
Greater, yet the distance is immense.
What can it do?

Forces lurk to imbibe its essence,
it quickens the descent to levels of
conspicuous fear.
Its flaccid heart trembles.
Where can it go?

It spies a light radiant with hope,
the emanation of one.
Together, the power is present;
the intrepid drop runs with the ocean.
It can do anything, it can go anywhere.

David Knueppel

The Way To The Light

He gives us all his love.
Through the wings of a dove.
He shows we are His own
At times when we feel alone.

We may feel our burden is heavy
He lightens our load and makes us ready.
Giving us strength for the day ahead
No matter where we may tread.

It may be night, it may be day
Where life takes us, we shall not dismay.
For He is there to be our guide
And shows us the way to the light.

Aurelia Perales Pitre

Sounds

The wind's gentle rustle
through the wood
The brook's soft
gurgle, understood

The silent sound
of a slithering snake
The deep low churgle
a green frog makes

A cricket calling
the way crickets woo
A small brown bird
singing its song too

A locust shedding
like the sound of corn
The joyful sound
of a child being born

A crack of lightening
from high above
The sound of silence
respect and love

Bonnie Morris Conrad

Will To Overcome

Forest fires rage
Through tinder-dry western lands
Nature's holocaust;

While heavy rains pour
Flooding the eastern cities
People seek high grounds.

And in the mid-west
The tornadoes havoc reek
Wrecking homes and towns;

Fire, rain and wind
When extreme or in excess
Dire destruction cause;

Some surely despair,
Others repair and rebuild
In spite of losses;

And the nation's strength
Dependent on this courage -
Will to overcome.

Hiroshi Minami

Soul Connection

Once connected by spirit and soul
throughout the universe and endless time
as souls attracted to heart and kind
endlessly searching in heart and mind
we choose to participate in change,
whether in joy or in pain
a bond of light, as if a golden cord
awaiting love or God's reward,
ascending all time and or space
to gaze into another's face...
...for acceptance
  recognition
    kindness
      friendship
        love.........

Christina Lynn Johnson

Nurtured

Leaves curled,
Tipped with brown.
Roots packed in crusted earth.
Trunk, once straight and strong
Now bent with age, neglect.

Watered, fed
With loving care,
Unbounded growth.
New life appears,
To live again.

A just reward.

Bette Leva

A Love Letter

They say you're planning a journey
To a Place where you've never been;
You've prayed for a fast departure
To stop all the struggles within.

My letter cannot reach you there—
So I'm sending it now with my prayers.
For your destination has no post office,
But neither does it have any cares.

When it's time for you to get on board
You'll arrive quickly, without fuss.
You'll get to see our Master first
And in bliss, wait peacefully, for us

And when the Lord says it's time
For us to join you above—
We'll run and laugh and sing His praise;
Living eternally in His love.

Avis Hilderbrand DeBrey

"One Hour Of Wealth"

I'd like to be rich for just one hour
  to change the world with money power!
Ravaged lives would be set free from
  prison bars of poverty.
New hope would come to those who've
  tried to raise a family and provide,
Forgotten souls that matter not, will
  "Shine like stars" in social spot!
Faded dreams of yesteryear, become
  reality; bright and clear
Money magic is a game that brings
  to some a certain fame; but
    sixty minutes of wealth indeed,
    could change the cause of human
    need.

Elsie Knolls

My Daughter

There is nothing more special
To a woman in need
Than the joy of a daughter
Made of her own seed.

She's born, oh so beautiful
To take home, all my own
To love with all my being
Even when she's full grown.

There's a wonderful joy
Way deep down inside
For me as her mother
My pride I can't hide.

She's growing up, oh so fast
Though she still likes to cuddle
She's at that vulnerable age
Where she must be yet subtle.

She relies on me now
For my guidance and love
And I'll always be there for her
To love and guide from above.

Elizabeth Sly

Poetry Must Be Love

Poetry is perfect peace for the soul
To bring love touching the heart
To also spread peace over the world
While giving relaxation for the mind!

Yes poetry has always existed
As creation was the start of poetry
Blue skies and rolling blue seas
Along with green grass and green trees!

The word "Poetry" came to meaning
A perfect photo of daily living
A pretty garden and a growing child
Shows how God bestows his love!

Doris L. Burleigh

Squirrel Tale

Sometimes a squirrel visits
To climb up in our tree,
His rippling tail in tow.

He rests among the branches,
Then spiraling leaves we see,
Distracting any foes.

His planned descent now hidden,
Approaching cautiously,
Across the yard he goes.
With bounding bounce and leaping,
His forepaws soon surround
The telephone wire pole.

Hind legs push, then forelegs pull,
Ascent in shinnied time,
To wires with purposed climb.

These lead to leafy shelter,
Opening to enclose
Behind him quietly.

Doris J. Cohoon

An Ode To Emma

It wasn't very nice of you
  To delay our poker game
Seems like out of the blue
  Your pains all came
    Oh! what are we going to do?

What chance do I have
  To get my money back?
With you in there
  Piled up in the sack.

The cards are cold
  My luck is too
So get back on your feet
  As fast a you can.

I'll just patiently wait
  I could not take advantage.
And hope that soon I'll hear
  You say, put your quarter in
  Deal the cards, let the game begin.

Annie Gentry

Best Friend

I'm so very lucky
To have a friend like you.
You're fun and understanding
And respect the things I do.
You've done so many things for me,
I can't thank you enough.
You helped me turn my life around
When things got really tough.
You're always there beside me
Knowing exactly what to say.
You've supported me more than you know
In each and every way.
I hope I've been there for you
As you have been for me.
If I had to choose a best friend,
I know who it would be.

Denise Hülsmeier

Him

  To feel his lips against mine,
  To kiss his neck all the time.
  I admire him so because
he makes me feel so good
inside, my feeling I just can't hide.
  I want to hug, kiss and
hold him tight; these feelings
I just can't fight.
  It's so delightful when
we are together, I wish
it could be forever.
  I want him to take
me into his arms and never
let me go, this romance
can't end - it can only grow.

Jodi Blachman

Harvest

I was too busy loving you
To traffic in rhythm and rhyme;
But now that you lie in ashes,
I heavily vintage time.

I'll pen into words our laughter,
Meter our pulse since we met,
Make every memory a poem,
And keep you with me yet!

Alice Lynton

Thoughts Of A Little Girl

I want to got to school today,
To learn the things that I should know.
To laugh, to run, to jump and play,
To have Tim pull my pretty bow.

I want to go to school today,
But I'm afraid of getting beat.
They won't let me kneel down to pray,
I'm scared to even cross the street.

I want to go to school today,
I haven't been at all this week.
I wish my fears would go away,
I want to play, "Go hide and seek".

I want to go to school today,
What happened to our jumping rope?
To skip and hop along the way,
But there are men out selling dope.

I did so go to school today,
In spite of cold, and wind and storm.
Blackboards are clean, books put away,
I wonder will I make it home.

John Mann

Where You Lead

Lord, give me strength today
to make it to the next.
Give me patience too, I pray,
and love through all the rest.
Turn my anger into love
and my sadness into joy.
Let me see the thing called life
as does my little boy.
Be my backbone when I weaken.
Be my wisdom when I flaw.
Let me withstand my trials;
show me my triumphs when I fall.
Hear my prayers I ask this day
and hear my special needs.
But most of all I pray, dear Lord,
take me where you lead.

Cathy Elizabeth Loch

The Song Writer

Inspiration, a song writer will need,
To make music with his musical reed.
Eyes rimmed with rings of red,
Working hard he feels close to dead.
He remains untidy, with chin unshaven,
His hair the color of a wing of a raven.
Pulsing music thrives in his head,
Simple thoughts weighing like lead.
Rhymes, notes, and many a jingle,
Often serve to make him tingle.
Patiently waiting for the words to come,
Deciding whether to sing or hum.
Ceaseless, unbroken his spirit
carries on. Nothing quite like it.
Love and mourning send him reeling,
But he knows there is nothing like this feeling.

Jennifer Kupper

Can Anyone Know?

Can Anyone know what she means
    To me?
Can Anyone know what she seems
    To be?
It's written so clearly down deep ,
    In my heart,
But the words and the phrases are so
    Hard to impart.
She's there in each task of my
    Busy life.
Only to make easier the struggle
    And strife,
Of each sorrow and tear that is
    Bound to be.
God send her, I know, to watch
    Over me.

JoAnne M. Gruley

My Mom

5 feet 2 eyes of green
To me she is a queen.
Blonde, spunky, and sweet
With a personality you can't beat.
She loves her coffee and cigarettes
And we sure love her with no regrets,
Her TV games are her device
She only eats like 3 little mice.
She's one in a million
A million in one.
And she's always called
me, "her little hon."
I love her a whole lot
She means the world to me,
No matter how old I get
She'll always still be
My Mommy.

Jan Mauldin

Why

When I was just a little boy
to me there was no difference.

We talked alike, we walked alike,
we even shared our toys.

Then one day I learned a difference
I hadn't known before.
the day my friend told me I
can play with you no more.

I cried that night in my mother's
arms, feeling cheap and low.

The pain my mother told me was
because of my black skin.

Stand tall she said be black and
show your pride.

Frances D. Thompson

Tribute To The Texas Oak

Trees all covered with dirt and dust
Underneath a hot blue sky,
Look like martyrs
With their claws dug deep
And their arms spread wide,
As if to say,
"You can't harm me,
You can only try!"

Jeannie Brymer-Roberts

"Dawn Of A New Life"

Whence I were A young man,
To now of middle years.

I focus on my new life,
Toward my retirement years.

For as a teen, I do recall,
My life t'was without fear.

For many times, I cheated death
you see, for I am still
Right here.

In close of Prose, I must not fear.
My time on earth, toward end come near,
But err I go, for you shall know
Make most of all your years.

Harry E. McEndree

Poetry Paints Pictures

Some people take an artist's brush,
To paint the things they see.
The sunset glowing in the west,
    a scarlet maple tree.
But mama always grabbed a pen.
She said she couldn't draw
And then - with word - she painted.
All the lovely things she saw.
When something special
    happened within our family
We know that mama would come up
With a bit of poetry.
Yes. Poetry paints pictures.
And I thank our God above
For the pictures my mother painted.
In Poetry framed with love!

Alice S. Orrell

Yesterdays

How do you learn to say good-bye
    to past precious moments
Yesterday - the toddler running into
    your arms laughing gleefully
The child growing into a teen
    and behold a young adult
All those wondrous years
    disappear so quickly
An emptiness remains - a void
    unwelcomed
The cycle of life, ever so fleeting
    and we are never ready
You give them away to new partners
    with joy, and a sense of loss
Behold! another miracle - a new
    life begins
A new generation - a joyous
    new journey and adventure
Oh - to live again the ecstasy
    of all my yesterdays.

Eleanor Stever

Puny Poets

I show a particular animus
To poets who are pusillanimous.
Dare they, professional or amateur,
Produce an iambic pentameter?

Anthony Gutowski

Free Like A Cloud

To be free like a cloud
To roam over the earth
To see the sun at rising,
A warm and beautiful birth.
To see the sun reposing
Into a peaceful sleep,
To cast luminous shadows
Over the shallow and the deep.

To be free like a cloud
To do anything I please
To sleep anytime I wanted
To be peacefully at ease.
To flow like the ocean
To be graceful and pure
To be free like a cloud
To be majestic and sure.

Anna Blair Thomson

What Are They Fighting For

It really is a pity
To see men go to war,
Engage in useless struggles,
"What are they fighting for?"

Nothing is really settled
But many lives are spent.
If the dead could only speak,
I'm sure wars would relent.

Men argue over land and rights
But I could give a hint.
I wonder if they ever thought
It's all God's firmament.

I often wonder how men feel
To start a raging war
And then wink at themselves and say,
"Tis me they're fighting for."

If heads of nations would forget
Their own selfish trend,
Then people would be happy
And all the wars would end.

Carl L. Richards

A Place For Lovers

I'd always thought to take him there
To sweetly share the beauty of it
Hoping that he might love it
Just because

Inside the room
No Mona Lisa graced a wall
No Venus stood serene and tall
But there were jewels everywhere
In crystal cases

A place that few had known to come
A place that we might call our own
A corner room, a secret room
A place for lovers

He was not charmed
Instead, he asked
To see the famous Samothrace
Down at the entrance landing
We ended there just standing
And waiting for the earth to move (it
didn't)
And then we walked out of the Louvre

Barbara Noel

A Job To Do

We have a job to do
    To teach the children
We can do our best to touch
    their lives.

We have a job to do
    To teach them self - respect
And how to face life best

They need us right now
    not tomorrow but today to
    teach them
What is right and wrong

We can't sit down on them
    We must teach them knowledge
    and encouragement
While we have the chance

Evan Farrior

"First Class"

From the dawn of my first day,
    to the sunset of
My final night, I will have
    been only a passenger
On life's grandest flight.

On the wingtips of an eagle,
    I have flown in the arms
Of an angel. I have soared on
    Loves strong current, and I
Plummeted into the
    fires of hell.

Love is the greatest adventure
    on life's grandest flight.
I have landed in hells burning
    pit, and I now face
The cold darkness of
    my final night.

Daniel Alexis Hunt Jr.

In Tune

If I, each day, give reverent thought
to things of God, and ask for naught
But what He offers me;
And then, by gentle words and deeds
I quietly just scatter seeds
Of Faith and Hope and Charity;
For me the sun will always shine,
And life, in tune with Life Divine,
Will be a symphony.

Barbara W. Baxter

Emotions

Emotions:	Are they yours or mine, To this we are blind, To myself they are hidden, From you unspoken.
Of Love:	It dare not mention, For sake of possession, So who is afraid And who is in need.
Within Us:	For to exist have we, But where lies the key, To light the flame Or plant the seed.

Anthony J. McCoy

Eternity's sunrise

The leaves bend and the roses peek
to touch my fears with green of tears
Long is lost
moments sway to dance my
thoughts inside my skull

Silver doors open wide
Lilacs leap to branches bowed
numbers hang of distance force
on cosmic light

Sweet sleep into waters move
Songs to a silent sun
    Awakens.

Jill Lys Shapiro

The Wall - The Replica

I've been to the U.S. Capitol
To visit the Memorial there
Although this one is half that size
The feeling is still — WE CARE.

There was a Green Beret
He was wounded 57 times
He received the Medal of Honor
For saving 14 of his guys.

He put his life on the line
He couldn't leave them behind
Although he was gravely wounded
He wanted them all to survive.

If he was perfectly able
Without all the aches and pains
He definitely would be willing
To do it all again.

His patriotism is special
His views and opinions rare
Oh what a world to live in
If we had more like him there.

Carole French

Season

Dolphins spread across
toast with tea in autumn
(Hindsight proved false
through foggy weather)
your breath - scent
of vanilla and honey
(foresight sent from
glorious mountains above)
sipping
the remaining drops
slow -
savoring
every last
sip
not wanting it
to end; and as the
smoke rises up
as plumage is feather - soft
(swinging envelopes
sing to any silent sign)

John Lehmus

466

Palmistry

I've spilled myself almost out.
Too much unseen support,
telling you you're fine
when I'm slowly not.

Much too much thinking
of you without your knowing;
too much silent sorrow
yet slightly savoring it too.

I feel this becoming permanent.
Becoming part of me
Like your face
haunting my heart,

Like the lines etched
into my fleshly palm,
and me vainly trying
to read my own destiny.

Ann Swider

Timothy

So often throughout history
True heroes remain nameless
Heaven has recorded their deeds
Each victory judged blameless
I remember a story
When chivalry overflowed
Of a boy who became a champion
When he fought the chilling snow
Dauntlessly he trudges a path
For his tiny sister to follow
To school, up a hill one day
And all of her tomorrows
Pausing if she cried for help
The only time he would
His eyes speaking volumes
A lifetime understood
Then silently he'd turn again
To face the future fearless
A paladin of brotherhood
My hero, so courageous

Annmarie Pearson

Cradle Death

Crumpled lights of passion
Tumble down her cheeks
Black silhouette against
The pale light shining moon
Pointed curves of motherhood
Scream quietly unheard
Streaks of dangling hair
Brush gently through space
Stairways of brilliant particles
Glimmer in the midnight sun
Stretching from her bosom
In a galactical umbilical cord
Sensual hints of sweet sweat
linger in the dark room of hot fusion
Creaking empty cream lace-covered cradle
Breaks her moment
A tear glistens
And falls on the lonely swollen flesh
The noxious tranquility of death returns

Emer Ann McInerney

Untitled

I sat on the edge of the dock
Turning over water
Fish, nibbling at my feet
The winds, slapped me in the face
Slowly my mind was slipping away
I felt myself drifting
Deep beneath the water
The darkness overcoming
The coldness freezing
I lie on the bottom
And watch her up above
Turning over water

Catherine Pearce

Cafe In South Texas

This gray haired waitress
twists open the blinds
and sunlight spills
over the tables
and vinyl booths...
For this she has no rag
so sits smoking
under the cool hum
of a ceiling fan
that shakes at its base
as if it would tear off
and go crashing through
the plate glass window
to slapslapslap new air.

Ed Holcomb

An Ode To Scrabble

Scrabble is a very good game,
Two people on this agree;
One of these is my friend,
The other happens to be me.

Whenever we do disagree,
To the dictionary we go;
And if we find the word,
We are always glad to know.

Is the word spelled "ei" or "ie"?
And what does that word mean?
Is there a plural to that word?
And how do you spell "cruisine"?
Some call the game Crabble,
But little do they know,
Even though we often crab,
The game makes our minds grow.

When this world is over,
And we meet on that distant shore,
Will I meet some of my friends?
And play Scrabble once more?

Clarice Pfefferle

Forever!!

Even though the time was short,
We shall never be apart,
You will always have a special
place inside of my heart,
You may be at the top or bottom,
but wherever you choose to be,
That place will always be
Special enough to boost me up
and set me Free!

Felicia McCloud

Time Capsule

To you, my dear descendants,
Two things I'll leave behind.
They'll make you pause in wonder
At the magic of my mind.

I'll place within this timeless space
A jug of wine so dear,
And by its side, all twinkling eyed,
My portrait, framed and clear.

So that at last when these frail bones
Are nothing more than dust,
My soul can look from realms unknown,
With undiminished lust,

And laugh to see that even then,
Despite the tears and pain,
The wine of life may yet be poured
By hands within a frame.

June Handeland

Bolero

Ravel's most perfect
unraveling of a melody
sound and color
as it traverses the orchestra
awakening the instruments
to its endless variations
and marching percussions.

Spring's most perfect
unraveling of a life wave
sound and color
as it traverses through nature
awakening life forms
to its endless variations
and marching percussions.

Ennio Rodriguez

Winter Masterpiece

Winter
unravels
autumn's
blazing tapestry,
weaving
her own
masterpiece
in quiet white
and shades of blue,
and decks it
with crystal.

Anna M. Moresi

Emptiness

Emptiness, craziness,
Vain meaninglessness.
Say what you will
This is how we live.
Of this I've had my fill,
And I have nothing more to give.
Time passes in this thing you call life,
Nothing but chatter and other strife.
Say what you will
This is how we live.
Emptiness, craziness
Vain meaninglessness

Jung Lee

Seed

To kill a seed inside of me
Very deep inside of me
A clinging vine that chokes
The child never allowed to be
Now traveling through the jungle
That the seed has now become
Trying to cut a path away
In order to reach the sun
For there is where the love will lie
And hold me in its ever grasp
Where truth will walk along with me
And tend the soil of growth
Where up will spring the child in me
To bloom in spirit and mind
And lay me down to sleep at night
Awaiting a new dawn of peace.

Brendan Rush

Shells

Shells tossed by the waves,
Visions of the week times in life.
The etched shells hang on, dearly
To the rocks which keep them alive,
But when waves turn to hate
The shells are torn from the rocks
Just like the believer who gives up.
The shells tossed on the shore,
Are picked up by tiny hands
As a memory of life.

Christy Prentice

"The Road"

The love of my life walked out on me
Walked to a new love
A love that I wished we had once again
To love and cherish is what we once said
Until death do us part
But neither one came.
We broke a vow that was meant to hold us
  Together forever
Now we both fell apart
I just wish we can work things out
Both know things will go wrong
So I wish you all the luck and love
  Out of my life.

Belvina Begay

The Base

As though you wonder, you wonder
was it ever important,
what was the base,
the main idea,

What was the base of the problem,
what is the moral,
what is the key to the moral,

As you travel,
travel through the base
the base is different,
different to many people,

The base is brought by struggle,
but up ahead you see another base,
the base is always different,

You explore through the base,
not knowing what is next,
you struggle, but you see it,
yet still in the base,
you know where you are,
the base of emotion

Frank Stroh

Untitled

Here we sit memories and me
Was it like that or
  just a dream
Scenes of such joy
  fill the being
Enough to share and
  lighten hearts.
Singing notes never
  heard before
Colors unfold on the stage
  of mind's love.
The pictures fade and blur.
Do memories grow old
Or is it me?

Cynthia Henderson

The Sea's Night Performance

Ocean waves,
Washing gently
And rhythmically
Upon the seashore,
Breaking the silence
Of the moonlit night,
Meeting little resistance,
Going in and out,
Time and time again,
Saturating the sand,
Leaving small treasures,
Seemingly rejected
By the sea,
As the only signs
Of the night's performance
Of the waves
Upon the shore.

A'Mae Cavett Sandifer

Untitled

Gentle
waves rolling in,
foaming in;
splashing, spraying
crashing in;
pounding, beating
hammering the shore
they come crashing, crashing in;
crashing,
crashing in,
in, in they come:
They recede;
I've gone.

Joy M. Peterson

Windows

Big, round, luminous yellow,
We are a furry, mellow fellow

Black pools on a sea of white,
We brightly shine with new found delight

Blankets of brown edged with green,
Loving, warm and never mean,

Blue, cool, fire and ice,
Hurt us most by being oh so nice

Windows, windows everywhere
Why do we care about windows
these windows to the soul,
I really, really do not know.....

Joy Amatury

Feelings

No man is an Island
We can't walk this road alone
Let's welcome others' talents
They can compliment our own.

Each of us is a link in a chain
That can either be broken or grow
By working together in faithfulness
The strength of the chain will show.

The mouth can be a two edged sword
We can tear each other down
The only way we know how it feels
Is when it comes back around.

Who is the greatest of us all?
I am, of course you'll say
It's easy to see someone else's faults
But have you walked on water today?

If you are a piece in the puzzle
Do the best you can
Satisfaction only comes
When you fit easily into the plan.

Frances Kerzman

Thank God Your Lord

Look around at all the things
we have to do and see
Have you ever thought about
how all of this could be?
Nature could not have evolved
all of these beautiful things.
It had to have been a Supreme Being,
to all of us he brings.
Thank God your Lord that
you enjoy all that He gives.
He didn't have to do it for us
because all of this is His.

Juli Carrillo

Tears Of Joy

It seemed like only yesterday
We held her in our arms.
As we counted all our blessings
And noted all her charms.

Was it only yesterday
She cried with shrieks of joy?
Where did all the time go
The diapers and the toys?

Honey, you grew up
Right before our eyes.
Into a lovely woman
That, no one can deny.

Today, my eyes are filled
With tears of joy and life.
As I watch my darling daughter
Become a young man's wife.

As she walks down the aisle
On her father's arm
I'm still counting all my blessings
And noting all her charms.

Janet L. Lundsberg

468

First Kiss

As we stared into each other's eyes,
we knew then that there was something
between us. Only for a moment we
realized we were in love. I looked
at him and he looked at me as a
rush of passion came over us. We
drew closer together. I closed my
eyes. I could feel my heart racing.
It seemed to be getting louder. I
felt he could hear. A rush of warm
air circled about us. We were
breathing faster. Suddenly, I felt
his lips pressing softly against
mine. It was something I had
never experience before. It made
me feel all tingly inside. I thought
to myself, if this is what it is like,
I'm glad I waited for my first kiss.

Elizabeth M. Johnson

The March Blizzard

One balmy day in early March
We started on a shopping spree.
Quite suddenly dark clouds appeared
And snowflakes tumbled softly down.

As anxiously we're homeward bound
The angry clouds began to swirl,
And soon the blizzard was full blown.
The temperature dipped far below.

Now progress could be made no more.
No rooms were found in hamlet inns;
The night was spent upon the floor
Just propped against a chair or wall.

At dawn the caravan began
Through unabated whirling snow.
The men tramped out the highway's edge
As slowly we processed toward home.

The devastation shocked the world
As unearthed body numbers rose
And livestock littered fields around.
Such fury has a springtime storm!

Dena D. Buckles

Over The Bridge

Over the bridge and up the ridge,
We walk with ease all the way,
With bare feet in the sand
We hold hand and hand
Not a stone to get in our way.

We feel the cool breeze trembling
Thru shrubs and trees,
The sea oats nod on our way
As the gulls wing their way
With chirping and play
To nest at the close of the day.

Back up to the ridge and over the bridge
As we reach the lights on the street
With the wind in our hair
The laughter we share
We know that our love is complete.

Chic Lail

Adam And Eve

If it wasn't for Adam and Eve
We wouldn't be here
Why can't we enjoy life
Like Adam and Eve
It is not ashamed to do it
Why can't we be like Eve
And satisfied Adam will be
That's what life is to enjoy
Your fruits of happiness
You will never regret it
Hurrah for Adam and Eve
They solved the population
Of this Great Old World
Amen

Joseph Matunas

Little Girl Lost

Together forever although
we're apart
see there's this special place
deep in my heart
where no one else can fit
quite as well.
In case you don't know
her name is Michelle
Even a distance as wide as
the sky
can never sever her soul
from I
and it doesn't matter if there's
sun or there's rain
together forever we
shall remain

Joseph Piacquadio

Pain Forever

I pause and stand and wish we
were hand and hand. Then the
sky turned gray, then I looked
away. The memories of you of once
had began to make me feel so sad.
The pain went through my heart like
it fell apart.
One minute your there, then your
gone. What in the heck is going on?
When you left us that day, her
heart began to crack and fray.
You said you would stand side by side,
and she was to be your bride.
Her love for you was true but,
over your head, it went through.
You have a heart made out of stone and
that's probably why you left us alone.
Well, now that I'm older,
I'm my own heart holder.

Cassandra

The Veil Of Tears

Somewhere at end of life's trail.
When all labors are to no avail
to consider the results of wasted years.
and leaving the gruesome veil of tears.
Looking back on past vain needs,
regretting life's unmerciful deeds -
Our soul in anguish nears journey's end,
We wish him our will to lend.
The clouds of sorrow come to a halt.
Seeing Jesus beyond the tumult,
and being joyful to end of our years.
Leaving behind this vail of tears.

Ethel May Lott

My Special Friend

We've walked and talked
We've laughed and cried
It didn't matter when
You were always at my side

We share our hopes and dreams
Our thoughts and prayers
It's nice to know
That the other cares

Hand in hand
Side by side
We can do anything
We only have to try

Cause when the going gets tough
That's really where we shine
That's why I'm glad
You're a friend of mine!

Janice Kuznicki

The Voice Of Apathy

I am but one person
What can I do?
I only know a little
Compared to all of you.
My voice is not that loud.
What could I even say?
My tiny little opinion
Couldn't do much any way.
I am not the only one
There are many who feel the same.
Remember I am but one person
And I don't want the blame.

Judith Gaito

Reflections From Within

Look in the mirror,
What do you see?
Hatred and anger,
All within thee.

See the deep furrows,
Across the brow?
How tense and so taut,
They all are now.

How stern is the chin,
The lips drawn tight.
The eyes are seething,
Oh, what a sight!

The muscles and joints,
All ache with pain.
To harbor this hate,
Is such a strain.

Forgive each other,
And God will thee.
Healthy and happy,
You both will be.

Jo Ann White

Loveless

Sorrow fills the air
Where happiness once was
life no longer is a care
forever just because

No romance is in my life
I'm only just a friend
now my heart is filled with strife
on a road that never ends

Corinna Lynn Willsie

"Jesus Is My Everything"

As we think about this matter
What does Jesus mean to you?
He has many names
In my poem, you'll see just a few.

When we are lonely
And feel we're drifting down an alley,
If we'll look to Jesus
He's The Lily of our Valley.

Sometimes we are so rushed
And get ourselves into a jam,
We can call upon Jesus
Because He is The Great I Am!

There are many times
We experience trouble and strife,
Again we can count on Jesus
For He is The Way, The Truth and Life.

If you do not know Jesus personally
As you Saviour, Lord and King,
You can accept HIM into your heart
Then HE can also be your Everything!

Janice M. Wilson

Dream

Can you be
What you've always dreamed of?
Could you do
What you've always wanted to?

Can you conquer?
Can you win?
Will you fail?
Will you try again?

Opportunity waits.
It calls to you.
Dare to listen.
Do what it commands you

The world will wait,
It will always be,
But things come to an end,
Like you and me.

We can dream
Our dreams can be
Live for tomorrow
Set your mind free!

Andrea Carmona

Generations

Life is easy when you're young,
when a sweet song is sung.
Life begins to come undone,
always busy on the run.
Later you fall right in love,
church bells ring wedding doves.
Then children come little ones,
as they grow laughter, tons.
High school, college, pursuing fun,
beaches, parties in the sun.
Now's their time to become,
united together as only one.
Grand kids are now my little ones,
they grow, too on the run.
Now it's time for the setting sun,
my time here is now done.
Life was easy when once young,
when a sweet song was sung.

Amy Cramer

Christmas Day

On Christmas Day, on Christmas Day,
when all the children laugh and
play, and every heart is light
and gay, on Christmas Day, on
Christmas Day.
On Christmas Day, most dreams
come true, God's way of saying,
"I love you." Not a time to be
untrue or a time to be blue.
God arose to make us free to
love, cherish and have piety.
Everything should just be fine,
if we let his great love shine.
Let's all sit together and pray,
On Christmas Day, on Christmas Day.

Dorothy Gross

Living Toys

I served my dolly Polly tea
When, golly, I began to see...
She started pouring tea for me!

Daisy doll, my Polly's guest
Who usually behaved the best,
Jumped and danced upon the chest!

My brother's truck began to roar
Up and down the bedroom floor —
And crashed into the closet door!

My teddy bear sat up in bed,
Scratched his furry little head,
Then slid and hid beneath the spread!

My doll house lights began to blink,
Its tiny lady gave a wink —
And sipped a drink at her wee sink!

My frowning clown began to grin,
my little top began to spin —
But all stood still when Mom walked in!

Dorothy J. Blacker

Lady Girl

I wonder what he sees
When he looks into your eyes
What is it What can it be
What does he recognize
Does he see the little girl
Who's crying out for love
Or does he see the woman
Who's trying to rise above
Does he see the little girl
Who's lost and all alone
Or does he see the woman
Who finally has grown

Georgette Laurent

Asheville

There are times
when I need you
if only to listen to my heart speak

times when your ear alone
can quench my voice

Where are you?
Can't you see I miss
the measured lunacy of your ways

the chance to trade absurdities
and know my brother?

Douglas E. Stackhouse

My Rock

Be the rock I lean on,
When hope is wearing thin.
Be the wish I dream on,
When the world starts closing in.

Be my port in stormy seas.
My shelter from the rain.
And when I'm crippled by my fears,
Be my walking cane.

Be my strength when I grow weak,
My blanket from the cold.
And when I'm lost and all alone,
Give me your hand to hold.

If our road is all up hill,
Will you carry me a while?
And if the tear drops cloud my eyes,
Be there with a smile.

Be the other half of me,
The stronger, wiser part.
And I will keep you safe and sound
Protected in my heart.

Brenda Webb

"Where Do I Go?"

Where do I go?
When I am almost
out of my mind
for love unreturned to me?
Love that was so near
and dear
that I felt could
last a lifetime
but seems like it is
now past
but not for me
but for he
and his new she
who took my place
so happiness is
now theirs
and loneliness is
once again mine.

Claudia Powell

My Dream

I had a dream
When I looked into your face
Was close to your body
Felt your warm embrace.

We laughed, talked,
Remembering things in the past
And the time we spent together
Went passed too fast.

It was a dream
For four lovely days
That will remain in my heart
Never to be taken away.

And if it should happen again
As I know it will
It will not be a dream
For our feelings will be for real.

Emily Warren

470

Hope Of Man

Sometimes I feel discouraged
When in your eyes I see
The tears of hunger, pain and death
A pleading to be free.

I wish a way to save you all
From a hopeless destiny
Knowing the source, but not the cure
For mankinds' agony.

So now we reap the bitter seeds
From sowing long ago
The fruits of man's own folly
But in my heart I know-

I cannot save you as a whole
But with each rising sun
I can look at those around me
And try to help just one.

DeLois Tittle

One Faded Rose

Mother told me about Aunt Alice
When she was young and gay
Was given a rose by her lover
Before he was called away.
How often I would see her
The rose pressed to her breast
As she rocked and looked at the picture
Of the man that she loved best.
The guns roared at St. Lo
Splitting the sky with their din
Alice's lover led the charge
A German bullet found him.
The years went by for Alice
She grew old and gray
Still she kept her faded rose
When all else had passed away.
Then one night she closed her eyes
And joined her lover in distant skies
And when the rose was found next day
It had crumbled to dust away.

Charlotte Anderson

To Bill

I miss you on a day like this
    when skies are dark and gray.

I so regret that God had said
    "I'm taking him away."

I miss our close embraces and
    I miss our laughter too...

Oh why did God decide right then
    that he was needing you?

But memories will linger,
    and the happy one's come through...

And time will heal the wounds and
    paint the gray skies back to blue.

I love you then... I love you now
    and time cannot erase

The look of you... the feel of you,
    the memory of your face.

Claire Bryan

Tomorrow

When we cease to contemplate the hours
When the gray clouds
convert to blue reflections
when the cold air
converts into a warm caress
when the color of skin
won't be more than the richness
that nature has given us
when there won't be violations of rights
nor abuse of trust
when pain will be only a distant memory
and not a piercing thorn
when the tear that rolls
will only fall for glory
when passion stays timid
for the disinterested delivery
of an absolute love
only until then
May we say that tomorrow has come.

Jose Luis Avila

A Turning Point

You have reached a moment in your life
When you must bid adieu
To thirty-nine, Jack Benny's line
And Aunt Matilda's too.

So many friends have bridged the realm
Experiencing the forty drama;
Leaving thirty-nine behind
Provoking heart felt trauma.

Don't waste your tears on thirty-nine,
Hark to what the ancient sages teach;
"Life does not begin 'til forty"
You must practice what they preach.

Strive to conquer all your fears;
Fulfill all dreams of earthly rolls,
What you learn is what you earn,
The culmination of your goals.

Don't look back, do visualize
The pleasure your future holds;
The best of times is yet to be
As the mystery of life enfolds.

Anita Moss

Brother

Where does time go?
When you're young
You swear it's moving too slow
So you try to grow-up
As fast as you can
But I watched my brother
Grow into a man he's 18 now
And gone from home it's hard for me
To accept he's grown
I'm his sister
Elder, by 10 years
And to watch him leave
Fills my eyes with tears
We're proud it's true
But still we're blue
We wish him the best
For-ever-more
For you see he's joined
The Marine Corp
We're very proud of you brother

Cheryl Harris

A Wise Old Man

I am sitting in a soft shade,
Where all that I can see,
Are rolling hills,
And daffodils,
From under my maple tree.

I look up at this old man,
With my brown young eyes,
It has heard all,
Every secret and squall,
As if its leaves were spies.

Its arms an intricate pattern,
With fingers each color and shade,
Yellow, orange, and red,
Soon to be shed,
Only to drift down and fade.

Alana Aldag

Untitled

Oh father,
where ever you are,
I have looked so long
for your hand.
My legs have grown strong through time,
and now
sadly I doubt,
if you I'll ever know.
But if by chance
there was a way,
to let you know
just one thing,
I'd tell you
that now,
I'm a man.

C. Righter

Nafta

What will come afta'?

Will it helpeth the trade
Where will goods be made
Can one crosseth the border
And keepeth the order
Can people be freed
From actions of greed?

One should be willing
To forfeit a shilling
When seeing a brother
In need of a mother

Who will turn mankind
To lift spirit and mind
Away from the dollar
As to become scholar
Making better earth place
For entire human race!

Blondell Overcash

Alone

Life is so unpredictable
with ever-changing tone.
Several instances
in a short span of time
Kindred souls have flown
the realm of the living
and left me
Walking here alone
with only memories.

Beulah M. Short

471

Return Of Spring

Soon it will be Spring again
Which brings to mind others when,
The hills and dales and meadow brooks
Changed their drab appearing looks.

Grotesque trees that once were bare
Have bursting bumps here and there;
Soon there will be leaves to cloak
Each and every branch's nook.

The bursting blooms of Springtime flowers
Offer pleasant fragrant dowers;
Daffodils and violets of wondrous hues
will nod their heads to me …. to you.

When frozen waters standing still
Turn to cool clear streams that spill;
Into creek and brook of every forest
There is nature …. at her best.

From window sills and doors ajar
City patches and fields afar;
We cannot help but feel this thing
Life's elixir …. living Spring.

Jean D. Lempek

To My Brother, Mark

As I think of you so dearly,
While I lie here in the dark.
I can still see your face so clearly,
my darling brother, Mark.

Why did you have to pass away
when I was only five?
We had so much fun together
when you were still alive.

But since our love for each other
was so true.
I know that someday in heaven,
I will be reunited with you.

And so my dearest brother, Mark,
I just wanted you to know
my great love for you
will always show.

Dana German

Wind Song

Gentle breeze blowing through the trees
    whispering words of love.
Tell me breeze, tell me please,
    what comes from up above.

Bring to me my loves gentle touch
    as you caress my hair.
Make it feel just such
    so I know he's always there.

Gentle breeze, listen, please,
    to what I have to say.
For me, you see, to be at ease
    I need to know today.

So, let me hear, loud and clear,
    what my love must say to me.
Let me hear the words so dear
    that our love will always be.

Angel Bennett

Untitled

One voice cries out to another,
Whispering words of pain.
Come give me your hand, brother,
And let peace remain.

O, world, be still.
Let peace remain.
For on this night,
We are blessed again.

Frances Oka

White Upon White Upon White

In Ivory White Towers all is still
White upon white upon white
And the energy rains down and in
White upon white upon white
And that is my spirit
White upon white upon white
And it fills this earthen vessel
White upon white upon white
Fills and extends into oblivion
White upon white upon white
Father I love thee
White upon white upon white
Mother I love thee
White upon white upon white
Child I love thee
White upon white upon white.

Judy MacGlaflin

God Is

God is the one
Who created all things
Great rivers and lakes
Even flowers in the spring

God is the one
Who made trees that stand tall
He made the four seasons
Winter, spring, summer and fall

God is the one
Who made mountains so high
He sprinkled the stars
through-out the blue skies

God is the one
Who made oceans and great seas
He made the wind to blow
In a soft summer breeze

God is the one
Who made all of mankind
To worship and obey him
and to love him at all times

Joan Olds

Untitled

I had a lovely grandchild.
Who often stayed with me.
She was from a broken home,
And I was a widow you see.
We each told a story at bedtime,
It could be made up or true.
Our love was there for each other;
So we were never sad nor blue.

Helen A. Bellah

Bosnia's Child

I know where the little boy is
who stepped on the mine
He is in the eyes of a child
who is now blind

He is there with the children
who's nights are lit up from the
mortars in the sky
Will we remember them all
when this war finally dies

He lays with a bloodied
child in the street,
Whose mother's tears run
on him as she weeps

He is there with a cold child
lying on the morgue floor
Shelling in his head,
no one will hear his laughter anymore.

He is there with the children that
are where he was before,
living or dead; they are children no more.

Amy Blair

Untitled

We bring lives to those
Who teach it
We bring the hopes
and dreams to people
Who mold them
We bring the most
precious cargo in
the world to their futures
We are school bus drivers

John Terase

Life

If life isn't worth living…..
……Why are we here then?

Elizabeth Zavala

Fly, Fly Away

Lightening Flash in skies of pitch
Why can you not resist,
    The senseless torture of a sparrow?
    Leave it be to greet tomorrow.
Mighty Thunder, I do wonder,
Why its cries do you cover?
    How can you be so cruel?
    Surely you must be a fool.
These actions you must both desist
On this I most surely do insist.
    The little bird must fly away
    For on its wings is the new day.
Gusty Wind, Gentle Breeze,
Guide it to its dreamed of tree.
    Blow the angry clouds behind
    Allow tomorrow, the sun to shine.
Little Sparrow, fly sure and strong
Past the storm where you belong.
    Into the light of a new day
    Away from the clouds, fly, fly away.

Eileen D'Amore

Look I Am Black

Look at me, what do you see
Why do you judge me
Because I am black.

Can the color of my skin
Tell you what's inside of me,
How I feel, my hurts, my sorrows

Look at me look deep inside of me
What do you see
I bleed red blood when my skin is
Broken, I laugh when I am happy
I cry when I am sad.

Look way pass the color of my skin
Look deep in my heart
You will find God within.

Johnnie M. Adams

The Lord's Forgiveness

Oh Lord when I die,
will I free to walk in?
Or will I be on the ground
crying from my sins.

Will you look at me
and say child this is home?
Or will I be waiting,
walking alone.

They say if I believe
you will forgive my sins
yes I believe,
May I come in.

I feel you at my hard times
I know you're there
I felt you carry me
When I thought no one cared.

Thank you for watching
every moved I make
now I can learn
from every mistake.

Debbie Haddon

Lost Love

No mountain too high
Will keep us a part.
No River too wide
Will keep me away
I will look for you
In everyone I meet,
I will think of you
every night and day
you will be on my mind
every moment of my life
until the day you are found.
You will always be my
Little one.
I love you
come home

Amy Brumley

"Lavender Forest"

I live in lavender forest
with elves dancing through the flowers
I flutter my rainbow wings
through the gentle rain
and meet my butterfly friends

Caitlin Elizabeth Greaney

"If I Could Change The Past"

What she might have been
will never be.
What she might have seen
she'll never see.
What she might have done
she'll never do.
What she might have learned
no one ever knew.

She never had the chance
to smell a red rose,
to run across a field,
or even blow her nose.

If I could change the past
my little girl would live.
A gift as great as that
I would be proud to give.
Yet, my mind took over
and my heart was pushed aside.
If I hadn't chosen to abort
She would not have died.

Charla Michelle Chavers

VACANCY

Red letters thump madly
Wind beats the lonely walls
The keeper sighs in grief
Special suite still vacant

Headlights penetrate the darkness
Watchful eyes focus with hope
The keeper wishes silently
Please fill my vacancy

A shadow emerges from the vehicle
Each step closer intensifies the moment
The keeper flings the door open
Lost friend on the doorstep

Can I fill your vacancy?

Jason A. Clever

Aged Wine

I may not have lived the
Wisdom of the ages
I may not see
The end of time

But I can use the
Wisdom of the ages
To light my path
Through many more moments
The moments of life and

I can see
Clear paths of tomorrow with
Aged wisdom and
Clear vision

To reach my goal
Solve any problem
Be all I can be

John Johnson

"The Letter"

Words
 written by you,
Fall on my heart
 like rain
 Upon thirsty earth.

Ann E. Walts

"Sea Psalm"

My mind is awash
With
The sound of the waves
That toss
In the tide by the shore
Of the sea.

With the smell
Of saltbrine:
It is here that I find
God has brought me
To a place, I can claim
For a time,
As mine.

Bob Head

Spooky

Yellow eyes peer from a mass of gray
with a questioning look.
Slowly, he melts into a shadow
and he is gone.
A soft touch on your leg
and his presence is known.
Clocks are set by his faithful return.
Time runs down and he is gone.
Forever.

Donna E. Seedarnee

Shadows I Walk

I walk my own shadow
With a raptured heart and
Scattered dreams.

Hours of pride
Swallowed by dusky skies and
Tangling wailing wind.

I hide my confusion
Sailing a strange vessel
Forming an unmarked ripple.

Commanded and ignored
I search to meet my soul
In the passing storm.

Irma Banales

Night Sounds

Cerulean sky painted
With alabaster clouds
Sunbathed lilies bloom near
Children playing hopscotch.

Pitch black night,
Moon glow silhouettes
Trees in the sky
A figure stands alone.

The lone figure longs to be
In that hopscotch world of children
To hear the music in their laughs and
Re-live the rainbow dreams of youth.

But she only hears chords of silence
Put to a heart beat rhythm
Of hollow and syncopated
Shades of grey.

Night breezes cold through
Frail bones and bitter heart
Struggles to find
What has been lost through time.

Joanne McDaniel

473

The Child I Long To Bear

With all my heart I love you,
With all my love I care,
With all the care I need you,
The child I long to bear.

Your brother and your sister
I love more than I can say,
The joy that they have brought me
Increases day by day.

And yet, somewhere deep inside,
I have a lonely spot,
It yearns to love another child,
For love is all I've got.

I pray someday I'll meet you,
And you can join us here,
With all my heart I'll love you,
With all my love I'll care.

Garnet 'Sam' Pauley

Autumn At Applethorp

There's an old deserted farm house,
    with apple trees abound.
With fat and tasty honey bees a
    buzzin' all around!

The old weather-beaten picnic
    table is just as I remember,
beneath the ancient apple trees
    as it was in late September.

The cool breeze that moves the creek
    along, plays a gentle tinklin' tune.
I'm kindly thankin' God today
    for a lovely afternoon!

Eleanor H. Foderaro

Life

Life is like a forest,
with deep and winding paths.
Life is one big question,
to which there is no answer.
But at the end of the
confusion, God sends
us his holy light, to
guide us out of our
forests in the darkness of
Life.

Amanda Dunburg

Mom

Mom, what a wonderful
    woman she was
    Who has passed on forever,
to that great home above.
    All thru her life,
she stood by her cross,
never leaving a moment
their pain, heartbreak or loss.
    She washed my face
And brushed my hair
Mom took good care of me,
with the most tender loving care.
    A woman like her,
there will be no other
You see, she wasn't really my mom;
She was my grandmother.

Betty Campbell

"Zingara"

Kiss the sacred stone for me,
With ladies do take tea,
Stroll upon the cobble stones,
Run barefoot by the sea.

Tickle guards until they blush,
And scale the castle stairs,
Play Rapunzel in The Tower,
And Shakespeare at the Fair.

Call Merlin from his hiding place,
And Robin from the wood,
Survey what once was Camelot,
And where true kings have stood.

Whence knights in shining armor gleamed,
And damsels feigned distress,
Where once a maiden graced her mount,
Clad only in blond tress.

Dance 'til dawn and sing their song,
While you're young and free,
And as I said when first you read,
Caress the stone for me.

Barbara Ann Zucchero

Morning Sunrise

The morning Sunrise of Sweet Desire.
With love straight from the heart.
A rose's petal isn't as soft as
your touch.
The fire warms up when we're close.
And a thousand armies aren't as
strong as our love for
Each other

Jennifer Brevoort

Each Sleeping Head

Thank you, Lord, for blessing me
With my loving family.
Each one is such a precious gift
That you have given me.

    And thank you, Lord for helping me
    Day in and day out.
    Sometimes I lost my patience,
    I know you heard me shout.

Then at the closing of each day
When they were all in bed,
I asked for your sweet blessing
Upon each sleeping head.

    I hope their actions please you,
    I tried to do my best
    To teach them love and kindness
    Before they left my nest.

They have children of their own now,
And when they're all in bed
I join with them in asking you
To bless each sleeping head.

Dorothy C. Gatto

"Human Will"

The will is strong
Yet flexible
A lesson in itself
For you who choose
A silent path
Gain knowledge
Peace and wealth

Clare Brady

Alone

All alone,
With no one to care,
All alone,
With no one to share.

All alone,
With the dark of the night,
All alone,
With no friend in sight.

All alone,
With no one to hear My cry,
All alone,
With no one to hear My sigh.

All alone,
With a heart full of love,
All alone,
With only Heaven above.

All alone,
Oh Lord, please hear My prayer,
All alone,
Oh Lord, I need someone to care.

Francis Carley

Truth

As I walk in the woods
    with the sunshine on my face,
I search for the inner peace
    that has eluded me for so very long.

Dusk begins to set in
    as the silver moon rises high,
emotions and thoughts
    cloud over in my mind.

Finally I reach the place
    that takes over my soul,
I speak out loud
    in the oh so silent night.

In the whispering hollow
    I await the truth,
for when I speak to the trees
    they respond with total honesty.

Jenny Gunther

Pleasing Others

Sometimes I really disappointment myself
With the way I carry on...
Always worrying about what others think
When I know that worrying is wrong.

You'd think that I'd know better
And that I wouldn't worry so
Because the only one I need to please
Is my saviour, don't know?

It's so much easier to please just One
Than a multitude of friends.
I'd be torn asunder
If I kept up with the trends.

Jesus is the only One
I should try to satisfy.
He alone can bring me peace
If I stay sweet in His eyes.

Jan Britt

Silent Love

A way
Without a word
To show
To live
A love
So sound
So sweet
To come
As one
A kiss
To blow
To embrace
Naturally
Silently
Lovely
Wanting
With silence
To understand
Quietly
Silent Love.

April C. Snyder

The Way Of The World

Long time ago when my hair was in curls
Wondering about the way of the world
Then my hair was fine and straight
Gotta figure out before it's too late

Now I'm wondering did I pass the test
Or did I just do what I knew best
I wish my hair was back in curls
It's too hard - the way of the world

Hattie Yvonne Johnson

Memories

Tears of memories, flowing down my face;
Wondering what was wrong -
Then realizing what it was...
Loneliness,
Like a mother bear, losing her cub.
Yes, it was loneliness -
A sad thing, but true.

Jaimee Thoelen

Love In The Air

A water droplet lies on earth
   yearning to be free
Looking up into the sky
   it flees the binding scree.

A cloud is passing overhead
   the droplet sees it clear,
He rises, rises, rapidly
   wanting to be near.

The droplet enters the cloud
   the cloud accepts his love,
Together they create a force
   rolling and twisting above.

The cloud begins to darken
   it rumbles with an angry sound,
It sends the droplet free again
   he is dropped onto the ground.

I was the droplet,
You were the cloud.

Hurst Bousegard, Jr.

Time Is

Time is a thief.
Years race by
Like a second-hand
Sweeping the clock.

Twenty -
When I first loved you -
Was only yesterday.
How brief life is.
How swift the pace.

Nowadays
Time is measured by heartbeats,
But love has not changed.
I am twenty
And you are twenty-eight.

Carlita McKean Pedersen

Easter

I talk in the language of spring.
Yellow flowers sprout from my tongue.

I spit blossoms and they float
like children's bubbles
in the warm air.

From my eyes that once held
tears sweet violets drip,
and my hair is a tangle of forsythia,
bright branches that dangle and dance
in the sun.

But beware the hands.

The hands sprout thorns
from the fingers.

They scratch at the palms,
made sore and red like red roses,
sore and red where the blood red
roses grow.

John Morrison

Birthday

Yes, my birthday
Yes, how I'm glad
Yes, I have one candle
On my cake
Yes, I got seven presents
Around me!
But, tomorrow I have
To wait 364 days
To be two

Aeri Chang

Untitled

Smile, my friends, for me.
Yes, I am gone.
Gone, but not dead.
For I am in another place.
A place among the living.
I am in a place where happiness
prevails and there's no time for tears.
So, you see, my friends,
do not mourn for my absentness.
Laugh, smile, and live, for yours.
For one day you will join me
and we will celebrate together.
But until that time,
you must live and remember.
For I am forever with you.

Edna L. Martorell

My Prayer

Dear Father,
Yesterday's gone forever
to it, I have said "Goodbye"
I can never again relive it,
no matter how hard I try.
Tomorrow will never come
that day I will never see.
I can never claim that time,
for it will never be.
Today, Right Now, Dear Father
is the only time I have got.
Please, Lord, help me to live it,
to cherish it and regret it, not.

Edrel Coleman

The Huntress

Taut as a bow string
yet fluid as the targeted deer
she blends, she ripples to patterns
she flows with the seasons,
she moves and is moved.
Part of, yet apart
she combines wisdom and innocence
youth and maturity, cunning and craft
to become the huntress.

She contradicts, she conforms
she melds into juxtaposition
and becomes one with her prey
answering only to her own goddess
in all things true to her nature.

Bill Chiquelin

New Life

The gradual awakening...is as a dream,
yet, not a dream!
Here I am, emerging,
the metamorphosis of a butterfly...
coming to life after lengthy slumber,
from darkness, into the light;
able to move...to expand my wings!
I am free...am free.

Clay Faro Parsons

Amends

Our regrets are not slight,
Yet we have naught to say?
We search for the light
And a much better way...

If the day holds pain
And the twilight unease,
The night finds no gain
And rest is not seized.

Make amends in twilight
And end the regret.
Prepare for the night,
With souls better set!

Lest over the years,
With flowers and stone,
Our too many tears
Is all we have sown!

Charles R. Jones

Palter

An illusion of my heart
    you are
and yet another scar

Your company aroused
    the depth of my soul
unleashing all self control
    of your artful
        toying of me

I know nothing of truths
    non-existent are these
        agreements with reality

With me ... you did palter
    and oh, how it saddens me
for the presence of one another
    was on excitement ...
        to my heart

Janet R. LaFountain

My Son My Son

You are my love
You are my joy
You are my one
And only boy

You are earth
You are sky
You can make
My heart fly

Your hair is sand
Your eye's are sea
Your precious love
Belongs to me

You are one
Your so much fun
Your my sun and sky
You are my fire fly
You are my son

Bill Verdon

For My Wish

As you take the first step today
You both will understand
It is God that put you two together
To give each other a guiding hand
To cherish and honor
For the rest of your life
The joy of two people
In love side by side
So thank God for the blessing
That he has brought your way
For you may never have
Another chance to say

Dorinda Standridge

Let Go Of Your Sorrow

So you want to be unhappy?
You want to be sad.
I feel pity for you
But I guess I should be glad.
Because if unhappiness is what you want
Who am I to say
That you should act or feel
Any other way.

Diane Marie

For Mother

I love you for the happiness
you bring to me each day.
I love you for the kindness
of your always thoughtful ways.
I love you for the tenderness
that lies within your heart.
I love you for the way you say
"I'll miss you" when we part.
I love you for your patience
when I do something wrong.
I love you for your laughter
that lingers like a song.
I love you for the gentle way
you cheer me when I'm sad.
I love you for the little things
you do to make me glad.
I love you for the faith and strength ....
that you have given me.
I love you for the beauty that you have
helped me see.
I love you for your love for me so
constant and so true.
But most of all I love you Mother dear ....
just because you're you.

Judy Sallee Kemp

"Death"

In Memory of Gregory Towers
    First you feel nothing, then
you feel pain, hate's inside you
you're kind of ashamed.
    You try holding on, but
there's no looking back, life
only seems like a big black crack.

    Then you fall into a deep
deep sleep, some people say
God will pick you off of your feet
    You want to go back, but
you know that you can't, so
you might as well face the facts.
    Life is living, death is
death. So make the choice
while you're ahead!!

Bree-Anne Carr

Dear Mother Earth,

You are the womb of my life.
You gave me so many brothers and
sisters.
You gave me so much food and toys,
So many wonders!
Thank you,

But,
How would I repay you?
I know, I love you.
I know, I should take care of you
with the passing time...

So,
if we together,
share uncompromising love for you
DEAR MAMA

You will stay,
healthier,
Younger,
Happy.
I promise I will.

Elizabeth Plater-Zyberk II

Rain - God's Tears

God's tears is the rain that
    You hear when it pours,
He's crying for people
    To open their doors,
He wants to come into your
    Heart to stay,
He is the truth and the life
    And the way,
So whenever you're feeling
    Sad and blue,
After the rain - comes
    Sunshine too
And God's rain will make
    A rainbow above,
To show us His pure and
    Everlasting love.

Dolores A. Miller

"You Make My Heart Sing"

Biking, you make my heart sing,
You jump everything, smoothly,
So common, let's go riding!

Hittin' the dirt,
Pumpin' up a tire,
Mud on my shirt,
The race is down to the wire!

To reach the top,
Better not stop,
Bearin' down on the pack,
Tearin' up the track!

The losers are crying,
Third place is sighing,
Second place tips his hat,
As I raise the trophy,
Everyone knows I did better
    than that!

Justin Piolunek

A Friend

A friend is there whenever
you need them
A friend makes you smile
whenever you see them

A friend helps you through
rough times anytime you feel
you did a bad crime

A friend comforts you whenever
you're tearing
A friend listens when you
need a good hearing

A friend can last a long time
and a friend shows they care by
showing different signs.

Friends come and friends go
but friends never turn their
backs and make you feel low.

Joyce L. Ferrer

A Poem For Mama (Grandmother)

So many times I've needed you,
you never let me down.
A great wonderful lady and a friend
was what I'd found.

So many times I think of you,
and all you've said and done.
You helped me see things differently,
without ever putting me down.

Your strong belief in God,
is what I admired in you the most.
The way you kept believing, though you
knew the end was close.

I never told you, "I Love You";
but, I knew you always knew,
whenever I'd need you, you'd always come
through.

So, at this time I will say "I Love You"
Mama Dear,
I know that you can hear me, because
your presence is ever near.

Brenda E. Jones

Man A Giant

Man you are a giant!
You raze mountains
stop rivers,
race faster than time.
But do these things
without asking from where
you came or why.
Ask not where you go
nor ask to stay.
Ask only for the strength
To live from day to day.

Juanita Dianda

"North End"

If you didn't live it
You won't understand my dream
It deals, not with houses
Or endless shades of green
It has to do with people
Who touched my very soul
They helped me find tomorrow
Helped to make me whole.
There was Tony and Mary upstairs
Emelia one floor below
So many people to love me
So many places to go.
You see, I was raised in the North End
And of all the places I've seen
Returning to yesterdays North End
Is the dream I dream.

Gennaro S. Pasquale

Untitled

If you could see inside of me
You would see the way things ought to be:
Justice served in every way,
Love and lust for everyday.
A girl for every boy hand in hand,
A friend for every lonely man.
Company down a dark alley way,
People that visit you from far away,
A vacation for every tired man
On a seashore in which to walk the sand.

Craig Ward

Shining Hope

Twinkle, twinkle little star
    your light is fading away.
You once shone so brightly,
    now falling from the night to day.
For all little stars must learn
    as many mistakes are made,
that every star had to do it's time
    it's the only way.
As a star you're responsible
    to all the other stars,
to help and guide in the right direction
    and thus you can't fall far.
If you continue to fall too far
    then you'll be out of place.
Your light will dim forever,
    and you'll die, cold..in space.
Search yourself, so you may find the
problems and the dreams
that keeps you falling from the night and
find your self-esteem.

LET'S TAKE OUR KINDS BACK FROM
THE STREETS.
MAKE SURE THEY KNOW WE ALL
MAKE A DIFFERENCE.

Morgan Martin

You're Always On My Mind

As the sun sets in the evening
Your memory
Keeps racin'
Always a flame burning

In the night sky
As the stars twinkle
Reminding me of the spark
That I see in your eyes

I lay my head to sleep
An angels glow appears
A vision with halo and wings
Showing love runs deep

The second my eyes open
All through the mornin'
Afternoon, all day long
It begins all over at dawn

This thinking of you on my mind
Consistently - constantly
With each and every thought
That you occupy all the time

Bryan Holzworth

The Gift

You are a special person to me,
You've taught me so many things.
You gave a gift to cherish and keep,
You gave the gift of wings.

The wings to soar up in the sky,
Toward a love never known before.
The wings of love, laughter and joy,
To extend and reach for more.

If I should come to a halt one day,
To find I have a broken wing.
The tool I need to repair my break,
Is the tool of love you shall bring.

But if there comes a time in life,
To say our forbidden good-bye's.
Remember you hold a place in my heart,
For being a part of my life.

Cindy Hogue

The Waiting Time

Your eyes speak volumes to me
Your soul whispers my name
I can see you - standing in the sunlight
    under the crystal clear skies -
As if you were right here, beside me
I wonder if you feel it too -
    the power that draws us together,
Or if it is only my own fantasy
    which fuels my longing.
I can hear your voice
    telling me all the possibilities
    you see in my eyes
As if you were right here, talking to me
And I wish I had seen them too,
    as I do now.
I hope that it is not too late
That this feeling does not die between us
    with the passage of time
That we were meant to wait.

Belynda Jullien

Rage Of Love

I knew you were true,
you've been there all the way through.
    You will do the best to defend,
All the way until the end.
    Well tonight is the night,
You will try will all your might.
    If you commit the crime,
You better serve the time.
    If you decide to use,
You're definitely gonna lose.
    I know inside you're real,
My heart, you would never steal.
    You're always in my dreams,
And you know what that means.
    I hope you will always learn,
Or else it will be my turn.
    My heart would be frayed,
And my soul would be decayed.
    I know you are sane,
So don't ever put me through the pain.

Deanna Triggs

Since You

In many ways I must confess
You've changed a million things for me.
I thank my God, and you I bless
For things above reality.

In battles lost and won I've fought
Convinced that both we're all in vain.
And sure that all things could be bought
With anything but grief or pain.

You stimulate in my poor soul
Almost a God's mentality.
And in a way you bought my soul
(Pray God this is not blasphemy).

For with this sight you gave to me
I see that naught has been in vain.
So much I can endure since thee
I pray the Lord, more grief! More pain!

Evelyn Hazelett

Mr. Blue Jay

Hey, Mr. Blue Jay,
Zoomin' thru the sky,
Divin' at my kittie,
Aimin' for her eye.

Tell your little baby,
"Get back up high."
We don't want to hurt him.
We just want him to go bye, bye.

Hey, Little Jay Bird,
Hopin' on the ground.
Kittie Cat's achasin',
Thinks a toy she's found.

You're way, way to little,
My kittie to be ateasin'
You better get aflyin',
While Kittie Cat's asneezin'.

Daddy's still adivin',
Mommy's joined in screechin',
Baby's still ahoppin',
Kittie Cat's asleepin'.

Judith K. Yoder

Never Lacking Love

How does he do it
Still my love
He plays the game
Like the person above

He has control
In the blink of his eye
It drowns the sorrow
But makes me cry

I love you
What does it mean
I can call on him
On him I can lean

Always and forever
Are the words we say
But when it come to it
Will he stay

He has my heart
Never to give it back
We can't return now
Our love can't lack

Morgan Neasby

Winter Art

Midnight
Still the snow swirls
through the blackness
on its journey downward
to paint my world in white.

Dancing
In fragile splendor
while here and there
a single snowflake gleams
like a ray of sunlight
glinting on an ocean swell.

Andante
It is a gentle snow
waltzing to soundless music
of old Vienna and Strauss
pausing, dipping, twirling,
glancing on pine needles
whitewashing my world.

Linda Hassett Veracka

Half Whirlwind

Something unborn in the
stiller childhood.

Awakening,
the early dead are lived.

The nighting pond,
the lit and lighting darkness,

Pass close in a
golden boat.

Half the sea is earth,
half whirlwind.

Paul Dietrich

A Lover's Rose

Delicate wine petals
Stood elegantly
Upon a slender
thorny stem
Watch the wine gush forth
Greeting the air in its blossom
Awakening you with its scent

For days it would smile
As the sun stroked its vase
But at night it would whisper
The song of fate

For in the morning
A nocturnal shadow lingers
The rose bows its head
And chokes

Michelle Prieto

"Setting"

Setting sun, so much
Stranger than I can see.

Setting sun, so different,
Unlike the night we find,

Dark, unbright, and without
thy light.

Marvin Gresham

A Drift Upon A Dream

Intruded on in restful slumber,
subconscious thoughts prevail.
Deliberately in wakefulness,
our inner feelings hailed.

In glimpses of a memory
retreat to yesterday;
of happy times, a long lost love
joy, laughter, or dismay.

This timeless space of selfishness
eluding every trespass;
A cleansing journey of the soul,
emotions forced to surface.

Inspiration sparks the dying embers;
of plans, and goals, to flames.
What once resigned to reminiscence,
breeds reason to sustain.

Cast inhibitions to the wind;
the dormant self's set free.
Embraced by bliss, in solitude;
a drift upon a dream.

Pamela J. Custeau

Rain

It rains.
Suddenly,
in the darkness
of the night
it rains.
Delightfully,
the drops
rhythm
a gentle sound.
Fresh.
A dance of pauses
that the wind
capriciously
intones.
There is
much abandon
in these light drops
and now the silence
has its own
intimacy.

Mario Vassalle

That's got to be the prettiest
sunset I've ever seen.
Majestic clouds of crimson
over trees no longer green.
The sun shines through the
rain, a crescent moon is high,
And as I turn from this mirage,
a rainbow blesses the sky.

Nicolette Larkin

The Tree

I perch on a strong and
supportive brownish grey root.
I can see that it's old and
has been worn. Wedges are
missing, and the sour apple-green
middle peers out of a hard
candy-like shell, that covers
the inner essence.
I stare up at the bold
chocolate brown spine of a
trunk. It sort of leans
toward the sun. Its long
armed branches grasp for the
suns rays, as the sweet
jungle-green leaves flutter
like butterflies in the wind
creating dark clusters of
shadows in the soft bitter
grass.

Kristy Ann Meyers

Lament

Like broken fragments from the past,
That exist in the corners of my mind
I recall sweet moments of an earlier time.

Before you left - leaving me bereft
Of all things loving and good
And in their stead-this sterile

Widowhood.

Ruth Sadkin

My Love For You

As I went through life I've often wondered, what kind of heaven God's placed us under? To see the cruelness of the earth, created by people - what is it worth? Where is the love and honest caring the trust and help and constant sharing. Will my life always be confused? Will I always feel abused? Can my hopes and dreams come true? Then it happened the day I met you. Someone out there who truly cared and protected me even if I was scared. A person who loves me every day and helps me out in every way. You've become so very special to me, I hope that this you truly see. You've made my life so complete. Having you is really sweet, I as your princess, you as my prince, my life has been changing ever since. We've seen good times and seen some bad. We've been very happy, and at times even mad, but through it all we come together, building a love that can withstand the weather, and make it through every day, to be loving you in every way to bring a smile to your face, and wanting to share a tender embrace. Making each day a happy start, in the hopes that we shall never part, I know through life I've had my health, but loving you I also have wealth, to care and love someone as I do you, I know my feelings are sincerely true, and whatever happens to come our way, my love for you will always stay. You'll be the one I always cherish, even after life has eventually perished.

Robin Greenwood

Memories

I would love to see the truth
played back on laser disk,
distortion free.
Not this eight millimeter stuff
in black and white.
That out of focus experience
I try to recall from childhood:
The birthday parties with homemade cake,
the rodeo parades,
me high up on a horse;
Christmas at Aunt Em's,
laughing, smiling, waving.
Spastic bursts of life
projected on the wall,
then packed away in boxes,
hauled up to the attic,
waiting to be exposed

Lou McGee

Untitled

What can I do since I must stop loving you?
Please tell me what I should do.
You think it's a joke; the feelings you felt you had to provoke.
You made me love you and I was so blind
to see there was no way you could ever
love me because of your family.
It isn't fair for you to tear my heart apart and not even care.
You never understood the way I felt:
the intensity of the passion you dealt.
I am in so very much pain. I sometimes feel my life is all rain.
If you ever loved me and if you still do,
then don't let me go.
I will never be stronger unless I have you with me forever.
I don't even know day from night any longer.
My life will become meaningless, I hate to confess.
But my weakness is showing; my insanity overflowing.
I will become one with all that is dark and bleak.
No light will fill my wall and eventually death will call,
and who will be there when I fall?
All you'll hear is a silent lull.

Lori M. James

A Pleasant Drive With Jesus

We ask in Jesus name that everyone relax and place your souls in the position of drive and slowly move to Deuteronomy 13:4 and walk after the Lord your God and fear him and keep his commandments and obey his voice and serve him and cleave unto him.

As you find yourself coasting in the neutral position we ask in 'Jesus' name that you think on Numbers 6:26 that the Lord will lift up his countenance upon thee and give thee peace.

Then go ahead and reverse yourself slowly, yes slowly into Revelation 2:26 and remember he that overcometh and keepeth my works unto the end to him will I give power over the nations.

And finally in Jesus name we ask as you park your souls you may want to go into two positions, one being that of Proverbs 16:3 commit thy works unto the Lord and thy thoughts shall be established and the other position being that of Psalms 69:30 I will praise the name of God with a song and will magnify Him with thanksgiving.

On the other hand, park yourself with prayer, lift the Lord with praise, patiently wait on him and you will receive prosperity along with God's promise and his promise is his word and his word does stand.
We ask in Jesus name that you restore these blessings.
This is a key to a pleasant drive with Jesus.

Margie Pettway

Sunset On The Beach

Walking along the golden beach
Powdered sand sifting between my toes,
Sweat bubbles forming on my wave-beaten body
And burnt skin peeling from my nose.

I trail along the waters edge
Wind is kneading through my silky hair,
As I look toward the sun I raise my hand
As if to catch the blinding glare.

I snap my fingers; the wind dies
I clap; the sun sinks from sight,
I turn and walk briskly away
For noon has now turned night.

Waves are breaking along the shore
The cool spray draws me near,
My sunburnt legs carry my naked body
Toward the blue-green depths without fear.

Robin Knight

I Knew

From the first time I sensed your
presence behind me
I knew
When I first felt your warm breath
On the back of my neck
I knew
When I felt your strong but ever
So gentle hands around me
I knew
As you pulled even closer causing me
to recognize and accept your
Strong manhood
I knew
And as I laid in bed that night with a
smile on my face, still lingering in
Your scent and your handsome face
Etched in my memory
I knew
But after all I knew, I never knew I would
Grow to love someone as special as you

Pamela Ballejos

Sunflower

Walking through the garden . . . Contentment comes from witnessing the power of flawless purity. Is the flower aware of the influence of its aroma?

In the mystery of stillness, blameless and carefree beauty lingers on her lips; and the enchanted whisper (The song that sweetens the sky and seduces the wind) brings imperishable delight to everyone and everything it touches, without exception. This breath of morning, this refreshment (The bringer of ancient youth), is the breath of the genuine, and knowledge that the path leads deep into totality.

Sensuous warmth emanates from the soul, and is now light from the delicate caress of vitality. Breathing burning flesh, this the perfect devastation; Smooth rich nakedness, this the immaculate majesty, is the symphony to which passion and elegance dance so exquisitely. The reason the silent rainbow continues to exit.

I am swimming in the meadow of simple harmony, where freedom shines eternal and the sweet melody sings throughout the measureless magnificence. In the center of this felicity lies the Sunflower. Her gentle smile: The reminder that heaven's glow is here on Earth. The assurance that bliss is deathless. The source of the spring of absolute wholeness rising inside of me. Unbridled immortal exhilaration has no captive, and flies freely. Your eyes then kissed my eyes. The clouds retreated. There is now nothing preventing golden brilliance from saturating my soul.

Tyler Blank

To The Man In The Moon

Hello up there, Mister Man in the Moon!
Pray what do you do all day?
When the sun is out and shines so bright,
Where do you go to play?

Do you ever play at Hide-and-Seek
With the stars that twinkle so?
They, too, disappear from my sight by day.
Mister Man, where do they go?

There are ever and ever so many stars.
There is only one of you.
Do you ever get lonesome Mister Man in the Moon?
Mister Man, do you ever get blue?

Ruth Broadaway

Unlike The Seasons (?)

I'm no longer in the Summer Solstice
preparing for the Autumnal Equinox
for I'm past all Solstitial Points
and beginning to feel it in all of my joints.

I've watched the Seasons change to age 77
all the while marveling at God in His Heaven
so I've broken my age down into Seasons
perhaps many will agree with my reasons.

SPRING: Stopped at 30 years after my birth
SUMMER: Ended after 49 years on this earth
AUTUMN: Lasting from age 50 to 80
WINTER: From age 80 to Eternity.

Loretta M. Hanneman

Untitled

I'm bored with my life, I need a big change
Priorities I will have to rearrange
It will be hard, not a strong girl am I.
I must give it my all or for sure I will die.
My life has been crazy the whole time thru
I will need all my strength and some extra too!
It took me this long to figure it out
The good things we keep and the bad we throw out!

Karyn Andersen

Untitled

When you're asleep
Problems are pushed away.
You just like there in peace.
You don't have to think about problems
You don't have to deal with people putting on some fake act,
Acting like they care, when you know they don't.
   You don't have to worry...
   You are asleep.
   You don't have to face reality...
   life...
   Pain...
   fear...
When you're asleep
Everything a fragment of your imagination...
just a dream,
it's all fake
you just lie there with no
hurt or pain.
If only we could sleep
forever.

Tina R. Gordon

For Sandy

A fresh ray of sunshine plays
   proudly along the valley's edge -
As horses and all the rare ones
   of the forest stand waiting by the hedge.
Gentle breezes blow
   through thinning clouds o'er head.
The early morning sky announces
   this day in blazing red.

Yes - nature can and often does
   reflect my mood - the inner me.
Today I'm filled with life, with love,
   dominated by wild and gentle thee.
The puffin we waited for appears
   and struts along the nearby shore.
Reminding me how rare real beauty is
   and that it's you and I truly do adore.

Thomas Fitzpatrick

A Summer's Garden

Tall larkspur in the garden,
Purple-robed ladies stiffly single.
Thin stemmed poppy by the gate,
Pink petticoated girls following, fluttering.
Tiny alyssum all in a row,
Waves of sweet smelling foaming, filling.
Stained glass butterflies roam-freely,
Sucking sweet juices-freely given.
Like you my love

F. Sinsa Baugh

Balloons On The River

Do you remember balloons on the river,
Red, and yellow, and green, that summer
We walked on the deck, and you tossed them over
So we could dance?

Do you remember, not one or two,
But a whole handful you had bought for me,
And laughed?

It was strange to think of balloons on the river,
Something that probably happened never before
In the course of the river and time.

Our balloons are gone forever
Floating down the endless river,
Yet all those gay balloons are mine.

Rilla A. Black

Days Dawning And Ending

I like to watch the sun come up on a new day,
Pushing all the remaining darkness away
Streaking the sky with beautiful hues.
And on this miracle I often muse.
The birds will stir from their nest
Awaking the flowers and all the rest
And at the dawning of each new day
I feel the need to close my eyes and pray
Thanking God for all this wonder and beauty
As I start my day and all its duty
So God make my life worthwhile,
Let me help someone today with a smile
Make me kind and gentle too.
And count all my blessings a new.
Toward the closing of each day
I have to talk to God and say.
Thank you for love and laughter.
And serious thoughts that come after
Thank you for the sun shine and rain
Even tho some hours are filled with pain.

Muriel Watson

Enchanted Land

In the morning the sun wakes up
Puts on his bright clothes
And walks across the sky all day...

In the evening under dreamy cloud covers
He changes to pink pajamas
And quietly slips away.

Scott Yancy

Life

It's full of pieces like a puzzle with one piece never
quite fitting in place.
It's never what you dream of as a child.
You let love come and go, you rise and you fall, your
problems always seeming to be of the worse proportion until
it passes.

As time goes along you realize what you need out of it,
always struggling to be a happy person, which is the hardest
task of it.

To deal with the everyday big problems and little pleasures.
You will pray to God when you're down and forget your
promises to him when you're up.

Wow, and here I am trying, trying to be me, too delicate for
where and who I am, because they don't make shelves for
feelings, only knick knacks.

Marie J. Caldwell

Alone

One solitary desert blossom
reaches slowly skyward,
feeling the cool evening breeze hit its gentle face.
Such are the joys of the hermit
who fishes upon the lake no others visit.
Such are the joys of independence;
the river which cuts its own path
through the dense forest of life.

Mark Andrew Stanford

Praise Of Fall

The colors of Fall have just arrived.
Reds and golds of leaves survived.

A beauty I see with wandering eyes.
Made even more brilliant by light from the skies.

Browns and yellows kissed by dew.
The mornings a splendid mixture of hue.

Mountains attest to falls excellent grace.
Clouds over the horizon, edge like white lace.

Imitations of colors we cannot perfect.
A joy to whom ever would like to detect.

Never would I miss the colors of fall.
Nor could I say my excitement would pall.

With each passing year I appreciate more.
Nothing more beautiful than a colorful tour.

A gift from nature to all people on earth.
No price could we place on this gift of great worth.

Roxy E. Carl

It's Never Too Late

Rising above the eastern horizon is a golden sun,
Reflected in amber waves of a foreign sea,
The dawning of a new day is begun,
For the people of an impoverished nation they now flee,

Escaping a rebel's hand,
Tearing away the fabric that held the nation as one,
Raping and devastating a depressed land,
Where prosperity is now long gone,

Huddled masses fill vessels venturing to a new and safer place,
Taking what morsels of their culture they can,
With tears that fall from the crevices of their face,
Weeping in sorrow for their homeland,

Hugging close to make room for all,
The boats set sail over the amber waves of fate,
Bringing the lost to America's beckoned call,
Where the liberty torch burns eternally, and it's never too late

Ronald E. Maples

I Have Forgotten

Wolf, wolf where have you gone?
Relative of our dogs with a beautiful song.
Lord of the Northern Forests, where are you?
    Oh, I have forgotten...
We have destroyed you by ignorance.

Great Bald Eagle, symbol of our country.
You are going the way of the Dodo.
    Why are you leaving?
Oh, I have forgotten...
Because of sickening chemicals we spray.

Mighty Elephant, largest on land,
    Why do you cry?
Oh, I have forgotten...
We have killed sisters for ivory.

Earth, our mother planet, stop playing hide and seek,
We need you. Where are you? Don't hide anymore.
    Oh, I forgot...
We have destroyed you.

Regina Shumaker

481

Our Garden

We have a secret place we go,
Renee and I.
That looks out over a quiet bay.
There's a beautiful garden there
With flowers of purple and gold, and pink
and blue that take your breath away.
There's a path that leads to the beach
below where we walk along the shore
And hunt for sea shells in the sun for
Renee and I.
We came upon three children playing in
the sand, they did not see us as we
walked by for they were busy
building dreams
And we were remembering.
We stopped to rest and watch the children
play and on the hill above
Our multicolored garden danced in the sun
for Renee' and I.

Ralph I. Wirick

The Cardboard Condominium

The cardboard condominium
  repels the rain,
   shrouds the sun,
    and blocks the breezes...

   But it cannot hide the tears;
    for the walls do have ears,
    and they hear the despair.

    And they heard the despair of
    all who preceded me.
    And they'll hear the despair
    of all who follow me.

    And they'll hear the despair
    until nature stops for lunch
    and it is a home no more.

    My cardboard condominium.

Ronald J. Surace

Memories Are Forever

You can almost see their youthful laughter
Riding high on ancient winds.
You can see their youthful faces
As they play where the river bends.

Playmates of your youth
At another time and place
You remember each and every name
As you fit it to a face.

So close your eyes and go
Back to where the river bends
And cavort once more with playmates
Where friendship never ends.
And memories are forever.

Vance A. Stroupe

Contemplation

When winter mist moves along the shore
Scarlet sunset darkens the silent seas
Solemn stillness breaks across the sky
Pale moonlight settles among the trees
Somehow we know the night blends into day
Forgive dear Lord the pain within my heart
Someday somewhere kindred spirits wait
To meet and greet on some distant shore

Robert E. Lee

The Pond

Slicing thru cool glass without cutting my hand,
Ripples dance around my fingers.
While staring at a clear, blue mirror, I see my reflection.
A tear drop streaks my cheek and silently falls.
It blends naturally with the water it hits.
Circles of waves surround the vertex and the water breathes with life.
I listen carefully to what it says, telling me to forget my present
And stop listening to my foolish heart.
So, angered by the knowledge of the condition of my soul,
I strike it with my fist and the water strikes back.
A splash hits my cheek where the tear had once been
To flout and laugh at my ignorance.
But soon the water calms down
As does my spirit and we become tranquil again.
Then, I slowly submerge my whole, shattered body
Into this pond, this blue hole of peace,
This grave that beckons me and calls my name,
Take one last, deep breath and finally
Exhale the last bit of life from me
As my body reunites with my tear.

Kim Bieber

"Rise"

Rise, Rise above your name, son.
  Rise above the sword.
  Rise above the mass of bodies, both dead and wounded
Soar, Soar above the labels, son.
  Soar above the compliments.
  Soar above the cries of doubt, disbelief, and disdain.
Dream, Dream to dare to dream to fly, son.
  Dream about your love.
  Dream that all the wars around you aren't there or anywhere.
Hear, Hear more than what you're told son.
  Hear beyond the lies.
  Hear until your ears bleed with pain, and then just listen.
Believe, Believe in all you see, son.
  Believe in nothing.
  Believe that you will rise, rise above your name.

Sean Robinson

The Spirit Of The Sixties

Dedicated to the Marchers on the Pentagon.
Rise up, rise up young people of America
Rise up as your forefathers did
The foreign enemy is gone, long gone
But the fight is now on against the Pentagon.

The French stormed the Bastille
The Russians took the Winter Palace
The American people will not be outdone
Rise up and march on the Pentagon.

This citadel of Militarism is not our heritage
Its aggressive spirits are foreign to our soul
America stands for peace, for peace alone
Rise up, rise up and march on the Pentagon.

Zorah E. Sheffner

God's Spice — Provincetown, MA

The green curved highway 6
Reaches the tip of the north hook,
Provincetown just hangs down
From the reversed rainbow.
Gray clouds smear over the harbor;
No sails, thunder roars.
In the streets tourists group, and wander.
The neons flash 99, 66, 69, and 96.

Thomas T. Lin

I Wish I Wasn't

I'm a slow, shy snail
Scared of the shovel in the little boy's pail.
Why did he choose me,
Out of all the others in the deep, blue sea?
I'm just a slow, shy snail.

The little boy's pail in my new home.
Mine, the shovel's, and the added stone.
Like a horse's stinky, stuffy stall,
I don't like it here at all.
I wish I wasn't a slow, shy snail all alone.

Each morning I receive a mouth full of sand
That the little boy pours into the pail from his hand.
This morning was special to me
For the little boy put in seaweed
Instead of a handful of sand.

The shovel, the stone, the seaweed and me,
Now are all free.
Thanks to the storm which swept up the pail and all,
Rescuing us from behind that metal wall.
The sea is where I want to be.

Lisa L. Griffith

Tortured Children

Tortured Children of windswept minds,
Scattered fears upon the vines.
Reaching for a past they know,
Always fearing to let go.

Tortured children of Social Grace,
Always feeling out of place.
Their empty eyes are dim and lost,
Forever more they pay the cost.

Tortured children of death and pain,
The kindred spirit of which they gain.
Battling a constant hell,
The thought of peace and love they dwell.

Tortured children of long ago,
In hopes to soon be found.
To find their souls of yesteryear,
That once have been of sound.

Renee J. Ehle

The Rat

Never underestimate the rat.
Scuttling across the floor
a hairy bead of mercury,
tiny nails make tic-tic-tic noises
on the linoleum.
Permanent grin across a pointed snout
show nasty incisors
gleaming, even in darkness
like his black scheming eyes
gnawing his way in
fighting his way out.
The clumsy paws of an anxious cat
mere cushions to the blows he's suffered.
Never underestimate the rat,
for though he dwells in filth,
he is master there.

Keith W. Harris

On The Earth's Edge I Take Notes In My Mind

Bushy tailed and tamed, squirrels solicit handouts of picnic pieces.
Sea otters skillfully dive delving for dinner from the deep.
as the babes learn from the elders and the moms tolerate their play.
Sea gulls skim the surface of the morning ocean whose calm is already
broken by divers daring the depths, lured by the sea's secrets.

Children in all sorts of flavors chance the rocks like goats not
  gazelles
stretching tall, out to harness the wind and the expanse
or crouch low to capture glimpses of sea stars and hermit crabs.
They move on, playing toetag with waves, skipping backwards,
arms drawing stay away circles in the air.
The dark circles of their pants legs tell who has won the game
at least once.

Parents pause,
indulging children with the tantalizing temptations of the ocean.
They sit, sanded, safely away from the foaming fingers of the waves,
trying to remember when they themselves played such games
and wondering why they stopped.

Loretta Strharsky

The Anguish Of Futility

Leopards and wild roses,
Sea-stars and hermit crabs,
Planet moons, a child's soft cheek.
They prospered here, full-blown and true to form.
God, how I grew to love them all!

I had heard a drunken voice from Earth.
"We follow no high and mighty one's advice!
We've made free choices as was our right.
Why be morose when time is running short?
Now, more than ever, the party must go on!"

Then your voice who has known me beckoned.
"Have you found the object of your searches?
Did you unlock the secrets of your being?
Dare you join in aid to Earth's dying races?
For them, you'll be a god in masquerade."

Can I endure this present desolation?
This panorama of despair?
Such living memories as I carry,
Can they sustain my soul?
My love, dear God, is my undoing!

Sondra Barnes

Winds Of Time

I know there's a quiet place that rests within my mind.
Searching, grasping those inner parts that flow on the winds of time.
Things that I remembered when I was very young.
Watering the pretty flowers in the bright morning sun.
Then off along the dusty path to adventures we'd just know.
It seems to me that it really wasn't that long ago.
Stopping and listening with great wonder.
The sound of oh, so distant thunder.
Soon the blowing grass, sighing breeze, waving trees.
The coming storm and the rustling leaves.
The all too soon of quickening rain.
Hurrying for the nearest shelter along the lane.
Spurring me on with each raindrop upon my face and brow.
Reaching shelter safely and knowing somehow.
It was just a normal rain on this summer day.
We hear the rolling thunder methodically going away.
Gazing out at green fields, flowing streams it becomes clear.
To give thanks to God for all those blessings and hold them dear.

Neva B. Meyers

Black On Grey

The night, as black as my mind is grey;
Searching, waiting, whispering from the corners of my mind.
A wind that blows so violent,
like the memories from my past.

The stars and moon that give some light,
Creep through my bedroom window.
It watches as I sleep, and as I breathe.
With each breath the light grows dimmer,
feeding from my silence.

And unknown are the hands that reach into my world.
They are bright, unlike the familiar darkness.
With it comes a brilliant light,
but I mustn't trust it.
Trusting would be giving in.
But yet with it comes a certain warmth,
some sort of innocence and kindness.

Could it be you really care,
and came to take away my darkness?

Kerri L. Simmons

Look, Jane, Look, Dick, Closely

Look, Jane. Look, Dick. Look and see.
See the birds. Hear their songs, to you and me.
Look mother. A child's smile, simple, free.
Look father, mothering the child, emotionally.
Up, up, up goes the plane.
Bring American children to Russia.
Up, up, up goes the plane.
Carry Russian children to the USA.
Look, Dick, look. Hands join as people come together.
Farm-aid, Band-aid, People-aid.
Help, help, help.
Look at all the volunteers.
Look in nursing homes, shelters too.
Look, Dick, Look, peacemakers, inspiring dreams.
Mother Theresa, Ghandi, Martin Luther King.
Look, Armenian relief, Chenobyl, whales are freed.
Look, Jane, look. Listen, Dick, listen.
Prayers of the people; songs of hope and peace.

Lorraine Rheault

More Than Just A Friend

I stand at the kitchen window where I
see your tiny grave beneath the oak tree.
You are Resting. I know.
My mind pictures you waiting there on the
rug when I open the door from being gone all
day, tail wagging with your nose inspecting
my packages.
At night my mind pictures you quietly
sneaking around to the side of the bed where I
lie wanting to get warm next to me.
Sometimes when I sat in that big chair crying
and feeling sorry for myself., you'd jump up
along side me with your eyes fixed on mine as
if to say; "Hey, I'm here, I love you, were fine!"
You sat and you listened so patiently
I can't bring you back and I suppose my
broken heart will mend with time, and yes;
It helps to remember your eyes saying to me;
Hey. I'm here! I love you. We're fine!

Tracy Lorelei Sullivan

The Gods

The Gods look down upon the world they created.
Seeing a lonely dark witch drawing life from the mortals around her.
Never knowing what was needed to make her life complete.

After watching awhile, they confer.
Finally reaching agreement, they take pity on this lost one.

Seeing the lone wolf following dead-end trails
in the woods bordering the witch's land.
His path suddenly turns in a direction he had yet to track.
Not knowing why, he continues on.

Coming to the edge of the woods he spies the witch
and cautiously watches from the safety of the trees.
The witch sensing something casts her spell of protection.

The wolf now changed into a man, steps boldly into the clearing.
The witch is mesmerized by his expressive eyes.
Seeing herself there not as a dark witch,
but a being of bright light.

They approach each other and as their minds touch,
their shattered existences become complete.
As they walk off together the Gods smile.

Nancie D. Geppert

Awaiting Victory

I'm walking the shores of Babylon Carrying a load entitled strife
Seeking, begging, and surrendering here I travail and heave for
new life. But a wall stands, blocking the womb

"Oh, can I be forsaken?" I cry. "Where is the hand whose
shadow I see?" In that shade, I have hidden in wait On the shores
of this desolate sea. Looking for the arm which delivers

It is here I have nursed on the manna And hungered, craved and starved
My plate has become faith and hope As I discard the fear which mars.
While I long for the arm which frees

Thrust unto a bed of thorns, I lay Watching the self I knew bleed away
The grace which only the desert brings Fills my wounds to face a
new day. As I seek the arm which delivers

I will travail till the time does arrive When the arm brings the
wall to the ground Then birth will come forth to the desert And
only Glory and Majesty will abound. Then I will walk the shores
of Babylon no longer.

Melody D. Yeazell

He'll Send Us A Rainbow

Our Father always knows when our world
   seems dim,
For He cares about us, and we're never
   forgotten by him.

He shares our sorrows, and feels our pains,
And, we know the sunshine follows the rain.

Though He wants us to cast our burdens upon him,
He knows when our hearts are sad before we tell Him; —

And, we can reach Him on His direct prayer line.
I've never been put "on-hold" a single time.

Many times, when I've felt lonely or blue,
A friend, somewhere, He'd already spoken to,

And, I'd be pleasantly surprised with a
   kind deed or word,
Because our Father mentioned me to them,
   and his leading, they heard.

Immediately, I'd feel better, and a rainbow I could see;
For I was reassured of His GREAT LOVE for you, and for me.

Marie Dudley

484

Looking Back To The Past

Looking back to the past today
Seems strange and so very far away
When the future seemed so pretty and clear
Now all the exists is pain and fear.

I remember thinking how great motherhood would be
Taking care of someone happy and carefree.
All the love in your heart you so wanted to give
All the things you wanted to change with just your will

Looking back at the past seems not so far away
Yet things are changing drastically every single day
How could it be that so many young hearts-
Have turned to stone.
With no remorse just bitter to the bone.

It's very painful to see how our young hearts -
Have transpired
To end in tragedy and rapid gunfire.

Pamela Robinson

A Sailors Bane

The ocean waves roll and roar
Sending white caps into the shore
Strong winds billowing the sails
Sailors hanging on to the rails
Lookout in the crowsnest faces west
Praying the waters will come to rest
Neptune is blowing his top this day
Controlling the waters as they spray
Over the deck and down the hatch
The sight of land sailors praying to catch
The strong winds subside to a breeze
Sailors arise from down on their knees
The ship sailing along without a groan
The crew of the ship sigh, "We're going home".

Ray F. Schroeder

Your Birthday

Your birthday is a gift of love
Sent from our Heavenly Father above
Another year He's kept you from all harm
That's because you're safe in His arms
Safe from all the world's fiery darts
That would only seek to tear you apart

So on this your birthday I know you're reminded of
God's Grace, His Mercy, AND Is Love
Extended to His servant who preaches His World
The Word that comes from a true and living God
So continue to preach the gospel and compel men to come
Continue to lift up Jesus
For He is the ONLY ONE!!!

Lastly, be encouraged by the work you do for our Lord
For He has faithfully promised us in His Word
Everlasting life for you and me
When we discharge our Christian duties for all to see
So work on Pastor 'til God says well done
The battle's fought—Praise God!!! Victory's won!!!

Mary J. Huntley

"Tomorrow I Pray If"

As I lay in my bed to sleep
Seriously in heart I pray
God safely in your arms I keep,
"Tomorrow I pray if."
Through all the joy and pain
the sounds and signs of death abound
still remains the same,
"Tomorrow I pray if."
Year after year, time and again
decisions are being made,
chances taken and a risk or two is lost always,
love grows, hate is surely to die together
sweetly all can find our mother divine
"Tomorrow I pray if."
Here dawn is gone a new day appears
we are happy in our hearts,
quietly we know how we won
no we are not out of danger
and our troubles are not at all gone
"Tomorrow I pray if."

Sheila Ann Spencer

Remembering Our American Heroes

They risked precious lives for love of their country,
Serving on land, on the sea, in the air;
Men and women assigned to awesome tasks
On far-off shores with unfamiliar names.
Their many brave deeds will one day appear
In books of history's heroic tales.
Their accomplishments at home and abroad
Are not forgotten by a proud nation
That sets aside time for remembering.

They sacrificed their lives to preserve freedom,
Determined to halt ruthless aggression.
Some returned home in stillness and silence,
While others found their peace on foreign soil.
No words of sympathy could stem the grief
Nor dry the tears of heartbroken loved ones.
With bugles sounding their haunting farewell,
Heroes too young to die were laid to rest,
Safely entrusted to God's loving care.

M. Elisabeth Steiner

Where Does My Story Begin?

My story don't begin with ropes and castration
Shackles and chains? Please... we had nations!!!!
Knew how to fly and cultivate land
    Built complex structures you still don't understand
The earth as the center of the solar system? Uh Uh....
    all you had to do was look on the walls of my tomb,
    it's all charted right there
    Nine planets, one star, all rotating in harmonious orbits.

Where does my story begin?....
IMHOTEP 2800 B.C. "Father Of Medicine"
    taught the Greeks a thing or two
    speaking of two.... 1 2 3 4 5 6 7
Yeah, we could count; developed a numbering system 8,000 years ago
Optics, Mathematics, Chemistry and yes even Physics;
we didn't leave a stone unturned
Did I hear someone say travel? Yea we traveled. Remember the
Shang dynasty of China?
1766 B.C. to 1,000 B.C.?
The ones they describe as "Black with oily skin?
Who do you think that was?
You know those Olmecs, who lived down in Mexico in 1,000 B.C.?
The ones with the large Negroid heads. Who do you think that was?
Where does my story begin?....
It begins with Power, Invention, Wisdom, Respect, Grace and Freedom.
Peace!

Ron Foley

In Memory Of David

We planned to grow old together, you and I,
Sharing space in some old folk's home.
Gliding in unoiled rocking chairs,
Aging, but not alone.

Then the silent stalker came
With epidemic rage.
He stole your life — in one fell swoop,
Denied your right to age.

And so I trudge the dreary path
Between loneliness and guilt,
For I still live, but you're resigned
To a name upon a quilt.

Nancy Geisler

Ariel At Piece

Inhabited by that cry she knew so well,
she called it by its name; she called it hell.
Sylvia, I wish you could see
what they have done to you.
Sugar on your tongue was like salt in a wound.
A red tulip to most was to you a bad dream.
No possible way they can know how you felt,
when time and time again
the plaster began to peel.
They glued you back together
or so you said.
When all you wanted was to be dead.
And now here comes the blank-faced nurse,
No peace in rebirth;
All peace in death.
Could all this be nine lives
or a curse?
I hope you are happy and at peace
with your Daddy's arms around you reached.

Lou Ann Hopper

My Dog, Baby

I have a dog named Baby,
She can be very lazy.
She sleeps all day, and sleeps all night,
But will bark if she hears us fight.
She can be playful when it comes to her ball,
and she'll play with you if you toss it.
But alone she'll roll over her ball if you're
    not available.
Baby is a very picky eater
Sometimes I have to hand feed her.
She can be so cute when she sits or begs,
Paws out front, sitting on her hind legs.
She greets me at the door step when I come
    home,
She wags her tail, which tells me "Welcome!"

Melanie Gonzalez

Woman In The Kitchen

The woman feels like a slave.
She cannot spare a dime, so she works on.
Smoke sizzles out of the pot on the stove.
She feels the vapor burn her hands.
The heat radiates through the room.
She stirs the cream.
She starts the wash in the basin.
She blots the sweat off her face.

Kathleen Thomas

The Longing Soul

Beauty of the Universe all showered upon her,
She captivated men of great Value and Valour:
Producers richest and directors many,
Rushed oft towards her ivory balcony.

Within a year they'd shot movies ten
Utilizing her acting talent to stun:
Her fabulous billions tempted many men,
For owning her came like cock around the hen.

Men of riches and fame stayed for awhile,
She enraptured all with her enthralling smile:
They loved her money and looks of honey,
Ne'er she found a loving heart from any.

Her charity homes in cities of the world,
Spoke volumes of her heart that was yet untold:
Aided victims of disaster, distress or disease,
None hadn't enjoyed her benevolent breeze.

Enormous money and eternal fame though earned
A loving heart only all she finally yearned;
Individuals' mania had her completely churned
A longing heart's desire by others couldn't be learnt.

Savarimuthu Sebastian

Indian Princess

With her long brown hair and large solemn eyes,
she dances in the rain each time the spirit cries.
Her father with feathers in his graying hair,
waits for the buffalo with out another care.
The princess was happy with her family and friends,
but, unfortunately, it came to an end.
Not much later on a Holy Day, white men came;
Looking for gold, their ticket to fame.
They massacred the buffalo,
as the Indians hid and watched the gruesome show.
The Indians have been moved from their land,
on to the land of the never-ending sand.
They have been moved again and again,
when will all this madness end?

Tiffany A. Roe

"A Motherless Child"

Her mother died when she was six years old,
She died during childbirth, she was told.

After the funeral her father did not delay,
Giving her to an Aunt who lived miles away.

Devastated that she was not the one her father would keep,
A motherless child cries herself to sleep.

Losing all her family within a week,
The motherless child's pain ran so very deep.

She was treated like a slave but she tried to be strong,
Yet within her heart she knew she never belonged.

About once a month she would see a wagon coming up the road,
She knew it was her father, her heart would almost explode.

He would visit a while and then start back toward home,
She would be left standing in the road crying alone.

Her father never took her home with him to stay,
And sixty-six years later she never understood his way.

I listen to a motherless child as tears flow down our cheeks,
My heart filled with compassion for my mother's pain still
    runs so deep.

And somewhere a motherless child cries herself to sleep.

Shirley J. Wynne

Spring Tears

Oh how she blooms in Spring and awakens forgotten dreams.
She floats on the wind spilling hope on every landscape.
Cursed memory don't cheat her purpose teasing me with sips of youth
Drown me, if you must, in success that has escaped me.
My lovely Springtime, don't awaken the world and forsake me.
Spring don't tempt me with your mischief of youth.
The laughter of the innocents is as infectious as it is condemning.
Spring don't let me believe in your endless possibilities.
The energy that now denies me and
    makes me choose simpler paths of truth.
Spring don't torture me with dreams of love.
You were mine to claim once.
Ever since... my search illusive, the quest, denied.
    She tempts me again -
I've strayed from the path.
    I shriek, at another season's change.
The truth I've found is false and comforting.
Don't look for me among Autumn's fury; I'll be here
Hiding in springtime's tragic tears.

Tempt Me.
Matthew Lester

"Ellen"

She has her mother's nose, they say
She has her daddy's eyes
And that space between her two front teeth
was destined by both sides.

She has her father's long slim legs
She has her mama's hair
Her impatience and incisiveness
come naturally from theirs

She has her mother's temper
She has her father's pout
Her ability to get her way
is uncanny without doubt

She has her father's steadfast calm
She has her mother's fury
Her charm outweighs her tendency
toward tantrums when she's angry

She is her mother's daughter
She is her daddy's girl
The rightful post she'll ever hold
God's treasure in their world
Patricia R. Weaver

"Coming to A Playground Near You..."

Small, red blanket covers her face.
She is cold.
    Still.

Hopscotch boxes' painted lines turn to chalk, choking her frame.
    "My little girl cried and no one came."
She couldn't even cry to her mama about the rips in her dress -
young girl's mouth clamped with rape.
    "She was my best friend."
Chain-link shadows, the only thing holding her body together.
Beauty and a buddy betrayed her in the schoolyard.
    "The killer was an acquaintance."
A gorgeous white dress, fifteenth birthday picture
painted in celebration.
Portrait now displayed in despair.

Small, red blanket of blood covers her stark, naked body.
She is cold.
    dead.
Little girl cries no more.
C. Valentino Puppione

Remembrance Of Martha

Today is her day to shine.
She smiles down at me with glowing eyes.
She twirls around in her gown and hat.

Her day comes and goes but her happiness stays.

Today I see her even happier.
Her daughter sitting next to her.
While she smiles at her husband because their last child is a son.

Today she lies in bed.
Begging to speak, but not able to.
She lies silent.
Only her eyes speak for her.

Today I only see her in one place.
In her daughter's eyes.
Nadia Urvina

"Tribute To Jessica"

She's faithful - friendly - devoted and cute -
She talks with her hands, because she's
    a mute.
In her heart she carries sorrow and tears -
Yet on the outside, she's ready to cheer.
She tells you of clouds that billow
    in the sky,
But she can not see, no matter how
    she tries.
She sits, not stands, for she can not
    walk - and you watch very
    carefully as she tries to talk.
Jessica tells of journeys she takes all
the time - I pray someday all her
    dreams will be mine.
    God made her so "Special" to cheer
up our lives. She does it each day
and helps keep us alive.
Marilyn Moore

The Quickening

Impervious to the struggles surrounding her,
she waits with unwavering patience
for the tender pushes
of the traveler within.

The event engages her completely,
as in a breathless flash she is swept up
by the intimate signals
from an innocent unknown.

Responding to the sweet speechless message
with smiling caresses over the heart,
the face she imagines
exists in all that is good.
Mary Larsen

Angels Angels

Angels, Angels up above, please show me the way to love.
Show me, show me the path that leads straight to his heart
that always pleads.
Angels, Angels can't you see
I need him so desperately.
Shining, Shining ever so bright
I see the stars that shine tonight.
Angels, Angels everyday guide and show me the way.
Then I wonder and it's clear to see, you are watching over me.
Angels, Angels everywhere you truly do care.
Guiding, Guiding me with strength and with love
You certainly do come from heaven above.
Theresa Santos

Grandma's Prayer

No longer could she breathe
She walked toward the beaming light
Her children were desperately crying,
"Mama, please don't leave us tonight!"

She could see her children touching
Her cold hands and silver hair
She heard God calling through the light
She asked, "God, did you hear my prayer?"

God replied, "Yes, every word.
I was with you when you were on your knees."
She said, "Does my family know I asked you
To guide them in times of need?"

"See them crying by my deathbed?
What is your reason for taking me?
My grandchildren need me, God.
What are their lives going to be?"

"I am the one that needs you in heaven.
There are many things we must do.
For it was you that lived for your grandchildren,
Not your grandchildren that live for you."

Katina Renee Frye

My Moma

I have always held my Moma close and dear to me.
She was always there when I needed her to be.

She was more than my Mother, she was also my friend.
When things got broken, she was first there to mend.

She raised this loving daughter and it took thirty-eight years.
Thru measles, mumps and chicken pox, marriage, kids, laughter
and tears.

Sometimes while looking in the mirror I never though that I would see
myself standing there, staring at my Moma, looking back at me.

Moma was strong when she needed yet at times, just like a child.
She never had to raise her voice, her temper was disciplined, but mild.

I didn't have a little girl, in which to share our name.
I gave my moma two grandsons, and she loved them just the same.

But now my Moma's gone, from this life, she's no longer a part.
But my Moma's not done, because she still lives in my heart.

Vikki Green

Lost Love

One day I met a pretty girl,
She was funny, cute and smart.
We walked together and talked together,
And soon she won my heart.
We started our life together
She was wonderful as could be.
She said "I love you truly,
You mean everything to me."
But soon, all that had changed and
She left me for another.
She broke my heart and I cried a lot,
I thought there was no other.
That could take the place of that beautiful girl.
That was my friend, my pal, and my lover.
I would like to say to this beautiful girl
That made my life a mess.
I hope your doing well in life,
And I wish to you my best.

Teddy Wiles Jr.

Thankful

A little girl was very ill,
She'd been that way so long.
Mother cared for her at home
Praying she'd grow strong.

Was medicine each quarter hour -
The Momma gave each one.
All thru the day and at night;
No calling, yet she would come.

Why don't you let her die one said?
She'd be better off you know.
But God did bless the loving care -
And health began to grow.

One day the doctor said "Give this child"
Anything she want's to eat.
And the maker did again restore -
The body to its feet!

I am that person;
And I owe so much...
To my sweet Mother,
And God healing touch.

Lillian Reed

Untitled

Sitting in my evening chair, moonbeam filling up the room
sheds light on clouded memories
old treasures brought anew

Memories of stepping stones I've walked on long ago
The strength I've gained from traveling on
through blinding, bitter snow

Ancient trees, strong and serene, I still hear their charming songs
The music of amorous days
in lush fields I've danced upon

Mother Earth and Father Sky, record keepers of it all
The seasons and the cycles
Such a joy to be involved

Contentment found in sitting here, in my evening chair
Reflecting on the miracles
with a smile from ear to ear

The mother and the father, below me and above
Know all my earnest footsteps
The truth, my soul, my love

Sheree Carroll

Lost In The Sky: A Moonlit Sonnet

Moonlit web of clouds lost in the sky, a lunar nightmare
Shooting through a galaxy of ice. The moon
Is a neon spider, dangling by a thread. I stare
At its white and ageless eye; it whispers my name. Its glowing dunes
Entice me to soar and touch its quivering
Black edge, but I am trapped under the lurking sky.
I listen to the stars as they are caught, one by one, shivering
In its topaz web. A mist covers the earth, hiding the mesh from
  my eye.
A crack of crimson thunder: Distant lightning erupts from nowhere;
The net is destroyed by the trembling rain.
My dripping eyes see the lonely moon; I want to be there,
Floating on the soft, crystal web, trapped with the stars. A train
In the distance pulls me back down.
Its hollow scream pulsates through this dark town.

Meri M. Harary

488

Games Of Torture

Horribly confined in such a small space,
Shouldn't it be hell that they call this place?
Deceiving shower look-a-likes,
Why not just puncture us with thorns and spikes?
Nerves shudder awaiting the torture,
Wrongly using cleanliness as a lure,
For, we're only humans scared out of our minds,
Trembling we await, is it water or gas we will find?
We use our strength to claw the brick wall,
Death awaiting us - Impossible to stand tall,
What is the obsession with persecuting a jew,
The oldest of torment - for Jesus is not new,
Silently scared - we await the end,
When suddenly water is what the faucets send,
Hearts are nervously aching and worn,
Fingers bleeding, and our nails are torn,
SS returning us to our beds for the night,
We can't leave or get out, security is tight,
So we save our fate for another day,
Wondering when in that pile of bodies we will lay.

Natasha Ann Young

Beginning Of A Journey

The plum trees had not yet begun to
show their pretty blossoms of white
and pink.

The birds with their white wings opened wide,
began knocking gently at each other's hearts.

The willow tree's branches swayed in the
gentle spring breeze,
making music only they could hear.

It was the beginning of a journey.
The coming together of two hearts.
A journey through a path of seasons
to come.

As the mystery of love continues
down a path now formed as one,
to add to the world as they
become one,
with all their love and devotion.

Michelle Croft

"Opposite"

Speaking to me with her eyes
Showing me her love in signs
I learned from her a gentle way
Whose silent world is everyday.

Her dainty hands that speak so softly
Is like a soft and gentle breeze
And when she signs the words "I love you"
I hold her close and we both can feel.

She shares with me my words of love
We smile to think we learned so much
From each other's opposite touch.
If everyone could feel our love
For sure, they will know
Their love comes from heaven above.

J. R. Edwards

Late August And Still No Rain

Prickly pear cactus pads, pale and yellowed,
Shriveled, like old unshaven faces,
Stand still in clumps of anticipation,
As survivors on rafts in a desert sea.

Dark pillow clouds sail heavy under gray,
While leaves, with not a quiver, wait.
Wait, for the dance to commence,
When neighbors sway and beats begin.

With a tap on one, and then another,
Drops lie dark, like coins, on dusty pads,
Anointing heads in a baptism of promise:
That skins will plump and firm with virile color.

But turquoise circles appear amid the billows,
Pushing, spreading against the shrouding gray.
Brave faces, craggy and still, listen: No drips, no drops.
And hope sails off... and into dry September.

Margaret Craig Chrisman

May We Know What We Are

Making the truth of us known.
Shuddering at what our Father told us.
He said: "No, you are not me."
What then could we be? cracks in the dust
that is us, afraid to bleed there —
No! We will bleed. We will bleed.
Develop hard hearts we'll never need,
blaming Father, who we stopped letting in.
Oh. I will say it again. Oh.
We have not earned our wings, and may.
We integrate it all as well as these billion years have
alone, and in our understanding, Father,
our anger then is laughter now, our anger now, is wind.

You called at 3 AM from a booth outside Asheville,
and said, "you're an angel."
You were leaving for the mesh of glassy-eyed streets.
The connection broken, I had to whisper "yes."

Yes.
Yes, Father, but you will not make our minds,
and we, may have eternity to pour our hearts.

Nik Morgan

Mystic Moon

Solemnly you shine down on the earth forming many kinds of silhouettes
As a still ball of light interrupting the darkness of night
With such intense beauty that for a moment the troubles of my mind
I seem to forget.
Glistening beams of blue listlessly brush the bare branches
of the season
Artfully casting dimly lit shapes like happy demons,
Yet rising steadily to greet the black sky, making way to wake
the red morning sun.
In mid-sky, at the midnight hour with your shades of blue-grey
silently shining through my window onto my face,
For a moment bringing my weary mind to a level of peace, presented
for me in your picture of such grace.
Into the twilight easing my emotions to a silent calm
This mystic moon intercepting the dawn
Briskly escaping over the horizon making way for the light of
this morning sun
While on the other side of the earth your beauty has just begun.

Linda D. Hutto

"Time"

Time is lonely, time is long
Since the day you walked into the sun
The sun grew dim, then shone again
But lacked the sparkle surrounding the rim.

Time,
The sparkle still shines, unable to be seen
It is charred, it is tattered
And hides with pain.

A special touch, a special love,
Can show the luster that remains
A special love few will know,
A special love only you will show.

Time can change,
With love that is shown
To be friendly and fast
Where time goes is unknown.

In time the sun will shine with a sparkling rim,
Living, loving and laughing again.
I look to the day of singing a song,
For now time is lonely, time is long.

Kelsey Kaelyn Kara

Father

This time that's passed has been so hard
Since you went away.

The feelings that we have inside
  No words could ever say.

We miss the presence that you had
And the love you showed in your own way.

It's especially hard at this time
Because it's Father's day.

Conversations are still spoken
as if you were still here.

Sometimes the pain is so very great
It's almost too much to bear.

We would give most anything
Just to have you here.

Rest assured father your
memory will never fade.

You're alive and well in our hearts and minds.
And there your sure to stay.

Kevin J. Abbott

Blue Sky And Calm Sea

Two years have passed
Since you went away
Time has gone by so fast
It seems like yesterday,
Only sometimes, when tears fall
And from some distant place I hear you call,
I cannot answer or go there,
For I know not why you call or from where,
So I must believe you are telling me
That where you are "blue is
  the sky and calm is the sea"

Verna M. Pomeroy

The Last Bird Cries

On that dark and dreary day by the seashore
Sits a lonely little girl whose heart has a
Hollow place within, but holds only a memory.
As she sits looking at the birds soar
Above the water she sees a face,
A face that smiles and watches the caps
On the waves fall onto the hot sand,
A face that laughs at the little fish jumping
And splashing.
Then the clouds part to show a sun that
Warms the land with not only its heat but its shine.
As the sun goes down it enters
The water where it sleeps with the
Fish. Then she knows that her lost one
Will always be with her just as the sun
Rises and sets. So she gets up as the
Last bird cries.

Rebeccah DeBlois

Untitled

As I pretend to pay attention,
Sitting in my English class.
It started day dreaming,
Waiting for the time to pass.

When my thoughts turned to you,
A friend of mine I truly trust.
I realized this was a thing I cherished,
And couldn't let it turn to dust.

I can't even count,
The number of friend I've had over the years,
But now when I think of it,
I start to shed my tears.

But then I come to reality,
And start thinking of today.
When my thoughts again turn to you,
And that you're just a phone call away.

So I guess what I'm saying,
Is I hope we always keep in touch.
This is really something,
That I would like very much.

Kris Krogstad

Angels

Angels are our friends who guide us with love,
Sitting on pillows made of clouds, they watch from above

Protecting us from danger and all that we fear,
It helps to know that these angels are always near

They wake us in the morning and kiss us good-night,
Hope and Love will be spread from them, so long as the sun shines its light

So the next time you hear a bell
And so gently it rings,

Think of the angel who was just granted his wings!

Noelle Pasatieri

Teenage Love

Feelings that are deep inside,
Something that I just can't hide,
You are my heart
And I hope we can make a new start,
We got's to be one and have a daughter or a son,
I want to live my life with you,
And I know you want the same thing too,
So get yourself together...
Don't let the system get you down forever.

Sue Hodge

Education In Alabama

A yellow stripe separated the black macadam - one side
slightly wider than the other. I walked in the gutted gully —
oil pigmented water pock marked puddles of mud. My ten-year-
old hands inspected the red lettering of a bent and rusted
Budweiser can. Faded, its label resembled the cold Alabama
clay. By the bus stop, I found a brown spot-rusted tool box near
the edge of the swamp. Like a small treasure chest, I broke the
clasp to open it. Inside, four puppies putrefied. Their skinned
bodies were swollen white and infected green. I didn't know
men used the pelts of runts for wallets and small leather purses. I
closed the metal coffin and sunk it in the swamp.

I was in third grade. Mrs. Williams wrote, in capital letters,
GOOD and BAD on a black board. Then, with yellow chalk,
drew a line between them. Making your bed, brushing your
teeth, eating your vegetables and caring for others were good.
Cursing, spitting and cheating were bad. On brown green-lined
paper I wrote, "Why Good's Better."

Walking home, after school, I scuffed my mud-caked Keds
and left brown strips across the yellow line. Behind
me the swamp's tar black surface still held the lesson of the day.
Ahead, the road stretched long like a black snake. At its tail
the yellow line faded, the two macadam columns appeared as one.

Marc Sharrar

Here I Am

As a child, everyone loved me because I was so innocent and
small but when I grew, I learned that innocent is only a
word for people who are unaware of the truth, I also learned
that being small only meant you didn't speak out for what you
believe in and who you cared about, so when I was neither,
people didn't seem to love me anymore…so how could I love
them back? Time passed and I felt alone but would not lose my
believes to join a crowed that had none, I always knew I was
different but people made it seem like being different was wrong,
so I didn't act like I cared…but really I was dying inside, yes, I
can feel hurt when I want too, and even sometimes I don't have a
choice though that is when my believes begin to grow even
stronger and I raise myself up and feel good, but other days I can
barely deal with my problems, I don't want to face them but I do.
I cry a lot in the middle of solving them sometimes, but that's
what makes me human, and yes maybe I do face these problems
alone but when the end is near I will relax and die with a smile
for I know that I've worked hard and tried my best but until then
my dreams are still out of reach and I must go on.

Kerstin Broughton

Pieces Of A Dream

Life - A piece of a dream
   Small pieces of an unfinished puzzle with no pieces ever the same
Each of us searching for our interlocking pieces of Life's puzzle.
   Some pieces - they never fit.
Others pieces - Never get tried.
   Yet, few ever fall into place.

Pursuing happiness is the CHALLENGE.
   Pain is the CONQUEROR.
You are the CONTROLLER.

Does this piece fit? It is too BIG? Is it to small?
   Or just doesn't really   at all?
                  FIT
No one is to say whether each piece will fit perfectly or not.
   You are the MAKER!
When the END is near, you'll know you have everything you've needed
   For your completed puzzle.

There'll be no more searching fitting or rearranging
   Your puzzle is finished and eternity is near
Your pieces of a dream are now…
   A dream gone by!

Paula Jones

CFS/FMS

Feelings of fear and discouragement
smother the joy I've lived this week-
Birthday cheerfulness has run away
like little wayward three-year-olds.
I feel lonely and scared again…
This cloudy, soulless beach is the scene I act in,
eroded by the wind, the wind, the wind…
The thick-lens glasses which focus my world
have blown off today, I see only colors - browns and grays
My bones and muscles ache and burn with unending pain.
An unseen band around my head is tightened by a hidden vise-
it makes me dizzy, off-balance and I stagger in the sand.
Gone are any boundaries, highway signs
the sun to tell me where to go; I'm frightened.
They say my mind may slowly die away-
They say my lost memories may never return.
Still others say it's all in my head, But
I'm living this "fiction", day after god-awful day…
this Chronic Fatigue Syndrome, this Fibromyalgia…
Joy is still here, but it's glazed with the colors of fear.

Linda D. Barnes

Untitled

Snow, cold and plain
Snow, sparkling and white
Snow, the fresh, alive, meaning of a perfect winter.
To look out a frosted window,
   only to see the deadness
   covered with a blanket.
To see a twenty-four hour day,
   And dream of a night that will never fall.
To awaken from a pretend sleep,
   In the dawning
   Of a sparkling, glowing earth,
   That is rising of the frozen angels downy.
Snow,
When you leave the earth's
   Barren ground,
   To walk on heaven's fluffy clouds.
Only to float back down,
   Within the melting of the days.

D. L. Karcher

Can We Go Swimming

It is spring it's getting hot,
   So can we go swimming?
Soon it will be summer then fall,
   After fall it will be winter again,
So can we go swimming?
   It's been a long time since we went in the pool.
Is it hot enough?
   Who cares if it's too cold.
If we can't go in the pool we will keep asking you,
   So please, if we can, we will try to be good,
So can we go swimming?
   Okay, go ahead,
But if it's too cold it won't be my fault.
   We know.
We went swimming and had so much fun.
   We stayed in the pool for over an hour.
It was a little bit cold,
   But we didn't care,
We were just happy that we could go swimming!

Summer Bezdek

Kyle

I dream of your young face in which I cannot see the mirror image,
So close yet so distant from my child of body.
Pain screeches through my tormented mind.
Yet distance is the sanity that keeps blind!
Forgive me for patiently waiting instead of on a steed charging.
I think daily of your peace, carefully contemplating deeds which
will not harbor envy.
To allow memories would be depletion of inner soul.
Lying, I grasp my heart in turbulent gasps of unrequited love;
Waiting for sweet youth to pass, tolerated only by visions of
welcoming arms outstretched to hungering maternal adoration.

Leverne H. Peterson

The Sacred Season

So Holy a place I chance upon,
So cold a day to crunch the snow,
Beneath my boots,
And wonder where I next shall shoot.

Not light enough, the air is still,
And yet I sense a presence still,
Of terraced shelters, vacant now,
Where man communed and once asked how,
To carve a village of clay and house,
And constructed dwellings, named Taos.

Where children's voices echoed remnant sounds,
Of laughter, giggles, sweet pronouns,
And women gathered to weave baskets,
Sorting seeds upon blankets.

A Baptism pouring begins to sleet,
In Snow I find I begin to weep,
Out a blessing
A witness, I am,
The Sacred Season....
                                    Commencing again.

Tresa Michele Niccoli

To America From The New Immigrant

   Oh! America! You were a dream,
So colorful, bubbly and frosty like cream;
I loved, I longed and waited to reach you,
the star spangled banner, beckoning like a rainbow;
The home of the brave, with freedom and liberty,
Oh! America, are you the land of opportunity?

I embrace you, oh the land of my dream,
I am the new pioneer, swimming against the stream;
"East is east and the west is west,
and the twain shall never meet,"
But America are you the true melting pot?
Brooklyn, Manhattan, they make me spellbound,
Man's highest achievement, oh! my adopted land;
The crime the violence, they make me scared,
But still I love you, for everything is shared;
Truly, I bow to you, thou the magnificent land,
Oh America, do you make me unwind?
I am the proud daughter of the east, so stunned,
To your new daughter, America, will you be kind?

Swarupa Rao

'Heaven'

I hear it has plenty of space.
So I'll keep running my race.
I hear the streets are paved with gold.
So when I get there I can take my stroll.
I hear the gates are made with pearls
Nothing like this you will ever see in this old world.
I hear the walls are made with the finest gem stones.

Surely when, I see this place I will not be alone.
Everyone who knows of this place will have already gone.

Sharon E. Emanuel

Heaven's Hotline

I heard heaven installed a hotline, 1-800-dial God;
So I dialed the number, although it did seem odd.
A recorded message answered, "You have reached the God hotline;"
From a touchtone phone press the right button at the right time.
Press one for prayer requests, two to save yourself;
Three for spiritual matters, four for healing and good health.
Press five for forgiveness, and six for information;
Please press the proper button for the line of your selection.
Just stay on the line if you have a rotary dial,
Someone will answer you, though it may take a while.
However if your call is of an urgent nature,
You might wish to try the following procedure:
Hang up the phone, get on your knees and open up your heart;
Pray directly to the Lord though you may not know where to start.
He will hear every word that you care to say,
And will surely answer you once you start to pray.
You'll have a direct connection, no hotline to impede,
God himself will answer your every want and need."

Patricia A. Hampson

For Mom

Spring has arrived and the flowers are in bloom this beautiful May.
So it's a wonderful time to show my love for you on this special
   Mother's Day;

We've eternally shared a special bond that words just can't describe.
And though times may change and circumstances arise, I know
   you're always by my side;

I know that God instills in all of us many special gifts.
And having your constant caring and support gives me an extra lift;

From the earliest that I can recall, you put us all above the rest.
From academics to playing bat and ball, you only asked that we
   do our best;

There's just a handful of the many things I wanted to say.
To let you know how much I cherish you in a very special way!

Kim Campbell

Love's Arrival

Tearful, anxious state of happiness...
So many emotions bombard my armored heart.

Unsure of how to define this fluttering feeling that
   resembles a high school crush...
      I just laugh at my plight.

Soothing, comforting and loving touch of healing...
      my heart welcomes you.

Yet this gentle hand of understanding and acceptance,
      confuses my fragile heart.
And this engulfing intimacy, brings a fearful feeling of joy.

With our new found gift, we are united by a common need
      desire, attraction and spirit.
And with slightest touch of two hands... a new love begins.

MAG

So Tired

I be so tired that I can't see straight,
so tired and my feet do surely ache.
So tired that simply thinking is a chore
my eyes want to close and my ears hear no more.

I be so tired that I can't taste what's going down my throat.
If I had a ticket and some cash, I'd still miss that boat.

My nose is so numb that I couldn't even smell
if the house was burning down or I was on my way to H_ _ _!

Well Father Time ain't gonna be proud of me,
cause I be so tired I can't even sleep.

Tiahuana D. Vaughan

The Last One

With pen in hand the mind races -
So much to talk about - yet nothing to say.
I've written about love, joy, peace, sorrow and death,
  the up's and down's, the in's and out's.
The pen wobbles, my tears fall.
The pain is unexplainable.
I stand before you a broken woman.
You have finally accomplished that.
My mind and body never rest anymore.
Your words have been like a knife -
The wounds are so deep, so open.
I see no way they can ever heal.
You've broken my heart, but more than that
  you've broken my spirit.
This is it, the end -
With the last word, I will lay down the pen,
- And I will write no more.

Mary Ellen Dietz

Masks

I have many masks I hide behind
So no one knows what's on my mind
The hurts, joys, pain, and strife
That come to me while living life
I hide behind so no can see
The hurts and disappointments inside of me
I hide the hurts also the joy
"Act like a man" they said "not a little boy"
So I made my masks I made them well
Then I looked at my mask and said this is swell
Now I'm safe behind my mask to keep it on isn't even a task
I couldn't show love or that I care
I sometimes rarely thought it isn't fair
Then one day I was surprised to find
My masks were shackles on my mind I looked at myself hard and
  I found
I made all the masks to which I was bound
Hiding behind my masks I was shocked to find I couldn't express
What was on my mind on that day I was surprised to see
My masks were much to small for me so finally my masks
I threw away and without them face the light of day

Terry M. Taylor (deceased)

submitted by Trevor M. Taylor (father)

And She Walks

And she walks
So quietly no soul can hear
Along her tightrope
Up in the sky
Above the world destruction
Insanity of life and love
Borrowing angel wings
To keep afloat
Poised with book of expectation on her head
Dreams of dancing
But carefully she walks in one straight line
Still no sound or sight of destination
Afraid to blink
Afraid of strain or slack
She must cajole the scared and lonely child
Within her breast
And smile incase someone sees her face
A cry suppressed by tears, suppressed by the weight
Of the rope
Pressing up against her tiny feet.

Kirsten Thorpe

Your Smile

Your smile is like an oasis
so refreshing, so cool.
So many of my days are filled
with dryness, emptiness, and boredom.
I drag on like a weary man on an endless journey...
but then I see your smile.
It lights up my soul like a
shooting star flashing across the sky.
It makes my burdens lighter, easier to bear.
I know I can't see your smile often,
so I picture it in my mind's eye.
It has tolerance, patience;
as though time didn't matter.
It's a smile that endures
all the rough edges of life
and emerges victorious.
It's a smile tinged with love, too.
I hope it will always be there for me,
because I'd go through a month of nightmares
as long as I could wake up to your smile.

Susan Rose

"When A Mother Dies"

My mother was a beautiful California red-head,
  So sensitive, so caring, so gentle, and yet sedate,
But the died and left this vale of tears
  Before she had reached the age of forty-eight.

She had brought six healthy children into this world
  But her oldest son, Francis, died in an accident, before she
  passed away,
And her next oldest, Oliver, was away working when she died,
  Which left the four youngest of us kids, who seemed to be
  in the way.

Our father then promptly, put us in the orphanage in L.A.
  Where we all went to different homes, and I went to stay
With a lady in pasadena, 'til she took me back to the orphanage,
  But by that time, my sister and two brothers had been taken away.

Then I went to live, where my older sister, Mary, was living,
  But she resented me now, because she was the first one there,
And I interfered with her new-found status as an "only child",
  So she tolerated me, but not because she cared.

Eventually we made a trip, with our guardian to a ranch in southern Cal.
  Where we stumbled, by accident, on our older brother, Fred,
  living there
And many years later, he found our younger brother, Robert,
  But not before twenty-one long years had passed, of hope and
  prayer

Martha Thompson

"Born To Live, Love, And Die"

As sure as we have lived and loved,
so surely some day must we also die.
But let us not fret or worry when,
for it is more comforting to know just why.

He places us here just for a visit,
and soon summons us back to His fold.
He also summons back our loved ones,
and it hurts, whether they are young or old.

Sometimes we doubt His reason for this,
but we know that He is always just.
If His plan for us is designed this way,
then live, love, and someday die we must!

J. B. White

Revelation

I awoke early this morning with thoughts filling my head -
So urgent did they seem to be - I sat straight up in bed...
I thought of all the Blessings that GOD had sent my way,
And how He'd been beside me, as I faced each dawning day.

No matter what the problems were; how hard might be the task,
It only took a fervent prayer - for guidance, and to ask
That GOD would let His will be done and give me strength to do
Whatever was His will for me. He always pulled me through.

Not always as I wanted it - but what He knew was best
I learned how to accept this, and leave to Him the rest.
Because you know, there's no one else on Earth to hear my plea
But GOD is here - thru Jesus Christ - to always answer me.

Nellie C. S. Robinson

A Mother's Love

So sweet and cherished right from the start.
So warm and giving straight from her heart.
To give equal shares, she can only try.
To be tried and tested as time goes by.
Her scars too numerous to even name.
Her God stays near to help ease her pains.
A Mother's Love;
Sometimes too tough, at first it seems.
Sometimes a swift kick gives vision to big dreams.
I'm sure this love's one only "God" can surpass.
I'm sure if there's more, our youths can last.

A Mother's Love;
In time you'll see it helped nurture
And make strong. So respect it now
Because when she's gone she's forever gone.

But at the end you will know, it was
The unselfish giving of that love
That lets her spirit forever
Live on.

Lewis Wright, Jr. II

Blind Man

If only I could see this place
so when curious eyes burn on my face
I could focus my dumb pupils, stare
these spheres back at them. It would only be fair.
I wonder what it's like to go outside
and squint and have to hide
them with cupped hands from the sun.
Would there be any less to overcome?

As I rest here on one side
of a bench, I do not want to hide
from whispers of a little child. No shame.
I do not mind the game
she plays to test my ghastly sight.
The motions of her hands might
sometimes even make me smile.
Now, she wants me to feel her profile
but the wiser voice takes her away
to teach her to be afraid
of me, to teach her how to pity.

Linda Abadjian

Untitled

I know you,
strength.
You are my biggest fear faced—
spontaneously and unpaced.
When I walk up to you and away, unscarred;
I then know you (as)
courage.

Valerie Johnson Cloud

"The Love I Want"

There is so much love in my heart.
So why am I lonely?
I just want to give a part...
I want to love one only.
Love is so hard to find.
Where can you go mingle?
I want to be with someone and have peace of mind.
I'm not happy being single.
Some may think I have everything.
Because I'm young and have my own.
But my phone doesn't even ring.
And most of the time I'm all alone.
All I want is to be with someone who has the same interest as me.
Sometimes I feel I'm asking too much.
I want a love that will forever be.
Now I'm beginning to feel it's impossible to find such.
But I'm going to keep my hope strong.
And I will find my true love one day.
If it's true love it can't be wrong.
It should last forever and a day.

Alastair

There Was A Method To My Madness

When you were a baby, I played for you the musical carousel,
so you'll be soothed, reassured, and not be afraid.

When you were a toddler, beginning to differ wrong from right,
I began to play the role that would set you off, on your way,
to lofty heights.

When I felt spooked and paralyzed, I closed my door so I can hide,
from you, the trepidation I felt inside. And at night, I turned the
lights off in your room, but in mine, I turned them on. You see,
my love, in actuality, and deep inside, I couldn't master the courage
I was trying to convey to you, I was much too petrified.

I wanted you to be confident where I was hesitant, strong where I
was weak.
To be convincing where I was vague, and assertive where I was
meek.

There wasn't anything or anyone I couldn't have short of you.
And, the only one who could ever have me, oh, my darling, was you.

Your brother raveled despondently, to have just a part of me.
But, he may just as well have been the man on the moon.

It was my ploy, baby, you're not to blame. It was produced
through love, acted by the heart, and with me the only cast.

Here is what I wanted you to be......
Here is what I wanted for you.....Infinity

Reema Ghuntos-Salloum

Mask Of Secrets

The mask I wear covers many secrets
Some of love and hatred.
Some of sorrow and pain,
And some of terrible lies.

I cannot bare to take my mask off,
But sometimes it's taken away.
When it is, only little is let out,
For that shall keep me safe.
I will only take off my mask for people I trust
And never for anyone else.

There are good secrets of love and friendship
and there are bad of hatred and lies.
For the secrets of sorrow and pain are of heart break and death
And things that never should of happened to me.

Someday I will dispose of this mask and tell all I know and feel.

Everyone has a mask of some kind or sort
Except the wise, because they left their mask behind long ago.

Kristina Hurkmans

New Wonders

Sometimes in life things happen
Some things you would like to change.
They do sometimes gappen.
Even when they are shortly out of range.
They turn out pretty and bright
They make the world go around
You learn to see they are all right
And sometimes bring new treasures to be found
They bring you happiness and love
They bring you joy and sorrow
They help you to see above
Whatever happens tomorrow
They show pain and tears
They bring new friendships to find.
Memories come into the years
Of every single different kind
A person makes you realize some things
You will grow out of home
This kind of love especially sings
A friendship all on its own.

Stacy Ring

The End

I saw a flash of light but never heard a sound.
Somehow my life had ended, I was no longer on the ground.
I had a place to go. I had someone to see.
I did not know where or who, a voice kept calling me.
I saw the roads before me, ones I thought I could not make.
But it soon became very clear, there was only one that I could take.
The way was long and hard though I did not seem to care.
The only thing that mattered was, I had to make it there.
When I saw what I had seen... that wonder before my eyes.
It was hard for me to really believe... somehow I had died.
The air was fresh and still, the light was a brilliant glow.
I felt a pleasant warmth that came from down below
I saw a figure before me It was someone I could not go by.
His presence there was puzzling me, I had to find out why.
He looked at me... smiled... and in a soothing voice He said,
"Don't be afraid... I won't hurt you, I'm only just a friend."
I asked my friend about my death and He just shook his head.
"The people down on Earth," He said, "Took the world to the end".

Michael Carnahan

That Special Person

There is a special person made for everyone on this earth,
Someone that's been created for us from our time of birth.
We are expected to find one another to share each others joys,
Then one day we are to marry, then raise children girls or boys.
As searching for the person made especially for you,
Thou must find the patron whose love for them is true.
True love is not defined by the things one does for you,
And true love cannot be judged by the way two people screw,
You cannot find your true love through ways listed in any books,
Nor can this love be found by the way this person looks.
Don't expect to find this person having them judged by your friends,
Instead you must search your heart for a love that extends.
Finding that special person may take a thousand tries,
But when found you'll know this person upon gazing in their eyes,
For if you look down deep enough you will find no lies,
Instead you'll see your freedom as it starts to rise.
This freedom will be found even if they aren't around,
For a persons freedom hunts them like a tracking hound.
So once you've found the person with your freedom in their life,
You've found the special person to be your husband or your wife.

Scott Douglas Stone

"Stay Gold"

Within your heart, something golden is true
Something golden, most never knew
Very few have it, they don't have a clue
Those who have it, all they would do

It is always there, any given day
Some who sees it, stands at bay
Some accept it, in a special way
Others want to, they do pray

It's called true love, a love from above
Delivered to you, by a silver white dove
There is nothing more, to know of
Than this love, that is called true love

Within ourselves, it is there
A rainbow so bright, so very rare
A love so golden, with so much flare
A love of one, that takes a pair

Two as one, it is so bold
So many things, could unfold
Within your heart, a love untold
Within your heart, you must stay gold!

Norman L. Detro

What Is Truth?

It's being honest and just
something that might be worthy of trust.
It's being frank, open, sincere and fair
being untrue will get you nowhere.
It's telling the truth that could be a task,
but honesty is the best policy, is there reason to ask?

It's uprightness of character no need to corrupt
unless you want someone to slowly erupt.
It's correctness and accuracy that will make it just right,
but don't play games, it might end in a fight.

Take it from me who has told some white lies,
it's better to be truthful, because it is easier to get by.
So when it comes to reality, fact and being true
the truth behind everything is up to you.

Michelle Holtman

A New Beginning

The flowers bloom, birds sing
Somewhere out in the world a
  young girl wakes.
Her life now full of hope and
  prosperity.
Addicted to drugs and alcohol,
  her life was messed.
Now she wakes every morning
  enjoying life and a second chance.
Just to be thankful she goes to
  the park and visits everyone
  and everything.
Her life renewed, refreshed.
She looks at life with a different view.
Joyful.
Happy.
Content.
A new beginning.

Liz Diedrich

Celia

My eyes blink and I arouse ever so slightly.
Soon I am drifting with only my mind's eye to guide my travels.
Like a bird I float through the air admiring the countryside.
I see rolling hills to the north and inviting gardens to the south.
I see a pond overflowing with water lilies and I descend to
    rest on its neighboring gazebo.
The intoxicating aroma of azaleas, roses, camellias, and magnolias
    overcome my senses.
Suddenly she appears and everything else fades...
The moonlight glistens on her light brown skin.
Her long white gown gently billows in the breeze and I am
    mesmerized by her beauty.
In an instant I realize that she is the essence of my dreams.
From her longing eyes, supple smile, and her soft, rounded
    breasts to the north,
To her beckoning southern valley where gentlemen only dream
    to travel.
A robin chirps nearby and she turns and then disappears.
I awaken and look around the room...
There she is...
She is my partner, my soul mate, my future, my wife,
And as I lean to greet her and our lips touch to start the new day,
I return to the garden and once again my dreams come true.

    Perry J. Jeffrey

Moonlight

    filtered through the gently moving clouds
  Speaking softly
of the space   many seek yet few find
  Lost in the maze of daily affairs
    rarely stopping to listen
      to the moonlight
        Speaking softly
          of a tale told throughout time
A tale of Love
A tale of Truth
A tale of Kindness
  words set against a starry sky
accented by the brilliant flash
 of the meteor racing through the night
    paying tribute with its very life
 to the moonlight
    Speaking softly

      Can you hear it?

    Russell O'Brien

Untitled

The brilliant orange sphere dipped below the cumulus border
spraying radiant pink and lavender across the horizon
Exposed to the New England town, the belly of the clouds
took but a hue of the grandeur, sustaining a stubborn grey
The pinnacle of the church steeple, peeling white,
pointed towards the heavens as if casting blame

A boy, with visions of promises made and pirates at sea
patiently waited, watching the traffic and clinging to faith
Lights flashed and passed as anticipation faded to despair
Clutching and sliding down the deeply gouged oak
the aging child's sneaker failed to hold the bark
His knee skidded and scraped, shivers proclaimed defeat

The tear, so long held back, swelled and spilled over
trailing his cheek with renewed zeal and validation
Bravely, the young man rubbed his eyes with soiled palms
Kicking the frozen earth, he stuffs his hands in his pockets
Glancing back, he spies a lone vehicle drift over the rise
Hope expands from desolation and deflates in anguish

Casting his held breath into the crisp air, his head hung
The path he wandered led to a house but less a home.

    Michael Hazard

The Old Man By The Sea

Angry surf lashes pathless sands. The old man walks
sprightly in rhythmic motion, azure winds etched in
his tanned, bearded face. His wiry body clad in
tattered blue, harmonious with twinkling eyes.

Musingly he proceeds, pattering prints of his bare
feet, observing cast away shells, sandcastles of loving
design crumbling, as dreams, slowly vanishing into
predestined time. His overgrown, snowy hair streaming.
A knapsack holds his most cherished possessions - the
wisdom of the ages of gleaming.

    Stefanie Kalinoski

Spring

Spring is like a sunset over a hill
Spring is like a bird flying by
Spring is like winning winter
Spring is like a whole new adventure of nature
Spring is like seeing fresh water
Spring is like a lot of bass
Spring is like falling into damp grass
Spring is like planting trees
Spring is like no more bad weather
Spring is like a fresh garden
Spring is like doing whatever you want
Spring is like taking a trip that is not cancelled by a winter storm
Spring is like having races against the wind
Spring is like feeling a nice breeze - not too cold
Spring is like riding your bike as long as you want
Spring is like seeing no more snow
Spring is like no more homework just recess
Spring is like having a lot of recess
Spring is like a whole New Year

    D. J. Ford

Creation

Anxiously awaiting mammoth trees.
Spring is so near in season,
awakening trees, stretching branches.
Buds are blooming so prettily,
dainty flowers are everywhere.
Intricate details in design showing beauty.
Suns splashing warmth on me,
it's all just in spring.
Take a peek just one,
explore the earth with curiosity,
tantalize your senses, enjoying it.
Just everywhere with fragrance.
Evidence of God's craftsmanship so wonderful,
joy all around us,
is always so perfectly for me.
Cardinals song very boisterously,
sweet to my ears every time.
I'm so very jubilant!

    Summer Lermon

JOY

It came like a hummingbird alighting a peony,
    Staying like a spider spinning its web.

Permeating the entire being,
    Rejoicing with what was, what is and what will be.

Seemingly, it is a rare and special gift,
    Arriving after processing several losses.

Bringing experienced reality,
    Centering was reached.

Is this brought inexplicable JOY?

    Lena Feiner

The Image

Into the fathomless well —
Spring of life —
Peering but not yet seeing.

The nadir holds mystery — and love.
Dark but not sinister,
Deep but not cold,
Fluid but not weak,
Calm but not stagnant,
These waters wash over me,
Healing me, enlivening me, supporting me.

The source is deep within — and pristine.
Truth but not finite,
Light but not shadow,
Pure but not simple,
Eternal but not unreachable,
This image comes to me,
Filling me, encouraging me, guiding me.
Into the fathomless well —
Spring of life —
Peering but not yet seeing.

Nancy J. Rainwater

Surrender

Red-hot it slashes through me
Stabbing licks of flame
Cutting with each drawn breath
Leaving me a gaping wound bleeding
A mass of nerve endings rubbing raw

Pain primal surrounds invades
In sleep pursues me
Relentless it lifts me up to slam me down
With searing dreams that crush

Haunting images their blank faces decades-old
Refused me love and worse
Savaged me ignoring my tortured cries

Then melds into now as
Long and loud I still scream
Beyond tears
In agony my lifelong constant

Too broken and weary to heal
I surrender
Now there is only the pain
I am no more

Kathy E. Hook

Innocents

Irrefutable vigorous passion
storm on my emotions.
My system is lightning,
inflamed, an erotic carnivore
rapid fire reverberating responding spreading.
Raging war against my eroticized maidenhood.
Surging hormones pierce,
my reasoning strong will.
Bleeding and weak it tries to consociate.
Scared tissue reach begging for help.
Lacking strength, utters a shrill cry.
GOD SAVE ME!
shrieking hormone laugh at their victory!
But from within a small voice is born,
Frail and wet it weeps, with Gods help.
Immediately silence is heard.
Then with newly impregnated force,
No, no, my body screams,
Virtue breaks forth and consoles my famished lioness.
I discover, with God's help I have won!!

Tiayu R. Hage

Friendship

We gazed, each upon the other and began to dance to the syncopated steps of desire. Slow was the rhythm; the air charged with the electricity that dancers feel upon surrendering thought to the hypnotic beat of an ever so sweet sound.

We danced. Now moving to an altered beat, our bodies involuntarily harmonized to the new score. Our minds were partially released from the old spell, and formed a new connection in time to the new beat. We swayed, enjoying the closeness while the dictates of our own minds began to echo.

We danced. The orchestra played now a changed melody. Through the cooled temperature of the other's body and the sharpening consciousness of the other's mind, we felt a connection remain. We enjoyed the new movement, for though different, it was fulfilling.

We danced. Staccato beats now filled the air. Laughter ceased. Instincts sharpened. Steps became broken. Our bodies struggled to retain what our minds had lost. In your eyes I saw the fear, the frustration, the passionate rage, which were the mirrored projections of my own eyes. We each turned, eager to walk away, to escape to solemnity's comfort.

The orchestra played on. Smooth sounds at once filled the air. We swayed, once again in time to the music; once again in time to each other. Laughter filled the air, connecting our minds by a different thread. You moved. I moved. Our steps not mirror images, but beautifully choreographed productions of our independent minds.

As we each looked into the eyes of the other, we then knew the truth. We had danced all the while, not to a variety of disconnected compositions but to one and only one splendid song; the title of which was friendship.

Valerie Straughn

She Sometimes Looks My Way

In the light of a room where neon
  Stirs the images of people into
A mix of moving cubes, cold as freon,
  I saw a glow begin to warmly issue.

Not a place for noticing the unique,
  A class room is the usher of bland
Objects and persons worth little critique.
  Yet, I see the wave, that flaming hand.

You defy the dull, witless working white
  That pervades the room and fills
The foggy faces, void of the power of sight.
  Your gestures come clean, no frills.

You work the night in ambulances, scurrying about
  The city in search of the hurt,
While I lay awake in torment, torn with mind-gout
  With the memory of a minor flirt.

Your early arrival, badge on your chest with pride
  Is the sign of commitment to a cause,
Progress, the rush to class after the night-ride.
  You look and leave my heart in pause.

Lewis Field

"Richard's" A Little Bake Shop

Tis a little Bake Shop with flavors of long ago,
Tasty treasures being, baked in ovens all aglow.
Plump fresh berries and fruits so tartly sweet,
Baked in cakes and muffins for another special treat.
OLD WORLD breads and bagels of forgotten days gone by,
Flavors waken taste buds and memories with a sigh.
A very special Bake Shop and a very welcome place,
RICHARD'S is its formal name, with a very friendly face.

Sunny Santry

A Special Man

This man I knew
stood tall and proud
spoke of forgiveness
and led a big crowd.

He knew he was of importance
but people did not believe
that this man could do so much
and that he had a dream to see.

He wished all people could live in harmony
So that we all could be free
and everyone would have rights
just like you and me.

So listen closely
you'll hear freedom ring
let the sound remind you
of Dr. Martin Luther King.

Nieves M. Aguon

Soldier Of Fate

Tranquility is hard to find, in my world of constant change.
Strength a virtue I wear as my shield, carrying me into war.

My casualties many, I crawl to my destiny. High above the
clouds of darkness, and rain, I fly on.
Physically not as whole, as when I started. Invisibly stitched,
and bandaged. I move on.

No strategy in mind, but my stature survives. I rise to the
challenge life bestowed upon me.
The map of my war, unclear, fogged with some fear. I fight on.

Gathering peace in my small victories. Vehemently pushing
aside enmity as my alliance. I stumble on.
Victorious in allowing amnesty, to the misconceptions I have,
of the soldier, I should be!

Lonnie Jean Frost Whipple

Depression

It sneaks up behind you slowly.
Sucking all the light from the world.
Sucking the laughter from your soul.

Its tentacles surround your heart.
Surround your mind.
Surround your being.

No one recognizes you anymore.
Your family. Your friends.
Your own reflection in the mirror.

Its grasp tightens. Your struggle weakens.
It drags you into the ebony pit
Down and down. Deeper and deeper.

Pain. . . Empty. . . Alone.

Kathy L. Nichols

My Mind

My mind is whirling with dangerous thoughts,
Strange, Weird, Wrong thoughts.
These horrible thoughts are buzzing
through my mind like bees,
flying, bumping into each other.
Stinging my mind every moment of everyday.
My mind soars like an eagle before the sunrise.
My mind is running with the cheetahs,
Faster and faster.
I can't stop, I can't slow down,
Or change the course.

Nesreen Mahmoud

Friends

They endure your chatter.
Suffer your vacation slides.
Loan you their car.
Sometimes feed your cat.

Then, one day you're feelin' low.
And there they are.

They offer helping hands.
Give you a great big smile.
Tell you how great you look.
Let you know they care.

Suddenly, you know things aren't so bad.
This too shall pass.

You count your blessings.
Feel that glow inside.
Voice your feeble thanks.
Wish you could do more.

You just hope they know.
You care for them as they for you.

Marjorie A. Crutchfield

What Are The Children?

Children are the seeds of immortality...
    sunshine for the soul...
    the ultimate true satisfaction.

They reflect the liquid sheen of innocence...
    the bubbling curiosity that makes the smallest event an
    adventure...

    The joyous excitement that spills over and affects everyone
    who is near...
    the sweet trust that bolsters confidence and self-esteem.

Who does not enjoy the mirroring of personality traits...
    the use of words...or the revealing qualities that show the
    world that this is your child indeed!

They are God's greatest tools to develop our patience, love,
    and sacrifice.

Ruth Swanson

"Flower Man"

Wiping the sweat from your brow
Swatting the dirt off your knees
Still holding on to your trowel
You step back to look at your first trees

Your tender hands have given all their worth
Now take the time to feel the fading sun
Come back to the arms of mother earth
Come, rest your body now that the job is done

So many seasons have come to pass
Leaving behind treasures of future's youth
Buried underneath fields of grass
Waiting for your to tend to their truth

All the colors will bloom in full array
Golden petals will shimmer with the dew
Your treasures will grow every passing day
With tomorrow's sun they'll shine anew

Tim Shelton

"If I Were To Write A Song..."

I'd begin at the end, and
swell the music into your ear backward, But
not by force. It would be like a wave brings
pebbles to the edge. I'd carry the little notes
like they were delicately written on paper, and
I'd take them to your heart; and I'd kiss you
  twice,
  once for the angels, and
  another for beauty.

  I'd arrange the colors on
A rhythm line like an "S" or a "C", and
those lines would fashion their magic around
your lips. The only other thing I'd do is
  cry for you,
  for a song like this
  would crack the radio
And cause the grace of deity to stop the
diseases of your mind. Those tears, mine,
would cause the song to start.
  And it would.

  William A. Herring

Laughter

Laughter tingled like an icicle
  Swinging in the wind
Sparkling like diamonds.
The resonance rich and ripe.

Our hero left us with a firm clasp of his hand
  and envisioned many bright tomorrows waiting to encircle
  friends and family.

Eyes bright, ablaze with hope
  the man turned and strode away
  engulfed in the madness and wilderness of war.

This hero of war returned dead to life on
  earth

No more tingling laughter which sounded like
  tinkling glass swaying in the breeze, no more handshake or
  eyes ablaze.

No chance to love
  Ruth Torres

Roses In The Dark

I am most certain roses never sleep.
Switch on the light
And you will see how bright
They stand. They are too proud to weep
Or bend. And shadows cannot sweep
A pall upon the flushing beauty which this night
Has freshened and made lustrous to delight
Those who a rendezvous with roses keep.

Do roses lie awake and dwell upon
The frogs which all night sing and frolic in the pond,
Or so much love the quiet time between
The hours of sunset and of dawn to feel serene?
Or do they choose this time to meditate
In patient solitude. Perhaps they only wait.

  Marjorie B. Walker

Free Gun

Gunshot
Takes my sight
Blackout is my night
Will I break?
Earthquake
Rips through my mind
Pain and hate the only survivors I find
Up in a pillar of flame, down in a storm of ash
It fills my mouth and nose with its taint
And brings back the past
Flashflood threatens
To carry me away
Hope
Keeps me hanging on for just another day
Will I ever win?
Fragments explode
Pierce my lungs and heart
Choke on my own blood, the world disintegrates apart
Serenity covers me like a shroud as the guns go silent
Did I win?

  A. Jeff Allen

The Contest

Across the field, the opponent waits, we here at home do too.
Teams sit quiet; sweat beads pop; jerseys stick like glue.
Stomachs knot, numbers blur, salt water stings the eyes;
But then the captains take the field; both teams, bands, crowd arise.

Anthem rings, it echoes back; stars and stripes a waver.
The crowd, the teams, the feel is there; sure it's a time to savor.
Sing out the words loud, clear and strong, emotion wells our eyes;
Same words, same song, same sweet refrain, yet goose bumps
  crawl our sides.

Song sung and o'er, the whistle shrills; adrenaline flows like light;
Contest begins, teams strain and groan, sweet victory in sight.
Win some, lose some, the way the saying goes;
But deep inside the hurt's for real; to lose, "Oh, Heavens No!"

Game is done, the die is cast; victors gloats in glory;
Losers weep and wail their loss, and therein lies the story.

  Marilyn P. Gulley

"My Youth"

Sadness and despair pity them.
  Tears of joy embrace them.
    The qualities of my youth linger, deeply rooted in my face.
    Ambitious memories fall flat, all hope is crushed.
      The ambiguousness of the night frightens me,
        Obscene gestures of the mind atrophy.
          Obscure desires await me amorous feelings reject me.
            The passion, total darkness,
              My character is altered, crippled inside
              My youth is destroyed.

  Michael Bingham

Painting

Paint you a picture?
Sure, what of?
Okay, try this on for size:
Lazy summer days blowing by like the wind.
Too big? Well...
Okay try this on for size:
The morning sun washed the room in a golden mellow light.
Too small? Well...
Okay, try this on for size:
You and I holding hands and smiling.
Oh, you're happy?
I wouldn't give it up for the world.
Paint it yourself.

  Marta Lucus

Snippets Of Time - Clare J. Morse

Listen! Do you hear the song of the cicada,
  telling nature to begin to rest

Do you see a tinge of gold or red in the leaves
  and the robin's empty nest

Look! South go the geese and ducks screaming,
for the young must learn to get into the vee.

My little chipmunk by the drain pipe, Mr. Rabbit,
Mrs. Squirrel wonder what winter will be.

  My fat black cat and I know:
We feel the gentle fall breeze came thru the window,
Midnight is curled in my lap as I sew,

Knowing our winter will be warm and cozy
With thoughts of Spring, warm sun, a pink posy

  C. Jeanne Brown

As Freedom Rings

Today, he closed his eyes for the final time,
telling those he loved:
"Now don't you cry
for I am glad to be in heavenly skies.
So far away from my earthly bound prison;
That shell of a man who could only rise
to a happy occasion in my mind.
My smile danced for me,
and my eyes sought the tops of trees.
Now, I have climbed one
and have looked down upon you.
What a wonderful sight I see!
I am running through the fields,
stretching my legs, and I am singing,
as freedom is ringing through my soul!
Grieve, if grieve you must!
But keep in mind, I'm a new man now,
I feel young and robust!
There's a new spring in my steps
and my freedom rings!"

  Tina Fayta

Ageless Tree

Ageless tree, branching to the north of the sea. As we grow old,
  not telling us of our destiny.
A woman of youth, bearing all the burdens of life
Facing the tranquility of losing one, physical youthfulness of life
Her heart full with thoughts and feelings she shall never share
Giving with love and the utmost care. Ageless tree, why does
  this have to be?
She can hear the rustling of your leaves, the sweetness in the
  early morning breeze.
Oh mighty tree, why does one not see? She is much greater now,
  because she has to be.
For it is true, she doesn't see as well, but age has given her
  plenty to tell.
It's true she can't move nearly as fast, but age has taught her to
  grow older with grace and class.
It is true her skin is not as smooth, but does that make her a fool?
She hasn't done anything wrong, but there she sits all alone..
When in reality she should be put upon a throne, for she has
  been the overseer for so long.
The young have forgotten, but time has not.
So ageless tree, tell us your secrets so we too can be set free.
To tell our children age is not destiny, it is a transformation from
  a sprouting bud.
To a garden of love, pairing off into the freshness of a flower
Drifting in the air, with peace and love without a care.
Farewell to my ageless tree, standing proud for all to see. Age
  is beautiful as can be.

  Sharon D. Adams

'Silent Footsteps'

Silence of your footsteps …
Tells me you are near,
I cannot see your image … A whisper I do hear,

A special surge of love within …
Truly, truly endures,
By your silent footsteps … around me which occurs

A soft touch on my shoulder …
I turn around to see,
Just an empty, vacant space … occupied only by me,

Your presence is around me … everywhere I go,
I know your silent footsteps …
By visions you often show

I never am alone … I'm free from all my fears,
It's by your silent footsteps …
That will guide me through the years,

My hands stretch forth to touch you…
I know you touch me back
Because your silent footsteps …
Will keep us all on track

  Shirley J. Russell

Man

His dream begins the same.
  Tempting the beast within his savage core.
  He gnaws his teeth upon the warm flesh encompassing her sex.

The dream continues.
  Wearing the mask of civility he speaks his words of eloquence.
  He pretends his appetite can be suppressed.

But still he craves the blood meat teeth and flesh.

The sleepwalkers.
  Roaming through the streets.
  He shudders at the thought he detests.

The enlightened being.
  Sharing her razor.
  He tickles his wrist in a gentle quest.

Always craving the blood meat teeth and flesh.

  Leila Ben-Joseph

Southern Night

The soft southern night,
Tender as a long remembered song,
Soothes and comforts
A young girl's heartache.
Blue mist rising
From a moon-sparkled lake
Wraps itself healingly
Around the silent heartbreak.
After a time, hearing the mockingbird's night call
Beckoning from above,
The heart calms and grows strong.
The hurt cannot resist
The glorious song,
And soon answers
With its own sweet song.
The soft southern night,
Tender as a long loved song,
Brings peace
To the girl in the moonlight.

  Walter L. Blumenthal

Our True Image

Owe no man anything but love
That does not mean that you will always please him
Be true to yourself first of all
Extend that truth, and then you will release him

"This above all to thine own self be true,"
As Shakespeare said - he must have known the plan
"And it must follow as the night the day
Thou canst not then be false to any man,"

Let us go on into the full expression
Of that pure image which the Father gave us
No longer building on some other form
Except the form of Christ given to save us,

Remove the garb that your love piled upon you
Don't hide your essence from your brothers' eyes
When you have cast off all those old dead fig leaves
You'll find in nakedness your beauty lies.

Allow your image to be blurred no longer
Because transparent for everyone to see
You will encourage others to be stronger
In their true image, which is you and me

Margaret Siracusa

Grandmother's Prayers

My grandmother would pray each night
That God would keep us in his sight
And hold us with his strong arm
Away from danger hurt and harm

When day was done and all were fed
And we were safely in our bed
She said "God watch them while they sleep.
And through the night their souls to keep"

She would get down on her knees
And asked the Lord for mercy please
On sinners who have lost their way
And bring them into the fold to stay

She prayed for our mothers and fathers too
To bless them and help them in all they do
To raise each child with patience and love
And to each one about God above

To wake us up in our right mind
And learn to leave our sins behind
Thank you God for grandmother's prayers
I cannot forget her love and her cares

Rosa J. Byrd

"Until The World Ends"

Although I prayed that you would stay
that horrible day came when you moved away.
The promise you made to keep in touch
    couldn't have meant very much.
I've written and called but you will not respond
I guess time has stolen our special bond.
It's been over a year but one thing isn't quite
clear - how I've survived without you here.
I thought for sure my life would end
the day that I lost my very best friend.
I just don't understand what went wrong
our friendship seemed so very strong.
I'm not going to say that you're to blame
I guess nothing can ever stay the same.
  But you said that you loved me
    and we would always be friends
And I will believe that until the world ends.

Tiffany Morici

Oh No!

You, my grandma who reached my heart
That ignited a flame in my eyes that will never part
But cannot be captured in these rhymes
A religious, peaceful woman who now flies with the doves
Up high in the blue, glittering sky
That has accepted you as an angel of the night

You are with the bright, golden face of the sun and bapuji
And looking upon me, please shed some light
For me all the shimmering sparkles of the stars, the moon and
candles are burnt out
All I seem to see is your innocent smile and
you sitting for pooja merrily
There is an unrefillable hole in my mind and soul, no doubt
I was hopeful to see your sweet face and soft hands once more
You were to live on forever I thought

And sounds of your voice, and braiding your hair are not vanished
    images
They are beautiful creations to look back on and reminiscence
Remembering you hurts, but I will not destroy internally and fall
You, in heaven gives me an incentive to put a proud smile up
on your youthful face
And make you glow at the sound of the name Rupa

All the tears in my eyes
Cannot show how fast a faithful heart dies

Rupa Mehta

Untitled

The first rule of all of life's game is this:
That in the field your name be list.
If with those who win, you would be writ,
Then all of yourself you must commit.
For if unused a part of you be,
Unfulfilled shall be your destiny.

God cries out, "Play! and damn the risk -
Why, to play 'gainst such numbers, is pure bliss."

To play is the all, the end is none;
Quick now, swift moves that shining sun.
Not a scrap of yourself must you hold back
Else your life's battle will feel that lack.
That bit of yourself unused, unworn,
Shall rust out, fade out and die unmourned.
What feckless fool would himself save -
To merely lie in a forgotten grave.

R L Rarey

Homecoming

The day you left was difficult for me
That is why I had to bring you back.
Your face brings memories of you dancing and laughing through
    the fields.
Shining so brightly, you were my world, my own personal sun
that shone warm light on me alone.
But you turned away from me and my world grew cold.
I didn't want to do it, but I did.
Then I missed you.

You're so dirty.
Don't worry, I will clean the blood and dirt and flesh
from beneath your fingernails.
I will change your torn and ill fitting clothes
and brush the leaves and worms from your hair.
This time will be better for us, my sweet.
You will shine again, I promise.

Rodney F. Macklin

The Battered

It happens in the midst, of the multitude of stress,
That leaves both parties always, severely depressed,
And yet the man can go on, to do it all again,
While the wife covers it up, and asks forgiveness, for his sins,

We all know that love, on us can leave its mark,
And yet to be the battered, can tear our world apart,
Also it can take our trust, our dreams totally shattered,
We never know when we've had enough, cause we're used to
  being the battered,

In a land taken by violence, it's part of the American way,
It's nothing for us to batter each other, we can only pray,
All the time we tell each other, let's stop the violence,
Only for us to be haunted, by the uncensored silence,

And now low and behold, help us on its way,
We are not alone, in this world that runs astray,
Let's all try to be as one, let's all try to gather,
Then the violence will be done, and no more being called...
The Battered
LaVon J. Ash Sr.

"Lack Of Money"

Oh, I never thought,
that money is important
so you could succeed,
I couldn't reach the goal, that I wanted to,
I couldn't go to college,
I finished High School,
I wanted to study, to stay in school
to write, be an author, an artist a star
to be something big, and who knows
someday be in the Hall of fame.
I was born not poor, but in the society
called the upper middle class,
then my father died and whatever we had,
properties and businesses, whatever we owned
so we could survived it has to be sold.
Then my dreams sank down to an endless drain
and whoever offer to give me some help,
they always expected something in return,
but this only happens to people like me,
for the lack of money, we never succeed.
Virginia Lopez

Lorelle

They never cared
That my heart lay elsewhere.
I sat for hours
Alone — but not alone
As I watched the waves roll on
And listened to their stories:
Some were sad and some were sweet.
Yes, they told me —-
The waves as they beat.
The clouds visited me and left and came again.
The birds sang their songs to me,
And I was concerned.
The winds were cool,
And the trees and I shook together.
I talked to the moon and the stars,
And they listened
And they were my friends.
But the people —-
Yes, the people:
I had acquaintances.
Tanya Keith Smith

Water Skies

The stark skies
that once harbored the late afternoon sun,
Now hold tightly to the frosted air
that freezes raindrops
into tiny beads of lace.

The lace that gracefully falls to the ground
in the same manner that
the hands of a loving father caress
the cheek of his newborn son.

The days will shorten with time,
the gray lake will freeze into a mirror
of reflections.
And I know I will wake up tomorrow,
only to see a new world before me.
Sarah Ingrid Savage

Forever's Ours

For never there was a love like ours
That runs so deep and true
All the happiness I know I owe to you
For never there was a love like ours
That was hidden away for so long
While all the time we knew together is where we belong
For never there was a love like ours
That stands the test of time
Forever I'm yours and you are mine
For never there was a love like ours
Together we'll be never to part
You're the only thing that fills my heart
For never there was a love like ours
Together our souls are wound so tight
Love has never been so right
For never there was a love like ours
Together we'll be forever and true
Together forever just me and you
Kristen Miller

"Stars"

A bright glimmering light, from afar
That shines on all the earth, is a star
When gloom and darkness, are all around
The stars shine their light, to brighten the ground
Its glittering rays, shine and light our way
In hopes that God will give us, a much brighter day
So clear and still, the stars can be
God made a star, so all man could see
The stars, just another gift of God's love
Like the Holy Spirit, in the form of a dove
So as you gaze upon the skies
Know that the stars, were for everyone's eyes
Trudy J. Jones

Sparkling Fall Days

Fall is my favorite time of year,
the air is sparkling, crystal clear.

My days are full of energy and zest,
I accomplish my goals and do my best.

My dogs seem to come to life and play.
You should see them run on a crisp, fall day.

The countryside is all aglow
with orange and gold to view.
It wakes up my senses from head to toe
and it can do the same for you too!

Oh, come and enjoy a glorious Fall day with me.
Then we'll sit by a crackling fire with a hot cup of tea.
Shirley F. Danzis

For Ryan

You're lying there so unaware of everything
That surrounds you. The russet specks reflect
Against the azure of your eyes; water

Sparkles when you giggle. Quite unexpectedly
Clear-blue tears suddenly submerge
Your eyes, telling me nothing, just intersecting

My bewilderment. A glittering star submerges
At the peak of mountains, symbolizing your
Innocence, twirling endlessly diverging —

Multicolored mobile suspended in mid-air, therefore
Attracting your attention like bees to honey.
It's so nice to see your healthy glow ashore

At nightfall, day after day. Journey
To anticipate the future, knowing what
Madness it holds. Closing my eye

To fantasy, the world woefully grins, smut
Echoing, "Three blind mice." Fond memories flashback —
Quickly discontinuing — unable to cut.

Karen L. Anctil

"Homelessness"

Some people, just don't seem to understand,…
that we all belong to the family of man;
Even if we're down on our luck…without a home,
Destined to wander the streets, that we roam.

Some people look down on us with shame…
And treat us like we have no name.
They secretly wish, we would disappear,
But, we all know; they only do it out of fear.

Maybe…just maybe…if they took the time,…
And got to know us…they would find,
That we only want someone to care, to give a helpin' hand;
So we can…again…join them in the family of man.

I guess people think that we've given up hope…
Because it seems, we just can't seem to cope,
But when you get as low as anyone can go;
It's a hard road up and so far to go!

Linda M. Matt

"Forever Our Love"

It is not often enough
that we take the time
to simply say "I love you"

Instead we only too often
dwell on the problems of our children
and extended families

They will most certainly survive
and better yet, thrive
without our constant intervention and bickering
over problems which we probably
cannot solve anyway

Let's try to stay focused on the one thing
that means the most to our current struggle,
our love and continued friendship.

Can we not walk through life as we once did
confident in the fact
that when we got married,
we married our best friend.

Our love is certainly forever.

Richard S. Lisi

Paths

Paths bring to mind trails in the woods
    That wind and wander.
Walkways in a garden
    Straight and narrow.
It's up to us which ones we will take,
    Today or tomorrow.

The paths of life are not so well defined.
They're not laid out like an old English garden.
We stumble along the twists and turns,
Not even aware, the paths are there.

Life's paths lead to happiness, to love,
    and to sorrow.
But we know not which one we follow.

Of the paths that I tread,
The ones I hold dear,
(And there are only a few)
Are the ones that led me to each
    and every one of you.

Marjorie H. Baker

"Grandmother"

A Grandmother is a treasure
That you never can replace;
She fills your life with memories
That you never can erase;
I remember Mondays when she's knock upon our door
We'd all come out running and almost knock her on the floor
And with her smiling face, she'd open her bag and say,
"Look what little goodies Nana has for you today."
She was always there to listen to what you had to say
And always give you good advice in her loving way
Her door is always open no matter what time of day
You can be sure of Nana, she'll never turn you away;
Her house is always spotless, you could eat right off her floor
And the stairs are always shinning right up to her front door.
And so we say to Jesus, we thank you once more
For giving us our grandmother to love and adore.

Bob Behm

"The Truth Lies In You"

If you look inside your heart; what is it
    that you truly see -
Is there that peace and contentment; is your
    life really what you want it to be.

Is the love that you need and want given to you -
remember there's a reason we touch each life we do.
Ask yourself can you settle for less when
    you know that you need and want more -
Can you go on pretending choosing not to open that door.

There's nothing wrong with fearing which road in life to choose -
life has no guarantees; taking any direction is taking a chance to lose
Be selfish this time and look only for yourself
    because only then will you know -
you've searched within to find that sometimes in life
    you have to let something go.

Being honest with yourself leaves your heart and mind full-
I ask you to do this regardless of what you find your answers to be.
Soul searching is never an easy thing to do -
but sometimes it's necessary because… the truth lies in you.

Polly Miller

Confusion

You are the center of a circle
That's closing in on you
but your hands are bound
and you can't breathe
like silence screaming in a dream
so you search for a reason of your existence
or someone to set you free.

Tara N. Smith

Vision

Is life a pretty garment
that's perfectly woven?
Or is it a music box that's been broken?
Dance, dance pretty ballerina, wave your magic wand.
Please take me far away, to the great beyond.
So I don't have to dance on my shattered world.
I thought the dance was over, but once the ballerina twirled.
Everything's all right, hold your breath, stay in your place.
Put on your mask made of lace, or you will fall in disgrace.

Linda M. Perkins

Silent Treasured Memories

The drawer is silently pulled open its true treasures are revealed,
The abundance of memories it holds are no longer to be concealed.
A small flowered jar with bobby pins, knee highs and some socks,
lingerie neatly folded and some jewelry in a box.

I caress each item fondly sighing deeply as tears descend,
These are the fragments of a life that has sadly reached its end.
I press each item to my cheek hoping to resurrect some life force,
As the silence deepens and surrounds me, I yearn to be able to
    reverse life's inevitable course.

Softly, quietly closing my eyes,
I strain to hear the sweet music and the laughter.
The summer wind blows through our hair,
As the sun dances on sea and sand to the false tune of happily
    ever after.

I now know that nothing lasts forever,
but memories drift like trails of smoke through my mind.
Each whisper echoing through the soft fog,
Leaving an uncontrollable gnawing ache behind.

Each drawer must be carefully opened for she would have wanted it
only that way, each item lovingly held and sorted, each memory
finally put away. And when the last task is done and the drawers
are forever silently closed, I turn and throw a final kiss to wish
her dear sweet peaceful repose.

Paula Pollack

Staying In The Rain

As I spade the earth in my spring garden,
the air grows damp and cool.
The maple's budding, moss-colored leaves turn toward heaven,
exposing their shiny, grass-green undersides, pirouetting in
unison, mouths open, like tiny robins in a nest.

The gray rain-laden clouds roll toward me,
as the cool, swift breeze ruffles my long skirt.
A few huge raindrops fall, clear and cold on my bare arms.
The rain falls faster, dancing on the pond, soaking and
straightening my hair.

Distant thunder rumbles, as spider webs of lightning
flicker far away.
I stretch out my arms, palms up.
Brown earth streaks to my elbows and I look up at the electric
sky, smiling as the rain stings my face.

White, streaking lightning stabs a wound on a thick walnut.
Thunder booms like a cannon releasing its load.
My body is drenched and my clothing is washed clean.
I am Artemis! Witness to this symphony of life!

Linda E. Case

The Rain Dance Of The Peacocks

The moon shines in all its glory,
The air is filled with a magical fragrance
The pearl like rain drops touch the ground softly.

A musk deer runs out in joy,
To celebrate the first rain of the season.
Crimson and pearl white lilies unfold in ecstasy!

A sudden flutter!
A sight so wonderful to behold,
A peacock in all its majesty, crest held upright
Its rainbow tail spread out like a bejewelled fan
Shimmering in the brilliant display of colors.
A vision of beauty!

The peacock dances the rain dance
Cries out for its mate.
Their dancing feet make the tingling sound of the anklet bells,
The graceful tilt of the peacocks' neck
The sudden movement of their wings
Brushing against each other
Fills the air with the lyrics of the bamboo flute.
Ecstatic in love, together they dance to greet the golden dawn!

Rima S. Gulshan

Dreams For Reality

Deception and lies spoken through your eyes;
    The art of betrayal beaten upon cries.
Visions of truth fall like rain;
    Your truth build my fathomless pain.
Us, my love, your conditional, eternities invincible,
    To this I inveigh to you my principles.
With correct two stand a forever one;
    With wrong, a dimension none.
My dreams confirming your reality;
    Now I stand impassable,
    Dream your feel.
Then my dreams twisted and finished;
    Dimension none, now vanished.
Speak truth and act the innocence;
    Like a mirror seems to be a reflectance.
If not, this I give to you is your
    forever.

Kelly Wahala

The Bear

In the Spring of '88
The Autumn of my life
I could hardly wait for the ice to leave the lake.

I'm going up the Pickeral River, to kill myself a bear.
I'm going up the Pickeral River, because I heard there were lots
    of bears there.

I went up the Pickeral River 'til I came to a waterfall
A prettier place
I never saw.

So I hunted for a day or two and none to my surprise,
I saw a bear standing there by the waterfall.

I fired my gun, but the bear didn't fall
I touched not a hair on that bear
    standing by the waterfall
So I came down the Pickeral River
    None the sadder for it all
I was glad I had missed that bear standing by the waterfall.

And if you're ever up the Pickeral River and come to the waterfall
I hope you chance to see the same old bear standing there by the
    waterfall.

Roy Wright

Coming Home

My mind was foggy, I could not see,
The beauty of the flowers that were beckoning to me
I was alone.

There were places to go, mountains to climb,
But don't you see, I had no time.

The birds sang sweet, the sky so clear,
I could not focus, nothing was near.
I was alone.

Then someone reached out and took my hand,
We walked, we talked,
Now I understand.

I paint the flowers that beckoned to me,
I paint the mountains I could not see,
I hear the birds and see the sky,
You gave me the choice to live or die.

I've found a haven, I've come home.
Thanks to that someone, I'm no longer alone.

LoRaine Murray

The Bubble Master

No one blows bubbles like Bobby McCate.
The bubbles he blows are simply just great.
He blows bubble birds, and animals galore,
bubble elephants, giraffes, and rhinos, and more.
He mixes up species with creatures and things,
like blowing bubble baby bears with airplane wings.
Bubble cat-owls and bubble fish-goons,
bubble baboons blowing bubble balloons.
The bubbles Bobby blows are like scenes from a play,
bubble boy blue asleep in the hay.
His bubbles are moving, his bubbles are alive,
he blew a bubble bumble-bee buzzing by its hive.
With a little soapy water his boy Bobby McCate,
blew a bubble dinner complete with fork and plate.
Before Bobby blew his best bubble of all,
he told us that magic could hear when we call.
Then Bobby blew a bubble bodacious,
with a house and a yard, and wide open spaces.
He climbed in the bubble and floated away.
I wonder if Bobby's bubble is still floating today.

William Brest

Summer Romance

She watched him sleep, the brown curls of his hair
the cat purring softly nearby
She wonders what life holds, and if he'll be there
and then she started to cry

How could she love him, they both had agreed
a Summer romance at best
but watching him sleep, the brown curls of his hair
she knew she had failed at the test

She hoped, dreamed and prayed, that one day she would wake
and find he'd been watching her too
that their Summer romance would be endless indeed
and maybe their love could be true

She watched him sleep, the brown curls of his hair
would he find love for her by and by?
Only the heart knows, and it can't be rushed
so till then she'll wait....and she'll cry.

Raeann Stacey Wilson

Friendship Between Two

Our friendship came into existence like an explosion
the cause should be recorded as a natural wonder
Because we were the only humans who made it happen
And time has only made us grow closer
From the start, You and I were to be friends.

We have learned to share each other's thoughts
So we may not be together, but we will never be apart.
Our friendship is so strong
Because it is part of our souls.

The words to explain our friendship
Are not easy to find
For our friendship is too strong for words
And can not easily be defined.

When our friendship started
God had already determined that it would last forever
It will not end due to the passage of time
Nor will anyone ever be able to stop it.

William Harris Danes

If Dried

And I wanted you to give me dried roses I could hang from
the ceiling or frame under glass.

But while I waited to have known you long enough to have
memorized everything about your hands and neck and the
patterns of your footsteps in the early morning hours,

I did not realize that a window had been closed and then a
curtain drawn on the field of grass absorbing and reflecting
the sun.

And the song innocence was played on a piano long since
closed. The notes I had thought were reverberating were
really just part of the music from the blackness of your eyes.

The roses you gave me though tied with your question were
not dried but as soft and fresh as skin.

And only dried roses last so the ones you gave me were soon
dead - unable to breathe in light through a closed window and
drawn curtain behind which the grass field, at least,
continues to grow and change and live.

Olivia Weber

By The Way

In modern times they come, buzzards, crucifix, the fury of the sun.
The charred wall where the dead are named torn down, a nation
was freed, united.

Walk backward, down the future, buy the past with gold, for
tomorrow is its prize. I once saw a man lost, find his way.

They call, they come, their minds full of dribble, pockets full of
drugs. Where did the light come from, the creator of the first dawn?

Little time to waste my friend, the borders must be breached, the
charge begun. I once heard the sound of tears fall, sounded like
dirt, when it hits the coffin lid.

The artists rise to lift the words in the morning, as gray light
spills over the sea, stealing small pieces of freedom. Cold takes
steel and makes it fire!

The poets words, soft, love stained songs of war, called mortal
by most men, but most men die before they live. I once had a
dream of wings for my voice.

Rockets and drugs don't mix, can cause problems if the day is
clear, wind is slow. The visions of tomorrow's thunder linger
with the lands of yesterday.

Call the number on the screen and you too can be saved from the fires
of Dante's Inferno; don't delay, act today. This offer won't last.

Robert Fortner

505

Bounce - Is The Thing

To win all the time - is the easy way.
The cheers, the applause and the accolades.
You can roll along "on top of the heap".
Honored by all you happen to meet.
You can reach the point where you really believe.
Your better than most by some divine creed
But the bounce is the thing - that shows true worth
For the fall and rebound is like a re-birth.
The harder the fall - the greater the height.
Is the mark of the man - with real insight.
It hurt when you fall - it's painful and dark
Feeling rejected and sad - you can't make the mark.
But, the bounce is the thing - that shows man is man
To soar to new heights - as best as he can.
For having not fallen - he'd never achieve
The height on the bounce - where he strives to be.
  So - let's all remember.
When you're down for the count -
Things will be better - if you only have bounce.

   William L. McCarthy

The End

The guns they rumble and they roar
The children all hidden under their floors
The bombs they fall, the missiles they fly
Oh! What wizards, you and I.
And when this all comes to pass
The cries and suffering, as humans gasp
3000 years of Peace To Share.
Ah! But not a human will be there.

   William A. Rhyan

Lonely Tonight

Hi Honey...It's late...and a little bit lonely, tonight;
The children are gone, but I'm doing alright...
I'm hearing the sound of the whistling wind;
I'm thinking of winter, and when it will end;
Remembering Summer...and all of our fun,
With every activity under the sun!
Breath-taking sunsets that end much too soon;
Skies full of stars, and our Idaho moon;
Bare feet on blacktop and tan, freckled skin;
Memories that make me want Summer again;
Things that I love, but... tonight, I feel blue,
Because all of these things just remind me of you.
It isn't life's pleasure that brings my heart cheer;
It's knowing you love me, and having you here...
Your voice in the hallway, your clothes on the floor;
Wet towels on the carpet and boots at the door;
Your quiet "Amen" when the prayers have been said;
Your snaggy old toenails that scratch me in bed!
My head on your shoulder makes everything right..
I'm trying to be brave, but... I miss you tonight.

   Rebecca Bryan-Howell

Parent's Delight

T'was the break of morn and a parent's delight,
The first day of school is in sight.
From all over the city they came with a roar,
Just to find out the school was no more.
As the bus unloaded letting the kids out,
What happen to all was the great shout.
The old school has seen its better day,
Made up of old mortar, brick and clay.
With the years it has passed to a well known fate,
To become a highway, suburb or lake.
Pass the old into the new, the kids are delighted
And the parents too.

   Laura C. Houston

The White Carnation

One bright and sunny Sunday in the merry month of May,
the children of my neighborhood, were observing Mother's Day.

Here comes Johnny, cried little Sue!
We all have red carnations .
What color have you?

Johnny looked down as sad as can be,
I'm wearing one of white, can't you see?
My mother died while giving birth to me.

I never knew my mother like you,
you or you but she was the grandest mother
for all she went through.

Come I'll show you where she's sleeping
if you want to see,
down yonder by the old oak tree.

When I touch this white carnation,
everything seems so warm and bright,
because this was her favorite color,
Immaculate White.

   Luther E. Bullock

As Seen From The Stalled "L"

Dirty grey back porches in the sun
The cloying steaming sultry heat
And people sitting motionless and quiet
An old man bent forward sleeping
The aged bones welcoming the warmth
Dreaming of what used to be and is no more

Suddenly the sky is dark
Lightning streaks the heavens and thunder rolls
And rain falls and thirsty earth
Drinks and little rivulets run down gutters
Like dribbles out of the corners of her mouth

Coolness comes and people smile
And talk begins
The oldster lifts his rheumy eyes
And moves inside to escape the chill
And goes to bed warmly covered
Awaiting death patiently

   Robert Galloway Sr.

Hustlin' And Bustlin'

'Twas early one morning while the family was sleepin',
The coffee was perkin' when the pager started beepin',
A D.O.N. with orders from the night before
And a home health nurse in a big uproar.
So it's gulp down the coffee and run out the door
Slip in a puddle the dog left on the floor.
While fussin' and cussin' climb into the van,
Drive quickly to work where trouble already began;
Orders stacked in the FAX machine tray,
The beginning of a real butt-busting 300 script day.
The phones start ringing and the computer did crash,
Yesterday's reports got thrown out with the trash.
Add grumpy customers, irate nurses and pious M.D.'s
It's enough to drive anyone to their knees.
But close your eyes and listen for the distant swooshing sound
Of wings-wind and surf —a VACATION comin' round!!!

   Maggie Garrison

An Empty Space

As I awaken with
the dawn's blue skies
I find myself weary
And not wanting to rise.

I find someone very special
on my mind every day
She left me, she's gone,
She passed away

She took a part of me
with her when she drew her last breath.
I never thought in my growing years
I would see her, before me face death.

There is a place in my heart
and my life that will not be filled by no other.
This special someone is no dearer to me,
Than anyone could be.
    She is my mother.
    Marsha L. Black

No Goodbye

Even tho I held you all day,
The day God took you from my side.
My heart won't stop aching,
Because I really didn't get to say goodbye.

Who would have ever known,
What was in store for you that night.
My Baby that I loved so much.
His life was gone not even time to fight.

It seems so strange that one small twist of fate,
Could take your life so fast.
How could I have ever known,
Our happiness wasn't going to last.

We all think we have forever,
To be with the ones we love.
Never stopping to think tomorrow.
God may want them up above.

So as the months and years go by,
The ache in my heart won't subside.
Because my little sweetheart,
There never was a goodbye.
    Martha Tirheimer

For You

Summer Breezes have come and gone, Autumn has followed suit
The days are longer now, and not as meaningless
Because my heart is full

With all my heart, I write what I feel, all of this for you
My love is a flower, much more than a rose; Its name is passion
It can be as strong as a tempest's fury
and yet as delicate as glass

I give my love to you, Forever, if you'll have it
All of this from me for you

Yesterday is taken, tomorrow belongs to us, we can face it now
    together
With dreams and a chest full of new hopes, things only get better.

I'll always be here, if you want me to
My heart is yours, I'll never leave you.

Sometimes I can't tell you how much I care, words get in the way
But feeling this strong always have to be said.
They are expressed and understood anyway

Can you feel my love for you, it is real.
This much I guarantee.
It is there now, and always will be.
For now, forever, and for eternity.
    Michael E. Nocivelli

Peace

Sun settles low over pine filled horizon
The day's business ends. A special night arrives.
Winter wind blows silently, hesitantly.
Snowy rabbit settles... waiting, nose twitching.
Crow perches expectantly, calm fills its heart.
Dire wolf bays longingly, hunger forgotten.
Timid animals gather. A star shines above.
Peace settles in the forest, no hate tonight.
All eyes aim Heavenward, A voice fills their hearts,
"Tonight is my Night. No need for haste or fright.
Love one another while My heart is open.
Men's cold hearts will close again after this night,
But, you My Children, live in My Blessed Light."
A star brightened in the sky, "Live in My Love!"
    Michael N. Yavorsky

Sometimes In My Darkest Hours

Sometimes, in my darkest hours, I wonder how to go on.
The depression pulls me down so low I can barely breath.
I wonder, 'Why do I feel this way? What is making me so sad?'
I can't find an answer. There simply isn't one.
I just have to live through it.
To some that sounds easy.
To those that know, it takes a lot just to get up in the morning.
One day at a time is not a choice; it's a must.
I'm luckier than some, I believe in God.
Even when I'm all alone, I'm not.
I pray for strength, for guidance.
And slowly, very slowly, the clouds lift.
For a while I'm fine.
Of course it comes again, but every time I get through it, I win.
And with every victory, I gain strength.
    Susan Scott

New Morning

The sky is red with the morning's glow,
The dew on the roses lay heavy,
As the sun peeps over the hill,
It is breaking morning on a new day.

As the red fades away,
The blue welcome sky appears,
I stand at my window,
Watching the nodding of the flowers against the warm
summer breeze.

The singing of the birds,
Seem to welcome me,
As I walk outside,
Giving my last yawn.

The new born blossoms give out their scent,
As mother nature came alive before my eyes,
I will stand still and enjoy this moment,
While giving thought to a new morning.
    Lawrence Sailors

Serenity

The young deer peeks from behind the high brush on the sloping
part of the hill. He moves gracefully into the field of tall grass,
pausing to gaze and listen. The tall rye, golden in color, shares
this friendship that only the breeze can touch and sigh. As
daylight brightens the darkness he moves closer to the yellow
lilies. A black cat, sitting still, looks down from the tree of apples.
The young deer alert to each sound, waits in silence and then
moves peacefully away.
    Michael Martocci

Little Bird

Ah, little bird, you are very kind.
The dew on the roses you sweeten for me
By bringing your love notes to my mind,
Sitting up there in the apple tree.

As in the Opera when lights are low,
A solemn hush as curtain is drawn—
So, little bird, when the moon fades low
You come forth, the soloist of the dawn.

Soft and low, sweet and trilling,
You awaken me from my dreams.
Lovely! Joyous! Daring notes swelling
'Till they must reach God, in Heavenly praise.

Ah! Little Bird, you are very kind,
For thusly you cheer my whole day along
By bringing your love notes to my mind
You, little bird, and your wonderful song.

Luma Bullock

The Dictator

Thus you lament, wotan, in the luminous dark,
the dispersal of the gods. Your fingers
clutch the crumbling walls; the palace
rocks and falls.
Once you were garbed in diamonds and rubies,
Your domain extended without limits,
Your voices thundered from every rock,
Your face gleamed from every star;
You rose like a wind, a typhoon
And murdered friend and foe alike,
With rage of speech you indicted the world
And confined your child to a ring of fire.
Now you are shadow,
Your prophecies sink in the rubble

In the nave of a church
Once struck by bombs,
Someone somewhere sings your end
"Away false god, you brought a storm of blood
And anguish to the earth;
Nourish yourself on solitude and never return."

Ronald Green

The Traveling Room

The weary faces fill the traveling room;
the eyes close to dreams and awake to the truth.
A part of the city rides within this tomb
with wisdom of age and candor of youth.

Voices, soft-spoken, tell a tale or two
as, stop-by-stop, they come and they go.
Each rider is home when the ride is through,
and they feel more secure with the friends that they know.

While two strangers converse of two separate lives,
they are close through the minutes they quietly spend.
He explains that a perfect life never deprives,
and she shares her own troubling truths with her friend.

There is more they could share, but the time has run out;
she steps down and she waves as she goes on her way.
His stop soon approaches, and he's thinking about
the lessons of life he has learned on this day.

I watch the man leave, wondering where his heart leads,
but before long my interest, as with the day, dies.
The city fades out with the dusk of life's needs,
as I turn from the window and close my tired eyes.

Roger L. Dutcher

Pain Never Leaves

The melody of my broken heart comes to a close,
The fall of tomorrow waits for another day,
Closing the gates of my heart to a painful crash,
Falling deep, to the pit of ground, not able to walk,
Night so filled with open arms, weak at reason,
Day rising to the full light of sunshine,
The day comes to the end of no ending battle,
My days are numbered to the bad fall that appears,
Greatly, I stand awake and humble to the beat of Death,
Pleading for the sorrow that has deeply found me,
Now has left me, for death,
The discussion of communication is over,
To the day of my death, I won't admit to my deepest secret,
Filling the void of space trying to replace my deepest pain,
The will to live is the will to die,
My friend, I have to spoken deeply from my true heart.

Kris Bens

Thoughts...While Sailing On The Changjiang (Yangtze)

Morning's coming
    the far off rooster crows.
The sound of chains
    and the boatman's cry.
My small bed rolls
    in the river's serge.

At last, I raise my head.
Faintly, through the mist,
    I see a light from a small boat, yonder.

In my half sleep,
    it must be you!
But, a thousand plus years have passed
    since the days of Tang.

Do you still watch,
    Old DuFu, over the waters of the Changjiang (Yangtze)?

Mary Erikson

Alone

How can a person describe
the feeling of loneliness?
A big empty room
no sound, no speech, no people
Just a small window
which outlooks over a vast sea of confusion.
Men scurrying around like mice,
Man-made objects tightly woven together
like a collage of steel and rubber.
One person, alone, looks into this window
and sees nothing.
Nothing but a reflection of oneself
with the tears slowly rolling
down his face.

Stacy Beth Katz

Wellspring

Love is the water that nourishes and enriches life.
The foolhardy try to grasp it tightly in their fists.
It slips through clenched fingers,
leaving only the damp memory of happiness.
The wise gather love in a gently cupped hand,
allowing it fill the palm with a sweet pool of delight,
to be savored for a lifetime.

Lugene Rosen

My Wish

For so long in my world there was no sun,
The flowers didn't grow.
There were no stars to shine at night,
And the moon, it had no glow.

I had no song in my heart to sing,
No evening lullabies.
The clouds were always waiting near
To darken all my skies.

I thought that if I wished enough
My wishes would come true.
And so I wished and wished and wished,
And finally there was you.

Now when the day is all but through
I set back, relax and think of you,
With all your ways so good and sweet
You give treasures that are mine to keep.

And often when I'm alone
I say a silent prayer,
And thank God over and over
That finally, there was you.

Pat Luttmann

Charm Carnation

She wore a jester's smile to her Masquerade Garden
The flowers of her mind's bed stirred with a gentle breeze
That only her best friends could truly appreciate

When wild winds launched her forward
It was just then that her garden's bouquet
Sneezed for the very first time

And the Wine from her Vine was dry beyond understanding
Yet sweet, like an unexpected Bloom
The fragrance of her smile was Ripe

Though she love all things Juicy
Those fruits of her lifestyle rang Bells of Thunder
Their chaotic chimes at times hilarious

HAVE YOU SEEN HER?
She roams the acres with a lightning bolt tame at her side
It divines a glimpse or three of a Time Not Yet Come
Life's Mystery is her Chosen Knowledge

Give her your children's souls as you have lent her yours
And life's magic will always be within a whisper
For she is the Charm Carnation
She rules the Masquerade Garden

Tammy L. Ward

To My Sons

Why I was blessed with you God only knows.
The fruits of labor, born to loving arms
To shelter you and keep you safe from harm.
Ten tiny fingers and ten perfect toes,
Skin smooth as silk, and the wonder of those
Blue eyes that shine when life presents its charms;
The quickness of their tears when it alarms;
The peacefulness of slumber when they close.
The promise of a brand-new world I see
Through your blue, sparkling eyes; my spirit lifts
Above the loneliness of being one.
I realize now who I was meant to be,
A mother to these two most precious gifts:
My life, my joy and comfort, my two sons.

Kelly A. Ray

The Funeral

Today, the day of
the funeral, our hearts
are filled with great
pain and sorrow, but
yet on the outside
somehow we managed
to crack a smile

Some may be real
and some maybe fake.
But yet we smile
You ask why we smile
when someone we
loved has just passed away?

You think we should weep?
We have and we will. For some it may take time,
but as for me I've come to realize
that our loved one is
in a much better place and is no longer
having to hurt and suffer.

And for that reason we should smile.

Melissa Renee Cauley

The Nature Of God

Peaceful is the day that shines,
The glorious sun that warms my soul of time.

Graceful is the wind that blows,
And the leaves that dance to the ground below.

Bountiful are the birds that sing sweet blessings
of harmony accord.

Joyful is the symphony of crickets with their tone-a-
praising up to the Lord.

Beautiful is God's glorious green earth,
And peaceful is everyday that shines like a new birth.

Wonderful is this place where I'm submerged; glorious
is his majestic peace.

Magnificent are these marvelous creations, and the name of
Jesus on every breeze.

Karen Lannon

Memory Of You

Memory's of you is when I look into the mirror of time and
remember the great things we used to do. Like when we walked
in the park at night, and I knew every thing was gonna be
alright. When you brought me flowers for when I was sad. You
always gave me the sweetest kiss, it always felt like sugar on my
lips. The way you made me feel when you held my hand, and
told me you loved me. I look into your eyes and I would never
see a disguise. The way you wrapped yourself around me when
we lay asleep. But now those days are over and unfortunate for
it was the way the breeze felt so freely. I stare out at the ocean
and cry til' my heart sings out "Come back to me so I can love
you ever so deeply"... But there's no answer.... Not a single
response... Just the sound of waves crashing down on the shore.
I look down at the sand and I felt it between my feet. The wind
blew through my hair as the sun began to set. Each day without
you would be like a eternity with suffer. But heh, what do I
know, these are only dreams. Dreams of love come and gone. I
looked up in time to see the last good-bye of the sun. As I started
to walk away, I realized that I was beginning to have memories
of you.

Nicole Davis

The Caterpillar Men

The silver dawn awakes,
The green dark forest is deep and still.
The silence shatters, like crystal,
As Caterpillars roll, on case-hardened steel.

Raker teeth scream through blue diesel smoke.
They rip in two a century of life
In minutes,
Death is delivered upon those pristine giants.

Choke-setters pause, a moment of silence.
Then they dance, set and nod,
As the cat-skinner snakes out the fallen splendor.

Fallers count and mark their conquests,
Thinking only of their logs, their numbers,
And their whiskey at five.

The birds are now gone.
And butterflies die,
Inside their cocoons.

Robert L. Fromm

My Chrissy

The bright smile.
The happy squeal.
The sloppy kiss "that's Chrissy".
They said, that she would never walk,
would never talk, would never learn.
But oh, how wrong they were.
She not only walked,
she ran and danced,
and wrapped everyone around
her finger
A happy surprise for every day,
Now she's up in Heaven.
In my heart I see the bright smile,
and hear her happy squeal.
I feel the sloppy kiss, My Chrissy gives to me.

Virgina Wallace

Untitled

As a mother you do more than your share
The income shows just how much you do care
You've always got a place you need to be
It makes me happy when that place is with me.

Today with me your precious time was spent
Even though you had your own work load pit
It made me feel special I came before
Your work load dealing with the rest of the world.

Your devotion to me shows that you care
When I have a need you are always there
As I grow older I see me in you
I'm sure you see the opposite as I do.

Kathy Peterson

The Poplar Tree

Glinting in the light of the late afternoon sun,
The leaves of the poplar gleam like silver spun.
In consort with the beckoning breeze,
They tinkle melodious, the moment to seize.
In harmony, the tree its arms upward lifts
To do obeisance to its Maker, the Giver of Gifts.

God, in His wisdom, chose this stately tree
To rise, when buffeted midst the tempest blow,
And free itself and straighter grow
To heights unknown, its destiny to know.

Miye Nishimoto

Rise And Sail

Wave at the opaque masquerade
The jerking marionette parade
They're dragged on mute with stupid grins
Some devilish hand controls their sins
Do not join the teaming jesters
Shining submissiveness darkly festers
Individuality's lost
They all gave in and paid the cost
Follow your skipping hopes and dreams
Light the blackness that fills their streams
Slice up their strings to set them free
Give them your eyes so they can see
Conformity is shackles cold
That bind the blind ones 'til their old
Don't dive into their "mainstream" jail
You have the wings so rise and sail

Kami D. Straining

The Joy Of It All

There is no joy like the joy of it all.
The joy of each precious moment of a tiny baby's eyes and
fingers uplifted into mine.
Joy, each explosion of Earth beauty assaulting itself
with its infinite uplifting right straight into my heart cave.
The joy of old lovers no longer bothered by old judgements,
but lost, never to be found in loving.
Joy, joy, joy, joy, Great God almighty this is unimaginable
longing joy!
The tender caressing healing hand of a mother's gift giving God
goodness into the distant suffering lost big-eyed frightened old man.
Flowing flows this goodness, this thoughtfulness,
that uses us like a farmer uses an old hoe.
This goodness, that will not die, that will not go away.
This reaching goodness growing like the shoots, fingers
feeling for the holes in concrete.
It cracks the hardest hard, it is what you long for,
it is what's always missing, what can't be bought.
And you my most precious darling, the joy as we lie, dying into
each others arms suspended and lost into this goodness.
Dying, we die and the rich goodness, our goodness, lives on.

Ron Bynum

Death By The Sea

'Twas stormy night, the wind swept howl,
the lightning crack the thunder growl

Our leaked ship, tossed to and fro,
the Sea was angry, with chaos and billow.

The Captain lay dead, by the mizzen's cracked fall
the mate by the wheel, stood mighty and tall.

'Twas hours it seemed, 'fore dawn's heaven light
the storm had passed, slipped away with the night.

We cast our dead, their souls to the deep,
many brave lads, lives lost, scarce a peep,

With stitching and axe, we set sail best we could,
our ships strong and mighty, for all that she withstood

Many men perished, that night brave and true
still, better the sea, than lost, lonely love.
  or brew.

Steven A. Wheeler

Man O'War

Born in Kentucky in a spring-snug barn,
the little colt rises and neighs.
With knobby knees and spindly legs,
he's an attraction for all to see.
With a deep chestnut coat, and a large white star,
They christen him...
Man O'War.

Raised in the blue grass and golden rod valleys,
he's become Beauty and Fire.
With no need for his momma he's taken away,
to train to be the racehorse,
he was bred and born to be.

In Belmont Park's saddling paddock,
he fights the bridle and the saddle.
Then he quivers as he hears the bugle.
He runs all his races as a champion should,
and lost only one to a horse named Upset.
He's the most honored horse in all the books,
the giant chestnut stud, who's christened...
Man O' War.

Marlo Gierczynski

If Only

If only you could know
The love I do not show.
It showers you and follows you wherever you may go.

If only you could feel
The love that's very real.
Naive of the pain that haunts me like a ghostly blade of steel.

If only I could scream
The chaos of my dream.
The fantasies I'll never live are never to be seen.

If only I had spoke
Of the tears that try to choke.
You'd change your mind, but it's too late-for now my heart is broke.

Kevin Veillette

Beauty

The beauty you possess is not in your face
The love in your heart
Is where it should be
Sometime we wish for the moon and the stars
But the light that they give is
All that they have
So by cleansing your heart
And finding your soul
The beauty you possess
Will shine just like gold
When you wake in the morning
You should say a pray
And remember him dearly all
through the year.

Rudranath Baldeosingh

Past Times

One day you have so many friends,
the next you have so few.
It's not what you did for them,
but what their doing for you.
When times are hard and things are rough,
friendship always seem to last.
But one day your friend will find another,
and you will be his past.

Stanley E. Kocanda

Passion Of Life

Passions of life can be many things.
The love of something and the joy that brings.
What is it that turns us on?
The passion for a moment and then it's gone.

Life and all its glory
A never ending variety of fact and story.
Oh how we as the human race.
Seem to lead a never ending pace.

For to love a some special thing.
Is a high in the mind of bird on the wing.
As they soar in the heaven so high.
Do they really know the joy of the sky?

For if humans could soar into such a way.
Oh how this would make joy for a day.
And the passions of life no matter what.
Would hold us up and out of a rut.

No matter what our passions of life,
The high of the feeling would dwarf all strife.
And no individual would ever again,
Bask in the glory of multitudes of sin.

So fact as it is and passions abound,
Would it be too much to play around,
With the idea that here on earth,
Heaven could become reality and not rebirth.

Lyell Thomas

The Days Of Fall

The days of Fall are drawing near -
The Master Painter, His canvas sets -
His colors are mixed, His brushes clear -
As Summer delivers its passing regrets.
The yellows, the browns and the purples, too
The trees stand ready to receive,
Their garb is adorned in dramatic hue -
Too beautiful to believe.
He turns the forest into a colorful scene
As the trees are gaily arrayed -
A riot of color, but hardly a green -
His rainbow is here displayed.
The leaves, thus dressed in their ballroom gown,
Prepared for their Dance of Death,
They dance in the wind and come tumbling down -
As they sigh with their dying breath.
To become a soft carpel for the cooling earth -
They rustle and shiver and shake -
The cold of the winter is nearing its birth -
The trees sleep - but in Spring, will awake.

Monty Montague

Duty Calls

The trumpets have sounded,
    the men are ready-Duty Calls;
The mission before us has been varied and challenging,
    the threat has been real-Duty Calls;
We are living the reality of a splendid history,
    our abilities and pride are worthy;
We will finish in glory for we are
    the last of a chosen few;
Our mission has not ended; however,
    the chapter with C Troop has been closed;
We have been the chosen vessels,
    we now go forward to begin a new legacy;
The threat to freedom has not diminished;
    The men are ready-Duty Calls.

Paul J. Wood

The Last Tiger

In the jungle or in the snow,
The mighty tiger has no foe.

Can you hear the tiger roar?
What will you do when he is never more?

Only man can cause his demise,
and it is him that I despise.

For man takes the tigers land, and kills his game
and soon the tiger will not remain.

How sad I feel the day will come,
when I must tell my son what man has done.

What will I do when the last tiger dies,
and how will I stop my daughters cries?

Man may build, and man can destroy,
but he must remember Gods creation is no toy.

Who are we to say who lives and what dies,
no-one hears the tigers cries.

Help me understand the tigers fate,
it is something I often contemplate.
        Lee D. Soule

My Dearest Love

O what earth and sun do see at last,
the moon and stars and heavens so vast.
A picture of a women, how time does tell,
with fainting eyes, this southern bell.

Speak to me without a word,
and whisper so softly, your voice is heard.
We are not blood, no sister to me,
but I love you dear, my sweet Eilene.

Your portrait I have hung on the wall,
taken before death did call.
My bride to be, you soon would be,
but death tried to take your love from me.

I feel you like I felt you then,
by my side until the end.
Stay with me, forever true,
this love of mine, is only for you.

I shalt not weep, but follow my heart,
for you my love, we seldom part.
One day my love, death will mend,
a heart that's forever yours until the end...
        Steven Ferrino

Wonders Of Life, Wonders Of Love

As the sun ascends into the sky
The moon descending into the horizon
So is our relationship
The fact that we depend upon one another
To live and make it
In unison with one another,
Life's miracles bring forth joy
So does our love in unison with each other
Does happiness employ
        LaRonda Pringle

The Searchers

January 28, 1986
The moon is crying tonight;
The sun will shine less bright
    on the morrows;
The flags will fly at half mast
    for seven days;
The jet streams across the sky at sundown
    are signalling good bye.
All are paying homage to the seven
    daring searchers of space.
The seven are there in space—they
    vanished with the Challenger in a ball of fire.
They are there in space—
Their faces in the clouds;
Their voices in the wind;
Their eyes in the stars.
The SEARCHERS.
        O'Dessa Birdwell

The End

Dark days, dark nights, the sun is gone
The moon no longer reflects its light
The stars now stare all the time
As they travel around to mark the time
They have worlds of their own
Where people live and love and call home
How could they take our sun away?
What did we do to pay this way?
What used to be the air we breathe
Is now a liquid, freezing sea
And it's much too cold for you and me
Excuse me now, but my joints are stiff
I'm frozen to the bone
It's much too cold to finish this poem
I consider the sun a real gift
        Nelson Erbs

Let It Snow

Alone with thoughts and falling snow;
The muffled softness, blanketing calm;
Whispers above and silence below,
The quiet and stillness a comforting balm.
Streetlights shining, the waltzing flakes fall,
Revealing a cosmos in a sodium glare.
The sidewalks slip and freeways crawl
To the gravely gaze of a snowman's stare.
Chimney puffing hickory smoked breeze,
Windowpanes gazing a crystals diffusion.
Longings and teardrops congeal and freeze
Numbing the mind to the solstice seclusion.
Sudden wind whips up a cutting lash
Slicing the air with razored chill.
Waltzing flake dancers tangoing flash
To a wintry melody, a whistling shrill.
        Peter M. Lyman

Chiconda

The tear on my cheek falls for her,
The pain in my heart grows deeper each day,
Her words are silent now, her pain is gone,
All her dreams are still,
But her memory shall live on,
Her smile so sweet, her eyes so warm,
Little Chiconda your fear is gone,
Your wings will carry you to a better place,
Now I will wait for the time,
When we will meet again,
    My little Indian friend,
        Chiconda!
        Patricia Huotari

Untitled

Once again I play the game the record spins around
the names have changed but not the plot
is it reality or not
the pain remains more clear than ever
every time it comes more clever
I always here about their sorrow when they say goodbye
can't they see the pain I feel makes me want to die
If not for the anger deep inside pity might overcome
I'd sit there brooding in despair with no where left to turn
but the rage inside me burns like fire embrace it and feel the burn
Prejudice and Ignorance feed it and make it strong
preconceived ideas and views they are so very wrong
If Color didn't matter and what counted was within
they might perceive me as I am not a stereotyped idea
Spawned in hatred, created in ignorance, nurtured by their fear
life is a broken record for those who don't comply
the endless song plays on and on for those who live the lie
When color no longer matters and characters comes into play
it may be then I'll press onward right now it's an endless replay!

H. Joseph Hayford

"The Angel's Lullaby"

My child, it is time to fold in your wings,
the night falls as the last sparrow sings.
Close your precious eyes,
for the sun has already been swallowed by the skies.
Hang your heavenly halo upon the wall,
the world in which you sleep in has heard your call.
Lay your head upon the clouds so white,
dream now with the stars that cover the night.
Hush my love, don't you pout,
a gentle wind has blown all the candles out.

Wander off into your dreamland,
the sandman is coming with enchanted sand.
You have knelt to say your prayers,
your mind is free with out any cares.

As the world around you begins to die,
Sleep now my child, for I've already sang you the angel's lullaby.

Tamera Joe Santic

From The Diary Of An Insomniac

I toss, I turn, I thrash about;
The night-time silence seems to shout.
My mind plays leapfrog without pause,
Etching my brain with fangs and claws.

I yearn to sleep, perchance to dream;
I'd welcome even a nightmare's scream.
I count sheep backwards, drink warm milk,
Play mood tapes of soothing silk.

I put these techniques to the test,
Prescriptions for "a good night's rest"
To still my body's anguished moves;
But nothing changes— not a thing improves.

I sigh for sleep to overtake me,
"Come, dear Morpheus, do not forsake me!"
The seconds, minutes, hours churn,
But still I thrash, and toss, and turn.

The final act of this tragic play:
As I hear the birds announce the day,
A heaviness starts in my eyes and mind,
But it's time to rise for the daily grind!

Ruth C. Goodman

Happy Haunted Halloween

Happy, haunted Halloween!
The only night when ghosts are seen.
When witches stir their brewing pots,
And Frankenstein rattles his rusty locks.

When dark clouds cover a bright orange moon,
and werewolves howl a mournful tune.
Candles glowing through Jack-o'-Lanterns
throw haunting shadows in scary patterns.

Ghosts and goblins and vampire bats,
Clowns and cowboys and witches' hats.
"Trick or Treat" is the battle cry
as costumed figures go passing by.

Upside down and inside out,
Right side up and turn about.
When nothing is as it really seems,
It's happy, haunted Halloween!

Sandra L. Reagan

Today We Bury Our Dead

Give us this day our daily dead
The overworked and underfed
The words that always go unsaid
Nothing on earth is sacred, and today we bury our dead.

Today we bury our dead, I say today we bury our dead
Why did we stay, we should have fled
Instead of cowering under the bed
Now we follow without being led
And today we bury our dead.

Divorced from the one we wed
The body severed from the head
The blood is bled, a tear is shed
Nothing is worthy of hatred, and today we bury our dead.

Today we bury our dead, I say today we bury our dead
Bathed in blood and showered in dread
Dressed in but a single thread
No use for water, no will for bread
Today we bury our dead, say we
But tomorrow they will bury me.

Ray Ostrowski

My Girl: Sonnet

When I think of the one in which I love,
The pain inside is like none on this earth.
For now she has gone to a place above,
And now my girl cannot even be heard.

Each night I lay in deep sorrow and weep,
Thinking of her in all possible ways.
Not even getting a good night of sleep,
Thinking of my girl in her better days.

Except those from above no one has seen,
Where my little lady reigns everyday.
I hope where she is at, she is the queen,
She wanted to be with those who had sway.

Now that my lady has gone to heaven,
She can rest with her eternal brethren.

Melissa Ann Swearingen

The Past

The Past. What a concept!
The Past. Where all our mysteries lie.
Unsolved.
The Past. Our sins and faults are hidden in it.
Without it, this world would not be a world,
But a chaotic hell.
Our Past. What a concept!
Thousands of lives, now deaths
Thousands of deaths now forgotten.
Our future lies ahead,
But our memories lie in the past.
And memories are what we are made of.

Terence O'Dwyer

The Death Of The Pride

Her sails were full of wind that day,
  the Pride sped on without delay.
All hands on deck to trim the sail,
  the pumps were working to empty the bail.

Her bow rose up to challenge the sea,
  she was so proud if only you'd see.
The decks were awash from stem to stern,
  but she was determined to hold course firm.

Then all of sudden like a wink of an eye,
  she had no thoughts she was going to die.
The savage wind grew into a squall,
  and then her tall sails began to fall.

And as she slipped beneath the sea,
  she cried, "No!, No!, don't let it be.
"Please give me a chance to save my crew,"
  she was so sad to take the few.

And as she rests beneath the sea,
  bring me back again she plead.
"Fill my sails with wind once more,
  I'm still the Pride, the Pride of Baltimore."

Sebastian Barbagallo

Beyond The Realm Of Day

What force remains and worked before, the two sides of the day?
The query pending, but answered not
In human method way.

They 'in the know' will search and tell, until explained away,
Every mystery so clear defined
The workings of the day.

Effect of cause to effect again, the higher mind might say!
Of bangs and apes to now and you
And thus so goes the day.

But what of night unknown to come... and night before the day?
Why won't (or can't) these epochs fall
In line with reason's way.

The tracer's trail to morning claims the first song of the day
The seer's path to nightfall bids on last note that will play

Alas still night hides singer safe from human method way,
Which in the day seeks clues to night...
But night defines the day.

The night both first and last provides for knowledge seeking way,
But reason alone shall never go
Beyond the realm of day!

Michael J. Armstrong

The Problem

Rabbits are hopping from to den,
The raccoons are high in the trees.
Fish are jumping, beavers are thumping,
And eagles are flying as free as can be.

The smell of garbage chokes up the air,
And people complain about weather.
Men are trying to keep children from crying,
And people don't know what's the matter.

The smell of sewage seeps up from the ground,
And trees lay bare from acid rain.
The river is brown, the forest lays down,
And people just keep on POLLUTING.

Rabbits are struggling to stay alive,
Raccoons are permanently grounded.
Fish are depleting, beavers retreating,
And eagles are falling out of the sky.

Matt Larson

Fishing Streamside

The spring at last has come, I wade the stream no more
The rod's pliant body flexes toward the farther shore
The trembling arc, the fluid pressure know,
The infinite feel of movement, the slippery rock below.
No longer the numb cold of a dark dawn feel
Nor hunger's appetite at evening's savory meal
The peace and the solitude as the graying ashes glow;
The presence at streamside where native ghosts
Of yesterday kneel to drink and stay
With a sense of oneness for all of life and living
And a gratitude for the bounty of the day.

Russell Landwehr

The Border

Our van pulls up to the border

A lookout post still stands
the same that bristled with machines guns
aimed at us those decades ago
now unmanned, it looks innocent as a judge's
stand left there after a long gone horse race
nothing remains to tell of my flight to freedom that cold
starless November night
not a shred of the corner of coarse coat claimed by skin-raking
barbs just the tough grass I pressed flat into under the
searchlight's stripping stare as I crawled forward out of my
carcassed homeland toward my unlikely and unknown future in a
country whose books I could not read

My sons stand with me now, eyes seeking to that time
each trying to reach back into their father's freedom fighting
days while the music connecting them to their headphones
keeps them in their own beat and time

Maryann Landon

Terminal Enigma

The wind blows and with it my spirit flies away...
The sun beats down, rotting, what was once my home.
Success at last. I feel brave, accomplished and at peace.
The anger, the loneliness, and the pain are all gone.
They claim I am stupid and weak; I leave now to prove them wrong.
For not many are strong enough to embark on this journey.
They would rather hide in the security of their meaningless lives.
Nevertheless, I do take this journey cautiously, and pray it is not
too late to ask God for His forgiveness of my sins and guidance
into Heaven.

Zora Huddleston

I Thought Last Night I Saw You Cry

Standing by a bridge on the edge of a river
the shadow of the redwood and the full moon and the memory of
someone that you once knew
I thought last night I heard you cry when you got ready for bed
you finished writing in your diary your last thought of the day
and you started to think of your journey
you want to let go with all the things that bundle you up in
     little parcels
the right shape to fit the convenience of space
the way the carry-on luggage fits under the seat of an airplane
you said to yourself it is ok it is not too bad it does not matter
you will soon get there and someone will be by the bridge of the
     next river
perhaps you cried because you miss him
but his space is the whole void with no boundary
and nothing to say that this is where things begin and this is
     where things end
you turned off the computer and you said to yourself that it does
     not matter
you never loved him anyway
you turned off the light and you went to bed
but last night you did not cry and now you wonder who did
and now you wonder why
maybe someday you will

M. Duong-van

Copley Square

Copley Square seemed so remote, a bit of old back bay,
The sheraton-plazas' table d'hote, tourists buses sight-
seeing in May,
I really knew not much at all, but I had heard a lot,
of the lowells', saltonstalls and lodges, h.cabot.
however, then, we met and all this changed and the square
is not the same,
for of all the places I have ranged, none so forbidding
is now so tame.
trinity church we sat within, old south sheltered us in the rain,
b.p.L. so quiet from the din, john hancock declaring
for boston again,
within a few blocks, cafes and chic shops, like an island
self-sufficing,
truly the mother of boston squares, a boston creme pie
with all the icing.
So, thank you my dear, for making it so, wither with you
'tis delightful to go, and
may we recall dear copley square, forever changing
his and hers to their.

Tom Short

The Sea, My Best Medicine

I sat on a bench, by the sea, watching
the ships go by. I wondered where they
were going and to what strange land to arrive
Wish I were on one, I fantasized
different countries, I would see, different
languages to listen to, how nice to romanticize
There is something quieting to watch the waves
roll in and lap against the shore, my
mind is tranquil and so relaxed, I'm never
ever bored.
When I'm uptight, and feel so tense, sitting
by the sea, makes so much sense
Right now my thoughts are calm, my memory lax
psychiatry I don't need and that's a fact
The sea after all is medicine for my nerves
My mind becomes free, I've forgotten time
Peace has taken over, I've reached my goal
My secret is released, it has been told
The sea has always been around forever
for all to behold

Otto Harris

Stopping The Tango

A whisper on the wistful wind,
The silent sounds of sadness.
Withered hopes with wilted wishes,
Shattered dreams of scattered sorrows.

Fists, fury, frenzy, fear,
Panic, peril, penance, pain.
The dance of anger tangos
Its rhythmic patterns - and on it goes.
Forefathers taught their children well,
An heirloom passed, but who would tell?

Remnants, rubble, revenge, rage,
Trembling, tattered, tension, tears.
We tango on for we must dance,
It is our heritage, our stance.
A mirror reflects an image known,
Is it the child or parent who's shown?

A whisper on the wistful wind,
Sifting strains of sadness spent.
We've won the war with welcome warning,
Silhouettes step softly, slowing as the Tango stills.

Kathi Kreinik

Night Walk

For: Steven Rigg
Female is captive in the hunt.
The sister of your desire, mates with infatuation.
Joined, appears to be an emptiness.
Inside the shallow, lies the gateway.

Nocturnal intruder of mystical sleep:
the asylum waits, where wise men cease to exist.
While apparitions falter in realms of fire,
the invisible traveller opens the door,
heading me through, the tunnel of light.
     An armillary of Time
Trespassers, Yankee scout
The drummer's footsteps; a forgotten waltz
     Lay with me.
I am wet with love for you.
Sounds of shots, moaning in the waking,
Wounds unable to heal.
Magnolia scent, pain pleasure,
     Cruelties suitor
Death is theirs to share.
     Make dark the light...

Century

The Snowstorm

Outside the wind is wailing,
The sky is paling,
While inside all is warm.

The ancient bell tolls
Meaning the death of another soul.
Another soul lost to the terrible storm.

The fireplace is hot and all gather close,
Not one daring to break the silence,
But all repeating to themselves a terrible prose.

They all know that they will die.
Once again the bell tolls,
Meaning death to all warmed by fire.

The whirling snow making all weird noise,
They now move closer to the leaping flames,
And without knowing are on the roaring pyre.

Such wailing, moaning, helpless sounds
As was never heard before.
Then the noise stops and they will worry no more.

Patricia A. Hoare

515

A New Life

Here I sit running my feet through
the soft and warm sand, surprisingly
in the middle of October.

The water glistening from the
suns reflection as the oceans waves
roll up on the shore.

A gentle breeze blows from side
to side and I watch a happy
couple walking by.

I feel a peace so deep in
my mind, as I picture future
moments with the life I have growing inside.

Naylee Sylvia

Appalachian Mountain Memories

Rising mist from the emerald mountains
The softness of the streams
Flowing where? I often wondered,
These were a young man's dreams.

Why must I journey from such beauty
So little time if seems
Is there more beyond these mountains?
These were a young man's dreams.

I travelled most this whole world over
I've encountered so many schemes
The world today with so many adversities,
Can spoil a young man's dreams.

I lie here now in my autumn years
And make peace with God supreme
I have come home to my mountain memories
And what's left of an old man's dreams.

As I think my final thoughts
Of mountains so serene
I close my eyes and rise with the mist
As in the young man's dreams.

Sid White

Hope

The close of another day.
The solitary moment when you watch light leave.
Wondering what the darkness will hold forth.
Comfort is found in the softness of the stars.
No points, these, like those drawn in books;
rather warm and light, fading into darkness.

I love the stars.
The planets are unseen and unkind
but the stars are willing to walk through the night with you,
to guide and direct,
to give hope that in all the darkness
there is still light somewhere.

Rodney D. Hambrick

Fonda

I searched Mr. Webster, but failed to find
The words I needed to make this rhyme.
So I just proceeded as best as I could,
And asked the Lord to see what He would
Have me say, since no words exist
To meet my need, so to Him I did insist
That He enlighten mine eyes to behold
The fact that surely must be told.
And this is what I heard Him say,
There exists none other this very day
Than our fond—— Fonda.

Mattie Hershey

When You're Down, Look Up

He descended down with two doves,
The Son of God from high above.
He carried the hope of Joy and Peace,
An innocent lamb with snow white fleece.
He traveled over their land,
Healing people with the touch of a hand.
He wanted to show them love of his Father,
They just shrugged and said, don't bother.
Prophets thought Him a threat and a scare,
Threw Him in jail, tortured and mocked Him there.
You would think that all was lost,
Especially when they nailed Him to a cross.
He said, forgive them for they know not what they do,
Filled with burdens and sins, He died for me and you.
THANK YOU JESUS!!!

Tony R. Sasser

The Last Day

The wind blows,
The sound of rustling leaves echo though the trees
The majestic stag knows,
Soon, winter brings the chilling freeze.
The water is cold,
Bringing life and quenching thirst.
The forest seems on hold,
The silence reaches the ear first.
A sniff of the air,
The scent of danger, something is wrong
What is there?
Panic and fear, the feeling are strong.
Run, jump, flee,
There must be an escape.
What can it be?
Something emerges from the landscape.
A flash of light, a loud thunderous sound.
No way to fight, already on the ground.
The warm blood flows, and life drains away.
The majestic stag knows, this is his last day.

Tony Larsen

Castles

The sun is shining very bright,
The sounds of splashing waves bring delight;
To the little boy on the beach,
With his bucket and shovel right in reach.

The world is his for the day,
So he can laugh, run, and play.

He builds a castle in the sand,
He builds it with his own little hand;
The sun goes down, now it's gone,
He's left the castle which he was so fond.

The moon comes up over the hill,
And shines on the earth so still.
The castle stands, all alone.

Toni L. Willi

To Be Your Lover

You'd penetrate my soul with your kiss-
the tender moments, the unbridled bliss.
To feel the fire which lights your soul, to hear
the thoughts that make you whole.
To know the intimacies of your heart, and find
solace in you even when we're apart.
To walk a path of life in ease, and only feel
a gentle breeze.
To love so completely you every way, and know
I'll love you more tomorrow than today.

Nicole Nordberg

Our Star

The star of friendship,
The star of light,
Forgetting the hardship,
And shining so bright.

The star of remembrance,
The star of good times,
Helping friendships enhance,
Through the sharing of minds.

The star of rapture,
The star king of the galaxy,
Keeping us together,
Behind the bars of camaraderie.

Look for our star every night before bed,
Remember your friends,
And the tears that were shed.

Remember
  Your
    Friends.
      R.Y.F.
Rachel Lamb

Crystal Blue Dawn Marie

Her crystal blue eyes shimmer and shine just like
the sun beaming down on a wave on the open sea,
their warm and kind and they glisten like diamonds
that are hard to find.

With her long tresses of chestnut with a hint of
blonde in between she's a ravishing beauty to
behold, she is truly an artist's dream.

Obsessed only with her beauty he works hard to
complete his new work of art that will be uncovered
in a gallery in the city, for everyone to see.

Will people who visit just see a sketch of a
ravishing woman, or will they go beyond the
sketch and see a real and pure heart of gold
that lies underneath.

This is a real person and I know her by name, the
woman in this sketch is Crystal Blue Dawn Marie.

Maryellen Gibney

A Silent Tear

I awoke this morning to the dawn of a new day.
The sun was bright.
The birds in song.
But then - I cried a silent tear.

A silent tear for the Mother
who today will lose a child.
A silent tear for the child
Who today will lose a friend.

A silent tear for all who,
on this glorious day will be
touched by the violence which
has taken hold of our world.

For such a short time we are
here on this earth.
We can find time to fight.
We can find time to hate.
But where is the time for peace?
Where is the time for love?

So today I cry a silent tear-
Before I say a silent prayer.

Lenora Moore

The Silence Of The Grave

Silence, silence you stand by her grave
  The time has come.
    It's here,
    It's now,
Your mother has gone away
You stand alone on this day.

No other generation is before you
No one to lean on, no one to run to.
    It's here,
    It's now,
You are no longer a child at play
Your mother has gone away.

So stand tall, carry the load
You are the one they turn to on life's road.
    It's here,
    It's now,
Hear the silence of the grave
Your mother has gone away.

Rita Dye

Supper Time

Come in, come in, it's supper time
the tired mother said
as standing at the door she counts each
childish windblown head

When the last child comes in on a rush of
noisy feet, each grubby little hand is
washed and then they take their seat.

"Let's all give thanks" the Mother said for
this our daily bread, every little head
is bowed as the prayer of thank is said.

No fancy food in on their plates, but each
will have his share.
And eat the food with gladness that mother has placed there.

Now mother has long since been gone, and
the house no longer stands.
The children are all scattered to places throughout the land.

But still each night at supper time, there echoes
through each mind, the call that was so
dear to them "Come in it's supper time.

Wilma Treat

When The Steel Comes In

Nature us removed when the steel comes in.
The trees are cut.
They bleed and plead, but
no one cares, no one sees the blood that is shed
When the trees fall to the ground.
Their cries are piercing, their pain, intense.
No one hears, no one sees how they sacrifice
for the steel that comes in.
The birds, they lose their homes
when the trees crash to the ground
and are carried away after decades of solitude
and strength.
The trees, they cry when they die, but no one hears,
no one sees, how hurt are the trees
when the steel comes in.

Suzen Bell

517

A Plea To A New Age

I am air; I am fire
The undulating red-blue flame of desire.

The lively breeze of burning hope for humanity,
That man may soon recover his sanity—

Before he destroys all the earth's vibrating choir,
Through his greedy macho vanity.

Let woman now take her place,
With her soft giving face.

To help solve human's fate,
By unleashing man's bitter hate.

May they recreate a loving race,
So that "HE" won't soon set the date.

Reach deep with in the "self" to the being higher,
Allow the air to fan the fire.

May man take a step beside and not before,
Equalled, "Humankind" would soar—

By replenishing earth's natural attire,
Or the end will be the horror.

Marsha L. Curry

Never Written - Never Read

I ponder as I walk Life's pathway
The virtues and the ills as I contrived
To not look back but make amends for errors
Made in my overzealous drive.

Many songs still echo in my heart
And prose still lingers..never said
Because of time I do not have..
Never written..never read.

The shadows lengthen in the twilight..
I won't let darkness interfere
With all my plans for deeds undone in daytime
And I am sad to see night all too near.

Mary Utt Bishop

It's Sunrise

It's quiet
The warm yellow glow spreading slowly over the land
A cock crows, a dog barks
The smell of perking coffee fills the air
Paper boys tossing papers on porches
It's sunrise

Mothers shouting, children screaming,
The slamming of doors
Hurried footsteps on the walk
Car alarms beeping, motors staring
It's sunrise

Suddenly it's quiet again
The streets are bathed in a warm yellow glow
A warm breeze caresses the trees
Somewhere a bird chirps, a phone rings
Muted conversations filter through paper-thin walls
The neighborhood relaxes, another work day begins
It's sunrise

Marshall Gonsky

The Perennial Trunk

I am so in love with you.
　　The way your body twists and turns.
The way you move around me
　　or wrestle in the night.

You provide a shelter for me
　　and give me the soul of my breath.

I love the way your smell permeates my nostrils.
And how when I touch you —
　　you quiver.

I love spending the night with you
　　and listening to your evening voice.
And as the sun rises —
　　you shake the sunlight through your limbs.

I watch as you flex your muscles
　　and attend to your development.
You elicit from me all responses of praise
　　and as I fold my arms around you,
　　sometimes you even weep.

For I am in love with a tree.

Mary M. Fredlund

Be Aware Of The Weapon

The weapon has many names.
The weapon, the gun can kill instantly.
The weapon, the tongue can kill eventually.
The weapon, the knife can kill slowly.
The weapon, the hands can kill surely.
Be aware of the rapist, who rape our little
Children and destroy their virginity.
Be aware of the drug pusher, who destroys
the mind of our young and old.
Be aware of the gambler, who destroys
the soul.
Be aware of the thief, who steals of
our hard work and labor.
Be aware of the starvation, for there's
no food on the table.
Be aware of Aids, the sneakiest
Weapon of them all.
Be aware, Be aware of these weapon all,
or by these weapons you will surely fall.

Margie Tart

Foolish Flight

Why have I sought in man to find
The wisdom that is God's alone,
To let blind vanity confine
The measure of my stepping stone.
When has my God proclaimed to me
A master of all wisdom great,
When has He given up the key
Or power to judge another's fate?
Ah, foolish me, to seek so far for truth and right
Not knowing that I held it in my blinded sight.

Oh, blinded sight, to seek so long
To find another to impart
The worlds to fit into my song
The meaning that is in my heart.
Oh, foolish me, whose flight has led
Around this weary universe
Back to that spot from which I fled
A lonely path I did traverse.
There was no earthly words to fit my melody
And God alone can answer to my rhapsody.

Sarah Andrews-Stark

Cave In

It's not the end but it's sure begun.
The world's caving in and my sanity is on the run.
I stepped up but fell behind.
I lost sight but was not blind.
It's not time but it sure feels right.
The world's caving in and my sanity has left me tonight.
I came close but I got nil.
I lost thought but I forgot not.
It's not for me but it sure must be.
The world's caving in and my sanity has gone again.
I try to hide but a place I cannot find.
I lose wisdom but keep my mind.
It's not this but it's sure not that.
The world's caving in and my sanity is not mine.
I should go now but I can't leave.
I could stay now but not as me.
The world's caving in. In on me.

Ken Gable

Eulogy

This morning
  the yellowest river of sunlight
  poured through my window

I watched
  as she danced across the floor
  warming the room to full measure
  breathing life into each and every particle she touched
  as the room sang to her brilliance.

This evening
  the dark seems so much darker as it sighs into midnight,
  this cool night breeze stirs ice across my skin
  as the quiet of this room cries mortal in its silence

  And all this,
  the price cuts so much deeper
  for having touched her brilliant morning.

And yet,
  even in the darkest hour of this night,
  I would not have missed the gift of her morning
  for all the world.

D. Jean Harding

Untitled

On summer days, as you walk through the sylvan glades,
The zephyrs whisper through the leaves and call your name.
Sunbeams light your path as you walk along your way,
Lending a rosy glow to your delicate cheeks.
Gracefully, the trees bow as you pass where they stand.
In the glens, grass gently sways a fanfare to you.
All the flowers incline their blossoms toward you,
Hoping to please your senses with their fragrances.
The stream, gleefully rushing down the mountainside,
Babbles of your loveliness to all listening.
Flying through the trees, the songbirds sing to nature,
Meriting your insurpassable comeliness.
Above the crags, eagles soar in salute to you.
Timidly, the animals peek from the bushes,
Holding their breath, hoping to catch a glimpse of you.
All of nature lauds your exceptional beauty,
Yet, so much more than all this is my love for you.

Walter R. Litton, Jr.

"Merely Meers (Kats)"

As she looked upon the wall, at the picture of Merely Meers.
Their faces were so sweet and small, their bodies oh so dear.
Oh so innocent were their eyes, she just loved their shape and size.
It was becoming so much clearer, when she walked a bit nearer.
It looked the same, or so she thought,
Was it not the picture that she had bought?
At closer look she almost perished.
At closer peek the one Meer she cherished,
It had its face the other way.
What had happened this very day?
It seemed that at the opening of the light,
They ran ever so quickly into sight.
And stood together in a pack, so she wouldn't send them back.
Was it the hurry, or perhaps the scurry?
They ran too fast to stand up tall.
The poster was falling off the wall.
Oh my, she let out with a yelp!
Don't just stand there, give us some help!

Rochelle Bromberger

Our National Past Time

Our heroes were Ruth and Gehrig
Then DiMaggio with all his grace
And Jackie Robinson showed the world
That he too should have his place

Later we cheered for Willie and Mickey
Till Aaron homered his way to fame
Our heroes took to the diamond
Just for the love of the game

Now our heroes don't hit home runs
Or chase fly balls to the wall
The stadiums are all empty and silent
No umpires yelling "Play Ball!"

For today the players go on strike
The owners say money is the reason
But children don't understand contract matters
So their computers must finish the season

This October brings no playoffs
They'll play no World Series this year
The game of baseball has forgotten our youth
And gives them no heroes to cheer

Michael J. Verrastro

My Dream

A dream I had, I hoped would stay
Then I got up and it went away......

I dreamed the world was all at peace
Hatred and wars all did cease.......

I could even hear the birds joyously sing
Love and kindness to all mankind bring..

Everyone joined in helping one another
  regardless, of race, creed, religion a
  Black sister or white brother...........

Unfortunately, my dream didn't last
The calm, love and serenity went much too
  fast.............................

If a dream can be so beautiful and life
  a nightmare
Let us all pray that peace, harmony love
  and all God's blessings we can share....

Rose Orlin

519

Lesson Love Teaches

If you are lucky you can find Love in the first step,
Then others go through defeats and learn they have to except,

Some will seattle for what turns out to be second best,
Whenever you find True Love you know you are blessed,

True Love isn't found in a store bottled as a potion,
When you are young you might have that silly notion,

But pure and True Love can't be bought or sold,
When you have True Love treat it like it's gold,

Wheels set in motion you may hear them grind,
The lesson Love teaches, it's not always blind,

There's no certain age telling when, or if you will have it,
All I know is, if True Love was an animal, I've been bit!!!

Pixie L. Burr

"Love From A Distance"

When I met you I knew that no one could ever tear us apart.
Then we went our distant ways and that nearly broke my heart.
Since we've went our distant ways I know my love for you has
Grown, the only problem with that is we only talk on the telephone.

The first time I saw your face I knew that I would always love
You, even though the miles are between us that still holds true.
As I sit here missing you and the tears run down my face,
The pain grows deeper and my heart begins to pick its pace.

Although the miles are between us and my heart is broken
In two, I just want to tell you that i will always love you.
There's only one kind of love that has trouble growing and
Gives so much resistance, it hurts to say but that's the kind
Of loves we have, love from a distance.

Maria Monica Eckhardt

Ink On Paper

There are poems about homes.
There are rhymes about climes.
(What is prose? No one knows.)
We have odes about toads,
And themes about schemes.
Is there a riddle about a fiddle?
Or a thesis about a rhesus?
Did someone write a verse
About the virtues of a nurse?
Ink on paper isn't worth much
If someone's fancy it does not touch.
Current events are seldom pretty,
I.E., newspaper stories: Often painful, dirty.
Stark reality of the good and bad;
But aren't death notices always sad?
Still—
Ink on paper isn't worth much
If someone's heart it does not touch.

Tom N. Tubbs

Mommie

There are things I say and don't mean.
There are things I don't say and wished I did.
There are things I do and wished I didn't and didn't do
things I wished I did.
I could go on with all the things I wished I didn't
do and all the things I wanted to say and didn't say.
I love them very much and hope they understand, that
things change as time goes by.
One thing that will never change, is I love my children for
what they are, and not for we want them to be.

Margaret Denni

Mid-Life Crisis

In memory of Louis DeSisto
I never thought at this mid-life age
There ever could be, yet another stage
My future was empty, and I was always blue
But then along, came a wonderful man named Lou.
He offered me a new life, with hope and joy and love
And I knew at that moment, there truly was a Lord above.
He was my king, I was his queen
And for ten beautiful years, we shared everything
Now that he's gone, there's no time to mourn
For he taught me how to live,
But above all, how to give.
So once again I'm alone, but never again will I be blue
All because of a wonderful man named Lou!

Pauline DeSisto

What Makes People Special

You make the days worthwhile, each day as I live
There is always a special smile that both of you give,
There is never a dull moment to pass the time away
We keep our love shining each kind and loving day.

It is a big reward to know that two can share so much
There are so many times that I've needed that special touch,
To love you is to know you, this is a special task you do
Your heart is full of love by the simple things you do.

You turn an occasion of hurt into a day a new
From a time of joy to a time of hurt you've always been there,
I guess I never really realize how much you really care
Thanks for sharing so much love, with a big, big heart.

To my parents I say to you: The beginning has yet to start.

Sonja L. Murphy

Jennic

Of all the flowers in the world and all the water in the sea
there is nothing as gracious as the beauty of thee
as the seasons pass on by
they leave a happiness that won't die
It happened in the summertime
when your love took my mind
from that day you came into my life
I realized, finally, I had met my wife
I was honest, told you the score
'cause I have never loved like this before
thousands of miles fall between
but letting you go can only be dreamed
I am you and you are me
we fit together so easily
we need a name for our relationship
you and me — JENNIC — yes that's it

Nicholas Lorenzo

If You Were A Rose

If you were a rose, I'd be the thorn,
    There to protect you from hands of harm.
If you were a rose, I'd be the dew,
    There to quench the thirst, and help to make new.
If you were a rose, I'd be the leaf,
    Helping you bring beauty to a world of grief.
If you were a rose, I'd be the sand,
    Nourishing your needs and giving a helping hand.
But God made the roses for us to view,
    To enjoy their beauty; and their beauty renew.
For with each sprouting bud, God has blessed that rose,
    And has shown that His love for us ever grows.

Miranda Kay Rawls

"No Time To Pray"

We have time for everything, all during the day.
There just isn't enough time to kneel down to pray.

Time for work. Time to play.
Time to go shopping. No time to pray.

Time for my friends to go to the mall.
Time for my neighbor just giving them a call.

Time for the T.V. which plays all day.
But not enough time to kneel down and pray.

Time for washing and moping the floor.
Time to answer the knock at the door.

Time for the mailman who want a little
Chat. No time for my sister to lend her a hat.

Time for the game on Friday night.
Time for the wrestling "Oh" that's right.

Time to do my chores each day. I still
didn't have time to pray.

All the time God gave you today.
You had enough time to kneel down and pray.

"But instead you throw it Away."

Martha Jones

The Garden Of My Heart

In the center of the garden of my heart
There lies a dying willow
A willow where I used to play
Like a fish jumping out of a flourishing creek
A willow that I used to climb
Like a gorilla hoping through the trees
In a wool coat of mist
A willow that I used to love.
Now that willow weeps
That willow weeps with sorrow.

When I look at that sorrow I see a bowl
Empty like the depths of a cavern.
When I look at that sorrow I see a child
Weeping like a rush of many waterfalls.
When I look at that sorrow I see a cage
Barring my way to joy.
When I look at that sorrow I see a door
Ready to close, ready to slam.
When I look at that sorrow I see black.

Yet when I look at you, that willow thrives and the sorrow dies.

Katherine Knapp

To My Childhood Love...

I've put you on a shelf in the back of my mind
there you are collecting cobwebs and dust.

Like an old doll I once had, you were a childhood love
Well, now I've found you and dusted you off.
When I did so, I realized that I'd grown up
and don't need that doll anymore. It's time to
cast it away with all my other past fantasies.

I compare you to my doll because like her you
did not love me back. If love isn't fed back into
the heart of where it is found it dries, but like
a lake with no rain to fill it.

However, I am grateful to you, for you have made me stronger.
Now I can face what lies ahead in the future
of the adult world. A world where there is no room for
fantasy but only reality. I can look into the future
now because the past has been forgotten and locked
away in the corners of mind.

D. Robinson

The Monster

When I was a small child
There lived under my bed
A big furry monster with
A green shaggy head.

Every evening, when bedtime neared
It was for my life that I feared
My Dad would look under my bed and say
"See honey, he has gone away"

But as soon as he shut my bedroom door
I knew my monster was back with me once more.
Causing me to spend my nights full of fright
Always wishing I could leave on my bedroom light

He finally left when I turned five
Leaving me happy to still be alive
Forgetting about him for many, many years
Until the night my son came to me in tears

Begging and pleading for me
To look under his bed
At the big furry monster
With the green shaggy head.

Margy Ahnen

Grandpa's Workshop

Out behind the little blue house in a city far away
There stands a little workshop where my grandpa would pass the day.
Maybe he would fix a fan or tighten screws in a clock.
And if the weather was just right he would work his magic on the earth.
In autumn when the leaves all turned he would come and show us
  his wonders.
But as the years came and went and the seasons ran together
He found something he couldn't outdo: The endless march of time.
And in time God took him back and left the workshop empty.
But when you go there in the day, you can almost see him working.
And in the garden, where the wonders grow, you can almost hear
  the wind carrying his words.
And tho I will never hear his laugh as I walk on God's green
  earth
He will be with me always.
In my heart, in my soul, and in my mind forever.

Nicole Gover

Peaceful Waters

I used to be angry like the sea.
There was a lot of hate in me.
My emotions were very intense.
Up and down they went without making sense.
My mind had crashed upon the rocks.
I could not make the ill feelings stop.

Then I reached the end of my rope.
I was despondent and had no hope.
I do not know what was wrong.
Then Christ came along.
He put in my heart His Song.
He soothed the pain with His healing balm.
Instead of churning, my soul is calm.
In Him, I have no cause to be alarmed.

I look to Him and not to earth.
For the measure of my worth.
The rage within me has ceased.
The waters of my being are overflowing with peace.

Susan Conner

Untitled

Once again my Friend, you answered my request.
There was no need to worry, my Friend you are the best.
You, Yourself have told me, I only had to ask.
It doesn't really matter, how great or small the task.
"Ask, and you shall receive,"
I only need to believe.
"Seek, and you shall find,"
Peace, for my heart and mind.
"Knock, and it shall be opened for you,"
All doors if my faith is true.
So many times you have been there when I needed a friend near,
Just knowing You were with me, eased my many fears.
The burdens that I have carried, seem so small when they compare,
With the burden of the cross, You once had to bear.
You showed me that You loved me, that Your love for me was true,
When You said, "Forgive them, for they know not what they do."
The gift of life You gave me, when upon the cross You died,
My life now has new meaning, with You by my side.

Sherry Bradford

Untitled

why don't you come over?
there's a cloud in my room
and I could use some blue sky
it might rain and you have the umbrella that would work
you could dance on over
with those short quick steps you make
(red shoes celebrating the motion)
I've got some capezios
our shoes make quite a pair
why don't you come over?
I'm not a richer burden but I might make one demand
be my leading lady and I'll pretend
I'm your leading man
if you could steal some moments
(hide them deep in your pockets)
I wouldn't tell
I'd put them in my collection
moments too soon turn to memories
so why don't you come over?

Michael R. Nastari

Sweet Inspiration

Meditation causes sweet inspiration deeply drawn from
these love letters I see before me.

Fragments of time oscillate an echo in my mind which
recalls our sweet, beautiful, and joyous moments together.

Here and there I sense a sudden explosion of love in the air.

So I reach for the warmth of a body that really isn't there.

I stare frequently at her empty and abandon chair wandering,
just wandering, if she was ever really there.

Thinking of her to bring brightness into a rainy day.

My nights are forever cold, my days always old.

Since she wandered astray heaven knows I long for her each
night and many times during my dreary day.

Thinking of her to remember all the beauty, warmth, and
loveliness which entered my life at the first sight of her face.

Now I find myself losing life's race.

Headed for an uncertain destination because I no longer
have my sweet inspiration.

Otis Wilson

Palms

Majestic frail towers. How do they stand?
These palms on the beach, jabbed into sand
silhouette trunks that flex, bend and lean
topped by a parasol of plastic like sheen

Torqued by gale, whipped by sea
seduced by sun, stirred by breeze
undaunted, proud with regal grace
strange, this product of nature
that seems out of place

If one were given time with a free hand
what could be the replacement design to enhance
these grenadier guardians tapering command
of elegant poise, with its awkward stance?

Larry Lawlor

Royal Majestic

I'm so sick of this place
  these rooms don't fit anymore

Shoes with no feet
  chairs holding shirts and pants
darkened T.V. screen
  "you know...I could break your neck
like this"
  translucent china collecting dust in
there boxes, maps on the walls,
  empty bottles, black blankets, books,
alarm clocks, lamps, "the floor's f***ed up"
  radios, blank papers, notebooks,

Loose connections...
  almost
certain meanings...almost...

Nothing does
  what it's supposed to do.

Kevin Finnen

Untitled

It used to seem so innocent
These traffic lights and incense candles
This foolish heart in love with you
But now I've changed and it's so strange
Standing here outside your door.
I guess I've been so long away
The molten tide of time has come
And altered all my dreams.
But still I feel
Beneath my skin
That somehow I belong to you
Please forgive me
All these crazy fantasies
It's just because you broke my heart
I didn't know what else to do.
I hope the world will understand
Wash away my tears and pain
Let me have one moments peace
Resting in your arms
Innocent once again.

Marcel Halewijn

On Time And Eternity

There was a time when time first came to be.
There was a time for man's first infancy.
Time then, time now and all the nows to be.
Till one last man and one last now shall close this history.
But then I know there yet remains for me.
My life, my hope, I meet my destiny.

Thomas J. Dowling

Eclipse

Truly, if the stars had eyes they still could not see;
They are blind to the feelings that are hidden within me.
The man in the moon surely could not alter my ways;
Because there are so many memories that I've gathered in past days.
If the oceans' wisest creatures could swim through my head;
They still would get lost-by my thoughts they're misled.
If all the birds in the sky were suddenly brought all together;
They would gain weight and lose flight and ruffle their feathers.
So if only our eyes could see deep in our hearts;
We'd only drown our emotions in a sea full of sharks.
So keep all your dreams and lock them inside;
Protect what your heart knows is true.
Then maybe one day when luck comes your way;
You'll find you have nothing to hide.

Timotheus Dumsha

My Kids

When I think about my kids my heart fills with pride. Just to
know they are my kids makes me happy inside. They have been
neglected, battered and bruised. Not once have they blamed me
or ever accused. They have been pushed aside and put off for
others I thought needed me more. Yet they were always there
for me to love and adore. When things go wrong and everyone
else is gone. There are my kids right where they belong. Beside
me are my kids to help me get through whatever life and myself
have put me though. They listen and hear every sad word I say
and when I'm hard on them they love me any way. Some say
they are spoiled and selfish I know but wherever I go my kids
will go. We'll stand together from this day on and never again
will I allow my kids to be done wrong. Dear Lord, please help
me to be the mother I should be, everyday remembering my kids
are a living part of me. I asked my father for a boy and girl.
Now I ask you father help me raise them in this world. Never
again dear Lord allow me to neglect them. Help me to be proud
of my kids until me life grows dim.

Lillian McLeod

Together

Though the skies are always blue,
they are never sad.
And I love you, and that ain't bad,
Lovers are loved, the whole world over,
Even when they are not knee deep in clover.

When you look out to the sea,
the sun shines on you and me.
A year has passed, We are still in love.
THE HONEYMOON IS GLORIOUS,
AS THE HEAVENS ABOVE.
Togetherness is beautiful, don't you see?
It really is great for you and me.

Willamette Sampino

Tears

Little drops of Water running from my eye's
They can be from laughter happiness, fear, hurt or pain
This time they fall for a very true and Dear Person
A person I love with every little piece of my heart
I cry for him - for his side I am being stripped away.

He is going to end his pain, but only add to mine
Why can't he see the love he and his family possess inside
Show him (somehow) how deeply everyone cares.
These little tears fill my heart
They drown the feelings deep inside.
I'm starting to feel numb, I can't live without him.
I'll have to if I'm carrying his child
I could kill myself but not a beautiful soul
Created out of love and happiness.
A soul like that, I could not close the door on.

Marie C. Schrankel Leftwich

Grandparents

My grandparents are loving and caring,
They both have stories worth sharing.

My grandma loves it when I want to help,
And when I make a mess, she never starts to yelp.

My grandpa always lets me watch TV,
Even if the Aggies are in favor 10-3.

My grandma bakes me yummy treats like pimento cheese,
And she forgives me even when I don't say "please."

My grandpa tells me stories of when he was in war,
And the tales he tells are really great; they're never really
  a bore.

Working with my grandma isn't much of a chore,
In fact when we're done, I ask her if there's more.

When I'm with my grandparents, it's almost like in heaven,
On a scale of 1-10, they're definitely an 11!

Lori Evans

Little Girl

I remember a little girl, who used to live with me
thought I could do anything
and sat upon my knee

She used to listen to my records, and I'd show her how to dance
that girl would follow me anywhere
if she had the chance

One day I turned around, and the little girl was gone
replaced by a pretty young woman
with someone else to depend upon

So now she is all grown-up, and the wedding date is set
suddenly I feel that I must grasp
every moment I can get

I'm very happy for her, she's found a love that's true
but I still get this feeling
and I must confess to you

There's a tiny part of me, about the size of a pearl
that wishes I could still grab hold
of that precious little girl

Julie Tuttle

Bondage

In the stillness of the dark room
thoughts of you away, fill my heart with gloom
the want and desire are very there
but possession I have none, for I am bare.

But I ask only this of you sweetheart
Confide in me, and know my only want and desire
Is for our love to never, ever depart.
By my will is strong, and I'll earn what we require

I have but one dream, to spend forever with you
work until I die, to fulfill you every wish
If this would show my love, I would gladly do.
for it would be worth it all, for just one small kiss.

To put my trust in one so kind
was not very difficult to do
for with your charm, you made me blind
and anxious for our first rendezvous

But now, alone and without you to hold,
I pray that one day soon
I won't be left out in the cold
But have you in my arms, and our love to resume.

Isaac T. Samaniego

Sea Calling

Mighty river flow
Sweeping the land
Gathering all in its
Outstretched hands
Of living flowing power.
Trees yield their branches
Fields yield their crops
Houses stand in the wash
That washes clean
Or stagnates with filth
And we, the people, wonder
How could we have forgotten
Its power and merciless rage
When gathered together for its
Mighty return to the sea.
The sea, calling it home
Calling the waters home.

M. C. M. Johnston

Memories Of Mom

My memories of mom are so
    sweet and clear.
I will cherish them always
    and keep them near.
I grow older as each day
    passes by.
Sometimes I wish to just
    sit and cry.
My memories of Mom are with
    me each day.
These are loving memories
    that shall never go away.
I love my mom, so precious and
    dear.
I pray that my memories will
    always be here.

J. W. Black

What Is A Father?

Fathers come in a variety of hues
tall, short, lean or fat,
Who give love to all of you
And referees many spats.

A father gains his strength
From the Father from above,
As he goes to all lengths
To show his children love.

A father can be a farmer,
Banker, lawyer or President,
But all try their best to keep
Their children from accidents.

Some fathers teach their kids
To play all kinds of ball,
Just as their fathers did
To swat one over the wall.

One girl stated in a letter,
Anyone can be a father,
But it takes someone special
To really be a dad.

Vera M. Wolf

God's Gifts

A baby's cry, a butterfly
    Tears of joy, a girl, a boy

Seniors walking hand in hand
    Shifting winds across the sand

Speckled birds, rows of trees
    Bluesy sky, falling leaves

Water falling, cooling, splashing
    Raindrops gentle, thunder crashing

Dog
    Cats
        Fishes, too

People friendly
    me... you...

Mary T. Mansfield

Tears

There was a time I cried.
Tears of love filled my eyes.
The feelings I had were
definitely strong. Then all
the sudden you were
gone. I loved you with all
my heart and you know
that is true I would have
done anything... I would
have died for you why
did you leave. You left me
alone when I needed you
most. Sometimes I still cry
but the tears that fall
from my eyes is tears that
make me remember the
first day we meet in early...
June

Misty Avery

Untitled

Who are those who are better
than I when I look out with mine?
What is more filled with color
When two of them outwardly shine?
Who can look at pretentious
And comprehend fully the real?
Who can laugh without laughter
And roll in their caves like a wheel?

Who can tell what is coming
Without ever a turn to behind?
Who can seem far away
While perceptively piercing your mind?
Who can vary so greatly
In color, in shape and in size?
Take good care of them. They hold
the key to the truth and the lies:
They're our eyes.

Peter G. Phillips

Friendship

There's a miracle called friendship
That dwells within the heart
And you don't know how it happens
Or when it gets its start.
But the happiness it brings you
Always gives a special lift
And you realize that friendship
Is God's most treasured gift.

Lee Lawrence Pierce

The Masterpiece

The most perfect machine,
    That ever was built
Required no tools,
    But was pieced like a quilt.

Little by little,
    It grew and grew
And then it was born,
    To a world that was new.

With all of its pieces,
    It needed no part
Only a tap,
    To get it to start.

And then it began,
    Its noisy beginning
With all its new gears,
    All perfectly spinning.

This perfect machine,
    That its parents are seeing
Is a beautifully made,
    New Human Being.

Kevin M. Campisi

On Retirement

Folks will tell you you've crossed
that Great Divine
That there is no turning back
That the years to retirement
are full of joy
But the years beyond are black.
Well!
Don't you listen to all that jazz
Don't you believe that stuff
Your second childhood will be a blast
I've been there,
I know
Sho Nuff!!!

Virginia I. Prest

The Rose

I saw, a wilted flower,
    that held, my curiosity,
there was,
    something in particular,
that really, attracted me.
    I stopped, for a moment,
for I really,
    had to see,
I looked,
    inside the flower,
to find,
    the beauty seed.
I saw,
    the seed of beauty,
that clearly before,
    wasn't there,
I just,
    had to, look inside,
for the rose, the rose
    to appear!

Marta Bolton

"My Dream"

My poem is a dream
that I dream every night
either with my eyes closed
or with them open wide

I dream with many people
like in a Carnival
it is not in this country
but is not very far

I think that I see turkeys
and also Christmas trees
I sense the smell of berries
the aroma of pine trees

Many children are praying
thanking God for their treats
young and old people dancing
happily on the streets

They all are eating mangoes
and peeling ripe bananas
it's Thanksgiving in Haiti
and Christmas in Havana!!!

Maria C. Sanchez

Seeing The Light

You are the light
that let me find my way
through the deep dark tunnels
I've buried myself in.

You put nothing but joy
in my life
Never any sadness from you
Never clouding my sun.
When it rains
you allow me to see
the rainbow.

If I had any guy
on this earth
I would not be happy
unless it was you.
Of course I love you
because you let me enjoy seeing
the light I have never
seen before.

Melissa A. Garcia

The Search

Empty is the heart,
that longs for another.
A void not filled,
by sibling, friend, or mother.
Thus begins a painful search,
for that missing piece of me.
Gazing at you,
a mirror image I see.
Where my path is going,
only God knows.
It's as uncontrollable,
as which way the wind blows.
Fate steers our paths,
on a collision course.
So to you my heart goes freely,
without remorse.
As I give you this gift,
I know my search is through.
My world is now filled,
with overpowering thoughts of you.

Stephen Tarmey

Love

It's the emotion inside
That makes you cry
When you are sad
It makes you feel glad
When you help someone out who is
Deprived of shelter and food
It touches your body and soul to
make it sing
To thee Almighty King
It gladdens your heart
through sorrow and pain
It makes you forgive someone you hate
It makes a woman's labor pain
turn into joy
When her child comes out
It's a word that
does so many things
In a human being's life
It's the start and the end
It's a word about the human heart

Robert Thorson

Fragment

When we went to tell my aged mother
that my brother
her first born
had died suddenly of a heart attack
we talked of other things first
avoiding the subject
but she had already disappeared
into a little front room
and was sitting straight up in a chair
waiting for it.

Trudi V. Wiley

The Beloved

Ruby-red are his lips
That quiver like a bow,
Releasing gentle streams of words
That wash away my woes.

Immaculate glistening pearls
Underneath them show,
Exuding a smile...
Lingering a while...

Ah! How I love him so!!!

Mariquita N. Tandoc

Autumn Leaves

It came to be, for me, one day,
that things in this life can
easily slip away, the autumn
leaves give way to bare branches
of winter,
And I am like the tree,
bare, cold, and shivering inside,
longing for a warmth and new growth,
I am moved for awhile,
but it is just the winds
of winter stirring inside of me,
then finally, the ice has melted
inside, and a feeling of new
growth over whelms me, on a
warm Spring day, life can
slip away, but for now, life
will grow some how,
then give way,
    to Autumn leaves

Robert Andrew

Love Is

Love is a warm summer breeze
That riffles gently in the trees

Love is a melodic tune
Whose dulcet strains
Augurs love's boon

Love is a fine wine
Whose bouquet stands
The test of time

Love is a sweet kiss
That fills one's heart with bliss

Love is a fleeting glance
That one's soul entrances

Love is a warm embrace
That flushes color to your face

Love is a spontaneous thought
That limns what love has wrought

Love is a sheepish grin
That mask's love's inner din

Love is many things
That from within our hearts take wing

Wilmot N. Grant

Joy In My Heart

There's a joy in my heart
That sorrow cannot reach
Wings that take me forward
When troubles slow my feet
There's a peacefulness that lifts me
When cares would hold me down
God's love and hope surrounds me
When I kneel upon the ground

Karen Morphis

She Was Pretty As A Lily

It was a fairy
that was pretty as a lily.
Her curry was too pretty,
it was pretty as a rosy.

She had a diadem,
which sparkled as stars.
Yet she was pretty as a lily.

Her hair was dark as a crow
and long as branches.
She was known as Filomina
in that rainbow forest.

As she walked by,
she smelled the pretty flowers,
and her hair, long as forever
sheds as leaves
by the cool breeze.

Kaniz Hussain

Wings Of Love

Oh song bird sing a song,
    that will calm my poor soul.
Sing it softly with words of love,
    from days of old.
Pour out your golden chords,
    so sweetly let them flow.
Sing out your words of love,
    and soar across the sky.
I'll keep them here within my heart,
    and never let them die.

Mable Jean Johnson

Where's The Magic?

It is not tricks or a tall black hat
That we, as educators need.
It's basic strategies and direction
From those who opt to "lead".
We need no more infusion,
Initiatives and such.
It's truth and more stability
That may provide that "magic touch".
How can we have expectations high
If the delivery system's not strong?
No quality products ensuing
When the infrastructure's wrong.
Magicians are quite entertaining
Providing a suspense-filled show,
But education is serious business
Shaping youth in the way they will grow.
If we want to be on the cutting edge,
We can't use a lamp or a genie,
The "magic touch" is deep inside
Be your own creative Houdini!

Myra Powell Spriggs

"Kids 1994"

What is wrong with kids today?
That's what you hear people say.
Do you know what they go through?
When they leave to go to school.

Are they safe out on the streets?
Can they trust people they meet?
When you ask "How was your day?"
They don't have too much to say.

So give them all the love you can.
Try to listen and understand.
Pray to God to keep them safe,
And bring them back to you today.

Patricia K. Stephens

"Whew"

Terrible, terrible things I see
The awesome stinger of a killer bee.

The giant teeth of a grisly bear
and purple pools
With shadows lurking there

The midnight scream
of an awful witch
A deep dark hole
as black as pitch.

The eerie sounds
in the woods at night
of crawly things
That want to bite.

Big long hands
approach my bed -
"Wake up, wake up, you sleepy head."
I'm saved again
from things so bad,
and the worst dream I ever had!

Pauline Herzberg

Leningrad 1942-43

Like a silent movie
the Babushkas wail
mouths open
circles of grief
sobs of sirens
at nightmare time
in
Leningrad.
Dead baby
buried at mother's breast
old woman
frozen to soldier son
ice white horse
awaiting the knife.
This spirit
these Russians
who took the death
and lived
in
Leningrad.

Sally Rainer

"Betrayal"

Surfaced at last the real ways,
the beliefs of countless years.
Many feelings in the midst of dreams,
have been swept away in tears.

So I may seem to cry,
with unnecessary pain.
I had hoped for the sun,
and all I got was rain.

As nature has betrayed me,
so have my friends.
I will no longer see neutral,
but will color them again.

I have come to the conclusion,
I trusted a created illusion.
One based on acceptance,
Of the color of my skin.

Deep down I have been sold,
to the highest bidder again.
Deep down I have failed to watch
for betrayal by a friend.

Lawrence E. Winston

It's Monday, Already!

How great, it's Friday
The best day of the week,
No more paperwork
Except under my feet.

Two days to recover
All sanity that was lost,
Only to blink three times
And you're back facing the boss.

Karen G. Moore

Amitie Sincere

To most of us we have spent
the best part of our lives with them.
Their memories touch us,
we smile to think of them.
We are not alike
yet our differences become us
in worlds where we knew
how to find ourselves.

Lindsay Miller

Untitled

Deserted and devastated
the boy stands taut
belittled and betrayed
the boy looks lost.
Just another lost soul
without a clue why.
The umbilical cord of support
severed from its source left to drift.

Mike Wilson

Newness of Life

The joy of Easter
the breath of spring

The resurrection of our saviour
The new life Jesus brings

Through the precious holy spirit
Our guide from beginning to end

We are even so gently led
by our Comforter and friend

Agape love floods our hearts
So much joy divine
Peace that passeth all understanding
Forever is yours and mine

Lois N. Butler

The Patient Rose

Early in the spring, on the trees,
   The buds turn into leaves,
And dandelions and daisies are
   Everywhere to be seen.

But, hidden in my memories,
   Is the most beautiful flower,
That brightens up my life,
   Even at the darkest hour.

It gives me strength each passing day,
   And I cherish it with all my heart,
And though it's many miles away,
   We will never be apart.

It gives me so much love each day,
   Much more than it knows,
For, this flower is you, my love,
   You are my patient rose.

Lisa Good

Summer Still

The heat even dulls
the buzz of the bees
as they float
above the rippling,
yellow grass.

I settle under a sturdy oak
with leaves still green
despite the sun's weakening grip -
for its roots are deep
and it slowly sucks
the hidden moisture of the earth.

Though sweat trickles to my nose,
I dare not blink -
less I miss this eclipse
of the day's confusion;
For like a movie set on pause,
stillness reveals
the Masterful details
that action blurs.

Linda Dunn

"Through The Looking Glass"

As I sit here all alone
The echo of the wind I hear,
It too lets out a moan
Because instead of love there's fear.

In the street of empty dreams,
I have made my bed to rest,
My eyes great pain have seen
Empty souls where sorrows nest.

Faceless people roam the world
Emotionless, love they have forgotten,
The fear has gotten to their hearts
Their minds forever rotten.

The world has filled with prejudice
As punishment they roam alone
Yet they think to live in bliss -
But how to love remains unknown.

Maria Tsucalas

Make Our Mark

The whippoorwill, bright daffodil
The esplanade in bloom...
The day is new, with people who
Will know they can assume...

That life will be a cacophony
A symphony of sound
And pleasant sight, both day and night
Enchantments that abound.

But whisper wind, it doth rescind
The pledge of happiness
No sacred vow, no promise how...
Instead it will confess...

If we bend and do intend
To stop along the way
Through golden bower, a work of power
We'll greet each bright new day

And when the sun has just begun
To make its downward arc
Warm colors melt, a reverence felt
We've strived to make our mark.

Narda Wade Curlee

From Tuesday To Thursday

In City

The tree is by the garden wall.
The gate, beside the tree,
is open, waiting for a friend
who waits to visit me.

The mail is slow, old fashioned,
relaxed and undertaxed, out here,
so I could write and, quietly say,
"Could you come to visit
for luncheon, and, the day?

The tree is by the garden,
and, I see the rising sun
is sending rays to warm the day;
I'm waiting for my fun.

Marilyn Higham

Only a Moment

The sun reflects some kind of magic
The glowing yellow-gold leaves
   give off a life-giving feeling
      as they take in their last moments
It cannot be put into words
   the beauty of nature's ways
The warmth
   the light
      the whisper
In a few days
   it will all be gone
but for only a moment
   as it will appear again
      in some other form
God's great love and beauty

Leslie C. Crow

The Moment

The more we're together,
the harder we fall.
This wasn't the plan... No Not at All.
To find something so precious, to hold,
to have the experience, to taste...
and then let go.
Never to be the same as you were before.
Unreal like a dream,
now I have to close that door.

Sharron Paramore

Leaving

Leaving the ones you love is
the hardest thing to do
you don't want to cry when you
leave but you have to
you tell them not to cry
but they do
you say you'll be back someday
but you don't know when
Deep down inside your doubtful
but you still have hope
you don't know if you'll ever
see them again
but they will always be there
In your thoughts, your dreams
and in your heart

Robyn M. Schindewolf

The Heart Is Like A Rose

As the rose's home is in the garden
the heart belongs in the body, and
the family is its garden.

As like the rose, the heart needs
sunshine, to get it out of the
darkness, and to make it grow.

The rose needs oxygen to make it
bloom every day and keep it alive,
as like the heart

Both need love, for without love
they could wither away to nothing.
The rose needs someone to tend to
the garden, to pull the weeds and
give it water.
As the heart needs someone to hold
and love it.

Without sunshine, oxygen, and
love both the heart and the rose
could shrivel up and disappear.

Peggy Lansberry

Hi-View

Height overlooks
   the intricate designs,
seventeen stories high
   I view the blueprint;
I see the valley
   much as Gods must do.
And if I never knew
   the secret of bird
the simple string
   that threads a nest,
or the faint loop
   of dew and silk
a spider flings -
   I would believe
the world was more toy
   than anything.

Verlejean Parker

Hope

Hope is like sunshine.
The kind of sunshine that
peaks through the clouds after a
long rain. You know it is too
bright for your eyes, but you search
for it anyway. Anticipating its
brilliance and the warmth it brings.

Lisa Conley

Her Last Roses

It was autumn,
The last week of October.
A gentle breeze was blowing.
There was a stillness in the air.
Each morning I picked from
Her garden,
One of her cherished roses,
That she had tended with care.
She examined them carefully.
There was a silence.
She looked at me and said,
"I am dying slowly with them,
And until we shall meet again
GOD LOVE YOU."

Mary Rose Shoemaker

Untitled

On a cold and snowy April day
The Lord called my love away
In the twinkling of an eye
No time to say a last "good-bye"

The day began like any other
We had no hint of the twilights sad-
We spent a day of work and pleasure
The last we'd ever spend together

So take time to tell the one you love
How much you do.
Before the Lord makes a call on you

It was the way he'd said - "Be
ready". "I'll call you away".
"You'll never know the time or day".

Now I'm left alone and blue
With all our dreams that can't
come true.

Norma J. Smith

527

Indian Night Wind

Briskly through the night
  the moon listens
As the leaves rustle,
  then whistle
Keeping feelings hidden
  deep within a smile.
Fresh, warm yet crisp,
  gentle, strong but bitter.
How the bittersweet grows now
  only to blossom.
Camouflaged by the golden leaves
  Blown aimlessly
With the help
  of the Indian Night Wind.

Katherine Mary Weller

Untitled

A golden aura envelops
the nightly firmament,
nudging awake slumbering plants
who unfold flowering petals
and sharpen colorful hues.
Songbirds blast joyous trumpets,
chorusing glorious rounds
that dance across tree tops.
Perched upon hidden poises
amongst dew misted foliage,
their crescendo builds
with steady confidence
towards thunderous ovation
that exalts heavenly glory.

This morning a man awakes;
today he will wed.
Outside he is welcomed by a pleading call.
Come plant your seeds in our fertile soils.
For surely your love was meant
to be the greatest in our garden.

Tom Monahan

The Chirping Of The Crickets

The chirping crickets,
The noise,
The never-ending noise

We follow the noise,
And we get trapped,
And we all die,

The crickets keep chirping,
And the crow keeps watching,
And the noise never ends.

Stephanie Deitz

Her Light Lives On

My mother passed away, today.
The sun was clouded;
the sky was gray.
The birds sang quietly,
throughout the day.
Words cannot express what to say,
when someone you love has gone away.
My heart is heavy with the loss;
yet, my spirits are high
knowing into God's hands she crossed.
Oh sweetest heart, oh sweetest song,
I know she has not truly gone;
for I will carry her "light" within,
all my life long.

Laraine F. Palumbo

The Interloper

Stark and black
The old house stands
Without doors and windows
Letting the wind sweep
Through the empty rooms

A dog has left mud-caked tracks
Across the front porch
Detouring during a sudden shower
Running ahead of a quail hunter
My mother's ghost
May have chased the dog away
With a broom as she stood in the doorway

All the other floors are swept clean
On this early winter morning
I see my father talking to strangers
As the old family farm fades away
Like the end of a silent movie
And the broken country road
Can't take me away fast enough

Look who is really the interloper!

Thomas A. Baker

"Knight"

Once believed in fairy tales
The once upon a time
The good you knew would soon prevail
The sun would always shine
The storm blew in
The story dimmed
The prince did not prevail
The knight in shinning armour
Bellowed out a wail
He lost his will
The earth stood still
The silence in the night
Now beaten down
He lost his crown
The dawning of the light.

Marci Walgren

Grandpa Loves You

This is from your grandpa
The one who scares you so
He really does love you
Just wanted you to know
It seems you do not like him
At least not every much
But you're way too young to worry
About men and boys and such
He's not real mean and ornery
He's not too bad at all
'Course maybe that's the reason
Your daddy got so tall
But one thing to remember
Next time you come to stay
That wonderful, loving Grandma
Won't be far away
And when she's round for certain
Things can't be all that bad
And if you still have doubts
Just ask you Mom and Dad.

Roy A. Cooper

Tree

The old tree stands alone now.
The others were all cut down.
Her branches are so droopy,
Her roots are turning grey;
She needs the sun upon her back;
To keep the chill away.
So proud and tall she use to be,
When birds were there to nest.
Now years have done there toll I fear!
She's dying like the rest.

Roseann Hughes-Burns

Where Did It Go

Where did it go?
The peace, the happiness,
the joy.

Did it go far away to some unknown
  place, forever
Or is it here
Waiting to be seen
by one whose heart is filled with doubt

Will it come or will it go
That, I do not know

For only time will tell,
where the peace and joy will be

Marissa Willenbring

The City Of Faded Dreams

Hollywood,
The popular theaters
The handprints in cement
The pink gold sidewalk
That were perfect, without a dent.

Could it be the same city
I visited last year?
Could the spray painted sidewalk
Be the same one that everyone cheered?

What happened to the heroes,
Who appeared on the silver screen?
What happened to the lovers
And the young starlets dreams?

Could it have been my imagination
Or was the city not all it seemed?
I'm not sure anyone knows what happened
To the faded city of dreams.

Monica Rowinski

A New Day

Bright golden streamers in the sky,
The promise of a new born day.
Upon a rosy tinted cloud
The dawn peeks in to waken me,
On silent swiftly moving wings.
Slow your fleeting pace
Oh day of regal splendor
So I may ponder on your worth.
What promise do you hold for me?
A tear, a sigh, or boundless joy
That leaps to unexpected heights?
Go then, on your swift winged journey
And I will stay behind
To live this brand new day.

Robert Fox

528

Eyes

The brilliance of anger
The quality of torture
They see through me,
They look straight through me.
Through my feelings,
Through my soul.
They tear at my flesh,
They scream at my brain
They never forgive,
They never forget.
They never let me be me.

Kate Rundstrom

Music (?)

The bulging veins, the popping eyes;
The squalls and shrieks that agonize.
Convulsive bodies, torsos bare,
Afoul with sweat and matted hair.
Crescendoing cacophony
Assailing ears, discordantly,
Plus frenzied beat beyond control—
And that, my friend, is Rock and Roll!

Willard V. Roberts

Ragpicker's Wine

The bitter grapes of the lonely man,
The streets his only vine,
His tears, they fill his empty cup
As he drinks the Ragpicker's Wine.

He lives and breathes in the dust
And his eyes I could not face
He filled me with an angry lust
To denounce this hopeless place.

Rage boils forth from deep inside
For his burden is too great,
The shuffle of the lonely soul's ride
Has filled me full of hate.

He drinks his cup of Ragpicker's Wine,
Yet he tires not it seems
He is too often hungry to dine
On his all-forgotten dreams.

Ragpicker's Wine filled my cup
I have drunk and now I am lost,
'Tis with the lonely man I must sup,
One drink and I have paid the cost.

Rose Fioretti

Father

Father
The strong one
Father
The leader
Father
The caretaker
Father
The giver
Father
The friend
Father
The sick
Father
The weak
Father
Dead
Father
I LOVE YOU!

Sharon Franklin

Singularity

A single rose in the garden,
the sun begins to slowly rise.
The rays beam down on it.
The rose slowly dies.

The petals begin to wilt,
they fall one by one.
Down, down, down they go,
the flowers life is done.

I realize the rose is like me,
I thought as time passed by.
Like the rose I must go,
I must also die.

I pondered a thought as I walked on.
I would anticipate that day.
Then, just as the rose, I thought,
I'll slowly fade away.

Melissa Dudich

Storm

The sky turned dark
The sun disappeared
I saw lightning in the distance
And heard thunder in my ears

I thought to myself
That the storm would be bad
It started to drizzle
Then to pour

I slowly got wet
Then slowly got soaked
The water was cold
Like a winters breeze

Then it stopped
The sun came out
And the clouds moved away
To bother me on another day

Tim Carmack

The Ocean

As I look across the water
the sun glistens a path for me
I cannot imagine the wonders
the sights there are to see.

Such peace as the water ripples
waves rushing into shore,
tranquility envelops my body,
troubles matter to me no more.

I close my eyes and listen,
as the ocean calls to me
Come walk along the shoreline
find peace and be free.

I think God must have been proud
when he finished on the sixth day,
I wonder what he was thinking
I wonder if he felt this way.

To live each day as this one
how wonderful that would be
Sitting along the shore,
just God, the ocean, and me.

Sherri A. Davis

To A Daughter From Her Mother

The rain seems to always fall,
The sun never seems to shine,
My smiles come so infrequently,
I wonder if anyone seems to mind.

This feeling comes over all of us,
At one time or another;
So it is alright to let me know,
To a daughter from her mother.

Life seems like it is too trying,
You may even want to give in,
The thing that is important to remember,
You do have the power to win.

At those times when you hear raindrops,
Especially when it is night,
Take a moment for yourself and smile
Because in the end everything will be
alright.

Laurie Fisher

The Cross

The symbol of the cross is life
The symbol of the cross is Christ
The symbol of the cross is love and pace
that's what this world really needs
   so remember
when in need he'll be there in deed
if the word of God you heed
he loves us one and all I know
with faith in him to heaven will go

Robert M. Carnathan

A Valentine For You My Love

I'll give my heart to you
The warmth and love inside
I'll share my thoughts with you
There's nothing I will hide
I'll be your closest friend
Go with you everywhere
And I'll be standing there
When hope is but a prayer
I'll praise you every day
Console you in the night
When you want to hold me
I won't put up a fight
I'll love you to the end
And longer if I can
If there's another life
Again I'll be your man
I'll walk you in the rain
The snow, dark and sunshine
February fourteenth
I'll be your valentine.

Thomas R. O'Brien

Seasons Of The Heart

In seasons of the heart,
There's a hunger which drives the soul.
Destiny, a wild heart beating-
With passion as the sun to paint
   the blushing dawn.
Shining upon the jewels of spirit.
Kissing precious beauty,
Leaving tender moments - gold.

Tara Stepnowski

Lonely And Tired

When will it go away?
The way I feel is so sad.
Is there anyone that loves me?
Tell me please, I need to know.
   I am hurting, someone
hold me. Sitting here, watching
my reflection in the puddle
fade away. The puddle seems
to get bigger as the tears from
my tired eyes fall.
   The dark is so peaceful
and quite. Thinking of everything
makes me want of cry and die.
   Why doesn't anyone love me?
Tell me why no one comes
to me and holds me?
   I am cold tired and lonely,
holding me is all I ask for.

Nancy Simmons

August Evening

The hot and dusty day has gone.
The wind has died down,
and now the darkness
comes creeping forth.
   With such swift wing beat
the snipes are seeking shelter,
and you and I,
we sit together closely
at the lakeside.
   We listen and relish
the rustling, living
silence of the evening.
   Slowly the golden sickle
of the harvest moon
sinks to the horizon
and the fairytale colors
are fading in the sky -

Olav Coln

Love

   Love is more than saying
the words I love you.
They can be said by anyone
and really not be true.
   Love is something special
felt by you and me.
It is deep inside our hearts
for only us to see.
   Love like this is new to me
it's hard to understand.
The way I fell in love with you
could never have been planned.
   Love like ours will last forever
there is no other way.
We've already planned our future
and that's the way it will stay.
   Love is what I hope to have
in my life forever.
I hope you are always with me,
I will leave you never!

Katie Griffin

The Days

Are you the best in the world?
   The world is cold to be told.
Hey what is this place?
A place full of faces
   Oh!, What can I say
Life is such a gay thing
such a fling, to make you sing.
   Your heart says
"How many days?"
   In this place
of such grace, face to face.
   With the challenge of life and death.
   I find the wreath
   upon my head
   "I am dead," as I said,
I have done no harm, I have done no harm.
So I go back to heaven's arms
   it pulls me in
   just not quite a sin.

Nicole Srur

To My Teacher With Love

Those carefree days came to an end.
   The years had swiftly passed.
Dreams of childhood now forgotten
   Graduation at last.

As I thought of the past eight years
   My heart with emotion filled.
I wished a gift for the teacher
   For values she instilled.

I penned a rhyme about our school
   Describing its quaint charm.
I wrote of school day happenings,
   Sunday school, church and farm.

Again the years had swiftly passed
   When at our alumni show
The teacher read my gift to her
   Fifty-one years ago.

Wilma Human

Personal Computer

Blank faced.
Then a surge.
You've turned me on again.
My face slowly brightens
as your fingers dance upon me.

You always know how to control me
to get exactly what you want.

You slowly begin to enter,
starting sparks shooting throughout me,
careful to touch just the right places.
Soon, you have me whirring and purring,
my face full of light,
giving you everything that you desire.

When you want nothing more from me,
you simply walk away.

The glow gently fades from my face.
I sit, still and quiet,
On the stand you built for me,
Waiting for the next time.
Waiting to be used again.

William J. Shugart

Our Last Love Game

You say you love me
Then leave me again
Stop playing these love game
Where I never win
I thought when I met you
Your feeling were true
You said you loved me
If I only knew
So when you get bored
Desperate, down, don't come to me
I won't be around
Because love is not a game
When the winner is you
Loves is an emotion
Shared between two

Mark A. Snowden

If You Cannot Accept Me

If you cannot accept me
Then leave me alone
Don't try to make me over
No matter what I do
I'll still be my ornery self
Accept me as I am.
For you will be fighting
Night and day
I don't need that
Nor do you
This is what attracted me to you
By me being myself
For I am unique within myself
Just as you are unique within yourself
As the old saying goes
Love me or leave me

Lois Broadway

The Bed

Are you sleeping,
there across the bed?

Can you tell me what thoughts run
through your head?

Do you love me still?
Still within your heart,
or do your feel the love for
that is your part.

Am I sleeping here
across the bed?

I'd like to tell you the thoughts
runnin' in my head.

I love you still,
still deep within my heart.

I know I love you.
It's not my part.

Are you sleeping
there across the bed.

PLEASE WON'T YOU TELL ME THE
THOUGHTS IN YOUR HEAD!!!

Phyllis Wetmore

Goodbye

I conceal my shame
There are bitter tears
   Shed not because; my love
was betrayed
   But rather because; to the
inner voice I had not obeyed
   of such a sincere
   heart
you are
    which in turn
has brought about a subtle naiveness.
We think we know each other
   ... yet in reality we are
   strangers
Too great our differences be
you're unaware
   but
    I can see
   Tokoya Cureton-Price

Five O'clock In The Morning

Five o'clock in the morning
There are no sounds but songs of birds.
Vapor floats on the pond slowly
Quiet
Just quiet
Suddenly, a fish leaps in the pond
Many circles spread calmly
And again
Quiet
Just quiet
One summer morning
Five o'clock
   Sakiko Takagi

Untitled

Silence prevails.
There is a mist that creeps
along the ground when you
speak.
There is a bird
that attaches
itself to song
when you enter.
And there is a chill,
a familiar tingle
when you appear.
Stay, my love,
and let us count the days
until we die,
together in one heart
our souls beating like a humming birds'
wings.
   Marjorie M. Wass

There We are Again

All I do is close my eyes,
   There we are again.
Oh, I loved you so.
   The old stories that you told
Went along with your guitar.
   All I do is close my eyes
And stories are retold,
   Ah, but the laughters still abounds.
Memories are what I have.
   All I do is close my eyes,
There we are again.
   Theresa M. Burgess

Shadow Wandering

Beyond the shadows
there is light
or so I am told
it exists
this peace of mind
this condition of happiness
where you feel
more than a piece of a puzzle
that one can not locate
where you belong
and it is put aside
perhaps saved for last efforts
making you the last one
the open space obvious
without challenge
or true attempt
at possibility
   Karen Damon

Rhonda

Since the time when we were womb mates
There's a special bond we've shared
Of tacit understanding
If one hurt, the other cared

Though many miles lie between us now
Our thoughts aren't far apart
When that cancer seized your liver
It also grabbed my heart

As twins we know of empathy
beyond a normal range
You know I'd take your pain as mine
And welcome the exchange

But God, I guess, knew better, 'cause
To claim the final laugh,
Has had the devil challenge
By far our stronger half.
   Ken Smyth

Always A Way

There's always a way to be happy.
   There's always a way to be glad.
Though everything may not please us,
   We should never for long be sad.

The changes we face unexpected,
   Turns in the road that seem wrong,
While sometimes the end of a dream,
   Need not mean a hush to our song.

Whatever our hopes and ambitions
   And plans for the days up ahead,
If some do not come to fruition,
   There always are others instead.

Around us is endless potential
   For pleasure and joy every day
To counteract those disappointments
   In matters that don't go our way.

And often we find, of our wishes,
   Some better to not have come true,
So thinking of all to be glad for,
   We should never for long be blue.
   Lucille Cast Mowat

Can You Hear

Grandpa, can you hear me
There's something I must say
I miss you more than ever
And the feeling grows each day
I know that your with God
And I talk to him each night
So I hope that you can hear me
When I tell him of my plight
I miss being near you
Although you left when I was young
I've climbed the human ladder
And I'm on the adulthood rung
And though I'm getting older
I could use you by my side
Cause whenever I was in trouble
You've shown me not to hide
A man of strength and wisdom you taught
me to be strong
Now I know the difference between what's
right and wrong
So one day I'll be with you and this is
what I've vowed
To always be your grandson and one day
make you proud.
   Leland James Carlton

"Man's Winds Of Time"

The winds of time have no tomorrow
they blow death or endless life

Pain, laughter, tears and joy
Man's enter strength and timeless strife

The sunshine's hot or cold as icy winter
Man's pride of self burns
his heartfelt center

The mind running deep with
an unspoken thought
Reaches for the promise of dreams
that can not be caught

Always the wind waits
softly blowing sand across the grave

When at last there comes an ending
man will have taken so much
more than he gave
   Patsy L. Stevenson

Barn Swallowing

The bugs were there.
They filled the air.
The look was rather itchy.
But swallows came,
And gulped their claim.
They swooped, and soared and circled.
And then with happy stomachs full,
And gnats in number shrinking,
The birds roamed home,
And went to sleep,
Their bird eyes hardly blinking.
   Michelle Metcalf

"Children"

Children are God's mortal angels.

They surrender
   their wings to our hearts
So that we may soar
   with love above the pain.
   Keith Testa

"You Are My Angel"

They say the angels in the sky
They say they have wings and fly
They say they are from another world
I think my angel is on earth

Nobody knows, nobody understands
There is something no one can explain
There is something you see and feel
But never know what it's called

Love feeling it's not even in the heart
That warm feeling to your gut
That kind of feeling that burns inside
A love surrounded by fiery light.

I love you like a son and a brother
I love you like a big strong father
I love you like a real friend
But most of all I love you as a lover

Sheila R. Crissi

Untitled

Such a flower of beauty —
this Iris that you see.

We sometimes call them flags
for they wave upon a breeze.

It is so very glorious
created by our God.

Vigorous, green and pretty
stemming from the sod.

Lovely blossoms come forth
when spring turns to summer,

Splendid colors touch us while
we gaze upon this wonder.

Returning again each year
delightful and all a new.

Heavenly Father,
we give all praise to You.

Ronald Smith

Birthday Greetings

To A Wonderful Mother

Birthday greetings to you I send;
This is my message, Mother dear.
May each one be happier
As you gather up the years.
May all the toil and drudgery
You've encountered all through life
Be worth all the happiness
You're having here tonight.

Birthday greetings, mother dear
This is my message tonight.
Though I worry you and vex you.
It is wished with all my might.
As you travel over life's rough seas,
Always striving to reach your goals,
Please remember, I'm always near
To help keep you from the shoals.

Rufus C. Little

Where Does It End?

Where does it end?
This judging the masses.
   Who can say.
"they" are good, and "they" are not?
I have not done well enough in
   my life.
What are the qualifications?

What is black,
And what is white?
Who wrote the rules,
And why do the grays hide these
   facts so well?
The answers lie deep within
Each person own soul.

Nikki L. Brayman

Going Home

We're all just passing by this way,
This world is not our home.
For we will leave this place one day,
Never more to roam.

And when the bell shall toll for us,
In just a little while,
A well spent life will send us on,
To glory with a smile.

We labor here to build ourselves,
A home up in the sky.
For from the moment we start to live,
We surely start to die.

So when our journey's at its end,
Our time has come and gone.
We'll know that we're assured a place
Somewhere around God's throne.

Wayne M. Lewis

Untitled

I'll wait for you only
Though I am lonely
You will find me here

If you come home sighing
You'll not see me crying
We'll laugh again Dear

I dream of you ever
No distance can sever
Two hearts so entwined

Between us the sea
But you're always with me
That's how our love is defined.

Lena Zaks

Seduction

I conceive that the butterfly
Though it tarries here and there
Flies free until the day it dies
Blithe spirits without care

And if with risk it might alight
There, on my palm it sits
And I could take away its flight
If I just close my fist

But mounted wings I do not prize
They should stretch and preen
And flit to gently hypnotize
Against a sky blue screen

Martin J. Schwartz

Gray Hair Mother

Sitting by my window
Thoughts trailing in the wind
Watching the whirlwind dust
Mom, how I wish you were here
I miss your special touch
Whispering, "This is God's Place."
When the storms come and go
Mom, thru all your pain you gave
Each of us, a comfort in love
'Till your final breath came
Your silver hair against satin
A smile you wore to heaven
I pray, I can give; what I received
Sitting here watching the storm
For Mom, thru many storms
You have traveled
With a peaceful heart and mind
Thru the howl of wind, you whisper
"This is God's Place."

Ruby C. Hanson

Passageways

A minstrel wandering
through the passageways of time,
heralding his vision
in a melody of rhyme.

Sometimes he grows weary
searching for the truth,
yearning for the lost love
he tasted in his youth.

Looking on a sea of faces
all blurred as in a dream;
Casting wishes to the heavens,
asking, "What does it all mean?"

His song's an inspiration
to the travelers of the night,
a hand reaching out
to share a spark of light.

The spark lives on eternally,
vibrating through the ages;
and returns again to fan the flame,
that forever blazes ....

Lisa Hopper

The Vagabond

How soon small voice, am I at ease
Till you unrest me with a breeze
Oh soul that run ahead of me
As clouds that search the sky
Thou searcheth for my destiny
I follow to thy cry
Precious promise ever be
Of visions thou hath tempted me.

William C. Dowd

Lucky

With our minds free
   to come and go
Never to know
   loneliness or despair
When the day is done
   our hearts beat as one
What do we care
   We're lucky

Peggie Ann Stafford

Life

Life is a mere struggle
Time verses time
To be popular, or wanted
Is everyone dream
but yet there are those
Who are unwanted it seems

We are put on this earth for a purpose
At birth of which we don't know
But hopefully you have completed it
Before it's your turn to go

So live each day to its fullest
And never look back again
That way you will know
You will live your life to its end.

Michael R. Breitkreutz

At The Very Tip Top

Hey, little bird at the
Tip top of the tree,
Why don't you come down
And sing that song to me?

You're at the top of that tree
A wonderful place.
There you're the envy
Of the whole human race.

You have two feet
The very same we,
But you also have wings
So there you can be.

I wish you'd come down
With your hap-hap-happy sound
And keep me company
Here on the ground.

But I'll understand if
We're not eye to eye...
I wish I could sit
Half way to the sky.

Margaurette Upshaw

Untitled

"Our relationship has taken a rest.
'Tis my time to be free,
As time is yours to do as you please.
Feelings are stronger than words,
Yet, those words were never spoken
The love...
    The warmth.
      The strength..
Is what made us what we are,
And together, there isn't a
thing in this world more
  beautiful"

Patricia Finik

"Enuff Of Yarnies"

Isn't shoes enuff
to shoun our graud an' bradden feet?
Why's tem sockins on abode
'tween skin an' rubbee meet?

All t'will cause us kinsmen grief,
with sweat an' foulish holes.
T' gaub of yarnies on our fief
is moolin, quite the droles.

Lindsay McDonald

Lost

She's gone away
To another time and place.
No one know for sure when, where or how.
She just up and left for now.

She's gone away
From mere thoughts and dreams,
Though some say she's just in bed,
And may very well be dead.

She's gone away
To an empty place with an empty face.
What sadness.
To be left in madness.

Nancy A. Kawtoski

My Journey For Happiness

I have journeyed on a long path
To find the person of my dreams
And now that the path had ended
My life is better than ever

I believe that our LOVE is strong
And will help us through our problems
We will live our lives carefully
Creating Peace and Harmony

Letting our friendship last so long
Has helped us belong together
In the good times and in the bad
Has created a love so strong

We will be for one another
Like the clouds are in the sky
Our love will last for always
As we live our lives together

Penny Campbell

Mission Bells

A little Swallow flying South
to get away from the cold, got
lost from the flock, "so WE Are
Told". Instead of South it flew
West, farther and farther away
from the rest.

Many Swallows joined it on the
way, as it flew day after day.
Soon they came to the place they
liked best. Here they decided to
stop and rest.

Capistrona was the place. After
resting they left with a tear,
promising to meet each and every
year. When the Mission Bells start
to ring, "Thousands Of Swallows
Return In The Spring".

Mamie Hodge

People

I feel so lucky
  to live in a place,
Where everyone I meet
  has a smile on their face.
There's a distinct definition
  of what's right and what's wrong.
The people are all
  so genuine and strong.
The community as a whole,
  takes care of one another.
They know what it means
  to love they brother.

Sandra Jackson

Reflections

I would give
to her,
the silver moon
of my dreams

I would dazzle her
with red rubies of the desert
or sprinkle star dust
in her hair,

    fore, in her eyes
    I have seen
    the ever changing colors
    of the ocean
      from emerald green
      to deep water blue,
      and I have felt
      the warmth
        of the sea.

Paul D. Hatch

Wedding Song

Why did I wait so long
To know that love had come
Into my heart so strong -
Waiting for love so long?

God pushed me straight to you
So that we both would choose
To let our love so true
Be blest for me and you.

If you would come with me
Then filled with grace, we'll see
All that our lives can be
When you are close to me.

So take me by the hand
And you will understand
Why God's chosen me and you
To live as one for two.

Let's join with God above
Seeking His precious love;
Finding the place where peace,
Faith, hope, and lovers meet.

Laura J. Suggs

Lord Help Me

Lord give me strength
To meet every day
All of the trouble
That comes my way.

Lord give me wisdom
To know what to do
In every decision
To be led by you.

Lord give me courage
When trials press sore,
To keep true to Thee
And to trust thee the more.

Lord help me to act
Every day that I live
Most pleasing to thee,
And a witness give.

We say we are Christians,
So may all the world see
By the way that I act,
Christ living in me.

Nora Shutt

Loneliness

Loneliness escapes
to pain
and drips
its sorrow
into another day.

I walk
alone into
an empty house
where I shut
the door,

As the hollowness
reverberates
and the silence
irks me,

And the night
never seems
to pass.

Laura J. Pyne

Why.....

To watch the blood flow from the eyes
To see the man guilty of lies
To understand the soul that dies
To understand just why I cry.

To see the tears of blood flow free
To ask what things you've done for me
To stop the pain I have from thee
To make you watch and learn and see.

To see the rose that is limp from fear
To try and get away from here
To take from you all you hold dear
To make you pay for all my tears.

That's why you suffer, why you burn
That's why you must shut up and learn
That's why you get what you have earned
That's why, because it is MY turn.

Tristi Mullett

Lawyers

What are lawyers for?
To take your money and say there's
The door.

The criminals I guess,
To confuse and make a mess.
Most could care less.

Now the good guy's wear a white
Hat while the criminals walks and use
You like a door mat.

Now is it true there is a special
Place for these people. It must
Be hell because I know it's not heaven.
They protect the criminal who rob the
Seven eleven.

The innocent don't have a chance even if
The lawyers pockets they enhance.

The lawyers drive there porsche
While the criminals go free of course.
The lawyers set around like fat cats
    I know they don't wear white hats

Patricia Hunt

"Not Just Blue"

From the deepest blue
To the champaign gold sky,
    Lurks a mysterious truth
In the mystical eye.

From the auburn haze
In the waking August sky,
    Lurks a brand new day
With bright new eyes.

From the peaceful shower
In the grayest sky,
    Lurks an array of color
In the imaginative eye.

From the diamond dust
In the midnight sky,
    Lurks a sea of hope
In the dreaming eye.

From the ruby setting sun
In the cool emerald eve,
    Lurks an inspiration
You just have to believe.

Katherine M. Knippen

"What Christmas Means"

Christmas Day brings lots of cheer
To the children every year.
And so grown up folks as well
All the great glad tidings tell.

Our Dear Lord was born this Day
In a manger far away
With no pillow for his head
and no blanket for his bed.

Let us thank our Lord above
For his kindness and his love
And be thankful that we are
Born of him "Our Guiding Star"

Mary Reynolds

Land Of Love

Won't you come with me,
To the land of love,
I'll hold you close to me.
There's a moon above,
In the land of love,
And there are stars,
To light our way, to happiness.
There are no regrets,
In the land of love,
Just dream your cares away.
We'll kiss and then,
We'll start all over again,
When you come with me,
To the land of love.

Mirslow Barbushack

Summer Is....

Summer is...
Watermelon rinds, a
honeysuckle breeze,
and lines at the ice cream parlor.

Summer is....
Neon lights flickering;
moths gathering;
heat rising.

Wendy Tutins

Night On The Mountain Top

Night comes quickly
To the mountains.
Hills turn purple,
Valley flood
With heavy shadows.
Sky and ocean stay alive,
Running with streams of flame
Until the sun goes down,
Seeming to drag
The whole sky with it.
A small white ship
Flares like a candle
And dies in the darkness.

Lucille J. Oosterhous

Untitled

Eyes of a broken chain
To the past, the present is beatitude
To the future, is to wonder
Is to wonder, is the present even there?
The souls beginning of the end
The end of the broken
Roads of travel beckon the soul
Dream child, dream
One less day remains
Run child, run
Stop forbearing the blame
Endeavor all dreams
One more day remains

Sandra L. Schoenitz

Release

Because of time, the ties did bind.
To watch you grow, and love the glow.
There is a peace, for this release.
We learn to cope, there's so much hope.
I had to train, to see you gain.
But don't you fret, the best is yet.
Inside it burns, so take your turn.
And in his light, you'll shine so bright.
So make your peace, and run this race.
You'll do your best, go pass the test,
Yes, go away, this pain won't stay.
There's too much love, from God above.
So reach way up, and fill your cup.

Mary E. Nelson

"Reflections"

My dear little Charlie,
Today -
I wiped your two year old nose
And fingerprints
From my living room mirror
Where you stand
To admire yourself,
Make funny faces,
And hold conversations
With the little boy you see
Reflected there.
Your special little friend.
Some day
All too soon,
You will be grown
And looking in the mirror
To be sure you look just right
For that special someone in your life
I really didn't want
To wipe away those little prints.

Naomi Etter Vint

"In A World Of Our Own"

In a world of our own
Together as two
Until death do us part
Only me and you

To go on forever
To live and to love
To correct all the wrongs
You're what I dream of

I'll do my best for you
I will always care
Place your hand into mine
You know I'll be there

Tell me what I can do
To make everything right
To bring you happiness
And to kiss you good night

In a world of our own you can be sure I'm
    here
If you are ever sad I'll wipe away every tear
    In a world of our own,
    Together we're alone.
    Mike Kazakaitis

My Kid

I brought my kid up RIGHT
Told him to treat everybody RIGHT
Stand up for what he thought was RIGHT
And say his prayers every NIGHT
But he got killed the other NIGHT
Trying to do what was RIGHT
Stand up for what he thought was RIGHT
He told the boy he didn't want to FIGHT
Tried to walk away and do what was RIGHT
But things just didn't work out RIGHT
You see my kid that I brought up RIGHT
Treated everybody RIGHT
Stood up for what was RIGHT
Prayed every NIGHT
Got killed LAST NIGHT
    Kenneth R. Everett Jr.

Vision Dream

Crazy as it seems
Truth is in my dreams.
My visions are real
I am what I feel.

Death and birth are one
Karma debts are done.
Time to sing my song
Hope it won't be long.

My brother, my friend
Love to all you send.
Share with me your ways;
There are better days.

Knowledge in our hearts
We've all the lost parts
Of a story seen
In a vision dream.
    Shirley Marcoux

Feelings

We seem to be like a dove,
Two birds that fall in love.
It's really hard for me to say,
Although it comes to mind each day.

We are able to share,
Our feelings that we care.
Inside of us is what matters,
But sometimes it all shatters.

Soon our feelings turn around,
All that we were to have found.
That our love for one another,
It's like a child to a mother.
    Melinda Smith

They Were Brothers

There were three but
two never met the other.
He was dead and gone before
the other two were even
a wonder.
The one as loud and humorous as can be.
The other shy and quiet.
The third we'll never know
because he's gone now.
Only two remain.
But, they were brothers.
They'll never meet but they
were still brothers.
    Tonya Potts

Metamorphosis

She lays a single egg
Under a milkweed leaf.
With tiny blacks, whites and yellows
They begin to release.
Shedding, spinning a silk pad
Its shell forms a home of green.
Struggling then hangs upside down
Drying limp wings.
A first sign of spring!
    Sandra J. Mader

No Capture

Personal wit
understanding everything
but undetractable peril.
Trouble is like a river roaring
over a high hill,
upward bound,
rushing steadily
pounding the rocky, scanty,
grass covered pavement,
a usual occurrence -
but not welcomed.
Everyday I can face
good fortune without a smirk,
but when it comes to trouble
I'm the wave that precedes
the tide
coiling, covering,
protecting me.
Escaping a life threat,
keeping trouble-free.
    Rochelle C. Dawkins

A Deceased One's Prayer

As I stand here in heaven
unpainful, unsad. I look down
at my loved ones and smile and
feel glad. I know that they love
me I know that they care, because
they visit my grave, but I am
not there. I am with you everywhere
you go. I understand it is
hard to part, but I am not
at my grave, I am living comfortably
inside your heart.
    Ron Henry II

Untitled

I thought I knew what pain was
    Until I heard an angel's whine,
I thought I knew what joy was,
    Until I saw a mother's smile,

I thought I knew what hate was
    Until I heard a murder's cry,
I thought I knew what love was
    Until I saw Christ die.
    Stina C. O'Leary

World Of Nature

My hair blows out behind me with the wind
Up and down ridges
like an eagle in flight,
My hearts soars.
Sunflowers, their bright yellow petals
open wide to the sun,
Sway in the wind.
Crickets chirp lazily in the grass.
Bees dive deep within flowers
Storing pollen for thy honey making.
I lift myself on wings of air
high above the trees tops,
up to the peaks and then on
up toward the heavens.
clouds tinted pink yellow and blue
with the sun-set waver before my eyes
and then are gone
a swirl of mist left in their wake,
like landmarks of what was there
and of what was to come.
    Katherine Michalak

My Prayer

I spoke to her but yesterday,
Upon her bed of pain,
And now today you've taken her,
To dwell in thy domain.

I tried so hard to help her,
There was naught that I could do,
And so dear, gentle, loving Lord,
You took her home with you.

You took away all of her pain,
Oh Lord! Help me to see,
That though my loss is very great,
She found new life with Thee.
    Norma G. Gutkowski

She

Silently she steals
upon unsuspecting terrain;
Gently she drops her cloak
as softly as rain.

Elusive as mist
She reaches out to the shore;
To climb her cliffs
and dance with the night once more.

From the lavender sky
the stars twinkle and glance;
Watching her beckon the moon
to join in her dance.

Now with a roar
and one majestic splash;
Her cliffs she climbs
with a caressing crash.

All too soon
and all too fast;
The SEA returns
to the abyss of her past.

Sheila M. Lazar

Blacksmith

Heart a bellows pushing blood of wind
Veins like rivers of molten ore
Soul a furnace topped full of coal
Life cold and raw upon the hearth

Will of a hammer beats out a form
Love a horseshoe worn and repaired
Marriage s spike joining the rails
Friend a fine axe finished and faithful

Hate a mere flash distorting the ore
Foe a mistake hastily formed
Faith be a file to hone a fine edge
Decisions just nails piecing together

Hope the beauty of metals unknown
Feelings an anvil beaten and worn
Murder a weapon fashioned from fear
Death the water carelessly thrown

Matthew M. Moomjian

Roses Are Red

Roses are Red
Violets and Blue
So am I without you

Roses are Red
violets never bend
do you know me because
I want to be your friend

Roses are Red
Stems are green
I think my hole life is
Just a dream

Roses are Red
violets are blue
Hello good bye
See you soon
because I all ready
miss you

Rachel Matula

Conversation In The Hallway

Alright, One Minute
Wait a Second-
Hold Your Horses

Yes?! What is it?
What do you mean?
How can this be?
How could this happen?

You must be Kidding!
Please be joking
You'd best be lying!

What a relief!
I can't believe you did that!
You scared me half to death.

Are we still friends?
Are you serious?
Of course not.

I'm just kidding,
Or so you think.

Suzanne Moore

Divorce

Love and a spring day
warm
full of promise
budding trees
love plants a garden
laughter rings out
merriment abounds
two souls merge

Now is winter
barren trees
dead benches
virgin snow
icicle tears
cold rejection
what was joined
is now asunder

Loretta E. Morrow

Golden Sunset Home

There they sit along the bench
Warm in winter sun
Saying little, maybe thinking
Caught in dreams of long ago,
Or vegetating-who would know?
Inside are some who still look out
Beyond four walls and yesterday
With warmth and light and gentle wit.
The lucky ones who grow old well.
Elsewhere there's noise and locomotion
Conversations harshly shouted
Talk of children live or dead
Great occasions half forgotten
Chronic ills and therapeutics.
Dull and grey this place to you
To them it is God's Waiting Room..

Orlin J. Scoville

Clock

The clock has hands and a face,
We have only time and space.
If the clock is slow it
Loses its pace,
If it's fast it hurries the race.

Sandra Bryant Weaver

"My Long Lost Brother"

Have you ever had a brother that
Wasn't so very neat
And always thought he could
never be beat.

Have you ever had a brother that
you wanted out of your hair
But now that he's married
And gone, it's like he wasn't
Even there.

Have you ever had a brother that
is at sea
And hope he's the same one
You wish him to be.

But even though he's not at home
I'll always feel that I'm on my own.

For that, I have my parents to thank.
That I don't have to face the
Future alone.

Misty Moody

Children

Watch them grow.
Watch them
Spread their wings.
They are like
Birds,
Flying high
   in the sky.
Flying free
With no care
   in the world.
You know why.
Because
They are children.

Sandra D. George

Being

From the heart of God
We join the clay
On the Master Potter's wheel
And with each revolution
Our spirits flow from the Source.
As Holy hands press life
Into our mortal form
Slowly we rise
Until our skin becomes thin
And transmuted.
Marked by lines of time
Our bodies are fired
In the kiln of tribulation
Until we are brittle.
The fragile green is garnished
By colors of the four seasons
And at last crumbles
Under the weight of being
To flow once again
Into the heart of God.

Robert L. Brown Jr.

We Shall

We shall take hand by hand.
We shall help people that need help.
We shall make this world a better place.
We shall try to succeed and work.
We shall be who we want to be.
We shall light up the world in a touch.
We shall do what we can.
We shall do all these great things.
We shall....

Karen Gorycki

Dual System

Alone,
    We walked the road
together.
Two
    Two by two,
we passed along.

Revolution and Generation
equaled procreation.
Time united the difference
of being and eternity.

Everyday rhythms,
    the tides,
    the hours
are humming the end,
then two-by-two
Again, will life be
    one.

Lesley Sagel

Not Forgotten

And here I sit
Wearing my crown
        of echoes
Lost in this confusion
trying to climb back up
        into the light
to find my way again

    It was perfect before
    just the way it should be

    I knew
    I understood

Now I'm lost
And where do I belong?

Living in my memories
Though I don't want to go.

Through that curtain
I long for the answer
for the candle to burn brighter
as time marches on
    willing.

Laura Shane

Fantasies

If all our little fantasies
    were rolled into one.
We'd hold our breath and float above
    the heads of everyone.
Escaping all the envy
    and petty jealousies.
As the angels we'd sail along
    in joyous ecstasy.
Instead we trudge along
    life's cruel way.
To travel down friendships path
    we have to bend and sway.
One day we'll build a nest
    up among the clouds.
Peace and quiet will be ours
    avoiding noisy crowds.
God will take us by the hand
    and teach us to travel on.
Down the road to happiness
    just where we belong.

Marguerite McFarland

I Should Have

Looking back I think,
What all I should have done,
Letters I should have written,
Or errands I should have run,
I was going to call him,
But now it is too late, you see.
For all my good intentions,
Are forever silenced within me

Maudelene Bailey

Untitled

What is LOVE?
What does it mean?
Is it something you've heard,
Or something you've seen?
Does it hurt you,
And make you cry?
Or does it make you happy
Like the birds in the sky?
Is LOVE something you eat,
Or something that you sew?
Is it something handmade,
Or do we really know?
Is LOVE in the air,
Or on the ground?
Is it in big cities,
Or in small towns?
This is what I think
LOVE might happen to be:
When two people share their love "to-
gether"
Like you do with me.

Robin Maria Sinkford

"Metamorphosis"

Where is the spark
What has happened to the feeling
Suddenly I'm adrift
Wondering why life has changed

Everything is the same
But I am not
Like a flower slowly opening
Petals wide to face the sun

Somehow the days are warmer
The breezes are cooler
The scents are keener
Immediate purpose is in the air

Freedom to do whatever I please
And yet so hard to determine
My wants and my needs
Were any of them even my own

Mary Ann Weeden

My Twiggy

    My Twiggy has gone to heaven
    Where all good dogs go.

    She left with a smile and a sigh
    of sadness and relief God knows.

I'll miss her more - oh, so much more
    than anyone can never know.

    Her sweet little ghost will have her
    walks with me each day.

    Sun, rain or blowing snow
    I'll always love my Twiggy so!

Rosette Schoff

Wondering

What if...
What if the human self-confidence
was not so easily shattered by
the blow of a harsh or bitter
word?

What if...

What if The entire human race
was not judged by the ignorant
view of the naked eye?

What if...

What if everyone was appreciated
and accepted for their talent
and mind?

What if we all had a friend?

What if hunger was a problem
easily solved?

What if.....

What if we all understood,
And we all knew a way?

Mollie Ables

My Grandkids

Oh! I wish that all could see
    what my grandkids have done for me.

Before their day
    I had the time
to sit and ponder.
    About what? I wonder.

Before their day
    I had the time
to sit and rest.
    From what? Can't guess.

Before their day
    I had the time
to sit and read.
    Read what? Beats me!

Since their day
    I have no time
to ponder, rest or read.
    I only have time
for four little people,
    and that's all the time I need.

Nancy Stallings

Untitled

God created such beauty
    when He created the earth
He created the sky
    so far and wide
        encompassing us all
He created the sun
    to shine by day
    the moon
        to glisten by night
He created more magnificence
    than can be imagined
He created
    rivers and valleys
        mountains and streams
He created man
    He created woman
    Such beauty indeed
God created such beauty
    when he created the earth
    After all, He created... you

Kaye Patrice Brooks

Early Dawn

In the quiet of the early dawn
when I awake
and meditate
and pray to God,
I feel so near and close to him
almost as if I share him all alone.
God created the heavens and the earth
for us to enjoy, not destroy.

As I look out over the city
the dawn is so beautiful
On a clear day, the heavens are quiet
peaceful and blue,
and in the evenings, there is a ray of
crimson hue.

When the city wakes up
all living things that breathe
shares God's world
Rosalie T. Long

Untitled

Sometimes
When I can't sleep at night
I think of you, My Lord
How you came
To an unwilling people
With loving admonitions
To guide them,
    To touch and heal.
And I wonder
How those who walked with you
Came so late
To understand your divine self.
How today so many
Forget those words
    of love, of compassion
And the giving of self.
I pray forgiveness for myself
For all who
Like those unwilling ones
Have not understood.
Neva Perry Rye

Day Dreams

The things I dream of
when I close my eyes,
are of soft music
and friendly goodbyes.

Mountains that are brown
near pastures of gold,
a peace truce that's new
and red wine that's old.

The things I dream of
when I close my eyes,
are of folk dances
under cloudless skies.

A home in the hills
in Europe's own land,
near sparkling waters
and miles of sand.

A minute of dreams
takes me far away,
from the stress of work
and tasks of the day.
Mindy Sue Miller

In The Future

In the future
when I go
where the rain doesn't rain
and the snow doesn't snow.

I'll be where the sun's up all day
and where the stars are made.

Don't forget me don't even start
cause I will always be in your heart

I must go I hate to say,
but we will met again someday
Wendy Finley

Dad

He was never there
    when I needed him
only his constant yelling.

As hard as I tried
    to please him
I could do no right

No matter what or how much
    I believed in something
He'd find it to be wrong
He always put me down

But it's different now
or supposed to be anyway

    I'm older
And he's tying to be my friend

    But Dad
You still put me down
Sue Secunde

Last Request

On that final judgement day
    when Jesus asked me
    what I had to say.
"To be with you my Lord
    to love and pray,
    with family, with friends,
    and needless to say,
    with all the people
    who led my way."
Louis W. Durnavich

Heart Of Emotions

Long have I wanted to see this day
When my heart is finally being fulfilled
Yearning for my heart to overflow
With the sparks of divine love from you

Seeing you, giving me this chance
To know what love really is
I am compelled to know myself
Though I may not understand what I see
Just being there with you
I am lost in your presence
While a new world begins to unfold

There is so much to say
But how can words describe
Something that can't be seen
But can only be felt
Through the Heart Of Emotions.
Souphanh Xayavong

Counting The Moments

Counting the moments
When the days are young
My love for you
Is as warm as the sun.

But when the days get older
And the moments get shorter
I love as much
Over and over.
Robert Haskins

When The Sun Sets

The sky goes on forever,
when the sun sets.

The clouds dance on the
horizon, when the sun sets.

The colors of the sky
will make your heart skip
a beat, when the sun sets.

The beauty will take your
breath away, when the sun sets.

Everything is peaceful, when
the sun sets.
Kourtney Whiteman

Puppies

Puppies are so cute and furry
when they see food they run in a hurry
Puppies love to chew on slippers
But they hate to be cut by clippers
They also love to play outside
when they do wrong they run and hide.
Puppies like to play in the house.
Except for when they see a mouse
They sometimes like to watch T.V.
But do not like to be stung by a bee
Puppies like to play with dog toys
Sometimes they are such joys
Puppies sometimes wear little coats
And they love to take rides on boats
They also love to take long walks
But hate it when their owner talks
Puppies love to sleep in your bed
And they love to be fed
This is why puppies are so special
That they deserve to lay on your bed
Melissa N. Tackett

Symphony

Every night's a symphony
when you listen to the forest
with the bullfrogs humming tenor
and spring peepers singing chorus
the opera lights come up
as the moon begins to glow
the night owl sounds the trumpet
as the crickets start the show
the cicadas keep the tempo
as the conductor leads them on
to sing through out the darkness
until the rising dawn
the opera lights go down
as the sun begins to rise
and nature finishes the show
with a sleepy lullaby
Sarah Davis

Jump In The Ring And Fight

Don't give up so easily
When things don't seem just right,
Don your gloves of courage
And put up a great big fight.

In this vast ring of life
Defeat, your challenger stands;
With courage, ability and strength
Prove you're the better man.

Hard blows may even knock you down,
But let not defeat win,
In this big bout of life
The out count is more than ten.

Neither a blanket of self-pity
Or an immense bowl of tears
Will win any kind of fight
In any number of years.

So crawl from under that blanket
And wipe those eyes dry,
Jump into the right of life
And give defeat a try.

Margaret E. Jackson

Thoughts About You

I am on top of the world
When you are with me

I am ever so peaceful
When I journey
Deep into your soul

Your smile radiates the sunshine
that reflects into my eyes

Your voice pulsates
through my brain white
expressing your deepest thoughts

Your heart reaches out
and touches mine in a beat

Just by being near
you make me feel loved
as I have never been before.

Lee Singley

Reason For Silence

Sometimes I don't respond
When you hand me your heart
Something sews my lips
Unable to part
The sweet words I hear
Are strangers to me
I don't quite know how
To accept their company
But I look in your eyes
So honest and true
And know a response
Is long overdue
So I search for the words
But none can be found
To convey the right meaning
The right feeling and sound
I'd rather just hold you
Expressing what I can't say
I'm saying I love you
In my own quiet way

Lisa Ulmer

God

There is a staircase to the sky,
Where God in His kingdom waits on high
For those of us whose time is done,
To be with Him and His son.

God looks down on us from heaven above,
And sends all of us, His fatherly love.
He fills our earthly needs,
And helps us with our daily deeds.

For God is there when we call,
And he can make the rain to fall,
Then send the sun to brighten our day,
And to help us on our way.

God went ahead with His plan,
To beautify all this land.
He made the ocean and the sea.
Then He made Adam and Eve.

So, for the days and the nights,
Let's give thanks to all the sights,
Because we all know,
That only God can make it so.

Bobi Brittain

If I Knew

If I knew,
Where I could find you.
I would go.
If I knew,
What you looked like.
I would look.
If I knew,
What you sounded like.
I would listen.
If I knew,
When you would meet me.
I would plan
If I knew,
Who you were.
I would ask about you.
Well I don't.
So do me a favor,
When you see me tell me.

Yolanda Salinas

An Old Tear-Stained Altar

It's an old tear-stained altar
where I pour my heart to you
An old tear-stained altar
where I can be renewed.

I've come in grief and sorrow
I've come in joy untold
I've come to meet the needs of others
And I've come to meet my own.

Here I found salvation
And victory from sin
Here I found your mercy
And felt your peace within

I've wept tears of pain and sorrow
Tears of joy and love
I've come to call you holy
And to lift your name above
This altar's full of memories
With stories from the past
And here I'll meet you daily,
'til I go home at last.

Norah L. Brock

Moving On

By the river I found a home
where living was easy and slow.
But I moved
to the mountains where the air
was cool and clean.
But I moved
down to the desert floor,
warmed to the bone all year.
But I moved
out to the oceans shore
with a tang of salt in the air.
But I moved
Inland where the farmlands lay,
you could smell that rich black loam.
But I moved
into a place with bright white light
where finally I found peace
and moved no more.

William E. Douglas

Tenderness

The carpet worn
where those walk most

The break of a wave
again and again
beats down the cliff

The rock erodes

What is left
but tenderness?

Build a wall
put up a dam
to be sure
that it doesn't happen
again and again

Now you're strong
you're at your best
but what do you have
without tenderness?

Tara Daughrity

Prayer Changes Everything

Prayer changes everything,
Whether big or small.
God is ready to listen,
Anytime we are ready to call.

It doesn't matter the time of day,
God is always there.
He's ready and willing to help you,
When you go to him in prayer.

It doesn't matter where you are,
He'll still be able to hear.
In church, at home, or in the car,
God is always near.

And when you feel like no-one cares,
That no-one has a heart to lend.
Just talk to God,
He'll always be your friend.

Prayer changes everything,
No matter what the test,
When we pray and talk to God,
He answers our requests.

Tracy Swift

539

Contentment

My anger subsides
  While I watch the tides
As they return once more
  And wash gently to shore.
They seem to set me free
  As they absorb my cares and
  carry them out to sea.
Things I wished for are not to be
  And I know God has better plans
  for me.
I am content, cleansed of doubt
  I sense the future as I look about.
Excited, lacking in fear
  For I know my God is ever near.
He is loving, caring, protecting
  from harm
I am free to function without alarm.

Margaret J. Delph

The Dark Way

I trudge a long dark lonely road
while the roiling mists around me swirl.
I do not feel, I do not care,
I'm by myself - no one to share -

Sometimes I sense there is a town
with crowds of people milling around.
I hear the music, laughter and talk
but I keep my eyes ahead as on I walk.

Sometimes friends walk with me a way;
I don't understand anything they say.
I only know I must press on,
for if I stop, I will be gone.

Veta F. Grossman

New Berries

You see those shiny new berries,
while you look at my dullness.
Poison though they care,
you leave me,
pure and harmless.
Looks draw you towards them,
leaving me
though I am safe.
The warnings I give do not stop you.
Closer and closer
to their trap you are drawn,
snared by their deceptive charms.
The risk has been taken,
and now
We shall see.

Lauren Campbell

Stars Are The Souls

Of The Universe

They penetrate the black forbidding
  with purest light and cast
  out the shadows that shroud
  our existence and fade our paths.

Their brilliance exceeds our eyes and
  can only be measured in the
  heart.

Follow your heart's path and their
  brilliance will live forever
  in you.

Tammy McCaskey

Untitled

The soft sweet sound of love
Whispers in my ear
It's talking about you
It is your name I hear

The soft sweet sound of love
Echoes thru my heart
It is a hollow sound
When we are apart

The soft sweet sound of love
Dances thru the trees
It's a sound of approaching love
When it's you and I it sees

The soft sweet sound of love
As sung by a bird
Is the most beautiful melody
My heart has ever heard

The soft sweet sound of love
I am pledging this to you
For now I have no heart
And you are blessed with two.

Martha Morgan

The House Of The Tragic Poet

Empty streets frozen in time
whispers of people
who exist no more

One poet
one voice
covered with ash

Thoughts never recorded still exist
like dust in the air
waiting to be inhaled

A curled body cowers in the corner
motionless
hands cover the face

The tragic poet
leaves a shadow of this mortal self
with open eyes blind to the world

Waiting
for someone to understand his plight

The mountain that once gave inspiration to
  his soul
steals life
leaving ashen remains of ancient memories

Saundra Norton

Winter

Winter is cold,
Winter is neat,
In Winter you need a source of heat.
Winter is fun,
Winter is snow,
In Winter you are to and fro.
Winter is bare trees,
Winter is no fleas,
In Winter lots and lots of things freeze.
Winter is dens,
Winter is pens,
In Winter you are with lots of friends.
Winter is cool,
Winter is school,
In Winter you shouldn't go in a pool.
Winter is gifts,
Winter is smiles,
In Winter you can decorate - miles.

Minal Patel

My Dad

A smile on his face a song in his heart
Whistling a tune right from the start

Doing his job gardening the land
on his knees hoe in hand.
Digging little furrows
as neat as could be,
Keep the water flowing
as soft as the breeze.

Pushing his hat back
with one little stroke, wiping his brow
as quick as he spoke.

Blue eyes sparkling aglow
telling a story for all to hear,
one last adventure before I go.

Light all around where it's never night,
familiar faces, what a beautiful sight.
Angels singing - sweet and dear
just waiting for me.....so near.

Home at last....one quick breath
time for me to take up my hoe for
gardening the land is my task!!!!!

Willene Domenichelli

Two Gates

  God's gate is big and
white for those whose
love is kind. The devils
gate is red and hard
for those whose love
is blind. I know you
went to heaven, for you
were very kind. And those
whose love is bare, is
always left behind.

Michelle Barr

Untitled

I will await the Lord
  Who cometh in the night
To bring peace forever more
  Blessed are those
Who have faith in abundance
  They and they alone
Will have solitude and happiness
  in the Lord.

Maxine Ann Klein

Crystal

Crystal, you're my little Sunshine
Who glistens with many colors,
  when you smile,
  and because you're you.
You're a rainbow after a rain,
  bringing hope, joy, and Love.
Crystal, you're my little Sunshine
Who captures my heart
Whom I want to surround with Love.
You're a bright eyed little girl,
  and what your future holds,
  only God knows.
Crystal, you're my little Sunshine
Who will stand firm to be a courageous,
  brave leader in your beliefs.
You're not a little girl who will stand for
  nothing,
  you'll stand for something.
Crystal, you're my little Sunshine

Margaret Mary Frolo

Am I Or Not?

I am NOT
Who I seem to be:
Sure of myself, secure;
Full of this life, and friendly;
Courteous, caring, kind.
I am...
   ...NOT,
Much of the time.

I am
Who and what I am:
Uncertain, shallow, scared;
Empty, angry, nasty, mean;
Selfish, silly, shaken.
I am
  (Sadly)
Most of my time.

Leroy H. Prescott

Dear

Dear who's never shed a tear
Who knows how not to live in fear
Tell me how could it be
You left so suddenly
You came into my life a light
Shining so extra bright
I only wish you never gone
So now I sing a sad, sad song.

Summer Welch

My Ferret

I have a ferret named Chewy
Who likes to play in the house
She loves going around and around
Like a little mouse
She loves playing with little toys
Chewing them a little at a time
She likes destroying everything
Like an innocent looking little criminal
She bites your ears and bites your toes
But she never bites your nose
When she bites it doesn't hurt
It tickles and tickles like a furry doll
She's very young and very cute
She bites on rubber boots
She plays outside in the sun
This little ferret is number one!

Malaika Schiller

Jesus Christ

Blessed, be Jesus Christ;
  Who paid the ransom sacrifice.
He was Love;
  Who came from above.

He manifested;
  in the flesh.
He strengthens man;
  to pass every test.

The Blood He shed;
  covers all believers head.
He lived on Earth;
  along with strife.
So All could receive;
  Eternal Life.

Minette Smith

Gone

Yesterday I had a friend
who talked and walked and made amends

We laughed and joked and reminiscence,
of our past, as little kids

We grew together year by year
as only friends would bear to hear

Places and parks and backyard games
That only friends can share the same

I lost my friend to greater means
of days remembered, are gone in me.

Lucy G. Benvenuto

Hate

Hate is an ugly word that most people,
whole dear. Hate is the only word most
people fear. But love has always
conquered hate, this is what I learn
to appreciate.

Renota Johns

Grandma??!!

I'm too young to be a grandma...
Why, my hair's not even gray!
You're just a child yourself, girl...
Or you were just yesterday.

Why couldn't you have waited?
You have so much life ahead;
I'm too young to be grandma,
That's what I've always said.

You stand there in defiant youth
And tell me you're full grown;
I'm too young to be a grandma...
Too bad...the seed is sown.

I watch you bloom and start to bulge
As the summer months progress...
I'm too young to be a grandma...
But I'll get used to it, I guess.

My flesh, my blood inside you
Is my heritage, you see...
So I'll be the "bestest" grandma...
Like my grandma was to me.

Rebecca S. Seefeldt

Untitled

If I love you now,
Will I love you forever?
Is forever for always,
Always I say, I love,
Always do I mean it?
Do I mean it now,
will I mean it forever?
Or is it the moment,
Or the hour,
Or my lifetime,
And four long it that?

Lynda Gathing

Ode To A Modern Office Building

I see you standing silent
Windows sparkling in the sunlight,
Story after story of windows
But not a soul in sight.

Are people looking out as they work?
Do they see my car idling there -
At the red light?
I cannot see in.

As I look up I wonder who they are,
A smile, a wave, might be nice.
Are they happy there -
In your prison of tinted glass?

Mary Rohan Foley

"Winter's"

The leaves are changing colors
winter's on the way.
I turn to my books to study more
winter's on the way.
The weather is much colder now
winter's on the way.
I miss my family
winter's on the way.
The days are getting shorter now
winter's on the way.
I mark the days by the exams I take
winter's on the way.
It's dark much earlier now
winter's on the way.
My mind begins to hibernate
winter's on the way.
My parent's love warms my day
I like winter.
I know I'll be okay.

Patrick Henry Engebretson

Beyond The Touch Of Love

To the surprise of deep compassion
with a commitment of deepest love
The dreams of mysterious knowledge
with touch beyond the touch of love.

When is our hearts on praying
knees cloth the joy of Jesus
Caress and understand.

How far beyond hopes and
peace does the crimson, blood
begin oh beyond the touch of
magic beyond the touch of sin
Beyond the touch of trouble
beyond the reach of his hand

So far beyond the touch of
love, this world failed to see
For in the eyes of my Savior
are tears of lost human beings.

Vera S. Reddic

The Red Rose

On a near hill a vulture sat
with burning throat and thrusting eye,
Until you came, and the red rose bloomed
pure against the pale green sky.

Thelma Bennett

Magic Scarecrow

Spooky scarecrow standing there.
With dried up straw instead of hair.
Guarding all that you prevail.
Held to a post with a giant nail.
Dirty rags and turned up hat.
Telling all the crows to scat.
Standing morning, noon and night.
Never having any fright.
Casting shadows everywhere.
Never knowing here from there.
Magic Scarecrow on the hill.
Come to life you never will.

Peter A. Paras

Christmas

Christmas is tradition
With it's green and red
But for some it is gray
For their loved one's are dead
Families get together
With their laughter and joy
And forget about the children
Who will never have a toy
Christmas is a feast
With the presents and good food
Some forget it is holy
And completely change the mood
Christmas is a holiday
And to some, a whole lot more
So have your good times and your thanks
But don't forget what it's for.

Linda S. Wainscott

To My Husband

We started out not long ago
With love, with trust, with care.
So let us try our very best
To hold these things we share.

For this ball of mud we live on
Is spinning much too fast.
So all too soon my darling
The present will be the past.

Mavis Anderson

Great Grandma

She walks in the moonlight
  With nowhere to go
Her hair glimmers in the night.
She walks as slow as a snail
  Treasuring every step
    Like it's her last.

She tries to talk but
  Nothing comes out.
  Her fragile hand
  Touches my face.

She tries to tell me something
  But I don't know what

I wake the next morning
  Feeling cold and sick.
Later that day I find out
  My great grandma is gone.

Is that what she was trying to tell me?

Macy Juhola

It's Real

Calm, cool, warm, lust
with passion explodes love
the wonder of time passing
fades into now
and I know it's real.

It feels so good to know
the care is fully there
to be as free as we allow
through good times
and bad.

It's oh so sweet
a kiss completes
the wanting need of arms
around my back, my heart.

I can't depart
the moment I saw you sitting there.
Something deep said that I'd care
about your love and warm embrace
please hold me tight
reach through this space.

Lauren Hayes

Desert's Eye

The desert is a thing of beauty
with sand that seems to glitter
Like eyes that watch your every move
like diamonds on a river

But the desert is a place of death
so quick and yet so sly
it could kill you at a moments notice
or just watch you with its eye

so watch your back
and do not cry
but keep out of reach
of its evil eye

and don't lose hope
or you will die
and forever be in the hands
of the desert's eye

Mona Ibrahim

An Ode To Life

What a beautiful thing life is!
Without it what would I be?
I'll tell you what,
a rock on the bottom of the sea.
To breathe fresh air,
what a wonderful thrill!
We need to breathe,
so be thankful for lung and gill.
With eyes so to see,
and ears which to hear.
A world without these,
would be a world full of fear!
But the greatest of our gifts,
is the gift of choice.
To have the right to decide,
and in life have a voice.

Matt Hanne

Lunar Perihelion

The moon
Won't be this close
For a thousand years.

So long
To wait
To see
  Something so beautiful.
  Will you wait
  That long
  For me?

Tabare Depaep

Untitled

Words Prevail
Words are words; no meaning
Just sound.
Words kill like bloody daggers
Words drain thoughts like a river.
Blessed are words that float like petals
  on the wind,
Soothing the heart
And sweetening the skin
Words do have meaning
It's hidden inside,
Behind a black curtain of eyes,
To pull the curtain aside
To search for the meaning
  is a mission.
Kill the fear of dispersing the numb;
Feel the cool air of reality;
Realize the potential -
And search for the meaning.

Victoria Lynn Fisher

Poetry

What is this, this Poetry?
Words with life, to be sure;
And beyond life, they endure.

Just say what you feel,
without fear;
If your rhyme is pleasing,
You'll find others near.

Ah, but there's more,
Much more than we know;
And who knows,
Where next we may go?

Or those good people,
That now in words exist;
Are with you always.

The pen is a knife,
And the ink my blood;
My soul it bleeds forth,
Into the flood.

And the paper, it waits...

Mark A. Glenn

Through The Eyes Of A Dead Boy

I gave my life,
yet it was not without a fight.
I look back now and see
that it was right.
To save another
was more worthwhile,
Than to live without
a single smile.

Tara McCrudden

"Choices"

If I left this hell
Would you shed a tear?
Would it be one of fear?
Fear because you might be next?
Always think it through,
Choose what is best.
We all live in fear
Because we know death is near.
We don't exactly know when or how,
But it is always there
And who it kills it really doesn't care.

Sarah Smith

"If You Knew"

If you knew how much I love you
Would you turn and walk away?
If you knew how much I cared for you
Would you feel the need to stay?
If you knew just how the words
Could never ever begin to say
How my love grows and grows for you
Each and every day.

Lisa S. Bailey

Phoenix

Free to write.
Write to free.
Too long have shackles of fear
And inhibition
Caged us like birds
With clipped wings.
Brush the clouds away
And soar to the skies.
As words descend to the page
Insight is released -
Our souls ascend like youthful phoenix
Ever immortal

Marjorie Ciruti Williamson

Homeward Bound

Home is too far...
   Years and years back...
And I can't catch up-
   Backward or forward-
I can't find home...
The backyard is gone-
   It left off the ground..
The bed will not sleep
   And babies don't cry-
Can't find my Sweetheart,
   Mommy, Daddy, Brother
The pain of loss..
   Is never end homesick-
No way to go home
   For that we knew is gone-
Forward this way different
   Then reach for tomorrow-
I see together, now-
   Sing........
Heaven will safe me home!

Lodie Payne

The Attics Of My Life

Underneath the roof
Yet above the living quarters,
My memories and curiosities
Thrive and linger.

Inside of a trunk
Covered with a film of dust,
Memories slowly unfold,
Oxidize, and rust.

Nightmares of death
Once were a reality,
Now seem trivial
Under Life's tree.

Tucked away
Under a box or two,
Are papers explaining
The life I never knew.

These are days
As I continue my strife,
Shuffling through
The attics of my life.

Lindsay Cherry

Lovers Wade

You mean so much,
Yet are slow to touch.
A will so tame, never in shame.
Please don't leave... Don't go away.

So precious your world,
In thoughts so frail.
So worthy your trust.
Sad love, sad love... Why? Just why?

Alone as you weep,
Into yesterday you wander.
A battered soul the ship you sail.
Come home... Please come home.

In Lovers Wade, your ship to hail.
In Lovers Wade, our love is made.

Mark R. Loiselle

Love

You can't identify it
Yet it means so much
It's not cut and dried
And something you can touch

Passion isn't it
For that fades away
Love stays around
And is here everyday

Wants and desires
Can't pass as love
Any more than peace
Can be called a dove

Kindness and charity
Keeps it flame high
Like putting wood on a fire
So it wont die

It's deeply ingrained
And lasts forever, what a world to live in
If we all got together, and fell in love
With each other.

Melvin J. Shaw

Two Sides Of A Coin

I flip it once and then again,
Yet results they always change,
I try to figure out its chance,
And then it seems to rearrange.

The coin is much like life sometimes,
For our chances always change,
And every single precious moment,
Can always seem to rearrange.

There is no folly in the coin,
It baffles all who try,
To predict in it our life and goals,
No one knows where the answer lies.

And so it may be hopeless at times,
To have something that is not concrete,
But I'll tell you more than once,
This life will give you harsher feats.

So go on living and not worrying,
About the flip of life and dreams,
For the outcome has been predetermined
And things are never what they seem.

Robinson John Kapano

Free

Why can't you understand how I feel.
You always act like I'm unreal.

I feel the pain, the sorrow too.
Of loving a man, a man like you.

You break my heart again and again,
always tearing from within.

Within my soul within my heart.
You always know when to start.

To start the pain, the tears to flow.
How is it you always know.

Know when and where it's so unfair.

Unfair to me, I need let free.

Free from pain, free from you.
I'm sick and tired of being blue.

So can't you see, I just want to be free.
And live my life just for me.

For me alone, and only me.
Oh God, I just want to free.

Rhonda K. Siegfried

My Son My Son

You are my love
You are my joy
You are my one
And only boy

You are earth
You are sky
You can make
My heart fly

Your hair is sand
Your eye's are sea
Your precious love
Belongs to me

You are one
Your so much fun
Your my sun and sky
You are my fire fly
You are my son

Bill Verdon

I'll Call You

If I need you, I'll call you.
You called my name,
I was there for you.
You wanted reassurance,
The pain was always there.
But you felt better
When you called my name.
I still hear your voice
Calling my name.
Even though you are not here anymore
It's not the same.
I'll always remember the phrase,
I'll call you.

Mazie Gurnari

"To Julie"

I will never hold
you close to my heart,
nor kiss your
little face,
or wipe away
your tears.

I pray someday
my soul
will know you,
the face of Innocence.
The sacred gift of
Love and Life
we never had a
chance to share.
I Love You, your Mother.

Patricia King

Oh Cruel Happiness

Oh cruel happiness
You fill our cup of life
With sweet Ambrosia
You let us sip
We are intoxicated with its sweetness
You warn us not of its illusions
And then too late
We wake to find it empty.

Rose M. Walker

Talent Of A Stranger

Talent of a stranger
you have yet to know my name!
Talent of a stranger my hand shall write,
your heart will open
your opinion of me
shall change-
Talent of a stranger
tears roll the same
way—
Pain hurts in our hearts—
Talent of a stranger
Life and death shall
not set us apart.
Talent of a stranger
my name is at the end...
It's love of my art
that I write with
my pen.

Tammy Jo Davidson

Grin And Lose Them

Did you ever try to do it?
You know it's tougher than you think,
It takes a special kind of person,
To lose his dentures down the sink.

We all know it's kind of maddening,
When for a plumber one must wait,
But it's harder to be patient,
If you've also lost your plate.

Must say he tried the best he could,
Though his fees were rather high,
I guess it still was worth it,
For I'm not just any guy.

And as he finished and was leaving,
Called him back quick as a wink,
Would you believe it's happened twice?
Once again they're down the sink!

Kathy Hopfinger

Blush Marks

for bec
No, it's too late
you sit there
the words still fresh on the air
the painting blood warm
pouring up in your face
how dare you leave your blush marks
all over my pulses
indelible as fire
imperious as love

Lowell P. Dabbs

Questions?

Who do you love? Are
you sure that it's me?

Am I the one you always
miss? Am I the one you long
to kiss?

Is it me you want to
be with, or is that just
some silly myth?

Can you tell me that I'm
the one? Can you promise
me will always have fun?

Promise me we'll have
plenty of time, promise me
you'll always be mine.

Melanie A. Mulvihill

Ninety-Two

So you are ninety-two.
You've seen so many grand things come,
And bad things too, pass by.
But all the changes you've
seen made, how grand.
From horse to space, well,
If you had ever thought it,
when you were only two.
That you would live to a
grand old age of ninety two, an see,
This worlds great changes
Take place, before your eyes.
Would you have believed it,
at the age of two.

Sandra Merfeld

Mommy's Girl

What ever happened to the barbie dolls
you used to love to play?
What ever happened to the tea parties
in Mommy's clothes all day?

What ever happened to Mommy's girl
she rocked upon her knee?
What ever happened to the time you had
that you used to share with me?

Now you're busy all the time
running to the mall
Or talking on the telephone
sitting in the hall.

Going places with your friends
and running here and there.
Mommy misses the time we had
although I know you care.

Just remember one little thing
that comes right from the heart
Mommy's girl you'll always be
like you were right from the start.

Melissa Wilkes

Into My Fairy Tale

Into my fairy tale,
you walked,
bringing chaos and indecision with you,
in from the night,
you stalked,
dragging death behind you,
death of a fairy tale.
Into my fairy tale,
you raged,
bringing the smell of evil with you.
Into my fairy tale,
you stormed,
and death rode behind you,
death of a fairy tale.
In from the night,
you stalked,
and coldness and evil came with you,
into my fairy tale,
you crashed,
and reality rode at your side.

Stacey L. Somero

Breaking The Skin

And far too fine to be a whim,
You were borne through special heart;
God must hold you close to Him,
The paragon of all His art;

And Time will spare you of its rage;
Your brand of beauty's not the type
To shrivel up and fall to age,
But flourish and grow ripe;

And Logic bids me to assume
That flesh will follow fleshly suit;
A womanhood thus brought to bloom
Could only bear the choicest fruit;

O! Seven Wonders, stand aside
And make room for your peer;
Posterity awaits a bride
And bids her now, draw near!

Ralph Scarpato

Vincent

Where are you?
You were here just a moment ago,
But it happened -
And now you are gone.
I remember when we would share things.
You talked to me.
Now your voice is gone.

Where are you?
Did you go far away?
Or are you still here, watching
Waiting in silence for me to find you.

You loved me once.
Do you love me still?

Where are you? Will you return?
Or will you stay in your world far away.
You are here, but you are gone.

Wherever you are
I love you
And in my mind's eye I see you still.

Rebecca Hargrove

"My Heart Remember"

My heart remembers
Your eyes all aglow,
Like springtime flowers
Sparkling in snow

My heart remember
It tells me so,
Moments to treasure
I loved you so,

Seasons have changed
They're come and gone,
Letters with tears on
Are yellowed and torn,

Our life together
Was not meant to be,
You found another
And forgot about me,

My heart remembers
The promises we made,
They were forever
But they to must fade.

Rosemond Miseraco

Someone Cares

I look into
your eyes my friend,
and worry about
what I see.
You say nothing
but I know
you too well.
You can't hide
anything from me.
You reach out,
silently asking if
anyone cares what
happens to you.
My answer to
your unasked question
is yes, my friend.
Someone does care
what happens to you.

Sheila Ellison

It'll Be Fine

You sit alone wishing all of
your thoughts were gone,
of that special person who
has passed on.
He is now way up high
in that great blue sky.
He's looking down upon you
hoping you'll be fine.
After a few days, he sees
that change in your life.
As he looks down he sees
that your okay, with a smile
on your face.
He now knows you'll be fine.
With his remembrance in mind.
You now know it's fine to smile
because your alive and that one
person who's gone would want
you to keep on having fun.

Rosemary Olson

"Ode To Arlo Frog"

Arlo, you're so brown and boggy,
You're my sweetest little froggy.
How I love your dangly toes,
Your skinny stripes along your nose.

I had you since you were a tad.
You ate your brothers, that was bad.
I wanted them to grow big too,
But that's okay, 'cause I've got you.

I named you for a singer of folka.
He didn't ever play a polka.
He just played my favorite trickles
Of Alice, guitars, and motorcicles.

You ain't a prince, you ain't a Kermit,
But, please, don't ever be a hermit.
'Cause I love to see you everyday.
Swimming and dancing, my froggy at play.

People say it can't be done,
but I think it would be fun
if I taught you how to speak,
To say more than just "reedeep."

Lindsay McDonald

Rainbows

Thru all the good and bad times,
You've been a rainbow to my soul,
You took me in and sheltered me,
When I had no where to go,
Our friendship had a rocky start,
But we found each other
In our hearts,
You've been there thru my times
Of strife,
And gave me courage in my life,
You are the person I'd like to be,
You give so much and more to me,
I thank you for the friendship,
And more than you'll ever know,
I thank you for the rainbows,
That you've given to my soul.

Sylvia Somer

Mirrored World

I see this figure
Who stares at me
And wonder who is she?
And why does she care?
And always look from in there?
Who could this person be?
I see her,
Does she see me
From inside that place?
Or is she simply looking through
At her own deeply saddened face?
Maybe her world is
Extraordinary!
Much different from our own
Where many happy souls all dwell
And no one is ever alone.
Except, perhaps, this one girl
Who's world to me comes clearer.
I notice this girl is just me
Imagining in front of the mirror.

Kristal Shurtz

Last Dance, One Leaf

I wind dance now
    through deep brown bronze
and skate the pools
    of light and space...
I race!
a twirl of points, I bend
    and lace the air
with motion form,
    (ahhh breeze, so warm)

A certain shade of year,
    a blend,
enraptures, captures summer sun,
    yet bursts a thrill with winter chill.
I take the stage
    by storm, I twirl -
through wind, I whirl,
    then drift to dream
a spiral fall;
    ...that was my shape
but so ends all.

Cheryl Peoples Perez

Love Remembered

Like the gracious fawn that makes its way
Through mounds of snow and fields of prey
To sip the water that's crystal clear
I quench my thirst when you are near

Like the butterfly that soars so high
To capture sunlight in the sky
My life with you is so sublime
I am glad you're near me all the time

Like the snow that covers all the earth
And sparkles like a diamonds birth
I reach for you in all that splendor
And captured love without surrender

Like the ground that covers all the earth
With you beneath I await rebirth
I'll wait until the day you say
Come join me love it's another day

And for now although you're far away
I see your face most everyday
I see your smile, I touch your lips
When I close my eyes I cherish this.

Francine J. Pucillo

Untitled

Have you ever watched the sun go down
Though many ways it could be,
It might have made my eyes go out
But it was hazy and I could see.
My thoughts almost came to a one time halt
And my eyes focused long and steady,
The evening breeze made it appear all colors
As it was still shining through the trees,
But it disappeared too fast for our lives to last
To leave this old world if we're not ready.

Elsie W. Huddleston

Flowers

There's a new flower bed on the hill.
Three precious little animals are resting there.
Unconditional love and devotion were their generous gifts to me.

Guilt, grief and loneliness are very devastating,
But fifty collective years of happiness
Measured against their infirmities minimizes my pain.

My love for them was not enough to combat the ravages of time
    and civilization;
And we are told that releasing our pets from pain is not only a
    responsibility,
But also an act of unconditional love.

I miss my little four-legs, but I know I will see them again.
My heart tells me that they are very near,
Without infirmities or pain, peaceful and happy.

The flowers are blooming in the new bed.
Nature is forever at work.

Bessie Callender Lott

"Stay"

I found my way to happiness
Through the deepness in your eyes
You made my life worth living for
Still, there's sadness I can't disguise

Though you made me laugh,
Sometimes your sweetness made me cry
The one thing I hope I never do,
Is have to say goodbye

Our distance apart didn't seem to break our way
But this feeling I have of eagerness
Makes md hope harder you would stay.

Jessica L. Wisniewski

Untitled

Walk with me along the brim of existence to the doorstep of dawn,
through the double glass door of light, through the corridor of
ambivalence, down the steps of regrets, along the cherry wood floors
of environmental ambiance, through the crack of economic challenge,
up the pipe of sex, into the tub of love, into the hall way of reality,
through the window of death... strange how life is like a doll house.

Barbara Latham

Untitled

For senus and blood are a thin vale of lace
What you wear in your heart, you wear on your face.
If for others you live, not how much you get,
but how much you give.
The false and deceit that you bare in your heart,
will not stay inside where it first had it start.
If you live close to God, in his infinite grace,
you don't have to tell it, it shows on your face.

Marian M. James

Tolling Bells

Bells tolling across the lake
Through the mist their voices sound.
Ringing triumphantly for a new day hath dawned.
Listen to their sweet melody;
Cheerfully awakening the hearts of men.

The beauty cast from these bells is of fair quality.
Like the brightness of gold,
The bells have their own class of beauty.
Like the sparkle deep in the heart of a diamond,
Yon bells reflect visions of delight.
Listen to them ring over mountains far and wide.

Tolling bells, listen to them ringing.
Wonderful to hear; almost like a song.
Listen to their message:
A new day hath dawned.

David Glenn Fambrough

A Letter From A POW Or MIA From Viet Nam

Today is my birthday I'm forty two, I feel that my life is almost
through. The months and years have passed me by some days
I'm blue and other days I cry. For you see, I was nineteen when
my chopper went down and the V.C. took me to this V.C.
compound, I've seen a lot of friends be put in the ground but I'm
here just on the outskirts of town. Sometimes I wonder if this is
all real it's been twenty years since I had a nice meal. I sit here
all along in this little cage of a cell for twenty two years it's been
a life's living hell. For almost every day I have been tortured or
beat sometimes they won't even let me speak, I'm not allowed to
talk and sometimes it's months before they let me out to walk,
most every night I don't sleep, I just sit here and softly weep. It
is dark in this cage the only light I get is from Saigon town while
the V.C. pass and make their round, sometimes when I cry they
call me a clown, they laugh because I weigh just 85 pounds. I
haven't heard a word or got a letter from home. I wonder if
anything and what went wrong. Did you get a telegram saying
I'm an MIA or dead? Did you call all the family in for it to be
read?

Please keep writing and praying for me no matter what you have
read I'm still here and not dead. Please write Hanoi and tell
them no matter what they said I'm a POW and no I'm not dead.
So I'll say goodbye and I'll wish and pretend that it won't be
long, till I see you again.

Caroline Franks

Water Song

Looking out
Through window panes of water flowing down
Eyes touch the rich green ground
Rivulets reflecting lullabies of hours softly spent
Love letters I have
Scent of rain and dew drops

Morning dew
Caress of lover's lips
Brushing mine
Finger tips tracing lines of horizons
Of the curve of my waist, hips and thighs
Flowing smooth lines
Beckoning sleep and dreams

Dreaming deep
The forest and the sound of falling rain
Against my window pane
In my heart's remembering
Lonely times of longing
Gentle arms to cradle me through
Storms to calm my waters

Catherine Moon

An Abused Child

A child's life consisting of abuse and neglect.
Throughout his life it will reflect.
A pleasant smile, so cheery and bright.
Causes him confusion; he only sees fights.
Spreading your arms to give him a hug
He pictures a hard swing from a boxing glove.
His parents expecting so much from him,
"He's just a child" what's wrong with them?
A child so precious, yet this abuse takes places.
It's here among us all ages, sex and race.

DeLaVerne Wong

Zephyrleaves

Floating along on a gentle breeze,
Thrown madly about by puffs of air,
Soaring skyward then tumbling down,
Falling softly to the ground.

Following a current, twisting and turning,
Raked up in the fall and sent swiftly burning,
Used to fill bags for Halloween,
They come in all hues - from brown to green.

As a child, I'll always remember
Those special days in late November,
When I found a huge pile and threw myself in
And found myself covered up to my chin.

Now as an adult, I still fancy at these,
Those myriads of shapes simply called leaves.

Andie Pollock

Come Dance With Me

Come dance with me
  till the morning's light.
The time is right.
Let us share the night.

Come dance with me
And laugh in delight.
Time will disappear,
fade with the night.

Come dance with me.
Dance away the fears and worries
  of hearts once broken.
We'll have the tokens - memories unspoken.

Come dance with me,
trust again.
Take my hand,
love again.

Brian L. Husted

To My Daughter Kathleen

Kathleen, you will leave us in a few months this year
To attend university while Topaze and I are here.
Your face, so full of beauty, will always be on my mind,
Sweet, smart, serene, gentle, and kind.
Your laughter is music for my soul
Your singing so soft with the voice of gold!
Monte Carlo will miss you for sure this time,
And they will remember - so divine!
Without Kathleen, the Cote d' Azur will suffer,
Both French and Italian just love her!
Genuine, caring, and eyes full of passion,
Lovely clothes and adornments one could not imagine.
Blue skies, cool sea, long clear vistas below,
She gazed, sighing, from her Monaco window.
On the Riviera, it is sad if you have never seen or met her,
Because once you have, you never forget her!

Helene Harris

Lady Liberty

Come forth tall ships of all nations
  to a land where free men dwell.
And bring with you a part of peace,
  for the men who in war have fought and fell.
Also bring with you thoughts of histories
  past, for you are free at last.
The sound of rockets are heard across
  the sea, giving tribute to this
  lands birth, and Lady Liberty.
I see Old Glory flying in the tallest
  mast, leading the mighty fleet
  into the worlds past.
Our countrymen look proudly past as
  the tall ships cross the bay,
  and with her lamp Lady Liberty
  sends them on their way.
And so it will be another one hundred
  years, the tall ships will meet
  again on these shores, where free
  men dwell, and history never ends.

John Bradley Hall

Suspension

My eyes glance skyward now and then
to catch a fleeting glimpse of luminous mass,

Be it a tremor of wings I hear of Celestial
Beings come to pass.

As my spirit soars upward a gentle strain
of rhythmic drops descend on me settle and melt.
Sunlit rays penetrate and are warmly felt
as an arch of color blinds my eyes

I plummet to earth in an unsuccessful try
to touch heaven in the breath of a sigh.

Jayne Hillyer

The Infant's Eyes

The light from his face was nothing
To cause one to cover the eyes,
To stand back in awe,
To stir the silent, secret places of the heart.

His was only a tiny infant face,
Smudged with dust here and there,
With small lips that quivered from the cold
And framed by straw-entangled hair.

Yet, something in the eyes
Told of worlds where light never fades,
Where warm winds blow
And tears never fall.

It was the eyes
That made the heart beat faster,
That held the mind spellbound,
That awakened dreams of eternal days,
Life unending,
Love forever everywhere.

Augustine John Moore

Stirring Thoughts

And now I lay my thoughts to rest.
To reap moment to moment all happiness.
If again my mind starts to wonder,
I will seek within the silence and splendor.
To calm all my emotion and thunder.
For only I have the power to be,
this calm person I admire in me.

Jennie Hornstein

Each Month Is Special

September is a splendid month,
to cherish and hold fast.
But memories of June, July and August
are great and will last
Until another Summer has come and past.
October is a coveted time,
We enjoy it fully all the while.
The gorgeous Fall colors are of the best
we enjoy November with all the rest.
December comes and we love the way
our hearts are stirred with what friends say.
God gives us Christmas to impart
our joys and blessings from the heart.
January and February are welcome now
we settle down to rest somehow.
March comes along good and strong
So is our hopes of April and Spring
and oh what a joy May can bring.
Thank you Lord for all the year
each month you give us is very dear.

Jewell King

A Visit To The Ruins

Cautiously they kneel
to dig and scratch and sift through time
each particle of stone or sand a clue, a find, a link

To polish and clean and catalog
Charging a fee to come and look
at shards of glass and sharpened stones

And if we look long enough, dig far enough, deep enough
Layers of living will all peel away
till everyone's bones lie under glass
vessels painstakingly restored.

Forgive us our interest in ancient ruins
Bodies in buffalo falling in piles, in detroit it's suicide
Serial killers stalk their prey and children burn the schools
Infants die at alarming rates, no one cares to mourn

And so we kneel and dig and sift
through broken bones and sharpened stones
missing the little tiny grains that cry in the night
for someone to come and fall through the holes
while we listen politely and never touch,
artifacts before our time.

Carolyn Hastings

His Death

'Tis like a spear
To disappear
In such a mind
So sweet and kind

I heard a whisper of a kiss
Ever softer than a hiss
Ever softer than it all
Leaving so quickly and down the hall

I felt so tiny, ever small
Wandering through that darkened hall
Yet, what did I see, in the darkness of night
I saw a shining, bright light

I looked into his hazel eyes
Thinking of the ocean's tides
So I sat down to cry
Wishing that I might die
I rested my head
As he...
    rested dead.

Joy O'Brien

The Sea

I walked to the sea this morning
To dispel my grief somewhat.

As I approached the water
I heard the rhythm of the waves

Making music of the sea
Always so pleasing to me.

I looked at the blue sky
So high, so wide!

In the East I saw a glow,
a beautiful glow

Making sunbeams dancing on the horizon
Forecasting another fine day on the beach.

Could heaven so beautiful?
Of course it could,
of course it could.

Blanche Brink Hammond

The Promise

We're promised that a certain day will come
To draw a veil across all we have known
And sounding its intent with loud "Amen"
Will lead us into heaven's eternity:

    There, souls vexed and almost spent
    Are nourished anew by the breath of God.

I'll not regret a change or fear that day.
I'm weary of counting worldly hours.
Come now! and let me join the company
Of those who are given five new senses:

    Faith and joy, grace, peace and love of Thee
    With your Son and my comforter, The Holy Spirit.

This is not an empty, fearful place.
Nothing has perished in the crossing.
All that I cherish is with me still, familiar in
This Seven-fold light. You are here. You have come:

    Closer than touch, your refuge for my love.
    Warmer than the sun, your comforting,
    Keeper of the promise.

Anne H. Gibson

Dreams

I lay down my head upon a pile of feathers,
To dream of a world where everything is perfect and
wishes of kids are most likely to happen.
I dream of a celebrated swimmer with a shining gold
medal draping from her neck.
Standing on top of the world, under a starred and
striped flag upon a pool deck.
Her muscles flaring, and her skin and hair dripping
off her many days of practices and fast paces.
Her family and coach so proud, wiping tears of joy and
devotion from their faces.
Open up my eyes, back to reality and life.
Waiting for another darkness filled with more dreams!

Elizabeth A. Watt

Quest

I want the arid desert,
To swim the depths of the sea,
To ski the sheer south face of Everest,
This wanton passion,
This forbidden desire,
To kiss caress to touch, to taste, to enter,
I have always wanted what I can't have,
I want you.

Jude T. Burke

The Search

For so long I've wondered; for so long I've been afraid;
To even come close to the realization of who I am.
I began a search for you, within, and I could find none.
You're not the easiest to find, but yet, I pursue.
I never give in, I don't think I could.
Though years have come, and years have passed;
I have no memory of you at last.
I try to reason, but sometimes it's so confusing;
The questions of the heart.
I long for one day to say: "The search is over,
You were with me all the while,"
Was I just too busy trying to reason,
That I could not accept?

Connie Register

The Search

To cover his faults of a weakened hour
To exhibit the strength of his manly power
To display his virtues upon request
And cherish the desires within his breast
To esteem the honor of man all grown
To nourish his thoughts as it were my own
To increase his thirst for things divine
And dream his dreams that too are mine

For he and I are one the same
The joys of life will be our aim
Through me he see his work as art
And to find myself, I search his heart

Doris Smith

The Infamous Will

I watched as each one entered
to gaze upon his shell
I thought they all were mourning
for the one I knew so well
They were extra nice to him
before he met his maker
They were quite taken by the smile on
his face as they complimented the undertaker
They all commented on the enormous
deeds that each one had done
I was so proud to know that he
was loved by everyone
I wonder if this place will be as
packed when I must reveal
That the gentleman to whom we were paying
our respects had a non-existent will.

Deborah D. Hatchett

God's Masterpiece

How great God is to all of us, here on earth below,
To hang His masterpiece for us, as Autumns come and go.

Each leaf in its own hue, is magic to behold,
As it flutters from the tree, to join the pile below.

The grandeur of the Season, with colors of every blend
Can only be painted by God, with His Almighty hand.

I wonder what God is thinking, when He takes that mighty brush
And begins to paint His masterpiece of beauty, for each of us?

I am certain that He is saying, " my child take my hand
Let me walk beside you, I'm sure you understand

By lending you a masterpiece of color, by night and day,
I am simply saying I love you, in yet another way".

Joyce Crowther

River Smoke

Scent of death and a distant hope
To live for dreams on a shredded rope
I saw your face in the river smoke
I saw this place in a distant dream
I threw my youth into a bloody stream
Can I blame it all in the things I've seen?
I will plant my seeds
Where my mind grows weak
And await the mighty tree, the mighty oak
Or an answer from the river smoke
I sleep at night and dream of fame
I try to hide my fear of shame
When things seem clear it always rains
Will I fall with the sun and rise with the moon?
Or will I sink in the ocean and die too soon?
This pain will live on until I grow immune
I will plant my seeds
Where my mind grows weak
And await the mighty tree, the mighty oak
Or an answer from the river smoke

Bill Ciprian

To Hurt Of Broken Vows

I took you my darling to be my loving wedded wife,
   to live together in holy matrimony for the rest of our life.
I vowed to love and honor you my dear precious heart,
   for as long as we live and till death do us part.
For better or worse we vowed to unite into one,
   for richer or poorer, until our days are done.
We vowed, through sickness and health to be side by side,
   for our love for each other surely he could not be denied.
We vowed to be true and loyal for as long as we live,
   for my darling, our love and our vows is all we had to give.
What God has joined together, let no woman put apart,
   but all our vow's were broken and broke our poor hearts.
As we travel through life with our memories and bitter tears,
   we must remember that we were living in our tender years.
But in love for the good times, we did foolish things,
   we didn't think of the heartaches that hurting each other brings.
So, if we can't have each other, please let us be friends,
   and may God have mercy as I face the bitter end.
For God will judge us by the broken vows, and things we have done,
   for all of the loving vows we made, we broke one by one.

James E. Bingham

Night Follows Day

I believe there's a way, to make it through the day.
To make it I must pray, that night comes quickly
   my way, Yes, night follows day
I look to the night to find my delight.
   When the night will come and we become one
   as we search to find our way when
   night follows day
I know this is the one to be my morning sun.
   To make the night all right and show me the way
   when night follows day
I see she is mine as we intertwine and
   become one in the bright day's sun.
   We will journey thru life - astride the strife
   I now know the way as I enter the day
   and need not delay until night follows day

Grady D. George

The Quest For Love

The quest for love in this world is so great as if it were sublime,
  To make one think that love is out of this world and therefore divine
What genius put so much love into a little sparrow or a Bob-o-Link,
  Which courts a maiden with a love song that only a bird could sing

One need only to watch the birds, as they build their little nest,
  With uncanny love whether they be a wren or a robin red-breast.
Whence this great engineering knowledge is placed in their little heads,
  And to design a worm in order that their baby birds would be fed,

But the God who made the bird that could replicate and multiply
  Can also have children that would live with Him forever on high.
There is a record of a plan that the Master Builder has been making.
  Where a loving God is singing a love song to hearts that are breaking.

  Ed Hutka

Legacy

Pinpoint bombing made it easy
To pretend there were no bodies
With missing arms or legs, no blood
Inside the buildings that silently imploded
  on TV screens.

And we could swell with pride and boast
  of our proficiency,
Our cleverness in devising these marvelous
  machines of war that
Killed with surgical precision and
Hid the evidence of our destruction under a cloud
  of dust.

But the broken bodies hidden in the rubble
Of buildings new and ancient force the
  question:
How clever are we, the people?
Are bombs of high efficiency
  Our most conspicuous legacy?

  Dorothy Miles

A Man

God decided, to make a man
To put in the garden to rule the land
He decided to make a woman too
He knew just how and what to do
A rib was taken from Adam's side
He made sis Eve big as a bride
They were put in the garden all rich with fear.
You can have everything you shear
There's one thing you better not try.
The day you do the day you die
Sis Eve wouldn't do what she was told
Her and the serpent ate the fruit up whole
Then she decided to have some fun
Got some more gave old Adam some
Old Adam just like us men folks will
Up and received what Eve had to give
This is true when you don't abide
One thing left where you can hide
Then my God came about
He went to the garden and put both of then out.

  Cornelius Baker

Asleep In The Arms Of The Master

My father didn't live this year
To see the many colors of fall
As the leaves turned their brilliant hues
Then fell down one and all.

And he won't notice, no he won't
The first few signs of winter coming;
The very first frost and the windshields
with ice, the chill factor in the wind
As the breezes are humming and we run
For the warmth within our houses.

He's asleep in the arms of the master,
No longer suffering with pain.
He's alive in our hearts and
Although we are apart, I know
He can feel my love.
I'm sure he knows how much we all miss him,
As we struggle to continue on our own.
He's asleep, so we won't weep
Because tomorrow, in eternity,
We'll see him once again.

  Carrie L. Collins

Through A Child's Eyes

Through a child's eyes the world's so bright
to see the stars light up the night.
Through a child's eyes I feel so free
that's how I want the world to be
We all are one
there's no races at all
Your don't get judged for being short,
fat skinny or tall.
Through a child's eyes everything seem
so free
I wish there was no such thing a slavery,
Yes, through a child's eyes I wish
we all could see
Where life is simple, so carefree
no poverty, no crime like a fantasy.
To see, through a child's eyes
you'd hate to come back to reality.

  Gale A. Goodman

Creation Myth

As the way is, so is the way it shall be.
To seek the bare essence, of the essence of all
is to the look inside as the inside looks out.
Toward the What will be.

There was a way, there is still away back.
To the Time that was before.
Not the time Before, The TIME before.
And the way back, that was way back is coming back.

The all around that was everywhere,
didn't here about it.
It doesn't seem to matter.
Overall it was very clear.

Ramble down dogs with no sparkle,
set out for a joyride.
On some forsaken planet,
swirling in a vortex they don't even understand.

The beat goes on, but nobody listens.
Because the lady in white won't let them play
with the rattle.
Pity, it was a nice rattle.

  Andrew De Cecco

The Image In The Stream

To come upon the image in the stream
to sense the fearsome feeling in the dream
and walk the decades waiting
for the image-flesh to visit
in the waning moments time allows,
and know the present as the past-

To draw upon the spirits from the stream,
to paint the image-face upon the dream
and live in currents reaching
deeply toward the image dreaming
in the waning moments time allows,
and form the present from the past-

To touch the image in the stream,
to touch the curl upon the face
a wisp about an eye;
it is as then, and was as now
a dream.

John Pitts

My Journey Is In Your Hands

To hide beneath your wings, oh Lord
To stand there, hidden, with complete delight
Brings joy to my hungry soul
and peace to my longing heart

Oh to fly as an Eagle
To soar among the clouds
Imparts trust and security
that can only be found in
Your Trusting Hands.

Yes, to guide me in ventures
that far surpass all my imaginations.

The joy set before me is ever glorious
It holds great promise of Your sovereignty
You alone shall guide me to the secret places
Into the high places we shall travel together
We shall journey to places too marvelous for words

Alone I cannot travel - but with my hand in Yours
I shall know Your presence and loving kindness
As we soar -

Billi Switzer-Aaron

I, The Demon, Vs. Myself, The Angel.

Sitting amongst the silence, listening
to the clatter inside my head. A battle
over good and evil. My focus towards
death is nothing new here. It is and
always will be a dominating force.
How can I get away from myself?
When I try to run away, it follows.
When I try to hide, it finds me.
When I turn on my stereo to drown
out its voice, it speaks to me through the music.
When I sedate my mind and body to escape its pain,
it screams for more. What keeps me going during
these turbulent and often desperate times?
Is it faith, hope or a hopeless faith?
Demons and Angels,
who will win?
I can never decide.

Gabriel Alvarado

A Feeling Of Not Being Real

The years pass by like a piece of string with a cat's toy attached
   to the end.
I grope for your hand in the darkness, and your hand is there,
   but it is as heavy as a thick book.
I look for you sometimes, and I recognize you by your eyes.
If only I could recognize myself as easily as I recognize you.
Our bodies come together, but I often feel that I am just a ghost
   of such thin shell and so little bit of soul.
We mold together but I am not really whole.
I sometimes look around me and see familiar things.
I feel so lost sometimes that these familiar possessions bury me
just as soft, black soil would be shoveled over my body.
Winter is still upon us, but then winter has held me back
   for ever so many years.
Do not lament the loss of my soul and do not shed you tears.
I never was, I do not live, I am not real.

Denise Riccardo

A Primer

After a bad harvest my father looks up
To the sky. My mother, too, as I find
Her arm. Maybe they want it bluer.
I want nothing, except the birds
But suddenly they are shadows on the ground.
My father, he stands like a big rock,
But my mother like a tree in the strong wind,
I shake to a remembered lullaby.
I think of a game, I will hide myself
From the sky. But my father, he begins
To talk to it in an angry voice.
I fear I will be found. I cry. "Hush!"
I hush, but I hear a louder, longer cry.

Benjamin V. Afuang

Destiny's Voice

Time has never been a friend
to those unable to defend
themselves from that which some call fate
they see their world disintegrate

They never stop to realize
the power they hold in their eyes
the vision to avoid the wrath
of walking down life's chosen path

From chances taken by a few
we've witnessed strength in form so true
not thinking that it can't be done
but forgiving on until they've won

While some things cannot be controlled
by man or woman, meek or bold
we have a say in what will be
our self-decided destiny

Arthur S. Rossin

Untitled

People become confused when women complain of being fat.
To us she is gauntly thin,
But to the person inside, the mirror has another side.
This side is twisted, distorted, confused.
Trapped in a body of relentless abuse.
To far, too many the ideal is unreal.
It is like a mirage in a desert.
We travel and become weak, searching and seeking
for something that will never be.
I tell you these words about your body straight from my heart.
You are a beautiful woman, don't tear your life apart.

Chloe Norton

Nature's Beauty Of The Rose

Love is like a rose, that opens with passion,
  to touch the velvet of its petal,
  the sweetness of its scent,
Makes you respond with, the greatest reaction.
  Feeling the sting of its thorn
  gives you pain of pleasure.
  Which travel thru the veins
  of its leafy treasure.
Just as the breeze may blow,
beneath the greenest of its leaves,
they stretch as though to grow.
  Rays of the sun that penetrate
  thru the beauty of its color,
  gives life something to appreciate.
To touch the roots with the morning dew
gives it life for its day a new.
  This natures beauty of the rose;
release the peace and pleasure of the heart
Now, in this quiet time to never be apart.

Alice R. Lopez

Just Wishing

Just wishing
To understand all that life has planned
Just wishing
To understand why some people find life grand
Able to bend with the wind, tolerate those that sinned
Just wishing
To remember just the best and forget all the rest
The world has been here a long time and always a hard climb
Just wishing
Better times are coming
Maybe we can wake up each morning humming
Just wishing
We have an ego fit to live with and
A job fit to work for
Then we score
Just wishing
For someone to love and be loved by
What a glorious high
Just wishing
We all have a faith to live by.

Frances Adissi

Before, Now And Forever

It's like somehow I expected
to wake up and find you gone
to have a fresh perspective on life
I was missing all along
Somehow I always thought
that losing you was right
so when you said you were leaving
I didn't put up a fight

Where can I go, when nowhere is sane?
Every corner of my world is filled with pain
each memory of you keeps echoing in my mind
and now you've left me so far behind

It's strange how this life of mine keeps moving on ahead
never stopping to look back at things I should have said
but my never changing soul will always be a part
of the past we made together, before I broke your heart

When someone becomes a part of your soul
they can never fully leave
and although you try to start again
it's only yourself you deceive

DeeAnnah Ghazarian

Death

May I take this opportunity to greet you
To welcome you with arms wide open
I know you feel the same about me
Though no words will be spoken

You don't have to come in night's cover
Nor must you overcome me in my sleep
For you must sense I long for you
I will not hesitate or hide or weep

Come on then. I grow weary of the wait
If you force me to seek you out
I might not come so willingly
But will fight you, of that there is no doubt

You were not here to take me
When I wanted you to be
So I will take my chances now on life
Turn me loose, set my mind and body free

Cheryl Ventura

The Gift Of Life

We give you the gift of life. I bring you to this point you are today. Your graduation, a gift of education, you'll carry along, long way.

As you start this life's journey we'll be there to help, but my dear daughter, your life is what you make of it, so make it worth these twelve years you just spent.

The years ahead should be used wisely, to prepare for your future life. So don't waste it away, for life goes fast as you grow older. Just remember what you've learned and what we've taught you.

The road ahead can get rocky, so further you're education as much as you can. Along with the gift of life, education is the gift of our human spirit....More precious than gold.

As your parents we give you these words from our hearts, we to have the gift of life and education, and wisdom to share with you on this very special graduation day.

Joan Weeks

Flash-Backs

Sand, so warm and golden, peeking up through the spaces
  between your toes.
Capturing minnows with an empty glass milk bottle.
Fragile baby shells of oysters and scallops found in the small
  ebb-tide pool.
Bluefish playing leap-frog and testing fate.
Sea gulls soaring and diving, catching bluefish in their beaks and
  leaving.
Puffy white clouds playing hide and seek with the sun.
Sun warming the air and dancing on the water.
The sea smelling so sweet and clean.
Caring hands building a sand-castle and washed away by an
  uncaring wave.
Idly sitting in a row boat.
Listening to the rhythm of the waves.
Hanging feet over the stern and feeling the tickle from the
  motion.
Watching your father bait your hook with a piece of shucked
  quahog.
Delight in his expression when your fishing rod suddenly jerks
  and bends.
Gleeful when he relates pride in "your catch".
Watching the sun drop into the ocean.
Being content, exhausted and in awe.

Grace M. Ganat

It Doesn't Matter

It doesn't matter that, I'm here today and gone
Tomorrow. I know there'll be lots of sorrow but,
Not for long, for I'll be gone and forgotten by all,
Except those who loved and cared for me most, and
Sometimes I think that they too shell forget me, until
Some occurrence reminds them of me as having been, but soon
After, forgotten again. So it doesn't matter that I'm here
Today and gone tomorrow

Herman E. Hawkins

Time Is

Always the day ahead is called TOMORROW.
TONIGHT is, has been, will be, and YESTERDAY was.
TIME IS, it's even in sorrow.
So relative, yet who can explain, nothing to hear or feel or touch,
IT was, has been, will be ours, however long or however much.
There is a TIME to live, a TIME to die, a TIME to love,
or for just letting IT pass by.
What it does is up to us.
So intangible and so indefinable,
No word or thought can explain,
Like the wind or falling rain.
Another of GOD'S wonders, ours to conceive
TIME IS always there to receive.
Today you are older than yesterday's grace
But TIME, my friend, gives tomorrow another face.

Betty Grace Pease Bruce

School Daze

To Shannon

Too long, too short, too loose, too tight,
Too baggie, too saggie, too dark, too light.

To Foley's, to Dillard's and ever K-Marts,
Teens hurry and scurry before school starts.

Across the land, repeated scenes
Of Moms buying their teen's blue jeans.

Jackie St. Cyr

Conservation's Call

Rescue this beautiful land carelessly being swept
   toward the raging sea.

Stop the rapid descent of topsoils into
   deep crevices, gullies swept.

Make stable the meadowed hills,
   green with verdant grasses.

Safeguard the vaulted sanctuary of the deer,
   deep within the forest glades.

Keep the broad savanna grasses gently swaying
   in the summer breezes.

Defend the refuge of the rabbit, quail, the winged
   dove, all creatures great and small.

So plead unborn generations in mimicked silence,
   preserve for us unspoiled paradises.

Each new dawn calls to faithful stewards, the
   guardians of a blessed land.

All this cherish, use wisely, and pass on
   to waiting hands.

A dream, a blessing, and a benediction...
   So plead our children.

John W. Flowers

The Meadow

Tiny spring blossoms reach to dark blue skies.
Tractor grinds methodically through fertile fields.
   -Birth in the meadow

Spiral blades turn rich earth clods
Heaped upon themselves, fodder for seedlings.
   -Life in the meadow

A deer bounds innocently from lush forests -
Bounds and cavorts with butterflies and blossoms
   -Joy in the meadow

Mechanical rumble dulls driver to all distractions.
Deer stops . . stares at noisy creature upon her.

Tractor swordblades bring her down.
   -Death in the meadow.

Bonnie B. Hall

Untitled

A woman ordinary but for a moment!
Transformed and given immortality.
...sight and mingling senses...
Only a cheek, the delicate angle of smoothness
conforming to the soft curve.
An instant drawn out of time
held immobile in true perfection.
Swept away in motion
but held forever in memory.

Gregory C. Linde

Who Will Help

Pain streaks tonight dark inner skies,
Traumas like lightning strike the heart,
Hurt and ache and cries inside
Make me wander paths leading no where.

What might I do that makes a difference?
Am I quiet, subdued, injured and broken
To remain in touch with that storm outside
Yet feel the fire searing within?

Where do I find an answer, solution, a clue?
Whom do I question? Whom do I seek?
Am I always a long-distance call away?
Do oceans stop me that I can't swim?

Then answers to empty separation
Leap the chasm of rejection,
Fill the craters of isolation
And bridge a mote swimming with fear.

Her love-strong words break out,
Streak, like arrows, a hurt-filled night
Winging across with piercing grace
To press, embrace and penetrate.

Gus Wilhelmy

One Is The Same As None For My Love

I Shall Never Find.

Your love is as twinkling starlight,
traveling thousands of years to reach our steady earth.
But as the earth waits, so will I.
Ever continuous, humbly waiting for your twinkle.
For that twinkle shall start my life anew.

Dan Hernesman

Apartment Pool Summer

A breathless breeze nudges the chair
Tree reflections fade into the surface of the water
Narcissus lies to baste the true self
Heat inebriation beckons drowsiness
Heavy air smothers movement
Lethargy flourishes
While slumber rises.
Darrell Pittman

Wondrous Things

Flowers that bloom
Trees that grow
Beautiful beyond anything I know
Fish that swim and birds that sing
These are wondrous things.

Clouds that float
Dew that glistens
Wondrously speaks to one who listens
Wind that blows and sweet smells brings
These are wondrous things.

Leaves that fall
Mists that creep
Light that brightens waters deep
Creatures that run or view earth from wings
These are wondrous things.

A Spirit within
A God who lives
A Savior who salvation gives
Let all that have breath sweet praises sing
To Him who created these wondrous things.
David G. Schulman

Riding The T

Steady reflections in its dark glass
Trigger mind and memory and
Flashes sharp and clear
Play my dream video
Over and over again

See my summer meadow
Watching warm bright hues
Of flowing garments touching
As two women dance an echo slow
To soft vibrations I still feel inside

See their model faces
Color lips lining a perfect
Secret smile, glazing eyes
Turn inbound as their hands move
In rhythm skin of pale members protruding

My mind is slow in seeing fall
Into place recognition and
While I question visions
Rather too bizarre
The music slips away
Erna Horn

Believe In Yourself

Others may bring you down
Try to keep you within their bounds
They fill your mind with negative beliefs
Keeping you from the goals you seek
There's only way you can break through this wall
You have to stand up and show them all
To do this may seem far away
That's why you have to stand up and believe in yourself today
Jacqueline McLevis

Up Stream

Casting up stream with the hatch in sight
Trout rising create such delight
To master the form with perfect precision
Will surface the fish despite my decision

In the shadows obstacles arise
The fly I've stretched out lost from my eyes
Surveying the spot where it should emerge
A splash instead and then a surge

To my demise I've missed the hit
Reluctant to forge I hold back a bit
Then cast a new where I've been before
With promise I know I'll bring one ashore

No matter whether I hook one or not
No matter if I forego the just spot
I've accomplished a feat that most will not try
The perfect display of casting a fly
Carrie E. Boyce

True Love

True love gives off a special aura all its own.
True love takes nothing but gives all.
True love forgives fully and without hidden resentments.
True love means you care enough to give of your best.
True love is from God for only God is TRUE LOVE.
Deborah Pengelly

Tell The Truth

Speaking the truth a rewarding performance indeed
Truth non-hazardous to the mind
Conducive to confidence, personality and integrity
Contributive elements to our populace society

Deceitful intentions lend to mistrust
Godless acts along a devious path
Speak truthfully and accept the consequences
As others may not be misjudged thru ruthlessness

Essence of innocence - tots - tell it as is
Occasionally surprisingly shocking but hilarious
Comparatively adults shamefully make up white tales
Persuasively believed for sake of peace

Let truth prevail for well-being and moral sense
Ideal for all concerned for just determinations
For all to be judged fairly and none to be hurt
So for goodness sake - "Tell the Truth"!
Angelo S. Massaro

Forever Real?

The many confusions there are in life
Trying to understand our love and all it's meant to be,
The hardship of forgiving a fallen love
Changing the feelings between you and me.

There comes a time when two loves must pass
Separated, taking their own route,
Once crossing the lane that lovers cross
Not knowing that things wouldn't work out.

There is a time when all must change
But if love is love, real and true,
The troubles of a once misleading relationship
Are fading from the darkest gray to blue.

With a renewed relationship comes many different experiences
New fascinations of lust, love, and thrill,
Opening the tenderness in one's mind and heart
Knowing their lives together are going to be forever real.
Anthony Harmon

Precious Love

Hidden from view, and closely guarded.
Tucked away from prying eyes.
Like a fragile piece of crystal —
Protected from carelessness and lies.

A look, a touch, and a sweet caress,
Whistling a tune and not knowing why.
Like the velvet touch of a rose petal —
Soft and sweet as a gentle sigh.

Things shared by both - precious and few,
Stolen moments of moonlight from above.
Like the notes of a haunting melody —
Shared by two in love.

Helen M. Oates

Overworked

Heavy-set eyelids; the weight of ten pounds
Two dragging arms, that linger to the ground
A dense passive posture, hunched over and slouched
A curvy shaped body, the amorphous mass, resembling a couch
Recollections in countless pursuit, concentration has been lost
A hazy-headed price to pay where time has been the cost.
Trudged steps are taken, the movement of two cinder-blocks
Concreted appendages that are bolted and joint-locked
Mind in full reason, but thoughts are confused
Energy never gained and yet, already used.
Cloudy objects are suspended in the air around your head...
Just one wink of sleep, in a cozy bed?
One wink of sleep, for this body of lead?
One wink of sleep, body sedated as if dead?
One wink of sleep?
One wink just shed!

Jaclyn Bloomer

My Little Boy

Hair like sunshine, eyes like the sea,
Two little rosy cheeks.
Always smiling, laughing, playing, my little boy.
Those carefree days are gone so fast
And the little boy has gone.
No more smiling, laughing, playing, no more rosy cheeks.
Time has taken the little boy
And changed him into a man,
Surrounded by darkness, gloom, and despair.
Taken away the eyes like the sea,
And turned them into a vacant stare.
Taken away the rosy cheeks,
And made them hollow and bare.
Darkness won't last forever,
Sunshine will return.
Those carefree days will come once again
And chase away the gloom.
For off in the distance I can see, hair like sunshine,
Eyes like the sea, two little rosy cheeks.
Always smiling, laughing, playing, my little boy.

Janet Rasnick

How quickly burn the stars which shined so bright
Until, at last, they flare across the night
We watch, with difficulty comprehending
All is all ever so slowly ending
Comes a time when all will be forgotten
Every struggle, grand and misbegotten
But we, less than masters of our here and now
Still seek, for love, for what life may endow
With hearts which flare, each in time and turn
Still strive, for hope, still risk, perchance to learn

David W. Sjoberg

Angels And Apricots

In springtime we planted an apricot tree,
Two little seeds, my small son and me,
Seeds that my sister gave us, you see,
Seeds from her very own apricot tree.
The rains came down and the bright sun shown.
We had an apricot tree of our own.
Then an angel came and whispered his need,
For the one who gave us the apricot seed.
The years fled by and the tree grew tall,
Green leaves in the spring, and russet in fall;
And the child grew too, as children do.
He dreamed the summer and winter time through.
And one spring day, mid the sun and the showers,
The tree burst forth with a garland of flowers,
Then as the summer began to unfold,
The apricot tree was covered with gold.
And I shed a tear for the one dear to me,
Who gave us our very own apricot tree.

Betty Toops

The Last

Two worlds separated by a tiny body of water
Two worlds, where there only is supposed to be one.
Sitting on the shore I can hear the water lapping against the rocks.
Calm and serene... perfect for a night like this
In the distance, the pounding of drums and the shuffling
of dancing feet are all that can be heard through
the wind in the trees.
They were pushed out. Forced to live in a place "given" to them.
They were here first. Why aren't we restricted to tradition
in a certain area of land?
Feathers, dances, chants, drums...
One leader and the rest followers: Trying to hold on,
trying to hold on to tradition the songs are sung and
the dances danced.
The "new people" will never understand
They dance and sing louder, louder, LOUDER...
Until the end — the drums fade, the chants grow
weaker; fading...fading... until finally it is gone.

Brendan C Shane

A Change Of Habit

She acts like a great Christian in Mass.
Under her habit she feels the slash of sin.
She walks down the hall as though with wisdom.
No one knows her feelings and decisions.
She can hardly wait for this big occasion.
Where she will get to bare her inner sensation.
The mighty event came, Oh how fast!
The nun wore a swim suit, and with class.
Bashfulness was in her eyes.
When she stepped out there was shock and suspense.
Was this a nun out of her inhabitants?
No one knew except I,
The bashfulness that was in her eyes.
Ready to suspend all caught up within.
The nun felt free,
And swam to her destiny.

Diane Griffin

The Retreat

Courage sought in the battle of love,
  Waged unkindly, loser maimed.
Forever doubtful, fears of wounds yet felt,
  The heart retreats.
A moment's victory. Eternal defeat.

Edward Alan Brutscher

"Bury Me In The Bluegrass."

Bury me in the Bluegrass,
  Under the Kentucky moon,
A top a hill, that shines like glass,
  Be it December, or be it June.

Bury me in the Bluegrass.
That's where I'll lay to rest,
  With Ma and Pa,
And good o'le Auntie Bess.

Bury me in the Bluegrass,
  Under the Kentucky star lit night.
With Coffee trees, standing at their best,
  I'll rest in peace, with sheer delight.

Bury me in the Bluegrass,
  Where the Kentucky flower grows
Where sun beams, are of solid brass,
  I'll lie in sweet repose.

Bury me in the Bluegrass,
  Be it January, or be it July.
Just bury me in my home sweet home
  In Kentucky when I die!

  Frances Farnstrom

Just Beyond Reach

Stereophonic voices swirl
Universal truths to tell
Vague silhouettes bring cataclysmic perils
  Just beyond reach

Marching furies beat out kaleidoscopic cadences
Nondescript tentacles smother undeclared intentions
Nomadic thoughts meander, ever at attention
  Just beyond reach

Emotions congregate
Listening for the stillness
Engulfment awaits
  Just beyond reach

Certain annihilation?
Gasping breaths of minuscule hope surface
Seeking re-creation
  Just beyond reach

  Andrea Jackson Huber

Remember Me

  Enter the cave of my past, walk the halls of loneliness with me until we reach the end of my innocence.

  Help me remember the child I was - the child I still long to be, the day I lost my innocence was the day pure hell began for me.

  My laughter was turned to tears, and in my head - which was pure as snow - perverted thoughts would begin to flow.

  Hold my hand as we wade through the river of fear, and when bad things hurt the tender child - remind me that you are near.

  Come through the horror quickly - it's the terror that grips me so - to stay there long would haunt us - believe me the frightened child knows.

  My hiding places are all around, they're dark and lonely too. The desperate child is so afraid, she doesn't know what to do.

  Protect me when the shadows snatch my world away - promise me the men that steal from me are not really here to stay.

  I'm willing now to let you see through the windows of my soul, the child in me is waiting for someone to love her and make her whole.

  Amy Holloway

The River Of Pain Flows

The hot white wax fell like the ax
Unto the place where the rose bed did lay.
The viper rode on the pale horse's shadow
As he came to claim his prey.
The life he lived he didn't have to give
When tempted by the mountain climber.
But he took the risk, accepted the kiss,
And lost count in his emotional timer.
Like a lonely child thrown out in the wild
He thought there was nothing to lose.
The viper stole the coveted soul
Of one who never learned how to refuse.
What he lost was the final cost
For the games that he played.
In the presence of smoke, he never awoke
As his mind grasped onto the final fade.
All of his pain flows in his veins
Which are hidden behind his crimson headband.
The rebel is gone, but the river lives on
Inside the needle clenched in his hand.

  Darin Strachan

Beautiful Snow

The snow fell quietly all around
upon the mountain and in the town.
The old familiar scenes fade from sight
to join the serenity of the night.

The earth lies white, so fluffy and still
from the frozen pond to the windswept hill.
While high in the heavens, the twinkling stars
in silence spread their lights afar.

The birds and the animals know they must endure
so they have found shelter and are safe and secure.
The snow has blanketed the ground for miles around
and from our forest friends we hear not a sound.

The magic of snow calms our souls
like velvet wings, contentments unfolds.
Our hurries began to cease
and within our hearts, we find sweet peace.

  Fannie Mae Evans

My Son

Chris, is sittin' in the city jail,
Waitin' for me, to make the bail,
Not realizin' the seriousness, of it all.

The big, young son of mine,
Has been, cryin' all the time,
Then yesterday, he finally, heard the call.

"Jesus, sweet Jesus!"
Help that boy, become a man,
Although you have his soul now,
There's so much he don't understand.

"Jesus, sweet Jesus!"
Yes, my son belongs to you,
Please guide him past this hell,
And let me borrow him, when your through.

"Jesus...oh Jesus!"
He's sixteen, yet going on ten,
Keep his hero dreams alive,
Don't let this child, go to, the pen.

  Danny Rucker

556

Grandpa

On a fishing dock he stands
Waiting for the Lord's Command

In shallow water or deep ravine
Reflections of his life are serene

Children from the neighborhood gather
I can hear the sound of laughter

Baseball mitts and canvas shoes
"Come join the fun, what have you got to loose?"

When they called out "Hey Tige"
He'd answer right back
"Gotta go, gotta go
No time to slack"

Some catches were big, others small
But Oh, the memories, top them all.

Deb Volkmer

The Hole In The Wall

Look over there, just what do I see, there seems to be a hole in
the wall. Big enough for the neck eye to see, there seems to be
someone looking out at me. I see a small boy child, dark and
small. In one hand he carries a spear, in the other I see grains of
falling sands. As one teardrop falls, he never says a word to me.
But his eyes tell it all. They tell me of the long journeys he had
traveled and the wars that lay ahead. His feet were covered with
mud, his hands were filled with sores dripping blood. He told
me of his people, he helped bury with just his hands. I had
turned my head just for a split second and this boy had changed
that fast into a man. Standing tall, I could now see anger in his
eyes. His chest spread wide, he told me of another journey that
was up ahead. That he would travel all alone once again. I
offered him a drink of water, a sip was all he took. Barely
wetting his dry lips. Then once again he spoke, but much
louder and bold. My people have come a long way. My people
have suffered severe lost and pain. My people will be.
Then he turned and smiled at me.

Constance Louderdale

Untitled

Memories of years gone by
wanting to magically
jump back in time

To a time of wonder, and things brand new
Amazing stories, you never knew
Hopscotch and tag were your main concern
Sitting at the camp site watching the fire slowly burn

The years full of first times, excitement in your eyes
Joyous laughter of the children fill the bright blue skies
A time of magic and amazement sitting with anticipation
When boys and girls all played together unknowing of discrimination

Skinned up knees and dirty jeans band-aids from head to toe
Put everything in the bedroom closet she won't look she'll never know
Come back down and look around sometimes I think we're blind
Lord how I wish for just one day we all could jump back in time

Jesse Arellano

You Never Me Say

You never me say, under the flower bed,
virgin...
Keep your tight hands around my waist
You never, me say, if God his Self gives me
some gold pot, golden man.
You never me say nothing untie me with your
robes of courage woman.
You never me say something, jump kill she
knifes me done.
Grip and give, glide me in and out again.

John Fiordelisi

Your Love, All Together...

Your love, all together, is the
warmest embrace. When we make love, it's the
glow on your face. When you look at me, you touch
my heart. Like every mate should do, just play the
perfect part. You're the perfect man for me, and I
realize that every time you touch my knee. Your warm
touch on my thigh makes me feel like I could just
die. I guess you could say that these first three months
have been really hard, but we've made our way through
it. You've pulled me out of my deep, dark pit. I want to
be a part of your perfect world, the cause of your
deepest thoughts, and the answer to all your problems.
I want to be the one you can hold and cuddle
up to at night. Cause holding you feels all the right.
Being wrapped in your arms so gentle, yet tight.
Just the sensation of your kiss makes my heart and face
glow ever so bright. I feel like the luckiest girl in the world.
I have the perfect man by my side to watch me glow. You
stick by me even through my worst decisions and talk me through
our fights. I'm glad you have the patients for me. I love you.

Becky Huntoon

Spirit Of Woman

The softness of a fluffy cloud of white,
Warmth of glowing embers in a fire,
Nurturing as the rays of sunlight, compassionate to all wrongs,
Loving enough to embrace the world.
She is a spirit that searches for peace
In an existence of great storms who steps past the horror of man's
Inhumanity to man to reach to the sky for a star.
Strength clothed in a garment of tenderness for all living things,
Bound with a string of endless energy to meet the challenge
Of hatred and abuse of this earth.
A mind that is filled with knowledge so vast as the drops of rain
That fill oceans, and yet is still held in bondage,
Censored, pushed back, to wait her turn to bask
In the equal glory of belonging.
You may bind her mouth, but can not stop her silent voice
That cries out against all injustice.
Step back, she is approaching, for equality, for freedom.
Stretching, clawing she will emerge, like a newly hatched bird,
To conquer the art of flying against howling winds
That her enduring spirit will finally calm.

Betty Jo Moore

The Child

The child sat that Sunday morning in the Lords house,
Wary of the fact she must be quiet, quiet as a mouse.
She looked around at all the grown up faces,
And wondered why she was here, of all places.
She looked at her mother and realized she wasn't listening to
    what was being said,
Instead her mother was thinking of errands and chores she was to dread.
But there sat the innocent child with those big blue eyes,
Who didn't yet understand responsibility, regret or grieving cries.
Slowly her eyes traveled to the statue of the handsome man with
    the open arms,
How kind and gentle he looked she thought, not once considering
    any harms.
Then it came to her, this is the one they call Jesus, yes it must be
    him,
He's the one that helps everyone at all times, no matter how
    bright or dim.
It was at that moment she reached out and blew him a kiss,
It was one that the Lord Jesus would surely not miss.

The child, a true example of life that was so right, so pure,
Is what God wants us to idolize, not something we must endure.
It is said that all the love of God is seen through a child,
Along with all your hopes and dreams however naive or wild.
But there is one thing you mustn't forget, I thought with a nod,
Each and every one of us is a child of God.

Dawn Collins

Ode To Leontyre Price

Not too long ago in a quiet little town
Was born a baby girl with eyes dark, lustrous brown.
The angels up in heaven were distressed to see her go,
But God said, "Send her down today, my gift to
   earth below."
The baby grew so straight and tall, but from
   the very start,
Celestial music seemed to flow from
   deep within her heart.
"I'll sing all over God's wonderful world, for
   that is His plan for me.
And every door will open wide, for God will
   give me the key."
It all came true, as the child foretold, for
   she's blessed our world with a voice of gold.
And so with the passing of each blissful day,
   the baby delights me more than I can ever say.

Evelyn Stevens

'I Wonder'

Something scurried there,
Was it a rabbit, or was it a hare?
Was it a gopher, or just a lazy loafer?
Was it an eagle, or a sea gull?
Was it a dog or a hog?
Was it a mouse, or just the shadow of a house?
Lookout!
There it goes again!
What was it?

Diana Lynn Scharp

In Time for Fun

The pink polka dotted giraffe
Was taking a hot bubble bath.
"Oh, I hope I get done
In time for the fun.
There's a party on the old jungle path."

She put on her frilly blue dress.
There was no time to sit down and rest.
"Oh, I hope I get done
In time for the fun.
There's a party and I am the guest."

She combed her long blonde curly hair
While she sat in a four-legged chair.
"Oh, I hope I get done
In time for the fun.
I wonder who else will be there?"

As she raced out the swinging front door
The hyenas did laugh and did roar.
"Oh yes you are done
Too early for fun.
The party's tomorrow at four!"

Eulalia A. Cylkowski

The Last Largo

Here ends that unfinished something. Some other thing
was to come before or after. Perhaps at the same time.
The shutter goes down and the picture reveals itself.
The likeness of a smile. On a close look, it's a grimace.
Remains to find out what's hidden behind the twist. The task
is to fill in what appears to be missing. Events to follow
each other in a semblance of approximation. All along
a figure on the rooftop blows a silent horn. The implants
make the memory system disintegrate even further. Now
the whole thing is more of a puzzle. Time is no object.
Try to solve the mystery or just stand by. Try to explain
the night or just look the other way. Comes the daylight.
No more stars.

Ilhan Mimaroglu

Stars Fall From The Sky

Staring from the cold rocks,
   watching the ebon waves tendril up the deserted beach.

Across the table sits an empty chair;
   one voice echoes in the silence.

My open hand grasps for its mate;
   unanswered,
it slips deeply into my pocket.

The clock ticks;
   sweeping hands anticipating nothing,
an eternal record of each falling tear.

A note;
   so many things left unsaid,
too many things left undone.

Bittersweet;
   remembrances of,
dreams for,
   hopes unfulfilled.

Silently,
   the liquid darkness enveloping,
the stars fall from the sky.

Charles R. Maynard

There Is No God?

As I sit here looking out my window,
watching the rain beat against the pane,
I marvel at the beauty of it all.
I know that it couldn't happen without the hand of God.

I look at the sun coming over the horizon
and wonder at how anything so beautiful could just happen.

Anyone who does not believe in a higher power cannot
comprehend how these things can be. One has to believe
in God to explain this beautiful phenomenon.

Anyone who has seen a beautiful setting sun and then say
"There is no God". I cannot fathom such a statement.

One has only to look about the landscape and know that
there had to be a divine hand in the making of such a
colossal setting "Of this I am sure.

Jean A. Ramsey

When The Sun Goes Down

I sat in the park one day,
Watching the sun sink with its golden ray.
My eyes wandered over the flower beds,
They were closing up getting ready to rest their weary heads.

I walked over to one place,
And found myself looking at a particular flower face.
It was different from the ones surrounding it,
And took up a space of only a little bit.

It was a tiny flower,
Yet I was amazed by its striking power.
It chose to grow with ones that were different,
But on staying there it was firmly bent.

Now it was encroaching upon night,
The flowers just a shadow in the moonlight.
A thought struck me as I stood there in the dark,
Looking around the silent park.

We wander in this world not happy with where we are,
And our travels may take us away far.
Each one searching for his claim to fame,
But once the sun goes down we are all the same.

Heather Hall

Friends In The Sky

Above the world, they look down on me.
Watching. Waiting,
Silent but alive with whispers only I can hear
Like friendly conversation to keep my spirits high
My soul alive
Their brightness bursts through the darkness
Like distant holes in the night
I'm never alone
Long as their twinkled eyes watch over me
Guide me to the songs of tomorrow
The life that I must live
The past that I must lead
The future that I must follow
They are the hopes. They are the dreams
   They are the stars
And I
  Am
   Their
Number one
  Fan

   Jason Worthley

Africa

Africa, mile by mile blowing away with the wind.
Water dancing off, never to return.
No grazing animals seen, bowing to the land.

Africa, the young slipping away in death.
Infants given life, but no hands to care for long.
The old sliding off in death leaving nothing behind, to give life.

Africa, throw away the old ways, embrace new ways.
Open the gate ways to life once more, working the land.
Bring back beauty, then wealth will come if throwing in
great love for human life.

   Charmaine R. Vogt

Happy Birthday

Happy birthday to you;
Way up there, beyond the blue;
Upon your cake, stands one lonely candle dear;
I put out the flame, with my tears;

This year would have been, forty seven;
This will be your seventh birthday, in heaven;
How many more, will I celebrate alone?
Are you waiting anxiously, for me to come home?

Keep counting our birthdays, we've spent apart,
But always knowing, we're there in our hearts
One day we'll celebrate, all the days we've missed,
So I'll keep lighting candles, make a big wish!

I wish upon candles, I wish upon stars;
I'll always keep you close, locked away in my heart,
I know you're there waiting, up there in the blue;
And I'm here darling, waiting to come to you;

When again we meet, on those golden streets;
It will be for Good, it will be for keeps;
No more tears, no more sorrows;
We'll always be together, we'll always have tomorrow;

   Bonnie Belle Frazier

Alone!

Locked within the boundaries of our minds
We are the masters of the dream

Creating release from anxious moments
And erasing our doubts and fears

Changing life, as it is, with the blinking of an eye
Reliving joyous memories we've experienced through the years

Traveling the highways of our, often longed for, past
Enjoying the infinite fantasies of our imaginary future

But, this world revolves around the living
And, if we never unlock the boundaries of our minds

To share with, yet, another master of the dream
We are forever - alone!!

   Cynthia Annette Moore

Flyin' High

As we float off into the sunset, traveling to the unknown,
We can look back and be so proud of how our love has grown.
We started out as two people so scared to let their feelings show,
But with trust and understanding, we've found there's no limit
   to where our love can go.
I've discovered I can turn to you when I need to talk,
Learning that if I should stumble, you'll pick me up and help
  me walk.
Often I wonder if you know just how much you mean to me...
Valentine's Day seemed to be the perfect time to try to make
  you see.
Every dream I have, every plan I make, has something to do
  with you.
You have made me believe that sometimes wishes do come true.
Our love has made me realize that with you is where I want to be,
Using everything we've learned to build a life together that
  will last through all eternity.

   Gail L. Overly

The Motion Of Love

A place in Florida is Kissimmee.
  We don't have to be there for you to kiss me.
You can kiss me in a diner!
  You can kiss me in a recliner!
You can sit in my lap!
  Get comfortable and take a nap!
I'll be comfortable and feel loved!
  I'm yours and you're my beloved!
Darling, I don't have much money.
  I'm rich when I have your love, Honey!
We can enjoy each sunset and each sunrise!
  We can look into each other's eyes!
We don't have to go to the beach!
  There's so much beauty in our reach!
The motion of the ocean stirs each wave!
  The motion of love stirs this Brave!
With you, I'm on cloud nine!
  With you, I always feel fine!
I feel like we're floating among stars above!
  You are my Star, I'm thinking of!

   Al Thomas

Francis

As we approached our deadened arrival
we had already known
our words had been locked inside the heads of many.
And to some it was jaded and foul.
But to some it was therapeutic and somewhat
sensible to contemplate.
That it would never dwindle, fade, or lack again.
From there birth to there death it led them to far off viscous wild
fantasies of death pain and boundless ignorance.
It all had once been listened to but now.....

   Jeff Gordo

My Broken Heart!

It all seem so perfect at the time
we fit so well together like poetry in rhyme-

But they say nothing last forever and at
one time it all fell apart you tried to
be so gentle and held me once more
before we said good-bye-

Yesterday I saw you with another girl
by your side I wanted to tell you I
love you but I just walked away
Leaving the tears inside.

Maybe someday somehow I'll cure my
broken heart but until then I love you
forever until death.

Christie Ann Gulick

The Highway

We each have a highway, a road that we follow.
  We go where it leads, this path of tomorrow.
No two are alike; each is unique.
  The horizon ahead, with its great mystique.
Along the way our road will split,
  and decisions made will determine fate:
Peaks and valleys and flat terrain,
  patches of gravel; areas of rain.
The path not chosen,
  missed opportunities never known.
Other highways we cross, too many to count,
  and the distance travelled, continues to mount.
As we travel along on this unpredictable adventure,
  We keep looking ahead to the end of our future.
We wish that this trip could go on forever,
  but alas 'tis true:
the highway we're using will end much too soon.

James Joseph Stein

Scene

In our lives we have seen fire and rain
we have seen laughter and pain
perhaps what we thought was quite a lot
We now must focus on something new that before we had not
It's about our world, one that's coming together one that is
  falling apart,
a world that is cold as ice yet has a warm inviting heart
a world whose people love so much but still have endless time to hate
whether it be black, white wrong or right we won't last long at
  that rate
so let us pull together and join hands as one
feeling the winds of freedom, no longer under the gun
we can do this, it has happened before
since history repeats itself, peace is knocking on our door
before we know it harmony will be ours to hold
a bright beacon of light in the dark and a blazing fire in the cold
so think twice before judging or turning your back on someone in need
with that we cannot help but grow as would a planted seed
Contrary to belief, the difference you make will be great
at this time it may seem far off but with love it is never too late
our future now holds us in its undecided hand
waiting patiently for our next move let us now take our stand.

Jeremias J. Stelter

Photo From A Time Capsule

Instead of hushy ocean sounds
we hear a surf of autos every day
our roses rust, our apple tree is dead
but out beyond the wired-over sky
sea, like a molten meadow twists
shudders and heaves and spurts out atom-balm
to reanoint that which was Earth
before Erectus rose to codify
all light and time
and claim he'd measured grace.

Doris Straus

Souls

We stand so close, but yet so far.
We hold hands but yet we don't touch.
We are very smart, but yet so confused.
We talk, but yet we are not heard.
We fit in, but yet are still rejected.
We try to love, but yet our hearts are still broken.
We try to make things make sense, but still cannot comprehend.
We try for the best, but yet still get the worst.
We try and have confidence, but yet there is no hope.
We travel so far, but yet it's not worth the trip.
And now that we've tried we stand tall and try not to cry.

Jean Henderson

All Halloween's Eve

All Halloween's Eve is coming again.
  We hope you've been expecting.
To join us once more in our halloween den.
  We won't take any rejecting.

A witch's coven (13 in all),
  Is waiting to do their duty.
They're planning on having a great big ball,
  With your flesh and blood as their booty.

Drac and the goblins, the werewolf, and friends
  Will be here to greet you at five.
Your costume, we hope, will give you the means,
  To come out of this alive.

So see you then, at the same old place,
  All covered with cobwebs and dust.
Bring baby along and an appetite too—
  For blood and guts — is a must.

Deanna C. Segal

A Tribute To Bill Christel

The wondering we felt we need not fear,
  We let it all out in one big tear.
We miss you more than you will ever know,
  But we'll be there to watch your children grow.
We know that you see us every day,
  And you show us your love in your own way.
To all who knew you, you were a GREAT GUY,
  But you bought all the time you had to buy.
You should know that you touched everyone's heart,
  That it's gonna be hard to be apart.
We have that memories that you left behind,
  We know that deep-down you were very kind.
Now that you're gone our lives are on standstill,
  But we want you to know, WE LOVE YOU, BILL!!!

Amy Marie Savage

God's Finger-Prints

God's finger-prints are everywhere,
We may not see them but they are there.
He made the world and you and I;
He made the stars shine in the sky;
He made the sun, the land and sea,
And made them all for you and me,
And His finger-prints are there
For He made all things with greatest care.
His finger-prints we may never see
But think how special it is to be
Made in His image, as was His plan,
And maybe wear the finger-prints of His hand.
His finger-prints we may never see
But we know with great love He made you and me,
So be proud of the earthly prints you now wear
For someday we may meet Him way up there,
And since no earthly finger-prints are the same,
Maybe when He calls our name,
And maybe if finger-prints we could compare,
Do you suppose they might match His when we
    get up there?

Eula H. Johnson

Where Has All The Quiet Gone?

Where has all the quiet gone?
We no longer try to hear the noise of a falling snow flake
The flapping of a birds wings
Or the growing of a leaf.

We miss the sign of one fulfilled, or the cats tongue as it
preens its coat.
We do not hear the flower as its petals open.
Or the rippling of a brook.

The sound of a frost covered leaf as it hits the earth with
a gentle crash.
Or a rain drop as it hits a puddle with a resounding splash.

No one speaks gently any more, they yell
Is it pent up rage that we cry so loud.

No one listens, though one soft whisper could perhaps catch
an ear.

Dorothy Klotzsche

In Loving Memory We Remember

We remember your beautiful and soulful eyes.
    We remember your bright and radiant smile.
We remember your good and kind nature.
    We remember your easy laugh and zest for life.

We remember your love for your family and country.
    We remember your strong sense of responsibility.
We remember your deep sense of dignity.
    We remember your unflinching sense of honor.

We remember your burning desire to serve your country.
    We remember your pride that you were a Marine.
We remember you were so young when you went away.
    We remember your battle was brief, but very brutal.

We remember our sadness in saying good-bye.
    We remember praying you had found eternal peace.
We remember to carry you in our heart.
    We remember you, always, with love as our hero.

Christine M. Van Hooft

America The Beautiful

Sing a song sing a new song
We shall sing to keep our jobs

Sing about taxes sing about welfare
Sing this or that it's not the essence for which we care

We sing about prayer we toot about reform
The importance is not implication, but perceived form

Sing the song veto the hymn
Look in the mirror is the important one him

Turn up the speaker and strike those chords
People listen to your stance and don't remember records

The house sings a top ten, but plays the oldies
If the audience knew the lyrics they would remove the cronies

Spend this and tax that whose radio could it be
Mr. distinguished gentleman look in the glass, say it is me

America The Beautiful is the song we all sing, it must stay on the books
Man please be gentile for our song is distinguished, it is
not sung simply for its looks

One day I learned you don't actually care
I looked in your mirror and you were the only one there

David A. Tubbs II

Then And Now

It shouldn't be so hard my son to be a man today.
We started out so naturally, but somehow lost our way.

It seems when we were three or so our path was crystal clear;
Our wants and needs were stated and were free from guilt and fear.

But a boy must have a father, son, to guide him on his way;
To show him how to be a man each and every day.

In the past I wasn't there for you; I left you on your own.
It's scary just to be a boy and have to act full grown.

But son, I want to change that past; I want to be your dad.
I want to share my thoughts with you; to comfort when you're sad.

I want to run and play with you; to walk along the beach.
To scale that misty mountain; the top, son, you will reach.

Arthur P. Garneau

Weaving

Life is a tapestry - in which we endure, sustain, love, hate.
We thread our way across a vast territory called living.
No maps - no one knows our exact road.
Our lives touch, intertwine, withdraw
Often turning sharply -
Turns filled with fear that penetrate the heart and mind,
Fabric roads rutted with nubs on which we stumble,
Rising again - only hope to walk with.
Are there no rules to life?
Where shall I find them?
Will tomorrow be a brighter day?
Adversity and failure are lessons;
Listen to the teacher.
The teacher's name is love.
Follow.
You will find a road of harmony, compassion, tenderness.
Trust your wisdom.
Life is a tapestry;
Weave your threads gently.

Carmen Engram

Retirement

In 1973 we decide to retire in warmer climate then Chicago,
We traveled many states for a perfect place to go.

After several months our mind was made,
It was time to consider the move before it all fades.

Mountain Home, Arkansas was our choice,
We were greeted in every way with great force.

We transferred our V.F.W membership in a month or sooner,
The members opened their hearts when they heard the rumor.

We got involved in all the activity,
Tired to build up the membership in the vicinity.

A few years later a Retiree Meals Program got started,
Volunteering was a key to all the good hearted.

Cooking and serving good food was the key to success,
With pride and joy it lasted fifteen years or less.

I also volunteer as a Pink Lady in the hospital,
Helping the sick and giving a helping hand is never dull.

I am still helping as I am needed,
Hope you enjoy my retirement poem when you read it.
Catherine Mytnik

"Waiting"

Life is a waiting game
We wait to be born — We wait for our name
We wait to crawl — to walk and to talk.

We wait for our teen- age years
With many unspoken fears
And when they come they are filled with woes
Never yes - but no-no-no's.

Then the middle years—the best of all
They come before the fall.
Oh - then the down hill wait begins
We lose our teeth — We lose our hair
We put on weight — and wait in despair,

We look up old friends — just to see
If they have aged as much as we
Then having seen — we say to ourselves
We are not sitting alone on the shelf.

The memories are many, the rewards are great
When we come to the end of our long wait
As we pass through the "Golden Gate," we see our Maker's face aglow
He smiles and says, "I've been waiting too, you know!"
Juanita J. Priest

Home Of The Brave

America the beautiful, home of the brave
what do these words mean to an illiterate former slave?

For four hundred years I fed your family,
plowed your fields, and even picked your corn.
For four hundred years you raped my mothers,
killed my fathers, and filled my heart with scorn.

You say I am American, I am not, I am much more
I am African American for the burdens that I wore

They tried to keep us down, to deep us close in sight
but there just was no stopping our African American plight

Many many years ago, I dropped my cotton seeds
instead I picked up a book and taught myself to read

So when you see me on the street
your pity you can save
for you are in the presence of an intelligent former slave.
Derrick W. Smith

Precious Moments

Hi! my dear little one and welcome to earth
We were chosen for you, at the moment of birth
What a blissful feeling to hold you my dear
When we look at you, we know heaven is here

Sleep on, my dear little one and never know fear
For your mommy and daddy will always be near.
We will love you and cherish you with all our might
And help raise an angel with the greatest delight!

You are our star, our guiding light.
You are a wonder! A beautiful sight!
So welcome again, o dear little child.
You light up our lives with your precious smile

You are our angel, our miracle of love
You have been sent from heaven above
You whimsical smile, your gentle touch
You magical eyes make us love you so much.

We have waited so long for this special hour,
God searched His garden, and picked you for our flower
We will raise you with honor and comfort and love
And lead you to God on the wings of a dove!
Catherine Coulton

Revenge Of Hansel And Gretel

Had they, the cruel parents, only wanted us dead?
Were they the only ones filled with hideous thoughts?
Could they have planned this all alone?
No.
It was he, the little bird, who took shelter from our grasp.
It was he who fell upon the bread crumbs,
Puzzling our minds,
Wanting us to burn in the ovens.
It is also he, the little bird, who is laid out before our eyes.
Gasping for another breath.
The little bird lays dormant at our feet.
We gaze on,
Overwhelmed with relief.
Our sling shots rest silently in our palms.
Revenge,
Revenge!
Could there have been another way?
Christine A. Snyder

A Poor Rich Man

If god had given me riches, instead of family,
What a poor old lonely rich man, I would surely be.

He's given me wives, sons and daughters, the very,
very best.
My grandchildren and their children, seem better
than the rest.

I would not trade the love we share
for all the gold mines anywhere.

Riches can buy you very much,
But they cannot buy a loving touch.

A child to cuddle and to coo,
A gift from God that's part of you.

A wife to hold in love's embrace,
To walk by your side in this life's race.

Memories that we like to share,
Many showing much love and care.

Many with riches, though they may try,
Cannot with their riches, happiness buy.

So, I thank God that He gave to me,
Instead of riches, a loving family.
John A. Keeton

Time

Time...the taker of tolls.
What a taskmaster!
Everyone must pay.

Time...where do you hide and wait
For the unwary traveller passing through your gate?

Methinks thou art a magic of a sort,
Everything and everyone comes under your spell.

Everyone and everything is constantly rising or falling,
Succumbing to...time.

Now is the time...tomorrow is late.
Wake up in your world!

Time...marches on.
        Carl W. Kirk

If People

If people didn't judge others by the color of their skin,
What a wonderful world we would live in.
If people looked inside the heart of everyone they see,
We would live in perfect harmony.
If people shared and people cared for others of every kind,
Everyone would have peace on their mind.
If people didn't vandalize a person's things because of their Race,

We would live in a very peaceful place.
If people treated others like they were their friend,
Our hurt world would be on the mend.
If people would listen to what children have to say,
They may help us on our way.
Children are our future whether you know it or not,
So don't teach us things that would hurt our world a lot.
If you listened well and understood what I said,
You can help others learn what you've read.

        Jessica Rosen

The Crossroads

When we meet at the crossroads
What hope we to find?

One look, then a whisper,
no need for design.

Oblivious to obligation and promises once vowed,
we relish the eternity, in this interval we're allowed.

Though someone's to suffer from our libidinous bond,
We savor the danger, of which we're more fond.

So our parting is torment, and the price we all pay,
for even she, the naive, will encounter someday...

When we meet at the crossroads.
        Christina M. Wimmer

Sitting In Slumber

As I sit in half slumber, I just have to wonder,
what will become of this day.

I'm halfway asleep and halfway aware,
as I look at the world through a cold bitter stare.

Will we wake up and see the problems we've got?
or sit here in slumber not caring whether or not.

Rainforests, AIDS, and nuclear bombs,
sitting in slumber will our lives go on?

So I'll sit here in slumber and pray for some hope,
and tell myself to keep trying to cope.

        Jason Jones

Blackness

Blackness.
What is it?

This one's white. This one's black.
They say as a matter of fact.
It could not only be the skin.
But it must be something close in kin.

Is it only the sounds that we hear,
The rat-tat-tat-tat of rhythm and blues?
Or the inner person that we fear,
That invisible man within?

Can we ever tell its true meaning?
Can any poet capture its feeling?

Black list, Black mail, Black face,
Black widow, Black sheep, Black race.
Black magic, Black plague, Black rage!
Black power?

Can one person define the essence of all time?
Blackness.
Not in such a few lines.
        Joe A. Carrol, Jr.

"What Is Life All About?"

What is life all about, all about?
What is life all about?

Life is a miracle, some people say,
It can bring us joy and pain in a day.
What is life all about?

Each new day is here for the asking,
With the sun in the sky, it's here for basking.
What is life all about?

Many people say, "life is for living,"
Others will say, "life is for giving,
Giving to others near and far,
Showing you care, no matter who they are."

Is this what life is all about?
Struggling to accept and not to doubt.
We are here now for what seems like a minute,
Life flies fast and how do we spend it?
Hopefully it is done with love,
With God's grace, a gift from above.
        Celestine L. Alvarez

A Mixed One

He sits on a bridge wondering
What is life all about? Can I go on?
Why so much hatred? So much racism
Feeling caught in the middle
Why are people the way they are?
Why can't they see an individual?
Not a black man, not a half breed.
Watching the water flow by,
Why fight a losing battle?
There no say-so on either side,
Just someone for both sides to talk about-
To make fun of-
What's the use of believing?
There's nothing to have faith in-
No one to talk to.
Looking at the water again, the last look of life.
Deciding he's not a winner, not a fighter
With a final breath, praying for God's forgiveness.
Good night!
        Gloria Ann Rayburn

The Wrong Ending

She glanced at him and held back tears.
What she saw confirmed her fears.
She knew they had to break apart,
But he was gone. He took her heart
She told herself he had to stay,
But in a flash he'd gone away.
They'd gone out to have some fun,
But he drank many more than one,
She tried to tell him that she'd drive.
Now she's lucky to be alive.
She glanced once more as they lowered him down,
She said good-bye and stared at the ground.
Now she knew he couldn't stay.
She never thought it would end this way.
With him in grave and her still above
All she knows is that she still feels love.

Beth Hall

Not Much Time

Everything goes on no matter
what time of year it is. Time
can never cease, so I can treasure
every moment.
Our world is turning into a
battle field. We have to stand
up as an individual, but all at
the same time stand together
as we are, and respect each others'
rights. Will we last? Or will we all
end up a faded memory? If you
were to ask, I'd say just be you
and do your best at that. And we'll
all get along!

Ginger Dean Knight

A Gift Of Giving

If you could give the world a gift.
    What would it be?
Bunches and bunches
    Of wonderful tress?
Peace on earth and mercy mild?
    Or loving parents for every child?
Would you visit people in the hospital?
    Or give gifts, that would let people do
    Things that are virtually impossible?
Like wings or magic powers.
    That would allow them, to jump upon
    the tallest towers!
If I could give the world a gift,
    It would be a gift of giving.
Giving to those who are poor or lonely,
    To help them keep on living.
When giving my gift to the world,
    First, the hungry I would feed.
Then give homes to the homeless,
    And love to those in need.

Jennifer Filbert

"My Kind Of Thank You Note This Poem Is"

I shall never forget, that warm summer night,
When a beautiful limo, shiny and white,
Flowed smoothly through traffic to "Catch 35",
Where the food was scrumptious, the music live.
How excited we gals were, to be off to the show,
To see Donnie Oz play "Technicolor Joe".
Every moment was great, what a wonderful thrill,
An evening to remember, you can bet I always will.
The limo, the food, the show, was such a generous treat,
Lucky me, for such gracious hostesses,
Thank you.......double sweet!

Eleanore A. Bufano

Crossroads

I met you at the Crossroads of my mind,
When all was lost. My soul was bruised and bare ...
All meaning stripped away ... raw nerves exposed ...
The pain too great ... the heart too numb to care.

Through weary years, the mind cannot endure
The anguish of the empty soul. In strife,
The hopes must perish and the dreams must die
And dry to dust along the path of life.

Pressed in by haunting darkness on each side,
My road, directionless, stretched far ahead ...
No goal to reach ... no challenge to be met ...
Each by-road tried ... to find it too was dead.

And then without a warning you were there
With arms outstretched to halt my hurtling flight.
I stopped at last ... with wonderment beheld
A Crossroad streaking brightly through the night.

All time stood hushed and still, in breathless awe ...
For in that moment I, once more, was free.
My mind tore off its shackles. I could choose
My road anew. You gave life back to me.

Christena B. Kern

Patchwork

Remember when life was easy and mellow.
When family and friends were precious.

The ice age is here in the heart of man.
We have reached the years of non-caring.

We stand knee deep in crowded loneliness.
To preserve our sanity we laugh out our emptiness.

Cultural freedom abounds... yet,
The freedom to scream is disallowed.

Doretha H. Bogan

Remembering Jason

I remember the time
When I didn't know you quite well
I remember the short time
I got to know you better
I remember your jokes
I remember your smile,
It just brightened my day
I remember your personality
It always wanted to play
Too bad those days can't continue to exist
Only in my mind, but as for you
Your only a mist
Jason, while you are in those floating skies
I hope you are having fun
You're in heaven
And your life has just begun

Alani Thompson

Our Holy Comforter

Trust in the Lord and don't ever fear for
When things seem darkest he's ever so near, near
when you call him just trust in his name
He'll make ways out of no way which you thought was in vain.
For there comes a time when our spirits are
low we feel it's an effort to trust in him so.
But knowing our hearts as he knows our minds
He'll lift all our burdens and give peace of mind.
So I wish you God speed and all that is best,
keep trusting in Jesus and he'll do the rest.

Frances Brown Johnson

I Drowned

To me, I felt as if I was drowning
When I look back today
I guess what I really want to say
Is that you could not even realize
That I was drowning right in front of you.

You could not even hear my cries
For help and for you to come to my aid.
You could not even hear my cries from a distance.

But when you saw that I was drowning
When you knew and sensed that I had given up the struggle
To survive and stay afloat
You said to yourself "Should I help him or should I just walk away?"
"Or should I just let him drown?"

You thought to yourself about the pain and suffering
I caused you in your life.
You said "God, what should I do?"
But when you finally realized what you wanted to do
It was too late for you and I.

I drowned before your eyes
No longer did you hear my cries simply because I died.
        Edwin Conde, Sr.

My Love For You

I love your green gorgeous eyes
when I look in them, I see there are no lies
The smoothness of your black hair
as you act like you don't care
I love you with my heart and soul
even if you weren't into rock and roll
You're all I dream about
Till the sun comes out
You're all I live for
And all I care for
You're so sweet
And hot as heat

My love for you is deep
Like a mountain steep
my love for you is strong
And nothing goes wrong
my love for you will always last
as the days go by fast
        Arieez Wattz

In Memory Of My Father: Missing You

Through cuts and bruises you were always my shield
When I needed a laugh you were always my heal
    You were there when tears came out of my eyes
Your guardian angels aroused you when you died
    Heartaches and pain now fill my days
Life doesn't seem right with you away
    From birth to death hearts reached out to you
You stuck to drugs, now where did it get you?
    A nice plaque, your body buried six feet deep
I can remember the days seeing you roam the streets
    Helplessly in need for love and attention
We gave you more of that, then I can even mention
    Missed by everyone, always in our hearts
Never thought this day would come that we would part
    But now we must all say our goodbyes
Tears of love and pain overflowing our eyes.
        Brandy Neumann

Hunting The Beast

I remember that clear, spring day
When I opened my soul to you.
I told you of my love and admiration,
Begged for your love in return.

And yes, you opened your soul to me.
Out of the dark recesses came forth a beast.
Its sharp, black talons tore at my flesh,
Swatting aside my precious feelings.

It ripped out my heart, devoured it whole
It tore apart my very soul,
Then left me empty and helpless.

But I survived.
My flesh healed, my soul mended.
And my feelings, one by one, returned.

Now I come to hunt your beast,
To bring it to its knees.
This time, I do not beg for love.
For love is nothing without a heart.

I come to take back my heart,
So I can love you once again.
        Donald G. Lipps, III

The Land Of Rig Rag Roo

I get a funny feeling that I will share with you
When I think about my visit to the land of Rig Rag Roo.

It's just beyond the mountains across a vinegar sea
Past the seven stop signs so, come along with me.

Now we're on our journey it's really not too far
Don't wear you boots or mittens come dressed the way you are.

There's the magic doorway the one we must go through
The one that leads to fun time in the land of Rig Rag Roo.

Look! See the chocolate flowers and the banana milk shake tree
and licorice covered fences and a cotton candy bee.

Parents never yell there and schools are out of place
You never take a shower or wash a dirty face.

You never have to go to bed or wash a cup or dish
And if you want a special thing just make a tiny wish.

The daytime lasts forever and the ice cream is the best
Behind each tree and rock you'll find a pirate's treasure chest.

Now you know I'm just pretending there's no land of Rig Rag Roo
But if you want to think there is it's really up to you.
        Jack Welch

Untitled

There are times when love turns to hate,
When words of sorry come a little too late.

There are seasons when leaves do not fall,
When proud, strong men refuse to stand tall.

There are ages when young turn to old,
When a flower withers after it unfolds.

There are spells when the seeing suddenly become blind,
When the unfeeling have your heart with theirs intertwined.

    Together they go
        hand-in-hand
            good versus evil
                Forever
        Heather Meyer

My Dad And Mushrooms

My dad used to take me mushroom hunting with him
  when I was just a kid.
He knew all the edible kinds; when they grew
  and where they were hid.
In the Fall, when the leaves blanketed the ground,
  was the best time of the year when they could be found.
There were the morels, or sponge mushrooms,
  found under the oak trees....
And the little clumps of yellow corn mushrooms
  found just before a freeze.
There were tall stately king mushrooms
  with a fringed crown all around;
Poking their heads up through the leaves....
  just waiting to be found.
I loved finding the pink bottoms, or sand mushrooms,
  down by the river's shore.
And on old rotten logs, hugh elephant ears
  weighing five pounds or more!
My dad is gone now, but the memories remain;
  perhaps when my time comes, we shall mushroom hunt again.

   Charles M. Wentworth

   (455 Sundoro Ct., Merritt Island, FL 32953)

To Him It Was A Game

Life was once a game
When I was the only one
But you say you want her too.

Don't you know silly boy
Life is not a game anymore
Don't you know you can't
have your cake and eat it too.

But I bet you don't see what
she is doing to you.
I bet you don't know how bad
I feel for you.
You probably think what I say isn't true

So if this is the game you feel is best for you
Then there is nothing more I can do for you.

   Carrie Pueblo

This House Of The Out Of Doors

In this great big house of the out of doors,
  when it comes to rain, it really pours.
The ground is the floor and the walls are high,
  they reach way up, where the roof is the sky.

The sun shines down through God's opening there,
  while buttercups nod and I their beauty share.
I hear blue birds singing out or'e the hills and dale.
  And the mocking bird perches on the old dinner bell.

I see the farmer plowing furrows by the way
  and I smell fresh turned earth all the live-long day.
The honeysuckle blooming sends fragrance all the while,
  and the mountain laurel is swinging like a child.

The birds, all are singing and every thing is gay,
  for soon we shall greet the merry month of May.
You keep your lovely cities and your fancy houses too,
  for I'm content to dwell at home under my roof of blue.

   Ataka Rhodes Royse

O My Good Friend

O my good friend why be so sore of heart?
When lo! The woeful moments pass you by!
Be of good cheer with someone else and start,
Greeting one's neighbors and true friends nearby.

Few acquaintances and alien faces,
Bear all their troubles and worries behind,
Meeting them often in various places —
At times you see, it's hard a friend to find.

Though heavy of heart and mind a-weary.
Release your spirit, cheer up all the while...
Loving God, befriending everybody,
By sharing with them a warm friendly smile.

Someday, somehow my friend you may recall,
In love, in want, your friends do not ignore,
A-rise what may, when troubles you befall,
Look unto God and then sorrow no more!

   Deogracias S. Dela Rosa

A Song For Erica

I was awakened in the wee hours of the morn
when my daughter came to me to say
that a child whose family we know
had died and gone away

Though I didn't know Erica personally
my heart felt a stabbing pain
to know one more innocent child
had been brutally slain

As I look at her picture
her eyes seem to say
why at such a young age
has my childhood been taken away

I was a good girl
and did what I was told
taking care of my siblings
though I was only ten years old

And if she could speak now, I'm sure she would say
treasure your children
love them and be wary
and please save them by any means necessary

   Juanita Alston

A Family Forever We Will Always Be Together....

A family forever, we will always be together
when someone is in despair, someone in the family is always there.
If we live near or far our love is still strong.
Sometimes hearts are broken but, they are always mended again
everyone in our family has a special bond, so that we may come
together as time goes on
Sometimes people laugh sometimes people cry but we all struggle
to be a family
When holidays are near all anger and sadness is forgotten as we
all share and cherish the special time we all spend together
before we all go our separate ways
We have happy times together decorating the Christmas tree
or Listening to old stories being passed on from person to person
Wise advice being given to everyone
Family is love that no one but each individual can understand
Family is a special honor in everyone's heart, but for different reasons
In my heart till the day I die, my family will always stay there
forever

   Charlotte Jacobs

Untitled

I remember long ago
When times seemed so rough
A time for dreams were at a low
To succeed was really tough

So many problems, so little hope
feelings of gloom both day and night
So many failures, feeling I'm such a dope
When will I see this so called light?

Well the present has come
And I'm much wiser and definitely older
I now realize I'm really not that dumb
But I'm definitely much bolder

Yes times are hard to succeed
But your choices are here
We all have our own life to lead
We just need to eliminate our fears

Barbara Rivera

My Grandma Loves Me

My grandma loves me, this I know.
When we go by she tells me so.
The first thing that happens, I buckle up sis.
Grammy says thank you, and blows me a kiss

Thank you grandma, for caring so much,
To teach us that seat belts are important to us.
Grandma says we must never forget, to buckle
our seat belts. Then we're all set.

My sister's still tiny, so she doesn't know
how important she is, and that I love her so.

So buckle up sissy, and I will too.
Off we go Grandma, let's go to the zoo.

Judy Hamilton Williams

1981

Empty Quest
When we were together,
it was like
    fuzzy slippers,
    a crackling fire in the fireplace,
    a mug of hot chocolate.
But I wanted fireworks, champagne, and
a trip to the top of the ferris wheel.
So, I turned to see, touch and experience
the excitement I felt I had missed.
When I turned back, it was too late-
you were gone, and I was alone.

Joan Bargmann

"Time"

Time, how fast it does pass,
When you measure it in days that have past.
One minute you are young and you wonder,
Where did the time go?
The first quarter you spend trying to learn,
The second trying to improve your career,
The third trying to get ahead, and
The last quarter you realize you have grown quite old.
And all the past means little now.
You just cherish the little time you have left and wonder.
Where did the time go?

Hugh T. Warmack

Birth Of A Poem

Have you ever experienced what it's all about
Whenever a poem says, "let me out"?
Why it's like opening a water spout
Just grab my pen and it all pours out.

My pen it knows just what to write
My goodness what a marvelous sight
Right before your eyes it comes right out
Sometimes it makes me want to shout.

Sometimes it silly, sometimes it's sad
Sometimes it's things that make you glad
The most marvelous feeling you ever had
But I never do want to make anyone mad.

There's poems about myself and some others
Sometimes it's my sisters, sometimes brothers
At times it's friends I have just met
But old friends poems are best ones yet.

I've written poems for the grandchildren too.
About things that happen and all that adieu
But friend I know and you do too
The best poems written was just for you.

Bettye Dansby

Birthdays

It's my birthday!
Where are the cake, the presents, the fanfare
All gone

Funny - such a to-do is often made of birthdays
    when you're small
Clowns, balloons, frosting on the tips of noses
They're needed just as much, if not more,
    when you're older
Yes, there is still a need for laughter, light
    heartedness, and sweetness of life
Still a need for clowns, balloons, and frosting

Jean Pulliam-Hurd

"Where The Angels Live"

There is a most wonderful place, where the angels live.
Where gold is forever and all the love everyone can give
The angels are surrounded with such a peace, love and serenity
And if you love my God, you could be there too for eternity
It's such a beautiful love, there's more than angels.
There are also beautiful pure white doves. I believe there are
colorful lights, of Gold, Silver, Red, Blue and Whites.
Such a place you can't imagine it all.
Where all the angels stand so tall.
Jesus is there with his arms, stretched out far.
Embracing all his people when they come home to him
like a beautiful shining star.
Jesus has no favorites, they are all the same.
If you can't go home with Jesus someday. That sure would be a shame.
The angels all flying around, taking care of people who
are heaven bound. I see the angels, with pure gold wings.
Flying around Jesus with so many wonderful songs they sing
It sure would be so wonderful someday. To live with the angels
in the most cherished precious way with Jesus holding out his
arms, to meet you with the highest of love and charm. So that's
where the angels live showing all the peace and love for
everyone to give.

Joyce Ann Lambeth

Where I Was Born

Way down South in Dixie Land
Where I was born in nineteen ten
I never knew until first grade school
That this was all the world I knew

As I passed from grade to grade
I soon found out this world is big
And when I reached young manhood
I pledge myself to see the world

If you can travel it will enrich your life
And see the world to compare yourself
With other people around the earth.
You will find you have a wonderful life

One must work to reach his goal
And every step along the way
Has a price that must be paid
If you ever reach your goal
You will have Paid that toll
    Edgar H. Kleckley

Grandpa's House

How sad it is to see an empty hill
Where my Grandpa's house used to be.
I had many memories on that farm.
The house went with the smoke
When it was burned down.
And was bulldozed and plowed.

I have memories of my Grandpa.
And that house,
And the way things used to be.

I have looked to the top of that hill many times,
And thought of all my memories
Of my Grandpa and grandma.
After my Grandpa died,
I look up at that barren hill,
And remember the times we had together.

It looks so sad and empty.
At the top of that hill,

Where my Grandpa used to be.
    Bret Pierce

For Peace Sake

Consider a world filled with peace,
Where one looks out for the other.
There would be no hatred or turmoil,
All mankind would be brothers.

It breaks my heart each time I hear,
Of another human demise.
For the sake of peace, love and understanding,
I'm afraid, no one gets the prize.

Tho some be troubled and filled with despair,
I've chosen to lift up my head.
For, I am, my brother's keeper,
At least that's what some have said.

But do they care enough to get involved.
By the look of things, I think not.
For if we truly loved one another,
All this violence would stop.

So I'll rise up and do my part,
to ensure the word gets out.
We're on a path to self-destruction,
To this, there is no doubt.
    Gene Austin Bowden

Where The Flowers Grow

I want to go,
Where the flowers grow,
Away from this sea of tears.

Where roses, lilies, and violets bloom,
A tree, a bush, a white mushroom,
Where all the scents will drown my fears.

This place is far and far away,
Yet now I know I cannot stay,
In this place of many cheers.

For I must go,
Back to my sea,
The sea of many tears.

But I will once again return,
To pick a flower or a fern.
For I will come again,
To the place where the flowers grow.
    Heather Prew

A Simple Man

I am just a simple man in a complicated time
where the forces of evil versus the forces of good,
so well disguised that I know not what I should.
I am just a simple man in a complicated time
within a dimension of black, white and gray.
I am desperately trying to find my way.
I am just a simple man in a complicated time
which is so confusing and ultimately misleading
that I know not what direction to proceed in.
The straight and narrow I often ponder,
but which way is it? I often wonder,
for I am but a simple man in a complicated time.
    Dwight L. Brown

A Letter Home

I left my roots up in Ohio,
  Where they had always been.
Then I headed South to Florida
  To try and start again.

They said, "There's lots of work in Florida,
  And plenty of things to do."
But the one thing I need, it doesn't have
  Sweetheart, it don't have you.

Now I've got a home in Florida
  And the money's rollin' in
I've got everything a man could need
  But there's an emptiness with in.

Well I've seen the sandy beaches,
  And I love the pretty view,
But none of these things mean a thing
  As long as I don't have you.

With love Jo-Jo
    1992
    Jo-Jo Bland

Rose

There's a Rose growing inside of me.
which the Father and Son is blooming
Some days, I'm beautiful and gentle,
Sweet as Jesus blesses me.

Other days, I'm like the thorn-having trials,
feeling hurt or hurting someone dearest to me;

But, I'm learning new things through the Lord's
earthly things,
The precious Rose the Father put in me.
    Elizabeth Miller

The Time Of The Ocean

Mysteries unfurled in the depths below
Where treasures and kingdoms may chance to go
Where untamed beauty cannot hide
A place where danger and excitement abide
Capped with white at the dusk of day
The tide travels home but does not stay
The wave makes a statement on the rocks with force
But the wind, the breeze, takes a separate course
A mystical moment for a couple to reminisce
Along the shore a refuge for bliss
Shimmering moonlight on the vastness beyond
A picture of memories far to fond
A peaceful vision for the eyes to behold
Although the deep is mighty and bold
The dimensions are truly majestic and grand
But through the test of time, it shall forever stand

Heather Marie Tippetts

The Mirror Of Your Mind

Where is the place
Where visions and reality interlace?
A place where
the curse of being mortal no longer makes
mistakes so hard to face?
Far away, where interpersonal traumas can be escaped.
A flight of fantasy
where I can be a master of the game,
not a perpetrator of those who watch and wait
but an elusive confident
of the perils of fate.
Reach into the realm of the unconscious
for clues to the answer
of this long standing debate.
Reach into the deep regions of the psyche,
to see what you can find
and make the future a reflection of
the mirror of your mind.

Denise Robinson

Son

My gypsy boy who likes to roam,
Wherever you go, you're special to me.
Strum your guitar, polish your chrome,
Ski the mountains, explore the sea.
It's really alright to be free -
If you (foresee and) not forget Gethsemane
Lord, as he speeds on thru the night
Please keep him ever in your sight.
For I love this son of sons
You gave to me,
And will someday return to Thee.

Joan Kuehl

Falling Leaves

The wind carried a sweet smell,
which blow the leaves as they fell,
Such a beautiful sight,
to see the leaves go to such heights,
The branches waved back and forth as a goodbye,
as the leaves ascended the branches held high.
For they knew they would grow back,
so the tree lowered the branches to give the leaves some slack.
The wind has gone still,
now the leaves pour over the hill.
The leaves are now tickled by rakes
and others are poked with stakes,
The leaves wish they where back home,
it would be better then being alone.

Angela Marie Bruaw

The Veil

Could we but glimpse beyond the veil
Which God, in wisdom cast:
To shield the soul and spare the heart
From that we cannot grasp

To see each day before it dawned
Unfolding with its care,
And never wonder nor be awed
By beauties hidden there;

To know each challenge in advance
Our future secret tests,
Would faith be strong....or would cold fear
Lay confidence at rest?

Frail Will of Man! Too insecure
To penetrate the veil,
For it protects the purpose of
The When, the Where, and How!

Gwen Mills

Dare To Dream

Dare to dream that vision unseen
Which others may fail to obtain
To see a rose unfold in the mid-winter's cold
Or the sun shining bright through the rain

Don't always conform to the usual norm
Or you may set yourself asunder
From far away places and happy young faces
Or lofty realms of wonder

Dare to dream though at times it may seem
The world has passed you by
If you dare to achieve in all you believe
Your dreams will never die

Should you find your succumbing to reality numbing
Then set yourself apart
From everyday care and if you should dare
Those dreams there in your heart

Not all would agree as a dreamer to be
Mere foolishness some deem
But this I hold to be true so I say to you
Be bold and dare to dream.

Gregory B. Packard

The Masterpiece

The meadow, mother nature's masterpiece,
Which she salted with myriad daises
And buttered with golden dandelions,
Felt the tide of wind
Crash over her calm meadow,
As brilliant pillars of light
Pierce down through the cloudy heavens.

Countless shades of greenwood,
Fringing the bottomland,
Darkly towers into the rumbling, black sky.

But on the north end,
Within a peaceful calm,
Lies a brooklet pouring forth
                    Through the forest
                              With a gentle ease.

Cassie A. Frank

To Daddy, On Receipt Of A Valentine

Thankee for the Valentine
  Which thee sent me today.
Though this daughter has grown up,
  She loves you, too, the same ole way.

She's past the days of a nickel a day,
  No longer buys penny candy;
And way beyond that allowance time
  When three dollars seemed mighty dandy.

Life's story is too long to relate,
  But the gist of mine on this special date:
From a happy home and the best of folks,
  Came this workin' gal (sob! -her throat, it chokes)

And, she wants it known, right now & forever,
  She loves you, too … will ever and ever.
So thankee, thankee, and, one more time…
  Daddy, I adore your Valentine!
    Betty Burdick Rutishauser

Latino

Latino, descendant of that Iberian race,
which with the sword and the cross,
sailed the ocean they called the Atlantic,
to conquer these immense continents.

Latino, that by force and bravery,
colonized both North and South,
of this rich and beautiful land,
that we call the Americas.

Latino, race of cultured and learned men,
which with the pen and the sword,
inscribed those Spanish names,
that our countries are still called.

Latino, from the United States,
to the deep South Tierra del Fuego,
we live, fight and die,
for a cause, liberty and justice.

Latino, legacy of our forefathers,
melodious language we speak,
carry yourself high and proud,
shout your name always; with firmness.....
    Angel A. Berrios

To My Valentine

It's time to remember St. Valentine's dart
Which years ago lodged in my heart.
Time again for the church bells to ring
And it's time again when my heart wants to sing.
Time, Lover Girl, to write you this letter
Time to tell you I'm feeling much better.
It's fifty-six years plus a couple of days
And I still love you, except in more ways.
Love, like a letter, starts with page one
But goes on and on — is never done.
The knot is tied first, and then the bow
Prettier yes, but more fragile — I know!
I am thankful beyond measure for Donald and Jean
And the countless other joys we have seen.
When you went away it was only for a time.
You will always be my Valentine.
    Franklin Finsthwait

Untitled

  The sun shines high in the dark night sky
while all of our babies are out getting high
the bums in the streets are teaching the truths
to our pitiful, formative youths

We don't know
What we're gonna do
the sex and the drugs are coming for you
and with all the problems in the world today
how do we know
why the sky has turned gray

When we watch our kids go off to play
in the hot burning sun of the mid day
they're gonna come back with cancer spots
and we'll laugh as they tell us the hooker was hot

What will we do
on that faithful may day
when all of our children are taken away.
    David Andrews

Picking

Today while I was watering the front yard, I was also picking berries.
While I was picking berries I thought of all the picking
I had done or the picking on me that I had endured.

I remember my brothers picking on me.

I picked cow chips, picked nails in the yard, picked berries,
picked on my brother, other boys, some smaller and some bigger.
So picking or being picked on is and has been part of my life.
I picked the mother of my children.
I helped pick their names.
I did not pick their spouses.

My picking days are about over.

I know better than to pick on my wife, or anybody bigger and
younger than I.

I have picked all my friends.
I have picked all my jobs, now I do what I can.

I used to pick my nose but I was broke of that.
I still pick weeds and trash, but my last hurrah is I can
still pick berries.
    Albert A. Riedel

Untitled

Hard for one to know the truth
While others believe the lies
Pain watching justice displaced
In order to rationalize
Hurts to see the love of man
Converted into despise
How? Keep the pieces of puzzle in space
So that one may keep earthly ties.

The mouth is salesman of the soul
words are the salesman's tools
If you cannot perceive the slant of the pitch
You're apt to be taken like fools

The ear is there to help the brain
  (mastermind of the goal)
The brain is there to code the waves
to form the object of the soul
The waves are the pieces of puzzle
that the brain could select for its end
But, the brain has developed dissonance
so there's little hope, my friend.
    Frances Hirsch

Flower Tree

The flower tree sits on a steep, steep hill,
While the snow covers its branches.
People watch it and think it has died for it looks so old and frigid.

Summer has sprung and the tree is looking lovely.
It is filled with tiny compounds of pink and white flowers,
Looking as soft and as perfect as colored clouds at sunset.

In a week of seven days the flowers have fallen,
For the tree does not share its beauty for long.
When the flowers are all gone it grows little green leaves
   to show it is alive.
The flowers still surround the tree,
But do not look as nice as when they were on it.

Soon the wind takes the flowers,
Like a kidnapper takes a child.

The tree becomes sad because it was once part of the flowers life,
But knows it will never see them again.
As it becomes sad it starts crying tears of leaves.

Letting the snow bury it for the one hundredth time,
The tree decides it can not take it any more,
And it slowly fades away.
It fades away into the land of darkness.

   Jodi Barnes

"When The Wind Cries"

Leaves rustling on the ground's cold back.
Whispering trees fade into screams
fading into cries shouted from the wind.

After a moment the sky breathes calmly again
blackness covers the desolate land
blanketing the night's cold.

The symptoms of fall released.
Life dies with each deep breath
The wind shall take.

Wind weathers voice not knowing
to be angry or content with existence
Its mood changes with time

Darkness retreats and light prevails
Revealing a land torn and destroyed
each time the wind cries

   Ed Lavin

The Petals Of A Rose

  Red for the beauty within our hearts.
White for the uncharted journeys and dreams we have.
  Black for the adventurous roller coaster ride we call life.
Yellow for the passions lurking inside each of us,
  Growing and becoming stronger with each passing moment,
Bringing light into our day,
  Letting young ones know if "he loves me" or not.
Glistening with dew each rainy mourn
  Never worrying, just wondering
What tomorrow will bring.
  When in bloom, its beauty is more wondrous than anything we
    could imagine.
Making itself visible to all
  The colors, bringing out the inner magic.
And even though its days are numbered
  It lives each day to the fullest
Having mysterious and mystical reflections.
  These wonders of beauty.
These petals of a rose.

   Jennie Mikkelsen

The Giants Great Valley

The Ocean crashes, the Ocean explodes in the night.
White sea gulls hover over the beach.
What Giant long ago dug this hole?
And dug ditches to irrigate the fields?
There are green plateaus in the great valley,
The crowded land is being washed away.
Eleven thousand green trees whistle and crack.
The wind rips the green spring leaves.
His warriors are the tornados.
His great Gardens have disintegrated away.
His mighty steed and subjects are gone.
Only a Great Ocean is left in his Power.
He Sits down and looks at the desolate, but beautiful land of his.
He can not see the future as it slowly slips away.
Who knows what will become of him now?

   Alex Gordon

I Wonder

I often wonder about the rescuers
Who are they and could I be one?

I wonder if I have the courage
To save another when death seems inevitable.

I wonder if I have the wisdom
To determine who is wrong and who is right.

I wonder if I have the power
To influence those that determine who will be saved.

I wonder if I have the skill
To do what is necessary to rescue a life.

I wonder if I am brave enough
To risk my own life to save that of another.

I wonder if I will ever be forced
To witness the loss of innocent lives.

I wonder what I can do now
To seal the answers for the pride of my children.

   Jennifer Brecht

After I Die

  I will know who threw the world into orbit
  Who built knowledge
  And who does it serve
If something is real how will we know
  In a box of true understanding
  Through it are visions from neighbors eyes
  A meaning from which we have drifted
Will the Gods accept us
  Their monsters
  Full of hate and greed
  Left in dirt for time to sort through
The chosen will know
  Those who have known
  Rise up
  Meet the souls Father
Are we on track
  How far have we excelled in wrong directions
  How far have we distanced ourselves
From original intentions

   Justin Hackman

This Woman: A Tribute To Deloris Easter-Russell

There's no other woman in this nation,
Who can serve as a greater inspiration.

On May 5, 1974, this woman gave birth
And introduced me to the Earth.

This woman taught me the values of life,
And the importance of finding a nice wife.

This woman works hard to succeed,
And provides three children with everything they need.

This woman is 37 years old,
And has a heart made of gold.

For twenty years,
This woman has brought me cheers.

This woman has raised me to respect others.
This woman is my mother.

Clarence E. Easter, Jr.

Ode To Cathy

To the sweetest girl I ever knew,
  Who fought the odds - and beat 'em, too;
Your courage an example I'll never forget,
  You lost the battle but won it yet.

You taught me how to fight and win
  And even how to start again!
From you my courage has been renewed.
  (You never seem to come unglued.)

You've shown the world your class, your style,
  Even though you're here but for awhile;
Thanks for the lesson of your life;
  You've shown me how to beat my strife.

  The eye of the storm
   Has come along.
  Thanks for showing me
   My right from wrong.

Gary Hooven

"We Will Sure Miss Granny"

Who makes the best sweet potato pie? Granny!!
Who fried the best chicken? Granny!!
Who makes the best peach cobbler? Granny!!
Who will watch the kids, when we go out for the evening?
Granny!!
Who will stay home from church when the kids are sicks?
Granny!!
Who never forgets your birthday or Christmas present? Granny!!
Who will slip you some spending money? Granny!!
"We Will Sure Miss Granny"
She was so special!!
She told us about boys.
She told us about girls.
She told us how we should obey our parents.
She told us always do your best in school.
She told us to take care of one another.
She told us to love one another.
But most of all she told about Jesus and how we all will go and
live with Him one day.
"Yes, we will sure miss Granny, but the memories of her love
and the good times will live on in our hearts forever.

Alline McElroy

Who Am I?

I invade the bodies of drug addict men
Who tie up their arms, shoot drugs in their veins;
Who share their used needles with drug addict brothers,
Have sex with their own wives, sweethearts or lovers.
I invade the bodies of innocent babes
Born of such tragic consensual unions,
And likewise, the bodies of bisexual men, who,
Infected themselves, then pass it to women.
I invade the bodies of all those who meet
To buy and sell flesh in the alleys and streets.
I invade the bodies of men who would render
Sexual performance to one of same gender.
I invade their lungs, their brains, their intestines,
Make them weak, drained and tired, gasping for breath.
I cover them head to toe with strange lesions
And leave them hopelessly praying for death.
I make them depressed, I cause them to cry,
I inflict massive suffering before they die.
I ravage their bodies, regardless of age,
A modern-day leprous plague, I am AIDS.

Barbara B. Williams

Guardian Angel

Mommy said I had a guardian angel
Who was always at my side
I looked for him all over. Now why does he hide?
It was hard for her to make me see
Or understand who he could be
There wasn't much she could say
So she explained it in this way
Little one I'm sure you know
What to do when Mom says no
Their's that little voice inside. That tell's you so
Your too small to understand
Conscience is your guide
Your little guardian angels there. He helps you to decide
Maybe you asked yourself
When you fell and bruised your knee. How could this happen
With my angel guarding me well he's always there
giving tender loving care. So if you use your reason
Think and do good deed's
Your little guardian angel
Takes care of all your needs.

Catherine Marin

Lament

Who'll be your love this time next year?
Who'll spend her nights in lonely tears?
I've had my share — now I'm thru'.
But I keep wond'ring — what gives with you?

I used to think one day you'd learn
Tho' fire is pretty, it can burn.
It may yet happen — what then?
Will you find it too late to make amends?

Why don't you stop your whirlwind rounds?
Give love a chance to gain some ground.
You might be surprised; you might suddenly be
Too much loved and in love to see
Any enchantment in bright burning blazes.
True love's glow defies all phrases of comparison.

Why don't you love me?
Why can't it be?

Cleo J. Frye

Hello World

Hello world,
Whom I can't see,
Can't touch
Can't feel,

Hello world,
Tis unto you I am held captive
Not to leave,
Not to talk,
Not even to breathe.

Even though your features and events are spectacular
Still I am not allowed,
Not allowed to look
Smell, or hear.

Goodbye world,
For soon I shall be leaving
And not returning
For this is my last look,
Last breath,
And these, my last words.

Adam Halford

A Baby's Lullaby

Rock a bye baby, young yet so ill,
Who's gonna pay the hospital bill?
Maybe you'll live and maybe you'll die,
We'll know for sure as time passes by.

Rock a bye baby, on the coke high,
Mama's an addict; baby, don't cry.
It's not your fault that life will be hell,
It's mama's mistake that baby's not well.

Rock a bye baby, small special dear,
Sure hope you make it through your first year.
I know it's hard to go through it all,
After some time you'll outgrow the withdrawal.

The shaking will stop, the cold chills will end,
From human touch you will probably fend.
You will stay sick from some type of germ,
Whether your life span is long or short term.

Danille Ann Schlosser

Soledad

Loneliness......
Why art thou embracing me
as if thou cares
comfortness you lack which makes
mine aching more painful
felt not as sweet sorrow but,
as bitter thwart, to which must be taken
for another day is tomorrow
Thine anguish felt deep in thine wrath
has awaken mine heart for unpleasantry
Let its beat retire to the cave
from which it comes; while mine cerebrum
records this tasteless episode.
And when tomorrow becomes yesterday
I will laugh
And be glad the day is done.

Janelle Wright

Passage To A Friend

Why do all good things suffer,
Why do all goods things die?
We're all here to live, love, and pass away.
Who's to reason why?

The one you love,
with all your heart,
has left you now,
Leaving you loose and part.

For in God's Kingdom,
There's a place for us,
To be together forever,
This is a must.

We've grown ever closer,
I gave it my best,
But now I'm afraid,
It's time that you rest.

And in this our darkest hour,
When our bodies can no longer mend,
In a warm and found remembrance
A passage to a friend.

Edward S. Cadugan

A Problem For Keeps

How do I get in the trouble I do?
Why do I keep on hurting you?
Trouble just seems to follow me around
Like a lost pup with its nose to the ground
Why can't I ever be good just for you?
Why do I never know just what to do?
When will I realize life ain't so bad?
And living at home, well I should be glad.
I was gone and on my own
Wishing that I was only back home
Just put up with me for our love is deep.
So I guess this little problem you'll
just have to keep.

Kimberly Sue Wells

Remembrances Of Times Gone By

Wake up! Get up! Times a wasting.
Why do you tarry so?
  Voices - softly, and gingerly speaking
  From the downstairs passageway,
Reassuringly offer comfort, security, and relief
  To a small child in her sleep.
No monsters abound, no creatures exist,
  My life is serene and blessed.
  With no threats of war, violence, nor death,
I securely revolve to adulthood through life's open door.
  Don't bother me with your banter.
Don't challenge me to believe
  That the world is hostile and changed.
  Leave me be! Leave me alone!
Lest I speak your name.
  Go — Cast down that heavy burden
That threat to my body and mind.
  Throw it away, void its existence
To some other place and time.

Cluster Payne

Shattered

I don't know why I have all this eye crying hurt in me.
Why does everyone yell and expect me to see?
I haven't a clue why I stay up till three crying,
Maybe it's me, or my heart that's just dying.
I try to be helpful and do what I can,
But all I have left is a two-buddy clan
Why does everything go the opposite way?
Why is it me, the one who will pay?
Why do things happen to me all the time?
I care about me, but they don't give a dime
Life to me, just ends in a rut,
It resembles the pain of salt in a cut.
Hate and pain and go ahead give her the blame
Is one reason why I feel all the shame.
I don't know what's right, but I wish that I knew,
So I can gather pieces of a broken heart, and escape the blue.

Jenny Offenbaker

Death

Death is something people seem to fear;
Why I do not know, for it is always near.
Death is a part of life or so more people say;
But all people die in a different way.
Some people die while they are still alive,
Searching for answers of how to survive.
Some will die by a twist of fate,
For it seems that death always has a date.
Others will die at their own hand,
Because they fear what they can't understand.
Some will die trying to save a friend;
The greatest example of love in the end.

Haley Sledge

Our Seven Astronauts Died Today,

The Ship Exploded And ...

A nation mourns and asks God, "Why"
"Why, Lord, do the good, the brave,
  the courageous have to die?"

"It's so early, they were young,
  had so much to teach and give
Would not the world be better for it
  if you had let them live?"

"Or does tragedy offer more
  than heartache, tears and pain,
Does it add a special lustre
  To the triumphs men attain?"

"Cause us to remember, dedicate
  our lives to worthy goals,
And the balm of dedication
  soothes our grieving souls?"

Jean S. Barto

Why Mom Why

Why Mom why, did the man drive so fast.
Why Mom why, did he hurt my pet.
Why Mom why, did she look at me with her soft
  brown eyes, so full of hurt and pain.
Why Mom why, couldn't I fix her hurt and take
  away her pain.
Why Mom why, couldn't she get up.
Why Mom why, doesn't she jump and play.
Why Mom why, doesn't God know she was my best
  friend and playmate.
Why Mom why, did He take away her pain.
Why Mom why, does He want her for a friend.
Why Mom why, did God take her away.
  Why Mom Why

Helen Y. Ford

The Winds Of Time

The winds of time, how briskly they blow!
Why they keep blowing
Is not ours to know

They start in the beginning
with sweet days of childhood dreams
And usher in adulthood, how cruel it all seems!

But this newfound maturity, I like it so much
Offering numerous experiences and feelings to explore,
the need to keep going - how I hunger for more!

The winds begin changing and the days become cold
I don't think I like it,
this time to grow old

Family and friends start slipping away
I find myself lonely
like being led astray

The winds of time, how briskly they blow
for why they keep blowing,
no one will ever know.

Christine Kowalczyk

I Was To Blame!

There once was a Scot, who pondered somewhat
Widening a thought, with Single Malt Scotch

The question of the tilt, that appears in his Kilt
Will only be known, by the tone of his lilt [Hm-Hm]

And to silence this [Hm-Hm], can only be done
With the mere squeeze, of a bag-pippin' mum

The gleam in his eye, sent her hopes on high
As she poured out a drop, arousing thoughts to the sky

Alas! Alas! Alas!, when all's said and done
All this reaction, with no Golden Band

She was "out of this world", this Scot did acclaim
She could really squeeze that bladder, I was to blame!

Clyde Wilson

Be Saved Sinner

My work is almost over, my life is almost gone,
Will you come and see me in my new home?
I will soon be with Jesus, my race here is run.
I've been so happy here, having so much fun,
Serving my Lord and helping my friends,
won't you come and go to that land
where there is no end?
You might think you're happy here
but oh, the joy can't compare with the
joy in Heaven, God wants you to share.
He has gone to prepare a place for you.
its beauties I can't tell,
Will you make your bed in Heaven
Or will you make it in Hell?
That awful place of torment, that everlasting fire,
Come now dear Sinner just as you are
Take Christ as your Savior
Praise him on high,
Then you'll be happy
When you come down to die

Eloise Perry Beckett

Mountains

Falling white mountains and professional skiers.
Wind and echoes and slushy snow falling.
Fresh air and pine trees.
Snow and ice and cocoa I bring along.
Cold, numb and blue.

Anthony Michael Halpern

Billowing Clouds

Billowing clouds across the skies
Windblown images to test our eyes

What artistic magic they display
Changing forms as though planned that way

Billowing clouds for all to see
Yet often unnoticed by you and me

What beautiful things and thoughts abound
If only we'd look up as well as down

Don Rodrigues

Seasons

I have felt the Bitter Cold that the
    Winter has to Hold.
I have felt the Warmth of Spring, and
    seen the Newness it brings.
I have felt the Heat of the Hot Sultry Summer.
I have felt the Chill, yet seen the
    Beauty in the Death of Fall.

I have felt the Malice of those who like
    the leaves of Fall, Remain Dormant on the ground.
I have felt the Fear of another Winter,
    but there are my Children to Guide Along the Way.
I have felt Pain, like a Tree in Spring
    as the New Branches Emerge.

I have felt the Joy of Their Budding in the Spring.
I have felt Their Pride as They Blossom in the Summer.
I have felt Their Sadness as Their Leaves
    Hit the GROUND in the Fall.

I have felt the Presents of Thee, because
    of this, I know What Will Be, Will Be,
(As I Am Me, and a Part of Thee.)???

Carol Boesen

Just Sitting Here Thinking

Just sitting here thinking of today
Wishing and praying that things turn out okay,
I once had an out of sight dream, that faded away quickly it seemed.
I am lucky just being alive
Because only the strong survive.
The world is a sick place to be
Sit back and observe you will see,
Fools are all around us you know
People are always on the go,
Families are growing apart, this is truly not smart
You should always love from the heart.
It is hard to find someone trustworthy to love,
Please send me someone from the heavens up above!
Just sitting here thinking of today
Feeling a little sad with dismay,
But everything will be okay and it will turn out a beautiful day.
Amen.

Betty J. Wright

Untitled

With dark comes light, with clouds come rain;
With love comes hate, with joy comes pain.
My heart and mind to you I give;
For you to keep, this life you live.
With good comes bad, with black comes white.
Our love evolves like day and night.
But keep in mind though it will not show;
My heart will break if you have to go.
So bear one thought, when you look above;
The infinity in heaven, represents my love.
So, with life comes death, with you comes me;
As long as you live, that's how it shall be.

Derhonda Owen

"Diamond Love"

Think of me as your diamond,
with a flawless love that glows.
Like the fire of the sun,
and such passion that knows.
No limits or boundaries,
to which I might love thee

With a love that surrounds you,
yet lets you be free.
Let me be your diamond,
and mold me to perfection,
To bring out my best,
accept no imitation.
Let me be the diamond that's captured your heart,
hard yet soft as ever.
And just like diamonds let us last,
to be in love forever.........................

Jesse L. Davis

"The World"

I see homeless people on the drift
With Bags and Bundles too heavy to lift
I see people of various colors and cultures
At nights, all heading for homeless shelters
And I feel sorry. Yes I feel so sorry
This World, it is not the place it used to be
Where is the love, the hope, the unity, justice and equality
The world today, what is happening to this world I say
There are signs of moral decay
As I am afraid of come what may
The sound of gunshots echo through the night
Abandoned babies crying out in fright
The grown-ups living worse than cats and dogs
And children whose lives were destroyed by drugs
And I feel sorry Yes, it makes me worry
This world, this is not the world we used to know
My heart is filled with pain and much sorrow, just thinking of
tomorrow
The world today, what is happening to this world at all
There are signs of moral decay
As this world keeps heading for a fall

Albert Bacchus

"Life"

Some say that life is a fragile thing,
with cardinals and doves and robins that sing.
They don't see the cruel things happen,
just pets and kids and things house broken.
They never really feel the pain,
as they think of what they'll gain.
They cannot possibly understand,
everything has pain, not just man.
They cut down trees and murder friends,
and wonder why their lives end.
Natures not just a thing that's there,
it has a job, to fix and repair.
We don't own this earth you see,
we rent it, it is not free.
We destroy and maim and cause great death,
While mother earth takes her last breath.

Jeff Strom

Untitled

Dear old spring has come at last
With flowers that are blooming ever so fast
Birds that are teaching their little ones to fly
While children go dancing and singing by.

Evelyn J. Ambach

Nature's Parade

Summer has passed, my dear Child,
With her array of colors so mild.
And, see? Here's Autumn in her russet-gold hue!
Do you not think she is beautiful, too?
Next is Winter in his snowy attire.
Enjoy watching him from the hearthside fire.
Spring comes last in her splendid green,
Presenting a lovely, breath-taking scene.
For, her finery reveals the wonderful rebirth
Of the leaves, the grass, and flowers of Earth.
The Parade has ended, but not for long;
Summer shall return, and with her a throng
Of people basking in the Summer sun,
Delighted with all of the Summer fun.
So, be happy, my Child, for it is true
That Nature's Parade is never through!

Ginger K. Lambert

Contentment

In a damp, dreary prison, so far away
    With high walls and strong iron gates,
Sits a man in a cold and narrow cell,
    And the hour of death he awaits.

They say he is lonely, they say he is ill
    And pity this man who is doomed,
With a guilty heart and a broken will,
    As he sits in the prison's gloom.

There is a cottage where roses bloom
    And a blue-eyed maiden roams,
She has chestnut hair and ruby lips;
    This dream cottage is her home.

She has forgotten the man in the cell -
    It was only a hideous dream;
She knew him once in happier days,
    Many lifetimes ago it seems.

In spirit he is in that cottage with her,
    While his body remains in hell;
He is not lonely and cares not about ills.
    I know - I'm that man in the cell.

Johannes Borgwardt

Teddy And You

He arrived that Christmas of seventy five and watched from your
crib with his big brown eyes
This was his child he knew in his heart her dreams and tears he
would forever be a part
His arms would cradle you as you slept peacefully there safe in
knowing he was your own special bear

The days flew by and as you grew teddy and I both knew
That soon our little girl would be grown and off to conquer the
world on her own

We sat in your room yesterday, teddy and I remembering all the
years gone by that special night when he came to be, I said a
little prayer as I placed him there take care of her teddy love and
keep safe he said that he would that he understood that the most
precious of gifts was this beautiful child

So today he is ready, He's almost like new he's stitched and sewed
He's got a brand new bow he's all set to go
His arms are ready to hug you again should you need someone to
lean on
Remember he's your own special friend

You make a good team teddy and you, I always knew in my
heart he would be going I wish I could too

The choice's you make are yours now alone but I want you to
know that there's no place like home for Teddy and you!

Glinda Stavrou

Welcome H.B.

Harry Benjamin - what a prize!
With his black, black hair and those
    beautiful black eyes.
He came to us a South American child-
an athletic body - a disposition so mild.
I've read God is good and God is great
It's certainly true, we have learned of late
Now he is two - with a mind of five
Aren't we lucky that he arrived?

Dorothy Klampert

Storm

    A cloud of darkness blankets the earth
with its ominous light
Trees stir in the cool winds and leaves blow
across the grass. Lightning flashes a brilliant
yellow in the distance bringing an evil glow to
objects on the ground. Thunder roars simultaneously
crackling loudly and booming faintly in
the distance. As tiny droplets of rain begin
to fall I cover myself with a thin gray
jacket. The sky metamorphosis from a
light gray to a deep rich blue. Thunder
and lightning echo in my ears and stings my
eyes. As the rain steadily pours down washing
the earth clean, I also feel it washing
my mind and soul of worries.

Heather Bryan

The Majestic Mountain

Before me stood the majestic mountain so high
    with the clouded invisible crest.
I yearned to reach that tortuous summit,
    taking my first step to conquer that awesome hill.
The gentle slope soon became more rugged as I struggled up
    until each step became life's awesome chore.
New hazards appeared as the stones loosened under foot,
    and plunged down into the abyss.
It no longer was a rapid climb to the top as I labored
    with abated breath, carefully watching each step.
Moving slower toward my hope and dream
    that seemed so far away
From my desire to reach the vaunted pinnacle,
    yet, if I cannot achieve my goal in life,
I can only say, that I tried my very best.

Evelyn McClellan

The Shaman

A fire reaching up to the heights,
    with the Shaman, singing by the flickering lights.
All sounds are still, there is no cause for rejoice,
    all are silenced by the medicine man's voice.
An ancient song, sung by his tribe long before,
    a song of a tribe that is no more.
He sings, the sadness pouring off his tongue in desolate tones,
    his family, his tribesmen, all gone, he is alone.
The stars one by one fall, sending sparks to the ground,
    such is their tears at the lonesome sound.
All at once he stops and begins to weep,
    then he is blessed with eternal sleep.

Brandy Nickerson

A Poet And His Pen

For Erica, and for my favorite poet, J. Shafer Taylor.
I see the hourglass has filled
With unfamiliar grains of sand;
The power now I summon
As I hold you, Stranger, in my hand.

Old friend you've grown so crippled
And you've somewhere lost your way;
It's been so long since last we met,
Have you no words to say?

Yes, my boy, you've been gone long,
I've missed your soft and kind caress;
I long to brighten your raging flame
And shape the thoughts that you confess.

My passion though, must rest in peace,
For it's not worthy of your heart;
There's so much catching up to do,
And I've no place to start.

Just promise me that each new sand
Will simply mark more of the same;
That from my box I'll look about
And always see that raging flame.

John Morrical

Beginning

And as the sun begins each day
with warmth and goodness
so should you;
for all life abounds
for your interest and pleasure.

If you but see without perceiving
You are not seeing.
If you but hear without listening
You are not hearing.
If you but touch without feeling
You have none.
And if you speak without thought or wisdom
Your words are but that.

So revel in each new day;
that your spirit may soar, your mind absorb,
and your body be made aware.

For today is but tomorrow
and tomorrow but the past.
All life is a beginning.

Bill Hagmaier

The World Without Me

I want to go around the world
Without anyone being able to see me,
  I want to walk around by
  myself and nobody fill my
  heart with glee.
I want to fill the death that is coming my way,
  I wait impatiently day by day,
I tend to always think of my only true friend, the end.
The end of the road, the end of my life,
  for I will never be someone's
  wife.
I will never have kids, I can not survive,
  why the hell am I still alive.
my life upon the world, upon the
earth is yet not to be known why,
  So as I lay here, tears shed from eye.
I wish I was I dead,
  Soon I'll be laying, upon my
  request, in my death bed.

Cynthia Hall

To: John   From: Darcie

It's been one year since you've been gone, one year
without my friend, and although the time has been
so long, I knew it would not be the end...

The day you left you took with you that special place
in my heart. So I would never forget you —
so we would never part...

I think about you every day, the wonderful times
that we shared. And because of these memories
that comfort me, I am no longer scared...

For I know that you watch over me — the angel
that was once my friend, to help me through my times
of trouble and be with me until the end...

I miss you, want and need to see you to know
that you are okay... To hug you and tell you that
I love you and miss you each and everyday...

But I know one day I will see you in heaven,
together once again, you can fool me with your
magic tricks and I can just be with my friend...

Darcie Raynor

One And Only

-Marriages of today seem to be out of convenience
-Without the future being thought of
-Marriages of today seem to be of pure lust
-Without the presence of true love

-Marriages of today seem to lack respect
-That each couple should give to one another
-Marriages of today seem to be self-centered
-Thinking of oneself and not the other

-Marriages of today seem to be falling apart
-Without trying to work things out
-Marriages of today make me think about the future
-About falling into the same old route

-As I sit back and think of these problems
-I get a bothersome frown upon my face
-Worrying about what might happen to my own marriage
-Hoping I'll stay in my wife's good Grace

-But when I think of my wife
-I no longer worry about marriages of today
-Because I know how wonderful she is
-And together, we'll always stay

Fred McIntyre

Peaceful Expiration

Into this world, we must enter. Out of this world, we must exit.
Witness the death of a physical body, the rebirth of a spirit.
It is then that you begin to realize,
Oh, how precious life really is.
But people rarely give it merit.
We, the living, go around mistreating others, being hateful,
Revenging, and brutally killing one another.
How can our people continue,
To behave in a negative manner towards the other?
When God only gives one earth life our fellow brother.
The above thoughts may enter the mind of those, who have watched
A loved one hanging on to life's last devastation.
Fearful of the unknown destination.
Oh, what joy in one experiencing a Peaceful Expiration.
Watching the exhale of the last breath of air.
Releasing all of the pain, suffering, and
Disappointments of life in Earth's living hell.
Oh, how beautiful it is to witness a beloved one hearing,
The sweet ringing of God's heavenly bell:
A Peaceful Expiration prevail.

Debbie Matthews

Women

Men do not understand women.
Women understand women.
They know the cares that keep their feet to the ground.
Chatter is a froth concealing that dark place where
Strength lies waiting. No woman tells everything.
That would be unthinkable!
Yet, women to women are transparent.
Eye-contact reveals all. They can shatter self-esteem
With a single glance. But most of all, they ache for one
Another with a universality of pain, counting each tear
As it drops into the ocean of sorrow, watching the
Concentric circles expand beyond the mind's grasp.
They tidy up after wars,
Sweeping the accoutrements of battle
Into the tear-strewn sea.
They mend bones, sew gashes.
Never ever count their losses,
For they would die. They
Die of them, anyway, but
Never count them, never, never.

Edith Spark Hollander

Wonder Why

Wonder why the sky is dark and gray only when I come out to play

Wonder why the world is round when all I see is flat ground
Wonder why my face looks sad when all around me people are glad

Never knowing, wondering why there must always be a sky

Wonder why my mommy cries when all I did was say goodbye

Wonder why my daddy screams when mommy forgets to clean
Wonder why the road looks so long when I know it ends just
   down the road

Never knowing, wondering why someone always has to cry
   someone always has to die
   someone always has to
      wonder why.

Jennifer Lynn

Live Each Day

We wake each day, to start a new.
Wondering about yesterday, how quick it was thru.

Time becomes more valuable, the older we get.
Like a long lost friend, who we never forget.

Living life to its fullest, with its up and downs.
Is truly a journey, which sometimes brings frowns.

How did we arrive, at this place where we are?
Look back on life's moments, for the answer's are not far.

One thing is certain, if we don't like our place.
Changing attitudes and beliefs,
makes all the difference in the race.

The race will end, one day that is certain.
Bringing all of life's moments, down like the final curtain.

When the curtain comes down, you can look back and say.
I have lived life to its fullest, and with no dismay.

John E. Wiltsey

Untitled

Just when you think you have someone they turn
you down. You thought they loved you, they just
turned around. Will I ever find anyone, that
question always lingers. You here a song and
you cry, but why? People tell me don't be sad.
He told me just to be his friend. Did he think
the pain would mend? About this line I will
never lie. True love will never die.

Amanda Lockwood

'Love'

What is Love?
   Wondering what it means
   So I asked from above
   If you're alone you're sad
   If you're two it is okay
   If you're three you're not free.
It is wonderful to say; I love you
When love is sure and true
Mind and body feels the greatest joy
When someone is sincere to you,
yes, my dear, I love you so.
   what is love?
It has many meanings to follow
Love of work, all that you want to pursue
I love the hills and the mountains,
I love my parents and also my friends.
   Counting all as far as I can see
   I love the clouds that are over me
   How happy I am that I was born today
   To love this wonderful world everyday.

Francisca F. Cacdac

July Twenty fourth

   It's on this day, just eleven
years ago,
   My parents went away with
reasons for me not to know.
   Leaving behind my brother and me,
   Both with puzzled minds and
questions with answers not to be.
   How could it happen to our Mom and Dad?
   Why would our creator take all
we ever had?
   How could we be so gifted with
parents such as they?
   Why was our happiness lifted and then
be taken away?
   We have struggled without parents
for eleven years,
   Still today, we cry alone with
breathless tears.
   No matter how many times we cry,
   The question remains unanswered WHY!!

Charles R. Gibson

Ode To A Friend

In passing you leave a void,
Yet, I know it must be so.
I still see your non-committed stare and,
Your voice haunts my dreams.
When I would not or could not give love,
You were patient.
Your love and companionship you gave without regret.
Your touch burned my soul,
And now you are gone.
But be patient still, my Friend,
For I know that we shall meet again.

Allen Wakefield

We Could Be Friends

We could be friends like friends are supposed to be
You picking up the phone calling me
To come over and play
Or take a walk
Finding a place to sit and talk
Or just to goof around like some friends do
Me picking up the phone calling you?

Jason J. Sargent

A Tribute To Retiring Teachers

Teachers are born, teachers are made,
 Yet so many among us never make the grade.
Totally committed, solely dedicated to the profession,
 Helping children learn was always your obsession.

Watching you in action on any given day,
 Provided the incentive to press on without delay.
Toiling, laboring with that ever-present smile,
 Unceasing, unrelenting, totally committed to walk another mile.

You have been a model, a colleague, a friend,
 Providing all co-workers with goals to ascend.
The words, "Thank you" seem so small and trite,
 To express gratitude stimulated these few thoughts to write.

Teaching children was always your first and greatest desire,
 Within your students you lighted on every burning fire.
It wasn't always easy building better skills,
 However, students success provided you with many thrills.

We shall miss you, your smile, your face,
 You tackled any task with so much style and grace.
Enjoy your retirement, one you have surely earned,
 You'll be remembered by many boys and girls who really learned.

Jamie Lynn Jinks

Violets In Love's View

Rapture in red and blue
You are my lovely dream
To capture you is simply divine
Surrender to me this dream of reality
This moment of suspense meets with sublime
Reach out to me, with your colorful spell
Endear to each other, for who can foretell
That our rapture is true, in the red and the blue
Your going and coming in violet loves view
Is surely to be a sign of you
It's only a daydream of red rapture in blue
This sunrise color scheme, is only a dream of you,
Hold on, all things are you care for me
Hold on, of my promise what is yet to be
I feel so, your love will ever shine
Since now I know sincerely, you are mine.
Hold on, hold on my love prayer, with this you renew
Hold on, hold on my memories of this are now true

John Ginard

The Love Of Old

You are a priceless treasure, that no man can change.
you are the foundation that carries our burdens, thoughts, and tears.

And even though, you may not think or walk the way you once did.
I love you now more than before, because now is where I know
you best.

You once gave of yourself so that I can be as I am.
Besides the love and gratitude I feel, I can now give you
my hand for support.

You once fed and clothed me, now I will do the same for you if
you allow me the chance.

You are angelic in your wisdom
 a giant in your strength
 stern in your ways
and precious in my heart.

Never look at what you lost, never linger on the past for too long.

Life exists in the present and the present is all we have.
Thank you for my illustrious past and present;
for the times we shared,
and let us pray for God to hold our futures.

Harriet L. Sheppard

To My Mother

Mother you feel you are not loved, but you are
You are the most important person by far
If it weren't for you I would not be
I am grateful to you, I hope you can see
You always know the right words to say
You are there for me each and every day
I know the sacrifices you have been through
Because now I'm a mother and have experienced them too
Each day that goes by, I love you more and more
You are the center of the family, the rock, the core
These feelings come from the bottom of my heart
You are my mother and you play the most important part
I think of everything you have done for me up to this day,
And here are some words I have been meaning to say.....
I love you and I thank you

Gina Luppino

Listen Carefully

I always tell all my children that this is how it is,
 You better pay attention 'cause there's going to be a quiz.
God made all the lil' children living on this earth,
 Then He chose the Virgin Mary for Our Holy Saviors birth.

We are the teacher, student, fool in each and every story,
 Each must find his own path to truth and light and glory.
Now we must all keep on learning until we get it right,
 Then all will stand before Him and He will judge who might.

Come live with Him in heaven for all e-ter-nity,
 That is why I tell my children with such cer-tain-ty.
Would you tell all your children that this is how it is;
 We must all pay attention 'cause there's going to be a quiz.

Candace Jansen

The Past...A Visitor

You come and surround me with "used to be's"
You bring your trunk loaded with memories.
When you come in the door, my eyes fill with tears,
As you clutter my rooms with your yesteryears.
You have some of my plans, faded and worn
And the dreams I loved best are tattered and torn.
You say to me, "Listen!—do you recall when...?"
And then you start telling your stories again!

The Future—seeing your shadow—just said,
"Don't let him depress you with old schemes that are dead!
I'll teach you new ways, if you want to learn how;
The Past has his place—but I'm here with you now."

Please, come in and visit — I don't mean to be rude...
But when you drop by, change your bad attitude!
Sure, we'll talk about yesterday, as life used to be
But let Here And Now speak! because he lives here with me.
He too has his ideas about great times ahead
So when YOU get moody I'll choose HIM instead!

Well, I think I have spent enough time with you,
So, now if you'll excuse me, I have things to do.

Gloria Jaime

Promises

You said we would be together forever and a day
You said your love would never, never ever stray
You promised me eternity and said it with a smile
You said our love would endure through all the long lost miles
You told me that your love for me was greater than all the seas
But now I see your love for me was nothing but a breeze
You told me that you would never leave but now I stand alone
You never saw how high I put you upon that precious throne
My life will never be the same I know now that we are no more
My life will not end here though for this is but a shore
And when I set sail to find a new, a new love that is true,
I will be sure to find a love who will say as well as do!

Amy V. Ortiz

My Friend Blaze

Dumped from a car, you were lost.
You came to my house, but not too far.
I let you in, we became best friends.
You would bark when we played,
chasing each other this and that way.
Then on that terrible morning you were hit.
Who ever done it didn't care.
It broke my heart to see you laying there.
I knew you were fading fast, no time to get you to the vet.
I had to load the rifle and I was crying.
I put the barrel to your head and said goodbye,
I pulled the trigger and watched you die.
Now your buried in your favorite place,
Don't have to suffer the pain.
You know that I loved you and always will
your memory will never die.

John Hacker

Untitled

Beautiful dreamer, someone's little special own.
You carry the essence of Divinity's indefinite throne.
All of God's light shines on you, yet your shadows are cast in stone.

You run with what you have so careless and free,
Unaware of the potential of control you have over me.
Frugal with your emotions, I still lean and let myself be.

Your beauty and presence intoxicate my head.
An addiction I both need and dread.
With you, both my mind and heart are fed.

A sheltered flow of release is outshined, and I withhold,
to respond to a baby, as it cries out to be told,
that traces of warmth can be found in blood so cold.

In taking what you need you leave the rest to bleed.
In taking what you need you leave the earth to reseed.
In taking what you need you leave the rest to bleed.

Chris Palko

Children Of The World

Yearning for a better tomorrow,
You created a vision ripe for sorrow.
For your vow we became children of the world.

Your vow was too hollow to comprehend,
Your vision was too shallow to mend,
Your tomorrow was but a tattered history.

We were innocent and young,
But you made us guilty of your wrong.
Our sentence was to be your vindication.

We played the wounds and the scars
In your theater of farce,
And broken heart was our cue.

In your world we shed no tears.
We only turned like tiny gears.
Spring-loaded tension drove us into oblivion.

Cry the helpless girls and boys,
"Love us not as your wind-up toys!"
We pray for a better tomorrow but dare not yearn.

Carl Yao

Untitled

Magic woman they call you mambo
you dance as you shake your gourd and mumble
as you stir in your black kettle
all your troubles will be settled

As you stir in your iron pot
the Hyssop, the Sage or Motherwort
your healing brews are in demand
you read the future in people's hand

You light your candles in the dark
and the Incense aroma begins to rise
For peace and love there's the smell of roses
or Myrrh to turn away evil eyes

Bathe your body in sweet spices
Rub on Bergamont for vibrations pure
Lock in your precious thoughts with meditation
Now relax as heavenly beings you lure

Full moon ... waning moon
New moon ... waxing moon
The answers are coming soon...soon...soon.... Magic woman

Doris Gilmer

To Aborted Babies Everywhere

To precious little babies, living in your mother's womb.
You didn't know it wasn't safe, you couldn't know your doom.
Your trembling little body felt the instruments so cold,
taking parts of your little body, piece by piece, we are told.

It could have been by suction, taking you from warmth into the cold.
Such horrible pain and suffering, no one will ever know.
Your tiny little fingers could have held mother's hand so tight.
She will never know the pleasure, she took away your right.

You will never say "I love you Mama" never give her a good night kiss.
No sound of little footsteps, gone the joy of childhood bliss.
She will never know the color of your eyes whether green brown or blue
Maybe a little girl with golden curls, hanging over a dimple or two.

You could have been a little boy, growing to a fine young man.
Making a minister, doctor or lawyer, maybe the president of our land.
Maybe a teacher or wise counselor, advising people as they go.
But of these darling little babies, these things we will never know.

But God looked down from Heaven, He heard your silent cry.
He felt the pain you suffered, His plan wasn't for you to die.
You are safe with Jesus now little rose buds to decorate God's throne.
There will be no murders in Heaven; you are safe with Him at home.

Beatrice Rogers

Neon Nevada Nirvada

You holler away on your steam train...
You drive away in your FORD BRONCO to the GOLD MINE of the
West, to the infested neon-light 'slot machine city'
You DIG for dust, you roll the dice...
Ahh!... GOLDEN RESIDUE in your sifter!
Ahh!... A nickel more in your empty pocket!
You keep on digging, you keep playing your pennies
The people push-they shove-they yell...
Greediness fills the polluted air
You're on a limitless voyage to the unknown, the UNDERGROUND
The rainbow pots of GOLD are within your reach
You crawl through the hot sandy deserts
The ashes fill your lungs, you start to dehydrate...
You drink some liquor... What a grand time you're having now!
The mining cars speed faster through the underground
Intoxicated with exuberance your cart becomes HEAVIER...
Your cup of chips OVERFLOWS, your cart derails and you CRASH!!!
GOLD DUST fills the air - your last infested breath
And the next cart comes through
EMPTY

Heather Dziamalek

Untitled

Beyond the graveyard of expired Volkswagens and tripped out buses,
You fly -
Beyond the planted caddies with their asses in the sky,
You turn your heads slowly and laugh. Laugh as you drive by,
Beyond the moonlit mountains where you can never get so high -
On you travel, singing songs, songs that make you cry.
Onward, onward, to a place called home.
The home in your minds eye.
It reaches out to grab you. It whispers, whispers, whispers,
till you sigh.
Every mile draws you nearer, earthbound yet you fly.
Hasten on young travelers, but you'll never get there faster,
even if you try.

Gary T. Harbour

Soldiers Of America

Soldiers of America, we're so proud of you!
You fought to stop aggression, you had a job to do.
Americans of every race, color and creed,
Came to serve the U.S.A. in her hour of need.

Soldiers of America, Army, Navy, Marines, Air Force,
Throughout Desert Storm, you stayed a steady course,
You stopped a bloody tyrant and saved a nation too!
Soldiers of America, we're so proud of you!

Soldiers of America, you did what was right,
For freedom and justice you stood up to fight.
Throughout the world, a message came through,
It's Best Not To Mess With the Red, White and Blue!
Soldiers of America, we're so proud of you!

Soldiers of America, you fought and some died
And when that happened, the whole nation cried.
You have the support, as well you deserve
Of America, the great nation you serve!
As you return there'll be jubilation and celebration, too
SOLDIERS of AMERICA, WE'RE SO PROUD OF YOU!

Doris Johnson Gaddis

Asking

I ask you for a drink,
    You give me acid rain.
I give you trees and flowers,
    for oxygen and beauty.
You choke me with chemicals,
    and give me much pain.
I give you the richest lands,
    for food and for God's creatures
to rome free.
    Again, you tear up my face,
with your machines and your modern design.
    You hunt God's creatures,
for your furs and your enjoyment.
    One thing I ask of you people,
that stand upon me.
    Do I have a future with thee?
I am the earth, which helps you to live.
Once I was strong, and now, I grow weak.
I am begging of you, people.
"Please", come help me.

Deanna Caudillo

To A Masterful Instructor

With all the graceful moves of a dance
You glide and intricately step into a stance.
With blinding speed and strength so deceptive
You daily inspire, encourage and challenge
Students to be more than just receptive.

With the sometimes-patience of a saint
You teach so well the art of making a feint.
Instilling discipline seems to be your goal
With your example, the mysteries of Karate
begin to unfold.

Preaching the need for self-defense
You stress the necessity for always being
On the carefully-executed offense.

Just a word of thanks that maybe rhymes
To a teacher who makes my child's
Self-confidence and self-esteem shine.

Jackie Campetti

Live Your Dream

Did you ever want for something
    you knew you could not have.
Did you ever try to reach for
    the things beyond your grab?

Did you ever have a dream
    you knew would not come true?
    But still you hold it close to your heart.
Cause it means so much to you.

Did you ever walk the extra mile
    you will only meet a few.
Those who go there are the one's who strive
To make their dreams come true.

My home is not a castle
I may never be a king.
    But without the hopes and dreams we keep
It would not be worth anything.

    A dream is a wish from deep inside
and what your mind can conceive.
    But if you keep your dreams alive
surely, your heart will believe...

Debra Hadley

You

You made me laugh
You made me cry
You made me sing
You made me lie
You made me so angry when you told me to chill
I wanted to scream but instead I was still.
You wanted blue jeans
I wanted dresses
You wanted short hair
I wanted long tresses
You went from Barbie and Ken and all of your toys
To make-up and hairdye and then came the boys.
You made me worry through many a night.
Hoping and praying, "Please God let her be alright.
You made me get gray hair before it was time
by showing me a nose hoop and tattoo
wasn't such a crime.
You make me think, "Can I take any more
then I hear footsteps outside
and you open the door...

Janice Carello

Black Beast

You stalk,
You pounce
Like a wild beast upon its prey.

You play hide-n-seek
With our children
And grab them in their prime.

Bete noir of life,
You lurk behind every moment;
You peer at each breath,
Watching, hoping for no more.

Go play somewhere else!
Go quietly and wait for youth to age.
Go dance around octogenarians and terminals.
Go!!!
Take your party to your darkness and send years of warning
Before your eminent return.

Ina Vahlsing Everman

The Day You Broke My Heart

The day that you broke my heart
You said someday we will be together once more.
I have been waiting for that special day
But that day still has not come
Every time I look into those baby blue eyes
My heart breaks all over again
One thing I can tell you, no matter how hard
I have cried or how much I hurt,
I'll wait for that special day, if I must.
With every second, with every minute,
Of every day my love for you grows stronger
But, I might as well face it,
That day is never going to come.
No matter if that day comes or if it doesn't,
I still have the memories.

But always remember,
I will never stop loving you.
No matter what.

Amanda Hughes

"You Are My Flag"

You are my flag, the flag I adore.
You show me the way, you teach me the score.
You give me the right
To adore your might.
When I see your red, white and blue,
I know what I am required to do.
I fought for your right to survive,
As many more, who are no longer alive.
They must not spit on you, they must not burn you,
No matter what the Supreme Court lets them do.
I will fight for your future, that you may remain
The star spangled banner that overflies our domain.
Our children must abide, too.
That is also theirs to do.
That they may live in peace, and with love,
As long as that banner waves high, on above.
Yes, It is my flag, and I share it with you,
All we Americans, happy, proud and true.
So, don't you rabble, make of it a rag,
Because, as I have said, "It is my flag".

Irving Schlesinger

Youth Of Disdain

Youth of disdain why is your heart so hollow
You show no love, your mind is so shallow
Saying you are a victim, protesting system
But are you truly afflicted, or just addicted

Gangbanger... Tagger... What's your epilogue
You loot, you shoot, yet never been flogged
Who's wrong, who's right, who will endure the fight
Who knows if their own will be the victim tonight

Of course society instill the rule
That to flog the youth is child abuse
Now they're taking drugs, staging mugs
Thrown in jail cells filled with bugs

Mother hold her head and mourn
Seeing the child that she had bourne
Youth of disdain... His fuse he blew
The positive repelled, but the negative doomed

Cleaveland C. Williams

Boreas

You are my constant companion.
You stir my blood until it pounds through my veins.
My spirit soars as the fragrance of your scent encases me.
You change with the seasons;
Your icy touch turns to gentle warmth.
After your heat robs me of my senses, you replenish me with life.
I search for you longingly.
To feel your fingers' strength as you caress my face takes my
   breath away.
Together we sigh—our auras in total harmony.
A whisper from you becomes a bellow until you howl my name
   incessantly.
A single scream from you and the essence of my being is withered.
I hear you moan outside my door at night while I am safe and warm—
though wanting.
What warnings do your words contain?
Your life is eternal.
Someday you will spread my ashes,
and we will be as one.

Jenniffer L. Poe

Secrets Of The North Wind

Gentle breezes? Forgive me - on days such as this,
you usually bring me comfort. But now, you agitate me.
No reason for this change as I can see.
You are blowing much too strong; I haven't a fair grip!
Look on into the future as you pass me by.
Display the glorious treasures we'll share.
If only I'd wait - I can't see you!
Something calls me and I must answer.
For it is like you - fast, furious, soft, gentle.
At times, it too aggravates me for reasons not yet told.
Even without me, you will go on-
Why should I be an obstinate figure?
I shall turn ... no! I shall move forward!
Somehow, we will always be; now that we've met.
We shall not part; how, when, could I
   find another
     place to be
        without finding
          you there with me?

Carol A. Roberts

Bliss Amiss

Your soul longs for it, but your mind knows not what it is.
Your heart knows it is good, your head says it's bliss.
Could it be you'll never know except I tell you this,
Jesus Christ the Son of God, the answer to all amiss.

David B. Cribbs

In October

There was a time in your mind
  you were in love with me.
With a special touch, I'd feel warmth on days crisp and cool.
I lay with you nestled close to me.
  Inside me I'd feel my child.

We would delight in the afternoons of October:
  speaking in quiet soft tones,
    walking along the beach feeling the sand beneath our feet.
You rested your head on my shoulder and I felt your soft hair.
The night would come
  I would feel desperate and in love in our separation.

Loving was like a dream.
We did love in October
  with leaves turning shades then falling to the ground.
Sky grey, the winter came
  and then you were gone.
    Don A. Roberts

My Dearest Friend

As years pass our friendship only grows stronger with time.
You were there from the beginning and I hope to see you
  to the end.
I have never had another who understood my feelings
  so completely.
One who never judged or criticized, but supported me fully.
You let me talk when I needed to, and you told me to shut up
  when it was what I needed to hear.
It was on your shoulders that I cried, and then placed the
  burden of my pain.
And you carried it so well.
You knew when to call, and you always lifted me with your
  encouraging words.

Your friendship has been the greatest gift that I ever received,
  and I truly love and thank you,
    my dearest friend.
    Caroldean K. Cummings

"It's All Good"

  Yeah, that's what he said, "It's All Good, don't
you worry," but he was the one crying, not me. I
looked in utter amazement. "She is gone" I thought.
"She's really gone." How can that be? He hugged me
and kept repeating those same words, "It's all good,
don't you worry. "But I had to worry, she left me. I
didn't know her as well as I wanted and I would never get
my chance. She was gone. I hadn't seen her in a long time.
When I finally saw her lying a sleep so
peacefully, dressed in her pale blue suit, her face looking
so beautiful, I didn't want to wake her, but I had to.
I touched her cold hands, stared at the golden beautiful
ring on her pretty, long brown fingers, I said to her,
"It's all good, grandma, It's all good, Because you
don't have to worry anymore."
    Adrienne Gantt

Summer's Challenge

Your dominance lures the soul to return repeatedly
  Your schizophrenic behavior is astonishing as we, share the emerald
water's beauty-
Lost in the mystical immensity
  The abrupt flounder against the wave crescendo's
    taunt moments, rapidly replacing the wooing of the magical
    embraces
You will always challenge my skills, my strength, my endurance, as
you lure me back repeatedly for another day of boating-
    Jessica C. Van Benthuysen

The Raven

Begin for us a dance of triumph
Young lovers: Tap your heels against these cold, smooth stones
Leap o'er the dark places to touch the green earth
Break down this fence that hides our wounds,
And run through the grey and silent crowd.

Sing for us an air of victory
Supplant the keen voice with gentle tune,
The sting of tears with quiet melody.
Now, dare to shout a song of life—
In this sinuous maze of paths worn thin.

Create for us a verse of conquest
Words weighted with wonder and hope,
Terms of meaning, filled with promise.
The tributes you speak go not unheard—
Still voices echo in our children's ears.

Mourn no more—we are set free
Our dark cageling has lost its hue;
The flaws of time have rattled its prison.
So let loose the dove that holds our dreams—
We have killed the raven that nests within.
    Don Wolford

"Promise To My Child"

To never see you again?
Your big, brown eyes and long soft hair,
Your little white teeth, the dimples in your face
All gone away forever?

Your giggles, your tears, your soft sweet voice
The patter of your feet, the clap of your hands
The beating of your heart against mine
Never to be heard again?

Oh, my little love, forgive me my impatience!
Impulsive words which hurt us both.
Dear God, look down upon us;
Please teach me love and patience.

Within my soul I know your preciousness;
The special joy you've brought to me.
To lose you - would not I too be lost?
For you are part of me.

As you wrap me in your tiny arms, I promise
Never again in anger to wish you gone.
For who could live without their heart,
After they have foolishly thrown it away?
    Datina M. Herd

Untitled

Allow Winter to freeze up
your doubts and insecurities,
so that Spring
will melt them away.

Allow Spring to give life
to good within your heart,
so that Summer
will urge its growth to the fullest.

Allow Summer to cook up
your ideas and turn them into goals,
so that Fall can be creative and decorate your path
that will lead you to them.

Allow Fall to insulate with patience
your dreams that lay in waiting,
so that as Winter moves in without mercy
he'll overlook their delicate bulbs.
    April Eve Bragg

583

The Light

Dear Lord,
Your love has always been the light of the world
Your love has always been a light for your people
And this light never shone more brightly
than when it became Sin and Death
On His head was placed a crown of thorn,
In the distance were the women who
came to see Him die, crying and ready to mourn,
The sweat and blood ran down my
Lord's face, for thirty pieces of silver He was sold
We can now receive God's free gift of grace,
In exchange I shall receive a crown of
gold; a righteous robe of white,
Because of the Bright Morning Star
Who always and forever will be my Light.

Hina N. Tripathi

Wow! You're All Grown Up!

Well Lamont, "by golly," another year has passed
You're all grown up and left, the 'teen-age' group at last
But here's a simple question; that is due a serious consult
You're not a 'teen-ager' any more, but still you're not an adult

Now I was just a-wondering; have you ever stopped to think?
Only from twenty-one and up; can vote or buy a stronger drink.
So twenty-is the turning point; of directions you must choose
You'll have to wait another year, to be in a grown man's shoes.

Up ahead lies years of strife
Which won't be complete without a wife
Then next will come a family; so start preparing now
Nothing is ever given to you; it's earned by the sweat of your brow

Sometimes there will be failures, of things you try to do.
But keep on pluggin'; don't give up, success will come to you.
SO, always remember God is with you, carefully guiding every step
For you never could have come this far without the "Master's help"

There's going to be all kinds of 'temptations to face you day by day
But you can over come them all; if you just take time and pray
You'll soon be twenty-one, and a new cycle in life will begin
"Please" don't smoke, drink or do drugs; or it'll quickly come to
    a tragic end:

Juanita Timms

The Game Of Life

With which team do you play?
You're born on the devils, but don't have to stay.
Because God loves you; He planned it that way.

He sent His son, as head of the team,
To coach you and help you; and on Him always lean.

With a coach such as Jesus who suffered all pain.
Who's team do you choose?
And what can you gain?

Jesus will come back for His team someday.
All those who have said, "For, Jesus, I'll play."

It's all in the game book, God's Holy Word.
The rules for His team and what they deserve.

To all of you on God's team today.
Remember you're judged!
How well do you play?

And when the big game is over and God's team called in.
How many did you coach?
How many did you win?

Bobbie J. Thomas

The Wrens Arc Coming Home

Welcome to my home my friends.
You're so much like my beautiful wrens.

That fly in so swift
But then again they drift
To the south in the morning
Just about the time of dawning.

I'll wait again sometimes 'til late
And at another exciting date

When I know I'll see my beautiful wrens,
Coming home again and bringing my friends.

Ellen Lineberry

A Friend Of Mine

You were always there to let me know you care.
You've always been there when I've been low
and helped guide me...which way to go.

You made me feel what no one else can.
You are, to me, a real man.

You gave me faith and courage
when life seemed dim..on a whim.

You've made me feel alive again.

You're a friend of mine,
a friend of mine
Until the
End of Time.

Joann Cardona

Always

Right I feel like I'm going to cry
You've been giving your love to another guy.
And I know it's foolish for me to throw my feelings away
But I love you babe always.

It's time for me to face reality
You've found another man to give you the love you need
And I know I should listen to what all my people say
But I love you babe always

I try to keep my cool and I hope things will turn out fine,
But it just keeps getting harder and harder making up my mind
To stay with someone who's cheating because I'm still in love
    with them
Can't make you have me if you don't want me and lady you want him

You try to snow me but it show's when I look in your eyes
You've been giving your love to another guy.
I want to pack my heart get up and walk right away
But I love you babe. Always

George Woods

The Broken Fly Swatter

Clipity, clipity, clot. There's a fly that I'd like to swat.
Zzz up here, zzz down there, please, give me just one shot.

Clipity, clipity, clot. Ah! She has finally come to a stop.
Now hold my breath, and take my aim at her on the table top.

Clipity, clipity, clot. Swish went my swatter to swat.
Away she flew with the greatest of ease, and utter frustration my lot.

Clipity, clipity, clot. Maybe, it's this broken swatter I've got.
Before this thing falls apart, I'll get her on the second stop.

Clipity, clipity, clot. Ah! There she goes for that one more shot.
Now easy does it and carefully aim, remember this is my last shot.

Clipity, clipity, clot. Swoosh, went my swatter to swat.
Bang! and it came all apart. Alas, she's dead, and not a single blot.

Anthony A. Gasparro

Sensuous Hands

They massage and cajole.
They excite, they control.
They are his tools, these magnificent hands.

They explore and invite.
They delight, they ignite!
They conjure lust, do these sensuous hands.

Their gentle caressing
Is kin to a blessing!
These hands belong to a sensitive man.

Kay Shaffer

Love Letters

I was reading all your love letters today
They had been ribbon tied and carefully put away
They are old you see, all from world war II
They tell the story of our love and how it grew
The beautiful innocence written in each word
Today's generation would find them absurd
In one you asked permission for our first kiss
In turn, I asked my mother if I be allowed to do this
Now the innocent boy who penned these lines to me
Has been called to heaven, and left me alone you see
I never knew they'd be a consolation in my golden years
And even as I read them my eyes still fill with tears

I think it's because we were so pure of mind
And today that virtue is so hard to find
We lived by your mother's teachings and God's good book
And we respected life and another's possessions we never took

It's sad to think these times have truly past
It's too bad that they could not last
I hope innocent love letters will last for a million years
And as their read with old hearts still bring beautiful tears

Kathleen Taylor

Four Freedoms

These four freedoms of flag and star are part and parcel of who we are!
They have forged this great foundation, this freedom base that
 we call nation.
To our founding fathers we proclaim: "WE ARE BLESSED
WHO ARE AMERICANS, AND LIVE WITH THESE FOUR
 FREEDOMS"...

FREEDOM OF WORSHIP, FREEDOM OF SPEECH,
 FREEDOM FROM WANT,
FREEDOM FROM FEAR, THESE FOUR FREEDOMS WE
 WILL TREASURE, DEAR!
In a world where tyranny may rush and reign, with our lives uphold our
freedom's claim, with our lives protect our fruited plain.
To our founding fathers we clearly say,

"WE ARE BLESSED WHO ARE AMERICANS; WE LIVE IN
 YOUR DEBT FOR
                F R E E D O M !"

These precious freedoms we enjoy today are from your hands
 given, in every way.
May this constitution guide us day by day. Freedom from want,
opportunity here, with courage and conviction, freedom from fear.
May we do our best to seed this land, with the fruit from these
 four freedoms.

Our children to stand for flag and star, having taught them it's
simply who we are! They will do their best to seed this land, with
the fruit from these four freedoms. And from these seeds, MAY ALL
PEOPLE GROW, THESE FOUR FREEDOMS TO REAP AND SOW!

Patricia L. Lindsay

Memories

Memories ...
they remain as a refrain
returning with the same tunes and images
the smell of scorched flesh
of bones like glowing embers
of flames shooting toward the sky
in search of God
unable to cope
he went on vacation
replaced by a sign
"For the duration
this office is closed."

Memories ...
my bouquet of grotesque flowers
interspersed with weeds of cruelty and greed
their shades of gray and ribbon of black sorrow

Memories ...
I cultivate them in solitude
for on these fortunate shores
few would fathom their pain

Vera Laska

Taint Over Till It's Over

By rights I should have married young and had a family.
They say, two can live as cheap as one but that I've got to see.
I'm lonely now and getting old and my hair's turning gray.
A funeral is down the road. I just don't know the day.

If I just had my "Druthers" I'd do things so differently.
I'd ask that pretty girl I loved to please, please marry me.
I hear that she's moved back to town and living down the street.
Rumor has it she's a widow and a man she'd like to meet.

Don't know if she'd remember me with all the years gone by.
I'd be a fool to pass her up. I think that I shall try.
She did remember me and so we're dating now and then.
I'd marry her most any time if she'd just tell me when.

She set the date and now we're just as happy as can be.
She has a daughter so I have a full time family.
Taint over till it's over, that's what they always say.
We make each other happy. There is no better way.

Taint over till it's over. That's what they always say.
It worked for me. It will work for you in a similar sort of way.
If you've had rough times, keep the faith, you're bound to have day.
Taint over till it's over. That's what they always say.

Lambert T. Jones

Graveyard Of Memories

The tombstones that encompass my feet have a forgotten memory.
They seem to just be there, does anybody care?
Thousands, maybe millions, who gave their life so that we may be free,
Are forsaken in the shifting sands of time.
How can we truly appreciate what these pioneers have done for us?
To this, I have no answer.
Everyday of our gracious lives we inhale and take in what our
 forefathers have done for us.
It is hard to imagine an America with a different face.

As wounds are revealed to us, on the outside and within,
We bandage our own to the best of our abilities....
Then we pause, and realize that together,
As a whole, a great big family, one mighty people, we may tend
 each other's wounds.
We owe much to those courageous Minuteman on that morn,
Where the smell of gunpowder and thundering booms of muskets could
 be distinguished through the heavy mistfall of uncertainty.
They gave us this unity, this spirit of togetherness.

Let us pray that we will always have this freedom, this liberty,
This country. So here we are, free at last - Now what do we do?

Matthew Saradjian

585

Friends Are Treasures

Friends and pearls, are one of a kind,
They stand alone, as they shine.
As the pearl slowly grows, within the shell,
Friendships develop, they're treasures to be held.

Friends are the supports, we need along the way,
To smooth the rough edges, that come into play.
Their laughter, their joy, brings a feeling of hope,
That life isn't bad, if we're prepared to cope.

Appreciate the friends, you know,
Your wealth will increase ... untold!
For friends are treasures, like a lovely pearl,
You collect and treasure them ... around the world.

Pat Sarin

Bird Song Symphonies

I hear the little birds up in the trees.
They start their days by singing symphonies.
They're teaching all the world a way of life;
By heralding the new day's golden light.

We sometimes ponder life's philosophies,
While all the time, the birds up in the trees,
Are proving faith and virtue conquer might.
Their singing changes darkness into light.

So, take your lesson from our feathered friends.
They worry not how each day's going to end.
They only use each moment at its best,
And, when the day is done, they've earned their rest.

Leona E. Murray

The Mesquite

From south of the border his offspring came.
They traveled with horses and cattle through
Heat, snow and rain.

They made many a hot meal, and warmed numerous
Hands on South Texas cowboys as they moved
Through the land.

Shaded many a creature from the not summer
Heat, and on cold winter nights they warmed near
Frozen feet.

Though they're numerous now there's something
Unique about the traveling thorny South Texas
Mesquite.

Terry K. Smith

The First Christmas

Almost two thousand years ago
They trudged through the snow.
When the Inn came into sight
They sought shelter for the night.

Mary was tired and worn,
Soon her babe would be born;
They were poor and had but a pittance
So at the Inn they were refused admittance.

"Perhaps the stable would do for the likes
of these two?"
Poor Joseph with Mary at his side,
Tired and weary from their long ride,
Went to the stable to rest and wait,
Time was short, the hour late.

Soon a star in the East did appear
(Never was it so brilliant, so clear)
To let the Wise men know that morn,
That to the world a Saviour was born.

A. Margaret Browell

What You Find In The Cafeteria

It started out in the building's cafeteria
They would sit and talk and I would listen to their voices and
watch their mannerisms which exposed bits and pieces of two
personalities
interwoven and charged by mystery, intelligence and surprisingly
childlike fancy.

Were they mid 20's? I waited every day for them to come and not
every day they did.
Since I did not know their names I chose two due to physicality.
I profoundly called them The Big Guy and the Little Guy.

The Big Guy was a Charleston Chew. I imagined
taking his hand, smiling sweetly and then pulling.
His arm would stretch and expand, curving this way and that
until it went around the table three times and I would turn to
face him and at the starting place he'd be standing, staring
straight at me — dumbfounded, while, the Little Guy who

looked like he came out of a Norman Rockwell painting but a closer
inspection of his clear blue eyes revealed the mischievousness
within, well he would look at me, and we would both laugh, and then
The Big Guy would laugh and we would all be amused.

Vicki Kligerman

The Moon And Stars

If the moon and stars could talk,
they'd tell you how many times I've wished upon them.
Wished that we could stay together for all eternity.

If the moon and stars could dance,
they'd dance the dance to my heart.

If the moon and stars could design themselves into a configuration,
they'd configurate a heart.
A heart to show you my heart belongs to you.

If the moon and stars could talk,
they'd scream, "I LOVE YOU."

Lori Ann Washburn

Questions In The Night

I lie in a bed of thoughts of you within a blackened room.
Thinking about your loneliness, or whether you're alone at all.

Are you nights filled with passion as you lay on your stomach,
while I lie lonely, Catatonic on my back?

Are your arms filled with a warm, waiting chest of another,
while my chest feels the night's chill rush through the window?

Do your fingers grasp the sweaty flesh of you Lover's Back,
  leaving your climatic marks?
While my fingers clinch my dry, lifeless pillows pretending they
  were you?

Are you breasts erect from your Lover's kiss and gentle touch?
While mine stand firm from another passing, flesh raising current.

Does she really lie alone as I do at night?
Does she finally have me?
Or, is it the Night's playful domination over me in a weakened state?

Robert J. Smith

Angels

One day as I was sitting in my yard, I saw what might be angels.
This is true. Only I could see them. I watching as they moved,
closer and closer, with shimmering halos above their heads.
They appeared to be a man and woman dressed in white satin robes.
As they spoke I scarcely heard a word, but I managed to hear my name.
Then with one wave goodbye, they each kissed my forehead and
spread their wings. As they soared away, I sat with wonder.
I've seen angels today...

Katherine Maxwell

A Final Farewell

The day is here, the one I swore, would never come.
This day of pain and fear, I alone could keep away.
I was the protector, the guardian. I failed.
My strength, my soul, everything I am, failed.
I stand before you, I stand beside you.
My soul as shattered as yours.
His time was brief, his courage unmatched.
The love in his soul, unmatched, his strength puts ours to shame.
Never was he a burden, he was our stability, our anchor ever our life.
Do you see in him everything we could not be. I do.
His love and caring, unconditional, free of the burdens
we put upon ourselves.
Today we must look back, reflect in his warmth, his innocence.
Free yourself of the pain, grow strong in his memory.
Learn to give of yourself as freely as he did.
Perhaps I was not his guardian, perhaps he was mine.
Now I am stripped of my armor.
Yet I must rebuild. To Ron, my guardian, my protector.
My heart and my soul are with you.
My love is forever, unconditional. To Ron, farewell.

Sharon Osenkowski

Craving

What does it mean?
This hunger I feel...
These feelings...with no words to attach...
    ...to describe...
    ...to express...
It is sensual; sexual, perhaps...
It feels like a longing
    for affection...for love...
    missed as a child
    - a feeling very ancient
      a need to be held
Felt as an adult, I interpret it as sex.
A need for passion, or passionate expression.
A need for another...a union built on trust.
Laugh if you must.
I will ignore you -
This is the true child of my heart.

Shannon Alderson

After The Spirit Comes

In Peace and Joy
This longing seems at least to rest
In a Spirit —
Seen . . . but for a moment,
To fill this soul with Love's own
    quiet quest for Life!
With what benign and tender movement!
    Grace!
Imposed (so lovingly)
That Mildness becomes the way!
And Chastity . . . the gift of self!
And Charity! . . . that thing of all account!
Whereby Love lives — and is lived —
    Diffusively —
        as of a Goodness . . .
Wrought with passion . . .
    . . . for fulfillment!

Mary I. Levack

The Rose

Once there was a rose so small and pure.
This rose, it grew, strong were its roots
and brilliant red were its petals blossoming in the sunlight.
This rose, it knew no harm as it was only nurtured.

After the rose bloomed, a strong winter storm
set in, blowing and ripping at its soft, red
petals, breaking and tearing at them.
But the rose survived though tattered and torn,
its roots were still strong.

The seasons they passed, long though they seemed,
this was the time for the rose to mend.
And so it did, day by day, pulling its strength from within.
The rose was not pure now but the rose was even stronger
and more beautiful than before.

The rose, now cautious, was careful to shut tight
when the weather grew cruel. It would only open
on the most beautiful days and even then, sometimes
the warmth was not enough to open it fearlessly.

In time the rose knew that a brilliant ray of sunlight would flood
its petals with warmth so right that its fear would vanish forever.

Kathy Nash

Ode To Christmas

Christmas is alive with the sounds of the season,
this time of year is festive for a good reason.

CHRIST was born this day by immaculate conception-
our LORD Father gave us His Son for our redemption.

The holidays bring us peace & joy
as we march to the beat of the lil' Drummer boy.

Lest we not forget to pray for those in need,
for Christmas is about caring and doing good deeds.

A time for families to rejoice,
knowing they were given a choice.

Those who believe in themselves and the Almighty
can stand proud, strong and tall.

Comfortable with the fact they will be sought
if they happen to stumble or fall.

Scott Michael Robichau

Joshua

Here I was age 70, he but a few hours old,
This tiny, precious baby put in my arms to hold.
A surge of love passed through me,
A thousand thoughts went through my mind —
They jumped to year 2060,
Then to the 70 years I'd left behind.
My childhood had been so simple —
The world moved at a slower pace
No computers, TV's, or video games —
Only Buck Rogers mystified outer space.
Only ships could take you overseas,
No planes travelled faster than sound,
Horse drawn sleighs made deliveries
When winter snows covered the ground.
But perhaps even back in the 20's when I was a child, I guess
Grandma's wondered how lives would be changed
By that simple phrase "That's Progress".

Dorothy Hokkanen Bayerl

587

Whole In Her Heart

As the coffin was lowered she watched through her tears;
this would be the ending of three very precious years.

She fell to her knees, overcome with grief,
"God, you stole my child, you hypocritic thief.

You claim to stand for love, then you kill the heart in me;
a tiny life has died, what reason could there be?"

She clung to the ground as a silence filled the air;
her pulse began to race and she knew that he was there.

He spoke to her soul and this is what he said,
"Oh ye of little faith, your child is not dead.

He lives with me in heaven for all eternity;
his eyes - they were shut, so that yours could see.

Today is the first time you've ever called my name,
from now on, my friend, your life won't be the same.

You cry for your baby who is more alive than you,
but fail to see yourself and what you need to do.

Give yourself to me, that you may know my joy,
and then one day I promise... you'll see your little boy.

He didn't die in vain for he saved your precious soul;
let me in your life and I will make you whole."
Lisa Stolhanske

Under The Lights

I walk under the lights down the road in my neighborhood
Though not alone as I go

The street lights on the poles light my path with a bluish
   fluorescent tint
In broad patches, not quite connected

The moon shines on the night from far off in the southeastern sky
Filling in the gaps from patch to patch

The two lights are my escorts through the cold darkness
Each casting a silhouette on the pavement

One shadow appears long and distorted anticipating me
Then retreating back, under my feet

The other remains constantly by my side through my travel
Never waxing or waning; constant

All three of us pilgrims move quietly to the warmth of home,
Though only one has been my companion
Michael Wood

Remembering You

Thinking back to how it was,
Thoughts of you are just because
Remembering when I used to cry,
Not forgetting your one last lie
Saying I would never let you go,
Screaming how much I love you so
Writing true love for all to see,
Dreaming our love was meant to be
Feeling my heart being broken in two,
The hurt lies there are growing, but what can I do?
Believing how much I thought you once cared,
But no ever forgetting the thoughts we both shared
Hearing you're happy, and found someone new
Questioning myself, will I get over you?
Trying to smile, just hearing your voice
You're going your way, but that is your choice
All of these things I have done, and I'll do so much more

Just always remember, It's you I adore
The last thing I'll write is remembering you,
Has been all my life, and it seems to be true!
Lorena Arias

Beach

Thinking of you the conclusion I reach
Thoughts of you remind me of a beach.
When thinking of the sand
It reminds me of the touch of your hand
reassuring me that you understand.
Sometimes your touch is soft sometimes rough
but sometimes just your touch is enough.
Next I think of the sea
it reminds me of how much you mean to me
The waves consist of white yes, sometimes we fight
Then I see the greenish-blue
I know your friendship will always be true.
I see the setting sun I remember all the times we had fun.
Then I see the skies I think of your eyes.
Next there are the clouds white and full of fluff
You try to be so tough
And when they are grey
You hold back the things you would like to say
When it rains I feel your pain
When the sun shines I know everything is fine.
Mickie Kenyon

Untitled

Immunity shines its force,
thresholds drown in struggle,
even the most cavalier,
wallow in melancholiness.

Access in unavoidable,
sages and jackals endure,
when the wrath strikes,
its trace stains.

Mending seems eternal,
pondering the way to clarity,
as ignorance clouds the mind,
and advice protrudes from the experienced.

To repeat the inevitable,
kills the previous,
I have found my new ending,
she doesn't
Salvatore Gugliara

He Was There

Dedicated to William Kyle Soule
He was with me through it all,
Through it all he was there.
For I know he cares,
He was there.
He was there at that very same moment holding my hand.
He knows just when to love me.
He's my everlasting friend.
He was there on that day of horror,
Standing right by my side,
For on that day my very best friend had died.
He was there when the time came,
To bury my loving friend.
He was there when I was crying,
He really understands.
Though I try and try,
I still can't comprehend,
Why he took away my very best friend.
But no matter what the reason,
I know he's always there
And that he'll always care.
He was there.
Rhonda Wright

A Family Facsimile

Together though it seems so odd. They share a special union.
Through many years, and growing kids, there is still a fire.
They walk hand in hand in life, their marriage is secure.
They love each other with passion true, and it shall never tire.

He is strong, and willful too. A man to lead the rest.
She is dainty, quite demure, and follows in his wake.
Together they have made a life, that none can come between.
No better life could I conceive, or possibly duplicate.

Their children always give them cause to break into a smile.
These are two most special kids. One precious girl, one handsome boy.
Within their hearts grows each a love which finds no limit ever.
They bring to light a special warmth, and truly bring out joy!

I see them all from quite a distance, each a careful work.
At once demure, strong-willed, secure, and even sort of shy.
For they harbor quiet peace no harm can 'ere befall;
Within their world, the sun is bright, and the only limit the sky!

Marcy Lynne Brown

Friendship Means So Much

We've been through a lot, through the years,
Through the pain, sadness, and tears.
Times of laughter, happiness, and peace,
As we grew older our friendship increased.
We've had our differences and our fights,
But it didn't matter who was right.
Periods of times that we've been mad,
We soon realized what a friendship we've had!
Remember the smiles, the laughs and the fun,
And the stupid, crazy things we've done.
We share everything from clothes, secrets, trust to dreams.
We are like sisters, well at least it seems.
Although you are leaving, our friendship is here,
Even though you are not near.
Don't ever forget me, always stay in touch,
I know I'm going to miss you so much,
Keep the memories close at heart.
Our friendship is too strong to come apart,
Friends forever is what we'll always be,
Because our friendship means so much to me.

Rossette M. Mones

Ode To The Ocean

Ocean of fire, the waters never cease
Throughout the days you bring me endless peace
But in anger you rise to cast your gale
Making my troubles flee with no avail
Ocean of security, draw me near
Bring my homeland to the wilderness here
The sea possessed beauty that spoke no word
But a song that my heart always heard
In the waking of night, the birds cry out
To feel the stormy waves gushing about
But amid the gentle currents I feel
A bonding of man before nature's heel
To combine our hearts into infinite joy
Actions of reason without a false ploy
Ocean of love, calling outward to me
Allow our hearts to once again be free
To build in vain a nation that can stand
Born of liberty from the tyrannical hand.

Lisa O. Wood

Animal Nightmares

Brute wings of owls appear in dreams of wild dogs,
Timber wolves still the elk of their night dreams,
Ospreys are afraid of slow-diving for herring,
Salmon peer at river passes as brown bear hover over noisy rapids.

Copperheads place fangs into eager hunters,
Butterflies kiss the architecture of giant cobwebs,
Porpoises swish in and out of green-grey water to avoid the
    greedy sharks,
Ants scurry in dream-sleep to carry human-like bodies into
    winter pantries.

Wolf eyes stare at rabbits larger than elephants,
Crows caw with cicadas' orchestrating noises as loud as tornadoes,
Fox cry to the long-haired, lop-eared rodent,
Fat whale spouts the sea to the flip-flopping clouds as migrating
    geese fly into unknown skies.

African lions offer up cubs to giant gazelles,
Heavy-horned moose fearfully search for food in empty fields
    covered with solid ice,
Hungry rat stares at wild cats peering from giant Swiss cheese holes,
A graceful swan hides in tall wild reeds as huge water snakes
    slither around its nest.

Darling baby doe watches dolefully as brown-tailed mama runs
    off alone,
Bushy-tailed beaver quivers as a purple turtle invades its beaver house,
Pink flamingo fans its feather while dancing on the back of a
    golden eagle
As the moon shimmers stealthily through a wind-whipped cloudburst.

Lillian Powis

The Circle And The Square

The square begins with corners blind
to all it holds. Inside we find.
secrets that hide the fears that bind.

There is a warning: we must heed
to the faint cries of those in need;
then yearning hearts will then concede.

A circle of love can then be sought
to right the wrongs that life has wrought.
Compassionate hearts to these we brought.

The edges soon begin to round,
when understanding hearts surround
this wanting life - a peace is found.

The choice is ours: the life we hold
depends upon the shape we mold.

Linda Davis-Holt

I Love To Run

I love to run, I love to run
To feel the earth beneath my feet
In rhythm with my heart they beat
Like mighty hammers pounding down
With lightning speed upon the ground
To feel the morning suns' embrace
The breeze that cools my sweating face
Like a blacksmiths' bellows my lungs cry out
And drown all noise in their silent shout
To continue on through fatigue and pain
And by sheer will, the goal obtain
To see the world go rushing by
To be at one with earth and sky
To feel, that if I stop, I'll die
To race toward the setting sun
I love to run, I love to run

Michael R. Watson

Moments

Some of life's moments are so precious,
to catch a glimpse as they go fleeting
leaves but to boggle one's mind at the
thought of another chance meeting.

The quickly passing of a cherished moment
leaves a trail of need and want behind.
We search, although knowing not where,
once again that fleeting moment to find.

A moment in time is relative to all,
if it be pleasant, it will also be speedy;
but if sorrowful, time will all but still,
it's human nature, for pleasure, to be greedy.

Hold on to your moments as long as you can,
enjoy them, savor them, share them if you will;
take what you wish from what life presents,
when the good stuff comes along, grab your fill.

Catch and hold on, fleeting as they may be,
you must catch those moments for yourself;
for when the moment has passed, only
memories are left in your heart on the shelf.

Marie Roberts

Heart Full Of Hate

Heart full of hate, in vain he will wait,
To enter the heavenly gate—
Never to see life's light,
To reach ecstatic heights

Heart full of hate, kills and maims
The gifts of love never gained
Oh woe is he, how can he not see,
The beauty around

How can I show, the way to go
To reach for the star, even though afar
For the gifts of life, love without strife
Friendship and glee,

The chains of hate broken,
  Free - Free - Free

Leatrice L. Marson

A Distant Love

From distant seas,
To far off lands
I walked upon foreign sands.

I sought thee out 'neath mast and sail,
I kept hope through threatening gale
And held my gaze to the morning pale.

Across cloudless azure blue
To the setting sun's reddish hue,
An immortal remembrance of you.

I gaze on the distant stars shimmering in the twilight
Stars aflame with passion, for your burning eyes, so bright
As twin beacons of hope in the night.

Traversing the wide expanse of space
I gazed at last on your beautiful face,
At last, I had come to my love, my place.

Nathan Scott Smith

Library Land

There's a wonderful land where I go by myself,
To forget every worry and care.
I just take a book from the library shelf,
Begin reading, and, "presto," I'm there!

I've been to the land of Arabian nights, and,
I've been through the Eskimo's cold.
I've been with the poor hungry beggar, and,
I've been to the lands of pure gold!

So, if you are weary, and tired, and sad,
And can find no happiness here,
Just take a book from the library shelf,
Begin reading, and, "presto," you're there!

Therian H. Williams Mendelsohn

Patience

To be the earth, to know a flower,
to gaze and see it as a tower.

Roots...
Through my soil they course,
as high above an eagle soars.

I wonder... I wish...
To breath the water to be a fish.
Or warrior up in a tree, feather in my hair,
gazing on the enemy, wondering if I dare... To pounce.
Or would I long to call him "brother"?
To taste the food cooked by his mother.

Why did we have to grow?..
To change?.. To build our bombs our poison waste?..
Or is this just another taste...
Of what we are?.. Have always been.

I need not wonder for I will know,
when above my body flowers grow... As towers.

Roots... Through my shell they course,
as high above my spirit soars.

Then, I will know.

Kevin J. Pranger

Eagle Eyes

An eagle swooping down from out of space,
To grasp within its talon sharp its prey,
You come to me in boldness and in grace,
You call and I am powerless to stay;
Your eyes tell of the crag's eternal fate,
But also of the tender downy cloud,
They speak of soaring up to Heaven's gate,
Of noble ventures that you have avowed;
They tell of things unknown and yet to know,
Those eyes so brilliant with emotion fired,
They bring to me the dream of love aglow,
And in the eagle's grasp, I'm firmly mired;
  Oh, take me to your side, bold, taloned friend,
  Begin my life, or quickly let it end.

Marian Sobel Levitt

Home

Some people say a home is just walls and a floor.
To me, it's part of my life.
Home is where the heart is and where you lay
To rest, home is the best place yet.
Big, tall, large, or small, 1 or 2 floors, three or four
Home should be a special place.
Good times, bad times or even sad times
and every holiday
Home is very special to me in a great big way.

Mark Washington

Life: An Unfortunate Dilemma

I wake up in the morning,
To hear mother snoring.
Step into the shower, to exit like a flower.
Eat my breakfast of bran,
Catch the bus if I can.
Get to school slightly late,
In a most serious state.
My notebooks are missing, so I contemplate skipping.
But by walked a lass, who enticed me to class.
I settled beside her, her kilt shifted higher!
But entered the teacher, leading a preacher.
Who saw me settled beside her, her kilt shifting higher!
Fearing suspension I withdrew,
I, wiping my brow, shouted, "Damn!"
Life: An unfortunate scam!
This day was nothing but a hassle,
Found my books but, lost my tassel.
Tomorrow: Hopefully a better day,
One by one they drift away.
My life, my life, forever stay.

Martin Miller

Years Ago

He wanders back to years ago and wishes he could stay
To hear the laughter of his love whom now has gone away.
"I'm happy here in years ago when we were young and free,
Look, come look with me, there's our names in that old oak tree."

"Yes I know they're hard to see from many seasons past,
But as I promised you my love I carved them in to last".
He wanders back from years ago, and feels the pain once more
For he is back into today and lets the tear drops flow.

"I'm sad and lonely in today I miss my one true love
And if again I find my way, years ago is where I'll stay".
If I close my eyes and pray" could I be taken there,
One more time to years ago to see my love with golden hair"?

With eyes closed tight he breathes a sigh that only he can hear
And in his heart, his leaping heart, he knows his love is near.
With pounding heart and tear filled eyes he reaches for her hand,
He's waited countless moments, countless as are grains of sand.

"Another dream it can not be, I know that I was there
I smelled the sweetness of a rose as I pinned it in her hair".
Emptiness is all they found when friends came to his door,
Dancing shadows from the moon beams, and a rose upon the floor....

Karen Kuerbitz

The Concert

I have come to see you tonight
    to hear the sounds and see the sights
Hoping to have a good point of view
    to watch and admire you
I envy the magical talent you have
    to reach into our minds and souls like you have
To bring such joy and pleasure to all
    who have come and packed the hall
To each of us in special ways
    you light our souls
        and help us through our days
To be so blessed just to hear your sounds
    and to have you all around
It might be hard for you to realize
    what pleasures your music makes materialize
Our dreams and hopes all come true
        when we listen
            to you
                the
            Moody Blues

Susan Rabbitt

Suicide

Have you ever wondered what it would be like to be dead,
To lay in a square box with no pillow for your head?
To live in a world all your own,
Without a place to call your home?

Will your new home be located in the sky,
Or will you live somewhere nearby?
Is that place the place you took your first breath,
Or is it the place of your horrible death?

Will there be stars where you stay,
Stars in which you can see all day?
Can you see people that you once knew,
Are they the ones gazing and crying over you?

Don't you wish you could communicate with your family and friends,
To explain as to why you took your life and put it to an end?
Instead you are forced to watch them suffer and cry.
Why did you do it, why did you have to die?

The time has come for you to depart,
You take one last look and the pain conquers your heart.
Suddenly all the light is gone and you are left alone,
In the cold, dark box that is now your permanent home.

Missy Wozny

Reflections Of Me

Miranda, you are the calm that I could never be
To look upon, you are the image of me
Eyes of brown, with specks of green, you were my first
If I felt more love, I would burst

Elizabeth, your name means gift from God
But I wasn't ready, so I felt sorrow, and I found this odd
You were my pain until my patience grew
And when it did, I saw you anew, I love you too

Danielle you are my soul and my life
I was looking for a Daniel, but your arrival met no strife
Only love which is plenty and free
My children, they are reflections of me

Penny Lawson

Tears Of The Land

There were some Cherokee people set;
To make the famous trail of tears,
October mourning for the Cherokee
There were not many left to tell
About these trails of tears, death, fear, no one ever gave a damn
Tell the people this is yours, later say, "This is mine"
Resettle in some distant place, worthless to the white man
Then fling the people from the land, their souls became tokens of
    the land
The white man came and took this land
Which linked the people on which it could stand
Some will live, some will subside, the white man shall always be
    around
Stalking the Indian man, on his own sacred land
Cherokee people were on the richest of these lands
The people have made a stand, there will be a time to have your land
No blood sweat, nor tears, a time of no more fears,
Of this hateful, unhealthy man, great spirits, uncommon to white men,
Shall guard the people of the land no more searching; this yours!
With no assuagement from the white man

Kenneth W. Cubine

Untitled

When you take that away - you take what I know, is mine
To me, my mind.
When you make me cover your eyes
You are blind, and cannot see my mind.
You make me change it all - my life behind, hid in my mind.

I cry to cover you - your blind soul
Push back all of which we know.
Quiet mouths of remembrance of hurt we still hold
Deep within our souls.
To say it, to forget but truly we know
Too much to ever hold.

I feel the pain as the day's show replays.
You say a forgiveness but still always
Reminders say and tell me how
Wrong I lay and will always stay.
It won't go away.

So when you take that, from me, Soul Blind
Not let to find a way of hiding
Only my mind, all I hear inside makes me insane to feel
The pain behind, my mistake, my mind.

Lori Lanice Anderson, 16 yrs. old

If I Were A Centimeter Tall...

If I were a centimeter tall,
to me nothing would be small.
Every thing to me would be gigantic,
I could ride around on the back of a tic.
I could ride on the wings of a very small bird,
I could yell real loud and wouldn't be heard.
I could be whatever I wanted to be,
But I'm afraid sometimes it might get lonely.
I would often get sad or even mad,
When someone stepped on me for it's me they can not see,
So if I was a centimeter tall,
I would not like it at all.
I would be too very very small
to ever go to the mall.
I would be too very little
to play the fiddle or rhyme a riddle.
I would be too very minny,
to ever go to a restaurant named Denny or lenny or even ginny.
I'm glad I'm not a centimeter tall
cause I wouldn't have any fun at all.

Savannah Hill

More Into My World

Come my dearest, dearest friend;
To my world of emotional Foreverland,
Where thoughts and feelings run with the tides
Of ever-expanding Seas of Life.

To the depths of love in the watery expanse,
Where no one has been, and probably never will;
For few experiences weave in and out,
Like miniature sea horses dancing in the sand,
Ever so delicate, so fragile, so beautiful.

Come with me, my dear; come to my island of love;
Where flourishing revelations and pursuits of dreams,
Bounce in the crests of waves, and pound in the hearts of the ones
Who dare to wash ashore.

Walk in my expanse of life, and tread in my footsteps on the windswept
Beaches of Eternity; for as each of us is just a pebble in the
Universe, we share the same crystals of all the sand
castles that were ever built.

For my castle is your castle, and the moat that surrounds the walls
Is drying up; and the inward cries beckon out to you,
To walk through the gate, And more into my world.

J. Duncan Rogde

"Susan"

If she would have taken the time to be a mother,
to nurture, to love - then maybe she would have discovered.

The meaning of love, the meaning of a home. But she thought
of herself and left them to roam.

Far away she traveled going different places, never seeing
the tears or the pain on their little faces.

Their life was in shambles, no place to call home. The
youngest died in a state funded home. She never came to say
her good-byes, everyone wondered if she even cried.

Her girls how they grew and stronger became - never once
saying her name.

All grown now - with families of their own, they've left her
behind to stand alone.

Patty Leaders

Insight

What should I do, would it be O.K.
to reveal my inner self through this poem
to some of you, or should I just make up
a rhyme and never mind if my words speak true?
Dare I bare my soul and let others know
how alone and insecure I feel at times and how
I sometimes worry about what tomorrow may
bring, or should I just let my true feelings
be a private thing?
Oh what the heck, why should I hide
myself inside and not let others see the
true me - So what if they don't like what
they see, at least I am being honest and
I am the only one who's really eternally stuck with me.

So how I see myself (not how others view
me) is of the most importance to me, for
if I go around putting myself down, then is
it fair to expect others to like everything
they see in me.

Shelbia Downing

Looking Back

I do not know why men would leave their homeland
To sail rough seas, to leave the land of fjords.
To go to places strange and yet unbroken,
To face the elements of woe and strife.

I cannot guess what urgent feelings gripped their hearts
As on this land they placed their eager feet.
Nor how their anxious minds raced forward far beyond,
To lands unclaimed and challenges to meet.

By rail and foot they ventured on to make their way
To those great territories yet untamed.
To test the earth and its great plan to give them life
And prove their worth by honest sweat and toil.

I can't imagine living in a house of sod,
Crude refuge from the wind and sun and cold.
Then praising God for luxury beyond their dreams
As now their families could unite again as one.

Our praise to God who gave them strength for every day
To guide His children and protect their lives.
Our roots gone deep in this beloved land now ours,
Transplanted lives — Our hopes and dreams revealed.

Lois B. Asp Janssen

Small Price To Pay

What a small price we are ask to pay,
To serve our Lord each day.

God's only son nailed to the cross,
So our souls would not be lost.

His pain cannot be measured,
With the gain we are able to treasure.

Praise God for the love He has for us,
In return, He asks for faith, prayer, and trust.

What a small price we are ask to pay.
When God gave Jesus that day!

Thank you God for being so grateful that all things;
Can be conquered through being faithful!

Timmy Turley

"Chase My Blues Away"

The rain you send day after day,
To simply chase my blues away.
The clouds they seem to say, hello to all the creatures far below.
The lightening comes to make its round as it makes its crackling sound.
The sun - it just goes in to stay to let the rain have its way,
The thunder - it comes to make its display.
The rain simply chases my blues away.
The rain brings peace when it comes.
It's not like its brother sun; that makes you want to laugh and play.
The rain simply chases my blues away.
The rain it may seem a little cold,
Might bring an aching to some people's soul.
But me, I just have to say, the rain simply chase my blues away.

Paul E. Puckett

Forever

The shore has the desire
To sip from the sea.
Its thirst unquenchable
Is something that must be.
Since the time of Genesis,
Millions of moons ago,
The shore drank greedily
From the waves to and fro.
Till the day of Armageddon,
When there will be no more,
Parched it still will be,
Sea must satiate shore.

I have immense longing
To enjoy life with you.
Giving you all my love is something I must do.
Since the time the sparrow sang,
Awakening my soul, to love and be with you
Was made my life's one goal.
Till the physical is no more, through whatever my be,
All my essence is yours. Your love was made for me.

Valerie G. Santana

The Duffer

The game of golf brings out in me
two virtues learned at my mother's knee -
tenacity and veracity.

When I strike the ball from off the tee
Then down the fairway repeatedly,
and search for my lost ball in the trees
it's obvious I have tenacity.

My final score no one will see,
so who can doubt my veracity!

Olivia C. Godat

Greater Than Gold

A moment I must take, I take for you,
to speak of feelings ever so true,
since Love is our binding right from the start,
it is true love, I endeavor, forever to impart.

When once and again communications fail,
it lets us know, how our feelings are frail,
yet, in spite of such erring, it is within us we must,
to seek to hold true love between us.

And so sometimes it is hard, and makes us feel sore,
to say we are sorry, has got to mean more,
to give in for pain, of emotion or pride,
it is compassion I seek and truth that I confide,

If not for love, there would be no shame,
we would play simply, a hide and seek game,
for in our love I desire, a treasure to behold
a love that is honored, a Love greater than gold....

Terrence Lee Taylor

Visions Through A Prism

When the fire lights a flame infernal
To stand by the gates of souls eternal

Captured by the light and the stars up above
Raindrops fallen on a new born dove

The sights and sounds of crystal tears
Running down like hopes and fears

The dawn of a new day more tests to arise
Some fail, some succeed with nothing to prize

The blackness that you see when you close your eyes
To take shimmering gold as the price one dies

But one thing stands the test of time
To the highest mountain our love will climb

Kathleen M. Curtis

Christmas Blessing

The star over Bethlehem showed the wisemen the way
To the lowly stable where the babe, Jesus, lay.
Jesus came to teach and an example to give,
That future generations should know how to live.
He told us to love, to respect, and to pray,
That we could join Him and His Father in heaven one day.

As we place a star atop our Christmas tree
We should remember to be light for others to see.
The blessings we have we should cheerfully share
With those who are less fortunate and have no one to care.

Our Christmas giving should not stop here.
Others need love and kindness thru out the year.
So as we say "Merry Christmas" and for next year, happiness,
Lets add a reverent and sincere, "God Bless".

Marjorie Nail

A Look Inside

Enlightenment fell upon me. A love relationship
triggered a feeling inside me. Sadness struck me.
Many spontaneous unstable acts followed me. I was lost in a
altered state of my own being...

A look inside alleviates feelings of worthlessness.
It's evident I grew to love life. The confusion that blinded
me no longer exist. It was essential for my existence to
overcome a natural journey...

A look inside gave a distraught female courage to move on.
I've gained knowledge from my triumph. I'm able to
conquer trails and tribulations, after my last yearly
defeat. It took one final look inside...

Michelle D. Clanton

Ocean And Earth

Foamy waves of ocean rushing
  To the shore day and night
As if telling the good earth
  "I love you with all my might.

But you stay cruelly quiet
  Remain as cold as it can be
My heart is full of love
  Can you ever feel and see?"
And finally says the earth
  "A big responsibility I have taken
To carry the world on my shoulder
  To be with you, will prove a destruction

Do not give the definition of love
  To something interfering with one's duty
And therefore, my dear ocean
  We can't and shouldn't be one in reality."

So the earth and the ocean
  Never became one physically
The waves of the ocean though
  Keep coming to the earth eternally
    Roop Prasad

Who Will Feed Us

Shackled by their poverty
To this arid and barren land
Souls stripped naked for all to see
Imploring with outstretched hands

Faceless forms in a dying world
Who roam so aimlessly
To beg a crumb from the rich man's feast
Denied their dignity

Bloated bellies and racks or ribs
Dull eyes hold a silent plea
What sound can reach an ear turned deaf
To this dreaded misery

The world may question when they die
How all this came to be
When life for nearly all the rest
Proclaimed humanity

The unseen horror of lives enmeshed
In the tight web of poverty
Will be a scar on mankind's heart
And damned in history
    Mary L. Casselberry

My Wife, My Mother, My Sister, My Friend

My wife, my mother, my sister, my friend
  to you our lasting love we send.
As my wife, you were with me for so many years
  but God has taken you and left me with tears.
But one by one, the tears will dry
  and wipe the sadness from my eye.
As my mother, no one could ever replace
  the laughter, the memories, and your smiling face.
As I go on each step of the day
  you'll be in my heart where you'll always stay.
As my sister, we grew up loving each other
  four sisters together, and one youngest brother.
We spit and we spat and we fought all along
  but deep in our hearts we knew we belonged.
As my friend, you were so giving
  so thoughtful and kind while you were living
Even though your road is at its end
  we'll always remember you as our friend.
    Nita L. Folsom

God's Call To Our Nation

God has called us to be nation
  To turn from this rebellious generation.
Call on him who gives us life
  He will guide us into everlasting life.

Blessed is the nation, whose God is their Lord.
And look to him who is our guard.
A nation of holy people that last
If to our faith, we will hold fast.

  His word will light and guide our way.
  Look to him and do not stray.
  Lay our burden at his feet,
  Rest in him and be complete

    Stand in the gap - guard our land
    According to God's plan.
    Lift our hearts in prayer;
    For the land we share.

  Blow the trumpet loud and strong.
  Be not afraid of those that do wrong;
  A watchman for the Lord.
  The Holy Spirit is our guard.
    Mary E. Hale

Simply Love

It should be so simple to describe my love.
To write words that rhyme and add a title above.

To share with my sweetheart these feelings within.
To show hope for the future and thanks for where we've been.

It should be so simple when you feel as I do.
Just state them clearly, these feelings for you.

How happy you've made me, all of these days,
being loving and caring and a thousand other ways.

It should be so simple to put it on paper,
How a party for St. Patty's day became a love maker.

How besides a lover, you became my best friend.
And with this combination, we can only win.

It should be so simple, and now I find it's true,
it's only simple because all my love belongs to you.
    Sylvia A. Lohr

Where Is Jennifer Today?

Today is my little girl's birthday
today Jennifer would be ten
She isn't here with us to celebrate
But I made her a cake again

Jenny disappeared when she was only four
we have not seen her since then
But every year on her birthday I bake her a cake
and I remember way back when

We've been looking for Jenny every single day
but we've been unable to find a clue
I wish I knew if she was still out there
So I could say, Jenny, we love you

So here I sit on your birthday, Jennifer
I wish you could see your beautiful cake
I wish you were here to blow out your candles
I wish your wish you could make

Here I am crying all over Jenny's cake
I have not a wish but something to say
God why-oh-why can't you tell us
Where is Jennifer today?
    Nicki Hardwick-White

To A Sunflower

Poets have written odes to flowers rare;
Told of the daffodils and crocuses,
And dainty flora blooming fragrantly:
The hyacinth, the lilac, and the rose,
Or Paris with a flower in her hair.

But who has written to the sunflower -
That King of Flowers kissed by Kansas sun?
O brave soldier of prairie field and plain,
You grow so sturdy, strong, and unafraid.

In youth, you stand erect and tall and proud;
You bring the sun to those in darkened cloud,
Reaching to kiss the gentle hand of God
And holding firm to fields of broken sod.

Your sunny face is always bright with smile;
You never sleep nor cease to guard the while
The gathering storm threatens all around;
And then you bow your head in silent prayer,
O King of Flowers kissed by Kansas sun!

Willard J. Madsen

"Vanessa King"

I use to sit alone at nights and wonder what
tomorrows might bring;

Contemplating over my life, not wanting to be
just same old everyday, Vanessa King.

I started recognizing the flow of thoughts and feelings,
that somehow possessed me;

I then began putting it down on paper, and setting it all free:

It was amazing, what I saw before my eyes;
Though, what I thought and felt within, was to me of no surprise.

"But, the flow of words, the form!" to see them all
down on paper,
Made me feel like a professional Jewel thief, after a
big successful caper.

"It glittered! it shined! it blew my mind!" It turned
me on to me;
It gave an insight of my life, as to what all that I could be;
Not excluding Vanessa, the Mother; Vanessa, The cook...
But gave hopes of being, Vanessa, the poet, who wrote a Book.
All poetic, about people, places and things;

Vanessa, who's more proud of Vanessa,
and enjoys more of being, Vanessa King...

Vanessa King

Untitled

Do you know what I feel for you?
Too scared to say I love you
Yet too in love to leave
Even though sometimes I should

What exactly do you feel for me?
Too scared to commit or just not ready
Do you mean to hurt me the way you do?
Too ignorant to care or just unaware

Every time I try to distance myself from you
You seem pop back into my life
Not quite sure what you want from me
I fall back in without even a second thought

Stability is what I need most
While you still go on with your games
My heart bleeds with aching pain
Am I your sanity or just another flame?

Karen Wallace

"Fly High"

Fly high, sweet lover, and let not the soil
touch your feet.
Fly high, sweet soul, and let not the wages
of life drag you down.
Fly high, sweet spirit, and let not the wild
take control.

Land gently, sweet lover, and rest your
weary body.
Land gently, sweet soul, and drink deep
the well of life.
Land gently, sweet spirit, and cradle
yourself in angel hands.

Beware the evil, let it not carry you
astray.
Beware the beasts, let them not cage you with
their claws.
And beware me, my lover, let me not drag you
down into my blackness.

Tara New

"Why"

So young, so talented, so hard to believe.
Touched our lives, how could he leave.

We talk about him like he's still here,
Trying to forget all the fear.

He left so soon, so much behind.
He'll stay forever in my mind.

Who could have guessed on March 31, 1993,
Someone would take him away from me.

Bang one gunshot, now he's gone.
In memories forever burned into our souls, he lives on.

I'll never forget, 28 years old, a master in arts.
The best actor to play all the parts.

Brandon Lee, the name of my heart,
You shall never part.

Try to bear the pain,
Cry like all the rain.

So now we grieve,
Cause we can't believe,
He's gone. He's given us so many memories.

Lisa Hegyes

True Constant Heart

Oh weary he of the true constant heart
travels far trying to find himself
In a shadow of facades
He looks beyond and finds only truth
He will see past the lies and find true love
Deep in his heart it lies
Only one really had the heart to believe
Only one
Off to her own adventure this one goes
And he of the true constant heart travels on without her
He will surpass all and become great
Through the use of his newly found tools
Creations that lived only in his mind will come to life
He will create, I say
And beauty the landscape
And the one who left on her own adventure
Will see and remember that he of the
true constant heart was once her friend

Teresa D. Gonzalez

Loving Family

She walks down a long and twisted road
trying to find herself, trying to get away
from the pain. Where can she turn? What
can she do? When all her parents do is
pile on the pain - making her feel as if
she's going insane. She looks into a
window pane of a lonely house, but to her
surprise she sees the love of a family;
something she's never experienced. Now
all she dreams of - all she wishes is to
be part of a loving, caring family. So
she leaves only to find herself young,
pregnant and married. Now that she is
really messed up what can she do?
She abandons her husband and child - only
to end up on the streets, raped, homeless
and alone. She leaves for a place where
She can be happy; for nothing can
harm her now and this would not be
only if she had a loving family.

Theresa Barbier

I Feel

I lived in the dark. Like an unsettled wave in the sea tossed and
turned by the wind, I was held and caged by the shadows of my
own fears. A protective shell enveloped my heart, my soul, my
mind. Always wanting to express the beauty that raged through
my body, but never knowing how. I laid dormant, cold, unable
to feel.

And then as gently as winter changes into spring you have come
and touched my life. A beam of pure light, soft and delicate,
strong and clear. At first I emerged ever so slowly, cautious not
to expose myself to your light lest my fragile wings would burn.

But you are patient and warm allowing me to unfold, recognizing
and delighting in my uniqueness. Through your honesty and
love, I fly in the brilliance of your ways. Carried on the breezes
of your being, I dance amongst a field of flowers by day and the
full moon by night.

Like a dream you are the passionate blessing in my life. You are
all the colors of the rainbow. Infinite hues fill my senses,
glowing richly, shining brightly. Radiant beams rush to the
depths of my soul. I feel life. I feel love. I feel you.

Lorilu Jackson

Daughter Of Midnight

Daughter of Midnight, thou art lovely.
T'was a time in the age of old that black was not counted fair
or if it were, it bore not beauty's name;
ignorance failed to see thy beauty.
But I my lady am not ignorant nor am I blind.
Thou art the fairest and most precious jewel of the Nile.
Thy fiery eyes of obsidian
have torched my heart and made my soul a burning ember.
I behold you, with hair so black,
that it seems to have been spun from the fabric of midnight.
And I know, not since the dawn of Cleopatra,
has the world seen such beauty.
Somehow it seems a sin
that I alone am allowed to gaze upon the Daughter of Midnight.
Dark, mysterious, sensual, and irresistible,
you are a beauty without a comparison.
I am unable to compare you to a summer's day,
nor to a midsummer's night,
and the beauty of a rose wanes before you.
You are the Daughter of Midnight, need I say more?

Kenneth Edmond Wolke Huddleston

A Dream

Like silvery strands of mist they flow
Twisting, turning, blurry, and slow.
Writhing with a sinister glow,
Or weeping with thoughts of sadness and woe.

They are the stuff that dreams are of,
The laughter, sadness, fear and love.
During the night while you sleep,
It is they who know your thoughts down deep.

The sounds that echo are barely words,
They fade away and are scarcely heard.
The mist envelopes all again,
And all is peaceful like a summer rain

Suddenly a darkness races,
And fear pursues with countless faces.
Evil smiles a hateful grin,
And a monster prepares to sink its teeth in.

Fading, fading, fading,
The dream is dissipating.
The blackness falls as quiet swells,
And the weary mind knows that all is well.

Rachel Ebert

Oh, Gentle Spirit

I extend a hand to caress John's cheek; the sinewy muscles of his
    jaw twitch and start.
In his tightly clenched hand John guards a toothbrush. Mine
    from the sink.
I have caused him concern as he searches my face for a glimmer of
    past,
Knowing, in practiced surrender, that none will come.

We sit quietly for John won't visit.
It's been a bad day. Too many people, his sagging shoulders infer.
In his stillness I detect his renown gentle spirit,
Now caught for the first time, the truly challenged victim.

The silent predator has seeped undetected into John's brain.
Stirring powerful memories into a fitful dance of brief recognition,
Before vanquishing them into still, deep waters of a waste chasm —
The one that harbors fetal haunts, out at home plate, and the first
    kiss.

I watch as John struggles; his eyes blink as if to rekindle a thought.
Like a young suitor desperate to ignite the passions of a disdainful
    love — only to be rejected.
Alzheimer's is an old-man disease — a distant phantom of senility.
How could it muster the charge to entrench the japer, the
    inventor, the lover, at 54?

Oh, gentle spirit, learned prayers go unanswered to pardon John's
    fears,
And reestablish the dignity and character of one so true. A man
    so needed.
"My brush," he whispers to me finally as he tickles the bristles
    with his finger tips.
I take respite that my father remembered the noun.

N.M. Niemann

A First Grade Treasure

A half eaten sandwich imprinted with teeth marks,
    Two missing ones, of course,
Crumpled pieces of paper of which he denies he knows the source.
A pencil with a chewed eraser—a monument to his dreamy thoughts,
A straw from lunch a week ago is twisted tight in knots.
A toy car with a missing wheel,
A wad of gum he'll try to conceal,
An overdue library book he forgot to return,
Loose crayons scattered without concern.
To most a sight which is quite grotesque,
But he'll proudly explain it's his first grade desk!

Suzanne L. Bailey

596

Euphoria

Love and happiness,
   two words,
two words synonymous with each other.

Love, like the dream that always comes,
   like the seashore we endlessly run.

Happiness,
      the horizon that seemingly has no end.
      the butterfly that goes and comes back to begin again.

Friendship,
      the flower that blooms, the
      clown that bears no gloom, the
      tie that always binds.

With these, people come together.
   With these, people stay together,
Whether in close proximity or miles apart.

   With these, memories begin, memories
like space, become large, vast and
      never ending, but unlike space,
never empty, always with a beginning.
      Dreams do come true.
         Samuel Miles

Symptom Of Discontent

Like a latent heat yet potent
Unabashed, unguarded and oft uninvited
It's like a stranger in the rain
Knocking at the door at inopportune moment

From afar it's a show of wisp
Swirling and curling in place
Suddenly, a dragon's tongue in frenzied dance
And a palpitation of uncultured wings

Akin at times to faceless mask
Nameless ritual its trademark
And for want of a suitable altar
The mind becomes its print of damask

On a course of denial
It plunders the mind in fitful abandon
Fed and nurtured by humongous ego
Its only prize is a betrayal
         Vincent O. Obe

"Prison In My Head"

In this life, trapped I am,
unable to end it by my own hand,
this worldly realm is so hard to take,
seems I'm never happy when I'm awake.

Some things make me happy and light of mind,
but those feelings seem few and hard to find,
seems that time goes by at such a fast pace,
when one crisis ends there's another to face.

When there's so much that's real and good,
why do I feel left out in the woods,
I live in a prison that's all in my head,
in my mind there's a demon that's constantly fed,

By memories and thoughts of the past,
when will those ghosts leave me at last,
'till they do I'll keep going on,
'till all the fight in me is gone.
         Steven N. Duarte

Cold Stone

Once again they met as strangers often do
unexpectedly unplanned
They exchanged greetings
never daring their eyes to meet
All the feelings and emotions that lay within
Stay imprisoned and bounded
By the hearts' unexpressed walls
Alike in so many ways
but neither found the time to discover
Time is hard to find in such a demanding world
So each occasion that came about
the tension between them remained
no feelings or emotions were shared
just cold hard walls between them
But now time stands still
as the hearts' unexpressed walls
break to pieces and finally explode
as she places a single rose
and a single tear
on her daddy's grave
         Sonya Thomas

The Journey

Pure, open fields welcome her to their
Untainted beauty.

Dressed in white, she is young,
Innocent and believing.

Rose cheeks brighten as she flies through
Trusting fields without a care.

The sun always shining;
Never blocked by uncertainties.

But that was before.
The invitation is now closed forever.

Trudging through the forest, virtue torn,
She heads on uncertain of her destination.

The sun is not in sight.
Her sins are covering it up.

Dirty face, spotted soul, she battles through
All the doom with her stained ideals.

Forever looking for the sun
And the innocence she lost.

Toughened by the falls
Kicking the broken halo aside as she goes...
         Sarah Blanchard

Alone

No one really knows how lonely alone can really be,
until you have been cast away to a life of misery...

When you have no one who cares, no one who loves you,
you act as though you don't care, but you know you really do...

Soon you wish each morning will be your last,
knowing you can end it all with a single shotgun blast...

But you hang in there, like a gambler, looking for that one big break,
really knowing in your heart, your own life you cannot take...

Yeah, you hang in there and roll with the punches life gives you
   each day,
because, you know that taking your own life is only a coward's way...
         Robert A. James

My Sister My Brother Dear

The race is not given to the swift nor to the strong but
unto those who can endure until the end. I see my sister
and she is not enduring too busy swiftly following that
downward rough road that looks so fair and bright but
tomorrow will come and there will be no light for another
child will come to be because of one careless night.

My brother I see you too are not enduring too busy being
funny and running. Though the drink and drugs you share will
surely make it hard for you to bare that you can not fly
away like a bird while my sister lies awake home wondering
which way you roamed and what tomorrow trails put her
under and saying not a word.

So today my brother, my sister dear let's start enduring
for today's fair bright light will not last through the
night, as my God from heaven above looks down on us. He
will give us wings to fly away like heavenly doves. If we
only would believe and start enduring. He will give us
light to last through the night.

Phyllis Blair

Soft Virgin Skin

Soft virgin skin
Untouched by sin
Smiling innocently at me
I think of you beneath me
like a hungry man staring through the glass
at sweet pastries baked by the mass
This man will go hungry today
for with his food he should not play
These thoughts are best unread
for surely they could wake the dead
These thoughts will be gone soon
Softly she will sleep alone in her room
Ignorant about his thoughts within
about her soft virgin skin

Ryan Lubbers

Untitled

Tears, uncontrollable tears,
unwanted, uncontrollable tears,
AGAIN!
And for what? For what I've lost? NO.
For what I've gained.
Love, respect, discipline, warmth, care,
but most importantly Leonor.
I may have lost a mother, father, friends, wealth, position, but
I have her. Dear, sweet, beautiful, Leonor.
Nothing or no one should or would even try to compare.
True it is that with her I have every thing I want, Need, but
would easily, happily exchange it just for her.
Brilliant, loving, caring, Leonor.
Filled with hopes and dreams for her Pride and joy her one
greatest reason for living. Her second chance!
Honest, fun-filled, radiant, glorious. A miracle!
A treasure of more value to me than life,
MY GRANDMOTHER, LEONOR!

Shauna M. Poete

A Fall Fantasy

The leaves are falling twisting
Turning towards the ground they are yearning.
For they have spent their time in the tree
a beautiful sight for all to see.
"Now they are tired and want to rest
of course the ground below looks best"
when the weather is better they all agree
only then shall we return to the tree.

Robert McDonald

"My Life"

I used to be a seed,
very fragile,
and watched carefully.

I was planted,
water was poured on me.
Each day I was fed a little more,
And then I started to grow.

Now I am a plant,
as fragile as the vase
I live in.

People walk by and admire my
arms, my legs, my body, and everything that follows.

I am as young as a newborn puppy,
Who hasn't opened its eyes.

I still have to grow,
get bigger and stronger,

I have plenty of time,
no need to hurry,

I am not ready to see the world.

Lia E. Lynch

Parking Lot Scarecrow

Face of hanging rock
violent in its uselessness
bent form robed in plain brown
wrapper sits enclosed, enthroned
jack-in-the-box turned sideways
ready with stern gaze and
spastic bellow-wishfully deterrent
of the five o'clock revolution
when metallic crustaceans snicker and growl
and his kingdom returns to gravel

William B. Hosp, Jr.

The Room

I sit here alone
waiting, watching
wondering
wanting
Longing to be ... to be,
anywhere but here
Alone.
I light up a cigarette and the flame from the match
illuminates the room like a firefly in a deepen wood.
Melancholy music drowns my thoughts,
numbing me to my emptiness, fulfilling my imagination, and
breaking the silence of this cold, dark, smoke filled room.
I sit here alone
waiting, watching
wondering
wanting
Longing to be ... to be,
anywhere but here
Alone.

S. Krista Owens

Aware - And A Prayer!

I pressed my cheek 'gainst the warm moist sod
"Tween the rows of stubble where the cattle had trod.
I knelt to drink from the tumbling brook
And winked at a rabbit when he stopped to look.
The fragrance of hay, fresh mown and baled,
Caressed my nostrils as I deeply inhaled.
This is God's land but He shares it with me.
May I keep it unspoiled, untroubled and free.

R. B. Curry

598

Waiting

Sitting silently, sulking
waiting, watching, brooding
watching for the day when he comes
waiting for the night that will bring him.

Shifting, moving, running, fleeing
escaping those that would have us
eluding the ones that will come.

Sleeping, dreaming, screaming, wailing
dreaming of those days gone by
screaming of the days to come.

Praying, wishing, hoping, pleading
praying for the Lord to save us
hoping that he will hear us.

Raheel Khan

Botanical Gardens

I feel awe at the various colors of fall.
Walking through the wide expanse of plants and grass,
I wish I could better remember the past.
Who would have thought death so beautiful?

William Horwitz

Abstracts

Words flowing and riding with the lightness of air
  Waltzing and dancing, oblivious to care.
Words hurting and squeezing, tensing and tightening
  Controlling the listener; encompassing and frightening.
Speak out and acknowledge — all must be clear.
  Imitation and pretense are valueless here.

Time stirring and jetting, knotting a course.
  Oh, recognized balancer of delight and remorse.
Time throbbing and breathing, expanding with fear.
  Oh, dominating scythe, suffocating seer!
Loosen your limits, allow space to seep in
  With faith and hope set a course to win.

Dreams sailing and gliding, drifting to earth
  Tickling and teasing, giggling with mirth.
Dreams skipping, playing, ignoring the rules
  Entangling and twisting, tightening its tools
Mingle, congeal, cement, my friends,
  Prove to the dubious our ingredients blend.

Noreen J. Rooney

Seasons Of Dryness

Seasons of dryness in a soul
Wandering aimlessly without any goal
Almost without any desires to share
Maybe, it is the absence of someone who would care

Going through the motions of living every day
Wondering if there is another delay
To something grand that could begin
But, hope is becoming pretty thin

Wanting so much more but not knowing what
Knowing that life is now in a rut
Hoping the answer is on the way
Attempting to keep indifference at bay

Waiting and waiting but not knowing for what
Promises from heaven but the door seems shut
Only God knows what is going on
It seems interest is almost dead and gone

The only hope that remains in a heart
Is that God will give life a new start
But, as for now, a soul can only wait
While life and dreams hesitate.

Vicki Hilton Brown

Hope

We call ourselves adults and believe it to be true
Wanting to be respected is an old desire, nothing new
However, sometimes being an adult is only a disguise
Worn by less deserving, often more pretentious than wise

Sometimes what was lacking in our childhood shows through
In rearing our babies, through them our dreams can still come true
Children need an example, but a life of their own to live
With nourishment and guidance we all have so much to give

When one starts living through oneself, an example can be set
Let others do the same and reach for goals that can be met
Time to take responsibility for our actions and point our finger less
Then hope will become an eraser and wipe out all the worldly mess

Kay Coop

In My Mind

In my mind I've kissed your lips at thousand times,
Wanting to kiss them a thousand more.
Passion and desire surge from each;
Emotions which extend from my love for you.

We pause for only a moment,
While looking into each other's eyes.
Still holding onto the passion;
Still holding you in my arms.

A smile forms on my face as you tell me you love me.
You smile as I tell you I feel the same.
We tell each other we will be together forever;
Swearing never to leave each others side.

My smile slowly disappears as do you.
I close my eyes as my head hangs low.
Tears begin to form, reality has come into play.
All this was just a dream; only true in my mind.

Norbert Velazquez

My Love For You

My love for you is like a summer's day,
Warming me from head to toe.
Or maybe it's like a shooting star
That sets the night a glow.

Perhaps it is a bright blue flame
That burns indefinitely.
My love has no beginning, no end,
It lasts eternally.

The way your face lights up the night
I want to tell you but I might
Reveal my feelings to you.
Still there is one thing that remains true.

There is nothing in this world that can compare
To the love I have for you.

Tom Brightman

The Lost Friend

I had a friend
We were as close as sisters
Then she met Michael
I was happy for her at first
But then she acted as if I didn't exist
I have told her how I felt
But it didn't help
Now they're engaged
I feel as if I have lost her forever
Please friend, come back to me. I miss you.

Penny Mercer

Edgar Allen Poe

Edgar Allen Poe,
was at times a morbid man.
When his feelings ran deep,
they spread out wide, like a great giant fan.
Then with pen and paper he would write,
sometimes 'til late, sometimes past midnight.
Let no one ever put his name down,
for to me he was a king, complete with crown.
Not of land or sea, with ships in motion,
but of intense thoughts, feelings, and emotions.
I cannot explain why he wrote like this,
I only know it gives me exuberant bliss.
He had a talent rare and he is my idol,
his works and his writings are my Bible.
He is famous in name and in heart,
his was a mysterious and emotional art.
His name and works forever linger on,
I can only hope that mine will, when I am gone.

Nancy E. Tolley

Always There

When my husband passed away, my future
was so dim; I felt my life was listless
to go on without him.
No one but I would ever know that half
my soul was gone; no one would see my
heart ache or feel the pain as long.
But mother, as she always done, was
standing there by me; her strength would
never vary, as everyone could see.
She's always tried to give me hope and
shield me from each pain; always willing
to give her all, never expecting gain.
I know today's her birthday, a day she
should be glad; but how can she be happy
when her only child is sad.
I wish I could erase the pain that she
now feels for me, and she could celebrate
her birthday with happiness and glee.
Mother is just a word they say, for one who gives us birth;
but she deserves all happiness that can be found on earth.

Nancy Calhoun-Medlock

Days With You

I can see my life slipping away,
Watching as I slide through one more day.
I wish the hours would creep but they go so fast,
Before I know it my present becomes past.

My yesterday was spent dreaming of you,
Enjoying the moments, the feelings so new.
My heartbeat quickens, a smile crosses my face,
Your arms hold me tight in just the right place.

My today was spent wanting you near,
To laugh with and cry with, my fears disappear.
I remember the time when we needed no words,
We spoke with our hearts, our actions were heard.

My tomorrow will be spent needing your love,
A gift most precious, sent from above.
Caring for you deeply, longing for your touch,
As time quickly passes, I miss you so much.

My days with you are so few and far,
I look to the sky to wish on a star.
Your todays and tomorrows are my silver and gold,
That I wish to have and always to hold.

Kathryne S. Allen

Mars In Flight

Puffs to sail and soar its height,
Wave abound its wingless flight.
Moments to be and love revealed,
Shores distant, across drifting hills.
Soft and sweet the sounds, seem to be,
Wondering channels that senses and sees,
Swiveling hearts, entwined in the glow,
Lights the yearning all hearts know.
Knowledge floats out the window
while emotions remain;
And cosmic beams delight the name,
Choices defined and gathered to conceal;
Enchanting melodies, serenade the deal,
Because, with lights to guide them, and
warmth to hide them, rights to shelter
them, and trials to define, and make them,
Life's promise is surely eternal

P.M. Graham

Soundless Sounds

Coming of day break-
Waves leaving the shore.

Darkness of night - the lightning of Stars
Sky meeting the horizon.
The falling of a tear drop
The breaking of a heart
Breaking of a promise - going back on your word
Hurting of someone's feelings - with words left unsaid

The silence when you find out how lonely alone can be.
Thinking of thoughts never brought forth to say
The last goodbye that was too late.

A hug or caress that could have meant so much more
The look in your eyes when you went out the door.

Miriam Burker

A Dedication To A Grandfather
Who Was Loved To No End

We're all wondering why,
We all have to say goodbye
To someone so great; the thought just makes us cry.
He'd do anything for you and I,
No matter who, what, when, where, or why
His memories were all great ones
And they'll never be forgotten.
Everybody loved him; and he loved you too
Especially his Munckin and his Sweethearts
And of course his friends too.
Nobody will ever forget him
And he'll never forget us
I'll never forget when he promised to be there he was, proud as
he ever could be.
He always did special things with everyone he knew
Everyone was special to him, especially you and I
So promise him never to let his special and great memories die
We love you and we'll miss you...
Unfortunately, this is goodbye.

Nicole Tibbs

What Have We Become?

In this current day and age,
  We are defined as imposter or mage.
  There is no median inbetween,
  Only two sides to an extreme.

Justice has no tolerance with crime as a whole,
  But the crimes go unpunished due to a
  technical loop-hole.

Corruption poisons our delegates eyes,
  And all their wrong-doings are cloaked
  in disguise.

The rights of our society have been twisted
  astray,
  That which is legal tomorrow may not
  be legal today.

Hope still lingers in the mist of our past.
  But the teachings of old are fleeting
  fast.

The question is coming, "What have we done?"
  But the answer is a reflection," Look at the
  race we've run."

  Trav Hill

Who Are You - - -

Who are you - - - I would like to know
We are different each day as we grow

Life's experiences mold us uniquely each day
And we are reminded of what acquaintances did say

Who are you - - - I would like to know
Knowing you will help both of us grow

Our learnings are the keys to success
Sharing what you know will make us the best

Who am I - - - I would like you to know
Listen and we both will grow

Share what you know about yourself and life
This will help other people make it through life

Who am I - - - I would like you to know
I am your friend and not your foe

Life's journey takes us down many trails
I was there when you thought you had failed

Who am I - - - I am you
Share who we are and we will be true

  Linda Taylor

The Splendid Building

Down twelve miles of highway, each side lined with stately trees,
we begin our descent towards church each Sunday Morning.

For it is a tranquil place where we love to go and commune in
beauty and purity. Its doors symbolize open arms that summon
the desperate, the recluse, the weary, the content, all can enter.
Some for solace, some in joy, and some for restoration.

Its steeple, magnificent and lofty; an emblem of life, truth and
love. The windows lighted; etched and stained in beauty; each
framed window glass an allegory. For these stories seem to heal
the deepest wounds. Yes, the doors that swing open, the steeple
that beckons and the windows that narrate the lessons, they all
make the splendid building a beloved sanctuary.

  Laura Goodman

The Birthday

A special day a special date, it's a birthday that
  we celebrate.
We will celebrate for years to come, but neglect to
  remember where we've come from.
If we could remember that special day, I wonder what
  things we would like to say.
I remember my head was sticking outside, when a man
  in a mask shook my head from side to side.
Then he turned me upside down, hanging by my feet,
and he hit me on my bottom and I began to weep.
Then he took a little ball, and stuck it in my nose,
and he was yelling, "It's a baby boy", then he
  counted all my toes.
So this is the world, I don't think I want to stay,
but then he put me in my mothers arms and it all
  became okay.
So if you can remember, just the way I do, then that
  tiny little baby, most probably
    was you.

  Richard Aloy

Looking Back

On the 12th of the 8th in the year double four
we couldn't even dream of fifty or more.
Yet here we are looking back on our life
for together we stayed through joy and through strife.

It wasn't a year and we had our first-born
a little man-child who our lives would adorn.
The youngster was born as red as a beet
we thought that an Indian had danced at our feet.

In another 6 years our second came 'round
enhancing our lives by a leap and a bound.
A good-natured young son who kept us so busy
with his running around and acting so dizzy.

13 years more and our daughter would be here
with her fairness and solace being so dear.
A lovely young girl with wings on her feet
rambunctious in nature but yet very sweet.

Our family has grown and not come apart
keeping us happy with kids dear to heart.
Our children have children as listed below
and we hope that the list continues to grow.

Happy 50th Anniversary
Wayne, Dee, Don, Shalai, Kevin, Diane, Stacy,
Chris, Dave, Susan, Tommy, Mike, Ashley

  Wayne E. Brenneman

Demise

Mother's death was our first experience with grief.
We dared not weep
Lest we join the wailing of the elders.
A few years later, father died.
The bulwarks were gone
and we would stray.
Since then a sister and brother have gone.
The remaining few accept the loss.
Bitterness we felt when death was new
has been cushioned by its recurrence.
Parental loss is much too great
to keep the siblings in a flock.
As a family lessens - so does its unity
and we become strangers
to be remembered on Christmas and birthdays....

  Paul Alicakos

Water Me...See Me Grow

You two followed me, through my life.
We drove through the smoothest roads,
and made it through the toughest hills.
You planted me, to present myself to the world.

Over the hot dry summer days,
you cooled me with your soothing words.
Through the chilly cold days, you warmed me with your heart.
Don't forget beating the strong snowy winter days,
you covered me like a blanket.
You watered me, and watched me grow.

I would have never forgotten the arguments,
and how we would fight over the strangest things,
but you always came up with the greatest solutions.
And if it weren't for you,
all the math problems would have been unsolved mysteries.
You gave me sunlight, to guide me through.

After all these years, of your generosity and soul,
thank you, is the most I can do.
A green-leafed plant myself,
would have never been green without you.

  Yue Xu

A 2,000 Year Old Thought

From a time of born, out across the sands
We erase our minds to the past, it travels within our hands
Only forgetting to the present, what we've tried not to remember
carrying a book of prophecies, withstanding time like an ember
So then hindsight must be learned, having had sinned, and
  questioning it too late
And why then are we living the torture, as people did during a
  past ethereal inquisition of fate
Not thinking about the future, it being 2,000 years like a chime
For whatever its worth, it's come in on the four winds of time
So looking into the future, gazing up upon a star
Could we see tomorrow whence, not knowing thence from hence,
  or how far

  Paul Bowman

Untitled

This morning the dawn poured a brilliant purple along the east.
We gazed, dazed in astonishment, through the lattice of hard-limbed
  oaks,
Through the twisted twiggeries of hickories, maples, pines.
We saw the wind tear the trembling trees and we heard its roaring
And the sound of its soaring, bearing the spark of an unseen sun.
On dark tides of the undulant sky, like crossed timbers of driftwood
Tossed a toy airplane toward the ragged beaches of the west.

The purple flushed, blushing with an orange mantled crest,
Flooding the hilltop woodland with a foaming copper haze.
When the horizon kindled clouds with pink and rose red flames
Then crowds of blackbirds swooped, scattering the debris of dawn;
Some sleepy sentinel of light pulled the covers off the night.
The sun blinked, hesitant, over the forest's dark vignette.
A lonely car chugged up the hillside road.

  Will Pigot

Paradise Lost

Paradise lost, Paradise found
  What has become of this madness we call the human race?
Paradise, no such thing ugliness and hatred will
  soon follow thee.
Fellow teachers, fellow friends show us the way
  for I cannot say.
Where will paradise begin and unhappiness end?

  Katie Weiderman

For My Late Husband

When we first met, we fell in love.
We had our ups and our downs.
God gave us the strength to come through it.
Then we married and promised to love one another forever.
You had always said you would never leave me.
But God came and took you away from me forever.
I still can't believe that you are
gone from my life for now and always.
But please know that I forgive and understand.
You were the most important person to me.
And I will always remain your wife forever.
Times are hard for me to go ahead.
But thanks to family and friends.
That help me get through a broken heart.
One day we will meet in heaven again.
And begin our lives all over.
We will then have all the joys and happiness we had before.
For us there will never be an ending.

  Rosina Paolicelli

Maze Of Time

Time enhances the labyrinth of life
We must travel the winding roads without direction
Hoping to turn the right way without a barricade
Expecting to endure all obstacles without complete failure
Praying not to accept the fools gold
And be banished from eternal freedom
To take the lighted path to happiness without remorse

For the everlasting will allow those who laugh
To bellow without hesitation

But time stalls us in the maze
Every doubt keeps us further away
Accepted temptation leaves us with punishment

Your heart is the chain
Your love is the key
Thus enabling you to bare the burden of the test

Alas
The reward
The golden crystal traveling in the hour glass

  Patrice Miller

Children Of The Forest

Once upon a time the forest was a happy place,
We played games, and, we had picnics there.

Then the clouds came - so quickly -
with a thickness and gloom beyond description.

The deafening thunder of guns
Permeated the peaceful rustle of the trees.
Screams of pain replaced the chirping of the birds.
Mass graves replaced picnic blankets and laughter.

Then silence presided once more
Over the desecrated forests.
Broken only by the hushed whispers of
Children's voices, and the rustling movement of branches in the
  shadows.

We own the forest now, we children.
Children only in name,
For we are children no more.
Our childhood was stolen,
Murdered with our families.

The friendly forest - our shelter,
Our home, our playground and our cemetery.

  L. Lilo Cohn

All Through The Years

All through the years as we come and go,
We think of life as going too slow but when you reach
the ripe old age of 71, you sorrowfully wish life had just begun.

We realize by now we can't change life
Although we've experienced a whole lot of strife.

There again, is the way life is, so
Enjoy each day as much as you can.

Not our decision but above it is his,
So weep not for mistakes and don't
Shed tears as that's the way life is,

For those who put thorns in our daily living,
Be ever and always kind and forgiving.

It pays much more than silver and gold
To stay with the Lord for blessings untold.

He will guide and direct us in all that we do.
To him always we should ever be true.

So always remember and never forget
The Lord our Saviour is the best friend we've met.

He will never forsake us in times of need
If only we have the faith of a Mustard seed.

Virginia Glenn Bris-sett Howerton

A Crown for Mama

Today I crown you Mother
Wear it for all you've done
It's from all your children
Your daughters and your sons

Each diamond represents mother
The years we've had with you
But first let us say mother
Just how much we love you

For when I sneezed my nose was wiped
You chased the monsters out my room at night
You cooked, ironed and never complained
And today we're here to honor your name

Secondly your grands were born
You nursed them like they were your own
Mothers are the strongest beings on earth
And aging just generates them new birth
This crown's like a halo around your greying hair
And no else could wear it so well

Nettie R. Geiger

Prairie Dog Town

Prairie grass blowing in the wind
Weaving, waving their message to send
Prairie dog stands on a mound of dirt
Looking so fat, slick and pert
Out on the wind he sends his bark
Calling for a mate to come for a lark
Over the wind they hear his call
Brother, friend, cousin and all
So many they come like a day in the park
They play all day and long after dark
Soon there will be pupletts all over the ground
And they will romp and play with a joyful sound
Next year they will be grown
With a new message to send
Over the grasses that weave and wave in the wind

Lillian E. Payton

If We Were...

If we were running the WHITE HOUSE, Mrs. President and First Man;
We'd raise many eyebrows as we went about our plan.

After about a day or two, the mister would declare;
Going to paint this old house blue and make the Oval office square.

Well into week number three, and paint can number twenty-one;
Suddenly he'd say that's enough for me, don't worry I'll get it done.

Leaving scaffolds hanging high, with paint brushes all askew;
Into the half white house he'd stride saying now what will I do.

Afraid to think what he's going to do next, I decide to set out and explore;
With presidential authority to flex, I ask, James, take me to the store.

But ma'am, says James, his eyes so wide, you can't as the nation's chief;
James, just take me to the store for the ride, I want to know where's the beef.

Into the market we go in D.C.. with my agents all about;
Love to shop in the A & P, as Mrs. Pres., it'll be fun no doubt.

With the men and I each taking a cart, up the aisle we all do walk;
Let the people know we do have heart, as I stop with them to talk.

Me in the White House is just a dream, ever so far fetched/
Great excitement it would seem, more than working in the luncheonette.

Phyllis Chartier

Truckers Lament

Worked hard all week and made lots of miles;
Went to the Post Office and came out all smiles.

'Cause there was enough to pay salaries and bills;
Even paid myself a little, and paid for my pills.

And after all that there was a little left over;
It began to look like I was in clover.

So I relaxed Friday Night, and then came the call -
"I'm broke down at the airport, she won't back up at all."

"And I didn't get unloaded, so I need another truck."
There's no one to go but me, ain't that just my luck?

So this question haunts me and fills me with dread.
How does a blasted truck know when I get a few bucks ahead.

And how to adjust so that what's broke or bent,
Will wind up costing my very last cent!

Robert C. Loyd

Ode To My Husband, Paul

My husband is a rockhound and he likes all kinds of rocks.
We've brought them home for thirty years and put them in a box,
Or on a shelf, or in a case, or even in a pile,
Which kept our little acreage very much in style.

With nature all around us, a tree, a rock, some dirt;
And in the wash sometimes I'd find rock dust upon a shirt.
He polished some, he displayed some, he traded even more
Until the garage was lined with rocks, with room just on the floor.

I never thought I'd see the day, he'd give the rocks away,
But since we're moving out of town he had to find some way
To keep the weight down when the movers came to load
The treasures we have gathered as we traveled down the road.

So he began to sort and pitch and pack and say to friends,
"Please take a rock to remember that our friendship never ends."
Neighbors on the corner hauled yard rock by the pounds
The University geology club took much right off the grounds.

And rockhounds right and left were delighted with their find,
As they chose the one just right for them, one of another kind.
So even though the piles are less, the boxes not so high,
He'll always like the rocks as much as he does coconut pie.

603   *Margaret Good*

Once Again

Once again...
We've misinterpreted our words,
We've misjudged the gentleness,
We've misread the smiles,
    Both of us confused, perhaps so wanting
        the notion of two being one.
We were excited, needing so much
    to entwine our lives,
        our families, our home, our work in one.
It's become overwhelming
    NOW...our soft spoken words,
        our caring love, our touch
    slowly beginning to diminish,
        turning our hearts upside down
            into a world of cold darkness.
May the fate of our love
    be strong enough to prevail,
        this journey through darkness
            until the rays of sunlight
                reach our hearts and warm our lives... ONCE AGAIN.

Melanie B. Starkman

What Is My Place

As I run this race... I really don't know my place,
  what are my boundaries... what is my space.
Should I slow my pace... am I allowed to get in my children's face,
For them I have tried to keep a solid home base,
  and to be there for them... just in case.
There was something that I could help them to face,
  but should I give them more space...
  do I need to be their ace...what is my place?

Being a parent really takes a toll,
  so if I think I can see what is up the road...
  and feel I know that the future holds...
  can I be straight forward and bold...
  do they need by me... to be told?

Am I allowed to scold... do I still have the right... to try to mold
  or do I need to loosen my hold?
When do I let my children leave the fold
  at what point... is being a parent stole...
  I'm standing... out here in the cold..
  and I really don't know my role... what is my place?

Virdajean Towns-Collins

Toys

When Jesus was a little boy
What did He play with, what kind of toy?
Did He make things out of wood
Shaping and building as best He could?
Did He play games with pebbles and stones
Or use the jugs to make musical tones?
Did He make statues out of clay?
Did He make pillows out of hay?
Did He use a stick to draw in the sand?
Did He hold the fireflies in His hand?
Did He call up echoes at the water well?
Did He gather up every pretty shell?
Did He climb up high on the tallest tree?
Did He ride on His father's little grey donkey?
Did He have his very own little pet?
Did He catch lots of fish with a fishing net?
Yes, I'm sure He played with all these things,
Such simple toys for the King of Kings.

Theresa Magnani

The Onyx Man

Young black male, what is your dream
What does your future hold
All your life is this what it is to be
Hassled by someone so ignorant and bold

You were beaten for what
The marks I see, there for show
Your eyes are black, your back was scratched
But when will the answers be told

White people their prejudices and insecurities
They hold the power, have the control
Why must you suffer and endure
The prejudices just because you're a black man

I never understood the plight of the black man
I could never walk in your shoes
I can never feel the injustices
I could never be you, the black man

Lynn Mac Paintsil

Intimate Strangers

My heart will never tell, cannot tell
what I am truly feeling inside for you.
We'll just live in our dream world.

Someday you may find the reality of that world.
It's exciting you don't know, yet sad
that the imaginary you and I
are the only ones that can ever be.

Oh, to take a walk with you in the rain!
The lights reflecting somewhat distorted on the pavement

None of this is real; not in this lifetime can it ever be.
We will remain strangers.
Intimate strangers with the same dream.

Tomorrow will never come.
Not the tomorrow we silently and so desperately await.

I hold you tightly, and pray that the world will go away,
letting us have just one night together.

Not until then can I let go of this ludicrous hope.
Under a blanket of stars we lay, together
Knowing this isn't real.

Karen S. Petrofsky

Vital Questions Of Our Time

Answers to the vital questions of our time...
What is it in the twittering and singing of the afternoon
birds so sublime?
What is it in the nectar that flows from you to me that
tranquils time?
Is it our garden we create in the tangle of limbs, yours and mine?
Was each of us, before the dawning of our time, withering on
a greying vine?
And do we, in the music of each caress, from a driven world digress?
And when we are breast to breast, breath to breath, essence
to essence, is it truth revealed or loneliness concealed?

When the singing birds stop to sleep, will we two pause and weep?
With the languorous rays of winter sun departed,
do we make sure our garden has been started?

And when we are the dear, dear departed, will we have locked
in our heavenward gaze an answer to the phrase, "Do you love me?"

These, are the vital questions... And when time is
complete, and the last star fallen in to its core, will we
two meet to discuss them more?

Rena Patton

Impossible Dream

What is a rose without thorns?
What is love without pain?
I live and I die at the same time
I live for the life your existence gives to me
I die because your loving presence is not here with me.
To live and to die, how ironic!
Our love is an impossible dream
a whole world separates us
condemning our love, but, Oh love!
There is so much joy in loving you
and there is so much pain in not having you
I cannot longer say which one is deeper
in loving you my whole being is uplifted
not having you is a torment burning my soul for my longing.
If our love is not destined to bloom in this garden
Hurry up, my Lord, fast forward the wheel of time
so my beloved and I can be together in the Eternal
beyond the stars, beyond time, together at last!
Where there are no more bridges
Oh, my sweet love, my twin soul, the greatest love of my life!!

Reina

The System

The system, the system, the system
What system may I ask?
The judicial system.
Is it fair for the human race,
or is it only for the white man's race.

Give us a break, wake up America
Do not be a disgrace upon the human race.
I have been watching,
the world is watching the picture we see,
is not very nice.

We the people have to stop this
or it will only get worst.
Wake up America, and stop this
nonsense before it's too late!

R. George Mellard

Quakes Of L. A. Valley

As I awoke and walked to my window to see,
What the day that's beginning is about to be.
The sky is clear, the sun is shining.
Below in the valley, the traffic is winding
Another beautiful, wonderful day,
As the birds and small animals scurry away.
Frightened by a hawk soaring high in the sky.
Circling around by the mountains so high.
As I look out over the trees of green
Everything seems peaceful and very serene.
But tell me old earth with beauty to end all.
Will it be here tomorrow or part of it fall.
Or could it tomorrow, when I awake
Start to rumble and move and shake.
The beautiful valley of mountains and lakes.
Are frightening and scary with your many earthquakes.
People, animals, birds and all run,
Everything feels like we are all done.
But I guess in our fright, we all do survive
You've done it before and we're still alive.

Scarlett Maglieri

Getting Over The Edge

In the moment drugs seem so grand
What they do to your mind is what we can't understand
They get you over the edge into kind of a euphoric feeling
But the next day you still have to face your problems
in a bigger way
Escaping is not the answer in the long run
Because you always have to wake up to yourself
Go within and do the work - address the issues
Look them straight in the eyes - allow yourself the freedom to cry
It cleanses your soul and gives you the strength to be
who you really are -
The person you were meant to be.
We are all here to teach each other to love ourselves
and give love freely
Getting over the edge is not a reason to escape -
It's a sign to keep growing
and to realize there's something wrong
Call a friend who cares and let it all out.
You will then have a natural high - a sense of well being
And you'll know why!

Sherry Stearn

Tim:

Written for the passing of Tim Block.
If only we had one more conversation...
What we would say, but then we said it all
in the years that we were friends.

Oh, dear heart; what a life mine has become.
You always knew the right things to say.
I need just one more conversation with you.
I got your legacy of accepting Christ;
You knew I would make the right decision.

We never told each other, what to do.
I wish the phone would ring, like it use to on Sunday night.
Why didn't you tell me how sick you were?
You didn't bore me with all the fever talk-hospital talk.
You called me to laugh, you need to forget.
You needed to remember those funny times.

I panicked the night you died, I really didn't think I
would live-racing heart.

Spinning, twirling-truths spilling forth.
You would have said, "Get a grip."
And then you would have told me, "That's a step
in the right direction." Start living, you have a second chance.

Marla Orton

Going Home

The vicious cycle begins at birth.
When a death approaches
I see my self worth.

Death is a mystery and it's also a must,
to those left behind it shakes our trust.

"Why did you leave me?" I cry in despair.
I'm turned upside down, it doesn't seem fair.

I toss and turn and cry through the night.
"Why am I here?" I can't see the light.

In whispers unnoticed I hear in my heart,
"Please don't give up, you must do your part."

Time is a healer I have often heard.
The struggle seems lighter as I take God's word.

Alas the cloud lifts as I hear you say,
"That wasn't my home, I was not meant to stay."

For death is no enemy, he's a friend - you see -
He carries us over to where we're all meant to be.

Kathy Holguin

"It Ends"

It is the time
When all other senses fail
The only thing that comes to mind
Is the great time I had last Saturday night
and how the smile lit up his face
When I told him so.
Life is filled with sweet caresses,
and whispered thoughts
That are held so close to the heart.
The only time reality shows itself
is those few moments that are spent apart.
But then it ends.
Without reason,
Or at least it seems
Without reason.
Those old memories and tender thoughts
are held even closer to the heart.
Hate exists.....but under the hate,
Love still holds true, not for him but for me.

Linda McClain

Winter Of Ninety-Four

Now I know what Shakespeare meant
when he wrote of the "Winter of Discontent".
But had he lived in ninety-four
he may have said a few things, and more!
As stop Damn Snow, Stop I Say,
try to appease the Gods some other way.
'stead of picks and shovels against
mountainous slopes, as we were mortals
just try to cope, and dig ourselves
from these mounds of cement,
let's pray for this winter of Discontent!

Rita H. Dolan

Roses And Memories

The last rose fell apart without warning
When I lightly touched its folds this morning.
The velvet petals fluttered to the ground
And scattered like pollen without a sound.
I remembered then last autumn when
We cut the last rose together,
And how each of us kissed the heart of it,
At the same moment vowing
To be in the garden by next fall
To find the last rose left upon the bush.
But time is never sentimental like roses
And the scattered petals that I tramp on now
Are my hopes of other autumns.

Paul Monroe

I Love Being Their Mother

With five beautiful daughters and one precious son,
When I open my eyes in the morning, my day's work begun.
I drove them here and took them there and
    never once complained
I knew I was a winner and had so much to gain.
God gave me strength and patience
    and I kept a tranquil mind
When I look at my children, I just
    burst with pride.
No other job on this earth, can compare to
    being a mother.
To know God trusted you, to raise his children
    and to love one another.
Now they are grown, some have children of
    their own and I look at them and think
I can't see them enough or do enough cause,
    I Love Being Their Mother

Rita Cottrell Weissenburger

The Search

The search for love has given me tears.
When I put aside my fears
Some things in life are so far, and so near.
When I find my love, I will keep her as a queen.
I don't know how much pain I can bear
Love is such a thing, it has wings.
I don't know what it takes and brings.
I know it will be some wonderful things.

Tarun Bhardwaj

A Mother's Growing Questions

Wasn't it just yesterday
When I taught them how to pray?

Wasn't it just last week
When they were playing in the creek?

Wasn't it just last year
When they were so little and Oh! so dear?

That's how I remember it today
And when I look at them, I say,

"My! You've grown so big..so strong
Where have all those growing years gone"?

Two little boys...born two years apart
The pride and joy of a young mother's heart

Dreams and fears...laughter and tears
All were looked after...in those growing years

Those two little boys are now all grown
Have wed and are raising families of their own

They teach their children as I taught them
To pray, to laugh, to be a friend

But wasn't it just yesterday when I taught them how to pray?

Wasn't it just last week when they were playing in the creek?...

Patti Ann Griffin

"I'll Think Of You"

When I see the first violet of the spring,
When I walk the trails and see everything
We planted, we cared for, and grew,
    Then I'll think of you.

When the dogwood blooms in white array.
And the redbud bursts forth at the dawn of day,
And all the flowers sparkle with dew
    Then I'll think of you.

When the autumn leaves begin to fall,
And I hear the wild geese give their call
As they fly against the sky so blue,
    Then I'll think of you.

When the first snowflakes come floating down
Covering the earth with its soft white gown
Making the tracks of the animals so true,
    Then I'll think of you.

Each night when I see the Evening star
Shining in the West, so very far,
I'll say a prayer, one I hope will come true,
Someday, my love, I'll be there with you.

Ruth T. George

Blue Plastic

How do you reach out in a superficial world
   When it's all you can do to survive
What do you do when you need a shoulder
   That you don't understand why you're alive
What happens when you can't seem to belong
   When your backyard is an alien place
What is there to say when no one will listen
   And words vanish without a trace
Where is love when there's no compassion
   When you are down and in everybody's way
Which way is ahead when there's no direction
   And you're lost when night blends into day
How do you rebuild when your world has crumbled
   When you have lost the ground that you needed
Why is it wrong to love and to be loved
   Why is desire the only thing heeded
How do you reach out in a cellophane world
   When self destruction is posh and not sick
I still want to tell you I need you and love you
   But you won't hear me through blue plastic

   Shirley Bolstok

Dreams

Imagination is the true elixir of life
When mixed together with faith and hope
All things become possible to any child

Our task is to challenge what we already know
Discover the thought that lies deep within our hearts
And pass on to all the children with whom we meet
The ability to let them believe in their dreams

For we are The Merchants Of Dreams
Bringing to life within four walls of darkness
An experience so elusive, so magical yet seemingly so real
A journey that is etched indelibly into all lifetimes.

For Dreams should not be taken to Heaven."

   Lynton V. Harris

About My Mother

She has this quiet strength that cannot be altered,
When she makes a decision, it won't be faltered.
She holds amazing beauty that just increases with the years,
She has a way about her that erases my doubts and fears.
She has always been there, waiting for my call,
When I least deserved it, she gave me her all.
She is the one I look up to, I know she doesn't know her worth,
I love her more than life itself, the one
who gave me birth, my mother, my friend,
the most beautiful lady on earth.

   Patricia Coffman

"Sleep"

In the mist of the night
When the moon becomes the light

The grass talk to the flowers
The trees breathe from underneath

There is a smell in the air of life
The unknown has set out in flight

The wild has found a place to rest
A mother just gave birth in her nest

The wind is shifting to the east
Many are dying in the street

If I wake up will I still be here
When I wake up will someone still care

If last night was just a smell of fresh air
Then I feel my needs are out there somewhere

   Rebecca Roby

Doe

She watched from the outside,
When she saw the herd around her,
And watched her own expressionless face,
Her gashed heart, that was black and bleeding.
The herd looked upon her,
The single doe in the meadow,
A single flower in a desert.
And the herd gazed lustfully,
And moved in on the doe, pursuing her like prey.
And the doe laughed, at their ignorance,
And cried, at their blindness.
The blind herd circled round her,
And stroked her silky coat.
And finally saw inside her.
Her black heart, almost motionless.
And bleeding.
And they backed away,
Mortified to see the blood,
Flowing from her heart,
Onto the meadow.

   Sarah G. Ambrose

Homeless

A homeless man; how can this be,
When the creator gave the whole world to me?
As a homeless man, I have no worth,
But a homeless king was born onto earth.

As a homeless man the world,
Would rather leave me alone.
But earth is just a dwelling,
And really no man's home.

Just a place until we're reborn,
And from our heart evil is torn.
For heaven is our home beyond this life, you see.
So who is really homeless, is it you or me?

From the hurt in my heart,
And the spirit of my Lord.
Help me, my brother,
To see life abroad.

In The Spirit
Time 2:45 am
Date 6-9-93

   Randy Vincent Hall I

The Heart of a Fair Beats Swift and Free

Magical picture books spring to life
When the raging turmoil of life leads you
to this gripping and intense world.
   The realm of childhood dreams.
Many dangers to take your breath away
where migrating clouds sweep the horizons
of dense woodlands filled with ancient
clear creeks of pebble. The brave and
gallant hero who brings you love,
romance, and suspense. Flowers of
exotic scent. Raging rivers and great
wars brought by kings and queens while
storms of mist curtain the plains. Stars
and blackness surge the skies opening
wide with slow deliberance. Wild
yet cunningly. Compacted tranquility.
Listen! The wind... there is always,
the wind...

   Natasha Ondarza

Spring

Spring is the awakening time of the year
When the sun becomes warm without any fear
The crocus have lifted their sleepy heads
As if nudged from their winter beds
The pussy willows begin to purr
And the buds on the trees begin to appear
As if given a sign from Heaven above
Like a door pushed open with a gentle shove
Birds are a twitter, their nests to be made
In a tree where soon will be shade
Folks in their yards are friendly and nice
The world has suddenly become a Paradise.

Marjorie L. Nadin

Beauty Of The Whole World!

Sweet things are beautiful.
When the sunlight strikes the
    apple of your eye,
You'll feel the beauty of the whole world.

Sweet things are beautiful.
When the moon in the sky starts
    smiling at you,
You'll feel the whole world twinkling its
    eyes to you.

Sweet things are beautiful.
When the snow starts falling down,
You'll feel that you're also falling down
    with the snow.

Sweet things are beautiful .
When the whole world looks green
    and white,
You'll feel - this is the solution of
    the FUTURE!!!

Keziah P. Chacko

My Perfect Child

As my children were born, I wanted them to be perfect.
When they were babies, I wanted them to smile
And be content playing with their toys.

I wanted them to be happy and to laugh continually,
Instead of crying and being demanding.
I wanted them to see the beautiful side of life.

As they grew older, I wanted them to be giving instead of selfish.
I wanted them to skip the terrible twos.
I wanted them to stay innocent forever.

As they become teenagers, I wanted them to be obedient and not rebellious,
Mannerly and not mouthy.
I wanted them to be full of love, gentle, and kind hearted.

"Oh God, give me a child like this," was often my prayer.
One day He did.
Some call her handicapped... I call her perfect!

Valerie J. Geary

Vacant Room

Trophies scattering a vacant room,
Where pain and loneliness had once loomed.
Poems were written, pictures drew,
writhing in anguish as only he knew.
A talented kid who was distraught,
a gun in possession, easily bought.
Crucify his pain is what he thought.
Bloodied trophies scattered a deserted room.

Kris Torkelson

"Heart In Bondage"

My soul became a slave to your heart
When this feeling came over me, I never want to part.
Handcuffed to you by sheer desire
The blaze is burning, my soul's on fire.

I'm tied to you by chains so sweet
My heart is open for you to greet.
The chains may tarnish, but never break
For to be bound to you would cure my heartache.

You'll crack the whips that sting my skin
The pain, you'll learn, is deep within.
I'll surrender all my love to you
I'll give up, give in, if that's what I must do.

The ropes you use will keep me true
There is a master and he is you
The rope will forever wrap around my soul
For your heart is my target yet not the goal.

The shackles surround me above and below
You've captured my heart, it will never let go.
My heart's in bondage and you are the key
Don't open the lock, never set me free.

Marjorie Stelmack

Untitled

Life is like a movie,
When you have a bad day
There is a nurse in the hallway

Live one day at a time
There is no other way - It's not a crime.

Some say I am full of hate
Then why am I never late at the gate
The fastest way is no way
So come out of the closet and say: "I'm gay"

Some say that I am
I don't give a damn
I don't want to live forever
Even though we are not together
I will wander alone - forever.

Lloyd L. Sowles

A Mother's Day Poem From Heaven

I remember a time not long ago
When you hugged me and held me so tight
And you didn't complain or get mad at me
When I kept you up all through the night.

You fed me and changed me and gave me a bath
And played with my fingers and toes.
You told me you loved me and Jesus did too
As you dressed me in cute little clothes.

Now I have left the world far behind
And I'm praising in glory above
In the presence of God and His Son our Lord
The Creator of true, perfect love.

My time with you was so short, it seems,
And I can't wait to see you again
When you come to Heaven after this life is through
I know I will be with you then.

When my brothers and sisters all come along,
What a glorious time it will be.
I know you will be the most wonderful mom,
As terrific as you were with me.

Paul J. Soos (& Josiah)

608

When Will You Know

When will you know old age is creeping on?
When your get up and go has gotten up and gone.

When you can't stand the kids' squeals and laughter
When you go into a room and say "Lord, help me to know what
 I'm here after."

When you go to the mailbox and stop half way down the road
When you remember the grass mowin and the taters need hoed

When you sit down to watch TV and hear the world news
And you wake when it's over from a relaxing snooze.

When you bite into a steak sandwich whether well done or rare
And when you take it from your mouth your teeth remain there.

When your wig is on the bed post and your teeth are in a cup
And when it gets harder each day for you to get up.

When arthritis has set in and affects every joint.
And you whisper, "Oh, Lord, what is the point"?

When you meet with your friends and tell your stories over and
 over again.
When the work piles up way past your chin.

You still love to meet people to visit and talk
Though some are like you they hardly can walk.

So for fun, food, and friendship, you can do like me
Join the local chapter of the A.A.R.P.

 Wayne Giacomo

Untitled

When the words of joy flow from the pen,
When your lips sing a song,
You will see him again;

When the sky has a rainbow,
When the flowers do bloom,
It will be him that enters the room.

When the river flows gently,
When the stars shine so bright,
The love in your eyes will be in his sight.

Let the gentle breeze lift your spirits,
Fill your soul with the sun,
His heart will belong to you,
When all this has been done.

 Kim Diane Dorsey

Zat Is Where I Was

In the flat world of Zat
where a friend and I sat
at the edge as we felt the sun's heat...
there the gravity pulls you up and not down,
so we sat on our head not our seat.

And the birds were all swimming.
The fish were all flying.
Your tears would evaporate
as you were crying.
(Now don't look at me as if I were lying!)

The world of Zat is a really cool place,
but they've cancelled most flights there
because of the space
that exists between earth and the city of Zat.
So, you probably never will sit where I sat!

 Sonja E. Patterson

Jesus Spared Their Lives

I heard my Savior traveled, to a wreck one winter day,
Where a Little Dodge Aries, had skid along the way.
When a mother and her daughter, were on their way back home,
And ice was on the highway, things started to go wrong.
The car approached the road, carrying laughs and joy inside.
No warning signs were flashing, to say danger was in this ride.
But after minutes passed, tragedy faced them eye to eye,
As the little Dodge Aries hit ice along the side.
The mother steered but lost control, and a Bronco came in sight.
The daughter called out mom, and reached to hold on tight.
I know they must have felt death had met them on this way
But Jesus rode beside them, and pushed that thought away.
He spared their lives this winter day, and I thank Him, yes I do.
For that daughter is my sister, and I'm that mother's daughter too.

 Karen Haley Wathen

Window To My Past

Up up on my tiptoes to reach and part the curtain over the window
where all my memories are stored
I see grandma in her colorful apron as she bakes cakes and pies
suddenly she stops and turns from her work
It seems as though she is thinking I'd better hurry because it
will soon be time for church
Grandma loved living things so she planted flowers and told me
how this one needs sun and the other needs shade
I didn't know and didn't really care but I was happy that grandma
had the knowledge and took the time to share
I see her with her well worn Bible in her hand
I can hear her gently saying read your Bible everyday
Because the solution to all of life's problems are only a chapter away
I can see grandma and I gliding back and forth in the front porch
swing where she'd tell me of her childhood and I'd ask all kinds
of things
As the curtain falls over this window I am reminded that I am
creating windows so that others who seek a warm memory may
stop and take a view.

 Vivian McCloud

I Took A Drive Today

My aging automobile led me to the countryside,
where every view danced of life!
The rolling hills revealed their prime -
orange, yellow, red.
Hues of an artists' pallet,
and I, the painter of dreams.
Horses trotting, wild flowers in bloom,
and the sweet scent of apples filled my air.
It was <u>my</u> air.
I drove as a queen;
looking, breathing, feeling...
the beauty of nature.
I long for the hills -
to recline, forget woes,
and love life.
I gathered plenty, yet not enough.
I must return, to share the glory.
Will you join me, friend?
Our journey will replenish your soul!

I took a drive today.

 Kathleen E. Gdula

609

The Heart Of Home

When life takes me away to places
  Where I have to be left out in the cold,
I reach inside myself for the warmth
  That I captured in the heart of home.

When sounds of laughter becomes forgotten
  And the feeling of caring becomes unknown,
I think back to the love and happiness
  That surrounded me in the heart of home.

When youthful vigor forsakes me
  And the wrinkles on my face describe me so,
I know it is time to nurture the seed
  That was planted within the heart of home.

Lorraine L. Terry

Serenity Of Life

Oh Dear Father, Take me back to the land where I belong
Where the skies are clear, no smog or pollution to fear...
Where the grass is green and the water is fresh and clean...
Take me back where there's no people standing on a corner fussing and
fighting to sell a drug no alleys to walk down to get mugged.

Take me back Oh Father, Take Me Back where the children can
run and play, and not duck or dodge in fear of that day.
Where there's no gangs waiting to kill another brother,
Who knows maybe yours sister, father or mother where...
Elders are respected and children are not neglected
When mothers stay out, sell their bodies.
Come home only to get rejected.

Take me back where I can live in peace.
Gather up My Community and have a feast.
Where I can live with humanity and not lose my sanity where...
My eyes won't be saddened when I see my brothers and sisters
who think they are free only to find out it's a conspiracy.

Oh Heavenly Father...
I live for that day when I can say I'm where I belong?
My native land, my home sweet home

Linda L. Phillips

Beggar Woman

She walks in the streets of indifference
where there is a covert concern for her bulging breast
but no reverence
for her bare body which is a roving jest

Her yielded nipples dry as a desert have no prospects of feed
for her baby's need
still she braves the burden of this world
silently unstirred

On her daily run for a penny from place to place
she is required to compromise her grace
that was given up for sheer survival
and *Zakat and **Ushar with their revival
haven't extended her what is her due
as her stew is shared by the few
who control its distribution
without caring for God's retribution.

And so with a sick surmise
I see the emptiness of her eyes
that tell a tale of poverty
without pricking anybody's sensitivity.

*Zakat is a compulsory contribution for charity at the rate of 2.5% by all Muslims in an Islamic State.
**Ushar is a levy of 10% on farm produce payable by all Muslims in an Islamic State.

Sikandar H. Khan

Our Children

When there is life, there is hope.
Where there is love, there is happiness.
Where there is dreams,
there is a chance.
Take away their dreams
you take their chance,
and hope to a better life.
Then there is no more love,
and then shall there be darkness.
Let them dream, believe in their thoughts.
  Have hope in them,
they are our future.
What becomes of them, is there
chance to succeed, to a better life.
Bring back the stars
for them to wish upon
And may we see a brighter day
in our children.

Susan Frank

The End

Everyday we get closer to death
whether it be 10 years or 20
A day has gone by,
A day taken away from our lives,
A day to mark off, subconsciously
counting down to the end.
So as I peer out yonder and look
at the melancholy sky, I feel its sorrow
For it hath had to watch over
our segregated world, our discriminating world;
Within this world we look down upon one another,
When Divinity is the only thing that
is above us.
So far from the end of this shrewd, cruel world
Yet nigh to our own ending.
This is why we ponder,
like a shadow creeping somberly
in the back of our minds
We stand alone, waiting, watching,
in awe, for the end.

Sarah Vasilas

"Sea Solace"

I love the Sea, I love the Sand, the Surf, the Sun and Moon
Whether it be at Midnight, at Morning or at Noon.

To walk the beach alone at the breaking of a day
Gives my mind a Solace, more than words could ever say.

And watching graceful Egrets strutting near the Water's end
Their footprints in the sand so fragile as they wend.

The Sea gulls flying overhead in their great formation
Causes eyes to follow their varied gyrations.

Far out on the horizon the ships sail on their way
As snowy clouds are forming and Dolphins are at play.

When the tide is washing in the Shells upon the sand
For me to find a Special one is a "Treasure in My Hand".

Now if you listen closely, the waves will talk to you
They may be saying that your "Wish will soon be coming true.

And even if it's raining and winds blow on the shore
I still stay on the beach to hear the Ocean's roar.

At times it's very angry, At times it's quite serene
But Utter fascination it will always hold for me.

For where else better in this world can you set your mind at ease
Than to spend a day in Solitude just "Listening To the Sea".

Rita Juracek

We Ask What Is Love?

Love is ...
  While I sleep with my body around you, I feel
    how fragile you are;
  While I sleep with your body around me, I feel
    your strength and it reminds me how fragile I am;
  When I see your smile it warms my body
    like the summer sun;
  When I look in your eyes I see our future so
    promising and bright;
  When I feel your love I know I am alive;
  For your love is my life and may I
    be blessed with it until my final breath.

Kevin M. McCrea

Essence

How passionately I have loved you ever so many years,
While my interminable search for love without you has been unyielding.
There is no time nor place for my mind to rest,
As images of you rage through it,
Like a tempest...a violent storm,
Every sense overwrought.

When the evening sun vanishes into the horizon, I lay wondering...
Why we allowed others to rule our destiny,
And wistfully I try to console this fragmented heart.
I whisper to myself, "it is God's will,"
But this consolation evokes no comfort.
The agony of your absence in unrelenting.

Has our sole chance for love indeed eluded us,
Leaving only your memories to savor?
And a return to yesteryear...would it be in vain,
Or could we once again flourish in the affinity of each other's arms?
I beg of you to fill my life with your life, fulfill my hunger,
For the beauty of your being and the warmth of your soul are
  the essence of my existence.

Mary Jo Bartone

Do Animals Go To Work?

Does the rooster tend the farm all day
while the sheep rakes the hay?
Does the horse make the rounds
To keep chickens from going astray?

Does the lion stare like a foreman
while the giraffe works the crane?
When the badger reports the news, he's never, ever tame.

Does the elephant sit in a rocking chair writing a quick report,
while a monkey searches his briefcase, looking for papers to sort?

Does the weasel walk the city streets picking up the garbage,
while the snake serves in the homeless shelter
dishing out yesterday's cabbage?

Does the mouse read a paper that he never really finishes,
while the zebra seems happy with the furniture she replenishes?

Does the coyote howl when he hears the news,
while rabbits all take different views?
When the raccoon's boss asks him to work,
Does he say "Yes, Sir!" without a shirk?

Questions have been raised, the answers seem to lurk
Only animals know if they really go to work.

Maxwell C. Pollock

Dream

The dream I had was in color: white.
White room and scared white faces.
White snow falling out of white sky,
White piles of paper cases.

Shaking hands of white-haired doctor,
Astounding glances of white-clothed nurses.
They were all looking at unbelievable something
They have not covered in their medical courses.

The color emerged: red, hot,
Pulsating often and loudly hoarse.
They were all looking at my broken heart
In the live body, which should be corpse.

The doctor said in a thin voice:
"Close incision, keep to the mark."
White knight appeared on the white horse,
Followed by a new color: pitch dark.

Lana Smile

A Father Proud

What matter of man can stand alone
Who bears such weight without a groan
Who leads his family all through life
All fret with sorrow, pain and strife

Who tries to smile when oft he can
But sporting the rod must take a stand
And raise his children to be upright
Yet comfort their fears in the still of night

Oh the pangs of being a father proud
Where making mistakes is not allowed
But setting examples of right is a must
If you're ever to gain your children's trust

But when it's all been said and done
And when life's race is finally run
I'll stand in line like all the rest
and tell the Lord "I did my best"

Ronald Rancilio

My Heart-Chillun

Gee, but we are blessed with a couple of "Kids"
Who like to call us Mom and Pop.
When someone objects and says,
"They are not yours by blood,"
We answer right from the start,
"Not by blood but by the heart."

Because, you see, the heart
Is what makes the blood go round
And when it quits,
The future is under the ground!

Well, then, maybe I can't
Call you my blood-kin kids
But, I betcha, I call you night and day,
My "Heart-Kin Chillun" every way.
And that makes me proud to say,
"I Love You" and also know
You love us in every possible way.

Richard L. James

Changed

These are not the friends I used to know;
  who stayed up all night laughing and talking
  about boys and love-the innocent things in life.
Gone are the days of purity and here are the days of darkness.
Drugs luring one friend in, sex appealing to another,
  and death trying to take its toll.
Greed, jealousy, and anger pulling at the bonds of friendship,
  loosening what may never be built up again.
Each one a victim of Satan's evil mind,
  each one blinded by the simplicity of sin.
And I, alone, approach them with God's love
  and a chance at a better way of life.
Rejected here, and turned away there;
  they do not see the consequences of their own deeds
My heart is breaking in two-time is running out.
I yearn for the old days-
  the days of love and kindness, of joy and happiness.
But I know they will never come again-
  too much has changed;
And my friends are not the friends I used to know.

Laurie Nicole Thompson

"Karen"

My thoughts are with Karen,
Who was a dear friend of mine.
She left me but not my heart,
Karen fought aids for nine years.

Without her my life seems lost,
For in my heart I bear a cross.
Her green eyes would shine so bright,
Her personality was out of sight.

She was strong and full of love,
Her courage was given to her from God above.
Now she's gone and at rest,
Friends and Family knew she was the best.

Karen taught me to be strong,
And when I feel real down.
She's in my heart,
Whether I'm home or out of town.

Always remember the good she did,
Not only for herself but for her kid.
Her son was the apple of her eye,
Remember her always and try not to cry.

Mary Massalongo

Forever And A Day

Now look around you, and what do you see,
who's picking up whom, now that's not how it should be,
have another beer or bottle of wine,
just keep looking, to see who you can find.
Now this is not love,
because it's not from above,
believe me, it's not from the heart,
with a beer or bottle of wine,
because that's no way to start.
Now stop and listen to what I say,
Must all friendships start this same way.
Now when true love appears,
it's not sought after
and you can't explain it one bit
because it's the flame in your heart that's been lit
and a person truly in love can't see,
because it's not the outward appearance, that they see.
Now this is the way it is with me
because it is only your heart that I see.

Robert V. Brown

Do You Know Me?

Who I am? I'm a young girl. "You're bright," a teacher says.
"Why can't you be more like __? (Fill in the blank; any name will do).
You'll never amount to anything," my dad says. Silence from mom ...

Who I am? I'm a teen, a prisoner in my home, allowed no friends.
School's my only refuge.
"Why can't you be more like __? (Fill in the blank; any name will do).
You'll never amount to anything," my dad says. Silence from mom ...

Who I am? I'm a mother at eighteen. A baby with a baby, but I'm free?
Got our own place, her dad and me.
"I knew you'd never amount to anything," my dad says.
Silence from mom ...

Who I am?
I've left him; he ain't going nowhere, and I've already been there.
I go home.
"So, you're back. I knew you'd never amount to anything," my dad says.
Silence from mom ...

Who I am? I'm a baby with a baby, yet I never had a childhood.
I feel old and weary, yet I'm still wet behind the ears,
I forge ahead, trying to stop that damned ringing in my ears,
"Why can't you be more like __? (Fill in the blank; any name will do).
You'll never amount to anything." And still silence from mom ...

Luz N. Ortiz

Michael Joseph

You were my Angel, so beautiful and fair,
Why did God take you, why couldn't He share?
You were so happy, so full of joy,
All that you wanted was to play with a toy,
Wires and machines, that is all that you knew,
Why did He take you, is He some kind of fool?
I hope that your happy and not in pain,
I'll never think your labor vain,
When you smiled it was so nice,
now why do I feel as cold as ice,
I just can't make it without you,
I just don't know how,
I just want some answers and I want them now.

Lisa Hoopengardner

Mr. Piano

Mr. Piano...
Why do people look at you
and only see black and white?
How can they not see
each individual key as a unique sound?
Why do people keep their eyes half closed?
If only, they would open
their eyes, their hearts and their minds,
they would see each song
as a beautiful masterpiece.
We are all beautiful Masterpieces,
We just exist
in a different Tune.

Rebecca McGrew

Through The Window Of The World

Through the window of the world what will I see?
Will I ever see peace become a reality?
I see crime, hatred, injustice all around
Will it ever end, will true peace ever be found?
Drugs taking our young generation one by one,
While others are in gangs just to have fun,
Small wars in countries after another
Does anyone really love their brother?
It saddens my heart as I see, through the
Window of the World will peace ever
become a reality?

Michelle D. Bailey

"My Beauty Inside"

I look at my face in the mirror, the truth becomes clearer, I know
    why in your heart I don't have a place, it's because I don't
    have a cover girl face.
My body is not small and slender, but I do have feelings and my heart
    is tender, I may not have beautiful blue eyes, but they can see
    and they do cry.
It's said beauty is only skin deep, so if to be beautiful I have to
    give up what's inside, what I have I'm going to keep, in my heart
    there's a lot of love but that you didn't see because
    you never tried.
Your eyes never saw my soul, perfectly you played the typical male
    role, you go along with the crowd just so you fit in, I guess
    that makes you feel proud.
To let everyone else think for you, never to yourself being true,
being like this you'll never know in your heart what you feel,
but at least I can say that I am real.

    Rebecca Callis

Crossroads

I often really wonder,
Why life seems like a dream,
My spirit blindly existing,
Can't help but cry out and scream,
I'm walking along a path in life,
Looks like a yellow brick road to me,
Because I encountered a crossroad,
That leads me to my destiny,
I admit I've taken the wrong road,
I just could not see the light,
I'm going to wake up and smell the coffee,
With the help of an angel tonight,
Must stop shedding tears of sorrow,
Look ahead and see straight,
I'm on a mission in life - to find my soul,
My hourglass says it's running late.

    Martha Garcia

My Sunshine

    The Sun that used to keep me warm has gone.
Will I ever again feel her dawn?
    I remember the warmth she brought my life.
Just her sight released all my strife.
    Now all I have is this cold, black, emptiness in her place.
All I have is this big, empty space.
    Will my Sun rise, once again, on me?
Will I ever be able again to see?
    The warmth of her beauty brought love to this loveless heart of mine.
Just the touch of her rays made me feel just fine.
    Everyday, I awaited her rise like the arrival of a new life.
How I wish I could have made her my wife.
    But, the Sun never shines on this heart of mine anymore.
It has frozen my heart to the Bitter core.
    I no longer see things clearly, it's all dark.
I long to hear that morning lark.
    But, until that day I will remain in this dark, cold world; that
is now home.
But forever, for my Sunshine, my heart shall roam.

    William Allen Gates

"Thursday's Child"

Who will love this mournful child, who cries alone?
Who will wipe her tears, and give her a home?
Who will mend her broken heart, make up for the past?
Who will say "It's not your fault," make her free at last?

Who will say "The debt is paid", it's ok to smile,
Who will say "You're special" and you're worthwhile.
Who will see within the rock, the gem that's inside?
Who will search for the child, though she tries to hide?

    Patti Taylor

Believe Embarrassment

Stairs / Stairs / I stare at them all
Will there ever be a top floor?
Should I find out before?

Chairs / Chairs / I stare as I wear them
Can there ever be a place to find peace?
Will I end up as well deceased?

This day is someday somewhere

Halls / Halls / I stall while around them
Will there ever be a final door?
Might I find it just a bore?

Walls / Walls / I crawl to them to keep away
Shall desperation's shadow be kind?
Will the smile I give be mine?

Fear / Fear / A tear falls from my lash
Am I helpless to the thoughts?
Is my mind tied up in knots?

Here / Here / What's near is so unclear
Will I rot and disappear?
If one can answer one can cheer

This was someone's someday.

    Timothy J. DeSoto

The Man In The Mirror

    When I look into the mirror, I see a man who is capable, willing, and determined. I see someone able to make his own decisions. I see someone who can accept his own actions and responsibilities as a mature adult. There, is a man with the ability to see beyond the empty shells of others and deal with the truth he finds.
    When I look into the mirror, I see a man willing to accept the consequences of his actions. I see someone tall, strong, and dignified in his stride. I see a man humble enough to welcome defeat as a chance to start the task over with new direction.
    And when I look into the mirror, I see a man determined to be somebody. I see someone who will try his all to become what he knows he can be. He is direct and confident in his ways and will always have his say. When I look into the mirror, I see a man who has learned a lot, and is still willing to learn with an open heart and an open mind.
    When I look, I am proud of that person, for he reflects the best in me.

    Michael Littlejohn

Forever Wind

Wind is a rustling symphony that strings across the sea
Wind is a reed-like melody that passes over me
There's wind forever, though I've gone by
There's wind forever, it's there - up high
And I am here - but I am dead,
While wind lolls its vespus above my head
Why should death take me when life holds so much
And why is there wind when its substance can't be touched
Why am I dead when I've done no wrong
And yet I lie dead while wind sighs its song

And forever and forever its breeze shall pass
Across my grave until the last
I've known no wind for countless years
But it laughs in life, while I cry silent tears
And I am gone for death is clever
But wind is there, it's there - forever.

    Raymond Muscarello

Untitled

All doors have locked.
Winds cry of lost love.
Old gardens grow new.
Guns pointed in the wrong.
Alterations split the heavens.
New and old generations grow old together.
Canopies of life stretched tight to survive one another.

Robert Britton

Vanishing Point

The water smooth as velvet.
Wings glide and flutter in the silence.
All around me, mist rises from the water.
No division is seen in this colorless evenness.
The earth and sky have vanished.
All appears to rise and disappear.
All that exists in this mid-state mind state is dissolution,
Wings, transformation.
A colorless radiance of invisibility.

Kalinda Sonriente

A Cold Winters Dream

If you ever lay down to sleep on a cold
winters night,
you can close your eyes and drift away
and there will be no fright.
For a dream is like a bird lost for ever
in its flight,
and with the dream within your grasp there
will always be a light.
A dream is like a distant, far and peaceful
land,
a dream of our Gods arm outstretched with an
open hand.
For in that hand the dream will show what
your mind can hold,
and though it is a winter's dream doesn't
mean it's cold.
And even though it's cold or lonely as sad
as it may seem,
it may hold warmth it may hold joy although
it's a winter's dream.

Kenny Higgins

Untitled

There stood an old rugged cur
With a tall spine and a small metal box
Today I gave to him one day of my life for a mere pittance
Where is my mansion?
Where is my metaphor for the sake of a dignified identity?
My flesh tone changes with my plight
Soon I will be a fledgling stereotype
Peeling away at some old tile floor
So that I may somehow find out where this all began
And who might be my savior?
None other than myself would be a ploy to be complacent
I'll not die apathetic
Nor will I die rich
But the small metal box surely will be full
Nice and heavy
A bag of wet sand to throw down at the flood

Nicholas Alexandros Sorlien

Crossroads

Crossroads we travel everyday we treat
with caution and near-sightedness.
Paralyzed by which way to go, we should
see a situation with an open mind and
nothing less.
You have to reach out without realizing
your limitations.
To build a formula which works for you
sometimes requires the simplest equation.
Having the basic necessities, a good head
and being who you want to be,
Are sometimes the easiest things for
an individual to oversee.

Michael A. Soltis

Dragon, Dragon

Dragon, dragon, what a grand creature are you.
With enormous scaled body,
And tail lashing about,
Is there anything you cannot do?

Dragon, dragon, what a deadly creature are you.
Armed with long killer claws,
And dagger sharp fangs,
Yet you hurt no one.

Dragon, dragon, what a magnificent creature are you.
Possessing gigantic leathery wings,
As white as winter snow,
Flying gracefully and freely in the sky.

Dragon, dragon, what a gentle creature are you.
One with nature and all living things,
Kind, loving and compassionate,
Befriending every creature of the earth.

Dragon, dragon, oh how I wish I could be you.
Living without worry in the world,
Soaring to where ocean meets sky,
A grand creature, free-spirited, wandering without end.

Ryan Patrick Fong

Reflection

He's gone again; we kissed goodbye parting at the train;
    with happy memories in my heart, I am alone again.
Duty calls my soldier as he hastened back to camp
    and in the lonely night I slowly light a lamp.
With longing in my heart; in the mirror's deep confine
    a woman's are searching this very soul of mine
For some sign of courage I may have left with him;
    and for a fleeting moment I saw the light grow dim.
Then the woman answered; that image in the glass
    "Fear not!" But keep your faith, time indeed will pass."
Oh, image does he know the depth of love I bear?
    Would that I might lighten his burden and each care!
A prayer rose to my lips, please send him home again!
    from view the image faded, as I heard a low "Amen."

Marjorie W. Lewis

Love Never Knows

Pondering, what will become of us,
Wondering, if we can just be,
Trusting, in the higher powers, of which rule our destiny,
Loving, your lips, your touch, your soul,
Caring, that we stay together and grow,
Accepting, the past and what was,
Anticipating, the future and what will be,
Knowing, we can be sure of nothing,
Yet, having faith always.

Maria E. Talcott

Mood Swings Of Nature

Strolling through a peaceful country lane,
With hazy sunshine filtering the clouds,
I felt the first few drops of summer rain
Hiding the sun from all its worshipping crowds.

The lake in sunlight - clear as shining glass.
No breath of wind to stir the summer air.
I feel beneath my hands the soft warm grass
And close my eyes in silent, secret prayer.

Thunder, lightning, rain and hail!
A blazing fire within the living room.
Outside, the wind is shrieking "Force is gale!"
Sounding just like the voice of doom.

The morning mist turns suddenly to rain,
And flowers raise their heads in gratitude.
The moment they have longed for, thought in vain
Has brought relief to their parched petals once again.

When I am with you, love, sun fills my heart.
There is no room for rain or stormy skies.
But at the moment when we have to part
I find the rain is falling from my eyes.

Patricia Gough Risk

With Praise And Thanksgiving For A Need Fulfilling

I have known you forever, yet I know you not at all.

You come suddenly into my life
With kindness, love, understanding,
And precious fleeting moments of intimacy.

My soul is aglow with the newness of your friendship
Born in a time of emptiness and sorrow.

You listen - and I hear.
The sound of my voice speaks from the depths of my inner being
With words I did not know were there.

You hold me - and we communicate anew
In silent conversation unspoiled by lips and tongue.

A look, a touch, a whispering kiss drifting across my face,
A gentling smile saying all and yet nothing, for all is said.
The emptiness of my heart fills with the joy of another's caring.

Oh, God, I thank Thee for this brief new glimpse of Your infinite way.

I am Me, We are You: Apart, and a part of each other;
Together alone, alone together...
The eternal integration of all that is.

No matter how long, how briefly, this closeness endures,
It is mine forever.

Ruth Pestalozzi Pape

Windy Night

The dark green pine trees blowing in the wind
    with leaves toppling over in little piles.

The splintering feeling of a cool breeze blowing
    against my face

The whipping of pine branches blowing down
    around my hair

The scenes of clouds floating like animals
    soaring in the heavens
Smelling sap dripping like drops of rain

Watching a stream carry fish and frogs
    and turtles to its destination
And at last the full moon bending down

Stephen Georgeson

What I'd Miss (A Child's Poem)

I'd miss the fun of playing games
With long time friends that I know well
I'd miss the faces that we'd make
And stories promised not to tell.

I'd miss the whispered phone calls to
My best pal who would always say
That anything I'd ever do
Would be accepted as okay.

I'd miss my family even more
Although I gripe about some acts
Of love and caring that I see
As bossy and as mean attacks.

I'd miss the mornings dark or bright
That tells me it's another day
For when I die there won't be that
And in its place I cannot say.

Selma Rubler

"Patsy"

The moonlight peeks in that musty old barn.
With me and Patsy beneath it.

Her mane glistens in the dark night.
A tint of pride shines in her eyes, oh, so bright.

She chews up her grain and looks up at me again,
Wondering what I am thinking as the crickets are singing.

The radio keeps playing. My memory goes back to those rodeo nights,
And I remember the way Patsy flew.
Racing around barrels, it had come from her heart,
Just like the other Patsy I knew.

My memory continues back in time
To a little girl singing Patsy Cline,
And hoping to become as famous.

Her teachers didn't agree with a singing career,
Musicians were amazed, and kids thought she was weird.
But today she lives in Nashville.

Her family was proud, the audience was in love.
As her music played aloud, she danced like a white dove.

That little girl was me. Tomorrow I'll be in another town or city,
but tonight I'm with Patsy, and both Patsy's are with me.

Kenni L. Jones

The Sentry

The sentry walks his post at night,
With mind alert and senses keen.
To catch a sound that isn't right,
And pierce the darkness of night's screen.

He walks then suddenly turns around,
And listens hard to hear.
A step that matches with his own,
To take him from the rear.

His comrades lie in weary sleep,
Their arms are all laid down.
They know the vigil well he'll keep,
For their lives and his own.

For he knows the peril of the night,
A knife thrust in the dark.
His life is gone without a fight,
The foe has found his mark.

Kenneth P. Sery

Shenandoah Indian Summer

A couple went canoeing down the Shenandoah
With nature's pleasures to explore.
The miracles of nature were all in array
Before their eyes on this lovely fall day.

As the canoeists meandered down the river through rocks,
And just before they came to a two foot drop,
They made a quick turn in the river's bend
And momentarily thought that their lives were at end.

The madam immediately looked down the river
To see who saw her develop a shiver.
All heads were turned in her direction
Seeing her face with a strawberry complexion.

This poor couple dragged the canoe to the shore
And emptied the water until there was no more.
Now that they were soaked from head to toe,
Down the river they went with more speedy row.

Finally, with well soaked shoes on squeaky feet,
The climbed to the top of the mountain peak.
They turned in their oars and away they went
Both agreeing that this was a day well spent.
  Martha Penney Butler

Changes

From birth to death, many changes do we face,
With no question, change affects every race,

  War to peace and back to war,
  Fighting for freedom, this is the core,

  Food to fertilizer, fertilizer to food,
  Without this cycle, we would all be doomed,

  Seasons change, tides roll in and out,
  More phenomena, that is what this is about,

Surrounded by things we cannot control,
Even more changes as we grow old,

  Changes exist as we make our plans,
  Plans are altered by change, do whatever you can,

  Complications set in with internal moves,
  Reactions to change affects our goals and moods,

  Before you know it, death will come,
  Then a new birth ... more changes ... but, we will be done,

Accept the cycle that life has to give,
Make the best of it, each day you live!
  Vanessa Lynn Piwtorak

The Wall

Once it stood with its power and might.
With people climbing over late in the night.

Looking for freedom and the dream of a new life.
Without stone or sword that could cut like a knife.

What man could give divide one piece into two?
That would make two brothers be just me and the other just you.

But now in the wall is a hole like a door.
And a piece of the wall stands no more.

The two brothers are together like the stars and the sun.
And what was two countries is again joined as one.

Like the influence of god and the bells in the steeple.
The power can be ran by the people.
  Scott Young

Catie

Tall and solid,
  with skin so ivory fair.
Sparkling eyes of cobalt blue,
  a bow in her yellow-ochre hair.
One mind, adult-like, yet is a child,
  is of great intelligence.
Emotions are high and quick,
  so sensitive and intense.
The questions are forever endless:
  "Why will boys be boys?
  Why do people fight in wars?
  Mom, why can't we afford more toys?"
Studies of Math and Spelling,
  writing stories is her best.
Reading, Art and Music,
  exceed above the rest.
Great fun can be dolls, baby brother or ballet,
  Oh! to draw and create!
"Grandma, No - I can't be still - for after all -
  I am just ALMOST eight!"
  Nancy A. Cryder

"Is Love Blind?"

"Love is blind", I've heard it said.
With this, I cannot agree,
But first, of what kind of love is this spoken,
  romantic or passionate love?

Though deep and wonderful this love may be,
  'tis not all "true love":
Within the spring there bubbles up a
  passion of the body,
Mixing indistinguishably with the waters
  of "true love".
Love of this fountain may be blind,
  but I doubt it—
'Tis more likely the lovers only close
  their eyes to shut all faults out.

Within the fountain of "true love" frailties
  can be seen;
But, it contains the waters of understanding
  and forbearance,
It's surest test of authenticity:
It seeks to give and share and not to gain.
  Verna Lee Wood

My Little House Built For Two

If I could have a little house
with trees around the side
I'd want a girl whose just like you
To be my loving bride

We could relax on a white fluffy rug
snuggle up tight and maybe make love
Watch the coals as their silhouettes dance
doesn't a fireplace add to romance

For every new born baby
We'll add a new bedroom
and sit around the fireplace babe
To plan the new playroom

We could eat our meals by candlelight
or sit under the stars
or else go out and hike around
The forest that's all ours

For if my every dream comes true
I'll build this little house for you
and we can start our lives again
and live happily ever after till the end of time.
  William Frizelle

616

Dear Dad

I was too young to know you when you lived
With us. The cries of frustration by mom
Were the earliest memories I hid,
For thou with infants three and plus a job
Full time has no easy life. Trips to bare
And dry land became commonplace. Spent weeks
In summer cannonballing at your fair
Sized abode: playing softball in the heat
Of August. But your interest went by
Like the time. Trips to Arizona were
No longer. Like a fisher reeling thy
Hope, you called almost often. Yet it's sure
To be fake, cast out again. All in vain,
This hope; to cut the line will ease the pain.

Scott Kacenga

The Golden Years

As she sits alone in her rocking chair,
With wrinkled hands and snow white hair,
The lines on her face are a mark of the years,
From many a smile and a lot of tears.
Her mind is wandering and she's thinking back,
Of sad times and happy times,
And of some things she's lost track.
As she thinks of her husband,
Who's been gone for years,
She gives a sigh and wipes away tears,
Her children and grandchildren she would so love to see,
But the old home place is where she wants to be,
Her heart is full of memories dear,
Their voices she can almost hear,
She feels alone, but she's not really alone,
A gentle voice whispers, calm your fears,
I'll he here with you, in your golden years.

Naomi R. Grooms

What Chair

In what chair will I sit, and become my world, bound
within my soul that I should never be enthralled
with what I cannot see, 'tis darkness that is not my
own, only a thorn that pierces the flesh, for in
darkness only have I sown, the distant stars are just
at reach and my hands long to touch but are tied
with angry ropes that burn into the heart,
In my chair I am banished never to walk, never to
reach the distance of the stars or the broken
heavens, in my chair I am a beggar and a thief if
I do not struggle against the bonds that hold
me in silence, for I will have stolen the hope and
begged even for silent life.

Nathan A. Comte

Thy Will Be Done

I watched with you throughout the night,
When your baby had ceased his earthly flight
Feeling your sorrow, so hard to endure
For one short moment, the earth was pure!

Surely the gates of Heaven were opened wide
As your child passed across the great Divide;
A warm, gentle light shone for him alone,
As the angels carried him to their home.

Time alone will ease the memory of your grief,
This tiny saint, whose mission so good, so brief!
A little child will lead you over the years,
With love and peace to wipe away your tears.

Mary Virginia Murphy

To Lisa Gaye

One afternoon, of summer's charm,
Without one thing to cause alarm,
Was spent with my darling, Lisa Gaye,
Who sat in her swing that wondrous day,
Dragging the earth with her barefoot toe,
As she idly swung to and fro.
She held on with one hand; then she rested her head
Against the rope and pensively said,
"Gram, where do birdths thleep? And why can't we fly
Up in the air, way up in the thky?
It'ths tho fun to thwing away up there...
I lub you, Gram, and your white hair."

Her golden brown pony tail hanging in curls,
Her blue, blue eyes with wonder for the world,
Glanced at me, and then lit up with a smile,
My lovely, my piquant, and dear grandchild.
She is so precious, she's only just four,
And never again will she be more
Hauntingly sweet, more lovable, and say,
"I lub you, Gram," in her own special way.

Melba Bryce

Don't Worry, I Still Remember You!

Every night I lay in my bed alone,
without you this house is not a home.

Why did you have to leave me and
go so very far away, I long for you
to be with me day after day.

Even though your gone, being alone
I have to make due,
But don't worry, I still remember you!

I walk along the lane and wonder
in my mind, if I look deep inside,
what I might find.

I will find you in ky heart, mind and soul.
I will find that I miss you and a heart
of solid gold.

To represent a love for just us two,
you've passed away, but don't worry,
I will always remember you.
I LOVE YOU!

Nicole Hebert

Memories Of Death

Your pains are so great, and last so long we
wonder how much can the human brain take. There's
no relief when you are really sick, we would love to
see all the pain, and the hurt go away real quick,
but that isn't in our control.

The days, and nights are so very long that you
feel like you are just hanging on, and on, but to us
the days and the hours are not long enough to share with you.

The dreams you have has no real meaning to
them, but it seems very real to someone who is very
ill. You may not be walking the way we would like,
but at least you are still talking, and please don't
give up the fight.

Marilyn L. Diamond

Nineteen

Sitting alone in my living room
Wondering if there's something I should do.
Is this what my life is going to be
My days and nights feeling so empty...
Am I a person only filling space
Just another life that's been misplaced.
There's plenty of time to chase my dreams,
The future is mine at age nineteen,

A few years pass as days go by
There are still those dreams behind my eyes.
Is this what my life is coming to,
Not really living just getting through,
Feeling more closed in than I used to be,
Should have lived my dreams from age nineteen.

Time rolls on with little change,
My empty nights are filled with pain. I feel boxed in and
I can't break free, but my four walls have been inside me.
The things I would give if I could relive my life from age
nineteen.
Too young the man to challenge destiny's hand,
Strong and scared at age nineteen.

M. L. Faulkner

Musings

She lay in her bed
Wondering what to do
Only one thing was on her mind,
Which boy should she choose?

One she had loved since the day they had met
Their time had been short, although well spent.
The other was a friend, an acquaintance well-known
He had called her one night to talk on the phone.

One she loved, the other she liked
One she would die for, and cry over all night.
The other was sweet and talked of grand things
But nothing ever seemed to come from these dreams.

As she drifted deeper and deeper into sleep,
She thought to herself, which one shall I keep?

Kanoe Sing

Untitled

Standing at a cross road,
Wondering which way to turn.
Wondering if there is a right way,
And praying to God that I will learn.

Looking to the left,
The sunshine shows no pain.
To the right there is a storm,
Hoping that I'm strong enough to face the rain.

Realizing that sunshine doesn't last,
That the storm can end.
And in choosing my way,
To escape my sadness and bring my heart to mend.

I cry out in confusion,
Terrified of my choice.
I wave goodbye to the sun,
And listen to my inner voice.

Melissa Himelrigh

I'd Be Happy!

If I but had at my command,
Words to make you understand;
And in some small way reveal,
Just exactly how I feel;
    I'd be happy.

If there were a way for me to show,
The things I'd like you to know;
If there were a way to start,
The story that's in my heart;
    I'd be happy.

If I could repay you all I owe,
For the friendship and love you bestow,
For sharing the little things you possess,
For each embrace and sweet caress;
    Then I'd be happy.

If you but knew how I aspire,
To satisfy this - my heart's desire,
Then you would know - from A to Z,
All the things I feel and see;
    And I'd be happy.

Pauline Pickering

A Child Of The Streets

A mother stands up on her feet, for she has to
work five days a week, she has three kids she
has to feed, and there is one who really needs
to hear her pled. For he's the child that's in
the street. She tries to hide the pain she
feels, for her eyes are red from shedding tears.
She never sleeps for fear she will hear the
cries and sounds of the streets.

For when she hears the shot's aloud, she jumps
to her feet and weeps out loud, please God,
please God I don't let that be my child. For
she get's down on her knees and pray out loud.
The child is mine where he is I can not say but
please don't let him leave me this way. For the
child is mine A child of the street but give him
courage to retreat.

For this is my child of the street.
I will not rest I will not sleep,
until I get my child back from the streets.

Thelma Smith

Walls Within

My hands tremble, body sweats, eyes flood with tears as I
wrench my inner man for something to write, some glimpse of
wisdom. Drained I crash to the floor, drop my pen and watch
it fall and hit the floor. As it hits, the sound of shattering
glass pierces my ears. I close my eyes and feel myself melt into
the floor. All around me I hear things fall and crumble away,
I am left lying in the dark on what seems to be a plateau.

Loneliness knows me by name and my soul cries out like a single
wolf in the moonlight. Like the wolf the only communication
I know is the echo of my own spirit's cry. I am always alone;
for even when I am surrounded by people I'm off in a distant
land. Living in a world created by myself, within myself.
I live there always and have for some time. Far too long.
trapped in that world, I try to escape; but walls built to keep
people out also keep me in. Pounding on the walls within I grow
tired and weak, but I continue pounding. My bloody hands tremble,
body sweats and my eyes flood with tears. Drained, I crash to
the floor. I later wake to the faint morning light, lying
on a plateau.

Sam Whitmore

618

With Pen In Hand

With pen in hand I am a
writer, a writer with so much
love and memories that are not
So easy to put into words.

With pen in hand, I am an artist,
that can bring out the beauty
that everyone keeps locked up inside.

With pen in hand I am a creator,
A creator that tries to create and
build up one's self-esteem, ones self
pride and create ones own self dignity.

With pen in hand almost anything is possible.

Michelle Smith

Like You And Me

In the library he will be found;
Writing and reading, not making a sound.

His, hair disarray; mix matched clothes;
A troubled look; glasses fixed on end of his nose.

The table before him, scattered with debris;
Books and papers as far as the eye can see.

His manner is contemplative, quiet and shy;
He is quite introverted, a bashful kind of guy.

A wealth of knowledge, he does possess;
Wisdom acquired, through earnestness.

No, his manner is not comely nor charismatic;
Most people avoid him; calling him a fanatic.

His closest friends are thoughts and words;
The now generation would call him a nerd.

To the literary world, he has few rivals;
They wait in anticipation for all his arrivals.

They call him a deep thinker, quanted with strife;
Saying his works will out live his life.

If, a man such as this, you should happen to see;
Judge him not; he may be a poet, like you and me.

Teresa Ann Bever

Just Another Junkie

I get lost in the midst of people
Yes me, who I really am
I'm a love junkie
Fiending for a fix
Love cures my heart
Takes away my pain
It vanishes the windows from my past
I cannot see through
Love causes mirrors to become opaque
I cannot see... me
This love thang
Becomes habitual
Needing this love from others
To know I'm loved becomes a risk
To give love back becomes a challenge I want more
Take my memories away I want more
Heal my wounded heart I need more
Give me a reason to breath
My mirrors begin to break
My life SHATTERED once again!

Martia Faulkner

"Remembering"

She's a pretty little picture of a darling little girl;
Yes, the "rose with sweetest petals yet unfurled."
She's the softest breath of angels, the rippling of the streams.
She's a part of the fulfillment of all my fondest dreams.

He is love and roguish laughter, like the babbling of a brook.
His whole world swirls about him, like a color picture book.
His eyes are dancing sunbeams on a cool fresh mountain lake
As he chases after rainbows, the kind that young hearts make.

He's a morning in the springtime, she, a summer afternoon —
— Still, along the way, my days have turned to years —
And I find myself returning, as I sit and rock alone,
And a fond, remembering smile breaks thru the tears.

Mildred Ahearn Turner

The Crucifix

I am created and molded with rough hands of a carpenter.
Yet am a God for those who plead with folded hands and a
     doused conscience.
A silver bug is pinned to my crosses, and doubted.
I preach a worship, unproven.

I represent, for some,
The damn which holds their waves stable.
Others, slandered as lost without me,
Require, simply,
The calmness their inner tides can reach alone.

Karen Perkins

Tropic Sun

Sultry breezes waft across the tranquil cove,
Yet do not disturb the branches of the palm,
That hang limp in the burning tropic sun.
High in the tree the vultures perch with wings outstretched
trying to remain cool, too tired to pursue the prey
that lies panting in the scorching mid-day sun.

The blazing sun is at its zenith and in its blistering heat
The very shadows cringe, shrivel and disappear.
Man too, sapped of energy and will, shuffles in
to seek the comfort of the shade and mops his brow
As salty streams run down the crevasses of his work - worn face.

An eerie silence falls upon the land as the earth holds its breath.
A shimmering haze rises from the surface of the stagnant pond
And the sky is filled with a thousand wings of snow-white gulls
that soar on high, screeching, riding the hot updrafts
Watching, mindless of the calm, yet sensing the change that's in
     the air.

Ruthven Benjamin

Far From Home

She's hundreds of miles away
Yet in my heart, she's with me everyday
She gives me the strength to carry on
She guides me to our future beyond
And I've always know deep down in my heart
That in my life, she's the biggest part
And I count the days till again we're together
When I can hug and kiss and gently caress her
And I will be whole and happy you see
When she smiles and boasts, my daddy loves me

Mark Archuleta

Trigger

I hold it in my hand, it's smooth and gleams;
Yet it's heavy and cold, full of broken dreams,
It's weight is my burden, its bullets my pain,
The hollows of my heart, the wracking of my brain;
It's power is in my hand, it's deadliness is my fears,
As I raise it to my head, I can feel the warm tears,
As I let my hand go I feel nothing inside,
There's no more regret, and there's nothing to hide.

Kathleen Farran

When Freedom Goes

The winds of war have long since gone,
  Yet little war'ry breezes blow,
Among the sentinels of stone,
  Where fallen warriors lay.

While the things, for which they fell,
  Man barters, sells or gives away,
And thinks that things are going well,
  If only he can have his way.

But some day soon will come a day,
  When man must face up to the news,
That all things done will have their way,
  And he must pay the price, and lose.

Robert T. Waddle, Sr.

Words

I finally realized why you seem so odd to me
yet so interesting
you can say words so easily
that I would never think of saying
and you say them to me
with such ease and happiness

You say things like "I care"
and "I miss you"
and you complement me endlessly
but it's so odd
and in other ways comforting

I try my hardest to say something in return
but I can think of nothing to say

Your complements and kindness
do not go unnoticed
and yet I do not know how to return the favors
or except them.

Mara Parkhurst

To Be The Fool...

My tears they fall
Yet they are full of emptiness
Or so it appears they are
My heart it bleeds
Yet the river of blood runs through nowhere
Or so it appears not to
My body and soul is for him
Yet I cannot make it appear to be
What I say is wrong, yet I cannot change it
Because if I did I would not be true
And to him, I cannot lie

To sit back and stay afraid is the hardest thing.
Afraid, afraid of what is to come—
More tears and the heartbreak
When the tears are full of sorrow and overflowing the dam
When the river of blood that ran through nowhere runs
  through everywhere
Disrupting the natural balance and making me impossible.
All in response to my own inability
My own blockage, my dam...of emotion and feeling.

Monique J. Manning

Truth

Thy heart of purity and pain,
Yet thou soul stands proud with such yearning,
With praise of hope and strength for the future,
If they could only see the love; that was born in them,
There would cease to be hurting and sickness,
Truth would be a new light shining throughout eternity,
As hope would be reborn in the very eyes of men,
People of all colors, yet of one creation would hold hands and cry,
Not of misery or pity, but of the triumph of faith,
Eyes shall bare truth to the same,
Death would have no envy or partner, but silence,
Peace what a journey that kills the minds of
men; yet saves their souls,
Not one person shall spare the rod of pain,
For the reflection of ones self is the killer of all men.

Latoya Anteva Morris

What Are You Afraid Of

What are you afraid of? Are you afraid of me? Are
you afraid of the love I feel for you, or the love you
feel for me.

Don't be afraid to love me. I'm not anymore. Don't be
afraid to love me, I'll only love you more....

Rita Angelopoulos

Untitled

Pen-see - (French) - A Reflection or Thought,
  You, always on my mind;
  Love is hard to find.

Ecstasy- rapturous delight, an overpowering emotions or exaltation,
  a state of sudden or intense feeling. The frenzy of poetic
  inspiration.
  This is what you do for me, -
  Your essence has set me free.

Nectarous - delicious or sweet.
  How can I say more;
  I'm like a kid in a candy store.

Nourish - To supply with what is necessary for life, to cherish.
  What I wish to give,
  What I need to live.

Yearn - To have a strong desire or longing for; but seems
unattainable
  I dream of being in your warm embrace;
  All dressed in Satin and lace.

Robert Gibbons Sr.

Black Woman's Struggle

Although their words may not be said with flair
You can bet if you listen the message is there
For she's a mixture of love for those who care
A furious hate for those who dare
To harm her children or her man
Forgetting the word can't and using can
When telling her children what they must do
In their life before they say "through"
A cleaner of houses not always her own
She's always striving to make her house a home
Molding and making day after day
Her family as if, it were made of clay
She knows what suffering really means
Yet she has pride fit for a Queen
She carries a lot deep within her soul
And she constantly strives to meet her goal
She's always pushing forward...No looking back
For the struggle has been rough for the woman who's Black

Wynna F. Elbert

Special Thanks

Thank you, God, for being my friend.
   You are always there so I can win.
Continuous blessings come from above:
   You send them, Lord, to show your love.

No way can anymore replace you, Lord!
   I sing your praise with full accord.
Problems come and problems go
   You are always there the path to show.

If only I could write a song,
   I'd sing your praise all day long!
I will keep on witnessing as I go,
   Doing my best your path to show

Thank you for Christ your son
   whereby the whole world could be won.
It is great to have a perfect God.
   It's good to know upon earth you did trod.

We know Christ was "God with man";
   On his promises I will always stand!
Give me grace and wisdom to know
   The person to whom you want me to go.
    William B. Kornegay

Negro Toes

Being exotics
   ...you are an object of fascination
   a curiosity of the streets
   the stuff of dreams, liable of lustful approaches

Being a cold climate
   ...it's not easy to warm friends
   excavation in the snow
   may freeze your negro toes
   only to uncover another cold heart

Of the new world...in a new world
   ...it's a cultural thing
   from dazed diversity to secular homogeneity
   from bold self-expression
   to muted or tentative individuality
   difficult to understand, pointless to question

Being of natural growth
   ...some toes pour
   into wooden shoes and call it a fit
   while others hang suspended
   from unnamed species of nut trees
    Margaret Mary McBride

Advice

Next time try using your head, he says
you are by now too abstract to see
danger lurking around your corners,
traveling the backroads trying to pretend
you do not know this street is raggedly feathered,
narrow and unpretty

How loudly can you fool your own seems, he says
you are no stranger to chains and links,
you know with every jab comes the blood,
welling up behind your eyes to flooding point
and no one would ever want a woman
who cries those sort of tears
I say these things to you (and more), he says
because I am your friend
    Meri Mayfield

Love Or Illusion

Love is a pillow I lowered my head
You are my dream come to my bed.

Life is a sensation a roaring red fire
Your a blooming rose you are my desire.

The world is our destiny we are born to be free
You are my fantasy please come to me.

This man that I see I know he's a steal
So I must ask myself is he for real.

My mind keeps wondering what should I do
of all my experiences the best has been you.

I try to be strong through all the confusion
This wonderful man could he be an illusion.

All talk on the outside inside frightened as a kitten
This beautiful man love has once bitten.

The torment the torture the sorrow the pain
Nothing can stop it not even the rain

You are the one my shining star
So now I am asking please don't drift too far.

If I can help I'll erase all your fears
Don't be afraid because I'm always here.
    Monica Santoyo

When You Walk With God

When you walk with God, you're never alone
   You are safe, wherever you go
You don't have to fear, the tug of the world
   It is easy for you to say "no".

When you walk with God, you're never alone
   For you've found the light and the way
You listen for guidance, then heed His call
   You know what to do and to say.

When you walk with God, you're never alone
   Know this as an actual fact.
While you're busy about God's business
   There is joy in your every act

When you walk with God, you're never alone
   You have courage wisdom and health
For these are the things which really count
   And more precious than good-looks or wealth

When you walk with God, you're never alone
   You understand your mission on earth
For walking with God, lets you comprehend
   The true reason for which there is birth
    Lavaughn Ogren

To You

To you who is in my thoughts,
You are the one I've sought.
The first time we met,
I did not see what you meant to me yet.
We hung out now and then,
Now I wish you were here again.
When you left I did not cry,
Until a couple of days went by.
Then I realized how far you've gone,
And all you left me were memories to pawn.
We write and call to keep in touch,
But, you should know I miss you very much.
    Kimberly Petro

621

My Dad

The room is full of silence, as no one will speak;
You can hear the mumble of the doctor
as your heart starts to get weak.
You know what he will say, so you close your ears so tight;
you wish that things would change, you wish he'd be all right.
you sit there hearing family say, "Everything's alright;"
well if everything's so perfect,
why won't he put up a fight.
If I could do anything
to help him win this fight,
I would be helping him everyday,
morning, noon and night.
But there's nothing I can do,
so I sit here helpless and alone,
and when all of this is over
this will soon be unknown.
But, I know God had his reasons
so I try to think it's alright—
But the room is still very silent
and the picture's out of sight.

Melyssa Claire Fields

In Your Shadows

Today I followed in your footsteps.
You didn't see me.
I was hidden in the shadows you always leave behind.
In your supposed solitude,
I saw the hopes and dreams and fears
you always try to hide.
I saw you (for the first time, really,)
and I think I understand now why;
why you struggle and scream and fight
against a world that wants to love and hold you.
(Hold you down, Hold you back - you say.)
And I don't blame you.
To soar you have to break free
leaving behind weighty people like me.
And I'm tired of running, and following, and failing
to try to keep pace with you.
So go.
I can't keep pace with you.
I've tried.

Stacey Hall

Dream

Dreams.
You dream with your eyes closed,
a blissful smile on your face, alone,
but in the company of friends
in a dream world.

But there are times
when you dream
with open eyes, open mind,
and an open heart.
You see,
there are things you can't see,
you can only feel them; the breeze
betraying its presence in rustling leaves,
the fragrance of flowers
wafting gently to you,
the warmth of friends
making your heart glow.

The warmth of friends
makes you dream with your eyes open,
as I do, when I'm with you.

Praveen Kumar

For My Son

Watching you grow throughout the years has brought me lots of joy.
You even brought me years of laughter when you were just a boy.
But now you've grown into a man with life's road just ahead.
Go forth my son and don't lose hope while through the years you tread.
Don't lose sight of goals and dreams when brick walls you may hit.
'Cause through it all you'll do just fine as long as you don't quit.
As I sit here with my memories, a tear or two may fall
For having you my son has been the greatest gift of all!!

Peggy A. Pickern

Beauty

You inspire my dreams to come alive every night,
You fill them with your beauty and chase away my fright,
In my dreams our souls are but one,
The love that we share will never come undone.
Like the stars need darkness to give off their shine,
I need you and your love to make life divine,

Making my nightmare turn into a dream,
Your beauty and love are all that they seem.
If ever I doubted how precious you are,
I now know I'm holding my very own star.
I realize how lucky I am to have you,
God's given me a gift - my one dream come true.

Tina Selleck

Please Stop Crying

Please stop, no need to cry,
You gave it your best, it was a good try.
My time was up, I had to go,
So please stop crying and feeling low.

It was just love that wasn't meant to be,
So please stop crying over me.
You should be glad, I'm moving on,
I'll be with you till the break of dawn.

Go home, you had a long day,
You gave in, you had your say.
I lost, but you fought and won,
Go on, my time is gone.

Tomorrow will be another day,
Where I'll forever lay.
Please don't cry and try to be glad,
Cause I don't want you to be sad.

I'm writing this but you don't know why,
Your asking why did you have to die.
I'm six feet deep and you'll be too,
Don't cry cause there's nothing you can do.

Wendy Wheeler

Lonely Teardrops Fall As I Think Of You!

Lonely teardrops fall as I'm lying here thinking of you. I remember the time you took me to the park and we stayed until it was completely dark. You're the only real thing I believed in. So when you left me, a part of me died. God took you from me and I can still see your smiling eyes and your laughter that always made me smile. I love you dad! And you mean so much to me that I know I'll never forget you. Lonely teardrops fall as I feel the pain that God inflicted in me. Some days are ok, but other days, all I feel is the emptiness of the love I felt for you. I remember your strong arms wrapped around me. When I felt sad, and you were always there when I needed you, and now I need you and you're not there. I miss you and will always love you. When I see you in my dreams, I know you're still with me and that's why lonely teardrops fall as I think of you.

Melissa Clarke

"Lady Luck"

Lady luck where have you gone
You have never deserted me this long
Come back and be my very best friend
I'll always love you to the end.

Since you left I am very much heartbroken
Make me believe our love was just a token
If ever there was a girl I love
It was you ladyluck my turtle dove

If need be I'll bow to you
Showing you my love is true
I'll never ever again be blue
As long as I live I'll always love you

Maybe I didn't treat you right
As usual two lovers will fight
But we have to forget and forgive
So that our love will long live

If ever ever I treat you wrong
Please don't take flight and be gone
I very much need you by my side
My love for you I can no longer hide

Patrick A. Bazil

"Rabbit"

Little rabbit with the great big ears; can
you hear my whispers?

And what about those big, big teeth?
Do they cut your lettuce leaf?

What job do you have for your big long
feet; do they keep you warm while you sleep?

No; I bet they help you jump! Or
warn of danger when you thump.

I can't forget your big pink eyes!
I know they sparkle; but can they
see good at night?

Most of all; what I like best; to touch
your fluffy white fur as you rest.

But, no rabbit would be complete;
without mention of his tail; tucked
all under so nice and neat!

Patricia Vigil

Helas

...And then I saw the picture of the stones, and
you in the village — those stones with
names of heroes no longer loved,
no longer remembered. And your
smile, still your smile and the
patchwork of defiance (your face opposite an
old threshold, an old window) and the
Sun — gold over your presence, and the
outside world, the killings, the
old lady wishing me peace during the
liturgy (you see, my memories are
immediate, no past or future, I do not have,
I think I never had, a picture of
my hometown, a snapshot of my old folks);
just transient images provoked by emotions, when
the journey is long, and time twists
used words towards new meanings, the hours
when all guests have gone, my book of hopes
temporarily closed and my
voice cheering the sound of your voice.

Marcilio R. Farias

Remembering

You left me abruptly with no sad good-byes
You left me abruptly with tears in my eyes
I dream of you nightly as soon as it's dark
I think of you daily with a spark in my heart
I'm ever so lonesome for your tender embrace
I long for your arms dear and a look at your face
I'll never forget you I'll not even try
I live for the day dear that I may die
I pray you'll be waiting with outstretched hand
I'll grasp it gently and together we'll stand
Together forever you and me
No more departures will there ever be

Nina Naomi Pescatrice

Eclipsed

I am but a shadow in your eyes.
You look at me, but you rarely see.
A darkened spot in your shining skies,
Unnoticed, and perhaps that shall always be.

You feel my presence standing close at hand.
You hear my thoughts, but do you understand
What I'm trying to say? Must it always be this way?

I could share your world if you'd but learn
One thing to do...
Let me come from the darkness and stand beside you.

Marchelle E. Cain

If You Would Look

Hello, you don't know me, but you see me on the street.
You look away and pass me by, praying I don't speak.
You think I am an animal, another useless case.
You would see I am as you if you would look into my face.

You think I was always homeless and always I will be,
I say the things that brought me here you refuse to see.
You feel that all we have to say are threats or alibis.
You would surely know the truth if you would look into my eyes.

You feel we are incapable of loving acts of kindness.
I pity you for prejudice has caused your moral blindness.
You feel within yourselves that we are worlds apart.
You'd find we are as brothers if you would look into my heart.

You feel we are all evil, something you should fight.
You think we hide away by day, and rob and kill by night.
I have no wicked mind, nor heart as black as coal.
You'd see the love of God if you would look into my soul.

You just cannot believe that I am human too.
I wish to give ten times as much as all I get from you.
I seek only a normal life, good friends, good health.
You would see me as I am if you would look into yourself.

Mark R. Montgomery

Angel Of Mine

Little angel of mine, when you are asleep,
you look so helpless and innocent,
know my little one that God has you in his care,
he will never leave you or forsake you.

Oh! Angel of mine, how peaceable you sleep.
I hope that those sweet dreams that you dream will come true.
For you are so precious to me. And I will always love you forever,
don't ever think that you will ever be alone, because Daddy God
will always hold and love you forever.

Angel! Angel! How beautiful you are.
When you are sleep. I know you have fears,
But believe me when I say, I will hold you and try to be the best
mother I can be to you and knowing that God will help me.
And know my angel that God will be with you always.

Patricia Martin

Reality

I have no time to dote and dream, what I want is reality,
you may call it foolish, I call it, agony of desire, I have not
always been as now, somewhere there a snare in every human
path my image deeply lies, my words I strangely mistrusted,
talk was serious and sober thoughts they were mature, letting
this mystery explode hesitating no longer, let my heart be still
a moment let me catch my breath,
we grow in age and love another when in reality we love together,
loving all the wrong things for all the right reasons and all the
right things for all the wrong reasons, I firmly do believe we were
destined to be, neither time and distance can't keep us apart,
crossing my path like a black cat, with little luck I wait the signs
and signals leaving my gate ajar, oh but youth is wild and age
is tame and pleasure comes in all ages, sometimes I'm frighten
but I'm ready, ready to learn the power of life,
and happy to be alive...

Luz Ares

Slowing Down

Pause and savor the joy of each day
You may never again pass along this way.

Marvel at the dove and the lowly sparrow,
Never let your view of life be sparse and narrow.

I watch you, my friend, scurry along your frantic pace;
I know well what you are missing, for I lost this race.

If you would but pause, and listen to my voice,
For I did not leave this world by choice.

The Lord gives us life and wisdom without measure;
But we must search for it, as we would a hidden treasure.

Slow down your steps and gaze on nature's beauty.
Make this your goal, rather than earthly duty.

Your spirit will soar, and your body glow with health,
A prize much greater than worldly wealth.

My sorrow will abate, and I will no longer mourn my pain,
Because my message to you will not have been in vain.

Nancy J. Hummer

The Crotchety Bluejay

Did you see the flash of the handsome Jay?
You must have heard him screeching away.
As he went flitting to the bird feeder.
He's got to be first, he thinks he's the leader.

He bullies his way among the feathered fowl
Though I doubt if he'd dare attack an owl.
A flash of blue, a glimmer of white
He's flying around as soon as it's light.

The Bluejay robs other nests of their young
That certainly wouldn't prove he's a hero unsung.
He likes to be out in all sorts of weather
But he screeches and fights when others gather.

Bluejays like to live among the oaks and pines
A feast of nuts and acorns is right down their line.
Their nests are bulky cups of sticks
Where they can hide from the fights they pick.

They are about eleven inches long
And they do occasionally burst into song
Even though screeching at an aggressive friend
Is more the Bluejay's nature upon which one can depend.

Mildred Asp

A Cry For Peace

To tell the story, all in all,
You must listen carefully, and I will not flaw,
There was never a time when I felt his grief,
Because as until now, there has been no peace.

When the war first started and the fighting had begun,
Sorrow filled the air, as this by far, was no fun.
When this was to end, as one knew,
We could only hope and pray, as the hatred grew.

Years had passed, when it came to a halt,
There was nothing left, as mankind was at fault.
All was at rest, on this place called Earth,
It was never this peaceful, except maybe birth.

I'm telling you this tale, so you can be warned,
To spare this world, so it won't be mourned.
I leave you these words, those you shouldn't forget,
So use them wisely, and there will be no regret.

Mike Martin

Daddy Why?

You say that you love me, is that really true?
You never once said to me, "My child how are you"?
I can't remember you ever throwing me a ball,
taking me for ice-cream or shopping at the mall. (Daddy Why?)

I would look at my friends with envy, as they embraced their
dads with hugs,
I would drop my head and walk away, in pain my heart did tug.
Mom did her best to bring the family through,
but there were things to be done that only Dad could do. (Daddy Why?)

As I grew up I learned the hard way, that in this world there's a
great price to pay
While living without a Father from day to day.
If I only had a dad whose arms I could run into,
I could rest in assurance that any harm to me no one could do.
(Daddy Why?)

Being rejected by anyone is a hard pill to swallow,
But God has helped me throughout the years, that's why His path
I will continue to follow.

Oh! how important it is, to have a father in the home,
Being the head and priest of your family is where you really belong.

A call to account will soon be required of you,
For the Stewardship that was rejected and your role of Fatherhood too.
(Daddy Why?)

But as long as there is breath in your body you still have the time,
to repent and say that you're sorry, and a new life together we
are sure to find. (Daddy it's time!)

Marie A. Moore

Winter

Winter...
    You snowbound warrior
    Exciting, yet frigid
    Dressed in soft reds and deep forest greens
    Accented with wintery whites
    Warmed by the memory of golden wheat..waving
    Treating us to delicious snow cream
        Freezing,
            exciting,
                dying,
In the dimness of the forest
In the lighting of a fire
Until, at last, you lie down
To rest, waiting for spring
To cover your cold and frigid hands.

Tracy Moore

624

Open Season

We saw the herd and pulse ran like a hart.
You nodded yer head and gave me a start.
I chased you about and we had some fun,
but something went wrong, it's over and done.

To me you were fawn, you were so young and tame.
n thought I was brawn, but to you I was game.
I did my duty and thought me the least.
I weren't no beauty, but you was a beast.

I gave you my all to have you so near,
I took the great fall fer a two legged deer.
You wore my jewel and dared lady luck,
Ya played me a fool and run off fer a buck.

He was a poach who oughta be fined,
Had an approach and ya musta been shined.
He won the roe and he took a bride,
It was a blow and I lost my hide.

I don't recall ever bein' so low,
But that's what I get fer making some doe.
Ya do pay a price for messin' around
And ya don't need a license fer gettin' shot down!

Kurt A. Kylloe

Untitled

You are older, it seems, than some people, and they call
you old. Old, old, old. You have wrinkles you do not cover
And your hair is gray and you have lived for something
like 74 years on this earth without much complaint.
There is nothing much to complain about.
But some people look at you and think you should
Stop now, rest now, grow old now, gracefully.
But you live gracefully enough you don't have time
to grow old.

You have a canoe. And that canoe has a river.
And that river does not end. And you watch the
river flow and watch it flow.
And watch the leaves change color, and watch your
hands turn eighty years old in the middle of a river
bend. You hike thirteen miles at the end of the day
And that is how you rest, that is how you rest.
So let the young ones sleep. Let the whole world
sleep. You will sleep when you have to.
You are crossing the water, crossing the water,
And there is so much water left to be crossed.

Mark A. Simonson

Feelings

Feeling, oh feelings, feelings of mine,
You seem to be with me all of the time.
You're in and you're out and always about,
And sometimes ,make me give out a shout.

The feelings are good more than they're bad,
But sometimes they seem to make us so sad.
Feelings are here both day and at night.
And really give us a reason to fight.

Feelings of love and hope and dreams,
Hit me like the flowing streams
So feeling oh feeling, feelings of mine
I think I will keep you around all the time.

No bad feelings can take mine away,
So you see that they're here to stay.
And feelings of bad I do not adore,
And they will never be any more.

Nancy I. Arbuckle

"Looking Into Your Own Eyes"

Sadness - it grows like thick black smoke, it grows. It
surrounds you, smoothers you, and chokes you. You can't
breath. Your eyes they hurt. Tears falling, you can't see.
Sadness like a pool of water, it drowns you. Your smile runs off
your face. Like a fire that grows and you can't put it out. It
feeds off of you, and burns down your world. You are very
small, like a seed that means nothing, no place to plant you.
Your soul as hollow as the hole you are in.
Your cry echoes off the sides and nobody hears.

Sadness - like climbing a tree that you know the most beautiful
thing is waiting for you at the top, and suddenly parts of the tree
start growing so rapidly you can't keep up. The top gets further
and further away. Still you keep up the pace till you can't climb
anymore. You sit and stare as your dream grows away from
you. You become a part of this tree like a limb. You grow with
it. You are like an October leaf that gets blown off the tree by a
small gust of wind. Winter comes and the snow covers you.
Finally the shimmering sun melts all the snow, and the wind
picks you up one more time only to crumble you into dust.

Tricia Topping

A Tribute To Parents

One beautiful day filled with sunshine and glory
You started life's greatest ever love story

You took the first step and joined your lives together
And a wonderful future you planned on forever

You created several children - a mixture of two
Each one containing a resemblance of you

You bathed us in love and taught us about life
And bandaged our knees and broke up the strife

You helped us in school and drove us to sports
And cheered and yelled as we were out on the courts

You taught us about values and how to stand on our own
And created a place we will always call home

You helped us leave the nest and softened the fall
By being caring and patient and always on call

You encouraged our dreams and helped us build goals
And tried to prepare us for life's many roles

You are the best parents that could ever be had
And we've never taken the time to thank you Mom and Dad

For being loving and supportive and making a home
And for being there always no matter how far we roam

Rosemarie Kasianiuk

From You To Me

When everything is said and done,
You still will be the only one.
I run to you when I am in need,
Strength and hope from you I always receive.

You listen, you speak, you understand,
And soon I can face, from which I ran.
You give me hope to face another day,
I listen to your words and hold on to what they say.

When you hold me near, my world seems brighter,
The problems that weigh me down, always seem lighter.
Do you cure my ills because you are so wise,
Or is it love that cures that I see in your eyes.
Whichever it is, please always be the one,
That I can turn to, to whom I can run.

Marion Abramowitz

The Plight Of Refugees

No matter how far you go back in history
You will always learn of the plight of refugees
As they discover there is no place to call their home
They are destined to flee and to forever roam

And history repeats itself time and time again
With refugees fleeing, losing relatives and friends
War has left them such a heavy burden to carry
Leaving most possessions behind, it is life that matters

Injustice prevails in times of war after war
And refugees must suffer more and more
The price of freedom is a high cost
With so many, many lives that are forever lost

Patricia Cox Napoli

Once In A Lifetime

Once in a lifetime
  You'll meet your one true love.
    Your knight in shining armor
      To light up the heavens above

For me, the light was different
  Flashing red and bright...
    It was accompanied by sirens
      Echoing in the night.

My knight was a fireman
  His armor was yellow-turned-black.
    He stole my heart away
      And, I've never looked back.

I have lived the American dream
  There's only one thing to say.
    I married one of the "America's Bravest"
      I wouldn't have had it any other way.

Linda K. Short

My Easter Island

If you have ever lived on an Island
You'll never be quite the same
You may look the same and talk
the same, but never in quite the same way
For life becomes more meaningful
and God's presence is always near
In the blue blue waters that surround
you to the pristine white clouds so clear
And at night the celestial heavens seem
to open up to the stars and the moon
comes out in its brilliance dropping
diamonds from the sky and in the
morning the loons cry out and the gulls
fly in and the sun comes up a deep
pink ball bringing the dawn of a
bright new day of hope and joy to all.
So - once you have lived on an Island
You'll never be quite the same.

Virginia Follett Easter

A Scared Generation

Sittin on the corner
Young and scared
Tryin to be cool
So the dealers won't attack
Pushed to the edge
Gun in pocket in case of emergency
Worries of being beat down
Common thoughts of making it in this world
Hope to live at least another decade
Too young to walk the streets
Old enough to care.

Kisha C. Danielson

For My Heart

For my heart needed you, and
  your liberty completed
    my freedom.

When we kissed,
  the sky reached out to us;
    it fell asleep over our souls.

The horizon secretly crept away
  with your absence, like
    the bird takes flight with eternity.

I received your voice as an
  echo of my mind.

I woke, and knew you were gone.
  The bird that once slept in our souls
    had flown away.

Robin A. Cagle

Untitled

Like a faceted crystal
Your light shines wherever directed.
Its energy creates love
When the brightness is perfected.
Friendship refracts the beams to bending dimensions:
A rainbow — the result of colorful intentions.

The gleam of your personality
Brightens my muddled existence —
Like a glowing, healing sphere
Floating without resistance.
Its clarity generates creativity
Resulting in ideas of great proportion:
Cognitions true and precise
Like an echo without distortion.

Crystalline attention offers sensitive interpretation
To those whose search for answers leads to your illumination.
The wisdom, courage, and strength you provide
Are qualities only part
That continue to grow and reside
In the contoured facets of my heart.

Tracy Stephenson

Touch Of Life

I want to touch all of you
Your most inner deepest you
To shower you with my most intimate caress
Together we can knock down all those walls
And illuminate all the darkness locked inside.

To want it as much as it wants you
All you have to do is care enough
Ask yourself, would you die for this sacred vow?
Until that time the world will suffer
The torment of life, that only you can change.

Without you I am hopeless
Only you can savor that forbidden fruit,
Will you share yourself with me?
You know me,
For I am life and the world around you.

Do you know who you are?
Do you care?
Do you care enough?
For if you don't...
I don't exist.

Sally J. Church

Granddaughter

You've come to that crossroad in your life,
Your no longer called a child.
But from tiny babe to sassy miss
O' how I've loved you all the while.
Together we have known joy,
We shared great sorrow too
But our love for one another,
Has always seen us through.
Sometimes your crazy antics,
Left me shuddering with fear,
But they never ever made you
Any less to me than dear.
As you continue down the road of life,
May God be there at your side,
To help you when you stumble,
And in your home abide.
My wish for you is happiness,
No matter what you do,
This comes from gram with all her love
And echo's papa's too.

Kay McDonnell

Eric

Sleep now my friend, your suffering is over,
your pain has come to an end.

Your young life was taken, a life that was hard,
your purpose is over, your soul is what GOD.

Oh how we'll miss you,
I wonder if you knew how much you meant,
No one could console you, in the time you had left.

Sleep now my friend Eric, your spirit at ease,
Your combat is over with a painful disease.

Although I grieve now, I know we will meet again,
you touched my life, I have lost a good friend.

Louise La Femina

"Time To Forget"

You're gone now. Time to forget
  Your shining face...
    And bright smile...
      Your calm nature...
        And wild whims...
          Your serious words...
            And cute sense of humor...
              Your soothing voice...
                And great big hugs...
                  Your passionate kisses...
                    And the love you gave me.

  You're gone now
  And you're so hard to forget
So I think I'll continue to remember that
  time in my life that you were a part
    of because it meant so much
      to me then as it does today.
        And so to me, it'll never be
          Time to forget.

Maria Moscatello

Good-bye

Good-bye my love. I have to let you go.
Your time has come to leave this world.
And travel to a new one.
Don't look back; just ahead.
My life will go on.
I'll remember you in so many ways
The first time we met, our eyes locked together.
And then our hearts.
The first time you gave me a kiss.
So soft
So natural.
The first time you said you loved me.
I felt the same way too.
You left my life so young. So much living to do.
Your memories will always be with me.
Do you watch over me at night.
Are you my angel from God.
Good-bye my love.

Tonya Bond

Diseased

   Look into these diseased eyes, let
your whole body go. Don't try to hold off,
let me take control. Let me enter your body,
let me taste your soul, let my poisoned
blood take control. Let this disease run
rampant through your veins. Let my hate and
passion make you feel this earthly pain. Enjoy
this disease, just lay back and smile. Think
of all the good things that make us humans
so wild. This disease that I have needs
to feed off your soul. It needs to feel
more hate and pain to stay in control. I'm
sorry if it hurts, but it only lasts a while.
Soon you will enjoy it, soon you will
be able to smile. You now have my disease;
your part of me. So pass it on to the
next victim, so that they can be diseased!

E. Joseph Foley

My Father's And Mother's Day

Although, you're my friends
You're also my closest, kin.
You're the ones, that God sent to me, from above,
Wrapped up with all his love,
While, in an orphanage, in a corner, all alone
Having no one, and no home,
He knew I needed someone to call, my very own.
God, also knew, I needed someone, to guide me from astray.

So, he blessfully, guided your footsteps my way.
So, I thank, God on this special day
for he gave me a wonderful
Father and mother, and in my heart
You'll, both always stay!
Happy father and mother's day

Kathy Hames

The Rainbow

Blue is for our heavenly church where God is so strong.
Yellow is for peace of mind that God can give to you.
Red is for his blood that he shed on Calvary.
White is for the robes that we will wear up there.
Gold is for the streets that we will walk upon.
Pink is for the rose's that bloom forever more.
Green is for the green, green grass that we may rest upon.
Pearl is for the pearly gates that we may walk thru.
Put them all together and they make the most beautiful rainbow
of all.

Thelma Burley

The Very Best Choice

You're the picture of health baby girl;
You're the apple of my eye.

You're the epitome of wealth baby girl;
An angel high in the sky.

My breast milk is the source of your nutrition and strength.
All these good things show up in your weight and your length.

I'm your reason for having a very healthy start.
The bond we are creating, we'll never want to part.

You love the warmth the closeness, the touch.
I love being needed; I enjoy it so much.

Doesn't cost a nickel although I don't mind;
It's just the best way to feed you that I could ever find.

Your Daddy is proud of the choice that I made.
It was a good decision; one that will never fade.

Call it nursing, breast-feeding, suckling
or nourishing; I know this way you will always be flourishing.

That loving look in your baby blue eyes
tells me what I know is true;

I've made the very best choice for you!
Lori Ann Walsh

Untitled

You light up my life as no other has done,
You're truly beyond compare;
Your smile, your touch, the love in your eyes,
There's not a jewel so rare.

Your beauty is the standard of judge,
All others just pale away;
And when I'm with you all darkness recedes
To eternal brightness of day.

But true beauty is that which comes from within,
It transcends that seen by the eye;
Your kindness, gentleness, your unselfish love
Is boundless as is the sky.

I had no chance! I was felled with a glance,
You captivated my heart;
And darkness hangs like a thick dark cloud
Whenever we're apart.

But I sing for joy when I see your face,
And I just want you to know;
These words of mine can't say it all,
Because I love you so.
Larry Arnold

Lovers And Friends

A stranger in the nighttime
You've become a friend,

Someone I somehow could understand

An artist's touch, a hunter's smile
Let's be lovers if only for a while.

A quiet loud, a gentle strong
Knowing right but choosing wrong.

It's the chase that feeds your heart,
I'll never know you...only a part.

I hope thoughts of me will never crowd your mind
And we will remain lovers and friends through the changes of time...
Zoe Zimmer

A Note To My Kindergarten Teacher

You are the beginning of what's about to unfold.
You're very important to what my future holds.
I'm impressionable, young, very much in need.
You are the planter, I am the seed.

This next year you will help me to grow,
watering nurturing, teaching me, what I need to know.
I know you'll be with me, only a little while each day.
For the rest of my life you are paving the way.

Will I like school? Or will it be a bore?
Will a little while be enough? Or will I want more?
Will you be there to praise me, whenever I try?
Will you be able to answer my questions, starting with why?

Will things get to you, will your patience wear thin?
Will I make you feel better with my silly grin?
Will you remember I appreciate the hard work that you do!
And what I become in life depends partially on you.

WHAT A BIG JOB! Such expectations of you.
I'm sure all would agree, not just anyone could do!
Mrs. Rudolph, you're special important to me.
I hope this poem helps you to see.
Katherine Lynn Zeis

Winter Blahs

(With Apologies To All Those Who Love Winter)

Wintertime, you sneaky wizard,
You've sent us yet another blizzard!
Though some may want to ski and sled,
I'd just like to stay in bed.

Wintertime, so dark and drear,
Oh how I wish that Spring was here.
My sniffles have sniffles, my back does ache,
From ice and snow, I need a break.

Wintertime, so dreadfully long,
Can wishing for Springtime be so wrong?
The warmth is gone from my down-filled vest,
And my furnace could certainly use a rest.

Wintertime leave, without hesitation,
I need to get out of hibernation!
I yearn to see the tulips grow,
I'd even like some grass to mow.

But winter's still here, alas and alack,
I'll put on my snuggies and crawl in the sack.
And with my bedtime prayers I'll sing,
Tomorrow is one day closer to Spring!!!
Pauline Randazzo

'Once Upon A Time'

Little old house at the side of the road
Shingles all weathered and worn
The curtains are gone from the windows
The shades hang all crooked and torn
It leans from its age and the weather
Dejected, lacking love and repair.

Now someone lived in this house by the road
Laughter from children was heard there
Sorrows and joys filled the air in that place
Life was lived and died inside there.

Now everyone's gone, moved on who knows where
And silence is felt everywhere
Some day when the wind blows cold and strong
Its leaning more obvious it seems
It will end in a pile with a shuddering sound
And leave all its memories and dreams.
Theresa Derkatch

Flight Of The Spirit

Athena sat in her cage looking out the window
Thinking there must be another world out there.

One day, Vincent came and quietly opened her door,
Gently took her out and cradled her in his hands,
Nurturing her, loving her, teaching her.
Slowly she gained her strength and her spirit grew.
She would sit in his hand and stretch her wings
And feel the warm breeze caress her.

There came days,
When she would take short flights,
Always to return to Vincent's nurturing hands.

Then came the day
When she knew that it was time to fly into the light:
It was time to wish Vincent happiness and peace;
It was time to feel her own strength;
A time for Athena to spread her wings.
Reach out into the universe and feel
Its love, its power, its strength....

Athena was free
She had learned to fly.
JoAnne Nemec

Shadow

Awake in a shadow
a shadow shinning through
from the light
the light from the window
the light from the moon
the bright, Glowing crescent moon
the shadow is towering
the shadow is delicate
This shadow, This silhouette I would
like to be
slender and willowy
the shadow is all around me
I am standing here looking at this figure
Upon the floor
For you see,
this shape I see is genuinely, indisputably,
unequivocally ME.
Jennifer Marabella

Stoplight Love

Pulled up at a stoplight
Acting real shy
Look over at this girl/guy
She caught my eye
Didn't know what to say
Time was running out
So I said stoplight love to you

So many times it happens
I just don't know what to say
My only trying to be friendly
They don't see it that way
You wouldn't even look
You wouldn't even turn
Now I understand
When they say passion really burns

So when you're at a stoplight
And there's a love for you
Say stoplight love
And they will feel it too
Stoplight love
Barbara Jean Brown

Emptied Arms

Lord, I kneel before you, with an armload of troubles,
and a head full of sorrow and a heart full of despair;

But, a spirit filled with praying, always hoping, never straying,
reaching out for just tomorrow, and the solace that is there.

For I know that You as Father, sometimes will that we should suffer,
and I'll always accept suffering for to dwell within Your love;

Still, I place my trust within You, knowing that You're there to
guide me, I will never cease my searching for direction from above.

So, I cast my cares upon You, for I know You'll take them from me,
lay me down to sleep in silence, free from danger and alarm;

And when morning comes, I'll thank You,
rise up early just to praise You;

Spirit singing, head-heart happy, lifting up my emptied arms!
Phyllis Hill

Happy Mother's Day Poem

MOM.....It's been long days.
But, yet, it's fun.
I thank you so,
for all you've done.
I can't explain the way it feels,
even though, I make big bills.
I try to help, but no one sees;
the work I've done just to please.
I see your face in my palm;
that you are glad to be my MOM.
Say, oh! How it's been.
You'll be within my little grin.
Happy Mother's Day.
Gloria Lisa Brooks

Polka Dot Blues

Down in dixie where the
Cotton grows
Picking cotton all in
A row
Singing as they go to
And fro
The polka dot blues.

Hear them singing to the
Tune of polka dot blues
Picking cotton by the score
Listen listen to that
Polka dot roar.
Down in dixie the song
They adore polka dot blues
Shirley Schlieman

"Sun #1"

When the sun comes up
Every morning, it looks down on me
To tell me I am free.
When the sun reaches above me
It watches over me like a angel.
When the sun finally sets in the west
It is telling I am safe for that day
And I should now rest up for another
Good day tomorrow.
John Nicosia

"Stand Off"

As he stands in the sand so brisk and so harsh;
His horse seems to wave in the heat of the day.
He cries, he screams, his tears fall gracefully.
An eagle in the sky feels pity on thee;
Why such a prey should fall, so easily to me
Is he too brisk, too tough for I to take?
Should we just blink eyes and go our own way?
Fly, fly, fly away - never to return.

Barry Mosher

Windowpains

Sitting on the padded seat looking out,
I saw the figure of a girl.
Only her face was distinguishable.
She was gazing at me intently
With a small sad smile on her thin lips.
Her long face looked pale and drawn,
Blending into the bleak grayness outside.
But it was her eyes that caught my attention.
Eyes of clear blue crystal
With deep dark centers.
Such sorrowful eyes I had never before seen.
They were broken, shattered
And pleading silently, hopelessly,
Begging for a loving touch.
So I reached out toward her,
Pressing my face up against the glass.
And then she was gone.
She just disappeared.

Julianna Johansen

Insecurity

Emotionally drained,
I sit staring blankly
Afraid of the emptiness I feel.
Terrorizing images rage in my memory

Things have changed
My peace has been devoured by time.
This hatred in my heart won't let me forget.

Awareness came all too soon.
Leaving behind a disaster
Raping my innocence
Security is a luxury I have never known.

Brandy Hestand

Butterfly

Butterfly, butterfly in the sky
Let's try to catch him, and learn how to fly.
Don't let him go or Oops!, Goodbye!
Butterfly, butterfly high in the sky.
Come down and be our pet, and teach us how to fly.
Don't open the box or Oops!, Oh, well goodbye!

Katie Billey

Life

Life is hard
Life is fun
Life is a lot of work
But you know it will be okey
Because you did your best today.

Derek Crasi

Empty Soldiers

Please don't empty another soldier I will lose my mind
old purses reek of a scent left behind

Half empty leaking on shoes worn for school
passed out at the kitchen table plate full of drool

Hidden in my winter coat pocket
soldiers drained burst verbally like a rocket

Afraid to stir in the night ahead
walk softly or you will wake the living dead

Who to confide in when their hearts are full of sauce
you will hear my slurred words I am the boss

So young and confused will I be the same
some siblings still play the game

Years have come and gone some good some bad
wish you were here now my soul feels so sad

I have come through it all emotionally distraught
recovery is the answer where life is taught

True love is here hopefully to stay
for some reason it ends I will be OKAY

Dottie Dunbar

Madeline

Oh ladybug
Sweet Bumble Bee
Who sleeps curled up
Tonight with me

Does Baby bug
In her cocoon
Dream of growing
Red hair soon

Or does her
Beating baby heart
Leap with joy
That she'll soon walk

And when will
Dearest Ladybug
Delight her Mommy
With a hug

Mary Herlihy

Friends

Friends can be forever, sometimes,
they are not, they can live close or they
can live apart. They can be people,
dolls, animals or anything. Friends
stick together day by day and always
stay. Friends no matter size, shape
or sound. Friend I finally realize
I will love you to the end.
So no matter how far or close I love you.

Tara Stanford

Voice Of Time

We come as a seed, with hope, trust and love.
We grow and grow till we are tall and strong.
We bend and twist as time goes along,
then we bloom with all our love in hopes we will be strong.
To share with you our thoughts of all Do's and Don'ts of time.
To give to you our knowledge and wisdom
that in hopes you will be strong.

Barbara A. Allen

630

Soul Love

I never felt love like
this.
I lay down upon your
bed, with your head gently
on my breast, my heart
pounding so!! Only once
to hear you whisper in
my ear I love you so.
This is a love that can
flower and grow. The time
we share as little as we
know? Will be cherished in
our lifetime and forever in
our souls!!

Donnel Gloster Sheffer

"Memories"

I want to give from the heart to show my love. Reaching inside,
way down deep, I find love beyond words. Beyond words I'll go.
To the mountains of smiles, the valleys of laughter and the rivers
of tears we've shared. The past is gone, today is here, and
tomorrow is only twenty-four hours away. Today is the beginning
of the tomorrows we call the past in the world of memories.
Keep all memories alive, good and bad; and tomorrow we will
share them once more.

Phyllis Maddix

Love's Destiny

Although we had our differences;
Although in our decisions; we had our differences'
Although we look like enemies'
Although our relationship has empathized'
Although there is a dead smile on our lips'
Although to me you stop wiggling your hips'
There is a hidden destiny.
You can't live without me.
When I am around' you light my fire.
I am sure' I light you fire.
Although through all our differences'
Although the rains have fallen' and never finishes'
Although we gave gifts'
Although we took back gifts'
Although we have seen our love's icon broken'
Although time passes slowly' with no token'
I still believe our destiny will get us together.
Our destiny will reject our false excuses' forever.

Hamdy H. El-Berry

The Paper Fairy

Look forth yonder
At the bark from the paper tree
At the youth of the stems
The blood it spills for me
Come to the meadow
The field of pollen
Don't wander too close
The tree has a hole you might fall in
The paper fairy so small and light
Lives in the paper tree almost every night
Until one day when the evil dogs came
Pulled out their machines
The forest to tame
They killed the fairy when they cut down her tree
So now no one is left to guard you and me
So late at night if you hear her plea
Don't be scared she died for you and me

Darren Lee Rowe

Realistic Dreams

In through the silence of the night,
I hear a phone ringing, can I be right?
I think I am still dreaming, but decide to open my eyes.
As I answer the phone, I turn to look at the sky,
Wondering, why do I hear your voice so shaken like the wind?
Unable to cry, you explain to me the uneasy journey you will
    be on.
It will be awhile before you get home,
Not to worry you tell me things will be.
Soon I will fly free, like an eagle, destination unknown.
Phone goes dead, the morning weather predicts stormy
    weather ahead.

Elysa D. Bray

The Goodbye Place

The sea gulls soar in the wind as she carries him out to sea.
Some turn around and start their day - he's gone, so now they're free.
Water crashes upon the rocks as tears stream down her face.
She sits, her face buried in her hands - this is the goodbye place.

Then one day they drift back in and hearts are filled with joy,
when daddy returns back home to his wife and little boy.
She smiles as they toss the ball - an innocent game of catch.
Yet in her heart and mind she knows the togetherness won't last.

It hurts to think about it but year after year it's true.
It's the place you go to pray to God to bring him back to you.
He does this for his country, while the Navy credits their gain.
What we're left with is a tear-stained face and a heart filled with
    pain.

Brenda L. Fraedrich

The Tale Of A Feather Duster

From the stately ostrich the plumes were plucked with care
To make the finest duster to be found anywhere.

Then the peddler took me, assembled in his wares
Sold me to the maid at home of Mrs. Dare.

The maid was very fussy and the house was very fine
So she had me dusting, dusting, DUSTING overtime!

I dusted in the attic — I dusted in the hall
I even dusted places where there was no dust at all!

Dusted all the knick-knacks from Italy and Spain
Then I dusted all of the golden picture frames.

I dusted and I dusted and the children came and went
I dusted and I dusted until my feathers bent.

Then the maid she shook me and said, "What can this be?"
This forlorn old duster is very, very worn and no more use to me.

Then she did something quite arrogant and rash
She picked me up and took me straight to the trash.

But when the trash man saw me, his eyes lighted up with glee
He'd found the perfect item of the Market of the Flea.

There a lady found me and gave a hearty cheer
She'd been looking for a duster almost a year.

Verlee T. Wise

631

Biographies
of
Poets

AARON, ALLAN D.
[Pen.] Allister, R. Aaron; [b.] January 30, 1960, Utah; [m.] Lynne Mehmert-Aaron; [ch.] Allister R. Aaron; [occ.] Orthopedic Surgeon; [pers.] My love for my wife and son provide the hues that color my paper canvas.; [a.] Chevy Chase, MD

ABBRUSOATO, DANA R.
[Pen.] Dayne; [b.] November 14, 1966, Johnstown, PA; [p.] Guy Thomas and Judity Renee Abbrusoto; [m.] Single; [ed.] Associate in Applied Science majoring in Early Childhood Education from Westmoreland Co. Community College, Blairsville Senior High School; [occ.] Preschool Teacher; [memb.] Saints Simon and Jude Catholic Church, F.H.A., H.E.R.O. Vice President 1984-1984; [hon.] March of Dimes Walk-a-thon, Award in Parliamentary Procedures; [oth. writ.] Several poems that I have chosen not to publish because of personal reasons.; [pers.] This poem is dedicated to Bradley W. Hustor who gave me the strength and inspiration to write and also taught me the depth of love; without him, the poem would not exist.; [a.] Blairsville, PA

ABELL, DONNA
[b.] July 26, 1932, Creston, Iowa; [p.] Dale G. and Beulah M. Conley; [m.] Richard E. Abell, May 19, 1948; [ch.] David L., Richard D., LuJana K.; [occ.] Artist; [memb.] Laurie Fine Arts Club, Ozark Brush and Palette, Inc., Versailles Assembly of God Church; [hon.] In Artistry; [oth. writ.] Many poems, songs, stories, card verses, articles on many subjects, etc.; [pers.] I write from the heart, hoping to inspire hope and encouragement to the readers. My writings for special occasions is on request. I try to bring forth the words and feelings for those who are unable to put their feelings into words.; [a.] Laurie, MO

ABLES, MOLLIE
[b.] August 31, 1981, Kernville, TX; [p.] Steve and Lynda Ables; [ed.] Currently at Peterson Middle School in Kerrville, TX; [memb.] National Honors Society, Youth Council of First United Methodist Church in Kerrville, TX; [hon.] Outstanding Musician of Starkey Elementary. Gold Medals in VIL Solo Violin; [oth. writ.] Several works of poetry, none of which have been published. (amateur writer); [pers.] Things only change if you take them to your own hands and make them. I like to remind people of that. As a youth, I'm part of the world's future. I want to make a difference. And I believe I can.; [a.] Kerrville, TX

ACKER, JEREMY D.
[b.] June 30, 1970, Motesto, CA; [p.] Peggy and Gary Acker; [occ.] Clerk for Dutch Haven, Lancaster Co., PA (Famous for Shoo Fly Pie); [memb.] 1993-1994 Vice President for English Club of Millersville University. Guitarist for progressive art-rock group Ritual.; [oth. writ.] Currently working on Alexander XL, Twenty Nothing, a picture book and diary of my tour through Canada and the U.S.; [pers.] I write because Gary Phillips told me to look through the window. I looked, and then through the brick, where ideas shattered into a million little pieces to be picked up.; [a.] Millersville, PA

ACKERMAN, STEPHANIE
[b.] March 20, 1971, Frankfurt, West Germany; [p.] Jim and Jan Ackerman, brother Jeff Ackerman and sister Jessica Ackerman; [ed.] Willman Sr. High, Willman, MN; St. Cloud Business College, St. Cloud, MN; [occ.] Full time, Live-in Nanny; [oth. writ.] Several poems written on childhood dreams, also write short stories.;

[pers.] I am influenced and inspired by the mountains and the ocean's beauty.; [a.] Silver Spring, MD

ADAMS, COURTNEY
[Pen.] Kitty Gunther; [b.] April 5, 1981, Cleveland, OH; [p.] Nancy and George Adams; [ed.] Breckville, Broadview Hts. Middle School; [occ.] Student; [memb.] Girl Scouts, Cleveland Orchestra Children's Choir, School Band; [hon.] G.S. Silver Award, Honor Roll and Merit Roll Academic Achievements, part of the Midwest Talent Search; [oth. writ.] Several other poems that haven't been published (as of yet), short stories from my childhood and now.; [pers.] I am what I am, and always have been, and always will be. Thank you to my dear friends, to Mrs. Nero, and to my boyfriends for all of your love and support. Many thanks mom and dad.; [a.] Broadview Heights, Ohio

AFIFI, ALY
[b.] June 6, 1956, Kafr Al-Sheikh, Egypt; [m.] Nancy Hill, 1991; [ch.] rima, Hannah; [ed.] Tanta University (BS) (BA) Cairo University (MA in Progress); [occ.] Editor; [oth. writ.] Numerous poems, critical pieces, and translations published in newspapers and magazines throughout the Arab World.; [a.] Nevada, MO

AFUANG, BENJAMIN
[b.] March 31, 1942, Laguna, Philippines; [m.] Maria Mirasol M. Afuang, December 11, 1966; [ch.] Brian, Maria Jasmin and Maria Katleya; [ed.] A.B. Journalism, University of Santo Tomas Manila, Philippines; [occ.] Editor, The Guam Tribune; [memb.] Philippine P.E.N.; [hon.] Works included in several literary anthologies in the Philippines; [oth. writ.] A collection of poems published in 1972; an art book published in 1975; articles and editorials in various Manila and Guam publications.; [pers.] For whom should one write? I write mainly for my brethren.; [a.] Agana, Guam

AGELLO, TERRIE LYNN HURD
[b.] September 13, 1978, Killeen, TX; [p.] Sherry and Gerald Hurr; [p.] Guardian: Shirley Gibbs; [ed.] Sophomore, Attending Smith County High School of Carthage, TN. I plan to go on to college to major in acting and music producing and writing.; [occ.] Student; [memb.] I've been in SADD, Stars, and 4-H. I took 6 years of ballet, I belong to Church of Christ and I want to be in the Sorority AKA when I get to college.; [hon.] 2nd place in Track, 4th place in beauty pageant, and have a B average in school. Write for my school newspaper.; [oth. writ.] I write short stories, plays, TV series, songs, and poetry. All my writings I treasure with all my heart and hope to share even more with the public soon.; [pers.] I'm inspired by all poets, and hope to have faith that someone can be inspired by me. Everything I write expresses my feelings to the world about issues that do occur and how it sounds read by other poets in our society.; [a.] Carthage, TN

AGUON, NIEVES
[Pen.] Navy, Cream Puff; [b.] October 10, 1980, Norfolk, VA; [p.] Roque and Balbina Aguon; [ed.] Went to Cottonwood Elementary and currently going to Fairview Junior High; [memb.] Student Academic Advisory Committee, Honor Society, Select Choir, Sprint Squad; [hon.] Student of the Month; [oth. writ.] A short story called "Stop The Violence, Increase The Peace"; [pers.] My writing is mainly about peace, love and being kind to other people; [a.] Bremerton, WA

ALARVA, ALFREDO P.
[Pen.] Fred Alarva; [b.] January 14, 1950, Philippines; [p.] Nemosio and Nieves Alarva; [m.] Naty R. Alarva, September 15, 1981; [ch.] Alexander and Alister; [ed.] B.S. in Accounting; [occ.] Data Control Tech. Sr., U.S. Postal Service; [hon.] High School Valedictorian; [a.] Daly City, CA

ALFORD, CHRISTINA
[b.] March 23, 1983, Denver, Colorado; [p.] Dean and Ginny Alford; [occ.] Student; [memb.] Little People of America; [oth. writ.] Several poems written, this is the first to be published.; [pers.] I'm a quadriplegic, confined to a wheelchair. I enjoy writing in my spare time I hope to be a screen writer when I grow up.; [a.] Aurora, CO

ALLEN, DANIEL NEAL
[b.] September 3, 1910, Sumter County, AL; [p.] Benjamin and Maggie F. Allen; [m.] Mildred P. Allen, July 22, 1939; [ch.] Three boys, two girls; [ed.] High school graduate, Ward High School; [occ.] Retired; [memb.] Christopher's Chapel United Methodist Church, Woodmen of the World, Trinity Senior Citizens; [pers.] This poem was written to introduce the Senior Citizen Singers.; [a.] Butler, AL

ALLEN, JANE E.
[b.] April 8, 1939, Dayton, Virginia; [p.] James and Stella Shull; [m.] William Allen, March 14, 1964; [ch.] Andrea Weathington, Lori Tatom, and Bryant Allen; [ed.] Harrisonburg High, James Madison Univ., Strayer Junior College; [occ.] Retired in April 94 after 35 years of Federal Service. Positions: Secretary; Editor/Writer; [memb.] Montgomery Branch of National League of Am Pen Women; Alabama Writers' Conclave; Press & Authors Club.; [hon.] Outstanding Civilian Career Service Medal; various writing awards for short stories, poems and articles; [oth. writ.] Several poems published in local newspapers; poem published in The Progressive Farmer; stories published in literary magazines; technical articles and human interest stories published in military newspaper; [pers.] I want to share my experiences and thoughts with others (poetry). I enjoy writing short stories about relatives and friends who are unusual. I also enjoy writing fictional stories with surprise endings. Goal: To entertain readers of all ages.; [a.] Wetumpka, AL

ALLEN, PAULINE L.
[b.] Middletown, CT; [m.] Charles E. Allen, Sr., August 21, 1951; [ch.] (7) David, Gary, Kathleen, Paula, Claudia, Constance, and Charles, Jr.; [ed.] Htfd High, MXCC (Middlesex Community College); [occ.] Therapeutic Recreation Director for Elderly; [hon.] St. James Church - Woman of the Year; Speech Contest Winner of Greater Htfd Chapter of ITT; President of Greater Htfd Prof and Business Women, President of Greater Htfd ITC; President of the St. James Women's Club; [oth. writ.] Former reporter for local newspaper: Weth-Rocky Hill Post; Cromwell Chronicle. Free-lance writer with many poems published in above local newspapers as well as articles features; [pers.] I believe "life" is a gift and that each day is an exciting adventure! How I wish there were more hours in a day! I also believe there's nothing, nothing on earth more important than family, my husband and wonderful (grown) children are my greatest friends; [a.] Rocky Hill, CT

ALLISON, RIKER
[b.] August 8, 1986, Parsippany, NJ; [p.] Wayne and

Christine Riker and Sister Michele; [ed.] 3rd Grade Student in Rockaway Meadow School in Parsippany, NJ, Teacher, Mrs. Shearman; [occ.] Student; [memb.] Gifted and talented program.; [hon.] 5 year dance award for jazz and gymnastics, student of the month award.; [oth. writ.] Published in 1994 edition of "Anthology of Poetry by Young Americans;" [pers.] I am only 8 years old and I like writing poetry because it is fun.; [a.] Parsippany, NJ

ALLMAN, LICIA L.
[b.] February 18, 1930, Italy; [p.] Vincent and Emilia Tinari; [m.] Robert G. Allman, July 1, 1961; [ch.] Robert, Vincent, Richard, Lee; [ed.] B.A. in Science; [a.] Philadelphia, PA

ALMGREN, ELFREDA M.
[b.] October 16, 1914, Minneapolis, MN; [p.] Anton and Valborg Jacobson (both deceased); [m.] Rudolph C. Almgren (deceased); [ch.] David L. Rudolph Jr.; [occ.] Retired; [hon.] Outstanding Lady Senior Citizen Mille Lacs Co. MN 1985; [oth. writ.] No other published work.; [pers.] Some of my verses are silly, some are sad, some are serious, but my thoughts are in them all.; [a.] Anoka, MN

ALSTON, JUANITA
[b.] August 3, 1952, Chicago; [p.] Ruby Fountain and William Parker; [ch.] Nichelle Monette and Tamika Kim

ALVARADO, GABRIEL GAMBOA
[Pen.] Gabriel A.; [b.] May 4, 1966, Los Angeles, CA; [p.] Carol and Hank Cosores/Xavier J. Alvarado; [ed.] Norte Vista High, Riverside; [occ.] Unemployed Poet; [hon.] Publication in Reflections of Light; [pers.] My personal fulfillment is when I can express my feelings and pass that experience onto the reader or the listener, who is fortunate to hear me at a poetry reading. Influences: James D. Morrison, and Henry Rollins; [a.] Rosemead, CA

ANDERSON, ARNOLD LEROY
[b.] August 31, 1949, Lakeland; [hon.] From talented associated companies, President Ted Rosen; [oth. writ.] I would like to have a chance and opportunity to share my gift and talent with people from all over the world. Since age of 11 year old I've been writing, now at age 45 yrs. old I am still writing. I was born with that gift and talent in my heart, no man can take it out my heart but Jesus himself.; [a.] Lakeland, FL

ANDERSON, BRADLEY G.
[Pen.] Meepzoo Adroit; [b.] December 10, 1964, Oakes, ND; [p.] Janice Irene Day, Clyde Arthur Anderson; [m.] Tial Anderson (Divorced), February 25, 1989; [ch.] Christopher Bradley Anderson; [ed.] High School Graduate Bonanza High 1983 LV, Nevada. Studied in Welding Technology and Automotive courses. Enjoyed working with hands; [occ.] Self employed writer/musician (helping mankind); [memb.] I have considered becoming a Mars--Musicians Against Racism - Sexism member. Also have a band but we have not named it yet. (Soon to be Adroit Corp); [hon.] Motorcycle off road racing trophies are all I have received, not very many but they mean an awful lot to me; [oth. writ.] Broken no cause, Lost touch, Chasing Dreams, Believe in Yourself. The young never cry Innocent, Why lie, Justice Prevails, Wake Up America, The Game, Atrocity, Haven't a Clue, Am I crazy, So quiet is the night, Playing Games, (Where Now), (Shame), Free Anger, Who Will Listen and many more; [pers.] I pray for the day, when not judged by color

of skin, sex, where from, is truly practiced world wide. Never give up, no matter how hard things get. Somewhere right beside you is the one who will see you through; [a.] Desert Hot Springs, CA

ANDERSON, CATHERINE D.
[Pen.] Catherine Moon; [b.] May 19, 1967, NYC; [ed.] Northern Valley Regional High School, Old Tappan, NJ, Ithaca College, Ithaca, NY, B.A. Philosophy and Religion; [occ.] Singer/Songwriter, acoustic musician; [memb.] Founder and member of the Women's Fold Project based in New Brunswick, NJ, (a collective of women songwriters and poets); [oth. writ.] Two self-released recordings, Catherine Moon "Soul on Fire" and Catherine Moon "Winter." Also on a compilation CD put out by the Women's Folk Project.; [pers.] Believe in yourself, hold steadfastly to your dreams, and all things are possible; that is my motto.; [a.] New Brunswick, NJ

ANDERSON, EULANHIE
[b.] January 10, 1941, Trinidad; [p.] Mr. and Mrs. Errol and Beryl Rosemir; [m.] Lio Anderson, December 18, 1971; [ch.] Patricia, Sherry, Richard, Roxann, Gregory; [ed.] St. Rose's High School and St. Joseph College; [occ.] Self Employed Catering.; [memb.] Trinidad and Tobago Red Cross Society.; [hon.] Red Cross Senior Cadet Honors List and several awards, senior class poetry award; [oth. writ.] Several school plays and poems.; [pers.] I am a realist, I have learned to deal with reality and to reject the impracticality of mankind. This way when you expect nothing, you are never disappointed. And to look at things as they really exist without any idealization.; [a.] Brooklyn, NY

ANDERSON, GLORIA C.
[b.] October 3, 1919, Texarkana, AR; [p.] Deceased; [m.] H. Edison Anderson (deceased), August 16, 1942; [ch.] Samuel E., Gloria Johnson, Ed Jr. (deceased); [ed.] Washington High, Diploma, Arkansas State College, Langston Univ, BA; [occ.] Retired Secretary; [memb.] AARP, Teacher Retirement of Prairie View, TX; [hon.] Write-up with poems, Forward Times, Houston; Book reviews, PVAMU Library, Lonnie Smith Library, Houston, Private home, Alexandria, VA. Awards: Army Reserve Officers Training Corps; Kiwanis Club, Prairie View; WR Banks Library, Prairie View. Plaque, Dept, Art, Music, Drama, PVAMU; [oth. writ.] Two collections of poetry presently writing family story for my grandchildren and great grandchildren; [pers.] I began writing overnight in 1973. My poems, unrevised and unplanned, evolve from mental images, dreams, and experiences of a lifetime. I am inspired by nature and humanity. I try to take nothing for granted in this life; [a.] Prairie View, TX

ANDREW, ROBERT BRUCE
[b.] June 7, 1962, Titusville, FL; [p.] Erwin and Margaret Andrew; [ed.] Astronaut High School, Data Processing Institute; [occ.] Computer Programmer; [oth. writ.] Small collection of unpublished poems and songs.; [pers.] I believe creativity and imagination are the key to life, and self expression is rarely experienced by most people, unfortunately, so let yourself shine.; [a.] Tampa, FL

ANDRUZZI, III JOSEPH
[b.] March 1, 1958, New York; [p.] Joseph and Barbara Andruzzi; [m.] Kris-Ann Andruzzi, July 18, 1992; [ed.] Somerset County Vocational and Technical Schools, Ducret School of Arts; [occ.] H.V.A.C. Technician; [memb.] Our Lady of Mercy Church; [hon.] Brown Belt Rank in Martial Arts; [oth. writ.] unpublished; [pers.]

Faith and fate walk hand in hand. It is what you believe, that which you shall become.; [a.] Somerset, NJ

ANGELIAS, ANTHONY
[Pen.] Tony Angelias; [b.] August 17, 1961, Waco, TX; [p.] Vincent Angelias Jr. and Florence Angelias; [m.] Patty Angelias, September 27, 1979; [occ.] Material Handler, Wainwright Industries; [pers.] No matter what your dream is, it can be realized if you're willing to pursue it regardless of obstacles in your path. To God I give the glory.; [a.] Azle, TX

ANTONETTI, MIGDALIA
[b.] August 21, 1944, Puerto Rico; [p.] Paul Silverstone and Isabel Antonetti; [ch.] Paula Haynes; [ed.] Herbert Lehman College BA Degree; [occ.] Housework; [memb.] Library of Congress; [oth. writ.] "The Teeth of The Lion" American Poetry Anthology, vol II, 2 Simmer '86 Ed by John Frost; [pers.] I try to express common human emotions such as love, fear, hope, despair. I think that the human mind is like a small child's. Every word in poetry should impress upon it a feeling of wonder; [a.] Bronx, NY

APILADO, CRYSTAL MARIE
[b.] January 4, 1981, Vallejo, CA; [p.] Emil Apilado, Yvonne Apilado; [ed.] Patterson Elementary, Federal Terrace Elementary, Vallejo Jr High, Winters Middle School; [occ.] Student; [pers.] With this being my first submittal being published, I am greatly excited. In my poems, I try to express any feelings I have at the moment. It's a good feeling when you see your poems touch someone's heart; [a.] Winters, CA

ARABY, CHRISTINE ANN
[Pen.] Christine McClain, Skie; [b.] August 6, 1974, California; [p.] Glen and Alice McClain; [ch.] Isabel Jean Troncin; [ed.] High School, also Institute of Children's Literature, unfinished. Next year plan on enrolling in Longridge Writer's Group; [occ.] Receptionist; [oth. writ.] Painted Soldier, first poem published in The Other Side of the Mirror. Various other poems also published. Short story and poems in High School magazines.; [pers.] I believe that dreams are very powerful, and they all have meaning. I believe in non-conformity, and I hate the words "politically correct." E.E. Cummings is my favorite poet. He stood for everything I believe in.; [a.] Riverside, CA

ARANA, IGNACIO
[Pen.] Iggy Arana; [b.] November 18, 1978, Florida; [p.] Julie Gonzalez, Ignacio Arana; [ed.] Christopher Columbus High; [occ.] Student; [oth. writ.] Personal poetry; [pers.] Through my writings, I try to express my reflections on life as well as address the questions and problems which it presents; [a.] Miami, FL

AREDON, DANIELLE
[b.] October 7, 1973, Brooklyn, NY; [p.] Jeffrey and Nadean Avedon; [ed.] Brunswick High, Cuyahoga College, Graphic Tech. Degree; [oth. writ.] Upon Request; [a.] Strongsville, OH

ARELLANO, JESSE
[b.] December 23, 1965, Ridgecrest, CA; [p.] Eliseo Arellano, Lupe Arellano; [ed.] Burrough High School, National Education Center; [occ.] Engineering Tech; [oth. writ.] I have written many poems, some were made into songs; [pers.] I wish the spirit of Christmas would last all year because only during that time do people seem to smile more and generally be good to each other; [a.] Ridgecrest, CA

ARMSTEAD, RODNEY
[b.] April 14, 1959, Pineville, LA; [p.] Lilly Frank (mother); [m.] Single; [ch.] Rodney and Brandon (2 sons); [ed.] Crosby High School Graduate; [occ.] Master Operator; [oth. writ.] Over a hundred poems but none published; [pers.] I try to write where all ages can understand and relate; [a.] Houston, TX

ARMSTRONG, MICHAEL J.
[b.] December 29, 1970, Washington, DC; [p.] George Charles and Jean Madeline Armstrong; [ed.] St. John's College High School, Washington, DC, Mount Saint Mary's College, Emmitsburg, MD; [occ.] Consulting Assistant - Price Waterhouse; [a.] Washington, DC

ARNOLD, DAVID
[b.] January 18, 1970, Jacksonville, FL; [ed.] Graduate of Riboult High School.

ARNOLD, LARRY
[b.] July 2, 1948, Akron, OH; [p.] Charles and Naomi Arnold; [m.] Stacie Arnold, January 2, 1994; [ch.] 3; [ed.] John R. Buchtel High, Akron, OH. Texarkana Community College; Texarkana, TX; FBI National Academy; [occ.] Deputy Sheriff - Bowie County, TX; [memb.] Texas Peace Officers Assoc; Christian Peace Officers Assoc; [oth. writ.] Other non-published poems; [a.] Redwater, TX

ARNOLD, REGINA
[b.] July 12, 1949, Marysville, KS; [p.] Mary Hosch, Bud Hosch; [m.] Darryl Arnold, August 21, 1993; [ch.] Michele Denise, Stephen Phillip; [ed.] Pleasant Hill High, Solano Community College; [occ.] Writer, productivity consultant; [oth. writ.] A Simple Solution To Finding A Job, co-authored with my husband, 1994, several newsletter articles for employment industry; [pers.] My writing has taught me unending faith. Leap...and the net will appear is my philosophy of life; [a.] Sebastopol, CA

AROCHO, DEBORAH
[b.] May 27, 1963, New York City, NY; [p.] Damaso Arocho, Lucrecia Quinones; [ed.] University of Puerto Rico; [occ.] Accounting; [pers.] A child's spirit is like a flower; nourish it, and it will blossom beyond limits; but please...do not break it, it is much too delicate.; [a.] New Britain, CT

ASHCRAFT, BUTCH
[b.] June 7, 1972, Hamilton, OH; [p.] Linda Thieken and Butch Ashcraft; [m.] Terra Ashcraft, October 17, 1992; [ch.] Jessica Rose Ashcraft; [ed.] Mississinewa High, 205 E.N. "H" St, Gas City, IN 46533; [occ.] I want to be a musician; [hon.] Athletics; [oth. writ.] The Wrath of God, Please Free My Mind. I am working on one right now; [pers.] When writing a song or poem let it come natural. Don't strain your mind. Too much strain can turn you insane. Anything natural always comes out top of the line; [a.] Gas City, IN

ATKIN, HELEN O.
[b.] February 14, 1908, Ithaca, NY; [p.] Robert H. and Helen M. Ogle (deceased); [m.] Philip T. Atkins, June 22, 1935 (deceased); [ch.] Philip O. and Melanie C.; [ed.] B.S. Education Howard University; [occ.] Retired Teacher; [memb.] Dunbar High School Alumni Class of 1925; Capitol Hill Poetry Club; Anawim Christian Life Community; St. Peter's Senior Citizens; Plymouth Senior Citizens; Phi Delta Kappa Sorority; "The G.P.T.'s" Social Club; [oth. writ.] Several plays and poetry for the schools where I taught and others; plays and poetry for

senior citizens and other events; many speeches for programs, retirements, events, etc.; [pers.] I have loved poetry as far back as I can remember and have read, learned, recited, and written it. I have never tried to publish anything but have freely shared whatever gift I have by reciting and writing whatever was asked of me. This has enriched me and given me joy.; [a.] Washington, D.C.

AUSTIN, BERNADETTE L.
[Pen.] B. L. Austin; [b.] April 28, 1947, Salisbury, MD; [p.] Mamie Williams and Thomas Carrigan; [m.] Randolph E. Austin, Sr, January 2, 1981; [ch.] Thomas, Randy Jr, Danielle, Roger, Nicole and Lintisha; [ed.] Salisbury High School, UMES (didn't complete); [occ.] Letter Carrier; [memb.] Center of Love COGIC NALC, Trustee for NALC; [hon.] Several letters of recognition from the Postal Service, award letter from Assistant Postmaster General, several safe driving awards; [oth. writ.] A Play that will be completed by February 1995, featured writer for JFKapers, several songs written for daughter and son's debut album and many poems written for my church; [pers.] I put God first in my life and everything else seems to flow smoothly. My church and family inspire me and are very supportive. I hope through my writings, I will make a big difference and inspire someone positively; [a.] VA Beach, VA

AVERILL, JEANNIE M.
[b.] May 6, 1959, Cottonwood, Ariz.; [p.] Tony and Vera Martinez; [m.] Dane C. Averill, August 23, 1985; [ch.] Dana Jean, Nathan and Gabriella (Averill); [ed.] Stagg High, Delta College; [occ.] Homemaker; [memb.] Southern Baptist; [oth. writ.] 14 other yet unpublished poems.; [a.] Stockton, CA

AZMON, EMANUEL
[Pen.] Emanuel; [b.] December 29, 1929, Jerusalem, Israel; [m.] Ziva Azmon, 1954; [ch.] Omer, Guy, Sela; [ed.] Ph.D Geology; [occ.] Prof of Geology, The Bengurion Univ of the Negev; [hon.] Allen Hancock Scholarship in Marine Geology, (USC, Los Angeles, 1958); [oth. writ.] 55 hours to the moon (A novel on the pre-Apollo period); [pers.] In this age of communication - super-highway, the poem is an instrument of communication and the poet is its skilled operator; [a.] Los Angeles, CA

BADEAUX, TREVIS R.
[b.] December 10, 1973, New Iberia, LA; [p.] Raymond F. and Elaine C. Badeaux; [ed.] New Iberia Senior High, Univ of Southwestern Louisiana; [occ.] Salesman, Anthony's Dept Store, New Iberia, LA; [oth. writ.] Several poems to be published in a collection upon my college graduation; [pers.] Do not fear what you don't understand, but understand what you fear. Always remember man is important; [a.] New Iberia, LA

BAHAMON (M.D.), JUAN E.
Born in La Plata, Colombia. 38 yrs old. Practices Neurology in TX. His poem "Sweetheart" was inspired by Mrs. Katy Bailey of Corpus Christi, TX

BAILEY, KRISCINDA A.
[b.] July 1, 1974, Rockdale Co, Conyers, GA; [p.] Beverly and Jackson Bailey - Artist. Note: My parents are commercial artists who painted the world's largest religious painting, 11'x1000' long, entitled, "The Life of Christ", as listed in the Guinness Book of World Records; [ed.] Georgia College - Bob Jones Univ Athens Techn School Nursing; [occ.] Student - Bob Jones Univ Nursing Program; [memb.] Thespian Society -

Epsilon Sigma - Alpha Sigma Kappa Rho - Baptist Church also their youth counselor; [hon.] Journalism Award, Spanish Award; [oth. writ.] Local Newspaper, High School paper - short stories, script writing; [pers.] Live life one day at a time and love the Lord with all your heart; [a.] Ruthledge, GA

BAILEY, LISA
[b.] April 29, 1965, Williamsburg, KY; [p.] Buddy and Shirley Sowder; [ch.] Kelsey Danielle Bailey; [ed.] Berea High; [occ.] Certified Customer Sales Representative; [pers.] I put a lot of myself in my poetry. I write from my feelings.; [a.] Greenville, SC

BAILEY, MAUDELENE
[b.] September 27, 1935, Connellsville, PA; [p.] Clarence & Agnes Kirchner; [m.] Arthur W. Bailery Sr., June 12, 1954; [ch.] Arthur Jr., Michael Bailey; [ed.] EHHS High; WCCC; NCHM & Polley Real Estate School. (Received Certification from the National Center of Housing Management in 1989 and continuing education in 1993.; [occ.] Resident Manager of Apts. & Licensed Real Estate & Notary; [memb.] Pennsylvania Assoc., of Notaries; [oth. writ.] Co-Wrote Music (1969) No poems published.; [a.] Mt. Pleasant, PA

BAILEY, SUZANNE L.
[b.] February 3, 1956, Camp Pendleton, CA; [p.] Garnett R. Bailey and Rita L. Bailey; [ed.] St. Andrews Priory School, Honolulu, Hawaii; College of William and Mary, Williamsburg, VA; [occ.] 1st Grade Teacher, Fairfax County Public School; [memb.] Phi Delta Kappa, Delta Kappa Gamma; [hon.] National Honor Society; Recognized for excellence in the teaching profession by nomination for the 1986 Teacher of the Year Award; Awarded Impact II Grant; [oth. writ.] Article - "All I Really Need to Know I Learned From Stevie" published in Challenge Magazine; [pers.] My life is like a patchwork quilt--each patch reflects special people, places, and times in my life. Woven with love, the quilt continues to weave its magic and warm my heart as I celebrate living; [a.] Centreville, VA

BAIRD, TONY L.
[b.] August 12, 1952, Gulf of Mexico; [pers.] I never knew, a drifting newborn awakening in the twilight of heroin from my mother's view. Given love by a grandfather who saw me through, until he died a decade later, leaving me in a sad state. Darkness fell around me in a sad state. Darkness fell around my grandmother's hate, touching my soul in Houston until I met my mate. Gary shared with me the danger of a gun she held out right. We were married 12/28/74, still holding on tight. I finished first a master degree in education for me. Gary studied hard to afford the engineering degree I see. We traveled near and far to Egypt, Greece and more...Then ten and thirteen years later, Justin Ryan and Derek Jordan I bore. Now we all have found our calling together. And today it is only getting better! I am now a traveler of time and space, exploring the realities of life with my soulmate.; [a.] Richmond, TX

BAKER, CORNELIUS
[b.] April 4, 1924, Lowell, FL; [m.] M. F. Baker, August 23, 1949; [ch.] 4; [ed.] 6, 6-40 last day in there, Reddick, FL read, chart first yr, Peter and Peggy, next, then first; [occ.] DAV and Volunteer and all works to make happy; [memb.] VFW, DAV, new hope UMC Citra Fla Mom and Dad, know how to work with 8 down to 80 up a family of 16 sisters and brothers, March 78 101 add on, 1-30-81, last old, 185 add on; [hon.] I am send-

ing them. My mother Leola H. Baker started the Church of God in Reddick, FL. They had the 67th A. now 86, This one now 94, please for the Church, send to it I will pay it, she passed October 25, 1979; [oth. writ.] I am sending you one I did today, I need your help please, use this one release form for all writings send me what's best and price, I will pay it; [pers.] Mom first she's beating my sis 1yr 6mo older than I had the baby must free her, by hitting her in the back, I did, take the baby Daisy, Dad, horse ate corn cobs, made her sick. The wire had her up nocuts yasir, where boys put your hand on it get to the house gery like a baby; [a.] Ocala, FL

BAKER, TAMMY MICHELE
[b.] November 12, 1977, Ft. Worth, TX; [p.] Kenneth and Denise Baker; [ed.] Attending High School; [memb.] Environmental Society, Speech and Drama Club, Student Council, Member of Who's Who Among American High School Students, Earth Force and National Honor Society; [a.] Alvarado, TX

BAKER, TINA M.
[b.] September 20, 1959, Redmond, OR; [p.] Rodney L. and Elouise Gregg; [m.] Divorced, March 4, 1977 to April 1992; [ch.] Odessa M., Kay Lynn M., Charlene M.; [ed.] Madras Senior High, Madras OR, Paraoptometric Assistance course, AOA CE Program; [occ.] Registered Optometric Assistant, Madras Vision Clinic, Madras OR; [memb.] American Optometric Association; [oth. writ.] Songs of Youth, American Poetry Press, July 1975; [pers.] I enjoy sharing my poetry and the many inspirations that life gives.; [a.] Bend, OR

BALES, JON
[Pen.] Bullet Bales; [b.] July 23, 1944, Glendale, CA; [m.] Juanice Bales, March 31, 1989; [ch.] Step, Ambur and Michele; [ed.] Notre Dame High, Rome, Italy, Cal State Univ., Northridge, Northridge, CA; [occ.] 4th grade teacher Mark Keppel Elementary School, Glendale, CA; [memb.] Pi Lambda Theta; S.C. Paleontological Society; CAL Teachers Assoc., CAL Nat'l Guard Assoc.; American Div. Assoc.; [hon.] Golden Edge Cinema Award; Hallmark Cards Golden Key Award; Magna Cum Laud, Dean's List; 4 Arcon's, C.I.B., Air Medal; Bronze Star, 17 Sr. Olympic Swimming Records; [a.] Glendale, CA

BALLEJOS, PAMELA
[b.] September 17, 1959, Parsons, KS; [p.] Edwin and Fern Jones; [ed.] LCHS graduate; [occ.] Instructor for the developmentally disabled; [memb.] Tribal member of the Cherokee Nation of Oklahoma; [pers.] There are no words so beautiful as those that come straight from the heart.; [a.] Vallejo, CA

BANFE, JUNE F.
[b.] Ansonia, CT; [p.] Ambrose and Vincenza Banfi; [ed.] Ansonia High School; Southern Ct. State University, New Haven; Univ. of Hartford; St. Joseph College, West Htfd., Santa Clara Univ., Calif.; [occ.] 5th grade teacher, Doolittle Elementary School, Cheshire, CT; [memb.] E.A.C., C.E.A., N.E.A., Education Assoc., Delta Kappa Gamma, Nat'l. Science Teacher's Assoc., Chesire Kiwanis Club; [hon.] Dean's List College; Past President, Kiwanis Club of Cheshire (1992 - 1993); Delegate and Elections Committee member at Kiwanis International Convention, Nice, France (June, 1993); [pers.] Poetry is the written reflection of the true emotions of the heart! I have been greatly influenced by the poets and writers of the Romantic Period in American Literature.; [a.] Chesire, CT

BARBAGALLO, SEBASTIAN
[b.] May 4, 1919, Baltimore; [p.] Frank and Anna Barbagallo; [m.] Elinor, October 31, 1969; [ch.] Seven: Ronald, Gary, Patricia, Cheryl, Michael, Jay, Scott; [ed.] Garrett Heights High School, 2 year night classes, John's Hopkins Univ. (Managerial Marketing Purchasing and Contracting; [occ.] Retired U.S. Govt. 38 yrs. as Scheduler Analyst; [memb.] Knights of Columbus, Holy Name, Society, at Our Lady of Fatima Church; [hon.] Several poems received letters from Presidents, Johnson and Reagan, Gov. Schaefer on some of my poems; [oth. writ.] Wrote poem about Vietnam War (Humble Man) about President Johnson-received letter from White House, also about the Challenger Disaster, (Response from beyond) also received letter from President Reagan, also send copies to families of astronauts. Received letter of thanks from the National Aeronautical Space Administration. I also wrote approx. twenty poems about family and friends, of which I delight writing about.; [pers.] I write poems on different events, spiritual love, disaster, happy moments. I enjoy writing poems as most of them tend to make people happy.; [a.] Baltimore, MD

BARBEE, JAMES M.
[b.] May 28, 1931, Concord, NC; [p.] Relus Barbee, Iola Barbee; [m.] La Vaughn Deese Barbee, August 12, 1950; [ch.] Cynthia Suzanne, Nancy Kay; [ed.] Hartsell High, Concord, NC; Valley College, San Bernardino, CA, National Academy of Broadcasting, Washington, DC; [occ.] Retired from US government; [memb.] First Baptist Church, Pensacola FL - various media associations, boards and panels representing government and private industry; [hon.] Various motion picture and television industry honors and awards for creativity in the production of programs used in the training of US and foreign military and civilian personnel; [oth. writ.] Children's book, media scripts, training manuals and reports; [pers.] I believe future accomplishments are directly related to past failures; therefore there is no better time for "new beginnings" than the present; [a.] Milton, FL

BARBEE-WOOTEN, DAPHNE E.
[b.] June 7, 1955, Madison, WI; [p.] Roudaba David, Lloyd A. Barbee; [m.] Andre' S. Wooten, September 1, 1985; [ch.] Alexis Anderson-Wooten; [ed.] J.D. University of Washington, B.A. University of Wisconsin; [occ.] Attorney, Writer; [memb.] Civil Rights Commission; [oth. writ.] Several poems and articles published in various magazines and newspapers.; [pers.] The world needs more love and understanding. Diversity is beautiful, let's explore and enjoy it.; [a.] Honolulu, HI

BARNES, CYNTHIA ANN
[b.] July 17, 1955, Washington, D.C.; [p.] Robert and Lucy Foster; [m.] Darwin O. Farmer, February 4, 1988; [ch.] Jewel and james; [ed.] b.s. (1991) in Business Management, University of Maryland, working on a master's degree; track; applied management.; [occ.] Manager in the Federal Government; [hon.] Received numerous plaques and certificates of appreciation for involvement and support of women's programs and efforts; [oth. writ.] Numerous poems; [pers.] Life has taught me to be thankful! I am!; [a.] Upper Marlboro, MD

BARNES, KRISTAL C.
[Pen.] Kristal C. Barnes or Kristal C. Marshall; [b.] September 18, 1968, San Gabriel, CA; [p.] Kathryn Hammer, James Marshall; [m.] Eric Barnes, September 7, 1991; [ch.] None except dog named Tippy; [ed.] Oswego High School, Oswego, KS, Labette Community College,

Parsons, KS, Pittsburgh State University, Pittsburgh, KS; [occ.] Mental Retardation Technician II at Parsons State Hospital and Training Center; [memb.] Student Psychology Association, Campus Christians; [hon.] Psi-Chi the National Honor Society in Psychology, Dean's List, attended Kansas Girl's State in 1985.; [pers.] What I'm searching for in my writing is passion; the passion of love, life, and Christ.; [a.] Parsons, KS

BARNES, SONDRA SCOTT
[b.] September 28, 1939, Tomborton, NC; [p.] IM and Jewel Scott; [m.] Ralph W. Barnes, July 10, 1965; [ch.] Karen, Scott; [ed.] Duke Univ, Univ of NC at Chapel Hill; [occ.] Retired child care educator, spiritual teacher; [pers.] This is a poem from my heart and my personal journey; [a.] Winston-Salem, NC

BARNETT, BILL
[b.] November 7, 1940, Alica, AR; [p.] Edgar and Linnie Barnett; [ed.] High School, Gideon High, Gideon, Missouri; [occ.] Owner of a Garage and Body Shop; [oth. writ.] Several, none published; my writings are inspired by something or someone.; [pers.] Youngest of 12 children, divorced. I try to express the good in all that's in God's earth. I attend Calvary Assemble of God Church.; [a.] Lawton, OK

BARR, LINDA
[b.] June 22, 1962, Oregon; [p.] Richard and Donna Barr; [m.] Kenneth Allen Capps; [ch.] Courtney Janai, Johnathan Adam; [ed.] Thomas Jefferson High; [pers.] Never stop treating people as individuals. And thus may the gap between race, creed, color, or generation be no more.; [a.] Puyallup, WA

BARR, MICHELLE M.
[Pen.] Micki; [b.] February 5, 1983, Clinton, IA; [p.] Glenn and Theresa Barr; Sister: Nicole, Brothers: Brian, Steve, Daniel, 1 cat Carmel; [ed.] Currently a student at Washington Middle School. Attended grade school at Henry Sabin and Jefferson Elementary; [occ.] Student at Washington Middle School; [memb.] Band (saxophone), chorus, and drama, currently. Also plays piano; [hon.] Received Honorable Mention in state PTA reflections program for a music composition. Placed in school and city competition; [oth. writ.] Books through Henry Sabin Story Station; [pers.] This poem was written for and dedicated to my late Uncle Don, who I miss very much; [a.] Clinton, IA

BARR, NICOLE J.
[Pen.] Nicki; [b.] July 24, 1984, Clinton, IA; [p.] Glenn and Theresa Barr; Sister: Michelle; Brothers: Steve and Daniel, 1 cat Carmel; [ed.] Currently in 5th gr at Henry Sabin Elementary. Also attended Jefferson Elementary and the YWCA kindergarten readiness; [occ.] Student; [memb.] Band (flute), learning piano, spring and fall soccer, and volleyball when in season; [hon.] Reflections of Light, PTA award for art work; [oth. writ.] Books through Henry Sabin Story Station; [pers.] This poem is dedicated to my cousin Carmen and my brother Daniel. There are no real monsters; [a.] Clinton, IA

BARRE, ANN
[b.] July 4, 1915, Portland, OR; [p.] Norris and Rose Lewis; [m.] Ernest Barre, September 30, 1924, March 24, 1962; [ch.] None - my life's regret; [ed.] My formal education however, essential for existence, has been extended by the school of life, which by far has been the better teacher; [occ.] Engineering support analyst; [memb.] Pearl Harbor Survivors Assoc, Huntington

Harbour Art Association; American Dental Assistance Assoc; Interior Designers Guild; [hon.] Many honors have been extended to me for having given of myself to others. My awards have been my many years of living life and learning its joys; [oth. writ.] Many fiction stories, also many poems. These have never been submitted for publication or rejection; [pers.] If I had but one wish it would be to extend to all humanity love and charity, to make the world a better place. To add a moment of happiness to a troubled life, would be the greatest achievement; [a.] Temecula, CA

BARRETT, DEBORAH
[b.] April 13, 1953, Houston, TX; [ch.] Chad Andrew; Matthew James; Jana Michele; [ed.] Lampasas High School, Lampasas, TX; Navarro Jr., College; Lamar University; Howard Payne Univ.; B.A. in Communications Disorders, Minor in Psychology; [occ.] Speech Pathologist; Troy BISD, Troy, TX; [memb.] Texas Speech and Hearing Assoc.; [hon.] Dean's List; Outstanding Student in Home Eco. H.S.; Quill & Scroll; Leading roll in college play.; [oth. writ.] A few songs and one other poem, none published or submitted for publication.; [pers.] I believe that all persons have value and worth given by a loving and heavenly father or creator. I strive to treat each person in that respect.; [a.] Temple, TX

BARTELL, NANCY L.
[b.] February 9, 1968, Evanston, IL; [p.] James and Justine Bartell; [ed.] Lake Zurich Senior High School, Miami Univ, Oxford, OH; [occ.] Retail Sales, Volunteer Junior High Youth Leader; [memb.] First Presbyterian Church, Evanston, IL; Zeta Tau Alpha Sorority; [oth. writ.] Mostly personal for friends written for various occasions, devotionals, etc; [pers.] Proverbs 3:5-6; [a.] Wilmette, IL

BARTLETT, FLORENCE LORRAINE
[b.] March 27, 1943, Wellsville, NY; [p.] William and Lela Shelley; [m.] Ronald Steven Bartlett, Sr, August 17, 1963; [ch.] Tracy Diane and Ronald Steven, Jr; [ed.] Wellsville High; [occ.] Homemaker; [pers.] There is no love more treasured in fantasy, than that which is unrequited and unattainable in reality; [a.] Marion, NC

BARTON, TRACY L.
[b.] November 25, 1962, Manchester, CT; [p.] Louis and Karen Barton; [m.] Hilary Barton, May 9, 1987 (divorce final in Jan.); [ch.] Amanda Elizabeth, Holly Michelle; [ed.] Harvard H. Ellis Tech.; [occ.] Torpedoman First Class in the U.S. Navy; [memb.] American Legion; [pers.] In life, when you stop to smell the roses, everything isn't always fresh and flowery.; [a.] Groton, CT

BARTONE, MARY JO
[b.] December 28, 1959, Dover, NJ; [p.] Dominic and Amelia Bartone; [ed.] Lenape Valley Regional H.S., Dover Business College; [occ.] President, The Silent Secretary Inc.; [pers.] I share with all of you this personal poem that has come from the very core of my heart. I am fortunate and exhilarated that my "hunger has been fulfilled," after 16 years, by the person who inspired this poem. L.L.L. to all, never stop believing!; [a.] Netcong, NJ

BASS, MICHELLE
[Pen.] Shelley Bass; [b.] January 20, 1981, Gales Creek; [p.] Craig and Elizabeth Boss, Oregon; [occ.] Student at Sisson Middle School in Mt. Shasta, CA; [oth. writ.] "You Should Know" and "Now I Love You," songs not published.; [pers.] I got started in writing songs and po-

etry when I was in 4th grade. Now I'm in 8th grade, and this is my first published poem and song.; [a.] Dunsmuir, CA

BATES, JENNIFER E.
[b.] November 9, 1971, Buffalo, NY; [p.] J. David and Mary Eick; [ch.] Devon, age 3; [ed.] GED received 6/89; some college (Austin Community College, Austin, TX); [occ.] Teacher's Assistant at Child Care Center; Free-lance writer; [memb.] Adoptee's Liberty Movement Association (ALMA); [oth. writ.] Poem previously published in The Space Between, Suicide Show, numerous other as yet unpublished works.; [pers.] I strive, through writing, to deal with human emotion, no matter how painful. My statement might be "The Truth Hurts." It does at times, but it also still needs to be explored and dealt with.; [a.] Overland Park, KS

BATTISTIZZI, EUGENIA C.
[b.] January 31, 1948, Shanghai, China;[p.] Sir Giulio and Eugenia Battistuzzi; [ed.] Graduate St. Helena High School, Empire College, Sanata Rosa Junior College; Associate Arts Degree; [occ.] School Secretary, Robert Louis Stevenson Middle School; [memb.] Member, California School Employees Assn., Chapter 287; Women's Missionary Union, First Baptist Church of St. Helena.; [oth. writ.] Various other poems. I am currently working on my autobiography entitled On Eagles Wings.; [pers.] I will strive to share with my readers the presence and mercy of God and the goodness of the people who have come in and out of my life.; [a.] St. Helena, CA

BAUGHER, GARY
[Pen.] Bill Grimm; [b.] April 51, U.S.A.; [ed.] U. of MI; B.A. Industrial Arts Assembler; [hon.] Troubleshooting Electric Vehicles; Sandbagging on Bowling League; [a.] Bloomfield Hills, MI

BAYER, JOANNE
[Pen.] Lucia Summer; [b.] August 25, 1980, Southampton, PA; [p.] Dennis and Irma Bayer; [ed.] Currently in 8th grade at Our Lady of Good Counsel School; [occ.] Student; [memb.] Counsel Gazette School Paper, Counsel Yearbook Staff, Choir; [hon.] 2nd Place O.L.G.C. Essay Contest, Region 11 C.Y.O. Softball "B" League, 1993, Runner-Up, Region II C.Y.O. Ginny Grey Sportsmanship Award, Certificate Award for Outstanding Achievements In Dramatic Arts, Certificate of Achievement for Excellence in O.L.G.C. Good Writers' Club; [oth. writ.] Several poems printed in the Counsel Gazette; [pers.] I like to write about what really happens in the world, like the killings, drugs, and other things that are killing Society! The truth sometimes hurts, but we have to tell others what is happening.; [a.] Southampton, PA

BEASLEY, AKENDUCA
[Pen.] Linda and Akenduca Beasley; [b.] June 1, 1949, Gilmer, TX; [p.] Earnie Beasley, Stafford Beasley; [m.] Divorced; [ch.] Ubora Reghi, Satchidananda; [ed.] Berkeley High School, Cal-State Univ Hayward; [pers.] When I write poetry the omnipotent speaks to me. The human spirit is one of the manifestations of the omnipotent spirit; poetry is the manifestation of the human and omnipotent spirit. The medium of poetry allows us to experience infinity; [a.] Oakland, CA

BEATRAND, ASHLEY
[b.] January 5, 1932, Detroit; [p.] Deceased, Ashley and Lillian B.; [m.] February 26, 1961, Divorced; [ch.] Earl and Colin; [ed.] 12th grade; [occ.] Retired (Ford Motor

Co.); [oth. writ.] How many works accumulated over the years. I suppose what is really here is exposure.; [pers.] "What is meant to be is what is." Have been influenced by: Kahil Gibran and Robert L. Stevenson.; [a.] Detroit, MI

BECKERMAN, LEON
[b.] January 29, 1942; Brooklyn, NY; [p.] Julius and Sophie; [ch.] David, Michael, Ilana; [ed.] Doctor of Philosophy, Education Administration - PhD; [occ.] High School Principal; [memb.] Suffolk County High School Principals Association; NASSP: National Association of Secondary School Principals; ASCD: Association for Supervision and Curriculum Development; [hon.] American Federation of School Administrators - Leadership Award; NY State-Jenkins Award presented by local PTSA; Port Jefferson Elks Distinguished Citizenship Award; Brookhaven Town Board Certificate of Appreciation; Commendation - Terryville Lions Club; Commendation VFW Post 1941; [oth. writ.] Articles in professional publications: NASSP Bulletin, Journal of Classroom Management, CAS Bulletin, Journal of Reading, New York State - Attendance Teacher; [pers.] I most appreciate the writings of Thoreau and Whitman; [a.] Eastport, NY

BECKETT, ELOISE PERRY
[b.] March 2, 1927, Huntington, WV; [p.] Okey and Rena Morrison Perry; [m.] Clythe Clinton Beckett, December 23, 1944; [ch.] Five, Sue Ellen, George Robert, Marcella, Darlene and Clyta; Seven Grandchildren, 2 girls and 5 boys; [ed.] 9th grade Milton High School and Sald Rock WV grade school; [occ.] Now a housewife formerly worked at Reliance Dress Factory and Huntington Tent and Awning and helped with farming; [hon.] 20 years church pen went to church all my life most every Sunday at Enon and Balls Gap. Gave my heart to God in January 25, 1953 at age 25, my husband and I play the Omni Card and sing at Church; [oth. writ.] I have written several poems and made about 32 books myself just to give my friends. I have written a beautiful song from the poem I sent to you and put my own music to it.

BECKMON, JON
[b.] Sometime, Somewhere; [pers.] I owe all I am to God; [a.] Boise, ID

BEHLE, PAUL F.
[b.] July 26, 1949, Adrian, ND; [m.] Kathie, June 19, 1976; [ch.] Charles, Austin and John; [ed.] BA, University of North Dakota; [occ.] Farmer; [pers.] I compose my songs and poems while working on the farm. They are reflections of a lifetime of thoughts and experiences. [a.] Adrian, ND.

BELL, HELEN J.
[Pen.] Helen Pope Bell; [p.] Charlie Pope (deceased), Mamie Pope; [occ.] Executive Secretary for a Real Estate Investment Trust; [oth. writ.] Several poems published in various editions of Poetic Voices of America; [pers.] I have loved poetry all my life. I wrote my first poem in Grammar School which was displayed on the school bulletin board. I have long since misplaced the poem, but I shall never forget the title, "The Four Seasons". Most of my poetry is still inspired from nature and the beauties of the world that surround us. I find great solace in poetry in music; [a.] Smyrna, GA

BELT, ANDREA J.
[b.] February 13, 1974, Louisville, KY; [p.] Carol and Andrew Belt; [ed.] Highview Baptist School and Univ

of Louisville. Pursuing a BA in English and a Masters in teaching; [occ.] Pre-school/day care teacher; [hon.] Phi Eta Sigma, Dean's List at Univ of Louisville; [oth. writ.] I enjoy writing poems and short stories as a form of self-expression; [pers.] This poem is dedicated to Lisa and Melissa for their inspirations, and friendship; and to my sister, Laura who encouraged me to enter the contest; [a.] Louisville, KY

BENEDETTO, JANET L.

[Pen.] Janet Lee; [b.] March 15, 1949, Bronx, NY; [p.] George and Hannah R. Schwartz; [m.] Michael X. Benedetto, June 9, 1968; [ch.] Justine Ellice and Danielle Marie; [ed.] High School of Performing Arts, George Washington High School; [occ.] Legal Secretary; [oth. writ.] Poems requested by other people for special occasions, high school yearbooks, cheerleading squads and poems written to honor people at "roasts," etc.; [pers.] Don't measure one's worth by what they have, but by the love they give.; [a.] Pleasant Valley, NY

BENNETT DR., LYNNE D.

[Pen.] Dominique Bennett; [b.] March 23, 1926, New York; [p.] Frank and Helen Klinker; [m.] Two Marriages, L. Manders, H. Bennett; [ch.] Adopted Nancy Manders, Nassau Community College; [ed.] Adelphi B.S., C.W. Post, M.S., Heed University, Doctorate in Psychology, Hebrew Union College, St. Brigets Theology School, Taught Children pottery at Hofstra University; [occ.] Retired Sexual Therapy Psychologist, writing a book on the needs and behavior of older citizens; [memb.] Sex information and educational council of the U.S. (SIECUS); [hon.] Dean's List, Nassau Community College, Graduated Cum Laude, Adelphi University; [oth. writ.] Published in Psychological Journal. My poems are from birth to old age sexual in nature accepting in old age.; [pers.] God is a relationship not a religion. I am studying the Bible to find truth. Psychology of Behavior is helpful, what it needs to be more helpful is incorporation of prayer.; [a.] Westbury, NY

BENNETT, THELMA H.

[b.] February 6, San Francisco, CA; [p.] Mervyn Martin, Violet Martin; [m.] The late Harold Bennett, June 12, 1960; [ed.] BA degree from Golden Gate Univ, San Francisco, CA; Major: Public Administration. (entered and graduated from college in mid-life); [occ.] Formerly Project Analyst, US Dept of Education - now retired; [memb.] Eleven-year member of Toastmasters, Int'l; [hon.] Graduated Cum Laude from Golden Gate; worked full-time while attending college. Toastmaster of year, 1986, Division C of National Capitol District; [oth. writ.] None published (haven't tried as yet). Am currently completing a course in writing children's stories with Inst of Children's Literature (Connecticut). Have written poetry for relaxation since childhood; [pers.] I believe that despite its stumbling, mankind is evolving toward a plane of true goodness and spirituality. I want to help that upward climb in any way I can; [a.] Annandale, VA

BENOIT, CAROL E.

[b.] March 27, 1942, Medford, Wisc.; [p.] Arnold A. and Olgan Trumm; [m.] Donald J. Benoit, October 6, 1962; [ch.] Derek, Douglas, David and Dawn; [ed.] Graduated Medford (W.) H.S. 5/60 some college; [occ.] Postal Clerk; [memb.] American Legion; [hon.] National Honor Society, Little League Service Awards, Postal Achievement Award; [oth. writ.] None published. This is my first attempt.; [pers.] My goal is to write books and/or stories for children. Currently enrolled in a correspondence course to pursue this objective.; [a.] Putnam, CT

BENSON, DARLENE

[b.] February 8, 1960, Utica, NY; [p.] Marlene and John De Iorio; [m.] James R. Benson, December 20, 1989 (second marriage); [ch.] Carrie Lynn Benson (stepdaughter), Gianni Paul Notaro and Brian James Benson (sons); [ed.] Clinton Central School, Nazareth College of Rochester (BA), Syracuse Univ (MSW); [occ.] Clinical and school social worker; [memb.] New York State School Social Workers Assoc (NYSSSWA), St. Mary's Catholic Church, Clinton, NY, Kirkland Art Center, Clinton, NY; [hon.] 1976 - 2nd place, NY State French Contest, 1992 1st place, Kirkland Art Center Walk; [oth. writ.] I have a book of poetry that I've worked on since I was in the second grade. Some caught attention during my high school years and were published in the local newspaper; [pers.] The poem in this book reflects the beauty of hope that went along with entering a second marriage. Most of my poetry is inspired by the works of Edgar A. Guest. I am so excited to be a part of this publication; [a.] Clinton, NY

BENSON, JESSICA

[b.] February 14, 1978, Houston, TX; [p.] Joy and Jerry Benson; [ed.] I'm a junior at Cypress Creek High School in Houston, TX; [memb.] I'm a youth representative at my church, and an active member of my church youth group.; [a.] Houston, TX

BENTLEY, SHAWN M.

[b.] October 31, 1963, St. George, VT; [p.] Marion and DeAnna Bentley; [m.] Becky Daives Bently, August 21, 1993; [ch.] none yet; [ed.] Bringham Young University, University of Chicago Law School; [occ.] Counsel, Senate Judiciary Committee; [memb.] Church of Jesus Christ of Latter-day Saints; [pers.] I consider myself a post-contemporary poet with romantic tendencies.; [a.] Arlington, VA

BERES, DANIELLE

[b.] November 22, 1982, Long Island, NY; [p.] Jean and Mitchell Beres; [ed.] Armstrong Elementary, currently attending Herndon Middle School; [occ.] student; [hon.] President's Award for Academic Achievement.; [a.] Reston, VA

BERGMAN, KORY

[b.] August 4, 1975, Florida; [p.] John and Rose Bergman; [ed.] Edward C. Reed High School, Southern Oregon State College; [oth. writ.] Poetry published in school literary magazines.; [pers.] Writing is my way of expressing my feelings towards different aspects of life. Writing about how I feel about what is going around me is a great release for me.; [a.] Ashland, OR

BERNIER, DWAYNE L.

[Pen.] "Chuckles"; [b.] December 23, 1963, Winslow, AZ; [p.] Ed and Lenora Bernier; [m.] Single; [ed.] Winslow High, Northern Pioneer College, Central Arizona College; [occ.] Hwy. Maint. Tech I., A.D.O.T. Winslow, AZ; [memb.] National Rifle Assoc.; [oth. writ.] Although this is my first poem that ever got published, I have several others that I wrote, at my home.; [pers.] I love to run and while I am running I become inspired and the creative juices just start flowing. Then I can't wait to get home to write them down.; [a.] Winslow, AZ

BERNSTEIN, MELISSA

[b.] April 18, 1975, Brooklyn, NY; [p.] Marvin Bernstein, Judith Bernstein; [ed.] North Miami Beach High School, Florida State University; [occ.] Student; [memb.] Florida State Hillel; [hon.] Phi Eta Sigma,

Dean's List, Florida Council of Teachers of English, National Council of Teachers of English; [oth. writ.] Poem published by Florida Council of Teachers of English, articles published by local newspaper; [pers.] "If I am not for myself, who is for me? If I am only for myself, what am I? If not now, then when?" - Hillel; [a.] Tallahassee, FL

BERRY, ANNIE V.

[Pen.] Anne Berry; [b.] July 29, 1917, Topeka, KS; [p.] Peter H. and Annie Baker; [m.] Dean O. Berry, July 13, 1982 (deceased Sept. 1990); [ch.] One, John (deceased 1977); [ed.] Eighth Grade, self educated in school of life.; [occ.] Retired Appt. Mgr.; [memb.] First Christian Church; [hon.] none; [oth. writ.] articles and poems; [pers.] I believe in God's Angels, I have many poems and written articles and given talks about their visitations to me.; [a.] Trenton, MO

BERTIN, HOWARD S.

[b.] April 3, 1984, TX; [p.] My Grandparents, Marion and Fausto Bertin; [ed.] I am in the 5th grade, I am in home school, San Marcos, CA; [occ.] Student, Concert Pianist; [memb.] I sing in the San Diego Children's Choir, I sing in the "North Coast" Singer's Chorus, I play guitar and harmonica in a "Blue Grass" Band. I play piano in a "Chamber Music Group" and do Piano Concerts for various clubs, etc.; [hon.] I composed a song and music, "Rainbow Day" when I was seven and for the "Reflections" statewide Fine Arts contest, my song took 2nd prize in the whole state. I composed a Ballet "Pleasant Dreams" for my dance class; and many other awards; [pers.] I love my music, dancing, drama and writing, especially writing music, my goal is to go to "Julliard Music School" and be a world famous concert pianist. Then someday also own a "Big Music Store" like my poem.

BETSCH, DEBORAH L.

[b.] November 27, 1957, Kennedy Tup.; [p.] Mr. and Mrs. Gregory W. Scharding; [m.] Louis A. Betsch, Jr., September 6, 1986; [ch.] Brittany Jean, Ashley Marie; [ed.] Moon Area Schools, High School Graduate; [occ.] Presently a full time homemaker; [oth. writ.] Our hometown paper published my poem regarding the committee office I held for the board.; [pers.] It gives me a great sense of pride to share my work with others. My family and friends have a deeper feel for the inner me! My heart and soul are reflected in my writing.; [a.] Corapolis, PA

BEVER, TERESA A.

[b.] December 29, 1952, Peoria, IL; [m.] Robert E. Bever, August 28, 1970; [ch.] Bradley and Brian; [ed.] 12th grade; [occ.] Free-lance writer; [pers.] Life is not about feelings, it's about being; [a.] Machesney Park, IL

BHARDWAJ, TARUN

[b.] December 26, 1978, India; [p.] Ravinder, Maheshwari Bhardwaj; [m.] Unmarried; [ed.] Grade 11 in high school; [occ.] Student; [memb.] Only school sponsored clubs; [hon.] Best Citizen Award; [oth. writ.] Poems published in high school magazine. A play dealing with substance abuse; [pers.] I would like to go to college to be a doctor. I would like to continue my writing skills in future; [a.] Elizabeth, NJ

BIANCANIELLO, LUKE

[Pen.] Luke; [b.] January 27, 1968, Rome, Italy; [p.] Maria, Amato Biancaniello; [ed.] North Shore College; [occ.] Deputy Sheriff, Boston, Mass., UPS Driver P/T; [memb.] American 82nd Airborne Assoc., Parachute

Club, Dept. Sheriff's Assoc.; [hon.] Dean's List; Military: Multi National Force and Observers Sinai, Egypt, Foreign Service Parachute Badge (Honduras) 1988; [oth. writ.] Several other poems not yet published.; [pers.] Tremendous praise to all war veterans, God Bless!; [a.] E. Boston, MA

BIERCE, CHERYL
[Pen.] Shari Bierce, Jeanna Diar (Gina); [b.] October 16, 1977, Painesville, OH; [p.] Richard Bierce, Mary Bierce; [ed.] Junior at Mentor High School; [occ.] Waitress at Friendly's; [oth. writ.] Articles in Universe Bulletin; [pers.] In my seventeen years of life, I honestly believe that there are three kinds of people in this world. Those who have a headache, those who cause a headache, and those who take Advil; [a.] Mentor, OH

BIESTERFELD, BONNIE
[b.] November 13, 1955, Farmingdale, NJ; [p.] Herbert and Verna Ritter; [m.] Joseph, July 6, 1974; [ch.] Stacy Lauren and Ashley Lynn; [ed.] Ocean Township High, NJ; [occ.] Homemaker and Community Volunteer; [oth. writ.] Short stories, poems and thoughts to ponder.; [pers.] My work comes from within influenced by my daily surroundings. I try to make poetry paint a picture of what we all might take for granted.; [a.] Coral Springs, FL

BILANYCH, ANN IRENE
[b.] August 19, 1928, Kent, Ohio; [p.] Pearl and Joseph Bilanych; [m.] Single; [ed.] Kent State High School, Kent, Ohio; B.S. in Educa., major: Business, Minor: Home Economics; [occ.] Secretary, plan to volunteer at Robinson Memorial Hospital Ravenna; [memb.] Former Member Children's Institute of Literature, Member Newman Center, Chapel, member North Shore Animal League; [hon.] Ran in election for county recorder; good experience; [oth. writ.] Aiming toward writing more poetry. Entered recipes for our local record-courier newspaper cookbook.; [pers.] My goal is to try to be of help to my family, friends and community and use any writing talent to share with others. Proud to be a first-generation Ukrainian. My parents were born in Austria and became citizens of the United States. At Kent State University I qualified to be a teacher and was offered a job but I went into the business world. Now I would like to get into being creative.; [a.] Kent, OH

BILLINGS, MARGARET
[Pen.] Lorraine Billings; [b.] October 9, 1936, Baltimore, MD; [p.] Lawrence Schriefer, Marie Schriefer; [m.] James Billings, January 14, 1953; [ch.] James Douglas, Theresa Dawn; [ed.] High School, Confraternity of Christian Doctrine (Archdiocese of Baltimore), Dundalk Community College; [occ.] Artisan, Homemaker; [memb.] St. Luke's Catholic Church, Women of the Moose (Edgemere, Chapter), Honors Assoc (Dundalk Community College); [hon.] Honors Program Appreciation Award, Outstanding Student Music Award, Dean's List; Dundalk Community College; [oth. writ.] Three short stories and sixteen poems published in Chimera's Literary Magazine (DCC) and two poems published in The Dundalk Eagle (community newspaper) over past ten years; [pers.] My writings are a reflection from the heart laced with sincerity, respect and often a sense of humor; intended to capture an audience from all walks of life; [a.] Baltimore, MD

BINGHAM, MICHELLE
[b.] January 16, 1979, Rexburg, ID; [p.] Kelly and Ruth Bingham; [ed.] Sophomore at Los Lunas High School in New Mexico; [occ.] Student, Summer Volunteer at

VA Hospital; [hon.] Honor Student, President of Mia Maid Class in the LDS Church; [a.] Los Lunas, NM

BIRDWELL, O'DESSA
[b.] February 3, 1911, Wanetta, OK; [p.] Frank and Maggie Murray; [m.] James W. (Red) Birdwell, June 1, 1941; [ch.] Benita, Murray and Judy Ann; [ed.] B.S. degree in Business, Life Elementary Certificate, H.S. Certificate renewed every 5 years.; [occ.] Retired in 1971 from Fletcher after 30 yrs.; [memb.] Nat'l Ed. Asso. Ret, Okla. Ret. Teach. Assoc., Commanche Co. Teach. Assoc., Okla. Historical Society, AARP, Fletcher Mt. View Family & Community Education Assoc. Church of Christ; [hon.] Mr. and Mrs. Fletcher of 1990, Citizenship, Fletcher School honored me for 30 yrs. tenure. "To a Mouse" and other poems on miscellaneous subjects as well as some stories.; [pers.] Cousin twice removed of Okla. Gov. Alfalfa Bill, William H. Murray, dated Wiley Post's brother, Arthur, in school with his brother Gordon and waved one of his aviation caps in a play at Maysville High.; [a.] Fletcher, OK

BISHOP, MARY UTT
[b.] February 21, 1915, Jacksonville, TX; [p.] Rev. Claude R. and Eugenia Meadows; [m.] George D. Utt (deceased), February 2, 1938; David E. Bishop (deceased); May 29, 1971; [ch.] Julie A. (Utt) Ford; [ed.] Sunset High School, McBride's Business College - Dallas, TX; [occ.] Self employed, bookkeeping, retired (30 yrs) Phinney, Hallman, Pulley and Coke, Attorneys; [memb.] Lifetime member International Society of Poets; National Association for Female Executives; Texas Historical Foundation; [hon.] World of Poetry Golden Poet 1990-1991-1992; Five Awards of Merit from WOP; Editor's Choice Award, National Library of Poetry "My Heart Remembers You" in Outstanding Poets of 1994; World's Who's Who of Women 13th Ed 94/95 - International Biog Inst Cambridge, England; Women's Inner Circle of Achievement, 2000 Notable Women, 7th Ed; American Biog Inst; [oth. writ.] "Steps of a Good Man" a biog of my father Claude R. Meadows, pub 1965; Genealogical History "Meadows and Related families" 1987; personal biography "From East Texas to Big "D"; poems - World of Poetry Anthology 1990; "Selected Works of Our World's Best Poets" 1991; "Our World's Favorite Poems" 1992; National Library of Poetry's Outstanding Poets of Dreams and Best Poems of 1995; [pers.] I am rewarded when others tell me they enjoy my poems and I hope I may continue to give pleasure through my poetic efforts. My inspiration was my father, a Baptist Minister who taught me to "love they neighbor as thy self" and you can't do better than that; [a.] Dallas, TX

BLACK, MARSHA LYNN
[b.] December 14, 1959, Milton, WV; [p.] Betty Jane Casey; [m.] Clinton Mack Black, March 20, 1988; [ch.] Alvis, Christopher, Corinna, David; [ed.] Milton High School; [occ.] Housewife and mother; [memb.] KYOWVA Genealogical Society; [oth. writ.] I have written other poems in my life but I have just stored them away; [pers.] I write my poems on what I feel in my life and in my heart, whether it be pain or happiness. But have never had one of them published until now; [a.] Milton, WV

BLACK, NANETTE
[b.] August 31, 1947, Jackson Co., AL; [p.] John D. and Willa Dean Inman; [m.] Jimmy Black, February 12, 1965; [ch.] Scott, Patrick, and Johnathan; [ed.] 8th grade at North Sand Mountain High School; [occ.] Housewife,

Saddlemaker for 29 years, help my husband; [hon.] Arts, Crafts; [oth. writ.] I Nanette Black has a book of poetry I have been writing for a long time and I would love to share this.; [pers.] I would love to touch a heart with my poetry, and words,, of love come free, so I write my mind and thoughts for all to read by Nanette Black; [a.] Flat Rock, AL

BLACK, RILLA
[b.] Quincy, IL; [p.] Deceased; [m.] Albert Black; [ch.] Diana, Linda and Robert; [ed.] Bachelor of Arts, Culber-Stockton College, Canton, MO; MA in English Literature, Chapman Univ, Orange, CA; [occ.] Housewife, student; [hon.] 1 poem in American Collegiate Poets/Anthology; [oth. writ.] I have a collection of other poems that have never been published; [pers.] I like to reflect a colloquial use of the language; [a.] Santa Ana, CA

BLANCO, MARK F.
[Pen.] Mark White; [b.] June 26, 1973, New Orleans, LA; [p.] Manny Blanco and Maria Medina; [ed.] Alfred Bonnebel High; [occ.] Musician, Office Clerk; [oth. writ.] "A Stolen Spot For A Stolen Mind;" "New Orleans;" [pers.] My writings are done with the purpose to promote thought of the human condition.; [a.] Metairie, LO

BLANKENSHIP, PAULA
[b.] January 25, 1944, Huron, TN; [p.] Eutra and Clyda Russell; [m.] Glen, August 16, 1961; [ch.] Rob, Tammy, Jay; [ed.] Lexington High School; [occ.] Employed with Dayco Inc., and Mary Kay Cosmetics; [pers.] I enjoy writing poetry that describes the natural beauty God has provided for us. It gives me pleasure to share my writings with family, friends, and all mankind.; [a.] Lexington, TN

BLOOMER, LOIS M.
[b.] December 6, 1924, Pgh., PA; [p.] Bertram and Hilda Fair; [m.] Harry E. Bloomer, December 27, 1946; [ch.] Beverly Jean Kasinec, Jeffrey A.; [ed.] Graduate from the school of Ed. from University of Pgh.; [occ.] Retired Elementary Teacher; [memb.] 1st United Methodist Church, Circle Bay Yacht Club, Kappa Kappa Gamma, Nashville Songwriters Assoc., International; [hon.] Honorary Education Society; [oth. writ.] In collaboration with my son, I have written several recorded songs. Among them, "Squeakin and a Creakin" which received the first runner-up award in the Inter-Mountain Song Writers Contest. I am looking for an illustrator for a children's book.; [pers.] I usually write metaphorically. My topics and styles range from limericks to serious social issues. I am interested in watercolor painting and other crafts. I enjoy people and life.; [a.] Fairview Park, OH

BLUSKE, EDYTHE
[b.] Februry 11, 1934, Minneapolis; [p.] Betty and Samuel Dolf; [ch.] Fred, Nancy, Pamela; [ed.] Attended University of Minnesota and Minneapolis College of Art and Design; [occ.] Free Lance Artist; [memb.] Humane Society of the United States, National Society of Tole and Decorative Painters, Inc.; [oth. writ.] Several poems published in "The Moccasin" when I was a member of The League of MN. Poets in the Sixties. Lately my only writing has been journaling.; [pers.] I write purely from my feelings from my heart. It's an emotional expression for me.; [a.] Minneapolis, MN

BOESEN, CAROL LEE
[b.] February 5, 1943; [p.] Victor LeRoy Johnson, Dorothy Marie Boden; [ch.] Cheryl, Bryan, Nathan, and Donnie; grandchildren, Saunna and Daniel; [occ.] Re-

tired from Nursing, Navy Reserve HMC P03; [oth. writ.] Several nonpublished poems; [pers.] My inspiration is due to my many experiences and life's changes.

BOGAN, DORETHA
[b.] March 31, Oxford, NC; [p.] McCoy Harris, Sallie Harris; [m.] Robert L. Bogan, September 15, 1959; [ch.] Jhana Rakelle, Vicki LaJuan; [ed.] A&T State U, NC, Wright State U, OH; [occ.] Homemaker; [oth. writ.] Many other poems several short stories; [pers.] I believe love of The Supreme Being, love of oneself and unconditional love of mankind forms the basis for the salvation of civilization; [a.] Ft Washington, MD

BOGDANOVS, NICK
[Pen.] Tinman; [b.] June 12, 1950, Paderborn, Germany; [p.] Nikolajs and Helene Bogdanovs; [ch.] Sons, Nicky and Kris, Daughter Bernadette; [ed.] Des Moines Tech. High, U.S. Marine Corps 4 yrs., 1968-1972, Cal. Paramed and Tech. College 1 yr., U.C. Riverside, Public Relations; [occ.] S.S. and V.A. Disability; [hon.] Chefs De Cuisine Palm Springs Respiratory Therapist tech.; [oth. writ.] On bathroom walls.; [pers.] We are all vessels carrying gifts to one another which God has bestowed on us.; [a.] Palm Springs, CA

BOGGS, JEFF
[b.] August 8, 1969, Lebanon, MO; [p.] Elmer and Jean Boggs; [ed.] Lebanon High School, Southwest Missouri State University, B.S. in Electronic Media; [occ.] Substitute teacher and "Professional Slacker."; [hon.] Lebanon Junior High School's "Fancy Phrases" Publication Poetry 1st Place; [oth. writ.] "The Song" which won first place in 1984's "Fancy Phrases." "Milinda" and "Scream It Now," not yet published, were debuted at the same poetry "slam" as "Vince Guaraldi is Okay." Also some articles for local newspapers.; [pers.] My poetry is influenced by the Best writers and a combination of the voice of rap, heavy metal and jazz. Written with poetry "slams" in mind.; [a.] Lebanon, MO

BOLDEN, BECKY J.
[Pen.] B.J.; [b.] September 8, 1944, Buffalo, NY; [p.] Thomas and Bessie Robinson; [m.] Divorced; [ch.] Tony, Scott, Phil; [ed.] Bennett High, California College Health Sciences; [occ.] Respiratory Care Practitioner x 28yr; [memb.] St. John United Methodist Church/Pontiac, MI/ AART, MSRT; [hon.] To be the proud mother of 3 very special boys and witness their metamorphosis into 3 wonderful men...my award...their friendship and love; [oth. writ.] Several poems, a few short stories; [pers.] I have been inspired to create many of my works after the experience of life's frequent traumas! Like music, I blend my words to soothe the soul; [a.] Waterford, MI

BOOHM, CARRIE PAIGE
[b.] December 16, 1981, Salem, OH; [p.] Bonnie and Clifton Boohm; [ed.] I attend East Liverpool Christian School. Am in 7th grade and a Student Council representative for my class; [memb.] I am a junior member of Pleasant Heights Baptist Church. Am involved in Word of Life Youth Club. Also play the piano; [hon.] Was chosen to represent my school class at the ASCI Speech Meets for 6 consecutive years and received a trophy for participating all through the elementary grades. Received the Principal's Award for Outstanding Christian Behavior for 3 yrs; [pers.] I wrote this poem in memory of my niece, Kaydee Jean Walker, who was born with Spina Bifida and Hydrocephalus, and died at the age of 6 1/2; [a.] Wellsville, OH

BOOK, BECKY
[b.] January 12, 1975, Colorado; [p.] Steve Book, Bonnie Di Leonardo; [ed.] Canon City High School, DeVry Inst of Tech; [memb.] International Thespians Society; [a.] Canon City, CO

BOONE, TRACEY
[Pen.] Same as above; [b.] January 27, 1961, Aurora,CO; [p.] Carl Mitchell, Geraldine Mitchell; [m.] Robert Boone, March 30, 1985; [ed.] Archer Elementary, Lincoln Middle School, Fort Clarke Middle, Eastside High School. Gainsville, FL; [occ.] Material Coordinator, Lutheran Med Center, Denver, Colorado; [memb.] Wheat Ridge Police Assoc, International Pen Pals; [hon.] Art awards for pencil and charcoal; [pers.] I look for the beauty in things. I feel giving unselfish love is one of the greatest feelings I have. The romance and beauty of the Victorian Era inspires me in my art and my writing; [a.] Denver, CO

BORDEN, PHILLIP
[Pen.] The Philosopher; [b.] October 20, 1970, New York City; [p.] Harold Borden, Sr, Keolota Borden; [m.] Joanne Borden, June 17, 1995; [ch.] None yet!; [ed.] [occ.] Security Officer; [hon.] Outstanding Achievement Awards in the following areas: Lotus 1,2,3, Mathematics, Science and Art; [oth. writ.] Wide selection of unpublished poetry; [pers.] This piece of poetry is dedicated to "Loisida", "AKA" the Lower East Side of Manhattan, (where I'm from). "L.E.S. - is more than what you think and see"; is my personal philosophy; [a.] Brooklyn, NY

BOROVSKI, CONRAD
[b.] December 4, 1930, Prettin, E. Germany; [p.] Jozef Borowski, M.D., Anna Iruszis, R.N.; [m.] Catherine Perrot, April 10, 1962; [ch.] Julia Madeline; [ed.] Abitur, UC Berkeley (B.A., M.A.), Universite'de Strasbourg, France (D. Litt.) 1960; [occ.] Foreign Correspondent; [memb.] ACLU, Common Cause, Greenpeace; [hon.] Prof. of the Year, Tau Delta Phi, San Jose State University, CA. 1966; elected Pres. of the AATG's Northern Calif. Chapter, 1984; [oth. writ.] Poems in German and English, Surrealistic stories in Dimension (Nose Critters, Angels in the Meadows, Speakers), articles on language and literature in English and in German in various journals.; [pers.] I'm a quixotic Sancho Panza who would have liked to be a Cervantes, although I still believe in courtly love...; [a.] Menlo Park, CA

BOSWORTH, SANDRA LEE
[b.] September 23, 1940, Grand Rapids, MI; [p.] Ronald and Helen DePuit; [ch.] Andrew Carl, Allison Lee; [ed.] Michigan State Univ; [occ.] Volunteer: International Spouse YMCA Program at Virginia Tech; [pers.] Lived abroad as spouse of Foreign Service Officer. This poem was written while living in Tunis, Tunisia.

BOTZKO, JEFFREY A.
[Pen.] I. L. DooRight, Willa U. DooRight; [b.] August 12, 1942, Zanesville, OH; [p.] Charles and Mary Masterson Botzko; [ed.] Burnham H.S., Sylvania, OH;; Watchtower Society, self educated; [occ.] Minister for True Christianity Evangelism, Akron, OH, President of Kind and Decent Music, writer and publisher of morally elevating songs and articles.; [pers.] I use my poems and songs to nudge people to think and act more humanly.; [a.] Akron, OH

BOURGEAU, ELLEN MARIE
[b.] May 13, 1950, Wallace, ID; [p.] Lyle and Dorothy

Babcock; [m.] Ronnie Lee Bourgeau, August 23, 1969; [ch.] David, Robert, Scott, Bryant, Tammy; 2 grandchildren, Christopher, Robert Lee; [ed.] Custer County High School, Inchelium H.S. Whitworth College; [occ.] Homemaker; [memb.] Girl Scouts, PTA, National Association of Parliamentarians; [a.] Missoula, MT

BOUVIER, ELIZABETH PHILBIN
[b.] March 9, 1978, Providence; [p.] Kathleen Philbin Dennis Bouvier; [ed.] Presently a Junior, Martha's Vineyard Regional High School; [occ.] Student; [memb.] E.C.H.O Youth Group, M.V. Drama Club, Seabreezes Lit. Mag.,; [oth. writ.] Who's Who Among American High School students for 2 consecutive years; [pers.] My writing is a personal expression of experiences in my life that I find to be profound. I use my creative resources as a positive outlet to address my inner emotions.; [a.] Oak Bluffs, MA

BOWLING-MATTHEWS, DEBBIE
[Pen.] Dibora; [b.] September 12, 1967, Akron, OH; [p.] Grady Jr. and Jessie Matthews; [ch.] No children; [ed.] University of Akron, "Bachelor's of Science in Elementary Education, Presently working on my masters in Elem. Administration.; [occ.] Teacher and writer; [memb.] The House of the Lord Church, Owner of Dibora Publishing Company; [hon.] Nominated as one of Ohio's outstanding (Educators for 1994. (top 10%) Ashland, Oil Teaching Award) Semi-finalist in 1994 North American Open Poetry Contest. Graduated Magna Cum Laude from Univ. Algrom 1990, Maintaining a 4.0 average in Master's Program 1993 - present; [oth. writ.] Why Polly Wants A Cracker. (Children's Rhyming Story/Coloring Book). It's a love thang! (Adult poetry book); [pers.] One should love and help others. This is one of the main purposes of human life. If you have God on your side, all things are possible.; [a.] Akron, OH

BOYCE, CARRIE E.
[Pen.] Ellen Carey; [b.] January 2, 1960, Southern, CA; [p.] Charles and Noreen Boyce; [occ.] Telecommunications Technician; [oth. writ.] Personal poem collection dating back to childhood.; [pers.] If we look hard enough, we will come to a conclusion that will prove beyond a shadow of a doubt who our greatest influence in life really is: our parents.; [a.] Albuquerque, NM

BOYER, E. DEAN
[b.] January 8, 1951, Cassville, MO; [p.] Louise and Millard boyer; [ed.] Cassville High School, Southwest Baptist Univ., 1 Term; [occ.] Singer/Entertainer at the Roy Clark Theatre, Branson, MO; [memb.] Branson Entertainers Guild; [hon.] "All American Music Awards Show," Bass Vocalist of the Year. As determined by nationwide "fan" voting, at the awards show in December of 1992.; [pers.] All our talents, whatever they may be, are gifts from God. What we do with them and how we use them are our gifts back to him.; [a.] Branson, MO

BRADSHAW, BETH A.
[b.] May 4, 1975, Waterloo, NY; [p.] Carman S. Bradshaw and Barry Bradshaw; [ed.] Studying to be an English teacher. In my second year; [occ.] Student at Villanova Univ; [memb.] Member of the Villanova Women's Basketball team, a Division I program; [a.] Villanova, PA

BRADY, CLARE
[Pen.] Broken Arrow; [b.] November 29, 1949, Michigan; [p.] Helen Alsop, Harry Brady; [m.] Ray E. Kimien,

May 12, 1978; [ch.] Raenn and Erik Kimmen; [ed.] Each day in life is our education; [occ.] Writer, mom, wife; [memb.] N.L. of Poetry; [hon.] Best Poets of the 90's; [oth. writ.] If in my mothers arms, Hum in will, In doubt, Evergreen, A Mothers Prayer for Retican; [pers.] The first step to success, is to have achievement in the second step!; [a.] Toledo, OH

BRADY, ELSIE L.
[b.] November 16, 1911, New Haven, Ind.; [p.] David and Bessie Conner; [m.] John H. Brady, August 27, 1929; [ch.] Bob, Dave, Melvin, John, Colleen, Stephen; [ed.] Two years high school; [occ.] Retired; [memb.] 1st Church of God, Ft. Pierce Florida and member of Senior Citizen of Okeechobee Lottie, Raulerson Center; [hon.] I won 3rd place in 4-H Sewing Bee Contest at age 12; [oth. writ.] I wrote only to entertain family and friends.; [pers.] I taught Sunday School for 52 years. I am a proud mother and grandmother of at least 75 children and counting.; [a.] Okeechobee, FL

BRAGG, APRIL EVE
[b.] April 21, 1971, Atlanta, GA; [p.] Frances E. Manry and David Lee Bragg; [m.] Rusty Maddox, August 18, 1994; [occ.] Commercial Printing, Typesetting Graphics (Hensley Printing); [hon.] Golden Poet 1989, World Of Poetry, Sacramento, CA; [oth. writ.] Local newspaper publication; [pers.] Honesty gives purpose and balance to your life. To practice it toward yourself and to others is the hardest virtue to master, but the greatest gift from God. To have patience, love, mercy and a sense of humor will ensure happiness and bring peace to your soul. Everything that I am and will ever be is due to God, and to all my elders, whom I love, respect and admire. [a.] Griffin, GA

BRAIDA, DOLLY
[Pen.] Dolly; [b.] April 17, 1937, San Francisco; [m.] Arthur Braida, August 25, 1962; [ch.] 2 sons; [ed.] High School; [occ.] Homemaker and Poet; [memb.] International Society of Poets; [hon.] Twice Editor's Choice Award; [oth. writ.] A book of poems which includes this one coming out this year hopefully, titled "From Sad Beginnings To Happy Endings;" [pers.] Wife, Mother, Grandmother, hope to write books for children to help in their education. Through my poems I hope to make a change in the world. From hate to love of one another.; [a.] San Francisco, CA

BRAINARD, VIRGINIA
[Pen.] Virginia Brainard; [b.] April 2, Shelby Co TX; [p.] John and Dora Ann Burns; [m.] Arthur A. Brainard, August 30, 1959; [ch.] Stephen C. Wray; [ed.] Bisby AZ High School, Western New Mexico Univ, Alan Lee School of Drama, Hollywood, Arthur Murray Gold Star Standard; [occ.] Dance instructor; [memb.] Arthur Murray Medalist Association, Starlighters Dance Club, Los Boiladores, Dance Club, Green Valley Women's club, Green Valley Elks Ladies, Presbyterian Church; [oth. writ.] Poems in "The Coming of Dawn", and "The Space Between", and in the "Green Valley News"; [pers.] I feel that when another person reads my poetry, we touch each other's feelings - faith and understanding exist between us; [a.] Green Valley, AZ

BRAMLET, ALICE J.
[b.] July 4, 1911, Graham, TX; [p.] Alvin Goethe, McGalliard Effie; [m.] J.D. Bramlet (deceased); [ch.] 4 children: 3 boys, 1 girl; [ed.] High School. Born on ranch, father raised mules for railroad. The mules hauled heavy things; [occ.] Retired; [pers.] I have dabbled with words

all of my life. I also paint. I have made a living selling my paintings. I paint in all mediums - I am crippled with arthritis; [a.] Taft, CA

BRAND, ALEX J.
[b.] April 25, 1957, Aberdeen, MD; [p.] Alex M. and Edith W. Brand; [m.] Susan Thomas, May 22, 1994; [ch.] Wade Greenberg Brand; [ed.] Manheim Twp. High School, Lancaster, PA, Tyler School of Art, BFA., Phila., PA; [occ.] Professional Artist/Craftsman; [pers.] I write in search of truth.; [a.] Corning, NY

BREEN, LAURA
[b.] July 22, 1978, Lawrence, MA; [p.] Cathy and Allan Breen; [ed.] Currently a student at North Andover High School, North Andover, MA; [occ.] Waitress; [memb.] High School literary magazine, "Bourbon Red," People for the Ethical Treatment of Animals, Amnesty International; [oth. writ.] Publication in high school magazine, Bourbon Red; [pers.] Thank you to Paul Moore for having confidence in my poems and in me.; [a.] North Andover, MA

BRENNAN, TONY
[b.] May 5, 1972, New York; [ed.] South Side High School, C.W. Post College; [occ.] Bartender, Private Investigator; [memb.] Human Race; [oth. writ.] Look Up You Fools, published in Looming's Arts and Crafts Magazine.; [pers.] Through imagination we achieve reality.; [a.] Long Beach, NY

BREST, WILLIAM A.
[b.] October 30, 1957; [p.] William and Collette Brest; [m.] Marie E. Deleon; [ch.] Storm Brest, Nick McCarthy; [ed.] John Marshall H.S., Cuyahoga Community College, Broadcasting and Electronics Tech. School; [occ.] Audio Visual Supervisor, Marriott Society Center Cleveland; [oth. writ.] Monsters and Dinosaurs (unpublished Children's poems) Ponder Rings (unpublished thoughts) The Consummate (unpublished fantasy novel) The evolution of Armageddon (unpublished S.F. novel); [pers.] This poem, from my collection monsters and dinosaurs, is very much like my writing. Like Bobby McCate, it seems I have been blowing bubbles, hoping to one day find the magic to create something solid enough to support my dreams.; [a.] Lakewood, OH

BRIANT, VERNON BUD
[b.] June 11, 1914, Dover, NJ; [p.] Wm. and Emma Briant; [m.] Almeda Y. Briant, September 2, 1961; [ch.] Deceased 6/92; [ed.] Dover High School, Some College; [occ.] Retired; [memb.] D.A.V., A.L. F.O.P. #10 NJ, Cincinnati Lodge #3, F&AM, AARP, N.J. Fire Chiefs Assoc., 112th F.A. Assoc., WW2, Lacey Twp. Republican Club, A.A. Scottish Rite Valley, Trenton; [hon.] Pact Fire Chief Mantoloking, NJ, PAC's BD Trustee, UM Church, F.R. NJ; [oth. writ.] Doc's Clocks, Honor of Late Brother in Law.; [pers.] My mother died 1924. At the age of 12 I wrote this poem.; [a.] Forked River, NJ

BRIGGS, KEVIN
[b.] Newark, NJ; [p.] Willie Head and Callie Briggs; Grandparents: Richard and Callie M. Briggs; [oth. writ.] Premiere Book, titled Visions By Briggs; [pers.] In an attempt to contribute to the finding of a cure against the destruction of mankind, I have shared in my writing through poetry, messages of hope and direction.; [pers.] The mind is in a state of being, that is superior, to which it is capable of comprehending.; [a.] Manhattan Beach, CA

BRINDLE, JULIA NANNETTE
[Pen.] Juli Carrillo; [b.] April 25, 1973, Austin, TX; [p.] Larry Brindie Sr., Brenda Allison; [m.] Chalio Carrillo, March 17, 1989; [ch.] Nancy, Billy, Michael; [occ.] Housewife, Mother; [hon.] Honored to be published in Reflections of Light.; [oth. writ.] All poems, short stories and drawings unpublished.; [pers.] Jehovah God, of course, is an exceptional inspiration and a little push from my Grandmother Marie Brindle, Thanks to my Mom and her great talent and Dad's intelligence.; [a.] Odessa, TX

BRINSON II, WILLIAM NEWELL
[b.] January 31, 1977, Washington, D.C.; [p.] William N. Brinson and Karen J. Trotter; [ed.] Thomas Store High School; [pers.] "Words are the most powerful things in the world, they can make your life limitless."; [a.] Waldorf, MD

BRISTOL, DANIEL J.
[Pen.] D. Joseph Bristol, Padmabodhi, Vimalakirti; [b.] September 17, 1969, Binghamton, NY; [p.] Irene Wicks, Daniel L. Bristol Jr.; [ed.] Bainbridge Guilford Central School, the school of hard knocks, pursuing college; [occ.] Wood carver, meditation teacher; [memb.] Purple Lotus Society, Theosophical Assembly; [hon.] Student of the Chinese Lama Grandmaster Lian Shen Sheng, Yen Lu; [oth. writ.] 12 notebooks of poetry, working on a fantasy saga, 14 books on philosophy and mysticism. All unpublished.; [pers.] Influenced by Dylan Thomas, Walt Whitman, and Friederich Nietzsche. Also by the teachings of Buddhism and Taoism. I write because I must. Writing is life explaining itself to itself.; [a.] Unadilla, NY

BRITTON, ROBERT
[Pen.] Rob; [b.] November 3, 1968, Lawrence, KS; [p.] Jon Britton, father; Cathy Williams, mother; [ed.] Lawrence High School, Graduated 1987; [occ.] Painter; [oth. writ.] Several personal writings; [pers.] To feel feelings that are not true to us, is to let feelings over power us, until we become powerless over our own minds.; [a.] Tulsa, OK

BROADWAY, ROBERTA
[Pen.] Lois Broadway; [b.] November 17, 1942, Aiken County, SC; [p.] Robert and Minnie Jeff; [ch.] Robert Broadway; [ed.] Franklin K. Lane H.S., College of New Rochelle, Long Island University; [occ.] Special Education Teacher, Brooklyn, NY; [oth. writ.] Several poems published in local newspaper the Caribbean American National Review, Famous Poets Anthology.; [pers.] I am like a river that runs deep and silently but swiftly throughout time. You will never know when I will change course because I am always moving. I see myself as a strong willed and caring person who is always ready to help someone in need.; [a.] Brooklyn, NY

BROOKINE, JOHNNY
[b.] May 26, 1964, Lower Bucks, PA; [p.] Sammuel and Floretta Brookine; [ed.] Bristol High, Bristol Borough, PA, Moody University, Free Spirits Seminar; [occ.] Uniform Trousers Tailor, Personal Weight Trainer; [memb.] American Drug Free Powerlifting Assoc., Islamic Hebrew, Holy Tabernacle Ministries, Missionary, Counselor; [oth. writ.] I've written poems for the Doylestown Poetry Club.; [pers.] To express what lies within myself; intimate inspiration, compassion that utilizes one's innocence and strength. To pursue a point of exquisite thoughts that set our inner person free, makes our dreams what we wish they could be.; [a.] Collegeville, PA

BROWN, ANDREW
[b.] February 1, 1975, Hartford, Conn.; [p.] Charles and Anita Brown; [ed.] First Assembly Christian School, Crichton College; [occ.] Operator, EFS National Bank; [pers.] I write about reality and people that touch me personally. I want other people to feel the pain and emotional suffering I see in my life and know that there is freedom in Jesus Christ from that anguish and heartache.; [a.] Memphis, TN

BROWN, GLADYS
[b.] October 4, 1929, Kellysville, WV; [p.] Frank Whitlow and Rebecca Hylton; [m.] Archie Brown, January 19, 1948; [ch.] Five Children; [ed.] High School, Nursing Assistant; [occ.] Homemaker; [oth. writ.] Children's names, Carlotta, Linda, Philip, Otto, Victoria; [pers.] I wrote this poem from the heart upon losing my dear mother in the year 1977.; [a.] Princeton, WV

BROWN, JANET MCNALLY
[b.] November 17, 1925, Portsmouth, OH; [p.] Floyd and Bessie McNally; [m.] Elmo G. Brown, June 8, 1947; [ch.] Ellen and Sallie; [ed.] 12 Grades, Graduate School of Cosmetology, Medical Secretary; [memb.] Church Group Sorority, Humane Society, Wild Bird Center.; [hon.] Placed in National Outrageous Humor Contest, Editor's Choice Award for poem "Night Skits" published in the National Library of Poetry At Day's End Edition; [oth. writ.] Poems, song lyrics, humorous articles in Fort Lauderdale, Sun Sentinel.; [pers.] Accomplished pianist and harmonica. I express the pure joy of expressing my innate creativity.; [a.] Sunrise, FL

BROWN JR., ROBERT L.
[b.] May 25, 1936, Cartersville, GA; [p.] Robert L. and Florine C. Brown; [ed.] A.B. Morehouse, Atlanta, GA, M.A.T. Purdue Univ., Lafayette, Ind.; Other study, Ohio State Univ., Columbus; [occ.] Retired Teacher, French & English; [memb.] AARP, GA Retired Teachers Assoc., Habitat for Humanity, Big Brothers - Big Sisters, Delton Little Theatre, Friends of The Library; [hon.] Ford Foundation Scholar 1953, Pi Delta Phi, Nat. French Honor Society, State Teacher of The Year for English 1980; [oth. writ.] Poems published in the Georgia English Counselor other poems published in Cat Tales, An anthology of Student/Faculty writings at Dalton High School; [pers.] In order to get something out of the bank, we must make deposits. Life is meaningful only when we give.; [a.] Dalton, GA

BROWN, KYEIMAH I.
[Pen.] Breach Mender; [p.] Deceased; [m.] Divorced; [ch.] Quivenia Shai Lee, Joseph Lee, Steven, Alan Brown; [ed.] Contra Costa College, San Pablo, California; [occ.] Corporal, Georgia State University Police Department; [pers.] My mission before I transcend into eternity is this, through the anointing of God transcribe spiritual poems objectively bringing the chosen lost into the knowledge of the "Gift of Salvation."; [a.] Stone Mountain, GA

BROWN, WARREN A.
[Pen.] Aloysius Peter; [b.] January 7, 1948, New Orleans, LA; [p.] Daniel Thomas and Lillian Gadison Brown; [m.] Mary Anne Reed-Brown, August 23, 1969; [ch.] Warren Anthony; Binta Niambi; Kafi Drexel; [ed.] Xavier University of Louisiana, B.A., English Educ., 1969; Columbia University Graduate School of Journalism, M.S.J., 1970; [occ.] Business Writer, Automotive Columnist, The Washington Post; [memb.] National Asso. of Black Journalists; Washington Association of

Black Journalists; Washington Automotive Press Assoc.; [pers.] New York Times Fellowship for Graduate Study, 1969; LA-Miss. AP Award for Investigative Reporting, 1970; Pulitzer Prize Nominee (with co-author Frank Swaboda), GM Series, Wash. Post; [oth. writ.] Published "All American Cars and Trucks," 1994, National Press Books; Column Syndicated in 167 Newspapers through LA Times, Wash. Post News Service; [pers.] My poetry is my freedom to explore things I find difficult to talk about, the interplay of sex, race, and love.; [a.] Arlington, VA

BROWN-HAYO, ANEISE
[Pen.] Anne Niesel B-Mayo; [b.] March 8, 1941, SC; [p.] Roley Brown, Gertrude Brown; [m.] November 19, 1961; [ch.] Timothy, Donna, Milton, Renee; [ed.] Lincoln High, 6 mts of Business Sch, Beauty Sch; [occ.] (Housewife) Retired; [memb.] American Legion Charmott, Profiles of Courage, Salutatorian, Biology Superior Accomplishment, Letter of Commendation from School, Honor Roll; [oth. writ.] Poems published in school newsletters, special poems by request, Mother's Day, Father's Day, Programs, Obituaries, etc; [pers.] I try to reach the elderly, young children, with simple poems, while conveying a message of reality, understanding hope and serenity to all who read my poems. Thank you; [a.] Ken Gardens, SC

BRUCE, BETTY GRACE
[b.] September 10, 1924, Nevada City, CA; [p.] Liston and Ada Roberts; [m.] William W. Bruce, March 22, 1986; [ch.] Steve, John, James Pease; [ed.] Graduate Sierra College; [occ.] Retired; [memb.] Member of First United Methodist Church, Santa Cruz - 40 yrs; National Association of Retired Federal Employees; Local Bridge Clubs; Methodist Women's Society; [hon.] Many years ago I was a PTA president for my sons, also very active in scouting, a den mother for Cub Scouts (3 times); [oth. writ.] Short stories, poems, free verse, humor; [pers.] I strive to bring people together. Also, I am a grandmother to eleven and a great grandmother to two. Just a plain, ordinary, hopefully, good citizen, who loves people; [a.] Capitola, CA

BRUTSCHER, EDWARD ALAN
[Pen.] Jack Wilder; [b.] December 9, 1969, Louisville, KY; [p.] Sally Brutscher; [m.] single; [ed.] Western High School; Univ of Louisville; [occ.] Child Care Worker; [memb.] National Guard Assn of KY; [pers.] Had it not been for the opportunity to fail, I would never have developed the moral courage to succeed; [a.] Louisville, KY

BRYAN, DAVID
[b.] October, 10, 1972, Durham, NC; [p.] Charles and Carol Bryan; [ed.] Durham High School, Univ of NC at Greensboro; [memb.] Phi Mu Alpha Sinfonia Fraternity, Habitat for Humanity, Boy Scouts of America; [hon.] Eagle Scout Award, 1990 Brightleaf Music Scholar, 1990 John Sprunt Hill Leadership Award - presented at high school commencement; [pers.] Being a song writer. I write lyrics that have deep spiritual significance to me. I try to pass that spirit on to my listeners, regardless of religious belief, in hopes that they will reflect and meditate on their own lives, producing some sense of spiritual fulfillment in themselves.

BRYAN, KARL R.
[b.] April 4, 1955, Washington, D.C.; [p.] Robert and Lucille Bryan; [m.] Alba M. Bryan, February 20, 1988; [ch.] Two; [ed.] High School, Richard Mont. Rockville,

MD; Traveling, Life Experience; [occ.] Carpenter, Furniture Designer, Missionary; [memb.] Local Church, Comm. Christian Church San Marcos, CA; [hon.] None; [oth. writ.] I've written a poem published in "The Cornerstone" and one in a local magazine. Also several editorial articles in local christian and secular papers.; [pers.] Things I see and deeply feel inspire me to write on life's tragedy's as well as joys. If I can wake a soul up and make him see or feel something before hidden, I know I've done my job and served my creator.; [a.] Escondido, CA

BRYANT, ERIN
[b.] December 12, 1979, Morristown, TN; [p.] Tim and Linda Bryant; [ed.] Currently Freshman in High School; [hon.] Beta Club, Track, Shotput and Discus Conference Champion; [oth. writ.] I write about things that I have dealt with in my life. This helps me take care of my pain.; [pers.] I believe that if you take time in any kind of relationship to be honest and caring you will learn to understand and relate to others.; [a.] Hendersonville, NC

BRYANT, JOHNETTA LEOLA
[Pen.] Sister Johnetta; [b.] January 2, 1957, Orrville, AL; [p.] Mildred and Charles Bryant; [ch.] One Grandchild: Dawn Lanay, Seven Children: Bernard, Sharell, Sol, Roberta, Colleena, Diane and Romeo; [ed.] I'm graduate of Northeastern in Detroit. Secretarial Skills for Sawyer.; [occ.] DCS and CNA and homemaker and writer; [memb.] I'm a member of Stephen Temple Church of God and Christ; [hon.] Award from Nashville Tennessee Recording Studio Years Ago.; [oth. writ.] Short stories in school; my teacher, Mr. Lunsford at Northeastern encouraged me to write.; [pers.] My future plan is to write a book and keep my poetry alive. This is the greatest of them all.; [a.] Mt. Clemens, MI

BRYMER-ROBERTS, JEANNIE
[b.] June 3, 1950, Austin, TX; [p.] Jake and Annie Brymer; [ch.] Christopher Paul Roberts; [ed.] John H. Reagan H.S., Nixon-Clay Business College; Austin Community College; [occ.] Administrative Technician, Texas Education Agency; [a.] Spicewood/Lake Travis, TX

BUCCO, JENNIFER LYNN
[b.] September 5, 1973, Highlands, NJ; [p.] Anthony and Carol Bucco; [ed.] Mater Dei High School, University of Massachusetts, Millersville University; [occ.] Student; [memb.] UMass Women's Varsity Swim Team 91-92, Millersville U. Women's Varsity Swim Team 92-94; [hon.] Captain MU's Swim Team 93-94; [oth. writ.] Several unpublished poems.; [pers.] My poetry reflects my personal experiences in life and love; two things that change constantly.; [a.] Highlands, NJ

BUCHANAN, PAULINE
[b.] April 13, 1926, Logging Camp, Montgomery County; [p.] Viola and Paul Buchanan; [m.] Not married; [ed.] GED at age 50 in 1976; [memb.] Member of First Baptist Church Willis. I am a Christian and this is how I live my life. Most of my poetry is Christian; [pers.] I am a victim of cerebral palsy and have fought it all my life. It is getting worse as I get older. I do my best to live a normal life. I try to find the bright side of life which isn't always easy.; [a.] Willis, TX

BUCK, ELLSWORTH C.
[b.] January 4, 1918, Roscoe, NY; [m.] Deceased; [ed.] Graduate Monticello High School, Monticello, NY;

[occ.] Retired; [memb.] BPOE 1545, Presbyterian Church; [oth. writ.] I just published a book of poems titled - People, Places and Events. It sells for $5.00 plus $1.00 s/h. It has sixty (60) pages with poems on both sides about Catskills and Sull Co and people; [pers.] I tell the truth about the happenings (golf tournaments) or anything else and reveal the good points in people; [a.] Swan Lake, NY

BUCKWALTER, LYDIA T.
[b.] September 21, 1948, Norristown, PA; [ed.] A.D. Eisenhower HS 1966, Beaver College BA 1970; [occ.] Elementary School Teacher, Arrowhead School; [a.] Creamery, PA

BUETER, BONNIE
[Pen.] Vivian Kate Cleste; [b.] May 9, 1979, Little Rock, Ark.; [p.] Randy and Patricia Bueter; [ed.] Student at Mount Saint Mary's Aca. for Girls; [occ.] Student, high school; [memb.] Debate team, stage manager for Community Theater, Student Council, FCA, Soccer; [hon.] 1st place in state in Mock Trials, President of the Sophomore Class, Officer of the Freshman Class in 93', I'm third place at Kanakuk Kamps, over 10 various leadership awards; [oth. writ.] Writing to me is a hobby. I have written several speeches and given several talks. I have been a guest writer for our school newspaper.; [pers.] Writing to me is a window into a new world. In life, unfortunately you can not experience everything, but through writing you can experience anything. You can also share those experiences with anyone who reads your work. I hope my work touches the imaginations of all those who read it; [a.] Little Rock, AR

BUFANO, ELEANORE A.
[b.] November 24, 1938, Chicago, IL; [m.] Single; [ch.] Laura Marie Evans, E. Eiric Spaw, Maria Ellen Koontz and John Robert Spaw; Ten grandchildren: Christopher D. Evans, Jennifer Y. Hanson also Jessica A., Heather M., Nicole F. Koontz, E. Eric Jr., Matthew K., & Scott P. Spaw, John (J.J.) Jr., & Gabriel N. Spaw; One great-grandchild: K.C. Lee Evans.; [ed.] G.E.D., Computer Course at Wright college; [occ.] Health Care/Companion for elderly woman.; [hon.] Partial Scholarship for High G.E.D. Scores; [oth. writ.] Several, never submitted poems and humorous lyrics set to well known songs.; [pers.] Greed unchecked, is wiping out the "Shades of Grey" from the classes, and the "Red, White and Blue" from our country.; [a.] Chicago, IL

BUFFINGTON, CHRISTINA M.
[b.] October 5, 1968, Annapolis, MD; [p.] Howard and Lee Buffington; [ed.] Archbishop Keough H.S., Anne Arundel Community College; [occ.] Customer Service Agent for US Air at BWI Airport; [memb.] Herald Harbor Volunteer Fire Dept. EMT; [oth. writ.] Have had poems published in Angelic Passages, a Nationally distributed newsletter. Also write personalized poems.; [pers.] Majority of my writings have an inspirational theme and reflect personal experiences that have touched me profoundly.; [a.] Crownsville, MD

BUGG, LAWRENCE
[Pen.] Todd Bugg; [b.] March 8, 1967, West Branch, MI; [p.] Larr and Nancy Bugg; [m.] Michelle Bugg, August 9, 1986; [ch.] Tiffany (7), Nichlas (5); [ed.] Fairview area school, Kirtland Community College; [occ.] H.B Tool Carbide "Machinist"; [oth. writ.] I have a whole book of other poems I wish to have some read.; [a.] Mid, MI

BULLER, KRISTIN M.
[b.] May 27, 1980, Lake Charles, LA; [p.] Rod A. and Karen R. Buller; [ed.] Currently attending 9th grade at Lumberton High School; [occ.] Student; [memb.] Flutist in band; [hon.] 2nd place - fourth grade poetry contest. Placed in AAAA dictionary VIL contest in 8th grade; [oth. writ.] Creative Writing for enjoyment and other various poems; [pers.] I try to portray moral values through my writings; at the same time making them an enjoyment for everyone who may read them; [a.] Lumberton, TX

BULLOCK, ROBERT B.
[b.] December 15, 1943, Detroit, MI; [p.] Esther G. Edwards/Robert T. Bullock; [ch.] Elisha, Robin, Gwen; [ed.] St. Emma Military Academy, Morehouse College, Wayne State Univ; [occ.] Property Manager of a thoroughbred Horse Farm; [memb.] Board of Directors Motown Historical Museum; [oth. writ.] (none published) songs, poems, philosophies; [pers.] "Seek the wealth of love and not the love of wealth"; [a.] San Jacinto, CA

BUMGARNER, ANGELA MARIE
[Pen.] E. J. and T. C. Love; [b.] August 7, 1977, NC; [p.] Donna Bolton, Darrell Bumgarner; [pers.] Only we can save ourselves, if not us then who else. Thank you Dawn. I love you Sis. Jessica, I miss you; [a.] Conover, NC

BURGESS, THERESA
[b.] November 29, 1958, Conn.; [p.] Milton and Robena Corbett; [m.] Michael Burgess, April 29, 1979; [ed.] Shelton High School, Sacred High University Valley Academy of Cosmetology; [pers.] I would like to dedicate my poem to my Dad Milton Corbett. He had a dream to be a writer also. I hope you're watching and are proud.; [a.] Shelton, CT

BURKE, JUDE THAD
[b.] May 20, 1957, Vacherie, LA; [p.] Irving and Rose Burke; [ed.] St. James High, Southern University; [occ.] Free Lance Poet; [memb.] Alpha Delta Mu Social Work Honor Society; [pers.] I am inspired in my writings by my first love, who will always be very dear to me, the late Lauren Claire Soper; [a.] New Orleans, LO

BURKE, KATHRYN A.
[b.] July 29, 1974, Kent; [ed.] Roosevelt H.S., Kent, 3rd yr. psych. major at Kent State (currently); [occ.] Residential and in home support staff for mentally and developmentally disabled persons.; [memb.] Volunteer for the Summit County Board of Mental Retardation and Developmental Disabilities; [oth. writ.] Several poems published in my senior year high school literary magazine, lots of love letters!; [pers.] I don't believe in re-writes.; [a.] Kent, OH

BURKEMPER, DIANE D.
[b.] October 14, 1955, Nebraska City, NE; [p.] Merle and Darlene Webber; [m.] Howard Burkemper, May 17, 1985; [ch.] Paul, Katie, Ryan, Joy, Molly; [ed.] South Page High, College of Lake County; [occ.] Deputy City Clerk, City of Zion, Illinois; [memb.] Municipal Clerks of Illinois, Lake County Literacy Program, Phi Theta Kappa Honors Fraternity; [hon.] Phi Theta Kappa, Daughters of the American Revolution (DAR) Good Citizenship Award; [oth. writ.] Numerous personal poems, greeting cards, unpublished children literature; [pers.] In a world being overcome with darkness, an expression of beauty through poetry is a light at the end of the tunnel; [a.] Zion, IL

BURRELL, PEGGY
[b.] January 24, 1967, Shamrock; [p.] Bennie and Mary Bennett; [m.] Divorced; [ch.] Aaron Quentin Burrell; [ed.] GED Diploma, Shamrock School District; [occ.] Mother; [memb.] Baptist Church; [hon.] In Art, Track, Church; [oth. writ.] None yet published, but I shall continue to write; I have several poems.; [pers.] I encourage all talented people to never give up hope. Your dream is yet to be fulfilled, dreams never die (mine never did).; [a.] Shamrock, TX

BURSELL, TAMMY RENEE
[b.] February 14, 1967, Bitburg, Germany; [p.] Relton and Eleanor Forrester; [m.] Kevin Allen Bursell, May 14, 1988; [ch.] Jessica, Kevin, Kristopher; [ed.] Jefferson High School; [occ.] School District 205, and Food Services; [hon.] Special Awards for helping children; [oth. writ.] Various poetry; [pers.] I enjoy writing poetry; it's very rewarding.; [a.] Rockford, IL

BURTON, RANDI RENEE
[b.] April 23, 1977, Grass Valley, CA; [p.] Debra and William Burton; [ed.] Bear River High School; [occ.] Student; [pers.] I would like to thank my family for sticking by me through all my problems. I love you. And to Charleen Rooney - I love you. B/F/F; [a.] Grass Valley, CA

BUTHER, LOIS N.
[b.] April 10, 1937, NY, NY; [p.] Mary Samuel Warner; [ch.] April R. Willis; [ed.] Practical Arts High; [occ.] PBX Operator, Neiman Marcus; [memb.] Pleasant Hill Baptist Church; [hon.] Keys of the Kingdom, Deliverance Class No 1; Deliverance Class No 2; Teacher's Training; Psalmist Certificate; Bethel Bible School 4 yrs; [oth. writ.] none published; [pers.] I write to praise our Lord Jesus who lifts and saves all who come to him; [a.] Jamaica Plain, MA

BUTLER, MARTHA (PENNEY)
[b.] June 28, 1923, Gadsden, AL; [p.] Henry and Fannie Penney; [ch.] Cindy Butler, Scott Butler; [ed.] Hokes Bluff High School, Athens College, BA Degree Dept of Agriculture Graduate School (3yrs); [occ.] Part time secretary; [memb.] Calvert Manor Garden Club, Accokeek Lioness Club; [hon.] Five awards with the National Park Service; [pers.] My writing reflects my love of nature and the works of our Supreme Artist; [a.] Accokeek, MD

BUTLER, PATRICIA
[b.] October 13, 1955, Drumright, OK; [p.] Richard and Betty Anderson; [m.] John butler, April 7, 1974; [ch.] Felicia Kay, LaWanda Patrece, Jonathan Ray, Kristina Joy, Joshua Daniel; [ed.] Drumright High, Central Vo-Tech; [occ.] Housewife; [memb.] Crossroads Cathedral Church; [oth. writ.] Several dynamic and encouraging short stories; [pers.] I strive to write to be an encourager to my many readers; [a.] Del City, OK

BYARD, ANDREA LEE
[Pen.] Angie, Andrea Darby; [b.] November 16, 1962, Philadelphia; [p.] Jeannetta and Lloyd Darby Sr.; [m.] Tracy Dean Byard, May 21, 1983; [ch.] Ashley Anne Byard, Kyle Ryan Byard; [ed.] John Bartram High School; Community College of Phila.; [occ.] Checkout Supervisor; [memb.] Governance Council, Deliverance Evangelistic Church, Home and School Association; [hon.] Who's Who Among America's High School Students, Honor Awards on Job, Cheerleading, Writing Short Children's Story Award, Outstanding Achievement

Award; [oth. writ.] Short stories, poems for daily news, scripts for plays, and now in the process of writing a movie made for television.; [pers.] I enjoy writing, I have been writing since I was ten years old. I get my inspiration from God first and my lovely mother whom I think passed her talent on to me. Poems are my favorite to write because I feel closer to God as he opens my heart and helps me put my feelings on paper.; [a.] Philadelphia, PA

BYE, DAYNA LEIGH
[b.] October 24, 1974, Aston, PA; [p.] David Bye and Shawn Bye; [ed.] Attended Northeast High School. During 12 grade, attended Cecil County Vocational School of Technology.; [occ.] ICT Group; Telemarketer; [hon.] English Honors, 1st place in Perryville Art Show, FBLA President; [pers.] I get great satisfaction by sharing my thoughts and emotions within my poetry. Not only have I been inspired by many books, but also my high school poetry teacher Mr. Connors and my mother.; [a.] Wilmington, DE

BYKOFSKY, ARI RUSSELL
[b.] August 3, 1979, Washington, DC; [p.] Susan Bykofsky, Marshall Bykofsky; [ed.] Woodrow Wilson High School; [occ.] 10th grade student; [oth. writ.] Unpublished poems such as "Painted Faces," "Where the Wild Things Roam," "In the Water," "Once Was, Always One," "Can I See It?" and "When One Kills"; [pers.] "Wash off the paint on your face"; [a.] Washington, DC

BYRD, ROSA J.
[Pen.] Mama Rosa; [b.] February 15, 1925, Richmond, VA; [p.] Eva and Junius Foster; [m.] Odell R. Byrd Sr., October 10, 1981; [ch.] Gloria Lucas Brenda Fisher, Ronald Cureton, Paul Johnson, 6 stepchildren; [ed.] Maggie Walker High School; [occ.] Retired from MCV Hospital, Office Serv. Asst.; [memb.] Golden Years Club, Usher Georgia Ross Board, Ada Lewis Missionary Circle #10 of Second Baptist Church; [oth. writ.] I have written about 30 poems. About 5 personal, some for my grandchildren, 12 have been copyrighted under "Poems from Moma Rosa's Pen" not published as yet.; [pers.] I was inspired by my friend Lun who gave me a few titles and told me to write my own poems. Some are spiritual and other varieties. Started around 1990 in my spare time.; [a.] Richmond, VA

CAIN, MARCHELLE F.
[Pen.] Sashell; [b.] March 15, 1948, Cleveland, OH; [ch.] Edward Lewis, Melvin Earl, Kandice Ann; [ed.] John Hay High School, Cleveland State Univ.; [occ.] Supervisor, Patient Admissions, Meridia Huron Hospital, E. Cleveland, OH; [oth. writ.] "You", A Mother's Love, Farewell, Reminiscing and several short stories; [pers.] My true desire is to write so that anyone who reads my writing can feel it as though they were writing it themselves.; [a.] Euclid, OH

CALDWELL, MARIE
[Pen.] Marie Lancaster; [b.] September 29, 1947, Tewksbury, Mass.; [p.] Frances Lancaster, Divorced 1985; [ch.] Mark Trevor and Dona Scott; [ed.] Bridgewater State College, Stone Hill College (Accounting) currently will attend Massasoit College January 6, 1995 for writing and tv production; [occ.] Painting contractor; [memb.] Post National Assoc. for Women in Construction, Contractor Assoc. of Boston, Nat. Assoc. of Minority Contractors, National Assoc. of Public Accountants; [hon.] Published in the September 1988 is-

sue of "Home Office Computing" for work in construction. Feature article entitled "A Woman Builds Her Own Place In Man's World." Documentary done on my life for cable channel while I was a contractor "1986;" [oth. writ.] "My Life and Just My Opinion" unpublished book about my life story. "Nina's Story" written for a contest with Ebony Magazine.; [pers.] Writing is easy when you're reflecting on your life and your feelings.; [a.] Canton, MA

CALLAGHAN, BRIAN JOSEPH
[b.] June 15, 1973, BRONX, NY; [p.] Joseph Patrick Callaghan, Ann Callaghan; [ed.] Plainview High School, St. Joseph's College, Trinity College Dublin; [occ.] Student; [pers.] I point out the areas of humanity and of myself through my writings. I have been influenced greatly by the Byronic hero and by the Irish dramatists such as Samuel Beckett and J. M. Synge.; [a.] Plainview, NY

CALLAHAN, ELIZABETH POOLE
[b.] Betty Callahan; [b.] November 15, 1920, Gary, WV; [p.] (adopted) Julia and Lewis Poole; [m.] Robert Callahan, November 16, 1974; [ch.] (1) daughter - Shirley Danison - 1st marriage (deceased 1975). By marriage, I have 7 grandsons and 1 granddaughter, 1 step daughter, son in law, 1 step son, and daughter in law. All I adore; [ed.] Graduate - Jefferson Sr High School, Rke, VA 1940 - 1 yr Bus School - 1 yr an Photo Artist. 12 yrs Study as concert violinist - seamstress; [occ.] Retired - Housewife - hobby; [memb.] Formerly - member of Swinging Stars - Square, Club 14 yrs L.V. NV - Also Butterfly Squares, also Camping Promenaders; [hon.] Won 1979 - 1st place for making the most beautiful square dance costume for spouse and - we wore in fashion show presented by Jackpot - square - Square Dance Club. Also won plaque - 1st place for most beautiful decorated mobile home in Meadows Park. I did entire job; [oth. writ.] Total poems to date - 110; [pers.] I strive to do unto others as I would have them do unto me. I try to be understanding courteous and helpful in any way humanly possible to all those I come in contact with; [a.] Las Vegas, NV

CALLIS, REBECCA
[b.] August 7, 1976, Baltimore; [p.] Darlene and James Callis; [ed.] Lansdowne High School entering Catonsville Comm. College in 1995; [occ.] Receptionist; [memb.] GreenPeace, PETA; [oth. writ.] Several personal writings, poems, short stories.; [pers.] Every one of my poems are based on my personal situations. Writing about a painful experience can sometimes help take the pain away. I am a fan of Robert Frost, Ella Whelleter Wilcox and Edgar Guest; [a.] Baltimore, MD

CALVANESE, KATHLEEN B. (BRUCE)
[Pen.] O'Hara Bruce; [b.] August 8, 1946, Pennsylvania; [p.] John Bruce, Marie Bruce; [m.] Anthony, March 9, 1975; [ch.] Dina Marie; [ed.] St. James, Carney Pt NJ, Glassboro State College, Glassboro, NJ; [occ.] Freelance Photo/writer, short stories; [memb.] Mothers Against Drunk Driving, Society to Protect Animals; [oth. writ.] Remembering Randy; [pers.] Love the Lord every day of your life and He will return your love in "Full Measure" for eternity.

CAMERON, DOROTHY REBECCA
[Pen.] Rebecca York; [b.] June 28, 1922, St. Louis, MO; [p.] Russell Hibner, Rebecca Hibner; [m.] Russell Cameron (deceased), December 31, 1977; [ed.] Jefferson Davis High graduate, of Houston, TX; [occ.] Retired

Telephone Operators of Hotel Utah, (Salt Lake City); [memb.] Utah Poetry Society; [hon.] Two poems accepted for Utah Sings (published only once every 10 years); [oth. writ.] 2 poems in Utah Sings (1960's) - 52 poems published in Salt Lake Tribune Newspaper - 2 poems published in Ideals Magazine; [pers.] It is said that "What you are is God's gift to you; what you make of yourself is your gift to God". I hope to be worthy of that precious trust and writing talent; [a.] Salt Lake City, UT

CAMP, DOROTHY VAN
[Pen.] Dorothy Gordon-Van Camp; [b.] May 4, 1938, Canville, IL; [p.] William and Orlis Gordon; [m.] Larry W. Van Camp, July 6, 1959; [ch.] Four children.

CAMPBELL, O'KEATHER T.
[Pen.] O.T. Campbell; [b.] June 20, 1956, Winston-Salem, NC; [p.] (the late) Herbert and Ida M. Thompson; [ch.] Herbert Samuel Campbell, Sertilya L. Campbell; [ed.] R.J. Reynolds Sr High School; [occ.] Information Processing Asst III, Forsyth County Dept of Social Services; [memb.] Missionary Board, Mt Nebo TVPH Church; [pers.] God is the beginning of life. Therefore, I strive to include life's struggles in the body of my writing so that in its closing man can see the poetry of God. I have been marvelously inspired by God, family and close friends; [a.] Winston-Salem, NC

CANGUREL, SUSAN
[b.] September 11, 1946, Madison, WI; [p.] John and Lois Murray; [m.] Mel Cangurel, April 8, 1985; [ch.] Lora Quezada, Julia Calorusso; [ed.] Ph.D., Century University in Business Administration; [occ.] Human Resources Director, RM Personnel, Inc., El Paso, TX; [memb.] El Paso Society of Human Resource Management; Epshrm Legislative Affairs CTE; Epshrm Audiovisual Chairman, National Society for Human Resource Management; Texas Association for Business; [hon.] Honors List for B.S. and Masters Degree; Received Certification as Senior Professional in Human Resources; [oth. writ.] Several poems and short stories published.; [pers.] I believe that writing should stretch one's mind and provide readers with the challenge for thought.; [a.] El Paso, TX

CANNATA, CHRISTINE R.
[Pen.] Penny Hope; [b.] May 14, 1969, Chicago, IL; [p.] James L. and Penny Malone; [m.] Michael D. Cannata, July 5, 1991; [ch.] Shawn Michael and Daniel James; [ed.] Gage Park High; [occ.] Mother and a beginning freelance writer/artist; [memb.] The Roman Catholic Church and an Anonymous Group to whom I am indebted to.; [hon.] Life and motherhood; [oth. writ.] This is my first publication and it is my hope to have many more in the days to come.; [pers.] As long as there is life, there will be more room to grow. More things to be gained, and greater loves to show.; [a.] Chicago, IL

CANTLEY, CHERYL A.
[b.] April 2, 1950, Quincy, FL; [p.] Joseph P. and Fannie L. Cantley; [ch.] Angela Carole and Michael Lee Elrod; [ed.] Chattahouchee High School; St. Petersburg Junior College; [occ.] Office Manager, Renker, Eich, Parks, Architects, St. Petersburg, FL; [memb.] First Baptist Church singles council; [oth. writ.] Personal poems written for beloved personal friends; [pers.] I believe our world and its inhabitants were created by a Supreme being to live in balance, harmony and peacefulness through a direct spiritual connection with our creator. Many of my poems are reflections of this purpose and God's love; [a.] St. Petersburg, FL

CANTRELL, PATRICIA BOLIN
[b.] March 13, 1928, Oakland, CA; [p.] Delia, Michael Mulhern; [m.] George Cantrell; [ch.] Nancy, Kenneth Robert; [ed.] St. Joseph's Presentation High School for Girls; [occ.] Retired; [hon.] High school: placed 1st in Oratorical Contest - East Bay, placed 3rd in oratorical contest - San Francisco Region; [oth. writ.] I have written several poems on various subjects especially nature; [pers.] I feel very in tune with the poems I write. The beauty that surrounds us. The Love that is in each person's heart; [a.] Walnut Creek, CA

CAPESTANY, SANDRA
[b.] July 20, 1964, Rio Piedras, PR; [p.] Roger Capestany, Ada Haddock; [m.] Adolfo Garcia, October 31, 1986; [ch.] Jeanette Musse, Toni E. Jamie Garcia; [ed.] Life has been my teacher, left school in high school, but managed to continue learning, especially through reading; [occ.] Mother and wife. (Creative Person); [memb.] PTA; [oth. writ.] Many, though not yet published; [pers.] I believe that the Lord blessed me with a gift. The gift to express myself through my poetry. Edgar Allan Poe is my inspiration; [a.] Bronx, NY

CAPOBIANCO, GLORIA
[b.] April 27, 1936, NYC; [p.] Madelena and Bruno Forte; [m.] Joseph, October 6, 1956; [ch.] Diane, Tina and Lisa; [ed.] Bushwick HS, 1 yr Rider College; [occ.] Housewife; [memb.] Ladies Auxil VFW, Sacred Heart League; [oth. writ.] None ever submitted for publication. Read on radio station; [pers.] I try to reflect laughter, truth and most human feelings; [a.] Howell, NJ

CAPRIA, KAREN S.
[b.] February 28, 1974, Brooklyn, NY; [p.] Ernest Capria, Nancy Capria; [ed.] John P. Stevens High School; University of Delaware; [occ.] Student at the Univ of Delaware: English Major; [memb.] National Honor Society in High School; [pers.] The focus of my poetry is usually on people's deep-felt emotions generally dealing with love and all its complications; [a.] Edison, NJ

CARDENAS, CARMEN A.
[b.] September 8, 1979, Long Beach, Ca; [p.] Victor & Pamela Cardenas; [ed.] Long Beach Polytechnic High School, during my freshman year, but now I am a sophomore at Aliso Niguel High School.; [occ.] Full time student; [memb.] "The "Artist's Guild" at Aliso Niguel; [oth. writ.] I've written several poems for myself, but I've never published them.; [pers.] For being only fifteen years old, I'd say I'm doing pretty good!; [a.] Laguna Niguel, CA

CARDONA, JOANN
[Pen.] Jody; [b.] January 29, 1944, Enid, OK; [p.] Mary Fine and Charles Fager; [m.] Dean Ardon Cardona, July 20, 1982; [ch.] Tammy, 11 yrs. (Student), Dena Joanne guerry, 25 yrs. (Schoolteacher); [ed.] High School; [occ.] Hair Dresser; [oth. writ.] "A Mother to a Daughter," "To My Baby," "The Red Raven," "No Road's Too Long."; [pers.] I strive to write what we feel, to give comfort to others as well as myself. When I am happy or in pain I do my best writing.; [a.] Cathedral City, CA

CAREY, JEANNE WILLIAMS
[b.] Rensselaer, NY; [m.] William J. Carey; [ch.] Eight, 5 boys, 3 girls; [ed.] M.A. in Public Service, University of San Francisco; [occ.] Teaching, writing; [memb.] Business, Professional Womens, University Women, D.A.R., D.A., Roger Wins Family Assoc., Juvenile Justice Commission, S.C. Historical Society, Waddell Creek

Assoc., Rancho del Oso Nature Assoc., CDA; [oth. writ.] Other published poems short stories, historical essays and stories; [pers.] The joy of living as seen in the vivid courage and bright hope of people should be chronicled so that others will take heart and realize it's a great life.; [a.] Santa Cruz, CA

CARLE, GLENN
[b.] May 26, 1975, Somersworth, NJ; [p.] Donald Carle, Alice Carle; [ed.] Restaurant Associate; [hon.] I won an award for a high school poetry contest. The poem was then put on my high school graduation program; [oth. writ.] Many unpublished poems; [pers.] I believe that everybody has a poem or story inside them. It's just up to them to put it on paper; [a.] Shapleigh, ME

CARMAN, RON
[a.] West Los Angeles, CA

CARMODY, KERIN LYN
[b.] April 28, 1956, Los Angeles, CA; [p.] Everett and Norma Carmody; [ed.] Pepperdine Univ; BA Journalism, BA Broadcast Communications Cum Laude; [hon.] The first recipient of the RTNA Award from a college student (Radio, Television, News Association) for radio documentaries while in college; [oth. writ.] Radio documentaries and copy writing, advertising collateral and brochures, several unpublished poems and short stories. [pers.] This poem is dedicated to the memory of Richard Rosenberg who was with me when I wrote it. His love, encouragement and constant belief in my creativity will remain within me forever; [a.] Norwalk, CT

CARPENTER, CRYSTAL SHAVON
[b.] March 9, 1979, Fairfax, VA; [p.] Antoenette M. Carpenter; [ed.] Sophomore Fairfax High School; [occ.] Student; [memb.] Strong Church Member; [hon.] I was previously in the Fairfax Gifted and Talented Program.; [pers.] As a teenager my goal is to go on to college and study foreign language.; [a.] Fairfax, VA

CARPENTER, SCOTT DAVID
[b.] June 13, 1970, Pittsburgh, PA; [m.] Fiancee: Tristen Herristrom; [ed.] Trenton State College, 1993; [occ.] Desktop Support Specialist, Millipore Corp., Bedford, M.A.; [memb.] Boston Computer Society; [oth. writ.] Feature writer for small newspaper in N.J.; [pers.] Writing has a two-fold purpose for me. One, it gives me an outlet for the words, phrases and sounds that clamor for attention inside my head. Two, writing helps to make sense of the vast emotions and experiences of life.; [a.] Allston, MA

CARR, DE ERICA
[Pen.] Muffin; [b.] April 28, 1982, Cleveland, OH; p Sheila Christmas/Derrick Carr; [ed.] I'm in the 7th grade - I am 12 yrs old. My school is Harry E. Davis Middle Village; [occ.] Student; [hon.] I made honor roll and perfect attendance this past June; [pers.] I like to write poems, I've been writing poems since I was 7 yrs old. As I get older I will write many poems; [a.] Cleveland, OH

CARR, LEILANI
[Pen.] Lonnie Carr; [b.] May 14, 1940, Breckin Ridge, Minn.; [p.] Billie H. and Beatrice G. Noyes; [m.] Richard T. Carr, February 5, 1965; [ch.] Michael Wayne, Sheri Lynn, Penny Leann, Richard William; [ed.] Arcata High, Arcata, CA; [occ.] Housewife; [memb.] American Cancer Society, Children's Hospital Fund, Paralyzed Veterans Association, Amvets Post #13 and IACT Sportsmans Club; [hon.] "Mother of the Year." given by

one of my daughters; [oth. writ.] Several poems given to family and friends, songs I've written, have been sung by local bands or by myself or my daughters.; [pers.] Even as a child I've enjoyed poetry and I've always enjoyed putting my words and thoughts to rhyme or song both on the religious or country side of music.; [a.] Waldorf, MD

CARSWELL, LEO D.
[b.] November 15, 1958, Jersey City, NJ; [p.] Ann Carswell and Leo Smith; [ed.] P.S. #32, Lincoln High, Jersey City, NJ; [occ.] Presser, Profession, Hairdresser; [pers.] I believe in what I write on paper. I also believe that when I take the pen to the paper that I must wait for honesty to embrace me.; [a.] Chase City, VA

CARTER, BRENDA
[b.] October 27, 1956, Vienna, MO; [p.] Ralph and Bonnie Wiles; [m.] Werner Carter, April 4, 1980; [ch.] Jason and Matthew Carter; [ed.] Hayden Heights Elem and Maries R-1 School, Vienna, MO; [occ.] Self made arts, crafts and poetry writing. Also homemaker; [memb.] Veterans Administration Fund and The Humane Society; Hobbies: I am an avid flower nut. My yard always blooms with a large variety of beautiful plants! Also love the outdoors - walking - camping and fishing too!; [oth. writ.] I have written poetry, prose, rhymes and stories, even some abstract; [pers.] Having the knowledge to write poetry is a gift from God. My poetry comes from within. It is what's in my heart!; [a.] Brumley, MO

CARTER, FRANCES
[b.] Iowa; [m.] Married; [ch.] Mother of three; grandmother of seven; [oth. writ.] I am currently creating a collection of writings on "What God Has Revealed In His Word"; [pers.] My poems, my songs plainly depict life as I know it. My desire is, for them, to bring good to others; [a.] Mooers, NY

CASE, LINDA EILEEN
[b.] November 5, 1949, Cumberland, MD; [p.] Bernard and Lora May Loar; [m.] Howard Anthony Case, September 20, 1968; [ch.] Melinda Joy, Camile Kathleen, Anthony Raymond; [ed.] Mount Savage High School, Mt. Sav., MD; BA/ED Marshall University, Huntington, WV, Specialties: French and General Science; 18 graduate hours in Secondary Education, Marshall University; [occ.] Substitute Teacher, Cabell County, WV; [memb.] Cabell Midland H.S. Band Boosters; [hon.] Gamma Beta Phi; Pi Delta Phi; National Dean's List; [pers.] I strive to reflect the beauty and perfection of nature in my poetry.; [a.] Barboursville, WV

CASSIDY, KIRA JEANNE
[b.] April 30, 1969, Greensboro, NC; [p.] Virginia and Gene Hilborn; [m.] Paul Cassidy, September 22, 1990; [ed.] North Penn High, Bradford College; [oth. writ.] I am currently working on a book of poems dedicated to the Goddess; [pers.] I strive for honesty and beauty and I hope to reflect the Goddess in my writing and in my life. I am inspired by artists who are not afraid to be themselves and I like to see artists grow through their work; [a.] Arlington, VA

CASTRO, ALISHA
[b.] August 9, 1978, Oceanside, CA; [p.] Raquel Tarango and Manuel Castro; [ed.] Junior at Rancho Buena Vista High School, Vista, CA; [memb.] Amnesty International; [hon.] Quality writing award 1993, Certificate of Achievement in a high school Ready Writers Project 1992; [oth. writ.] Poems not published.; [pers.] At 16 I

am still young and exploring through new experiences. One saying that I have deeply believed in is that "good things come to those who wait."; [a.] Oceanside, CA

CAUDILL, DEANNA
[b.] May 17, 1979, Tell City, IN; [p.] Charles and Linda Caudill; [ed.] New Albany High School; [occ.] Student; [oth. writ.] Poem published in Junior High Schools "Freshman Book of Poems."; [pers.] I dedicate this poem to my grandfather, Charlie Caudill (1918-1994), and I thank my God for the talent he has blessed me with.; [a.] New Albany, IN

CAULEY, MELISSA RENEE
[Pen.] Melissa Cauley; [b.] March 21, 1979, Enterprise, AL; [p.] DeWayne and Renna Cauley; [m.] Single; [ed.] New Brockton High School; [occ.] Student; [pers.] I write poems from things that happen. That gives me a motive for writing.

CECIL, ELVIA SALDIVAR
[b.] May 31, 1948, Albion, MI; [p.] Rosalinda Arevalos and Aniceto Saldivar; [m.] Widowed; [ch.] Katherine J., Cecil Sanchez; [ed.] Brownsville High, Univ of Kansas, Del Mar College; [occ.] Student; [oth. writ.] Volumes of unsubmitted poetry and prose; [pers.] Philippians 4:13. I hope to instill in my students the joy of expressing oneself through whatever creative talents God has given all of us; [a.] Corpus Christi, TX

CHAKRABARTI, ISHAN
[b.] September 6, 1985, N. Delhi, India; [p.] Partha and Tapashi Chakrabarti; [ed.] 4th grade at Nottingham Country Elementary School, Katy, Texas; [occ.] Student; [oth. writ.] "The Turtle From Outer Space" published in "The Statesman," Calcutta, India. "The Polite Tornado" and "The Dangerous Ocean Adventure" all adventure stories.; [pers.] I like to read about nature and science, especially dinosaurs, volcanoes, space and geography. I am nine years old and like to play the violin. I like to write science fiction stories.; [a.] Katy, TX

CHANG, JANICE MAY
[b.] May 24, 1970, Loma Linda, CA; [p.] Belden Shiu-Wah and Sylvia tan Chang; [ed.] Ph.D. International University, 1994; N.D. The Clayton School of Natural Healing, 1993; J.D. LaSalle University, 1993; B.A. California State University, San Bernardino, 1990; [occ.] Doctor, Lawyer, Psychologist; [memb.] American College of Legal Medicine; American Naturopathic Medical Association; American Psychology, Law Society; American Society of Law, Medicine, and Ethics; Association of Trial Lawyers of America; California Trial Lawyers Association, Medical Law Section; [hon.] Editor's Choice Award, 1994. Listed in: Who's Who in California, 1992, 1995; Who's Who in U.S. Writers, Editors, and Poets, 1992-3; [oth. writ.] Writingscapes: An Approach to Creative Writing, 1991; Psychological Ramification of Child Sexual Abuse, 1993.; [pers.] Poetry is the most expressive form of revealing ourselves. It captivates the inherent beauty and speaks truthfully about our world.; [a.] Loma Linda, CA

CHASE, EVE LEWIS
[b.] May 17, Columbus, OH; [p.] William T. Doris and Catherine Lewis; [m.] Harry Lee Chase; [ed.] Ohio State University - Journalism; [occ.] Legal Secretary; [oth. writ.] Features, news articles and column; "Eve's Dropping" during 10 year journalistic career; [pers.] I am pleased to see a renewed appreciation of poetry with rhyme and meter.; [a.] San Francisco, CA

CHERNISHOVA, Ph.D., KAYA
[ed.] St. Louis University; University of San Francisco (undergrad); Professional School of Psychology (grad); Univ. of California, Berkeley Campus (grad); Grad. Seminars, Golden Gate University, S.F.; [occ.] Practiced Marriage and Family Therapy and Counseling; [memb.] Univ. of California Alumni Assoc.; [hon.] B.A., MPH., Ph.D. (Psychology) Dean's List.; [oth. writ.] Several poems in "Bozart," short essays in local publications.; [pers.] While living in Korea and Japan I was impressed by the gentle beauty of Asian literature. I am a follower of the great thinker, Dr. Albert Schweitzer who taught reverence for all forms of life as were all equal inhabitants of the universe. Since age 15 I have painted in pastels and exhibited in private showings.; [a.] San Francisco, CA

CHERRIER, LISA FL.
[b.] July 19, 1962, Torrance, CA; [p.] Richard and Fleta Thomas to whom I dedicate this poem; [m.] Engaged to Daniel Brown (currently divorced; [ch.] Cory Cherrier 9 and Kameran Cherrier 7; [ed.] West High School, El Camino College, Victor Valley College, Real Estate Principles; [occ.] Entrepreneur; [memb.] American Blood Donor, (Riverside & San Bernardino Counties); [oth. writ.] This was a first! Inspired by the most loving and supportive parents, that many people and children long and pray for, I dedicate to you.; [pers.] I love you Mom and Dad. Thanks to my children, I send all my love and hope to dedicate my next poem to them (The bright lights of my life).; [a.] Lake Hausu City, AZ

CHERRY, LINDSAY
[b.] April 11, 1977, Auburn, IN; [p.] David and Bobbie Cherry; [ed.] Alan C. Pope High School in Marietta, GA; [memb.] First Presbyterian Church; [hon.] National German Honor Society, National Honor Society, National Beta Club, Who's Who in American High Schools; [oth. writ.] Several poems dealing with love, loss, and hope.; [pers.] Relationships are the key to life. Find them, develop them, and learn to love them for what they are truly worth.; [a.] Marietta, GA

CHEWNING, DEBORAH M.
[b.] July 1, 1967, Washington, D.C.; [p.] Della K. Chewning; [ed.] Suitland High, Suitland, MD, Strayer College - Bachelors of Science - Computer Information Systems, WDC; [occ.] Computer Specialist; [memb.] Galilee Baptist Church and - New Members Ministry of Galilee Baptist Church; [hon.] President's List and Honor Roll 1992; [oth. writ.] Unpublished poems - "Rise Up All Ye Women", "Black, Beautiful and Born Again", and "Women on the Move, But Where Are We Going"; [pers.] "Every good gift and every perfect gift is from above, and cometh down from the father of lights..." (James 1:17). [KJV] My gift of writing is inspired by God, and I'm grateful and honored to be blessed with such a gift to uplift and console the hearts of mankind; [a.] Temple Hills, MD

CHINCHILLO, JEAN BELL
[b.] "Granny Jean"; [b.] April 9, 1912, Boston, MA; [p.] Sarah (London) and Roy Bell; [m.] June 25, 1939, deceased 3/9/93; [ch.] Ten children, 10 great grandchildren, Joyce Griffin and Janet Siemasko; [ed.] Revere High, Boston University, Malden Business School; [occ.] Homemaker and writer; [memb.] National Library of Poetry; [hon.] Golden Poet Award 1991 by Eddie Cole; [oth. writ.] First book published 1988, "The Caterpillar and Other Poems for Children." I am presently working on two stories, "Mr. Crickadoodle's Secret, and "Soolie,

the boy from the planet Euranus," also a volume of "Poetic Stories" and Editor's Awards 1991, 1993, 1994 received; [pers.] Poem "My Love" published by the National Library of Poetry dedicated in memory of my husband Tory.; [a.] Revere, MA

CHODOBA, NICK
[b.] October 19, 1969, NY; [p.] Vaziaica Chodoba; [ed.] Queens College, CUNY; [pers.] Concentration on the senses brings humanity out of the information age. The only sane response to the global village is schizophrenia.; [a.] Woodhaven, NY

CHOLEWA, PAULA KAY
[b.] July 4, 1966, Belen, NM; [p.] Paul and Leonella Montano; [m.] Don, February 4, 1989; [ch.] Madeline Rose; [ed.] High School Education, U.S. Air Force, October 23, 1984 through September 1, 1991; [occ.] Mother, homemaker, volunteer worker.; [hon.] Air Force, Good Conduct Medal, Air Force Achievement Medal; [oth. writ.] Several poems, short stories, One published in high school yearbook.; [pers.] I owe my inspiration to my partner and to my shadow--Thank you Don and Madeline.; [a.] Cheyenne, WY

CHONG, SUNJU CHOI
[b.] May 5, 1960, Korea (South); [p.] Suh Kyoon Cho, Ktoo Seek Chong (Korea); [m.] Kwan Chong, April 5, 1984; [ch.] Lillian, Jane, Christopher, Eileen; [ed.] Jeon buk National Univ. (Korea), M. Div. in Garrett Evangelical Theological Seminary (Evanston); [occ.] Full time student for a doctorate in pastoral counseling at Chicago Theological Seminary; [memb.] Calvary United Methodist Church; [oth. writ.] Several poems published in the Korean Newspaper, an article for a magazine.; [pers.] I believe that life is the journey with the ultimate questions of meaning, beauty and truth. My writing is based on my passion to find experiential answers for them.; [a.] Chicago, IL

CHRISMAN, MARGARET CRAIG
[b.] January 20, 1931, Evanston, IL; [p.] John Merrill and Amelia Henderson Baker; [m.] William H. Chrisman, April 17, 1989; [ch.] Amelia, Janet, Peter, Katherine, Emily; [ed.] Evanston, Township High School, Northwestern University B.S., Harvard University, M.Ed.; [occ.] Principal, AZMECO Investment, Scottsdale, Arizona, Real Estate and Securities investments; [memb.] Junior League of Phoenix, Achievement Rewards for College Scientists, Harvard Club of Phoenix, Habitat for Humanity International, YMCA, Planned Parenthood.

CHURCH, CHERYL W.
[b.] July 3, 1966, Baltimore, MD; [p.] Kenneth N. Wheeling and Vonda J. McVicker; [m.] Arthur C. Church, April 21, 1991; [ch.] Chelsea Robin and Arthur, Jr (AJ); [ed.] C.Milton Wright High, Beaver Creek High, Wilkes Community College; [occ.] CNA, Ashe Services for Aging, Jefferson, NC; [memb.] Ashe Developmental Day School Board Member, Autism Society of North Carolina, Smart Start Committee; [pers.] I wrote this poem for my 3 year old, developmentally delayed, mildly autistic, daughter. She has given me so very much more, than I am deserving of. Thank you Chelsea; [a.] West Jefferson, NC

CLAMPET-LUNDQUIST, MERRILL
[b.] August 1, 1970, Orange, CA; [p.] Wesley Lundquist, Margaret Lundquist; [m.] Susan Clampet-Lundquist, June 11, 1994; [ed.] Eastern College; St. Davids, PA -

BA Sociology; [occ.] Social Worker; [memb.] Amnesty International; [hon.] Dean's List; Magna Cum Laude; [oth. writ.] Several poems have been published in other anthologies, including "Tumbleweed" a "She Lives In Her Heart/Magic Happen"; [pers.] My father once told me that if I shoot it more than twice, I was playing with it (rarely do I shake it more than twice now). I, therefore, believe that serious poetry requires a sense a humor...we must be able to laugh at that which makes us cry; [a.] Philadelphia, PA

CLANCY, CAROL
[b.] October 25, 1964, Cleveland, OH; [ed.] MA in English from Cleveland State Univ; BA in English and Psychology from Baldwin-Wallace College; [pers.] For me, poetry is an expression of truth, often times truth that cannot be told any other way. For this reason, I believe that poetry plays a very important role in our world, and especially in this society; [a.] Lakewood, OH

CLANTON, MICHELLE D.
[Pen.] U. Shelc; [b.] June 6, 1971; [p.] Denise and Thomas Clanton Sr.; [ed.] King High, Watterson School of Technology; [occ.] Medical Assistant, Medical College of Pennsylvania; [memb.] Bright Hope Baptist Church, YMCA; [oth. writ.] Several unpublished poems; [pers.] I'm blessed with relatives and friends who encourage me. My faith in God reassures me. Every life experience is a lesson with theory for you to indulge in.; [a.] Roslyn, PA

CLARK, CASSANDRA J.
[Pen.] Cassandra; [b.] January 9, 1980, Honolulu, HI; [p.] Christine Clark Voeghtly and Ronald Voeghtly; [ed.] Scobee Elementary, Stinson Middle School and Marshall High School; [occ.] Student; [memb.] Band and Basketball Clubs in middle school. Basketball, swimming and Student Artist Clubs in high school; [hon.] Outstanding student. Star player on her middle school basketball and track and field teams. Honor Chair and Solo Contest 1st Place Winner for both the baritone and clarinet for middle school band. Recipient of many firsts for her excellent swimming skills for youth summer swimming programs; [oth. writ.] Has written over 56 other poems reflecting her personal beliefs and feelings. To date this is her first published poem; [pers.] My poetry reflects my teenage years and problems in our society. It enables me to get my feelings out in a creative way. Emotionally deep and meaningful poetry interests me in the same sense that certain words can be other people's feelings, also; [a.] San Antonio, TX

CLARK, JANNIE B.
[b.] April 30, 1935, Carrollton, KY; [p.] Roy and Muriel Floyd; [m.] Roger R. Clark, September 19, 1987; [ch.] William Daniel and Robert Taylor Butler; [ed.] Charlestown High School, Indiana University; [occ.] Retired Real Estate Broker; [memb.] Ind. State Federation of Poetry, Southern Ind. Poetry Society, Eastern Star, Life Member American Legion, Life Member V.F.W., Life Member D.A.V., Life Member P.O.W., husband is a former P.O.W.; [hon.] First Place in State Contest in 1990 & 1991. Lots of Honorable Mention. Several awards from the V.F.W.; [oth. writ.] Published in Voices in the Wind Vol 3, Wisdom of the Heart, 1990 Poetic Voices of America, 1991 Golden Anniversary Anthology of I.S.F.P., 1991 Poetic Calendar, Southern Indiana Quill, On The Threshold of a Dream Vol 3, My own book Efforts of an Aspiring Poet 1993; [pers.] I was inspired to write poetry by my mother. It is to her I dedicate all my poems.; [a.] Scottsburg, IN

CLARK, TANYA DIANE
[b.] June 16, 1972, Columbus, MS; [p.] Larry Speed, Mary Virginia Speed; [m.] David Clarke, February 2, 1993; [ch.] Larry Leon Clark; [ed.] Eau Gallie High School, East Mississippi Community College; [occ.] Housewife, Custom Home Designs; [pers.] I use my writing as a way to express my feelings and emotions about experiences that have happened in my life, which in turn helps me improve myself; [a.] Vernon, AL

CLARKE, YVONNE
[b.] March 22, 1959, Philadelphia, PA; [p.] John Thomas and Ineatha S. Clarke; [m.] Single; [ch.] Anthony Ray and Roquois Yvonne; [ed.] South Phila High Motivation and Community College of the Air Force; [occ.] Inquiry Specialist; [memb.] Greater Mt. Nebo AME Church; [hon.] Various US Air Force military honors, ribbons and awards; [oth. writ.] "Love is Interatmosphere", "Conception", "Mom", "Abuse", and "Good Bye".

CLAY, LINDSAY M.
[b.] April 8, 1983, Tucson, AZ; [p.] William and Katrina Clay; [a.] Tucson, AZ

CLAYTON, CHERYL E.
[b.] June 9, 1975, Westwooa, NJ; [p.] William F. and Elizabeth H.K. Clayton; [ed.] River Dell High School, Rider University; [occ.] Student; [memb.] Venture, Rider's Literary Magazine, Greenpeace; [hon.] Dean's List; [oth. writ.] Many poems written in high school for creative writing classes.; [pers.] I feel that my work is greatly influenced by studying the great poets of past times. The majority of my reading comes from 16th century poets, namely Shakespeare and Donne, and poets from the romantic era. For me writing poetry is an escape and a wonderful emotional release.; [a.] Oradell, NJ

CLEMENTS, KATHLEEN D.
[b.] January 26, 1941, Buffalo, NY; [p.] John J. Dolan, Katherine G.; [m.] Gerald W. Clements, May 24, 1980; [ed.] Mt. St. Mary Academy, Kenmore, NY; D'Youville College, Buffalo, NY, BS ED, Rank II Western Kentucky Univ, Bowling Green, KY; [occ.] Teacher - Junior High English, St. Martha School, Louisville, KY; [memb.] NCEA 1980-Present, NCTE 1980-1984, GLEC - 1944 ACE, (National Catholic Education Assoc), (National Council Teachers of English), (Greater Louisville English Council), (Academy of Catholic Educators); [hon.] Who's Who Among America's Teachers 1994; [pers.] I look for the beauty of God everywhere, and aim to develop a love for writing and self-expression in my students; [a.] Louisville, KY

CLOUGH, PRISCILLA M.
[b.] May 20, 1908, Dorchester, MA; [p.] Samuel Clough; [m.] Johnima Johnson; [ch.] Nima Andersen; [ed.] Girls Latin School, Boston Univ. School of Journalism; [occ.] Retired; [memb.] John Clough Genealogical Society, Daughters of the American Revolution, West Roxbury Historical Society, Roslyn Senior Citizen Club; [hon.] Too numerous too mention; [oth. writ.] Biographical sketches, publicity, correspondents; [pers.] At age 12 I was asked to go to Hollywood to become a child actress. Parents refused.; [a.] Roslindale, NH

COBB, KAREN RENAY
[Pen.] Tracey Pearson; [b.] May 29, 1980, Oxford, MS; [p.] Mr. and Mrs. Tommy Cobb; [ed.] Lafayette Junior High School and in the 8th grade; [occ.] Help in the fam-

ily restaurant; [oth. writ.] Got some in the process (poems) but first three that I have sent in.; [pers.] Many romance poems that I've read have really given me a start on how I want to start out. From then on I write from the heart, on how I feel about romance, people and everyday life etc.; [a.] Oxford, MS

COBLE, FRANCES ROSS
[b.] September 30, 1908, Washington, C.H., OH; [p.] Alfred H. W. Ross, Amma Jones Ross; [m.] Hoyt Lorenzo Coble (deceased); [ed.] Colo State Teachers College, Greeley, Colony BA, MA, Further study Univ of Minn; [occ.] Retired; served until retirement as registrar at Winston-Salem Stat Univ, Winston-Salem, North Carolina; [memb.] Wentz Memorial United Church of Christ, Golden Soror and Life Member of Alpha Kappa Alpha Sorority, American Association of Retired Persons (AARP), National Council of Negro Women, IN; [hon.] Professor Emeritus, Winston-Salem State Univ, Winston-Salem, NC; [oth. writ.] In collaboration with two other writers, a History of Winston-Salem State Univ covering the first 100 years (1892-1992) is in progress; [a.] Winston-Salem, NC

COHEN, JOE
[b.] November 13, 1971, Thousand Oaks, CA; [p.] Michael S. and Eileen T. Cohen; [ed.] 3 years of Cal Poly, San Luis Obispo Journalism Major; [occ.] Slave to the grind; [memb.] Quill and Scroll Society, Readers Digest Subscription (ha, ha); [hon.] Newbury Park Award of Excellence in Writing, Best On-Air Personality KCPR 91.3 F.M.; [oth. writ.] Poems published in FIZGIG and Neopoliton magazine. Columns published in the Prowler and Mustang Daily (Cal Poly's Paper) I'm looking to publish book of 200 of my poems.; [pers.] If you would like to read more of my words, send a SASE and I'll share them. If you want to publish your words, write my P.O. Box and I'll explain how you can.; [a.] Marro Bay, CA

COHN, LILLIAN L.
[Pen.] Lilo; [b.] November 21, 1931, Berlin, Germany; [p.] Horbert and Hilde Klopstock; [m.] Daniel H., October 4, 1953; [ch.] Allan L. Cohn and Scott H. Cohn; [ed.] Nicholas Senn High School, Chicago Art Institute & National Louis Univ.; [occ.] Freelance Artist and Writer; [memb.] Holocaust Association of Child Survivors, N.O.W. (Nat'l Organization Women) Na'Amat USA; [hon.] Honorable Mention; Art Institute College Scholarship Competition. Graduate with Highest Honors; National Louis University, Evanston, IL 1983; [oth. writ.] "A Shadow Over My Life," (Book) Green Publishing House, Jerusalem, Israel; [pers.] I deplore man's inhumanity to man.. Both during the holocaust and through time immemorial. We must remember, we must teach and we must be aware to stop evil in its tracks everywhere.; [a.] Glenview, IL

COHOON, DORIS J.
[b.] December 7, 1929, Oak Park, IL; [p.] Everett and Edith Cohoon; [ed.] American Academy of Art, Eastern Illinois University, University of Illinois and Iowa, Control Data Institute, Community Colleges in St. Louis and Mattoon; [occ.] Sales Clerk, Wal-Mart Super Center; [pers.] With our creator and universe as teachers, our minds know no boundaries in growth.; [a.] Mattoon, IL

COLE, NATALIE L.
[b.] October 11, 1964, Bangor, ME; [p.] Charles J. and Jacqueline A. Cole; [ed.] Wichita Falls High School, Midwestern State Univ; [occ.] Professor of English,

Venion Regional Junior College, W.F., TX; [hon.] Academic Ribbon and Daughters of the American Revolution Medal, JROTC, Wichita Falls High School (1983); [oth. writ.] MA in English thesis: The Waste Land: "After the first death, there is no other"; [pers.] Je suis ceque je suis, je ue suis pas ce que je suis; si je tais ceque je suis, jeve serais pas ce que je suis. Que suis-je? The message in this french comendrum is that originality is the soul of one's existence. Individuality is the measure of the individual.; [a.] Wichita Falls, TX

COLEMAN, EDREL KELLY
[b.] November 5, 1918, Seminary, MS; [p.] Mack Kelly and Emma Kelly (Deceased); [m.] Victor S. Coleman, May 8, 1939 (recently deceased), May 8, 1939; [ch.] Janet Coleman Mitchell; [ed.] B.S. Kansas State University in Education; [occ.] Retired Educator; [memb.] Charlotte County Retired Educators; Right to Breath; Pt. Charlotte United Methodist Church. Before retiring I was active in many, many community activities. Belonged to many organizations.; [hon.] Alaska "Mother of the Year" "Military Wife of the Year," for all five Military Branches, Who's Who Among American's Best Teachers, Honored Merits Award, City of Fairbanks, Nominee for "Woman of the Year" of the International Federation of women Guest of Mrs. Pat Nixon at White House Toured with Art Linkletter and his Entourage, Guest on many Art's "House Party Shows"; [oth. writ.] Your Son Abe, poem. It is an answer to the poem "Nancy Hanks." "Packing My Suitcase for Heaven" (Poem) Monthly articles "Patterns for Living" Many plays and skits. I am now writing my autobiography.; [pers.] It is not what people give to me, in honor praise or commendations; It is what I give to others to help unfold their life's aspirations.; [a.] Pt. Charlotte, FL

COLES, JR., EPIFANIO C.
[Pen.] Philip P. Nash; [b.] May 1, 1950, Manila, Philippines; [p.] Epifanio Coles, Sr., and Adoracion Coles; [m.] Roselyn Zausa-Coles, June 10, 1978; [ch.] Yasmin Katrina, Lea Kristina, Rex Oliver, Roselle Karmina; [ed.] Araullo High School, Genetical Engineering, Mapua Institute of Tech., Bachelor of Arts, Philippine Christian University, Master in Management, Philippine Christian University; [occ.] Businessman, Management Consultant; [memb.] Philippine Foundation for Public Administration, Philippine Historical Assoc., AHS Alumni Association in America; [hon.] President's and scholar, PCU Honor Student, Phil. Christian Univ., First Place, Poem Writing Contest, PCU, Award of Recognition, World of Poetry, Inc.; [oth. writ.] Several poems published in Manila Newspaper and Magazine.; [pers.] "The days will pass, and the poets will rest, but their verses remain ever changing, until next year's reckoning."; [a.] Santa Ana, CA

COLLINS, C. T.
[b.] December 17, 1926, Boston, MA; [p.] Dana and Miriam (Nee Rice); [m.] Tess (Nee Cooley), October 26, 1985; [ch.] Richard and Bruce (previous marriage); [ed.] Norwich Univ 1 yr. Grad Denver Univ BS in Bus Ad (Hotel and Rest Mngmt); [occ.] Actor. Retired from Hotel business after 30 yrs to take up writing and acting. Wrote my first poem "Final Curtain" while in intensive care. Became a professional actor on film, T.V. and stage. Took some writing courses at Bakersfield High (CA); Denver Univ and LA Comm College. Have written several poems under the title Nostalgia and Other States of Mind (This poem included.); [hon.] Best Actor-Comedy and Best Actor-Drama 1979; [oth. writ.] Travel and Misc articles for magazines and newspapers; [a.] San Clemente, CA

COLLINS, CARRIE LINDA
[Pen.] China Doll; CLC; [b.] December 16, 1958, El Paso, TX; [p.] (the late) Robert L. Clark, Sr. and (the late) Joyce E. Clark; [m.] Mitchel Anthony Collins, October 11, 1985; [ch.] Cheyenne Lynn Collins; [ed.] Wm H. Burges HS - El Paso, TX, Univ of TX at El Paso; Delaware St College, Rutgers - The State Univ of NJ and Thomas Edison St Col; [occ.] Homemaker/writer; [memb.] Delta Sigma Theta Sorority, Inc; Literary Volunteers of America; Second Bapt Church, Mt Holly, NJ; [hon.] Honorary Mentions from World of Poetry organization. Poems, articles published in HS and college, Dean's List - Del State College; Wheel of Fortune Contestant, 1989; [oth. writ.] Currently working on 2 novels and a compilation of my poetry; [pers.] Maya Angelou and other great women poets have been my mentors; the love of God and reading His word, the Bible have been my inspiration; and the love and encouragement of my family has kept me going forward. I seek to uplift myself through others; [a.] Pittsburgh, PA

COLLINS, DWIGHT
[Pen.] Vincent; [b.] July 22, 1954, New York; [p.] Gloria and Edward; [occ.] Consultant and romantic, A knight in shining armor, An angel; [pers.] Stephanie is my world, Emily is an island, They are my universe and my inspiration.

COLLINS, RANDALL LEE
[b.] May 28, 1963, Junction City, KA; [p.] Richard C. Collins, Margaret Hawkins; [m.] Sherrie M. Collins, May 17, 1994; [ch.] Chloe E. Collins; [ed.] Hayfield Secondary School, Western Michigan University, University of Detroit School of Law.; [occ.] Senior Law Attorney, Berrien County Legal Services; [memb.] Michigan State Bar Association, Senior Nutrition Services Board of Directors, Southwestern Aging Network; [oth. writ.] Various poems, love songs, short stories.; [pers.] I live everyday with the hope that I will find beauty in every experience; and I am rewarded with finding such beauty in the simplest of things.; [a.] Niles, MI

COLLINS, VIRDA JEAN
[Pen.] Virdajean Towns-Collins; [b.] June 9, 1938, Grenada, Miss.; [p.] Geraldine Norwood, Louis Towns; [m.] John R. Collins, August 23, 1978; [ch.] Paul, Phillip, Perry; [ed.] Crane Tech High Night School; [occ.] Retired Postal Clerk; [memb.] Mall Walkers; [oth. writ.] Several poems, and profiles of family members in rhyme.; [pers.] I strive to make my poems rhyme, and to reflect the positive, and to tell the truth.; [a.] Chicago, IL

COLONNA, JOANN
[b.] September 15, 1946, Brooklyn, NY; [m.] Frank S. Colonna; [ch.] Remy Gili, Step daughter Diane Parrella; [occ.] Own and operate restaurant; [memb.] Vice President Son's of Italy, Community Associations; [hon.] Achievement Award for Community Services; [oth. writ.] Commentaries about local government activity in our local news paper "Osceola News Gazette."; [pers.] What induces me to write, are my true feelings and belief. In this world every person does make a difference. If we reach out and touch one or one hundred people. At least we've reached out and touched.; [a.] Brooklyn, NY

COLWELL, ALEXANDER PETER
[b.] April 1, 1981, Washington, D.C.; [p.] James C. and Judith K. Colwell; [ed.] Currently an 8th grader at Takoma Park Middle School. Graduate of the Montgomery County French Immerson Program (K-6th gr.); [oth. writ.] Journal entries and assignments for school.;

[pers.] The writings of Edgar Allen Poe were the inspiration for this poem. Maybe I will try to become a professional writer someday but at age 13, I am not yet sure.; [a.] Takoma Park, MD

COMER, NILES U.
[b.] November 1, 1967, Wilmington, DE; [p.] James W. (deceased) and Sandy James; [ed.] Bishop McGuinnes High School, Marymount University (currently); [occ.] Adm. Ass't.; National Assoc. of State Board of Education; [memb.] Brazilian American Cultural Institute; [hon.] "Tomorrow's Leaders Today," Public Service Award 1993, Public Allies Civic Award, 1986 Winston-Salem Civic Assoc.; [oth. writ.] Several volumes of unpublished poems, a few published free-lance articles in newspapers.; [pers.] Writing poetry is my way of seeking and creating justice, peace, beauty, and truth. Writing is a vacation that I am held accountable for, and must use in the service of the most vulnerable and broken in our society.; [a.] Washington, D.C.

CONDER, LOIS MILDRED SNELLING
[b.] May 16, 1924, Zebra, MO; [p.] Elisha and Flora Snelling; [m.] James C. Conder I, November 9, 1940; [ch.] Sandee Janes, James C. II, Welby Williams; [occ.] Retired; [pers.] Work and play, love and pray. These are words I've always tried to live by. Love is the most important to love God first, your spouse and children next to God. If you don't love God first you can't love people.; [a.] Prescott Valley, AZ

CONKLIN-CERF, PATRICIA BUTLER
[Pen.] P.B. Cerf; [b.] May 5, 1939, Baltimore, MD; [p.] Anna and Wilmer T. Butler; [m.] Kenneth A. Cerf; [ch.] Raised 6 children; [ed.] Valencia Community College, Univ of Baltimore; [occ.] Caseworker for member of congress; [memb.] Leaders Council of Winter Park, Florida; Daughters of the American Revolution; Member of the Women's International Writers Guild; [hon.] Listed in "Who's Who and Why of Successful Florida Women" and "The Directory of Distinguished Americans"; [oth. writ.] Play entitled "Jesus Last Supper" Library of Congress catalog card #86-083230, copyright 581-576, 23 Jan 1984; [pers.] Each day offers opportunities to grow and help others. I try to smile often, apologize quickly and forgive readily limiting my regrets - for life is so short and so fragile; [a.] Maitland, FL

CONLEY, LISA DONEL
[b.] November 24, 1969, Milwaukee, Wisc; [p.] Irene and Cecil Conley; [ed.] Shorewood High School, Clark Atlanta University; [occ.] Nursing Assistant, Geriatric Center at Emory Telerecruiter, American Red Cross; [hon.] Volunteer Service Award, Dean's List; [oth. writ.] Previously published in Tears of Fire.; [pers.] Everything I write is inspired by love, the people I've loved, those who have loved me and even the love I've lost.; [a.] Atlanta, GA

CONNER, SUSAN
[b.] April 13, 1948, Washington, D.C.; [p.] Joseph and Dorothy Breedlove; [ch.] Theresa Lynn; [ed.] Cynthia Warner School, Mars Hill College, Marjorie Webster Jr. College; [occ.] Customer Service Rep. in Real Estate office.; [memb.] Church of God of Prophecy, a servant of Jesus Christ; [oth. writ.] Have been published in local magazine, in anthology, Eternal Echoes published nationally, written book, Solitude, poems and prayers copyrighted by Library of Congress.; [pers.] Jesus Christ writes my poems and prayers, I'm just the recorder.; [a.] Bethesda, MD

CONNORS, ROBERT
[b.] December 22, 1951, Phila., PA; [p.] John Connors; [m.] Claire Connors, September 24, 1988; [ch.] Neil Alexander; [ed.] University of Louisville Master of Science; [occ.] Computer Systems Analyst; [hon.] Dean's List, National Honor Society; [oth. writ.] Several poems published in college and local papers.; [pers.] Think life is a test for improvement of each spirit; who has as many chances as it takes.; [a.] Burtonsville, MD

CONROY, MARY
[Pen.] Mary O. Connell; [b.] October 10, Ireland; [p.] Patrick O. Connell and Kathleen McCarthy; [m.] William Thomas Conroy, April 18, 1940; [ch.] Kathleen Merrell and William M. Conroy; [ed.] High School in Ireland, Nursing at Los Angeles Jr. College, Creative Writing Orange Coast College, Pharmacology Compton College; [occ.] Crossing Guard, City of Newport Beach; [memb.] Classic Friends Club, Our Lady Queen of Angels, Catholic Church; [hon.] Pictures taken up on the moon and congratulations for poems; [oth. writ.] Poems for Allen Shepard, First Man in Space, Named, Our Changing Era, Poem for Astronauts, Armstrong, Collins, and Aldrin, First landing on the moon, titled "Our American Men on the Moon;" [pers.] I keep in close touch with family, son and daughter and six grandchildren; [a.] Del Mar, CA

COOK, WILLIAM
[b.] December 20, 1936, Otsego, WV; [p.] James M. and Haydla Cook; [m.] Toula B. Cook, May 29, 1971; [ed.] Bachelor's Degree, CPA; [occ.] Treasurer; [memb.] Eckankar, Science of Spirituality, IL CPA Society; [hon.] National Honor Society; [oth. writ.] "Earth Cries", "Transformation", "The Silence of Sound", "Quest"...and other poetry; [pers.] Sooner or later, now or beyond the measurement of time, all souls will journey home having learned all that pain can teach, all that love can realize, all that dreams can bring; [a.] Batavia, IL

COOLBAUGH, MARGARET D.
[b.] February 6, 1917, New Albany, PA; [p.] William and Jessica Caster Dunbar; [ed.] Athens, PA High School 1936; [occ.] Retired; [memb.] Independent Baptist Church, Towanda, PA, GTE Sylvania Women's Club, Towanda, PA; [oth. writ.] Through the Eyes of A Child, Biographical The Way Things Were, Comparing yesterday and today, My Thoughts Wise and Otherwise.; [pers.] Most of my poetry reflects my belief in, and love for God. Some are patriotic, some whimsical. Some just for fun. I have had some published in our local newspaper and several in the Baptist Bulletin; [a.] Towanda, PA

COOP, KATHRYN E.
[Pen.] Kay Coop; [b.] February 27, 1943, Missouri; [p.] Kenneth and Neta Madison; [m.] David H. Coop, California; [ch.] Kevin and Krystal; [occ.] Real Estate Agent; [memb.] National Assoc. of Realtors Calif. Assoc. of Realtors, Greater Long Beach Assoc. of Realtors, Vice-Chair Grievance Comm. Board of Directors NLB/BA Club; [hon.] Who's Who Registry of Global Business Leaders, Certified Residential Specialist, Graduate Real Estate Institute; [oth. writ.] Co-authored with spouse Real Estate Course; [pers.] Have written poetry for many years for personal enjoyment and as yearly presentation at office year end meetings.; [a.] Long Beach, CA

COOPER, AUDREY
[b.] August 2, 1931, Phila. PA; [p.] Augustus and Maetee Gray; [m.] Charles Cooper, November 13, 1962 (deceased); [ch.] Maetee, Sheila, Laverne Donzell; [ed.] Cardoza High; [occ.] Correspondent for various organizations; [oth. writ.] Poems published in various anthologies.; [pers.] I strive to inform that God's grace and mercy is for all and He can empower us to rise above our faults.

COOPER, BILLIE A.
[b.] October 25, 1927, Missouri; [p.] W.S. and Sarah Cooper; [ed.] Univ of Colorado; [occ.] Retired Telecommunications Specialist; [memb.] Valley View Bible Church; DAR; [hon.] Beta Gamma Sigma; [oth. writ.] Poems and other writings in church publications; [a.] Phoenix, AZ

COOPER, JAMIE M.
[b.] April 19, 1979, Portland, OR; [p.] Mike and Cathy Cooper; [ed.] View Acres Elem, McLoughlin Jr Hg, a sophomore at Clackamas Hg School as of 1994; [occ.] Student; [memb.] Camp Fire boys and girls Drama Club in Jr High; [hon.] Read-a-Thon at school, Certificate of Award for Academic Improvement, the TAG (talented and gifted) program grades (k-8th); [oth. writ.] Poems and short stories, movie scripts and plays for fun at home; [pers.] I think to tell the "truth" in my poems; [a.] Milwaukie, OR

COOPER, JENEAN
[b.] February 6, 1948, Asher, Oklahoma; [p.] Vinita and Earl Cooper; [ch.] Trevin Cooper; [ed.] B.F.A. in Acting, Director at the University of Oklahoma, M.A. in English Traditional Studies at Central State University; [occ.] Co-owner of Zarcon RoCo Publishing co., Spring, TX; [memb.] Broadcast Music Inc., Nashville, TN; [hon.] Recognized for Environmental and American Indian issues by Ned McWherter, Governor, Tenn., Phil Bredesen, Mayor Nashville, Bruce Todd, Mayor, Austin, TX, Dallas Morning News; Austin American Statesman; San Bernardino Sun; Dean's Honor Roll; [oth. writ.] Four original musical compositions have aired nationally.; [pers.] On my road through life it has been better to take a chance on the path to greatness than to follow the safe highway to mediocrity.; [a.] Seminole, FL

CORDELL, PATRICIA
[b.] February 12, 1941, Austin, TX; [p.] Avna LaRue and Gragy Lee Leggett; [m.] Lenn Olen Cordell, June 23, 1958; [ch.] Vickie L. Wilms, Darrell R. Cordell; [son-in-law] David; [daughter-in-law] Diane; [grandch.] Billy L. Sutton, Kandice L. Sutton, Bobby J. Cordell, Chip C. Cordell; [ed.] Leander High, 2 Years, Art Instruction School, I paint in oils, I've been an artist for over 7 years.; [occ.] Writer Children's Manuscripts; [oth. writ.] I'm being published at this time, through High Tech Distributors, Idaho Springs Co., Children's Stories. I'm not sure of the title of my book yet. The Pub. Co. has at this time 5 manuscripts of mine.; [pers.] At this time I am in completion of a collection of my poems for Chapbook, that I will be sending out to Still Water Press, Galloway NJ. My poetry comes from the heart, my guide is God. He has given me this talent to pass along his greatness through my work. "I thank God;" [a.] Belton, TX

COTONE, MARY HAGERTY
[Pen.] William C. Hagerty; [b.] July 4, 1904, Boston; [p.] Mary Cashman, William J. Hagerty; [m.] Cleo Hagerty, October 23, 1926; [ch.] Mary E., William M., Anne L.; [ed.] BC High, BC College, Art School, Exeter School of Art.

COULTON, CATHERINE
[Pen.] Aunt Kate, To everyone; [b.] March 18, 1917, Newark, NJ; [p.] Leonard and Vita Gino; [m.] Deceased, Edgar Coulton, February 25, 1967; [ed.] Received education in the community where I was trained to be a Num and Teacher, Order of The Religious Teachers Philippines; [memb.] Our Lady Queen of Prack Church, The Nine Choirs of Angels; [hon.] Recognition from the Board of Education for guiding children in the lunch room and the playground; [oth. writ.] Composed a poem to commemorate the death of my precious little niece Jennifer who passed away at the age of 6 weeks. Also composed a poem for my beautiful niece Valarie to commemorate her graduation.; [pers.] I spent 30 years as a teacher, dealing with all types of children. Even now I see hundreds of little faces marching before me. May God bless each one. If I had to do it all over again, I would not change a thing!; [a.] North Arbington, NJ

COUSINS, IVAN E.
[b.] November 26, 1929, Baileyville, ME; [p.] Mr. and Mrs. Omar Cousins; [m.] Dorothy (Stetson) Cousins, June 25, 1954; [ch.] 4, married; [ed.] 3 years college (Eastern Nazarene College); [occ.] Retired; [memb.] Church of the Nazarene.

COWAN, RONNIE
[b.] June 14, 1941, Atlanta; [p.] Deceased; [m.] Helen Cowan, September 9, 1972; [ch.] none; [ed.] High School, Sylvn High, and Southern Bus. University; [occ.] Senior Mail Clerk at National Data Corp.; [memb.] Brightstar United Methodist Church; [hon.] One Five Year, One Ten Year, Service Award Nat. Data, Army Commendation Metal, Certificate of Appreciation Award, and a award for 25 years service in the Army Reserves, no absences or tardies; [pers.] I would like to reiterate this, to people, believe in one's self and strive for achievement.

COX, EDGAR
[b.] October 3, 1916, Cloverport, TN; [p.] William and Birdie Cox (deceased); [m.] Emma Cox (deceased), March 3, 1944; [ed.] 1 yr. college; [occ.] Retired; [pers.] Worked in space program for 25 years, on a team that designed and built first space ship. Also was a member of the launch team, for all the moon landings.

COX, REV. WILLIAM SHERMAN
[b.] March 1, 1910, Arkansas; [oth. writ.] None...This one poem was written for the 40th anniversary of the Hillcrest Children's Home in Hot Springs, Arkansas which my ex-wife founded with her friend. Co-founder, Rev. Pauline Guy Bullock who wrote a book entitled The First 17 children in the home. She asked me to write something for the book and I chose to do a poem and turn Hillcrest around to The Quest. Mrs. Bullock has since copyrighted the book and is free to let you see it; [pers.] Should I win a small award, please refund Mrs. Bullock $20 and make the check out for the remainder to The Hillcrest Children's Home, Hot Springs, AR with a note: in memory of Rev. William Sherman Cox.

CRAIG, JEANETTE LYNN
[Pen.] Jenny Craig; [b.] December 25, 1965, Agana, Guam; [p.] Ann G. and James E. Craig Jr.; [ch.] Kenneth, Michael, Brandon and Jeffrey; [ed.] Edmondson Sr. High; Coppin State College; [occ.] Fingerprint Specialist Maryland State Police Headquarters; [memb.] Pobo's Ladies Club, St. Edward's Church; [hon.] Outstanding Community Service Award; Black History Month Essay Contest, first place, 1981, 1982 and 1983;

[oth. writ.] Several poems and essays from previous contest entries.; [pers.] My writing is inspired through personal thought and/or personal life experiences.; [a.] Baltimore, MD

CRANK, GREG
[b.] September 8, 1975, Laurenceburg, IN; [p.] Ronald Crank; [ed.] Jac-Cen-Del High School; [occ.] Unemployed; [memb.] Future Farmers of America; Osgood First Baptist Church; [oth. writ.] Poems not yet published, but I am trying; [pers.] I write my feelings better than I speak them. I love you Samantha. I really love to write and hope someday I will be paid to do it.; [a.] Osgood, IN

CREASEY, ELAINE ANN
[b.] July 23, 1939, Waterbury, CT; [p.] Marie and Jerome Rovelli; [m.] Divorced; [ch.] Jerriann Hope, Dana Marie; [ed.] Sacred Heart Elementary; Sacred Heart High School; [occ.] Homemaker; [oth. writ.] Short stories; [pers.] I have never submitted anything before so this is my first publication. Like my Dad I am a dreamer, and I would like to believe that where would the world be, but for its dreamers!; [a.] Waterbury, CT

CRIMO, ROSANNE M.
[Pen.] R. M. Crimo; [b.] January 29, 1966; Highland Park, IL; [p.] Robert and Christine Crimo; [ed.] DePaul University, Chicago, B.A.; [a.] Chicago, IL

CRISP, CATHERINE SALERNO
[Pen.] Catherine Rose; [b.] February 1, 1953, Brooklyn, NY; [p.] Alphonse Salerno; Antoinette Majorana Parrish; [ch.] Ray Stephen; [ed.] Sunset High; Richland Jr. Col.; [occ.] Freelance Photographer, Secy., Recpt.; [memb.] Tarrant County Poetry Assoc.; The Smithsonian Assoc.; The Nature Conservancy; Nat'l. Wildlife Fed., Nat'l Geographic Society; [hon.] Honorable Mention Certificates from The World of Poetry and the Nat'l Authors Registry; [oth. writ.] "The Poem;" "Poetry on Buses;" published in anthologies. Interviews and articles published in The West Texas Sound; [pers.] Life's own experiences has been my greatest motivator and teacher (as trite as it sounds), with its painful awakening's, to its hidden beauties, and the delicate balance of it all.; [a.] Arlington, TX

CRISSI, SHULAMITH RACHEL
[Pen.] Sheila R. Crissi; [b.] November 11, 1955, Israel; [p.] Jacob and Rita Zacut; [m.] S. Crissi, December 19, 1977; [ch.] Edith, Jack, Arik, Ron, David; [ed.] High school, art school - Israel; [occ.] Artist, writer, a mother; [memb.] American Heart Assoc, American Lung Assoc, YMCA Denver Co, JCC Denver, CO; [pers.] True love is the key between a couple. The power of faith, spirit and mind can move mountains; [a.] Denver, CO

CRIVELLI II, LOUIS S.
[b.] June 16, 1975, Trenton, NJ; [p.] Ann and Louis Crivelli; [ch.] Brother: Marco Crivelli; [ed.] Notre Dame High School, Muhlenberg College; [occ.] Student; [memb.] Chambersburg Little League, Lehigh Valley Institute of Italian Culture, Tau Kappa Epsilon Fraternity, Immaculate Conception Church; [hon.] Comcast Cable Outstanding Youth Leader Award, Merit Award in Science; United States Marine Corps, Al-Mercer County Place Kicker; [oth. writ.] Several unpublished poems, short stories and essays.; [pers.] I draw inspiration from the world around me and the people in it, especially my family. I am also inspired by my own dreams and imagination. The poem in this book was inspired by my late father.; [a.] Trenton, NJ

CROFT, JOHN
[Pen.] Kozz; [b.] May 6, 1970, Toronto, Ontario Canada; [p.] John Sr. and Virginia Croft; [ed.] 1988, Graduated, Houston TX High School for the Performing and Visual Arts, currently completing B.M. Performance and B.A. Religious Studies; [occ.] Student and Macintosh Computer Consultant; [memb.] American Federation of Musicians; [hon.] 1980-1987 Co-assistant Winner of Houston Independent School District Solo Competition (Classical Cello), currently attending Penn State University on a performance scholarship; [pers.] This poem was written when I was in high school, 2 weeks after the space shuttle Challenger disaster; [a.] State College, PA

CROWLEY, WILLIAM K.
[b.] December 31, 1962, Michigan; [p.] June Crowley; [occ.] US Submarine Service; [memb.] Lifetime Member International Society of Poets; [oth. writ.] Several poems published by the National Library of Poetry, selected for Contemporary Poets on Tape 1994; Island of Guam, MI

CRUZ, MARGUERITA ANNA
[Pen.] M.C. Libertine; [b.] December 17, 1973, Oceanside, NY; [p.] Nikki Long, Leo Cruz, The Germands; [m.] Christopher R. Miller, to wed 9/16/95; [ch.] Metallica Love McInturff; [ed.] James Wood High, Majored Business Education, Winchester, VA, Creative Writing, Journalism, Edited Newspaper, and Reporter on Staff; [occ.] Auto Auction Lot Engineer; [memb.] Evil Fate Book of Writings.; [oth. writ.] Several Bands, including two of my own carrying literature. My life as a mime, book. Yourself book, and my many years of personal hand art with poetry and songs written to music.; [pers.] My fingers paint the rock that will be thrown by all men and women, in any part of madness. The words, once read, breathe the touch of curessence. Inspired by the world's transformation around myself.; [a.] Bunker Hill, West VA

CUBINE, KENNETH WAYNE
[Pen.] Kenneth W. Cubine; [b.] December 18, 1964, Colman, TX; [p.] Amelia and Tommy; [ed.] New London or West Trusk High, Massage Thr Wellness Skills; [hon.] High School 3rd place in poems; [oth. writ.] Back in high school; [pers.] I have epilepsy. If it was not for a good friend, this poem would not have been as good. He is like my big brother to me. This poem is for the people of the lands; [a.] Venus, TX

CUPPER, JACK
[b.] February 4, 1920, Tyrone, PA; [p.] Rufus and Cordelia Cooper; [m.] Carol R. Cupper, May 25, 1975; [ch.] Carol, Pamela, Gary, Greg, David, Karen; [ed.] Tyrone High Studied writing and art at Elizabethtown College, Elizabethtown, PA; [occ.] Landscape and wildlife artist; [memb.] Member of several environmental organizations, such as National Audubon Society, Sierra Club and Pine Creek Headwaters Protection Group. The latter was founded by the author.; [hon.] Chosen to display art at numerous art museums and competitive shows selected to display art at Fredricksburg, Texas 150th anniversary, spring of 1995; [oth. writ.] Since 1979 have written a newspaper column titled, Painting along with Jack, published by Texas and Pennsylvania Newspapers.; [pers.] I am committed to nature, to its preservation and I hope my poetry and paintings will serve to remind all people to cease destroying our planet, lest we destroy ourselves.; [a.] PA

CURETON-PRICE, TOKOYA
[b.] March 24, 1962; [p.] Mildred and James Cureton; [m.] Verner A. Price, February 12, 1985; [ed.] High School, Flint Academy College, Attended Northern Michigan University; [occ.] Respiratory Care Practitioner and Dept. of Heath and Human Services, Hearing Reporter Contractor; [memb.] CCT, Certified Cardiographic Technologist, American Association for Respiratory Care; [pers.] Individuals are reflections of their experiences, therefore it should be our mission to positively affect others. This could mean the difference between a down trodden or an uplifted soul.; [a.] Marquette, MI

CURLEE, NARDA
[b.] August 3, 1947, Seattle, WA; [m.] Divorced for 15 years; [ch.] Robert, James, Debra and Melissa; [ed.] Ballard High, Class of '65 and two years at the University of Washington. Also, dance training since age 3; [occ.] Along with my daughters, I own and operate the Narda Elaine Studio of Dance, we teach ballet, tap, polynesian, jazz, lyrical and hip-hop; [memb.] Northgate Kingdom Hall of Jehovah's Witness; [hon.] I've won cash prizes twice for my poetry (100.00 and 400.00); [oth. writ.] I have written over 25 manuscripts (most being on the order of American Indian Historical-Based Fiction. One day soon I plan to seek an agent to handle my properties and I'll hope for the best.; [pers.] I find that writing (be it poetry, songs or manuscripts) is a very relaxing form of recreation.; [a.] Seattle, WA

CURRAN, WILLIAM
[b.] October 8, 1949, Boston; [p.] Stephen and Helen; [ed.] College, Grad, some grad. school; [occ.] Office Worker; [a.] Boston, MA

CURTIS, KATHLEEN
[Pen.] Kat Curtis; [b.] January 24, 1974, Elmhurst, IL; [pers.] Limitless imagination. Everlasting. Creativity. These things mixed with nature, love, loyalty, life, self-sacrifice, magic, fantasy and the mystical, combine to become the kind of poetry that captures us all. Thank you to the few people who reminded me of who I really am. Carpe Diem! Believe! [a.] Wheaton, IL

CUSHING, YUKA J.
[b.] August 8, 1977, Anchorage, AK; [p.] Harold and Tazuko Cusing; [ed.] Attending K-12, Alternative School; [pers.] I'll have fun, fun, fun till my mommy takes the Subaru away. Word to that. Thanks to everyone.; [a.] Anchorage, AK

CUSTEAU, PAMELA J. SERGE
[b.] March 9, 1963, Connecticut; [p.] Michael C. Serge, Emma D. (Baker) Serge; [m.] Thomas A. Custeau, May 25, 1985; [ch.] Kyle t. Custeau, Kevin M. Custeau; [ed.] Lewis S. Mills High School, Burlington, CT; [occ.] Commercial Loan Clerk, The Merchants Bank, Burlington VT; [pers.] "Adrift Upon A Dream" was written for my sister, Susan A. McGinnis, who's encouragement and love is always unconditional, and ever present. There's a side of each of us with talents, abilities, hopes and dreams, do all that's in your power to encourage it to surface; [a.] St. Albans, VT

CYR, LORNA MORRIS
[Pen.] L.M.C., Ink; [b.] June 17, 1944, Portland, ME; [p.] Norman and Ina Morris; [m.] George F. Cyr, October 25, 1969; [ch.] Mark M. Cyr; [ed.] Plainville High School, Tunxus Community College, Connecticut School of Broadcasting; [occ.] Advertising, Public Relations,

The Bristol Press Publishing Company, Newspapers; [memb.] Connecticut Aviation and Space Education Council, Young Astronauts council, St. Paul High School, PTO Republican Town Committee; [hon.] Special Recognition Certificate, Young Astronauts Council, Life Office Management Certificate; [oth. writ.] Short stories, various small magazines, editorials, editor, Ct. Aviation Space Education Council (ASEC Newsletter); [pers.] Children are like gifts to earth, they must be treasured and not cast aside.; [a.] Bristol, CT

D'AMELIO, JOHN C.
[Pen.] J. L. D'Amelio; [b.] February 23, 1972, Philadelphia; [p.] John Sr. and Ran; [m.] Not yet; [ed.] Pemberton High School, Burlington County College; [occ.] Student; Print Operator; [hon.] Not Yet; [oth. writ.] Poems published in the Best New Poems, Poet's Guild; other poems in American Poetry Annual, the Amherst Society 1994.; [pers.] I like to bring out the unique side of every situation. The side most people don't consider. The abnormal side, yet then again, what is normal?; [a.] Philadelphia, PA

DALONZO, NICHOLAS A.
[b.] August 1, 1964, East Liverpool, OH; [p.] Joseph and Margaret Dalarzo; [m.] Jacki Walsh Dalonzo, September 27, 1986; [ch.] One boy, Nicholas Joseph 12/22/93; [ed.] Associates Degree, Jefferson Technical College (Radiologic Technology) (X Ray Tech), Diploma, Wellsville High School; [memb.] A.R.R.T. American Registry of Radiologic Technologists; B.P.O.E. Benevolent and Protective Order of Elks (Past Exalted Ruler); [pers.] My inner most feelings, of the people I love, are expressed through my poems. I find it much easier than telling them in person.; [a.] Wellsville, OH

DAMIEN, PAUL G.
[b.] August 12, 1961, Hartford, CT; [ed.] Newport/Pacific High School, Foley Belsaw Institution; 1992 The National Locksmith Publishing Company; 1994; [occ.] Locksmith, Westminister Preparatory High School, Simsbury, Ct.; [memb.] World Wildlife fund, National Park and Conservation Assoc., The Wilderness Society, The Environmental Defense Fund; [hon.] Born an American (1961) Registered American Voter, 10/14/1980; [pers.] "We should all try not to use the now, so that the future, will have its now, for its self; beyond now!" I am inspired by; Frost, Whitman, Longfellow; [a.] Collinsville, CT

DAMM, PETER
[b.] November 13, 1949, Michigan; [ed.] B.A. with honors, Univ. of Michigan in English Literature; Masters Program in Creative Writing, Fiction, San Francisco State Univ., Ph.D., Clinical Psychology, The Wright Institute, Berkeley, CA; [occ.] Clinical Psychology and Writing; [oth. writ.] Poems, fiction, articles for magazines and newspapers; [pers.] My work draws upon the magic and mystery of the natural world in concert, and often conflict, with the bubbling uncertainties, dreams, and determinations of human kind, the interplays of life.; [a.] Berkeley, CA

DANIEL, CALVIN
[Pen.] Mr. C.; [b.] October 9, 1940, Johns, AL; [p.] Arthur Daniel, Vera Daniel; [m.] Valerie M., May 26, 1986; [ch.] Rosalind, Cal, Jr., Billy, Bernard, Jay; [ed.] Westfield High School, Park College, Golden Gate Univ; [occ.] Computer Specialist with the Dept of Defense; [memb.] Amvets, Golden Gate Alumni Assn, Springfield Civic Assn, Masonic Lodge, Majestics Club; [hon.] Win-

ner in a poetry contest a few years ago (1988); [oth. writ.] Numerous poems published in local papers in various cities; [pers.] I strive to seek a oneness in mankind in my writings; [a.] Springfield, VA

DANIEL, FRANCES MARION
[Pen.] F. Marion Daniel; [b.] November 11, 1933, Orlando, FL; [p.] Oscar and Lucille Daniels; [m.] Cabell Walton Daniel, August 10, 1966; [ch.] none; [ed.] College Graduate, B.S. Degree, Fla. A&M Univ, Tallahassee, FL 1961, Jones High School 1952 graduate; [occ.] Retired Elem. Teacher, Self Employed, owner Dan and Fran's Limousine Service and corner produce seasonal market.; [memb.] Christ Episcopal Church; Girl Scout Leader Troop 636 Halifax, VA, VA Skyline Girl Scout Council, Girl Scouts of USA Lifetime Membership, Vestry member church Jr. Warden of church, work with United Way last 3 years, chairman, res. for town neighborhoods; [hon.] Retirement Award for 25 years Outstanding Service as a teacher 1991. United Way Awards 3 different years 1991-1993; [oth. writ.] Have written many poems, mainly on family members and friends. Also have written poems for Elem. graduating class.; [pers.] Since around fifth grade I loved writing. I would often go to some place where it was very quiet to write. Being a child, I really didn't know what I wanted to write about. Since I retired I start putting my feelings on paper as to how I remembered family members and friends. Also liked writing poetry because teaching reading, get involved greatly.; [a.] Halifax, VA

DANIELSON, KISHA C.
[b.] February 15, 1976, E. Elmhurst, NY; [p.] Leo and Annie Danielson; [ed.] Forest Lake Academy, Oakwood College; [occ.] Student, Oakwood College; [memb.] Oakwood College Wind Ensemble, Literature Evangelist Training Center; [hon.] Who's Who Among American High School Students award, selected to go to the National Leadership Convention in Washington, DC; [pers.] I strive to use the talent that God has given me. I have been greatly influenced by the author and poet, Maya Angelou; [a.] Casselberry, FL

DANLAG, DONALD A.
[b.] Philippines; [ed.] Ph.D. University of San Augustine, Post Doctoral at Pepperdine University, M.A. University of Iloilo, A.B., B.S.E.; [occ.] Security (Federal) Officer, Former College Professor (Philippines); [memb.] Delta Mu, YMCA; [hon.] Jose Rizal Scholar, Outstanding Contributor to News Magazine "Philippines" Free Press; [oth. writ.] College textbooks; [a.] Glendale, CA

DANNA, NICOLE
[b.] December 17, 1987, San Diego, CA; [p.] Christine Schroeder and Charles Danna; [ed.] 6th grade, Carmel Del Mar School, San Diego, CA; [occ.] Student; [hon.] 1st place Del Mar Fair, Drawing 1993, Special Award Youth, Art Del Mar Fair 1994, Carmel Del Mar School - Authors Tea 1994; [oth. writ.] None of my writings have been published yet; [pers.] I endeavor to put grace and familiarity into my writings; [a.] San Diego, CA

DANSBY, BETTYE
[b.] June 5, 1928, Lamon, CO; [p.] Harry and Margaret Atwood; [m.] Olen Dansby (2nd Husband), August 6, 1977; [ch.] 3 daughters, Roberta, Terrill and Linda (children of 1st husband-now deceased); [ed.] 2 yrs Community College Degree in Real Estate; [occ.] Retired Housewife; [oth. writ.] I have written several poems. None published. I write them for my own personal satisfaction and enjoyment. One enclosed, title: Baker's Dozen;

[pers.] Poetry is just a part of being me. It's just there. In my daily thoughts, meditations, and experiences, I find myself seeking to put things in rhyme or poetic form. Then when I sit down to write - it just comes out. Hence my birth of a poem included in this book; [a.] Calera, OK

DARBY, JEANNETTA L.
[b.] July 6, 1938, Chatta, TN; [p.] Walter L. Brown, Mildred Brown; also a beloved step-father Benjamin Wilson; [m.] Lloyd C. Darby, Sr., September 2, 1956; [ch.] Denise, Renee, Lloyd Jr. Andrea Lee, Clarissa Anne; [occ.] Homemaker, care-giver, self employed homemaker; [memb.] Deliverance Evangelistic Church; [oth. writ.] Poem written in church bulletin, also poem chosen and published in another poetry contest. Sparrowgrass - Treasured Poems of America; [pers.] For, "God has made my Tongue the pen of a ready writer". I give glory and honor to Him, and my Lord and Saviour Jesus Christ, who is my greatest inspiration; [a.] Philadelphia, PA

DAVIES, CLUSTER
[Pen.] Cluster Payne; [b.] September 2, 1951, Halifax, VA; [p.] Van and Eliza Farrar; [m.] Darrell Davies, August 14, 1993; [ch.] Andrea Janelle, Alvin Eugene; [ed.] George Washington High Univ. of Maryland; [occ.] Program Analyst, U.S. Navy, Department of Defense; [memb.] Parents and Teachers Assoc.; [oth. writ.] Several poems submitted for publication by various editors.; [pers.] I enjoy writing emotional and humanistic poetry. I have been influenced and truly appreciate the works of Maya Angelou and Elizabeth Browning.; [a.] Clinton, MD

DAVIS, ADRIENNE
[b.] July 14, Philadelphia; [p.] Kenneth F. and Ethel F. Davis; [ed.] MA, History, New Mexico State University, Las Cruces, NM; [occ.] Writer, the Boing Company; [a.] Seattle, WA

DAVIS, JEAN
[b.] May 9, 1946, St. Helens, OR; [hon.] Nominated for Hayward Award (Amateur Athlete) Leading Jockey in the state of OR 4 years. Golden Poet Award 3 yrs. Numerous Leading Jockey titles; [oth. writ.] 4 poems published/World of Poetry/poem published HBPA magazine. Article published/Williamatte Week/Publication pending/Vantage Press for book of poetry; [pers.] The world happenings need to be put into poetry in hopes the majority will read it and wake up. We must start loving the world and each other or we will have nothing; [a.] Troutdale, OR

DAWKINS, ROCHELLE C.
[b.] February 12, 1972, Washington, D.C.; [p.] Charlene Turner and George Baldwin; [m.] Mr. Sean R. Dawkins, July 22, 1994; [ch.] Sean R. Dawkins, Jr., "Little Russell"; [ed.] Anacostia Senior High and the University of the District of Columbia (Student); [occ.] Media Librarian; [hon.] I am greatly honored to let the Lord work through me and very elated that He has allowed me to discover one of my talents, which is an award in and of itself.; [oth. writ.] I currently have numerous unpublished works that will hopefully come to be recognized.; [pers.] "Money is but a piece of paper that does not increase the quality of life, but the quantity of the things in it."

DAYANANDA, NILU
[b.] November 23, 1979, London, England; [p.] Mala and Upali Dayananda; [ed.] Previously attended Our

Lady of Good Counsel School. Currently attending Mount Saint Mary Academy.; [pers.] I would like to thank my mother, for her unending encouragement and my friends for inspiring me more than they will ever know.; [a.] Little Rock, AR

DE ANGELIS, DONNA MARIE
[b.] January 10, 1961, Harrisonville, MO; [p.] Bessie and Howard Russell; [m.] Ray A. DeAngelis, March 4, 1991; [ch.] Dylan Anthony; [ed.] Temple City High, CA; Citrus College, CA; [occ.] I perform various duties -- NY Post Prod Facility; [hon.] 2nd place in a UNISEF Poster Contest; 2nd place in Arts and Crafts Show, Dean's List; [oth. writ.] "The Lulla Bye Blues"; Lyrics to a song I wrote for my son Dylan (unpublished); [a.] Lake Carmel, NY

DEATON, MARENE
[b.] January 31, 1929, San Angelo, TX; [p.] B. J. and Clara Olsen Hudson; [m.] Robert Dwight Deaton, December 12, 1948; [ch.] Darril Wayne, Marlene, Ronald Dean; [ed.] Bracken Ridge H.S., San Antonio, TX; Odessa Jr. College, TX; Cuyahoga Community College, Cleveland, OH, Baylore UN., TX; Cleveland State UN., OH, BA, Ma Cum Laude In education; [occ.] Co-Owner Mobile Home Park with husband, semi-retired; [memb.] Lakeshore Baptist Church Weatherford, TX; [hon.] Honor Graduate, Cuyahoga Community College, OH; Cum Laude Master's Degree in Education, Cleveland State UN., OH; [oth. writ.] None Published; [pers.] Primary focus in life and poetry is on the depths of love expressed toward mankind by God through the sacrifice of His son Jesus the Messiah, in our stead, for our sins. He is the true light of the world from which all others reflect.; [a.] Weatherford, TX

DEETJEN, JANETTE ROSS
[Pen.] Jan Ross; [b.] May 1, 1928, Oak Park, IL; [p.] Joseph and Grace Ross; [m.] James Deetjen, September 18, 1948; [ch.] Barbara Herzoa, Cheryl Thuente, David Deetjen, Lois Palmer, Mary Jungenberg; [ed.] B.A. Barat College, Lake Forest, IL; [occ.] Artist, writer; [memb.] Charter Member, Natl. Museum of Women in the Arts; [hon.] Graduated Cum Laude; [oth. writ.] I am presently working on a book.; [pers.] Poetry has always been integral with the art that I do; there is within a kindred spirit that speaks to the seeing, the speaking, the being heard or seen. The poem, the painting, the sculpture are often companions.; [a.] Menominee, MI

DEGAN, ADELINE TINKOVICZ
[b.] June 15, 1927, Cleveland, OH; [p.] Valentine and Josephine Tinkovicz; [m.] Charles H. Degan, November 20, 1948 (deceased); [ch.] Patrick C. Degan; [ed.] St. Wendelin High, American Business Institute, American Medical Technology Education Institute; [occ.] Retired Legal Secretary; [memb.] National Assoc. of Legal Secretaries, Louisiana Assoc. of Legal Secretaries, New Orleans Assoc. of Legal Secretaries; [oth. writ.] Published book of poetry "Shades In Rainbow," Songs published, poems in American Poems Anthology; [pers.] To turn words into treasures of thought is a continuing ambition.; [a.] New Orleans, LA

DEHNICK, PHILIP
[b.] January 14, 1927, Plasantville; [p.] Joseph and emma Dehnick, NJ; [m.] Renee, January 6, 1979; [ch.] Dorothy Pearce, Barbara Jacobs, Joseph Dehnick; [ed.] B.A. Yale Univ., Ed.D Temple Univ.; [occ.] Retired Educator; [pers.] I hope that my poetry will, at best, give others models for reconciling their feelings and goals to the same

of the people in their lives and to their environment and at least, give utterance to my own attempts to do so.; [a.] Ventnor, NJ

DEITSCHEL, DANIEL J.
[b.] August 11, 1975, Elk Grove, IL; [p.] Joseph Deitschel, Carol Deitschel; [ed.] College sophomore; [occ.] Audio-Visual Circulation Worker; Schaumburg Township District Library; [oth. writ.] Poems published in Utah, Nebraska, Pennsylvania, New York, and California. Poems published in college newspaper; recently completed first novel, entitled Pryde's Corner; over 300 poems and 10 short stories; [pers.] My poems often involve themes such as artifice, metacognition, and strange humor and/or observation. My greatest influences have been Hawthorne and Poe; [a.] Schaumburg, IL

DELA ROSA, DEOGRACIAS S.
[Pen.] Deo - Acias; [b.] March 23, 1919, Clhveria, Masbate, Philippines; [p.] Leon P. Dela Rosa, Froilana S. Dela Rosa; [m.] Rosita Alimuin Dela Rosa, September 26, 1953; [ch.] Edgar, Blanca, Virginia, Ramon, Romeo, Rosalie, Gina, Zylma and Jerry; [ed.] Baybay Academy (High) Pakil, Laguna, Phil; Eastern Laguna College, Paete, Laguna, Phil; [occ.] (none) Disabled Army Veteran of World War II; [memb.] Veterans Federation of the Philippines, American Legion; [pers.] Whatever a man says and does, either privately or publicly, he is judged in actions and character constituted as vital records of himself - who...he is; [a.] National City, CA

DENNI, MARGARET
[b.] May 13, 1940, Bronx; [p.] Caroline and Robert Cartland; [m.] Constant Denni, May 23, 1959; [ch.] Margaret, Constant, Kathleen, Robert; [ed.] Far Rockaway High School in Far Rockaway, Rockaway Beach; [occ.] Housewife; [oth. writ.] Children Stories, still trying to get them published.; [pers.] I love to make the little ones happy, so I make up stories or I tell them what happened to me and my sisters when I was little. So far they love it.

DERKATCH, THERESA WESTFALL
[b.] March 16, 1923, Canada; [p.] Mary and John Westfall; [m.] Peter A. Derkatch, July 3, 1948; [ch.] Judith, Patricia, Michael, Deborah, Timothy, Marilyn, Jeffrey, Gregory and Marianne; [ed.] Nursing degree; [occ.] Nursing, Annapolis Hospital, Wayne, MI; [oth. writ.] I have written several other poems and short stories that have not been submitted; this is my first entrance; [pers.] My writings reflect personal real life episodes and deep feelings of life and family. [a.] Garden City, MI.

DERRICO-WHITE, RITA J.
[b.] November 17, 1956, Birmingham, Alabama; [p.] Nathaniel and Pethenia Derrico; [m.] Eddie A. White Jr., June 4, 1983; [ch.] Jeffrey Todd, Kyrstine Arielle; [ed.] John F. Kennedy High, Grand Hills, CA,; University of Maryland, Europe; Cameron University, Lawton, OK; Ultimate Goal: Pursuing Ph.D in Social Psychology; [occ.] Administrative Secretary; [memb.] Several Community and Social Organizations, Lakeview Terrace Baptist Church, CA; Greater Galilee Baptist Church, Lawton, OK; [oth. writ.] None published.; [pers.] There's a loving and powerful spirit that lives within each of us. Once that spirit is nourished and set free, it leads you to places where dreams come true--where your purpose for living is then revealed. This is dedicated to my son Jeff.; [a.] Lawton, OK

DESOTO, TIMOTHY JOHN
[Pen.] Dripper; [b.] September 6, 1970, San Francisco, CA; [p.] David and Anne DeSoto; [ed.] AA Specializing in Commercial Art; [occ.] Commercial Art, Communication, Surreal Painter, Computer Arts; [oth. writ.] Currently piecing several screenplays, novels along with poems mixed with music.; [pers.] Writing is a hobby I stumbled on when I became isolated from my visual work. Although I have no training in creative writing, I find myself improved as enjoyment claims me.; [a.] Watsonville, CA

DHANIFO, ALICIA
[b.] Pasadena, CA; [p.] Alice and Clarence J. Floyd; [ch.] 1 son and 1 daughter; [ed.] MFA - UCLA MP/TV Prof (major). Minor - African American studies and Ethnic dance; [occ.] Writer/producer - Goldenisles Theatrical Youth Organization; [memb.] UCLA Alumni and The Screen Actors Guild; [hon.] Howard Kock/Roger Berstock Award. Ronald McDonald House. Dean's List (one semester) guest speaker at the Rotterdam Film Festival in 1980 and in Florence Italy; [oth. writ.] "Belly Dance For Fitness and Fun" (video), "Information Gathering Techniques" (training film) "To Be Young" (musical/dance) the American scenes for the movie "Summer Affair". "Tomas Goes to His Bilingual Class"; [pers.] I believe in God and the universal brotherhood and sisterhood. I believe that love is the greatest and only power. I believe that each of us should strive to become better each day; [a.] Pasadena, CA

DIAMOND, LISA DIANN
[b.] May 8, 1965, Poplar Bluff, MO; [p.] George May and Minnie May; [m.] Brian K. Diamond, October 31, 1987; [ed.] Neelyville High School, Three Rivers Community College; [oth. writ.] Several poems on various themes.; [pers.] I wrote the poem Summer Storm when I thought there was no chance at being with the man I loved. I am happy to say that today that man is my husband.; [a.] Fisk, MO

DIAMOND, MARILYN LOUISE
[b.] August 4, 1956, Revere, Mass.; [p.] Mr. and Mrs. William M. Diamond; [ed.] Cotting School for Handicapped Children. A school that goes from first to 12th grade.; [occ.] Not working at this time; [memb.] Cotting School Alumni, Cerebral Palsy Assoc.; [hon.] None at this time, but I write to show my feelings of beautiful poetry that is still alive.; [oth. writ.] I have many short stories, and poems that are unpublished at this time, but I'm working on it.; [pers.] I really do enjoy writing short stories, and poetry. I hope that we the people can keep the art of writing alive. I love the idea of writing my thoughts on paper for the whole world, to share my feelings or life.; [a.] Chelsea, MA

DIANDA, JUANITA
[b.] April 7, 1926, Butte, Montana; [p.] Adolfo and Lina Dianda; [m.] Fernando R. Leyva, November 9, 1946; [ch.] Four; [ed.] Courses in Writing, English, Drama, Strayer College 1944, Catholic University, Washington, D.C., Georgetown University, Washington, D.C.; [occ.] None, secretarial part time; [memb.] National Honor Society; [oth. writ.] Essays and poems in Spanish. Founder and editor of publication.; [pers.] The poem is the perfect veil for the soul, sensitive and shy, there, from some concealed to some revealed with music words laid bare thoughts not easily shared.; [a.] Washington, D.C.

DIANNE, SHIREEN
[b.] East Pakistan; [ed.] BA Mass Communication Univ of Hartford, Hartford, CT; [occ.] Freelance Photographer; [memb.] The Editor's Guide to Freelance Photographers. Advertising photographers of America. Who's Who in Photography in 1992; [hon.] Dean's List. Published in local newspaper - photo story, poems published in East Pakistan's weekly magazine; [oth. writ.] Also produced a bi-monthly feature program and wrote the screen play, on a cable television channel; [pers.] I was influenced by my maternal grandfather who was a great poet and a writer. He inspired me at an early age. I hope to continue to write poems in future; [a.] Middletown, CT

DICK, BARBARA J.
[b.] April 1, 1946, Norfolk, VA; [p.] Darius and Garnet T. Lively Cooper; [m.] Henry Dick, Jr, August 3, 1968; [ch.] None. 3 birds - 2 dogs, 7 fish; [ed.] Fairborn High School, Fairborn, OH class 1965; [memb.] ISP International Poetry Society, BMI Broadcast Music, Inc; [hon.] Editor's Choice Award - Are you my friend? (Outstanding Poets of 1994) Certificate of Merit - can you describe a rose?; [oth. writ.] Many songs. 1. Walk Hand in Hand -(Coming of Dawn); 2. Are you my friend? (Outstanding Poets of 1994); 3. Can You Describe a Rose? (Selected Works of Our World's Best Poets); [pers.] I have been influenced by my only sister Carol Garrison of Lexington, KY. Who always told me! "How Do You Know You Don't Like Something if you haven't tried it." So I tried poetry and I found it is "Good Thing"; [a.] Miamisburg, OH

DIEHL, STEPHANIE
[b.] May 8, 1980, Niagara Falls; [p.] Christopher Diehl and Iris Huntoon; Grandparents: Earl and Ellen Maloney; [ed.] Abate Elementary Gaskill Junior High School, and now I'm a 9th grader at Niagara Catholic Senior High; [occ.] On the Honor Roll; [memb.] JV Basketball Team; [hon.] Awarded the Lions Club Award three years in a row; [oth. writ.] Poems which include; Friendship Is A Powerful Thing, Our Friend And Father, Happy Thoughts, The One I loved, and A Wintery Walk; [pers.] I'm very thankful that God has given me so many talents, writing being just one. My surroundings are what really inspire me! [a.] Niagara Falls, NY

DIETRICH (JR), JOHN
[b.] July 8, 1969; Dayton, OH; [p.] John and Elizabeth Dietrick; [ed.] Eastern High School - Louisville, KY; [occ.] Song Writer; [memb.] Historical Society of Henry County, Tennessee; and Four Rivers Music Group in Murray, KY; [pers.] Juliet Hettinger's "Wheatfields", Debbie Elmer's and Richard Robinson's faith, God, music, and the good and bad in mankind are my inspiration. "Creativity sees no failure"; [a.] Buchanan, TN

DIETRICH, JUDY
[b.] August 23, 1952, Sheboygan, WI; [p.] Glenroy and Theresa Greuel; [m.] Ronald dietrich, July 3, 1972; [ch.] Jennifer, Jonathan, Jessica; [ed.] Holy Family Academy, Manitowoc, Wis.; [occ.] Clerk; Enterprise Printing, Owner/Manager; Craft Business, "Pinecone Creations;" [memb.] Heritage Foundation, Yosemite Fund; [hon.] "Woman of the Year Award" in my Catholic parish 1982.; [oth. writ.] Several poems published in local newspapers and high school anthology.; [pers.] There is so much in life to celebrate and experience; joys and sorrows, feelings, relationships, loves, children, family, faith, challenges and constant change. I enjoy writing about all of these little things.; [a.] Plainfield, IL

DIGENNARO, PETE
[Pen.] Peter Ertol; [b.] June 4, 1970, Waterbury, CT; [p.] Maria and Anthony DiGennaro; [ed.] Wolcott High School, Bentley College, English major, Management minor; [occ.] Freelance Writer, Musician; [memb.] Fairfield Country and Darien County Poets Association; [oth. writ.] Three books: Screaming Silent Symns, The Festival of the Flame, Ricochet Thunderstorm, 2 1/2 yrs.; Journalism New Age Album, The Stillness Moving; [pers.] Live the Live Missile; Hope is waiting, Faith is knowing.; [a.] Prospect, CT

DINKEL, LINDA MAE
[b.] October 27, 1960, Colby, Kansas; [p.] August and Mary Mader; [m.] Steven Dinkel; [ch.] Benjamin James, Mary Katherine and Andrew Steven; [occ.] Full time wife and mother, free time writer; [memb.] St. Mary's Church, St. Mary's School Council. Concerned Women for America Member; [pers.] Life is a gift from our creator above. What I do or become knows no limited resource with Him as my guide. Words we can share in life, like His touch, and heal many.; [a.] Ellis, KS

DION, ALAN H.
[b.] August 16, 1960, Philadelphia, PA; [p.] Samuel, Sylvia; [ed.] Springfield High School, Drexel University, B.S. in Business Administration; [memb.] Board Member, Global Education Motivators; [pers.] Ideas are in the wind. Reach up and grab one. e-mail: 70721.2432@Compuserve.Com; [a.] Philadelphia, PA

DISHMAN, ROBERTA
[b.] July 6, 1928, Logan Co., Mallory, W.VA; [p.] Ala and Sarah B. Crockett; [m.] Frank H. Dishman, July 5, 1946; [ch.] Elva Faye, Elda Kaye, Franklin D., James Lee, and Evelyn Aileen; [ed.] Graduated Big Creek High School 1946; attended Beckley College, Concord College and Bluefield State College; [occ.] Homemaker, retired educator of compensatory reading and math at Berwind Elementary School; [memb.] Canebrake Free Will Baptist church; Canebrake Women's Auxiliary, Adult Bible Class of Canebrake F.W.B., Sunday School.; [hon.] National Honor Society 1946, Golden Poet Award 1990; Adult Bible Class Teacher (from 1979 to 1994) 15 years. Selected for Who's Who in American Education 1994-95.; [oth. writ.] Articles to local newspapers; article to a professional journal; children's book, Impy the Salamander; numerous other poems for family and friends; Christmas plays for my church; book Bulletin Board Brighteners.; [pers.] Writing is one of my favorite past times. In everything I write, there is a ray of sunshine, a positive note, just as Christ is my ray of Sunshine.; [a.] Squire, WV

DODELIN, VERA M.
[b.] March 2, 1949, Camden, NJ; [p.] Joe Pritchett; [ed.] St. Paul's Elem, Wildwood Catholic High School, D'Youville College for Special Education, Trenton State College for Masters in Sp. Education; [occ.] Teacher of The Handicapped Educ. Mentally Retarded Children; [memb.] "Share-A-Care" founder 1989, ARC board member 1992, 1993; [hon.] Award from Dept of Human Services for contribution to children in need, neglected and abused, Women's Club award for Comm Service. Teacher of The Year, County 1992 Teacher of The Year, Finalist in State Teacher of The Year. Acknowledgement from Gov. Florio and Pres Bush 1990 for Outstanding Comm Serv. NJ State Federation of Colored Women's Club award for Outstanding Service to Afro American children; [oth. writ.] "A Poem of Friendship", "Watching and Waiting" and many other poems published in local newspapers and contest won for the 2 above; [pers.] The trust and faith in God and your own abilities will carry you through hard times. An education is essential and belief in your fellowman will gain you much rewards; [a.] Lawnside, NJ

DONALDSON, JOHN
[b.] Age 22, Hyattsville, MD; [ed.] DeMatha High School, University of North Carolina at Chapel Hill; [oth. writ.] I write the show Allone. If you would read, call or write.; [a.] Chapel Hill, NC

DONOVAN, SHIRLEY E.
[Pen.] Shirley E. Sliter-Donovan; [b.] December 19, 1926, Deposit, NY; [p.] Nancy Adams, John Millard Sliter; [m.] James L. Donovan, 1946-1968; [ch.] Six, Kathleen, John, James, Thomas, William, Nancy; [ed.] H.S. Nursing Education, Ongoing Study of Life and Self Betterment; [occ.] Retired; [memb.] AARP, Participant On-Stage, an actor amid a massive cast in our world's play entitled, this is my life, attested to by Shakespeare; [oth. writ.] Published by National Library of Poetry and Contemporary Poets of America and Britain. Poems of Letters and Verse as well, on occasion to friends, etc.; [pers.] Aware from earliest memory of my yen to compose and express with a pen. I take time now.; [a.] Syracuse, NY

DORSEY, KIM DIANE
[b.] November 16, 1957, Wichita, KS; [p.] Larry and Shirley Overstreet; [m.] William P. Dorsey, August 7, 1993; [ch.] Brian, Kristin, Shayne Gibson; [ed.] West High, Wichita, KS; [occ.] Office Specialist, Kansas Corporation Commission, Wichita, KS; [oth. writ.] 1973-1975 West Word (High School Newspaper); [pers.] Applaud all you do and are, as you will always be your best audience; [a.] Wichita, KS

DOSS, CHARITY
[b.] November 11, 1979, Indep, MO; [p.] Troi Rhoades and Kenneth Doss; [ed.] Fort Osage Jr. High School, Buckner MO, freshman; [occ.] Student, babysitter; active with literary arts; [memb.] Future Business Leaders of America, Pep Club, Speech, healthy spiritual well-being, careers and business courses; [hon.] Reflections contest - (poem), Honor Student, Homeliving 1st place award, Sports awards; [oth. writ.] Unpublished (large) collection of writings; [pers.] I just thank God for the special gift he has given me. I believe I can bring light, hope, and understanding to the world with His help!; [a.] Independence, MO

DOTHEROW, SANDRA CAMPBELL
[Pen.] Sandra C. Dotherow; [b.] August 26, 1942, Los Angeles, CA [p.] Anna C. Langford and Alfred Tennison Langford; [m.] William Davis Dotherow, February 5, 1963; [ch.] Patricia Ann, William Scott, Christopher Wayne; [ed.] Palm Beach High School; Orange County Vocational School (Graduated L.P.N.); Hope and Help Health Care Training Program (HCW); Mid-Florida Technical Institute (Security Officer Certification Training; and Hotel Security Training). Studied for short period with the Institute of Children's Literature.; [occ.] Health Care Worker; Part-Time Convention Assist; Part-Time Licensed Security Officer for Conventions.; [occ.] Poems published in local retirement newsletter; articles printed in Washington, D.C. Paper; In the North Carolina African-American Newsletter; and in the hope and help center of Orange County's Newsletter. The H&H Center is also printing two of my poems.; [pers.] Reaching out to others is what I do best. Joy is the by-product

of sharing my thoughts and love in writing. God is my inspiration. Spreading happiness is my goal.; [a.] Orlando, FL

DOTSON, CONSTANCE RAE
[b.] September 4, 1970, Cleveland, OH; [p.] Ronald and Shirley Carter; [m.] Randl E. Dotson, June 9, 1994; [ch.] none; [ed.] James Ford Rhodes High School; [occ.] Homemaker; [pers.] My poems are inspired by everyday life...Being, past, present and future. I'm deeply appreciative of this one. Thanks to my husband.; [a.] Cleveland, OH

DOUGLASS, EMILY JANE
[b.] August 25, 1976, El Paso, TX; [p.] James Robert and Edna Jane Douglass; [ed.] Eastwood High School (El Paso) attended McMurray Univ. (Abilene, TX) currently transferring to University of Texas at El Paso; [occ.] Full time college student; [oth. writ.] Poetry published in Penny Whittle Press for children, when in elementary school; poems published in high school literary magazine, senior year (Reville); [a.] El Paso, TX

DOZIER, LAURIE
[b.] June 21, 1966, Cleveland, OH; [p.] Shirley Dozier and R.C. Clay; [ed.] East High School; [occ.] Senior Underwriting Asst.; [oth. writ.] Various Editorial pieces for the high school newspaper.; [pers.] I base my writing on my own life experiences, creating an equal balance of elation, melancholy and wonder. I've been greatly influenced by Rudyard Kippling, Robert Frost, Edgar Allen Poe and the songwriter "Sting;" [a.] Cleve, OH

DRAPER, AUDIE ALAN
[Pen.] A. Alan Draper; [b.] May 18, 1958, San Barnardino, CA; [p.] Samuel K. and Velma R. Draper; [m.] Divorced, July 24, 1977 to August 1985; [ch.] Audie Lee Draper; [ed.] Self Educated; [occ.] Calligrapher; [oth. writ.] Several unpublished poems and musical arrangements, and one published short story entitled "In the Mind's Eye" in the softcover book, Reflections from Within (U.W. Extension); [pers.] My poetry reflects the hopelessness of life without the true light of life, Jesus Christ.; [a.] Portage, WI

DROESCH, AUDREY
[Pen.] A. Elizabeth Droesch; [b.] January 27, 1980, New York, NY; [p.] Vigee and Thomas Droesch; [ed.] Currently a freshman at Darien High School; [hon.] Jack Caswell Award for excellence in English and grammar (8th grade), 3rd place Northeast Division winner for DAR essay on the Bill of Rights (5th grade), one of the highest scoring participants in the State of Connecticut in the 1993 SAT math and verbal talent search (7th grade); [oth. writ.] Numerous stories, essays, poems, and articles in school newspapers; [pers.] I try to tap into that part of you which responds to feelings and makes the poetry almost sacred to you in that it made you realize something about yourself or the world around you. I believe that everyone has the capacity to respond to things emotionally and the better you can do that, the more you will know of human nature. Everyone strives for acceptance and love, and even if you get hurt in your struggle, you will be better off in the end, because otherwise your heart would be stagnant and lose the precious power it has as a window to the world.; [a.] Darien, CT

DUARTE, STEVEN N.
[b.] March 15, 1951, Pomona, CA; [p.] Nick and Donna Duarte; [m.] Pam Duarte, December 31, 1986; [ch.] Melissa Brook, Michelle Rene, Nickolas Eugene; [ed.]

Lynwood H.S. Rowland, H.S. Santa Clara H.S., U.S. Army; [occ.] House Painter, among other things; [memb.] None; [hon.] Santa Clara H.S. poetry book and this one. Never really entered or showed many people my work.; [oth. writ.] Have been writing poems, lyrics and short themes since 1960. Never knew if I should do things with this, or how.; [pers.] Although my writing tends to be on the dark side, I do write some on the lighter side, it's all definitely feelings. As for influences, I feel Lord Byron, Edgar A. Poe.; [a.] San Louis Obispo, CA

DUBE, RAY
[b.] May 23, 1976, Berlin, NH; [p.] Paul and Priscilla Dube; [ed.] Berlin High School, University of Alaska Fairbanks; [occ.] Student; [memb.] Catholic Student Assoc. UAF, UAF Circle K Club, NRA; [hon.] Danforth Award, DAR Good Citizen Award (1993), listed in Who's Who Among American High School Students; [oth. writ.] Several poems and short pieces of work.; [pers.] My works are derived from my experiences and feelings, especially my love of nature; [a.] Berlin, NH

DUDRA, GLORIA ELIZABETH
[Pen.] Gloria Buckanell; [b.] November 2, 1922, Nashua, NH; [p.] Rev. and Mrs. S.Z. Angeledes (deceased); [m.] Stephen P. Dudra, January 25, 1945; [ch.] Elizabeth Theresa Trach; [ed.] Elementary through High School, Graduated from Morris High School in Bronx, NY, January 25, 1942; [occ.] Church Day Care Assistant; [memb.] First Assembly of God Church, Daytona Beach, FL; [hon.] Special Art Certificate from Scholastic Magazine, presented in 1941; [pers.] The pen is mightier than the sword. It put down on parchment and paper what no sword could ever produce: The Holy Bible and the Constitution of the United States of America.; [a.] Daytona Beach, FL

DUFFICY, THOMAS F.
[b.] July 3, 1960, Chicago, IL; [p.] Mary and Maurice Dufficy; [ed.] Quigley South High School, Loyola University; [occ.] Theology Teacher, Queen of Peace High School; Burbank, IL; [pers.] People and experiences have shaped my character. Writing helps shape my soul. I thank Denise Brendal for her inspiration and friendship.; [a.] Chicago Ridge, IL

DULEY, CINDY
[b.] August 11, 1962, Great Falls, MT; [p.] Denis Chase and Lois Brown; [m.] Carl Duley, June 27, 1987; [ch.] One son, Lucas Duley age 2 1/2; [ed.] Cascade High School, Cascade, MT, Montana State University, B.S. in Elementary Education from UW, River Falls; Masters in Reading, UW, River Falls 1995; [occ.] Teacher, Grade One at Alma Elementary; [memb.] WSRA, Wisconsin State Reading Association; IRA, International Reading Association; St. Croix Valley Reading Council; [oth. writ.] Newspaper and newsletter articles published locally; poetry; many reviews and papers; [pers.] I believe that everyone is a writer and has a story to tell. As an educator, I feel that we need to provide a nurturing and supportive environment to allow children to become all they can be.; [a.] Alma, WI

DUMSHA, TIMOTHY ERIC
[Pen.] Timotheus; [b.] May 11, 1972, Baltimore, MD; [p.] Maria Cortina and Joseph Dumsha; [ed.] Diploma Northeast High School; [occ.] U.S. Merchant Marine; [hon.] Fifth publication with National Library of Poetry; [oth. writ.] Have my own personal compilation of about sixty poems and verses which was created in 1993 at "New Life For Youth; Christian Bible Program; that I

attended for one year.; [pers.] One must never give up hope for attaining lost dreams, and strive for what's best in self and in helping others around you.; [a.] Glen Burnie, MD

DUNAWAY, JOHN B.
[b.] September 17, 1927, Oklahoma City, OK; [p.] Jack and Velma Dunaway; [m.] Mary Louise M. 1954-1987 and Ina Lynne, April 5, 1989; [ch.] Between us, 12 children, 31 grandchildren, 1 great-granddaughter; [ed.] Miami HS; NEO A&M College, Miami (Assoc. Arts) Doctor of Veterinary Medicine, Okla State Univ.; Command and General Staff College, Army Reserve; [occ.] Retired as Vet. med. Off. USDA and Infantry Lt. Col. U.S. Army Reserve; [memb.] Ina Lynne and I do volunteer work together; Meals on Wheels, Dobson Museum, Parish Council. We're both Certified mediators for Okla Supreme Court Alternate Dispute Resolution System. Tanglefooters Round Dance Club, Joplin, MO. I'm Financial Secretary for local Knights of Columbus Council; Ina Lynne belongs to Altar Society.; [hon.] Our children and grandchildren are our proudest honor.; [oth. writ.] Light poetry and short humorous articles, never published--reprinted for kids and grand kids.; [pers.] The poem was written at the time as an expression of deep feelings. One can't judge his own work and I simply wondered what professionals might think of the work.; [a.] Miami, OK

DUNBAR, PATRICIA
[b.] December 3, 1953, Ft. Eustis, VA; [p.] Sterlie and Ruby Walker; [m.] Jerome Lee Dunbar, November 5, 1993; [ed.] Eastern HS; Trinity College (DC); [occ.] Legal Secretary; [a.] Seabrook, MD

DUNBURG, AMANDA
[b.] October 13, 1979, Texas City, TX; [p.] William Dunburg, Judith Dunburg; [ed.] Freshman at Catholic Central High School, Steubenville, OH; [memb.] Yearbook Staff, Christian Concern Club, Foreign Language Club, Academic Team; [oth. writ.] Many different poems, stories and plays none of which were ever published; [pers.] Writing, for me, is an excellent way to unleash emotions; [a.] Brilliant, OH

DUNCAN, MAOMI
[b.] May 8, 1979, Abington, PA; [p.] C. Fred and Royal Duncan; [ed.] Freshman in High School, Cherry Hill High School East; [occ.] Student; [memb.] Active member of school's poetry club called Demogorgon; [pers.] Life is one big mystery where people try to find themselves, but in fact they already are themselves.; [a.] Cherry Hill, NJ

DUNHAM, SHEILA
[b.] June 18, 1994, Steubenville, OH; [p.] Mr. and Mrs. Robert L. Featherston; [m.] Divorced; [ch.] Dominique K. and Stephen R. Dunham; [ed.] Steubenville High and University of the District of Columbia English Major; Also attended Montgomery College Rockville, MD; [occ.] Legal Secretary/Probate Law COBB, Howard, Hayes and Windsor, Washington, D.C.; [memb.] Greater Mount Calvary Holy Church, Washington, D.C.; [oth. writ.] This is my first writing; [pers.] Every individual is successful by his or her own merits; one should always remember that success is relative and should not be judged by outside forces; a successful person can always find good in others.; [a.] Rockville, MD

DUNLAP, RACHEL KAY
[b.] August 24, 1974, Clifton, NJ; [p.] Alice Smith and Roger Dunlap; [oth. writ.] Flaming Images, Painful Endings, Special Things, A Thought on Life, Life, The Beginning or the End and many others not yet available.; [pers.] The only influence I have toward my poems comes from true experiences in my life.; [a.] Belleville, NJ

DUNLAP, SONJA
[pers.] "Everyone wants to believe they have one purpose in life." Mine is: Be Happy, enjoy the good and bad times. This short stay on earth is just borrowed; [a.] Chicago, IL

DUNLOP, RIKK
[b.] January 23, 1962, Chicago Heights, IL; [ed.] Rich East High School, Prairie State College; [occ.] Material Handling Specialist; [memb.] Park Forest Poets and other writers; [oth. writ.] Poems and short stories; [pers.] In my poetry and short stories, I attempt to reach the readers heart and soul by writing about the subtle, the soft, and the forever special experiences of life; [a.] Park Forest, IL

DUNN, PHYLLIS CHRISTINA
[Pen.] Phyllis Christina Dunn; [b.] July 1, 1925, Dover Village; [m.] Michael Spooner and Venezia Spooner, June 7, 1949; [ch.] Ramon Dunn and Colleen Downs; [occ.] Physical Fitness Instructor; Owner of White House Uniform Stores; [oth. writ.] Have written other poems; [a.] Rocky River, OH

DUONG-VAN, DR. MINH
[Pen.] Mrchaos; [ed.] PhD Physics, Cornell Univ; [occ.] Prof of Physics President, CKAOTIX, Inc; [hon.] 1981 "Man of Science and the Future", Encyclopedia Brittanica, 1981; [oth. writ.] "Physics of Chaos" book; [pers.] "You have to have chaos in yourself in order to give birth to a dancing star. Thus spoke Z. Nitzche; [a.] Menlo Park, CA

DUONOLA, ELAINE
[b.] December 31, 1969, Canada; [p.] Sofia and Dimitrios; [m.] Kenneth Duonola, Valentine's Day 2/14/92; [oth. writ.] Poem published in 1987, "World Poetry Anthology" poem published in 1989 "World Treasury of Great Poems."; [pers.] My dreams, thoughts and desires are endless. Kenny, I love you always. My beautiful Mom and Dad, God Bless You! My life is filled with love and I thank God every day.; [a.] Mount Vernon, NY

DURKEE, DAVID M.
[b.] July 4, 1970, Bennington, VT; [p.] Linda and George E. Durkee Jr.; [ed.] Hoosick Falls, Central School, Plattsburgh State University, Hudson Valley Community College; [occ.] Student of poetry, writing, and literature, writing tutor; [memb.] Nu Theta Gamma Fraternity, Amnesty International, Z Platt Literary Society; [hon.] Dean's List (HVCC); [oth. writ.] Many other poems which will, perhaps, be published someday.; [pers.] Once, if I remember well, my life was a feast where all herbs opened and all mines flowed. Rinbaud.; [a.] Plattsburgh, NY

DURKEE, MRS. DOROTHY
[b.] March 13, 1916, Drain, OR; [p.] Harvest and Ena Ramsdell; [ed.] Univ of California, graduated 1939 -- Decorative Arts; [occ.] Retired. When I was working, I worked in offices, mostly; [pers.] I'm retired and living in Half Moon Bay, CA in a senior complex of 58 people.

We came here in March, 1992 and my husband, sadly, had cancer and passed away in January 1993. We had been married 50 years. Half Moon Bay is a beautiful place to live--a little coastal town with people who have a wonderful community spirit. My philosophy is to try to be kind and friendly to others, keep a positive attitude and recognize and enjoy the little every day pleasures and treasures that life freely gives us; [a.] Half Moon Bay (about 25 or 30 miles south of San Franciso), CA

DURNAVICH, LOUIS
[b.] February 24, 1942, Blue Island, Illinois; [p.] Louis and doris Durnavich; [m.] Rosemarie (Alfano) Durnavich, August 4, 1961; [ch.] Steven, Therese, Tony, Don, Jimmy, Brian; [ed.] Thornton High, Moraine Valley College; [occ.] Senior Operations Manager A&R Security Services Inc.; [memb.] Past United States Jaycees; [hon.] Jaycees of the Year; [oth. writ.] "Via Con Dios" poem published in local newspaper; [pers.] "To thank all the people who led my way." So my family and I could enjoy the God given freedom we have today.; [a.] Richton Park, IL

DYE, RITA, G.
[b.] April 28, 1945, Plainview, TX; [p.] Joe and Beth Stubblefield; [m.] A.J. Dye, July 1965; [ed.] West Tex State Univ; [occ.] Artist--Exhibiting in area galleries; [memb.] Valley Art Assoc, Brunswick Art Assoc, Y-Me Cumberland Valley, volunteer work at the Cancer Center; [hon.] Awards in local Art Shows. Paintings in Brunswick Train Museum, and area business and Dr's offices; [oth. writ.] Poems and songs not published. Working on a book to be completed at a later date; [pers.] Reach for new experiences - they hope make you a more interesting person; [a.] Brownsville, MD

DZIAMALEK, HEATHER
[b.] March 10, 1971, Milford, CT; [p.] Richard and Margaret Dziamalek; [ed.] West Haven High, Central Ct. State University; [occ.] Swim Instructor/Assistant Swim Coach, West Haven Park and Rec.; [memb.] Appalachian Mountain Club; [hon.] Athletic Swimming Awards (High School and Collegiate), Piano Competition Awards; [oth. writ.] Articles for CCSU Recorder and article in the Durango Herald, Colorado; [pers.] I am a traveling westward vagabond and was recently inspired by the Beats and the Colorado Rocky Mountains with my very dear friend Kristin Talaias who was my support through it all.; [a.] West Haven, CT

DZIUK, JOSETTE C. H.
[b.] December 6, 1982, Los Angeles; [p.] Eugene R. P. Dziuk; [m.] Mariefe F.V. Dziuk; [ed.] Grade 6 at Holy Trinity School, Los Angeles, Calif.; [occ.] Student; [hon.] Recipient of a 1st prize trophy, award in 1992 (grade 4) in an essay writing contest of "What a Teacher Means to Me" For the Entire Glenfeliz Boulevard School. Recipient of Principal Awards for both of short stories written in 1993 when she was in grade 5, "Halloween" and "Jurassic Park" which also won 1st prize in a contest; [oth. writ.] 2 short stories, Jurassic Park and Halloween; poems: What Happened At The Mall; Leaves; My Favorite Hero; [pers.] I hope to achieve great success and become worthy enough to be a role model for all people.; [a.] Los Angeles, CA

EARL, MAURICE
[b.] August 14, 1950, Phila., PA; [p.] James and Dorothy Earl; [ch.] Tamika, Monique, Maurice; [memb.] Disabled American Veterans, American Legion; [hon.] Semi-Finalist, 1994 North American Open Poetry Con-

test; [oth. writ.] Numerous poems and inspirational verses.; [pers.] Write now, for what you feel can be seen and felt by others who read you works.; [a.] Jenkintown, PA

EASTERLING, MIRIAM W.
[b.] November 6, 1960, Jackson, MS; [p.] Albert E. and Nan Willson; [m.] Lauernon Earl Easterling, January 4, 1981; [ch.] (3) Sammy, Andy, Chris; [ed.] Oak Grove High School, William Carey College - secretarial science - Univ of Southern MS - specialed; [occ.] Transcriptionist with Hattiesburg Clinic; [oth. writ.] Personal poems and cards to one's I love and know. Poems for special occasions or to go in the church bulletin; [pers.] Jesus is the foundation for my poems and the gift of writing; [a.] Hattiesburg, MS

EAVES, SARA
[b.] July 25, 1931, Barnetts Creek, KY; [p.] W. R. Reynolds, Vergie Sturgell, Deceased; [ch.] Lelia Gretchen and James Carlisle (deceased); [ed.] High School, plus course in creative writing and sociology; [occ.] Part Time Caregiver; [oth. writ.] Poems and one short story.; [pers.] There is something worth loving in everyone.; [a.] Tampa, FL

EBY, CYNTHIA L.
[b.] August 5, 1954, Mt. Home, ID; [p.] Kaye Medsker of TX and Kenneth C. Eby of AK; [ch.] Crystal Diane Stephens, Cassandra Michelle Grieger, Rachael Adele Grieger, and Jamilynn Renee Grieger; [ed.] Dunbar High, Ft Worth, TX, Thomas College, Waterville, ME; [occ.] Over the road truck driver; [memb.] American Legion Ladies Auxiliary; [oth. writ.] Several poems in manuscript form; [pers.] The time I'm most inspired to write is during my driving time. Going across the country side gives me strong senses of beauty and warm feelings of awe; [a.] Darlington, WI

ECKHARDT, MARIA MONICA
[Pen.] Monyka Ippich; [b.] July 23, 1972, Bretten, Germany; [p.] Otto and Mirella Ippich; [m.] Douglas C. Eckhardt, April 24, 1993; [ed.] Bangor Area High School, Warren County School of Nursing; [occ.] Student Nurse; [memb.] New Jersey Association of Licensed Practical Nursing; [hon.] None; [a.] Oxford, NJ

EDMONDS, ROBIN JAYNE
[b.] November 26, 1981, Wichita, KS; [p.] Reggie and Marsha Edmonds; [ed.] Hulsing Elementary, Michigan Malcolm Elementary, Maryland John Hanson Middle, Maryland Johnson Jr., High, Florida; [occ.] Student; [memb.] Student Council; Youth Advisory Committee for Florida Region of Reorganized Church of Jesus Christ of Later Day Saints; [hon.] Hobbies: Student of the piano and violin; [pers.] I hope to become an attorney as my career choice.; [a.] Melbourne, FL

EDWARDS, BETTY SUE
[b.] June 2, 1950, Anniston, AL; [p.] Loyd and Betty Frier; [m.] James Edwards, April 28, 1966; [ch.] Lisa, Michael, Marie; [ed.] Hokes Bluff School; [occ.] Homemaker and Grandmother.; [oth. writ.] Mostly just poems for my family and friends.; [pers.] I try to accomplish something in life that my family and friend will be proud of. To Tisha, Suzanne, Jamie.; [a.] Piedmont, AL

EDWARDS, JUDY
[b.] New York City; [m.] Robert Edwards; [ch.] Barbara and Ricky

EDWARDS, VIRGINIA LUCILE
[b.] July 15, 1915, Brunswick County, VA; [p.] Daisy Braswell and James Frank Edwards; [ed.] B.A. George Washington Univ., Arts Design; [occ.] Retired; [hon.] Graduated High School at age 14; [oth. writ.] Numerous; [pers.] Through the years I have wanted to mark the important events of our family reunions, births, deaths, homecomings, marriages, partings with little stories, poems, illustrations. My aim has always been to capture the spirit of the event in words, to keep the event with us, to trap all of the fleeting emotions of the world in words that will live on forever, beyond our lives.; [a.] Washington, DC]

ELAM-BLANCHARD, TERI
[Pen.] Teri L. Elam/TLE/Teri; [b.] June B. Elam, John L. Elam, Jr; [m.] Alexis Daryl Blanchard, November 26, 1994; [ed.] Glenn Hills High School, Augusta, Georgia, Tuskegee Univ, Alabama; [occ.] Claim Specialist, State Farm Insurance Co; [memb.] National Assoc of Female Executives, Alpha Kappa Alpha Sorority, Inc; [oth. writ.] Poems published in local newspaper and employer magazine; [pers.] My writings reflect my daily experiences and those around me. My poetic influence are Nikki Giovanni and Maya Angelou; [a.] Norcross, GA

ELBERT, WYNNA FAYE
[b.] October 25, 1944, Columbia, MO; [p.] Savannah Tapp, Ernestine Tapp; [m.] Significant Other: Thomas Walker; [m.] Divorced; [ch.] Larry, Dwayne, Debra, Kevin, Robin, George; [ed.] Frederick Douglass High School, Stephens College: AA, BA University of MO, Columbia: MS; [occ.] Recreation Supervisor, Columbia Parks & Recreation Dept.; [memb.] MO Parks & Recreation Assoc.; National Recreation & Parks Assoc.; Frederick Douglass Coalition & Alumni Assoc.; Dr. Martin Luther King Memorial Assoc.; University of MO, Columbia Alumni Assoc.; [hon.] Outstanding Service Award, 1981, 83, 84; Community Service Award, 1984; Support & Superior Commitment Award, 1985; Exemplary Black American Award, 1987; Foster Parent Appreciation, 1985 through 1994; Dr. Martin Luther King Award, 1988.; [oth. writ.] Published poetry in the "Community Voice" a community newspaper; various articles for individual community activities.; [pers.] As a Black female I feel that I have a particular sense for the struggles of my people and the social ills that affect them. My writings reflect those concerns.; [a.] Columbia, MO

ELLINGTON, GRANT
[Pen.] Grant; [b.] March 1, 1979, Jackson, TN; [p.] Cindy Tate and Robert E.; [ed.] I am a 10th grade student attending Milan High School; [occ.] None; [hon.] I once won a poetry contest and got my poem placed in an Anthology of Poetry by Young Americans book: 1991 Edition; [oth. writ.] "Where Can I Go"; [pers.] I enjoy writing poems, but I do not do it regularly.; [a.] Milan, TN

ELLIOTT, JENNIFER LEE
[b.] September 17, 1966, Lakeland, Florida; [p.] Dalton R. (deceased) and Sarah E. Harris; [m.] J. David Elliott, September 15, 1990; [ch.] Ryan Christian, Shane Anthony and Jordan Christopher; [ed.] Lakeland High, Tampa Business College; Marketing A.S.; [occ.] Advertising Specialist, WTMV TV-32, Tampa, Florida; [hon.] Dean's List 1992; [oth. writ.] Several other poems published in school newspaper, and personal writings.; [pers.] My intention to share with the common soul, the expressions of one; the emotions of many, to in my absence

pass along a memento of a full life, enjoyed and well lived. Influences: Loving husband, children, the best mother a daughter could want.; [a.] Lakeland, FL

ELLIS, LEONARD R.
[Pen.] Lenny Ellis; [b.] June 9, 1947, Chicago, IL; [p.] Rosario and Alton Ellis; [ed.] 18 Semester Hours of College, Philosophy, Psychology, Japanese, Sociology and Literature; [occ.] Disabled Veteran; [memb.] Paralyzed Veterans of America (PVA). Hospitalized Veterans' writing project. International Society of Poets.; [hon.] 6 Awards from "World of Poetry." "Certificate of Award" for Outstanding Achievement in Creative Writing from the "Hospitalized Veterans' writing project."; [oth. writ.] 4 poems published in PVA magazine. 2 poems published in Veterans' Voices. 2 poems published in World of Poetry.; [pers.] Be yourself, never give up.; [a.] Albuquerque, NM

EMANUEL, SHARON E.
[Pen.] Shyrun; [b.] June 9, Houston, TX; [p.] Occie Emanuel (father), Freddie Phillips (mother); [ed.] Evan E. Worthing Sr. High Univ of Houston; Houston, Community College; [occ.] US Postal Service Career Employee 13 yrs; [memb.] First Elizabeth Missionary Baptist Church; Deaf Communications. I am currently enrolled in sign language; [hon.] Perfect Attendance Special Achievement Awards; Conservation Sick Leave Awards; Sick Leave Pins; [oth. writ.] Which are nonpublished; The Cost - Choice. The Wind Wings - The Walk and many more including one entitled "The Book"; [pers.] I enjoy writing. It is relaxing to my mind. I am greatly influenced by other poetry writers. Writing to me is creativity; [a.] Houston, TX

EMBRY, PATTY VERDE
[b.] March 21, 1945, Lebanon, MO; [p.] Erna and Cleo Stokes; [m.] Darrell Embry, April 6, 1963; [ch.] one son, 31 years old; [ed.] High School in Lebanon College Business Con. Drury Springfield, MO; [occ.] Activity Director, Lebanon Care Center; [memb.] Nat. Appaloosa Club, Community Theater Gp., Eureka methodist Church, Rader, MO; [oth. writ.] Many poems for family and friends; [pers.] I was raised on a farm at Rader, MO where most of my family still lives. I always included a personal poem to family friends on special occasions.; [a.] Lebanon, MO

EMMERLING, FLOYD
[b.] March 3, 1927, Cabot, AR; [p.] Andrew and Laura (Fildes) Emmerling; [m.] Sarah (Phelps) Emmerling, January 29, 1994; [ch.] David Andrew, Laura Kay and Sherri Lynn; [ed.] B.A. Degree, Ouachita Baptist University, B.D. Degree Southwestern Baptist Theo Seminary, M.Div. 1962, Southwestern Bapt. Theological Sem., Certified Clinical Hypnotherapist; [occ.] Retired, Fee Base Chaplain, VA Hospital; [memb.] Bee Branch Baptist Church; [oth. writ.] Several Christmas poems and various other themes some published in newspapers.; [pers.] I tend to see the meanings of life expanded and enriched by observing the opposites and the contrasts.; [a.] Bec Branch, AR

ENGEBRETSON, PATRICK HENRY
[Pen.] Henre Engebretson; [b.] June 26, 1974, Minnesota; [p.] Larry and Marge Engebretson; [ed.] Currently a sophomore at North Dakota State University, Enrolled in the college of Psychology; [occ.] Student; [memb.] Member of Delta Upsilon Fraternity at NDSU, Newman Center; [oth. writ.] Numerous personal writings but this is my 1st publication; [pers.] Everything I have, and all

that I will be, I owe to my family. I may write the words but they're the inspiration. At least I got the easy job!; [a.] Cass Lake, MN

ENGLISH, ROBERT G.
[b.] August 12, 1945, Portland, OR; [p.] Mr. and Mrs. Samuel English; [ed.] 12 yrs. high school, 2 yrs. college, 4 yrs. Army; [occ.] Poet, Author, Photographer, Poetry in Print; [memb.] World of Poetry 1991-1992, International Society of Poetry an Lifetime Member Stormbelt Paris, France; [oth. writ.] Only Yours! Susanna My Rose, Poetical Jest-My Gestful World, The Dream Catcher, All published by Carlton Press Inc.; [pers.] Reflections of light, conjuring colors out of sight, poetry in print never out of tint.; [a.] Albuq., NM

ENGO, ANNE E.
[b.] July 16, 1942, Elia and Arthur Damers; [m.] Henry, September 9, 1961; [ch.] Henry, Lydia, Michael, Brian, Dennis; [ed.] Richmond Hill, HS; [occ.] Secretary - Suffolk County Police Dept. Information Bureau; [memb.] Order of Carmel Discalced Secular - Formation Director, Former Girl Scout Leader; [hon.] Class Artist - Swimming Medals; [oth. writ.] Articles for the Police Dept Magazine - Shield 307 - Poem published in Secular Carmelite Magazine; [pers.] I strive to see God in all things and to show His love and mercy to all mankind. St. John of the Cross is my favorite poet; [a.] Shirley, NY

ERSKINE, PHYLLIS A.
[b.] January 9, 1940, Chicago, IL; [p.] Frank R. and Olive A. Erskine; [occ.] Executive Assistant; [pers.] Much of my writing reflects a believe that there is more to life than this earthly experience and we place too much emphasis on material rather than spiritual wealth.; [a.] Orlando, FL

ESTES, HOLLIE
[Pen.] Brennan McCall; [b.] November 27, 1967, Philadelphia; [p.] Joseph and Charlotte Zimmerman; [ed.] BA Psychology, Beaver College; [occ.] Social Worker, Foster Children; [oth. writ.] Various unpublished works.; [pers.] To do the best I possibly can each and everyday. To convey emotion with my writing.; [a.] Phila., PA

ETHRIDGE, WENDY LEE
[b.] April 8, 1976, Brownsville, PA; [p.] Kathy Lee Ethridge, Gary Lee Ethridge; [ed.] Three Rivers Community Technical College full time criminal justice students; [occ.] Full time college student major: criminal justice; [memb.] Was member of FFA in high school; [hon.] Student of the month many times in junior high; in high school got a trophy in animal science; [oth. writ.] Poems as a child, but not published; [pers.] Even when things get rough, look to God and always think positive; [a.] Norwich, CT

EVANS, SHAUN C.
[b.] March 5, 1969, Harrisburg, PA; [p.] Wenfra and Edith T. Evans; [ed.] Oxon Hill High School, U. of MD, Eastern Shore; [occ.] Videographer, I record weddings, receptions and parties for the Pros, full service party professionals, Ramada buffet attendant, bartender's assistant and busboy. Assured painting, tile layer and painter.; [hon.] Radio Assoc. of Delmarva (Maryland) Scholarship 1992, Certificate of Achievement, Telecommunications, 1992.; [oth. writ.] Published poems in the Maryland Review; poems and short stories.; [pers.] Most people make the mistake of judging the speaker instead of the message or the artist instead of the art. The mes-

sage and or the art should be judged only on it's merit.; [a.] Fort Washington, MD

EVERETT (JR), KENNETH R.
[b.] August 18, 1956, Dallas, TX; [p.] Kenneth Everett, Ruby Crowder Everett; [m.] Keena Sledge Everett, February 20, 1983; [ch.] Kamilyah; [ed.] Hamilton Park Elementary, Northwood Jr. High, Richardson High Richland College AA Degree, East Texas State BS Degree; [occ.] Teacher (Algebra) WH Adamson High School; [oth. writ.] Be You Rich or Be Your Poor (Get an education and you have a little more); Respect the Black Women; Kids Killing; Another Brother Beat Down; Problems; Never Give Up; Life; Thinking About Killing Yourself; [pers.] What ever you thinking about doing think about it before you do it; [a.] Dallas, TX

EVERS, GENE
[Pen.] Gene Alexander Evers; [b.] March 26, 1951, 516-785-1319; [p.] Pauline Stein, Lee Evers; [ed.] 4 years Liberal Arts at Nassau C.C., Stony Brook University, State U. at Old Westbury, Made The Nursing Program at Nassau Community College (N.C.C.); [occ.] Scriptwriter, writer of lyrics, producer of games.; [hon.] Made dean's list and honor roll at Hicksville Jr. Hs.; [oth. writ.] Assorted poems, lyrics and movie script.; [pers.] I believe the way to truth and freedom for the individual and humanity, is through the perception of the mind, to the gates of the understanding to the love of the heart. Influenced by Socrates love of truth.; [a.] Bethpage, NY

FAGLIANO, ANN
[b.] February 6, 1952, Oakland, CA; [p.] Tony and Dina Vignale; [m.] John Fagliano, January 28, 1973; [ch.] Laura, Lisa and David; [ed.] High School, 12 yrs. of Catholic Education, St. Augustine's 1-8, Holy Names High 9-12; [occ.] Homemaker, Taxi, Mom, Wife; [memb.] Italian Club, M.S. Society; [oth. writ.] Special occasions birthday 40th's, 16th, 50 years of marriage, high school graduations; [pers.] To my entire family: I wish everyone true and everlasting happiness. For all the love you have given me, try and share your hearts with others.; [a.] Castro Valley, CA

FAGUNDES, KRISTINA
[b.] February 25, 1977, Mountain View, CA; [p.] Dinah DiBernardo and Ricardo Fagundes; [ed.] Graduating from Gunderson High School in San Jose, CA; [memb.] Gunder's Senior Women (president); [hon.] I have won awards for excellent academics. (Golden Book Award); [pers.] Work hard, have fun, and smile. It makes you feel better; [a.] San Jose, CA

FALCO, RITA J.
[b.] May 22, 1957, Derby, CT; [p.] Walter and Clara Krupa; [m.] Frank, May 28, 1983; [ed.] Attending Porter and Chester for Medical Assistant Program in Statford; [occ.] Attending Porter and Chester for Medical Asst.; [hon.] Inventory; [pers.] Don't dwell on past transgressions, but look forward to each day and make the best of every situation.; [a.] Seymour, CT

FAMBROUGH, DAVID GLENN
[b.] October 17, 1963, Gadsden, AL; [p.] Jack and Nadine Fambrough; [ed.] Sardis High, Gadsden State Junior College, Mobile College, Southwestern Baptist Theological Seminary; [occ.] Student, Chaplain, Night Receptionist; [hon.] Theta Alpha Kappa, Alpha Chi, Religion Area Award, Who's Who 1991-92. President's List, Dean's List; [pers.] My writings are from a broad base of topics and come about as a result of experiences

or emotions. I credit God with the abilities and accomplishments that have been mine; [a.] Fort Worth, TX

FARMER, KAREN
[b.] July 20, Chester, SC; [p.] Mr. and Mrs. William N. Farmer; [ch.] Son, Christopher, age 15 1/2; [ed.] Brockman Jr., High Chester, SC, Rabren Co. High Clayton, GA, Erwin High School, Asheville, NC, AB Tech. Asheville, NC; [occ.] Certified Nursing Assist. Deerfield Retirement Community, Asheville, NC; [hon.] My biggest reward in life is my son Chris; [oth. writ.] Published book of poems from the heart. Several published in newspapers as well as writing for people for gifts for their graduating children. Many poems about people at work for our employee of the month.; [pers.] I write simple, so young and old can relate and enjoy. I'm plain like the ivory soap girl. Always had a knack for rhyme and writing is the best way I have of expressing myself.; [a.] Skyland, NC

FARNSTROM, FRANCES MARIE
[Pen.] Frances Farnstrom; [b.] September 13, 1942, Cincinnati, OH; [p.] Eugene and Anna Bacheier; [m.] Daniel Lee Farnstrom, March 23, 1968; [ch.] Christine, Carla, and Daniel Scott; [ed.] High school (completed) 2 yrs later GED 1985; [occ.] Homemaker; [memb.] St. Joseph's Church, WIBC (Women's International Bowling Congress); Hobbies: bowling, gardening and writing poetry; [oth. writ.] Several poems--about 70--all still unpublished; [pers.] I'm an earthy person. I enjoy the simple things in life. I stay true to myself and never try to be something other than what I am; [a.] Dingches, KY

FAULKNER, M.L.
[b.] October 3, 1968, LaFolleette, TN; [p.] Johnny and Pancheta Faulkner; [ed.] Jellico High, East Tennessee State University, Southern College of Optometry; [occ.] Entrepreneur, Optometry Student; [memb.] Various; [hon.] Various; [oth. writ.] First Publication; [pers.] Experience, appreciate, reflect...Life. Never limit yourself, accomplish dreams, and laugh as often as possible.; [a.] Memphis, TN

FAWKES, RICHARD D.
[b.] April 6, 1918, Otho, Iowa; [p.] Clement and Catherine; [m.] December 19, 1943; Deceased; [ch.] Four; [ed.] High School; [occ.] Retired; [a.] Phoenix, AR

FAYTA, TINA ELIZABETH
[b.] January 5, 1966, Jackson County, Scottsboro, AL; [p.] Ernest and Christine Stirling Swearengin; [m.] Michael E. Fayta, May 6, 1989; [ed.] Thornridge High School; [occ.] Homemaker; [oth. writ.] Article in Day by Day with Jesus by Father John Catoir; [pers.] I am thankful to God for my talents, and the ability to express my feelings through my pen. I am also thankful for Mrs. McCue, an English teacher in High School for assigning the class to a spiral book of poetry. She helped me to discover my talent.; [a.] Joliet, IL

FEDERNOK, JAMES P.
[b.] April 27, 1926, Mishawake, IN; [p.] Andrew and Elsie Federnok; [m.] Justine M., September 26, 1953; [ed.] Mishawaka High School, Indiana Univ - several courses; [occ.] Retired - Indiana State Police Officer; [memb.] Pioneers of the Indiana State Police, VFW - Post 360.

FEE, JOSEPH P.
[Pen.] Brother Joe, or Joe Fee; [b.] October 1, 1910, Pittston, PA; [p.] Thomas F. and Mary M. Fee; [m.] Alice Kahn Fee, October 23, 1933; [ch.] One, Patricia; [ed.] Pittston High and Numerous Seminars, RE. the food industry (I worked 43 yrs. in the food industry before retirement); [occ.] Retired; [memb.] Knights of Columbus, National Restaurant Association, Friendly Sons of St. Patrick; [oth. writ.] I have a collection of approx., 30 other poems. All are about either my family or my church, I did a lot of them re. holidays, i.e., St. Patrick's Day, XMAS, Thanksgiving, Valentine Day, and just plain people; [pers.] I am 84 years old, I have been writing poetry since 1986. I have no explanation for the interest. I just started.; [a.] Richmond, VA

FEINER, LENA ARLENE M.
[Pen.] Lena Feiner; [b.] March 23, 1937, Spring Green, WI; [ed.] M.A. in Library Science, M.A. in Organizational Development, B.A. Alverno College; [occ.] Finance/Business; [memb.] National Association of Female Executives; Carl G. Jung Society, Evanston, IL; American Library Assoc.; [hon.] Research grant to Indiana Univ., Summer 1976. Listed in Who's Who of American Women, 1987/88; Listed in Directory of Library and Information Professionals, 1988.; [oth. writ.] Guide to Women's Studies Sources In the Elizabeth M. Cudahy and Julia D. Lewis Libraries, 1985. Article: "Frameworking in Cooperative Collection; Development, "Illinois Libraries, v.71, #1, 1989; Women An Inquiry Approach, Proceedings of the American Theological Librarians Assoc.; [pers.] One's love is as deep as one's art, try to make all of living life and art. Life motif: light, airy and cheerful.; [a.] Chicago, IL

FELLNER, HEIDI
[b.] April 8, 1975, Kingsville, TX; [p.] Michael and Carol Fellner; [ed.] Sturgis High School, Northern State University; [occ.] Student; [memb.] Honors Society, Masquers; [hon.] Outstanding Freshman of the Year, NSU, Sturgis Young Woman of the Year 1993; [oth. writ.] Poems and short stories published in college anthologies and student papers.; [a.] Aberdeen, SD

FENTON, LELA MAE
[b.] February 10, 1934, Tulsa, OK; [p.] Ida Mae Tinker and Sylvester Revard Fenton; [ed.] B.A.; Mt. Mary College; Milwaukee, WI, M.A. Cardinal Stritch College, Milwaukee, WI; [occ.] Life Enhancement Center (for holistic health) co-director; [memb.] National Association of Catholic Chaplains, Network (for social justice), Life/Ministry Task Force (Sisters of Sorrowful Mother) Board of Directors; St. Joseph's Hospital, Marshfield, WI, Osage Nation; [oth. writ.] Destroy Not the Wheat, Narrative History of the Sisters of the Sorrowful Mother, various articles for newsletters.; [pers.] I believe that life can be fuller and happier when we take the responsibility to see what is good and create environments capable of promoting happiness.; [a.] Crandon, WI

FERRARA, LISA
[b.] September 6, 1976, Quincy, MA; [p.] Louise and Ilona Ferrara; [occ.] Aspiring Artist; [pers.] Don't believe what others think of you, only what you believe of yourself.; [a.] Quincy, MA

FERRELL, STEVEN
[b.] February 21, 1975, Atlanta; [p.] Shirley and Jerry Ferrell; [m.] Single; [ed.] Student; [occ.] Student; [oth. writ.] Demented Thoughts, 1st edition 1992; [pers.] Father died when I was a little over 2 years of age. Moved

from Atl, GA to Stillwell, OK. Lived with mother. 2 half sisters and 1 half brother. Poem is about my uncle Ronnie, dad's brother.

FESKO, DIANE
[b.] September 25, 1948, New York City; [p.] Carmela and Jack Antonini; [m.] Single; [ed.] Fordham University, New York City College; [occ.] Financial Manager, Montefiore Medical Center; [memb.] Sierra Club; [pers.] All the good that comes from my poetry published or not; belongs to John, Michael and Dorothy with my love and thanks for a second childhood.; [a.] New York, NY

FICARELLA, PEARL
[b.] October 9, 1915, Kathryn, ND; [p.] Oscar Sanders, Zella Sanders; [m.] Deceased; [ed.] Greenbush High and Warroad Teacher Training, in Minn, elementary piano keyboard harmony, bank bookkeeping, many classes in electronics, vocal singing in LA; [occ.] Teaching, piano, care of elderly and babies; [memb.] At present: Lyric Chorus - Emeritus College in Santa Monica. Many choirs down through the years, Conservative Baptist Church, sons of Norway; [hon.] A trophy for competing in singing "Granada", as a solo in competition. I felt honored when chosen to sing it on stage of big Alaskan cruise ship; [oth. writ.] I have assembled picture albums on the Psalms, on Proverbs, and written in modern day English the corresponding scripture passages to go with each picture. Am now preparing for picture album on New Testament; [pers.] These picture albums are dedicated to my son, daughter and grandchildren, and others. Spreading the word, and telling the Good News, our only hope, is of utmost importance; [a.] Los Angeles, CA

FIELD, LEWIS
[b.] 1958, Ft. Worth, TX; [m.] 1978; [ch.] 3; [ed.] BA History, U Texas at Arlington; MA History, U of Houston; [occ.] Asst Professor of History; [pers.] I believe that those things which reside in our hearts have value, and in sharing them we all become both teachers and learners; [a.] San Antonio, TX

FIELDS, VINCENT
[b.] March 25, 1975, Bristol Memorial, VA; [p.] Larry and Anna Fields; [ed.] Graduated from Lebanon High School, attending Virginia Highlands Community College, I plan to transfer to a university and major in Physical Therapy; [occ.] Student and part time inventory clerk at Green Seed Inc.; [memb.] Future Farmers of America, 4-H, Member of Springfield Baptist Church; [hon.] President of FFA, Lebanon Chapter, State Competition, Virginia High School League Varsity Baseball; [oth. writ.] None published; [pers.] Inspiration is a valued tool in any profession to any walk of life. The National Library of Poetry has inspired me to use a talent not normally used. I hope my work will do the same, for somebody else. Thank you.; [a.] Lebanon, VA

FILBERT, JENNIFER ELIZABETH
[Pen.] Jen, Jennie, "Wey," Jennie Beth; [b.] April 30, 1981, Eugene, OR; [p.] Tod and Lori Filbert; [ed.] Karshner Elem (K); All Saints Catholic Private School (1,2); Mt. View Elem. (3-6), Edgemont Jr. High (7,8); [occ.] Full time student; [memb.] Honors Society; P.A.L.; [hon.] Honors Society; P.A.L; 1st Place in School in "Reflections" 93 art and was sent to district level; placed in literature, Reflections 94 (and was sent to district level with this poem); [oth. writ.] Several stories throughout these past years.; [pers.] Can't we all just get along?! Peace!!!; [a.] Puyallup, WA

FILHO, SEBASTIAO PEREIRA CORDEIRO
[Pen.] S. Cordeiro, March 12, 1939, Santo Antonio do Ica, Amazonas, Brazil; [p.] Sebastiao Cordeiro and Francisca P. Cordeiro; [m.] Graziela Martins Cordeiro, June 9, 1973; [ch.] Rodolfo (19), Tatiana (16), Rafael (13); [ed.] BA in Economics by Federal Univ of Pernambuso and BA in Phylosopy by Catholic Univ of Pernambuco, Brazil; [occ.] Finance Department at Brazilian Aeronautical Commission attached to Brazilian Embassy; [pers.] I look for originality and the goodness of the Almighty; [a.] Fairfax, VA

FINCH, CHRIS
[b.] November 25, 1973, Utah; [p.] John and Vida Finch; [ed.] Orem High, Deury Institute of Technology; [occ.] Student; [hon.] 2nd place V.I.C.A. Welding Contest; [oth. writ.] Many other poems not yet published.; [pers.] Oh Captain my Captain, remember the man and his sword.; [a.] Phoenix, AZ

FINKE, BLYTHE FOOTE
[ed.] B.A., International Affairs, University of California, Berkeley; B.B. Woodbury Business College, Los Angeles; German (read and speak); French, Spanish, Chinese (some); [occ.] United Nations and New York City Correspondent for the U.S. Information Agency; American Foreign Service Information Officer and Writer/Editor, Administrator in Austria, Germany, Turkey, Washington, D.C., Administrator, International Cultural exchange Program, New York; Radio News Commentary Writer, Japan; Director of Public Relations, Broilyn Public Library System (52 libraries); Editor, Shell Oil Company house organ; Employee and Industrial Relations, Union Oil Company; Freelance assignments for media and organizations; volunteer for International Council of Women, National Council of Women (USA), Foreign Policy Association, United Nations Association, and U.N. delegate.; [oth. writ.] Over 20 educational books in print; newspaper and magazine features; [memb.] Member of National Press Club, Overseas Press Club of America, American Society of Journalists and Authors, Council of Writers Organizations, Travel Journalist Guild, Women in Communications. Listed in Who's Who; [a.] Fort Belvoir, VA

FINKELMAN, SOL
[Pen.] Sol The Sage; [b.] February 6, 1918, Warsaw, Poland; [p.] Sam and Rosa Finkelman; [m.] Gay Carol Finkelman, December 31, 1985; [ed.] BBA Bernard B College, UUNY; [occ.] Retired; [oth. writ.] Book - Death and Grief; Love, Sex, and Marriage (not necessarily in that order); [a.] Lakeland, FL

FINN, CHRISTINE FRANKLIN
[b.] March 23, 1952, Mineola, NY; [m.] Eugene Patrick Finn, September 26, 1986; [ed.] Fordham Univ BA, JD; [occ.] Attorney; [oth. writ.] Poetry; [pers.] Love is stronger than death; [a.] Moloun, NY

FINSTHWAIT, FRANKLIN MCKEAGE
[b.] July 31, 1909, Cherry Tree, PA; [p.] Deceased; [m.] September 25, 1937 (deceased); [ch.] Donald and Jean; [ed.] Amherst College; [occ.] Retired; [memb.] Old Presbyterian Meeting House, Alexander VA; [pers.] My wife, Eleanor Hoover Finsthwait and I became engaged February 14, 1937 (Valentine's Day) She died August 16, 1992. My poem was written on St. Valentine's Day 1993 after nearly 56 years of marriage.

FIORDELISI, JOHN
[b.] January 22, 1967, Bridgeport, CT; [p.] John and Phyllis Fiordelisi; [ed.] BA in English, with concentration in journalism from Univ of Connecticut, 1988; [occ.] Self employed; [oth. writ.] Currently working on poetry compilation, short story collection and two mini-novels; [pers.] Most everything one needs to know about being a moral being is in the Bible; the reminder is in Atlas Shrugged; [a.] Stamford, CT

FISHER, LINDA J.
[p.] Pauline and Kenneth Ennis; [m.] Donald E. Fisher, January 3, 1969; [ch.] Kelley, Kristen, Denise; [ed.] Graduate of Rockland Public School System; [occ.] Employed at Graphic Developments in Hanover, MA; [hon.] I have the distinct honor of being mother to three wonderful daughters, all of whom I am very proud of.; [oth. writ.] "Where Are You" dedicated to my mother and other parents who have passed away, but will always be loved and missed by their children.; [pers.] If I am able to touch even one person with my writing, to make them think for a moment, to laugh for a moment, or even to cry for a moment, that poem was worth writing. May we all ride in the limousine of happiness in life.; [a.] Rockland, MA

FITCH, HOWARD MERCER
[b.] December 23, 1909, Jeffersonville, IN; [p.] J. Howard and Kate Girdler Fitch; [m.] Jane Rogers McCaw, December 25, 1930; Nancy Dolt, April 28, 1984; [ch.] Catherine Druitt, Jane Butterworth, M.D.; [ed.] U. of KY BS, MS in Mech. Engr. U. of Louisville J.D. Magna Cum Laude; [occ.] Retired; [memb.] AM. Academy of Arbitrators, ASME, ASHRAE, KY Bar Assoc., SAR, Filson Club, Arts Club Past President, Rotary Club, KY Soc. Natural History, KY Photographic Assoc., St. Francis in the Fields Episcopal Church; [hon.] 1973 1st prize poetry, Arts Club poem published "Sat. Review of Literature."

FITZGERALD, HANNAH
[Pen.] J. H. Kemper; [b.] November 18, 1942, Savannah, GA; [p.] David and Louisa Bonam; [m.] Charles Fitzgerald, April 28, 1973; [ch.] Tina, Harvey, David, Lisa, Mia, Joy, Nehomia, and Ben; [ed.] High School; [occ.] Housewife; [memb.] Orlando Christian Center Church, I am that I am Charter. Afro American Historical Genealogical Society Inc.; [oth. writ.] Several poems and few songs.; [pers.] I can do all things through Jesus Christ who strengthens me. I'm inspired by God and all he made.; [a.] Orlando, FL

FITZPAJTRICK, THOMAS H.
[Pen.] Horace Bliffcliff; [b.] November 18, 1941, West Palm Beach, FL; [p.] Eunice G. Farrell Fitzpatrick and John J. Fitzpatrick; [m.] Sandra Steele Fitzpatrick, March 2, 1985; [ch.] K.B., Phinney, Foster, Klancy; [ed.] B.S., Boston College; [occ.] Manager of Management Communications, Digital Equipment Corp.; [memb.] U.S. Marine Corps, Retired Officers Assoc., Boston Marathon Ten Finishes Club; [hon.] Dean's List, Delta Sigma Pi; [oth. writ.] Several poems yet to be published; Children's Story, "Creatures Move To Moist New Berry" currently in progress.; [pers.] Carpe Diem, as the glass is always half full! Dog is man's best friend.!; [a.] West Newbury, MA

FLEMING (AMAN), CHARLOTTE, ANN
[Pen.] Char; [b.] April 17, 1942, Grafton, WV; [p.] Mary E. and George B. Fleming; [m.] Blaine P. Aman, Jr; [ch.] John Jr, Warder II, Teresa; [ed.] High School; [occ.] Certified Nursing Aide Administrative; [pers.] This is for you mother who will always be with me.

FLEMING, MARJORIE FOSTER
[Pen.] Marjorie Foster Fleming, Jarjorie Foster Hondermark, Marjorie Foster; [b.] September 12, 1920, Cheltenham, PA; [p.] Major B. and Helen V. Foster; [m.] Paul S. Fleming, May 6, 1961; [ch.] John and David Hundermark; [ed.] Oak Lane Country Day School, Cheltenham High School, Ursinus College. Attended: Temple Univ (advertising) Pierce Business College, Cheltenham Twsp Art Center (Courses in painting, photography, day work, creative writing) Chelt Adolt school 8 yrs music; [occ.] Homemaker, writer painter, sculptress, musician; [memb.] Cheltenham Tsp Art Center; [hon.] WWII Army Navy "e" Aard from Major Samuels of Phila for contribution to evening bulletins 4th of July celebration (special events dept). Red Cross for occupational therapy (Valley Forge Army Hospital (WW II). Special duty stage door canteen hostess for members of Purple Heart. 1st prize in creative sewing; [oth. writ.] Poetry, plays, short stories, May pageant editor, House organ (Art Center) and assisted in writing scripts for TV and radio productions. Presently writing auto-biography; [pers.] I believe God has given us a purpose to fulfill which may or may not be revealed. I think that if we are able to use our experiences with both "Good" and "Bad" toward enhancing our spiritual growth, and if we then act for "Good" and with "Love" we will be "Happy". Voila, we have one step up on the stairway to Heaven; [a.] Crystal Lake, IL

FLEMING, PATRICIA
[Pen.] Pat Fleming; [b.] October 19, 1955, Lufkin, TX; [p.] W.I. and Faye Capps; [m.] David Fleming, June 2, 1979; [ch.] Lesa, Kara and Keli; [ed.] Lufkin High School, Lufkin, TX; [occ.] Commercial Lines Ins., CSR, Bill Russell Ins. Agency, Austin, TX; [memb.] Insurance Women of Austin, Round Rock Community Choir, Cedar Valley Middle School Band Booster; [hon.] Graduated Cum Laude 1974 High School; [oth. writ.] Several poems have won honorable mention in various poetry contests; one poem published.; [pers.] I have loved poetry since it was introduced to me in the third grade. Most of my writings are inspired by the family that I love so much. "A Man of Pure Gold" was written for my Dad on his 70th birthday.; [a.] Round Rock, TX

FLEMING, RICK
[b.] August 9, 1947, Oakland, Calif.; [p.] William and Cornelia Fleming; [m.] Debi Fleming, February 27, 1993; [ch.] Cindi, Billy, Kim, Creed, Evan, Matthew, Ryan, Jason; [ed.] Tennyson High, Chabot Jr. College; [occ.] President/CEO Titusville Area Chamber of Commerce; [memb.] Jaycees, Rotary, Masons, D.A.V., V.F.W.; [hon.] JCI Senatorship #37271; Calif. Jaycee of the Year (1982, 1984); U.S. Jaycees Recruiters Hall of Fame Inductee (1984); Listed in Outstanding Young Men of America (1983), Who's Who in the West (1992-93), and Who's Who in California (1993); [a.] Titusville, FL

FLETCHER, DIANNE
[b.] January 5, 1968, Siloam Springs, Ark.; [p.] James O. and Dorothy Norris; [m.] Henry Fletcher, July 1, 1988; [ch.] Letitia, Amanda, Bethany, Cassandra; [ed.] Watts Public High School; [occ.] Housewife and mother; [pers.] When I write words on paper. It helps me through the hard and lonely times in my life. My heart has the strongest influenced for my words and my life.; [a.] Watts, OK

FLOWERS, STAN
[b.] April 21, 1966, Carrollton, GA [p.] Paul and Pearl Flowers; [m.] Sherry Lynn Flowers, June 14, 1986; [ch.] Leah and Zachary Flowers; [ed.] High School Grad and 3 years college in Electricity; [occ.] Lineman at Greystone Power Corp., Douglasville, GA (10 years); [memb.] 1st Pentecostal Church in Villa Rica, GA; [oth. writ.] In memory of my Father, He Abides, My Children, etc...(lots of untitled); [pers.] I like everyday, one day at a time, in hope of another day to thank God for, and to enjoy my children.; [a.] Villa Rica, GA

FLYNN, SEAN HENRY
[b.] August 23, 1961, Grangeville, ID; [p.] Daren Henry Flynn, Mryna M. Flynn; [m.] Dawn S. Flynn, January 3, 1987; [ch.] Shannon Anita Flynn; [ed.] High School, US Coast Guard Correspondence Machinery Technician Courses; [occ.] Maintenance Technician; [hon.] Honorably Discharged Veteran after 6 years in the US Coast Guard, Two Good Conduct Awards; [pers.] When you have the desire to do something good, do it; [a.] Longmont, CO

FOGEL, TINA E.
[b.] August 5, 1958, Brooklyn, NY; [p.] Sylvia and Jorah Fogel; [ed.] High School of Art and Design Katherine Gibbs Secretarial College; [occ.] Legal Secretary; [pers.] Life can very often be a painful struggle. writing helps to soothe the heart and remind me of the beauty that was there in addition to the sadness.

FOISIE, DONALD ROBERT
[b.] November 22, 1931, Nashua, NH; [p.] Deceased; [m.] Rita Priscilla Bergeron Foisie, September 13, 1952; [ch.] Donna, David, Danny; [ed.] EPA Certification, Ferris State Univ., Graduate of Non-Commission Officers, Germany Certificate received in Air Conditioning and Heating, Military Police and Intelligence School, Germany; [occ.] Self-employed (Heating and Air Conditioning); [memb.] Past President and current member of Texas; Lonestar Chapter of Korean War Veterans, Veterans of Foreign Wars, Post 8790 Houston, TX, Lamb of God, Lutheran Church, United Way Committee Member; [hon.] Purple Heart Recipient, Combat Infantry Badge (total of 9 military awards received) Numerous top-sales awards received as well as sales training awards; [oth. writ.] Numerous other poems such as "I Am the American Flog" and "The Small Pocket Bible" These poems have been distributed around the world and published in local newspapers.; [pers.] I primarily write poetry to reflect American patriotism while at the same time, instill in those who were not there a sense of reality and a more in depth understanding of the combat veteran's emotions.; [a.] Humnble, TX

FOLEY, RON
[b.] May 14, 1968, Detroit, MI; [p.] Alma and eugene Foley; [ed.] B.A. Western Michigan Univ.; [occ.] Television Producer, Music Composer for film and video games; [memb.] Black Filmaker Foundation, Urban League, Eugene B. Redmond Writer's Club; [hon.] M.L.K. Jr., Scholarship; [oth. writ.] Over (60) Inspirational Audio Programs for youth; various journals and publications.; [pers.] Start your dream with what you have and god will fill in the blanks.; [a.] Detroit, MI

FOLLIS-LEHR, SYLVIA G.
[b.] December 5, 1946, Houston, TX; [p.] Thomas A. Follis, Aleen D. Mosley, Birthmother, raised by wonderful stepmother, Jenny Faye Follis; [m.] Jerry Wilson Lehr, December 19, 1986; [ch.] Melinda, Allena, Ellen, Ronald, Christopher; [ed.] Klein High, Spring, TX., T.H. Harris Voc. Tech., Opelousas, LA, Lee College, Baytown, TX.; [occ.] Grandmother, Homemaker, Student, Retired

Hair Stylist; [memb.] Recently returned to Texas after living many years in Louisiana. There I was involved with the first Assembly of God Church at Pearl River, LA. Loved to enter music competitions. Was introduced into the Little Theater Group of Slidell, LA. Intermingling Make-Up and Acting; [hon.] Trophies in Music Competitions; [oth. writ.] Several poems. A few of which were published in the church paper. Have written the words to several songs along with daughter Melinda, the guitarist of the family.; [pers.] Most of my writings come from my own life situations. I know that many of the things that I put on paper are truly inspired by God. I always feel that I have an angel, (who gets, up very early in the morning, I must add) and this angel tells me to "take notes." And I do!; [a.] Baytown, TX

FORD, AMY
[b.] October 27, 1959, Abington, PA; [p.] Roz and Henry Schaeffer; [m.] Mark Ford, September 6, 1987; [ed.] Solebury School, Philadelphia College of Art, Private Music Study with Master Art Weinstein; [occ.] Musician, Teacher, Massage Therapist; [memb.] American Massage Therapy Assoc.; [hon.] Hamill Gillespe Award, Dean's List; [oth. writ.] Many songs and poems in various styles; [pers.] My writing spans and formats. I perform my music solo and with bands as well as hosting poetry readings. My subject matter is my interpretation of life.; [a.] Quakertown, PA

FORD, D. J.
[b.] February 23, 1985, Yonkers, NY; [p.] Laurie and David Ford; Brother: Daniel Ford (7yrs); Sister: Kayde Lyn Ford (2yrs); [ed.] 3rd grade Fulmar Road Elementary School - Mahopac New York; [occ.] Student; [memb.] Mahopac Soccer Association; Mahopac Basketball Assoc; Mahopac Baseball Assoc; Fulmar Track Team; [hon.] Fulmar Finest; [oth. writ.] I wish; [pers.] I like writing poems and stories. My 2nd grade teacher, Mr. Murphy - Third grade Teachers, Ms. Baker, Ms. Bertram, Ms. Kristopherson really encouraged me to write my best poem ever.

FORD, HELEN YVONNE (BIDWELL)
[b.] October 27, 1925, Sturgis, MI; [p.] Leon and Leona Bidwell; [m.] Francis Ford, August 12, 1950; [ch.] Elizabeth, Thomas and Melinda; [ed.] 12 yrs, Certified Phy Tech; [occ.] Adult Nursing Care; [memb.] Wesllyen Ladies Fellowship; [pers.] Write poems for self. Believe in God and country, caring for the ill and doing for others; [a.] Coldwater, MD

FOREMAN, TERRY P.
[b.] March 8, 1957, Martinez, CA; [ed.] San Jose State University, Los Medanos Police Academy, Diablo Valley College; [occ.] Police Officer & Professional Golfer; [oth. writ.] Numerous poems and other works not yet reviewed for publication.; [pers.] I wish for people to see, through my writings, that we all hold, in our hearts and in our minds, the brass ring to our dreams, no matter what life puts on the table.; [a.] Antioch, CA

FORTNER, ROBERT
[b.] January 26, 1956, Binghamton, NY; [m.] Ilene Fortner, April 4, 1984; [ch.] Shayla Ayn and Guthrie Montana; [ed.] Aslem Broome Community College; [occ.] Rhythm Guitar and song writer for devastation masters.; [hon.] EOP Academic Achievement Award 92 & 93, Garret News Service Award 93-94; [oth. writ.] Other poems published in local newspapers, a collection of sci-fi and horror short stories, a manuscript (Celsor's Quest), articles in local publications.; [pers.] It is the po-

ets, not the politicians, who change the world. Poetry (including songs) is the weapon of Knights of Truth. My influences include Woody Guthrie, Bob Dylan, William S. Burrough, Kafka; [a.] Binghamton, NY

FORTUNE, ROBERT E.
[b.] November 14, 1960, Bad Kreuznach, Germany; [p.] Ray and Sue Fortune; [ed.] Timberline High School, Central Texas College; [occ.] Senior Instructor, JROTC, Marmion Military Academy, Aurora, IL; [memb.] Non-Commissioned Officer's Association; [oth. writ.] Silent Memories, in Dusting Off Dreams, Quill Books; Dreams in At Day's End, The National Library of Poetry; [pers.] My new wife Cheryl is the inspiration of all my poems.; [a.] Aurora, IL

FOSTER, JANN MARIE
[b.] August 8, 1950, Minneapolis, MN; [p.] Lowell and Marion Foster; [ch.] Jennifer Hope, age 21; [ed.] B.A. Journalism, Univ. of Minnesota; [occ.] Technical/ Freelance writer; [oth. writ.] Many poems published in National Poetry Journals. Two poetry books published. Two genealogy books published.; [pers.] Poetry is one of the most personal ways of expression available to humankind. Poetry must evolve from the various senses, and the perception of these senses is the path to writing fine poetry.; [a.] Minneapolis, MN

FOWLER, SHARON HACKNEY
[Pen.] S.H.; [b.] October 9, 1951, Williamson, WVA; [p.] Kennie and Fairy Hackney; [m.] Phil Fowler, November 12, 1987; [ch.] Three; [ed.] High school completed, two years journalism school; [occ.] Write for Williamson Daily News, Williamson, WVA; [hon.] Poet's awards 4, Ashment Award for History around Kentucky, World of Poetry Awards; [oth. writ.] Books and short stories, news paper articles around KY; [pers.] When all find something in life you feel deep into you soul that you enjoy to do it, writing is mine an I enjoy it deeply.; [a.] Bethel Ridge, KY

FOWLER, SUSANNE M.
[Pen.] Susan Jayne; [b.] October 25, 1959, Elgin, IL; [p.] DeForest and JoAnne Jayne; [m.] Kevin Fowler, November 19, 1988; [ch.] Tiffany, Holly, Jacqueline, Kevin; [ed.] Mooseheart High School Graduate, Cosmetologist License, Real Estate License, Institute of Children's Literature, etc.; [occ.] Self-employed.; [memb.] Holy Angels Church; [hon.] National Honors Society, All State Track & Field Award, N.A.F.E., and H.S. Athletic Hall of Fame (*First Female to receive this award at my H.S.); [oth. writ.] Yes, both poetry and dramatic works. I also write, edit, and publish a small newsletter packed with information that I've researched.; [pers.] I love to write, and strive to do my best. I enjoy opening my mind and writing my thoughts; always have.; [a.] Aurora, IL

FOX, ROBERT
[b.] June 15, 1927, Schenectady, NY; [p.] Nicholas J. and Mabel Brower Fox; [m.] Lorraine C. Fox, April 12, 1980; [ch.] Sharon Lapalme, Dawn Erardy, Cindy Grillo, Robert J., Virg Hill; [ed.] High School, Electronics School, US Navy, Welding School; [occ.] Special Products Division, C & M Corp, Wauregan, CT (Wire and Cable); [memb.] Lutheran Church, AARP; [hon.] World War Two Medals: American Victory, China Service and Asiatic-Pacific Theater, Expert Rifle Badge; [oth. writ.] Have written several other short poems; [pers.] Served in US Marine Corps 1945-6 in China. Also US Navy 1947-50 at Chicago and Hickam Field, Hawaii; [a.] Brooklyn, CT

FRAEDRICH, BRENDA
[Pen.] Brenda Wiebers; [b.] August 18, 1974, Sterling, CO; [p.] John and Mary Wiebers; [m.] Thaddeus Fraedrich, October 3, 1992; [ed.] Fleming High School, Northeastern Jr. College, Three Rivers Community Technical, Aims Community College; [occ.] Certified Nursed Aid, Emergency Medical Technician; [memb.] Future Business Leaders of America; Future Homemakers of America; Volleyball; Basketball; Yearbook; Journalism; School Play; [hon.] Voice of Democracy 2nd and 3rd places; Editor of School Yearbook; Co-Editor of Cat-Tales (Journalism); Honor Roll; Who's Who Among American High School Students; [oth. writ.] School newspaper; Voice of Democracy Contest; Personal Collection of Poems; [pers.] I try not to take life too serious. My theory, stop and smell the roses! It's the little things in life that mean so much...but don't do it alone. Take your best friend by the hand.; [a.] Uncasville, CT

FRANEY, BEVERLY LOUISE
[b.] June 22, 1973, Nashville, IL; [p.] Fred and Arlene Franey; [ed.] Graduated from Central High School; attended Southeast Missouri State Univ; graduated from Youth With A Mission (a missionary training school); [occ.] Work at JC Penny Jewelry and watch repair; [hon.] An Editor's Choice Award for Fallen Clown. An Editor's Choice Award For Fallen Cross; [oth. writ.] Fallen Clown and Fallen Cross; [pers.] I wish to exemplify God's love and concern for people in my poetry; [a.] Cape Girardeau, MO

FRANK, CHERIE
[Pen.] Cherie; [b.] July 22, 1962, Mercy Hospital, Oklahoma City, OK; [p.] Lloyd and Evelyn Frank,; [m.] Isaiah 34:16; [ch.] Megan and Melora; [ed.] Union High school graduate, 13 year student. Tulsa, OK 1 yr. College; [occ.] American Airlines Payroll; [memb.] Higher Dimensions, Tulsa, OK; [hon.] Voted Christian Girl of the Year. Class of 1980 Union High School; [oth. writ.] My journal to my daughters.; [pers.] John 3:16 for god so loved the world the He gave His only begotten Son, that Whoever believes in Him should not perish but have everlasting life. John 1:17 for the law was given through Moses, but Grace and Truth came through Jesus Christ!; [a.] Tulsa, OK

FRANK, JEREMY
[b.] June 26, 1980, Spokane, WA; [p.] Robert and Deborah; [ed.] In high school; [occ.] Student; [memb.] National Junior Honor Society, 4-H, Nez Perce Tribe; [hon.] Won a poetry contest with same poem, 6th grade top award, Spokane Regional contest, read poem over radio, received $100.00 Savings Bond, community recognition; [oth. writ.] I keep journals and write poems and short stories for my pleasure; [pers.] I feel good when I can make people laugh. Most of my writing reflects humor and the fun side of life and people. [a.] Newnan, WA.

FRANK, STEPHANIE
[Pen.] Stephanie Frank; [b.] October 2, 1969, Salt Lake City, UT; [p.] Andrew and Mildred Detmer; [m.] David Frank, December 21, 1987; [ch.] Carrie Lynn Frank; [ed.] St. James the less (1-8), Bellarmine Jefferson High School (9-12); [occ.] Housewife, mother and secretary for the family business; [oth. writ.] I have written many poems but this is my first one to be published; [pers.] I write all of my poems with special feeling straight from my heart. My mother and I have both inspired each other; [a.] Sunland, CA

FRANKLIN, JO M.
[Pen.] Jo Marie; [b.] Joseph C. Herron and Ellmae Wynn; [m.] Robt E. Franklin, June 28, 1956; [ed.] High school graduate; [occ.] JC Penney, 16 yrs, 1994 cashier/clerk/ stocker. Jack of all trades, master of none; [hon.] Still searching; [oth. writ.] Poems and skits for school / employer: JCP. Poems written for store newsletter. I have also written 2 sequels to my poem "Family". The 2nd is "My Family and Me", but the third is yet to have a title; [pers.] For me, writing is fun, whether its poems or short stories. I enjoy writing words that make people happy or just feel good. This makes me feel good; [a.] Wichita, KS

FREDERICK, SHIRLEY
[b.] October 25, 1936, Dover, NH; [occ.] Reading teacher, Rapid City Area Schools; [oth. writ.] A volume of poems and photographs of the Black Hills and Yellowstone is in production; [pers.] Using images from nature I reflect on the human condition. The Black Hills, Jackson Hole, Yellowstone, and the Sonoran Desert are my favorite sources.; [a.] Rapid City, SD

FREEMAN, CHARLES H.
[Pen.] Chuck Freeman; [b.] April 22, 1947, Tuscon, AZ; [p.] Neal and June Freeman; [m.] Jacquelynne Hurlbut, June 2, 1992; [ch.] Chase Matthew and Rachel; [ed.] High School, 3 years college; [occ.] Const. Super.; [pers.] Life is a road filled with rocks and pot holes. As you pass this way you can either avoid the rocks and holes or take the time to move the rocks and fill the holes. I'll do the latter.; [a.] W. Plains, MO

FRENCH (JR), R. W. "BOB"
[Pen.] Bob French; [b.] July 27, 1940, Villa Grove, IL; [m.] Divorced; [ch.] 3 sons; [ed.] 2 yrs college, Univ of IL and Univ of AR, Little Rock; [occ.] Arch/Eng Design Coordinator for Univ of AR Medical Sciences; [pers.] I write poems for the emotional release that soothes my soul for yet another day in search of serenity in this life; [a.] Little Rock, AR

FRIEDMAN, MELANIE
[b.] May 19, 1950, So. Bend, IN; [p.] Laverne and Dorothy Cyrier; [ch.] Kimberly (24), Tamara (22), Gregory (20); [ed.] John Adams High School, Vogue Beauty School, Bert Roger's School of Real Estate; [occ.] Licensed Broker/Salesperson, Real Estate sales in Florida; [memb.] Board of Realtors, Vice President of Villa Manor Condo Assoc; [oth. writ.] An anthology of poetry book: A Place of Springs By Tabby House Books 1992. I placed 14 poems of my work in that. And a new release to be out in early spring of 1995 will carry another selection of my work; [pers.] My writings are personal experiences of my own life. "I believe that everything happens for a good reason, whether good or bad its for the best"; [a.] Port Charlotte, FL

FROMM, ROBERT LYELL
[b.] May 10, 1949, Hart, MI; [p.] Alfred and Jean Fromm; [ed.] Western Mich Univ, Kalamazoo, MI; [occ.] Photographer/songwriter; [memb.] Friends of Photography, National Academy of Songwriters, Northern California Songwriters Assoc, Los Angeles Songwriters Showcase; [hon.] Honorable Mention in Professional Category for Photography at Santa Cruz County Fair in 1986-1990; [oth. writ.] Other poems include: Visitors, 8th Air Corp, Sojourn, "No Problems". Songs include: "Touch of Texas", "They Live On", western songs; [pers.] Is to raise the levels of awareness about our fragile balance and relationships on this planet earth where

we reside. The ancient forests must be saved for our first and foremost goal; [a.] Santa Cruz, CA

FROST, BERNICE WILLIAMS
[b.] August 4, 1957, Choctaw County, Alabama; [p.] Hazel Lee Williams and Walter Louis Williams, Sr; [ch.] Bernadette Cherie Edwards, John Tyler Edwards, Jr.[ed.] 1st through 8th grade (East Choctaw Jr High School) 9th through 12th Choctaw Co High School. Graduated in 1976; [occ.] Customer Service Rep for JC Penny Co (Meridian, MS); [memb.] I belong to the Millwood Primitive Baptist Church and is very active in my community. I am a member of the High Energy Social Club here in my town; [oth. writ.] I love writing poetry and other short stories. My children have recited them in Church on occasions. I recently had one published this year in the Choctaw Advocate (newspaper here in my town), concerning a dear uncle of mine that passed away; [pers.] I have always wanted to be heard or noticed in some way. I do believe that if ever given the chance I could and would make a difference. Not only in my life but in someone else's life as well; [a.] Pennington, AL

FRY (JR.), HAROLD E.
[Pen.] H. E. Fry; [b.] October 2, 1949, San Diego, CA; [p.] Harold E. Fry, Sr., Melva J. Michaelson; [m.] Kathleen J. Fry 'nee (frei), February 12, 1972; [ch.] Jon, Harold Fry; [ch.] Jon, Harold, Fry; [ed.] Beloit Memorial, Beloit, TX, Lee College Baytown, TX, New York Regents College, Albany, NY; [occ.] Licensed Vocational Nurse (LUN), ACLS, working in outpatient surg; [memb.] American Diabetes Assoc, National Rails to Trails Conservatory; [oth. writ.] I have written several hundred poems yet this is my first publication; [pers.] Poetry has been a way for me to express life as I've seen it, felt it, and tasted it, and to express gratitude to those who have given me so much in this life; [a.] LaPorte, TX

FRY, STEVE
[b.] October 23, 1957, NY, NY; [p.] William and Linda Berglum Fry; [ch.] "Rocky" (Siberian Husky); [ed.] Wilton High School, Wilton, CT, Norwalk Community College, CT, CT Center for Massage Therapy; [occ.] Massage Therapist; [pers.] My poetry reflects a personal interest in mystical experience, and the perception of beauty in creation. I hope to honor the individual guest for self-discovery and unity, with all it's challenges as well as rich rewards.; [a.] New Canaan, CT

FRYE, KATINA RENEE
[b.] March 11, 1975, Greensboro, NC; [p.] Charles and Gloria Frye; [ed.] Liberty Academy High, Alamance Community College; [occ.] Secretary, TRC Staffing Services, Greensboro, NC; [hon.] College Diploma High Honors; [oth. writ.] Poems published in Reba McEntire's fan club newsletter; [pers.] To me writing is one of the greatest gifts given. I enjoy writing poems, songs and short stories. In my writings, I express the loneliness of being an only child, the emptiness of never having grandparents and the values I place on life. When I put my feelings on paper, I know they will be remembered and be an heirloom to hand down to my future children. I take pride knowing I've touched someone's heart when I see a tear shed or a smile generated by my writings.; [a.] Reidsville, NC

FUELBERG, NANCY F.
[Pen.] Nan Fuelberg; [b.] February 22, 1947, Burton, TX; [p.] W.O. and Ida Bell Rauch; [m.] Gene Arthur Fuelberg, June 24, 1967; [ch.] Kristine K. Fuelberg -

Morris; [ed.] Round Top - Carmine High School, Blinn College, Univ of Houston; [occ.] Homemaker; [memb.] Lamb of God Lutheran Church, 100 Club of Houston; [oth. writ.] Poems: "To My Brother at War" and "Pray for the POW's", published in the Brenham Banner Press. Essay: "Red Neck Girl" published in the magazine - The Houston Post; [pers.] My poems are personal. They are my emotions "laid bare". Sometimes they are worth sharing; [a.] Houston, TX

FULLER, MAXCINE
[Pen.] Mack; [b.] July 31, 1940, Diboll, TX; [p.] Malissia Randolph and Paul Fred; [ch.] Beverly, Anita, Tyrone and Crystal; [ed.] H. G. Temple High, Valerie Hurd Beauty and Business College; [occ.] Custodian DJH School; [memb.] Perry Chapel CME Church. Actively supports church functions and community programs; [oth. writ.] Second chance, poems that I have not published.; [pers.] When I write I express my views of the twist and turns of life which seem a lot straighter with Wisdom influenced by Maya Angelou; [a.] Diboll, TX

FURSTENBERG, CHRISTINE
[b.] March 3, 1953, Coatesville, PA; [p.] Malcolm R. and Virginia S. Wagner; [m.] Ronald K. Furstenberg, February 14, 1991; [ch.] Debra, Amy, John and Matthew (also, step children: Scott, April, and Melanie); [ed.] Big Spring High School, Cumberland Perry Technical School; [occ.] Accounts Receivable Valve Maintenance Corporation; [memb.] Holy Redeemer Catholic Church; [hon.] Graduated with distinguished honors. Member National Honor Society; [oth. writ.] Various unpublished poems for my own enjoyment.; [pers.] I have always been influenced by literature and music. As photographs reflect pieces of time, poetry and music reflect pieces of emotion.; [a.] Odessa, TX

GAARN, EILEEN SHANNON
[b.] May 23, 1949, NYC; [p.] James and Augusta Shanic; [m.] Francis D. Gaarn, Jr., August 20, 1948; [ch.] Kathryne, Christopher, Cecilia; [ed.] Our Lady of Lourdes, NYC, The Assissium, NYC; [oth. writ.] Myriad Prose and Reflections; [pers.] Having grown up on the West Side of Manhattan in the 1930's and 40's, reading provided me with the passport to far a way places that lay beyond the horizon. I believe my writings still have that essence of romance where now, all is just a day or two journey away.; [a.] G. Barrington, MA

GADDIS, DORIS ANN JOHNSON
[b.] July 27, 1948, Lancaster, PA; [p.] Pearl and Charles Johnson; [ch.] Charles Arthur Gaddis; [occ.] Bachelor of Education 1972 Univ of Akron, Graduate Work, Ohio State, Ashland Univ; [occ.] Teacher; [memb.] National Council for History Education, Ohio Council for Social Studies, National Council for the Social Studies, Boy Scouts of America, Girl Scouts, PTA, St. Paul Lutheran Church; [hon.] Education Honor Fraternity, Deans List, Ashland Oil Golden Apple Award, Boy Scout Award of Merit, Second Place-Ohio Council of Economics - BP American Award, Presenter National Middle School Association Convention, Presenter Lazotte Reading Council, Presenter National, Regional and State Social Studies Conventions, Consultant-National Council for History Education; [oth. writ.] Snowball, The Special Christmas Present. A darling story about a puppy's silly antics as he searches for a family to love. Presently in the process of searching for the right publisher. I have also written numerous Teaching Units and Seminars on Creative Teaching; [pers.] Each time I return to the United

States, following an international trip, I realize how great it feels to be truly free! I feel a tremendous debt of gratitude to the men and women who fought and often died to preserve all precious freedom! The United States may not be perfect but it is head and shoulders above all the more than thirty countries I've been lucky enough to visit!; [a.] Sharon Center, OH

GALARZA, ALEJANDRA MATUS
[b.] March 24, 1944, AZ; [p.] Francisca and Guadalupe Matus; [m.] Deacon Frank G. Galarza, October 6, 1962; [ch.] Theresa Figueroa, Frank Galarza, Jr, Gilbert Galarza, Lael Galarza, Rosann Luna, Jason Galarza, Carmen Galarza, Olga Galarza and 9 grandchildren; [ed.] Mesa Community College, Arizona Stat Univ (in progress); [occ.] Prevention Specialist at Frank Elementary School, Guadalupe, AZ; [oth. writ.] In process of publishing poetry concerning women's issues in fall 1994. The publication will be titled "Fragmented Woman" and will be bilingual. Two scripts "MAYA" and "Breaking the Walls"; [pers.] My close friends have influenced and inspired my writings. I have found my own identity as an Indo-hispanic author and script writer. My spirituality is also reflected in my writings; [a.] Tempe, AZ

GALIC, SPIRO I.
[b.] September 22, 1961, Yugoslavia; [p.] Ilija and Danka Galic; [ed.] Technical School Center, "Slavko Zardin" Bihac; University of Belgrade, School of Mechanical Engineering, South Suburban College; [hon.] State finalist in academic competition graduate assistant to the mathematics and statistics professor; [oth. writ.] High level of proficiency in the metric system research, measurement and recording of materials strengthens. Mechanical drawing and reading of Mech. Blue Prints.; [pers.] I have been greatly influenced by the early romantic poets.; [a.] Crown Point, IN

GALLANT, ARTHUR
[b.] May 3, 1914, Brooklyn, NY; [p.] Fay and Louis Gallant (deceased); [m.] Martha (deceased), September 25, 1948; [ch.] Kenneth Stuart; Judith; [ed.] BA - History - Geo Washington - UDC MA in Public Administration - American Univ DC; [occ.] Former government employee - Navy Dept; retired; [memb.] The Academy of Political Science, American Academy of Political and Social Science, Eastern Area Recreation Advisory Board, Montgomery County, MD; [oth. writ.] I did five (5) book reviews on Public Administration for the "Annals" of the American Academy of Political and Social Science; [pers.] As an Octogenarian, I'm just beginning to learn and like poetry. My unpublished poems reflect experiences during the depression years (29-39) and World War II. Navy Veteran; [a.] Silver Spring, MD

GALLEGOS, MANDI
[b.] March 17, 1976, San Antonio, TX; [p.] Victor M. and Martha A. Gallegos; [nephew] Jeffery A. Flores; [sister] Martha M. Gallegos; [ed.] Santa Barbara High School, Santa Barbara City College; [occ.] Student at Santa Barbara City College; [hon.] Award of Honor of Outstanding Achievement in Writing; [oth. writ.] This will be my first published poem, with many more waiting in the wings.; [a.] Santa Barbara, CA.

GANZER, SUZAN T.
[b.] May 17, 1961, Chicago, IL; [p.] Adam and Jenny Ganzer; [ed.] Lyons Township High School, Lagrange, IL; and The Art Institute of Fort Lauderdale, Florida; [occ.] Artist, Office Manager, Songwriter; [oth. writ.]

Many poems for the people I care about, some have become words for songs. I'm working on the completion of my first children's book.; [pers.] The words I write, speak and sing are reflections of my heart and mind. When others truly hear my words, they have heard my heart. I feel I have shared something glorious. For me, this is the meaning of success.; [a.] Western Springs, IL

GARBER, NATHAN
[b.] December 14, 1965, Sault Ste. Maire; [p.] Joseph and Delores Garber; [m.] Melissa Diane Garber, June 1, 1991; [ed.] Sault Ste. Maire High, Sault Ste. Maire, MI; [occ.] Delivery Driver; [memb.] Teamsters Local 33; [pers.] I owe my thanks for this opportunity to my wife Melissa, without her this honor would not be possible. I remember, as a child, listening to poetry by candlelight. Thank you Dad for opening my eyes to this great gift.; [a.] Delmar, DE

GARCIA, DE ANN M.
[b.] March 13, 1972, Cleveland, OH; [p.] Wanda Snyder, Charles Snyder; [m.] Garcia, Samuel, October 20, 1990; [ed.] Wilson High Y. Oh Mary Crest Boarding School Ind OH; [occ.] Red Robin N. Olmsted OH; [hon.] Principle's Award; [oth. writ.] This is my first publication; [pers.] I've been inspired by the good and bad of my life, and the determination to understand life as it is through my writing; [a.] Cleveland, OH

GARCIA, MARTHA
[Pen.] Madom O; [b.] October 30, 1967, Chicago; [ch.] Valerie and Samson Garcia; [occ.] Material Handler Rich Corp 6200 Milford St. Niles (Chgo), [oth. writ.] Diamond Angels, Reflections (poems); Last Sands of Time; [pers.] Life is like a puzzle. It's up to you to put the pieces in the proper order. If you pass the test, I believe you move on to a higher existence; [a.] Chicago, IL

GARCIA, MICHAEL A.
[b.] May 13, 1956, Pontiac, Michigan; [p.] Israel and Mary Garcia; [m.] I've never committed matrimony, nor do I have children.; [ed.] Academy of Dramatic Art; Eastern Michigan University; [occ.] Storyteller & Performance Artist; [memb.] National Storytelling Association; Writers' Theatre-Chicago; [hon.] Eight-time National championship speaker for the National Forensics Association; storyteller for the National Geographic Society film series Where On Earth; First Voice in the critically acclaimed Chicago production of Dylan Thomas's Under Milk Wood.; [oth. writ.] This is my first published piece of writing.; [pers.] As an actor and storyteller I actually appreciate the great benevolence of written works. We need this benevolence in our lives, you can't shoot a gun and write a poem at the same time.; [a.] Chicago, IL

GARCIA, RICHARD
[Pen.] Dick Garcia; [b.] April 26, 1938, Honolulu, HI; [p.] Rose Skelton (mother); [m.] Divorced; [ed.] Kaimuki High School dropped out after junior year to join Army. Received GED while in the Army. A brain Mind course called "Alpha Cybernetics"; [occ.] Artist/Photographer; [oth. writ.] "Sunset" a poem published by "The National Library of Poetry," in their anthology, "The Space Between."; [pers.] Back in 1972, I took a Brain Mind course called "Alpha Cybernetics". It changed my life completely, that it was controlled by our thoughts and beliefs. That negative positive thoughts creative negative or positive realities. So choose wisely my friends.; [a.] Honolulu, HI

GARCIA, SID J.
[b.] May 1, 1959, Loveland, Colo.; [p.] Carrie Castaneda; [ed.] Graduated Loveland High School; [occ.] Sams Dist. Loveland, Colo.; [hon.] Junior high and high school awards in English; [oth. writ.] I am just finishing up a book I wrote (a science fiction thriller.) I hope to someday have published.; [a.] Loveland, CO

GARDNER, MATTHEW
[b.] October 25, 1952, Troy, NY; [p.] Francis and Viola Gardner; [m.] Deborah, July 7, 1975, (Divorced); [ch.] Tyshina, Amissa, Rakeea, Matthew; [ed.] Troy High School, Butera School of Art; [occ.] Custodian Boston Schools; [oth. writ.] Songs that have been copyrighted including Blackrose; [pers.] I would like to, eventually, be a songwriter professionally. Thank you to the National Library of Poetry for letting me share my work.; [a.] Dorchester, MA

GARRISON, MAGGIE
[b.] June 3, 1950, Lyons, GA; [p.] Jim H. and Melba Harrison; [m.] William E. Garrison Sr., August 29, 1970; [ch.] William Jr. and Melissa Gayle; [ed.] Winter Havan High School, Winter Haven, FL; South-Eastern College and the Assembly of God, Lakeland, FL; [occ.] Certified Pharmacy Technician, Nursing Home Pharmacy; [memb.] FL Pharmacy Assoc., FL Society of Hospital Pharmacist, FL Notary Public, FL Pharmacy Technician Assoc.; [a.] Haines City, FL

GARVAN, JANE NICODEMUS
[b.] August 17, 1977, New York, NY; [p.] (deceased) Dorothy Townsend and L.C. Nico Bemus; [m.] (deceased) Anthony Brady Garvan, June 15, 1940; [ch.] 1 son - 7 daughters; [ed.] St. Timothy, Catonsville, MD, now located at Stevenson, MD, 4 yrs, college prep, 2 yrs at Columbia Univ (extension); 2 yrs, Albemtus Magnus, New Haven CT; [occ.] Learning to Fly; [pers.] I remember being born on the dining room table in our small New York apartment. My next big thrill was seeing Charles Lindbergh flying at 50 feet fog bound for Paris, France in his "Spirit of St. Louis". Finally and always so exciting the births of our children head first and healthy. All 8 of them.

GARZA, LAURIE MELISSA
[b.] June 13, 1978, Los Angeles, CA; [p.] Crisoforo and Gale Garza; [ed.] Kindergarten - 8th grade - St. Paul the Apostle School; currently - 10th grader - Marymount High School, Los Angeles, CA; [memb.] Teenetles Service Organization of Orthopedic Hospital; Drama Club; Christian Service Representative; Yearbook Committee; [hon.] High School: California Scholarship Federation; Honor Roll; Basketball Coaches Award; St. Paul's: graduated with Bronze Medal for Academic Excellence and Citizenship; Service Award; Athletic Commendation for Sportsmanship in Basketball; [oth. writ.] "Anxiety", poem I wrote that was published in the Anthology of Poetry by Young Americans in 1993; [pers.] I want to promote understanding and tolerance of different cultures through my writings. Also, even during difficult times, I strive to do my best and see good in others; [a.] Los Angeles, CA

GASCOYNE, RUSS
[b.] June 13, 1976, Melrose Park; [p.] Robert and Pat Gascoyne; [occ.] Musician and Poet; [oth. writ.] Abode, no hope, etc. on my bands demo which is called Untaken; [pers.] I don't believe in good or bad luck, I think whatever happens, happens and it happens for a reason. So I stay happy and accept it.; [a.] Addison, IL

GASTELUM, ANGELO EMILE
[b.] August 6, 1978, La Joua, CA; [p.] Michele Gastelum; [ed.] Eleventh Grade, High School (last attended) Boys Town High, Boys Town, Nebraska; [occ.] I have no current occupation; [hon.] I have never been recognized for any of my literature.; [oth. writ.] I have given life to several prose and free verse collections but never have I attempted to have my work published.; [pers.] My only statement is that as writers we must strive for perfection, but as humans we cannot possibly deny ourselves. What we see and how we feel.; [a.] San Diego, CA

GATHING, LYNDA
[Pen.] Zola Uhuru; [b.] November 1, Chicago.; [p.] Lucille Overton; [m.] Ahmed Gathing, November 1, 1994 (high school sweetheart); [ch.] 1st Marriage Erick, Anthony and Nicole Jackson; [ed.] Graduated from Calumet in 1970, Most Outstanding Student in Afro-American Society. Attended Kennedy-King College, but left because of marriage and children; [occ.] Health Unit Clerk in Metro Hospital; [memb.] Sexual Assault Victims Advocate Outreach Ministry at Church; [oth. writ.] I have written many poems, some were published in high school where I took Journalism. But most I just write and keep.; [pers.] My favorite poet, Nikki Giovanni say's "I am a poet, my job is to write poetry." So I do my job and write poetry and now I even have a published poem.; [a.] Chicago, IL

GATTO, DOROTHY
[b.] April 7, 1928, Brooklyn, NY; [p.] Edward Clougher, Anne Clougher; [m.] Thomas Gatto, June 17, 1950; [ch.] Chuck, Nora, Tom, Mary, Eddie, Anne and 13 grandchildren; [ed.] Washington Irving HS, Metropolitan Hosp School of Nursing; [occ.] Retired RN; [oth. writ.] Several other poems. This is the first to be published; [pers.] Poetry is my way of communicating with God and sharing my feelings with family and friends; [a.] NY, NY

GEARY, VALERIE J.
[b.] March 20, 1945, Bakersfield, CA; [p.] Marion and Bertha Mitchell; [m.] Kenneth L. Geary, January 18, 1964; [ch.] Michael Geary, John Geary, Joshua Geary, Gloria Willson, Suzanna Geary, Jeana Geary; [ed.] East High, Bakersfield College; [occ.] Family Resource Specialist; [memb.] Bakersfield Community Church; [oth. writ.] Editor of "The Connection". Articles in "Above Rubies" magazine published worldwide, and many newspapers across the US and Canada; [pers.] I give glory to Jesus Christ for inspiring me to write concerning the world of special needs; [a.] Bakersfield, CA

GECKOS, MARGARET J.
[b.] April 22, 1930, Isle of Tinos, Greece; [p.] James and Irene Kouvaras; [m.] Gus J. Geckos, July 23, 1961; [ch.] Marietta, John, Rena; [ed.] DePaul University, Ph.B., Columbia Teachers College, M.A.; [occ.] Elementary School Teacher; [memb.] National Education Assoc.; [hon.] I consider it the greatest of all honors to be permitted the opportunity to awaken in children the joy, beauty and power of well-crafted words which when strung together artfully can express the noblest ideals and emotions of man.; [oth. writ.] Poems for classroom use, designed to serve as models to inspire an instruct children to write their own. Writer of Curriculum Units, Sunday School Teaching Materials, Editor of Church publication, Ghost Writer for church Officials.; [pers.] A poet is one who is inspired by beauty and truth, one who reaches deep into his won soul and speaks for humanity from the depths of his heart.; [a.] Potomac, MD

GEERTS, JERRI
[b.] September 25, 1963, Ft. Worth, TX; [p.] Robert J. and the late Dorothy Barclay; [m.] Jerry Geerts, June 1, 1985; [occ.] Manager of retail store; [oth. writ.] Currently working on a book.; [a.] Jacksonville, FL

GEIGER, NETTIE R.
[b.] September 30, 1940, Irmo, SC; [p.] Mr. & Mrs. John H. Pollock; [m.] Charles L. Geiger, Sr, February 17, 1960; [ch.] Charles, Jr, Ivan R.; grandson: Vincent; [ed.] Rich-Lex High School, 1958. I co-wrote Alma mater, Anthem wrote school literature, and other literary plays; [occ.] Disabled (arthritis and asthma) worked 25 yrs as cafeteria cook, Dist #5 School, Irmo, SC; [memb.] Home Society, Hopewell AME Missionary and Program Advisor of Hopewell AME Church, White Rock, SC; [hon.] I co-wrote our school Alma, Anthem in 1956 (I think was the year). "Hail to Rich-Lex". I was born and raised in Irma, SC. When I was three, my goal in life was to be a famous poet and inventor; [oth. writ.] Two poems in local newspapers. Several poems for funeral Homes in Columbia, SC Obituaries. Two songs on Tape by a recording company, which add music and male and females singing the lyrics; [pers.] I love reading and writing, but I love Paul Dunbar poems. A part of Black History's greatest minds. Although I have a variety of different subjects. I like writing (slave poems) I call them, I have a Slave Dictionary, just give me pen and paper; [a.] Irmo, SC

GEISLER, NANCY L.
[b.] January 7, 1944, Van Nuys, CA; [p.] Lucille and Byron Pedersen; [ch.] Krista Irene, Werner George; [ed.] Canadian Academy (Kobe, Japan), California State University at Northridge; [occ.] Word Processor; [hon.] Dean's List, Golden Key National Honor Society; [oth. writ.] Poems, non fiction essays, biographical interview, editorials; [pers.] I am strongly influenced by romantic poets. Am interested in topics covering issues such as AIDS. Overcoming hardship and tragedy and finding a meaning for life.; [a.] Salem, OR

GENDRON, SHEILA MANDELL
[b.] January 29, 1953, NYC; [m.] Dan Gendron, 1988; [ch.] Girl age 6, Boy age 3; [ed.] Life; [occ.] Husband and I own watch repair company; [pers.] My poetry has always been a catharsis for my sadness and an enhancement for my joys.; [a.] Sandpoint, ID

GEORGE, MARY A.
[Pen.] Mag; [b.] November 7, 1947, Utica, NY; [p.] Alice M. McShea; [ch.] Five, ages 10 - 24; [ed.] St. Elizabeth Hospital School of Nursing, 3 yr. Diploma Program R.N., High School, DeSales, Utica, NY; [occ.] Director of Recruitment Admissions; [oth. writ.] Non published writings only; [pers.] My writings are reflections of a middle aged woman in the height of change and growth; fed by my experiences of the death of a marriage and the birth of my newly released soul.; [a.] New Hartford, NY

GEORGE, RUTH T.
[b.] November 22, 1913, Clark County, KY; [p.] Mr. and Mrs. Roger Talbott; [m.] Arthur J. George, March 1, 1941 (deceased); [ch.] Carol Conley and Chad Conley; [ed.] North Middleton High School, B.S. Eastern KY, University, M.A. Ohio Un. Athens; [occ.] Retired School Teacher, Homemaker, Sunday School Teacher; [memb.] Christian Church, Eastern Star, Golden Alumni, Ohio U., 60 yr. Alumni Eastern Kentucky Colonel, Kappa Delta Pi, Pi Theta, AARP, and others; [hon.] Valedictorian of Sr. Class High School, Teaching Fellowship to

Ohio Univ., Outstanding Athlete in Basketball and many others; [oth. writ.] Poems about life in Kentucky, Masters Thesis "Classroom Teachers Guide to Child Growth in Creative Art" many articles in Athens Messenger, poetry book and numerous others.; [pers.] Education Philosophy "Teach the child to live today so he may meet the problems of tomorrow." When teaching Art at Rio Grande College, "God is the basis of an Art, no one can duplicate his glorious colors" but we can try. Life Philosophy: I count not my age by years, I live, but by happiness to others I give, the friends I make the good I do, the little things that day by day bring cheer to others along the way. I count each birthday one more mile upon the road of things worth while.; [a.] McArthur, OH

GEORGESON, STEPHEN N.
[b.] January 7, 1961, Worcester, MA; [p.] Nicholas and Aristea Georgeson; [m.] Dawn Georgeson, May 6, 1990; [ed.] Bachelor of Science, Northeastern Univ; [occ.] Special Security Assistant; [memb.] Chairman, Finance Committee - Rice Memorial Baptist Church, Order of Ahepa; [oth. writ.] Varies poems during grade school, high school; [pers.] Step back and notice and admire all of God's creations; [a.] Clinton, MA

GERBAN, KANDY STEWART
[Pen.] Kandy Stewart; [b.] February 9, 1966, Norman, OK; [p.] Kenneth L. and Jeanne K. Stewart; [m.] Walter J. Gerban, July 23, 1993; [ch.] Misty Autumn; [ed.] San Antonio College; [occ.] Writer/motion picture producer; [pers.] Glorify the Lord in all that you do.; [a.] Converse, TX

GHARZOZI, CAROL
[b.] 1978, Scarb, General; [p.] Mary and Simon Gharzozi; [ed.] Grade 10 and eleven; [occ.] Student; [memb.] Zoological Society; [oth. writ.] Rainbow of the World, Mountain Peak.

GHAZARIAN, RICHARD
[Pen.] Richie Shock; [b.] September 14, 1971, Savannah, Georgia; [p.] Richard Ghazarian Sr., and Linda Ghazarian; [ed.] Brentwood High, New York Institute of Technology Old Westbury Campus; [occ.] Lead Singer & Co-Song Writer of Photon Recording Artists "Side Show Virus"; [hon.] Dean's List, National Honor Society, Presidential Academic Fitness Award; [oth. writ.] Various songs used on the Photon Power Disc and to be used on Sideshow Virus' Debut Album.; [pers.] I believe in taking chances because if you do what you have always done you will get what you have always gotten. I also believe I am a creation of my environment so if at any time in my life there is controversy over any of my actions the person pointing the finger at me should realize that three point back at them.; [a.] Brentwood, NY

GHUNTOS-SALLOUM, REEMA
[b.] June 16, 1951, Jordan, Middle East; [p.] Speredon and Latifeh Salloum; [ch.] Laurice and Charles; [ed.] AAS in Business, Onondaga Community College, Graduated w/honors; [occ.] Jr. Accountant; [hon.] 1990 "Award of Merit Certificate" through the "Great Annual World of Poetry" contest. 1991 "Golden Poet Award" through the same.; [oth. writ.] Will be published in the anthology, "Seasons to Come," in the Spring of 1995, through the National Library of Poetry.; [pers.] God did not create man equal for the sake of balance. Yet, we must render equal treatment to maintain the balance in God's creation.; [a.] Clay, NY

GIARDINO, TARA MARIE
[b.] July 11, 1978, Gloversville, NY; [p.] Paul and Robin Giardino; [ed.] Junior at Mayfield Central School; [oth. writ.] I have been writing poetry for three years. This poem "Can't Let Go" I had written in 2/94 while going through chemo treatments.; [pers.] I have been fighting my cancer for 14 mos., now I write poetry to pass along to other people to be strong and positive as I have been.; [a.] Gloversville, NY

GIBB, DAVE
[b.] February 13, 1941, Pittsburgh, PA; [p.] John and Ann Gibb; [m.] Divorced; [ch.] Daughter, Danielle; [ed.] McKeesport High School, Associates Degree, Business Management, LaSalle; [occ.] Operations Manager U.S. Air, Laguardia Field, NY; [memb.] Kiwanas Club, New York; [hon.] Numerous Team and Individual Softball awards, New York Softball League; [oth. writ.] Numerous romantic writings.; [a.] Flushing, NY

GIBNEY, MARY ELLEN
[Pen.] Silent Angel; [b.] September 27, 1955, Brooklyn, NY; [p.] George and Anna Mitchell; [m.] Fiancee: Anthony Jacobson; [ch.] Dawn Marie Gibney; [ed.] Grover Cleveland High School, Drake Business School; [oth. writ.] Several unpublished poems that I hope to have published in the near future.; [pers.] I've always been a spiritual person and also a romantic, so when I write, I write from the heart.

GIBSON, GEORGE W.
[b.] June 14, 1917, Edina, MN; [p.] John H. and Grace D. Gibson; [m.] Marjorie H., June 10, 1949; [ch.] Anne Elizabeth and Carol Lynne; [ed.] Carleton College and Univ of MN BA 1948 BS 1950; [occ.] Retired (Harvard Univ Faculty); [memb.] Cotuit (Mass) Historian Assoc, Cotoit Civic Assoc; [hon.] Cited in Who's Who in Education, Who's Who in Libraries, Who's Who in the East; Chris Award - Columbus Film Festival (Educational Oscar) for Excellence in Film Production; [oth. writ.] Articles - Mechanix Illustrated Harvard Business Review, Educational Screen, North Islander Cape Code News, Cape Code Times; writer-producer of fifteen 16mm sound educational motion pictures, composer/lyricist, musician; [pers.] "All the World's a stage". "This above all-to thine own self be true."; [a.] Cotuit, MA

GILLILAND, DOUG
[Pen.] Lone Wolf, Righteous Rider; [b.] November 2, 1977, Florida; [p.] Deborah Ann Gilliland and Robert Earl Stevens; [ed.] In 11th grade Hendersonville High School; [occ.] Bilo Bagboy/Stock; [memb.] FCA Club, Literary Club, African American Club; [oth. writ.] None published but, "Nothing, Love, Terry, No More, Last Chance, Eyes of Steel, Failure, Anger, Dreams, are always dreams and many more."; [pers.] I was born in Florida but I now live in NC. I have written many poems and I am hoping to get them published. My writings are based upon fact and are usually sad. Poetry to me is a way to escape the pains this world loves to inflict on your soul. My poetry comes from my heart and I thank Sandy Forman for helping take it a step farther.; [a.] Horse Shoe, NC

GILMAN, TAMARA A.
[b.] October 3, 1947, Lorain, Ohio; [p.] Janice and Thomas Lyons; [m.] Barry Martin Gilman, June 10, 1972; [ch.] James Matthew, Jonathan Michael; [ed.] Lorain High School 1965, Northwestern University, B.A. 1969, Cornell University, M.I.L.R. 1972, Harvard Business School, M.B.A. 1976, Harvard Business School, D.B.A.

1981; [occ.] Professor and Consultant: Business Administration; [a.] Lexington, MO

GILMER (BOHANNON), DORIS
[b.] Cleveland, OH; [p.] Deceased; [m.] Sam Bohannon, Married 1945, again in 1994; [ch.] 3 adults - Carole, Gayle, Chester; [ed.] Neotarion College of Philosophy, Kansas City, MO; John Carroll Univ ordained minister - 1952; [occ.] Retired; [memb.] Mt. Zion Women's Fellowship; Eliza Bryant Senior Citizens Organizations; [hon.] Interracial Plaque Awarded from the Catholic Diocese; listed in Who's Who in Black, America 1974, Establishment of Doris Gilmer Scholarship Award in Zimbabwe, Africa; [pers.] Only one life it soon will past only what's done for Christ will last; [a.] Cleveland, OH

GILMER, WILLIAM D.
[b.] July 17, 1927, Kingsport, TN; [p.] William R. and Stella D. Gilmer; [m.] Carlene Kearns Gilmer, September 1, 1951; [ch.] Cindy G., Norman, Tad, Chuck, and Debbie; [ed.] Kingsport City Schools, Dobyans-Bennett High School, Duke University B.S., 1950, Forestry School, M.F., 1951; [occ.] Retired from paper and lumber industry as logging, wood handling and lumber sales; [memb.] Society of American Foresters, American Pulpwood Assoc, College Place U. Methodist Church, Boys Scouts of America, PTA President and Council Pres, U.S. Navy in 1940's, Scoutmaster 18 years; [hon.] Boss of the year 1975, Chairman of Harvesting Committee, A.P.A., Lifetime Membership in P.T.A., Lifetime Membership U. Meth., Founded Square Dancing Group in Brunwich, GA; [oth. writ.] Technical articles in journal of forestry and American Pulpwood Assoc., 30 prodigious Christmas Letters that are being bound to serve as our family history.; [pers.] I love folk songs and music and the land and people that produce them. My poem was inspired by a mountain fiddler, Claude Greer. I try to reflect a love for all folks and the beauty of nature in my writings.; [a.] Levoir, NC

GINGRAS, FLORENCE
[b.] November 23, 1938, Brooklyn, NY; [m.] Rudolph L. Gingras; [ch.] Jason S. Gingras; [ed.] C.W. Post College, Hofstra Law School; [occ.] Attorney, Retired; [hon.] Pi Gamma Mu, Phi Eta, C.W. Post Under-graduate non-traditional student academic achievement award in political science.; [a.] Hendersonville, NC

GINSBURG, BARBARA L.
[b.] July 11, 1942, Neustadt, Germany; [p.] Hans-Erich Leppin, Frieda Leppin; [m.] Jeter M. Watson, December 24; [ed.] U. of Hamburg, Sorbonne; UNC, Chapel Hill, N.C., Rice University; [occ.] Writer, Photographer, Journalist; [memb.] Hand Workshop, Richmond, VA, Virginia Museum of Fine Arts, Virginia Society of Photographic Arts, LACUS (Linguistic Assoc. of America/Canada); [hon.] Stipend "Rice Publ. Program, Student participant in Rice U. Studies in Photography, Houston Arts Council Grant; and many other awards; [oth. writ.] Poems and narratives; [pers.] Began as photographer, artist, and academic expressing (and doing research) on visual and verbal narratives and when to express just that, am particularly drawn to rhythmic progression, want to write short stories; [a.] Ashland, VA

GIOIA, ILONA J.
[b.] March 28, 1947, Germany; [p.] Jim and Ilona Barker; [m.] Anthony Gioia, June 4, 1971; [ch.] Nicholas (son); [ed.] Bladensburg Sr High 1965, BS Univ of MD 1969; [occ.] Founder/Ex Director Bio-Aerobics, Inc. Ilona Gioia taught studio arts, on the secondary level, in the Maryland Public School system, from 1969-1970. In 1971, she developed the studio fine arts curriculum at Queen Ann School - (A private prep school in Upper Marlboro, MD) and taught art there until 1977. In 1989 Ilona founded the Fitness Instructor Training Assoc (FITA) Training Program and wrote its extensive training manual; [memb.] American Heart Assoc, American Council on Exercise, Exec Safety Assoc, East Coast Alliance Aerobic Fitness Professionals, International Dance Exercise Assoc; [hon.] Special Recognition Award - American Heart Assoc - 1992 (raised $40+ M!); Gold Certificate Award - Int'l Dance Exercise Assoc - 1986; Outstanding Service - Bowie Recreation Council - 1989; Special Recognition Award - American Heart Assoc - So MD Div - 1991; Special Recognition Award - American Heart Assoc Maryland Affiliate - 1992; [oth. writ.] Many, but not published as yet.

GIRARD, MARCI
[b.] April 14, 1974, New York, NY; [p.] Roberta and Joseph Girard; [ed.] Bishop Eustace Preparatory, presently a Junior Midshipman, will graduate with a BS in Marine Transportation, as an Ensign in USNR, and with a USCG 3/M license; [hon.] Academic Awards; Varsity Crew for the Academy's nationally ranked Sailing Team; Received Sextant Award for an outstanding job of her Sea Year.; [oth. writ.] This is my first poem ever submitted, but I have been writing extensively as a hobby.; [pers.] I have spent a year traveling abroad on US flag merchant ships as a cadet.; [a.] Medford, NJ

GLASSER, POLLY
[b.] No! I just "grew"!, Methuen, MA; [p.] George and Annie Haddad; [m.] Donald F. Glasser, September 21, 1958; [ch.] Kenneth Bradley, Beverly Hope, Laurie Lynn; [ed.] Boston Univ, BS in BA; [occ.] Senior Manuscript Editor at Harvard Business School, Boston, MA; [memb.] St. Margaret's Church in Burlington, MA, Phi Beta Gamma Nu; [oth. writ.] Just zillions of humorous poems to friends, family, colleagues, professors, my dentist, my doctor, my husband, my kids...and you!!; [pers.] Life is full of heavy duty. Stop and smile. Enjoy its beauty! Hard work brings success, but "dazies". Sometimes lets us "smell the daisies"; [a.] Burlington, MA

GLENN, JASON
[b.] July 27, 1976, Tulsa, OK; [occ.] Student at Oklahoma State Univ; [oth. writ.] A personal compilation of poems titled Glimpses; [pers.] To know and to grasp those things that are not immediately convenient for the senses, acutes the senses and makes them sensitive enough to receive the unknown; [a.] Stillwater, OK

GODFREY, MARILYN MC GOWAN
[b.] August 8, 1923, Mexico, TX; [p.] CB and Lela Falling McGowan; [m.] Floyd Wilson Godfrey, March 23, 1951; [ed.] Bachelor of Arts and Master of Arts degrees - Sam Houston State Univ, Huntsville, TX; [occ.] Retired elementary music teacher; [memb.] Chamber of Commerce past president; United Fund, past president; [hon.] Citizen of the Year, 1977 and 1985; (past pres) Delta Kappa Gamma; Daughters of the American Revolution, Regent First United Methodist Church Missions Chairman, Administrative Board; Annual Conference Delegate; Staff-Parish Committee; District Steward; Choir Soloist; [oth. writ.] None, except other poems; [pers.] I try to express my faith in God and my love of life and concern for others in my writing; [a.] Gladewater, TX

GOLDING, HELEN L.
[Pen.] Jacobie Louise Meyers; [b.] September 1, 1962, Lincoln, ME; [m.] William E. Golding, January 14, 1984; [ch.] 2 boys - 7 & 8; [ed.] High School graduate; [occ.] Secretary / CNA; [hon.] My poem (Remember Me) was published in the Bangor Paper called (the Weekly) the 1st poem ever to be in this local paper for Bangor, ME on Jan 20, 1995. For a 5 yr old girl that died of Starvation by her mother in Nov 1994; [oth. writ.] I have written over 120 Lyrics poems on issues of child abuse. I have been published in the Amherst Society Poetry Book (Be careful); [pers.] I believe that children are our future. Someone has to stand up for their rights, in order for them to speak out. And break the silence of child abuse of any kind; [a.] Bangor, ME

GOLDMAN, BARRY
[b.] August 6, 1950, NYC; [p.] Pauline and Leo; [ch.] Brian R. Goldman; [pers.] I would like to dedicate this poem to my son Brian who has been loving and caring and given me much inspiration.

GOLDMAN, JACKIE
[b.] February 14, 1982, Brooklyn, NY; [p.] Vic and Hattie; [oth. writ.] A poem published in 1993 in an Anthology and in several newspapers and magazines; [pers.] As an only girl out of 5 brothers and only 12 yrs. old, I would like to say to everyone, dreams come true and never give up.;

GOLDTHWAIT, DAVID
[b.] May 22, 1970, Augusta, Georgia; [p.] John and Barbara Goldthwait; [ed.] B.A. English Lit. UCSC, B.A. Creative Writing UCSC 1992; [occ.] Office Manager at Health Software Company; [oth. writ.] Walking Down Golgotha, collection of poems; [a.] Santa Cruz, PA

GOLTON, DR. MARGARET A.
[b.] January 12, 1909, Cleveland, OH; [m.] Eugene G., April 15, 1934, deceased 12/77; [ed.] Case Western Reserve Univ, B.A. Mather College, M.S.W., SASS (Now Mandel), Ph.D. Mandel/SASS; [occ.] Social Psychotherapist, marriage counselor, parent guidance; [memb.] numerous; [hon.] Mather Congenial Citation for Outstanding Achievement, Melbourne Austria Poetry Society, Roll of Honor; [pers.] A lifetime for What is basic, what is universal in the human estate from which a planet at peace may be invented.; [a.] Euclid, OH

GOLTZ, JOSEPH FRANCIS
[b.] February 23, 1961, Phoenix, AZ; [p.] Eugene Goltz, Rosemary Goltz; [ed.] Lawrenceburg High School, Northern Kentucky Univ, Montgomery College, Rockville, MI; [occ.] Freelance Artist, Musician; [memb.] Valley Cruisers Car Club, East Coast Chapter; [hon.] Who's Who Among American High School Students, Hoosier Scholar, National Honor Society, Most Outstanding Artist Award Lawrenceburg High School; [pers.] Love God, love your neighbor - this is the stuff the universe is made of; [a.] Silver Spring, MD

GOMEZ, CHRISTOPHER J.
[b.] July 23, 1974, Denver, CO; [p.] Sammy and Mary Gomez; [ch.] Michael Chase Moloy; [oth. writ.] Several unpublished poems and short stories.; [pers.] Wrote this poem in a time a young lady broke my heart and took our child away. I don't have any hard feelings, though I would love to see him everyday.; [a.] Masa, AZ

GONZALES JR., ROY
[Pen.] Chapo; [b.] April 11, 1973, Roswell, NM; [p.] Roy H. and Sylvia Gonzales; [ed.] Foswell High, Eastern New Mexico University; [occ.] telerecruiter, United Blood Services; [memb.] Delta Epsilon Chi, Gateway Christian Church; [hon.] Various academic scholarships, Delta Epsilon Chi President, Marketing competition recognition; [oth. writ.] Several poems to personal friends.; [pers.] I get all my inspiration from Jesus Christ. Writing things that really touch people has always been a lifetime goal of mine.; [a.] Roswell, NM

GONZALEZ, MELANIE JOY
[Pen.] Yeppers; [b.] August 24, 1977, Sierra Madre; [p.] Louis and Sally Gonzalez; [ed.] Nogales High School; [occ.] Customer Service; [hon.] Honor Society, Honor Roll, Essay Contest (50 words or less); [oth. writ.] Essay contest (50 words or less) at Golf 'N Stuff. (was 12 years old); [pers.] I love writing creatively. I write my stories that I can use my imagination on. Children have a lot to do with influencing my writings.; [a.] West Covina, CA

GONZALEZ, TERESA D.
[b.] January 20, 1976, Los Angeles, CA; [p.] Valentine and Teresa Gonzalez; [ed.] Went to John Marshall H.S. and am now attending the University of California at Riverside.; [occ.] Student (1st year); [hon.] Graduated with honors from high school; [oth. writ.] I have written many poems including one in Spanish. I have also written a couple of stories (they are at a more horrific nature); [pers.] I dedicate this poem to the person in whose yearbook it resides. A person for whom I will always have an infinite amount of love.; [a.] Los Angeles, CA

GOOD, DANA C.
[Pen.] Sky --- Lovebug --- Rainbow; [b.] August 10, 1973, Aiken; [m.] James Mikel Good, Jr, June 14, 1993; [ed.] South Aiken High, Phillips Jr College; [pers.] I try to write about the things that effect the youth and the older generation of America. I write to reflect the goodness. Sadness and the evil in our world. I've been influenced by Jim Morrison and our history in America; [a.] Aiken, SC

GOOD, LISA
[Pen.] Lisa Conn; [b.] May 3, 1970, Kettering, OH; [p.] Wayne Conn, Katie Dougan; [m.] Todd Good, June 9, 1990; [ed.] Graduated from West Carrollton High June 1988, 2 years of Study at Wright State University; [occ.] Cosmetician at Kroger; [hon.] Award for being Editor of High School Creative writing publication. Various Awards for my school work, grade point average of 3.5 through school; [oth. writ.] Over 300 poems that remain unpublished.; [pers.] I would like to thank everyone who has encouraged my writing. I would also like to say a special thanks to Florence Cox, "Though you're gone, you're not forgotten.; [a.] Meammisburg, OH

GOODMAN, GALE
[b.] October 8, 1964, Philadelphia, PA; [p.] Alice and Kenneth Goodman; [m.] Timothy Stewart, Sr.; [ch.] Alicia, Kenny and Joey; [occ.] Homemaker and student; [memb.] Emlen Home and School Ass; [hon.] Educating Children For Parenting Service Award, Certificate of Service, Outstanding and Effective Services to Students and Teachers at Emlen School; [oth. writ.] Children stories for my children as they are learning to read; [pers.] If you write from the heart there is no wrong way, because God will lead you; [a.] Philadelphia, PA

GOODMAN, JOSHUA IAN
[Pen.] Ian Black; [b.] February 11, 1978, Dubuque, IA; [p.] Gregory George and Marilyn Kay; [ed.] Junior in high school, Central High School; [occ.] Dishwasher at Perkins Family Restaurant; [memb.] Boy Scouts of America; [hon.] Academic Excellence Award: May 11, 1994; Eagle Scout attained March 29, 1992; [oth. writ.] Publish regularly for magazine known as "Make Talk"; [pers.] I believe that life is only what you see it as. Life is poetry in motion, and so many blind themselves to that poetry by chaining themselves to every day problems. There is beauty in everything; [a.] St. Joseph, MO

GOODMAN, LAURA
[b.] August 1, 1924, Hampton, VA; [p.] Deceased; [m.] Charles E. Goodman, Rev., December 17, 1978; [ch.] Brenda, Edward, Sherian, Michael; [ed.] George P. Phenix High, Golden Gate Univ, AA, St Leo College, BA; [occ.] Retired; [memb.] The Int'l Assoc of Ministers' Wives and Ministers' Widows, Inc. New Elam Baptist Church (Church School Teacher), National Literacy Society; [hon.] Superior Performance Award - US Civil Service; [oth. writ.] None published; [pers.] May the good I do be nestled in the hearts of others and foster love, hope and encouragement.

GORDON, ROBERT
[b.] April 24, 1969, Belleville, NJ; [p.] Blanche I. Gordon; [ed.] State Univ of New York at Albany; [occ.] Contract Negotiator; [memb.] Museum of Natural History Assoc; [pers.] I believe that only true suffering and emotional pain can create a truly beautiful literary piece; [a.] Staatsburg, NY

GORDON, TINA
[b.] August 3, 1978, St. Louis, MO; [ed.] Lutheran High North; [pers.] Poetry can not just be read, it must be understood. Experienced...and absorbed. If not, it is simply senseless. Words on paper, having no affect on the mind or soul; [a.] Maryland Hts, MO

GORMAN, TODD ALAN
[b.] March 21, 1978, Houston, TX; [p.] Marilynn and Fred Gorman; [ed.] High school at Alexander Smith Academy; [occ.] Student at Alexander Smith Academy; [memb.] National Youth Leadership Conference, Key Club; [a.] Houston, TX

GOSTIN, TANYA
[b.] August 27, 1978, Fredonia, KS; [p.] Roy and Charletta Gostin; [ed.] Junior in High School; [occ.] Student; [memb.] Staff writer on the school newspaper; [oth. writ.] Several poems; [pers.] I try to put what I am feeling in my writing, I try to live by the quote "I may not control the wind, but I can control my sails."; [a.] Fredonia, KS

GOTT, ELIZABETH MARJORIE
[b.] May 17, 1983, Princeton, NJ; [p.] J. Richard Gott, III and Lucy Polland Gott; [ch.] Maurice Hawk School, K-1 Dutch Neck School, 2-3 Upper Elementary School, 4-6 (West Windsor-Plainsboro School System); [occ.] Student; [memb.] Math League 5th grade; [hon.] 5th grade class spelling bee winner's certificate; [oth. writ.] "A Witch's Pet," a story chosen for the Maurice Hawk Short Literary Magazine, The Hawk's Eye in 1990. "Inauguration" and "Should Kids Vote?" in 4th grade class newspaper, The Papciak Press on January 22, 1993.; [pers.] I like to write, read, draw cartoons and architectural plans. I wrote my poem, "Sunrise and Moonset" in honor of my wonderful grandfather, J. Richard Gott, Jr.; [a.] Princeton Junction, NJ

GOWALLIS, HEATHER
[Pen.] H. L. Davenport; [b.] September 6, 1970, Fairfax, VA; [p.] Richard and Vicki Davenport; [m.] Tom Gowallis, October 29, 1994; [ed.] Fallbrook Union High, Marshall University, WVA; [occ.] Proofreader/Editor, Global Associates, Arlington, VA; [memb.] Communications Society, Gymnastics Federation Alumni, Marshall University Alumni; [hon.] Honor Society, College Dean's List, Founding Member of The Marshall Communications Society; [oth. writ.] Several poems and screen plays including "The Bye-Cycle."; [pers.] I wish only to evoke emotions from my writings. Special people and places are forever.; [a.] Arlington, VA

GRAFFAM, AMANDA DAWN
[b.] August 22, 1982, Norway; [p.] Patricia Murphy, Mark Graffam; [ed.] Currently a 7th grader at Oxford Hills Junior High School; [occ.] Student; [memb.] I've taken jazz dance w/art moves for four years, continental math league, interest club; [hon.] I've been an honor roll student since 4th grade. Math award, music awards; [oth. writ.] Personal writings; [pers.] Through my writing I try to show people fears and emotional pain caused by others. I would like to help people be aware of the emotional pain they inflict on others; [a.] Harrison, ME

GRAHAM, MONETTE
[Pen.] M & M Graham; [m.] Larry D. Graham; [ch.] Christopher D. Graham; [ed.] W. S. High, Charleston Southern Univ, and Boston Univ; [occ.] Counselor; [a.] Kingsland, GA

GRANTHAM, CINDY
[Pen.] C.A. Grantham; [b.] July 14, 1959, Dallas, TX; [p.] Betty A. Grantham; [ed.] Lancaster High School 1973-1977, Univ of TX at Arlington 1977-1982; [occ.] Tennis Teaching Professional/Aspiring Author; [memb.] Tennis Competitors of Dallas; United States Tennis Assoc 1982-Present; United States Professional Tennis Assoc 1982-1992; [hon.] Elected to Grapevine/Colleyville Community Education Dept - Director of Advertising - Public Relations 1992 - Selected as a Loan Executive for United Way Campaign 1993; [oth. writ.] Several poems in which are unpublished. At present but awaiting opportunity; [pers.] I strive desperately to write poetry with feeling in which everyone can enjoy and be influenced. The simplest pleasures in life are the most complex to write about; [a.] Arlington, TX

GRAVES, RITA
[Pen.] Rita Palumbo Graves; [b.] August 9, 1950, Bainbridge, Georgia; [p.] Colonel (Ret.) Rocco Palumbo (USAF), Margaret Cloud Palumbo; [m.] Kenneth Phillip Graves, December 20, 1980; [ch.] Any Marie, Brandon Carter, Kimberly Denise; [ed.] Robinson High School, Bixby Business College, ISC Medical/Dental; [occ.] Homemaker; [pers.] We will pass this way but once. Therefore, any good we may do let us do it now, for we shall never pass this way again.; [a.] Elkins Park, PA

GRAVES, SHANA N.
[b.] January 29, 1975, Alkhobar, Saudi Arabia; [p.] Charles and Janice Graves; [ed.] Jakarta International School, Mississippi State University; [memb.] University Honors Council, Blackfriars Drama Society; [hon.] Phi Eta Sigma, Dean's List; [oth. writ.] Poems published in Honors Newsletter (UHP Chronicle), article published in Freethought Today.; [pers.] I write from my heart, giving life to the words within.; [a.] Ms. State, MS

GREEN, RONALD
[b.] October 2, 1918, England; [p.] Fred and Doris Green; [ed.] N.Y.U., G.I. Bill of Rights; [occ.] Retired; [memb.] American Legion; [pers.] I am glad about the National Library of Poetry. This Society needs the pure light of poetry as witness.; [a.] Brooklyn, NY

GREEN, SCOTT DUNCAN
[b.] July 21, 1970; [p.] William and Karen Green; [ed.] Binghamton Univ, class of 1993; [occ.] Youth Counselor Wyoming Conference Children's Home; [pers.] Through poetry I try to create images that takes life in the readers mind. My words don't really try to "say" anything; but at their best they alter the way readers see, hear and feel; [a.] Binghamton, NY

GREENWOOD, ROBIN
[b.] September 9, 1962, Redbank, NJ; [p.] Walter and Deanna Greenwood; [m.] Thierry Smith, October 16, 1993; [ed.] Freehold Twsp. High School Freehold Vocational School; [occ.] Beauty Consultant/Manager of Elizabeth Arden Cosmetics; [oth. writ.] A small collection of poems I've written since I was seventeen, which I treasure.; [pers.] I reflect my true feelings and emotions in all my poems. they are a part of me as well as all of me. They are all written to and about someone special who has touched my life.; [a.] Toms River, NJ

GREGG, ANGEL
[b.] February 24, 1976, Augusta, GA; [p.] Micha and Ralph Gregg; [ed.] East Anchorage High, currently University of Anchorage, AK; [occ.] File Clerk, receptionist; [hon.] Congressional Scholar, AWANA Leadership, Who's Who among American High School Students; [oth. writ.] Several poems, none published.; [pers.] My poems comes straight from the heart, I put all personal trauma into words, it helps me to deal with it.; [a.] Anchorage, AK

GREGG-RABBITT, TAMMY A.
[b.] March 4, 1967, Cleveland, OH; [p.] George M. and Shirley A. Gregg; [m.] Edward Rabbitt, October 30, 1993; [ch.] Megan Anne Gregg; [ed.] Parma High School, Tri-C Community College; [memb.] Cleve. Zoological Society; [pers.] My goal is to make mankind more appreciative of the world and animals around them. And to raise my child with an environmentally conscious attitude.; [a.] Cleveland, OH

GRESHAM, MARVIN
[b.] January 9, 1956, Chicago; [p.] Florence and Willie Gresham; [m.] Diana Marie Gresham; [m.] January 22, 1992, Latrice, Valerie, Trinnelta, King, Cherie, David Gresham; [ed.] Bowen High School, James N. Thorp Elementary; [occ.] Carpenter; [pers.] I search for the goodness in mankind and with these emotional feeling within. I wish with all my heart and help from God to find it. I'm motivated by God and self; [a.] Chicago, IL

GRETENCORD, JASON
[b.] July 9, 1981, Terre Haute, IN; [p.] Steven and Kathryn; [ed.] grade 7; [occ.] Student; [memb.] Drama Club; [pers.] This is my first poem. My poetry helps me sort the confusion of adolescence.; [a.] Terre Haute, IN

GRIFFIN, MATTHEW
[b.] October 24, 1966; [occ.] Broadcast Technician; [memb.] Army Reserve, NARTE (National Association of Radio and Telecommunication Engineers); [pers.] The pen is mightier than the sword, but not as fast.; [a.] Concord, NC

GRIFFIN, WETZEL, TAYLOR ANN PATRICIA
[Pen.] Patti Ann Griffin, O.G. Nanna; [b.] July 24, 1940, Milwaukee, WI; [p.] Thomas J. Taylor, Ruth A. McArthur; [m.] Lawrence P. Griffin; [ch.] David William Scott Arthur Wetzel; [ed.] Riverside H.S. University of Wisconsin, Milwaukee; [occ.] Writer; [oth. writ.] Several articles and poems of Americana Nostalgia published in Good Old Days and Reminisce Magazine.; [pers.] Never give up, no matter what obstacles there are or how old you become! Hang on to your dreams, with God's help and your willingness they will come true! I know; it happened to me. It can happen to you; [a.] Minneapolis, MN

GRIMES, SHARI LYNN
[b.] May 2, 1960, Washington, DC; [p.] Sallie D. Boicar and Earl C. Wright; [m.] Harry J. Grimes, Jr (Biff), April 24, 1987; [ch.] Tammie - 13, Amie - 11, Kellie - 6, Sallie - 3; [ed.] Lackey High School; [occ.] Child Care Provider; [memb.] Indian Head Baptist Church; [a.] LaPlata, MD

GROOMS, NAOMI R.
[b.] August 21, 1931, Cynthiana, OH; [p.] George and Callie Anderson; [m.] Elbert Grooms, Jr., August 4, 1950; [ch.] June, Beverly, Robert, Wayne, Jane; [ed.] Western High school; [occ.] Housewife; [pers.] I enjoy reading and writing about life's experiences. I always like to read things that create a picture in my mind. I hope my writing might act as a paint brush in the minds of other people.; [a.] Latham, OH

GROSEK, JACOB ROBERTS
[b.] April 6, 1982, Johnson City, NY; [p.] Robert and Patricia Grosek; [ed.] Attending Chenango Valley Jr High School; [occ.] Student; [oth. writ.] Promises - soon to be published in Songs on the Wind.

GROSSMAN, VETA F.
[b.] November 18, 1929, Sheridan, Wyo.; [p.] Julia A. and Author L. Barrett; [m.] John Grossman, November 25, 1948; [ch.] John A. and Madeline K.; [ed.] Grade and High School in Lodge Grass, Montana. One Year at Eastern Montana State, Billings, Montana majored in Journalism.; [occ.] Semi-retired, over 35 years as executive secretary/bookkeeper.; [memb.] Have a private pilot's license SEL; [pers.] Communication comes in many forms; poetry can be heart-to-heart.; [a.] Livingston, MT

GRUSS, DENNIS F.
[Pen.] "D"; [b.] August 25, 1949, Huntington, NY; [p.] Louise and Frederick Gruss; [ch.] Jason; [ed.] Life's Experiences; [oth. writ.] My feelings are my writings.; [pers.] Life is like clay make sure before you mold it and let it dry. It is the way you want it.; [a.] Deer Park, NY

GUERRERO, LYDIA
[b.] October 9, 1980, Fullerton, CA; [p.] Ismael and Bertha Guerrero; [ed.] Kofa High School; [occ.] Student of Kofa High School; [memb.] Drama Club, Renaissance Team; [hon.] Honor Roll; [pers.] I want people to stop taking life for granted. I want them to think twice before they use the word "tomorrow"; [a.] Yuma, AZ

GUGLIARA, SALVATORE
[b.] August 17, 1972, Brooklyn, NY; [p.] Ernesto and Catherine; [ed.] B.S. Business Marketing at Marist College, Poughkeepsie, NY, High School, Monsignor Farrell; [occ.] Clerk at the Commodities Exchange, Company name Dapco; [memb.] Sigma Phi Epsilon Fraternity; [pers.] Thank you Lord for everything in my life and to my inspiration, Sherri.; [a.] Staten Island, NY

GUNTER, DANNY W..
[b.] January 21, 1970, Kansas City; [p.] Earl W. Gunter, Vernetta R. Lungstrum; [ed.] Turner High School; [occ.] Inventory Control Clerk; Fleming Foods; [oth. writ.] It Doesn't Matter published in the Space Between; [a.] Independence, MO

GUSTKEY, NIKOLE ELAINE
[b.] September 24, 1978, Johnstown, PA; [ed.] Conamaugh Valley High School; [occ.] Student; [memb.] Sacred Heart Youth Choir, Drama club, Who's Who is American Math Honors, CVHS Band CVHS Chorus, St. John's Adult choir; [pers.] The poems that I write are from my deepest inner feelings; [a.] Johnstown, PA

GUTIERREZ, GARY M.
[b.] May 26, 1973, Manila Philippines; [p.] Raymundo and Ofelia Gutierrez; [ed.] Holy Rosary Academy, Far Eastern University, Manila, Philippines; [occ.] Office Assistant, Alpha Investment, Mgmt. Inc.; [hon.] Graduate with Honors; [oth. writ.] Poems published in our High School paper, and one of the literary articles in our school paper. (The Rosarian); [pers.] I wish to share my talent to everybody who's interested, and further develop my God given talent and extend my knowledge in poetry.; [a.] Elmhurst, NY

HADLEY, DEBRA
[b.] January 28, 1958, Mass.; [oth. writ.] Poems for special occasions. Poems of feelings. Poems in newspapers.; [pers.] I enjoy writing about everyday emotions, whether good or bad. I have been and will always be deeply touched by the life and works of Reginald Dwight.

HAECKEL, JAIME ANN
[b.] September 18, 1959, Indianapolis, IN; [p.] Joseph and Evelyn Carleton; [m.] John Haeckel, February 14, 1978; [ch.] Jason and Melissa Haeckel; [ed.] Hamilton High Los Angeles Portland Community College on The Oregon Coast; [occ.] Student of Psychology; [memb.] I am a member of Women's violence intervention support group Lincoln City, OR; [hon.] Dean's List, Oregon State Fair Winner for cooking, canning, baking, poetry and crochet baby dresses; [oth. writ.] Poetry state fair winner 1994. Writing published for local newspaper, and currently working on a research paper for publication; [pers.] I have been greatly influenced by my wonderful teacher Jane Thielsen, and many fine poets of the northwest and elsewhere.; [a.] Lincoln City, OR

HAGGERTY, MARK
[b.] August 8, 1948, Providence, RI; [p.] Donald M. and Jane C. Haggerty; [ed.] Associate in Arts - Comm Col of RI (1970), Shindler Fellow - Fuller Museum of Art - Brockton, MA (1985), BFA - Art Inst of Boston (1990), Graduate Level Human Development Course - Eastern Nazarene Col - 1992; [occ.] Poet/songwriter/illustrator; [memb.] Lifetime Charter Member - Intern'l Soc of Poets, New England Writer's Network, Boston Atheneum, Guild of Boston Artists, Harvard Univ Art Museums Secular Franciscan Order Holy Name Society, Air Force Sergeant, Assoc Legion of Mary; [hon.] NLP - "Sound of Poetry" and "Visions" tape series 93-94 "Outstanding Poets" 1994, "Best Poems" 1995 Editor's Choice Awards 93-94, Intn'l Poet of Merit Award (ISP) 1994, 1st prize No Greater Love Day Poetry Competition - Brockton, VA Hosp - 1977, Sparrowgrass Poetry Forum's "Treasured Poems of America"; [oth. writ.]

Children's Book "Slippy Sloth" Vantage Press 1993 (other books are being prepared). Numerous poems about love nature, friendship, spirituality and tranquility; [pers.] Ah! To pass for just a few dreamy moments into the world of "One Hundred Fine"; [a.] Brockton, MA

HAIGLER, MELINDA
[b.] August 16, 1979, Marshville; [p.] Karen and Edward Haigler; [ed.] Union Elementary School, East Union Middle School, Forest Hills High School; [memb.] Church and or the Flagline Honor Society; [hon.] None, I have never entered; [oth. writ.] none; [pers.] I am only 15 years old and write in my spare time or as a hobby.; [a.] Marshville, NC

HAITHCO, WILLIAM H.
[b.] February 7, 1923, Saginaw, MI; [p.] William J. and Lady Dabney Haithco; [ch.] Wm. H., II, Shari Lin Clarke, Rev. Jai S. Haithco; [ed.] BS Physiology and Pharmacology MSU BS Pharmacy U of MI; [occ.] Retired Pharmacist; [memb.] American Lung Association; Michigan Pharmacists Assoc; Delta College Committee of "100"; Univ of MI Alumni Assoc; Mid MI Dispute Resolution Center Board of Directors; Chairman, Saginaw County Parks and Recreation Commission (also its founder 1969); Chairman, Saginaw County Parks Fund Advisory Board; MI Pharmacists Political Action Committee; MI Pharmacy Foundation; [hon.] GD Searle and Co,/US Pharmacist Service to the Community Award; JC Penney Golden Rule Award; MI Parks and Recreation Distinguished Service Award; MI Credit Union Person of the Year Ronald Wilde Award; AH Robins Bowl of Hygeia Outstanding Community Service Award; Gordon F. Goyette, Jr Humanitarian Award; National Parks and Recreation Volunteer Service Award; American Lung Assoc of MI Volunteer Recognition Award; [oth. writ.] "The Sights and Sounds of Christmas"; [pers.] What a man does for himself will die with him; What a man does for others will live forever; [a.] Saginaw, MI

HAJJAR, KATERINA
[b.] February 13, 1984, Silver Spring, MD; [p.] Nick and Sophie Hajjar; [ed.] Elementary School 5th grade.; [occ.] Student at East Bradford Elem. in West Chester, PA; [pers.] I live at home with my mother, father, brother and two hamsters, I like to read, write, great at babysitting and loves to cook.; [a.] West Chester, PA

HALL, BETH
[b.] December 9, 1978, Mason City, IA; [p.] Allen and Kathryn Bencker; [ed.] Student at Robbinsdale Cooper Senior High school; [memb.] World Citizens Club at Cooper High School; [hon.] A-Honor Roll at Robbinsdale Cooper High School; [pers.] My writing comes straight from my heart, and I always strive to stand for what I believe in. I am always influenced by the events in my life.; [a.] Robbinsdale, MN

HALL, BONNIE
[b.] June 18, 1942, Lynchburg, VA; [m.] Thomas R. Hall, September 19, 1993; [ed.] B.A. Lynchburg College, M.A. Virginia Commonwealth University; [occ.] Teacher, English, John Rolfe Middle School; [memb.] Virginia Association of Teachers of English; [a.] Richmond, VA

HALL, CYNTHIA
[b.] March 26, 1977, Jacksonville, FL; [p.] Wylena and Herschel Hall; [ed.] High School; [occ.] Student; [memb.] Chess Club Burroghs High School, Ridgecrest, CA; [hon.] Sabor on Sabor Day for being Lt. in a JROTC

(Army) at North Atlanta High, Atlanta, GA; [oth. writ.] I do not have any other published.; [pers.] If at first you don't succeed, try, try again has been the best motto for me.; [a.] Ridgecrest, CA

HALL, DELIA G.
[b.] Richmond, VA; [p.] Henry Claiborne and Annie Duncan Gregory; [m.] George H. Hall.; [ch.] George Claiborne Hall and Gregory Harwood Hall; [ed.] Longwood College, B.S. Farmville State Teachers College, Graduate Work University of Virginia; [occ.] Housewife (retired public school teacher); [pers.] I write as a hobby. My poetry is a product of my experiences and associations with other people. Poetry writing gives me great pleasure.; [a.] King George, VA

HALL, JAMES E.
[b.] February 28, 1944, Sedalis, MO; [m.] Divorced; [ch.] James D. (24), Leslie (21); [ed.] BA - United States International Univ - Cal Western Univ - Humanity 1967 - San Diego, CA; Master of Divinity - Iliff School of Theology 1970 - Denver, CO; [occ.] Senior Pastor - Hemet United Methodist Church - Hemet, CA; [memb.] Rotary Int'l, 12 step programs; [oth. writ.] Unpublished poetry; [pers.] at 49 I found that I had the ability to write and express myself in new and different ways. Life is turning better at 50; [a.] San Jacinto, CA

HALL, LENA G.
[Pen.] Gee/Gen; [b.] December 10, 1939, Hale Co.; [p.] Mr. and Mrs. Jim Hall; [ch.] Toney, Tronda, Randy; [ed.] B.A. Elementary Education, Stillman College, University of Alabama (extra studies); [occ.] Teaching; [memb.] T.E.A., A.E.A., N.E.A., Member of Mt. Sinai Church in the Big Sandy Community; [hon.] Who's Who Among America's Teachers, Jackson State Teacher Hall of Fame representative from Englewood Elementary; [pers.] I strive for the "best," through thinking hard and working hard using my "special" gift.; [a.] Moundville, AL

HALL, MANDY M.
[b.] December 11, 1975, Rivendale, GA; [ch.] Mason Lee Hall; [ed.] Lovejoy High School; [occ.] Legal Secretary, James W. Studdard; [hon.] Lovejoy High School Honors, Lovejoy High School Senior Chorus Award, Golden Poets Award of 1992; [oth. writ.] Several poems and research articles for my school newspaper, including a personal biography.; [pers.] Life is virtuous; as long as you are.; [a.] Jonesboro, GA

HALL, THRASHER PAUL
[b.] September 1, 1910 (died: Feb 9, 1994), Chicago, IL; [p.] Thrasher Hall, Amalia Linda Hall; [m.] (dec'd) Victoria Hall, January 30, 1943; [ed.] MA Education 1948, MA English 1950 De Paul Univ; [occ.] (Early) Prof Engr Radio Engr CBS, High School Teacher Taft Chicago Public Schools; [oth. writ.] The Ballad of the Thirteen Million, 1940; First Satire on Men and Nations; Black Beauty Revisited (Highlights in Verse); Collections of Poems: 56 original poems accepted for Master's thesis (English) 1950; Maxima et minima II TCP Hall 1968; Alabastron 1973; Dragon Teeth (Booklet of poems and epigrams) 1985; Phantoms -- The Spinning Planets 1987; [pers.] (From thesis) "Here are admitted poems of escape. They are conscious efforts to produce beauty by idea, by image, by rhythm, and by rhyme...they are distillates of reality...They are keys to that world of Corot where old mossed Woods sleep, where forest streams laugh and swains sing...they are petite tableaux, brush strokes of color done with a pen. They are meant to be bound in jeweled morocco, to be read beneath Tuscan moons..."; [a.] Park Ridge, IL

HALVORSON, JEAN
[b.] December 20, 1956, Mpls, MN; [p.] Trygue Halvorson, Clara Halvorson; [ed.] South High, Calvary Bible College (both Mpls, MN); [occ.] Pastor, Majesty Tabernacle - Mpls, MN; Secretary - distribution center; [memb.] Evangelistic Missionary Fellowship (where received ordination -- ordination with Evangelistic Missionary Fellowship), Alcoholics Victorious; [hon.] National Honor Society, South High; Minnesota Office Education Association - 1st place Speech - Citywide; Dean's List - Bible School; [oth. writ.] Booklets copyrighted at Library of Congress - "Step up to Victory"; "Help Me, Lord, I Cannot Hold On Any Longer"; various Bible study sections, ministerial sermons for 13 years; [pers.] As a pastor - shepherd, I hope the scope of my poems shows people the great love and tenderness of the Great Shepherd. I have been challenged by writers of the Christian faith (Spurgeon, Finney, Lewis) and Helen Steiner Rice; [a.] Minneapolis, MN

HAMMELL, GRANDIN K.
[b.] May 6, 1912, Brooklyn, NY; [p.] Charles E. and Marian McQueen; [m.] Catherine E. Hammell (deceased) August 13, 1933; [ch.] Joan L. Peterson, Karen A. Brown, Grandin G. Hammell, Michael S. Hammel; [ed.] Red Bank, New Jersey High, University of Richmond, VA, American Academy of Dramatic Arts, Carnegie Hall New York; [occ.] Writer, publisher author; [memb.] Lady Lake, Florida Methodist Sigma Phi Epsilon Fraternity Founder Monmouth Players Rumson, NJ, Founder Diamond Bar, Calif. Player, Honorary Seabee, Former Board of Education Rumson, NJ; [oth. writ.] Woman of Destiny, Publisher Zebra Books, went into fourth printing, was on B. Dalton's best seller list, being considered for film. Christmas series syndicated by Tribune and Register syndicate. Published the Sure Way to Get Job Interviews. Two other novels The Boss's Lover and Loud Wails the Wind being considered by publishers.; [a.] Port Charlotte, FL

HAMMOND, BLANCHE BRINK
[b.] April 27, 1904, Killbuck, OH; [p.] Harold S. and Elva Brink; [m.] Harry S. Hammond, November 1931; [ch.] Connie, Harold, Nancy, Jane, Jon; [ed.] BS Wooster College, Wooster, OH, graduated 1926; [memb.] PEO, Central Christian Church - Marion, OH; [hon.] Awesome Mother (5), (18) grandmother, (17) great grandmother; [oth. writ.] Poems and short stories journals of family history covering 90 yrs (although legally blind, she has written beautifully for many yrs - she is a wonderful example to her family; [pers.] I believe one should never give up, do the best one can, and keep in touch with God; [a.] Pensacola Beach, FL

HAMPSON, PATRICIA A.
[b.] July 22, 1938, E. Stroudsburg, PA; [p.] William J. and Martha E. Fenimore; [m.] Erwin S. L. Hampson; [m.] November 1, 1959; [ch.] Ann, Diane, Susan, Kathy and Gary; [ed.] Meyers High School, Carnegie Inst. of Medical Technology, and Boston University.; [occ.] Floral Designer and Independent Tax Preparer; [memb.] First Presbyterian Church, former Deacon and Sunday School teacher, Director for 25 yrs. Youth Talent Program Sayreville Recreation Dept. Grange, Former 4H and Girl Scout Leader.; [hon.] The greatest award is having a kid I helped come back and say "Thanks Mrs. H."; [oth. writ.] Currently at work on a book of poetry and essays titled "Views From A Mind Out Of Step With The Times." Occasional poems written for the "Lamplighter."; [pers.] Some people march through life to the beat of a different drum, me, I seem to walk a line

that's slightly out of plumb. (Excerpt from "Out of step"); [a.] Sayreville, NJ

HANKIN, MAX A.
[b.] March 29, 1914, Philadelphia; [m.] Janet F. Hankin, October 31, 1937; [ed.] Completed one year of college and had to leave due to death of father.; [occ.] Retired farmer and developer; presently writing poems of which all earnings from the sale of the books are contributed to: The Perry Como Fund for Children at the Duke University Medical Center.; [hon.] U.S. Navy League Award, Greater Willow Grove Chamber of Commerce Exempler Award, Golf Club Champion, Hidden Springs Golf & Country Club, Meadowlands Country Club, Warrington Country Club; [oth. writ.] Sponsor, Ladies Professional Golf Association of America Tournament; [pers.] Max Hankin, Poet-Philosopher, an exceptional man who has led an extraordinary life. The verses in this collection are universal in scope, lending a quality of grace to the endeavors and sentiments of our everyday existence. Max puts much thought and imagination into his poems; people are often surprised when they learn that the characters and the situations portrayed in his poems are often based on facts and only sometimes based on fiction. [a.] Horsham, PA

HANKS, BONNIE MARIE
[b.] January 19, 1947, Poplar Bluff, MO; [p.] Paul Fleming, Ruby Fleming; [ch.] (1 daughter) Angie L. Hanks; [pers.] I dedicate this poem to my mother Ruby Marie Fleming, who was a loving and caring mother and grandmother. I deeply regret she passed away 10-5-94. With my warmest love, I dedicate this poem in her memory. Her daughter: Bonnie Hanks; [a.] Poplar Bluff, MO

HARARY, MERI M.
[b.] July 11, 1969, Brooklyn, NY; [p.] Al and Helen Harary; [ed.] B.A., English, Cum Laude, University of Hartford, Presently enrolled in graduate program in education; [occ.] Administrative Assistant, Yale University; [memb.] Principal Flute, West Haven Symphony; [hon.] 2nd place in poetry, University of Hartford's writing contest, 1991; Schoen Scholarship for Community Service and Leadership; Soloed (on flute) with the Connecticut Chamber Orchestra and the New Haven Youth Orchestra; [oth. writ.] Essays, short stories, plays and many poems; [pers.] I like to write poems that evoke universal feelings.; [a.] Hamden, CT

HARDEN, JENNIFER R.
[b.] September 29, 1973, New Orleans, LA; [p.] Joyce Harden; [ch.] Jamisha Harden; [ed.] Urban League Academy, Booker T. Washington High School, Sidney Colliar; [occ.] Homemaker; [hon.] Principals Honor Roll, Philis Wheatly Award, Presidential Academic Fitness Awards Program; [oth. writ.] Several poems in school year; [pers.] You can only get to better days once you make it through the night. Because no day will come until the dark of night; [a.] New Orleans, LA

HARDING, DEBORAH JEAN
[Pen.] D. Jean Harding; [b.] June 27, 1050, Columbus, OH; [p.] Bob and Marcia Doudna; [m.] Jim R. Harding, January 1, 1986; [ch.] Jesse James, Matt, Barry; [ed.] BA in Psychology, WTAMU, MA in Psychology, Counseling from WTAMU; [occ.] Counselor, Instructor, Musician, Songwriter, Poet; [memb.] American Psychological Assoc., Amarillo Women's Network, Psy Chi, Alpha Chi, American Assoc. of Clinical Hypnotherapist; [hon.] Alpha Chi Scholarship Award, Psy Chi Scholarship

Award, Psy Chi Scholarship Award graduated Summa Cum Laude with Honors in Psychology; [oth. writ.] Published songs: "Working Girl," "Tell Me Easy," "That Man," Poetry: "The Pasture," "Full Circle," "With All My Heart," in Different Path articles. "Volunteers," American Journal of Hospice Care, Biography; [pers.] Be open and aware! Life is being connected, simplicity rich with meaning. The gentle fall of a golden leaf may point the way in one's journey, stay alert.; [a.] Amarillo, TX

HARDY, MARGARET
[Pen.] Herritage McLewean; [m.] Harold Hardy, October 26, 1962; [ch.] James Hardy, Carol Hardy; [ed.] New Hanover High, HBC, UMC; [occ.] Part Owner of K & S Dist.; [oth. writ.] Local Newspapers, one book of poems in print.; [pers.] Always look for the positive, the good. Do your best, forget the rest.; [a.] Kinston, NC

HARE, MARYLOU
[b.] September 12, 1968, Tamuning, Guam; [p.] Herminio T. and Carmen R. Villapide; [m.] Marick O. Hare, September 12, 1991; [ch.] none; [ed.] Inaratan Jr. High; Oceanview High; University of Guam; [occ.] Data Entry for Western Pioneer Ins. Company; [pers.] I live each day with "love that lightens my hear" and I thank my husband Marick O. Hare who has encouraged me, but I also thank my parents who has also guided me every step of the way.; [a.] Hayward, CA

HARGETT, ANDREA
[b.] July 2, 1969, Enid, Oklahoma; [p.] Albert Lee and Gloria Butler; [m.] Delwin Hargett, April 29, 1989; [ed.] Helena-Goltry (Oklahoma) High School. Attended Phillips University; [occ.] Receptionist/Secretary, Professional Building, Pratt, KS; [memb.] American Quarter Horse Association; [hon.] High School Salutatorian, Horse Show Awards; [oth. writ.] A poem in South Wind, an area publication for local hospice.; [a.] Pratt, KS

HARLESS, SARA L.
[b.] August 10, 1981, Orlando, FL; [p.] Bill and Joyce Harless; [pers.] I am in 8th grade at Crystal River Middle School in Crystal River, Florida. My parents and language art teachers are very happy to see that I am a semifinalist. When I write poetry, I usually write about nature.; [a.] Lecanto, FL

HARMAN, ERIC
[b.] June 26, 1968, Pittsburgh, PA; [p.] Marge and Jim Harman; [pers.] The poem, passed away, is dedicated to the memory of Rick Renna, a kinder soul among men.

HARMON, ANTHONY W.
[b.] July 31, 1974, Salem, NJ; [p.] Deborah Harmon; [b.] July 31, 1974, Salem, NJ; [p.] Deborah Harmon; [ed.] Salem High School; [occ.] U.S. Army; [hon.] Army Service and National Defense Ribbon; [oth. writ.] Several poems published in high school newsletters.; [pers.] I've always enjoyed writing poetry. Now it's like a dream to have my work published, in where everyone can enjoy it.; [a.] Salem, NJ

HARO, ALANA LEE
[b.]; February 7, 1976, Salem, Oregon; [m.] Felix Robert Haro II, June 9, 1994; [ch.] None as yet; [ed.] Ontario High School, Ontario, Oregon; [hon.] Certificate of Merit from Taylor Publishing and Gayle Kerr. Certificate of Accomplishment from Larry Van Auken and Owaches. Honor Roll every quarter at O.H.S.; [oth. writ.] The End, published through Ontario High School's Owaches.;

[pers.] PN, I survive myself by expressing my emotions into a portal of poetry. P.S. There is a happiness for everyone, with faith and love there can be a smile in every heart.; [a.] Ontario & Salem, OR

HARRELL, JOSIE B.
[Pen.] Jone' Morrison; [b.] September 25, 1925, Boley, OK; [p.] Eddie L. Johnson and Lillie M.; [m.] Lester Harrell, February 23, 1970; [ed.] Boley High School, Langston Univ, San Jose State College; [occ.] Care giver; [pers.] I have always wanted to be a writer. At present I am enrolled in the Long Ridge Writer's Group. Hope my first manuscript will be superb; [a.] Albuquerque, NM

HARRIS, JANIE ROGERSON
[Pen.] Janie Bear, October 5, 1935, Martin County; [p.] Ethel and Gilbert Rogerson; [m.] Clay Winfield Harris, December 18, 1954; [ch.] Nannette Harris Stephenson (husband-JC Stephenson); Julia Nicole and Cameron (grandchildren); [ed.] 1-12 at Bear Grass School, 2 yrs at Martin Community College - graduated with second highest honors both schools; [occ.] Retired teacher assistant, Farm-wife and "Nanny" to my grandchildren; [memb.] Different farm organizations during school it was different titles too many to mention. Anything relative to art and music were foremost on my mind and membership; [hon.] In school honors were Beta Club, Monogram Club, "Princess Bear Grass". In my working as a teacher assistant for 19 yrs -- Tooth Fairy Queen at Dental Health Week; [oth. writ.] A poem about "Martin County" published earlier years in a book of poetry. I have written articles of my travels and the articles were published in our local enterprise paper in Williamston, NC; [pers.] My poems are about people or places dear to me. I have only one time to live and pass through this world. The best and most of anything I can ever do is to help people in my way - not to suite my equal half of whom 40 years of married life I have spent, but to help the people who need it; [a.] Williamston, NC

HARRIS, KYLUS
[p.] Emma G. Harris; [ed.] Mattamuskeet HS, Swan Quarter North Carolina; [occ.] Entrepreneur; [memb.] Le Detroit Baptist Church, Oxon Hill, MD; [oth. writ.] Poetry on T-shirts by Just a Phase, Washington, D.C.; [pers.] A change in life starts with us. And a touch of grandma's old ways; [a.] Oxon Hill, MD

HARRIS, MYRTLE PAULSEN
[Pen.] God's Love Myrtle Harris; [b.] April 19, 1929, Conn.; [p.] George and Sadie Kastner; [m.] Leonard Paulsen Sr., Donald Harris; [ch.] Diane, Leonard, Louise; [ed.] What the Lord has gave me, plus 8 grade in school; [memb.] Born Again Christian member of the Lords Family; [hon.] If I have any, it would be in the eyes of the Lord, May the Lord bless you all; [oth. writ.] Numerous poems; [pers.] In the front of my books I put down what I was praying about. The Lord gave me the words to all of my songs and poems. This is the work of the Lord, I'm just a worker of His. Different is what they called Him. Is in memory of Burley Rodgers. For He was one of God's Children; [a.] Vanzant, ME

HARSHBERGER, SANDY
[b.] November 30, 1941, Altoona, PA; [p.] Jack and Ethel Ramey; [m.] Donald T. Harshberger, February 20, 1965; [ed.] High school graduate, some college credits; [occ.] Executive Secretary Altoona Area School District; [memb.] Altoona Alliance Church (Deaconess); [hon.] Have won several poetry contests; [oth. writ.] The Up-

per Room, Progress Magazine, Progress Magazine, The Villager, Blair County Arts Festival Poetry Contest, "New Day", "The Night", "Spring Fever"; World of Poetry, "World's Best Loved Poems Anthology"; Blue Mountain Arts, Greeting Card "My Friend, On Valentines Day You Deserve to Know How Great You Really Are"....., "Best Friends Are Forever, "My Friend, I Don't Know What I'd Do Without You"; Whispers In The Wind, National Library of Poetry; The Saturday Evening Post; Reflections of Light, National Library of Poetry; [pers.] My philosophy is to live each day to the fullest and serve the Lord any way I can. I can be summed up in the Proverb "If of thy worldly goods thou art Bereft; and of thy slender store, two loaves alone to thee are left. Sell one, and with the dole, buy hyacinths to feed thy soul; [a.] Altoona, PA

HART, ELEANOR F.
[b.] October 8, 1939, Rockville, MD; [p.] Theodore and Ida Harris; [m.] Maurice Hart, August 15, 1965; [ch.] Cheryl, David, Jason; [ed.] Carver Sr. High, Eastern Michigan University; [occ.] Executive Secretary, Word Processor; [memb.] Heritage Pen Writers; Trinity Church Layreader, Lay Minister, Evangelism Commission and Vestryperson, N.A.A.C.P; National Honor Society; [hon.] Voice of Democracy Oratorical Pgm.; N.A.A.C.P 1st Place Distinguished Service Award; Award, Pride In Excellence; Featured in Jan/Feb 1992 Missioner Ser.; [oth. writ.] Currently writing first book, "Hushabye Baby"; several poems, none currently published (some poems have been published in church newsletters and work newsletters); [pers.] Give love to all and no one refuse.; [a.] Westland, MI

HASKINS, ROBERT
[Pen.] Bob Haskins; [b.] June 11, 1958, Monroe, MI; [p.] Helen Haskins-Stura and Howard Haskins; [ed.] Dundee Community Schools, Monroe Community College; [occ.] Senior Adjustor; [memb.] Tang So Do, Tae Kwon Do, Calvary Baptist Church; [oth. writ.] Several poems published in local newspapers, articles for Monroe Evening News and local church publications.; [pers.] I like to write from the heart. Some of the simple things never change they go un touch personal and spiritual.; [a.] Dundee, MI

HATCH, PAUL D.
[b.] December 22, 1946, North Platte, NE; [p.] Frank and Lydia Hatch; [m.] Christine, (divorced); [ch.] Lisa Marie, Andrew Franklin, Daniel William; [ed.] Univ of Nebraska Omaha; [occ.] Trichologist; [memb.] Viet Veterans of America; Nebraska Poets Assoc; [oth. writ.] "The Hazards of Fences" 1978 (poetry book). Several poems published in local newspapers, in addition to several poetry readings sponsored by Nebr Poets Assoc; [a.] St. Louis, MO

HATZ, MELANIE J. IRWIN
[b.] September 8, 1952, Joliet, Illinois; [p.] William B. Irwin, James Lackey; [m.] Donald Alvin Hatz, June 15, 1974; [ch.] David Alan, Deborah Lynn, Kiane Marie; [ed.] Minooka Community High School, Joliet Junior college; [occ.] Housewife, Mother Psych Readings, Poetry all occasions, cake decorating; [memb.] Parapsychology Club, Graphology Club, American Heart Assoc., Cancer Research; [hon.] Citizen of the Year 1969, various awards for charity work, cake decorating award, Montgomery Wards; [oth. writ.] Poems for any occasion, local newspapers; [pers.] I am but a yellow rose my friendship is waiting to be picked.; [a.] New Lenox, IL

HAUGHTON, MARGIE DUDLEY
[b.] December 5, 1921, North Carolina; [p.] Lewis and Tinie Tyson Dudley; [ch.] Robert and Daniel Haughton, Annel Haughton Williams; [ed.] A.B. East Carolina Univ., M.S. Samford Univ., A.A. (Advanced Study in Education U.A.B); [occ.] Retired Educator; [memb.] Canterbury United Methodist Church, Phi Delta Kappa; [oth. writ.] Short stories and essays (none published) ideas for novels an plays.; [pers.] Enjoy reading, esp. biography, autobiography, inspirational and mystery. I have four adorable granddaughters.; [a.] Birmingham, AL

HAUSAN, KENDRA
[b.] September 9, 1972; [p.] Lillie Hausan, Kenian Hausan; [memb.] 700 Club: The Christian Broadcasting Network; [pers.] This poem was written when I was experiencing a personal dilemma. This poem was inspired by and written as a dedication to God. It was written to encourage others that whatever situation they are facing, God wants them to know that he cares and is there to help them; even if he seems far away; [a.] Bronx, NY

HAYES, JUDITH
[b.] May 6, 1949, Culver City, CA; [p.] Stan and Rose Abramson; [m.] Michael L. Hayes, April 24, 1970; [ch.] Sasha and Annabelle; [ed.] 2 years college, sociology major at Pierce College, Certified Childbirth Educator of Bradley Method; [occ.] Writer, Editor, Educator, Wife, Mother, Public Speaker; [memb.] Church on the Way, Van Nuys, CA; [oth. writ.] Co-wrote and edited a book with Ray Breson, called "Create in me a Clean Heart" published by Thomas Nelson in 2/95.; [pers.] I love to write and to share, to give hope and faith to others. I have a strong belief in God which I am sure is a recurring theme in my writing and in my life.; [a.] Chatsworth, CA

HAYFORD, HOWARD J.
[Pen.] Cax; [b.] February 5, 1977, Akron; [p.] Howard and Sudi Hayford; [occ.] Student; [pers.] Life is a game meant to be played.; [a.] Kent, OH

HAYNES, ALICE
[Pen.] Alice R. Haynes; [b.] July 8, 1944, Miss.; [p.] Deceased; [m.] So, dearly; [ch.] Audrey 28 (computer), Allen 27 (Army), Lindsey 24 (nurse); [pers.] My child Leslie was killed 11/92 for no reason. The poems that I have written were for my boyfriend. Lord knows they were from my heart.; [a.] Chicago, IL

HEAD, BOB
[b.] July 9, 1952, Salinas, CA; [p.] C.K. "Bud" Miller, Julie Miller; [m.] Divorced; [ed.] Salinas High School, Hartnell College; [occ.] Southern Gospel Singer, Freelance Writer, currently employed as a Salesman; [pers.] "I consider my writing ability to be a Divine Gift. In writing: I attempt to share insights on life from both a spiritual and physical perspective"; [a.] Salinas, CA

HEATH, RAINY
[b.] August 4, 1978, Phoenix, AZ; [p.] Ted and Vicki Kimelman; [m.] Still looking; [ed.] Sophomore at North Canyon High School; [occ.] Student; [memb.] Peer Counselor; [hon.] Dean's List; [pers.] I've been writing poems since I was six. I am now 16 and I will continue writing till I can no longer lift my hand. [a.] Phoenix, AZ.

HEERING, WILLIAM ARTHUR
[b.] February 18, 1948, El Paso, TX; [p.] Henry and Jan Herring; [m.] Kay K. Herring, June 10, 1972; [ch.]

Kindra, Teresa, Carolyn, Joanna; [ed.] BA, Texas A&M University, 1971; [occ.] Artist; [memb.] President, Knickerbocker Artists, New York; [hon.] Nominated in 1993 by the Governor of Texas for a Presidential Appointment to become the Chairman of the National Endowment for the Arts; [oth. writ.] Author of book "The Wonderful Madness of becoming a horse of a different color" (Red Tree Pub., Co., Box 223, Clint, TX 79836, 915-852-1913; [pers.] I live and work by the light of the bright morning star.; [a.] El Paso, TX

HEFFNER, RAY GEORGE
[Pen.] "Kool Ray"; [b.] November 10, 1937, Philadelphia; [p.] Ida and George Heffner; [m.] Joanne Lena Morreale, September 7, 1957; [ch.] Ray, Tony, Joe, Joanne, Lisa, Charlotte; [ed.] North Catholic 5 yrs., Apprentice School for Electrician; [occ.] Electrician, Construction; [memb.] "Warlock's M.C." 1%er "W.F.F.W" Life Time Member, "Elfis and James Dean"...Member; [hon.] Most likely not to succeed; [oth. writ.] Several poems I write to Lady Friends, people in need.; [pers.] "Make someone happy," "Take time...to make time" Sad and lonely poems; [a.] Philadelphia, PA

HEIDI, RIMANICH
[b.] March 13, 1945, Gdansk, Poland; [p.] Eva and Georg Bludau, Germany; [m.] Rudolph Rimanich - a born New Yorker, June 30, 1973; [ch.] Michael; [ed.] In Germany, equal to High School and two yrs college in the USA. Worked as a Medical Assistant in Germany; [occ.] Living since 1982 here in the USA and working as Nurses Aid; [oth. writ.] A few poems published in German newspapers; [pers.] I always loved to read and write poetry. For me, writing a poem is the expression of my innermost feelings and thoughts as well as my search for an answer to the meaning of Life; [a.] Middle Village, NY

HEIFNER, JANET RAE
[b.] September 15, 1971, Okinawa; [p.] Marvin and Carol Heifner; [ed.] 1994 graduate of Southwest Missouri State University (SMSU) degree in psychology and bio-medicine; [occ.] Psychologist Technician; [memb.] (SMSU) Southwest Missouri State University Psychology Club, Mountaineering Society, Vice President of SMSU Taekwondo Club; [hon.] National broadcast winner, VFW Speech Winner, I have had the honor of lecturing for the health classes of Southwest Missouri State University; [oth. writ.] "Tidal Wave" published, "Sea of Love," published "Guidance," "Friendship;" [pers.] I want to be able to do what I do best, and not have to stop until I've made a difference. I have to write what I feel because I could never say it out loud.; [a.] Springfield, MO

HELBERG, EDNA
[b.] November 14, 1916, Sioux Falls, SD; [p.] Earl and Anna Thompson; [m.] Melvin G.F. Helberg (deceased), November 3, 1934; [ch.] David W. and Judy Ann Benson, 4 grandchildren - 6 great grandchildren; [ed.] Grade school - high school - some college courses; [occ.] Retired from NW Bell. Supervisor; [memb.] National Travel Club, AARP, Telephone Pioneers, Life Goes On Group - Methodist Church Groups; [hon.] So far only thanks from friends and family as this is the first I've entered in competition; [oth. writ.] Poems for great grandchildren using letters in their names. Poems honoring neighbors and friends - spur of the moment poems at parties; [pers.] I like light hearted poems and complimentary; [a.] Sioux Falls, SD

HELMBRECHT, HEIDI
[b.] September 27, 1980, Salem; [p.] John and Jean Helmbrecht; [ed.] High School Freshman; [memb.] Student Council, Health Careers Club, Drama Club and Walnut Street Journal; [hon.] American Legion Medal; [oth. writ.] Life's Lesson which was published in Anthology of Poetry by Young Americans.; [pers.] I give all my love to my mom, dad, grandparents, Natalie, Michelle, and everyone else who has supported me through the years.; [a.] Salem, NJ

HELMERICK, GREGORY ALAN
[Pen.] Greg Helmerick; [b.] Larry and Sharron Helmerick; [ed.] Tucson High School, Red Rocks Community College; [hon.] National Honor Society; [oth. writ.] Several unpublished poems; [pers.] Nature and emotions play the largest role in my writings. I often combine the two; [a.] Conifer, CO

HENDERSON, EVELYN L.
[b.] April 19, 1951, Fresno, CA; [p.] Lem and Louise Reese; [m.] Patrick Henderson; [ch.] Duncan Jones, Kyle Jones, Sara Henderson; [ed.] Fresno High School, Fresno City College; [occ.] Instructional Aide, Special Day Class at Sierra High School; [memb.] Sierra Lutheran Church; [hon.] Dean's List High Honors AS Degree in Child Development; [oth. writ.] None, 1st attempt.; [a.] Auberry, CA

HENRY (II), RONALD R.
[Pen.] Ron Henry; [b.] October 10, 1981, Marlton, NJ; [p.] Ronald R. Henry, Sr, Deborah L. Henry; [ed.] Bell Oaks Upper Elementary School, Bellmawr, NJ; [occ.] Student; [memb.] Bellmawr Baseball Little League; Bellmawr Tigers Football; Academically Talented Class; Bell Oaks Chorale; Bell Oaks Band; [hon.] Honor Roll Student for last 3 yrs; DARE Program Awards; Spelling Awards; [pers.] My poem ("As I stand here in Heaven") is dedicated to my Poppi (William F. Henry) with everlasting love and remembrance; [a.] Bellmawr, NJ

HENSON, PATRICIA SUSAN
[b.] May 10, 1944, Dallas, TX; [p.] Joseph and Minnie Hart; [m.] Richard Douglas Henson, September 3, 1961; [ch.] Theresa Davis, Richard Henson Jr., Bryan Anderson; [grandch.] Joshua and Beau Davis; [hon.] My good friends; [oth. writ.] Parables and greeting cards for friends and family.; [pers.] To do unto others as you would have them do unto you.; [a.] Keizer, OR

HERNANDEZ, JANETTE E.
[b.] February 10, 1939, Calestine, IL;[p.] Joy Dennis and Frances Dennis Powers; [m.] Henry G. Hernandez, August 15, 1961; [ch.] Rowena Poirrier, David; [ed.] Robinson High, Connet Hernandez Barnes Hospital School of Nursing; [occ.] Registered nurse, Pasadena, TX; [memb.] Austin Ave. Baptist Church; [pers.] My life's greatest influence has been my mother, who's every act and gesture was punctuated by a "just right" and mixture of courage, kindness and grace. Although departed from this life. She lives on the hearts of those who's lives she so deeply touched.; [a.] Pasadena, TX

HERSEY, LINDA D.
[b.] August 18, 1945, Fairfield, OH; [p.] Marshal V. and June H. Hersey; [ed.] Dreux American High (France); Cortez High (Arizona); Northern Arizona University (B.S./Communications) American Management Assoc. and Future Enterprises, (Info. Technology Education); [occ.] Editor/Publishing; [memb.] American Women in Radio and Television; Broadcasters Promotion Assoc.,

USCC/NCCB Personnel Relations Review Board; Past State Chair Nevadan's for Equal Rights; [hon.] National Journalism Honorary, Alpha Phi Gamma,; Honors Program NAU; [oth. writ.] Several poems published in newspapers; wrote daily newspaper column for 2 yrs. in "Las Vegas Review Journal," contributing feature writer to local newspaper.; [pers.] We should try to remember to walk softly among the wonders of the earth, taking only that which we replenish and balancing life with the flow of life. For we are merely the caretakers.; [a.] Columbia, MD

HERSHEY, KARMEN
[b.] January 7, 1969, Monticello, IA; [p.] Dennis and Sandy Bayne; [m.] George Hershey, Jr., September 30, 1989; [ch.] Cavan, Nathan, Adrienne; [ed.] Monticello High, Hamilton Business College, currently attending Kirkwood Community College; [occ.] Part time student; [memb.] Education Majors Club; [hon.] Graduated with honors from high school and from Hamilton Business College; [oth. writ.] I have only written for my own family and my own personal pleasure.; [a.] Center Point, Iowa

HESTAND, BRANDY J.
[b.] April 18, 1979, Leavenworth, KS; [p.] Mattie Fischer, Darryl Hestand; [ed.] I am currently in the 9th grade; [occ.] Student; [oth. writ.] "Insecurity" has been my only entry, but I have many other poems; [pers.] I believe you can never really find happiness until you recognize your own true feelings; [a.] Olathe, KS

HIGHAM, MARILYN S.
[Pen.] Sybil Brown; [b.] September 14, 1941, Tolland County, Conn.; [p.] James and Dorothy G. Brown; [m.] Deceased John Lawrence Higham, December 14, 1964; [ch.] Lars Christopher Higham; [ed.] Hodge Podge, High School Graduate, Southern Conn. State College, Housewife, Mother, Educator member of National Library of Poetry; [occ.] Retired; [oth. writ.] I believe infants are born of defined sex and combined gender until disturbed, that all children believe in goodness and in justice and, for the sake of justice should be educated. I like four line poetry.; [pers.] One love for life, whether husband or wife, leaves space for a friend and, defense against the gore.; [a.] Seymow, CT

HIILSMEIER, DENISE
[b.] April 19, 1977, Clifton, TX; [p.] Don and Debra Hillsmeier; [ed.] Currently a senior at Morgan High School; [occ.] Student; [pers.] I've written poetry for several years and would like to have a book published someday.; [a.] Hico, TX

HILL, BEULAH MAE
[b.] January 17, 1941, Dunn, NC; [p.] Lillie and John Spears; [m.] Rudolph Hill, December 29, 1963; [ed.] Harnet High School in Dunn, NC and Essex County Tec. in Newark, NJ; [occ.] Housewife; [memb.] Franklin-St. John's United Methodist Church, a member of the United Methodist Women; [hon.] Certificate of Credit Essex County Vocational School (Nurse's Aide); [oth. writ.] None, this is my first writing; [pers.] To try and give, as much love and express love in all my writings that I can, and why not! Love is free.; [a.] Newark, NJ

HILL, VALERIE
[b.] February 2, 1955, Cleveland, OH; [p.] Mary (deceased) and Benjamin Hill; [m.] Rev. Charlie Hill, Jr., May 10, 1975; [ch.] Erik, Andrea, Sondra, Tiffany Charlie (C.J.); [occ.] Mother, homemaker, minister's

wife, caregiver, writer; [oth. writ.] Encouragement to you inspirational writings; [pers.] I look forward to a time when people are not judged by the color of their skin but by the content of their heart and minds. Too many times we look at things as black and white, but God made us all in living color. So we should learn to live together and love one another; [a.] East Cleveland, OH

HINGSON, JUDITH NOEGEL
[Pen.] Judy; [b.] November 12, 1956, Lake City, FL; [p.] Berkley L. and Atma Kennedy Noegel, Mr. and Mrs. B.L. Noegel; [m.] Henry Hingson, September 25, 1993; [ed.] High School, (Columbia High) attending College through correspondence, ICS; [occ.] Medical Clerk; [memb.] AGE (Union) through work.; [pers.] I strive to reflect hope and joy of mankind in my writing. I have been greatly influenced by the elderly who are confined to nursing facilities.; [a.] Live Oak, FL

HOBSON, MILDRED
[b.] November 9, 1945, Brooklyn, NY; [p.] Kenneth Hodge, Doris Hodge; [m.] Francis Hobson, September 10, 1978; [ch.] Katherine, Mary, Frank, Kenneth; [ed.] HS of Fashion Industries, Univ of Texas at El Paso (UTEP); [occ.] English major/creative writing, Educ minor, UTEP Sr., grad May 1995; [memb.] The IO Foresters, St. Stephen Catholic Church, Rutus Magazine on Campus (UTEP); [pers.] I attempt to address the importance and worth of every human being in my writing. I have great admiration for the satirical writers of the 18th century during the time of the Enlightenment; [a.] El Paso, TX

HOFFMAN, DEBORAH MARIE
[b.] February 13, 1960, Rochester, MN; [p.] Donald and Margaret; [occ.] Licensed Practical Nurse; [oth. writ.] Several other poems; [pers.] "A Birthday Wish For Adam" was written in loving memory of my nephew. Adam so enriched my life. Born 11, 1987, he died May 9, 1993 hours after a tragic backyard accident. I thank God for blessing my life with Adam, and for the gift of self expression I have discovered. My poetry has enabled me to share my innermost feelings and to reach out to others.; [a.] Rochester, MN

HOFFMAN, SCOT
[b.] December 21, 1970, Aiken, SC; [p.] Patricia Hoffman; [occ.] Assistant Operator for Trumbull Asphalt Division of Owens Corning Fiberglass; [pers.] Being a man and a blue collar worker, poetry gives me an emotional outlet and a chance to ponder many things. Some foolish, some serious; [a.] Medina, OH

HOLDEN, WILLIAM J.
[Pen.] Bill Holden; [b.] August 30, 1971, Binghamton, NY; [p.] Frederick and Patricia Holden; [ed.] Chenago Valley High School, Broome Community College, Binghamton University; [occ.] Production Assistant, WMGC, TV34, Binghamton, NY; [memb.] American Bowling Congress (ABC); [hon.] Dean's List; Blue Ribbon, Arnot Art Contest, 298 Game Ring, American Bowling Congress; [oth. writ.] Two vignettes published in a campus literary magazine.; [pers.] Writing creatively reminds me that I am alone. That's what we are in life; alone.; [a.] Binghamton, NY

HOLDER, PENELOPE E.M.
[Pen.] Maxine Dagley; [b.] January 29, 1936, India; [p.] Maxwell and Joan Perkins; [m.] Maxwell R. Holder, Jr, October 31, 1992; [ch.] Nicola, Kimberly, Michael, Elizabeth; [ed.] 2 yrs college--English Literature; [occ.]

Executive Secretary; [memb.] Beta Sigma Phi, Rosewell Historical Society, Rosewell Arts Alliance; [hon.] Speech Ntn'l Poetry Contest 1954; [pers.] To be the best I can be as a person, mother, wife, friend and live one day at a time; [a.] Roswell, GA

HOLLAR, LAURA
[Pen.] Laura; [b.] February 5, 1968, Asheville, NC; [p.] James Robinson, Shirley Cox; [m.] Alan Q. Hollar, April 13, 1991; [ch.] James Michael, Laramie Quenton; [ed.] Morristown Hamblen High School East; [occ.] Housewife; [oth. writ.] Several other poems unpublished, that I would like to have recognized; [pers.] I started writing home-made birthday cards for family members, and that led me to start writing poems of my inner feelings and experiences; [a.] Weaverville, NC

HOLZMAN, ADAM
[b.] September 23, 1968, Long Island, NY; [m.] Cheryl Ann Holzman, August 11, 1990; [ch.] Scott Joseph; [ed.] Barry Univ, BS in Elementary Education; Nova Univ, MS in Elementary Education; 1st year student, Doctoral Program in Curriculum and Instruction, Florida International Univ; [occ.] Professional Educator, Crestview Elementary School, Miami, FL; [memb.] Association of Supervision and Curriculum Development, Impact II Teachers Network, United Teachers of Dade, Florida Education Association/United, American Federation of Teachers; [hon.] Dade County Public Education Fund/Impact II Grant, Citibank Success Fund Grant, Finalist for College Student of the Year, as selected by Florida Leader magazine; [oth. writ.] "Opera Ghost Writing" Teacher Resource Guide, published by Impact II Teachers Network, based on "The Phantom of the Opera"; [pers.] I would like to thank Cheryl and Scott, Joe and Carole Palmese, and Joe and Diane Giliberti for their constant support and encouragement. I love you; [a.] Fort Lauderdale, FL

HOOPENGARDNER, LISA JO
[Pen.] M. J. Worth; [b.] May 23, 1965, Pt. Pleasant, NJ; [p.] Joseph and Helen Hoopengardner; [Fiance] Donald Worth; [ch.] Joseph Lorenzo, Michael Joseph, Steven Tyler, Nicole Kristen; [ed.] Toms River High School North; [occ.] Full time mom; [oth. writ.] My own personal poem; [pers.] The poem that's printed is my dedication to my son whom past away. He was a very sweet kind hearted little boy full of love. This is just one of many ways for me to tell him, "I love you"; [a.] S. Toms River, NJ

HOOTMAN, JENNIFER
[b.] July 16, 1973, Peoria, IL; [p.] Gary and Lynda Hootman; [ed.] Morton High School, Illinois Central College, Bradley University; [occ.] Student; [hon.] Who's Who Among American High School Students, All-American Scholar, Dean's List, Phi Theta Kappa, Phi Kappa Phi, Phi Alpha Theta, Gamma Beta Chapter; [pers.] Do not conform any longer to the pattern of this world, but be transformed by the renewing of your mind. Rom. 12:2; [a.] Morton, IL

HOPKINS, OMAR F.
[b.] December 27, 1956, New Castle, IN; [p.] Robert C. and Betty I. Hopkins; [m.] Cathy D. Hopkins, June 29, 1990; [ch.] Brittany Danielle Hopkins; [ed.] Graduated Hagerstown Jr./Sr. High, Hagerstown, IN; [occ.] Dietary Driver, Richmond State Hospital, Richmond, IN; [memb.] None; [oth. writ.] Dust on the Bible, St. Mary's Catholic Church, Richmond, IN; Two poems written for funerals of family members; Christmas poem published

for my mother in local newspaper during my military service.; [pers.] The poem that you have read is dedicated to my loving wife and my first born child. May we have many more.; [a.] Richmond, IN

HORN, ERNA
[b.] January 1, 1964, Emmer, The Netherlands; [p.] Ewold Horn and Aalderika E.M. Horn-Huls; [ed.] G.S.G. Emmen, M.T.S. Vakschool Schoonhoven both in the Neverlands; [occ.] Silversmith, Traveller; [oth. writ.] I have always found myself being captured by words, only recently have I discovered the fascinating process and joy of releasing my own thought journal writing and poetry.; [pers.] The most important strength in my life, instilled by my family and 30 years of living, is this deep, deep, love and respect for mother natures abundance. I reach out and share this feeling is what I have to do.; [a.] Brookline, MA

HORNETT, THOMPSON
[b.] August 21, 1975, Tahlequah; [p.] Judy Tinker, Mother; [ed.] Muskogee High, Haskell Indian Junior College; [memb.] Cherokee National; [a.] Muskogee, OK

HORTON, ROXANNE MARIE
[b.] May 23, 1967, OK; [p.] Elias and Linda Zietounce; [m.] Shawn Horton, December 25, 1984; [ed.] B.A. Criminal Justice, pursuing; [occ.] U.S. Army, Artist; [memb.] N.R.A.; [hon.] President's List three times at Mira Costa College; [oth. writ.] Short story published in "Tidepools" a literary journal in Southern, CA.; [pers.] Those who seek answers to their questions believe they are wise, those who question the answers are the wisest of all, they admit how little they know.; [a.] El Paso, TX

HORWITZ, WILLIAM
[b.] January 10, 1946, St. Louis; [p.] Harold and Henrietta Horwitz; [m.] Abby Klein, August 1, 1971; [ch.] Harris Saul Horwitz, Pallas Hannah Horwitz; [ed.] St. Louis Country Day, Harvard AB 67, Yale M Phil '69, Phd. '71; [occ.] Treasurer Blumstein's Brides House; [memb.] Harvard Club of St. Louis, Yale Club of St. Louis; [hon.] Woodrow Wilson Fellow, John Harvard Honorary Scholar, Yale Univ Fellow Assoc Professor, Dept of Classics, Univ of Oklahoma (retired); [oth. writ.] Numerous articles on the Hebrew Bible, Canaanite Scribal Practices, and the history of writing; [pers.] I strive to increase my understanding of humanity and to appreciate the beauty that surrounds me. Robert Frost has influenced my poetry; [a.] St. Louis, MO

HOUGHAM, DUANE FREDERIC
[b.] January 1, 1916; [p.] Grover Cleveland and Edna Etta Miller Hougham; [m.] I am a bachelor, never married; [m.] None; [ed.] Graduated Ft. Collins High School 1934, Bachelors Degree, Colo State U. 1934, degree was in Botany, Masters Degree, Colo. State U. in Chemistry.; [ed.] Have taught in grade schools and high schools, throughout the country, taught Chemistry at Florida State Univ., Utah State Univ. and Colo. State Univ., traveled to China, Japan, Taiwan, Honolulu, Poland, Turkey; [memb.] Methodist Church, Toastmasters, Senior Writer's Club in known as International Center of CUS; [pers.] Read your Bible, love your neighbor, get rid of drug and alcohol and act like a human being rather than some impudent monkey.; [a.] Ft. Collins, CO

HOUNSHELL, MELANIE LYNN
[Pen.] Nan Butler; Myrtle Hayes; [b.] April 26, 1955, Zanesville, Ohio; [p.] Glen H. and Verna Jean Ash; [m.]

Bob L. Hounshell, October 14, 1989; [ch.] Carrie Jo Hounshell, Sarah Lynn Hounshell, Stepchildren; [ed.] Terre Haute South Vigo High School, Indiana State University BA & MS; [occ.] Library Media Specialist, Institute for the Study of Developmental Disabilities, Bloomington, IN; [memb.] AIME (Association for Indiana Media Educators); GSA (Girl Scouts of America); AFBF (American Farm Bureau Federation Church of Christ; [hon.] Phi Kappa Phi; [oth. writ.] A few poems published in local church newsletters.; [pers.] I have been greatly influenced by the western writers, Zane Grey and Louis L'Amour. I am a great lover of nature and the wilderness, and feel most at home when out-of-doors.; [a.] Orleans, IN

HOUSTON, LAURA C.
[Pen.] L. C. Houston; [b.] December 1, 1948, Cambridge, MA; [p.] Arthur and Elizabeth Di Stasio; [m.] Henry (Sam) Houston, February 2, 1970; [ch.] Angelique Caroline, Martinique Ann; Grandson, Samuel S. Melton; [ed.] Cambridge High and Latin, Wright State University, Central Missouri State University; [occ.] Secretary, Treasurer Houston Appraisal Services, Inc.; [memb.] Literacy Volunteers of America; [oth. writ.] One poem published in, Today's Great Poems.; [pers.] My children and grandchildren are a gift I cherish. They have been my inspiration and encouragement to expand my horizons.; [a.] Shalimar, FL

HOWARD, WANDA
[b.] July 23, 1960; Fayetteville, NC; [p.] Margaret Koonce; [ch.] Sara Ann; Seventy-First Senior High, Barclay College, ICS, [memb.] North Shore Animal League, American Cancer Society; [oth. writ.] Several poems, unpublished; [pers.] As a teenager, I began writing poems over the years, my writing has served as a kind of "release" for me; [a.] Modesto, CA

HOWELL, MARY LOU
[b.] November 16, 1934, Boca Grande, FL; [p.] Clarence R. Kohn, Mellie T. Kohl; [m.] Carroll J. Howell, April 4, 1980; [ch.] Mellie, Steve, Allan, Jimmy, Laura; [occ.] CNA; [pers.] What I want for the person that reads this poem is to ponder on the words lonely road. An let lash of us do some road construction and make this lonely road a super highway to Jesus.

HUBBARD, EVERETT R.
[b.] March 10, 1956, Baltimore, MD; [p.] Claudie and Juanita Hubbard; [ch.] Tiffany M. Hubbard; [pers.] I'm currently writing a book titled "The Sensitivity of a Man", which contains thoughts, prose and poems about life, my interaction with God, Myself and Women. If there are any publishers interested in reading my manuscript they can contact me. I like to end by saying, "The light of love seeks not the heart which hides behind the shadow of it's own despair. For love doesn't want to find those who don't want to be found"; [a.] Baltimore, MD

HUDDLESTON, ELSIE WINFRED
[Pen.] Winfred Huddleston; [b.] June 18, 1920, Gallatin, TN; [p.] Bessie Wagoner and Andrew Carter; [m.] Roy Lee Huddleston Sr. Deceased, August 9, 1942; [ch.] Roy Jr., Andrew, Steven, Marc, Nancy, Diane; [ed.] Gallatin High School, Lebanon Beauty Institute, Active life as busy homemaker.; [occ.] None, single, retired, widow; [memb.] Tenn, Extension Homemakers, Carroll Club; Member Cedar Grove Baptist Church, Women's Missionary Society; [pers.] I would like for people being aware of the Lords beauty and creation, life being short not to be ready, also this poem and others I may write will give hope to many.; [a.] Labanon, TN

HUDDLESTON, KENNETH EDMOND WOLKE
[b.] January 15, 1967, New Albany, IN; [ed.] BS Univ of Maryland Univ College; [occ.] US Postal Service Annapolis, MD; [hon.] Naval Achievement Medal, Southwest Asian Service Medal with Bronac Star. Golden Poet Award 1989 - World of Poetry Assoc; [oth. writ.] Several poems published in a "small" poets publication in my former home state; [pers.] I believe a writer must believe in rugged individualism...he or she must constantly strive for excellence in all that they do. Success will eventually come to those that work for it. I've been influenced/inspired by Edgar Allan Poe, T.S. Elliot and Joseph Smith...A little known poet but a wonderful teacher; [a.] Edgewater, MD

HUFF, VALERIE J.
[b.] March 27, 1941, England; [p.] Walter and Christine Cooke; [m.] Lloyd C. Huff Ph.D., April 2, 1'966; [ch.] Amanda and Lesley Huff; [ed.] Educated in England, Registered Nurse with Post Graduate Diploma in Midwifery; [occ.] Reg. Nurse specializing in Reproductive Endocrinology and Infertility; [memb.] American Fertility Society, European Society of Human Reproduction and Embryology.; [oth. writ.] 2nd prize poem, British Digest Illustrated, Spring 1994.

HUGHES, BEVERLY
[b.] May 23, 1952, Milwaukee; [p.] Rev. Joe L. and Lucy Hughes; [m.] Divorced; [ch.] Herman Lamont Ramsey; [ed.] Custer High School, Milw. Area Tech College, University Milwaukee Wisconsin, Utopian School of Ministerial Training, International Christian and Ministerial Bible School; [occ.] (CEO) Operator for Milwaukee Police Department or Booker; [memb.] Elder Utopian Pentecostal Church, Associate Minister Inter Christian Ministerial Assoc., God Victorious Partner, Children Prayer and Scripture Instructor, Assoc. Minister in International Bahama Faith Ministries; [hon.] Award from Mayor of Milwaukee for volunteer work with families that are victims of homicide. Award Social Development Services Milw. for volunteer work with families victim of homicide, many plaques from career youth development agency where I counsel family members; [oth. writ.] Written poems for mother's of deceased children, for programs honoring people, Christian Magazine, Women Magazine, Newspaper, Some of Jeffery Dahmer Victims, Prisoners, for school; [pers.] My inspiration comes from Jesus who helps me to deal with the winds of adversaries, worries and pressures of this world. He helps me to face the social problems that confronts me by sharing in love the gift of poetry which helps others to see Christ in me and to trust and believe in God.; [a.] Milwaukee, WI

HUGHES, GENE
[b.] March 15, 1946, Peru, IN; [p.] Betty and Herbert (dec.) Hughes; [m.] Bea Hughes, July 31, 1965; [ch.] Joe, Mark, Teri, Becky; [ed.] Mentone High School; [occ.] Job Controller, RR Donnelley & Sons, Inc.; Athletic Trainer, Tippecanoe Valley, H.S.; [memb.] Indiana Athletic Trainers Assoc., Indiana Volunteer Fireman's Assoc.; [a.] Mentone, IN

HUGHES-BURNS, ROSEANN
[b.] August 31, 1946, Brockton, MA; [p.] Thussa Pianella; [ch.] Toni Ann O'Neil, Hal Hughes, Amy Hughes; [ed.] Oriskany Central High School - Oriskany, NY, Mohawk Valley Community College, Utica, NY; [occ.] Mental Hygiene Therapy Aide; [oth. writ.] Write many poems for family and friends; [pers.] My poems come from an inner part of my soul, that no one can enter but me; [a.] Stittville, NY

HUMMEL, HEATHER
[b.] January 17, 1980, LaGrange, IL; [p.] Kenneth and barbara Hummel; [ed.] I'm a freshman at Plainfield High School; [occ.] student, competitive figure skater; [memb.] ISIA, USFSA; [hon.] Child's Play Theater performed a poem of mine when I was in fifth grade entitled "Green Beans" ; [oth. writ.] Various poems I have written in my spare time.; [pers.] Write whatever is in your heart to write. You will be surprised in how good it is. Don't be afraid to chase your dreams.; [a.] Plainfield, IL

HUMMER, NANCY J.
[b.] February 9, 1931, Cleveland, OH; [p.] Helen and Harvey Ryan; [m.] Ronald G. Hummer, January 5, 1950; [ch.] Cheryl, Mark, David, John; [ed.] Graduate of Heights High School; [occ.] Housewife; [memb.] St. Noel Church, International Organization of Couples for Christ; [hon.] Scholarship from Euclid General Hospital for L.P.N., School of Nursing, received an A+ in English Composition at Lakeland Community College, Chosen to write composition for contest "Student Writers at work" Bedford Books, St. Martin's Press.; [oth. writ.] Composition for "Student Writer's at Work," Bedford Books, St. Martin's Press. Composition published in "Touch of Class" book for Lakeland Community College; [pers.] I thank the good Lord for showing me, in these later years, that I could write. I wish to convey a deep, uplifting message to mankind.; [a.] Willoughby Hills, OH

HUMPHREY, SHANNON
[b.] October 1, 1976, Syracuse, NY; [p.] Martin Humphrey and Kathleen Grannis; [ed.] Presently a senior at Cloverleaf High School; [occ.] Cashier at Miller Bros Grocery Store; [memb.] Member of the National Honor Society; in the Cloverleaf High School Marching Band (4yrs); [hon.] I'm a second year Letterman in Academics; [pers.] I try to reflect real-life situations in my writing. I hope to open people's eyes to what is really going on in the world around us; [a.] Lodi, OH

HUNT, PATRICIA
[b.] September 22, 1941, Auburndale; [p.] John and Rhoda Sterling; [m.] Thomas Hunt, July 7, 1984; [ch.] Joseph and Patricia (Patty); [ed.] Auburdale High, Business School 2yrs., Cosmetology, completion for teaching; [occ.] Owner and operator of beauty shop.; [memb.] Hair Style of the Month Club; [hon.] Advisory Committee for Ridge Vo-Tech; [oth. writ.] Abused, a child divorce through a child's eyes. In the past local newspaper.; [pers.] My daughter and I have had a lot of pain from the unbelievable things that has happened to her because of lawyers not doing their job. Writing poetry is one way to release the pain.; [a.] Winter Haven, FL

HUNTER, DON
[Pen.] Hunter; [b.] March 29, 1947, Dearborn, MI; [p.] Anthony and Marg; [m.] Divorced; [ch.] 2 Jeff and Laurie; [ed.] BA Mgt and Psych, MA counseling; [occ.] District Mgr Oil Co; [pers.] I believe that poetry is an expression of an author's true beliefs and experiences in life; [a.] Brighton, MI

HURLEY, DOUGLAS
[b.] January 29, 1974, Joliet, Illinois; [p.] Patricia Hurley; [ed.] David Crockett High; [occ.] Paralyzed from the waist down; [oth. writ.] I have a binder filled with a number of interesting poems for which many have enjoyed reading.; [pers.] I believe in having a dream and trying all that's possible to reach this dream by writing poetry it allows me to express my dreams, thoughts and opinions; [a.] Elizabethton, TN

HURT, BONNIE L.
[b.] October 19, 1949, Hart, Co; [p.] Clarence Philpott, Lillie Philpott (deceased); [m.] Jerry R. Hurt, December 15, 1971; [ch.] Jeremy Ray, Jerianna Nicole; [ed.] Pleasure Ridge Park High School; [memb.] Highland United Methodist Church Pathfinders; [hon.] The National Library of Poetry; [oth. writ.] Just started writing poetry two years ago. I have several poems of my own work. A true gift from God; [pers.] My poems reflect spiritual and personal growth through the trials of daily life of the poet; [a.] Cave City, KY

HUSSAIN, KANIZ
[Pen.] Eva; [b.] August 8, 1978; Bangladesh; [p.] Mohammed A. and Faxilatun N. Hussain; [ed.] High School (11th grade); [occ.] Student; [hon.] Dean's List; [oth. writ.] Participated with several poem competitions; [pers.] I try to reflect from my writing is that I want to make a drug free and peaceful society.; [a.] Paterson, NJ

HUSTED, BRIAN LLOYD
[b.] December 7, 1953, Des Moines, IA; [p.] Mr. and Mrs. George and Doris Husted; [m.] Cherly K. Husted, September 6, 1992; [ch.] Brian and Sean Eddy, and April, Brian, and Brent Husted; [ed.] Bachelor of Business Management and Mechanical Engineering Senior status, Univ of IA and Concordia College; [occ.] Avionics, Duncan Aviation; [memb.] Doeden's Dancers, Model AirCraft Club; [hon.] Other artistic accomplishments: Artist of oil painting private collection ("Man Crying", "Ships", "Lighthouse"). Received college credit/recognition for poetry life-learning, after submitting a paper and collection of "romantic" poetry; [oth. writ.] When I met Cheryl, who is now my wife, I was interested in dancing. From this chapter of my life came more poetry, and the involvement with the artistic expression of country dance. A poem, inspired by romance intertwined with dancing, was written and given to our dance instructor and friend. Later the poem was published in a local country dance publication; [pers.] Poetry is an expression of my feelings and thoughts, and writings may revolve around what is happening of importance in my life, or around issues in society. I write to capture and encapsulate my feelings in a rewarding and expressive manner; [a.] Lincoln, ME

HYATT, ANNE-MARIE
[b.] November 25, 1978, Livonia, MI; [p.] Kathleen and Daniel Hyatt; [ed.] I'm currently in 10th grade at Millbrook High.; [memb.] Millbrook Madrigals, Millbrook Masquers; [pers.] I would like to thank all of my loved ones and everyone that encouraged me in my work. I write about personal experiences, and beliefs. It is nothing special or great, but it is something. Maybe someone out there will appreciate my work.; [a.] Raleigh, NC

IBRAHIM, MONA
[b.] October 8, 1981; [p.] Maureen and Abel Ibrahim; [ed.] Sofar Commack Middle School and Meadows Elementary; [oth. writ.] I have written about 15 poems and stories hopefully soon to be published; [pers.] I've always had a lot of support from my loving parents and dear sister. I try to set a good example for my little brother and younger and more impressionable friends. Therefore, I must say I dedicate my poem to all of these who believed I could do it; [a.] Huntington, WV

INGERSOL, STEVEN LEE
[b.] November 19, 1957, Bartlesville, OK; [p.] John and Sue Ingersol; [m.] Deanna Ingersol, August 5, 1993; [ch.] Stepdaughter, Jessica Owen; [ed.] East Central High School, Tulsa, OK; [occ.] Cook, Diamond Restaurant, Virginia; [oth. writ.] "Grandpas Gone", Cats Don't Keep Score, I only yell out Bingo in my dreams, ten day hold, Has anybody seen Kim Lee?, Ballad of Magee McGee, Dimes for Dollar Signs, Samarilla by morning, when you left last night you left more than me; [pers.] I suppose that every American Soldier that has fallen in battle is kinda like Jesus, they gave up their life so others might live and live more abundantly; [a.] Norfolk, VA

INGRAM, JOYCE
[b.] July 30, 1950, Akron, OH; [p.] Henry and Alistine Ingram; [ch.] Monica and Marcia Armstead; [ed.] BA in Sociology, Univ of Akron; [occ.] Case Management Supervisor - AAoA, 10B; [memb.] Fairlawn Kiwanis, Arlington Church of God, Alpha Kappa Alpha Sorority; [pers.] Daily treat each person as if it is the last time that you will see them.

IRELAND, FRANK L.
[b.] 1918, Los Angeles; [m.] Married 52 years; [ch.] Three children, 4 grandchildren and 2 great grandchildren; [ed.] High School, A.A., B.S., and M.S.Ed from U.S.C. with Phi Delta Kappa membership. Completed internship and personal therapy and had 1 year and dissertation to go for Ph.D. degree in clinical psychology; [occ.] Worked at Lockheed Aircraft and spent 20 years in the Crime Laboratory of the Scientific Invest. Div. of the Los Angels Police Dept., Special Agent and Instructor in U.S. Army W.W. II counter Intelligence Corp.; [oth. writ.] Many lectures; [pers.] Hobbies and interests have been pictorial photography and oil painting. I was a technical advisor for 22 moving pictures; several for Mervin LeRoy. I did volunteer work as a therapist and manager and have letters of thanks and congratulations from Ronald Reagan and Harry Truman.

ISAMAN, BARBARA SOUCY
[b.] April 2, 1949, Lacawanna, NY; [p.] Rob Roy and Alvina Olver; [m.] Edward J. Isaman, Sr, November 4, 1989; [ch.] Thomas Olver, Patrick Manning, Matthew Bender; Stepmother of Edward, David Jason, Lionel, Thomas, Stacy; plus 11 grand children; [occ.] Stringer - Okeechobee News; [a.] Olean, NY

JACKSON, DAWN
[b.] November 26, 1972, Waterbury, CT; [p.] Jeffrey and Peggy Dupre; [m.] Michael Jackson, December 27,1992; [ed.] Kaynor Tech; [memb.] V.I.C.A.; [hon.] Semi-finalist for a fashion design contest, semi-finalist for a Mother's day Poetry contest three times.; [oth. writ.] Three Mother's Day poems were published in a local newspaper.; [pers.] I hope to give off a warm feeling to people who read my poems nd to see what I see when I write my poetry to give such feelings is a gift to me as smile on there face is a smile on mine.; [a.] Waterbury, CT

JACKSON, MARGARET E.
[b.] Richmond, VA; [p.] Bertha and Joseph Jackson; [ed.] Virginia Union University, Richmond, VA; Trinity College, Wash., D.C., Oxford University, Oxford, England. George Washington University, Wash. D.C., Roehampton Inst., London, England; [occ.] Science Resource Teacher, Garrison Elem. School, Washington, D.C.; [memb.] National Science Teachers Assoc., American Assoc., for Advancement of Science. District of Columbia Science Educators, National Geographic Assoc.; [hon.] 1994

Presidential Award for Excellence in Science and Mathematics Teaching (State Award); Biography Appears in 1994-95 World Who's Who of Women and 1991 International Leaders of achievement; 1985 D.C. National Association of Conservation , Teacher of the Year; 1981 District of Columbia Science Educators Assoc. Award; 1980 Joint Board of Science and Engineering Education Award.; [oth. writ.] Many; [pers.] It is going to be it is up to me.; [a.] Washington, D.C.

JACKSON, SANDRA
[b.] July 26, 1939, Montgomery, AL; [p.] Clara and Ferrill Cochran; [m.] William L. Jackson, Jr., December 26, 1959; [ch.] William L. III, Andrew Scott; [ed.] Jacksonville Univ, Jacksonville, FL; [occ.] Housewife; [memb.] Beta Sigma Phi, Shining Mountain Extension Club; [a.] Pray, MT

JACKSON-CHRISTIE, EARTHA L.
[b.] December 26, 1943, Miami, FL; [p.] Estella and Leroy Jackson; [m.] Richard Langford Christie, November 29, 1962; [ch.] Five; [ed.] A.A. in Education, BED in Special Education and Master's in Education; [occ.] Varying Exceptionalities Teacher.; [memb.] Honor Society; University of Miami, Director of Community School activities, Parenting and teacher Assistant Director; [hon.] Torch of Education Award; Recognition of Pioneers of Education; [pers.] Extract from the past and build on the future.; [a.] Miami, FL

JACOBINI, MARSHALL
[b.] March 30, 1982, Ft. Worth, TX; [p.] Frank and Susan Jacobini; [ed.] Attending the Oakridge School, A private school, I am in the Seventh Grade; [occ.] Student; [hon.] TASMEA, Solo Score of (1), PSMEA All Region Choir.

JACOBSEN, MILDRED
[b.] December 29, 1914, Fox, Mich.; [p.] Marie and Birger Petersen; [m.] Einar Jacobsen, December 12, 1936; [ch.] Janet, Carol, Joan, Penelope; [ed.] High school, 1 yr. of college; [occ.] Retired Nurse's Aide; [hon.] Received Honorable Mention for poem "Old Era, New?" Major poets chapter. Environment Contest 1972. Have one poem published in The Great Treasury of Poems.; [oth. writ.] Wrote several articles for the Herald Leader (a newspaper) during the 2nd World War.; [pers.] Have always liked to write, started when I was about ten years old. Write about many subjects.

JACOBSON, EDNA F.
[b.] December 22, 1915, Boston, MA; [p.] Rae Jacobson, Alex J.; [ed.] High school - chemistry courses in college to get my professional rating working as a chemist in the defense dept; [occ.] Retired; [memb.] (ACS) American Chemical Society, (ASTM) American Society for Testing and Materials. Many government commendations for excellence in my work; [hon.] Lundell Bright Memorial Award (ASTM), Certificate of Honorary Membership (ASTM), Listed 200 Women of Accomplishment - England "Who's Who of American Women 1976"; [pers.] I'm grateful for having had the most wonderful mother. Her teachings of love and kindness to all was my greatest lesson in life.

JAGGER, TARRILYNN
[b.] December 6, 1957, Wichita Falls, TX; [p.] Eugene and Jo Wall; [m.] Robert Larry Jagger, August 15, 1981; [ed.] BAAS, Computer/Business (currently working on BA Math, expected Grad Sep. 96); [occ.] Paraprofes-

sional II, Math VRJC, SAFB, TX; [memb.] Sike Senter Fashion Guild; Alpha Lambda Delta, Phi Chi Theta, DPMA; [hon.] Ventriloquist, Plus Size Model; University Honor Roll; [oth. writ.] None (Just in school); [pers.] My goal is to foster a love for learning and ignite inner experience.; [a.] Wichita Falls, TX

JAMES, JACINTH CAROLE
[b.] July 3, 1968, Jamaica, WI; [p.] Tren and Gloria James; [ed.] West Indies College, Jamaica, WI, Ramapo College, NJ; [occ.] Student; [memb.] Pre-low Society, Ramapo College of NJ; [oth. writ.] Another completed poem and working on another.; [pers.] I believe that God is the giver of all good things; and my ability to write is a gift from Him and I am merely an instrument used in His grand design for humanity.; [a.] Mahwah, NJ

JAMES, STELLA
[b.] February 21, 1948, Memphis; [p.] Freddie L. and Lorena Jefferson; [m.] Calvin, April 1, 1982; [ch.] Angela, Anthony, Alysia and Artemis (deceased); [ed.] Mitchell Road High, (self); [occ.] Business Owner (Self); [memb.] Westwood Community C.O.G.I.C., Milemore Community Development Org., Commission Against Senseless Killing (C.A.S.K); [oth. writ.] God's trying to tell us something, The wake Up Call, Our Fallen Children, Which way to Hell, The Foreign Affair Teachers, and many, many more.; [pers.] My goal is to reach into the subconscious mind of people and awaken them to reality. I write the truth as I see it from my point of view. Then put it in poem form, so as to interest others too.; [a.] Memphis, TN

JANOSIK, KRISTIN
[b.] May 19, 1975, Parma, OH; [p.] Richard and Barbara Janosik; [ed.] Parma Sr. High School, currently attending Cuyahogo Community College. In the fall of 1995 I am transferring to Baldwin Wallace College. Afterwards, I plan to further my education in graduate school and obtain a Masters Degree in Psychology.; [occ.] Supervisor for Carrols Corporation; [hon.] National Honor Society while attending Parma Sr. High, Dean's List at Cuyahoga Community College; [oth. writ.] None published; [pers.] Always strive for the best. I believe if you are strong and believe in yourself, you can accomplish anything.; [a.] Parma, OH

JAQUINTO, FRANCINE
[b.] October 11, 1960, Manhattan, NY; [p.] John and Carmen Jaquinto; [m.] Single; [ed.] High School Graduate; [occ.] Assembler liner at Accurate forming Corp.; [hon.] Achieving as a member of the sixth and eight grade concert chorus; [pers.] Everyone has a unique way of being themselves. And to expressing their viewpoints and values to survive the world we live in.; [a.] Sussex, NJ

JARMAN, CHERYL LYNN
[Pen.] Cheryl Jarman; [b.] July 15, 1956, Jacksonville, NC; [p.] Edward and Lorraine Jarman; [m.] Divorced; [ch.] Jamie Bland, Amanda Bland; [ed.] White Oak High School, Coastal Carolina Comm. College; [occ.] Disabled/Multiple Sclerosis; [memb.] M.S.A.A., Multiple Sclerosis Assoc. of America; [hon.] Volunteer work for P.E.E.R.S. Working with abused and handicapped children; [oth. writ.] Poems for friends and loved ones. My friends and M.S. leader Sharon Plain encouraged me with my writing.; [pers.] I have always enjoyed reading, especially poems. My own ones are my way of reflecting how I feel. And I hope they can inspire others.; [a.] Richlands, NC

JAYASURIYA, B.A., M.A., Ph.D., REV. LUKE
[b.] February 20, 1929, Colombo, Sri Lanka; [p.] M. Andrew F. Jayasuriya and Elizabeth Perera Jayasuriya; [ed.] B.A. in Philosophy, M.A. in Education, Ph.D. in Philosophy of Religion at the Papal Athenaeum, Kandy, Sri Lanka, The Fordham University, Bronx, NY; [occ.] Priest retired from active work; [oth. writ.] Published in Vernacular; Poem Mihira, Life of St. Maria Goretti, Life of St. Ignatius of Loyola; [pers.] He that cares not, humanity bears not. In my future writings I wish to portray human life under two aspects; a) in its reality from "within," and b) as a mystical entity.

JEFFERS, SHIRLEY A.
[Pen.] Shirley Jeffers; [b.] August 20, 1938, Atkins, AR; [p.] Virgil and Reatha Moore; [m.] Leon M. Jeffers, November 23, 1958; [ch.] Sheryl A., Cathy L., Debra R.; [ed.] Wichita High School North Wichita, KS; [occ.] Learjet Inc, Wichita, KS; [oth. writ.] Spring, Freedom, Memories, Cruisin at 55, My brother and his dog Blue, my brother, in our little room and several others.; [pers.] I like to reflect in my poems on personal memories, nature, family, friends, and enjoy putting these into words.; [a.] Sedgwick, KS

JEFFERSON, JEANETTE H.
[Pen.] J. Harris Jefferson; [b.] January 9, 1943, Missouri; [p.] Mr. and Mrs. A. J. Harris; [m.] John L. Jefferson, December 20, 1969; [ch.] Cynthia, Kevin and Patrice Jefferson; [ed.] A.S. Degree Nursing from Columbia College, Columbia, MO 1991; [occ.] RN Retired disabled, RN Volunteer, Patient Education; [memb.] none current; [hon.] Chancellor Staff Recognition Award Univ. of MO for attending service 1983 Outstanding Patient Education award U. of MO Hosp. Clinics, 1992; [oth. writ.] Public Lynching of O.J. Simpson from Plantation U.S.A., Save the Children, Salute to Maya Angelou, Can't Legislature Must Demonstrate, Morality, Death By Racism; [pers.] Since my illness 5/93, severe stroke, I am an aspiring poet for social change to save our children, our nation and mankind. There is a sincere desire to do something or write something to make a difference.; [a.] Columbia, MO

JEFFREY, PERRY J.
[b.] September 30, 1958; Scottsboro, AL; [p.] E. James Jeffrey, Ella Jeffrey; [m.] Celia M. DeLeon-Suarez, September 24, 1988; [ed.] Auburn Univ, Indiana Univ, Univ of the State of NY; [occ.] Registered Nurse; [oth. writ.] Hopeful to have two children's books published in the near future - "Our Trip to the Operating Room" and "Seasons of Change - A Holiday Memory"; [pers.] I write fore my own personal enjoyment and to hopefully both bring joy and possibly help to others. I am inspired by this possibility; [a.] Fairfax, VA

JENKINS (III), JACKSON
[Pen.] Jack Jenkins, III; [b.] October 19, 1969, Hagerstown, MD; [p.] Jackson Jenkins, Jr., Deborah Jenkins; [ed.] South Hagerstown High School; [occ.] Maintenance, Martins Food; [memb.] Board of Directors, Little League of Halfway, American Film Inst; [oth. writ.] Several writings in local newspaper; [pers.] To me, poetry is the perception of emotions through any form of communication; [a.] Hagerstown, MD

JENKINS, BRIAN
[b.] October 4, 1978, Rockville Centre, NY; [p.] Tom and Gale Jenkins; [ed.] Westhampton Beach, H.S., 10th Grade; [occ.] Student; [memb.] Varsity Soccer Team, Certified Red Cross Lifeguard; [hon.] National Junior Honor Society; 2nd Honors, Ancient Order of Hibernians, Irish History Essay Contest, Suffolk County Long Island, New York; [oth. writ.] "Seascapes" Student writing collection, Westhampton Beach; [a.] Manorville, NY

JENKINS, ROSE MARIE
[Pen.] RoseMarie J.; [b.] March 28, 1943, Washington, DC; [p.] Alfred and Mary Dintino; [m.] Franklin Marvin Jenkins, March 27, 1961; [ch.] Franklin, Anthony, Renatta, Christina, John and Jimmy; [ed.] Suitland High, six years dance, "LS Willer"; [occ.] Homemaker, looking to all needs of family and relatives; [memb.] Collected for many charities and donated also, member of, "Our Lady Help Christians Church"; [hon.] Danced on Channel 5 "Uncle Brooke's Show" made audition steel pier Atlantic City, to dance in line; [oth. writ.] Many writings, unpublished at this time; [pers.] All of my writings are the personal stories of life, as well as the many happenings of everyday life; [a.] Waldorf, MD

JEWEL, SARAH
[Pen.] Elizabeth Devore; [b.] May 13, 1977, Washington, D.C.; [p.] Kathryn and Harold Jewel; [memb.] National Junior Art Honor Society; [oth. writ.] Melancholy Reality, Progression, Inspiration; [pers.] Life has turmoil and life has pain, but none of it is without meaning or lesson. Sir Isaac Newton said that "For every action there is an equal and opposite reaction." For every mistake there is an equally important lesson to be learned.; [a.] Bethesda, MD

JEWELL, BARBARA
[b.] January 28, 1947, Tucson, AZ; [p.] Bill Peterson, Bette Hargrove Negri; [m.] David Jewell, June 25, 1992; [ch.] Roger, Tracey, Brandeis; [ed.] BA Social Ecology, Univ of California; [occ.] Retired 911 communications dispatcher / contented mountain lady; [hon.] Dean's List Univ of California, Social Ecology Advisory Board, nomination for dispatcher of the year 1991; [pers.] Exploration is the life blood; [a.] Shingletown, CA

JIMENEZ, MARIA DEL SOL
[Pen.] Maria del Sol; [b.] June 10, 1977, Santurce, P.R.; [p.] Eduardo Jimenez, Migdalia Cruz; [ed.] Colegio Rosa-Bell; [occ.] Student; [memb.] National Honor Society; [hon.] Honor Award and Fidelity Award; [oth. writ.] A collection of more than 100 poems written by me but not published.; [pers.] I am inspired in all kinds of love for love holds everything.; [a.] San Juan, P.R.

JINKS, JAMIE LYNN
[b.] August 11, 1981, Savannah, Georgia; [p.] Larry and Maxine Jinks; [ed.] Hesse Elem., Hodge Elem., Scott Middle; [hon.] Honor Roll, an award from American Academy of Poetry, a trophy from National Youth Sports Program Summer 1992, a trophy for making Honor Roll during 6th grade year.; [oth. writ.] A poem published in Anthology of Poetry by Young Americans; [a.] Savannah, GA

JOHNS, RENOTA
[b.] January 30, 1957, Illinois; [p.] Helen and Torrez Indellco; [m.] Loren Johns, October 18, 1985; [ch.] Three; [ed.] High School Grad, De Paul University College, Taylor Business School; [occ.] Postal Worker; [memb.] No Place; [oth. writ.] Mirror Images, No One Knows My Anger Or My Grief, Hate Is An Ugly Word.; [pers.] Life has so many problem kids, adults my poems are to reflect this, with all the abuse, mistrust and lack of love.; [a.] Gary, IN

JOHNSON (III), AUGUSTUS W.
[b.] August 25, 1947, Brooklyn, NY; [p.] Augustus and Rosalie Johnson (Deceased); [m.] Divorced; [ch.] Clifton Wesley and Christian Whitney; [ed.] High school graduate, three months Spanish I - Nassau Community College Garden City, NY; [occ.] Distribution - Window Clerk - US Postal Service; [oth. writ.] Is There Still Time, published in American Collegiate Poets, 1987; [a.] Roosevelt, NY

JOHNSON, DOLORES
[Pen.] Dee McGirt; [b.] Savannah, Georgia; [m.] W. J. Johnson (Deceased); [ch.] Vance, Lisa, Phillip, Marlene; [ed.] Jane Addams "Nursing School"; [occ.] Jehovah's Witness Bible Teacher; [oth. writ.] Poems's written of a personal nature to relatives and friends, one article for newsletter "Sears Ears."; [pers.] My poems reflect everyday life, my love of God and humor. I've been greatly influenced by real life experiences both personal and through the pages of the Bible, which truly tells the Greatest Story Ever Written; [a.] Peekskill, NY

JOHNSON, HATTIE YVONNE
[Pen.] Hattie Bryant; [b.] August 10, 1957, B'ham, AL; [p.] Rev. Alfonzy and Helen Bryant; [ch.] Chakea Rucker, Stephanie Rucker; [ed.] Carver High School, Southern Junior College of Business; [occ.] Clerk Stenographer, State of Alabama; [memb.] B'ham Association of Rehab Secretaries; [pers.] I try to reflect in my poetry, the heart and souls of real people and how they deal with life situations.; [a.] Birmingham, AL

JOHNSON, JAMIE WILSON
[b.] April 19, 1976, Wilkes Co, NC; [p.] Tony and Cereda Johnson; [ed.] Harrisburg High School; [occ.] Employee - Tyson Foods; [oth. writ.] Many poems and several short stories; [pers.] Writing is my true form of self expression. I write in words how I feel and what I see; [a.] Harrisonburg, VA

JOHNSON, JUDITH LYNN
[b.] August 30, 1959, Lansing, Mich.; [p.] James and Juanita Johnson; [ch.] Christian James Johnson; [ed.] Escondido High, Palomar College Grossmont College; [occ.] Self-employed in sheet metal fabrication and woodworking; [memb.] His Church Christian Fellowship; [oth. writ.] Although unpublished: numerous poems and children's songs.; [a.] Escondido, CA

JOHNSON, MICHAEL J.
[b.] May 30, 1970, Baltimore, MD; [p.] Felix L. Johnson, Jr., Elizabeth G. Johnson; [m.] Lisa L. Holmes (divorced), October 19, 1990; [ch.] Terrell C. Johnson (6), Kimani O. Johnson (4); [ed.] Baltimore City College, school with no walls and no halls, CCB - 2 yrs; [occ.] Jack of all trades, master of none; [memb.] Human race; [hon.] My sons and being present when my youngest was born into our world; [oth. writ.] A lot of love letters, short stories, and poems; [pers.] Never let anyone steal your dreams. Whatever you do in life make sure you tried your best!!!; [a.] Richmond, VA

JOHNSON, SHADA
[b.] September 14, 1947, Orange, TX; [p.] Buddy Crew, Anne Crew; [ch.] Sloan Terese and Amy Druanne; [occ.] Medical Technician, Beach Cities Dialysis, Gardena, CA; [pers.] Writing to me is a sharing of my soul with all who read my words. It is my favorite thing to do; [a.] Redondo Beach, CA

JOHNSON, THOMAS A.
[b.] December 24, 1933, Bainbridge, GA; [p.] Willie and Alice Johnson; [m.] Jean Lee, December 26, 1958; [ch.] Thomas II, Brandon, Tammy; [ed.] Bainbridge High School, Mercer Univ., BA Post Graduate Studies, Business; [occ.] Property Manager, Real Estate; [memb.] Phi Delta Theta, The Retired Officers Assoc., Rotary International; [hon.] Who's Who Among Global Business Leaders 1994; [a.] Pensacola, FL

JOHNSON, VICTORIA
[Pen.] Vicki Johnson; [b.] January 8, 1930, Savannah, GA; [p.] Amy and John Cain; [m.] Late Samuel Johnson, August 8, 1947; [ch.] Louise Allen, Norman, Michael; [ed.] H.S. Grad, YWCA Trade, Beauty Culgure; [occ.] Retired, worked 12 yrs. as a hairdresser. 21 yrs. as a high school teachers aide.; [memb.] Retired member of DC 37 Union, Baptized Roman Catholic, Active Member of Choir, Active member of Church; [hon.] Received awards for poetry, Honorable Mention, Silver and Gold; [oth. writ.] Started to write poems after death of husband 1971, the writing filled the loneliness and the children at H.S. liked to read them. Monotonous Site, Changing Gears, many more.; [pers.] I like to write poems to make young and old aware of all that's around. Everyday things we take for granted.; [a.] New York, NY

JOHNSON, WILLIAM D.
[b.] July 11, 1966, Toledo, OR; [p.] Ted Johnson, Bonnie Johnson; [m.] Divorced; [ed.] McNary High School, personal in depth study of many varied subjects self taught; [occ.] Self employed, DBA Schnook's Restaurant; [memb.] ORA, NFIB, US Chamber of Commerce, North Salem Business Assoc; [oth. writ.] This is the first poem I have published, though I have a personal collection of ninety three pieces to date. Two short stories published in Goldstar Magazine, and I am slowly writing a fantasy trilogy; [pers.] I have been accused of being a hopeless romantic, I plead guilty. I strive to bring forth the intensity of human emotion in a thought provoking format; [a.] Salem, OR

JOHNSON-BOBO, ADELE C.
[Pen.] Gadge Bobo; [b.] May 6, 1929, Tampa, FL; [m.] John Bobo, January 24, 1988; [ch.] Sander Johnson, grandchild Kjel Julie Storozynsky, grandchild Azura and Tara also Liza Bobo and Brian Bobo; [ed.] Glendale H.S., USC BA; CSUN, MA Living Tao Seminars, Workshops; china and bali Study Tours; Bodywork Sioma/Psyche Integration; [occ.] Tai Ji Dancer; Mind/Body Therapist; Perennial Student and Educator; [memb.] Living Tao Foundation; NEA; CTA; Screen Actors Guild; AFTRA; Equity; Delta Gamma; Zeta Phi Eta; [oth. writ.] Poetry and Lyrics yet unpublished.; [pers.] I believe it is incumbent on each person to create, direct, and cast the script of his/her own life. In our script we must always play the leading role. And as we live the questions of our lives while awaiting the answers, we can select a mode of joy and love with which to enrich ourselves as well as those around us.; [a.] Northridge, CA

JOHNSTON, PATRICIA DUNKEL
[b.] November 3, 1926, Rochester, NY; [p.] Wilbur and Georgia Dunkel; [m.] Arthur Johnston; [ch.] Margaret, Georgia, Bill, Elizabeth; [ed.] B.S. Wellesley College, M.A. Columbia University; [occ.] Retired; [memb.] Dramatists Guild; [oth. writ.] Robert and Elinor, a play Mistress Lidian, a musical The Pilgrim's Progress, a musical.

JOHNS-GIBSON, JANETTE C.
[b.] December 2, 1957, Jamaica West Indies; [p.] Cynthia and Uriah Johns; [m.] Separated; [ch.] Natasha A. Gibson; [ed.] PH.D 1996 Organizational Communications Howard Univ., M.Ed Curriculum Development 1991; B.A. Language Arts 1984, J.W.I. Dip. in Ed. Excelsior Teacher's College; [occ.] Teacher of English, Ventures In Education, Coordinator, Ballou S.H.S. Washington, D.C.; [memb.] District of Columbia Teacher of English Council; Assoc. for Supervision and Curriculum Development; Educational Testing Services Reader; [hon.] Outstanding Teacher SY 1990, D.C. Public School Sys., Proposal writing awarded $3,000.00, Tutorial 1600, Video Producer for McDonald's Corporation; [oth. writ.] Article on "Gonzalez, Bob Marley replica" unpublished, National Art Gallery, Kingston, Jamaica; [pers.] With my fingers I try to weave together the fabric of human emotions. I dig deep for all those hidden feelings that if not exposed will destroy our very presence. I write so that my beautiful gem, Natasha will shine and conquer the evils of pretentious emotions.; [a.] Washington, D.C.

JONAS, MARIA LEIGH
[Pen.] Destiny Lewis; [b.] March 24, 1978, Columbia, SC; [p.] Faye and Larry Jonas; [ed.] Mount Vernon High School; [memb.] American Heart Association, S.A.D.D., German Club, Future Business Leaders of America, Math Team, National Honor Society, Debate Team, Young Astronauts, Young Readers of Virginia; [hon.] Honor Roll, English Student of the Year, (8th Grade) 1991-92, Semi-Finalist of the Congress Budestag exchange between Germany and the U.S.A.; [oth. writ.] Several articles for the teen newsletter of my church youth group, one poem in my high school's literary magazine 1994.; [pers.] I strive to illustrate complex deeper meanings of simplistic literature through familiar language and events.; [a.] Alexandria, VA

JONES, CHARLES R.
[b.] June 23, 1944; [m.] Virginia W. Jones, December 26, 1966; [ch.] Susan and Jennifer; [pers.] One life is not enough to get it right.; [a.] Germantown, MD

JONES, DIANE LYNN
[b.] April 20, 1956, Endicott, NY; [p.] Daniel and Clara Fredenburg Sr., [m.] Michael Lee Jones, May 29, 1983; [ch.] Frederick, David, Diane, Betty; [occ.] Personal Care Aide II for the elderly and Children Since 1980; [memb.] Women of the Moose NY, since 1985, 4-H, Girl Scout; [hon.] My 1st poem I ever sent to any one to look at out of Ton's of poems and year's of writing.; [pers.] I have been greatly influenced by my best friend Mrs. LuAnn Ford of Newark Valley, NY. She made me believe in myself. Thank you LuAnn and I thank my precious Lord again for giving me a new life.

JONES, FREDERICK
[Pen.] Fred Ricks; [b.] May 2, 1954, New Orleans; [p.] Alvin and Priscilla Jones; [m.] Rita Hunt, engaged; [ch.] Two sons; [ed.] 12th grade; [occ.] Confined; [oth. writ.] I've written an uncountable amount of material. Plays, movie scripts, poetry, songs, articles of various types, quotes and most of my material has never been reviewed by anyone.; [pers.] Compassion is not in the heart who sees the suffering of others, but rather the one who feels it. I view the world through the eyes of righteousness and my words are sheer inspirational.; [a.] Vidalia, LA

JONES, MARTHA
[Pen.] Martha; [b.] May 9, 1940, Riceboro, GA; [p.]

Mr. and Mrs. Charlie Brown; [m.] Mr. Toney Jones, July 6, 1968; [ch.] Dorothy, Toney Jr., Julian, Linda, Annie, Charles, Eloise, Anthony, Edward; [ed.] Cuyler Junior High School, Savannah, GA; [occ.] Housewife; [memb.] Member of Mt. Carmel Holiness Church Riceboro, GA; [oth. writ.] Several poems published in the Church of Christ, upon the Rock of the Apostolic, Faith local newsletter.; [a.] Midway, GA

JONES, OSCAR AR.
[Pen.] Alastair; [b.] March 26, 1965, Phila.; [p.] Oscar and Gracie Jones; [ed.] Melrose Acad. (Elem.), LaSalle College H.S., Temple Univ., West Chester Univ.; [occ.] Senior Distribution work for Phila. Gas Works; [memb.] Phila Catholic Forensics League; [hon.] Several awards in Phila. Catholic Forensics League, Finalist in WDAS radio in Phila. "Claim Your Culture" contest; [oth. writ.] I am now starting a book of poetry, I have gotten published: "By Myself," "If Ever I Will Miss Someone," "Should I?" "The Forbidden."; [pers.] Life is too short to judge others.; [a.] Phila., PA

JUBELIRER, ARMY R.
[b.] February 1, 1953, Brooklyn, NY; [p.] Murray and Laurette Lehrer; [m.] Robert A. Jubelirer, July 25, 1976; [ch.] Matthew Aaron and Rebecca Emily; [ed.] Middletown H.S.; B.S. Pennsylvania University 1975; M.A. Temple University 1978; Degree: Speech and Language Pathologist; [occ.] Freelance writer, Homemaker, Speech and Language Pathologist; [memb.] American Speech and Hearing Assoc. (ASHA); [hon.] Dean's List, Honor Society, D.A.R. Award; [oth. writ.] Articles for the Keneseth Israel "Bulletin" of Elkins Park, PA. Articles for local publications and newspapers.; [pers.] My children are my greatest fans! The sparkle in their eyes and their gentle encouragement keep my pen moving! My mother provided the spiritual depth necessary to write from the heart.; [a.] Huntingdon Valley, PA

JUDICE, DAVID
[Pen.] Frank - Edward; [b.] March 20, 1958, Lake Charles, Louisiana; [p.] Richard and Anne Lowther Judice; [ed.] B.A. Degree in Journalism Advertising, Louisiana State Univ., Baton Rouge, LA in 1981, Graduate of A.M. Barbe High School, 1976 in Lake Charles, LA; [occ.] Math & Algebra and English Language Teacher and private tutor in Los Angeles, CA; [memb.] Nat'l Audubon Society, Louisiana State Univ. Alumni Association Screen Actors Guild, Los Angels World Wildlife Fund, The Nature Conservancy, St. Joseph's Lakota Indian School, SD, Boy Scouts of America; [hon.] Eagle Scout Award, Boy Scouts of America; [oth. writ.] Several poems published in the 1994 Nat'l. Kidney Foundation of So. California Poetry Revival Anthology. Also, poem to be published in upcoming Summer 1995 edition of "Treasured Poems of America" anthology, Sparrowgrass Poetry Forum, WV; [pers.] "I do not know what I may appear to the world, but to myself I seem to have been only like a boy playing on the sea-shore, and diverting myself in now and then, finding a smoother pebble or a prettier shell than ordinary, whilst the great ocean of truth lay all undiscovered before me.; [a.] Los Angeles, CA

JYLES, CLEVE ESTHER MC SWAIN
[Pen.] Shot; [b.] April 28, 1942, Greenwood, MS; [p.] Rev. and Mrs. Cleve Robert Jyles; [m.] Divorced; [ch.] Gloria, Ronald, Sherry, Benjamin, Rhonda, Tanya, Darrell, and Cornealous; [ed.] Eureka High School, Jones County Jr College; [occ.] Child Care Provider, MAP Heardstart Center; [memb.] Heroines of Jerico, 700 Club

Life Study Fellowship; [oth. writ.] One song; [pers.] Under the guidance of the Holy Spirit I write. I have been greatly influenced by my father Rev. Cleve Robert Jyles and the most wonderful and inspiring Mya Angelo and Helen Steiner Rice; [a.] Richton, MS

KALISER, SYLVIA
[b.] May 10, 1939, Philadelphia, PA; [ch.] Helene, Cheralyn, Paul; [ed.] South Philadelphia High, and Life; [occ.] Human Resources Spec Payroll Unit; [hon.] Was Home and School President of Francis Scott Key Elementary School. Received three awards for having a summer reading program in my home for 5 summers; [oth. writ.] Had articles published in Phila newspapers which centered on keeping Francis Scott Key Elementary School open; [pers.] I love watching children. We can learn so much from them. I believe if we treat them with respect they will pass that on to their friends and family. I try to treat them not as children, but as people; [a.] Philadelphia, PA

KALITZ, REGINA
[Pen.] Gina; [b.] January 24, 1977, Darby, PA; [p.] Robert and Edna Kalitz; [ed.] Cardinal O'Hara High School, Our Lady of Charity Grade School; [occ.] Student; [hon.] Numerous academic honors throughout nine years of grade school; [oth. writ.] Several poems published in Dialogues (school magazines); [pers.] Special thanks to my family and friends for believing in me.; [a.] Brookhaven, PA

KALLASY, EDNA
[Pen.] ED, only by sister; [b.] June 23, 1926, Utica, NY; [p.] Otto and Hilda Dellers; [m.] Louis A. Kallasy, July 4, 1966; [ch.] Jo Ann, Bob, Tony, Joseph; [ed.] Oriskany Central School, Utica School of Commerce; [occ.] Owner of Edna's Restaurant, 25 yrs. (cook) 50 years total; [memb.] Oneida County, Liquor Dealers Assoc., Eagles Club; [oth. writ.] Memoriums to my father.; [pers.] I tend only to put things on paper when I am sad or scared. When people are sick or in trouble, I try to send them a note of cheer by writing.; [a.] Utica, NY

KALLISON, Ph.D., SARAH RUSH
[b.] November 23, 1953, Salt Lake City, Utah; [p.] Elizabeth and Leonard Rush, M.D.'s; [m.] Steven G. Kallison, M.D., May 30, 1987; [ch.] Eli Rush Kallison (born June 12, 1990); [ed.] B.A. with distinction in literature, Phi Beta Kappa from Yale Univ., 1975., Ph.D, California School of Professional Psychology 1985.; [occ.] Clinical Psychologist.

KARPOUAGE, LINDA
[b.] February 3, 1981, Trenton, NJ; [p.] Raymond Karpouage, Carol Karpouage; [ed.] I am finishing my last year at Reynolds Middle School; [occ.] Student.; [pers.] I believe that you don't need other people to help you get through life, as long as you have faith in yourself.; [a.] Yardville, NJ

KASZUBSKI, CAROL
[b.] March 25, 1927, New York; [p.] William and Mathilda Schatz; [m.] Stanley (deceased), May 28, 1948; [ed.] Graduated from Bayside HS in Queens; [occ.] Retired. Formerly secretary to Production Control Mgr of Manufacturing Plant in L.I. City; [memb.] Have been an officer of the Utopia Improvement Civic Assn for 20 yrs and President for past 10 yrs. Have produced a monthly newsletter for the Assn for 13 yrs working with city, state and fed representatives, police, community boards, etc. to protect the quality of life of our commu-

nity; [oth. writ.] Have compiled many of my own poems for the past forty years, but never submitted any for possible publication; [a.] Flushing, NY

KATSAMPES, GEORGE G.
[b.] April 6, 1925, Zanesville, OH; [p.] Constantine and Jasmine Katsampes; [m.] Leitsa Katsampes, October 26, 1958; [ch.] Jasmine Davlantes, Peter Katsampes, Maria Medlij; [ed.] High School, Sparta, Greece; [occ.] Retired, Ex-Restaurant Manager and Dentistry; [memb.] American Hellenic Educational Progressive Assoc., Holy Trinity Greek Orthodox Church, Chairman Grand Rapids Cyprus Committee; [hon.] Order of Ahepa, District Lodge Award of Meritorious Service; [oth. writ.] Several articles published in local newspaper, "Grand Rapids Press" and in the "National Herald" Greek-American Daily Newspaper in New York; [pers.] I have the motivation to explore and expose the wrongs, the immortality and therefor the wish to thrust the righteousness for the benefit of humanity, the Christian principles and the philosophical thoughts of the Ancient Greek philosophers influenced me to write.; [a.] Grand Rapids, MI

KAULILI, DEBBY
[b.] February 4, 1964, Koloa, Kauai; [p.] Mr. Springwater and Mrs. Marjorie Kaulili; [ed.] Kauai High, Kauai Community College, and Leeward Community College; [occ.] Graphic Artist/Lithographic Stripper and Cook; [hon.] Dean's List, and Talent Search America, and Honor Roll; [oth. writ.] American Lung Association Newsletter, Lyric writing.; [pers.] I like to thank my Mom and Calabash Sister, Sylvia for broadening my perspective in life. Life has its ups and downs but we must survive and persevere; [a.] Honolulu, HI

KAYE, DANIEL SEAN
[b.] September 18, 1967, Purley, England; [p.] Dr. Yvonne Kaye, Samuel Kaye; [m.] Wendy Snyder (as of 9-17-95); [ed.] Abington High, Penn State Univ, Temple Univ, Columbia Pacific Univ; [occ.] Freelance cartoonist for several area publications; [memb.] Belong to many charitable institutions such as the National Tuberous Sclerosis Assoc, PAL, Special Olympics, American Assoc of State Troopers, Fraternal Order of Police, Clean Water Action, Greenpeace, Children International, among others; [hon.] First teenage radio show host in Pennsylvania, citizenship award from Abington High; [oth. writ.] Have had my comic strip, "Abyssburg", published in several publications for the last five years, illustrated two books, written opinion pieces and features for newspapers, and wrote political/social satire; [pers.] Investigate yourself. Take the time to really know what you want out of life and how far you are willing to go to get it. Then, be consistent. It will probably be difficult, but as long as you are aware of that the challenge will not be insurmountable; [a.] Abington, PA

KEKE, ARNO
[ed.] UCLA, class of 85; [occ.] Foreign Correspondent: Soccer Action magazine; [oth. writ.] A Decade In The Blood, published in 1991, is an illustrated, autobiographical account of the 1980's, which includes fifteen original poems.; [pers.] Special recognition for inspiring the poem, which appears in this anthology, should go to Bionca and Bruce Seven.; [a.] El Monte, CA

KELLER, JOE
[b.] May 9, 1978, Wichita; [p.] Jerry and Sharon Keeler; [ed.] Junior at Bluestem High School; [occ.] Martial Arts Instructor; [memb.] Eldorado Martial Arts Academy;

[hon.] 4.00 GPA, 1993, Martial Arts Student of the Year; [oth. writ.] Poem: A light, essays: The Loss of My Childhood, My Grandpa, Rest in Peace.; [pers.] I dedicate this poem to my parents: Sharon Keeler and Jerry Keeler. Also, I'd like to thank my brothers and sisters for spending so much time with me.; [a.] Lenon, KS

KELLEY, STEPHEN D.
[Pen.] Ace; [b.] July 23, 1972, West Hamlin; [p.] Ivan and Connie McCoy; [ed.] Buffalo - Wayne High School, Nashville Auto - Diesel College; [occ.] Sales Representative, McCoy Freightliner, Kenova, WV; [oth. writ.] Tears of a Clown, Day Dream Star, and several more, but none have been published or recognized other than "Dream"; [pers.] Be true to yourself, and you will never have to lie about yourself; [a.] Kenova, WV

KELLOGG, PAULA C.
[b.] October 31, 1979, Augsburg, Germany; [p.] Greg and Jane Kellogg; [ed.] Currently enrolled as a freshman at East Coweta High School; [occ.] Student; [memb.] Astronomy Club, Drama Club; [oth. writ.] Numerous unpublished poems; [a.] Newnan, GA

KELLY, JOSEPH B.
[b.] August 23, 1942, Charleston, WVA; [m.] Linda Schoben Kelly, August 16, 1964; [ch.] Sean Kelly, Kimberly Szatkiewicz; [ed.] North Hills H.S., Pittsburgh, PA, Michigan State Univ., Antioch Univ., Yellow Springs, OH; [occ.] Therapist and Pastor; [memb.] American Counseling Assoc., American Mental Health Counselor Assoc., International Association of Addictions and Offender Counselors, Religious Society of Friends; [oth. writ.] Several articles for friends publications; [pers.] All for the glory of God.; [a.] Cedar, MI

KEMP, JUDY SALLEE
[b.] October 13, 1944, Kentucky; [p.] Alma Shoemaker, Sallee, Brane/Lyons M. Sallee; [m.] Donald R. Kemp, January 11, 1964; [ch.] Gina C. Kemp - Hutto BA, MA; [occ.] Bookkeeper, Cardiology of Georgia; [pers.] I have always know that I was blessed with a good mother. I am pleased to honor her with this poem; [a.] Decatur, GA

KENNA, HENDRYK Z.
[b.] May 16, 1930, Plymouth County, Terryville, Conn.; [p.] Irene Smolenska-Thomas and Chester Kenna; [m.] rita Preciado Kenna, August 19, 1959; [ch.] Julieta Irene K. DeLutz, Thomas Henry, Francis Xavier, Walter Anthony; [ed.] Chelsea Senior High, U.S.M.C., Dept. of State, Foreign Service, Wash. D.C., UCLA, Dept of Def., Def. Mapping Agency, Inter-American Geodetic Survey, Panama Canal Company, Panama Canal; [occ.] Writer, poet administration; [memb.] K of C; [hon.] Two M.A. Senate Official Citations, One AARP Recognition, One Mayoral Commendation, U.S. Southern Command and Def. Dept., Awards plus several high honors and Awards from the Dept. of State, Foreign Service During over 30 yrs in the Diplomatic Corps and Dept. of Defense; [oth. writ.] Several local newspaper articles and stories.; [pers.] Inspired by a few teachers, nuns and friends, I have written for years, to make people happy and entertain them, or teach; [a.] Chelsea, MA

KERN, CRISTENA BRYSON
[b.] October 1919, Silver Lake, New Hampshire; [p.] Kenneth and Beulah Spencer Bryson; [m.] October 1943; [ch.] Bruce, Kristina, Gregory; [ed.] College of Wooster, B.A., Baldin-Wallace B.S. of ED., Kent State, Graduate work in Special Education, Cleveland School of Art;

[occ.] Retired Teacher (Language/Math); [hon.] In First Women Officer's Class at Northampton, Mass. in 1942, a LT (J.G.) in WAVES at Cape May, Stationed at CM Naval Base during WWII; [pers.] Just as a symphony follows a strict, prescribed form, and is not an aimless succession of beautiful chords, I feel that a poem should follow a rhythmic cadence and a rhyme pattern, and not just be a successor of beautiful words.

KERR, RENA GLENN
[b.] May 28, 1920, Roswell, NM; [p.] Mr. and Mrs. D.A. Glenn; [ch.] Lyndol Leon Cook (son); [ed.] Sacred Heart High School, NM; Univ. of New Mexico, Albuquerque, NM, Albuquerque Business College, NM; French and German classes in California UCLA and Univ. of Irvine Extension; [occ.] Retired; [memb.] University Women Chamber of Commerce, C.D.M. Cal., National Artists Assoc., World Affairs Council of Orange County, Christian Women's Club, Toastmasters Club, International Cultural Assoc., International Children's Laureates, Listed in Blue Book of East and Blue Book of Los Angeles, CA; [oth. writ.] Newspaper articles in several newspapers, New York, New Mexico, and California.

KERRICK, JAMES
[Pen.] Cadwallader; [b.] April 10, 1927, Alamogordo, NM; [ed.] MA, Literature; [occ.] Retired; [memb.] SPEBSQSA; [hon.] 20 year pin, volunteer weather observer, NOAA; [oth. writ.] Seaman's Prayer (poem), Beaucatcher Hill: A Musical Comedy Sledge (novel); Sin City (one act play), Death Came Twice (novellette); various poems and dramatic monologues; Fastest Gun in the West; (musical comedy in progress); [pers.] I explore the intense inner relationships between two people, especially man and woman, that goes beyond mere sex. I am influenced by the humor of Mark Twain, Will Rogers and American Folklore live close to nature and thus ever impending disaster.; [a.] Hi Rolls, Mt. Park, NM

KESKAR, SONIYA P.
[b.] June 13, 1981, New Jersey; [p.] Prabhakar and Sandhya Keskar; [ed.] 8th grade student at Fort Clarke Middle School (wrote poem in the 7th grade); [occ.] student; [hon.] Straight - A, Honor Roll student since 1st grade; [pers.] I enjoy reading and writing. Some of my hobbies include: classical Indian dance and American Jazz dance. I have been dancing since I was 3 yrs old; [a.] Gainesville, FL

KETCHAM, GRACE M.
[b.] January 30, 1917, New York; [p.] Olof and Marie Olson; [m.] Widowed 1977; [ch.] 4 sons: Kenneth, Louis, Roger, Gary - Surname Bal Bo; [ed.] BS Ed, Hofstra, 56; MS Ed Hofstra '60; [occ.] Retired Teacher taught in No Bellmore, NY, Shirley, NY, Central Islip, NY; [memb.] New Hope Church, Shirley, NY, Accuracy in Media; [pers.] I am concerned with promoting good human relationships and cultural understanding through education and example; [a.] Shirley, NY

KETCHAM, PAMELA
[Pen.] Julian St. Michael; [b.] March 3, 1952, MI; [p.] Mr. and Mrs W.C. King; [m.] David Ketcham, Sr, April 8, 1987; [ch.] Scott-22, Michelle-21, Eric-19, David-9, Ashley-7; [ed.] 1-12, now attending writers institution; [occ.] Writer; [oth. writ.] Through a Child's Eyes, book (River of Dreams - ISBN-1-5617256-4) Journey's End (short story) Good Morning Pa Pa (short story); [pers.] Reach for the moon, if you grab a few stars along the way that's fine, but don't stop reaching for the moon; [a.] Thomaston, GA

KEVIN, VEILLETTE
[b.] April 18, 1978, Waterbury, CT; [p.] Andre Veillette, Joby Veillette; [ed.] St. Margaret Grammar School, Wilby High School; [memb.] RADD (Recreational Alternatives to Drinking and Drugs); [hon.] Talented and Gifted Program, Who's Who Among American High School Students; [oth. writ.] A poem published in School Literary Magazine, other unpublished poems and short stories; [a.] Waterbury, CT

KIDDER, LORRAINE
[Pen.] Laurie Newington; [b.] October 17, 1952, Hastings, MI; [p.] Jack and Sally Newington; [m.] Harry D. Kidder Sr., November 26, 1977; [ch.] Harry D. Kidder Jr., Carrie Stevens; [ed.] Hastings High School, Graduated 1980 at Hastings Adult Education; [occ.] Homemaker, Disabled; [memb.] I am the member of the Hastings Apostolic Tabernacle Church; [oth. writ.] I have many poems and writings that have never been published or seen or read by the public.; [pers.] I am just a woman who has a heart full of love and compassion and serve our Lord Jesus and would like to give his love.; [a.] Hastings, MI

KIENZLE, DE
[b.] January 18, 1994, Lehr, ND; [p.] Jacob and Fred Ricka Kienzle; [ed.] High School, Nurses School, Certified Registered Nurse Anesthetist; [occ.] Retired; [memb.] AARP, NARFE, American Diabetes Association; [pers.] "The lower planes are designed to give us the run-around, to drive us finally through despair - to the golden moment of light and awareness of the Big Picture"; [a.] Poplar Bluff, MO

KIHLE, THOMAS BLAINE
[Pen.] Blaine Thomas; [b.] April 14, 1965, El Cajon, CA; [p.] Irv Hoffman, Betty Hoffman; [m.] Dorene Marie Kihle, March 4, 1989; [ch.] Korey Robert, Trevvor Thomas; [ed.] San Marcos High Palomar College; [occ.] Retail, musician/writer, poet, lyricist; [memb.] San Diego Blood Bank Bone Marrow Donor; [hon.] Honor Role one yr ceramics; semi-finalist 1994 North American Open Poetry Contest, scheduled publishing summer 1995, anthology, (Reflections of Light); [oth. writ.] Several unpublished songs, lyrics, poems; [pers.] Quote "Doesn't thou love life than do not squander time" Ben Franklin. I am influenced by experiences in my life. Favorites John Barley Corn by Roberts Burns, Harvard Classics Fight the Good fight Humanity!; [a.] Murrieta, CA

KILDUFF, BARRY
[b.] October 2, 1960, Norwood, Mass.; [p.] Ruth and James; [ed.] Xauerion Bros. H.S.; [occ.] Foreman; [pers.] I can make many lyrics better than the original.

KIM, AUSTIN DALE
[b.] September 12, 1971, Seoul, Korea; [p.] Hak Sung Kim and Myung Hee Kim; [m.] Single; [ed.] Tustin High School, California University of Long Beach; [occ.] Full time student; [memb.] Orange Korean Evangelical Church, Korean Christian Fellowship, Korean Student Association, Asian American Student Assoc.; [hon.] California Scholastic Federation, 4 Year Honor Roll, 3 year Varsity Letter in Tennis and Golf. Tae Kwon Do Junior Olympics Gold Medalist. Southern California Evangelical Church Volleyball Championships Gold Medalist; [oth. writ.] None; [pers.] I strive to live my life in God's will and His magnificent glory. For I am truly nothing without Him. I write what is deep within my heart because that is the only way true sincerity is expressed.; [a.] Tustin, CA

KIM, REV. DR. BO-JOONG
[Pen.] BJ; [b.] July 24, 1948, Seoul, Korea; [m.] Young-Sook, April 5, 1975; [ch.] James, Sun-Hea; [ed.] Han-Yang University, B.S., Drew University, Theological School, Wesley Theological Seminary, M.Div and D.Min.; [occ.] Minister/Pastor; [memb.] Wesley Foundation Campus Ministry, Monday-Club of United Methodists, Northern New Jersey Annual Conference; [hon.] The Best Man of the Year, Jaycees, The Distinguished Lieutenant, R.O.T.C.; [oth. writ.] Articles on Religion and Race, Doctorate Paper on A Cross-Cultural Ministry Model, Journals on Personal Faith Journey; [pers.] I would like to share all experiences of my life with other people, so that we may life this life on earth through "The way, and the truth." I do my best to accomplish what is good and beautiful for this life.; [a.] Clifton, NJ

KING, CONSTANCE H.
[b.] May 21, 1894, Hetland, SD; [p.] Willoughby Mullins, Laura Tuttle; [m.] John W. King (deceased 1961), August 16, 1916; [ch.] Three daughters; [ed.] High school, both in Canada and in Los Angeles in 1913 and Normal School in Canada; [occ.] No occupation; [memb.] In the Retired Teachers, the Republican Women's Assoc here in Port Charlotte, FL also First Christian Church here; [oth. writ.] One book The Three Horizons in 1980. Really my life history. Fourth book. My fourth horizon 1980 - 1990. I am now doing my 1990 to 2000.

KING, GLENNGO A.
[b.] January 19, 1952, Brooklyn, NY; [p.] James A. King, Sarah King; [ed.] High School of Art and Design, The Cooper Union School of Art, Hunter College; [occ.] Art Teacher, NYC Bd of Ed, Actor/Puppeteer; [memb.] Actors' Equity Assoc, SAG and AFTRA, The Puppeteers of America, United Federation of Teachers; [oth. writ.] Several poems published in local art journals; [pers.] I strive to elevate global consciousness using many local cosmic ingredients including language, art, music, puppetry, dance, etc. I have been greatly influenced by a multi-national array of poets and writers, known and unknown; [a.] Brooklyn, NY

KING, JANET E.
[b.] July 3, 1935, Everette, MA; [p.] Dorothy J. Bickford, Peter H. Padovani; [m.] George L. King, February 14, 1985; [ch.] Catherine Janet and David Scott; [ed.] High school.

KING, MONTY A.
[Pen.] Monty; [b.] February 1, 1978, Bellingham, WA; [p.] Dan and Carolyn King; [ed.] High School Sophomore; [occ.] High School Student; [pers.] This poem was inspired while my cousin was serving in the United states Army in Saudia Arabia during the Gulf War.; [a.] Houston, TX

KING, NICOLE
[b.] July 25, 1980, San Angelo, TX; [p.] Linda Hearn, Michael and Diana Shear; [ed.] I have graduated from Ballinger Elementary and Junior High School. I have recently begun my Freshman year at Ballinger High School. High school student; [memb.] I am a member of Seventh Street Baptist Church in Ballinger, TX. At school, I am a member of Future Homemakers of America (FHA) and Rotary Interact; [hon.] I have won trophies each year for the last five years for art in FPPC. I have received awards for outstanding service in music, also a medal for Division 1 vocal solo. I have received awards for UIL, honor roll, outstanding girl in moth and

performance choir. This year I have also received the President's Educational Award and the Presidential Academic Effort Award; [oth. writ.] I have written several other poems, a short story, and a song, but until now, I have not attempted publication of any; [pers.] To me poetry is my way of expressing feelings when those around me do not seem to be listening; [a.] Ballinger, TX

KINKOL, JONATHAN R.
[b.] April 30, 1977, Chapel Hill, NC; [p.] Dr. Elizabeth Bendeich and Dr. Richard Konkol; [ed.] I am a senior at Lincoln High School, Portland, OR; [occ.] Student; [hon.] National Scholastic Honors Society; [oth. writ.] None published.; [pers.] I generally use my poetry to explore my own emotions.; [a.] Portland, OR

KIRK, CARL WALTER
[Pen.] Cal Kirk / Thoughtful; [b.] August 16, 1914, Olyphant, PA; [p.] (late) Walter Kirk and Elizabeth Lake-Kirk; [m.] Eleanor Louise Welch-Kirk (divorced), Carol Rosalee Muschette-Kirk (present wife), February 14, 1991; [ch.] (2 daughters) Judith Ann, Suzanne Eleanor; [ed.] Olyphant High School, PA; Power School of Business, Scranton, PA; U of Penn (Wharton School of Finance); [occ.] Retired Building Contractor, President and Chief Executive Officer; Dolb Construction; States Construction of NJ and President Board of Trustees of Elder Osceola Presbyterian Church, NJ; President Bd of Dirs Cerebral Palsy Assn in NJ; New Jersey State President Cerebral Palsy Assn; Member A. Masonic Lodge #127, NJ; Member Scottish Rite Temple 32 Mason, NJ; Member Crescent Shrine Temple, NJ; Institutional Rep Troop 44, boys scouts of America, Clark, NJ; [hon.] Bronze Medal from Union County, NJ; Cerebral Palsy Assn for Years of Service as member of board of directors; 1st runner up award, American Poets Society; [oth. writ.] Several poems published in The Scranton (PA) Times (1930's and 1940's). Poetic citations to many individuals over the years; Hundreds of poets being prepared for publication; [pers.] From Biblical text: "Do justly, love mercy, walk humbly with thy God"; [a.] Takoma Park, MD

KITTINGER (SR.), WALTER L.
[b.] November 6, 1944, Cleveland; [p.] Lewis and Florence; [m.] Nancy, January 5, 1993; [ch.] Tracie, Walter Jr., Vincent, Tammy; [ed.] Went to 10th grade; [occ.] Truck Driver; [oth. writ.] Personal poems, once I enterer your contest before but forgot the name of the poem; [pers.] Memories are pleasant reflections of the past, seen by the minds eye; [a.] Cleveland, OH

KLASINSKI, JAMIE
[b.] August 9, 1978, KC, KS; [p.] Marguerite and Richard Klasinski; [ed.] Shawnee Mission South High School class of 1996; [hon.] Blue ribbon in district competition for 2 poems; [oth. writ.] Several other poems; [pers.] It makes me proud to see others feel for my poems. I love to read poetry and my passion lies with writing it. I thank all of my family and friends for their support.; [a.] Overland Park, KS

KLATT, LLOYD E.
[b.] November 3, 1911, Ohiowa, NE; [p.] John and Maude Klatt; [ed.] High school grad. Two full yrs business college; [occ.] Retired; [memb.] West Salem United Methodist Church.

KLEIDER, ERIN A.
[b.] May 2, 1968, Racine, WI; [p.] Richard and Maxine Anderson; [m.] Kelly Kleider, June 13, 1992; [ed.] B.A. Eng. Lit. SFSU, currently pursuing an MA in Eng. Lit. at SFSU.; [occ.] Graduate Student; [memb.] Art Deco Society of Calif.; [a.] San Francisco, CA

KLEIN, MAXINE ANN
[b.] Peshtigo, Wisc.; [p.] John and Mary Scholten; [m.] The late Edward Klein, October 31, 1933; [ch.] Edward and Mary; [ed.] High School, Piano 8 years, and singing 2 years private lessons; [occ.] Home; [memb.] Daughters of American Revolution Church also taught class at St. Mary's (children) Sunday.; [hon.] Citation of Merit in recognition of outstanding effort in behalf of American Red Cross, June 1944 signed by Mayor Arnold H. Klenty, also knitted 12 sweaters for World War II Soldiers; [oth. writ.] Many more; [pers.] My son is a graduate of Marquette Univ. and employed by the Milwaukee Court House. Federal Bldg., Police Protection.; [a.] West Allis, WI

KLEIST, JOANNE
[b.] Reedsburg, WI; [p.] Edward and Alice Brunhoefer; [ch.] Marie; granddaughter: Lauren; [ed.] Bachelor of Science in Education/Concordia Teachers College, Kiver forest IL - Master of Arts / Michigan State Univ; Specialist in Administrative Leadership / Univ of WI - Milwaukee; [occ.] Executive Director - Curriculum and Instruction, Waukesha Schools; [memb.] American Association of School Administrators, Phi Delta Kappa, Assoc for Supervision and Curriculum Development; [hon.] Selected to be member of State Commission on Schools for the 21st Century (1990). Selected to participate WI German Studies Program including 2 weeks study in Germany (1988-1990). Participated I/D/E/A fellows program since 1985; [oth. writ.] Published "Curriculum Development that really works" (1983), "Plan for Vacation Time Now" (1974); Inhouse: Position Paper on Grouping and Grouping Practices at Elementary Level (1991); Non-published: Other poetry; [pers.] I would like to achieve a balance of writing for enjoyment and writing for work; [a.] Waukesha, WI

KNAPP, KATHERINE
[b.] March 5, 1981, San Francisco; [p.] Anna Maria Knapp and Vernon Jacobs; [ed.] Presently in the 8th grade; [occ.] Student; [hon.] Academic: Honor roll and President's List; [oth. writ.] Short stories essays, poems and songs, all unpublished; [pers.] I'm a kid with ambitions.

KOCH, CRYSTAL
[Pen.] Crystal Bemiss (maiden-name); [b.] April 2, 1975, Okinawa, Japan; [p.] William Bemiss and Jill Bemiss; [m.] Larry Koch, December 4, 1993; [ed.] High school diploma; [occ.] Housewife; [oth. writ.] Several, but none that have been published. It's basically been just a hobby; [pers.] I mostly just write things out of thought when I think up a topic for a poem. I write it down and think of things from there.

KOCH, LETA
[b.] January 12, 1945, Denton, TX; [m.] Steven Koch, Organic Farmer; [ed.] Business, Social Work; [occ.] Executive Director for battered Women's Shelter, Sexual Assault Abuse Program and Program for Unlearning Violence; [oth. writ.] Poetry, short stories, dinner theatre mysteries and children's plays. Local paper publications and other poetry compilations.; [pers.] Everyone is a story-everything you see can be told to others in an interesting way!; [a.] Pottsboro, TX

KOLOM, AARON L.
[b.] May 17, 1921, Chicago, IL; [p.] Louis Kolom; Ethel Nee Levy; [m.] Serita Kolom, November 17, 1993; [ch.] Barry; Elana; Halyse; [ed.] MSAE, Hero, USC; BSME - IL Inst of Tech Post grad courses; [occ.] Retired Aerospace Eng; [memb.] Beth Jacob and Adat Shalom Congregations; Amer Inst Aeronautics and Astronautics; [hon.] NASA Public Service Medal; Summa Cum Laude - USC; Honor Mah of All Depts - IIT; Two Engineering Patents; Who's Who: In the West, American Universities and Colleges; [oth. writ.] Other poems and articles; letters to editor, etc; [pers.] Derive satisfaction and if you can, enjoyment from meeting the challenge of whatever your lot is in life; [a.] Los Angeles, CA

KOONTZ, SHIRLEY M.
[b.] April 10, 1938, Chambersburg, PA; [p.] Laura R. Cooper Gray; [m.] Robert William Koontz, January 19, 1979; [ch.] Jerri L. Haines; Peter A. Harrison; Robin Englehart; Robert W. Koontz, Jr.; [ed.] Chambersburg Area H.S., Fine Arts 10 yrs. Adult Night Classes (oil painting) Numerous Sales, Marketing & Mgmt. Courses; [occ.] Public Relations, Howard Johnson Lodge, Chambersburg; [memb.] Spirit of Christ Comm. Church, Chambersburg, PA; [hon.] I used to exhibit works of art at Harpers Ferry, WV and also locally with the Chambersburg Art Alliance. I have won ribbons and sold art work.; [oth. writ.] I have been writing poetry since my teen years for my own pleasure and the pleasure of friends and relative.; [pers.] I believe the Lord gives each person their own special gifts and talents and allows each of us the opportunity to develop them.; [a.] Chambersburg, PA

KOSTKA, LAURA
[b.] September 28, 1965, Oak Park, IL; [p.] Janice and Roger Kostka; [ed.] Hinsdale Central H.S., University of Illinois at Urbana Champaign; University of Kansas, Nearing Completion of MBA Program; [occ.] Beta Specialist, Informix; [memb.] Alpha Chi Omega; [hon.] Dean's List, Freshman Honors at U of I; National Honor Society and Who's Who Among High School Students at Hinsdale Central H.S.; [oth. writ.] Several poems published in high school contest, article published in local newspaper.; [pers.] My writing often occurs as I reflect on life and situations special to me or others.; [a.] Kansas City, MO

KRAMER, KEVIN WAYNE
[b.] November 17, 1957, Elgin, IL; [ch.] Damian, Brittani, Ashley; [ed.] Elgin High. Elgin Comm College McHenry College; [occ.] Engineering, IL State Toll Highway Authority; [hon.] Purple Heart, Honorable Mention USMC; [oth. writ.] Several poems for Northwest Comm Hospital, New Directions. Auto-biography; [pers.] After a long bout with depression, I've learned, strength comes from inside, love is where we look for it, peace comes from above, happiness comes from all three combined; [a.] Lake In The Hills, IL

KRATZ, ANNICA
[Pen.] Annica Kratz; [b.] October 22, 1970, Sweden Kristinehamn; [p.] Tore and Kerstin Kratz; [pers.] "I strive to express what I have experienced in life, and beyond the door of the unseen"; [a.] Tampa, FL

KRIEG, ROBERT L.
[Pen.] Robert Louis Krieg the Ist; [b.] November 25, 1973, St. Mary's, PA; [ed.] Penn State University; [occ.] Student of Forestry; [pers.] This work was inspired by and dedicated to Ms. Julie Lynn Schmidt of Biglerville, PA

KROMAS, KIM
[b.] January 10, 1958, Cocoa Beach, Florida; [p.] James Kromas, Marina Petumenos; [ed.] Bachelor of Science 1987, Doctor of Chiropractic 1987, Los Angeles College of Chiropractic; [occ.] Chiropractic; [memb.] American Business Women, California Chiropractic Association, American Association of Drugless Practitioners; [hon.] Woman of the Year 1988; [oth. writ.] Nutritional articles for quarterly newsletter, Anorexia, Bulimia and Bulimarexia, Schizophrenia and Allopathic Treatment; [pers.] This poem was written out of pure emotion, without editing, proving that our hearts and should can always express our deepest feelings. All we have to do is listen.; [a.] Rancho Palos Verdes, CA

KROUSE, INGRID
[Pen.] Baroness Von Hellenstein; [b.] May 4, 1944, Heidenheim, Germany; [p.] William and Lore Holt; [ch.] Nikole, Alexis, Kai; [occ.] Office Manager, Times Newspaper; [pers.] I am, therefore I think.; [a.] Fairfax, VA

KRUK, HARRY
The name is a non de plume, the author wishes no credit for the poem, but he would want the readers to be aware that each mark in the poem symbolizes three free haircuts given at old age homes and orphanages, a period counts as one, an exclamation point counts as two. Over two thousand haircuts were given free of charge. At today's prices for a haircut this poem symbolizes approximately sixteen thousand dollars worth of charity. The author's philosophy is simple, his main desire is that someone may benefit by his existence, and that his life may cause no one to suffer hardship, be there a God or not, it doesn't matter. He places no copyright on the poem, so that anyone who desires to print it may do so; [a.] Dryden, MI

KUBIAK, MOLLY MARGARET
[b.] May 29, 1984, Evanston, IL; [p.] Samuel and Margaret Kristen Kubiak; [ed.] 5th Grade, Tuckahoe Elementary School, Arlington, VA; [occ.] Student; [memb.] Girl Scouts, Rainbows; [hon.] Honor Student; [a.] Atlanta, GA

KUPISZEWSKI, TONY EDWARD
[Pen.] Tone; [b.] June 17, 1941, Chicago; [p.] Helen and Edward Kupiszewski; [ed.] 8 yrs. gammer, 4 yrs. High School; [occ.] Supervisor, Plastic Capaction, Chicago, IL; [oth. writ.] World of Poetry Contests; Several poems in contest won Awards of merit Certificates. A record recorded from Columbine Records Corp. for one poem.; [pers.] I want to reflect the love everyone should have for there brother.; [a.] Chicago, IL

LA CROSS, JANET
[Pen.] The Universal Unicorn; [b.] November 14, 1957, Hartford, CT; [p.] Elaine Irish, Reginald La Cross (deceased); [ed.] Somers High - EOC (College Prep Courses); [occ.] Disabled; [memb.] MADD; [oth. writ.] Several unpublished works. This is my first unpublished poem; [a.] Enfield, CT

LA PRELL, LILLIAN
[b.] January 11, 1909, Buffalo, NY; [p.] Natalie and Fred Feirbend; [m.] Ambrose, September 28, 1940 (deceased); [ed.] Grammar School and 1 year of business school, I started working at age 14 and worked until 65; [occ.] Retired after 20 years as secretary for Marine Midland Bank in Buffalo, NY; [memb.] Did a lot of babysitting as a young girl and told the children stories that I made up and they loved it. I was told I should write a book and include all the stories I made up.; [hon.] Last year I met three of the youngsters that I sat and they said they still remember the stories I told them. They never forgot them after all these years.

LABAS, CHRISTIAN VLADIMIR
[b.] March 5, 1976, Trieste, Italy; [p.] Zvonko M. and Melania Labas; [occ.] Christian died April 10, 1994 of an unrecognized infection while undergoing chemotherapy for Burnitt Lymphoma that was diagnosed on March 9, 1994; [hon.] Maryland High School Certificate of Merit. The Christian V. Labas winner of NCTE Achievement in Writing Award. Nominated for the Jefferson Scholarship at UVA. Accepted as a Notre Dame Scholar, Maryland American Legion Boys State, Offer of appointment to the US Naval Academy, Governor citation for the NCTE Achievement in Writing; [oth. writ.] The Path Ahead (3-2-94), Twelve, Christian A La Canterbury Tale; [a.] Rockville, MD

LABATO, ANTHONY
[b.] December 29, 1962, Newark, NJ; [ed.] B.S. Environmental Design; Landscape Architecture; Cook College; Rutgers University; [occ.] Construction Project Manager, Environmental Remediation; [a.] Freehold, NJ

LACKEY, ALAINA ELISE
[b.] May 26, 1982, Tulsa, OK; [p.] James Daniel Lackey and Terri Lynn Lackey; [ed.] I've gone to school at Kiefer Elementary and am presently in the 7th grade; [occ.] Student at Kiefer Junior High; [memb.] I am a member of FCA, (Fellowship of Christian Athletes), Cheerleader for Kiefer Junior High School, And a number of Kiefer High School Band. I play the Clarinet. I attend First Grace Church in Glennpool, Oklahoma; [hon.] Best in Class Outstanding Band Award, 4 medals at Sand Springs Band Competition, Two Ribbons and a spirit stick in Cheerleading. Also, Cheerleading Captain in 6th grade. Won 3rd Sapulpa Vo-Tech art contest, Also school awards for Honor Roll and other classes; [pers.] I try to get young people to be wise about their choices and to follow their dreams in life; [a.] Kiefer, OK

LAFOUNTAIN, JANET
[b.] January 3, 1956, Plattsburgh, NY; [p.] Edward E. and Mildred Q. Raymond; [m.] James J. LaFountain, February 14, 1991; [ed.] Plattsburgh Sr. High, completed college courses; Clenton Community College, Asnuntuck Community College.; [occ.] Assistant Manager/Retail (Hardlines); [oth. writ.] My poem, "A Mask to Shed" was published in the "New American Poetry Anthology" in 1988. I have a personal collection of poetry I've written, not yet published.; [pers.] Take life and consume all the emotional morsels you can, sot that you will be able to taste every experience. I write in hopes that my writings will be an emotional morsel for all who reads them.. a tasty experience.; [a.] Somers, CT

LAMAR, MARIA E.
[b.] December 11, 1952, Philadelphia, PA; [p.] Rozell Pough, Mildred Bailey; [m.] Warren Lamar, July 28, 1979; [ch.] Eric Lee; [ed.] Germantown High, LaSalle University, Cheyney University, Gwynedd, Mercy College; [occ.] Secretary, Martin Luther King High School, Phila., PA, Certified Elementary Teacher; [memb.] Youth Aid Panel; helping Juveniles to become productive citizens; [pers.] The mirror is the looking glass of life, always reflect a positive image.; [a.] Philadelphia, PA

LAMBERT, GINGER
[b.] March 13, 1931, Brooklyn, NY; [p.] Mary A. Kaufman; [m.] James M. Lambert, February 17, 1962; [ch.] Patrice, Brian, Malcolm, Michael; [ed.] St. Joseph Catholic High School, Marshall (College); [occ.] Program/Clerk typist, Dept. of Veterans Affairs, Huntington, WV; [hon.] Certificate of Volunteer Remedial Reading Tutor; Special Contribution Awards at the U.S. Dept. of Veterans Affairs; [oth. writ.] Several, two of which were published in local paper's "Poetry Corner" (1976 & 1977). Wrote article in Church Magazine. Compiled H.S. Reunion program book, aided by my committee.; [pers.] I write about whatever inspires me at the moment, family, friends, other people...; [a.] Huntington, WV

LAMBETH, JOYCE ANN
[b.] April 29, 1951, Alvin, TX; [p.] T. K. and Dorothy Ann Lambeth; [m.] Divorced, February 1, 1967; [ch.] Marci Gale Berkman 25, Patricia Ann Strawn 23, Patricia Ann Strawn 23; [oth. writ.] Alvin High School; [oth. writ.] I have many more poems, copyrighted but I've never been published. I never knew where or how.; [pers.] I have struggled most of my life since I was 10 yrs. old. But I have beautiful children, March, Gale and Patricia and four precious grandchildren God has blessed me with and I write deep from my heart and soul from a precious higher power.; [a.] Alvin, TX

LAMMERT, EMILY
[b.] September 7, 1979, Cincinnati, OH; [p.] James and Ellen Lammert; [occ.] Student at: Carmel High School; [memb.] Student Council, Art Club, Volunteer, Chicago Botanic Garden; [pers.] I am always in search of meaning.; [a.] Vernon Hills, IL

LANDRUM, HUGH RANDOLPH
[b.] November 26, 1921, Victoria, VA; [p.] William and Gertrude Landrum; [m.] Joyce Landrum, February 1, 1947; [ch.] Cindy and Will; [ed.] American Univ., Washington, D.C., B.A. Music; Graduate work in Math; [occ.] Retired; [pers.] Too frequently experience clouts us hard, makes us wince and sometimes does not teach. No doubt it fails because of what's left out: when it strikes we hardly know just what it is we undergo!; [a.] Fredericksburg, VA

LANDWEHR, RUSSELL
[b.] May 1, 1919, Elizabeth, NJ; [p.] Henry and Dolly Landwehr; [m.] Frances Latawiec, February 23, 1947; [ch.] (3) Val (son), Jan (dau), Tad (son); [ed.] Linden High, Newark School of Fine and Industrial Arts, Academy of Arts (Newark, NJ), Newark College of Engineering; [occ.] Retired; [memb.] Somerset County Historical Society, Association of American Boyers, American Littoral Society; [pers.] Retired Artist-Draftsman, chiefly interested in researching and writing biographies of ancestors, genealogy, with an occasional poem or artwork; [a.] Linden, NJ

LANE, M.D., WENDY S.
[Pen.] W. S. Lane; [b.] January 11, 1959, Washington, D.C.; [p.] Ruth and Benjamin Karp; [m.] Ronald W. Lane, M.D., August 21, 1983; [ch.] William Gregory, Benjamin Cameron, Rebecca Susan; [ed.] Yale University (1976-1980), Dartmouth Medical School (1980-1984); Fellowship: Maine Medical Center (University of Vermont); [occ.] Physician (Endocrinologist); [memb.] American Board Internal Medicine, American Diabetes Association, Endocrine Society, Boston Athletic Association; [hon.] Undergraduate, Honors in English Letters (Yale U.); [pers.] Hampton Falls, NH

LANE, SHARON K.
[b.] March 25, 1948, Greencastle, IN; [p.] Russell and Jessie Coleman; [m.] Robert E. Lane, April 17, 1987; [ch.] Shannon, Derek, Jessica, Jonathan, Joseph and Sean; [ed.] Greencastle High, Indiana State University; [occ.] Household Engineer; [memb.] Youngstown United Methodist Church; [oth. writ.] One poem published in local newspaper. Have written a collection of approximately 150 poems, put in book form, not yet published. My husband and I write songs together for a hobby.; [pers.] This is a 25 year dream come true. I have two grand-daughters, Andrea and Sarah, and a 3rd grandchild on the way. If I should never accomplish anything else, I am satisfied to have the honor of having my poem in this book! This is the inheritance I leave behind for all my children and grandchildren, and future generations.; [a.] Terre Haute, IN

LANG, FLORENCE
[b.] September 26, 1914, Memphis, TN; [m.] J.C. Lang; [ch.] Carolyn Woodson and Sylvia Lang; [ed.] High School; [occ.] McDonnell Douglas; [memb.] Blessed Hope Bible Church M.E.S.A. (Mercantile Bank); [oth. writ.] A few other poems written in early years, Lessons from the Bible.; [a.] St. Louis, MO

LANGE, RICK
[b.] December 26, 1965, New Hartford, NY; [p.] Richard and Phyllis; [oth. writ.] I have an unpublished children's book called Bouncing Thoughts; [pers.] I'd like to thank my grandfather, Reginald, for his continuous support. A friend once said to me, "Our feet are planted in the earth. Our arms are stretching toward the heavens. And our souls are anywhere we want them to be". I think that's true; [a.] Brewerton, NY

LARKIN, NICOLETTE LENORE
[b.] November 5, 1962, Annapolis, MD; [p.] Robert and Beatrice Larkin; [m.] Single; [ch.] Walter Somerby and Joan Elizabeth Cooke; [ed.] South River High School, life is the greatest teacher; [occ.] Postal Jerk, I mean "clerk" U.S.P.S., Bulk Mail Center, Capitol Heights, MD; [pers.] Genesis, Chapter 9, Verses 12-16, To God be the glory. Praise the Lord.; [a.] Edgewater, MD

LARSEN, MARY
[Pen.] Mary Egan Larsen; [ed.] B.A., M.A. Special Education; [occ.] Special Education Teacher; [memb.] Council for Exceptional Children; [oth. writ.] Started writing in 4th grade. Poems published in school magazines and yearbooks. Editor of school literary magazine.; [pers.] I believe communication is the key to a better world. I write about the experiences and feelings that all people share but I especially try to address issues affecting children and families.

LARSON, IRENE MARY
[b.] September 19, 1921, Lynd, Minn.; [p.] Andrew and Marry Larron; [m.] Single; [ed.] High School Graduate; [occ.] Retired, Disabled, M.S.

LARSON, JOHNNYE BELINDA
[Pen.] Johnnye Larson; [b.] July 29, 1963, Wilson, OK; [p.] Frank and Linda Carriker; [m.] Frank Joel Larson, August 23, 1990; [ch.] Pamela, Leanna, T.J.; [ed.] Wilson High, Wilson, OK, So-Ok Area Vo-tech, Ardmore, OK, NCTC Gainsville, TX; [occ.] Licensed Vocational Nurse; [memb.] Grace Temple Baptist Church, Denton, TX, Preschool Sunday School Teacher; [oth. writ.] Personal Journaling; [pers.] Thanks to all who believed in fairytales, and to Mom and Dad for the love they have

shown to all their daughters equally. Thanks to a very understanding husband.; [a.] Denton, TX

LASKOWITZ, PEARL LIEBMAN
[b.] January 28, 1910, Orange, NJ; [p.] Isidor Liebman and Sarah Klein (both deceased); [m.] Irving Laskowitz, January 27, 1946 (deceased); [ch.] One daughter, Janice Serena Laskowitz; [ed.] High School Graduated; [occ.] Retired; [memb.] Hadassah for many years and many others; [hon.] Poet Laureate of the Theater Club of the Air, New York World Telegram and numerous others; [pers.] Poetry, compositions, articles, plays; [pers.] Gardens, like people, grow with care, with lots of sun and rain and air, Wholesome plants, from wholesome seed, With here and there an ugly weed That saps the strength from other shoots, Until it's lifted by its roots, and banished by a watchful hand, Then, once more healthy brows the land. With weeding out of crime and evil, With banishment of human weevil, With lots of air and sun and rain, People, like gardens, grow and gain; [a.] Newark, NJ

LAWLER, KEVIN A.
[b.] May 22, 1941, Nyack, NY; [p.] Mary J. Lawler; [m.] Anne B. Lawler, July 15, 1964; [ch.] Nancy and Joe Donahue, Leanne (2), Grace (1 1/2), Beth and Deron Koval, Christopher (1 1/2), Christin Lawler; [ed.] Xavier HS, NYC, Holy Cross College, Worcester, MA; [occ.] Disabled, Multiple Sclerosis; [memb.] Nat'l Assoc of Realtors GRI, Instructor, Church of the Presentation; [pers.] "Choose the day when you will serve. As for me and my home, we will serve the Lord".

LAZAR, SHEILA M.
[b.] November 23, 1941, Los Angeles, CA; [p.] Michael and Beatrice Shanahan; [m.] Wayne J. Lazar, August 21, 1971; [ed.] MBA, College of Notre Dame Belmont, Calif.; [pers.] Words are the keys that unlock the passions of the heart.; [a.] Belmont, CA

LEADERS, PATTY
[b.] September 23, 1948, Wolfboro, NH; [m.] Skip Leaders; [ch.] Mellisa, Susan, Chanda and step-daughter Colette; [occ.] Low-Temp Refrigeration, Inc.; [pers.] With out the encouragement from my husband I would never have written this poem.; [a.] Orlando, FL

LEBEL, KEVIN T.
[b.] March 3, 1967, Lynn, MA; [m.] Karen L. Lebel, October 2, 1994; [ch.] Stephen Bethune, Shawn Quigley; [ed.] Peabody Vocational High, US Army 1985-1988; [occ.] Teamsters Warehousemen, Part time musician; [oth. writ.] Hundreds of unpublished works of poetry and songs.; [pers.] I try to concentrate on the negatives of life to open ways for mankind to find solutions. People need to open their eyes to reality; [a.] Plaistow, NJ

LEE, JENNIFER L.
[b.] March 16, 1985, Niles, MI; [p.] David and Loretta Lee; [ed.] Attends Ballard Elementary School. Currently in the fourth grade.; [memb.] Student Council Representative.; [hon.] Received many spelling awards.; [a.] Niles, MI

LEE, LORIE ANN
[b.] January 26, 1978, Uniondale, NY; [p.] Melvin and Gertrude Lee; [ed.] South Shore Christian School; [occ.] student; [memb.] National Honor Society, Long Island Fund for Women and Girls, St. John's Episcopal Church Youth Group, St. John's Episcopal Church Acolyte Guild; [hon.] High Honor Roll, Who's Who Among

American High School Students, Congressional Youth Scholar; [oth. writ.] Poems published in Anthology of Poetry for Young Americans; [a.] Uniondale, NY

LEEKS, TRACYE
[Pen.] Tracye Linette; [b.] October 17, 1971, New Jersey; [p.] Sandra and Leslie Ware; [ed.] Brooklyn Technical High, Prairie View A&M University, Lincoln University; [occ.] 2nd Grade Teacher, Christ Lutheran School; [memb.] Zeta Phi Beta Sorority Inc., Kappa Delta Phi; [hon.] Miss Black Int'l 1993-4, Dean's List 1990-1993; [pers.] To whom much is given, much is required.; [a.] Jamaica, NY

LEET, JAMIE D.
[b.] October 2, 1978, Sedalia, MO; [p.] Pamela and Jack Leet; [ed.] Currently 10th grade in Otterville, High School R-6; [occ.] Student; [memb.] Cheerleader 93", Dance Studio 90-92" and Swim Team 85-89"; [hon.] Sewing Award, Cheerleading Awards, State District Awards, State District Award in Music, Choir Award, Chorus Award, Honor Roll; [oth. writ.] Written several poems but no others have been published.; [pers.] I encourage everybody to find their secret talent, whatever that may be, and try to use it.; [a.] Otterville, MO

LEFEBVRE, CHRISTIN
[Pen.] Gabrielle McCloud; [b.] March 26, 1968, Meriden, CT; [p.] Eric and Bonnie Moore; [ch.] Ashleigh Lefebvre; [ed.] Currently attending Quinnebaugh Valley Community and Technical College, majoring in English and Communications; [occ.] Operators Secretary at Crabtree & Evelyn, Ltd.; [hon.] Publications in the National Library of Poetry's Anthology entitled "Reflections of Light."; [oth. writ.] Several short stories published in newsletters. I have also written product write-ups and sell sheets for my company.; [pers.] For me, the challenge of writing is to provoke my readers into experiencing vivid feelings, moods and visions. The interpretations of my reality are expressed as I lead them by the hand through a complex maze of carefully chosen metaphors and descriptive phrases. My satisfaction comes from successfully prompting an emotional response, stirring the waters of their imagination.; [a.] Grosvenordale, CT

LEGERWOOD, BARBARA
[b.] Washington, DC; [ch.] 3 (grown), 6 grandchildren; [ed.] AB (Liberal Arts), Howard Univ, Washington, DC, New York City public schools; [pers.] I am living in Maryland but I left my heart in DC; [a.] Maryland

LEMPEK, JEAN D.
[b.] September 15, 1912, Chicago; [p.] Walter and Maryann Banasiak; [m.] William Alexander Lempek, July 30, 1932, (deceased); [ch.] Lorraine Mary; [ed.] St. Joseph's Teachers Academy, Stevens Point, Wisconsin, Courses in Business Management furthered my education in Chicago, Illinois.; [occ.] Retired Business Professional; [memb.] American Assoc., of Retired Persons, Polish National Alliance of America, MacNeal Coronary Club; [oth. writ.] Unpublished Poems; [pers.] My husband and I became successful in various business enterprises. We also enjoyed the arts of music and photography. In our many travels throughout the United States the sheer beauty of nature ultimately instilled in me the desire to express my feelings through poetry.; [a.] Chicago, IL;

LEONARD, STEPH
[Pen.] Tienne (pronounced T.N.); [b.] February 23, Philadelphia, PA; [p.] Edward T. and Dorothy C. Leonard. Raised by my beloved grandmother Bertha M. Campbell and my Aunt Florence and Uncle Sam Asher; [ed.] Lankenau School, Central Bucks High School, and St. Joseph's College; [occ.] Due to severe accident, writing is my only occupation; [memb.] Elizabeth Taylor AIDS Foundation Sponsor, Greater Guild Sponsor for a number of years; [hon.] Blue Ribbons at Horse Show at Gwynedd Farms and, once, had Helen Hayes, the 1st Lady of the American Theatre, See me in a play at Totem Pole Playhouse in Rural PA; [oth. writ.] Have had my poetry published in an anthology by Lincoln B. Young and also included in two collections "The Poet" published by Doris Nemetty. Collaborate w/a friend writing songs. Am currently writing a novel and a cook book along with poetry and short stories; [pers.] My Philosophy of life was best expressed by Tennessee Williams in his play Night of the Iguana, "Nothing human is alien to me, save cruelty or violence". I love writing and the theater; [a.] Lansdale, PA

LEVACK, MARY I.
[b.] November 12, 1937, Glens Falls, NY; [p.] Theresa McDonnell and Harold Levack; [ed.] St. Mary's Academy, Glen Falls, NY, Siena Heights College, Adrian Mich., Michigan State University, E. Lansing; [occ.] Diagonal Minister in the Methodist Church; Director of Music; [memb.] Fummwoa; Tuesday Musicare of Detroit; "Wrangler" is an ecumenical clergy fellowship founded in the early 1900's by Rheinhold Nibube; [hon.] First Woman President of "Wranglers" 1993, M. Music in Piano Performance from MSU; [oth. writ.] A few brief discarded poems, a few songs.; [pers.] "Words written or spoken in truth have power to create, resolve, heal and make whole." "Goodness is diffusive of itself."; [a.] birmingham, MI

LEVERING, RICHARD
[b.] January 22, 1933, LaPlata,MD; [p.] Olga and Charles Levering; [m.] Arline Levering, April 12, 1959; [ch.] Allison and Robert; [ed.] St. Johns College, Annapolis, MD; C.W. Post College, Long Island, NY; [occ.] Correction Officer Sergeant, Nassau County Correctional Center; [memb.] American Legion Post 948, Retired Captain USAF; [oth. writ.] Contributed poems to Corrections News Letter and American Legion Newsletter, poem published in "Perspectives" book of poems by Iliad Press.; [pers.] I am touched by the romance of life and a desire to pass this emotion on.; [a.] Bellmore, NY

LEWIN, GREGORY A.
[b.] October 7, 1967, Bluefields, Nicaragua; [p.] Austin and Daphnie Lewin; [m.] Dina Hodgson Lewin, November 21, 1991; [ed.] High Point High; [occ.] Commissioning Officer; [oth. writ.] Wrote several poems for the International Committee at High Point, including the Year Book; [pers.] In my writing I try to express exactly what I see and feel from the bottom of my heart.; [a.] Silver Spring, MD

LEWIS, MARJORIE W.
[b.] September 29, 1913, Philadelphia, PA; [p.] Elsie Stearly Winchell and Samuel Dickson Winchell; [m.] Don E. Lewis, May 23, 1942; [ch.] Son, Dickson Winchell Lewis; [ed.] Upper Darby High, 1930 and Palmer Business College 1932; [occ.] Retired; [memb.] Lifetime Member of International Society of Poets and Advisory Board.; [hon.] Was Salutatorian of Class at Palmer; Presidential Award for Red Cross Instructor in World War II, etc.; [oth. writ.] Newspaper reporter and feature writer with former Upper Darby News and Phila. Bulletin and other local papers.; [pers.] From Academics to secretary and after our son's birth combining motherhood and journalism at home, culminating in my love of poetry in travels with my husband and upon his retirement his challenge that he would cook if I would hang on to my dream and write. Always unable to resist a challenge I went for it.; [a.] Havertown, PA

LEWIS, MICHAEL HARRY
[b.] April 1, 1968, Washington, D.C.; [m.] Charlette Kim lewis, November 5, 1993; [ch.] Britany Marie Forster; [ed.] Northwestern High School, United States Airforce; [pers.] I would like to take this moment to thank the Lord for blessing me with the gift of creative and artistic expression. I love you father with all of my heart.; [a.] Lanham, MD

LEWIS, WAYNE MC CARTHY
[b.] May 2, 1953, Crewe, VA; [p.] Earnest and Mozella Lewis; [m.] Gloria C. Lewis, July 26, 1975; [ch.] Aretha M., Valerie A., LaShonda M.; [ed.] Nottoway High School, Nottoway, VA - Class of 1971; [occ.] Correctional Officer Nottoway Correctional Center, Burkeville, VA; [memb.] New Bethel Baptist Church Choir, Worshipful Master of Evergreen Lodge #131, Free and Accepted Masons, Inc, Crewe, VA; [a.] Crewe, VA

LILLIE, BRIAN NORRIS
[Pen.] Brian Norris; [b.] August 23, 1973, Los Gatos, CA; [ed.] Los Gatos High School, Santa Barbara City College; [occ.] Clothing Designer for "Kind Minor" and "Virgo Luster"; [oth. writ.] Numerous poems and short stories; Wall writings; Currently writing first full length novel; numerous musical projects; [pers.] I attempt to lyrically capture the exact moment I am surrounded in smiles, sunsets, and music are my passion which lead to my inspiration. Live the moment, and be the action!!!! [a.] Los Gatos, CA

LILLIE, WILLIAM MICHAEL DAVID
[Pen.] Mike; [b.] December 15, 1979, Millington, TN; [p.] Jerry F. Lillie and Barbara A. Lillie; [ed.] Attending Kofa High School; [occ.] Student; [memb.] Member of Kofa's wrestling Team, Baseball Team and Football Team. Miyama Ryu Ju-Jutsu School. St. Francis Youth Group; [hon.] Received several honors certificate. Certified Training in Combat Ju-Jutsu. Honor Student; [pers.] Some things in life cannot be changed. So accept them; [a.] Yuma, AZ

LIN, JO-ANN SANCHEZ
[b.] August 2, 1951, New York, NY; [p.] Jennie Pazos and William Sanchez; [m.] Juan Lin, December 24, 1976; [ch.] Adrian; [ed.] B.A. Suny at Stony Brook; [occ.] Writer; [oth. writ.] Unpublished Manuscripts: London Bridge, Carousel Top and three one act plays.; [pers.] Blood, sweat and tears.; [a.] Chestertown, MD

LIND, JOSEPH A.
[b.] March 18, 1962, Chignik Lake, AK; [p.] Fred and Annie Lind; [m.] Cynthia H. Lind, January 21, 1983; [ch.] Timothy J. Lind, Elizabeth Ann L.; [ed.] Bristol Bay High School, graduated May, 1980. AAS Human Services - Dec 1994, Univ of Alaska Anchorage; [occ.] Aftercare Counselor, singer - song writer - musician; [memb.] Alaska Song writers Assoc 1986-87-88-89-90; [hon.] Billboard Song Writers Contest. Honorable Mention in 1991 and 1993 for songs: "Alaskan Life", "I Feel For You Baby" and "Heart of Gold"; National Dean's List 1992-93-94; [pers.] "Everything has a reason - just ask." [a.] Anchorage, AK

LINDE, GREGORY C.
[b.] January 22, 1954, Minneapolis, MN; [p.] Carl and Marjorie Linde; [m.] Lisa Ann Linde, December 7, 1991; [ch.] Katie, Nick, Cobi Linde; [ed.] Hopkins High School, University of Minnesota, William Mitchell Law School; [occ.] Attorney; [memb.] Minn. Bar Association, Minneapolis Assoc. of Realtors; [a.] Minnetonka, MN

LINDO, JAYE SHELTON
[b.] July 31, 1961, Fort Ord, CA; [p.] Stanley D. and Edith J. Shelton; [m.] Robert and Alwin Lindo, August 8, 1987; [ch.] Nicole E. and Krystal E. Lindo; [ed.] Northwestern Sr. High; [occ.] Customer Service Manager for Leading Convention; [memb.] Decorator; [oth. writ.] Several poems; [pers.] I believe in looking for the light within me.; [a.] Cheverly, MD

LINDSAY, PATRICIA
[b.] March 1, 1946, Sharon Hill, PA; [p.] James J. and Eleanor M. Leahy; [m.] James E. Lindsay, June 7, 1989; [ed.] Wildwood Catholic H.S., Glassboro State College (limited Term); [occ.] Author Book Title "It Comes Down to Wanting Something" writer, homemaker; [memb.] The Concord Coalition, National Republican Party Comm., Library of Congress, National Member, Oxford club; [hon.] Miss Cape May County, NJ 1964, Miss America Pageant Preliminary, NJ State Level; [oth. writ.] Formerly a staff writer, recording artist, Jamie Records and Publishing Co., Phila., PA formerly a member of "BMI" (Broadcast Music Inc.) currently, freelancing.; [pers.] If you know no boundaries of imagination or abilities, you can accomplish anything (Author of Quote, My Husband); [a.] White Haven, PA

LINEBERRY, M. ELLEN
[Pen.] Ellen Lineberry (maiden); [b.] April 13, 1934, Randloph County; [p.] Hilda P. Lineberry and Hobard Roscoe Lineberry (deceased); [m.] Divorced; [ch.] Janet Ellen, Counselor, Criminal Justice System; [ed.] Grays Chapel High, Pfeiffer College; [occ.] Self, President El-Wim Associates, Inc., for 26 years.; [memb.] Grays Chapel United Methodist Church, Human Society of the United States; [oth. writ.] Several poems, none published, this is my first entry; [pers.] I began writing poetry almost two years ago. My inspiration was like a bump in the night, a light from heaven so to speak. I write from my heart with a story to tell. I hope others are inspired by my work as told in a literary way. I am an advocate of the animal rights crusade and have been all of my life, even as a child. My make a wish is that the human race will come to have equal respect for the animal kingdom. My daughter has been and is a constant inspiration and friend in my life. I dedicate this poem to her. I never met a dog I didn't like.; [a.] Greensboro, NC

LITTLE, RUFUS C.
[b.] January 29, 1926, Concord, NH; [p.] Robert B. and Evelyn V. Little; [m.] Single; [ch.] Zoie V. Little, Honorary and Robert E. Little, Adopted; [ed.] Grad., Concord High School 1944; [occ.] Retired Worked in lumber and bldg. materials for 45 yrs., 31 yrs. at Concord Lumber Co. in Concord, NH; [memb.] N.H. Historical Society, Concord, NH, Mt. Dora Hist. Society, Mt. Dora, FL, Immanuel Community Church, Concord, NH, Community Congr. Church Mt., Dora, FL.; [hon.] None; [oth. writ.] Many, too numerous to list.; [pers.] Very interested in poetry, especially such as Helen Steiner Rice has written as well as others like her.; [a.] Mount Dora, FL

LITTLEJOHN, MICHAEL
[Pen.] Richard Allen; Sinbad; [b.] November 19, 1978, Cleveland, OH; [p.] Christine and Leroy Littlejohn; Inspiration: Nikki Giovanni; [ed.] Garrett A. Morgan Cleveland School of Science; John f. Kennedy High School. (both in Cleveland, OH); [occ.] Junior in High School; [memb.] Case Western Reserve University Upward Bound, SD P.S.H.D.; Lee Road Baptist Church Youth Group (both in Cleveland, OH); [hon.] National Honors Society; [oth. writ.] Several writings in school newspapers, historical writings in The Plain Dealer (both in Cleveland, OH); [pers.] "Perseverance is the key to unlock the doors of your future"; [a.] Cleveland, OH

LITUAK, KATHY
[b.] May 5, 1944, Kavcay, Hungary; [p.] Magda and Imre Miselbach; [m.] Augustine Litvak, November 14, 1964; [ch.] Salvador, David; [ed.] Dunalastair, Santiago Chile School of Chemistry and Pharmacy Santiago, Masters of Science Long Island U, NY; [occ.] Assoc Editor, American Hospital Foumulary Service; [memb.] ASHP, Beth El Synagogue; [hon.] Valedictorian in Dunalastair, Summa Cum Laude, Univ of Chile, Dean's List Long Island Univ; [oth. writ.] Short stories, poems; [pers.] I write, because I have fun doing it; [a.] Bethesda, MD

LITZ, JAMES CHARLES
[Pen.] Artist "J.C. Litz; [b.] September 17, 1948, Buffalo, NY; [p.] Thomas Sr. and Barbara Litz; [m.] Beverly Jean Litz, July 12, 1986; [ed.] Mother of Divine Grace Elem., Cleveland Hill, High School Graduated 1967; [occ.] World Renowned Primitive Naive Unschooled Artist; [memb.] Museum of American Art, NY, Cooperstown Art Assoc, Burchfield Penny Art Museum, Buffalo Arts Council; [hon.] All my visuals are art paintings, Partners Press Award All Bright Knox Art Museum 1988; Cooperstown Art Assoc., National Exhibition First Prize Award July 1990, many other smaller awards in exhibitions I have entered my paintings; [oth. writ.] Children's books written and illustrated by James C. Litz, Title "Harold The Happy Hobo" 1993. This book has not been published "A View From My Backyard Porch" May 2, 1987; [pers.] Within every human being there is an ability for creativity. It must be motivated by the individual through His own experiences in life and expressed in his own form of art!; [a.] Depew, NY

LIVERANI, CHRISTINE
[b.] December 31, 1971, Manhattan, NY; [p.] Sandra and Edward Liverani; [ed.] Siena College (Bachelor of Arts in English) Loudonville, NY; High School, Immaculate Heart Academy; [occ.] Graduate Student of Journalism; [memb.] Coalition for the Homeless, Big Brothers, Big Sisters; [hon.] Dean's List, Siena College Ambassador's Club, Most Accomplished Speaker in Department Forum; [oth. writ.] Several letters to the editor of local newspaper, 2 short stories published in college publication; [pers.] Ambition to step in the shoes of God and achieve the nobility of the most wretched beggar.; [a.] Stony Point, NY

LIZZIO, MADELYN D.
[Pen.] Madelyn D. Mc Carson; [b.] October 4, 1953, Long Island; [m.] Frank P. Lizzio, November 15, 1980; [ch.] Nicole Marie, Frank James; [ed.] South Side Sr., High School of visual Arts, N.Y.C., N.Y.; [occ.] Artist; [pers.] We all have the freedom to write, whether it be personal or public. When we choose to exercise this right we allow our voices to be heard. In the words of Kahlil Gibran: Wisdom is not in words; Wisdom is meaning within words.; [a.] Rockville Centre, NY

LLOYD, PETER M.
[b.] July 23, 1963, London, England; [p.] Carmen L. Lloyd; [ed.] Boys and Girls High School, Baruch College; [occ.] Railroad Clerk, New York City Transit Authority; [memb.] Mt. Zion Tabernacle Christian Mission Church; [pers.] I live by the Philosophy of treating others the way I would like to be treated. I appreciate the good people who I have met in my life, and I have learned not to take them for granted. Jesus Christ is my hero.; [a.] Brooklyn, NY

LO GIOCO, LORI-ANN
[b.] December 6, 1972, Paterson, NJ; [p.] Chief Frank J. LoGioco and Carol A. LoGioco; [ed.] Clifton High School, Bergen Community College; Univ of MD College Park; [memb.] Gamma Phi Beta Sorority, Alpha Phi Omega Service Fraternity; [a.] Clifton, NJ

LOBO, IVA ANJOS
[b.] September 14, 1946, Soa Paulo Brazil; [p.] Augusto S. Anjos and Maria Alencar Anjos; [m.] Rosaluo Santos Lobo, December 8, 1987; [ed.] Blair High, Wilson Center, ESL; [occ.] Babysitter, Children Samantha Balser, Hannah G. Weiss and Mari Beth Weiss; [oth. writ.] Several poems and songs not published yet.; [pers.] I do enjoy writing about it, love, justice, freedom, human rights, better world and democracy.; [a.] Manassas, VA

LODET, MONICA RAYMON
[b.] April 26, 1958, Natchitoches, Louisiana; [p.] Bill Raymon Sr. and Dorothy J. Raymon; [ch.] Pet, Tigger; [ed.] Natchitoches Central High School, Northwestern State University; [occ.] Special Attendant to the Elderly; [memb.] Turtle Creek After Care; [oth. writ.] Poem published in 1984 by Quill Books; [pers.] My desire is to please God through my writing. Therefore I feel if I give unconditional love someday I'll receive it. Of all the things I've seen and done the greatest reward has come by connecting with the spirit through my poems. The poem, Under the bridge of the Word was inspired by actual experience, I was homeless, alcoholic and addict but by the Grace of God I'm in Recovery today.; [a.] Dallas, TX

LOGAN, BILL JR.
[Pen.] William Mills; [b.] March 23, 1948, Gaffney, SC; [p.] B.L. Logan and Julia Logan; [m.] Patricia Ann, December 18, 1966; [ch.] Darren Scott, Stephanie Francene; [ed.] Benjamin E. Mays High School, Rutledge College; [occ.] Trainer/ISO 9000 Specialist, Hoechst Calenese Corp., Spartanburg, SC; [memb.] Veterans of Foreign Wars; Pleasant View United Methodist Church, Chairperson; Sickle Cell Anemia Foundation; [hon.] Navy Commendation Medal with Combat V.; [oth. writ.] Poems for the Sickle Cell Anemia Foundation, Pleasant View United Methodist Church, and the Hoechst Celanese Corporation.; [pers.] My writing comes from deep within the inner thoughts of what I see and feel.; [a.] Spartanburg, SC

LOGSDON, TOBY
[b.] June 14, 1972, Oregon; [p.] Dr. Richard Logsdon, Julie Logsdon; [ed.] High School, BS in Psychology (California Luthern Univ); [occ.] Student (soon to be a seminary student); [hon.] Dean's List, Santa Lucia Award, 1988 Nevada State High School Soccer Champions, 1991-92 Sophomore Class Vice-President; [oth. writ.] Had poems published in the Morning Glory, California Lutheran University's annual All American rated publication; [pers.] All praise and thanks be to God, not only for blessing me with the ability to express myself

with words, but for taking all the darkness out of my life and replacing it with truth. Thank you, Father, for blessing me with a supportive, loving, Christian family. Special thanks to Kay McGarvey; [a.] Las Vegas, NV

LONDON, MICHAEL
[b.] March 13, 1950, San Jose, CA; [p.] John and Marie; [m.] Susan London, February 18, 1995; [ed.] Tennyson High, Hayward CA, University of Cal. at Santa Barbara; [occ.] Musician, recording artist/voice-over artist; [memb.] A.F. of M., A.F.T.R.A.; [hon.] Gold Record Awards, Stephen Bishop, "Bish" Carless, "On and On"; [oth. writ.] Pop song and country catalogs published by "Pen and Sword Music."; [pers.] "Between the conscious and unconscious lies the mind of an artist. This mind is unfettered and eternal."; [a.] Castro Valley, CA

LONDON, REV. LAWRENCE
[Pen.] Larry London; [b.] February 1, 1921, Des Moines, Iowa; [ed.] Convert to Catholic Church 1937 Delay desire for religious lifestyle until after WW II military service with USCG in Hawaii. After two years college enter Capuchin Franciscan Order for 5 years, Father's death causes change to diocesan seminary to help mother. Ordained priesthood 1953. Celebrate first Mass at Poor Clare Monastery Rockford, IL of Rockford diocese. Serve in parish ministry (plus 5 years as hospital chaplain) 40 years. Live contemplative religious life with Lebh Shoemea Community, Sarita, TX for first retirement year.; [oth. writ.] Many unpublished poems; [pers.] "My poems reflect my desire to discern, express and proclaim the presence of One, who is greater than ourselves and all creation, still personally and intimately within and among us. The ground of being and constant source of new life. Hope for all peoples fulfillment in divine providence."; [a.] Rockford, IL

LONG, ANDREW JAMES
[Pen.] A.J. Long; [b.] March 4, 1970, Lincoln Park, MI; [p.] Judith R. Long, Ronald J. Long; [m.] Lynda Marie, March 26, 1995; [ch.] Chelsey Noel Anderson; [ed.] Thunderbird HS, Northern Ariz Univ, Glendale Comm College; [occ.] US Coast Guard Active; [hon.] Various military commendations and medals; [oth. writ.] Have been writing for approx 5 yrs. Have never submitted anything before now; [pers.] I use poetry writing as a channel to keep everything in live that is random; organized; [a.] Phoenix, AZ

LONG, R.N., ROSALIE T.
[Pen.] Rosalie Tyler Long; [b.] May 20, 1924, South Carolina; [p.] Geneva McMillan Tyler and Robert Tyler; [m.] Deceased, Forezene C. Tyler Long, May 16, 1946; [ch.] Jerelyn, Rosalyn, and Kathy; [ed.] Booker T. Washington High, Cola. Hospital School of Nsg. Diploma; B.A. Mary Mount, Man. College, MPS.C.W. Post/L.I. Univ., NY; [occ.] Retired R.N., (Reg. Prof. Nurse); former Nursing and Hospital Admin; [memb.] Chi Eta Phi Sorority (Nat. Nurses); American Lung Assoc., Abyssian Baptist Church Building Fund. Comm., Chairperson Women's Day Committee; Democratic National Committee, Wash. D.C.; [hon.] Senior Citizens Recognition Awards, Recognition award for outstanding achievement in Education, Nursing and Hospital admin.; [oth. writ.] High school and nursing reunion speeches, several poems unpublished; [pers.] I strive to reflect my thankfulness to God, for the gifts he endowed to me, in my poems and writings.; [a.] Bronx, NY

LOOSE, IAN M.
[b.] October 27, 1978, Reading, PA; [p.] William J. and Susan A. Loose; [ed.] 9th grade student at Burns Jr High; [oth. writ.] This is my first poem I ever submitted for publication.

LOPEZ, VIRGINIA
[b.] September 21, 1927, PR; [p.] Mr. and Mrs. Raymond Gutierrez; [m.] Jose R. Lopez (deceased), March 13, 1957; [ch.] 9; [ed.] Ponce High School (12); [occ.] I work part time in a recreation center; [memb.] AARP - Lifestudy Fellowship - Sacred Heart of Jesus; [hon.] Five or six from World of Poetry whose founded in 1975 by John Campbell; [oth. writ.] Poems, novels, songs (some of my lyrics at Peer International Corp). I used to dance and sing in a club, in Bklyn, NY; [pers.] My writing poems, or stories are inspired by personal, family and friends daily lives. It helps me a lot to go on with my life.

LORENZ, LARRY K.
[Pen.] Killer (as in Lady); [b.] February 10, 1960, St. Louis, MO; [p.] Richard and Shirley Lorenz; [m.] Roxane Lorenz, June 16, 1984; [ch.] Danielle, Jake; [ed.] Riverview Gardens High School; [occ.] Machinist/ Trainer at Alco Controls, St. Louis; [memb.] Lodge #1345 I.A.of M.; [pers.] Do something in your life before your life does you in, so when you look back on your life and see where you've been..., you're satisfied! These are my words to live by.; [a.] St. Louis, MO

LORENZ, RUTH E.
[Pen.] Sara Stina Dalson/S.S. Lord; [b.] August 14, 1918, Saginaw, MI; [p.] Hulda and Lisle Grimes; [m.] Lyle R. Lorenz, August 24, 1940; [ch.] Michelle; [ed.] John Marshall High, Ohio State University; [occ.] Retire, from NASA Lewis Research Center was head of report typing unit during WWII; [hon.] Special Achievement Award from NASA in 1973 as the only female staff member of the Job Classification Branch of Personnel during reduction in force years.; [oth. writ.] French poems published in high school mag., unpublished book length epic poem, short stories and poems.; [pers.] The writing of poetry is good therapy.; [a.] North Olmstead, OH

LORINO, ERIN MORONEY
[b.] April 19, 1962, Laurelton, NY; [m.] Richard Lorino, October 20, 1984; [ch.] Daniel Ross Lorino; [pers.] I live a quiet life in the small town of Forestburgh, NY with my husband Richard and son Daniel. It is here where we all strive to help each other achieve our goals in life. Whether it be my husband's wood sculpting or my son's school activities or my being able to write what I feel in my heart. We all are there for each other, and for this bond of family I am able to express myself through my writing.; [a.] Forestburgh, NY

LOYD, CHARLES KEVIN
[b.] June 26, 1963, Roanoke, VA; [p.] Charles E. and Margaret Loyd; [ed.] Fauquier High; [occ.] Construction, Equipment Operator; [oth. writ.] Several unpublished poems; [pers.] I believe in freedom, love, and the simple country way of life. I oppose oppression by government or individual, and wish for a return to traditional values and to God.; [a.] Amissville, VA

LOYD, ROBERT C.
[b.] March 15, 1927, Iredell County, NC; [p.] Rufus and Cordia Loyd; [m.] Sara Lea Campbell, November 29, 1949; [ch.] Martha Karen; [ed.] High School plus several home study courses in Traffic Management, Electronics, Etc.; [occ.] Retired, Operating Small Air Freight

Distribution Company; [memb.] Masonic Lodge, Order of the Eastern Star, Gideons Intnl.; [hon.] Past Master, Past Patron, Past District Deputy Grand Patron, Past District Deputy Grand Lecturer; [oth. writ.] Poems and songs in local distribution. Have memoirs consisting of numerous short pieces written in style of Whaley, Grizzard, Porch et al. Looking for publisher for same.; [pers.] Qualify yourself as an expert in one or more fields. Your expertise will be in demand sometime.; [a.] Statesville, NC

LUCAS, MACHELE
[b.] May 19, 1981, Antioch Memorial Hospital; [p.] Gary Lucas, Mari Bourret; [a.] Hapine, OR

LUCRETIA, SCREEN WILLIAMS
[Pen.] Lucretia Screen; [b.] December 31, 1934, Bayonne, NJ; [p.] Mr. and Mrs. Earl Screen; [m.] Nathaniel Williams, February 2, 1952; [ch.] Patricia, Denise, Nathaniel, Jeffrey, Cheryl, Annette and Celeste; [ed.] 11th; [occ.] Tech Clerk for New York Telephone Company; [memb.] AARP, Pioneers.

LUFTGLASS, SCOTT BRIAN
[b.] June 8, 1979, New York City; [p.] Michael and Stephanie Luftglass; [ed.] Sophomore at Freehold Township, International Studies High School; [occ.] Student; [memb.] Junior Statesmen of America, The Forensics Team, The Hugh O'Brian Youth Foundation Representative, The Octagon Public Service Club, Temple Shaari Emeth Confirmation Class, Drama Club House Tickets Committee Johns Hopkins City; [hon.] Hanover Park Forensics 1st Place Extemporaneous Speaking, Renaissance Honor Scholar; [oth. writ.] Poems published in Iguana Crossing Literary Magazine 1994 and The Book of Life 1994.; [pers.] What good is knowledge if it cannot be shared. I believe that literature is a fundamental basis for communications essential for the future, yet important to reflect on the past.; [a.] Marlboro, NJ

LULGJURAJ, VICTORIA
[Pen.] "Vicky"; [b.] May 10, 1977, Queens, NY; [p.] Nikolla and Lula Lulgjuraj; [ed.] I am presently a high school high honor student at Washingtonville High. I plan to further my education in college; [pers.] Poetry invites you to a new way of seeing with the mind and eyes, which makes you become a part of a poets experiences and feelings, and that's what makes the love of poetry for me; [a.] Campbell Hall, NY

LUND, DON
[b.] 1934, Norma, ND, but was nurtured and raised in the Puget Sound area of Washington State; [ed.] Univ of Washington (class of "62"); [occ.] Retired teacher; [pers.] Family advocate, teacher, and friend to youth and nature. Enjoys writing essays, poetry and song as an emotional and philosophical outlet for personal expression and edification. Thus far, this has been the only offered for public scrutiny. Most valued accomplishment: Longevity of marriage to wife Fells, and the character outcome of three sons and three daughters.

LUNDSBERT, JANET
[b.] February 24, 1945, Chicago, IL; [p.] Jerome and Georgiana Patera; [m.] Gary Lundsbert, August 12, 1972; [ch.] Andrew Jerome, Julie Anne; [ed.] J. Sterling Morton West High School; [occ.] Part-time Social Secretary; [memb.] Newcombers Club of Lake Bluff/Lake Forest, Lake Forest Women's Club, St. Mary's Catholic Church Guild; [oth. writ.] Poems written for family and friends; [pers.] I am greatly influenced by my family and

friends and the events that take place in our lives at that time.; [a.] Lake Forest, IL

LUSSIER, KIMBERLY P.
[Pen.] Kim Lussier; [b.] July 30, 1964, Lawton, OK; [p.] Mr. and Mrs. Dale Perkis; [m.] Eric A. Lussier; [ch.] Dakota Lee; [oth. writ.] February comes with deep regret, A day, a month we wont forget. It broke our hearts to loose you but you did not go alone, a part of us went with you the day God called you home, so many times we needed you, so many times we cried. If love could have saved you, you would have never died; [pers.] I wrote don't cry now mom, because I now live, in memory of Blake Dillon Camp, my son who died February 4, 1991, who gave so much to be so little, age 6 years.; [a.] Lawton, OK

LYNCH, JENNIFER C.
[Pen.] J.C. Lynch; [b.] December 4, 1973, Sarasota, FL; [p.] Frank and Nancy Lynch; [ed.] Humanities High School, NY, NY; Florida State Univ, Tallahassee FL; [occ.] Full time student majoring in English; [oth. writ.] Several poems published in local magazines; [pers.] For me, poetry is my escape from the everyday experience. It allows me to express my inner most feelings; [a.] Tallahassee, FL

LYNCH, PATRICIA A.
[Pen.] Patricia Henigin Lynch; [b.] March 14, 1943, Jamaica, NY; [p.] Gerard and Rita McMashon Henigin; [m.] Joseph L. Lynch, August 20, 1972; [ch.] Stefanie Siobhan, Elizabeth Mary, Nathaniel Joseph; [ed.] Our Lady of Wisdom Academy; St. Joseph College; Bread Loaf School of English, Middlebury College; [occ.] English teacher, Northwest Catholic High School, West Hartford, CT; [memb.] NCEA, NCTE, MLA, Mark Twain Foundation, Hill-Stead Museum; [oth. writ.] Other poems published in newsletters; poems and dramatic monologue used in retreat programs; short stories.; [pers.] The beauty of life as "gift" in all its varied shades of experience is at the core of my poetic song, that and of its Giver. My poems remind me of who I am, of what I have received, and of what I have yet to give.; [a.] Simsbury, CT

MAC KILLIGAN, COURTNEY A.
[b.] August 14, 1982, Portland, ME; [p.] Gayle Asmussen, Wm MacKilligan; [ed.] Sea Road Elementary Middle School of the Kennebunks; [occ.] Student; [a.] Kennebunk, ME

MAC WILLIAMS, MARY
[b.] March 2, 1955, South Bend, IN; [p.] Ned Mac Williams, Barb Mac Williams (deceased); [ed.] Oak Park River Forest HS, Northern Arizona U (2 yrs) and College DuPage, IL; [occ.] Outpatient Pharmacy Tech; [pers.] I believe that there is good in all people, but in 1984 I was a victim of abuse and here wrote how I felt. I've made a better life for myself with help and tons of support and now, again. I believe there is still good in all; [a.] Chicago, IL

MACCULLOCH, HOLLEY NOELLE
[Pen.] The "MAC;" [b.] December 30, 1978, Ottawa, KS; [p.] Tom and Cheryl Bramlette; [memb.] Monica's School of Dance Show Troupe Dancer; vocalist with Rob Davis; L.S. Swim Team; National Forensics League; [hon.] Dancer in Las Vegas w/Monica's Dance Troop; National Forensics League Competitor; L.S. Swim Team; [oth. writ.] Many other poems and prose, creative writings and quotes.; [pers.] I love to write about death and

after-worlds. Many people fear death but I am fascinated with it. "Death is a futuristic memory." [a.] Lee's Summit, MO

MACK, KARI REGINA
[Pen.] Regina Mundy; [b.] August 8, 1968, Lexington, KY; [p.] Doug and Helen Mack; [ed.] Henry Clay High School, Lexington, KY; [occ.] Transit Bus Driver; [hon.] Graduated from high school at age 15 in top 10%, National Honor Society, Beta Club, Yearbook Staff, Speech Team; [oth. writ.] About 60 or 70 other poems; [pers.] My poetry is a means of expressing my deep fears, hopes and feelings; [a.] Park Hills, KY.

MADISON, YVONNE
[b.] November 13, 1952, Ukiah, CA; [p.] George, Eleanore Madison; [m.] Divorced; [ed.] Workman, LaPuente High; [occ.] Disabled; [hon.] Have had one poem published in National Library of Poetry book; [oth. writ.] Various poems different subjects; [pers.] Have always been big fan of Stephen King, so wrote poem as my tribute to him; [a.] Baldwin Park, CA

MAGEE, PAMELA ALICE
[b.] March 20, 1943, Bridgewater, MA; [p.] Benjamin Crawshaw, Jessie Crawshaw; [m.] Harold A. Magee, September 21, 1978; [ed.] Bridgewater High School; [occ.] Housewife/retired. Was food service manager for Interstate United in IL; [memb.] New England Genealogical Society also Lincolnshire Genealogical Society, England, St. Paul's Episcopal Church, Montrose, CA; [oth. writ.] None published - most writings have been used for special people and occasions also for personal; [pers.] Because of all I have comes from my Lord Jesus, I try to reveal His wisdom and to whom all things reflect His Glory. In quietness and thanksgiving poetry is revealed. I was greatly influenced from reading poetry throughout my younger years; [a.] Montrose, CO

MAGLIERI, SCARLETT
[Pen.] Scarlett Lee; [b.] November 16, 1925, Chicago, IL; [p.] Wm. and Carol Tribolete; [m.] Mario Maglieri, November 3, 1947; [ch.] Three, Eleven grandchildren, three great grandchildren; [ed.] High School; [ed.] High School; [occ.] Housewife; [hon.] In school won ribbons and awards, for art work. Also wrote some poetry and once wrote a play that was given by the school.; [oth. writ.] None ever published; [pers.] At my age (69, next week) I am both pleased and surprised! I wrote this in a matter of 10 or 15 minutes one morning as I drank my coffee. Now in my later years I would like to write more.; [a.] Los Angeles, CA

MAGNANI, THERESA
[b.] May 27, 1934, New York City; [m.] Alfred Magnani; [ch.] Seven Children; [occ.] IBM Retiree; [memb.] St. Paul's Prish Council and Youth Committee; Beverly Crest Homeowners Assoc., in Yonkers; [oth. writ.] A portfolio of unpublished poems, short stories, and essays all with a spiritual and moral point of view.; [pers.] My desire is to make God and the spiritual life within us more of a reality in our lives, more meaningful, more important and to offer some ways to achieve this, especially for the young.; [a.] Yonkers, NY

MAGUIRE, EVELYN Z.
[b.] May 12, 1906, Hopewell Township, Bedford County, PA; [p.] James Hayes and Annie Price Zimmerman; [m.] John T. Maguire (deceased), June 11, 1938; [ch.] Janet Hess, Carolyn Kerr, Mary Ann Maguire; [ed.] Hopewell High School, Millersville State Normal School, Juniata

College, Penn State University, University of Vermont, University of MD; [occ.] Stroke survivor since 1989; retired math teacher; formerly corporate treasurer of Capitol Trailways; [memb.] Colonial Park United church of christ, Soroptimist International of Harrisburg, PA Inc.; [hon.] Valedictorian in high school; honorable mention in math at Millersville graduation; essay contest in high school on "Care and Feeding of Birds."; [oth. writ.] Poetry for church, friends, and relatives. My first published article was in the Everett Press and concerned the report of an animal born in the neighborhood "sired by a Guernsey Steer."; [pers.] My grandfather was an Englishman from Herefordshire, and he read and recited a great deal of works from British writers (for example, Shakespeare and "Bobby" Burns) to entertain me as I was growing; [a.] Mechanicsburg, PA

MAHAKIAN, LINDA
[b.] March 3, 1952, S.F., CA; [p.] Orville Jarman and Mary Jarman; [m.] Fred Mahakian, April 24, 1970; [ch.] One daughter - Jennifer - 22 yrs old; [oth. writ.] Two of my poems were published in a local collection of women's writing; [pers.] Writing poetry is such a release of emotional energy for me and in many ways has been my salvation. I am so honored and this is such a thrill for me to be a part of your 1995 book "Reflections of Light". My daughter, Jennifer, has also been such a part of my inspiration; [a.] Fremont, CA

MAHAR, KELLEY
[b.] August 19, 1967, Cleveland, OH; [occ.] Medical Student; [a.] Cleveland, OH

MAIDMENT, FRED
[Pen.] John Maidmente; [b.] January 8, 1981, Lexington, SC; [p.] Sandra H. and Frederick H. Maidment; [ed.] Lilburn Elem., Ebenezer Elem., Cedar Crest Middle School, Classes at Labanon Valley College; [occ.] Student; [memb.] Boy Scouts, Civil Air Patrol; [hon.] Citation American Diabetes Assoc., Presidential Commendation, Arrow of Light, Presidential Academic Fitness Award (3), Johns Hopkins U., 7th Grade Math and Verbal Talent Search; [oth. writ.] Currently writing a novel, non-published short stories.; [pers.] Winners don't do drugs.; [a.] Lebanon, PA

MAJID, MARIAM, MARI AL
[b.] March 8, 1973, Kabul, Afghanistan; [p.] Khadija, Tabibi, Abdul, Hakim, Al Majid; [ed.] Associate Degree, currently transferred to American Univ; [occ.] Administrative's Assist for int'l import and export firm; [oth. writ.] Working on my book about my experiences of escaping Afghanistan, at a very young age with family; [pers.] I have been inspired by the word love itself to write poetry. In this day and age, poetry and love are not taken very seriously; for me poetry is the essence of divine love. Love is not complete without poetry. I strive to speak for the broken hearted through my poetry; [a.] Falls Church, VA

MAJOR, ALAN
[b.] June 21, 1968, Mdpls., Indiana; [p.] Alvis and Mary Major; [ed.] Emmerich Manual High School, Purdue University, B.A. in Ed., California Lutheran Univ., MA in Ed.; [occ.] Assistant Basketball Coach at California Lutheran Univ., Graduate student; [memb.] National Assoc., Basketball Coaches; [oth. writ.] None published. This poem is first. Many other poems in personal collection.; [pers.] I want my poems to bring the reader right where I am at any given moment, so they may feel what I feel.; [a.] Thousand Oaks, CA

MAKSIN, MELISSA T.
[Pen.] Me; [b.] August 21, 1964, Florence, SC; [p.] Mrs. Grover L. Mehaulic, Mr. Jim Tunstall; [m.] 1984, widowed 1992; [ch.] Brandon Maksin (11/23/88); [ed.] Manager - The Phone Doctor (Family Business); [hon.] The first thing that comes to my mind is my son, Brandon. The second is that I was selected as a semi-finalist and that my poem will be published in the Reflections of Light; [pers.] When I feel it so strongly within my heart, the words flow onto paper; [a.] Florence, SC

MALDONADO, GERTRUDE
[Pen.] Trudy; [b.] July 9, 1966, Brooklyn, NY; [ch.] Jasmine Else Lopez 5/11/93; [ed.] Murray Bergtraum H.S., College of New Rochelle; [occ.] Administrative Assistant; [memb.] National Association for Female Executives; [oth. writ.] Accumulation of over 50 poems waiting to be discovered.; [pers.] My inspiration for writing comes from moments of solitude wherein I lose myself waiting to express my feelings and emotions.; [a.] Bronx, NY

MALINOWSKI, MIKE
[b.] February 13, 19868, Norristown; [p.] Barbara Browislaus Malinowski; [ed.] Souderton, H.S.; [occ.] Self Employed Contractor; [oth. writ.] Several poems, in process of novel at present.; [pers.] I intend to become successful through hard work and determination. I will help anyone I can to succeed along the way.; [a.] Allentown, PA

MALONE, JUYNNE
[Pen.] Juynne; [b.] June 29, 1930, New York; [p.] George Lohr, Louise Lohr; [m.] John Patrick Malone, June 11, 1949; [ch.] Colleen Mac Avoy; [ed.] Grover Cleveland High; [occ.] Retired Exec Secy; [oth. writ.] Article for Science of Mind Magazine; [pers.] I write mainly on self discovery, expressing the freedom that comes from awareness and acceptance of life's situations, hoping to help others in their own walk-through life; [a.] Brentwood, NY

MALTZ, AARON
[b.] April 4, 1970, Hayward, CA; [p.] Stephen and Maureen Maltz; [ed.] Hayward High School, Humboldt State Univ, Chabot College - AA. Presently attending Hayward State Univ; [occ.] Full time student studying to be a recreation therapist; [memb.] Conservation Unlimited, Rainforest Action Group, Student Advocacy for the Deaf, Animal Welfare Group, Humboldt State Ambassadors; [hon.] Youth Citizenship Award, qualified in high school league cross-country and track and field competition, Assoc of Arts Degree; [oth. writ.] Self published own collection of poetry entitled, Poetry From Life Underneath. Have written three poems in Spanish. Have had submitted article to campus paper at Humboldt State and Hayward State; [pers.] Like to play with words, thoughts and ideas for rhyme, metaphor, and diversion; [a.] Hayward, CA

MAMINGI, NLANDU
[b.] August 27, 1953, Boma; [p.] Nzita Mamingi and Mundayi Zala; [m.] Nsona Levo; [ch.] Matumuene Nlandu, Zola Nlandu and Mundayi Nlandu; [ed.] Colonie Scolaire de Boma, National University of Saire, Institute of Social Studies, The Hague State University of New York at Albany; [occ.] Consultant, The World Bank; [memb.] American Economic Assoc., American Statistical Assoc., Econometric Society, African Findna and Economics Assoc.; [oth. writ.] Lobata, unpublished poetry book, Les Oublies, Gloire Atoimamere, unpub-

lished poetry book, I am also a native son (poetry book under preparation); [a.] Rockville, MD

MANBY, BURR
[b.] January 25, 1922, Battle Creek, MI; [p.] Charles J. and Amber Manby; [m.] Joyce Manby; [ch.] Joseph, Mia; [ed.] Battle Creek Central, H.S., B.S. Degree, Hillsdale College, Hillsdale, MI; [occ.] Retired; [a.] Flossmoor, IL

MANN, JASON
[Pen.] Jayson Matthew; [b.] May 11, 1974, Harrisburg, IL; [p.] Ed and Glenna Mann; [ed.] Southeastern IL College; [occ.] Student/English Major; [hon.] Egyptian Shrine Scholarship; [oth. writ.] Many unpublished poems; [pers.] I use my poetry as an emotional and creative release. My influences are my cousin, my environment, and my disability. My favorite writers include Poe, King and Seuss; [a.] Harrisburg, IL

MANN, JOHN E.
[b.] March 24, 1926, Camden, SC; [m.] Jean Tucker Mann; [ch.] Patricia, John Jr., Helen, Stuart and Scott; [ed.] BA Park College, Parville, MO - MPA U of OK, Norman OK - Longridge Writers Group, Danbury CT; [occ.] Retired Army Officer, Personnel Director Prince George County MD, Business Manager of an independent school; [hon.] Silverstar, Legion of Merit with two oak leaf clusters, Distinguished Flying Cross, Bronze Star with 3 oak leaf clusters; [oth. writ.] Poem "A Train Trip South" published by the Natn'l Library of Poetry in the anthology "At Days End" 1994; [a.] Largo, MD

MANNING, FERNANDA "PATRICIA"
[Pen.] Patricia Manning - Pat Benton; [b.] April 29, 1944, White Plains, NY; [p.] Rachel Allen; [m.] Louroy B. Manning, September 18, 1960; [ch.] Rhea Lewis, Rodney, Zoe & Toby Manning; [ed.] GED - Middlesex Community College; [occ.] Licensed Practical Nurse; [memb.] Nursing Journals; [hon.] Perfect Attendance in Nursing School; [oth. writ.] Unpublished poems; [pers.] Be not judgmental of others for their beliefs or lifestyles. Always believe in yourself; [a.] Old Saybrook, CT

MANNING, STEPHEN B.
[b.] April 10, 1964, Chester, PA; [p.] Denis Manning, Ed and Agnes James; [ed.] BA, Psychology, UC Irvine, Ocean View HS, Monsignor Bonner HS; [occ.] Supervisor for house of retarded adults; [hon.] Theology and world cultures awards - Monsignor bonner HS; Employee of Quarter - Impact Systems - winner 1994; [oth. writ.] A Whisper To Some (A View From The Edge), At the Height of Your Existence (Best poets) Book NLP; [pers.] Never...ever...never...ever... never...ever...never...ever...never...ever quit this life; continue on children.

MAPLES, RONALD E.
[b.] August 30, 1949, Missouri; [m.] Nancy J. Maples; [ed.] Master of arts in Anthropology and Sociology; [occ.] Case Worker at Daniel Memorial, Inc.; [pers.] The spirit is set free in the birth of its time.; [a.] Jacksonville, FL

MARCUM, BETTY KING
[b.] April 17, 1959, Cincinnati; [p.] Frances Audrey Scott and Dewey King; [m.] George David Marcum, September 20, 1980; [ch.] no children, 1 dog (Cowboy), 2 cats (Patches and Orea); [ed.] Holy Cross Luth School, Detroit. Somerset High School. Somerset, KY; [occ.] Certified Medical Assistant; [pers.] Knowledge of all things

is unimportant. So long as you use the knowledge you do possess to enrich the world in which you live; [a.] Louisville, KY

MARDEN, COURTNEY
[b.] October 31, 1976, Newton, MA; [p.] Charlotte and Donald Marden; [ed.] Holliston High School, St. Anselm College Class of 1998; [occ.] Student in freshman year at college; [memb.] Varsity softball pitcher at St. Anselm; [hon.] Many All-Star and MVP awards in softball while in high school; [a.] Holliston, MA

MARGARET, PAUL A.
[b.] March 14, 1923, Ft. Dodge, IA; [p.] Avilla and John Paul; [m.] Never married; [ed.] M.A. in Education, M.A. in Theol.; [occ.] Retired from lifelong teaching administration. Currently Director of Interreligious Senior Center.; [memb.] Altrusa Club of Des Moines, Community Services Ctr., Shepherds Center of Greater Des Moines; Formerly teachers organizations and ASTD (training org.); [hon.] Early years college scholarships. Later years helping others do so.; [oth. writ.] First efforts; six poems published in Elder hostel "Poems" Univ. of Iowa 1993. Local bank published my "Floods of 93' in Senior Newsletter.; [pers.] Thus far I've written only from depth of feelings (s) and as I reach into mine, touch others.; [a.] Urbandale, IA

MARIE-BENNETT, MARVIN E.
[b.] December 4, 1912, Prescott, AZ; [p.] Grant Bennett; [m.] Catherine, February 1, 1946; [ch.] Charles, Richard, Walter, Floyd; [ed.] 6th Grade; [occ.] Retired Cowboy; [hon.] Mule Skinner First Paid Entertainer at Grand Canyon, AZ 1930 in Top Ten Calf Roper in 1931; [a.] Mayer, AZ

MARKLEY, STEVE
[b.] August 24, 1973, Lancaster, PA; [p.] Deb Markley, Don Markley; [ed.] McCaskey High School, currently enrolled at Millersville Univ; [occ.] Myrtle digger/nursery laborer, Minder's Nursery; [hon.] Dean's List; published in Millersville's "White Buffalo". Family and Friends; [oth. writ.] Several poems published in Millersville's "White Buffalo"; [pers.] Inspiration comes to me as I sweat in the field with my pitchfork. Physical labor has given me the truth and purity that I attempt to convey in my writing; [a.] Lancaster, PA

MARSH (II), GORDON E.
[b.] July 26, 1948, Jamestown, NY; [ed.] Jamestown High School, Jamestown Community College; [occ.] Disabled Veteran; [memb.] American Legion, Disabled Vets, War Vets, Fraternal Order of Eagles Jamestown Community College Un-commoners; [hon.] Phi Theta Kappa, Dean's List, Theatre Excellence Award, Two-Language and Literary Festival Awards, JCC Alumni Scholarship Award; [oth. writ.] Several poems, short stories, and plays; [pers.] Unkept promises make deep wounds; [a.] Paisley, FL

MARSHALL, CYNTHIA M.
[Pen.] CM Marshall; [b.] May 26, 1960, Gettysburg, PA; [p.] Agnes I. and Bill and Marlene Gillespie; [m.] Bruce Marshall, September 12, 1992; [ch.] Michael, Brett, Lisa; [ed.] High School Graduate, Catoctin High School, Thurmount, MD; [occ.] Data Input Admissions, Mount Saint Mary's College, Insurance Billings, Christine Curley, MD, PC; [hon.] Athletic awards in high school; professional honors in employment; [pers.] I try to live a life of caring for others, and for animals; I like the little things, they mean the most.; [a.] Fairfield, PA

MARSHALL, ROCKY
[b.] November 8, 1963, Blounstown, FL; [p.] Mary Elliott and Jimmy Marshall; [oth. writ.] I have written a number of poems that reflect on my life, thoughts and dreams. But "Drifting Back" is my first and only poem to be published so far.; [pers.] I have very little education, therefore time has been my teacher and life itself, is my influence. Every day to me is a journey, a test of faith, and strength. To write about it is the only way I've found to conquer the fear of living it.; [a.] Tallahassee, FL

MARSHALL-LINDEN, RACHEL L.
[b.] April 29, 1955, Lynn, MA; [p.] Robert and Doris Linden; [m.] Cary S. Linden-Marshall, July 11, 1977; [ch.] Lukas Sparhawk and Emmo Morgen; [ed.] University of New Hampshire, P.S.C.; [occ.] Mother, Writer, Artist; [memb.] Planetary Citizens, International Wildlife Coalition; [hon.] Cum Laude Graduate; [oth. writ.] A small part of something, the collected poetry of Rachel L. Linden-Marshall.; [pers.] Greatly inspired by other poets and writers; but it is the love of my family, friends and the intrigue of this planet which inspire me the most.; [a.] Danvers, MA

MARSON, LEATRICE L.
[b.] May 23, 1926, Trenton, NJ; [p.] Mary and Orestes De Cavalcanti; [m.] Robert J. Marson, September 26, 1953; [ch.] Glenn, Bruce, Jeanine; [ed.] Jonathan Dayton Regional High; [occ.] Homemaker; [memb.] Literacy Volunteer of America; Silver Wings Flying club 1951; [pers.] The killing of 200+ Arabs by a deranged Jewish man in Israel prompted the title of my poem and the worlds. It saddens me when I read about the many tragedies that occur due to violet feelings. Despite difficult obstacles that can happen during life's journey, we must have perspective and a good attitude.; [a.] Cranford, NJ

MARTIN, MICHAEL
[b.] April 23, 1974, Cleveland, OH; [p.] Karen Bumpus; [ed.] Hauken High School, Ohio State Univ; [occ.] Full-time student; [pers.] I want to thank God for giving me the rare talent of expressing feelings into words. I also want to thank my mother for being there and believing in me. I love you Ma; [a.] Warrensville Hts, OH

MARTIN, PATRICIA
[b.] January 10, 1954, Boston, MA; [p.] Leroy and Gracie Martin; [ch.] One child, Diondra; [ed.] Finish high school; [occ.] Airand driver and homemaker; [memb.] Belong to Harvest Christian Fellowship Church; [oth. writ.] 20 poems that have not been published; [pers.] I really like to write poems and hope to publish more, I have been so inspired by other poets; [a.] Riverside, CA

MARTIN, RAYFUS
[Pen.] Ray Martin; [b.] January 12, 1930, Franklinton, LA; [p.] Archie and Alma Martin; [m.] Elnora L. Martin; [ch.] Mechelle D. Martin; [ed.] Washington Parish High school, Southeastern University, B.A. Degree English and History, Master's Degree, Administration and Supervisor; [occ.] Retired Educator after 32 yrs.; [memb.] New Jerusalem Baptist Church, Phi Delta Kappa Fraternity, L.A. Historical Society, L.A. Education Assoc., L.A. Municipal Assoc., Eureka Lodge #27, F&AM State of LA; [hon.] First Black American elected to Franklinton's Town Council, Received Silver star for having been elected 5 consecutive 4 year terms in 1992.; [oth. writ.] Have written some poems and short stories (never published) to encourage students to become interested in writing. Assisted High School classmate in

writing lyrics, for class song. Am now writing a book.; [pers.] It is my desire to continue to live a clean and decent life before God and man. I believe that if mankind turns back to God, many of our ills in society will be cured. God and education is the Answer. Poets Langston Hughes and Robert Frost have influenced me.; [a.] Franklinton, LA

MARTIN, ROGER
[b.] September 3, 1925, Gloucester, MA; [p.] Capt R.H. Martin and Ellie E. Martin; [m.] Ann O. Martin, September 23, 1990; (married Joan Fertig - 1954-1989 - deceased); [ch.] Christopher, Rachel, Mari; [ed.] Rockport High/Boston Museum School, Boston, MA; [occ.] Artist - Poet; [hon.] Honors grad: Boston Museum School 1950. Rockport Poet Laureate for Life 1991. Prof Emeritus, Montserrat College of Art, Beverly MA; [oth. writ.] Child Life Magazine, Gloucester Daily Times, Gloucester, MA, Boston Sunday Globe, North Shore Magazine, Beverly, MA; [pers.] I use poetry to explore ideas that refuse transposition to the easel; [a.] Rockport, MA

MARTOCCI, MICHAEL
[b.] December 1, 1924, HTFD, CT; [p.] Domonick and Rose Martocci; [m.] Arlene Martocci, 1954; [ch.] Paul, Stephen, Michael, Rose, David; [ed.] Bulkeley High School, University of HTFD, Manchester Community College; [occ.] Retired - Temp at Travelers Ins Co; [memb.] SPEBSQSA - Knights of Columbus; [oth. writ.] Article for the Hartford Courant, a booklet on coin collecting, also a show review for Goodspeed Opera House; [pers.] Poetry brings me a contentment and peacefulness that is very appealing. I love the prose and poetry of Donald Hall and Raymond Carver; [a.] So. Windsor, CT

MASCARO, JOSEPH R.
[b.] March 19, 1934, Utica, NY; [m.] Carolyn J. Mascaro, May 3, 1977; [ch.] Jason Edward Mascaro; [ed.] Georgetown Univ. and Siena Coll. B.A., Syracuse Univ. Coll of Law LL.B.; [occ.] Attorney; [oth. writ.] Various poems, short stories and plays.; [a.] Utica, NY

MASTERS, BETTE
[b.] May 7, 1931, Portsmouth, VA; [p.] Chester Orvis and Myrtle Kimball; [m.] Michael E. Masters, August 19, 1990; [ch.] Leslie, Tracey, Gina and Chris; [ed.] St. Petersburg Sr High; [occ.] Housewife; [oth. writ.] Only for my own personal reading; [a.] Perris, CA

MATHEWS DR., VIVIAN
[b.] November 24, 1910, Waterloo, WI; [p.] Charles (Architect) and Amanda Hintz Archie (Vocalist); [m.] Dr. Willis Mathews, February 20, 1942; [ch.] Willis A. (Artist), Charles J. (Executive), Monie Ruth (Teacher); [ed.] U. of Wisconsin, BA, BS, MA, Ph.D., taught at Univ., Chattanooga, Univ. of Wisconsin, Wayne State U.; [occ.] Retired Teacher; [memb.] Sigma Psi (graduate honorary), Sigma Delta Epsilon (Woman Honorary) Lakeside Pallette Club, Eastern Star; [hon.] Oil Painting Awards, Hand Quilting Awards, Poetry Awards; [oth. writ.] Amanda Archies Cookbook; "Archie Clan" (Archie Genealogy) published poetry; Children's Readers. Histology & Developmental History of the Ovotestis of Lymnaea Stagnalis Lillena.; [pers.] To me, writing poetry is the same as weeding my flower beds. I hope to produce something beautiful that others can also enjoy.; [a.] St. Clair Shores, MI

MATUNAS, JOSEPH
[Pen.] Big Joe Tunas; [b.] August 23, 1909, Eliz., NJ; [p.] Julia and Frank Matunas Sr.; [m.] Mary and Elsie Matunas, July 29, 1939 - October 26, 1985; [ch.] No children; [ed.] 7th grade night school, had to go to work, 11 yrs. old, to support family, I made myself a good education by reading; [occ.] Chief Specialist and Specialized in Machinery and Tooling; [memb.] N.G. Junior Police Lieutenant had a squad to guard high schools, regular school also accident reports, robber reports. I was athletic type, jogging, every week 5 miles a weight lifter; [hon.] A medal from N.G. Merit Award and was company mechanic had to service automatic 45, I was a wrestler and boxer, loved sports; Worked G.M. in NJ, Lead Man on Machines and Tooling was my specialty. Had to take exam every month, had to maintain an average 97.5 in order to maintain my position.; [pers.] Had a lot of different jobs worked for China, under Col-Chin and Col Mau, plus had to train Chinese how to operate machine and had photo taken and sent to China.; [a.] Linder, NJ

MAY, CHRISTY
[b.] September 5, 1975, Akron, OH; [p.] John and Kay May; [ed.] 1994 Graduate Brecksville High; [occ.] Student. Univ of Akron; [oth. writ.] Commencement speech 1994. This is my first published work. I hope to someday publish my own anthology; [pers.] "Wish upon a star, remember that wish through all your days, and you will find success"; [a.] Akron, OH

MAY, MARIA MICHELLE
[b.] May 28, 1979, Opelika, AL; [p.] Samuel and Kimberly May; [ed.] I am currently in the 10th grade in High School; [occ.] Student in High School; [hon.] Honor Student; 1st place in a musical ensemble at a State convention of Texas; [oth. writ.] My short story won fourth place at a State Convention in Texas.; [pers.] I would like to give all the honor and glory to the Lord for my ability to write. (try to portray a sense of great feeling in my poems.); [a.] Falfurrias, TX

MAYE, MICHAEL P.
[Pen.] Christopher Rossy; [b.] February 4, 1969, Auburn, NY; [p.] Mr. and Mrs. Thomas C. Maye; [oth. writ.] Essay on the philosophy of universal love.; [pers.] It is the duty and obligation of a cultured and refined individual, to recognize, appreciate, and to express the infinitude of beauty and splendor that surrounds the individual, in universal symbols and images, through the sublime medium of the creative arts.; [a.] Buffalo, NY

MAYES, KATHLEEN M.
[b.] September 13, 1955, Lock Haven, PA; [p.] Robert and Jane Biley; [m.] Paul A. Mayes, June 28, 1975; [ch.] Jonathan P., Robert A., Lori M.; [ed.] Undergraduate, Shippensburg Univ., PA, 1988 B.S. Elem. School, 1993 M.S. Reading Western Maryland College, Westminster, MD; [occ.] Teacher 8th grade reading Gettysburg, PA; [hon.] 1994 Who's Who Among American Teachers, nominated by a former student; [pers.] Life is a choice, while we may not always enjoy what happens to us, we can affect the future by the decisions we make today. We must strive to show kindness and compassion for each person we encounter as we pass through our days. The difference we make in the world may not be noticeable to us today, but sometime, somewhere in the future, those choices will be gratefully acknowledged.; [a.] Gettysburg, PA

MAYNARD, CHARLES R.
[Pen.] C. R. Maynard; [b.] September 5, 1966, Lorain, OH; [p.] Frank Maynard, Kathleen Maynard; [ed.] Cleveland State Univ: [occ.] Asst Director, Mkt Support Services, Univ Hospitals of Cleveland; [memb.] Sierra Club, Cleveland Museum of Art, World Wildlife Federation, Nature Conservancy; [oth. writ.] Articles for local magazine, children's stories, adult fiction; [a.] Lorain, OH

MC ARDLE, KELLY
[b.] June 20, 1968, HAWTHORNE, CA; [p.] Ronald and Francine McArdle; [ed.] Canyon High, Antelope Valley College, Currently at Univ of California, Riverside; [occ.] Student at the Univ of Calif at Riverside; [memb.] Alpha Gamma Sigma, Alpha Iota; [hon.] Ed Walsh Service Scholarship Dean's List, Graduation from Antelope Valley College with high honors; [pers.] This writing is dedicated to my family for their unconditional love and support. Without which this poem would not have been possible. I also wish to thank my good friend, Karen Perry, for her assistance in writing this poem; [a.] Riverside, CA

MC BRIDE, MARGARET MARY
[Pen.] M3; [b.] November 11, 1953; [p.] Mr. and Mrs. Lee Andrew McBride I; [m.] Jon Helge Volstad, December 31, 1992; [ch.] Marton Leander Volstad; [ed.] BS Biology, Brandeis Univ, Waltham, MA; MS Fish and Wildlife Science Oregon State Univ, Corvallis, OR; [occ.] Fishery Biologist; Assistant Project Leader Maryland Fisheries Resources Office, US Fish and Wildlife Service, Annapolis, MD; [memb.] American Fisheries Society; [hon.] Outstanding Young Women of America, 1981 Publication; Visiting Scientist at the Inst of Marine Research, Bergen, Norway, June 1990-June 1991; [oth. writ.] Scientific writings, a personal diary, and other poems; [pers.] I have kept a personal diary since age 11 in order to clarify recognition of my thoughts regarding the events which shape my existence, and consequent feelings regarding these events which determine my character. However, in later years I have found greater pleasure, and challenge, in exploring the expression of my thoughts in an abbreviated, artful, and somewhat abstract form. Self expression as a tool of self realization is redeemed through recognition of what has gone before us and glorified in our vision of what is to come.

MC CLOSKEY, KERRI
[b.] March 22, 1978, Queens, NY; [p.] Patricia, James McCloskey; [ed.] I'm in the 11th grade attending East Meadow High School; [memb.] A perspective club which is the only public place my writings are seen. I attended youth group too; [oth. writ.] I have over a million writings from a very young age til now. I write of feelings and experiences; [pers.] I love to write and it's my only material talent and I hope to one day go somewhere with it. I also hope to get a scholarship to a college with it; [a.] East Meadow, NY

MC CORKELL, ROBERT A.
[b.] August 11, 1956, Akron, IA; [p.] Step Father - James P. Six, Natural Parents - Edward V. and Joan R. McCorkell; [m.] Graciela G. McCorkell, October 20, 1979; [ch.] Christina M. McCorkell, Nancy A. McCorkell; [ed.] Gladstone High School, Citrus College: Trade Classes; [occ.] Tool and Die Maker; [hon.] Beautification award from the city of Santa Fe Springs, CA; Numerous Awards from the Boy Scouts of America High School Sports; [oth. writ.] I enjoy giving poems to friends and family last Christmas. I built a Christmas

tree with poems for my family; [pers.] Poetry is personal, it's from your heart and it makes you feel good. I encourage everyone to spend a little time with your own hearts and feelings and put it to words; [a.] Santa Fe Springs, CA

MC CREA, KEVIN M.
[b.] April 30, 1965, Philadelphia, PA; [p.] Margaret McGoigan and John McGoigan, Jr; [m.] Marie J. McCrea (my best friend), October 7, 1989; [ed.] GED (high school equivalent), BA Temple Univ Phila PA, JD Widener Univ School of Law, Wilmington, DE; [occ.] Attorney at Law; [memb.] Pennsylvania Bar New Jersey Bar, Federal District Court of New Jersey Federal Court Eastern District of PA 3rd Circuit Court of Appeals, ABA Philadelphia Bar Assoc; [hon.] Dean's List Temple Univ; [pers.] Don't waste time you cannot get it back. Strive to love and do a little better everyday; [a.] Philadelphia, PA

MC DANIEL, JOANNE LAURA
[b.] January 16, 1971, Painesville, OH; [p.] Helen A. and the late James E. McDaniel; [ed.] Riverside High School, 1989; Cleveland State Univ, 1994; [occ.] Reconcilement Clerk, Bank One; [memb.] Residence Hall Assoc 1990-1994; Student Conduct Committee, 1992; North East Ohio Housing Officers, Cleveland State Univ Band, 1994; [hon.] Resident Assistant of the Year, 1994; Dean's List; Editor, Viking Hall Newsletter, 1993-1994; [oth. writ.] Personal journal writings, inspirational thoughts and other observations; [pers.] What I hear, think, see and feel, I write. It all comes from the heart; [a.] Painesville, OH

MC ELROY, CORDELIA
[b.] April 15, 1917, Ardmore, OK; [p.] Willie and Jewell Herweck (deceased); [m.] George B. McElroy, Jr. (1913-1972), September 6, 1934; [ch.] WM (Bill) BSA Executive, CB III (Mack) Prosecuting Atty, M. Eileen - Teacher, Education Ranger High School; [occ.] Retired; [memb.] Lamar Baptist Church - no longer active or a member of any political, charity, social, youth or school organizations; [hon.] No awards. Honors - mother of three wonderful children, grandmother of thirteen and great grandmother of seven; [oth. writ.] Never submitted before. My poems are about God, nature, babies, husbands, teenagers, animals, emotions and imagination. True to life comical and serious; [pers.] In this troubled world, I hope to remind everyone of all the love and beauty in the simple things of life; [a.] Wichita Falls, TX

MC GUIGAN, CHRISTINE
[b.] January 25, 1967, Evanston, IL; [p.] John T. McGuigan and Rosemary Bernardo McGuigan; [m.] single; [ed.] William Paterson College - graduated in 1991 - BA in English; [occ.] Substitute teacher for Bergen County; [memb.] People for the Ethical Treatment of Animals; [hon.] Dean's List, 1990-91, National Dean's List. Winner of WPC 1991 Feminist Essay Contest; [pers.] With my writing, I hope to open the door of possibilities to others. I want to break through the limited ways in which we see and judge things; [a.] Lyndhurst, NJ

MC GURK, CARRIE
[b.] November 13, 1979, Silver Spring, MD; [p.] Peter McGurk, Bernice Richmond; [ed.] Currently 10th grader at Paint Branch High School; [occ.] Student; [pers.] I strive to reflect the greatness of "life" in my poetry. I most enjoy writing about life and love; [a.] Burtonsville, MD

MC INERNEY, EMER ANN
[b.] June 19, 1968, Dublin, Ireland; [ed.] BSc Trinity College, Dublin, Ireland; [occ.] Unemployed (by choice); [oth. writ.] I have had children's; stories published; several poems and articles also published.; [pers.] I'm Irish, female, agnostic, short, tv addict, straight, non-political, theoretical, vegetarian, single, a generation X product. I like to off-load with a burst of poetry. Will only be discovered when I'm dead.; [a.] San Francisco, CA

MC MCLUNEY, TAMIA WYNETTE
[Pen.] Mia; [b.] June 12, 1979, Shelby, NC; [p.] Donald and Cynthia McCluney; [ed.] K-5 Grade Elizabeth School, 6th-8th grade Crest Middle School. I am now in the 10th grade at Crest High School; [occ.] I help my father teach karate in Tae Kwon Do; [memb.] In school, I am a member of the DECA, FBLA Club and a homeroom representative, also a peer helper for CODAP. At church I am in the youth group and in the choir; [hon.] In 1984, I started taking karate from my father. In 1987, I was awarded the Junior Martial Artist of the Year Award. My picture is in the karate to win book by: J. Allen Queen. Page 96 I got my Black Belt in 1992. In 1991-1994, I was a Competitor of the Year in the Jr Girls Kata Division; [a.] Shelby, NC

MC NEELY, ESTHER NAOMI
[b.] September 19, 1913, Stockton, MO; [p.] Rev. James Jeffries; [m.] Forest McNeely, September 20, 1933; [ed.] Grade school, and high school writing class by mail; [occ.] Housewife; [memb.] Church, Aux Cox Medical Center; [hon.] Lamar Mo 1st Lady Carpenter in 1928. Book, for poem in Fair Play Mo paper in 1929; [oth. writ.] Several unpublished poems and storybook.

MC NICHOLS, THELMA
[b.] February 3, 1923, Metropolis, IL; [p.] Ben Burnham, Virgie Burnham; [m.] Lavern McNichols, November 21, 1942; [ch.] France Louise, Steven Lavern; [ed.] Joppa High School; [occ.] Part time bookkeeper; [memb.] Lighthouse Assembly of God Church; [oth. writ.] Poems used in our church bulletin; [pers.] I have always loved poetry. I like my writings to reflect the good things of life. Sometimes I write about a friend or relative; [a.] Metropolis, IL

MC SWEENEY, JOE
[b.] December 18, 1974, Bronx, NY; [p.] Ira and Angela McSweeney; [ed.] Currently enrolled in Rockland Community College for liberal arts; North Parkland High School; [occ.] The Orchards of Conklin, a farm market owned by the Conklin family; [memb.] Sierra Club; [oth. writ.] As yet unpublished; Play around in the areas of short stories, poetry, playwriting, and beginning a novel; [pers.] We do create our own realities, live in our own world that others can perceive only if we allow them too let go your mask and breathe the fragrant airs of infinite freedom; [a.] Gamerville, NY

MCCARTHY, KELLY C.
[b.] March 21, 1971, Chestertown, MD; [p.] Lois and Jerry McCarthy; [ed.] 1989 grad Kent County High School, MD, 1993 grad. B.A. English Virginia Tech; [occ.] Graphics Administrator Siemens Rolm Communications; [memb.] NAFE, AAUW, TBE National Honorary Band Sorority; [oth. writ.] Poem "October Morning" published in Kent County News, Chestertown; Currently working on collection of poems to be titled Laughing with the Daffodils; [pers.] I believe a ready smile coupled with a hearty laugh promotes a positive enthusiastic "I can" attitude that will get you furthest in any direction in life.; [a.] Reston, VA

MCCLENDON, GLORIOUS
[b.] March 1, 1954, Grady, Ark.; [p.] Charley & Ethel Williams; [ch.] Loyeatta and Marteen Spencer; [ed.] High School Grad.; [occ.] U.S. Postal Clerk; [memb.] Lakewood Church, Houston, TX; [oth. writ.] Several unpublished poems.; [pers.] My one desire is to show our Father God's great love for us all in both my life and my writing.; [a.] Houston, TX

MCCOY, REX V.
[b.] July 3, 1955, Newcastle, Wyoming; [p.] Rex W. and Edith F. McCoy; [m.] Laura J. McCoy, March 17, 1994; [ch.] Renee Marie, Rochelle Marie, Raquel Marie, Regina Marie, Taylor Nicole, Rex Ryan; [ed.] Inglewood High, Life; [occ.] District Manager, Retail Cutlery; [hon.] Fatherhood; [oth. writ.] Editorials published in local newspapers, collection of unpublished poems.; [pers.] All living creatures leave footprints, mine are poems.; [a.] Palmdale, CA

MCDONALD, CHANEL J.
[b.] March 3, 1983, Key West, Florida; [p.] Malcolm and Trina McDonald; [ed.] 6th grade; [occ.] Mommy's Little Helper.

MCDONALD, RITA C.
[b.] June 16, 1933, Bethel Twsp., PA; [p.] Catherine and Frank McDonald; [ed.] BSE St. John College, MA John Carroll University, OH, M.A. St. Charles Barremeo, PA; [occ.] Assistant Procurator of India Mission and Writer for Christ our life series Loyola Press was English Teacher for 32 years; [memb.] N.D.E.A,; [oth. writ.] Jesus Kit, publication for Loyola Press, Christ Our Life Series, Words of Life, published out of Canada, Poems have been in the Notre Dame Connection, a monthly magazine; [pers.] In most of my poems I reflect the soul's search for meaning in one's life journey. My favorite poet is the Indian Poet Rabindranath Tagore; [a.] Chardon, OH

MCELROY, ALLINE
[Pen.] Alline Chandler McElroy; [b.] October 13, 1937, Chicago; [p.] Nathan and Alice Chandler; [m.] Herbert C. McElroy, April 4, 1970; [ch.] Raymond Edward, Carla Elizabeth, Gregory Alan; [ed.] Lucy Flower High, Jones Commercial Business, Crane Jr. College, Triton College; [occ.] Office Coordinator for Illinois Star Police; [memb.] Stone Temple Baptist Church, Better Boys Foundation Scholarship Program.; [oth. writ.] "My Reflection" a copy of this was sent to you.; [pers.] Family, It's so important. The little things we do for each other are so important. You can feel it in your heart and remember them for ever; and this makes me write.; [a.] Bellwood, IL

MCFALLS, DAVID G.
[b.] August 11, 1967, Springfield, PA; [ed.] B.S. Business Administration, B.S. Special Education; [occ.] Special Education Teacher and Youth Pastor; [oth. writ.] Two poems published in American Arts Association Anthologies.; [pers.] I hope that I may share this gift of poetry with others, in order to bring glory to God, through his son, Jesus Christ.; [a.] Morton, PA

MCFARLAND, MARGUERITE
[b.] September 16, 1926, Wachita, AK; [p.] Wesley and Mallissa Price; [m.] C.M. McFarland, July 234, 1986; [ch.] Carol Lee Drake; [ed.] Galena Park High, Galena Park, TX; [occ.] Ladies Handbags Mfg., Self Employed; [memb.] American Legion Auxiliary, Honor Society of Above, City Federation of Ladies Clubs Eastern Star;

[oth. writ.] Large collection but none have been published. My friend sent this one in.; [pers.] I like people. Everybody has beauty, mirth, sorrow, a little bit of the devil and lots of goodness. My friends get lots of chuckles from the way I see them.

MCGREGOR, SARAH LYNN
[b.] November 19, 1981, Burlington, VT; [p.] Michael and Cynthia McGregor; [ed.] Currently in 8th grade at Colchester Middle School. (currently on Honor Roll); [memb.] Student Council, Girls Auxiliary for VFW, Volunteer for Adult Day Program at Visiting Nurse Association; [hon.] Continued Excellence in and dedication in creative writing, continued effort of excellence in physical education, excellence in effort for all studies, (Colchester school system), winner of DARE contest, 3rd place, 200 meter Dash, Third place 100 meter dash, eighth place softball throw, 1991 Hershey Track Meet, 2nd place 200 meter dash, fourth place, softball throw, long jump, 100 meter dash, VRPA State Track Meet; [oth. writ.] Poems published in book Anthology of Poetry by Young Americans, article for the Colchester Chronicle.; [pers.] Influenced by Robert Warren who's philosophy is "In the end the poem is not a thing to see; it is, rather, a light by which we may see and what we see is life."; [a.] Colchester, VT

MCGUIRE, CHRISTY
[b.] January 19, 1970, Mankato, MN; [p.] Carol and James Menge, Joe McGuire; [ed.] Hastings High, North Dakota State University; [occ.] student; [pers.] At the moment I looked down and smiled at my caterpillar, I could feel God smiling at all of us.; [a.] Fargo, ND

MCINTYRE, FRED
[b.] April 21, 1965, Lancaster, SC [p.] Butch and Louise McIntyre; [m.] April McIntyre, April 14, 1990; [ed.] Associate In Science Art Sandhills Community College, Bachelor In Mechanical engineering At North Carolina State University; [occ.] Mechanical Engineer, Specializing In Vibration Analysis at Norfolk Naval Shipyard; [memb.] I only write poetry for my wife or about weightlifting which are my two(2) lovers. So I am a member of Team Flex which is a body building and powerlifting team in VA Beach, VA; [hon.] My only honor is my wife whom sent in this poem I wrote without me knowing as a surprise.; [oth. writ.] My two favorite poems which were too long for this contest are "April Flower" about my wife and "Big Iron" about weight lifting.; [pers.] I believe in order for a person to be whole, one must be versatile and well rounded. This is why I'm an Engineer, Competitive Body Builder and Power Lifter and part time Poet.; [a.] Chesapeake, VA

MCLAUGHLIN, JR. MICHAEL E.
[b.] September 11, 1969, Lowell; [p.] Michael Sr. and Donna McLaughlin; [ed.] Lowell High School, Providence College; [a.] Lowell, MA

MCLEVIS, JACQUELINE
[b.] May 4, 1972, Anchorage, AK; [p.] Ronald and Lorraine McLevis; [occ.] Student/Nurses Aide; [memb.] Fit For Life; [hon.] National Honor Society; [oth. writ.] I have a poem published in the American Collegiate Anthology book of poets, fall 1993 edition.; [pers.] Writing poetry to me is very relaxing. My inspiration comes from the people around me.; [a.] Akeley, MN

MEDLER, CLIFFORD
[b.] August 11, 1955, L.A. Calif.; [p.] Elnatan & Elinor Medler; [m.] Brenda Lee Medler; [ch.] Tyree, Cody,

Bailey, Cayden; [ed.] High School; [occ.] Well drilling; [oth. writ.] Mountain Green, Rio Grandie, Meadow, The Rock. Available through me.; [pers.] I write of the miracle of nature as it applies to ourselves. Expressions of love through song.; [a.] Heber, VT

MEEK, MARSHA A.
[Pen.] Marsha Ann Hatfield Meek; [b.] May 18, 1941, South; [p.] Roland B. Hatfield (deceased) J. B. Cocanour, Lorraine M. Perry Cocanour; [ch.] Wm. L. Payne, Jr. (deceased), Lori Payne Rice; [ed.] High School; [occ.] Part time substitute at school; [memb.] Life Christian Center; [hon.] I have had the honor of being a mom to the most handsome, intelligent loving son, and the most beautiful intelligent loving daughter, and they have decorated my life with precious grandchildren; [oth. writ.] numerous poems; [pers.] My writings have been inspired through my feelings of joy, pain, and everyday life experiences of myself and others. Only this pst 5 years have I shred with others the words of my heart, knowing that only by giving of your life have you truly lived. Letter writing is a favorite daily pastime with me as my close family, and also several grandchildren live on the West Coast. I love animals and I stand in awesome wonder of God's creation that surrounds me.; [a.] Newalla, OK

MEEKS, WILLIAM WOOD
[Pen.] Bill Meeks; [b.] December 8, 1974, San Antonio, TX; [p.] Mr. Larry and Mrs. Shirley Meeks; [ed.] Pine Tree High School, Kilgore Junior College will attend UT at Austin in Fall of 1995; [occ.] Assistant Manager at Signs and More; [memb.] Manion's Militaria Mail Auction Texas Military Collectors Assoc; [hon.] Phi Theta Kappa, High School Honor Roll, Kilgore College Scholarship Recipient, United States Achievement Academy, Who's Who; [pers.] Hopefully, my goals and honorable social status will guide me through my life. My lifetime wish is to become a lawyer and pursue a career in politics; [a.] Longview, TX

MEIN, ERIC A.
[b.] November 25, 1974, Rome, NY; [p.] Kathleen and Roy Mein; [ed.] Meade Senior High, University of Maryland at College Park; [occ.] Full time undergraduate at U. of MD; [memb.] Role Playing Game Assoc. Network; [hon.] Dean's List; [pers.] I believe, like Poe, that poetry should be about beauty. The fact that my conception of beauty is sometimes abhorrent to others does not disturb me.; [a.] Arnold, MD

MEIS, ROSE MARIE
[b.] December 9, 1971, Hays, KS; [p.] Earnest and Pauline Meis; [ed.] Hays High, Bryan Inst; [occ.] Distributor Sales and Service Rep, Globe Envelope and Forms, Wichita, KS; [hon.] Valedictorian - Bryan Inst; [a.] Wichita, KS

MELARO, MARIE A.
[b.] May 14, 1927, Oakmont, PA; [p.] John B. and Rose E. Melaro; [ed.] Oakmont HS - Hood College - Duquesne Univ - U of Pittsburgh - Pinkerton Bus Sch; [occ.] Retired HS Language Teacher (PA and MD Certification); [memb.] Democratic Party - Roman Catholic Church; [hon.] American Legion Medal Award; Honor Society (2yrs); Editor HS Paper; Literary Editor HS yr book; Honor Grad (HS) - College: Dean's List; Feature Writer Coll Newspaper and Frederick News" (Local paper); CH UN Interest Group; Hood Delegate to UN; State CH UN MD and DC Region; Ch CCUN; Ch Twin Boro's Beauty Pageant (Verona and Oakmont); Twin Boros Secretary; Speaker on Language Instruction at PA St Ed Assoc

Conference; [oth. writ.] Publications in American Mercury; Christians Science Monitor; Progressive Tchr; Family Digest; Today's Catholic Teacher; [pers.] Life is what we make of it; we shape our own destiny; [a.] Silver Spring, MD

MENDELSOHN, THERIAN H. WILLIAMS
[Pen.] Terri Ann Malone; [b.] June 1, 1930, Cleveland, OH; [p.] Theodore and Inez Williams; [m.] Lawrence Medley, January 1950; [ch.] Laurene Winifred and Tanya Elizabeth; [ed.] One yr college; [occ.] Retired Word Processor / Office Associate; [memb.] Universal Life Church, Inc; [hon.] Honorary Doctor of Divinity; [oth. writ.] The Mendelsohn Educator: Prophecy Edition, Secular Editions, and Basic Religion Editions: Report/Newsletters. Book: When God Says "No!"; Book: 20th Century Poems; Religious and Secular Sheet Music; [pers.] The poem herein, was written circa 1939, when I was about nine years old, then in Cleveland, OH; [a.] Cincinnati, OH

MERCADO, JAIME
[Pen.] Jay Mercado; [b.] May 15, 1947, Camry, PR; [p.] Carmelo Mercado and Eugenia Diaz; [m.] Eileen Feliciano, January 26, 1969, divorced July 1991; [ch.] (son) Jaime; [ed.] HS grad - Brooklyn, NY 1964; [occ.] Tenant/Landlord Relations Representative; [memb.] Viet Vets of NYC (former); [hon.] Military US Navy Letter of Commendation, National Defense Medal, Viet Nam Service Medal, Honorable Discharge; [oth. writ.] "Broken Promises, Forgotten Dreams". An anthology of essays, short stories and poems (unpublished); [pers.] I only fear ignorance and hate; [a.] New York, NY

MERCED, SANDRA L.
[Pen.] Sandra Helms-Merced; [b.] February 15, 1962, San Bernadino, CA; [p.] Jack and Jan Helms; [m.] Edgar N. Merced, November 15, 1991; [ed.] Military Family, I served ten years 82-92, my husband is still serving in the Army.; [occ.] Watchmaker/Repair; [hon.] ARCOM, Army accommodation medal for Desert Shield/Storm; [oth. writ.] I have many other poems, this is the first that was sent in "By my mother" to be published.; [pers.] I write mainly to express myself, and to put my feelings on paper, in hopes that someone may read it, and realize that they are not alone with their thoughts.; [a.] Hephgibah, GA

MEYERS, KRISTY
[Pen.] Kristy Ann Meyers; [b.] July 16, Jackson Memorial Hospital, Miami; [p.] Legal Guardians, Martin and Nancy Sehleifer; [ed.] I'm a student in a private school called Developmental Resource Center in South Miami; [occ.] I sometimes work at my uncle's office of (Ad Productions) making 5 dollars an hour.; [memb.] I have one membership for the Museum of Science. I believe is almost expired and I will become a member of Coconut Grovey Children's Theatre soon.; [hon.] I have been awarded one gigantic horseback riding trophy and one trophy for school of outstanding excellence, and another trophy for having good grades in school; [oth. writ.] I haven't gotten any other poetry writings published.; [pers.] I think poetry is the most beautiful thing. I like to write poetry very often. When I get older I'm going to become a writer for a couple of years and then teach for the 7th or 8th grade.; [a.] Miami, FL

MICHALAK, KATHERINE
[b.] June 5, 1985, Ft. Collins, CO; [p.] Deborah and Joseph Michalak; [ed.] I am in the 4th grade and have been home schooled my entire life; [oth. writ.] I have written

other poems in the past and last year I started a newsletter named the World Hawk and Eagle; [pers.] I believe that poetry speaks and that the words must merge to write your feelings as well as flowing in a smooth patterns reflecting thoughts and emotions from the writer, yet holding its substance; [a.] Crestone, CO

MICHALSKI, JAMES
[Pen.] Jimi; [b.] December 23, 1960, Kenmore, NY; [p.] Edward and Jane Michalski; [occ.] Video Technician; [pers.] I have many unpublished poems of this nature. I have a note pad on my headboard, as most of my writing comes directly from my dreams. I find the conscious mind to be quite amused with stories from the sub conscious.; [a.] Tonawanda, NY

MICHEL, MELODY
[b.] August 29, 1985, Washington, D.C.; [p.] Mother, Eva Michel; [ed.] Grade 3, Galway Elementary School; [occ.] Student; [memb.] Spencerville Seventh Day Adventist Church Primary Division.; [hon.] Author Award for Excellence in Story Writing, 1994; Award of Excellence for Outstanding Achievement in English, 1994.; [oth. writ.] My Day At Busch Gardens; When in Grade 2 at Spencerville Junior Academy; several poems and short stories not yet published.; [pers.] I like writing because I can use my imagination. I also like music and have composed several scores for the piano.; [a.] Silver Spring, MD

MICHIE, DELSA H.
[b.] December 19, 1908, Afton, Wyoming; [p.] John and Mary Hardman; [m.] Monroe Michie, April 29, 1932 (deceased 1976); [ch.] Coy, Rex, Mark, Evan, Allan; [ed.] College Degree, taught elementary grades and Jr. High 23 years in Utah and Idaho; [occ.] Retired; [memb.] L.D.S. Church, A Conservative Republican. Have held many church and community positions. My parents and husband were farmers. I love farm life and small communities.; [hon.] Very few except for my poetry.; [oth. writ.] Many poems and a few articles.; [pers.] My life has been the simple life of a country gal with the usual joys and sorrows. I have tried to reflect these experiences and emotions, hoping it may help others.; [a.] Washington, UT

MIDDLETON, JANELLE N. WRIGHT
[Pen.] Janelle Middleton; [b.] November 26, Queens, NY; [p.] Marlene Wright-McKoy; [m.] Herb Middleton, October 15, 1994; [ch.] Bobby L. Wright, Tisha and Daniel Middleton; [ed.] Andrew Jackson H.S., Katharine Gibbs Jr. College; [pers.] Your past is always with you. Learn from it. Because the future has yet to come.; [a.] Gutte Berg, NJ

MIDDLETON, MARGARET LENORA
[Pen.] Len Jackson; [b.] September 27, 1924, D.C.; [p.] Margaret and Lenwood; [m.] Raymond Middleton, May 15, 1974 (deceased); [ch.] Linda and Raymona; [ed.] Cardoza High, Margaret M. Washington Vocational School; [occ.] Retired; [memb.] D.C. Chapter of United Ostomy Association, Inc.; [oth. writ.] Poems I have not yet entered. I am currently writing a book with the same title I entered in your contest "The Other Me."; [pers.] I have been a victim of Crohn's Disease since the age of 38 (32 yrs.). I am now 70, I underwent open heart triple by-pass surgery on 6/29/94. I am an Ostomate; [a.] Washington, D.C.

MILES, SAMUEL C.
[Pen.] Dedea, Sam, Sammie; [b.] February 20, 1955, Galveston, TX; [p.] Eddie Gayle Miles, George Louis Miles; [m.] Never married; [ch.] none. 3 sisters, 1 brother; [ed.] Crenshawn High, Gateway Community College, California Business College, Upward Bound Program Univ at Long Beach; [occ.] Health Unit Coordinator, currently disabled; [memb.] National Assoc of Health Clerk - Coordinators, Black Student Union at Gateway, Unit Coordinators Council, several support groups. Attend spiritual retreats; [hon.] Trophies for dancing; [oth. writ.] Several poems for personal collection. Never published. Would someday like to have them all published as a book, as a collection entitled "Myself, My Silent Self"; [pers.] I reflect the hurt and pain, hope, love and goodness of relationships (friendship, love relationships) especially those of the gay community. My inspiration comes from all that surrounds me and also my spirituality. Also by my best friend Allen Perry; [a.] Phoenix, AZ

MILLAR, ROBERTO
[b.] June 10, 1953, PA; [p.] Leticia Sostre; [ed.] Los Angeles High, West L.A. College, American Academy of Dramatic Arts; [occ.] Writer of Screenplays; [memb.] "Not waste a whole lifetime, while I am alive..."; [hon.] "Best Actor" for the production of "Sweeney Todd" while in college at West L.A. College in 1972, proclaimed citizen of the world; [oth. writ.] "Color Me Blue" 1988, "Stickman" 1992, both are screenplays; [pers.] My passion is to comprehend truth beyond human beliefs, thinking and feelings--I am a mystic of natural philosophy, compelled to uncover rather than to discover. [a.] Los Angeles, CA.

MILLER, ELIZABETH A.
[b.] April 2, 1938, Utica, NY; [p.] Stephen and Martha Pavlovich; [m.] Norman D. Miller, May 10, 1958; [ch.] Brian, Kimberly, Audrey; [ed.] New York Mills Central School, New York Mills, New York; [occ.] Bookkeeper and Co-Owner of Breaky and Miller Distributing, Sauquoit, NY; [memb.] Cassville Baptist Church, Mohawk Valley Christian Women's Group, Hamilton College Golf Club; [pers.] My inspiration for my poetry comes from my Lord and God.; [a.] Sauquoit, NY

MILLER, FRANCIS W.
[b.] January 29, 1946, Jackson, Mississippi; [p.] Francis W. Miller and Sarah Carmen Therrill; [m.] Linda Ann Miller, April 24, 1971; [ch.] 2 sons, James and Joseph; [ed.] Undergrad, Major Finance, Minor Economics, Masters Business Admin., Accounting, Hofstra University, all degree's; [occ.] Investment Broker; [oth. writ.] Out of Control, a novel, unpublished; The Care and Feeding of Your "Stock Broker" expect publication May 1995; Numerous unpublished poems written for and to family and friends; [pers.] It's easy to write then write and write and even write some more, but poetry forces a choice of words that lift straight from the heart and drive right to the core!; [a.] Port Jeff Station, NY

MILLER, HELDIA B.
[b.] 1934, Swannanoa, North Carolina; [a.] Florida

MILLER, MINDY SUE
[Pen.] Mindy Miller; [b.] September 12, 1970, Perth Amboy, NJ; [p.] Francine and Milton Miller; [m.] Dr. Daniel Eisenman McGuire, MD, July 3, 1994; [ed.] (MA) Boston University, BA 1992, (NYC) Columbia University, MS, Social Work, 1994; [occ.] Social Worker; [memb.] Neve Shalom Synagogue, NASW, Psi Chi.; [hon.] Dean's List (Boston U.); [oth. writ.] I have

a collection of several recent poems. One poem (a holiday poem) was published in a paper when I was about 12 and was on the radio as well! Now that I finished my masters, I want to get back into poetry again.; [pers.] I have given poems to friends...designing poems about our friendship, which they loved. I love more than anything, a beautiful poem that rhymes!; [a.]j Chicago, IL

MILLER, POLLY ANNY
[b.] July 23, 1961, Greenville, SC; [ed.] South Florence High, Florence-Darlington Technical College, Denmark College; [occ.] Radiation Safety Technician, Calvert Cliffs Nuclear Power Plant Safety Committee; [hon.] Bachelor of Arts of Friendship Award, Certificate of Achievement from the National Academy for Nuclear Training; [pers.] Writing poetry allows me to express the feelings in my heart which might not otherwise be exposed to others.; [a.] California, MD

MILLER, TODD
[Pen.] T.U.K.E/The Unknown Explorer; [b.] February 21, 1963, Westwood, NJ; [p.] Dorothy Andrews, Gary Miller; [ed.] Metaphysics, Earth Sciences; [occ.] Dock Maintenance TNT Red Star Express, Newark, NJ; [memb.] Association for Research and Enlightenment; [pers.] Out of chaos and confusion comes order and creativity.; [a.] Elizabeth, NJ

MILLINER, LOUISE ENDIAKA M. JEWELL
[Pen.] Endiaka Jewell Milliner; [b.] October 25, Cleveland, OH; [p.] John and Marie Jewell; [ch.] Maurice, Walter, Lamont; [ed.] East Technical High School, Cleveland Dental and Medical Inst, Glendale Community College; [occ.] Medical Receptionist; [memb.] A Mission Donor, Aid The Children,, Lupus Society, Give to Cancer Society; [hon.] Award for honorable mention for my poem true gems; [oth. writ.] True gems, Isn't it a shame, inventor of African-American Heritage Pride Collectors Plates; [pers.] I truly hope my black brothers and sisters will come together and love and respect each other. And also that all races will learn to live in peace; [a.] Altadena, CA

MILLNER, TEILA
[b.] March 27, 1984, Portsmouth, VA; [p.] Mary Allen and Wayne Millner; [ed.] Belshaw Elementary School; [occ.] Student, Belshaw Elementary School; [memb.] Pallen's Martial Arts, Academic Achievers; [hon.] Honor Student, Academic Achievers; [oth. writ.] Young Authors Book; [pers.] Believe in yourself and others will too.; [a.] Antioch, GA

MILLS, FIORE
[b.] Lenore Fiore Mills; James Mills; [ed.] Scranton Central High School, York College of Pennsylvania; [occ.] Student at York College of Pennsylvania; [a.] York, PA

MILLS, KELLY MARIE
[b.] October 25, 1979, Houston, TX; [p.] Wilton and Lynn Mills; [ed.] Presently, 9th grade student of Nacogdoches High School, Nacogdoches, TX; [occ.] Student; [memb.] Member First Baptist Church, Nacogdoches, TX; [hon.] B Honor Roll, Cheerleader; [oth. writ.] Sometimes; [pers.] The mood I am in sets the mood for my writing, i.e., if I am in a happy mood, my writing is about happy feelings, etc. if I am sad, my writing has a sad tone. I write what I feel - thoughts that come from my heart. If the words don't come at once, give it time and use words that are my own; [a.] Nacogdoches, TX

MINICH, CONNIE F.
[Pen.] "Connie"; [b.] October 19, 1950, Mayport, PA; [p.] Mr. & Mrs. Myron R. Troup; [m.] Melvin G. Minich, July 13, 1970; [ch.] Gina R. Minich (bush), Barbara S. Minich (Cotherman); [ed.] High School Diploma; [occ.] Food Service Clarion Hospital; [hon.] H.E.A.R.T. Award from Clarion Hospital in which I work.; [oth. writ.] Poems just for my family and local newspapers.; [pers.] I want to convey the fact; that it's better to love and show peace than to fight and create violence.; [a.] Mayport, PA

MINISSALE, ADILE
[b.] September 3, 1939, Philadelphia, PA; [p.] Annette and Arthur Ciarlante; [m.] Dr. Anthony A. Minissale, November 9, 1963; [ch.] Anthony Joseph, Angela Maria; [ed.] Academy of Notre Dame, de Namur, Temple University; [occ.] Participating member Montgomery Cty., Assn. for the Blind; [memb.] Until recently when I became severely sight impaired, I was a coordinator for the Mayor's Commission on Literacy and served on a committee at Immaculate College to promote higher education among minority students; [hon.] National Spanish Honor Society, Dean's List; [oth. writ.] Several circulated articles on spirituality and the integrated personality.; [pers.] Life is a gift, and gratitude for that gift leads us to the discovery that we are greater than our circumstances.; [a.] Gladwyne, PA

MISCIO, CAROL A.
[b.] February 15, 1945, NY; [p.] Joseph and Julia O'Donnell; [m.] Charles M. Miscio, August 24, 1965; [ch.] Charles and Lisa; [ed.] B.A. Brooklyn College graduate studies; George Washington University; [occ.] Self employed owner: Celestial Connections; [memb.] Zonta Club of Fairfax County, Great Falls Business Professional Women, United Way Board Member; [pers.] Treasure and celebrate the human spirit.; [a.] Ashburn, VA

MISENER, RICHARD S.
[b.] April 27, 1957, Cleveland; [p.] Roy and Gerry Misener; [ch.] Jeffrey Brandon - Matthew Stephen; [ed.] Ongoing. I don't think anyone can say that they have learned all that they need; [oth. writ.] I am just now putting together what I've written over the years into a collection; [pers.] I really started writing after my sons were born. They have enriched my life so much that from them my inspiration flows; [a.] N. Olmstead, OH

MITCHELL, DWAYNE P.
[b.] November 23, 1961, Gary, IN; [p.] Lieutenant and Joyce Mitchell; [ed.] Indiana University, Bloomington, B.A. Forensic Studies 1984, B.A. Afro American Studies 1981; [occ.] Insurance Executive, Los Angeles, CA; [memb.] Kappa Alpha Psi Fraternity, Scottish Masonry; [pers.] The very sense of love starts between a mother and her child.

MITCHELL JR., MARK DOUGLAS
[b.] July 29, 1975, Tyrone, PA; [p.] Caroline Sue Webb; [ed.] Tyrone Area High School; presently a sophomore at Penn State University, University Park, PA; [occ.] Sophomore at Penn State University majoring in Elementary Education; [hon.] Who's Who Among American High School Students, Junior and Senior Year of High School, National Dean's List, Freshman Year, American College Students; [oth. writ.] Poems written during my junior year of high school (none published); [pers.] In becoming an elementary teacher, I hope I can positively formulate young people's lives for the better. If I

can influence one young life as Jerry Sandusky, founder of the "Second Mile" has mine, I will have achieved something.; [a.] Tyrone, PA

MITCHELL-GILKEY, TRUDY ANN
[b.] July 19, 1965, Little Rock, AR; [p.] George H. and Rosa M. Mitchell; [m.] Divorced, October 1, 1988; [ch.] Lauren Camille Gilkey; [ed.] Hazen High School; Univ. of South Carolina, Columbia; [occ.] Juvenile Justice Administration; [oth. writ.] A variety of poetry/songs read to small coffeehouse local audiences.; [pers.] To pay attention is to see poetry in everything that is.; [a.] Columbia, SC

MODARELLI, MATTHEW RHODES
[Pen.] M.R. Modarelli; [b.] November 16, 1973, NC; [p.] Robert O. and Carolyn Modarelli; [ed.] High school: Bellarmine Prep, Tacoma, WA; Virginia Military Inst Lexington, VA - 2nd Classmen; [occ.] Student; [memb.] Varsity Football and Lacrosse at Virginia Military Inst. School newspaper editor, drug and alcohol counselor. Air Force contracted cadet; [hon.] $8,000 Athletic Talent Scholarship to Virginia Military Inst; [oth. writ.] Not yet released; [pers.] My work is a reflection of the struggle between God, man, and love. I wish to portray a positive message in the institutions of religion; [a.] Tacoma, WA

MOGER, GEORGETTE
[b.] July 2, 1977, Long Island, NY; [p.] Dorothy and Ken Moger; [ed.] High School (Charlotte High); [occ.] Secretarial work, auto dealership; [memb.] High school art club, high school writers club; [oth. writ.] Several poems and charcoal portrait published in local literature magazines. Three articles submitted and accepted to local paper.; [pers.] I've kept two years resolutions on completing one, two hundred page journals out per month. Inspirations and influences. William S. Burroughs, Sylvia Plath, and E. E. Cummings.; [a.] Punta Gorda, FL

MOLINA, NELSON
[b.] March 24, 1956, New York, NY; [p.] Santos and Carmen Molina; [m.] Candida Molina, August 25, 1984; [ch.] Nelson Nathaniel Molina; [ed.] Hoboken High, Rutgers University; [occ.] Computer Operator/Pgmr. Austin Nichols Company Incorporated.; [memb.] Spanish Trinity Baptist Church; [oth. writ.] I have written other poems and songs which are presently being prepared for publication.; [pers.] I strive to relay all which is good, morally sound, and founded in Gods word the Bible, especially the greatest gift of all, the love of Jesus. Some of my inspirations comes from songs I've heard on love, life's experiences and the Bible.

MONDAY, MICHELLE FABRE
[b.] August 22, 1967, Richmond, VA; [p.] Mrs. Virginia Elder; [ed.] Associate Degree in Executive Secretary from Erie Business Center; [occ.] Secretary/Waitress; [pers.] Life is too short. If you see or want something, go for it. If you never take changes, you're not living life to the fullest.; [a.] Union City, PA

MONTGOMERY, JOSEPH M.
[b.] December 2, 1907, Co. Bluffs, IA; [p.] Charles Henry Montgomery; [m.] Maurene E. Montgomery, November 10, 1935; [ch.] 3; [ed.] College (BA), graduate studies, military schools; [occ.] retired; [memb.] Mason, Lion's Club, Hi 12, Toastmaster, Des Moines Garden Club, Men's Club (church), US Army Officers Club (TROA), Iowa Alumni Assoc; [hon.] Published 2 poems written many articles for newspaper, local maga-

zines; [oth. writ.] Family history for our three children and 13 grandchildren; [pers.] I write poetry for those who enjoy the "love of living". I have written over 100 poems. Four have been published and many have been read to groups; [a.] Des Moines, IA

MONTGOMERY, MARK R.
[Pen.] Hawkeye; [b.] April 3, 1957, Tripoli, Libya; [p.] Jarvis and Faye Matheney; [ch.] Jessica Montgomery; [ed.] Cookeville High School; [occ.] Truck Driver; [pers.] I hope to end the myth that homeless people choose to be so.; [a.] Cookeville, TN

MONTGOMERY, RICHARD E.
[Pen.] Rickey; [b.] February 7, 1967, New Brunswick, NJ; [p.] Gladys Montgomery, Samuel Montgomery; [ed.] Franklin High School graduate, Somerset, NJ; [memb.] Macedonia Church of God in Christ. Somerset, NJ; [oth. writ.] I write for Churches on different acco; [pers.] I would like to write so that others can find comfort and relief, enjoyment and encouragement as they read. I write all occasions; [a.] Somerset, NJ

MONTOYA, LORRAINE D.
[Pen.] Lorrie; [b.] May 24, 1953, Rawlins, WY; [p.] Steven F. Montoya Sr. and Mary E. Montoya; [ch.] Kimberly Campos, Valerie Campos; [ed.] B.A. Elementary Education from University of WY, M.A. Elementary Education, Emphasis in Spanish from U. of NM; [occ.] Bilingual/ESL Resource Teacher; grades K-3; [memb.] IRA (International Reading Association); TESOL, Teaching English Second Other Language; [hon.] Sundin Scholarship; Zonta Award, Youth Opportunity Grant. Nominated for Teacher of the Year Award by Channel 7 News in Alb., New Mexico; [oth. writ.] Some personal poems at home, but have not been published.; [pers.] To reach our children especially now in times of so much crime, violence and abuse they may encounter at home in their lives. For they are the future that will lead us in the next generation.; [a.] Albuquerque, NM

MONTOYA, MICHAEL F.
[b.] September 23, 1969, Albuquerque, NM; [p.] Hermon and Cecilia; [ed.] B.S. Education; [occ.] Teacher, Special Ed., Coach Varsity Track; [memb.] National Triathalon Federation; [hon.] Top age grouper S.W. Triathalon Series; [pers.] Life is too short to sit on a coach and watch it pass you by, get involved.

MOORE, ANDREA
[b.] June 25, 1967, Boonton, NJ; [p.] Beverly C. Politowicz; [m.] Edward S. Moore, September 26, 1987; [ch.] Edward Seth and Ryan Mitchell; [ed.] Hackettstown High School and Warren Co Vocational Technical School; [occ.] Wife and Mother and Poet; [pers.] "Always keep a dream in mind!" [a.] Greendell, NJ

MOORE, EMMANUEL
[b.] December 26, 1971, Liberia; [p.] Mr. and Mrs. James Yarsiah; [ed.] Freshman (TMC), graduated May 10, 1992, St. Patrick's High School - Liberia; [occ.] Student; [memb.] First Baptist Church, Cleveland; Baptist Student Union (TMC Branch); Royal Ambassador (New Georgia Baptist Church - Liberia); TMC Choir; TMC Soccer Team; 2nd All Region Team (Region 17) Soccer; [hon.] Meritorious Conduct (1987-1992); Honor Roll Award (1987-1992); Best French Student (10th grade - 1988); Best Christian Principles' Student (10th grade-1988) Salutatorian (Class of '92); Best Social Studies Student (12th grade 1992); [oth. writ.] Personal: Mother and Child; Is Your Life a Channel of Blessing?;

[pers.] All that I am today, I owe it to my dear mother, Mrs. Clara H. Yarsiah. I dedicate all my works to her; [a.] Cleveland, GA

MOORE, KAREN G.
[b.] October 21, 1946, Brooklyn, NY; [m.] Divorced; [ch.] Traci L. Moore; [ed.] H.S. grad, some college; [occ.] Smith Barney Sales Asst to Managing Director in Brokerage Firm; [memb.] Strap Hangers Campaign, Red Cross and Memorial Sloan Blood Donor; [pers.] We are all God's children; therefore, we should only be judged by Him!; [a.] Brooklyn, NY

MOORE, KIMBERLEY A.
[b.] March 8, 1969, Sumter, SC; [p.] Marsha and Fraser Boykin; [m.] Rusty Lee Moore, May 18, 1991; [ch.] Russell Fraser Moore; [ed.] Sumter High School, currently attending Central Carolina Technical College; [memb.] Westside Baptist Church; [pers.] My poetry is inspired by my wonderful family, especially my beloved son, Russell Fraser; [a.] Sumter, SC

MOORE, LISA MICHELE
[b.] February 7, 1971, Baltimore, MD; [p.] Catherine Day-Moore, Jerry Moore; [ch.] Mark Timothy williams, II; [ed.] Frederick Douglass Senior High; [occ.] Handle Operator, Sweet-heart Cup Co, Owings Mills, MD; [memb.] Perkins Square Baptist Church's Soup Kitchen Ministry; [hon.] Graduated in Top Five Percentile of my Class; [oth. writ.] "Snake" (poem), 1980; [pers.] Poetry is a way for me to express my private thoughts; [a.] Baltimore, MD

MOORE, MARIE A.
[Pen.] Rita Moore; [b.] June 18, 1957, Montgomery, AL; [p.] Elizabeth and Edward Humphrey; [m.] David F. Moore, June 18, 1981; [ch.] David Emmanuel Moore; [ed.] Shaw High School; [occ.] Private home health care nurse; [memb.] Full Gospel Evangelistic Center, Parent Committee for the Boy Scouts Assoc. FGEC Discipleship Ministry. The Firm Believer's Prayer Group; [hon.] Merit and Honor Roll student from high school; [oth. writ.] Various poems written on several occasions, such as weddings; anniversaries; funerals, friendships, etc; [pers.] My poetry is inspired writings revealing the hidden hurts in the hearts of mankind defining healing through truth, and spiritual progression. I am greatly influenced by the lives and conversation of people; [a.] Cleveland, OH

MOORE, MEGHAN COLLEEN
[b.] May 8, 1982, Stamford, CT; [p.] Michael and Colleen Moore; [ed.] Newfield Elementary School and I am now attending Turn of River Middle School; [memb.] Kids in Motion gymnastics travel team, Turn of River cross country team.; [hon.] Presidential Academic Fitness award, Graduation, winner of class essays, and Honor Roll Student; [oth. writ.] Graduation essay winner of my class. Only a few poems "A Cry" is my first to be published.; [pers.] If life is made up of different doors, writing is my exit.; [a.] Stamford, CT

MOORE, NORMA
[b.] March 20, 1920, Niagara Falls, NY; [p.] Margaret Powers Myeve; [m.] Frederick J. Moore (deceased June 1969), February 3, 1945; [ch.] 9 children, 14 grandchildren; [ed.] Niagara Falls High School, courses in adult education and community college; [occ.] Foster Grandparent in Headstart Program; [hon.] A poem entitled "Free-at Last" was given honorable mention and published in "Bridges to the Past", a collection of poems of

senior citizens of Niagara County 1994; [oth. writ.] This poem is one taken from a book titled "Horizons" an autobiography of the author's inner life written in prose and poetry which has been mailed to publishers for publication consideration; [pers.] Two events in my life - my husband's death at 50 and the death of my son 3 years later led me into expressing my emotions in poetry and the impact everything has had on my spiritual and human existence; [a.] Niagara Falls, NY

MOORE, SUZANNE M.
[b.] June 2, 1978, Boston, Massachusetts; [p.] Ann Marie Tobey and Patrick D. Moore; [ed.] Currently attending the South Carolina Governor's School for Science and Mathematics; [memb.] U.S. Chess Foundation, National Beta Club, South Carolina Junior Academy of Science; [pers.] I have come to the conclusion that there lies within every man, some good, in every heart, some love, in every life, some hope. Only ignorance and prejudice stand in the way of what could be.; [a.] Hartsville, SC

MOORE, TRACY L.
[Pen.] Tracy; [b.] March 6, 1979, North Carolina; [p.] John T. and Sandra T. Moore; [ed.] Sophomore at Kinston High School, Kinston, NC; [occ.] Student; [memb.] Who's Who National Spanish Club, Prep Club, Spanish Club, Anchor Club, Hospital Junior Volunteers, Students Against Drunk Driving, Junior Civitans; [hon.] Honor Roll, Academic Achievement Award 1993-94; [a.] Kinston, NC

MOORE, VIOLA JUNE
[b.] June 15, 1939, Big Run, WV; [p.] Lee and Pauline Dulaney; [m.] Robert Oran Moore, Sr, July 2, 1960; [ch.] Reda Ann, Robert Oran, Jr; [ed.] Pine Grove High; [occ.] Homemaker; [memb.] Pleasant Heights Baptist Ladies Missionary Fellowship Secretary; [pers.] Life is day-by-day living and we need God and people to make our lives richer. It's my desire to weave this truth into my writing; [a.] East Liverpool, OH

MORELLI, CLAUDIA ANGELA
[b.] April 16, 1969, Yonkers, NY; [p.] Frank and Antonietta Morelli; [ed.] Sacred Heart High School, College of Mount Saint Vincent, Institute of Children's Literature; [occ.] Establishing a writing career in children's stories for magazines and books.; [memb.] Associated Humane Societies.; [hon.] I have received a diploma certifying that I have met all the requirements to write for children and teenagers.; [oth. writ.] I have written several unpublished short stories for middle-grade readers.; [pers.] Writing poetry enables me to express my true beliefs and deepest emotions.; [a.] Yonkers, NY

MORESI, ANNA M.
[b.] Warsaw, NC; [p.] Claude and Rosabell Rouse; [m.] Kenneth L. Moresi, April 5, 1964; [ch.] none; [ed.] John Small Grammar, Washington High, Little Washington, NC, Merritt business, Oakland, CA, San Leandro High Adult; [occ.] Home Engineer and Secretary to Husband; [memb.] Past member Peninsula Hospital Auxiliary, Information Desk; [oth. writ.] I have written hundreds of poems about nature and everyday things I see and hear. Some are visual, attended a writers workshop for two years. Some of my poems were published in two booklets. I own copyrights.; [pers.] One of my favorite and best poems, "That Old Which," was published in the Mill Brae Sun at Halloween a few years ago.; [a.] Millbrae, CA

MORGAN, JEAN
[b.] April 25, 1959, Long Island, NY; [p.] John and Mabel Lindquist; [m.] Douglas Morgan, June 8, 1985; [ch.] Alyssa Marie, Krista Mae; [ed.] Babylon Jr. Sr. High School; [pers.] My writing is influenced by the love and experiences I've shared with my friends and family; [a.] Oakdale, NY

MORGAN, MARTHA M.
[b.] July 24, 1967, Akron, OH; [p.] Daniel and Martha Morgan; [m.] James Terry, October 31, 1994; [ch.] Danyelle Kymberly Terry; [ed.] Stanton High School, Kent State University; [occ.] Homemaker Child Care Provider; [memb.] National Honor Society; [hon.] Dean's List; [pers.] I try to express my thoughts and feelings about life and daily living in my writing. Each of my poems is different in content and style, but all come from within.; [a.] Kent, OH

MORGAN, NIK
[Pen.] Nik M. Orfaos, Nikos Morgos; [b.] April 7, 1968, San Francisco; [p.] Nancy and Larry Morgan; [ed.] Student University of NC at Asheville Creative Writing Program; [occ.] Actor, playwright and chief advisor for 8th Wonder Magazine; [memb.] NC Writer's Network; [hon.] Francis P. Hulme playwrighting Award, Thomas Wolfe Fiction Award, Carl Sandburg Poetry Award, Hemingway Days Short Story Contest, Honorable Mention and semi-finalist for the 1992 Heekin Fellowship; [oth. writ.] Antennae Blues, a long short story published in two issues of Gray Magazine; Moogy Don't Give A Shit in UNCA's 1992 Fury Magazine and Clear Eyed Crazy and Caved In On a Big Strong Girly in the 1993 Fury, both short stories.; [pers.] It is important to heal the sicknesses in the psychology of our culture with responsible artistry.; [a.] Asheville, NC

MORGAN, SHIRLEY O.
[b.] May 14, 1930, Baltimore, MD; [p.] William and Helen O'Brien; [ch.] David, John, Jane; [ed.] BA Western Reserve University, MA Case Western Reserve University; [occ.] Publisher Chagrin Valley Times, a local weekly newspaper; [oth. writ.] Articles, travel book, poems; [pers.] For many years I have ridden horseback in our local Amish country. I always feel to be in a time warp. I admire their pace of life, their industry and their tremendous family solidarity; [a.] Gates Mills, OH

MORGAN, VIOLET A.
[b.] February 1909, St. Paul, MN. At the age of nine contracted Infantile Paralysis and spent the next eight years in and out of Gillette Children's Hospital undergoing numerous operations on her legs to combat the affects of the disease; [m.] Harold R. Morgan, 1932; [ch.] Gloria, born in 1933; In 1939 she entered the tubercular hospital in Cannon Falls, MN. She volunteered for various experimental operations and was released in 1942 as an 'arrested case' of T.B.; She was divorced in 1943 and died in 1952 at the age of 43. She was survived by her daughter and ten month old grandson, Lloyd Bruce.

MORGAN, VIOLET A.
[b.] February 1909, St. Paul, MN. At the age of nine, she contracted polio. For the next eight years she underwent numerous operations on her legs. Although crippled she was able to limp along on her own power. She married Harold Morgan in 1932 and they had their only child, a daughter Gloria, in 1933. In 1939 she got t.b. She entered Mineral Springs Tubercular Sanatarium in Cannon Falls, Minnesota. She volunteered for experimental procedures and operations. After spending three years in

the hospital, she was pronounced, 'arrested' and allowed to return home. After World War II she and her husband were divorced. She retained custody of their daughter and on a very meager income from child support and alimony, raised her daughter alone. Her interest in writing developed while in the hospital as a child, creating a weekly newsletter of interest to the young inmates. Her education ended after the ninth grade. Being unable to continue her education she read avidly. Edgar Allan Poe her favorite author. Many of her poems reflect his influence on her own writing. She celebrated the birth of her grandson, Lloyd Bruce, in September of 1951. Ten months later she died. She was 43 years old.

MORGANS, JAY
[b.] September 30, 1975, Wilkes-Barre, PA; [p.] Mary Anne Mulcahy, Robert Morgans; [m.] The Amaranth; [ed.] Almost nearly most of high school, GED, Frags College; [occ.] Guitarist, vocalist for Shedding Blue; [memb.] The Drug Free New Youth; [hon.] My girlfriend smiles at me a lot and sometimes other people do too.; [oth. writ.] Poems published in Scranton, PA's Ergo magazine, published in The Thesaurus, self-published Flight of the Bluejay; [pers.] Live, Love, Learn; [a.] Hudson, PA

MORICI, TIFFANY
[b.] December 23, 1975; [ed.] Destrehan High Graduate; [pers.] I dedicate "Until the World ends" to my friend and Mentor Gail Batchelor who helped me through the darkest year of my life. 1992-93; [a.] Destrehan, LA

MORIN, JEANNE
[b.] March 31, 1980, Tunkhannock, PA; [p.] George Morin, Mary Ann Morin; [ed.] Currently a 9th grade student at Benton High School; [hon.] Winner of DAR essay contest. Winner in "Young Voices of Pennsylvania" poetry contest with "The Dragon Flight"; [pers.] I write for fun and enjoy writing. I have no message to expound in my poems. People may interpret them as they like; [a.] Stillwater, PA

MORPHIS, KAREN J.
[b.] June 24, 1951, Galion, OH; [p.] Lawrence and Myrtle Kelogg; [m.] Joseph R. Morphis, May 28, 1994; [ch.] Dustin, Charles and Derek Davis; [ed.] Galion High; [occ.] Timeshare Inspector / Warehouse Clerk; [oth. writ.] A personal collection of poems; [pers.] My poems are a result of the peace, joy and strength of the Lord working in my life; [a.] Crossville, TN

MORRIS, ANANDA
[b.] November 21, 1962, Knoxville, TN [p.] Donald and Cora Chamberlain; [m.] Guy Morris, July 2, 1983; [occ.] Pharmacy Technician; [pers.] We always hold close to our hearts, these that make us laugh, or hold us when we cry, or gives us precious memories we can call upon at any time. I was lucky enough to get all of this from one person. My dear Granny, thank you for allowing me to share.; [a.] Knoxville, TN

MORRIS, LA TOYA ANTEVA
[Pen.] Toy Anteva; [b.] February 6, 1977, Charlottesville; [p.] Alonza and Joyce Morris; [ed.] I am a senior at Louisa county high school. I hope to attend Radford Univ in the fall of 1995; [occ.] Student, Dietary Aid; [memb.] French Club President at my school, NAACP, Minority Achievement Committee; [oth. writ.] I have several other poems I would like to publish; [pers.] I write about my feelings, hopes, and the greatest treasure of all "equality"; [a.] Louisa, VA

MORROW, LORETTA E.
[b.] November 4, 1939, Cleveland, OH; [p.] Alfred and Loretta Mack; [m.] Divorced; [ch.] Eileen, Jennifer, Joyce, Keith and Lauren; [ed.] Notre Dame College, Cuyahoga Community College; John Hay High School; [occ.] English Teacher; [memb.] Pi Lambda Theta; [hon.] Dean's List - Pall Mall Society; [oth. writ.] Poems published in College publication and in Dusting Off Dreams by Quill Books; [pers.] I have a special interest in writing about the dynamics of human relationships; [a.] Cleveland Heights, OH

MOSCATELLO, SHANA
[b.] November 21, 1976, Stanhope; [p.] Gil and Kristine Moscatello; [ed.] Senior at Lenape Valley High School, will attend Bloomsburg University of Pennsylvania in the fall of 95; [occ.] Student; [memb.] Student Council, Peer Leader, Literary Magazine National Honor Society, French Honor Society, Gifted and Talented Program; [hon.] Creative Writing Award, Principal's Award, Award for Excellence in Humanities; [oth. writ.] Essays published in Literary Magazine, Articles published in school newspaper.; [pers.] Poetry is a way for me to express myself. I am influenced by music and the works of other poets.; [a.] Stanhope, NJ

MOVILLA, GISELA
[b.] December 3, 1962, Puerto Rico; [p.] Jose Fco Serrano, Julie Otto; [m.] Arturo F. Movilla, March 5, 1983; [ch.] Frances, Melissa and Fabian; [ed.] Papa Juan High School, P.R.; [p.] Cosmetologist; [oth. writ.] Book: (Beyond the Truth) (unpublished), collection of poems (unpublished); [pers.] I write what I feel, because writing makes my soul free - letting others identifying themselves with my poems; [a.] Ozone Park, NY

MUCKLE, KIRK
[b.] October 8, 1958, Elmhurst, NY; [p.] George and Althea (Boyd) Muckle; [m.] Divorced, September 20, 1994; [ch.] Christopher Corey Muckle; [ed.] New York University (Film Studies) Suny of Science and Forestry, BS, BLA Syracuse University, BS SUNY at Farmingdale, AAS; [occ.] Architectural Designer Artist; [memb.] Municipal Art Society of NY, Architectural League of NY; [hon.] NEA Student Fellowship, 1981; [pers.] "I seek through my poetry to enlighten society to me, tragic beauty of the human condition.; [a.] Iselin, NJ

MUIRHEAD, JANET
[Pen.] Janet Lee; [b.] April 2, 1934, Baltimore, MD; [m.] Robert Muirhead; [ch.] Two married daughters - Kim and Kathy. Three grandchildren - Kristin, John and Colby; [ed.] Eastern High School, Baltimore, MD; [occ.] Retired; [memb.] Coquina Presbyterian Church and Choir; [oth. writ.] Inspirational poems from the Bible's New Testament Books of John, James, Matthew, Luke, and other inspirational poems; [pers.] It is with great joy and awe that I write poems about some of the writers of the New Testament. Now that I am retired, I hope to write more; [a.] Ormond Beach, FL

MULLEN, MARY M.
[b.] May 9, 1948, Omaha, NE;[p.] Louise and Robert Nachtigall; [m.] William Thomas Mullen, November 13, 1993; [ch.] Matthew, Laura Christopher; [ed.] One Year College; [occ.] Retail Supervisor, [m.] Smithsonian Inst., United States Equestrian Team; [hon.] I've been awarded ribbons for Equestrian competition in Dressage and Jumping, and three wonderful children, some years ago; [oth. writ.] I have volumes I have written for my own

fulfillment and hopeful other souls someday.; [pers.] My desire is that through my writing I can touch other hearts and souls perhaps, a spot no one has touched before.; [a.] Cumberland, MD

MURPHY, CHARLOTTE
[b.] May 26, 1943, Philadelphia, PA; [p.] Frank and Elizabeth Iacono; [m.] Frank J. Murphy, August 26, 1961; [ch.] Lisanne, Frank Jr., Steven and Charlotte Ann; [ed.] Saint Maria Goretti High School; [occ.] Receptionist, Tioga Pipe Supply Co., Inc.; [oth. writ.] Article in Patroness Magazine, Honorary mention for short stories pending publication.; [pers.] Expressing my thoughts on paper is the ultimate challenge, successful completion is the ultimate satisfaction.; [a.] Philadelphia, PA

MURPHY, JEFF
[b.] May 14, 1958, Castro Valley, CA; [p.] Bill Murphy and Georgia Murphy; [m.] Susan Vandruff, June 6, 1987; [ch.] Megan, Larkyn, Jasper; [ed.] Quincy High School, Hartwood College of the Natural Healing Arts; [occ.] Massage Therapy, Ricki Master Rock Mason, Home schooling parent; [memb.] I, as all I'm a member of creation and the light that connects us all.; [oth. writ.] Poems, short stories, children's books.; [pers.] I see my reflection in all around the woods, the water, the people seeing that which reflects back in what I try/attempt to write about.; [a.] Quincy, CA

MURPHY, JOY
[b.] September 24, 1974, Evergreen Park, IL; [p.] Isaiah and Carrie Murphy; [ed.] George W. Curtis Elem, George H. Corliss High, PTC Career Inst, Kennedy King College; [occ.] Certified nursing assistant/student; [memb.] Antioch Missionary Baptist Church, Broadcasting Club; [hon.] English Awards; [oth. writ.] Several poems and essays in my personal notebook, kudos to IBM in high school paper; [pers.] Life isn't always what you make it, but the effort you put into it; [a.] Chicago, IL

MURPHY, SONJA
[b.] October 6, 1972, Hattisburg, MS; [p.] Webber and Martha Murphy; [ed.] Petal High, Jones County Junior College, Mississippi State University (B.B.A May 1995); [occ.] Student; [memb.] Pi Sigma Epsilon, Student Alumni Council; [hon.] Who's Who Among High School Students, Outstanding High School Students of America, Mu Alpha Theta; [pers.] I try to express my feelings through my poems and other writings. I feel this is a way to share things with others.; [a.] Petal, MS

MURRAY, BRIAN J.
[b.] November 5, 1967, Piscataway, NJ; [p.] Barry and Judy Murray; [ed.] High School, Some College at Community College of Phila.; [occ.] Disabled due to brain tumors since 2/92, on 10/30/94; [hon.] Won 1st prize in photo contest sponsored by the Philadelphia Zoo. The Camera shop in 1982; [oth. writ.] Various unpublished poetry.; [pers.] My poetry is inspired by the people I write about. Each person brings a different meaning to my life. One Immortal Soul was written for Ann Doyle.

MURRAY, JUANITA MYERS
[Pen.] Nits Myers; [b.] June 8, 1926, Eddiceton, MA; [p.] Oga Myers and Luay Robinson; [m.] Floyd Aaron Murray, July 3, 1961; [ch.] Daniel Lee, Myrtle Lee; [ed.] High School and welding course; [occ.] Housewife, holding my family together; [memb.] The Bompy Baptist Church. Also the middle child in a family of nine. Mother sid I was the one God gave her to teach the younger ones about the older ones.; [hon.] My three year old great

granddaughter said I was the "Best Nana in the whole wide world and that she would be my best friend, always."; [oth. writ.] I wrote a poem in honor of my parents which was published in our weekly county paper The Advocate, I will send it if you want me to. It is special.; [pers.] I have C.H.F. and must take too many pills, I think. but my doctor says I have to have them and I have a lot of living to do. Sure hope I can leave our world a better place.; [a.] Meadeville, MS

MURRAY, LEONA E.
[b.] June 15, 1918, Detroit, MI; [p.] Oliver Troy, Eva Troy; [m.] George V. Murray, July 24, 1937; [ch.] Seven daughters and six sons; [ed.] Assoc Degree MCCC; [occ.] Retired Nursery School Teacher. Retired Law Firm Sec'ty; [memb.] Christian Women's Assoc, Church Altar Soc, ATRC, Tekakwithan Soc, Right to Life of Michigan; [hon.] Dean's List; [oth. writ.] Poems published in "Poetic Voices of America", newspapers, Church Bulletins. Childrens' book currently to make rounds of publishers. Lyric poem published by Four Star Music Co; [pers.] The laughter and innocence of children, the wisdom and patience of the elderly, and the beauty of nature has inspired my poems, songs and writings; [a.] Roseville, MI

MUSCARELLO, CHERYL
[b.] October 17, 1944, Chicago, IL; [p.] William and Charline McGowan; Parents In Law: Stephen and Ruby Muscarello; [m.] Stephen C. Muscarello, Jr., July 26, 1969; [ch.] Victoria Charline/Stephen C. III; [ed.] Kelly High School; [occ.] Insurance Agent, Northwestern Mutual Life, Mitchell Agency, Chicago, IL; [memb.] Women's Auxiliary V.F.W. Holiday, Florida; [pers.] If you love people, you will love life.; [a.] Chicago, IL

MUSCARELLO, RAYMOND
[b.] July 6, 1937, Brooklyn, NY; [p.] Sebastian and Maria Muscarello; [ed.] Abraham Lincoln High, NY Univ, Studied Journalism, Dean's List; [occ.] Worked with Bennet Serf and Dorothy Hillgaelen Broadcasting on TV; [hon.] Had many honors and awards; [pers.] Unfortunately Raymond died 3 months before graduating NYU at the age of 20. He lived with his parents at the time of his death from cerebral hemorrhage; [a.] Brooklyn, NY

MUSILLAMI, SHIRLEY
[Pen.] Shirley Sunshine; [b.] March 27, 1927, Des Plaines, IL; [p.] Albert and Genevieve Sengstock; [ch.] Albert; [ed.] 2 yrs. College, Chicago Musical College, Roosevelt College; [occ.] Retired, Volunteer Church Pianist, Neighborhood Grandma; [memb.] North Brook 7th Day Adventist Church; [pers.] Shirley Sunshine try to spread joy in little ways to those who's life she touches, spreading the love of God to everyone in little acts of kindness.; [a.] Des Plaines, IL

MUSSER, JULIANNE
[b.] February 22, 1977, Duarte, CA; [p.] Diane and Bill Johnson and Richard and Frances Musser; [ed.] Columbia River High and Early Admission Clark College; [occ.] Student; [hon.] Exceptional Peer Education; [pers.] John J. Davis was my inspiration in writing this poem because I admire his strength and courage in his unyielding fight against AIDS. He is greatly missed.; [a.] Vancouver, WA

MUTISYA, BENEDETTE
[Pen.] Mbula Mutisya; [b.] June 1, 1978, East Africa, Kenya; [p.] Raphael K. Mutisya, Fidelma H. Mutisya;

[ed.] Still attending Millbrook High School; [pers.] I have noticed that writing poetry has become part of me. Writing poetry is a part of relieving tension and stress. It makes me feel like being in a different dimension in this universe; [a.] Raleigh, NC

MYERS, HOLLY
[b.] June 26, 1979, Rock Valley, IA; [p.] Cary and Donna Myers; [ed.] Dell Rapids High School; [occ.] Student at Dell Rapids High School (Sophomore); [memb.] Peer Helper's Writers Group, RCYF; [oth. writ.] Several poems published in the local Writer's Group book. Three poems have been used as lyrics by a local musician.; [pers.] I try to put a little of myself into every poem and keep it reality based so everyone understands it and relates.; [a.] Dell Rapids, SD

MYERS, ROSE M.
[Pen.] Rosellea Wine; [b.] May 25, 1969, Wooster, OH; [p.] Anna M. Meadows; [m.] Single; [ed.] Graduated from East High School in Cleve. OH in 1988.; [occ.] Cashier for Convenient Food Market; [memb.] National Honor Society; [pers.] I'm wise, I love life and I love beautiful scenery. I try to reflect all the beautiful things of life within my poetry.; [a.] Lakewood, OH

NAGY, CHRISTOPHER
[Pen.] Christopher Turner; [b.] June 17, 1971, Trenton, MI; [p.] Dennis Nagy, Catherine Nagy; [ed.] Trenton High School, Eastern Michigan Univ; [occ.] Journalist/Student; [memb.] Society of Collegiate Journalists; [hon.] Echo Staff Writer: Summer 1994; [pers.] I like to find the simple truth in what is real; [a.] Ypsilanti, MI

NAKATA, DANETTE A.
[b.] August 10, 1955, Honolulu, HI; [p.] Joseph and Katherine Gomes; [m.] Marvin S. Nakata, June 1, 1982; [ch.] Azsa; [ed.] W.R. Farrington High; [occ.] Kahala Hilton's Room Service Ordertaker; [pers.] Bonding with nature has inspired my work. To understand differences in mankind, makes me believe that is why we are here, no matter the turmoil peace comes from within.; [a.] Honolulu, HI

NAPOLI, PATRICIA
[Pen.] Patricia Cox Napoli; [b.] February 27, 1938, Pittsburgh; [p.] George and Agnes Cox; [m.] Joseph Napoli, November 12, 1966; [ch.] Angelo 26, Maria 24, Joey 18; [ed.] Corres Degree, Palmer Institute of Authorship, Children's Stories, Art Degree; [occ.] Former Legal Secretary and Notary Public; [memb.] St. Francis of Assisi Welcoming Committee, St. Francis Prayer Group, Int'l Society of Poets, Poet's Guild, Children's Book Writers Society, Int'l Society Authors and Artist; [hon.] Poet of Merit, Int'l Society of Poets, Certificate of Merit, Poet's Guild, Iliad Literary Award, Iliad Press, Amer. Legion Medal, Award Diocese of Catholic Education; [oth. writ.] Best New Poems 1994, Best Poems 1995, Musings, Poetic Voices of America, Westbury Anthology, Amer. Poetry Anthology, Voices of Many Lands, Echoes of Yesterday, Edge of Twilight, Dark Side of the Moon.; [pers.] Writing is a talent that never grows stale for the mind is always at work and eager to put those thoughts on paper.; [a.] Springfield, PA

NASTARI, MICHAEL R.
[b.] May 24, 1949, San Francisco, CA; [ch.] Stefanie Angela, Nicole Marie; [oth. writ.] Poems, prose, music.; [pers.] I write so this inner voice may speak of the common ground on which all of us temporarily walk.; [a.] San Mateo, CA

NEEDY, TAMARA L.
[b.] October 24, 1970, Murray, Kentucky; [p.] Kahla Smith; Dan and Patricia Needy; Siblings: (sister) Crystal Ward; (brother) Craig Engel; [ed.] Arvada High School, Colorado State Univ; [oth. writ.] A collection of over 60 poems; [pers.] My poetry has always been a reflection of my soul, and I am eternally grateful to my family and friends for holding up that mirror and being my inspiration; [a.] Arvada, CO

NELMS, RENEE
[b.] July 7, 1972, Cecil and Sylvia Dean; [m.] Michael Nelms, December 16, 1989; [ch.] Brandon and Bradley Nelms; [ed.] White Co High; [occ.] Housewife; [memb.] Mt. View Baptist Church; [pers.] I love to read and write poetry. Most of my poetry reflects the love for my family; [a.] Cleveland, GA

NELSON (JR.), MAC ARTHUR
[b.] April 23, 1970, Baton Rouge, LA; [p.] MacArthur and Jeanette Nelson, Sr; God-Parents: Mr. Alex and Nora Palmer; [ed.] Rosenwalk High School, Tulane Univ, Santa Monica College; [occ.] Computer Systems Analyst - Home Savings of America, Model; [memb.] Knights of St. Peter Claver, St. Augustine Church - New Roads, Louisiana; [hon.] Editors Choice Award for River of Dreams; [oth. writ.] Publications in local newspaper magazine, high school graduation poem; [pers.] "Eternity - The power to share something with others that will last forever"; [a.] Inglewood, CA

NELSON, AUGUSTA D.
[Pen.] Gussie; [b.] February 13, 1924, Sidney, Montana; [p.] Clifton and Loma Sparks; [m.] November 18, 1949 (deceased); [ch.] Mark and Joel; [ed.] High School; [occ.] Retired from Librarian; [memb.] RLDS Church, Audubon Society for the People (political); [oth. writ.] Poetry, short stories; [a.] Independence, MO

NELSON, CLAUDIA M.
[Pen.] Elizabeth Everest; [b.] March 19, Oconomowoc, WI; [p.] Stanley and Monica Frey; [ch.] Anita Marie (21 yrs); [ed.] BA Legal Assistance/BA Management and Communications Concordia Univ; [occ.] Assistant to President and CEO, GE Medical Systems; [memb.] Great Lakes Hemophilia Foundation, GE Elfun Society, NAACP; [hon.] GE Group Executive Award, GE Management Award, Circle of Friends (Hemophilia Foundation); [oth. writ.] "The Environmental Office", The Secretary Magazine; [pers.] Don't delay -- today make a list of 100 things to do before you die. Then do them! It will make your time in this world extraordinary!; [a.] Waukesha, WI

NELSON, MARY
[b.] January 15, 1951, Bethesda, MD; [p.] George and Evelyn Hamilton; [m.] John Edward Nelson, August 31, 1977; [ch.] Nichele Nelson, Keysha Nelson; [ed.] McKinley Tech High School, DC Teacher College; [occ.] Principal, Rhema Christian Center School; [hon.] Dean's List, Teacher Award at Given's Bible College; [oth. writ.] Unpublished; [pers.] That my gifts and talents remain God inspired; that I might reflect his perfection in my writing; [a.] Washington, DC

NELSON, SALLY
[Pen.] Sarah Hillabush; [b.] April 24, 1934, Batavia, NY; [p.] Gladys and David Hillabush; [m.] Jack Nelson 2nd marriage, February 21, 1981; [ch.] Linda Lee, Daniel John, John Matthew, Kimberly Anne, Jody J.; [ed.] South Byron High and a lifetime of experiences.;

[occ.] Retired from workforce, full time housewife.; [memb.] Clarendon Historical Society; [pers.] I love poetry, as they are words of wisdom and feelings from the soul. There is a personal and individual beauty in every persons life experiences, if they are put into words of poetry. The same experience lived by 100 people, will have 1000 different versions.; [a.] Holley, NY

NEMEC, JOANNE
[b.] July 26, 1938, Oak Park, IL; [p.] Josephine and Joseph Veverka; [ed.] AA degree College of DuPage; [hon.] Phi Theta Kappa, High honors; [pers.] A dream - a thought - can create our reality. [a.] Lombard, IL

NERO, STEVEN D.
[b.] August 20, 1974, Akron, OH; [p.] David and Jennie Nero; [ed.] Green High School, Akron University; [occ.] Firestone Country Club; [hon.] Father Diederich Award, Veteran's of Foreign Wars National A.F.J.R.O.T.C. Award National Sojourners A.F.J.R.O.T.C. Award; [pers.] Writing gives me a special opportunity express my thoughts and feelings in my own personal way.; [a.] Akron, OH

NETHERY, BERNICE
[b.] May 17, 1919, Milam, TX; [m.] Charles A. Nethery, September 26, 1938; [ch.] Pat, Jim, Janet, Ken; [ed.] B.S. Degree, SFASU; Med SFA Post Graduate; Professional Counselor Cert., SFA; Professional Librarians Certificate; Certified Social Worker; [occ.] Part time social worker; [memb.] Alpha Chi; PTA; TSTA Delta Gamma of Delta Kappa Gamma Hospital Auxiliary; [hon.] Dean's List, Who's Who in American Women, Leader in Secondary Education, Leader in American Elem. and Secondary Education, Teacher of Year, National Honor Society of Hemphill High School, named Bernice Nethery Chapter; [oth. writ.] Poems published in local newspapers; in state religious publication; in National Poetry Anthology. Writes occasional poems for many outstanding people and organizations such as MADD; [pers.] I believe that life is a special gift to be used to benefit them to glorify God.; [a.] Milan, TX

NEVELS, BOB
[b.] December 4, 1945, Jackson, MS; [p.] (deceased) Robert E. Nevels, Marjorie Nevels; [m.] Lorene Schrock-Nevels, August 22, 1992; [ch.] Step-children: Eric Schrock, Chad Schrock, Hans Schrock, Britt Schrock; [ed.] Ph.D. MS - Univ of Southern MS; MA, BS - Mississippi College; [occ.] Clinical Psychologist, Mississippi State Hospital and private practice; Adjunct Faculty - Mississippi; [memb.] American Psychological Assoc; American Assoc for Marriage and Family Therapy; Southeastern Psychological Assoc; Jackson Astronomical Assoc; Wells United Methodist Church; [hon.] Favorite Professor - Austin Peay State Univ - 1984; President's List; Dean's List; [oth. writ.] Professional journal articles in psychology; poems in literary magazines; [pers.] I reject post-modernism; I believe in absolutes. The great task of my life is learning to love as Jesus loved; [a.] Ridgeland, MS

NEVIS, EVELYN
[b.] February 13, 1911, Nevada City, CA; [p.] Frank and Lottie Naake; [m.] Deceased, Abner Ruhkala, January 23, 1931; [ch.] JoAnne and Jack Ruhkala; [ed.] Roseville High, American River College; [occ.] Retired, McClellan AFB California (23 yrs. Communications); [memb.] Community Covenant Church, Toast Mistress Club, Sierra View Country Club, now retired.; [oth. writ.] Short stories, none published.; [pers.] I try to express my own feelings in my writings.; [a.] Roseville, CA

NEWMAN, GLENDA
[b.] July 2, 1949, Mobile, AL; [p.] Glenn and Louisa Davis (deceased); [m.] Philip Noel Newman, October 18, 1980; [ch.] Leticia Ann Pruitt, Katrinia Marie Pruitt; [ed.] Murphy High, Southwest State Technical College; [occ.] Homemaker; [memb.] University Baptist Church Media Committee; [oth. writ.] Several poems written and shared with my church family.; [pers.] Poetry is my release mechanism from life's ups and downs; for pleasure, healing and growing, the therapeutic value is overwhelming. I give God the glory.; [a.] Mobile, AL

NEWPORT, GEORGE WILLIAM
[b.] July 15, 1952, Windsor, VT; [p.] George Joseph Newport, Jr, Barbara Lucy Newport; [m.] 2 x, June 1971, March 30, 1979; [ed.] High school and Fayetteville Technical Community College; [occ.] Writer - Administrative Assistant - Mechanic; [memb.] National Railway Historical Society, Special Forces Association; [oth. writ.] Auto-biographical, 7 Combat Tours; [pers.] It is my wish that people will read my writings and realize that this horror we glorify and call war should not continue; [a.] Cumberland, NC

NEWTON, LULY
[b.] January 2, 1929, Council Bluffs; [p.] Mr. and Mrs. W.B. Whittington; [m.] Gerald Newton, September 1, 1989; [ed.] 7th grade; [occ.] Housewife; [oth. writ.] Many others.

NGUYEN, BATONG
[b.] May 19, 1971, Vietnam; [p.] Huong Nguyen; [ed.] Salem High, NRI School of computer programming; [occ.] Free-lance proofreading at home profession; [memb.] Choirs at First Baptist Church of Salem; [hon.] NRI School of Computer Programming; Achievement Award with high honors, received 4 certificate awards at Beachmont School; [oth. writ.] Songs writers and most favorite is poetry; [pers.] In our lives, we're all have gifts provided by God. We must use the gifts to reach out our fellow man; [a.] Salem, OR

NICHOLAS, CHARLES VINCENT
[Pen.] May 20, 1975, Manatee County, FL; [p.] Vincenza and William Nicholas; [ed.] Graduate of Fairfield High School 1993; [occ.] Aspiring Musician an poet, construction; [oth. writ.] Several unpublished poems.; [pers.] I endeavor to try to let people feel the confusion I feel about the way life is and the way human-kind is letting the world slip from us. My writings are inspired by life and feelings.; [a.] Fairfield, CT

NICHOLAS, WILLADENE L.
[Pen.] Willadene; [b.] March 12, 1910, Streator, IL; [p.] Almyron C. and Etta Dunbar Kelly; [m.] Widow of Ray T. Nicholas, December 25, 1932; [ch.] Ray T. Nicholas, Jr., Sally Martens, and Gayle Dene Bohne; [ed.] Princeville, IL, H.S., Monmouth, Monmouth College, and University of Illinois, Urbana, IL; [occ.] Retired Teacher, Artist, Writer and poet; [memb.] United Protestant Church, Grayslake Garden Club, Tenth District Federation of Women's Clubs, NFWC, Old Plank Road Questers, D.A.R., A.A.R.P., Grayslake Historical Society, Village Afternoon Unit of Homemakers Extension.; [pers.] Grayslake Woman of the Year Award, Gold Jury Award from University of IL, many awards in Lake County Fair Art Show.; [oth. writ.] Published 4 books of poetry; [pers.] I believe in kindness to and understanding of others; daily appreciation, things created in nature and the profound thoughts developed in the creative minds of mankind.; [a.] Grayslake, IL

NISHIMOTO, MIYE
[Pen.] Mia Nishimoto; [b.] April 28, 1926, Brawley, CA; [m.] Jim Nishimoto, November 1, 1953; [ch.] Becky Jean Roberts, Paul Nishimoto, Kay Cragg; [ed.] Poston High, Poston, CA and Antelope Valley College, Lancaster, CA; [occ.] Retired from the field of social services; [memb.] Lancaster Presbyterian Church, Lancaster, CA and Antelope Valley Literacy Council, in Lancaster, CA; [hon.] Dean's List, Antelope Valley College; [oth. writ.] I have entered none, as yet, but hope to in the foreseeable future; [pers.] God promises that if we walk in faith, and abide by His principles governing our thoughts and actions, He will direct our paths, leading to unexpected blessings in our lives.; [a.] Lancaster, CA.

NOBLES, JACK C.
[b.] June 27, 1940, Hattiesburg, MS; [p.] J.K. and Allie Dye Nobles; [m.] Linda Kay Doty Nobles, December 21, 1973; [ch.] Shane Nobles and Lisa Nobles Baehle; [ed.] 1958 Graduate of Forrest County AHS, Brooklyn, MS; [occ.] Transportation Dispatcher, Ingalls Shipbuilding, Pascaqoula, MS; [pers.] I enjoy writing about experiences of today and yester years; [a.] Pascaquola, MS

NOCIVELLI, MICHAEL
[b.] July 2, 1967, Somerville; [p.] Edward J. and Hazel Nocivelli; [m.] Michelene Nocivelli, November 2, 1991; [ch.] Samantha; [ed.] Somerville High School, University of Massachusetts, Boston; [occ.] Retail Manager; [memb.] RPGA, Former Boy Scout; [hon.] High School Spring Writing Festival, Honorable Mention 1983, Spring Writing Festival, 2nd place 1984, Northeast Language Award, Italian 1985, Brookstone Customer Service Gold Coin (4 times); [oth. writ.] Short stories in horror and fantasy genre, Leather, The Hanging, Penance, Princess, Epic poem Armageddon; [pers.] Having something published is achieving immortality. Hundreds of years from now someone will read my poem in a dusty library, and wonder for a second who I was.; [a.] Medford, MA

NOE, JEANETTE C.
[b.] September 24, 1918, Garden City, KS; [p.] W. E. Cavey and Meyers; [m.] Charles L. Noe, July 5, 1941; [ch.] Charles J. and Kathryn A.; [ed.] High School, Wichita Business College; [occ.] Retired; [memb.] Presbyterian Local and State Hospital Auxiliary, New Mexico, P.E.O. Sisterhood, Tri-County Genealogical Society; [hon.] Achievement Awards, Hospital Auxiliary New Mexico; [oth. writ.] Unpublished poetry; [pers.] The incongruity of life! The word "somewhere" in the last verse is an appeal to all mankind to seek for the "somewhere", so man may walk in peace.; [a.] Leonard, TX

NOLAN, ELEANOR A.
[b.] December 3, 1933, Calkin, PA; [p.] Horace Dennis, Evelyn Rutledge; [m.] Divorced; [ch.] Five, Seven Grandchildren; [ed.] Hancock High School, Oneonta State University, BA Psychology, Leaf Council on Alcoholism (to obtain education to be a certified alcoholism counselor; [occ.] Case Manager, Family Service Society of Yonkers, Yonkers, NY; [memb.] National Assoc. for Female Executives, National Assoc., of Realtors, Westchester Bd. of Realtors, (I have an Assoc. Broker's License); [hon.] National Honor Society (H.S.); [oth. writ.] Letters to the Editor (usually of a political nature); [pers.] I have been working on excellence in personal and professional growth. My poems are a product of this experience.; [a.] Tarrytown, NY

NORDBERG, NICOLE MARIE
[Pen.] Nadja Newberg; [b.] December 10, 1972, Abington, PA; [p.] Toni Trachtman, David Trachtman; [ch.] Hannah Kathryn; [ed.] Upper Merion Area High School, Temple Univ; [occ.] Home Health Care Giver and Journalism Student; [hon.] Most recently, I have been recommended for Temple's honor program by one of my intensive writing course instructors. Although a great honor; I declined; [oth. writ.] Several poems and two short stories not yet submitted for publication; [pers.] My greatest inspiration for my writings comes from my hopes and dreams for the future; [a.] Swedesburg, PA

NORIEGA, MARCO A.
[Pen.] M. Antonio Catarino; [b.] January 2, 1968, Mercedees, TX; [p.] Jacinta R. Noriega; [ch.] Bullet Easter; [ed.] Mercedes High School; [occ.] ATP (MHMR Assistant), San Antonio State School; [oth. writ.] Written over 80 songs and poems; [pers.] My writing has not changed the world around me but it does keep changing the world I'm in. Suzanne Vega has truly influenced me; [a.] San Antonio, TX

NORRELL, GLYNA
[Pen.] Zoe; [b.] April 25, 1952, Weatherford, TX; [p.] Bill and Jolita Cooper; [ch.] Josh Norrell 25 yrs.; [ed.] Bachelor of Business, Bachelor of Education, Texas Christian University; [occ.] Third Grade Elementary Teacher; [oth. writ.] Book of Poetry: Love In Bloom by Zoe.

NOSS, JOHN A.
[b.] April 13, 1976, Lakenheath AFB, UK; [p.] John F. Noss and Susan L. Simmons; [ed.] Holmes High School, Texas A&M University, Southwest Texas Junior College, University of Texas at San Antonio; [occ.] Student; [memb.] American Numismatic Association, United States Cycling Federation, National Off Road Bicycle Association; [oth. writ.] First poem published in O.W. Holmes High School's Polaris; [pers.] All of my literature is inspired by Taffy. (Not the Candy). In a world filled with beginnings, why can't we live through an end?; [a.] San Antonio, TX

NYCE, LORI ANN
[b.] March 17, 1970, Harrisburg, PA; [p.] Lloyd and Georgianna Nyce; [ed.] Central Dauphin East High School; Lebanon Valley College; [occ.] Circulation Assistant; East Shore Area Library, Harrisburg, PA; [hon.] Magna Cum Laude, Phi Alpha Epsilon, Dean's List, Who's Who in American Colleges and Universities, College Honors; [a.] Harrisburg, PA

O'BRIEN, JOY DE ANNE
[Pen.] Joy; [p.] October 27, 1980, Inglewood , CA; [p.] Joni Kohr and Craig O'Brien; [ed.] Preschool through 8th at Faith Lutheran (pre-7th) and Trinity Lutheran (8th) Schools; [occ.] 9th grade student at Red Bluff Union High School; [memb.] Cheerleading - 5,7, and 8th handbells; 5,8, and 9th, currently in dance and drama; [hon.] Honor Roll and Honorable Mention Trophies for cheerleading and National and Presidential Physical fitness Awards (5,6 grade); [oth. writ.] Many other poems written for pleasure, and expression, also a few printed in my elementary school's newsletter; [pers.] This poem was written when I was in 5th grade, inspired by mixed feelings for a certain boy in my class. I'd just like to take a little space to thank Steve Hamilton; [a.] Cottonwood, CA

O'BRIEN, THOMAS ROBERT
[Pen.] T. Robert O'Brien; [b.] April 3, 1958, Abington, PA; [p.] Savilla O'Brien, Harry O'Brien; [m.] Kathleen McKay-O'Brien, June 4, 1994; [ch.] Jennifer Lynn, Kaycie Lee; [ed.] Holy Martyrs, Enfield Jr. High Springfield Sr. High PA; [occ.] Quality Assurance Agent, Kmart Corp; [oth. writ.] Three poems selected for an anthology of poetry. One poem recited and broadcasted on a local radio station that won a prize. Currently working on a book of poetry; [pers.] I am motivated by words of love and romance that touch the heart of others. It pleases me more to give smiles and warmth to someone else; [a.] Levittown, PA

O'CONNOR, JANICE
[b.] April 17, 1944, Oneonta, NY; [p.] Willard and Louise Becraft; [ch.] Cynthia, Michael, Candace, Colleen; [ed.] Whitesboro High School, Boces School of Nursing; [occ.] Licensed Practical (Psychiatric) Nurse at St. Elizabeth Hospital; [hon.] Vice President of my Nursing Class; [oth. writ.] A poem which was published in our local newspaper. A poem published in "Woman's World" Magazine; [pers.] I write mostly for fun and personal satisfaction. I am continually inspired by the people who are nearest and dearest to my heart.; [a.] Remsen, NY

OBRAN, MARK F.
[b.] July 25, 1959, Lorain, OH; [pers.] I feel we should teach our children and each other; that we have a choice, to love with the heart, and to be truthful. Remember that nothing's free.

ODOM, JOSEPH
[b.] October 10, 1975, Oakdale, LA; [p.] Arblee and Darlene Odom; [ed.] Elizabeth High School, attending Louisiana College; [memb.] Louisiana College Student Foundation; [hon.] Summer staff at Dry Creek Baptist Camp; [pers.] I try to show God's love in my writings, since He is the one who inspires me; [a.] Oakdale, LA

OH, DAVID
[b.] April 11, 1978, Sao Paulo, Brazil; [p.] Gin Hwa Yang Oh, Yong Yun Oh; [ed.] Stuyvesant High School; [occ.] Student; [pers.] Without pain their is no art; [a.] Bayside, NY

OH, SOYOUNG
[b.] February 12, 1981, Toronto, Canada, Ontario; [p.] Mootak and Ali Jung Oh; [ed.] Ridge Ranch Elementary School, East Brook Middle School (currently 8th grade); [hon.] Student of the Year, North Jersey Spelling Bee Finalist, Johns Hopkins Talent Search, First place in poetry contest, Math counts, tile part of Wall of Harmony; [oth. writ.] Articles for school newspaper, The Est Brook Eagle; [a.] Paramus, NJ

OLDS, JOAN PAULINE
[b.] July 2, 1933, Cleveland, OH; [p.] Charles and Pauline Cunningham; [m.] A.D. Olds (deceased), September 19, 1959; [ch.] Brenda Joyce Cook; [ed.] Southern OH College (GED), Certified Office Specialist; [occ.] Retired; [memb.] Order of the Eastern Star, Sharon Temple Missionary Baptist Church - Commissioner - Membership Evangelism/Directress-Baptist Training Union - BTU; [hon.] Southern Ohio College (Kings Skills Center) - Student of the Phase, Perfect Attendance, Academic Achievement. (Inner City Nursing Home) Volunteer Certificates - (1988); [oth. writ.] Several unpublished poems; [pers.] I strive to share the gift that God has given to me, to inspire others; [a.] Cleveland, OH

OLIGER, STACEY
[b.] November 22, 1977, Woodside, NY; [p.] Mary and Robert Oliger; [ed.] Attending LaGuardia Community College; [occ.] Student Aid for Auxiliary Services for High Schools; [hon.] Received a certificate for writing at my graduation ceremony from G.E.D.h; [oth. writ.] Several poems including one that was published in grade school.; [pers.] I write poems to express my feelings to others and sometimes to myself.; [a.] Woodside, NY

OLSZYK, ALLISONBETH
[b.] July 14, Groton, CT; [p.] Peter R. Olsyzk and Kathleen N. Hart; [ed.] Dodd Jr. High, current Highland Elementary St. Thomas Day School; [occ.] Student; [pers.] This is my first time ever being published. Not including the school newspaper. At age 13 this is quite an honor.; [a.] Cheshire, CT

OLTMANNS, RACHEL JEAN
[Pen.] Chloe Norton; [b.] November 29, 1979, SLC, Utah; [p.] Ken and Shirley Oltmanns; [ed.] Freshman at Tooele High School, Tooele, Utah; [memb.] Jazz-In-It dance and gymnastic team; [hon.] Various awards in gymnastics and dance competitions; [oth. writ.] Various poems and short stories; [pers.] Life isn't what you make of it, it's how you see it; [a.] Tooele, UT

OLUBANDEWO, DR., JOSEPH O.
[b.] April 16, 1945, Oro Ago, Nigeria; [p.] Solomon and Leah Olubadewo; [m.] Victoria Ibidunni Olubadewo, August 20, 1971; [ch.] Dele, Seyi, Bodurde, Wole; [ed.] Ph.D. in Pharmacology from Vanderbilt Univ., Nashville, TN, B.SC (Hons) in Chemistry from Ahmadu Bello Univ., Zaria, Nigeria; [occ.] Professor of Pharmacology of Toxicology; [memb.] Amer. Soc. Pharmacology and Exptl. Therap. (ASPET); Amer. Assoc. Univ. Professors (AAUP); New York Acad. Sciences; Member of Suburban Baptist Church in New Orleans, LA; [hon.] Amer. Heart Assoc., TN, Affiliate Fellow; Afr-Amer. Graduate (AFGRAD) Fellow; Recipient of Imperial Chemical Co. Award for Best Graduate Chemistry Major; [oth. writ.] Numerous manuscripts published in refereed scientific journals.; [pers.] My poems are attempts to express God's perspective on mankind's self-made problems.; [a.] New Orleans, LA

ORDONEZ, ROSEMARY
[b.] August 17, 1968, Bronx, NY; [p.] Justo and Jilma Ordonez; [ed.] St. Thomas Aquinas Elementary Aquinas High school, Marymont Manhattan College; [occ.] Social Service Coordinator; [memb.] NAACP, Black Task Force On Child Abuse and Neglect, Lambert New Hope; [pers.] Writing poetry is a time of fulfillment for me, and a new beginning for me, as I dream new dreams and accept new challenges. Always strive to make your dreams a reality.; [a.] Bronx, NY

ORI, ANTHONY
[Pen.] T. J. Allen; [b.] May 1, 1980, Waokegan; [p.] James Craig, Gerri Batalia (raised by grandparents); [ed.] High School Freshman; [occ.] Student; [memb.] Splitlog Baptist Church; [oth. writ.] Other poetry as yet unpublished.; [pers.] I am a 14 year old boy. I strive to be the best I can be. I take my innermost thoughts and try to express them on paper. I have Tourette Syndrome and writing poetry helps me deal with everyday life.; [a.] Goodman, MO

ORR, VICKY
[b.] October 29, 1958, Cleveland, OH; [p.] Louis Samuels and Mable Slaughter; [m.] Samuel U. Orr, Sr, November 19, 1983; [ch.] Jason Brandon and Samuel U; [ed.] Shaker High, Cuyahoga C. College; [occ.] Preschool teacher/writer; [oth. writ.] I manage my own greeting card business (small scale). This poem is my first published piece. I've created several original card stylings which I am researching now with great consumer response; [pers.] To God my father, I offer all the praise. The gift of creativity comes from a source much greater than myself; [a.] Cleveland, OH

ORRELL, ALICE S.
[b.] December 23, 1905, Watertown, CAN; [p.] Albert W. Skilton; [m.] James B. Orrell, May 9, 1926; [ch.] Margaret, Mary, Sue, Richard; [ed.] BA in Elementary Education (1959), Stetson University, DeLand, FL; [occ.] Retired School Teacher; [memb.] Assembly of God Church, Ozark, MO; [hon.] Current MS. Missouri Health Care Queen 1994; [oth. writ.] "Mama Spouts Poetry" a published book of original poems. Published in 1982; [pers.] "Wear Out or Rust Out" With Gods help I prefer to wear out, never rust out.; [a.] Springfield, MO

ORTIZ, LUZ N.
[b.] Puerto Rico; [ed.] Presently attending Baruch College, Major: English; [occ.] Student; [oth. writ.] Several articles for the ticker, Baruch College's Day Student Paper; Article for Dollars and Sense, The Baruch College Business Review; Poetry for the Reporter, Baruch's Evening Student Paper; [a.] Brooklyn, NY

OSBORNE, TANYA B.
[Pen.] Tara Poinier; [b.] October 1, 1972, Ann Arbor, MI; [p.] Lois Osborne; [m.] Timothy Mansfield, November 25, 1995; [ed.] West Jefferson High School, Our Lady of Holy Cross College, (BSN - Nursing); [occ.] Student Nurse, Our Lady of Holy Cross College; [memb.] Who's Who of American High School Students, National Honor Society; [pers.] You must have lived your work in order to live through your work - or your readers will never grasp the reality that inspired you to write it; [a.] Terrytown, LA

OTTERSTROM, JIM
[b.] November 14, 1945, Santa Monica, CA; [p.] Claude Hampson, Lois Hampson; [m.] Peggy Sue Otterstrom, September 16, 1979; [ch.] James Walker, Jamie Grier; [ed.] Birmingham High, Pierce College, San Bernardino Valley College; [occ.] Postal Clerk, Big Bear Lake, CA; [memb.] Nature Conservancy, Environmental Defense Fund, Wilderness Society, Sierra Club, National Parks Conservation Assoc; [hon.] "Gold-Award" recipient for leadership - 1990 United Way Combined Federal Campaign "Eagle Award" recipient - 1992 and 1994 United Way, Combined Federal Campaign; [oth. writ.] Several commentary pieces published in local newspapers, poetry published in trade-union paper. Novel in progress; [pers.] This form of poetry is an anomaly for me. I usually write strong pro-environmental essays or semi-autobiographical stories. My strongest literary influence is the late Edward Abbey.; [a.] Big Bear City, CA

OVERCASH, BLONDELL
[b.] December 24, 1929, Cab-Count, NC; [p.] Rose and Andrew Self; [m.] Demps Ray Senior, 1949; [ch.] Four; [ed.] 12 yrs. Public School, several curses at local community college, Beginning Art Cert., Adult Growth and Parent Ed. (AGAPE) Trained NA (11 yrs. exp); [occ.] Retired; [memb.] NCWN; [hon.] Golden Poet, Honor-

able Mentions, Third Prize w/World of Poetry (now no longer publishing); [oth. writ.] Three poems published in "The River's Edge," "Oak Leves" (one poem), (songwriter also); [pers.] True knowledge is to know but not to tell abruptly; [a.] China Grove, NC

OWEN, KEITH
[b.] June 27, 1973, Nashville, TN; [p.] Holly and David Owen; [ed.] Fayetteville Technical Community College; [occ.] Commercial Art Student; [memb.] National Art and Advertising Design Club, Student Government; [hon.] My family's love.; [pers.] I'd like to thank Joan and Pat Riley, Billy Malone, Ramona Dewitt and Nanette Chism for everything. And I'd like to ask everyone to stop the violence. My pain runs deep enough.; [a.] Fayetteville, NC

OWENS, S. KRISTA
[Pen.] S. Krista Manley; [b.] November 2, 1975, Seneca, SC; [p.] Deborah S. Manley; [ed.] Graduate Seneca High School, Currently a Sophomore at College of Charleston Studying Spanish and Education; [occ.] Full time student; [memb.] National Beta Club, Interact Club, Spanish Club, High School Cheerleader; [hon.] Who's Who Among American High School Students for 4 years, Top 10% of Class in Oconee County, SC, Academic Letter; [oth. writ.] Many other unpublished works.; [pers.] Life is poetry.

OYEWOLE, DEJI
[Pen.] Dejoy; [b.] April 26, 1956, Nigeria; [p.] Dotun and Lape Oyewole; [m.] Imo Annette Oyewole, December 31, 1983; [ch.] Jumoke and Seni; [ed.] School of visual Arts, New York, Boston University Massachusetts.; [occ.] Writer; [hon.] Boston University Dean's Award for Multi-Media Research Project Presentation, "Aliens in New York."; [oth. writ.] "Quandary or Purgatory," a collection of poems, "Incarceration," "The Kidney Factor."; [pers.] If it's a tunnel you'll get out of it; look for a light and heat out of it. If it's a cave you'll live in it; settle down and meditate in it.; [a.] Silver Spring, MD

PABON, ELLAMARIE
[b.] February 25, 1965, Camden, NJ; [p.] Joan Marie Silver, Edward C. DeVault, Jr; [m.] Robert B. Pabon, August 27, 1994; [ch.] Nicole Renee DeVault, Tiffany Joan DeVault; [ed.] Maple Shade High, Omega Inst; [occ.] Homemaker, mother and wife; [hon.] DDD Training Certificate, Medical Assistant Certificate; [oth. writ.] Several poems which never have been published; [pers.] Most of my writings are based on the happy and sad moments of my life. I have been wonderfully influenced by my mother and her own writings; [a.] Glassboro, NJ

PACHECO, ORLANDO E.
[b.] October 23, 1954, Caracas, Venezuela; [p.] Carmita and Enrique Pacheco; [m.] Rosa Pacheco, November 26, 1988; [ed.] Bishop McNamara High School, Case Western Reserve University, B.A. Georgetown University, M.A., University of the Witwatersrand, Ph.D.; [hon.] Phi Beta Kappa; [oth. writ.] Academic articles on South African and Nigerian political/military affairs.; [pers.] Our relationship with God must be intimately personal: a covenant love. Otherwise, one tends to languish amidst impersonal abstractions and deepening isolations.; [a.] Brandywine, MD

PACKARD, GREGORY
[b.] June 5, 1960, Lancaster; [p.] Ruth and Brent Packard; [m.] Jolynn M. Packard, June 19, 1987; [ch.] Sarah, Brandi, Kristi; [ed.] Graduate of Manheim Central School District; [occ.] Production Worker at Burle Ind. Lancaster, PA; [memb.] Trinity Baptist Church; [hon.] I received two Editor's Choice Awards and a separate award for being judged in the top 2% of poems received. I've also had work published in "Outstanding Poets of 1994"; [oth. writ.] I've had several poems published by the "National Library of Poetry" an have been writing for two years as a past time.; [a.] Manheim, PA

PAINTSIL, LYNN MAC
[Pen.] A.G. O'Donnell; [b.] June 17, 1954, Pennsylvania; [p.] Gwen Jones and Francis O'Donnell; [m.] Divorced; [ch.] Christopher Michlovsky Stacey Mac Paintsil; [ed.] High School, New Heyes Comp, Liverpool England, Eton Lodge Liverpool, England; [pers.] Dream in color and reach for the sky. I was influenced by a dear friend, Mike who gave me encouragement to pursue my dreams.; [a.] Lindenwold, NJ

PALASEK, JACQUELINE
[b.] March 13, 1965, Smithtown, NY; [p.] John P. and Helene Palasek; [ed.] Half Hollow Hills High School East, State University of New York at Farmingdale, University of Stony Brook.; [occ.] Claims Examiner, Allstate Insurance Company; [memb.] The Long Island Greenbelt Conference, Sierra Club Legal Defense Fund, Political Action Team, Regional.; [pers.] In this universe of eternal travel, we are only passing through this life to get to the next phase. Always remember to take notes as you go.; [a.] Dix Hills, NY

PALMER, AMIE MARIE
[b.] November 12, 1968, NY; [p.] Virginia Birkmier, Don Palmer; [ch.] Amaranda Lynn Palmer; [ed.] Polytechnic High, Riverside Community College; [occ.] Transcript Clerk, Riverside Community College; [memb.] American Red Cross, Citizens Patrol of Moreno Valley California; [oth. writ.] I've written many other poems, lyrics, and recently I wrote a one act play called, "Terry and Michelle in High School"; [pers.] I have always enjoyed writing. My theater Professor, Patricia Scarborough, encouraged me to write a one act play this year, 1994. I will keep on writing forever; [a.] Moreno Valley, CA

PALMER, CONNIE
[b.] January 31, 1953, Nyssa, Oregon; [p.] Reinie and Charlene Bashon; [m.] Rick Ralmer, June 23, 1969; [ch.] Dusty, Billy and Travis; [ed.] Harper, Oregon; [occ.] Housewife; [oth. writ.] Several personal poems and children's poems; [pers.] I find that feelings from the heart, mind and soul are best expressed through poetry.; [a.] Prairie City, OR

PALMER, FLORENCE BRECKENRIDGE
[Pen.] Loren Palmer, Breckenridge Palmer; [b.] 1908, Winsted, CT; [p.] Allison and Louise Palmer; [ed.] Gilbert High, Elmira College, B.A.; [occ.] Retired Editor Teacher, Iran 1931-34; [memb.] American Assoc. Univ. Women; [hon.] AAUW Ed. Foundation named Grant; [oth. writ.] A Taste of Poetry, poems; Private Printings 1960-1990; [pers.] Poetry is emotion recollected in tranquility.; [a.] Elgin, IL

PANKONIN, CHRISTOPHER
[b.] Jan 6, 1978, Bonn, Germany; [p.] Vernon Pankonin, Gladys Pankonin; [pers.] Much love to my inspiration, Wendi Jeanette Walker; [a.] Springfield, VA

PAOLICELLI, ROSINA
[b.] January 27, 1943, Bronx, NY; [p.] Louise and Frank Adams; [m.] Leonard (deceased 3/11/93), October 21, 1978; [ed.] Graduated high school, Central Commercial 1960; [occ.] Retired, cannot work anymore; [pers.] I decided to write the poem so that my husband will always be remembered. This is not only for myself, but for other people who have lost someone dear to them; [a.] Brooklyn, NY

PARAS, PETER ANTHONY
[Pen.] Peter Paras, Peter A. Paras; [b.] March 8, 1984, Cleveland, OH; [p.] Dr. and Mrs. Antonios Paras; [occ.] Student; [oth. writ.] The Piano, Trip Up In Time - short stories. Also several other poems, most recently books before bed; [pers.] I use my writings as a way to express my feelings. There's a saying that I have..."Time, it's infinite in amount, but never enough!" Also, "If in doubt, look to a world of fantasy"; [a.] Westlake, OH

PARKER, VALERIE L.
[b.] May 16, 1949, Suburb of Detroit, Mich.; [p.] Mr. and Mrs. Fred Parker; [m.] Mr. Al Skero, October 10, 1992; [ed.] Ohio University, Athens, Ohio, BSED, ARM, (Accredited Resident Mgr.) from Institute of Real Estate Mgt. Chicago, TX, Real Estate Salesman's License #0431225; [occ.] Realtor, Ft. Bend County and Harris County, TX; [memb.] Ohio University Alumni Assoc., Ft. Bend Assoc. of Realtors, Texas Assoc. of Realtors, National Assoc., of Realtors, Institute of Real Estate Mgt.; [hon.] Top Office Salesperson, over 30 agents; [oth. writ.] Working on a book of Children's poetry to hopefully be published as "Months of Fun with Poetry;" [pers.] I began a career in property mgt. after six successful years of teaching, after 14 years of managing and supervising commercial, residential and homeowners associations, I shifted my career to listing and selling homes. In a world of stress, traffic and crime, I feel the sanctuary of your own home is the most important item I help anyone with.; [a.] Houston, TX

PARRISH, CRYSTAL
[Pen.] Cali Girl (Cali = C.A.); [b.] November 25, 1978, California; [ed.] At this time in my life, I am now attending Branson High School in Missouri. I'm in the 10th grade; [occ.] Hope to become a famous writer and singer. Working at it now; [hon.] July 23, 1993, I won 1st prize in an Art Contest in Warren, OH, at age 14. I received in 1994 a 2nd place All State Choral Medal for Chorus Teacher, Mrs. Cleal; [oth. writ.] I started writing poetry and other forms of writing art in the summer of 1992. I have many writing notebooks; [pers.] Life is like one obese classroom. You must "Live Alive", as late Jim Morrison put it. Penetrate the dawn, taste the night stars, experience your life, have freedom. Be true to all, and your self; [a.] Branson, MO

PASATIERI, NOELLE MARIE
[b.] December 12, 1979, Brooklyn, NY; [p.] Michael Pasatieri/Linda Alcantara; [ed.] Good Shepherd Elementary School, Saint Saviour High School; [occ.] Student; [memb.] Drama Club, French Club, Earth Club, National Honors Society; [hon.] First Honors, Veronica Radioli Award, Computer Award; [oth. writ.] Articles for school newspaper - "Skyline"; [pers.] Always follow your dreams and reach for the stars. My writings are all reflections of the things and people I love and hold close to my heart; [a.] Brooklyn, NY

PASQUALE, GENNARD S.
[b.] July 23, 1941, Boston; [p.] Frank and Caroline; [ed.]

BS in Ed; [occ.] Science teacher; [memb.] MFT, NEA; [oth. writ.] Several poems published in newspapers and yearbooks; [pers.] I love the idea of taking a thought and making it sing; [a.] Somerville, MA

PASSALACQUA, WILLIAM E.
[Pen.] Bill Passalacqua; [b.] June 2, 1962, Geneva, NY; [p.] Sam and Marie (deceased) Passalacqua; [ed.] Geneva High School, SUNY Cobleskill, Norwich University; [occ.] Assistant Commandant of Cadets, Norwich University, VT; [memb.] United States Army 1988-1994; [hon.] Army Meritorious Service Medal, ROTC Distinguished Military Graduate, Dean's List; [pers.] I try to reflect life of the common man in my writing. I draw upon my personal experiences in life.; [a.] Northfield, VT

PASTORE, ROBERT LOUIS
[b.] May 9, 1969, New York; [p.] Angelo Pastore, Anne Pastore; [ed.] John Adams High School; [occ.] Unemployed due to illness; [hon.] Scholastic excellence in all subjects, Tripe C Award, Science Medal; [pers.] If you don't experience the struggle...you can't acquire the strength; [a.] Howard Beach, NY

PATTERSON, SHARON L.
[b.] August 1, 1947, Kansas City, MO; [p.] Betty Hendrix and E.L. Hendrix, Jr.; [m.] LTC Garry D. Patterson, December 12, 1981; [ch.] Jacob Patterson, Joseph Milliman, Jeremy Milliman; [ed.] Eastern Hills High, University of Texas at Arlington; [occ.] Independent Beauty Consultant; Part time teacher (formerly taught school for 18 years) History and French; [memb.] Round Rock Chapel, National Guard Assoc. of Texas; [hon.] Top Girl Graduate, 1965; Teacher of the Year, 1971, Essay Winner 1994 Lancer Contest, Dean's List; [oth. writ.] Seasons of the Soul, Make Me Laugh In Rhyme, When They Call Me Names, Out Of The Ordinary, Let No Man Despise Thy Youth; [pers.] I love to encourage others to look for hope and strength when life's bridges are broken.; [a.] Round Rock, TX

PATTON, RENA S.
[b.] January 2, 1947, Germany; [p.] Joseph and ruth Shalman; [m.] Fred Benson, July 2, 1994; [ch.] One; [ed.] B.A. English, M.A. English, M.A. Education; [occ.] English teacher, South Gate Senior High, LAUSD; [memb.] Toastmaster International; [hon.] Distinguished Toastmaster"; [oth. writ.] Various poems; [pers.] Writing poems is the way I freeze feeling or sensation for later examination and understanding. Poems are an instant couchstone to the past; [a.] Long Beach, CA

PAULEY, GARNET
[Pen.] Sam; [b.] March 3, 1945, Buffalo, NY; [p.] George and Norma Biersbach; [m.] Raymond Pauley, (second), November 6, 1985; [ch.] Shawn Michael and Kelly Ann; My Sister Marilyn; [ed.] Buffalo East High School; [occ.] Wife, mother and Nuclear Research Development assembly technician; [oth. writ.] Various other unpublished works throughout my lifetime.; [pers.] At the end of my first marriage there was a chance I might be pregnant with my third child. Even knowing that the timing was bad, I wanted the baby very much. As it turned out, there was no child, only an emptiness, which inspired me to express my feelings in writing.; [a.] Grand Island, NY

PAYNE, LODELL RAMSOWER
[Pen.] Lodie; [b.] September 27, 1934, Wharton, TX; [p.] Read and Lavine Ramsower; [m.] Lee Payne, Au-

gust 19, 1952; [ch.] (5) Leedell, Tye Ann, Tabby, Dal and Ray; [ed.] Wharton High. Mostly "School of Hard Knocks and Seat of Pants". Training, continuing education: Interior Design, Window Coverings Quest for Excellence, Tapes: How to Sell, Merchandise management; [occ.] Self employed, owner, interior dressings designer, custom window coverings; [memb.] St. Catherine's Catholic Church, former choir leader. Eucharistic Minister, Civic Club, Window Covering Professionals. "Human of the world"; [hon.] Honors graduate...First prize medals: Oboe, singing, twirling, most beautiful. County Fair: Blue Ribbon, Lemon Pie! Won KTRH Radio singing contest. Houston Press, Loveliest Mother 1960. From kids and grandkids: "World's Best Mom"; [oth. writ.] My pencil has done some real good stuff through the years wrote songs and poems, never enough. When in "Cry - Sis", sad and glad. Titles, such as these, good and bad: Honey Bear, Living Today and Job Well Done, The latter 'bout family strife and fun. Wrote this song for 42 years. Laughing, crying through my tears. Last verse penned August 31, 1994, When half of me, my spouse, went forward, different, forevermore; [pers.] I like meeting faces made out of races, Painted in every hue. `Cause the best part of selling to get your heart swelling, Is to see what all folks do. They are hirers and buyers, drivers and divers; Preachers and teachers of Kung Fu. I'm arranging and changing my banquet of faces. I race to finish on time. I keep my eyes open, but can't seem to find, In all of my longest of long, long years, I can't find true white...Oh dear!; [a.] Houston, TX

PAYNE, RANDY
[b.] September 18, 1975, Danville, IL; [p.] Ron Payne, Janet Payne; [ed.] Georgetown - Ridge Farm High School; [pers.] The poem's that I have written are about the many feelings people experience in their lives. Mine included; [a.] Westville, IL

PAYNE, RONNIE LEE
[b.] August 4, 1970, Danville, IL; [p.] Ronald and Janet Payne; [m.] Shawn Payne, September 17, 1994; [ed.] Westville High, ITT Technical Institute; [occ.] Communications Field Engineer; [pers.] I write only to express my inner feelings and emotions.; [a.] Villa Park, IL

PAYNE, SHALA R.
[Pen.] Shala Payne; [b.] February 11, 1965, Ft. Scott, KS; [p.] Howard and Billie Kay Payne; [ed.] Associates Degree in Nursing Bachelors Degree in Science of Nursing presently Master's Student in Master's in the Science of Nursing; [occ.] Registered Nurse; [memb.] Reserve Officers Association, Sigma Theta Tau, Gamma Upsilon Chapter; [pers.] I want the world to be aware of the beauty and happiness the man I love brings into my world. Even though he inspires me to write what is in my heart and soul, I could never truly capture what he gives me on a piece of paper.; [a.] Arcadia, KS

PEARL, GENEVIEVE LYON
[b.] September 11, 1942, Wichita, KS; [p.] Marie A. William T. Lyon; [ch.] Alesha M. Lyon; [ed.] High School; [occ.] I work for the Bd of Ed here in Wichita, KS.

PEASE, GWENDOLYN TRIMBELL
[b.] June 30, 1932, Spring Grove, MI; [p.] Vincent and Olga Havig Trimbell; [m.] Morgan A. Pease, Jr, November 18, 1951; [ch.] Susan Carroll, Sally Adamson, Cynthia Oldham, Morgan Pease III and Martin Pease; [ed.] Graduate - Union Univ School of Nursing, Schenectady, NY; [occ.] Registered Nurse, Charge Nurse

- BNH, Valatie, NY; [memb.] Christian Women's Club, 4-H Club Leader - 28 yrs; [hon.] Golden Poet Awards, World of Poetry 1988-1991, "Frozen Rosebuds", 4th National Prize; [oth. writ.] Numerous poems printed - "Chatham Courier", "Register Star", "The Advertiser", World of Poetry books - 37 volumes; [pers.] Inspire and promote our youth; [a.] Castleton, NY

PEIRCE, MARGOT
[b.] December 17, 1941, Phila., PA; [p.] Wilmont Grant Peirce, Jr.; [m.] Margaret Ann Phelps; [ed.] As far as 8th grade, Devereux Foundation; [occ.] Laundry Attendant Guest Quarters Hotel in Chester Brook; [memb.] Greater Philadelphia Puppetry Guild, speaking for ourselves; [hon.] Employee of the Month, Embassy Suites Hotel in Chesterbrook, October 1986 Nature, thinking etc.; [oth. writ.] No other writings, except "There is only one time we can make our choices, and it is in the here and now.; [pers.] I strive to spread the gospel of Jesus Christ to all mankind.; [a.] Wayne, PA

PELHAM, JOHN CHARLES
[b.] September 22, 1920, Magnolia, MS; [p.] Mabel Ruth and John Mann Pelham; [ed.] Graduate of Spring Hill College and the Univ of Alabama. Also completed full apprenticeship in ship building, and steel fabrication; [occ.] Consulting engineering and fabrication. Owned and operated plants for 30 yrs in ship building and steel fabrication 55 yrs; [memb.] Erectors Association, American Arbitration Association; [oth. writ.] Presently working on an eight part poem entitled "Songs of the Workers". Have completed several poems never submitted for publication; [pers.] Poetry will never be widely appreciated until there is less blank verse and more lyrical poetry addressed to the average reader on subjects of greater and wider interest; [a.] Springfield, VA

PELUSO, WANDA
[b.] December 2, 1931, Philadelphia, PA; [p.] Wanda and Martin Lundy (both deceased); [ch.] Robert and Philip; [ed.] Frankford High School, Philadelphia, PA; [occ.] Retired; [memb.] Peta - People Against (experiments and torture to animals); [oth. writ.] Four poems were published in the Philadelphia Daily News recently; [pers.] Writing poems in the Autumn of My Life, I will try to reflect only on the beauty and goodness of our human families and our four legged friends; [a.] Philadelphia, PA

PEREZ, ELENA I. CHARNECO
[b.] October 11, 1929, Moca, PR; [p.] Santiago y Eduviges; [m.] Comusto Acosta Marrero, March 1, 1952; [ch.] Jaime, Irise, Robert, Edwin, Joshua, Wilfredo; [ed.] Graduate of high school in the school of Aguadilla PR Jose D Diego; [occ.] Mistress of House. In my home I study medicine, natural; [memb.] American Cross of PR. I am member of Presbyterian Church Life Study Fellowship of USA; [hon.] I received a gold pin when I graduated elementary school in social science. An award in the Caserio when was celebrating a crowd of little girls here where I lived; [pers.] I strive to reflect things that occur, success that pass good or bad and I take the pen and write some words as a poem; [a.] Mayaguez, PR

PERIFIMOS, MARY
[b.] December 28, 1947, Queens, NY; [p.] Harry and Georgia Perifimos (deceased); [ed.] Grover Cleveland High School, Hunter College; [occ.] Admin. Asst. to the Executive Director of the Hearst Foundation; [memb.] Hellenic Univ. Club of NY, Holy Trinity Cathedral Fel-

lowship; [hon.] Dean's List; [oth. writ.] I have written an anthology of love poems entitled "Poems from the Heart" from which The Flame and The Fire is a part of and which I hope to publish. I have also written spiritual poems and have written song lyrics in both Greek and English.; [pers.] I am a person who needs to express my feelings and I have found that I am able to release feelings of joy, elation and sadness in my writings and songs. I feel people should release their feelings and not hold them inside and for me writing about them give me this release.; [a.] New York, NY

PERKINS, ANTHONYE EARLE
[Pen.] a.e. Perkins; [b.] September 26, 1961, Berkeley, CA; [p.] Arnold and Patricia Perkins; [m.] Pamela Denin Perkins, June 23, 1991; [ed.] berkeley High, Alameda College, Oakwood College, "Real Life"; [occ.] Writer, Videographer, Public Speaker, Video Production Instructor; [memb.] Atlanta Olympic committee-Host Broadcast Training Program, "The Men of Distinction" Zeta Alpha Psi; [hon.] Dean's List, Honor Roll, National Aeronautics and Space Administration Certificate of Appreciation, Certificate of Appreciation Outstanding Service Award, Oakwood College United Students Movement; [oth. writ.] Several poems published in local newspapers, international journals and magazines, anthologies and newsletters.; [pers.] I give God all the honor and praise for all of my achievements. He is my strength and inspiration. Without him, I'm nothing. I dip the pen of creativity into the inkwell of my soul and write upon the pages.; [a.] Huntsville, AL

PERKINS, PATRICIA ANN
[Pen.] Samantha Rivers; [b.] July 26, 1942, North St. Paul, MN; [p.] Howard and Charlotte Patterson; [m.] Ronald E. Perkins, July 9; [ch.] Rebecca, Scott, Pamela, Richard; [ed.] High School, and Flex Lab, College Classes "Computer" 6 credits; [occ.] Motel Owner; [memb.] Double-Day, Literary Guild, Mystery Book Club; [oth. writ.] 190 unpublished poem's, several short stories, presently working on a novel.; [pers.] My present short stories seem to lean towards the Alfred-Hickcock Style, did it happen or was it just a dream.; [a.] Brainerd, MN

PERRON, MARJORIE
[Pen.] Ma'ire'ad Ni'Bhran; [b.] December 6, 1941, Brooklyn, NY; [p.] Evelyn and Robert Perron; [ch.] Jessie and Sarah; [ed.] B.A. in Humanities Dowling College, Oakdale, NY, attended Mulloy College, Rockville Center and was graduate from the Academy of St. Joseph Brentwood; [occ.] Probation Officer; [memb.] Probation Officer's Assoc., Fraternal Order of Police, Police Assoc., Gerry Tobin Irish Language School; [hon.] Sigma Tau Delta, The International Honor Society of English; [oth. writ.] None that have been published, other than in the PTA newsletter.; [pers.] I hope to the take the structure and idiom of the Irish Language and blend it with American English. My mission is to keep alive the memory of the Gods and Heroes of the Colts. My idols are W. B. Yeats and Augd'n U' Rathaille and my dear friend and mentor, the poet Aaron Kramer; [a.] East Islip, NY

PERRY, EDWARD MICHAEL JAMES
[Pen.] James Midnight; [b.] June 8, 1977, Worcester, MA; [p.] Earl Dwight Perry, Cynthia Perry; [ed.] Currently a high school senior; [occ.] Restaurant Work; [oth. writ.] Several unpublished works of horror fiction, currently residing in my word processor; [pers.] "Do not study a shadow and ignore the light that causes it to be". Dedicated to Kelly Klink and Eve Comtois-Davis; [a.] Worcester, MA

PERSONS, SUSAN L.
[b.] November 24, 1952, Canadaiqua, NY; [p.] Shirley Wilson King; [m.] Joseph N. Persons, March 25, 1985; [ch.] Derrick Tuell, July 21, 1971; [ed.] Naples High, Naples FL, Lake City Community College, Lake City, FL; [occ.] Insurance Solicitor 25 yrs.; [memb.] Lake City, Columbia County Humane Society, First Presbyterian Church, Lake City Community Concert Assoc., Venture Touring Society, Boy Scouts of America Troop Committee, Friends of the Library-Lake City; [hon.] National Honor Society 1969-1970 Naples, FL; [pers.] God has given me a loving family, Indian heritage, special friends, and books, I try to use all these gifts to see good in everyone, to count my blessings, and to try to make a difference in this life.; [a.] Lake City, FL

PETELL, TERESA S.
[b.] October 20, 1956, Greenville, SC; [p.] The Late Judy Gail Coleman and John J. Tucker; [m.] Roy W. Petell, May 6, 1988; [ch.] Amanda Gail Singleton (13); [ed.] Greer High School; [occ.] Housewife; [hon.] None other than this.; [oth. writ.] Two poems published in our local newspaper. I would like to see my poem to, and in memory of my mother, without whom this poem would not have been possible.; [pers.] I enjoy the poems of Alice E. Chase, and Helen Steiner-Rice. I write about feelings, people and nature.; [a.] Greer, SC

PETTWAY, MARGIE E.
[b.] October 4, 1956, Birmingham, AL; [p.] Mr. and Mrs. Julian Pettway, Jr; [ed.] Presently attending American Univ, Washington, DC; Major: Liberal Arts Communications; [occ.] Directorate Secretary, Planning and Integration, Defense Information Systems Agency; [memb.] Member of Greater Mount Calvary Holy Church, Pastors Alfred and Susie Owens; [pers.] Nominated as Secretary of the Year. Received a Special Act Award; [oth. writ.] Another poem, numerous speeches songs written monthly; [pers.] It is my desire that the 'me' decrease so that my Beloved Lord and Saviour Jesus Christ can increase a new 'Me' in 'Me' Daily; [a.] Washington, DC

PFEISTER, CARLENE M.
[b.] March 18, 1969, Middletown, NY; [m.] Thomas E. Pfeister, October 7, 1989; [ed.] Port Jervis High School; Orange County Community College; [occ.] Physical Therapist Assistant; [memb.] Crohn's and Colitis Foundation of America; [hon.] Graduated with honors and in top 10% of my class, from High School. Graduated from college with an Associates Degree in Physical Therapy Assisting; [oth. writ.] Several poems/lyrics and short stories for personal enjoyment and possible future publication; [pers.] Be kind, warm, and giving from the heart, and it will always come back to you ten fold; and love others unconditionally - including yourself; [a.] Ferndale, NY

PFUND, JOHN GEORGE
[Pen.] Jack Pfund; [b.] May 15, 1902, Youngstown, OH; [p.] John Conrad and Sophie Jacob Pfund; [m.] Mary D. Diehl, August 17, 1926 to December 19, 1994; Helen Duckley, June 11, 1986; [ch.] J. Richard and Janet Golden; [ed.] Eighth grade elementary, two quarters (no credit) at Youngstown College; [occ.] Retired; [oth. writ.] I have a good "show-people" poem of about thirty lines. Are you interested.; [pers.] I like to be a nice guy, the king pin and a sport, but when a double eagle flies the coop, my fun budget comes up short. "Jack." Wife's comment: send a check you cheap skate, just once, settle out of court.

PHILLIPS (M.D.), PHILIP B.
[Pen.] Phil; [b.] July 16, 1915, Siloam Springs, AR; [p.] Rev. and Mrs. E.G. Phillips; [m.] Kathleen Thomas Phillips, June 23, 1942; [ch.] Phil Jr, Thomas M. and Mark B.; [ed.] BS, MBA, JD, LT CDR USNR Ret, BS-MD-Anesthesiologist; BS-Univ of the Ozarks 1935, Univ of AR Med Sch MD 1941; [occ.] Retired Capt USN '41-'63, retired psychiatrist (1992); [memb.] Fla Psychiatric Assoc, Southern Psychiatric Assoc, APA; Int'l Seniors Golf Assn; Pensacola Country Club, Pers Fea; Mexican Seniors Golf Assoc; [hon.] Legion of Merit and Combat "V" - 1944, Purple Heart, Commendation Ribbon 1953 and 7 others; [oth. writ.] Many medical papers (20-25), fun poems for golf friends; [pers.] Strong belief in education and support capital punishment for felons. Much travel - 20 trips to Europe. Duty in Japan during Korean War visited Russia 1978. Have played 293 golf courses; [a.] Pensacola, FL

PHILLIPS, PETER G.
[b.] April 1, 1957, Dublin, Ireland; [p.] Edward and Eileen Phillips; [m.] Frances Morrisroe, August 9, 1980; [occ.] Musician, Singer/Song Writer; [oth. writ.] Several songs, some published (various publishing companies) and many more poems. One children's book.; [pers.] I don't know why I write in rhyme, and only time will tell if twas or wasn't wasted time in fishing, wishing well.; [a.] Burbank, IL

PICKERN, PEGGY A.
[pers.] This poem is dedicated to my sons, Joe and Mike. They have filled my life with love, hope and joy.

PICKETT, VIRGINIA N.
[b.] August 25, 1968, Lebanon, TN; [p.] Gayle King and the late Billie H. Pickett; [ed.] Smyrna High School (diploma); [occ.] Parman Corporation/Cashier; [oth. writ.] I have other writings but never had them enter in any poem contest or anything else; [pers.] I always wondered were I got the idea to write because I assumed nobody in my family did but my grandmother told me recently that she used to write in her younger years. I don't have to have awards, honors or memberships to write about things that I feel or real to me. I believe she is one of the reasons why I have a gift like this; [a.] Nashville, TN

PIERCE, LEE L.
[Pen.] Lee Pierce; [b.] February 26, 1927, New York, City; [p.] Helen Lee and John T. Lawrence; [m.] Allen B. Pierce, July 26, 1962; [ch.] W. Shelby and Allen L. Pierce; [ed.] Concord Academy, Barmole College, NYC, Summer courses at U. of Mexico, Catholic University, Chile; Conn. College for Women, Tufts Univ.; [occ.] Lecturer "Dows from Many Lands, Writer, Real Estate; [memb.] Museum of Fine Arts Boston, Met Museum, NYC, Met Opera, NYC, various theater groups, time share weeks on the Cape, Newport, RI2, Sedona, AZ; [hon.] Bicentennial award in 1976 for multi-media historical pageant "Tea and Tyranny" which brought together 6 schools (public, private and parochial) all ages (8 yrs. to 80) performed at Harvard's Loeb Theater, now known as the Art, Cambridge, MASS. (AM Repertory Theater); [oth. writ.] Short stories, poetry, and now working on doll stories (true and historical involving dolls); [pers.] To put back beauty into children's lives (and all ages) through poetry, drama and music and to encourage all ages to share without fear, friendships from the world over.; [a.] Cambridge, MA

PIERCE, MILDRED FLOY
[b.] November 13, 1942, Dunlap, TN; [p.] Cecil L. and Mattie Dean; [m.] Larry L. Pierce, February 29, 1980; [ch.] Julia Eleen, Deana Lynn, Fletcher Lee, Guy Alan and Lydia Mamo; [ed.] Kirkman High School, Chattanooga, TN, Chattanooga State Community College; [occ.] Self employed boutique; [oth. writ.] Many poems published in local newspaper; self published a collection of Christmas poetry, children's stories in poetic form; [pers.] My greatest desire is to convey feelings that capture and express the beauty of our world and love between mankind; [a.] Chattanooga, TN

PILC, HEIDE MARIE
[Pen.] Heide Howard-Pilc; [b.] December 8, 1940, Germany; [p.] Ernest and Wilmi Baunach; [m.] Robert Pilc, August 11, 1983; [ch.] One daughter, several step children; [ed.] Eleonaren Schule College Worms Rhine, Germany; Cuest College, San Luis Obisop and Continuing Education Courses; [occ.] Jazz Reporter; Housewife; Temp-Secretary; [memb.] Piedmont Writer's Group; Member of Organizations for German-Jewish Relations; Activist for the Advancement of Jazz and Classical Music; [hon.] 3rd prize non-fiction award from East Bay Writers' Roundtable, 1994; Translator's Award from Musical Sciences, 1966; [oth. writ.] Jazz-related articles; short stories and non-fiction; reviews on art for various publications in Germany and the U.S.; [pers.] My writings speak of the struggle for survival in all aspects of life. I'm a survivor of WWII and my childhood experiences have taught me the importance of universal love and understanding of other cultures.; [a.] Oakland, CA

PITTMAN, B. CARTER
[b.] October 13, 1962, Seminole, TX; [p.] Bill and Bonnie Pittman; [ed.] High school graduate, attended Texas Tech Univ, Lubbock, TX as well as SLV Area Vocational School in Alamosa, Colorado. Military Training (US Army); [occ.] Forest Service Firefighter, soon to be a government contractor; [memb.] American Legion; [hon.] (Military) Army Commendation Medal, Army Achievement Medal, (2 ea) Good Conduct Medal, Army Service Ribbon, Overseas Service Ribbon. (Forest Service) Certificate of Merit, Volunteer Award, Safety Awards (College) Dean's List; [oth. writ.] I have written 6 country and contemporary songs, most of which are in the process of getting copyrights. One song has been copyrighted, entitled "Lonely Won't Leave Me Alone". I also have 2 other poems. None have been published yet; [pers.] Live several lifetimes within your lifetime. Never limit yourself to only one occupation and or lifestyle. Let no one tell you can't do something - prove them wrong. Turn a bad experience into a blessing - write a song or poem about it. Keep faith in God and in yourself. You can't lose; [a.] Carrizozo, NM

PITTMAN, JESSICA LEIGH
[b.] January 26, 1981, Belhaven, NC; [p.] Alfred and Vickie Pittman; [ed.] Mattamuskeet Middle School, 8th grade; [occ.] Student; [pers.] Sensitivity is admired, so don't be afraid to show it.; [a.] Scranton, NC

POE, RICHARD ROBERT
[b.] November 22, 1961, Oklahoma; [p.] Robert and Jaqueline Poe; [m.] Helene Poe, April 29, 1989; [ch.] Alexander Poe; [ed.] Regis College; [occ.] Real Estate Developer; [memb.] Napa Valley Country Club, Olympic Club, San Francisco, Board Member YMCA; [hon.] Citizenship Award, Tulsa, OK; [oth. writ.] Include unpublished my stories, novels, short stories and screen plays.; [pers.] Everyday is a new beginning. My writing reflects the Rejuvenation of the human spirit.; [a.] Napa, CA

POLING, CHRISTINA
[Pen.] Christina L. Poling; [b.] July 7, 1980, Barbarton; [p.] Kim Grim, Weldon Poling; [ed.] 7th grade; [occ.] Student; [pers.] I have been inspired to write my poems by Susan Wismar and Robert Bucy. They are my best friends, and have taught me how to believe in myself and to love life. I want to thank them both.; [a.] Wadsworth, OH

POLLOCK, ANGELA SOLOMON
[Pen.] Andie Pollock; [b.] August 16, 1956, Baytown, TX; [p.] Kathryn Solomon; [m.] David Pollock; [ch.] Michael, Stephanie; [ed.] BA Anthropology, Texas A&M Univ, MS Sociology, Valdosta State Univ; [occ.] Writer, sociologist; [memb.] Georgia Sociological Assoc, BETA Sigma Phi Int'l; [oth. writ.] Children's Stories, poems, songs, humorous articles; [pers.] The opportunity to share one's talent with humanity is truly a precious gift.

POPLAWSKI, JAMES J.
[Pen.] 10523 Crockett; [b.] May 18, 1946, Bridgesport, CT; [p.] John and Sophie M. Poplawski; [ed.] 1 1/2 Valley Jr. College, 2 1/2 L.A. Trade Technical College, no degree; [occ.] Inventory Cycle Clerk for Burbank Aircraft; [memb.] Since 1976, Cousteau Society of Norfolk and VA, Mac Arthur Committee Honor, Duty, Country in Human Rights, "People Who Care"; [pers.] You give from the heart you get from the heart. We must save the plant quotation from honorable Jacquos Yves Cousteau "It's Our Duty."; [a.] Sun Valley, CA

POULIN, CATHERINE MARIA
[Pen.] Maria Kai Poulin; [b.] December 17, 1961, Honolulu, HA; [p.] Philamina M.K. and Larry K. Schrader; [m.] Stephen K. Poulin, November 12, 1981; [ch.] Steven K. and Joseph R. Poulin; [occ.] School bus driver, Brandywine Bus Lot for Prince Georges.; [memb.] I am a member of the Oxon Hill Ladies Auxiliary Fire Department, Station 21; [oth. writ.] My poems come from many of my own experiences. They've allowed me to hold onto a part of myself I wasn't ready to reveal. So World War III, is my first published poem.; [pers.] I believe communication and togetherness can overcome any hardship, and only strengthen our successes. And that belief, is the foundation of my poetry.; [a.] Bryans Road, MD

POWERS, GREGORY A.
[Pen.] G.A.Powers; [b.] December 20, 1969, Erie, PA; [p.] Beth Thompson, Richard Powers; [pers.] My two obsessions are truth and dreams; without these, I am nothing; [a.] Girard, PA

POWIS, LILLIAN
[b.] March 9, 1929, Sangerville, ME; [p.] Alice and Bert Braden; [m.] Earl Powis, June 8, 1974; [ch.] 2 sons (adults); [ed.] 2 yrs college, majored in English and English Lit, Certificate Outstanding Employee; [occ.] Travel Agent; [memb.] Petaluma Woman's Club; AARP; ABWA; ARTA (Assoc of Retired Travel Agents) St. James Church in Petaluma; [hon.] Commendations from Dept of Army; [oth. writ.] Articles travel trade magazine, poetry in college; [pers.] Love writing poetry about unusual subjects. Wrote many technical pieces for Dept of Army while in Civil Service; [a.] Petaluma, CA

POYNER, JAMES R.
[b.] February 14, 1950, Brockville, Ontario; [p.] Walter and Irma Jean Poyner; [ed.] B.A. English, Millikin University, Decatur, IL; [occ.] File Clerk, Elek-Tek, Inc., Skokie, ILL.; [memb.] 4th Presbyterian Church of Chi-

cago, Northwestern Society of Model Railroaders, Habitat for Humanity Volunteer; [hon.] Dean's List; [oth. writ.] Several unpublished novels awaiting the patient eye of a quality-minded editor!; [pers.] My works are not vulgar, erotic or loud, because I want my writing to be judged for its merit, not its sensationalism.; [a.] Chicago, IL

PRANGER, KEVIN J.
[Pen.] Kevin Jose Pranger; [b.] January 15, 1964, Fresno, CA; [p.] Byron K. and Connie Pranger; [ed.] San Joaquin Memorial High School; Fresno City College; Berean College of the Assemblies of God; [occ.] Manufacturing Technician, Grundfos Pumps Corp., Fresno, CA; [memb.] World Vision; Pacific Latin American, Assemblies of God; Family Worship Center, Missions Committee, Sanger, CA; [pers.] All that I am, all that I have, and all that I will be is due solely to the grace of my Lord Jesus Christ. His name be exalted.; [a.] Clovis, CA

PRENTICE, CHRISTY
[b.] March 14, 1974, Arcadia, CA; [p.] Lyndel and Deana Prentice; [ed.] California State Univ - San Bernardino: English Major, Children's Inst of Literature, Long Ridge Writers' Group; [occ.] Preschool Teacher, Full time student, Free-lance writer; [memb.] Anne of Green Gables Kindred Spirits Society, The Michael Sweet Fan Club; [hon.] Dean's List; [pers.] I could say that the pen conforms to the talent of my hand, but in reality my pen and hand, a united fixture, simplex trace what God has already outlined; [a.] Apple Valley, CA

PRESKENIS, PAUL E.
[b.] August 25, 1951, Philadelphia; [m.] Debbie DeCicco (Soulmate); [ch.] (1) Children International; [oth. writ.] Poems, short stories; [pers.] From the moment I first became aware of my own existence I began searching for the reason for it and the search continues to this day. I doubt that mankind can comprehend the truth.; [a.] Green Creek, NJ

PRIEST, JUANITA JOYCE
[b.] March 11, 1917, Mt. Vernon, Ohio; [p.] John Galvin and Shrilda Jane Griffin; [m.] James Ray Priest, August 19, 1979; [ch.] Gary Eugene, Joyce Elaine; [ed.] Marion High, Business College; [occ.] Retired from Superior Metal Products as Executive Secretary; [memb.] Mississinewa Camera Club, Lakeview Wesleyan Church; [hon.] First, second and third awards in photography at Indiana State Fair, Indianapolis, Indiana; [oth. writ.] Many poems for my own enjoyment and my families.; [pers.] I try to express my deepest feelings on just basic things in life.; [a.] Marion, IN

PRIEST, LYDIA P.
[b.] September 13, 1940, NY; [p.] William A. Pallme and Haley K. Pallme (deceased); [m.] Walter S. Priest, September 25, 1965 (deceased); [ch.] Nora C. Priest, Katherina Priest Hugel (Kate and Jeff have two children; [ed.] M.A. George Washington University, M.A. Andover Newton Theological School; [occ.] Retired on disability former English Teacher and Pastors Assistant; [memb.] Secular Franciscan Order, Stoke Club, and others; [hon.] Honors in English Literature, University of Edinburgh, Scotland, and many other awards; [oth. writ.] None published, other than in local newspaper where my husband and I published.; [pers.] I'm trying to communicate a sort of earthy transcendence. My models are J. R. Tolkin, C.S. Lewis and anonymous haiku poets.; [a.] Gloucester, MA

PRINGLE, LA RONDA
[b.] December 11, 1964, Inkster, MI; [p.] Thelbert Pringle, Major Pringle; [ch.] Brittany LaRonda, Aaron II; [ed.] Hamilton J. Robichaud High; [occ.] Medical Coordinator, Parkgrove Group Home, Westland, MI; [hon.] National Honor Society; [pers.] To give and have love, for myself and my children that is my life's goal; [a.] Romulus, MI

PROSPER, GUY DAVID
[Pen.] G. David Prosper; [b.] April 10, 1974, Port Au Prince, Haiti; [p.] Josseline and Guy Prosper; [ed.] Quisqueya Christian High School, College of William and Mary; [occ.] Student; [a.] Williamsburg, VA

PUCILLO, FRANCINE J.
[b.] December 3, 1946, Brooklyn; [p.] Madeline and William Sisniewski; [m.] Arthur, December 3, 1988; [ed.] Product of the Sisters of the Good Shepherd of Brooklyn and Huntington, NY; [occ.] Housewife; [p.] I will always want to say a word to turn a head, wipe a tear, bring a smile and share it with the world. I love to share my thoughts and write it in a way that is universal.

PUCKETT, PAUL E.
[Pen.] Rickey; [b.] September 10, 1959, Tallulah, LA; [p.] Mr. & Mrs. Wilbert Puckett; [m.] Diana M. Puckett (8-25-61), May 16, 1992; [ch.] Eric D. Hardy and Tavaris Johnson; [ed.] Thomastown High, Florida Univ; [occ.] Account Executive, Ford Sign Company; [memb.] Greater Progressive COGIC: Mass Choir and Brotherhood Committee; [pers.] I strive each day to understand the awesome powers of the Lord. I was greatly influenced by Paul L. Dunbar and Norman V. Peale; [a.] Fort Worth, TX

PUGLISI, DONNA
[Pen.] Poetry in Motion; [b.] December 16, 1950, San Diego, CA; [p.] Frank and Mae Waterman, Wis.; [m.] Fred Puglisi, December 16, 1987; [ch.] Three Stepchildren, 2 grandsons; [ed.] Stevens Point State University, Wisconsin Major: Dance/Drama Communications; [occ.] Writer, Poetry In Motion, for business, personal poetry for any occasion, weddings, etc.; [hon.] Nat'l Honor Society, Dance Club President, Quill and Scroll Society; [oth. writ.] Poetry in Motion, a collection of poems for any occasion, working on a book Feeling sexy and Over 40!; [pers.] A talent is truly a blessing from God! I was greatly influenced to write poetry by my mother. I believe poetry should come from the heart and either make people look into themselves and be happy or to better themselves.; [a.] Ashburn, VA

PULLUM, ANTANUS
[Pen.] A.S.P.; [b.] September 4, 1971, Las Vegas, NV; [p.] James and Gertrude Pullum; [m.] Girlfriend: Kevylon Mason; [ed.] Southern Nevada Community College, Arizona State University; [occ.] Free-lance Writer; [pers.] My writing reflects society seen through my eyes.; [a.] Atlanta, GA

PUPPIONE, CHRISTOPHER RICHARD VALENTINO
[Pen.] C. Valentino Puppione; [b.] August 31, 1974, Hayward, CA; [p.] Richard and Cynthia Puppione; [ed.] Moreau High School, Castro Valley High School, CSU Long Beach, Diable Valley College, Sonoma State University; [occ.] Host at The Olive Garden; [oth. writ.] Hundreds of poems, tucked away in notebooks, with a few proudly pinned up on my wall.; [pers.] I thank my parents, Rich and Cindy, my teachers, Barbara Glass and

Betty Solomon, and dedicate my writings to my friends, grandparents and siblings.; [a.] Rohnert Park, CA

PURYEAR, CAMETRA
[b.] January 31, 1972, Arlington, VA; [p.] Shirley Puryear; [ed.] Mount Vernon High, Virginia State Univ (Senior); [occ.] Full-time Student; [memb.] New Generation, Accounting Club, Restoration Ministries; [oth. writ.] Destiny, Where To?, The Battle Has Begun, Who Am I?; [pers.] I strive to reflect sincerity, reality, and express emotions to allow the reader to relate and become personally and emotionally involved with what is taking place. I am influenced by real life situations; [a.] Alexander, VA

PURYEAR, HELENA M.
[Pen.] Helena Puryear; [b.] June 5, 1964, South Boston, VA; [p.] Owen Puryear, no known mother; [ch.] Chadwick Mitchell Daniel; [ed.] Chadwick Mitchell Daniel; [ed.] Danville Christian School, Southside College; [oth. writ.] Something in my heart; Why; [pers.] I write to bring hope, mainly to influence this generation. My son and my fiance' are my inspiration. My poems reflect courage and inner strength. I have God to thank for this. I would like the piece I wrote "She Knows" dedicated to my son Chad Daniel; [a.] Halifax, VA

PYNE, LAURA JEANNE
[b.] August 20, 1962, N.J. USA; [p.] Ann and James R. Pyne; [ed.] B.A. English and Philosophy, University of Rochester; [occ.] Director of Marketing and Sales Archives Mgmt. Ctrs.; [memb.] Night Heron Poets Society, Help various battered women's shelters; [hon.] MVP, U. of R. Women's Tennis Team; [oth. writ.] Much Poetry; [pers.] Life is short, follow your dreams. Believe in yourself and be who you are, who is anyone else to inflict their way upon you, who really knows? Spousal abuse must stop to provide balance in the home and on the planet.; [a.] Stuart, FL

QUACH, LOUIE LINH
[b.] August 11, 1972, Saigon, Vietnam; [p.] Hung Nam Quach, Ly Thi Trang; [ed.] Oakland High School, Univ of California at Berkeley; [occ.] Forestry Aide (CDF), Jackson Demonstration State Forest, Fort Bragg, CA. Hydrologic Technician USFS; [memb.] Member of Society of American Foresters, California Alumni Association; [hon.] Academic Excellent for the Golden State Examination. President Academic Fitness Award for Outstanding Academic Achievement. Won 1st place in Boom Run and 3rd place in Limber Pole and Pole Climb; [a.] Poems published in Oakland High School's Oak Leaves Magazine and UC Berkeley's Timber 1994 Edition; [pers.] I hope my poems bring out the feelings that people have, but were afraid to express them; [a.] Oakland, CA

QUEZADA, EVA E.
[b.] March 1952; [ed.] M.A., English as a Second League; B.A., Linguistics University of Arizona; [occ.] Adult ESL Teacher and Coordinator; [memb.] CATESOL, Women Educators; [hon.] University of Arizona Dean's List; [pers.] Shakespeare and the Bible have influenced my life greatly. Shakespeare for his genius description of human nature. The Bible for its revelation of God's divine nature and love toward man.

QUINN, KARA POPPY
[b.] January 4, 1981, Leonardtown, MD; [p.] Joyce and Chuck Quinn; [ed.] Kingsway Christian Academy; [a.] Moyock, NC

RABBITT, SUSAN
[b.] June 9, 1949, Woodstock, IL; [m.] Joe Rabbitt, August 6, 1977; [ed.] Completing my BA, at Western Illinois University. High School Bryan Adams, Dallas, Texas, Texas Woman's University, El Centro Jr., College, Dallas; North Texas Univ.; Northern IL, University, Dekalb, IL; [occ.] Student; [oth. writ.] Poetry published in high school through the Creative Writing Club. A poem published in college, at Texas Woman's Univ.; [pers.] Thanks to my husband, friends and family who have supported me throughout the years. To the Moody Blues whose music has inspired me, to be my best and to never give up your dreams.; [a.] Lincoln, IL

RACE, DOTTIE
[Pen.] E. Race; [b.] February 13, 1937, Cleve., OH; [m.] richard, February 12, 1955, Mark and Kimberly; [oth. writ.] many unpublished poems.; [pers.] My poetry is swayed by the person it is for. If it makes them happy, I've received much more. Sending a message of humor or some joy is like giving a needy child a long awaited toy. Poetry is my antidote regarding things unkind, it keeps my sense of humor and aids a healthy mind. I hope that others try their hand in writing what they choose. It's giving unto others while ridding their own blues. I've never read a poem except the ones I write. Nor have I had a lesson that could have shed some light.; [a.] Parma, OH

RACKI, SHERRI
[b.] February 14, 1980, Worcester, Mass.; [p.] Robert and Pamela Racki; [ed.] Hollywood Hills High; [occ.] Student; [memb.] French Club; [hon.] Numerous awards received for poems entered in county competition; [oth. writ.] Article published in nationally syndicated column. Article published in international magazine. An article published in local newspaper.; [pers.] In my poems I try to leave the meaning up to the reader.; [a.] Hollywood, FL

RADUNZ, ELAINE
[b.] March 1948, Litchfield, Minn.; [p.] Charles and Mae Delp; [m.] Richard Radunz, November 4, 1967; [ed.] Litchfield High Graduate; [occ.] 3M factory worker, Hutchinson, Minn.; [pers.] This was taken from a larger poem I wrote to my husband's brothers and sisters after the loss of both their parents in one year. It was wrapped and sent with a teddy bear made from a chenille bedspread found at the house while I was cleaning. It was my Easter gift to them in hopes that they too should have hope.

RAGONA, MARY ANN
[b.] May 8, 1948, Queens, NY; [p.] Martha and Stephen Malack; [m.] Vincent Ragona, July 5, 1969; [ch.] Vincent Jr. and Joseph; [ed.] Queensborough Community, Suffolk Community, St. Joseph's College; [occ.] Executive Director and Chief Administrative Officer LI Gasoline Retailers Assn; [memb.] L.I. Association - Environmental and Energy Committee; Bd of Director - Literary Volunteers of America; [hon.] Community Service Award - Nassau Technological Center; [oth. writ.] Editor - LIGRA Bulletin; [pers.] Doer's get things accomplished!; [a.] Medford, NY

RAINSTEIN, MARGARET
[b.] 1960, Vilnius, Lithuania, Immigrated to the U.S. in 1976; [m.] Married; [ch.] Two Children; [occ.] Programmer/Analyst in a Major New York Bank; [pers.] Began writing poetry at age 33, both in Russian and English.

RAKOCZY, ANGELA
[b.] June 24, 1978, Monroe, MI; [p.] Barbara E. and Paul M. Rakoczy; [ed.] Clinton High School; [occ.] Student; [pers.] Nobody gets to live life backwards. Look ahead - that's where your future lies; [a.] Clinton, MI

RAMIREZ, JENNIFER
[b.] December 28, 1973; [pers.] This poem is dedicated to James L. Minoque, October 26, 1963 - November 12, 1994. May you find the peace you couldn't find here.

RAMPONI, PETER C.
[b.] November 14, 1955, Quincy, MA; [p.] Peter and Nancy Ramponi; [m.] Susan (Disalvio) Ramponi, Ma 24, 1980; [ch.] Michael 13, Steven 11, Matt 10; [ed.] Quincy High School, Quincy Junior College, Northeastern; [occ.] Computer Consultant; [memb.] Director Quincy Youth Basketball Coach, Saint Joseph's of Quincy Boys Basketball, Quincy Little League Baseball Coach.; [oth. writ.] Many unpublished poems. That I wish to share.; [pers.] Everyone is a poet. Poetry is the means by which people express the world to themselves.; [a.] Quincy, MA

RANARD, JAMES MATTHEW
[b.] October 15, 1971, Bloomington, IN; [p.] Stephen and Terri Payton; [m.] Girlfriend: Brandy Ann Collins; [ed.] Basic High School (Edgewood High); [occ.] Installs Satellite Communications Systems; [oth. writ.] Many unpublished works of various styled poetry.; [pers.] I believe poetry is a direct statement from the soul, sometimes expressing the pain, nonetheless a beautiful form of art for many to enjoy.; [a.] Bloomington, IN

RANDALL, JOAN
[b.] November 9, 1933, Elgin, IL; [ch.] Richard, Cynthia, Catherine, Margaret, Patricia and Robert; Grandchildren: Stephanie, William, Christine, Frances, Billy F., Katherine, Andrew, Alexander; [ed.] St. Scholastic High School; [occ.] Supervisor: Enco Mfg. Co.; [memb.] High School Camera Club; [hon.] Scholastic Art Award, Gold Medal for Illinois State Speed Roller Skating; [pers.] Dedicated to my family. Thank you for your love and support of me and everyone around you. I'm so proud of you. May God bless you.; [a.] Stickney, IL

RANDAZZO, JANET
[b.] November 24, 1957, Cleveland, OH; [p.] Gene and Rhoda Thomasson; [m.] Pete Randazzo, November 22, 1980; [ch.] Renee Lynn, Debra Marie; [ed.] West Geauga High School '76; [pers.] I write for pleasure and try to capture the gifts that nature brings to me.; [a.] Highland Hts., OH

RANGATORE, CHRISTINA
[Pen.] Sunshine Love; [b.] November 16, 1973, Lewiston, NY; [p.] Joseph and Helen Rangatore; [ed.] Niagara Falls High School; [occ.] Day Care Teacher YMCA; [memb.] YMCA; [oth. writ.] A poem published in other anthologies. Article in Niagara Falls Gazette; [a.] Niagara Falls, NY

RANKIN, ANNIE LOIS
[b.] August 27, 1930, Houston, TX; [p.] John Marshall and Bessie Melissa Dagley; [m.] Levi D. Ranfkin, January 28, 1950; [ch.] Dolana Lynn Rankin; [ed.] Ass. Degree in Liberal Arts College of the Mainland, Texas City, TX; [occ.] Harris County Sheriff Department, Classification Dept.; [memb.] Texas Real Estate Broker; [hon.] I graduated in the top quarter of John H. Reagan Sr. High

School in 1948 out of 500 students; [oth. writ.] A few short stories, and poetry and one novel.; [pers.] I like to write and enjoy human interest topics both old and modern. I get a lot of enjoyment from any poem by Robert Frost and hope to do some other writings of my own on the female desperation in the feature, that I have encountered in the jail.; [a.] Houston, TX

RAO, SWARUPA
[b.] August 27, 1954, Bangalore, India; [p.] Dr. Nadigkrishna Murthy and Shakuntala Nadig; [m.] Dr. Venkatesh Rao, December 11, 1980; [ch.] One daughter, Manasa; [ed.] M.SC (Botany), Ph.d (Indian Dance); [oth. writ.] Short stories for children.; [pers.] I want to develop as an inter cultural communicator. Deeply interested in Indian Culture and Philosophy; [a.] West Babylon, NY

RAPSHER, BRUCE
[b.] July 23, 1960, Philadelphia; [ch.] Charles and Lois Papsher; [ed.] Temple University, DePaul University; [occ.] Salesman, Seabrook Wallcovering; [memb.] Involved with Chicago Cares and Habitat for Humanity; [oth. writ.] I have written several short stories and many poems.; [pers.] I try to write from my experience and heart.; [a.] Chicago, IL

RASMUSSEN, NORMAN
[b.] January 26, 1920, Brooklyn, NY; [p.] Hans and Elvira Rasmussen; [m.] Marilyn Rasmussen, June 4, 1943; [ch.] Michael, Guy, John, Danny; [ed.] Tilden High School, Brooklyn; [occ.] Retired industrial painter; [memb.] VFW, American Legion; [pers.] I read poetry for pleasure and write poems for fun. I am a bookworm and amateur oil painter; [a.] Lanoka Harbor, NJ

RATTCLIFF, KEVIN G.
[b.] September 26, 1958, St. Martinville, LA; [p.] Howard J. and Rita (Wiltz); [m.] Lucille Arceneaux, March 27, 1981; [ch.] Megan E., Nicholas J., Mark A.; [ed.] St. Martinville High, Louisiana State University, University of Maryland; [occ.] Project Engineer, (GSA) General Services Administration; [memb.] Deacon Board Hillcrest Baptist Church, The Arc, The Forresters.; [hon.] Service Awards, Draper Elementary 1986, 1987; Performance Award, GSA, 1993; National Capital Barbecue Battle, Finalist 1993, 4th Place 1994.; [oth. writ.] Feature writer for Quarterly Corporate Newsletter, Other poems and essays (unpublished); [pers.] My writings reflect my view as the external optimist. My philosophy, what you say is not as important as how others interpret it.; [a.] Clinton, MD

RAWLS, MIRANDA
[b.] May 28, 1994; [p.] Randall and Darius Rawls; [ed.] Winfield City High School, My future plans are to attend Auburn University, Auburn, AL; [occ.] Junior, Winfield City High school, Winfield, AL; [memb.] Spanish Club, FBLA; [hon.] William Moore National Honor Society, Winfield City High School Science Fair Exhibit Winner.; [oth. writ.] Poem, The Journey of Life, published Axolotl 1994, Winfield City High School; Short story, Memories of a Soldier, published Axolotl 1994, Winfield City High School; [pers.] Goals are never reached with good intentions, for it is procrastination that keeps you from turning dreams into realities.; [a.] Brilliant, AL

RAY, JERRY F.
[b.] September 25, 1933, Ada, OK; [p.] Clifford Ray, Flonnie Ray; [m.] Rosemarie Elisabeth Ray (nee

Feuerabendt), October 7, 1957; [ch.] Susanne Felicia and Cynthia Clarissa; [ed.] Polytechnic HS, SF, CA, Academy of Stenographic Arts, SF; [occ.] Court Reporter (retired); [oth. writ.] Personal recollections; Highland Spins; [pers.] In my golden years, I wish to leave something behind for those who follow; [a.] Daly City, CA

RAYBURN, GLORIA ANN
[b.] June 30, 1976, Rowan County; [p.] Arthur and Kathy Rayburn; [ed.] Laurel Elementary, Lewis County Junior High School, and Lewis County High School; [pers.] My poems come from thoughts in my head. I don't concentrate on the writing, I just go with the flow and revise later; [a.] Vanceburg, KY

RAYNER, SARA BETH KRISTINE
[Pen.] S.K. Lachlan; [b.] December 28, 1967, Detroit, MI; [p.] Roberta A. Rayner, Gordon N. Rayner; [ed.] Valparaiso Univ and Tampa College; [occ.] Entrepreneur and inventor; [oth. writ.] Several songs and musical compositions, essays in Valparaiso's Freshman Journal; [pers.] Only that the more I learn, the less I understand. Not original, I know, but screamingly true.

RAYSOR, ANGELO
[b.] August 21, 1961, Jersey City; [p.] Lucille and Daniel Raysor; [ed.] Ferris High School, Wiley College; [occ.] Construction Worker (General Work); [memb.] Third World Assoc. Club from high school, Allah (God) Club; [hon.] Omega Flange Fraternity, Honors Convention from College (Wiley) Careerworks, Trade School; [oth. writ.] I write poems for relatives and friends when I have time. I love writing Anthologies.; [pers.] Mom and Dad: I appreciate Pete Grudagnino for elevating and motivating my thoughts which enable me to keep writing. Plus my brother Dennis Raysor; [a.] Jersey City, NJ

REAGAN, SANDRA LEE
[b.] September 12, 1948, Troy, OH; [p.] William L. and Norma J. Booher; [ch.] Robert E. Reagan and grandson Damen S. Reagan; [ed.] Tippechanoe High School, Tipp City, OH 1966; [occ.] Certified Medical Transcriptionist Upper Valley, Medical Centers, Troy, OH; [memb.] American Assoc. for Medical Transcription; [hon.] Certified Medical Transcriptionist 1990, Licensed Optician 1976 to 1990; [oth. writ.] Poem published in Young America Sings By The National High School Poetry Anthology 1965; Guest Editorial for The Dispensing Optician in January 1982, personal poems for birthdays, weddings, special occasions, personal release, etc.; [pers.] Most of my poetry deals with romance and/or expressing joy and or sorrow of every day life as well as writing for special events. I am an avid reader of historical romances (England, The South and West) from 1500-1900's; [a.] Piqua, OH

REAMS, JENNIFER
[b.] January 1, 1983, Washington, PA; [p.] Catherine P. and Timothy W. Reams; [a.] Claysville, PA

REAMY, JAMES
[b.] June 24, 1964, San Diego; [pers.] It is the mystery and subtleties of life that move me. Those impressions and expressions that are deeply sensed and felt, I come to have a greater appreciation for through the writing of poetry; [a.] San Diego, CA

REAVES, TONIE L.
[Pen.] Shatonie Reaves; [b.] November 25, 1971, Greensboro, NC; [p.] Harry Reaves, Sheila Reaves; [ed.] Page Senior High School, NC A & T State Univ; [occ.]

Radio Disc Jockey, Business Manager for Theatrical Company; [memb.] Pershing Riffle, TBMP - Broadcast Association, Network 90' Organization; [hon.] McLendon Award, Who's Who (high school), Spanish Poetry Award; [oth. writ.] Articles for "CIPHER" magazine at NC A&T, music playlist, musical lyrics; [pers.] My writings reflect what I see and my inner thoughts and feelings; [a.] Greensboro, NC

RECKNER, KATHY K.
[Pen.] Kat; [b.] July 12, 1963, Toccoa, GA; [p.] J.R. Smith and Annie L. Roberts; [m.] Russell E. Reckner, September 10, 1988; [ch.] Not yet; [ed.] West High, Denver CO; TGSA, Hilsborough Community College, PHCC; [occ.] Owner/operator specialized home day care, Wesley Chapel, FL; [memb.] World Wildlife Fund, National Wildlife Fund, the Wilderness Society, Teachers of Young Children Assoc; [oth. writ.] I have a book of unpublished poems. Because of the success of Stallion of Zeus. I may submit others also. I am currently working on a booklet of humor; [pers.] I am very active in taking care of the Earth and all the creatures who live here. I teach the children, reduce, reuse and recycle and friends of Earth Programs. Because its their future at stake; [a.] Wesley Chapel, FL

REDNOUR, RITA K.
[b.] May 5, 1960, Fort Thomas, KY; [p.] Elmer and Marlene Kon Knight; [m.] Floyd A. Rednour, March 17, 1987; [ch.] Nicholas A. Rednour; [ed.] General; [occ.] Housewife; [memb.] Cub Scout Leader; [oth. writ.] None published; [pers.] My family inspires me and causes me to strive to be the best in whatever I attempt; [a.] New Orleans, LA

REED (III), WINSTON H.
[b.] February 17, 1971, Kirksville, MO; [p.] Winston Jr, Rebecca Mae; [ed.] Foran High School; [oth. writ.] Have written six books of poetry; [pers.] I write because I like to do so. I am very influenced by Link Wray; [a.] Shelton, CT

REED, LILLIAN
[b.] June 25, 1922, Ewing, IN; [p.] C.F. and Caroline Abbott; [m.] Theran O. Reed, June 25, 1940; [ch.] Jerry and Dorothy; [ed.] Scottsburg High; [occ.] Retired; [memb.] New Providence Baptist Church, Assoc. Sec. Scott Co., Hymn Sing Assoc., Children's worker in many churches with mission work as team member of Lay Renewal Ministry; [hon.] High School Honor Roll; [oth. writ.] Local news items for Scott Co. Journal for several years. Presently retired, correspondent for U.S. Shoe Factory, Madison, IN, "Footnotes" while working.; [pers.] I'm leaving a lot of family history and bits of blessings nd encouragement for my loved ones in poetry. I want to be a blessing in someone's life as my work is read.; [a.] Scottsburg, IN

REEVE, JUDY
[b.] March 13, 1950, Houston, TX; [p.] Bruce Reeves, May 17, 1988; [ed.] robert E. Lee High School, GED U. of H., some College; [occ.] Homemaker; [memb.] U.S. Holocaust Museum Society, Houston Genealogical Society, Honorary Member Krewe of Olympus, Inner Loop Alternatives Bowling League, IGBO/WIBC; [hon.] NAMES Project Houston (Aios Quilt); [pers.] I write about what I know, life, more specific, my life. It is sometimes frightening, always enlightening...strengthening.; [a.] Bellaire, TX

REGISTER, CONNIE
[b.] December 18, 1973, Lake City, FL; [p.] Tony Harvey and Joann Adams; [m.] Ricky Lynn Myatt Jr., April 22, 1995; [ch.] Talia Chrystene Thomley; [ed.] Columbia High School, Lake City, FL also At-Home Professions, Fort Collins, CO; [occ.] Medical Transcriptionist; [hon.] Secretary in District 21 Cooperative Education Clubs of Florida, May 2, 1991.; [pers.] If you can take whatever life may hand you, and from it try to fashion something good; your life will be rewarding and fulfilling, and nothing good will ever pass you by. Poetry to me, is my reward and my fulfillment.; [a.] Lake City, FL

REID, PATRICIA A.
[b.] February 26, 1963, Chester, SC; [p.] John and Jessie Reid; [ed.] Winnsboro High School, Columbia Junior College, New Destiny Christian Center attending University of Baltimore; [occ.] Commercial Lines Technician, USF&G, Baltimore, MD; [memb.] Alpha Nu Omega Sorority; [oth. writ.] Various inspirational poems.; [pers.] Take time and examine your heart because out of it flows the issues of your life.; [a.] Columbia, MD

REINHARD, MADELEINE ELISABETH
[b.] June 13, 1914, Waterbury, Conn.; [p.] Elizabeth Lawton, John Raynor; [m.] Theodore G. Reinhard, September 5, 1936; [ch.] Joanna S. Calabro, Patricia Desiderio; [ed.] Wilby High; [memb.] Christ Chapel Episcopal Church; [hon.] Valedictorian; [oth. writ.] Numerous Poetry throughout my lifetime spanning 80 years.; [pers.] Throughout my lifetime by the spanning 80 years.; [pers.] Throughout my lifetime I have been inspired by the day to day experiences along the pathways of life.; [a.] Cheshire, CT

REINHEIMER, BYRON A.
[b.] December 28, 1929, Milwaukee; [p.] Byron M. and Irene A. Reinheimer; [m.] Betty Lou Reinheimer, February 10, 1951; [ch.] Two; [ed.] BA - Accounting; [occ.] 38 yrs Insurance Sales -- semi-retired; [pers.] In 1973 at age 42, I accepted the Lord Jesus Christ as my personal savior. Until this glorious day, I never wrote a poem. Now I write poems to glorify my Lord.

RENZ, LINDA N.
[m.] Joseph H. Renz; [ed.] Senior at Virginia Commonwealth Univ, Richmond, VA - Eng Maj; [occ.] Full time student; [hon.] Golden Key National Honor Society, Dean's List; [oth. writ.] A Litany of Poems: I write in my spare time; [pers.] My poetry is totally inspired by the people in my life especially my nieces and nephews, and the places I love in America; [a.] Sandston, VA

REYES (II), BENITO CRISANTO
[Pen.] Benito or Crisanto; [b.] January 23, 1974, Houston, TX; [p.] Benito C. and Maria H. Reyes; [m.] Cassandra Moreno-Reyes, Valentines Day 1994; [ch.] Daughter - Ariel Alyssandra Reyes (2); [ed.] High School, Aldine Sr High, Houston, TX; [occ.] Deck Seaman, USN; [memb.] US Navy, Boost Officer Ascension Program; [hon.] This publication is my first honor and award; [oth. writ.] Many computer disks full of undiscovered works; [pers.] If not for the support of my mother (whom notified me of the contest) and the inspiration of my wife, I would probably never be published; [a.] Any Naval Base, The World

REYNOLDS, MARY AGNES
[b.] June 20, 1922, Killingly, Conn.; [p.] John Lacey and Jane Dowling Lacey; [m.] Charles B. Reynolds, November 26, 1942; [ch.] Five, 2 girls, 3 boys; [ed.] Three years high school; [occ.] retied; [hon.] 1st prize on this poem $10.00 "What Christmas Means"; [oth. writ.] I wrote a few poems in high school and received "A" on them.

RHAE, RENNE
[b.] June 21, 1945, San Diego, CA; [p.] Francis J. Stammen, Mary Kaye; [occ.] Artist, Writer; [oth. writ.] Although not published, often art patrons have requested short essays reflecting the feelings or thoughts interwoven throughout the work. It becomes a personal reflection of the viewer.; [pers.] My own commitment includes manifesting visually what comes to me in thought. Paintings and writing capture the essence of that illusion to nurture self-satisfaction, and hopefully, to move others in thought and feelings.; [a.] San Diego, CA

RHYMER, VALENCIA
[b.] October 22, 1971, St. Thomas USVI; [p.] Carmena Turnbull; [ed.] Bauder College, AS Travel and Tourism Management; [occ.] Reservation Agent for Carnival Airlines; [hon.] Dean's List; [pers.] My poem is a direct reflection of society; [a.] Fort Lauderdale, FL

RICAPITO, CHRISTIE
[b.] December 26, 1975, Upper Darby, PA; [ed.] Cardinal O'Hara H.S.; Currently pursuing a B.A. in Theatre at Temple University; [occ.] Student; [memb.] Temple University Honors Society; [hon.] Dean's List, University Scholar, and faculty Honors at previous college; Southampton College; past chairperson of the Southampton Coffee House, which I opened in Fall of 1993.; [oth. writ.] Several poems published in high school literary magazine, Dialogs.; [pers.] This poem reflects my hope for experiences of discovery and transition. My deepest love and thanks to Matthew, M512, M523 and Julie for changing my life in so many ways.;[a.] Broomall, PA

RICCIO, DEBORAH J.
[b.] June 8, 1960, New Haven, CT; [m.] Divorced; [ch.] Two, Dawn 7 months, Paul 7 years; [ed.] Completed High School; [occ.] Daycare provider; [hon.] Citizens Award; [a.] Hamden, CT

RICHARDS, CARL L.
[p.] Rev. Lewis and Tama Richards (deceased); [m.] Barbara Carter Richards, April 10, 1948; [ch.] Carter L., Terri G., Tama G.; Grandchildren: Anu O. Meacham, Arienne D. Richards; [ed.] Dover High, Dover, OH, College BA, Grad school MA Western Reserve U; [occ.] Retired School Teacher; [hon.] Dean's List, Sen Mer Rekh Jennings Scholar, WWII, EIO Honorable Discharge; [oth. writ.] Collection in Philosophy In Poetic Verse (unpublished poems); [pers.] In my writings, I try to make a philosophical statement by using poetic verse; [a.] Cleveland, OH

RICHARDSON, JAYSON WADDE
[b.] September 3, 1971, Corydon, IN; [p.] Ellie Schilling-Morris and Eugene Richardson, currently attending Indiana University Kokolho, currently attending IUPUI; [occ.] Full time student working on a masters in education; [hon.] Dean's List; [pers.] The greatest gift an individual can bestow upon the next generation is thought.; [a.] Logansport, IN

RICHEY, DARIN E.
[b.] May 12, 1967, Tampico, IL; [p.] Paul and Linda Richey; [m.] Lisa M. Richey, June 27, 1992; [ch.] none; [occ.] Auto Technician Ruges Subaru Rhinebeck, NY; [pers.] Hopefully, my poetry will reflect to others that we must not listed to the darker side of ourselves and that there is always a way to the light.; [a.] Wappingers Falls, NY

RIDEOUT, STEPHANIE
[b.] January 23, 1979, Chambersburg Hospital; [p.] Mervin and Evander Richardson; [pers.] I thank God for my talent and the people who influenced me the most I thank them.; [a.] Chambersburg, PA

RIGHTER, CHIP
[Pen.] C. Righter; [b.] October 28, 1954, Baltimore, MD; [p.] Beatrice S. Schmidt; [m.] Single; [ed.] Towson High School, Park Street Collegiate Institute, Essex College, President of Mercedes Benz; [occ.] California Benz and Founder of President of The Breakaway Skate Center, Inc.; [memb.] Founder of the Dolphin Conservation Group in Newport Beach, CA, keeps the awareness of the dolphin population and status with an annual fund raiser; [hon.] My spare time is spent teaching hockey to children, both ice hockey and roller hockey, and clothing and feed those on skid row here in L.A. the awards I have received are general ones in appreciation for volunteering; [oth. writ.] I have won other contests before through Essex College in 1975 and some have been in local papers. I am currently working on my own book of poetry.; [pers.] There isn't a gift more precious to give, than your time.; [a.] Newport Beach, CA

RITCHIE, JOANNE
[b.] November 2, 1972, Dover, NJ; [p.] Homer and Stephanie Pennell; [m.] Bruce Ritchie, October 8, 1994; [ed.] Graduated Seabreeze Senior High; [occ.] Homemaker; [memb.] Eagle Gold Card Club; [hon.] Graduated with honors, honorable mention in Seabreeze art show, voted most creative 1989; [oth. writ.] unpublished book of my own original poems.; [pers.] Special thanks to my parents, and my husband, my inspiration. I couldn't do it without you.; [a.] Daytona Beach, FL

RIVERA, DEMETRIO
[b.] December 22, 1944, Puerto Rico; [p.] Angel Rivera, Lydia Garcia; [m.] Ana M. Rivera, July 19, 1965; [ch.] Dwight D., Diana M. Doreen; [ed.] Montclair State University, BA Psychology, Social Studies, Paralegal; [occ.] Building Maintenance, City of Tampa; [memb.] North American Fishing Club; [hon.] MVP, Coach of the Year (soft and baseball) bowling, also trophies and plate of recognition for poetry; [oth. writ.] Short stories, songs, proverbs and hundreds of poetry in spanish.; [pers.] In my poems, I try to transmit the understanding of love an care through the feeling of sadness and joyfulness. Philosophical Sta. "Any tear through the cry of pain or any smile in any face for joy, shown the emotions to be human and still alive."; [a.] Tampa, FL

RIVINO, HEATHERLYNN
[b.] January 10, 1975, Derby, CT; [p.] Sharon and Les Rivino; [ed.] Currently enrolled at St. Joseph's College. Attended Derby High School; [occ.] Nursing Assistant; [hon.] Certificate of Award for High Honors and perfect attendance at Connecticut Business Inst, Nursing Assistance Program; [oth. writ.] None published; [pers.] Writing is my salvation. Being able to express my emotions and beliefs with the world is my most precious gift from God; [a.] Derby, CT

ROBARE, MARIA
[b.] July 7, 1975, Plattsburgh, NY; [p.] Glenn Robare and Pauline Robare; [ed.] High school diploma from AuSable Valley Central School. Attending college at Clinton Community in Plattsburgh; [occ.] College student; [memb.] I have a membership with Columbia House and with Sterling Magazines; [hon.] When I was younger, I was awarded first prize for a picture I drew in 1st grade; [oth. writ.] I wrote a poem about "Sisters", "Mother", and "Boys"; [pers.] I hope to write more poems, have a good education and job, I hope to meet the guy of my dreams and have children someday; [a.] Keeseville, NY

ROBERSON, KAREN
[Pen.] Elaine Carin; [b.] September 23, 1966, Raleigh, NC; [p.] John Godwin, Jean Tant; [ch.] Derek Roberson; [occ.] Freelance Artist, Author; [hon.] National Scholastic Art Gold Key Award, 1982. Awarded 1st place short story writing contest, JMS, Alburqurque, NM 1980; [oth. writ.] Pursuing publication of Revelations, illustrated collection of poetry and Midnight Cries, fiction novel.; [pers.] My work tends to question or shed light on, negative societal behaviors and their sometimes permanent effects all in an attempt to influence a personal, positive change in societies actions and/or attitudes; [a.] Clayton, NC

ROBERTO, LEONARD
[b.] July 20, 1970, Bridgeport, CT; [ed.] Fairfield College Prep, Univ of Connecticut; [oth. writ.] One full volume of poetry awaiting publication titled "Afterimage"; [pers.] I am inspired by images and memories. Taking something that seems "normal" or innocuous and placing it in a new light is my goal in writing. I also use poetry as a release for anger and pain; [a.] Bridgeport, CT

ROBERTS, CANDY
[b.] March 3, 1970, Springfield, MO; [p.] Bill Roberts, Sandra Roberts; [m.] (soon to be) John Fulks, May 1995; [ed.] Phillips Junior College - AAS Degree; [occ.] Janitor/Housekeeper; [hon.] Graduated from junior college Magna Cum Laude; made President's or Dean's List every semester; [oth. writ.] Several poems published in Junior College paper; [pers.] Don't ever give up on your dreams, life is too short for regrets; [a.] Springfield, MO

ROBERTS, CECILIA M.
[b.] August 24, 1928, San Francisco, CA; [ed.] George Washington HS, Marquette Univ BA, Univ of Kentucky MA, PhD; [occ.] Retired; [memb.] Mensa, Intertel, ISPE; [hon.] Pi Gamma Mu, Alpha Kappa Delta, Phi Beta Kappa; [oth. writ.] Book: Doctor and Patient - 1975, many articles; [a.] Laurel, MD

ROBERTS, WILLARD V.
[b.] April 5, 1915, North Bend, WA; [p.] Clyde and Ethel Roberts; [m.] Marguerette, June 20, 1936; [ch.] Judith, 4 grand and 9 great grand; [ed.] high school; [occ.] Retired Operating Engineer and Musician; [memb.] International Operating Eng., City of Seattle Eng. Dept.; [oth. writ.] As publishers don't seem eager to publish unknown poets, I have had 5 books of my poems printed through the years to give to family and friends mostly short, humorous verse.; [pers.] Flowery, blank verse leaves me cold. I like rhythm and rhyme. I have also composed many songs and lyrics.; [a.] Salem, OR

ROBERTSON, MELINDA
[b.] July 12, 1979, Des Moines, IA; [p.] Vance and Jeannie Robertson; [ed.] Sophomore at Collins-Maxwell High School; [occ.] Student; [memb.] Maxwell Christian Church; [oth. writ.] Well over one hundred poems and a book of poems, Poems From The Heart, but not yet published; [pers.] Life has given me many troubles. My writing of poetry has helped me have the courage and the strength to work through the problems I have had; [a.] Maxwell, IA

ROBIDEAUX, AMY
[b.] March 24, 1938, Eunice, LA; [p.] A.L. and Isabel (Dardeau) Guillory; [m.] divorced; [ch.] Jason, Joel, Jeanmarie, John; [ed.] Master's Elem Educ - Special Educ Certification - Univ of South Western Lafayette, LA; [occ.] Director of Special Services/Jr High Resource Teacher, Our Lady of Fatima School, Lafayette, LA; [memb.] Council for exceptional children. American Council on Learning Disabilities; [hon.] Teacher of the year - Our Lady of Fatima School, Diocese of Lafayette; [oth. writ.] Personal essays on learning disabilities (unpublished); [pers.] Age brings its blessings. Wisdom begins to set in -- discernment becomes clearer, and life is more precious; [a.] Lafayette, LA

ROBINSON, ELLA S.
[b.] April 16, 1943, Wedowee, AL; [p.] Less and Mary E. Scaks; [m.] Deceased; [ch.] John W. Robinson, Jr.; [ed.] Wedowee High, Alabama State University, B.S., University of Nebraska, Ph.D; [occ.] Professor of English, Tuskegee University, Tuskegee Institute, AL; [memb.] African Literature Assoc., MLA Modern Language Assoc., Life Time Membership NAACP, Stephen Mission Methodist Church; [hon.] High School Valedictorian, Listed in Who's Who of American Women 1979-80, Who's Who in the South and Southwest 1980-81, Who's Who Among Black Americans 1988; [oth. writ.] Articles "The World of Bessie Head" "Myth as Regeneration in Aime Cesairne's Poetry," 1,500 poems in anthologies and placed in the Archives Love Library Univ. of NE poems in Black Scholar.; [pers.] I celebrate life, honesty and the exquisite moment in my poetry. I have been greatly influenced by Aime Cesaire.; [a.] Montgomery, AL

ROBINSON, PATRICIA
[Pen.] Patricia Rose; [b.] June 4, 1940, New Haven, CT; [p.] John and Helen O'Brien; [m.] John L. Robinson, September 18, 1982; [ch.] John, Scott, Trisha, Tracy; [ed.] High School; [occ.] I'm a very busy Mom and Grama; [oth. writ.] Although I have other poems, this is the first one I have entered. I enjoy writing as a hobby but I do not have the free time as I would like to have.; [a.] East Haven, CT

RODOLPH, PAULINE M.
[b.] June 26, 1915, Randlett, OK; [p.] Frank and Helena Linkugel; [m.] James E. Rodolph, November 13, 1933; [ch.] Mrs. Jeanne Boland, Mrs. Kay Stephen, Mrs. Linda Mann; [ed.] Walters High School, Cameron Junior College, Texas Wesleyan College; [occ.] Retired from Forth Worth Public Schools; [memb.] Ryanwood Baptist Church; Phi Theta Kappa; [hon.] Class Poetess - Walters Public School; Dean's List - Cameron College; Phi Theta Kappa Fraternity; [oth. writ.] Several stories; music/chorus (music and words) for a statewide TV convention. Many poems in local newspapers; [pers.] To honor my Lord in all things I write, and to read my Bible through - Genesis to Revelation - every year; [a.] Fort Worth, TX

RODRIQUES, DON
[b.] March 19, 1933, Oakland, CA; [p.] Wm. and Gladys Rodriques; [m.] Divorced, 1969-1989; [ch.] Darin (26) and Darice (24); [ed.] BA San Francisco State 1963 and one year graduate work, U.C. Berkely School of Social Work 1964; [occ.] Retired Child Welfare Worker from Alameda County 3/93; [memb.] Fremont Ballroom Dance Club; "Beyond War" 1988-1991; Service Employee's International Union 1965-1993; YMCA "Indian Guides" (father son program) '75-'79 U.S. Army (Cook) '51-53; [oth. writ.] Editor "Social Work News" at S.F. State 1962-'63. Various "Letters to Editor" regarding social/political matters.; [pers.] I have strong feelings about social/political issues, parenting and relationships. I believe in working toward non-violent resolutions of human conflict.; [a.] Fremont, CA

ROE, TIFFANY
[b.] March 17, 1980, Lexington, KY; [p.] Donald Ray and Sherry Lynn Roe; [ed.] 9th Grade in High School; [occ.] Student at Kickapoo High School; [oth. writ.] Numerous titles yet to be published.; [pers.] Don't underestimate the influence of your family.; [a.] Springfield, MO

ROGDE, JAMES DUNCAN
[Pen.] J. Duncan Rogde; [b.] October 28, 1949, Houston, TX; [p.] Mr. and Mrs. William J. Rogde; [m.] Patricia A. Rogde, December 29, 1972; [ch.] Amber Kristen, Allison Leigh; [ed.] Lamar High School, University of Houston, BBA 1972; [occ.] Director of Materials Mgt., Memorial Hospital, Nacogdoches, TX; [memb.] First church of the Nazarene Board Member; [oth. writ.] Other writings that were written for enjoyment and shared with family and friends.; [pers.] I strive to be the best husband and father to my family, and a christian example to others. I write for enjoyment and to reflect the beauty, greatness and mysteries of our world.; [a.] Nacogdoches, TX

ROGERS, CYNTHIA JEAN
[Pen.] Cindy Rogers; [b.] January 27, 1969, Waukesha, WI; [p.] Ron and Judy Low; [m.] James Wesley Rogers, September 2, 1989; [ed.] Lebanon High School, Lebanon, MD; [occ.] Factory worker at Marathon Electric, Lebanon, MO; [memb.] St. Francis De Sales Catholic Church; [hon.] National Science Merit Award, Spring of 1985, I was a sophomore in high school.; [oth. writ.] Presently under a songwriter's contract out of New York City. They have accepted one of my songs and are putting lyrics to it. I am also taking a home course in writing Children's Books.; [pers.] As a writer, I am continuously studying my surroundings. I have learned more about people, animals and the environment world wide. Most of my writings come from my deep feelings from past and present experiences.; [a.] Lebanon, MO

ROHRER, SHEILA B.
[b.] November 9, 1959, Mooresville, NC; [p.] Mary and Hoyt Beam; [m.] Jeffrey C. Rohrer, June 26, 1982; [ch.] Jason (11) and Stephen (8); [ed.] Completed 3 yrs of undergraduate study at UNC - Chapel Hill; 2 yrs at Presbyterial Hospital School of Radiologic Technology, Charlotte, NC; [occ.] Radiologic Technologist Registered (Computed Axial Tomography); [memb.] American Registry of Radiologic Technologists; American Society of Radiologic Technologists; Riverside United Methodist Church; Agape Women's group; [pers.] I have always loved to think of life's simplest tasks in beautiful ways. Even the most mundane of chores, gets done a little faster if a little excitement is added.; [a.] Camden, NC

RONKAINEN, TRACEY
[b.] December 19, 1978, Clinton, Iowa; [p.] Greg and Debi Ronkainen and Kathleen Menning; [ed.] Redondo Union High School; [occ.] student; [memb.] USFSA, ISIA; [hon.] Most Inspirational, Academic Achievement, Presidential Academic Fitness Award, Best Citizenship, Citizenship Award for Outstanding honor, service, courage, leadership, scholarship, companionship from Lions Club; [a.] Hermosa Beach, CA

ROONEY, NOREEN
[b.] December 10, 1925, Detroit; [p.] Albert G. Hamming, Viola Hamming; [m.] Divorced-Deceased; [ch.] Terrence, Douglas, Brian, Karen; [ed.] St. Anthony Hi (Detroit) Western Michigan (Kalamazoo), (Major in English, minor in Psychology and Science); [occ.] Retired - Former TV Editor - Detroit Free Press; [memb.] AWRT - Detroit Chapter; [hon.] Who's Who of American Women - tenth edition 1977/78, Detroit Free Press Publishers Club - Feb 1989; [oth. writ.] Article - Michigan History Magazine; [pers.] To strive for: Dignity, Maturity, Integrity, Compassion; [a.] St. Clair Shores, MI

ROSALES, MARIA CHRISTINA OLAGUE
[Pen.] Turtle; [b.] September 9, 1945, El Paso, TX; [p.] Marcela Olague and Pablo Olague; [m.] Antonio Rosales, May 20, 1967; [ch.] Felipe Antonio Rosales, Aida Christina Rosales-Salazar, Annabel Christina Rosales, Urias; [occ.] Superintendent's Secretary, Chamizal National Memorial, National Park Service, Department of Interior; [pers.] This poem is a result of the wonderful feeling of being a grandmother. The poem is dedicated to all my grandchildren who I consider a blessing from God to us.; [a.] El Paso, TX

ROSARIO, MARQUEZ T.
[b.] February 11, 1974, Cleveland, OH; [p.] Jose and Julita Rosario; [ed.] Cleveland St. Ignatius High School, Cleveland State Univ; [occ.] Electrical Engineering Student, Cleveland State Univ; [memb.] Member of National Technical Assoc; Former Member of Cleveland Music Federation, and former member of Junior Council of World Affairs; [hon.] Participated in 1992 Cuyahoga Community College Senior's Best Short Story and Poetry Competition; [oth. writ.] Editor in Chief of Vista, high school literary magazine; [pers.] Striving to be the best, learning all the way, that knowledge can be found every single day. Thank you to God, to my parents, and to all my family and friends; [a.] Cleveland, OH

ROSE, MARGARET JO
[b.] January 10, 1932, Vicksburg, MS; [p.] Frank William Meyer, Catherine May Lassiter Meyer (deceased); [ch.] Anne Catherine, Jean Marie, Patrick Michael; [ed.] St. Francis Xavier Academy - Vicksburg, MS, Sacred Heart School - Memphis, TN; St. Louis Univ Extension; Mercy Junior College; Webster College - Webster Groves, MO; [occ.] Retired teacher, McRae's Customer Service; [memb.] Mercy Associate, St. Michael Catholic Church, AARP.

ROSENBERGER, MARGARET A.
[b.] Oct. 30, Micanopy, FL; [p.] Eugene David and Lillian Rosenberger; [m.] Single; [ed.] Attended Stetson Univ., Graduated Univ. of Florida, BAE and MED, Attended Santa Fe Community College, Speaking Class Univ of Heidelberg, Germany; [occ.] Retired Elementary School Principal; [memb.] Numerous; [hon.] Graduated from U. of F with honors, and many others; [oth. writ.] Too many to mention; [pers.] I believe in doing what I can to

help and serve mankind, young and older. It is hoped that my life and writings will reflect the goodness of God and mankind while considering the past, present, and future generations.; [a.] Gainesville, FL

ROUSSEL, JUAQUIN OMAR
[Pen.] Jake Roussel; [b.] December 1, 1981, San Antonio, TX; [p.] Daniel and Beverly Roussel; Brother: Husain Roussel; [ed.] Attended Pre-school through 5th grade at Aukamm Elementary School, in Wiesbaden, Germany 6th til present, at Murchison Middle School, in Austin, TX; [occ.] Student (8th grader); [memb.] American Heart Assoc; [hon.] Honor Roll, Student Council Member, Presidential Academic Fitness Award, and Shell Oil Student Recognition Award; [oth. writ.] Poems published in Sparks '89 European Edition (DODDS Schools), Glimpses 90-91 Aukamm School Edition, and Austin American Statesman '93; [pers.] There is a hidden talent in all us, some of us just have to look a little deeper to fine it! My greatest influence is my family and friends; [a.] Austin, TX

ROWE, CARRIE BELLE
[b.] October 31, 1943, Burgaw, NC; [p.] John Douglas and Sarah Rowe; [m.] Thomas Wilson, James Bruce, Adell Henderson, now single; [ch.] Douglas and Gene Wilson, and Elizabeth Bruce; [ed.] Burgaw High School; [occ.] Art dept at a label printing company in Burgaw, NC; [memb.] Several Historical Societies in Eastern, NC; My hobbies are genealogy and photography and raising plants; [oth. writ.] Numerous unpublished poems, article in Wilmington Morning Star; [pers.] I enjoy the Ogden Nash style of poetry. Poets seem to run in my family. They say I may have descended from Nicholas Rowe, Poet Laureate of England. William Blake was supposed to be an ancestor of my great grandmother, Martha E. Blake; [a.] Burgaw, NC

ROWE, WENDY
[Pen.] Wendy Bowker Rowe; [b.] April 4, 1961, Stevenage, England; [p.] Derek Bowker, Josephine Rowe; [ed.] Florence Township Memorial High School; [occ.] Restaurant manager; [memb.] Fountain of Life Center Church; [oth. writ.] This is my first to be published, but have written 3 novels, and several other poems; [pers.] I am grateful to my close friends for encouraging me to continue writing; [a.] Roebling, NJ

ROYSE, ATAKA RHODES
[b.] February 17, 1925, Florence, AL; [p.] Wm. H. and Myrtle Rhodes; [m.] Ralph Royse, June 6, 1987; [ch.] Mark Adam, Paul Aaron; [ed.] High School, Nursing; [occ.] Housewife, S.S. Teacher; [memb.] Independent Fellowship; [hon.] Hospital Corp. of America, Humanitarian Award, Distinguished Service Award, Nazarene, Spotlighted Newspapers; [oth. writ.] Poem in Ann. School Book., Special Tributes, Dedications, Award Services; [pers.] I strive to beauty, hope and praise in my writings. My mother was my early mentor and I learned to love and deliver with oral perfection from her. I am indebted to the poets who have gone before me.; [a.] Tulsa, OK

RUANE, JOSEPH
[b.] June 4, 1964, Ireland; [p.] Tomas and Flor; [m.] Regina, September 30, 1989; [ch.] Shane Joseph/Dylan Thomas; [ed.] St. Patrick's National School, St. Gerald's College, Castlebar Co Mayo Ireland; [occ.] Painting Contractor; [oth. writ.] Poetry and short stories for Irish News newspaper. Few articles for local newspaper (Ireland); [pers.] "Learn how to walk before you take your

first step, because a circle is a nothing, framed by an endless line".

RUBIN, ANN ROSALINE
[Pen.] Ann R. Rubin; [b.] August 12, 1905, New Bedford, MA; [p.] Dora and Fisher Wolfson; [m.] Gabriel J. Rubin M.D., September 6, 1928 (Pediatrician) deceased; [ch.] Sheila Judith Eckastein and Deborah Merle Rubin (deceased); [ed.] Wolleley College, Radcliff College, M.A., Columbia Univ., Univ. of Berlin; [occ.] Retired; [memb.] Brownie Leader, PTA President, School Advisory Council, and many others; [hon.] World of Poetry Golden Poet of 1990 for poem "My Private Room;" World of Poetry Golden Poet of 1991 for poem "In Transit;" and many others; [oth. writ.] Published in T.G. Quarterly Magazine and other writings; [pers.] My poetry is autobiographical and deals with personal experiences and feelings. Have traveled extensively abroad, the Mid-East and S. America as well throughout the U.S.A.; [a.] Olmsted Township, OH

RUBIN, NAOMI GREIFER
[b.] June 8, 1919, Hartford, CT; [p.] Joseph L. Greifer and Minnie L. Greifer; [m.] Alfred Rubin, November 25, 1951; [ch.] Jennifer, Steven, Lydia; [ed.] Graduation with honors; BA Northern MI Univ; MA Northwestern Univ; [occ.] Housewife, (formerly instructor of English); [memb.] American Assoc of Univ Women; Various Book Clubs and Writing Clubs and Community Clubs; [pers.] My poems deal with persons deepest concerns, written, I hope, in poetic language; [a.] Naperville, IL

RUCKER, DANNY A.
[Pen.] Alfonse; [b.] February 4, 1950, Charleston, W.VA; [p.] Donald D. Rucker (deceased) and Norma L. Duncan, stepfather Charles E. Duncan; [m.] Divorced; [ch.] Sean Lee Rucker and Chris Alan Rucker; [ed.] Graduated from St. Albans High School in St. Albans High in St. Albans, W.VA in 1968, was discharged honorably from the Navy in 1970.; [occ.] Airframes Tire and Wheel, Specialist, CD QCI and part time Leadman B, The Tire Shop; [memb.] Winfield Baptist Church, The Bailey Baptist Church; [hon.] No honors, but I would like to thank God, my two sisters: Mrs. Donna L. Brillhart in Meridian, MS. & Mrs. Melinda B. Ray in Huntington, W.V. and my sons Sean and Chris, I love you all very much.; [oth. writ.] "Why?" & "On Calvery" are two other poems that were suppose to be published in other editions of Hardbound Volumes produced by National Library of poetry; poems published in several Baptist Church; [pers.] My ninth grade english teacher asked us to write a poem for a literature assignment and she encouraged me to continue writing, especially my mother, family, encouraged me while I was young and my sons kept me going. I've written over 500 poems and songs since I was in the 9th grade.; [a.] Meridian, MS

RUFFIN, LEE E.
[Pen.] Rosalfie Fay; [b.] November 13, 1943, Lynn, MA; [p.] James S. and Helene Adrian; [ch.] Paula H. Vargo, James P. Monahan, Jr., Jason L. Ruffin; [ed.] BFA Drama, Musical Theater from The Boston Conservatory; graduate work in English: Salem State College; [memb.] American Guild of Variety Artists; AFLCIO; NYC American Federation of Musicians; Local 126; The Boston Conservatory Alumni; Assn. Board of Directors; [oth. writ.] Several poems published in local newspapers and a collection of short stories titled "Monuments."; [pers.] Lee is a former Middle Eastern dancer who performed in New England under the name of "Kleanthi."

At present, she performs as an actor and singer of jazz standards under her stage name of Rosalie Fay. Daytime, Lee teaches Drama, English, and Music in the public schools.; [a.] Lynn, MA

RUPERT, LAVERNE H.
[Pen.] My middle name: Laverne; [b.] A long time ago; [p.] Jane Mize and Perry Peters; [m.] John D. Rupert, October 16, in Springfield, IL; [ch.] Five sons and one daughter; [ed.] Eight years of college after children were in school...a lot of night school but it was great!; [occ.] After becoming a widow in 1986, I have been a part-time nurse, generally for seniors; [memb.] Choir in Spring Arbor Church. Missionary Circle; for years on the Speakers Roster for Woman's Clubs up and down the West coast, from So. California to Fairbanks, AK. For a number of years I helped put five of my children through college, Univ and Grad School; [hon.] My greatest honor and award was seeing my children grow up to be good citizens, and productive members of society and now raising their own children to be the same. My five sons are all in the professions; [oth. writ.] Articles for religious publications as well as secular mags. My first published poem was when in high school in Scribblers Magazine; [pers.] I enjoy writing songs, most of them in my files, some from many years ago. A half dozen have been copyrighted. My goal each day is to made a difference in someone's life...A word of encouragement, a smile, a thoughtful deed, planned or spontaneous. Also volunteer hospital work; [a.] Spring Arbor, MI

RUSSELL, BRENDA LYNN
[Pen.] Mrs. Brenda Russell; [b.] April 28, 1963, Joliet, IL; [p.] Gordon and Caryl Johnson; [m.] Robert Mark Russell, March 1, 1994; [ed.] A.A. in Elementary Education from Joliet Junior College; B.A. in Elementary Education from the College of St. Francis; [occ.] Babysitter; [pers.] I've always enjoyed writing poetry. If's more than a release of tension; it's a beautiful way to express my feelings.; [a.] Peonte, IL

RUSSELL, PATRICIA
[Pen.] Pat, Trici, Bay, and Queen; [b.] November 30, 1953, Bridgetown, NJ; [p.] Rev. Wilbert and Margie Russell; [m.] Eddie G. Jacob Sr. (Deceased), February 23, 1974; [ch.] Alexander Russell, Eddie G. Jacobs Jr., William J. Green, Stepson; [ed.] Bridgeton Senior High, Cumberland Co. College, JT.PA Training School; [occ.] Disable; [memb.] Embeneze Baptist Church; [hon.] Honor with nine brothers and sisters and nine grandchildren. Once deceased brother; [oth. writ.] Several poems that music has been put to by Hollywood Artists Record Company and Five Star Music Masters Co.; [pers.] To let every one know that without God where would we be and hoping that my writing will reflect on someone's life.; [a.] Bridgeton, NJ

RUSTEN, KEVIN
[b.] January 1, 1961, Washington, DC; [p.] George Rusten, Ruby Rusten; [m.] Cynthia Rusten, July 14, 1992; [ch.] Kevin Davon; [ed.] Parkdale High School; [occ.] Warehouse Order Filler, Staford Paper Co, Landover, MD; [memb.] Church of the Nativity Committee, Local Union 449; [hon.] The Golden Gloves 80 AAU, Diploma in Machine Architecture, On-the-Job Awards, Forklift; [oth. writ.] Several poems unpublished. Time Is Ticking, A Grandmother's Love, Life and Death, It's a Father's Cry. I have wrote several eulogies for family members and friends; [pers.] I strive to write poems that penetrate the soul. I like to force on the concept of reality, things that's are happening right now; [a.] Silver Spring, MD

RUTON, MILDRED K.
[Pen.] Mildred Marsh Ruton; [b.] November 2, 1906, Bridgeport, OH; [p.] Joseph Clarence Marsh, Pearl Fonner Marsh (both deceased); [m.] Edgar H. Ruton (deceased), October 15, 1947, [ch.] Larry, Bill (Bill-deceased); [ed.] Graduate of Wheeling High School 1925. Back then college didn't seem necessary and we couldn't afford it; [occ.] Retired when I was 62 yrs of age. I am now 88; [memb.] Chapter 305 Order Eastern Stars - Silver Club of Newark of Newark (was a former President of same); [hon.] Won Trophy for 2nd place in local senior citizens spelling bee. My husband and I travelled in show business anolater in life we operated a country music park in this area. He died in 1958 and I operated it alone for 8 yrs alone (20 yrs in all); [oth. writ.] Nothing published. I did not try tho. I wrote poems since I was a child. I've written stories in rhyme for my own enjoyment about things I was learning to cook and made into disasters. I use them in my routine as a standup comedian currently; [pers.] I like to see and hear people laugh. They need it these days that's way I donate my comedy at the Senior Center when they want me to do so; [a.] Newark, OH

RYAN, ELEANOR F.
[Pen.] Eleanor Blanchat Ryan; [b.] September 28, 1910, Vermilion, OH; [p.] Josephine and George Blanchat; [m.] James M. Ryan, August 11, 1936; [ch.] Thomas Patrick Ryan; [ed.] Vermilion High School, Vermilion, OH, Ursuline College for Women, Cleveland Hts., OH, Graduate: Ohio Wesleyan Univ., Delaware; [occ.] Retired, Freelance Art Designer, Bookkeeper and Advertising Mgr. of family owned Crystal Beach Park; [memb.] St. Mary Catholic Church, Chi Omega Sorority, Long time former member of Nat'l Assoc., of Univ. Women; [hon.] Bachelor of Arts Degree in Fine Arts majoring in design. Delta Phi Delta, National Honorary Art Fraternity; [oth. writ.] Poem submitted is one of two poems composed to supplement slides and commentary of the History of Crystal Beach Park (1907-1962). Presented as program for Historical Groups.; [a.] Vermilion, OH

SADAKA, JENNIFER
[b.] August 12, 1976, Livingston, NJ; [p.] Adnan and Connie Sadaka; [ed.] Queen of Peace High School LaSalle Univ; [occ.] Student LaSalle Univ; [hon.] Featured in 1992-93 and 1993-94 editions of "Who's Who Among High School Students". Received the Harry Dorfman Journalism Scholarship i 1994; [oth. writ.] Several poems published in literary magazines, articles for The Star Ledger; [pers.] "Every day we're standing in a time capsule, Racing down a river from the past, Every day we're standing in a wind tunnel, Facing our future coming fast"; [a.] Newark, NJ

SADOFF, JOHNNY
[b.] May 13, 1984, Washington, D.C.; [m.] James and Elizabeth Sadoff; [ed.] I am a 5th grader at the Evergreen School in Kensington, Maryland. I have attended Evergreen since I was 5 years old.; [occ.] Student; [memb.] I am an active member of the U.S. Chess Center in Washington, D.C. and the Silver Spring Boys Club in Silver Spring, Maryland.; [hon.] I have received several awards from participating in local chess tournaments.; [oth. writ.] I have written several other poems and stories. Example: A poem is as small as a rock and as beautiful as a rose.; [pers.] I had many questions I could not find the answers to. Writing poetry was my answer.; [a.] Washington, D.C.

SAGUNSKY, CINDY L.
[Pen.] Lee Van Zagun; [b.] October 25, 1967, Appleton, WI; [p.] Mike and Donna Werner, Gary Sagunsky; [ed.] Appleton High School East, American Institute of Banking, University of Illinois Chicago; [memb.] National Honor Society, Chicago Cares, National Association of Female Executives; [oth. writ.] I have been writing since I was 9 years old, only recently have I felt compelled to allow strangers to read my work.; [pers.] I enjoy sharing my personal reflections of life if only to evoke an emotional response or to inspire and direct others.; [a.] Midlothian, IL

SALAHU-DIN, DEBORAH T.
[b.] June 26, 1959, Baltimore, MD; [p.]Edward Taylor, Doretta Jones Taylor; [m.] Derrick Amin; [ch.] Janna Saran Amin; [ed.] Coppin State College; Salisbury State Univ; [occ.] Writing Specialist; National Council of Teachers of English; African-American Writer's Guild; [hon.] Congressional Achievement Award for Dedicated Community Service, 1992; [oth. writ.] Contributing writer to Notable Black American Women, 1993; [pers.] Writing is at once personal and sacred, then too, public and profane. It at once consoles and pacifies, then too violates and provokes. The water that nurtures the gentle lilac nourishes the deadly night shades. Writing unites all of this and is therefore one and good; [a.] Salisbury, MD

SAMUELS, SOPHIA
[b.] August 26, 1971, St. Andrew, JA, WI;[p.] Everald and Eulalee Samuels; [ed.] Waterford Secondary School, Taylor Bus. Inst.; [occ.] Personal Care Aid, Olsen Kimberly Quality Care, NY; [hon.] Perfect Deans List [oth. writ.] Unpublished songs and poems.; [pers.] It doesn't matter what the situation may be, people will always relate to songs and poems, because there is always apart of us that goes untold and unknown, but revealed in a poem and a song.; [a.] Central Islip, NY

SANCHEZ, MARIA CRISTINA
[Pen.] Mery Mendez-Sanchez; [b.] October 24, 1952, Alquizar Havana, Cuba; [p.] Luis and Julia Mendez; [m.] Candido Sanchez, November 27, 1976; [ch.] Cesar Jesus, Monica Cristina, Isabel Cristina; [ed.] LA Santa Infancia Catholic School, Superior School (Alquizar), Hialeah High School, Miami Dade Community College; [occ.] School Clerk, Hialeah Elem. School, Hialeah, Florida; [memb.] Parent, Teacher Assoc., Hialeah Elementary Social Committee, United Office Personal of Dade; [hon.] Hialeah Elem. PTA Outstanding Service, 1991.; [oth. writ.] Several poems published in Gibson Greeting Cards, and many unpublished.; [pers.] I like to create poems that influence mankind to look at life with a better perspective and believe in God's power.; [a.] Hialeah, FL

SANDERS, GEORGE & PAT
[b.] Age 72 & 59; [hon.] 7/4/91 Lions Club Appreciation Award to George Sanders for Reciting "The Sleeping Giant" to thousands at outdoor arena on 50th anniversary year of the Japanese attack 12/7/41; [oth. writ.] Poetry, The Mustard Seed, The Last Goodby, The Sleeping Giant, Guadalcanal, My Guardian Angel, Thank You, Dad; [pers.] The Homecoming is a true life story of a W.W.II Vet., survivor of Pearl Harbor and Guadalcanal, who upon medical discharge in 1945, with Battle Fatigue (P.T.S.D) was unable to find or hold a job for the rest of his life. He lived in causes as a hermit and never readapted to society. War kills bodies, but also minds.; [a.] Huffman, TX

SANDERS, KATHLEEN PRISCILLA
[Pen.] Priscilla Sands; [b.] February 14, 1953, Huntington Beach, CA; [p.] Charles Olney, Oma Rider; [ch.] Donnie L. Stamps; [occ.] Legal Assistant, McCaffrey and Tawwater Law Firm; [pers.] Behold all creatures of the land and sea, they are man's greatest treasure; [a.] Oklahoma City, OK

SANDHOLT, BARBARA L (MAGUIRE)
[Pen.] Bobby Mack; [b.] August 3, 1916, Belmont, MA; [p.] Mary Louise and Maurice Maney; [m.] 1. Herbert E. Maguire (died 1980), February 18, 1939; Soren Sandholt - 1982, May 20, 1982; [ch.] Moira, Ardan, Sheila Maguire and step - Carol and Richard Sandholt; [ed.] High School for Girls, Bryant Stratton, Business College - various courses at Harvard and Radcliffe; [occ.] Retired since 1967, formerly manager research corp - now volunteering in county; [memb.] Vice Pres and Charter Member former - Bus and Prof Women's Club, Administrative Organizations in Boston, MA; Limited activities due to ill health; [hon.] Volunteerism Awards; [oth. writ.] Letters to editor, publisher in local newspapers; [pers.] I am an avid reader starting at age 4. I have 17 grandchildren and 7 g/grandchildren who fill my life with love abundantly; and I love making new friends; [a.] Port Charlotte, FL

SANDY
[pers.] Dedication: For those who strived, whose journey has not been merely an inspiration, love always lights the way. (many...thanks!)

SANTIAGO, MARIA T.
[Pen.] Tere; [b.] April 25, 1945, Aguada, Puerto Rico; [p.] Manuel Santiago, Juan Rico Alers; [m.] Murray Eisenberg, April 25, 1987; [ch.] Dara and Kent; [ed.] A class short of an Assoc Degree in Accounting; [occ.] Order Filler; [oth. writ.] Several poems, prose and essays all unpublished; [pers.] I am a romantic trying to see and fulfill the best that life can offer to me; [a.] Chicago, IL

SANTIC, TAMERA S.
[Pen.] T.S.S.; [b.] August 22, 1980, Urburn, Wash.; [p.] Betty and Joe Santic; [ed.] I am in 9th grade at White River High School Buckley, Wash.; [hon.] Young Authors Award in 1990.; [oth. writ.] I have other poetry and stories.; [pers.] I write poetry to express my feelings.; [a.] Buckely, WA

SARDELLI, DR. WILFRED G.
[b.] May 6, 1932, Rhode Island; [m.] Sandra; [ed.] BS Electrical Engineering, MS Business Administration, Ph.D. Management Information Systems; [occ.] Vice President, Business Strategies; [memb.] IEEE, Advisory Board - George Washington Univ, Engineering Board - Univ of Rhode Island, Healthcare Information and Management Systems Society; [oth. writ.] Management Theory, Business Strategies, Poems, Music; [hon.] Presidents Award - Management Excellence, Registered Professional Engineer, Billion Dollar Club; [pers.] I know my talents are a gift from God.

SARDI, ANDREW
[b.] August 6, 1963, Milford, CT; [m.] Linda Sardi; [ed.] Currently an English Major at Yale University; [a.] Derby, CT

SAVARIMUTHU, SEBASTIAN
[Pen.] Bastin; [b.] June 18, 1945, Vallam (India); [p.] Savarimuthu, Chinnammal; [m.] Stella Sebastian, Au-

gust 17, 1977; [ed.] Gov't High School, Vallam - 613403 (India), Rajah Serfoji College, Thanjavur, Tamil Nadu, India; [memb.] American Heart Assoc; [oth. writ.] "Mild Child and Wild Man" published in India in 1967. Several poems on environment and wild life preservation have been published; [pers.] I prefer to write on the neglected humans of any kind - Race, nationality. No more barrier for my writing - happiest, peaceful humankind I foresee very soon; [a.] Chevy Chase, MD

SAWYER, LESLIE I.
[Pen.] Leslie Nunamaker Sawyer; [b.] November 6, 1959, Portsmouth, VA; [p.] Walter and Ruby Nunamaker; [m.] Divorced; [ch.] Margaret Eloise Sawyer; [ed.] Graduated class of 1978 Wilson High School, Portsmouth; [occ.] Self employed; [oth. writ.] Published with N.L. of Poetry; [pers.] That's ok; [a.] Portsmouth, VA

SCALETTY (C.S.J.), SISTER MARIE
[b.] July 4, 1908, Parsons, KS; [p.] Mr. and Mrs John Scaletty (deceased); [ed.] BS and RN St. Louis Univ, St. Louis, MO; [occ.] Retired Nurse-Teacher, Nazareth Living Center, St. Louis, MO; [oth. writ.] Several poems published in local publications; [pers.] I am a nun - 86 yrs old. I love nature and I love to write about it. I am retired and keep busy helping the elderly. I also play the piano and the organ; [a.] St. Louis, MO

SCAMACCA JR., SAMUEL J.
[Pen.] Fohyer Zohiny; [b.] August 3, 1958, New Brunswick, NJ; [p.] Sam and Dot Scamacca; [m.] Camille Perillo; [ed.] Metuchen High, East Brunswick Tech.; [occ.] Electrician; [oth. writ.] Many songs and poems not yet published.; [pers.] Reality hits hard sometimes, experience's in my life and the people around me inspire most of my work. I think emotions run deep within souls of human creation. When I write, I try to make the hidden realities surface and perhaps make an unseen truth visible.; [a.] East Brunswick, NJ

SCARBOROUGH, BRENDA L.
[b.] November 18, 1970, Phelps, Wisconsin; [p.] Mary Lou and Jimmie Bolgiano; [m.] Edmund C. Scarborough, November 29, 1991; [ch.] Christian M. Scarborough; [ed.] Bartlett High School, Fayetteville Technical Community College, University of Alaska, Anchorage; [occ.] Student, Associate Degree in Nursing; [a.] Fayetteville, NC

SCHABERT, JASON DAVID
[Pen.] Sticks; [b.] March 23, 1969, Alameda, CA; [p.] Daniel Schabert, Antonia Schabert; [ed.] Encinal High, Navy Fireman School, Computer Learning Center; [occ.] Printer Operator, USL Capital, San Mateo, CA; [oth. writ.] Several letters published in the small local paper; [pers.] I hope to make a musical career with my poetry talents. I have over one hundred and twenty poems currently, all written about various topics, mostly inspired by personal experiences; [a.] Alameda, CA

SCHAIBLE, BUNA REYNOLDS
[b.] June 19, 1940, Nashville, TN; [p.] Horace and Edna Choate Reynolds; [m.] Armin Schaible, December 29, 1961; [ch.] 2 daughters: Sandra and Conny; [ed.] Springfield High, Springfield, TN and Fall's Business College, Nashville, TN; [occ.] Walburg State Bank in Walburg, TX; [memb.] Member First Baptist Church in Springfield, TN, Member German/American Clubs in Houston, TX; [hon.] Lifetime Membership in Texas PTA for Several Years of Volunteer Work in Schools; [oth. writ.]

Several poems inspired by the death of my only son who died at an early age. My poems are like letters to him and say the things I would say if I could see him again.; [pers.] To great people with a smile can add love to the heart. My real feelings are reflected in my poetry, like light reflected in a mirror.; [a.] Walburg, TX

SCHANFIELD, FANNIE S.
[b.] December 25, 1916, Minneapolis, MN; [p.] Mary and Simon Schwartz; [m.] Abraham Schanfield, Aug. 28, 1947; [ch.] Moses, David, Miriam Kieffer; [ed.] Univ. of Minnesota Continuing Ed. for Women; [occ.] Retired, Bookkeeper, Homemaker, Community Volunteer; [memb.] Hadassah, Bnai Emet Women's League, League of Women Voters, Jewish Community Center, Council of Jewish Women; [hon.] Hadassah President Award, Hennepin County Citation of Honor, Jewish Comm. Ctr. Volunteer of Yr. Service Award, Community Housing & Service, Distinguished Service Award; [oth. writ.] Booklet of My Thoughts, story Ma, I wrote It all Down, several poems; [pers.] My mother said to me, Every mother should have a baby girl and I think so too. Most of my writing reflect care and concern for children; [a.] Minneapolis, MN

SCHAUFLER, PATRICIA
[Pen.] Panajack; [b.] August 16, 1935, IL; [p.] Charles and Evelyn Smith; [m.] Edward, December 25, 1977; [ch.] Rita; Terry, Teresa Ann; John; grandchildren: Zac, Michelle, Dylan, Rachel, Julia; [ed.] Associate Degree in Science, working on student - BA in Science. Certified CMT, ART; [occ.] College student at Southern Nevada Community College; [memb.] The American Association for Medical Transcription; American Health Information Association; English Club; Phi Theta Kappa, Student Health Information Technology Assoc; [hon.] Dean's List 1990-1994; Student of the Month 1994. Ambassador for Phi Theta Kappa 1993-1994; [oth. writ.] Local newspaper. Several stories and poems published in, "The Lyceum Spotlight". Also for National Spiritualist Assoc of Churches; [pers.] I write to express my love for family, friends, God and strangers I haven't met yet. I feel I need to express positive thoughts to all who seek; [a.] Las Vegas, NV

SCHEFLER, LISA
[Pen.] Ricki; [b.] April 15, 1977, New York; [p.] Arthur and Maria Schafler; [ed.] Palm Springs North Elem. Miami Lakes Middle Junior High, American Senior High; [occ.] Student; [memb.] Future Homemakers of America; [hon.] Do The Right Thing Award, Several Awards in Citizenship and English; [pers.] Influences have been many, my parents, my teachers and my friends but, my most important has been my mother for she taught me to never let anything or one stand in the way of my dreams.; [a.] Pialean, FL

SCHEUTZOW, WILLIAM
[b.] October 12, 1971, Cleveland, OH; [p.] William and Geraldine; [m.] Divorced; [ch.] William III, Paige Marie Scheutzow; [pers.] A person experiences many good and bad situations in their lifetime. A wise person takes this knowledge and learns from it. Note: life is what inspires my writing and music.; [a.] Parma, OH

SCHILLER, MALAIKA
[b.] May 5, 1984, Washington, DC; [p.] Libambu Schillert and John Schiller; [ed.] 5th grade; [occ.] Student; [hon.] Reflections contest; [oth. writ.] Poems and stories; [a.] Arlington, VA

SCHIMMING, JACOB DANIEL
[b.] April 3, 1976, Fort Atkinson, WI; [p.] Laurie and Steve Rohloff, David Schimming; [ed.] Lomira High School, Lomira WI, Nogales High School, Nogales, AZ; [occ.] Student; [hon.] Honor Roll Student numerous times, awarded 2 metals for academic achievement, won 2nd place for 2D mixed media in the 1991 Fond du Lac Noon Optimist Junior Art Exhibit.; [pers.] Strive for a little bit of perfection in everything you do.; [a.] Rio Rico, AZ

SCHLADWEILER, SISTER MARY JOYCE
[b.] August 6, 1913, Farmer, S.D.; [p.] Joseph and Anna Schladweiler; [ed.] Bachelor of Philosophy, Cardinal Stritch College, Milw., Reading Specialist from University of Chicago (Master's Degree); [occ.] Adult Education (One-on-One); [memb.] WSRA, Wis. State Rdg. Assoc.; IRA, International Rdg. Assoc.,; [hon.] Teacher of the Month, Today's Catholic Teacher May, 1977; Awards from Nat'l Library of Poetry; [oth. writ.] Articles for WSRA Journal for Reading Teacher, for Journal of Reading; Catholic School Journal (out of print now); [pers.] Education is work and pays off dividends well, for time and eternity, or the human mind is a most precious resource, waste it not.; [a.] Milwaukee, WI

SCHLESINGER, IRVING
[Pen.] "Red"; [b.] April 22, 1922, New York, NY; [p.] Charles and Clara; [m.] Helen Schlesinger, May 24, 1945; [ch.] Alan Henry, Charles Steven; [ed.] High School Graduate, Abraham Lincoln H.S., Brooklyn, NY; [occ.] Retired; [memb.] 1st Marine Div. Assn, Marine Corps League, Disabled American Veterans, Tamaral Veterans Committee, Vars, Vaeac Sr. Albany, Ny; [hon.] 12,000 Hours Voluntary Duty, Veterans Affairs Voluntary Service; [oth. writ.] To my wife on her birthday. A Volunteers Desire; [pers.] It is far greater to give than to receive; [a.] Tamarac, FL

SCHMIDT, AUDREY C.
[Pen.] Maiden name, Cazzetta, grandfather changed to Caserta; [b.] January 31, 1923, Chalmette, LA; [p.] Cecila Riess and Daniel Cazzetta; [m.] Louis J. Schmidt, August 10, 1941; [ch.] 4, 6 grandchildren, 1 great grandchild; [occ.] Housewife and Painter; [hon.] Sold paintings, but never entered a contest before of any kind.

SCHMITZ, GEORGIANA
[Pen.] Georgie; [b.] November 14, 1938, Cicero, IL; [p.] Goerge and Connie Hradecky; [m.] Lawrence A. Schmity, February 11, 1961; [ch.] Jeffrey Joseph, Kevin Michael; [oth. writ.] Several poems: in a book: Words in Motion from a Bleeding Heart, in memory of Erica; Book: Tomorrow Never Came.; [pers.] Showing how art can come from adversity and pain.; [a.] Westchester, IL

SCHNEIDER, EVELYN S.
[Pen.] Evelyn Schneider; [b.] April 26, 1923, Cleveland, OH; [p.] Deceased; [m.] July 10, 1949, Deceased; [ch.] Francine Katz and Steven Schneider; [ed.] High School, 2 yrs. night school George Washington, D.C.; [occ.] Retired; [memb.] ORT, City of Hope; [oth. writ.] About 100 or more poems; [pers.] Worked as Administrative Secretary in Budget Bureau, Executive Office of the President, knew Vice President Henry Wallace, helped to set up the Embassy of Israel when recognition come from UN; [oth. writ.] Washington, D.C.

SCHOENITZ, SANDRA L.
[b.] March 20, 1971, McClure Ohio; [p.] Heinz and Judy Schoenitz; [ch.] Ashley Nichole; [ed.] Fayetteville Technical Community College, Robeson Community College; [occ.] full time Nursing Student (RCC); [memb.] American Heart Assoc., BAP; [hon.] President's List (RCC); [oth. writ.] Book, Passage Through The Broken Chain; [pers.] Special thanks to Sam Zahran for inspiring me. You have shown me the true beauty of literature.; [a.] Fayetteville, NC

SCHRAMM, MODINE G.
[b.] September 23, 1917, Lydia, SC; [p.] Duncan and Naoma Galloway; [m.] Dr. Robert J. Schramm, March 6, 1943, (deceased); [ed.] Lydia High School, Bowens Business College, B.S., Columbia, S.C., Lake Erie College, B.A., Painesville, Ohio; Eastern Connecticut State Univ., M.A.; [occ.] Retired; [memb.] American Name Society, League of Women Voters, AARP, National Committee to Preserve Social Security and Medicare, Member of Greater Hartsville (S.C.) Chamber of Commerce); [oth. writ.] Articles in the Willimantic chronicle (Newspaper), Willimantic, Ct., plus some poetry. Two articles in the Connecticut Onomastic Review, a branch of American Name Society; [pers.] If life hand you lemons, make sweetened lemonade.; [a.] Hartsville, SC

SCHUETT, KURT C.
[b.] August 6, 1974, Oak Park, IL; [p.] Arthur and Crystal Schuett; [ed.] St. Paul's Lutheran; Lyons Township High School; Culver-Stockton College; [occ.] College Student; [memb.] Lambda Chi Alpha Fraternity, Culver Stockton College Baseball Team, IFC (Inter-Fraternity Council at Culver-Stockton); [hon.] Myron F. Johnson Scholarship, Shannon Hall Scholarship, Phi Eta Sigma, Dean's List, Creative writing student of the Year, Outstanding Pledge Scholarship Award; [oth. writ.] Several poems recently submitted to local college anthologies; published work in the American Goat.; [pers.] I attempt to write and create material that "anyone and everyone can enjoy; I also tend to lean towards the comical and sensual aspects of human nature in my writing, "Crayola" was an interesting "new" theme for me.; [a.] Canton, MO

SCHULMAN, DAVID
[b.] January 3, 1969; [p.] George and Patti Schulman; [occ.] Business Owner, Lawn Maintenance, Landscape; [oth. writ.] A collection of poems from which wondrous things came. A short story entitled The Tree.; [pers.] The Lord Jesus has changed my life and given me a peace that only He could give. It is my desire to give Him the glory through my writing. He has given me the ability. If you enjoyed this oem, praise God and seek Him in all things!; [a.] Fairfax, VA

SCHULZ, ODRA TWYLITA CURRY
[b.] September 1, 1947, Custer, KY; [p.] Raymond and Louise Curry; [ch.] Troy Daniel DeMuth; [ed.] Jefferson Community College, Lou., KY; [occ.] Registered Nurse; [oth. writ.] Long poems and short stories; [pers.] My mother encouraged my artistic and creative ability. She herself was talented. My brothers and sisters tell me I'm good. My son is always supportive. My thanks to all of my family.; [a.] Louisville, KY

SCHWARTZ, ERIC
[b.] December 31, 1971, East Chicago, IN; [p.] Ward and Bessie Schwartz; [ed.] West Aurora High School, Waubonsee Community College, College of Dupage; [occ.] Clean houses; [memb.] Comedy Troupe, "Strange's" Band: "Jack"; [oth. writ.] This is my first publication I have written several unpublished one act plays, a screen play called "Romancing Death" and have written countless comedy sketches and song lyrics.; [pers.] Try to be good to each other.; [a.] Aurora, IL

SCHWARTZ, NETTIE YANOFF
[b.] October 19, 1909, Louisville, KY; [p.] Hyman and Bessie Yanoff; [m.] Sol Percy Schwartz, July 5, 1932; [ch.] Jean Trager, Neil M. Schwartz, Susan Cohen; [ed.] BS degree, Univ of Louisville 1957, Master of Education, May 1976, Louis Art Center - Center for Photographic Studies; [occ.] Retired Writer - artist; [memb.] National Council of Jewish Women - Life member Hadassah - Life Member Mizarchi; Ky Teachers Retirement Org; [hon.] State Chairman of KY for Youth Art Month 1971; won National Grand Youth Art Month - $500 cash award for promoting art education in KY, only junior high school art teacher in KY to serve with 28 art teachers administrators and college personnel, KY Art Education Council 1972; [oth. writ.] Painting with a needle - Doubleday and Co 1972-6mo later went into 2nd printing. Written: Ancient Crafts/for Modern Times - 20 crafts in history of each. Been around world 2 times, writing about travels; "Poetry and Verses for Children", "More Truth than Poetry", "Happiness for all Ages" and more on word processor. is my therapy since stroke.; [a.] Louisville, KY

SCIOLLI, GABRIEL
[b.] December 10, 1935, Geneva, Switzerland; [occ.] Economist; [oth. writ.] Three books of poetry in Italian, author's mother language. P.S. Spleen written originally in English; [a.] Bethesda, MD

SCOTT, SUSAN G.
[b.] April 5, 1961, Dallas, TX; [p.] Bill and Gavy Lumpkin; [m.] Delroy E. Scott, July 9, 1988; [ed.] Mesquite High School, Eastfield Jr College; [pers.] Poetry can set off a range of emotions. It can be inspiring, uplifting, or just plain sad. But as long as a poem makes you feel something, it has done it's job; [a.] McMinnville, OR

SCOTT, TEKEAH CHARLIKA
[Pen.] Charlika and Chipmunk; [b.] September 15, 1980, Washington, DC; [p.] Towona Scott and Charles Kirksey; [ed.] Orr Elementary and Francis Jr. High Higher Achievement Program (HAP) (7 yrs); [occ.] Volunteer Tutor (Biology) Francis Jr. High School, Washington, DC; [memb.] Francis Jr. High School - Choir, Drama Club, Foreign Language Club; Tutoring Program (Biology), Basketball Team and the Alpha Phi Kappa Beta Sorority; [hon.] 1994 - 1st place poster contest at Francis Jr. High. 1991 and 1992 2nd place Oratorical Contest - City Wide ($300.00 Savings Bond Each); [oth. writ.] Various short poems and essays for contests; [pers.] In the mist of the violence in our society with adolescents in my age group (14) killing each other, I strive to reflect positiveness through my writings, the oratorical speeches I've given, as well as, the speeches I plan to give in the future. I will continue to give something back to my peers by volunteering my time as a tutor (biology), assisting students that are less biologically inclined. I have been greatly influenced by the arts (all kinds), which I feel makes it possible to laugh in a sometimes frowning world; [a.] Washington, DC

SEAMAN, EILEEN A.
[b.] May 29, 1961, Elmira, NY; [p.] Donald and Rita Seaman; [ed.] Nazareth College of Rochester, BS, Syracuse Univ, MS; [memb.] American Speech - language, Hearing Assoc, Our Lady of Lourdes Religious Education Teacher; [hon.] Who's Who Among Students in American Universities and Colleges, Magna Cum Laude degrees; [oth. writ.] Several pieces in Nazareth College's Literary magazine Verity; [pers.] Live one day at a time and make it a masterpiece; [a.] Elmira, NY

SEARLES, FRANCES
[b.] June 6, 1948, Phila., PA; [p.] Charles and Catherine Searles; [ch.] David Maurice Royster; [ed.] Attended Weber State College and Community College of Phila.; [occ.] Typist and Admin. Office Worker; [memb.] Holy Tabernacle Ministries and others; [hon.] Received award for Outstanding Achievement or IBM Keyboard printers and computers from United States Airforce; [oth. writ.] Since being inspired by the National Library of Poetry I've written other poems such as when the wind blows, unborn child, knowledge which I hope I'll be able to publish soon.; [pers.] I cam from a family of 5 sisters and two brothers. My brother Charles Searles is a well known famous artist in Phila.; [a.] Phila., PA

SEELIG, IRA C.
[b.] QQueens, NY; [p.] Gus - Rose Seelig; [ch.] Charles, Gwendolyn; grandchildren (8) - Sean, Sara Slattery, Roxanne Dugan; [occ.] Retired NY City Police Officer. My youth was spent overseas during World War II. I spend my time painting and writing; [hon.] My poetry has been read in public - re: The Sculptors Guild "A Salute To New York"; [oth. writ.] Thought - Rhyme - Comment. "Ode To A Silent Wall", "Valid Measure", etc; [pers.] I hope my poetry will give solace to others; [a.] Douglaston, NY

SELKIRK JR., ALEXANDER M.
[b.] October 2, 1943, Jamaica, New York City; [p.] Alex and Anne Selkirk; [m.] Joanne P. Selkirk, July 21, 1976; [ch.] Marianne C. and Victoria L. Selkirk; [ed.] Saint John's Univ., B.A. Political Science 1965; New York Law School Juris Doctor 1970; New York University School of Law, Master of Flaws in Trade Regulation 1973; [memb.] NYS Bar Asso., Suffolk County Bar Assoc., N.Y. Army National Guard, and many others; [hon.] Winner Nathan Burkan memorial Competition at NY Law School 1968 & 1969, NYS Civil Service Employees Assoc., Brotherhood Essay Award 1969, Named in Who's Who in American Law, Who's Who in the east, International Men of Achievement, International Who's Who of Intellectuals; [oth. writ.] Articles published in New York State Bar Assoc. Journal, Nassau Lawyer, Cases and Comment, Ronkonkoma review, Our Place; [pers.] My poem is dedicated to all the unselfish people who generously donate blood to save the life of others and to the blood service who tirelessly labor to make the precious gift of life available to all who need it.; [a.] Holbrook, NY

SELLARS, EVE
[b.] April 19, 1953, Cairo, Georgia; [p.] betty and Odysseas Sellars; [ed.] Studied business at MPC (Monterey); [occ.] Promoter of Celebrity Invitational that benefit charities.; [hon.] Started Eve Shampoo at age 17 that became a major contender in the Health Food Industry.; [oth. writ.] The Little Orphan Piglet, The Watermelon Dream, The Falling Star, The Sugar Tree, Melancholy Butterfly, A Day at the Beach; [pers.] It is important that we remember we are spiritual beings first. I find peace in my knowledge of this when my moral being is perturbed!; [a.] Tiburon, CA

SELTZ, DORIS M.
[b.] April 30, 1933, NYC; [p.] Hazel and John Murray; [m.] David D. Seltz, December 29, 1962; [ch.] David, Anne, Laura; [ed.] BA Wellesley 1955; [occ.] Disabled, Aroke '89; [oth. writ.] Column in a Sew Business Magazine for 10 yrs.

SERAFIN, JASON KENNETH
[b.] September 28, 1971; Paterson, NJ; [p.] Frank and Sandra Serafin; [ed.] Garfield High School, Kean College of New Jersey (Union, NJ); [occ.] Computer System Technologist, Roseland, NJ; Influences: Edgar Allan Poe; James Douglas Morrison; [hon.] NJ All State First Team Football: Defensive End; 4-time Dean's List; Most influential open poetry speaker (within Kean College's) "writing poetry" class); [oth. writ.] Several hundred poems, ideas, quotes, short stories and my personal opinions on certain feelings and behaviors of myself and others; [pers.] My poems are aimed to influence and penetrate inner most feelings and thoughts. If my particular writings influence at least one person, than my personal goal is obtained. I would like to thank my parents, my brother - Frank, and sister - Jolene and lastly - a true friend who has inspired and encouraged me to publish my poems, Frank Kurdyla; [a.] Garfield, NJ

SERKLAND, DAN
[pers.] i have to go to school, i have to go to work, i have to pay for my car, i have to go to college; i feel trapped and life is a cage.

SHAFER, JOYCE E.
[b.] August 3, 1928, Wisner, LA; [p.] Alva and Lester Evans; [m.] Deceased; [ch.] Beaux, JoLynn and Al Davis; [occ.] Retired, Co-ordinate Children's Bible Club, Hospital Visitation, Sing with a group that travels called God's Recycled Angels, Writing Children's Book.; [pers.] To live the balance of my life for others and pass on my christian Heritage to children in a stressful world.; [a.] Pineville, LA

SHAHEEN, MAHDI A.
[b.] January 15, 1962, Saudi Arabia; [p.] A.F. Shaheen and Sadia Shaheen; [m.] Divorced, July 8, 1988; [ed.] B.S. Management Information Systems, University of Arizona, Tucson, AZ, May of 1985; [occ.] Vice-President for Body Nature'l Inc., Brownsville, TX; [memb.] Brownsville Chamber of Commerce on the Board for International Business Development.; [oth. writ.] Unconditional love, tec. about 30 poems and short stories, also commercials made for T.V. I hope I will be discovered by some producers to publish all my writings.; [pers.] There are a lot of great people out there but the sad part, that we all afraid to come out of our shell and get hurt, but we have to take a chance in life, one way or another. Life is to short to live in fear.; [a.] Harlinger, TX

SHANFIELD, LOUISE S.
[Pen.] Louise Sprague; [b.] July 30, 1926, Yardville, NJ;[p.] Sterling and Hazel Sprague; [m.] William Shanfield; [ch.] Linda Bosse, Wayne Dunfee; [ed.] Upper Freehold Regional High School, Selective Insurance School; [occ.] Retired Insurance Broker; [memb.] Trustee Allentown United Methodist Church, Past State President N. J. Mutual Insurance Women; [hon.] N.J. Insurance Woman Award, Grand Prize Winner "Heart of Dreams" Poetry Anthology; [oth. writ.] Several poems published in various anthologies.; [pers.] I want to share the message of my heart with the reading public. Toghert let us enhance the joy of living.; [a.] Princeton, NJ

SHANHOLTZER, SHARON J.
[b.] December 27, 1954, Euclid, OH; [p.] Eugene and Doris Shanholtzer; [p.]: William Werkley; [ch.] Shane and Aimee Obuchon; [ed.] South Plantation High School, Sheridan Vocational (Florida); [occ.] Assistant - Crowe Rope, Warren, ME; [pers.] I wrote this poem for a man I met 19 yrs ago and had not been in touch with in 17 yrs until this last May, 1994. He is now my partner/lover and we're together again - I'd also like to thank my parents for all their love and support. I love you!; [a.] Union, ME

SHANNON, ETHEL M.
[b.] Fremond, OH; [p.] Edith Laura and Albert Merl Bauders; [m.] Married; [ch.] Two; [memb.] Baycrafters; [pers.] I enjoy watercolor painting, sewing, gardening and miniatures. I have been interested in poetry since grade school. A favorite poem is Trees. I am inspired to write about the beauty of the outdoors.; [a.] Bay Village, OH

SHAPIRO, HAROLD
[b.] 1942, New York; [p.] George, Frances; [m.] Rochelle Lee, 1978; [ch.] Brett, Jonathan; [ed.] M.S. Brooklyn College; [occ.] Teacher; [a.] Woodmere, NY

SHARP, DIANA LYNN
[b.] March 20, 1956, Canton, IL; [p.] Clyde D. Hill and Evla Lee Hill; [m.] Robert K. Scharp, October 4, 1986; [ed.] Canton Senior High School, Associate of Art, Spoon River College, Bachelor of Arts, Augustana College; [occ.] Flight Attendant for Transworld Airlines; [memb.] Alpha Phi Omega Alumni; [hon.] Deans List; [oth. writ.] An original poem "You" was selected and set to music by the Canton Senior High Chorus, it was performed in concert.; [a.] Bridgeton, MO

SHARP-D'ESOPO, CHERYL
[Pen.] Cheryl Sharp; [b.] October 7, 1947, Boston, MA; [p.] Charles and Mary Munroe; [m.] Mr. Sandy D'Esopo, October 7, 1989; [ch.] Cora S. Sharp; [ed.] Cambridge High and Lation, Northeastern University, University of Hartford.; [occ.] Director of Facilities, Hartford Region YWCA; [memb.] Leadership Greater Hartford Alumni Association, The Recovery Club.; [oth. writ.] One of my poems was selected for a poetry reading at the Greater Hartford Arts Festival.; [pers.] Writing is an emotional cathartic for me. I write because I have so many stories to tell.; [a.] Windsor, CT

SHARRAR, MARC
[b.] August 7, 1972, New Cumberland, PA; [p.] Thomas and Dyanne Sharrar; [ed.] Stroudsburg High School, Penn State University, Dean's List; [occ.] Student; [oth. writ.] Several poems published in magazines.; [pers.] I think of life as a series of lessons that furthers our understanding of ourselves and the world around us. I try to capture these moments in my writing and reflect upon how these lessons affect us.; [a.] Hagerstown, MD

SHASKEVICH, MICHAEL
[b.] January 25, 1929, Dubrovnik; [p.] Vladimir and Smiljka; [m.] Anna; [ch.] Helen and Nicholas; [ed.] M.A. University of Wisconsin, Madison, Wisc.; [occ.] Retired; [oth. writ.] Several books in Yugoslavian Language. Number of poems and stories in newspapers.; [pers.] Quiet family man.; [a.] Clicops, IL

SHAW, MELVIN J.
[b.] March 22, 1918, Bovard, PA; [p.] Melvin Joseph, Edith May; [m.] (1) Helen Guba, (2) Ruth Jones; [ch.]

Bonnie Louise, Brian Paul, Brad Michael; [ed.] High school; [occ.] Retired from Air Force and Postal Service; [memb.] Air Force Sergeants Assoc and AARP; [pers.] Mother Nature wants all of us to stop and smell her flowers. If we do that, maybe then we will stop harming her; [a.] Utica, NY

SHEFFNER, ZORAH E.
[b.] February 8, 1910, Lithuania; [p.] Julius and Eva; [m.] Betty; c Yahdi and Edwin; [ed.] Civil and Structural Engineer; [occ.] Consulting Structural Engineer; [memb.] Structural Engineer Assoc., of Southern California; [oth. writ.] Several papers on engineering problems at international conferences.; [pers.] It is never too late.; [a.] Los Angeles, CA

SHELTON, TIM
[b.] March 28, 1967, Aurora, IL; [p.] Bonita Coffman Shelton and Glenn Shelton; [ed.] Oswego High School, MacCorrmac Jr. College, College of Du Page; [occ.] Press Operator; [memb.] Du Page Art League; [hon.] Various places of ribbons in the Illinois Sandwich Fair 1981-1994; [oth. writ.] This is my first published piece but have years of others all about.; [pers.] Thanks to my friends and family for your love, inspiration and honesty, to aspiring poets, look to life music and your imagination for your poems. Never be afraid to show off your work and always try like hell.; [a.] Montgomery, IL

SHERMAN, ROBERT
[b.] January 7, 1952, Hawthorne, CA; [p.] Harry Sherman, Rosalie Sherman; [m.] Phunsi Sherman, June 1, 1984; [ch.] Brian and Keith; [ed.] Inglewood High El Camino Junior College, UCLA extension; [occ.] California Certified Nursery Professional Armstrong Garden Center; [memb.] Greater South Bay Audiophile Society, Los Angeles County Arboretum; [hon.] Police Involvement Award. Aided Police in apprehending a suspect; [pers.] I enjoy writing poetry because it is an avenue for sharing my feelings with other people; [a.] Walnut, CA

SHERRELL, MICHAEL WINSTON
[b.] June 6, 1950, Chicago, IL; [p.] Robert and Katie Sherrell; [m.] Laverne Sherrell, January 17, 1980; [ch.] Jennifer Sherrell; [ed.] De La Salle Inst, Wilson Jr College, US Army, Kennedy King Jr College, Chicago St Univ; [occ.] Juvenile Attendant, Cook County Juvenile Detention Center; [oth. writ.] Short fiction unpublished stories; [a.] Chicago, IL

SHIN, MARIE
[b.] May 16, 1982, Burlingame; [p.] Chung Shin and Young Hu Shin; [ed.] I'm a seventh grader at St. Robert's School, located in San Bruno in San Mateo County; [hon.] I won the Milbrae Lions Club essay contest in fifth grade and I won again in 6th grade. In fifth I won 1st place, and in 6th I won Honorable Mention; [pers.] I am a cheerful talkative person. I detest boring lectures and math. My poems or stories are usually inspired by my teachers or my hyper friends.; [a.] San Bruno, CA

SHINE, BARBARA J.
[b.] June 13, 1944, San Francisco, CA; [p.] Jesse Luther Shine and Iva Frances Dombrow; [ch.] Amy, Gary, Michael Leffingwell; [ed.] Fresno City College, Fresno, CA; Univ of Alaska, Anchorage, AK; [occ.] Accountant; [memb.] American Society of Women Accountants; [hon.] ASWA Scholarship 1994; [oth. writ.] Great poems of the Western World, vol II pg 319 "Growing Pains" under Barbara Peterson; [a.] Anchorage, AK

SHIVPRASAD, GHIRE CHANDRA
[Pen.] Leon; [b.] October 22, 1977, New Amsterdam (Guyana); [p.] Cyril and Merlin Shivprasad; [ed.] High School Grad, Attained eight subjects at the Caribbean Examination Council Exam; [occ.] Cashier; [hon.] Honored along with others, all five years high school as 80% and above student; [pers.] I try to make myself and most of all my family happy in everything I do. I have been greatly influenced by those who worked hard to achieve their goals despite the race and nationality, God bless them; [a.] Richmond Hill Queens, NY

SHORS (II), JOHN
[b.] March 4, 1969, Des Moines, IA; [p.] John and Patsy; [ed.] Colorado College - BA in English (1991); [occ.] Writer; [oth. writ.] I have recently completed the fantasy novel Moonset Over Dryden, which will be available in August of 1995 (Northwest Publishing Inc). This novel is the culmination of several years work and I have high hopes for its success. Currently I am in the midst of writing an account of my extensive travels throughout Asia; [pers.] Prior to living in the orient for two years, I was fortunate enough to visit many other regions of the world. Time spent abroad has influenced my writing in a number of ways. Equally important, it has given me the insight to appreciate much of the freedoms that Americans (myself included) often take for granted. With this enlightenment also comes the knowledge that America still has a great deal of problems all of which need our immediate attention; [a.] Des Moines, IA

SHORT, LINDA
She is a lifelong resident of Princeton, West Virginia and derives her ideas from her husband, the Asst Chief and a volunteer fireman with the East River Volunteers for over 25 yrs. She has a collection of poetry, all dedicated to the "Greatest Fire-fighters Alive - The Fighting 105". Her inspiration came from her sister-in-law who lost her battle with cancer in 1993 and always believed in her abilities to accomplish her dreams.

SHORTRIDGE, BEULAH DAVIS
[b.] August 25, 1934, Grundy, VA; [p.] Coy and Laura Dawson Davis; [m.] Edd H. Shortridge, November 18, 1955; [ch.] David, Rebecca, Douglas; [ed.] High School, 2 yrs. bible College have taught Sunday School for 42 years in the same church; [occ.] Homemaker and volunteer work.; [memb.] Have been active in PTA of our schools, having served as an officer; [oth. writ.] I write many things, mostly poetry and short articles. I have written a 3 act play, "Ruth of the Plains" about my early life and my desires.; [pers.] I try to write to encourage and inspire those who read to be the very best possible. I must feel inspired to write before it is effective. My desire is to help those who are hurting. I now help out a Funeral Home owned by my youngest son. It was for him that I wrote this poem. This had been his life's dream. This became a reality last year. I, along with my family, attend the Fookland Pentecostal Church where we are charter members.; [a.] Vansant, VA

SHOTTS, QUIENTANA L.
[Pen.] Sunnie Grace; [b.] December 29, 1970, Amory, Miss.; [p.] Larry W. and Melissa Shotts; [ed.] General Education Diploma; [occ.] Little Debbie Snack Cake Distributor; [memb.] Church; [pers.] With Jesus as my personal savior I am enlightened to express my view of the wonderful life he has give me.; [a.] Hamilton, AL

SHUMAKER, REGINA
[b.] August 23, 1976, Milford, MA; [p.] Virginia

Barreiro; Bill Miller (step); [ed.] Norfolk Agricultural High School; [memb.] North Shore Animal League, Columbia House Record Club; [hon.] School's Honors Programs (Teens on Privileges (T.O.P.S.J); F.F.A. (Future Farmers of America) Green Hand Award, numerous first place ribbons at county firs.; [oth. writ.] A few other poems. All unpublished, a school poem entitled "The Search;" [pers.] When I write I write about what I know and how I feel. I don't write often, but when I do, it's mostly on the spur of the moment. I can't dwell on what I write until I finish writing because if I do, I might lose the poems meaning.; [a.] Milford, MA

SIEGFRIED, RHONDA K.
[b.] September 30, 1968; [p.] Rev. and Mrs. Robert Wittlinger; [m.] David A. Siegfried, Jr, April 28, 1990; [ch.] (son) Jesse A. Siegfried; [ed.] Susquenita High School, Thomas Inst Business School; [occ.] Text prep operator, PA Blue Shield, Camp Hill, PA; [memb.] St. Paul's Lutheran Church; [a.] Duncannon, PA

SIEMON, LULA M.
[b.] June 24, 1912, KY; [p.] Chas and Nancy Shaw; [m.] NM Siemon, July 3, 1930; [ch.] 6; [ed.] Eighth grade; [occ.] Housewife/widow.

SIFORD, SANDRA L.
[b.] January 16, 1952, Indiana, PA; [p.] Anthony Menoskey and Helen Gromley; [m.] Paul O. Siford, September 24, 1980; [ch.] Nicole Marie and Paula Jo (stepchildren); [ed.] Purchase Line High School - Class of 70; [oth. writ.] This is my first; [pers.] I enjoy poetry and writing it. I usually write about the things that are happening around me. In this case, the death of my youngest brother, Dave, and explaining death and angels to his son, Branden; [a.] Cherry Tree, PA

SILBERGELD, SAM
[b.] March 1, 1918, Wengrov, Poland; [p.] Frieda and Hyman Silbergeld, June 22, 1952; [ch.] Four; [ed.] Ph.D U. of IL (Biochemistry), MD, Duke University; [occ.] Semi retired physician, researcher, psychiatrist, university professor; [memb.] Numerous scientific medical organizations; [hon.] Leadership Citation of Blackburn Univ, IL; [oth. writ.] Scientific papers, contributions in newspapers; [pers.] Know thyself; [a.] Garrett Park, MD

SILVER, ALICE MOOLTEN
[b.] October 18, 1935, New York City; [p.] Dr. Sylvan E. Moolten and Dr. Isabel M. London; [m.] Alan Silver, August 14, 1960; [ch.] Daniel Alan 29, Paul London 28; [ed.] Bardard College, P.S. 6 NYC, Highland Park High School; [occ.] Writer, previously Medical Abstracter Laboratory Technician, Administrative Assistant in husband's business.; [memb.] ACLU, NOW, Museum of Natural History, NYC; [hon.] Piano Audition Award, Newark, NJ approx. 1950.; [oth. writ.] Published in Philosophical Library, co-author scientific medical articles and many other publications; [pers.] Political and medical background, grandfather Socialist Congressman from Lower East Side, NYC, parents Physicians. I am vitally interested not only in idealistic principles but also in humanistic behavior man's humanity to man.; [a.] Highland Park, NJ

SILVERMAN, RALPH J.
[b.] May 2, 1912, Providence, RI; [p.] Dora and Harry Silverman; [m.] Late Sarah Altagen in June 1925; [ch.] Arnold Nathan silverman married to Barbara (Fox) Silverman, One Daughter married, three children two boys one girl; one son Mark Married to Joan, Bruce

Stanly, two daughters Sara and Lanee; [ed.] Self educated, courses in writing, history, literature; [memb.] B'nai B'rith was International Commissioner continuing education. President on local levels, Editor B'nai B'rith Bulletin; President of the San Francisco Humanities, Inc anon profit foundation, Master of Starr King Lodge FAAM (masons); Awards from State Senate for activity in commemorating the Holocaust. Active in the community; [oth. writ.] Some essays, mostly poems: Egotist, Noise The Wind Random Thoughts, Morning, The Ship On The Horizon..; [pers.] I study (do not practice) mysticism write somewhat in that vein am looking to condense the essence of life within twenty lines.

SILVIA, JUDY MURR
[b.] Wausau, WI; [ch.] Lien Jr. and Scott; [ed.] Striving to complete my degree in International Development Management; [occ.] Commercial Leasing Agent; [memb.] National Peace Corps Assoc., and Returned Peace Corps Volunteers of Washington. Council of Commercial Realtors, International Committee.; [hon.] Honor Student, Board Member, Council of Commercial Realtors; [pers.] I enjoy writing poetry about our spiritual life and strive to reflect God's goodness.; [a.] Fairfax, VA

SIMES, R. PATRICK
[b.] March 5, 1967, Ephrata, PA; [p.] Mr. and Mrs. Robert Simes; [m.] Fiancee Laura White; [ch.] Tiffany and Sasha; [ed.] National Registry of EMT/Paramedic Wilkes University; [occ.] Full time student, self employed painter; [memb.] Registry of National EMT/Paramedic, March of Dimes, Red Cross; [hon.] Dean's List; [oth. writ.] "Trespassing" (poem), "Progress" (short story); [pers.] Writing with complete openness, places no limits upon a writer.; [a.] Nanticoke, PA

SIMMONS, OMAR
[Pen.] Oskee; [b.] February 16, 1968, Phila, PA; [ch.] Cherelle Simmons; [oth. writ.] Many other poems and songs; [pers.] Children are neither good or bad they only follow their Host, could be TV, parents or radio which ever they see the most; [a.] Phila, PA

SIMMS, STACHA TEXON
[b.] October 6, 1974, Brooklyn; [oth. writ.] Written 91 poems in 3 years, "Not Yet Lone," first publication so far.; [pers.] I write of who people want to be and who I really am.; [a.] New York, NY

SIMONSON, MARK A.
[b.] July 28, 1953, Bronx, NY; [p.] Addison and Ernestine Simonson; [m.] Valerie L. Simonson, July 28, 1990; [ch.] Natasha, William, Terrance; [ed.] Evander Child's High School, Trinity Valley Community College, Ventura College, Hofstra University; [occ.] Placement Director Concorde Career Institute, Studio City, CA; [memb.] Fortune Society; [oth. writ.] Prisoners of Love, locally published.; [pers.] The world's future is dedicated by our past and present. To know where we are going, as a result of the past, we need to consult our seniors.; [a.] Hicksville, NY

SIMPSON, LEE ANN MARIE
[Pen.] Annie; [b.] December 17, 1961, Des Moines, IN; [p.] Carolyn Jeffries (McAllen, TX); [m.] Dennis Michael Simpson (Prof. Musician) December 10, 1993; [ch.] Amanda Gail, Derek Michael, Keith Allen; [ed.] McAllen High, Business Administration, Lenexa, KS, English Major Sedalis, MO, Fluent in Spanish and too analytical for my own good.; [occ.] Central Missouri

News, Sedalia, Missouri; [oth. writ.] I have compiled years of poetry and other styles of writing or better worded, I might say much of my life has been lived out-instrumental of pen and paper. I have never tried to publish a writing.; [pers.] A poet is a person who is alone in many ways, who struggles desperately within himself to resolve or understand life's meaning and through poetry he is able to reach out and share his experiences, not always offering hope or answers but simply revealing a very personal option of coping.; [a.] Sedalia, MO

SINCLAIR, LILY
[m.] Widow; [ch.] One son, three daughters; [ed.] Life; [occ.] Designer and Art Collector; [memb.] Museum Trustee; [oth. writ.] I am an artist internally feeling the world as painted with vivid colorful strokes, hearing its sounds as rhythms and movements.; [pers.] Poetry for me is the brushstroke of the word.; [a.] San Francisco, Woodside, CA

SINGH, KRISHNADAI
[p.] Kris Singh; [b.] November 11, 1960, Guyana; [p.] Rampersand and Mahadai Singh; [ed.] Univ of Guyana; CPA, State of MD; [occ.] Accountant; [oth. writ.] Poems and short stories not published; [pers.] I like to write about life's experiences, to which anyone can relate. My influences were primarily the English poets of the 19th and early 20th century; [a.] Rockville, MD

SINGLEY, LEE
[b.] November 11, 1975, Houston, TX; [p.] Cora Holley; [ed.] Franklin County High, Patrick Henry Community College; [oth. writ.] Poems published in Franklin County High School's Literary Magazine throughout high school. Published in the Animo, 1994 edition of FCHS annual; [pers.] Never stop dreaming - a child's dreams become an adults realities; [a.] Henry, VA

SINKFORD, ROBIN MARIA
[b.] October 18, 1961, Columbus, OH; [p.] Louis and Vivian Sinkford; [ed.] London High School, Central Ohio Joint Vocational School; [occ.] Computer Operator for Ohio Dept. of Transportation; [memb.] Body of Christ Tabernacle Church, Cols., OH; [pers.] I thank Jesus christ, who is the head of my life, for giving me the gift of writing poems. Also, thanks to my pastors: Brian Keith and Donna Williams, for being an inspiration in my life.; [a.] Galloway, OH

SINSABAUGH, FRANCINE
[Pen.] Sinsa Bauah; [b.] September 16, 1928, Paris France; [p.] Milo and Elisabeth Lewis; [m.] Art Sinsabauah, June 1957; [ch.] Elisabeth and Katherine; [ed.] Art Institute of Chicago, Certificate of U of I at Urbana, BA, MA 6th year; [occ.] Teacher, Artist Jr. College, Dest. 118; [memb.] Art Leagues, NEA, Delta Kappa Gamma; [hon.] Many in the Art Filed, Commissions, Shows, etc. None in writing as yet!; [oth. writ.] Several poems to newspapers other Anthologies, use writing as part of my teaching.; [pers.] The little wonders of everyday show me the relationship between us all.; [a.] Dannille, IL

SIRACUSA, MARGARET
[b.] March 19, Ireland; [p.] Daniel and Bridget O'Driscoll; [m.] Vincent Siracusa, May 30, 1970; [ed.] Primary and secondary education in Ireland Nursing School in London, England; [occ.] Registered Nurse - private duty in New York City; [memb.] Member "Research Institute of Self Evolvement"; [pers.] I wish to inspire others to become their true selves and not the self formed by illusions and traditions; [a.] New York, NY

SLAUSON, MICHELLE A.
[b.] March 8, 1954, Long Island, NY; [p.] Irving/Margaret Sack; [occ.] Hotel Service Industry; [pers.] For Scott from whom my inspiration comes.; [a.] Tahoe, CA

SLUSHER, MRS. ELEANOR J.
[p.] John T. and Ethel S. Jones; [m.] J. Kenneth Slusher, June 14, 1941; [ed.] Christiansburg VA High School. Virginia Intermont College, Bristol, VA. Radford Univ, Radford, VA. Bachelor of Science degree. Double language major (English and French). Minor -psychology; [occ.] Homemaker - (retired); [memb.] Hayes Barton Baptist Church, Townsend Couples' Sunday School Class, Round Table Group, Tea and Talk (non-fiction) Book Club Neighborhood Garden Club; [hon.] Sigma Sigma Sigma (Social) Sorority, Pi Gamma Mu - (scholastic sorority), Dean's List, Publication of my poem by National Library of Poetry; [oth. writ.] Essays. Memorials on the death of a person. Resolutions on the retirement of people in public office; [pers.] Interested in all aspects of nature. The beauty of words has always appealed to my mind and heart. They are very important in the total development of a person's life. Words -- poetic words -- are visual encyclopedias of excitement!; [a.] Raleigh, NC

SMALL, THOMAS G.
[b.] November 12, 1956, Tyler, TX; [p.] Robert James and Mary Luins Small; [m.] Marcia G. Flanigan, December 10, 1983; [ed.] Brookline High; Brookline, MA, Cornell University, School of Hotel and Restaurant Management; [occ.] Chef and Organic Food Distributor; [oth. writ.] Collection of poems titled Playing On Waves; [pers.] I strive to initiate recognition that we are all more than brothers: there is no we, just God.; [a.] Charlestown, WV

SMALLEY (SR.), JOE A.
[b.] July 8, 1936, Gallup, NM; [p.] Helen and Royal Smalley; [m.] Divorced, 1957 ended 1990; [ch.] Four boys; [ed.] Four yrs college - no degree; [occ.] Truck Driver - Race Horse Trainer; [memb.] Use to be in the Elks, the Catholic Church, etc. Had to quit them all; [oth. writ.] 2 books started A Period of Time, Whatever Happened to Smalejo; [pers.] I intend to write about life - just the way it was and is now. Peoples feelings for that is the essence of life as I see it; [a.] Milan, MN

SMITH, CAROLYNE
[b.] April 28, 1979, Jacksonville, FL; [p.] Laura Y. and Richard W. Smith; [ed.] Robert E. Lee High School; [memb.] Camp Fire Girls and Boys; [hon.] Best Handwriting in Second Grade in the whole County; [oth. writ.] I keep a book of poems to myself.; [pers.] I write with my feelings and feel with my heart. My heart is filled with love from my friends; Lissa, Leslie, Alex and many more.; [a.] Jacksonville, FL

SMITH, CORY
[b.] August 28, 1994, St. Johns Hospital; [p.] Von and Mary Smith; [ed.] Still in High School; [memb.] FFA, Other Worlds Club, and Brown County Antique, Machinery Assoc.; [hon.] Manner Award, Several for my antique tractor.; [oth. writ.] Crying Black, Ancient in Name, Beast of the Abyss, In Tombed, Immortal Evil; [pers.] I like to bring out the evil side of life; the Black Perils of Death.; [a.] Morkleville, IN

SMITH, DALE, RONALD
[Pen.] Ron Smith, Tin Man; [b.] April 1, 1942, Hot Springs, AR; [p.] Lee Smith, Faye Smith; [m.] Sharon Ann Smith, October 92; [ch.] Tasha, Shannon, Dale Jr; [ed.] Hot Springs High, UAPB, Univ AR Pine Bluff; Computer Drafting Riverside Vo-tech; Computer Accounting Riverside Vo-tech; [occ.] Retired USMC; [memb.] Disabled American Veterans; [oth. writ.] Deer Hunting -- Beginners or Experienced book, also two western books; Revenge of a Halfbreed; MACOBA - The Halfbreed. One song: Heaven for a Home. Various poems and articles; [pers.] I enjoy bringing my readers interest. Their compliments are rewards to me and most certainly a sense of accomplishment; [a.] Lake Hamilton, AR

SMITH, DONNA J.
[b.] October 10, 1953, Akron, OH; [p.] John & Lucille Ford & Craig L. Roberts; [m.] Stanford A. Smith, June 17, 1972; [ch.] Stanford A. Smith II and Lezly N. Smith; [ed.] Buchtel High School and extensive Professional Development courses.; [occ.] Administrative Assistant; [oth. writ.] Several other writings. My writing draws me into my own quiet world reveling my deepest inner being. They are as much a part of me as a physical self.; [a.] Akron, OH

SMITH, ERIC J.
[b.] September 27, 1973, Fairmont, West Virginia; [p.] Laura Smith; [ed.] Currently an undergrad student at Rutgers University in New Jersey; [a.] Whitehouse Station, NJ

SMITH, JACOB D.
[Pen.] Jacob D. Smith; [b.] November 16, 1960, Marrero, LA; [p.] Carolyn Smith and Jacob D. Alwell; [ed.] GED; [pers.] I try to write my poetry with love and care, or sometimes just to make people aware, In life there's always hope, Even though at times it's an uphill slope, Through love and understanding we will complete, An existence where pain and hatred are obsolete.; [a.] Jackson, MS

SMITH, JACQUELINE
[b.] February 24, 1930, Aurora, MO; [p.] Edward D. and Mamie Ruhl; [m.] S. J. Smith, February 8, 1974; [ch.] Dr. R.E. Burnett, Lexington, KY, Mrs. Bill (Jacquie Sue) Evans, Elk Creek, MO; [ed.] Aurora High School; [occ.] Retired from State of Missouri, Court Clerk, Greene County, Springfield, Missouri; [memb.] Association of Retired Missouri State Employees; Southern Baptist Belief.; [oth. writ.] My first entry in poetry contest. Short stories of my childhood which I intend to submit for publication.; [pers.] My sisters, Mrs. June Rushing, Albuquerque, NM and Mrs. Mildred Indermill, Chattanooga, TN (deceased) and I cherished memories of our Christian Parents. They are my inspiration.; [a.] Springfield, MO

SMITH, JEAN
[b.] August 19, 1944, Dallas, TX; [p.] Albert and Edith Gunthrie; [m.] Ken Smith, April 9, 1983; [ch.] Laura Anne, Matthew Kenneth; [ed.] Crozier Tech. High; [occ.] On Special Assignment for Union/Management Venture at AT&T; [memb.] Agape New Testament Church, Communications Workers of America Local 6260; [oth. writ.] A book of unpublished poems.; [pers.] My poems are written from my heart above things I've learned and people I know.; [a.] Quinlan, TX

SMITH, JENNIFER CHRISTOPHER
[b.] May 23, 1980, Chicago, IL; [p.] Robert and Jeanne; [ed.] Sandburg Jr. High, graduated 1994, Culver Woodcraft Camps graduated 1993; [occ.] Student, Culver Girls

Academy; [hon.] Culver Woodcraft Camp, Gold C Award 1993, Culver All Star Soccer Team 1993; [pers.] My poetry is a extension of my personal feelings at the moment as well as feelings and reflections of my experiences.; [a.] Highland Park, IL

SMITH, JOHN WILLIAM
[b.] NY, NY; [m.] Betty Thomas-Smith, 1959; [ch.] Karla, Erick; [ed.] B.A. Sociology, M.A. Education; [occ.] President, Consortium of Small, School Districts, Inc.; [oth. writ.] Recently self-published a series of works on urban life.; [pers.] A poet tries to present life unencumbered by false images, sometimes the poet succeeds.

SMITH, JOSIE GOODRICH
[Pen.] Josie Goodrich Stevens; [b.] November 15, 1896, Maryland; [p.] Marewillis and Katie Goodrich; [m.] December 28, 1928, Deceased; [ed.] B.A. Morgan College, M.A. New York University, Seminars: Yale U., Temple U., Observation, Johns Hopkins, Columbia U.; [occ.] Humanities Institute, Oxford U., Retired; [memb.] Roman Catholic Church, Metropolitan Opera Guilds, MD Historical Society, MD Public Television, Nat. Urban League, Habitat for Humanity; [hon.] Teacher of the Year, First female lecture in parish, First in city to serve on committee to evaluate secondary education, Member of committee to formulate program and select test; [oth. writ.] Teaching Book: English Is A Becoming.., Articles: English Journal, Articles: Balto. Bulletin; Poems in Anthologies, Presentations for Lectures; [pers.] "Of the power expect performance. Unless the student excel the master, civilization dies."; [a.] Baltimore, MD

SMITH, MINETTE
[b.] December 16, 1949, St. Louis, MO; [p.] Fred and Clendell Henry; [m.] Divorced twice; [ch.] Johnny Johnson, Melodie Smith-Wells, Michelle Smith; [ed.] Graduate of Class of 1967 from O'Fallon Technical High School; [occ.] Homemaker; [memb.] Mt. Airy M.B. Church, Poets Alley Workshop of St. Louis, MO, Director, Shirley Lefleur. I am 1st Vice President of the Mt. Airy M.B. Mission Society, Rev. Charles J. Brown Sr., Pastor; [hon.] Recognition as a Sunday School Teacher of the Mt. Airy M.B. Church; [oth. writ.] Several poems and a Christmas play that are unpublished.; [pers.] My life is in the Lord's hands. My writing style has been reborn like my lifestyle. My poems are Holy Ghost inspired with reference to God's Holy Word.; [a.] St. Louis, MO

SMITH, RANDY
[b.] September 26, 1961, Richmond, CA; [p.] Ken and Barbara Smith; [m.] Michelle Smith, February 15, 1992; [ch.] Tiffany and Kenny Smith; [ed.] Richmond High School; Contra Costa College; [occ.] Production Worker; [memb.] The Sure Foundation Church; [oth. writ.] Some unpublished poems.; [pers.] I try to write about life's good and bad times and how they make me feel.; [a.] Oroville, CA

SMITH, ROBERT J.
[b.] April 3, 1967, North Tarrytown, NY; [p.] Donald and Myrtle Smith; [ed.] Ossining High School, Westchester Community College, Univ of Maryland; [occ.] Litigation Paralegal; [hon.] Outstanding Author for the Office of Minority Students at Univ of Maryland (1989); [oth. writ.] Several essays written for contests at the Univ of Maryland; [pers.] "To the greatest inspiration a man can have; woman"; [a.] Alexandria, VA

SMITH, THELMA
[Pen.] Zellie; [b.] October 4, 1958, Baltimore Co.; [p.] Henrietta and Henderson Smith; [ed.] Overlea Sr. High School; [pers.] I try to reflect in my writing. The things that I feel in my Heart. And the thing's that I have seen in my life time. And the hopes and dreams that I wish to happen.; [a.] Baltimore, MD

SMITH-THOMPSON, PHYLLIS Y.
[Pen.] Shy Mistique; [b.] August 24, 1948, Baltimore, MD; [p.] James R. and Lillian V. Gee Smith; [ch.] Kelly and Kevin Crockett, Tiffany Thompson; [ed.] B.S. Sociology University of MD, Edmondson High School; [occ.] Accounting Group Leader; [hon.] Golden Poet Award, 1985-1987 and 1989, Honorable Mention for numerous poetry entries.; [oth. writ.] Several poems published in a number of poetry collections by World of Poetry Press.; [pers.] Writing is the release of stress, emotions, ideas and fantasy. What a wonderful outlet!; [a.] Baltimore, MD

SNYDER, CHRISTINE
[b.] June 27, 1972, Park Ridge, IL; [p.] Rita and Carl Snyder, Jr.; [ed.] Alvernia High School, Notre Dame High School, DePaul University, Northeastern University; [occ.] Billing Supervisor, Global Midwest, Elk Grove Village, IL; [hon.] 3 Years Honor Roll Student at Alvernia H.S. inducted into Who's Who Among High School Students for 3 years.; [oth. writ.] Poem published in the Oxford of Newman; [pers.] Writing poetry has opened many new doors in my mind helping me to see beyond the obvious.; [a.] Norridge, IL

SOAPE, NITA
[b.] May 28, 1957, Rusk County; [p.] Mr. and Mrs. W. L. St. Clair Jr.; [m.] Russell Soape, November 9, 1988; [ch.] Gary, Jennifer, Shay, Kipp Soape; [ed.] Graduated High School 1975; [occ.] Housewife; [pers.] To live each day of my life to the fullest, and to enjoy it with my family and friends.; [a.] Henderson, TX

SOLLOCK, PATRICIA D.
[b.] June 16, 1968, Lake Jackson, TX; [p.] Daniel and Florence Dannhaus; [m.] M. B. Sollock, October 12, 1985; [ch.] Austin, autumn and Ashton; [ed.] Huntsville High School; Brazosport College; [occ.] Writer/Homemaker; [pers.] I strive to stir emotions in the souls and minds of readers. If I do not do this, I have failed.; [a.] Lake Jackson, TX

SOMERO, STACEY
[b.] January 11, 1979, Peterborough, NH; [p.] Boone and Anne Somero; [ed.] Currently in the tenth grade at Mascenic Regional High School in New Ipswich, NH; [occ.] Cook at Irena's Restaurant in New Ipswich, NH; [oth. writ.] I have a collection of poetry that is not yet published, just waiting.; [pers.] Don't regret the time it took to go through any period of life, good or bad, if you learned it was worth it. Learning is living.; [a.] New Ipswich, NH

SONDERGAARD, SUSANNE
[b.] May 11, 1976, Luxembourg; [p.] Soren and Patricia Sondergaard; [ed.] Rungsted Gymnasium, Denmark; currently student at Georgetown Univ.; [a.] McLean, VA

SOOS, PAUL J.
[b.] December 13, 1964, Cleveland, OH; [p.] Joseph P. and Nancy Soos; [m.] Debra Soos, April 27, 1991; [ch.] Joshiah Christopher (5/11/92 - 7/3/92); [ed.] Nordonia High, Cuyahoga Community College, University of

Akron; [occ.] Account Executive, The Telephone Exchange, Chargrin Falls, OH; [memb.] MENSA; Faith Fellowship Church; Promise Keepers; [hon.] Founding Vice President, Sigma Tau Gamma Fraternity, Delta Mu Chapter; National Merit Semifinalist; Who's Who Among American High School Students; [oth. writ.] Several poems and numerous music lyrics for various groups; [pers.] My writing all stem from situations I have experienced personally. It is my hope that all who read them are blessed in some way. There is hope, even in darkness!; [a.] Aurora, OH

SORLIEN, NICHOLAS ALEXANDROS
[b.] December 3, 1967, Minneapolis, MN; [ed.] BFA in Sculpture and Drawing from Oklahoma State University, with special emphasis on Philosophy; [pers.] I am presently obsessed with finding the purpose of human existence relative to the universe. I am attempting to discover this through the venues of poetry, sculpture, drawing, painting, philosophy, science, et al.; [a.] St. Paul, MN

SOUSA, ANN MARIE
[b.] January 25, 1974, New Brunswick, NJ; [p.] Diane Veith; [m.] Hadrian Sousa, August 2, 1994; [ed.] Ridge High School, Stonehill College; [occ.] Student; [pers.] In loving memory of my sister Kristen Veith who will never be forgotten. Also, I thank my wonderful husband for his support.; [a.] Basking Ridge, NJ

SOUTHERLAND, CAROL E.
[b.] February 3, 1933, Washington, NJ; [p.] Theodore and Laurina Havens; [ch.] David and Susan Southerland; [ed.] Washington High, NYACK College, Art Instruction School; [occ.] Retired-Emergency Dispatcher; [memb.] Hunterdon Art Center and Warren County Community Singers; [oth. writ.] Poetry for special events and personal greeting cards and songs; [pers.] Feeling that talent is God given to each as He wills, it is my desire to stir feelings of sadness, concern, happiness, or pleasure and see pictures through words; [a.] Washington, NJ

SOWLES, LLOYD L.
[Pen.] Luther Krane; [b.] August 11, 1963, San Diego, USA; [ed.] Madison High, MESA College; [occ.] Laundry Working Lead; [memb.] American Management Assoc, Pro Rodeo Hall of Fame; [pers.] This poem is dedicated to John Davis. He died in 1987 in New York. A majority of the words are His. To all who are in the closet, its time to open the door and walkout.

SPENCER, SHEILA ANN
[Pen.] Silence; [b.] May 7, 1949, Okla., City, OK; [p.] Mattie and Chester Lowe; [m.] Harry B. Spencer Jr., December 8, 1968; [ch.] Three, ages 22, 21, 5; [ed.] 12, music, sewing, child care, nurse aide, swimming, horseback riding and computer operator; [occ.] Director Information Operator; [memb.] Catholic Church Assumption Speeches, Volunteer work, visit the sick. Volunteer to care for children in hospital for the sick. A two hour reading to the blind. And P/T work in a nursing home.; [hon.] Georgetown University Pin for helping patients and others as well. I was also given a T-Shirt to go along with it. I was also given an award for Parent of the Year Award; [pers.] Life is very precious and when I wrote the poem it is a very deep meaning within my life. A new day is to live to see another one and to be blessed again to lay in your bed and pray again.; [a.] Washington, D.C.

SPETH, CORY
[b.] April 24, 1978, Davenport, IA; [p.] Connie and Dale Speth; [ed.] Presently a junior at Bettendorf High School in Bettendorf, Iowa; [hon.] Bettendorf High School Academic Letter Winner; Honor Roll, 2 years running; [pers.] If you're determined to succeed, success is inevitable.; [a.] Bettendorf, IA

SPRINGS, EDNA ROSHELL
[Pen.] Roshell Springs; [b.] December 7, 1960, Halifax, Virginia; [p.] William E. Majors, and Mary C. Bouldin; [m.] Eli Springs Jr.; [ch.] Wendy Juanita, Marcus Gabriel, Kyle Tremaine; [ed.] Halifax County Senior High School; [oth. writ.] Many unpublished poems.; [pers.] I have encountered the endurance of the encounter, but I still have much to endure, and much to encounter.; [a.] FPO, AP

SPRINKLES, LISA GILLESPIE
[b.] November 9, 1970, Alamosa, CO; [p.] Rueben and Linda Gillespie; [m.] James D. Sprinkles, February 29, 1992; [ch.] Jaimie Nicole Sprinkles - age 14 months; [ed.] Albany High, Hardin - Simmons Univ, and Angelo State Univ; [occ.] Student, homemaker and mom; [memb.] National Honor Society, Sigma Tau Delta, Fellowship of Christian Athletes; [hon.] DAR Good Citizens Award, Lions Club Sweetheart, Salutatorian, Dean's List, U/L Editorial Writing State Qualifier; [oth. writ.] One poem published in the Angelo State Journal - The Oasis; [pers.] To write poetry is to reach out and touch souls. My goal is to introduce those I touch to the love of god, who is the source of my inspiration and talent. I write for His glory; [a.] San Angelo, TX

SQUIRES, MICHAEL EVERETT
[Pen.] Michael Jacob Esquire; [b.] December 29, 1958, Lawton, OK; [p.] James F. and Irene R. Squires; [ed.] Bachelor of Arts, Kent State Univ (Degree in Philosophy, BA); [occ.] Specialist, National Inst of Standards and Technology, Gaithersburg, MD; [memb.] Deutsche Dichter (German Poets), Munchen, Deutschland; [hon.] CFC Awards, 1990, Washington, DC; [oth. writ.] "Sayings from the Squire...(in the steps of my forefathers)" a philosophical essay copyrighted 1993 "Existence is the Nihilist's Foe" a philosophic treatise copyrighted 1994; [pers.] To delve into lyrical interpretations, that is my reason for writing; [a.] Thurmont, MD

ST. CLAIR, EUGENE
[b.] May 14, 1927, Taylor Co., KY; [p.] Mr. and Mrs. R. L. St. Clair; [m.] Doris St. Clair; [ch.] Dee Dee Davis; [ed.] Two Yr. Campbellsville College; [occ.] Retired, T.G.T.; [a.] Campbellsville, KY

ST. CYR, JACKIE
[b.] March 27, 1931, Houston, TX; [p.] Louis G. and Irene (Marcovich) St. Cyr; [ch.] Sharon Page Wolfe and Steven B. Campbell; Grandchildren: Stephanie Page, Shannon Christine Page, Louis Martin Campbell, Jen and Lynn Wolfe; [ed.] Stephen F. Austin High School - Houston, TX, Univ of Houston - Houston, TX; [occ.] Retired from Southwestern Bell Telephone 1992, Dallas, TX; [memb.] Haltom City and Watauga Senior Citizens; Telephone Pioneers of America; numerous PTA's; US Figure Skating Assn, (63-66); [hon.] National Honor Society (48-49) two 1st place and one 3rd place ribbons, Senior Citizens Services Art Shows 1993 and 1994; one of 20 Poetry Finalists 1994 / Ft Worth Senior Citizens Poetry Contest; [oth. writ.] Limerick "Joe Todd's Dilemma" published in book At Day's End, The National Library of Poetry (1994), p 441; [pers.] The poem,

"School Daze" here in published in Reflections of Light (1995) was inspired by and dedicated to my 13 year old granddaughter, Shannon Christine Page, while on a "shopping spree"; [a.] Haltom City, TX

STAFFORD, PEGGIE ANN
[b.] October 9, 1937, New Jersey; [p.] Conrad Dewey and Margaret Helen Quinn; [m.] Half-a-Buck (Edward), July 9, 1961; [ch.] Four; [ed.] By life experience; [occ.] Daily Survival; [memb.] Grandparents, Babysitting Society; [hon.] Having loved and giving birth; [oth. writ.] Letters in the sand.; [pers.] I dedicate my poem to Half-a-Buck for giving me a lifetime of unconditional love.; [a.] Wayside, NJ

STALLINGS, NANCY
[b.] March 20, 1955, Paris, TX; [p.] Curtis and Nina Malone; [m.] James Stallings, May 1, 1953; [ch.] James Mitchell and Sharon Micaela; [ed.] Paris High School; [occ.] Homemaker; [memb.] Ridglea Baptist Church, Fort Worth, TX; [oth. writ.] No published writings, except one poem in my local newspaper. I have a home library of poems and children's short stories; [pers.] My writing is inspired by my love of God and my family; [a.] Fort Worth, TX

STALLWORTH, DUANA DAVIS
[Pen.] Annie Beatrice; [b.] September 21, 1954, Richmond, CA; [p.] Ann B. Davis and William P. Davis; [m.] Nelson Hosea Stallworth, September 3, 1983; [ch.] Reana Rashida and Rhosea Ranice; [ed.] El Cerrito High School, Contra Costa College; [occ.] Secretary; [memb.] Calvary Temple Church of God in Christ, PTA; [hon.] Graduated with honors, Dean's List; [pers.] My inspiration for writing comes from my mother. Langston Hughes is my favorite author/writer; [a.] Richmond, CA

STAMBAUGH, DEBORAH
[b.] April 10, 1966, Amarillo, TX; [ed.] BS Environmental Science, Univ of St. Thomas; [occ.] Health, Safety and Environmental Affairs Data Analyst Solvay America, Inc; [memb.] Houston World Affairs Council; [hon.] Phi Sigma Tau, Alpha Sigma Lambda, Dean's List; [oth. writ.] Songs, poems, short stories and two novels in the making; [a.] Houston, TX

STANDRIDGE, DORINDA
[Pen.] Dee, Devo; [b.] January 29, 1961, Harvey, IL; [p.] Hershel and Emmer Milligan; [m.] Jerry Standridge, September 15, 1984; [ch.] One child Melinda Phillips, and two stepchildren; [ed.] GED, went to Shoal's Community College; [occ.] Barber/Cosmetologist; [hon.] Dean's & President's List, Outstanding Student of Year, 1st place winner in the National Competition for "Promotional Bulletin Board" with VICA Outstanding Achievement and Certificate of Recognition and appreciation from Shoals Community College; [oth. writ.] I have received two Honorable Mention Awards for two of my poems and I mostly write for me and my love ones, and friends.; [pers.] I have always tried to find the goodness in all mankind. And through my husband and daughter, I found the peace and love of silence that I write down as poetry. In memory of my father my love is forever.; [a.] Florence, AL

STANGEL, DARLA
[b.] September 12, 1959, Mason City, Iowa; [p.] LeRoy and Bonnie Williamson; [ch.] Robbie, Jason, Travis, Derek; [oth. writ.] I've written many poems, all for my own use. Everything I've written, are of my own feelings and life experiences. I have a hard time expressing

myself verbally, and it gives me peace of mind to write it down.; [pers.] I want to dedicate this poem to Dale Winter. The man who came into my life and made it wonderful. You've inspired me like no other. I love you, sweetie!; [a.] Clear Lake, IA

STANLEY, BARBARA J. COCHRAN
[Pen.] Cochran, Sisco, Panter, Thomas, Stanley; [b.] April 11, 1943, East Liverpool, OH; [p.] Augustus (Gus) and Jennie Cochman; [m.] Widow; [ch.] Daniel, Marsha, Howard, David Sisco; [ed.] Completed freshmen yr, Westgate Jr. High; [occ.] Unemployed; [memb.] Honorable Member of the Society of Poets, First Assembly of God; [hon.] Golden Poet Awards 1984 Through 1991 World of Poetry. Also 9 Honorable Mention Certificates; [oth. writ.] Published in the World of Poetry Press: Editions, World of Poetry anthology, Our Worlds Most Beloved Poems, Great Poems of the Western World, World Treasury of Golden Poems, several others; [pers.] My writings I feel are inspirational, and are very much similar to the works of the late and great Helen Steiner Rice. I write to uplift and bring joy and peace to others; [a.] East Liverpool, OH

STATEN, JENNIFER
[b.] November 18, 1977, Tyler, TX; [p.] Larry and Debra Staten; [ed.] Bullard High School; [occ.] Student; [memb.] Key Club, National Honor Society, Band, Majorette; [hon.] 1993-94 Sophomore of the Year, Member of the most outstanding majorette line in the 1994 Texas Rose Festival; [a.] Bullard, TX

STEARN, SHERRY
[b.] August 2, 1965, Lancaster; [p.] Craig and Jean Stearn; [m.] Single; [ed.] Manheim Township High School, Lancaster Business School, Various Acting Schools in New York; [occ.] Model and actress also currently taking classes for acting; [memb.] Highland Presbyterian Church; Aftra/Sag; [oth. writ.] I am currently writing a Sci-Fi thriller and have a library of poetry from years of trying to find true love.; [pers.] I have found inner peace through my writing and hope the world around me can find outer peace through love and communication.; [a.] NY City, NY

STEFANEAS, OLGA
[b.] September 20, 1975, Chicago, IL; [p.] Lambros and Christina Stefaneas; [ed.] Lane Technical High School, DePaul Univ; [occ.] Student; [memb.] United Hellenic Organization; [hon.] Dean's List, Alpha Lambda Delta Honor Society, Honorable Mention for Law Week Essay Contest by the American Bar Assoc (YLS), Third place in city-wide Shakespearian Oratory competition; [oth. writ.] Several articles published in the DePaulia Student newspaper, including poetry; Time Magazine letter to the editor; [pers.] The poetry I create comes from the depth of my soul and is highly influenced by my cultural background. Writing poetry allows me to expand my inner feelings and personal passions without any barriers; Chicago, IL

STEFFENS, IRENE MARIE
[p.] Irene O'Donnell and Eric Hoecker; [m.] Robert Steffens (deceased); [ch.] Annie Laurie and Roberta; [occ.] Registered Nurse (retired); [hon.] Highest Average; Nursing Arts Award; Editor of Nursing School Yearbook; [oth. writ.] Other poetry, unpublished, wrote reviews for a Book Club; [pers.] I owe my love for poetry to my brother, Professor Eric L. Hoecker, who taught me to read before I started school. Then took me to join the library.; [a.] Brattleboro, VT

STEIN, JAMES JOSEPH
[b.] February 13, 1967, Detroit, Michigan; [p.] William J. and Patricia A. Stein; [ed.] Churchill High, Schoolcraft College, Lawrence Technological University; [occ.] Microfilm Courier, Great Lakes Technologies Corp., Livonia, MI; [memb.] Phi Theta Kappa, Statue of Liberty, Ellis Island Foundation; [hon.] Business Honor Student, Listed in Who's Who Among American High School Students 1984-1985 19th ed., Vol. V; [pers.] Through my writing, I want to remind people that life is precious. I wish every person would take some time to enjoy the beauty of this world.; [a.] Livonia, MI

STENROTH, SIGNE
[b.] March 20, 1914, Finland; [p.] Karla and Maria O. Gabrielson; [m.] Dag E. Stenroth, June 4, 1938 (deceased); [ch.] John Lennart (Carol Olof, Bertel Edward deceased); [ed.] Upton High School, Becker College, Evening Div.; [occ.] Retired Office Worker; [memb.] Christ United Methodist Church; [hon.] Valedictorian; [oth. writ.] Poems listed in local newspapers, short articles in same.; [pers.] I try to spread joy, and help those around me in my retirement village.; [a.] Vineyard Haven, MA

STEPHENSON (JR.), JOHN
[b.] May 10, 1957, Long Island, NY; [p.] John Stephenson, Joan Stephenson; [ed.] West Albany High School, Brigham Young Univ; [occ.] Freelance Artist, Writer, Political Cartoonist; [oth. writ.] Numerous volumes of unpublished poetry, a first novel: 'The Call of Azoth' (Fantash) near completion; [pers.] If you want to write: read! Increase your vocabulary and be inventive. Learn from others, but don't use others writings to judge your own, I'm grateful for those who have encouraged me, and my family; [a.] Long Island, NY

STEVINSON, MICHAEL J.
[b.] September 3, 1972, Rahway, NJ; [p.] Ronald and JoAnne Stevinson; [ed.] Rahway High Way, Kean College of New Jersey; [occ.] Student; [memb.] Greenpeace, Amnesty Int'l; Poems published in student publication, 1992; [pers.] "Beyond a certain point there is no return. This point has to be reached" - KAFKA; [a.] Rahway, NJ

STEWART, JUDY LYNN
[Pen.] ABBA's Child; [b.] December 20, 1959, Morgan City, LA; [p.] Shirley Dupy; [m.] David Bryan Stewart, August 5, 1989; [ch.] Jolie, Larry and Jonathan; [ed.] High School Equivalency; [occ.] Homemaker, and student at the victoria College, Victoria, TX; [memb.] Paralyzed Veterans of America, Focus on the Family, and Concerned Woman of America; [oth. writ.] Poem published in local newspapers.; [pers.] My writing is inspired by God and by the beauty of his creations. To God be the glory.; [a.] Smiley, TX

STEWART, KATHY METZE
[b.] March 14, 1958, Stuttgart, Germany; [p.] Melvin L. Metze, I, Alberta K. Metze; [m.] Howard Stewart; [ch.] Garrison Albert, 1 yr; [ed.] Irmo High School, Columbia College (BA), Univ of South Carolina (M.Ed); [occ.] Special Education Teacher, SC Department of Juvenile Justice, Columbia, SC; [memb.] St. Paul AME Church, Irmo, SC; [pers.] My writings are truly a gift from God. He creates and I pen. He placed the piece printed her in my heart a few days after the sudden death of my beloved mother; and the words resounded in my spirit until I put them on paper. To Him be all the glory!! [a.] Irmo, SC

STEWART, RUBY
[b.] April 2, 1926, Baltimore, MD; [p.] Mr. & Mrs. Daniel McClain; [m.] James T. Stewart, October 29, 1950; [ch.] Michael, Lark, and Wynston; [ed.] BS Medical Research; [occ.] Sr. Job Service - Employment for those over 55; [memb.] Medical - ASCP - Mt ASCP HMT; [hon.] City Art awards for drawings; art shows charcoal pen and ink; [oth. writ.] Scientific - Spinal Cord Injury - Brain Studies; [pers.] I write from the heart, things that touch me, happiness or sadness; [a.] Philadelphia, PA

STILLEY, SHEILA N.
[b.] December 29, 1968, Chicago, IL; [p.] Richard and Evelyn Nelson; [m.] Donald T. Stilley, Jr, February 4, 1989; [ch.] Amber (4), Brandon (20 mos); [ed.] Belair High, El Paso, TX; [occ.] Housewife, mother of two; [hon.] Certificates from the colonels wife Mrs. Ruth, support group activities; [oth. writ.] Personal poems, nothing else ever entered; [pers.] A soldier's life will always take...was written for my husband, while gearing up to deploy for Haiti. I do love and support Donald 100%.

STOCKBERGER, NICOLA
[b.] December 28, 1968, Los Angeles, CA; [p.] Olivia and Joseph Skenandore; [m.] Robert Ellsworth Stockberger III, October 14, 1990; [ch.] Robert Ellsworth Stockberger IV; [ed.] UC Irvine, Cal State Northridge, Miraleste High School; [occ.] Homemaker, Lakota beadworker; [pers.] I write poetry for my personal enjoyment and it is a way for me to express my life experiences. It brings me pleasure to express my thoughts, feelings and human emotions.; [a.] Palmdale, CA

STOETZER, JASON
[Pen.] Ron M. Rozhenko; [b.] April 21, 1974, Miami, FL; [ed.] Coral Gables Sr High, Miami-Dade Community College; [occ.] Student and nightclub promoter/entertainer; [hon.] Dean's List; Student Writer's Award for Excellence in Language Arts; honored in Miami-Dade County Arts and Letters Day 1994; [oth. writ.] Published poems in Miambience, a local literary magazine for student writers; [pers.] It is my conviction that the arts not only serve as an objective lens through which humanity may judge and view itself, but also a mealer, which serves humanity on an individual level by communicating the need to understand human experience as both unique and universal; [a.] Miami, FL

STOLHANSKE, LISA
[b.] July 19, 1973, Robbinsdale, MN; [p.] Dennis and Terry Stolhanske; [ed.] Robbinsdale Cooper High School; St. Cloud State University; [occ.] Student, Psychology Major; [memb.] Psi Chi Psychology Club; [hon.] Dean's List at St. Cloud State for 3 1\2 years; [oth. writ.] Two poems published in the Roundelogy, a high school poetry book; have written 50 or so other poems that have not been read by anyone.; [pers.] Most of the poems that I write reflect my deep belief in God and in love. My family, friends, and boyfriend give me all the inspiration I need to write, but all the credit for the finished piece goes to God.; [a.] New Hope, MN

STOLTZ, DR. DONALD R.
[b.] August 13, 1935, Philadelphia, PA; [m.] Phyllis, July 15, 1962; [ed.] Attended Central High School in Philadelphia, graduated 1953. Attended Temple University in Phila.; [occ.] Physician; [memb.] American Osteopathic Assoc., PA Osteopathic Assoc, American Physicians, Art Assoc.; [hon.] Dog Writers Association of America, February 13, 1983, "But Mom Didn't Like Dogs"; [oth. writ.] Norman Rockwell and The Saturday Post, 3 Volumes, 1976 and 1994, The Advertising World of Norman Rockwell 1 Volume, 1981 Albert Staehle American's Annual Illustrator, Collectors Showcase, 1991. The Three Cavaliers, U.S. Art Magazine 1992; [pers.] Accomplished author, artist, poet, lyricist and authority on American Illustration. He has written 6 children's books, dozens of poems and many short stories. He has lectured extensively on American Illustration and has written many magazine articles. He has a large practice of family medicine in Philadelphia with an office decorated with his art work. He is married and has 3 children, a daughter in advertising, a daughter in the art field and a son who is his associate in medicine.

STONE, GILLIAN M.
[b.] July 16, 1938, Wallasey, Cheshire, England; [p.] Jean and Kenneth Gran; [m.] Gilbert D. Stone; [m.] July 9, 1970; [ch.] Deborah and Karami; [ed.] Boarding School, England. Secretarial College, England; [occ.] Housewife; [hon.] Bronze Medal Elocution, Silver Medal - Acting (London Academy of Music and Dramatic Art); [pers.] I lived in Jos, N. Nigeria for 18 years among the Biron Tribe, designated Pagan because they were generally resistant to missionary influence. I was impressed by their happy acceptance of an extremely harsh life. I have never attempted, until now, to publish my poems; [a.] Grand Junction, CO

STONE, SCOTT DOUGLAS
[b.] October 29, 1994, Dearborn, MI; [p.] Walter D. and Bernice E. Stone; [m.] Divorced; [ed.] Waterford Mott High School, North Western Vocational Education Center U.S. Army (Food Service Specialist); [occ.] Landscaping and snow removal for Spartan Landscaping; [hon.] Honorable Discharge from the Military; [oth. writ.] Two other poems for the National Library of Poetry.; [pers.] I write down poetry as it comes to my head, and a lot of people have admired my poems! I can only dream of becoming rich and famous some day.; [a.] Lincoln Park, MI

STOPPEL, REBECCA
[b.] July 10, 1966, Portales, NM; [p.] Julio and Maria Rodriguez; [m.] Robert Alan Stoppel, March 5, 1985; [ch.] Robert A. Stoppel, Jr. and Kimberly; [ed.] Calhoun Community College - rec'd AA in accounting and gen ed..Currently attending Athens State College, pursuing BA in accounting; [occ.] Student and part-time restaurant work; [memb.] PTA at McDonnell Elementary; [pers.] I am an avid reader and lover of medieval history, literature, and poetry. I believe peace can be achieved by the most simplistic pleasures in this technological society in which we live. My philosophy is: "Life is poetry and we are the poets!"; [a.] Huntsville, AL

STORK, CASEY
[b.] July 15, 1985, Austin, TX; [p.] Randy and Kelly Stock; [ed.] Attending LaGrange, Intermediate School in LaGrange, TX; [occ.] Student; [memb.] Warda 4-H, Texas Pork Producers Assoc; [hon.] Many; [oth. writ.] Many poems and stories; [pers.] Wants to attend Texas A & M Univ in animal science or veterinary medicine; [a.] LaGrange, TX

STORK, JESS PAPANEK
[Pen.] Jo Papanek; [b.] July 19, 1983, Wausau, Wisconsin; [p.] Paul and Sharon Papanek Stork; [ch.] Wausau Montessori School, Wausau, WI; Weston Elementary School, Schofield, WI; Lowden Elementary

School & Greenview Upper Elementary School, South Euclid, Ohio.; [occ.] Sixth Grade Student; [memb.] Daisy & Brownie Girl Scout Troop #13, Schofield, WI; Woodson YMCA, Wausau, WI; Bethany Lutheran Church, Aniwa, WI; St. Stephen Lutheran Church, Wausau, WI; Brownie, Junior & Cadette Girl Scout Troop #1087, South Euclid, OH; Bethlehem Lutheran Youth Group, Cleveland Heights, OH; [hon.] "Best Religious Story" in First Grade Class at Weston El. School, 1990. Citizenship Award, 1991; Most Improved Award & second Place in Bike Rodeo, 1992; Academic Achievement & Helping Hands Awards, 1993 at Lowden El. School. Greenview "Student of the Month" September, 1994. 1994 Marble Champion, Hale Farm Camp, Bath, OH.; [pers.] I am grateful to all my teachers who encouraged my writing, especially Miss Margaret Pempek in Schofield. Wisconsin and Miss Laura Bianchi, Mrs. Rachel Berry, Mrs. Lisa Krosin, Mrs. Amy Herzenstein, Miss Laura Ayers and Mr. Dave Englander in South Euclid, Ohio; [a.] South Euclid, OH

STOTT, GREGORY
[b.] October 14, 1971, Bryan Mawr, PA; [p.] Leslie Stott, Ronald Stott; [ed.] Owen J. Roberts High, Millersville Univ of Pennsylvania; [occ.] Book store clerk; [hon.] Dean's List; [oth. writ.] Poems published in White Buffalo literary magazine, and George Street Carnival magazine; [pers.] I try to observe the recurring patterns in Nature. I believe that all life is sacred, from the lowly worm to the "noble" man; [a.] Pottstown, PA

STRACHAN, DARIN
[b.] February 16, 1976, Cincinnati, OH; [p.] Brian Strachan, Pamela Strachan; [ed.] Hudson High School, 1994; [occ.] Student, Ohio Univ, College of Communications; [a.] Cuyahoga Falls, OH

STRAHL, NICKY
[b.] October 24, 1978, Des Plains; [p.] Sue and rick Strahl; [ed.] Libertyville High School; [occ.] High School Student, part time kennel attendant.; [memb.] Smithsonian, Holy Cross Lutheran Church; [oth. writ.] A variety of poems, not published.; [pers.] The earth is just a place we call home. I believe, but where we stay is our own, fantastical worlds of imaginations.; [a.] Libertyville, IL

STRAUGHN, VALERIE
[b.] December 7, 1962, Brooklyn, NY; [p.] Nel and Charles Straughn; [ed.] Brooklyn Technical High School; Vassar College, Hofstra University School of Law; [occ.] Attorney, on behalf of Homeless Population; [memb.] American Bar Association, New York, Country Trial Lawyers Association; [oth. writ.] I have written several poems but I have never before entered any contests or submitted any poems for publication.; [pers.] The study of human nature, with all of its many spectacular intricacies, will always provide me with the richest and most tantalizing of subjects. Here in lies the source of my passion for life.; [a.] New York, NY

STRAUSS, GLORY
[Pen.] "Glory"; [ch.] (Four) Jim, Lind, Vicki, Cyd; [ed.] Miami Dade Jr. College - Life Lab; [occ.] Writer - Artist, "My Own Continuing" journal "since 1975"; [memb.] Amnesty International Unity, American Indian Relief Council, others; [oth. writ.] Poetry book - "There is a Space Inside of Me" - "Silly Dilly" a series of 3 completed and 2 unfinished children's books - "Silently I Speak" - thoughts along my journey - "And a Mini-Series" - I am a star - I am a Rain Drop - ...A Tree -- a

Cloud...Lightening. I also have written a continuing journal of my our journeys since 1975 - consisting of many, many books; [pers.] The writings in my books were created while in pursuit of the essence of life's meaning. I am compelled to share what meaning I have found with the lovers, the searchers and the dreamers; [a.] Newberry, FL

STREET, ANNA
[b.] September 4, 1977, Sacramento, CA; [p.] Barbara and Robert T. Street; [ed.] Will graduate from Hiram Johnson West Campus High School in June 1995.; [memb.] School newspaper "The West Side" Varsity Soccer Team.; [pers.] I use poetry to express my feelings, especially when its something I don't feel like talking about. Between tomorrow's dream and yesterdays regret is today's opportunity.; [a.] Sacramento, CA

STRIBLING, BETTY J.
[b.] April 23, 1927, Omaha, NE; [p.] John and Marie James; [m.] 1948; [ch.] Mary, David, Christine, Pat, Mark, Esther; [ed.] Bachelor of Science in Health Arts; Reg Psychiatric Nurse; [occ.] Retired; [oth. writ.] Several poems published in Great Poems of Our Times by the National Library of Poetry; [pers.] I try to create images that excite, soothe or stimulate in my poetry. Using words to make pictures leaves a wide range media; [a.] Chicago, IL

STRICKLIN, CHRIS R.
[b.] January 28, 1972, Shelby, AL; [p.] Gary and Patsy Stricklin; [m.] Terri D. Stricklin, June 11, 1994; [ed.] Shelby County High School, United States Air Force Academy; [occ.] Pilot, USAF; [a.] Sheppard Air Force Base, TX

STROM, JEFF
[b.] August 7, 1977, Louiston, Maine; [p.] George and Lynda Strom; [ed.] Junior in High School; [occ.] Student at Meridan Senior High; [memb.] Boy Scouts; [hon.] Baseball and assorted scholarship awards; [pers.] Our goal, to reach the heavens, to share knowledge, but first to believe. I have been influenced by fantasy and science fiction authors.; [a.] Sanford, MI

STUBBLEFIELD, JULIE P.
[Pen.] Julia S. Field, Julie Pimental, Emma Stubblefield; [b.] September 28, 1965, Fayetteville, NC; [p.] Ltc. Rodney and Dorothy Pimental; [m.] F. Fee Stubblefield, Jr., August 24, 1985; [ch.] Matthew Fee 9/10/92; Emma Dorothy Claire 7/19/94; [ed.] Richland NE High, Clemson University, Portland State University, Portland State University B.S. Degree and Post Graduate Studies in Literature; [occ.] Mother and Writer.; [memb.] Women in the Arts Museum, The Heritage Foundation, Beaverton Foursquare church, Concerned Women of America.; [hon.] Who's Who American High Schools, Dean's List, Magna Cum Laude Graduate; [oth. writ.] Working on other poems, short stories, children's literature and a play.; [pers.] To be able to put into words a deeply felt feeling or impression and evoke in others the same feeling is difficult and precisely what I strive to do. I believe genuine Art is beautiful and uplifts the soul and originates with God.; [a.] Portland, OR

STUCKEY, KATHERINE RUNKLE
[Pen.] Katherine Stuckey, November 18, 1902, Littleton, IL; [p.] Robert and Cora Runkle, April 12, 1925; [ch.] Three daughters, nine grandchildren; [ed.] Western Academy, Western Illinois Univ, 1961; [occ.] Retired, teacher and homemaker; [memb.] United Church of Altona,

Rebecca Parke Chapter NSDAR, Retired Knox Co Teachers, Home Extension, Local Unit; [hon.] Poetry award - Illinois Women's Club. Several honorable mention in watercolor at local shows; [oth. writ.] Several poems published in Knox College 'Step Ladder'. Some essays published in "Tales From Two Rivers IV" published by Two Rivers Art Council, Macomb, IL; [pers.] My goal in poetry writing is simple truth as I have seen it, in clear language that all can understand; [a.] Altona, IL

STURGEON, H. MACK
[b.] August 3, 1954, Enid, OK; [p.] Lawrence R. Sturgeon, Elaine Sturgeon; [m.] Shelly Jo Sturgeon, April 17, 1990; [ch.] Tanner Scott Sturgeon; [ed.] Helena High School, Oklahoma State Univ Colorado State Univ, Seminole Ja Co; [occ.] Public Horse Trainer and Special Operations Div for Wrangler Corporation; [memb.] Helena Christian Church (Helena, OK), Oklahoma Cattleman's Assoc, Charter Member Oklahoma Horseman's Assoc; [hon.] (My honors include) Being born and raised in Oklahoma and being able to write words that amuse, and entertain people from time to time. (My awards include) My wife and son, and my family and friends; [oth. writ.] Contributing poet in a book entitled (Cowboy Poetry Collection), Horsemans Lament - Speedhorse Publications, Inc.; [pers.] Train your soul to sympathy your life to prayer and your hands to helpfulness. My grandmother Goldia Sturgeon wrote down this that many years ago in a Feed and Seed Book; [a.] Seminole, OK

STURGIS, MARCIA J.
[b.] August 29, 1949, Ardmore, OK; [p.] A.J. Everett and Oral Everett; [m.] Jere A. Sturgis, March 9, 1985; [ch.] Byron, Andrea and Lindsay; [ed.] Enid High School, plus continuing educational courses; [occ.] Investments; [oth. writ.] Produce column for church organizational newsletter; personal experience articles published in the Lutheran Witness magazine.; [pers.] My stories and poems are reflections of personal experiences and outside influences. I desire to portray "snapshots" of time.; [a.] Tulsa, OK

STURR, JENNIFER
[b.] October 23, 1968, New Hartford, NY; [p.] Bernard and Sylvia Sturr; [ed.] Bachelor of Arts; English State University of New York at Plattsburgh, Plattsburgh, NY; [occ.] Technical Writer, Electrovert USA Corp.; [memb.] Society of Technical Communications; [hon.] Member; Omicron Delta Kappa, National Leadership Honor Society; [a.] Osage Beach, MO

SUDWEEKS, KORRIE T.
[b.] March 1, 1962, Ogden, VT; [p.] Connie and Paul Thorpe; [m.] Trevor, May 21, 1981; [ch.] Brandon, Brooke, Christian; [ed.] Clearfield High School, Utah Technical College, UNLV; [occ.] Fitness Instructor, Life Centre Health Club, Sandy, VT; [memb.] U.S.G.F. & NAWGT Gymnastic Judging Assoc., AFAA Fitness Certification; [oth. writ.] Several poems published in local newspapers; [pers.] I have written many of my poems about personal experiences with life and spiritual awareness.; [a.] Sandy, VT

SULLIVAN, JAY CHRIS
[b.] February 10, 1952, Orange, CA; [p.] Howard and Beverly Sullivan; [ed.] B.S. Agriculture, University of Arizona, Tucson, 1976; [occ.] Horticulturist; [memb.] Coachella Valley Hiking Club; [hon.] U/A Dean's List (Top 10% of Class); Alpha Zeta Fraternity; Most Popu-

lar Senior, May 1976; [oth. writ.] I have an unpublished book of over 100 poems and song lyrics and a set-up to each explaining why I wrote it and who I know that inspire me.; [pers.] I have voted in every election since I became legal at age 18. Last year I switched to the new Greens Party because they have a philosophy similar to the Native American Indians: Man needs to balance his culture with the natural work in order to survive.; [a.] Indo, CA

SULLIVAN, LOWELL
[b.] June 6, 1955, Columbus, OH; [p.] Donald Sullivan, Nancy Sullivan; [m.] Stan Wickham, February 14, 1991 (domestic partnership); [ed.] Washington - Lee Univ ('77); [occ.] Disabled - AIDS; [memb.] Metropolitan Community Church; [pers.] As a gay man in a committed relationship and as a gay father, much of my writing tries to reflect the need for a more tolerant society. My illness lends an urgency to that message; [a.] San Francisco, CA

SULLIVAN-STAPLES, MARGARET K.
[Pen.] Margaret K. Staples; [b.] February 16, 1927, Frederick, MD; [p.] Margaret/Denmead Kolb; [m.] Geo. M. Staples, July 17, 1993; [ch.] 3 (George, Stephen, Andrea); [ed.] Hannahmore Acad, Reisterstown, MD; Mt Vernon College, Wash, DC; [occ.] Writer; [memb.] Samuel Chase Chapel DAR; Eastern Shore Writers Assn; Coastal Hospice of Eastern Shore; [oth. writ.] Former journalist, Norfolk Naval Base newspaper - Soundings; Former journalist, Salisbury, MD - Daily Times, articles in regional magazines newspapers; [pers.] My poems reflect my philosophy environmental concern, feminine freedom of choice, government integrity; [a.] Berlin, MD

SUMMERS, WAYNE J.
[Pen.] Jody Summers; [b.] April 3, 1955, New Orleans, LA; [p.] Donald A. and Louise F. Summers; [ch.] Kelsey D. Summers; [ed.] BGS Psychology/English University of Kansas; Whitehave grade school, Memphis, TN; Whitehave high school (2 yrs.) Springwoods High School, Houston, TX; [occ.] President Klean Heart Inc., Pet Products; [memb.] Aircraft Owners and Pilot's Association, American Taekwondo Association, World Kuk Sool Association, Riverbend Baptist Church; [hon.] Gymnastics Scholarship to University of Kansas, Runner Up to the Junior Olympic Nationals from Texas in Gymnastics 1973; [oth. writ.] Various poems and a novel in progress.; [pers.] He who does not risk cannot be free. People, like vegetables, are either growing...or dying.; [a.] Austin, TX

SUPLEE, DIANA
[Pen.] Dina Fabiani; [b.] September 16, 1923; [p.] Katrina and Frank Brewster; [m.] Charles J. Suplee; [ch.] David Long, Wayne, PA; [ed.] West Chester Univ. for Julliard, Combs College, Dr. Mus. Arts; [occ.] Composer, Painter, Writer; [memb.] Tampa Bay Composers Forum, Cecilian Music Society, Sarasota Music Teach Assoc.; [hon.] Carnegie Hall Recital, TV appearances: Opera Theatre, Mike Douglas, Show; [oth. writ.] "Dynamics in Arts" column for newspaper, "Vocal Vitamins," tips, exercises, literary anthology for better speaking and singing.; [pers.] My nature is basically optimistic but my artistic expressions cover a wide range of styles, moods.; [a.] Sarasota, FL

SUTMAIER (III), MICHAEL J.
[Pen.] Trip; [b.] June 27, 1979, Tampa, FL; [p.] Michael and Lana Sutmaier; [ed.] Engineering Academy at Tampa Bay Technical High School; [occ.] Student - 10th

grade; [hon.] Principal and High Honor Awards; [oth. writ.] Many poems and short stories that I have never tried to get published; [pers.] I try to bring out people's deepest emotions and imagination. My greatest influence is a beautiful woman named Ingrid F.; [a.] Tampa, FL

SUTTON, ROBERT JOSEPH
[Pen.] Joey Sutton, Seawind; [b.] September 5, 1968, Bamberg County, South Carolina; [p.] John and Louise Corson; [ed.] Bamberg, Ehrhardt High School University of South Carolina; [occ.] Paramedic; [memb.] South Carolina E.M.S., Educators Assoc., American Heart Association; [hon.] Highest State Test Average from Paramedic Class; [oth. writ.] Numerous poems on a wide variety of subjects/situations.; [pers.] I like to write about what I feel deep inside, what I have been through, something that may help others cope with similar circumstances are what they are going through.; [a.] Bamberg, SC

SWARTZ, JOSHUA
[b.] July 6, 1975, Wayne, NJ; [p.] Robert R. Swartz, Emilie A. Swartz; [ed.] Working towards creative writing major; [occ.] Student, Butokan Karate Instructor; [memb.] Butokan Karate Club, United Synagogue of America; [hon.] Many awards for martial arts, completed army, archaeological, and intense language programs in Israel; [oth. writ.] Songs, short stories, and other poetry pursuing publication as well as writing for magazines; [pers.] One who talks more than listens will not get very much out of life.; [a.] El Paso, TX

SWEARINGEN, MELISSA
[b.] January 24, 1977, Crossville, TN; [p.] William and Nancy Swearingen; [ed.] Bledsoe County High School, Joint Enrollment, Chattanooga State Community College; [memb.] National Beta Club 3 yrs., Beta Epsilon 2 yrs., 4-H Club 4 yrs., 4-H Honor Club 4 yrs., FTA (Future Teachers of America) 4 yrs., Executive Student Council Member, Future Nurses of America 4 yrs., Sequatchie Akaliyeti Reading Counsel 2 yrs.; [hon.] Bledsoe's Sweetheart 1994-95, Honor Roll 4 yrs., President of FTA, Secretary of Beta Club, Treasurer of Ex. Student Council, Graduation Pianist 4 yrs., National Anthem Soloist 4 yrs., Who's Who of American High School Student s 4 yrs.; [oth. writ.] Sequatchie Valley Electric Co-Op Essay Contest Winner 1994, Aug. TN Magazine. School Newspaper Staff. Wrote 2 books one in 1989, the other in 1991. I won a gold metal in County on both books, and a bronze in 1989, and silver in 1991 on State Levels.; [a.] Pikeville, TN

SWEENEY, SARA E.
[b.] June 10, 1917, Pitman, NJ; [p.] Edward, Lillie Drew; [m.] John F. Sweeney, June 24, 1939; [ch.] John Irvin, Sheila Gay, William Patrick, Michael Francis; [ed.] Cape May High School, Cape May, NJ; [occ.] Retired; [memb.] Catholic Daughters, St. Peters, Riverside, NJ, various senior clubs; [hon.] An editor for "The Inkwell" Cape May High School, Cape May, NJ; [oth. writ.] Poems in "The Inkwell" and several newspapers; [pers.] I love to watch people. I try to find the good in them. Despite "Little Things". My life has been wonderful; [a.] Burlington, NJ

SWIFT, TRACY R.
[b.] March 3, 1971, Leitchfield, KY; [p.] Dennis and Ada Nugent; [m.] Anthony L. Swift, August 12, 1989; [ed.] A graduate of Grayson Co. High; [occ.] Inspector, I.M.S. Manufacturing; [pers.] Poetry has always been a part of my life. I've been writing poems since I was a

child, and to have one published has been a life long dream.; [a.] Leitchfield, KY

SWITZER-AARON, BILLI
[b.] February 16, 1951, Indiana; [p.] William B. and Virginia K. Switzer; [m.] Gregory J. Aaron (Lt Colonel, USAF Retired); [m.] March 15, 1970; [ch.] Jason Patrick - Kristin Dawn - Joshua Nicholas; [ed.] Fountain Central High Sch, attended Purdue Univ; [occ.] Homemaker; [oth. writ.] Until now, my writings have remained private and unpublished. I am presently compiling my poems for future publication; [pers.] My writings come from my daily experiences in life. My inspiration is from my relationship with Jesus Christ, My Lord. I strive to express myself in a very open and deeply honest manner, hoping to touch and inspire others who have traveled a similar road in life; [a.] Lubbock, TX

SYLVIA, NAYLEE
[Pen.] Naylee Ann Sylvia; [b.] April 25, 1973, Falmouth Hospital; [p.] Renee and Dennis Sylvia; [ch.] Steven Gregory Packish; [ed.] Elementary School, High School, CNA Certification and HHA Certification; [occ.] (CNA) Certified Nurses Aid; [memb.] Union; [hon.] Elementary school awards in English (writing skills); [oth. writ.] My poetry is all kept in a personal portfolio and has been for a long time; [pers.] I want my poetry to inspire and give great hope. I have expressed my feeling through poetry since age 10 and have a great need for writing poetry; [a.] Martha's Vineyard Island, MA

TACKETT, YVONNE
[b.] February 18, 1938, Colson, KY; [p.] Ochra Sexton, Della Amburgey; [m.] Efford Tackett, April 28, 1960; [ch.] Alan Duane; [ed.] Whitesburg High; Mercy College; [occ.] Assistant Director -Medical Record Department Children's Hospital of Michigan; [memb.] American Health Information Management Assoc; Little Ida Regular Baptist Church.

TAKABE, HISAMITSU
[Pen.] Takabe; [b.] November 19, 1971, Tokyo, Japan; Kyoko Takabe; [ed.] Sundai High School in Tokyo. Ramapo College of New Jersey; [oth. writ.] Several poems published in school magazine and PHP magazine in Japan, also short novels and essays in school papers.; [pers.] This poem is dedicated with my love to Lt. Mikel. I have always been influenced by Kenji Miyazawd a great Japanese poet and novelist of 50's.; [a.] Rutherford, NJ

TALIAFERRO, JUNE C.
[Pen.] Jonathan David; [b.] July 5, 1931, Washington, DC; [p.] Frederick D. and Helen Y. Williams; [m.] Henry L. Taliaferro (deceased); [m.] November 30, 1950; [ch.] Gail Y. and Guy L. Taliaferro; [ed.] Cardozo High School; Short stay LaSalle Extension Univ (Accounting) Schools of Ministry; Life-time Bible student; [occ.] Ordained Minister for the Lord Jesus Christ; [memb.] Elder/New Convent Church of The Lord Jesus Christ under Pastor Juanita E. Turner; Concerned Women for America, Prison Fellowship Fort Totten Civic Assoc; [hon.] Ordained Minister for the Lord Jesus Christ, Merit Award for Poetry (Dynamic Poetic Concepts), Prison Ministry Award (DC Dept of Corrections), Life Member PTA, Valedictorian; [oth. writ.] 2 books of verse: Moods Intermingled: 1975; Jesus Is His Name: 1992 (under Pen name, Jonathan David); Play: He Is Alive; Essays: under, "The Other Side of the Coin"; [pers.] I write under the inspiration of the creative ministry of the Lord Jesus Christ. I am so thankful to be used as His secretary; [a.] Washington, DC

TALLMAN, EVELYN T.
[b.] November 13, 1922, So. Westerlo, NY; [p.] Mrs. Hazel Mabie; [m.] January 23, 1940; [ch.] Mr. Ralph R. Tallman; [ed.] Greenville High School, Diversey Parkway, Chicago, IL; [occ.] Retired Cook and Baker; [memb.] Social Security Pension with the benefits.; [hon.] Golden Poetry Gram; [oth. writ.] The Albany Times Union I wrote food recipes.

TAMPLEN, ANNIE
[b.] May 22, 1980, Henryetta, OK; [p.] Ralph W. Tamplen; Patricia Smith; [ed.][oth. writ.] I am a freshman at Schulter High School; [hon.] Board of Education, Honor Student; [a.] Schulter, OK

TANNER, JENNIFER
[b.] November 26, 1969, Atlanta, GA; [p.] Mr. and Mrs. J. F. Fisher III; [m.] Charles Todd Tanner, June 20, 1992; [ch.] Todd Zachary Tanner; [ed.] B.A. English/University of Georgia; [occ.] Housewife, but would like to further my education in the future; [memb.] Sigma Kappa Sorority; [pers.] I plan on continuing my education in a master's program sometime in the future. Meanwhile, I will continue to write poetry and novels.; [a.] San Diego, CA

TANTILLO, CRAIG C.
[b.] June 11, 1971, Flushing, NY; [p.] Michael and Barbara Tantillo; [m.] Sara Harrison; [ch.] Jade Elizabeth; [ed.] West Islip High School, University of Story Brook; [occ.] Student; [oth. writ.] Several poems unpublished in school newspapers.; [pers.] I began writing as a hobby and it has become an addiction. My writings interpret my perception of life and all of its peculiarities.; [a.] Mastic Beach, NY

TAYLOR, ALEXANDRA RENEE
[Pen.] ART; [b.] February 6, 1978, Youngstown, OH; [p.] Priscilla Taylor; [ed.] Port Allen High; [memb.] Beta Club Secretary, L.I.F.E. Club President, 4-H Club Vice-President, Drama Club, FBLA Club, Talent Search, Biology Club; [hon.] Principle's List, English I Award, Spanish Award, Track Trophies, Cheerleading Trophies, First Place in Parish Poetry Contest; [pers.] Personal poems written in a journal.; [pers.] My writing is a reflection of my life. My initials spell the word out, therefore I believe my poems are not only a work of art, but a work of A.R.T.; [a.] Port Allen, LA

TAYLOR, TERRENCE L.
[Pen.] Terry Taylor; [b.] September 26, 1968, Winter Park, FL; [ed.] High School Honors Graduate Naval "A" School, College Degree (in pursuit of); [occ.] Power Plant Aux. Operator, Ft. Pierce, FL; [hon.] High School (Awarded) Nominated Artist of Year, Navy-Awarded Art Award, various active duty awards received from Gulf War, Dean's List; [oth. writ.] In pursuit of writing a book, personal poetry portfolio; [pers.] To dream a dream and find the means.; [a.] Pt. St. Lucie, FL

TEDD, BARBARA
[Pen.] Tedd Hughes; [b.] April 12, 1924, Cazenovla, NY; [m.] William Tedd, 1944 (deceased); [ch.] William, Bruce, Virginia; [ed.] High School; [occ.] Retired, ED. Volunteer (Docent) at Burnet Park Zoo, Syracuse; [memb.] Life Member Neowahga Chapter O.E.S., Cazenovla, NY, Smithsonian, National Geographic Society, World Wildlife Fund.; [oth. writ.] Several poems, a short essay published in Zoo paper. I also write skits for Zoo Clowns.; [pers.] I have been writing since my teens. Subjects vary. Wheels start spinning in my head and I must write immediately.; [a.] Baldwinsville, NY

TELOWITZ, NIKKI
[b.] December 12, 1967, Oceanside, WY; [p.] Harvey and Dianne Telowitz; [ed.] Freeport High School, Dowling College; [occ.] Full-time college student; [hon.] Dean's List, Dowling College; [oth. writ.] Various short stories and poems; [pers.] "In memory of my father, Harvey Telowitz, whose love and kindness will live on in my heart, and my writing; [a.] Oakdale, NY

TENCZA, LAWRENCE M.
[Pen.] "Sal"; [b.] May 21, 1963; [m.] Michelle Tenza, July 30, 1993; [ed.] Culinary Inst. of America; [occ.] Pastry Chef; [pers.] This poem was written for an ex-girlfriend who I was madly in love with about 7 years ago. Today she is my beautiful wife. I love you always and forever Michelle.

TESTA, KEITH
[Pen.] Le Poete Sombre; [b.] May 31, 1956, Brooklyn, NY; [m.] Lauren Testa, July 17, 1993; [ch.] Nicole; [occ.] Mailman; [hon.] 1) Golden Poet Award (1991), 2) Silver Poet Award (1990) -- World of Poetry; [oth. writ.] Published in following journals: 1) The Pen, 2) Word and Image Press, 3) Felicity, 4) World Poetry Anthology, 5) Great Poems of Today; [pers.] Our blood is wet with ancient and somber Greek ideas. I have been greatly influenced by Rimbaud, Shelley and Poe; but my wife, Lauren, is my eternal muse; [a.] Whitestone, NY

THEUERKAUF, SHARON
[b.] October 14, 1951, Menominee, MI; [p.] Ben and Alice Milelas; [m.] Fiance; Richard L. Marcin, I wrote my couples poem for him; [ed.] 1969 graduate of Menominee High School; [oth. writ.] I have written 36 other poems, some of the titles are: Illness, Families, Sin, Wishes, Hope, Guardian Angels, Hurt, Promises, Divorce, Alone, Fathers, Prayers and Freedom to name some; [pers.] I hope my poems will in some way help people through good and bad times in their lives and with the help of God.; [a.] Menominee, MI

THIELEN, GREGORY
[b.] July 17, 1966, Richmond, VA; [p.] R. Henry and Lucy Thielen; [m.] Elizabeth Thielen; [ed.] BA in English Literature at Arizona State Univ, MFA in Creative Writing at Arizona State Univ; [a.] Tempe, AZ

THILL, JANET M.
[b.] August 10, 1961, Marshalltown, IA; [p.] Roland Thill, Betty Dannen; [ed.] West Marshall High, Ellsworth Community College; [pers.] This poem was written for my parents who gave me the courage and strength to walk.; [a.] Milwaukee, WI

THOLENAAR-PANAIT, KARINA
[b.] October 10, 1968, Santo Domingo, Dominican Republic; [p.] Francis and Tachy Tholenaar; [m.] Vily Panait, October 30, 1992; [ed.] Santa Teresita High (In Dom. Rep.) Brookdale College, Lincroft, NJ, Travel Agents International, Ocean, NJ; [occ.] Hostess, Water Lot Cafe Restaurant (at the Oyster Point Hotel in Red Bank); [oth. writ.] Hundreds of Poems, which I am starting to translate them to english. (Cruel Grave was originally in Spanish). None published so far. This is the first time I submit my work.; [pers.] I started writing when I was 13. My writing is a reflection of my feelings and the way I think about the world. I live for love, peace, understanding, justice, passion and I feel sorrow, hurt, loneliness, madness, and that's what my writing is about.; [a.] Eatontown, NJ

THOMAS, BOBBIE J.
[b.] September 3, 1936, Crane, Texas; [p.] Crystal K. and Mable Lightfoot; [m.] Everett R. Thomas (Deceased), June 27, 1958; [ch.] Harold, Janice, Ronald, Donald; [ed.] Crane High School; [occ.] Retired; [oth. writ.] Some poems never submitted for publication.; [pers.] My poems were written as inspired.; [a.] Odessa, TX

THOMAS, FLORENCE L.
[Pen.] FLT; [b.] April 26, 1939, Brooklyn, NY; [p.] George and Vivian Barney; [m.] Divorced; [ch.] One Son Ronald, 1 Grandson Desean; [ed.] Computer Development, Certificate Awarded; [memb.] Ebenezer Missionary Baptist Church, Hushing, NY; Rev. T.P. Mitchell, Pastor; [hon.] This is my first honor (contest). Though I have written numerous poems for church, and have been honored and awarded spiritually; [oth. writ.] Jewell, Heaven, Operator, The Test, Bang! Bang! Bang!; [pers.] This poem (Little Sister & Brother) was meant to reach everyone. The key world: "Think." I feel if we use our "Thinking Power." So many situations, could be awarded.; [a.] NY, NY

THOMAS JR., HENLEY C.
[b.] October 11, 1969, Warrenton, VA; [p.] Henley and Betty Thomas; [ed.] B.S. in Psychology from Shenandoah University; [pers.] We all have keys, a key to a house, a key to a car, yet poetry is a key to my imagination.; [a.] Marshall, VA

THOMAS, VAUDALINE
[Pen.] Virginia Vaudaline Thomas; [b.] February 22, 1916, Sweetwater, TX; [p.] Deceased, Claude and Marguerite Rogers; [m.] T.T. Thomas, July 1, 1934 (deceased); [ch.] Toby (deceased), James, Mondel; [ed.] Sweetwater High School, Hardin-Simmons B.S., Texas-Tech Masters; [occ.] Retired Teacher, 32 years teaching; [memb.] T.STA, A.A.R.P, Lubbock Retired Teachers Assoc., storytelling Club (Lubbock) Northside Church of Christ; [hon.] Certification of Appreciation, TX Health Volunteers, Certificate of Appreciation from Lubbock Retired Teacher, Sweetwater Classroom President; [oth. writ.] Books "Straight Way to Heaven," "Terms Related to the Exceptional," "Plum Creek Memorabilia," "My Teaching Experience; Poem, Sharing My Dreams, won a free trip to NY City; [pers.] I write tributes for family and friends. I plan programs for senior citizens, I write programs, poems etc., for senior citizens. I wrote program for church; [a.] Lubbock, TX

THOMPSON, FRANCES L.
[b.] April 23, 1918, Sask, Canada; [p.] Deceased; [m.] Tammy Thompson, November 21, 1987; [ch.] Bill Lewellen, Sandra Bodeker, Ron Lewellen, Hazel Brunkow; [ed.] Washington High in Portland, OR; LPN Training in Montana (Lewistown); [occ.] Retired Licensed Practical Nurse from the Federal Government; [memb.] First Church of the Nazarene, Salem, OR; [hon.] Two Certificates of Merit: 1. From the Indian Health Service upon retirement after 14 years of dedicated service to the Indian community. 2. From the US Dept of Health, Education, and Welfare in grateful appreciation for many years of faithful and loyal service to the gov't of the United States; [oth. writ.] Poems in church bulletins and for each of my children. Also for fellow employees; [pers.] The Lord has inspired me to write many poems and some songs over the years for my own souls satisfaction, and I strive to honor Him and be an encourager to others; [a.] Salem, OR

THOMPSON, KAREN B.
[Pen.] Miss Debbie T.; [b.] October 7, 1967, St. Johnsbury, VT; [p.] Linda and Otis Thompson; [ed.] Lyndon Institute High School; [occ.] Business owner, stand-up comedian; [pers.] My life is a series of dreams waiting to come true, with my assistance they now live. I eagerly look forward to the birth of more!; [a.] Lyndonville, VT

THOMPSON, MOSES
[b.] August 15, 1970, Kingston, Jamaica, WI; [occ.] Owen and Beryl Thompson; [m.] Single; [ed.] Prospect Heights High School, University of Rochester; [occ.] Mechanical Engineer; [memb.] National Society of black Engineers (NSBE), Key Club; [hon.] Valedictorian 1988, Chancellor Roll of Honor, Urban League Scholar, Metropolitan Museum Gold Medalist (Art), Member of The Year (NSBE), Math and Physics Gold Medalist; [oth. writ.] Several poems published in school newspapers.; [pers.] I strive to understand what people "Think" and not what they "Say." I think that ones imagination is the strongest tool known to man. I try to exercise my imagination in my poetry and my paintings.; [a.] Springfield Gardens, NY

THORNHILL, RANDY
[b.] January 25, 1977, Fairfax, VA; [p.] Kathy and Randy Thornhill; [m.] Mike Thornhill; [ed.] Seminole High; [occ.] Lead vocals in band, poet, songwriter; [memb.] Artistic Progressions, Ten Club, The Crow Club; [oth. writ.] Underground newspapers, etc.; [pers.] In a world of rape, murder, racism and starvation it's good to know that people can read my poetry and feel alive for a change, like that.; [a.] Seminole, FL

THORSON, ROBERT
[Pen.] Robert E. Thorson; [b.] June 30, 1969, Appleton, WI; [p.] Lester and Jerry Thorson; [occ.] Mill Worker; [memb.] Musician.

TIDMAN, GINEVRA GINN
[b.] December 28, 1910, Ironton, OH; [p.] Fred and Helen Ginn; [m.] Two, both deceased; [ch.] Navy Captain Jim Callaway, Helen Callaway Hall and Holly Callaway Grobe; [ed.] BA Degree, major in Journalism, U of MI, 27 hrs towards Masters, Marshall U, Huntington, WV; [occ.] Retired, Huntington Dist, US Army Corps of Engineers, 39 yrs, 35 yrs of which served as editor employee newspaper, Castle Comments; [memb.] Am Pen Women, AAUW, Pan Hellenic, Toastmistress, YWCA Bd of Directors, Huntington Planning Commission, Deacon, First Presbyterian Church; [hon.] Castle Comments in 1984 won first place for a special Veterans Issue in the entire Corps of Engineers. Later on 2nd place in the Army-wide prestigious Keith L. Ware award for the same newspaper; [oth. writ.] One first and two second place awards in West Virginia Writers, Inc. contests, plus several Honorable Mentions, all have been published in anthologies. Published in the following magazines: Wild, Wonderful West Virginia, Huntington Quarterly; national Family Safety and Health; Marshall Univ Alumnus. Also published in one hardback, "What the Mountains Yield. "Short story won an award in a Mountain State Press contest and was published in an anthology; [pers.] Writing is tough but rewarding. Mostly it is not a team effort. You struggle alone. But if you are truly a writer, you are always composing something in your mind - in the still dark reaches of the night, etc. And then when something like this poetry contest comes along you are rewarded for your agony!; [a.] Huntington, WV

TIMMONS, RAILYN JANEL
[b.] June 12, 1980, Dover Del; [p.] Donna Spencer and Ray Timmons; [ed.] Cape Henlopen High School, 9th grade; [occ.] Student; [oth. writ.] I have written many other poems; [pers.] I love to write poems b/c it gives me a chance to let out how I feel. I hope to continue to write poems, until I no longer can; [a.] Ellendale, DE

TIRHEIMER, MARTHA
[b.] October 1, 1937, Los Angeles; [p.] Tames and Irene Sudberry; [m.] Raymond Tirheimer, September 4, 1965; [ch.] 10; [ed.] Now attending CA State San Bernardino Senior in Psychology; [occ.] Housewife; [memb.] Soroptimist, PTA; [hon.] Like membership in PTA, Dean's list at Fullerton College; [oth. writ.] Several poems for bereaved parent group, book of love poems; [pers.] I try to reflect on life and convey my thoughts on paper, so other people may read and see a reflection of similar thoughts that they are unable to write down; [a.] Running Springs, CA

TITCOMB, ROSE
[b.] March 16, 1974, San Francisco; [p.] Lydia and Martin Titcomb; [ed.] Interlochen Arts Academy, The Williston Northampton School, and presently College of Marin; [occ.] Student; [pers.] When I write, I write to untangle my tangled thoughts. To me feelings tangled and confused, sometimes is not so terrible. It just means I am living. Basically, that is what my poetry is all about, living, from the core of my heart.; [a.] San Francisco, CA

TONERI, JUDY
[b.] April 4, 1958, Everett, WA; [p.] Bevan Toneri, Judy Toneri; [ed.] BA - Business Administration - Western WA Univ; BA - Special Education - Western Wash U; MA - Elementary Education - Troy State Univ; [occ.] Second Grade Teacher, Glenwood Elementary School, Lake Stevens, WA; [memb.] Phi Delta Kappa Member, YMCA; [hon.] President's List 4-06PA Master's Program, Troy State Univ; Recognized for Outstanding Volunteer Work in Pyongtack, South Korea, 1991; Nominated by parents for US West Outstanding Teacher Program, 1988; [pers.] Embrace your past as part of your uniqueness, welcome your future with an open heart, free spirit, and soul, live in the present, making each day an adventure; [a.] Everett, WA

TOOPS, BETTY ANTRIM
[b.] September 16, 1927, Forsythe, IL; [p.] Alonzo and Rosalie Bennett Antrim; [m.] James J. Troops, June 3, 1945; [ch.] Phillip, Sandra, Vernon, Jay; [ed.] Graduated Neoga High School 1945, some creative writing classes, Lakeland College, Mattoon, IL; [occ.] Retired, Wife, Mother, Homemaker; [memb.] National League of American Pen Women, Past Vice President of Mattoon Chapter; [oth. writ.] "You Might as Well Laugh" copyright 1980 Prairie Poet Books, Charleston, IL; [pers.] I like to sort out the way I feel about events that move me deeply by writing poems about them sometimes I write about the way I would like them to be rather than the way they are why not?; [a.] Neoga, IL

TORKELSON, KRIS
[b.] June 1, 1977, Wichita, KS; [p.] David and Robin Torkelson; [ed.] Sr at Catoosa High School; [hon.] Who's Who in High School Teenagers - Principal's Honor Roll at Grand Island High School; [oth. writ.] Unpublished book of poems, which I hope one day will be published; [pers.] "I write what I see and feel, real poetry doesn't say anything it just ticks off the possibility's and opens all the doors"; [a.] Tulsa, OK

TORRES, NICK
[b.] January 29, 1983; [p.] Eric and Corinne Torres; [m.] Single; [ed.] Frank Elementary School, Nevitt Elementary School; [occ.] student in 5th grade.; [hon.] Good Citizenship, Good reading and writing award.; [pers.] I enjoy poems because it helps me relax.; [a.] Phoenix, AZ

TORRES, RUTH
[b.] Fairmont, NC; [p.] James Alton and Nora Barnes; [m.] Raul, May 14, 1966; [ch.] Bob; [ed.] Mastbaum Vocational HS; Community College of Philadelphia; [occ.] Legal Secretary; [memb.] Trinity Methodist Church; [hon.] Highest honors, Assoc Degree; [oth. writ.] Shadows on the Wall (poem) published: Days End; Poetry drafts/story drafts; [pers.] My metamorphosis took longer than that of the caterpillar who emerged to become a beautiful monarch butterfly. Now that my rebirth has begun, I can take wing and soar; [a.] Philadelphia, PA

TRACY, MEEGAN
[b.] August 14, 1970, Fairfax, VA; [p.] John and Lesley Tracy; [ed.] University of Maryland, University College; [memb.] Ski Club of Washington, D.C.; [pers.] I try to treat everyone with love and kindness.; [a.] Bethesda, MD

TRASK, DEANNA
[pers.] There will always be those to guide our footsteps when the teardrops won't let us see.

TRAVERSE, VERNON LEE
[b.] December 8, 1957, Owosso, MI; [p.] Howard Traverse, Marge Traverse; [m.] Marie Blazo-Traverse; [ch.] Eric Traverse; [ed.] St. Charles High, Michigan State Technical College; Also, Durham Technical Community College; [occ.] Machinist; [memb.] Saginaw Bay Church of God, Eagles Club; [oth. writ.] Several poems published with newspapers about God and love and romance; [pers.] I write to show my son God is for all. Also, we all have God in us some way!

TRIGGS, DEBORAH
[b.] October 15, 1966, Smithtown, NY; [p.] William and Barbara Fogelberg; [m.] Robert Triggs, April 22, 1990; [ch.] Jessica Triggs; [ed.] Seton High Christendom College, Northern Virginia Community College; [occ.] Dental Hygienist; [memb.] American Dental Hygienists Association; [hon.] NVCC - Magna Cum Laude, Dean's List, Hu - Friedy's Golden Scaler Award; [pers.] Have faith in your writing ability. With much perseverance, your efforts will be rewarded; [a.] Woodbridge, VA

TRIMBLE, VICKY N.
[Pen.] Taz; [b.] May 25, 1973, St. Charles, MO; [p.] Shelia June Trimble and Guy R. Trimble; [ed.] Portageville High School, Hickey Business School; [occ.] Paralegal; [pers.] My writing comes from my heart. I write about things that have happened to myself or my friends and family.; [a.] Overland, MO

TRINKLE, JOANNE E.
[b.] April 21, 1970, Philadelphia, PA; [p.] Edward and Isabel Trinkle; [ed.] Currently enrolled in Bachelors/ Masters Program at Syracuse University in School of Social Work; [occ.] Employment Specialist for persons with Disabilities; [pers.] My goal is that my writing would be used to facilitate change for persons who have been degraded or treated unfairly. To give a contribution to the greater society by touching individuals in my life's work.; [a.] Syracuse, NY

TUMEY, JENNIFER
[b.] January 24, 1975, New York City; [p.] Wayne Tumey, Linda Tumey; [ed.] Babylon High, Nassau Community College, currently transferring; [occ.] College student; [memb.] Student Council in high school, currently pledging for position on college newspaper staff; [hon.] Principles List, Honor Roll, and Regents Diploma from High School. Currently pledging Phi Theta Kappa Honor Society with a 3.5 average; [oth. writ.] Many other poems published in both high school and college newspapers; [pers.] Since the age of nine, I have expressed my feelings through poetry. There is no better way to reach another's heart; [a.] Babylon, NY

TURLEY, TIMOTHY
[pers.] Praise Jesus for all things. Through Him all things are possible; [a.] Huntington, WV

TURNER, CHRISTOPHER J.
[Pen.] C. J., Doc; [b.] June 22, 1964, Munich, W. Ger.; [p.] Joseph L. and Juanita Turner; [ed.] Graduated Russell County High Attending, Mid Continent Baptist Bible College; [occ.] Motel Worker and U.S. Army National Guard; [memb.] NCOA, AUSA, EANG-KY, Reidland Baptist Church, Moose Club; [hon.] Army Achievement Medals, Army Commendation Medals, Expert Field Medical Badge, Combat Medical Badge; [pers.] Jesus Christ is the only way into Heaven.; [a.] Paducah, KY

TURNER, DAVID J.
[b.] September 13, 1963, Boscobel, WI; [p.] Lloyd L. and Pearl C. Turner; [ed.] Hamilton High School, Sussex, WI; [occ.] Owner, Progressive Printing and Advertising; [oth. writ.] Four books of poems, prose, and lyrics...never published; [pers.] I write from inside myself...How I felt yesterday. What I feel today. How I may feel tomorrow; [a.] Waukesha, WI

TURNER, LOIS BAGGETTE
[b.] May 15, 1918, Manning, SC; [p.] Robert C. and Elizabeth R. Baggette; [m.] O. Blount Turner, Jr., January 6, 1940; [ch.] Elizabeth T. Darling, Joseph B. Turner; Grandchildren: Scott, David, Madeline Turner, Laura Darling; Great Grandson: Dakota Andrew Turner; [occ.] Retired Teacher; [ed.] Manning, SC High, Barton College; [hon.] None Recently; [oth. writ.] Several Poems; [pers.] I write for my own pleasure about my experiences and thoughts.; [a.] Silver Spring, MD

TURPEN, CYNTHIA
[b.] September 12, 1978, Phoenix, AZ; [p.] Charles and Nancy Turpen; [ed.] Freshman at Tempe High School; [occ.] Student; [memb.] Freshman Volleyball Player, school newspaper, and active in numerous school activities.; [hon.] 4.0+ G.P.A., Honors classes and Golden Scholar; [oth. writ.] To Eric, published in at Day's End. Many school publications; [pers.] When I sit down and write a poem it is usually always about someone who means a great deal to me. I feel relieved and extremely proud of myself after I have successfully written a good poem. I'm glad I have the opportunity to share my poems with others.; [a.] Tempe, AZ

TUTTLE, JULIE
[b.] April 28, 1965; Bloomfield, IA; [p.] Joe Jones and Linda LaRue; [m.] Patrick Tuttle, June 12, 1987; [ch.] Phillip Dean, Wayland Robert and Tricia Nicole; [ed.] Davis Co High School till 1981 - received GED from Indian Hills Comm College in 1985; [occ.] Mother - homemaker - babysitter - aspiring songwriter; [hon.]

Editor's Choice Award from the National Library of Poetry in 1994. Being chosen for publication in "Best Poems of 1995" Having my first song recorded; [oth. writ.] Love is - published in "Tears of Fire". "Howdy" a tribute song to Minnie Pearl, recorded in Nashville by Lulu Roman. Many unpublished poems and songs; [pers.] Wishes: something wanted - only wished for - expected to happen by luck. Dreams: Something desired - strived for - made happen by labor; [a.] Birmingham, IA

TYLER, FRANCINE
[Pen.] Francine Weathersby; [b.] July 2, 1957, Natchez, MS; [p.] Lindsay and Imogene Weathersby; [m.] Bobby L. Tyler, February 26, 1982; [ch.] Wendy Shonta, Byron Lamar, Kelley Waddell; [ed.] Franklin High, Meadville, MS Jackson State University, Watterson Career Com.; [occ.] Residential Trainer Aide; [memb.] Heroines of Jericho; [oth. writ.] Several poems waiting to be published.; [pers.] I put God at the head of my life, for without him nothing is possible. Writing comes a daily living thing for me, I only wish I had pursued it sooner.; [a.] Oakdale, LA

UCMAN, FRANK A.
[b.] July 10, 1943, Herminie #2, Penna.; [p.] Anton and Alice ucman; [m.] Ruth Gremminger, Ucman, November 23, 1950; [ch.] Robert Collin and Barbara Ellen ucman; [ed.] Sewicidey Township High School, University of Pittsburgh and Robert Morris; [occ.] Retired from Dept. of Interior, National Park Service in Washington, D.C.; [memb.] Veterans of Foreign Wars, Acme Lodge #83, Ancient Accepted Scottish Rite, American Contract Bridge League, Leven Green Presbyterian Church; [oth. writ.] "Soldier Boy," a fictionalized novel of World War II, being published by Quixote Publications, slated for release during March, 1995.; [pers.] Soldier Boy's theme is the futility of war, paying tribute to all brothers-in-arms who gave up their lives in the most devastating carnage ever on earth. god help us keep it from ever happening again!; [a.] Trafford, PA

UDEN, CAROL
[Pen.] Elaine Horton; [b.] April 14, 1970, New York; [p.] Joan and Ken Simons; [m.] Dale Uden, May 20, 1989; [ed.] Emily Ann Uden age 4; [pers.] I feel children are a special gift given to special people and those that don't treasure that, don't understand the gift.; [a.] Yuma, AZ

URBAN, JEFF
[b.] July 25, 1969, Whavehouse Pt. CT; [p.] Raymond and Suzanne Urban; [ed.] Palmyra High School, United States Naval Academy, University of Missouri, Columbia; [occ.] Student, Univ. of Missouri; [oth. writ.] Currently in the process of writing a novel dealing with my years at the Academy and ultimately my separation from that institution.; [pers.] I used to think fate was guiding my life when things were going well. My poem is a result of that fate being shattered. Learning and excepting your new fate is the key.; [a.] Columbus, MO

URBAN, MAGGIE ANN
[b.] May 31, 1979, Cleveland, OH; [p.] Diane Miller and William Urban; [ed.] Sophomore at Vermilion High School; [occ.] Student; [pers.] My poetry comes from my thoughts and feelings.; [a.] Vermilion, OH

URIEGAS, JULIA
[Pen.] Juls; [b.] August 2, 1973, Houston, TX; [p.] Frank and Esther Munoz; [m.] Steven Uriegas, August 5, 1994;

[ed.] Graduated Sam Houston High with honors; [occ.] Secretary; [oth. writ.] Several poems I've written throughout the years.; [pers.] My writing is a treasure to me. And I'm grateful to my husband for all his support and encouragement throughout the years of my writing.; [a.] Houston, TX

VALICENTI, ELIZABETH
[b.] Canton, NY; [p.] Samuel and Ida Kaplan; [m.] Pasquale W. Valicenti (died May 1983), June 21, 1952; [ed.] Graduate, Rogers High, Newport, RI; Courses at George Washington University, Washington, D.C.; Poetry and Writing at Georgetown U., Washington, D.C., Poetry Workshops by teacher from Georgetown U.; [occ.] Retired from business; now occupied with the arts--Japanese Brush Painting at the Smithsonian; Voice at Levine School of Music; Poetry and Writing; [memb.] Smithsonian, Washington Opera; Washington Performing Arts Society; Kennedy Center; Hebrew Home of D.C.; [hon.] First Place for Poetry, Creative Writing Festival 1989, $75.00. (Washington, D.C.); [oth. writ.] "Safari In Kenya, East Africa," recently submitted to Travel Holiday for possible publication (Oct. 1994 NYC); [pers.] Without the encouragement to enter your contest, from my dear friends, Margaret beck and Sylvia MacKinnon, I may not have entered. For this, I thank them.; [a.] Washington, D.C.

VAN CLEVE, JERRY R.
[b.] November 5, 1952, Middletown, Ohio; [p.] Jesse and Marcella Van Cleve; [m.] Josephine M. Brannon Van Cleve, August 29, 1981; [ch.] Chad Jeremy, Jerry Thomas, Joseph Brannon; [ed.] Lemon Monroe High; [occ.] Truck Driver; [oth. writ.] T.G.I.F.; Rags to Riches; I Have A Confession; The Lovin Store; He'll Never Know; It's An Autobiography; I Hope You'll Come Back Home Someday; I'm Just A Man; This Is My Song; The Call; I Don't Live On No Gulf Course; [pers.] Country music and ballads have captured my heart. No matter if it's happy or sad, it must relate to the common working class. Hopefully it not only has a message, but is a learning experience.; [a.] Middleton, OH

VAN HOOFT, CHRISTINE M.
[Pen.] Chris Van Hooft; [b.] November 16, 1956, Fall River, MA; [p.] Edward and Dorothy Rego; [m.] Richard Van Hooft, October 5, 1984; [ed.] Bridgewater, Raynham Regional High School; [memb.] National Organization for Women, Massachusetts Audobon Society; [pers.] Strive to be true to yourself, carry love in your heart, and never fear risk or change.; [a.] Sharon, MA

VAN PRAET, MARIEA T.
[b.] October 3, 1940, N. Ireland; [p.] John and Ellen Josephine McDonell; [m.] Camiel Gustav Van Praet, May 8, 1992; [ch.] Lorraine, Therese, Kieran Fraser (Gillian-Elsie Corina); [ed.] Kilkeel Technical College, N. Ireland; [occ.] Homemaker; [memb.] American Cancer Society Inc., The Arthritis Foundation, National Heart Council, The Nature Conservancy; North Shore Animal League; [pers.] I like to write what I feel and see and hope to create a greater awareness of the world around us.; [a.] Sarasota, FL

VANARSDALE, CINDY T.
[b.] August 1, 1960, St. Louis, MO; [p.] Harvey and Pat Totsch; [m.] Bruce Vanarsdale, October 8, 1982; [ch.] Anthony Bruce (11) and John Alexander (3); [ed.] St. Benedict Elementary, Foley High, Univ of Montevallo; [occ.] Self employed screen printer, T-Shirt line called

"Sancta-T's"; Religious: Anti-abortion; [oth. writ.] Several other selections unpublished; [pers.] Through both my writing and T-Shirts I want to touch the hearts of people who have grown callous and insensitive to the innocent; [a.] Foley, AL

VANDIVER, PAUL
[b.] September 14, 1979; [p.] Janet and Charles Vandiver; [ch.] Two sisters: Nicola and Natalie Vandiver; [ed.] Freshman, Lexington High School; [occ.] Tip Top Exxon and Student; [memb.] Former Pentathlon Team, 4-H reporter and in charge of Westover's School News; [oth. writ.] Short stories and poems; [pers.] My friend April Leon convinced me to send my poem to you, so I have her to thank a great deal. None of my work has been publicly printed, but I hope some of it will be in the future.

VARNADORE, RODNEY
[p.] Ann and Talmadge Varnadore; [b.] September 26, 1969, Winter Haven, FL; [ed.] Auburndale Sr. High, Polk Community College, United States Marine Corps.; [occ.] Incarcerated, North Carolina, Dept. of Corrections; [hon.] Music scholarship to Polk Community College; [oth. writ.] Several non-published poems.; [pers.] To give relief to people who might not see the light to happiness; without the materialistic attribute. Moreover, Disposing Cognitive Distortions and recognizing "Change" as human development. "Being contempt is in the eye of the beholder."; [a.] Auburdale, FL

VARNER, ELIZABETH PETTIT
[b.] July 10, 1924, Wilkes-Barre, PA; [p.] Fred S. and Charlotte Lewis Pettit; [m.] George Wilson Varner, September 29, 1951; [ed.] James M. Coughlin High School, Wilkes-Barre, PA, 1942. Wyoming Seminary Dean School of Business, Secretarial Course, 1943; attended Manchester Community College, Manchester, CT for extra courses periodically; [occ.] Retired Executive Secretary, The Travelers Insurance Company, Hartford, CT; [memb.] St. James' Episcopal Church, Glastonbury, CT. Treasurer, VFW Post 7659 Ladies' Auxiliary, Glastonbury, CT; National Honor Society - 1942; [oth. writ.] Occasional letters in local papers; once had letter published in Life Magazine's Letters to the Editor; [pers.] "And this above all, to thine own self be true and it must follow, as the night the day, thou canst not then be false to any man." William Shakespeare; [a.] Glastonbury, CT

VAUGHAN, GWENDOLYN ADDIE MORRIS
[Pen.] Gwen Morris-Vaughan; [b.] March 17, 1967, Portsmouth, VA; [p.] Jesse and Marie Morris; [m.] Ernest Purvis Vaughan, November 25, 1955; [ch.] Robin Leslie, Beverly Rae; [ed.] I.C. Norcom High, Courses at Norfolk St. Univ., Old Dominion Univ., and Tidewater Community College; [occ.] Retired; [memb.] 3rd Baptist Church, Sunday School Teacher, Choir Member, member of Women's Guild, Children's Ministry Council Counselor; [hon.] Sect'y Former Port Norfolk East Condo Assoc.; Former Sect'y Martin Luther King Steering Committee (local). Sect'y I.C., Norcom Class of 55, Award of Merit Certificate, World of Poetry, Eddie Lou Cole, Poetry Editor and Senior Judge; [oth. writ.] Wrote song for National Motto "Miss School, Miss Out" Luke 2:52 (9/17/91) local Award of Merit Certificate, World of Poetry for "Help Wanted" PS. 1:1-2, Honorable Mention (2/28/87) Published 2 lines "Grit" publications. Paraphrased jester Hairston's "Great God A'Mighty" for church choir (local) 2/16/88; [pers.] Poetry is Bible based, God-given and scripturally relevant. Inspired by the Holy Spirit of God.; [a.] Portsmouth, VA

VAUGHN, MRS. IRIS ANN
[Pen.] Candi; [b.] August 18, 1961, Camden, NJ; [p.] Elzora and John Diggs; [m.] Mr. Willie Vaughn (In Heaven), August 18, 1984; [ch.] Jeri, Brook and Courtney; [ed.] Williamstown High, Gloucester County Voc Tech, Gloucester County College; [occ.] Nurse; [memb.] Open Door Faith Ministries, Salvation Army, Heal The World, Save The Children, Foster Parent Assoc, PTA, PTO, DARE; [hon.] HS Honor Roll, College Dean's List, Becoming a grandmommy for the first time in December 1994; [oth. writ.] Full poetry collections awaiting publishing; [pers.] "If I never achieve anything else, I hope to show the world one thing through my poetry; Love." I dedicate this to my husband, Willie and my pop-pop, Ross Pratt; [a.] Williamstown, NJ

VELASQUEZ, MARIA
[Pen.] Raven; [b.] April 27, 1966, Juan Velasquez, Catalina Velasquez; [ed.] Bassett High School, ELAC (East Los Angeles College), FIDM (Fashion Inst of Design and Merchandising); [hon.] Dean's List; [pers.] As a romantic, I am free to explore the many possibilities of feelings in my writing. The early romantic poets were always an inspiration to me; [a.] LaPuente, CA

VELAZQUEZ, NORBERT
[b.] September 6, 1971, New York; [p.] Luz Velazquez, Manuel Velazquez; [ed.] Hunter College; [occ.] Operations Supervisor, Popkin Software and Systems, Inc; [oth. writ.] The Space Between; [pers.] You'll always have your memories and dreams. No one can take those away from you; [pers.] New York, NY

VERACKA, LINDA M.
[Pen.] Linda Hassett Veracka; [b.] November 19, 1946, Revere, MA; [ch.] John, Leta; [ed.] Msgr. Ryan Memorial, Dorchester, MA, Bridgewater State College, Bridgewater, MA (Soph); [occ.] Full-time student; [memb.] Dean's List; [hon.] New England Press Assoc. 1st place, special category, 1991 for newspaper issue following the murder of a 13 year old by her next door neighbor.; [oth. writ.] 10 years journalism, including hard news, features, sports.; [pers.] I live my life constantly working to achieve balance between reason and passion.; [a.] Kingston, MA

VERGARA, IRENIO
[b.] September 22, 1921, Philippines; [p.] Castor and Teodora Vergara, March 18, 1944; [ch.] Ed. Glenn, Arnold, Aida and Irene; [ed.] High School; [occ.] Insurance Salesman, Retired; [memb.] AARP, PTA, and many others; [hon.] Certificate of Award from Lafayette Life Ins. Co., Certificate of Award from Governor George Ariyoshi, A Plaque of Distinguish and Devoted Service as UFCH Convention Chair and many more.; [oth. writ.]q Essays, affidavits, poems; [pers.] As trained in english writing in any "English 100" I believe age doesn't stop me from learning more. The more I write the more I pursue learning variety of subjects. I also learned journalism.; [a.] Kaunakauai, HI

VERMONT, DONNA MARIE
[b.] May 12, 1963; Boonton, NJ; [p.] Pasquale Vermont - Lucyena Vermont; [ed.] County College of Morris, Randolph, NJ; Degree: Associate in Applied Science, Concentration: Nursing; [occ.] Registered Nurse; [pers.] During my nursing education, I developed a keen sense of delivering patient care with my "head, heart, and hands". We, as human beings, need to acquaint ourselves with this "trio", and passionately exercise it during the ebb's and flows of our lives; [a.] Howell, NJ

VERNON, CYNTHIA L.
[Pen.] C. L. Vernon; [b.] June 18, 1958, Newark, NJ; [p.] Liba and Margaret Vernon; [ed.] High School graduate - 1976 - Tioga Central High Sch, Tioga Center, NY; [oth. writ.] Additional poetry - unpublished as yet. Ghost writer with my sister, Lisa Vernon on short stories - Sci Fi and Fantasy; [pers.] Poetry is a release for me. It helps me organize my thoughts and get in touch with me; [a.] Binghamton, NY

VERUCCI, EVELYN A.
[b.] January 16, 1962, Wilmington, DE; [p.] James and Frances Verucci; [m.] Divorced; [ch.] David Carl and Crystal Marie Russnak; [ed.] Glasgow High; [occ.] Legal Secretary; [hon.] Honor Roll in High School; won scholarship to Control Data Institute in Arlington, VA; [pers.] The most important thing in lie to me is to teach your children good moral standards and that they are worthy of love.; [a.] Delaware City, DE

VINE, JUDITH
[b.] December 23, 1944, Detroit, MI; [p.] Ruth and Charles Rader; [m.] George Vine; [m.] April 8, 1990; [ch.] Betsy Share, David Share, Allen and Amy Vine, Michael Vine, Sandy and Michael Baumhaft, Nikki Baumhaft and Jason Baumhaft; [ed.] BS - Wayne State Univ, MA Michigan State Univ; [occ.] Publicist; [memb.] Michigan Recreation and Park Association, Hadassah; [hon.] Michigan Volunteer Leadership Award; [oth. writ.] Articles published in local newspaper; script for video production aired on cable television; [pers.] All voices need to be heard. Poetry, the inner voice, flows through one's fingertips into the framework of language. When I write poetry, my inner voice shares its thoughts and ideas; [a.] West Bloomfield, MI

VINSON, EDWARD A.
[Pen.] Thomas Rafferty; [b.] November 5, 1943, Charleston, SC; [p.] Edward and Elizabeth Vinson; [m.] Constance H. Vinson; [ch.] Josander, Eric, Nicole, Ralph, Quentin; [ed.] BA, MSW, Jewis studies; [occ.] Volunteer pastoral counseling, maritime mercy ministries; [memb.] Ministerial Assn and Christian Boaters Assn; [oth. writ.] Under the Influence: A Coming of Age (a trilogy); Within Thy Gates; Within The Viel; Meditations On A Miracle; various booklets and songs; [pers.] The enclosed poem is an example of the river of song God puts in hearts by His indwelling Spirit when people ask His Son Jesus or Yeshua to live in them, forgive them, and make them "new creations"; [a.] Gloucester Pt, VA

VISCONTY, ELIZABETH VICTORIA
[b.] July 23, 1975, Manhattan, NY; [p.] Emil and Norma Visconty; [ed.] Cardinal Gibbons High, B.C.C. North Campus Major: Pre-Optometry; [occ.] Medical Assistant at South Florida Eye Institute; [oth. writ.] One poem published in B.C.C.'s art magazine P'an Ku, "Falling of the Edge."; [pers.] I base my poems on my inner feelings, thoughts, and dreams. I also write about what I see around me and the stresses of everyday life. My favorite poets are: John Donne, Percy Bysshe Shelley, and John Keats.; [a.] Ft. Lauderdale, FL

VOGELSANG, JACQUELINE
[Pen.] Jacqueline; [b.] I am of a certain age; [p.] Birdie and Basil Carlton Davis; [m.] I am divorced; [ch.] Crystal and Michael; [ed.] Baxley High School, reading and world travel; [occ.] Retired, Vogel Marine Supply Co. I am a newly published writer, just local newspapers, mostly opinion pieces, two poems published. I'm proud that TNLOP accepted one of my poems. I love reading and writing; [a.] Mandarin, FL

VOLKART, NANCY ALICE
[Pen.] Nanc/Nancy Volkart; [b.] November 14, 1952, Jackson, Minn.; [p.] Lawrence and Hazel Kusler; [m.] Jere L. Volkart, July 17, 1976; [ch.] Hope Darcy and Joshua Lee; [ed.] Atwater Public School; [occ.] Domestic Engineer; [oth. writ.] Story in Dakota Magazine, poem in local newspaper, craft and art tips and Easter Story.; [pers.] Whatever comes from my thoughts and heart goes on paper; I have the need to write truth and good positive things in our lives.; [a.] Watertown, SD

VOLPE, EILEEN R.
[b.] August 23, 1942, Fort Morgan, CO; [p.] Earl and Ellen Moore; [m.] David P. Volpe Sr. (divorced), July 28, 1965; [ch.] David Peter Jr., Christina Marie; [ed.] Ft. Morgan High School, Northeastern Jr. College, University of N. Colo., California State University-L.A.; [occ.] Special Education Resource Teacher--Saugus H.S., Saugus, CA; [memb.] Daughters of American Revolution, Council for Exceptional Children, California Teacher's Association, National Teacher's Association, Phi Delta Kappa; [hon.] Dean's List, Kappa Delta Pi-Education Honorary; [oth. writ.] Published winner of VFW Essay Contest--"Civil Defense An American Institution," poem published in local newspaper, children's stories--Children's Institute of Writing; [pers.] My life and surroundings are reflected in each verse; combining the past with the present. American poets of the nineteenth century have been and will continue to be an influence on my life.; [a.] Santa Clarita, CA

VON DOLLN, GEORGETTA
[b.] May 4, 1963, Columbus, OH; [p.] Thomas Collier, Lena Collier; [m.] Edward von Dolln, February 20, 1993; [ed.] Lancaster High, Circleville Bible College, Mt. Vernon Nazarene College (Ohio); [occ.] Child care; [memb.] Church of the Nazarene (Bellows Ave) Ohio, Columbus Christian, Writers Association; [pers.] My goal in writing poetry is to reflect on the goodness of life as well as to offer love and hope to every individual who reads it; [a.] Grove City, OH

VOORHIES, PAULINE
[Pen.] "Billie" Voorhies; [b.] October 24, 1922; [p.] Numa and Mamie Pierce; [m.] P.J. Voorhies (deceased), September 18, 1944; [ch.] Four, three living, a twin died at age 2; [ed.] High School, Business School and some College Courses; [occ.] Assistant Librarian at Cathedral-Carmel School; [memb.] Member Oakbourne Country Club, City Club of Lafayette, Member of First Methodist Church, Choir Member; [pers.] I endeavor to express the deep longing that lives in all of us. So the heart and soul of the poet is poured out in the written lines. After reading you'll come to know me...just as I am.; [a.] Lafayette, LA

VOSS, JUDY
[b.] July 2, 1953, Malone, New York; [p.] Carlton and Shirley Fairchild; [m.] Paul Voss; [ch.] Jimmy and Matt; [ed.] Brushton, Moira Central School, State University of New York at Canton, California State University at Chico; [occ.] Registered Nurse; [memb.] Association of Operating Room Nurses; [pers.] I wish the gift of laughter and sense of humor to those who have neither but could benefit from both.

WADDLE SR., ROBERT T.
[b.] February 26, 1922, Sante Fe Trail, Dodge City, Kansas; [p.] George William and Agnes Marie Waddle; [m.] Jean Crissman Riley, Nov. 1945; [ch.] Marcia Jean Crissman, Robert Jr. and Marie I; [occ.] Retired USAF

1964; [hon.] A chest full of ribbons and medals from 22 yrs in the military; [oth. writ.] Written life story called "Footsteps through Life," a few poems and grandpa stories from my memories of growing up in the great depression, my military years, and life since then; [hon.] God gave us a perfect world and allows us to direct our own footsteps through life.; [a.] Salton City, CA

WAGNER, MARLENE JO
[Pen.] M. J. Wagner; [b.] December 5, 1949, Harrisonville, MO; [p.] Wm. and Carol Carroll; [m.] Michael E. Wagner I; [ch.] Shelly 23, Mike 12, Matt 5; [ed.] CMSU, B.S. Graphic Arts, Technology & Management; [memb.] C.H.A.D.D.; [hon.] Outstanding Support Staff Member of the Year at Griffith Elementary in the Ferguson/Florissont School District 1992; [oth. writ.] A.D.D. My poem used to open conferences and workshops on Attention Deficit Disorder in St. Louis, MO; [pers.] Always do everything 100% without hurting anyone, or anything esp. Earth, but children are earth's greatest asset that must be educated and nurtured with a sense of love and kindness.; [a.] Florissant, MO

WAKEFIELD, ALLEN
[b.] September 21, 1938, Kalamazoo, MI; [ed.] Kalamazoo Central High school, Western Michigan University; [occ.] Retired Postal Clerk, Co-Publisher and Editor of The Grass Roots Review, (a literary review by and for working people; [a.] Comstock, MI

WAKEFIELD, SHARRON E.
[b.] December 20, 1948, Maryland; [p.] Gerry and Arden Cardner; [m.] X Samuel D. Wakefield, July 19, 1966; [ch.] Donald, Mike, Brad; also 4 beautiful grand girls: Melanie, Ashley, Brittany, Brooke; [occ.] Nurse Aid; [hon.] A poem in another book - "Want"; [oth. writ.] "Want!"; Our Western World's Greatest Poems '83; [pers.] I write what comes from my heart; [a.] Akron, OH

WALKER, MARJORIE B.
[b.] November 8, 1915, Chicago; [p.] Mr. and Mrs. Owen E. Brumbaugh; [m.] Franklin E. Walker, May 10, 1941; [ch.] James, Lauri and Robert; [ed.] Roosevelt HS Chicago, various night school college courses; [occ.] Retired legal sec'y; Note: resided in Fremont, MI - 49 yrs - in Ohio 1 yr; [oth. writ.] Only poetry; [pers.] Take time to listen and to smell the roses along the way. A rose garden is as lovely at night as in day time.

WALKER, PEYTON
[b.] August 7, 1979, Gainesville, GA; [p.] Micki and Tony Walker; [ed.] Attended Gainesville City Schools; [occ.] Student; [hon.] Oratorical Speech Winner/Optimist Club; [oth. writ.] Reflection; For Fears of Night; Moon; A Song Keeps Playing In Mind; Darkness; Dancing Lily; Eyes Closed; Another Realm; Distant; A Chance; Blue Sphere; A Life For All; [pers.] Thanks to Mother Earth, for giving me wings. I have been greatly influenced by poets Paul Simon, and Edgar Allan Poe.; [a.] Gainesville, GA

WALKER, RONALD ALFRED
[b.] Bronx, NY; [p.] Maurice and Vera (Deceased); [m.] Alma, December 11, 1965 (divorced 1989); [ch.] Lisa, Stephan; [ed.] Graduate High School, Bronx, NY, Theo Roosevelt; [occ.] Freelance Writer, Essayist; [oth. writ.] Several essays covering humanitarian subjects and profiles of authors and literary works.; [pers.] Literature is to all men, I believe, a rescuer from darkness...a stronghold of hope to our highest aspirations, and a refuge of

reason to our most impassioned thoughts.; [a.] Binghamton, NY

WALLACE, DOROTHY A.
[b.] September 11, 1942, Wright County, MO; [p.] Stephen Foster Dudley, Lois Breman Dudley; [m.] Widow; [ch.] Michael Dean Huckaby, David Lee Wallace; [ed.] Mansfield High School, Mansfield, MO, Drury College and Southwest Missouri State Univ, Springfield, MO; [occ.] Special Education Administrator, Mansfield R-IV Schools, Mansfield, MO; [memb.] Council for Exceptional Children, Council of Administrators of Special Education, Missouri State Teachers Assoc, Network for Women in Administration, American Sales Assoc; [oth. writ.] Articles for local newspapers, family histories for the Wright County History Book and Douglas County History Book; [a.] Mansfield, MO

WALLACE, JOE DON
[b.] June 15, 1982, Pine Bluff, AK; [p.] Don Wallace and Rebecca Myhand; [ed.] Seventh Grade Student, Rison Junior High School; [occ.] Student; [memb.] Library Club, Boy Scouts, Drug Awareness Club, Student Council, Rison Wildcat Marching Band, First Presbyterian Church of Pine Bluff Ark., Gifted and Talented; [hon.] Presidential Award, School Honor Award; [oth. writ.] Glory to God (Dedication Poem); [pers.] Poetry is a way in which I express my feelings for life, and I love the expressions on my readers face whether it be tears, or a smile.; [a.] Pine Bluff, AR

WALSH, ZIONE
[b.] 1955; [ed.] Engineering and Physics; [occ.] Fifteen years in the Wall Street as Telecommunications Specialist; [hon.] Many awards and honors for poetry; [oth. writ.] Numerous writings; [pers.] Zione's love for life is evident in her writing. Her belief is that most people spend the majority of their lives existing and not partaking in life. Her Philosophy is: "I don;t mind the idea of dying; I am more concerned with missing the participation of being human." "My life is now and my spirit is forever." As for poetry--"The job of the poet is to render the world--to see it and report it without loss, without perversion. No poet ever talks about feelings. Only sentimental people do." Mark Van Doren

WALTERS, EUGENIA
[b.] October 13, 1918, Fulton, Howard Co.,; [p.] Eugene and Edna Marlow Walters; [ed.] St. Mary's Female Seminary Jr. College, St. Mary's City, MD, A.A. Degree, George Washington, Univ, Wash. D.C. AA, BGS, M.A. Higher Ed. Admin.; [occ.] Retired U.S. Office of Ed. Washington, D.C., Grant Specialist; [memb.] Phi Delta Kappa, MD Retired Teachers Assoc., MD Historical Society and many others; [hon.] Awarded Sesquicentennial Distinguished Service Award by St. Mary's College of MD; [oth. writ.] Poetry; [pers.] Since retiring in 1983, I have been active on several city committees and have for the last few years tutored as a volunteer, persons with reading disabilities.; [a.] College Park, MD

WALTMAN, CASEY
[b.] May 11, 1977, Anchorage, AK; [p.] Kathy Russell and Harry Waltman; [ed.] Currently in 11th grade at Chugiak High School, Chugiak, AK; [oth. writ.] Several poems and short stories.; [a.] Wasilla, AK

WARD, CRAIG DAVID
[b.] November 2, 1974, Augusta, ME; [p.] David and Suzanne Ward; [ed.] High School graduate, Winthrop High School; [pers.] My writings are inspired from many

different things. Fantasy, dreams, experience, mystery, romance, I find poetry a very easy expression. All you need is a muse and a pencil.; [a.] N. Monmouth, ME

WARD, TAMMY L.
[b.] May 8, 1958, Hartford, CT; [p.] Patricia and Walter Ward; [ed.] A.S. Business Administration 1979, University of Hartford, C.R.M.C. Accreditation, Certified Radio Marketing Consultant; [occ.] Art Dealer/Consultant; [memb.] Unitarian Universalist Church, Wadsworth Atheneum, National Organization for Wormen, National Museum of Women in the Arts; [oth. writ.] I write song lyrics, short stories, feature articles, navel articles and radio commercials in addition to poetry.; [pers.] Always...trust your instincts. Listen to your inner voice, be open to positive outside influences and bring your dreams to destiny; [a.] Bloomfield, CT

WASHBURN, LORI ANN
[b.] August 31, 1967, Minerial Wells, TX; [p.] Lyle & Claudia Washburn; [m.] Tye Koch, October 4, 1994; [ch.] Muzette C. Washburn; [ed.] Berryhill High, Career Point Business School, Tulsa County Area Vo-Tech,Tulsa Junior College; [occ.] Computer Operator, Free Lance Writer; [oth. writ.] A Salem Breeze Published in Quill Books of Poetry 1988.; [pers.] All of the poetry I write is about my life and the feelings I have had. Writing is the way I express my views of life, love and death. I love all types of poets and poetry, I enjoy all forms of the writing world and find all writers to be enjoyable.; [a.] Tulsa, OK

WASHINGTON, DENECE
[b.] September 24, 1969, Salisbury, MD; [p.] Shirvon Stanford and Donald Washington; [ch.] Derrick, DeJanne, Mychael; [ed.] Parkside High School; [occ.] Primary Unit Assistant, at Peninsula Regional Med. Ctr. Salis, MD; [pers.] In my life I have been through so much pain and so much unkindness, that in my children I find love, joy and peace. My influences on my writing is what I have been through and where I'm going.; [a.] Hebron, MD

WATKINS, DAPHNE C.
[b.] July 5, 1981, Newport News, VA; [ed.] Benjamin Syms Middle School; [occ.] Student; [memb.] National Science Foundation; Student council Assoc. (SCA); Oratorical Expo; Federal Women's Program, (FWP) "Take Our Daughters to Work Foundation;" Vision of Charm and Manners; [hon.] Honor Roll Society; Jump Rope Contest 1991; Fiction Writing Workshop, 1994; Young Author's Celebration 1992 & 1993; Essay/Poster Contest 1994; Presidential Physical fitness 1990-1994; [pers.] Never ever take "no" for an answer; [a.] Hampton, VA

WATTS, DELORES
[b.] Tennille, GA. She moved to Newark, NJ at the age of ten, under the guidance of her mother, Mrs. Velma D. Watts. Therefore, Ms. Watts considers her self a native of the city of Newark. She received her elementary and high school education from the Newark Public School System. Ms. Watts earned a BA Degree and two Teaching Certifications from Jersey City State College. One certification in Elementary Education and the other in the field of Cosmetology. Her first published work appeared in an anthology entitled Contemporary Poets of America - 1984, published by Dorrance and Company. The title of the work is "A Christmas Prayer", a poem/prayer that concerns itself with the inspiration of the true Christmas Spirit as well as focusing on a religious con-

troversy as to whether one should or should not celebrate the birth of Christ Jesus. The primary objective of her works are to aid the spiritual aspects of mankind. Delores dedicates this particular work, `Poverty', to her son Jonathan.

WAVRUNEK, SHARON
[b.] August 20, 1963, Green Bay; [p.] Rose Mary and Edward; [m.] Single; [ch.] None; [ed.] Luxemburg, Casco High School; IBA College of Cosmetology; [occ.] Disabled; [a.] Luxemburg, WI

WAYMON, FLORA LEWIS
[Pen.] Mel; [b.] January 7, 1925, Vienna, GA; [p.] Abbie L. and Willie C. Lewis; [m.] Albert Waymon, Sr., January 8, 1944; [ch.] Eleven; [ed.] High School; [occ.] Housewife; [memb.] Zion Hill Baptist Church, Leslie, GA; [oth. writ.] Variety of poems relating to family, family honors, special occasions and expressions, none published.; [pers.] I enjoy writing sentimental poems; poems expressing joy, happiness, fear and hope. I was influenced early in life by my mother, who was a very talented writer, but never had her works published.; [a.] Americus, GA

WAYNE, LENER
[Pen.] Dr. Wayne Lener MBA, PhD; [b.] December 19, 1954, Brooklyn, NY; [p.] Gerald Lener, Rina Lener; [ed.] Rutgers Univ, Fairleigh Dickenson Univ, Greenwich Univ; [occ.] Statistician, Author, Lecturer Consultant; [memb.] Mensa, Washington Statistical Society; [oth. writ.] Several texts in statistics and statistical sampling, seventy-five poems; [pers.] To touch the heart, mind and spirit of a woman of wisdom, warmth and beauty to share a life partnership of joint fulfillment; [a.] Bellevue, WA

WEATHERMAN, GREG
[b.] October 1, 1965, Denver, CO; [p.] J.W. Virginia Nelson; [ed.] Haughton HS; Haughton LA, Jefferson County Comm Coll; Louisville, KY; [occ.] Cook; [oth. writ.] JCCC school publication; [pers.] Listen To The Music; As You Like It; You Don't Need a Weatherman to Know Which Way The Wind Blows; Carry On; [a.] Falls Church, VA

WEATHERMAN, GREG
[b.] October 1, 1965, Denver, CO; [p.] J.W. and Virginia Nelson; [ed.] Haughton HS - LA; LA Tech Univ LA; Jefferson County Comm Coll - Louisville, KY; [occ.] Cook; [oth. writ.] Some writings in a Journal for Jefferson County Comm Coll; [pers.] Listen to the music as you like it. You don't need a weatherman to know which way the wind blows...Carry on; [a.] Falls Church, VA

WEAVER, LINDA
[Pen.] L. Weaver; [b.] September 26, 1948, Burton, OH; [p.] Freeman and Ida Byler; [m.] Jake P. Weaver, May 25, 1972; [ch.] 1 daughter 3 sons; [occ.] Housewife and mother.; [oth. writ.] I write a weekly newsletter to The Budget printed in Sugarcreek, OH; [pers.] I enjoy writing and poems are "spur of the moment" happenings. My goal is to write a book someday.; [a.] Middlefield, OH

WEAVER, SANDRA JUNE
[Pen.] Sandra Bryant Weaver; [b.] April 7, 1950; [ch.] Arthur and Christopher Axtell; [ed.] AA degree, PhD in MOM; [occ.] Aspiring Writer and Poet; [pers.] We all have a poem inside us waiting to be written. My inspiration is British literature and all poets; [a.] Houston, TX

WEBER, KEVIN R.
[b.] May 10, 1972, Flint, Michigan; [p.] Janice Brown & Lawrence Weber; [ed.] Flushing High School, Michigan State University (BA in English, 1995); [occ.] Student: Michigan State University, Teacher Education Program; [memb.] Quill and Scroll; [hon.] Dean's List (MSU); [oth. writ.] Volumes of yet unpublished personal literature.; [pers.] I have been greatly influenced by the "Best Generation" writers and Diane Wakoski. In my poetry, I struggle to understand the universe and my place in it. I strive for a "personal mythology" in my art, uniting the common and the mysterious.; [a.] Grand Rapids, MI

WEED, MEL
[b.] Detroit, MI; [hon.] Citation Award, City of Madison Hgts, MI, for the physical capture of a criminal in flight of police while committing a burglary; [oth. writ.] "Do You Feel Like Me!" a book published in the category of self-help, "Cloud Nine With An Angel" a feature song released on single cassette (recording artist, producer and writer), also lecturing in category of self-help; [pers.] "It matters not in what parts of the world we live, what language we speak or the period of time which we have lived, we all share the experience of life." Why can art, music and literature cross all barriers of time, language and prejudice? "People have a desire to identify with the expressed feelings of others"; [a.] Detroit, MI

WEIDERMAN, KATIE
[b.] January 19, 1982, Ft. Leonardwood, MO; [p.] Karin and Robert Weiderman; [ed.] McAuliffe Elementary, Saunders Middle, Central Jr. High; [occ.] Student at Central Jr. High; [memb.] ADT Dance School; [hon.] Accelerated Reader Award; [pers.] I'm very proud of myself since I'm only 13 years old, I still can't believe I did this!; [a.] Anchorage, AK

WELDON, RICK L.
[b.] September 23, 1953, Atlanta, GA; [p.] Leon and Beatrice Weldon; [ch.] Ashley Weldon; [ed.] Shaw High School, East Cleveland Ohio, Ohio University, Athens Ohio; [occ.] Director of Sales and Marketing; [memb.] American Heart Assoc., American Karate Association; [hon.] Father; [oth. writ.] Most exposure has been through oral presentation of poems ranging from political to romantic to philosophical to just plain old fun stuff.; [pers.] My goal is to emotionally and spiritually identify with my readers but at the same time challenge beliefs.; [a.] Savana, GA

WELLS, FRANK
[b.] Holley, FL; [p.] Johna and Ella Wells; Attended Holley School. Had to quit school at age 16 because father died of sugar diabetes. Had to help (work) raise 5 younger brothers and sisters. [m.] Mamie Lou Rayburn, 1932, school teacher at Holley School; [ch.] Sherman, Billy Frank, Marilyn and Carolyn (twins) and Sara Lou; Served in 2nd Marine Division, World War II in the Pacific. After war worked with civil service at Eglin AFB for 25 yrs. Retired 1969. Auxiliary Deputy with Sheriff's Office for 3 yrs. Security Guard at Holley by the Sea 3 1/2 yrs. Wife, Mamie Lou died of cancer 1975. Remarried Jane Bishop - school teacher. Widowed in July 1993. Hobbies - gardening and woodworking shop. [memb.] Scottish Rite, York Rite, Shriner, Eastern Star, Amaranths, Past President of Holley - Navarre Chamber of Commerce (2 yr award) Navarre Kiwanis - Vice President, WWII Veteran, Member of Disabled American Veteran, Member and Deacon of Billory Baptist Church,

American Legion. [hon.] 3 battle stars, Bravery ribbon from President Roosevelt; [pers.] Love to write poetry. Have written other poems.

WENTWORTH, CHARLES MARVIN
[Pen.] Chas. M. Wentworth/Charles Wentworth; [b.] September 14, 1924, St. Louis, MO; [p.] Charles Melvin and Hulda F. Wentworth; [m.] Violet B. Stenzinger-Wentworth, October 6, 1944; [ch.] Eric Charles and Michael James; [ed.] Graduate of Washington University, Engineering College, St. Louis, MO 1960.; [occ.] Retired Senior Industrial Artist, currently teaching art.; [memb.] Central Brevard Art Association; International Society of Marine Painters; Artists Forum; Brevard Art Center and Museum; Brevard Zoo; Central Brevard Genealogical Society; [hon.] Received over 90 awards for watercolor painting in juried exhibitions, including "Best of Shows."; [oth. writ.] As a freelance writer and photographer for Florida Today Newspaper (Sunday Sunrise Section) in the 1970's; Had many articles published relating to sports in Florida. Also had many articles published in local press concerning art exhibits.; [pers.] I have never read much poetry. About two years ago, I began dreaming at night in verse and wrote the words down on a pad on the lamp table next to my bed. In the morning, I would read what I'd written: recompose, add, and refine it.; [a.] Merritt Island, FL

WEST, GAIL L.
[b.] April 25, 1950, Beloit, WI; [p.] Jack and Betty Brusberg; [m.] Dr. Pres West, December 30, 1972; [ch.] Kerry, Laura, Scott; [ed.] B.S. and M.A. Northwestern University; [occ.] Speech Therapist, Storyteller, Puppeteer; [memb.] Zeta Phi Eta; Woman's Board of Presbyterian Homes.; [a.] Evanston, IL

WEST, JACQUELINE
[Pen.] Jackie; [b.] Harlem; [p.] Florence Douglas; [m.] Harold West, Jr., June 30, 1985; [ch.] Kawana J. Harper; [ed.] B.S. York College, Cum Laude, A.A.S. Medgar Evers College; [occ.] Supervisor Maintenance Operations; [memb.] Who's Who Among American Professionals; [hon.] Kappa Delta Pi, Cum Laude Graduate; [a.] Hyattsville, MD

WESTMORELAND, KAREN
[b.] May 12, 1975, Howell; [p.] Stan and Jenny Westmoreland; [ed.] Howell High School, I am currently a sophomore at Michigan State University majoring in English Education; [memb.] Michigan State University Honors College; [pers.] This poem is dedicated to Merrie Sigro, the voice that has saved me over many cups of tea. In memory of your father and mine. I love you Daddy!; [a.] Howell, MI

WHARTON, CARL
[Pen.] Xdous; [b.] August 30, 1979, Phila., PA; [p.] Roland and Hattie Wharton; [ch.] Brother: Roger Wharton; [ed.] Overbrook High, Temple Univ. Real Estate; [oth. writ.] Several poems published in local newspapers, Philadelphia Tribune and Poetry Plus; [pers.] All I want is for all African people (worldwide) to gain a knowledge of self, and to use that knowledge, wisdom and understanding to uplift us all.; [a.] Phila., PA

WHATLEY, LARRY N.
[Pen.] L.N.W.; [b.] July 26, 1961, Floyd County, GA; [p.] Joseph and Catherine Whatley; [m.] Tammie L. Whatley; [ch.] Kathlyn A. Whatley; [pers.] There are several reasons for my writing. One of the reasons that I'll say stands out from the rest is it's a gift from God. I

feel we should do our best with what God has given us; [a.] Rome, GA

WHEAT, DEBORAH NICHOLS
[b.] September 30, 1950, Baltimore, MD; [p.] Paul Lincoln and Anne Bryant Nichols; [m.] William Burton Wheat, May 26, 1967; [ch.] Jeff, Christine, Karen, Paul, Timothy; [ed.] Picayinne High, currently working on a Bachelors Degree in Speech Pathology at University of Southern Mississippi; [occ.] Housewife, Mother, Student; [hon.] Dean's List; [oth. writ.] Several short articles for the local newspaper, usually based upon my strong convictions on current issues. Some poetry published in a Gulf Coast Anthology.; [pers.] I write poetry as both hobby and therapy. Most of my writing reflects a soul's struggle to burst its boundaries, and to express my joy of life. My favorite poets are Emily Dickinson and Sara Teasdale; [a.] Carriere, MS

WHEELER, BETTY K.
[b.] Warren, PA; [p.] Arthur and Katheryn Hamblin; [m.] Betty was a widow at age 19. She has raised 2 children on $2,000 a year. She writes from experience and her insight into the human heart. Despite hardships, she has a positive attitude and loves people, words and feelings!; [hon.] Honor Certificates in songwriting; [oth. writ.] copyrighted booklet "Ideals that touch us Close To Home"; [a.] Meadville, PA

WHEELER, EARL B.
[b.] July 29, 1926, Corrigan, TX; [p.] Joel Wheeler, Maggie Wheeler; [m.] Marggie Fuller, July 12, 1968; [ed.] Under twelfth grade (9th). I am a surviving twin, lost my twin brother in 89. I was born with foil on my face; [occ.] Was #1 machinist, but I'm retired on disability; [memb.] DAV and member of Missionary Baptist Church and am the last of four Wheeler boys. Still have two sisters in immediate family; [hon.] None except kind deeds and do unto others as you have them do unto you, and live a Christian life as possible; [oth. writ.] None, but was saddened because my mother was sick and sat down and wrote this poem in 1973. Recently saw your ad and decided to send it in, 1994; [pers.] I am now 68 yrs old and totally disabled since 1959. I love poems, and like to read, as I sit day after day. I have lung problems and ill health as a whole. Happy my poem was selected; [a.] Groves, TX

WHEELER, STEVEN ALEXANDER
[Pen.] Shadow; [b.] October 9, 1966, Sanford, FL; [p.] Lee A. and Vivian S. Wheeler; [m.] Rochelle Denise Wheeler, July 27, 1990; [ch.] Steven Lee Wheeler; [ed.] Associate of Arts, Seminole Community College; [occ.] United States Coast Guard Officer; [pers.] There are too many extremes in the world today, too many rights or wrongs. The middle is a good place to be, you're never very far from home. Be centered, be well, and be careful. Sleep with one eye open and a pen at your side.; [a.] Coos Bay, OR

WHEELESS, ANGELA
[b.] January 24, 1974, Cincinnati; [p.] Jim and Maxine Wheeless; [ed.] Union High School, OK; CLC Language Inst, Tokyo, Japan; Univ of Washington, WA; [occ.] Student at the Univ of Washington; [oth. writ.] Several poems published in a school anthology book; [pers.] Only by acknowledging our faults can we strive to change them. We are all guilty. When each individual is at peace with themselves, only then can we be at peace with one another; [a.] Seattle, WA

WHIPPLE, LONNIE JEAN
[Pen.] Lonnie Jean Frost; [b.] February 6, 1956, Rochester, MN; [p.] Ercell E. Frost II, and Doris Frost; [m.] Kevin J. Whipple, October 15, 1977; [ch.] Naomi Jean, Jarrod James; [ed.] Life; [occ.] Parenting; [memb.] National Multiple Sclerosis Society; [hon.] Motherhood, Certificate of Appreciation from the Rochester School Board, Julie Monday School of Dance; [oth. writ.] Poems, school newspaper, short stories.; [pers.] I love you all, but my journey here on earth is short. Let my last word, touch, smile, be the best it can be. Remember to always dream, strive and conquer!; [a.] Rochester, MN

WHITE, J. B.
[b.] September 6, 1930, Carlstadt, NJ; [p.] James B. and May White; [m.] Patricia (deceased Aug 23, 1994), January 29, 1955; [ch.] James W. White, Donna Spiegel; [ed.] East Rutherford High, North Carolina State; [occ.] Retired; [memb.] Life member VFW #7095, Masonic Lodge #259, and various charities; [pers.] Always write from the heart and the mind.

WHITEHEAD, RICHARD
[Pen.] R.P. Whitehead; [b.] January 6, 1950, Crown Point, IN; [p.] Mr. and Mrs. Arthur Whitehead; [m.] Roberta, May 17, 1975; [ch.] Megan (11), Ricky (13); [ed.] Manchester College - '72 N. Manchester, IN; [occ.] Bus Manager; [a.] Hudson, OH

WHITEMAN, KOURTNEY J.
[b.] November 17, 1982, North Kansas City, MO; [p.] Kurt E. and Deborah S. Whiteman; [ed.] Inman Elementary - 6th grade; [occ.] Student, poet; [hon.] Special Recognition: "DARE Essay" (poem form), "Cluster" program Nixa, MO for the gifted and talented; [oth. writ.] Published poem in "The Anthology of Poetry By Young Americans" - 1993 Edition; [pers.] I try to excel in everything I do; [a.] Nixa, MO

WHITMORE, LOUISE E.
[b.] July 9, 1930, Tacony Section of Phila; [p.] (late) Viola Clayton and (late) James Johnson; [m.] Leonard H. Whitmore, Jr (Music Therapy Director at Delaware State Hospital, June 22, 1957; [ch.] Leonard H. Whitmore, 3rd - Retail Manager; Renee L. Whitmore - Teacher; [ed.] Distinguished and Valedictorian of Kensington High School - BS in Education, West Chester Univ - MS in Education, West Chester Univ - MS in Education - Temple Univ -Phila; [occ.] Retired from Palmyra, NJ School System - taught 39 yrs (also taught in Contesville, PA); [memb.] Retired Member of PA Reflexology Assoc, National Education Assoc and NJ Education Assoc; Member of Star of Hope Bapt Church; National Assoc of Music Therapy, Inc; [hon.] Chapel of Four Chaplains for outstanding service to all people regardless of race or faith Palmyra Education Assoc - for enhancing peace and brotherhood throughout her career. Campbell AME Church for dedicated service to church and community 1972 "Teacher of the Year" plaque awarded by her students; [oth. writ.] Educational Game - "Together Juntamente"; [oth. writ.] Songs of Hope; Peace on Earth for , All Mankind" (has 21 translations) Spanish - "Paz en la Tierra Para Toda Humanidad"; "God's Gift to Man"; "God Says They're All Mine"; "With God We can Do Anything"; "Stand Up And Cheer For Jesus"; "Message and Cheer"; [pers.] Trust God, and He will solve any problem you have!; [a.] Bensalem, PA

WHITT, MARCELLA
[Pen.] Girl; [b.] April 6, 1935; [m.] October 22, 1954; [ch.] Rick, Shawna, Stephen Kirk; [occ.] Small Business Owner; [oth. writ.] As a rule, I only write personal poems for my relatives; [a.] McRae, AR

WILEY, ROBERT L.
[b.] January 13, 1918, Van Alstyne, TX; [p.] John and Beulah (deceased); [m.] Mary F. Wiley (retired school teacher and now Professional Artist), February 22, 1941 (54 yrs); [ch.] Linda Kay and (Ronald Lee-deceased); [ed.] H.S., Strayers College, Student and Instructor-Grayson County College, 20 yrs. Continue to study writing at Austin College, Sherman, TX. Retired in 1974 as Industrial Engineer, also retired Chief Warrant Officer, and Captain USAR, over 40 years of service WWII and Korea. [occ.] Writing my autobiography and short stories. Devote time to Artistic woodworking. [memb.] First United Methodist Church, Sherman Art League, Sherman City comprehensive Planning Committee, Texoma Planning Commission for the Aging, Grayson County College, Senior Avocational-Vocational Education Board, Lifetime member of the Retired Officers' Assn, National Assn of Federal Employees, American Association of Retired Persons; [hon.] Publication of Short Stories, Grayson County College Year Books 1989-1994, Star Awards for Autobiographical Storywriting "Telling Our Stories," Austin College, Sherman, TX 1992-1994; [oth. writ.] Several stories published in local newspaper, writings of my woodworking are published in books throughout the United States, Shopsmith Inc.; [pers.] My inspiration for writing has come from my Professors and Instructors. My personal thought is that "Something simple made well is more rewarding than something complex made poorly;" [a.] Sherman, TX

WILHALMENA, WILLIAMS
[b.] September 25, 1915, Levi, TX; [p.] Sidney and Edna Stamps; [m.] Clifford W. Williams (deceased), August 1, 1937; [ch.] Alan, (Sharon) Rae, James; [ed.] BA from U of Northern Colorado at Greely. Speech and languages education certificate; [occ.] Retired homemaker/teacher; [memb.] Common Cause, Southern Poverty Law Center Klan Watch; Moral Rearmament; U. Methodist Committees; Foundation For A Global Community (formerly Beyond War); Oregon Writers Colony; [hon.] Paeblo, CO HS National Honor Society (c'est assez-c'est tout); [oth. writ.] "Occasional" as an occasion or a cause calls for it. (prose - or doggerel - or serious elegaic!); [pers.] I write poems upon inspiration. I speak from a strong belief in the perfectibility of human-kind. Often express my humor regarding our human predicaments (viz "And Other Losses", on thinning hair - and other losses to bewail or bear). Influenced by all poets and poetic prose. Words everyday play things; [a.] Portland, OR

WILHELMY, GUS
[b.] February 17, 1935; [p.] George and Emily Wilhelmy; [m.] Mary Vallely, September 1, 1990; [ch.] Rochelle, Rebecca, Todd; [ed.] Good Counsel High, Passionist Academic Inst, Univ of MI, Univ of WI; [occ.] Fund Raising Consultant; [memb.] National Society of Fund Raising Executives, American Marketing Assoc, American Management Assoc, Chicago Assoc of Technical Assistance Providers; [pers.] I feel poetry touches deep down into the innermost person and allows mankind to reveal its unique, tragically wonderful self.

WILKES, MELISSA
[b.] April 15, 1960, Huntington, WVA; [p.] Earl Dean and Joyce Ann Patterson; [m.] Timothy Wilkes, November 28; [ch.] Patty, George, Kevin, Michael; [ed.] I graduated at C-K High School no further education; [occ.] Housewife and mom; [oth. writ.] I have written a book in which I am trying to get published. Carlton Press wanted it but I could not get the subsidy for it. The title is Everyday Windows.; [pers.] I just write different poems from my heart about the happiness and the sadness which life has to offer us.; [a.] Catlettsburg, KY

WILKINS, RAYANNA MARCHE
[b.] November 8, 1983, Philadelphia, PA; [p.] Cynthia and Jonathan Lee Wilkins; [ed.] Presently Hill Freedom School of Humanities, Phila., PA; [memb.] New Bethel A.M.E. Church of Germantown, Phila., PA, Young Adult Choir, Junior Usher Board, Acolyte, YPD Secretary (Young Peoples Dept.), Sunday School Secretary; [hon.] Honors Award, Bronze Medal and Black History Reading Achievement Award for participation in the Black Oratorical Contest, Membership Certificate for the Fell Academics Plus Program; Certificate of Achievement for Instrumental Music, Science Fair Participation Award, Women in Science and Engineering (Wise), Letter from President Clinton and many other awards; [oth. writ.] Many others; [pers.] I would like to thank NLP for selecting my poem for publication and many thanks to teachers, church members, my pastor, family and friends for support. I would like to thank my two mentors Maya Angelou and Edgar Allen Poe. Most of all I thank God and my mother who always encourages me.; [a.] Philadelphia, PA

WILKINSON, CARL
[b.] December 30, 1961, Mobile, AL; [p.] Brenda Wilkinson, Bill Wilkinson; [m.] Christine Wilkinson, August 27, 1988; [ch.] Grey Poupon (Yorkshire Terrier); [ed.] C.F. Vigor High, USNR - 8 1/2 yrs, honorable discharge; [occ.] Sprinkler maintenance, Villas of Rainberry Lakes HO Assoc; [hon.] Meritorious Service Medal, 100% Drill Attendance Awards; [oth. writ.] Many unpublished poems and several children's stories in the Dr. Seuss style are awaiting standard publishing contracts; [pers.] Inspired by Dr. Seuss, I strive to touch the emotions of experiences we all have felt at one time or another. My dream is to share my work with the world; [a.] Lake Worth, FL

WILLIAMS, ANNIE L.
[b.] February 26, 1935, McCall, SC; [p.] James and Fannie McCrae; [m.] James T. Williams, December 31, 1977; [ch.] Cassandra, Franklin, Terry, David, Charles; [ed.] Carpozo High School, George Washington University (1 yr.); [occ.] Retired; [memb.] Straightway Church of Christ, Missionary Board; [hon.] Special Achievement Awards from the Dept. of Labor; [oth. writ.] Some other writings not published.; [pers.] My writing is a reflection of my personal experiences. I have been blessed in many areas, and I am inspired to put it in writing.; [a.] Washington, D.C.

WILLIAMS, BARBARA B.
[Pen.] Lillian Bagby; [b.] September 10, 1935, USA; [p.] Earl Williams and Lillian Bagby; [ed.] B.S. Degree Long Island University; [occ.] Physician's Assistant; [memb.] AAPA; [hon.] Honorable Mention for song lyrics in contest; [oth. writ.] All unpublished poems, stories, song poems; [pers.] Poverty, crime, drug addiction, AIDS are social ills of man, over which I have no control. By writing about them I allow others to share and experience the pain, and hopefully move those who can change things to do so.; [a.] Union, NJ

WILLIAMS, JONES D.
[Pen.] Dino; [b.] December 4, 1967, Chicago, IL; [p.] Johnny Williams, Darlene Johnson; [m.] Karen Williams, April 17, 1993; [ch.] Karl, James, Williams (KJ); [ed.] Polatine High, GED; [occ.] Manager for Mobil Oil Company; [hon.] Manager of the Year 1990; [oth. writ.] High School Year Book; [pers.] My writings are mostly about feelings and I try to make people understand these feelings with the words I use; [a.] Elgin, IL

WILLIAMS, JUDITH
[b.] Chicago, IL; [ed.] Bachelor's Degree from the Univ of Illinois-Urbana; [occ.] Formerly a teacher of English and Spanish. I am currently a graphic artist and proofreader for a small composition house; [hon.] Honors in Liberal Arts and Sciences with distinction in the curriculum, Sigma Delta Pi Spanish National Honorary Fraternity; [pers.] I love a poem that's cleanly written and compact, each image distilled to its essence, every idea pared to its core, with word choice and placement critical. However, along with this economy of language and precision in thought, the poem must flow gracefully and be rich in interpretation. Disciplining oneself to compose such a poem can be likened to the artist who's told by a particularly tough taskmaster, "using as few brush strokes as possible, create a masterpiece"; [a.] Wildwood, NJ

WILLIAMS, JUDY MAE HAMILTON
[b.] June 3, 1945, Cincinnati, OH; [p.] John C. and Mary E. Hamilton; [m.] Carl G. Williams, July 8, 1963; [ch.] Lesha, Deborah, Alain, Jennifer; [ed.] Hughes High School - Cincinnati, OH; [occ.] Interior decorating and home remodeling; [memb.] Member of Chamber of Commerce, Volunteer for transporting elderly to appointments, and errands; [hon.] I am an advocate for the promotion of the Made in America label. I believe in our products and our people. I feel this is important for the security of our economy; [pers.] I have been a wife and mother my whole life. I came from a family of 14 sisters and brothers. Which I might add I helped raise half of them. My father was ill, my mother had to work. I love children. I am very concerned for their safety.

WILLIAMS, KEVIN MORRELL
[Pen.] Kevin; [b.] April 17, 1957, S.F. CA; [p.] Oscar and Lorraine Williams; [ed.] J. Eugene McAteer High School, City College, San Francisco; [pers.] Talent, In the name of the Father. Motivation by Claude Jenkins the muse.; [a.] San Francisco, CA

WILLIAMS, RALFRALOME HOPE COLLINWOOD
[Pen.] Cleveland Chabaska Williams; [b.] January 2, 1964, Kingston, Jamaica; [p.] Oswald Williams, Delores Hibbert; [m.] Marcia Higgs-Williams; [ch.] JoBeth, Dontue, Charina, Chevette, Marsha; [ed.] Trench Town Comprehensive High; [occ.] Composer of Songs, Artist, Painter; [memb.] Jamaica Institute of Art, Jamaica Council of Human Rights, Spartan Health Club; [oth. writ.] Short comic books, writer of songs for various artists, including my spouse Marcia who is vocal artist by profession. Cartoon drawings submitted to LA Times; [pers.] The fear of the Lord, is the beginning of Wisdom, and the way to victory is to hold on steadfastly, in faith. Unlock the wisdom of the heart and mind, and focus deeply on the principles of life.", [a.] Los Angeles, CA

WILLIAMSON (M.D.), D. L.
[Pen.] Dr. D'Gang; D'Gang; July 29, 1956, NYC; [p.] Analy dia Torres, James Williamson; [ed.] St. Edmono's High, St. John's University , Mt Sinai Medical School, University of Medicine and Dentistry, Master Program Mt. Sinai Medical Center; [occ.] Physician in training. Fellow in 1 care HIV/AIDS Master's in benenal preventive medicine; [memb.] American College Physicians, New York State Medical Society; American Medical Assoc; [hon.] National Health Services Scholarship; National Research Service Award; [oth. writ.] Muscluskaletal Oncology - Adult Oncology; Poetry, short stories, essays; [pers.] I live for the moment, enjoy life and found calling to take care of HIV/AIDS pts. My writings are hobbies and reflective of work experiences and community; [a.] NY, NY

WILLIAMSON, MARJORIE CIRUTI
[b.] March 30, 1938, Goose Creek, TX; [p.] Manuel and Rosa Ciruti; [m.] David L. Williamson; [ed.] Robert E. Lee - Baytown; BA from Howard Payne Univ; MA from Univ of Texas; [memb.] Delta Kappa Gamma; General Federation of Women's Clubs; National Council Teachers of English, International Reading Assn; [hon.] Who's Who in Amer Colleges/Universities; Winner State PTA Scholarship; Recipient of Member in Print Award from Delta Kappa Gamma; [oth. writ.] Published in English in Texas; The Writing Teacher; The Reading Teacher; [pers.] Everyone has a "story" to tell; therefore, everyone has something about which to write; [a.] Baytown, TX

WILLIARD, BOB
[b.] November 24, 1972, Piedmont, CA; [ed.] Presently a student at Arizona State Univ studying communication; [memb.] USTA, BOB, Comedy Committee of Memorial Union Activity Board, Cast member and editor of "Bleep U Productions", FBFG; [hon.] Dean's List, founder and president of BOB Fraternity ASU Chapter; [oth. writ.] Article for the "Grapeville" journal; [pers.] I love to play with words; [a.] Tempe, AZ

WILSON, CHERYL D.
[b.] August 5, 1970, Asheville, NC; [p.] Larry Adlis, Linda Collins; [m.] Kelly Wilson, June 24, 1988; [ch.] Christopher David, Jessica Caitlin; [ed.] Granby High School, Norfolk, VA; [occ.] Freelance Writer and Mother.; [a.] Tulsa, OK

WILSON, CLYDE
[b.] November 8, 1920, Alameda, CA; [p.] Melva and Clyde Wilson Sr.,; [m.] Barbara Wilson, June 26, 1943; [ch.] Karna, Clyde II, Dean, Janinne; [ed.] Alameda High School; [occ.] Printer/ Lithographer; [hon.] Patent Holder, U.S. Patent #3,752,766; [pers.] "May Your Mettle Surpass The Crucible of Challenge and Change;" [a.] Moraga, CA

WILSON, EMERSON M.
[Pen.] E. M. Wilson; [b.] December 13, 1931, NY, NY; [p.] James and Helen Wilson; [ed.] B.S./M.S. State University at Oneanta, NY; [occ.] Retired sales for Wal Mart.

WILSON, JANICE
[b.] March 20, 1946, Oconee County, GA; [p.] Mr. and Mrs. J.R. Manders; [m.] Altrin N. Wilson, November 24, 1965; [ch.] Daughter (living), son (deceased); [ed.] Grades 1-12, Watkinsville Elementary School, Oconee County High School; [occ.] At the present time I am on disability through Athens-Clarke County, GA (worked 18 yrs in the Clerk of Superior Court's Office); [memb.]

I am an active member of Mars Hill Baptist Church; [memb.] I write Community News for Mars Hill which is published weekly in "The Oconee Arrow" which is located here in the County in which I reside; [pers.] My first inclination to write poetry was a tribute to my little deceased son. After this, I began to write poems for family members for their birthdays; also some other tributes to friends who passed away and these were used in the funeral service; [a.] Watkinsville, GA

WILSON, MARVIN P.
[b.] October 7, 1957, Wilmington, NC; [p.] Marvin and Guineveve Wilson; [ed.] BA, Economics, Business Management, NC State Univ; MS, Systems Management, Univ of Southern CA; AAS Financial Management, Community College of the Air Force; [occ.] Budget Analyst, Defense Printing Service; [hon.] US Air Force: Meritorious Service Medal, Commendation Medal with One Oak Leaf Cluster, Achievement Medal; [oth. writ.] Poems "Nature Held Captive" and "Ode to the Forgotten Soldier"; [a.] Fairfax, VA

WILSON, OTIS
[Pen.] O. O. Wilson; [b.] September 16, 1960, Massillion, OH; [p.] Charles and Emma Wilson; [m.] Deborah Wilson, February 2, 1982; [ch.] Valerie and Nicole Wilson; [ed.] Handley High, Southern Union College; [occ.] Minister; [oth. writ.] The trouble with Marriage a tract.; [pers.] Seek ye, First the Kingdom of God and His righteousness.; [a.] Wadley, AL

WIMMER, CHRISTINA M.
[b.] August 1, 1969, Livingston, NJ; [p.] Joseph George and Erna Hein; [ed.] Boca Raton Academy, BS Elementary Education from Univ of South Florida, 1991; [occ.] 4th grade ESOL teacher, Cypress Elementary; [memb.] Advent Lutheran Church, Nat'l Education Assn, Broward Teachers Union, American Lung Assn; [hon.] West Boca Raton Kiwanis Club Youth Leadership Award, 1987, Palm Beach Pathfinder Nominee for Choral Music, 1987; [oth. writ.] "Drama In Life" published in the National Library of Poetry's anthology entitled At Day's End. Collection of personal poetry dating from 1984 to present; [pers.] I believe that once in every lifetime you meet the person who makes your life complete. For me, I reflect on what was, eternally hoping for what should be, here and now; [a.] Boca Raton, FL

WINFREE, STEPHANIE DENISE
[b.] June 30, 1974, Philadelphia, PA; [p.] Linwood Winfree, Barbara Winfree; [ed.] Ridley Senior High, Millersville Univ; [memb.] Millersville Univ Gospel Choir, SAAS/Success for African American Students (Mentoring Program); [pers.] "I breathe, therefore I can". I admire the poetry of Maya Angelou a great deal; [a.] Folsom, PA

WINIARSKI, PATTY
[Pen.] Mrs. Wyno; [b.] April 15, 1952, Oak Park, IL; [p.] Patrick and Therese Kelly; [m.] John Wayne Winiarski, February 16, 1974; [ch.] Joe, Jeff, Dan, Mary; [ed.] Immaculate High, St. Francis Hospital School of Nursing; [occ.] Reg. Nurse, wife and mother; [memb.] P.T.A., Booster Club, Home and School Assoc., C.C.W. of Our Lady of Mercy Church; [pers.] I dedicate my writing to my children for they have provided me with their love and many growing up experiences to share with the world.; [a.] Aurora, IL

WININGER, ROBERT EUGENE
[b.] February 23, 1971, Silver Spring, MD; [p.] Bob and Melba Wininger; [ed.] Marcus High, Lewisville High, Berkner High, Richland Community College, Texas Tech Univ; [occ.] Full time student; [oth. writ.] Several poems and short stories; [pers.] All the glory that is bestowed upon me is because of God! For I am third and He is first, while others are second. My favorite scripture: Luke 1:37 "For nothing is impossible with God!" [a.] Richardson, TX

WINN, JOHN D.
[b.] November 23, 1965, Trenton, MI; [p.] Carlanna F. Lieb, John T. Winn; [ed.] Theodore Roosevelt High, Wyandotte, MI; [occ.] Customer Advocate; [oth. writ.] Currently working on story of Middle Class American who discovers spiritual awareness and reaches a high plain, redefining his view of the world; [pers.] If one does not dream, how could it possibly come true; [a.] Ecorse, MI

WINSTON, LAWRENCE E.
[Pen.] L.E.W.; [b.] August 14, 1946, Detroit, MI; [p.] Robert and Ruby Winston; [m.] Joanne Winston, April 2, 1971; [ch.] Kathleen Nichols; Ian Winston; [ed.] Rogers High (Toledo, O) Univ of Toledo; Southern Illinois Univ; [occ.] Hospital Administration O, Environmental Svcs; Walter Reed AMC; [memb.] American Society for Healthcare Environmental Services (ASHES); [hon.] Numerous military awards; [oth. writ.] Several poems published in high school literary magazine; [pers.] To write poetry is to be in touch with one's soul; [a.] Lorton, VA

WOJNOWICH, SANDY
[b.] November 3, 1962, Lincoln County, USA; [ch.] Valerie and Sonia; [oth. writ.] Beyond the pain (poetry) Dark Side of the Moon.; [pers.] Another place and time.

WOLLSCHLAGER, SSND, JO
[b.] May 25, 1941, Evergreen Pk., IL; [p.] Joseph and Emily Wollschlager; [ed.] B.S., M.S. Ed., MSA; [occ.] Business Management and Financial Consulting; [memb.] School Sisters of Notre Dame, Provincial Assembly Advisory Board, National Assoc. of Church Board Business, Joilet Diocese Business Admin.; [oth. writ.] Numerous poems; [pers.] My writing informs me of my deeper spiritual experience; the words flow out before my conscious intellect catches them; [a.] Evergreen Park, IL

WONG, RON
[b.] December 21, 1931, Fresno, CA; [p.] Ray and Ruth Wong; [ch.] Gary Hunter, Julie, Christy, Carina, Lara and Sabrina; [ed.] John Marshall High, University of Southern California; [occ.] Pediatric Dentist; [memb.] Rotary International, Delta Sigma Delta, National Archery Association; [hon.] National Dental Honorary, Omicron Kappa Upsicon, Wescott Gold Medalist in Flight Archery - Amateur Champion USA 1984; [oth. writ.] Univ So Calif Dental "Pedodontic Laboratory Manuel", Contributing Editor "US Archer" Contributing Photographer "Town and Country" magazine; [pers.] Harmony in nature - humanity and God - "Haiku Style". My poetic preference in composing - poetry.

WONG, STANLEY
[Pen.] SW1; [b.] December 24, 1975, Vietnam; [p.] Hoa Dung & Lee Wong; [ed.] Francis Lewis High School, Bernard M. Baruch College; [occ.] Secretarial Assistant; [memb.] Hoby Leadership Association Baruch's Student

Body Government (DSSG), Asian Student Association, "Rising Star" Student Leadership; [hon.] Three time Silver Honors, Physical Fitness Award, Two Time Certificate of Award, Seven Time Varsity Track Awards, Certificate of Achievement, Math Recognition Award, and Certification of Cooperation in Gov; [oth. writ.] Articles for the Francis Lewis Patriot, Poems published in yearbook; [pers.] The existence of life is an issue of living each day to the fullest extent. The way I see it, each day will be filled with happiness, basked in a eternal reverie of joy. Accomplishing this, I shall relinquish all my anger, burden, and passion. Taking everything the way it is, without strings attached and let my conscience be my guide; [a.] Bellerose, NY

WOOD, LISA ORLENA
[b.] August 31, 1973, Washington, DC; [p.] Gary and Stella Wood; [m.] single; [ed.] Northern VA Community College, Potomac Senior High School; [occ.] Part-time student, full-time cleaning services; [memb.] National Honor Society (briefly about a year-had to get out because of too much stress); [hon.] 2 academic awards; 1st place in Spanish dramatic reading contest; [oth. writ.] Over 20 poems (that may prove to be published); [pers.] Poetry has been an "escape from the present" for me. It has in turn helped me to define what I felt and to find myself; [a.] Woodbridge, VA

WOOD, PAULA
[b.] May 14, 1978, California; [p.] Paul and Jheri Wood; [ed.] Still attending High School; [occ.] Student; [memb.] SADD; [oth. writ.] A few more personal poems.; [pers.] Everyone is hurt by something. This poem shows how I was hurt by love disguised as friendship.; [a.] Sylva, NC

WOOD, VICKI S.
[Pen.] Pepper; [b.] July 25, 1951, Wteruliet, MI; [p.] Jesse and Jessica DeMay; [ch.] Fawn Marie Wier and "Dusty" Dustin Sean Wier; [ed.] Hartford High, Lakeshore High, St. Joseph Beauty College, A.C.T. Travel School; [memb.] Michigan Lupus Foundation, St. Paul Lutheran Church; [hon.] First Place Awards, in Piano, 13 awards in hair styling; [oth. writ.] Just my own personal poetry to share.; [pers.] I enjoy sharing my poetry. I always say..."Keep your eyes on the face of the Lord. Give him all of your troubles and burdens and ask for His help. Never be afraid to ask for his help for he is always there for you.; [a.] Coloma, MI

WOODARD, FRANCES PHELPS
[Pen.] Wind Song; [b.] January 18, 1925, Portsmouth, VA; [p.] Earnest Linwood Phelps and Edna Rowland Phelps; [m.] Ray O'Neal Woodard, January 29, 1943; [ch.] Brenda Raye Woodard and Ray O'Neal Woodard Jr.; [ed.] Woodrow Wilson High School, Extensive Training by Fed. Gov't.; [occ.] Retired from Federal Gov't., Norfolk Naval Shipyard, Portsmouth, VA., as Budget Analyst with 38 years of service; [memb.] Charter member of Believers Baptist Church, Chesapeake, VA; Teacher of Gleaner SS class. Birthright member of the Nansemond Indian Tribal Assoc., Inc. Chesapeake, VA Charter Member of the National Museum of the American Indian, Smithsonian Inst., Wash. D.C. and many others; [hon.] Outstanding and Superior Award from Fed. Gov't. for on job performance. Editor's Choice for Outstanding Achievement in Poetry by the National Library of Poetry, Golden Poet Award, Awards of Merit and many others.; [oth. writ.] Poems published in local newspapers, several published in Nansemond Indian Tribe program booklet of annual festivals. Several poems published in World of poetry books and many others.; [pers.]

All I am, All I have, All I ever hope to be... I now and forever dedicate to the Lord Jesus Christ for His use and glory, absolutely, unconditionally, now and forever. I thank him for this gift to write poetry that he has given to me, and also for the greatest gift of all, life eternal.; [a.] Portsmouth, VA

WOODRUFF, GENE L
[Pen.] Gene L Woodruff-Rohrer; [b.] August 8, 1954, Troy, PA; [p.] Leon A. and Ruby Kent Woodruff; [m.] Robert R. Rohrer, April 18, 1992 (deceased 11/11/92); [occ.] Disabled due to HIV Disease; [memb.] Universalist Unitarian Church of Towanda, PA, Church Secretary; [oth. writ.] Feature Writer, Eagle's Cry, Elmira, New York, Guest Speaker/Educator HIV/AIDS and Grieving, some poetry written for World AIDS Day 1993, as well as articles on religion and Gay Concerns, Endless Mountains Weekend News, Mansfield, PA; [pers.] Loving and committed relationships are on display for all of us as long as we are not blinded by prejudice. When outsiders saw how we loved each other, and sex was out of the picture, the perception of perversion was replaced by the realization that even this love was God given.; [a.] Troy, PA

WORLAND, JENNAFER
[Pen.] Jenna; [b.] September 13, 1981, Barstow, CA; [p.] Gary and Connie Worland; [ed.] Henderson Elem., Barstow Middle School; [occ.] Student; [pers.] The heart that holds a dream is the one which will change the world.; [a.] Barstow, CA

WOSS, BARBARA A.
[b.] August 31, 1952, Nanticoke, PA; [p.] Florence and Howard Balliet; [m.] Michael Woss, September 1, 1973 (Deceased 8/29/91); [ch.] Lee Ann, Stacy; [ed.] Northwest Area High School Graduate; [occ.] Housewife; [memb.] Lifetime Member of the International Society of Poets; [hon.] Semi-Finalist 1993 ISP Conference, Editor's Choice Award 1992; [oth. writ.] Lost Love, published in NLP Anthology Where Dreams Begin, 1992; [pers.] I like to write about personal experiences because they come from the heart; these are to what most people can relate. I can't and won't write about something I don't know about or have not experienced.; [a.] Wilkes-Barre, PA

WRIGHT (JR.), LEWIS
[b.] October 20, 1963, Cleveland, OH; [p.] Carolyn Wright and Muhammad Shabazz; [m.] Katherine M. Wright, July 30, 1988; [ch.] Rico (12), Lewis (8) and Neyko (4); [ed.] High School (West Technical); [occ.] Textile Srvs, for Univ Hosp of Cleveland; [memb.] Amateurs Bowling Assoc; [hon.] Winner of Four Bowling Tournament Championships; [oth. writ.] Only private poems, none have been published. This is my first submission; [pers.] My poems are inspired by the everyday joys and pains of my life and the people around me. And even the troubles of my black culture; [a.] Cleveland, OH

WRIGHT, BRIAN
[b.] April 16, 1975, Denville, NJ; [p.] Barbara and William Wright; [ed.] Denville Township Schools - Morris Knolls High School, Denville, Rutgers (pre-med) New Brunswick, NJ (present soph); [occ.] Student; [hon.] Sumaua Awards, Varsity Basketball Capt, Varsity Baseball, Sigma Phi Epsilon Fraternity; [a.] Denville, NJ

WRIGHT, CHARALAYNE
[b.] November 9, 1963, San Francisco, CA; [ed.] B.A., San Francisco State Univ.; [a.] Daly City, CA

WRIGHT, MARK BRIAN
[Pen.] Markus Crash; [b.] October 1, 1966, Cortland, NY; [ch.] Zeth James Wright; [ed.] Data Entry Self Taught, Graduate 1985 at Dryden Central High School; [occ.] Data Entry at NCC Industries, Cortland, NY; [hon.] English Achievement Award in High School Senior Year; [oth. writ.] Music and lyrics written and performed publicly, also many works unpublished, including children's songs and stories.; [pers.] My love for God and my family are always an influence in my writing, as I strive to reflect my inner emotions in words that are easy for everyone to identify with. I have also been influenced by several 19th century writers.; [a.] Cortland, NY

WRIGHT, MICHAEL L.
[Pen.] Johnathan Erik Michaels; [b.] April 18, 1955, Dumas, TX; [p.] Cecil and Larena Wright; [m.] Teresa Jean (Harris) Wright, December 14, 1974; [ch.] Christopher, Terra, Erik; [ed.] Dumas H.S., Some College Hrs., Amarillo College; [occ.] Mechanic, John Deere; [hon.] Past Member and Master Councilor Order of De Molay's; [oth. writ.] Poems: "Thanks" being printed in Voices of America 1995 Ed. and "Cause and Effect" being printed in Musings Latest Edition 94-95; [pers.] I am as passionate in my anger as I am my friendships. If you will apply that method of approach to all items of life, you will have a full life.; [a.] Belvidere, IL

WRIGHT, MICHELLE RENEE
[b.] March 8, 1966, Monroe, Louisiana; [p.] Maggie Bell Moore Wright; [m.] Robert Wiley III, January 3, 1993; [ed.] Louisiana Business College, Delta High School; [occ.] "United States Navy" Disbursing Clerk Third Class; [hon.] Letter Commendation from Admiral Kelly United States Navy; [pers.] I've always written from the heart, it greatly expresses my feeling of what's going on with my life at the time.; [a.] USS Willamette, FPO AP

WYE, JONATHAN BURLINGAME
[Pen.] J.B.; [b.] July 30, 1979, Washington, D.C.; [p.] Chris and Jean Wye; [ed.] Peabody, Watkins, Stuart-Hobson, Woodrow Wilson High; [occ.] Student; [pers.] One's greatest follower is himself.; [a.] Washington, D.C.

WYNNE, SHIRLEY JEAN
[Pen.] Jean Wynne; [b.] March 8, 1951, Kittrell, NC; [p.] Beatrice and Barker Wynne; [ed.] Vance County High School, Vance Granville Community College; [occ.] Computer Operator, Ameritech; Roseville, MI; [hon.] Beta Club, Dean's List, Who's Who in American Colleges and Universities; [oth. writ.] I write poems for family and friends reflecting the stories that they tell me. I have never submitted anything until now for publication.; [pers.] I write from personal experiences and compassionate stories told to me by others. I write from the heart with Guidance from God.; [a.] Oak Park, MI

YASPARRO, ROSEMARY MUNTZ
[b.] October 18, Cynthiana, KY; [p.] Florence and Dean Muntz; [m.] Joseph Yasparro, October 4, 1969; [ed.] Buena Vista High School and Goergetown College; [hon.] Dean's List; [oth. writ.] Many other poems; [pers.] Poetry is music without tones and paintings without colors, yet it can grasp the human heart and wring the emotions with a powerful hand. It is my ambition to publish a book of my own poetry.; [a.] Lynbrook, NY

YATES, WILLIAM
[b.] September 30, 1945, Wake County; [ed.] I have 15 yrs of education; [occ.] Writer, salesman, common collar man; [memb.] Lifetime member of senior citizens.

YEAGER, HEIDI L.
[b.] July 6, 1984, Natick, MA; [p.] Patricia and David Yeager; [ed.] I'm in Elementary School in grade five; [occ.] Student; [memb.] MSPCA; [hon.] I've got a few awards in art.; [oth. writ.] I wrote a poem for my grandmother when she passed away.; [pers.] This was the first time I've ever entered a poetry contest. I was so glad I did. I'm honored to be chosen one of the semi-finalists.; [a.] Framingham, MA

YLINIEMI, DAR LAYNE L.
[b.] May 5, 1945, Santa Rose, CA; [m.] Richard, May 8, 1965; [ch.] Rick, Laura, Duey, Leann, Levi, Ron; [occ.] LPN at Green Pine Acres Nursing Home in Menahga; [pers.] My poetry is inspired by my husband and family. I am a devoted Grandma, mother, wife and nurse. I am considering for my next writing how to depict life as an elderly resident of a nursing home; [a.] Menahga, MN

YODER, JUDITH K.
[Pen.] Grandma Judy; [b.] March 16, 1947, Williamsburg, IA; [p.] Russell and Miriam Yoder; [m.] Divorced; [ch.] Anita Kay, Shannon Marie; [ed.] Iowa Mennonite School (high school), Hesston College, Hesston, KS, Home Ec and Child Development was major; [occ.] Writing children's books, working towards publication; [oth. writ.] I have four manuscripts looking for publications: Sticks and Stones, Cat Book, Bird Book, and Farm Books. I am currently working on My Guardian Angel; [pers.] I write books and poems that are fun, encourage children's imagination, that deal with fears and problems in a positive and safe manner; [a.] South Bend, IN

YORK, ANNE MC KENNA
[b.] April 17, 1971, Meadowbrook, PA; [ed.] University of Delaware; [pers.] A life of learning is the only life worth living; [a.] Huntingdon Valley, PA

YORK, REBECCA
[b.] February 5, 1958, Kansas City, MO; [p.] Allen Dee and Ramona York; [ch.] Sarah E. Conner and Jonathan J. Conner; [ed.] Stockton High School, Stockton, MO; Evangel College, Springfield, MO; Burge School of Nursing, Springfield, MO; [occ.] Certified Activity Director at the Ash Grove Nursing Home, Inc. Ash Grove, MO; [memb.] A.D.A.M., Activity Directors Assoc. of Missouri; Member of the Hillside Baptist Church, "Servant's Heart" musical duet; [oth. writ.] Several unpublished poems and songs; [pers.] Do your best each and every day. Trust in the Lord to direct your path.; [a.] Ash Grove, MO

YOUNG, NATASHA ANN
[b.] December 19, 1968, Silver Spring, MD; [p.] John Young, Josephine Young; [ed.] Woodward High School, Montgomery College; [occ.] Property Manager, Self-employed, Young Associates (Solomons, MD); [oth. writ.] I have only just begun. If I can change the life of just one person for the better, only then will I be able to achieve success in my life; [a.] Solomons Island, MD

YOUNG, WILLIAM K.
[Pen.] Tiger William; [b.] March 20, 1982, Knox County, OH; [p.] Ruth Eileen Young; [ed.] Currently in seventh grade; [occ.] Student; [memb.] Junior membership in the National Geographic Society; Central Christian Church; Olympia Sales Club; Friendly Farmers 4H Club; [hon.] 4H Superior Award Ribbons, Honor Roll at School; [oth. writ.] "The Beast," "Journey of Legends," "Animal Catalog"; [pers.] I shoot animals with a camera, not a gun; [a.] Heath, OH

ZAHORA, LORI ANN
[b.] October 4, 1968, Bronx, NY; [p.] Carol J. Austie and Richard J. Zahora; [ed.] Graduate of Port Jervis High School, Orange County Comm. College; [occ.] Day Hab Facilitator; [hon.] Belts up to orange w/stripe in Tang Soo Do; [pers.] My poem was inspired by people who have influenced me deeply and I would like to say, "Thank You."; [a.] Port Jervis, NY

ZAKS, LENA
[b.] Senior Citizen; [m.] Widow; [ch.] One Son; [ed.] Music Studies trained by Isaac Levine of the Levine School of Music. Later became his assistant.; [occ.] Piano teacher; [memb.] Chicago Area Music Teacher Association, Illinois State Music Teacher's Assoc., Music Teacher's National Assoc.; [oth. writ.] Many unpublished poems.; [a.] Chicago, IL

ZAVALA, ELIZABETH
[b.] January 10, Puerto Rico; [p.] Aida Rodriguez, Jacinto Zavala; [pers.] I thank God for my talents and thank my family for the inspiration. Because I write what is in my heart, there are no boundaries, regulations or standards that I go by.; [a.] Boston, MS

ZEHRING, JIMMIE D.
[Pen.] Daisy Bones; [b.] November 7, 1959, Bucyrus, OH; [p.] Red and Audrey Zehring; [ch.] Mumdi Zehring; [ed.] Twelfth grade, Wynford High School; [occ.] Disabled construction worker, restoring cabinets; [memb.] Church of Christ of Upper Sandusky, OH; [hon.] Wheel Chair Olympics; [pers.] This came true because of my friend, who I think the world of. She believes in me. True and close friendship is very rare these days. Thank you. (Daisy); [a.] Bucyrus, OH

ZEIS, KATHERINE LYNN
[b.] November 19, 1961, Cincinnati, OH; [p.] Ken Montgomery - Grace Hayes; [m.] Jeffrey Zeis, June 1, 1991; [ch.] Jennifer, Victor, Matt, Amy, Emily, Michael; [ed.] Learned most from people around me; [occ.] Licensed practical nurse; [hon.] Birth certificates of my children; [oth. writ.] Personal enjoyment and for others. Greeting cards (homemade); answer machine messages; [pers.] I believe you learn through other people. I hope I teach something good!; [a.] Cincinnati, OH

ZENIERIS, JER
[Pen.] Jay Zee; [b.] May 7, 1961; [m.] Petros Zenieris, September 21, 1990; [ch.] Alexander; [occ.] Adult Basic Education Instructor, Resa III, Charleston, WV; [oth. writ.] Kikli, a fiction novel that I am attempting to get published.; [pers.] I attempt through my writing to help uplift the human spirit. I believe that in spite of cultural differences we are similar, in that, we are all bound together by the light. It is my hope to reflect this in my writing.; [a.] Charleston, WV

ZIELINSKI, C. JEANENE
[b.] March 4, 1959, Abilene, TX; [p.] A.J. and Marie Harrell; [m.] Russell J. Zielinski, April 28, 1994; [ch.] Jarod J. Bell, Melissa M. Bell; [ed.] High school graduate 1977, Peru Central School, Peru, NY; graduate - John W. Harold Educational Center 1977; [occ.] Hair Salon owner and Cosmetologist; [memb.] Peru Central School Alumni Assoc; [oth. writ.] Local newspaper. Opening reading for Peru Central School 1993 graduation ceremony. Working on book of poetry presently; [pers.] My purpose is to make us think about where we have come from, where we are and to try to inspire the drive to get to where we want to be; [a.] Peru, NY

ZWEIG, MAUREEN HOGAN
[b.] April 3, 1947, Long Beach, CA; [p.] Charles Matthew and Helen Hayes Hogan; [m.] Stephan Zweig, MD, April 13, 1982; [ch.] Denise Kathlene, Timothy John, Michael Jacob; [ed.] Orange Glen High - Escondido, CA, Long Beach City College, Nursing Degree; [occ.] Homemaker/writer; [oth. writ.] Book in progress. My grandmother's life as told through her poetry - written by her from 1919 - 1956 approx; [pers.] When I can remember to look back, I see more clearly where I'm going; [a.] Pacific Palisades, CA

Index
of
Poets

Index

A

Aaron, Allister R.   138
Abadjian, Linda   494
Abbett, Christopher G.   284
Abbott, Kevin J.   490
Abbruscato, Dana   311
Abell, Donna, Jayne Cottrell   295
Ables, Mollie   537
Abramowitz, Marion   625
Abruzzese, Corrie   320
Acevedo, Hortencia   323
Acker, Jeremy D.   170
Acosta, Chris   128
Acton, Kathy   389
Adams, Ashley   442
Adams, Courtney   141
Adams, Gail   36
Adams, Jill H.   144
Adams, John   156
Adams, Johnnie M.   473
Adams, Linda   99
Adams, Lois J.   243
Adams, Lynne E.   254
Adams, Sharon D.   500
Adinolfi, Helen   268
Adipietro, Sara   244
Adissi, Frances   552
Adkins, E. M.   230
Afifi, Aly   46
Afuang, Benjamin V.   551
Agrimi-Hayes, Margo   227
Aguon, Nieves M.   498
Ahmels, Harriet   166
Ahn, Peggy   247
Ahnen, Margy   521
Al Majid, Mariam   192
Alan, Gary S.   288
Alarva, Fred P.   336
Alastair   494
Albert, John   330
Aldag, Alana   471
Alderson, Shannon   587
Aldrich, Judy   431
Alexander, Joris   324
Alexander, Virginia   248
Alford, Christina Lea   135
Alicakos, Paul   601
Allen, A. Jeff   499
Allen, Barbara A.   630
Allen, Daniel Neal   421
Allen, Jane E.   308
Allen, Kathryne S.   600
Allen, Lucy I.   20
Allen, Pauline L.   403
Allen, Shernise Alexa   200
Allen, Sue   85
Allman, Licia L.   240
Almgren, Elfreda M.   324
Aloy, Richard   601
Alston, Juanita   566
Alvarado, Gabriel   551
Alvarez, Celestine L.   563

Aman, Charlotte   140
Amarandei, Otilia   249
Amatury, Joy   468
Ambach, Evelyn J.   575
Ambrose, Lisa   382
Ambrose, Sarah G.   607
Amero, Anthony V.   153
Amundson, Beau Allen   134
Anctil, Karen L.   503
Anderegg, Brad   421
Andersen, Karyn   480
Anderson, A. L.   75
Anderson, Bradley   307
Anderson, Charlotte   471
Anderson, Christine   61
Anderson, Eulanhie   287
Anderson, Gloria C.   37
Anderson, Heath   44
Anderson, Kristi   220
Anderson, Kristina D.   357
Anderson, Lori Lanice,   592
Anderson, Mary Lou   213
Anderson, Mavis   542
Anderson, Mildred   189
Anderson, Ruth   241
Andrew, Robert   525
Andrews, Dana L.   449
Andrews, David   570
Andrews-Stark, Sarah   518
Andruzzi III, Joseph   119
Angelias, Anthony   417
Angelopoulos, Rita   620
Anneski, Adeline E.   279
Anthony, Linda J.   385
Antonetti, Migdalia   87
Anzalone, Jo   118
Apilado, Crystal-Marie   63
Araby, Christine   136
Arana, Iggy   29
Arbuckle, Nancy I.   625
Archer, Lois   346
Archie, Sharese   218
Archuleta, Mark   619
Arellano, Jesse   557
Ares, Luz   624
Arias, Lorena   588
Armiger, Milton W.   234
Arms, Janis Hunt   278
Armstead, Rodney   96
Armstrong, Christine   159
Armstrong, Michael J.   514
Arnold, Gerald   330
Arnold, Larry   628
Arnold, Regina   105
Arocho, Deborah   117
Arredondo, JoAnn   183
Arteaga, Claudia   454
Arthur, Burt K.   58
Arthur, Frank   39
Arthur, Truth   210
Ash Sr., LaVon J.   502
Ashcraft, Butch   127
Askew, Irma L.   302
Asp, Mildred   624
Aszman, Melodie Ann   213
Atkins, Helen Fiske   24
Aucoin, Heather   186

Augusta, James H., Sr.   305
Aulson, Bill   37
Austin, Bernadette L.   280
Avaricio, Sylvia Sol   26
Avedon, Danielle   422
Averill, Jeannie   325
Avery, Christina M.   459
Avery, Misty   524
Avery, Quientana L.   255
Avila, Jose Luis   471
Azmon, Emanuel   31

B

Babcock, Douglas Thomas   269
Bacchus, Albert   575
Bacso, Jennifer   141
Badeaux, Trevis R.   249
Baer, Donna C.   29
Bahamón, Juan E.   412
Bailey, John G.   417
Bailey, Kriscinda   255
Bailey, Lisa S.   543
Bailey, Maudelene   537
Bailey, Michelle D.   612
Bailey, Suzanne L.   596
Bailiff, Lee   87
Bainter, April   448
Baird, Toni   18
Baker, Barbara   453
Baker, Christine   116
Baker, Cornelius   550
Baker, M. L.   254
Baker, Marjorie H.   503
Baker, Marolyn E.   378
Baker, Tammy   370
Baker, Thomas A.   528
Baker, Tina   216
Balcarcel, Rebecca   257
Baldeosingh, Rudranath   511
Baldwin, Dani McNeil   436
Bales, Jon   430
Ballard, Brenda D.   263
Ballejos, Pamela   479
Ballinger, Dorothy   332
Banales, Irma   473
Banerjee, Gopal H.   7
Banerjee, Kaustab   253
Banez, Jose Patricio   279
Banfe, June F.   118
Bannister, Stephen W.   108
Barbagallo, Sebastian   514
Barbee, James M.   267
Barbee-Wooten, Daphne   140
Barber, Heidi E.   34
Barbier, Theresa   596
Barbushack, Mirslow   534
Bargmann, Joan   567
Barlow, Amber Dawn   458
Barnes, Candace   133
Barnes, Charlotte M.   319
Barnes, Cynthia A.   456
Barnes, Jodi   571
Barnes, Kristal C.   244
Barnes, Linda D.   491
Barnes, Sondra   483
Barnett, Bill   419

Barnick, Susan   91
Barr, Ellen   304
Barr, James K.   4
Barr, Linda M.   254
Barr, Michelle   540
Barr, Nicole   260
Barré, Ann R.   143
Barrett, Deborah A.   428
Barron, Tania   407
Bartee, Patti Fairchild   388
Bartell, Nancy L.   232
Bartholomey, David   148
Bartkoski, Amanda   297
Bartlett, Florence L.   319
Barto, Jean S.   574
Barton, Tracy L.   218
Bartone, Mary Jo   611
Bashiruddin, Catherine   265
Basile, Lillian K. Wells   21
Bass, Shelley M.   398
Bassham, Denise   40
Bastian, Tish   384
Bates, Jennifer E.   32
Battaglia, Jessica   442
Battistuzzi, Eugenia   299
Batts, James Clark   16
Baucom, Chastity M.   322
Baugh, Diane Gerber   140
Baugh, F. Sinsa   480
Baugher, Gary M.   61
Baunach, Esther Ilona   10
Baxter, Barbara W.   466
Bay, Ailene   314
Bayer, Dorothy E.   121
Bayerl, Dorothy Hokkanen   587
Bayles, James C.   336
Bayless, Gina M.   175
Bazil, Patrick A.   623
Bazos, Kiri   358
Beach, Ollis L.   409
Beal, Rhonda L.   199
Beall, Nannie E.   405
Bear, Miranda Running   253
Beard, Evelyn Jeanette   435
Beard, Pepper   259
Beasley, Akenduca   50
Beaubien, Marilyn   102
Beavers, Melodie   228
Beck, Carrie Emily   421
Becker, Luba   220
Becker, Phil H.   394
Beckerman, Leon   217
Beckett, Eloise Perry   574
Beckman, Kristin   387
Beckmon, Jon   323
Beebe, Harold W.   141
Beebe, Sarah   393
Beeram, Sapna   368
Begay, Belvina   468
Behle, Paul   262
Behling, Erica L.   274
Behm, Bob   503
Bell, Elizabeth Bradner   9
Bell, Helen Pope   443
Bell, John W., Jr.   411
Bell, Mark   200
Bell, Martha   411

Bell, Robert L.   385
Bell, Suzen   517
Bellah, Helen A.   472
Bellew, Donna   122
Belt, Andrea J.   54
Ben-Joseph, Leila   500
Benedetto, Janet L.   294
Benjamin, Ruthven   619
Bennett, Angel   472
Bennett, Brian   55
Bennett, Lois   348
Bennett, Marvin   94
Bennett, Stefanie   377, 378
Bennett, Thelma   541
Benoit, Carol E.   178
Bens, Kris   508
Benson, Barbara J.   264
Benson, Darlene Delorio   291
Benson, Jack L.   62
Benson, Jessica   267
Benson, William O.   74
Bentley, Charles S.   135
Bentley, Shawn M.   15
Benvenuto, Lucy G.   541
Beohm, Carrie P.   443
Beres, Danielle   412
Bergeron, Cindy Rose   310
Bergeron, Matt   13
Bergman, Kory   256
Berkowitz, Jay   261
Bernhard, Janice L.   56
Bernier, Dwayne   148
Bernstein, Melissa Joy   249
Berrios, Angel A.   570
Berry, Annie   188
Berry, Sandra L.   237
Bertin, Howard   184
Bertini, Pat   96
Bertrand, Ashley   459
Besaw, Kristy M.   392
Besen, Jane   39
Betsch, Deborah L.   456
Bever, Teresa Ann   619
Bey, Yillie   381
Beynon, Jessica   461
Bezdek, Summer   491
Bhardwaj, Tarun   606
Biancaniello, Luke   103
Biberos, Adelaida   136
Bidwell, Angela   295
Bieber, Kim   482
Bierce, Shari   378
Biesterfeld, Bonnie   416
Bilanych, Ann   318
Bildson, Gloria Fowler   139
Bilis-Bastos, Kate F.   347
Billey, Katie   630
Billings, Lorraine   391
Bilstad, Gayle   444
Binder, Nancy R.   189
Bingham, Alexander D.   322
Bingham, James E.   549
Bingham, Michael   499
Bingham, Michelle   76
Birdwell, O'Dessa   512
Bishop, Angel J.   130
Bishop, Mary Utt   518

Bishop, Raymond C.   97
Bishop, Rosemary   360
Bissi   47
Bitner, Dorothy West   125
Bixler, Lindsey   387
Blachman, Jodi   464
Black, E.   313
Black, Helen E.   149
Black, J. W.   524
Black, Marsha L.   507
Black, Nanette   259
Black, Rilla A.   480
Blackard, Brandi   37
Blacker, Dorothy J.   470
Blackwell, Renee   215
Blair, Amy   472
Blair, Phyllis   598
Blake, Bonnie   124
Blake, Haynesly R.   282
Blake, Joan   47
Blancas, Maria   212
Blanchard, Sarah   597
Blanchfield, Joseph J.   134
Blanco, Mark F.   207
Bland, Jo-Jo   568
Blank, Heather   125
Blank, Karin   97
Blank, Tyler   480
Blankenship, P. J.   396
Blauvelt, Jamie   288
Bloomer, Jaclyn   555
Bloomer, Lois   341
Bluesky   235
Blumenberg, Theodore A.   375
Blumenthal, Walter L.   500
Blumline, August G.   157
Bluske, Edythe M.   123
Bobb, Donald E.   421
Bobo, Gadge   456
Bobo, Gwen   70
Bockian, Edith   19
Bodine, Jody   31
Bodman, Nikola   229
Bodrie, Tammy   196
Boelig, Sarah   101
Boerem, Kerrie   402
Boesen, Carol   575
Bogan, Doretha H.   564
Bogart, Christine E.   331
Bogdanovs, Nick   380
Boggs, Jeff   146
Boiteux, Carl   52
Bolden, Becky J.   158
Boling, Allison   281
Bolls, Bobby W.   280
Bolstok, Shirley   607
Bolt, Kimberly   353
Bolton, Marta   524
Bommarito, Joseph   430
Bond, Tonya   627
Bone, Jamie E.   334
Bonini, Lacey D.   397
Bonner, Matthew   375
Bonnick, Stephanie R.   348
Bonsu, Clement   182
Book, Becky   156
Boone, Francine Thornton   14

Boone, Tracey   367
Borden, Phillip   227
Borgwardt, Johannes   576
Borne, Jane S.   139
Borovski, Conrad   337
Bosch, Sharon A.   361
Bossone, Richard S.   372
Bosworth, Sandra Lee   411
Botelho, Thomas   375
Bottoms, Ruth Bucher   206
Botts, Henry   126
Botzko, Jeff   64
Bourassa, Beth   129
Bourgeau, Ellen   451
Bousegard, Hurst, Jr.   475
Boutwell, Muriel C.   215
Bouvier, Elizabeth   125
Bowden, Gene Austin   568
Bowden, Kathryn   345
BoWell, Bonnie   118
Bowen, Dale C.   181
Bowermaster, Tara   101
Bowers, Suphrina L.   375
Bowhay, Samara L.   409
Bowman, Johnny   460
Bowman, Paul   602
Boyce, Carrie E.   554
Boyd, David P.   41
Boyd, Kelli B.   352
Boyer, Dean   54
Bradford, Bret Matthew   418
Bradford, Sherry   522
Bradley, Tom   361
Bradshaw, Beth Anne   68
Brady, Clare   474
Brady, Elsie   172
Bragg, April Eve   583
Bramlet, Alice J.   432
Brand, Alex   148
Brand, Karen P.   233
Brandafino, Darlene   322
Brandts, Danielle   261
Brannon, Courtney   64
Brannon, Jayne Lynn   425
Brantley, Bobbi   62
Brasel, April   321
Braun, Heather   6
Braun, Theresa   405
Bray, Elysa   631
Brayman, Nikki L.   532
Brazwell, Christian D.   337
Brazzeal, Amanda   328
Brecht, Jennifer   571
Breen, Jennifer   167
Breen, Laura   245
Brehse, Tami   249
Breitkreutz, Michael R.   533
Brennan, Jeanmarie   335
Brennan, Nicole   216
Brennan, Tony   94
Brenneman, Wayne E.   601
Breslin-Blake, Rose L.   15
Brest, William   505
Brettschneider, Mildred Shavelson 360
Brevoort, Jennifer   474
Brewer, Angie   30
Briant, V. B.   242

Bridgers, John D.   330
Bridgett, Shirley   113
Briggs, Chelsy Z.   454
Briggs, Irene E.   164
Briggs, Kevin   90
Briggs, Paul Michael   114
Brightman, Tom   599
Briles, Marie   409
Brinson II, William   104
Briski, Diane   287
Bristol, Daniel J.   34
Britt, Jan   474
Brittain, Bobi   539
Britton, Grace Odom   454
Britton, Robert   614
Broadaway, Ruth   480
Broadway, Lois   530
Brock, Norah L.   539
Brock, Suzanne   235
Broker, Leonilla   208
Bromberger, Rochelle   519
Brookins, Johnny   327
Brooks, Gloria Lisa   629
Brooks, Kaye Patrice   537
Brooks, Loretta M.   211
Broughton, Kerstin   491
Browell, A. Margaret   586
Brown, Andrew   50
Brown, Barbara Jean   629
Brown, C. Jeanne   500
Brown, Carolyn A.   324
Brown, Chandra   445
Brown, Charlton   38
Brown, Donald E.   22
Brown, Donna S.   275
Brown, Dwight L.   568
Brown, Edward J.   71
Brown, Gladys   178
Brown, Jacqueline L.   452
Brown, Janet McNally   293
Brown, Jessica   32
Brown, Joy   163
Brown Jr., Robert L.   536
Brown, Lorraine L.   380
Brown, Marcy Lynne   589
Brown, Robert V.   612
Brown, Vicki Hilton   599
Brown, Warren   377
Brownell, Randi   348
Bruaw, Angela Marie   569
Brubaker, Barbara J.   163
Bruce, Betty Grace Pease   553
Bruce, Charles   61
Brumley, Amy   473
Bruni, Jessica Lynn   46
Bruns, Sister Barbara   129
Brutscher, Edward Alan   555
Bryan, Claire   471
Bryan, David   441
Bryan, Heather   576
Bryan, Karl   392
Bryan-Howell, Rebecca   506
Bryant, Erin   283
Bryant, Heather   166
Bryant, Johnetta   168
Bryce, Melba   617
Brymer-Roberts, Jeannie   465

Bryson, Nethus 201
Bucco, Jennifer 319
Buchanan, Briget 334
Buchanan, Japhus E. 37
Buchanan, Pauline 243
Buck, Bill 179
Buck, Ellsworth C. 326
Buckles, Dena D. 469
Buckwalter, Lydia T. 250
Bueter, Bonnie 440
Bufano, Eleanore A. 564
Buffington, Christina 312
Buffington, Kristy 386
Bugg, Todd 398
Buitron, Barbara S. 335
Bukowski, Marie D. 244
Buller, Kristin 110
Bullock, Luma 508
Bullock, Luther E. 506
Bullock, Robert B. 75
Bumgarner, Angela 172
Bunger, James D. 429
Bunker, Jo Ann 126
Buoye, Misti 198
Burgener, Irene J. 154
Burgess, Michelle 349
Burgess, Theresa M. 531
Burkart, Karen Elizabeth 395
Burke, Jude T. 548
Burke, Kathryn 245
Burkemper, Diane 145
Burker, Miriam 600
Burleigh, Doris L. 464
Burley, Amanda 146
Burley, Thelma 627
Burnett, Benjamin R. 314
Burr, Pixie L. 520
Burrell, Paul L. 393
Burrell, Peggy 383
Burris, Cora M. 177
Bursell, Tammy Renee 390
Burt, Ayanna N. 150
Burt, Essie B. 453
Burt, Stan C. 189
Burton, Edith L. 276
Burton, Randi 259
Bush, Patricia 370
Buske, Laura 344
Buss, Herbert G. 172
Buss, Natalie 257
Butler, Dolores R. 123
Butler, Helen M. 168
Butler, Jeanne M. 185
Butler, Lois N. 526
Butler, Martha Penney 616
Butler, Michael 258
Butler, Patricia 258
Buttler, Gabe 334
Byard, Andrea 176
Bye, Dayna Leigh 66
Byers, Valerie Ann 238
Bykofsky, Ari 297
Bynum, Ron 510
Byrd, Kelly 340
Byrd, Lisa Marie 265
Byrd, Rosa J. 501

C

Caboon, David C. 137
Cacciotti, Valencia 386
Cacdac, Francisca F. 578
Cadogan, W. A. 242
Cadugan, Edward S. 573
Cagle, Robin A. 626
Caimens, Richard M. 22
Cain, Marchelle E. 623
Calame, Marie 253
Caldwell, Edith 42
Caldwell, Marie J. 481
Calhoun-Medlock, Nancy 600
Callaghan, Brian 45
Callahan, M. Elizabeth Poole 190
Callis, Rebecca 613
Calmes, M. 363
Calvanese, Kathleen Bruce 406
Cameron, Dorothy R. 307
Campanella, Carla 56
Campbell, Betty 474
Campbell, Kim 492
Campbell, Lauren 540
Campbell, Lori 233
Campbell, O'keather T. 103
Campbell, Penny 533
Campbell, Susan D. 399
Campetti, Jackie 581
Campisi, Kevin M. 524
Cangurel, Susan 98
Cannon, Angela M. 11
Cannon, Pat 357
Cantley, Cheryl A. 56
Cantrell, Patricia 239
Capen, Phyllis 402
Capestany, Sandra 390
Capobianco, Gloria 58
Capria, Karen S. 252
Capriccioso, David 39
Caprice, Joanne C. 27
Caran, S. M. 95
Caratachea, Viviana 257
Carbo, Margaret 239
Cardenas, Carmen 52
Cardin, Nathan 245
Cardona, Joann 584
Cardone, Alycia 140
Cardwell, Nicole 366
Carello, Janice 581
Carey, Jeanne W. 431
Carey, Peter 95
Carini, Anna 51
Carl, Roxy E. 481
Carle, Glenn 175
Carley, Francis 474
Carlson, Dana 185
Carlson, Susan T. 192
Carlton, Leland James 531
Carmack, Tim 529
Carman, Ron 73
Carmody, Kerin L. 243
Carmona, Andrea 470
Carnahan, Michael 495
Carnathan, Robert M. 529
Carney, A. E. 12
Carpenter, Crystal Shevon 71

Carpenter, Nancy L. 411
Carpenter, Scott 188
Carr, Bree-Anne 476
Carr, DeErica Angelita 136
Carr, Lonnie 402
Carr, Virginia 251
Carrigan, DeNeese 273
Carrillo, Juli 468
Carrol, Joe A., Jr. 563
Carroll, Daron M. 182
Carroll, Sheree 488
Carruth, Julie 279
Carson, Jeremy 55
Carson, Maryanne 199
Carswell, Leo 195
Carter, Angela 321
Carter, Brenda 125
Carter, Candy 124
Carter, Frances 139
Carter, Isebella 337
Carter, Jamie 460
Carter, Terri S. 388
Case, Linda E. 504
Casey II, Charles L. 280
Casey, Marie P. 405
Casey, Mary Lou 216
Caskie, Erna B. 267
Cass, Rebecca J. 257
Cassandra 469
Casselberry, Mary L. 594
Cassell, Louise 202
Cassidy, Kira Jeanne 6
Castelino, Cecilia 165
Castillo, Donna 276
Castillo, Terri Parker 233
Castro, Alisha 49
Castro, Jennifer 64
Catarino, M. Antonio 405
Caudill, Deanna 454
Caudill, Gregory 44
Caudillo, Deanna 581
Cauley, Melissa Renee 509
Caulfield, Gary J. 452
Cecil, Elvia Saldivar 289
Cecil, Kathleen 86
Centavo 331
Center, Brad 430
Century 515
Ceresa, Peter A. 346
Cerf, P. B. 74
Chacko, Keziah P. 608
Chaffee, Dorothy 63
Chakrabarti, Ishan 451
Chaloff, Marjory L. 391
Chand, Kishan 396
Chang, Aeri 475
Chang, Janice M. 309
Chao, Ning 200
Chaple, Matthew 339
Charles, Holly 169
Charles, Irisdeane H. 436
Chartier, Phyllis 603
Chase, John A. 148
Chavers, Charla Michelle 473
Chavis, Micheal J. 240
Chernick, Cheryl 272
Chernishova, Kaya 84

Cherrier, Lisa Louise 382
Cherry, Dwayne 130
Cherry, Lindsay 543
Chewning, Deborah M. 298
Chezum, Sharon 200
Chiang, Judy 128
Chiaradio, Diana L. 149
Chilson, Ruby 402
Chinchillo, Jean G. 307
Chiquelin, Bill 475
Chism, Pauline 235
Choi-Chong, Sunju 347
Cholewa, Paula Kay 258
Chou, Eileen 182
Chouinard, Gilbert P. 447
Chrisman, Margaret Craig 489
Christensen, A. Sherman 18
Christianson, Beth 285
Christie, Eartha L. 175
Church, Cheryl W. 154
Church, Eleanor Louise 26
Church, Sally J. 626
Ciaglia, Joseph 292
Cilibraise, Lisa A. 338
Ciotti, Antoinette M. 141
Cipperly, Ian 295
Ciprian, Bill 549
Claiborne, Brenda 307
Clampet-Lundquist, Merrill 8
Clancy, Karen 249
Clanton, Michelle D. 593
Clapp, Rebekah 262
Clark, Janet 140
Clark, Jannie B. 333
Clark, John Henry 311
Clark, Ruth H. 74
Clark, Tanya Diane 410
Clarke, Melissa 622
Clarke, Yvonne 251
Claus, Michelle 99
Clay, Lindsay M. 85
Clayton, Cheryl 171
Clegg, Donna M. 128
Clemann, Elizabeth 140
Clements, Jan 303
Clements, Kathleen D. 106
Clever, Jason A. 473
Click, Anita Gayle 463
Clinkscales, Jal 288
Cloud, Valerie Johnson 494
Clough, Priscilla M. 76
Cobb, Karen 396
Coble, Frances R. 68
Cobos, Eve 304
Codding, David 323
Coderre, Anna F. 142
Coey, Vicky 204
Cofane, Michael 235
Coffee, Jill 313
Coffman, Patricia 607
Cohen, Joseph A. 313
Cohn, L. Lilo 602
Cohoon, Doris J. 464
Coker, Leigh A. 247
Colacino, Elaine H. 315
Colberg, Shawn 88
Colburn, John E. 30

Cole, Dorothy Spicer   154
Cole, Natalie   12
Coleman, Darlene   133
Coleman, Edrel   475
Coles Jr., Epifanio C.   135
Collander, Eric E.   27
Collings, Darron   57
Collins, C. T.   16
Collins, Carrie L.   550
Collins, Colleen   179
Collins, Dawn   557
Collins, Dwight Vincent   279
Collins, Erica H.   457
Collins, George W.   313
Collins, Patricia H.   115
Collins, Randall L.   229
Collitt, Josephine L.   462
Coln, Olav   530
Colonna, JoAnn   28
Colwell, Alex   12
Comer, Niles U.   88
Compton, Amy   118
Comte, Nathan A.   617
Concello, John   442
Conde, Edwin, Sr.   565
Conder, Lois Snelling   206
Conley, Lisa   527
Conlin, Liberty Rice   84
Connally, William   390
Conner, Susan   521
Connor, Nancy   196
Connors, Bob   453
Conrad, Bonnie Morris   463
Conry, Ebee   428
Cook, Charles E.   120
Cook, Jessica   419
Cook, Lori Ann   107
Cook, William Wayne   390
Coop, Kay   599
Cooper, Audrey   56
Cooper, Billie A.   24
Cooper, Doris L.   305
Cooper, Jamie   321
Cooper, Jayson   147
Cooper, Jenean   187
Cooper, Ronald   192
Cooper, Roy A.   528
Corbo, Joseph   176
Corcoran, Juliet   132
Cordeiro, S. P.   399
Cordero, Will   378
Cordova, Roger D.   409
Corff, William   22
Corman, Heather   422
Corr, Edwin G.   5
Coscarella, James H.   294
Coscarello, Barbara A.   312
Cosgrove, William C.   253
Coté, Cheryl S.   298
Cotone, Mary   197
Cottle, Carol A.   261
Coulton, Catherine   562
Cousins, Ivan E.   299
Couto, Dianna   52
Cowan, Ronnie   350
Cox, Addy   160

Cox, Edgar   29
Cox, Micheal R.   400
Cox, Ruth   221
Craft, Carla   133
Crago, Mary   229
Craig, Jenny   450
Craig, Kelly A.   382
Craigie, Chris   142
Cramer, Amy   470
Crank, Greg   141
Crash, Markus   394
Crasi, Derek   630
Creasey, Elaine A.   173
Crescenzo, Joseph P.   139
Crews, Efrem   320
Cribbs, David B.   582
Crick, Victoria   220
Crimo, Rosanne M.   236
Crissi, Sheila R.   532
Crivelli II, Louis S.   188
Crobaugh, Emma   8
Croft Jr., John C. R.   43
Croft, Michelle   489
Crombie, Donald   331
Cromer, Deborah   462
Cromwell, Judith A.   40
Crosby, Monica   373
Cross, Doug   172
Crothers, Joseph W.   320
Crouch, David Wayne   427
Crow, Jennifer   428
Crow, Leslie C.   527
Crowe, Irene Glass   416
Crowley, Diana   336
Crowley, William   247
Crowther, Joyce   549
Crum, Annabelle   302
Crumpton, Nannie Sue   402
Crutchfield, Marjorie A.   498
Cruz, Joey   321
Cruz, Marji   113
Cryder, Nancy A.   616
Cubine, Kenneth W.   591
Culbertson, Jennifer   318
Culp, Mildred L.   247
Culver, Angela   318
Cummings, Caroldean K.   583
Cunnigham, Ken   245
Cunningham, Anthony E.   276
Cupit, Jane   118
Cupper, Jack   278
Curbeaux, Aridith G.   412
Curcuru, Jennifer   462
Cureton-Price, Tokoya   531
Curlee, Narda Wade   527
Curram, William   403
Curry, Marsha L.   518
Curry, R. B.   598
Curtis, Kathleen M.   593
Curtis, Kim   209
Curtiss, A.B.   172
Curto, James   124
Cushing, Yuka   102
Custeau, Pamela J.   478
Cvar, Anne S.   324
Cylkowski, Eulalia A.   558

D

D   389
Dabbs, Lowell P.   544
Dagley, Maxine   246
Dailey, Margaret   245
Daines, Anna   172
Daka, John   447
Dalbow, Harry   122
Daleo, Anthony   24
Dallas, John E.   50
DaLonzo, Nicholas A.   224
Dalrymple, Michelle   88
D'Amelio Jr., John   220
Damien, Paul G.   377
Damm, Peter   401
Damon, Gloria   25
Damon, Karen   531
D'Amore, Eileen   472
Dandridge, Herbert S.   164
Danek, Bess   272
Danes, William Harris   505
Daniel, Calvin   320
Daniel, F. Marion   340
Daniels, Abbey   139
Danielson, Kisha C.   626
Danielson, Patria E.   250
Danlag, Donald A.   33
Danna, Nicole   210
Dansby, Bettye   567
Danzis, Shirley F.   502
Darby, Jeannetta Louise Brown   415
Darcy, Dixie   446
Daremo   92
Darkes, Linda   364
Daughrity, Tara   539
Davenport, H. L.   315
Davenport, Kenneth L.   249
Davey, Anne R.   120
Davey, Carl Joseph   57
Davey, Eleanor E.   126
Davidson, Del   441
Davidson, LaDena   252
Davidson, Tammy Jo   544
Davis, Adrienne   14
Davis, Alice S.   281
Davis, Earnest N.   145
Davis, Iris H.   132
Davis, J. Max   234
Davis, Jean   299, 424
Davis, Jennifer K.   321
Davis, Jesse L.   575
Davis, Kristin L.   408
Davis, Nancy Estell   112
Davis, Nicole   509
Davis, Rod   240
Davis, Sarah   538
Davis, Sherri A.   529
Davis-Holt, Linda   589
Dawkins, Rochelle C.   535
Dawson, H. Marie James   113
Day, Martha Louise   356
Dayananda, Nilu   245
De Cecco, Andrew   550
De Cola, Dolores   269
De Luca, Richard J.   14
De Menna, Helen   119

Deale, Ali   17
Dean, Bobby   45
DeAngelis, Donna M.   49
DeAngelis-Parent, Fran   267
Deardorff, Dora McClure   319
Deaton, Marene   230
DeBaldo-Thode, Elizabeth C.   128
DeBar, Kay   395
DeBlois, Rebeccah   490
DeBrey, Avis Hilderbrand   464
Decker, Allison   330
Deetjen, Jan Ross   119
Degan, Adeline Tinkovicz   135
Dehnick, Phil   357
Deitschel, Dan   187
Deitz, Stephanie   528
del Pilar, Maria   260
del Sol Jimenez, Maria   234
Dela Rosa, Deogracias S.   566
Delaney, Amy J.   432
Dell, Irene Prater   25
Delos, Bernard   3
Delph, Carmen   149
Delph, Margaret J.   540
DeMars, Joseph T.   277
Demasi, Joseph C.   116
DeMicco, Jennifer   448
Dempsey, Jack W.   290
Denman, Billy E.   261
Denni, Margaret   520
Depaep, Tabare   542
DePiero, Gail A.   336
Derhammer, Linda   189
Derkatch, Theresa   628
DeRosa, Christine   313
Derrick, Shelleen S.   78
Derrico-White, Rita Joy   380
Derryberry, Mary Margaret   260
Derstine, Cheryl A.   70
DeSantis, Rosemary   384
DesChene, Helen P.   460
DeSisto, Pauline   520
DesMeules, Morgan Metzger   387
DeSoto, Timothy J.   613
Detro, Norman L.   495
DeUrso, Roberta   213
Deutscher, Kay V.   81
DeVine, Geraldine   301
Devore, Ed   175
Dhanifu, Alicia F.   448
Diamond, Lisa Diann   94
Diamond, Marilyn L.   617
Dianda, Juanita   477
Dianne, Shireen   258
DiBella, Jan A.   16
DiBetta, Paul   215
Dick, Barbara J.   171
Dickey, Christopher Steven   57
Dickinson, Christine A.   297
Diedrich, Liz   495
Diehl, Sheila   358
Diehl, Stephanie L.   362
Diener, Russell   368
Dietrich, Judy   188
Dietrich, Paul   478
Dietz, Mary Ellen   493
DiGennaro, Peter   17

Dimberg, Kristen   194
Dimeglio, Cathy H.   39
Dinerstein, Edith   123
Dinga, Lindsey Leigh   235
Dinkel, Linda   457
Dion, Alan H.   462
Dirzuweit, Joyce Moretz   167
Dishman, Roberta C.   392
Dismukes, Patty   246
Doan, David I.   438
Dobbs, Adam   130
Dodds, Irene   63
Dodds, John   144
Dodelin, Vera M.   374
Doggett, Amie Claire   316
Dolan, Rita H.   606
Domanski, Robin   374
Domenichelli, Willene   540
Donaldson, John   140
Donna, June E.   183
Donofrio, Annette   159
Donovan, Marvis   244
Doolin, Rick   109
Doombadffe, Annebi   320
Doranzo, Joan   121
Dorsey, Kim Diane   609
Dos Santos, Fred   331
Doss, Charity   329
Dotherow, Sandra C.   94
Doty, Terry   249
Doud, Amy Marie   329
Douglas, William E.   539
Douglass, Emily   412
Douglass, Helen L.   21
Douglass, Karen   89
Dovalina, Nancy   94
Dowd, William C.   532
Dowling, Susan   388
Dowling, Thomas J.   522
Downey, Megan   410
Downing, Shelbia   592
Dows, Teresa   202
Doyle, Erin Chaye   70
Draper, A. Alan   313
Drennan, Della Rae   432
Droesch, Audrey   146
Duan, Jenny   172
Duarte, Steven N.   597
Dube, Ray   89
Dubin, Minna   231
Dudich, Melissa   529
Dudley, Marie   484
Dudra, Gloria E.   302
Dufficy, Thomas   81
Dufrechou, Jason   52
Duke, Sarah K.   234
Duley, Cindy   460
Dumas, Claudia B.   136
Dumsha, Timotheus   523
Dunaway, John B.   443
Dunbar, Dottie   303
Dunbar, Mike   405
Dunbar, Patricia   224
Dunburg, Amanda   474
Duncan, Lorene   260
Duncan, Naomi   243
Duncan, Susan   234

Dunham, Sheila   213
Dunigan, Juane   29
Dunlap, Ellen Stone   269
Dunlap, Rikk   9
Dunlap, Sonja   230
Dunn, Karen   346
Dunn, Linda   526
Dunn, Phyllis Christina   397
Dunson, Yvonne D.   239
Duong-van, M.   515
Duonola, Elaine   462
Duran, Belkis   176
Durben, Steven M.   76
Durio, F. Joann   256
Durkee, David   23
Durkee, Dorothy   63
Durnavich, Louis W.   538
Dutcher, Roger L.   508
Duvall, Michelle Lynne   203
DuVaul, Stacey   343
Dye, Rita   517
Dziamalek, Heather   580
Dziuk, Josette Corinne H.   438

E

Earl, Maurice   384
Earl-Dudley, Patricia   369
Easter, Clarence E., Jr.   572
Easter, Virginia Follett   626
Easterling, Miriam W.   79
Eaves, Sara   372
Ebert, Julia   141
Ebert, Rachel   596
Ebli, Geri   158
Ebner, Martha E.   235
Eby, Cynthia L.   142
Eccles, Janet S.   314
Echols, Lillian V.   262
Eckdale, Paul   234
Eckhardt, Maria Monica   520
Eddy, Frank C.   336
Edmonds, Robin   341
Edmonson, Brenda Lee   284
Edwards, Betty   328
Edwards, Dawn   434
Edwards, J. R.   489
Edwards, Susan   204
Edwards, Todd   363
Edwards, Victoria   78
Edwards, Virginia L.   257
Egeler, Walter A.   245
Ehle, Renee J.   483
Ehlers, John Thomas   282
Eichenberg, Nicole   255
El-Berry, Hamdy H.   631
Elam, Teri L.   86
Elbert, Wynna F.   620
Elder, Everett   31
Eleni, Sianis   383
Elin, Marty   214
Ellington, Grant   459
Elliott, George   303
Elliott, Jennifer   143
Elliott, Jonathan C.   306
Elliott, Mary Frances   402
Elliott, Robyn Joule   81

Ellison, Donald H.   148
Ellison, Jessica O.   419
Ellison, Sheila   545
Ely, Todd C.   212
Emanuel, Margaret   101
Emanuel, Sharon E.   492
Embry, Patty   91
Emery, Dawn   460
Emery, Jessica   126
Emmerling, Floyd   435
Engebretson, Patrick Henry   541
Engel, Erica   164
Engle, Richard W.   97
English, Deborah   168
Engo, Anne E.   183
Engram, Carmen   561
Enrico, Florence   32
Epes, W. Perry   10
Erbs, Nelson   512
Erickson, Lindsey   224
Erikson, Mary   508
Erskine, Kit   372
Erskine, Phyllis A.   198
Erwin, Elizabeth Stiles   53
Esguerra, Angeli   166
Eskra, Beverly   282
Eskridge, Kenneth   362
Esposito, Edward M.   331
Esposito, Peter J.   220
Estabrook, Gordon A.   167
Ethridge, Wendy   364
Evans, Amy   330
Evans, Doris   261
Evans, Dorothy Mae   285
Evans, Fannie Mae   556
Evans, Irene M.   128
Evans, Lori   523
Evans, Michael D.   238
Evans, Shaun   74
Evans, Tiffany   238
Evans, Winifred   258
Everett Jr., Kenneth R.   535
Everett, L. B.   388
Everman, Ina Vahlsing   582
Evers, Gene   59
Everson Sr., Thomas M.   96
Ewing, Helen Ruth   290
Eyrich, Julie   319

F

Fabicon, Ismael F.   461
Fabiszewski, Jeffrey Jc.   25
Fackrell, Denise   154
Fagliano, Ann   455
Fagundes, Kristina   101
Fairchild, Charles D.   335
Fairchild, Don   21
Fairclough, Allisandra   431
Fakankun, D'aria   156
Falco, Rita Jean Krupa   372
Fambrough, David Glenn   546
Fargnoli, Brian   261
Farias, Marcilio R.   623
Faries, Sherree   192
Farinella, Helen   306
Farmer, Gregory A.   18

Farmer, Karen   109
Farmer, Kathy L.   345
Farnstrom, Frances   556
Farrah, Martina G.   406
Farran, Kathleen   620
Farrar, C.   463
Farrior, Evan   466
Fassbender, Ann   136
Fauci-Morosky, Patricia A.   99
Faulconer, Diana   173
Faulkner, M. L.   618
Faulkner, Martia   619
Favreau, Carol   275
Fawkes, Richard D., Sr.   109
Fayta, Tina   500
Federnok, James P.   291
Fee, Joseph Patrick   174
Feiner, Lena   496
Feingersh, Adele   271
Feldman, Cathy D.   35
Feldman, Moe   95
Feldstein, Tracy   192
Fellner, Heidi   324
Fenton, Lela Mae   102
Ferguson, Carol   158
Fernandez, Lucio B.   8
Ferrara, Lisa   115
Ferrell, Lynda D.   211
Ferrell, Steven   89
Ferrer, Joyce L.   476
Ferrino, Steven   512
Fesko, Diane   287
Fiadzigbe, Tafa   78
Ficarella, Pearl   77
Field, Julia S.   282
Field, Lewis   497
Fields, Mary Major   208
Fields, Melyssa Claire   622
Fields, Vincent   82
Fierro, Irene Sandy   324
Filbert, Jennifer   564
Filmore, Ann Mills   147
Filteau, Mark   248
Finch, Chris   146
Fincher, Joseph   324
Finik, Patricia   533
Finke, Blythe Foote   427
Finkelman, Sol   19
Finley, Wendy   538
Finn, Christine   18
Finnen, Kevin   522
Finnigan, Laurie   403
Finsthwait, Franklin   570
Fiordelisi, John   557
Fioretti, Rose   529
Fischer, Buck   438
Fisher, Connie E.   186
Fisher, Florence L.   129
Fisher, Jack   124
Fisher, Joseph   11
Fisher, Laurie   529
Fisher, Linda   225
Fisher, Steven T.   235
Fisher, Victoria Lynn   542
Fitch, Howard M.   5
Fitzgerald, Betty M.   143
Fitzgerald, Jean   152

Fitzgerald, Nehemia C. 212
Fitzgerald, Tom 256
Fitzherbert, Jason 445
Fitzpatrick, Thomas 480
Flanagan, Lawrence 26
Fleming, Marjorie Foster 79
Fleming, Patricia 211
Fleming, Rick 360
Fletcher, Dianne 316
Flint, Lori 78
Floccari, Joey 309
Flora, Marsha 94
Florsek, Carina L. 414
Flowers, Joe J. 53
Flowers, John W. 553
Flowers, Stan 363
Flynn, Charly 124
Flynn, Michelle 236
Flynn, Sean H. 189
Foderaro, Eleanor H. 474
Fogel, Tina 373
Foisie, Donald Robert 296
Foley, E. Joseph 627
Foley, Helen M. 177
Foley, Mary Rohan 541
Foley, Ron 485
Follis-Lehr, Sylvia G. 214
Folsom, Nita L. 594
Fong, Ryan Patrick 614
Fontannay, Danielle M. 69
Forbes, Florrie J. 161
Forcum, Jennifer 26
Ford, Amy 43
Ford, D. J. 496
Ford, Helen Y. 574
Ford, Patricia A. 248
Foreman, Terry P. 369
Fortner, Robert 505
Fortune, Fanta 160
Fortune, Robert E. 108
Fossum, Carl 336
Foster, Clarence O. 462
Foster, Jann Marie 186
Foster, Margaret Baker 17
Foster, Susan Rena 196
Fountain, Ruth Johnson 20
Fowler III, John A. 314
Fowler, Oliver E. 80
Fowler, Sharon 96
Fowler, Susanne M. 239
Fox, Karen C. 410
Fox, Peter 403
Fox, Robert 528
Fraedrich, Brenda L. 631
Franchino, Angela 177
Franey, Beverly 131
Frank, Cassie A. 569
Frank, Cherie 320
Frank, Jeremy 266
Frank, Stephanie 388
Frank, Susan 610
Franklin, Jo 277
Franklin, John 5
Franklin, Sharon 529
Frankowiak, Pamela M. 98
Franks, Caroline 546
Fransaw, I'Yanda Harris 61

Frazier, Bonnie Belle 559
Frazzetta, Joseph 281
Frederick, Shirley 73
Fredlund, Mary M. 518
Freeman, Charles H. 324
Freeman, Michael R. 244
French, Carole 466
French, Robert W., Jr. 210
Friedenberg, Nicole 408
Friedrichs, Esther 314
Frisby, Erika E. 294
Fritz, Mary 193
Frizelle, William 616
Froggett, Daniel 441
Frolo, Margaret Mary 540
Fromm, Robert L. 510
Frost, Bernice 288
Fry, H. E. 299
Fry, Steven 19
Frye, Cleo J. 572
Frye, Doris V. 423
Frye, Katina Renee 488
Fryman, Bridget 36
Fuelberg, Nancy E. 208
Fuentes, Gloria S. 308
Fukuyama, Aimee 334
Fulda, Joseph S. 460
Fuller, Don 304
Fuller, Maxcine 92
Fultz, Ruth Barnsdale 338
Funderburk, David 165
Funderburk, Elisabeth 131
Furstenberg, Christine 424
Futch, Lisa 222

G

Gaarn, Eileen S. 134
Gable, Ken 519
Gabriel, Ann 444
Gaddis, Doris Johnson 581
Gadell, Mandi 342
Gaenzle, Pat 77
Gaeth, Ben 45
Gahan, Marica 367
Gaito, Judith 469
Gajarsa, Arthur J. 62
Galarza, Alejandra M. 328
Galarza, Gregoria 312
Galassi, Mark 92
Galer, Eilleen Gardner 157
Galic, Spiro I. 343
Gallagher, Julia 149
Gallagher, Renelda 240
Gallant, Arthur 328
Gallar, John 64
Gallegos, Mandi 262
Galloway Sr., Robert 506
Galvin, Lisa 388
Ganat, Grace M. 552
Ganger, Connie S. 334
Gannon, Edward J. 168
Gantt, Adrienne 583
Ganzer, Suzan T. 202
Garber, Linda 82
Garber, Nathan S. 223
Garcia, DeAnna 121

Garcia, Dede 448
Garcia, Martha 613
Garcia, Melissa A. 525
Garcia, Michael A. 457
Garcia, Mike 81
Garcia, Rico 72
Garcia, Santos M. 390
Garcia, Sid J. 231
Gardner, Matthew A. 400
Gardner, Teresa A. 232
Garneau, Arthur P. 561
Garneau, Coleen 426
Garrahan, Richard 3
Garrison, Maggie 506
Garry, Mary Jane, CSJ 346
Gartner, Marilyn 347
Garton, Joanne 7
Garvan, Jane Nicodemus 316
Garvey, Max W. 226
Garza, Laurie 345
Garza, Maria L. 225
Gascoyne, Russ 80
Gasparro, Anthony A. 584
Gastelum, Angelo Emile 63
Gates, William Allen 613
Gatewood, June S. 141
Gathing, Lynda 541
Gatto, Dorothy C. 474
Gay, Barbara R. 326
Gdula, Kathleen E. 609
Geary, Valerie J. 608
Geckos, Margaret J. 386
Geigel, Bernice 296
Geiger, Nettie R. 603
Geisler, Nancy 486
Gelhaus, Hilda 311
Gendron, Sheila Mandell 19
Gentry, Annie 464
George, Grady D. 549
George, Gretchen 184
George, Ruth T. 606
George, Sandra D. 536
George, Stephan A. 190
Georgeson, Stephen 615
Geppert, Nancie D. 484
German, Dana 472
Germano, Jennifer 446
Gernaga, Wira 409
Gesell, Carolyn W. 445
Gessitz, George 327
Gharzouzi, Carol 120
Ghazarian, DeeAnnah 552
Ghazarian, Richard 402
Ghuntos-Salloum, Reema 494
Giacomo, Wayne 609
Giancola, Christopher C. 433
Giardino, Tara M. 389
Gibb, Dave 42
Gibbons Sr., Robert 620
Gibbs, Paula J. 406
Gibney, Maryellen 517
Gibson, Anne H. 548
Gibson, Charles R. 578
Gibson, George W. 337
Gibson, Joseph Brook 437
Gierczynski, Marlo 511
Gilbert, Russell 72

Giles, Carolyn Markel 41
Gilliam, Frankie 319
Gilliland, Douglas Lee 59
Gillis, Cynthia 66
Gilman, Tamara 373
Gilmer, Doris 580
Gilmer, William D. 256
Gilmour, Terry 355
Ginard, John 579
Gingras, Florence 45
Ginsburg, Barbara L. 458
Gioia, Ilona 333
Girard, Marci 401
Girdham, Glenn F. 127
Gist, Alice Sunday 51
Giterman, Muriel Rail 243
Gladwin, Eleanor P. 26
Glasco, Carol Williams 436
Glass, Robert B. 210
Glasser, Polly 74
Glaude, Grace C. 312
Glenn, Jason Michael 13
Glenn, Mark A. 542
Gliesmann, Tonya 201
Godat, Olivia C. 593
Godfrey, James 279
Godfrey, Marilyn McGowan 398
Gogiel, Leonard 246
Golden, Donna 427
Golding, Helen L. 155
Goldman, Barry 148
Goldman, Gary 412
Goldman, Jackie 134
Goldrick, Victoria 237
Goldthwait, David 268
Golton, Margaret A. 389
Goltz, Joseph 11
Gomez, Christopher J. 437
Gonder, Laurie B. 344
Gonsalves, R. D. D. 338
Gonsky, Marshall 518
Gonzales Jr., Roy 86
Gonzalez, Diego 137
Gonzalez, Melanie 486
Gonzalez, Teresa D. 595
Good, Dana C. 69
Good, Donald M. 47
Good, Lisa 526
Good, Margaret 603
Goodknight, Misti 241
Goodman, Gale A. 550
Goodman, Joshua Ian 48
Goodman Jr., Hugh 176
Goodman, Laura 601
Goodman, Mary R. 203
Goodman, Ruth C. 513
Gordo, Jeff 559
Gordon, Alex 571
Gordon, Elizabeth 146
Gordon, Harry W. 428
Gordon, Robert S. 194
Gordon, Tina R. 480
Gordy, Gene 51
Gorman, Nita 400
Gorman, Todd Alan 457
Gorycki, Karen 536
Gosnell, Robert F. 352

Gott, Elizabeth Marjorie   51
Gotur, Manorama   25
Gould, William M.   241
Gover, Nicole   521
Grabowski, Valerie L.   197
Gracia, Bridget   143
Graesser, Melissa   245
Graffam, Amanda   461
Graham, Bill   35
Graham, Charles F.   30
Graham, Dacia   56
Graham, Dianne M.   134
Graham, Jennifer Karalee   140
Graham, Monette M.   370
Graham, P.M.   600
Graham, Roberta   377
Graham, Thomas W.   97
Grant, Barbara   307
Grant, Cornelia Kay   423
Grant, Genevieve   181
Grant, Wilmot N.   525
Grantham, Cindy   286
Grappel, Robert D.   114
Graves, Hazel McNeal   333
Graves, Rita Palumbo   354
Graves, Shana N.   244
Graves, William W.   114
Gravlee, Deborah Willett   157
Gray, Alex   132
Greaney, Caitlin Elizabeth   473
Greeley, Christopher   318
Green, Bryan   426
Green, Lorella   264
Green, Lucille Ann   374
Green, Marilynn   79
Green, Renee L. F.   215
Green, Ronald   508
Green, S. Duncan   251
Green, Vikki   488
Greene, Allison Laytin   6
Greene, Darius La Mar   65
Greenway, Tammy   206
Greenwood, Robin   479
Greer, Melanie   114
Greer, Samantha A.   258
Gregg, Angel   278
Gregg, Grace W.   131
Gregg, Lois   228
Gregg-Rabbitt, Tammy A.   252
Gregory, Evelyn Scott   184
Greiner, Charles F.   121
Gresham, Gary D.   265
Gresham, Marvin   478
Gretencord, Jason   32
Greyerbiehl, Mary   80
Griffin, Diane   555
Griffin, Helen   129
Griffin, Johnna J.   152
Griffin, Katie   530
Griffin, Norma Jean   80
Griffin, Patti Ann   606
Griffis, Jennifer   143
Griffith, Carolyn B.   411
Griffith, Lisa L.   483
Griffor, Darlene M.   445
Grigg, Elizabeth H.   461
Grimes, Shari L.   228

Gronsbell, Joshua   329
Grooms, Naomi R.   617
Grosek, Jake   120
Gross, Dorothy   470
Gross, Jacqueline   128
Grossman, Veta F.   540
Gruber, Laura   250
Gruenebaum, Ruth   226
Gruley, JoAnne M.   465
Guatelli, Rose M.   349
Guelde, Lisa   195
Guerrero, Aliete O.   21
Guerrero, Lydia   227
Guesman, Kate   266
Guevara, George   268
Gugliara, Salvatore   588
Guilmette, Patricia E.   241
Gulick, Christie Ann   560
Gulley, Marilyn P.   499
Gulshan, Rima S.   504
Gunes, Darlene Anne   171
Gunn, David H.   27
Gunter, Danny W.   302
Gunther, Jenny   474
Gurnari, Mazie   544
Gurrera, V. A.   245
Gustin, Tanya   109
Gustkey, Nikole   401
Guthre, Bill   135
Gutierrez, Gary   455
Gutkowski, Norma G.   535
Gutowski, Anthony   465
Guttormson, Thelma   393
Guyer, James T.   460

H

Haag, Victor J.   251
Hacker, John   580
Hacker, Leona E.   266
Hackl, Edda H.   459
Hackman, Justin   571
Haddon, Debbie   473
Hadley, Debra   581
Haeckel, Jaime Ann   67
Hage, Kristin E.   5
Hage, Tiayu R.   497
Hager, Kristopher M. R.   397
Haggerty, Mark W.   243
Hagmaier, Bill   577
Haigler, Melinda M.   396
Hailey, Janelle   280
Haines, Ronald L.   97
Hairston, Polly   89
Haithco, William H., Sr.   250
Hajjar, Katerina E.   221
Hale, James P.   183
Hale, Mary   395
Hale, Mary E.   594
Hale, Patsy   72
Halewijn, Marcel   522
Haley, Brian   118
Halferty, Erin   441
Halford, Adam   573
Halfpenny, Donna   321
Hall, Beth   564
Hall, Bonnie B.   553

Hall, Cynthia   577
Hall, Delia G.   433
Hall, Emily Davina   36
Hall, Heather   558
Hall I, Randy Vincent   607
Hall, James E.   180
Hall, John Bradley   547
Hall, Lena G.   351
Hall, Linda J.   350
Hall, Mandy M.   250
Hall, Robie Glenn   23
Hall, Stacey   622
Hall, Thrasher   18
Hallett, Jennie   462
Hallman, Stefanie Joy   103
Halme, Elna S.   268
Halpern, Anthony Michael   574
Halvorson, Jean   270
Hambrick, Rodney D.   516
Hamby, Thomas N.   255
Hamel, Joseph L.   171
Hames, Kathy   627
Hamilton, Evelyn   170
Hammell, Grandin K.   278
Hammer, Joanne   288
Hammond, Blanche Brink   548
Hampson, Patricia A.   492
Hamric, Ramona E.   378
Handeland, June   467
Handelman, Stacy   256
Haney, Daniel L.   165
Haney, Patricia E.   373
Hankin, Max A.   368
Hankins, Thora Snow   379
Hanko, Pamela S.   408
Hanks, Bonnie   314
Hanne, Matt   542
Hanneman, Loretta M.   480
Hannig, Elaine S.   454
Hansbury, Barbara   265
Hansen, Jayme   284
Hanson, Ruby C.   532
Hanson, Stacy   399
Harary, Meri M.   488
Harbour, Gary T.   581
Harden, Jennifer   143
Harder, Danny   159
Harding, D. Jean   519
Hardman Jr., Charles J.   270
Hardwick-White, Nicki   594
Hardy, Margaret   379
Hare, Dawn   420
Hare, Marylou V.   239
Hargett, Andrea Buller   43
Hargrove, Rebecca   545
Harkins, Rachel   197
Harless, Sara L.   236
Harlin, Kate   82
Harman, Eric   282
Harmon, Anthony   554
Haro, Alana   415
Harold, David L.   28
Harper, Michael J.   217
Harpster, Angela   51
Harrell, Josie B.   455
Harris, Cheryl   471
Harris, Daniel Bradley   62

Harris, Frances M.   184
Harris, Helene   547
Harris, Janie R.   62
Harris, Jennifer   321
Harris, Keith W.   483
Harris, Kylus   389
Harris, Lorraine R.   223
Harris, Lynton V.   607
Harris, Marilyn Anita   256
Harris, Natalie   192
Harris, Nicole L.   391
Harris, Otto   515
Harris, Sheila M.   381
Harrison, Barbara   441
Harrison, Echo   38
Harrison, Kathryn L.   403
Hart, Eleanor F.   290
Hart, Kristen   232
Hartman, Harlan   332
Hartness, Dianne   151
Harvath, Bonnie   433
Harvey, Joyce   330
Haskins, Robert   538
Hassan, Mani   241
Hastings, Carolyn   548
Hatch, Paul D.   533
Hatchett, Deborah D.   549
Hatz, Melanie J.   373
Haughton, Margie Dudley   196
Haun, Lisa P.   397
Hausan, Kendra   349
Haven, Charlotte A.   286
Hawkins, Herman E.   553
Hawkins, Steven W.   347
Hawn, Miriam   393
Haydon, Nancy   100
Hayes, Donna R.   291
Hayes, Judith   6
Hayes, Judy   327
Hayes, Lauren   542
Hayes, Ruby   407
Hayford, H. Joseph   513
Haynes, Alice   325
Haynes, Lynne   380
Hazard, Michael   496
Hazelett, Evelyn   477
Head, Bob   473
Heard, Lydia   397
Heath, Cindy   53
Heath, Rainy   263
Hebert, Nicole   617
Hebets, Caryn L.   179
Heckathorne, John P.   145
Hedrick, Sheri   393
Heerssen Sr., Wesley William   389
Heffernan, James   281
Heffner, Ray G.   245
Hegge, Allison   437
Hegyes, Lisa   595
Heifner, Janet   60
Heiss-Moses, June R.   451
Helberg, Edna T.   178
Heller, Tovah   241
Helling, Nick   206
Helmbrecht, Heidi   327
Helmerick, Greg   136
Helms-Merced, Sandi   386

Hemple, Florence L.   173
Henderson, Cynthia   468
Henderson, Evelyn   181
Henderson, Jean   560
Henderson, Marina   359
Henderson, Sherry L.   393
Hendren, Merlyn Churchill   384
Hendrickson, Wendy   194
Henkel, David L.   327
Henry, Audrey Baie   450
Henry II, Ron   535
Henry, James   325
Henson, Patricia Susan   83
Herd, Datina M.   583
Heric, Douglas E.   31
Herlihy, Mary   630
Herlihy-Chevalier, Barbara   52
Herman, Nanette   387
Hernandez, Andy R.   323
Hernandez, Janette E.   456
Hernesman, Dan   553
Herold, Courtney R.   53
Herring, William A.   499
Herrmann, A. Bernard   382
Herron, Kim   287
Hersey, Linda D.   100
Hershey, Karmen   393
Hershey, Mattie   516
Herskowitz, Mara   400
Hervey, Brekka J.   118
Herzberg, Pauline   526
Hestand, Brandy   178, 630
Hickerson, Stacy L.   390
Hicks, Angela L. (Clawson)   68
Hicks, Grace Roberson   9
Hicks, Ranita   107
Hicock, Claire Waeber   13
Higgins, Kenny   614
Higham, Marilyn   527
Highsmith, Iris   298
Hiilsmeier, Denise   464
Hilal, Basem E.   439
Hilderhoff, Holly   132
Hill, Beulah   296
Hill, Gladys L.   415
Hill, Josephine C.   318
Hill, Lisbeth   108
Hill, Phyllis   629
Hill, Savannah   592
Hill, Trav   601
Hill, Valerie   102
Hiller-Siemiatkoski, Wendi   253
Hillerich, A. E.   105
Hillyer, Jayne   547
Himelrigh, Melissa   618
Hines, Melissa   347
Hirsch, Frances   570
Hirschfeld, Fritz   160
Hirst III, John J.   417
Hisamitsu, Takabe   401
Hitsman, Marion   257
Hitt, Owen   245
Ho, Can N.   29
Hoare, Patricia A.   515
Hobart, Lori   408
Hockensmith, Nancy   342
Hockett, C. C.   107

Hoddinott, Thomas F.   222
Hodge, Mamie   533
Hodge, Sue   490
Hodges, Montana   246
Hodson, Pat   236
Hodzic, Migdat I.   344
Hoeltje, Peter J.   386
Hoer, P. K.   241
Hoff, Kimberly   102
Hoffman, Deborah Marie   438
Hoffman, Scot Thomas   410
Hofmans, Sean   237
Hogan, Jim   150
Hogan, Laura Renee   256
Hogle, Kristine   266
Hogue, Cindy   477
Holcomb, Ed   467
Holden, Bill   54
Holey, Misty   221
Holguin, Kathy   605
Hollabaugh, Shelly   257
Hollander, Edith Spark   578
Hollar, Laura M.   356
Hollinger, Gerda M.   451
Holloway, Amy   556
Holmes, Nicole   105
Holtman, Michelle   495
Holtschlag, Karen   406
Holzman, Adam   434
Holzworth, Bryan   477
Homer, Melissa   385
Honeycutt, William   403
Honto, Trisha Lee   369
Hoobler, Elizabeth U.   166
Hood, Bridgette N.   287
Hook, Amy   331
Hook, Kathy E.   497
Hoopengardner, Lisa   612
Hooper, Sara Ella   222
Hootman, Jennifer   296
Hooven, Gary   572
Hopfinger, Kathy   544
Hopkins, Omar Edward   208
Hopper, Christine K.   267
Hopper, Lisa   532
Hopper, Lou Ann   486
Horack, Leslie F.   353
Horalek, Edward   127
Horn, Erna   554
Hornett, Thompson Peter   238
Hornstein, Jennie   547
Horton, Angela C.   325
Horton, Roxanne   379
Horwitz, William   599
Hosp, William B., Jr.   598
Hougham, Duane F.   306
Hounshell, Melanie Lynn   259
Houston, Laura C.   506
Howard, Gregory T.   145
Howard, Linda S.   352
Howard, Rick   382
Howard, Wanda   394
Howe, Jane   320
Howell, Gerard A.   9
Howell, Mary L.   402
Howerton, Virginia G. B.   603
Hroch, Gladys W.   177

Hubbard, Everett R.   60
Huber, Alison   31
Huber, Andrea Jackson   556
Huddleston, Elsie W.   546
Huddleston, Kenneth E. Wolke   596
Huddleston, Rhonda   242
Huddleston, Zora   514
Hudler, Tonya M.   356
Huff, Valerie J.   261
Hughes, Amanda   582
Hughes, Beverly   31
Hughes, Elisabethe   321
Hughes, Gene   271
Hughes, James E., Sr.   139
Hughes, Keith   102
Hughes, Patricia E.   385
Hughes-Burns, Roseann   528
Hughs, Brenda L.   158
Hui, Jackson C.   295
Hull, Willie Jean   257
Human, Wilma   530
Hummel, Heather   61
Hummer, Nancy J.   624
Humphrey, Shannon Marie   98
Humphrey-Leonard, Elizabeth J.   139
Humphreys, Elizabeth (Benda)   11
Humphreys, Janet Hartley   337
Hunsicker, Julie   131
Hunt, Allison   333
Hunt, Jennifer Marie   436
Hunt Jr., Daniel Alexis   466
Hunt, Patricia   534
Hunter   36
Hunter, Barbara Eugenia   45
Hunter, Melvin P.   351
Hunter, Penelope Jacobsen   401
Hunter, Ruth   248
Huntley, Mary J.   485
Huntoon, Becky   557
Huot, Janie E.   184
Huotari, Patricia   512
Huotari, Timothy J.   223
Hurd, Terri Lynn   350
Hurkmans, Kristina   494
Hurley, Douglas James   6
Hurst, Elizabeth   132
Hurt, Bonnie L.   452
Huseth, Dianne Tharaldson   337
Hussain, Kaniz   525
Husted, Brian L.   547
Hutka, Ed   550
Hutt, Alice M.   117
Hutto, Linda D.   489
Hyatt, Anne-Marie   135
Hymer, Heather   135
Hynes, Jean   129

I

Ibex, Jeanette   145
Ibrahim, Mona   542
Ichikawa, Lona Terumi   221
Ihlenfeldt, Nancy   253
Ineich, Heather   446
Ingersol, Stephen   232
Ingino, Joan D.   459
Ingle, Karen   225

Ingram, Joyce   158
Ingrasciotta, Philip   93
Innis, Anna   422
Inostroza, Carolina   311
Ireland, Frank L.   300
Irvin, Marianne Fanelli   192
Irving, Sarah   237
Isaman, Barbara Soucy   272
Isasi, Danielle   328
Isham, Jean   182

J

Jaarsma, Julie   152
Jabbarnezhad, Jamshid   3
Jackson, Barry   411
Jackson, Cassandra   300
Jackson, Dawn   319
Jackson, Hannah M.   308
Jackson, Holly   48
Jackson, Laura A.   254
Jackson, Lorilu   596
Jackson, Margaret E.   539
Jackson, Preston L., Sr.   378
Jackson, Richard Dana   404
Jackson, Sandra   533
Jackson, Verna   84
Jaco, Anna   141
Jacobini, Marshall   359
Jacobs, Charlotte   566
Jacobs, Doris   144
Jacobs, Eric P.   416
Jacobsen, Mildred   255
Jacobson, Edna F.   40
Jagger, Tarrilynn   72
Jaime, Gloria   579
Jakubowski, Rae Ann Joy   254
James, Blaise   335
James, Jacinth   54
James, Lindsey   367
James, Lori M.   479
James, Marian M.   546
James, Richard L.   611
James, Robert A.   597
James, Sarah   394
James, Stella   200
Jan, Ann Marie   44
Jannick, Peggy   258
Jansen, Candace   579
Janssen, Lois B. Asp   592
Jaquez, Eunice Anne   316
Jaquinto, Francine   329
Jaramillo, Gerri   157
Jardin, Bronwyn Anne Best   261
Jarecke, Jeanne   150
Jarman, Cheryl   133
Jarsulic, Helen   30
Jaspers, Koralee Helen   87
Jayapathy, Raman   259
Jayasuriya, Luke   246
Jayson, Tricia   396
Jean, Betty   333
Jeffers, Shirley   104
Jefferson, J. Harris   348
Jefferson, Vanessa Sharie   379
Jeffery, Mary H.   241
Jeffrey, Perry J.   496

Jenkins, Barbara 461
Jenkins, Brian 334
Jenkins, Charleen 431
Jenkins III, Jackson M. 54
Jenkins, Jasmine 30
Jenkins, Rose Marie 383
Jenkins, Valeria W. 73
Jennings, Nedra La Shawn 259
Jensen, Marjorie H. 346
Jensen, Patricia 199
Jerset, April 459
Jessup, Geraldine 162
Jessup, Jeremy 324
Jester, Sue 74
Jewel, Sarah E. 362
Jewell, Barbara Lee 5
Jinks, Jamie Lynn 579
Jobe, C. Merla 361
Johansen, Julianna 630
Johns, Missy 85
Johns, Renota 541
Johns-Gibson, Janette C. 67
Johnson, Aaron P. 297
Johnson III, Augustus W. 324
Johnson, Christina Lynn 464
Johnson, Christine 117
Johnson, Collette 118
Johnson, Dolores 22
Johnson, Elizabeth M. 469
Johnson, Eula H. 561
Johnson, Frances Brown 564
Johnson, Freddy 169
Johnson, Hattie Yvonne 475
Johnson, John 473
Johnson, Judith L. 322
Johnson, Larry D. 114
Johnson, Lawrence F. A. 386
Johnson, Leqia G. 221
Johnson, Mable Jean 525
Johnson, Micheal T. 115
Johnson, Ron L. 22
Johnson, Rosalie C. 97
Johnson, Sandra R. 258
Johnson, Shada 257
Johnson, Shannon M. 400
Johnson, Shirley 73
Johnson, Tamika 263
Johnson, Thomas A. 214
Johnson, Vicki 385
Johnson, Victoria 389
Johnson, Wava T. 251
Johnson, William D. 194
Johnston, Earl W. 153
Johnston, M. C. M. 524
Johnston, Mable Glover 392
Johnston, Patricia Dunkel 202
Johnston, Richard 238
Jonas, Maria L. 259
Jones, Annie 264
Jones, Brenda E. 477
Jones, Brenda Mae 169
Jones, Charles 118
Jones, Charles R. 475
Jones, Courtney 43
Jones, Diane Lynn Fredenburg 155
Jones, Fredrick 67
Jones, Jason 563

Jones, Jenni 65
Jones, Jessica 174
Jones, Julie 328
Jones, Kenni L. 615
Jones, Lambert T. 585
Jones, Martha 521
Jones, Paula 491
Jones, Tina Nicole 73
Jones, Trudy J. 502
Jones, Wilbur P. 404
Jordan, Jaime 37
Jowett, Jeremy 147
Jozsa, Veronika 360
Juarez, Cynthia P. 121
Jubelirer, Amy 57
Judice, David 9
Juhola, Macy 542
Jullien, Belynda 477
Juracek, Rita 610
Jurkowski, Regan 369

K

Kacenga, Scott 617
Kady, Joyce 68
Kainu, Audrey C. 48
Kalinoski, Stefanie 496
Kaliser, Sylvia 206
Kalitz, Regina 237
Kallasy, Edna 443
Kallison, Sarah Rush 10
Kane, Grace S. 124
Kantor, Anatole 151
Kanz, Cynthia D. 34
Kapano, Robinson John 543
Kapinos, Minna L. 371
Kaplan, Morton H. 236
Kara, Kelsey Kaelyn 490
Karcher, D. L. 491
Karpovage, Linda 407
Karpovich, Todd 342
Karr, Adam R. 312
Kashary, Rebecca A. 224
Kasianiuk, Rosemarie 625
Kasper, Andrea 187
Kasprzak, Andrew B. 293
Kassouf, Philippe 82
Kasubick, Christina 54
Kaszubski, Carol 441
Katalinic, Keri 78
Katemopoulos, Mildred J. 396
Katsampes, George 47
Katz, Stacy Beth 508
Kaulili, Debby 132
Kawtoski, Nancy A. 533
Kaye, Daniel Sean 140
Kazakaitis, Mike 535
Keating, Jacquilyn M. L. 137
Keck, Sylvia 188
Keeler, Joe 130
Keeran, Vicky 255
Keeton, John A. 562
Keezer, Dorothy 328
Keist, Barrington W. 436
Keith, Caroline E. 90
Kellam Sr., Thomas B. 408
Kelley, Stephen D. 355

Kellogg, Charles 71
Kellogg, Paula 407
Kelly, John 274
Kelly, Joseph B. 274
Kemen, Mary 408
Kemp, Judy Sallee 476
Kemp, Marjorie Josephine 388
Kemper, Jeffrey 59
Kendall, Jennifer 121
Kendall, Martha 390
Kenderes, Laura Lee 89
Kendrick, Cheryl 134
Kenna, Hendryk Zenon 187
Kennard, Ddoris 325
Kennedy, Kelly 74
Kent, Lucy 245
Kenyon, Mickie 588
Kern, Christena B. 564
Kerr, Rena Glenn 404
Kerrick, James 326
Kersmarki, Steve 363
Kerzman, Frances 468
Kerzman, Jami 130
Keskar, Soniya 76
Kesler, Andrea 459
Kester, Rachel E. 405
Ketcham, Grace M. 463
Ketcham, Pamela 349
Ketterer, Nathalie 242
Kettering, Brian 119
Keys, Yvonne 368
Khan, Farida 336
Khan, Raheel 599
Khan, Sikandar H. 610
Khwaja, Khatija 407
Kidder, Laurie 226
Kienzle, De 450
Kihle, Thomas 358
Kihn, Ryan 260
Kilcooley, Helen 55
Kilduff, Barry 122
Kilham, Stephanie 357
Killen, Karen M. 249
Kim, Austin Dale 305
Kim, Bo-Joong 430
Kim, Johnny 439
Kimzey, Carol 284
Kinchner, Mary E. 338
Kindilien, Melissa 399
King, Anthony J., Sr. 310
King, Cheryl L. 269
King, Constance H. 423
King, Curtis 422
King, Floyd W. 122
King, Glenngo Allen 129
King, Harry R. F. 422
King, Janet 437
King, Jewell 548
King, Monty 205
King, Nicole 83
King, Patricia 544
King, Terri 354
King, Vanessa 595
Kirby, Shannon 240
Kirk, Carl W. 563
Kirke, Olive B. 352
Kirkpatrick, Katherine 229

Kite, Jerldine 435
Kittinger, Walter L. 106
Klampert, Dorothy 576
Klasinski, Jamie 303
Klassen, Karen Amber 213
Klatt, Lloyd E. 373
Kleckley, Edgar H. 568
Kleider, Erin A. 301
Klein, Maxine Ann 540
Kleynenberg, Sara 91
Kligerman, Vicki 586
Klotzsche, Dorothy 561
Knapp, Katherine 521
Knaus, Laura 240
Knight, Ginger Dean 564
Knight, Robin 479
Knighton, Jennifer 320
Knippen, Katherine M. 534
Knolls, Elsie 464
Knowdell, Virginia 251
Knueppel, David 463
Kocanda, Stanley E. 511
Koch, Crystal 275
Koch, Leta 114
Koehler, Cody 178
Koenty, Shirley M. 354
Koeppel, David 316
Kolom, Aaron 437
Komperda, Dorothy 462
Konkol, Jonathan 454
Konzel, Theresa 242
Kornegay, William B. 621
Kosch, Donna L. 34
Kostka, Laura 254
Kotyk, Nicole Marie 409
Koury, Mandi M. 201
Kovacs, Frances 135
Kovelman, Gloria 433
Kowalczyk, Christine 574
Kozora, Crystal 47
Kramer, Adeline M. 294
Kramer, Jacob 435
Kramer, Kevin W. 368
Kratz, Annica 120
Kratz, Christine 312
Krause, David A. 332
Krause, Ingrid 136
Krause, Joan S. 66
Krause, Shara 236
Kregar, Carolyn 274
Kreinik, Kathi 515
Krieg, Robert Louis 356
Krieger, Joan W. 24
Krist, William 237
Kritzman, C. 243
Krogstad, Kris 490
Kromas, Kim 364
Kropp, Skipp 364
Kruck, Carol M. 142
Krueger, Ione 313
Krupinski, Katie 410
Kubiak, Molly Margaret 338
Kuehl, Joan 569
Kuerbitz, Karen 591
Kulhanek, Mary Jo 407
Kulkey, Michelle 369
Kulp, Steven D. 403

Kumar, Praveen 622
Kumar, Sharath 191
Kunes, Christina 280
Kupiszewski, Tony E. 90
Kupper, Jennifer 465
Kuznicki, Janice 469
Kvingedal, Harriet Trehus 64
Kyle, Lidi Mary 252
Kylloe, Kurt A. 625

L

La Chapelle, L. V. 406
La Femina, Louise 627
Labas, Christian V. 133
LaBato, Anthony 149
LaBelle, Irene F. 119
Lachlan, S. K. 4
Lackey, Alaina 40
LaCross, Janet M. 285
Ladet, Monica Raymo 112
Ladwig, Emily Klare 287
LaFountain, Janet R. 476
Lail, Chic 469
Laird, Christie 161
Laison, Johnnye Belinda 135
Lam, Quan 209
Lamar, Maria E. 341
Lamb, Cindy 461
Lamb, Rachel 517
Lambert, Allan H. 297
Lambert, Ginger K. 576
Lambeth, Joyce Ann 567
Lamm, Erin 63
Lammert, Emily 312
Lamplen, Annie 292
Lance, Mary Jo (Wood) 79
Land, Morgan 396
Landis, Gordon R. 461
Landon, John R. 296
Landon, Maryann 514
Landrum, Hugh 124
Landwehr, Russell 514
Lane, Sharon K. 215
Lane, W. S. 7
Lang, Florence 161
Lange, Rick 105
Langsdorf, Doris 137
Langton, Carrie L. 62
Langworthy, Jerome 302
Lanham, James 449
Lannon, Karen 509
Lansberry, Peggy 527
Lansenderfer, Crystal 125
Lantz, Rose A. 211
LaPrell, Lillian 391
Laprocino, Gary 427
Lapworth, Tiffany 384
Larkin, Nicolette 478
LaRocque, Joseph 319
Larsen, Mary 487
Larsen, Tiffany Lei 93
Larsen, Tony 516
Larson, Irene Mary 326
Larson, Matt 514
Lash, Billie 56
Lashbrook, Lee 75

Laska, Vera 585
Laskowitz, Pearl Liebman 103
Lasky, Michelle 389
Lastowicka, Mark 396
Laszlo, Cleo 275
Latham, Barbara 546
Laughead, Kurtis 240
Launius, Teri 74
Laurence, Waustella 89
Laurent, Georgette 470
LaValley, Erin M. 447
Lavin, Ed 571
Lawler, Kevin 410
Lawlor, Larry 522
Lawrence, Joyce 325
Lawson, Clifford (Jack) 434
Lawson, Penny 591
Laycock, Neta Walker 207
Lazar, Sheila M. 536
Lazarus, Carolyn 263
Lea, Stephanie M. 247
Leach, Cathy 337
Leaders, Patty 592
Leasure, E. V. 203
Lebel, Kevin T. 207
Lecocq, Nancy 199
Ledford, Kris 221
Lee, Alitroi Brandon 129
Lee, Chia 36
Lee, Courtney 419
Lee, DJ 256
Lee, Janet 435
Lee, Jennifer L. 322
Lee, Jung 467
Lee, Lorie-Ann 365
Lee, Paul M. 353
Lee, Robert E. 482
Leeks, Tracye 343
Leet, Dana 427
Leet, Jamie 180
Legerwood, Barbara 311
Lehmus, John 466
Leiser, Janet Diane 276
Lejeune, Laura T. 256
LeMarie, Pauline 253
Lembeck, Jennifer M. 335
Lemoyne, Crystal 129
Lempek, Jean D. 472
Lenart, Tessa 370
Lener, Dr. Wayne 85
Lenius, Tom 255
Lenkey, Rob 392
Lentz, Kathleen M. 244
Lermon, Summer 496
Leslie, Mitchell 228
Lester, Matthew 487
Letson, Frances 44
Lev, Abe 164
Leva, Bette 464
Levack, Mary I. 587
Levering, Richard 8
Levine, Joseph 263
Levitt, Marian Sobel 590
Lewallen, Barbara 314
Lewin, Gregory A. 430
Lewis, Kristen L. 401
Lewis, Marjorie W. 614

Lewis, Wayne M. 532
Lewis-Chase, Eve 16
Liao, Angela 165
Liberona, Helena 306
Ligotti, Joann 308
Liljeqvist, Alysha 27
Lillie, William 239
Limarenko, Maria 385
Lin, Jo-Ann Sanchez 458
Lin, Thomas T. 482
Lincoln, J. D. 237
Lind, Joseph A. 155
Lind, Susan Weddell 110
Linde, Gregory C. 553
Linden-Marshall, Rachel L. 401
Linder, Lezlie M. 110
Lindo, Jaye 314
Lindow, Maren 391
Lindsay, Andrew 420
Lindsay, Dennis P. 451
Lindsay, Patricia L. 585
Lineberry, Ellen 584
Link, Andrea 299
Linton, Lisa Salvata 398
Lippman, Robert Thomas 203
Lipps, Donald G., III 565
Lisa, Jennifer 317
Lishinsky, Joyce E. 134
Lisi, Richard S. 503
List, John 279
Little, Gloria M. 431
Little, Rufus C. 532
Littlejohn, Michael 613
Litton, Walter R., Jr. 519
Litvak, Kathy 228
Litz, James Charles 458
Liu, Linda 347
Liverani, Christine 304
Lizzio, Madelyn D. 86
Lloyd, Doris 320
Lloyd, Joyce J. 277
Lloyd, Peter M. 190
Lloyd, Sylvia 342
Loar, Kimberly 395
Lobo, Iva Anjos 311
Loch, Cathy Elizabeth 465
Lockhart, Angelee 274
Lockwood, Amanda 578
Loewinger, Rose 255
Logan, Bill, Jr. 289
Logiacco, Nicholas 240
LoGioco, Lori Ann 219
Logsdon, Toby 220
Lohr, Mary R. 348
Lohr, Sylvia A. 594
Loiselle, Mark R. 543
Lollman, Kristina Rose 381
Lombardi, Helen M. 43
Lombardo, Andrew M. 293
Lonas, Nina F. 392
London, Lawrence 253
London, Michael 399
Long, Andrea 430
Long, Andrew James 326
Long, Frances E. 326
Long, Lawrence 262
Long, Rosalie T. 538

Long, Stuart 248
Long-Heaton, Tracy 355
Loose, Ian 318
Lopez, Alice R. 552
Lopez, Virginia 502
Lordi, Patricia 254
Lorenz, Larry 393
Lorenz, Ruth E. 4
Lorenzo, Len 95
Lorenzo, Nicholas 520
Lorino, Erin Moroney 66
Lothridge, Angela 305
Lott, Bessie Callender 546
Lott, Ethel May 469
Lottermoser, Kelly 239
Lough, Greg 317
Loughrey, Tammi 191
Louissaint, Calvin 122
Lovas Sr., Eugene E. 144
Lovato, Idulia F. 42
Loveland, Gladys 35
Lovett, Kim 260
Lowe, Kathleen 254
Loyd, Kevin 193
Loyd, Robert C. 603
Loyko, Margaret R. 394
Lubbers, Ryan 598
Lucas, Catherine 412
Lucas, Machelle L. 403
Lucas, Marjorie L. 218
Lucas, Steve M. 350
Lucus, Marta 499
Luftglass, Scott Brian 198
Luick, Elizabeth 322
Lukather, Elizabeth Burt 8
Lulgjuraj, Victoria 211
Lund, Don 120
Lundsberg, Janet L. 468
Luppino, Gina 579
Lussier, Kimberly 248
Luther, Garland L. 162
Luttmann, Pat 509
Luttner, Amy 130
Lutz, Jay 58
Lutzi, Kathy 190
Luzier, Lisa 411
Lykins, Leah A. 193
Lyle, Minnie Jane 197
Lyman, Peter M. 512
Lyn, Tabor 234
Lynch, James 315
Lynch, Jennifer C. 413
Lynch, Lia E. 598
Lynch, Patricia Henigin 8
Lynch, Thomas L. 387
Lynn, Jennifer 578
Lynton, Alice 464
Lyttle, John S. 143

M

M. M. J. 344
Macauley, Gloria D. 128
MacCulloch, Holly 120
MacGlaflin, Judy 472
Macieiski, Ellen 448

Mack, Kari R. 262
Mackenzie, Louise L. 356
Mackey, Sarah 376
MacKilligan, Courtney A. 316
Macklin, Rodney F. 501
MacWilliams, Mary 77
Maddix, Phyllis 631
Maddrey Jr., Roosevelt 210
Madeira, Nancy 353
Madejczyk, JoAnna L. 131
Mader, Sandra J. 535
Madison, Yvonne 340
Madsen, Willard J. 595
Maes, Felicia 50
MAG 492
Magee, Erin 325
Magee, Pamela Alice 243
Maglalang, Carlos Rodrigo 127
Maglieri, Scarlett 605
Magnani, Theresa 604
Magnusen Jr., Harold M. 460
Maguire, Evelyn Z. 290
Mahakian, Linda 99
Mahar, Kelley A. 113
Mahmoud, Nesreen 498
Maida, Clarissa 65
Maidment, Fred 57
Majba, Christen 286
Major, Alan 313
Maksin, Melissa T. 339
Malafronte, Deborah Murray 60
Malcomson, Betty J. 297
Maldonado, Gertrude 414
Maldonado, Raul 190
Malinowski, Mike 400
Mallon, Walter 220
Malone, Juynne 300
Maloney, Robert J. 404
Maltz, Aaron 23
Manby, Burr 426
Mancini, Edward 6
Maness, Charles V. 142
Manial, Brad 186
Manis, Beulah 314
Mann, Anthony 269
Mann, John 465
Mann, Peggy Jo 369
Manning, Monique J. 620
Manning, Patricia 227
Manning, Stephen D. 237
Mannion-Sass, Kathleen 343
Mansfield, Mary T. 524
Manszewski, Sharon 100
Manuel, Jennifer O. 295
Maples, Ronald E. 481
Marabella, Jennifer 629
Marable, Paul D., Jr. 23
Marasinghe, Gayathri E. 420
Marchant, Anyda 447
Marcoux, Shirley 535
Marcum, Betty 334
Marcum, Calvin C. 51
Marello, Jhane E. 414
Margo, Gay 138
Marhevko, Nicole 246
Marie, Diane 476
Marin, Catherine 572

Marinaccio, Jaime 163
Markert, Patricia 96
Markiewicz, Norbert F. 193
Markley, Steve 342
Markman, Pamela 366
Markow, Alli 411
Marlowe, Cynthia Koncki 233
Marquez, Helen 63
marsh II, gordon e. 334
Marshall, Bruce 126
Marshall, C. M. 239
Marshall, Marna J. 398
Marshall, Mary Carolyn 390
Marshall, Rocky 217
Marson, Leatrice L. 590
Martin, Cynthia 327
Martin, Dennis 119
Martin, Elaine 459
Martin, Janine 7
Martin, Jeremy 329
Martin, Michael 101
Martin, Mike 624
Martin, Morgan 477
Martin, Patricia 623
Martin, Rayfus 400
Martindale, Cam 310
Martinek, Adeline 24
Martinez, Genaro 458
Martinson, Cindy Jackels 425
Martocci, Michael 507
Martorell, Edna L. 475
Masaniello, Christen 332
Mascaro, Joseph R. 432
Masecar, Jeanne 429
Mason, Betty D. 272
Mason, Phyllis L. 374
Massalongo, Mary 612
Massaro, Angelo S. 554
Massei, Dennis A. 418
Massey, Eleanoir 335
Masters, Bette 144
Mathews, Ivy 322
Mathews, Vivian Archie 235
Mathieson, Heather M. 449
Matt, Linda M. 503
Matthews, Debbie 577
Matthews, Emmy 137
Matthews, Tara 384
Mattix, Velva 84
Matula, Rachel 536
Matunas, Joseph 469
Matuska, Donna 317
Matute, Adela 449
Mauldin, Jan 465
Maxwell, Florence E. 135
Maxwell, Katherine 586
Maxwell, Linda 379
May, Christy A. 142
May, Maria Michelle 239
Maye, Michael P. 109
Mayer, Jerome David 23
Mayes, Kathleen 78
Mayfield, Meri 621
Maynard, Charles R. 558
Mayo, Aneise Brown 271
Mazujian, Drew 125
Mazza, Colleen Renee 170

Mazzarella, B. M. 380
Mazzoni, Mary 240
McAdam, Robert E. 93
McAfee, Jill Randolph 423
McArdle, Kelly 371
McBride, Margaret Mary 621
McBride, Velma 402
McBryde, Judy 137
McCabe, DeLila Mize 327
McCabe, James 126
McCain, Emily B. 270
McCall, Brennan 121
McCallar, C. James, Jr. 83
McCandless, Michelle 408
McCarthy, Kelly C. 111
McCarthy, William L. 506
McCaskey, Tammy 540
McClain, Linda 606
McClellan, Evelyn 576
McClellan, Karen R. 250
McClendon, Glorious 453
McCloskey, Kerri 253
McCloud, Felicia 467
McCloud, Gabrielle 422
McCloud, Vivian 609
McCluney, Tamia 222
McClure, Douglas Stormont 47
McComb, Darhla 176
McCorkell, Robert A. 405
McCoy, Anthony J. 466
McCoy, Rex V. 409
McCray, Billy 126
McCrea, Kevin M. 611
McCrudden, Tara 542
McCulloh, Wanda 90
McCutcheon, Amanda Jo 170
McDaniel, Joanne 473
McDermott, Jason 167
McDonald, Chanel 155
McDonald, Eileen 132
McDonald, Gloria A. 273
McDonald, Lindsay 533, 545
McDonald, Rita C. 207
McDonald, Robert 598
McDonnell, Kay 627
McDougall, Bernadette 286
McDowell, Sandra Lea 371
McElroy, Alline 572
McElroy, Cordelia 312
McElroy, Sarah Lynn 346
McEndree, Harry E. 465
McFalls, David G. 418
McFarland, Marguerite 537
McFarlane, Darlene 323
McGee, Lou 479
McGoun, Liz 256
McGregor, Sarah Lynn 251
McGrew, Rebecca 612
McGuigan, Christine 297
McGuire, Christy 155
McGuire, Darlene A. 123
McGurk, Carrie Ann 294
McInerney, Emer Ann 467
McIntyre, Fred 577
Mckay, Judith Ann 272
McLamb, Gordon 315
McLaughlin Jr., Michael 242

McLeod, Lillian 523
McLevis, Jacqueline 554
McMillan, Mathes J. 397
McNair, Bobby 332
McNeely, Esther N. 267
McNeill, Craig 138
McNichols, Thelma 90
McSheehy, Libby 230
McSparen, Art 53
McSwain, Cleve Esther 416
McSweeney, Joe 117
Meacham, Caitlyn 326
Meadows, Thelma L. 392
Meares, Julie L. 462
Mecham, Judy 273
Medler, Clifford M. 121
Meek, Marsha Ann Hatfield 96
Meeks, Bill 154
Mehta, Rupa 501
Mein, Eric A. 418
Meis, Rose M. 392
Mejia, Ricardo M. 248
Melaro, Marie A. 213
Mellard, R. George 605
Melton, Jessica 283
Meltzer, Ruth K. 395
Mendelsohn, Therian H. Williams590
Mendoza, Yolanda 93
Mengersen Sr., Joseph 304
Menser, Kenneth Ray 218
Mentasti, Toni 189
Mentzer, Joyce 302
Mercado, Jaime 152
Mercer, Bryan 131
Mercer, Penny 599
Mercer, R. 395
Merfeld, Sandra 544
Merriman, Wendy S. 350
Merritt, Floyd E. 168
Messick, Jennifer 330
Metcalf, Michelle 531
Meurer, Kim 225
Meyenburg, Timothy J. 198
Meyer, Angel 171
Meyer, Heather 565
Meyer, Jennifer L. 133
Meyers, Kristy Ann 478
Meyers, Neva B. 483
Meyerson, Karen A. 100
Mezo, Kathryn J. 257
Miceli, Constance 457
Michaels, Darnell Vaughn 61
Michalak, Katherine 535
Michalek, Amy 445
Michalski, James 131
Michalski, Julie 415
Michaud, Monique C. 390
Michel, Melody 248
Michelli, Dorothy 122
Michie, Delsa 125
Mickle, Thomas H. 362
Middleton, Margaret L. 106
Mielcarek, Linda 391
Miele, Michael A. 217
Mihalek, Kathy 236
Mikkelsen, Jennie 571
Miles, Dorothy 550

Miles, Samuel 597
Millar, Roberto 265
Miller, Autumn 288
Miller, Beth L. 337
Miller, Colleen 120
Miller, D. G. 366
Miller, Dolores A. 476
Miller, Elizabeth 568
Miller, Francis W. 421
Miller, Kerry L. 106
Miller, Kristen 502
Miller, Lindsay 526
Miller, Martin 591
Miller, Mindy Sue 538
Miller, Patrice 602
Miller, Polly 503
Miller, Sarah 246
Miller, Sharon 221
Miller, Todd 389
Miller, Victoria 243
Milliner, Louise Endiaka 219
Millner, Teila L. 256
Mills, Fiore 10
Mills, Gwen 569
Mills, Kelly Marie 204
Mills, Pauline 366
Mimaroglu, Ilhan 558
Minami, Hiroshi 463
Minich, Connie 188
Minissale, Adele R. 418
Mink, Lillian A. 394
Minor, Sheila L. 209
Minter, Angela 153
Miraglia, Ann 139
Mirville, Wilfrid 397
Misener, Richard S. 238
Miseraco, Rosemond 545
Mitchell, Alexa 162
Mitchell, Dwayne 128
Mitchell Jr., Mark 395
Mitchell-Gilkey, Trudy Ann 345
Mixa, Thomas 206
Modarelli, Matthew R. 207
Modic-Coon, Ella 69
Moger, Georgette 161
Mohr, Jacci 169
Mokracek, Evelyn L. 338
Molina, Nelson 201
Monagan, George 12
Monahan, Tom 528
Monday, Michelle 384
Mones, Rossette M. 589
Monismith, Mary 112
Monroe, Margaret Jo 202
Monroe, Paul 606
Montague, Monty 511
Montgomery, Joseph M. 46
Montgomery, Mark R. 623
Montgomery, Richard 191
Montour, Jessica 285
Montoya, Lorraine 79
Montoya, Michael 231
Moody, Mary H. 391
Moody, Misty 536
Moomjian, Matthew M. 536
Moon, Catherine 546
Moore, Andrea 328

Moore, Augustine John 547
Moore, Betty Jo 557
Moore, Cynthia Annette 559
Moore, Eli 55
Moore, Emmanuel 182
Moore, Eve 118
Moore, Karen G. 526
Moore, Kimberley A. 351
Moore, Lenora 517
Moore, Lisa 199
Moore, Lola 410
Moore, Marie A. 624
Moore, Marilyn 487
Moore, Meghan 350
Moore, Norma 409
Moore, Suzanne 536
Moore, Tracy 624
Moore, Viola June 238
Mooty, Toi Lynn 340
Moragne, Donald Carroll 323
Morales, Jessica 274
Moreira, Lucinda 15
Morelli, Claudia Angela 289
Moresi, Anna M. 467
Morgan, Jean 432
Morgan, Leola M. 199
Morgan, Martha 540
Morgan, Nik 489
Morgan, Pamela Rae 111
Morgan, Shirley O. 14
Morgan, Susan 254
Morgan, Violet A. 80
Morgan-Wiles, Donnie 159
Morgans, Jay 41
Morici, Tiffany 501
Morin, Jeanne 317
Morissette, Barbara A. 152
Morphis, Karen 525
Morrical, John 577
Morris, Alisa 329
Morris, Ananda D. 159
Morris, Joan 38
Morris, Kathy 208
Morris, Latoya Anteva 620
Morris, Pamela 263
Morris-Cyr, Lorna 236
Morrison, John 475
Morrison-Wesley, Christina 130
Morrow, Angelica 283
Morrow, Loretta E. 536
Mortland, Margaret 365
Moscatello, Maria 627
Moscatello, Shana 368
moses, douane 67
Mosher, Barry 630
Mosher, Roxanne 360
Moss, Anita 471
Moss, Cheryl Ann 49
Moten, Phyllicia 107
Motter, Katie 188
Mounts, Marla 259
Moustakas, Anastasia Spiris 147
Mowat, Lucille Cast 531
MSJ 333
Muckle, Kirk 234
Muhart, Seana Kay 20
Muhich, Matt 238

Mulford, Larry Dee 355
Mullen, Mary 249
Mullen, Michael 410
Mullett, Tristi 534
Mulloy, Joan 185
Mulvihill, Melanie A. 544
Munden, Kenneth J. 387
Mundo, Margaret 247
Munson, Jennifer 319
Muronaga, Jayson 170
Murphy, Brian 452
Murphy, Charlotte 320
Murphy, Coralysa 156
Murphy, Erika 13
Murphy, Jeff 417
Murphy, Jennifer J. 435
Murphy, Joy 306
Murphy, Mary Virginia 617
Murphy, Sandy 218
Murphy, Sonja L. 520
Murray, Brian J. 134
Murray, Charles R. 163
Murray, Juanita Myers 317
Murray, Leona E. 586
Murray, LoRaine 505
Murray, Theresa D. 395
Murray, Vanessa 214
Murray, Walter 392
Muscarello, Cheryl A. 309
Muscarello, Raymond 613
Mushoyan, Elizabeth 186
Musillami, Shirley 217
Musser, Julianne 128
Mustill, Gloria 157
Mutisya, Benedette 277
Myers, Holly 330
Myers, Juanita R. 264
Myers, Margaret Story 365
Myers, Rose M. 244
Myrick, Marjorie 397
Mytnik, Catherine 562

N

Nadin, Marjorie L. 608
Nadzan, Linda Jean, RSM 115
Nagy, Christopher 121
Nail, Marjorie 593
Nakata, Danette A. 335
Napoli, Patricia Cox 626
Nash, Kathy 587
Nastari, Michael R. 522
Navarra, Jennifer 323
Navarro, David R. 333
Nave, William J. 98
Neal, Darlene 424
Neal, George F. 300
Neary, Nellie 72
Neasby, Morgan 478
Necak, Pete 251
Needy, Tamara L. 195
Neill, Meredith 353
Neiman, Norma 407
Nelms, Renee 91
Nelson, Augusta 291
Nelson, Carol 116
Nelson, Claudia M. 26

Nelson, Eric Byron 298
Nelson, Jenny 322
Nelson, Karyn C. 231
Nelson, MacArthur, Jr. 376
Nelson, Mary E. 534
Nelson, Sally J. 359
Nemec, JoAnne 629
Nero, Steven D. 74
Nethery, Bernice 41
Neu, Heidi 169
Neumann, Brandy 565
Nevels, Bob 18
Nevis, Evelyn C. 275
New, Tara 595
Newhall, Diana Forrester 283
Newman, Brandi Ralain 315
Newman, Glenda 17
Newport, George William 292
Newsom, Georgia L. 285
Newsom, Robert C. 255
Newton, Luly 406
Newton, Stephanie 385
Nguyen, Batong 315
Niccoli, Tresa Michele 492
Nicholas, Charles V. 71
Nicholas, Willadene L. 86
Nichols, Beatrice Kelley 305
Nichols, Joy 289
Nichols, Kathy L. 498
Nickerson, Brandy 576
Nicosia, John 629
Nielsen, Brian 120
Nielsen, Sandra Star Schif 365
Niemann, N.M. 596
Nimbach, Eric 4
Nimmo, Doug 129
Nishimoto, Miye 510
nitta, alida-ruth 333
Nobles, Jack C. 182
Nocivelli, Michael E. 507
Noe, C. Terry 24
Noe, Jeanette C. 165
Noegel-Hingson, Judith 161
Noel, Barbara 466
Nolan, Eleanor A. 165
Noon, Clayton 287
Nordberg, Nicole 516
Nordin, Barbara 39
Noreault, Dianne 160
Norris, Brian 9
Norris, Gayle 67
Norris, James W. 437
Norstrand, I. F. 196
Northcutt, Helen 45
Northup, Betty Grace 117
Norton, Chloe 551
Norton, Saundra 540
Noss, John A. 138
Noyes, Zena 219
Nudleman, Fauvette 429
Nuzzo, Louis J. 341
Nyce, Lori Ann 250

O

Oates, Helen M. 555
Obe, Vincent O. 597

OBran, Mark F.   248
O'Brien, Joy   548
O'Brien, Russell   496
O'Brien, Thomas R.   529
O'Connor, Janice   446
O'Connor, Maureen   385
Odle, Beth   122
Odom, Joseph   119
O'Donnell, Phil   375
O'Donnell, Richard   377
O'Dwyer, Terence   514
Offenbaker, Jenny   574
Ogburn, Donna M.   277
Ogren, Lavaughn   621
Oh, David   456
Oh, Soyoung   92
Ohlrich, Julianne H.   117
Oka, Frances   472
Olague-Rosales, Cristina   69
Olds, Joan   472
O'Leary, Stina C.   535
Oliger, Stacey   377
Olivos, Valeria   348
Oller, Nora D.   255
O'Lone, Kelly   225
Olson, Rachel   203
Olson, Rosemary   545
Olszyk, Allisonbeth   142
Olubadewo, Joseph O.   447
O'Malley, April Simon   307
O'Malley, Ronan C.   376
Ondarza, Natasha   607
O'Neal, Brenda Faye   133
O'Neill, Jeanne   150
Oosia   10
Oosterhous, Lucille J.   534
Opara, Juliana   159
Opelka Jr., William J.   99
Ordonez, Rosemary   206
Oresto, Andrew   178
Ori, Anthony   66
Orlin, Rose   519
Orr, Vicky L.   252
Orrell, Alice S.   465
Orta, Eric   322
Ortega, Joseph L.   315
Ortiz, Amy V.   579
Ortiz, Luz N.   612
Orton, Marla   605
Osborne, Tanya B.   112
Osenkowski, Sharon   587
Ostrowski, Ray   513
Oswald, Louis C.   90
Otterstrom, Jim   463
Overcash, Blondell   471
Overly, Gail L.   559
Overpeck, John   277
Overstreet, Dicky   285
Owen, Derhonda   575
Owen, Keith   200
Owens, Jean M.   449
Owens, Leah   353
Owens, S. Krista   598
Oyewole, Deji   459
Ozanich, Ruth S.   96

P

Pabon, Ellamarie   268
Pace, Louise L.   86
Pacheco, Orlando E.   15
Packard, Gregory B.   569
Paintsil, Lynn Mac   604
Paladini, Cindi   417
Palanca, Ramon G.   403
Palasek, Jacqueline M.   43
Palko, Chris   580
Palmer, Amie   35
Palmer, Connie   164
Palmer, Florence Breckenridge   423
Palmer, Mary B.   197
Palumbo, Laraine F.   528
Pankonin, Chris   335
Pankratz, Roberta Marie   411
Paolicelli, Rosina   602
Pape, Ruth Pestalozzi   615
Papineau, Melissa L.   381
Paradowski, Donna   420
Paramore, Sharron   527
Paras, Peter A.   542
Parbs, Robert C.   20
Pardo, David   24
Paris, Evelyn R.   177
Parise, Linda   211
Parker, Courtney   315
Parker, Eugenia L.   444
Parker, Sara M.   25
Parker, Valerie L.   91
Parker, Verlejean   527
Parkhurst, Mara   620
Parks, Heather E.   309
Parks, Martha   208
Parks III, Richard   260
Parmley, Helma Sophia   117
Parrish, Crystal   310
Parsons, Clay Faro   475
Parsons, Phelps E.   209
Partee, Tony Anthony, Sr.   115
Paruszkiewicz, Jessica   181
Pasatieri, Noelle   490
Paschal, Raymond   366
Pasquale, Gennaro S.   477
Passalacqua, William E.   201
Pastore, Robert Louis   110
Patel, Anita   179
Patel, Minal   540
Patrick, Patrice L.   388
Patterson, Diane Bryce   42
Patterson, Sharon L.   104
Patterson, Sonja E.   609
Patton, Rena   604
Paul, Angela   323
Paul, Cherlyn   30
Paul, Christie   123
Paul, Dorothy   162
Paul, Margaret A.   228
Paulchell III, Joseph T.   136
Pauley, Garnet 'Sam'   474
Pavlakis, Jamie   58
Pavloff, Patricia E.   73
Payeur, Normalea Rabeka   226
Payne, Cluster   573
Payne, Lodie   543

Payne, Randy   384
Payne, Ronnie   92
Payne, Shala   109
Payton, Lillian E.   603
Paz-Ligorria, Elizabeth   71
Pearce, Catherine   467
Pearl, Genevieve Lyon   310
Pearson, Annmarie   467
Pearson, Tim   247
Pease, Gwendolyn Trimbell   68
Pecaut, Waynette   221
Pedersen, Carlita McKean   475
Peirce, Marrgot   392
Peluso, Wanda   405
Pendergast, Denise   119
Pengelly, Deborah   554
Penn, Laureen   359
Pennell, Joanne   322
Pennell Sr., Ernest L.   320
Pennington, Amy   321
Pensa, Patrizia   365
Perez, Cheryl Peoples   545
Perez, Elena Iris Charneco   461
Perez, Susan   357
Perifimos, Mary M.   233
Perkins, Anthonye E.   13
Perkins, Cyndi   137
Perkins, Karen   619
Perkins, Linda M.   504
Perkins, Patricia Ann   410
Perkins, Terry L.   225
Perron, Marjorie   407
Perry, Benny J.   33
Perry, Edward D.   119
Perry, Edward Michael James   34
Perry, Jason M.   151
Perry, Tory   215
Persons, Susan L.   366
Pescatrice, Nina Naomi   623
Pesock, Ivy   301
Petell, Teresa S.   76
Peters, Konrad   261
Peterson, Joy M.   468
Peterson, Kathy   510
Peterson, Leverne H.   492
Peterson, Robert   404
Petranek, Rose Marie   238
Petrausch, Julie   181
Petro, Kimberly   621
Petrocy, Karen   113
Petrofsky, Karen S.   604
Petruna, Pam   110
Pettee, Andrea Marie   444
Pettway, Margie   479
Pettyjohn, Barbara E.   144
Pfautz, Sheri   394
Pfefferle, Clarice   467
Pfeister, Carlene M.   423
Pfund, Jack   67
Phillips, Glen E.   329
Phillips, Linda   92
Phillips, Linda L.   610
Phillips, Michelle   92
Phillips, Peter G.   524
Phillips, Philip B.   197
Phillips, Serina J.   222
Phipps, Claire A.   149

Phouthone, Cathy   121
Piacquadio, Joseph   469
Pickering, Pauline   618
Pickering, Vera   13
Pickern, Peggy A.   622
Pickett, Virginia   102
Pierce, Alice D.   46
Pierce, Bret   568
Pierce Jr., Anthony W.   163
Pierce, Lee Lawrence   524
Pierce, Mildred Floy   219
Pietrzak, Tana   210
Pigot, Will   602
Pilc, Heidemarie   10
Pillsbury, Craig   143
Pinciaro, Joe   291
Pinkney, Ernette B.   138
Piolunek, Justin   476
Pipenhagen, Anne   316
Pitre, Aurelia Perales   463
Pittman, B. Carter   452
Pittman, Darrell   554
Pittman, Donna   283
Pittman, Jessica Leigh   275
Pitts, John   551
Pitts, Jonathan W.   48
Piwtorak, Vanessa Lynn   616
Plater-Zyberk II, Elizabeth   476
Player, Geraldine   184
Pledger, LaJuan   111
Poe, Jenniffer L.   582
Poe, Richard Robert   241
Poe, Stella   97
Poete, Shauna M.   598
Pointer, Suzanne   240
Poling, Christina   309
Pollack, Paula   504
Pollock, Andie   547
Pollock, Maxwell C.   611
Pomeroy, Verna M.   490
Ponce, Dino A.   176
Poplar, Harriet   11
Poplawski, James J.   138
Post, Joseph M.   15
Potter, Dorian   148
Potts, Tim   194
Potts, Tonya   535
Poulin, Catherine M. K.   185
Powdrell, Elena   139
Powell, Barbara S.   304
Powell, Claudia   470
Powers, G. A.   404
Powis, Lillian   589
Poyner, James R.   333
Praeger, Donald   426
Pranger, Kevin J.   590
Prasad, Roop   594
Prashker, Cheryl   269
Prats III, Hugh A.   123
Prejzner, Marek   386
Prendergast, Jim   144
Prentice, Christy   468
Prentice, Margaret Johnson   341
Prescott, J.   59
Prescott, Leroy H.   541
Preskenis, Paul E.   362
Prest, Virginia I.   524

Presti, Denise Butler   38
Prew, Heather   568
Price, Jim   170
Price, Kay   376
Price, Kevin   252
Price, Lillian   249
Price, Timothy J.   75
Priest, Juanita J.   562
Priest, Lydia   379
Prieto, Michelle   478
Pringle, LaRonda   512
Pritzlaff, Donna   413
Prochaska Jr., Danny   121
Prohm, Leona Susan   212
Prosper, G. David   12
Pucillo, Francine J.   545
Puckett, Nadine   398
Puckett, Paul E.   593
Pueblo, Carrie   566
Puglisi, Donna   270
Pulliam-Hurd, Jean   567
Pullum, Antanus   291
Puma, Gina   174
Puppione, C. Valentino   487
Purich, Skip   76
Purser, Robert Walter   399
Puryear, Cametra   338
Puryear, Helena   419
Putty, Lee   196
Pyne, Laura J.   534

Q

Quatroche, Barbara   152
Quezada, Eva   317
Quezada, Gloria A.   119
Quigley, Mary Lenore   87
Quinn, Carina   413
Quinn, Ellen   138
Quinn, Poppy   401

R

Rabbitt, Susan   591
Race, Dottie Macik   161
Racki, Sherri   411
Racko, Samantha   251
Radeke, Mark E.   370
Radunz, Elaine   442
Ragona, Mary Ann   355
Rahn, Margaret   388
Rainer, Sally   526
Rainey, Kevin   372
Rainstein, Margaret   396
Rainwater, Nancy J.   497
Rait, Norma   360
Rakoczy, Angela   33
Raleigh, Doug   173
Ralph   254
Ramirez, Carmen M.   424
Ramirez, Jennifer   318
Ramnarine, Mala   85
Ramos, Marina   264
Ramponi, Peter   235
Ramsey, Jean A.   558
Ramsey, Valerie   387
Ranard, James M.   137
Rancilio, Ronald   611

Randall, Joan   138
Randazzo, Jan   413
Randazzo, Pauline   628
Rangatore, Christina   177
Rankin, Annie Lois   164
Rao, Swarupa   492
Rapsher, Bruce   414
Rardin, Lauren   387
Rarey, R L   501
Rasmussen, Faith   336
Rasmussen, Norman   104
Rasnick, Janet   555
Ratcliffe, Sheila P.   209
Ratnaike, Eunice   55
Rauch, Joshua   69
Raven   216
Rawls, Miranda Kay   520
Ray, Ginny   132
Ray, Heather   153
Ray, Jerry F.   458
Ray, Kelly A.   509
Rayburn, Gloria Ann   563
Raynor, Darcie   577
Raysor, Angelo   140
Rea II, Lawrence A.   195
Read, William A.   246
Reagan, Sandra L.   513
Reams, Jennifer   311
Reamy, James   132
Reaves, Gene L.   131
Reaves, Shatonie L.   344
Reckner, Kathy K.   347
Reddic, Vera S.   541
Rednour, Rita K.   404
Reed, Karen   100
Reed, Lillian   488
Reed, Maureen   390
Reed, Winston H. III   354
Reeder, Jane   337
Reel, Carol   267
Reese, Jeanette   158
Reese, Melanie   359
Reeves, Charlotte   458
Reeves, Judy   295
Regan, Shannon   252
Register, Connie   549
Reichenbach, Amy K.   69
Reid, Leah   76
Reid, Patricia A.   72
Reifer, Blanche   263
Reilly, Regina M.   264
Reina   605
Reinhard, Madeleine   345
Reinheimer, Byron A.   151
Reiss, Angela   426
Renz, Linda   358
Reres, Dawn J.   324
Resler, Whitney, Age 10   239
Reuss, Thomas   356
Reyes, Cris   327
Reyes, Ryane   246
Reynolds, Allison   266
Reynolds, Delila   48
Reynolds, Hazel   455
Reynolds, Mary   534
Rhae, Renne   258
Rheault, Lorraine   484

Rhoden, Betty Williams   37
Rhodes, Ben   23
Rhodes, Willie V.   252
Rhyan, William A.   506
Rhymer, Valencia   369
Ricapito, Christie   456
Riccardo, Denise   551
Riccio, Deborah J.   271
Riceardi, Michael   111
Rich, Samuel   403
Richards, Carl L.   466
Richardson, Bernice   453
Richardson, Daniel A.   32
Richardson, Debra M.   38
Richardson, Gloria J.   265
Richardson, Jayson W.   151
Richardson, Mary   192
Richey, Darin E.   175
Richmond, Bridget Katherin   144
Richter, Adelaide   66
Richter, Gregory   448
Rico, Jose Domingo   293
Ridge, April S.   174
Riedel, Albert A.   570
Riegel, John E.   317
Righter, C.   471
Righthouse, Helen A.   183
Riker, Allison   412
Rimanich, Heidi   146
Rimar, Robin   348
Ring, Stacy   495
Riolo, Sarah E.   87
Risk, Patricia Gough   615
Ristau, Heidi   321
Rittgers, Daisy   125
Rivera, Barbara   567
Rivera, Demetrio   439
Rivera, Rachelle   103
Roadifer, V. R.   255
Robare, Maria Ann   190
Robbins, Joanne   140
Roberson, Karen E.   244
Roberto, Leonard J.   191
Roberts, Candy   419
Roberts, Carol A.   582
Roberts, Cecilia M.   167
Roberts, Don A.   583
Roberts, Kenneth   402
Roberts, Marie   590
Roberts, Willard V.   529
Robertson, Julie A.   119
Robertson, Melinda   91
Robichau, Scott Michael   587
Robideaux, Amy   317
Robinette, Dawn J.   32
Robinson, Alfred E.   442
Robinson, D.   521
Robinson, Delesia   311
Robinson, Denise   569
Robinson, Dora   272
Robinson, Dr. Byron C.   32
Robinson, Ella   145
Robinson, Lulabelle T.   363
Robinson, Nellie C. S.   494
Robinson, Pamela   485
Robinson, Patricia A.   236
Robinson, Robert, Jr.   398

Robinson, Sean   482
Roble, Edwin F., Jr.   25
Roblyer, Pamela Wolfe   93
Roby, Rebecca   607
Roche, Patrick   395
Rochford, David   3
Rodgers, Christine   157
Rodolph, Pauline M.   388
Rodrigues, Don   575
Rodriguez, Ennio   467
Rodriguez, Esmeralda P.   70
Roe, Tiffany A.   486
Rogde, J. Duncan   592
Rogers, Beatrice   580
Rogers, Craig   462
Rogers, Cynthia   171
Rogers, Jessica   65
Rogers, Sharon Paula Ruiz   249
Rohrer, Sheila   203
Rollins, Rebecca   240
Romano, Melora   75
Ronkainen, Tracey   205
Rood, Jacqueline S.   311
Rooney, James   452
Rooney, Noreen J.   599
Roppolo, Jason   334
Rosado Rodriguez, Roberto B.   205
Rosario, Mark   341
rose, catherine   439
Rose, Gina   152
Rose, James Perry   443
Rose, Josephine   457
Rose, Margaret Jo   77
Rose, Susan   493
Rosen, Jessica   563
Rosen, Lugene   508
Rosenberger, Margaret A.   392
Ross, C. M.   271
Ross, Judith D.   157
Ross, Tammi   396
Rossi, Tirzah   384
Rossin, Arthur S.   551
Rotariu, George J.   131
Roth, Kerry   195
Rothleutner, Kathleen J.   198
Roulston, Ellie   35
Roussel, Jake O.   453
Rowe, Carrie Belle   421
Rowe, Darren   631
rowe, james t.   455
Rowe, Wendy   224
Rowinski, Monica   528
Royalty, G. E.   105
Royd-Sykes, Susan   95
Royer, Marty Rae   266
Royls, Suzanne   195
Royse, Ataka Rhodes   566
Rozane, Albert   41
Rozinski, Bert   136
Ruane, Joseph   281
Rubenstein, Deborah Bass   318
Rubin, Ann R.   65
Rubin, Naomi Greifer   260
Rubler, Selma   615
Rucker, Danny   556
Rucker, Millicent   387
Rudert, Ashlee   286

Rudoy, Irene 432
Rudy, Patrick 409
Ruffin, Lee E. 406
Ruffin, Vince 340
Ruhl, Delores 180
Ruhl, Paul G. 99
Ruiz, Barbara 305
Rundstrom, Kate 529
Rupert, Laverne 378
Rupley, Janine 153
Rush, Brendan 468
Rush, William V. 249
Rushefsky, Leah 260
Rushing, Tommy 361
Russell, Brenda Lynn 41
Russell, Ellen 290
Russell, Jane Dexter 51
Russell, John McGreevy 131
Russell, Patricia 385
Russell, Shirley J. 500
Russell, Tom 86
Russert-Kraemer, L. 9
Russin, Marjorie Perry 384
Russom, Pearl M. 248
Rusten, Kevin D. 233
Rutherford, Deborah J. 434
Rutherford, Shannon 83
Rutishauser, Betty Burdick 570
Rutkowski, Joseph J. 117
Ruton, Mildred Marsh 229
Ryan, Eleanor Blanchat 414
Ryan, Teresa Donoher 339
Rye, Neva Perry 538

S

Sacco, Lisa A. 397
Sacharski, Gail 142
Sadaka, Jennifer Rose 301
Saddlemire, Michele 371
Sadkin, Ruth 478
Sadoff, Johnny 285
Saffle, Winnie 236
Safka, Pauline 242
Sagel, Lesley 537
Sagunsky, Cindy L. 126
Sailors, Lawrence 507
Saint-Gaudens, James Douglas 177
Sajorda, Cherilyn Anne M. 180
Salahu-Din, Deborah T. 181
Salemi, Joseph 303
Salera, John R. 413
Salinas, Yolanda 539
Salmons, Dixie Ann 440
Salo, Jannine 428
Salvato, Nicholas G. 15
Samaniego, Isaac T. 523
Samartino, Rachele 90
Sampino, Willamette 523
Sample, Glenda 437
Sampson, John P. 301
Sams, Anita L. 455
Sams, Christian K. 330
Samuels, Sophia 83
Sanchez, Chris 170
Sanchez, Jackie 270
Sanchez, Maria C. 525

Sanchez, Reymundo 226
Sanders, G. & P. 226
Sandholt, Barbara L. 294
Sandifer, A'Mae Cavett 468
Sands, Priscilla 376
Sanghavi, Sarah 380
Sang'iewa, Yvette 362
Santana, Valerie G. 593
Santer, Benjamin D. 416
Santiago, Maria T. 257
Santic, Tamera Joe 513
Santoro, Alta Mae 176
Santos, Chona 71
Santos, Denise Michele 273
Santos, Theresa 487
Santoyo, Monica 621
Santry, Sunny 497
Saradjian, Matthew 585
Sardelli, Wilfred G. 406
Sardi, Andrew 458
Sargent, Jason J. 578
Sarin, Pat 586
Sarnataro, Henry T. 27
Sarvary, Erik C. 308
Sasser, Tony R. 516
Sasso, Kathleen K. 77
Sauter, Kristen 244
Savage, Amy Marie 560
Savage, Sarah Ingrid 502
Savage, Sylvia Vicker 391
Sawyer, Leslie 202
Sayler, Mary Harwell 209
Scaletty, Marie 404
Scamacca, Samuel J., Jr. 91
Scarborough, Brenda L. 143
Scarbrough, Claudia M. 122
Scarbrough, Dorothy 137
Scarlett, John A. 151
Scarpato, Ralph 544
Scenti, John 270
Schabert, Jason 150
Schachter, David 143
Schaible, Buna M. 179
Schanbeck, Theresa 385
Schanfield, Fannie S. 463
Schappel, Katy 112
Scharp, Diana Lynn 558
Schatzman, Martin 397
Schaufler, Patricia 219
Schefler, Lisa Maria 361
Scheirer, Louise I. 339
Schenck, Teresa Moreland 82
Schenk, Tanya 104
Schenks, Jim 125
Scheutzow, William R., Jr. 223
Schiller, Malaika 541
Schimmel, Allyson 127
Schimming, Jacob 138
Schindewolf, Robyn M. 527
Schiwart, Joyce H. 138
Schladweiler, Mary Joyce 116
Schlesinger, Irving 582
Schlieman, Shirley 629
Schlosser, Danille Ann 573
Schmainda, Frank A. 434
Schmidt, Audrey 329
Schmidt, Hope M. 293

Schmitt, Sarah Jean 112
Schmitz, Georgiana 127
Schmoll, David C. 45
Schneider, Danielle 449
Schneider, Evelyn 54
Schoenitz, Sandra L. 534
Schoff, Rosette 537
Scholz, Laura L. 200
Scholz, Maria 251
Schoonover, Marjorie A. 244
Schrader, Jolene J. 317
Schramm, Modine G. 374
Schrankel, Marie C. Leftwich 523
Schreiber, Dorothy 122
Schroeder, Margaret L. 22
Schroeder, Ray F. 485
Schuck, Christina 146
Schuett, Kurt C. 109
Schulman, David G. 554
Schwarck, Poncheena Kay 401
Schwartz, Eric P. 434
Schwartz, Martin J. 532
Schwartz, Nettie Yanoff 349
Schwarzbach, Ruth 340
Sciaky, Dolsa 303
Sciolli, Gabriel 7
Scott, Crystal A. 445
Scott, Gwendolyn 294
Scott, LaKesha M. 107
Scott, Nancy Craig 248
Scott, R. L. 198
Scott, Susan 507
Scott, Tekeah C. 383
Scoville, Orlin J. 536
Seale, Doreene S. 174
Seaman, Eileen A. 458
Searles, Frances 296
Sears, Maynard J. 3
Sebastian, Savarimuthu 486
Secor, Dawn 313
Secunde, Sue 538
Seedarnee, Donna E. 473
Seefeldt, Rebecca S. 541
Seelig, Ira C. 123
Seemungal, Sesha 247
Segal, Deanna C. 560
Segraves, Kimberley A. 398
Seifrit, Bambie 144
Seipel, Gary W. 162
Seitz, Jennifer 174
Selesky, Debra 117
Self, Albertine 153
Seligman, Rebecca K. 19
Selkirk Jr., Alexander M. 413
Sellars, Eve 306
Selleck, Tina 622
Seltz, Doris M. 425
Selva, Shelly Della 214
Sementelli, Vicki 204
Semmelrogge, Kate 222
Sendroff, Vera K. 193
Senevey, Leslie 21
Senft, Jennifer 173
Senn, Robert Louis 386
Serafin, Jason Kenneth 285
Serafini, Lisa 81
Sergeant, Courtney 307

Serkland, Dan 328
Serrano, Gisela Movilla 150
Serrano-Figueroa, Gladys 49
Sery, Kenneth P. 615
Sessions, Betty Sue 124
Shade, Tisa 250
Shadoe 123
Shafer, Joyce E. 331
Shaffer, Kay 585
Shaheen, Mahdi A. 374
Shane, Brendan C 555
Shane, Laura 537
Shane, Stefan 357
Shanholtzer, Sharon J. 231
Shanks Jr., Edmund J. 174
Shanley, Jason 327
Shannon, Ethel M. 440
Shapiro, Harold 463
Shapiro, Jill Lys 466
Sharman, Elizabeth 29
Sharp-D'Escopo, Cheryl 432
Sharrar, Marc 491
Shaskevich, Michael 394
Shaw, Cassandra 326
Shaw, Clara May 459
Shaw, Melvin J. 543
Sheehan, Dorothy 460
Sheets, Dana 298
Sheffer, Donnel Gloster 631
Sheffner, Zorah E. 482
Shelton, Amanda 64
Shelton, Andrew 273
Shelton, Samuel Dewayne 75
Shelton, Tim 498
Shephard, Carolyn Ann 290
Shepherd, Marion M. 6
Sheppard, Harriet L. 579
Sheridan, Robert 7
Sherman, Carrie 299
Sherman, Jennifer 160
Sherman, Robert 400
Sherr, Harry B. 186
Sherrell, Michael Winston 111
Sherrill, Barbara 332
Sherrod, Rene 259
Sherwood, Fay M. 458
Shevlin, Erin 175
Shin, Marie 256
Shine, Barbara 305
Shinko, Kelly Marie 396
Shipp, Alma 287
Shirley, Shirley R. 376
Shivprasad, Ghire C. 173
Shoemaker, Chris C. 425
Shoemaker, Mary Rose 527
Shoemaker, Stacie 229
Shoop, Charles W. 48
Shors II, John D. 427
Short, Beulah M. 471
Short, Linda K. 626
Short, Tom 515
Shortridge, Beulah 132
Shropshire, Betty R. 152
Shugart, William J. 530
Shumaker, Regina 481
Shuman, Neil M. 223
Shurtz, Kristal 545

Shutt, Nora   533
Sias, Rosie   242
Siegel, Marjorie S.   235
Siegfried, Rhonda K.   543
Siemon, Lula Shaw   83
Siford, Sandra L.   114
Sigler, Lora Ann   4
Sigmon, Gertrued Hickin   439
Silbergeld, Sam   358
Siller, David G.   34
Silver, Alice Moolten   39
Silverman, Ralph J.   401
Silvia, Judy G.   446
Simes, R. Patrick   408
Simmons, Gage   325
Simmons, Jenniffer   133
Simmons, Kerri L.   484
Simmons, Nancy   530
Simmons, Omar K.   354
Simms, Stacha   235
Simonson, Mark A.   625
Sims, Mignon   204
Sinclair, Lily   251
Sing, Kanoe   618
Singh, Kris   361
Singleton, Debbie   126
Singley, Lee   539
Sinkford, Robin Maria   537
Sipes, Amber   178
Siple-Derouchie, Denise   58
Siracusa, Margaret   501
Sisk, Juanita   414
Sjoberg, David W.   555
Skierski, Janelle   269
Skinner, Lynne Louise   251
Sklar, Steve   358
Skleros, M.   406
Skyles, Margaret   112
Slabic, Chris   34
Slanicka, Linda   205
Slauson, Michele   400
Sledge, Haley   574
Sleight, Helen Sue   371
Sliter-Donovan, Shirley E.   219
Slover, Jay   314
Sluka, Jill   151
Slusher, Eleanor J.   46
Sly, Elizabeth   464
Small III, James E.   49
Small, Thomas G.   108
Smalley Sr., Joe A.   436
Smart, Ramona   393
Smile, Lana   611
Smilnyak, Norman E.   381
Smith, Bonnie S.   462
Smith, Brenda   302
Smith, Bryant T.   442
Smith, Carl A.   317
Smith, Carolyne   138
Smith, Colleen Tuthill   436
Smith, Cory   116
Smith, Derrick W.   562
Smith, Donna J.   277
Smith, Doris   549
Smith, Eric J.   459
Smith, Eric T.   450
Smith, Ethel   147
Smith, Heather Lee   316
Smith, Helen   331
Smith, Jacob D.   440
Smith, Jacqueline   429
Smith, Jane Parker   126
Smith, Jean   425
Smith, Jennifer C.   436
Smith, Jessica Christiana   334
Smith, John William   4
Smith, Josie Goodrich   46
Smith, Matthew B.   355
Smith, Melinda   535
Smith, Meredith E.   400
Smith, Michelle   619
Smith, Minette   541
Smith, Nathan Scott   590
Smith, Norma J.   527
Smith, Randy   239
Smith, Rhonda A.   399
Smith, Robert J.   586
Smith, Ronald   532
Smith, Sarah   543
Smith, Tanya Keith   502
Smith, Tara N.   504
Smith, Terry K.   586
Smith, Thelma   618
Smith, Troy   88
Smith, Virginia K.   352
Smithson, Clyde   452
Smothers, Laurie C.   384
Smuda, Jennifer D.   123
Smyth, Ken   531
Snelgrove, Elizabeth   415
Snell, Jeanne   450
Snipe, Indira   141
Snodgrass, Hillary A.   59
Snowden, Mark A.   530
Snyder, April C.   475
Snyder, Christine A.   562
Snyder, Gayle Elaine   325
So, Taiwon   230
Soape, N.   390
Sobola, Denise L.   166
Soborowski, Margaret   407
Sola, Janet S.   338
Soles, J. V.   104
Solie, Emily D.   301
Sollock, Patricia D.   399
Soltis, Michael A.   614
Somer, Sylvia   545
Somero, Stacey L.   544
Sommer, Greg   66
Sommers, Charles R.   446
Sondergaard, Susanne   250
Soner, Jerry   136
Sonriente, Kalinda   614
Soos, Paul J. (& Josiah)   608
Sorlien, Nicholas Alexandros   614
Sosbe, Nicole   366
Soule, Lee D.   512
Sousa, Ann Marie   271
Southerland, Carol E.   128
Southern, Travis   364
Souza, Nadine   212
Sowles, Lloyd L.   608
Spaeth, Jennifer   332
Sparino, Rebeccar Todd   190
Spear, Kathleen   94
Spears, Clara   130
Spears, Joseph   142
Specht, David Lee   329
Specht, John A.   120
Spector, Rachel Stewart   339
Speer, Garrick E.   65
Spencer, Carolyn   326
Spencer, Michael W.   87
Spencer, Sheila Ann   485
Spendlove, Mishayla   242
Speth, Cory   329
Spielvogel, Tamra   84
Spivack, Gershon   431
Sprague, Louise   232
Spriggs, Myra Powell   526
Springs, Edna R.   28
Spurlin, Doralee   155
Spurlock, Charles A.   57
Spurrier, Mary   260
Spyrou, Spyros   16
Squires, Michael Everett   106
Squires, Raymond O.   350
Srur, Nicole   530
St. Clair, Eugene   123
St. Cyr, Jackie   553
Stack, D. Dale   196
Stackhouse, Douglas E.   470
Stafford, Peggie Ann   532
Stallings, Nancy   537
Stallworth, Duana Davis   50
Stambaugh, Deborah   69
Standish, Lorraine   82
Standridge, Dorinda   476
Stanford, Mark Andrew   481
Stanford, Tara   630
Stangel, Darla   168
Stanley, Barbara J. Cochran   424
Stanley, Brianne   275
Stanley, Molly   368
Stannard, Richard   242
Starkman, Melanie B.   604
Starks, Dawn W.   139
Staten, Jennifer   446
Statler, Erma C.   149
Stavely, Samantha   408
Stavrou, Glinda   576
Steadman, Veda Nylene   361
Stearn, Sherry   605
Steckler, Morgan Herman   372
Steele, Joy M.   187
Steele, Milly   255
Stefaneas, Olga   377
Steffens, Irene Marie   42
Stefon, Matt   368
Stein, James Joseph   560
Stein, Richard   252
Steinberg, Gideon   162
Steiner, M. Elisabeth   485
Stelmack, Marjorie   608
Stelter, Jeremias J.   560
Stemper, Alan   433
Stenger, Carl J.   180
Stenroth, Signe O.   104
Stepanek, Laura E.   359
Stepanich-Reidling, Kisma K.   16
Stephen, Joan   289
Stephens, Leanna   191
Stephens, Patricia K.   526
Stephenson Jr., John   292
Stephenson, Tracy   626
Stepnowski, Tara   529
Steuermann, Margaret   243
Stevens, Evelyn   558
Stevenson, Evelyn Floria   31
Stevenson, Julie D.   123
Stevenson, Patsy L.   531
Stever, Eleanor   465
Stevinson, Michael   115
Stewart, Florence B.   327
Stewart, Jane M.   133
Stewart, Judy   286
Stewart, Kandy   217
Stewart, Kate   15
Stewart, Kathy Metze   360
Stewart, Lee D.   80
Stewart, Lori   246
Stewart, R.   224
Stieber, Laurie A.   342
Stiegelmeyer, Iradell   53
Stiffler, Barbara J.   169
Still, Patsy H.   105
Stillwell, Dave   121
Stires, Jean   67
Stock, Charles Frederick   129
Stockberger, Nicola   346
Stockle, Jeni   433
Stoetzer, Jason   452
Stokell, Barbara   50
Stokes, Alberta Evans   280
Stolhanske, Lisa   588
Stoltz, Dr. Donald R.   21
Stone, Coral L.   292
Stone, Elizabeth   338
Stone, Gillian M.   279
Stone, Scott Douglas   495
Stoppel, Rebecca T.   99
Storey, Beth   67
Stork, Casey   327
Stork, Jess   146
Stott, Gregory H.   51
Stout, Gretchen   335
Strachan, Darin   556
Strahl, Nicky   85
Straining, Kami D.   510
Strait, Shane   258
Strange, Julia Margaret   11
Straub, Lisa Frazier   216
Straughn, Valerie   497
Straus, Doris   560
Strauss, Glory   33
Streck, Rachel   189
Street, Anna   293
Streit, Jonathan   444
Strharsky, Loretta   483
Stribling, Betty Jean   276
Stricklin, Chris R.   282
Stringer, Paul V.   253
Stroh, Frank   468
Strom, Jeff   575
Strom, Jennifer   315
Stroupe, Vance A.   482
Stucke, Amber   233
Stuckey, Katherine   409

Stucki, Tina M. 223
Sturgis, Carol 447
Sturgis, Marcia J. 372
Sturm, Carol A. 426
Stutzman, Carie 323
Styer, Kevin 341
Subers, Karen 237
Suduba, Darlene 301
Sudwecks, Korrie 350
Sugawara, Michiyo 229
Suggs, Laura J. 533
Suggs, Teresa 231
Sullivan, Edward T. 416
Sullivan, Jay Chris 428
Sullivan, Joan 144
Sullivan, Lowell 235
Sullivan, Margaret K. 194
Sullivan, Tracy Lorelei 484
Summer, Lucia 127
Summerkamp, Hazel 429
Summers, Wayne J. 393
Super, Nicole 410
Suplee, Diana Fabiani 456
Surace, Ronald J. 482
Sutliff, Dawn 332
Sutmaier III, Michael Joseph 340
Sutton, Jimmie Nell Bush 124
Sutton, Joey 417
Svey, Mike 359
Svoboda, Kerri Jo 197
Swalm, Dora 163
Swanson, Anita 268
Swanson, Ruth 498
Swartz, Cheryl L. 316
Swartz, Joshua F. 451
Swearingen, Melissa Ann 513
Sweeney, Sara E. 405
Sweigart, Rebecca J. 364
Swenson, Alanna 284
Swider, Ann 467
Swift, Tracy 539
Swigart, Eugene Calvin 132
Swinderman, Frances 335
Switzer-Aaron, Billi 551
Sybert, William 85
Sylvia, Naylee 516

T

Tabassum, Jawaid 320
Tackett, Melissa N. 538
Tackett, Yvonne 107
Tafua, Anthony V. 299
Takagi, Sakiko 531
Talcott, Maria E. 614
Taliaferro, June C. 326
Tallman, Evelyn T. 439
Tamrie, Tesfaye 100
Tandoc, Mariquita N. 525
Tanner, Jennifer 128
Tanner, Lee 393
Tanner, W. Louise 352
Tantillo, Craig 310
Tapper, Jacalyn 62
Targowski, Francis A. 308
Tarmey, Stephen 525
Tart, Margie 518

Tartamella, John 315
Tarulli, Cheryl 142
Tatum, Lance 227
Taylor, Alexandra Renee' 334
Taylor, Donn E. 3
Taylor, Duane 186
Taylor, G. Warren 102
Taylor, Gertrude M. 14
Taylor, Jackie 131
Taylor, Kathleen 585
Taylor, Linda 601
Taylor, Michelle 352
Taylor, Patti 613
Taylor, Terrence Lee 593
Taylor, Terry M. 493
Teague, Scott L. 19
Teague, Theresa 411
Teaters, Dorothy A. 441
Tedd, Barbara H. 293
Teed, Richard M. "Rik" 338
Teeter, Floyd 167
Telowitz, Nikki 406
Temes, Terrence 234
Tencza, Lawrence M. 106
Terase, John 472
Terry, Lorraine L. 610
Test, Kelley Joan 193
Testa, Keith 531
Theuerkauf, Sharon 389
Thielen, Gregory 20
Thill, Janet M. 273
Thoelen, Jaimee 475
Thomas, Al 559
Thomas, Bobbie J. 584
Thomas, Florence Lorraine 284
Thomas Jr., Henley C. 323
Thomas, Kathleen 486
Thomas, LaMarr 23
Thomas, Laura 198
Thomas, Lorrie A. 367
Thomas, Lyell 511
Thomas, Sonya 597
Thomas, Vaudaline 205
Thomason, S. Joseph 5
Thompson, Alani 564
Thompson, Carol L. 185
Thompson, Frances D. 465
Thompson, Frances L. 139
Thompson, Karen B. 371
Thompson, Laurie Nicole 612
Thompson, Lori Danielle 247
Thompson, Martha 493
Thompson, Moses A. 226
Thompson, Nichole 409
Thompson, Phyllis Y. Smith 342
Thompson, Whisper 266
Thomson, Anna Blair 466
Thornhill, Randy D. 98
Thorpe, Kirsten 493
Thorson, Robert 525
Thrasher, Diana M. 306
Tian Li Chin, Cheryl 440
Tibbs, Nicole 600
Tidman, Ginevra Ginn 459
Tieger, Laura 210
Tiemeyer, Erin 130
Tienne 343

Till, Justin 150
Timmons, Railyn 391
Timms, Juanita 584
Tippetts, Heather Marie 569
Tirheimer, Martha 507
Titcomb, Rose 351
Tittle, DeLois 471
Toliver, Aaron, Jr. 281
Tolley, Nancy E. 600
Tomlinson, Emma Jo 163
Tomlinson, Kay 229
Toneri, Judy 17
Toops, Betty 555
Topping, Tricia 625
Torchenaud, Jude 278
Torkelson, Kris 608
Torn, Rhoda 388
Torquemada, Debra 283
Torres, Anthony 300
Torres, Nick 193
Torres, Ruth 499
Torrison, Aaron J. 6
Tougaw, Laura 105
Tovar, Elisa 18
Tower, Jennifer 429
Towns-Collins, Virdajean 604
Tracy, Meegan 214
Transou, Larry 100
Trasy, Anjali G. 58
Traverse, Vernon 375
Traywick-Jones, Andrea 36
Treadway, Myrtle A. 404
Treat, Wilma 517
Trezek, Lacey A. 381
Triggs, Deanna 477
Triggs, Deborah 273
Trimble, Rochelle 103
Trimble, Vicky N. 207
Trinkle, Joanne E. 438
Tripathi, Hina N. 584
Tripp, Mary 401
Troesch, Mirjam 261
Troilo, Barbara Carol Kares 116
Trotter, Phil 113
Trutner, William 399
Tsucalas, Maria 527
Tubbs II, David A. 561
Tubbs, Tom N. 520
Tucker, Gary D. 33
Tucker, Jenni 435
Tuma, Brian G. 429
Tumey, Jennifer 332
Tuohey, Margaret 88
Turley, Timmy 593
Turner, Christopher J. 55
Turner, Corinne 49
Turner, David J. 183
Turner, Edith Cox 156
Turner, John E. 14
Turner, Lois B. 406
Turner, Mildred Ahearn 619
Turpen, Cynthia M. 185
Tutins, Wendy 534
Tuttle, Julie 523
Tyler, Francine 180

U

Ucman, Frank 42
Uden, Carol 274
Ulmer, Lisa 539
Umberger, Lara 82
Underside, Carla Jo 322
Unruh, Michael R. 88
Upshaw, Margaurette 533
Urban, Jeff 278
Urban, Maggie 387
Uribe, Maribell 108
Uriegas, Julia A. 137
Urvina, Nadia 487

V

Vacovec, Beth 59
Vail, Chuck 422
Vail, Michelle 398
Vair, Janet A. 42
Valdez, Chantae 438
Vale, Arthur M. 155
Valentino, Anthony 124
Valenzuela, Angie 430
Valicenti, Elizabeth 133
Valverde, Ramon C. 243
Van Arsdale, Donna S. 326
Van Benthuysen, Jessica C. 583
Van Camp, Dorothy J. 312
Van Cleve, Jerry R. 143
Van Damme, Yvonne 365
Van Dyke, Jeffrey L. 168
Van Fossen, Sarah 408
Van Hooft, Christine M. 561
Van Middlesworth, Diane 309
VanArsdale, Cindy 331
Vandiver, Jerry 319
VanMeter, Sharon 228
VanPraet, Mariea 201
Varnadore, Rodney 205
Varner, Elizabeth Pettit 283
Vasilas, Sarah 610
Vassalle, Mario 478
Vasseur, Sheila F. 238
Vaughan, Gwen Morris 274
Vaughan, Susan Boyle 397
Vaughan, Tiahuana D. 492
Vaughn, Iris Ann 147
Vedder, Dale A. 121
Veillette, Kevin 511
Velazquez, Norbert 599
Ventura, Cheryl 552
Veracka, Linda Hassett 478
Verdon, Bill 476, 543
Vergara, Irenio C. 160
Vergith, Kenneth E. 243
Verhegghe, Leslie 231
Vermont, Donna Marie 303
Vernon, C.L. 315
Verrastro, Michael J. 519
Verucci, Evelyn A. 50
Vessa, Gladys B. 130
Vidales, Mona A. 382
Vidanoff, Stephanie N. 345
Vigil, Patricia 623
Vine, Judith 44

Vinson, E. A. 75
Vinson, Elizabeth A. 35
Vint, Naomi Etter 534
Vint, Peggy 395
Visconty, Elizabeth 172
Visnaw, Debbie 420
Visser, Kathryn R. 262
Vivona, Michelle 102
Vlasic Jr., Nickolas A. 381
Vogelsang, Jacqueline 30
Vogt, Charmaine R. 559
Vogt, Richard J. 191
Volk, Everett 124
Volkart, Nancy 108
Volkmer, Deb 557
Volpe, Eileen R. 444
Voltz, Judy Merriman 272
von Dolln, Georgetta 57
von Tobel, Barbara 449
Vondall, Valda M. 370
Vonnegut, Sarah 387
Voorhies, Billie 127
Voss, Judy 116

W

Wackerle, Lloyd E. 351
Waddle, Robert T., Sr. 620
Wade, Harry J. 415
Waggoner, Chris 60
Wagner, Marlene J. 191
Wagstaff, Sherida 380
Wahala, Kelly 504
Wainscott, Linda S. 542
Waitkus, Beth 447
Wakefield, Allen 578
Wakefield, Sharron 409
Waldon, Clara Faye 461
Walgren, Marci 528
Walker, Christy W. 133
Walker, Marjorie B. 499
Walker, Mark 367
Walker, Peyton 242
Walker, Ronald Alfred 20
Walker, Rose M. 544
Walker, Shycole D. 93
Walker, Willie H. 383
Wall, Jennifer 312, 419
Wallace, Dorothy A. 52
Wallace II, Joe Don 319
Wallace, Karen 595
Wallace, Virgina 510
Walling, Amanda 323
Wallis, Carol L. 150
Wallover, Amanda 295
Walser, Jeremy H. 447
Walsh, Ashley P. 29
Walsh, Bryan T. 56
Walsh, David A. 60
Walsh, David Boncic 132
Walsh, Jason C. 292
Walsh, Lori Ann 628
Walsh, Zione 234
Walters, R. Eugenia 242
Walters, Wanda C. 204
Waltman, Casey 434
Walts, Ann E. 473

Ward, Craig 477
Ward, Harold B. 413
Ward, L. M. 392
Ward, Sandy M. 383
Ward, Tammy L. 509
Warmack, Hugh T. 567
Warner, Linda 84
Warren, Cynthia L. 268
Warren, Emily 470
Washburn, Lori Ann 586
Washington, Denece 317
Washington, Ella 289
Washington, Mark 590
Washington, Robert L. 386
Wass, Marjorie M. 531
Waters, Carolyn 164
Wathen, Karen Haley 609
Watkins, Daphne C. 318
Watson, Joy C. 131
Watson, Julie 28
Watson, Michael R. 589
Watson, Muriel 481
Watson, Sam L. 351
Watt, Elizabeth A. 548
Watts, Debbra L. 332
Watts, Delores 68
Wattz, Arieez 565
Wavrunek, Sharon 250
Waymon, Flora 426
Wean, Ellen 40
Weatherman, Greg L. 329
Weaver, Linda 252
Weaver, Patricia R. 487
Weaver, Sandra Bryant 536
Webb, Brenda 470
Weber, Kevin 407
Weber, Olivia 505
Weber, T. G. 405
Wedding, Brian K. 418
Weed, Mel 343
Weeden, Mary Ann 537
Weekes, Joseph S. 166
Weekley, Glenda 154
Weekley, Mary A. 82
Weeks, Joan 552
Weiderman, Katie 602
Weinberg, Donn (1972) 28
Weinberg, Nicole 219
Weissenburger, Rita Cottrell 606
Welch, Jack 565
Welch, Marie E. 395
Welch, Summer 541
Welding, Allen E. 461
Weldon, Rick L. 366
Wellbank, Joseph H. 318
Weller, Katherine Mary 528
Wells, Clay A. 53
Wells, Janet 118
Wells, John Frank 279
Wells, Kimberly Sue 573
Wells, Raymond L. 255
Wenger, Grace 335
Wente, Charles J. 414
Wentworth, Charles M. 566
Werber, Maxine 252
West, April 311
West, Gail L. 117

West, Jacqueline 154
West, Shelly Lee 367
Westfall, Angie 335
Westmoreland, Karen 110
Weston, Peggy Wells 195
Wetmore, Phyllis 530
Whalen, Shirley M. 222
Wharton, Carl (xdous) 44
Wharton, Muriel 364
Whatley, Douglas Reagan 291
Wheat, Deborah Nichols 17
Wheeler, Betty 38
Wheeler, Earl B. 166
Wheeler, Leesa A. 72
Wheeler, Steven A. 510
Wheeler, Wendy 622
Wheeless, Angela 276
Whipple, Lonnie Jean Frost 498
Whirl, Larry L. 349
White, Cheryl 337
White, J. B. 493
White, Jo Ann 469
White, Joyce E. 454
White, Lisa A. 212
White, Sara 399
White, Sid 516
Whitehead, Roberta 77
Whiteman, Kourtney 538
Whitlock, Dave 127
Whitmore, Louise E. 217
Whitmore, Sam 618
Whitney, Karin Cathryn 394
Whitt, Marcella 241
Wicker, Judy K. 461
Wiedenhaefer, Brian 183
Wiemer, Brittany 316
Wightman, Jonna B. 317
Wilbanks, Sam 351
Wilburn, Shirley Taylor 98
Wildt, Dorothy Koeller 158
Wiles Jr., Teddy 488
Wiley, Robert L. 227
Wiley, Trudi V. 525
Wilhelmy, Gus 553
Wilhoite, Lucinda 339
Wilkes, Melissa 544
Wilkey, Ross 247
Wilkins, Lynn 106
Wilkins, Rayanna M. 189
Wilkinson, Carl 156
Wilkowski, Theresa 111
Willenbring, Marissa 528
Willey, Vickie L. 343
Willi, Toni L. 516
Williams, Annie L. 323
Williams, Barbara B. 572
Williams, Brian Bernard 33
Williams, Charlene 271
Williams, Cleaveland C. 582
Williams, Danny 425
Williams, Domestric 312
Williams, Donald J. 298
Williams, Hattie B. 292
Williams, James D. 63
Williams, Jeannette 325
Williams, Judith 275
Williams, Judy Hamilton 567

Williams, Kathy 89
Williams, Kevin 79
Williams, Lucretia Screen 386
Williams, Wilhalmena 81
Williamson, Cassidy 329
Williamson, D. L. 346
Williamson, Marjorie Ciruti 543
Williard, Bob 336
Wills, J. J. 394
Willsie, Corinna Lynn 469
Wilson, Borghild 458
Wilson, Cheryl Diane 443
Wilson, Clyde 574
Wilson, Emerson M. 321
Wilson, James 440
Wilson, Janice M. 470
Wilson, Jo 48
Wilson, Liane 356
Wilson, Marvin P. 204
Wilson, Mike 526
Wilson, Otis 522
Wilson, Raeann Stacey 505
Wiltberger, Grace E. 318
Wiltsey, John E. 578
Wimmer, Christina M. 563
Wines, Stacie 106
Winfree, Stephanie D. 391
Winiarski, Patty A. 344
Wininger, Robert 218
Winn, John D. 330
Winne, Laura E. 254
Winston, Lawrence E. 526
Winters, Laura 236
Wireman, Elaine 134
Wirick, Ralph I. 482
Wise, Verlee 631
Wisniewski, Jessica L. 546
Wittenberg, Jonah 141
Wittenstein, W. Andreas 115
Wogan, Diana 423
Wojnowich, Sandy 396
Wolf, Vera M. 524
Wolf, Zolene 398
Wolfe, Esther Skinner 328
Wolford, Don 583
Wolicki, Erica 65
Wolk, Ed 137
Wollschlager, Jo 325
Wong, DeLaVerne 547
Wong, Ron 250
Wong, Stanley 232
Wood, Holly 423
Wood, Lisa O. 589
Wood, Michael 588
Wood, Paul J. 511
Wood, Paula 383
Wood, Robert E. 104
Wood, Robyn M. 395
Wood, Verna Lee 616
Wood, Vicki S. 199
Woodard, Frances P. 420
Woodie, Lisa-Kurtz 76
Woodruff, Emily 177
Woodruff-Rohrer, Gene L. 56
Woods, George 584
Woods, Terry B. 222
Woodward, Jason Kalakaua 27

Wooldridge, Wendy D. 101
Worland, Jennafer 187
Worthley, Jason 559
Woss, Barbara A. 38
Wozny, Missy 591
Wright, Betty J. 575
Wright, Brian 296
Wright, Carol A. 34
Wright, Charlayne 276
Wright, Christina Leigh 138
Wright, Janelle 573
Wright, Lewis, Jr. II 494
Wright, Michael L. 194
Wright, Michelle 250
Wright, Rhonda 588
Wright, Roy 504
Wroblewski, Linda T. 409
Wyatt-Mackay, Joan 180
Wye, Jonathan 334
Wynn, Ian 330
Wynne, Shirley J. 486

X

Xayavong, Souphanh 538
Xu, Yue 602

Y

Yai, Youlim 238
Yancy, Scott 481
Yanez, Christopher 185
Yang, C. W. 247
Yank, Brian 70
Yao, Carl 580
Yaros, C. L. 354
Yaros, Joanne M. 300
Yasparro, Rosemary Muntz 5
Yavorsky, Michael N. 507
Ybarra, Geneva 178
Yeager, Edith A. 40
Yeager, Heidi L. 442
Yeager IV, James F. 47
Yeazell, Melody D. 484
Yliniemi, Darlayne L. 288
Yoder, Judith K. 478
York, Ann F. 122
York, Irving 4
York, Rebecca 95
Young, Diana A. 415
Young, Florence 125
Young, John D. 70
Young, Natasha Ann 489
Young, Scott 616
Young, Tara 216
Young, William K. 84
Yray, Joyce 424
Yuan, Tien Lin 81
Yuengst, Todd 362
Yurick, Kelly 78

Z

Zahora, Lori Ann 339
Zaks, Lena 532
Zamrzla, Jessica 126
Zavala, Elizabeth 472
Zeglin, Leann M. 363
Zehring, Jimmie D. 179
Zeis, Katherine Lynn 628
Zeller, Peter James, II 95
Zenieris, Jer 60
Zerbian, Cary 336
Zickau, Amy C. 450
Zielinski, C. Jeanene 391
Zimmer, Zoe 628
Zinan, Dorothy 60
Zoland, Anna Marie 284
Zucchero, Barbara Ann 474
Zucchetto, James 162
Zweig, Maureen Hogan 230